Contents

ON THE ROAD

SAMI SERT / GETTY IMAGES ©
ÉCLAIRS DISPLAY IN A PATISSERIE

Contents

UNDERSTAND

SURVIVAL GUIDE

SPECIAL FEATURES

Welcome to France

France seduces travellers with its unfalteringly familiar culture, woven around cafe terraces, village-square markets and lace-curtained bistros with their plat du jour chalked on the board.

Cultural Savoir Faire

France is about world-class art and architecture. It seduces with iconic landmarks, rising stars and a cultural repertoire that is staggering in volume and diversity. And this is where the beauty of *la belle France* lies: when superstars such as Mademoiselle Eiffel, royal Versailles and the celebrity-ridden French Riviera have been ticked off, there's ample more to thrill. France is, after all, the world's top destination. Some 85 million visitors flock to the land of the Gauls each year to feast on its extraordinary wealth of museums, galleries, ateliers (artist workshops) and hands-on cultural experiences.

Gastronomy

Food is of enormous importance to the French and the daily culinary agenda takes no prisoners: breakfasting on warm croissants from the *boulangerie,* stopping off at Parisian bistros, and market shopping are second nature to the French – and it would be rude to refuse. But French gastronomy goes far deeper than just eating well. Its experiential nature means there is always something tasty to observe, learn and try. Be it flipping crêpes in Brittany or clinking champagne flutes in ancient Reims cellars, the culinary opportunities are endless.

Art de Vivre

The rhythm of daily life – dictated by the seasons in the depths of *la France profonde* (rural France) – exudes an intimacy that gets under your skin. Don't resist. Rather, live the French lifestyle. Embrace the luxury of simple, everyday rituals being transformed into unforgettable moments, be it a coffee and croissant in the Parisian cafe where Sartre and de Beauvoir met to philosophise, a stroll through the lily-clad gardens Monet painted, or a walk on a beach in Brittany scented with the subtle infusion of language, music and mythology brought by 5th-century Celtic invaders.

Outdoor Action

The *terroir* (land) of France weaves a varied journey from northern France's cliffs and sand dunes to the piercing blue sea of the French Riviera and Corsica's green oak forests. Outdoor action is what France's lyrical landscape demands – and there's something for everybody. Whether you end up walking barefoot across wave-rippled sand to Mont St-Michel, riding a cable car to glacial panoramas above Chamonix, or cartwheeling down Europe's highest sand dune, France does not disappoint. Its great outdoors is thrilling, with endless opportunities and the next adventure begging to be had. *Allez!*

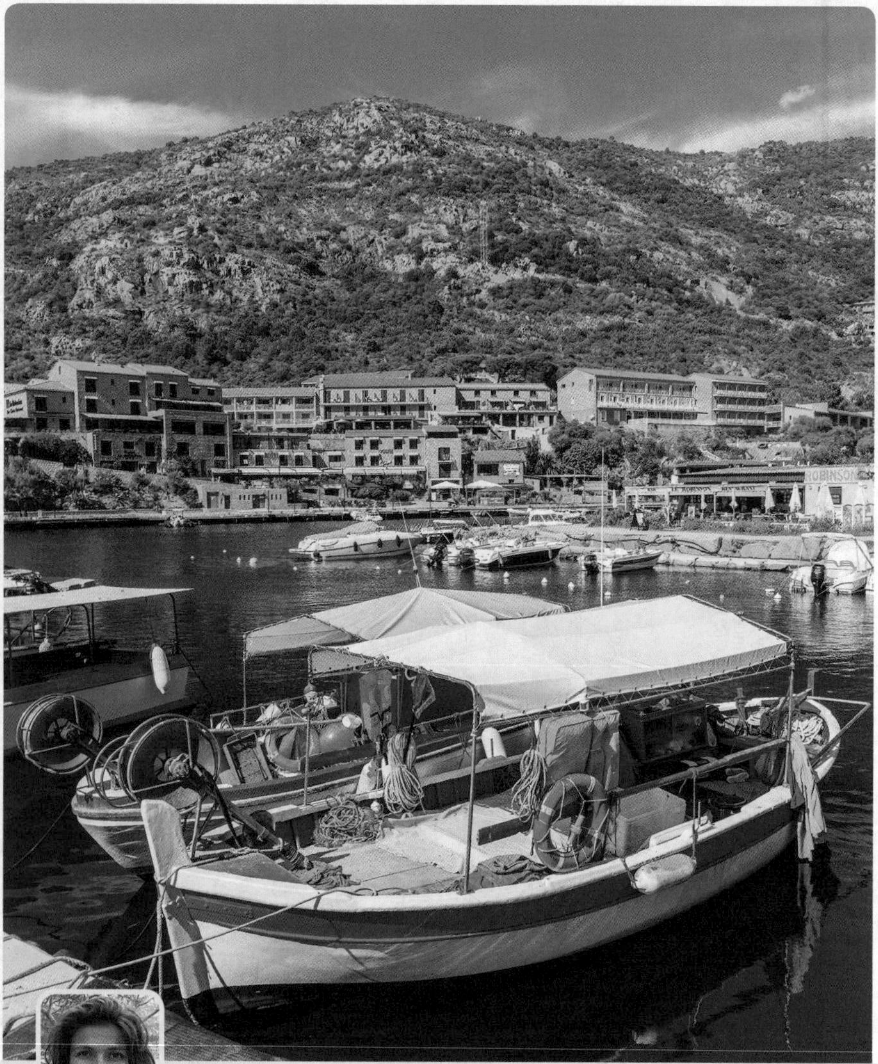

Why I Love France

By Nicola Williams, Writer

France has been home for decades yet I still feel on holiday – French *art de vivre* (art of living) is just too good. From my Haute-Savoie house on Lake Geneva's southern shore, the Jura's dark-green hills and *un café* in the wisteria-draped village bar are my wake-up call. Weekends of endless possibilities punctuate the gentle rhythm of village life: art museums in Lyon and Paris, alpine hiking and skiing, paddle boarding on the glittering lake, road trips to Beaujolais and Burgundy and other regions so different they could be another country. France's sheer variety is amazing.

For more about our writers, see p1000

Above: Moored fishing boats, Porto (p884), Corsica

France

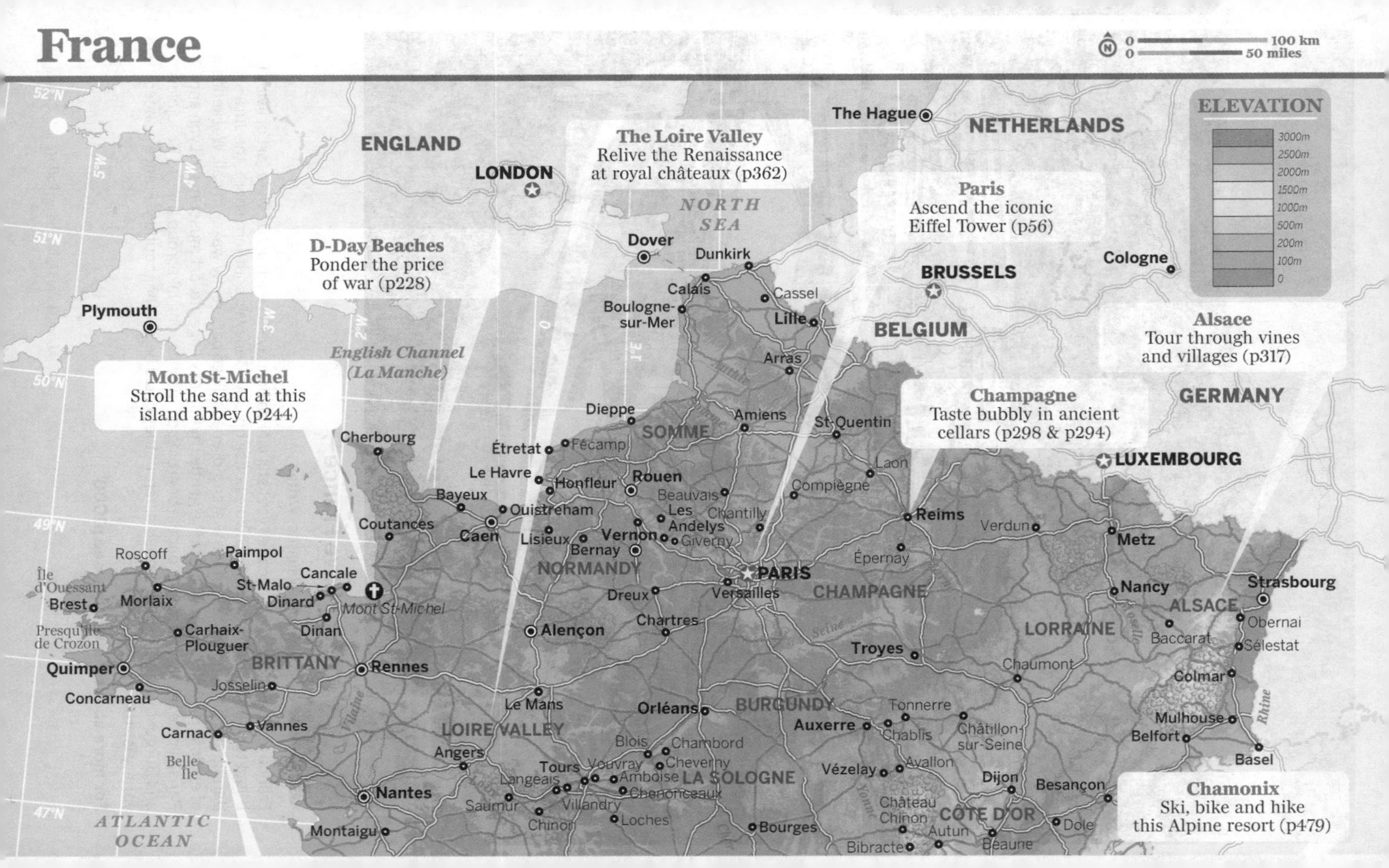
0 100 km
0 50 miles
ELEVATION
3000m
2500m
2000m
1500m
1000m
500m
200m
100m
0
The Loire Valley
Relive the Renaissance at royal châteaux (p362)
Paris
Ascend the iconic Eiffel Tower (p56)
D-Day Beaches
Ponder the price of war (p228)
Alsace
Tour through vines and villages (p317)
Mont St-Michel
Stroll the sand at this island abbey (p244)
Champagne
Taste bubbly in ancient cellars (p298 & p294)
Chamonix
Ski, bike and hike this Alpine resort (p479)
ENGLAND
LONDON
NETHERLANDS
The Hague
BRUSSELS
BELGIUM
Cologne
GERMANY
LUXEMBOURG
NORTH SEA
English Channel (La Manche)
ATLANTIC OCEAN
Plymouth
Dover
Dunkirk
Calais
Cassel
Boulogne-sur-Mer
Lille
Arras
Dieppe
Amiens
St-Quentin
SOMME
Cherbourg
Étretat
Fécamp
Le Havre
Honfleur
Rouen
Laon
Compiègne
Beauvais
Reims
Bayeux
Ouistreham
Caen
Coutances
Lisieux
Bernay
Vernon
Les Andelys
Giverny
Chantilly
Verdun
Metz
Roscoff
Paimpol
Île d'Ouessant
Brest
Morlaix
St-Malo
Cancale
Dinard
Dinan
Mont St-Michel
NORMANDY
PARIS
Versailles
Épernay
CHAMPAGNE
Nancy
ALSACE
Strasbourg
Presqu'île de Crozon
Carhaix-Plouguer
Quimper
BRITTANY
Rennes
Alençon
Dreux
Chartres
Troyes
LORRAINE
Baccarat
Obernai
Sélestat
Concarneau
Josselin
Le Mans
Orléans
BURGUNDY
Chaumont
Colmar
Vannes
Carnac
LOIRE VALLEY
Angers
Tours
Langeais
Saumur
Chinon
Villandry
Vouvray
Amboise
Blois
Chambord
Cheverny
Chenonceaux
Loches
LA SOLOGNE
Auxerre
Chablis
Tonnerre
Châtillon-sur-Seine
Mulhouse
Belfort
Basel
Rhine
Belle Île
Nantes
Montaigu
Bourges
Vézelay
Avallon
Dijon
Besançon
Château Chinon
Autun
Bibracte
CÔTE D'OR
Beaune
Dole
Seine
Loire
Yonne
Vilaine
Moselle
52°N
51°N
50°N
49°N
47°N
5°W
4°W
3°W
2°W
0
1°E

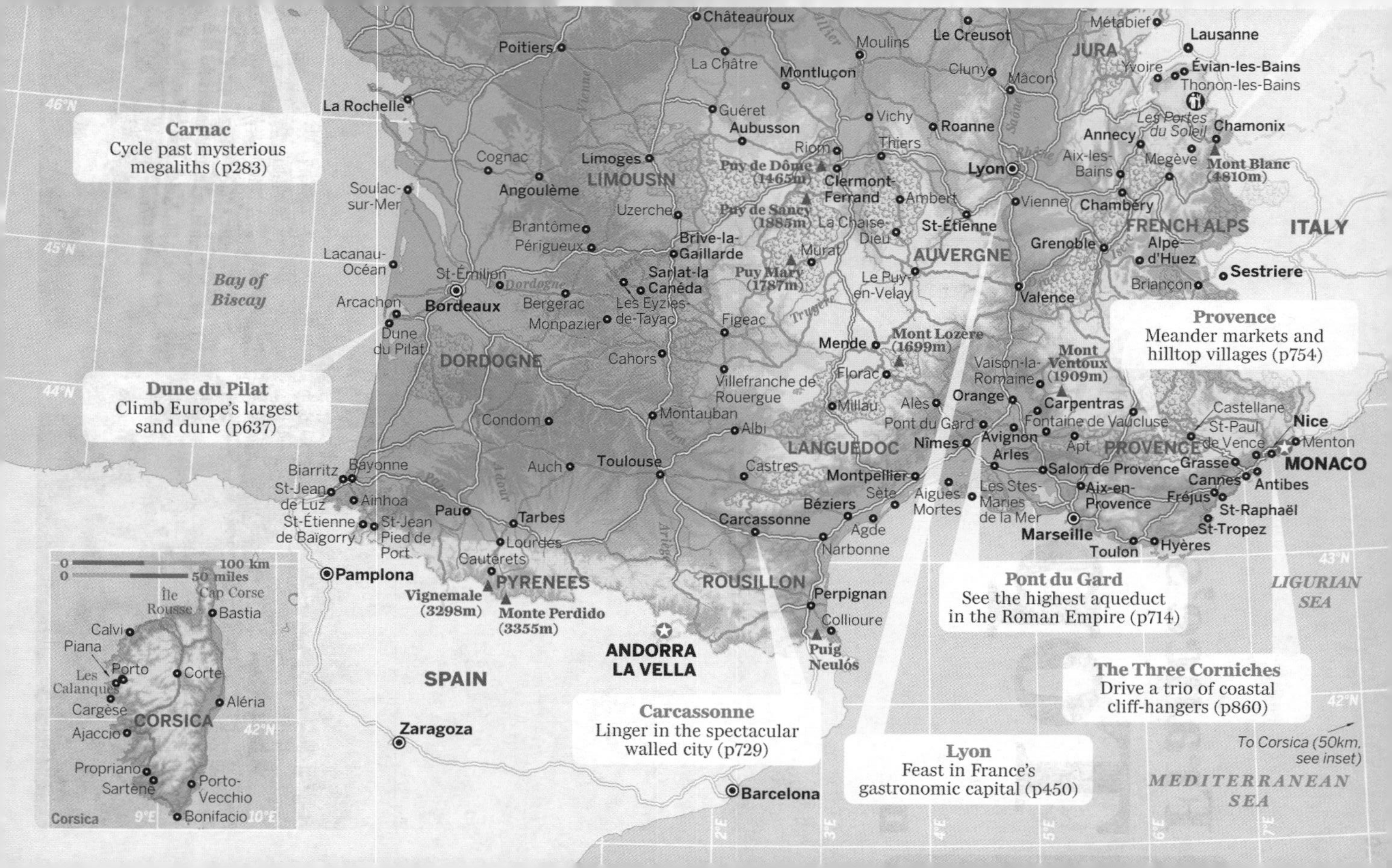

Carnac
Cycle past mysterious megaliths (p283)
Dune du Pilat
Climb Europe's largest sand dune (p637)
Provence
Meander markets and hilltop villages (p754)
Pont du Gard
See the highest aqueduct in the Roman Empire (p714)
The Three Corniches
Drive a trio of coastal cliff-hangers (p860)
Carcassonne
Linger in the spectacular walled city (p729)
Lyon
Feast in France's gastronomic capital (p450)
Bay of Biscay
LIGURIAN SEA
MEDITERRANEAN SEA
To Corsica (50km, see inset)
SPAIN
ITALY
ANDORRA LA VELLA
MONACO
LIMOUSIN
DORDOGNE
AUVERGNE
LANGUEDOC
ROUSILLON
PYRENEES
PROVENCE
FRENCH ALPS
JURA
Châteauroux
Poitiers
La Rochelle
La Châtre
Montluçon
Moulins
Le Creusot
Cluny
Mâcon
Métabief
Lausanne
Yvoire
Évian-les-Bains
Thonon-les-Bains
Les Portes du Soleil
Chamonix
Mont Blanc (4810m)
Annecy
Aix-les-Bains
Megève
Chambéry
Grenoble
Alpe-d'Huez
Briançon
Sestriere
Guéret
Aubusson
Vichy
Roanne
Thiers
Riom
Puy de Dôme (1465m)
Clermont-Ferrand
Lyon
Cognac
Limoges
Angoulême
Soulac-sur-Mer
Uzerche
Ambert
Vienne
Puy de Sancy (1885m)
La Chaise-Dieu
St-Étienne
Brantôme
Périgueux
Brive-la-Gaillarde
Murat
Puy Mary (1787m)
Lacanau-Océan
St-Émilion
Bordeaux
Sarlat-la Canéda
Les Eyzies-de-Tayac
Bergerac
Monpazier
Le Puy-en-Velay
Valence
Arcachon
Dune du Pilat
Figeac
Cahors
Mende
Mont Lozère (1699m)
Florac
Villefranche de Rouergue
Vaison-la-Romaine
Mont Ventoux (1909m)
Orange
Carpentras
Fontaine de Vaucluse
Castellane
St-Paul de Vence
Nice
Menton
Millau
Alès
Pont du Gard
Avignon
Apt
Nîmes
Arles
Montauban
Condom
Albi
Grasse
Cannes
Antibes
Auch
Toulouse
Castres
Montpellier
Aigues Mortes
Les Stes-Maries de la Mer
Salon de Provence
Aix-en-Provence
Fréjus
St-Raphaël
St-Tropez
Biarritz
Bayonne
St-Jean de Luz
Ainhoa
Pau
Tarbes
Sète
Béziers
Agde
Carcassonne
Narbonne
Marseille
Toulon
Hyères
St-Étienne de Baïgorry
St-Jean Pied de Port
Lourdes
Cauterets
Pamplona
Vignemale (3298m)
Monte Perdido (3355m)
Perpignan
Collioure
Puig Neulós
Zaragoza
Barcelona
Adour
Dordogne
Vienne
Allier
Saône
Rhône
Isère
Drôme
Tarn
Truyère
Ariège
Vézère
46°N
45°N
44°N
43°N
42°N
2°E
3°E
4°E
5°E
6°E
7°E
0 100 km
0 50 miles
Île Rousse
Cap Corse
Bastia
Calvi
Piana
Porto
Les Calanques
Corte
Cargèse
Aléria
CORSICA
Ajaccio
Propriano
Sartène
Porto-Vecchio
Bonifacio
Corsica
9°E
10°E

France's Top 15

1

Eiffel Tower

1 More than seven million people visit the Eiffel Tower (p61) annually – and from an evening ascent amid twinkling lights to lunch in one of the restaurants, every visit is unique. Pedal beneath it, skip the lift and trek up it, munch a crêpe next to it, snap a selfie in front of it, ice-skate on the 1st floor in winter or visit it at night. Best up are the special occasions when all 324m of the iconic tower glows a different colour.

Mont St-Michel

2 The dramatic play of tides on this abbey-island in Normandy is magical and mysterious. Said by Celtic mythology to be a sea tomb to which souls of the dead were sent, Mont St-Michel (p245) is rich in legend and history, keenly felt as you make your way barefoot across rippled sand to the stunning architectural ensemble. Walk around it alone or, better still, hook up with a guide in nearby Genêts for a dramatic day hike across the bay.

KISZON PASCAL / GETTY IMAGES ©

2

DYZIO / SHUTTERSTOCK ©

3

GUIZIOU FRANCK / GETTY IMAGES ©

4

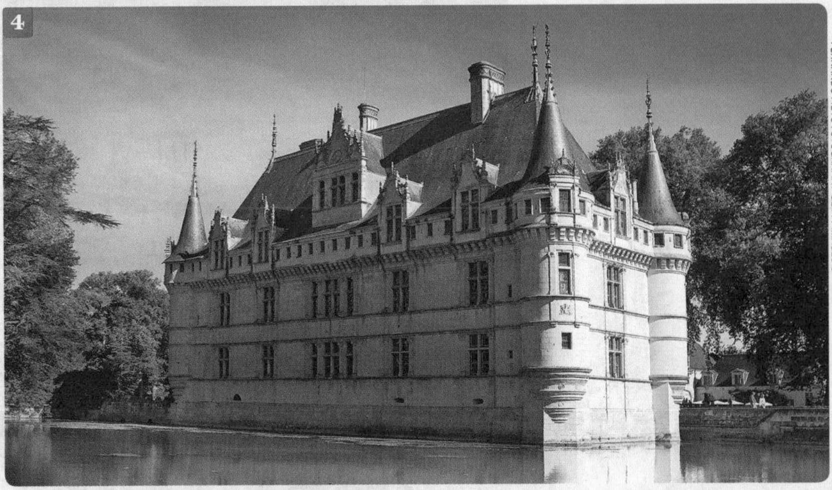

FERNANDO FIETO FOTOGRAFÍA / GETTY IMAGES ©

Champagne

3 Known-brand Champagne houses in the main towns of Reims and Épernay are famed the world over. But – our tip – much of Champagne's finest liquid gold is created by passionate, small-scale *vignerons* (winegrowers) in drop-dead-gorgeous villages – rendering the region's scenic driving routes the loveliest way of tasting fine bubbly amid rolling vineyards. Our favourite: exploring the region's best Champagne museum, the Musée de la Vigne et du Vin (p305), in Le Mesnil-sur-Oger, followed by a tasting and lunch in the village at Le Mesnil.

Loire Valley Châteaux

4 If it's pomp and splendour you're after, this valley is the place to linger. Flowing for more than 1000km into the Atlantic Ocean, the Loire is one of France's last *fleuves sauvages* (wild rivers) and its banks provide a 1000-year snapshot of French high society. The valley is riddled with châteaux (p386) sporting glittering turrets and ballrooms, lavish cupolas and chapels. If you're a romantic seeking the perfect fairytale castle, head for moat-ringed Azay-le-Rideau (pictured), Villandry and its gardens, and less-visited Château de Beauregard.

CHRISTIAN KOBER / GETTY IMAGES ©

ALEXANDER DEMYANENKO / SHUTTERSTOCK ©

Chamonix Action

5 The birthplace of mountaineering and winter playground to the rich, famous and not-so-famous, this iconic ski resort in the French Alps has something for everyone. Snowsport fiends fly down slopes on skies or boards in order to savour the breathtaking views of Mont Blanc and surrounding mountains. But there's absolutely no obligation to do so: non-skiers can hop aboard the Aiguille du Midi (p479) cable car – and onwards to Italy aboard the Télécabine Panoramic Mont Blanc – for the ride of a lifetime above 3800m.

Dune du Pilat

6 The Dune du Pilat (p637) is a 'mountain' that has to be climbed. Not only is the coastal panorama from the top of Europe's largest sand dune a stunner – ogle at the Banc d'Arguin bird reserve and Cap Ferret across the bay – but nearby beaches have some of the Atlantic Coast's best surf. Cycle here from Arcachon and feast afterwards on locally farmed oysters and *crepinettes* (local sausages) at a 1930s hunting lodge redesigned by Philippe Stark, aka the-place-to-be-seen La Co(o)rniche.

The Three Corniches, Nice

7 It's impossible to drive this dramatic trio of coastal roads (p860), each one higher and with more hairpin bends than the next, without conjuring up cinematic images of Grace Kelly, Hitchcock, the glitz of Riviera high life, and the glamour of the Monaco royal family – all while absorbing views of the sweeping blue sea fringing Europe's most mythical coastline. To make a perfect day out of it, shop for a picnic at the Cours Saleya morning market before leaving Nice.

Carcassonne at Dusk

8 That first glimpse of La Cité's sturdy, stone, witch's-hat turrets above Carcassonne (p729) in the Languedoc is enough to make your hair stand on end. To properly savour this fairy-tale walled city, linger at dusk after the crowds have left, when the old town belongs to its 100 or so inhabitants and the few visitors staying at the handful of lovely hotels within its ramparts. Don't forget to look back when you leave to view the old city, beautifully illuminated, glowing in the warm night.

7

ROCHUS / SHUTTERSTOCK ©

8

MATTEO COLOMBO / GETTY IMAGES ©

SHAK / BUDGET TRAVEL ©

ALPSKIER / BUDGET TRAVEL ©

AGNES LEUNG / GETTY IMAGES ©

D-Day Beaches

9 A trip to these peaceful, broad stretches of fine sand and breeze-blown bluffs is one of France's most emotional journeys. On 6 June 1944, beaches here became a cacophony of gunfire and explosions, the bodies of Allied soldiers lying in the sand as their comrades-in-arms charged inland. Just up the hill from Omaha Beach, the long rows of symmetrical gravestones at the Normandy American Cemetery & Memorial (p230; pictured) bear solemn, silent testimony to the horrible price paid for France's liberation from Nazi tyranny.

Pont du Gard

10 This Unesco World Heritage Site (p714) near Nîmes in southern France is gargantuan: 35 arches straddle the Roman aqueduct's 275m-long upper tier, containing a watercourse that was designed to carry 20,000 cu metres of water per day. View it from afloat a canoe on the River Gard or jig across the top. Oh, and don't forget your swimming gear for some post-Pont daredevil diving and high jumping from the rocks nearby. Flop afterwards on a floating deck a little way downstream.

Markets in Provence

11 No region is such a market-must. Be it fresh fish by the port in seafaring Marseille, early summer's strings of pink garlic, Cavaillon melons and cherries all summer long or wintertime's earthy 'black diamond' truffles, Provence thrives on a bounty of local produce – piled high each morning at the market. Every town and village has one, but those in Aix-en-Provence (p776) and Antibes are particularly atmospheric. Take your own bag to stock up on dried herbs, green and black olives marinated a dozen different ways, courgette flowers and tangy olive oils.

OLE HOUEN / SHUTTERSTOCK ©

BONCHAN / SHUTTERSTOCK ©

Hilltop Villages

12 Impossibly perched on a rocky peak above the Mediterranean, gloriously lost in back country, fortified or château-topped… Southern France's portfolio of *villages perchés* is vast and impressive, and calls for go-slow touring. Most villages are medieval, built from golden stone and riddled with cobbled lanes, flower-filled alleys and hidden squares silent but for the glug of a fountain. Combine a village visit with lunch alfresco – La Table de Ventabren (p782) near Aix-en-Provence is one such dreamy address that you'll never want to leave.

Gordes (p809)

Lyonnais Bouchons

13 The red-and-white checked tablecloths and decades-old bistro decor could be anywhere in France. It's the local cuisine that makes Lyon's *bouchons* (bistros) unique, plus the quaint culinary customs, such as totting up the bill on the paper tablecloth, or serving wine in a glass bottle wrapped with an elastic band to stop drips, or the 'shut weekends' opening hours. Various piggy parts drive Lyonnais cuisine (p463), but have faith – this French city is said to be the gastronomic capital of France. Dine and decide.

Andouillette (pig-intestine sausage)

Carnac Megaliths

14 Pedalling past open fields dotted with the world's greatest concentration of mysterious megaliths (p283) gives a poignant reminder of Brittany's ancient human inhabitants. No one knows for sure what inspired these gigantic menhirs, dolmens, cromlechs, *tumuli* and cairns to be built. A sun god? Some phallic fertility cult? Post-ride, try to unravel the mystery from the soft-sand comfort of La Grande Plage, Carnac's longest and most popular beach, with a 2km-long stretch of pearly white sand.

OSCITY / SHUTTERSTOCK ©

14

Alsatian Wine Route

ANNEKA / SHUTTERSTOCK ©

15

15 It is one of France's most popular drives – and for good reason. Motoring in this far northeast corner of France takes you through a kaleidoscope of lush green vines, perched castles and gentle mist-covered mountains. The only pit stops en route are half-timbered villages and roadside wine cellars, where fruity Alsace vintages can be swirled, tasted and bought. To be truly wooed, drive the Route des Vins d'Alsace (p329) in autumn, when vines are heavy with grapes waiting to be harvested and colours are at their vibrant best.

Need to Know

For more information, see Survival Guide (p947)

Currency
Euro (€)

Language
French

Visas
Generally not required for stays of up to 90 days (or at all for EU nationals); some nationalities need a Schengen visa.

Money
ATMs at every airport, most train stations and on every second street corner in towns and cities. Visa, MasterCard and Amex widely accepted.

Mobile Phones
European and Australian phones work, but only American cells with 900 and 1800 MHz networks are compatible; check with your provider before leaving home. Use a French SIM card to call with a cheaper French number.

Time
Central European Time (GMT/UTC plus one hour)

When to Go

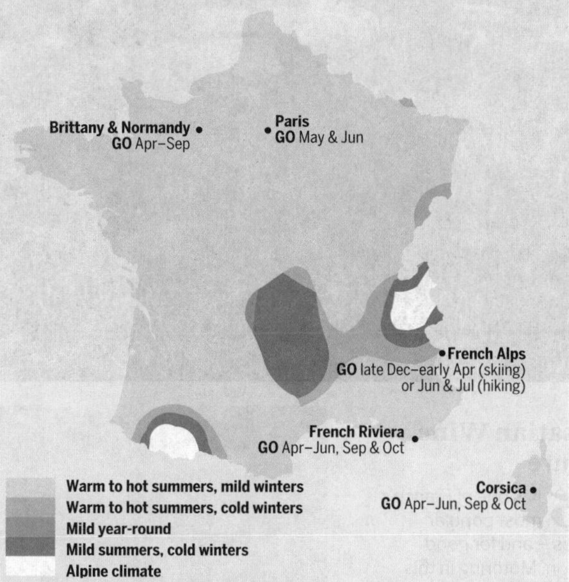

High Season
(Jul & Aug)

- Queues at big sights and on the road, especially August.
- Christmas, New Year and Easter busy.
- Late December to March is high season in Alpine ski resorts.
- Book hotels and tables in the best restaurants well in advance.

Shoulder
(Apr–Jun & Sep)

- Accommodation rates drop in southern France and other hot spots.
- Spring brings warm weather, flowers and local produce.
- The *vendange* (grape harvest) is reason to visit in autumn.

Low Season
(Oct–Mar)

- Prices up to 50% lower than high season.
- Sights, attractions and restaurants open fewer days and shorter hours.
- Hotels and restaurants in quieter rural regions (such as the Dordogne) are closed.

Useful Websites

France.fr (www.france.fr) Official country website.

France 24 (www.france24.com/en/france) French news in English.

Paris by Mouth (www.parisbymouth.com) Dining and drinking; one-stop site for where and how to eat in the capital with plenty of the latest openings.

David Lebovitz (www.davidlebovitz.com) American pastry chef in Paris and author of several French cookbooks; insightful postings and great France-related articles shared on his Facebook page.

French Word-a-Day (http://french-word-a-day.typepad.com) Fun language learning.

Lonely Planet (www.lonelyplanet.com/france) Destination information, hotel bookings, traveller forum and more.

Important Numbers

France country code	☎33
International access code	☎00
Europe-wide emergency	☎112
Ambulance (SAMU)	☎15
Police	☎17

Exchange Rates

Australia	A$1	€0.70
Canada	C$1	€0.69
Japan	¥100	€0.72
NZ	NZ$1	€0.64
UK	UK£1	€1.26
US	US$1	€0.76

For current exchange rates see www.xe.com

Daily Costs

Budget: Less than €130

- Dorm bed: €18–30
- Double room in a budget hotel: €90
- Admission to many attractions first Sunday of month: free
- Lunch *menus* (set meals): less than €20

Midrange: €130–€220

- Double room in a midrange hotel: €90–190
- Lunch *menus* in gourmet restaurants: €20–40

Top end: More than €220

- Double room in a top-end hotel: €190–350
- Top restaurant dinner: *menu* €65, à la carte €100–150

Opening Hours

Opening hours vary throughout the year. We list high-season opening hours, but remember that longer summer hours often decrease in shoulder and low seasons.

Banks 9am to noon and 2pm to 5pm Monday to Friday or Tuesday to Saturday

Restaurants Noon to 2.30pm and 7pm to 11pm six days a week

Cafes 7am to 11pm

Bars 7pm to 1am

Clubs 10pm to 3am, 4am or 5am Thursday to Saturday

Shops 10am to noon and 2pm to 7pm Monday to Saturday

Arriving in France

Aéroport de Charles de Gaulle (Paris; p962) Trains, buses and RER suburban trains run to the city centre every 15 to 30 minutes from 5am to 11pm, after which night buses kick in (12.30am to 5.30am). Fares are €9.75 by RER, €6 to €17.50 by bus, €8 by night bus or a flat fare of €50/55 for the 30-minute taxi ride to right-/left-bank central Paris (15% higher 5pm to 10am, and Sundays).

Aéroport d'Orly (Paris; p962) Linked to central Paris by Orlyval rail then RER (€12.05) or bus (€7.50 to €12.50) every 15 minutes between 5am and 11pm. Or T7 tram to Villejuif-Louis Aragon then metro to the centre (€3.60). The 25-minute journey by taxi costs €35/30 to right-/left-bank central Paris (15% higher between 5pm and 10am, and Sundays).

Getting Around

Transport in France is comfortable, quick, usually reliable and reasonably priced.

Train Run by the state-owned SNCF (p963), France's rail network is first-class, with extensive coverage of the country and frequent departures.

Car Away from cities (where a car is hard to park) the car comes into its own. Drive on the right. Be aware of France's 'priority to the right' rule.

Bus Cheaper and slower than trains. Useful for remote villages that aren't serviced by trains.

Bicycle Certain regions – the Loire Valley, the Lubéron and Burgundy – have dedicated cycling paths, some along canal towpaths or between orchards and vineyards.

For much more on **getting around**, see p964

First Time France

For more information, see Survival Guide (p947)

Checklist

- Check passport validity and visa requirements
- Arrange travel insurance
- Check airline baggage restrictions
- Book accommodation; reserve big-name restaurants
- Buy tickets online for the Louvre, Eiffel Tower et al
- Download France-related travel apps and music

What to Pack

- Travel plug (electrical adapter) for France's two-pin plugs
- Sunscreen, sunhat and sunglasses (southern France)
- Rainproof jacket and umbrella (northern France)
- Pocket knife with corkscrew – most French wines have corks (pack this in your checked-in luggage)
- Walking shoes – for mountains, hilltop villages, cobbled streets and pedestrian old towns
- Light scarf or sarong – to cover bare shoulders in churches
- An adventurous appetite (a French culinary necessity)

Top Tips for Your Trip

- Almost every village and town has a weekly morning market brimming with fruit, veg and other regional produce – and there's no finer opportunity for mingling with locals! Take your own shopping bag or basket.
- To get the best out of a French road trip, avoid *autoroutes* (highways) and main roads. Opt for back roads and country lanes that twist past farms, châteaux, vineyards and orchards – scenic routes are highlighted in green on road maps (print and digital) published by French cartographer Michelin (www.viamichelin.com).
- For local dining experiences, avoid restaurants that tout a *'menu touristique'* or display a sample meal of plastic food outside. While it might be tempting to favour restaurants with a menu in English, the very best (and best-loved by locals) rarely offer a translation.

What to Wear

- It might be the cradle of haute couture, but Paris sports a mixed bag of styles. To avoid standing out from the urban crowd, smart-casual is the way to go. The further south you are, the more relaxed fashion becomes. Even so, no bikini tops or bare male chests *s'il vous plaît*, unless you're on the beach.
- Dress up rather than down in nicer midrange restaurants, clubs and bars – no jeans and sneakers, unless you're at the local village bar (though black or 'smarter' jeans will probably be OK).

Sleeping

Be it a fairy-tale château, a boutique hideaway or floating pod on a lake, France has accommodation to suit every taste and pocket. If you're visiting in high season, reserve ahead.

- **B&Bs** Enchanting properties with maximum five rooms.
- **Camping** From wild and remote, to brash resorts with pools.
- **Hostels** New-wave hostels are design-driven, lifestyle spaces with single/double rooms as well as dorms.
- **Hotels** Hotels embrace every budget and taste.
- **Refuges and Gîtes d'Étape** Huts for hikers on trails in mountainous areas.

Cent Savers

➡ **Eat cheap** Lunchtime *formules* (two courses) and *menus* (three courses) in restaurants are a snip of the price of evening dining.

➡ **Discount admission** City museum passes provide cheaper admission to sights.

➡ **Savvy sleeping** It's cheaper for families staying in hotels to ask for a double room with extra bed rather than a triple. Families of four or more will find self-catering accommodation cheaper.

➡ **Picnic perfection** With its bucolic scenery and outstanding produce, France is picnic paradise. Buy a baguette from the *boulangerie* (bakery) and fill it with Camembert, pâté or charcuterie (cold meats). Finish sweet with macarons (Paris), buttery *Kouign amann* (Breton butter cake), cherries (southern France) or – for blue-blooded gourmets – Champagne and Reims' *biscuit roses*.

Bargaining

With the exception of the odd haggle at the market, little bargaining goes on in France.

Tipping

Restaurant and bar prices include a 15% service charge in the bill, so tipping is not expected. Many locals do, however, show appreciation for good service by leaving a small 'extra' tip for waitstaff. For more information, see p954.

Phrases to Learn Before You Go

English is increasingly widespread in Paris, Nice and other big tourist-busy cities, but step into *la France profonde* (rural France) and you'll need those French phrases you mastered before setting off. See Language (p973) for more information.

1 **What are the opening hours?**
Quelles sont les heures d'ouverture?
kel son lay zer doo·vair·tewr

French business hours are governed by a maze of regulations, so it's a good idea to check before you make plans.

2 **I'd like the set menu, please.**
Je voudrais le menu, s'il vous plait.
zher voo·dray ler mer·new seel voo play

The best-value dining in France is the two- or three-course meal at a fixed price. Most restaurants have one on the chalkboard.

3 **Which wine would you recommend?**
Quel vin vous conseillez?
kel vun voo kon·say·yay

Who better to ask for advice on wine than the French?

Etiquette

➡ **Conversation** Use the formal *vous* when speaking to anyone unknown or older than you; the informal *tu* is reserved for close friends, family and children.

➡ **Churches** Dress modestly (cover shoulders).

➡ **Drinks** Asking for *une carafe d'eau* (free jug of tap water) in restaurants is acceptable. Never end a meal with a cappuccino or cup of tea. Play French and order *un café* (espresso).

➡ **French kissing** Exchange *bisous* (cheek-skimming kisses) – at least two, but in some parts of France it can be up to four – with casual acquaintances and friends.

Eating

In cities there are a multitude of places to eat. To dine fine and eat local, book ahead, particularly for weekend dining. In rural France, the same goes for *bonnes tables* (literally 'good tables') and Sunday lunch, always a fiesty, afternoon-long affair.

➡ **Restaurants and bistros** Range from unchanged for a century to contemporary minimalist; urban dining is international, rural dining staunchly French.

➡ **Brasseries** Open from dawn until late, these casual eateries are great for dining in between standard meal times.

➡ **Cafes** Ideal for breakfast and light lunch; many morph into bars after dark.

What's New

Louvre Renewal
The Musée du Louvre has embarked on a 30-year renovation plan to make the labyrinthine art gallery more user-friendly. A snazzy new entrance hall and improved navigation are top priorities. (p65)

City of Wine
No single address evokes the history, culture and savoir-faire of French viticulture quite like Bordeaux's sparking new Cité du Vin, shaped like a golden decanter on the banks of the Garonne River. (p622)

Museum of Man
Paris' revamped anthropological museum, the Musée de l'Homme, traces the evolution of humankind through smarter exhibits, an updated layout and five-star Eiffel Tower views from its 2nd-floor cafe. (p61)

Lascaux IV
Laser technology has been used to re-create – for the first time ever – the entire collection of prehistoric paintings found in the Grotte de Lascaux. Lascaux IV, at Montignac's brand-new Centre International de l'Art Pariétal, will be a dazzling, digital-smart experience. (p582)

SkyWay Monte Bianco
Peerless views of Mont Blanc, Matterhorn and Vallée Blanche can be ogled at aboard this spectacular cableway of rotating cars, linking Pointe Helbronner (3452m) with Courmayeur in Italy. (p481)

Cité Internationale de la Tapisserie
Antique to modern tapestry worldwide is the fascinating, eye-pleasing focus of this grand new space in Aubusson, with museum, exhibitions and resident contemporary artists. (p587)

Aeroscopia
Be awed by huge aircraft in the birthplace of the Airbus at this new aviation museum near Toulouse. (p693)

Historial Jeanne d'Arc
Learn the story of Joan of Arc through brilliant, cinematic displays inside the actual medieval chambers in Rouen where the young French peasant girl was tried and condemned in 1431. (p213)

Gluten-free Greatness
Thanks to the opening of Chambelland *boulangerie* in Paris, gluten-free bread and cakes in the capital are suddenly as great as those of any traditional French bakery. Watch the trend spread across France… (p132)

Châteaux by Design
World-class architects are turning heads in the wine world: new Bordeaux wine cellars by Sir Norman Foster and Jean Nouvel for age-old winegrowers such as Château Margaux and Château La Dominique are dazzling. (p636)

Baie de Somme
All along the one-time Western Front in the Somme and French Flanders, new memorials, museums and monuments continue to mark the centenary of key WWI events (until 2018). (p197)

For more recommendations and reviews, see lonelyplanet.com/france

If You Like...

Gorgeous Villages

There is no humbler pleasure than exploring villages of gold stone, pink granite or whitewash. Cobbled lanes ensnare ornate fountains, flowery squares and houses strung with wisteria, vines or drying peppers.

Pérouges Day trip it from Lyon for cider and sugar-crusted *galettes* between yellow-gold medieval stone. (p470)

St-Émilion A medieval village perched dramatically above Bordeaux vines. (p633)

St-Jean Pied de Port Ancient pilgrim outpost en route to Santiago de Compostela in Spain. (p662)

Yvoire On Lake Geneva's southern shore, this Savoyard village is a privileged address. (p493)

The Luberon A part of Provence lavishly strewn with hilltop villages; red-rock Roussillon is pure brilliance. (p807)

Èze Fuses a stunning hilltop village with sweeping Riviera panoramas. (p861)

Wine Tasting

Be it tasting in cellars, watching grape harvests or sleeping *au château,* French wine culture demands immediate road-testing.

Bordeaux The Médoc, St-Émilion and Cognac set connoisseurs' hearts aflutter. (p622)

Burgundy Sample renowned vintages in Beaune, the Côte d'Or and Chablis. (p404)

Châteauneuf-du-Pape Vines planted by 14th-century popes yield southern France's most illustrious red. (p804)

Gigondas Taste raved-about reds in this gold-stone village in Provence, or try the equally luscious poulsard reds from Arbois-Pupillin, in the Jura. (p807)

Route des Vins d'Alsace Pair wine tasting with castle-topped villages in this storybook region, rich in rieslings, pinots and sylvaners. (p329)

Beaujolais Gentle cycling and wine tasting through vine-ribboned hills near Lyon. (p466)

Castles

The Loire Valley is the prime stop for French châteaux, dripping in gold leaf. But venture elsewhere and you'll be surprised by what hides behind lumbering stone walls.

Versailles France's largest and grandest château, a stone's throw from Paris. (p162)

Chambord Renaissance country-getaway castle where French kings and queens had a ball. (p374)

Azay-le-Rideau Classic French château with moat, turrets and sweeping staircase. (p389)

Villandry The formal French gardens framing this Renaissance Loire Valley château are glorious. (p385)

Cathar fortresses Now ruined, these dramatic, heat-sizzled hilltop castles in Languedoc evoke 13th-century persecution. (p749)

Château de Foix A château in Vallée de l'Ariège with amazing views of the Pyrenees. (p684)

Coastal Paths

From white cliff to red rock, pebble cove to gold sand strip, France's coastline is dramatically different. Explore on a windswept *sentier du littoral* (coastal trail), scented with sea salt and herbal scrub.

St-Tropez This *sentier du littoral* leads from fishing coves to celebrity-laced sands. (p851)

Bandol Stride the coast between inland vines and waterfront rock formations. (p859)

Chemin de Nietzsche Spectacular, steep rocky footpath near Nice where the German philosopher once hung out. (p860)

Corsica Hike from Bonifacio to a lighthouse, or past Genoese watchtowers along Cap Corse's Customs Officers' Trail. (p871)

Côte d'Opale Savour opal blues from windwept clifftops near Cap Blanc-Nez and Cap Griz Nez. (p190)

Breton island capers Fall in love with Brittany's Belle Île or Île d'Ouessant; hobnob with Parisians on chic Île de Ré. (p284)

Île de Porquerolles Mediterranean island beauty strung with sea-facing cycling and hiking trails. (p858)

Markets

Art-nouveau hangar or tree-shaded village square... French markets spill across an enticing mix of spaces. Every town and village has one – they operate in the mornings, at least once a week. Bring your own bag.

Les Halles This market and Croix Rousse are Lyon's two buxom market divas, endowed with stalls heaving with fruit, veg, meat and runny St Marcellin cheese. (p460)

Place des Lices No town square is as celebrity-studded as St-Tropez. (p851)

Marché des Capucins Enjoy oysters and white wine at Bordeaux's Saturday-morning market. (p631)

Uzès Languedoc's most splendid farmers market. (p715)

Carpentras This Friday-morning *marché* steals the Provençal market show. (p805)

Les Halles Victor Hugo Lunch with locals on the 1st floor of Toulouse's covered food market. (p694)

St-Girons Riverside extravaganza of food, crafts, antiques and delectable Pyrenean produce. (p684)

JUSTIN FOULKES / LONELY PLANET ©

VISUALCORRUPTION / GETTY IMAGES / ISTOCKPHOTO ©

Top: Flat bottomed boat, Marais Poitevin (p613)

Bottom: Goat cheese at Les Halles de Lyon (p460)

Islands & Beaches

The country's 3200km-long coastline morphs from white chalk cliffs (Normandy) to treacherous promontories (Brittany) to broad expanses of fine sand (Atlantic Coast) and pebbly or sandy beaches (Mediterranean Coast).

Îles d'Hyères France's only marine national park and a pedestrian paradise fringed with near-tropical beaches. (p858)

Plage de Pampelonne Stars love this hip beach in St-Tropez, darling, and for good reason – it's glam and golden. (p851)

Île de Ré Follow the flock from Paris to this chic, beach-laced island off France's west coast. (p615)

Belle Île Its name means 'Beautiful Island' and that is just what this island off the coast of Brittany is. (p284)

Plage de Palombaggia Near Porto-Vecchio, this is a Corsican beauty to die for, along with nearby Plage de Santa Giulia. (p895)

Les Landes Surfers' secret backed by dunes on the Atlantic Coast. (p648)

Côte d'Opale Rousing, wind-buffeted beaches across from the white cliffs of Dover. (p190)

Incredible Train Journeys

There is nothing quite like watching mountains, valleys, gorges and rivers jog past kaleidoscope-style from the window of an old-fashioned steam train or mountain railway.

Train du Montenvers Ride this historic rack-and-pinion train from Chamonix to Montenvers, then catch a cable car to the Mer de Glace, France's biggest glacier. (p481)

Tramway du Mont Blanc Travel in the shade of Europe's biggest mountain aboard France's highest train from St-Gervais-Le Fayet. (p487)

Le Train Jaune Mind-blowing Pyrenean scenery aboard a mountain train in Roussillon. (p750)

Train des Pignes Narrow-gauge railway from Nice. (p832)

Chemin de Fer Touristique du Haut-Quercy Savour the sun-baked vineyards, oak forests and rivers of the Lot in southwest France aboard a vintage steam train. (p599)

La Vapeur du Trieux Journey riverside on this steam train from Breton harbour to an artists' village. (p264)

Rural Escapes

Solitude is sweet and if you know where to go, there's ample opportunity to stray off the beaten track and play Zen *sans* the crowds.

Marais Poitevin Paddle in perfect peace by boat through this tranquil, bird-filled wetland dubbed 'Green Venice'. (p613)

Vallée d'Aspe The 21st century has yet to reach this quiet valley, sprinkled with tiny hamlets in the Pyrenees. (p675)

Essoyes Watch vine-streaked landscapes of Champagne fade into watercolour distance in this riverside village, Renoir's summer home. (p315)

Le Crotoy The mood is laid-back and the panorama superb in this picturesque fishing town on the northern bank of the Baie de Somme. (p197)

Forêt de Paimpont Recharge your batteries in this immense Breton forest, far away from the coastal crowds. (p289)

Ota and Evisa Rolling hills, chestnut groves and picturesque villages in the Corsican hills above Porto. (p885)

Domaine de la Palissade Trek on horseback through this remote, coastal nature park in the Camargue, kissed pink by salt pans and flamingos. (p785)

Massif des Maures Chestnut forest, right next door to but a million miles away from the French Riviera glitz. (p854)

Mountain Vistas

On sunny days, views from atop France's highest mountains are breathtaking. Cable cars and mountain railways often take out the legwork.

Aiguille du Midi, Chamonix If you can handle the height (3842m), unforgettable summit views of the French, Swiss and Italian Alps await. (p479)

Pic Blanc, Alpe d'Huez Scale the 3330m peak year-round by cable car – magical views ripple across the French Alps into Italy and Switzerland. (p516)

Massif de l'Estérel, French Riviera Stupendous views of red rock, green forest and big blue – only on foot! (p849)

Ballon d'Alsace See where Alsace, Franche-Comté and Lorraine converge from this rounded, 1247m-high mountain. (p344)

Puy de Dôme, Auvergne Gulp at extinct volcanoes, pea-green and grassy, from this wind-swept summit reached by foot or cog railway. (p544)

Cirque de Gavarnie Near Lourdes, a mind-blowing mountain amphitheatre ringed by icy Pyrenean peaks. (p676)

Month by Month

TOP EVENTS

Festival d'Avignon, July

Fête du Citron, February

Fête des Lumières, December

Cannes Film Festival, May

Monaco Grand Prix, May

January

With New Year festivities done and dusted, head to the Alps. Crowds on the slopes thin out once school's back, but January remains busy. On the Mediterranean, mild winters are wonderfully serene in a part of France that's mad busy the rest of the year.

Vive le Ski!

Grab your skis, hit the slopes. Most resorts in the Alps, Pyrenees, Jura and Auvergne open mid- to late December, but January is the start of the ski season in earnest. Whether a purpose-built station or Alpine village, there's resorts to match every mood and moment. (p44)

Truffle Season

No culinary product is more aromatic or decadent than black truffles. Hunt them in the Dordogne and Provence – the season runs late December to March, but January is the prime month.

February

Crisp cold weather in the mountains – lots of china-blue skies now – translates as ski season in top gear. Alpine resorts get mobbed by families during the February school holidays and accommodation is at its priciest.

Nice Carnival

Nice makes the most of its mild climate with this crazy Lenten carnival. As well as parade and costume shenanigans, merrymakers pelt each other with blooms during the legendary flower battles. Dunkirk in northern France celebrates Mardi Gras with equal gusto. (p825)

Fête du Citron

Menton on the French Riviera was once Europe's biggest lemon producer, hence its exotic Fête du Citron. These days it has to ship in a zillion lemons from Spain to sculpt into gargantuan carnival characters. (p869)

March

The ski season stays busy thanks to ongoing school holidays (until mid-March) and warmer temperatures. Down south, spring ushers in the bullfighting season and *Pâques* (Easter).

Féria d'Arles

No fest sets passions in France's hot south blazing more than Féria d'Arles, held at Easter in Arles to open the bullfighting season. There are four days of street dancing, music, concerts alfresco and bullfighting. (p782)

April

Dedicated ski fiends can carve glaciers in the highest French ski resorts until mid-April or later at highest altitudes. Then it's off with the ski boots and on with the hiking gear as peach and almond trees flower pink against a backdrop of snow-capped peaks.

Fête de la Transhumance

During the ancient Fête de la Transhumance in April or May, shepherds walk their flocks of sheep up to green summer pastures; St-Rémy de Provence's fest is the best known. Or head to villages in the Pyrenees and Auvergne to witness this transit. (p790)

Fêtes de Jeanne d'Arc

Orléans residents have celebrated the liberation of their city by Joan of Arc since 1430. Festivities include a four-day medieval market, costume parades, concerts and, on 8 May, a cathedral service and military parade (including tanks). (p367)

May

There is no lovelier month to travel in France, as the first melons ripen in Provence and outdoor markets burst with new-found colour. Spring is always in.

May Day

No one works on 1 May, a national holiday that incites summer buzz, with *muguets* (lilies of the valley) sold at roadside stalls and given to friends for good luck. In Arles, Camargue cowboys prove their bull-herding and equestrian skills at the Fête des Gardians. (p782)

Pèlerinage des Gitans

Roma flock to the Camargue on 24 and 25 May and again in October for a flamboyant fiesta of street music, dancing and dipping their toes in the sea. (p787)

Festival de Cannes

In mid-May, film stars and celebrities walk the red carpet at Cannes, Europe's biggest cinema extravaganza. (p836)

Monaco Grand Prix

How fitting that Formula One's most glamorous rip around the streets is in one of the world's most glam countries at Monaco's Formula One Grand Prix. (p868)

June

As midsummer approaches, the festival pace quickens alongside a rising temperature gauge, which tempts the first bathers into the sea. Looking north, nesting white storks shower good luck on farmsteads in Alsace.

Fête de la Musique

Orchestras, crooners, buskers and bands fill streets with free music during France's vibrant nationwide celebration of music on 21 June (www.fetedelamusique.culture.fr).

Paris Jazz Festival

No festival better evokes the brilliance of Paris' interwar jazz age than this annual fest in the Parc de Floral. (p107)

July

If lavender's your French love, now is the time to catch it flowering in Provence. But you won't be the only one. School's out for the summer, showering the country with teems of tourists, traffic and too many *complet* (full) signs strung in hotel windows.

Tour de France

The world's most prestigious cycling race ends on av des Champs-Élysées in Paris on the third or fourth Sunday of July, but you can catch it for two weeks before all over France – the route changes each year but the French Alps are a hot spot. (p108)

Bastille Day

Join the French in celebrating the storming of the Bastille on 14 July 1789 – countrywide there are fireworks displays, balls, processions, parades and lots of hoo-ha all round.

Festival d'Avignon

Rouse your inner thespian with Avignon's legendary performing-arts festival. Street acts in its fringe fest are as inspired as those on official stages. (p795)

Jazz à Juan

Jive to jazz cats in Juan-les-Pins at this mythical Riviera music fest, which has been around for 50-odd years. Jazz à Juan requires tickets, but the fringe 'Off' part of the music festival does not. (p842)

Festival de Cornouaille

Traditional Celtic music takes over the Breton town of Quimper during this inspiring summer festival in late July. (p275)

August

It's that crazy summer month when the French join everyone else on holiday. Paris, Lyon and other big cities empty; traffic jams at motorway toll booths test the patience of a saint; and temperatures soar. Avoid. Or don your party hat and join the crowd!

Celts Unite!

Celtic culture is the focus of the Festival Interceltique de Lorient, when hundreds of thousands of Celts from Brittany and abroad flock to Lorient to celebrate just that. (p286)

Bubbles!

There's no better excuse for a flute or three of bubbly than during the first weekend in August when Champagne toasts its vines and vintages with the Route du Champagne en Fête. Free tastings, cellar visits, music and dancing. (p314)

September

As sun-plump grapes hang heavy on darkened vines and that August madness drops off as abruptly as it began, a welcome tranquillity falls across autumnal France. This is the start of France's *vendange* (grape harvest).

Rutting Season

Nothing beats getting up at dawn to watch mating stags, boar and red deer at play. Observatory towers are hidden in woods around Château de Chambord. (p374)

Braderie de Lille

The mountains of empty mussel shells engulfing the streets after three days of mussel-munching have to be seen to be believed. Then there's the real reason for visiting Lille in the first weekend in September – its huge flea market is Europe's largest. (p186)

October

The days become shorter, the last grapes are harvested and the first sweet chestnuts fall from trees. With the changing of the clocks on the last Sunday of the month, there's no denying it's winter.

Nuit Blanche

In one last ditch attempt to stretch out what's left of summer, Paris museums, monuments, cultural spaces, bars, clubs and so on rock around the clock during Paris' so-called White Night, aka one fabulous long all-nighter! (p108)

November

It's nippy now. Toussaint (All Saints' Day) on 1 November ushers in the switch to shorter winter opening hours for many sights. Many restaurants close two nights a week now, making dining out on Monday a challenge in some towns.

Beaujolais Nouveau

At the stroke of midnight on the third Thursday in November the first bottles of cherry-red Beaujolais *nouveau* wine are cracked open – and what a party it can be in Beaujolais, Lyon and other places nearby! (p469)

December

Days are short and it's cold everywhere bar the south of France. But there are Christmas school holidays and festive celebrations to bolster sun-deprived souls, not to mention some season-opening winter skiing in the highest-altitude Alpine resorts from mid-December.

Alsatian Christmas Markets

Visitors meander between fairy-light-covered craft stalls, mug of *vin chaud* (warm mulled wine) in gloved hand, at Alsace's traditional pre-Christmas markets.

Fête des Lumières

France's biggest and best light show, on and around 8 December, transforms the streets and squares of Lyon into an open stage. (p457)

Itineraries

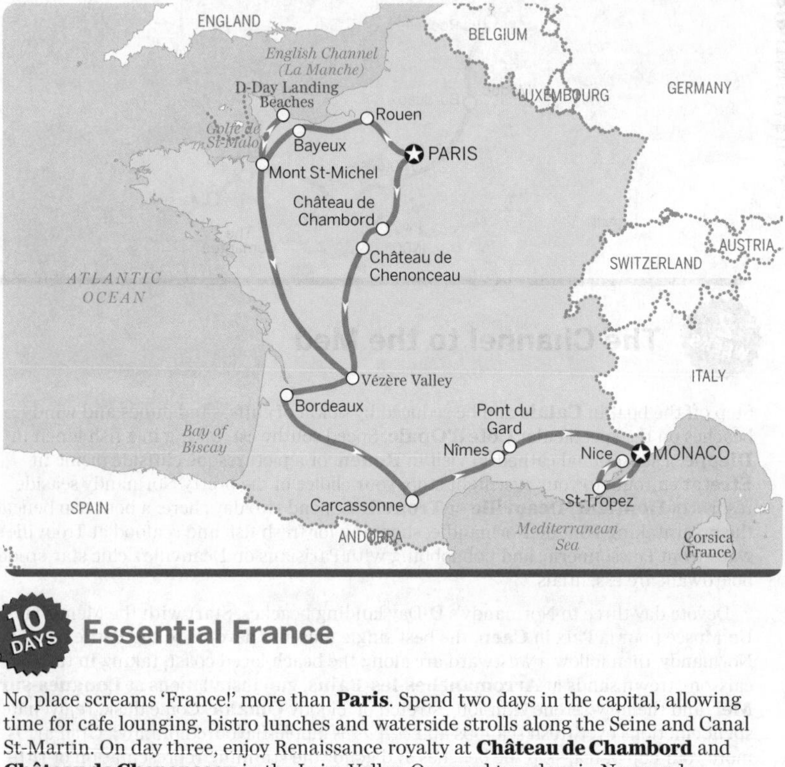

10 DAYS Essential France

No place screams 'France!' more than **Paris**. Spend two days in the capital, allowing time for cafe lounging, bistro lunches and waterside strolls along the Seine and Canal St-Martin. On day three, enjoy Renaissance royalty at **Château de Chambord** and **Château de Chenonceau** in the Loire Valley. Or spend two days in Normandy, marvelling at **Rouen's** Notre Dame cathedral, the **Bayeux** tapestry, sea-splashed **Mont St-Michel** and – should modern history be your passion – the **D-Day landing beaches**.

Day five, zoom south to view world-class cave art in the **Vézère Valley**. Key sites are around the towns of Les Eyzies-de-Tayac-Sireuil and Montignac. Or base yourself in Sarlat-la-Canéda, showcasing some of France's best medieval architecture with a fabulous food market to boot. Day seven, experience 12 hours in **Bordeaux**, not missing wine tasting in the stunning La Cité du Vin. Next day, drive three hours to the walled city of **Carcassonne**, Roman **Nîmes** and the **Pont du Gard.** Finish on the French Riviera with a casino flutter in Grace Kelly's **Monaco**, a portside aperitif in Brigitte Bardot's **St-Tropez** and a stroll through Matisse's **Nice**.

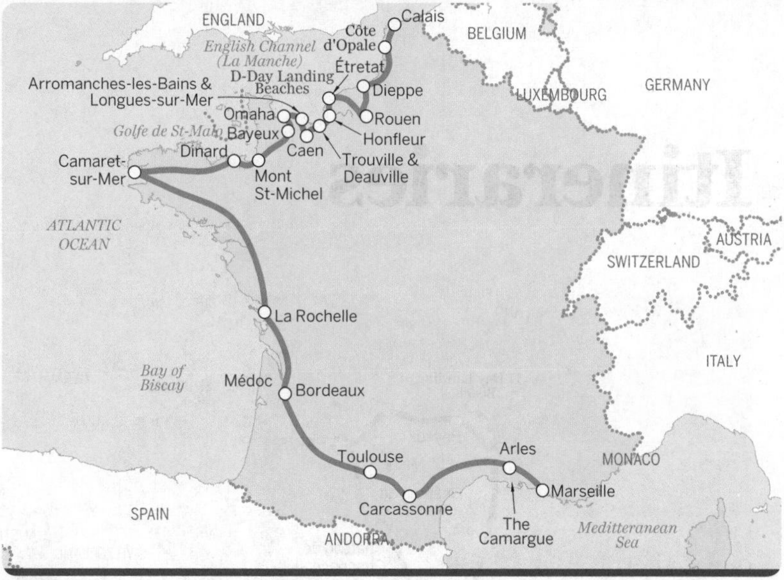

2 WEEKS The Channel to the Med

Step off the boat in **Calais** and be seduced by 40km of cliffs, sand dunes and windy beaches on the spectacular **Côte d'Opale**. Speed southwest, taking in a fish lunch in **Dieppe**, a sensational cathedral visit in **Rouen**, or a picturesque cliffside picnic in **Étretat** en route to your overnight stop: your choice of the pretty Normandy seaside resorts of **Honfleur**, **Deauville** or **Trouville**. Spend two days here: a boat trip beneath the breathtaking Pont de Normandie, shopping for fresh fish and seafood at Trouville's waterfront Poissonnerie, and hobnobbing with Parisians on Deauville's chic star-studded boardwalk are essentials.

Devote day three to Normandy's D-Day landing beaches. Start with the Mémorial – Un Musée pour la Paix in **Caen**, the best single museum devoted to the Battle of Normandy, then follow a westward arc along the beach-laced coast, taking in the caisson-strewn sands at **Arromanches-les-Bains**, gun installations at **Longues-sur-Mer**, and the now-serene 7km-long stretch of 'bloody **Omaha**'. Come dusk, rejuvenate spent emotions over fresh scallops and *calvados* (apple-flavoured brandy). Or, if art is more your cup of tea, skip the beaches and go for the stunning representation of 11th-century warfare embroidered across 70m of tapestry in **Bayeux**.

Day four and iconic **Mont St-Michel** beckons – hiking barefoot across the sands here is exhilarating. End the week in Brittany with a flop in an old-fashioned beach tent in **Dinard** and a bracing stroll on spectacular headlands around **Camaret-sur-Mer**.

Week two begins with a long drive south to chic **La Rochelle** for a lavish seafood feast. Spend a night here, continuing the gourmet theme as you wend your way south through Médoc wine country to **Bordeaux**. Next morning, stop in 'ville rose' **Toulouse** through which the undisputed queen of canals, Canal du Midi, runs, and/or **Carcassonne** before hitting the Med. The Camargue – a wetland of flamingos, horses and incredible bird life – is a unique patch of coast to explore and Van Gogh thought so too. Follow in his footsteps around **Arles**, before continuing onto the ancient, enigmatic and totally fascinating port city of **Marseille**.

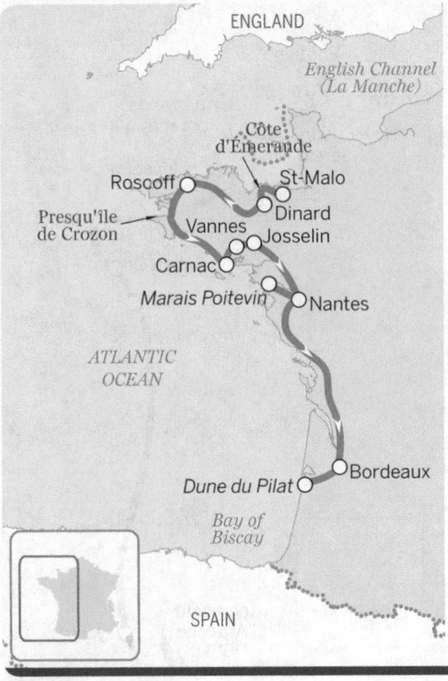

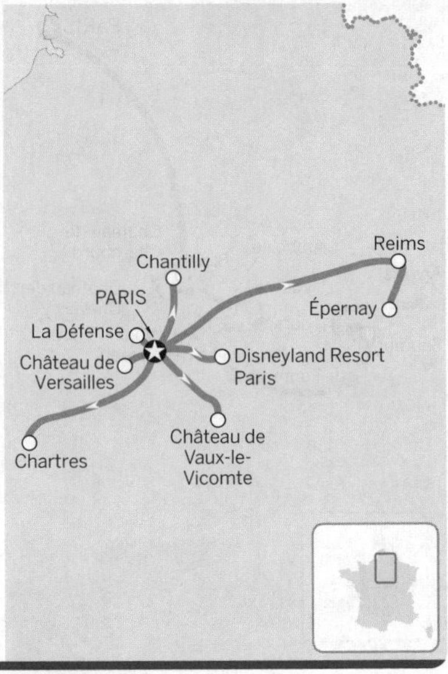

1 WEEK Brittany to Bordeaux

It starts fresh off the boat in **St-Malo**, a walled city with sturdy Vauban ramparts that beg exploration at sunset. Linger at least a day in this attractive port. Walk across at low tide to Île du Grand Bé and lap up great views atop a 14th-century tower in pretty St-Servan. Motor along the Côte d'Émeraude the next day, stopping in **Dinard** en route to **Roscoff** 200km west. Devote day four to discovering Brittany's famous cider and megaliths around **Carnac**, the enchanting medieval town of **Vannes** overlooking the glittering island-studded Golfe du Morbihan, and the turreted medieval castle in **Josselin**. Push south along the Atlantic coast, stopping in **Nantes** if you like big cities (and riding mechanical elephants), or continuing to the peaceful waterways of Green Venice, aka the **Marais Poitevin**. **Bordeaux** is your final destination for day six, from where a bevy of Bordeaux wine-tasting trips tempt. End the journey on a high atop Europe's highest sand dune, **Dune du Pilat**, near oyster-famed Arcachon.

1 WEEK A Week Around Paris

Day one has to be France's grandest castle, **Château de Versailles**, and its vast gardens. Second day, feast on France's best-preserved medieval basilica and the dazzling blue stained glass in **Chartres**, an easy train ride away. Small-town **Chantilly** is a good spot to combine a laid-back lunch with a Renaissance château, formal French gardens and – if you snagged tickets in advance – an enchanting equestrian performance.

On the fourth day, catch the train to elegant **Reims** in the heart of the Champagne region. Scale its cathedral for dazzling views before tucking into the serious business of Champagne tasting. Dedicated bubbly aficionados can hop the next day to **Épernay**, France's other great Champagne city.

On day six, enjoy a lazy start then catch an afternoon fountain show at **Château de Vaux-le-Vicomte**, followed by a candlelit tour of the château. End the week with a look at futuristic **La Défense** or, for those with kids, **Disneyland Resort Paris**.

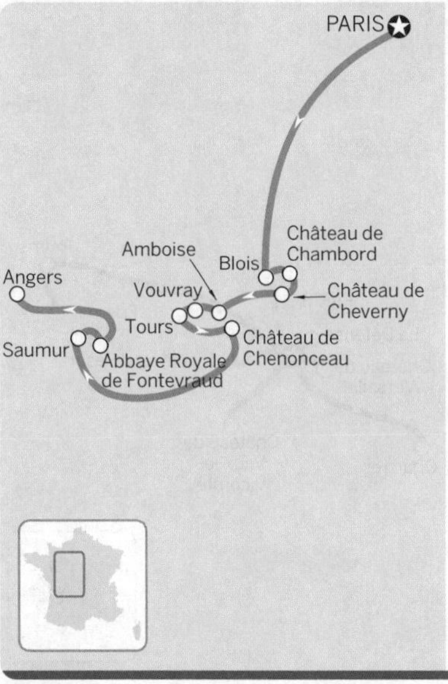

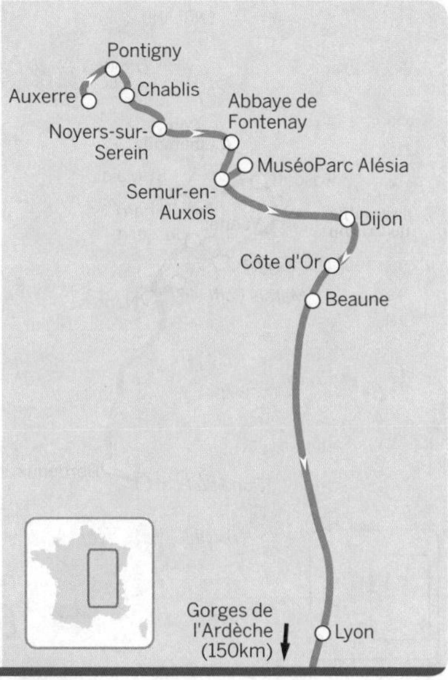

5 DAYS Along the Loire Valley

For five days of aristocratic pomp and architectural splendour, there is no finer destination than the château-studded Loire Valley. Make your first base the regal city of **Blois**, from where you can maximize the limited amount of time you have by hooking up with an organised château tour: queen of all castles **Château de Chambord** and the charmingly classical **Château de Cheverny**, with its extraordinary furnishings and dramatic hound-packed kennels, make a great combo. Day three, follow France's longest river southwest to **Amboise**, final home of Leonardo da Vinci. If wine is a love, build some *dégustation* (tasting) of local **Vouvray** wines in vineyards into your itinerary on the way to solidly bourgeois **Tours**, an easy hop from Amboise. From here **Château de Chenonceau** is beautifully strung across the River Cher 34km east. End your trip with France's elite riding school in **Saumur** and the movingly simple abbey church **Abbaye Royale de Fontevraud** – or push on northwest to **Angers** with its black château and Apocalypse tapestry. Château de Verrières in Saumur is a befitting overnight address in this château-rich neck of the woods.

6 DAYS Burgundy & Beyond

Red-wine lovers can enjoy the fruits of Burgundy with this itinerary. Begin in the Roman river port of **Auxerre**, 170km southeast of Paris. Explore its ancient abbey and Gothic cathedral, and cycle along towpaths. On day two consider an easy bike ride to a wonderful piece of Cistercian architecture in pretty **Pontigny**, 25km north. Stay overnight or push on to **Chablis**, where more bike rides and gentle hikes between Burgundy vineyards await – allow ample time to taste the seven *grands crus* of this well-known wine-making town. Day four, meander south to the picture-postcard village of **Noyers-sur-Serein**, then head east to the breathtaking, Unesco-listed **Abbaye de Fontenay**, before winding up for the night in **Semur-en-Auxois**, 25km south. **MuséoParc Alésia**, where Julius Caesar defeated Gaulish chief Vercingétorix in 52 BC, is not far from here and makes for a fascinating day out. On the last day, discover **Dijon** and its beautiful medieval and Renaissance buildings. From here, should you have more time, take a road trip through the wine-making area of **Côte d'Or** to **Beaune**, or south to **Lyon** in the Rhône Valley and beyond to the rugged **Gorges de l'Ardèche**.

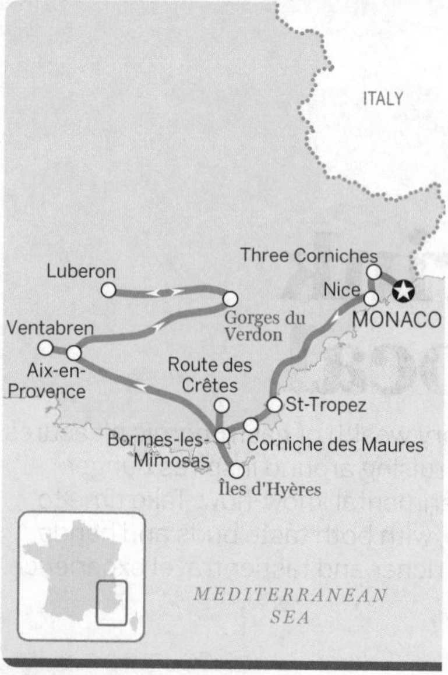

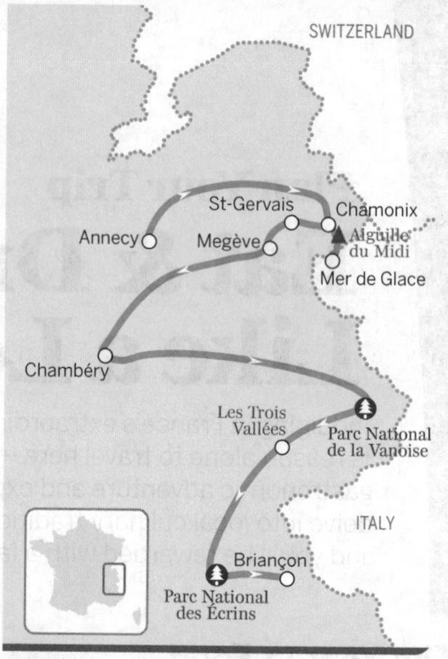

10 DAYS The South of France

For sun, sea and celebrity action, hit France's hot south. Start in **Nice**, star of the coastline that unfurls in a pageant of belle-époque palaces and iconic sands. Drive along the Riviera's trio of legendary **corniches** – coastal views are mind-blowing – and on day three take the train to glitzy **Monaco**. Then move to fishing port **St-Tropez** where million-dollar yachts jostle for space with street artists. Rise early the next morning for the place des Lices market and frolic away the afternoon on the sand at Plage de Pampelonne. Day six is a toss-up between a dramatic drive along the **Corniche des Maures** to **Bormes-les-Mimosas** and the staggering **Route des Crêtes** mountain pass, or a boat trip to the *très belle* **Îles d'Hyères**. Head inland next to **Aix-en-Provence**, a canvas of graceful 19th-century architecture, stylish cafes and hidden squares. From Aix, it's a hop and a skip to **Ventabren** where lunch or dinner alfresco at La Table de Ventabren is what eating in Provence is all about. Devote your last two days to the wild **Gorges du Verdon**, Europe's largest canyon, two hours' drive northeast, or the gentler **Luberon** with its bounty of photogenic hilltop villages.

5 DAYS Spring in the Alps

A trip to the French Alps often translates as one week of skiing in one place. Yet take time to explore the region after the snow has melted – spring or early summer is best – and you'll be pleasantly surprised. Warm up with old-town ambling, lakeside strolling and warm-weather swimming in fairy-tale **Annecy**, a beautiful medieval town just 45km from Geneva, Switzerland. Day two, shift to **Chamonix** at the foot of Mont Blanc, Europe's highest peak: ride a cable car up to the **Aiguille du Midi** or, if the sky is not crystal-clear, ride a cog railway up to the **Mer de Glace** glacier. Yet more unforgettable views of Mont Blanc seduce along hiking trails in the chic, picturesque Alpine villages of **St-Gervais and Megève**. Let the adrenalin rip, or push on via the ancient Savoyard stronghold of **Chambéry** to the **Parc National de la Vanoise**, where spectacular mountain biking in **Les Trois Vallées** will please the most jaded outdoor junkie. A fitting finale to your Alpine foray is the stunning drive through the **Parc National des Écrins** to **Briançon**, perhaps the loveliest of all the medieval villages in the French Alps, famous for its Vauban fortifications.

Plan Your Trip

Eat & Drink Like a Local

Indulging in France's extraordinary wealth of gastronomic pleasures is reason alone to travel here – cruising around inspires hunger, gastronomic adventure and experimental know-how. Take time to delve into local culinary tradition, with both taste buds and hands, and you'll be rewarded with a far richer and tastier travel experience.

The Year in Food

Feasting happens year-round, and what's cooking changes with the seasons.

Spring (March–May)

Markets burst with asparagus, artichokes and fresh goat's cheese, Easter cooks up traditional lamb for lunch, and the first strawberries redden.

Summer (June–August)

Melons, cherries, peaches, apricots, fresh figs, garlic and tomatoes brighten market stalls. Breton shallots are hand-harvested, and on the coasts, diners gorge on seafood and shellfish.

Autumn (September–November)

The Camargue's nutty red rice is harvested. Normandy apples fall from trees to make France's finest cider and the chestnut harvest begins in the Ardèche, Cévennes and Corsica. In damp woods, mushrooming and the game season begins.

Winter (December–February)

Nets are strung beneath silvery groves in Provence and Corsica to catch olives. Markets in the Dordogne and Provence sell black truffles, and in the Alps, skiers dip into cheese fondue. Christmas means Champagne and oysters, foie gras, chestnut-stuffed turkey and yule logs.

Food Experiences

Meals of a Lifetime

- **Restaurant Guy Savoy** (p136) Triple-starred Paris flagship of Guy Savoy, at home in the gorgeously refurbished neoclassical Monnaie de Paris.
- **Le Bistrot** (p485) Gastronome paradise in Chamonix, French Alps.
- **Le Vieux Logis** (p568) Local Dordogne products, including seasonal truffles, crafted into creative cuisine; in season, join a truffle hunt or the chef at the truffle market.
- **Le Coquillage** (p260) Triple-starred Michelin temple set to French perfection in a château in Brittany; cooking school too.
- **La Fleur de Sel** (p242) A celebration of the underrated culinary riches of Normandy, prepared by a talented Honfleur native in his hometown.
- **Auberge du Père Bise** (p499) Alpine bounty and the fruits of Lake Annecy raised to rare heights by Sophie Bise, scion of a long line of chefs.

Cheap Treats

- **Croque monsieur** Toasted ham and cheese sandwich; cheesy *croques madames* are egg-topped.
- **Chestnuts** Served piping hot in paper bags on street corners in winter.

➡ **Socca** Chickpea-flour pancake typical to Nice in the French Riviera.

➡ **Pan bagnat** Crusty Niçois tuna sandwich dripping in fruity green olive oil.

➡ **Flammekueche** *(tarte flambée* in French) Alsatian thin-crust pizza dough topped with sour cream, onions and bacon.

➡ **Ice cream** By the best *glaciers* (ice-cream makers) in France: Berthillon (p131) in Paris, Fenocchio (p831) in Nice; Glaces Geronimi (p884) or Raugi (p875) in Corsica; La Martinière (p619) in St-Martin de Ré. Myrtle, chestnut, lavender, artichoke or camembert ice anyone?

➡ **Crêpes** Large, round, thin sweet pancakes cooked at street-corner stands while you wait.

➡ **Galettes** Savoury, gluten-free pancakes, made with buckwheat flour and typically served with *fromage* (cheese) and *jambon* (ham).

➡ **Pastilles de Vichy** Ubiquitous little sweeties with a history of healing powers!

➡ **Beignets au brocciu** Corsican deep-fried doughnuts, sweet or savoury, filled with the island's local cream cheese.

Dare to Try

➡ **Andouillette** Big fat sausage made from minced pig intestine; try it in Troyes or Lyon, France's gastronomic heart and known for its piggy cuisine.

➡ **Oursins** (sea urchins) Caught and eaten west of Marseille in February.

➡ **Epoisses de Bourgogne** Create a stink with France's undisputed smelliest cheese from Burgundy.

➡ **Escargots** (snails) Eat them in Burgundy, shells stuffed with garlic and parsley butter, and oven-baked.

➡ **Cuisses de grenouilles** (frogs' legs) Catching wild frogs and frog farming have been outlawed in France since 1980, but frogs' legs are imported from Southeast Asia, ensuring this French culinary tradition is alive and kicking.

➡ **Foie** (liver) Die-hard aficionados in the Dordogne eat fresh fattened duck or goose liver, raw and chilled, with a glass of sweet Monbazillac wine.

➡ **Pieds de cochon** (pig trotters) Just that, or go for the oven-baked trotters of a *mouton* (sheep) or *veau* (calf).

➡ **Presskopf** Alsatian head cheese or brawn, made with a calf or pig's head.

Local Specialities

Gourmet appetites know no bounds in France, paradise for food lovers with its varied cuisine, markets and local gusto for dining well. Go to Burgundy for hearty wine-based cooking, Brittany and the Atlantic Coast for seafood, and Basque Country for a slice of Spanish spice.

Normandy

Cream, apples and cider are the essentials of Norman cuisine, which sees mussels simmered in cream and a splash of cider to make *moules à la crème normande* and tripe thrown in the slow pot with cider and vegetables to make *tripes à la mode de Caen*. Creamy Camembert is the local cow's milk cheese, and on the coast *coquilles St-Jacques* (scallops) and *huîtres* (oysters) rule the seafood roost. Apples are the essence of the region's main tipples: tangy cider and the potent *calvados* (apple brandy), exquisite straight or splashed on apple sorbet.

Burgundy

Vine-wealthy Burgundy honours a culinary trinity of beef, red wine and Dijon mustard. Savour bœuf bourguignon (beef marinated and cooked in young red wine with mushrooms, onions, carrots and bacon), followed by the pick of Burgundy AOC cheeses. Or eat a snail, traditionally served by the dozen and oven-baked in their shells with butter, garlic and parsley – mop the juices up with bread.

Wine tasting in the Côte d'Or vineyards, source of world-famous Côte de Nuits and Côte de Beaune wines, is obligatory when in Burgundy; laid-back Irancy, less known around the globe but much-loved by locals, is an insider favourite.

The Dordogne

This southwest region is famous for its indulgent black truffles and poultry, especially ducks and geese, whose fattened livers are turned into *pâté de foie gras*, which, somewhat predictably, comes straight or flavoured with Cognac and truffles. *Confit de canard* and *confit d'oie* are duck or goose joints cooked very slowly in their own fat. Snails are another tasty treat – savour one stuffed with foie gras. Walnuts from the region's abundant walnut groves go into *eau de noix* (caramel-coloured walnut liqueur).

Lyon

All too often Lyon is dubbed France's gastronomic capital. And while it doesn't compete with France's capital when it comes to variety of international cuisine, it certainly holds its own when it comes to titillating taste buds with the unusual and inventive. Take the age-old repertoire of feisty, often pork-driven dishes served in the city's legendary *bouchons* (small bistros): breaded fried tripe, big fat *andouillettes* (pig-intestine sausage), silk-weaver's brains (a herbed cheese spread, not brains at all) – there is no way you can ever say Lyonnais cuisine is run of the mill. A lighter, less meaty speciality is *quenelle de brochet,* a poached dumpling made of freshwater fish (usually pike) and served with sauce Nantua (a cream and freshwater-crayfish sauce).

Equally fine is the Lyonnais wine list where very fine Côtes de Rhône reds vie for attention with local Brouilly and highly esteemed Mâcon reds from nearby Burgundy. In *bouchons,* local Beaujolais is mixed with a dash of blackcurrant liqueur to make a blood-red *communard* aperitif.

Alsace

No Alsatian dish is more classic than *choucroute alsacienne* or *choucroute garnie* – sauerkraut flavoured with juniper berries and served hot with sausages, bacon, pork and/or ham knuckle. It's meaty, Teutonic and served in *winstubs* (traditional Alsatian taverns). *Wädele braisé au pinot noir* (ham knuckles braised in wine) also come with sauerkraut. Crack open a bottle of light citrusy sylvaner, crisp dry Alsatian riesling or full-bodied pinot noir to accompany either, and round off the filling feast with a *tarte alsacienne,* a scrumptious custard tart made with local fruit such as mirabelles (sweet yellow plums) or *quetsches* (a variety of purple plum). Beer might be big in Alsace but it's a big no-no when it comes to sauerkraut.

Sweet tooths will adore Alsatian gingerbread and Kougelhopf (sugared, ring-shaped raisin cake).

Provence & the Riviera

Cuisine in this sun-baked land is laden with tomatoes, melons, cherries, peaches, olives, Mediterranean fish and Alpine cheese. Farmers gather at the weekly market to sell their fruit and vegetables, woven garlic plaits, dried herbs displayed in stubby coarse sacks, and olives stuffed with a multitude of edible sins. *À la Provençal* still means anything with a generous dose of garlic-seasoned tomatoes, while a simple *filet mignon* sprinkled with olive oil and rosemary fresh from the garden makes the same magnificent Sunday lunch it did generations ago.

Yet there are exciting culinary contrasts in this region, which see fishermen return with the catch of the day in seafaring Marseille; grazing bulls and paddy fields in the Camargue; lambs in the Alpilles; black truffles in the Vaucluse; cheese made from cow's milk in Alpine pastures; and an Italianate accent to cooking in seaside Nice.

Bouillabaisse, Marseille's mighty meal of fish stew, is Provence's most famous contribution to French cuisine. The chowder must contain at least three kinds of fresh saltwater fish, cooked for about 10 minutes in a broth containing onions, tomatoes, saffron and various herbs, and eaten as a main course with toasted bread and *rouille* (a spicy red mayonnaise of olive oil, garlic and chilli peppers).

The fish stew *bourride* is similar to bouillabaisse but has fewer ingredients, a less prescriptive recipe, and often a slightly creamier sauce. It's customarily served with *aïoli* (garlic mayonnaise).

When in Provence, do as the Provençaux do: drink pastis. An aniseed-flavoured, 45%-alcohol drink, it was invented in Marseille by industrialist Paul Ricard in 1932. Amber-coloured in the bottle, it turns milky white when mixed with water. An essential lunch or dinner companion is a chilled glass of the region's irresistibly pink, AOC Côtes de Provence rosé wine.

Brittany

Brittany is a paradise for seafood lovers (think lobster, scallops, sea bass, turbot, mussels and oysters from Cancale) as well as kids, thanks to the humble crêpe and *galette,* an ancient culinary tradition that has long-ruled Breton cuisine. Pair a sweet wheat-flour pancake or savoury buckwheat *galette* with *une bolée* (a stubby terracotta goblet) of apple-rich Breton cider, and taste buds enter gourmet heaven. Royal Guillevic and ciders produced by the Domaine de Kervéguen are excellent quality,

artisanal ciders to try. If cider is not your cup of tea, order a local beer like Coreff or non-alcoholic *lait ribot* (fermented milk). *Chouchen* (hydromel), a fermented honey liqueur, is a typical Breton aperitif.

Cheese is not big, but *la beurre de Bretagne* (Breton butter) is. Traditionally sea-salted and creamy, a knob of it naturally goes into crêpes, *galettes* and the most outrageously buttery cake you're likely to ever taste in your life – *kouign amann* (Breton butter cake). Bretons, unlike the rest of the French, even butter their bread. Butter handmade by Jean-Yves Bourdier – buy it at his shop in St-Malo (p257) – ends up on tables of top restaurants around the world.

Seaweed is another Breton culinary curiosity, and 80% of French shallots are grown here.

Languedoc-Roussillon

No dish better evokes Languedoc than *cassoulet,* an earthy cockle-warming stew of white beans and meat that fires passionate debate. Everyone knows best which type of bean and meat hunk should be thrown in the *cassole,* the traditional earthenware dish it is cooked and brought to the table in. Otherwise this region's trademark cuisine *campagnarde* (country cooking) sees fishermen tending lagoon oyster beds on the coast, olives being pressed in gentle hills inland, blue-veined 'king of cheeses' ripening in caves in Roquefort, geese and gaggles of ducks fattening around Toulouse, sheep munching in salty marsh meadows around Montpellier, and mushrooms growing in forests.

In Uzès, *croquignoles* (shortbread biscuits adorned with a sweet almond or hazelnut and covered in orange syrup after baking) are a sweet treat. A Spanish accent gives cuisine in neighbouring Roussillon a fiery twist of exuberance.

Basque Country

Among the essential ingredients of Basque cooking are the deep-red Espelette chillies that add bite to many dishes, including the dusting on the signature *jambon de Bayonne,* the locally prepared Bayonne ham. Eating out in this part of France near Spain is a delight thanks to its many casual *pintxo* (tapas) bars serving garlic prawns, spicy chorizo sausages and other local dishes tapas-style. Wash the whole lot down with a glass of local cider *(sidrea* in Basque), lighter, sweeter and more

MENU DECODER

Carte	Menu, as in the written list of what's cooking, listed in the order you'd eat it: starter, main course, cheese then dessert.
Menu	Not at all what it means in English, *le menu* in French is a two- or three-course meal at a fixed price. It's by far the best-value dining and most bistros and restaurants chalk one on the board. Lunch *menus* – usually incredibly good value – occasionally include a glass of wine and/or coffee; dinner *menus* in gastronomic restaurants sometimes pair a perfectly matched glass of wine with each course.
À la carte	Order whatever you fancy from the menu (as opposed to choosing a fixed *menu*).
Formule	Not to be confused with a *menu, une formule* is a cheaper lunchtime option comprising a main plus starter or dessert.
Plat du jour	Dish of the day, invariably good value.
Menu enfant	Two- or three-course kids' meal at a fixed price (generally for children up to the age of 12); usually includes a soft drink.
Menu dégustation	Fixed-price tasting *menu* served in many top-end restaurants, consisting of five to seven modestly sized courses.
Amuse-bouche	A complimentary savoury morsel intended to excite and ignite taste buds, served in top-end and gastronomic restaurants at the very beginning of a meal.
Entrée	Starter, appetiser.
Plat	Main course.
Fromage	Cheese, accompanied with fresh bread (never crackers and no butter); always served after the main course and *before* dessert.
Dessert	Just that, served *after* cheese.

sparkling than ciders in northern France, best poured in a glass at arm's length. *Izarra* is a much-loved herbal liqueur.

Basques love cakes, especially *gâteau basque* (layer cake filled with cream or cherry jam). Then there's Bayonne chocolate...

Corsica

The hills and mountains of the island of Corsica have always been ideal for raising stock, and the dense Corsican underbrush called the *maquis* is made up of shrubs mixed with wild herbs. These raw materials come together to create aromatic trademark Corsican dishes like *stufatu* (fragrant mutton stew), *premonata* (beef braised with juniper berries) and *lonzo* (Corsican sausage cooked with white beans, white wine and herbs).

How to Eat & Drink

It pays to know what and how much to eat, and when – adopting the local culinary pace is key to savouring every last exquisite moment of the French day.

When to Eat

➡ **Petit déjeuner (breakfast)** The French kick-start the day with a *tartine* (slice of baguette smeared with unsalted butter and jam) and *un café* (espresso), long milky *café au lait* or – especially kids – hot chocolate. In hotels you get a real cup but in French homes, coffee and hot chocolate are drunk from a cereal bowl – perfect bread-dunking terrain. Croissants (eaten straight, never with butter or jam) are a weekend treat along with brioches (sweet breads), *pains au chocolat* (chocolate-filled croissants) and other *viennoiserie* (sweet baked goods).

➡ **Déjeuner (lunch)** A meal few French would go without. The traditional main meal of the day, lunch translates as a starter and main course with wine, followed by an espresso. Sunday lunch is a long, languid affair taking several hours. Indeed, a fully fledged, traditional French meal – *déjeuner* or *dîner* – can comprise six courses, each accompanied by a different wine. Standard restaurant lunch hours are noon to 2.30pm.

➡ **Aperitif** The *apéro* (predinner drink) is sacred. Urban cafes and bars get packed out from around 5pm onwards as workers relax over a chit-chat-fuelled *kir* (white wine sweetened with blackcurrant syrup), glass of red or beer. Come weekends, a leisurely noon-time *apéro* before lunch is equally acceptable – and oh so pleasurable.

➡ **Goûter** An afternoon snack, devoured with particular relish by French children. A slab of milk chocolate inside a wedge of baguette is a traditional favourite.

➡ **Dîner (dinner)** Traditionally lighter than lunch, but a meal that is increasingly treated as the main meal of the day. Standard restaurant times are 7pm to 10.30pm.

Where to Eat

➡ **Auberge** Country inn serving traditional fare, often attached to a small hotel.

➡ **Ferme auberge** Working farm that cooks up meals from local farm products; usually only dinner and frequently only by reservation.

➡ **Bistro** (also spelled *bistrot*) Anything from a pub or bar with snacks and light meals to a small, fully fledged restaurant.

➡ **Neobistro** Trendy in Paris and large cities where this contemporary take on the traditional bistro embraces everything from checked-tablecloth tradition to contemporary minimalism.

➡ **Brasserie** Much like a cafe except it serves full meals, drinks and coffee from morning until 11pm or later. Typical fare includes *choucroute* (sauerkraut) and *moules frites* (mussels and fries).

➡ **Restaurant** Born in Paris in the 18th century, restaurants today serve lunch and dinner five or six days a week.

➡ **Buffet** (or *buvette*) Kiosk, usually at train stations and airports, selling drinks, filled baguettes and snacks.

➡ **Cafe** Basic light snacks as well as drinks.

➡ **Crêperie** (also *galetterie*) Casual address specialising in sweet crêpes and savoury *galettes* (buckwheat crêpes).

➡ **Salon de thé** Trendy tearoom often serving light lunches (quiche, salads, cakes, pies and pastries) as well as green, black and herbal teas.

➡ **Table d'hôte** (literally 'host's table') Some of the most charming B&Bs serve *table d'hôte* too, a delicious homemade meal of set courses with little or no choice.

➡ **Winstub** Cosy wine tavern in Alsace serving traditional Alsatian cooking and local wines.

➡ **Estaminet** Flemish-style eatery of Flanders and *le nord*, cooking up regional fare.

Plan Your Trip

Travel with Children

Be it the kid-friendly extraordinaire capital or rural hinterland, France spoils families with its rich mix of cultural sights, activities and entertainment – some paid for, some free. To get the most out of travelling *en famille*, plan ahead.

Best Regions for Kids

Paris

Interactive museums, choice dining for every taste and budget, and beautiful parks at every turn make the French capital a top choice for families.

Normandy

Beaches, boats and some great stuff for history-mad kids and teens give this northern region plenty of family lure.

Brittany

More beaches, boats, pirate-perfect islands and bags of good old-fashioned outdoor fun.

French Alps & the Jura Mountains

Winter in this mountainous region in western France translates as one giant outdoor (snowy) playground – for all ages.

French Riviera & Monaco

A vibrant arts scene, a vivacious cafe culture and a beach-laced shore riddled with seafaring activities keeps kids of all ages on their toes.

Corsica

Sailing, kayaking, walking, biking, or simply dipping your toes or snorkel in clear turquoise waters: life on this island is fairy-tale *belle* (beautiful).

France for Kids

Savvy parents can find kid-appeal in almost every sight in France. Skip the formal guided tour of Mont St-Michel, for example, and hook up with a walking guide to lead you and the children barefoot across the sand to the abbey; trade the daytime queues at the Eiffel Tower for a tour after dark with teens; don't dismiss wine tasting in Provence or Burgundy outright – rent bicycles and turn it into a family bike ride instead. The opportunities are endless.

Museums & Monuments

Many Paris museums organise creative ateliers (workshops) for children, parent-accompanied or solo. These are themed, require booking, last 1½ to two hours, and cost €5 to €20 per child. French children have no school Wednesday afternoon, so most workshops happen at this time, weekends and daily during school holidays. Most cater for kids aged seven to 14 years, although art tours at the Louvre start at four years and at the Musée d'Orsay, five years.

Countrywide, when buying tickets at museums and monuments, ask about children's activity sheets – most have something to hook kids. Another winner is to arm your gadget-mad child (from six years) with an audioguide. Older children can check out what apps a museum or monument might have for smartphones and tablets.

Outdoor Activities

Once the kids are out of nappies, skiing in the French Alps is the obvious family choice. Ski school École du Ski Français (www.esf.net) initiates kids in the art of snow plough (group or private lessons, half or full day) from four years old, and many resorts open fun-driven *jardins de neige* (snow gardens) to children from three years old. Families with kids aged under 10 will find smaller resorts including Les Gets, Avoriaz (car-free), La Clusaz, Chamrousse and Le Grand Bornand easier to navigate and better value than larger ski stations. Then, of course, there is all the fun of the fair off-piste: ice skating, sledging, snowshoeing, mushing, indoor swimming pools…

The French Alps and Pyrenees are prime walking areas. Tourist offices have information on easy, well-signposted family walks – or get in touch with a local guide. In Chamonix, the cable-car ride and two-hour hike to Lac Blanc followed by a dip in the Alpine lake is a DIY family favourite; as are the mountain-discovery half-days for ages three to seven, and outdoor-adventure days for ages eight to 12 run by Cham' Aventure (p479). As with skiing, smaller places such as the Parc Naturel Régional du Massif des Bauges cater much better to young families than the big names everyone knows.

White-water sports and canoeing are doable for children aged seven and older; the French Alps, Provence and Massif Central are key areas. Mountain biking is an outdoor thrill that teens can share – try Morzine. Or dip into some gentle sea kayaking around *calanques* (deep rocky inlets), below cliffs and into caves in the Mediterranean, a family activity suitable for kids aged four and upwards. Marseille in Provence and Bonifacio on Corsica are hot spots to rent the gear and get afloat.

TOP WEBSITES

➡ **Familiscope** (www.familiscope.fr) Definitive family-holiday planner: endless activity, outing and entertainment listings.

➡ **Tots to Travel** (http://totstotravel.co.uk) Self-catering properties vetted by a team of trained mums.

➡ **Baby-friendly Boltholes** (www.babyfriendlyboltholes.co.uk) This London-based enterprise specialises in sourcing charming and unique family accommodation.

➡ **Baby Goes 2** (www.babygoes2.com) Why, where, how-to travel guide aimed squarely at families.

Entertainment

Tourist offices can tell you what's on – and the repertoire is impressive: puppet shows alfresco, children's theatres, children's films at cinemas Wednesday afternoon and weekends, street buskers, illuminated monuments after dark, an abundance of music festivals and so on. Sure winners are the *son et lumière* (sound-and-light) shows projected on some Renaissance châteaux in the Loire Valley; the papal palace in Avignon; and cathedral facades in Rouen, Chartres and Amiens. Outstanding after-dark illuminations that never fail to enchant include Paris' Eiffel Tower and Marseille's MuCEM.

Dining Out

French children, accustomed to three-course lunches at school, expect a starter *(entrée)*, main course *(plat)* and dessert as their main meal of the day. They know the difference between Brie and Camembert, and eat lettuce, grated carrot and other salads no problem. Main meals tend to be meat 'n' veg or pasta, followed by dessert and/or a slice of cheese. Classic French mains loved by children include *gratin dauphinois* (sliced potatoes oven-baked in cream), *escalope de veau* (breaded pan-fried veal) and *boeuf bourguignon* (beef stew). Fondue and *raclette* (melted cheese served with potatoes and cold meats) become favourites from about five years, and *moules frites* (mussels and fries) a couple of years later.

Children's *menus* (fixed meals at a set price) are common, although anyone in France for more than a few days will soon tire of the ubiquitous spaghetti bolognaise or *saucisse* (sausage), or *steak haché* (beef burger) and *frites* (fries) followed by ice cream that most feature. Don't be shy in asking for a half-portion of an adult main – restaurants generally oblige. Ditto in budget and midrange places to ask for a plate of *pâtes au beurre* (pasta with butter) for fussy or very young eaters.

Bread, specifically slices of baguette, accompanies every meal and in restaurants is brought to the table before or immediately after you've ordered – to the glee of children who wolf it down while they wait. Watch for the fight to ensue over who gets the *quignon* (the knobbly end bit, a hit with teething babies!).

It is perfectly acceptable to dine *en famille* after dark providing the kids don't run wild. Few restaurants open their doors, however, before 7.30pm or 8pm, making brasseries and cafes – many serve food continuously from 7am or 8am until midnight – more appealing for families with younger children. Some restaurants have high chairs and supply paper and pens for children to draw with while waiting for their meal.

France is fabulous snack-attack terrain. Parisian pavements are rife with crêpe stands and wintertime stalls selling hot chestnuts. Savoury *galettes* (pancakes) make for an easy light lunch, as does France's signature *croque monsieur* (toasted cheese and ham sandwich) served by most cafes and brasseries. *Goûter* (afternoon snack), devoured after school around 4.30pm, is golden for every French child and *salons de thé* (tearooms) serve a mouth-watering array of cakes, pastries and biscuits. Or go local: buy a baguette, rip off a chunk and pop a slab of chocolate inside.

Baby requirements are easily met. The choice of infant formula, soy and cow's milk, nappies (diapers) and jars of baby food in supermarkets and pharmacies is similar to any developed country, although opening hours are more limited (few shops open Sunday). Organic *(bio)* baby food is harder to find.

Drinks

Buy a fizzy drink for every child sitting at the table and the bill soars. Opt instead for a free *carafe d'eau* (jug of tap water) with meals and *un sirop* (flavoured fruit syrup) in between – jazzed up with *des glaçons* (some ice cubes) and *une paille* (a straw). Every self-respecting cafe and bar in France has dozens of syrup flavours to choose from: pomegranate-fuelled grenadine and pea-green *menthe* (mint) are French-kid favourites, but there are peach, raspberry, cherry, lemon and a rainbow of others too. Syrup is served diluted with water and, best up, costs a good €2 less than a coke. Expect to pay around €1.50 a glass.

Children's Highlights

Gastronomic Experiences

➡ **Ladurée, Paris** Indulge in cakes too beautiful to eat over afternoon tea at this historic tearoom. (p117)

➡ **Berthillon, Paris** Ice cream in dozens of different crazy flavours; other master ice-cream makers include Geronimi (p884) and Raugi (p875) in Corsica; Fenocchio (p831) in Nice; La Martinière (p619) in St-Martin de Ré. (p617)

➡ **Meert, Lile** Waffles with sweet vanilla cream, served since the 18th century. (p183)

➡ **La Cité du Vin, Bordeaux** Grape-juice tasting; parents taste the alcoholic equivalent. (p622)

➡ **La Bicyclette Bleue, La Dombes** Frogs' legs and a lakeside bike ride. (p469)

➡ **La Caracole, near Alès** (☎04 66 25 65 70; www.lacaracole.fr; St-Florent-sur-Auzonnet; adult/child €6/4; ⊙tours 3pm Sun Jul & Aug, by reservation other times) Snail discovery and tasting at Languedoc snail farm and museum.

➡ **Moutarderie Fallot, Beaune** Hand-mill mustard seeds with stone at this mustard factory. (p419)

➡ **Musée du Champignon, Saumur** Get acquainted with fabulous fungi at the mushroom farm in a cave. (p398)

➡ **L'Atelier du Chocolat, Bayonne** Watch chocolate being made in this Basque chocolate factory and museum. (p645)

Energy Burners

➡ **French Alps and Pyrenees** Skiing, snowboarding, sledging and dog-mushing (from four years). (p474)

➡ **Aiguille du Midi, Chamonix** Scale this mountain peak by gondola and cross glaciers into Italy (from four years). (p479)

➡ **Île de Ré** and **Île de Porquerolles** Explore an island by bike (over five years) or parent-pulled bike trailer (over one year). (p617 and p858)

➡ **Gorges du Verdon, Gorges du Tarn and Gorges de l'Ardèche** White-water sports (over seven years). (p817, p739 and p472)

➡ **Pont du Gard, Nîmes** Canoe (over seven years) beneath a Roman aquaduct, or along the Dordogne River around La Roque Gageac. (p714)

➡ **Parc National des Cévennes, Languedoc** Donkey trek (over 10 years) like Robert Louis Stevenson. (p737)

ADMISSION PRICES

There is no rule on how much and from what age children pay – many museums and monuments are free to under 18 years. In general, under fives don't pay (a noteworthy exception is Paris' must-do Cité des Sciences et de l'Industrie which costs from two years). Some museums offer money-saving family tickets, worth buying once you count two adults and two children or more.

➡ **Camargue, Provence** Ride horses with cowboys. (p778)

➡ **Acrobastille, Grenoble** Zip between trees on wires (from five years). (p510)

➡ **Val Thorens, French Alps** Fly along the world's highest zip wire (from eight years). (p501)

➡ **Domaine du Rayol, Corniche des Maures** Embark on a snorkelling safari on the French Riviera or snorkel off island shores on Porquerolles, Port-Cros and Corsica (from six years). (p856)

Best Free Stuff

➡ **Fort St-Jean, Marseille** Crazy about castles? No fortress is finer to explore. (p755)

➡ **Route des Vins d'Alsace, Alsace** Watch fairy tales come to life before your eyes in half-timbered, castle-topped villages. (p329)

➡ **Montpellier Parc Zoologique, Montpellier** Great city zoo. (p719)

➡ **Dune du Pilat, Atlantic Coast** Run wild on the largest 'sandcastle' any child is ever likely to see. (p637)

➡ **Festival Off, Avignon** World-class freebie festival that kids love; Lyon's Fête des Lumières (p457) and the Carnaval de Nice (p825) are other memorable favourites. (p795)

➡ **Maison Natale de Pierre Fermat, Toulouse Area** Learn about the life and works of 17th-century mathematician Pierre de Fermat through puzzles and games at this fun house museum. (p702)

Wildlife Watch

➡ **Pointe du Hourdel, Baie de Somme** Admire colonies of sandbank-lounging seals in northern France. (p198)

➡ **Parc National de la Vanoise, French Alps** Come face-to-face with ibex, chamois and cuddly, kid-pleasing marmots. (p506)

➡ **Parc National du Mercantour, Parc Animalier des Monts de Guéret and Parc du Gévaudan** Wolves.

➡ **Réserve Ornithologique du Teich, near Arcachon** Observe storks and kingfishers. (p638)

➡ **Centre de Réintroduction Cigognes & Loutres, Hunawihr** Discover the springtime joy of hatchling storks in Alsace. (p337)

➡ **Réserve de Bisons d'Europe, Mende** Watch European bison at close quarters. (p745)

➡ **Parc des Oiseaux, Les Dombes** Marvel at hundreds of local and exotic birds at this well-organised bird park near Lyon. (p469)

➡ **Belvédère des Vautours, Haut-Languedoc** Watch vultures soar through mountain skies in the wild Parc Naturel Régional des Grands Causses; the Parc National des Pyrénées (p674) and the Gorges du Verdon (p816) in Provence are other spots vultures love. (p741)

Rainy Days

➡ **Musée des Égouts, Paris** Romp through sewage tunnels with rats. (p95)

➡ **Musée Océanographique de Monaco** Stunning museum with aquarium dating to 1910. (p863)

➡ **Le Petit Musée Fantastique de Guignol, Lyon** Immerse yourself in the enchanting world of puppetry. (p451)

➡ **Aquarium La Rochelle** This Atlantic Coast aquarium is among France's finest; find others in Paris, Boulogne-sur-Mer, St-Malo, Montpellier, Brest, Lyon and Biarritz. (p613)

➡ **Les Catacombes, Paris** Ogle at thousands upon thousands of skulls (from 14 years). (p96)

➡ **Aven Armand, Languedoc** Discover the world's largest collection of stalactites. (p741)

➡ **Vézère Valley, Dordogne** Play cavemen in caves riddled with prehistoric art. (p575)

➡ **Cité de l'Océan, Biarritz** Delve into the depths of the ocean in southwest France. (p645)

➡ **Micropolis, near Millau** Inspect insects, lots of insects, in Languedoc. (p744)

➡ **Musée du Bonbon Haribo, Uzès** Sweeter than sweet, sweet museum. (p716)

➡ **Planète Musée du Chocolat, Biarrtiz** Handmade chocs, frothy hot chocolate and

the Basque Country history of the cacao bean. (p647)

➡ **Le Train Jaune, Pyrenees** Watch spectacular Pyrenean scenery unfold aboard this mythical mountain train. (p750)

Tech Experiences

➡ **Les Machines de l'Île de Nantes** Fly on a heron or ride a house-sized mechanical elephant at this fantastical workshop like no other. (p606)

➡ **Cité des Sciences, Paris** Sign up for a hands-on science workshop at the capital's leading science museum (from three years). (p79)

➡ **Palais de la Découverte, Paris** The other key address for budding young scientists (from 10 years) in the capital. (p65)

➡ **Le Vaisseau, Strasbourg** Science is never boring at this interactive science and technology museum in northern France. (p323)

➡ **Jean Luc Lagardère Airbus factory, Toulouse** Learn how planes are built (from six years). (p693)

➡ **Cité de l'Automobile and Cité du Train, Mulhouse** Enter wannabe-mechanic heaven. (p346)

➡ **Funiculaire du Capucin, Massif Central** This 100-year old funicular is one mighty cool way to climb the mountain of Le Mont-Dore. (p546)

Hands-On History & Culture

➡ **Jardin du Luxembourg, Paris** Time-travel to 1920s Paris: chase vintage sailboats with a stick like Parisian kids did a century ago. (p96)

➡ **MuséoParc Alésia, Burgundy** Relive the battle between Julius Caesar and Vercingétorix at Alésia in 52 BC at this first-class museum. (p423)

➡ **Grasse, Provence**) Become acquainted with the fine art of perfume in Grasse. (p845

➡ **Chantier Médiéval de Guédelon, Burgundy** Play medieval builders for real at this medieval construction site. (p430)

➡ **Ludo, Pont du Gard** Go Roman (over five years) near Nîmes in Provence. (p714)

➡ **Romagne '14-'18, Lorraine** Learn about WWI on battlefields near Verdun with an excellent guided walk for kids. (p361)

➡ **Cité des Machines du Moyen Age, Larressingle** Watch medieval siege machines in action. (p705)

➡ **Château de Chambord, Loire Valley** Search for virtual golden coins on a HistoPad (tablet computer) treasure hunt. (p374)

➡ **Ecomusée d'Alsace** Fascinating excursion into Alsatian country life and its time-honoured crafts. (p346)

Planning

When to Go

Consider the season and what you want to do/see: teen travel is a year-round affair (there's always something to entertain, regardless of the weather), but parents with younger kids will find the dry, pleasantly warm days of spring and early summer best suited to kidding around the park – every town has at least one *terrain de jeux* (playground).

France's festival repertoire (p26) is another planning consideration.

Accommodation

In Paris and larger towns and cities, serviced apartments equipped with washing machine and kitchen are suited to families with younger children. Countrywide, hotels with family or four-person rooms can be hard to find and need booking in advance. Functional, if soulless, chain hotels such as Formule 1, found on the outskirts of most large towns, always have a generous quota of family rooms and make convenient overnight stops for motorists driving from continental Europe or the UK (Troyes is a popular stopover for Brits en route to the Alps). Parents with just one child and/or a baby in tow will have no problem finding hotel accommodation – most midrange hotels have baby cots and are happy to put a child's bed in a double room for a minimal extra cost.

In rural France, family-friendly B&Bs and *fermes auberges* (farmstays) are convenient. For older children, tree houses decked out with bunk beds and Mongolian yurts create a real family adventure.

Camping is huge with French families: check into a self-catering mobile home, wooden chalet or tent; sit back on the verandah with glass of wine in hand and watch as your kids – wonderfully oblivious to any barriers language might pose – run around with new-found French friends.

Plan Your Trip
Outdoor Activities

France takes outdoor activities and elevates them to a fine art. In the birthplace of the Tour de France, the cycling is world class; in Mont Blanc's backyard, the skiing is second to none. And everywhere the hiking – from Corsica's coastal wilds to the volcanic cones of Auvergne – is, ah, just magnifique.

Best Outdoor Experiences

Best Off-Piste Descent

Whoop as you make a 2800m vertical descent on La Vallée Blanche in Chamonix – it's the ride of a lifetime.

Best Long-Distance Hike

Scale the wildest heights of the Pyrenees on the GR10, taking you from the Mediterranean to the Atlantic.

Best Cycling

Cruise past turreted châteaux and trace the curves of France's longest river in the Loire Valley.

Best Surf

Grab your board and hit the fizzing surf on the Atlantic Coast. Hossegor, north of Bayonne in French Basque Country, is big-wave heaven.

Best Kayaking & Canyoning

Make a splash in the astonishingly turquoise water of the Gorges du Verdon, Europe's largest canyon.

Skiing & Snowboarding

Just whisper the words 'French Alps' to a skier and watch their eyes light up. These mountains are the crème de la crème of European skiing, with the height edge, Mont Blanc views and more phenomenal pistes than you could ever hope to ski in a lifetime. Return time and again and you'll still never ski them all!

When to Go

The ski season goes with the snow, generally running from early or mid-December to around mid-April: the higher you go, the more snow-sure the resort and the longer the season. Crowds and room rates skyrocket during school holidays (Christmas, February half-term, Easter), so avoid these times if you can. There is summer glacier skiing in two resorts: Les Deux-Alpes and Val d'Isère (Espace Killy) from roughly mid-June to August.

Skiing & Snowboarding Destinations

Two of the world's largest ski areas are in France – Les Portes du Soleil, with 650km of runs, and Les Trois Vallées, with 600km of runs – as well as Europe's highest resort, Val Thorens (p503), at 2300m. Crowned by Mont Blanc, Chamonix skiing is the

stuff of legend, especially the do-before-you-die La Vallée Blanche (p482), a high-level 2.8km off-piste descent. Speed is of the essence in the glacier-licked free-rider favourites of Les Deux Alpes and Val d'Isère, as well as Alpe d'Huez, where the brave can tackle Europe's longest black run, the 16km La Sarenne.

Beginners and intermediates will find tamer skiing and boarding in the Pyrenees and Le Mont-Dore in Massif Central. Cross-country *(ski de fond)* is big in the thickly forested Jura, the host of the famous Transjurassienne race (p519), and at the Espace Nordique Sancy (p546) in the Massif Central, with 250km of trails to glide and skate on.

Ski Passes, Tuition & Equipment Hire

Prices for ski passes *(forfaits)* covering one or more ski areas vary according to the popularity of the resort, but can be anything from €32 to €54 per day and €120 to €282 per week (six days). Most passes are now hands-free, with a built-in chip that barriers detect, and can be prebooked online – a wise idea if you want to beat the slopeside queues. Children usually pay half-price and under-fives ski for free (bring proof of age).

All-inclusive rental will set you back around around €34/180 per one/six days for skiing or snowboarding equipment, and €15/65 for cross-country. Most resorts have one or more ski schools with certified instructors. Group lessons cost roughly €45/170 for one/six half-days. Kids can start learning from the age of four.

More Information

- **Where to Ski and Snowboard** (Chris Gill and Dave Watts; www.wheretoskiandsnowboard.com) Up-to-the minute guide to the slopes.
- **If You Ski** (www.ifyouski.com) Resort guides, ski deals and the lowdown on ski hire and schools.
- **Météo France** (www.meteofrance.com) Weather and daily avalanche forecast during the ski season.
- **École du Ski Français** (ESF; www.esf.net) The largest ski school in the world, with first-class tuition. Search by region.
- **France Montagnes** (www.france-montagnes.com) Official website of French ski resorts, with guides, maps, snow reports and more.

SKI RUN CLASSIFICATIONS

- **Green** Easy-peasy runs for absolute beginners.
- **Blue** Gentle, well-groomed runs for novices.
- **Red** Intermediate – groomed but steeper and narrower than blue runs.
- **Black** Difficult runs for experts, often with moguls and steep, near-vertical drops.

Hiking & Walking

When to Go

There is some form of walking available year-round in France. Spring and autumn are great seasons to hike in Corsica and on the French Riviera, which swelter in summer. The season is short and sweet in the Alps, running from mid-June to September.

Hiking & Walking Destinations

Hikers have a high time of it in the Alps, with mile after never-ending mile of well-marked trails. Lifts and cable cars take the sweat out of hiking here in summer. Chamonix (p479) is the trailhead for the epic 10-day, three-country Tour de Mont Blanc, but gentler paths, such as the Grand Balcon Sud (p482), also command Mont Blanc close-ups. Some of the finest treks head into the more remote, glacier-capped wilds of the Parc National des Écrins (p520), with 700km of trails – many following old shepherd routes – and the equally gorgeous Parc National de la Vanoise (p506).

But the Alps are tip-of-the-iceberg stuff. Just as lovely are walks threading through the softly rounded heights of the Vosges and through the forest-cloaked hills of Jura spreading down to Lake Geneva. The extinct volcanoes in the Auvergne, interwoven with 13 Grandes Randonnées (long-distance footpaths), and the mist-shrouded peaks and swooping forested valleys of the Parc National des Pyrénées (p674) offer fine walking and blissful solitude. In the Cévennes, you can follow in Robert Louis Stevenson's footsteps on the GR70 Chemin de Stevenson (p736) from Le Puy to Alès – with or without a donkey.

Corsica is a hiker's paradise – the GR20, the 15-day trek that crosses the island north to south, is one of France's most famous, but there are dozens of shorter, easier walks. Or combine walking with swimming on the *sentiers littoraux* in the Alpes-Maritimes. More bracing hikes await on the GR21 skirting the chalky cliffs of Côte d'Albâtre in Normandy, the Côte d'Opale's GR120 taking in the colour-changing seascapes of the English Channel, and Brittany's Presqu'île de Crozon peninsula with 145km of signed trails woven around rocky outcrops and clear ocean views.

More Information

- **Club Alpin Français** (French Alpine Club; www.ffcam.fr) Has guides for Alpine sports and manages 127 *refuges* (mountain huts).
- **IGN** (www.ign.fr) Topographic maps covering every corner of France, plus walking guides. The hiker's best friend.
- **GR-Infos** (www.gr-infos.com) Multilingual site with route descriptions and maps for France's long-distance trails.
- **Parcs Nationaux de France** (French National Parks; www.parcsnationaux.fr) Official site for info on France's seven national parks.
- **Cicerone** (www.cicerone.co.uk) Walking guides to Haute Savoie, Dordogne, Languedoc, Massif Central and Corsica among others.

Cycling & Mountain Biking

When to Go

Slip into a bicycle saddle to maximise breezes when the heat turns up. Summer is prime time for road cycling on the coast and mountain biking – *vélo tout terrain* (VTT) – in the French Alps and Pyrenees, with the season running from mid-June to September. Elsewhere, there's some form of cycling available year-round, be it in vine-ribboned valleys or along France's great waterways.

Cycling & Mountain Biking Destinations

France is fabulous freewheeling country, with routes leading along its wooded valleys and mighty rivers begging to be explored in slow motion. The options are boundless, but among the best are the soothingly lovely Loire Valley, where **Loire à Vélo** (www.loireavelo.fr) maintains 800km of signposted routes from Cuffy to the Atlantic; the peaceful towpaths shadowing the 240km, Unesco-listed Canal du Midi (p695), many of which form part of the stunning **Canal des 2 Mers en Vélo** (http://en.canaldes2mersavelo.com) cycling route linking the Atlantic with the Med via canals; and Provence's 236km **Autour du Luberon** *véloroute* (bike path) linking one gold-stone village to another. Pair wine tasting with a pedal through the vines in Burgundy (www.burgundy-by-bike.com), Bordeaux, the Beaujolais region, the southern Rhône Valley or the Route des Vins d'Alsace. Bicycle trails also crisscross the sun-baked Île de Ré, dangling off the Atlantic Coast.

Naturally, if you're up for a challenge, the gruelling inclines and exhilarating descents of the Alps and Pyrenees will appeal. Resorts such as Alpe d'Huez, Morzine and Les Deux Alpes are downhill heaven, as is the Parc National des Pyrénées, where ski stations open up to mountain bikers in summer with *sentiers balisés* (marked trails) and obstacle-riddled bike parks for honing technique. Most cable cars let you take your bike for free or a nominal fee with a valid lift pass.

Bike hire is widely available and costs from €10 per day for a classic bike to €35 for a top-of-the-range mountain bike or ebike, and even as high as €40 to €90 for the sort of high-end road bike you'd want to tackle a mountainous section of Le Tour. Tourist office websites are a good first port of call for route maps and itineraries.

More Information

- **Cycling France** Your definitive Lonely Planet guide to cycling in France, with elevation charts, itineraries for all fitness levels and detailed maps.
- **Fédération Française de Cyclisme** (French Cycling Federation; www.ffc.fr) Going strong since 1881, this is the authority on competitive cycling and mountain biking in France.
- **VeloMap** (www.velomap.org) For free Garmin GPS cycling maps.
- **Véloroutes et Voies Vertes** (www.af3v.org) The inside scoop on 250 signposted *véloroutes* and *voies vertes* (greenways), plus an interactive map to pinpoint them.

Adventure & Water Sports

Kayaking & Canoeing

Kayaking and canoeing are available up and down the country, with some of the best options (including the looking-glass Lake Annecy) in the French Alps, the Vézère Valley, the Dronne, the River Gard and the Gorges de l'Ardèche. Startlingly turquoise water and sheer, forest-cloaked cliffs make the Gorges du Tarn and Gorges du Verdon highly scenic spots for a paddle. Sea kayakers prefer the ragged, cove-indented Parc National des Calanques and Corsica's islet-speckled waters.

Expect to pay around €10 to €15 for kayak or canoe rental per day, and €25/50 for a half-/full-day excursion.

Surfing & Kite-Surfing

The wave-thrashed, wind-lashed Atlantic Coast – Arcachon and Cap Ferret, for instance – and the French Basque Country make surfers swoon. You'll find some of Europe's best surf in ocean-battered Biarritz and nearby Hossegor, which hosts the 10-day Quiksilver Pro France on the ASP World Surfing Tour in late September and early October. Group lessons are available everywhere for between €30 and €40. For surf spots and schools, visit www.surfingfrance.com.

Kite-surfers, meanwhile, catch breezes on the French Riviera and Corsica (around Porto-Vecchio), where outfits offer courses as well as equipment rental.

Stand-Up Paddleboarding

Grab a board, bring along your balance and a Zen mind, and away you go –

NATIONAL PARKS AT A GLANCE

PARK	FEATURES	ACTIVITIES	WHEN TO GO
Parc National des Cévennes	wild peat bogs, granite peaks, ravines & ridges bordering the Massif Central & Languedoc (910 sq km); red deer, beavers, vultures, wolves, bison	walking, donkey trekking, mountain biking, horse riding, cross-country skiing, caving, canoeing, botany (2250 plant species)	spring & winter
Parc National des Écrins	glaciers, glacial lakes & mountaintops soaring up to 4102m in the French Alps (1770 sq km); marmots, lynx, ibex, chamois, bearded vultures	walking, climbing, hang-gliding & paragliding, kayaking	spring & summer
Parc National du Mercantour	Provence at its most majestic with 3000m-plus peaks & dead-end valleys along the Italian border; marmots, mouflons, chamois, ibex, wolves, golden & short-toed eagles, bearded vultures; Bronze Age petroglyphs	Alpine skiing, white-water sports, mountain biking, walking, donkey trekking	spring, summer & winter
Parc National de Port-Cros	island marine park off the Côte d'Azur forming France's smallest national park & Europe's first marine park (700 hectares & 1288 hectares of water); puffins, shearwaters, migratory birds	snorkelling, birdwatching, swimming, gentle strolling	summer & autumn (for birdwatching)
Parc National des Pyrénées	100km of mountains along the Spanish border (457 sq km); marmots, izards (Pyrenean chamois), brown bears, golden eagles, vultures, buzzards	Alpine & cross-country skiing, walking, mountaineering, rock climbing, white-water sports, canoeing, kayaking, mountain biking	spring, summer & winter
Parc National de la Vanoise	postglacial mountain landscape of Alpine peaks, beech-fir forests & 80 sq km of glaciers forming France's first national park (530 sq km); chamois, ibex, marmots, golden eagles; bearded vultures	Alpine & cross-country skiing, walking, mountaineering, mountain biking	spring, summer & winter

cruising on a stand-up paddleboard across glittering Alpine lakes (Lake Annecy is a scenic favourite), around island fortresses in the Atlantic and from one *calanque* (rocky outlet) to another in the Med. This is the new way to explore in style, and pretty much anyone can do it. Rent boards for fun along the Promenade des Anglais in Nice on the French Riviera, or sign up for a more serious ocean encounter on the Atlantic Coast with Antioche Kayak (p618) near La Rochelle; in Corsica with Bonif' Kayak (p894) or Club Nautique d'Île Rousse (p880); or in Sète with Kayak Med (p725). Life jackets and waterproof containers are generally provided. Expect to pay €10 to €15 per hour for board rental and from €25 per hour for tuition.

Rock Climbing & Via Ferrate

For intrepid souls, the holy grail of rock climbing is France's highest of the high: 4810m Mont Blanc. Chamonix guide companies organise ascents of this monster mountain, as well as five-day rock-climbing courses in the surrounding Alps. On a less daunting scale, you'll find rock climbing on sandstone ridges in the Forêt de Fontainebleau (p170) on Paris' fringes, in the jagged pinnacles of Corsica's L'Alta Rocca, and in the thickly wooded Parc National des Cévennes.

If you are less experienced but fancy flirting with climbing, *via ferrate* (fixed-rope routes) lace the Alps, Pyrenees, Cévennes and Corsica. Guide companies charge around €50 for half-day escapades.

Canyoning & White-Water Rafting

For a thrill, little beats throwing yourself down a foaming river in a raft or a waterfall while rappelling – cue white-water rafting and canyoning. Canyoning operators are found in mountainous, ravine-riddled areas – from the French Alps to Aiguilles de Bavella (p897) in Corsica.

White-water rafting is another sure-fire way to get the heart pumping. France's most scenic options on this front include the cliff-flanked limestone wilderness of the Gorges de l'Ardèche (p472) and the mind-blowingly spectacular Gorges du Verdon, Europe's largest canyon, where you can also hydrospeed and gorge float. A half-day outing for either activity will set you back around €50.

Scuba Diving

Scuba divers bubble below the glittering surface of the Mediterranean. Among France's top dive sites are the Massif de l'Estérel on the French Riviera, with its WWII shipwrecks and pristine waters, and the Reserve Naturelle de Scandola (p885), Îles Lavezzi and Mérouville (Bonifacio) in Corsica, the latter for close encounters with groupers. Starfish and wrasse are often sighted on dives in St-Jean de Luz in the French Basque Country. A single dive will set you back around €40; all equipment is provided.

Paragliding

Many a peak, perfect thermals, and glacier-frosted mountains and forests to observe while drifting down to ground level attract paragliders to Alpine resorts such as Chamonix. Lake Annecy is another favourite in the Alps, while the Valllée d'Aspe is a good launch pad in the Pyrenees. In the Massif Central, there's paragliding off the top of Puy de Dôme. Tandem flights with a qualified instructor cost anything between €65 and €220.

Regions at a Glance

Few appreciate quite how varied France is. The largest country in Europe after Russia and Ukraine, hexagon-shaped France is hugged by water or mountains along every side except its northeastern boundary – an instant win for lovers of natural beauty, the coast and great outdoors. Winter snow sports and summer hiking 'n' biking rule the Alps in eastern France and the Pyrenees lacing the 450km-long border with Spain in the southwest. For *très belle* beach holidays, the coastal regions of Normandy and Brittany (northern France), the Atlantic Coast (with oyster-rich islands and waves for surfers), Corsica, and the French Riviera (Côte d'Azur), Provence and Languedoc-Roussillon on the hot Mediterranean deliver every time. Then there's food and wine, most exceptional in Burgundy, Provence, the Dordogne and Rhône Valley.

Paris

Food
Art
Shopping

Bistro Dining

Tables are jammed tight, chairs spill onto busy pavements outside, dishes of the day are chalked on the blackboard, and cuisine is simple and delicious. Such is the timeless joy of bistro dining in the capital.

Museums & Galleries

All the great masters star in Paris' priceless portfolio of museums. Not all the booty is stashed inside: buildings, metro stations, parks and other public art give *Mona* a good run for her money.

Fashion & Flea Markets

Luxury fashion houses, edgy boutiques, Left Bank designer-vintage and Europe's largest flea market: Paris really is the last word in fabulous shopping.

p56

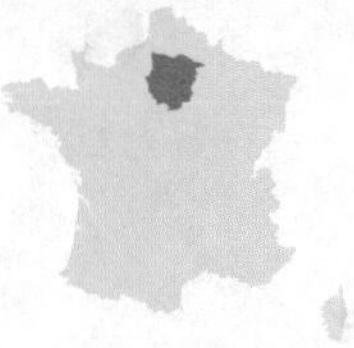

Around Paris

Châteaux
Cathedrals
Green Spaces

A Taste of Royalty

Château de Versailles – vast, opulent and *very* shimmery – has to be seen to be believed. Fontainebleau, Chantilly and Vaux-le-Vicomte are other addresses in French royalty's little black book.

Sacred Architecture

Chartres' cathedral, near Paris, is one of Western architecture's greatest achievements, with stained glass in awesome blue – at its most dazzling on sunlit days.

Urban Green

Parisians take air in thick forests outside the city: Forêt de Fontainebleau, an old royal hunting ground, is a hot spot for rock climbing and family walks. Chantilly means manicured French gardens and upper-class horse racing.

p160

Lille, Flanders & the Somme

Architecture
History
Coastline

Flemish Style

Breaking for a glass of strong local beer between old-town meanders around extravagant Flemish Renaissance buildings is a highlight of northern France. Lille and Arras are the cities to target if you have limited time.

Gothic to WWI

Amiens evokes serene contemplation inside one of France's most awe-inspiring Gothic cathedrals, and emotional encounters in WWI cemeteries.

Coastal Capers

Hiking along the Côte d'Opale – a wind-buffeted area of white cliffs, gold sand and ever-changing sea and sky – is dramatic and beautiful, as is a Baie de Somme bicycle ride past lounging seals.

p178

Normandy

Food
Coastline
Battlefields

Calvados & Camembert

This coastal chunk of northern France is a pastoral land of butter and soft cheeses. Its exotic fruits: Camembert, cider, fiery *calvados* (apple brandy) and super-fresh seafood.

Cliffs & Coves

Chalk-white cliff to dune-lined beach, rock spire to pebble cove, coastal path to tide-splashed island-abbey Mont St-Michel: few coastlines are as inspiring.

D-Day Beaches

Normandy has long played a pivotal role in European history. But it was during WWII's D-Day landings that Normandy leaped to global importance. Museums, memorials, cemeteries and endless stretches of soft golden sand evoke that dramatic day in 1944.

p211

Brittany

Food
Walking
Islands

Crêpes & Cider

These two Breton culinary staples are no secret, but who cares? Devouring caramel-doused buckwheat pancakes in the company of homemade cider is a big reason to visit Brittany.

Wild Hikes

With its wild, dramatic coastline, islands, medieval towns and thick forests laced in Celtic lore and legend, this proud and fiercely independent region promises exhilarating walks.

Breton Beauties

Brittany's much-loved islands, dotted with black sheep and crossed with craggy coastal paths and windswept cycling tracks, are big draws. Don't miss dramatic Île d'Ouessant or the very aptly named Belle Île.

p250

Champagne

Champagne
Walking
Drives

Bubbly Tasting

Gawp at a Champagne panorama from atop Reims' cathedral then zoom in close with serious tasting at the world's most prestigious Champagne houses in Reims and Épernay.

Vineyard Trails

Nothing fulfills the French dream like day hikes through neat rows of vineyards, exquisite picture-postcard villages bedecked in flowers and a gold-stone riverside hamlet right out of a Renoir painting.

Majestic Motoring

No routes are more geared to motorists and cyclists than the Champagne Routes, fabulously picturesque and well-signposted driving itineraries taking in the region's wealthy winemaking villages, hillside vines and traditional cellars.

p294

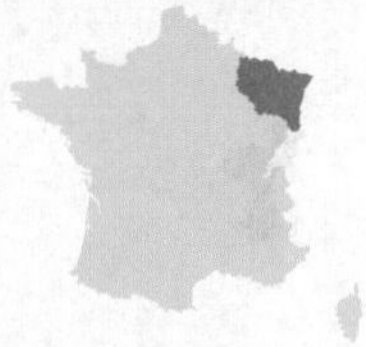

Alsace & Lorraine

Battlefields
City Life
Villages

Emotional Journeys

Surveying the dazzling symmetry of crosses on the Verdun battlefields is painful. Memorials, museums, cemeteries, forts and an ossuary mark out the journey.

Urban Icons

With the sublime (Strasbourg's cathedral) to the space-age (Centre Pompidou in Metz), this chunk of France steals hearts with its city squares, architecture, museums and Alsatian dining.

Chocolate-Box Villages

There is no lovelier way of getting acquainted with this region than travelling from hilltop castles to stork-nest-blessed farms to half-timbered villages framed by vines – with your foot on the pedal. Slow is the pace.

p316

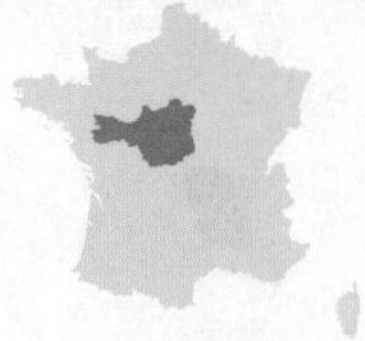

Loire Valley

Châteaux
History
Cycling

Royal Architecture

Endowed with structural and decorative gems from medieval to Renaissance and beyond, the Loire's lavish châteaux sweep most visitors off their feet.

Tempestuous Tales

This region is a storyteller: through spectacular castles, fortresses, apocalyptic tapestries and court paintings, the gore and glory, political intrigue and scandals of medieval and Renaissance France fabulously unfold.

Riverside Trails

The River Loire is France's longest, best-decorated river. Pedalling riverside along the flat from château to château is one of the valley's great joys – not to mention tasting the fruits of vineyards along its banks.

p362

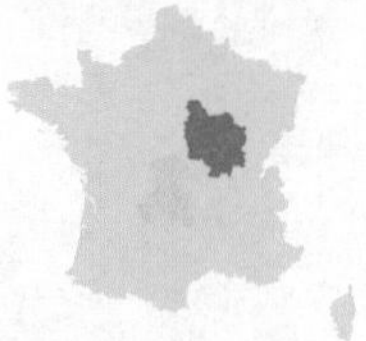

Burgundy

Wine
History
Outdoors

Reds & Whites

Mooch between vines and old-stone villages along the *grand cru* vineyard route. But this region is not just about Côte d'Or reds. Taste whites in Chablis and Mâcon also.

Medieval History

Nowhere is Burgundy's past as one of medieval Europe's mightiest states evoked more keenly than in the dashingly handsome capital Dijon. Complete the medieval history tour with abbeys Cluny and Cîteaux, Fontenay, Tournus, Vézelay and Autun.

Great Outdoors

Hiking and biking past vineyards or cruising in a canal boat is the good life. Pedal the towpath to gloriously medieval Abbaye de Fontenay, open a bottle of Chablis and savour the best of Burgundy.

p404

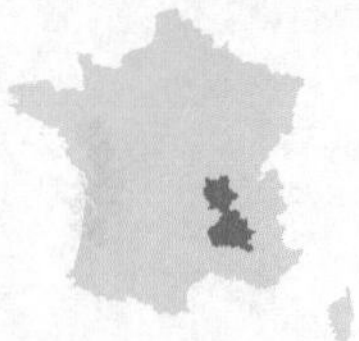

Lyon & the Rhône Valley

Food
Roman Sites
Cycling

Famous Flavours

No city in France excites taste buds more than Lyon. Savour local specialities in a checked-tableclothed *bouchon* (Lyonnais bistro), washed down by Côtes de Rhône wine poured from a Lyonnais *pot* (bottle).

Roman Remains

Not content with lavishing two majestic amphitheatres on Lyon (catch a concert after dark during Les Nuits de Fourvière – magical!), the Romans gifted the Rhône Valley with a third in jazz-famed Vienne.

Two-Wheel Touring

Pedalling between vineyards in Beaujolais country or around lakes swamped with bird life in La Dombes is a simple pleasure of valley life.

p448

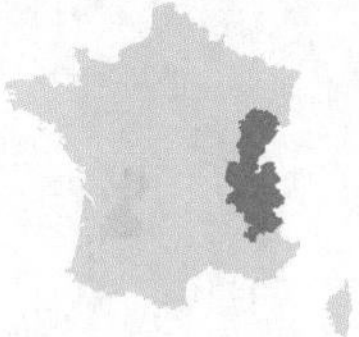

French Alps & the Jura Mountains

Food
Outdoors
Farmstays

Culture & Cuisine

Fondue is the tip of the culinary iceberg in this Alpine region, where cow's milk flavours dozens of cheeses. Around chic Lake Annecy, chefs woo with wild herbs and lake perch.

Adrenaline Rush

Crowned by Mont Blanc (4810m), the French Alps show no mercy in their insanely challenging ski trails and mountain-bike descents. Did we mention Europe's longest black downhill piste and the world's highest zip line?

Back to Nature

Feel the rhythm of the land with an overnight stay on a farm. Bottle-feed calves, collect the eggs, eat breakfast in a fragrant garden or before a wood-burning stove, and feel right at home.

p474

Auvergne

Volcanoes
Architecture
Outdoors

Volcanic Landscape

The last one erupted in 5000 BC but their presence is still evident: mineral waters bubble up from volcanic springs in Vichy and Volvic; volcanic stone paints Clermont-Ferrand black; craters pocket the hills in the Parc Naturel Régional des Volcans 'd'Auvergne.

Belle Époque

A string of early 20th-century spa towns including Vichy and La Bourboule add understated elegance to this region's otherwise deeply provincial bow.

Hiking & Skiing

Walking is the best way to explore this unique landscape – an uncanny, grass-green moonscape of giant molehills crossed with trails. Then there are the little-known ski slopes of Le Mont-Dore.

p532

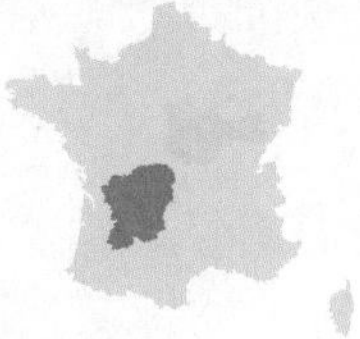

The Dordogne, Limousin & the Lot

Food
Hilltop Towns
Cruises

Mouth-Watering Markets

Black truffles, foie gras and walnuts… Gourmets, eat your heart out in this fertile region, where the fruits of the land are piled high at weekly markets.

Mighty Bastides

Not only is Dordogne's collection of fortified 13th-century towns and villages a joy to explore, valley views from the top of these clifftop *bastides* are uplifting. Start with Monpazier and Domme.

Meandering Waterways

Be it in a canoe, raft or *gabarre* (flat-bottomed boat), cruising quietly along the rivers is an invitation to see *la belle France* at her most serene.

p557

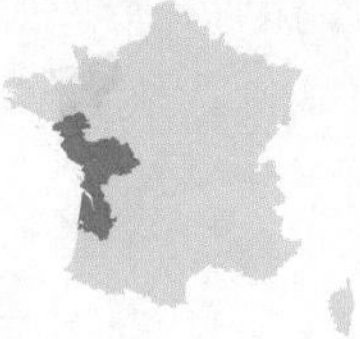

Atlantic Coast

Port Towns
Wine
Outdoors

Town Life

Make a hip dining rendezvous in an old banana-ripening warehouse in Nantes, or take in bright-white limestone arcades and islands in the fortified port of La Rochelle, and brilliant art museums in wine-rich Bordeaux.

Wonderful Wines

France's largest wine-growing region, Bordeaux, encompasses the Médoc with its magnificent châteaux and medieval hamlet of St-Émilion. The wine is wonderful (not to mention the Cognac).

Rural Retreats

Paddling emerald-green waterways in the Marais Poitevin, pedalling sun-baked Île de Ré and wandering between oyster shacks in Arcachon Bay are what this tranquil region is all about.

p604

French Basque Country

Food
Activities
Culture

Culture & Cuisine

This exuberant region beneath the mist-soaked Pyrenees evokes Spain with its fiestas, bullfights, traditional *pelota* (ball games), tapas and famous Bayonne ham.

Surf's Up

Riding waves in the glitzy beach resort of Biarritz or on surfer beaches in Les Landes are good reasons to visit this sun-slicked coastal region, snug in France's most southwestern corner.

A Timeless Pilgrimage

For centuries pilgrims have made their way across France to the quaint walled town of St-Jean Pied de Port, and beyond to Santiago de Compostela in Spain. Do the same, on foot or by bicycle.

p639

The Pyrenees

Outdoors
Scenery
History

Outdoor Action

Make Parc National des Pyrénées your playground. Vigorous hikes to lofty heights, good-value downhill skiing and racy white-water sports will leave you wanting more.

Jaw-Dropping Views

France's last wilderness has rare flora and fauna, snow-kissed peaks, vulture-specked skies, waterfalls and lakes. Top views include those from Pic du Jer, Pic du Midi, Lescun, Cirque de Gavarnie, Lac de Gaube and pretty much every valley going.

Rare & Holy Cities

That same elegance that saw well-to-do 19th-century English and Americans winter in Pau still attracts guests today. Then there is sacred Lourdes, a provincial pilgrim city.

p664

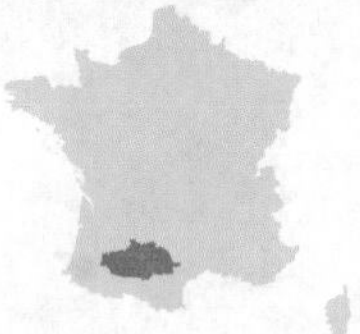

Toulouse Area

Food
History
Cruises

Cassoulet & Armagnac

Try Le Genty-Magre restaurant for Toulouse's best *cassoulet* – this classic bean-stew dish simmers on the stove in most kitchens. Begin the experience with an aperitif and end with an Armagnac brandy.

Towns with Tales

Red-brick Toulouse's historic mansions, quintessential fortified town Montauban, Gothic Albi, Moissac's Romanesque abbey: this compact region is packed with historical tales and historic architecture.

Canal du Midi

Pop a cork out of a bottle of Vin de Pays d'Oc and savour the go-slow, lush-green loveliness of the Canal du Midi. Stroll or pedal its towpaths, soak in a spa, or simply rent a canal boat and drift.

p687

Languedoc-Roussillon

Culture
Roman Sites
Outdoors

Neighbouring Spain

Roussillon is a hot, dusty, lively region, long part of Catalonia at the eastern end of the Pyrenees. Celebrate a traditional fiesta in Perpignan, and modern art and *sardane* (Catalan folk dance) in Céret.

Aqueducts & Amphitheatres

Nîmes' amphitheatre and the Pont du Gard are two of the Roman Empire's best-preserved sites. Catch a show in Nîmes, canoe on the Gard.

Footpaths & Waterways

Try canoeing beneath the Pont du Gard, cycling towpaths to Carcassonne, boating the Canal du Midi, climbing up to Cathar fortresses, donkey trekking in the Cévennes, or hiking gorges in Haut-Languedoc.

p707

Provence

Food
Villages
Modern Art

Eating & Drinking

Sip pastis over *pétanque* (boules), spend all evening savouring bouillabaisse (fish stew), mingle over buckets of herbs and marinated olives at the market, hunt truffles, and taste Bandol reds and Côtes de Provence rosé.

Sensual Sauntering

Travelling *à la provençal* is a sensual journey past scented lavender fields and chestnut forests, through apple-green vineyards and silvery olive groves, and around markets, chapels and medieval villages perched on rocky crags.

Avant-Garde

Provence itself is an art museum and has the roll-call to prove it: Matisse, Renoir, Picasso, Cézanne, Van Gogh and Signac all painted and lived here.

p754

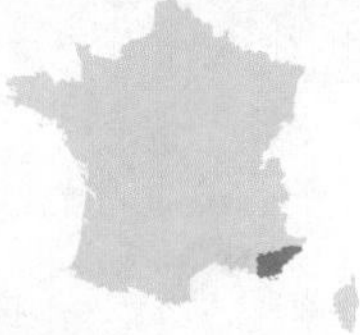

The French Riviera & Monaco

Seaside Resorts
Glamour
Coastline

Coastal Queen

Urban grit, old-world opulence, art that moves and a seaside promenade everyone loves – Nice, queen of the French Riviera, will always be belle of the seaside ball.

Party Time

Enjoy the Riviera high life: trail film stars in Cannes, watch Formula One, meet high society in Monaco, guzzle champers in St-Tropez, frolic in famous footsteps on sandy beaches, dine between priceless art, dance til dawn...

Magnificent Scenery

With its glistening sea, idyllic beaches and coastal paths, this part of the Med coast begs wonderful walks. Cicadas sing on Cap Ferrat, while the sun turns the Massif de l'Estérel red.

p820

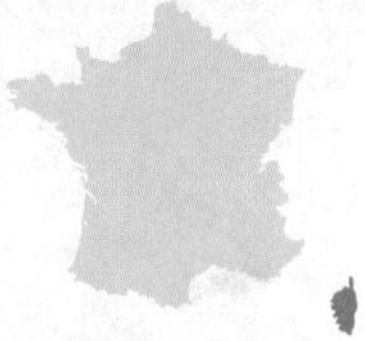

Corsica

Drives
Hiking
Boat Trips

Postcard Home

Corsican coastal towns are impossibly picturesque – alley-woven Bastia, Italianate Bonifacio, celeb-loved Île Rousse, chichi Calvi – but it is the hair-raising coastal roads that wend their way past medieval Genoese watchtowers and big blue views that really scream, 'Send a postcard home!'

Great Outdoors

Hiking high-altitude mountain trails once the preserve of bandits and *bergers* (shepherds) is a trail-junkie favourite, as are the cliffhanging Gorges de Spelunca and the pink, ochre and ginger Les Calanques de Piana.

The Big Blue

Nowhere does the Med seem bluer. Hop on deck in Porto, Bonifacio or Calvi for a boat excursion, or view sapphire waters through a mask while snorkelling.

p871

On the Road

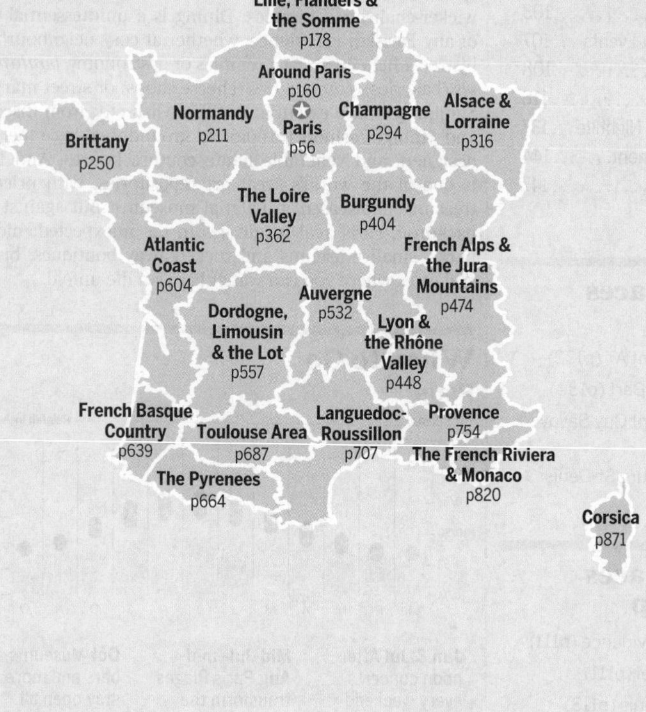

Lille, Flanders & the Somme p178
Around Paris p160
Paris p56
Normandy p211
Champagne p294
Alsace & Lorraine p316
Brittany p250
The Loire Valley p362
Burgundy p404
Atlantic Coast p604
French Alps & the Jura Mountains p474
Auvergne p532
Dordogne, Limousin & the Lot p557
Lyon & the Rhône Valley p448
French Basque Country p639
Toulouse Area p687
Languedoc-Roussillon p707
Provence p754
The French Riviera & Monaco p820
The Pyrenees p664
Corsica p871

Paris

POP 2.2 MILLION

Includes ➡

Best Places to Eat

- ➡ Restaurant AT (p132)
- ➡ Le 6 Paul Bert (p130)
- ➡ Restaurant Guy Savoy (p136)
- ➡ 52 Faubourg St-Denis (p123)

Best Places to Sleep

- ➡ Hôtel Providence (p111)
- ➡ Joke Hôtel (p111)
- ➡ Hôtel Exquis (p113)
- ➡ Les Piaules (p112)
- ➡ L'Hôtel (p115)

Why Go?

Paris has a timeless familiarity for first-time and frequent visitors, with instantly recognisable architecture – the Eiffel Tower, the Arc de Triomphe guarding glamorous Champs-Élysées, gargoyled Notre Dame cathedral, lamplit bridges spanning the Seine and art-nouveau brasseries spilling onto wicker-chair-lined terraces. Dining is a quintessential part of any Parisian experience, whether at cosy neighbourhood bistros, Michelin-starred temples or gastronomy, *boulangeries* (bakeries), *fromageries* (cheese shops) or street markets. Shopping is also essential in this stylish city, from discount and vintage fashion through to groundbreaking emerging designers and venerable haute couture houses. And Paris is one of the world's great art repositories, with priceless treasures showcased in palatial museums. But against this backdrop, Paris' real magic lies in the unexpected: hidden parks, small museums and tucked-away boutiques, bistros and cafes where you can watch Parisian life unfold.

When to Go

Paris

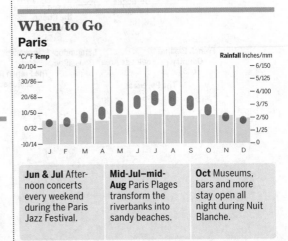

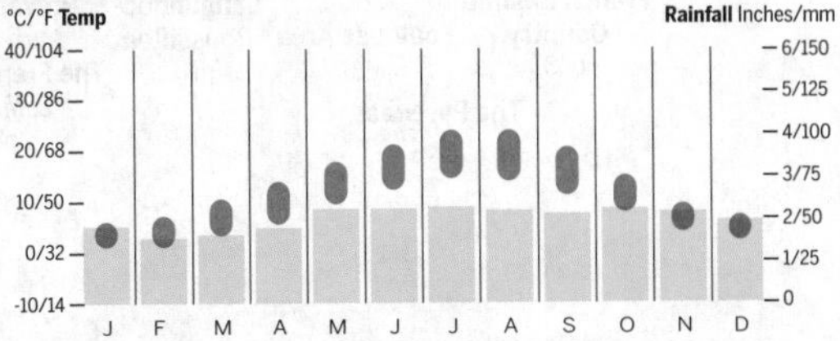

Jun & Jul Afternoon concerts every weekend during the Paris Jazz Festival.

Mid-Jul–mid-Aug Paris Plages transform the riverbanks into sandy beaches.

Oct Museums, bars and more stay open all night during Nuit Blanche.

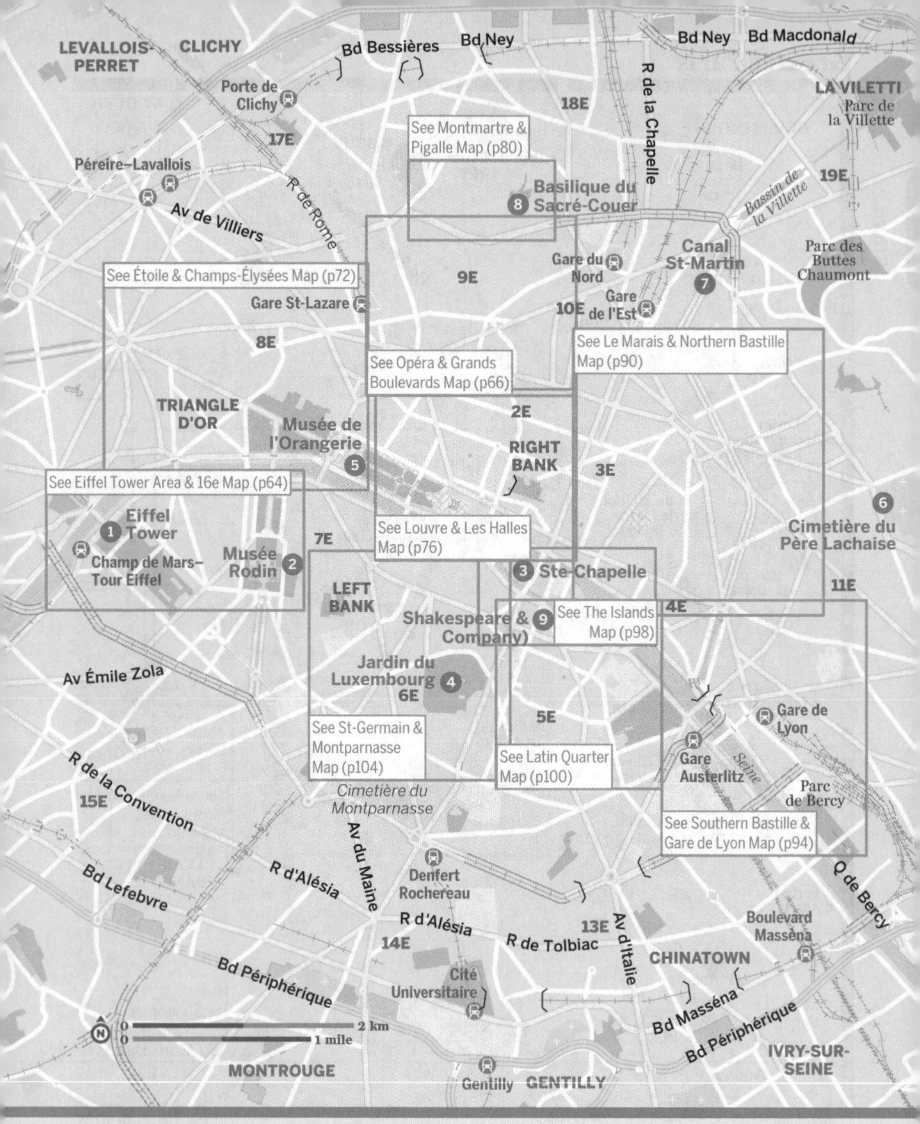

Paris Highlights

1 **Eiffel Tower** (p61) Ascending at dusk for the best views of the City of Light.

2 **Musée Rodin** (p96) Indulging in a Parisian moment in the sculpture-filled gardens of this art museum.

3 **Sainte-Chapelle** (p87) Taking in the magical sparkle of stained glass in the sun.

4 **Jardin du Luxembourg** (p96) Lounging with locals in the city's most popular park.

5 **Musée de l'Orangerie** (p74) Marvelling at Monet's *Water Lilies*.

6 **Cimetière du Père Lachaise** (p83) Paying respects at the world's most visited cemetery.

7 **Canal St-Martin** (p79) Ducking and diving across old swing bridges and towpaths.

8 **Basilique du Sacré-Cœur** (p75) Admiring the city of Paris laid out at your feet.

9 **Shakespeare & Company** (p131) Attending a reading at this mythical bookshop and hobnobbing over coffee after.

Greater Paris

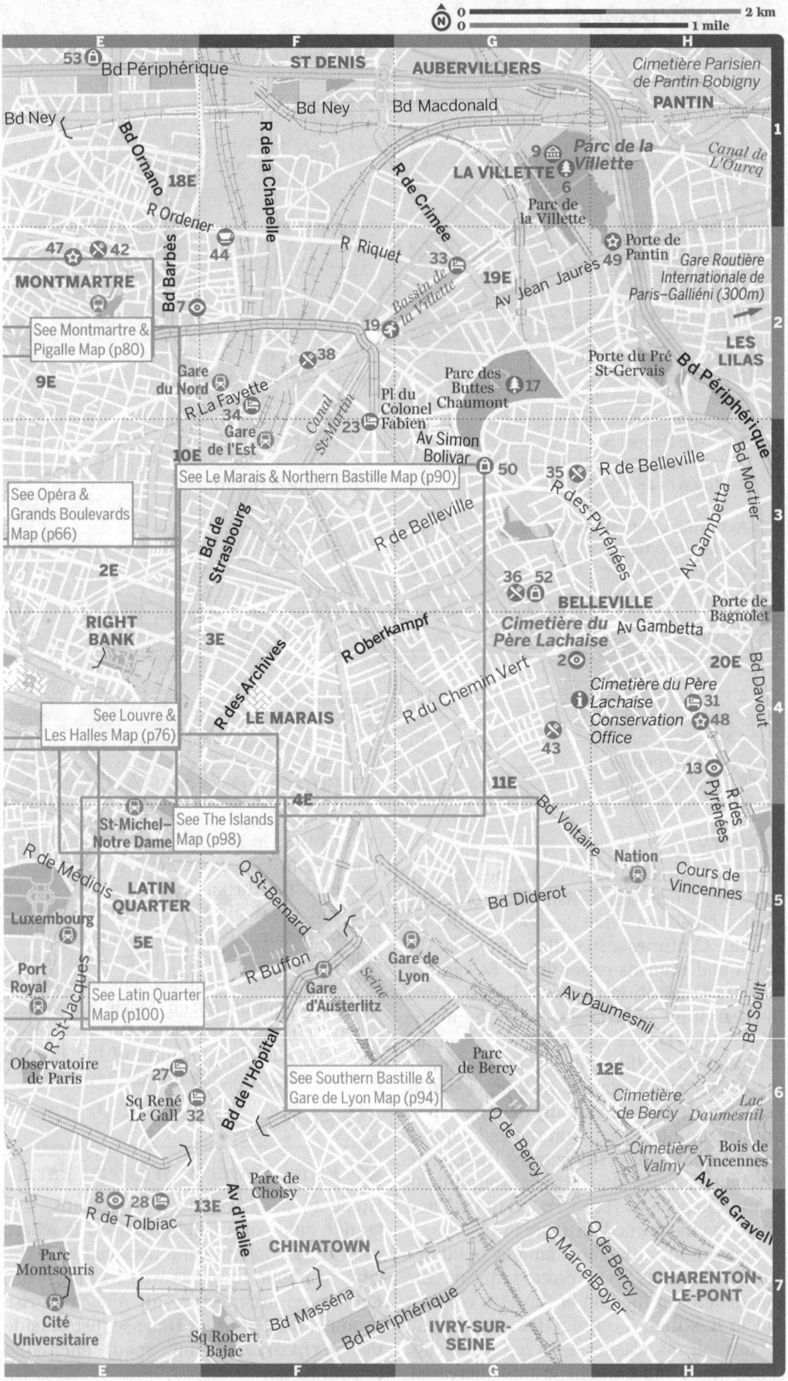
0 2 km
0 1 mile
E
F
G
H
1
2
3
4
5
6
7
53
Bd Périphérique
ST DENIS
AUBERVILLIERS
Cimetière Parisien de Pantin Bobigny
PANTIN
Bd Ney
Bd Macdonald
Bd Ornano
R de la Chapelle
R de Crimée
9
Parc de la Villette
LA VILLETTE
6
Canal de L'Ourcq
18E
R Ordener
Parc de la Villette
44
R Riquet
Porte de Pantin
49
Gare Routière Internationale de Paris–Galliéni (300m)
47
42
MONTMARTRE
Bd Barbès
33
Bassin de la Villette
19E
Av Jean Jaurès
7
19
See Montmartre & Pigalle Map (p80)
LES LILAS
38
Gare du Nord
Porte du Pré St-Gervais
Bd Périphérique
9E
R La Fayette
34
Canal St-Martin
Pl du Colonel Fabien
23
Parc des Buttes Chaumont
17
Gare de l'Est
Av Simon Bolivar
10E
50
35
R de Belleville
Bd Mortier
See Le Marais & Northern Bastille Map (p90)
R des Pyrénées
Av Gambetta
See Opéra & Grands Boulevards Map (p66)
Bd de Strasbourg
R de Belleville
2E
36
52
BELLEVILLE
Porte de Bagnolet
RIGHT BANK
3E
R Oberkampf
Cimetière du Père Lachaise
Av Gambetta
2
20E
Bd Davout
R des Archives
R du Chemin Vert
Cimetière du Père Lachaise Conservation Office
31
48
See Louvre & Les Halles Map (p76)
LE MARAIS
43
13
11E
R des Pyrénées
4E
St-Michel–Notre Dame
See The Islands Map (p98)
Bd Voltaire
Nation
R de Médicis
Cours de Vincennes
LATIN QUARTER
Q St-Bernard
Bd Diderot
Luxembourg
5E
Gare de Lyon
R Buffon
Seine
Port Royal
R St-Jacques
See Latin Quarter Map (p100)
Gare d'Austerlitz
Av Daumesnil
Bd Soult
Observatoire de Paris
27
Bd de l'Hôpital
Parc de Bercy
See Southern Bastille & Gare de Lyon Map (p94)
12E
Sq René Le Gall
32
Cimetière de Bercy
Lac Daumesnil
Q de Bercy
Cimetière Valmy
Bois de Vincennes
Parc de Choisy
Av de Gravell
8
28
R de Tolbiac
13E
Av d'Italie
Q de Bercy
Q MarcelBoyer
Parc Montsouris
CHINATOWN
CHARENTON-LE-PONT
Cité Universitaire
Bd Masséna
Bd Périphérique
IVRY-SUR-SEINE
Sq Robert Bajac

Greater Paris

Top Sights
1 Cimetière du Montparnasse D6
2 Cimetière du Père Lachaise G4
3 Les Catacombes D6
4 Musée d'Orsay D4
5 Musée Marmottan Monet A4
6 Parc de la Villette G1

Sights
7 Brasserie la Goutte d'Or E2
8 Brasserie La Parisienne E7
9 Cité des Sciences G1
10 Fondation Louis Vuitton A3
11 Île aux Cygnes B4
12 Jardin d'Acclimatation A2
13 La Manufacture 111 .... H4
14 Le Ballon Air de Paris A5
15 Les Berges de Seine D4
16 Musée Dapper B3
17 Parc des Buttes-Chaumont G2
18 Statue of Liberty Replica B5

Activities, Courses & Tours
19 Canauxrama F2
20 Le Chalet des Îles A3
21 Le Cordon Bleu B5

Sleeping
22 BVJ Champs Élysées C2
23 Generator Hostel F3
24 Hôtel de la Loire D6
25 Hôtel Eldorado D2
26 Hôtel Félicien A5
27 Hôtel Henriette E6
28 Hôtel Saint Charles E7
29 Hôtel Vic Eiffel C5
30 Le Bellechasse D4
31 Mama Shelter H4
32 Oops E6
33 St Christopher's Canal G2
34 St Christopher's Gare du Nord F2
Sublim Eiffel .... (see 29)

Eating
35 Au 140 .... G3
36 Chatomat G3
37 Hugo Desnoyer A4
38 La Bulle F2
39 L'Atelier B D6
40 Le Beurre Noisette B6
41 Le Grand Pan C6
Le Petit Pan .... (see 41)
42 Soul Kitchen E2
43 Yard G4

Drinking & Nightlife
44 Café Lomi F2
45 Coutume D5
46 St James Paris B3

Entertainment
47 Au Lapin Agile E2
48 La Flèche d'Or H4
49 Philharmonie de Paris H2

Shopping
50 Belleville Brûlerie G3
51 Fromagerie Laurent Dubois B5
52 Koché G3
53 Marché aux Puces de St-Ouen E1

History

Paris was born in the Seine in the 3rd century BC, when the Parisii tribe of Celtic Gauls settled on what is now the Île de la Cité. Centuries of conflict between the Gauls and Romans ended in 52 BC, and in AD 508 Frankish king Clovis I made Paris the seat of his united Gaul kingdom. In the 9th century France was beset by Scandinavian Vikings. In the centuries that followed, these 'Norsemen' started pushing towards Paris, which had risen rapidly in importance. Construction had begun on the cathedral of Notre Dame in the 12th century, the Louvre was built as a riverside fortress around 1200, Sainte-Chapelle was consecrated in 1248 and the Sorbonne opened its doors in 1253.

Many of the city's most famous buildings and monuments were erected during the Renaissance at the end of the 15th century. But in less than a century, Paris was again in turmoil, as clashes between Huguenot (Protestant) and Catholic groups increased, culminating in the St Bartholomew's Day massacre in 1572. Louis XIV (the Sun King) ascended the throne in 1643 at the age of five and ruled until 1715, virtually emptying the national coffers with his ambitious building and battling. His greatest legacy is the palace at Versailles. The excesses of Louis XVI and his queen, Marie Antoinette, in part led to an uprising of Parisians on 14 July 1789 and the storming of the Bastille prison – triggering the French Revolution.

Sights

Eiffel Tower & Western Paris

Home to *very* well-heeled Parisians, this grande dame of a neighbourhood is where you can get up close and personal with the city's symbolic tower as well as more contemporary architecture in the high-rise business district of La Défense just outside the *périphérique* (ring road) encircling central Paris.

PARIS IN...

Two Days

Kick off with a morning cruise or tour, then concentrate on the most Parisian of sights and attractions: **Notre Dame**, the **Louvre**, the **Eiffel Tower** and the **Arc de Triomphe**. In the late afternoon have a coffee or glass of wine on the **av des Champs-Élysées** before making your way to Montmartre for dinner. The following day take in such sights as the **Musée d'Orsay, Sainte-Chapelle, Conciergerie, Musée National du Moyen Âge** or **Musée Rodin**. Dine in soulful St-Germain before hitting the Latin Quarter's jazz clubs.

Four Days

Be sure to visit at least one Parisian street market and consider a cruise along **Canal St-Martin**, bookended by visits to the **Cimetière du Père Lachaise** and **Parc de la Villette**. By night, take in a concert, opera or ballet at the **Palais Garnier** or **Opéra Bastille**, and a bar and club crawl in Le Marais and its vibrant surrounds.

One Week

With one week in the French capital, you can see a good many of the major sights covered in this chapter and take excursions from Paris proper further afield to areas around Paris such as **Versailles**.

★Eiffel Tower LANDMARK

(Map p64; ☎08 92 70 12 39; www.tour-eiffel.fr; Champ de Mars, 5 av Anatole France, 7e; adult/youth/child lift to top €17/14.50/8, lift to 2nd fl €11/8.50/4, stairs to 2nd fl €7/5/3, lift 2nd fl to top €6; ⏰lifts & stairs 9am-12.45am mid-Jun–Aug, lifts 9.30am-11.45pm, stairs 9.30am-6.30pm Sep–mid-Jun; Ⓜ Bir Hakeim or RER Champ de Mars–Tour Eiffel) No one could imagine Paris today without it. But Gustave Eiffel only constructed this elegant, 320m-tall signature spire as a temporary exhibit for the 1889 World's Fair. Luckily, the art nouveau tower's popularity assured its survival. Prebook tickets online to avoid long ticket queues.

Lifts ascend to the tower's three floors; change lifts on the 2nd floor for the final ascent to the top. Energetic visitors can walk as far as the 2nd floor using the south pillar's 704-step stairs.

Parc du Champ de Mars PARK

(Map p64; Champ de Mars, 7e; Ⓜ École Militaire or RER Champ de Mars–Tour Eiffel) Running southeast from the Eiffel Tower, the grassy Champ de Mars – an ideal summer picnic spot – was originally used as a parade ground for the cadets of the 18th-century **École Militaire**, the vast French-classical building at the southeastern end of the park, which counts Napoléon Bonaparte among its graduates. The steel-and-etched-glass **Wall for Peace memorial** (www.wallforpeace.com), erected in 2000, is by Clara Halter.

★Musée du Quai Branly MUSEUM

(Map p64; ☎01 56 61 70 00; www.quaibranly.fr; 37 quai Branly, 7e; adult/child €9/free; ⏰11am-7pm Tue, Wed & Sun, 11am-9pm Thu-Sat; Ⓜ Alma Marceau or RER Pont de l'Alma) No other museum in Paris so inspires travellers, armchair anthropologists and those who simply appreciate the beauty of traditional craftsmanship. A tribute to the diversity of human culture, Musée du Quai Branly presents an overview of indigenous and folk art. Its four main sections focus on Oceania, Asia, Africa and the Americas. An impressive array of masks, carvings, weapons, jewellery and more make up the body of the rich collection, displayed in a refreshingly unique interior without rooms or high walls.

Palais de Chaillot HISTORIC BUILDING

(Map p64; place du Trocadéro et du 11 Novembre, 16e; Ⓜ Trocadéro) The two curved, colonnaded wings of this building (built for the 1937 International Expo) and the terrace in between them afford an exceptional panorama of the **Jardins du Trocadéro**, the Seine and the Eiffel Tower. The eastern wing houses the standout **Cité de l'Architecture et du Patrimoine** (www.citechaillot.fr; adult/child €8/free; ⏰11am-7pm Wed & Fri-Mon, to 9pm Thu), devoted to French architecture and heritage, as well as the **Théâtre National de Chaillot** (www.theatre-chaillot.fr), staging dance and theatre. The western wing houses the **Musée de la Marine** (Maritime Museum; www.musee-marine.fr; adult/child €8.50/free; ⏰11am-6pm Wed-Mon) and the **Musée de l'Homme**

FAST FACTS

Area 105 sq km

Local industry Commerce, manufacturing, technology, tourism

Signature drinks France's finest are all here; don't miss a Bloody Mary from inventor Harry's New York Bar (p139).

(Museum of Humankind; www.museedelhomme.fr; adult/child €10/free; ⏲10am-6pm Thu-Mon, to 9pm Wed; Ⓜ Passy, Iéna).

Aquarium de Paris Cinéaqua AQUARIUM
(Map p64; www.cineaqua.com; av des Nations Unies, 16e; adult/child €20.50/13; ⏲10am-7pm; ⓂTrocadéro) Paris' aquarium, on the eastern side of the Jardins du Trocadéro, has a shark tank and 500-odd fish species to entertain families on rainy days. Three cinemas screen ocean-related and other films (dubbed in French, with subtitles). Budget tip: show your ticket from the nearby Musée de la Marine or the Musée Guimet to get reduced aquarium admission (adult/child €16.40/10.40).

★**Musée Guimet des Arts Asiatiques** ART MUSEUM
(Map p72; ☎01 56 52 54 33; www.guimet.fr; 6 place d'Iéna, 16e; adult/child €7.50/free; ⏲10am-6pm Wed-Mon; Ⓜ Iéna) France's foremost Asian art museum has a superb collection. Observe the gradual transmission of both Buddhism and artistic styles along the Silk Road in pieces ranging from 1st-century Gandhara Buddhas from Afghanistan and Pakistan to later Central Asian, Chinese and Japanese Buddhist sculptures and art. Part of the collection is housed in the nearby **Galeries du Panthéon Bouddhique** (19 av d'Iéna, 16e; ⏲10am-5.45pm Wed-Mon, garden to 5pm) with a Japanese garden.

Musée Dapper ART MUSEUM
(Map p58; ☎01 45 00 91 75; www.dapper.com.fr; 35 rue Paul Valéry, 16e; adult/child €6/free; ⏲11am-7pm Wed, Sun & Mon, to 10pm Fri & Sat; Ⓜ Victor Hugo) Focused on African and Caribbean art, this jewel of a museum is an invitation to leave Paris behind for an hour or two. Exhibits rotate throughout the year, but the permanent collection is superb: ritual and festival masks and costumes accompanied by several video presentations. The auditorium hosts film screenings, concerts, storytelling and other cultural events.

Palais de Tokyo ART MUSEUM
(Map p72; www.palaisdetokyo.com; 13 av du Président Wilson, 16e; adult/child €10/free; ⏲noon-midnight Wed-Mon; ⓂIéna) The Tokyo Palace, created for the 1937 Exposition Universelle, has no permanent collection. Rather its shell-like interior of concrete and steel is a stark backdrop to interactive contemporary-art exhibitions and installations. Its bookshop is fabulous for art and design magazines, and its eating and drinking options are magic.

Musée d'Art Moderne de la Ville de Paris ART MUSEUM
(Map p72; www.mam.paris.fr; 11 av du Président Wilson, 16e; ⏲10am-6pm Tue, Wed, Fri-Sun, 10am-10pm Thu; ⓂIéna) FREE The permanent

MUSEUM DISCOUNTS & PASSES

Almost all museums and monuments in Paris have discounted tickets *(tarif réduit)* for students and seniors (generally over 60 years), provided they have valid ID. Children often get in for free; the cut-off age for 'child' is anywhere between six and 18 years. EU citizens under 26 years get in for free at national monuments and museums.

Paris Museum Pass (www.parismuseumpass.com; 2/4/6 days €48/62/74) Gets you into 50-odd venues in and around Paris; a huge advantage is that pass holders usually enter larger sights at a different entrance meaning you bypass (or substantially reduce) ridiculously long ticket queues.

Paris Passlib' (www.parisinfo.com; 2/3/5 days €109/129/155) Sold at the **Paris Convention & Visitors Bureau** (p155) and on its website, this handy city pass covers unlimited public transport in zones 1 to 3, admission to some 50 museums in the Paris region (aka a Paris Museum Pass), a one-hour boat cruise along the Seine, and a one-day hop-on hop-off open-top bus sightseeing service around central Paris' key sights with **L'Open Tour** (☎01 42 66 56 56; www.paris.opentour.com; 1-day pass adult/child €32/16). There's an optional €15 supplement for a skip-the-line ticket to levels one and two of the Eiffel Tower, or €21.50 for all three Eiffel Tower platforms.

collection at Paris' modern-art museum displays works representative of just about every major artistic movement of the 20th and (nascent) 21st centuries, with works by Modigliani, Matisse, Braque and Soutine. The real jewel, though, is the room hung with canvases by Dufy and Bonnard. Look out for cutting-edge temporary exhibitions (not free).

Flame of Liberty Memorial MONUMENT
(Map p72; place de l'Alma, 8e; M Alma Marceau) This bronze sculpture, a replica of the one topping the Statue of Liberty, was placed here in 1987 as a symbol of friendship between France and the USA. More famous is its location, above the place d'Alma tunnel where, on 31 August 1997, Diana, Princess of Wales, was killed in a car accident. Graffiti remembering the princess covers the entire wall next to the sculpture.

Grande Arche de la Défense LANDMARK
(www.grandearche.com; 1 Parvis de la Défense; M La Défense) La Défense's landmark edifice is the marble Grande Arche, a cube-like arch built in the 1980s to house government and business offices. The arch marks the western end of the *axe historique* (historic axis), though Danish architect Johan-Otto von Sprekelsen deliberately placed the Grande Arche fractionally out of alignment. After several years of renovations, access to the roof is expected to reopen in 2017.

Champs-Élysées & Grands Boulevards

Baron Haussmann famously reshaped the Parisian cityscape around the Arc de Triomphe, from which 12 avenues radiate like the spokes of a wheel, including the glamorous Champs-Élysées. To its east are gourmet shops garlanding the Église de la Madeleine, the palatial Palais Garnier opera house and the Grands Boulevards' art nouveau department stores.

★ **Arc de Triomphe** LANDMARK
(Map p72; www.monuments-nationaux.fr; place Charles de Gaulle, 8e; adult/child €12/free; 10am-11pm Apr-Sep, to 10.30pm Oct-Mar; M Charles de Gaulle–Étoile) If anything rivals the Eiffel Tower as the symbol of Paris, it's this magnificent 1836 monument to Napoléon's victory at Austerlitz (1805), which he commissioned the following year. The intricately sculpted triumphal arch stands sentinel in the centre of the Étoile ('Star') roundabout. From the viewing platform on top of the arch (50m up via 284 steps and well worth the climb) you can see the dozen avenues.

DON'T MISS

MUSÉE MARMOTTAN MONET

This **museum** (Map p58; 01 44 96 50 33; www.marmottan.fr; 2 rue Louis Boilly, 16e; adult/child €11/6.50; 10am-6pm Tue-Sun, to 9pm Thu; M La Muette) showcases the world's largest collection of works by impressionist painter Claude Monet (1840–1926) – about 100 – as well as paintings by Gauguin, Sisley, Pissarro, Renoir, Degas, Manet and Berthe Morisot. It also contains an important collection of French, English, Italian and Flemish illuminations from the 13th to 16th centuries.

Avenue des Champs-Élysées STREET
(Map p72; 8e; M Charles de Gaulle–Étoile, George V, Franklin D Roosevelt or Champs-Élysées–Clemenceau) No trip to Paris is complete without strolling this broad, tree-shaded avenue lined with luxury shops. Named for the Elysian Fields ('heaven' in Greek mythology), the Champs-Élysées was laid out in the 17th century and is part of the *axe historique,* linking place de la Concorde with the Arc de Triomphe. It's where presidents and soldiers strut their stuff on Bastille Day, where the Tour de France holds its final sprint, and where Paris turns out for organised and impromptu celebrations.

Place de la Concorde SQUARE
(Map p72; 8e; M Concorde) Paris spreads around you, with views of the Eiffel Tower, the Seine and along the Champs-Élysées, when you stand in the city's largest square. Its 3300-year-old pink granite obelisk was a gift from Egypt in 1831. The square was first laid out in 1755 and originally named after King Louis XV, but its royal associations meant that it took centre stage during the Revolution – Louis XVI was the first to be guillotined here in 1793.

Grand Palais ART MUSEUM
(Map p72; 01 44 13 17 17; www.grandpalais.fr; 3 av du Général Eisenhower, 8e; adult/child €15/1; 10am-8pm Sun, Mon & Thu, to 10pm Wed, Fri & Sat; M Champs-Élysées–Clemenceau) Erected for the 1900 Exposition Universelle (World's Fair), the Grand Palais today houses several exhibition spaces beneath its huge 8.5-tonne

Eiffel Tower Area & 16e

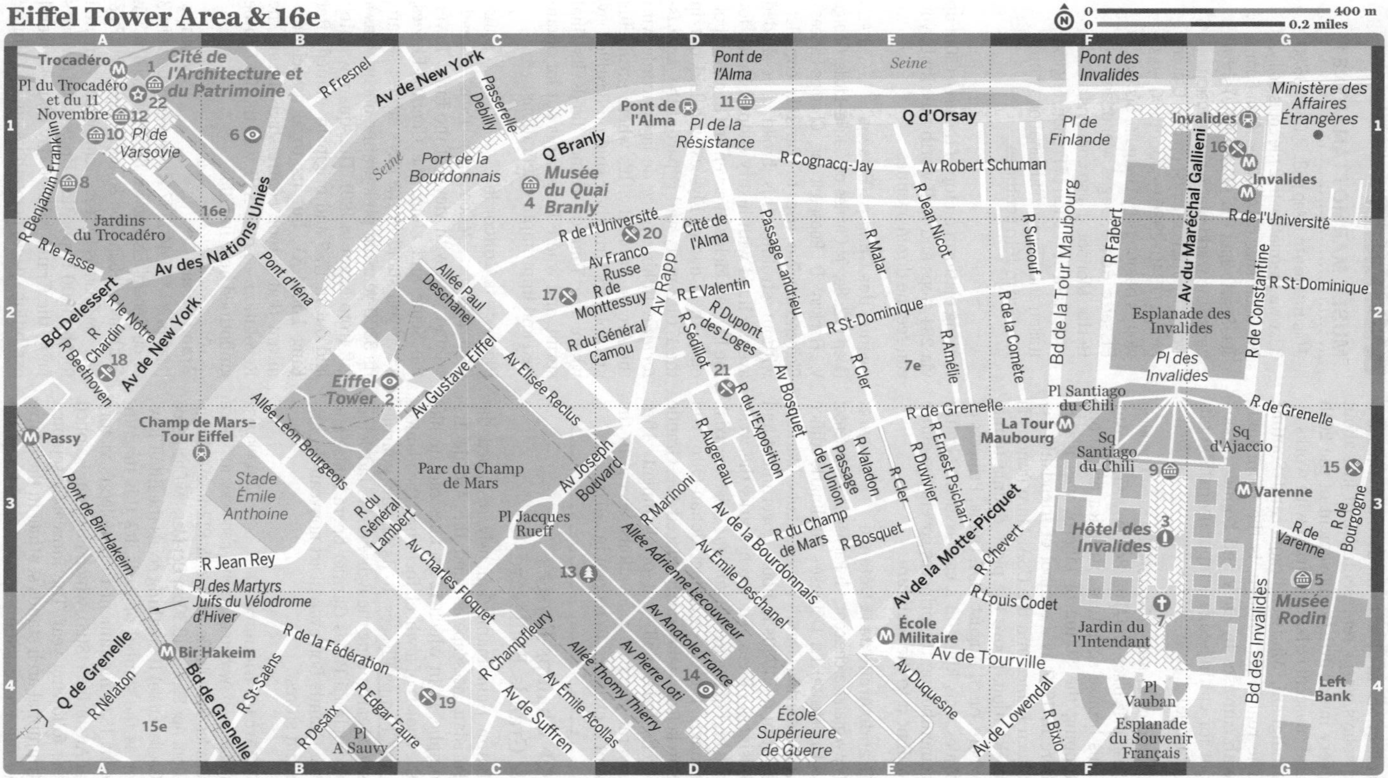

Eiffel Tower Area & 16e

Top Sights

1 Cité de l'Architecture et du Patrimoine ... A1
2 Eiffel Tower ... B2
3 Hôtel des Invalides ... F3
4 Musée du Quai Branly ... C1
5 Musée Rodin ... G3

Sights

6 Aquarium de Paris Cinéaqua ... B1
7 Église du Dôme ... F4
8 Musée de la Marine ... A1
9 Musée de l'Armée ... F3
10 Musée de l'Homme ... A1
11 Musée des Égouts de Paris ... D1
12 Palais de Chaillot ... A1
13 Parc du Champ de Mars ... C3
14 Wall for Peace Memorial ... D4

Eating

15 Besnier ... G3
16 Chez Françoise ... G1
17 Firmin Le Barbier ... C2
18 L'Astrance ... A2
19 Le Casse Noix ... C4
20 Les Deux Abeilles ... D2
21 Les Fables de la Fontaine ... D2

Entertainment

22 Théâtre National de Chaillot ... A1

art nouveau glass roof. Some of Paris' biggest shows (Renoir, Chagall, Turner) are held in the Galeries Nationales, lasting three to four months. Hours, prices and exhibition dates vary significantly for all galleries. Those listed here generally apply to the Galeries Nationales, but always check the website for exact details. Reserving a ticket online for any show is strongly advised.

Petit Palais ART MUSEUM

(Map p72; 01 53 43 40 00; www.petitpalais.paris.fr; av Winston-Churchill, 8e; permanent collections free; 10am-6pm Tue-Sun; M Champs-Élysées–Clemenceau) FREE This architectural stunner was built for the 1900 Exposition Universelle, and is home to the Musée des Beaux-Arts de la Ville de Paris (City of Paris Museum of Fine Arts). It specialises in medieval and Renaissance objets d'art, such as porcelain and clocks, tapestries, drawings, and 19th-century French painting and sculpture; it also has paintings by such artists as Rembrandt, Colbert, Cézanne, Monet, Gauguin and Delacroix. The cafe here has lovely garden seating.

Palais de la Découverte SCIENCE MUSEUM

(Map p72; www.palais-decouverte.fr; av Franklin D Roosevelt, 8e; adult/child €9/7; 9.30am-6pm Tue-Sat, 10am-7pm Sun; M Champs-Élysées–Clemenceau) Attached to the Grand Palais, this children's science museum has excellent temporary exhibits (eg moving lifelike dinosaurs) as well as a hands-on, interactive permanent collection focusing on astronomy, biology, physics and the like. Some of the older exhibits have French-only explanations, but overall this is a dependable family outing.

★ **Palais Garnier** OPERA HOUSE

(Map p66; 08 25 05 44 05; www.operadeparis.fr; cnr rues Scribe & Auber, 9e; adult/child unguided tours €11/7, guided tours €15.50/11; unguided tours 10am-5pm, to 1pm on matinee performance days, guided tours by reservation; M Opéra) The fabled 'phantom of the opera' lurked in this opulent opera house designed in 1860 by Charles Garnier (then an unknown 35-year-old architect). Reserve a spot on an English-language guided tour or take an unguided tour of the attached museum, with posters, costumes, backdrops, original scores and other memorabilia, which includes a behind-the scenes peek (except during matinees and rehearsals). Highlights include the Grand Staircase and horseshoe-shaped, gilded auditorium with red velvet seats, a massive chandelier and Chagall's gorgeous ceiling mural.

Louvre & Les Halles

Paris' splendid line of monuments, the *axe historique* (historic axis; also called the grand axis), passes through the Tuileries gardens before reaching IM Pei's glass pyramid at the entrance to the world's most visited museum, the Louvre. Nearby, the Forum des Halles shopping mall has recently emerged from a much-needed makeover.

★ **Musée du Louvre** MUSEUM

(Map p76; 01 40 20 53 17; www.louvre.fr; rue de Rivoli & quai des Tuileries, 1er; adult/child €15/free; 9am-6pm Mon, Thu, Sat & Sun, to 9.45pm Wed & Fri; M Palais Royal–Musée du Louvre) Few art galleries are as prized or daunting as the Musée du Louvre, Paris' pièce de résistance no first-time visitor to the city can resist. This is, after all, one of the world's largest and most diverse museums. Showcasing 35,000 works of art – from Mesopotamian, Egyptian and Greek antiquities to masterpieces by artists such as da Vinci,

Opéra & Grands Boulevards

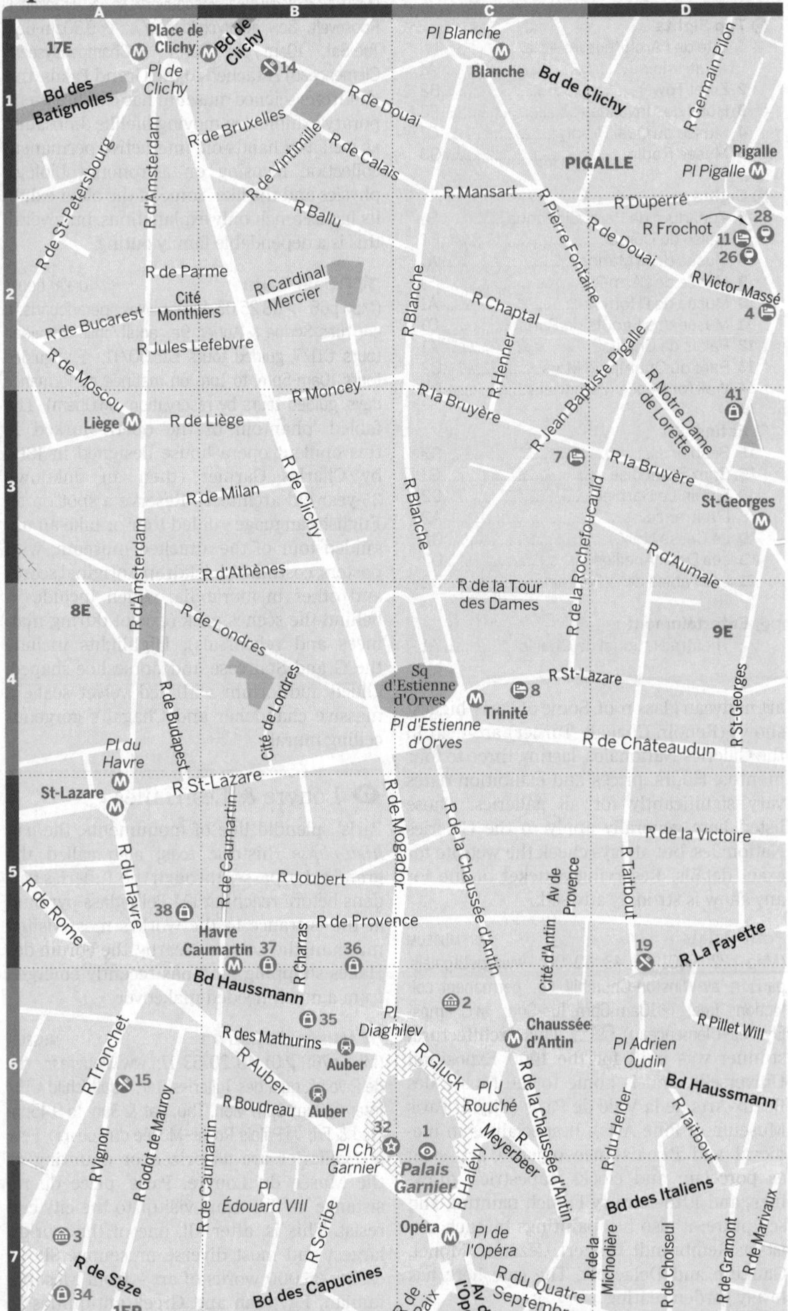

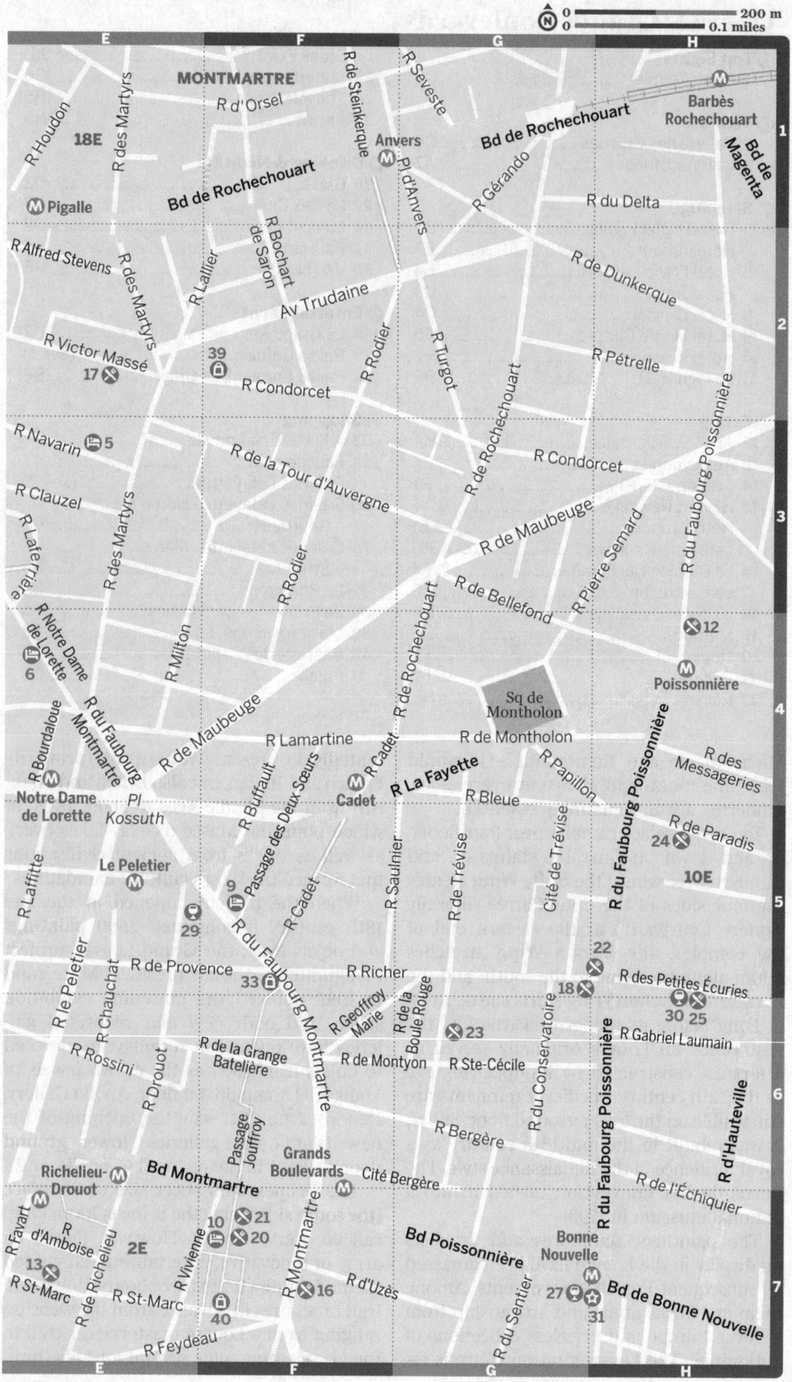
0 200 m
0 0.1 miles
MONTMARTRE
18E
R Houdon
R des Martyrs
R d'Orsel
R de Steinkerque
R Seveste
Anvers
Bd de Rochechouart
Barbès Rochechouart
Bd de Magenta
Pigalle
Pl d'Anvers
R Gérando
R du Delta
R Alfred Stevens
R Bochart de Saron
R Lallier
Av Trudaine
R de Dunkerque
R Victor Massé
17
39
R Condorcet
R Rodier
R Turgot
R Pétrelle
R du Faubourg Poissonnière
R Navarin
5
R de la Tour d'Auvergne
R de Rochechouart
R Condorcet
R Clauzel
R Laferrière
R de Maubeuge
R Pierre Semard
R de Bellefond
12
R Notre Dame de Lorette
6
R Milton
Poissonnière
Sq de Montholon
R Bourdaloue
R du Faubourg Montmartre
R Lamartine
R de Montholon
R des Messageries
Notre Dame de Lorette
Pl Kossuth
R Buffault
Passage des Deux Sœurs
R Cadet
Cadet
R La Fayette
R Papillon
R Bleue
R de Paradis
24
Le Peletier
R Laffitte
9
R Saulnier
R de Trévise
Cité de Trévise
10E
29
R de Provence
R Richer
22
33
R des Petites Écuries
18
30
25
R le Peletier
R Chauchat
R Geoffroy Marie
R de la Boule Rouge
23
R du Conservatoire
R Gabriel Laumain
R Rossini
R de la Grange Batelière
R de Montyon
R Ste-Cécile
R Drouot
R d'Hauteville
R Bergère
Passage Jouffroy
Grands Boulevards
Richelieu-Drouot
Bd Montmartre
Cité Bergère
R de l'Échiquier
21
10
20
R Favart
R d'Amboise
2E
R Vivienne
Bd Poissonnière
Bonne Nouvelle
13
R de Richelieu
R St-Marc
R St-Marc
40
16
R d'Uzès
27
31
Bd de Bonne Nouvelle
R du Sentier
R Feydeau
E
F
G
H
1
2
3
4
5
6
7

Opéra & Grands Boulevards

Top Sights
1 Palais Garnier C6

Sights
2 Galerie des Galeries C6
3 La Pinacothèque A7

Sleeping
4 Grand Hôtel Pigalle D2
5 Hôtel Amour E3
6 Hôtel France Albion E4
7 Hôtel Joyce C3
8 Hôtel Langlois C4
9 Hôtel Monte Carlo F5
10 Hôtel Vivienne F7
11 Le Pigalle D2

Eating
12 Abri H4
13 Aux Lyonnais E7
14 Crêperie Pen-Ty B1
15 Helmut Newcake A6
Hôtel Amour .... (see 5)
Lafayette Gourmet .... (see 35)
16 Le Camion Qui Fume F7
17 Le Pantruche E2
18 L'Office G5
19 Mamou D5
20 Noglu F7
21 Racines F7
22 Richer H5
Steak Point .... (see 35)
23 SuperNature Cantine G6
24 Tricycle Store H5
25 Vivant H6

Drinking & Nightlife
26 Glass D2
27 Le Rex Club G7
28 Lulu White D2
29 PanPan E5
30 Vivant Cave H6

Entertainment
31 Le Grand Rex H7
Palais Garnier .... (see 1)
32 Palais Garnier Box Office B6

Shopping
33 À la Mère de Famille F5
34 Fauchon A7
Galeries Lafayette .... (see 2)
35 Galeries Lafayette - Home & Gourmet B6
36 Galeries Lafayette - Men's Store B5
37 Le Printemps B5
38 Le Printemps de l'Homme A5
39 Maison Kitsuné F2
40 Passage des Panoramas F7
41 Pigalle D3

Michelangelo and Rembrandt – it would take nine months to glance at every piece, rendering advance planning essential.

Today the palace rambles over four floors, up and down innumerable staircases, and through three wings: the **Sully Wing** creates the four sides of the Cour Carrée (literally 'Square Courtyard') at the eastern end of the complex; the **Denon Wing** stretches 800m along the Seine to the south; and the northern **Richelieu Wing** skirts rue de Rivoli. Long before its modern incarnation, the vast Palais du Louvre originally served as a fortress constructed by Philippe-Auguste in the 12th century (medieval remnants are still visible on the lower ground floor, Sully); it was rebuilt in the mid-16th century as a royal residence in the Renaissance style. The Revolutionary Convention turned it into a national museum in 1793.

The paintings, sculptures and artefacts on display in the Louvre have been amassed by subsequent French governments. Among them are works of art and artisanship from all over Europe and priceless collections of antiquities. The Louvre's raison d'être is essentially to present Western art (primarily French and Italian, but also Dutch and Spanish) from the Middle Ages to about 1848 (at which point the Musée d'Orsay takes over), as well as works from ancient civilisations that formed the West's cultural foundations.

When the museum opened in the late 18th century it contained 2500 paintings and objets d'art; the 'Grand Louvre' project inaugurated by the late president Mitterrand in 1989 doubled the museum's exhibition space, and both new and renovated galleries have opened in recent years devoted to objets d'art such as the crown jewels of Louis XV (Room 66, 1st floor, Apollo Gallery, Denon). Late 2012 saw the opening of the new Islamic art galleries (lower ground floor, Denon) in the restored Cour Visconti.

The richness and sheer size of the place (the south side facing the Seine is 700m long) can be overwhelming. However, there's an array of innovative, entertaining self-guided thematic trails (1½ to three hours; download trail brochures in advance from the website) ranging from a Louvre masterpieces trail to the art of eating, plus several for kids (hunt

lions, galloping horses). Even better are the Louvre's self-paced multimedia guides (€5). More-formal, English-language guided tours depart from the **Hall Napoléon**, which has free English-language maps.

For many, the star attraction is Leonardo da Vinci's *La Joconde,* better known as *Mona Lisa* (Room 6, 1st floor, Denon). This entire section of the 1st floor of the Denon Wing, in fact, is hung with masterpieces – rooms 75 and 77 have enormous French paintings from Ingres, Delacroix *(Liberty Leading the People)* and Géricault *(The Raft of the Medusa),* while rooms 1, 3, 5 and 8 contain transcendent pieces by Raphael, Titian, Botticini and Botticcelli. On the ground floor of the Denon Wing, take time for Michelangelo's *The Dying Slave* and Canova's *Psyche and Cupid* (Room 4).

But don't rush by the treasures from antiquity: both Mesopotamia (ground floor, Richelieu) and Egypt (ground and 1st floors, Sully) offer fascinating insights into ancient civilisations, as seen in the *Code of Hammurabi* (Room 3, ground floor, Richelieu) and the *Seated Scribe* (Room 22, 1st floor, Sully). Also worth a look are the mosaics and figurines from the Byzantine Empire (lower ground floor, Denon), which merge into the state-of-the-art Islamic collection in the Cour Visconti, and of course the armless Greek duo, the *Venus de Milo* (Room 16, ground floor, Sully) and the *Winged Victory of Samothrace* (top of Daru staircase, 1st floor, Denon).

Also of note are the gilded-to-the-max Napoleon III Apartments (1st floor, Richelieu), Dutch masters Vermeer (Room 38, 2nd floor, Richelieu) and Rembrandt (Room 31, 2nd floor, Richelieu), and the 18th- and 19th-century French painting collection (2nd floor, Sully), which features iconic works like Ingres' *The Turkish Bath* (off Room 60).

The main entrance is through the 21m-high **Grande Pyramide**, a glass pyramid designed by the Chinese-born American architect IM Pei. If you don't have the Museum Pass (which gives you priority), you can avoid the longest queues (for security) outside the pyramid by entering the Louvre complex via the underground shopping centre **Carrousel du Louvre** (www.carrouseldulouvre.com; 99 rue de Rivoli, 1er; 8.30am-11pm, shops 10am-8pm;). You'll need to queue up again to buy your ticket once inside; buying tickets and renting an audioguide online will save you time.

DON'T MISS

PARIS FOR CHILDREN

Musée en Herbe (01 40 67 97 66; www.musee-en-herbe.com; 23 rue de l'Arbre-Sec, 1er; €6; 10am-7pm Fri-Wed, to 9pm Thu; ; M Louvre Rivoli, Châtelet) is one of the city's great backstreet secrets. This children's museum, which moved to a new, larger locale in 2016, is a surprise gem for art lovers of every age, not just kids. Its permanent exhibition changes throughout the year and focuses on the work of one artist or theme through a series of interactive displays.

Captions are in English as well as French, children get a *jeu de piste* (activity sheet) to guide and entertain, and additional workshops and guided visits for kids and adults – think hands-on art workshops, afternoon tea, early-evening aperitifs and so on (€6 to €10, reserve in advance) – add to the playful experience.

Tickets are valid for the whole day, so you can come and go as you please. The centrepiece of the Carrousel du Louvre is the glass Pyramide Inversée, also by Pei.

Les Arts Décoratifs ART MUSEUM

(Map p76; www.lesartsdecoratifs.fr; 107 rue de Rivoli, 1er; adult/child €11/free; 11am-6pm Tue-Sun, to 9pm Thu; M Palais Royal–Musée du Louvre) A trio of privately administered collections – Applied Arts, Advertising and Fashion & Textiles – sit in the Rohan Wing of the vast Palais du Louvre. They are collectively known as the Decorative Arts; admission includes entry to all three. For an extra €2, you can scoop up a combo ticket that also includes the **Musée Nissim de Camondo** (63 rue de Monceau, 8e; adult/child €9/free; 11am-5.30pm Wed-Sun; M Monceau, Villiers) in the 8e.

★ **Jardin des Tuileries** PARK

(Map p76; 7am-11pm Jun-Aug, shorter hours Sep-May; ; M Tuileries, Concorde) Filled with fountains, ponds and sculptures, the formal 28-hectare Tuileries Garden, which begins just west of the Jardin du Carrousel, was laid out in its present form in 1664 by André Le Nôtre, who also created the gardens at Vaux-le-Vicomte and Versailles. The Tuileries soon became the most fashionable spot in Paris for parading about in one's finery. It now forms part of the Banks of the Seine Unesco World Heritage site.

The Louvre

A HALF-DAY TOUR

Successfully visiting the Louvre is a fine art. Its complex labyrinth of galleries and staircases spiralling three wings and four floors renders discovery a snakes-and-ladders experience. Initiate yourself with this three-hour itinerary – a playful mix of Mona Lisa obvious and up-to-the-minute unexpected.

Arriving in the newly renovated **Hall Napoléon** 1 beneath IM Pei's glass pyramid, pick up colour-coded floor plans at an information stand, then ride the escalator up to the Sully Wing and swap passport or credit card for multimedia guide (there are limited descriptions in the galleries) at the wing entrance.

The Louvre is as much about spectacular architecture as masterly art. To appreciate this zip up and down Sully's Escalier Henri II to admire **Venus de Milo** 2, then up parallel Escalier Henri IV to the palatial displays in **Cour Khorsabad** 3. Cross room 1 to find the escalator up to the 1st floor and the opulent **Napoleon III apartments** 4. Next traverse 25 consecutive galleries (thank you, floor plan!) to flip conventional contemplation on its head with Cy Twombly's **The Ceiling** 5, and the hypnotic **Winged Victory of Samothrace sculpture** 6, which brazenly insists on being admired from all angles. End with the impossibly famous **The Raft of the Medusa** 7, **Mona Lisa** 8 and **Virgin & Child** 9.

TOP TIPS

» **Floor Plans** Don't even consider entering the Louvre's maze of galleries without a Plan/Information Louvre brochure, free from the information desk in the Hall Napoléon

» **Crowd dodgers** The Denon Wing is always packed; visit on late nights Wednesday or Friday or trade Denon in for the notably quieter Richelieu Wing

» **2nd floor** Not for first-timers: save its more specialist works for subsequent visits

MISSION MONA LISA

If you just want to venerate the Louvre's most famous lady, use the Porte des Lions entrance (closed Wednesday and Friday), from where it's a five-minute walk. Go up one flight of stairs and through rooms 26, 14 and 13 to the Grande Galerie and adjoining room 6.

Napoleon III Apartments

1st Floor, Richelieu

Napoleon III's gorgeous gilt apartments were built from 1854 to 1861, featuring an over-the-top decor of gold leaf, stucco and crystal chandeliers that reaches a dizzying climax in the Grand Salon and State Dining Room.

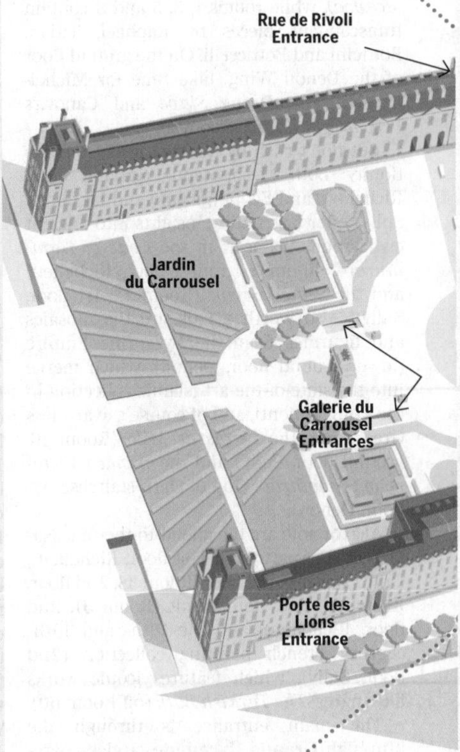

The Raft of the Medusa

Room 77, 1st Floor, Denon

Decipher the politics behind French romanticism in Théodore Géricault's *Raft of the Medusa*.

DEA/G.DAGLI ORTI/GETTY IMAGES ©

Mona Lisa
Room 6, 1st Floor, Denon
No smile is as enigmatic or bewitching as hers. Da Vinci's diminutive *La Joconde* hangs opposite the largest painting in the Louvre – sumptuous, fellow Italian Renaissance artwork *The Wedding at Cana*.

Cour Khorsabad
Ground Floor, Richelieu
Time travel with a pair of winged human-headed bulls to view some of the world's oldest Mesopotamian art. **DETOUR»** Night-lit statues in Cour Puget.

The Ceiling
Room 32, 1st Floor, Sully
Admire the blue shock of Cy Twombly's 400-sq-metre contemporary ceiling fresco – the Louvre's latest, daring commission. **DETOUR»** *The Braque Ceiling*, room 33.

CY TWOMBLY FOUNDATION/GETTY IMAGES ©

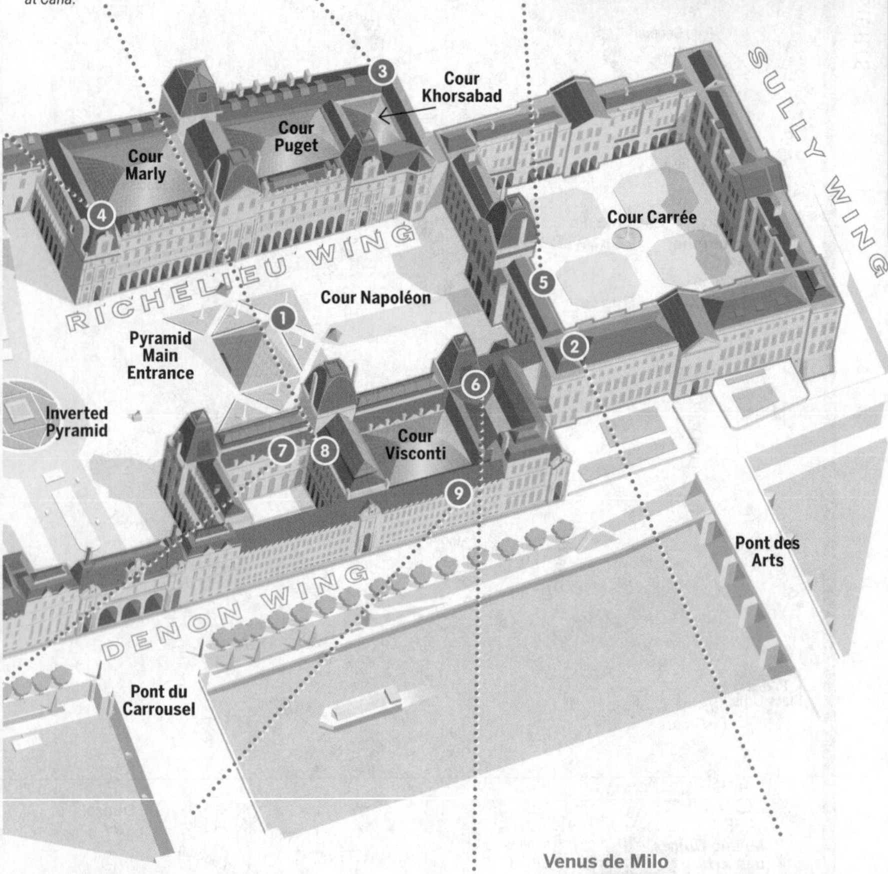

SUPERSTOCK/GETTY IMAGES ©

Virgin & Child
Grande Galerie, 1st Floor, Denon
In the spirit of artistic devotion save the Louvre's most famous gallery for last: a feast of Virgin-and-child paintings by Da Vinci, Raphael, Domenico Ghirlandaio, Giovanni Bellini and Francesco Botticini.

Winged Victory of Samothrace
Escalier Daru, 1st Floor, Sully
Draw breath at the aggressive dynamism of this headless, handless Hellenistic goddess. **DETOUR»** The razzle-dazzle of the Apollo Gallery's crown jewels.

Venus de Milo
Room 16, Ground Floor, Sully
No one knows who sculpted this seductively realistic goddess from Greek antiquity. Naked to the hips, she is a Hellenistic masterpiece.

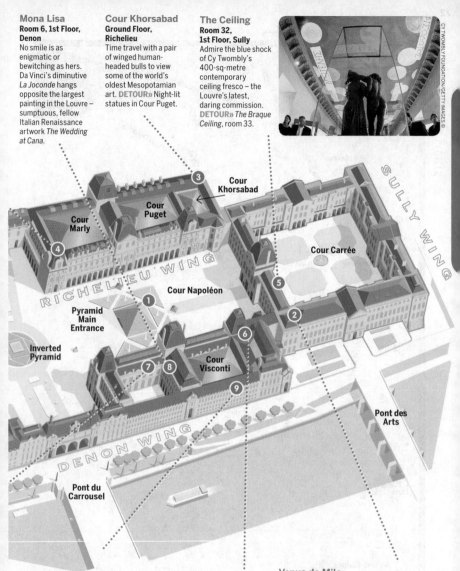

JOHN SONES SINGING BOWL MEDIA/GETTY IMAGES ©

Étoile & Champs-Élysées

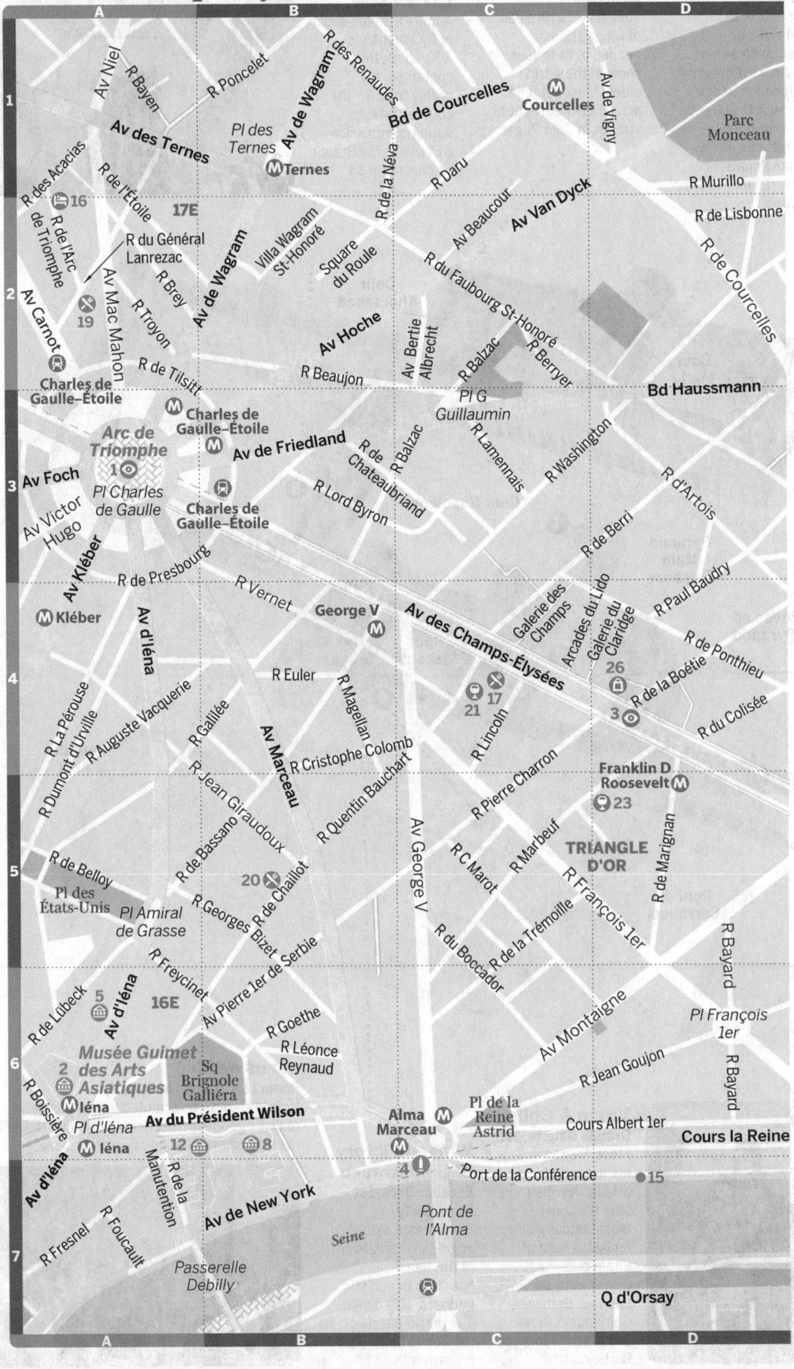

R Poncelet
R des Renaudes
Av de Wagram
Bd de Courcelles
Courcelles
Av de Vigny
Parc Monceau
Av Niel
R Bayen
Av des Ternes
Pl des Ternes
Ternes
R de la Néva
R Daru
R Murillo
R de Lisbonne
R des Acacias
16
R de l'Étoile
17E
Av Beaucour
Av Van Dyck
R de l'Arc de Triomphe
R du Général Lanrezac
Villa Wagram St-Honoré
Square du Roule
R du Faubourg St-Honoré
R de Courcelles
R Brey
Av Mac Mahon
Av Carnot
19
R Troyon
Av Hoche
Av Bertie Albrecht
R Balzac
R Berryer
R de Tilsitt
R Beaujon
Charles de Gaulle–Étoile
Pl G Guillaumin
Bd Haussmann
Arc de Triomphe
1
Av de Friedland
R de Chateaubriand
R Lamennais
R Washington
R d'Artois
Av Foch
Pl Charles de Gaulle
R Lord Byron
Av Victor Hugo
R de Berri
Av Kléber
R de Presbourg
R Vernet
George V
Av des Champs-Élysées
Galerie des Champs
Arcades du Lido
Galerie du Claridge
R Paul Baudry
Kléber
Av d'Iéna
R de Ponthieu
R Euler
R Magellan
21
17
26
R de la Boétie
3
R du Colisée
R La Pérouse
R Dumont d'Urville
R Auguste Vacquerie
R Galilée
Av Marceau
R Cristophe Colomb
R Lincoln
R Pierre Charron
Franklin D Roosevelt
23
R Jean Giraudoux
R Quentin Bauchart
Av George V
R de Bassano
R C Marot
R Marbeuf
TRIANGLE D'OR
R de Marignan
R de Belloy
Pl des États-Unis
20
R de Chaillot
R Georges Bizet
Pl Amiral de Grasse
R François 1er
R de la Trémoille
R du Boccador
R Bayard
R Freycinet
Av Pierre 1er de Serbie
R de Lübeck
5
16E
Av Montaigne
Pl François 1er
R Goethe
R Léonce Reynaud
Musée Guimet des Arts Asiatiques
2
Sq Brignole Galliéra
R Jean Goujon
R Boissière
Iéna
Pl d'Iéna
Av du Président Wilson
Alma Marceau
Pl de la Reine Astrid
Cours Albert 1er
Cours la Reine
12
8
R de la Manutention
4
Port de la Conférence
15
Av de New York
Pont de l'Alma
Seine
R Fresnel
R Foucault
Passerelle Debilly
Q d'Orsay
A
B
C
D
1
2
3
4
5
6
7

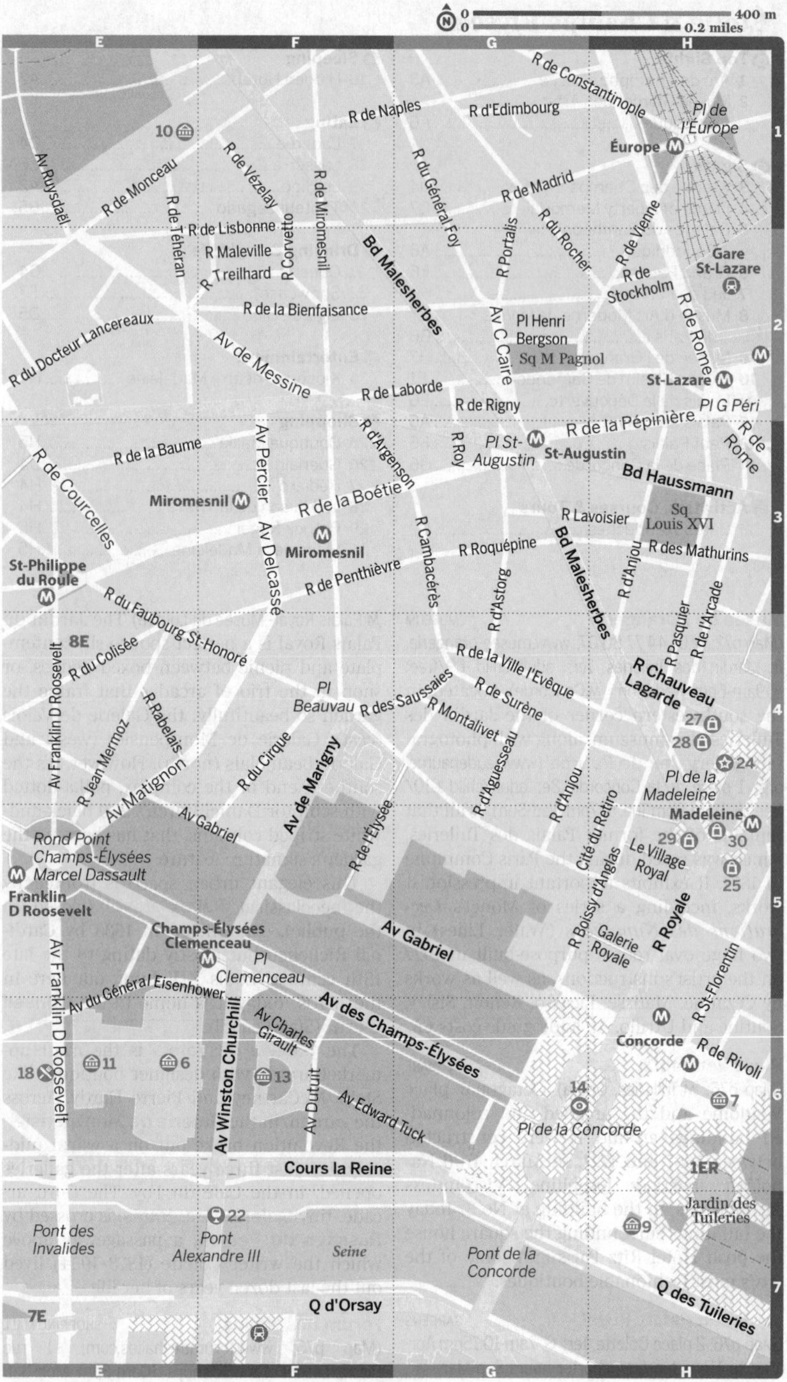
0 400 m
0 0.2 miles
E
F
G
H
1
2
3
4
5
6
7
R de Constantinople
Pl de l'Europe
Europe
R de Naples
R d'Edimbourg
10
Av Ruysdaël
R de Monceau
R de Vézelay
R de Miromesnil
R du Général Foy
R de Madrid
R de Téhéran
R de Lisbonne
R Maleville
R Treilhard
R Corvetto
Bd Malesherbes
R Portalis
R du Rocher
R de Vienne
R de Stockholm
Gare St-Lazare
R de la Bienfaisance
Av C Caire
Pl Henri Bergson
Sq M Pagnol
R de Rome
R du Docteur Lancereaux
Av de Messine
R de Laborde
St-Lazare
R de Rigny
Pl G Péri
R de la Pépinière
R de Rome
R de la Baume
Av Percier
R d'Argenson
R Roy
Pl St-Augustin
St-Augustin
Bd Haussmann
R de Courcelles
Miromesnil
R de la Boétie
R Cambacérès
R Lavoisier
Sq Louis XVI
Av Delcassé
Miromesnil
R Roquépine
R d'Anjou
R des Mathurins
St-Philippe du Roule
R de Penthièvre
R d'Astorg
R de l'Arcade
R du Faubourg St-Honoré
R Pasquier
8E
R du Colisée
R de la Ville l'Evêque
R Chauveau Lagarde
Av Franklin D Roosevelt
Pl Beauvau
R des Saussaies
R de Surène
R Rabelais
R Montalivet
27
28
24
R Jean Mermoz
R du Cirque
Av de Marigny
R d'Aguesseau
R d'Anjou
Pl de la Madeleine
Av Matignon
Cité du Retiro
Madeleine
Av Gabriel
R de l'Élysée
29
30
Rond Point Champs-Élysées Marcel Dassault
R Boissy d'Anglas
Le Village Royal
25
Franklin D Roosevelt
Champs-Élysées Clemenceau
Av Gabriel
Galerie Royale
R Royale
Pl Clemenceau
R St-Florentin
Av du Général Eisenhower
Av des Champs-Élysées
Av Charles Girault
Concorde
R de Rivoli
Av Franklin D Roosevelt
Av Winston Churchill
18
11
6
13
14
7
Av Dutuit
Av Edward Tuck
Pl de la Concorde
Cours la Reine
1ER
Jardin des Tuileries
22
9
Pont des Invalides
Pont Alexandre III
Seine
Pont de la Concorde
Q d'Orsay
Q des Tuileries
7E

Étoile & Champs-Élysées

Musée de l'Orangerie MUSEUM

(Map p72; ☎01 44 77 80 07; www.musee-orangerie.fr; Jardin des Tuileries, 1er; adult/child €9/free; ⏲9am-6pm Wed-Mon; Ⓜ Concorde) Located in the southwestern corner of the Jardin des Tuileries, this museum, along with photography gallery **Jeu de Paume** (www.jeudepaume.org; 1 place de la Concorde, 8e; adult/child €10/free; ⏲11am-9pm Tue, to 7pm Wed-Sun), is all that remains of the former Palais des Tuileries, which was razed during the Paris Commune in 1871. It exhibits important impressionist works, including a series of Monet's *Decorations des Nymphéas* (Water Lilies) in two huge oval rooms purpose-built in 1927 on the artist's instructions, as well as works by Cézanne, Matisse, Picasso, Renoir, Sisley, Soutine and Utrillo. An audioguide costs €5.

Place Vendôme SQUARE

(Map p76; Ⓜ Tuileries, Opéra) Octagonal place Vendôme and the arcaded and colonnaded buildings around it were constructed between 1687 and 1721. In March 1796 Napoléon married Josephine, Viscountess Beauharnais, in the building at No 3. Today the buildings surrounding the square house the posh Hôtel Ritz Paris and some of the city's most fashionable boutiques.

Jardin du Palais Royal GARDENS

(Map p76; 2 place Colette, 1er; ⏲7am-10.15pm Apr-May, to 11pm Jun-Aug, shorter hours Sep-Mar; 🚹; Ⓜ Palais Royal–Musée du Louvre) The Jardin du Palais Royal is a perfect spot to sit, contemplate and picnic between boxed hedges, or shop in the trio of arcades that frame the garden so beautifully: the Galerie de Valois (east), Galerie de Montpensier (west) and Galerie Beaujolais (north). However, it's the southern end of the complex, polka-dotted with sculptor Daniel Buren's 260 black-and-white striped columns, that has become the garden's signature feature.

This elegant urban space is fronted by the neoclassical **Palais Royal** (closed to the public), constructed in 1633 by Cardinal Richelieu but mostly dating to the late 18th century. Louis XIV hung out here in the 1640s; today it is home to the **Conseil d'État** (State Council).

The **Galerie de Valois** is the most upmarket arcade with designer boutiques like Stella McCartney and Pierre Hardy. Across the garden, in the **Galerie de Montpensier**, the Revolution broke out on a warm mid-July day, just three years after the galleries opened, in the Café du Foy. The third arcade, tiny **Galerie Beaujolais**, is crossed by **Passage du Perron**, a passageway above which the writer Colette (1873–1954) lived out the last dozen years of her life.

Forum des Halles SHOPPING MALL

(Map p76; www.forumdeshalles.com; 1 rue Pierre Lescot, 1er; ⏲shops 10am-8pm Mon-Sat;

Ⓜ Châtelet–Les Halles) Paris' main wholesale food market stood here for nearly 800 years before being replaced by this underground shopping mall in 1971. Long considered an eyesore by many Parisians, the mall's exterior was finally demolished in 2011 to make way for the new golden-hued translucent canopy, unveiled in 2016. Below, four floors of stores, cafes and a cinema extend down to the city's busiest metro hub.

★Église St-Eustache CHURCH
(Map p76; www.st-eustache.org; 2 impasse St-Eustache, 1er; ⏲9.30am-7pm Mon-Fri, 9am-7pm Sat & Sun; Ⓜ Les Halles) Just north of the gardens snuggling up to the city's old marketplace, now the bustling Forum des Halles, is one of the most beautiful churches in Paris. Majestic, architecturally magnificent and musically outstanding, St-Eustache has made spirits soar for centuries.

★Centre Pompidou MUSEUM
(Map p90; ☎01 44 78 12 33; www.centrepompidou.fr; place Georges Pompidou, 4e; museum, exhibitions & panorama adult/child €14/free; ⏲11am-10pm Wed-Mon; Ⓜ Rambuteau) The Centre Pompidou has amazed and delighted visitors ever since it opened in 1977, not just for its outstanding collection of modern art – the largest in Europe – but also for its radical architectural statement. The dynamic and vibrant arts centre delights with its irresistible cocktail of galleries and cutting-edge exhibitions, hands-on workshops, dance performances, cinemas and other entertainment venues. The exterior, with its street performers and fanciful fountains (place Igor Stravinsky), is a fun place to linger.

Montmartre & Northern Paris

Montmartre's lofty views, wine-producing vines and hidden village squares have lured painters from the 19th century onwards. Crowned by the Sacré-Cœur basilica, Montmartre is the city's steepest *quartier* (quarter), and its slinking streets lined with crooked ivy-clad buildings retain a fairy-tale charm. The edgy neighbourhoods of Pigalle and Canal St-Martin are hotbeds of creativity and have true grit: both squirrel away a treasure trove of fashionable drinking, dining and shopping addresses that every Parisian hipster adores.

★Basilique du Sacré-Cœur BASILICA
(Map p80; ☎01 53 41 89 00; www.sacre-coeur-montmartre.com; place du Parvis du Sacré-Cœur; dome adult/child €6/4, cash only; ⏲6am-10.30pm, dome 8.30am-8pm May-Sep, to 5pm Oct-Apr; Ⓜ Anvers) Although some may poke fun at Sacré-Cœur's unsubtle design, the view from its parvis is one of those perfect Paris postcards. More than just a basilica, Sacré-Cœur is a veritable experience, from the musicians performing on the steps to the groups of friends picnicking on the hillside park. Touristy, yes. But beneath it all, Sacré-Cœur's heart is gold.

★Le Mur des je t'aime PUBLIC ART
(Map p80; www.lesjetaime.com; Sq Jehan Rictus, place des Abbesses 18e; ⏲8am-8.30pm Mon-Fri, 9am-8.30pm Sat & Sun May-Aug, to 7.30pm Sep-Apr; Ⓜ Abbesses) Few visitors to Paris can resist a selfie in front of Montmartre's 'I Love You' wall, a public art work created in a small city-square park by artists Frédéric Baron and Claire Kito in the year 2000. The striking wall mural made from dark-blue enamel tiles features the immortal phrase 'I love you!' 311 times in 250 different languages. Find a bench beneath a maple tree and brush up your language skills romantic Paris-style.

Musée de Montmartre MUSEUM
(Map p80; ☎01 49 25 89 39; www.museedemontmartre.fr; 12 rue Cortot, 18e; adult/child €9.50/5.50; ⏲10am-6pm; Ⓜ Lamarck-Caulaincourt) One of Paris' most romantic spots, this enchanting 'village' museum showcases paintings, lithographs and documents illustrating Montmartre's bohemian, artistic and hedonistic past – one room is dedicated entirely to the French cancan! The museum is in a 17th-century manor where several artists, including Renoir and Raoul Dufy, had their studios in the 19th century. You can also visit the studio of pioneering female painter Suzanne Valadon, who lived and worked here with her son Maurice Utrillo and partner André Utter between 1912 and 1926.

Clos Montmartre VINEYARD
(Map p80; 18 rue des Saules, 18e; Ⓜ Lamarck-Caulaincourt) No, it is not a hallucination. If only to confirm Montmartre's enchanting village-like atmosphere the *quartier* even has its own small vineyard. Planted in 1933, its 2000 vines produce an average of 800 bottles of wine a year. Each October the grapes are pressed, fermented and bottled in Montmartre's town hall, then sold by auction to raise funds for local community projects.

Louvre & Les Halles

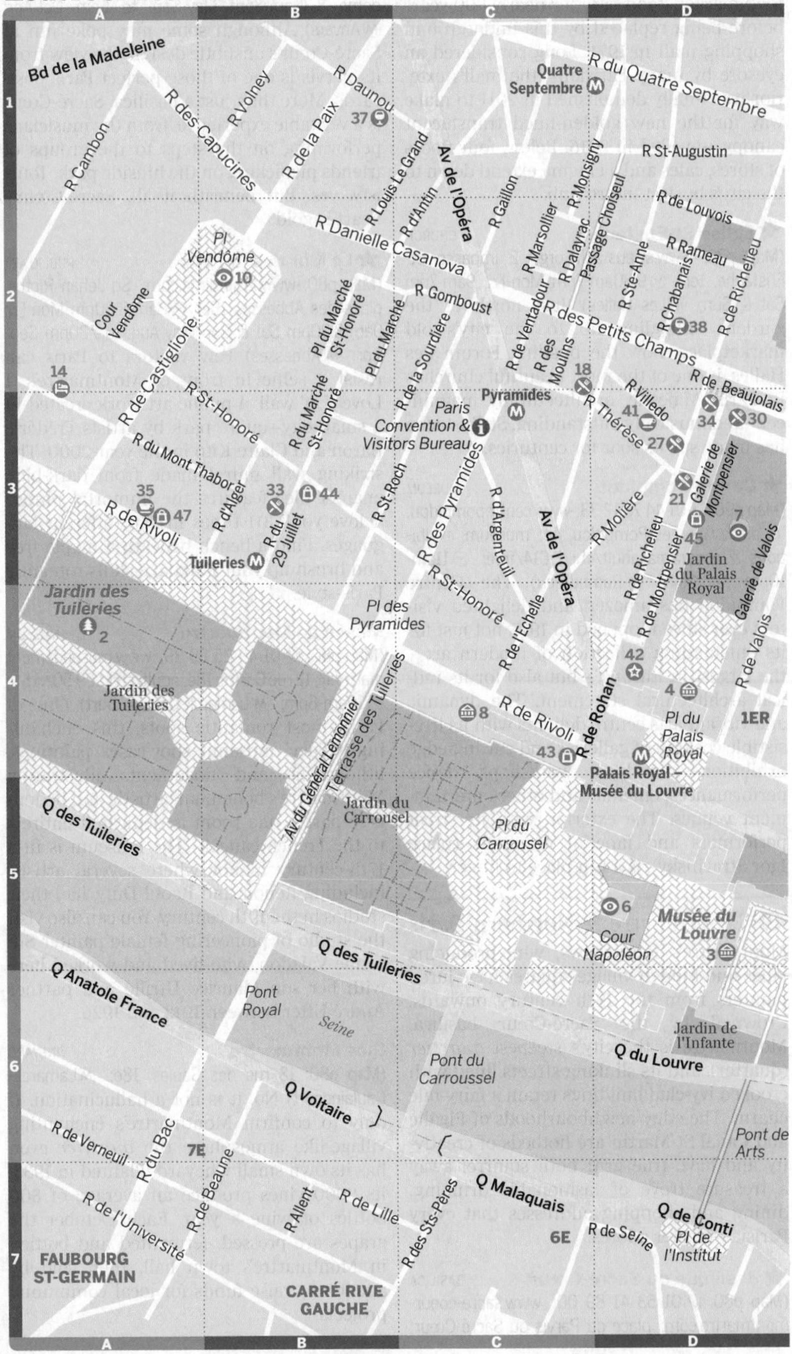

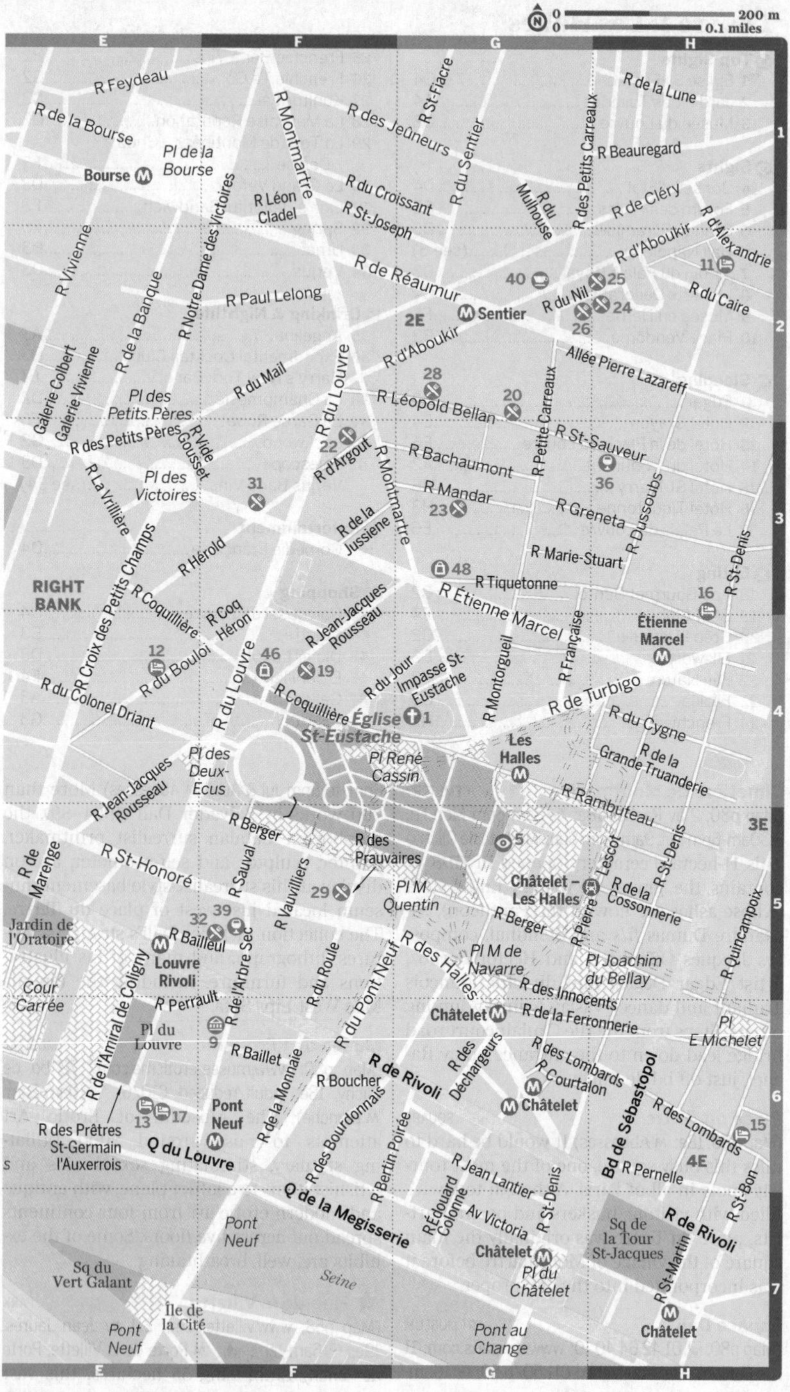
0 200 m
0 0.1 miles
E
F
G
H
1
2
3
4
5
6
7
R Feydeau
R de la Bourse
Pl de la Bourse
Bourse
R Vivienne
R de la Banque
R Notre Dame des Victoires
R Léon Cladel
R Montmartre
R des Jeûneurs
R St-Fiacre
R du Sentier
R du Croissant
R St-Joseph
R du Mulhouse
R des Petits Carreaux
R de la Lune
R Beauregard
R de Cléry
R d'Alexandrie
R d'Aboukir
R de Réaumur
R Paul Lelong
Sentier
2E
R du Nil
R du Caire
Allée Pierre Lazareff
R d'Aboukir
Galerie Colbert
Galerie Vivienne
R du Mail
R du Louvre
Pl des Petits Pères
R des Petits Pères
R Vide Gousset
R Léopold Bellan
R Petits Carreaux
R St-Sauveur
R d'Argout
R Bachaumont
R La Vrillière
Pl des Victoires
R Mandar
R Greneta
R Dussoubs
R de la Jussiene
R Marie-Stuart
R St-Denis
R Croix des Petits Champs
R Hérold
R Tiquetonne
RIGHT BANK
R Coquillière
R Coq Héron
R Jean-Jacques Rousseau
R Étienne Marcel
Étienne Marcel
R du Bouloi
R du Jour
Impasse St-Eustache
R Montorgueil
R Française
R du Colonel Driant
R Coquillière
Église St-Eustache
R de Turbigo
R du Cygne
Les Halles
Pl des Deux-Écus
Pl René Cassin
R de la Grande Truanderie
R Jean-Jacques Rousseau
R Rambuteau
3E
R Berger
R des Prauvaires
R de Marenge
R St-Honoré
R Sauval
Châtelet – Les Halles
R Lescot
R St-Denis
R de la Cossonnerie
R Vauvilliers
Pl M Quentin
Jardin de l'Oratoire
R Bailleul
R de l'Arbre Sec
R Berger
R Pierre
R Quincampoix
Louvre Rivoli
R des Halles
Pl M de Navarre
Pl Joachim du Bellay
R de l'Amiral de Coligny
R du Roule
R du Pont Neuf
R des Innocents
Cour Carrée
R Perrault
Châtelet
R de la Ferronnerie
Pl du Louvre
Pl E Michelet
R Baillet
R des Lombards
R de la Monnaie
R Boucher
R de Rivoli
R des Déchargeurs
R Courtalon
Bd de Sébastopol
Châtelet
R des Lombards
Pont Neuf
R des Bourdonnais
R des Prêtres St-Germain l'Auxerrois
Q du Louvre
R Bertin Poirée
R Jean Lantier
R Pernelle
4E
R St-Bon
Q de la Megisserie
R Édouard Colonne
Av Victoria
R St-Denis
Sq de la Tour St-Jacques
R de Rivoli
Pont Neuf
Châtelet
Pl du Châtelet
R St-Martin
Sq du Vert Galant
Seine
Châtelet
Île de la Cité
Pont Neuf
Pont au Change
1
5
9
11
12
13
15
16
17
19
20
22
23
24
25
26
28
29
31
32
36
39
40
46
48

Louvre & Les Halles

Top Sights
1 Église St-Eustache....G4
2 Jardin des Tuileries....A4
3 Musée du Louvre....D5

Sights
4 Conseil d'État....D4
5 Forum des Halles....G5
6 Grande Pyramide....D5
Hall Napoléon....(see 6)
7 Jardin du Palais Royal....D3
8 Les Arts Décoratifs....C4
9 Musée en Herbe....F6
10 Place Vendôme....B2

Sleeping
11 Edgar....H2
12 Hôtel Crayon....E4
13 Hôtel de la Place du Louvre....E6
14 Hôtel du Continent....A2
15 Hôtel St-Merry....H6
16 Hôtel Tiquetonne....H3
17 Le Relais du Louvre....E6

Eating
18 Ace Gourmet Bento....C2
19 Beef Club....F4
20 Crêpe Dentelle....G2
21 Ellsworth....D3
22 Fée Nature....F3
23 Filakia....G3
24 Frenchie....H2
25 Frenchie Bar à Vins....H2
26 Frenchie To Go....G2
27 Kunitoraya....D3
28 La Mauvaise Réputation....G2
29 La Tour de Montlhéry – Chez Denise....F5
30 Le Grand Véfour....D3
31 Lina's Beautiful Sandwich....F3
32 Spring....F5
33 Uma....B3
34 Verjus....D3

Drinking & Nightlife
35 Angelina....A3
36 Experimental Cocktail Club....H3
37 Harry's New York Bar....B1
38 La Champmeslé....D2
39 Le Garde Robe....F5
40 Lockwood....G2
41 Telescope....D3
Verjus Bar à Vins....(see 34)

Entertainment
42 Comédie Française....D4

Shopping
43 Carrousel du Louvre....C4
44 Colette....B3
45 Didier Ludot....D3
46 E Dehillerin....F4
47 Galignani....A3
48 Kiliwatch....G3

Cimetière de Montmartre CEMETERY
(Map p80; 2 av Rachel, 18e; 8am-6pm Mon-Fri, 8.30am-6pm Sat, 9am-6pm Sun; M Place de Clichy) This 11-hectare cemetery opened in 1798. It contains the graves of writers Émile Zola (whose ashes are now in the Panthéon), Alexandre Dumas *fils* and Stendhal, composers Jacques Offenbach and Hector Berlioz, artist Edgar Degas, film director François Truffaut and dancer Vaslav Nijinsky, among others. Steps from the rue Caulaincourt road bridge lead down to the entrance on av Rachel, just off bd de Clichy.

Place du Tertre SQUARE
(Map p80; 18e; M Abbesses) It would be hard to miss this busy square, one of the most touristy spots in all of Paris. Although today it's filled with visitors, buskers and portrait artists, place du Tertre was originally the main square of the village of Montmartre before it was incorporated into the city proper.

Espace Dalí ART MUSEUM
(Map p80; 01 42 64 40 10; www.daliparis.com; 11 rue Poulbot, 18e; adult/child €11.50/6.50; 10am-6pm, to 8pm Jul & Aug; M Abbesses) More than 300 works by Salvador Dalí (1904–89), the flamboyant Catalan surrealist printmaker, painter, sculptor and self-promoter, are on display at this surrealist-style basement museum located just west of place du Tertre. The collection includes Dalí's strange sculptures, lithograph, and many of his illustrations and furniture, including the famous Mae West Lips Sofa.

Musée de l'Érotisme MUSEUM
(Map p80; www.musee-erotisme.com; 72 bd de Clichy, 18e; adult/reduced €10/6; 10am-2am; M Blanche) The Museum of Erotic Art attempts to raise around 2000 titillating statuary, stimulating sexual aids and fetishist items to a loftier plane, with antique and modern erotic art from four continents spread out across five floors. Some of the exhibits are, well, breathtaking.

★ **Parc de la Villette** PARK
(Map p58; www.villette.com; 211 av Jean Jaurès, 19e; 6am-1am; ; M Porte de la Villette, Porte de Pantin) Embracing 55 hectares, this vast

city park is a cultural centre, kids playground and landscaped urban space at the intersection of two canals, the Ourcq and the St-Denis. Its futuristic layout includes the colossal mirror-like sphere of the Géode cinema and the bright-red cubical pavilions known as *folies*. Among its themed gardens are the Jardin du Dragon (Dragon Garden), with a giant dragon's tongue slide for kids, the Jardin des Dunes (Dunes Garden) and Jardin des Miroirs (Mirror Garden).

Cité des Sciences SCIENCE MUSEUM

(Map p58; ☎01 56 43 20 20; www.cite-sciences.fr; 30 av Corentin Cariou, 19e, Parc de la Villette; adult/child €9/7, La Géode €12/9; ⏲10am-6pm Tue-Sat, to 7pm Sun, La Géode 10.30am-8.30pm Tue-Sun; 👪; Ⓜ Porte de la Villette) This is the city's top museum for kids, with three floors of hands-on exhibits for children aged two and up, special-effect cinema **La Géode**, a planetarium and a retired submarine. Each exhibit has a separate admission fee (combined tickets exist), so research online beforehand to work out what's most appropriate. Be sure to reserve tickets in advance for both weekend and school-holiday visits, plus for the fabulous **Cité des Enfants** educative play sessions (1½ hours, ages two to seven years or five to 12 years) year-round.

Parc des Buttes-Chaumont PARK

(Map p58; rue Manin & rue Botzaris, 19e; ⏲7am-10pm May-Sep, to 8pm Oct-Apr; Ⓜ Buttes-Chaumont, Botzaris) This quirky park is one of the city's largest green spaces; its landscaped slopes hide grottoes, waterfalls, a lake and even an island topped with a temple to Sybil. Once a gypsum quarry and rubbish dump, it was given its present form by Baron Haussmann in time for the opening of the 1867 Exposition Universelle. The tracks of an abandoned 19th-century railway line (La Petite Ceinture, which once circled Paris) run through the park.

Le Marais, Ménilmontant & Belleville

Fashionable bars and restaurants, emerging designers' boutiques, the city's thriving gay and Jewish communities, and some excellent art and history museums all squeeze into Le Marais' warren of narrow medieval lanes. Neighbouring Ménilmontant has some of the city's most happening nightlife, while hilly Belleville is a vibrant multicultural neighbourhood with interesting dining and drinking spots and one of Paris' most colourful and raucous street markets.

> DON'T MISS
>
> ### CANAL ST-MARTIN
>
> The tranquil, 4.5km-long **Canal St-Martin** (Map p90; Ⓜ République, Jaurès, Jacques Bonsergent) was inaugurated in 1825 to provide a shipping link between the Seine and Paris' northeastern suburbs. Emerging from below ground near place République, its towpaths take you past locks, bridges and ordinary Parisian neighbourhoods. Come here for a romantic stroll, cycle, picnic lunch or dusk-time drink. Linger on the iron footbridge by the intersection of rue de la Grange and quai de Jemmapes to watch the vintage road bridge swing open to let canal boats pass.

★**Musée National Picasso** ART MUSEUM

(Map p90; ☎01 85 56 00 36; www.museepicassoparis.fr; 5 rue de Thorigny, 3e; adult/child €12.50/free; ⏲11.30am-6pm Tue-Fri, 9.30am-6pm Sat & Sun; Ⓜ St-Paul, Chemin Vert) One of Paris' most beloved art collections is showcased inside the mid-17th-century Hôtel Salé, an exquisite private mansion owned by the city since 1964. Inside is the Musée National Picasso, a staggering art museum devoted to the eccentric Spanish artist, Pablo Picasso (1881–1973), who spent much of his life living and working in Paris. The collection includes more than 5000 drawings, engravings, paintings, ceramic works and sculptures by the *grand maître* (great master), although they're not all displayed at the same time.

Hôtel de Ville ARCHITECTURE

(Map p90; www.paris.fr; place de l'Hôtel de Ville, 4e; Ⓜ Hôtel de Ville) FREE Paris' beautiful town hall was gutted during the Paris Commune of 1871 and rebuilt in neo-Renaissance style between 1874 and 1882. The ornate façade is decorated with 108 statues of illustrious Parisians, and the outstanding temporary exhibitions (admission free) inside in its **Salle St-Jean** almost always have a Parisian theme.

During most winters from December to early March, an ice-skating rink is set up outside this beautiful building, creating a real picture-book experience.

Musée Cognacq-Jay MUSEUM

(Map p90; www.cognacq-jay.paris.fr; 8 rue Elzévir, 3e; ⏲10am-6pm Tue-Sun; Ⓜ St-Paul, Chemin Vert)

Montmartre & Pigalle

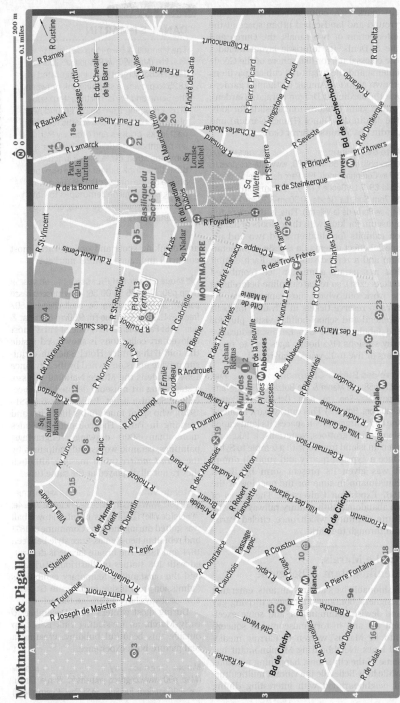

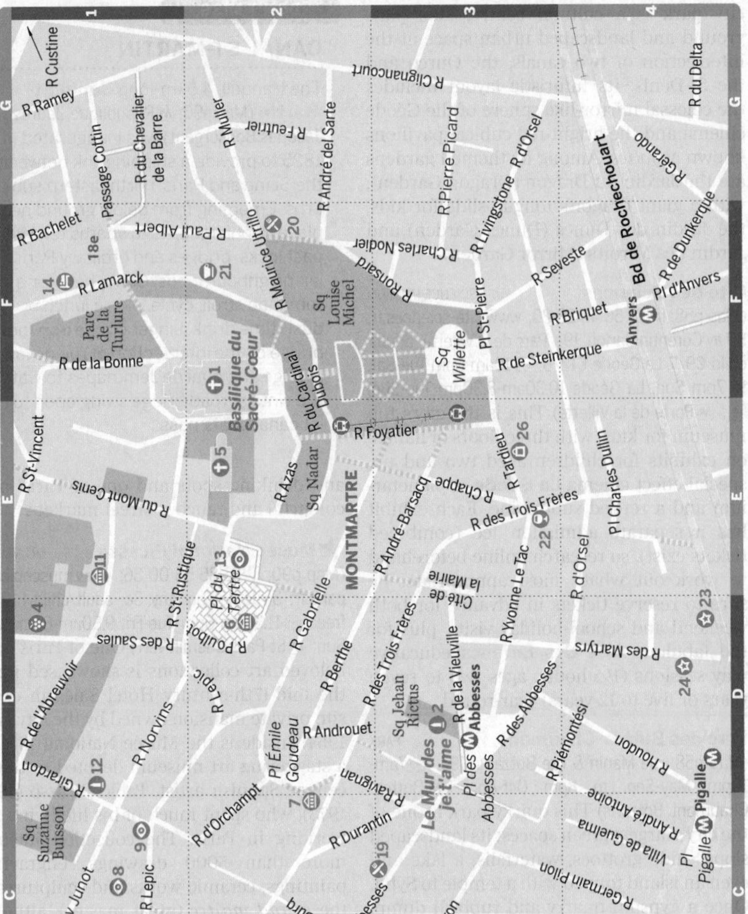

Montmartre & Pigalle

Top Sights

1 Basilique du Sacré-Cœur F2
2 Le Mur des je t'aime D3

Sights

3 Cimetière de Montmartre....A2
4 Clos Montmartre.... D1
5 Église St-Pierre de Montmartre....E2
6 Espace Dalí D2
7 Le Bateau Lavoir C2
8 Moulin Blute Fin C1
9 Moulin Radet C1
10 Musée de l'Érotisme....B3
11 Musée de Montmartre E1
12 Passe-Muraille.... D1
13 Place du Tertre....E2

Sleeping

14 Ermitage Hôtel F1
15 Hôtel Particulier Montmartre.... C1
16 Joke Hôtel....A4

Eating

17 Jeanne B B1
18 Le Dépanneur....B4
19 Le Grenier à Pain....C3
20 L'Été en Pente Douce F2

Drinking & Nightlife

21 Hardware Société....F2
22 Le Progrès....E3
Le Très Particulier ....(see 15)

Entertainment

23 La Cigale.... D4
24 Le Divan du Monde.... D4
25 Moulin Rouge....A3

Shopping

26 Belle du Jour....E3

FREE This museum inside Hôtel de Donon displays oil paintings, pastels, sculpture, objets d'art, jewellery, porcelain and furniture from the 18th century assembled by Ernest Cognacq (1839–1928), founder of La Samaritaine department store, and his wife Louise Jay. Although Cognacq appreciated little of his collection, boasting that he had never visited the Louvre and was only acquiring collections for the status, the artwork and objets d'art give a good idea of upper-class tastes during the Age of Enlightenment.

★ Place des Vosges SQUARE

(Map p90; 4e; Ⓜ St-Paul, Bastille) Inaugurated in 1612 as place Royale and thus Paris' oldest square, place des Vosges is a strikingly elegant ensemble of 36 symmetrical houses with ground-floor arcades, steep slate roofs and large dormer windows arranged around a leafy square with four symmetrical fountains and an 1829 copy of a mounted statue of Louis XIII. The square received its present name in 1800 to honour the Vosges *département* (administrative division) for being the first in France to pay its taxes.

Maison de Victor Hugo MUSEUM

(Map p90; www.musee-hugo.paris.fr; 6 place des Vosges, 4e; ⌚10am-6pm Tue-Sun; Ⓜ St-Paul, Bastille) FREE Between 1832 and 1848 the writer Victor Hugo lived in an apartment in Hôtel de Rohan-Guéménée, a townhouse overlooking one of Paris' most elegant squares. He moved here a year after the publication of *Notre Dame de Paris* (The Hunchback of Notre Dame), completing *Ruy Blas* during his stay. His house is now a museum devoted to the life of this celebrated novelist and poet, with an impressive collection of his personal drawings and portraits. Temporary exhibitions command an admission fee.

★ Musée des Arts et Métiers MUSEUM

(Map p90; www.arts-et-metiers.net; 60 rue de Réaumur, 3e; adult/child €8/free; ⌚10am-6pm Tue, Wed & Fri-Sun, to 9.30pm Thu; 👪; Ⓜ Arts et Métiers) The Arts and Crafts Museum, dating to 1794 and Europe's oldest science and technology museum, is a must for anyone with kids – or an interest in how things tick or work. Housed inside the sublime 18th-century priory of St-Martin des Champs, some 3000 instruments, machines and working models from the 18th to 20th centuries are displayed across three floors. In the attached church of St-Martin des Champs is Foucault's original pendulum, introduced to the world at the Universal Exhibition in Paris in 1855.

Musée d'Art et d'Histoire du Judaïsme MUSEUM

(Map p90; ☎01 53 01 86 62; www.mahj.org; 71 rue du Temple, 4e; adult/child €8/free; ⌚11am-6pm Mon-Fri, 10am-6pm Sun; Ⓜ Rambuteau) To delve into the historic heart of the Marais' long-established Jewish community in Pletzl (from the Yiddish for 'little square'), visit this fascinating museum inside Hôtel de St-Aignan, dating from 1650. The museum traces the evolution of Jewish communities from the Middle Ages to the present, with particular emphasis on French Jewish history. Highlights include documents relating to the Dreyfus Affair, and works by Chagall, Modigliani and Soutine. Creative workshops

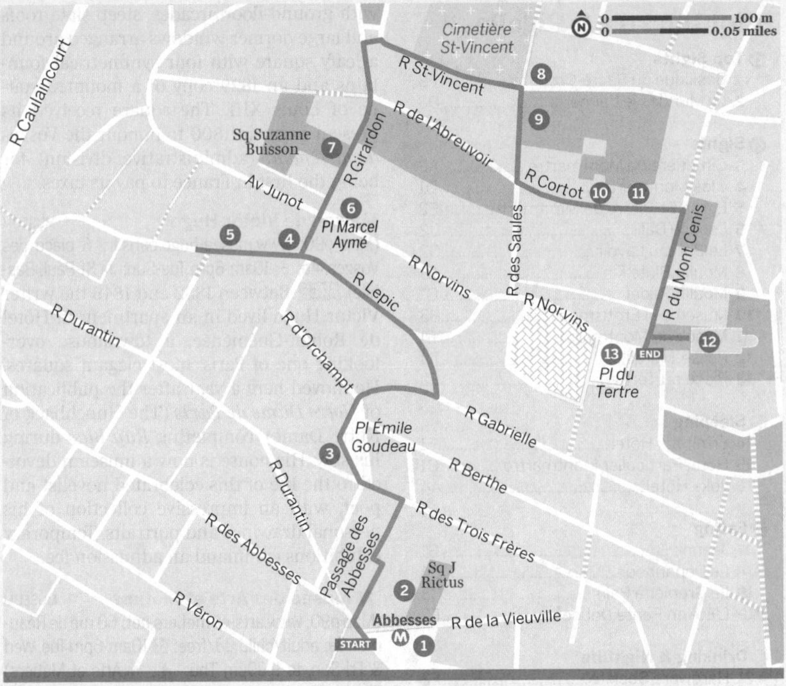

City Walk
Mythic Montmartre

START ABBESSES METRO STATION
END PLACE DU TERTRE
LENGTH 1KM; ONE HOUR

Begin on **1 place des Abbesses**, where Hector Guimard's art-nouveau metro entrance (1900) still stands. Beneath a maze of gypsum mines, it is one of Paris' deepest metro stations. Learn how to say 'I love you!' in another language at **2 Le Mur des je t'aime** (p75), hidden in a park, Sq Jehan Rictus, on place des Abbesses.

Head up to place Émile Goudeau. At No 11bis you'll find **3 Le Bateau Lavoir**, where Max Jacob, Amedeo Modigliani and Pablo Picasso – who painted his *Les Demoiselles d'Avignon* (1907) here – once had studios. Continue the climb up to Montmartre's two surviving windmills: **4 Moulin Radet** (now a restaurant) and **5 Moulin Blute Fin**. The latter became the open-air dance hall Le Moulin de la Galette, immortalised by Renoir in his 1876 tableau *Bal du Moulin de la Galette* (in the Musée d'Orsay).

Just north on place Marcel Aymé, watch a man pop out of a stone wall. This **6 Passe-Muraille statue** portrays Dutilleul, the hero of Marcel Aymé's short story *Le Passe-Muraille* (The Walker Through Walls). Aymé lived in the adjacent building from 1902 until 1967. Continue to Sq Suzanne Buisson, home to a **7 statue of St-Denis**, the 3rd-century martyr and patron saint of France beheaded by Roman priests.

After passing by Cimetière St-Vincent you'll come upon the celebrated cabaret **8 Au Lapin Agile**, with a mural of a rabbit jumping out of a cooking pot by caricaturist André Gill. Opposite is **9 Clos Montmartre** (p75), a vineyard dating from 1933.

Uphill is Montmartre's oldest building. One-time home to painters Renoir, Utrillo and Raoul Dufy, it's now the **10 Musée de Montmartre** (p75). Continue on past composer **11 Eric Satie's former residence** (No 6) and turn right onto rue du Mont Cenis; you'll soon come to historic **12 Église St-Pierre de Montmartre**. End on busy **13 place du Tertre** (p78), the former main village square.

for children, adults and families complement excellent temporary exhibitions.

★ Mémorial de la Shoah MUSEUM
(Map p90; www.memorialdelashoah.org; 17 rue Geoffroy l'Asnier, 4e; ⏲10am-6pm Sun-Wed & Fri, to 10pm Thu; Ⓜ St-Paul) FREE Established in 1956, the Memorial to the Unknown Jewish Martyr has metamorphosed into the Memorial of the Shoah – 'Shoah' is a Hebrew word meaning 'catastrophe' and it's synonymous in France with the Holocaust. Exhibitions relate to the Holocaust and German occupation of parts of France and Paris during WWII. The actual memorial to the victims of the Shoah stands at the entrance. The wall is inscribed with the names of 76,000 men, women and children deported from France to Nazi extermination camps.

★ Cimetière du Père Lachaise CEMETERY
(Map p58; ☎01 55 25 82 10; www.pere-lachaise.com; 16 rue du Repos & 8 bd de Ménilmontant, 20e; ⏲8am-6pm Mon-Fri, 8.30am-6pm Sat, 9am-6pm Sun, shorter hours winter; Ⓜ Père Lachaise, Gambetta) The world's most visited cemetery, Père Lachaise, opened in 1804. Its 70,000 ornate and ostentatious tombs of the rich and famous form a verdant, 44-hectare sculpture garden. The most visited are those of 1960s rock star Jim Morrison (division 6) and Oscar Wilde (division 89). Pick up cemetery maps at the **conservation office** (Bureaux de la Conservation; ⏲8.30am-12.30pm & 2-5pm Mon-Fri) near the main bd de Ménilmontant entrance. Other notables buried here include composer Chopin; playwright Molière; poet Apollinaire; and writers Balzac, Proust, Gertrude Stein and Colette.

Bastille & Eastern Paris

Fabulous markets, intimate gourmet bistros and some cutting-edge drinking and dancing venues make this neighbourhood one of the best places to discover the Parisians' Paris. And the area has ample creative quirks too: think interesting boutique shopping and a disused 19th-century railway viaduct with artist studios below and an elevated park (Promenade Plantée) on top, clearly made with green weekend walks in mind.

Place de la Bastille SQUARE
(Map p90; 12e; Ⓜ Bastille) The Bastille, a 14th-century fortress built to protect the city gates, is the most famous Parisian monument that no longer exists. Nothing remains of the prison it became under Cardinal Richelieu, which was mobbed on 14 July 1789, igniting the French Revolution. Today it's a skirmishly busy roundabout, with flying traffic around the 52m-high **Colonne de Juillet** in its centre. The unmissable green-bronze column is topped by a gilded, winged Liberty, and revolutionaries from the uprising of 1830 are buried beneath.

MUSÉE CARNAVALET

Currently closed for renovations until at least 2019, Paris' history museum rambles over a pair of remarkable *hôtels particuliers* (private mansions), the 1560-built **Hôtel Carnavalet** (23 rue de Sévigné, 3e) and 1688-built **Hôtel Le Peletier de St-Fargeau**. For more information, see www.carnavalet.paris.fr.

Promenade Plantée PARK
(La Coulée Verte René-Dumont; Map p94; cnr rue de Lyon & av Daumesnil, 12e; ⏲8am-9.30pm May-Aug, to 5.30pm Sep-Apr; Ⓜ Bastille, Gare de Lyon) The disused 19th-century Vincennes railway viaduct has been reborn as the world's first elevated park, planted with a fragrant profusion of cherry trees, maples, rose trellises, bamboo corridors and lavender. Three storeys above ground, it provides a unique aerial vantage point on the city. Access is via staircase and it starts just south of place de la Bastille on rue de Lyon. Along the first section, above av Daumesnil, chic art-gallery-workshops squat gracefully beneath the arches to form the Viaduc des Arts (p150).

La Manufacture 111 CULTURAL CENTRE
(Map p58; ☎01 40 33 01 36; www.manufacture111.com; 111 rue des Pyrénées, 20e; ⏲6-10pm Fri, noon-10pm Sat, noon-8pm Sun, but variable; Ⓜ Maraîchers) A massive 1500-sq-metre former garage now houses this cutting-edge urban cultural centre. Street art and hip-hop are at the heart of its temporary exhibitions, events and soirées, which can be anything from a music gig to live painting and performances. Here you can also catch a food truck, art workshops, a bookshop and the most creative Sunday brunch in town (11.30am to 3pm, €25). Check its Facebook page or Twitter feed for updates.

The Islands

Paris' geographic and spiritual heart is here in the Seine. The larger of the two inner-city

Cimetière du Père Lachaise

A HALF-DAY TOUR

There is a certain romance to getting lost in Cimetière du Père Lachaise, a grave jungle spun from centuries of tales. But to search for one grave among one million in this 44-hectare land of the dead is no joke – narrow the search with this itinerary.

From the main bd de Ménilmontant entrance (metro Père Lachaise or Philippe Auguste), head up av Principale, turn right onto av du Puits and collect a map from the **Bureaux de la Conservation** ❶.

Backtrack along av du Puits, turn right onto av Latérale du Sud, scale the stairs and bear right along chemin Denon to New Realist artist **Arman** ❷, film director **Claude Chabrol** ❸ and **Chopin** ❹.

Follow chemin Méhul downhill, cross av Casimir Périer and bear right onto chemin Serré. Take the second left (chemin Lebrun – unsigned), head uphill and near the top leave the footpath to weave through graves on your right to rock star **Jim Morrison** ❺. Back on chemin Lauriston, continue uphill to roundabout **Rond-Point Casimir Périer** ❻.

Admire the funerary art of contemporary photographer **André Chabot** ❼, av de la Chapelle. Continue uphill for energising city views from the **chapel** ❽ steps, then zig-zag to **Molière & La Fontaine** ❾, on chemin Molière.

Cut between graves onto av Tranversale No 1 – spot potatoes atop **Parmentier's** ❿ headstone. Continue straight onto av Greffülhe and left onto av Tranversale No 2 to rub **Monsieur Noir's** ⓫ shiny crotch.

Navigation to **Édith Piaf** ⓬ and the **Mur des Fédérés** ⓭ is straightforward. End with lipstick-kissed **Oscar Wilde** ⓮ near the Porte Gambetta entrance.

TOP TIPS

➡ **Say 'Cheese!'** Père Lachaise is photography paradise any time of day/year, but best are sunny autumn mornings after the rain.

➡ **Guided Tours** Cemetery lovers will appreciate themed guided tours (two hours) led by entertaining cemetery historian Thierry Le Roi (www.necro-romantiques.com).

BRUNO DE HOGUES / GETTY IMAGES ©

Chopin, Division 11

Add a devotional note to the handwritten letters and flowers brightening the marble tomb of Polish composer/pianist Frédéric Chopin (1810–49), who spent his short adult life in Paris. His heart is buried in Warsaw.

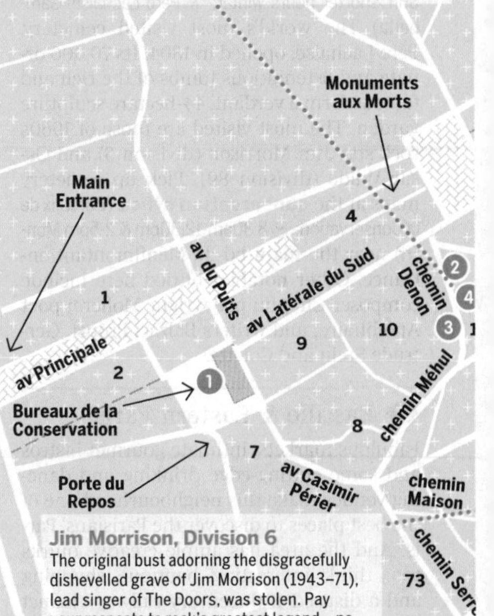

Jim Morrison, Division 6

The original bust adorning the disgracefully dishevelled grave of Jim Morrison (1943–71), lead singer of The Doors, was stolen. Pay your respects to rock's greatest legend – no chewing gum or padlocks please.

DAN HERRICK/ GETTY IMAGES ©

84
Porte Gambetta Entrance
av des Combattants Étrangers morts pour la France
Crematorium
88
av Circulaire
av Tranversale No 3
89
14
Chapel
51
50
8
av Tranversale No 1
av de Saint Morys
av Tranversale No 2
93
92
chemin Bertholié
24
21
chemin Molière
25
11
av Greffülhe
av de la Chapelle
7
20
9
42
94
26
10
41
95
6
Rond-Point Casimir Périer
39
av Pacthod
Commemorative war memorials
14
12
97
13
chemin Lauriston
5
76
96
6
5
chemin Lebrun
av Circulaire
Porte de la Réunion

André Chabot, Division 20

Contemporary photographer André Chabot (b 1941) shoots funerary art, hence the bijou 19th-century chapel he's equipped with monumental granite camera in preparation for the day he departs – and a QR code.

BRUNO DE HOGUES / GETTY IMAGES ©

Molière & La Fontaine, Division 25

Parisians refused to leave their local *quartier* for Père Lachaise so in 1817 the authorities moved in popular playwright Molière (1622–73) and poet Jean de la Fontaine (1621–95). The marketing strategy worked.

BRUNO DE HOGUES / GETTY IMAGES ©

Oscar Wilde, Division 89

Homosexual Irish writer Oscar Wilde (1854–1900) was forever scandalous: check the enormous packet of the sphinx on his tomb, sculpted by British-American sculptor Jacob Epstein 11 years after he died.

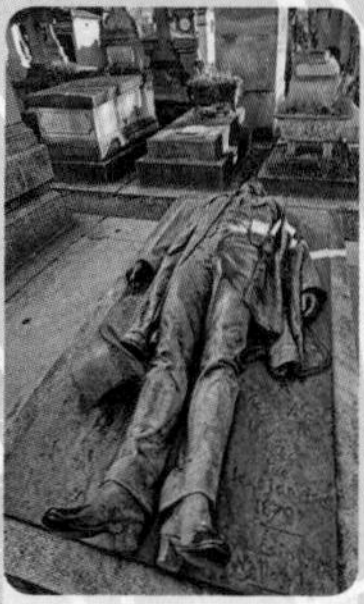

BRUNO DE HOGUES / GETTY IMAGES ©

Monsieur Noir, Division 92

Cemetery sex stud Mr Black, alias 21-year-old journalist Victor Noir (1848–70), was shot by Napoléon III's nephew in a botched duel. Urban myth means women rub his crotch to boost fertility.

Édith Piaf, Division 97

The archbishop of Paris might have refused Parisian diva Édith Piaf (1915–63) the Catholic rite of burial, but that didn't stop more than 100,000 mourners attending her internment at Père Lachaise.

ALAN COPSON / GETTY IMAGES ©

Mur des Fédérés, Division 76

This plain brick wall was where 147 Communard insurgents were lined up and shot in 1871. Equally emotive is the sculpted walkway of commemorative war memorials surrounding the mass grave.

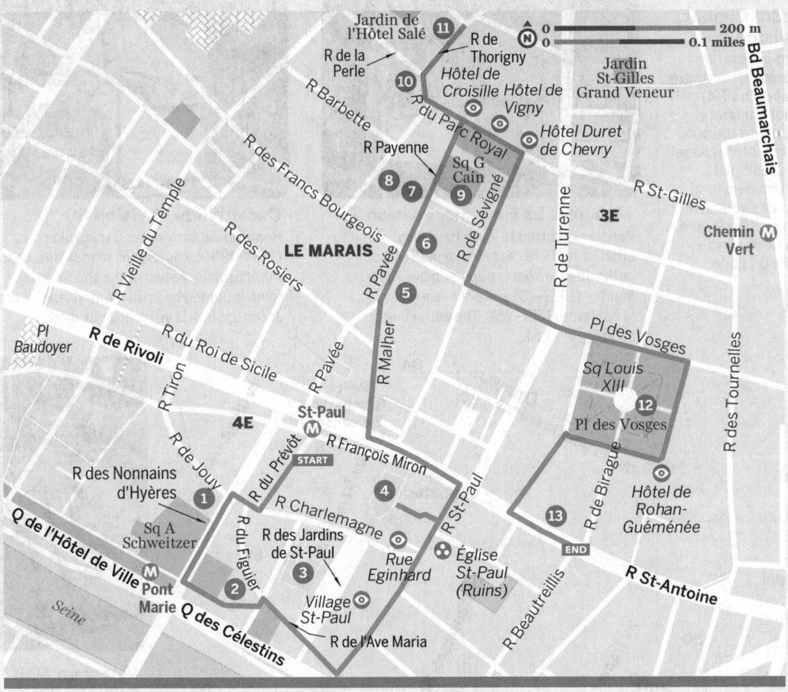

City Walk
Medieval Marais Meanderings

START METRO ST-PAUL
END HÔTEL DE SULLY
LENGTH 2KM; 1½ HOURS

While Henri IV was busy having place Royale (place des Vosges) built, aristocrats were commissioning gold-brick *hôtels particuliers* (private mansions) – the city's most beautiful Renaissance structures that lend the Marais a particular architectural harmony.

From rue François Miron, walk south on rue du Prévôt to rue Charlemagne. To the right at 7 rue de Jouy stands majestic 1 **Hôtel d'Aumont**, built around 1650 for a financier. Continue along rue des Nonnains d'Hyères and turn left onto rue de l'Hôtel de Ville. At 1 rue du Figuier is 2 **Hôtel de Sens**, the oldest Marais mansion, with geometric gardens and a neo-Gothic turret. Begun around 1475, it was built as digs for the archbishops of Sens. It was restored in mock Gothic style in 1911.

Continue southeast along rue de l'Ave Maria, then northeast along rue des Jardins de St-Paul. To the left, two truncated towers are all that remain of Philippe-Auguste's 3 **Enceinte**, a fortified wall built in 1190 and once guarded by 39 towers. Cross rue Charlemagne, duck into rue Eginhard and follow it to rue St-Paul and 4 **Église St-Paul St-Louis** (1641). At the end of rue St-Paul, turn left, then walk up rue Malher and rue Pavée, the first cobbled road in Paris. At No 24 is the late Renaissance 5 **Hôtel Lamoignon**, built for Diane de France (1538–1619), the legitimised daughter of Henri II.

North along rue Payenne is the back of the 6 **Musée Carnavalet** (p81); the Revolutionary-era 'Temple of Reason' 7 **Chapelle de l'Humanité** at No 5; and the rear of the 8 **Musée Cognacq-Jay** (p79). From grassy 9 **Sq George Cain** opposite 11 rue Payenne, walk northwest to more spectacular 17th-century *hôtels particuliers:* 10 **Hôtel de Libéral Bruant** and 11 **Hôtel Salé**, crammed with Picassos, at 5 rue de Thorigny.

Retrace your steps to rue du Parc Royal, walk south down rue de Sévigné and follow rue des Francs Bourgeois eastwards to end with sublime 12 **place des Vosges** (p81) and 13 **Hôtel de Sully**.

islands, the Île de la Cité, is dominated by the magnificent cathedral Notre Dame. Serene little Île St-Louis is graced with elegant apartments and hotels, and charming eateries and boutiques.

★ Cathédrale Notre Dame de Paris CATHEDRAL

(Map p98; ☎01 42 34 56 10; www.cathedraledeparis.com; 6 place du Parvis Notre Dame, 4e; cathedral free, adult/child towers €8.50/free, treasury €2/1; ⏲cathedral 8am-6.45pm Mon-Fri, to 7.15pm Sat & Sun, towers 10am-6.30pm Sun-Thu, to 11pm Fri & Sat Jul & Aug, 10am-6.30pm Apr-Jun & Sep, 10am-5pm Oct-Mar, treasury 9.30am-6pm Apr-Sep, 10am-5.30pm Oct-Mar; Ⓜ Cité) Paris' most visited unticketed site, with upwards of 14 million visitors per year, is a masterpiece of French Gothic architecture. The focus of Catholic Paris for seven centuries, its vast interior accommodates 6000 worshippers.

Highlights include its three spectacular rose windows, treasury, and bell towers (www.monuents-nationaux.fr), which can be climbed. From the North Tower, 400-odd steps spiral to the top of the western façade, where you'll find yourself face-to-face with frightening gargoyles and a spectacular view of Paris.

★ Sainte-Chapelle CHAPEL

(Map p98; ☎01 53 40 60 80, concerts 01 42 77 65 65; www.monuments-nationaux.fr; 4 bd du Palais, 1er; adult/child €8.50/free, joint ticket with Conciergerie €15; ⏲9.30am-6pm Thu-Tue, to 9pm Wed mid-May–mid-Sep, 9.30am-6pm Mar–mid-May & mid-Sep–Oct, 9am-5pm Nov-Feb; Ⓜ Cité) Try to save Sainte-Chapelle for a sunny day, when Paris' oldest, finest stained glass is at its dazzling best. Enshrined within the Palais de Justice (Law Courts), this gemlike Holy Chapel is Paris' most exquisite Gothic monument. Sainte-Chapelle was built in just six years (compared with nearly 200 years for Notre Dame) and consecrated in 1248.

The chapel was conceived by Louis IX to house his personal collection of holy relics, including the famous Holy Crown (now in Notre Dame).

Conciergerie MONUMENT

(Map p98; www.monuments-nationaux.fr; 2 bd du Palais, 1er; adult/child €8.50/free, joint ticket with Sainte-Chapelle €15; ⏲9.30am-6pm; Ⓜ Cité) A royal palace in the 14th century, the Conciergerie later became a prison. During the Reign of Terror (1793–94) alleged enemies of the Revolution were incarcerated here before being brought before the Revolutionary Tribunal next door in the **Palais de Justice**. Top-billing exhibitions take place in the beautiful, Rayonnant Gothic **Salle des Gens d'Armes**, Europe's largest surviving medieval hall.

Pont Neuf BRIDGE

(Map p98) Paris' oldest bridge, ironically named 'New Bridge', has linked the western end of Île de la Cité with both riverbanks since 1607, when the king, Henri IV, inaugurated it by crossing the bridge on a white stallion.

View the bridge's arches (seven on the northern stretch and five on the southern span), decorated with 381 *mascarons* (grotesque figures) depicting barbers, dentists, pickpockets, loiterers etc, from a spot along the river or afloat.

Latin Quarter

So named because international students communicated in Latin here until the French Revolution, the Latin Quarter remains the hub of academic life in Paris. Centred on the Sorbonne's main university campus, graced by fountains and lime trees, this lively area is also home to some outstanding museums and churches, along with Paris' beautiful art deco mosque and botanic gardens.

★ Musée National du Moyen Âge MUSEUM

(Map p100; www.musee-moyenage.fr; 6 place Paul Painlevé, 5e; adult/child €8/free, during temporary exhibitions €9/free; ⏲9.15am-5.45pm Wed-Mon; Ⓜ Cluny–La Sorbonne) The National Museum of the Middle Ages holds a series of sublime treasures, from medieval statuary, stained glass and objets d'art to its celebrated series of tapestries, *The Lady with the Unicorn* (1500). Throw in the extant architecture – an ornate 15th-century mansion (the Hôtel de Cluny), and the *frigidarium* (cold room) of an enormous Roman-era bathhouse – and you have one of Paris' top small museums. Outside, four medieval gardens grace the northeastern corner; more bathhouse remains are to the west.

★ Panthéon MAUSOLEUM

(Map p100; www.monum.fr; place du Panthéon, 5e; adult/child €8.50/free; ⏲10am-6.30pm Apr-Sep, to 6pm Oct-Mar; Ⓜ Maubert-Mutualité or RER Luxembourg) Overlooking the city from its Left Bank perch, the Panthéon's stately neoclassical dome stands out as one of the most recognisable icons on the Parisian skyline. An architectural masterpiece, the interior is impressively vast. Originally a church and now a mausoleum, it has served since 1791 as the resting place of some of France's

Notre Dame

TIMELINE

1160 Maurice de Sully becomes bishop of Paris. Mission: to grace growing Paris with a lofty new cathedral.

1182–90 The **choir with double ambulatory** ① is finished and work starts on the nave and side chapels.

1200–50 The **west façade** ②, with rose window, three portals and two soaring towers, goes up. Everyone is stunned.

1345 Some 180 years after the foundation stone was laid, the Cathédrale de Notre Dame is complete. It is dedicated to notre dame (our lady), the Virgin Mary.

1789 Revolutionaries smash the original **Gallery of Kings** ③, pillage the cathedral and melt all its bells except the great bell Emmanuel. The cathedral becomes a Temple of Reason then a warehouse.

1831 Victor Hugo's novel *The Hunchback of Notre Dame* inspires new interest in the half-ruined Gothic cathedral.

1845–50 Architect Viollet-le-Duc undertakes its restoration. Twenty-eight new kings are sculpted for the west façade. The heavily decorated **portals** ④ and **spire** ⑤ are reconstructed. The neo-Gothic **treasury** ⑥ is built.

1860 The area in front of Notre Dame is cleared to create the parvis, an alfresco classroom where Parisians can learn a catechism illustrated on sculpted stone portals.

1935 A rooster bearing part of the relics of the Crown of Thorns, St Denis and St Geneviève is put on top of the cathedral spire to protect those who pray inside.

1991 The architectural masterpiece of Notre Dame and its Seine-side riverbanks become a Unesco World Heritage Site.

2013 Notre Dame celebrates 850 years since construction began with a bevy of new bells and restoration works.

Virgin & Child
Spot all 37 artworks representing the Virgin Mary. Pilgrims have revered the pearly-cream sculpture of her in the sanctuary since the 14th century. Light a devotional candle and write some words to the *Livre de Vie* (Book of Life).

North Rose Window
See prophets, judges, kings and priests venerate Mary in vivid blue and violet glass, one of three beautiful rose blooms (1225–70), each almost 10m in diameter.

Choir Screen
No part of the cathedral weaves biblical tales more evocatively than these ornate wooden panels, carved in the 14th century after the Black Death killed half the country's population. The faintly gaudy colours were restored in the 1960s.

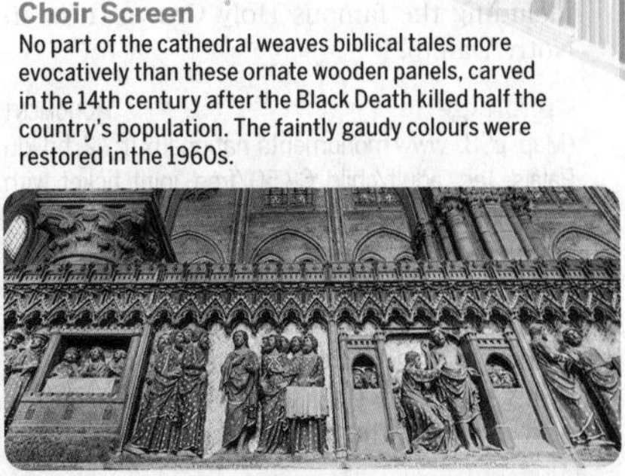

JOHN SONES SINGING BOWL MEDIA/GETTY IMAGES ©

DE AGOSTINI/C. SAPPA/GETTY IMAGES ©

BARBARA VAN ZANTEN/GETTY IMAGES ©

Treasury
This was the cash reserve of French kings, who ordered chalices, crucifixes, baptism fonts and other sacred gems to be melted down in the Mint during times of financial strife – war, famine and so on.

Great Bell
The peal of Emmanuel, the cathedral's great bell, is so pure thanks to precious gems and jewels Parisian women threw into the pot when it was recast from copper and bronze in 1631. Admire its original siblings in Square Jean XXII.

Chimera Gallery
Scale the north tower for a Paris panorama admired by birds, dragons, grimacing gargoyles and grotesque chimera. Nod to celebrity chimera Stryga, who has wings, horns, a human body and sticking-out tongue. This bestial lot warns off demons.

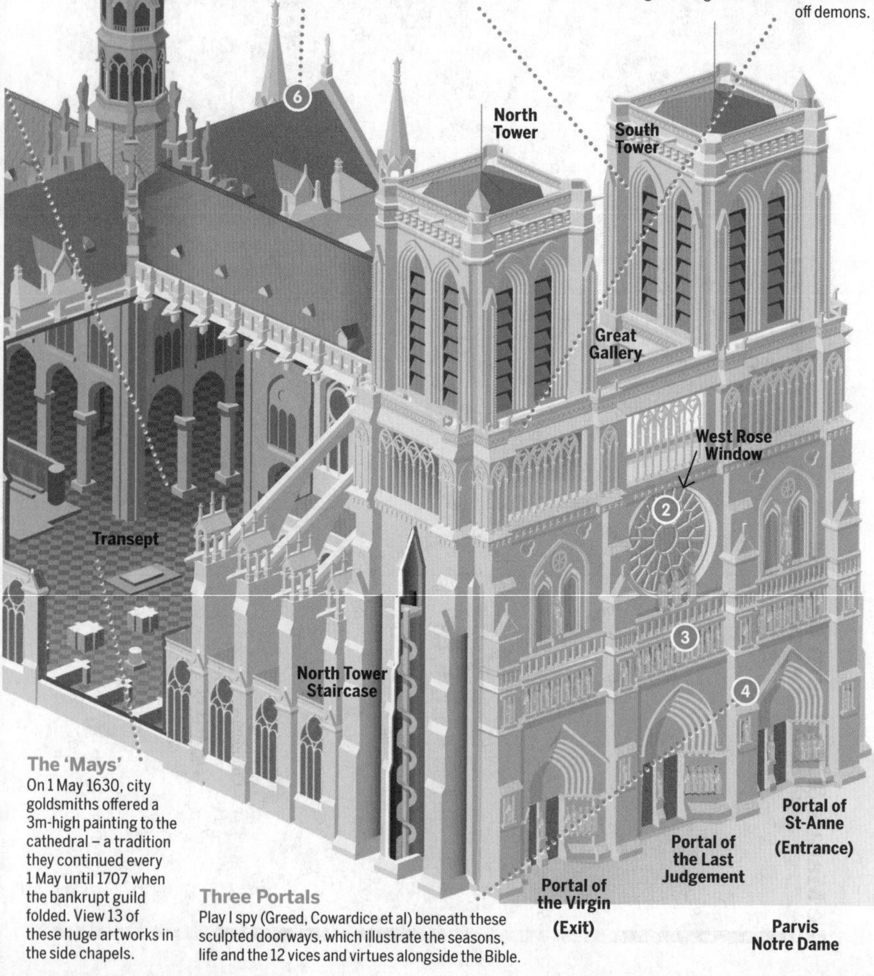

The 'Mays'
On 1 May 1630, city goldsmiths offered a 3m-high painting to the cathedral – a tradition they continued every 1 May until 1707 when the bankrupt guild folded. View 13 of these huge artworks in the side chapels.

Three Portals
Play I spy (Greed, Cowardice et al) beneath these sculpted doorways, which illustrate the seasons, life and the 12 vices and virtues alongside the Bible.

Le Marais & Northern Bastille

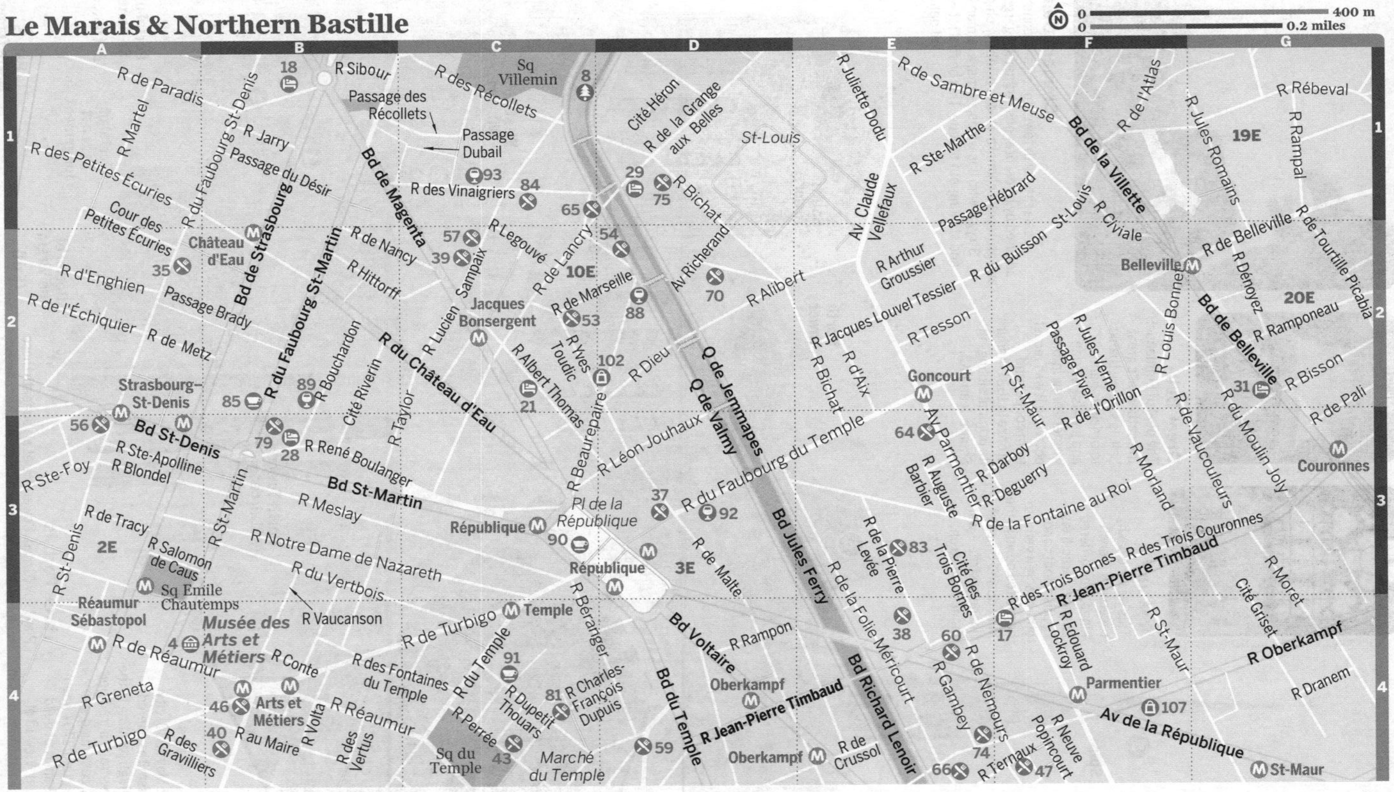

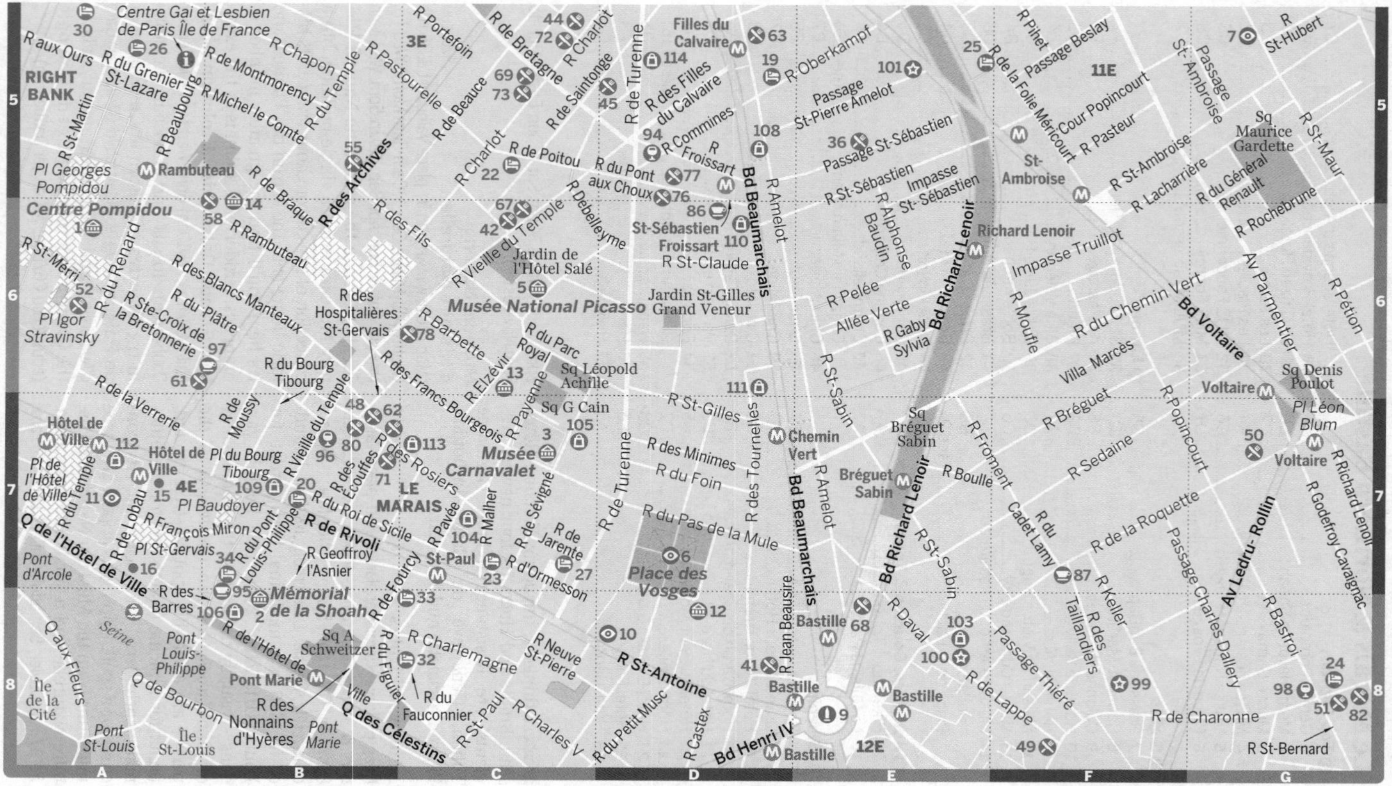
RIGHT BANK
3E
4E
11E
12E
LE MARAIS
Centre Pompidou
Musée National Picasso
Musée Carnavalet
Place des Vosges
Mémorial de la Shoah
Centre Gai et Lesbien de Paris Île de France
Pl Georges Pompidou
Pl Igor Stravinsky
Jardin de l'Hôtel Salé
Jardin St-Gilles Grand Veneur
Sq Léopold Achille
Sq G Cain
Sq A Schweitzer
Sq Bréguet Sabin
Sq Maurice Gardette
Sq Denis Poulot
Pl Léon Blum
Pl de l'Hôtel de Ville
Pl Baudoyer
Pl St-Gervais
Pl du Bourg Tibourg
Hôtel de Ville
Rambuteau
Filles du Calvaire
St-Sébastien Froissart
Chemin Vert
Bréguet Sabin
Richard Lenoir
St-Ambroise
Voltaire
St-Paul
Pont Marie
Bastille
Seine
Pont d'Arcole
Pont Louis-Philippe
Pont Marie
Pont St-Louis
Île de la Cité
Île St-Louis
Q aux Fleurs
Q de Bourbon
Q de l'Hôtel de Ville
Q des Célestins
Bd Beaumarchais
Bd Richard Lenoir
Bd Voltaire
Bd Henri IV
Av Parmentier
Av Ledru-Rollin
R de Rivoli
R St-Antoine
R des Archives
R de Bretagne
R Vieille du Temple
R des Francs Bourgeois
R de Turenne
R du Temple
R Rambuteau
R de la Roquette
R de Charonne
R St-Martin
R St-Merri
R du Renard
R aux Ours
R du Grenier St-Lazare
R Beaubourg
R de Montmorency
R Michel le Comte
R Chapon
R Portefoin
R Pastourelle
R de Beauce
R Charlot
R de Saintonge
R de Poitou
R des Filles du Calvaire
R Commines
R Froissart
R du Pont aux Choux
R Debelleyme
R de Braque
R des Fils
R des Blancs Manteaux
R du Plâtre
R Ste-Croix de la Bretonnerie
R des Hospitalières St-Gervais
R Barbette
R Elzévir
R du Parc Royal
R Payenne
R du Bourg Tibourg
R de Moussy
R de la Verrerie
R des Écouffes
R des Rosiers
R du Roi de Sicile
R Pavée
R Malher
R de Sévigné
R de Jarente
R d'Ormesson
R de Fourcy
R Geoffroy l'Asnier
R François Miron
R du Pont Louis-Philippe
R de Lobau
R des Barres
R de l'Hôtel de Ville
R des Nonnains d'Hyères
R du Figuier
R du Fauconnier
R Charlemagne
R Neuve St-Pierre
R St-Paul
R Charles V
R du Petit Musc
R Castex
R Jean Beausire
R des Tournelles
R des Minimes
R du Foin
R du Pas de la Mule
R St-Gilles
R St-Claude
R Amelot
R Oberkampf
Passage St-Pierre Amelot
Passage St-Sébastien
R St-Sébastien
Impasse St-Sébastien
R Alphonse Baudin
R Pelée
Allée Verte
R Gaby Sylvia
R St-Sabin
R Froment
R Boulle
R Daval
R de Lappe
Passage Thiéré
R des Taillandiers
R Keller
R du Cadet Lamy
R Sedaine
R Bréguet
Villa Marcès
R Moufle
R du Chemin Vert
Impasse Truillot
R Popincourt
Passage Charles Dallery
R Basfroi
R Godefroy Cavaignac
R Richard Lenoir
R St-Bernard
R Pétion
R St-Maur
R Rochebrune
R du Général Renault
R Lacharrière
R St-Ambroise
Passage St-Ambroise
R Pasteur
Cour Popincourt
R de la Folie Méricourt
Passage Beslay
R Pihet
R St-Hubert
1 2 3 5 6 7 9 10 11 12 13 14 15 16 19 20 22 23 24 25 26 27 30 32 33 34 36 41 42 44 45 48 49 50 51 52 55 58 61 62 63 67 68 69 71 72 73 76 77 78 80 82 86 87 94 95 96 97 98 99 100 101 103 104 105 106 108 109 110 111 112 113 114
A B C D E F G
5 6 7 8

Le Marais & Northern Bastille

Top Sights

1 Centre Pompidou A6
2 Mémorial de la Shoah B8
3 Musée Carnavalet C7
4 Musée des Arts et Métiers A4
5 Musée National Picasso C6
6 Place des Vosges D7

Sights

7 Brasserie BapBap G5
8 Canal St-Martin C1
9 Colonne de Juillet E8
10 Hôtel de Sully D8
11 Hôtel de Ville A7
12 Maison de Victor Hugo D8
13 Musée Cognacq-Jay C6
14 Musée d'Art et d'Histoire du Judaïsme B6
Place de la Bastille .... (see 9)

Activities, Courses & Tours

15 Bike About Tours A7
16 La Cuisine Paris A7

Sleeping

17 Cosmos Hôtel F4
18 Grand Amour Hôtel B1
19 Hôtel Beaumarchais D5
20 Hôtel Caron de Beaumarchais B7
21 Hôtel du Nord – Le Pari Vélo C2
22 Hôtel du Petit Moulin C5
23 Hôtel Emile C7
24 Hôtel Exquis G8
25 Hôtel Fabric E5
26 Hôtel Georgette A5
27 Hôtel Jeanne d'Arc C7
28 Hôtel Providence B3
29 Le Citizen Hotel D1
30 Les Bains A5
31 Les Piaules G2
32 MIJE Fauconnier C8
33 MIJE Fourcy C8
34 MIJE Maubuisson B7

Eating

35 52 Faubourg St-Denis A2
36 Au Passage E5
37 Blend D3
38 Blue Valentine E4
39 Bob's Juice Bar C2
40 Bob's Kitchen B4
41 Brasserie Bofinger D8
42 Breizh Café C6
43 Broken Arm C4
44 Café Pinson C5
45 Candelaria D5
46 Cantine California B4
47 Chambelland F4
Chez Alain Miam Miam .... (see 69)
48 Chez Marianne B7
49 Chez Paul F8
50 CheZaline G7
51 Clamato G8
52 Dame Tartine A6
53 Du Pain et des Idées C2
54 Fric-Frac D2
Grand Amour Hôtel .... (see 18)
55 Hank B5
56 Hero A3
57 Holybelly C2

greatest thinkers, including Voltaire, Rousseau, Braille and Hugo. Its four newest 'residents' are Resistance fighters Germaine Tillion, Genèvieve de Gaulle-Anthonioz, Pierre Brossolette and Jean Zay.

Jardin des Plantes GARDENS

(Map p94; www.jardindesplantes.net; place Valhubert & 36 rue Geoffroy-St-Hilaire, 5e; ⌚7.30am-8pm Apr-Oct, 8am-5.30pm Nov-Mar; Ⓜ Gare d'Austerlitz, Censier Daubenton, Jussieu) Founded in 1626 as a medicinal herb garden for Louis XIII, Paris' 24-hectare botanic gardens – visually defined by the double alley of plane trees that run the length of the park – are an idyllic spot to stroll around, break for a picnic (watch out for the automatic sprinklers!) and escape the city concrete for a spell. Upping its appeal are three museums from the Muséum National d'Histoire Naturelle and a small **zoo** (www.mnhn.fr; 57 rue Cuvier, 5e; adult/child €13/9; ⌚9am-6pm Mon-Fri, to 6.30pm Sat & Sun Easter-Oct, to 5pm Nov-Easter).

Muséum National d'Histoire Naturelle MUSEUM

(Map p100; www.mnhn.fr; place Valhubert & 36 rue Geoffroy-St-Hilaire, 5e; ⌚10am-5pm Mon & Wed-Fri, to 6pm Sat & Sun Apr-Sep, 10am-5pm Wed-Mon Oct-Mar) Despite the name, the Natural History Museum is not a single building, but a collection of sites throughout France. Its historic home is in the Jardin des Plantes, and it's here you'll find the greatest number of branches: taxidermied animals in the excellent **Grande Galerie de l'Évolution** (adult/child €9/free; ⌚10am-6pm Wed-Mon; Ⓜ Censier Daubenton); fossils and dinosaur skeletons in the **Galeries d'Anatomie Comparée et de Paléontologie** (adult/child €7/free; Ⓜ Gare d'Austerlitz); and meteorites and crystals in the **Galerie de Minéralogie et de Géologie** (adult/child €6/free; Ⓜ Censier Daubenton).

★ Institut du Monde Arabe ARCHITECTURE, MUSEUM

(Arab World Institute; Map p100; www.imarabe.org; 1 place Mohammed V, 5e; adult/child €8/4; ⌚10am-6pm Tue-Thu, to 9.30pm Fri, to 7pm Sat & Sun; Ⓜ Jussieu) The Arab World Institute was jointly founded by France and 18 Middle Eastern and North African nations in 1980, with the aim of promoting cross-cultural dialogue. In addition to hosting concerts, film screenings and a research centre, the stunning landmark is also home to a museum and temporary exhibition space.

Mosquée de Paris MOSQUE

(Map p100; ☎01 43 31 14 32; www.la-mosquee.com; 2bis place du Puits de l'Ermite, 5e; adult/child €3/2; ⌚9am-noon & 2-7pm Sat-Thu Apr-Sep, 9am-noon & 2-6pm Sat-Thu Oct-Mar; Ⓜ Place Monge) Paris' central mosque, with a striking 26m-high minaret, was completed in 1926 in an ornate art deco Moorish style. You can visit the interior to admire the intricate tile work and calligraphy. A separate entrance leads to the wonderful North African–style **hammam** (admission €18, spa package from €43; ⌚10am-9pm Mon, Wed, Thu & Sat, 2-9pm Fri), **restaurant** (mains €15-26; ⌚kitchen noon-2.30pm & 7.30-10.30pm) and tearoom (p142), and a small *souk* (actually more of a gift shop). Visitors must be modestly dressed.

Musée de la Sculpture en Plein Air MUSEUM

(Map p100; quai St-Bernard, 5e; Ⓜ Gare d'Austerlitz) FREE Along quai St-Bernard, this open-air sculpture museum (also known as the Jardin Tino Rossi) has more than 50 late-20th-century unfenced sculptures, and makes a great picnic spot. A salad beneath a César or a baguette beside a Brancusi is a pretty classy way to see the Seine up close.

Southern Bastille & Gare de Lyon

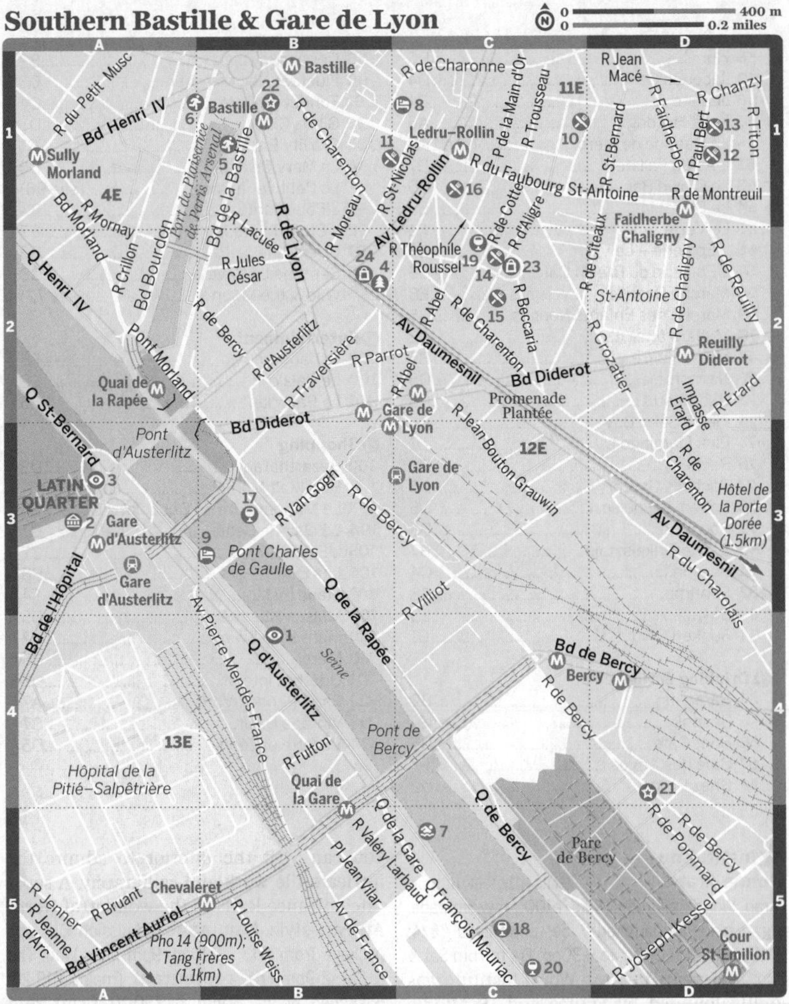

St-Germain & Les Invalides

Literary buffs, antique collectors and fashionistas flock to this legendary part of Paris, where the presence of writers such as Sartre, de Beauvoir and Hemingway still lingers in historic cafes, and exquisite window displays entice shoppers into tiny specialist stores and chic boutiques.

★Musée d'Orsay MUSEUM

(Map p58; www.musee-orsay.fr; 62 rue de Lille, 7e; adult/child €12/free; ⏲9.30am-6pm Tue, Wed & Fri-Sun, to 9.45pm Thu; Ⓜ Assemblée Nationale or RER Musée d'Orsay) The home of France's national collection from the impressionist, postimpressionist and art nouveau movements spanning from 1848 to 1914 is the glorious former Gare d'Orsay railway station – itself an art nouveau showpiece – where a roll-call of masters and their world-famous works are on display.

Top of every visitor's must-see list is the museum's painting collections, centred on the world's largest collection of impressionist and postimpressionist art.

Southern Bastille & Gare de Lyon

Les Berges de Seine PROMENADE

(Map p58; btwn Musée d'Orsay & Pont de l'Alma, 7e; information point noon-7pm Sun-Thu, 10am-10pm Fri & Sat May-Sep, shorter hours Oct-Apr; Ⓜ Solférino, Assemblée Nationale, Invalides) A breath of fresh air, this 2.3km-long expressway turned riverside promenade is now a favourite spot to run, cycle, skate, play board games or take part in a packed program of events. Equally it's simply a great place to hang out – in a Zzz shipping-container hut (reserve at the information point just west of the Musée d'Orsay), on the archipelago of floating gardens, or at the burgeoning restaurants and bars (some floating aboard boats and barges).

Musée des Égouts de Paris MUSEUM

(Map p64; http://equipement.paris.fr/musee-des-egouts-5059; place de la Résistance, 7e; adult/child €4.40/3.60; 11am-5pm Tue & Wed May-Sep, 11am-4pm Tue & Wed Oct-Dec & Feb-Apr; Ⓜ Alma Marceau or RER Pont de l'Alma) Raw sewage flows beneath your feet as you walk through 480m of odoriferous tunnels in this working sewer museum. Exhibitions cover the development of Paris' waste-water-disposal system, including its resident rats (there's an estimated one sewer rat for every Parisian above ground). Enter via a rectangular maintenance hole topped with a kiosk across the street from 93 quai d'Orsay, 7e.

The sewers are closed when rain floods the tunnels. Toy rats are sold at its gift shop.

Monnaie de Paris MUSEUM

(Map p98; 01 40 46 56 66; www.monnaiedeparis.fr; 11 quai de Conti, 6e; Ⓜ Pont Neuf) The 18th-century royal mint, the Monnaie de Paris – still used by the Ministry of Finance to produce commemorative medals and coins – houses the Musée de la Monnaie (Parisian Mint Museum), showcasing the history of French coinage from antiquity onwards. The overhaul of this sumptuous neoclassical building, with one of the longest façades on the Seine, incorporates interior streets, the restoration of an aristocratic townhouse built by Jules Hardouin Mansart in 1690, and Guy Savoy's flagship restaurant (p136) and courtyard brasserie.

★ Église St-Germain des Prés CHURCH

(Map p98; www.eglise-stgermaindespres.fr; 3 place St-Germain des Prés, 6e; 8am-7.45pm; Ⓜ St-Germain des Prés) Paris' oldest standing church, the Romanesque St Germanus of the Fields, was built in the 11th century on the site of a 6th-century abbey and was the main place of worship in Paris until the arrival of Notre Dame. It's since been altered many times, but the **Chapelle de St-Symphorien** (to the right as you enter) was part of the original abbey and is believed to be the resting place of St Germanus (496–576), the first bishop of Paris.

Église St-Sulpice CHURCH

(Map p98; www.pss75.fr/saint-sulpice-paris; place St-Sulpice, 6e; 7.30am-7.30pm; Ⓜ St-Sulpice) In 1646 work started on the twin-towered

Church of St Sulpicius, lined inside with 21 side chapels, and it took six architects 150 years to finish. It's famed for its striking Italianate façade with two rows of superimposed columns, its Counter-Reformation-influenced neoclassical decor and its frescoes by Eugène Delacroix – and its setting for a murderous scene in Dan Brown's *The Da Vinci Code*.

You can hear the monumental, 1781-built organ during 10.30am Mass on Sunday or the occasional Sunday-afternoon concert.

★Jardin du Luxembourg PARK

(Map p98; www.senat.fr/visite/jardin; numerous entrances; Ⓜ Mabillon, St-Sulpice, Rennes, Notre Dame des Champs or RER Luxembourg) This inner-city oasis of formal terraces, chestnut groves and lush lawns has a special place in Parisians' hearts. Napoléon dedicated the 23 gracefully laid-out hectares of the Luxembourg Gardens to the children of Paris, and many residents spent their childhood prodding 1920s wooden **sailboats** (30/60min €2/3.30; ⏲Apr-Oct) with long sticks on the octagonal **Grand Bassin** pond, watching puppets perform *Punch & Judy*–type shows at the Théâtre du Luxembourg (p147), and riding the *carrousel* (merry-go-round) or **ponies** (rides €3.50; ⏲3-6pm Wed, Sat, Sun & school holidays).

★Musée Rodin MUSEUM, GARDEN

(Map p64; www.musee-rodin.fr; 79 rue de Varenne, 7e; adult/child museum incl garden €10/7, garden only €4/2; ⏲10am-5.45pm Tue & Thu-Sun, to 8.45pm Wed; Ⓜ Varenne) Sculptor, painter, sketcher, engraver and collector Auguste Rodin donated his entire collection to the French state in 1908 on the proviso that they dedicate his former workshop and showroom, the beautiful 1730 Hôtel Biron, to displaying his works. They're now installed not only in the magnificently restored mansion itself, but in its rose-filled garden – one of the most peaceful places in central Paris and a wonderful spot to contemplate his famous work *The Thinker*. Prepurchase tickets online to avoid queuing.

★Hôtel des Invalides MONUMENT, MUSEUM

(Map p64; www.musee-armee.fr; 129 rue de Grenelle, 7e; adult/child €11/free; ⏲10am-6pm Apr-Oct, to 5pm Nov-Mar, hours can vary; Ⓜ Varenne) Flanked by the 500m-long Esplanade des Invalides lawns, the Hôtel des Invalides was built in the 1670s by Louis XIV to house 4000 *invalides* (disabled war veterans). On 14 July 1789, a mob broke into the building and seized 32,000 rifles before heading on to the prison at Bastille and the start of the French Revolution.

Admission includes entry to all Hôtel des Invalides sights. Hours for individual sites often vary – check the website for updates.

In the **Cour d'Honneur**, the nation's largest collection on the history of the French military is displayed at the **Musée de l'Armée**. South is **Église St-Louis des Invalides**, once used by soldiers, and **Église du Dôme** which, with its sparkling golden dome (1677–1735), is one of the finest religious edifices erected under Louis XIV and was the inspiration for the United States' Capitol building. It received the remains of Napoléon in 1840: the extravagant **Tombeau de Napoléon 1er**, in the centre of the church, comprises six coffins fitting into one another like a Russian doll. Scale models of towns, fortresses and châteaux across France fill the esoteric **Musée des Plans-Reliefs**.

Atmospheric classical concerts (ranging from €5 to €30) take place regularly here year-round.

Montparnasse & Southern Paris

Despite some architectural eyesores, fabled Montparnasse has surviving brasseries from its mid-20th-century heyday and re-energised backstreets buzzing with local life. The largely residential 15e harbours some beautiful hidden parks, while the 13e is home to edgy street art and Paris' largest Chinatown, filled with Asian grocers and eateries.

★Les Catacombes CEMETERY

(Map p58; www.catacombes.paris.fr; 1 av Colonel Henri Roi-Tanguy, 14e; adult/child €12/free; ⏲10am-8pm Tue-Sun; Ⓜ Denfert Rochereau) Paris' most macabre sight is its underground tunnels lined with skulls and bones. In 1785 it was decided to rectify the hygiene problems of Paris' overflowing cemeteries by exhuming the bones and storing them in disused quarry tunnels and the Catacombes were created in 1810.

After descending 20m (via 130 narrow, dizzying spiral steps) below street level, you follow the dark, subterranean passages to reach the ossuary (2km in all). Exit back up 83 steps onto rue Remy Dumoncel, 14e.

★Cimetière du Montparnasse CEMETERY

(Map p58; www.paris.fr; 3 bd Edgar Quinet, 14e; ⏲8am-6pm Mon-Fri, 8.30am-6pm Sat, 9am-6pm

Sun; Ⓜ Edgar Quinet) Opened in 1824, Montparnasse Cemetery, Paris' second largest after Père Lachaise, sprawls over 19 hectares shaded by 1200 trees, including maples, ash, lime trees and conifers. Among its illustrious 'residents' are poet Charles Baudelaire, writer Guy de Maupassant, playwright Samuel Beckett, sculptor Constantin Brancusi, painter Chaim Soutine, photographer Man Ray, industrialist André Citroën, Captain Alfred Dreyfus of the infamous Dreyfus Affair, actress Jean Seberg, and philosopher-writer couple Jean-Paul Sartre and Simone de Beauvoir, as well as legendary singer Serge Gainsbourg.

Tour Montparnasse VIEWPOINT

(Map p98; www.tourmontparnasse56.com; 33 av du Maine, 15e; adult/child €15/9.50; ⏲9.30am-11.30pm daily Apr-Sep, to 10.30pm Sun-Thu, to 11pm Fri & Sat Oct-Mar; Ⓜ Montparnasse Bienvenüe) Spectacular views unfold from this 209m-high smoked-glass-and-steel office block, built in 1973. (Bonus: it's about the only spot in the city you can't see this startlingly ugly skyscraper, which dwarfs low-rise Paris.) A speedy lift/elevator whisks visitors up in 38 seconds to the indoor observatory on the 56th floor, with multimedia displays. Finish with a hike up the stairs to the 59th-floor open-air terrace (with a sheltered walkway) and bubbly at the terrace's Champagne bar.

Musée Bourdelle MUSEUM

(Map p98; www.bourdelle.paris.fr; 18 rue Antoine Bourdelle, 15e; ⏲10am-6pm Tue-Sun; Ⓜ Falguière) FREE Monumental bronzes fill the house and workshop where sculptor Antoine Bourdelle (1861–1929), a pupil of Rodin, lived and worked. The three sculpture gardens are particularly lovely, with a flavour of belle époque and post-WWI Montparnasse. The museum usually has a temporary exhibition (attracting an admission fee) going on alongside its free permanent collection.

Île aux Cygnes ISLAND

(Isle of Swans; Map p58; btwn Pont de Grenelle & Pont de Bir Hakeim, 15e; Ⓜ Javel–André Citroën or Bir Hakeim) Paris' little-known third island, the artificially created Île aux Cygnes, was formed in 1827 to protect the river port and measures just 850m by 11m. On the western side of the Pont de Grenelle is a soaring one-quarter scale **Statue of Liberty replica**, inaugurated in 1889. Walk east along the Allée des Cygnes – the tree-lined walkway that runs the length of the island – for knock-out Eiffel Tower views.

LOCAL KNOWLEDGE

ROMANCING IN PARIS

Chestnut, yew, black walnut and weeping willow trees grace picturesque **Square du Vert-Galant** (Map p98; place du Pont Neuf; ⏲24hr; Ⓜ Pont Neuf) at the westernmost tip of the Île de la Cité, along with migratory birds including mute swans, pochard and tufted ducks, black-headed gulls and wagtails. Sitting at the islands' original level, 7m below their current height, the waterside park is reached by stairs leading down from the Pont Neuf. It's romantic at any time of day but especially in the evening watching the sun set over the river.

Docks en Seine CULTURAL CENTRE

(Cité de la Mode et du Design; Map p94; www.citemodedesign.fr; 34 quai d'Austerlitz, 13e; ⏲10am-midnight; Ⓜ Gare d'Austerlitz) Framed by a lurid-lime wave-like glass façade, a transformed Seine-side warehouse now houses the French fashion institute, the Institut Français de la Mode (hence the docks' alternative name, Cité de la Mode et du Design), mounting fashion and design exhibitions and events throughout the year. Other draws include an entertainment-themed contemporary art museum **Art Ludique-Le Musée** (www.artludique.com; adult/child €16.50/11; ⏲11am-7pm Mon, 11am-10pm Wed-Fri, 10am-10pm Sat & Sun), along with ultra-hip bars, clubs and restaurants and huge riverside terraces.

Bois de Vincennes PARK

(blvd Poniatowski, 12e) In the southeastern corner of Paris, Bois de Vincennes encompasses some 995 hectares. Originally royal hunting grounds, the woodland was annexed by the army following the Revolution and then donated to the city in 1860 by Napoléon III. A fabulous place to escape the endless stretches of Parisian concrete, Bois de Vincennes also contains a handful of notable sights, including a bona fida royal chateau, **Château de Vincennes** (http://www.chateau-de-vincennes.fr; av de Paris, Vincennes; guided tour adult/child €8.50/free; ⏲10am-6pm mid-May–mid-Sep, to 5pm mid-Sep–mid-May; Ⓜ Château de Vincennes), with massive fortifications and a moat.

The Islands

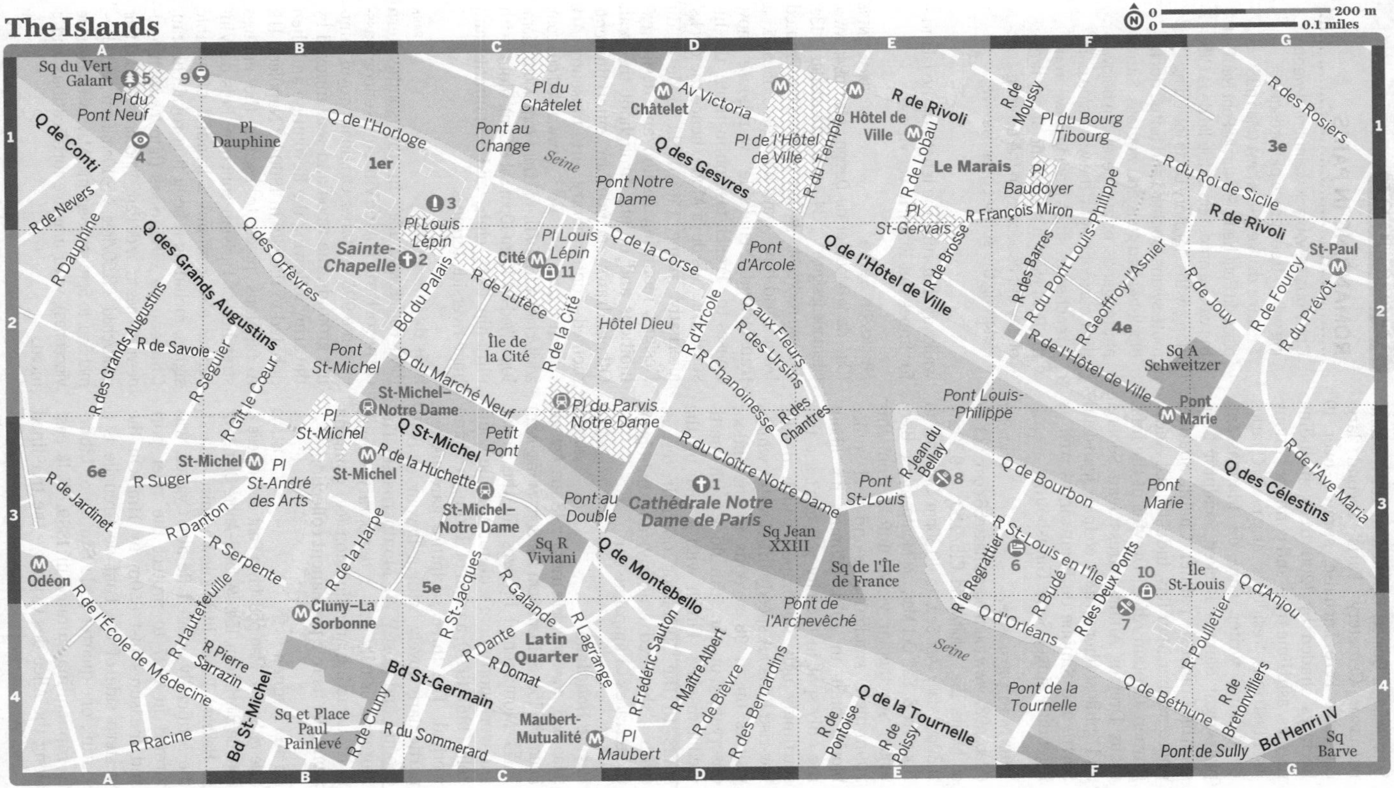
200 m
0.1 miles
Sq du Vert Galant
Pl du Pont Neuf
Q de Conti
Pl Dauphine
Q de l'Horloge
1er
Pl du Châtelet
Pont au Change
Seine
Châtelet
Av Victoria
Q des Gesvres
Pont Notre Dame
Pl de l'Hôtel de Ville
R du Temple
Hôtel de Ville
R de Rivoli
R de Lobau
Le Marais
R de Moussy
Pl du Bourg Tibourg
Pl Baudoyer
R François Miron
Pl St-Gervais
R de Brosse
3e
R des Rosiers
R du Roi de Sicile
R de Rivoli
St-Paul
R de Nevers
R Dauphine
Q des Grands Augustins
Q des Orfèvres
Pl Louis Lépin
Sainte-Chapelle
Bd du Palais
Cité
R de Lutèce
Q de la Corse
Pont d'Arcole
Q de l'Hôtel de Ville
R des Barres
R du Pont Louis-Philippe
R Geoffroy l'Asnier
R de Jouy
R de Fourcy
R du Prévôt
4e
Sq A Schweitzer
R des Grands Augustins
R de Savoie
R Séguier
R Gît le Cœur
Pont St-Michel
Île de la Cité
R de la Cité
Hôtel Dieu
R d'Arcole
Q aux Fleurs
R des Ursins
R Chanoinesse
R des Chantres
R de l'Hôtel de Ville
Pont Louis-Philippe
Pont Marie
Q du Marché Neuf
St-Michel–Notre Dame
Pl St-Michel
Q St-Michel
Petit Pont
Pl du Parvis Notre Dame
R du Cloître Notre Dame
R Jean du Bellay
Pont St-Louis
Q de Bourbon
Q des Célestins
R de l'Ave Maria
6e
R de Jardinet
R Suger
St-Michel
Pl St-André des Arts
R de la Huchette
Pont au Double
Cathédrale Notre Dame de Paris
Sq Jean XXIII
R Danton
R Serpente
R de la Harpe
St-Michel–Notre Dame
Sq R Viviani
Q de Montebello
Sq de l'Île de France
R St-Louis en l'Île
R le Regrattier
Île St-Louis
Q d'Anjou
Odéon
R de l'École de Médecine
R Hautefeuille
R Pierre Sarrazin
Cluny–La Sorbonne
5e
R St-Jacques
R Galande
Pont de l'Archevêché
R Budé
R des Deux Ponts
Q d'Orléans
R Poulletier
Latin Quarter
R Dante
R Domat
R Lagrange
R Frédéric Sauton
R Maître Albert
R de Bièvre
R des Bernardins
Bd St-Germain
Bd St-Michel
Sq et Place Paul Painlevé
R de Cluny
R du Sommerard
R Racine
Maubert-Mutualité
Pl Maubert
Q de la Tournelle
R de Pontoise
R de Poissy
Pont de la Tournelle
Q de Béthune
R de Bretonvilliers
Pont de Sully
Bd Henri IV
Sq Barve

The Islands

Top Sights

1 Cathédrale Notre Dame de Paris........D3
2 Sainte-Chapelle..................................C2

Sights

3 Conciergerie..C1
4 Pont Neuf..A1
5 Square du Vert-Galant........................A1

Sleeping

6 Hôtel Des Deux-Îles............................F3

Eating

7 Berthillon..F4
8 Café Saint Régis..................................E3

Drinking & Nightlife

9 Les Jardins du Pont-Neuf....................A1

Shopping

10 38 Saint Louis.......................................F3
11 Marché aux Fleurs Reine Elizabeth II...C2
Marché aux Oiseaux....................(see 11)

Paris' largest, now state-of-the-art zoo, the **Parc Zoologique de Paris** (Zoo de Vincennes; www.parczoologiquedeparis.fr; cnr av Daumesnil & rte de Ceinture du Lac, 12e; adult/child €22/14; 9.30am-7.30pm summer, shorter hours rest of year; MPorte Dorée), is also here, as is the magnificent botanical park **Parc Floral de Paris** (www.parcfloraldeparisjeux.com; Esplanade du Chateau de Vincennes or rte de la Pyramide; adult/child €5.50/2.75; 9.30am-8pm summer, shorter hours rest of year; ; MChâteau de Vincennes), with exciting playgrounds for older children. The wood also has a lovely lake, with boats to rent and ample green lawns to picnic on.

Activities

Cycling

Everyone knows that the Tour de France races up the Champs-Élysées at the end of July every year, but you don't need Chris Froome's leg muscles to enjoy Paris on two wheels. Between the Paris bike-share scheme Vélib' (p157) and the hundreds of kilometres of urban bike paths, cycling around the city has never been easier. Sign up for one of the great city **bike tours** (Map p90; 06 18 80 84 92; www.bikeabouttours.com; 4 rue de Lobau, 4e, Vinci Parking; MHôtel de Ville) or hire a bike (p157) yourself. Some streets are closed to vehicle traffic on Sundays – great news for cyclists! Bring your own helmet.

Skating

The next most popular activity after cycling has to be skating, whether on the street or on ice. Rent a pair of in-line skates at **Nomadeshop** (Map p94; 01 44 54 07 44; www.nomadeshop.com; 37 bd Bourdon, 4e; half-/full day from €5/8; 11am-1.30pm & 2.30-7.30pm Tue-Fri, 10am-7pm Sat, noon-6pm Sun; MBastille) and join the Friday-evening skate, **Pari Roller** (Map p98; www.pari-roller.com; place Raoul Dautry, 14e; 10pm-1am Fri, arrive 9.30pm; MMontparnasse Bienvenüe), that streaks through the Paris streets, or join the more laid-back Sunday-afternoon skate, **Rollers & Coquillages** (Map p94; www.rollers-coquillages.org; 37 bd Bourdon, 4e; MBastille). During the winter holidays several temporary outdoor rinks are installed around Paris – the most famous are located in front of the Hôtel de Ville and on the 1st floor of the Eiffel Tower. See www.paris.fr for locations.

Swimming

If you want to go swimming at either your hotel or in a public pool, you'll need to don a *bonnet de bain* (bathing cap) – even if you don't have any hair. You shouldn't need to buy one ahead of time as they are generally sold at most pools. Men are required to wear skin-tight trunks (Speedos); loose-fitting Bermuda shorts are not allowed.

Piscine Joséphine Baker SWIMMING
(Map p94; 01 56 61 96 50; http://equipement.paris.fr/piscine-josephine-baker-2930; quai François Mauriac, 13e; adult/child pool €3.60/2, sauna €10/5; 7-8.30am & 1-9pm Mon, Wed & Fri, 1-11pm Tue & Thu, 11am-8pm Sat, 10am-8pm Sun; MQuai de la Gare) Floating on the Seine, this striking swimming pool is style indeed (named after the sensual 1920s American singer, what else could it be?). More of a spot to be seen than to thrash laps, the two 25m-by-10m pools lure Parisians like bees to a honey pot in summer when the roof slides back.

Boules

Don't be surprised to see groups of earnest Parisians playing *boules* (France's most popular traditional game, similar to lawn bowls) in the Jardin du Luxembourg and other parks and squares with suitably flat, shady patches of gravel. The **Arènes de Lutèce** (Map p100; www.arenesdelutece.com; 49 rue Monge, 5e; 8am-9.30pm Apr-Oct, to 5.30pm Nov-Mar; MPlace Monge) FREE *boulodrome* in a 2nd-century Roman amphitheatre in the Latin Quarter is a fabulous spot to absorb the scene. There are usually places to play at Paris Plages (p108).

Latin Quarter

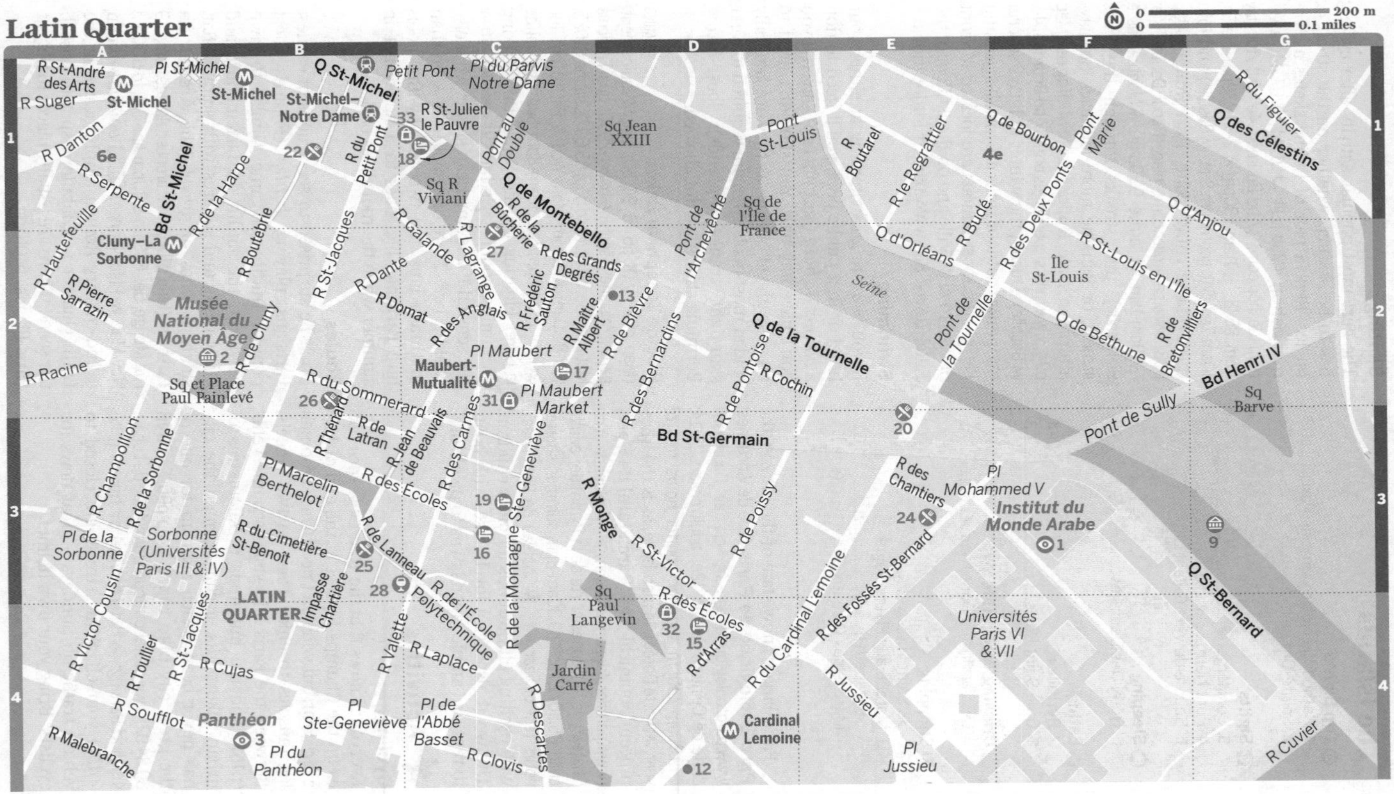

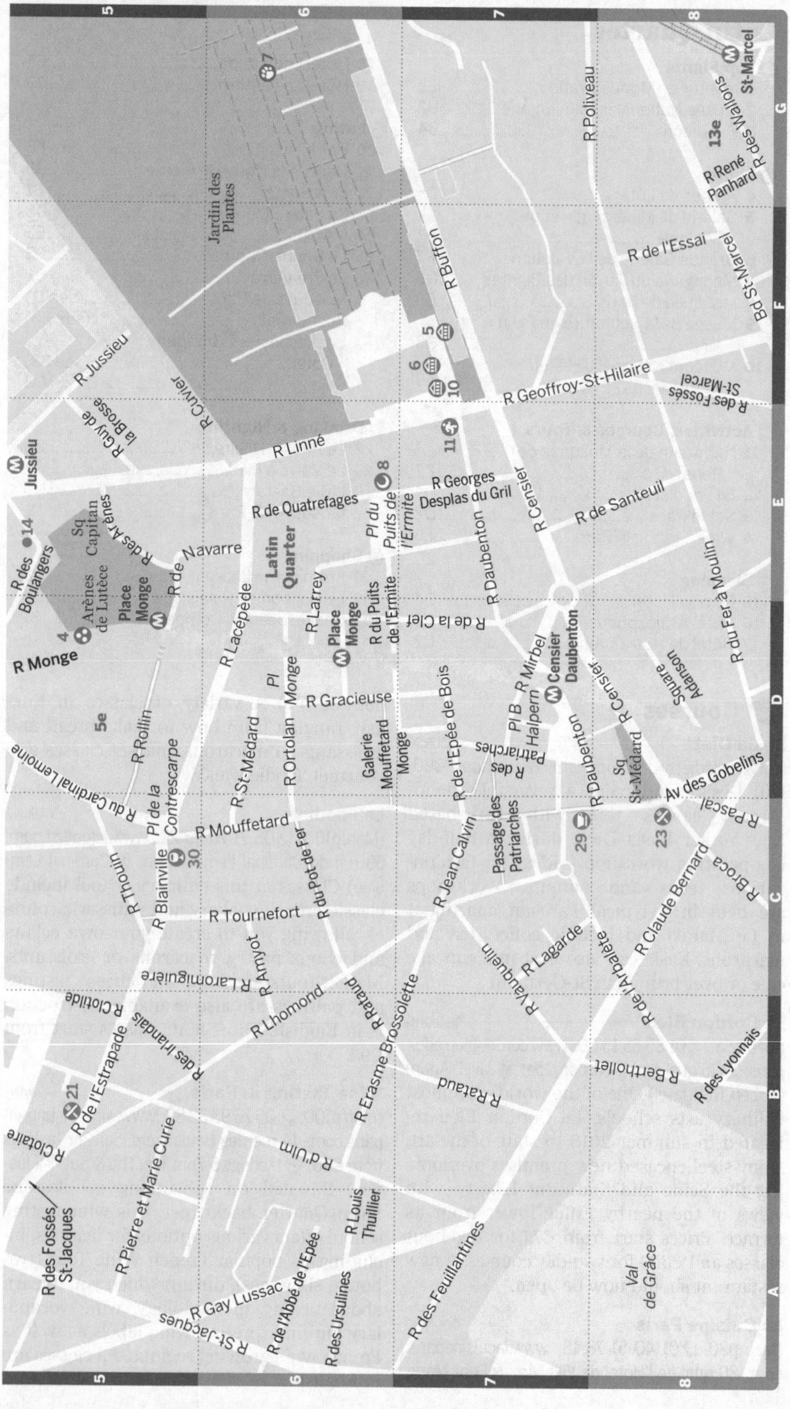
Jardin des Plantes
R Cuvier
R Jussieu
R Guy de la Brosse
Jussieu
R Linné
R Geoffroy-St-Hilaire
R des Fossés St-Marcel
R Buffon
R de l'Essai
R Poliveau
R René Panhard
R des Wallons
13e
Bd St-Marcel
St-Marcel
Sq Capitan
Arènes de Lutèce
R des Arènes
R des Boulangers
R de Navarre
Place Monge
R Monge
R de Quatrefages
R Georges Desplas du Gril
Pl du Puits de l'Ermite
R du Puits de l'Ermite
Latin Quarter
R Lacépède
R Larrey
R de la Clef
R Daubenton
R Censier
R de Santeuil
R du Fer à Moulin
Square Adanson
Censier Daubenton
R Mirbel
Pl B Halpern
R des Patriarches
Passage des Patriarches
R de l'Epée de Bois
Galerie Mouffetard Monge
R Gracieuse
Pl Monge
R Ortolan
R St-Médard
Sq St-Médard
Av des Gobelins
R Pascal
R Broca
R Claude Bernard
R de l'Arbalète
R Lagarde
R Vauquelin
R Berthollet
R des Lyonnais
R Rataud
R Erasme Brossolette
R Jean Calvin
R Mouffetard
R Rollin
R du Cardinal Lemoine
Pl de la Contrescarpe
5e
R Thouin
R Blainville
R Tournefort
R du Pot de Fer
R Amyot
R Laromiguière
R Lhomond
R Clotilde
R des Irlandais
R de l'Estrapade
R Clotaire
R des Fossés St-Jacques
R Pierre et Marie Curie
R d'Ulm
R Louis Thuillier
R Gay Lussac
R St-Jacques
R de l'Abbé de l'Epée
R des Ursulines
R des Feuillantines
Val de Grâce
4
5
6
7
8
10
11
14
21
23
29
30
A
B
C
D
E
F
G

Latin Quarter

Top Sights
1 Institut du Monde Arabe....F3
2 Musée National du Moyen Âge....B2
3 Panthéon....B4

Sights
4 Arènes de Lutèce....D5
5 Galerie de Minéralogie et de Géologie....F7
6 Grande Galerie de l'Évolution....F7
7 Ménagerie du Jardin des Plantes....G6
8 Mosquée de Paris....E6
9 Musée de la Sculpture en Plein Air....G3
10 Muséum National d'Histoire Naturelle....F7

Activities, Courses & Tours
11 Hammam de la Mosquée de Paris....E7
12 Le Foodist....D4
13 Set in Paris....D2
14 Wine Tasting in Paris....E5

Sleeping
15 Familia Hôtel....D4
16 Hôtel Atmosphères....C3
17 Hôtel de Notre Dame....C2
18 Hôtel Esmeralda....C1
19 Hôtel La Lanterne....C3

Eating
20 Bar à Vins AT....E3
21 Café de la Nouvelle Mairie....B5
22 FrogBurger....B1
23 La Salle à Manger....C8
24 L'AOC....E3
25 Le Coupe-Chou....B3
26 Le Pré Verre....B2
Mosquée de Paris....(see 11)
Restaurant AT....(see 20)
Shakespeare & Company Café....(see 33)
27 Sola....C2

Drinking & Nightlife
28 Le Pub St-Hilaire....B3
29 Le Verre à Pied....C7
30 Little Bastards....C5
Mosquée de Paris....(see 11)

Shopping
31 Fromagerie Laurent Dubois....C2
32 Le Bonbon au Palais....D4
33 Shakespeare & Company....C1

Courses

Kasia Dietz COURSE
(www.kasiadietzworkshops.com; workshops €90-120) Design and paint a reversible, hand-printed canvas tote with Paris-based New Yorker Kasia Dietz during a half-day bag-painting workshop – ideal for fashion-curious teens and parents. Workshops are held in a typical Parisian apartment in Le Marais and include coffee, tea and macarons. Kasia can also host in a cupcake cafe or over brunch in St-Germain.

Le Cordon Bleu COOKING
(Map p58; ☎01 85 65 15 00; www.cordonbleu.edu/paris; 13-15 quai André Citroën, 15e; Ⓜ Javel–André Citroën, RER Javel) One of the world's foremost culinary arts schools, Le Cordon Bleu relocated in summer 2016 to state-of-the-art, shiny steel-encased new premises overlooking the Seine and Statue of Liberty, with views of the nearby Eiffel Tower from its terrace. Prices start from €75 for two-hour classes and €360 for two-day courses. A new restaurant should now be open.

La Cuisine Paris COOKING
(Map p90; ☎01 40 51 78 18; www.lacuisineparis.com; 80 quai de l'Hôtel de Ville, 4e; Ⓜ Pont Marie, Hôtel de Ville) A variety of classes in English, ranging from how to make bread and croissants to macarons, market classes and gourmet 'foodie walks'.

Le Foodist COOKING
(Map p100; ☎06 71 70 95 22; www.lefoodist.com; 59 rue du Cardinal Lemoine, 5e; Ⓜ Cardinal Lemoine) Classes at this culinary school include classic French cookery and patisserie courses, allowing you to create your own éclairs and choux pastry, macarons or croissants. Market tours and wine and cheese tastings and pairings are also available. Instruction is in English. Three-hour classes start from €95.

Wine Tasting in Paris WINE
(Map p100; ☎06 76 93 32 88; www.wine-tasting-in-paris.com; 14 rue des Boulangers, 5e; 2hr tastings from €60; ⊙tastings 5-7pm Tue, Thu & Sat; Ⓜ Jussieu) Situated on a winding cobblestone Latin Quarter backstreet, this wine-tasting school offers various options for tastings, including its popular French Wine Tour (two hours, six wines), during which you'll learn about tasting methodology, wine vocabulary and interpreting wine labels as well as French wine-growing regions. All classes are in English.

WORTH A TRIP

BOIS DE BOULOGNE

The 845-hectare **Bois de Boulogne** (Map p58; bd Maillot; M Porte Maillot) owes its informal layout to Baron Haussmann, who, inspired by London's Hyde Park, planted 400,000 trees here in the 19th century. Along with various gardens and other sights, the park has 15km of cycle paths and 28km of bridle paths through 125 hectares of forested land.

Be warned that the area becomes a distinctly adult playground after dark, especially along the Allée de Longchamp running northeast from the Étang des Réservoirs (Reservoirs Pond), where all kinds of prostitutes cruise for clients.

The Bois de Boulogne is served by metro lines 1 (Porte Maillot, Les Sablons), 2 (Porte Dauphine), 9 (Michel-Ange-Auteuil) and 10 (Michel-Ange-Auteuil, Porte d'Auteuil), and the RER C (Avenue Foch, Avenue Henri Martin). Vélib' stations are found near most of the park entrances, but not within the park itself.

Jardin d'Acclimatation (Map p58; www.jardindacclimatation.fr; av du Mahatma Gandhi; €3, per attraction €2.90; 10am-7pm Apr-Sep, to 6pm Oct-Mar; M Les Sablons) Families adore this green and flowery amusement park on the northern fringe of wooded Bois de Boulogne. There are swings, roundabouts and playgrounds for all ages (included in the admission fee), as well as dozens of attractions such as puppet shows, boat rides, funfair rides, a small water park, pony rides, a little train and so on, which you pay extra for.

Le Chalet des Îles (Map p58; 01 42 88 04 69; Carrefour du Bout des Lacs; 30/60/90/120min €6/10/15.50/19, plus €50 deposit; noon-5pm Mon-Fri, 10am-6pm Sat & Sun mid-Feb–Oct; M Avenue Henri Martin) Rent an old-fashioned rowing boat to paddle around Lac Inférieur, the largest of Bois de Boulogne's lakes – romance and serenity guaranteed.

Parc et Château de Bagatelle (rte de Sèvres à Neuilly, 16e; adult/child Jun-Oct €6/3, Nov-Apr free; 9.30am-8pm, shorter hours winter; M Porte Maillot) These enclosed gardens, originally designed as the result of a wager between Marie-Antoinette and the Count of Artois, frame the 18th-century **Château de Bagatelle** (rue de Sèvres à Neuilly; adult/child €6/free; tour 3pm Sun Apr-Oct; M Porte Maillot), built for the younger brother of Louis XVI. Magnificent irises bloom in May, roses from June to October, and – perhaps most majestically of all – water lilies in August.

Pré Catelan (Catelan Meadow; rte de Suresnes, 16e; 9.30am-8pm, Jardin Shakespeare 2-4pm, shorter hours winter; M Ranelagh) FREE This garden area within Parc de Bagatelle squirrels away the wonderful Jardin Shakespeare, where plants, flowers and trees mentioned in Shakespeare's plays are cultivated. Watch for summertime performances in the garden's small open-air theatre.

Jardin des Serres d'Auteuil (av de la Porte d'Auteuil, 16é; 8am-8.30pm summer, shorter hours otherwise; M Porte d'Auteuil) FREE Located at the southeastern end of the Bois de Boulogne are these impressive conservatories, which opened in 1898 and are home to a large collection of tropical plants. The new Stade Roland Garros (p107) has begun expansion into the gardens; they will remain open, but visitors should expect construction through at least 2020.

Stade Roland Garros-Musée de la Fédération Française de Tennis (www.fft.fr; 2 av Gordon Bennett, 16e; M Porte d'Auteuil) The world's most extravagant tennis museum will be closed until stadium renovations are complete (2020).

Fondation Louis Vuitton (Map p58; www.fondationlouisvuitton.fr; 8 av du Mahatma Gandhi, 16e; adult/child €14/5; 10am-8pm Sat-Thu, to 11pm Fri; M Les Sablons) Designed by Frank Gehry, this striking contemporary-art centre opened its doors in late 2014. Emerging behind the Jardin d'Acclimatation, the glass-panelled building thus far has proven more interesting than the temporary exhibits it has hosted. Check online for the latest exhibit.

Tours

★Parisien d'un Jour – Paris Greeters WALKING
(www.greeters.paris; by donation) See Paris through local eyes with these two- to three-hour city tours. Volunteers – mainly knowledgeable Parisians passionate about their city – lead groups (maximum six people) to their favourite spots. Minimum two weeks' notice is needed.

St-Germain & Montparnasse

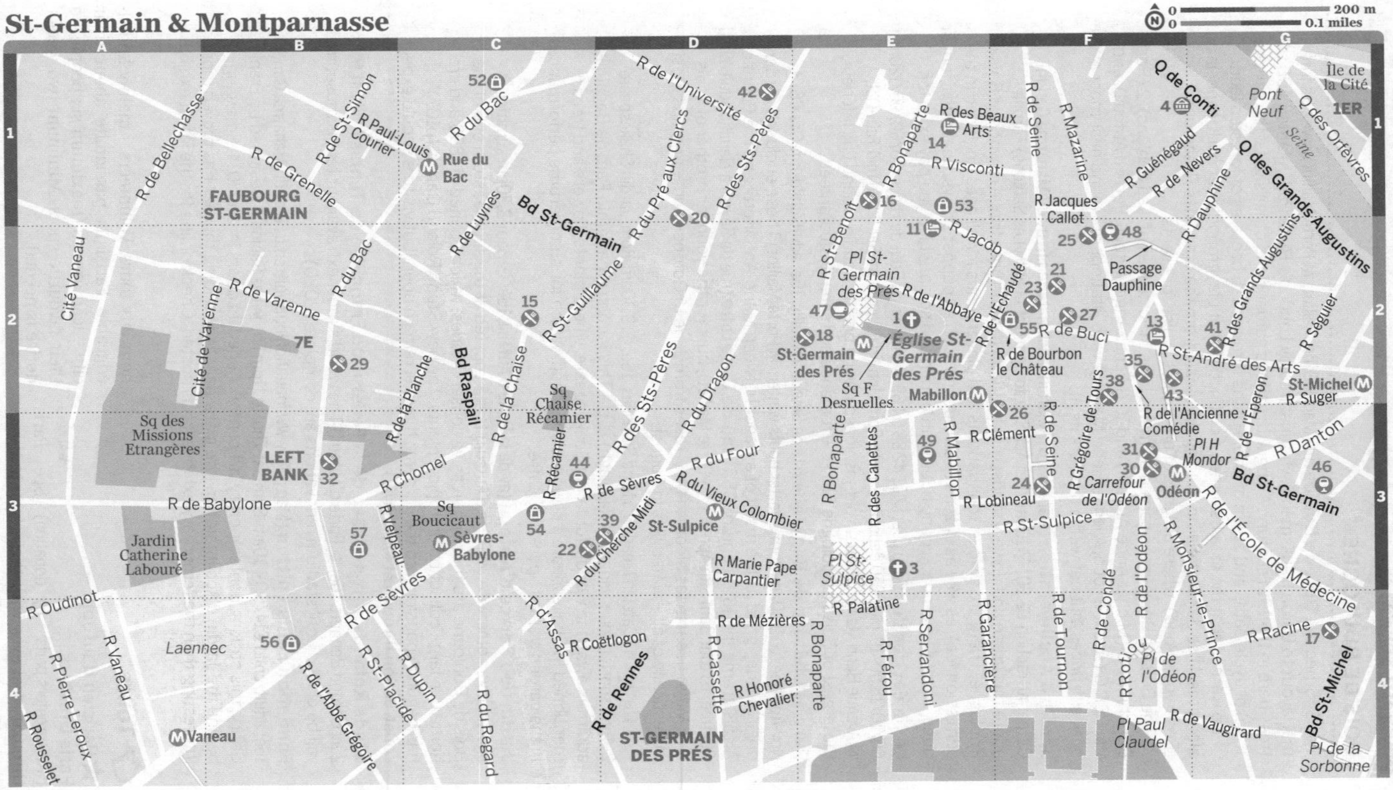

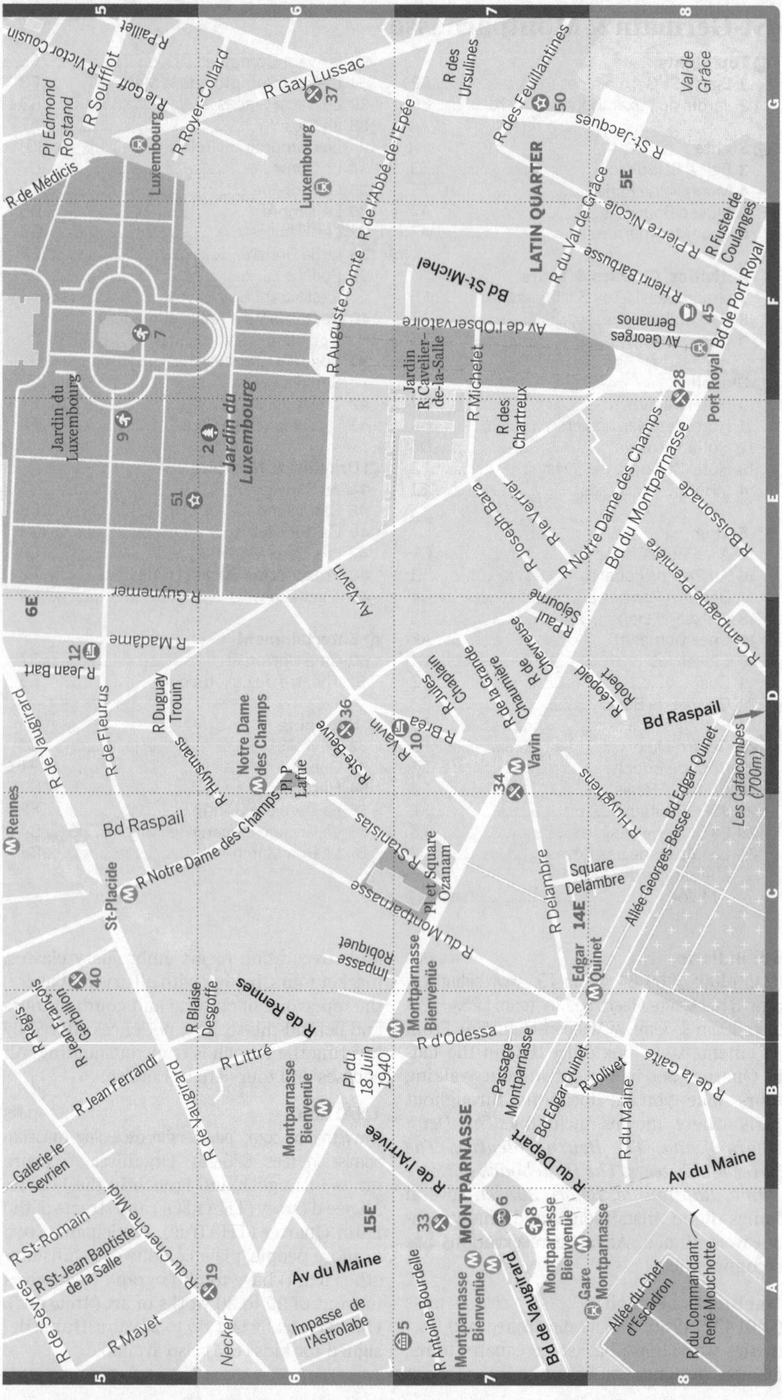
Jardin du Luxembourg
Jardin du Luxembourg
LATIN QUARTER
MONTPARNASSE
6E
5E
14E
15E
R de Médicis
Pl Edmond Rostand
R Soufflot
R Victor Cousin
R Paillet
R le Goff
R Royer-Collard
R Gay Lussac
R des Ursulines
R des Feuillantines
Val de Grâce
R St-Jacques
R du Val de Grâce
R Pierre Nicole
R Henri Barbusse
R Fustel de Coulanges
Bd de Port Royal
Port Royal
Av Georges Bernanos
Bd St-Michel
Av de l'Observatoire
R de l'Abbé de l'Épée
R Auguste Comte
Jardin R Cavelier-de-la-Salle
R Michelet
R des Chartreux
R Joseph Bara
R le Verrier
R Notre Dame des Champs
Bd du Montparnasse
R Boissonade
R Campagne Première
R Guynemer
R Madame
R Jean Bart
R de Vaugirard
R de Fleurus
R Duguay Trouin
R Huysmans
Notre Dame des Champs
Pl P Lafue
R Ste-Beuve
R Vavin
R Bréa
R Jules Chaplain
R de la Grande Chaumière
R de Chevreuse
R Paul Séjourné
R Léopold Robert
Bd Raspail
Les Catacombes (700m)
Vavin
R Huyghens
Bd Edgar Quinet
Allée Georges Besse
Square Delambre
R Delambre
Edgar Quinet
R Stanislas
Pl et Square Ozanam
R du Montparnasse
Impasse Robiquet
Montparnasse Bienvenüe
R d'Odessa
Passage Montparnasse
R Jolivet
R de la Gaîté
R du Maine
Av du Maine
R de Rennes
Rennes
St-Placide
R Blaise Desgoffe
R Littré
R Régis
R Jean François Gerbillon
R Jean Ferrandi
Pl du 18 Juin 1940
R de l'Arrivée
R du Départ
Galerie le Sevrien
R St-Romain
R St-Jean Baptiste de la Salle
R du Cherche Midi
R de Sèvres
R Mayet
Necker
Impasse de l'Astrolabe
R Antoine Bourdelle
Bd de Vaugirard
Gare Montparnasse
Allée du Chef d'Escadron
R du Commandant René Mouchotte
Luxembourg
2
5
6
7
8
9
10
12
19
28
33
34
36
37
40
45
50
51
A
B
C
D
E
F
G

St-Germain & Montparnasse

Top Sights
1 Église St-Germain des Prés ... E2
2 Jardin du Luxembourg ... E6

Sights
3 Église St-Sulpice ... E3
4 Monnaie de Paris ... F1
5 Musée Bourdelle ... A7
6 Tour Montparnasse ... A7

Activities, Courses & Tours
7 Grand Bassin Toy Sailboats ... F5
8 Pari Roller ... A7
9 Pony Rides ... E5

Sleeping
10 Hôtel Danemark ... D7
11 Hôtel des Marronniers ... E2
12 Hôtel Perreyve ... D5
13 Hôtel St-André des Arts ... F2
14 L'Hôtel ... E1

Eating
15 À la Petite Chaise ... C2
16 Au Pied de Fouet ... E1
17 Bouillon Racine ... G4
18 Brasserie Lipp ... E2
19 Chez Dumonet ... A6
20 Clover ... D1
21 Cosi ... F2
22 Cuisine de Bar ... C3
23 Freddy's ... F2
24 Gérard Mulot ... F3
25 Goût de Brioche ... F2
26 Huîtrerie Regis ... F3
27 JSFP Traiteur ... F2
28 La Closerie des Lilas ... F8
29 La Pâtisserie des Rêves ... B2
L'Amaryllis de Gérard Mulot ... (see 24)
30 L'Avant Comptoir ... F3
31 L'Avant Comptoir de la Mer ... F3
32 Le Bac à Glaces ... B3
33 Le Clos Y ... A7
Le Comptoir du Relais ... (see 30)
34 Le Dôme ... D7
35 Le Procope ... F2
36 Le Timbre ... D6
37 Les Papilles ... G6
38 Little Breizh ... F2
39 Poilâne ... D3
Restaurant Guy Savoy ... (see 4)
40 Restaurants d'Application de Ferrandi ... C5
41 Roger la Grenouille ... G2
Semilla ... (see 23)
42 Treize ... D1
43 Un Dimanche à Paris ... F2

Drinking & Nightlife
44 Au Sauvignon ... C3
45 Caffé Juno ... F8
46 Castor Club ... G3
47 Les Deux Magots ... E2
48 Prescription Cocktail Club ... F2
49 Tiger Bar ... E3

Entertainment
50 Café Universel ... G7
51 Théâtre du Luxembourg ... E5

Shopping
52 Deyrolle ... C1
53 Gab & Jo ... E1
54 Hermès ... C3
55 La Dernière Goutte ... F2
56 La Grande Épicerie de Paris ... B4
57 Le Bon Marché ... B3

Set in Paris WALKING
(Map p100; 09 84 42 35 79; www.setinparis.com; 3 rue Maître Albert, 5e; 2hr tours €25; 2hr tours 10am & 3pm; M Maubert-Mutualité) From its cinema-style 'box office' HQ in the Latin Quarter, Set in Paris' two-hour walking tours take you to locations throughout Paris where movies including *The Devil Wears Prada, The Bourne Identity, The Three Musketeers, The Hunchback of Notre Dame, Ratatouille, Before Sunset,* several James Bond instalments and many others were filmed. Advance reservations are recommended.

Meeting the French COURSES, TOURS
(01 42 51 19 80; www.meetingthefrench.fr) Cosmetics workshops, backstage cabaret tours, fashion designer showroom visits, French table decoration or art embroidery classes, market tours, baking with a Parisian baker – the repertoire of cultural and gourmet tours and behind-the-scene experiences offered by Meeting the French is truly outstanding. All courses and tours are in English.

THATLou TOURS
(www.thatlou.com; per person excluding museum admission fees €20-25) Organises treasure hunts in English and French in the Louvre, Musée d'Orsay (THATd'Or) and streets of the Latin Quarter (THATrue). Participants (two or more people, playing alone or against another team) have to photograph themselves in front of 20 to 30 works of art ('treasure'). Hunts typically last 1½ to 2 hours. Hunts designed for kids (€15) also available.

Fat Tire Bike Tours CYCLING
(☎01 85 08 19 76; www.fattirebiketours.com; tours from €32) Offers both day and night bicycle tours of the city, both in central Paris and further afield to Versailles and Monet's Garden in Giverny.

Left Bank Scooters TOURS
(☎06 78 12 04 24; www.leftbankscooters.com; 3hr tours per 1st/2nd passenger from €150/50) Runs a variety of scooter tours around Paris, both day and evening, as well as trips out to Versailles and sidecar tours. Car or motorcycle licence required. Also rents scooters (p158).

Bateaux-Mouches BOATING
(Map p72; ☎01 42 25 96 10; www.bateauxmouches.com; Port de la Conférence, 8e; adult/child €13.50/6; Ⓜ Alma Marceau) The largest river cruise company in Paris and a favourite with tour groups. Cruises (70 minutes) run regularly from 10.15am to 10.30pm April to September and 13 times a day between 11am and 9.20pm the rest of the year. Commentary is in French and English. It's located on the Right Bank, just east of the Pont de l'Alma.

Canauxrama CRUISE
(Map p94; www.canauxrama.com; adult/child €18/9) Seasonal 2½-hour cruises depart from the **Bassin de la Villette** (Map p58; 13 quai de la Loire, 19e; Ⓜ Jaurès) near Parc de la Villette and from the Port de l'Arsenal; summertime evening weekend cruises are particularly enchanting. Boats go at a leisurely pace, passing through four double locks, two swing bridges and an underground section (livened up somewhat by an art installation). Gourmand and thematic cruises too.

Festivals & Events

January

Paris Cocktail Week COCKTAILS
(www.pariscocktailweek.fr; ⏲Jan) Each of the 50-plus cocktail bars all over the city that take part in late January's Paris Cocktail Week creates two signature cocktails especially for the event. There are also workshops, guest bartenders, masterclasses and food pairings. Sign up for a free pass for cut-price cocktails.

April

Foire du Trône FUN FAIR
(www.foiredutrone.com; ⏲Apr-Jun; Ⓜ Porte Dorée) Dating back some 1000(!) years, this huge fun fair is held on the Pelouse de Reuilly of the Bois de Vincennes from around Easter to early June.

May & June

Paris Beer Week BEER
(www.laparisbeerweek.com; ⏲May) Craft beer's popularity in Paris peaks during Paris Beer Week, held during the first week of May, when over 150 events take place across the city's bars, pubs, breweries, specialist beer shops and other venues.

French Open TENNIS
(www.rolandgarros.com; ⏲May-Jun; Ⓜ Porte d'Auteuil) The glitzy Grand Slam tournament Les Internationaux de France de Tennis hits up from late May to early June at **Stade Roland Garros** (www.billetterie.fft.fr; 2 av Gordon Bennett, 16e, Bois de Boulogne).

Fête de la Musique MUSIC
(www.fetedelamusique.culturecommunication.gouv.fr; ⏲21 Jun) This national music festival welcomes in summer on the solstice with staged and impromptu live performances of jazz, reggae, classical and more. Held at venues all over the city.

Marche des Fiertés LGBT
(Gay Pride March; www.gaypride.fr; ⏲Jun or Jul) Late June's colourful, Saturday-afternoon Marche des Fiertés through Le Marais to Bastille celebrates Gay Pride Day with over-the-top floats and outrageous costumes.

Paris Jazz Festival MUSIC
(www.parisjazzfestival.fr; ⏲Jun-Jul; Ⓜ Château de Vincennes) Free jazz concerts swing every Saturday and Sunday afternoon in June and July in the Parc Floral de Paris during the Paris Jazz Festival. There is a park entry fee for adults/under 25s of €6/3.

UP, UP, UP & NOT AWAY

Drift up and up with **Le Ballon Air de Paris** (Map p58; ☎01 44 26 20 00; www.ballondeparis.com; Parc André Citroën, 2 rue de la Montagne de la Fage, 15e; adult/child €12/6; ⏲9am-9pm May-Aug, shorter hours Sep-Apr; Ⓜ Balard, Lourmel). This helium-filled balloon in Parc André Citroën remains tethered to the ground as it lifts you 150m into the air for spectacular panoramas over Paris. The balloon plays an active environmental role, changing colour depending on the air quality and pollution levels. From September to May, the last 'flight' is 30 minutes before the park closes. Confirm ahead any time of year as the balloon doesn't ascend in windy conditions.

July & August

Paris Plages BEACH

(www.paris.fr; ⌚mid-Jul–early Sep) From mid-July to early September, 'Paris Beaches' take over the Right Bank between the Louvre, 1er, and Pont de Sully, 4e; and the Rotonde de la Villette and rue de Crimée, 19e. All beaches are open from 8am to midnight.

Bastille Day CULTURAL

(⌚14 July) The capital celebrates France's national day with a morning military parade along av des Champs-Élysées, accompanied by a fly-past of fighter aircraft and helicopters. *Feux d'artifice* (fireworks) light up the sky above the Champ de Mars by night.

Tour de France SPORTS

(www.letour.com; ⌚Jul) The last of 21 stages of this prestigious, 3500km-long cycling event finishes with a race up av des Champs-Élysées on the third or fourth Sunday of July – as it has done since 1975.

September & October

Jazz à la Villette MUSIC

(www.jazzalavillette.com; ⌚Sep; MPorte de Pantin) This super, two-week jazz festival in the first half of September has sessions in Parc de la Villette, at the Cité de la Musique and at surrounding venues.

Nuit Blanche CULTURAL

(www.paris.fr; ⌚Oct) From sundown until sunrise on the first Saturday and Sunday of October, museums and recreational facilities such as swimming pools stay open, along with bars and clubs, for one 'White Night' (ie 'All Nighter').

Fête des Vendanges de Montmartre WINE

(www.fetedesvendangesdemontmartre.com; ⌚Oct) This five-day festival held during the second weekend in October celebrates Montmartre's grape harvest with costumes, speeches and a parade.

December

Le Festival du Merveilleux CULTURAL

(www.arts-forains.com; ⌚Dec-Jan; MCour Saint-Émilion) Normally closed to the public, the magical private museum Musée des Arts Forains, filled with fairground attractions of yesteryear, opens for 11 days from late December to early January, with enchanting rides, attractions and shows.

Sleeping

Paris has a wealth of accommodation for all budgets, but it's often *complet* (full) well in advance. Reservations are recommended year-round and essential during the warmer months (April to October) and all public and school holidays.

Although marginally cheaper, accommodation outside central Paris is invariably a false economy given travel time and costs. Choose somewhere within Paris' 20 *arrondissements* (city districts) to experience Parisian life the moment you step out the door.

Eiffel Tower & Western Paris

Not surprisingly, this very chic neighbourhood has little in the way of midrange accommodation. If you're in the mood for boutique luxury, however, you're in the right place.

★**Hôtel Félicien** BOUTIQUE HOTEL €€€

(Map p58; ☎01 55 74 00 00; www.hotelfelicienparis.com; 21 rue Félicien David, 16e; d €280-330, ste from €470; ❄@📶; MMirabeau) The price–quality ratio at this chic boutique hotel, squirrelled away in a 1930s building, is outstanding. Exquisitely designed rooms feel more five-star than four, with 'White' and 'Silver' suites on the hotel's top 'Sky floor' more than satisfying their promise of indulgent cocooning. Romantics, eat your heart out.

Hôtel Molitor HISTORIC HOTEL €€€

(☎01 56 07 08 67; www.mltr.fr; 2 av de la porte Molitor, 16e; d from €490, ste €560-750; ❄@📶🏊; MMichel Ange Molitor) Famed as Paris' swishest swimming pool in the 1930s (where the bikini made its first appearance, no less) and a hot spot for graffiti art in the 1990s, the Molitor is one seriously legendary address. The art deco complex, built in 1929 and abandoned from 1989, has been restored to stunning effect.

Champs-Élysées & Grands Boulevards

Hôtel France Albion HOTEL €

(Map p66; ☎01 45 26 00 81; www.albion-paris-hotel.com; 11 rue Notre Dame de Lorette, 9e; s/d/q from €107/127/227; ❄📶; MSt-Georges) For the quietest night's sleep, go for a room facing the courtyard of this neat-as-a-pin budget hotel. Its rooms all have private bathrooms and, for Paris, are decently sized (doubles

from 14 sq metres), and staff are eager to please. The location, near Opéra, is excellent.

Hôtel Monte Carlo HOTEL €
(Map p66; ☎01 47 70 36 75; www.hotelmontecarlo.fr; 44 rue du Faubourg Montmartre, 9e; s €88, d €130-140, tr €176; ; Ⓜ Le Peletier) A unique budget hotel, the Monte Carlo is a fabulous deal, with 20 colourful, personalised rooms and a great neighbourhood location. The cheaper rooms don't have private bathroom facilities, but overall it outclasses many of the other choices in its price range. Prices for a double drop below €100 out of season.

Hôtel Joyce DESIGN HOTEL €€
(Map p66; ☎01 55 07 00 01; www.astotel.com; 29 rue la Bruyère, 9e; d €200-235; ; Ⓜ St-Georges) Located in a lovely residential area between Montmartre and Opéra, this place has all the modern design touches (iPod docks, individually styled rooms, a skylit breakfast room fitted out with old Range Rover seats) and makes some ecofriendly claims – it relies on 50% renewable energy and uses organic products.

Hôtel Langlois HISTORIC HOTEL €€
(Map p66; ☎01 48 74 78 24; www.hotel-langlois.com; 63 rue St-Lazare, 9e; s €150-160, d €180-190; ; Ⓜ Trinité) Built in 1870, this 27-room hotel has kept its charm, from the tiny caged elevator to sandstone fireplaces (sadly decommissioned) in many rooms, as well as some original bathroom fixtures and tiles. Room 64 has wonderful views of Montmartre's rooftops.

Hidden Hotel BOUTIQUE HOTEL €€€
(Map p72; ☎01 40 55 03 57; www.hidden-hotel.com; 28 rue de l'Arc de Triomphe, 17e; d €389-454; ; Ⓜ Charles de Gaulle–Étoile) The Hidden is one of the Champs-Élysées' best secrets. It's serene, stylish, reasonably spacious, and it even sports green credentials: the earth-coloured tones are the result of natural pigments (no paint), and all rooms feature handmade wooden furniture, stone basins and linen curtains surrounding the beds. The queen-size 'Emotion' rooms are among the most popular.

Louvre & Les Halles

The area encompassing the Musée du Louvre and the Forum des Halles is very central, but don't expect to find tranquillity or many bargains here. While it is more disposed to welcoming top-end travellers, there are some decent midrange places and even a budget pick or two to choose from.

ACCOMMODATION BOOKING SERVICES

Lonely Planet (www.lonelyplanet.com/france/paris/hotels) Reviews of Lonely Planet's top choices.

Paris Hotel Service (www.parishotelservice.com) Boutique hotel gems.

Paris Hotel (www.hotels-paris.fr) Well-organised hotel booking site with lots of user reviews.

Room Sélection (www.room-selection.com) Select apartment rentals centred on Le Marais.

Paris Attitude (www.parisattitude.com) Thousands of apartment rentals, professional service, reasonable fees.

Hôtel Vivienne HOTEL €
(Map p66; ☎01 42 33 13 26; www.hotel-vivienne.com; 40 rue Vivienne, 2e; d €100-150, tr & q €200; ; Ⓜ Grands Boulevards) This refurbished two-star hotel is amazingly good value for Paris. While the 45 rooms are not huge, they have all the mod cons; some even boast little balconies. Family rooms accommodate up to two children on a sofa bed.

Hôtel Tiquetonne HOTEL €
(Map p76; ☎01 42 36 94 58; www.hoteltiquetonne.fr; 6 rue Tiquetonne, 2e; d €80, without shower €65; ; Ⓜ Étienne Marcel) What heart-warmingly good value this 45-room cheapie is. This serious, well-tended address has been in the hotel biz since the 1900s and is much loved by a loyal clientele of all ages. Rooms range across seven floors, are spick and span, and sport an inoffensive mix of vintage decor – roughly 1930s to 1980s, with brand-new bathrooms and parquet flooring in recently renovated rooms.

★**Edgar** BOUTIQUE HOTEL €€
(Map p76; ☎01 40 41 05 19; www.edgarparis.com; 31 rue d'Alexandrie, 2e; d €235-295; ; Ⓜ Strasbourg St-Denis) Twelve playful rooms, each decorated by a different team of artists or designers, await the lucky few who secure a reservation at this former convent/seamstress workshop. 'Milagros' conjures up the magic of the Far West, while 'Dream' echoes the rich imagination of childhood with surrealist installations. Breakfast is served in

the downstairs restaurant, and the hidden tree-shaded square is a fabulous location.

★Hôtel Crayon BOUTIQUE HOTEL €€
(Map p76; ☎01 42 36 54 19; www.hotelcrayon.com; 25 rue du Bouloi, 1er; s/d €203/229; ❄ 📶; Ⓜ Les Halles, Sentier) Line drawings by French artist Julie Gauthron bedeck walls and doors at this creative boutique hotel. *Le crayon* (the pencil) is the theme, with 26 rooms sporting a different shade of each floor's chosen colour – we love the coloured-glass shower doors, and the books on the bedside table guests can swap and take home. Online deals often slash rates by up to 50%.

Hôtel de la Place du Louvre BOUTIQUE HOTEL €€
(Map p76; ☎01 42 33 78 68; www.paris-hotel-place-du-louvre.com; 21 rue des Prêtres St-Germain l'Auxerrois, 1er; d €230-290; ❄ 📶; Ⓜ Pont Neuf) Not to be confused with the Relais du Louvre next door, this chic choice has just 20 rooms split across five floors – a couple on each floor are lucky enough to ogle the majestic Louvre across the street. Decor is contemporary and stylish, with lots of white and oyster grey to show off those enviable views to perfection.

Hôtel du Continent DESIGN HOTEL €€
(Map p76; ☎01 42 60 75 32; www.hotelcontinent.com; 30 rue du Mont-Thabor, 1er; s/d €187/277; ❄ 📶; Ⓜ Concorde) For a hotel designed by Christian Lacroix and located a block from the Jardin des Tuileries, this globetrotter's pick is a reasonable deal. Granted, rooms facing the street can be slightly noisy, but the colorful motifs and themed floors (each is dedicated to a particular continent or pole) will add a bit of *haute-couture* mystique to your stay.

Hôtel St-Merry HISTORIC HOTEL €€
(Map p76; ☎01 42 78 14 15; www.saintmerrymarais.com; 78 rue de la Verrerie, 4e; d €180-240, tr €286; ❄ 📶; Ⓜ Châtelet) The interior of this 12-room hostelry, with beamed ceilings, church pews and wrought-iron candelabra, is a neo-Goth's wet dream; you have to see the architectural elements of room 9 (flying buttress over the bed) and the furnishings of room 12 (choir-stall bed board) to believe them.

Montmartre & Northern Paris

Montmartre, encompassing the 18e and the northern part of the 9e, is one of the most charming neighbourhoods in Paris and a good place to base yourself. Every taste and budget is well catered for and many hotels have a view – of Montmartre and Sacré-Cœur or the Paris skyline stretching away to the south; check top-floor availability when deciding where to stay. Accommodation in Pigalle has upped its game recently, with a brilliant choice of stylish and boutique, 'lifestyle' addresses on offer.

★Generator Hostel HOSTEL €
(Map p58; ☎01 70 98 84 00; www.generatorhostels.com; 11 place du Colonel Fabien, 10e; dm €23-42, d €112-218; ❄ @ 📶; Ⓜ Colonel Fabien) A short walk from the water, this buzzing hostel is a shout-out to design, street art and French *art de vivre* (art of living). From the stylish ground-floor cafe-restaurant and 9th-floor rooftop bar (spot Montmartre!) to the basement club and supercool bathrooms with 'I love you' tiling, this overwhelmingly contemporary hostel is sharp. Dorms have USB sockets, and the best doubles have fabulous terraces with views.

Hôtel Eldorado HOTEL €
(Map p58; ☎01 45 22 35 21; www.eldoradohotel.fr; 18 rue des Dames, 17e; s €70-120, d €80-140, tr €100-160; 📶; Ⓜ Place de Clichy) Bohemian Eldorado is one of Paris' greatest finds: a welcoming, reasonably well-run hotel with 33 colourfully decorated and (often) ethnically themed rooms above the Bistro des Dames restaurant, with a private garden. Unfortunately rooms facing the back will probably be quite noisy as they look out onto the restaurant terrace – earplugs may be a good idea. Cheaper-category singles have washbasin only. Breakfast costs €9.

BVJ Champs Élysées HOSTEL €
(Map p58; ☎01 42 67 20 40; www.bvjhotel.com; 12 rue Léon Jost, 17e; dm/d €30/70; 📶; Ⓜ Courcelles) Set in the historic studio and *hôtel particulier* (private mansion) of painter Henri Gervex (1852–1929), this hostel retains a period feel with original moulding and parquet floors throughout. Its 24 spacious rooms sleep two to 10 people, bathroom is shared, and the courtyard garden with empire furnishings and original Henri Gervex fresco is utterly gorgeous. Rates include sheets and breakfast.

St Christopher's Gare du Nord HOSTEL €
(Map p58; ☎01 70 08 52 22; www.st-christophers.co.uk/paris-hostels; 5 rue de Dunkerque, 10e; dm €15-50, d €96-240; @ 📶; Ⓜ Gare du Nord) Steps from Gare du Nord, St Christopher's is a modern backpacker hostel with six floors of

light-filled rooms (600 total). Dorms sleep four, six, eight or 10 but beds are pricey unless you reserve months in advance. Facilities include laundry, female-only floor and Belushi's bar and restaurant with live music and a buzzing happy hour (5pm to 10pm). No kitchen; breakfast included.

St Christopher's Canal HOSTEL €
(Map p58; ☎ 01 40 34 34 40; www.st-christophers.co.uk/paris-hostels; 159 rue de Crimée, 19e; dm €15-50, d €96-240; @ 📶; M Riquet, Jaurès) This is one of Paris' best, biggest (300 beds) and most up-to-date hostels, with modern design and four sizes of dorms (four to 12 beds, mixed and female floors). Doubles come with or without en suite bathroom. Other perks include canalside cafe, bar, bike rental and organised day trips. Daily prices vary wildly; reserve in advance to secure reasonable prices. No kitchen.

Hôtel du Nord – Le Pari Vélo HOTEL €
(Map p90; ☎ 01 42 01 66 00; www.hoteldunord-leparivelo.com; 47 rue Albert Thomas, 10e; s/d/q €73/86/125; 📶; M République) This quaint address has 24 rooms decorated with flea-market antiques and 10 bikes for guests to borrow to ride around town. Beyond the bric-a-brac charm, Hôtel du Nord's other winning attribute is its prized location near place République. Ring and wait to enter. Breakfast costs €8.

★ Joke Hôtel DESIGN HOTEL €€
(Map p80; ☎ 01 40 40 71 71; www.astotel.com/hotel/joke-hotel; rue Blanche, 9e; s/d €129/150; ❄ @ 📶; M Place de Clichy, Pigalle) No joke. This hotel is a serious contender for Paris' best-value, most fun address. Play 'scrabble' or spin the wheel of fortune above your bed each night, hunt for coins stuck in the floor, and generally frolic in the youthful ambience and striking design of this fabulous, childhood-themed hotel. Rates include breakfast and all-day complimentary drinks, cakes and fruit.

★ Le Pigalle DESIGN HOTEL €€
(Map p66; ☎ 01 48 78 37 14; www.lepigalle.paris; 9 rue Frochot, 9e; d €140-340; ❄ @ 📶; M Pigalle) This offbeat lifestyle hotel evokes the spirit of hipster Pigalle today. Edgy design reflects the neighbourhood's legendary nightlife, while carefully thought-out details like a postcard taped on the bathroom wall and a key ring jangling with Paris souvenirs add unique homely touches to the 40 stylish rooms. Each has an iPad loaded with music, and larger rooms have vintage turntables with an eclectic vinyl collection.

The ground-floor bar and restaurant is a happening space, with DJs spinning tropical music two nights a week and Sunday brunch packing out the place from 11am. Kudos for the good-value 'Pigalle 12' rooms – actually twins with bunk beds.

★ Hôtel Providence BOUTIQUE HOTEL €€
(Map p90; ☎ 01 46 34 34 04; www.hotelprovidenceparis.com; 90 rue René Boulanger, 10e; d from €170; ❄ 📶; M Strasbourg-St-Denis, République) This luxurious hideaway, in a 19th-century townhouse in the increasingly trendy 10e, is exquisite. Its 18 individually decorated rooms come with rich House of Hackney velvet wallpaper and vintage flea-market finds; the smallest rooms are not nearly as 'Mini' (by Paris standards) as the name suggests. Utterly glorious is the bespoke cocktail bar gracing each room, complete with suggested recipes and ingredients.

Hôtel Amour BOUTIQUE HOTEL €€
(Map p66; ☎ 01 48 78 31 80; www.hotelamourparis.fr; 8 rue Navarin, 9e; d €170-230; 📶; M St-Georges, Pigalle) Craving romance in Paris? The inimitable black-clad Amour ('Love') features original design and nude artwork in each of the rooms, some more explicit than others. The icing on the cake is the hip ground-floor bistro with summer patio garden, a tasty spot for breakfast, lunch or dinner and everything in between. Rooms don't have a TV, but who cares when you're in love?

Grand Amour Hôtel DESIGN HOTEL €€
(Map p90; ☎ 01 44 16 03 10; www.hotelamourparis.fr; 18 rue de la Fidelité, 10e; s/d from €145/230; 📶; M Château d'Eau) Younger sister to Pigalle's Hôtel Amour, this hipster lifestyle hotel mixes vintage furniture from the flea market with phallic-symbol carpets and the striking B&W nude photography of graffiti artist André Saraiva. The result is an edgy hideaway for lovers in one of the city's most up-and-coming neighbourhoods. Breakfast is served in the hotel bistro, a trendy drinking and dining address in itself.

Ermitage Hôtel HISTORIC HOTEL €€
(Map p80; ☎ 01 42 64 79 22; www.ermitagesacrecoeur.fr; 24 rue Lamarck, 18e; s/tr/q €105/160/180, d €125-140; @; M Lamarck-Caulaincourt) Located in a 19th-century townhouse, family-run Ermitage is a quaint 12-room B&B in the shadow of Sacré-Cœur. The traditional-style rooms are simple but

attractive, with floral-patterned fabric on the walls and antique furnishings that convey a yesteryear charm. Like many addresses in this area, the upper floors have good views.

★Hôtel Particulier Montmartre BOUTIQUE HOTEL €€€
(Map p80; ☎01 53 41 81 40; www.hotel-particulier-montmartre.com; 23 av Junot, 18e, Pavillon D; d from €390; ❄@📶; Ⓜ Lamarck-Caulaincourt) This secret mansion in Montmartre, hidden behind a high wall, only has five rooms – or should we say, lavishly large designer suites peppered with retro curiosities found in flea markets. Guests have free access to the exclusive *pétanque* (similar to the game of bowls) pitch next door, but it's the hotel garden and fashionable cocktail bar that really stuns. Weekend brunch (€38) is equally hot; reservations essential.

To find the hotel, tucked down an old stone-paved alley, ring the buzzer outside the unmarked black gated entrance at No 23.

★Grand Hôtel Pigalle BOUTIQUE HOTEL €€€
(Map p66; ☎01 85 73 12 00; www.grandpigalle.com; 29 rue Victor Massé, 9e; d from €275; ❄@📶; Ⓜ Pigalle) 'Bed and beverage' is the thrust of this elegant and outrageously hip hotel in South Pigalle, or 'SoPi' to those in the know. Love child of the Experimental group who pioneered cocktails in Paris, this is a sophisticated lifestyle hotel with cocktail 'minibars' in its 37 beautifully crafted rooms and a fabulous restaurant–wine bar with Italian chef Giovanni Passerini in the kitchen.

🛏 Le Marais, Ménilmontant & Belleville

In a part of Paris as fashionable as Le Marais, accommodation is naturally chic. All budgets are well catered for – in that sassy, boutique manner Paris does so well. Moving east into the ethnically diverse 'hood of Ménilmontant and Belleville, pickings are not quite so rich or varied, and prices inevitably drop. Hot tip: Belleville has a fantastic hostel with swish doubles, rooftop terrace and skyscraper views of Paris.

★Les Piaules HOSTEL €
(Map p90; ☎01 43 55 09 97; www.lespiaules.com; 59 bd de Belleville, 11e; dm €23-58, d €130-200; @📶; Ⓜ Couronnes) This thoroughly contemporary hostel is the Belleville hot spot to mingle with locals over Parisian craft beer, cosy up in front of the wood-burner with a good book, or lap up sun and stunning views from the 5th-floor rooftop terrace. Dorms are bright and cheery, with custom bunks and ample bedside plugs, but it's the sleek all-white rooftop doubles everyone really gushes over.

MIJE Fourcy HOSTEL €
(Map p90; ☎01 42 74 23 45; www.mije.com; 6 rue de Fourcy, 4e; dm/s/d/tr incl breakfast €33.50/55/82/100.50; 📶; Ⓜ St-Paul, Pont Marie) Sweep through the elegant front door of this *hôtel particulier* and congratulate yourself on scoring such magnificent digs. Fourcy welcomes guests with clean rooms and a summer garden to breakfast/hang out in. It's one of three Marais hostels run by the Maison Internationale de la Jeunesse et des Étudiants – the others are **MIJE Le Fauconnier** (Map p90; 11 rue du Fauconnier, 4e; @📶) and **MIJE Maubuisson** (Map p90; 12 rue des Barres, 4e; @📶).

Cosmos Hôtel HOTEL €
(Map p90; ☎01 43 57 25 88; www.cosmos-hotel-paris.com; 35 rue Jean-Pierre Timbaud, 11e; s €66, d €72-82, tr €93; 📶; Ⓜ République) Cheap, brilliant value and just footsteps from the nightlife of rue JPT, Cosmos is a shiny star with retro style on the budget-hotel scene. It has been around for 30-odd years but, unlike most other hotels in the same price bracket, Cosmos has been treated to a thoroughly modern makeover this century. Breakfast costs €8.

★Hôtel Georgette DESIGN HOTEL €€
(Map p90; ☎01 44 61 10 10; www.hotelgeorgette.com; 36 rue du Grenier St-Lazare, 3e; d from €190; ❄📶; Ⓜ Rambuteau) Clearly seeking inspiration from the Centre Pompidou around the corner, this sweet little neighbourhood hotel is a steal. The lobby is bright and appealing, and rooms are a decorative ode to either Pop Art, Op Art, Dada or New Realism with lots of bold colours and funky touches like Andy Warhol–inspired Campbell's-soup-can lampshades.

★Hôtel Jeanne d'Arc HOTEL €€
(Map p90; ☎01 48 87 62 11; www.hoteljeannedarc.com; 3 rue de Jarente, 4e; s/d/q €120/195/420; 📶; Ⓜ St-Paul) About the only thing wrong with this gorgeous address is everyone knows about it; book well in advance. Games to play, a painted rocking chair for tots in the bijou lounge, knick-knacks everywhere and the most extraordinary mirror in the breakfast room create a real 'family home' air in this 35-room house.

Hôtel Fabric DESIGN HOTEL €€
(Map p90; ☎01 43 57 27 00; www.hotelfabric.com; 31 rue de la Folie Méricourt, 11e; d from €240; ❄📶; Ⓜ Oberkampf) Four-star Hôtel Fabric is a stylish ode to its industrial heritage as a 19th-century textile factory. Steely pillars prop up the red-brick lounge area with *table d'hôte* (set menu at fixed price) dining table and vintage touches including a Singer sewing machine. Darkly carpeted corridors open onto 33 crisp, bright rooms with beautiful textiles and ubercool cupboards (upcycled packing crates!). Breakfast costs €18.

Hôtel Emile DESIGN HOTEL €€
(Map p90; ☎01 42 72 76 17; www.hotelemile.com; 2 rue Malher, 4e; d €135-218; ❄📶; Ⓜ St-Paul) Prepare to be dazzled – literally. Retro B&W, geometrically patterned carpets, curtains, wallpapers and drapes dress this chic hotel, wedged between boutiques and restaurants in Le Marais. Pricier 'top floor' doubles are just that, complete with breathtaking outlooks over Parisian roofs and chimney pots. Breakfast, included in the price, is on bar stools in the lobby; open the cupboard to find the 'kitchen'.

Hôtel Caron de Beaumarchais BOUTIQUE HOTEL €€
(Map p90; ☎01 42 72 34 12; www.carondebeaumarchais.com; 12 rue Vieille du Temple, 4e; d €210-250; @📶; Ⓜ St-Paul) The attention to detail at this unique 19-room themed hotel, decorated like an 18th-century private house, is impressive. From the period card table set as if time stopped halfway through a game, to the harp and well-worn sheet music propped on the music stand, the decor evokes the life and times of the 18th-century playwright after whom the hotel is named.

Hôtel Beaumarchais DESIGN HOTEL €€
(Map p92; ☎01 53 36 86 86; www.hotelbeaumarchais.com; 3 rue Oberkampf, 11e; s/d/tr €150/210/260; 📶; Ⓜ Filles du Calvaire) This brighter-than-bright 31-room design hotel, with its emphasis on sunbursts and bold primary colours, is just this side of kitsch. But it makes for a bright Paris experience. There are monthly art exhibitions and guests are invited to the *vernissage* (opening night). The boutiques and bars of Le Marais are a two-minute walk away. Good-value rates online.

★ **Les Bains** DESIGN HOTEL €€€
(Map p90; ☎01 42 77 07 07; www.lesbains-paris.com; 7 rue du Bourg l'Abbé, 3e; d from €392; ❄@📶; Ⓜ Étienne Marcel, Rambuteau) Probably Paris' most fabulous lifestyle hotel, Les Bains opened in 1885 as thermal baths frequented by the literary likes of Marcel Proust. In 1978 the baths morphed into the Bains-Douches nightclub – an iconic address made famous by David Bowie, Mick Jagger and a host of other rock stars and celebs. Today's hotel remains rock-star hot. Its 39 rooms are a showcase of vintage treasures, luxury fabrics and eclectic design touches. Concerts and DJs fill its club Wednesday to Saturday evening (11pm to 5am), and hipsters enliven its restaurant for Sunday brunch (€48). Breakfast costs €25.

★ **Hôtel du Petit Moulin** BOUTIQUE HOTEL €€€
(Map p90; ☎01 42 74 10 10; www.hoteldupetitmoulin.com; 29-31 rue de Poitou, 3e; d €250-395; 📶; Ⓜ Filles du Calvaire) This scrumptious 17-room hotel, a bakery at the time of Henri IV, was designed from head to toe by Christian Lacroix. Pick from medieval and rococo Marais (rooms sporting exposed beams and dressed in toile de Jouy wallpaper), or more modern surrounds with contemporary murals and heart-shaped mirrors just this side of kitsch.

Bastille & Eastern Paris

★ **Mama Shelter** DESIGN HOTEL €
(Map p58; ☎01 43 48 48 48; www.mamashelter.com; 109 rue de Bagnolet, 20e; s/d/tr from €89/99/139; ❄@📶; 🚌76, Ⓜ Alexandre Dumas, Gambetta) This former car park was coaxed into its current zany incarnation by uber-designer Philippe Starck. Its 170 cutting-edge rooms feature iMacs, catchy colour schemes, polished-concrete walls and free movies on demand. A rooftop terrace, pizzeria, and huge restaurant with live music and Sunday brunch only add to its street cred. Book as early as possible to get the best deal. Breakfast is €16.

The drawback? Mama Shelter is a hike from both central Paris and the nearest metro stop, but bus 76 from the centre via place de la Bastille drops you at the door.

★ **Hôtel Exquis** DESIGN HOTEL €€
(Map p90; ☎01 56 06 95 13; www.hotelexquisparis.com; 71 rue de Charonne, 11e; d/q from €178/404; ❄📶; Ⓜ Charonne) Surrealism is the theme of this excellent-value, three-star hotel near place de la Bastille and a cluster of top-choice dining addresses. A unique work of surrealist art decorates each room, where beautiful colour palettes, designer lighting and bathrooms with twinkling tile lights woo guests.

Rates drop by as much as 50% in low season; check online for deals. Breakfast is €12.

★Hôtel l'Antoine DESIGN HOTEL €€€
(Map p94; ☎01 55 28 30 11; www.hotelantoine-bastilleparis.com; 12 rue de Charonne, 11e; s/d €280/380; ; MBastille) Few hotels evoke the local 'hood quite like three-star, 38-room Antoine. A showcase for stunning contemporary decor by Christian Lacroix, its five floors reflect a different aspect of the Bastille – the 1950s, nightlife at the mythical **Balajo** (Map p90; www.balajo.fr; 9 rue de Lappe, 11e; variable), romance, technology – where the French designer once lived. A luxury candle boutique fills part of the lobby and there's a basement sauna and fitness room.

The Islands

The islands are a delightful place to stay but choice is limited and budget accommodation nonexistent.

Hôtel Des Deux-Îles HISTORIC HOTEL €€
(Map p98; ☎01 43 26 13 35; www.deuxiles-paris-hotel.com; 59 rue Saint-Louis en l'Île, 4e; s/d from €210/240; ; MPont Marie) A venerable 17th-century building shelters this intimate hotel with a vaulted stone guest lounge with a massive open fireplace and 17 spacious rooms with patterned wallpaper, screen-printed fabrics, original Portuguese *azulejos* (blue-and-white ceramic tiles) in some bathrooms, and ancient wooden beams. Breakfast (€14) is available in the lounge and, unusually for the same price, in the privacy of your room.

Latin Quarter

This lively neighbourhood has plenty of options in all price categories. Some areas, especially just across the bridge from Notre Dame and around place St-Michel, are exceptionally central. Note that the months of March to June and October are very busy with students and professors attending conferences and seminars, so book well ahead if you're visiting then.

Hôtel Esmeralda HOTEL €
(Map p100; ☎01 43 54 19 20; www.hotel-esmeralda.fr; 4 rue St-Julien le Pauvre, 5e; s/d/tr from €85/125/150; ; MSt-Michel) Tucked away in a quiet street with million-dollar views of Notre Dame (choose room 12!), this no-frills place is about as central to the Latin Quarter as it gets. At these prices, the 19 rooms are no great shakes (the cheapest singles have washbasin only) but they're popular – book well ahead.

★Familia Hôtel HOTEL €€
(Map p100; ☎01 43 54 55 27; www.familiahotel.com; 11 rue des Écoles, 5e; s €110, d €134-152, tr €191, f €214; ; MCardinal Lemoine) Sepia murals of Parisian landmarks, flower-bedecked windows and exposed rafters and stone walls make this friendly third-generation family-run hotel one of the most attractive 'almost budget' options on this side of the Seine. Eight rooms (on the 2nd, 5th and 6th floors; there's a lift/elevator) have little balconies offering glimpses of Notre Dame. Breakfast costs €7.

Hôtel La Lanterne BOUTIQUE HOTEL €€
(Map p100; ☎01 53 19 88 39; www.hotel-la-lanterne.com; 12 rue de la Montagne Ste-Geneviève, 5e; d/ste from €170/390; ; MMaubert-Mutualité) A stunning swimming pool and *hammam* (Turkish steambath) in a vaulted stone cellar, a topiary-filled courtyard garden, contemporary guest rooms (some with small balconies) with black-and-white photos of Parisian architecture, and amenities, including Nespresso machines, and an honesty bar make this a jewel of a boutique hotel. Breakfast (€19) lets you choose from hot and cold buffets and includes Mariage Frères teas.

Hôtel Atmosphères DESIGN HOTEL €€
(Map p100; ☎01 43 26 56 02; www.hotelatmospheres.com; 31 rue des Écoles, 5e; s/d/tr/ste from €126/144/174/229; ; MMaubert-Mutualité) Striking images by award-winning French photographer Thierry des Ouches are permanently exhibited at this haven, where cocooning rooms evoke different Parisian 'atmospheres', such as 'nature', 'monuments', the metro-inspired 'urban' and colourful *salon de thé* (tearoom)–style 'macaron'. There's a small gym and a sauna as well as an honesty bar. Breakfast costs €16.

Hôtel de Notre Dame BOUTIQUE HOTEL €€
(Map p100; ☎01 43 26 79 00; www.hotel-notre-dame-charmeparis.com; 19 rue Maître Albert, 5e; d from €240; ; MMaubert-Mutualité) Regular deals mean this charming boutique hotel invariably sits within midrange territory and offers excellent value for its location in a quiet street near Notre Dame. Some of its stylish rooms have rain showerheads, while others have deep tubs (with coloured fibre-optic lighting that you can change

according to your mood). There's an on-site sauna and small gym.

St-Germain & Les Invalides

St-Germain is one of the most quintessentially Parisian neighbourhoods and there are some enchanting history-steeped jewels and swish designer digs. On the downside, accommodation invariably doesn't come cheap here. Les Invalides is less epicentral and more residential but alas no cheaper.

Hôtel St-André des Arts HOTEL €
(Map p98; ☎01 43 26 96 16; www.hotel-saintandre-desarts.fr; 66 rue St-André des Arts, 6e; s/d/tr/q €95/115/156/181; ; Odéon) Located on a lively, restaurant-lined thoroughfare, this 31-room hotel is a veritable bargain in the centre of the action opposite the beautiful glass-roofed passage Cour du Commerce St André. The rooms are basic and there's no lift/elevator, but the public areas are very evocative of *vieux Paris* (old Paris), with beamed ceilings and ancient stone walls, and rates include breakfast.

Hôtel Perreyve HOTEL €€
(Map p98; ☎01 45 48 35 01; www.perreyve-hotel-paris-luxembourg.com; 63 rue Madame, 6e; s/d €152/197; ; Rennes) A hop, skip and a jump from the Jardin du Luxembourg, this welcoming 1920s hotel is superb value given its coveted location. Cosy, carpeted rooms have enormous frescoes; on the ground floor, start the day in the pretty breakfast room with herringbone floors and fire-engine-red tables and chairs.

Le Bellechasse DESIGN HOTEL €€
(Map p58; ☎01 45 50 22 31; www.lebellechasse.com; 8 rue de Bellechasse, 7e; s/d €197/206; ; Solférino) Fashion (and, increasingly, interior) designer Christian Lacroix' entrancing room themes – including St-Germain, with brocades, zebra striping and faux-gold leafing; Tuileries, with *trompe l'œil* and palms; and Jeu de Paume, with giant playing-card motifs – give the impression you've stepped into a larger-than-life oil painting. Mod cons include docking stations and 200 TV channels. Rates include a glass of Champagne.

Hôtel des Marronniers HOTEL €€
(Map p98; ☎01 43 25 30 60; www.hoteldesmarronniers.com; 21 rue Jacob, 6e; s/d/tr/q from €139/169/239/289; ; St-Germain des Prés) At the end of a small courtyard 30m from the main street, this 37-room hotel has a delightful conservatory leading on to a magical garden. From the 3rd floor up, rooms ending in 1, 2 or 3 look on to the garden; the rooms on the 5th and 6th floors have views over Paris' rooftops.

Hôtel Danemark BOUTIQUE HOTEL €€
(Map p98; ☎01 43 26 93 78; www.hoteldanemark.com; 21 rue Vavin, 6e; d €195-220; ; Vavin) In a peaceful location near the Jardin du Luxembourg, this stone-walled hotel has 15 scrumptious, eclectically furnished rooms. All are well soundproofed and at least 20 sq metres, which is bigger than many Parisians' apartments. Also unlike many residential apartments, all have bathtubs. Breakfast (€11) is served in the atmospheric vaulted cellar.

★ **L'Hôtel** BOUTIQUE HOTEL €€€
(Map p98; ☎01 44 41 99 00; www.l-hotel.com; 13 rue des Beaux Arts, 6e; d from €325; ; St-Germain des Prés) In a quiet quayside street, this award-winning hostelry is the stuff of romance, Parisian myths and urban legends. Rock- and film-star patrons fight to sleep in room 16, where Oscar Wilde died in 1900 and which is now decorated with a peacock motif, or in the art deco room 36 (where entertainer Mistinguett stayed once), with its huge mirrored bed.

Montparnasse & Southern Paris

Oops HOSTEL €
(Map p58; ☎01 47 07 47 00; www.oops-paris.com; 50 av des Gobelins, 13e; dm/d €43/115; ; Gobelins) A candyfloss-pink lift/elevator scales the six colourful floors of Paris' first 'design hostel'. Good-size four- to six-bed dorms and doubles (from €27 and €70, respectively, outside high season) have en suites and are accessible all day. Some have Eiffel Tower views. Breakfast is included; there's also a self-catering kitchen, luggage room and lockers. No credit cards; no alcohol allowed.

Hôtel de la Loire HOTEL €
(Map p58; ☎01 45 40 66 88; www.hoteldelaloire-paris.com; 39bis rue du Moulin Vert, 14e; s €80, d €85-90, tr €105, apt €140; ; Alésia) Obviously at these prices don't expect luxury but do expect a warm welcome and clean, colourful en suite rooms (18 all-up) at this budget hotel of old. The lovely villagey location near Denfert-Rochereau makes it easy to reach both major airports and Gare du Nord, and there's a pretty table-set garden. The kitchen-equipped apartment sleeps four.

★ Sublim Eiffel DESIGN HOTEL €€

(Map p58; ☎01 40 65 95 95; www.sublimeiffel.com; 94 bd Garibaldi, 15e; d from €146; ; Sèvres-Lecourbe) There's no forgetting what city you're in with the Eiffel Tower motifs in reception and rooms (along with Parisian street-map carpets and metro-tunnel-shaped bedheads) plus glittering tower views from upper-floor windows. Edgy design elements also include cobblestone staircase carpeting (there's also a lift/elevator) and, fittingly in *la ville lumière* (the City of Lights), technicoloured in-room fibre-optic lighting. The small wellness centre/*hammam* offers massages.

Off Paris Seine HOTEL €€

(Map p94; www.offparisseine.com; 20-22 Port d'Austerlitz, 13e; d/ste from €160/400; ; Gare d'Austerlitz) If you like the idea of being gently rocked to sleep (not to mention staying right on the Seine), book into Paris' first floating hotel, an 80m-long catamaran-design structure by the Pont Charles de Gaulle with a panoramic 400-sq-metre sun terrace, 15m-long swimming pool, bar, lounge, and 54 stunningly appointed rooms and four even more stunning suites.

Hôtel Vic Eiffel BOUTIQUE HOTEL €€

(Map p58; ☎01 53 86 83 83; www.hotelviceiffel.com; 92 bd Garibaldi, 15e; s/d €190/220; ; Sèvres-Lecourbe) A short walk from the Eiffel Tower, with the metro on the doorstep, this pristine hotel has chic orange and oyster-grey rooms (two of which are wheelchair accessible). Classic rooms are small but perfectly functional; Superior and Privilege rooms offer increased space. All have Nespresso coffee-making machines. Rates plummet outside high season. Breakfast, served in an atrium-style courtyard, costs €14.

Hôtel Saint Charles HOTEL €€

(Map p58; ☎01 45 89 56 54; www.hotel-saint-charles.com; 6 rue de l'Espérance, 13e; s/d/tr/q €170/200/240/280; ; Corvisart) Live like a local at this Butte aux Cailles hotel, located on a quiet, village-like street yet close to the area's lively bars and restaurants. Some of its 57 streamlined, contemporary rooms with aubergine tones have balconies; communal outdoor areas include a timber-decked terrace and fern- and conifer-filled garden.

★ Hôtel Henriette DESIGN HOTEL €€€

(Map p58; ☎01 47 07 26 90; www.hotelhenriette.com; 9 rue des Gobelins, 13e; s/d from €169/249; ; Les Gobelins) Interior designer Vanessa Scoffier scoured Paris' flea markets for over a year sourcing unique pieces, such as Platner chairs and 1950s lighting, to give each of these 32 rooms a one-of-a-kind twist. The results are spellbinding, as is the light-bathed, glassed-in atrium, and adjoining plant-filled stone courtyard graced with wrought-iron furniture and a dazzling star made from multicoloured lightbulbs.

Eating

The inhabitants of some cities rally around local sports teams, but in Paris, they rally around *la table* – and everything on it. Pistachio macarons, shots of tomato consommé, decadent bœuf bourguignon, a gooey wedge of Camembert running onto the cheese plate...food is not fuel here, it's the reason you get up in the morning.

Eiffel Tower & Western Paris

In addition to the pickings of the 16e *arrondissement,* the many restaurants of Les Invalides and the buzzing market street of rue Cler, 7e, are a short walk from the Eiffel Tower. For a truly memorable experience, dine in the icon itself.

Les Deux Abeilles CAFE €

(Map p64; ☎01 45 55 64 04; 189 rue de l'Université, 7e; lunch menu €22, salads €14-18; 9am-7pm; Alma or RER Champ de Mars–Tour Eiffel) There is no lovelier sanctuary from the Eiffel Tower crowds than this old-fashioned tearoom, the elegant love child of a mother-and-daughter team who greet regulars with a *bisou* (kiss). Delicious homemade cakes and *citronnade* (ginger lemonade) aside, the Two Bees cook up quiches, tarts and salads ensuring every table is full by 1pm. Breakfast and brunch available too.

Traiteur Jegado FAST FOOD €

(Map p72; ☎01 47 20 23 83; www.traiteur-jegado.fr; 45 rue de Chaillot, 16e; mains per kg €11-31; noon-2pm Mon-Fri; Alma Marceau, George V) The sign outside this busy canteen-style *traiteur* (caterer) simply reads *'plats cuisinés'* (cooked dishes), but there's no missing this top-choice takeaway address – just look for the lunchtime line snaking halfway down the street. Delicious salads, starters and hot dishes are prepared in the no-frills kitchen, then bagged to go.

Firmin Le Barbier FRENCH €€

(Map p64; ☎01 45 51 21 55; www.firminlebarbier.fr; 20 rue de Monttessuy, 7e; mains €26-35; noon-

FOOD BLOGGERS & USEFUL WEBSITES

David Lebovitz (www.davidlebovitz.com) Former Bay Area pastry chef who relocated to Paris in 2004. Good insight and recommendations.

Le Fooding (www.lefooding.com) The French movement that's giving Michelin a run for its money. Le Fooding's mission is to shake up the ossified establishment, so expect a good balance of quirky, under-the-radar reviews and truly fine dining.

La Fourchette (www.thefork.com) Website offering user reviews and great deals of up to 50% off in Paris restaurants.

Gilles Pudlowski (www.gillespudlowski.com) Indefatigable French (and French-language) food critic and author of the *Pudlo Paris* and *Pudlo France* guides.

Paris by Mouth (www.parisbymouth.com) Capital dining and drinking; one-stop surf for deciding where to eat.

2pm Wed-Fri & Sun, 7-10.30pm Wed-Sat; Ⓜ Pont de l'Alma) This brick-walled bistro was opened by a retired surgeon turned gourmet, and his passion is apparent in everything from the personable service to the wine list. The menu is traditional French (sirloin steak with polenta, decadent bœuf bourguignon), while the modern interior is bright and cheery with an open kitchen. Find it a five-minute walk from the Eiffel Tower. Reserve.

★ Hugo Desnoyer MODERN FRENCH €€€
(Map p58; ☎01 46 47 83 00; www.hugodesnoyer.fr; 28 rue du Docteur Blanche, 16e; mains from €28; ⏲restaurant 11.30am-3.30pm Tue-Sat, 8-11pm Wed; Ⓜ Jasmin) Hugo Desnoyer is Paris' most famous butcher and the trip to his shop in the 16e is well worth it. Arrive by noon or reserve to snag a table and settle down to a *table d'hôte* (set menu at a fixed price) feast of homemade terrines, quiches, foie gras and cold cuts followed by the finest meat in Paris – cooked to perfection *naturellement*. Another branch, Steak Point, is located in the basement of Galeries Lafeyette Gourmet.

★ L'Astrance GASTRONOMIC €€€
(Map p64; ☎01 40 50 84 40; 4 rue Beethoven, 16e; lunch menus €70-150, dinner €230; ⏲12.15-1.15pm & 8.15-9.15pm Tue-Fri; Ⓜ Passy) It's been over 15 years since Pascal Barbot's dazzling cuisine at the three-star L'Astrance made its debut, but it has shown no signs of losing its cutting edge. Look beyond the complicated descriptions on the menu – what you should expect are teasers of taste that you never even knew existed. Reserve one to two months in advance.

Champs-Élysées & Grands Boulevards

The Champs-Élysées area is known for its big-name chefs (Alain Ducasse, Pierre Gagnaire) and culinary icons (Taillevent), but there are a few under-the-radar restaurants too, where Parisians who live and work in the area dine on a regular basis. Rue de Ponthieu, running parallel to the Champs-Élysées, is a good spot to hunt for casual eateries, bakeries and cafes.

Head to the Grands Boulevards for a more diverse dining selection – everything from hole-in-the-wall wine bars to organic cafes.

★ Ladurée PATISSERIE €
(Map p72; www.laduree.com; 75 av des Champs-Élysées, 8e; pastries from €1.50; ⏲7.30am-11.30pm Mon-Fri, 8.30am-12.30am Sat, 8.30am-11.30pm Sun; Ⓜ George V) One of the oldest patisseries in Paris, Ladurée has been around since 1862 and was the original creator of the lighter-than-air macaron. Its tearoom is the classiest spot to indulge on the Champs. Alternatively, pick up some pastries to go – from croissants to its trademark macarons, it's all quite heavenly.

Lafayette Gourmet FOOD COURT €
(Map p66; bd Haussmann, 9e; ⏲9.30am-8pm Mon-Sat, to 9pm Thu; Ⓜ Havre Caumartin or RER Auber) This one-stop shop for all of Paris' most decadent indulgences (Pierre Hermé macarons, lemon-yuzu eclairs, foie gras, bean-to-bar chocolate, wine and Champagne) also has a gourmet food court where you can feast on delicacies as varied as oysters, charcuterie, dim sum and sizzling steaks from Hugo Desnoyer's **butcher shop** (mains €14-26; ⏲noon-7.30pm Mon-Sat).

LOCAL KNOWLEDGE

BEST BOULANGERIES

Poilâne (Map p98; www.poilane.com; 8 rue du Cherche Midi, 6e; ⌚7.15am-8.15pm Mon-Sat; Ⓜ Sèvres-Babylone) Turning out distinctive wood-fired sourdough loaves since 1932.

Besnier (Map p64; 40 rue de Bourgogne, 7e; ⌚7am-8pm Mon-Fri Sep-Jul; Ⓜ Varenne) Watch baguettes being made through the viewing window.

Du Pain et des Idées (Map p90; www.dupainetdesidees.com; 34 rue Yves Toudic, 10e; pastries from €1.50; ⌚6.45am-8pm Mon-Fri; Ⓜ Jacques Bonsergent) Traditional bakery near Canal St-Martin with an exquisite 1889 interior.

Au 140 (Map p58; www.au140.com; 140 rue de Belleville, 20e; sandwiches €3-5; ⌚7am-8pm Tue-Fri, 7.30am-8pm Sat, 7am-7pm Sun; Ⓜ Jourdain) Crunchy-to-perfection baguettes and gourmet, wood-fired-oven breads.

Le Grenier à Pain (Map p80; 38 rue des Abbesses, 18e; sandwiches €3-4.10; ⌚7.30am-8pm Thu-Mon; Ⓜ Abbesses) Perfect Montmartre picnic stop.

Huré (Map p90; ☎01 42 72 32 18; www.hure-createur.fr; 18 rue Rambuteau, 3e; sandwiches €5-10; ⌚6.30am-8.30pm Tue-Sat; Ⓜ Rambuteau) Contemporary bakery with a graffitied wall.

★ Richer NEOBISTRO €€

(Map p66; www.lericher.com; 2 rue Richer, 9e; mains €19-20; ⌚8am-midnight; Ⓜ Poissonière, Bonne Nouvelle) Run by the same team as across-the-street neighbour **L'Office** (2-/3-course lunch menus €22/28, dinner menus €27/34; ⌚noon-2.30pm & 7.30-10.30pm Mon-Fri), Richer's pared-back, exposed-brick decor is a smart setting for genius creations like trout tartare with cauliflower and tomato and citrus mousse, and quince and lime cheesecake for dessert. It doesn't take reservations, but it serves up snacks and Chinese tea, and has a full bar outside meal times. Fantastic value.

Mamou NEOBISTRO €€

(Map p66; ☎01 44 63 09 25; www.restaurant-mamou.fr; 42 rue Taitbout, 9e; 2-course lunch €19, mains €20-26; ⌚noon-2.30pm Mon-Fri, 7.30-10.30pm Wed-Sat; Ⓜ Chaussée d'Antin) Fans of *haute cuisine* sans *haute* attitude should seek out this casual bistro by the Palais Garnier. Romain Lalu, who previously worked at the Parisian icon Lasserre, runs the kitchen, and diners can expect all the playful flavour combos of a chef free to follow his whims. Excellent natural wine selection. Reserve ahead.

Le Hide FRENCH €€

(Map p72; ☎01 45 74 15 81; www.lehide.fr; 10 rue du Général Lanrezac, 17e; 2-/3-course menus €27/35; ⌚6-10.30pm Mon-Sat; Ⓜ Charles de Gaulle–Étoile) A perpetual favourite, Le Hide is a tiny neighbourhood bistro serving scrumptious traditional French fare: snails, baked shoulder of lamb with pumpkin purée or monkfish in lemon butter. Unsurprisingly, this place fills up faster than you can scamper down the steps of the nearby Arc de Triomphe. Reserve well in advance.

Louvre & Les Halles

The dining scene in central Paris is excellent, and there is no shortage of choices, from eat-on-the-go bakeries to casual foodie favourites to Michelin-starred cuisine. By all means reserve a table at a big-name restaurant, but also try wandering market streets like rue Montorgueil or, for something different, sample ramen or udon at one of the innumerable Japanese noodle shops along rue St-Anne.

Frenchie To Go FAST FOOD €

(Map p76; www.frenchietogo.com; 9 rue du Nil, 2e; sandwiches €11-14; ⌚8.30am-4.30pm Mon-Fri, 9.30am-5.30pm Sat & Sun; 📶; Ⓜ Sentier) Despite the drawbacks – limited seating, eye-poppingly expensive doughnuts – the fast-food outpost of the burgeoning Frenchie (p122) empire is a wildly popular destination. Bilingual staff transform choice ingredients (eg cuts of meat from the Ginger Pig in Yorkshire) into American classics like pulled-pork and pastrami sandwiches, accompanied by cornets of fries, coleslaw and pickled veggies.

Le Camion Qui Fume FAST FOOD €

(Map p66; www.lecamionquifume.com; 168 rue Montmartre, 2e; burgers €9-11; ⌚11am-11pm Sun-Thu, to midnight Fri & Sat; Ⓜ Grands Boulevards) The sedentary outpost of the famous food truck, Le Camion Qui Fume has staked a claim on burger-happy rue Montmartre, and

judging by the late-night crowds, business is good. The Camion's claim to fame is gourmet burgers made with high-grade French beef and freshly baked buns, but you'll also appreciate the draught beer, friendly service and smothered chilli cheese fries.

Filakia FAST FOOD €

(Map p76; ☎01 42 21 42 88; www.filakia.fr; 9 rue Mandar, 2e; souvlaki €7; ⏰11.30am-3pm & 6.30-10.30pm Mon-Fri, 11.30am-10.30pm Sat; Ⓜ Les Halles, Sentier) On the prowl for a quality €10 meal? Look no further than this upbeat souvlaki spot off rue Montorgueil. It's more French then Greek, but that's a minor detail – what really counts is the excellent pita bread, hand-cut fries (€3) and selection of finger-licking locavore fillings (including a vegetarian zucchini and feta option).

Dame Tartine CAFE €

(Map p90; ☎01 42 77 32 22; 2 rue Brisemiche, 4e; tartines €9.90-13.50; ⏰9am-11.30pm; 📶; Ⓜ Hôtel de Ville) One of the few reasonable dining options near the Centre Pompidou, Dame Tartine makes the most of its lively location across from the whimsical Stravinsky Fountain. Don't expect miracles on the culinary front, but its speciality – the *tartine* (open-face sandwich) – will hit the spot after a morning in the museum.

Lina's Beautiful Sandwich SANDWICHES, SALADS €

(Map p76; www.linasparis.com; 50 rue Étienne Marcel, 2e; sandwiches €5.50-6.90; ⏰8.30am-6pm Mon-Fri, 9am-6.30pm Sat; ❄📶; Ⓜ Sentier, Bourse) For made-to-measure sandwiches built from five different bread types and countless fillings and dressings, there is no better address than this large, hip, contemporary space with bags of comfy seating. Serves breakfast too.

Crêpe Dentelle CRÊPERIE €

(Map p76; ☎01 40 41 04 23; 10 rue Léopold Bellan, 2e; crêpes €5-15, lunch menu €11.50; ⏰noon-3pm & 7.30-11pm Mon-Fri; 👪; Ⓜ Sentier) Named after a style of crêpe that's as delicate as fine lace *(dentelle)*, this is probably not the place to go if you're starving. However, it is an excellent choice for a light and inexpensive lunch, and is certainly the best bet for crêpes near the Louvre. Arrive by 12.15pm or you may not get a seat.

Ace Gourmet Bento KOREAN €

(Map p76; 18 rue Thérèse, 1er; lunch €9-13; ⏰noon-10pm Mon-Sat; Ⓜ Pyramides) It's as cheap as chips – a mug of sweet lemon tea gets you change from €2 – and you can eat in or take away. In the heart of Paris' Japantown, this place is a bijou Korean canteen-bistro with bright white walls, flowery pop-art deco and an unbeatable-value lunch deal.

Kunitoraya JAPANESE €

(Map p76; www.kunitoraya.com; 1 rue Villedo, 1er; noodles €10-20; ⏰noon-5.30pm & 7-11.15pm Thu-Tue; Ⓜ Pyramides) Some of Paris' best udon (thick Japanese noodles) is what this buzzing brick-walled address is all about. Grab a seat at one of the communal tables and watch the young chefs strut their stuff over steaming bowls laced with battered prawns, sweet duck and curry. Arrive well before 1pm (or 8pm) or risk leaving disappointed. Cash only and no reservations.

Uma FUSION €€

(Map p76; ☎01 40 15 08 15; www.uma-restaurant.fr; 7 rue du 29 Juillet, 1er; 2-/3-course lunch €25/29, mains €23-25; ⏰12.30-2.30pm & 7.30-10.30pm Tue-Sat; Ⓜ Tuileries) Embark on a culinary voyage at Uma, where chef Lucas Felzine infuses contemporary French sensibilities with Nikkei: Peruvian-Japanese fusion food. The lunch menu comes with two exquisitely prepared starters (think ceviche with daikon radish or smoked duck with lychees and *huacatay*); grab a table upstairs to spy on the open kitchen. Mezcal, pisco and vodka cocktails served until 1.30am. Reserve.

Racines FRENCH €€

(Map p66; ☎01 40 13 06 41; www.racinesparis.com; 8 Passage des Panoramas, 2e; mains €24-32; ⏰noon-2.30pm & 7.30-10.30pm Mon-Fri; Ⓜ Grands Boulevards, Richelieu-Drouot) Snug inside a former 19th-century *marchand de vin* (wine merchant's; look up to admire the lovely old gold lettering above the door), Racines (meaning 'Roots') is an address that shouts Paris at every turn. Shelves of wine bottles curtain the windows, the old patterned floor smacks of feasting and merriment, and the menu chalked on the blackboard is straightforward.

Noglu MODERN FRENCH €€

(Map p66; ☎01 40 26 41 24; www.noglu.fr; 16 Passage des Panoramas, 2e; mains €16-25; ⏰noon-3pm Mon-Sat, 7.30-10.30pm Tue-Sat; 🖉; Ⓜ Richelieu-Drouot, Grands Boulevards) Gluten-free kitchens are hard to find in France, but that's only one of the reasons that Noglu is such a jewel – this chic address builds on French tradition (bœuf bourguignon) while simultaneously drawing on newer culinary

The Seine

The lifeline of Paris, the Seine sluices through the city, spanned by 37 bridges. Its Unesco World Heritage–listed riverbanks offer picturesque promenades, parks, activities and events, including sandy summertime beaches. After dark, watch the river dance with the watery reflections of city lights and tourist-boat floodlamps.

Paris' riverbanks have been reborn with the creation of Les Berges de Seine (p95). On the Right Bank, east of the Hôtel de Ville, 1.5km of former expressway now incorporates walkways and cycleways. Even more revolutionary is the completely car-free 2.3km stretch of the Left Bank from the Pont de l'Alma to the Musée d'Orsay (linked to the water's edge by a grand staircase that doubles as amphitheatre seating).

A resounding success since it opened in 2013, this innovative promenade is dotted with restaurants and bars (some aboard boats), chessboard tables, hopscotch and ball-game courts, a skate ramp, kids' climbing wall, a 100m running track and floating gardens on 1800 sq metres of artificial islands (complete with knotted-rope hammocks where you can lie back and soak up the river's reclaimed serenity).

The Seine's riverbanks are where Parisians come to cycle, jog, inline skate and stroll – staircases along the banks lead down to the water's edge.

SEINE-SIDE HIGHLIGHTS

Picnics Idyllic spots include the Musée de la Sculpture en Plein Air (p93) and Square du Vert-Galant (p97).

Bridges Stroll the historic Pont Neuf (p87), or busker-filled Pont St-Louis or Pont au Double (p146).

Beaches Lounge along summer's Paris Plages (p108).

Islands The Île de la Cité and Île St-Louis (p130) are enchanting; the Île aux Cygnes (p97) is a little-known gem.

Cruises Board Bateaux-Mouches (p107) or hop on and off the Batobus (p157).

1

PIERRE JEAN DURIEU / SHUTTERSTOCK ©

1. Statue in Square du Vert-Galant (p97), Île de la Cité
2. Cathédrale Notre Dame de Paris (p87), beside the Seine
3. Pont Neuf (p87), Île de la Cité

3

GARDEL BERTRAND / HERMIS.FR / GETTY IMAGES ©

LUCIANO MORTULA / GETTY IMAGES / ISTOCKPHOTO ©

trends from across the Atlantic to create some devilishly good pastries, vegetarian plates, and superb pizzas and salads. Don't skip the chocolate-passion tart. Reserve.

La Tour de Montlhéry – Chez Denise TRADITIONAL FRENCH €€
(Map p76; ☎01 42 36 21 82; 5 rue des Prouvaires, 1er; mains €23-28; ⏰noon-2.30pm & 7.30pm-5am Mon-Fri; Ⓜ Châtelet) The most traditional eatery near the former Les Halles marketplace, this boisterous old bistro with red-chequered tablecloths has been run by the same team for 30-some years. If you've just arrived and are ready to feast on all the French classics – snails in garlic sauce, veal liver, steak tartare, braised beef cheeks and housemade pâtés – reservations are in order. Open till dawn.

Beef Club STEAK €€
(Map p76; ☎09 54 37 13 65; www.eccbeefclub.com; 58 rue Jean-Jacques Rousseau, 1er; mains €24-48, lunch €28; ⏰noon-2pm Mon-Fri, 7.45-11pm daily; Ⓜ Les Halles) No steakhouse is more chic or hipper than this. Packed ever since it threw its first T-bone on the grill in spring 2012, this beefy address is all about steak, dry aged and prepared to tender perfection. The vibe is hip New York and the downstairs cellar bar, the Ballroom, shakes a mean cocktail courtesy of the cool guys from the Experimental Cocktail Club (p138).

La Mauvaise Réputation MODERN FRENCH €€
(Map p76; ☎01 42 36 92 44; www.lamauvaisereputation.fr; 28 rue Léopold-Bellan, 2e; 2-/3-course lunch menu €18/22, mains €16-24; ⏰noon-2.30pm Mon-Fri, 7.30-10.30pm Tue-Sat; 📶; Ⓜ Sentier) The name alone – Bad Reputation (yep, also a Georges Brassens album) – makes you want to poke your nose in and see what's happening behind that bright-orange canopy and oyster-grey façade just footsteps from rue Montorgueil. The answer is great bistro cooking and warm, engaging service in a catchy designer space with coloured spots on the wall and fresh flowers on each table.

Aux Lyonnais LYONNAIS €€
(Map p66; ☎01 58 00 22 06; www.auxlyonnais.com; 32 rue St-Marc, 2e; lunch menu €34, mains €24-34; ⏰noon-2.30pm Tue-Fri, 7.30-10.30pm Tue-Sat; Ⓜ Richelieu-Drouot) This is where top French chef Alain Ducasse and his followers 'slum' it. The venue is an art nouveau masterpiece that feels more real than movie set; the food is perfectly restructured Lyonnais classics, such as quenelles (creamed fish or meat shaped like a dumpling) and blood sausage.

★ Verjus MODERN AMERICAN €€€
(Map p76; ☎01 42 97 54 40; www.verjusparis.com; 52 rue de Richelieu, 1er; prixe-fixe menu €68; ⏰7-11pm Mon-Fri; Ⓜ Bourse, Palais Royal–Musée du Louvre) Opened by American duo Braden Perkins and Laura Adrian, Verjus was born out of a wildly successful clandestine supper club known as the Hidden Kitchen. The restaurant builds on that tradition, offering a chance to sample some excellent, creative cuisine in a casual space. The tasting menu is a series of small plates, using ingredients sourced straight from producers. Reserve well in advance.

If you're just after an aperitif or a prelude to dinner, the downstairs **Verjus Bar à Vins** (47 rue de Montpensier, 1er; ⏰6-11pm Mon-Fri) serves a handful of charcuterie and cheese plates. For lunch or a casual dinner, don't miss nearby **Ellsworth** (www.ellsworthparis.com; 34 rue de Richelieu, 1er; 2-/3-course lunch menu €20/26, mains €11-15; ⏰12.30-2.30pm Tue-Sat, 7-10.30pm Mon-Sat, 11.30am-3pm Sun).

★ Frenchie BISTRO €€€
(Map p76; ☎01 40 39 96 19; www.frenchie-restaurant.com; 5-6 rue du Nil, 2e; prix-fixe menu €68; ⏰7-11pm Mon-Fri; Ⓜ Sentier) Tucked down an alley you wouldn't venture down otherwise, this bijou bistro with wooden tables and old stone walls is iconic. Frenchie is always packed and for good reason: excellent-value dishes are modern, market-driven and prepared with just the right dose of unpretentious creative flair by French chef Gregory Marchand.

The only hiccup is snagging a table: reserve well in advance; arrive at 6.30pm and pray for a cancellation (it does happen); or share tapas-style small plates with friends across the street at **Frenchie Bar à Vins** (6 rue du Nil. 2e; dishes €9-23; ⏰7-11pm Mon-Fri). No reservations at the latter – write your name on the sheet of paper strung outside, loiter in the alley and wait for your name to be called.

Spring MODERN FRENCH €€€
(Map p76; ☎01 45 96 05 72; www.springparis.fr; 6 rue Bailleul, 1er; prix-fixe menu €84; ⏰6.30-10.30pm Tue-Sat; Ⓜ Palais Royal–Musée du Louvre) One of the Right Bank's talk-of-the-town addresses, with Chicago-born Daniel Rose in the open kitchen and stunning food. It has no printed menu, meaning hungry gourmets put their appetites in the hands of the chefs and allow multilingual waiting staff to reveal what's cooking as each course is served. Reserve well in advance.

LOCAL KNOWLEDGE

BEST ORGANIC

SuperNature (Map p66; ☎01 47 70 21 03; www.super-nature.fr; 12 rue de Trévise, 9e; mains €15.50; ⌚noon-2.30pm Mon-Fri, 11.30am-3.30pm Sun; Ⓜ Cadet, Grands Boulevards) 🌿 Funky cafe with clever veggie creations.

Fée Nature (Map p76; ☎01 42 21 44 36; www.feenature.com; 67 rue d'Argout, 2e; plat du jour €8.50; ⌚noon-4pm Mon-Fri; 📶; Ⓜ Sentier) Thinking green north of Les Halles.

Soya (Map p90; ☎01 48 06 33 02; www.facebook.com/soyacantinebio; 20 rue de la Pierre Levée, 11e; weekday lunch menu €15-22, brunch €27; ⌚7-11pm Tue, noon-3.30pm & 7-11pm Wed-Fri, 11.30am-11pm Sat, 11.30am-4pm Sun; 🖉; Ⓜ Goncourt, République) Uber-cool *cantine bio* in an industrial atelier.

Bloom (Map p94; ☎01 43 72 87 88; www.bloom-restaurant.fr; 25 rue de la Forge Royale, 11e; 2-/3-course lunch menu €13/15.50; ⌚noon-3pm Tue-Fri, to 4pm Sat & Sun; 🖉; Ⓜ Ledru-Rollin) 🌿 Local, organic and *fait maison* (homemade) on a quiet street opposite a park.

Café Pinson (Map p90; ☎09 83 82 53 53; www.cafepinson.fr; 6 rue du Forez, 3e; mains €14; ⌚9am-10pm Mon-Fri, 10am-10pm Sat, noon-6pm Sun; 📶🖉; Ⓜ Filles du Calvaire) 🌿 Enchanting lifestyle cafe between designer boutiques in the trendy Haut Marais.

Season (Map p90; www.season-paris.com; 1 rue Charles-François Dupuis, 3e; mains €15-20; ⌚8.30-1am Mon-Sat, to 7pm Sun; Ⓜ Temple) 🌿 Hipster all-day address in Le Marais.

Le Grand Véfour TRADITIONAL FRENCH €€€
(Map p76; ☎01 42 96 56 27; www.grand-vefour.com; 17 rue de Beaujolais, 1er; lunch/dinner menu €115/315; ⌚noon-2.30pm & 7.30-10.30pm Mon-Fri; Ⓜ Pyramides) This 18th-century jewel on the northern edge of the Jardin du Palais Royal has been a dining favourite of the Parisian elite since 1784; just look at who gets their names ascribed to each table – from Napoleon and Victor Hugo to Colette (who lived next door). The food is tip-top; expect a voyage of discovery in one of the most beautiful restaurants in the world.

Montmartre & Northern Paris

★52 Faubourg St-Denis MODERN FRENCH €
(Map p90; www.faubourgstdenis.com; 52 rue du Faubourg St-Denis, 10e; mains €16-20; ⌚8am-midnight, kitchen noon-2.30pm & 7-11pm; 📶; Ⓜ Château d'Eau) This thoroughly contemporary, neighbourhood cafe-restaurant is simply a brilliant space to hang out in at any time of day. Be it for breakfast, coffee, a zingy fresh-sage infusion, dinner or drinks, 52 Faubourg, as locals call it, gets it just right. Cuisine is modern and creative, and the chef is not shy in mixing veg with fruit in every course – including dessert. No reservations.

★Holybelly INTERNATIONAL €
(Map p90; www.holybel.ly; 19 rue Lucien Sampaix, 10e; breakfast €5-11.50, lunch mains €13.50-16.50; ⌚9am-6pm Thu, Fri, Mon, from 10am Sat & Sun; Ⓜ Jacques Bonsergent) This outstanding barista-run coffee shop and kitchen is always rammed with a buoyant crowd, who never tire of Holybelly's exceptional service, Belleville-roasted coffee and cuisine. Sarah's breakfast pancakes served with egg, bacon, homemade bourbon butter and maple syrup are legendary, while her lunch menu features everything from traditional braised veal shank to squid *à la plancha*.

Breakfast is served until noon weekdays and all day at weekends; lunchtime is noon to 3pm. No reservations.

★Soul Kitchen VEGETARIAN €
(Map p58; www.soulkitchenparis.fr; 33 rue Lamarck, 18e; lunch menu €13.50; ⌚8.30am-6pm Tue-Fri, 10am-6.30pm Sat & Sun; 📶🖉👪; Ⓜ Lamarck-Caulaincourt) This vegetarian eatery with shabby-chic vintage interior and tiny open kitchen is as soulful as its name suggests. Market-driven dishes include feisty bowls of creative salads, homemade soups, savoury tarts, burritos and wraps – all gargantuan in size and packed with seasonal veggies. Round off lunch or snack between meals on muffins, cakes and the finest mint-laced *citronnade maison* (homemade lemonade) in town.

Families, note: feel free to rifle through the playful content of the sage-green 'games' cupboard.

Fric-Frac SANDWICHES €
(Map p90; http://fricfrac.fr; 79 quai de Valmy, 10e; sandwiches €11.50-14.50; ⌚noon-3pm & 8-11pm

DON'T MISS

TOP THREE FOOD MARKETS

If you only get to one open-air street market in Paris, **Marché Bastille** (Map p90; http://equipement.paris.fr/marche-bastille-5477; bd Richard Lenoir, 11e; ⏲7am-2.30pm Thu, 7am-3pm Sun; Ⓜ Bastille, Richard Lenoir) – stretching between the Bastille and Richard Lenoir metro stations – is among the city's very best.

Built in 1615, **Marché des Enfants Rouges** (Map p90; 39 rue de Bretagne & 33bis rue Charlot, 3e; ⏲8.30am-1pm & 4-7.30pm Tue-Fri, 4-8pm Sat, 8.30am-2pm Sun; Ⓜ Filles du Calvaire) is Paris' oldest covered market. It is secreted behind an inconspicuous green metal gate – and for good reason. A glorious maze of 20-odd food stalls selling ready-to-eat dishes from around the globe, it is a great place to come for a meander and munch with locals. Grab a Moroccan couscous or Caribbean platter and consume at communal tables.

All the staples of French cuisine can be found in chaotic **Marché d'Aligre** (Map p94; http://marchedaligre.free.fr; rue d'Aligre, 12e; ⏲8am-1pm Tue-Sun; Ⓜ Ledru-Rollin), a street market and real favourite with Parisians: cheese, coffee, chocolate, wine, charcuterie, even Tunisian pastries. At weekends follow locals into the historic covered market hall – signposted **Marché Beauvau** (Map p94; place d'Aligre, 12e; ⏲9am-1pm & 4-7.30pm Tue-Fri, 9am-1pm & 3.30-7.30pm Sat, 9am-1.30pm Sun; Ⓜ Ledru-Rollin) – on place d'Aligre for a glass of white wine and platter of freshly shucked oysters. The morning flea market **Marché aux Puces d'Aligre** (p150) takes place on the square.

Tue-Fri, noon-11pm Sat, noon-7pm Sun; Ⓜ Jacques Bonsergent) Traditional snack croque monsieur (a toasted cheese and ham sandwich) gets a contemporary makeover at this quayside space. Grab a toasted sandwich to munch on along the canal banks or eat in: gourmet Winnie (Crottin de Chavignol cheese, dried fruit, chestnut honey, chives and rosemary) and exotic Shaolin (king prawns and Thai chutney) are among the creative combos served with salad and fries.

★Tricycle Store — FAST FOOD €

(Map p66; www.letricycle.fr; 51 rue Paradis, 10e; hot dogs €5; ⏲noon-6pm Mon-Fri, to 4pm Sun; 📶🖉; Ⓜ Poissonnière) What began life as a hot-dog stand on wheels – three wheels to be precise – pedalled around town by flame-haired Coralie and partner Daqui has now morphed into a fully fledged shop with upstairs seating. Dogs are 100% vegetarian with names inspired by hip-hop artists. House special Dogtor Dre is a corn and smoked-soya sausage smothered in creamy avocado, coriander, onions and tomato.

Sunken Chip — FAST FOOD €

(Map p90; ☎01 53 26 74 46; www.thesunkenchip.com; 39 rue des Vinaigriers, 10e; fish & chips €12-14; ⏲noon-2.30pm & 7-10pm Tue-Fri, noon-3.30pm & 7-10pm Sat & Sun; Ⓜ Jacques Bonsergent) It's hard to argue with the battered, fried goodness at this ideally located fish 'n' chip shop near Canal St-Martin. Nothing is frozen here: it's all line-caught fish fresh from Brittany (three varieties per day), accompanied with thick-cut chips (peeled and chopped *sur place*), brown malt vinegar and minty mushy peas. Pickled eggs and onions are optional. Takeaway is available.

Rococo — KEBAB €

(Map p90; www.rococokebab.fr; 10 rue du Faubourg St-Martin, 10e; kebabs €9, lunch menu €12; ⏲noon-midnight; 📶🖉; Ⓜ Strasbourg-St-Denis, Jacques Bonsergent) With its black minimalist interior and creative kebabs to eat in or to go, Rococo casts a great new spin on fast food. Everything from the tasty bread buns and pickles to the tangy herb salsa and aubergine caviar doused on the meats is homemade. Meats are spit-roasted and marinated in orange and mustard, and lemon and spices among others.

Le Dépanneur — AMERICAN €

(Map p80; ☎01 48 74 48 74; www.facebook.com/LeDepanneur; 27 rue Pierre Fontaine, 9e; burgers €17; ⏲10am-2am; 📶; Ⓜ Pigalle) Burgers, tacos and tequila is the holy grail at this Californian diner in the buzzing heart of Pigalle, worth a port of call for its brilliant people-watching pavement terrace – or rather 'ubercool alfresco lounge' with low wooden tables and stools. Creative meal-sized salads (kale with caramelised almonds, apple, Parmesan and zesty lemon dressing) and veggie burgers pad out an otherwise meaty menu.

Hero KOREAN €

(Map p90; www.heroparis.com; 289 rue St-Denis, 2e; cocktails €8-12, chicken €12.50-18; ⌚noon-2.30pm & 7-11pm Tue-Sun; Ⓜ Strasbourg-St-Denis) The creative team behind Le Mary Céleste (p140) and Glass (www.glassparis.com) are behind this unique drinking and dining space. Hero cooks up *yangnyeom* (crispy fried Korean chicken) in sweet and sour, garlicky or fiery *gochu yang* sauces. Tasty salads and snacks pad out the menu, all to be washed down with a truly fabulous cocktail or shot of traditional Korean *soju* (distilled rice liquor).

L'Été en Pente Douce CAFE €

(Map p80; ☎01 42 64 02 67; 23 rue Muller, 18e; mains €10.30-18.30; ⌚noon-midnight; Ⓜ Anvers) Parisian terraces don't get much better than 'Summer on a Gentle Slope' (named after the 1987 French film): a secret square wedged in between two flights of steep staircases on the backside of Montmartre, in a neighbourhood that's very much the real thing. Quiches, giant salads and classic dishes like Niçois-style stuffed veggies make up the menu.

Bob's Juice Bar VEGETARIAN €

(Map p90; ☎09 50 06 36 18; www.bobsjuicebar.com; 15 rue Lucien Sampaix, 10e; juices €4-7.50, bagels €4.50; ⌚7.30am-3pm Mon-Fri, 8.30am-4pm Sat; 🖉; Ⓜ Jacques Bonsergent) Craving a protein shake or green smoothie? This pocket-sized space with bags of rice flour and flaxseed lining the walls is the original hot spot in Paris for smoothies, cold-pressed organic juices, vegan breakfasts, hummus sandwiches, gluten-free muffins and generously filled bagels.

Pink Flamingo PIZZA €

(Map p90; ☎01 42 02 31 70; www.pinkflamingopizza.com; 67 rue Bichat, 10e; pizzas €11.50-17; ⌚7-11.30pm Mon-Thu, noon-3pm & 7-11.30pm Fri-Sun; Ⓜ Jacques Bonsergent) Once the weather warms up, the Flamingo unveils its secret weapon – pink helium balloons that the delivery guy uses to locate you and your perfect canal-side picnic spot (GPS not needed). Order a Poulidor (duck, apple and chèvre) or a Basquiat (Gorgonzola, figs and cured ham), pop into **Le Verre Volé** (http://leverrevole.fr; 67 rue de Lancry, 10e; mains €15-25; ⌚bistro 12.30-2pm & 7.30-10.30pm, wine cellar 9am-1am) across the canal for the perfect bottle of vino and you're set.

Crêperie Pen-Ty CRÊPERIE €

(Map p66; ☎01 48 74 18 49; 65 rue de Douai, 9e; galettes €3-10.90, crêpes €3.90-8.90; ⌚noon-2.30pm & 7.30-11pm Mon-Fri, 12.30-4pm & 6.30-11.30pm Sat, 12.30-4pm & 6.30-10.30pm Sun; Ⓜ Place de Clichy) Hailed as the best crêperie in northern Paris, the Pen-Ty is worth the detour. Book ahead, and don't miss the selection of authentic Breton aperitifs like *chouchen* (a type of mead) and *pastis marin* (an aniseed and seaweed liquor). Savoury *galettes* (made with buckwheat flour) and sweet crêpes are pricier in the evening and at weekends. There is a takeaway window too.

★ Grand Amour Hôtel NEOBISTRO €€

(Map p90; ☎01 44 16 03 30; www.hotelamourparis.fr; 18 rue de la Fidélité, 10e; 2-course lunch €18, mains €14-22; ⌚8am-12.30am; 📶🖉; Ⓜ Gare de l'Est) Track down in-the-know Parisians in this hipster neobistro beneath Hôtel Grand Amour, an address that is rapidly turning the 10e into *the* place to be in Paris. Breakfast – French, English or vegetarian – opens the day, followed by an enticing mix of food served all day: think vegetarian risotto, pastrami sandwiches, hake roasted with parsnip and avocado, or steak and fries.

★ La Bulle MODERN FRENCH €€

(Map p58; ☎01 40 37 34 51; www.restolabulle.fr; 48 rue Louis Blanc, 10e; 2-/3-course lunch menu €18.50/24, dinner menus €43 & €55; ⌚noon-2.30pm & 7.30-10.30pm Mon-Sat; Ⓜ Louis Blanc) It's worth the short detour to this contemporary corner bistro with oyster-grey façade, lime-green seating on a sunny pavement terrace, and talented young chef Romain Perrollaz in the kitchen. His cuisine is creative and strictly *fait maison* (homemade), with lots of tempting combos like beef with dill-spiked spelt risotto or pork *pot au feu* with old-time veg, watercress and peanut vinaigrette.

★ Matière à. MODERN FRENCH €€

(Map p90; ☎09 83 07 37 85; 15 rue Marie et Louise, 10e; 2-/3-course lunch menu €19/23, dinner menu €44; ⌚noon-2.30pm & 7.30pm-1am Mon-Fri, 7pm-1am Sat; Ⓜ République) The short but stunning seasonal menu changes daily at this unique space. *Table d'hôte*-style memorable dining for no more than 14 is around a shared oak table lit by dozens of naked light bulbs. In the kitchen is young chef Anthony Courteille, who prides himself on doing everything *fait maison* (homemade), including bread and butter to die for. Reservations essential.

Abri NEOBISTRO €€

(Map p66; ☎01 83 97 00 00; 92 rue du Faubourg Poissonnière, 9e; lunch/dinner menus €26/46;

⌚12.30-2pm Mon, 12.30-2pm & 8-10pm Tue-Sat; Ⓜ Poissonnière) It's no bigger than a shoebox and the decor is borderline nonexistent, but that's all part of the charm. Katsuaki Okiyama is a seriously talented chef with an artistic flair, and his surprise tasting menus (three courses at lunch, six at dinner) are exceptional. On Monday and Saturday, a giant gourmet sandwich is all that's served for lunch. Reserve well in advance.

Vivant MODERN FRENCH €€

(Map p66; ☎01 42 46 43 55; http://vivantparis.com; 43 rue des Petites Écuries, 10e; mains €23-29; ⌚noon-2pm & 7-10.30pm Mon-Sat; Ⓜ Poissonnière, Bonne Nouvelle) Simple but elegant dishes – creamy burrata, crispy duck leg with mashed potatoes, foie gras and roasted onion – showcase the carefully sourced ingredients used at this small but chic restaurant, inside a century-old exotic-bird shop with a stunning ceramic wall and ceiling. Swiss-born Pierre Jancou is a natural-wine activist and at least one glass of *vin* is an essential part of the meal here. Reserve ahead.

Hôtel Amour BISTRO €€

(Map p66; ☎01 48 78 31 80; www.hotelamourparis.fr; 8 rue Navarin, 9e; mains €17-24; ⌚8am-midnight; 📶; Ⓜ St-Georges, Pigalle) Attached to the arty 'Love' Hotel, this bistro is the hipster address in Pigalle in which to eat and drink at any time of day. Food covers most tastes and cuisines, from grilled scallops in hazelnut and celery cream or truffle-laced macaroni cheese to simple steak tartare, bacon burgers and fish 'n' chips. Weekend brunch (around €20) buzzes and the summer patio garden is prime real estate.

Le Marais, Ménilmontant & Belleville

Packed with restaurants and bistros of every imaginable type, Le Marais is one of Paris' premier dining neighbourhoods with many addresses requiring an advance reservation. Despite the huge concentration of eating addresses, new openings pop up seemingly every week. Multi-ethnic Belleville is tops for tasty Asian fare. Looking east, some of Paris' hippest addresses in the Bastille and Eastern Paris neighbourhood are easy walking distance from Cimetière du Père Lachaise – perfect for lunch or dinner post-grave walking.

★Breizh Café CRÊPERIE €

(Map p90; www.breizhcafe.com; 109 rue Vieille du Temple, 3e; crêpes & galettes €6.50-18; ⌚11.30am-11pm Wed-Sat, to 10pm Sun; Ⓜ St-Sébastien-Froissart) It is a well-known fact among Parisians: everything at the Breton Café (*breizh* is 'Breton' in Breton) is 100% authentic, rendering it the top spot in the city for authentic crêpes. Be it the Cancale oysters, 20 types of cider or the buttery organic-flour crêpes, everything here is cooked to perfection. If you fail to snag a table, try **L'Épicerie** (⌚11.30am-9pm) next door.

★Jacques Genin PATISSERIE €

(Map p90; ☎01 45 77 29 01; 133 rue de Turenne, 3e; pastry €9; ⌚11am-7pm Tue-Sun; Ⓜ Oberkampf) Wildly creative *chocolatier* Jacques Genin is famed for his flavoured caramels, *pâtes de fruits* (fruit jellies) and exquisitely embossed *bonbons de chocolat* (chocolate sweets). But what completely steals the show at his elegant chocolate showroom is the *salon de dégustation* (aka tearoom), where you can order a pot of outrageously thick hot chocolate and legendary Genin *millefeuille*, assembled to order.

★Chez Alain Miam Miam SANDWICHES, CRÊPERIE €

(Map p90; www.facebook.com/ChezAlainMiamMiam; 39 rue de Bretagne & 33bis rue Charlot, 3e, Marché des Enfants Rouges; sandwiches €8; ⌚9am-3.30pm Wed-Fri, to 5.30pm Sat, to 3pm Sun; Ⓜ Filles du Calvaire) Weave your way through the makeshift kitchens inside Marché des Enfants Rouges (p124) to find Alain, a retired baker with grey surfer locks and T-shirt with attitude. Watch him prepare you a monster sandwich or *galette* (savoury pancake) on a sizzling crêpe griddle from a bespoke combo of fresh, organic ingredients – grated fennel, smoked air-dried beef, avocado, sesame salt and carefully curated honeys.

★Candelaria MEXICAN €

(Map p90; ☎01 42 74 41 28; www.candelariaparis.com; 52 rue de Saintonge, 3e; tacos €3-5; ⌚12.30pm-11pm Sun-Wed, 12.30pm-midnight Thu-Sat, bar 6pm-2am; Ⓜ Filles du Calvaire) You need to know about this terribly cool *taqueria* to find it. Made of pure, unadulterated hipness in that brazenly nonchalant manner Paris does so well, clandestine Candelaria serves delicious homemade tacos, quesadillas and tostadas in a laid-back setting – squat at the bar in the front or lounge out back around a shared table with bar stools or at low coffee tables.

Come dark, the party kicks off with occasional DJ sets, tastings, post-gallery drinks and some of the best cocktails (€12 to €13) in town. Regulars swear by the Bloody Mary and cocktail-fuelled brunch, served until 4pm on weekends.

Sacha Finkelsztajn DELI €
(Map p90; ☎01 42 72 78 91; www.laboutiquejaune.com; rue des Rosiers, 4e; pasties & sandwiches from €4; ⏲10am-7pm Wed-Mon; Ⓜ St-Paul) Tempting smells waft from the canary-yellow façade of this third-generation delicatessen and bakery, opened by a Polish couple in 1946. Viennese apple strudel, *borek* (pasties) oozing warm goat's cheese, Yiddish sandwiches, plain or meaty *latkes* (fried potato cakes traditionally eaten at Hanukkah), and *pirojki* with cabbage, aubergine or spinach are some of the Eastern and Central European specialities baked by their grandson today.

Miznon ISRAELI €
(Map p90; ☎01 42 74 83 58; 22 rue des Écoffes, 4e; pita sandwiches €9-12; ⏲noon-1.30pm Sun-Fri; Ⓜ Hôtel de Ville) Parisians cannot get enough of this hip, shabby-chic hang-out whose big sister is none other than the Tel Aviv restaurant of celebrity Israeli chef Eyal Shani. Push your way past the grocery crates and cauliflowers to the bar; order a pita or lamb kebab, or a side of the finest hummus in town.

Do not leave without ending on a sweet *banane au chocolat* pita.

Okomusu JAPANESE €
(Map p90; ☎01 57 40 97 27; www.okomusu.com; 11 rue Charlot, 3e; mains €11-17; ⏲7-10.30pm Tue, noon-2.30pm & 7-10.30pm Wed-Sun; 🌿; Ⓜ St-Sébastien-Froissart) Once full – which happens within seconds of young Japanese chef Hiroko Tabuchi opening her *table d'hôte* – the door is amusingly wedged shut with a spoon. All eyes are then on the chef as she deftly whips up her speciality *okonomiyaki* (a wheat-flour patty with cabbage, chives, ginger, dried fish shavings and pork, prawn or squid), while diners sit hungrily at the bar. Vegetarians can order the non-meat version.

L'Epicerie – Le Verre Volé DELI €
(Map p90; ☎01 48 05 36 55; www.leverrevole.fr; 54 rue de la Folie Méricourt, 11e; sandwiches €4.50-6.90; ⏲11am-8pm Mon-Sat; Ⓜ Oberkampf) This mouthwatering deli, a hop and a skip from trendy rue Oberkampf, serves gourmet sandwiches to take away or eat around a shared table inside the upmarket *épicerie* (grocer) run by the savvy Verre Volé team. Take your pick of one of 15 cheeses and dozens of tempting cold meats from France, Italy and Spain, or go for a creative *sandwich du jour*.

Broken Arm CAFE €
(Map p90; ☎01 44 61 53 60; 2 rue Perrée, 3e; mains €7.50-18.50; ⏲9am-6pm Tue-Sat, lunch noon-3.30pm; 📶; Ⓜ Temple, Arts et Métiers) Kick off with a fresh apple, kiwi and mint juice and congratulate yourself on scoring a table – inside or out – at this overpoweringly hipster address where chic Marais folk lunch after making an appearance in the adjoining concept store. The menu is limited but packed with goodness: imaginative salads, cold platters and cakes. Between meals, snack on designer *tartines* (open sandwiches).

Nanashi FUSION €
(Map p90; ☎09 60 00 25 59; www.nanashi.fr; 57 rue Charlot, 3e; bentos €14-19; ⏲noon-3pm & 7.30-11pm Mon-Fri, noon-4pm & 7.30-11pm Sat & Sun; Ⓜ Filles du Calvaire) An address that packs a punch in the Haut Marais, this hip industrial space with large street-facing windows and concrete floor is ubercool, ultrahealthy and brilliant value. Pick from the creative salads, soups and bento boxes – always one meat, one fish and one veggie option – chalked on the board. Don't miss the freshly squeezed, frothy-topped apple, carrot and ginger juice.

Bob's Kitchen PANCAKES €
(Map p90; www.bobsjuicebar.com; 74 rue des Gravilliers, 11e; pancakes €5-10; ⏲8am-3pm Mon-Fri, to 4pm Sat & Sun; 🌿; Ⓜ Arts et Métiers) If it's pancakes US-style you're after without a spot of cow's milk in sight, Bob's your man (although you might be hard pushed to even get in this tiny space, let alone snag a seat). Sweet and savoury pancakes, milk- and gluten-free, alongside one of the most creative vegetarian lunch menus in town that changes daily and flits all over the globe.

Robert et Louise TRADITIONAL FRENCH €
(Map p90; ☎01 42 78 55 89; www.robertetlouise.com; 64 rue Vieille du Temple, 4e; mains €13-21; ⏲7-11pm Tue & Wed, noon-3pm & 7-11pm Thu-Sat, noon-11pm Sun; Ⓜ St-Sébastien-Froissart) This 'country inn' with red gingham curtains offers simple and inexpensive French food, including *côte de bœuf* (side of beef for two or three people, €46) cooked on an open fire. Arrive early to snag the farmhouse table next to the fireplace – the makings of a real jolly Rabelaisian evening.

Cantine California AMERICAN €

(Map p90; ☎09 81 15 53 13; www.cantinecalifornia.com; 46 rue de Turbigo, 3e; burgers €15; ⏲11.30am-3pm & 7.15-10.30pm; Ⓜ Arts et Métiers) This American eatery run by American-Canadian-born, Paris-raised Jordan Feilders is worth a pit stop, if only because it's the offspring of Paris' first organic food truck (that hit the city streets in 2012). Creative burgers made from organic French beef, tacos and jumbo salads are served in a startlingly simple and very wooden interior with central bar, wood-chip tables and bench seating.

Rachel's AMERICAN €

(Map p90; ☎01 44 61 69 68; www.facebook.com/RachelsParis03; 25 rue du Pont aux Choux, 3e; mains €16-25, brunch €18.50; ⏲noon-2pm & 7.30-10.30pm Mon-Fri, noon-4pm & 7.30-10.30pm Sat, noon-4pm Sun; Ⓜ St-Sébastien-Froissart) What started life as a showcase for the cakes of American-Bulgarian-Austrian trio Rachel, Maria and Birke is now a full-blown restaurant cooking up gutsy US burgers, meal-sized salads and warm gourmet sandwiches in homemade brioche buns. Everything comes in two sizes – small or large – and weekend brunch packs the Dorothée Meilichzon–designed interior to bursting. Sampling Rachel's famous cheesecake (€7/4.50 to eat in/take away) has become a Parisian rite of passage.

★ Pierre Sang Boyer MODERN FRENCH €€

(Map p90; ☎09 67 31 96 80; http://pierresangboyer.com; 55 rue Oberkampf, 11e; 2-/3-/5-course lunch €20/25/35, 4-/6-course dinner €35/50; ⏲noon-3pm & 7-11pm Tue-Sat; Ⓜ Oberkampf) *Top Chef* finalist Pierre Sang Boyer stars at his kitchen restaurant where foodies sit on bar stools and watch the French–South Korean chef perform. Cuisine is modern French with a strong fusion lilt, and the vibe is fun and casual. If the place is full, nip around the corner to Sang's 'atelier' annex on rue Gambey.

★ Au Passage BISTRO €€

(Map p90; ☎01 73 20 23 23; www.restaurant-aupassage.fr; 1bis passage St-Sébastien, 11e; small plates €7-14, meats to share €18-70; ⏲7-11.30pm Mon-Sat; Ⓜ St-Sébastien-Froissart) Spawned by talented Australian chef James Henry, who went on to open Bones then Parisian bistro Belon in Hong Kong, this *petit bar de quartier* (neighbourhood bar) is still raved about. Pick from a good-value, uncomplicated choice selection *of petites assiettes* (small plates designed to be shared) featuring various market produce – cold meats, raw or cooked fish, vegetables and so on. Advance reservations essential.

★ Le Clown Bar MODERN FRENCH €€

(Map p90; ☎01 43 55 87 35; www.clown-bar-paris.fr; 114 rue Amelot, 11e; mains €25-30; ⏲noon-2.30pm & 7-10.30pm Wed-Sun; Ⓜ Filles du Calvaire) Le Clown is a historic monument next to the city's winter circus, the Cirque d'Hiver (1852), and is practically a museum with its ceramics, mosaics, original zinc bar and purist art deco style. This legendary address, which has been a restaurant for decades, now serves up fabulous modern French cuisine and excellent natural wines for a jovial crowd. Its pavement terrace gets packed out on sunny days.

If you fail to snag a table for lunch or dinner, return between meals to admire the decor while you enjoy an early morning *café* with regulars (the bar opens at 8am) or a glass of *vin naturel*.

Chatomat MODERN FRENCH €€

(Map p58; ☎01 47 97 25 77; 6 rue Victor Letalle, 20e; mains €15-20; ⏲7.30-10.30pm Tue-Sat & 1st Sun of month; Ⓜ Ménilmontant, Couronnes, Père Lachaise) No dinner address is worth the trek to Belleville more than this contemporary bistro with plain white walls, post-industrial flavour and bags of foodie buzz. In the kitchen of the old shop turned restaurant, Alice and Victor cook up just three starters, three mains and three desserts each night – and none disappoint. Book in advance.

Brasserie Bofinger BRASSERIE €€

(Map p90; ☎01 42 72 87 82; www.bofingerparis.com; 5-7 rue de la Bastille, 4e; menus €31 & €56; ⏲noon-2pm & 6.30pm-midnight Mon-Sat, noon-11pm Sun; 👪; Ⓜ Bastille) Founded in 1864, Bofinger is reputedly Paris' oldest brasserie, though its polished art nouveau brass, glass and mirrors indicates redecoration a few decades later. Specialities include Alsatian-inspired dishes like *choucroute* (sauerkraut), oysters (from €27.90 for a dozen) and magnificent seafood platters (€29.90 to €122). Ask for a seat downstairs beneath the *coupole* (stained-glass dome). Kids are catered for with a €14.50 children's *menu*.

Jeanne A DELI €€

(Map p90; ☎01 43 55 09 49; www.jeanne-a-comestibles.com; 42 rue Jean-Pierre Timbaud, 10e; 2-/3-course lunch €19/23, dinner €23/27; ⏲10am-10.30pm; Ⓜ Parmentier, Oberkampf) Be it for breakfast, lunch, *goûter* (the traditional French afternoon snack) or dinner, Jeanne

FAST FOOD IN LE MARAIS

If you want to grab a bite on the move, you won't do better than the following:

Blend (Map p90; www.blendhamburger.com; 3 rue Yves Toudic, 10e; burgers €9-14, lunch menu €15; noon-11pm; ; République) This gourmet burger bar is easy to spot by the hungry crowd outside waiting for a table or a takeaway. Blend is a small, smart, black-and-wood space serving the best bijou-sized burgers in town. Buns are homemade, meat is *à la* celebrity butcher Yves-Marie Le Bourdonnec and a delicious veggie option involves smoked tofu, bulgar, smoked cheddar and honey mustard.

Hank (Map p90; 09 72 44 03 99; http://hankburger.com; 55 rue des Archives, 3e; menus €11.80 & €13.80; noon-10pm; ; Hôtel de Ville, Rambuteau) If you prefer yours sans meat, hit Hanks for a veggie burger. The stylish space is a pleasure to linger in and the kitchen works strictly with fresh, organic and, where possible, local produce.

L'As du Fallafel (Map p90; 34 rue des Rosiers, 4e; takeaway €6-8.50; noon-midnight Sun-Thu, to 5pm Fri; St-Paul) The lunchtime queue stretching halfway down the street says it all. Join the line for kosher, perfectly deep-fried falafel (chickpea balls) and turkey or lamb shawarma sandwiches.

Kraft Hotdog (Map p90; http://krafthotdog.com; 15 rue des Archives, 4e; hot dogs €3.50-5.50; noon-11pm Mon-Thu & Sun, noon-midnight Fri & Sat; Hôtel de Ville) Parisians can't get enough of the gourmet hot dogs rolled out of this New York–style deli. Dogs come in four types, plus a choice of sides including nachos. Our current fave: a hot dog smothered in coleslaw, guacamole and honey mustard.

Rachel's Grocery (Map p90; www.facebook.com/RachelsParis03; 20 rue du Pont aux Choux, 3e; sandwiches €6.50-15.50; 10am-10pm; St-Sébastien-Froissart) Hit this retro US grocery for build-your-own hotdogs made from American black Angus beef and gourmet sandwiches to take away. Sarnies range from a classic BLT to spicy southern fried chicken, pastrami, double-smoked mackerel or a Real McCoy, a monster-sized steak-and-egg sandwich.

A – whose twin sister, **Jeanne B** (Map p80; 61 rue Lepic, 18e), lives in Montmartre – delivers. This deli restaurant cooks up delicious homemade tarts, salads, terrines and giant seasonal artichokes. Tasty meats roasted on the *rôtisserie* (spit) can also be taken away. Interior decor is red, white and blue, and there is a €15 children's *menu*.

Blue Valentine MODERN FRENCH €€

(Map p90; 01 43 38 34 72; http://bluevalentine-restaurant.fr; 13 rue de la Pierre Levée, 11e; 2-/3-course lunch menu €21/45, dinner menu €41-60; 7-10pm Wed, noon-2pm & 7-10pm Thu-Sun; République) This thoroughly modern bistro with retro 1950s decor in the gourmet 11e lures a hip crowd. Well-crafted cocktails are married perfectly with the exquisite dishes of Japanese chef Terumitsu Saito, flavoured with edible flowers and a profusion of herbs. The menu is small – just three dishes to choose from per course – but memorable.

Le Dauphin BISTRO €€

(Map p90; 01 55 28 78 88; 131 av Parmentier, 11e; small plates €3.50-18; 6pm-2am Tue-Sat; Goncourt) Advance reservations are essential at this buzzing 'tapas' bar, very much a temple to taste and good looks with its stark white marble, glitzy mirrors and series of small plates that promise to thrill. Prep your taste buds for clams with coffee and cauliflower; foie gras with haddock and quince; tandoori squid; or cider-marinated chorizo. Excellent wine list too.

Chez Marianne JEWISH €€

(Map p90; 2 rue des Hospitalières St-Gervais, 4e; mains €18-25; noon-midnight; St-Paul) Heaving at lunchtime, Chez Marianne translates as elbow-to-elbow dining beneath age-old beams on copious portions of felafel, hummus, aubergine purée and 25-odd other *zakouski* (hors d'oeuvre). Fare is Sephardic rather than Ashkenazi (the norm at most Pletzl eateries), not Beth Din kosher. A hole-in-the-wall window sells felafel in pita (€7) to munch on the move.

Bastille & Eastern Paris

CheZaline SANDWICHES €

(Map p90; 85 rue de la Roquette, 11e; sandwiches €5.50-8; 11am-5.30pm Mon-Fri; Voltaire) A

former horse-meat butcher's shop (*chevaline,* hence the spin on the name) is now a fabulous deli creating seasonally changing baguettes filled with ingredients like ham and house-made pesto. Other delicacies include salads and homemade terrines. There's a handful of seats (and plenty of parks nearby). Prepare to queue.

Miss Lunch at Première Pression Provence CAFE €
(Map p94; ☎01 53 33 03 59; www.lunchintheloft.com; 3 rue Antoine Vollon, 12e; 2-course lunch menu €15.50, mains €12-15; ⏲12.30-2.30pm & 7-10.30pm Thu & Fri, noon-2.30pm Wed & Sat; Ⓜ Ledru-Rollin) This quaint cafe with tables outside overlooking a quiet leafy square is perfect for lunch after shopping at Marché d'Aligre. Cook and visual artist Claude Cabri, aka Miss Lunch, is the creative talent behind this pocket-sized address, backed by Première Pression Provence founder Olivier Baussan. Cuisine is market-driven and rich in AOC-rated cold-pressed *huile d'olive* (olive oil) from Provence.

Yard MODERN FRENCH €
(Map p58; ☎01 40 09 70 30; www.yardparis.com; 6 rue de Mont Louis, 11e; 2-/3-course lunch menus €16/19, mains €15-18; ⏲noon-2.30pm & 8-10.30pm Mon-Fri, tapas 6pm-midnight Mon-Fri; Ⓜ Philippe Auguste) This modern bistro near the Père Lachaise cemetery is squirrelled away in a former construction yard, hence its name. The short but inventive *menu* changes daily, incorporating seasonal dishes such as spring lamb with leeks or a wintery wild boar *mijoté* (stew) with olives and polenta. Sit at the bar to watch the chefs cook in the tiny open kitchen.

Le Bistrot Paul Bert BISTRO €€
(Map p94; ☎01 43 72 24 01; 18 rue Paul Bert, 11e; 2-/3-course lunch/dinner menu €19/41; ⏲noon-2pm & 7.30-11pm Tue-Sat; Ⓜ Faidherbe-Chaligny) When food writers list Paris' best bistros, one name that consistently pops up is Paul Bert. The timeless vintage decor and perfectly executed classic dishes like *steak-frites* and hazelnut-cream Paris-Brest pastry merit booking ahead. Look out for its siblings in the same street: **L'Écailler du Bistrot** (22 rue Paul Bert, 11e; weekday lunch menu €19, mains €17-34) for seafood; La Cave Paul Bert (p142), a wine bar with small plates; and **Le 6 Paul Bert** (6 rue Paul Bert, 12e; 2-/3-course weekday lunch menu €18/19, 4-course dinner menu €44, mains €24-26) for modern cuisine.

Chez Paul BISTRO €€
(Map p90; ☎01 47 00 34 57; www.chezpaul.com; 13 rue de Charonne, 11e; 2-/3-course lunch menu €18/21, mains €17-27; ⏲noon-12.30am; Ⓜ Ledru-Rollin) This is Paris as your grandmother knew it: chequered red-and-white napkins, faded photographs on the walls, old red banquettes and traditional French dishes that could well make your hair curl: pig trotters, *andouillette* (a fiesty tripe sausage), *tête de veau et cervelle* (calf head and brains) and the like. Less offal: a steaming bowl of *pot au feu* (beef stew).

★**Dersou** NEOBISTRO €€€
(Map p94; ☎09 81 01 12 73; www.dersouparis.com; 21 rue St-Nicolas, 12e; 5-/6-/7-course tasting menu incl drinks €95/115/135; ⏲7.30pm-midnight Tue-Fri, noon-3.30pm & 7.30pm-midnight Sat, noon-3.30pm Sun; Ⓜ Ledru-Rollin) Leave any preconceptions you might have at the door, ignore or enjoy the brutishly understated decor, and be wooed by the creative fusion cuisine of Taku Sekine. Much of the seating is at the counter, meaning first-class views of the Japanese chef at work, and options are limited to tasting menus, with each course exquisitely paired with a bespoke cocktail. Reservations essential.

★**Septime** MODERN FRENCH €€€
(Map p90; ☎01 43 67 38 29; www.septime-charonne.fr; 80 rue de Charonne, 11e; lunch menus €28 & €55, dinner menu €58; ⏲7.30-10pm Mon, 12.15-2pm & 7.30-10pm Tue-Fri; Ⓜ Charonne) The alchemists in Bertrand Grébaut's Michelin-starred kitchen produce truly beautiful creations, while blue-smocked waitstaff ensure culinary surprises are all pleasant ones: each dish on the menu is a mere listing of three ingredients, while the mystery *carte blanche* menu puts your taste buds in the hands of the innovative chef. Snagging a table requires planning and perseverance – book three weeks in advance.

For a pre- or post-meal drink, drop by its nearby wine bar **Septime La Cave** (3 rue Basfroi, 11e). For stunning seafood tapas, its sister restaurant **Clamato** (tapas €7-20; ⏲7-11pm Wed-Fri, noon-11pm Sat & Sun) is next door.

The Islands

Île St-Louis is a pleasant if pricey and often touristy place to dine. Otherwise barren of decent eating places, Île de la Cité has a handful of lovely addresses on its western tip. Self-caterers will find a couple of *from-*

ageries (cheese shops) on rue St-Louis en l'Île, 4e, as well as a small supermarket.

★Berthillon ICE CREAM €
(Map p98; www.berthillon.fr; 31 rue St-Louis en l'Île, 4e; 1/2/3 scoops take away €3/4/6.50, eat-in €4.50/7.50/10.50; ⏲10am-8pm Wed-Sun, closed Aug; Ⓜ Pont Marie) Founded here in 1954, this esteemed *glacier* (ice-cream maker) is still run by the same family today. Its 70 all-natural, chemical-free flavours include fruit sorbets such as blackcurrant or pink grapefruit, and richer ice creams made from fresh milk and eggs, such as salted caramel, *marrons glacés* (candied chestnuts) and Agenaise (Armagnac and prunes), along with seasonal flavours like gingerbread.

★Café Saint Régis CAFE €
(Map p98; www.cafesaintregisparis.com; 6 rue Jean du Bellay, 4e; breakfast & snacks €3.50-14.50, mains €18-32; ⏲8am-2am; 📶; Ⓜ Pont Marie) Waiters in long white aprons, a white ceramic-tiled interior and retro vintage decor make hip Le Saint Régis (as regulars call it) a deliciously Parisian hang-out any time of day – from breakfast pastries to mid-morning pancakes, lunchtime salads and burgers and early-evening oyster platters. Come midnight it morphs into a late-night hot spot.

Latin Quarter

From chandelier-lit palaces loaded with history to cheap-eat student haunts, the 5e *arrondissement* caters to every budget and culinary taste. Rue Mouffetard is famed for its food market and food shops, though you'll have to trek down side streets for the neighbourhood's best meals.

★Shakespeare & Company Café CAFE €
(Map p100; www.shakespeareandcompany.com; 2 rue St-Julien le Pauvre, 5e; dishes €4-9.50; ⏲10am-6.30pm Mon-Fri, to 7.30pm Sat & Sun; 📶; Ⓜ St-Michel) Instant history was made when this light-filled, literary-inspired cafe opened in 2015 adjacent to magical bookshop Shakespeare & Company (p150), designed from long-lost sketches to fulfil a dream of late bookshop founder George Whitman from the 1960s. Its primarily vegetarian menu (with vegan and gluten-free dishes available) includes homemade bagels, rye bread, soups, salads and pastries, plus Parisian-roasted Café Lomi coffee. Picnic hampers (named 'A Moveable Feast' and including a short story) are in the works.

Bar à Vins AT MODERN FRENCH €
(Map p100; ☎01 56 81 94 08; http://atsushitanaka.com; 4 rue du Cardinal Lemoine, 5e; dishes €12-16; ⏲7pm-2am Tue-Sun; Ⓜ Cardinal Lemoine) Six to eight wines are available by the glass at this cellar wine bar, but the real reason to come is the chance to try the incomparable cuisine of chef Atsushi Tanaka, whose Restaurant AT (p132) is upstairs, at bargain prices. Cold (only) dishes served here might include raw beef with powdered and puréed smoked artichokes, or ribboned beetroot and fennel.

FrogBurger BURGERS €
(Map p100; www.frogburger.com; 18 rue St-Séverin, 5e; burgers €11-13, sides €3.50-5; ⏲11.30am-11pm Sun-Thu, to midnight Fri & Sat; Ⓜ St-Michel) Frog-Pubs (famed for its Parisian microbreweries) is behind this cut-above spot sizzling up burgers including Revolution (beef, smoked pulled pork and coleslaw), da Vinci (beef, Serrano ham, mozzarella and pesto mayo), Crunchy Chicken (with rocket, cheddar and salsa) and Veggie (halloumi, red peppers and grilled mushrooms), with gluten-free bun options and Frog's own-brewed beers.

La Salle à Manger TRADITIONAL FRENCH €
(Map p100; ☎01 55 43 91 99; 138 rue Mouffetard, 5e; mains €10-15, weekend brunch €22; ⏲8.30am-6.30pm; Ⓜ Censier Daubenton) With a sunny pavement terrace beneath trees enviably placed at the foot of foodie street rue Mouffetard, the 'Dining Room' is prime real estate. Its 360-degree outlook – market stalls, fountain, church and garden with a playground for tots – couldn't be prettier, and its salads, *tartines* (open sandwiches), tarts and pastries ensure packed tables at breakfast, lunch and weekend brunch.

★Café de la Nouvelle Mairie CAFE €€
(Map p100; ☎01 44 07 04 41; 19 rue des Fossés St-Jacques, 5e; mains €12-32; ⏲kitchen 8am-midnight Mon-Fri; Ⓜ Cardinal Lemoine) Shhhh... just around the corner from the Panthéon but hidden away on a small, fountained square, this narrow wine bar is a neighbourhood secret, serving blackboard-chalked natural wines by the glass and delicious seasonal bistro fare from oysters and ribs *(à la française)* to grilled lamb sausage over lentils. It takes reservations for dinner but not lunch – arrive early.

Les Papilles BISTRO €€
(Map p98; ☎01 43 25 20 79; www.lespapillesparis.com; 30 rue Gay Lussac, 5e; 2-/3-course menus

GLUTEN-FREE ESSENTIALS

In a city known for its bakeries, it's only right there's **Chambelland** (Map p90; ☎01 43 55 07 30; www.chambelland.com; 14 rue Ternaux, 11e; lunch menu €12; ⏰9am-8pm Tue-Sun; Ⓜ Parmentier) – a 100% gluten-free bakery with serious breads to die for. Using rice and buckwheat flour milled at the bakery's very own mill in southern France, this pioneering bakery creates exquisite cakes and pastries as well as sourdough loaves and brioches (sweet breads) peppered with nuts, seeds, chocolate and fruit. Make a meal of it and stop here for lunch at one of the handful of formica tables in this youthful space, strewn with sacks of rice flour and books. There is always a salad (summer) or homemade soup (winter) on the boil, served of course with a designer chunk of crunchy focaccia, perhaps of brown linseed-laced loaf. Or grab a sandwich – to eat in or take away.

Combining the French genius for pastries with a 100% gluten-free kitchen, **Helmut Newcake** (Map p66; ☎09 81 31 28 31; www.helmutnewcake.com; 28 rue Vignon, 9e; lunch menus €9.30-13.50; ⏰11.30am-7pm Mon-Sat; Ⓜ Madeleine) is one of those Parisian addresses that some will simply have to hang on to. Eclairs, fondants, cheesecake and tarts are some of the dessert options, while you can count on lunch (salads, quiches, soups, pizzas) to be scrumptious and market driven. Takeaway only.

from €20/35, mains €18-35; ⏰noon-2pm & 7-10.30pm Tue-Sat; Ⓜ Raspail or RER Luxembourg) This hybrid bistro, wine cellar and *épicerie* (specialist grocer) with a sunflower-yellow façade is one of those fabulous Parisian dining experiences. Meals are served at simply dressed tables wedged beneath bottle-lined walls, and fare is market driven: each weekday cooks up a different *marmite du marché* (market casserole). But what really sets it apart is its exceptional wine list.

Le Pré Verre — BISTRO €€

(Map p100; ☎01 43 54 59 47; www.lepreverre.com; 8 rue Thénard, 5e; lunch menu €14.50, mains €20; ⏰noon-2pm & 7.30-10.30pm Tue-Sat; 📶👶; Ⓜ Maubert-Mutualité) Noisy, busy and buzzing, the Delacourcelle brothers' jovial bistro plunges diners into the heart of a Parisian's Paris. At lunchtime join the flock and go for the fabulous-value *formule dejéuner* (lunch menu), which might feature truffle chestnut soup, pollack and purple carrots, and for dessert pineapple minestrone, served with a glass of wine and loads of ultracrusty, ultrachewy baguette (the best).

Le Coupe-Chou — FRENCH €€

(Map p100; ☎01 46 33 68 69; www.lecoupechou.com; 9 & 11 rue de Lanneau, 5e; 2-/3-course menus €27/33; ⏰noon-2pm & 7-10.45pm Sep-Jul, 7-10.45pm Aug; Ⓜ Maubert-Mutualité) This maze of candlelit rooms inside a vine-clad 17th-century townhouse is overwhelmingly romantic. Ceilings are beamed, furnishings are antique, open fireplaces crackle and background classical music mingles with the intimate chatter of diners. As in the days when Marlene Dietrich dined here, advance reservations are essential. Timeless French dishes include Burgundy snails, steak tartare and bœuf bourguignon.

L'AOC — TRADITIONAL FRENCH €€

(Map p100; ☎01 43 54 22 52; www.restoaoc.com; 14 rue des Fossés St-Bernard, 5e; 2-/3-course lunch menus €21/29, mains €19-34; ⏰noon-2pm & 7.30-11pm Tue-Sat; Ⓜ Cardinal Lemoine) *'Bistrot carnivore'* is the strapline of this ingenious restaurant concocted around France's most respected culinary products. The concept is Appellation d'Origine Contrôlée (AOC), the French precursor to Europe-wide AOP, meaning everything has been reared or produced according to strict guidelines. The results are outstanding. Choose between favourites (steak tartare) or the rotisserie menu, ranging from roast chicken to suckling pig.

★Restaurant AT — GASTRONOMIC €€€

(Map p100; ☎01 56 81 94 08; www.atsushitanaka.com; 4 rue du Cardinal Lemoine, 5e; 4-/6-course lunch menus €35/55, 12-course dinner tasting menu €95; ⏰12.15-2pm & 8-9.30pm Tue-Sat; Ⓜ Cardinal Lemoine) Trained by some of the biggest names in gastronomy (Pierre Gagnaire included), chef Atsushi Tanaka showcases abstract artlike masterpieces incorporating rare ingredients (charred bamboo, kohlrabi turnip cabbage, juniper berry powder, wild purple fennel, Nepalese Timut pepper) in a blank-canvas-style dining space on stunning outsized plates. Just off the entrance, steps lead to his cellar wine bar, Bar à Vins AT (p131).

★Sola FUSION €€€

(Map p100; ☎dinner 01 43 29 59 04, lunch 09 65 01 73 68; www.restaurant-sola.com; 12 rue de l'Hôtel Colbert, 5e; menus lunch €48-78, dinner €98; ⏰noon-1.30pm & 7.30-9pm Tue-Sat; Ⓜ St-Michel) Pedigreed chef Hiroki Yoshitake combines French technique with Japanese sensibility, resulting in gorgeous signature creations (such as miso-marinated foie gras on *feuille de brick* served on sliced tree trunk). The artful presentations and attentive service make this a perfect choice for a romantic meal – go for the full experience and reserve a table in the Japanese dining room downstairs.

St-Germain & Les Invalides

The picnicking turf of the Jardin du Luxembourg is complemented by some fabulous places to buy picnic ingredients. Even if it's not picnic weather, the neighbourhood's streets are lined with everything from quintessential Parisian bistros to chic designer restaurants and flagship establishments with Michelin-starred chefs. Some charming places hide inside Cour du Commerce St-André, a glass-covered passageway built in 1735 to link two *jeu de paume* (old-style tennis) courts.

Le Bac à Glaces ICE CREAM €

(Map p98; www.bacaglaces.com; 109 rue du Bac, 7e; ice cream per 1/2/3 scoops €3.50/4.50/5.50; ⏰11am-7pm Mon-Fri, to 7.30pm Sat; Ⓜ Sèvres-Babylone) Apricot and thyme, lemon and basil, strawberry and rose, and a triple hit of orange, Grand Marnier and chocolate are among the 60 flavours of all-natural ice creams at this luscious *glacière* (ice-cream maker). A cloud of Chantilly sugar-whipped cream costs an extra €0.50.

★Goût de Brioche PATISSERIE €

(Map p98; www.goutdebrioche.com; 54 rue Mazarine, 6e; brioche €4-7; ⏰8.30am-7.30pm Tue-Fri, 8am-7.30pm Sat & Sun; Ⓜ Odéon) After relocating his eponymous triple-Michelin-starred restaurant (p136) to the Monnaie de Paris complex, Guy Savoy and his pastry chef, Christian Boudard, opened this nearby boutique specialising in light, fluffy brioche loaves in savoury flavours ranging from Parmesan to mushroom, Lorraine (with ham) and duck, and sweet varieties such as chocolate, pink praline, pistachio and apricot, and ginger confit with cashew nuts.

Little Breizh CRÊPERIE €

(Map p98; ☎01 43 54 60 74; 11 rue Grégoire de Tours, 6e; crêpes €4.70-12; ⏰noon-2.15pm & 7-10.15pm; 🌶; Ⓜ Odéon) As authentic as you'd find in Brittany, but with some innovative twists (such as Breton sardines, olive oil and sun-dried tomatoes; goat's cheese, stewed apple, hazelnuts, rosemary and honey; smoked salmon, dill cream, pink peppercorns and lemon), the crêpes at this sweet spot are infinitely more enticing than those sold on nearby street corners. Hours can fluctuate; book ahead.

L'Avant Comptoir FRENCH TAPAS €

(Map p98; www.hotel-paris-relais-saint-germain.com; 3 Carrefour de l'Odéon, 6e; tapas €5-10; ⏰noon-midnight; Ⓜ Odéon) Squeeze in around the zinc bar (there are no seats and it's tiny) and order off the menu suspended from the ceiling to feast on amazing tapas (crab custard tarts with Pernod foam, Iberian ham or salmon tartare croquettes, duck confit hot dogs, blood-sausage macarons, and prosciutto and artichoke waffles), with wines by the glass, in a chaotically sociable atmosphere.

For seafood tapas, head to neighbouring **L'Avant Comptoir de la Mer** (tapas €4-30; ⏰noon-11pm), or for gourmet bistro dining, try for a lunchtime table or evening reservation at **Le Comptoir du Relais** (☎01 44 27 07 97; 9 Carrefour de l'Odéon, 6e; mains €14-39, dinner menu €60).

Au Pied de Fouet BISTRO €

(Map p98; ☎01 43 54 87 83; www.aupieddefouet.com; 3 rue St-Benoît, 6e; mains €9-12.50; ⏰noon-2.30pm & 7-11pm Mon-Sat; Ⓜ St-Germain des Prés) At this tiny, lively, cherry-red-coloured bistro, wholly classic dishes such as *entrecôte* (steak), *confit de canard* (duck cooked slowly in its own fat) with creamy potatoes and *foie de volailles sauté* (pan-fried chicken livers) are astonishingly good value. Round off your meal with a *tarte Tatin* (upside-down apple tart), wine-soaked prunes, or deliciously rich *fondant au chocolat*.

L'Amaryllis de Gérard Mulot PATISSERIE €

(Map p98; www.gerard-mulot.com; 12 rue des Quartre Vents, 6e; dishes €6.60-20, lunch menu €25; ⏰11am-6.30pm Tue-Sat; Ⓜ Odéon) Pastry maestro Gérard Mulot has three boutiques in Paris, including one nearby at **76 rue de Seine** (⏰6.45am-8pm Thu-Tue), but this branch also incorporates a *salon de thé* (tearoom) where you can sit down to savour his famous fruit tarts on the spot. Other dishes include quiches, gourmet salads, omelettes

and more filling lunch meals including a meat or fish *suggestion du chef*.

Treize CAFE €

(Thirteen – A Baker's Dozen; Map p98; ☎01 73 77 27 89; 16 rue des Sts-Pères, 7e; mains €13-15, brunch menus €10-21; ⏰10am-6pm Tue-Sat; ✎; Ⓜ St-Germain des Prés) Pass through a passageway, cross a cobbled courtyard and at the very end you'll find the latticed doors of Treize, a charming contemporary cafe turning out savoury pies, creative salads and cakes (including heavenly carrot cake), along with unique tea blends, and coffee by Parisian roaster Coutume (p144). Most of the food is organic or free range and made on-site.

JSFP Traiteur DELI €

(Map p98; 8 rue de Buci, 6e; dishes €3.70-6.20; ⏰9.30am-8.30pm; ✎; Ⓜ Mabillon) Brimming with big bowls of salad, terrines, pâté and other prepared delicacies, this deli is a brilliant bet for quality Parisian 'fast food' such as quiches in a variety of flavour combinations (courgette and chive, mozzarella and basil, salmon and spinach...) to take to a nearby park, square or stretch of riverfront.

Cuisine de Bar SANDWICHES €

(Map p98; www.cuisinedebar.fr; 8 rue du Cherche Midi, 6e; dishes €9.20-13.50; ⏰8.30am-7pm Mon-Sat, 9.30am-3.30pm Sun; 📶; Ⓜ Sèvres-Babylone) As next-door neighbour to one of Paris' most famous bakers, this isn't your average sandwich bar. Instead, between shopping in designer boutiques, it's an ultrachic spot to lunch on open sandwiches cut from that celebrated Poilâne bread (p118) and fabulously topped with gourmet goodies such as foie gras, smoked duck, gooey St-Marcellin cheese and Bayonne ham.

La Pâtisserie des Rêves PATISSERIE €

(Map p98; http://lapatisseriedesreves.com; 93 rue du Bac, 7e; ⏰9am-8pm Tue-Sat, 9am-6pm Sun; Ⓜ Rue du Bac) The most extraordinary cakes, far too beautiful to eat, are showcased beneath glass domes at this contemporary 'patisserie of dreams' of big-name *pâtissier* Philippe Conticini. Each season has different fruit tarts, such as citrus and quince in winter, and rhubarb and berries in spring and summer.

Cosi SANDWICHES €

(Map p98; 54 rue de Seine, 6e; sandwich menus €10-15; ⏰noon-11pm; 📶✎; Ⓜ Mabillon) A local institution for a quick, cheap sandwich fix like tandoori turkey and coleslaw, black-olive tapenade and roast tomato or blue cheese and walnuts. Eat in its upstairs dining room or take away to a park. Classical music plays in the background and the homemade foccacia is still warm from the oven. Sandwich *menus* include a salad or dessert plus drink.

★Clover NEOBISTRO €€

(Map p98; ☎01 75 50 00 05; www.clover-paris.com; 5 rue Perronet, 7e; 2-/3-course lunch menus €28/42, 3-/5-course dinner menus €58/73; ⏰12.30-2pm & 7.30-10pm Tue-Sat; Ⓜ St-Germain des Prés) Dining at hot-shot chef Jean-François Piège's casual bistro is like attending a private party: the galley-style open kitchen adjoining the 20 seats (reserve ahead!) is part of the dining-room decor, putting customers at the front and centre of the culinary action. Light, luscious dishes span quinoa chips with aubergine and black sesame to cabbage leaves with smoked herring *crème* and chestnuts.

★Bouillon Racine BRASSERIE €€

(Map p98; ☎01 73 20 21 12; www.bouillonracine.com; 3 rue Racine, 6e; weekday lunch menu €16, menus €31-42; ⏰noon-11pm; 👪; Ⓜ Cluny-La Sorbonne) Inconspicuously situated in a quiet street, this heritage-listed 1906 art nouveau 'soup kitchen', with mirrored walls, floral motifs and ceramic tiling, was built in 1906 to feed market workers. Despite the magnificent interior, the food – inspired by age-old recipes – is no afterthought but superbly executed (stuffed, spit-roasted suckling pig, pork shank in Rodenbach red beer, scallops and shrimps with lobster coulis).

★Semilla NEOBISTRO €€

(Map p98; ☎01 43 54 34 50; 54 rue de Seine, 6e; lunch menu €24, mains €20-50; ⏰12.30-2.30pm & 7-10.45pm; Ⓜ Mabillon) Stark concrete, exposed pipes and an open kitchen (in front of which you can book front-row 'chef seats') set the factory-style scene for edgy, modern, daily changing dishes such as pork spare ribs with sweet potato and cinnamon, mushrooms in hazelnut butter, and trout with passionfruit and ginger (all suppliers are listed). Desserts here are outstanding. Be sure to book.

If you haven't made a reservation, head to its adjoining walk-in wine bar, **Freddy's** (small plates €5-15; ⏰noon-midnight), serving small tapas-style plates.

★Chez Françoise TRADITIONAL FRENCH €€

(Map p64; ☎01 47 05 49 03; www.chezfrancoise.com; Aérogare des Invalides, 7e; 2-/3-course men-

us from €28/33, oysters per half-dozen €15.50-29; ⏲noon-3pm & 7pm-midnight; Ⓜ Invalides) Buried beneath the enormous Air France building but opening to a retractable-roofed terrace, this old-school 1949-opened restaurant – a favourite with parliamentary workers from the Assemblée Nationale – recalls the early glamour of air travel, the era when it was established at this former off-site terminal for transiting passengers. Specialities include *entrecôte de bœuf* and sublime oysters.

★Huîtrerie Regis SEAFOOD €€

(Map p98; http://huitrerieregis.com; 3 rue de Montfaucon, 6e; dozen oysters from €16; ⏲noon-2.30pm & 6.30-10.30pm Mon-Fri, noon-10.45pm Sat, noon-10pm Sun; Ⓜ Mabillon) Hip, trendy, tiny and white, this is *the* spot for slurping oysters on crisp winter days. The oysters come only by the dozen, along with fresh bread and butter, but wash them down with a glass of chilled Muscadet and *voilà,* one perfect lunch. A twinset of tables loiter on the pavement; otherwise it's all inside. No reservations, so arrive early.

Chez Dumonet BISTRO €€

(Joséphine; Map p98; ☎01 45 48 52 40; 117 rue du Cherche Midi, 6e; mains €25-42; ⏲noon-2.30pm & 7.30-9.30pm Mon-Fri; Ⓜ Duroc) Fondly known by its former name, Joséphine, this lace-curtained, mosaic-tiled place with white-clothed tables inside and out is the Parisian bistro of many people's dreams, serving timeless standards such as confit of duck, *millefeuille* of pigeon, and grilled *châteaubriand* steak with Béarnaise sauce. Be sure to order its enormous signature Grand Marnier soufflé at the start of your meal. During truffle season (November to March), though, it's hard to go past its aromatic truffle menus (€49 to €105).

Les Fables de la Fontaine GASTRONOMIC €€

(Map p64; ☎01 44 18 37 55; www.lesfablesdelafontaine.net; 131 rue St-Dominique, 7e; 2-course lunch menu €25, mains €21-29; ⏲noon-2.30pm & 7-10.30pm; Ⓜ École Militaire or RER Pont de l'Alma) Prices at this Michelin-starred restaurant are a serious bargain and the lunchtime *menu* (available midweek only) is an absolute steal. Chefs Julia Sedefdjian and David Bottreau create true works of art: on-the-shell oysters in vivid green cucumber jelly with green apple and lemon caviar; almond-crusted veal with mashed artichokes and king trumpet mushrooms; and banana soufflé with rum ice cream.

LOCAL KNOWLEDGE

RUE CLER

Pick up fresh bread, sandwich fillings, pastries and wine for a picnic along the typically Parisian commercial street rue Cler, 7e, which buzzes with local shoppers, especially on weekends.

Interspersed between the *boulangeries* (bakeries), *fromageries* (cheese shops), grocers, butchers, delis and other food shops (many with pavement stalls), lively cafe terraces overflow with locals too.

Le Timbre NEOBISTRO €€

(Map p98; ☎01 45 49 10 40; www.restaurantletimbre.com; 3 rue Ste-Beuve, 6e; 3-course lunch menu €26, 3-/4-/5-course dinner menus €36/43/49; ⏲noon-3pm & 7.30-11pm Tue-Sat; Ⓜ Vavin) As tiny as the postage stamp for which it's named, Le Timbre is run by husband-and-wife team Charles Danet (in the kitchen) and Agnès Peyre (front of house) and has a local following for its daily changing menu of original dishes (caramelised endives with Parmesan *crème* and brioche; and turbot and clams with marinated cabbage and potato terrine).

Un Dimanche à Paris FUSION €€

(Map p98; ☎01 56 81 18 18; www.un-dimanche-a-paris.com; 4-8 Cour du Commerce St-André, 6e; menus lunch/dinner/brunch from €29.50/32/38; ⏲restaurant 7-10pm Tue, noon-2pm & 7-10pm Wed-Sat, 11am-7pm Sun; Ⓜ Odéon) Inside the beautiful covered passageway Cour du Commerce St-André, this 'chocolate concept store' incorporates a boutique (where you can order a decadently rich hot chocolate), patisserie classes (from €50), a tearoom and a restaurant serving chocoholic dishes like ricotta-filled pasta in hazelnut and white-chocolate broth, prawns with cocoa and candied pineapple, and seared beef with Brazilian-chocolate *jus*. Hours can vary.

Restaurants d'Application de Ferrandi GASTRONOMIC €€

(Map p98; www.ferrandi-paris.fr; 28 rue de l'Abbé Grégoire, 6e; menus Le Premier lunch/dinner €25/40, Le 28 lunch €30-32, dinner €30-45; ⏲by online reservation, closed school holidays; Ⓜ St-Placide) Founded in 1920 by Paris' chamber of commerce and industry, Ferrandi is arguably France's most prestigious culinary school, turning out a who's who of industry professionals. You can taste these future Michelin-starred chefs' creations at bargain

prices at the school's two training restaurants, Le Premier (focusing on classical French cookery) and Le 28 (high-level gastronomy), overseen by Ferrandi's esteemed professors.

Roger la Grenouille TRADITIONAL FRENCH €€
(Map p98; ☎01 56 24 24 34; 26-28 rue des Grands Augustins, 6e; menus lunch/dinner €27.50/32, mains €18-29.50; ⌚noon-2pm & 7-11pm Mon-Fri, noon-11pm Sat; Ⓜ St-Michel) Scattered with frog sculptures, B&W pictures of 1920s Paris and an array of old lamps, time-worn, sepia-coloured institution 'Roger the Frog' serves nine varieties of frogs' legs, including *à la Provençale* (with tomato) and *Normande* (cooked in cider and served with apple). If you're squeamish about devouring Roger, alternatives include dishes such as veal kidneys or lamb shanks.

Brasserie Lipp BRASSERIE €€
(Map p98; ☎01 45 48 53 91; 151 bd St-Germain, 6e; mains €22-38; ⌚8.30am-1am, kitchen 11.45am-12.45am; Ⓜ St-Germain des Prés) Waiters in black waistcoats, bow ties and long white aprons serve brasserie favourites like *choucroute garnie* (dressed sauerkraut) and *jarret de porc aux lentilles* (pork knuckle with lentils) at this illustrious wood-panelled establishment. (Arrive hungry: salads aren't allowed as meals.) Opened by Léonard Lipp in 1880, the brasserie achieved immortality when Hemingway sang its praises in *A Moveable Feast*.

★ **Restaurant Guy Savoy** GASTRONOMIC €€€
(Map p98; ☎01 43 80 40 61; www.guysavoy.com; Monnaie de Paris, 11 quai de Conti, 6e; lunch menu via online booking €110, 12-/18-course tasting menus €420/490; ⌚noon-2pm & 7-10.30pm Tue-Fri, 7-10.30pm Sat; Ⓜ Pont Neuf) If you're considering visiting a three-Michelin-star temple of gastronomy, this should certainly be on your list. The world-famous chef needs no introduction (he trained Gordon Ramsay, among others) but now his flagship, entered via a red-carpeted staircase, is ensconced in the gorgeously refurbished neoclassical Monnaie de Paris (p95). Monumental cuisine to match includes Savoy icons like artichoke and black-truffle soup with layered brioche.

Montparnasse & Southern Paris

Since the 1920s, bd du Montparnasse has been one of the city's premier avenues for enjoying Parisian pavement life, with legendary brasseries and cafes. The down-to-earth 15e cooks up fabulous bistro fare – key streets are rues de la Convention, de Vaugirard, St-Charles and du Commerce, and south of bd de Grenelle.

For Asian food, try Chinatown's avs de Choisy and d'Ivry and rue Baudricourt. The villagey Butte aux Cailles, 13e, south of Corvisart metro station, is chock-a-block with interesting addresses. Uberhip restaurants hide inside the Docks en Seine (p97).

L'Atelier B BURGERS €
(Map p58; www.latelierb.fr; 129 rue du Château, 14e; burgers €11-13; ⌚noon-2.30pm & 6pm-2am Tue-Sat; Ⓜ Pernety) The best thing about this brilliant spot isn't the late closing time, friendly service or even the cocktails, wine and beers, but the burgers themselves. Choices include Mon Bougnat (black Angus, confit onion, rocket and blue cheese), Mon Basse Cour

PARIS' OLDEST RESTAURANT & CAFE

St-Germain claims both the city's oldest restaurant and its oldest cafe.

À la Petite Chaise (Map p98; ☎01 42 22 13 35; www.alapetitechaise.fr; 36 rue de Grenelle, 6e; menus lunch/dinner €25/33, mains €21; ⌚noon-2pm & 7-11pm; Ⓜ Sèvres-Babylone) hides behind an iron gate that's been here since it opened in 1680, when wine merchant Georges Rameau served food to the public to accompany his wares. Classical decor and cuisine (onion soup, foie gras, duck, lamb and unexpected delights like venison terrine with hazelnuts) make it worth a visit above and beyond its history.

Le Procope (Map p98; ☎01 40 46 79 00; www.procope.com; 13 rue de l'Ancienne Comédie, 6e; 2-/3-course menus from €21/28; ⌚11.30am-midnight Sun-Wed, to 1am Thu-Sat; 👪; Ⓜ Odéon), the city's oldest cafe welcomed its first patrons in 1686, and was frequented by Voltaire, Molière and Balzac et al. Its chandeliered interior also has an entrance onto the 1735-built glass-roofed passageway Cour du Commerce St-André. House specialities include coq au vin, calf's-head casserole in veal stock, calf kidneys with violet mustard, and homemade ice cream.

(chicken, aubergine, red onion, pickles and homemade barbecue sauce) and Mon Bia (chickpea patty, coleslaw, spinach, mushrooms and brie).

★Le Clos Y MODERN FRENCH €€

(Map p98; ☎01 45 49 07 35; www.leclosy.com; 27 av du Maine, 15e; 2-/3-course lunch menus €26/31, 4-/6-course dinner menus €45/65; ⊙noon-2pm & 7.30-10pm Tue-Sat; Ⓜ Montparnasse Bienvenüe) One of Paris' rapidly rising star chefs Yoshitaka Ikeda creates utterly original *menus* that change daily but might start with foie gras ice cream and move on to perch sashimi with beetroot, apple and powdered olive oil; green peas in pea jelly with mascarpone; smoked salmon and egg with raspberry foam; and Madeira-marinated beef with butternut squash and carrot purée.

★Le Grand Pan NEOBISTRO €€

(Map p58; ☎01 42 50 02 50; www.legrandpan.fr; 20 rue Rosenwald, 15e; mains €16-29; ⊙noon-2pm & 7-11pm Mon-Fri; Ⓜ Porte de Vanves) Red-leather banquettes, gorgeous mosaic-tiled floors and dark-timber tables set the stage for an atmospheric Parisian dining experience. The blackboard menu changes daily but stalwarts include foie gras ravioli with truffle shavings, *côte de veau* with cream sauce, and a chocolate cylinder filled with vanilla mousse and drizzled with salted caramel sauce. Its small-plates restaurant, **Le Petit Pan** (www.lepetitan.fr; 2-/3-course lunch menu €15/20, small plates €4-16), is directly opposite.

★Le Beurre Noisette NEOBISTRO €€

(Map p58; ☎01 48 56 82 49; 68 rue Vasco de Gama, 15e; 2-/3-course lunch menus €23/32, mains €18; ⊙noon-2pm & 7-10.30pm Tue-Sat; Ⓜ Lourmel) *Beurre noisette* (brown butter sauce, named for its hazelnut colour) features in dishes such as scallops with cauliflower purée, and tender *bœuf fondante* with artichokes, courgette and carrot at pedigreed chef Thierry Blanqui's neighbourhood neobistro. Other treats include homemade blood sausage with apple compote. Filled with locals, the chocolate-toned dining room is wonderfully convivial – be sure to book.

★Le Casse Noix MODERN FRENCH €€

(Map p64; ☎01 45 66 09 01; www.le-cassenoix.fr; 56 rue de la Fédération, 15e; 2-/3-course lunch menus €21/28, 3-course dinner menu €35; ⊙noon-2.30pm & 7-10.30pm Mon-Fri; Ⓜ Bir Hakeim) Proving that a location footsteps from the Eiffel Tower doesn't mean compromising on quality, quantity or authenticity, 'the nutcracker' is a neighbourhood gem with a cosy retro interior, affordable prices, and exceptional cuisine that changes by season and by the inspiration of owner-chef Pierre Olivier Lenormand, who has honed his skills in some of Paris' most fêted kitchens. Book ahead.

La Closerie des Lilas BRASSERIE €€

(Map p98; ☎01 40 51 34 50; www.closeriedeslilas.fr; 171 bd du Montparnasse, 6e; mains restaurant €28-55, brasserie €24-33; ⊙restaurant noon-2.30pm & 7-11.30pm, brasserie noon-12.30am, piano bar 11am-1.30am; Ⓜ Vavin or RER Port Royal) Brass plaques tell you exactly where Hemingway (who wrote much of *The Sun Also Rises* here) and luminaries like Picasso, Apollinaire, Man Ray, Jean-Paul Sartre and Samuel Beckett stood, sat or fell at the 'Lilac Enclosure' (opened 1847). It's split into a late-night piano bar, upmarket restaurant and more lovable (and cheaper) brasserie with a hedged-in pavement terrace.

Le Dôme BRASSERIE €€€

(Map p98; ☎01 43 35 25 81; 108 bd du Montparnasse, 14e; mains €44-66.50, seafood platters €75; ⊙noon-3pm & 7-11.30pm; Ⓜ Vavin) A 1930s art deco extravaganza of the formal white-tablecloth and bow-tied waiter variety, monumental Le Dôme is one of the swishest places around for shellfish platters piled high with fresh oysters, king prawns, crab claws and much more, followed by traditional creamy homemade *millefeuille* for dessert, wheeled in on a trolley and cut in front of you.

Drinking & Nightlife

For the French, drinking and eating go together like wine and cheese, and the line between a cafe, *salon de thé* (tearoom), bistro, brasserie, bar, and even *bar à vins* (wine bar) is blurred. The line between drinking and clubbing is often nonexistent – a cafe that's quiet midafternoon might have DJ sets in the evening and dancing later on.

Eiffel Tower & Western Paris

Ogling the illuminated Eiffel Tower aside, being in the wealthy and predominantly residential 16e after dark doesn't translate to much when it comes to buzzing bars and clubs. The pace picks up around Palais de Tokyo, and the lively bars and cafes of St-Germain are a short walk away.

LOCAL KNOWLEDGE

BEST PAVEMENT TERRACES

Chez Prune (Map p90; 71 quai de Valmy, 10e; ⏲8am-2am Mon-Sat, 10am-2am Sun; Ⓜ République) The boho cafe that put Canal St-Martin on the map.

Café des Anges (Map p90; ☎01 73 20 21 10; www.cafedesangesparis.com; 66 rue de la Roquette, 11e; ⏲7.30am-2am; Ⓜ Bastille) Wrap up in a ginger blanket and live the Paris dream.

L'Ebouillanté (Map p90; http://ebouillante.pagesperso-orange.fr; 6 rue des Barres, 4e; ⏲noon-10pm summer, to 7pm winter; Ⓜ Hôtel de Ville) On sunny days there is no prettier cafe terrace.

Les Jardins du Pont-Neuf (p145) Glam floating bar with Seine-side terrace seating.

★St James Paris BAR

(Map p58; ☎01 44 05 81 81; www.saint-james-paris.com; 43 av Bugeaud, 16e; drinks €15-25; ⏲7pm-1am Mon-Sat; 📶; Ⓜ Porte Dauphine) It might be a hotel bar, but a drink at St James may well be one of your most memorable in Paris. Tucked behind a stone wall, this historic mansion opens its bar each evening to nonguests – and the setting redefines extraordinary. Winter drinks are in the library, in summer they're in the impossibly romantic garden.

Champs-Élysées & Grands Boulevards

The Champs-Élysées is home to a mix of exclusive nightspots, tourist haunts and a handful of large dance clubs that party all night. As a rule, you'll want to look as chic as possible to get in the door.

PanPan BAR

(Map p66; ☎01 42 46 36 06; 32 rue Drouot, 9e; ⏲11am-2am Mon-Fri, 6pm-2am Sat; Ⓜ Le Peletier) This unassuming locals' hang-out doesn't even bother with a sign, but it keeps things interesting with a variety of activities throughout the week. Favourites include the cocktail workshop on Mondays (where you learn to mix your own, in French, *bien sûr*) and the Thursday-night *aperitivo* (from 7pm), where you can nibble on quiche, charcuterie and the like for €1.

Zig Zag Club CLUB

(Map p72; www.zigzagclub.fr; 32 rue Marbeuf, 8e; ⏲11.30pm-7am Fri & Sat; Ⓜ Franklin D Roosevelt) Some of the hippest electro beats in western Paris, with star DJs, a great sound and light system, and a spacious dance floor. It can be pricey, but it still fills up quickly, so don't start the party too late.

Showcase CLUB

(Map p72; www.showcase.fr; Port des Champs-Élysées, 8e; ⏲11.30pm-6am Thu-Sat; Ⓜ Invalides, Champs-Élysées–Clemenceau) This gigantic electro club has solved the neighbour-versus-noise problem that haunts so many Parisian nightlife spots: it's secreted beneath the Pont Alexandre III bridge alongside the Seine. Unlike other exclusive Champs backstreet clubs, the Showcase can pack 'em in (up to 1500 clubbers) and is less stringent about its door policy, though you'll still want to look like a star.

Louvre & Les Halles

The area north of Les Halles is a prime destination for night owls. Cocktails predominate, but you'll also find wine and Champagne bars, studenty hang-outs, open-till-dawn local dives and a smattering of fun nightclubs. Rue Montmartre, rue Montorgueil and rue St-Sauveur are the best streets to explore.

★Lockwood CAFE

(Map p76; ☎01 77 32 97 21; 73 rue d'Aboukir, 2e; ⏲8am-2am Mon-Sat, 10am-4pm Sun; Ⓜ Sentier) A happening address for hip coffee lovers. Savour beans from the Belleville Brûlerie during the day, brunch on weekends and well-mixed cocktails in the subterranean candle-lit *cave* (wine cellar) at night.

★Experimental Cocktail Club COCKTAIL BAR

(Map p76; 37 rue St-Saveur, 2e; ⏲7pm-2am; Ⓜ Réaumur-Sébastopol) Called ECC by trendies, this fabulous speakeasy with a black curtain for a façade and an old-beamed ceiling is effortlessly hip. Oozing spirit and soul, the cocktail bar – with retro-chic decor by American interior designer Cuoco Black and sister bars in London and New York – is a sophisticated flashback to those *années folles* (crazy years) of Prohibition New York.

Cocktails (€13 to €15) are individual and fabulous, and DJs set the space partying until dawn at weekends. It's not a large space, however, and fills to capacity quickly.

Le Garde Robe WINE BAR
(Map p76; ☎01 49 26 90 60; 41 rue de l'Arbre Sec, 1er; ⏲12.30-2.30pm Mon-Fri, 6.30-midnight Mon-Sat; Ⓜ Louvre Rivoli) Le Garde Robe is possibly the only bar in the world to serve alcohol alongside a detox menu. While you probably shouldn't come here for the full-on cleansing experience, you can definitely expect excellent, affordable natural wines, a casual atmosphere and a good selection of eats, ranging from the standard cheese and charcuterie plates to more adventurous veg-friendly options.

Harry's New York Bar COCKTAIL BAR
(Map p76; ☎01 42 61 71 14; 5 rue Daunou, 2e; ⏲noon-2am; Ⓜ Opéra) One of the most popular American-style bars in the prewar years, Harry's once welcomed writers like F Scott Fitzgerald and Ernest Hemingway, who no doubt sampled the bar's unique cocktail and creation: the Bloody Mary. The Cuban mahogany interior dates from the mid-19th century and was brought over from a Manhattan bar in 1911. There's a basement piano bar called Ivories where Gershwin supposedly composed *An American in Paris* and, for the peckish, old-school hot dogs and generous club sandwiches to snack on. The occasional advertisement for Harry's that appears in print still reads 'Tell the Taxi Driver Sank Roo Doe Noo'.

Le Rex Club CLUB
(Map p66; www.rexclub.com; 5 bd Poissonnière, 2e; ⏲midnight-7am Thu-Sat; Ⓜ Bonne Nouvelle) Attached to the art deco Grand Rex cinema, this is Paris' premier house and techno venue where some of the world's hottest DJs strut their stuff on a 70-speaker, multidiffusion sound system.

Montmartre & Northern Paris

★ **Lulu White** COCKTAIL BAR
(Map p66; www.luluwhite.bar; 12 rue Frochot, 9e; ⏲7pm-3am Mon-Sat; Ⓜ Pigalle) Sip absinthe-based cocktails in Prohibition-era New Orleans surrounds at this elegant, serious and supremely busy cocktail bar on rue Frochot; several more line the same street, making for a fabulous evening out. Should you be wondering, Lulu White was an infamous African-American brothel owner in early 20th-century New Orleans.

★ **Gravity Bar** COCKTAIL BAR
(Map p90; 44 rue des Vinaigriers, 10e; ⏲7pm-2am Tue-Sat; Ⓜ Jacques Bonsergent, Gare de l'Est) Catching the wave is the theme behind this trendsetting, surfing- and water-sports-themed bar near Canal St-Martin. Indeed, the stunning wave-like interior crafted from soft wood threatens to distract from the business at hand – serious cocktails, best partaken in the company of some excellent tapas-style small plates (€5 to €12).

★ **Le Très Particulier** COCKTAIL BAR
(Map p80; ☎01 53 41 81 40; www.hotel-particulier-montmartre.com; 23 av Junot, 18e, Pavillon D; ⏲6pm-2am Tue-Sun; Ⓜ Lamarck-Caulaincourt) There is possibly no more enchanting spot for a summertime al fresco cocktail than Le Très Particulier, the utterly unique and clandestine cocktail bar of Hôtel Particulier Montmartre (p112). Ring the buzzer at the unmarked black gated entrance to get in and make a beeline for the 1871 mansion's flowery walled garden bar with conservatory-style interior. DJs spin tunes from 10pm every Friday and Saturday.

★ **CopperBay** COCKTAIL BAR
(Map p90; www.copperbay.fr; 5 rue Bouchardon, 10e; ⏲6pm-2am Tue-Sat; Ⓜ Strasbourg-St-Denis, République) This sleek, faintly playful cocktail bar's floor-to-ceiling windows, polished pale-wood decor and glistening copper fixtures and fittings inject a generous dose of design flair into proceedings. The cocktail menu mixes classics with house specials like the fig-and-blackberry Black Julep.

★ **Hardware Société** COFFEE
(Map p80; ☎01 42 51 69 03; 10 rue Lamarck, 18e; ⏲9am-4.30pm Thu-Mon, kitchen 9am-3.30pm

DON'T MISS

THE MOST FAMOUS HOT CHOCOLATE IN TOWN

Clink china with lunching ladies, their posturing poodles and half the students from Tokyo University at **Angelina** (Map p76; 226 rue de Rivoli, 1er; ⏲8am-7pm Mon-Fri, 9am-7pm Sat & Sun; Ⓜ Tuileries), a *grande dame* of a tearoom dating to 1903. Decadent pastries are served here, against a fresco backdrop of belle époque Nice, but it is the superthick, decadently sickening 'African' hot chocolate (€8.20), which comes with a pot of whipped cream and a carafe of water, that prompts the constant queue for a table at Angelina.

Thu-Mon; 📶; Ⓜ Château Rouge, Lamarck-Caulaincourt) With its black-and-white floor, Christian Lacroix butterflies fluttering across one wall and perfect love-heart-embossed cappuccinos, there's no finer spot around the Sacré-Cœur to linger over superb barista-crafted coffee (yes, that is a Slayer espresso machine). This is the Paris outpost of Melbourne's Hardware Société, with feisty breakfasts and brunches cooked up by Di and Will complementing the coffee.

Baranaan CAFE, COCKTAIL BAR
(Map p90; ☎01 40 38 97 57; www.elaichicafe.com; 7 rue du Faubourg St-Martin, 10e; ⏰cafe 3pm-12.30am Tue-Thu & Sun, 3pm-1.30am Fri & Sat, bar 6.30pm-2am Mon-Sat; 📶; Ⓜ Strasbourg-St-Denis, Jacques Bonsergent) One address, two ubercool identities: by day Baranaan is the hip **Elaichi Café**, serving tasty vegetarian food and lassi, chai and fresh juices in a smart contemporary setting. Come dusk, the space morphs into one of Paris' most exciting new-wave cocktail bars, serving Indian cocktails and well-filled naan breads to a keen hipster crowd. Check Baranaan's Facebook page for events and happenings.

Vivant Cave WINE BAR
(Map p66; ☎01 42 46 43 55; www.vivantparis.com; 43 rue des Petites Écuries, 10e; ⏰5pm-midnight Mon-Fri; ⓂPoissonnière, Bonne Nouvelle) This stylish wine bar, sister to neighbouring gourmet bistro Vivant (p126), is an ode to natural wine. Linger over a glass at the polished, Carrara marble bar or reserve a table in advance to make an evening of it over a casual dinner (mains €20 to €25). Bottles to go too.

Le Progrès BAR
(Map p80; 7 rue des Trois Frères, 18e; ⏰9am-2am; Ⓜ Abbesses) A real live *café du quartier* perched in the heart of Abbesses, the Progress occupies a corner site with huge windows and simple seating and attracts a relaxed mix of local artists, shop staff, writers and hangers-on. It's great for convivial evenings, but it's also a good place to come for meals (mains €17.90 to €20.50), coffee and well-priced cocktails (€9).

> **ℹ DRINKING REAL ESTATE**
>
> Drinking in Paris essentially means paying the rent for the space you take up. So it costs more to sit at a table than to stand at the counter, more for coveted terrace seats, more on a fancy square than a backstreet, more in the 8e than the 18e.

Le Marais, Ménilmontant & Belleville

Le Marais is a spot par excellence when it comes to a good night out, the lively scene embracing everything from gay-friendly and gay-only to bourgeois arty cafes, eclectic bars and raucous pubs. Rue Oberkampf and parallel rue Jean-Pierre Timbaud are hubs of the Ménilmontant bar crawl, a scene that is edging out steadily through cosmopolitan Belleville.

★**Le Mary Céleste** COCKTAIL BAR
(Map p90; www.lemaryceleste.com; 1 rue Commines, 3e; ⏰6pm-1.30am; ⓂFilles du Calvaire) Predictably there's a distinct nautical feel to this fashionable, ubercool cocktail bar in Le Marais. Snag a stool at the central circular bar or play savvy and reserve one of a handful of tables (in advance online). Cocktails (€12 to €13) are creative and the perfect partner to a dozen oysters or your pick of tapas-style 'small plates' designed to be shared (€8 to €15).

★**Fluctuat Nec Mergitur** CAFE
(Map p90; ☎01 42 06 44 07; http://fluctuat-cafe.paris; place de la République, 10e; ⏰7.30am-2am; 📶; ⓂRépublique) No address guarantees a fuller immersion into local life than Fluctuat (formerly Café Monde et Média), all shiny, new and rebranded with an edgy name after a kitchen fire in February 2015 wrecked the popular cafe and after-work hot spot. Its enviable location on pedestrian esplanade place de la République means it's always buzzing with Parisians chatting over drinks.

The cafe's name – 'tossed but not sunk' in Latin – is a reference to the city's resilience and unbroken spirit following the terrorist attacks that took place near the square in 2015.

★**Wild & the Moon** JUICE BAR
(Map p90; www.wildandthemoon.com; 55 rue Charlot, 3e; ⏰8am-7pm Mon-Fri, 10am-7pm Sat, 11am-5pm Sun; Ⓜ Filles du Calvaire) A beautiful crowd hobnobs over nut milks, vitality shots, smoothies, cold-pressed juices and raw food in this sleek new juice bar in the fashionable Haut Marais. Ingredients are fresh, seasonal and organic, and it is one of the few places in town where you can have moon porridge

GAY & LESBIAN PARIS

Le Marais, especially the areas around the intersection of rue Ste-Croix de la Bretonnerie and rue des Archives, and eastwards to rue Vieille du Temple, has been Paris' main centre of gay nightlife for some three decades and is still the epicentre of gay and lesbian life in Paris. There's also a handful of bars and clubs within walking distance of bd de Sébastopol. The lesbian scene is less prominent than its gay counterpart, and centres on a few cafes and bars in Le Marais, particularly along rue des Écouffes. Bars and clubs are generally all gay- and lesbian-friendly.

By far the biggest event on the gay and lesbian calendar is Gay Pride Day, in late June, when the annual **Marche des Fiertés** (www.gaypride.fr) through Le Marais to Bastille provides a colourful spectacle, and plenty of parties take place.

Year-round, check gay and lesbian websites or ask at gay bars and other venues to find out about events.

Best Drinking & Nightlife

Open Café (Map p90; www.opencafe.fr; 17 rue des Archives, 4e; ⏲11am-2am; Ⓜ Hôtel de Ville) The wide terrace is prime for talent-watching.

Gibus Club (Map p90; ☎01 47 00 59 14; www.scream-paris.com; 18 rue du Faubourg du Temple, 11e; ⏲11pm-7am Thu-Sat; Ⓜ République) One of Paris' biggest gay parties.

La Champmeslé (Map p76; 4 rue Chabanais, 2e; ⏲4pm-dawn Mon-Sat; Ⓜ Pyramides) Cabaret nights, fortune-telling and art exhibitions attract an older lesbian crowd.

Queen (Map p72; ☎01 53 89 08 90; www.queen.fr; 79 av des Champs-Élysées, 8e; ⏲11.30pm-6.30am; Ⓜ George V) Don't miss disco night!

Guided Tours

For an insider's perspective of gay life in Paris and recommendations on where to eat, drink, sightsee and party, take a tour with the **Gay Locals** (www.thegaylocals.com; 3hr tour from €180) – two long-time residents who lead tours of Le Marais in English, as well as private tours of other popular neighbourhoods and customised tours based on your interests.

More Information

Centre Gai et Lesbien de Paris Île de France (CGL; Map p90; ☎01 43 57 21 47; www.centrelgbtparis.org; 63 rue Beaubourg, 3e; ⏲centre & bar 3.30-8pm Mon-Fri, 1-7pm Sat, library 6-8pm Mon-Wed, 5-7pm Fri & Sat; Ⓜ Rambuteau, Arts et Métiers) is the single best source of information for gay and lesbian travellers in Paris, with a large library of books and periodicals and a sociable bar. Also has details of hotlines, helplines, gay and gay-friendly medical services and politically oriented activist associations, plus they can provide details of transgender resources and workshops

or avocado slices on almond and rosemary crackers for breakfast.

★ **Le Petit Fer à Cheval** BAR

(Map p90; www.cafeine.com/petit-fer-a-cheval; 30 rue Vieille du Temple, 4e; ⏲9am-2am; Ⓜ Hôtel de Ville, St-Paul) A Marais institution, the Little Horseshoe is a minute cafe-bar with an original horseshoe-shaped zinc bar from 1903. The place overflows with regulars from dawn to dark. Great *apéro* (predinner drink) spot and great WC – stainless-steel toilet stalls straight out of a Flash Gordon film (actually inspired by the interior of the *Nautilus* submarine in Jules Verne's *20,000 Leagues under the Sea*).

L'Étoile Manquante BAR

(Map p90; www.cafeine.com/etoile-manquante; 34 rue Vieille du Temple, 4e; ⏲9am-2am; Ⓜ Hôtel de Ville, St-Paul) With its fabulous pavement terrace, spilling onto rue Ste-Croix de la Bretonnerie, the Missing Star is a trendy, gay-friendly bar with a retro interior topped by starlit vaults.

Bespoke COCKTAIL BAR

(Map p90; http://bspk.fr; 3 rue Oberkampf, 11e; ⏲noon-2am Tue-Sun; Ⓜ Filles du Calvaire) Particularly handy for guests staying at Hôtel Beaumarchais next door, this design-driven space is a sweet, late-night drink call. In keeping with the image its name evokes,

LOCAL KNOWLEDGE

BEST COFFEE

Belleville Brûlerie (Map p58; ☎09 83 75 60 80; http://cafesbelleville.com; 10 rue Pradier, 19e; ⏰11.30am-5.30pm Sat; Ⓜ Belleville) Ground-breaking roastery with Saturday-morning tastings and cuppings.

Boot Café (Map p90; 19 rue du Pont aux Choux, 3e; ⏰10am-6pm; Ⓜ St-Sébastien-Froissart) A fashionable must, if only to snap the enchanting façade.

Caffé Juno (Map p98; www.caffe-juno.com; 58 rue Henri Barbusse, 5e; ⏰9am-7pm Mon-Sat; 📶; Ⓜ Raspail or RER Port Royal) 🍃 Aromatic little Latin Quarter roaster.

Telescope (Map p76; ☎01 42 61 33 14; 5 rue Villedo, 1er; ⏰8.30am-5pm Mon-Fri, 9.30am-6pm Sat; Ⓜ Pyramides) It may be small, but it packs a punch.

Fondation Café (Map p90; www.facebook.com/fondationcafe; 16 rue Dupetit Thouars, 3e; ⏰8am-6pm Mon-Fri, 9am-6pm Sat & Sun; Ⓜ Temple) Belleville beans on a buzzing terrace with Le Marais trendies.

Café Lomi (Map p58; ☎09 80 39 56 24; www.cafelomi.com; 3ter rue Marcadet, 18e; ⏰10am-7pm; Ⓜ Marcadet Poissonniers) Coffee roastery and cafe in the multi-ethnic La Goutte d'Or neighbourhood.

cocktails are its thing – sipped over shared small plates (€6 to €9) and excellent sweet potato fries. Check out the leather-belt wall!

Bastille & Eastern Paris

Place de la Bastille has become increasingly crass over the years, but it invariably draws a crowd, particularly along rue de Lappe just east, which is literally lined with bars. Continue further east and the options become much more stylish and appealing.

★La Cave Paul Bert WINE BAR
(Map p94; ☎01 58 53 30 92; 16 rue Paul Bert, 11e; ⏰noon-midnight, kitchen noon-2pm & 7.30-11.30pm; Ⓜ Faidherbe-Chaligny) It is strictly no reservations and standing only at the latest addition to the gourmet Paul Bert empire. This bijou wine bar has eight wines by the glass (predominantly French; €5 to €8), and cheeses, charcuterie, anchovies etc to nibble on. The real gourmet action kicks in at 7.30pm: stylish small plates of devilled eggs with truffles, veal sweetbreads with clams and more.

★Le Baron Rouge WINE BAR
(Map p94; ☎01 43 43 14 32; 1 rue Théophile Roussel, 12e; ⏰10am-2pm & 5-10pm Tue-Fri, 10am-10pm Sat, 10am-4pm Sun; Ⓜ Ledru-Rollin) Just about the ultimate Parisian wine-bar experience, this place has barrels stacked against the bottle-lined walls. As unpretentious as you'll find, it's a local meeting place where everyone is welcome and it's especially busy on Sunday after the Marché d'Aligre (p124) wraps up. All the usual suspects – cheese, charcuterie and oysters – will keep your belly full. For a small deposit, you can fill up 1L bottles straight from the barrel for under €5.

★Concrete CLUB
(Map p94; www.concreteparis.fr; 60 Port de la Rapée, 12e; ⏰10pm-7am; Ⓜ Gare de Lyon) This hugely popular, wild-child club with different dance floors lures a young international set to a boat on the Seine, firmly moored by Gare de Lyon. Notorious for introducing an 'after-hours' element to Paris' somewhat staid clubbing scene, Concrete is the trendy place to party all night until sunrise and beyond. Watch for all-weekend events with electronic dance music around the clock.

Admission is usually free before midnight. Check for world-class electro DJ events on its Facebook page.

Latin Quarter

★Little Bastards COCKTAIL BAR
(Map p100; 5 rue Blainville, 5e; ⏰6pm-2am Mon-Thu, to 4am Fri & Sat; Ⓜ Place Monge) Only house-creation cocktails are listed on the menu at uberhip Little Bastards – among them Fal' in Love (Beefeater gin, cranberry juice, lime, mint, guava purée and Falernun clove-, ginger- and almond-syrup), Be a Beet Smooth (Jameson, coriander, sherry, egg white and pepper) and Deep Throat (Absolut vodka, watermelon syrup and Pernod) – but they'll also mix up classics if you ask.

Mosquée de Paris TEAROOM
(Map p100; www.la-mosquee.com; 39 rue Geoffroy-St-Hilaire, 5e; ⏰9am-11.30pm; Ⓜ Censier Daubenton) Sip a sweet mint tea and nibble on a *pâtisserie orientale* between trees and chirping birds in the courtyard of the

tearoom of Paris' beautiful mosque, the Mosquée de Paris (p93).

Le Verre à Pied CAFE

(Map p100; http://leverreapied.fr; 118bis rue Mouffetard, 5e; 9am-9pm Tue-Sat, 9.30am-4pm Sun; M Censier Daubenton) This *café-tabac* is a pearl of a place where little has changed since 1870. Its nicotine-hued mirrored wall, moulded cornices and original bar make it part of a dying breed, but it epitomises the charm, glamour and romance of an old Paris everyone loves, including stallholders from the rue Mouffetard market who yo-yo in and out.

Le Pub St-Hilaire PUB

(Map p100; 2 rue Valette, 5e; 3pm-2am Mon-Thu, 4pm-5am Fri & Sat; M Maubert-Mutualité) 'Buzzing' fails to do justice to the pulsating vibe inside this student-loved pub. Generous happy hours last from 5pm to 9pm and the place is kept packed with a trio of pool tables, board games, music on two floors, hearty bar food and various gimmicks to rev up the party crowd (a metre of cocktails, 'be your own barman' etc).

St-Germain & Les Invalides

St-Germain's Carrefour de l'Odéon has a cluster of lively bars and cafes. Rues de Buci, St-André des Arts and de l'Odéon enjoy a fair slice of night action with arty cafes and busy pubs, while place St-Germain des Prés buzzes with the pavement terraces of fabled literary cafes. Rue Princesse attracts a student crowd with its bevy of pubs, microbreweries and cocktail bars.

Les Invalides is a day- rather than nighttime venue, with government ministries and embassies outweighing drinking venues. Particularly in summer, however, look out for bars along Les Berges de Seine (p95).

★ **Les Deux Magots** CAFE

(Map p98; www.lesdeuxmagots.fr; 170 bd St-Germain, 6e; 7.30am-1am; M St-Germain des Prés) If ever there was a cafe that summed up St-Germain des Prés' early 20th-century literary scene, it's this former hang-out of anyone who was anyone. You will spend *beaucoup* to sip a coffee in a wicker chair on the terrace shaded by dark-green awnings and geraniums spilling

DON'T MISS

ARTISAN BREWERIES

Young microbrewery **Brasserie BapBap** (Map p90; 01 77 17 52 97; www.bapbap.paris; 79 rue St-Maur, 11e; guided tours €10; 5-7pm Mon-Fri, 2-7pm Sat; M St-Maur), whose name means 'Brassée à Paris, Bue à Paris' (Brewed in Paris, Beloved in Paris), brews craft beer in an early 20th-century warehouse turned garage with an Eiffel-style metal structure. Saturday brewery visits (one hour; book online) include a peek at the filtering, boiling, whirlpool and fermentation tanks in the Brew House where the beer comes to life, plus tastings. If the brewery is shut when you pass by, nip into neighbouring **Hop Malt Market** (Map p90; 01 55 28 77 24; www.facebook.com/hmmarket75; 79 rue Saint-Maur, 11e; 9.30am-2pm & 3.30pm-1.30am; M St-Maur) to buy some bottles.

No address is such an earthy reflection of the gutsy, multiethnic *quartier* of La Goutte d'Or than **Brasserie la Goutte d'Or** (Map p58; 09 80 64 23 51; www.brasserielagoutte-dor.com; 28 rue la Goutte d'Or, 18e; 5-7pm Thu & Fri, 2-7pm Sat; M Château Rouge). This craft brewery, with brewmaster Thierry Roche at the helm. In business since 2012, it turns to the local 'hood for inspiration: spicy red beer Château Rouge is named after the local metro station; fruity India pale ale L'Ernestine evokes the street where La Goutte d'Or's early beers were brewed in the early 1900s; aromatic and bitter La Môme is a nod to a local restaurant. Guided tours are free and include tastings around a simple chipboard bar.

After founding organic brewery Brasserie Artisanale du Luberon in Provence in 2011, Jean Barthélémy Chancel launched his Parisian craft brewery, **Brasserie La Parisienne** (Map p58; 09 52 34 94 69; www.brasserielaparisienne.com; 10 rue Wurtz, 13e; tours €15; tours by reservation; M Glacière), in 2014. Look out for its brews (a bio white and blonde, classic red, stout, white and blonde, as well as eight speciality and seasonal beers, such as an IPA, Belgian white ale, Scottish Export and coffee-infused stout) around town, or try them during a two-hour brewery tour (in French), which includes eight tastings. Book tour tickets at http://reservation.tourisme-valdemarne.com/474-1761-visite-et-degustation-de-biere-a-la-brasserie-la-parisienne.html.

CLUBBING WEBSITES

Track tomorrow's hot 'n' happening soirée with these finger-on-the-pulse Parisian nightlife links:

Paris DJs (www.parisdjs.com) Free downloads to get you in the groove.

Paris Bouge (www.parisbouge.com) Comprehensive listings site.

Parissi (www.parissi.com) Search by date, then *la before, la soirée* and *l'after*.

Tribu de Nuit (www.tribudenuit.com) Parties, club events and concerts galore.

from window boxes, but it's an undeniable piece of Parisian history.

★Tiger Bar COCKTAIL BAR
(Map p98; www.tiger-paris.com; 13 rue Princesse, 6e; ⏲6pm-2am Tue-Sat; Ⓜ Mabillon) Suspended bare-bulb lights and fretted timber make this split-level space a stylish spot for specialist gins (45 different varieties). Its 24 cocktails include a Breakfast Martini (gin, triple sec, orange marmalade and lemon juice) and Oh My Dog (white-pepper-infused gin, lime juice, raspberry and rose cordial and ginger ale). You can also sip Japanese sake, wine and craft beer.

★Coutume COFFEE
(Map p58; www.coutumecafe.com; 47 rue de Babylone, 7e; ⏲8am-7pm Mon-Fri, 10am-7pm Sat & Sun; 📶; Ⓜ St-François Xavier) 🌿 The dramatic improvement in Parisian coffee in recent years is thanks in no small part to Coutume, artisan roaster of premium beans for scores of establishments around town. Its flagship cafe – a bright, light-filled, postindustrial space – is ground zero for innovative preparation methods including cold extraction and siphon brews. Fabulous organic fare and pastries too.

Au Sauvignon WINE BAR
(Map p98; www.ausauvignon.com; 80 rue des Sts-Pères, 7e; ⏲8am-11pm Mon-Sat, 9am-10pm Sun; Ⓜ Sèvres-Babylone) Grab a table in the evening light at this wonderfully authentic *bar à vins* or head to the quintessential bistro interior, with an original zinc bar, tightly packed tables and hand-painted ceiling celebrating French viticultural tradition. A plate of *casse-croûtes au pain Poilâne* – toast with ham, pâté, terrine, smoked salmon and foie gras – is the perfect accompaniment.

Castor Club COCKTAIL BAR
(Map p98; 14 rue Hautefeuille, 6e; ⏲7pm-4am Tue-Sat; Ⓜ Odéon) Discreetly signed, this underground cocktail bar has an intimate upstairs bar and 18th-century cellar with hole-in-the-wall booths where you can sip superb-value cocktails (custom made, if you like) and groove to smooth '50s, '60s and '70s tracks. Very cool.

Prescription Cocktail Club COCKTAIL BAR
(Map p98; www.prescriptioncocktailclub.com; 23 rue Mazarine, 6e; ⏲7pm-2am Mon-Thu, 7pm-4am Fri & Sat, 8pm-2am Sun; Ⓜ Odéon) With bowler and flat-top hats as lampshades and a 1930s speakeasy New York air to the place, this cocktail club – run by the same mega-successful team as Experimental Cocktail Club (ECC; p138) – is very Parisian-cool. Getting past the doorman can be tough, but, once in, it's friendliness and old-fashioned cocktails all round.

☆ Entertainment

Catching a performance in Paris is a treat. French and international opera, ballet and theatre companies and cabaret dancers take to the stage in fabled venues, and a flurry of young, passionate, highly creative musicians, thespians and artists make the city's fascinating fringe art scene what it is.

Cabaret

Whirling lines of feather-boa-clad, high-kicking dancers at grand-scale cabarets like cancan creator Moulin Rouge are a quintessential fixture on Paris' entertainment scene – for everyone but Parisians. Still, the dazzling sets, costumes and dancing guarantee an entertaining evening (or matinee).

Tickets to these spectacles start from around €90 (from €200 with dinner) and may include a half-bottle of Champagne for an extra €10. Reserve ahead.

Moulin Rouge CABARET
(Map p80; ☎01 53 09 82 82; www.moulinrouge.fr; 82 bd de Clichy, 18e; show €105-130, dinner show from €190; ⏲shows 9pm & 11pm summer, 9pm Sun-Thu, 9pm & 11pm Fri & Sat winter; Ⓜ Blanche) Immortalised in the posters of Toulouse-Lautrec and later on screen by Baz Luhrmann, Paris' mythical cabaret club twinkles beneath a 1925 replica of its original red windmill. Yes, it's rife with bus-tour crowds. But from the opening bars of music to the last high cancan-girl kick, it's a whirl of fantastical costumes, sets, choreography and Champagne.

Book in advance online and dress smart (jacket and tie is advised for men, but not obligatory). No entry for children under six.

Live Music

Festivals for just about every musical genre ensure that everyone gets to listen in. Street music is a constant in this busker-filled city, with summer adding stirring open-air concerts along the Seine and in city parks to the year-round serenade of accordions.

★Philharmonie de Paris CONCERT VENUE
(Map p58; ☎01 44 84 44 84; www.philharmoniedeparis.fr; 221 av Jean Jaurès, 19e; ⏲box office noon-6pm Tue-Fri, 10am-6pm Sat & Sun; Ⓜ Porte de Pantin) This major complex, comprising the new Philharmonie 1 building by architect Jean Nouvel and the neighbouring Philharmonie 2 building (previously called Cité de la Musique), hosts an eclectic range of concerts in its main 1200-seat Grande Salle and smaller concert halls. There's every imaginable type of music and dance, from classical to North African and Japanese.

★Café Universel JAZZ, BLUES
(Map p98; ☎01 43 25 74 20; www.cafeuniversel.com; 267 rue St-Jacques, 5e; ⏲9pm-2am Mon-Sat; 📶; Ⓜ Censier Daubenton or RER Port Royal) Café Universel hosts a brilliant array of live concerts with everything from bebop and Latin sounds to vocal jazz sessions. Plenty of freedom is given to young producers and artists, and its convivial relaxed atmosphere attracts a mix of students and jazz lovers. Concerts are free, but tip the artists when they pass the hat around.

La Flèche d'Or LIVE MUSIC
(Map p58; ☎01 44 64 01 02; www.flechedor.fr; 102bis rue de Bagnolet, 20e; Ⓜ Alexandre Dumas, Gambetta) Just over 1km northeast of place de la Nation in a former railway station on central Paris' outer edge, this awesome music venue hosts both indie rock concerts and house/electro DJ nights. The Golden Arrow – named for the train to Calais in the 1930s – has a solid reputation for promoting new talent.

Badaboum LIVE MUSIC
(Map p90; www.badaboum-paris.com; 2bis rue des Taillandiers, 11e; ⏲cocktail bar 7pm-2am Wed-Sat, club & concerts vary; Ⓜ Bastille, Ledru-Rollin) Formerly La Scène Bastille and freshly refitted, the onomatopoeically named Badaboum hosts a mixed bag of concerts on its up-close-and-personal stage, but focuses on electro, funk and hip-hop. Great atmosphere, super cocktails and a secret room upstairs.

Le Bataclan LIVE MUSIC
(Map p90; www.bataclan.fr; 50 bd Voltaire, 11e; Ⓜ Oberkampf, St-Ambroise) Le Bataclan, built in 1864 and Maurice Chevalier's debut venue in 1910, is one of the city's most mythical concert, theatre and dance halls, drawing

DON'T MISS

DRINKS & DANCING AFLOAT

Island life became more glamorous with the opening of ultra-chic **Les Jardins du Pont-Neuf** (Map p98; www.jdp9.com; quai de l'Horloge, 1er; ⏲7pm-2am Tue-Sat; 📶; Ⓜ Pont Neuf), a floating cocktail bar aboard a barge moored by the Pont Neuf. Decked out with art-nouveau-inspired decor including rattan furniture and hanging plants, its two vast terraces overlook the Seine. There's also a dance floor; check the website for upcoming soirées.

Le Batofar (Map p94; www.batofar.org; opp 11 quai François Mauriac, 13e; ⏲bar noon-midnight, club 11.30pm-6am; Ⓜ Quai de la Gare, Bibliothèque) , a much-loved, red tugboat, has a rooftop bar that's terrific in summer, and a respected restaurant, while the club underneath provides memorable underwater acoustics between its metal walls and portholes. It's known for its edgy, experimental music policy and live performances from 7pm, mostly electro-oriented but also incorporating hip-hop, new wave, rock, punk or jazz. Happy hour is 5pm to 8pm. Food is served at the restaurant from noon to 2pm and 7pm to 11pm May to September (shorter hours from October to April).

Another floating *boîte* (club) is **La Dame de Canton** (Map p94; www.damedecanton.com; opp 11 quai François Mauriac, 13e; ⏲7pm-2am Tue-Thu, to dawn Fri & Sat; Ⓜ Bibliothèque). Aboard a three-masted Chinese junk with a couple of world voyages under its belt, this place bobs beneath the Bibliothèque Nationale de France. Concerts cover pop and indie to electro, hip-hop, reggae and rock; afterwards DJs keep the crowd hyped. There's also a popular bar and restaurant with wood-fired pizzas served on the terrace from May to September.

French and international rock and pop legends. At the time of research it was closed for building works following the shocking 2015 terrorist attacks, when gunmen burst into the venue during a concert, opening fire on the crowd and killing 89 people.

Le Divan du Monde LIVE MUSIC

(Map p80; ☎01 40 05 06 99; www.divandumonde.com; 75 rue des Martyrs, 18e; ⏰variable; Ⓜ Pigalle) Take some cinematographic events and *nouvelles chansons françaises* (new French songs). Add in soul/funk fiestas, air-guitar face-offs and rock parties of the Arctic Monkeys/Killers/Libertines persuasion and stir with an Amy Winehouse swizzle stick. You may now be getting some idea of the inventive, open-minded approach at this excellent cross-cultural venue in Pigalle.

La Cigale LIVE MUSIC

(Map p80; ☎01 49 25 89 99; www.lacigale.fr; 120 bd de Rochechouart, 18e; tickets €25-75; Ⓜ Anvers, Pigalle) Now classed as a historical monument, this music hall dates from 1887 but was redecorated 100 years later by Philippe Starck. Artists who have performed here include Rufus Wainwright, Ryan Adams and Ibrahim Maalouf.

Cinema

The film-lover's ultimate city, Paris has some wonderful movie houses to catch new flicks, avant-garde cinema and priceless classics.

Foreign films (including English-language films) screened in their original language with French subtitles are labelled 'VO' *(version originale)*. Films labelled 'VF' *(version française)* are dubbed in French.

Pariscope and *L'Officiel des Spectacles* list the full crop of Paris' cinematic pickings and screening times; online check out http://cinema.leparisien.fr.

First-run tickets cost around €11.50 for adults (€13.50 for 3D). Students and over 60s get discounted tickets (usually around €8.50) from 7pm Sunday to 7pm Friday. Discounted tickets for children and teens have no restrictions. Most cinemas have across-the-board discounts before noon.

La Cinémathèque Française CINEMA

(Map p94; www.cinemathequefrancaise.com; 51 rue de Bercy, 12e; ⏰noon-7pm Mon & Wed-Sat, 10am-5pm Sun; Ⓜ Bercy) This national institution is a temple to the 'seventh art' and always screens its foreign offerings in their original versions. Up to 10 movies a day are shown, usually retrospectives (Spielberg, Altman, Eastwood) mixed in with related but more obscure films.

Le Grand Rex CINEMA

(Map p66; www.legrandrex.com; 1 bd Poissonnière, 2e; tours adult/child €11/9; ⏰tours 10am-6pm Tue-Sun, 2-6pm Mon; Ⓜ Bonne Nouvelle) A trip to 1932 art deco cinematic icon Le Grand Rex is like no other trip to the flicks. Screenings aside, the cinema runs 50-minute behind-the-scene tours (English soundtracks available) during which visitors – tracked by a sensor slung around their neck – are whisked up (via a lift) behind the giant screen, tour a soundstage and get to have fun in a recording studio.

DON'T MISS

BUSKERS IN PARIS

Paris' gaggle of clowns, mime artists, living statues, acrobats, in-line skaters, buskers and other street entertainers can be loads of fun and cost substantially less than a theatre ticket (a few coins in the hat is appreciated). Some excellent musicians perform in the long echo-filled corridors of the metro, a highly prized privilege that artists audition for. Outside, you can be sure of a good show at the following:

Place Georges Pompidou, 4e The huge square in front of the Centre Pompidou.

Pont St-Louis, 4e The bridge linking Paris' two islands (best enjoyed with a Berthillon ice cream in hand).

Pont au Double, 4e The pedestrian bridge linking Notre Dame with the Left Bank.

Place Joachim du Bellay, 1er Musicians and fire-eaters near the Fontaine des Innocents.

Parc de la Villette, 19e African drummers at the weekend.

Place du Tertre, Montmartre, 18e Montmartre's original main square is Paris' busiest busker stage.

Theatre

The majority of theatre productions in Paris, including those originally written in other languages, are – naturally enough – performed in French. Only occasionally do English-speaking troupes play at smaller venues in and around town. Consult *Pariscope* or *L'Officiel des Spectacles* for details.

Théâtre du Luxembourg THEATRE
(Map p98; www.marionnettesduluxembourg.fr; Jardin du Luxembourg; tickets €6; usually 2pm Wed, Sat & Sun, plus 4pm daily during school holidays; M Notre Dame des Champs) You don't have to be a kid or be able to speak French to be delighted by marionette shows, which have entertained audiences in France since the Middle Ages. The lively puppets perform in the Jardin du Luxembourg's little Théâtre du Luxembourg. Show times can vary; check the program online and arrive half an hour ahead.

Comédie Française THEATRE
(Map p76; www.comedie-francaise.fr; place Colette, 1er; M Palais Royal–Musée du Louvre) Founded in 1680 under Louis XIV, this state-run theatre bases its repertoire around the works of classic French playwrights. The theatre has its roots in an earlier company directed by Molière at the Palais Royal.

Opera & Ballet

France's Opéra National de Paris and Ballet de l'Opéra National de Paris perform at Paris' two opera houses, the Palais Garnier and Opéra Bastille. The season runs between September and July.

Palais Garnier OPERA, BALLET
(Map p66; 08 92 89 90 90; www.operadeparis.fr; place de l'Opéra, 9e; M Opéra) The city's original opera house is smaller than its Bastille counterpart, but has perfect acoustics. Due to its odd shape, some seats have limited or no visibility – book carefully. Ticket prices and conditions (including last-minute discounts) are available from the **box office** (cnr rues Scribe & Auber; 11am-6.30pm Mon-Sat).

Opéra Bastille CLASSICAL MUSIC
(Map p94; 01 40 01 19 70, 08 92 89 90 90; www.operadeparis.fr; 2-6 place de la Bastille, 12e; guided tours €15; box office 2.30-6.30pm Mon-Sat; M Bastille) This 3400-seat venue is the city's main opera hall; it also stages ballet and classical concerts. Tickets go on sale online up to two weeks before they're available by telephone or at the box office. Standing-only tickets (*places débouts;* €5) are available 90 minutes before performances begin. By day, explore the eyesore opera house with a 90-minute guided tour backstage; check hours online.

THEATRE & CONCERT TICKETS

Buy tickets for concerts, theatre performances and other cultural events at *billetteries* (box offices) in branches of **Fnac** (08 92 68 36 22; www.fnactickets.com), or by phone or online.

Or pick up half-price tickets for same-day performances of ballet, opera and music at **Kiosque Théâtre Madeleine** (Map p72; opposite 15 place de la Madeleine, 8e; 12.30-8pm Tue-Sat, to 4pm Sun; M Madeleine).

Shopping

Paris has it all: broad boulevards lined with international chains, luxury avenues studded with designer fashion houses, famous *grands magasins* (department stores) and fabulous markets. But the real charm lies in strolling the city's backstreets, where tiny speciality shops and quirky boutiques selling everything from strawberry-scented wellington boots to heaven-scented candles are wedged between cafes, galleries and churches.

Bastille & Eastern Paris

Bastille and eastern Paris are not really known for shopping, but a select choice of unique boutiques and specialist shops will delight. Key fashion brands have stores on trendy rue de Charonne and near Gare de Lyon, and arts and crafts are tucked under the arches of a disused aqueduct.

La Manufacture de Chocolat FOOD
(Map p90; www.lechocolat-alainducasse.com; 40 rue de la Roquette, 11e; 10.30am-7pm Tue-Sat; M Bastille) If you dine at superstar chef Alain Ducasse's restaurants, the chocolate will have been made here at Ducasse's own chocolate factory (the first in Paris to produce 'bean-to-bar' chocolate), which he set up with his former executive pastry chef Nicolas Berger. Deliberate over ganaches, pralines and truffles and no fewer than 44 flavours of chocolate bar.

1
FROMAGERIE
LA FROMAGERIE
BOUCHERIE
Charcuterie

2
LADUREE

BRUNO DE HOGUES / GETTY IMAGES ©

1. Marché d'Aligre (p124) 2. Ladurée patisserie (p117), Champs-Élysées 3. Galeries Lafayette (p150)

Paris Shopping

Paris has it all: broad boulevards lined with flagship fashion houses and international labels, famous *grands magasins* (department stores) and fabulous markets. But the real charm of Parisian shopping lies in strolling the backstreets, where tiny speciality shops and quirky boutiques sell everything from strawberry-scented wellington boots to heaven-scented candles.

Fashion is Paris' forte. Browse *haute couture* creations in the Étoile and Champs-Élysées neighbourhood (p150), particularly within the Triangle d'Or (Golden Triangle). For original streetwear and vintage gear, head for Le Marais, particularly the Haut Marais (p151). Small boutiques fill St-Germain's chic streets (p153). You'll also find adorable children's wear and accessories. Parisian fashion doesn't have to break the bank: there are fantastic bargains at secondhand and vintage boutiques, along with outlet shops selling previous seasons' collections, surpluses and seconds by top-line designers.

But fashion is just the beginning. Paris is an exquisite treasure chest of gourmet food (including cheeses, macarons and foie gras), wine, tea, books, beautiful stationery, art, art supplies, antiques and collectables. Ask for *un paquet cadeau* – free (and very beautiful) gift wrapping offered by most shops.

UNIQUE SHOPPING EXPERIENCES

Passages couverts Paris' 19th-century glass-roofed covered passages were the precursors to shopping malls.

Flea markets Lose yourself in the maze of *marchés* (markets) at the enormous Marché aux Puces de St-Ouen (p155).

Street markets Scores of colourful street markets take place every week.

Grands magasins One-stop department-store shopping in resplendent art nouveau surrounds.

Viaduc des Arts ARTS & CRAFTS
(Map p94; www.leviaducdesarts.com; 1-129 av Daumesnil, 12e; hours vary; M Bastille, Gare de Lyon) Located beneath the red-brick arches of Promenade Plantée (p83) is the Viaduc des Arts, a line-up of craft shops where traditional artisans and contemporary designers carry out antique renovations and create new items using traditional methods. Artisans include furniture and tapestry restorers, interior designers, cabinetmakers, violin- and flute-makers, embroiderers and jewellers.

Marché aux Puces d'Aligre MARKET
(Map p94; place d'Aligre, 12e; 8am-1pm Tue-Sun; M Ledru-Rollin) Smaller but more central than Paris' other flea markets; here you can rummage through boxes of clothes and accessories worn decades ago, as well as assorted bric-a-brac.

Champs-Élysées & Grands Boulevards

Global chains line the Champs-Élysées, but it's the luxury fashion houses in the Triangle d'Or and on rue du Faubourg St-Honoré that have made Paris famous. The area around Opéra and the Grands Boulevards is where you'll find flagship *grands magasins* (department stores).

Galeries Lafayette DEPARTMENT STORE
(Map p66; http://haussmann.galerieslafayette.com; 40 bd Haussmann, 9e; 9.30am-8pm Mon-Sat, to 9pm Thu; ; M Chaussée d'Antin or RER Auber) Grande dame department store Galeries Lafayette is spread across the main store (whose magnificent stained-glass dome is over a century old), men's store and homewares store, and includes a gourmet emporium (p117).

Catch modern art in the first-floor **gallery** (www.galeriedesgaleries.com; 1st fl, Galeries Lafayette; 11am-7pm Tue-Sat; M Chaussée d'Antin or RER Auber) FREE, take in a **fashion show** (bookings 01 42 82 30 25; 3pm Fri Mar-Jun & Sep-Dec by reservation), ascend to a free, windswept rooftop panorama, or take a break at one of its 24 restaurants and cafes.

Le Printemps DEPARTMENT STORE
(Map p66; www.printemps.com; 64 bd Haussmann, 9e; 9.35am-8pm Mon-Wed & Fri-Sat, to 8.45pm Thu; ; M Havre Caumartin) Famous department store Le Printemps encompasses Le Printemps de la Mode (women's fashion) and **Le Printemps de l'Homme** (men's fashion; rue de Provence, 9e), both with established and up-and-coming designer wear, and Le Printemps de la Beauté et Maison (beauty and homewares), offering a staggering display of perfume, cosmetics and accessories. There's a free panoramic rooftop terrace and luxury eateries, including Ladurée.

Guerlain PERFUME
(Map p72; spa 01 45 62 11 21; www.guerlain.com; 68 av des Champs-Élysées, 8e; 10.30am-8pm Mon-Sat, noon-7pm Sun; M Franklin D Roosevelt) Guerlain is Paris' most famous parfumerie, and its shop (dating from 1912) is one of the most beautiful in the city. With its shimmering mirror and marble art deco interior, it's a reminder of the former glory of the Champs-Élysées. For total indulgence, make an appointment at its decadent spa.

À la Mère de Famille FOOD & DRINKS
(Map p66; www.lameredefamille.com; 35 rue du Faubourg Montmartre, 9e; 9.30am-8pm Mon-Sat, 10am-1pm Sun; M Le Peletier) Founded in 1761, this is the original location of Paris' oldest chocolatier. Its beautiful belle époque façade is as enchanting as the rainbow of sweets, caramels and chocolates inside.

Place de la Madeleine FOOD & DRINKS
(Map p72; place de la Madeleine, 8e; M Madeleine) Ultragourmet food shops garland place de la Madeleine; many have in-house dining options too. Notable names include truffle dealers **La Maison de la Truffe** (www.maison-de-la-truffe.com; 10am-10pm Mon-Sat); luxury food shop **Hédiard** (www.hediard.fr; 9am-8pm Mon-Sat); mustard specialist **Boutique Maille** (www.maille.com; 10am-7pm Mon-Sat); and Paris' most famous caterer, **Fauchon** (www.fauchon.fr; 10am-8.30pm Mon-Sat), selling incredibly mouthwatering delicacies, from foie gras to jams, chocolates and pastries. Check out the extravagant chocolate sculptures at **Patrick Roger** (www.patrickroger.com; 10.30am-7.30pm).

Latin Quarter

★ **Shakespeare & Company** BOOKS
(Map p100; 01 43 25 40 93; www.shakespeareandcompany.com; 37 rue de la Bûcherie, 5e; 10am-11pm; M St-Michel) Shakespeare's enchanting nooks and crannies overflow with new and secondhand English-language books. The original shop (12 rue l'Odéon, 6e; closed by the Nazis in 1941) was run by Sylvia Beach and became the meeting point for Hemingway's 'Lost Generation'. Readings by emerg-

ing and illustrious authors take place at 7pm most Mondays. There's a wonderful cafe (p131) and various workshops and festivals.

★ Le Bonbon au Palais SWEETS
(Map p100; www.bonbonsaupalais.fr; 19 rue Monge, 5e; ⏲10.30am-7.30pm Tue-Sat; Ⓜ Cardinal Lemoine) Kids and kids-at-heart will adore this sugar-fuelled *tour de France*. The school-geography-themed boutique stocks rainbows of artisan sweets from around the country. Old-fashioned glass jars brim with treats like *calissons* (diamond-shaped, icing-sugar-topped ground fruit and almonds from Aix-en-Provence), *rigolettes* (fruit-filled pillows from Nantes), *berlingots* (striped, triangular boiled sweets from Carpentras and elsewhere) and *papalines* (herbal liqueur-filled pink-chocolate balls from Avignon).

Fromagerie Laurent Dubois CHEESE
(Map p100; www.fromageslaurentdubois.fr; 47ter bd St-Germain, 5e; ⏲8am-7.45pm Tue-Sat, 8.30am-1pm Sun; Ⓜ Maubert-Mutualité) One of the best *fromageries* in Paris, this cheese-lover's nirvana is filled with to-die-for delicacies, such as St-Félicien with Périgord truffles. Rare, limited-production cheeses include blue Termignon and Tarentaise goat's cheese. All are appropriately cellared in warm, humid or cold environments. There's also a **15e branch** (Map p90; 2 rue de Lourmel; Ⓜ Dupleix).

Le Marais, Ménilmontant & Belleville

Le Marais boasts excellent speciality stores and an ever-expanding fashion presence. Hip young designers have colonised the upper reaches of the 3e towards rue Charlot as well as rue de Turenne. Meanwhile, rue des Francs Bourgeois and, towards the other side of rue de Rivoli, rue François Mirron in the 4e, have well-established boutique shopping for clothing, hats, home furnishings and stationery. Place des Vosges is lined with very high-end art and antique galleries with some amazing sculptures for sale.

★ Maison Kitsuné FASHION & ACCESSORIES
(Map p90; ☎01 58 30 12 37; https://shop.kitsune.fr; 18 bd des Filles du Calvaire, 11e; ⏲10.30am-7.30pm Mon-Sat, 11am-6pm Sun; Ⓜ Filles du Calvaire) One of the city's most fashionable labels for men and women, Maison Kitsuné pulls out all the stops with its flagship store in Le Marais. The glorious white space evokes a Californian villa with its seamless maze of rooms, culminating in a magnificent white marble staircase leading downstairs to the Parisian brand's very own **Café Kitsuné** on rue Amelot.

> **ℹ LES SOLDES**
>
> Paris' twice-yearly *soldes* (sales) generally last five to six weeks, starting around mid-January and again around mid-June.

★ Merci CONCEPT STORE
(Map p90; ☎01 42 77 00 33; www.merci-merci.com; 111 bd Beaumarchais, 3e; ⏲10am-7pm Mon-Sat; Ⓜ St-Sébastien-Froissart) A Fiat Cinquecento marks the entrance to this unique concept store, which donates all its profits to a children's charity in Madagascar. Shop for fashion, accessories, linens, lamps and nifty designs for the home; and complete the experience with a coffee in its hybrid used-book-shop-cafe or lunch in its stylish basement **La Cantine de Mercia** (soups €8-10, salads & tarts €10-17).

★ Paris Rendez-Vous CONCEPT STORE
(Map p90; www.rendezvous.paris.fr; 29 rue de Rivoli, 4e; ⏲10am-7pm Mon-Sat; Ⓜ Hôtel de Ville) Only the city of Paris could be so chic as to have its own designer line of souvenirs, sold in its own ubercool concept store inside Hôtel de Ville (city hall). Shop here for everything from clothing and homewares to Paris-themed books, toy sailing boats and signature Jardin du Luxembourg Fermob chairs. *Quel style!*

★ L'Éclair de Génie FOOD
(Map p90; http://leclairdegenie.com; 14 rue Pavée, 4e; ⏲11am-7pm Mon-Fri, 10am-7.30pm Sat & Sun; Ⓜ St-Paul) You will never look at a simple éclair again after visiting the swish boutique of highly creative pastry chef Christophe Adam. Exquisitely filled and decorated éclairs are displayed with military precision in rows beneath glass. Like fashion, flavours change with the seasons. Count on between €5 and €7 a shot.

★ Les Exprimeurs ARTS, SOUVENIRS
(Map p90; www.lesexprimeurs.fr; 4 rue du Pont Louis-Philippe, 4e; ⏲9am-1pm & 2-6pm Tue, Thu & Fri, 9am-noon Wed, 11am-1pm & 2-7pm Sat; Ⓜ Hôtel de Ville) For an exquisite paper cut-out of the Eiffel Tower, a bookmark shaped like the Panthéon rooftop or a quality sketchbook or ink pen, look no further than this wonderful

stationery shop. It sells both fabulously classy souvenirs as well as daily essentials.

★**Made by Moi** FASHION, HOMEWARES

(Map p90; ☎01 58 30 95 78; www.madebymoi.fr; 86 rue Oberkampf, 11e; ⊙2.30-8pm Mon, 10am-8pm Tue-Sat; Ⓜ Parmentier) 'Made by Me', aka handmade, is the driver of this appealing boutique on trendy rue Oberkampf – a perfect address to buy unusual gifts. Mooch here for women's fashion, homewares and other beautiful objects like coloured glass carafes, feathered head dresses, funky contact-lens boxes and retro dial telephones. The ultimate Paris souvenir: 'Bobo brunch' scented candles by Bougies La Française.

★**L'Éclaireur** CONCEPT STORE

(Map p90; ☎01 48 87 10 22; www.leclaireur.com; 40 rue de Sévigné, 3e; ⊙11am-7pm Mon-Sat; Ⓜ St-Paul) Part art space, part lounge and part deconstructionist fashion statement, this shop is known for having the next big thing first. Two tons of wooden planks, 147 TV screens and walls that move to reveal the men's and women's collection all form part of the stunning interior design by Belgian artist Arne Quinze.

Koché FASHION & ACCESSORIES

(Map p58; www.koche.fr; 8 Cité du Labyrinthe, 20e; ⊙by appointment; Ⓜ Ménilmontant) Koché, with an atelier far from the madding fashion crowd in edgy Ménilmontant and rapidly rising designer Christelle Kocher at the helm, is the name that rocked Paris Fashion Week in 2016. Contemporary street art and traditional French craftsmanship heavily influence the funky, ready-to-wear street gear that mixes denim, jersey and other easy fabrics with elaborately crocheted feathers, chiffon, beads and sequins.

Louvre & Les Halles

The 1er and 2e *arrondissements* are mostly about fashion. Indeed the Sentier district is something of a garment heaven, while rue Étienne Marcel, place des Victoires and rue du Jour flaunt prominent labels and shoe shops. Nearby rue Montmartre and rue Tiquetonne are the streets to shop for streetwear and avant-garde designs; the easternmost part of the 1er around Palais Royal, for fancy period and conservative label fashion.

★**Didier Ludot** FASHION & ACCESSORIES

(Map p76; ☎01 42 96 06 56; www.didierludot.fr; 19-20 & 23-24 Galerie de Montpensier, 1er; ⊙10.30am-7pm Mon-Sat; Ⓜ Palais Royal–Musée du Louvre) In the rag trade since 1975, collector Didier Ludot sells the city's finest couture creations of yesteryear in his exclusive twinset of boutiques, hosts exhibitions and has published a book portraying the evolution of the little black dress.

Passage des Panoramas SHOPPING ARCADE

(Map p66; 10 rue St-Marc, 2e; ⊙6am-midnight; Ⓜ Bourse) Built in 1800, this is the oldest covered arcade in Paris and the first to be lit by gas (1817). It's a bit faded around the edges now, but retains a real 19th-century charm with several outstanding eateries, a theatre from where spectators would come out to shop during the interval, and autograph dealer Arnaud Magistry (at No 60).

Galignani BOOKS

(Map p76; ☎01 42 60 76 07; http://galignani.com; 224 rue de Rivoli, 1er; ⊙10am-7pm Mon-Sat; Ⓜ Concorde) Proudly claiming to be the 'first English bookshop established on the continent', this ode to literature stocks French and English books and is a good spot to pick up just-published titles.

Kiliwatch FASHION & ACCESSORIES

(Map p76; ☎01 42 21 17 37; http://espacekiliwatch.fr; 64 rue Tiquetonne, 2e; ⊙10.30am-7pm Mon, to 7.30pm Tue-Sat; Ⓜ Étienne Marcel) A Parisian institution, Kiliwatch gets jam-packed with hip guys and gals rummaging through racks of new and used streetwear. Startling vintage range of hats and boots plus art and photography books, eyewear and the latest sneakers.

Colette CONCEPT STORE

(Map p76; www.colette.fr; 213 rue St-Honoré, 1er; ⊙11am-7pm Mon-Sat; Ⓜ Tuileries) Uber-hip is an understatement. Ogle designer fashion on the 1st floor, and streetwear, limited-edition sneakers, art books, music, gadgets and other high-tech, inventive or plain unusual items on the ground floor. End with a drink in the basement 'water bar' and pick up free design magazines and flyers by the door for some of the city's hippest happenings.

E Dehillerin HOMEWARES

(Map p76; www.e-dehillerin.fr; 18-20 rue Coquillière, 1er; ⊙9am-12.30pm & 2-6pm Mon, 9am-6pm Tue-Sat; Ⓜ Les Halles) Founded in 1820, this extraordinary two-level store – think old-fashioned warehouse rather than shiny, chic boutique – carries an incredible selection of professional-quality *matériel de cuisine* (kitchenware). Poultry scissors, turbot

DON'T MISS

PARISIAN BOUQUINISTES

With some 3km of forest-green boxes lining the Seine, containing over 300,000 second-hand, often out-of-print, books, rare magazines, postcards and old advertising posters, Paris' *bouquinistes*, or used-book sellers, are as integral to the cityscape as Notre Dame. Many open only from spring to autumn (and many shut in August), but year-round you'll still find some to browse.

The *bouquinistes* have been in business since the 16th century, when they were itinerant peddlers selling their wares on Parisian bridges – back then their sometimes subversive (eg Protestant) materials would get them in trouble with the authorities. By 1859 the city had finally wised up: official licenses were issued, space was rented (10m of railing) and eventually the permanent green boxes were installed.

Today, *bouquinistes* (the official count ranges from 200 to 240) are allowed to have four boxes, only one of which can be used to sell souvenirs. Look hard enough and you just might find some real treasures: old comic books, forgotten first editions, maps, stamps, erotica and prewar newspapers – as in centuries past, it's all there, waiting to be rediscovered.

poacher, professional copper cookware or Eiffel Tower–shaped cake tin – it's all here.

Montmartre & Northern Paris

There are a growing number of boutiques in the Pigalle area – the ultimate cool souvenir is a 'Pigalle' hoodie – but by far the finest strips for fashion lovers are rue Beaurepaire and rue de Marseille by Canal St-Martin. Montmartre has its fair share of souvenir shops aimed squarely at tourists in search of Eiffel Tower key rings, but for discerning shoppers there are some exquisite specialist boutiques selling everything from handcrafted jewellery to antique perfume bottles and vintage fashion.

★Pigalle FASHION & ACCESSORIES

(Map p66; www.pigalle-paris.com; 7 rue Henry Monnier, 9e; noon-8pm Mon-Sat, 2-8pm Sun; M Pigalle) Blend in with local hipsters with a hoodie emblazoned with the B&W Pigalle logo from this leading Parisian menswear brand, created by wild-child designer and amateur basketball player Stéphane Ashpool, who grew up in the 'hood.

★Maison Kitsuné FASHION & ACCESSORIES

(Map p66; www.shop.kitsune.fr; 68 rue Condorcet, 9e; 1.30-7pm Mon-Sat, noon-6.30pm Sun; M Pigalle) Paris fashion label Kitsuné is the secret to looking effortlessly French. Shop here for ready-to-wear fashion, accessories and must-have everyday items for men and women.

★Belle du Jour FASHION & ACCESSORIES

(Map p80; www.belle-de-jour.fr; 7 rue Tardieu, 18e; 10.30am-1pm & 2-7pm Tue-Fri, 10.30am-1pm & 2-6pm Sat; M Anvers) Be whisked back in time to the elegance of belle époque Paris with this sweet-smelling Montmartre shop specialising in perfume bottles. Gorgeous 19th-century atomisers, smelling salts and powder boxes in engraved or enamelled Bohemian, Baccarat and Saint-Louis crystal jostle for the limelight with more contemporary designs. Whether you're after art deco or art nouveau, pink-frosted or painted glass, it's here.

Bazartherapy GIFTS & SOUVENIRS

(Map p90; www.bazartherapy.com; 15 rue Beaurepaire, 10e; 11am-7.30pm Tue-Sat, 2-7pm Sun; M Jacques Bonsergent) Should you have no idea what to take back home, hit this ubercool neo-bazaar, packed to the rafters with a mesmerising display of knick-knacks for every age, style and budget. Think toys, games, ornaments, candles, stationery, useful (and useless) gadgets, bath salts, coffee tables, decorative household items – the list is endless.

St-Germain & Les Invalides

The northern wedge of the 6e between Église St-Germain des Prés and the Seine is a dream to mooch with its bijou art galleries, antique shops, stylish vintage clothes shops, and designer boutiques (Vanessa Bruno, Isabel Marant et al). St-Germain's style continues along the western half of bd St-Germain and rue du Bac with a striking collection of contemporary furniture, kitchen and design shops. Gourmet food and wine shops galore make it a foodie's paradise.

Le Bon Marché DEPARTMENT STORE

(Map p98; www.bonmarche.com; 24 rue de Sèvres, 7e; 10am-8pm Mon-Wed & Sat, to 9pm Thu & Fri;

Ⓜ Sèvres-Babylone) Built by Gustave Eiffel as Paris' first department store in 1852, Le Bon Marché is the epitome of style, with a superb concentration of men's and women's fashions, beautiful homewares, stationery, books and toys as well as chic dining options.

The icing on the cake is its glorious food hall, **La Grande Épicerie de Paris** (www.lagrandeepicerie.com; 36 rue de Sèvres, 7e; ⏲ 8.30am-9pm Mon-Sat).

★Gab & Jo CONCEPT STORE
(Map p98; www.gabjo.fr; 28 rue Jacob, 6e; ⏲ 11am-7pm Mon-Sat; Ⓜ St-Germain des Prés) Forget mass-produced, imported souvenirs: for quality local gifts, browse the shelves of the country's first-ever concept store stocking only made-in-France items. Designers include La Note Parisienne (scented candles for each Parisian *arrondissement*, such as the 6e, with notes of lipstick, cognac, orange blossom, tuberose, jasmine, rose and fig), Marius Fabre (Marseille soaps), Germaine-des-Prés (lingerie), MILF (sunglasses) and Monsieur Marcel (T-shirts).

Hermès CONCEPT STORE
(Map p98; www.hermes.com; 17 rue de Sèvres, 6e; ⏲ 10.30am-7pm Mon-Sat; Ⓜ Sèvres-Babylone) A stunning art deco swimming pool now houses luxury label Hermès' inaugural concept store. Retaining its original mosaic tiles and iron balustrades, and adding enormous timber pod-like 'huts', the vast, tiered space showcases new directions in home furnishings, including fabrics and wallpaper, along with classic lines such as its signature scarves. There's also an appropriately chic cafe, Le Plongeoir (the Diving Board).

Deyrolle ANTIQUES, HOMEWARES
(Map p98; www.deyrolle.com; 46 rue du Bac, 7e; ⏲ 10am-1pm & 2-7pm Mon, 10am-7pm Tue-Sat; Ⓜ Rue du Bac) Overrun with creatures including lions, tigers, zebras and storks, taxidermist Deyrolle opened in 1831. In addition to stuffed animals (for rent and sale), it stocks minerals, shells, corals and crustaceans, stand-mounted ostrich eggs and pedagogical storyboards. There are also rare and unusual seeds (including many old types of tomato), gardening tools and accessories.

La Dernière Goutte WINE
(Map p98; ☎ 01 43 29 11 62; www.laderniereggoutte.net; 6 rue du Bourbon le Château, 6e; ⏲ 3-8pm Mon, 10.30am-1.30pm & 3-8pm Tue-Fri, 11am-7pm Sat; Ⓜ Mabillon) 'The Last Drop' is the brainchild of Cuban-American sommelier Juan Sánchez, whose tiny wine shop is packed with exciting, mostly organic French *vins de propriétaires* (estate-bottled wines) made by small independent producers. Wine classes lasting two hours (seven tastings)

LOCAL KNOWLEDGE

VINTAGE JACKPOT

Fashionistas keen to save a bob will be in heaven in Le Marais where a small but highly select choice of boutiques sell top-quality vintage:

Violette et Léonie (Map p90; ☎ 01 44 59 87 35; www.violetteleonie.com; 114 rue de Turenne, 3e; ⏲ 1-7.30pm Mon, 11am-7.30pm Tue-Sat, 2-7pm Sun; Ⓜ Filles du Calvaire) So chic and of such high quality that it really does not seem like secondhand, Violette et Léonie is a first-class *depôt-vente* boutique specialising in vintage. Shop in its wonderfully spacious concept store or online.

Odetta Vintage (Map p90; www.odettavintage.com; 76 rue des Tournelles, 3e; ⏲ 2-7.30pm Tue-Sat, 3-7pm Sun; Ⓜ Chemin Vert) Odetta specialises in luxury vintage from the 1960s to 1980s. If you're going to find a runway sample, it's here. Think women's shoes, accessories and clothing fashion, as well as the odd piece of remarkable vintage furniture.

Vintage Désir (Map p90; 32 rue des Rosiers, 4e; ⏲ 11am-9pm; Ⓜ St-Paul) Always stuffed to the gills with clothing and customers, this tiny shop on rue des Rosiers is a top spot to pick up quality pieces without breaking the bank. No credit cards and, yes, the name above the shop reads 'Coiffeur' (hairdresser) because that's what this charming old space used to be.

Mam'zelle Swing (Map p90; www.mamzelleswing.com; 35 rue du Roie de Sicile, 4e; ⏲ 2-7pm Mon-Sat; Ⓜ Hôtel de Ville) Polka-dot swing dresses, pointed stilettos and fabulous costume jewellery catch the eye at this secondhand shop selling vintage fashion from 1920 to 1960. The overwhelming friendliness and advice of super-stylish owner Bérénice are gold.

take place in English from Wednesday to Saturday (€55 per person); check the website for the program.

The Islands

Île St-Louis is a shopper's delight for craft-filled boutiques and tiny, charming specialist stores. Head to Île de la Cité for souvenirs and tourist kitsch.

★Marché aux Fleurs Reine Elizabeth II MARKET
(Map p98; place Louis Lépin, 4e; 8am-7.30pm Mon-Sat; M Cité) Blooms have been sold at this flower market since 1808, making it the oldest market of any kind in Paris. On Sunday, it transforms into a cacophonous bird market, the **Marché aux Oiseaux**.

★38 Saint Louis FOOD & DRINKS
(Map p98; 38 rue St-Louis en l'Île, 4e; 8.30am-10pm Tue-Sat, 9.30am-4pm Sun; M Pont Marie) Not only does this contemporary, creamy white-fronted *fromagerie* run by a young, dynamic, food-driven duo have an absolutely superb selection of first-class French *fromage* (cheese), it also offers Saturday wine tastings, artisan fruit juices and prepared dishes to go such as sheep's-cheese salad with truffle oil, and wooden boxes filled with vacuum-packed cheese to take home.

Information

DANGERS & ANNOYANCES

In general, Paris is a safe city and random street assaults are rare. The city is generally well lit and there's no reason not to use the metro until it stops running, at some time between 12.30am and just past 1am (2.15am on weekends). Many women do travel on the metro alone, late at night, in most areas.

Pickpocketing is typically the biggest concern. *Always* be alert and take precautions: don't carry more money than you need, and keep your credit cards, passport and other documents in a concealed pouch, a hotel safe or a safe-deposit box.

Metro Safety

- Metro stations best avoided late at night include Châtelet–Les Halles and its seemingly endless corridors, Château Rouge, Gare du Nord, Strasbourg St-Denis, Réaumur Sébastopol, Stalingrad and Montparnasse Bienvenüe.
- *Bornes d'alarme* (alarm boxes) are located in the centre of each metro/RER platform and in some station corridors.

DON'T MISS

MARCHÉ AUX PUCES DE ST-OUEN

A vast flea market, the **Marché aux Puces de St-Ouen** (Map p58; www.marcheauxpuces-saintouen.com; rue des Rosiers; variable; M Porte de Clignancourt) was founded in the late 19th century. It's said to be Europe's largest market, and has more than 2500 stalls grouped into 15 *marchés* (market areas), each with its own speciality (eg Paul Bert for 17th-century furniture, Malik for clothing, Biron for Asian art). There are miles upon miles of 'freelance' stalls; come prepared to spend some time.

MEDICAL SERVICES

American Hospital of Paris (01 46 41 25 25; www.american-hospital.org; 63 bd Victor Hugo, Neuilly-sur-Seine; M Pont de Levallois) Private hospital with emergency 24-hour medical and dental care.

Hertford British Hospital (01 46 39 22 00; www.british-hospital.org; 3 rue Barbès, Levallois; M Anatole France)

Hôpital Hôtel Dieu (01 42 34 82 34; www.aphp.fr; 1 place du Parvis Notre Dame, 4e; M Cité) One of the city's main government-run public hospitals; after 8pm use the emergency entrance on rue de la Cité.

Pharmacie Les Champs (01 45 62 02 41; Galerie des Champs-Élysées, 84 av des Champs-Élysées, 8e; 24hrs; M George V)

TOURIST INFORMATION

Paris Convention & Visitors Bureau (Office du Tourisme et des Congrès de Paris; Map p76; www.parisinfo.com; 27 rue des Pyramides, 1er; 7am-7pm May-Oct, 10am-7pm Nov-Apr; M Pyramides) The main branch is 500m northwest of the Louvre. It sells tickets for tours and several attractions, plus museum and transport passes. Also books accommodation.

Getting There & Away

AIR

Aéroport de Charles de Gaulle (CDG; 01 70 36 39 50; www.aeroportsdeparis.fr) Most international airlines fly to Aéroport de Charles de Gaulle, 28km northeast of central Paris. (In French the airport is commonly called 'Roissy' after the suburb in which it is located.)

Aéroport d'Orly (ORY; 01 70 36 39 50; www.aeroportsdeparis.fr) Aéroport d'Orly is located 19km south of central Paris but, despite being

closer to the centre than CDG, it is not as frequently used by international airlines and public transport options aren't quite as straightforward. If you have heavy luggage or young kids in tow, consider a taxi.

Aéroport de Beauvais (BVA; ☎08 92 68 20 66; www.aeroportbeauvais.com) Aéroport de Beauvais is 75km north of Paris and is served by a few low-cost airlines – but before you snap up that bargain, consider if the post-arrival journey is worth it.

BUS

Gare Routière Internationale de Paris-Galliéni (☎08 92 89 90 91; 28 av du Général de Gaulle) The city's international bus terminal is in the eastern suburb of Bagnolet; it's about a 15-minute metro ride to the more central République station.

TRAIN

Paris is the central point in the French rail network, Société Nationale des Chemins de Fer Français (SNCF), with six train stations that handle passenger traffic to different parts of France and Europe. Each is well connected to the Paris public transport system, the Régie Autonome des Transports Parisiens (RATP). To buy onward tickets from Paris, visit a station or go to Voyages SNCF (www.voyages-sncf.com). Most trains – and all Trains à Grande Vitesse (TGV) – require advance reservations. As with most tickets, the earlier you book, the better your chances of securing a discounted fare. Main-line stations in Paris have left-luggage offices and/or *consignes* (lockers) for a maximum of 72 hours.

Gare du Nord (rue de Dunkerque, 10e) Trains to/from the UK, Belgium, northern Germany, Scandinavia and Moscow (terminus of the high-speed Thalys trains to/from Amsterdam, Brussels, Cologne and Geneva and the Eurostar to London); trains to the northern suburbs of Paris and northern France, including TGV Nord trains to Lille and Calais.

Gare de Lyon (bd Diderot, 12e) In eastern Paris, the terminus for trains from Provence, the Alps, the Riviera and Italy. Also serves Geneva.

Gare de l'Est (bd de Strasbourg, 10e) For trains to/from Luxembourg, parts of Switzerland (Basel, Lucerne, Zürich), southern Germany (Frankfurt, Munich) and points further east; regular and TGV Est trains to areas of France east of Paris (Champagne, Alsace and Lorraine).

Gare d'Austerlitz (bd de l'Hôpital, 13e) The terminus for a handful of trains from the south, including services from Orléans, Limoges and Toulouse. High-speed trains to/from Barcelona and Madrid also use Austerlitz. Current renovations will continue until 2021.

Gare Montparnasse (av du Maine & bd de Vaugirard, 15e) The terminus for trains from the southwest and west, including services from Brittany, the Loire, Bordeaux, Toulouse, and Spain and Portugal. Some of these services will eventually move to Gare d'Austerlitz (by 2021 once refurbishment is complete).

Gare St-Lazare (esplanade de la Gare St-Lazare, 8e) The terminus for trains from Normandy. Located in Clichy, northwestern Paris.

Getting Around

TO/FROM THE AIRPORTS

Aéroport Charles de Gaulle

Bus

There are six main bus lines.

Le Bus Direct line 2 (€17; one hour; every 30 minutes, 5.45am to 11pm) Links the airport with the Arc de Triomphe via the Eiffel Tower and Trocadéro. Children under four years travel free.

Le Bus Direct line 4 (€17; 50 to 80 minutes; every 30 minutes, 6am to 10.30pm from the airport, 5.30am to 10.30pm from Montparnasse) Links the airport with Gare Montparnasse (80 minutes) in southern Paris via Gare de Lyon (50 minutes) in eastern Paris. Under fours travel free.

Noctilien bus 140 & 143 (€8 or four metro tickets; line 140 1¼ hours, line 143 two hours; hourly, 12.30am-5.30am) Part of the RATP night service, Noctilien has two buses that go to CDG: bus 140 from Gare de l'Est, and 143 from Gare de l'Est and Gare du Nord.

RATP bus 350 (€6; 70 minutes; every 30 minutes, 5.30am to 11pm) Links the airport with Gare de l'Est in northern Paris.

RATP bus 351 (€6; 70 minutes; every 30 minutes, 5.30am to 11pm) Links the airport with place de la Nation in eastern Paris.

Roissybus (€11.50; one hour; from CDG every 15 minutes, 5.30am to 10pm & every 30 minutes, 10pm to 11pm; from Paris every 15 minutes, 5.15am to 10pm and every 30 minutes, 10pm to 12.30am) Links the airport with the Opéra.

Taxi

➡ A taxi to the city centre takes 40 minutes. From 2016, fares have been standardised to a flat rate: €50 to the Right Bank and €55 to the Left Bank. The fare increases by 15% between 5pm and 10am and on Sundays.

➡ Only take taxis at a clearly marked rank. Never follow anyone who approaches you at the airport and claims to be a driver.

Train

CDG is served by the RER B line (€10, approximately 50 minutes, every 10 to 20 minutes),

which connects with the Gare du Nord, Châtelet–Les Halles and St-Michel–Notre Dame stations in the city centre. Trains run from 5am to 11pm; there are fewer trains on weekends.

Aéroport d'Orly

Bus

Two bus lines serve Orly:

Le Bus Direct line 1 (€12; one hour, every 20 minutes 5.50am to 11.30pm from Orly, 4.50am to 10.30pm from the Arc de Triomphe) Runs to/from the Arc de Triomphe (one hour) via Gare Montparnasse (40 minutes), La Motte-Picquet and Trocadéro. Under fours travel free.

Orlybus (€8, 30 minutes, every 15 minutes, 6am to 12.30pm from Orly, 5.35am to midnight from Paris) Runs to/from the metro station Denfert Rochereau in southern Paris, making several stops en route.

Taxi

A taxi to the city centre takes roughly 30 minutes. Standardised flat-rate fares since 2016 mean a taxi costs €30 to the Left Bank and €35 to the Right Bank. The fare increases by 15% between 5pm and 10am and on Sundays.

Train

There is currently no direct train to/from Orly; you'll need to change halfway. Note that while it is possible to take a shuttle to the RER C line, this service is quite long and not recommended.

RER B (€12.05, 35 minutes, every four to 12 minutes) This line connects Orly with the St-Michel–Notre Dame, Châtelet–Les Halles and Gare du Nord stations in the city centre. In order to get from Orly to the RER station (Antony), you must first take the Orlyval automatic train. The service runs from 6am to 11pm (less frequently on weekends). You only need one ticket to take the two trains.

Aéroport Paris-Beauvais

Shuttle (€17, 1¼ hours) The Beauvais shuttle bus links the airport with metro station Porte de Maillot. See the airport website for details and tickets.

BICYCLE

The **Vélib'** (☎01 30 79 79 30; www.velib.paris.fr; day/week subscription €1.70/8, bike hire up to 30/60/90/120min free/€1/2/4) bike-share scheme puts 23,600 bikes at the disposal of Parisians and visitors for getting around the city. There are some 1800 stations throughout Paris, each with anywhere from 20 to 70 bike stands. The bikes are accessible around the clock.

➡ To get a bike, you first need to purchase a one- or seven-day subscription. There are two ways to do this: either at the terminals found at docking stations or online.

➡ The terminals require a credit card with an embedded smart chip (which precludes many North American cards), and, even then, not all foreign chip-embedded cards will work. Alternatively, you can purchase a subscription online before you leave your hotel.

➡ After you authorise a deposit (€150) to pay for the bike should it go missing, you'll receive an ID number and PIN code and you're ready to go.

➡ Bikes are rented in 30-minute intervals. If you return a bike before a half-hour is up and then take a new one, you will not be charged.

➡ If the station you want to return your bike to is full, log in to the terminal to get 15 minutes for free while you find another station.

➡ Bikes are suitable for cyclists aged 14 and over, and are fitted with gears, an antitheft lock with key, reflective strips and front/rear lights. Bring your own helmet (they are not required by law).

➡ P'tits Vélib' is a bike-sharing scheme for children aged two to 10 years, with bike stations at seven sites, including Bois de Bologne, Bois de Vincennes and Les Berges de Seine. Child helmets are always provided.

Rentals

Most rental places will require a deposit (usually €150). Take ID and your bank or credit card.

Au Point Vélo Hollandais (☎01 43 54 85 36; www.pointvelo.com; 83 bd St-Michel, 5e; per day €15; ⊙10.30am-7.30pm Mon-Sat; Ⓜ Cluny-La Sorbonne or RER Luxembourg)

Freescoot (☎01 44 07 06 72; www.freescoot.com; 63 quai de la Tournelle, 5e; bike/tandem/electric bike per day from €20/35/40; ⊙9am-1pm & 2-7pm mid-Apr–mid-Sep, closed Sun & Wed mid-Sep–mid-Apr; Ⓜ Maubert-Mutualité)

Gepetto et Vélos (☎01 43 54 19 95; www.gepetto-velos.com; 59 rue du Cardinal Lemoine, 5e; per day €16, child seat €5; ⊙9am-2pm & 3-7pm Tue-Sat year-round plus 10am-2pm & 3-7pm Sun mid-Apr–mid-Sep; Ⓜ Cardinal Lemoine)

Paris à Vélo, C'est Sympa (☎01 48 87 60 01; www.parisvelosympa.com; 22 rue Alphonse Baudin, 11e; half-day/full day/24hr from €12/15/20, electric bikes per half-day/full day/24hr €20/30/40; ⊙9.30am-1pm & 2-6pm Mon-Fri, 9am-7pm Sat & Sun Apr-Oct, shorter hours winter; Ⓜ St-Sébastien-Froissart)

BOAT

Batobus (www.batobus.com; adult/child 1-day pass €17/10, 2-day pass €19/10; ⊙10am-9.30pm Apr-Aug, to 7pm Sep-Mar) runs glassed-in trimarans that dock every 20 to 25 minutes at nine small piers along the Seine: Beaugrenelle, Eiffel Tower, Musée d'Orsay, St-Germain des Prés, Notre Dame, Jardin des Plantes/Cité de la Mode et du Design, Hôtel de Ville, Musée du Louvre and Champs-Élysées.

TOURIST PASSES

The Mobilis and Paris Visite passes are valid on the metro, RER, SNCF's suburban lines, buses, night buses, trams and Montmartre funicular railway. No photo is needed, but write your full name and date of use on the ticket. Passes are sold at larger metro and RER stations, SNCF offices in Paris, and the airports.

Mobilis Allows unlimited travel for one day and costs €7.30 (two zones) to €17.30 (five zones). Buy it at any metro, RER or SNCF station in the Paris region. Depending on how many times you plan to hop on/off the metro in a day, a *carnet* (book of 10 tickets) might work out cheaper.

Paris Visite Allows unlimited travel as well as discounted entry to certain museums and other discounts and bonuses. The 'Paris+Suburbs+Airports' pass includes transport to/from the airports and costs €24.50/37.25/52.20/63.90 for one/two/three/five days. The cheaper 'Paris Centre' pass, valid for zones 1 to 3, costs €11.65/18.95/25.85/37.25 for one/two/three/five days. Children aged four to 11 years pay half price.

Navigo Pass If you're staying in Paris for longer than a few days, the cheapest and easiest way to use public transport is to get this combined travel pass that allows unlimited travel on the metro, RER and buses for a week, a month or a year. Since September 2015, passes now cover all of the Île-de-France (that is, all zones).

Buy tickets online, at ferry stops or at tourist offices. You can also buy a two- or three-day Paris À La Carte Pass that includes L'Open Tour buses for €45 or €49.

CAR & MOTORCYCLE

Paris' electric-car-share program, Autolib' (www.autolib.eu), is similar to bike-share scheme Vélib': pay €9 per half hour to rent a GPS-equipped car in 30-minute intervals, plus €1 per reservation. Its 3800 cars (most of which have more than a little wear and tear) can be picked up/dropped off at 1000 stations around the city and are designed only for short hops; the car battery is good for 250km. Carry your driving licence and photo ID.

Scooters

Cityscoot (www.cityscoot.eu; per minute/100 minutes €0.28/25; ⏲7am-11pm) Since summer 2016, electric mopeds with a top speed of 45km/h are available to rent as part of Paris' scooter-sharing scheme (similar to the Autolib' car-sharing program), with all bookings via smartphones.

Freescoot (☎01 44 07 06 72; www.freescoot.com; 63 quai de la Tournelle, 5e; 50/125cc scooters per 24hr €55/65; ⏲9am-1pm & 2-7pm mid-Apr–mid-Sep, closed Sun & Wed mid-Sep–mid-Apr; Ⓜ Maubert-Mutualité) Rents 50/125cc scooters in various intervals. Prices include third-party insurance as well as helmets, locks, rain gear and gloves. You must be at least 23 years old and leave a credit card deposit of €1000.

Left Bank Scooters (☎06 78 12 04 24; www.leftbankscooters.com; 50/125/300cc scooters per 24hr €70/80/100) Rents Vespa XLV scooters including insurance, helmet and wet-weather gear. To rent a scooter, you must be at least 20 years old and have a car or motorcycle licence. Credit-card deposit is €1000. Scooter tours also available.

PUBLIC TRANSPORT

Bus

Paris' bus system, operated by RATP, runs from 5.30am to 8.30pm Monday to Saturday; after that, certain evening-service lines continue until between midnight and 12.30am. Services are drastically reduced on Sunday and public holidays, when buses run from 7am to 8.30pm.

Metro & RER

Paris' underground network is run by RATP and consists of two separate but linked systems: the metro and the Réseau Express Régional (RER) suburban train line. The metro has 14 numbered lines; the RER has five main lines (but you'll probably only need to use A, B and C). When buying tickets consider how many zones your journey will cover; there are five concentric transport zones rippling out from Paris (5 being the furthest); if you travel from Charles de Gaulle airport to Paris, for instance, you will have to buy a zone 1–5 ticket.

For information on the metro, RER and bus systems, visit www.ratp.fr. Metro maps of various sizes and degrees of detail are available for free at metro ticket windows; several can also be downloaded for free from the RATP website.

➡ The same RATP tickets are valid on the metro, the RER (for travel within the city limits), buses, trams and the Montmartre funicular.

➡ A ticket – white in colour and called *Le Ticket t+* – costs €1.90 (half price for children aged four to nine years) if bought individually and €14.50 for adults for a *carnet* (book) of 10.

- Tickets are sold at all metro stations. Ticket windows accept most credit cards; however automated machines do not accept credit cards without embedded chips (and even then, not all foreign chip-embedded cards).
- One ticket lets you travel between any two metro stations (no return journeys) for a period of 1½ hours, no matter how many transfers are required. You can also use it on the RER for travel within zone 1, which encompasses all of central Paris.
- Transfers from the metro to bus or vice versa are not possible.
- Always keep your ticket until you exit from your station; if you are stopped by a ticket inspector, you will have to pay a fine if you don't have a valid ticket.

TAXI

- The *prise en charge* (flagfall) is €2.60. Within the city limits, it costs €1.04 per kilometre for travel between 10am and 5pm Monday to Saturday (*Tarif A;* white light on taxi roof and meter).
- At night (5pm to 10am), on Sunday from 7am to midnight, and in the inner suburbs the rate is €1.27 per kilometre (*Tarif B;* orange light).
- Travel in the city limits and inner suburbs on Sunday night (midnight to 7am Monday) and in the outer suburbs is at *Tarif C,* €1.54 per kilometre (blue light).
- The minimum taxi fare for a short trip is €6.86.
- Flat fees have been introduced for taxis to/from the major airports, Charles de Gaulle (p156) and Orly (p157).
- There's a €3 surcharge for taking a fourth passenger, but drivers sometimes refuse for insurance reasons. The first piece of baggage is free; additional pieces over 5kg cost €1 extra.
- Flagging down a taxi in Paris can be difficult; it's best to find an official taxi stand.
- To order a taxi, call or reserve online with **Taxis G7** (☎01 41 27 66 99, 3607; www.taxisg7.com), **Taxis Bleus** (☎08 91 70 10 10, 3609; www.taxis-bleus.com) or **Alpha Taxis** (☎01 45 85 85 85; www.alphataxis.fr).
- An alternative is the private driver system, Uber taxi (www.uber.com/cities/paris), whereby you order and pay via your smartphone. However, official taxis continue to protest about the service and there have been instances of Uber drivers and passengers being harassed.

Around Paris

Includes ➡

Best Places to Eat

➡ Le Jardin des Plumes (p168)
➡ Le Tripot (p177)
➡ La Cour (p167)
➡ L'Axel (p171)
➡ Le Vertugadin (p173)

Best Places to Sleep

➡ La Ferme de la Canardière (p172)
➡ Le Grand Monarque (p176)
➡ La Guérinière (p170)
➡ Le Clos Fleuri (p168)
➡ Hôtel de Londres (p173)

Why Go?

Whether you're taking day trips from Paris or continuing further afield, a trove of treasures awaits in the areas around the French capital.

The Île de France *région* – the 12,000-sq-km 'Island of France' shaped by five rivers – and surrounding areas contain some of the most extravagant châteaux in the land. At the top of everyone's list is the palace at Versailles, the opulence and extravagance of which partly spurred the French Revolution, but the châteaux in Fontainebleau and Chantilly are also breathtaking. Many beautiful and ambitious cathedrals are also here, including the glorious cathedral crowning the medieval old city of Chartres. In Giverny, Monet's home and gardens provide a picturesque insight into the inspiration for his seminal paintings.

Yet Paris' surrounds don't only hark back to the past. Also here is every kid's favourite, Disneyland Resort Paris, which now has more attractions than ever.

When to Go

Chartres

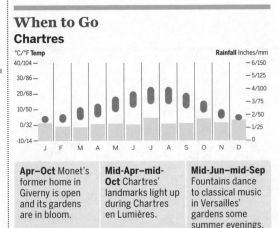

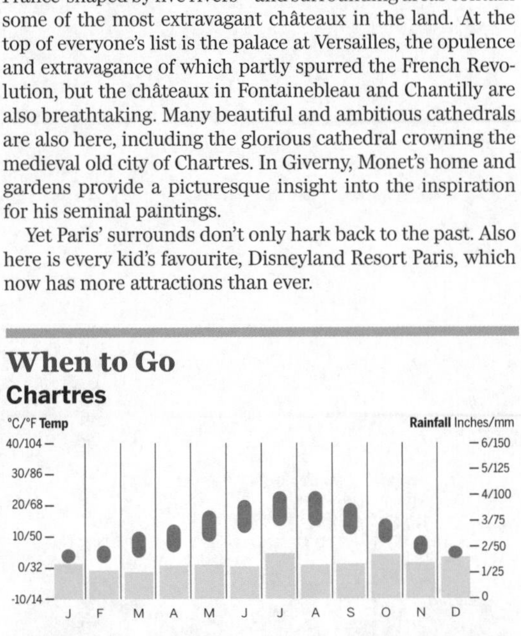

Apr–Oct Monet's former home in Giverny is open and its gardens are in bloom.

Mid-Apr–mid-Oct Chartres' landmarks light up during Chartres en Lumières.

Mid-Jun–mid-Sep Fountains dance to classical music in Versailles' gardens some summer evenings.

Disneyland Resort Paris

It took almost €4.6 billion to turn the beet fields 32km east of Paris into Europe's first Disney theme park. What started out as Euro-Disney in 1992 today comprises the traditional Disneyland Park theme park, the film-oriented Walt Disney Studios Park, and the hotel-, shop- and restaurant-filled Disney Village. And kids – and kids-at-heart – can't seem to get enough.

Sights

Basic one-day admission fees at **Disneyland Resort Paris** (☎hotel 01 60 30 60 30, restaurant 01 60 30 40 50; www.disneylandparis.com;

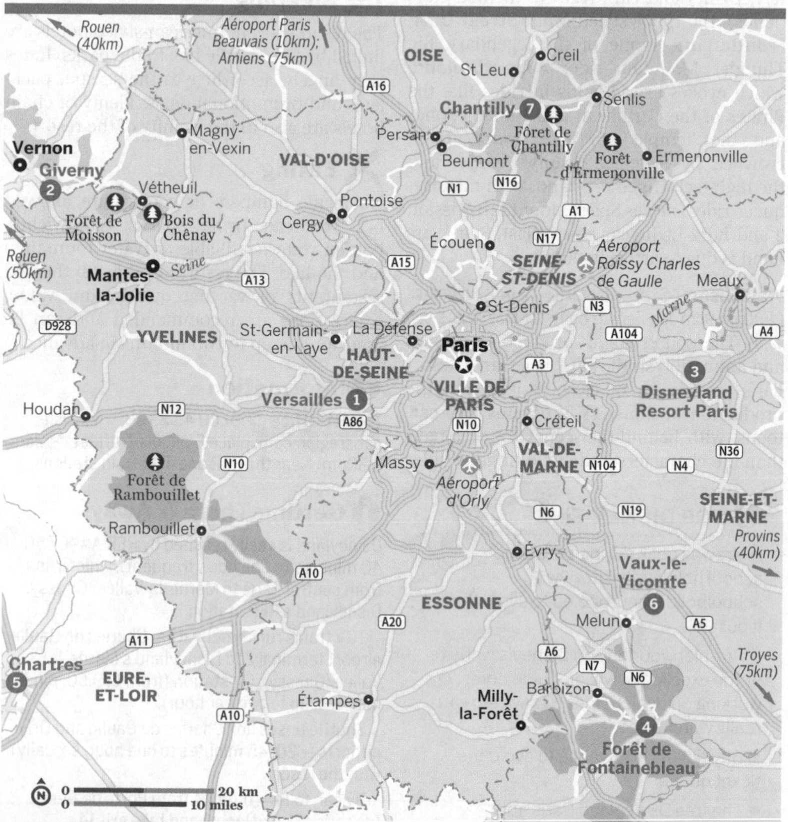

Around Paris Highlights

❶ **Château de Versailles** (p163) Reliving the glory of the 17th- and 18th-century kingdom of France at the opulent palace.

❷ **Maison et Jardins de Claude Monet** (p167) Strolling through the life-size impressionist masterpiece of Monet's garden in Giverny.

❸ **Disneyland Resort Paris** (p161) Following an adorable chef, rat Rémy, aboard the Ratatouille ride.

❹ **Forêt de Fontainebleau** (p170) Hiking, cycling, horse riding or rock-climbing in one of France's loveliest forests.

❺ **Cathédrale Notre Dame** (p174) Gazing at hypnotic blue stained-glass windows at the awe-inspiring cathedral in Chartres.

❻ **Château de Vaux-le-Vicomte** (p171) Visiting this 17th-century château by candlelight.

❼ **Château de Chantilly** (p171) Viewing the artworks inside the lake-set château where its namesake whipped cream was created.

adult/child 1 day single park €69/62, 1 day both parks €84/77, 2 days both parks €139/126) include unlimited access to attractions in either Disneyland Park or Walt Disney Studios Park. A multitude of multiday passes, special offers and packages are always available.

Disneyland Park AMUSEMENT PARK
(⌚10am-11pm May-Sep, to 7pm Oct-Apr, hours can vary) Disneyland Park has five themed *pays* (lands): the 1900s-styled **Main Street USA**; **Frontierland**, home of the legendary Big Thunder Mountain ride; **Adventureland**, which evokes exotic lands in rides like the Pirates of the Caribbean and Indiana Jones and the Temple of Peril; **Fantasyland**, crowned by Sleeping Beauty's castle; and the high-tech **Discoveryland**, with massive-queue rides such as Space Mountain: Mission 2 and Buzz Lightyear Laser Blast. Star Wars Land is due to arrive in 2022.

Walt Disney Studios Park AMUSEMENT PARK
(⌚10am-9pm Jun-Sep, to 6pm Oct-May, hours can vary) The sound stage, production backlot and animation studios at Disneyland Resort Paris provide an up-close insight into the production of films, TV programs and cartoons, with behind-the-scenes tours, larger-than-life characters and spine-tingling rides like the Twilight Zone Tower of Terror, as well as the outsized Ratatouille ride, based on the winsome 2007 film about a rat who dreams of becoming a top Parisian chef and offering a multisensory rat's perspective of Paris' rooftops and restaurant kitchens aboard a trackless 'ratmobile'. Marvel Land, inspired by the comics, is due to arrive in 2023.

TOP DISNEY TIPS

- Crowds peak during European school holidays; visit www.schoolholidayseurope.eu to avoid them if possible.
- Pre-plan your day on Disney's website or the excellent www.dlpguide.com, working out which rides, shows etc you really want to see.
- Buy tickets in advance to avoid the ticket queue.
- The free Disneyland Paris app provides real-time waiting time for attractions but note that free wi-fi is only available in limited areas within the park.
- Once in, reserve your time slot on the busiest rides using FastPass, the park's ride reservation system (limited to one reservation at a time).
- Disney hotel guests are often entitled to two 'Magic Hours' in Disneyland Park (usually from 8am May to October) before opening to the public, although not all rides run during these hours.

Sleeping

The resort's seven American-styled hotels are linked by free shuttle bus to the parks. Rates vary hugely, according to the season, packages and promotional deals. Plenty of chain hotels are also in the vicinity of the resort.

Eating

No picnic hampers or coolers are allowed but you can bring snacks, sandwiches, bottled water (refillable at water fountains) and the like. The resort also has 29 themed restaurants of varying quality and value; reservations are recommended and can be made online up to two months in advance.

Information

Tourist Office (☎01 60 43 33 33; www.visitparisregion.com; place François Truffaut; ⌚9am-8.30pm) Near the RER and TGV train stations.

Getting There & Away

Disneyland is easily reached by RER A4 (€7.50, 40 minutes to one hour, frequent), which runs from central Paris to Marne-la-Vallée/Chessy, Disneyland's RER station.

TGV trains run directly from Charles de Gaulle airport terminal 2 to Disneyland's Marne-la-Vallée/Chessy TGV station (from €19.50, nine minutes, up to two per hour).

Shuttle buses link Charles de Gaulle and Orly airports (€20, 45 minutes to one hour, six daily) with the resort.

By car, follow route A4 from Porte de Bercy (direction Metz-Nancy) and take exit 14.

Versailles

POP 87,434

Louis XIV transformed his father's hunting lodge into the monumental Château de Versailles in the mid-17th century, and it remains France's most famous and grand palace. Situated in the leafy, bourgeois suburb of Versailles, about 22km southwest of central Paris, the Baroque château was the kingdom's political capital and the seat of the royal court from 1682 up until the fateful events

of 1789 when revolutionaries massacred the palace guard. Louis XVI and Marie Antoinette were ultimately dragged back to Paris, where they were ingloriously guillotined.

Sights

★Château de Versailles PALACE

(☎01 30 83 78 00; www.chateauversailles.fr; place d'Armes; adult/child passport ticket incl estate-wide access €18/free, with musical events €25/free, palace €15/free; ⏲9am-6.30pm Tue-Sun Apr-Oct, to 5.30pm Tue-Sun Nov-Mar; Ⓜ RER Versailles-Château–Rive Gauche) Amid magnificently landscaped formal gardens, this splendid and enormous palace was built in the mid-17th century during the reign of Louis XIV – the Roi Soleil (Sun King) – to project the absolute power of the French monarchy, which was then at the height of its glory. The château has undergone relatively few alterations since its construction, though almost all the interior furnishings disappeared during the Revolution and many of the rooms were rebuilt by Louis-Philippe (r 1830–48).

Some 30,000 workers and soldiers toiled on the structure, the bills for which all but emptied the kingdom's coffers.

Work began in 1661 under the guidance of architect Louis Le Vau (Jules Hardouin-Mansart took over from Le Vau in the mid-1670s); painter and interior designer Charles Le Brun; and landscape artist André Le Nôtre, whose workers flattened hills, drained marshes and relocated forests as they laid out the seemingly endless gardens, ponds and fountains.

Le Brun and his hundreds of artisans decorated every moulding, cornice, ceiling and door of the interior with the most luxurious and ostentatious of appointments: frescoes, marble, gilt and woodcarvings, many with themes and symbols drawn from Greek and Roman mythology. The King's Suite of the Grands Appartements du Roi et de la Reine (King's and Queen's State Apartments), for example, includes rooms dedicated to Hercules, Venus, Diana, Mars and Mercury. The opulence reaches its peak in the Galerie des Glaces (Hall of Mirrors), a 75m-long ballroom with 17 huge mirrors on one side and, on the other, an equal number of windows looking out over the gardens and the setting sun.

The current €400 million restoration program is the most ambitious yet, and until it's completed in 2020, at least a part of the palace is likely to be clad in scaffolding when you visit.

Château de Versailles Gardens & Park GARDENS

(www.chateauversailles.fr; place d'Armes; free except during musical events; ⏲gardens 8am-8.30pm Apr-Oct, to 6pm Nov-Mar, park 7am-8.30pm Apr-Oct, 8am-6pm Nov-Mar) The section of the vast gardens nearest the palace, laid out between 1661 and 1700 in the formal French style, is famed for its geometrically aligned terraces, flowerbeds, tree-lined paths, ponds and fountains. The 400-odd statues of marble, bronze and lead were made by the most talented sculptors of the era. The English-style Jardins du Petit Trianon are more pastoral and have meandering, sheltered paths.

Oriented to reflect the sunset, the **Grand Canal**, 1.6km long and 62m wide, is traversed by the 1km-long Petit Canal, creating a cross-shaped body of water with a perimeter of more than 5.5km.

On the southwestern side of the palace, the **Orangerie**, built under the Parterre du Midi (Southern Flowerbed), shelters tropical plants in winter.

The gardens' largest fountains include the 17th-century **Bassin de Neptune**, a dazzling mirage of 99 spouting gushers 300m north of the palace, whose straight side abuts a small pond graced by a winged dragon (Grille du Dragon). On the same days as the Grandes Eaux Musicales fountain displays, the Bassin de Neptune flows for 10 minutes.

At the eastern end of the Grand Canal, the **Bassin d'Apollon** was built in 1688. Emerging from the water in the centre is Apollo's chariot, pulled by rearing horses.

Domaine de Marie-Antoinette PALACE

(Marie Antoinette's Estate; www.chateauversailles.fr; Château de Versailles; adult/child €10/free, with passport ticket free; ⏲noon-6.30pm Tue-Sun Apr-Oct, to 5.30pm Tue-Sat Nov-Mar) Northwest of Versailles' main palace is the Domaine de Marie-Antoinette. Admission includes the pink-colonnaded **Grand Trianon**, built in 1687 for Louis XIV and his family to escape the rigid etiquette of the court; the ochre-coloured 1760s **Petit Trianon**, redecorated in 1867 by consort of Napoléon III, Empress Eugénie, who added Louis XVI-style furnishings; and the 1784-completed **Hameau de la Reine** (Queen's Hamlet), a mock village of thatched cottages where Marie Antoinette played milkmaid.

Versailles Stables STABLES

(av Rockefeller; www.bartabas.fr) The Grandes Écuries (Big Stables) are the stage for the

Versailles

A DAY IN COURT

Visiting Versailles – even just the State Apartments – may seem overwhelming at first, but think of it as a house where people ate, drank, worked, slept and conspired and you'll be on the right path.

Some two decades into his long reign, Louis XIV began turning his father's hunting lodge into a palace large enough to house his entire court (to keep closer tabs on the 6000-strong army of courtiers). Sparing no expense, the Sun King employed the greatest artists and craftspeople of the day and by 1682 he'd created the most extravagant dormitory in history.

The royal schedule was as accurate and predictable as a Swiss watch. By following this itinerary of rooms you can recreate the king's day, starting with the **King's Bedchamber** 1 and the **Queen's Bedchamber** 2, where the royal couple was roused at about the same time. The royal procession then leads through the **Hall of Mirrors** 3 to the **Royal Chapel** 4 for morning Mass and returns to the **Council Chamber** 5 for late-morning meetings with ministers. After lunch the king might ride or hunt or visit the **King's Library** 6. Later he could join courtesans for an 'apartment evening' starting from the **Hercules Drawing Room** 7 or play billiards in the **Diana Drawing Room** 8 before supping at 10pm.

VERSAILLES BY NUMBERS

- **Rooms** 700 (11 hectares of roof)
- **Windows** 2153
- **Staircases** 67
- **Gardens and parks** 800 hectares
- **Trees** 200,000
- **Fountains** 50 (with 620 nozzles)
- **Paintings** 6300 (measuring 11km laid end to end)
- **Statues and sculptures** 2100
- **Objets d'art and furnishings** 5000
- **Visitors** 5.3 million per year

CHRISTOPHE LEHENAFF/GETTY IMAGES ©

Queen's Bedchamber
Chambre de la Reine
The queen's life was on constant public display and even the births of her children were watched by crowds of spectators in her own bedchamber. **DETOUR »** The Guardroom, with a dozen armed men at the ready.

LUNCH BREAK

Diner-style food at Sister's Café, crêpes at Le Phare St-Louis or picnic in the park.

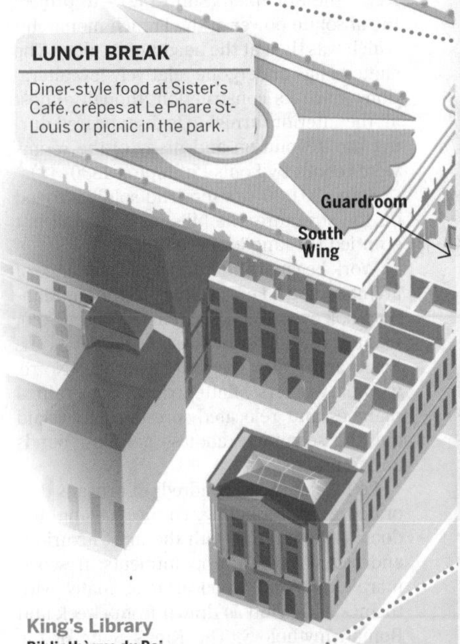

King's Library
Bibliothèque du Roi
The last resident, bibliophile Louis XVI, loved geography and his copy of *The Travels of James Cook* (in English, which he read fluently) is still on the shelf here.

DEA/G. DAGLI ORTI/GETTY IMAGES ©

SAVVY SIGHTSEEING

Avoid Versailles on Monday (closed), Tuesday (Paris' museums close, so visitors flock here) and Sunday, the busiest day. Also, book tickets online so you don't have to queue.

JOHN ELK/GETTY IMAGES ©

DENNIS JOHNSON/GETTY IMAGES ©

King's Bedchamber

Chambre du Roi

The king's daily life was anything but private and even his *lever* (rising) at 8am and *coucher* (retiring) at 11.30pm would be witnessed by up to 150 sycophantic courtiers.

Hall of Mirrors

Galerie des Glaces

The solid-silver candelabra and furnishings in this extravagant hall, devoted to Louis XIV's successes in war, were melted down in 1689 to pay for yet another conflict. **DETOUR»** The antithetical Peace Drawing Room, adjacent.

Council Chamber

Cabinet du Conseil

This chamber, with carved medallions evoking the king's work, is where the monarch met his various ministers (state, finance, religion etc) depending on the days of the week.

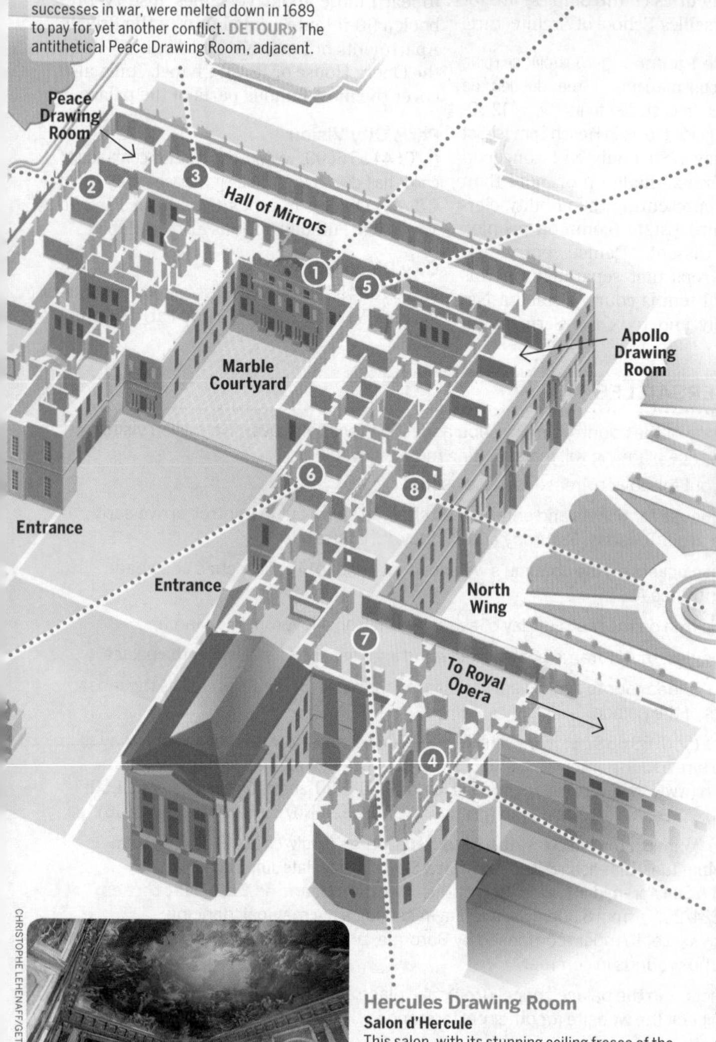

CHRISTOPHE LEHENAFF/GETTY IMAGES ©

Diana Drawing Room

Salon de Diane

With walls and ceiling covered in frescos devoted to the mythical huntress, this room contained a large billiard table reserved for Louis XIV, a keen player.

Royal Chapel

Chapelle Royale

This two-storey chapel (with gallery for the royals and important courtiers, and the ground floor for the B-list) was dedicated to St Louis, patron of French monarchs. **DETOUR»** The sumptuous Royal Opera.

CHRISTOPHE LEHENAFF/GETTY IMAGES ©

Hercules Drawing Room

Salon d'Hercule

This salon, with its stunning ceiling fresco of the strong man, gave way to the State Apartments, which were open to courtiers three nights a week. **DETOUR»** Apollo Drawing Room, used for formal audiences and as a throne room.

prestigious **Académie du Spectacle Équestre** (Academy of Equestrian Arts; ☎01 39 02 62 75; training session adult/child €12/9; ⏰by reservation). It presents spectacular **Reprises Musicales equestrian shows** (Musical Equestrian Shows; adult/child from €25/16; ⏰6pm Sat, 3pm Sun), for which tickets sell out weeks in advance; book ahead online. In the stables' main courtyard is a new manège where horses and their riders train. Show tickets and training sessions include a stable visit.

The Petites Écuries (Little Stables) are today used by Versailles' School of Architecture.

Salle du Jeu de Paume HISTORIC BUILDING
(www.versailles-tourisme.com; 1 rue du Jeu de Paume; admission free, guided tours €9; ⏰12.30-5.45pm Tue-Sun, guided tours in French 3pm 1st Sat of month) In May 1789 Louis XVI convened the États-Généraux, made up of more than 1118 deputies representing the nobility, clergy and the Third Estate (common people), to moderate dissent. Denied entry, the Third Estate's reps met separately on this 1686-built royal tennis court, formed a National Assembly and took the Serment du Jeu de Paume (Tennis Court Oath), swearing not to dissolve it until Louis XVI accepted a new constitution. Less than a month later, a mob in Paris stormed the prison at Bastille.

Tours

Château de Versailles Guided Tours TOURS
(☎01 30 83 77 88; www.chateauversailles.fr; Château de Versailles; tours €7, plus palace entry; ⏰English-language tours 9.30pm Tue-Sun) To access areas that are otherwise off limits and to learn more about Versailles' history, prebook a 90-minute guided tour of the Private Apartments of Louis XV and Louis XVI and the Opera House or Royal Chapel. Tours also cover the most famous parts of the palace.

Paris City Vision BUS
(☎01 44 55 61 00; www.pariscityvision.com; adult/child half-day tour including palace entry from €75/49) Guided minibus trips from Paris to Versailles. Full-day options also available.

City Discovery BUS
(☎09 70 44 52 90; www.city-discovery.com) Offers various Versailles trips from Paris starting

TOP VERSAILLES TIPS

Versailles is one of the country's most popular destinations, with over five million visitors annually; advance planning will make visiting more enjoyable.

➡ Monday is out for obvious reasons (it's closed).

➡ By noon, queues for tickets and entering the château spiral out of control: arrive early morning and avoid Tuesday, Saturday and Sunday, its busiest days.

➡ Prepurchase tickets on the château's website or at Fnac (p147) branches and head straight to Entrance A.

➡ Versailles is free on the first Sunday of every month from November to March.

➡ Prams/buggies, metal-frame baby carriers and luggage aren't allowed in the palace.

➡ Pre-book a guided tour to access areas that are otherwise off limits as well as the most famous parts of the palace.

➡ The **estate** (☎01 39 66 97 66; www.versailles-tourisme.com) is so vast that the only way to see it all is to hire a four-person **electric car** (per hour €32; ⏰Feb-Dec) or hop aboard the **shuttle train** (www.train-versailles.com; adult/child €7.50/5.80, audioguide per person €1.50; ⏰year-round); you can also rent a **bike** (per hour €7.50; ⏰Feb-Nov) or **boat** (per hour €16).

➡ Try to time your visit for the **Grandes Eaux Musicales** (adult/child €9/7.50; ⏰11am-noon & 2.30-4pm Tue, 11am-noon & 3.30-5pm Sat & Sun mid-May–late Jun, 11am-noon & 3.30-5pm Sat & Sun Apr–mid-May & Jul-Oct) or the after-dark **Grandes Eaux Nocturnes** (adult/child €24/20; ⏰from 8.30pm Sat mid-Jun–mid-Sep), truly magical 'dancing water' displays – set to music composed by Baroque- and classical-era composers – throughout the grounds in summer.

➡ Organ concerts in the palace chapel (free) take place at 3pm, 3.30pm and 5.30pm Thursdays; check the website for other performances.

➡ Audioguides are included in admission.

➡ Free apps can be downloaded from the website.

from €53/29 per adult/child. Other options from Paris include Versailles/Giverny (from €185/118), Fontainebleau (from €65/40) and Disneyland Resort Paris (including entry to both parks from €88/67).

Eating

★La Cour CAFE €

(☎01 39 02 33 09; www.versailles-lacour.fr; 7 rue des Deux Portes; 2-/3-course lunch menus €14/16, Sunday brunch €22; ⊙noon-6pm Tue-Sat, 11am-3pm Sun) Framed by a royal-blue façade and painted with giant flower murals inside, this charmer is hidden in a little courtyard that fills with tables in warm weather. Everything is made fresh daily, including quiches, salads, sandwiches, pastries and OJ. Book ahead for Sunday brunch, which features smoked salmon and dill cream, scrambled eggs with feta, and pancakes with maple syrup.

La Table du 11 GASTRONOMIC €€

(☎09 83 34 76 00; www.latabledu11.com; 11 rue St-Honoré; 2-/3-course lunch menus €29/38, 5-/7-course dinner menus €49/65; ⊙12.30-1.45pm & 7.30-9.30pm Tue-Sat) For an appropriately sumptuous meal in this stately town, Michelin-starred La Table du 11 fits the bill. The contemporary interior has snowy-white-clothed tables; dishes on the daily changing *menu* might include shellfish and *stracciatella di bufala* (shredded buffalo cheese), line-caught whiting from Brittany with pak choi and cauliflower, or Argentinian beef with pumpkin and *burratina* (milk-filled mozzarella). It's just across from Versailles' grandiose Cathédrale St-Louis de Versailles.

Angelina CAFE €€

(www.angelina-paris.fr; Domaine de Marie-Antoinette, Château de Versailles; light dishes €16-30, mains €24-36; ⊙10am-6pm Tue-Sun Apr-Oct, to 5pm Tue-Sun Nov-Mar) Eateries within the Versailles estate include tearoom Angelina, famed for its decadent hot chocolate. Stop by for pastries, light dishes such as quiches, charcuterie platters and salads, or filling meals such as truffle ravioli, beef with sweet potato mash or hot smoked salmon. In addition to this branch by the Petit Trianon, there's another inside the palace.

Information

Tourist Office (☎01 39 24 88 88; www.versailles-tourisme.com; 2bis av de Paris; ⊙10am-6pm Mon, 9am-7pm Tue-Sun Apr-Oct, 9am-6pm Tue-Sat, 11am-5pm Sun & Mon Nov-Mar) Sells the passport to Château de Versailles and detailed visitor's guides.

Getting There & Away

BUS

Bus 171 (www.phebus.tm.fr; €2 or one t+ metro/bus ticket, 35 minutes) links Paris' Pont de Sèvres metro station (15e) with place d'Armes at least every 15 minutes from around 6am to 1am.

CAR & MOTORCYCLE

Follow the A13 from Porte d'Auteuil and take the exit marked 'Versailles Château'.

TRAIN

RER C5 (€4.20, 40 minutes, frequent) goes from Paris' Left Bank RER stations to Versailles-Château–Rive Gauche station. The less convenient RER C8 links Paris with Versailles-Chantiers station, a 1.3km walk from the château.

SNCF operates regular trains from Paris' Gare Montparnasse to Versailles-Chantiers, and from Paris' Gare St-Lazare to Versailles–Rive Droite, 1.2km from the château. Both cost €3.55 and take 14 to 20 minutes.

Giverny

POP 518

The tiny country village of Giverny, 74km northwest of Paris, is a place of pilgrimage for devotees of impressionism, and can feel swamped by the tour-bus crowd in the summer months. Monet lived here from 1883 until his death in 1926, in a rambling house – surrounded by flower-filled gardens – that's now the immensely popular Maison et Jardins de Claude Monet. Note that it's closed from November to Easter, along with most accommodation and restaurants, so there's little point visiting out of season. If you are here between Easter and October, however, you're in for a treat.

Be aware that the village has no public toilets, ATMs or bureaux de change.

Sights

★Maison et Jardins de Claude Monet MUSEUM, GARDEN

(☎02 32 51 28 21; www.fondation-monet.com; 84 rue Claude Monet; adult/child €9.50/5.50, incl Musée des Impressionnismes Giverny €16.50/8.50; ⊙9.30am-6pm Easter-Oct) Monet's home for the last 43 years of his life is now a delightful house-museum. His pastel-pink house and Water Lily studio stand on the periphery of the **Clos Normand**, with its symmetrically laid-out gardens bursting with flowers.

Monet bought the **Jardin d'Eau** (Water Garden) in 1895 and set about creating his trademark lily pond, as well as the famous **Japanese bridge** (since rebuilt).

The charmingly preserved house and beautiful bloom-filled gardens (rather than Monet's works) are the draws here.

Draped with purple wisteria, the Japanese bridge blends into the asymmetrical foreground and background, creating the intimate atmosphere for which the 'painter of light' was renowned.

Seasons have an enormous effect on Giverny. From early to late spring, daffodils, tulips, rhododendrons, wisteria and irises appear, followed by poppies and lilies. By June, nasturtiums, roses and sweet peas are in flower. Around September, there are dahlias, sunflowers and hollyhocks.

Combined tickets with Paris' Musée Marmottan Monet (p63) per adult/child cost €20.50/12, and combined adult tickets with Paris' Musée de l'Orangerie (p74) cost €18.50.

Musée des Impressionnismes Giverny ART MUSEUM
(☎02 32 51 94 65; www.mdig.fr; 99 rue Claude Monet; adult/child €7/4.50, incl Maison et Jardins de Claude Monet €16.50/8.50; ⏰10am-6pm Easter-Oct) About 100m northwest of the Maison et Jardins de Claude Monet is the Giverny Museum of Impressionisms. Set up in partnership with the Musée d'Orsay, among others, the pluralised name reinforces its coverage of all aspects of impressionism and related movements in its permanent collection and temporary exhibitions. Reserve ahead for two-hour **art workshops** (€12.50 including materials) offering an introduction to watercolour, drawing, sketching or pastels. Lectures, readings, concerts and documentaries also take place regularly.

Sleeping & Eating

Le Clos Fleuri B&B €€
(☎02 32 21 36 51; www.giverny-leclosfleuri.fr; 5 rue de la Dîme; s/d €93/98; ⏰Apr-Oct; P 📶) Big rooms with king-size beds and exposed wood beams overlook the hedged gardens of this delightful B&B within strolling distance of the Maison et Jardins de Claude Monet. Each of its three rooms is named after a different flower; green-thumbed host Danielle speaks fluent English. Cash only.

La Pluie de Roses B&B €€
(☎02 32 51 10 67; www.givernylapluiederoses.fr; 14 rue Claude Monet; s/d/tr/f €120/135/193/251; P 📶) You'll be won over by this adorable private home cocooned in a dreamy, peaceful garden. Inside, the three rooms (two of which can accommodate families) are so comfy it's hard to wake up. Superb breakfast on a verandah awash with sunlight. Payment is by cash only.

La Musardière HOTEL €€
(☎02 32 21 03 18; www.lamusardiere.fr; 123 rue Claude Monet; d €85-99, tr €125-149, f €149, 3-course menus €26-36; ⏰hotel Feb–mid-Dec, restaurant noon-10pm Apr-Oct; P 📶) This two-star 10-room hotel dating back to 1880 and evocatively called the 'Idler' is set amid a lovely garden less than 100m northeast of the Maison et Jardins de Claude Monet. Breakfast costs €11. In season, savouring a crêpe in its restaurant is a pleasure. Family rooms sleep three or four people.

★**Le Jardin des Plumes** MODERN FRENCH €€€
(☎02 32 54 26 35; www.jardindesplumes.fr; 1 rue du Milieu; 3-course/tasting menu €48/75, mains €32-48; ⏰12.15-1.45pm & 7.15-9pm Wed-Sun, hotel closed Mon & Tue Nov-Mar; 📶 👪) This gorgeous sky-blue-trimmed property's airy white dining room sets the stage for chef Eric Guerin's exquisite, inventive and Michelin-starred cuisine, which justifies the trip from Paris alone.

It also has four rooms (€180 to €200) and four suites (€290 to €350) that combine vintage and contemporary furnishings. It's less than 10 minutes' walk to the Maison et Jardins de Claude Monet.

Information

Tourist Office (☎02 32 64 45 01; www.normandie-giverny.fr; 80 rue Claude Monet; ⏰10am-5.45pm Easter-Oct) By the Maison et Jardins de Claude Monet.

Getting There & Around

The closest train station is at Vernon, from where buses, taxis and cycle/walking tracks run to Giverny.

BICYCLE

Rent bikes (cash only) at the **Café L'Arrivée de Giverny** (☎02 32 21 16 01; 1 place de la Gare, Vernon; per day €15; ⏰7am-11pm), opposite the train station in Vernon, from where Giverny is a signposted 5km along a direct (and flat) cycle/walking track.

BUS

Shuttle buses (€8 return, 20 minutes, four daily Easter to October) meet most trains from Paris at Vernon. There are limited seats, so arrive early for the return trip from Giverny.

TAXI

Taxis (☎02 32 51 10 24) usually wait outside the train station in Vernon and charge around €15 for the one-way trip to Giverny. There's no taxi rank in Giverny, however, so you'll need to phone for one for the return trip to Vernon.

TRAIN

From Paris' Gare St-Lazare there are up to 15 daily trains to Vernon (€14.70, 45 minutes to one hour), 7km to the west of Giverny. Trains also run to/from Rouen in Normandy (€13, one to 1½ hours, at least every two hours).

Fontainebleau

POP 15,408

Fresh air fills your lungs on arriving in the smart town of Fontainebleau. It's enveloped by the 200-sq-km Forêt de Fontainebleau, which is as big a playground today as it was in the 16th century, with superb walking and rock-climbing opportunities. The town grew up around its magnificent château, one of the most beautifully decorated and furnished in France. Although it's less crowded and pressured than Versailles, exploring it can still take the best part of a day. You'll also find a cosmopolitan drinking and dining scene, thanks to the town's lifeblood, the international graduate business school INSEAD.

Sights

★Château de Fontainebleau PALACE

(☎01 60 71 50 70; www.musee-chateau-fontainebleau.fr; place du Général de Gaulle; adult/child €11/free; ⏲9.30am-6pm Wed-Mon Apr-Sep, to 5pm Wed-Mon Oct-Mar) The resplendent, 1900-room Château de Fontainebleau's list of former tenants and guests reads like a who's who of French royalty and aristocracy. Every square centimetre of wall and ceiling space is richly adorned with wood panelling, gilded carvings, frescoes, tapestries and paintings.

Visits take in the **Grands Appartements** (State Apartments), which contain several outstanding rooms. An informative 1½-hour audioguide (included in the price) leads you around the main areas.

The first château on this site was built in the early 12th century and enlarged by Louis IX a century later. Only a single medieval tower survived the energetic Renaissance-style reconstruction undertaken by François I (r 1515–47), whose superb artisans, many of them brought from Italy, blended Italian and French styles to create what is known as the First School of Fontainebleau. The *Mona Lisa* once hung here amid other fine works of art in the royal collection.

During the latter half of the 16th century, the château was further enlarged by Henri II (r 1547–59), Catherine de Médicis and Henri IV (r 1589–1610), whose Flemish and French artists created the Second School of Fontainebleau. Even Louis XIV got in on the act: it was he who hired landscape artist André Le Nôtre, celebrated for his work at Versailles, to redesign the gardens.

Fontainebleau was beloved by Napoléon Bonaparte, who had a fair bit of restoration work carried out. Napoléon III was another frequent visitor. During WWII the château was turned into a German headquarters. After it was liberated by Allied forces under US General George Patton in 1944, part of the complex served as the Allied and then NATO headquarters from 1945 to 1965.

The spectacular **Chapelle de la Trinité** (Trinity Chapel), the ornamentation of which dates from the first half of the 17th century, is where Louis XV married Marie Leczinska in 1725 and where the future Napoléon III was christened in 1810. **Galerie François 1er**, a jewel of Renaissance architecture, was decorated from 1533 to 1540 by Il Rosso, a Florentine follower of Michelangelo. In the wood panelling, François I's monogram appears repeatedly along with his emblem, a dragon-like salamander. The **Musée Chinois de l'Impératice Eugénie** (Chinese Museum of Empress Eugénie) consists of four drawing rooms created in 1863 for the Asian art and curios collected by Napoléon III's wife.

The **Salle de Bal**, a 30m-long ballroom dating from the mid-16th century that was also used for receptions and banquets, is renowned for its mythological frescoes, marquetry floor and Italian-inspired coffered ceiling. Its large windows afford views of the Cour Ovale (Oval Courtyard) and the gardens. The gilded bed in the 17th- and 18th-century **Chambre de l'Impératrice** (Empress' Bedroom) was never used by Marie Antoinette, for whom it was built in 1787. The gilding in the **Salle du Trône** (Throne Room), which was the royal bedroom before the Napoléonic period, is decorated in golds, greens and yellows.

As successive monarchs added their own wings to the château, five irregularly shaped courtyards were created. The oldest and most interesting is the **Cour Ovale** (Oval Courtyard), no longer oval but U-shaped due to Henri IV's construction work. It

incorporates the keep, the sole remnant of the medieval château. The largest courtyard is the **Cour du Cheval Blanc** (Courtyard of the White Horse), from where you enter the château. Napoléon, about to be exiled to Elba in 1814, bade farewell to his guards from the magnificent 17th-century double-horseshoe staircase here. For that reason the courtyard is also called the Cour des Adieux (Farewell Courtyard).

Château de Fontainebleau Gardens & Park GARDENS

(24hr) FREE On the northern side of the Château de Fontainebleau is the formal Jardin de Diane, created by Catherine de Médicis. Le Nôtre's formal, 17th-century Jardin Français (French Garden), also known as the Grand Parterre, is east of the Cour de la Fontaine (Fountain Courtyard) and the Étang des Carpes (Carp Pond). The informal Jardin Anglais (English Garden), laid out in 1812, is west of the pond. Excavated in 1609, the Grand Canal pre-dates the canals at Versailles by more than half a century.

Sleeping & Eating

For fabulous *fromageries* (cheese shops), head to rue des Sablons and rue Grande.

La Guérinière B&B €

(06 13 50 50 37; balestier.gerard@wanadoo.fr; 10 rue Montebello; d/f incl breakfast €70/€100;) This charming B&B provides some of the best-value accommodation in town. Owner Monsieur Balestier speaks English and has five en suite rooms, each named after a different flower and dressed in white linens and period furniture; some have wooden beams. Breakfast includes homemade jam and zesty marmalade. Two family rooms are available.

Dardonville PATISSERIE, BOULANGERIE €

(www.dardonville-fontainebleau.com; 24 rue des Sablons; 7am-1.30pm & 3.15-7.30pm Tue-Sat, 7am-1.30pm Sun) Melt-in-your-mouth macarons, in flavours like poppy seed and gingerbread, cost just €4.80 per dozen (per dozen!) at this beloved patisserie-*boulangerie* (bakery). Queues also form out the door for its amazing breads.

Crêperie Ty Koz CREPERIE €

(01 64 22 00 55; www.creperiety-koz.com; 18 rue de la Cloche; crêpes & galettes €3-12.80; noon-2pm & 7-10pm Tue-Thu, noon-2pm & 7-10.30pm Fri & Sat, noon-2pm Sun) Tucked away in an attractive courtyard, this Breton hidey-hole cooks up authentic sweet crêpes and *simple* (single thickness) and *pourleth* (double thickness) *galettes* (savoury buckwheat crêpes). Wash them down with traditional Val de Rance cider.

Le Ferrare BRASSERIE €

(01 60 72 37 04; 23 rue de France; 2-/3-course menus €12.30/13.90; 7.30am-4pm Mon, to 10.30pm Tue-Thu, to 1am Fri & Sat;) Locals pile into this quintessential bar-brasserie, which has a blackboard full of Auvergne specialities and bargain-priced *plats du jour* (daily specials; €10.80).

★L'Axel GASTRONOMIC €€

(01 64 22 01 57; www.laxel-restaurant.com; 43 rue de France; 3-/5-/7-course menus €33/55/90; 7.15-9.30pm Wed, 12.15-2pm & 7.15-9.30pm Thu-Sun) Chef Kunihisa Goto caught the atten-

FORÊT DE FONTAINEBLEAU

Beginning just 500m south of the Château de Fontainebleau and surrounding the town, the 200-sq-km Forêt de Fontainebleau (Fontainebleau Forest) is one of the prettiest woods in the region. The many trails – including parts of the **GR1** and **GR11** – are excellent for jogging, walking, cycling and horse riding; Fontainebleau's tourist office stocks maps and guides.

Rock-climbing enthusiasts have long come to the forest's sandstone ridges, rich in cliffs and overhangs, to hone their skills before setting off for the Alps. There are different grades marked by colours, starting with white ones, which are suitable for children, and going up to death-defying black boulders. The website Bleau.info (www.bleau.info) has stacks of information in English on climbing in Fontainebleau. Two gorges worth visiting are the **Gorges d'Apremont**, 7km northwest near Barbizon, and the **Gorges de Franchard**, a few kilometres south of Gorges d'Apremont. If you want to give climbing a go, contact **Top Loisirs** (01 60 74 08 50; www.toploisirs.fr; 1 rue de Montchavant, Ecuelles; 9am-6pm, hours can vary) about equipment hire and instruction; pick-ups in Fontainebleau are possible by arrangement. The tourist office also sells comprehensive climbing guides.

tion of foodies far and wide since opening here and he's since gained a Michelin star for his astonishing creations incorporating unlikely but ultimately amazing flavour combinations: sea urchin and black-truffle soup; sesame-crusted sweetbreads with langoustines; sea bass with coco beans, Iberian ham and chilli purée; and strawberries with shortbread and green-tea chiffon cake sorbet.

Information

Tourist Office (☎01 60 74 99 99; www.fontainebleau-tourisme.com; 4 rue Royale; ⊙10am-6pm Mon-Sat, 10am-1pm & 2-5pm Sun May-Oct, 10am-6pm Mon-Sat, 10am-1pm Sun Nov-Apr; 📶) In a converted petrol station west of the château, with information on the town and forest.

Getting There & Away

Importantly, train tickets to Fontainebleau/Avon are sold at Paris' Gare de Lyon's SNCF Transilien counter/Billet Ile-de-France machines, *not* SNCF mainline counters/machines. On returning to Paris, tickets include travel to any metro station.

Up to 40 daily SNCF Transilien (www.transilien.com) commuter trains link Paris' Gare de Lyon with Fontainebleau/Avon station (€8.85, 35 to 60 minutes).

Local bus line A links the train station with Château de Fontainebleau (€2), 2km southwest, every 10 minutes; the stop is opposite the main entrance.

Vaux-le-Vicomte

The privately owned **Château de Vaux-le-Vicomte** (☎01 64 14 41 90; www.vaux-le-vicomte.com; D215, Maincy; adult/child château & gardens €15.50/13.50, garden only €9.50/6, candlelight visits incl entry €19.50/17.50; ⊙10am-6pm Mar-early Nov, 11am-6.30pm Sat & Sun early Nov-Feb, candlelight visits 5-11pm Sat May-Sep) and its fabulous formal gardens, 20km north of Fontainebleau and 61km southeast of Paris, were designed and built by Le Brun, Le Vau and Le Nôtre between 1656 and 1661 as a precursor to their more ambitious work at Versailles.

The château's beautifully furnished interior is topped by a striking dome. Don't miss the stables' collection of 18th- and 19th-century carriages, or if at all possible, a candlelight visit.

During the same period as candlelight visits, there are elaborate jeux d'eau (fountain displays) in the gardens from 3pm to 6pm on the second and last Saturday of the month. In the vaulted cellars an exhibition looks at Le Nôtre's landscaping of the gardens.

The beauty of Vaux-le-Vicomte turned out to be the undoing of its original owner, Nicolas Fouquet, Louis XIV's minister of finance. It seems that Louis, seething that he'd been upstaged at the château's official opening, had Fouquet thrown into prison, where the unfortunate *ministre* died in 1680.

There are two on-site restaurants and a bar.

Getting There & Away

Vaux-le-Vicomte is not an easy place to reach by public transport. The château is 6km northeast of Melun and 15km southwest of Verneuil-l'Étang.

Melun is served by RER line D2 from Paris (€8.20, 30 minutes, frequent).

Trains link Paris' Gare de l'Est (direction Provins; €8.40, 35 minutes, hourly) to Verneuil-l'Étang, from where the **Châteaubus shuttle** (☎01 64 14 41 90; ⊙ adult/child return day €10/5, evening €25/20) runs to the Château de Vaux-le-Vicomte hourly from Easter to early November (20 minutes).

At other times you'll have to take a **taxi** (☎06 77 99 02 98; www.taxi-lionel-rozay-brie.fr). One-way day/evening prices are €15/26 from Melun, and €26/45 from Verneuil-l'Étang.

By car, follow the A6 from Paris and then the A5 (direction Melun), and take the 'St-Germain Laxis' exit. From Fontainebleau take the N6 and N36.

Chantilly

POP 11,368

The elegant old town of Chantilly, 50km north of Paris, is small and select. Its imposing, heavily restored château is surrounded by parkland, gardens and the Forêt de Chantilly, offering a wealth of walking opportunities. Chantilly's racetrack is one of the most prestigious hat-and-frock addresses in Europe, and deliciously sweetened thick *crème Chantilly* was created here.

Sights

Château de Chantilly CHÂTEAU
(☎03 44 27 31 80; www.domainedechantilly.com; domain pass adult/child €17/10, domain & show pass €30/22; ⊙10am-6pm Apr-Oct, 10.30am-5pm Wed-Mon Nov-Dec & Feb-Mar) A storybook vision amid an artificial lake and magnificent gardens, the Château de Chantilly contains a superb collection of paintings within the Musée Condé.

Left shambolic after the Revolution, the greatly restored château consists of two attached buildings, the Petit and Grand Châteaux, which are entered through the same

vestibule. The estate's Grandes Écuries are just west. A little train around the estate costs €5/3 per adult/child; four-person golf carts are also available for hire (€31 per hour).

The **Petit Château**, containing the Appartements des Princes (Princes' Suites), was built around 1560 for Anne de Montmorency (1492–1567), who served six French kings as *connétable* (high constable), diplomat and warrior, and died doing battle with Protestants in the Counter-Reformation. The highlight here is the **Cabinet des Livres**, a repository of 700 manuscripts and more than 30,000 volumes, including a Gutenberg Bible and a facsimile of the *Très Riches Heures du Duc de Berry,* an illuminated manuscript dating from the 15th century that illustrates the calendar year for both the peasantry and the nobility. The **chapel**, to the left as you walk into the vestibule, has woodwork and stained-glass windows dating from the mid-16th century.

The attached Renaissance-style **Grand Château**, completely demolished during the Revolution, was rebuilt by the Duke of Aumale, son of King Louis-Philippe, from 1875 to 1885. It contains the **Musée Condé**, a series of 19th-century rooms adorned with paintings and sculptures haphazardly arranged according to the whims of the duke – he donated the château to the Institut de France on the condition the exhibits were not reorganised and would remain open to the public. The most remarkable works, hidden in the Sanctuaire (Sanctuary), include paintings by Filippino Lippi, Jean Fouquet and (it's thought) Raphael. Guided tours (€45 minutes; €3) of the lavish Appartements Privés du Duc et de la Duchesse d'Aumale (the duke and duchess's private suites) are available in English by prior reservation.

Château de Chantilly Gardens GARDENS

(admission incl in domain pass, gardens & park only adult/child €8/5; ⌚10am-8pm Apr-Oct, 10.30am-6pm Wed-Mon Nov-Dec & Feb-Mar) The wondrous gardens of the Château de Chantilly encompass the formal Jardin Français (French Garden), with flowerbeds, lakes and a Grand Canal all laid out by Le Nôtre in the mid-17th century, northeast of the main building; and the 'wilder' Jardin Anglais (English Garden), begun in 1817, to the west. East of the Jardin Français is the rustic Jardin Anglo-Chinois (Anglo-Chinese Garden), created in the 1770s.

The foliage and silted-up waterways of the Jardin Anglo-Chinois surround the **hameau**, a mock village dating from 1774, whose mill and half-timbered buildings inspired the Hameau de la Reine (Queen's Hamlet) at Versailles. *Crème Chantilly* (sugar-whipped cream) was invented here.

Grandes Écuries STABLES

(Grand Stables; www.domainedechantilly.com; 7 rue du Connétable) The Grandes Écuries, built between 1719 and 1740 to house 240 horses and more than 400 hounds, stand west of the château near Chantilly's famous hippodrome (racecourse), inaugurated in 1834. The stables house the **Musée Vivant du Cheval** (Living Horse Museum; ☎03 44 27 31 80; ⌚10am-6pm Apr-Oct, 10.30am-5pm Wed-Mon Nov-Dec & Feb-Mar), included in domain-only and domain and show pass admissions. Displays range from riding equipment to rocking horses to artworks.

Every visitor, big and small, will be mesmerised by the one-hour **equestrian show** (adult/child €21/17.50; ⌚2.30pm Wed-Mon early Apr-late Oct), included in the combined domain and show pass.

The stables' pampered equines live in luxurious wooden stalls built by Louis-Henri de Bourbon, the seventh Prince de Condé, who was convinced he would be reincarnated as a horse (hence the extraordinary grandeur).

Forêt de Chantilly FOREST

Once a royal hunting estate, the 63-sq-km Forêt de Chantilly is criss-crossed by walking and riding trails. Long-distance trails here include the **GR11**, which links the Château de Chantilly with the town of **Senlis**; the **GR1**, from **Luzarches** (famed for its cathedral, parts of which date from the 12th century) to Ermenonville; and the **GR12**, which heads northeast from four lakes known as the Étangs de Commelles to the Forêt d'Halatte. Chantilly's tourist office stocks maps and guides.

Sleeping

La Ferme de la Canardière B&B €€

(☎03 44 62 00 96; www.fermecanardiere.com; 20 rue du Viaduc; s/d incl breakfast from €130/150; P 📶 🏊) Delicately embroidered cushions, country-style furnishings and a colour scheme of soft creams and beiges cast a romantic air over this family-run property, which is everything a French B&B should be. In summer allow plenty of time for breakfast on the terrace before plunging into the pool.

Hôtel de Londres HOTEL €€
(☎01 64 22 20 21; www.hoteldelondres.com; 1 place du Général de Gaulle; d €132-188; ❄@🛜) Classy, cosy and beautifully kept, the 16-room 'Hotel London' is furnished in warm reds and royal blues. The priciest rooms (eg room 5) have balconies with dreamy château views. Breakfast is €16.

Eating

Marché Decouvert MARKET €
(place Omer Vallon; ⊙8.30am-12.30pm Wed & Sat) Chantilly's twice-weekly open-air market is good for picking up picnic fare.

ID Cook L'Atelier Gourmand DELI €
(www.idcook-chantilly.fr; 78 rue du Connétable; ⊙10.30am-2pm & 4-8pm Tue-Fri, 10am-8pm Sat, 10.30am-1.30pm Sun) If it's not market day (and even if it is), this deli is a fabulous spot to pick up ingredients for a forest picnic. Charcuterie, smoked and marinated fish, foie gras, pre-made salads, preserves, cheeses, breads, chocolates, beer, wine and much more cram the shelves.

Le Café Noir CAFE €
(☎03 44 60 58 75; 5 place Omer Vallon; mains €9.50-16.50, 2-/3-course menus €19.50/25.50; ⊙kitchen noon-11.30pm Mon-Sat; 🛜👪) There's a terrace on the pavement out front of this sociable cafe but the best alfresco dining is in the umbrella-shaded cobbled courtyard. (If the weather's not behaving, head to the cherry-red skylit interior.) Dishes range from salmon in *beurre blanc* sauce to *entrecôte* with garlicky potato *dauphinoise*; lighter bites include salads, tartines and croques madame and monsieur.

Le Boudoir FRENCH €
(☎03 44 55 44 49; www.leboudoir-chantilly.fr; 100 rue du Connétable; lunch menu €11.50, dishes €4.50-10; ⊙11am-6pm Mon, 10am-7pm Tue-Sat, 11am-7pm Sun) As a certified partner of Parisian gourmet emporium Fauchon (p150), you can be sure of the quality at this charming tearoom. Strewn with comfy sofas, it's a perfect place to try *crème Chantilly* in all its decadence (on hot chocolate topped with lashings of the stuff) or to enjoy a light lunch (salads, savoury tarts and so on).

Le Vertugadin TRADITIONAL FRENCH €€
(☎03 44 57 03 19; www.vertugadin.com; 44 rue du Connétable; 3-course menu €32, mains €18-38; ⊙7.15-10pm Tue, noon-2pm & 7.15-10pm Wed-Sat, noon-2pm Sun) Old-style and elegant, this ode to regional cuisine – meat, game and terrines accompanied by sweet onion chutney; steak with foie gras and truffles with mashed potatoes and apple – fills a white-shuttered townhouse. A warming fire roars in the hearth in winter, and summer welcomes diners to the walled garden.

La Capitainerie TRADITIONAL FRENCH €€
(☎03 44 57 15 89; www.domainedechantilly.com; Château de Chantilly; 2-/3-course menus €28/32, mains €19-27, dishes €4-12.50; ⊙lunch noon-3pm, snacks noon-5.45pm Apr-Oct, lunch noon-3pm, snacks noon-4.45pm Wed-Mon Nov-Dec & Feb-Mar) Beneath the vaulted stone ceiling of the Château de Chantilly kitchens, La Capitainerie captures history's grandeur and romance. Fare is traditional and includes *crème Chantilly* at every opportunity.

CHÂTEAU DE WHIPPED CREAM

Like every self-respecting French château three centuries ago, the palace at Chantilly had its own *hameau* (hamlet) complete with *laitier* (dairy), where the lady of the household and her guests could play at being milkmaids. But the cows at the Chantilly dairy took their job rather more seriously than their fellow bovines at other faux *crémeries* (dairy shops), and the *crème Chantilly* served at the hamlet's teas became the talk (and envy) of aristocratic 18th-century Europe. The future Habsburg emperor Joseph II paid a clandestine visit to this '*temple de marbre*' (marble temple), as he called it, to taste it himself in 1777.

Chantilly (or more properly *crème Chantilly*) is whipped unpasteurised cream with a twist. It's beaten with icing and vanilla sugars to the consistency of a mousse and dolloped on berries.

Information

Tourist Office (☎03 44 67 37 37; www.chantilly-tourisme.com; 73 rue du Connétable; ⊙9.30am-12.30pm Tue, 9.30am-12.30pm & 1.30-5.30pm Mon & Wed-Sat) Can help with accommodation and has details of walks through town, along Chantilly's two canals and around the racecourse, as well as walking and mountain-bike trails in the forest.

Getting There & Away

Paris' Gare du Nord links with Chantilly-Gouvieux train station (€8.70, 25 to 40 minutes) by

DON'T MISS

THE HOLY VEIL

The most venerated object in Chartres' cathedral is the **Sainte Voile**, the 'Holy Veil' said to have been worn by the Virgin Mary when she gave birth to Jesus. It originally formed part of the imperial treasury of Constantinople but was offered to Charlemagne by the Empress Irene when the Holy Roman Emperor proposed marriage to her in 802. Charles the Bald presented it to the town in 876; the cathedral was built because the veil survived the 1194 fire.

hourly-or-better SNCF commuter trains. High-speed TGV trains are planned to arrive in 2020.

Driving from Paris, the fastest route is via the Autoroute du Nord (A1/E19); use exit 7 ('Survilliers-Chantilly'). The N1 then N16 from Porte de la Chapelle/St-Denis is cheaper.

Chartres

POP 40,216

Step off the train in Chartres, 91km southwest of Paris, and the two very different steeples – one Gothic, the other Romanesque – of its glorious 13th-century cathedral loom above. Follow them to check out the cathedral's dazzling blue stained-glass windows and its collection of relics, including the Sainte Voile (Holy Veil) said to have been worn by the Virgin Mary when she gave birth to Jesus, which have lured pilgrims since the Middle Ages.

After visiting the town's museums, don't miss a stroll around Chartres' carefully preserved old city. Adjacent to the cathedral, staircases and steep streets lined with half-timbered medieval houses lead downhill to the narrow western channel of the Eure River, romantically spanned by footbridges.

Sights

Allow 1½ to two hours to walk the signposted *circuit touristique* (tourist circuit) taking in Chartres' key sights. Free town maps from the tourist office also mark the route.

★**Cathédrale Notre Dame** CATHEDRAL
(www.cathedrale-chartres.org; place de la Cathédrale; ⏲8.30am-7.30pm daily, also to 10pm Tue, Fri & Sun Jun-Aug) One of Western civilisation's crowning architectural achievements, the 130m-long Cathédrale Notre Dame de Chartres is renowned for its brilliant-blue stained-glass windows and sacred holy veil. Built in the Gothic style during the first quarter of the 13th century to replace a Romanesque cathedral that had been devastated by fire – along with much of the town – in 1194, effective fundraising and donated labour meant construction took only 30 years, resulting in a high degree of architectural unity.

Today, it is France's best-preserved medieval cathedral, having been spared postmedieval modifications, the ravages of war and the Reign of Terror.

The cathedral's west, north and south entrances have superbly ornamented triple portals, but the west entrance, known as the **Portail Royal**, is the only one that predates the fire. Carved from 1145 to 1155, its superb statues, whose features are elongated in the Romanesque style, represent the glory of Christ in the centre, and the Nativity and the Ascension to the right and left, respectively. The structure's other main Romanesque feature is the 105m-high **Clocher Vieux** (Old Bell Tower), also called the Tour Sud (South Tower). Construction began in the 1140s; it remains the tallest Romanesque steeple still standing.

A visit to the 112m-high **Clocher Neuf** (New Bell Tower; adult/child €7.50/free; ⏲9.30am-12.30pm & 2-6pm Mon-Sat, 2-6pm Sun May-Aug, 9.30am-12.30pm & 2-5pm Mon-Sat, 2-5pm Sun Sep-Apr), also known as the Tour Nord (North Tower), is worth the ticket price and the climb up the long 350-step spiral stairway. Access is just behind the cathedral bookshop. A 70m-high platform on the lacy flamboyant Gothic spire, built from 1507 to 1513 by Jehan de Beauce after an earlier wooden spire burned down, affords superb views of the three-tiered flying buttresses and the 19th-century copper roof, turned green by verdigris.

The cathedral's 176 extraordinary stained-glass windows, almost all of which date back to the 13th century, form one of the most important ensembles of medieval stained glass in the world. The three most exquisite windows, dating from the mid-12th century, are in the wall above the west entrance and below the rose window. Survivors of the fire of 1194 (they were made some four decades before), the windows are revered for the depth and intensity of their tones, famously known as 'Chartres blue'.

In Chartres since 876, the venerated **Sainte Voile** (Holy Veil) – a yellowish bolt of

silk draped over a support, which is believed to have been worn by the Virgin Mary when she gave birth to Jesus – is displayed at the end of the cathedral's north aisle behind the choir.

The cathedral's 110m **crypt** (adult/child €3/2.40; ⌚up to 5 tours daily), a tombless Romanesque structure built in 1024 around a 9th-century predecessor, is the largest in France. Thirty-minute tours in French

Chartres

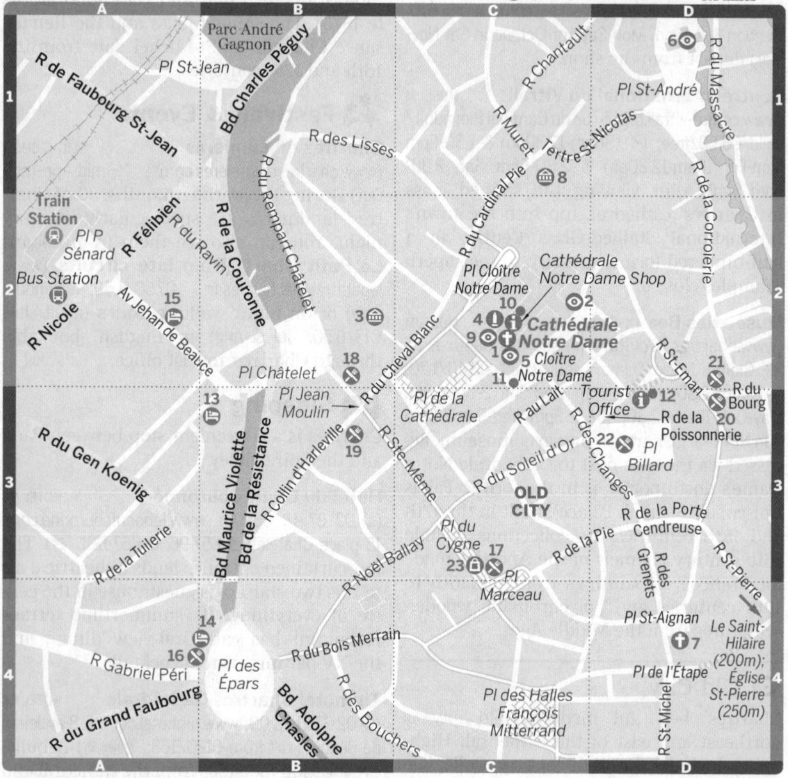

Chartres

Top Sights
1 Cathédrale Notre Dame C2

Sights
2 Cathédrale Notre Dame Crypt C2
3 Centre International du Vitrail B2
4 Clocher Neuf C2
5 Clocher Vieux C2
6 Collégiale St-André D1
7 Église St-Aignan D4
8 Musée des Beaux-Arts C1
9 Portail Royal C2

Activities, Courses & Tours
10 Cathédrale Notre Dame Tours C2
11 Le Petit Chart' Train C2
12 Night Walking Tours D3

Sleeping
13 Hôtel du Bœuf Couronné B3
14 Le Grand Monarque B4
15 Timhotel Chartres Cathédrale A2

Eating
16 Georges A4
17 La Chocolaterie C3
18 La Passacaille B2
19 Le Tripot B3
20 Les Feuillantines D3
21 L'Escalier D2
22 Marché Couvert D3

Shopping
23 Flower Market C3

(with a written English translation) start at the cathedral-run **shop** (☎02 37 21 59 08; ⊙8.30am-7.30pm) selling souvenirs, from April to October. At other times they begin at the shop below the Clocher Neuf in the cathedral.

Guided tours of the cathedral, in English, with Chartres expert **Malcolm Miller** (☎02 37 28 15 58; millerchartres@aol.com; tours €10; ⊙noon & 2.45pm Mon-Sat Apr-Oct, noon Sat Nov-Mar) depart from the shop.

Centre International du Vitrail MUSEUM
(www.centre-vitrail.org; 5 rue du Cardinal Pie; adult/child €6.50/free; ⊙9.30am-12.30pm & 1.30-6pm Mon-Fri, 10am-12.30pm & 2.30-6pm Sat, 2.30-6pm Sun) After viewing the stained glass in Chartres' cathedral, nip into the town's International Stained-Glass Centre, in a half-timbered former granary, to see superb examples close up.

Musée des Beaux-Arts MUSEUM
(www.chartres.fr/culture/musee-des-beaux-arts; 29 Cloître Notre Dame; adult/child €3.40/1.70; ⊙10am-12.30pm & 2-6pm Wed-Sat, 2-6pm Sun May-Oct, 10am-12.30pm & 2-5pm Wed-Sat, 2-5pm Sun Nov-Mar) Chartres' fine-arts museum, accessed via the gate next to Cathédrale Notre Dame's north portal, is in the former Palais Épiscopal (Bishop's Palace), built in the 17th and 18th centuries. Its collections include 16th-century enamels of the Apostles made for François I, paintings from the 16th to 19th centuries and polychromatic wooden sculptures from the Middle Ages.

Old City

Chartres' beautiful medieval old city is northeast and east of the cathedral. Highlights include the 12th-century Collégiale St-André (place St-André), a Romanesque church that's now an exhibition centre; rue de la Tannerie and its extension rue de la Foulerie, lined with flower gardens, mill-races and the restored remnants of riverside trades: wash houses, tanneries and the like; and rue des Écuyers, with many structures dating from around the 16th century.

Église St-Pierre CHURCH
(place St-Pierre; ⊙10am-5pm) Flying buttresses hold up the 12th- and 13th-century Église St-Pierre. Once part of a Benedictine monastery founded in the 7th century, it was outside the city walls and thus vulnerable to attack; the fortress-like, pre-Romanesque bell tower attached to it was used as a refuge by monks, and dates from around 1000. The fine, brightly coloured clerestory windows in Église St-Pierre's nave, choir and apse date from the early 14th century.

Église St-Aignan CHURCH
(place St-Aignan; ⊙8.30am-6pm) Église St-Aignan is interesting for its wooden barrel-vault roof (1625), arcaded nave and painted interior of faded blue and gold floral motifs (c 1870). The stained glass and the Renaissance Chapelle de St-Michel date from the 16th and 17th centuries.

Festivals & Events

Chartres en Lumières LIGHT SHOW
(www.chartresenlumieres.com; ⊙mid-Apr–mid-Oct) During the warmer months, 30 of Chartres' landmarks are spectacularly lit every night. You can also see them from aboard **Le Petit Chart' Train late circuits** (www.lepetittraindechartres.fr; €7.50/4.50; ⊙hours vary) or on **night walking tours** (adult/child €13/6.50; Jul & Aug) in English, bookable through Chartres' tourist office.

Sleeping

Chartres is a convenient stop between Paris and the Loire Valley.

Hôtel du Bœuf Couronné HOTEL **€€**
(☎02 37 18 06 06; www.leboeufcouronne.com; 15 place Châtelet; s €57-96, d €67-121;) The red-curtained entrance lends a theatrical air to this two-star Logis guesthouse in the centre of everything. Its summertime terrace restaurant has cathedral-view dining and the XV bar mixes great cocktails.

Timhotel Chartres Cathédrale HOTEL **€€**
(☎02 37 21 78 00; www.timhotel.com; 6-8 av Jehan de Beauce; d/f from €120/168; P) A bulls-eye location footsteps from the cathedral and train station, 48 rooms (some with cathedral views) and on-site parking make this hotel a winning trifecta. Staff are welcoming, rooms are spacious and there's a small, private rear terrace. Breakfast costs €15. Rates are up to 50% cheaper on the hotel's website.

Le Grand Monarque HOTEL **€€€**
(☎02 37 18 15 15; www.bw-grand-monarque.com; 22 place des Épars; d €145-215, f €275; @) With teal-blue shutters gracing its 1779 façade, stained-glass ceiling and treasure trove of period furnishings and old photos, the refurbished Grand Monarque (with air-con in some rooms) is a historical gem and very central. Hydrotherapy treatments are available at its spa and its restaurant, Georges, has a Michelin star. Staff are charming.

Eating

Marché Couvert MARKET €

(place Billard; 7am-1pm Wed & Sat) Food shops surround the covered market, just off rue des Changes south of the cathedral. The market itself dates from the early 20th century.

La Passacaille ITALIAN €

(02 37 21 52 10; www.lapassacaille.fr; 30 rue Ste-Même; 2-/3-course menus €16.80/19.80, pizzas €11.70-15.20, pasta €10.50-15.50; 11.45am-2pm & 6.45-10pm Thu & Sun-Tue, 11.45am-2pm & 6.45-10.30pm Fri & Sat;) This welcoming spot has particularly good pizzas (try the Montagnarde with tomato, mozzarella, Reblochon cheese, potatoes, red onions, cured ham and *crème fraîche*) and homemade pasta with toppings including *pistou* (pesto) also made on the premises. Tables spill onto the square out front in summer.

La Chocolaterie PATISSERIE €

(www.lachocolaterie-chartres.com; 2 place du Cygne; dishes €3.80-5.50; 8am-7.30pm Tue-Sat, 10am-7.30pm Sun & Mon) Soak up local life overlooking the open-air **flower market** (8am-1pm Tue, Thu & Sat). This tearoom/patisserie's hot chocolate and macarons (flavoured with orange, apricot, peanut, pineapple and so on) are sublime, as are its sweet homemade crêpes and miniature madeleine cakes.

★ **Le Tripot** BISTRO €€

(02 37 36 60 11; www.letripot.wixsite.com/chartres; 11 place Jean Moulin; 2-/3-course lunch menus €15/18, 3-course dinner menus €29.50-45, mains €13.50-22; noon-1.45pm & 7.30-9.15pm Tue & Thu-Sat, noon-1.45pm Sun) Tucked off the tourist trail and easy to miss, even if you do chance down its narrow street, this atmospheric space with low beamed ceilings is a treat for authentic and adventurous French fare like saddle of rabbit stuffed with snails, and grilled turbot in truffled hollandaise sauce. Locals are onto it, so book ahead.

Les Feuillantines MODERN FRENCH €€

(02 37 30 22 21; 4 rue du Bourg; menus €23.50-33.50, mains €19-22; noon-1.30pm & 7-9.30pm Tue-Sat) Take a seat in the sleek interior or under a market umbrella in the rear courtyard to dine on superb dishes such as sea bream with potatoes and tomato emulsion, bacon-wrapped veal with lentils, roast duck with butternut squash and cider *jus*, before finishing with its house-specialty chocolate sphere served with orange sorbet and sweet Chantilly cream.

L'Escalier BISTRO €€

(02 37 33 05 45; 1 rue du Bourg; 2-/3-course menus €18/22; noon-3pm & 7-10pm;) On a steep corner near its namesake staircase in Chartres' hilly old city, this deceptively large, very local restaurant has a wonderful terrace for summertime dining and is worth the pre- or post-meal climb for its short but superb menu (foie gras platters, succulent steaks and classic desserts like crème caramel). Look out for live jazz performances.

Le Saint-Hilaire MODERN FRENCH €€

(02 37 30 97 57; www.restaurant-saint-hilaire.fr; 11 rue du Pont St-Hilaire; 3-course menus €29.50-49; noon-2pm & 7-9.30pm Tue-Sat) At this pistachio-painted, wood-beamed charmer, local products are ingeniously used in dishes such as scallops in hazelnut and foie gras sauce. Don't miss its lobster menu in season, or the aromatic cheese platters any time of year. A two-course lunch menu from Tuesday to Friday costs €19.

Georges GASTRONOMIC €€€

(02 37 18 15 15; www.bw-grand-monarque.com; 22 place des Épars; 4-course menu from €75, 8-course tasting menu €95, mains €38-41; noon-2pm & 7.30-10pm Tue-Sat) Even if you're not staying at the lavish hotel Le Grand Monarque, its refined Georges restaurant is worth seeking out for its Michelin-starred multicourse menus and mains such as ginger-marinated salmon with pickled veggies and crustacean bouillon, or blackberry-marinated roast lamb with chestnut purée and green beans. Desserts (confit of grapefruit with Campari gelato, for instance) are inspired.

Information

Tourist Office (02 37 18 26 26; www.chartres-tourisme.com; 8-10 rue de la Poissonnerie; 10am-6pm Mon-Sat, to 5pm Sun) Housed in the historic Maison du Saumon, with an exhibition on Chartres' history. Rents 1½-hour English-language audioguide tours (€5.50/8.50 for one/two) of the medieval city as well as binoculars (€2), fabulous for seeing details of the cathedral close up.

Getting There & Away

Frequent SNCF trains link Paris' Gare Montparnasse (€16, 55 to 70 minutes) with Chartres, some of which stop at Versailles-Chantiers (€13.50, 45 to 60 minutes). The bus station is next to the train station.

If you're driving from Paris, follow the A6 from Porte d'Orléans (direction Bordeaux–Nantes), then the A10 and A11 (direction Nantes) and take the 'Chartres' exit.

Lille, Flanders & the Somme

POP 5.97 MILLION

Includes ➡

Best Places to Eat

- Meert (p183)
- La Sirène (p191)
- La Marie Galante (p191)
- Het Kasteelhof (p188)

Best Places to Sleep

- Hôtel Marotte (p206)
- L'Hermitage Gantois (p183)
- La Corne d'Or (p189)
- Les Tourelles (p198)

Why Go?

True, a tan is easier to come by along the Mediterranean, but when it comes to culture, cuisine, beer, shopping and dramatic views of land and sea – not to mention good old-fashioned friendliness – the home territories of the Ch'tis (residents of France's northern tip) and the Picards compete with the best France has to offer. In Lille and French Flanders, a down-to-earth Flemish vibe mixes easily with French sophistication and savoir faire. In Picardy and the Somme, WWI memorials and cemeteries marking the front lines of 1914 to 1918 often render visitors speechless with their heartbreaking beauty. Nearby, the underrated cities of Arras, Amiens and Laon captivate with their Gothic and Flemish architectural treasures, while the hearts of nature lovers will soar along the sublime Côte d'Opale and the estuaries of the Baie de Somme. Just outside greater Paris, Compiègne preserves the dazzle of Napoléon III's Second Empire.

When to Go

Lille

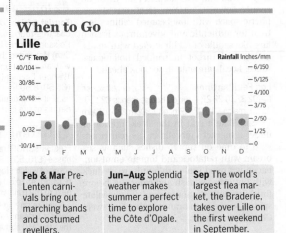

Feb & Mar Pre-Lenten carnivals bring out marching bands and costumed revellers.

Jun–Aug Splendid weather makes summer a perfect time to explore the Côte d'Opale.

Sep The world's largest flea market, the Braderie, takes over Lille on the first weekend in September.

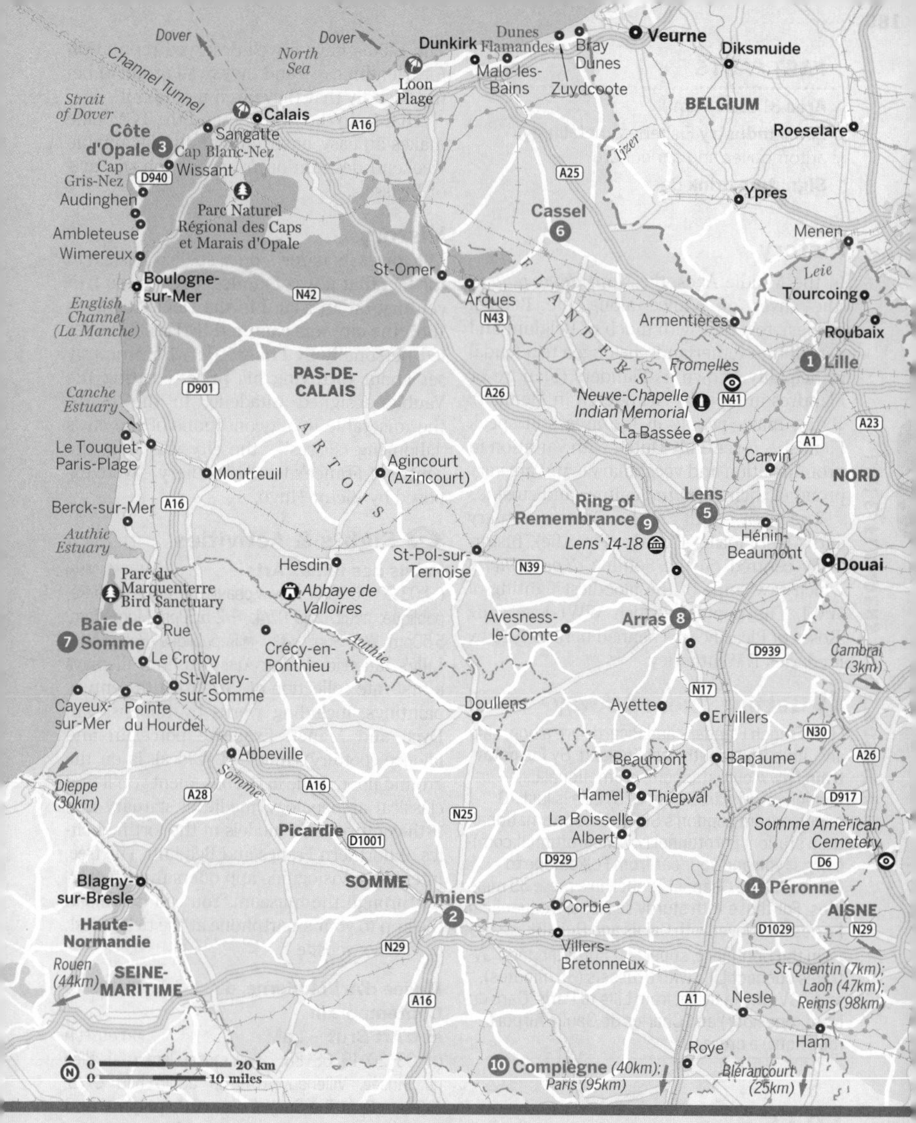

Lille, Flanders & the Somme Highlights

1 Lille's old town (p181) Exploring centuries-old alleyways and chic boutiques

2 Amiens (p205) Marvelling at the Gothic cathedral.

3 Côte d'Opale (p190) Rambling the spectacular, windswept coast.

4 Historial de la Grande Guerre (p200) Pondering the horror of WWI in Péronne.

5 Louvre-Lens museum (p190) Immersing yourself in 5000 years of civilisation at this innovative museum.

6 Cassel (p187) Enjoying Flemish landscapes, architecture and cuisine in this pretty hilltop town.

7 Baie de Somme (p197) Touring this magical area and spotting seals on sandbanks.

8 Arras (p188) Joining the bustle of the Saturday market at gorgeous Place des Héros.

9 Ring of Remembrance memorial (p202) Reflecting on the human price of WWI's hellish Western Front.

10 Compiègne (p208) Revelling in elegant architecture and fine food.

FAST FACTS

Area 31,813 sq km

Local industry Fisheries, metallurgy, automobiles and agriculture

Signature drink Beer

History

In the Middle Ages, the Nord *département* (the sliver of France along the Belgian border), together with much of Belgium and part of the Netherlands, belonged to a feudal principality known as Flanders (Flandre or Flandres in French, Vlaanderen in Flemish). Today, many people in the area still speak Flemish – essentially Dutch with variation in pronunciation and vocabulary – and are very proud of their *flamand* culture and cuisine.

The area south of the Somme estuary and Albert forms Picardy (Picardie), historically centred on the Somme *département*, which saw some of the bloodiest fighting of WWI. The popular British WWI love song 'Roses of Picardy' was penned here in 1916 by Frederick E Weatherley.

Getting There & Away

Lille, French Flanders and Picardy are a hop, skip and jump from southwest England. By **Eurostar train** (www.eurostar.com; promotional Lille–London return fares from €78) Lille is just 70 minutes from London's St Pancras International train station. Eurotunnel (www.eurotunnel.com) can get you and your car from Folkestone to Calais, via the Channel Tunnel, in a mere 35 minutes. For those with sturdy sea legs, frequent car ferries link Dover with Calais and Dunkirk.

On the Continent, superfast Eurostar and TGV trains connect Lille with Brussels (35 minutes), and TGVs make travel from Lille to Paris' Gare du Nord (one hour) and Charles de Gaulle Airport (one hour) a breeze.

LILLE

POP 231,500

Lille (Rijsel in Flemish) may be France's most underrated major city. In recent decades this once-grimy industrial metropolis, its economy based on declining industries, has transformed itself into a glittering and self-confident cultural and commercial hub. Highlights for the visitor include an attractive old town with a strong Flemish accent, three renowned art museums, stylish shopping, some excellent dining options and a cutting-edge, student-driven nightlife scene. The Lillois have a well-deserved reputation for friendliness – and they're so proud of being friendly that they often mention it!

Thanks to the Eurostar and the TGV, Lille makes an easy, environmentally sustainable weekend destination from London or Paris or Brussels.

History

Lille owes its name – once spelled L'Isle – to the fact that it was founded, back in the 11th century, on an island in the Deûle River. In 1667, the city was captured by French forces led personally by Louis XIV, who promptly set about fortifying his prize, creating the Vauban-designed Citadelle. In the 1850s, the miserable living conditions of the city's 'labouring classes' – the city was long the centre of France's textile industry – were exposed by Victor Hugo.

Sights & Activities

Palais des Beaux Arts ART MUSEUM

(☎03 20 06 78 00; www.pba-lille.fr; place de la République; adult/child €7/4; ⏲2-5.50pm Mon, 10am-5.50pm Wed-Sun; 👪; Ⓜ République Beaux-Arts) Lille's illustrious Fine Arts Museum displays a first-rate collection of 15th- to 20th-century paintings, including works by Rubens, Van Dyck and Manet. Exquisite porcelain and faience (pottery), much of it local, is on the ground floor, while in the basement you'll find classical archaeology, medieval statuary and 18th-century scale models of the fortified cities of northern France and Belgium. The free, interactive Visioguide app offers five itineraries through the museum. You can download the app to your smartphone at the ticket desk or via the website.

Musée d'Art Moderne, d'Art Contemporain et d'Art Brut – LaM ART MUSEUM

(☎03 20 19 68 88; www.musee-lam.fr; 1 allée du Musée, Villeneuve-d'Ascq; adult/child €7/5; ⏲10am-6pm Tue-Sun) Colourful, playful and just plain weird works of modern and contemporary art by masters such as Braque, Calder, Léger, Miró, Modigliani and Picasso are the big draw at this renowned museum and sculpture park in the Lille suburb of Villeneuve-d'Ascq, 9km east of Gare Lille-Europe. Take metro line 1 to Pont de Bois, then bus L4 six stops to 'LAM'.

La Piscine Musée d'Art et d'Industrie ART MUSEUM

(☎03 20 69 23 60; www.roubaix-lapiscine.com; 23 rue de l'Espérance, Roubaix; adult/child €5.50/

free; ⏲11am-6pm Tue-Thu, 11am-8pm Fri, 1-6pm Sat & Sun; Ⓜ Gare Jean Lebas) If Paris can turn an outmoded train station into a world-class museum (the Musée d'Orsay), why not transform an art-deco municipal swimming pool (built 1927–32) – an architectural masterpiece inspired by a combination of civic pride and hygienic high-mindedness – into a temple of the arts? This innovative museum, 12km northeast of Gare Lille-Europe in Roubaix, showcases fine arts (paintings, sculptures, drawings) and applied arts (furniture, textiles, fashion) in a delightfully watery environment.

Wazemmes AREA
(Ⓜ Gambetta) For an authentic taste of grass-roots Lille, head to the ethnically mixed, family-friendly *quartier populaire* (working-class quarter) of Wazemmes, 1.7km southwest of place du Général de Gaulle, where old-school proletarians and immigrants from Africa live harmoniously alongside penurious students and trendy *bobos* (bourgeois bohemians).

The neighbourhood's focal point is the cavernous Marché de Wazemmes, Lille's favourite food market. The adjacent outdoor market is the place to be on Sunday morning – it's a real carnival scene! Rue des Sarrazins and rue Jules Guesde are lined with shops, restaurants and Tunisian pastry places, many owned by, and catering to, the area's North African residents.

Wazemmes is famed for its outdoor concerts and street festivals, including La Louche d'Or (The Golden Ladle; 1 May), a soup festival that has spread to cities across Europe.

Maison Natale de Charles de Gaulle MUSEUM
(☎03 59 73 00 30; www.maison-natale-de-gaulle.org; 9 rue Princesse; adult/child incl audioguide €6/free; ⏲10am-noon & 2-5pm Wed-Sat, 1.30-5pm Sun) The upper-middle-class house in which Charles de Gaulle was born in 1890 is now a museum, run by the Nord *département*, presenting the French leader in the context of his times, with an emphasis on his connection to French Flanders. Displays include de Gaulle's dainty baptismal robe and some evocative newsreels.

Musée de l'Hospice Comtesse ART MUSEUM
(☎03 28 36 84 00; 32 rue de la Monnaie; adult/child €3.60/free, audioguide €2; ⏲2-6pm Mon, 10am-6pm Wed-Sun) Housed in a remarkably attractive 15th- and 17th-century poorhouse, this museum features ceramics, earthenware wall tiles, religious art, 17th- and 18th-century paintings and furniture, and a new exhibit on the history of Lille. A rood screen separates the Salle des Malades (Hospital Hall) from a mid-17th-century chapel (look up to see a mid-19th-century painted ceiling).

Citadelle FORTRESS
(https://citadellelille.fr; Vauban-Esquermes quarter; 🚌12) At the northwestern end of bd de la Liberté, this massive, star-shaped fortress was designed by renowned 17th-century French military architect Vauban after France captured Lille in 1667. Made of some 60 million bricks, it now serves as the headquarters of the 12-nation, NATO-certified Rapid Reaction Corps – France. Outside the 2.2km-long ramparts is central Lille's largest public park – children will love the playground, amusement park and small zoo (free).

Tours

The tourist office (p186) runs a variety of guided tours.

Citadelle Walking Tour WALKING
(av du 43e Régiment d'Infanterie; €7.50; ⏲3pm & 4.30pm Sun Jun-Aug, 3rd Sun of month Sep-May; 🚌12) The only way to see the inside of the Citadelle, usually a closed military zone, is to take a one-hour tour (in French); sign up at the tourist office up to seven days ahead and bring a passport or national ID card. Tours begin at the Citadelle's main entrance, the Porte Royale.

Vieux Lille Walking Tour WALKING
(☎03 59 57 94 00; www.lilletourism.com; adult/child €11.50/9.50; ⏲in English 10.15am Sat, in French 3pm daily) Takes in the highlights of Lille's 17th- and 18th-century old town. Reservations and departures at the tourist office.

Flanders Battlefields Tour BATTLEFIELD TOUR
(☎03 59 57 94 00; www.lilletourism.com; €69; ⏲1-6pm Sat Apr-Oct, Wed-Sat Nov-Mar) Takes you to Fromelles' museum and Australian

LILLE CITY PASS

Available in versions valid for 24/48/72 hours (€25/35/45), the **Lille City Pass** gets you into almost all the museums in greater Lille and affords unlimited use of public transport. The 72-hour option throws in sites around the Nord-Pas de Calais *région*, including Arras, Dunkirk and Cassel, and free use of regional TER trains for 24 hours. Available at the Lille tourist office or through its website.

Lille

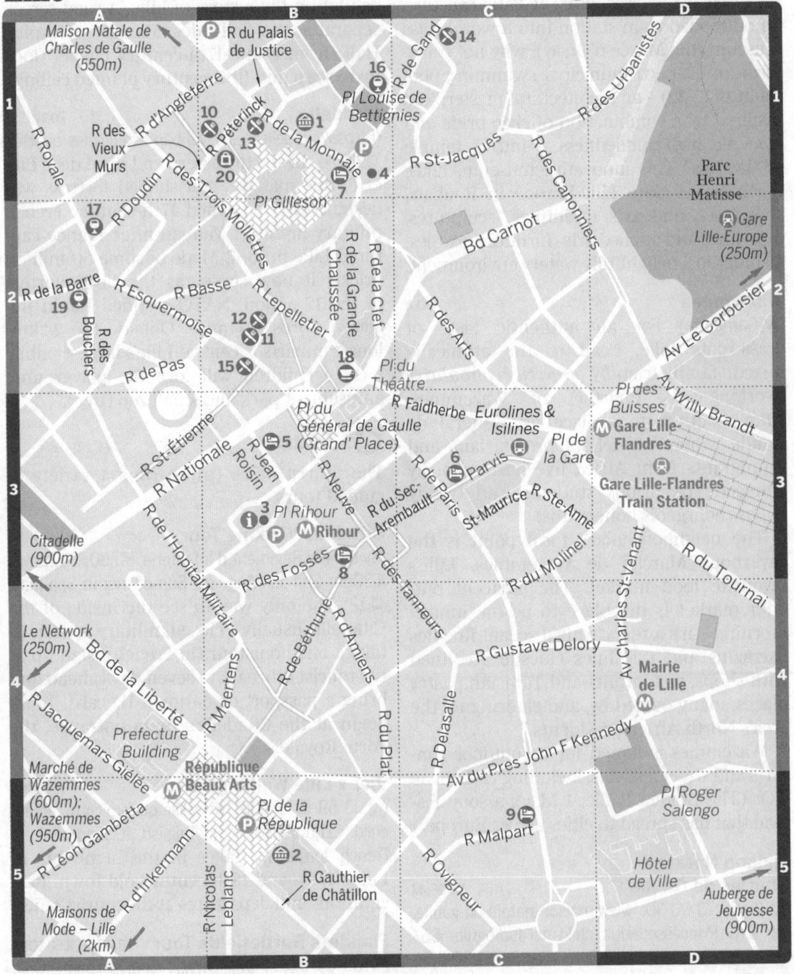

memorials and the Belgian city of Ypres. Tours depart from the tourist office, which handles reservations.

Festivals & Events

Marché de Noël CHRISTMAS MARKET

(www.noel-a-lille.com; place Rihour; late Nov-30 or 31 Dec) In the lead-up to Christmas, decorations and edible goodies are sold at the Marché de Noël.

Sleeping

At most hotels, room rates drop significantly on Friday, Saturday and Sunday nights and during French school holidays, including July and August.

Auberge de Jeunesse HOSTEL €

(03 20 57 08 94; www.hifrance.org; 235 bd Paul Painlevé; dm incl breakfast & sheets €25; ; MPorte de Valenciennes) The good news is that Lille has a youth hostel, opened in 2015, with a façade sporting the colours of Europe. The bad news is that while all 55 rooms have showers, only 12 have attached toilets, and instead of faucets the showers have annoying timer-buttons. Wi-fi is available in the lobby.

Furnishings are spartan, with metal bunk beds, foam mattresses and American-high-

Lille

school-style lockers. Situated 1.7km south-east of Gare Lille-Flandres.

Grand Hôtel Bellevue HISTORIC HOTEL €€
(☎03 20 57 45 64; www.grandhotelbellevue.com; 5 rue Jean Roisin; d €100-200; ❄@📶; Ⓜ Rihour) Opened in 1913, this grand establishment has 60 spacious rooms with high ceilings, all-marble bathrooms, gilded picture frames and a mix of inlaid-wood antiques and ultra-modern furnishings. For an extra €20 you can have fine views of place du Général de Gaulle – a bargain! Doubles as the honorary consulate of Brazil.

Hotel Kanaï HOTEL €€
(☎03 20 57 14 78; www.hotelkanai.com; 10 rue de Béthune; d €70-170; ❄@📶; Ⓜ Rihour) In the heart of the city centre's pedestrian zone, this hotel has 31 modern rooms in brown, white and prune. All come with coffee makers, attractive tiled bathrooms, crisp linen and excellent bedding; *Privilège* rooms are quite spacious. Breakfast includes fresh-squeezed orange juice, a nice touch. No lift. The entrance is on rue de la Vieille Comédie.

Hôtel de la Treille HOTEL €€
(☎03 20 55 45 46; www.hoteldelatreille.com; 7-9 place Louise de Bettignies; d €90-140; 📶) In a superb spot smack in the middle of Vieux Lille, a few steps from dining and shopping options galore. The 42 stylish rooms, totally redecorated in 2014, offer views of the lively square out front, the cathedral or a quiet interior courtyard.

Hôtel Brueghel HOTEL €€
(☎03 20 06 06 69; www.hotel-brueghel-lille.com; 5 parvis St-Maurice; d €98-150 Mon-Thu, €82-110 Fri-Sun; 📶; Ⓜ Gare Lille-Flandres) The wood-panelled lobby has charm in spades, as does the tiny, old-fashioned lift that trundles guests up to 62 quiet rooms with modern furnishings and art posters on the walls. Some south-facing rooms have sunny views of the adjacent church.

★ **L'Hermitage Gantois** HOTEL €€€
(☎03 20 85 30 30; www.hotelhermitagegantois.com; 224 rue de Paris; d €170-434; P@📶🏊; Ⓜ Mairie de Lille) This five-star hotel creates enchanting, harmonious spaces by complementing its rich architectural heritage, such as the Flemish-Gothic façade, with refined ultramodernism. The 89 rooms are sumptuous, with Starck accessories alongside Louis XV–style chairs and bathrooms that sparkle with Carrara marble. The still-consecrated chapel dates from 1637; a 12m pool and *hammam* opened in 2015.

Eating

Lille has a flourishing culinary scene. Keep an eye out for *estaminets* (traditional Flemish eateries, with antique knick-knacks on the walls and plain wooden tables) serving Flemish specialities.

Dining hot spots in Vieux Lille include rue de Gand, home to small, moderately priced French and Flemish restaurants, and rue de la Monnaie and its side streets, alleys and courtyards.

★ **Meert** PATISSERIE €
(☎03 20 57 93 93; www.meert.fr; 27 rue Esquermoise; waffles from €3; ⏲ shop 9.30am-7.30pm Tue-Sat, 9am-1pm & 3-7pm Sun, tearoom 9.30am-10pm Tue-Sat, 9am-6pm Sun; 📶; Ⓜ Rihour) Famed for its *gaufres* (waffles) made with Madagascar

vanilla, Meert has served kings, viceroys and generals since 1761. The sumptuous chocolate shop's coffered ceiling, painted wooden panels, wrought-iron balcony and mosaic floor date from 1839. Inside, the historic *salon de thé* is a delightful spot for a morning Arabica or a mid-afternoon tea. Also has a French gourmet restaurant.

Le Bistrot Lillois FLEMISH €

(☎03 20 14 04 15; 40 rue de Gand; mains €12.50-15.20; ⏲noon-2pm & 7.30-10pm Tue-Sat) Dishes both Flemish and French are served here under hanging hops. The highlight of the menu is *os à moëlle* (marrow bone); Flemish dishes worth trying include *carbonade flamande* (braised beef slow-cooked with beer, onions, brown sugar and ginger bread) and *potjevleesch* (jellied chicken, pork, veal and rabbit; served cold). Call ahead for dinner, or arrive promptly at 7.30pm.

La Petite Table MODERN FRENCH €

(☎03 20 55 60 47; www.lapetitetable-vieuxlille.com; 59 rue de la Monnaie; mains €11.20-15.80; ⏲noon-2.30pm Tue-Sun, 7.30-10pm or 10.30pm Tue-Sat; Wi-Fi) Inspired by the 34 countries he visited during nine years in the French navy, chef Arnaud Duhamel – a Lonely Planet fan – prepares both Flemish favourites and dishes inspired by the tastes he encountered in the Americas, Africa and around the Indian Ocean. A favourite of locals in search of good value.

Au Vieux de la Vieille FLEMISH €

(☎03 20 13 81 64; www.estaminetlille.fr; 2-4 rue des Vieux Murs; mains €12-15; ⏲noon-2pm & 7-10pm daily, to 10.30pm Fri & Sat; Wi-Fi) Hops hang from the rafters at this *estaminet*, where specialities include *carbonade flamande* and *Welsh au Maroilles* (toast and ham smothered with Maroilles cheese melted in beer). From about March to October, there's outdoor seating on picturesque place aux Oignons.

Le Comptoir 44 NEOBISTRO €

(☎03 20 21 03 63; www.comptoir44-lille.fr; 44 rue de Gand; 2-/3-course lunch menus €19/24, dinner menus €32; ⏲noon-2.30pm & 7-10.30pm; Wi-Fi) Prepared according to the motto *'La bonne cuisine est honnête, sincère et simple'* (Good food is honest, sincere and simple), the dishes on offer at this rustic-chic bistro change every two or three months as *produits du saison* (seasonal products) become available. Dining here is like eating *chez grand-mère* (at grandma's house).

La Petite Cour FLEMISH €

(☎03 20 51 52 81; www.lapetitecour-lille.fr; 17 rue du Curé St-Étienne; lunch menus €16-19, dinner menus €29; ⏲noon-2pm & 7.30-10.30pm Mon-Thu, to 11.30pm Fri & Sat; Wi-Fi; Ⓜ Rihour) Serves a tempting array of both Belgian- and French-Flemish staples, meat and fish dishes and salads, in either the atmospheric, brick-walled dining room or the lovely inner courtyard. The menu changes frequently according to what's available fresh in the markets.

Self-Catering

Marché de Wazemmes MARKET €

(place de la Nouvelle Aventure; ⏲9am-1pm Tue-Thu, 9am-7pm Fri & Sat, 7am-2pm Sun & holidays; Ⓜ Gambetta) This beloved foodie space is 1.7km southwest of the tourist office in the working-class quarter of Wazemmes. Open-air stalls add to the fun on Tuesday, Thursday and especially Sunday from 7am to 1pm.

Fromagerie Philippe Olivier CHEESE €

(☎03 20 74 96 99; www.philippeolivier.fr; 3 rue du Curé St-Étienne; ⏲2.30-7.15pm Mon, 9am or 10am-7.15pm Tue-Sat; Ⓜ Rihour) An excellent source of perfectly aged cheeses.

Drinking & Nightlife

The small, stylish venues along rue Royale and rue de la Barre are popular with chic 30-somethings. A university-age crowd descends on the bars along rue Masséna (750m southwest of the tourist office) and rue Solférino, as far southeast as Marché Sébastopol. In warm weather, cafes in place du Général de Gaulle and place du Théâtre are fine spots to sip beer.

L'Illustration Café BAR

(☎03 20 12 00 90; 18 rue Royale; ⏲12.30pm-1am Mon-Wed, 12.30pm-3am Thu & Fri, 3pm-3am Sat, 3pm-1am Sun) Adorned with art-nouveau woodwork and changing exhibits by local painters, this laid-back bar attracts artists, musicians, budding intellectuals and teachers in the mood to read, exchange weighty ideas or just shoot the breeze. The mellow soundtrack mixes jazz, blues, indie rock, French *chansons* and African and Cuban beats. Check the Facebook page for details on concerts.

Morel & Fils CAFE

(31-33 place du Théâtre; ⏲9am-11pm Mon-Sat, 2-8pm Sun; Ⓜ Rihour) This chic cafe-brasserie, renovated in 2016, incorporates eclectic ornamentation from its former life as a lingerie shop founded way back in 1813. In the

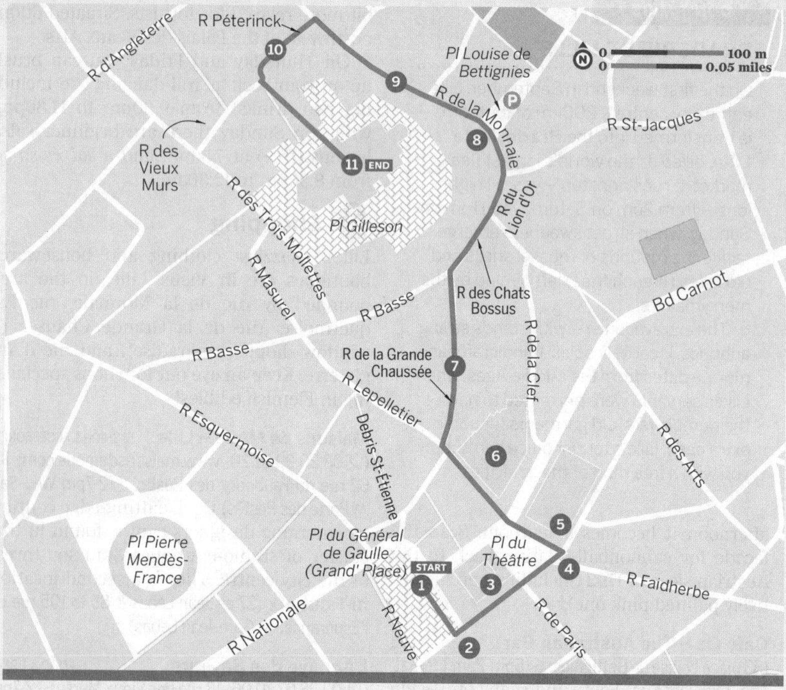

Walking Tour
Lille Discovery Stroll

START PLACE DU GÉNÉRAL DE GAULLE
END CATHÉDRALE NOTRE-DAME-DE-LA-TREILLE
LENGTH 1KM; ONE HOUR

The best place to begin a discovery stroll through Lille's Flemish heart is the city's focal point, 1 **place du Général de Gaulle** (the Grand' Place), where you can admire the 1932 art-deco home of 2 **La Voix du Nord** (the leading regional newspaper), crowned by a gilded sculpture of the Three Graces. The goddess-topped victory column (1845) in the fountain commemorates the city's successful resistance to the Austrian siege of 1792. On warm evenings, Lillois come here to stroll, take in the urban vibe and sip a strong local beer. The adjacent 3 **Vieille Bourse** (old stock exchange), ornately decorated with caryatids and cornucopia, is a Flemish Renaissance extravaganza. Built in 1653, it consists of 24 separate houses set around a richly ornamented interior courtyard that hosts a used-book market. In the afternoon, locals gather here to play *échecs* (chess). Just east of the Vieille Bourse, impressive 4 **place du Théâtre** is dominated by the Louis XVI–style 5 **Opéra** and the neo-Flemish 6 **Chambre de Commerce**, topped by a 76m-high spire sporting a gilded clock. Both were built in the early 20th century. Look east along rue Faidherbe and you'll see Gare Lille-Flandres at the far end. Vieux Lille (Old Lille), justly proud of its restored 17th- and 18th-century brick houses, begins just north of here. It's hard to believe, but in the late 1970s much of this quarter was a half-abandoned slum. Head north past the outdoor cafes to 7 **rue de la Grande Chaussée**, lined with Lille's chicest shops. Continue north along 8 **rue de la Monnaie** (named after a mint constructed here in 1685), whose old brick residences now house boutiques and the 9 **Musée de l'Hospice Comtesse**. Turning left (west) on tiny 10 **rue Péterinck** and then left again will take you to the 19th-century, neo-Gothic 11 **Cathédrale Notre-Dame-de-la-Treille**, which has a strikingly modern (some would say jarring) west façade (1999) that looks better from inside or when illuminated at night.

DON'T MISS

BRADERIE DE LILLE

On the first weekend in September, Lille's entire city centre – 200km of footpaths – is transformed into the **Braderie de Lille**, billed as the world's largest flea market. It runs nonstop – yes, all night long – from 2pm on Saturday to 11pm on Sunday, when street sweepers emerge to tackle the mounds of mussel shells and old *frites* (French fries) left behind by the merrymakers.

The extravaganza – with stands selling antiques, local delicacies, handicrafts and more – dates from the Middle Ages, when Lillois servants were permitted to hawk their employers' old garments for some extra cash. Lille's tourist office can supply you with a free map of the festivities.

afternoon it becomes a tearoom. Scan the façade for cannonballs dating back to the Austrian siege of 1792 (including one suggestively painted pink one).

Café Oz – The Australian Bar PUB

(33 place Louise de Bettignies; ⌚5pm-2am Tue-Sat, 2pm-midnight Sun) Footy and rugby on a wide screen, Australiana on the walls and cold bottles of Cooper's Pale Ale – what more could you ask for? Hugely popular with English speakers, including students, this place is packed when DJs do their thing from 9pm to 2am on Friday and Saturday nights. Has a great warm-season terrace. Happy hour is 5pm to 9pm.

Vice & Versa GAY

(☎06 38 75 07 53; 3 rue de la Barre; ⌚3pm-1am Mon-Wed, 3pm-3am Thu-Sat, 4pm-3am Sun) Rainbow blazes are displayed proudly at this well-heeled, sophisticated bar, which is as gay as it is popular (and it's very popular). Decor includes brick walls, a camp mirror ball and lots of red and green laser dots.

Le Network CLUB

(☎03 20 40 04 91; www.lenetwork.fr; 15 rue du Faisan; some nights incl 1 drink €10, until 1am women free; ⌚9.30pm or 10.30pm-7am Tue-Sat, 7.30pm-7am Sun; Ⓜ République Beaux Arts) Central Lille's hottest discotheque has two dance floors, three bars, plenty of flashing lights and space for 700 revellers. On most nights the music is three-quarters house and electronic and a quarter R&B. The door policy is pretty strict – locals dress up – but tends to be a bit more relaxed for tourists. Situated 600m northwest of the Palais des Beaux Arts.

On Thursday and Friday you can brush up on your rock 'n' roll dancing (€6 including two drinks) from 9.30pm to 11.30pm, while on Sunday there are beginner salsa lessons (free) at 7.30pm and a *soirée salsa* from 8.30pm to 12.30am.

Shopping

Lille's snazziest clothing and housewares boutiques are in Vieux Lille, in the area bounded by rue de la Monnaie, rue Esquermoise, rue de la Grande Chausée (a window-shopper's paradise!) and rue d'Angleterre. Keep an eye out for shops specialising in Flemish edibles!

Maisons de Mode – Lille FASHION & ACCESSORIES

(☎03 20 99 91 20; www.maisonsdemode.com; 31-62 rue du Faubourg des Poste; ⌚2-7pm Wed-Sat; Ⓜ Porte des Postes) Cool, cutting-edge couture by emerging designers can be found in this cluster of studio-boutiques 3km southwest of the city centre. There's a second location in **Roubaix** (27 av Jean Lebas & 85 to 105 rue de l'Espérance; Ⓜ Gare Jean Lebas).

L'Abbaye des Saveurs FOOD & DRINK

(☎03 28 07 70 06; 13 rue des Vieux Murs; ⌚2-7pm Mon & Tue, 11am-7pm Wed-Sat, 11am-1.30pm Sun) A beer-lover's dream, this little shop features dozens of artisanal brews from both the French and Belgian sides of the border.

Information

The **tourist office** (☎03 59 57 94 00; www.lille-tourism.com; place Rihour; ⌚9am-6pm Mon-Sat, 10am-4.30pm Sun & holidays; Ⓜ Rihour) is inside what's left of the Flamboyant Gothic-style Palais Rihour, built in the mid-1400s. It has free city maps, an excellent map (€3) outlining walking tours of five city *quartiers*, and details on Lille's rich cultural life.

Getting There & Away

AIR

Aéroport de Lille (www.lille.aeroport.fr) Linked to destinations around France and southern Europe by a variety of low-cost carriers. To/from the city centre (Euralille shopping mall), you can take a shuttle bus (€8, 20 minutes, hourly).

BUS

Isilines and Eurolines (☎Eurolines 08 92 89 90 91, Isilines 08 92 89 12 00; www.eurolines.com; 23 parvis St-Maurice; ⌚9am-6pm Mon-Fri, 10am-noon & 2-5pm Sat; Ⓜ Gare Lille-Flandres) Offer cheap domestic and international bus travel. Destinations served by Isilines include

Paris' Gallieni bus station (€9, 2¾ hours, four daily), Charles de Gaulle Airport (€9, 2½ hours, three daily), Nantes (€25, eight hours, one daily) and Strasbourg (€15, nine hours, one daily). Eurolines' international buses run to cities such as Brussels (€19, 1½ hours), Amsterdam (€34, five hours) and London (€36, five hours, four daily; by day via the Channel Tunnel, at night by ferry). The bus stop for both – and for Ouibus, the SNCF's new bus service – is 750m northeast of the office, just outside Gare Lille-Europe on bd de Turin.

TRAIN

Lille's two main train stations, Gare Lille-Flandres and newer Gare Lille-Europe, are 400m apart on the eastern edge of the city centre. They are one stop apart on metro line 2.

Gare Lille-Europe (📶) Topped by what looks like a 20-storey ski boot, this ultramodern station handles Eurostar trains to London, TGV/Thalys/Eurostar trains to Brussels-Midi, half of the TGVs to Paris Gare du Nord and most province-to-province TGVs. Has a children's playground on the street (upper) level.

Gare Lille-Flandres (📶) This old-fashioned station, recently spruced up, is used by half of the TGVs to Paris Gare du Nord and all intra-regional TER services.

Brussels-Midi By TGV €30, 35 minutes, at least a dozen daily; by regular train €22.50, two hours.

Charles de Gaulle Airport €45 to €63, one hour, at least hourly.

London (St Pancras International) By Eurostar €110 to €180, 90 minutes, 10 daily.

Nice-Ville €155, 7½ hours, one direct daily.

Paris Gare du Nord €50 to €67, one hour, 16 to 24 daily.

Getting Around

BICYCLE

L'Atelier Vélo (☎ 03 20 78 80 63; 10 av Willy Brandt; 7-speed/electric per day €6/20; ⏰ 9.30am-1pm & 2-5.45pm or 6.15pm Tue-Sat; Ⓜ Gare Lille-Flandres) Rents seven-speed and electric bicycles, does repairs, sells used bikes, and has cycling maps.

CAR & MOTORCYCLE

The only cheap parking near the city centre is next to the Citadelle at the **Champ de Mars** (www.transpole.fr; av Cuvier; per 3hr/day €2/4; ⏰ 24hr, staffed 7am-8pm Mon-Sat).

PUBLIC TRANSPORT

Lille's two speedy metro lines (1 and 2), two tramways (R and T), two Citadine shuttles (C1, which circles the city centre clockwise, and C2, which goes counterclockwise) and many urban and suburban bus lines – several of which cross into Belgium – are run by Transpole (www.transpole.fr). Transpole has an **information office** (☎ 03 20 40 40 40; ⏰ 7am-7pm Mon-Fri, 8am-6.30pm Sat; Ⓜ Gare Lille-Flandres) in the Gare Lille-Flandres metro station.

In the city centre, metros run every two to four minutes until about 12.30am. Useful metro stops include those at the train stations, Rihour (next to the tourist office), République Beaux Arts (near the Palais des Beaux Arts), Gambetta (near the Wazemmes food market) and Gare Jean Lebas (near La Piscine).

Tickets (€1.60, plus €0.20 for a reusable ticket) are sold on buses but must be purchased *before* boarding a metro or tram; there are ticket machines at each stop. A Pass' Journée (24-hour pass) costs €4.80 and needs to be time-stamped each time you board; two- to seven-day passes are also available. A Pass Soirée, good for unlimited travel after 7pm, costs €2.20.

FLANDERS & ARTOIS

Cassel

POP 2300

Perched at the summit of French Flanders' highest hill – though at 176m it's hardly Mont Blanc – the fortified, quintessentially Flemish village of Cassel offers panoramic views of the verdant Flanders plain.

Because of its elevated position, Cassel served as Maréchal Ferdinand Foch's headquarters at the beginning of WWI. In 1940 it was the site of intensive rearguard resistance by British troops defending Dunkirk during the evacuation.

Cassel's citizens are enormously proud of Reuze Papa and Reuze Maman, the resident giants, who are feted each Easter Monday. A bagpipe festival is held on a weekend in early to mid-June.

Sights

The **Grand' Place**, Cassel's focal point, is ringed by austere red-brick buildings with steep slate roofs.

Musée de Flandre ART MUSEUM
(☎ 03 59 73 45 60; www.museedeflandre.lenord.fr; 26 Grand' Place; adult/child €5/free; ⏰ 10am-12.30pm & 2-6pm Tue-Fri, 10am-6pm Sat & Sun) Has a worthwhile, well-presented collection of Flemish art, both old and modern, including some eye-popping canvases in the 15th-century Flemish primitive style and two dramatic paintings of the Battle

of Cassel (1677). For kids there's a play area with books. Audioguides are free.

Moulin LANDMARK

(3 rue St-Nicolas) Ten generations ago, wheat flour was milled and linseed oil pressed in windmills just like this one, perched on the highest point in town to catch the wind. In the 19th century, the region's skyline was dotted with 2000 such structures. Because of complicated town politics, the mill was closed in 2016.

Sleeping & Eating

Hôtel Le Foch HOTEL €

(☎03 28 42 47 73; www.hotel-foch.net; 41 Grand' Place; s/d €62/71; 🛜) Has six spacious rooms, some with views of the square, and antique-style beds. The restaurant serves traditional French cuisine; *menus* are €15 to €25.

★ **Het Kasteelhof** FLEMISH €

(☎03 28 40 59 29; http://lvermeersch.free.fr/kasteelhof; 8 rue St-Nicolas; mains €7-12; ⏲noon-9pm Thu-Sun) At the 'highest *estaminet* in Flanders', facing Cassel's hilltop windmill, you can quaff Flemish beer (including Kassels Bier, only available here), sip *vin de chicorée* (made with red wine and chicory) and dine on dishes such as *carbonade* (braised beef stewed with beer). For dessert, try yummy *crème brulée à la chicorée*. The tiny shop sells Flemish edibles.

Taverne Flamande FLEMISH €

(☎03 28 42 42 59; www.taverne-flamande.fr; 34 Grand' Place; menus €13.50-21, Sun menu €29.80; ⏲noon-2pm & 7-9pm Thu-Mon, noon-2pm Tue) Features a classic 1933 dining room with red banquettes, red-and-white checked tablecloths and, on cold days, a crackling fire. Specialities include *carbonade*, *waterzooi* (chicken and vegetable stew) and *potjevleesch*. When it's warm you can dine on a sunny terrace with panoramic views.

Information

Tourist Office (☎03 28 40 52 55; www.cassel-horizons.com; 20 Grand' Place; ⏲9.30am-noon & 1.30-5.45pm Tue-Fri Oct-Mar, plus Sat Apr-Sep) Can supply you with a walking tour of the town. May soon have a new online address.

Getting There & Away

Cassel is midway between Calais (59km) and Lille (49km). The village is served by trains from Dunkirk and Lille, but the station is 3km downhill from the centre and there's no public transport.

Arras

POP 41,200

An unexpected gem of a city, Arras (the final 's' is pronounced), the former capital of Artois, is worth seeing mainly for its exceptional ensemble of Flemish-style arcaded buildings – the main squares are especially lovely at night – and two subterranean WWI sites. The city makes a good base for visits to the Battle of the Somme memorials.

Sights & Activities

★ **Grand' Place & Place des Héros** SQUARE

Arras' two ancient market squares, the Grand' Place and the almost-adjacent, smaller place des Héros (also known as the Petite Place), are surrounded by 17th- and 18th-century Flemish Baroque houses topped by curvaceous Dutch-style gables. Although the structures vary in decorative detail, their 345 sandstone columns form a common arcade unique in France. Like 80% of Arras, both squares – especially handsome at night – were heavily damaged during WWI, so many of the gorgeous façades were reconstructed after the war.

Hôtel de Ville HISTORIC BUILDING

(☎03 21 51 26 95; place des Héros; belfry adult/child €3/2, boves tour €5.30/3.10, combined ticket €7/4; ⏲10am-noon & 2-6pm, boves closed 3 weeks Jan) Arras' Flemish Gothic city hall dates from the 16th century but was completely rebuilt after WWI. Four *géants* (giants) – the newest, Ami Bidasse, was 'baptised' in 2015 – live in the lobby. For a panoramic view, hop on a lift (plus 43 stairs) up the 75m-high belfry. Or, for a less expansive perspective, head down into the slimy *souterrains* (caves) under the square, also known as *boves*, which were turned into British command posts, hospitals and barracks during WWI.

Tours of the *boves* (40 minutes, three to six daily; in English upon request) generally begin at 11am, with at least two more departures in the afternoon. Tickets are sold at the tourist office (on the ground floor).

Carrière Wellington HISTORIC SITE

(Wellington Quarry; ☎03 21 51 26 95; www.explorearras.com; rue Arthur Delétoille; adult/child €6.90/3.20; ⏲10am-12.30pm & 1.30-6pm, closed Jan) Staging ground for the spring 1917 offensive, Wellington Quarry is a 20m-deep network of old chalk quarries expanded during WWI by tunnellers from New Zealand. Hour-long guided tours in French and

English combine imaginative audiovisuals, evocative photos and period artefacts. Signs painted in black are British and from WWI; those in red are French from WWII, when the site was used as a bomb shelter. Situated 1.4m south of the train station; follow signs to the 'Carrière'.

Sleeping

Hôtel Diamant HOTEL €

(03 21 71 23 23; www.arras-hotel-diamant.com; 5 place des Héros; d €82-96, apt €135-160;) This 12-room hotel, in one of the city's most desirable locations, enjoys a homey, B&B-like atmosphere. You can see the Petite Place from six of the rooms, all of which are themselves quite *petit* (small). There's no lift. Also rents out two fully equipped apartments with space for five or six in the townhouse next door.

Hôtel Les 3 Luppars HOTEL €

(03 21 60 02 03; www.hotel-les3luppars.com; 49 Grand' Place; d/f €85/105;) Occupying the Grand' Place's only non-Flemish-style building (it's Gothic and dates from the 1400s), this hotel has a private courtyard and 42 rooms, 10 of them with fine views of the square. The decor is uninspired, but the location is great and the atmosphere is homey. All the showers were redone in 2016. Amenities include a sauna (€6 per person).

★ La Corne d'Or B&B €€

(03 21 58 85 94; www.lamaisondhotes.com; 1 place Guy Mollet; d incl breakfast €125-155;) Occupying a magnificent *hôtel particulier* (private mansion) built in 1748, this very romantic B&B is filled with antiques, art and books on WWI. Some of the five imaginatively designed rooms and suites still have their original woodwork and marble fireplaces. Australian host Rodney, formerly of Australia's Department of Veterans' Affairs, is a great resource.

Grand Place Hôtel DESIGN HOTEL €€

(03 91 19 19 79; www.grandplacehotel.fr; 23 Grand' Place; d €99-135, family apt €135-165;) Opened in 2015, this sleek, stylish establishment has just 12 very comfortable rooms, whose decor mixes bright primary colours with snowy whites. All beds are king size. Also has a loft (€220) with space for six.

Eating

Lots of restaurants are tucked away under the arches of the Grand' Place, place des Héros and rue de la Taillerie.

Open-Air Market MARKET €

(place des Héros, Grand' Place & place de la Vacquerie; 8am-1pm Wed & Sat) The Saturday market is really huge.

Café Georget BISTRO €

(03 21 71 13 07; 42 place des Héros; plat du jour €9.50, sandwiches from €3.50; 8am-9pm daily;) Madame Delforge has been presiding over this unpretentious old-time cafe – and preparing dishes *comme à la maison* (as she would at home) – since 1985. Drop by for a trip back to the France of François Mitterrand.

Assiette au Boeuf STEAK €

(03 21 15 11 51; www.assietteauboeuf.fr; 56 Grand' Place; mains €16.90; noon-2.30pm & 7-11pm) Hugely popular with locals for its great-value steaks.

Le Petit Rat Porteur BRASSERIE €

(03 21 51 29 70; www.lepetitratporteur.fr; 11 rue de la Taillerie; mains €10-18.20, lunch menu €14; noon-2pm & 7-9.30pm Tue-Sat, noon-2pm Sun) Much appreciated for its marvellous vaulted cellar and friendly staff, this buzzing brasserie serves fun local food and has fantastic deals for lunch. In addition to lots of salads, you can dine on regional standards including *potjevleesch* and *waterzooi*.

La Faisanderie GASTRONOMIC €€

(03 21 48 20 76; www.restaurant-la-faisanderie.com; 45 Grand' Place; menus €28.50-55; noon-1.30pm Tue, Wed & Fri-Sun, 7-9pm Tue-Sat) Long appreciated by local gourmands, this formal restaurant, in a superb vaulted brick cellar, serves a range of French classics prepared with carefully selected ingredients.

Information

Tourist Office (03 21 51 26 95; www.explore-arras.com; place des Héros; 9am or 10am-6pm or 6.30pm Mon-Sat, 10am-1pm & 2.30-6.30pm Sun, closed noon-2pm Oct-Mar;) Inside the *hôtel de ville*. Has details on WWI battle sites and centennial events in 2017 and 2018.

Getting There & Away

BICYCLE

Arras à Vélo (06 29 71 61 91; www.arras-avelo.com; per day €10; 10am-5pm) rents electric bicycles, convenient for getting to the Vimy memorials 10km north of town. Bicycle pickup is at place du Théâtre.

TRAIN

Arras' station is 750m southeast of the two main squares.

Amiens €13.10, 45 minutes, five to 10 daily.

Lens €4.60, 15 minutes, 12 to 27 daily.

Lille-Flandres €11.50, 40 minutes, 14 to 23 daily.

Paris Gare du Nord (TGV) €37 to €58, 51 minutes, seven to 13 daily.

Lens

POP 32,600

Long known mainly for its towering black slag heaps, this former coal-mining town – nearly flattened during WWI – has little to offer visitors except for a brash new branch of Paris' renowned Louvre.

Sights

★Louvre-Lens ART MUSEUM

(☎03 21 18 62 62; www.louvrelens.fr; 99 rue Paul Bert; multimedia guide €3; ⊙10am-6pm Wed-Mon) FREE The innovative Louvre-Lens, opened to much fanfare in 2012, showcases hundreds of treasures from Paris' venerable Musée du Louvre in state-of-the-art exhibition spaces. The centrepiece, the 120m-long Galerie du Temps, displays a semi-permanent collection of 200-plus judiciously chosen objects – some of them true masterpieces – from the dawn of civilisation to the mid-1800s. Unlike that of the original Louvre, the collection here does not overwhelm and can easily be taken in and savoured in a single afternoon.

The glass-walled Pavillon de Verre is used for themed temporary exhibits (admission fee required) that change three times a year. For kids 11 and under there are 1½-hour art workshops (in French).

Getting There & Away

Lens is a quick 40km southwest of Lille and 18km north of Arras. It is served by TGV trains from Paris' Gare du Nord (€40, 1¼ hours, five or six daily) and regional TER trains from Lille-Flandres (from €8.30, 45 minutes, at least hourly) and Arras (from €4.60, 15 minutes, 12 to 27 daily).

CÔTE D'OPALE

Stretching from the Belgian border to the Baie de Somme (Somme estuary), the 140km-long Opal Coast – named for the ever-changing interplay of greys and blues in the sea and sky – features lofty chalk cliffs, rolling green hills, windswept beaches, scrub-dotted sand dunes and charming seaside towns. If you're coming from England, the area offers a breathtaking and sublimely beautiful introduction to France. Indeed, the shore here has been a favourite of British beach-lovers since the Victorian era.

The coast is dotted with the remains of Nazi Germany's Atlantic Wall, a line of fortifications and artillery emplacements built to prevent the Allied invasion that in the end took place in Normandy. The Third Reich didn't last a thousand years, but these massive, reinforced-concrete bunkers just might.

Calais to Boulogne

The most spectacular section of the Côte d'Opale is between Calais and Boulogne-sur-Mer. This 40km stretch, a mirror image of the White Cliffs of Dover, can be visited by car (take the D940), on foot (the GR120 trail, marked with red and white blazes, hugs the coast) or by local bus.

To the south, the relatively flat coastline is broken by the estuaries, wetlands and tidal marshes created by the Canche, Authie and Somme Rivers. Much of this area is privately owned – and used for hunting ducks and teals – but there are several attractive beach resorts and plenty of excellent spots for birdwatching and seal spotting.

Sights

Cap Blanc-Nez LANDMARK

Southwest of Calais, just past Sangatte, the coastal dunes give way to cliffs that culminate in windswept, 134m-high Cap Blanc-Nez, which affords breathtaking views of the Bay of Wissant, the port of Calais, the Flemish countryside (pockmarked by Allied bomb craters, such as those on the slopes of Mont d'Hubert) and the distant chalk cliffs of Kent. A grey stone obelisk honours the WWI Dover Patrol. Paths lead to a number of massive WWII German bunkers.

Cap Gris-Nez LANDMARK

Topped by a lighthouse and a radar station that keeps track of the more than 500 ships that pass by here each day, the 45m-high cliffs of Cap Gris-Nez are only 28km from the white cliffs of the English coast. The name, which means 'grey nose' in French, is a corruption of the archaic English 'craig ness', meaning 'rocky promontory'. The area is a stopping-off point for millions of migrating birds. The parking lot is a good starting point for hikes.

Musée du Mur de l'Atlantique MUSEUM
(Atlantic Wall Museum; ☎03 21 32 97 33; www.batterietodt.com; rte du Musée, Hameau de Haringzelle, Audinghen; adult/child €8.50/5; ⏰10am-5.30pm daily, to 7pm Jul & Aug, closed mid-Nov–early Feb) Oodles of WWII hardware, including a massive, rail-borne German artillery piece with a range of 86km, are on display at this well-organised museum, housed in a colossal German pillbox. Situated 400m off the D940 from the Maison du Site des Deux Caps tourist office. Last admission one hour before closing.

Musée 39-45 MUSEUM
(☎03 21 87 33 01; www.musee3945.com; 2 rue des Garennes, Ambleteuse; adult/child €8.50/5.50; ⏰10am-6pm Apr-Oct, weekends only Mar & Nov, closed Dec-Feb) Popular period songs accompany visitors as they stroll past dozens of life-size tableaux of WWII military and civilian life. Also screens archival films. The dashing but wildly impractical French officers' dress uniforms of 1931 hint at possible reasons that France fared so badly on the battlefield in 1940.

Brasserie Artisanale des 2 Caps BREWERY
(☎03 21 10 56 53; www.2caps.fr; ferme de Belle Dalle, Tardinghen; tours €4.50; ⏰10am-7pm Tue-Sat, 3-7pm Sun Jul & Aug, 10am-noon & 2-5pm Tue-Sat Sep-Jun) Historic farm buildings deep in the countryside house one of northern France's best microbreweries. Sample and buy here, or look for 2 Caps, Blanche de Wissant and Noire de Slack in area pubs. Brewmaster Christophe Noyon offers occasional 90-minute tours. Situated 1.5km along the D249 from Tardinghen's church.

Dunes de la Slack LANDMARK
Just south of Ambleteuse along the estuary of the tiny Slack River, the area's wind-sculpted sand dunes are covered with – and stabilised by – clumps of marram grass and brambles such as privet and wild rose. The best way to appreciate the undulating landscape is to follow the marked walking paths that criss-cross the area.

Tours

Eden 62 HIKING
(☎03 21 32 13 74; www.eden62.fr; ⏰mid-Feb–Oct) Organises free two-hour nature walks several times a week; they're in French, but tourists, including families, are welcome. No need to reserve – just show up at the meeting point.

WORTH A TRIP

DUNKIRK

In 1940, Dunkirk (Dunkerque) – the name means 'church of the dunes' in Flemish – became world famous thanks to the heroic evacuation of Allied troops. Destroyed by German attacks, it was rebuilt after the war – though, alas, during one of the most uninspired periods in the entire history of Western architecture. Thus, while the modern city has precious little charm, it does offer visitors worthwhile museums, a family-friendly beach and colourful pre-Lent carnivals.

Sleeping & Eating

Hôtel-Restaurant L'Escale HOTEL €
(☎03 21 85 25 00; www.hotel-lescale.com; 1 rue de la Mer, Escalles; d €72-87.50, q €106; ⏰closed early Jan-early Feb; 📶) Welcoming and cosy-modern, this family-run hotel in the heart of Escalles (population 280) has 44 rooms spread across three buildings. The restaurant serves French classics (especially fish) that you can wash down with a local craft beer. Book through the website for the best deals.

★**La Marie Galante** SEAFOOD €€
(☎03 21 83 02 32; 173 rue Edouard Quenu, Audresselles; menus €17.20-30.90; ⏰11.30am-2pm & 6.30-8.30pm Tue-Sun, closed Dec & Jan; 🖉) A gem for lovers of fish and seafood. All the sea creatures on the menu are local, but the sole, crab and lobster were landed right here in Audresselles. Seafood platters are €18.50 to €56. Situated one long block west of the D940.

★**La Sirène** SEAFOOD €€
(☎03 21 32 95 97; www.lasirene-capgrisnez.com; 376 rue de la Plage, Audinghen; mains €16-25.50, menu €29.50; ⏰noon-2pm & 7.30-9pm Tue-Sat, noon-2pm Sun Apr-Aug, shorter hours other months, closed mid-Dec–mid-Jan; 📶) Snuggled at the foot of Cap Gris-Nez, this much-loved hideaway serves only the freshest food, all of it sourced from Audresselles and Boulogne-sur-Mer. Picture windows offer glorious sea views. Reserve ahead in summer and for Sunday lunch.

Le Normandy GASTRONOMIC €€
(☎03 21 35 90 11; www.lenormandy-wissant.com; place de Verdun, Wissant; menus €24.50-36; ⏰noon-2pm & 7-8.30pm, closed Thu late Oct-late Mar; 📶) Trained in some of the world's top restaurants, chef Didier Davies – his grandfather came to France from Wales during

WWI – specialises in fish and seafood, including grilled sea bass. In the same family for five generations, this classy establishment also has 20 hotel rooms. On clear days you can see the outline of Dover Castle from here.

Information

Maison du Site des Deux Caps (03 21 21 62 22; www.lesdeuxcaps.fr; cnr D940 & D191, Hameau de Haringzelle, Audinghen; 10am-12.30pm & 2-5.30pm Apr-Sep, closed Mon Oct-Dec, Feb & Mar, closed Jan) Opened in 2014, this place serves as an information centre for the 'two capes', ie the area around and between Cap Blanc-Nez and Cap Griz-Nez. Rents out bicycles, both regular (per half-/whole day €7/10) and electric (€10/15), and sells hiking maps.

Wissant Tourist Office (03 21 82 48 00; www.terredes2capstourisme.fr; 1 place de la Mairie, Wissant; 9.30am-noon & 2-6pm Mon-Sat, 10am-1pm & 3-6pm Sun Jun-Sep, 10am-noon daily & 2-6pm Mon-Fri Oct-May) Has excellent English brochures and can help find accommodation.

Getting There & Away

The northern section of the Côte d'Opale, between Calais and Boulogne-sur-Mer, is served by bus 505, operated by **Oscar** (http://oscar.pasdecalais.fr) and **Voyages Inglard** (03 21 96 49 54). It runs three times a day; the fare is €1.

Calais

POP 73,450

As Churchill might have put it, 'Never in the field of human tourism have so many travellers passed through a place and so few stopped to visit'. More than 30 million people on their way to and from England travel via Calais each year, but precious few decide to stop – pity the local tourist office as it tries to snag a few of the Britons racing south to warmer climes – but in fact the town is worth at least a brief stopover.

A mere 34km from the English port of Dover (Douvres in French), Calais makes a convenient launching pad for exploring the majestic Côte d'Opale.

Sights

Cité Internationale de la Dentelle et de la Mode — MUSEUM

(International Centre of Lace & Fashion; 03 21 00 42 30; www.cite-dentelle.fr; 135 quai du Commerce; adult/child €5/3.50; 10am-5pm Wed-Mon) Innovative and surprisingly interesting exhibits trace the history of lace making – the industry that once made Calais a textile powerhouse – from hand knotting (some stunning samples are on display) through the Industrial Revolution. The highlight is watching a century-old mechanical loom with 3500 vertical threads and 11,000 horizontal ones bang, clatter and clunk according to instructions provided by perforated Jacquard cards. Signs are in French and English. Situated 500m southeast of the town-hall building.

Burghers of Calais — STATUE

(place du Soldat Inconnu) In front of Calais' ornate city hall stands the first cast of Rodin's famous sculpture *Les Bourgeois de Calais* (The Burghers of Calais; 1895), which portrays six local leaders (burghers) as they surrender to besieging English forces (the year is 1347) knowing that they will soon be executed – but hoping that their sacrifice will mean their fellow Calaisiens will be spared.

Edward III's wife, Philippa of Hainault, persuaded the English king that killing the hostages would be bad karma, so in the end both the brave burghers and the people of Calais survived.

Musée Mémoire 1939–1945 — MUSEUM

(03 21 34 21 57; www.musee-memoire-calais.com; Parc St-Pierre; adult/child incl audioguide €6/5; 10am-5pm Mon & Wed-Sat Oct, Nov & Feb-Apr, daily May-Sep) Housed in a massive concrete bunker built as a German naval headquarters, this WWII museum displays thousands of period artefacts, including weapons, uniforms and proclamations. Situated in the middle of flowery Parc St-Pierre, next to a *boules* ground and a children's playground.

Beffroi de Calais — TOWER

(Belfry; 03 21 46 20 53; place du Soldat Inconnu; adult/child €5/3; 10am-noon & 2-5.30pm, closed Mon Oct-Apr) Gilded statues glint in the sun atop Calais' 78m-high belfry, inaugurated in 1925, which like the adjacent *hôtel de ville* melds Flemish and Renaissance styles. An elevator whisks you to the top, where you can admire 360-degree views.

Beaches

Blériot Plage — BEACH

West of Calais, 8km-long Blériot Plage, broad and gently sloping, is named for pioneer aviator Louis Blériot, who began the first ever trans-Channel flight from here – it lasted 27 minutes – in 1909.

THE GIANTS

In far northern France, *géants* (giants) – wickerwork body masks up to 8.5m tall animated by people inside – emerge for local carnivals and feast days to dance and add to the merriment. Each has a name and a personality, usually based on the Bible, legends or local history. Giants are born, baptised, grow up, marry and have children, creating, over the years, complicated family relationships. They serve as important symbols of town, neighbourhood and village identity. Medieval in origin – and also found in places such as Belgium, the UK (www.giants.org.uk), Catalonia, the Austrian Tyrol, Mexico, Brazil and India – giants have been a tradition in northern France since the 16th century. More than 300 of the creatures now 'live' in French towns. France and Belgium's giants were recognised by Unesco as 'masterpieces of the oral and intangible heritage of humanity' in 2005.

Dates and places to see them appear in the free, annual poster-brochure *C'est quand les géants?*, available at tourist offices and online at www.calendrier-des-geants.eu.

Calais Beach BEACH

The singularly riveting attraction at Calais' cabin-lined beach is watching huge car ferries as they sail majestically to and from Dover.

Sleeping

Centre Européen de Séjour HOSTEL €

(03 21 34 70 20; www.auberge-jeunesse-calais.com; av Maréchal de Lattre de Tassigny; s/tw incl breakfast €32/49; ; 3, 5) Great for meeting fellow travellers, this efficiently run, 164-bed youth hostel is just 200m from the beach. It features a bar, a lounge area and modern (if soulless) one- to three-bed rooms; bathrooms are attached but shared by two rooms.

Hôtel Meurice HOTEL €

(03 21 34 57 03; www.hotel-meurice.fr; 5-7 rue Edmond Roche; d €74-114, f €135;) Sure to delight fans of retro, this once-grand, 39-room hotel has an impressive lobby staircase, old-time furnishings, a Hemingwayesque bar and an authentic 1950s vibe. Rates are cheapest if reserved by telephone or email.

Le Cercle de Malines B&B €€

(03 21 96 80 65; www.lecercledemalines.fr; 12 rue de Malines; d incl breakfast €85-125, q €150;) Built in 1884, this stately townhouse has been elegantly furnished in a modern spirit, with generous public areas and a lovely back garden. Our choice among the five spacious rooms is 'La Leavers', with its claw-footed Victorian bath-tub. Situated 1.2km south of the tourist office on a quiet street behind the main post office.

Eating

Calais is an excellent spot for a first or last meal in France. Restaurants ring place d'Armes, Calais' main public square, and can also be found along adjacent rue Royale.

★Histoire Ancienne BISTRO €€

(03 21 34 11 20; www.histoire-ancienne.com; 20 rue Royale; menus €17.90-32; noon-2pm Mon, noon-2pm & 6-9.30pm Tue-Sat;) Bistro-style French dishes, made with fresh ingredients, are served in a classic dining room that feels like 1930s Paris. Our favourites include mushroom cream soup and pepper-steak flambé with brandy. Service is prompt and friendly.

Le Grand Bleu MODERN FRENCH €€

(03 21 97 97 98; www.legrandbleu-calais.com; 8 rue Jean-Pierre Avron; menus €18-47; noon-2pm & 7-9pm Thu-Mon, noon-2pm Tue) Run by talented *avantgardiste* chef Matthieu Colin (formerly of Paris institution Ledoyen), this eatery – renovated in 2016 – is known for its *cuisine élaborée* (creatively transformed versions of traditional dishes) made with fresh local products. The weekday *menus* offer fabulous value. Book a table on the luminous verandah to enjoy harbour views.

Information

Tourist Office (03 21 96 62 40; www.calais-cotedopale.com; 12 bd Georges Clemenceau; 10am-5pm or 6pm, closed Sun Sep-Apr;) Has brochures on Calais and the Côte d'Opale and sells the discount Visit'Pass (€11). It's just north across the bridge from the train station.

Getting There & Away

The hovercraft are long gone, but you can still cross the English Channel by ferry, car-train or rail.

BOAT

Each day, 45 car ferries from Dover dock at Calais' car-ferry terminal, situated about 1.5km northeast of place d'Armes. As of 2016 it was patrolled by CRS riot police and surrounded by high, concertina-topped fences to prevent asylum seekers from stowing away on ferries to the UK.

Two companies, **P&O Ferries** (☎ 03 66 74 03 25; www.poferries.com) and **DFDS Seaways** (☎ 02 32 14 68 50; www.dfdsseaways.co.uk), operate regular trans-Channel services. P&O accepts foot passengers; DFDS only takes passengers with vehicles.

Shuttle buses (€2, almost hourly from 10.30am or 11am to about 6pm) link quai du Rhin (around the corner from the train station), with the car-ferry terminal. Departure times are posted.

BUS

Bus 505, run by **Oscar** (p192) and **Voyages Inglard**, makes three runs daily along the breathtaking Côte d'Opale coastal road (D940), stopping in Wissant (35 minutes) and other coastal communities en route to Boulogne-sur-Mer (1½ hours). The fare is €1 no matter how far you go. The bus stop, marked by a blue-and-yellow sign, is right outside Gare Calais-Ville.

CAR & MOTORCYCLE

To reach the Channel Tunnel's high-security vehicle-loading area at Coquelles, about 6km southwest of Calais' town centre, follow the road signs on the A16 to 'Tunnel Sous La Manche' (Tunnel Under the Channel) and get off at exit 42.

TRAIN

Calais has two train stations, linked by regional TER trains and SNCF buses (both €2.40).

Gare Calais-Fréthun A TGV station 10km southwest of town near the Channel Tunnel entrance; has direct TGVs to Paris' Gare du Nord (€53 to €80.50, 1¾ hours, four to eight daily) as well as the Eurostar to London St Pancras (€101 to €239, one hour, three daily).

Gare Calais-Ville In the city centre; has direct services to Boulogne-sur-Mer (€8.50, 21 to 39 minutes, 13 to 25 daily) and Lille-Flandres (€19, 1¼ hours, 12 to 22 daily).

Boulogne-sur-Mer

POP 42,780

The country's most important fishing port, Boulogne-sur-Mer makes a pretty good first stop in France, especially if combined with a swing north along the Côte d'Opale. The

Boulogne-sur-Mer

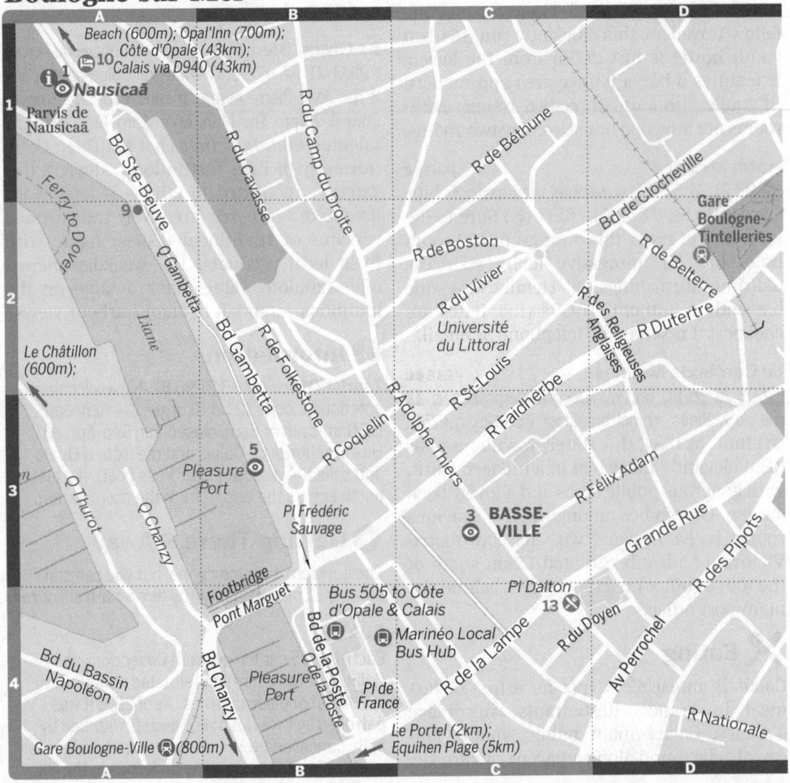

Basse-Ville (Lower City) is a bustling but uninspiring assemblage of postwar structures, but the attractive Haute-Ville (Upper City), perched high above the rest of town, is girded by a 13th-century wall. The biggest draw is Nausicaā, one of Europe's premier aquariums.

Sights

★Nausicaā AQUARIUM
(☎03 21 30 99 99; www.nausicaa.co.uk; bd Ste-Beuve; adult/child €19/12.50; ⏰9.30am-6.30pm Sep-Jun, to 7.30pm Jul & Aug, closed 3 weeks Jan) At this world-class aquarium, huge tanks with floor-to-ceiling windows make you feel as though you're swimming with the sharks – and with more than 1000 other species, including sea turtles, California sea lions, South American caimans and African penguins, some of them hatched right here. Kids of all ages will find ecologically conscious exhibits and activities to engage them, including fish petting, feeding sessions and sea-lion shows (one to three a day). A new land-reptiles section opened in 2016.

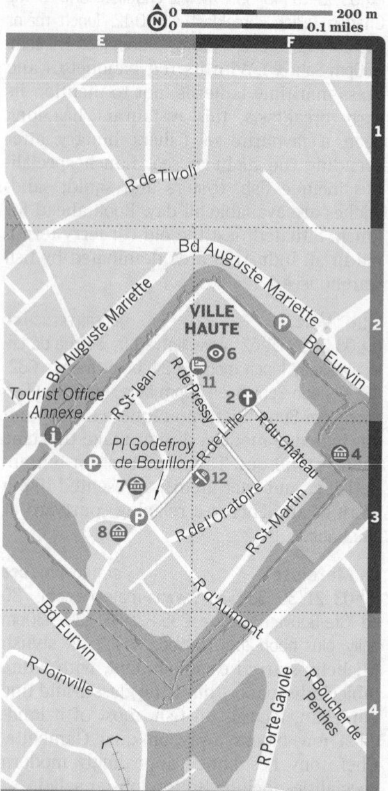

Haute-Ville HISTORIC SITE
(Ville Fortifiée) Boulogne's hilltop Upper City is an island of centuries-old buildings and cobblestone streets. You can walk all the way around this 'Fortified City' atop the ancient stone walls – look for signs for the Promenade des Remparts. **Basilique Notre Dame** (rue de Lille; ⏰10am-noon & 2-5pm, closed Mon Sep-Mar), its towering, Italianate dome visible from all over town, is an improbably tall structure built from 1827 to 1866; the vast, partly Romanesque crypt reopened in 2015 after extensive renovations.

The cultures of five continents meet and mingle inside the **Château-Musée** (Castle Museum; ☎03 21 10 02 20; 1 rue de Bernet; adult/child €5/free; ⏰museum 10am-12.30pm & 2-5.30pm Wed-Mon, courtyard 7am-7pm daily), one of the few places on Earth where you can admire Egyptian antiquities (some brought here by pioneering Boulogne-born Egyptologist Auguste Mariette) set alongside 19th-century Alaskan Inuit masks, and compare pre-Columbian ceramics from Peru with Grecian urns. A 4th-century Roman wall is thrown in for good measure, and all this is housed in a 13th-century fortified castle.

Among the impressive buildings around place Godefroy de Bouillon are the neoclassical **Hôtel Desandrouin** (17 rue du Puits d'Amour), built in the 1780s as a private

Boulogne-sur-Mer

Top Sights
1 Nausicaā A1

Sights
2 Basilique Notre Dame F2
3 Basse-Ville C3
4 Château-Musée F3
5 Fishing Port B3
6 Haute-Ville F2
7 Hôtel de Ville E3
8 Hôtel Desandrouin E3

Activities, Courses & Tours
9 Boat Excursions A2

Sleeping
10 Hôtel La Matelote A1
11 Les Terrasses de l'Enclos F2

Eating
La Matelote .... (see 10)
12 L'Îlot Vert F3
13 Marché C4

mansion and later used by Napoléon; and the brick **Hôtel de Ville** (8am-noon & 1.30-5.30pm Mon-Fri), built in 1735, with its square medieval belfry (the ground floor is accessible through the town hall's lobby).

Basse-Ville AREA

Boulogne's thriving economic heart is the Basse-Ville (Lower Town), centered on the Grande Rue and rue Adolphe Thiers. To encounter the city's long-time commercial bedrock, commercial fishing, head to the quay used by small fishing boats. Hungry seagulls dive and squawk overhead as they survey the **market stalls** (quai Gambetta; 7am-early afternoon) and the *poissonniers* (fishmongers) selling freshly landed *cabillaud* (Atlantic cod), *carrelet* (plaice) and sole – Boulogne's most important commercial fish – as well as *bar* (sea bass), mullet, *raie* (skate) and turbot.

Beaches

Boulogne's wide **beach** begins just north of Nausicaā aquarium, across the mouth of the Liane from a whirring wind farm on the former site of a steelworks. Other fine beaches include **Le Portel**, 2.5km southwest of Boulogne (take bus C), and **Equihen Plage**, about 5km to the south (take bus A). All are easily accessible by bike.

Tours

Boat Excursions BOATING

(06 48 49 42 26; www.boulogne-promenade-en-mer.com; 92 quai Gambetta; adult €11-33, child €8-19; Apr-Sep) The best way to discover Boulogne's fishing harbour and the magnificent Côte d'Opale is by taking a one- to four-hour *promenade en mer* (boat excursion). Departure times depend on sea conditions.

Sleeping

Opal'Inn HOTEL €

(03 21 32 15 15; www.hotel-opalinn.com; 168-170 bd Ste-Beuve; s €65, d €85-125;) The interior here is solid if unexciting, but the location is great: just 200m from Nausicaā aquarium and across the street from the beach. Lilac, taupe and chocolate hues give the 42 rooms, some with sea views, instant appeal. All the bathrooms were recently renovated.

Les Terrasses de l'Enclos B&B €€

(03 91 90 05 90; www.enclosdeleveche.com; L'enclos de l'Évêché, 6 rue de Pressy; d incl breakfast €75-120;) An imposing 19th-century mansion next to the basilica has been turned into Boulogne's most elegant accommodation. The five rooms are spacious, comfortable and full of old-time character.

Hôtel La Matelote HOTEL €€

(03 21 30 33 33; www.la-matelote.com; 70 bd Ste-Beuve; d €130-265 Fri & Sat, €105-208 Sun-Thu;) Boulogne's plushest hotel offers old-world character, professional service and amenities such as a *hammam*, a dry sauna and a tiny Jacuzzi pool. The 35 rooms are decorated in rich tones of gold, milk chocolate, maroon, cream and brass and have modern wooden furnishings; six have balconies.

Eating

In the Haute-Ville you'll find a number of restaurants along rue de Lille. For obvious reasons Boulogne is an excellent place to dine on fresh fish – everything except salmon and tuna is likely to have been landed locally.

★**Le Châtillon** SEAFOOD €

(03 21 31 43 95; www.le-chatillon.com; 6 rue Charles Tellier; breakfast €6.80-12, lunch mains €12-24, menus €22; 5am-4.30pm Mon-Fri, 4am-1.30pm Sat;) With its red banquettes and brass maritime lanterns, not to mention its early breakfasts, this restaurant has long been a favourite of fishers hungry after spending the night at sea. Lunch specialities include fish, oysters and squid; sandwiches are available all day. Book ahead for lunch. Situated past the old car-ferry terminal in an industrial area dominated by fish warehouses.

L'Îlot Vert MODERN FRENCH €€

(03 21 92 01 62; www.lilotvert.fr; 36 rue de Lille; weekday lunch menus €24, other menus €32-48; noon-2pm & 7-9.30pm Mon, Tue & Thu-Sat, noon-2pm Sun) 'Bistronomique' cuisine and cutting-edge modern design make this chic eatery stand out. The *carte* is short but appetising, and each item is presented like a work of art. There's a relaxing courtyard at the back.

La Matelote GASTRONOMIC €€€

(03 21 30 33 33; www.la-matelote.com; 80 bd Ste-Beuve; menus €35-82; 7.30-9.30pm daily, plus noon-2pm Fri-Wed;) This stylish Michelin-starred establishment, with white tablecloths, paper-thin wine glasses and fine porcelain, focuses on fish, most of it landed a few blocks away on quai Gambetta. Chef Tony Lestienne's appealingly modern specialities include Breton lobster salad.

Self-Catering

Marché FOOD MARKET €
(place Dalton; 8am-1pm Wed & Sat) A lively fruit and vegetable market.

Information

Tourist Office (03 21 10 88 10; www.visit-boulogne.com; parvis de Nausicaā; 10am-12.30pm & 2-5.30pm Mon-Sat year-round, plus 10.30am-1pm & 2.30-5pm Sun Apr–mid-Nov;) Helpful staff and plenty of English brochures (eg on the Côte d'Opale). Will move to a nearby location in 2017.

Tourist Office Annexe (www.visitboulogne.com; square Mariette Pacha; 10.30am-12.30pm & 2-5pm Mon-Sat Jul, Aug & Easter school holidays) Just outside the Haute-Ville.

Getting There & Around

BICYCLE

Cycléco (03 91 18 34 48; forum Jean Noël, quai de la Poste; per hour/day from €1/5) Hires out regular and electric bicycles in the warm season, ideal for getting to the beaches at Equihen Plage and Le Portel.

BUS

Bus 505, run by **Oscar** (p192) and **Voyages Inglard** (p192), runs from Boulogne's place de France (quai 19) to Calais via the gorgeous Côte d'Opale (€1 all destinations).

TRAIN

The main train station, **Gare Boulogne-Ville**, is 1.2km southeast of the Basse-Ville (take bus F). Destinations with direct services include:

Amiens €21.70, 1½ hours, seven to nine daily.

Calais-Ville €8.50, 21 to 39 minutes, 13 to 25 daily.

Lille-Flandres or Lille-Europe €22.90 to €35, one hour, five to eight daily.

Paris Gare du Nord €38.50 to €71, two to three hours, five to eight daily.

BAIE DE SOMME

Famed for its galloping tides and the seals that lounge on the Pointe du Hourdel sandbanks, this sparkling estuary – at 72 sq km it is the largest in northern France – affords delightful, watery views as the cycle of the tides reveals and hides vast expanses of marshland and sand. The area's wetlands provide hugely important habitats for hundreds of bird species. You can explore the bay by boat, kayak, outrigger canoe and – at low tide with a guide – on foot.

Both Le Crotoy, on the northern bank, and St-Valery-sur-Somme, on the south side, make excellent bases for exploring the area. Offering a good range of hotels, B&Bs, eateries and shops, they are becoming increasingly popular with Parisian weekenders.

Le Crotoy

POP 2150

Occupying a wonderfully picturesque spot on the northern bank of the Baie de Somme, laid-back Le Crotoy is a lovely place to relax. Jules Verne wrote *Twenty Thousand Leagues Under the Sea* (1870) while living here.

Activities

Promenade en Baie WALKING
(03 22 27 47 36, 06 28 05 13 02; www.promenade-en-baie.com; 5 allée des Soupirs; adult/child 2hr walk €12/6, 3hr walk €15/7, 5hr walk €18/7; 9am-12.30pm & 2-5pm, closed afternoons Dec & Jan) This experienced operator runs excellent two- to eight-hour guided walks

OFF THE BEATEN TRACK

ABBAYE DE VALLOIRES

Nestled in the bucolic Authie valley, this strikingly beautiful medieval **abbey** (03 22 29 62 33; www.abbaye-valloires.com; Argoules; tour & gardens adult/child €14/9; tours 2-7 times daily mid-Mar–11 Nov), rebuilt between 1687 and 1756, is well worth a detour for its harmonious Cistercian architecture and Baroque interiors. One of northern France's most intact old monasteries, the complex includes cloister, sacristy, chapter house and refectory. Among the church's furnishings are a magnificent organ loft and a wrought-iron choir screen. The landscaped gardens, great for strolling, envelop visitors in an ethereal calm.

The complex has been owned since the 1920s by an NGO that still runs foster and nursing homes on the premises, which is why visitors must join a guided tour; call ahead for details on English tours. Year-round, the abbey welcomes overnight guests in 20 large, simply furnished rooms and suites; doubles cost €55 to €90, while quads are €150. The abbey is a circuitous 25km northeast of Le Crotoy.

WORTH A TRIP

PARC DU MARQUENTERRE BIRD SANCTUARY

An astonishing 300 species of bird have been sighted at this 2-sq-km **bird sanctuary** (03 22 25 68 99; www.parcdumarquenterre.fr; 25bis chemin des Garennes, St-Quentin-en-Tourmont; adult/child €10.50/7.90, binoculars €4/2; 10am-5pm mid-Feb–mid-Nov, Sat & Sun only mid-Nov–mid-Feb), an important migratory stopover between the UK, Iceland, Scandinavia and Siberia and the warmer climes of West Africa. Three marked walking circuits (2km to 6km) take you to marshes, dunes, meadows, freshwater ponds, a brackish lagoon and 13 observation posts. Year-round, the park's friendly guides – they're the ones carrying around telescopes on tripods – are happy to help visitors spot and identify birds. One-hour guided introductory walks (free) begin daily at 10.30am and 2pm; call ahead if you'd like a tour in English (the guide coordinator, Alexander Hiley, is British). The immediate vicinity has a number of lovely day-hike paths, including Sentier des Crocs (15km). The park rents out bicycles (€15/11 for a whole/half day) for rides in the area, eg Circuit de l'Avocette. The park is 10km northwest of Le Crotoy. Allow at least two hours for a visit.

through and around the estuary, including seal-watching rambles at Pointe du Hourdel. Departure times depend on the tides.

Sleeping & Eating

★Les Tourelles HOTEL €€
(03 22 27 16 33; www.lestourelles.com; 2-4 rue Pierre Guerlain; d €93-138; closed 3 weeks Jan;) Overlooking Le Crotoy's beach, this atmospheric old-time hotel has 35 rooms, 13 with fabulous bay views; try no. 33, which occupies one of the cone-roofed *tourelles* (turrets). Five rooms are accessible by lift. Kids aged four to 14 can stay in a dormitory with 10 bunks (€31 per child including breakfast). The restaurant serves excellent coastal cuisine (mains €16 to €18), most of it locally sourced, and offers veggie options.

Getting There & Away

The SNCF train station in Noyelles-sur-Mer, 9km southeast of Le Crotoy, has direct services to Amiens (€11.40, 40 minutes, four or five daily) and Boulogne-sur-Mer (€12.60, 50 minutes, five or six daily). From late March to early November, two to six steam trains a day, run by the not-for-profit **Chemin de Fer de la Baie de Somme**, link Noyelles-sur-Mer with Le Crotoy.

St-Valery-sur-Somme

POP 2700

More fashionable and busier than Le Crotoy, St-Valery-sur-Somme – still a cargo and fishing port as late as the 1980s – has a charming maritime quarter, a pocket-size walled city and an attractive seaside promenade.

The colours of St-Valery-sur-Somme are the colours of maritime Picardy: the deep brick reds of the houses and sea hues that range from sparkling blue to overcast grey are accented by dashes of red, white and blue from flapping French flags, just like in an impressionist seascape.

Activities & Tours

A 3.5km promenade runs along the waterfront. The **Sentier du Littoral**, marked with yellow blazes, takes walkers west to Le Hourdel (8km) and around the bay to Le Crotoy (15km). Grey and harbour seals can often be spotted off **Pointe du Hourdel**, 8km northwest of town.

Tides (http://maree.info) have long set the pace of maritime life here and still do, at least as far as outdoor activities on the bay are concerned. High tide is a whopping 8m to 11m above low tide; high tides with a coefficient of 100 or more submerge the entire bay, including the salt marshes. The nearest swimming beach is at **Cayeux-sur-Mer**.

Chemin de Fer de la Baie de Somme TOURIST TRAIN
(CFBS; 03 22 26 96 96; www.cfbs.eu; quai Lejoille; adult/child return to Le Crotoy €14/10.50; daily late Mar-early Nov, weekends only Feb & Dec) Kids and adults alike relish an old-time train ride! Staffed by passionate volunteers, the not-for-profit CFBS runs one to three round trips a day around the bay to Le Crotoy and, on some days, west to Cayeux-sur-Mer. Visitors travel on trains assembled from the CFBS' collection of historic steam and diesel engines, carriages, wagons and autorails, all dating from 1889 to 1954.

Baliseur Somme II BOATING
(06 70 65 95 44; www.baliseursomme2.com; quai Lejoille; adult/child 1hr €12/8, 2hr €20/13; Apr-Sep) A *baliseur* (buoy tender) in use in the Baie de Somme from 1950 to 1999,

the *Somme II* now offers one- to two-hour cruises around the bay, including sunset excursions. Owned and operated in part by the Somme *département*.

Rando-Nature en Somme WALKING
(☎03 22 26 92 30; www.randonature-baiedesomme.com; quai Perret; adult €12-15, child €5; ⏲daily Mar-Oct, less often Nov-Feb) This well-regarded outfit offers guided nature walks on the estuary, including Traversons la Baie ('we cross the bay'; three hours) and Les Phoques et la Baie (seal-watching at Pointe du Hourdel; 2½ hours). Circuits begin at seven *points de rendez-vous* around the bay – the website has details. Reserve ahead.

Maison des Guides KAYAKING
(☎06 18 42 71 16; www.guides-baiedesomme.com; quai Jeanne d'Arc; 1/2/3hr €20/30/50; ⏲daily by reservation) Known for following best practice concerning animal welfare, Matthieu Cornu leads excellent kayak and outrigger-canoe excursions on the bay, including an environmentally aware, three-hour seal-watching trip.

Bateaux de la Baie de Somme BOATING
(☎07 83 25 08 14, 03 22 60 74 68; www.bateau-baie-somme.com; quai Perret; adult €12-20, child €8-13; ⏲late Mar–mid-Nov & school holidays Feb) Offers boat excursions around the bay lasting 45 minutes to two hours. For some real excitement, go seal-watching on a 12-person open-air Zodiac (€35 per person for 1½ hours). Departure times are determined by the tides.

Sleeping

Sophie et Patrick Deloison B&B, APARTMENT €
(☎03 22 26 92 17, 06 24 49 04 64; sp.deloison@gmail.com; 1 quai du Romerel; s/d incl breakfast €42/52, apt €50-75, 5-person lofts €143) Right in the centre, this welcoming B&B feels like a warm, soft nest. The two traditional-style rooms are simple yet attractive, with flea-market antiques and knick-knacks from yesteryear. Sophie and Patrick also rent out three spacious apartments with loads of character. No wi-fi except in loft. Reserve by email or phone.

Relais Guillaume de Normandy HISTORIC HOTEL €
(☎03 22 60 82 36; www.relais-guillaume-de-normandy.com; 46 quai du Romerel; d €79-93, tr €89-100; ⏲closed mid-Dec–mid-Jan;) Right on the waterfront in a mock Tudor mansion from the early 1900s, this vintage hotel has a five-storey tower and period touches such as a mosaic entryway and creaky wooden stairs. Half the 14 rooms have bay views. The excellent restaurant serves traditional French cuisine. Reserve well ahead in summer and on weekends.

Hôtel Les Pilotes BOUTIQUE HOTEL €€
(☎03 22 60 80 39; www.lespilotes.fr; 62 rue de la Ferté; d town view €70-170, bay view €100-200;) You have to walk under a lobby chandelier made entirely of white feathers to get to this hotel's 25 rooms, which sport 1960s-inspired furnishings and decor; the best come with fetching views of the bay through the large windows. Breakfast (€11) is sumptuously locavore.

Au Vélocipède B&B €€
(☎03 22 60 57 42; www.auvelocipede.fr; 1 rue du Puits Salé; d/tr incl breakfast €99/140;) Two townhouses facing the church are now a swish B&B. The eight supremely comfortable rooms are huge, with naked wooden floors, hip furnishings and modern slate-and-cream bathrooms. Those up in the attic (Vélo 3 and Vélo 4) are especially romantic. Cash only.

Eating

Le Bistrot des Pilotes NEOBISTRO €€
(☎03 22 60 80 39; www.lespilotes.fr; 37 quai Blavet; lunch/dinner menus from €19/25; ⏲noon-2.30pm & 7-9.30pm Wed-Sat, noon-2.30pm Sun Feb-Jun & Sep-Dec, daily Jul & Aug) Market-fresh cuisine with a twist, outdoor tables on the waterfront, a good selection of seafood dishes and Picard classics, and great *mousse au chocolat* make this place a perennial favourite.

Au Vélocipède MODERN FRENCH €€
(☎03 22 60 57 42; www.auvelocipede.fr; 1 rue du Puits Salé; mains €16-19; ⏲noon-6pm Sun, Mon & Wed-Fri, noon-6pm & 7.30-9pm Sat Easter–mid-Nov, weekends mid-Nov–early Jan & early Feb-Easter;) Rustic-chic in decor and foodie in spirit, this restaurant – and, after 3pm, tearoom and wine bar – serves creative, contemporary locavore cuisine and exquisite homemade cakes and pastries. Situated in the Cité Médiévale just inside the Porte de Nevers.

Information

Tourist Office (☎03 22 60 93 50; www.tourisme-baiedesomme.fr; 2 place Guillaume Le Conquérant; ⏲9.30am or 10am-12.30pm & 2.30-6pm daily Apr-Sep, closed Mon Oct-Mar;) Has details on outdoor activities and excellent English brochures, including cycling maps. Sells tickets for guided walks of the estuary.

Getting There & Away

By car, St-Valery-sur-Somme is 67km northwest of Amiens and 15km around the bay from Le Crotoy. The closest SNCF train station is 8km to the east in Noyelles-sur-Mer, which has direct services to Amiens (€11.40, 40 minutes, four or five daily) and Boulogne-sur-Mer (€12.60, 50 minutes, five or six daily). From late March to early November, two to six steam trains a day, run by the not-for-profit **Chemin de Fer de la Baie de Somme** (p198), link Noyelles-sur-Mer with St-Valery-sur-Somme.

BATTLE OF THE SOMME, FLANDERS & ARTOIS MEMORIALS

The Battle of the Somme has become a symbol of the meaningless slaughter of WWI, and its killing fields – along with those of the Battle of Arras and Western Front sectors further north – have since become sites of pilgrimage. Each year, thousands of visitors from Australia, Canada, Great Britain, New Zealand, South Africa and other Commonwealth nations follow the **Circuit du Souvenir** (Remembrance Trail; www.somme-battlefields.com).

Through 11 November 2018, solemn ceremonies and dedications throughout the region will commemorate the centenary of important WWI events and battles.

Convenient bases for exploring the area include Amiens, Arras and the small towns of Péronne, Albert and Pozières.

Sights

★ Historial de la Grande Guerre MUSEUM
(Museum of the Great War; ☎03 22 83 14 18; www.historial.org; Château de Péronne, Péronne; adult/child incl audioguide €9/4.50; ⏲9.30am-5pm, closed Wed Oct-Mar, closed mid-Dec–mid-Feb) The best place to begin a visit to the Somme battlefields – especially if you're interested in WWI's historical and cultural context – is the outstanding Historial de la Grande Guerre in Péronne, about 60km east of Amiens. Located inside the town's fortified medieval château, this award-winning museum tells the story of the war chronologically, with equal space given to the German, French and British perspectives on what happened, how and why.

The museum displays a unique collection of visually engaging material, including period films and the bone-chilling engravings by Otto Dix, which captures the aesthetic sensibilities, enthusiasm, naive patriotism and unimaginable violence of the time. The proud uniforms of various units and armies are shown laid out on the ground, as if on freshly (though bloodlessly) dead soldiers.

Battle of the Somme Memorials

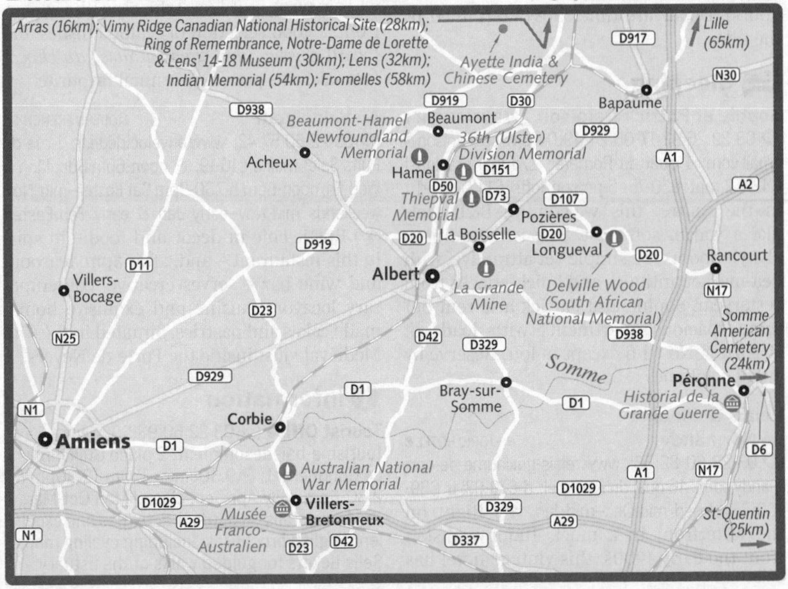

COMMONWEALTH CEMETERIES & MEMORIALS

Almost 750,000 soldiers, airmen and sailors from Great Britain, Australia, Canada, the Indian subcontinent, Ireland, New Zealand, South Africa, the West Indies and other parts of the British Empire died during WWI on the Western Front, two-thirds of them in France. They were buried where they fell, in more than 1000 military cemeteries and 2000 civilian cemeteries that dot the landscape along a wide swath of territory – 'Flanders Fields' – running roughly from Amiens and Cambrai north via Arras and Béthune to Armentières and Ypres (Ieper) in Belgium. French and German war dead were reburied in large cemeteries after the war. American war dead of the world wars were either repatriated (61%) or reburied in large cemeteries near where they fell (39%).

The focal point of each Commonwealth cemetery, tended by the Commonwealth War Graves Commission (www.cwgc.org), is the Cross of Sacrifice. Many of the headstones, made of Portland limestone, bear moving personal inscriptions composed by family members. Most cemeteries have a bronze Cemetery Register box that contains a visitors book, in which you can record your impressions, and a booklet with biographical details on each of the identified dead (Americans who died fighting with British forces can be spotted by their addresses). Some larger cemeteries also have a bronze plaque with historical information.

New exhibits (open from early 2017) include one on the role of Australian forces in liberating Péronne.

★Beaumont-Hamel Newfoundland Memorial MEMORIAL

(☎03 22 76 70 86; www.veterans.gc.ca; Beaumont-Hamel; ⊙Welcome Centre 11am-5pm Mon, 9am-5pm Tue-Sun) This evocative memorial preserves part of the Western Front in the state it was in at fighting's end. The zigzag trench system, which still fills with mud in winter, is clearly visible, as are countless shell craters and the remains of barbed-wire barriers. Canadian students based at the Welcome Centre, which resembles a Newfoundland fisher's house, give free guided tours on the hour (except from mid-December to mid-January). Situated 9km north of Albert; follow the signs for 'Memorial Terreneuvien'.

The memorial to the 29th Division, to which the volunteer Royal Newfoundland Regiment belonged, stands at the entrance to the site. On 1 July 1916, this regiment stormed entrenched German positions and was nearly wiped out; until a few years ago, a plaque noted bluntly that 'strategic and tactical miscalculations led to a great slaughter'. A path leads to an orientation table at the top of the Caribou mound, where a bronze caribou statue is surrounded by plants native to Newfoundland.

★Vimy Ridge Canadian National Historic Site MEMORIAL

(☎03 21 50 68 68; www.veterans.gc.ca; Vimy; ⊙visitor centre 11am-5pm Mon, 9am-5pm Tue-Sun) Right after the war, the French attempted to erase all signs of battle and return northern France to agriculture and normalcy. The Canadians took a different approach, deciding that the most evocative way to remember their fallen was to preserve part of the crater-pocked battlefield exactly the way it looked when the guns fell silent. As a result, the best place to get some sense of the hell known as the Western Front is the chilling, eerie moonscape of Vimy.

Of the more than 66,000 Canadians who died in WWI, 3598 lost their lives in April 1917 taking Vimy Ridge. Its highest point – site of a heavily fortified German position – was later chosen as the site of Canada's national WWI memorial, built from 1925 to 1936. It features 20 allegorical figures, carved from huge blocks of white Croatian limestone, that include a cloaked, downcast female figure representing a young Canada grieving for her dead. The names of 11,285 Canadians who 'died in France but have no known graves', listed alphabetically and within each letter by rank, are inscribed around the base.

A new **Visitor Educational Centre**, set to open for the centenary of the battle (9 April 2017), is staffed by bilingual Canadian students who run free guided tours of reconstructed tunnels and trenches; a self-guided-tour brochure should be ready by 2017. In the surrounding forest, the zigzag trench system is clearly visible, as are countless shell craters. Because human remains still lie buried among the trees, the entire site has been declared a graveyard.

Vimy Ridge is 11km north of Arras. A taxi from Arras costs about €25 one way (€30 on Sunday), or you can cycle along secondary roads to get here.

★Fromelles (Pheasant Wood) Cemetery & Museum CEMETERY, MUSEUM
(☎03 59 61 15 14; www.musee-bataille-fromelles.fr; rue de la Basse Ville, Fromelles; museum adult/child €6.50/4; ⌚cemetery 24hr, museum 9.30am-5.30pm Wed-Mon) The death toll was horrific – 1917 Australians and 519 Britons killed in just one day of fighting – yet the Battle of Fromelles was largely forgotten until 2008, when the remains of 250 of the fallen were discovered. They are now buried in the Fromelles (Pheasant Wood) Cemetery, the first new Commonwealth cemetery established in half a century. Next door, the excellent Musée de la Bataille de Fromelles, opened in 2014, evokes life in the trenches with reconstructed bunkers, photographs and biographies.

On 19 July 1916, a poorly planned offensive using inexperienced Australian and British troops was launched to divert German forces from the Battle of the Somme. After the surviving Australians retreated to their pre-battle front lines, hundreds of their comrades-in-arms lay wounded in no man's land. For three days the survivors made heroic efforts to rescue them, acts of bravery commemorated by the *Cobbers* sculpture in the Australian Memorial Park, 2km northwest of the museum. Ross McMullin, writing for the Australian War Memorial (www.awm.gov.au), describes the battle as 'the worst 24 hours in Australia's entire history'.

It is likely that one of the soldiers on the victorious German side was a 27-year-old corporal in the 16th Bavarian Reserve Infantry Regiment named Adolf Hitler.

After the failed and catastrophic assault, the Germans buried many of the Australian and British dead in mass graves behind their lines. Most were reburied after the war, but five pits were not found for more than 90 years. DNA testing has established the identity of 144 Australians.

The excellent 'Battle of Fromelles Walking Guide' has details on a 10km walking or driving tour of 10 WWI sites near Fromelles, which is 17km west of Lille.

★Ring of Remembrance MEMORIAL
(Anneau de la Mémoire; Ablain-St-Nazaire; ⌚9am-4.15pm, to 5.30pm or 6.30pm Apr-Sep) It's hard not to be overwhelmed by the waste and folly of the Western Front as you walk past panel after panel engraved with 580,000 tiny names: WWI dead from both sides who are listed in strict alphabetical order, without reference to nationality, rank or religion. Across the road from the memorial, inaugurated in 2014, is a vast French military cemetery, Notre-Dame de Lorette; 6000 unidentified French soldiers are interred in the base of the Lantern Tower (1921).

Lens' 14-18 Museum MUSEUM
(☎03 21 74 83 15; www.lens14-18.com; 102 rue Pasteur, Souchez; audioguide €3; ⌚10am-5pm Oct-May, to 6pm Jun-Sep) FREE Inaugurated in 2015, this superbly designed WWI museum, housed in four black concrete cubes, provides an excellent introduction to WWI on the Western Front. The highlight is over 300 extraordinary photos of daily life and death in the trenches, carefully selected by historians from French, British and German archives; also on display are about 60 hours of archival film. Situated 2km west (down the hill) from the Ring of Remembrance (Notre-Dame de Lorette), on a hill overlooking Lens.

Musée Franco-Australien MUSEUM
(Franco-Australian Museum; ☎03 22 96 80 79; www.museeaustralien.com; 9 rue Victoria, Villers-Bretonneux; adult/child €5/3; ⌚9.30am-5.30pm Mon-Sat Mar-Oct, to 4.30pm Nov-Feb) Some 2400 Australian soldiers were killed or wounded in the April 1918 assault that wrested Villers-Bretonneux from German control. In the 1920s, Australian children donated funds to rebuild the town's primary school, creating bonds of friendship that remain strong to this day. Part of Victoria School is now a museum featuring highly personal artefacts donated by Australian ex-servicemen and their families. Situated 20km east of Amiens via the D1029.

Somme American Cemetery CEMETERY
(www.abmc.gov; Bony; ⌚9am-5pm) In late September 1918, just six weeks before the end of WWI, American units – flanked by their British, Canadian and Australian allies – launched an assault on the Germans' heavily fortified Hindenburg Line. Some of the fiercest fighting took place near the village of Bony, on the sloping site now occupied by the 1844 Latin crosses and Stars of David of this serene cemetery. Situated 24km northeast of Péronne, mostly along D6, and 18km north of St-Quentin along D1044.

One regiment of the 27th Infantry Division, a National Guard unit from New York, suffered 337 dead and 658 wounded on a single day. The names of 333 men whose remains were never recovered are inscribed on the walls of the Memorial Chapel, reached through massive bronze doors. The small Visitors' Building (turn left at the flagpole) has information on the battle.

Thiepval Memorial MEMORIAL

(☎03 22 74 60 47; www.cwgc.org; Thiepval; ⏱museum 9.30am-5pm, closed mid-Dec–mid-Jan) Its silhouette instantly recognisable from afar, this 45m-high memorial to the missing of the Somme is inscribed with the names of more than 72,000 British and South African soldiers whose remains were never recovered or identified. Designed by Edwin Lutyens, it was built from 1928 to 1932 on the site of a German stronghold that was stormed on 1 July 1916, the bloody first day of the Battle of the Somme. The adjacent joint French and Commonwealth cemetery expresses Franco-British fraternity in death as in life.

At the time of writing, a new museum, run by Péronne's outstanding Historial de la Grande Guerre, was set to open in mid-2016. The visitor centre's bookshop has an excellent selection of English books on WWI. Situated 7.5km northeast of Albert along the D151.

36th (Ulster) Division Memorial MEMORIAL

(Ulster Tower Memorial; ☎03 22 74 87 14; D73, Thiepval; ⏱10am-5pm Tue-Sun Mar-Nov, closed Dec-Feb) FREE The 5000 Ulstermen who perished in the Battle of the Somme are commemorated by this Gothic-style tower, an exact replica of Helen's Tower at Clanboye, County Down, where the Ulster Division did its training. Dedicated in 1921, it has long been a Unionist pilgrimage site; a black obelisk known as the Orange Memorial to Fallen Brethren (1993) stands in an enclosure behind the tower. Situated 1.3km northeast of the Thiepval Memorial.

In a sign that historic wounds are slowly healing, in 2006, for the 90th anniversary of the Battle of the Somme, the Irish Republic issued a €0.75 postage stamp showing the overwhelmingly Protestant 36th Division in action on this site.

Virtually untouched since the war, nearby Thiepval Wood can be visited on a guided tour (donation requested); call ahead for times and dates.

Neuve-Chapelle Indian Memorial MEMORIAL

(www.cwgc.org; cnr D947 & D171, Richebourg) The evocative Mémorial Indien, vaguely Moghul in architecture, records the names of 4700 soldiers of the Indian Army who 'have no known grave'. The 15m-high column, flanked by two tigers, is topped by a lotus capital, the Imperial Crown and the Star of India. The units (31st Punjabis, 11th Rajputs, 2nd King Edward's Own Gurkha Rifles) and the ranks of the fallen – sepoy (infantry private), havildar (sergeant) – engraved on the walls evoke the pride, pomp and exploitation of the British Empire. It is situated 30km west of Lille.

La Grande Mine LANDMARK

(Lochnagar Crater Memorial; www.lochnagarcrater.org; La Boisselle; ⏱24hr) Just outside the hamlet of La Boisselle, this enormous crater looks like the site of a meteor impact. Some 100m across and 30m deep, it was created on the morning of the first day of the First Battle of the Somme (1 July 1916) by about 25 tonnes of ammonal laid by British sappers in order to create a breach in the German front lines. Situated 4km northeast of Albert along the D929.

Ayette Indian & Chinese Cemetery CEMETERY

Towards the end of WWI, tens of thousands of Chinese labourers were recruited by the British government to perform noncombat jobs in Europe, including the gruesome task of recovering and burying Allied war dead. Some of these *travailleurs chinois* (Chinese labourers), as well as Indians who served with British forces, are buried in this Commonwealth cemetery, which is 29km northeast of Albert, just off the D919 at the southern edge of the village of Ayette.

Many Chinese labourers died in the Spanish flu epidemic of 1918–19. Their gravestones are etched in Chinese and English with inscriptions such as 'A good reputation endures forever', 'A noble duty bravely done' and 'Faithful unto death'. The nearby graves of Indians are marked in Hindi or Arabic.

Australian National War Memorial MEMORIAL

(☎03 21 21 77 00; www.ww1westernfront.gov.au; Villers-Bretonneux) During WWI, 313,000 Australians – 7% of the country's entire population – volunteered for overseas military service; 46,000 met their deaths on the Western Front (14,000 others perished elsewhere). The names of 10,982 Australian soldiers whose remains were never found are engraved at the base of the Australian National War Memorial's 32m-high tower, which stands atop a gentle hill where Australian and British troops repulsed a German assault in April 1918.

The viewing area atop the tower, damaged by German gunfire in 1940, affords panoramic views of a large Commonwealth cemetery and the one-time battlefield. The Anzac Day Dawn Service is held here every 25 April

WWI SITES RESOURCES

Tourist offices can supply you with some excellent English-language brochures, including *Sites of the First World War – the Guide, The Great War Trail in Artois* and *The Australians in the Somme*, as well as a free multilingual map, *The Great War Remembered*. For online information:

- www.centenaire-somme.com
- www.remembrancetrails-northernfrance.com
- www.cwgc.org
- www.somme-battlefields.com
- www.ww1westernfront.gov.au
- www.greatwar.co.uk

at 5.30am. The Sir John Monash Centre, an interpretive centre scheduled to open for the centennial of the battle (April 2018), is being built behind the tower. The memorial is 2km north of Villers-Bretonneux along the D23.

Delville Wood MEMORIAL
(South African National Memorial & Museum; 03 22 85 02 17; www.delvillewood.com; Longueval; 10am-4pm Tue-Sun, closed Dec & Jan & South African holidays) The memorial (1926) and star-shaped museum (1986), a replica of Cape Town's Castle of Good Hope, stand in the middle of Delville Wood, where in July 1916 the 1st South African Infantry Brigade was nearly wiped out in hand-to-hand fighting that literally obliterated all the trees. In 2016, the names of all the South Africans, both black and white, who died in WWI were inscribed on a memorial wall.

During the 1916 offensive, pre-existing paths through Delville Wood were named for well-known streets in London and Edinburgh. Today, the area is still considered a cemetery because so many bodies were never recovered. Inside the museum, apartheid-era bronze murals portray black members of the South African Native Labour Corps (blacks were banned from combat roles) without shirts – despite the often chilly European weather! The Mémorial Sud-Africain is 13km east of Albert.

Tours

Tourist offices can help book tours of battlefield sites and memorials. Respected tour companies include **The Battlefields Experience** (03 22 76 29 60; www.thebattleofthesomme.co.uk), **Chemins d'Histoire** (06 31 31 85 02; www.cheminsdhistoire.com), **Sacred Ground Tours** (06 75 66 59 02; www.sacredgroundtours.com.au), **Terres de Mémoire** (03 22 84 23 05; www.terresdememoire.com), **True Blue Digger Tours** (06 01 33 46 76; www.trueblue-diggertours.com), and **Walkabout Digger Tours** (06 64 54 16 63; http://walkaboutdiggertours.free.fr).

Sleeping & Eating

Amiens and Arras have a good range of accommodation options, but a growing number of visitors choose to stay in small hotels or B&Bs in towns closer to the battlefields such as Péronne, Albert or Pozières.

★ **Au Vintage** B&B €
(06 83 03 45 26, 03 22 75 63 28; www.chambres-dhotes-albert.com; 19 rue de Corbie, Albert; d incl breakfast €65-85;) This delightful B&B, in a brick mansion from 1920, has five atmospheric rooms with old wooden floors, antique furnishings and marble fireplaces. Evelyne and Jacky are delightful, cultured hosts who enjoy sharing their knowledge about the battlefields with their guests. Reserve well ahead. Situated about 500m southwest of Albert's basilica.

Butterworth Farm B&B €
(03 22 74 04 47, 06 22 30 28 02; www.butterworth-cottage.com; rte de Bazentin (D73), Pozières; d incl breakfast €65; P) Beloved by Australians and Brits, this B&B is run by Bernard, the mayor of Pozières, and his wife, Marie. The five fresh, well-tended rooms occupy part of the owners' grandparents' family farm. There's a garden filled with flowers and herbs for lounging in, and breakfasts are copious. Situated half a block off the D929 on the southbound D73 (towards Bazentin).

La Basilique HOTEL €€
(03 22 75 04 71; www.hoteldelabasilique.fr; 3 rue Gambetta, Albert; d €89-99; @) In the heart of Albert right across the square from the basilica, this well-kept hotel has 10 neat rooms with French windows and bright bathrooms. The in-house French and Picard restaurant specialises in *cuisine du terroir* (regional specialities made with quality local ingredients) such as duck breast with sour-cherry sauce.

Hôtel Le Saint-Claude HOTEL €€
(03 22 79 49 49; www.hotelsaintclaude.com; 42 place du Commandant Louis Daudré, Péronne; d €86-112;) Originally a *relais de poste* (coaching inn), the Saint-Claude is in the centre of Péronne just 200m from the His-

torial. The 40 contemporary rooms are decorated in adventurous colours and have ultra-modern bathrooms.

Information

Péronne Tourist Office (☎03 22 84 42 38; www.hautesomme-tourisme.com; 16 place André Audinot, Péronne; ⏰10am-noon & 2-5pm or 6pm Mon-Sat Sep-Jun, plus 9am-12.30pm & 1.30-6.30pm Sun Jul & Aug) Has excellent English brochures on the battlefields and rents out bicycles. Situated 100m up the hill from the Historial de la Grande Guerre.

Albert Tourist Office (☎03 22 75 16 42; www.tourisme-paysducoquelicot.com; 9 rue Gambetta, Albert; ⏰9am-12.30pm & 1.30-5pm or 6.30pm Mon-Fri, 9am-noon & 2-5pm or 6.30pm Sat Sep-Apr, plus 9am-1pm Sun May-Aug) Has abundant information on the battlefields and rents out bicycles.

Getting There & Away

You'll need your own transport (a car or bike) to visit most of the Somme memorials. Bicycles can be rented at the tourist offices in Péronne (€5 per day) and Albert.

One exception is Villers-Bretonneux, which has rail services to/from Amiens (€4, 11 minutes, four to seven daily). The train station is 600m southeast of the Musée Franco-Australien (take rue de Melbourne) and 3km south of the Australian National War Memorial (a round-trip taxi ride from Villers-Bretonneux costs around €20).

Albert is also served by trains. It is linked to Amiens (€7, 20 minutes, seven to 18 daily) and Arras (€8, 23 minutes, five to 11 daily).

PICARDY

Amiens

POP 137,030

One of France's most awe-inspiring Gothic cathedrals is reason enough to spend time in Amiens, the comfy, if reserved, former capital of Picardy where Jules Verne lived for the last 34 years of his life. The mostly pedestrianised city centre, tastefully rebuilt after WWII, is complemented by lovely green spaces along the Somme River. Some 28,000 students give the town a youthful feel.

Amiens is an excellent base for visits to many of the Battle of the Somme memorials.

Sights & Activities

★Cathédrale Notre Dame CATHEDRAL

(place Notre Dame; north tower adult/child €5.50/free, audioguide €4; ⏰cathedral 8.30am-5.15pm daily, north tower to mid-afternoon Wed-Mon) The largest Gothic cathedral in France (it's 145m long) and a Unesco World Heritage Site, this magnificent edifice was begun in 1220 to house the skull of St John the Baptist. Connoisseurs of architecture rave about the soaring Gothic arches (42.3m high over the transept), unity of style and immense interior, but for locals the highlight is a 17th-century statue known as the Ange Pleureur (Crying Angel), at the far end directly behind the over-the-top Baroque high altar.

The octagonal, 234m-long labyrinth on the black-and-white floor of the nave is easy to miss as the soaring vaults draw the eye upward. Part of the skull of St John the Baptist, framed in gold and jewels, can be seen in the *trésor* (treasury). Plaques in the south transept honour American, Australian, British, Canadian and New Zealand soldiers who perished in WWI.

To get a sense of what you're seeing, it's worth hiring an audioguide (45 to 75 minutes), available in six languages, at the tourist office (across the square). Weather permitting, visitors willing to brave 307 steps can climb the north tower for spectacular views; tickets are sold in the boutique to the left as you walk through the west façade. The cathedral is closed to visitors during religious ceremonies, including marriages.

A free 45-minute light show bathes the cathedral's façade in vivid medieval colours nightly from mid-June to the third weekend in September, and from early December to 1 January; the photons start flying at 7pm in winter and sometime between 9.45pm (September) and 10.45pm (June) in summer.

Maison de Jules Verne MUSEUM

(☎03 22 45 45 75; www.amiens.fr/maison-jules-verne; 2 rue Charles Dubois; adult/child €7.50/4, English audioguide €2; ⏰10am-12.30pm & 2-6pm Mon & Wed-Fri, 2-6pm Sat & Sun year-round, plus 2-6.30pm Tue, from 11am Sat & Sun mid-Apr–mid-Oct) Jules Verne (1828–1905) wrote some of his best-known works of brain-tingling – and eerily prescient – science fiction under the eaves of this turreted home, where he lived from 1882 to 1900. The models, prints, posters and other items inspired by Verne's fecund imagination afford a fascinating opportunity to check out the future as he envisioned it over a century ago, when going around the world in 80 days sounded utterly fantastic. Most signs are in French and English; a detailed English guidebook is available at the ticket desk.

Musée de Picardie MUSEUM
(☎03 22 97 14 00; www.amiens.fr/musees; 48 rue de la République; adult/child €5.50/free; ⏲10am-noon & 2-6pm Tue-Sat, to 9pm Thu, 2-7pm Sun) Housed in a dashing Second Empire structure (1855–67) with a jaw-droppingly impressive central room, the Picardy Museum is surprisingly well endowed with archaeological exhibits, medieval art and Revolution-era ceramics.

Tour Perret TOWER
(place Alphonse Fiquet) Long the tallest building in western Europe, the reinforced concrete Perret Tower (110m), facing the train station, was designed by Belgian architect Auguste Perret (who also planned postwar Le Havre) and completed in 1954.

Hortillonnages BOATING
(☎03 22 92 12 18; apsseh@wanadoo.fr; 54 bd Beauvillé; adult/child €6/4; ⏲1.30-5pm Apr-Oct) Amiens' market gardens – some 3 sq km in extent – have supplied the city with vegetables and flowers since the Middle Ages. Today, their peaceful *rieux* (waterways), home to seven working farms, more than 1000 private gardens and countless water birds, can be visited on 12-person boats whose raised prows make them look a bit like gondolas. Get there at 1.30pm to avoid long lines.

From mid-June to mid-October, the Hortillonages host art installations accessible on foot, by bicycle or by rental *barque* (boat).

Sleeping

Le Quatorze B&B €
(☎06 16 89 19 87; www.lequatorze.fr; 14 av de Dublin; d incl breakfast €75; 📶) Laure offers the perfect B&B experience, with five snug rooms full of old-time touches (original tiles, family photos, wooden flooring, marble fireplaces). Situated 1.5km southeast of the train station in the historic Quartier Anglais, a little piece of England built in the 1890s for the British managers of a textile factory (part of Sebastian Faulks' novel *Birdsong* is set here).

Amenities include a full kitchen, a washing machine and an English-style back garden. Two rooms' private bathrooms are situated across the hall.

Hôtel Victor Hugo HOTEL €
(☎03 22 91 57 91; www.hotel-a-amiens.com; 2 rue de l'Oratoire; d €49-65; 📶) This bargain-priced, family-run hotel has a Victor Hugo–era vibe and 10 simple but comfortable rooms. Best value, if you don't mind a long stair climb, are rooms 7 and 8, under the eves on the top floor, which offer rooftop views and lots of natural light.

Hôtel Le St-Louis HOTEL €
(☎03 22 91 76 03; www.amiens-hotel.fr; 24 rue des Otages; d €84-98, f €155-200; 📶) The 24 rooms, half of them completely renovated in 2015, are quiet, spacious and pleasingly modern; most come with king-size beds. Rooms with street views get more natural light.

Grand Hôtel de l'Univers HOTEL €€
(☎03 22 91 52 51; www.hotel-univers-amiens.com; 2 rue de Noyon; d €95-125; @📶) Built in 1846, this venerable, Best Western–affiliated hostelry has a superb parkside location. The 40 rooms, set around a three-storey atrium, are immaculate and very comfortable; those on the 2nd floor come with balconies. Spacious corner rooms such as no. 26 are flooded with natural light.

★**Hôtel Marotte** BOUTIQUE HOTEL €€€
(☎03 60 12 50 00; www.hotel-marotte.com; 3 rue Marotte; d €165-300, q €365-435; ❄@📶) Modern French luxury at its most elegant and romantic. All 12 light-drenched rooms are huge (at least 35 sq metres), but the two sauna suites (100 sq metres), sporting one-piece stone bath-tubs weighing 1½ tonnes, are really luxury apartments.

Eating

Le T'chiot Zinc BISTRO €
(☎03 22 91 43 79; 18 rue de Noyon; menus €15.90-29.90; ⏲noon-2.30pm Mon-Sat & 7-10.30pm Tue-Sat; 📶) Inviting, bistro-style decor reminiscent of the belle époque provides a fine backdrop for tasty, home-style French and Picard cuisine, including fish dishes and *caqhuse* (pork in a cream, wine vinegar and onion sauce).

Le Quai BRASSERIE €
(☎03 22 72 10 80; www.restaurant-le-quai.com; 13 quai Bélu; weekday menus €14-18, other menus €20-25; ⏲noon-2pm & 7-10pm Mon-Thu & Sun, to 11pm Fri & Sat, closed Mon winter) With its zesty decor, reasonable prices and lovely riverside terrace, Le Quai is a great place to sample traditional French and Picard dishes with a modern twist – for example, the *burger spécial Quai*, piled with coppa pork, cheddar and Maroilles sauce.

Tante Jeanne CRÊPERIE €
(☎03 22 72 30 30; www.restaurant-tantejeanne.com; 1 rue de la Dodane; mains €9.90-16.90, lunch menus €16.50; ⏲noon-2pm & 7-10pm Mon-Sat, noon-10pm Sun; 📶) A fine spot for a light meal, with

Amiens

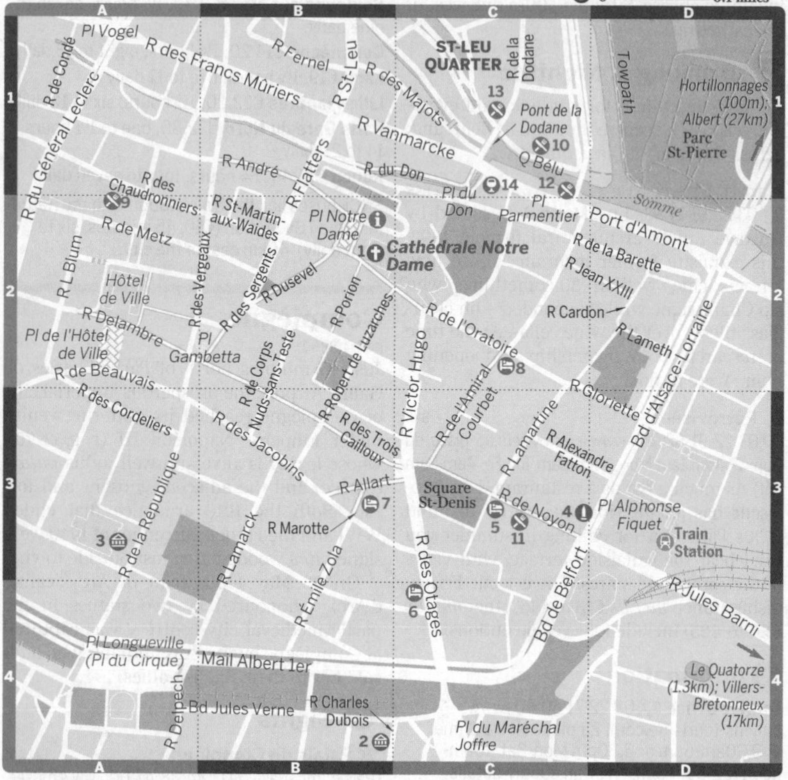

Amiens

Top Sights
1 Cathédrale Notre Dame B2

Sights
2 Maison de Jules Verne B4
3 Musée de Picardie A3
4 Tour Perret C3

Sleeping
5 Grand Hôtel de l'Univers C3
6 Hôtel Le St-Louis C4
7 Hôtel Marotte B3
8 Hôtel Victor Hugo C2

Eating
9 Covered Market A2
10 Le Quai C1
11 Le T'chiot Zinc C3
12 Marché sur l'Eau C1
13 Tante Jeanne C1

Drinking & Nightlife
14 Le Rétroviseur C1
Marott' Street .... (see 7)

galettes (gluten-free because they're buckwheat) available both savoury (13 kinds) and sweet (20 kinds). Also has meal-size salads, soups and Flemish and Picard dishes.

Self-Catering

Marché sur l'Eau FOOD MARKET €
(place Parmentier; ⏲to 1pm Sat) Fruit and veggies grown in the Hortillonnages are sold at this one-time floating market, now held on dry land. On the third Sunday in June, producers don traditional outfits and bring their products to market in high-prowed boats, like in the olden days.

Covered Market MARKET €
(Halles du Beffroi; rue de Metz; ⏲9am-1pm & 3-7pm Tue-Thu, 9am-7pm Fri & Sat, 9am-12.30pm

Sun) Two dozen stalls sell picnic supplies, including cheese. Situated 500m due west of the cathedral.

Drinking & Nightlife

Amiens' nightlife – for students and everyone else – is centred on quai Bélu and, across the river, at place du Don.

Marott' Street WINE BAR

(☎03 22 91 14 93; 1 rue Marotte) Designed by Gustave Eiffel's architectural firm in 1892, this exquisite former insurance office now attracts chic, well-off 30-somethings who sip Champagne while suspended – on clear-glass tiles – over the wine cellar. At the time of research, both ownership and opening hours were in flux.

Le Rétroviseur BAR

(☎03 22 91 92 70; www.leretroviseur.fr; place du Don; ⏲4pm-1am Mon, 11am-3am Tue-Fri, 4pm-3am Sat) As much a bar as a restaurant, Le Rétroviseur has an interior that brings to mind 1930s Paris, but for chilling in summer you can't beat the canalside terrace, with views of the cathedral's spires. The eclectic French dishes (lunch *menus* €13 to €16, other *menus* €20 to €25) include four veggie options.

Information

Tourist Office (☎03 22 71 60 50; www.amiens-tourisme.com; 23 place Notre Dame; ⏲9.30am-6pm or 6.30pm Mon-Sat, 10am-noon & 2-5pm Sun; 📶) Can supply details on the Somme memorials (including minibus tours), centennial events in 2017 and 2018, and cultural events such as marionette shows.

Getting There & Around

BICYCLE

The nonprofit **Vélo Service** (Buscyclette; ☎09 80 82 44 00; www.buscyclette.fr; 13 place Alphonse Fiquet; per day/weekend €3/7; ⏲9am-7pm Mon-Sat) rents regular, electric and kids' bikesfrom the sunken back courtyard of Tour Perret.

CAR & MOTORCYCLE

There's free parking four blocks east of the cathedral along rue Lameth, rue Cardon, rue Jean XXIII and rue de la Barette.

To hire a car to tour the Somme memorials, try **Avis** (☎03 22 91 31 21; www.avis.fr; 11 rue St-Martin-aux-Waides); it's usually possible to pick up your car at the train station.

TRAIN

Amiens is an important rail hub, with the following direct services:

Arras €13.10, 45 minutes, seven to 15 daily

Boulogne-sur-Mer €21.70, 1½ hours, seven to nine daily

Compiègne €14.20, 1¼ hours, eight to 13 daily

Laon €19, 1½ hours, five to 11 daily

Lille-Flandres €22.20, 1½ hours, six to 12 daily

Paris Gare du Nord €22.80, one to 1½ hours, 14 to 21 daily

Rouen €21.40, 1¼ hours, four to seven daily

SNCF buses link the train station with the Haute Picardie TGV station (€10, 45 minutes, six to eight daily), 40km east of the city.

Compiègne

POP 40,860

Just 40 minutes north of Paris' Charles de Gaulle Airport, the prosperous 'imperial city' of Compiègne reached its glittering zenith under Emperor Napoléon III (r 1852–70), whose legacy is alive and well in his *palais* (palace) and the adjacent gardens and forests. Both the 1918 armistice that ended WWI and the French surrender of 1940 were signed in a wooded area just outside town.

On 23 May 1430, Joan of Arc (Jeanne d'Arc) – honoured by two statues in the partly medieval city centre – was captured at Compiègne by the Burgundians, who later sold her to their English allies.

Sights

★Palais de Compiègne PALACE

(Palais Impérial; ☎03 44 38 47 00; www.musee-chateau-compiegne.fr; place du Général de Gaulle; adult/child €7.50/free; ⏲10am-6pm Wed-Mon, Grands Appartements 10am-noon & 1.30-4pm or 5.15pm Wed-Mon) This 1337-room palace, originally built for Louis XV, hosted Napoléon III's dazzling hunting parties, which drew aristocrats from all around Europe. A single ticket grants access to the sumptuous Grands Appartements, where highlights include the empress's bedroom and a ballroom lit by 15 chandeliers (English audioguide available); the Musée du Second Empire, illustrating the lives of Napoléon III and his family; and the Musée de la Voiture, featuring vehicles that pre-date the internal combustion engine.

The Musée de l'Impératrice, which stars Eugénie (Napoléon III's wife), will be closed for renovations until at least 2018. From about April to mid-November, you can have lunch or a drink in the Jardin des Roses (rose garden). Almost all parts of the palace are now wheelchair accessible.

Stretching southeast from the château, the 20-hectare, English-style Petit Parc links up with the Grand Parc and the Forêt de Compiègne, a forest that surrounds Compiègne on the east and south and is criss-crossed by rectilinear paths. The area is a favourite venue for hiking and cycling (maps and bike-rental details available at the tourist office) as well as horse riding.

Mémorial de l'Internement et de la Déportation – Camp de Royallieu MUSEUM
(Internment & Deportation Memorial; ☎03 44 96 37 00; www.memorial-compiegne.fr; 2bis av des Martyrs de la Liberté; adult/child incl English audioguide €3/1.50; ⏲10am-6pm Wed-Mon) Situated about 3km southwest of the city centre, the French military base of Royallieu was used as a Nazi transit and internment camp from 1941 to 1944; three of the 24 original barracks now house a moving memorial museum.

The majority of the estimated 54,000 men, women and children held here – mainly political prisoners (especially communists) and *résistants* but also some 3000 Jews – were marched to Compiègne's train station for the trip east to concentration and extermination camps, including Auschwitz; more than half never returned. A special section with less harsh conditions housed 500 American civilians, interned as 'enemy aliens'.

Clairière de l'Armistice HISTORIC SITE
(Armistice Clearing; ☎03 44 85 14 18; www.musee-armistice-14-18.fr; adult/child €5/3; ⏲10am-5.30pm Apr-Sep, closed Tue Oct-Dec, Feb & Mar, closed Jan) The armistice that put an end to WWI was signed in a thick forest 7km northeast of Compiègne, inside the railway carriage of the Allied supreme commander. On 22 June 1940, in the same railway car, the French were forced to sign the armistice that recognised Nazi Germany's domination of France. These momentous events are commemorated with monuments, memorabilia, newspaper clippings and 800 stereoscopic (3D) photos.

Taken to Berlin for exhibition, the railway carriage used in 1918 and 1940 was destroyed in April 1945 on Hitler's personal orders lest it be used for a third surrender – his own. The wooden rail wagon now on display is of the same type as the original, though some of the interior furnishings, hidden during WWII, were the ones actually used in 1918.

Sleeping & Eating

Hôtel du Nord HOTEL €€
(☎03 44 83 22 30; www.hoteldunordcompiegne.com; 1 place de la Gare; s/d from €82/92; 📶) This well-run establishment has 20 quiet, compact rooms, some with balconies and river views. Downstairs, La Table d'Elisa serves French *gastronomique* cuisine with a creative twist.

Les Halles du Grenier à Sel FOOD MARKET €
(cnr rue des Lombards & place du Change; ⏲7am-7pm Tue-Sat; ✍) Gourmet fruit, veggies, cheeses, wines and prepared dishes, sold inside a one-time salt store built in 1784.

Les Accordailles BISTRO €
(☎03 44 40 03 45; www.les-accordailles-restaurant.fr; 24 rue d'Ulm; menus €13-25; ⏲noon-2.30pm & 7-10.30pm Tue-Sat, noon-2.30pm Sun; ✍) Facing the Palais de Compiègne, this cosy, informal little bistro serves traditional French and Picard cuisine made with fresh organic ingredients purchased from small producers. The wines and liqueurs are organic, too.

★Bistrot du Terroir FRENCH €€
(☎03 44 40 06 36; www.bistrot-du-terroir.fr; 13 rue Eugène Floquet; lunch menus from €17.90, other menus €23.90-30.90; ⏲noon-2pm & 7-10pm Mon-Thu, to 11pm Fri & Sat) Tucked away on a side street near the tourist office, this cosy place serves excellent French cuisine created using fresh seasonal products. Mains often include *carré d'agneau rôti* (roasted rack of lamb).

Bistrot de Flandre BISTRO €€
(☎03 44 83 26 35; www.bistrotdeflandre.fr; 2 rue d'Amiens; menus €22-30; ⏲noon-2.30pm & 7.30-10.30pm Mon-Sat, noon-2.30pm Sun; 📶) Ask locals for restaurant recommendations and chances are they'll mention this place, known for its modern bistro-style *cuisine de passion*, all of it homemade using fresh ingredients. Semi-formal, with white tablecloths and crystal.

WORTH A TRIP

A FRENCH-AMERICAN MUSEUM

The Americans and the French have had an ardent but prickly affair for more than two centuries. **Musée Franco-Américain** (☎03 23 39 14 71; http://museefrancoamericain.fr; Château de Blérancourt, Blérancourt), which should now have reopened after a decade of archaeological excavations and renovations, showcases that relationship through art, historical exhibits and the Jardins du Nouveau Monde, planted with 'exotic' flowers (in bloom May to September), shrubs and trees native to the Americas. Situated 32km northeast of Compiègne.

Information

The centrally located **tourist office** (☎03 44 40 01 00; www.compiegne-tourisme.fr; place de l'Hôtel de Ville; ⏰9.15am-12.15pm & 1.45-5.15pm or 6.15pm Mon-Sat Nov-Easter, plus 10am-12.15pm & 2.15-5pm Sun Easter-Oct) abuts the 16th-century, Flamboyant Gothic *hôtel de ville*, whose tower holds aloft three figures that sound the quarter-hour.

Getting There & Away

Compiègne's train station, 1km northwest of the château, has direct services to Paris' Gare du Nord (€15.40, 50 to 75 minutes, at least hourly) and Amiens (€14.20, one to 1½ hours, nine to 14 daily).

Laon

POP 25,300

Enclosed within a 7km-long wall pierced by three fortified gates, Laon's medieval Ville Haute (Upper City) boasts a magnificent Gothic cathedral and no fewer than 84 listed historic monuments, the densest concentration anywhere in France. The narrow streets, alleyways and courtyards reward keen-eyed wandering. About 100 vertical metres below sits the Ville Basse (Lower City), completely rebuilt after being flattened in WWII.

Laon served as the capital of the Carolingians until the dynasty's demise in 987 at the hands of Hugh Capet (founder of the Capetian dynasty), who for some reason preferred ruling from Paris.

About 20km south of Laon along the D18, the 30km-long ridge known as the Chemin des Dames was the site of fierce fighting during WWI. The centenary of the Second Battle of the Aisne, a bloody French offensive, will be commemorated here in spring 2017.

Sights

Cathédrale Notre Dame CATHEDRAL

(⏰9am-6pm, later in summer) A model for a number of its more famous Gothic sisters – Chartres, Reims, Dijon and Paris' Notre-Dame among them – this medieval jewel was built (1150–1230) in the transitional Gothic style on Romanesque foundations. The 110m-long interior, remarkably well lit, has three levels of superimposed columns and arches, and a gilded wrought-iron choir screen; some of the stained glass dates from the 12th century. To fully appreciate the splendid interior, rent an audioguide (€5) next door at the tourist office.

Inside the west façade, a plaque commemorates 'one million dead of the British Empire who fell in the Great War'. Tours (€3) of one of the cathedral's five towers are held at 2pm on Saturday and Sunday; sign up at the tourist office.

Sleeping & Eating

Hôtel Les Chevaliers HOTEL €

(☎03 23 27 17 50; 3 rue Sérurier, Ville Haute; s/d €63/69, family ste €81; 📶) The foundations of this romantic, 13-room hostelry, right around the corner from the Ville Haute's *hôtel de ville*, date from the 12th century. Rooms 6, 11 and 12 have exposed beams, brick walls and great views. Excellent location, good value.

La Maison des 3 Rois B&B €€

(☎03 23 20 74 24; www.lamaisondes3rois.com; 17 rue St-Martin, Ville Haute; d incl breakfast €95-120; 📶) Nestled in a beautifully renovated *maison de maître* (nobleman's house) whose foundations date from the 14th century, this gem has five spacious rooms, each with its own personality. Ideal for families. Situated 700m west of the cathedral.

Estaminet Saint-Jean REGIONAL CUISINE €

(☎03 23 23 04 89; www.estaminetsaintjean.com; 23 rue St-Jean, Ville Haute; lunch menus €10-12.50, other menus €25; ⏰noon-2pm Tue-Sun, 7-9.30pm Tue & Thu-Sat) Specialising in Flemish and Picard cuisine accompanied by your choice of 30 beers, this old-fashioned neighbourhood eatery is especially good value for lunch.

Information

Tourist Office (☎03 23 20 28 62; www.tourisme-paysdelaon.com; place du Parvis, Ville Haute; ⏰10am-6pm Apr-Sep, 10am-noon Wed-Sat & 2-5.30pm daily Oct-Mar; 📶) Can supply you with an excellent walking-tour map of Laon (free) and audioguides (€5) for walks around the cathedral (one hour) and the Cité Médiévale (medieval city; one to four hours). The City Pass de Laon (€10) may save you some cash. Guided tours are in French, but some guides may speak English. Situated next to the cathedral in a 12th-century hospital; ask to see the vaulted Gothic hall downstairs.

Getting There & Around

The train station, in the Ville Basse, has direct services to Paris' Gare du Nord (€24.10, 1½ hours, eight to 14 direct daily), Amiens (€19, 1½ hours, four to 12 daily) and Reims (€10.40, 40 minutes, three to 12 daily). The Ville Haute is a steep 20-minute walk from the train station – stairs begin at the end of av Carnot – but it's more fun to take the **Poma funicular railway** (return €1.20; ⏰every 5min 7am-8pm Mon-Sat), which whisks you from the station to the upper city in just 3½ minutes.

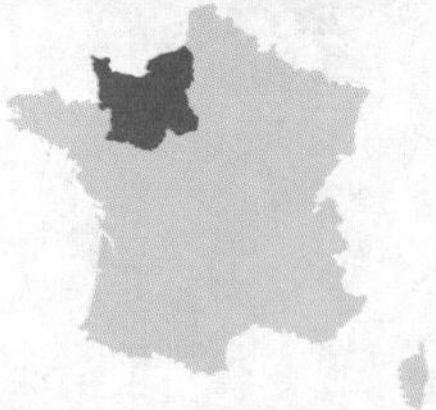

Normandy

POP 3.4 MILLION

Includes ➡

Best Places to Eat

- ➡ La Fleur de Sel (p242)
- ➡ L'Espiguette (p216)
- ➡ Marché aux Poissons (p238)
- ➡ Alchimie (p227)

Best Places to Sleep

- ➡ Hôtel de la Chaîne d'Or (p225)
- ➡ Hôtel de Bourgtheroulde (p216)
- ➡ Detective Hôtel (p222)
- ➡ La Petite Folie (p241)

Why Go?

From the Norman invasion of England in 1066 to the D-Day landings of 1944, Normandy has long played an outsized role in European history. This rich and often brutal past is brought vividly to life by the spectacular island monastery of Mont St-Michel; the Bayeux Tapestry, world-famous for its cartoon scenes of 11th-century life; and the cemeteries and memorials along the D-Day beaches, places of solemn pilgrimage. Lower-profile charms include a variety of dramatic coastal landscapes, lots of pebbly beaches, some of France's finest museums, quiet pastoral villages and architectural gems ranging from Rouen's medieval old city – home of Monet's favourite cathedral – to the maritime charms of Honfleur to the striking postwar modernism of Le Havre. Camembert, apples, cider, cream-rich cuisine and the very freshest fish and seafood provide further reasons to visit this accessible and beautiful region of France.

When to Go

Rouen

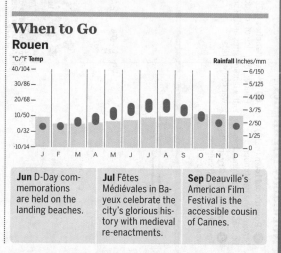

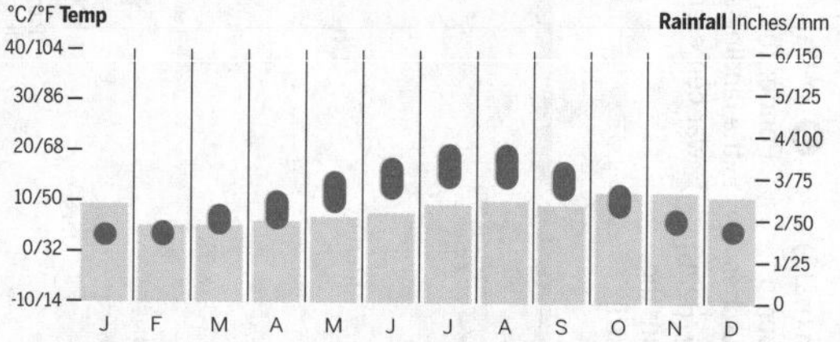

Jun D-Day commemorations are held on the landing beaches.

Jul Fêtes Médiévales in Bayeux celebrate the city's glorious history with medieval re-enactments.

Sep Deauville's American Film Festival is the accessible cousin of Cannes.

Normandy Highlights

1 **Rouen's old town** (p213) Stroll among half-timbered houses and Gothic churches.

2 **Bayeux Tapestry** (p225) Travel back to 1066 with the world's oldest comic strip.

3 **D-Day Beaches** (p228) Ponder the price of freedom at the landing sites and nearby war cemeteries.

4 **Mont St-Michel** (p244) Watch the tide rush in from the ramparts and the extraordinary monastery.

5 **La Fleur de Sel** (p242) Feast at some of Normandy's best eateries, such as La Fleur de Sel in charming Honfleur.

6 **Le Havre** (p222) Experience postwar modernism at its most elegant.

7 **Étretat** (p222) Marvel at the famous twin cliffs and free-standing limestone arches.

SEINE-MARITIME

The Seine-Maritime *département* stretches along the chalk-white cliffs of the Côte d'Albâtre (Alabaster Coast) from Le Tréport via Dieppe to Le Havre, France's second-busiest port (after Marseille). Its history firmly bound up with the sea, the region offers visitors a mix of small seaside villages and dramatic cliff-top walks.

When you fancy a break from the bracing sea air, head inland to the lively, ancient metropolis of Rouen, a favourite haunt of Monet and Simone de Beauvoir and one of the most intriguing cities in France's northeast.

Rouen

POP 111,000

With its soaring Gothic cathedral, beautifully restored medieval quarter, excellent museums and vibrant cultural life, Rouen is one of Normandy's most engaging destinations.

The city has had a turbulent history. It was devastated by fire and plague several times during the Middle Ages, and was occupied by the English during the Hundred Years War. The young French heroine Joan of Arc (Jeanne d'Arc) was tried for heresy and burned at the stake in the central square in 1431. And during WWII, Allied bombing raids laid waste to large parts of the city, especially south of the cathedral.

Sights & Activities

North of the cathedral, parts of the city centre – especially between rue de la République and rue Jeanne d'Arc – still have a distinctly medieval aspect, with half-timbered buildings and cobblestone streets. Alleyways worth exploring include tiny **rue des Chanoines**, just 90cm wide.

At the tourist office, audioguides (€5) of the city and the cathedral are available in seven languages.

Cathédrale Notre Dame CATHEDRAL
(www.cathedrale-rouen.net; place de la Cathédrale; 2-7pm Mon, 9am-7pm Tue-Sat, 8am-6pm Sun Apr-Oct, shorter hours Nov-Mar) Rouen's stunning Gothic cathedral, built between the late 12th and 16th centuries, was famously the subject of a series of canvases painted by Monet at various times of the day and year. The 75m-tall **Tour de Beurre** (Butter Tower) was financed by locals in return for being allowed to eat butter during Lent – or so the story goes.

A free sound-and-light spectacular is projected on the facade every night from June (at 11pm) to late September (at 9.30pm).

★ **Historial Jeanne d'Arc** MUSEUM
(02 35 52 48 00; www.historialjeannedarc.fr; 7 rue St-Romain; adult/child €10/7; 10am-6pm Tue-Sun) For an introduction to the great 15th-century heroine and the events that earned her fame – and shortly thereafter condemnation – don't miss this excellent new site. It's less of a museum, and more of an immersive, theatre-like experience, where you walk through medieval corridors and watch (and hear via headphones) the dramatic retelling of Joan's visions, her victories, the trial that sealed her fate, and the mythologising that followed in the years after her death.

Musée des Beaux-Arts ART MUSEUM
(02 35 71 28 40; www.mbarouen.fr; esplanade Marcel Duchamp; 10am-6pm Wed-Mon) FREE Housed in a grand structure erected in 1870, Rouen's outstanding fine-arts museum features canvases by Rubens, Modigliani, Pissarro, Renoir, Sisley (lots) and, of course, several works by Monet. There's also one jaw-dropping painting by Caravaggio.

Panorama XXL GALLERY
(www.panoramaxxl.com; Quai de Boisguilbert; adult/child €10/7; 10am-7pm May-Sep, to 6pm Oct-Apr) In a large, circular column on the waterfront, Panorama XXL lives up to its oversized name, with one massive 360-degree exhibition inside that offers in-depth exploring of one vast landscape, created with photographs, drawings, digital images and recorded audio. Past years have featured Amazonia, Ancient Rome and Rouen in 1431 – often with sunrise and sunset creating different moods, as well as storms. A 15m-high viewing platform in the middle of the room gives a fine vantage point over the scene.

Place du Vieux Marché SQUARE
The old city's main thoroughfare, rue du Gros Horloge, runs from the cathedral west to place du Vieux Marché. This is where 19-year-old Joan of Arc was executed for heresy in 1431.

Gros Horloge CLOCK TOWER
(rue du Gros Horloge; adult/child €7/3.50; 10am-1pm & 2-7pm Tue-Sun Apr-Oct, to 6pm Nov-Mar) Spanning rue du Gros Horloge, the Great Clock's Renaissance archway has a gilded, one-handed medieval clock face on each

Rouen

0 200 m
0 0.1 miles

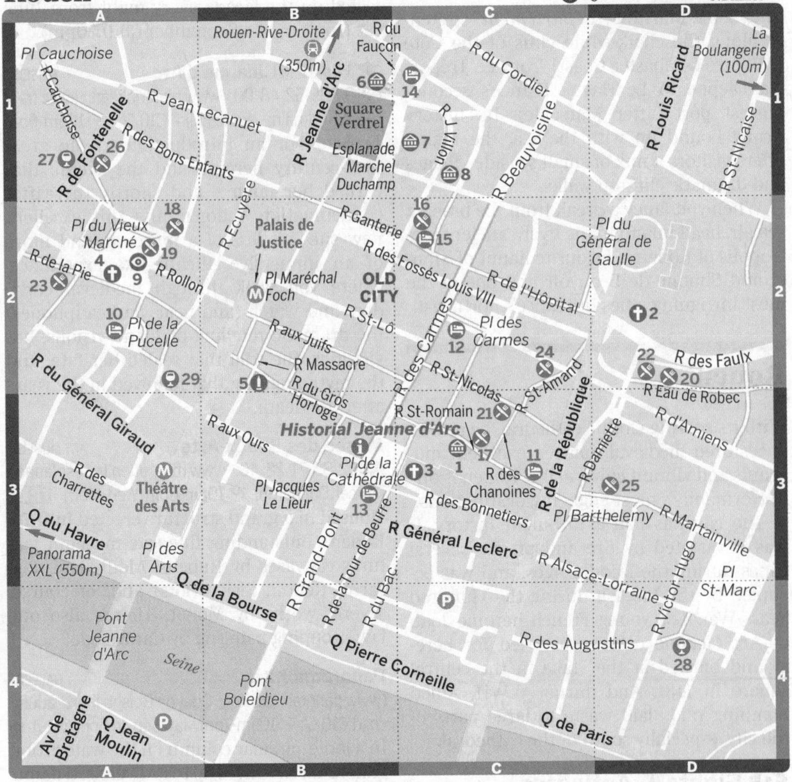

Rouen

Top Sights

1 Historial Jeanne d'Arc C3

Sights

2 Abbatiale St-Ouen D2
3 Cathédrale Notre Dame C3
4 Église Jeanne d'Arc A2
5 Gros Horloge B2
6 Musée de la Céramique B1
7 Musée des Beaux-Arts C1
8 Musée Le Secq des Tournelles C1
9 Place du Vieux Marché A2

Sleeping

10 Hôtel de Bourgtheroulde A2
11 Hôtel de la Cathédrale C3
12 Hôtel des Carmes C2
13 Hôtel Le Cardinal B3
14 Hôtel Morand C1
15 Le Vieux Carré C2

Eating

Bar à Huitres .... (see 19)
16 Citizen C2
17 Dame Cakes C3
18 Gill Côté Bistro A2
19 Hallettes du Vieux Marché A2
20 La Cornaëlle D2
21 La Rose des Vents C3
22 Le P'tit Bec D2
23 Les Nymphéas A2
24 L'Espiguette C2
25 Made in Normandy D3
26 Minute et Mijoté A1

Drinking & Nightlife

27 La Boîte à Bières A1
28 Le Saxo D4
29 Les Berthom A2

side. High above, a Gothic belfry, reached via spiral stairs, affords spectacular views. The excellent audioguide is a great introduction to Rouen's colourful history and is available in eight languages.

Église Jeanne d'Arc CHURCH
(place du Vieux Maré; ⏲10am-noon & 2-6pm, closed Fri & Sun mornings) Dedicated in 1979, the thrillingly bizarre Église Jeanne d'Arc, with its fish-scale exterior, marks the spot where 19-year-old Joan of Arc was burned at the stake in 1431.

Musée de la Céramique MUSEUM
(☎02 35 71 28 40; www.museedelaceramique.fr; 1 rue du Faucon; ⏲2-6pm Wed-Mon) FREE The Ceramics Museum, housed in a 17th-century building with a fine courtyard, is known for its 16th- to 19th-century faience (tin-glazed earthenware) and porcelain. Don't miss sculptural pieces such as the exquisite celestial sphere (1725) on the upper floor.

Musée Le Secq des Tournelles MUSEUM
(☎02 35 71 28 40; www.museelesecqdestournelles.fr; 2 rue Jacques Villon; ⏲2-6pm Wed-Mon) FREE Home to one of the world's premier collections of wrought iron, this riveting museum showcases the extraordinary skills of pre-industrial iron- and locksmiths. Housed in a desanctified 16th-century church.

Abbatiale St-Ouen CHURCH
(place du Général de Gaulle; ⏲10am-noon & 2-6pm Tue-Thu, Sat & Sun) This 14th-century abbey is a marvellous example of the Rayonnant Gothic style. The entrance is through the lovely garden on the south side, facing rue des Faulx.

Sleeping

★ La Boulangerie B&B €
(☎06 12 94 53 15; www.laboulangerie.fr; 59 rue St-Nicaise; s from €67, d €77-92, q €154; P) Tucked into a quiet side street 1.2km northeast of the cathedral, this adorable B&B, above an historic bakery, has three bright, pleasingly decorated rooms, adorned with artwork and attractive details (such as exposed beam ceilings). Your charming host Aminata is a gold mine of local information. Parking available for €5; breakfast is included.

Le Vieux Carré HOTEL €
(☎02 35 71 67 70; www.hotel-vieux-carre.com; 34 rue Ganterie; r €65-70;) Set around a little medieval courtyard, this quiet, half-timbered hotel has a delightfully old-fashioned *salon de thé* (tearoom, open 3pm to 7pm) and 13 small, practical rooms, all recently renovated.

Hôtel des Carmes HOTEL €
(☎02 35 71 92 31; www.hoteldescarmes.com; 33 place des Carmes; d €62-75;) This sweet little hotel, built in 1850, offers 12 smallish but pleasant rooms that get cheaper the higher you climb (there's no lift). The annexe has two spacious suites. The oil paintings are by the owner's wife, who also designed the decor.

Auberge de Jeunesse Robec HOSTEL €
(☎02 35 08 18 50; www.fuaj.org; 3 rue de la Tour; dm €25-35; ⏲reception 8-11.45am & 5.30-10pm;) The two- to eight-bed rooms at this modern, 88-bed hostel are comfortable and functional. It's set 2km east of the cathedral off route de Darnétal; from the city centre, take bus T2 or T3 to the 'Auberge de Jeunesse' stop.

Hôtel Morand HOTEL €
(☎02 35 71 46 07; http://morandhotel.com; 1 rue Morand; s/d from €49/68;) This budget-friendly place has simple rooms with wood floors, stiff mattresses and basic furnishings (though the in-room electric kettle is a nice touch). The cheapest quarters have a shower and sink only, with other shared facilities down the hall. Friendly service and a good location (with discounted parking at a nearby garage).

Les Cabanes du Clos Masure COTTAGE €€
(☎07 70 36 84 21; www.cabanesclosmasure.fr; 873 rue du Bornier; r €140) For something completely different, you can lodge in the treetops, in one of four all wood cabins located some 30 minutes outside of Rouen. It's also a working farm with cows and chickens running about, and a good choice for families with small children (cabins are small but cosy and sleep up to six).

Hôtel de la Cathédrale HOTEL €€
(☎02 35 71 57 95; www.hotel-de-la-cathedrale.fr; 12 rue St-Romain; s/d/tr/q from €85/95/145/165; @) Hiding behind a 17th-century half-timbered facade, this atmospheric hotel has 27 rooms with old-time French decor and modern bathrooms; most overlook a quiet, plant-filled courtyard.

Hôtel Le Cardinal HOTEL €€
(☎02 35 70 24 42; www.cardinal-hotel.fr; 1 place de la Cathédrale; s €78-98, d €88-118;) Facing the cathedral's famous west facade, this 15-room hotel is one of best midrange deals in central Rouen. All but two of the bright rooms have romantic cathedral views, and eight come with balconies or terraces.

WORTH A TRIP

JUMIÈGES

With its ghostly white-stone ruins glowing against bright green grass and dark green trees, the **Abbaye de Jumièges** (☎02 35 37 24 02; www.abbayedejumieges.fr; Jumièges; adult/child €6.50/free; ⏰9.30am-6.30pm mid-Apr–mid-Sep, 9.30am-1pm & 2.30-5.30pm mid-Sep–mid-Apr) is one of Normandy's most evocative medieval relics. The church was begun in 1020, and William the Conqueror attended its consecration in 1067. The abbey declined during the Hundred Years War but enjoyed a renaissance under Charles VII, flourishing until revolutionaries booted out the monks in 1790 and allowed the buildings to be mined for construction material.

Jumièges is 28km from Rouen. To get to here, take the west-bound D982 and then, from Duclair, the D65.

Hôtel de Bourgtheroulde LUXURY HOTEL €€€
(☎02 35 14 50 50; www.hotelsparouen.com; 15 place de la Pucelle; r €195-254; P❄📶🏊) Rouen's finest hostelry (now owned by the Marriott) serves up a sumptuous mix of early 16th-century architecture – Flamboyant Gothic, to be precise – and sleek, modern luxury. The 78 rooms are spacious and gorgeously appointed. Amenities include a pool (19m), sauna and spa in the basement, and a lobby bar with live piano music on Saturday evening.

Eating

Rouen's main dining district, home to dozens of eateries and cafes, is around place du Vieux Marché and adjacent place de la Pucelle. East of the cathedral, there's a row of classy little restaurants along the northern side of rue Martainville, near Église St-Maclou.

Citizen CAFE €
(4 Rue de l'Écureuil; mains €7-12, Sat brunch €22; ⏰9am-7pm Mon-Fri, from 11am Sat) Citizen is undeniably hip with its chunky wood communal tables, industrial fixtures and groovy tunes playing overhead. More important than the surrounds are the coffee, which is the best in town, and the tasty bites on hand (granola, fresh fruit and *fromage blanc* for breakfast; smoked salmon salad for lunch), plus beers from Brooklyn Brewery. Outdoor seating on the plaza.

Bar à Huitres SEAFOOD €
(place du Vieux Marché; mains €10-16, oysters per half-dozen/dozen from €10/17; ⏰10am-2pm Tue-Sat) For remarkably fresh seafood, grab a seat at the horseshoe-shaped bar at this casual but polished eatery located inside Rouen's covered market. Specials change daily based on what's fresh, from giant shrimp to dorado and fillet of sole, all cooked up to perfection. Don't neglect the restaurant's namesake – the satisfying *huîtres* (oysters) with several different varieties on offer.

La Cornaëlle CREPERIE €
(☎02 35 08 53 75; 174 rue Eau de Robec; crêpes €8-12; ⏰noon-3pm & 7-10pm Tue-Sat, noon-3pm Sun) Arched ceilings, pale stone walls and some low-playing blues set the scene for an enjoyable night nibbling on delicious savoury *galettes*, while sipping some of the fizzy local cider. Finish off with a decadent dessert crêpe (try the *poêlée Normande* with apples, caramel, cream and flambéed *calvados*).

La Rose des Vents MODERN FRENCH €
(☎02 35 70 29 78; 37 rue St-Nicolas; mains €16; ⏰noon-3pm Tue-Sat) Tucked away inside a secondhand shop, this stylish establishment is hugely popular with foodies and hipsters. Patrons rave about the two lunch mains, which change weekly according to what's available in the market. They can usually whip up something for vegetarians as well. Reservations are recommended.

L'Espiguette BISTRO €
(☎02 35 71 66 27; 25 place St-Amand; weekday lunch menu €13, mains €17-24; ⏰noon-10pm Tue-Sat) This charmingly decorated eatery serves excellent bistro classics (think osso buco, filet of sole, beef tartare), with the day's offerings scribbled on a chalkboard. Grab a seat at one of the outdoor tables on a warm day. It's quite popular with locals, so reserve ahead, even at lunchtime. Speaking of which, the lunch *menu* is a great deal.

Dame Cakes PATISSERIE €
(☎02 35 07 49 31; www.damecakes.fr; 70 rue St-Romain; lunch menu €16-20, tea & cake menu €9; ⏰10.30am-7pm Mon-Sat; 🍴) Walk through the historic, early 20th-century facade and you'll discover a delightfully civilised selection of pastries, cakes and chocolates. From noon to 3pm you can tuck into delicious quiches, *gratins* and salads in the attached *salon de thé* (tearoom). Lovely.

Le P'tit Bec MODERN FRENCH €
(☎02 35 07 63 33; www.leptitbec.com; 182 rue Eau de Robec; mains €12-15; ⏰noon-2.30pm Mon-Sat,

7-10.30pm Thu-Sat, plus 7-10.30pm Tue & Wed Jun-Aug;) The down-to-earth menu is stuffed with *gratins* (cheese-topped dishes), salads, *œufs cocottes* (eggs with grated cheese baked in cream) and homemade pastries.

Made in Normandy FRENCH €€
(02 35 14 07 45; www.lemadeinnormandy.fr; 236 rue Martainville; lunch menu €13-15, dinner menu €19-23; noon-2pm & 7-9.30pm Thu-Mon) A candle-lit, semi-formal restaurant that serves outstanding French and Norman dishes, including succulent beef, Dieppe-style seafood stew and rich crème brulée.

Minute et Mijoté BISTRO €€
(02 32 08 40 00; http://minutemijote.canalblog.com; 58 rue de Fontenelle; lunch menus €16.50-21, dinner menus €26-31; noon-2pm & 7.45-10pm Mon-Sat) This smart bistro, with its retro decor, is a long-time favourite dining spot in Rouen. The menu is limited (just two seafood and two meat plates per night on average), but the chef uses quality ingredients, prepared with care, and it's great value overall.

Gill Côté Bistro BISTRO €€
(02 35 89 88 72; www.gill.fr; 14 place du Vieux Marché; menus €23-30; noon-3pm & 7.30-10.30pm) Sleek contemporary design, traditional French and Lyonnaise cuisine, and first-rate wines by the glass are featured at this popular bistro, under the tutelage of renowned chef Gilles Tournadre. On warm days, the outdoor tables overlooking the Église Jeanne d'Arc are the best place to be.

Les Nymphéas GASTRONOMIC €€€
(02 35 89 26 69; www.lesnympheas-rouen.com; 7-9 rue de la Pie; weekday lunch menu €27, other menus €44-74; 12.15-2pm Tue-Sun, 7-9pm Tue-Sat) With its formal tables arrayed under 16th-century beams, Les Nymphéas has long been a top address for fine dining. Young chef Alexandre Dessaux serves up French cuisine that manages to be both traditional and creative. Reservations are a must on weekends.

Self-Catering

Hallettes du Vieux Marché MARKET €
(place du Vieux Marché; 7am-7pm Tue-Sat, 7.30am-1pm Sun) A small covered market with an excellent *fromagerie* (cheese shop).

Drinking & Nightlife

The bars and cafes around place du Vieux Marché and in the old town buzz from noon until the early hours. Rouen is also the centre of Normandy's gay life.

Les Berthom BAR
(60 rue de la Vicomte; 5pm-midnight Sun-Wed, to 2am Thu-Sat) Beer lovers should pay a visit to this sleek brewpub near the Vieux Marché. You'll find a changing selection of beers on tap (nine or so at a time, with good Belgian abbey-style ales dominating the list). It's a lively spot for a drink, with bartenders cranking up the beats as the night progresses.

Le Saxo BAR
(02 35 98 24 92; www.facebook.com/le.saxo.rouen; 11 place St-Marc; 5pm-2am Mon-Sat) Le Saxo swings to jazz, blues, rock, reggae and world music, with free concerts by local bands on Friday and Saturday from 10pm to 1.30am (except in July and August). It hosts jazz jam sessions every other Thursday from 9pm. Serves 13 beers on tap and 120 by the bottle.

La Boîte à Bières BAR
(www.laboiteabieres.fr; 35 rue Cauchoise; 5pm-2am Tue-Sat;) This friendly, often-crowded establishment, with walls plastered with memorabilia, is affectionately known as BAB. It serves 15 or so beers on tap and another 230 in bottles, including local *bières artisanales* (microbrews).

Information

Tourist Office (02 32 08 32 40; www.rouentourisme.com; 25 place de la Cathédrale; 9am-7pm Mon-Sat, 9.30am-12.30pm & 2-6pm Sun May-Sep, 9.30am-12.30pm & 1.30-6pm Mon-Sat Oct-Apr) Housed in a 1500s Renaissance building facing the cathedral. Can provide English brochures on Normandy and details on guided tours in English (July and August). Rouen's only exchange bureau is at the back.

Getting There & Around

BICYCLE

Cy'clic (08 00 08 78 00; http://cyclic.rouen.fr; 5am-1am), Rouen's version of Paris' Vélib', lets you rent a city bike from 20 locations around town. Credit card registration for one/seven days costs €1/5, plus a deposit of €150. Use is free for the first 30 minutes; the 2nd/3rd/4th and subsequent half-hours cost €1/2/4 each.

BUS

Rouen is not very well served by buses, although there's a useful, but very slow, service to Le Havre (€2, three hours, four to five daily) from the bus station.

TRAIN

The train station, **Rouen-Rive-Droite**, is 1.2km north of the cathedral. In the city centre, train

tickets are available at the **Boutique SNCF** (cnr rue aux Juifs & rue Eugène Boudin; ⌚12.30-7pm Mon, 10am-7pm Tue-Sat). Direct services:

Caen €28, 1¾ hours, five or six daily

Dieppe €12.20, 45 minutes, 10 to 16 daily Monday to Saturday, seven Sunday

Le Havre €16, one hour, 16 to 19 daily Monday to Saturday, nine Sunday

Paris' Gare St-Lazare €24.10, 1¼ hours, 25 daily Monday to Friday, 13 to 18 Saturday and Sunday

Dieppe

POP 30,600

A seaside resort since 1824, Dieppe hasn't been chic for over a century, but the town's lack of cuteness and pretension can be refreshing. During WWII, the city was the focal point of the only large-scale Allied raid on Nazi-occupied France before D-Day.

Dieppe was one of France's most important ports in the 16th and 17th centuries, when ships regularly sailed from here to West Africa and Brazil. Many of the earliest French settlers in Canada set sail from Dieppe.

Sights & Activities

Château-Musée MUSEUM

(☎02 35 06 61 99; www.dieppe.fr; rue de Chastes; adult/child €4.50/free; ⌚10am-noon & 2-5pm Wed-Mon Oct-May, 10am-6pm Jun-Sep) Built between the 14th and 18th centuries, this imposing cliff-top castle affords spectacular views of the coast. Inside, the museum explores the city's maritime history and has a remarkable collection of carved ivory. Another highlight: local scenes painted by artists such as Pissarro and Renoir between 1870 and 1915, when Dieppe was at the height of its popularity with the fashionable classes.

Cité de la Mer MARITIME MUSEUM

(Estran; ☎02 35 06 93 20; www.estrancitedelamer.fr; 37 rue de l'Asile Thomas; adult/child €7/50/4; ⌚9.30am-6pm Mon-Fri, 9.30am-12.30pm & 1.30-6pm Sat & Sun) The 'City of the Sea' brings Dieppe's long maritime and fishing history to life, with kid-friendly exhibits that include model ships and a fish-petting *bassin tactile*. Sea creatures native to the English Channel swim in a dozen aquariums. Ask for an English-language brochure at the ticket desk.

Dieppe Canadian War Cemetery CEMETERY

(www.cwgc.org) Many of the Canadians who died in the Dieppe Raid of 1942 are buried at this peaceful site framed by rolling fields. Situated 4km towards Rouen; from the centre, take av des Canadiens (the continuation of av Gambetta) south and follow the signs.

Beach BEACH

(👪) Dieppe's often-windy, 1.8km-long beach is covered with smooth pebbles. The vast lawns were laid out in the 1860s by that seashore-loving imperial duo, Napoléon III and his wife, Eugénie. The area has several play areas for kids.

Tours

Ville de Dieppe BOATING

(☎06 09 52 37 38; www.bateau-ville-de-dieppe.com; quai Henri IV; adult/child from €9/5.50; ⌚weekends & school holidays Apr-Nov & mid-Jul–mid-Aug) Boat excursions (35 minutes) along the dramatic cliffs of the Côte d'Albâtre.

Sleeping

Villa Les Capucins B&B €

(☎02 35 82 16 52; http://villadescapucins.jimdo.com; 11 rue des Capucins; s/d/tr/q incl breakfast €80/100/130) This B&B, run by a retired lady, is a good surprise, not least for the marvellous sense of peacefulness that wraps the property – yet just a two-minute walk east of the harbour. The three rooms are nicely appointed with antique furniture, framed artwork and homey touches, and the ravishing landscaped garden is a great spot to unwind after a bout of sightseeing.

Les Arcades HOTEL €

(☎02 35 84 14 12; www.lesarcades.fr; 1-3 arcades de la Bourse; d €74-90; 📶) Perched above a colonnaded arcade from the 1600s, this well-managed establishment enjoys a great location across the street from the tourist office. The decor, in tans and browns (with intriguing polka-dot carpeting), is nothing to write home about, but 12 of the 21 rooms have fine port views.

Hôtel de la Plage HOTEL €€

(☎02 35 84 18 28; www.plagehotel-dieppe.com; 20 bd de Verdun; d €77-119; P 📶) One of several somewhat faded places along the seafront, this hotel has 40 modern, mod-con rooms of varying shapes and sizes; those at the front have balconies and afford knock-out views of the sea. Parking €8.

Eating

Quai Henri IV, along the north side of the harbour, is lined with touristy restaurants.

Le Turbot NORMAN €

(☎02 35 82 63 44; 12 quai Cale; mains €18-27, menu €16; ⏰12.15-2.30pm & 7.15-9.30pm Tue-Sat) This family-run Norman bistro decked out in sea paraphernalia serves outstanding seafood. Fresh-off-the-boat dishes, such as monkfish, Dover sole, scallops, and ray in cream sauce and capers, vie with deftly prepared meat dishes. At €16, the prix-fixe *menu* (which also includes a buffet selection of seafood entrées) is good value.

L'Huîtrière SEAFOOD €

(☎02 35 84 36 20; rue de la Mer (D75), Pourville; mains €12-31; ⏰10am-8pm Fri-Sun Easter-Sep, plus Mon-Thu Jul-Sep) Housed in a dilapidated, mid-20th-century concrete building with fantastic sea views, the renowned 'oystery' serves the freshest seafood for miles around, though don't come looking for bargains. Sandwiched between the D75 and the beachfront.

À La Marmite Dieppoise SEAFOOD €€

(☎02 35 84 24 26; 8 rue St-Jean; menus €21-44, mains €17-36; ⏰noon-2pm Tue-Sun, 7-9pm Tue-Sat) A Dieppe institution, this eatery is celebrated for its hearty *marmite dieppoise* (cream-sauce stew made with mussels, prawns and four kinds of fish – though you can also order it with lobster), served in a rustic dining room. Other specialities include Normandy-style fish and, from October to May, scallops.

Les Voiles d'Or GASTRONOMIC €€€

(☎02 35 84 16 84; www.lesvoilesdor.fr; 2 chemin des Falaises; mains €33-38, lunch menu €38, dinner menu €55; ⏰noon-1pm Wed-Sun, 8-9pm Wed-Sat) For cutting-edge cuisine made from top-quality ingredients, this Michelin-starred place is worth seeking. Chef Christian Arhan has a soft spot for local seafood but the menu also includes savoury meat dishes. Just next door is Villa Bali-Dieppe (same owners), an excellent B&B featuring three rooms decorated in a Balinese style (doubles €130). It's near Église Notre-Dame de Bon Secours.

ℹ Information

Tourist Office (☎02 32 14 40 60; www.dieppetourisme.com; Pont Jehan Ango; ⏰9am-1pm & 2-5pm Mon-Sat year-round, plus 9.30am-1pm & 2-5.30pm Sun May-Sep) Has useful English brochures on Dieppe and nearby parts of the Côte d'Albâtre.

NORMAN CUISINE

Normandy may be the largest French region without even a single vineyard, but its culinary riches more than make up for the dearth of local wines – and besides, any self-respecting Norman would rather wash down a meal with a pitcher of tart cider or *calvados* (apple brandy).

Normandy is a land of cream, soft cheeses, apples and an astonishingly rich range of seafood and fish. Classics to look out for include *coquilles St-Jacques* (scallops), available from October to May, and *sole dieppoise* (Dieppe sole). Don't forget your *trou normand* ('Norman hole'), the traditional break between courses of a meal for a glass of *calvados* to cleanse the palate and improve the appetite for the next course!

ℹ Getting There & Away

BOAT

DFDS Seaways (www.dfdsseaways.co.uk) runs trans-Channel car ferries linking Dieppe's **ferry terminal** (Terminal Transmanche; quai de la Marine), on the eastern side of the port's entrance channel, with the English port of Newhaven.

TRAIN

The train station is just south of the harbour. Services:

Le Havre €25.30, two to three hours, eight to 11 daily

Paris' Gare St-Lazare €33, two to three hours, nine daily Monday to Friday, two to four Saturday and Sunday

Rouen €12.20, 45 minutes, 10 to 16 daily Monday to Saturday, seven Sunday

To get to Paris and Le Havre, you have to change trains in Rouen.

Côte d'Albâtre

Stretching along Norman coast for 130km, the vertical, bone-white cliffs of the Côte d'Albâtre (Alabaster Coast) are strikingly reminiscent of the limestone cliffs of Dover, just across the Channel. The dramatic coastline, sculpted over eons by the wind and the waves, is dotted with attractive villages, fishing harbours, resort towns, pebbly beaches and lovely gardens.

If you're driving west from Dieppe, take the beautiful tertiary roads near the coast (eg the D75, D68, D79, D211 and D11), which pass through verdant, rolling countryside, rather

than the inland D925 and D940, which is where road signs will try to direct you.

For a lovely coastal drive: feast on oysters in Pourville-sur-Mer before cruising to scenic Varengeville; Veules-les-Roses, a cute village with a seafront boardwalk; and handsome St-Valery-en-Caux, whose attractions include a yacht harbour and a lovely beach. Continue to Veulettes-sur-Mer and Les Petites Dalles before reaching Fécamp.

On the plateau above the cliffs, walkers can follow the dramatic long-distance **GR21 hiking trail** (www.gr-infos.com/gr21.htm), which parallels the coast from Le Tréport all the way to Le Havre. *Le Pays des Hautes Falaises* (Land of the high cliffs), a free map available at tourist offices, details 46 coastal and inland walking circuits ranging from 6km to 22km.

Cyclists might want to stop by a tourist office to pick up *Véloroute du Littoral,* a free map detailing coastal bike routes.

ST-VALERY-EN-CAUX

This delightful coastal village, 32km west of Dieppe, has a large fishing and pleasure port, a lovely beach and half a dozen hotels. It is also the site of a **Franco-British WWII cemetery**. In January 1945, a runaway troop train crashed here, killing 89 American soldiers.

Sleeping & Eating

La Maison des Galets HOTEL €

(02 35 97 11 22; 6 rue des Remparts, St-Valery-en-Caux; s €50, d €70-80;) The spacious lobby is classic 1950s, with leather couches and lovely sea panoramas. Upstairs, the 14 rooms are simply furnished, with nautical touches and shiny, all-tile bathrooms. Situated 100m west of the casino.

Hôtel Henri IV HOTEL €€

(02 35 97 19 62; 16 rue du Havre; d from €63;) This amiable, well-located 19-room hotel has a medley of rooms, the best of which have views over the boats bobbing in the harbour. Some of the furnishings are a bit worn, but the building has character (with exposed beam ceilings in some rooms), and the renovated bathrooms are in tip-top shape.

Restaurant du Port SEAFOOD €€

(02 35 97 08 93; 18 quai d'Amont, St-Valery-en-Caux; menus €27-46, mains €17-45; 12.15-2pm Tue-Sun, 7.30-9pm Tue-Wed, Fri & Sat) A treat for lovers of fish and seafood. À la carte offerings include oysters, fresh crab and turbot marinated in hollandaise sauce. The seafood platters (€43) are a sight to behold.

Getting There & Away

Most travellers arrive in St-Valery-en-Caux by car. If you're relying on public transport, bus 61 (€2, four to seven daily, one hour) provides regular service to/from Dieppe.

FÉCAMP

POP 29,000

Fécamp is a lively fishing port with an attractive harbour, dramatic cliffs and a long monastic history. It is best known for producing Bénédictine, a fiery 'medicinal elixir' concocted here by a Venetian monk in 1510. Lost during the Revolution, the recipe was rediscovered in the 19th century.

Sights & Activities

Abbatiale de la Ste-Trinité ABBEY

(place des Ducs Richard; 9am-7pm Apr-Sep, 9am-noon & 2-5pm Oct-Mar) Built from 1175 to 1220 by Richard the Lionheart, towering Abbatiale de la Ste-Trinité was the most important pilgrimage site in Normandy until the construction of Mont St-Michel, thanks to the drops of Jesus' blood that, legend has it, miraculously floated to Fécamp in the trunk of a fig tree. Across from the abbey are

THE DIEPPE RAID

On 19 August 1942 a mainly Canadian force of over 6000, backed up by 300 ships and 800 aircraft, landed on 20km of beaches between Berneval-sur-Mer and Varengeville-sur-Mer. The objectives: to help the Soviets by drawing Nazi military power away from the Eastern Front and – so the film *Dieppe Uncovered* revealed in 2012 – to 'pinch' one of the Germans' new, four-rotor Enigma encoding machines (the effort failed). The results of the Dieppe Raid were nothing short of catastrophic: 73% of the men who took part ended up killed, wounded or missing-in-action. But lessons learnt at great cost here proved invaluable in planning the Normandy landings two years later.

For insights into the operation, visit Dieppe's **Memorial du 19 Août 1942** (www.dieppe-operationjubilee-19aout1942.fr; place Camille St-Saëns; adult/child €3.10/free; 2-6.30pm Wed-Mon late May–Sep, 2-6pm Sat, Sun Apr–mid-May & Oct–mid-Nov, closed mid-Nov–Mar).

the remains of a fortified **château** built in the 10th and 11th centuries by the earliest dukes of Normandy. Situated 1.5km east of the beach.

Palais de la Bénédictine LIQUEUR FACTORY
(☎02 35 10 26 10; www.benedictinedom.com; 110 rue Alexandre Le Grand; adult/child €8.50/3.50; ⊙tickets sales 10.30-11.30am & 2.30-4.30pm mid-Dec–mid-Apr, longer hours mid-Apr–mid-Dec, closed early Jan–mid-Feb) This ornate, neo-Renaissance factory, opened in 1900, is where all the Bénédictine liqueur in the world is made. Self-guided tours take you to a mini-museum of 13th- to 19th-century religious artworks and then to the production facilities (visible through glass), where you can admire copper alembics and touch and smell some of the 27 herbs, many from East Asia and Africa, used to make the famous *digestif*. There's a tasting at the end.

Les Pêcheries MUSEUM
(Cité des Terre-Neuvas; quai Capitaine Jean Recher) Set to open in 2017, Fécamp's new flagship museum will showcase local history, the town's fishing industry, artists who were active here, and traditional Norman life. The dramatic, glassed-in observation platform on top offers great views of town. Situated in the middle of the harbour, 300m northwest of the tourist office.

Beach BEACH
Fécamp's 800m-long, smooth-pebble beach stretches southward from the narrow channel connecting the port with the open sea. In July and August, you can rent catamarans, kayaks, paddle boats and windsurfers.

Cap Fagnet VIEWPOINT
The highest point on the Côte d'Albâtre, Cap Fagnet (110m) towers over Fécamp from the north, offering fantastic views up and down the coast. The site of a German *blockhaus* and radar station during WWII, today it's topped by a chapel and five wind turbines (there's a plan to erect 83 more turbines offshore). Cap Fagnet is a 1.5km walk from the centre.

Sleeping

Hôtel Vent d'Ouest HOTEL €
(☎02 35 28 04 04; www.hotelventdouest.tm.fr; 3 rue Gambetta; d/tr/q €65/85/95) Small and welcoming, with a smart breakfast room and 15 pleasant rooms decorated in yellow and blue. Call ahead if you'll be checking in after 8pm. Situated 200m east (up the hill) from the port, next to Église St-Étienne.

Camping de Renéville CAMPGROUND €
(☎02 35 28 20 97; www.campingdereneville.com; chemin de Nesmond; tent & 2 adults from €14; ⊙Apr-Oct) Dramatically situated on the western cliffs overlooking the beach, this campground also rents out two- and six-people chalets (from €280 per week). In July and August, the tent rate goes up to €17.

Le Grand Pavois HOTEL €€
(☎02 35 10 01 01; www.hotel-grand-pavois.com; 15 quai de la Vicomté; d €105-150; P ᯤ) This reliable three-star hotel has a fine location overlooking the marina, and is within an easy stroll to the beach. The welcome is warm, and the spacious rooms have attractive furnishings and comfortable mattresses, though the big windows – and the view! – are undoubtedly the best features.

Eating

Tourist-oriented crêperies and restaurants, many specialising in fish and mussels, line the south side of the port, along quai de la Vicomté and nearby parts of quai Bérigny.

Le Daniel's FRENCH €€
(☎02 76 39 95 68; 5 place Nicolas Selle; lunch menus €15-17, dinner menu €24-40; ⊙noon-2pm Thu-Tue, 7-9pm Mon & Thu-Sat) Tucked down a narrow lane away just a short stroll from the marina, this delightful spot serves up market-fresh fare that highlights delicacies from the region including Valmont trout, creamy rich oysters and braised veal. The service is warm, and the plates are beautifully presented – great value. Just be sure to call ahead for a table in this tiny spot.

La Marée SEAFOOD €€
(☎02 35 29 39 15; www.restaurant-maree-fecamp.fr; 77 quai Bérigny; mains €17-27; ⊙noon-2pm Tue-Sun, 7.30-8.30pm or later Tue, Wed, Fri & Sat) Fish and seafood – that's all that matters at La Marée, Fécamp's premier address for maritime dining. Locals claim that you won't find better seafood anywhere in town.

Information

Tourist Office (☎02 35 28 51 01; www.fecamptourisme.com; quai Sadi Carnot; ⊙9am-6pm Mon-Fri, 10am-6pm Sat & Sun; ᯤ) Has useful English-language brochures and maps, an iPad you can use to surf the internet, and free luggage lockers. Situated at the eastern end of the pleasure port, across the parking lot from the train station.

DON'T MISS

VEULES-LES-ROSES

With its wonderfully relaxing atmosphere and lovely setting, Veules-les-Roses is one of the Côte d'Albâtre's gems. The pebbly beach is never too crowded and the flowery village is supremely picturesque, with elegant mansions and an imposing church. The small river running through the village adds to the bucolic appeal. Look out for the *cressonnières* (ponds where watercress is grown). Situated 8km east of St-Valery-en-Caux.

Getting There & Around

BICYCLE

The tourist office rents bicycles for €9/14/40 per day/weekend/week.

BUS

Scenic bus 24, operated by **Keolis** (☎02 35 28 19 88; www.keolis-seine-maritime.com), goes to Le Havre's train station (€2, 1½ hours, seven or more daily) via Étretat and various small villages. The tourist office has schedules.

TRAIN

Fécamp's train station is a block east of the eastern end of the pleasure port. Destinations:

Le Havre €9.30, one to 1½ hours, eight to 15 daily

Paris' Gare St-Lazare €35, 2¾ hours, six to nine daily

Rouen €15.30, 1½ hours, 10 to 13 daily

You usually have to change trains at Bréauté-Beuzeville, connected to Fécamp by an 18km rail spur.

ÉTRETAT

POP 1500

The small village of Étretat's dramatic scenery – it's framed by twin cliffs – made it a favourite of painters such as Camille Corot, Eugène Boudin, Gustave Courbet and Claude Monet. With the vogue for sea air at the end of the 19th century, fashionable Parisians came and built extravagant villas. Étretat has never gone out of style and still swells with visitors every weekend.

Sights & Activities

The pebbly **beach** is separated from the town centre by a dyke. To the left as you face the sea, you can see the **Falaise d'Aval**, renowned for its free-standing arch – compared by French writer Maupassant to an elephant dipping its trunk in the sea – and the adjacent **Aiguille**, a 70m-high spire of chalk-white rock rising from the waves. Further along the cliff is a second natural arch known as **La Manneporte**. To reach the plateau above, take the steep footpath from the southwestern end of the beachfront.

To the right as you face the sea towers the **Falaise d'Amont**, atop which a memorial marks the spot where two aviators were last seen before attempting to cross the Atlantic in 1927.

The tourist office has a map of trails around town and can also provide details on sail-powered cruises aboard a **two-masted schooner** (March to October).

Sleeping

★**Detective Hôtel** HOTEL €

(☎02 35 27 01 34; www.detectivehotel.com; 6 av Georges V; d €59-129; 📶) Run by a former detective, this clever establishment was inspired by the deductive exploits of Sherlock Holmes and Hercule Poirot. Each of the 14 charming rooms bears the name of a fictional gumshoe whose time and place have inspired the decor. In some, the first mystery you'll face is how to find the secret door to the hidden bathroom. Utterly original.

Information

Tourist Office (☎02 35 27 05 21; www.etretat.net; place Maurice Guillard; ⏰9.30am-6.30pm mid-Jun–mid-Sep, 10am-noon & 2-6pm Mon-Sat mid-Sep–mid-Jun, Sun during school holidays) Situated inside the town hall.

Getting There & Away

Étretat is 16km southwest of Fécamp and 28km northeast of Le Havre.

Keolis Scenic bus 24 (seven or more daily) goes to Le Havre's train station (€2, one hour) and to Fécamp (€2, 30 minutes).

Le Havre

POP 176,000

A Unesco World Heritage Site since 2005, Le Havre is a love letter to modernism, evoking, more than any other French city, France's postwar energy and optimism. All but obliterated in September 1944 by Allied bombing raids that killed 3000 civilians, the centre was completely rebuilt by the Belgian architect Auguste Perret, whose bright, airy modernist vision remains, miraculously, largely intact. Attractions include a museum

full of captivating impressionist paintings, a soaring church with a mesmerising stained-glass tower, and hilltop gardens with views over the city. Le Havre is a regular port of call for cruise ships.

Sights & Activities

★Musée Malraux ART MUSEUM

(MuMa; ☎02 35 19 62 72; 2 bd Clemenceau; adult/child incl audioguide €5/free; ⏲11am-6pm Mon & Wed-Fri, to 7pm Sat & Sun) Near the waterfront, this luminous modern space houses a fabulous collection of impressionist works – the finest in France outside Paris – by masters such as Monet (who grew up in Le Havre), Pissarro, Renoir and Sisley. You'll also find works by the Fauvist painter Raoul Dufy, born in Le Havre, and paintings by Eugène Boudin, a mentor of Monet and another Le Havre native. There's a cafe with fine views over the harbor. MuMa is 1km southeast of the tourist office, at the southwestern tip of the city centre.

Église St-Joseph CHURCH

(bd François 1er; ⏲10am-6pm) Perret's masterful, 107m-high Église St-Joseph, visible from all over town, was built using bare concrete from 1951 to 1959. Some 13,000 panels of coloured glass make the soaring, sombre interior particularly striking when it's sunny.

Stained-glass artist Margaret Huré created a cohesive masterpiece in her collaboration with Peret, and her use of shading and colour was thoughtfully conceived, evoking different moods depending on where the sun is in the sky – and the ensuing colours created by the illumination.

Jardins Suspendus GARDENS

(rue du Fort; gardens free, greenhouses €2; ⏲10.30am-8pm Apr-Sep, to 5pm Oct-Mar) An old hilltop fortress a bit over 1km north of the tourist office has been transformed into a beautiful set of gardens, whose greenhouses and outdoor spaces feature exquisite flowers, trees and grasses from five different continents. There are fine views over the harbour.

It's a 30-minute uphill walk from the centre, or you can catch bus no 1 along bd François I near the beach.

Appartement Témoin ARCHITECTURE

(☎02 35 22 31 22; 181 rue de Paris; adult/child €5/free; ⏲tours 2pm, 3pm, 4pm & 5pm Wed, Sat & Sun, plus 2pm & 3pm Mon, Tue, Thu & Fri Jun-Sep) Furnished in impeccable early-1950s style, this lovingly furnished bourgeois apartment can be visited on a one-hour guided tour that starts at 181 rue de Paris (Maison du Patrimoine), a block north of Le Volcan.

Le Volcan CULTURAL CENTRE

(Espace Oscar Niemeyer; ☎02 35 19 10 10; www.levolcan.com; place Charles de Gaulle; ⏲library 10am-7pm) Le Havre's most conspicuous landmark, designed by Brazilian architect Oscar Niemeyer and opened in 1982, is also the city's premier cultural venue. One look and you'll understand how it got its name, which means 'the volcano'. After extensive renovations, the complex reopened in 2015, with a new concert hall and an ultramodern *mediathèque* (multimedia library). Situated at the western end of the Bassin du Commerce, the city centre's former port.

Sleeping

There are several hotels right around the train station.

Hôtel le Petit Vatel HOTEL €

(☎02 35 41 72 07; www.lepetitvatel.com; 86 rue Louis Brindeau; s/d €52/62; @🛜) One block west of Le Volcan, this place earns high marks for its comfortable rooms, good location and exceptionally kind staff. Rooms get decent natural light, the mattresses are new, and the tiled bathrooms are spick and span. There's a small, sunny lounge on the ground floor (with an iPad and computer for guests' use).

Hôtel Oscar HOTEL €

(☎02 35 42 39 77; www.hotel-oscar.fr; 106 rue Voltaire; s from €55-65, d €63-83; 🛜) A treat for architecture aficionados, this bright and very central hotel brings Auguste Perret's mid-20th-century legacy alive. The rooms are authentic retro, with hardwood floors and large windows, as is the tiny 1950s lounge. Reception closes at 8.30pm. Situated across the street from Le Volcan.

★Hôtel Vent d'Ouest BOUTIQUE HOTEL €€

(☎02 35 42 50 69; www.ventdouest.fr; 4 rue de Caligny; d €100-150, ste €170, q €215, apt €185; 🛜) Decorated with maritime flair, this stylish establishment has nautical memorabilia downstairs, and cheerfully painted rooms upstairs with sisal flooring and attractive furnishings; ask for one with a balcony. There are lovely common areas where you can while away the hours with a book when the weather inevitably sours, including an enticing cafe-bar with leather armchairs.

Eating

You'll find a concentration of restaurants along pedestrian-friendly Rue Victor Hugo, one block north of Le Volcan. There's another cluster of restaurants in Quartier St-François, the area just south of the Bassin du Commerce – check out rue de Bretagne, rue Jean de la Fontaine and rue du Général Faidherbe.

Halles Centrales FOOD MARKET €
(rue Voltaire; ⊙8.30am-7.30pm Mon-Sat, 9am-1pm Sun) Food stalls at Le Havre's main market include a patisserie, a *fromagerie* and many tempting fruit stands; there's also a small supermarket. Situated a block west of Le Volcan.

★ **La Taverne Paillette** BRASSERIE €€
(☎02 35 41 31 50; www.taverne-paillette.com; 22 rue Georges Braque; lunch menu €15, mains €16-26; ⊙noon-midnight daily) Solid brasserie food is the order of the day at this Le Havre institution – think big bowls of mussels, generous salads, gargantuan seafood platters and, in the Alsatian tradition, eight types of *choucroute* (sauerkraut). Situated five blocks north of Église St-Joseph, at the northeast corner of a park called Le Square St-Roch.

Les Pieds Dans L'Eau SEAFOOD €€
(☎02 35 47 97 45; promenade de la Plage; mains €13-20; ⊙noon-10pm) Amid the many simple restaurants set on the beach promenade, this place always draws a crowd for its reasonably priced seafood plates and ample prix-fixe *menus*. The mussels (served seven different ways) are a highlight, as are the oysters and grilled *dorade*.

Information

Maison du Patrimoine (☎02 35 22 31 22; 181 rue de Paris; ⊙1.45-6.30pm year-round, plus 10am-noon Apr-Sep) The tourist office's city centre annexe has an exhibition on Perret's postwar reconstruction of the city.

Tourist Office (☎02 32 74 04 04; www.lehavretourisme.com; 186 bd Clemenceau; ⊙2-6pm Mon, 10am-12.30pm & 2-6pm Tue-Sun) Has a map in English for a two-hour walking tour of Le Havre's architectural highlights and details on cultural events. Situated at the western edge of the city centre, one block south of the La Plage tram terminus.

Getting There & Away

BOAT

Le Havre's car ferry terminal, situated 1km southeast of Le Volcan, is linked with the English port of Portsmouth via **Brittany Ferries** (www.brittany-ferries.co.uk). Ferries depart daily from late March to early November.

BUS

The bus station is next to the train station.

Bus Verts (☎09 70 83 00 14; www.busverts.fr) Heading south, bus 20 (four to six daily) goes to Honfleur (€4.15, 30 minutes) and Deauville and Trouville (€6.25, one hour).

Keolis (p222) For the Côte d'Albâtre, take scenic bus 24 (seven or more daily) to Étretat (€2, one hour) and Fécamp (€2, 1½ hours).

TRAIN

The train station, **Gare du Havre**, is 1.5km east of Le Volcan, at the eastern end of bd de Strasbourg. The tram stop out front is called 'Gares'. Destinations include:

Fécamp €9.30, one to 1½ hours, eight to 15 daily

Paris' Gare St-Lazare €35, 2¼ hours, 15 daily Monday to Friday, seven to nine Saturday and Sunday

Rouen €16, one hour, 16 to 20 daily Monday to Saturday, 10 Sunday

Getting Around

Two modern tram lines run by LiA (www.transports-lia.fr), link the train station with the city centre and the beach. A single ride costs €1.70; travelling all day is €3.80.

Location de Vélos rents out **bicycles** (two hours/half-day/full day €3/4/7) at two sites, including the train station and a shop on 9 ave René Coty, one block north of the Mairie du Havre.

EURE

From Rouen, lovely day trips can be made to the landlocked Eure *département* (www.eure-tourisme.fr). The 12th-century Château Gaillard in Les Andelys affords a breathtaking panorama of the Seine, while the beautiful gardens of Claude Monet are at Giverny, 70km southwest of Rouen.

Les Andelys

POP 8200

Some 40km southeast of Rouen, on a hairpin curve in the Seine, lies Les Andelys (the 's' is silent), crowned by the ruins of Richard the Lionheart's hilltop castle.

Sights

Château Gaillard CHÂTEAU
(☎02 32 54 41 93; adult/child €3.20/2.70; ⊙10am-1pm & 2-6pm Mon & Wed-Sun, 2-6pm Tue late

Mar-Oct) The now-ruined Château Gaillard, built with unbelievable dispatch between 1196 and 1198, secured the western border of English territory until Henry IV ordered its destruction in 1603. The tourist office has details on tours (€4.50, in French with English-speaking guides), held at 4.30pm daily and at 11.30am on Sunday. Year-round entry to the château grounds is free.

Sleeping & Eating

Hôtel de la Chaîne d'Or HOTEL €€
(☎02 32 54 00 31; www.hotel-lachainedor.com; 27 rue Grande, Petit Andely; s €79, d €95-150, f €160; P 📶) Packed with character, this little hideaway is rustically stylish without being twee. The 12 rooms are spacious, tasteful and romantic, with antique wood furnishings and plush rugs; some are so close to the Seine you could almost fish out the window.

Restaurant de la Chaîne d'Or GASTRONOMIC €€€
(☎02 32 54 00 31; www.hotel-lachainedor.com; 25 rue Grande, Petit Andely; weekday lunch menus €23-30, other menus €49-65, mains €30-36; ⊙noon-2pm & 7.30-8.30pm Thu-Tue year-round, closed Sun dinner & Tue mid-Oct–mid-Apr) A classy French restaurant that's one of the best for miles around. Specialities include risotto with scallops, and heart of braised veal with polenta. For dessert, end with local favourite *tarte aux pommes flambées au Calvados* (flambéed apple pie). Reservations are recommended.

Information

Tourist Office (☎02 32 54 41 93; www.lesandelys-tourisme.fr; rue Raymond Phélip; ⊙10am-noon & 2-6pm Mon-Sat, 10am-1pm Sun, shorter hours Oct-Mar) In Petit Andely. Ask here about walking routes around town.

Getting There & Away

To reach the main Eure town of Les Andelys, take a train to Gaillon-Aubevoye, and hop on bus 290 (€2) for the 30-minute onward journey.

CALVADOS

The Calvados *département* (www.calvados-tourisme.com) stretches from Honfleur in the east to Isigny-sur-Mer in the west and includes Caen, Bayeux and the D-Day beaches. The area is famed for its rich pastures and farm products, including butter, cheese, cider and an eponymous apple brandy.

Bayeux

POP 13,900

Two cross-Channel invasions, almost 900 years apart, gave Bayeux a front-row seat at defining moments in Western history. The dramatic story of the Norman invasion of England in 1066 is told in 58 vivid scenes by the world-famous Bayeux Tapestry, embroidered just a few years after William the Bastard, Duke of Normandy, became William the Conqueror, King of England.

On 6 June 1944, 160,000 Allied troops, supported by almost 7000 naval vessels, stormed ashore along the coast just north of town. Bayeux was the first French town to be liberated (on the morning of 7 June 1944) and is one of the few places in Calvados to have survived WWII practically unscathed. Bayeux makes an ideal base for exploring the D-Day beaches.

These days, it's a great spot to soak up the gentle Norman atmosphere. The delightful, flowery city centre is crammed with 13th- to 18th-century buildings and a fine Gothic cathedral.

Sights

A 'triple ticket' good for all three of Bayeux' outstanding municipal museums costs €15/13.50 for an adult/child.

★**Bayeux Tapestry** TAPESTRY
(☎02 31 51 25 50; www.bayeuxmuseum.com; rue de Nesmond; adult/child incl audioguide €9/4; ⊙9am-6.30pm Mar-Oct, to 7pm May-Aug, 9.30am-12.30pm & 2-6pm Nov–Feb) The world's most celebrated embroidery depicts the conquest of England by William the Conqueror in 1066 from an unashamedly Norman perspective. Commissioned by Bishop Odo of Bayeux, William's half-brother, for the opening of Bayeux' cathedral in 1077, the 68.3m-long cartoon strip tells the dramatic, bloody tale with verve and vividness.

★**Musée d'Art et d'Histoire Baron Gérard** MUSEUM
(MAHB; ☎02 31 92 14 21; www.bayeuxmuseum.com; 37 rue du Bienvenu; adult/child €7/4; ⊙9.30am-6.30pm May-Sep, 10am-12.30pm & 2-6pm Oct-Apr, closed Jan–mid-Feb) Opened in 2013, this is one of France's most gorgeously presented provincial museums. The exquisite exhibitions cover everything from Gallo-Roman archaeology to medieval art to paintings from the Renaissance to the 20th century, including a fine work by Gustave Caillebotte. Other

DON'T MISS

PONT DE NORMANDIE

This futuristic **bridge** (car one way €5.40), opened in 1995, stretches in a soaring 2km arch over the Seine between Le Havre and Honfleur. It's a typically French affair, as much sophisticated architecture as engineering, with two huge inverted-V-shaped columns holding aloft a delicate net of cables. Crossing it is quite a thrill – and the views of the Seine are magnificent. In each direction there's a narrow footpath and a bike lane.

highlights include impossibly delicate local lace and Bayeux-made porcelain. Housed in the former bishop's palace.

Cathédrale Notre Dame CATHEDRAL
(rue du Bienvenu; ⏲8.30am-7pm) Most of Bayeux' spectacular Norman Gothic cathedral dates from the 13th century, though the crypt (take the stairs on the north side of the choir), the arches of the nave and the lower parts of the entrance towers are 11th-century Romanesque. The central tower was added in the 15th century; the copper dome dates from the 1860s.

Conservatoire de la Dentelle LACE WORKSHOP
(Lace Conservatory; ☎02 31 92 73 80; http://dentelledebayeux.free.fr; 6 rue du Bienvenu; ⏲9.30am-12.30pm & 2.30-5pm Mon-Sat) FREE Lacemaking, brought to Bayeux by nuns in 1678, once employed 5000 people. The industry is long gone, but at the Conservatoire you can watch some of France's most celebrated lacemakers create intricate designs using dozens of bobbins and hundreds of pins; a small shop sells some of their delicate creations. The half-timbered building housing the workshop, decorated with carved wooden figures, dates from the 1400s.

Musée Mémorial de la Bataille de Normandie MUSEUM
(Battle of Normandy Memorial Museum; ☎02 31 51 46 90; www.bayeuxmuseum.com; bd Fabien Ware; adult/child €7/4; ⏲9.30am-6.30pm May-Sep, 10am-12.30pm & 2-6pm Oct-Apr, closed Jan–mid-Feb) Using well-chosen photos, personal accounts, dioramas and wartime objects, this first-rate museum offers an excellent introduction to the Battle of Normandy. The 25-minute film is screened in both French and English.

Bayeux War Cemetery CEMETERY
(bd Fabien Ware) The largest of the 18 Commonwealth military cemeteries in Normandy, this peaceful cemetery contains 4848 graves of soldiers from the UK and 10 other countries, including a few from Germany. Across the road is a memorial to 1807 Commonwealth soldiers whose remains were never found; the Latin inscription across the top reads: 'We, once conquered by William, have now liberated the Conqueror's native land'.

Sleeping

Les Logis du Rempart B&B €
(☎02 31 92 50 40; www.lecornu.fr; 4 rue Bourbesneur; d €60-105, tr €110-130; 📶) The three rooms of this delightful *maison de famille* ooze old-fashioned cosiness. Our favourite, the Bajocasse, has parquet flooring, a canopy bed and Toile de Jouy wallpaper. The shop downstairs is the perfect place to stock up on top-quality, homemade cider and *calvados* (apple brandy). Two-night minimum stay.

Hôtel d'Argouges HOTEL €€
(☎02 31 92 88 86; www.hotel-dargouges.com; 21 rue St-Patrice; s/d/tr/f €115/132/175/205; ⏲closed Dec & Jan; P📶) Occupying a stately 18th-century residence with a lush little garden, this graceful hotel has 28 comfortable rooms with exposed beams, thick walls and Louis XVI–style furniture. The breakfast room, hardly changed since 1734, still has its original wood panels and parquet floors.

Villa Lara BOUTIQUE HOTEL €€€
(☎02 31 92 00 55; www.hotel-villalara.com; 6 place de Québec; d €190-360, ste €390-520; P❄📶) Newly constructed in the past decade, this 28-room hotel, Bayeux's most luxurious, sports minimalist colour schemes, top-quality fabrics and decor that juxtaposes 18th- and 21st-century tastes. Amenities include a bar and a gym. Most rooms have cathedral views.

Eating

Local specialities to keep an eye out for include *cochon de Bayeux* (a local heritage pig breed). Near the tourist office, along rue St-Jean and rue St-Martin, there are a variety food shops and cheap eateries.

★**La Reine Mathilde** PATISSERIE €
(47 rue St-Martin; cakes from €2.50; ⏲9am-7.30pm Tue-Sun) This sumptuously decorated patisserie and *salon de thé* (tearoom), ideal for a sweet breakfast or a relaxing cup of

Bayeux

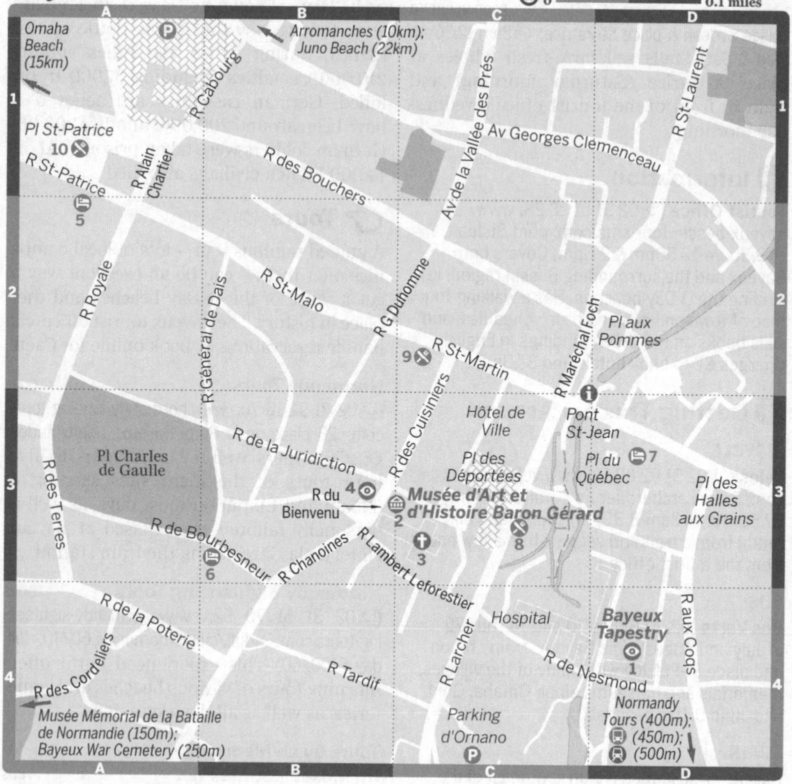

afternoon tea, hasn't changed much since it was built in 1898.

Au Ptit Bistrot MODERN FRENCH €€

(☎ 02 31 92 30 08; 31 rue Larcher; lunch menu €17-20, dinner menu €27-33, mains €16-19; ⊙ noon-2pm & 7-9pm Tue-Sat) Near the cathedral, this friendly, welcoming eatery whips up creative, beautifully prepared dishes that highlight the Norman bounty without a lick of pretension. Recent hits include chestnut soup, duck breast and bulgur with seasonal fruits and roasted pineapple, and black cod with spinach and spicy guacamole. Reservations essential.

Alchimie MODERN FRENCH €€

(lunch menu €12) On a street lined with restaurants, Alchimie has a simple but elegant design that takes nothing from the beautifully presented dishes. Choose from the day's specials listed on a chalkboard menu, which might include hits like *brandade de morue* (baked codfish pie). It's a local favourite, so call ahead.

Bayeux

Top Sights
1 Bayeux Tapestry D4
2 Musée d'Art et d'Histoire Baron Gérard C3

Sights
3 Cathédrale Notre Dame C3
4 Conservatoire de la Dentelle B3

Sleeping
5 Hôtel d'Argouges A2
6 Les Logis du Rempart B3
7 Villa Lara D3

Eating
8 Au Ptit Bistrot C3
9 La Reine Mathilde C2
10 Marchés A1

Self-Catering

Marché FOOD MARKET €
(place St-Jean & place St-Patrice; 8am-12.30pm Wed & Sat) Stalls sell farm-fresh edibles at place St-Patrice (Saturday morning) and right in front of the tourist office (Wednesday morning).

Information

Tourist Office (02 31 51 28 28; www.bayeux-bessin-tourisme.com; pont St-Jean; 9.30am-12.30pm & 2-6pm) Covers both Bayeux and the surrounding Bessin region, including the D-Day beaches. Has a walking-tour map of town and bus and train schedules, and sells books on the D-Day landings in English. Charges €2 to book hotels and B&Bs.

Getting There & Around

BICYCLE

Vélos (02 31 92 89 16; www.velosbayeux.com; 5 rue Larcher; per half-/full day from €7.50/10; 8am-8.30pm) Year-round bike rental from a fruit and veggie store a few paces from the tourist office.

BUS

Bus Verts (p224) Buses 70 and 74 (bus 75 in July and August) link Bayeux' train station and place St-Patrice with many of the villages, memorials and museums along Omaha, Gold and Juno D-Day beaches.

TRAIN

Bayeux' train station is 1km southeast of the cathedral. Direct services include:

Caen €7, 20 minutes, at least hourly

Cherbourg €18.10, one hour, almost hourly

Pontorson (Mont St-Michel) €25, 1¾ hours, three daily

To get to Deauville, change at Lisieux. For Paris' Gare St-Lazare and Rouen, you may have to change at Caen.

D-Day Beaches

Code-named 'Operation Overlord', the D-Day landings were the largest seaborne invasion in history. Early on the morning of 6 June 1944, swarms of landing craft – part of an armada of more than 6000 ships and boats – hit the beaches of northern Normandy and tens of thousands of Allied soldiers began pouring onto French soil.

The majority of the 135,000 Allied troops who arrived in France that day stormed ashore along 80km of beaches north of Bayeux code-named (from west to east) Utah, Omaha, Gold, Juno and Sword. The landings on D-Day – known as *'Jour J'* in French – were followed by the 76-day Battle of Normandy, during which the Allies suffered 210,000 casualties, including 37,000 troops killed. German casualties are believed to have been around 200,000; another 200,000 German soldiers were taken prisoner. About 14,000 French civilians also died.

Tours

A guided minibus tour – lots of local companies offer them – can be an excellent way to get a sense of the D-Day beaches and their place in history. The Bayeux tourist office can handle reservations or book online for Caen.

Normandy Tours TOURS
(02 31 92 10 70; www.normandy-landing-tours.com; 26 place de la Gare, Bayeux; adult/student €62/55) Offers well-regarded four- to five-hour tours of the main sites starting at 8.15am and 1.15pm on most days, as well as personally tailored trips. Based at Bayeux' Hôtel de la Gare, facing the train station.

Normandy Sightseeing Tours TOURS
(02 31 51 70 52; www.normandy-sightseeing-tours.com; adult/child morning €60/40, full-day €100/60) This experienced outfit offers morning tours of various beaches and cemeteries, as well as all-day excursions.

Tours by Le Mémorial – Un Musée pour la Paix BUS
(02 31 06 06 45; www.memorial-caen.fr; tour morning/afternoon €65/85; 9am & 2pm Apr-Sep, 1pm Oct-Mar, closed 3 weeks in Jan) Excellent year-round minibus tours (four to five hours), take in Pointe du Hoc, Omaha Beach, the American cemetery and the artificial port at Arromanches. There are cheaper tours in full-size buses (€45) from June to August. Rates include entry to Le Mémorial – Un Musée pour la Paix. Book online.

Getting There & Away

Bus Verts (p224) links Bayeux' train station and place St-Patrice with many of the villages along the D-Day beaches.

Bus 70 (two to four daily Monday to Saturday, more frequently and on Sunday and holidays in summer) goes to Colleville-sur-Mer (Omaha Beach and the American Cemetery; €2.10, 35 minutes); some services continue to Pointe du Hoc near Cricqueville en Bessin and Grandcamp-Maisy (both €4.15).

Bus 74 (bus 75 in July and August; three or four daily Monday to Saturday, more frequently

The Battle of Normandy

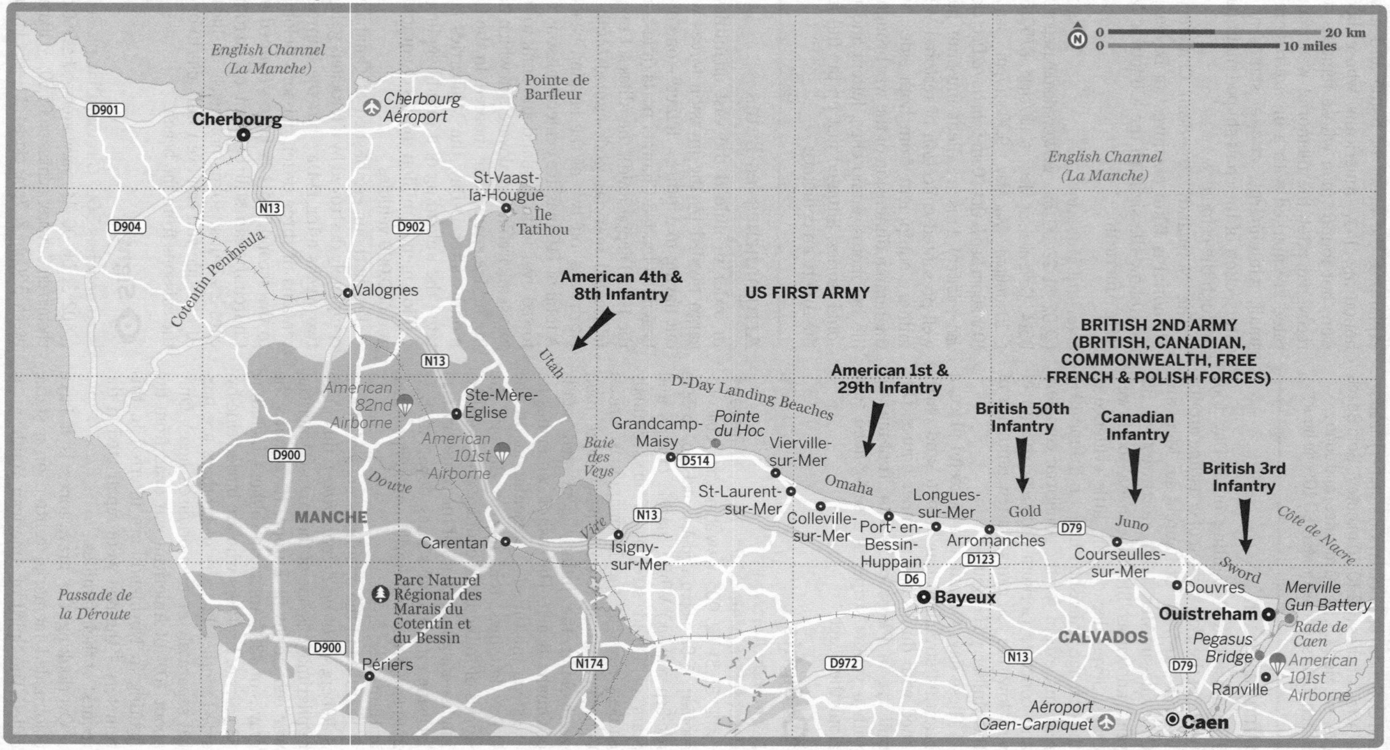

and on Sunday and holidays in summer) heads to Arromanches (€2.10, 10 minutes), Gold Beach (Ver-sur Mer; €3.10, 30 minutes) and Juno Beach (Courseulles-sur-Mer; €3.10; one hour).

Omaha Beach

The most brutal fighting on D-Day took place on the 7km stretch of coastline around Vierville-sur-Mer, St-Laurent-sur-Mer and Colleville-sur-Mer, 15km northwest of Bayeux, known as 'Bloody Omaha' to US veterans. Seven decades on, little evidence of the carnage unleashed here on 6 June 1944 remains, except for the American cemetery and concrete German bunkers, though at very low tide you can see a few remnants of the Mulberry Harbour.

These days Omaha is a peaceful place, a beautiful stretch of fine golden sand partly lined with dunes and summer homes. **Circuit de la Plage d'Omaha**, trail-marked with a yellow stripe, is a self-guided tour along the beach.

Sights

Normandy American Cemetery & Memorial MEMORIAL

(☎02 31 51 62 00; www.abmc.gov; Colleville-sur-Mer; ⏲9am-6pm mid-Apr–mid-Sep, to 5pm mid-Sep–mid-Apr) White marble crosses and Stars of David stretch off in seemingly endless rows at the Normandy American Cemetery, situated on a now-serene bluff overlooking the bitterly contested sands of Omaha Beach. The visitor center has an excellent multimedia presentation on the D-Day landings, told in part through the stories of individuals' courage and sacrifice. English-language tours of the cemetery, also focusing on personal stories, depart daily at 2pm and, from mid-April to mid-September, at 11am.

Featured in the opening scenes of Steven Spielberg's *Saving Private Ryan*, this place of pilgrimage is one of the largest American war cemeteries in Europe. It contains the graves of 9387 American soldiers, including 33 pairs of brothers who are buried side-by-side (another 12 pairs of brothers are buried separately or memorialised here). Only about 40% of American war dead from the fighting in Normandy are interred in this cemetery – the rest were repatriated at the request of their families.

Overlooking the gravestones is a large colonnaded memorial centred on a statue called The Spirit of American Youth, maps explaining the order of battle and a wall honouring 1557 Americans whose bodies were not found (men whose remains were recovered after the memorial was inaugurated are marked with a bronze rosette). A small, white-marble **chapel** stands at the intersection of the cross-shaped main paths through the cemetery.

The Normandy American Cemetery & Memorial is 17km northwest of Bayeux; by car, follow the signs to the 'Cimetière Militaire Americain'.

Overlord Museum MUSEUM

(☎02 31 22 00 55; www.overlordmuseum.com; D514, Colleville-sur-Mer; adult/child €7.50/5.50; ⏲10am-6pm Mar-May, 9.30am-7pm Jun-Aug, 10am-6pm Sep & Oct, 10am-5pm Nov & Dec, closed Jan–mid-Feb) This excellent museum has a well-presented collection of restored WWII military equipment from both sides, with the human dimension of the war brought to life by photos, audio clips, letters and personal stories. Situated just up the hill from the American cemetery.

Arromanches-les-Bains

In order to unload the vast quantities of cargo needed by the invasion forces without having to capture – intact! – one of the heavily defended Channel ports (a lesson of the 1942 Dieppe Raid), the Allies set up prefabricated marinas, code-named **Mulberry Harbours**, off two of the landing beaches. A total of 146 massive cement caissons were towed over from England and sunk to form two semicircular breakwaters in which floating bridge spans were moored. In the three months after D-Day, the Mulberries facilitated the unloading of a mind-boggling 2.5 million men, 4 million tonnes of equipment and 500,000 vehicles.

The harbour established at Omaha was completely destroyed by a ferocious gale just two weeks after D-Day, but the impressive remains of three dozen caissons belonging to the second, **Port Winston** (named after Churchill), can still be seen off Arromanches-les-Bains, 10km northeast of Bayeux. At low tide you can even walk out to one of the caissons from the beach.

Sights

Arromanches 360° Circular Cinema CINEMA

(☎02 31 06 06 44; www.arromanches360.com; chemin du Calvaire; admission €5.50; ⏲10am-between 5.30pm & 7pm, closed 3 weeks in Jan &

THE BATTLE OF NORMANDY

In early 1944, an Allied invasion of continental Europe seemed inevitable. Hitler's disastrous campaign on the Russian front and the Luftwaffe's inability to control the skies over Europe had left Germany vulnerable. Both sides knew a landing was coming – the only questions were where and, of course, when.

Several sites were considered by Allied command. After long deliberation, it was decided that the beaches along Normandy's northern coast – rather than the even more heavily fortified coastline further north around Calais, where Hitler was expecting an attack – would serve as a surprise spearhead into occupied Europe.

Code-named 'Operation Overlord', the invasion began on the night of 5 June 1944 when three paratroop divisions were dropped behind enemy lines. At about 6.30am on the morning of 6 June, six amphibious divisions stormed ashore at five beaches, backed up by an unimaginable 6000 sea craft and 13,000 aeroplanes. The initial landing force involved some 45,000 troops; 15 more divisions were to follow once successful beachheads had been established.

The narrow Straits of Dover had seemed the most likely invasion spot to the Germans, who'd set about heavily reinforcing the area around Calais and the other Channel ports. Allied intelligence went to extraordinary lengths to encourage the German belief that the invasion would be launched north of Normandy: double agents, leaked documents and fake radio traffic, buttressed by phony airfields and an entirely fictitious American army group, supposedly stationed in southeast England, all suggested the invasion would centre on the Pas de Calais.

Because of the tides and unpredictable weather patterns, Allied planners had only a few dates available each month in which to launch the invasion. On 5 June, the date chosen, the worst storm in 20 years set in, delaying the operation. The weather had improved only marginally the next day, but General Dwight D Eisenhower, Allied commander-in-chief, gave the go-ahead: 6 June would be D-Day.

In the hours leading up to D-Day, French Resistance units set about disrupting German communications. Just after midnight on 6 June, the first Allied troops were on French soil. British commandos and glider units captured key bridges and destroyed German gun emplacements, and the American 82nd and 101st Airborne Divisions landed west of the invasion site. Although the paratroops' tactical victories were few, they caused confusion in German ranks and, because of their relatively small numbers, the German high command was convinced that the real invasion had not yet begun.

Mon mid-Nov–mid-Feb) The best view of Port Winston and nearby Gold Beach is from the hill east of town, site of the popular Arromanches 360° Circular Cinema, which screens archival footage of the Battle of Normandy; it is run by Caen's Le Mémorial – Un Musée pour la Paix (p234).

Musée du Débarquement MUSEUM
(Landing Museum; ☎02 31 22 34 31; www.musee-arromanches.fr; place du 6 Juin; adult/child €7.90/5.80; ⏰9am-12.30pm & 1.30-6pm Apr-Sep, 10am-12.30pm & 1.30-5pm Oct-Dec, Feb & Mar, closed Jan) Down in Arromanches itself and right on the beach, the Musée du Débarquement makes for a very informative stop before visiting the beaches. Dioramas, models and two films explain the logistics and importance of Port Winston. Written material is available in 18 languages.

Juno Beach

Dune-lined Juno Beach, 12km east of Arromanches around Courseulles-sur-Mer, was stormed by Canadian troops on D-Day. A Cross of Lorraine marks the spot where General Charles de Gaulle came ashore shortly after the landings. He was followed by Winston Churchill on 12 June and King George VI on 16 June.

Sights

Juno Beach Centre MUSEUM
(☎02 31 37 32 17; www.junobeach.org; voie des Français Libres, Courseulles-sur-Mer; adult/child €7/5.50, incl guided tour of Juno Beach €11/9; ⏰9.30am-7pm Apr-Sep, 10am-5pm Oct-Dec, Feb & Mar, closed Jan) Juno Beach's only specifically Canadian museum, the non-profit Juno Beach Centre, has multimedia exhibits on

1

LES FORCES ALLIEES
DEBARQVENT SVR CETTE
PLAGE QV'ELLES NOMMENT
OMAHA BEACH ET LIBERENT
L'EVROPE 6 JVIN 1944
THE ALLIED FORCES
LANDING ON THIS
SHORE WHICH THEY CALL
OMAHA BEACH LIBERATE
EVROPE JVNE 6th 1944

2

DENNIS K. JOHNSON / GETTY IMAGES ©

1. D-Day Monument, Omaha Beach (p230) 2. Sherman tank, Utah Beach (p234) 3. Normandy American Cemetary (p230)

Normandy D-Day Sites

The bravery and sacrifice of Operation Overlord – the 6 June 1944 Allied landings known in history as D-Day – is still a palpable presence in Normandy, and nowhere more so than on the broad, quiet beaches: Utah, Omaha, Gold, Juno and Sword. Still dotted with German pillboxes, these beaches were where American, British, Canadian, Commonwealth, Polish, Free French and other soldiers stormed ashore in the early morning, beginning the long-awaited liberation of France.

As you gaze out over the brilliant golden sand from the Normandy American Cemetery, a place of solemn pilgrimage, or the Channel coast's quiet seaside villages, it's hard to picture the death and heroism that occurred here – but a number of excellent museums help put the world-changing events into historical and human context.

UNMISSABLE D-DAY BATTLE SITES

Omaha Beach (p230) Site of the landings' most ferocious fighting, 'bloody Omaha' shouldn't be missed.

Normandy American Cemetery & Memorial (p230) This vast war cemetery is extraordinarily moving.

Le Mémorial – Un Musée pour la Paix (p234) The best single museum devoted to the Battle of Normandy.

Bayeux War Cemetery (p226) The largest of Normandy's Commonwealth war cemeteries is next to a memorial for the many men whose remains were never found.

Canada's role in the war effort and the landings. Guided tours of Juno Beach (€5.50) are available from April to October.

Bény-sur-Mer Canadian War Cemetery CEMETERY

(www.cwgc.org) The Bény-sur-Mer Canadian War Cemetery is 4km south of Courseulles-sur-Mer near Reviers.

Longues-sur-Mer

Part of the Nazis' Atlantic Wall, the massive casemates and 150mm German guns near Longues-sur-Mer, 6km west of Arromanches, were designed to hit targets some 20km away, including both Gold Beach (to the east) and Omaha Beach (to the west). Over seven decades later, the mammoth artillery pieces are still in their colossal concrete emplacements – the only in-situ large-calibre weapons in Normandy. For details on the tours in English (adult/child €7/3), available from April to October, contact the on-site **Longues tourist office** (02 31 21 46 87; www.bayeux-bessin-tourisme.com; Site de la Batterie; 10am-1pm & 2-6pm, closed Nov-Mar). The site itself is always open.

Parts of the classic D-Day film *The Longest Day* (1962) were filmed both here and at Pointe du Hoc. On clear days, Bayeux' cathedral, 8km away, is visible to the south.

Utah Beach

Situated midway between Bayeux and Cherbourg, this beach – the Allies' right (western) flank on D-Day – stretches for 5km near the village of La Madeleine. It was taken, with only light resistance, by the US 4th Infantry Division. D-Day events are commemorated by a number of monuments and the impressive **Musée du Débarquement de Utah Beach** (Utah Beach Landing Museum; 02 33 71 53 35; www.utah-beach.com; Ste-Marie du Mont; adult/child €8/4; 9.30am-7pm Jun-Sep, 10am-6pm Oct-May, closed Jan), a few kilometres inland in Ste-Marie du Mont.

Caen

POP 109,300

Founded by William the Conqueror in the 11th century, Caen – capital of the Basse Normandie region – was 80% destroyed during the 1944 Battle of Normandy. Rebuilt in the 1950s and '60s in the utilitarian style in vogue at the time, modern-day Caen nevertheless offers visitors a walled medieval château, two ancient abbeys and a clutch of excellent museums, including a groundbreaking museum of war and peace.

Sights

★Le Mémorial – Un Musée pour la Paix MEMORIAL

(Memorial – A Museum for Peace; 02 31 06 06 44; www.memorial-caen.fr; esplanade Général Eisenhower; adult/child €20/17; 9am-7pm daily early Feb-early Nov, 9.30am-6.30pm Tue-Sun early Nov-early Feb, closed 3 weeks in Jan) For an insightful and vivid account of the entire war, with special focus on the Battle of Normandy, the best place to head is Le Mémorial, one of Europe's premier WWII museums. It's a hugely impressive affair, using film, animation and audio testimony, as well as

POINTE DU HOC

At 7.10am on 6 June 1944, 225 US Army Rangers under the command of Lieutenant Colonel James Earl Rudder scaled the impossibly steep, 30m-high cliffs of Pointe du Hoc. Their objective was to disable five 155mm German artillery guns perfectly placed to rain shells onto the beaches of Utah and Omaha. Unbeknownst to Rudder and his team, the guns had been transferred inland shortly before, but they nevertheless managed to locate the massive artillery pieces and put them out of action. By the time the Rangers were finally relieved on 8 June – after repelling fierce German counterattacks for two days – 81 of the rangers had been killed and 58 more had been wounded.

Today the **site** (02 31 51 90 70; www.abmc.gov; 9am-6pm mid-Apr–mid-Sep, to 5pm rest of year), which France turned over to the US government in 1979, looks much as it did right after the battle, with the earth still pitted with huge bomb craters. The German command post (topped by a dagger-shaped memorial) and several concrete bunkers and casemates, scarred by bullet holes and blackened by flame-throwers, can be explored. As you face the sea, Utah Beach is 14km to the left. A visitor centre with multimedia exhibits opened in 2014.

a range of original artefacts, to graphically evoke the realities of war, the trials of occupation and the joy of liberation. It is situated 3km northwest of the city centre, reachable by bus 2 from place Courtonne.

Château de Caen CHÂTEAU
(http://musee-de-normandie.caen.fr; 8am-10pm; P) FREE Looming above the centre of the city, Caen's castle – surrounded by massive battlements and a dry moat – was established by William the Conqueror, Duke of Normandy, in 1060. Visitors can walk around the ramparts and visit the 12th-century **Église St-Georges**, which holds an information centre with interactive exhibitions, and the **Échiquier**, which dates from about 1100 and is one of the oldest civic buildings in Normandy.

The **Jardin des Simples** is a garden of medicinal and aromatic herbs cultivated during the Middle Ages, some of them poisonous. There are also two worthwhile museums in the castle grounds, and a good restaurant-cafe.

Musée des Beaux-Arts ART MUSEUM
(Fine Arts Museum; 02 31 30 47 70; www.mba.caen.fr; adult/child €3.50/free, incl temporary exhibition €5.50; 9.30am-noon & 2-6pm Wed-Mon) This excellent and well-curated museum takes you on a tour through the history of Western art from the 15th to 21st centuries, including works depicting landscapes and interiors found around Normandy. The collection includes works by Rubens, Tintoretto, Géricault, Monet, Bonnard, Boudin, Dufy and Courbet, among many others. Situated inside the Château de Caen.

Abbaye-aux-Hommes ABBEY
(Abbaye-St-Étienne; 02 31 30 42 81; rue Guillaume le Conquérant; church free, cloisters €2; church 9.30am-1pm & 2-7pm Mon-Sat, 2-6.30pm Sun, cloister 8.30am-5pm Mon-Fri, 9.30am-1pm & 2pm-5.30pm Sat & most Sun) Caen's most important medieval site is the Men's Abbey – now city hall – and, right next door, the magnificent, multi-turreted **Église St-Étienne** (St Stephen's Church), known for its Romanesque nave, Gothic choir and William the Conqueror's rebuilt tomb (the original was destroyed by a 16th-century Calvinist mob and, in 1793, by fevered revolutionaries). The complex is 1km southwest of the Château de Caen; to get there by car, follow the signs to the 'Hôtel de Ville'. Access the cloisters via the adjoining Hôtel de Ville.

OFF THE BEATEN TRACK

NATURE WATCH

Inland from Utah Beach, to the south and southwest, is the 1480-sq-km **Parc Naturel Régional des Marais du Cotentin et du Bessin** (www.parc-cotentin-bessin.fr), a vast expanse of waterways, marshes, moors and hedgerows. The Maison du Parc (visitor centre) is in Saint-Côme-du-Mont, 50km west of Bayeux just off the N13.

For details on hiking and cycling in the park and elsewhere in the Manche *département*, visit www.manche-tourism.com and click on 'Walks, Rambles & Rides'.

Abbaye-aux-Dames ABBEY
(Abbaye-de-la-Trinité; 02 31 06 98 98; place Reine Mathilde) Highlights at the Women's Abbey complex, once run by the Benedictines, includes **Église de la Trinité** – look for Matilda's tomb behind the main altar and the striking pink stained-glass windows beyond. Free tours (at 2.30pm and 4pm daily) take you through the interior, but you can snoop around the courtyard and the church on your own at other times, except during Mass. Situated 600m east of the Château de Caen.

Sleeping

Hotel Bristol HOTEL €
(02 31 84 59 76; www.hotelbristolcaen.com; 31 rue du 11 Novembre; r from €70;) Located about 1km south of the Château, the Hotel Bristol has well-maintained contemporary rooms with comfortable beds and huge windows. It's the friendly and welcoming service, however, that sets this place apart from other similarly priced options.

★**La Maison de Famille** B&B €€
(06 61 64 88 54; www.maisondefamille.sitew.com; 4 rue Elie de Beaumont; d €70-95, q €110-135; P) Wow! This four-room B&B, overflowing with personality and charm, occupies three floors of an imposing townhouse 500m west of the Château de Caen. Added perks include a lovely breakfast, a peaceful garden and private parking.

Hôtel des Quatrans HOTEL €€
(02 31 86 25 57; www.hotel-des-quatrans.com; 17 rue Gémare; d from €100;) This typically modern hotel has 47 comfy, unfussy rooms in white and chocolate. Promotional deals are often available online. It's in a great location near the Château.

Caen

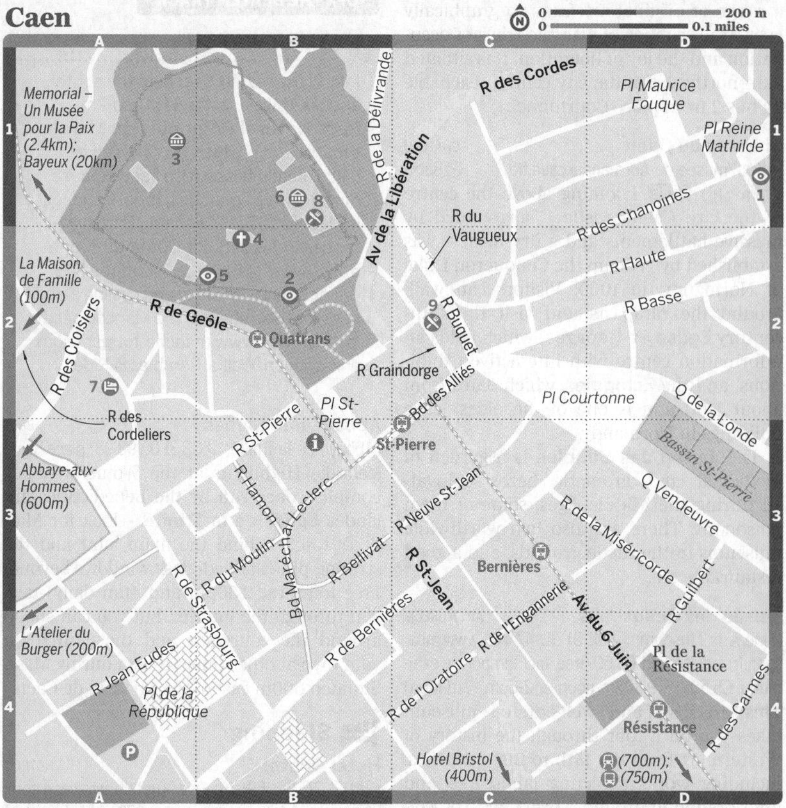

Caen

Sights

1 Abbaye-aux-Dames D1
2 Château de Caen B2
3 Échiquier A1
4 Église St-Georges B2
5 Jardin des Simples B2
6 Musée des Beaux-Arts B1

Sleeping

7 Hôtel des Quatrans A2

Eating

8 Café Mancel B1
9 Le Bouchon du Vaugueux C2

Eating

L'Atelier du Burger BURGERS €

(☎ 02 31 50 13 44; www.latelier-duburger.fr; 27 rue Écuyere; mains €8-9; ⊙ noon-2.30pm & 7-11.30pm Mon-Sat) Near the end of bar-lined rue Écuyere, this place whips up juicy, thick burgers piled high with guacamole, grilled onions and other toppings. There's also a veggie option (though no patty, just grilled vegetables). It's a casual place: order at the counter, grab your own drink, and take a seat amid the stone-walled back room, or on the small terrace.

Café Mancel NORMAN €€

(☎ 02 31 86 63 64; www.cafemancel.com; Château de Caen; menus €18-36; ⊙ noon-10pm Tue-Sat, to 2pm Sun) In the same building as the Musée des Beaux-Arts, stylish Café Mancel serves up delicious, traditional French cuisine – everything from pan-fried Norman-style beefsteak to hearty Caen-style *tripes*. Has a lovely sun terrace, which also makes a fine spot for a drink outside of busy meal times.

Le Bouchon du Vaugueux NORMAN €€

(☎ 02 31 44 26 26; www.bouchonduvaugueux.com; 12 rue Graindorge; lunch menu €16-24, dinner menu €22-34; ⊙ noon-2pm & 7-10pm Tue-Sat) The giant

wine cork marks the spot at this tiny *bistrot gourmande* (gourmet bistro), which matches creative modern cooking with a first-rate wine selection (from €4 a glass), sourced from small producers all over France. Staff are happy to translate the chalk-board menu. Reservations recommended.

Information

Tourist Office (☎02 31 27 14 14; www.caen-tourisme.fr; 12 place St-Pierre; ⊙9.30am-6.30pm Mon-Sat, 10am-1pm Sun Apr-Sep, 9.30am-1pm & 2-6pm Mon-Sat Oct-Mar) Helpful and efficient, with a thick brochure of all sights, and a several self-guided walking itineraries.

Getting There & Around

BICYCLE

V'eol (☎08 00 20 03 06; www.veol.caen.fr; 1st 30min free), Caen's answer to Paris' Velib', has 350 bicycles available at 40 automatic stations. The only problem is you need to sign up in advance (one week/year €1/15).

BUS

Bus 20 and bus 39 (aka Prestobus), run by Caen-based **Bus Verts** (☎08 10 21 42 14; www.busverts.fr; place Courtonne; ⊙7.30am-7pm Mon-Fri, 9am-7pm Sat), link the bus station (next to the train station) with Deauville and Trouville (€5.15, two hours, four to seven daily), Honfleur (bus 20, €7.25, 2½ hours, seven to 13 daily; bus 39, €12, one hour, one or two daily) and Le Havre (bus 20, €10.25, 2½ hours; bus 39, €17, 1½ hours, six to 10 daily). When arriving or departing, your Bus Verts ticket is valid for an hour on Caen's local buses and trams.

Twisto (www.twisto.fr) Local bus 61 links Caen with the ferry port of Ouistreham.

BOAT

Brittany Ferries (www.brittany-ferries.co.uk) links the English port of Portsmouth with Ouistreham, 14km northeast of Caen.

TRAIN

The train station is 1.5km southeast of the Château de Caen. Services include:

Bayeux €7, 15 to 20 minutes, hourly

Cherbourg €23, 1¼ hours, eight to 15 daily

Deauville & Trouville (via Lisieux) €15, 11 daily Monday to Friday, four to six daily Saturday and Sunday

Paris' Gare St-Lazare €37, two hours, 13 daily

Pontorson (Mont St-Michel) €29, two hours, two to three daily

Rouen From €28, 1½ hours, five to seven direct daily

Trouville & Deauville

The twin seaside towns of Trouville-sur-Mer (population 4800) and Deauville (population 3800), 15km southwest of Honfleur, are hugely popular with Parisians, who flock here year-round on weekends – and all week long from June to September and during Paris' school holidays.

Chic **Deauville** has been a playground of well-heeled Parisians ever since it was founded by Napoléon III's half-brother, the Duke of Morny, in 1861. Expensive, flashy and brash, it's packed with designer boutiques, deluxe hotels and meticulously tended public gardens, and hosts two racetracks and the high-profile American Film Festival.

Unpretentious **Trouville** is both a veteran beach resort, graced with impressive mansions from the late 1800s, and a working fishing port. Popular with middle-class French families, the town was frequented by painters and writers during the 19th century (eg Mozin and Flaubert), lured by the 2km-long sandy beach and the laid-back seaside ambience.

Sights & Activities

In Deauville, the rich and beautiful strut their stuff along the beachside **Promenade des Planches**, a 643m-long boardwalk that's lined with a row of 1920s cabins named after famous Americans (mainly film stars). After swimming in the nearby 50m **Piscine Olympique** (Olympic swimming pool; ☎02 31 14 02 17; bd de la Mer, Deauville; weekday/weekend from €4/6; ⊙10am-2pm & 3.30-7pm Mon-Sat, 10am-4pm Sun, closed 2 weeks in Jan & 3 weeks in Jun), filled with seawater heated to 28°C, they – like you – can head to the **beach**, hundreds of metres wide at low tide; walk across the street to their eye-popping, neo-something mansion; or head down the block to the spectacularly Italianate **casino**.

Trouville, too, has a waterfront **casino**, wide **beach** and **Promenade des Planches** (boardwalk). At the latter, 583m long and outfitted with Bauhaus-style pavilions from the 1930s, you can swim in a freshwater swimming pool and windsurf; there's also a playground for kids. Trouville's most impressive **19th-century villas** are right nearby.

Musée Villa Montabello MUSEUM
(☎02 31 88 16 26; 64 rue du Général Leclerc, Trouville; adult/child €3/free, Sun free; ⊙2-5.30pm Wed-Mon Apr–mid-Nov, from 11am Sat, Sun &

holidays) In a fine mansion built in 1865, this municipal museum recounts Trouville's history and features works by Charles Mozin, Eugène Isabey and Charles Pecrus. Situated 1km northeast of the tourist office, near the beach (and signed off the beach).

The two towns and beach scenes play a starring role in the impressionist works in the small permanent collection. There's also a short film (in French only), vintage travel posters from the 1930s, some early 20th-century clothing and black-and-white photos of beach-goers from days long past. The 1st floor features temporary exhibitions, with changing shows every three months or so.

Festivals & Events

Deauville is renowned for **horse racing** at two *hippodromes* (racetracks): **La Touques** for flat races and **Clairefontaine** (www.hippodrome-deauville-clairefontaine.com) for flat, trotting and jumping races (steeplechases and hurdles). For details on events dates and venues, see www.deauvillecheval.com and www.hippodromesdedeauville.com.

Deauville American Film Festival FILM
(www.festival-deauville.com) Deauville has a fair bit of Beverly Hills glitz so it's an appropriate venue for a festival celebrating American cinema; founded in 1975. Held for 10 days from early September; tickets cost €30 for one day or €150 for the whole festival.

LOCAL KNOWLEDGE

FRESH OYSTERS

Marché aux Poissons (Fish Market; bd Fernand Moureaux, Trouville; 8am-7.30pm) is *the* place in Trouville to head for fresh oysters with lemon (from €9 to €16 a dozen) and many other maritime delicacies. Even if you don't have access to a kitchen, there's cooked peel-and-eat shrimp, mussels, sea urchins and scallops, which you can enjoy on the tables out front. It's located on the waterfront 250m south of the casino.

Poissonnerie Pillet Saiter (www.poissonnerie-pilletsaiter.fr; bd Fernand Moureaux, Trouville; oysters per dozen €10-15; 8am-7.30pm), proud of having operated its own fishing boat since 1887, sells platters of seafood (by weight) and oysters (by the six or dozen) that you can eat at little tables.

Deauville Asian Film Festival FILM
(www.deauvilleasia.com) Running since 1999, this festival shows films from East, Southeast and South Asia. Held for five days in early March; one day/whole festival tickets cost €12/35.

Sleeping

La Maison Normande HOTEL €
(02 31 88 12 25; www.maisonormande.com; 4 place de Lattre de Tassigny, Trouville; d €55-85, q €120-130;) The 17 rooms in this late-17th-century Norman house vary considerably in size and style but all, though uninspiring, are eminently serviceable and offer good value. Situated six short blocks inland along rue Victor Hugo from Trouville's waterfront, across the street from Église Bonsecours.

L'Espérance HOTEL €€
(02 31 88 26 88; www.lesperancehoteldeauville.com; 32 rue Victor Hugo, Deauville; d €70-140;) Hidden away inside an elegant townhouse, beyond the lovely public areas, are 10 doubles decorated with excellent taste. Prices at this family-run gem change day by day according to demand. Situated in the heart of Deauville, a block north of place Morny.

Eating

L'Essentiel FUSION €€
(02 31 87 22 11; 29 rue Mirabeau; lunch menu €20-28, dinner menu €60, mains €23-34; noon-2pm & 7.30-11pm Thu-Mon) One of Deauville's top dining rooms, L'Essentiel serves up an imaginative blend of French ingredients with Asian and Latin American accents. Start off with codfish croquettes with sweet potato aioli before moving on to scallops with broccoli yuzu, or wagyu flank steak with roasted turnips and smoked cashew juice.

Les Vapeurs BRASSERIE €€
(02 31 88 15 24; 160 bd Fernand Moureaux, Trouville; mains €17-32; noon-10pm) Across from the fish market, Les Vapeurs has been going strong since 1927. The huge menu is a showcase for seafood platters, mussels in cream sauce, grilled haddock and classic brasserie fare (like steak tartare). It's served amid old-time ambience, with black-and-white photos, a touch of neon and wicker chairs at the outdoor tables in front.

Tivoli Bistro BISTRO €€
(02 31 98 43 44; 27 rue Charles Mozin, Trouville; menu €30; 12.15-2.30pm & 7.15-9.30pm Fri-Tue)

OFF THE BEATEN TRACK

ROUTE DU CIDRE

Normandy's signposted, 40km Route du Cidre, about 30km south of Deauville, wends its way through the **Pays d'Auge**, a rural area of orchards, pastures, hedgerows, half-timbered farmhouses and stud farms, through picturesque villages such as Cambremer and Beuvron-en-Auge. Signs reading 'Cru de Cambremer' indicate the way to 17 small-scale, traditional *producteurs* (producers) who are happy to show you their facilities and sell you their home-grown apple cider (about €3.50 a bottle), *calvados* (apple brandy) – affectionately known as *calva* – and *pommeau* (a mixture of apple juice and *calvados*).

Traditional Normandy cider takes about six months to make. Ripe apples are shaken off the trees or gathered from the ground between early October and early December. After being stored for two or three weeks, they are pressed, purified, slow-fermented, bottled and naturally carbonated, just like Champagne.

Normandy's AOC (Appellation d'Origine Contrôlée) cider is made with a blend of apple varieties and is known for being fruity, tangy and slightly bitter. You can enjoy it in crêperies and restaurants throughout Normandy.

You won't find a cosier place in Trouville than this much-loved hideaway, tucked away on a narrow side street a block inland from the riverfront. It's famous for its delicious *sole meunière* (Dover sole) and exquisite homemade terrine.

Information

Deauville Tourist Office (☎02 31 14 40 00; www.deauville.org; place de la Mairie; ⌚10am-6pm Mon-Sat, 10am-1pm & 2-5pm Sun) Has a trilingual walking-tour brochure with a Deauville map and can help find accommodation. The website has details on cultural events and horse races. Situated 800m west of the train station along rue Désiré le Hoc.

Trouville Tourist Office (☎02 31 14 60 70; www.trouvillesurmer.org; 32 bd Fernand Moureaux; ⌚10am-6pm Mon-Sat, 10am-1.30pm Sun Sep-Jun, 9.30am-7pm Mon-Sat, 10am-6pm Sun Jul & Aug) Has a free map of Trouville and sells brochures for two self-guided architectural tours (€3.50) and two rural walks (€1) of 7km and 11km. Situated 200m north of pont des Belges.

Getting There & Around

Deauville and Trouville are linked by pont des Belges, which is just east of Deauville's train and bus stations, and, near Trouville's Casino, a passenger ferry (*bac*; €1.20) that runs at high tide and a footbridge (€0.50) that's open at low tide; the ferry and footbridge operate daily from mid-March to September and on weekends and during school holidays the rest of the year.

AIR

Ryanair links tiny Deauville-Normandie airport, 7km east of Trouville, with London Stansted Airport twice a week (more frequently in summer).

BICYCLE

Les Trouvillaises (☎02 31 98 54 11; www.lestrouvillaises.fr; place Foch; bicycle per hour/day €5/14; ⌚9am-7pm mid-Mar–Oct) Based near Trouville's Casino (next to the footbridge/passenger ferry to Deauville), Les Trouvillaises rents out a variety of two- and four-wheel pedal-powered conveyances, including bicycles, tandems and carts, for both adults and children.

BUS

Deauville and Trouville's joint bus station is next to the Trouville-Deauville train station.

Bus Verts (p224) Bus 20 goes to Caen (€5.15, two hours, seven to 12 daily), Honfleur (€2.10, 30 minutes, four to seven daily) and Le Havre (€6.25, 1¼ hours, four to seven daily).

TRAIN

The Trouville-Deauville train station is in Deauville right next to pont des Belges (the bridge to Trouville). Getting here usually requires a change at Lisieux (€6.80, 20 minutes, nine to 11 daily), though there are two or three direct trains a day to Paris' Gare St-Lazare (€35, two hours). Destinations that require a change of trains include Caen (€14.50, 1¼ to two hours, six to 11 daily) and Rouen (from €25, 1¼ to two hours, five to eight daily).

Honfleur

POP 8200

Long a favourite with painters such as Monet, Normandy's most charming port town is a popular day-trip destination for Parisian families. Though the centre can be overrun with visitors on warm weekends and in summer, it's hard not to love the rugged maritime charm of the Vieux Bassin (old

harbour), which evokes maritime Normandy of centuries past.

In the 16th and 17th centuries, Honfleur was one of France's most important ports for commerce and exploration. Some of the earliest French expeditions to Brazil and Newfoundland began here, and in 1608, Samuel de Champlain set sail from Honfleur to found Quebec City.

Sights & Activities

Honfleur is spread around the roughly rectangular Vieux Bassin and, along its southeast side, the Enclos, the once-walled old town. Église Ste-Catherine is northwest of the Vieux Bassin (up the hill).

Honfleur is superb for aimless ambling, especially if you have a walking map from the tourist office. One option is to head north from the Lieutenance along quai des Passagers to **Jetée de l'Ouest** (Western Jetty), which forms the west side of the Avant Port, out to the broad mouth of the Seine. Possible stops include the **Jardin des Personnalités**, a park featuring figures from Honfleur history; the beach; and **Naturospace** (☎02 31 81 77 00; www.naturospace.com; bd Charles V; adult/child €9/7; ⊙9.30am-1pm & 2-5.30pm Feb-Nov, closed Dec-Jan), a lush greenhouse filled with free-flying tropical butterflies and birds that's situated 500m northwest of the Lieutenance.

The tourist office also has audioguides (€5; in English, French and German) for a 1½-hour walking tour of town.

Le Pass Musées (adult/student late Jun-early Oct €12/9, other times €10.50/7.50) gets you into all four municipal museums for less than the price of two.

Vieux Bassin HISTORIC SITE

The old harbour, with its bobbing pleasure boats, is Honfleur's focal point. On the west side, quai Ste-Catherine is lined with tall, taper-thin houses – many protected from the elements by slate tiles – dating from the 16th to 18th centuries. The **Lieutenance** (12 Place Ste-Catherine), at the mouth of the old harbour, was once the residence of the town's royal governor. Just northeast of the Lieutenance is the **Avant Port**, home to Honfleur's dozen fishing vessels, which sell their catch at the **Marché au Poisson** (Fish Market; Jetée de Transit; ⊙8am-noon or later Thu-Sun).

Small children will get a kick out of a ride on the carousel, situated opposite the Lieutenance.

Église Ste-Catherine CHURCH

(place Ste-Catherine; ⊙9am-5.15pm or later) Initially intended as a temporary structure, this extraordinary wooden church was built by local shipwrights during the late 15th and early 16th centuries after its stone predecessor was destroyed during the Hundred Years War. Wood was used so money would be left over to strengthen the city's fortifications. From the inside, the remarkable twin naves and double-vaulted roof resemble two overturned ships' hulls. Situated a block southwest (up the hill) from the northern end of the Vieux Bassin.

★**Les Maisons Satie** MUSEUM

(☎02 31 89 11 11; www.musees-honfleur.fr; 67 bd Charles V & 90 rue Haute; adult/child €6.20/free; ⊙10am-7pm Wed-Mon May-Sep, to 6pm Oct-Apr) Like no other museum you've ever seen, this complex captures the whimsical spirit of the eccentric avant-garde composer Erik Satie (1866–1925), who lived and worked in Honfleur and was born in one of the two half-timbered *maisons Satie* (Satie houses). Visitors wander through the utterly original rooms, each hiding a surreal surprise, with a headset playing Satie's strangely familiar music. Situated 350m northwest of the northern end of the Vieux Bassin.

Musée Eugène Boudin ART MUSEUM

(☎02 31 89 54 00; www.musees-honfleur.fr; 50 rue de l'Homme de Bois; adult/child Jun-Oct €7.50/free, Nov-May €5.80/4.30; ⊙10am-1pm & 2-6pm Wed-Mon Jun-Oct, 2.30-5.30pm Wed-Mon & 10am-noon Sat & Sun Nov-May) Features superb 19th- and 20th-century paintings of Normandy's towns and coast, including works by Dubourg, Dufy and Monet. One room is devoted to Eugène Boudin, an early impressionist painter, born here in 1824, whom Baudelaire called the 'king of skies' for his luscious skyscapes.

Musée de la Marine MARITIME MUSEUM

(☎02 31 89 14 12; www.musees-honfleur.fr; quai St-Etienne; adult/child €4.20/free, incl Musée d'Ethnographie €5.30/free; ⊙10am-noon & 2-6.30pm Tue-Sun Apr-Sep, 2.30-5.30pm Tue-Sun, 10am-noon Sat & Sun mid-Feb–Mar, Oct & Nov, closed Dec–mid-Feb) Has model sailing ships, nautically themed engravings and watercolours, and a case that examines Honfleur's role in the 17th- and 18th-century *traite négrière* (slave trade). Situated on the eastern shore of the Vieux Bassin, in the deconsecrated 13th- and 14th-century Église St-Étienne.

OFF THE BEATEN TRACK

CAMEMBERT COUNTRY

Some of the most enduring names in the pungent world of French *fromage* come from Normandy, including **Pont L'Évêque**, **Livarot** and, most famous of all, **Camembert**, all of which are named after towns south of Honfleur, on or near the D579.

It's thought that monks first began experimenting with cheesemaking in the **Pays d'Auge** area of Normandy sometime in the 11th century, but the present-day varieties didn't emerge until around the 17th century. The invention of Camembert is generally credited to Marie Harel, who was supposedly given the secret of soft cheesemaking by an abbot from Brie on the run from revolutionary mobs in 1790. Whatever the truth of the legend, the cheese was a huge success at the local market in Vimoutiers, and the *fabrication* of Camembert quickly grew from cottage production into a veritable industry. The distinctive round wooden boxes, in which Camembert is wrapped, have been around since 1890; they were designed by a local engineer to protect the soft disc during long-distance travel.

If you're interested in seeing how the cheese is made, you can take a tour of the **Maison du Camembert** (☎02 33 12 10 37; www.maisonducamembert.com; adult/child €3.50/1.50; ⏰10am-noon & 2-5pm daily May-Sep, Wed-Sun Apr & Oct, closed Nov–late Mar), an early-19th-century farm restored by Président, one of the largest Camembert producers. It's in the centre of the town of Camembert, about 60km south of Honfleur.

Musée d'Ethnographie et d'Art Populaire Normand MUSEUM
(☎02 31 89 14 12; www.musees-honfleur.fr; rue de la Prison; adult/child €4.20/free, incl Musée de la Marine €5.30/free; ⏰10am-noon & 2-6.30pm Tue-Sun Apr-Sep, 2.30-6.30pm Tue-Fri, 10am-noon & 2.30-5.30pm Sat & Sun mid-Feb–Mar & Oct-late Nov, closed late Nov–mid-Feb) Offers a glimpse of domestic and economic life in 16th- to 19th-century Normandy through traditional costumes, furniture and housewares. Situated around the corner from Musée de la Marine, in two adjacent 16th-century buildings: a one-time prison and a house.

Sleeping

Hôtel du Dauphin HOTEL €
(☎02 31 89 15 53; www.hoteldudauphin.com; 10 place Pierre-Berthelot; d €90-130, tr €160; 📶) Behind a 17th-century slate and half-timbered facade, this hotel and its various annexes have a mix of rooms, some rather worn and designed around unusual themes (macarons, for instance). The best have views of the cathedral. There is also one room for guests with limited mobility. The grotty carpeting on the stairs and dimly lit corridors may deter you.

★ La Petite Folie B&B €€
(☎06 74 39 46 46; www.lapetitefolie-honfleur.com; 44 rue Haute; d incl breakfast €145-195, apt €195-275; 📶) Penny Vincent, an American who moved to France from San Francisco, and her French husband Thierry are the gracious hosts at this elegant home, built in 1830 and still adorned by the original stained glass and tile floors. Each room has a different design, with original artwork, and the best are filled with vintage furnishings and overlook the pretty garden.

The lovely common areas make a fine spot for an evening glass of wine. La Petite Folie also rents nicely designed apartments on the same street.

Le Fond de la Cour B&B €€
(☎06 72 20 72 98; www.lefonddelacour.com; 29 rue Eugène Boudin; d €100-150, cottage €165-225; 📶) Watched over by a dog, a cat and some chickens, the rooms here (including a studio and a cottage, which sleeps up to four) are light, airy and immaculate. The energetic Amanda, a native of Scotland, goes to great lengths to make you feel at home. Breakfast, with eggs, croissants, crêpes, and jams, is included in all room rates.

Les Maisons de Léa BOUTIQUE HOTEL €€€
(☎02 31 14 49 49; www.lesmaisonsdelea.com; r €190-375) Set in a grand 16th-century mansion facing the Église Ste-Catherine, this highly regarded boutique hotel has attractively designed rooms and friendly service, but it's the extensive facilities that are the real draw, including a tea salon, a relaxing spa (guests have free use of the *hammam*) and a top-end restaurant.

La Maison de Lucie BOUTIQUE HOTEL €€€
(☎02 31 14 40 40; www.lamaisondelucie.com; 44 rue des Capucins; d €170-200, ste €250-330; 🅿📶) This marvellous little hideaway has just

nine rooms and three suites, which ensures intimacy. Some of the bedrooms, panelled in oak, have Moroccan-tile bathrooms and boast fantastic views across the harbour to the Pont de Normandie. The shady terrace is a glorious place for a summer breakfast. There's a chic jacuzzi in the old brick-vaulted cellar. No lift.

Eating

Some of Honfleur's finest restaurants, many featuring dishes plucked from the sea, are on place Hamelin and adjacent rue Haute, both just west of the northern end of the Vieux Bassin. There are more options up around Église Ste-Catherine. Budget places with watery views line quai Ste-Catherine, along the western side of the Vieux Bassin. East of the Vieux Bassin, there are more restaurants along rue de la Ville.

Honfleur's dining spots often fill up, especially for dinner on weekends and during school holidays, so it's a good idea to phone in a reservation.

La Cidrerie CREPERIE €

(☎02 31 89 59 85; 26 place Hamelin; mains €8-12; ⊙noon-2.30pm & 7-9.30pm Thu-Mon) For an inexpensive and casual meal, La Cidrerie is a great option, serving up a winning combination of piping hot *galettes* and fizzy Norman ciders served in bowls. You can choose from over a dozen savoury options, then finish with a dessert crêpe (try one with homemade caramel sauce). There's also warm cider – perfect if (when) the weather sours.

Bistro des Artistes FRENCH €€

(☎02 31 89 95 90; 30 place Berthelot; mains €20-28; ⊙noon-2.30pm & 7-9.30pm Thu-Tue) Anne-Marie Carneiro is a one-woman show at this tiny eatery near Église Ste-Catherine. She greets guests, waits tables and cooks. Though she may sometimes come across as brusque, the dishes here are magnificent, and everything is made in-house, including the hearty bread brought to your table after you arrive.

L'Endroit FRENCH €€

(☎02 31 88 08 43; 3 rue Charles et Paul Bréard; weekday lunch menus €25, other menus €30, mains €24-29; ⊙noon-1.30pm & 7.30-9pm Thu-Mon) In an eclectic and artfully designed space with an open kitchen, L'Endroit serves beautifully prepared dishes that showcase the bounty of Normandy fields and coastline. The menu is limited, with just a few roasted meats and seafood dishes on offer each night, but the high-quality cooking, friendly service and appealing surrounds (including a secret roof terrace for smokers) rarely fail to impress.

Au P'tit Mareyeur FRENCH €€

(☎06 84 33 24 03; www.auptitmareyeur.fr; 4 rue Haute; lunch/dinner menus €29/36; ⊙noon-2pm & 7-10pm Thu-Mon, closed Jan) Arrayed under 17th-century beams, this 'semi-gastronomique' restaurant serves up Norman-style fish and langoustine, foie gras and a famous *bouillabaisse honfleuraise* (fish and seafood stew made with potatoes and saffron; €35); some of the side dishes feature South Indian spices. There is also an upstairs dining area. Situated two blocks northwest of the northern end of the Vieux Bassin.

L'Homme de Bois FRENCH €€

(☎02 31 89 75 27; 30-32 rue de L'Homme de Bois; menus €24-36, mains €19-48; ⊙noon-2.30pm & 7-9.30pm daily) The rustic interior, complete with a fireplace, provides a relaxing backdrop for the locally caught fish, either grilled or prepared with delicate traditional sauces; *homard breton* (blue lobster) from the Carteret area; and excellent French-style steaks. Situated four short blocks northwest of the northern end of the Vieux Bassin.

Le Gambetta FRENCH €€

(☎02 31 87 05 01; 58 rue Haute; menus €26-36, mains €19-38; ⊙noon-1.45pm & 7.15-9pm Wed-Sun) This traditional restaurant takes pride in resurrecting old recipes, some from the early 20th century, others from the Middle Ages. Specialities include fish (three-quarters of it locally caught), meat prepared on a *plancha* (grill) and scrumptious desserts. Four short blocks northwest of the northern end of the Vieux Bassin.

★La Fleur de Sel GASTRONOMIC €€€

(☎02 31 89 01 92; www.lafleurdesel-honfleur.com; 17 rue Haute; menus €32-62; ⊙noon-1.30pm & 7.15-9pm Wed-Sun) Honfleur-raised Vincent Guyon cooked in some of Paris' top kitchens before returning to his hometown to make good and open his own (now celebrated) restaurant. Guyon uses the highest quality locally sourced ingredients and plenty of invention (with roast meats and wild-caught seafood featuring ginger and kaffir-lime vinaigrettes, Camembert foams and hazelnut tempura) in his beautifully crafted dishes. Reserve ahead.

SaQuaNa GASTRONOMIC €€€
(02 31 89 40 80; 22 place Hamelin; menus from €100; 12.30-2.30pm & 7.30-9.30pm Thu-Sat) This celebrated two-Michelin-starred restaurant dazzles with its exquisite, brilliantly inventive dishes. Chef Alexandre Bourdas trained in Japan (*sakana* means fish in Japanese, but also plays on French artistry in the realm of 'SAveur (flavour), QUalité (quality) and NAture'), and he brings elements of the Far East to incredibly fresh, locally sourced ingredients.

Self-Catering

Marché FOOD MARKET €
(place Ste-Catherine; 9am-noon Wed & Sat) A traditional food market on Saturday, a *biologique* (organic) market on Wednesday. There's usually a vendor selling made-to-order crêpes. Situated next to Église Ste-Catherine.

Information

Tourist Office (02 31 89 23 30; www.ot-honfleur.fr; quai Lepaulmier; 9.30am-12.30pm & 2-6pm Mon-Sat Sep-Jun, 9.30am-7pm Jul & Aug, also 10am-5pm Sun Easter-Sep;) Has a free map detailing three enjoyable walking circuits, audioguides (€5; in English, French and German) for a walking tour of town, and bus schedules. Internet access costs €1 for 15 minutes. Situated a long block southeast of the Vieux Bassin, inside the ultra-modern Médiathèque (library) building.

Getting There & Away

BUS

The **bus station** (quai Lepaulmier), two blocks east of the tourist office, has schedules posted in the window. **Bus Verts** (p224) services include Deauville and Trouville (€2.50, 30 minutes, four to seven daily), Caen (bus 20, €8.55, 2½ hours, seven to 13 daily; bus 39, €12, one hour, one or two daily) and Le Havre (€4.85, 30 minutes, four to six daily).

TRAIN

To catch the train (eg to Paris), take the bus to Deauville (18km from Honfleur) or Le Havre (25km from Honfleur).

MANCHE

The Manche *département* (www.manche-tourisme.com) encompasses the entire Cotentin Peninsula, stretching from Utah Beach northwest to Cherbourg and southwest to magnificent Mont St-Michel. The peninsula's northwest corner has unspoiled stretches of rocky coastline sheltering tranquil bays and villages. The fertile inland areas, crisscrossed by hedgerows, produce an abundance of beef, dairy products and apples.

The British crown dependencies of Jersey and Guernsey lie 22km and 48km offshore, respectively.

Cherbourg

POP 41,000

At the tip of the Cotentin Peninsula, the port city of Cherbourg plays host to French warships, transoceanic cargo ships, cruise liners, yachts and passenger ferries from Britain and Ireland. It's a far cry from the romantic locale portrayed in Jacques Demy's 1964 musical film *Les Parapluies de Cherbourg* (The Umbrellas of Cherbourg), but it's home to an outstanding aquarium-cum-sea-museum.

During WWII, Cherbourg's port was destroyed by the Germans shortly after D-Day to prevent it from falling into Allied hands.

Sights

★**Cité de la Mer** AQUARIUM
(02 33 20 26 69; www.citedelamer.com; allée du Président Menut, Gare Maritime Transatlantique; adult/child €18/13; 9.30am-6pm or 7pm, closed in Jan, may be closed Mon in winter;) Cherbourg's art-deco Gare Maritime Transatlantique (Transatlantic Ferry Terminal), built from 1928 to 1933, was designed so travellers could walk from their train directly to their ocean liner. These days it is still used by cruise ships such as the *Queen Mary 2*, but most of the complex houses a fine aquarium featuring Europe's deepest fish tank. The complex is situated 1km northeast of the tourist office.

Sleeping

Auberge de Jeunesse HOSTEL €
(02 33 78 15 15; www.fuaj.org; 55 rue de l'Abbaye; dm incl breakfast €23; reception 9am-1pm & 6-11pm; @) Located 1km northwest of the tourist office, this excellent, 99-bed hostel is housed in the French navy's old archives complex. Rooms have two to five beds; there's a small kitchen for self-caterers. To get there, take bus 3 or 5 to the Chantier stop.

Hôtel de la Renaissance HOTEL €
(02 33 43 23 90; www.hotel-renaissance-cherbourg.com; 4 rue de l'Église; d €65-80, f €85-115;) Staff here are very welcoming, and most of the 12 large, well-kept rooms have great views

LOCAL KNOWLEDGE

THE RED BALL

Equal parts gallery, wine bar and taxidermy shop, **Le Ballon Rouge** (9 rue du Port; ⏲10.30am-1pm & 3-8.30pm Tue, Thu & Sat, 4-8.30pm Wed, 10.30am-1pm & 3pm-1am Fri) near the waterfront embodies Cherbourg's most creative side. Stop in for a look at the changing artwork for sale, chat with the quirky owner, and enjoy an evening tipple amid half-deflated balloons, stuffed foxes and wildly eclectic tunes played on vinyl (from alt rock to old French marching songs).

of the port. Situated 400m northwest of the tourist office. Reception closes at 8.30pm.

Ambassadeur Hôtel HOTEL €€
(☎02 33 43 10 00; www.ambassadeurhotel.com; 22 quai de Caligny; s/d from €45/54; ❄📶) This good-value three-star has a great central location across from the marina, and pleasant modern rooms, with white stucco walls, big windows (that keep out street noise) and high-quality mattresses. Friendly service.

Eating

Restaurants can be found along quai de Caligny, a block or two north of the tourist office, and along the streets leading inland from there, including rue Tour Carrée.

Le Commerce BRASSERIE €
(42 François la Vieille; mains €12-16; ⏲11am-midnight Mon-Sat) When you (or your wallet) need a break from gourmet dining, head to this brash and boisterous brasserie, with pan-fried salmon, steak, chicken fajitas and other filling dishes. It's a local favourite of all ages – and all hours of the day.

Au Tire-Bouchon FRENCH €€
(☎02 33 53 54 69; www.restaurant-autirebouchon.com; 17 rue Notre-Dame; lunch menus €12.20-14.20, mains €15-22; ⏲noon-2pm & 7-10pm Tue-Sat) At this convivial bistro and wine bar, specialities include oysters, *tartines* (open sandwiches, €11 to €12) and the *salade tire-bouchon* (a salad with ham, foie gras and salmon). Au Tire-Bouchon is a bit hard to find – from quai de Caligny, follow the signs to 'Parking Notre-Dame'.

Le Plouc 2 FRENCH €€
(☎02 33 01 06 46; 59 rue du Blé; menus €21-38; ⏲noon-2pm Tue-Fri & Sun, 7-9.30pm Mon-Sat) Locals keep coming back for Le Plouc 2's creative versions of traditional French favourites, prepared with seasonal ingredients and served in a cosy, wood-beamed dining room.

Le Pily GASTRONOMIC €€€
(☎02 33 10 19 29; www.restaurant-le-pily.com; 39 Grande Rue; menus €43-78; ⏲noon-1.45pm & 7-9pm Tue-Sat) The young chef Pierre Marion is at the helm of Cherbourg's best restaurant. Expect a lively menu of seafood and meat dishes, with great care taken in the balancing of flavours.

Information

Tourist Office (☎02 33 93 52 02; www.cherbourgtourisme.com; 14 quai Alexandre III; ⏲9.30am-7pm Mon-Sat, 10am-5pm Sun mid-Jun–mid-Sep, 10am-12.30pm & 2-6pm Mon-Sat mid-Sep–mid-Jun) Has useful information on visiting the city, the Cotentin Peninsula and D-Day sites, and can help with accommodation. Situated on the west side of the Bassin de Commerce (inner harbour), two blocks south of the bridge.

Getting There & Around

BOAT

Cherbourg's **ferry terminal** is 2km northeast of the tourist office. A free shuttle-bus service, coordinated with ferry schedules, links the ferry terminal with the parking lot across the Pont Tournant (bridge) from the city centre.

Brittany Ferries (www.brittany-ferries.co.uk) Has services to the English ports of Poole and Portsmouth.

Irish Ferries (www.irishferries.com) Goes to the Irish ports of Rosslare and Dublin.

Stena Line (www.stenaline.ie) Sails to Rosslare.

TRAIN

The train station is at the southern end of Bassin du Commerce (inner harbour), just west of the new Les Éléis shopping mall. Direct services:

Bayeux €18.10, one hour, 15 daily Monday to Friday, eight to 10 Saturday and Sunday

Caen €23, 1¼ hours, eight to 15 daily

Paris' Gare St-Lazare €52, three hours, eight daily Monday to Friday, four or five daily Saturday and Sunday

Pontorson (Mont St-Michel) €31, 2½ to 3½ hours, three to five daily (via Lison)

Mont St-Michel

POP 44

It's one of France's most iconic images: the slender spires, stout ramparts and rocky slopes of Mont St-Michel rising dramati-

cally from the sea – or towering over sands laid bare by the receding tide. Despite huge numbers of tourists, both the abbey and the narrow alleys below still manage to transport visitors back to the Middle Ages.

The bay around Mont St-Michel is famed for having Europe's highest tidal variations; the difference between low and high tides – only about six hours apart – can reach an astonishing 15m. The Mont is only completely surrounded by the sea every month or two, when the tidal coefficient is above 100 and high tide is above 14m. Regardless of the time of year, the waters sweep in at an astonishing clip, said to be as fast as a galloping horse.

History

Bishop Aubert of Avranches is said to have built a devotional chapel on the summit of the island in 708, following his vision of the Archangel Michael, whose gilded figure, perched on the vanquished dragon, crowns the tip of the abbey's spire. In 966, Richard I, Duke of Normandy, gave Mont St-Michel to the Benedictines, who turned it into a centre of learning and, in the 11th century, into something of an ecclesiastical fortress, with a military garrison at the disposal of both abbot and king.

In the 15th century, during the Hundred Years War, the English blockaded and besieged Mont St-Michel three times. The fortified abbey withstood these assaults and was the only place in western and northern France not to fall into English hands. After the Revolution, Mont St-Michel was turned into a prison. In 1966, the abbey was symbolically returned to the Benedictines as part of the celebrations marking its millennium. Mont St-Michel and the bay became a Unesco World Heritage Site in 1979.

In recent decades, sand and silt have been building up around the causeway – built in 1879 – linking the Mont to the mainland, threatening to turn the island into a permanent peninsula. To restore the site's 'maritime character', in 2014 the causeway was replaced by a slender, 2km bridge designed to allow the tides and the River Couësnon (kweh-*no*) – whose new *barrage* (dam) stores up high-tide water and then releases it at low tide – to flush away accumulated sediments. For the latest, see www.projetmontsaintmichel.fr or drop by the dam's **observation platform**, across the street from the place du Barrage shuttle-bus stop.

Sights & Activities

The Mont's one main street, the **Grande Rue**, leads up the slope – past cheesy souvenir shops and eateries – to the abbey. The staircases and tiny passageways that meander up the hill from the Grande Rue – one, opposite Restaurant La Croix Blanche, is just 50cm wide – will take you to the diminutive parish church, a tiny cemetery and other Mont-sized surprises. Finding your way around is easier if you pick up a detailed map of the Mont at the tourist office or the abbey's ticket counter.

Be prepared for lots of steps, some of them spiral – alas, it's is one of the least wheelchair-accessible sites in France.

Abbaye du Mont St-Michel ABBEY
(☎02 33 89 80 00; www.monuments-nationaux.fr; adult/child incl guided tour €9/free; ⌚9am-7pm, last entry 1hr before closing) The Mont's star attraction is the stunning architectural ensemble high up on top: the abbey. Most areas can be visited without a guide, but it's well worth taking the one-hour tour included in the ticket price; English tours (usually) begin at 11am and 3pm from October to March, with three or four daily tours in spring and summer. You can also take a 1½-hour audioguide tour (one/two people €4.50/6), available in six languages.

Benedictine monks hold services in the abbey at 6.50am from Tuesday to Friday; at 7.50am on Saturday, Sunday and holidays; at 11.15am on Sunday; at noon from Tuesday to Saturday; and at 6.20pm from Tuesday to Friday.

From Monday to Saturday from mid-July to August, there are illuminated *nocturnes* (night-time visits) with live chamber music from 7pm to midnight.

Église Abbatiale CHURCH
(Abbey Church) Built on the rocky tip of the mountain cone, the transept rests on solid rock, while the nave, choir and transept arms are supported by the rooms below. This church is famous for its mix of architectural styles: the nave and south transept (11th and 12th centuries) are solid Norman Romanesque, while the choir (late 15th century) is Flamboyant Gothic.

La Merveille HISTORIC SITE
(The Marvel) The buildings on the northern side of the Mont are known as 'The Marvel'. The famous **cloître** (cloister) is surrounded by a double row of delicately carved arches

Mont St-Michel

TIMELINE

708 Inspired by a vision of **St Michael** ❶, Bishop Aubert is inspired to 'build here and build high'.

966 Richard I, Duke of Normandy, gives the Mont to the Benedictines. The three levels of the **abbey** ❷ reflect their monastic hierarchy.

1017 Development of the abbey begins. Pilgrims arrive to honour the cult of St Michael. They walk barefoot across the mudflats and up the **Grande Rue** ❸ to be received in the almonry (now the bookshop).

1203 The monastery is burnt by the troops of Philip Augustus, who later donates money for its restoration and the Gothic 'miracle', **La Merveille** ❹, is constructed.

1434 The Mont's **ramparts** ❺ and fortifications ensure it withstands the English assault during the Hundred Years War. It is the only place in northern France not to fall.

1789 After the Revolution, Monasticism is abolished and the Mont is turned into a prison. During this period the **treadmill** ❻ is built to lift up supplies.

1878 The Mont is linked to the mainland by a **causeway** ❼.

1979 The Mont is declared a Unesco World Heritage Site.

2014 The causeway is replaced by a bridge.

TOP TIPS

➡ Pick up a picnic lunch at the supermarket in La Caserne to avoid the Mont's overpriced fast food.

➡ Allow 45 minutes to an hour to get from the new parking lot in La Caserne to the Mont.

➡ If you step off the island pay close attention to the tides - they can be dangerous.

➡ Don't forget to pick up the Abbey's excellent audioguide – it tells some great stories.

JOHN ELK/GETTY IMAGES ©

ÎLOT DE TOMBELAINE

Occupied by the English during the Hundred Years War, this islet is now a bird reserve. From April to July it teems with exceptional birdlife.

Treadmill
The giant treadmill was powered hamsterlike by half a dozen prisoners, who, marching two abreast, raised stone and supplies up the Mont.

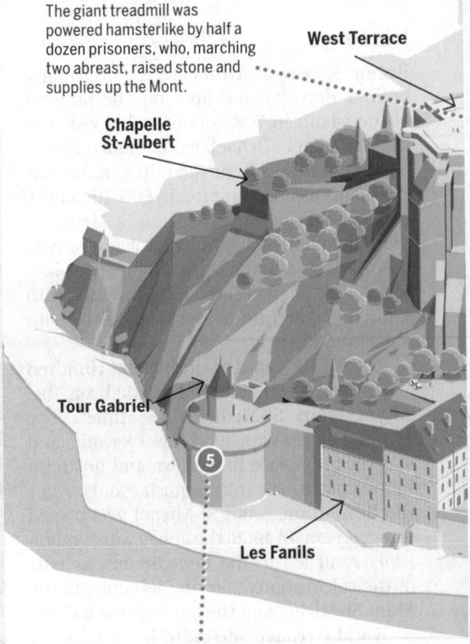

Ramparts
The Mont was also a military garrison surrounded by machicolated and turreted walls, dating from the 13th to 15th centuries. The single entrance, Porte de l'Avancée, ensured its security in the Hundred Years War. Tip: Tour du Nord (North Tower) has the best views.

ROCCO FASANO/GETTY IMAGES ©

Abbey

The abbey's three levels reflect the monastic order: monks lived isolated in church and cloister, the abbot entertained noble guests at the middle level, and lowly pilgrims were received in the basement. Tip: night visits run from mid-July to August.

HUGHES HERVA/GETTY IMAGES ©

St Michael Statue & Bell Tower

A golden statue of the winged St Michael looks ready to leap heavenward from the bell tower. He is the patron of the Mont, having inspired St Aubert's original devotional chapel.

IZZET KERIBAR/GETTY IMAGES ©

La Merveille

The highlights of La Merveille are the vast refectory hall lit through embrasured windows, the Knights Hall with its elegant ribbed vaulting, and the cloister (above), which is one of the purest examples of 13th-century architecture to survive here.

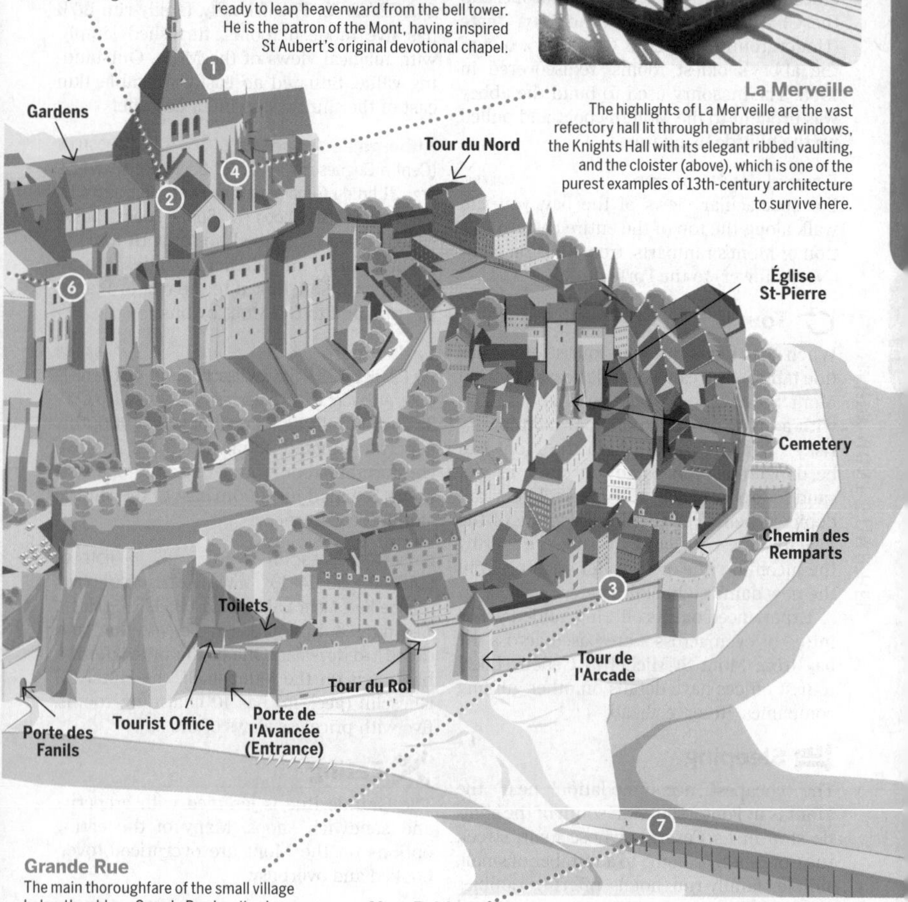

Grande Rue

The main thoroughfare of the small village below the abbey, Grande Rue has its charm despite its rampant commercialism. Don't miss the famous Mère Poulard shop here, for souvenir cookies.

DAVID TOMLINSON/GETTY IMAGES ©

New Bridge

In 2014, the Mont's 136-year-old causeway was replaced by a bridge designed to allow seawater to circulate and thus save the island from turning into a peninsula.

GNOPARUS/SHUTTERSTOCK ©

BEST VIEWS

The view from the Jardin des Plantes in nearby Avranches is unique, as are the panoramas from Pointe du Grouin du Sud near the village of St-Léonard.

resting on granite pillars. The early-13th-century, barrel-roofed **réfectoire** (dining hall) is illuminated by a wall of recessed windows – remarkable given that the sheer drop precluded the use of flying buttresses. The Gothic **Salle des Hôtes** (Guest Hall), dating from 1213, has two enormous fireplaces.

Other features to look out for include the **promenoir** (ambulatory), with one of the oldest ribbed vaulted ceilings in Europe, and the **Chapelle de Notre Dame sous Terre** (Underground Chapel of Our Lady), one of the abbey's oldest rooms, rediscovered in 1903. The masonry used to build the abbey was brought to the Mont by boat and pulled up the hillside using ropes.

Chemin des Remparts WALKING

For spectacular views of the bay, you can walk along the top of the entire eastern section of Mont's ramparts, from Tour du Nord (North Tower) to the Porte du Roy.

Tours

When the tide is out (the tourist office has tide tables), you can walk all the way around Mont St-Michel, a distance of about 1km, with a guide (doing so on your own is very risky). Straying too far from the Mont can be dangerous: you could get stuck in wet sand – from which Norman soldiers are depicted being rescued in one scene of the Bayeux Tapestry – or be overtaken either by the incoming tide or by water gushing from the new dam's eight sluice gates.

Experienced outfits offering guided walks into – or even across – are based across the bay from Mont St-Michel in Genêts. Local tourist offices have details on other guiding companies. Reserve ahead.

Sleeping

The cheapest accommodation near the Mont is in Pontorson, 7km south of the shuttle stop in La Caserne, whose main street, rue Couësnon, is home to a number of small, simple, family-run hotels offering doubles for as little as €40. Pontorson is linked with the rest of France by train and with La Caserne by bus (€3.20), the D976 and the Voie Verte walking and cycling route.

The most convenient hotels – most run by chains – are in La Caserne, 2km south of the Mont itself. The only way to drive into La Caserne is to get a gate code when you make your reservation. If you stay here or in a nearby B&B – several offer superb value – you'll save the €12 parking fee.

If you opt to stay up on the Mont itself, you'll have to park at La Caserne, take the shuttle with your luggage, and then walk to your hotel.

Vent des Grèves B&B €

(Estelle 02 33 48 28 89; www.ventdesgreves.com; 7-9 chemin des Dits, Ardevon; s/d/tr/q incl breakfast €42/52/62/72) This friendly, family-run B&B has five modern rooms, furnished simply, with magical views of the Mont. Outstanding value. Situated an easily walkable 1km east of the shuttle stop in La Caserne.

Auberge de Jeunesse HOSTEL €

(Centre Duguesclin; 02 33 60 18 65; www.fuaj.org; 21 bd du Général Patton, Pontorson; dm €15; reception 8am-noon & 5pm-8.30pm, hostel closed Oct-Mar) A 62-bed hostel with four- to six-bed rooms and kitchen facilities. Situated in Pontorson, linked to the rest of France by train and to the Mont by bus.

La Jacotière B&B €€

(02 33 60 22 94; www.lajacotiere.fr; 46 rue de la Côte, Ardevon; d incl breakfast €75-90, studio €80-95; P) Built as a farmhouse in 1906, this superbly situated, family-run B&B has five comfortable rooms and one studio apartment. Situated just 300m east of the shuttle stop in La Caserne.

Hôtel Du Guesclin HOTEL €€

(02 33 60 14 10; www.hotelduguesclin.com; Grande Rue, Mont St-Michel; d €95-125; closed Wed night & Thu Apr-Jun & Oct–mid-Nov, hotel closed mid-Nov–Mar) One of the most affordable hotels on the Mont itself, the Hôtel Du Guesclin (geck-*la*) has 10 charming rooms, five with priceless views of the bay.

Eating

The Grande Rue is jammed with crêperies and sandwich shops. Many of the eating options on the Mont are overpriced, overbooked and overbusy.

Crêperie La Sirène CREPERIE €

(Grande Rue; crêpes €4-11; 11.45am-5pm Sep-Dec & mid-Feb–Jun, to 9.30pm Jul & Aug, closed Jan–mid-Feb) Situated at the bottom of the Grande Rue, up a 15th-century staircase from the souvenir shop.

Super Marché SUPERMARKET €

(La Caserne; 9am-7.30pm) Good for picnic supplies. Has a shuttle stop out front.

Les Terrasses Poulard FRENCH €€
(☎02 33 89 02 02; www.terrasses-poulard.fr; Grand Rue; menus €19-29; ⊙noon-2pm & 7-9pm) Amid cast-iron chandeliers and copper pots hung from the walls, this bright and buzzing, always packed eatery serves up the usual assortment of bistro classics, as well as *galettes* (including a more affordable *galette* menu for €16). The waterfront views are a bonus.

Information

La Caserne Tourist Office (☎02 14 13 20 15; www.bienvenueaumontsaintmichel.com; La Caserne parking lot; ⊙10am-6pm) Run by the company that built the new bridge and parking lot, this *centre d'information* has lots of brochures, a free screening about Mont St-Michel, left-luggage lockers and an ATM.

Mont St-Michel Tourist Office (☎02 33 60 14 30; www.ot-montsaintmichel.com; ⊙9am-12.30pm & 2-6pm Sep-Jun, 9am-7pm Jul & Aug) Has an *horaire des marées* (tide table) posted, changes money and sells an excellent detailed map of the Mont (€3). Next door are toilets and an ATM. It's situated just inside Porte de l'Avancée, up the stairs to the left.

Getting There & Away

For all manner of details on getting to the Mont, see www.bienvenueaumontsaintmichel.com.

BUS

Intercity buses stop next to the Mont's new parking lot in La Caserne, very near the shuttles to the Mont.

Bus 1 (every hour or two, more frequently in July and August), operated by **Transdev** (☎02 14 13 20 15), links La Caserne with the village of Beauvoir (€3.20, five minutes) and the train station in Pontorson (€3.20, 18 minutes); times are coordinated with the arrival in Pontorson of some trains from Caen and Rennes

Keolis Emeraude (☎02 99 26 16 00; www.destination-montsaintmichel.com) Has buses to the train stations in Rennes (€15, 1¼ hours, four daily) and Dol de Bretagne (€8, 30 minutes, one or two daily); times are coordinated with TGVs to/from Paris.

CAR & MOTORCYCLE

Visitors who arrive by car must leave their vehicles in one of the new parking lots (two/24 hours €6/12) situated a few hundred metres east of La Caserne's hotel strip. Luggage can normally be left in lockers in the adjacent tourist office building – though at the time of research these lockers were not operational owing to security concerns.

TRAIN

The town of Pontorson, 7km south of the La Caserne parking area, is the area's main rail hub. Services from Pontorson include:

Bayeux €25, 1¾ hours, three daily

Caen €29, 1¾ hours, three daily

Cherbourg €31, 2½ to 3½ hours, three to five daily (via Lison)

Rennes €15, one hour, three or four daily

Getting Around

The new parking area next to La Caserne is 2.5km south of Mont St-Michel. To get from there to the Mont, you can either walk or take a free shuttle that lets you off 300m from the Mont's main gate. Shuttles run 24 hours a day – regularly from 7am to 1am, when summoned by phone after that. Count on spending 45 minutes to an hour to get from the parking lot to the abbey.

BICYCLE

In La Caserne, the **Hôtel Mercure** (☎02 33 60 14 18) rents out bicycles for €4.90/16.80 for one hour/all day.

Brittany

POP 3.27 MILLION

Includes ➡

Best Places to Eat

- ➡ Le Moulin de Rosmadec (p279)
- ➡ Breizh Café (p257)
- ➡ Restaurant de Roscanvec (p287)

Best Places to Sleep

- ➡ Le 14 Saint-Michel (p289)
- ➡ La Maison Pavie (p261)
- ➡ Le Keo – La Maison des Capitaines (p271)

Why Go?

Brittany is for explorers. Its wild, dramatic coastline, medieval towns and thick forests make an excursion here well worth the detour off the beaten track. This is a land of prehistoric mysticism, proud tradition and culinary wealth, where fiercely independent locals celebrate Breton culture, and Paris feels a long way away indeed.

The entire region (Breizh in Breton) has a wonderfully undiscovered feel once you go beyond world-famous sights such as stunning St-Malo, regal Dinard and charming Dinan. Unexpected Breton gems – including the little-known towns of Roscoff, Quimper and Vannes, the megaliths of Carnac, the rugged coastlines of Finistère, the Presqu'Île de Crozon and the Morbihan Coast – all demonstrate that there's far more to Brittany than delicious crêpes and homemade cider. Brittany's much-loved islands are also big draws – don't miss its two stars: dramatic Île d'Ouessant and the aptly named Belle Île.

When to Go

Brest

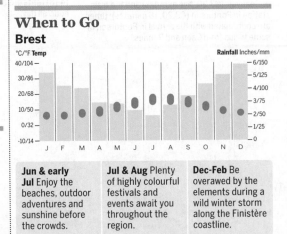

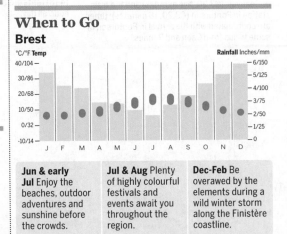

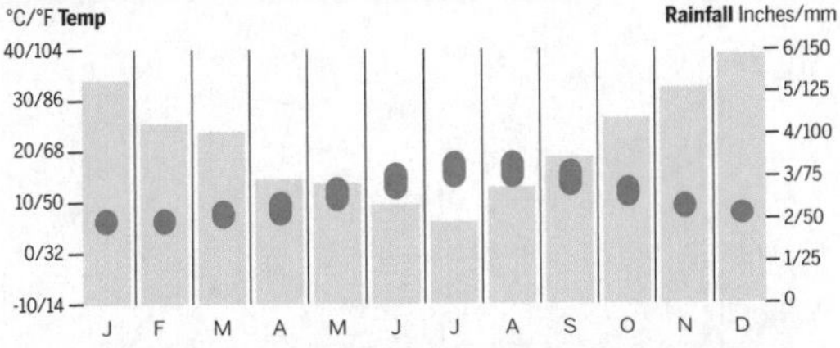

Jun & early Jul Enjoy the beaches, outdoor adventures and sunshine before the crowds.

Jul & Aug Plenty of highly colourful festivals and events await you throughout the region.

Dec-Feb Be overawed by the elements during a wild winter storm along the Finistère coastline.

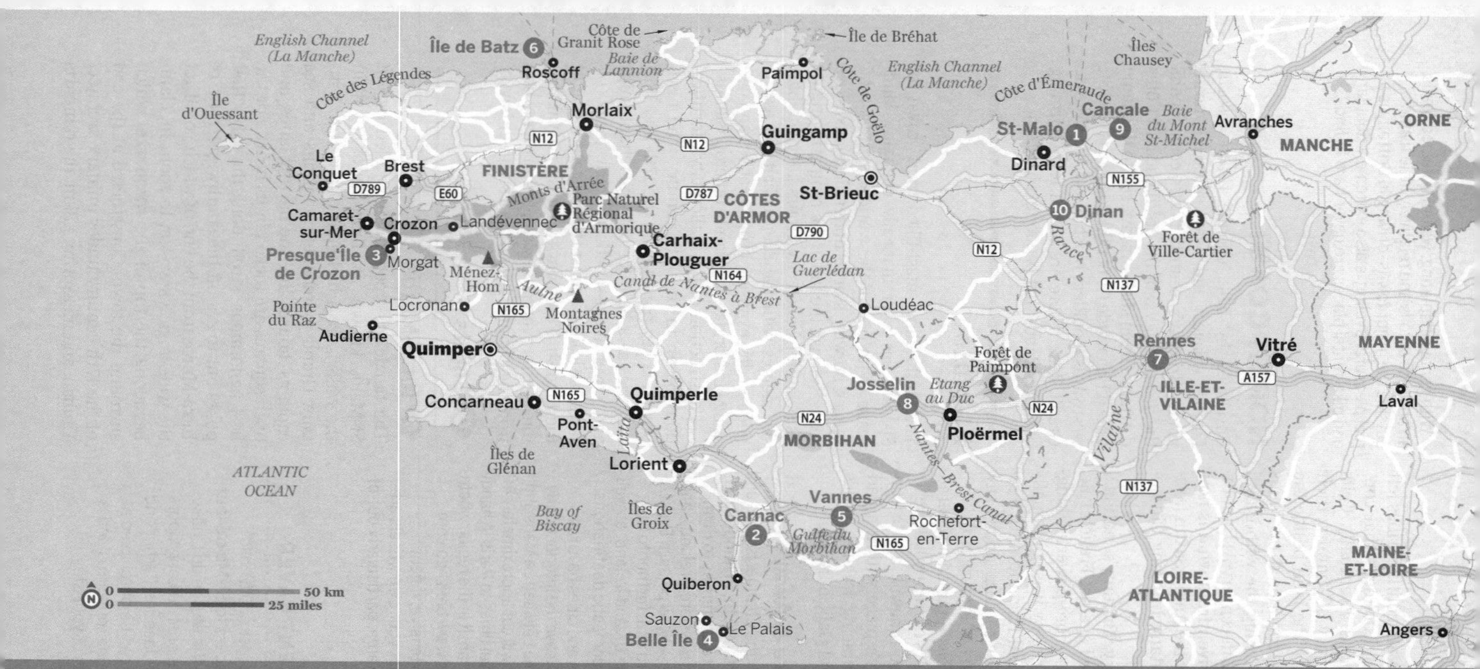

Brittany Highlights

1 **St-Malo** (p252) Strolling along historic ramparts at sunset with panoramic views.

2 **Megaliths** (p282) Cycling past fields full of prehistoric megaliths around Carnac.

3 **Coastlines** (p272) Exploring the magical Presqu'Île de Crozon and Pointe du Raz.

4 **Belle Île** (p284) Getting away from it all and frolicking in sun and sea.

5 **Vannes** (p286) Joining a vibrant Breton city in its *joie de vivre*, history and coastal sights.

6 **Île de Batz** (p266) Hiking and biking to your heart's content on this car-free islet.

7 **Rennes** (p292) Having a gastronomic holiday in one of France's great foodie cities.

8 **Josselin** (p288) Touring the turreted medieval castle over the fairy-tale forest village.

9 **Cancale** (p260) Tucking into freshly shucked oysters on a casual harbourfront.

10 **Dinan** (p261) Getting lost in the higgledy-piggledy old town.

History

Brittany's earliest known neolithic tribes left a legacy of menhirs and dolmens that continue to baffle historians. Eventually, Celts arrived in the 6th century BC, naming their new homeland Armor ('the land beside the sea'). The region was conquered by Julius Caesar in 56 BC. Following the withdrawal of the Romans in the 5th century AD, another round of Celts – driven from what is now Britain and Ireland by the Anglo-Saxon invasions – settled in Brittany, bringing Christianity with them.

In the 9th century, Brittany's national hero Nominoë revolted against French rule. Wedged between two more-powerful kingdoms, the duchy of Brittany was continually contested by France and England until a series of strategic royal weddings finally saw the region become part of France in 1532.

However, Brittany has retained a separate regional identity. There's currently a drive for cultural and linguistic renewal, and a consciousness of Brittany's place within a wider Celtic culture embracing Ireland, Wales, Scotland, Cornwall and Galicia in Spain.

Getting There & Away

Ferries link St-Malo with the Channel Islands and the English ports of Portsmouth, Plymouth and Poole. From Roscoff there are ferries to Plymouth (UK) and Cork and Rosslare (Ireland), and Bilbao (Spain). Alternatively, airports in Brest, Quimper, Rennes, Dinard and, further to the south, Nantes, serve the UK and Ireland, as well as other European and domestic destinations.

Brittany's major towns and cities have rail connections, but routes leave the interior poorly served. When the TGV line between Le Mans and Rennes opens in 2017, it will cut approximately 40 minutes off the train travel times to Paris. A handy website for calculating transit in the region whether by train, bus or boat is www.breizhgo.com.

The bus network is extensive, if generally infrequent, meaning that your own wheels are the best way to see the area, particularly out-of-the-way destinations.

ST-MALO CENT SAVER

A **combined ticket** (per adult/child €13/6) gives you access to St-Malo's four major monuments: the Musée du Château, Musée International du Long Cours Cap-Hornier, Musée Jacques Cartier and Mémorial 39–45. It can be purchased at any of the participating museums and is valid for the duration of your stay.

With gently undulating, well-maintained roads, an absence of tolls and relatively little traffic outside the major towns, driving in Brittany is a real pleasure. Cycling is also extremely popular, and bike-rental places are never hard to find.

NORTH COAST

Enveloped by belle époque beach resorts, fishing villages and wave-splashed headlands, Brittany's central north coast spans the *départements* of Ille-et-Vilaine and Côtes d'Armor. Green shallows give rise to the name Côte d'Émeraude (Emerald Coast) to the east; westwards, boulders blush along the Côte de Granit Rose. There are also a few charming offshore islands that beg for exploration.

St-Malo

POP 46,589

The enthralling mast-filled port town of St-Malo has a dramatically changing landscape. With one of the world's greatest tidal ranges, brewing storms under blackened skies see waves lash the top of the ramparts ringing its beautiful walled city. Hours later, the blue sky merges with the deep cobalt sea as the tide recedes, exposing broad beaches and creating land bridges to granite outcrop islands.

Construction of the walled city's fortifications began in the 12th century. The town became a key port during the 17th and 18th centuries as a base for both merchant ships and government-sanctioned privateers (pirates, basically) against the constant threat of the English. These days, English arrivals are tourists, for whom St-Malo, a short ferry hop from the Channel Islands, is a summer haven.

Sights

Intra-Muros

The tangle of streets in the walled city of St-Malo, known as Intra-Muros ('within the walls'), are a highlight of a visit to Brittany. Grand merchants' mansions and sea captains' houses line the narrow lanes, and open squares are tucked in its heart. For the best panoramas, stroll along the **jetty** that pokes out to sea off the southwestern tip of Intra-Muros from the end of which you'll get the wide-angle view – or, to zoom in, clamber along the top of the **ramparts**, which surround the town. Constructed at the end of the 17th century under military architect Vauban, and measuring 1.8km, the ramparts

St-Malo & St-Servan

Top Sights
1 Fort National B1
2 Mémorial 39–45 .... A5

Sights
3 Fort de la Cité d'Alet A4
4 Île du Grand Bé & Fort du Petit Bé A2
5 Musée International du Long Cours Cap-Hornier A5

Sleeping
6 Camping de la Cité d'Alet A5
7 Le Valmarin B5

Eating
8 Le Bulot B5

can be accessed at several points, including at all the main city gates.

Though you'd never guess it from the cobblestone streets and reconstructed monuments in 17th- and 18th-century style, during August 1944, the battle to drive German forces out of St-Malo destroyed around 80% of the old city, which has been painstakingly restored since then.

Cathédrale St-Vincent CATHEDRAL
(place Jean de Châtillon; ⌚9.30am-6pm) The city's centrepiece was constructed between the 12th and 18th centuries. During the ferocious fighting of August 1944, the cathedral was badly hit; much of its original structure (including its spire) was reduced to rubble. The cathedral was subsequently rebuilt and reconsecrated in 1971. A mosaic plaque on the floor of the nave marks the spot where Jacques Cartier received the blessing of the bishop of St-Malo before his 'voyage of discovery' to Canada in 1535.

Musée d'Histoire de St-Malo MUSEUM
(☎02 99 40 71 57; www.ville-saint-malo.fr/culture/les-musees; Château; adult/child €6/3; ⌚10am-12.30pm & 2-6pm daily Apr-Sep, Tue-Sun Oct-Mar) Within **Château de St-Malo**, built by the dukes of Brittany in the 15th and 16th centuries, this museum looks at the life and history of the city through a hodgepodge of nautical exhibits, model boats and marine artefacts. There are displays on the city's cod-fishing heritage, paintings, and info on famous locals, including Cartier, Surcouf, Duguay-Trouin and the writer Chateaubriand. The castle's lookout tower offers eye-popping views of the old city.

St-Malo & St-Servan

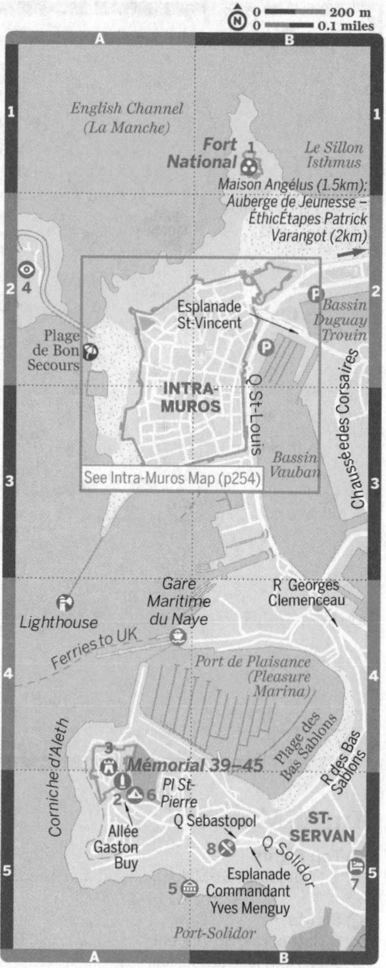

La Demeure de Corsaire HISTORIC BUILDING
(☎02 99 56 09 40; www.demeure-de-corsaire.com; 5 rue d'Asfeld; adult/child €5.50/4.50; ⌚10-11.30am Mon-Sat, 2.30-5pm daily Jul, Aug & school holidays, to 3pm Tue-Sun rest of year, closed Dec & Jan) This 18th-century mansion and historic monument was once owned by corsair (privateer) François Auguste Magon. Guided tours are in French, but descriptions are available in English.

Beyond the Walls

The pretty fishing port of St-Servan sits 2km south of the walled city.

Intra-Muros

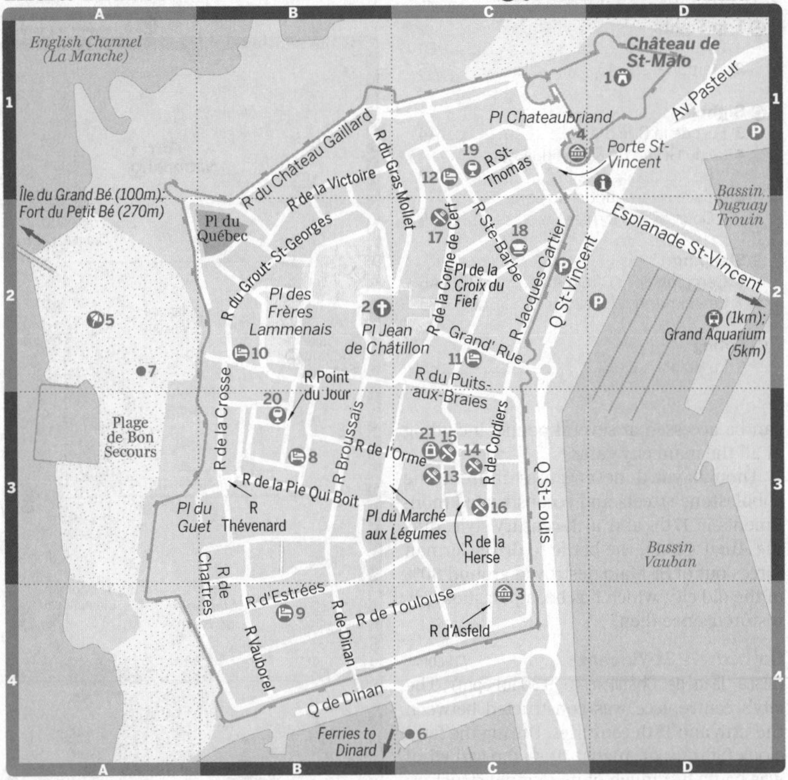

Intra-Muros

Top Sights

1 Château de St-Malo D1

Sights

2 Cathédrale St-Vincent B2
3 La Demeure de Corsaire C4
4 Musée d'Histoire de St-Malo C1
5 Plage de Bon Secours A2

Activities, Courses & Tours

6 Compagnie Corsaire C4
7 Les Corsaires Malouins A2

Sleeping

8 Accroche Cœur B3
9 Hôtel Quic en Groigne B4
10 Hôtel San Pedro B2
11 La Maison des Armateurs C2
12 Le Nautilus C1

Eating

Bistro Autour du Beurre .... (see 21)
13 Breizh Café C3
14 Halle Au Blé C3
15 L'Absinthe C3
Le Bistro de Jean .... (see 17)
16 Le Cambusier C3
17 Le Chalut C2

Drinking & Nightlife

18 La Cafe du Coin d'en Bas de la Rue du Bout de la Ville d'en Face du Port... La Java C2
19 L'Alchimiste C1
20 L'Aviso B3

Shopping

21 La Maison du Beurre Bordier C3

★**Fort National** RUINS

(www.fortnational.com; adult/child €5/3; ⏱Easter, Jun-Sep & school holidays) The St-Malo ramparts' northern stretch looks across to the remains of this former prison, built by Vauban in 1689. Standing atop a rocky outcrop, the fort can only be accessed at low tide. Check online or with the tourist office for tour times.

★**Mémorial 39–45** MONUMENT

(☎02 99 82 41 74; www.ville-saint-malo.fr; Fort de la Cité d'Alet, St-Servan; adult/child €6/3; ⏱guided visits 10.15am, 11am, 2pm, 3pm, 4pm & 5pm Jul & Aug, 2.30pm, 3.15pm & 4.30pm Tue-Sun Apr-Jun & Sep, shorter hours Oct) Constructed in the mid-18th century, **Fort de la Cité d'Alet** FREE was used as a German base during WWII. One of the bunkers now houses this memorial, which depicts St-Malo's violent WWII history and liberation, and includes a 45-minute film in French (not shown on every tour). Some guided visits are conducted in English; call ahead to confirm times.

Musée International du Long Cours Cap-Hornier MARITIME MUSEUM

(Museum of the Cape Horn Route; ☎02 99 40 71 58; www.ville-saint-malo.fr; Tour Solidor, quai Sébastopol, St-Servan; adult/child €6/3; ⏱10am-12.30pm & 2-6pm daily Apr-Sep, closed Mon Oct-Mar) Housed in the 14th-century **Tour Solidor**, this museum presents the life of the hardy sailors who followed the dangerous Cape Horn route around the southern tip of South America. It also offers superb views from the top of the tower.

Grand Aquarium AQUARIUM

(☎02 99 21 19 00; www.aquarium-st-malo.com; av Général Patton; adult/child €16.50/12; ⏱9.30am-9pm mid-Jul–mid-Aug, 9.30am-8pm early Jul & late Aug, 10am-6pm mid-Jan–Jun & Sep-Dec; 👪; 🚌C1, C2) This aquarium about 4km south of the city centre features a 'Nautibus' ride – a simulated descent aboard an underwater submarine – and a *bassin tactile* (touch pool), where kids can fondle rays and turbots. The exhibits on local marine life, tropical reefs and mangrove forests are also very strong. Allow around two hours for a visit. Bus 1 from the train station passes by every half-hour.

Beaches

You can splash in the protected tidal swimming pool west of the city walls at **Plage de Bon Secours** or climb its ladder to jump off into the sea. St-Servan's **Plage des Bas Sablons** has a cement wall to keep the sea from receding completely at low tide. The much larger **Grande Plage** stretches northeast along the isthmus of Le Sillon. Spectacular sunsets can be seen along the stretch from Grande Plage to Plage des Bas Sablons. Less-crowded **Plage de Rochebonne** is another 1km to the northeast.

> DON'T MISS
>
> **ÎLE DU GRAND BÉ & FORT DU PETIT BÉ**
>
> At low tide, cross the beach to walk across Plage de Bon Secours to the rocky islet **Île du Grand Bé**, where the great St-Malo-born, 18th-century writer Chateaubriand is buried. About 100m beyond the islet is the privately owned, Vauban-built, 17th-century **Fort du Petit Bé** (☎06 08 27 51 20; www.petit-be.com; ⏱by reservation). The owner runs 30-minute guided tours (adult/child €5/3) in French; leaflets are available in English. Once the tide rushes in, the causeway remains impassable for about six hours; check tide times with the tourist office.

Activities

★**Compagnie Corsaire** BOATING

(☎08 25 13 81 00; www.compagniecorsaire.com; Cale de Dinan; ⏱Apr-Sep) Compagnie Corsaire runs four-hour *pêche en mer* (deep-sea fishing) trips (€42.90). Boat tours and ferries leave from just outside Porte de Dinan and include: Bay of St-Malo (adult/child €20.90/12.50, 1½ hours), Bay of Cancale (adult/child €24.90/15), Dinan (adult/child €33/26.40), Île Cézembre (adult/child €15.20/9.10) and Îles Chausey (adult/child €34.30/20.60). Check online for schedules and itineraries.

Les Corsaires Malouins KAYAKING

(☎02 99 40 92 04; www.kayakdemer35.fr; Plage de Bon Secours; guided tours €25-32; ⏱Jul-Sep) The broad bay combined with beautiful sea- and landscapes make St-Malo prime sea-kayaking turf. This outfit runs guided trips around the bay for all levels.

Sleeping

Intra-Muros

Hôtel San Pedro HOTEL €

(☎02 99 40 88 57; www.sanpedro-hotel.com; 1 rue Ste-Anne; s €65-69, d €75-83; P 📶) Tucked at

the back of the old city, the San Pedro has a cool, crisp, neutral-toned decor with subtle splashes of yellow paint, friendly service, great breakfast, private parking (€10) and a few bikes available for free. It features 12 rooms on four floors served by a miniature lift (forget those big suitcases!); two rooms come with sea views.

Le Nautilus HOTEL €
(☎02 99 40 42 27; www.hotel-lenautilus-saint-malo.com; 9 rue de la Corne de Cerf; s €50-70, d €60-94; ⊙Feb-Nov; 📶) With efficient, friendly service and comfortable albeit smallish rooms, this super-central two-star abode offers excellent value. The decor has been freshened up with smartly finished bathrooms and light yellow walls. The elevator is an unexpected bonus for a hotel in this price range.

Accroche Cœur B&B €€
(☎06 07 10 80 22, 02 99 40 43 63; www.accrochecoeursaintmalo.fr; 9 rue Thévenard; d incl breakfast €125-145; 📶) Is this St-Malo's best-kept secret? There are five upper-crust *chambres d'hôte* in this solid townhouse tucked into a side street in the historic centre. Top of the heap is the vast Brieg suite, which is suitable for a family, but the Mac Low, which boasts polished wood beams, elegant furniture and sparkling bathroom, isn't a bad backup.

Hôtel Quic en Groigne HOTEL €€
(☎02 99 20 22 20; www.quic-en-groigne.com; 8 rue d'Estrées; d €90-130; ⊙mid-Feb–Dec; P 📶) This exceptional hotel has 15 rooms that are the epitome of clean, simple style. Not only is it good value, but it offers excellent service and an ideal location on a quiet, old-town street just a few metres from a beach. The icing on the cake: the convenience of secure parking (€14; five spaces only) in a city where parking can be downright hellish. No lift, but there are only two floors.

★ La Maison des Armateurs HOTEL €€
(☎02 99 40 87 70; www.maisondesarmateurs.com; 6 Grand Rue; d €110-210, f/ste from €190/230; ⊙closed Dec; ❄📶) No language barrier here – La Maison des Armateurs is run by a helpful French-American couple. Despite the austere granite-fronted setting, the inside of this sassy four-star hotel is all sexy, modern minimalism: modern furniture throughout, gleaming bathrooms with power showers and cool chocolate, pale orange and neutral grey tones. Families can plump for the super-sized suites. Check the website for deals.

Beyond the Walls

Camping de la Cité d'Alet CAMPGROUND €
(☎02 99 81 60 91; www.ville-saint-malo.fr; allée Gaston Buy, St-Servan; 2-person tent €16; ⊙Apr-mid-May & Jul–mid-Sep; 📶) Perched on a peninsula, this campground has panoramic 360-degree views and is close to beaches and some lively bars.

Auberge de Jeunesse – Éthic Étapes Patrick Varangot HOSTEL €
(☎02 99 40 29 80; www.centrevarangot.com; 37 av du Père Umbricht, Paramé; dm incl breakfast €24.50; P@📶) This efficient hostel scores high on amenities, with a well-equipped communal kitchen, a restaurant, a bar, laundry service, private parking and free sports facilities. It has 285 beds, with each room accommodating two to five beds and an en-suite bathroom. It's in a calm neighbourhood, a five-minute walk from Plage de Rochebonne. Take bus 3 from the train station.

★ Maison Angélus B&B €€
(☎02 99 40 66 79; www.maisonangelus.com; 82 av Pasteur; d incl breakfast €115-130; 📶) This three-room B&B, housed inside a tastefully restored 19th-century building, is a tranquil respite from the crowds of the walled city, and it's ideally situated just a two-minute stroll from the Grande Plage. You'll love the cosy lounge areas and the backyard garden oasis. Your Italian hosts, Giulio and Cristina, complete the charming picture and serve a delicious breakfast and a superb Italian dinner (€40).

★ Le Valmarin HISTORIC HOTEL €€
(☎02 99 81 94 76; www.levalmarin.com; 7 rue Jean XXIII, St-Servan; d €115-165, f €150-230; P 📶) If you're yearning for an aristocratic atmosphere then this peaceful 18th-century mansion should do the job nicely. It has 12 high-ceilinged rooms dressed in late-19th-century style, and glorious gardens full of flowers and shade trees. Minus: some bathrooms feel a bit dated. It's a soothing escape from the St-Malo hubbub, on the edge of the village-like St-Servan quarter.

Eating

St-Malo boasts superb places to eat, but also beware of the many mediocre tourist-style eateries (mainly those around the Porte St-Vincent and Grande Porte). For a seat at the best restaurants in town, it's essential to book ahead in high season and on weekends.

Market mornings are Tuesday and Friday in the Intra-Muros at the **Halle au Blé** (⏲ 8am-1pm Tue & Fri) market hall.

★Breizh Café CRÊPERIE €

(☎ 02 99 56 96 08; www.breizhcafe.com; 6 rue de l'Orme; crêpes €9-13; ⏲ noon-2pm & 7-10pm Wed-Sun) This will be one of your most memorable meals in Brittany. The creative chef combines traditional Breton ingredients and *galette* and crêpe styles with Japanese flavours and brilliant textures and presentation. Seaweed and delightful seasonal pickles meet local ham, organic eggs and roast duck. Save room for dessert, notably the transcendent Amuse-Crêpe: a crêpe roll (like a sushi roll) of melted Valrhona chocolate and ginger-caramel made with *beurre salé* (salted butter).

Le Bulot BISTRO €€

(☎ 02 99 81 07 11; www.lebulot.com; 13 quai Sébastopol, St-Servan; mains €15-19, lunch/dinner menus €14/25; ⏲ noon-2pm daily, 7-10pm Mon-Sat) A laid-back neighbourhood bistro with a modern feel and views over the Port-Solidor in St-Servan (best appreciated on sunny days from the restaurant's raised wooden terrace). There's a short menu of tasty French classics such as *brandade de morue* (salt cod purée) and chicken marinated in lemon.

L'Absinthe MODERN FRENCH €€

(☎ 02 99 40 26 15; www.restaurant-absinthe-cafe.fr; 1 rue de l'Orme; lunch menus €19, dinner menus €29-60; ⏲ noon-2pm & 7-10pm) Hidden away in a quiet street near the covered market, this fab eatery is housed in a 17th-century building. Ingredients fresh from the market are whipped into shape by talented chef Stéphane Brebel, and served in cosy surrounds. The wine list is another hit, with an all-French cast from white to red and rosé.

Le Cambusier MODERN FRENCH €€

(☎ 02 99 20 18 42; www.cambusier.fr; 6 rue des Cordiers; mains €19-25, dinner menu €35; ⏲ noon-2pm Thu-Tue, 7-9pm Mon, Tue & Thu-Sat) With its ambient lighting, honey-coloured parquet flooring and large B&W shots of fishermen enlivening the dining room, Le Cambusier can do no wrong. Run by a talented husband-and-wife team, it's known across the city for its upmarket take on classic French cuisine. Since *madame* is also a sommelier, let things rip with the list of well-chosen French tipples.

DON'T MISS

FRANCE'S MOST FAMOUS BUTTER

Bistro Autour du Beurre (☎ 02 23 18 25 81; www.lebeurrebordier.com; 7 rue de l'Orme; lunch menu €19, mains €18-24; ⏲ noon-2pm Tue-Sat, 7-10pm Thu-Sat) showcases the cheeses and butters handmade by the world-famous Jean-Yves Bordier; you'll find his **shop** (⏲ 9am-1pm & 3.30-7.30pm Tue-Sat, 9am-1pm Mon & Sun) next door. His products are shipped to renowned restaurants around the globe. At the bistro, the butter sampler (€15 in the shop, but included in meals) and bottomless bread basket are just the start to creative, local meals that change with the seasons.

The establishment is in one of the few remaining completely intact buildings from before WWII and the shop has an interesting exhibit on butter history around the world and in Brittany.

Le Chalut SEAFOOD €€

(☎ 02 99 56 71 58; 8 rue de la Corne de Cerf; mains €27-29, menus €29-79; ⏲ 12.15-1.15pm & 7.15-9.15pm Wed-Sun) This unremarkable-looking establishment is, in fact, St-Malo's most celebrated restaurant, with one Michelin star. Its kitchen overflows with the best the Breton coastline has to offer – buttered turbot, line-caught sea bass, crab and scallops. Feel like splashing out? Plump for the 'all lobster' menu.

Le Bistro de Jean BISTRO €€

(☎ 02 99 40 98 68; 6 rue de la Corne de Cerf; mains €19-20, menus €20; ⏲ noon-1.45pm Mon, Tue, Thu & Fri, 7-9.45pm Mon-Sat) Peer through the windows of this lively, authentic bistro to see where locals head for flavourful cuisine, based on fresh ingredients. Expect duck breast, lamb shanks and succulent line-caught sea bass, as well as excellent home-made desserts.

Drinking & Nightlife

★L'Aviso BAR

(12 rue Point du Jour; ⏲ 6pm-2am) This cosy place serves more than 300 beers, mostly from Brittany and Belgium, with more than 10 – including two Breton beers – on tap. If you can't decide, ask the friendly owner/connoisseur. It's the laid-back place with a cockatiel on the loose and jazzy tunes in the air.

La Cafe du Coin d'en Bas de la Rue du Bout de la Ville d'en Face du Port... La Java CAFE
(☎02 99 56 41 90; www.lajavacafe.com; 3 rue Ste-Barbe; ⊙8.51am-11.32pm daily mid-Jul–mid-Aug, shorter hours rest of year) The word 'eccentric' might have been coined to describe this extraordinary (and insanely named) cafe. Think part-museum, part-toyshop and a work of art from an ever-so-slightly-twisted mind. Traditional French accordion music plays and the eyes of hundreds of dolls and puppets keep watch from shelves. And the drinks? Ah, well they're actually quite sane – 100 different kinds of coffee and beer.

L'Alchimiste BAR
(7 rue St-Thomas; ⊙5pm-1am Tue-Sun) Mellow tunes fill this magical place lined with old books. Take a seat at the bar draped with a red-tasselled theatre curtain, on the carved timber mezzanine (including a pulpit) or in the wood-heated basement.

Information

Tourist Office (☎08 25 13 52 00; www.saint-malo-tourisme.com; esplanade St-Vincent; ⊙9am-7.30pm Mon-Sat, 10am-6pm Sun Jul & Aug, shorter hours Sep-Jun; 📶) Just outside the walls, near Porte St-Vincent. Has smartphone app, a good map (€1), transport info and loads of local advice.

Getting There & Around

BICYCLE

Rent bicycles and different sized scooters at **Cycles Nicole** (☎02 99 56 11 06; www.cyclesnicole.com; 11 rue du Président Robert Schuman, Paramé; bicycle/scooter per day €12/30; ⊙9am-noon & 2-6.45pm Tue-Sat).

BOAT

Brittany Ferries (www.brittany-ferries.com) sails between St-Malo and Portsmouth, and **Condor Ferries** (www.condorferries.co.uk) runs to/from Poole via Jersey or Guernsey, with connections to Portsmouth. Ferries leave from the **Gare Maritime du Naye**, 1km south of the Intra-Muros, which is served by the town-centre *navette* (shuttle).

Compagnie Corsaire (p255) runs a Bus de Mer shuttle service (adult/child return €8.30/5.50, 10 minutes, at least half-hourly) between St-Malo and Dinard, April to September. Outside the July/August peak season, both frequency and cost fall.

BUS

All intercity buses stop at the bus station alongside the train station. **Keolis St-Malo** (www.ksma.fr) has local buses, and services to Cancale (€1.30, 30 minutes). **Illenoo** (www.illenoo-services.fr) services run to Dinard (€2.70, 30 minutes, hourly) and Rennes (€6, one to 1½ hours, three to six daily). **Tibus** (☎08 10 22 22 22; www.tibus.fr) buses serve Dinan (€2, 50 minutes, three to eight daily).

TRAIN

St-Malo trains include:

Dinan €10.30, one hour, six daily (requiring a change in Dol de Bretagne)

Paris Montparnasse €45 to €79, 3½ hours, three direct TGVs daily

Rennes €15, one hour, roughly hourly

Dinard

POP 10,438

Visiting Dinard 'in season' is a little like stepping into one of the canvases Picasso painted here in the 1920s. Belle époque mansions built into the cliffs form a timeless backdrop to the beach dotted with blue-and-white-striped bathing tents and the beachside carnival. Views across to St-Malo are brilliant.

Out of season, when holidaymakers have packed up their buckets and spades, the town is decidedly dormant, but wintry walks along the coastal paths are spectacular.

Beaches

Framed by fashionable hotels, a casino and neo-Gothic villas, **Plage de l'Écluse** (Grande Plage) is the perfect place to shade yourself in style by renting one of Dinard's trademark bathing tents. Reproductions of Picasso's paintings are often planted in the sand here in high summer. When the Plage de l'Écluse gets too crowded, savvy Dinardais take refuge at the town's smaller beaches, including **Plage du Prieuré**, 1km to the south, and **Plage de St-Énogat**, 1km to the west.

Sleeping & Eating

Some of Dinard's best restaurants are attached to hotels, such as **Castelbrac** (☎02 99 80 30 00; www.castelbrac.com; 17 av George V; d €270-500; ❄@📶), which serves top-notch fish and seafood. Dinard's weekly open-air markets are on Tuesday, Thursday and Saturday on esplanade de la Halle.

Camping Le Port Blanc CAMPGROUND €
(☎02 99 46 10 74; www.camping-port-blanc.com; rue du Sergent Boulanger; site per 2 adults from €24.60; ⊙Apr-Sep; 📶) You'll find this camp-

BRETON LANGUAGE REDUX

Throughout Brittany you'll see bilingual Breton street and transport signs, and many other occurrences of the language popping up. Even though all Breton speakers also speak French, this is seen as an important gesture to normalising the use of a language that has been stigmatised (and even banned) throughout much of the early and mid-20th century.

Historically speaking, Breton is a Celtic language related to Cornish and Welsh, and more distantly to Irish and Scottish Gaelic. Following on from the French Revolution, the government banned the teaching of Breton in schools, punishing children who spoke their mother tongue. Between 1950 and 1990 there was an 80% reduction in Breton usage.

The seeds of the language's revival were planted in the 1960s, particularly after France's May 1968 protests, driven by the younger generation rebelling against the oppression of their cultural heritage. Bringing about the rebirth of the language, no longer passed on generationally, wasn't straightforward. As Breton is more often spoken than written (with regional differences in both within Brittany), settling on a standardised language for teaching in schools remains a complex issue.

Breton now extends beyond its former boundaries. Originally, Basse Bretagne (Lower Brittany, in the west) spoke variants of the Breton language, while Haute Bretagne (Upper Brittany, in the east, including areas such as St-Malo) spoke Gallo, a language similar to French. But today you'll find Breton signage in Rennes' metro stations and many other parts of the east as well.

ground close to the beach, about 2km west of Plage de l'Écluse. There's direct access to another beach.

Hôtel de la Plage HOTEL **€€**
(☎02 99 46 14 87; www.hoteldelaplage-dinard.com; 3 bd Féart; d €78-140; 📶) Attractive, fresh rooms with modern bathrooms and an enviable location a stone's throw away from the beach make this one of the best deals in town. Pricier rooms boast terrific sea views.

★Le Balafon MODERN FRENCH **€€**
(☎02 99 46 14 81; www.lebalafon-restaurant-dinard.fr; 31 rue de la Vallée; mains €17-24, lunch menu €18, dinner menus €29-39; ⏰noon-2pm & 7-9.30pm Tue-Sat, noon-2pm Sun) Away from the seafront tourist bustle, this quality, modern, neighbourhood bistro serves freshly made meals using produce from the nearby market. The lunch *menu* consists of a couple of well-chosen and presented dishes. It's totally unpretentious, well priced and many locals rate it the best place in town. In fair weather, sit in the inviting courtyard.

ℹ Information

Tourist Office (☎02 99 46 94 12; www.dinard-tourisme.com; 2 bd Féart; ⏰10am-12.30pm & 2.30-6pm Tue-Sat; 📶) Books accommodation for free, runs walking tours, offers maps of self-guided tours of Dinard's architecture.

ℹ Getting There & Away

AIR

Dinard–Pleurtuit–St-Malo Airport (www.dinard.aeroport.fr; Pleurtuit), 6.5km south of Dinard, is served by **Ryanair** (www.ryanair.com) with flights to/from London Stansted, East Midlands and Guernsey. There's no public transport; a daytime/evening taxi from Dinard to the airport costs around €17/25.

BOAT

Compagnie Corsaire (p255) runs a Bus de Mer shuttle service (adult/child return €8.30/5.50, 10 minutes) between St-Malo and Dinard, April to September, operating at least half-hourly. Outside July/August, both frequency and cost fall.

BUS

Illenoo (www.illenoo-services.fr) buses connect Dinard and the train station in St-Malo (€2.70, 30 minutes, hourly). Le Gallic bus stop, outside the tourist office, is the most convenient. Several buses travel to Rennes (€6, two hours).

Cancale

POP 5332

Tucked into the curve of a shimmering shell-shaped bay, the idyllic little fishing port of Cancale, 14km east of St-Malo, is famed for its offshore *parcs à huîtres* (oyster beds) that stretch for kilometres around the surrounding coastline. The excellent oysters are

DON'T MISS

FRESH OYSTERS

One of the most authentic seafood experiences you'll ever have awaits you in Cancale. Local fishermen sell their catch directly from stalls of **Marché aux Huîtres** (12 oysters from €4; ⏲9am-6pm) clustered by the Pointe des Crolles lighthouse. Point to the ones you want, and they'll be shucked, dashed with lemon and served before your eyes, and *voilà*, one perfect lunch. Oysters are numbered according to size and quality.

shipped all over northern France. There's no real beach, but the waterfront is a relaxing place to stroll and soak up the atmosphere. You can also drive or hike to Pointe du Grouin, a stunning headland and a nature reserve about 7km north of town.

Sights

Ferme Marine FARM

(☎02 99 89 69 99; www.ferme-marine.com; corniche de l'Aurore; adult/child €7/3.70; ⏲guided tours in English 2pm, in French 11am, 3pm & 5pm Jul–mid-Sep, 3pm only mid-Feb–Jun & mid-Sep–Oct) Learn about the art of *ostréiculture* (oyster farming) at this well-organised museum a couple of kilometres southwest of the port.

Sleeping

★Les Chambres Breizh Café B&B €€

(☎02 99 89 61 76; www.breizhcafe.com; 7 quai Thomas; d incl breakfast €118; 📶) You'll need to book early to bag your spot at this delightful *maison d'hôte* right on the harbourfront. It offers five fancy rooms all christened after apple varieties, ranging from coquettish Guillevic (balcony, views of the oyster parks) to sexy Kermerien (full frame bay views, gleaming bathrooms) and amply sized Rouget de Dol (a two-room suite, ideal for families).

La Pointe du Grouin HOTEL €€

(☎02 99 89 60 55; www.hotelpointedugrouin.com; Pointe du Grouin; d €95-116, ste €129-169; ⏲Apr–mid-Nov; P📶) A gracious welcome and cracking sea views are first to greet you at this family-owned abode poised on a rocky promontory at Pointe du Grouin, a few kilometres north of town. The 15 rooms are bright, comfy and designed to harmonise with the sea and sky just outside your window. The attached restaurant is equally popular. For outdoorsy types, there's a coastal path just in front.

Eating

Oysters, oysters, oysters! This is the place to sample them, fresh from their cosy beds. In addition to the daily oyster market (see box, left), there is a Sunday open-air market and an evening market on Thursdays in July and August.

★Breizh Café CREPERIE €

(☎02 99 89 61 76; www.breizhcafe.com; 7 quai Thomas; mains €5-14; ⏲noon-10pm Sat-Wed) Not your average crêperie, the Breizh Café is renowned for its gourmet crêpes and *galettes* made from organic flours. The cappuccino-and-cream decor gives it a fresh, modern feel, and the crêpes are really first-class. Where else could you savour a *galette* stuffed with langoustines and cheese? Wash it all down with a tipple from their range of top-notch local ciders.

Le Troquet SEAFOOD €€

(☎02 99 89 99 42; www.restaurantletroquet-cancale.fr; 19 quai Gambetta; mains €18-39, lunch menus €28, other menus €41; ⏲noon-2pm & 7-9pm Sat-Wed, daily Jul & Aug) Of the dozens of waterside restaurants you can find at the port, this sleek contemporary *troquet* (bistro) run by *artisan cuisinier* Laurent Helleu is the pick of the shoal. His *raison d'être* is locally bought, market-fresh ingredients, cooked with a minimum of fuss to bring out their natural flavours. Unsurprisingly in Cancale, seafood features heavily. Don't miss the killer *far Breton* (Breton cake).

Côté Mer SEAFOOD €€

(☎02 99 89 66 08; www.restaurant-cotemer.fr; 4 rue Ernest Lamort; mains €18-27, lunch/dinner menus from €24/30; ⏲noon-1.30pm & 7.30-9pm Mon & Thu-Sat, noon-1.30pm Sun & Tue) A fine waterfront position south of the downtown din makes this well-regarded restaurant a must for seafoodies. A big picture window gives lovely views of the bay, while inside, terracotta tiles, crisp white tablecloths and the odd colourful painting conjure a quietly stylish feel.

★Le Coquillage GASTRONOMIC €€€

(☎02 99 89 64 76; www.maisons-de-bricourt.com; D155, rte du Mont St-Michel, Le Buot; lunch menu €35, other menus €75-140; ⏲noon-2pm & 7-9pm) Super-chef Olivier Roellinger's sumptuous restaurant is housed in the impressive Château Richeux, 4km south of Cancale. Roellinger's creations have earned him three

Michelin stars (though he renounced them in 2008), and the food takes in the culinary highlights of Brittany and Normandy, all beautifully cooked and imaginatively served. He also offers cooking courses and deluxe accommodation around Cancale. Book well ahead.

Information

Tourist Office (02 99 89 63 72; www.cancale-tourisme.fr; 44 rue du Port; 9.30am-1pm & 2.30-6pm or 7pm;) At the top of rue du Port. In July and August there's an annexe on quai Gambetta.

Dinan

POP 11,440

Set high above the fast-flowing Rance River, the narrow cobblestone streets and squares lined with crooked half-timbered houses of Dinan's old town are straight out of the Middle Ages – something that's not lost on the deluge of summer tourists; by around 6pm, though, someone waves a magic wand and most of them vanish and a sense of calm overtakes the town.

Sights & Activities

Château-Musée de Dinan MUSEUM
(02 96 39 45 20; rue du Château; adult/child €5/free; 10am-6.30pm Jun-Sep, shorter hours rest of year, closed Jan & Feb) The town's museum is atmospherically housed in the keep of Dinan's ruined 14th-century château. It showcases the town's history and has information sheets in various languages.

★Tour Ste-Catherine TOWER
FREE The 14th-century Tour Ste-Catherine is just east of Basilique St-Sauveur and beyond the tiny **Jardin Anglais** (English Garden), a former cemetery and nowadays a pleasant little park. The 16m-high tower has great views over the viaduct and port.

Basilique St-Sauveur CHURCH
(place St-Sauveur; 9am-6pm, closed during services) The soaring chancel of the Basilique St-Sauveur is Flamboyant Gothic, but the south side of the church is Romanesque. The church contains a 14th-century gravestone in its north transept reputed to cover the heart of Bertrand du Guesclin, a 14th-century knight noted for his hatred of the English and his fierce battles to expel them. Ironically, today Dinan has one of the largest English expat communities in Brittany!

Tour de l'Horloge TOWER
(02 96 87 02 26; rue de l'Horloge; adult/child €4/2.50; 10am-6.30pm Jun-Sep, 2-6pm Apr-May) Climb up to the little balcony of this 15th-century clock tower whose chimes ring every quarter-hour. A few paces to the north, take in the half-timbered houses overhanging **place des Cordeliers** and **place des Merciers**, which mark the heart of the old town.

Vieux Pont HISTORIC SITE
Be sure to head downhill to the Vieux Pont (Old Bridge). To get there, descend the steep cobbles of **rue du Jerzual** and **rue du Petit Fort**, two of the best-preserved streets in Brittany. Both are lined with art galleries, antiques shops and restaurants. From here, the bridge, a pretty little **port**, hemmed by restaurants and cafes, extends northwards, and the 19th-century **Viaduc de Dinan** soars high above to the south.

Festivals & Events

Fête des Remparts MEDIEVAL FESTIVAL
(www.fete-remparts-dinan.com) No fewer than 100,000 visitors join Dinannais townsfolk dressed in medieval garb for the two-day Fête des Remparts, held in late July every even-numbered year.

Sleeping

Camping Municipal Châteaubriand CAMPGROUND €
(02 96 39 11 96; 103 rue Chateaubriand; per adult/tent/car €3.10/3.70/3.10; Jun-Sep) This campground at the foot of the ramparts is the closest to the old town.

★La Maison Pavie B&B €€
(02 96 84 45 37; www.lamaisonpavie.com; 10 place St-Sauveur; d incl breakfast €105-155; P) If you ever dreamt of staying in a 15th-century half-timbered house, look no further than this sumptuous B&B in the heart of Dinan. The building's medieval character and historic ambience have been lovingly preserved while modern comforts and designer fittings have been added – you have to see the architectural elements and furnishings of the rooms to believe them.

The private garden at the back is a delight, and dinner can be arranged (€35). The house once belonged to Auguste Pavie, a French 'plenipotentiary' in Asia.

Hôtel Arvor HOTEL €€
(02 96 39 21 22; www.hotelarvordinan.com; 5 rue Pavie; d €82-155, tr/f from €125/160; Feb-Dec;

1

2

Breton Coast

BORIS STROUJKO / SHUTTERSTOCK ©

1. City walls and beach, St-Malo (p252) 2. Fresh oysters (p260) from the Breton coast 3. Côte de Granit Rose (p265)

3

Brittany's rugged coastline is one of the region's best-kept secrets. With brilliant sandy beaches framing traditional fishing villages, rocky cliffs towering above the churning swell of the North Atlantic, and loads of outdoor activities to keep you occupied, there's plenty to discover.

Superb Stretches of Sand

Don't associate Brittany with beaches? Think again... Yes, the water may be freezing, but the sand is spectacular and the backing sublime at St-Malo (p252) and Quiberon (p282). Alternatively, find your own patch of sand on the beaches of Belle Île (p284).

Hiking the Coasts

Get out into nature on the coastal hiking trail from Morgat to Cap de la Chèvre (p272). For a challenge, walk the 45km coastal path on Île d'Ouessant (p270) or the 95km path around Belle Île (p284).

Coastal Villages

Find your own quiet bliss in the village life of charming Camaret-sur-Mer (p274), the fishing port of Roscoff (p265) and, our personal favourite, oyster-rich hideaway Cancale (p259).

Island Life

Take the ferry to Île d'Ouessant (p270), with its rugged coastal path and great activities, or head out of season to Belle Île (p284), the southern coast's star. To get off the beaten track, head to Île de Batz (p266).

Get Active!

You can dive, windsurf and hire catamarans in Dinard (p258); canoe or kayak in Paimpol (p264), St-Malo (p252), Îles de Glénan (p277) and Quiberon (p282); and hire bikes pretty much anywhere, though we recommend Presqu'île de Crozon (p272) and any of Brittany's islands. You can also learn to surf at schools (p284) around Brittany.

(P 📶) It's hard to believe that this sleek establishment was once a Jacobin convent. Expect thoroughly modern bathrooms, a few fancy decorative touches and calm colour tones. The charming tearoom is a great place to relax after a long day's sightseeing. Service is excellent and it's an all-round good deal. There's (limited) private parking (€8).

Eating

Crêperie Ahna CREPERIE €
(☎02 96 39 09 13; 7 rue de la Poissonnerie; mains €9-18; ⏲noon-2pm & 7-9.30pm Mon-Sat) This elegant scarlet eatery has been run by the same family for four generations and deserves its reputation as one of the best crêperies in town. Unusual delights include a *galette* with duck and snail butter (better than it sounds!). They also serve grilled meats and excellent ice creams.

La Courtine BISTRO €€
(☎02 96 39 74 41; 6 rue de la Croix; mains €15-18, lunch menus €13; ⏲noon-1.30pm Thu-Tue, 7.45-11.30pm Mon & Thu-Sat) Just steps from the animated place Duclos is this snug bistro with wood beams and stone walls serving classic French dishes. Its *souris d'agneau confite au cidre* (lamb shank stewed in cider) is not to be scoffed at. It also has a list of well-chosen French tipples, available by the glass.

Le Cantorbery TRADITIONAL FRENCH €€
(☎02 96 39 02 52; 6 rue Ste-Claire; mains €17-26, menus €33-42; ⏲noon-1.45pm Thu-Tue, 7-9.30pm Mon, Tue & Thu-Sat) This intimate restaurant in a 17th-century house is perfect for wining and dining your beloved over a romantic meal. Its traditional menu – based on beef, grilled fish and seafood, including *coquilles St-Jacques* (scallops) from St-Brieuc – changes with the seasons.

Information

Tourist Office (☎02 96 87 69 76; www.dinan-tourisme.com; 9 rue du Château; ⏲9.30am-7pm Mon-Sat, 10am-12.30pm & 2-6pm Sun; 📶) Free map in several languages plots two walking itineraries around town. In the 16th-century Hôtel Kératry.

FINISTÈRE CENT SAVER

The **Passeport Culturel** (http://passeport.culturel.finistere.fr) booklet covers 31 sights in the Finistère region. The first sight is full price, but each subsequent sight is discounted or, once in a while, free. Available free at participating sights.

Getting There & Away

BUS

Buses leave from place Duclos and the bus station. **Illenoo** (☎08 10 35 10 35; www.illenoo-services.fr) runs several daily services:

Dinard €3.80, 30 minutes
Rennes €6, 1¼ hours

TRAIN

Change in Dol de Bretagne:

Rennes from €15.70, 1¼ hour, nine daily
St-Malo €10.30, one hour, five daily

Paimpol

POP 7667

Set around a former fishing harbour, now a boating harbour, Paimpol is rich in history. It was the one-time home port of the Icelandic fishery, when the town's fishermen would set sail to the seas around Iceland for seven months or more at a stretch. Pierre Loti's 1886 novel *Pêcheur d'Islande* (An Iceland Fisherman) describes the experience. Paimpol is also rich in legends – the fishermen lost at sea are recalled in folk tales and *chants de marins* (sea shanties).

Sights & Activities

Enquire at the tourist office about canoeing and kayaking operators.

★**La Vapeur du Trieux** TOURIST TRAIN
(☎02 96 20 52 06; adult/child return €26/13; ⏲May-Sep) Steam-engine buffs and lovers of fine scenery will be in seventh heaven aboard the chuffing carriages of this 1922 steam train that plies the old railway line between Paimpol and the artists' town of Pontrieux, where there's time for a pleasant meal and a stroll before the return journey. Reserve at least one day ahead. The train was suspended at the time of research for track improvements.

Abbaye de Beauport ABBEY
(☎02 96 55 18 58; www.abbaye-beauport.com; rte de Kérity; adult/child €6/3.50; ⏲10am-7pm) If you have wheels (or you're up for a glorious 1½-hour walk along the seashore from the town harbour), head 3.5km east of Paimpol to this romantic 18th-century abbey. It hosts art and sculpture exhibitions. En route, stop at the Pointe de Guilben for beautiful bay views. The tourist office has a free map.

Musée de la Mer MARITIME MUSEUM
(Sea Museum; ☎02 96 22 02 19; www.museemer-paimpol.com; 11 rue Labenne; adult/child €4.50/free; ⏲10.30am-12.30pm & 2-6.30pm) This excellent little museum in a former cod-drying factory charts the Paimpol region's maritime history. Peruse nautical artefacts, from seine nets and canvas sails to vintage posters and fishing outfits.

Sleeping & Eating

Paimpol's Tuesday-morning **market** spreads over place Gambetta and place du Martray. On weekends, vendors sell freshly shucked oysters at quai Duguay Trouin.

Hôtel de la Marne HOTEL €
(☎02 96 16 33 41; www.hoteldelamarne-paimpol.fr; 30 rue de la Marne; d €65-100; P 📶) This granite inn ranks as highly in the dining stakes as it does in the sleeping. All rooms are beautifully modernised and the restaurant cooks up top-notch regional cuisine (*menus* from €29) with tip-top presentation and ace desserts. It's 650m southwest of the harbour.

Information

Tourist Office (☎02 96 20 83 16; www.paimpol-goelo.com; place de la République; ⏲9.30am-7.30pm Mon-Sat, 9.30am-12.30pm & 4.30-6.30pm Sun Jul & Aug, closed Sun Sep-Jun; 📶) Sells local rambling guides.

Getting There & Away

BUS

Tibus (p258) runs buses to and from St-Brieuc (€2, 1½ hours). In summer, most continue to Pointe L'Arcouest.

TRAIN

There are five daily trains between Paimpol and Guingamp (€7.90, one hour), where you can pick up connections to Brest, St-Brieuc and Rennes.

FINISTÈRE

The country's westernmost *département*, Finistère (www.finisterebrittany.com) has a wind-whipped coastline dotted with lighthouses and beacons lashed by the waves. The name Finistère literally comes from 'end of the earth' (the Latin *Finis Terræ*). Swaths of this beautiful land are preserved in the **Parc Naturel Régional d'Armorique** (www.pnr-armorique.fr).

Finistère's southern extent, called Cornouaille, takes its name from early Celts who sailed from Cornwall and other parts of Britain to settle here, and today it is a centre of Breton language, customs and culture.

Wild and mysterious, the Finistère is, for many people, the most enticing edge of an already enticing region.

> **DON'T MISS**
>
> **NATURAL WONDER**
>
> Running along the coast from Penvern to Trégastel and Ploumanach lies one of Brittany's natural wonders: a coastline of pink, salmon and russet-coloured granite known as the **Côte de Granit Rose**. Plan time to walk among the marvellously shaped and hued natural boulders and the sepia and coral-coloured beaches.

Roscoff

POP 3523

If you sail in by ferry, Roscoff (Rosko in Breton) provides a captivating first glimpse of Brittany. Granite houses dating from the 16th century line the pretty docks, and the town is surrounded by emerald-green fields producing cauliflowers, onions and artichokes.

Sights & Activities

★Église Notre Dame de Kroaz-Batz CHURCH
(place Lacaze-Duthiers; ⏲9am-noon & 2-7pm) The most arresting sight in Roscoff is this unique church at the heart of the old town. With its spectacular Renaissance belfry rising above the flat landscape, the 16th-century Flamboyant Gothic structure is one of Brittany's most impressive churches.

Le Jardin Exotique de Roscoff GARDENS
(☎02 98 61 29 19; www.jardinexotiqueroscoff.com; Le Ruveic; adult/child €6/3; ⏲10am-7pm Jul & Aug, shorter hours Sep-Nov & Mar-Jun, closed Dec-Feb) Wander through 3500 species of exotic plants (many from the southern hemisphere) at this impressive garden. It's a well-sign-posted half-hour walk southeast from the town centre.

Maison des Johnnies MUSEUM
(☎02 98 61 25 48; 48 rue Brizeux; adult/child €4/free; ⏲tours 11am, 3pm & 5pm Tue-Fri mid-Sep–mid-Jun, 3pm & 5pm mid-Jun–mid-Sep) Photographs at this popular museum trace Roscoff's roaming onion farmers, known as 'Johnnies', from the early 19th century. A

WORTH A TRIP

ÎLE DE BATZ

The Roscoff area may be light on beaches, but don't despair; skip across to the fabulous offshore island of Île de Batz and you'll find brilliant sand beaches (without the crowds). The largest and best beach is **Grève Blanche** on the northern shore.

A half-day is all you need to walk around this tiny speck of paradise (no cars allowed) but we suggest that you spend a night on the island to soak up its divine atmosphere. For more information, check www.iledebatz.net.

Ferries (adult/child return €9/4.50, bike €8.50, 15 minutes each way) between Roscoff and Île de Batz run every 30 minutes between 8am and 8pm in July and August, with less frequent sailings the rest of the year. Bicycles can be rented on the island for around €10 per day.

visit is by guided tour only. Call ahead, tour times change.

Sleeping

Camping Aux Quatre Saisons CAMPGROUND €
(☎02 98 69 70 86; www.camping-aux4saisons.fr; allée des Chènes Verts, Perharidy; sites €15.70; ⏲Easter-Sep; 📶🏊) Close to a sandy beach in the grounds of a lovely 19th-century mansion, this campground is approximately 3km southwest of Roscoff.

★Hôtel aux Tamaris HOTEL €€
(☎02 98 61 22 99; www.hotel-aux-tamaris.com; 49 rue Édouard Corbière; d €85-120; ⏲mid-Jan–Dec; 📶) This smart, family-run place in an old granite building overlooking the water at the western end of town is an excellent choice, with well-equipped, light, seabreeze-filled rooms, all with a pleasant maritime aura and yacht sails for ceilings. Rooms with sea views cost more. Expect locally sourced goodies at breakfast (€7 to €11). Bikes for hire.

La Résidence des Artistes HOTEL €€
(☎02 98 69 74 85; www.hotelroscoff-laresidence.fr; 14 rue des Johnnies; d €95-120; ⏲closed Dec & Jan; 📶) Bored with Breton character? This sassy hotel with a 'boutique-on-a-budget' feel might be just the ticket. Colour-coordinated, bright and modern, all the rooms here are slightly different and there's a piano in the arty reception area. The staff speak English and it's on a central, quiet street (close to a free car park).

Le Temps de Vivre BOUTIQUE HOTEL €€
(☎02 98 19 33 19; www.letempsdevivre.net; 19 place Lacaze Duthiers; d €153-200; 📶) This glamorous place is hidden away in a lovely stone mansion complete with its own tower just opposite the church. With fantastic sea views from some rooms, a great blend of modern and traditional decor, plus friendly staff, this is one of Roscoff's best options. Family rooms are available.

Chez Janie Hôtel HOTEL €€
(☎02 98 61 24 25; www.chezjanie.fr; 5 rue Gambetta, Le Port; d €99-124; ⏲mid-Feb–mid-Nov; 📶) You couldn't wish for a better Roscoff base than this refreshingly simple hotel perched above Chez Janie's bistro. The layouts are a bit awkward, but each room has a maritime-themed poem painted on the wall, and the bathrooms are in top nick. The sea-view rooms looking out over the postcard-pretty old port are well worth the extra cost.

Eating

Crêperie Ty Saozon CREPERIE €
(☎02 98 69 70 89; https://tisaozon.com; 30 rue Gambetta; mains €5.50-8.50; ⏲6.30-9pm Mon-Wed, Fri & Sat) Watch the making of handmade artisan crêpes and *galettes*, then devour them at this award-winning crêperie in the heart of the old town. You'll love the homey, intimate atmosphere.

★Le Surcouf BRASSERIE €€
(☎02 98 69 71 89; www.surcoufroscoff.fr; 14 rue Amiral Réveillère; lunch menus €13, dinner menus €19-80; ⏲11.30am-1.30pm & 6.30-9.30pm) Bang in the heart of Roscoff, this brasserie serves excellent seafood. You can choose your own crab and lobster from the window tank, tuck into the classic fish soup or opt for a heaping platter of fresh shellfish. Plate-glass windows keep things light and bright, and the dining room has a steady chatter.

★Le Brittany GASTRONOMIC €€€
(☎02 98 69 70 78; www.hotel-brittany.com; blvd Ste-Barbe; menu €58) Splash out on the best of Breton seafood at this Michelin-starred restaurant on the seafront at the east end of town. Chef Loïc Le Bail sources top local ingredients and crafts creative, artfully presented dishes in a formal dining room with views of the sea. There's also a hotel (doubles €150 to €320) and spa.

Information

Tourist Office (02 98 61 12 13; www.roscoff-tourisme.com; quai d'Auxerre; 9.15am-12.30pm & 1.30-7pm Mon-Sat, 10am-12.30pm & 2.30-7pm Sun Jul & Aug, 9.15am-noon & 2-6pm Mon-Sat Sep-Jun;) Next to the lighthouse.

Getting There & Away

BUS

The bus and train stations are together on rue Ropartz Morvan. Buses (www.viaoo29.fr) also depart from the ferry terminal (Port de Bloscon) and pass by the town centre.

Brest €2, 1½ to two hours, up to four daily

Morlaix €2, 40 minutes, several daily

BOAT

Boats leave from Port de Bloscon, about 2km east of the town centre.

Brittany Ferries (Roscoff 02 98 29 28 13, reservations in UK 0871 244 0744; www.brittany-ferries.com) links Roscoff to Plymouth, England (five to nine hours, one to three daily), Cork, Ireland (14 hours, one weekly April to October), and Bilbao, Spain (21 hours, one weekly, no sailings mid-July to early August).

Irish Ferries (Roscoff 02 98 61 17 17, Rosslare, Ireland +353 53 913 3158; www.irishferries.com) sails to Rosslare, Ireland (17½ hours, five weekly).

TRAIN

Nine trains and SNCF buses go to Morlaix (€6.40, 35 minutes), where you can make connections to Brest, Quimper and St-Brieuc.

Morlaix

POP 16,263

At the bottom of a deep valley sluicing through northeastern Finistère, Morlaix is an engaging town that makes a good gateway to the coast. The narrow, finger-like town centre is filled with ancient half-timbered houses that spill down to a small port at the end of a large coastal inlet. Towering above all else is an arched 58m-high viaduct built in 1861 to carry the Brest–Paris railway. During daylight hours you can walk along the lower level for a great view of the town.

Sights & Activities

Église St-Melaine CHURCH

(6 place des Otages; 9am-noon & 2-6pm) The late-15th-century Flamboyant Gothic Église St-Melaine features a star-studded barrel-vaulted roof and polychrome wooden statues, including those of St Peter and the eponymous St Melaine.

Musée de Morlaix MUSEUM

(02 98 88 68 88; www.musee.ville.morlaix.fr; place des Jacobins; adult/child €4.60/free; 10am-12.30pm & 2-6pm Jul-Sep, 10am-noon & 2-5pm Tue-Sat Oct-Jun) The area's history, archaeology and art are showcased at this museum, which also incorporates the beautifully preserved half-timbered house nearby, La Maison à Pondalez.

La Maison à Pondalez HISTORIC BUILDING

(02 98 88 68 88; 9 Grand Rue; incl in ticket for Musée de Morlaix; 10am-12.30pm & 2-6pm Jul-Sep, 10am-noon & 2-5pm Tue-Sat Oct-Jun) This beautifully restored half-timbered house dating back to the 16th century is a typical example of a Morlaix *maison à pondalez* (house with an inner gallery and spiral staircase).

Château du Taureau FORTRESS

(02 98 62 29 73; www.chateaudutaureau.com; adult/child €14/7; Mar-Sep) Sail out to this petite prison-fortress, constructed in the 16th century by Vauban, on a small islet in the Bay of Morlaix. Most departures are from Kelenn beach in Carantec (15km northwest of Morlaix), while a few leave from the port of Diben in Plougasnou (17km north of Morlaix). Check online for schedules.

Maison de la Duchesse Anne MUSEUM

(02 98 88 23 26; www.mda-morlaix.com; 33 rue du Mur; adult €2; 11am-6pm Mon-Sat, 2-6pm Sun Jul & Aug, 11am-6pm Mon-Sat May, Jun & Sep) This 15th-century home (which, despite the name, has nothing to do with Duchess Anne) is one of the finest examples of the local building style. The highlight is a staircase

DON'T MISS

CAIRN OF BARNENEZ

The **Cairn of Barnenez** (02 98 67 24 73; www.barnenez.fr; Plouezoc'h; adult/child €5.50/free; 10am-6.30pm May-Aug, 10am-12.30pm & 2-5.30pm Sep-Apr) is an enormous ancient series of tombs set spectacularly overlooking the Bay of Morlaix, on the edge of the modern-day village of Plouezoc'h, 10km north of Morlaix. Built between 4500 and 3900 BC, the cairn measures 75m and comprises two sets of tombs, built in successive eras, but attached to each other. You can walk through the centre of the cairn, where it was once, amazingly, used as a source of stones in the 1950s.

engraved with the faces of the building's patron saints.

Tours

Le Léon à Fer et à Flots BOATING
(☎02 98 62 07 52; www.aferaflots.org; adult/child €32/17; ⊙Apr-Sep) A great way to see the area by land and sea, this tour combines a boat trip through the islands of the Baie de Morlaix and a picturesque train trip between Roscoff and Morlaix.

Sleeping

Ty Pierre B&B €
(☎07 81 26 03 17, 02 98 63 25 75; http://lenaj.free.fr/typierre/index.htm; 1bis place de Viarmes; s/d/tr with shared bathroom incl breakfast €35/50/65; ⊙Mar-Dec; 📶) Knick-knacks and artefacts picked up by Pierre-Yves Jacquet on his Asian travels now decorate this quirky *chambre d'hôte's* five spacious rooms. At this price there's no lift (count on climbing up three or four floors), and most rooms don't have their own bathroom (they're just along the wide corridors). All in all, it's very simple but practical. Dinner are available (€20).

★ **Manoir de Ker-Huella** B&B €€
(☎02 98 88 05 52, 06 18 23 07 63; http://manoirdekerhuella.monsite-orange.fr; 78 voie d'accès au port; d incl breakfast €95; P📶) Built in 1898 by the then-director of the railways (the train station is very close by), this wonderful greystone manor house set in park-like gardens above the town is now a well-run *chambre d'hôte*. Despite the size of the building, there are actually only four guest rooms, all named after heroines from classic novels.

Eating & Drinking

Rue Ange de Guernisac has several enticing restaurants. Morlaix' excellent **Saturday market** fills the centre of the old town all day.

Grand Café de la Terrasse BRASSERIE €
(☎02 98 88 20 25; 31 place des Otages; mains €12-20; ⊙8am-midnight Mon-Sat) In the heart of town, Morlaix's showpiece is this 1872-established brasserie with an original central spiral staircase. Sip tea, coffee or something stronger, or sup on classic brasserie fare. The outdoor area abuts a busy road.

Le Viaduc REGIONAL CUISINE €€
(☎02 98 63 24 21; www.le-viaduc.com; 3 rampe St-Melaine; mains €16-26, lunch menu €16, other menus €31; ⊙noon-1.30pm & 7-9.30pm Tue-Sat, noon-1.30pm Sun Sep-Jun, noon-2pm & 7-10pm daily Jul & Aug) A sterling reputation props up this ode to contemporary Breton cuisine, framed by a stylish interior featuring grey-stone walls, wood-panelled ceilings and groovy lighting. On the menu are fish and meat dishes, all skilfully cooked and presented.

Le Tempo BAR
(☎02 98 63 29 11; quai de Tréguier; ⊙10am-1am Mon & Wed-Fri, 10am-3pm Tue, 5pm-1am Sat) Locals pile into this quintessential bar-brasserie overlooking the harbour. It has a blackboard full of brasserie staples and plenty of brews on offer. Well worth the detour.

Information

Tourist Office (☎02 98 62 14 94; www.tourisme-morlaix.fr; 10 place Charles de Gaulle; ⊙9am-7pm Mon-Sat, 10am-6pm Sun Jul & Aug, 9am-12.30pm & 2-6.30pm Mon-Sat Sep-Jun; 📶) Has a map of walking itineraries around town.

Getting There & Away

Morlaix is on the main Paris train line. The renovated bus-train transfer station opens from 2017.

Brest €11.50, ¾ hour, 16 daily

Paris Montparnasse €30 to €96, four hours, 7 daily

Roscoff €6.40, 30 minutes, SNCF bus or train, 7 daily

Brest

POP 143,458

A major port and military base, Brest is big, bold and dynamic. Destroyed by Allied air attacks during WWII, Brest was swiftly rebuilt after the war, in a utilitarian manner. Though it won't win any beauty contests, it's a lively port and university town, home to an elaborate aquarium and the gateway to the sea-swept Île d'Ouessant.

Sights & Activities

★ **Océanopolis** AQUARIUM
(☎02 98 34 40 40; www.oceanopolis.com; port de Plaisance du Moulin Blanc; adult/child €20.30/13.10; ⊙9.30am-7pm mid-Jul–mid-Aug, 10am-5pm Tue-Sun mid-Aug–Mar, 9.30am-6pm Apr–mid-Jul, closed Jan; P👪; 🚌3) Much more than just an aquarium, this enormous 'aquatic world' is divided into three pavilions containing polar, tropical and temperate ecosystems. Highlights are the shark tanks, mangrove and rainforest sections, colourful tropical reefs, seals and the penguin display.

The numerous films and interactive displays are educational for children and adults alike. It's about 3km east of the city centre; take bus 3 from place de la Liberté.

Buying tickets at the tourist office (for a discount) or online allows you to skip queues (long in summer). Many displays have an English translation; a €1 multilingual audioguide is also available.

Musée de la Marine MUSEUM
(Naval Museum; ☎02 98 22 12 39; www.musee-marine.fr; rue du Château, Château de Brest; adult/child €6/free; ⏰10am-6.30pm Apr-Sep, 1.30-6.30pm Wed-Mon Oct-Mar, closed Jan) Learn about Brest's maritime military history at this museum housed within the fortified 13th-century Château de Brest, which was built to defend the harbour on the Penfeld River. Following the 1532 union of Brittany and France, both the castle and its harbour became a royal fortress. The castle was heavily refortified by Vauban in the mid-17th century with his trademark combination of ramparts and defensive towers. From its ramparts, there are striking views of the harbour and the naval base.

Tour Tanguy MUSEUM
(☎02 98 00 87 93; place Pierre Péron; ⏰10am-noon & 2-7pm Jun-Sep, 2-5pm Wed, Thu, Sat & Sun Oct-May) FREE Inside this 14th-century tower, displays on Brest's history include a sobering reminder of what Brest looked like on the eve of WWII. One display documents the visit of three Siamese ambassadors in 1686, who presented gifts to the court of Louis XIV; rue de Siam was named in their honour.

Les Vedettes Azenor BOATING
(☎02 98 41 46 23; www.azenor.fr; Port de Commerce & Port de Plaisance; adult/child from €15/11; ⏰Apr-Sep) This well-regarded cruise operator offers 1½-hour to full-day cruises around the harbour, the naval base and Camaret-sur-Mer two or three times daily from both the Port de Commerce (500m south-east of the Château de Brest) and the Port de Plaisance (opposite Océanopolis).

Festivals & Events

Astropolis MUSIC
(www.astropolis.org) Brest's electronic music fest in early July.

Les Jeudis du Port MUSIC
(Harbour Thursdays; www.brest.fr; ⏰7.30pm-midnight Thu mid-Jul–late Aug) Plan to be in Brest on a Thursday night during summer, when Les Jeudis du Port fills the port with live rock, reggae and world music, as well as street performances and children's events.

> **OFF THE BEATEN TRACK**
>
> **ARGOL CIDER**
>
> Argol is a quaint village, with Église Saint-Pierre et Saint-Paul's historic parish close dating to 1576. Just outside the close, look for the 3m statue of King Gradlon, star of many Breton folk tales. Legend has it that his daughter, Dahut, died in Argol. **Maison du Cidre de Bretagne** (www.maisonducidredebretagne.fr; ⏰tours 3pm Fri-Wed Jul & Aug, Tue only Jun & Sep, by reservation Oct-May) produces cider, apple juice and vinegar. A visit takes you from the orchard to production and, of course, you get to taste it too. It also has two-hour introductory cider-making classes (€20).

Sleeping

Hôtel de la Rade HOTEL €
(☎02 98 44 47 76; www.hoteldelarade.com; 6 rue de Siam; d from €69; 📶) Right in the centre of town, this good-value place has smart and stylishly simple rooms with tiny, yet functional, bathrooms. Rooms at the back have superb views onto the harbour and the couple who manage it are very welcoming. Secure parking is available for bicycles. Prices drop to €49 in July and August.

Hôtel Continental HOTEL €€
(☎02 98 80 50 40; www.oceaniahotels.com; rue Émile Zola; d €120-155; ❄📶) Every business-person's favourite base in Brest, this retro downtown hotel offers plenty of atmosphere, thanks to its monumental art-deco lobby, stained-glass windows and 73 large, luminous and tidy rooms. Considerable reductions on room rates at weekends.

Eating & Drinking

Le Potager de Mémé ORGANIC €
(☎09 51 44 14 78; www.lepotagerdememe.com; 44 rue de Lyon; mains €7-12, menus €15-17; ⏰11.30am-2.30pm Mon-Sat, 7-9pm Fri & Sat) A fabulous lunch address wedged between shops, Le Potager de Mémé (Grandma's vegetable garden) is uber-cool, ultra-healthy and great value. Pick from zesty salads, soups, tarts and savoury *tartines* (slices of bread with toppings), all made with locally

sourced, organic products. Mmmm, vegetarian quiche with sheep's-milk cheese.

Ô Zinc MODERN FRENCH €

(☎02 98 43 08 52; 48 rue de Lyon; mains €13-18, lunch menus €16-18; ⏲noon-2pm Tue-Sat, 7.45-10pm Thu-Sat) This contemporary bistro with a pinch of post-industrial flavour (think suspended lamps, zinc table tops and walls done up in greys) cooks up just a few starters, three or four mains and a handful of desserts – and none disappoint.

La Chaumière MODERN FRENCH €€

(☎02 98 44 18 60; www.lachaumiere-brest.com; 25 rue Émile Zola; mains €12-20, menus €17-31; ⏲noon-2pm Mon-Fri, 7.30-9pm Tue-Sat) Creative cuisine is what makes this modern-meets-traditional restaurant with a big fireplace and contemporary furnishings stand out. Breton chef René Botquelen turns out succulent concoctions prepared with top-quality ingredients. Plump for the excellent crab with turnip, cooked in a sweet-and-sour sauce.

Le Crabe Marteau SEAFOOD €€

(☎02 98 33 38 57; www.crabemarteau.fr; 8 quai de la Douane; mains €21-33; ⏲noon-2.30pm & 7-10.30pm Mon-Sat) This eatery down by the port is famous for one thing and one thing only: crab (served with potatoes), savoured on a terrace facing the island ferries or in a rustically nautical interior. The menu also includes oysters and freshly caught fish.

Blind Piper PUB

(95 rue de Siam; ⏲2pm-2am) This legendary spot is a beauty – part Irish pub, part French bar, furnished in rich burnished wood and nautical bits-and-bobs. Has billiards upstairs.

Information

Tourist Office (☎02 98 44 24 96; www.brest-metropole-tourisme.fr; place de la Liberté; ⏲9.30am-7pm Mon-Sat, to 1.30pm Sun Jul & Aug, 9.30am-6pm Mon-Sat Sep-Jun; 📶) Helpful. Runs guided tours in summer. Sells discounted tickets to local attractions.

Getting There & Away

AIR

Brest's **airport** (BES; ☎02 98 32 86 00; www.brest.aeroport.fr), 10km northeast of town, has regular domestic and international flights. These include Finist Air flights to Île d'Ouessant; Air France flights to Paris, London and Lyon; Ryanair flights serving Marseille; Flybe flights to Birmingham, Dublin and Southampton; easyJet flights to Lyon and London; Aegean Air flights to Crete; and Vueling flights to Barcelona.

A Bibus (www.bibus.fr) shuttle connects the airport to the Tram line A at Porte de Guipavas (€1.50, seven to 10 per day). Buy tickets onboard. A taxi to the centre costs around €22 by day, €32 at night.

BOAT

Ferries to Île d'Ouessant leave from Port de Commerce.

Le Brestoâ (☎07 78 37 03 23; www.lebrestoa.com) connects Brest's Port de Commerce with Le Fret on the Crozon Peninsula (one way adult/child €9/7, 30 minutes, twice daily Tuesday to Sunday April to September).

BUS

Brest's **bus station** (☎02 98 44 46 73; www.viaoo29.fr; place du 19e Régiment d'Infanterie) is beside the train station, and buses serve the whole region.

Le Conquet €2, 45 minutes, six daily

Roscoff €2, 1½ hours, four daily

TRAIN

For Roscoff, change trains at Morlaix; Brest is the terminus of the Paris train line.

Morlaix €11.50, 45 minutes, 16 daily

Paris Montparnasse €50 to €96, 4½ hours, around seven daily

Quimper €18.10, 1½ hours, SNCF bus or train 11 daily

Rennes €31 to €44, 2¼ hours, 7 daily

Île d'Ouessant

POP 891

There is an old Breton saying, *'Qui voit Molène, voit sa peine, qui voit Ouessant, voit son sang'* ('Those who see Molène, see their sorrow, those who see Ouessant, see their blood'), and it's true that on a wild stormy winter day there's a real end-of-the-world feeling to the Île d'Ouessant (known as Enez Eusa in Breton, meaning 'Island of Terror', and Ushant in English). However, if you come on a sunny day, the place can seem like a little paradise, with turquoise waters, abundant wildflowers and not much to do but walk and picnic. The peace and calm of the island is best experienced by hiking its 45km craggy coastal path or hiring a bike and cycling.

While the island can be visited as a day trip (as masses of people do) it's an unusual and other-worldly feeling to stay over.

Sights

Musée des Phares et des Balises LIGHTHOUSE, MUSEUM
(Lighthouse & Beacon Museum; ☎02 98 48 80 70; www.pnr-armorique.fr; Phare du Créac'h; adult/child €4.30/3; ⏰10.30am-6pm Jul & Aug, 11am-5pm Apr-Jun & Sep, 1.30-5.30pm Tue-Sun Oct-Mar) The black-and-white-striped Phare de Créac'h is one of the world's most powerful lighthouses. Beaming two white flashes every 10 seconds and visible for more than 60km, it serves as a beacon for more than 50,000 ships entering the Channel each year. At its base is the island's main museum, which tells the story of these vital navigational aids. There are also displays devoted to the numerous ships that have been wrecked off the island.

Écomusée d'Ouessant MUSEUM
(Maison du Niou Huella; ☎02 98 48 86 37; www.pnr-armorique.fr; adult/child €3.80/2.80; ⏰10.30am-6pm Jul & Aug, 11am-5pm Apr-Jun & Sep, 1.30-5.30pm Tue-Sun Oct-Mar) Two traditional local houses make up this small ecomuseum. One re-creates a traditional homestead, furnished like a ship's cabin, with furniture fashioned from driftwood and painted in bright colours to mask imperfections; the other explores the island's history and customs. Joint ticket with Museé des Phares et des Balises is €7.

Sleeping

Auberge de Jeunesse HOSTEL €
(☎02 98 48 84 53; www.auberge-ouessant.com; Lampaul; dm incl breakfast €21.50; ⏰reception 7.30am-1pm & 6-8pm Feb-Nov; 📶) This friendly hostel on the hill above Lampaul has two- to six-person rooms and a small communal kitchen. Sheets cost an extra €5.30 per stay. It's popular with school and walking groups; reservations are essential.

La Duchesse Anne HOTEL €
(☎02 98 48 80 25; www.hotelduchesseanne.fr; Lampaul; r €49-60; ⏰Mar-Oct; 📶) Idyllically set on a cliff next to Baie de Lampaul on the edge of town, this hotel has unpretentious yet neat doubles, of which four have staggering sunset-facing sea views. It also boasts one of the island's best restaurants (*menus* €16 to €19) with a terrace overlooking the ocean.

★Le Keo – La Maison des Capitaines B&B €€
(☎06 01 39 67 08; www.lekeoouessant.com; Lampaul; d incl breakfast €75-95; ⏰Apr-Oct; 📶) This welcoming B&B in the heart of Lampaul fills a refurbished townhouse, and adds a dash of style to the accommodation scene. Its interior brims with creative trappings and its four rooms all boast unique decor. Two have swoon-inducing sea views, and one features a *lit clos* (traditional Breton bed). The fantastic breakfast room has original wood panelling, and there's a lovely small garden.

Ti Jan Ar C'hafe HOTEL €€
(☎02 98 48 82 64; www.tijan.fr; Kernigou, Lampaul; d €99; ⏰mid-Feb–mid-Nov; 📶) This haven of peace feels more like a B&B than a proper hotel and it's all the better for it. Rooms come in a swirl of different colours but they're normally loud and vivid, and two are tucked beneath the sloping roof. Superb breakfast (€10) in a sun-lit verandah overlooking a bijou back garden. It's 500m east of Lampaul.

Eating

Ty Korn SEAFOOD €
(☎02 98 48 87 33; Lampaul; mains €11-30; ⏰noon-1.30pm & 7.30-9.30pm Tue-Sat) The ground floor of this hyperfriendly place is a bar serving Breton black-wheat beers (made from the same *blé noire* as Breton *galettes*). Upstairs there's an excellent restaurant where seafood is a speciality. Save room for their divine *tiramisu breton* (biscuit with apples, mascarpone and salty caramel sauce). Opening hours can vary, though the bar stays open until 1am.

Ar Piliguet MODERN FRENCH €€
(☎02 98 03 14 64; Lampaul; mains €17-30, lunch menu €19; ⏰noon-2pm & 7-9pm Wed-Sun Mar-Oct, daily Jul & Aug) For picturesque, flavour-rich dining, head to Ar Piliguet, beautifully set in a traditional house behind the tourist office. Dishes are packed with fresh, local ingredients – enjoy them on the small terrace or in a snug interior full of stone and artistic flourishes. The lunch *menu* is outstanding value.

Information

Tourist Office (☎02 98 48 85 83; www.ot-ouessant.fr; place de l'Église; ⏰9am-6.30pm Mon-Sat, 10am-12.30pm Sun mid-Jul–mid-Aug, 10am-noon & 2-6pm Mon-Sat rest of year; 📶) Sells walking brochures and has information on operators offering horse riding, sailing and other activities.

Getting There & Away

AIR

Finist Air (☎02 98 84 64 87; www.finistair.fr) flies from Brest's airport to Ouessant in a mere 15 minutes. There are two flights daily on weekdays and one on Saturdays (one way adult/child €70/41).

BOAT

Ferries for Île d'Ouessant depart from Brest and the tiny town of Le Conquet (Brittany's most westerly point). **Penn Ar Bed** (☎08 10 81 00 29; www.viaoo29.fr) buses link Brest with Le Conquet (€2, 45 minutes, hourly).

In high summer, reserve ferry tickets at least two days in advance and check in 45 minutes before departure to avoid enormous lines.

Penn Ar Bed (☎02 98 80 80 80; www.pennarbed.fr) sails from the Port de Commerce in Brest (2½ hours), from Le Conquet (1½ hours) and from Camaret-sur-Mer (one hour). Boats run between the first two and the island two to five times daily from May to September and once daily between October and April. Boats run from Camaret two to six times per week in July and August, and once weekly in May, June and early September. Prices (return adult/child €35/28) fall in winter. A bike costs €15.30.

Finist'mer (☎08 25 13 52 35; www.finist-mer.fr; adult/child return €34/26.50) runs high-speed boats from Le Conquet (40 minutes), Lanildut (35 minutes) and Camaret (1½ hours) one to three times per day.

Presqu'île de Crozon

Stretching westwards into the Atlantic, the anchor-shaped Crozon Peninsula is one of the most scenic spots in Brittany. In previous centuries, this multifingered spit of land was a key strategic outpost; crumbling forts and ruined gun batteries can still be seen on many headlands, but these days it's the tucked-away coves, superb beaches, awesome panoramas, charming B&Bs and clifftop trails that attract thousands of visitors in summer.

Landévennec

POP 359

The Aulne River flows into the Rade de Brest beside the pretty village of Landévennec, home to the ruined Benedictine **Abbaye St-Guenolé**. The abbey **museum** (☎02 98 27 35 90; www.musee-abbaye-landevennec.fr; Landévennec; adult/child €5.50/3; ⏰10.30am-7pm daily Jul-Sep, shorter hours Mar-May & Oct, closed Nov-Feb) records the history of the settlement, founded by St Guenolé in 485 and the oldest Christian site in Brittany. Nearby, a new abbey is home to a community of monks, who run a little shop selling home-made fruit jellies.

Crozon & Morgat

POP 7909

The peninsula's largest town, Crozon is the area's practical hub, but though the town centre is pleasant enough there's little reason to hang around. On the water 2km south, Morgat was built as a summer resort in the 1930s by the Peugeot brothers (of motor-vehicle fame), and it retains something of the feel of that period. It's one of the prettier resorts in this part of Brittany, with colourful houses piled up at one end of a long sandy beach that has very safe bathing.

Sights & Activities

Cap de la Chèvre NATURAL SITE

The peninsula's most southerly point, Cap de la Chèvre is 8km south of Morgat, and offers stupendous panoramas of the Baie de Douarnenez and the Pointe du Raz. You'll be amazed by the contrast between the Mediterrean-like eastern side of the peninsula and the much wilder western shore, which is clearly Atlantic.

Pointe de Dinan NATURAL SITE

Wow! The cliffs of Pointe de Dinan, 6.5km west of Crozon, provide a dramatic outlook over the sands of Anse de Dinan and the rock formations locally known as the Château de Dinan, which is linked to the mainland by a natural archway.

★Coastal Hike WALKING

The coastline between Morgat and Cap de la Chèvre is gorgeous. Beyond the marina at the southern end of Morgat's beach, the coastal path offers an excellent 13km hike (part of the GR34) along the sea cliffs to Cap de la Chèvre, taking in some of the most scenic spots in the area. It takes roughly five hours to complete (one way), but you can also walk smaller sections.

The route takes you past an old fort and through sweet-scented pine forests overlooking numerous little coves (most inaccessible) with water that, on a sunny day, glows electric blue. Be sure to pause at the picture-perfect **Île Vierge** – you'll be smitten with this idyllic cove lapped by turquoise waters and framed by lofty cliffs. The lazy summer-

day feel is dramatically shattered on reaching Cap de la Chèvre and the wind-exposed, western side of the peninsula.

Vedettes Rosmeur BOATING
(☎06 85 95 55 49; www.grottes-morgat.fr; quai Kador, Morgat; adult/child from €14/9) This outfit operates 45-minute and one-hour boat trips to the colourful sea caves along the coast. It also takes in the lovely Île Vierge.

Beaches

Morgat has a picturesque beach that's popular with families. To the west, there's sunbathing aplenty on the 2km-long **Plage de la Palue** and nearby **Plage de Lostmarc'h**, but swimming is forbidden due to strong currents. Further north, **Plage de Goulien** is another wonderful stretch of golden sand.

Festivals & Events

Festival du Bout du Monde MUSIC
(Festival of the End of the World; www.festivalduboutdumonde.com) Morgat's place d'Ys area hosts this world music fest for three days in early August.

Sleeping

★ **Kastell Dinn** CABIN €
(☎02 98 27 26 40, 06 62 52 96 61; www.sejour-insolitebretagne.com; Kerlouantec; d €57-90) Looking for something extra special? This marvellous little hideaway in the tiny hamlet of Kerlouantec, 2km southwest of Crozon, won't disappoint. It offers two free-standing units set in decommissioned fishing boats (yes!) and one *roulotte* (caravan), as well as two rooms in a traditional Breton *longère* (long house). There's also a fully equipped shared kitchen. Incredibly atmospheric.

Les Pieds dans l'Eau CAMPGROUND €
(☎02 98 27 62 43; www.campinglespiedsdansleau-crozon.fr; St-Fiacre; per person/tent/car €4.50/5/2.50; ⏲mid-Mar–mid-Oct) 'Camping feet in the water' (almost literally, at high tide) is one of 16 campgrounds along the peninsula.

Hôtel de la Baie HOTEL €
(☎02 98 27 07 51; www.hoteldelabaie-crozon-morgat.com; 46 bd de la Plage, Morgat; d €49-88, studio €97;) One of the *very* few places to remain open year-round, this friendly, family-run spot on Morgat's promenade has renovated rooms, some with views over the ocean, and is one of the best deals around.

Eating

★ **Saveurs et Marées** SEAFOOD €€
(☎02 98 26 23 18; 52 bd de la Plage, Morgat; lunch menus €15-19.50, dinner menus €19.50-46; ⏲noon-2pm & 7-10pm Tue-Sun) Our pick of Morgat's clutch of restaurants has sweeping windows with fabulous views of the sea from its breezy contemporary dining room and sunny terrace. Tuck into consistently good, locally caught seafood (including succulent lobster).

★ **Le Mutin Gourmand** REGIONAL CUISINE €€€
(☎02 98 27 06 51; www.lemutingourmand.fr; place de l'Église, Crozon; menus €29-68; ⏲noon-1.30pm Wed-Sun, 7-8.45pm Tue-Sun Jul & Aug, closed Sun dinner rest of year) No, there's no sea view (it's in Crozon town centre), but this is the gourmet choice in the area. With its intimate dining room, charming welcome and delicious cuisine, Le Mutin Gourmand has honed the art of dining to perfection. The chef works with local, carefully chosen ingredients, so whatever season it is, you'll be in for a treat.

The associated **Le Bistrot du Mutin**, in a nearby annex, has very affordable *menus* (lunch *menu* €19).

Information

Crozon Tourist Office (☎02 98 27 07 92; www.tourisme-presquiledecrozon.fr; bd de Pralognan la Vannoise, Crozon; ⏲9.30am-12.30pm & 2-7pm Mon-Sat, 10am-1pm Sun Jul & Aug, 9.30am-noon & 2-6pm Mon-Sat Sep-Jun) Housed in the former railway station, on the main road to Camaret.

Morgat Tourist Office (☎02 98 27 29 49; www.morgat.fr; place d'Ys, Morgat; ⏲9.30am-12.30pm & 3-7pm Mon-Wed, 2.30-7.30pm Thu-Sun Jul-Aug, 9.30am-noon Mon Jun & Sep) Overlooks the promenade at the corner of bd de la Plage.

Getting There & Around

BICYCLE

Rent a bike in summer at the open-air stall in front of Morgat's tourist office for €12 per day, or year-round with **Point Bleu** (☎02 98 27 22 11; www.point-bleu.fr; 10 bvd Pierre Mendes, Crozon; per day €12; ⏲9.30am-noon & 2-7pm Mon-Sat, 10am-noon Sun).

BUS

Penn Ar Bed (www.viaoo29.fr) bus 34 connects Crozon with Camaret-sur-Mer and Le Faou, and bus 37 goes to Quimper. There's no public transport in Morgat.

Camaret-sur-Mer

POP 2647

At the western edge of the Crozon Peninsula, Camaret is a classic fishing village – or at least it was early in the 20th century, when it was France's largest crayfish port. Nowadays, abandoned fishing boats dot the attractive harbour, which is populated by clanking yacht masts and lined by cafes. Overlooked by a 17th-century red-brick watchtower, Camaret remains an enchanting spot that attracts artists who run an ever-increasing number of galleries throughout town.

Sights

★Pointe de Pen-Hir NATURAL SITE

Three kilometres southwest of Camaret, this spectacular headland is bounded by steep, sheer sea cliffs. On a peninsula known for its breathtaking scenery, this might be the most impressive lookout of them all. The series of offshore rock stacks are known as **Tas de Pois**. There are also two WWII memorials, and just inland 80 neolithic menhirs comprise the **Alignements de Lagatjar**. There are plenty of short walks in the area, as well as a handful of small cove beaches.

Chapelle Notre-Dame-de-Rocamadour CHURCH

(⌚10am-5pm daily, Sat & Sun only during school holidays) Its timber roof like an inverted ship's hull, the 17th-century Chapelle Notre-Dame-de-Rocamadour honours the miraculous icon in The Lot region's Rocamadour (and was a pilgrimage stop on the way there). The interior is dedicated to the sailors of Camaret, who have adorned it with votive offerings of oars, lifebuoys and model ships.

Information

Tourist Office (☎02 98 27 93 60; www.camaretsurmer-tourisme.fr; 15 quai Kléber; ⌚9.15am-noon & 2-6pm Mon-Sat, plus 10am-noon Sun Jul & Aug) On the waterfront.

Getting There & Away

BOAT

Le Brestoâ (www.lebrestoa.com) connects Brest's Port de Commerce with Le Fret on the Crozon Peninsula (one way adult/child €9/7, 30 minutes, twice daily Tuesday to Sunday April to September).

Penn Ar Bed (www.pennarbed.fr) sails between Camaret and Île d'Ouessant (return adult/child €34.60/27.70, one hour) two to six times per week in July and August, and weekly in May, June and early September. Also has high-season boats to Île de Sein.

BUS

Five buses daily run from Quimper to Crozon (€2, 1¼ hours), continuing to Camaret (€2); up to four go from Camaret and Crozon to Brest (€2, 1¼ hours, daily).

Quimper

POP 66,926

Small enough to feel like a village, with its slanted half-timbered houses and narrow cobbled streets, and large enough to buzz as the troubadour of Breton culture and arts, Quimper (kam-pair) is Finistère's thriving capital. With some excellent museums, a history of faience (pottery) production, one of Brittany's loveliest old quarters and a delightful setting along the Odet River, Quimper deserves serious exploration.

Sights & Activities

★Cathédrale St-Corentin CHURCH

(place St-Corentin; ⌚8.30am-noon & 1.30-6.30pm Mon-Sat, 8.30am-noon & 2-6.30pm Sun) At the centre of the city is Quimper's Gothic cathedral with its distinctive dip in the middle where it was built to conform to the land, said to symbolise Christ's inclined head as he was dying on the cross. Construction began in 1239, but the cathedral's dramatic twin spires weren't added until the 19th century. High on the west facade, look out for an equestrian statue of King Gradlon, the city's mythical 5th-century founder.

★Musée Départemental Breton MUSEUM

(☎02 98 95 21 60; www.museedepartemental-breton.fr; 1 rue du Roi Gradlon; adult/child €5/free; ⌚9am-12.30pm & 1.30-5pm Tue-Sat, 2-5pm Sun Sep-Jun, 9am-6pm daily Jul & Aug) Beside the Cathédrale St-Corentin, recessed behind a magnificent stone courtyard, this superb museum showcases Breton history, furniture, costumes, crafts and archaeology, in a former bishop's palace.

Musée des Beaux-Arts ART MUSEUM

(☎02 98 95 45 20; www.mbaq.fr; 40 place St-Corentin; adult/child €5/3; ⌚10am-6pm Jul & Aug, 9.30am-noon & 2-6pm Wed-Mon Apr-Jun, Sep & Oct, shorter hours Nov-Mar) The ground-floor rooms of the town's main art museum are home to 16th- to 20th-century European paintings, and upper levels include a room dedicated to Quimper-born poet Max Jacob with sketches by Picasso. There's also a section devoted to the Pont-Aven school.

Quimper

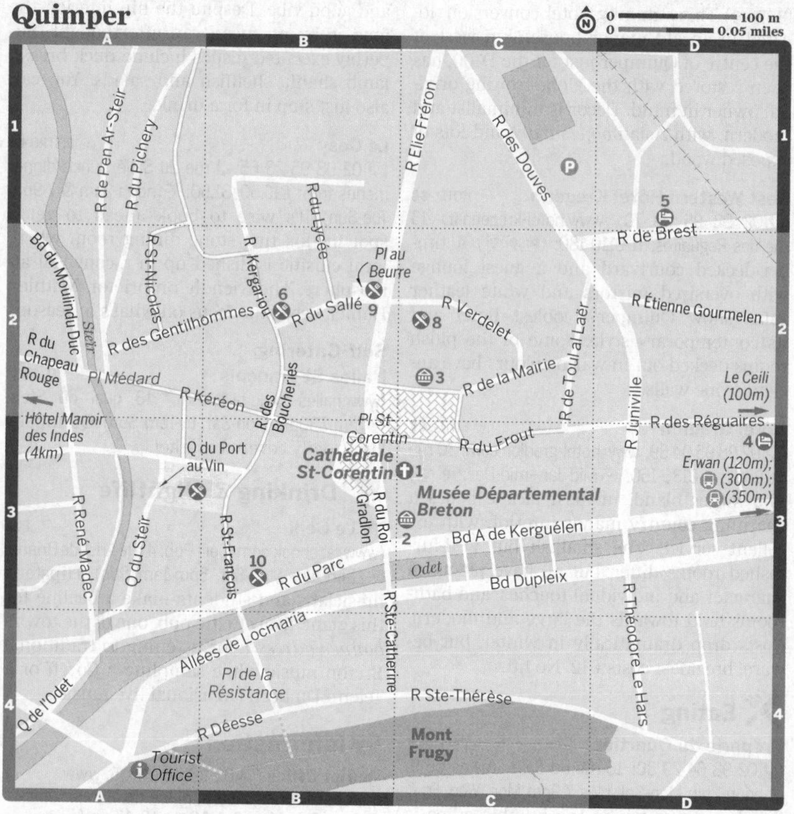

Vedettes de l'Odet BOATING

(☎02 98 57 00 58; www.vedettes-odet.com; adult/child from €28/17; ⊙Apr-Sep) Vedettes de l'Odet runs boat trips, including one around the îles Glénan and one from Quimper's Port de Corniguel along the serene Odet estuary to Bénodet. You can stop for a look about Bénodet and then hop on a boat back.

Festivals & Events

Thursdays at Jardin de l'Évêché PERFORMING ARTS

Head to the Jardin de l'Évêché on Thursday evenings from mid-June to mid-September to take in traditional Breton music and dance.

Festival de Cornouaille CELTIC

(www.festival-cornouaille.com) A celebration of traditional Celtic music, costumes and culture takes place over six days in late July. Other events take place around town during this time as well.

Quimper

Top Sights

1 Cathédrale St-Corentin C3
2 Musée Départemental Breton C3

Sights

3 Musée des Beaux-Arts C2

Sleeping

4 Best Western Hôtel Kregenn D3
5 Hôtel Gradlon D1

Eating

6 Crêperie du Quartier B2
7 Halles St-François A3
8 La Krampouzerie C2
9 Le Cosy B2
10 L'Épée B3

Sleeping

Hôtel Manoir des Indes HOTEL €€

(☎02 98 55 48 40; www.manoir-hoteldesindes.com; 1 allée de Prad ar C'hras; s €125-160, d €155-190;

(P wifi pool) This stunning hotel conversion, located in an old manor house 5km west of the centre of Quimper just off the D100, has been restored with the globe-trotting original owner in mind. Decor is minimalist and modern, with Asian *objets d'art* and lots of exposed wood.

Best Western Hôtel Kregenn HOTEL €€
(☎02 98 95 08 70; www.hotel-kregenn.fr; 13 rue des Réguaires; d €110-180; P ❄ wifi) A timber-decked courtyard and a guest lounge with oversized mirrors and white leather sofas show Quimper's coolest hotel and its contemporary style. Some of the plush rooms decked out in warm colours have ancient stone walls.

Hôtel Gradlon HOTEL €€
(☎02 98 95 04 39; www.hotel-gradlon.com; 30 rue de Brest; d €130-150; ⊙mid-Jan–mid-Dec; P wifi) The rather bland, modern facade belies a charming country manor interior, with excellent service. The smallish but well-furnished rooms differ, but all have plenty of character and individual touches, and bathrooms tend towards the large and modern. Costs drop dramatically in winter, but beware, breakfast costs €12. No lift.

Eating

Crêperie du Quartier CREPERIE €
(☎02 98 64 29 30; 16 rue du Sallé; mains €6-9; ⊙noon-2pm Mon-Sat, plus 7-9pm Mon, Wed, Fri & Sat) In a town where the humble crêpe is king, this cosy stone-lined place is one of the best. Its wide-ranging menu includes a *galette* of the week and, to follow up, you can go for a crêpe stuffed with apple, caramel, ice cream, almonds and chantilly.

La Krampouzerie CREPERIE €
(☎02 98 95 13 08; 9 rue du Sallé; mains €4-9; ⊙11.45am-3pm & 6.45-10pm Tue-Sat) Crêpes and *galettes* made from organic flours and regional ingredients such as *algues d'Ouessant* (seaweed), Roscoff onions and homemade ginger caramel are king here. Tables on the square out front create a street-party atmosphere.

★**L'Épée** CAFE €€
(☎02 98 95 28 97; www.quimper-lepee.com; 14 rue du Parc; mains €12-24, lunch menus €24, other menus €29-46; ⊙brasserie noon-2.30pm & 7-10.30pm, cafe 10.30am-midnight) A Quimper institution – it's one of Brittany's oldest brasseries – L'Épée hits the mark with its buzzy, contemporary dining areas, efficient service and good vibe. Despite the hip interior, the food is by no means an afterthought. Superbly executed dishes include duck breast, lamb shank, shellfish and salads. You can also just stop in for a drink.

Le Cosy BISTRO €€
(☎02 98 95 23 65; 2 rue du Sallé; lunch/dinner menus from €16.50/31.50; ⊙noon-2pm & 7-9pm Tue-Sun) It's wise to book ahead to get a spot in this tiny stone dining room where local cuisine is dished up in a convivial atmosphere. The friendly proprietor, Mathieu Hamel, keeps the focus on what's in season.

Self-Catering

Halles St-François MARKET
(www.halles-cornouaille.com; 16 quai du Steir; ⊙7am-7.30pm Mon-Sat, to 1pm Sun) Quimper's large, daily covered market.

Drinking & Nightlife

★**Le Ceili** PUB
(www.facebook.com/Ceili.Pub; 4 rue Aristide Briand; ⊙11am-1am Mon-Sat, 5pm-1am Sun) Hipsters, musicians and students make a beeline for this giant, lively Celtic pub, one of the town's *bonnes adresses* for listening to traditional Breton music while sampling a Coreff or a Telenn Du beer. Occasional live music.

Information

Tourist Office (☎02 98 53 04 05; www.quimper-tourisme.com; place de la Résistance; ⊙9am-7pm Mon-Sat, 10am-12.45pm & 3-5.45pm Sun Jul & Aug, 9.30am-12.30pm & 1.30-6.30pm Mon-Sat Sep-Jun, plus 10am-12.45pm Sun Apr-Jun & Sep; wifi) Sells the Pass Quimper (€12), which gives admission to four museums, sights or tours from a list of participating organisations.

Getting There & Away

AIR

Quimper's **airport** (UIP; www.quimper.aeroport.fr), 10km southwest of town, has direct flights to Paris, Figari (Corsica) and London. It is served by QUB (www.qub.fr) bus 25 from Quimper.

BUS

Penn Ar Bed (p272) has regular buses to Brest (€6, 1¼ hours), Concarneau (€2, 45 minutes) and Camaret-sur-Mer (€2). The bus station is next to the train station.

TRAIN

Quimper is on major lines to Vannes, Rennes and Paris, and a minor line north to Landerneau and Brest:

Brest €18.10, 1½ hours, SNCF bus or train 11 daily
Nantes €38.60, 2½ hours, three direct daily
Paris Montparnasse €30 to €96, 4¾ hours, nine direct daily
Rennes €31 to €44, 2½ hours, 11 direct daily
Vannes €18 to €27.50, 1½ hours, 15 daily

Concarneau

POP 19,568

The sheltered harbour of Concarneau (Konk-Kerne in Breton), 24km southeast of Quimper, radiates out from its trawler port, which brings in close to 200,000 tonnes of *thon* (tuna) from the Indian Ocean and off the African coast (the adjacent Atlantic is too cold). Jutting out into the port, and circled by medieval walls, the supremely picturesque old town – Ville Close – is memorable, and one of Brittany's popular spots in summer, though the town itself is rather bland.

The coast to the west of Concarneau is fun to explore if you have your own wheels, as it's cut by inlets and dotted with picturesque harbours such as Ste-Marine (a good place to stop for a coffee or meal in one of the port cafes). Concarneau is also a jumping-off point for the Îles de Glénan.

Sights

★Ville Close (Walled City) HISTORIC SITE

This special walled town, fortified in the 14th century and modified by the architect Vauban two centuries later, sits on a small island linked to place Jean Jaurès by a stone footbridge. Just past the citadel's **clock tower** and main gate, look out for the 18th-century **Maison du Gouverneur**. It's one of the access points for strolling the ramparts. As you continue, rue Vauban leads to place St-Guénolé, passing stone houses converted into shops, crêperies, ice-cream stalls and galleries.

The eastern side of the island has a small hilly park, and there's a passenger ferry (€1) that runs across the inlet to the opposite quay at place Duquesne. The Ville Close is thronged in summer and on weekends.

★Musée de la Pêche MARITIME MUSEUM

(Fisheries Museum; ☎02 98 97 10 20; www.musee-peche.fr; 3 rue Vauban; adult/child €5/free; ⏰10am-7pm Jul & Aug, 10am-6pm Tue-Sun Apr-Jun & Sep, 2-5.30pm Tue-Sun Feb, Mar, Nov & Dec, closed Jan) This excellent museum, just inside the main western gate of the Ville Close, delves into Concarneau's seafaring traditions using everything from archive film to scale models and vintage boats. You can even clamber aboard the museum's very own fishing vessel, the retired *L'Hémérica*, permanently docked just outside the city walls.

Beaches

Concarneau's best beach is **Plage des Sables Blancs**, 1.5km northwest of the town centre; take bus 3, northbound, from the tourist office. There are lifeguards on duty in summer. **Plage du Cabellou**, about 7km south of town, is a decent spot for sunbathing and swimming, with views back to Concarneau; take bus 2, southbound, which continues all the way to scenic **Pointe du Cabellou**.

Activities

★Vedettes de l'Odet BOATING

(☎02 98 57 00 58; www.vedettes-odet.fr; Port de Plaisance, Concarneau) Runs boat tours from April to September including to the **Îles de Glénan** (adult/child €35/18) – a cluster of nine little islands surrounded by waters so blue they look like they've dropped out of the South Pacific. The islands sit about 20km south of Concarneau and have good diving and kayaking opportunities. In July and August, four-hour river trips (adult/child €28/17) sail from Concarneau along the gorgeously scenic estuary of the River Odet.

Sleeping

Auberge de Jeunesse Éthic Étapes HOSTEL €

(☎02 98 97 03 47; www.aj-concarneau.org; quai de la Croix; dm incl breakfast €17.70; 📶) Fall asleep listening to the waves at this functional waterfront hostel at the southern tip

WORTH A TRIP

ÎLES DE GLÉNAN

Sapphire waters, idyllic white-sand beaches and no crowds. Bora Bora? No. Îles de Glénan. This archipelago of around a dozen mini-islands lies just 20km south of Concarneau and never fails to impress in fine weather. Visitors are only allowed on Île de St-Nicolas. **Vedettes de l'Odet** runs scenic cruises around the islands from Concarneau and other coastal towns. Optional activities include sea kayaking and glass-bottom-boat tours.

of Concarneau. Digs are in four- to six-bed dorms. Extras include a wraparound barbecue terrace, a self-catering kitchen and pastries for breakfast.

Les Sables Blancs BOUTIQUE HOTEL €€
(☎02 98 50 10 12; www.hotel-les-sables-blancs.com; place des Sables Blancs; d €135-235;) Right on the 'white sands' of the beach from which it takes its name (1.5km northwest of the centre), this contemporary hotel has tastefully decorated rooms with fabulous sea views and an excellent restaurant. The catch? The 'standard' rooms are a bit boxy and we found the prices somewhat inflated in summer.

Hôtel de France et d'Europe HOTEL €€
(☎02 98 97 00 64; www.hotel-france-europe.com; 9 av de la Gare; d €102-110, tr/q €123/145; P) This fairly sterile but comfortable and serviceable place is just two blocks north of the harbour. There's no 'wow' factor – just plain, good-value lodging in a handy location. Precious perks include private parking (car/bicycle per day €8/4) and a shady terrace.

Eating

Tourist-focused cafes, pizzerias and crêperies line the waterfront, and there are more inside the walls of Ville Close.

There's a **covered market** on place Jean Jaurès and a busy **open-air market** in the same square on Monday (smaller) and Friday (larger) mornings.

Le Petit Chaperon Rouge CREPERIE €
(☎02 98 60 53 32; 7 place Duguesclin; mains €4-12; noon-1.30pm Tue-Sun, 7.15-9.15pm Tue-Sat) Avoid the crêperies of the Ville Close, which leave a lot to be desired; instead, opt for this cute venture just inland from the seafront, near the tourist office. The setting is cosy, and there's a bumper selection of savoury *galettes* and sweet crêpes.

Le Flaveur MODERN FRENCH €€
(☎02 98 60 43 47; 4 rue Duquesne; lunch menus €16-19, dinner menus €25-54; noon-1.30pm Tue-Fri & Sun, 7.15-9.15pm Tue-Sat) One of Concarneau's top tables, Le Flaveur is tucked down a quiet street near the harbour. Meals range from strictly local dishes through to more generally French dishes and occasional use of products from further afield. The menu changes regularly – if it's available, how about the *pigeonneau royal* (royal pigeon), endorsed by locals as 'almost gastronomic' (ie delectable but affordable)?

Information

Tourist Office (☎02 98 97 01 44; www.tourismeconcarneau.fr; quai d'Aiguillon; 9am-12.30pm & 2-6pm;) Has information on walking and cycling circuits in the area.

Getting There & Away

L'Été Évasion (☎02 98 56 82 82; www.autocars-ete.com) runs up to 10 buses (€2) daily between Quimper and Quimperlé, calling by Concarneau.

Pont-Aven

POP 2901

Breton villages don't come much prettier than Pont-Aven, a former port and mill town cradled at the end of a wooded creek about 20km east of Concarneau. In the 19th century, its charms were discovered by artists. American painters were among the first to uncover it, but things really took off when France's Paul Gauguin and Émile Bernard set up a colony here in the 1850s and captured the beauty of the little village and the surrounding countryside.

Since the 1960s, Pont-Aven has again become a magnet for artists seeking fresh air and country inspiration. Today there are about 60 galleries around town.

Sights

★Musée des Beaux-Arts de Pont-Aven ART MUSEUM
(☎02 98 06 14 43; www.museepontaven.fr; place de l'Hôtel de Ville; adult/child €7/free; 10am-7pm Jul & Aug, 10am-6pm Tue-Sun Apr-Jun, Sep & Oct, 2-5.30pm Tue-Sun Mar, Nov & Dec, closed Jan) For an insight into the town's place in art history, stop by this well-organised museum which was completely renovated from 2012 to 2016. Gallery size has doubled, and interactive exhibits delve in to the life and art of Gauguin and others. Temporary exhibitions also bring masterpieces to town, and there is a garden and shop.

Sleeping

Les Ajoncs d'Or HOTEL €
(☎02 98 06 02 06; www.ajoncsdor-pontaven.com; 1 place de l'Hotel de Ville; d €68-75, tr/q €85/95;) A good deal for Pont-Aven, this venerable hotel has undergone quite a few sprucings, and they've all been for the better. The rooms feature cosy beds, tiled bathrooms and nice furnishings, all kept clean and presentable. There's an attached restaurant.

Castel Braz B&B €
(☎02 98 06 07 81; www.castelbraz.com; 12 rue du Bois d'Amour; d incl breakfast €70-90, studio per week €450; 📶) This towering 19th-century house smack dab in the centre of Pont-Aven has four stylish rooms that are all different, with attractive colour schemes and excellent bathrooms.

Eating

★**La Chocolaterie de Pont-Aven** TEAROOM €
(☎02 98 09 10 47; www.lachocolateriedepont-aven.com; 1 place Delavallée; sweets from €2.50; ⏰10am-7.30pm Jul & Aug, 10am-1pm & 2.30-7.30pm Tue, Thu-Sun Sep-Jun) *Au revoir,* diet. This mouth-watering patisserie-*chocolaterie* with an adjacent *salon de thé* has a wide assortment of goodies. Irresistable.

★**Sur Le Pont** MODERN FRENCH €€
(☎02 98 06 16 16; www.surlepont-pontaven.fr; 11 place Paul Gauguin; mains €16-23, lunch/dinner menus from €25/32; ⏰12.30-2pm Thu-Tue, 7.30-9pm Thu-Mon) You couldn't wish for a more perfect setting, lodged in a stylishly renovated building by the Pont-Aven bridge. A just-so palette of cool greys, beiges, blacks and whites creates the feel of an elegant bistro, and the mood is relaxed and joyous. Dishes are refined takes on Breton cooking with an emphasis on seafood.

The gastronomic sister restaurant, **Le Moulin de Rosmadec** (☎02 98 06 00 22; www.moulinderosmadec.com; venelle de Rosmadec; mains €32-49, menus €46-81; ⏰12.30-2pm Tue-Sun, 7-9pm Tue-Sat, closed Tue lunch Oct-Feb), is just around the corner.

Information

Tourist Office (☎02 98 06 04 70; www.pontaven.com; 5 place de l'Hôtel de Ville; ⏰10am-12.30pm & 2-6pm Mon-Sat, 10am-1pm Sun, closed Sun Oct-Mar; 📶) To see the spots where the masters set up their easels, pick up a free walking-trail map from the tourist office, which can also help with accommodation.

MORBIHAN COAST

In the crook of Brittany's southern coastline, the Golfe du Morbihan (Morbihan Coast; www.morbihan.com) is a haven of islands, beaches, oyster beds and bird life. The area is perhaps best known for its proliferation of magnificent and mystifying Celtic megaliths – a must for a visit to Brittany. They rise majestically throughout most of the *département.*

Carnac

POP 4334

With enticing beaches and a pretty town centre, Carnac would be a popular tourist town even without its collection of magnificent megalithic sites, but when these are thrown into the mix you end up with a place that is unmissable on any ramble through Brittany. Predating Stonehenge by around 100 years, Carnac (Garnag in Breton) also tops it with the sheer number of ancient sites found in the vicinity, making this the world's greatest concentration of megalithic sites. There are no fewer than 3000 of these upright stones erected between 5000 and 3500 BC.

Carnac, some 32km west of Vannes, comprises the old stone village Carnac-Ville and, 1.5km south, the seaside resort of Carnac-Plage, which is bordered by the 2km-long sandy beach.

Beaches

Not only is Carnac a fantastic open-air museum that appeals to culture vultures, it's also a superb playground for beachy types. **La Grande Plage** is Carnac's longest and most popular beach and is excellent for sunbathing – it's a 2km-long stretch of white sand 2km south of Carnac-Ville. To the west, **Plage de Légenèse** and **Plage de St-Colomban** are smaller and quieter. St-Colomban appeals to windsurfers.

Sleeping

Camping des Menhirs CAMPGROUND €
(☎02 97 52 94 67; www.lesmenhirs.com; 7 allée St-Michel, Carnac-Plage; adult/site from €9/33; ⏰mid-May–late Sep; 📶🏊) Carnac and its surrounds have more than 15 camping grounds, including this luxury complex of 100-sq-metre sites. Just 300m north of the beach, this is very much the glamorous end of camping, with amenities such as a sauna and cocktail bar!

Le Ratelier INN €
(☎02 97 52 05 04; www.le-ratelier.com; 4 chemin du Douet; d with/without bathroom €72/62; P📶) This vine-clad former farmhouse, now an eight-room inn with low ceilings, fabric-covered walls and traditional timber furnishings, is in a quiet street south of the church. The cheapest rooms have showers only and shared toilets. Those with private bathrooms

Golfe du Morbihan and Presqu'île de Quiberon

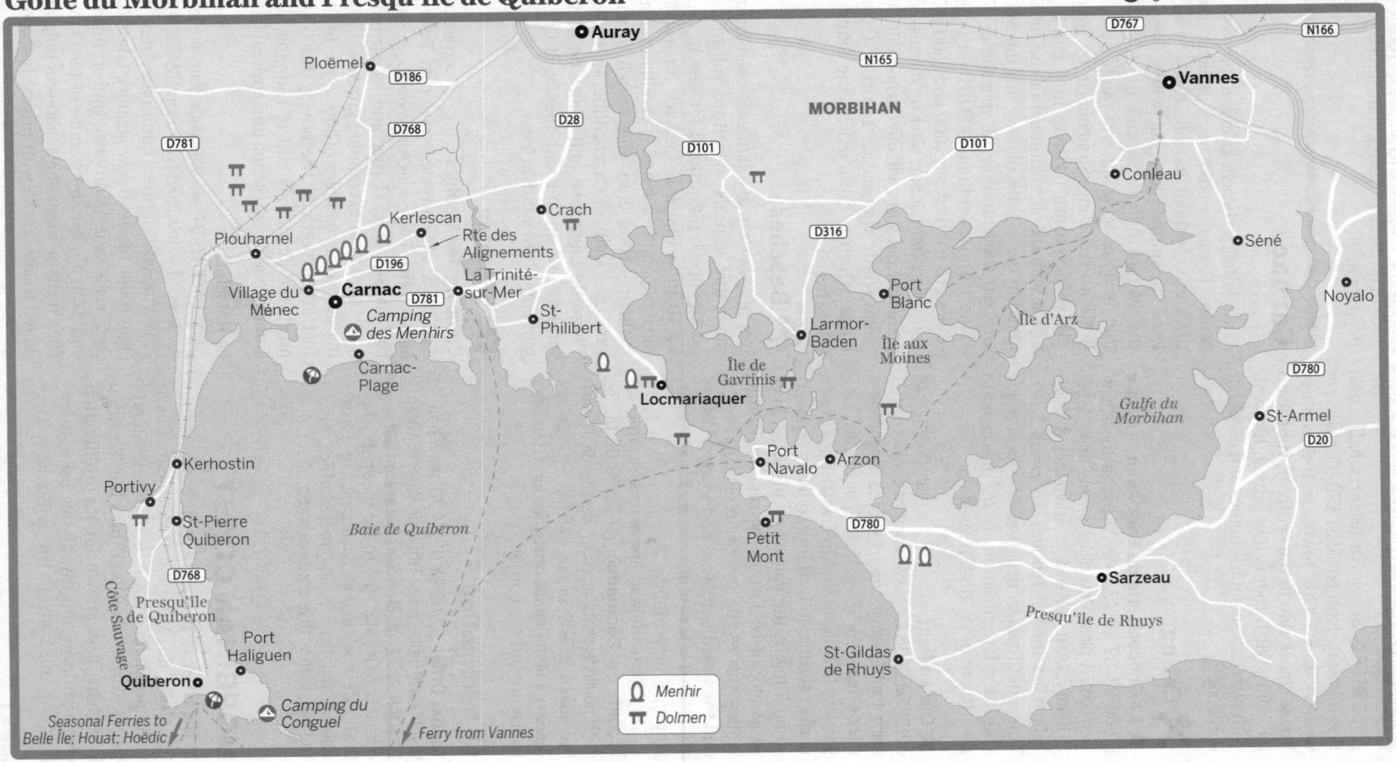
0 5 km
0 2.5 miles
Auray
Vannes
MORBIHAN
Ploëmel
Plouharnel
Village du Ménec
Carnac
Kerlescan
Rte des Alignements
La Trinité-sur-Mer
Crach
St-Philibert
Camping des Menhirs
Carnac-Plage
Locmariaquer
Île de Gavrinis
Larmor-Baden
Port Blanc
Île aux Moines
Île d'Arz
Conleau
Séné
Noyalo
St-Armel
Gulfe du Morbihan
Port Navalo
Arzon
Petit Mont
Sarzeau
Presqu'île de Rhuys
St-Gildas de Rhuys
Baie de Quiberon
Kerhostin
Portivy
St-Pierre Quiberon
Presqu'île de Quiberon
Côte Sauvage
Port Haliguen
Quiberon
Camping du Conguel
Seasonal Ferries to Belle Île; Houat; Hoëdic
Ferry from Vannes
D781
D186
D768
D196
D28
D101
D316
D767
N165
N166
D780
D20
Menhir
Dolmen

DON'T MISS

GOLFE DU MORBIHAN

Around 40 islands peep out from the shallow waters of the Morbihan gulf, which forms a breathtakingly beautiful inland sea that's easily accessible from Vannes. Some islands are barely sandy specks of land, while others harbour communities of fishermen, farmers and artistic types seduced by the island lifestyle. The bay's largest island is the 6km-long Île aux Moines. Nearby Île d'Arz is smaller – just 3km long and 1km wide – but it's the most scenic of the lot and features secluded sands and coastal walks. Tempted to stay? Both islands have a slew of B&Bs and eateries.

Lots of companies offer scenic cruises and ferry services to Île aux Moines and Île d'Arz and beyond. In high season, check with **Navix** (p286) and **La Compagnie du Golfe** (☎02 97 01 22 80; www.compagnie-du-golfe.fr; Vannes; cruise adult/child from €16.50/11.50; ⏰Apr-Sep). Year-round **Bateaux-Bus du Golfe** (☎02 97 44 44 40; www.ile-arz.fr; adult/child return €10.20/5.60; ⏰6.30am-8pm) runs 10 to 14 boats per day between Vannes port or Conleau and Île d'Arz. **Izenah Croisières** (☎02 97 26 31 45; www.izenah-croisieres.com; adult/child return €5/2.70) runs boats from the port at Baden to Île aux Moines year-round.

Locmariaquer Megaliths (☎02 97 57 37 59; www.site-megalithique-locmariaquer.fr; rte de Kerlognan, Locmariaquer; adult/child €5.50/free; ⏰10am-7pm Jul & Aug, 10am-6pm May & Jun, 10am-12.30pm & 2-5.15pm Sep-Apr), an unusual neolithic site on the eastern edge of the village of Locmariaquer (13km south of Auray), sits in an area rich in dolmens. This one features three distinct forms. A giant broken menhir (20m long and the tallest in Western Europe) was made from a type of granite that indicates it was transported (how!?) several kilometres. The Table des Marchand dolmen boasts an incredible geometric carving in its interior. And an enormous tumulus covers multiple graves. The site was once used as a quarry and a car park, but has since been reconstructed in spectacular style. There is no public transport.

One of the most special neolithic ruins along the Morbihan coast is **Cairn de Gavrinis** (☎02 97 57 19 38; www.morbihan.fr/gavrinis/; Île de Gavrinis; boat trip & tour adult/child €18/8; ⏰9.30am-12.30pm & 1.30-6.30pm Apr-Sep), a giant cairn out on the island of the same name. Dating from 4000 BC and measuring more than 50m in diameter, the beautifully situated tomb is well known for the profusion of intricate engravings on it. You access the site on a 15-minute boat trip from the harbour at Larmor-Baden (14km southeast of Auray), and it's important to reserve tickets in advance.

feel a tad compact due to the cubicle shower and toilets plonked in the corner. The **restaurant** (lunch/dinner *menus* from €19/34) is renowned for its fresh seafood.

★Plume au Vent B&B €€
(☎06 16 98 34 79; www.plume-au-vent.com; 4 venelle Notre Dame, Carnac-Ville; d/q incl breakfast €95/155; 📶) Forget about tacky seaside hotels, this two-room B&B on a *venelle* (little street) in the town centre is more like something from an interior-design magazine. It's all mellow shades of blues and greys, hundreds of neatly bound books, knick-knacks discovered washed up on the high-tide line and polished cement showers and sinks. A great find.

Eating

Chez Marie CREPERIE €
(☎02 97 52 07 93; 3 place de l'Église, Carnac-Ville; mains €6-13, menus €10-15; ⏰noon-2pm & 7-10pm Wed-Sun) Established in 1959, this Carnac institution churns out savoury *galettes* and sweet crêpes in a charmingly traditional stone house opposite the church. Connoisseurs recommend its flambéed specialities, especially the Arzal *galette*, with scallops, apples and cider.

★La Côte GASTRONOMIC €€€
(☎02 97 52 02 80; www.restaurant-la-cote.com; impasse Parc Er Forn, Kermario; lunch menu €26, dinner menus €37-83; ⏰12.15-2pm Wed-Sun, 7.15-9.15pm Tue-Sun) Top recommendation on the Morbihan Coast goes to this Carnac restaurant run by Carnacois *maître-cuisinier* Pierre Michaud, who has won plaudits for his inventive cuisine that combines the very best Breton ingredients. The setting is another drawcard, with an elegant dining room and a soothing terrace overlooking a small fish pond. Find it in a quiet property close to the Alignements de Kermario.

Information

Tourist Office (☎02 97 52 13 52; www.ot-carnac.fr; 74 av des Druides, Carnac-Plage; ⏰9.30am-7pm Mon-Sat, 3-7pm Sun Jul-Aug, 9.30-12.30pm & 2-6pm Mon-Sat, 3-6pm Sun Apr-Jun & Sep, shorter hrs rest of yr; 📶) Also has an office at Carnac-Ville, next to the church. Excellent map of nearby neolithic sites. Has a smartphone app.

Getting There & Around

BICYCLE

Hire bikes and cycle buggies from **A Bicyclette** (☎02 97 52 75 08; www.velocarnac.com; 93bis av des Druides, Carnac-Plage; bicycle per day

DON'T MISS

CARNAC'S MYSTERIOUS MEGALITHS

Two perplexing questions arise from the Brittany's neolithic menhirs, dolmens, cromlechs, tumuli and cairns. Just *how* did the original constructors hew, then haul, these blocks (the heaviest weighs 300 tonnes), millennia before the wheel and the mechanical engine reached Brittany? And *why*? Theories and hypotheses abound, but common consensus is that they served some kind of sacred purpose – a spiritual impulse like that behind so many monuments built by humankind.

Just north of Carnac there is a vast array of monoliths set up in several distinct alignments, all visible from the road, though fenced for controlled admission. There are also several spectacular sites around the Golfe du Morbihan, including **Cairn de Gavrinis** (p281), **Locmariaquer Megaliths** (p281) and **Cairn de Petit Mont** (☎06 03 95 90 78; www.morbihan.fr/petit-mont; Arzon; adult/child €7/3; ⏰11am-6.30pm Jul & Aug, 2.30-6.30pm Thu-Tue Apr-Jun & Sep).

The main information point for the Carnac alignments is the **Maison des Mégalithes** (☎02 97 52 29 81; www.menhirs-carnac.fr; rte des Alignements, D196; tour adult/child €6/free; ⏰9.30am-8pm Jul & Aug, 10am-5pm Sep-Apr, 9am-6pm May & Jun), which explores the history of the site and has a rooftop viewpoint overlooking the *alignements*. Sign up for a one-hour guided visit; times vary considerably depending on the time of year, but they run several times a day (in French) during the summer. English tours are available once a week in July and August – call the Maison des Mégalithes to confirm times.

Due to severe erosion, the sites are fenced off to allow the vegetation to regenerate, and certain areas are accessible only by guided tour. However, from October to March you can wander freely through selected parts – the Maison des Mégalithes has maps of what's currently open.

The best way to appreciate the stones' sheer numbers is to walk or cycle between the Ménec and Kerlescan groups, with menhirs almost continuously in view. Between June and September, seven buses a day run between the two sites, as well as Carnac-Ville and Carnac-Plage. The Carnac-Ville tourist office has an excellent map of all the nearby sites.

Opposite the Maison des Mégalithes, the largest menhir field – with 1099 stones – is the **Alignements du Ménec**, 1km north of Carnac-Ville. From here, the D196 heads northeast for about 1.5km to the equally impressive **Alignements de Kermario** (parts of which are open year-round). Climb the stone **observation tower** midway along the site to see the alignment from above.

The **Tumulus de Kercado** lies just east of Kermario and 500m to the south of the D196. It's the massive burial mound of a neolithic chieftain dating from 3800 BC. Deposit your fee (€1) in an honour box at the entry gate. About 300m east of the Kercado turnoff along the D196 lies the parking area for the **Géant du Manio**. A 15-minute walk brings you to it, the highest menhir in the complex.

The easternmost of the major groups is the **Alignements de Kerlescan**, a smaller grouping also accessible in winter.

Tumulus St-Michel, 400m northeast of the Carnac-Ville tourist office, and accessed off the D781 at the end of rue du Tumulus, is a gigantic burial mound with a church on top. It dates back to at least 5000 BC and offers sweeping views (exterior access only).

Be sure to visit the **Musée de Préhistoire** (☎02 97 52 22 04; www.museedecarnac.fr; 10 place de la Chapelle, Carnac-Ville; adult/child €6/2.50; ⏰10am-6.30pm Jul & Aug, 10am-12.30pm & 2-6pm Wed-Mon Apr-Jun & Sep, shorter hours Oct-Mar) in Carnac-Ville to see the incredible neolithic artefacts found throughout the region.

from €10, buggy per hour from €8) down near the beach.

BUS

The main bus stops are in Carnac-Ville, outside the police station on rue St-Cornély, and in Carnac-Plage, beside the tourist office. **Tim** (☎08 10 10 10 56; www.morbihan.fr; ticket €2) runs a daily bus (line 1) to Auray, Vannes and Quiberon (€2).

Quiberon

POP 5112

Quiberon (Kiberen in Breton) sits at the southern tip of a thin, 14km-long peninsula, called the **Presqu'île de Quiberon**, flanked on the western side by the rocky, wave-lashed **Côte Sauvage** (Wild Coast). The setting is superb, with a heady mix of lovely beaches and rugged inlets, but the town itself is quite tacky, and finding a parking spot is like looking for a pot of gold at the end of a rainbow. Even so, it's wildly popular in summer and is also the departure point for ferries to Belle Île. For outdoorsy types, there are plenty of water sports available, from diving and snorkelling to sea kayaking and *char à voile* (sand yachting).

Activities & Tours

Conserverie La Belle-Iloise CANNERY TOUR
(☎02 97 50 59 08; www.labelleiloise.fr; zone d'Activités Plein Ouest, bd Plein Ouest; ⊙tours 10am, 11am, 3pm & 4pm Mon-Fri, 11am & 3pm Sat) FREE Take a 45-minute guided tour of this former sardine cannery before replenishing your supplies of tinned tuna, mackerel, sardines and fish spread in the adjacent shop. It's north of the train station.

La Grande Plage BEACH
La Grande Plage is a family-friendly beach; bathing spots towards the peninsula's tip are less crowded.

Sillages KAYAKING
(☎06 81 26 75 08; www.kayak-sillages.com; 9 av de Groix, St-Pierre-Quiberon; adult/child from €20/17; ⊙daily by reservation) What about a morning paddle far from the crowds along the Côte Sauvage? This reputable outfit based in St-Pierre-Quiberon (look for the 'Base Nautique') runs guided kayaking tours for all levels – beginners are welcome.

Sleeping & Eating

Camping du Conguel CAMPGROUND €
(☎02 97 50 19 11; www.campingduconguel.com; bd de la Teignouse, Plage Conguel; sites €29-54; ⊙Apr-Oct; 📶🏊) This splashy option with an aqua park that has water slides is one of the peninsula's 15 campgrounds. Just 2km east of the town centre, it's beside Plage du Conguel. There are also caravans to rent.

★ **Le Petit Hôtel du Grand Large** BOUTIQUE HOTEL €€
(☎02 97 58 31 99; www.lepetithoteldugrandlarge.fr; 11 quai St-Ivy, Portivy; d €115-135; 📶) This intimate, sassy hotel is a soothing escape from the Quiberon hubbub, offering six spiffy, well-lit rooms facing the sea. Top choices are room 4, with its bathroom set in a turret, and room 5, for its wide balcony. Gastronomic bliss is dished up at the elegant restaurant downstairs (lunch/dinner menus from €30/55), which blends playful Breton classics in a jumble-shop chic setting.

It's in Portivy, an adorable, quiet seaside town a few kilometres north of Quiberon.

Le Vivier SEAFOOD €
(☎02 97 50 12 60; Côte Sauvage; mains €8-25; ⊙noon-3pm & 7-8pm Tue-Sun Feb-Nov, plus Mon in Jul & Aug) The food is almost secondary at this convivial eatery dramatically perched on a small cliff on the Côte Sauvage; bookings are essential for the top tables, squeezed onto a sunny terrace hovering above the rocky coastline. The menu is plain and unpretentious – think salads, mussels, smoked fish and shellfish. From central Quiberon, follow the signs north to 'Côte Sauvage' for about 2km.

Restaurant de La Criée SEAFOOD €€
(☎02 97 30 53 09; 11 quai de l'Océan; mains €20-30, menus €19-25; ⊙12.15-2pm Tue-Sun, 7.15-9pm Tue-Sat) On the harbourfront, La Criée has long been a favourite among fish lovers. Nautically themed and run by a talented team, the seafood here is a cut above most of Quiberon's bistros. Dover sole, fillet monkfish, brill cooked with apples, and red mullet in a fennel sauce all feature.

Information

Tourist Office (☎02 97 50 07 84; www.quiberon.com; 14 rue de Verdun; ⊙9am-7pm Mon-Sat, 10am-1pm & 2-5pm Sun Aug, shorter hours rest of year; 📶) Between the train station and La Grande Plage.

Getting There & Away

Cyclomar (☎02 97 50 26 00; www.cyclomar.fr; 47 place Hoche; touring/mountain bikes per day from €9.50/11, scooters incl helmet per

day from €39.50) Around 200m south of the tourist office. Hires out touring and mountain bikes as well as scooters – insurance costs extra. Runs an operation from the train station during July and August.

Cycles Loisirs (☎ 02 97 50 31 73; www.cyclesloisirs.free.fr; 32 rue Golvan; touring/mountain bikes per day from €9.50/13) Hires out bicycles; 200m north of the tourist office.

BOAT

Compagnie Océane (☎ 02 97 35 02 00, 08 20 05 61 56; www.compagnie-oceane.fr; adult/child return €34.50/18.50) runs ferries between Quiberon and Belle-Île, and Houat and Hoëdic islands. Park at Sémaphore car park 1.5km north of the harbourfront, and take the free shuttle to the port.

BUS

Quiberon is connected by **Tim** (p283) bus line 1 with Carnac (45 minutes), Auray (1¼ hours) and Vannes (1¾ hours). Buses stop at the train station and at place Hoche, near the tourist office and the beach.

TRAIN

In July and August only, a train runs several times a day between Auray and Quiberon (€6.40, 45 minutes). In June, an SNCF bus service links Quiberon and Auray train stations (€3.65, 50 minutes) at least seven times a day.

Belle Île

POP 5270

Belle Île (in full, Belle-Île-en-Mer, 'beautiful island in the sea') does indeed live up to its name: rugged cliffs and rock stacks line the island's west coast while picturesque pastel ports nestle along the eastern side. For sunbathers and outdoorsy types, there is no shortage of lovely beaches and activities.

Accessed by ferries from Quiberon, the island sees its population swell tenfold in summer. But as it's Brittany's largest offshore island (at 20km by 9km), there's room to escape the crowds.

Belle-Île has two main settlements: the main port of Le Palais is on the east side of the island, while smaller (and even more charming) Sauzon is in the northeast.

> **CATCHING THE WAVE**
>
> Feel like hitting the waves crashing on the wild shore of Brittany, but not sure how? Head to surf school at one of 12 outfits around Brittany (see www.ecole-surf-bretagne.fr for details). Courses range from a 1½-hour session (€35) to a full-time weeklong session (€260).

Sights & Activities

Citadelle Vauban & Musée d'Art et d'Histoire FORT, MUSEUM

(☎ 02 97 31 85 54; www.citadellevauban.com; Le Palais; adult/child €8/5; ⏱ 9am-7pm Jul & Aug, shorter hours Sep-Dec & Feb-Jun) The dramatic citadel, strengthened by the architect Vauban in 1682, dominates little Le Palais port. Inside, the museum's displays concentrate on the history of the island's defensive system, though there are also sections on the local fish trade and island life. There's also a hotel and restaurant.

★ **Aiguilles de Port Coton** NATURAL SITE

Just off the western side of the island, these magnificent rock stacks that resemble *aiguilles* (needles) are a must-see for panorama-lovers and photographers. The name Port Coton comes from the way the sea foams around the rocks, creating foam like cotton wool. These dramatic rock formations were depicted in a series of famous canvases by Claude Monet.

Pointe des Poulains NATURAL SITE

The island's northernmost point juts out at Pointe des Poulains. Flanked by craggy cliffs, this windswept headland is Belle Île's loftiest lookout, and was once the home of renowned actress Sarah Bernhardt. Her former fortress home is open to the public from April to October.

Grotte de l'Apothicairerie CAVE

Belle Île's fretted western coast has spectacular rock formations and caves including Grotte de l'Apothicairerie, where waves roll in from two sides.

Vives Eaux KAYAKING

(☎ 02 97 31 00 93; www.vives-eaux.fr; chemin de Port Puce, Sauzon; tours adult/child from €34/24, rental per hr €11; ⏱ May-Oct) Explore the bays, rugged inlets and tucked-away coves at a gentle kayaking pace. This outfit runs excellent guided tours.

Beaches

Belle Île is blessed with some lovely beaches, the largest of which is the 2km-long **Plage des Grands Sables**, spanning the calm waters of the island's eastern side. **Plage de Donnant**, on the opposite side of the island, is more secluded, but swimming is

OFF THE BEATEN TRACK

TREETOP SLEEP

For the ultimate eco-escape, don't miss eccentric **Dihan** (02 97 56 88 27; www.dihan-evasion.org; Kerganiet, Ploëmel; tent/cabin incl breakfast from €70/150), a guesthouse secluded in a leafy dell outside Ploëmel (follow the black signs from the village), 8km north of Carnac. Run by fun-loving Myriam and Arno Le Masle, a farmhouse and barn house the guest rooms, while the grounds shelter yurts, bubble tents and tree houses. Guests can fire up the barbecue and dine beneath a pergola.

Should nature call, there are biodegradable dry toilets (you'll find brightly tiled bathrooms and a sauna in the reception building).

Rates include breakfast, which is a combination of organic, fair-trade and local artisanal produce, such as *caramel au beurre salé* (Breton salted caramel spread). Fabulous *tables d'hôte* (meals that are a combination of Myriam's Breton, Mauritian and Indian heritage; by reservation) take place in the converted *cidrerie*, where pianist Arno hits the keys and bands sometimes drop by. You can also rent bikes (€12 per day) or book a massage (one hour €170).

very dangerous due to riptides. Sheltered **Plage d'Herlin**, on the south side, is better for children.

Sleeping

Camping Bordénéo CAMPGROUND €
(02 97 31 88 96; www.bordeneo.com; Bordénéo, Le Palais; adult/car/site €7.35/2.70/11.35; Apr-Sep;) This modern, well-equipped campground is beautifully sited in Bordénéo, about 2km northwest of Le Palais off the road to Sauzon. The heated pool is a plus, and there are mobile homes for hire.

Auberge de Jeunesse HOSTEL €
(02 97 31 81 33; www.fuaj.org/belle-ile-en-mer; Haute Boulogne, Le Palais; dm from €16.80; Apr-Sep; @) This modern, well-equipped but charmless, 96-bed, HI-affiliated hostel with a self-catering kitchen is to the north of the citadel. Its rooms are all twins with bunk-beds and shared toilets. Meals are available.

Les Tamaris HOTEL €
(02 97 31 65 09; www.auxtamaris.fr; 11 allée des Peupliers, Sauzon; d €55-88, q €95; P) A breath of fresh air, this well-priced simple hotel on the inland outskirts of Sauzon has plenty of rural charm but no sea views. Rooms are basic, colourful and comfortable, and the owners are charming. Transfers to/from walking trailheads can be arranged for €2.50 per person, and bikes are available for hire (€11).

Hôtel Vauban HOTEL €
(02 97 31 45 42; www.hotel-vauban-belleile.com; 1 rue des Remparts, Le Palais; d €80-98;) This comfy place, with 16 multicoloured rooms splashed with driftwood, is perched high on Le Palais' ramparts, with jaw-dropping views of the harbour below. Cheaper rooms don't have sea views. The owners do hiking packages, which include several nights' stay and all meals, including a picnic lunch.

★**La Villa de Jade** B&B €€
(02 97 31 53 00; www.villadejade.com; Taillefer, Le Palais; d incl breakfast €160-200, house per week incl breakfast €1200; P) Manuel and Valérie are the widely travelled, bilingual couple behind La Villa de Jade. This one-of-a-kind, gorgeous B&B in a stunningly renovated villa could not be more superbly placed – it's slap bang on a clifftop with plunging views of the sea, 2km north of Le Palais. Its three rooms ooze charm with their mix-and-match furniture, family photos, colourful touches and wood floors.

Eating

Les Embruns CREPERIE €
(02 97 31 64 78; www.creperielesembruns-sauzon.fr; quai Jospeh Naudin, Sauzon; mains €5-11; noon-9.30pm Apr-Oct) The harbourfront is lined with tempting restaurants but this crêperie is one of the best. It prepares perfectly buttered Breton crêpes and *galettes*, as well as scrumptious fillings such as *oranges confites maison* (homemade candied orange), and finger-licking ice creams. Most ingredients are organic and locally sourced. In summer, tables spill onto a pavement terrace.

Le Verre à Pied BISTRO €
(02 97 31 29 65; 3 place de la République, Le Palais; mains €13-20, lunch menus €16-19; noon-2pm & 6-10pm Thu-Tue Feb-Dec) This convivial bistro in central Le Palais is blessed with a lovely courtyard that's a perfect spot for a relaxed

WORTH A TRIP

BRETON FEST

Celtic communities from Ireland, Scotland, Wales, Cornwall, Isle of Man and Galicia in northwest Spain congregate with Bretons at the **Festival Interceltique de Lorient** (www.festival-interceltique.com) over 10 days in early August. Upwards of 600,000 people descend on the city of Lorient, about 30km northwest of Carnac, so book well ahead if you're planning to stay in town.

feed or tipple in summer. The food isn't starry, but it's fine for a heaping kettle of mussels or *tartine* (slice of bread with toppings), as well as Breton far cake for dessert.

★**Le Café de la Cale** BRASSERIE €€
(☎02 97 31 65 74; http://cafedelacale.pagecom.fr; quai Guerveur, Sauzon; mains €17-31, lunch/dinner menus €20/28; ⏰12.15-2pm & 7.30-9.30pm mid-Feb–Oct) This snazzy brasserie with a superb terrace overlooking Sauzon's harbour outshines most others with its relaxed mood, attentive service and creative take on seasonal produce. Seafood features prominently; tuck into an expertly prepared *lieu* (pollack) or ask for the *plateau de fruits de mer,* brimming with shellfish.

Information

The **tourist office** (☎02 97 31 81 93; www.belle-ile.com; quai Bonnelle, Le Palais; ⏰9am-1pm & 2-7pm Mon-Sat, to 1pm Sun Jul & Aug, shorter hours rest of year; 📶) is on the left as you leave the ferry in Le Palais, and it's stocked with lots of local maps and brochures.

Getting There & Away

Travelling to Belle Île can involve a bit of planning, as taking a car on the ferry is prohibitively expensive for a short trip (a small car starts at €170 return *plus* passenger fares) and needs to be booked well ahead, even outside peak season.

The shortest crossing to Belle Île is from Quiberon. **Compagnie Océane** (p284) operates car/passenger ferries (45 minutes) year-round, and fast passenger ferries to Le Palais and Sauzon in July and August. There are up to 10 crossings a day in July and August. Fares and frequencies are reduced off-season.

It is also possible to make the trip from Vannes (and Locmariaquer and Port-Navalo) on **Navix** (☎08 25 13 21 00; www.navix.fr; ⏰Apr-Sep), which operates ferries to Le Palais three to five times per week from April to September (adult/child return €30/25 from Vannes, 2½ hours).

Vannes

POP 53,558

What a beauty! Overlooking the Golfe du Morbihan, Vannes is one of the unmissable towns of Brittany. Spectacular fortifications encircle Vannes' meandering alleys and cobbled squares, and lead down to a sparkling marina lined with cafes and townhouses. The city still preserves much of its medieval atmosphere, but it's a long way from being a museum piece. It has a lively bar and restaurant scene year-round, and it's also an excellent base for exploring the glittering island-studded Golfe du Morbihan and nearby neolithic sites.

Sights

★**Ramparts** HISTORIC SITE
Vannes' old town is surrounded by massive ramparts, which are in turn lined by a moat and, on the eastern edge, flower-filled gardens. Tucked away behind rue des Vierges, stairs lead to the accessible section of the ramparts from which you can see the black-roofed **Vieux Lavoirs** (Old Laundry Houses) along the water. Or walk rue Francis Decker, on the wall's eastern exterior, to take it all in.

Musée d'Histoire et d'Archéologie MUSEUM
(☎02 97 01 63 00; www.mairie-vannes.fr; 2 rue Noé; adult/child €6.30/4.30; ⏰1.30-6pm Jun-Sep) Housed inside the 16th-century Château Gaillard, this small but excellent museum contains precious neolithic artefacts unearthed throughout the region.

Cathédrale St-Pierre CATHEDRAL
On the eastern side of place Henry IV looms the 13th-century Gothic Cathédrale St-Pierre. Inside, look for paintings of St Vincent Ferrier, a preacher and saint who died in Vannes is 1419.

La Cohue – Musée des Beaux-Arts ART MUSEUM
(☎02 97 01 63 00; www.mairie-vannes.fr; place St-Pierre; adult/child €4.60/free; ⏰1.30-6pm daily Jun-Sep, Tue-Sun Oct-May) Opposite the cathedral, the building called La Cohue has variously been a produce market, a law court and the seat of the Breton parliament. Today it's a well-curated museum of fine arts, displaying 19th-century paintings, sculptures and engravings, and rotating exhibitions of cutting-edge contemporary art.

Maison de Vannes et Sa Femme HISTORIC BUILDING
On the corner of rue Noë and rue Pierre Rogue, look for the famous Maison de Vannes et Sa Femme, which sports a timber carving of a portly 16th-century shop owner and his equally well-endowed wife.

Sleeping

★ Le Bretagne HOTEL €
(☎02 97 47 20 21; www.hotel-lebretagne-vannes.com; 36 rue du Mené; d €62;) Nothing much to look at from the outside, but the 12 rooms inside are a steal. Although on the small side, they're neat as a pin and bright, and have cutting-edge colours, excellent bedding and sparkling bathrooms. Top picks are rooms at the back, with stupendous views of the ramparts. Service is friendly.

Hôtel de France HOTEL €
(☎02 97 47 27 57; www.hotelfrance-vannes.com; 57 av Victor Hugo; d €72-95; P) This simple hotel near the train station caters for a business crowd, so it feels faceless in places, but the facilities are solid and the location very convenient. The best of the 30 rooms overlook a small garden at the back.

★ La Villa Garennes B&B €€
(☎06 76 01 80 83; www.hotel-lebretagne-vannes.com; 3 rue Monseigneur Tréhiou; d incl breakfast €75-105;) A stone's throw from the ramparts, this very attractive option has five charmingly and uniquely decorated rooms in a handsome stone building. They're light, airy and furnished with great taste, and breakfasts come in for warm praise.

Best Western Le Roof HOTEL €€
(☎02 97 63 47 47; www.le-roof.com; 10 allée des Frères Cadoret, Presqu'île de Conleau; s €117-156, d €139-180; P) Yes, yes, we know it's a Best Western, but this 40-room abode is ideal if it's a smart, efficient seaside retreat that you're after – it lies 4.5km southwest of Vannes' medieval centre, on the shoreline of Presqu'île de Conleau, and overlooks a small beach. Rooms vary in size and style; don't even consider one without a view of the Golfe.

★ Hôtel Villa Kerasy BOUTIQUE HOTEL €€€
(☎02 97 68 36 83; www.villakerasy.com; 20 av Favrel-et-Lincy; d €149-220, ste from €348; closed mid-Nov–mid-Dec; P) From the outside this looks like nothing more than a large Breton house, but once beyond the entrance you'll discover an exotic world of spices and far-away tropical sea ports. Rooms are individually decorated in Indian and Far Eastern styles and the garden, which is crowded with Buddha statues and ponds filled with lazy koi carp, are a little slice of Sri Lanka or Japan.

Eating

★ Dan Ewen CREPERIE €
(☎02 97 42 44 34; 3 place du Général de Gaulle; mains €4-10, menus €12-18; 11.30am-2pm & 6.30-9pm Mon-Sat) A near-life-size statue of a smiling Breton lady bearing a tray greets you at the entrance of this popular stone and dark-wood crêperie. Generous fillings include frangipane, or flambéed options topped with *crème Chantilly*. And, don't forget to order a *boule* (gobblet) of local cider.

Brasserie des Halles BRASSERIE €
(☎02 97 54 08 34; www.brasseriedeshallesvannes.com; 9 rue des Halles; mains €11-22, menus €16-29; noon-2.30pm & 7-11pm) Atmospherically set in a 16th-century building in the heart of the old town, this buzzing brasserie has a varied menu of fish and meat dishes, as well as pastas, salads and shellfish. It's an equally good spot for a drink while browsing the art, and its popular with families.

★ Restaurant de Roscanvec GASTRONOMIC €€€
(☎02 97 47 15 96; www.roscanvec.com; 17 rue des Halles; lunch menu €25, dinner menus €53-75; 12.15-2pm Tue-Sun, 7.45-9.15pm Tue-Sat Jul & Aug, also closed Tue Sep-Jun) Hidden in the timber-frame houses of the old city, this stellar restaurant is overseen by one of Britanny's most talented names, Thierry Seychelles, whose cooking has been championed by most of the major culinary critics. Rightly so: his trademark six-course 'Hedonist Menu' combines seasonal French classics with global flavours, and the lunch *menu* is a gourmet steal! Book ahead.

Drinking & Nightlife

Le Verre à L'Envers BAR
(6 place du Général de Gaulle; 4pm-1am Tue-Sat) A mature, in-the-know set favours this pearl of a place just outside the ramparts. Snag a seat on the terrace to soak up the street atmosphere or snuggle up in the pocket-sized room. Knock back a wine by the glass or a beer, and graze on an excellent cheese or charcuterie (cured meats) platter. But the real queen of the drinks card is the mojito – simply the most devilish in town.

WORTH A TRIP

ROCHEFORT-EN-TERRE

For an architectural trip into the Middle Ages, make a beeline for Rochefort-en-Terre. It's a photogenic town of narrow, cobbled streets and lovely squares lined with granite mansions, slate-roofed houses and flower-filled window boxes – not to mention a smattering of art galleries and crêperies. Its picture-book perch on a rocky outcrop above the River Gueuzon is enchanting, though it can be packed in summer. As befits any medieval Breton town, it also boasts a lovely castle, which is not open to the public, but has a sci-fi/fantasy museum in one of its out-buildings. The town's superb church was originally built in the 10th century. It's best visited on a day trip – there are loads more sleeping options in Vannes and Josselin. TIM (www.morbihan.fr) bus 9 serves Vannes (€2, 1¼ hours, four daily).

Paddy O' Dowd's PUB
(23 rue Ferdinand le Dressay; ⏲5pm-2am) Get the beers in at this popular pub overlooking the harbour. The terrace is a chilled spot for summertime imbibing. Arrive late for a truly eclectic crowd, including lots of students, and an atmosphere that can go from quiet tippling to raucous revelry.

Information

Tourist Office (☎08 25 13 56 10, 02 97 47 24 34; www.tourisme-vannes.com; quai de Tabarly; ⏲9.30am-7pm Mon-Sat, 10am-6pm Sun Jul & Aug, 9.30am-12.30pm & 1.30-6pm Mon-Sat Sep-Jun;) In a modern building on the marina. Has a smartphone app.

Getting There & Away

BUS

The small bus station is opposite the train station. Tim (www.morbihan.fr) has services throughout the region, including line 1 to Carnac (€2, 1¼ hours) and on to Quiberon (€2, two hours), and line 9 to Rochefort-en-Terre (€2, 1¼ hours).

TRAIN

Vannes is on the train line running east to Quimper and west to Rennes, Nantes or Paris. When the TGV line between Le Mans and Rennes opens in 2017, it will cut approximately 40 minutes off the train travel times to Paris.

Nantes €23.40, 1½ hours, five direct daily
Quimper €18 to €27.50, 1½ hours, 15 daily
Paris Montparnasse €40 to €94, 3¾ hours, eight direct daily
Rennes €22.50, one to 1½ hours, 14 daily

EASTERN & CENTRAL BRITTANY

The one-time frontier between Brittany and France, fertile eastern Brittany fans out around the region's lively capital, Rennes. Central Brittany conceals the enchanting Forêt de Paimpont, sprinkled with villages and ancient Breton legends.

Josselin

POP 2626

The storybook village of Josselin lies on the banks of the River Oust, 43km northeast of Vannes, in the shadow of an enormous, cone-turreted 14th-century castle that was the long-time seat of the counts of Rohan. Today, visitors in their thousands continue to fall under its spell. The little town's heart is place Notre Dame, a beautiful square of 16th-century half-timbered houses.

Sights

★Château de Josselin CASTLE
(☎02 97 22 36 45; www.chateaujosselin.com; place de la Congrégation; adult/child €9/5.50; ⏲11am-6pm daily mid-Jul–Aug, 2-6pm Apr–mid-Jul & Sep, 2-5.30pm Sat & Sun only Oct) Guarded by its three round towers, the extraordinary town château is an incredible sight that remains the home of the Rohan family today. Beyond the entrance gate, the castle fans out into tree-filled grounds and a central courtyard, which affords a great view of the castle's Flamboyant Gothic facade and the river below. The château is filled with treasures, including a medieval-style dining room, a 3000-tome library and a grand *salon* filled with Sèvres porcelain, Gobelins carpets and an astronomical clock.

The interior can only be visited by guided tour: there is one English-language tour per day in July and August; otherwise you can ask for a leaflet in English.

Basilique Notre Dame du Roncier CHURCH
(place Notre Dame; ⏲9am-6pm) Parts of the Basilique Notre Dame du Roncier date from the 12th century, including its Romanesque pillars. The 60m tower, however, was built in 1949. Superb 15th- and 16th-century stained

glass illuminates the south aisle. If you're lucky you'll be there while the organist is playing the 17th-century organ.

Musée de Poupées MUSEUM
(Doll Museum; 02 97 22 36 45; www.chateaujosselin.com; 3 rue des Trente; adult/child €8/5.30; 11am-6pm daily mid-Jul–Aug, 2-6pm Apr–mid-Jul & Sep, 2-5.30pm Sat & Sun only Oct) Part of the grounds of the Château de Josselin, this quirky museum has a collection of more than 3000 vintage dolls and puppets amassed by Herminie de Rohan around the turn of the 20th century. A combination ticket for the Musée de Poupées and the château costs €14.80/8.80.

Sleeping & Eating

★ **Le Clos des Devins** B&B €
(06 88 84 77 05, 02 97 75 67 48; www.leclosdesdevins.com; 11 rue des Devins; d incl breakfast €60-68;) A beautiful 18th-century private mansion complete with fabulous walled garden underpins this gem of a *chambre d'hôte,* 250m north of the church. Conscientious owner, Madame Astruc, has artfully decorated rooms with both modern touches and charming antiques. Each room has its own personality; our favourite is the Abricotine, which has a drop-dead-gorgeous roof terrace overlooking the garden.

Domaine de Kerelly Camping CAMPGROUND €
(02 97 22 22 20; www.camping-josselin.com; Bas de la Lande, Josselin-Guégon; site for 2 people €16; Apr-Sep;) This peaceful spot is 2km west of Josselin, on the south bank of the River Oust. It offers plenty of shady spots to pitch your tent.

★ **Le 14 Saint-Michel** B&B €€
(02 97 22 24 24, 06 89 37 26 07; www.le14st-michel.com; 14 rue St-Michel; incl breakfast s €75-95, d €85-105, f €113-140;) This outstanding *chambre d'hôte* fills a grand townhouse right in the historic centre. Spacious, stylish rooms (including a two-room suite for families) ooze romance, and there's a superb garden at the back. Breakfast is sumptuous, and the welcoming hostess, Viviane, also does *tables d'hôte* (€28) with local, seasonal products. It's a haven of charm and serenity, and some rooms have views of the countryside.

La Table d'O MODERN FRENCH €€
(02 97 70 61 39; 9 rue Glatinier; lunch/dinner menus from €13/30; noon-1.30pm Mon-Sat, 7.30-8.45pm Tue & Thu-Sat) This pleasant family-run place offers an interesting and varied menu of local cooking with a sprinkle of fusion on top, making it a local favourite. The sweeping views of the town and valley from the terrace are fantastic for a summer lunch. It's 250m west of the château.

Information

Tourist Office (02 97 22 36 43; www.josselin-communaute.fr; 21 rue Olivier de Clisson; 10am-6pm Jul & Aug, 10am-noon Tue-Sat, 1.30-5.30pm Mon-Sat Apr-Jun & Sep, shorter hrs Oct-Mar;) Offers a useful map of local sights and list of *chambre d'hôtes*.

Getting There & Away

Keolis Armor (02 99 26 16 00; www.keolis-armor.fr) runs several daily buses to Rennes (€15.30, 1½ hours), and SNCF has buses to Rennes (€15.30) as well. The nearest train station is in Pontivy, also served by Keolis buses.

Forêt de Paimpont

The Paimpont Forest is about 40km southwest of Rennes, and is legendary for being the site of Brocéliande, the place where King Arthur received his magic sword, Excalibur, from the Lady of the Lake. It's also the magical forest where she entombed Merlin. Although some dispute the link between Paimpont and the mythical Brocéliande, Paimpont is a magical setting all the same and local stories and themes focus on those medieval tales. The best base for exploring the forest is the lakeside village of Paimpont.

Activities

Some 95% of the forest is private land, but the tourist office, beside the 13th-century **Église Abbatiale** (Abbey Church) in Paimpont, has a free map outlining a 62km-long driving circuit with numerous short walks along the way that are accessible to the public. It also sells more-detailed walking and cycling guides, and has guided tours (adult/child from €7.50/4) in summer. Some areas are closed for hunting in winter, and the tourist office has a map showing what's open.

Sleeping & Eating

La Corne de Cerf B&B €
(02 99 07 84 19; http://corneducerf.bcld.net; Le Cannée; s/d/tr incl breakfast €55/63/83; Apr-Nov;) For garden lovers – flowers all around – and history vultures, Annick and Robert's gorgeously restored village house is cool, quiet and elegantly homey. Each room

has its own clear personality (we fell for Emeraldine, decked out in blue shades), comfortable beds, soft colours and privacy. This authentic rural haven is in Le Cannée, about 3km south of Paimpont.

Camping Municipal de Paimpont CAMPGROUND €
(☎02 99 07 89 16; www.camping-paimpont-broceliande.com; rue du Chevalier Lancelot du Lac, Paimpont; site/adult/car €3.60/4/2; ⊙Apr-Sep) Campers can set up their tents at this rural campground, 800m north of Paimpont.

★ **Le Relais de Brocéliande** HOTEL €€
(☎02 99 07 84 94; www.le-relais-de-broceliande.fr; 5 rue du Forges, Paimpont; d €105-136; P 📶) In an historic but thoroughly modernised building, this hotel attracts a varied foreign clientele, drawn by the comfy guest rooms – clean and bright with excellent bedding and gleaming bathrooms – and the efficient staff. Perks include a renowned **restaurant** (lunch *menus* €15-18, dinner *menus* €30-38) serving fresh, seasonal cuisine, and a top-notch spa.

Les Forges de Paimpont TRADITIONAL FRENCH €€
(☎02 99 06 81 07; www.restaurant.forges-de-paimpont.com; Les Forges, Plélan-le-Grand; lunch menu €16, dinner menus €21-34; ⊙noon-2pm Wed-Sun, 7-9pm Wed-Sat; P) This rustic country inn with a cosy interior owes its reputation to a menu that's rooted in the traditions of the *terroir*. The excellent value €23 set menu may include quail, deer, duck, pigeon or grilled ribsteak. Find the restaurant in the hamlet of Les Forges, near Plélan-le-Grand, 4km southeast of Paimpont.

Information

Tourist Office (☎02 99 07 84 23; www.tourisme-broceliande.com; place du Roi Judicaël, Paimpont; ⊙9.30am-noon & 2-7pm Apr-Sep, to 6pm Oct-Mar; 📶) Beside the Abbey Church. Runs guided tours of the forest on weekends in summer, has maps of forest walks, and has a 45-minute free film screening.

Getting There & Away

Compagnie Illénoo (www.illenoo-services.fr) bus line 1a connects Paimpont and Rennes (€4.90, one hour, nine per day Monday to Saturday). It's easiest to explore the forest with your own wheels.

Rennes

POP 217,309

A crossroads since Roman times, Brittany's vibrant capital sits at the junction of highways linking northwestern France's major cities. It's a beautifully set-out city, with an elaborate and stately centre and a superb medieval quarter that's a joy to get lost in. At night, this student city has no end of lively places to pop in for a pint and its restaurants are also superb.

Sights

Cathédrale St-Pierre CATHEDRAL
(rue de la Monnaie; ⊙9.30am-noon & 3-6pm; M République, Ste-Anne) Crowning Rennes' old town is the 17th-century cathedral, which has an impressive, if dark, neoclassical interior.

Palais du Parlement de Bretagne LAW COURTS
(☎reservations 02 99 67 11 66; place du Parlement de Bretagne; adult/child €7.20/free; M République) This 17th-century former seat of the rebellious Breton parliament has, in more recent times, been home to the Palais de Justice. In 1994 this building was destroyed by a fire started by demonstrating fishermen. It was reopened in 2004 after a major restoration and now houses the Court of Appeal. Daily guided tours (request in advance for a tour in English) take you through the ostentatiously gilded rooms. Tour bookings must be made through the tourist office.

★ **Musée des Beaux-Arts** MUSEUM
(☎02 23 62 17 45; www.mbar.org; 20 quai Émile Zola; adult/child €5/free; ⊙10am-5pm Tue-Fri, 10am-6pm Sat & Sun; M République) Extensive collections span the 15th century to the present, plus there is a section devoted to antiquities. The Pont-Aven school is featured, as is a 'curiosity gallery' of antiques and illustrations amassed in the 18th century. It also hosts ever-changing temporary exhibitions.

Champs Libres CULTURAL CENTRE
(☎02 23 40 66 00; www.leschampslibres.fr; 10 cours des Alliés; pass for all sights adult/child €9.50/5.50; ⊙noon-7pm Tue-Fri, 2-7pm Sat & Sun; M Charles de Gaulle) Rennes' futuristic cultural centre is home to the **Musée de Bretagne** (www.musee-bretagne.fr), with displays on Breton history and culture, and **Espace des Sciences** (www.espace-sciences.org), an interactive science museum, along with a planetarium, a temporary exhibition space and a library.

Rennes

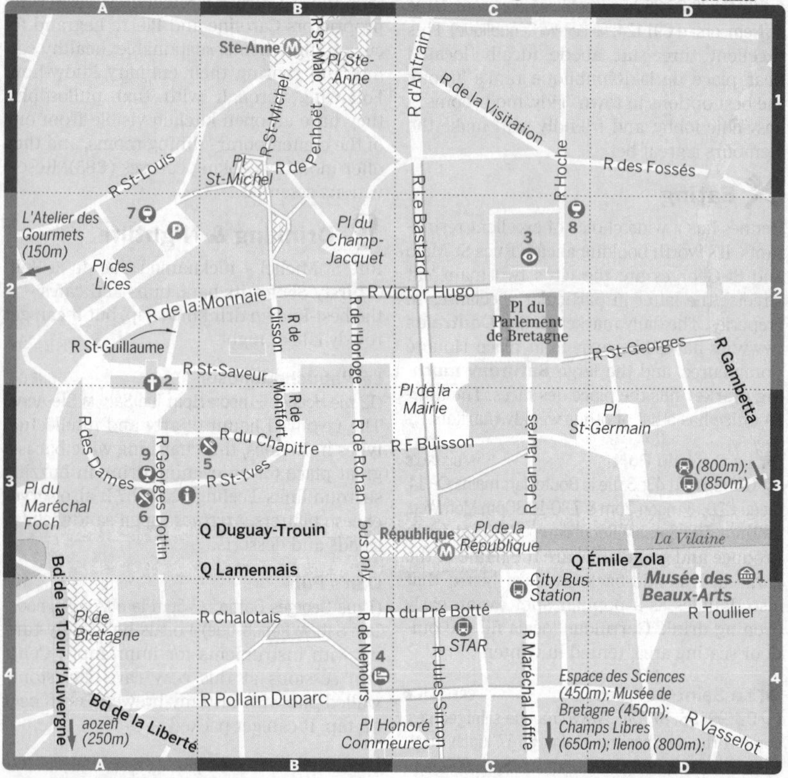

Festivals & Events

Les Mercredis du Thabor CULTURAL

Traditional Breton dancing and music take place in Rennes' beautiful Parc du Thabor on Wednesdays during June and July.

Tombées de la Nuit PERFORMING ARTS

(www.lestombeesdelanuit.com) Rennes' old town comes alive during this music and theatre festival in the first week of July. They are also partnered with Dimanche à Rennes, which offers a year-round program on Sundays.

Les Transmusicales de Rennes MUSIC

(www.lestrans.com) In early December, Rennes hosts one of France's biggest indie music festivals at venues all across the city.

Sleeping

Auberge de Jeunesse HOSTEL €

(02 99 33 22 33; www.hifrance.org; 10-12 canal St-Martin; dm incl breakfast €22.50; 7am-1am, closed late-Dec–mid-Jan; ; Ste-Anne) Rennes' well-equipped youth hostel has a self-catering kitchen and a canalside setting 2km north of the centre. Take bus 12 from place de la Mairie.

Rennes

Top Sights
1 Musée des Beaux-Arts D3

Sights
2 Cathédrale St-Pierre A2
3 Palais du Parlement de Bretagne C2

Sleeping
4 Hôtel de Nemours B4

Eating
5 La Saint-Georges B3
6 Le Café du Port A3

Drinking & Nightlife
7 Le Bar'Hic A2
8 Le Nabuchodonosor C2
9 Oan's Pub A3

★**Hôtel de Nemours** HOTEL €€
(☎02 99 78 26 26; www.hotelnemours.com; 5 rue de Nemours; d €91-124; ❄ 📶; Ⓜ République) This excellent three-star abode ideally located near place de la République ranks among the best options in town. Tidy, mod rooms, a cosy-chic lobby, and friendly staff make the Nemours a great bet.

Eating

Rennes has a wide choice of excellent restaurants. It's worth booking ahead. Rues St-Malo and St-Georges are the city's two main 'eat streets'; the latter in particular specialises in crêperies. The daily market **Halles Centrales** (www.les-halles-liberte.fr) is at place Honoré Commeurec, and the large **Saturday morning market** fills the place des Lices. The tourist office has a list of other weekly markets.

★**Le Café du Port** BISTRO €
(☎02 99 30 01 43; 3 rue le Bouteiller; mains €9-14, menu €20; ⏲noon-2pm & 7.30-10.30pm Mon-Wed, to 11pm Thu-Sat; Ⓜ République) Market-fresh produce and great value are the name of the game at this laid-back, modern bistro that also doubles as a popular spot for an early evening drink. Garrulous locals fill the outdoor seating area, tented in winter.

★**La Saint-Georges** CREPERIE €
(☎02 99 38 87 04; www.creperie-saintgeorges.com; 11 rue du Chapitre; mains €5-17, lunch menu €12; ⏲noon-2pm & 7-10.30pm Tue-Sat; Ⓜ République) Where most crêperies play on the twee old-Breton style, this one takes a totally eccentric approach – with its purple, green and gold furnishings and luxurious chairs, this place looks more like a glam Ibizan chill-out club. The crêpes themselves are creative, well presented and loaded with flavour.

★**L'Atelier des Gourmets** TRADITIONAL FRENCH €€
(☎02 99 67 53 84; www.latelierdesgourmets-rennes.fr; 12 rue Nantaise; mains €16-17, lunch menu €13, dinner menus €29; ⏲noon-1.30pm & 7.30-9.30pm Tue-Thu, to 10pm Fri & Sat; Ⓜ République) This smart bistro garners serious accolades in a city where talent is in no short supply. The chef has created a hidden institution in the heart of Rennes, adeptly blending the best of high-end bistro fare with solid regional cuisine. The menu is quite succinct.

★**aozeñ** GASTRONOMIC €€€
(☎02 99 65 64 21; www.aozen-restaurant.com; 12 rue de l'Arsenal; menus €49-80; ⏲8-10pm Tue-Sat; Ⓜ République) One of Rennes' shining stars (and they've earned a Michelin star)! aozeñ's proprietors Caroline and Pierre Legrand focus on ingredients, sustainable, healthy eating, and sharing their culinary know-how. Following through with that philosophy, they have an open kitchen visible from one of the contemporary dining rooms, and they offer monthly cooking courses (€85). Reservations essential.

Drinking & Nightlife

Rue St-Michel – nicknamed 'rue de la Soif' (Thirsty St) for its bars, pubs and cafes – is the best-known drinking strip, but it can get rowdy late at night.

Le Nabuchodonosor WINE BAR
(12 rue Hoche; ⏲noon-11pm Tue-Sat; Ⓜ Ste-Anne) The favoured haunt of arty and intellectual types in Rennes, this charming wine bar is a great place for an evening drink in buzzing surroundings. Feeling peckish? It also serves cheese platters, *tartines* (open sandwiches), salads and desserts.

Oan's Pub PUB
(1 rue Georges Dottin; ⏲5pm-1am Mon-Fri, noon-1am Sat; Ⓜ République) Locals habitually turn up with instruments for impromptu Celtic jam sessions at this cosy cave-like, stone-walled pub with Brittany-brewed Coreff beer on tap. It can get packed.

Le Bar'Hic BAR
(24 place des Lices; ⏲5pm-3am Tue-Sat, 9pm-3am Sun & Mon; Ⓜ Ste-Anne) This inviting bar is a good place for getting a bit of local vibe. It fills up at night, when students and young hipsters stream in for the music events – usually live bands. Earlier in the evening it's much quieter. In warm weather, bag a seat on the terrace and watch the world go by.

Information

Tourist Office (☎02 99 67 11 11; www.tourisme-rennes.com; 11 rue St-Yves; ⏲9am-6pm Mon-Sat, 11am-1pm & 2-6pm Sun; 📶; Ⓜ République) The tourist office offers an audioguide to the city, smartphone apps and a walking map (€.20). Staff can book accommodation.

Getting There & Away

AIR

Rennes' **airport** (RNS; ☎02 99 29 60 00; www.rennes.aeroport.fr) is 8km southwest of the city centre. It offers direct flights to many domestic and European destinations. Bus 57 connects place de la République and the airport, every 20 minutes daily. A taxi costs about €20.

BUS

The bus station is adjacent to the train station. **Illenoo** (☎08 10 35 10 35; www.illenoo-services.fr) offers many daily services in eastern Brittany, including the following:

Dinan €6, 1½ hours, 14 daily Monday to Friday, six Saturday, five Sunday

Dinard €6, two hours, 14 daily Monday to Friday, six Saturday, five Sunday

Paimpont €4.90, one hour, nine daily Monday to Friday, five Saturday

STAR (☎09 70 82 18 00; www.star.fr; 12 rue du Pré Botté) Rennes' efficient local bus network. Tickets (single journey €1.50, 24-hour pass €4) are interchangeable with the metro.

TRAIN

Rennes is a major transport hub for northeast France. By early 2017, Rennes will have brand new TGV tracks to Le Mans, cutting travel times to the east by about 40 minutes. As part of this, the Rennes station is being completely rebuilt. Until it is complete (due in 2019), the area around the station is chaotic; plan for extra time. It's easiest to reach by metro, since the streets are often blocked by construction. Destinations:

Brest €31 to €44, 2¼ hours, seven daily

Dinan from €15.70, 1¼ hours, nine daily

Nantes €26.30, 1¼ hours, nine daily

Paris Montparnasse €40 to €86, 2¼ hours, 24 daily

Quimper €31 to €44, 2½ hours, 11 direct daily

St-Malo €15, one hour, roughly hourly

Vannes €22.50, one to 1½ hours, 14 daily

Vitré

POP 18,080

With its narrow cobbled streets, half-timbered houses and colossal castle topped by witch's-hat turrets, Vitré rivals Dinan as one of Brittany's best-preserved medieval towns – with fewer tourists and a more laissez-faire village air than most. The modern outskirts are sprawling, but the centre is precious.

Sights

Château de Vitré CASTLE

(☎02 99 75 04 54; place du Château; adult/child €6/free; ⏰10am-6pm Jul & Aug, 10am-12.30pm & 2-6pm Apr-Jun & Sep, shorter hours Oct-Mar) Vitré's medieval castle rises on a rocky outcrop overlooking the River Vilaine, and is one of the most impressive in Brittany – a real fairy tale of spires and drawbridges. Beyond the twin-turreted gateway, you'll find a triangular inner courtyard and a warren of semi-furnished rooms. Don't miss the top of the tower of San Lorenzo where paintings by Raoul David and others re-imagine Vitré. The château was originally built in 1060, and expanded in the 14th and 15th centuries.

Sleeping

Le Minotel HOTEL €

(☎02 99 75 11 11; www.leminotel.fr; 47 rue de la Poterie; s €54, d €64-74, t €80, f €90; 📶) Near the train station and the medieval castle, this 15-room hotel is superb value given its coveted location. Freshly maintained rooms are decked out in beige and chocolate hues with modern bathrooms. Opt for the dearer rooms, which are more spacious than the pocket-sized cheaper ones. Cheerful breakfast room, too.

Hôtel du Château HOTEL €

(☎02 99 74 58 59; www.hotelduchateauvitre.fr; 5 rue Rallon; s €51-64, d €57-70, tr €68, q €71; P 📶) Wake up to the aroma of freshly baked bread and, on upper floors (choose room 12, 14 or 15!), fantastic vistas of the castle at this family-run hotel at the base of the ramparts. The rooms are simple and the bathrooms minuscule, but the friendly owners are a great source of local information; there's a nice courtyard for breakfast (€9).

Eating

Auberge du Château CRÊPERIE €

(☎02 99 75 01 83; 34 rue d'En Bas; mains €6-13; ⏰noon-2pm Tue-Sun, 7-9pm Tue-Sat) For crêpes, salads and *tartines*, look no further than the Auberge du Château, which occupies an atmospheric timber-framed house. There's outdoor seating in summer.

Auberge St-Louis TRADITIONAL FRENCH €€

(☎02 99 75 28 28; www.aubergesaintlouis.fr; 31 rue Notre-Dame; menus €18-34; ⏰noon-1.45pm & 7-9.15pm Tue-Sun) Just steps from Notre-Dame church, Auberge St-Louis is as much about ogling original 18th-century decor – check that dark-wood panelling, man! – as feasting on good-value French classics such as grilled kidney veal, duck breast and lamb shanks.

Information

Tourist Office (☎02 99 75 04 46; www.bretagne-vitre.com; place Général de Gaulle; ⏰9.30am-12.30pm & 2-6.30pm Mon-Sat, 10am-12.30pm & 3-6pm Sun Jul & Aug, shorter hours rest of year; 📶) Right outside the train station.

Getting There & Away

Frequent trains travel between Vitré and Rennes (from €8.20, 20 to 35 minutes, 23 per day). Three direct trains a day serve Paris Montparnasse (€40 to €76, two hours).

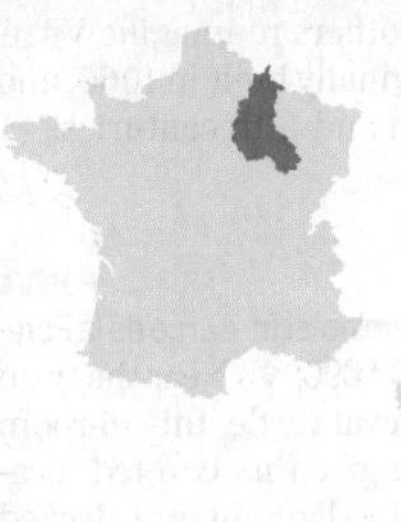

Champagne

POP 1.3 MILLION

Includes ➡

Best Places to Eat

- ➡ Anna-S – La Table Amoureuse (p300)
- ➡ Racine (p300)
- ➡ La Grillade Gourmande (p308)
- ➡ Claire et Hugo (p312)
- ➡ Le Valentino (p312)

Best Places to Sleep

- ➡ Les Telliers (p299)
- ➡ Château Les Crayères (p299)
- ➡ Le Relais St-Jean (p311)
- ➡ La Villa Eugène (p307)
- ➡ Hostellerie La Montagne (p314)
- ➡ Les Avisés (p305)

Why Go?

Champagne arouses the senses: the eyes feast on vines parading up hillsides and vertical processions of tiny, sparkling bubbles; the nose breathes in damp soil and the heavenly bouquet of fermentation; the ears rejoice at the clink of glasses and the barely audible fizz; and the palate tingles with every sip. The imagination and the intellect are engaged as Champagne cellar visits reveal the magical processes – governed by the strictest of rules – that transform the world's most pampered pinot noir, pinot meunier and chardonnay grapes into this Unesco World Heritage–listed region's most fabled wines.

Despite the prestige of their vines, the people of Champagne offer a warm, surprisingly easy-going welcome, both in the stylish cities and along the Champagne Routes, which wend their way through villages to family-run cellars and vineyards.

When to Go

Reims

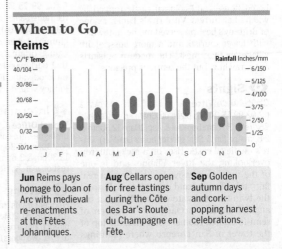

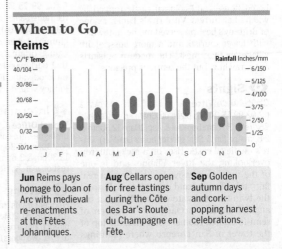

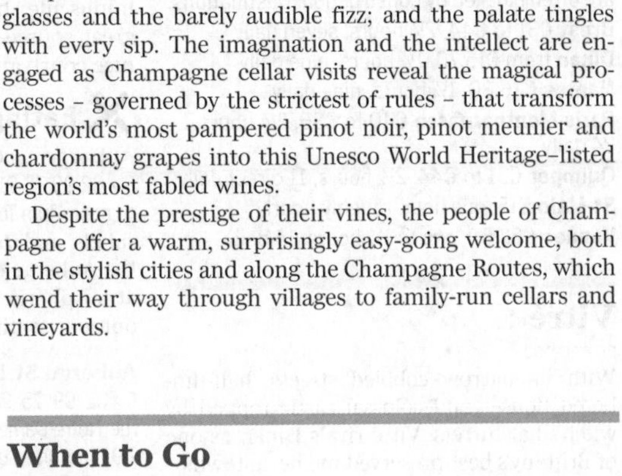

Jun Reims pays homage to Joan of Arc with medieval re-enactments at the Fêtes Johanniques.

Aug Cellars open for free tastings during the Côte des Bar's Route du Champagne en Fête.

Sep Golden autumn days and cork-popping harvest celebrations.

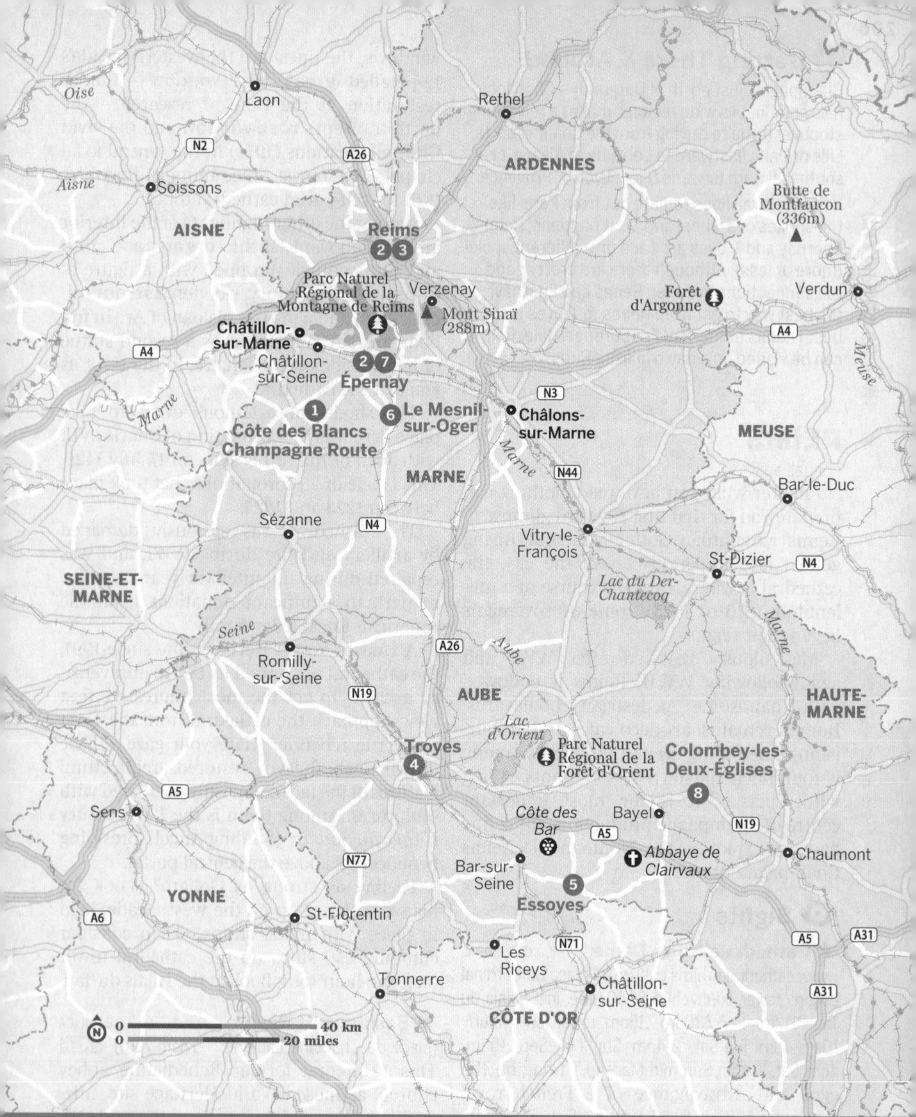

Champagne Highlights

1 Côte des Blancs Champagne Route (p304) Ramble through hillside vineyards and comely villages.

2 Épernay (p306) Toast the end of a cellar tour with a glass of fizz.

3 Cathédrale Notre Dame (p296) Climb the tower of Reims' Gothic wonder.

4 16th-Century Troyes (p309) Slip back to the Middle Ages in half-timbered streets.

5 Atelier Renoir (p315) Tread in Renoir's impressionistic footsteps in pretty-as-a-painting Essoyes.

6 Musée de la Vigne et du Vin (p305) Marvel at Champagne-making techniques in Le Mesnil-sur-Oger.

7 Avenue de Champagne (p306) Revel in the mansions and Champagne houses on Épernay's grandest avenue.

8 Mémorial Charles de Gaulle (p314) Immerse yourself in mid-20th-century France.

Getting There & Around

Champagne, just north of Burgundy's Châtillonnais and Chablis wine regions, makes a refreshing stopover if you're driving from the Channel ports, Lille or Paris eastward to Lorraine or Alsace, or southeastward towards Dijon, Lyon or Provence.

France's rail lines radiate out from Paris like the spokes of a wheel and, as it happens, Reims, Épernay and Troyes are each on a different spoke (more or less). Although there are pretty good rail connections between Reims and Épernay, the best way to get from Reims to Troyes is by bus. Thanks to the TGV Est Européen line, Reims can be visited on a day trip from Paris.

REIMS

POP 186,505

No matter what you have read, nothing can prepare you for that first skyward glimpse of Reims' gargantuan Gothic cathedral. Rising golden and imperious above the city, the cathedral is where, over the course of a millennium (816 to 1825), some 34 sovereigns began their reigns.

Meticulously restored after WWI and again following WWII, Reims is endowed with handsome pedestrian boulevards, Roman remains, art-deco cafes and a flourishing fine-dining scene that counts among it four Michelin-starred restaurants. Along with Épernay, it is the most important centre of Champagne production, and a fine base for exploring the Montagne de Reims Champagne Route.

Sights

★Cathédrale Notre Dame CATHEDRAL

(www.cathedrale-reims.culture.fr; place du Cardinal Luçon; tower adult/child €7.50/free, incl Palais du Tau €11/free; ⌚7.30am-7.15pm, tower tours hourly 10am-4pm Tue-Sat, 2-4pm Sun May-Sep, 10am-4pm Sat, 2-4pm Sun mid-Mar–Apr) Imagine the egos and extravagance of a French royal coronation. The focal point of such bejewelled pomposity was Reims' resplendent Gothic cathedral, begun in 1211 on a site occupied by churches since the 5th century. The interior is a rainbow of stained-glass windows; the finest are the western facade's 12-petalled **great rose window** – under restoration at the time of research – the north transept's **rose window** and the vivid **Chagall** creations (1974) in the central axial chapel. The tourist office rents audioguides (€6) for self-paced cathedral tours.

Among the other highlights of the interior are a flamboyant **Gothic organ case** (15th and 18th centuries) topped with a figure of Christ, a 15th-century wooden **astronomical clock**, and a **statue** of Joan of Arc in full body armour (1901); there's a second statue of her outside on the square, to the right as you exit the cathedral.

The single most famous event to take place here was the coronation of Charles VII, with Joan of Arc at his side, on 17 July 1429. This is one of 25 coronations that took place between 1223 and 1825.

The cathedral was seriously damaged by artillery and fire during WWI, and was repaired during the interwar years, thanks, in part, to significant donations from the American Rockefeller family.

A Unesco World Heritage Site since 1991, the cathedral celebrated its 800th anniversary in 2011. To get the most impressive first view, approach the cathedral from the west, along rue Libergier. Here your gaze will be drawn to the heavily restored architectural features of the façade, lavishly encrusted with sculptures. Among them is the 13th-century *L'Ange au Sourire* (Smiling Angel), presiding beneficently above the central portal.

Feeling as strong as Goliath? (Look for his worn figure up on the west facade, held in place with metal straps.) Then consider climbing 250 steps up the cathedral tower on a one-hour tour. Book at the Palais du Tau.

★Basilique St-Rémi BASILICA

(place du Chanoine Ladame; ⌚8am-7pm) FREE This 121m-long former Benedictine abbey church, a Unesco World Heritage site, mixes Romanesque elements from the mid-11th century (the worn but stunning nave and transept) with early Gothic features from the latter half of the 12th century (the choir, with a large triforium gallery and, way up top, tiny clerestory windows).

Next door, **Musée St-Rémi** (53 rue Simon; adult/child €4/free; ⌚2-6.30pm Mon-Fri, to 7pm Sat & Sun), in a 17th- and 18th-century abbey, features local Gallo-Roman archaeology, tapestries and 16th- to 19th-century military history. The abbey church is named in honour of Bishop Remigius, who baptised

FAST FACTS

Area 25,606 sq km

Local industry Viticulture, agriculture, metallurgy

Signature drink Champagne

Clovis and 3000 Frankish warriors in 498. The 12th-century-style chandelier has 96 candles, one for each year of the life of St Rémi, whose tomb (in the choir) is marked by a mausoleum from the mid-1600s.

★Palais du Tau MUSEUM
(www.palais-du-tau.fr; 2 place du Cardinal Luçon; adult/child €7.50/free, incl cathedral tower €11/free; ⏲9.30am-12.30pm & 2-5.30pm Tue-Sun) A Unesco World Heritage Site, this lavish former archbishop's residence, redesigned in neoclassical style between 1671 and 1710, was where French princes stayed before their coronations – and where they threw sumptuous banquets afterwards. Now a museum, it displays truly exceptional statuary, liturgical objects and tapestries from the cathedral, some in the impressive, Gothic-style Salle de Tau (Great Hall). Treasures worth seeking out include the 9th-century talisman of Charlemagne and Saint Remi's golden, gem-encrusted chalice, which dates to the 12th century.

Musée des Beaux-Arts ART MUSEUM
(8 rue Chanzy; adult/child €4/free; ⏲10am-noon & 2-6pm Wed-Mon) Lodged in an 18th-century abbey, this museum's rich collection stars one of four versions of Jacques-Louis David's world-famous *The Death of Marat* (yes, the bloody corpse in the bath-tub), 27 works by Camille Corot (only the Louvre has more), 13 portraits by German Renaissance painters Cranach the Elder and the Younger, lots of Barbizon School landscapes, some art-nouveau creations by Émile Gallé, and two works each by Monet, Gauguin and Pissarro.

Musée Hôtel Le Vergeur MUSEUM
(www.museelevergeur.com; 36 place du Forum; adult/child €5/free; ⏲2-6pm Tue-Sun) Highlights in this 13th- to 16th-century townhouse include a series of furnished period rooms (kitchen, smoking room, Napoléon III's bedroom), some engravings by Albrecht Dürer and a stunning Renaissance facade facing the interior garden.

Musée de la Reddition WAR MUSEUM
(12 rue Franklin Roosevelt; adult/child €4/free; ⏲10am-noon & 2-6pm Wed-Mon) The original Allied battle maps are still affixed to the walls of US General Dwight D Eisenhower's headquarters, where Nazi Germany, represented by General Alfred Jodl, surrendered unconditionally at 2.41am on 7 May 1945, thus ending WWII. Displays include military uniforms and photographs. A 12-minute film is screened in French, English and German.

DON'T MISS

ART DECO REIMS

The vaulted **Halles du Boulingrin** (rue de Mars; ⏲food market 7am-1pm Wed, 7am-1pm & 4-8pm Fri, 6am-2pm Sat) were a symbol of Reims' emergence from the destruction of WWI when they began service as the city's main food market in 1929. Following a major restoration project, the Halles were reopened in all their art-deco glory in September 2012. Besides sheltering a food market, they provide a unique backdrop for exhibitions and cultural events.

Thanks to a donation from the US-based Carnegie Foundation, the lobby of the **Bibliothèque** (2 place Carnegie; ⏲10am-1pm & 2-7pm Tue, Wed & Fri, 2-7pm Thu, 10am-1pm & 2-6pm Sat) boasts gorgeous 1920s mosaics, stained glass, frescos and an extraordinary chandelier – duck inside for a look. The tourist office also has a brochure on art-deco sites around Reims.

Porte de Mars HISTORIC SITE
(Mars Gate; place de la République) For a quick trip back to Roman Gaul, check out the massive Porte de Mars, a three-arched triumphal gate built in the 2nd century AD. The gate was undergoing total renovation at the time of writing and was expected to reopen in all its glory in late 2016.

Cryptoportique HISTORIC SITE
(place du Forum; ⏲2-6pm Jun-Sep) FREE One of Reims' Roman standouts, the below-street-level Cryptoportique is thought to have been used for grain storage in the 3rd century AD.

☞ Tours

★Taittinger CHAMPAGNE HOUSE
(☎03 26 85 45 35; www.taittinger.com; 9 place St-Niçaise; tours €17-45; ⏲9.30am-5.30pm, shorter hours & closed weekends Oct-Mar) The headquarters of Taittinger are an excellent place to come for a clear, straightforward presentation on how Champagne is actually made – there's no claptrap about 'the Champagne mystique' here. Parts of the cellars occupy 4th-century Roman stone quarries; other bits were excavated by 13th-century Benedictine monks. No need to reserve. Situated 1.5km southeast of Reims centre; take the Citadine 1 or 2 bus to the St-Niçaise or Salines stops.

Reims

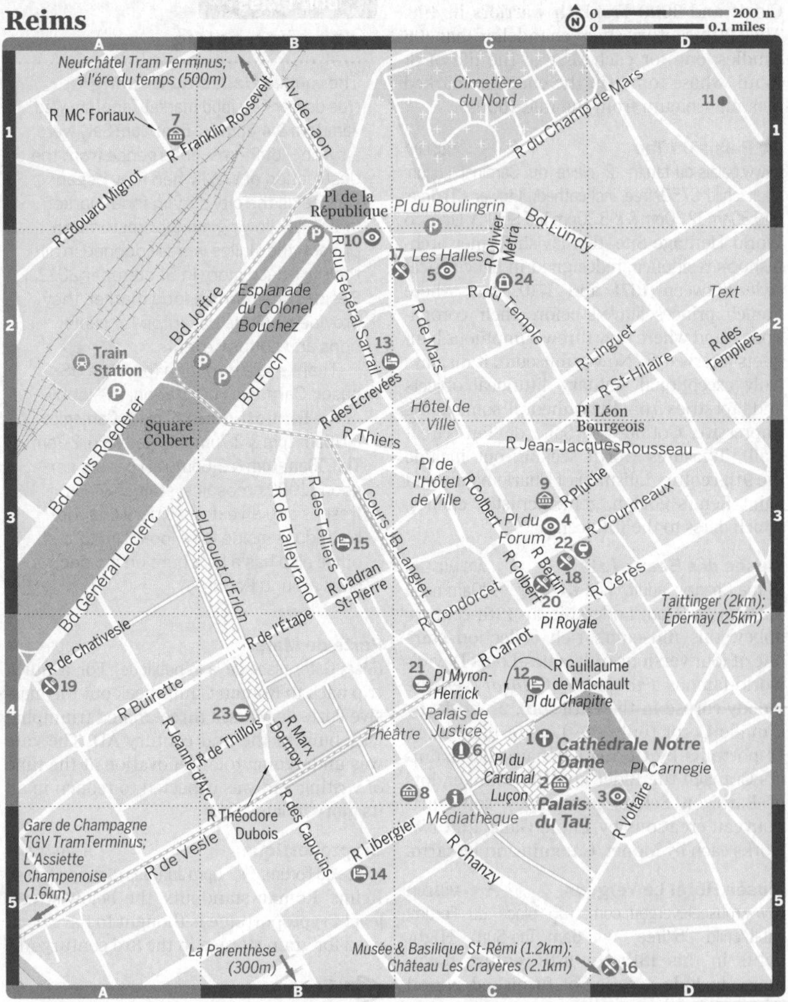

Mumm CHAMPAGNE HOUSE

(☎03 26 49 59 70; www.mumm.com; 34 rue du Champ de Mars; tours incl tasting €20-45; ⊙tours 9.30am-1pm & 2-6pm daily, shorter hours & closed Sun Oct-Mar) Mumm (pronounced 'moom'), the only *maison* in central Reims, was founded in 1827 and is now the world's third-largest producer (almost eight million bottles a year). Engaging and edifying guided tours take you through cellars filled with 25 million bottles of fine bubbly and conclude with a tasting. Wheelchair accessible. Phone ahead if possible.

Festivals & Events

Fêtes Johanniques CULTURAL

Reims pays homage to heroine Joan of Arc with medieval re-enactments on the first weekend in June. The line-up is packed with activities from jousting and street markets to falconry and craft displays.

Sleeping

Chambre d'Hôte Cathédrale B&B €

(☎03 26 91 06 22; 21 place du Chapitre; s/d/tr without bathroom €55/65/80) The cathedral bells are your wake-up call at this sweet and simple B&B. Rooms are immaculate and

Reims

old-fashioned, with stripy wallpaper, heavy wood furnishings and shared bathrooms.

Hôtel Azur B&B €
(☎03 26 47 43 39; www.hotel-azur-reims.com; 9 rue des Ecrevées; s €55-85, d €69-99, tr €99, q €109; P 📶) Slip down a sidestreet in the heart of Reims to reach this petite B&B, which extends a heartfelt welcome. Rooms are cheerfully painted and immaculately kept, and breakfast is served on the garden patio when the sun's out. There's no lift, so be prepared to lug your bags.

★ **Les Telliers** B&B €€
(☎09 53 79 80 74; http://telliers.fr; 18 rue des Telliers; s €67-84, d €79-120, tr €116-141, q €132-162; P 📶) Enticingly positioned down a quiet alley near the cathedral, this bijou B&B extends one of Reims' warmest *bienvenues*. The high-ceilinged rooms are big on art-deco character, and handsomely decorated with ornamental fireplaces, polished oak floors and the odd antique. Breakfast costs an extra €9 and is a generous spread of pastries, fruit, fresh-pressed juice and coffee.

La Parenthèse B&B €€
(☎03 26 40 39 57; www.laparenthese.fr; 83 rue Clovis; min 2-night stay d €180-240; 📶) Tucked away in the backstreets of old Reims, this little B&B has got everything going for it. The rooms are tastefully done with wood floors and bursts of pastel colour, and all come with kitchenettes. The good-natured owner will squeeze in a cot if you ask.

La Demeure des Sacres B&B €€
(☎06 79 06 80 68; www.la-demeure-des-sacres.com; 29 rue Libergier; d €145, ste €220-245; 📶) Nuzzled in an art deco townhouse close to the cathedral, this B&B harbours four wood-floored rooms and suites, with pleasing original features like marble fireplaces and free-standing bath-tubs. The Royal Suite has cracking cathedral views. Homemade treats (preserves, crêpes and the like) appear at breakfast, which is included in the room rate. There is a secluded garden for post-sightseeing moments.

★ **Château Les Crayères** LUXURY HOTEL €€€
(☎03 26 24 90 00; www.lescrayeres.com; 64 bd Henry-Vasnier; d €395-755; P ❄ @ 📶) Such class! If you've ever wanted to stay in a palace, this romantic château on the fringes of Reims is the real McCoy. Manicured lawns sweep to the graceful turn-of-the-century estate, where you can play golf or tennis, dine in two-Michelin-starred finery, and stay in the lap of luxury in exuberantly furnished, chandelier-lit interiors – all at a price, naturally.

L'Assiette Champenoise BOUTIQUE HOTEL €€€
(☎03 26 84 64 64; www.assiettechampenoise.com; 40 av Paul-Vaillant-Couturier, Tinqueux; r €245-360, ste €470-780) Occupying a stout mansion, this five-star pad is often fully booked with gastronomes, here for the three-Michelin-starred restaurant. Modern-minimalist rooms and suites sport a smattering of designer flourishes. Swishest of all is the Terrace Suite with private whirlpool. There's a chic bar for predinner drinks and an indoor

PASS REIMS

The great-value **Pass Reims** (€9), available at the tourist office, gives you entry to a museum of your choice, an audioguide tour of the city, plus discounts on activities such as Champagne house visits.

pool. It's 2km west of central Reims in the suburb of Tinqueux.

Eating

A tempting array of delis, patisseries and chocolatiers line rue de Mars, near Halles du Boulingrin. Place du Forum is a great place to watch the world drift languidly by at bistros, cafes and bars with pavement seating.

à l'ère du temps CRÊPERIE €
(03 26 06 16 88; www.aleredutemps.com; 123 av de Laon; lunch menu €10, mains €7-14; 11.45am-2pm & 6.45-9.30pm Tue-Sat) A short stroll north of place de la République brings you to this sweet and simple crêperie. It does a roaring trade in homemade crêpes, buckwheat *galettes* and gourmet salads.

La Cave aux Fromages CHEESE €
(12 place du Forum; 8.30am-1pm & 3.30-7.30pm Tue-Sat) Run by the knowledgeable Charlet family, this fabulous shop is *fromage* heaven, with cheeses carefully sourced from all four corners of France. Among them is the regional speciality Cendré de Champagne, a creamy, smoky cheese matured in beech ash.

Anna-S – La Table Amoureuse TRADITIONAL FRENCH €€
(03 26 89 12 12; www.annas-latableamoureuse.com; 6 rue Gambetta; 3-course lunch €17.50, dinner menus €29-47; noon-1.30pm & 7-9pm Tue & Thu-Sat, noon-1.30pm Wed & Sun) So what if the decor is chintzy – there is a reason why this bistro is as busy as a beehive. Friendly service and a menu packed with well-done classics – Arctic char with Champagne jus, fillet of veal in rich, earthy morel sauce – hit the mark every time. The three-course lunch is a steal at €17.50.

Brasserie Le Boulingrin BRASSERIE €€
(03 26 40 96 22; www.boulingrin.fr; 29-31 rue de Mars; menus €20-29; noon-2.30pm & 7-10.30pm Mon-Sat) A genuine, old-time brasserie – the decor and zinc bar date back to 1925 – whose ambience and cuisine make it an enduring favourite. From September to June, the culinary focus is on *fruits de mer* (seafood) such as Breton oysters. There's always a €9.50 lunch special.

l'Alambic FRENCH €€
(03 26 35 64 93; www.restaurant-lalambic.fr; 63 bis rue de Chativesle; mains €14-23; noon-2pm & 7-9.30pm Tue-Fri, 7-9.30pm Sat & Mon;) Ideal for an intimate dinner, this vaulted cellar dishes up well-prepared French classics – along the lines of home-smoked trout with horseradish, cod fillet with Champagne-laced *choucroute*, and pigeon served two ways with Reims mustard sauce. Save room for terrific desserts such as *crème brûlée* with chicory ice cream. The *plat du jour* is a snip at €11.

★ l'Assiette Champenoise GASTRONOMIC €€€
(03 26 84 64 64; www.assiettechampenoise.com; 40 av Paul-Vaillant-Couturier, Tinqueux; menus €95-255; noon-2pm & 7.30-10pm Thu-Mon, 7.30-10pm Wed) Heralded far and wide as one of Champagne's finest tables and crowned with the holy grail of three Michelin stars, L'Assiette Champenoise is headed up by chef Arnaud Lallemen. Listed by ingredients, his intricate, creative dishes rely on outstanding produce and play up integral flavours – be it Breton lobster, or milk-fed lamb with preserved vegetables. One for special occasions.

★ Racine JAPANESE €€€
(03 26 35 16 95; www.racine.re; 8 rue Colbert; menus €39-90; noon-1.30pm & 7-9pm Thu-Mon) With strong Japanese roots and a generous pinch of love for his adopted home, chef Kazuyuki creates menus that sing with bright flavours and are delivered with finesse at slick, monochrome Racine. They're listed in the modern, ingredient-driven way, so turbot with squash and pistachio, pineapple with lemon and Champagne ice-cream, and the like. Insiders are whispering Michelin star...

Drinking & Nightlife

Le Wine Bar by Le Vintage WINE BAR
(http://winebar-reims.com; 16 place du Forum; 6pm-12.30am Tue-Thu to 1.30am Fri & Sat) This bijou wine bar is a convivial spot to chill over a glass of wine or Champagne (some 500 are offered) with a tasting plate of charcuterie and cheese. The friendly brothers that own the place are happy to give recommendations.

Café du Palais CAFE
(www.cafedupalais.fr; 14 place Myron-Herrick; 9am-9.30pm Tue-Sat) Run by the same family since 1930, this art-deco cafe is *the* place

to sip a glass of Champagne. Lit by a skylight is an extraordinary collection of bric-a-brac ranging from the inspired to the kitsch.

Waïda TEAROOM

(5 place Drouet d'Erlon; ⏲7.30am-7.30pm Tue-Fri, 7.30am-8pm Sat, 8am-2pm & 3.30-7.30pm Sun) A tearoom and confectioner with old-fashioned mirrors, mosaics and marble. This is a good place to pick up a box of Reims' famous *biscuits roses,* traditionally nibbled with Champagne, rainbow-bright macarons and divine *religieuses* (cream-filled puff pastries).

Shopping

Trésors de Champagne WINE

(www.boutique-tresors-champagne.com; 2 rue Olivier Métra; ⏲2-7pm Tue & Wed, 10.30am-12.30pm & 2-7pm Thu & Fri, 10am-7pm Sat) Strikingly illuminated by Champagne bottles, this swish new wine boutique-cum-bar plays host to 28 vintners and more than 170 Champagnes. There is a different selection available to taste each week. Keep an eye out, too, for tasting workshops posted on the website.

Information

The **tourist office** (☎03 26 77 45 00; www.reims-tourisme.com; 6 rue Rockefeller; ⏲10am-6pm Mon-Sat, 10am-12.30pm & 1.30-5pm Sun) has stacks of information on the Champagne region and Reims (plus free city maps).

Getting There & Away

Reims train station, 1km northwest of the cathedral, was renovated in 2010; the bullet marks on the facade date from both world wars. Frequent services run to Paris Gare de l'Est (€19 to €63, 46 minutes to one hour, 12 to 17 daily). Direct services also go to Épernay (€7, 20 to 42 minutes, 16 daily) and Laon (€10.40, 36 to 47 minutes, three to nine daily). The journey to Troyes (€37 to €83, 2½ to 3½ hours, 10 daily) involves at least one change.

CHAMPAGNE ROUTES OF THE MARNE

The Champagne Routes of the Marne département wend their way among neat rows of hillside vines, through hilltop forests and across lowland crop fields. Along the way, they call on wine-making villages and hamlets, some with notable churches or museums, others quite ordinary, most without a centre or even a cafe. At almost every turn, beautiful panoramas unfold and small-scale, family-run Champagne wineries welcome travellers in search of bubbly.

Many producers prefer that visitors phone ahead but, if you haven't, don't be shy about knocking on the door. More and more young *vignerons* (winegrowers) speak English. Almost all producers are closed around the *vendange* (grape harvest, from late August to October), when bringing in the crop eclipses all other activities.

Montagne de Reims Champagne Route

Linking Reims with Épernay by skirting the Parc Natural Régional de la Montagne de Reims, a regional park covering the forested Reims Mountain plateau, this meandering, 70km route passes through vineyards planted mainly with pinot noir vines. Villages are listed in the order you'll encounter them if starting out from Reims.

MAKING FIZZ

Champagne is made from the red pinot noir (38%), the black pinot meunier (35%) or the white chardonnay (27%) grape. Each vine is vigorously pruned and trained to produce a small quantity of high-quality grapes. Indeed, to maintain exclusivity (and price), the designated areas where grapes used for Champagne can be grown and the amount of wine produced each year are limited.

Making Champagne according to the traditional method (*méthode champenoise*) is a complex procedure. There are two fermentation processes, the first in casks and the second after the wine has been bottled and had sugar and yeast added. Bottles are then aged in cellars for two to five years, depending on the *cuvée* (vintage). During the two months in early spring that the bottles are aged in cellars kept at 12°C, the wine turns effervescent. The sediment that forms in the bottle is removed by *remuage,* a painstakingly slow process in which each bottle, stored horizontally, is rotated slightly every day for weeks until the sludge works its way to the cork. Next comes *dégorgement:* the neck of the bottle is frozen, creating a blob of solidified Champagne and sediment, then removed.

Routes of the Marne

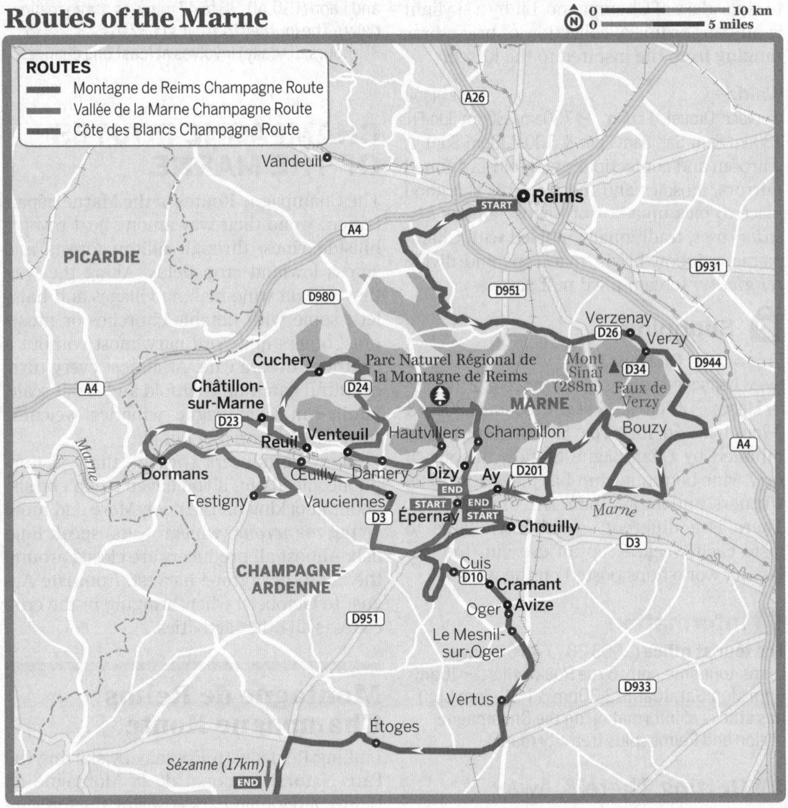

Verzenay

POP 1048

With vines spreading like a ribbed blanket over the hillsides and top-of-the-beanstalk views from its lighthouse, Verzenay makes an attractive stop on the Montagne de Reims Champagne Route. Its vines are planted mostly with pinot noir grapes – 100% *grand cru*.

Sights & Activities

Phare & Musée de Verzenay VIEWPOINT

(Verzenay Lighthouse; www.lepharedeverzenay.com; D26; lighthouse adult/child €3/2, museum €8/4, combined ticket €9/5; ⏲10am-5pm Tue-Fri, to 5.30pm Sat & Sun, closed Jan) For the region's best introduction to the art of growing grapes and the cycles of the seasons, head to the **Phare de Verzenay**, on a hilltop at the eastern edge of the village. Exactly 101 spiral stairs lead to the top of the lighthouse, constructed as a publicity stunt in 1909, which rewards visitors with unsurpassed 360-degree views of vine, field and forest – and, if you're lucky, a tiny TGV zipping by in the distance.

The Sillery sugar mill, visible on the horizon, turns an astounding 16,000 tonnes of beets (a major regional crop) into 2600 tonnes of sugar each day! After brushing up on the seasonal processes involved in Champagne production in the museum, stop by the tasting room for a glass of fizz (there are 30 varieties to sample).

Jardin Panoramique GARDENS

FREE Verzenay's Jardin Panoramique demonstrates the four authorised techniques for tying grapevines to guide wires.

Étienne and Anne-Laure Lefevre CHAMPAGNE HOUSE

(☎03 26 97 96 99; www.champagne-etienne-lefevre.com; 30 rue de Villers; ⏲9-11.30am & 1.30-5.30pm Mon-Sat) Étienne and Anne-Laure Lefevre run group tours of their family-owned vineyards and cellars – if you're on your own, ring

ahead to see if you can join a pre-arranged tour. There are no flashy videos or multimedia shows – the emphasis is firmly on the nitty-gritty of Champagne production.

Parc Natural Régional de la Montagne de Reims

The 500-sq-km Montagne de Reims Regional Park is best known for a botanical curiosity, 800 mutant beech trees known as faux de Verzy (see http://verzy.verzenay.online.fr). To get a good look at the trees, which have twisted trunks and branches that hang down like an umbrella, take the Balade des Faux forest walk from 'Les Faux' parking lot, 2km up D34 from Verzy (situated on D26).

Across D34, a 500m gravel path leads through the forest to a *point de vue* (panoramic viewpoint) – next to a concrete WWI bunker – atop 288m-high Mont Sinaï.

Squirrelled away deep in the forest is the **Perching Bar** (www.perchingbar.eu; Forêt de Brise-Charrette, Verzy; ⏲noon-2pm & 4-8pm Wed-Sun mid-Apr–mid-Dec), a slick, Nordic-cool treehouse that commands broad views over valley and vine – and we just love those swings! It's accessed via wooden walkways raised above the trees. Your €17 gets you a glass of Champagne. The bar champions both the *grandes maisons* and small producers.

Vallée de la Marne Champagne Route

A stronghold of pinot meunier vines, this 90km itinerary winds from Épernay to Dormans, heading more or less west along the hillsides north of the River Marne, then circles back to the east along the river's south bank. The GR14 long-distance walking trail and its variants (eg GR141) pass through the area.

Hautvillers

POP 789

Perched above a sea of emerald vines and ablaze with forsythia and tulips in spring, Hautvillers is where Dom Pierre Pérignon (1638–1715) is popularly believed to have created Champagne. The village is one of Champagne's prettiest, with ubiquitous medieval-style wrought-iron signs providing pictorial clues to the activities taking place on the other side of the wall.

Astonishing vineyard views await a few hundred metres north of the centre along route de Fismes (D386); south along route de Cumières (a road leading to D1); and along the GR14 long-distance walking trail (red-and-white markings) and local vineyard footpaths (yellow markings).

Sights

Volière des Cigognes Altavilloises BIRD SANCTUARY

(D386) FREE Hautvillers is twinned with the Alsatian town of Eguisheim, which explains why several storks (including one rare black one) live here, an easy 500m walk towards Épernay from place de la République. It's a great opportunity to get a close-up view of these majestic birds. In most years, storklings hatch here in late April and May.

Abbaye Saint-Pierre d'Hautvillers CHURCH

The good Dom Pérignon's tomb is in front of the altar of the Église Abbatiale, adorned with 17th-century woodwork.

Drinking & Nightlife

★ **Au 36** WINE BAR

(www.au36.net; 36 rue Dom Pérignon; ⏲10.30am-6pm Tue-Sun, closed Christmas-early Mar) This slinky wine boutique has a 'wall' of Champagne, innovatively arranged by aroma, and a laid-back upstairs tasting room. A two-/three glass tasting costs €12/16, while a six-glass tasting for two people costs €36. A tasting platter of Champagne specialities costs €18.

Information

The attractive main square is place de la République. Here you'll find the helpful **tourist office** (☎03 26 57 06 35; www.tourisme-hautvillers.com; ⏲9.30am-1pm & 1.30-5.30pm Mon-Sat, 10am-4pm Sun, shorter hours in winter), where you can pick up excellent free maps for several vineyard walks. One-hour guided tours cost €3 (with a Champagne tasting €5).

Châtillon-sur-Marne

POP 845

Sloping picturesquely down a hillside and braided with vines, this village's biggest claim to fame is as the hometown of Pope Urban II. A map panel on central place Urbain II details an 11km, four-hour vineyard walk. Its cellars also produce Champagnes worth lingering for.

Sights

Albert Levasseur CHAMPAGNE HOUSE

(☎03 26 58 11 38; www.champagne-levasseur.fr; 6 rue Sorbier, Cuchery; ⏲9am-noon & 2-5pm Mon-Fri, Sat by appointment) You're assured a warm –

and English-speaking – welcome and a fascinating cellar tour at Albert Levasseur, run by a friendly Franco-Irish couple, which turns grapes grown on 4.2 hectares into 35,000 to 40,000 bottles of Champagne each year. Try to phone or email ahead if possible – but if not just drop by and knock. Situated in the hamlet of Cuchery (population 438), 7.5km northeast of Châtillon-sur-Marne on D24.

Pope Urban II STATUE

The highest point in Châtillon-sur-Marne is crowned by a 25m-high statue of Pope Urban II, dedicated in 1887, a particularly successful local boy (1042–99) best known to history for having launched the bloody First Crusade. The orientation table near the base offers excellent views of the Marne Valley and is a super spot for a picnic.

Sleeping

Domaine du Moulin de l'Étang B&B €€

(☎03 26 58 72 95; Moulin de l'Étang; d €109-125; P 📶) Ah, such peace! This squat 18th-century farmhouse B&B reclines in the prettiest setting of vineyards and pond-speckled gardens. Rooms are furnished in nouveau-rustic style, with stone walls, earthy hues and natural fabrics. The lovely owner prepares great breakfasts and can advise on local Champagne *dégustations* (tastings).

Information

The **tourist office** (☎03 26 58 32 86; www.tourisme-chatillon-marne.fr; 4 rue de l'Eglise; ⏲10am-1pm & 2.30-6.30pm Tue-Sun, 2.30-6.30pm Mon, shorter hours Oct-Mar) has plenty of info on the village and the surrounding region.

Œuilly

POP 612

Blink and you'll miss dinky Œuilly, on the Vallée de la Marne Champagne Route, but that would be a shame. This cute grey-stone village, flower-draped in summer, is topped by a 13th-century church and home to a museum spotlighting winegrowing life of yore.

To get a sense of winegrowing life a century ago, drop by the **Écomusée d'Œuilly** (www.ecomusee-oeuilly.fr; cour des Maillets; adult/child €7/4; ⏲tours 10.30am & 2pm Wed-Mon) whose three sections showcasing traditional viticulture methods and country life include a schoolroom, c 1900.

Côte des Blancs Champagne Route

This 100km route, planted almost exclusively with white chardonnay grapes (the name means 'hillside of the whites'), begins along Épernay's majestic av du Champagne and then heads south to Sézanne and beyond. The gently rolling landscape is at its most attractive in late summer and autumn.

Avize

POP 1936

Right in the heart of Blancs des Blancs country and surrounded by rows of immaculately tended vines, which yield the chardonnay grapes that go into producing some of the world's finest fizz, Avize is lauded far and wide for its outstanding Champagnes. It's home to the Champagne High School of Wine Making and the renowned Sanger Cellars.

Sights

Sanger Cellars CHAMPAGNE HOUSE

(☎03 26 57 79 79; www.sanger.fr; 33 rue du Rempart du Midi; tour incl 2-/4-/9-flute tasting €10/17.50/30, full-day masterclass €60; ⏲8am-noon & 2-5pm Mon-Fri) At the Sanger Cellars, tours of the Avize Viti Campus' impressive production facilities take in traditional equipment and the latest high-tech machinery, such as a gadget that removes sediment from the necks of bottles after *remuage* (riddling) by an automated *gyropalette*. Tours include a tasting.

Champagnes are sold at the discounted *prix départ cave* (cellar-door prices) and profits are reinvested in the school. The entrance is on the D19; if the door is locked, push the intercom button.

Avize Viti Campus CHAMPAGNE HOUSE

(Champagne High School of Wine Making; www.avizeviticampus.fr; rue d'Oger) Many past, present and future Champagne makers learn, or are learning, their art and science at the Avize Viti Campus run by the Ministry of Agriculture. As part of their studies, students produce quite excellent bubbly, made with grapes from some of Champagne's most prestigious parcels and sold under the label Champagne Sanger (www.sanger.fr). Sanger was established shortly after WWI, and the name is from 'sans guerre' ('without war'), pronounced sahn-*gher*.

MORE BUBBLES ALL ROUND

Around 55% of the Champagne sold each year is popped open, sipped and savoured in France itself. That doesn't leave much for the rest of us, especially when you consider how many bottles are wasted naming ships and showering victorious football players. But help is at hand. Faced with rising worldwide demand, the government body that regulates where Champagne can be grown has proposed expanding the area – currently 327 sq km – for the first time since 1927. From 2017, 40 very lucky villages are likely to start planting their very first official Champagne vines. Not surprisingly, the exact delineation of the new vineyards has been hugely controversial, not least because the value of land declared Champagne-worthy will rise by up to 30,000%, to about €1 million per hectare!

Large *maisons* (Champagne houses) with global brand recognition send a high percentage of their production to other countries (Moët & Chandon, for example, exports 80% of its bubbly). But the region's 4800 small producers (known as *récoltants-manipulants* because they both harvest the grapes and turn the juice into wine) continue to serve an almost exclusively domestic clientele.

The global thirst for French fizz shows no sign of waning – 2015 was a record year for Champagne sales, with 312 million bottles sold and a rise of around 3% from 2014, thanks to growing demand from export markets, buoyant currencies and increased sales in France. Coupled with the fact that the region was finally awarded Unesco World Heritage status, it seems that Champagne does indeed have every reason to celebrate.

Église St-Nicolas CHURCH

(rue de l'Église (D10)) Once the abbey church of a Benedictine convent, Église St-Nicolas mixes Romanesque, Flamboyant Gothic and Renaissance styles. From here, aptly named rue de la Montagne leads up the hill (towards Grauves), past an oversized Champagne bottle, to Parc Vix (D19), which affords panoramic vineyard views; a map sign details a 6.5km, two-hour walk through forest and field.

Sleeping & Eating

Les Avisés HISTORIC HOTEL €€€

(☎03 26 57 70 06; www.selosse-lesavises.com; 59 rue de Cramant, Avize; d €250-390) Housed in a splendid neoclassical manor, Les Avisés is a touch of class in the heart of Champagne. Overlooking the park or vineyards, rooms manage the delicate act of combining historic and contemporary, with muted colours and clean lines. Regional cuisine is prepared with flair and served with top-quality wines (some produced on the estate) in the intimate restaurant (*menus* €30 to €60).

Oger

POP 592

The tiny hamlet of Oger is known for its *grand cru* fields, prize-winning flower gardens and the **Musée du Mariage** (www.champagne-henry-devaugency.fr; 1 rue d'Avize, D10; adult/child €8/free; ⌚9.30am-noon & 2-6pm Tue-Sun). Featuring colourful and often gaudy objects associated with 19th-century marriage traditions, highlights include a tableau of newlyweds in their nuptial bed – but they're not alone, for they've been woken up early by family and friends bearing Champagne, chocolate and broad smiles. The collection was assembled by the parents of the owner of Champagne Henry de Vaugency (founded 1732), an eighth-generation Champagne grower. An explanatory sheet in English is available. The price of entry includes a Champagne tasting.

Le Mesnil-sur-Oger

POP 1077

This comely winegrowing village on the Côte des Blancs Champagne Route is among the most famous, with 100% of its chardonnay vines producing the superlative *grand cru* Champagnes. It's worth the pilgrimage alone for an insight into Champagne making and its history at the Musée de la Vigne et du Vin.

Activities

★Musée de la Vigne et du Vin TOUR

(☎03 26 57 50 15; www.champagne-launois.fr; 2 av Eugène Guillaume, cnr D10; adult incl 3 flutes €12; ⌚tours 10am Mon-Fri, 10.30am Sat & Sun) This is so outstanding that it's worth planning your day around a two-hour tour. Assembled by a family that has been making Champagne since 1872, this extraordinary collection of century-old Champagne-making equipment includes objects so aesthetically ravishing

CHAMPAGNE TYPES

Blanc de Blancs Champagne made using only chardonnay grapes. Fresh and elegant, with very small bubbles and a bouquet reminiscent of 'yellow fruits' such as pear and plum.

Blanc de Noirs A full-bodied, deep golden Champagne made solely with black grapes (despite the colour). Often rich and refined, with great complexity and a long finish.

Rosé Pink Champagne (mostly served as an aperitif), with a fresh character and summer fruit flavours. Made by adding a small percentage of red pinot noir to white Champagne.

Prestige Cuvée The crème de la crème of Champagne. Usually made with grapes from *grand cru* vineyards and priced and bottled accordingly.

Millésimé Vintage Champagne produced from a single crop during an exceptional year. Most Champagne is non-vintage.

that you'll want to reach out and touch them. Among the highlights is a massive 16-tonne oak grape press from 1630. Reservations can be made by phone or through the website; tours are available in French and English.

Sleeping & Eating

Champagne Baradon Michaudet B&B €

(☎03 26 57 19 70; www.champagne-baradon-michaudet.com; 58 Grand'Rue; s €72-82, d €79-89, tr €91, q €111; P) Stay with the Champagne makers at this attractive little B&B, with four rooms and one *gîte* (self-catering apartment) big enough to accommodate a family. The decor is delightfully old school, with florals, flounces and wood beams, and it's not every day you find *grand cru* Champagne in your minibar! The friendly hosts put on a generous spread at breakfast.

La Gare FRENCH €€

(☎03 26 51 59 55; www.lagarelemesnil.com; 3 place de la Gare; menus €18-26; ⏲noon-1.30pm Mon-Wed, noon-1.30pm & 7-9pm Thu-Sat; 👪) Decked out like a station, La Gare prides itself on serving bistro-style grub prepared with seasonal produce, simple as pork tenderloin with cider and potatoes, grilled salmon with hollandaise and beef cooked in red wine. There's a €9 menu for *les petits*.

ÉPERNAY

POP 23,529

Prosperous Épernay, the self-proclaimed *capitale du Champagne* and home to many of the world's most celebrated Champagne houses, is the best place for touring cellars and sampling bubbly. The town also makes an excellent base for exploring the Champagne Routes.

Beneath the streets in 110km of subterranean cellars, more than 200 million bottles of Champagne, just waiting to be popped open on some sparkling occasion, are being aged. In 1950 one such cellar – owned by the irrepressible Mercier family – hosted a car rally without the loss of a single bottle!

Sights

★Avenue de Champagne STREET

Épernay's handsome av de Champagne fizzes with *maisons de champagne* (Champagne houses). The boulevard is lined with mansions and neoclassical villas, rebuilt after WWI. Peek through wrought-iron gates at Moët's private **Hôtel Chandon**, an early 19th-century pavilion-style residence set in landscaped gardens, which counts Wagner among its famous past guests. The haunted-looking **Château Perrier**, a red-brick mansion built in 1854 in neo-Louis XIII style, is aptly placed at number 13! The roundabout presents photo ops with its giant cork and bottle-top.

★Moët & Chandon CHAMPAGNE HOUSE

(☎03 26 51 20 20; www.moet.com; 20 av de Champagne; adult incl 1/2 glasses €23/28, 10-18yr €10; ⏲tours 9.30-11.30am & 2-4.30pm Apr–mid-Nov, 9.30-11.30am & 2-4.30pm Mon-Fri mid-Nov–Mar) Flying the Moët, French, European and Russian flags, this prestigious *maison* offers frequent one-hour tours that are among the region's most impressive, offering a peek at part of its 28km labyrinth of *caves* (cellars). At the shop, you can pick up a 15L bottle of Brut Impérial for just €1500; a standard bottle will set you back €31.

Mercier CHAMPAGNE HOUSE

(☎03 26 51 22 22; www.champagnemercier.fr; 68-70 av de Champagne; adult incl 1/2/3 glasses €14/19/22 Mon-Fri, €16/21/25 Sat & Sun, 12-17yr €8; ⏲tours 9.30-11.30am & 2-4.30pm, closed mid-Dec–mid-Feb) France's most popular brand was founded in 1847 by Eugène Mercier, a trailblazer in the field of eye-catching publicity stunts and the virtual creator of the cellar tour. Everything here is flashy, including the 160,000L barrel that took two decades to

build (for the Universal Exposition of 1889), the lift that transports you 30m underground and the laser-guided touring train.

Champagne Georges Cartier CHAMPAGNE HOUSE
(☎03 26 32 06 22; www.georgescartier.com; 9 rue Jean Chandon Moët; adult incl 1/2 glasses €12/16, 2-glass Grand Cru €22, 3-glass vintage €35; ⏲tours 10.30am, noon, 2.30pm, 4pm Tue-Sun) Hewn out of the chalk in the 18th century, the warren of cellars and passageways at Champagne Georges Cartier is incredibly atmospheric. Look out for the fascinating graffiti (both in French and German) dating to when they were used as bunkers during WWII. Tours are followed by a tasting of the *maison*'s Champagnes.

Tours & Courses

Champagne Domi Moreau BUS
(☎06 30 35 51 07, after 7pm 03 26 59 45 85; www.champagne-domimoreau.com; 11 rue de Bas, Mancy; tours €30; ⏲tours 9.30am & 2.30pm except Wed, Sun & Aug) Nathalie and Max run scenic and insightful three-hour minibus tours, in French and English, of nearby vineyards. Pick-up is across the street from the tourist office. Call ahead for reservations.

Villa Bissinger WINE
(☎03 26 55 78 78; www.villabissinger.com; 15 rue Jeanson, Ay; 2hr workshop €25; ⏲2.30pm 1st Sat of month Apr-Nov) You can taste Champagne anywhere but you might get more out of one of the two-hour workshops (in French) at Villa Bissinger, home to the International Institute for the Wines of Champagne. Besides covering the basics like names, producers, grape varieties and characteristics, workshops include a tasting of four different Champagnes. The institute is in Ay, 3.5km northeast of Épernay. Call ahead to secure your place.

Sleeping

La Villa St-Pierre HOTEL €
(☎03 26 54 40 80; www.villasaintpierre.fr; 1 rue Jeanne d'Arc; d €57-95, q €105-115;) Expect a warm, family-style *bienvenue* and a friendly yap from the shih tzus at this early 20th-century townhouse turned B&B. The 11 simple rooms retain some yesteryear charm, with chintzy florals and wooden furnishings. Breakfast (€8) includes a tantalising array of pastries.

Magna Quies B&B €€
(☎06 73 25 66 60; http://magnaquies-epernay.jimdo.com; 49 av de Champagne; d/tr/q €140/180/200; P) Nestled in a shuttered manor house on the av de Champagne, this family-run B&B extends the warmest of welcomes. The trio of sunny, wood-floored rooms command fine views of the vineyards. Rates include a generous breakfast spread of pastries, fresh fruit and cold cuts.

Hôtel Jean Moët HISTORIC HOTEL €€
(☎03 26 32 19 22; www.hoteljeanmoet.com; 7 rue Jean Moët; d €140-205, ste €230-260;) Housed in a beautifully converted 18th-century mansion, this old-town hotel is big on atmosphere, with its skylit tearoom, antique-meets-boutique-chic rooms and cellar, C. Comme (p308). Spa treatments and a swimming pool await after a hard day's Champagne-tasting.

Le Clos Raymi HISTORIC HOTEL €€
(☎03 26 51 00 58; www.closraymi-hotel.com; 3 rue Joseph de Venoge; s €120, d €170-190;) Staying at this atmospheric place is like being a personal guest of Monsieur Chandon of Champagne fame, who occupied this luxurious townhouse over a century ago. The seven romantic, parquet-floored rooms – styles include Provençal, Tuscan and colonial – have giant beds, high ceilings and French windows. In winter, there's often a fire in the art-deco living room.

Parva Domus B&B €€
(☎06 73 25 66 60; www.parvadomusrimaire.com; 27 av de Champagne; d €120;) Brilliantly situated on the av de Champagne, this vine-swathed B&B is kept spick and span by the amiable Rimaire family. Rooms have a countrified feel, with wood floors, floral fabrics and pastel colours. Sip a glass of house Champagne on the terrace or in the elegant living room.

★**La Villa Eugène** BOUTIQUE HOTEL €€€
(☎03 26 32 44 76; www.villa-eugene.com; 84 av de Champagne; s €160-177, d €216-343, ste €380-398; P) Sitting handsomely astride the av de Champagne in its own grounds with an outdoor pool, La Villa Eugène is a class act. It's lodged in a beautiful 19th-century town mansion that once belonged to the Mercier family. The roomy doubles exude understated elegance, with soft, muted hues and the odd antique. Splash out more for a private terrace or four-poster bed.

Eating

Épernay's main eat street is rue Gambetta and adjacent place de la République. For picnic fixings, head to rue St-Thibault.

DON'T MISS

DOM PÉRIGNON

Everyone who visits Moët & Chandon invariably stops to strike a pose next to the statue of Dom Pérignon (c 1638–1715), after whom the *prestige cuvée* is named. The Benedictine monk played a pivotal role in making Champagne what it is – perfecting the process of using a second, in-the-bottle fermentation to make ho-hum wine sparkle. Apparently, he was so blown away by the result that he rhapsodised about 'tasting the stars'.

Pâtisserie Vincent Dallet PATISSERIE €
(www.chocolat-vincentdallet.fr; 26 rue du Général Leclerc; pastries €2.70-4.50, light meals €8-18; 7.30am-7.45pm Tue-Sun) A sweet dream of a chocolaterie, patisserie and tearoom, with delectable pralines, macarons and pastries. A *champenoise* speciality is the 'Baba', vanilla cream topped by a cork-shaped pastry flavoured with Champagne. *Café gourmand,* coffee with a selection of mini desserts, is €8.90.

★**La Grillade Gourmande** FRENCH €€
(03 26 55 44 22; www.lagrilladegourmande.com; 16 rue de Reims; menus €19-59; noon-2pm & 7.30-10pm Tue-Sat) This chic, red-walled bistro is an inviting spot to try chargrilled meats and dishes rich in texture and flavour, such as crayfish pan-fried in Champagne and lamb cooked in rosemary and honey until meltingly tender. Diners spill out onto the covered terrace in the warm months.

Le Théâtre FRENCH €€
(03 26 58 88 19; www.epernay-rest-letheatre.com; 8 Place Pierre Mendès; menus €20-51; noon-2pm & 7.30-9pm Mon & Thu-Sat, noon-2pm Tue & Sun) Sidling up to Épernay's theatre, Le Théâtre raises a curtain on a delightfully old-school brasserie with splashes of high-ceilinged art-nouveau charm. The Belgian chef, Lieven Vercouteren, prides himself on using superb seasonal produce in *menus* that might begin, say, with pheasant terrine with juniper berries and move on to mains such as tender leg of lamb with seasonal vegetables

Chez Max FRENCH €€
(03 26 55 23 59; www.chez-max.com; 13 av AA Thevenet, Magenta; 3-course lunch menu €15.50, dinner menus €23-41; noon-1.30pm & 7.30-9.30pm Tue & Thu-Sat, noon-1.30pm Wed & Sun) No fuss, no frills, just good old-fashioned French cooking and a neighbourly vibe is what you'll get at Chez Max. Dishes including confit of duck leg and sea bass with Champagne sauce hit the mark every time.

La Cave à Champagne REGIONAL CUISINE €€
(03 26 55 50 70; www.la-cave-a-champagne.com; 16 rue Gambetta; menus €20-38; noon-2pm & 7-10pm Thu-Mon;) 'The Champagne Cellar' is well regarded by locals for its *champenoise* cuisine (snail-and-pig's-trotter casserole, fillet of beef in pinot noir), served in a warm, traditional, bourgeois atmosphere. You can sample four different Champagnes for €28.

Drinking & Nightlife

It may come as little surprise that the tipple of choice in Épernay is Champagne, and it's as readily available (and almost as reasonably priced) in the bars dotted about town as wine is elsewhere. Central Rue Gambetta is a fine starting point for a night on the fizz.

★**C. Comme** WINE BAR
(www.c-comme.fr; 8 rue Gambetta; light meals €7.50-14.50, 6-glass Champagne tasting €33-39; 10am-8.30pm Sun-Wed, to 11pm Thu, to midnight Fri & Sat) The downstairs cellar has a stash of 300 different varieties of Champagne; sample them (from €6 a glass) in the softly lit bar-bistro upstairs. Accompany with a tasting plate of regional cheese, charcuterie and *rillettes* (pork pâté). We love the funky bottle-top tables and relaxed ambience.

Information

Tourist Office (03 26 53 33 00; www.ot-epernay.fr; 7 av de Champagne; 9am-12.30pm & 1.30-7pm Mon-Sat, 10.30am-1pm & 2-4.30pm Sun, closed Sun mid-Oct–mid-Apr;) The super-friendly team here hand out English brochures and maps with walking, cycling and driving tour options. They can also make cellar visit reservations. Free wi-fi.

Getting There & Around

BICYCLE

The tourist office rents out bicycles (city/children's/tandem/electric bicycles €18/11/27/30 per day). Pick up cycling maps and map-cards (€0.50) here.

TRAIN

The **train station** (place Mendès-France) has direct services to Reims (€7, 24 to 37 minutes, 14 daily) and Paris Gare de l'Est (€24 to €65, 1¼ hours to 2¾ hours, eight daily).

TROYES

POP 61,220

Troyes has a lively centre that's graced with one of France's finest ensembles of half-timbered houses and Gothic churches. Often overlooked, it's one of the best places in France to get a sense of what Europe looked like back when Molière was penning his finest plays and the Three Musketeers were swashbuckling. Several unique and very worthwhile museums are another lure.

Troyes does not have any Champagne cellars. However, you can shop in its scores of outlet stores stuffed with brand-name clothing and accessories, a legacy of the city's long-time role as France's knitwear capital.

Sights

The tourist offices in Troyes can supply you with a 1½-hour **audioguide tour** (€6) of the old city in French, English, German, Italian or Dutch.

★16th-Century Troyes HISTORIC QUARTER

Half-timbered houses – some with lurching walls and floors that aren't quite on the level line many streets in the old city, rebuilt after a devastating fire in 1524. The best place for aimless ambling is the area bounded by (clockwise from the north) rue Général de Gaulle, the Hôtel de Ville, rue Général Saussier and rue de la Pierre; of special interest are (from southwest to northeast) rue de Vauluisant, rue de la Trinité, rue Champeaux and rue Paillot de Montabert.

★Cathédrale St-Pierre et St-Paul CATHEDRAL

(place St-Pierre; 9am-noon & 1-5pm Mon-Sat, 11.30am-5pm Sun) All at once imposing and delicate with its filigree stonework, Troyes' cathedral is a stellar example of champenois Gothic architecture. The flamboyant **west façade** dates from the mid-1500s, while the 114m-long interior is illuminated by a spectacular series of 180 **stained-glass windows** (13th to 17th centuries) that shine like jewels when it's sunny. Also notable is fantastical **baroque organ** (1730s) sporting musical *putti* (cherubs), and a tiny **treasury** (open July and August only) with enamels from the Meuse Valley.

Maison de l'Outil et de la Pensée Ouvrière TOOL MUSEUM

(www.maison-de-l-outil.com; 7 rue de la Trinité; adult/child €7/3.50; 10am-6pm daily, closed Tue Oct-Mar) Worn to a sensuous lustre by generations of skilled hands, the 11,000 hand tools on display here – each designed to perform a single, specialised task with exquisite efficiency – bring to life a world of manual skills made obsolete by the Industrial Revolution. The collection is housed in the magnificent Renaissance-style Hôtel de Mauroy, built in 1556. Videos show how the tools were used and what they were used for. A catalogue in English is available at the reception.

Musée d'Art Moderne ART MUSEUM

(www.musees-troyes.com; 14 place St-Pierre; adult/child €5/free; 10am-1pm & 2-6pm Tue-Sun Apr-Oct, to 5pm Nov-Mar) Housed in a 16th- to 18th-century bishop's palace, this place owes its existence to all those crocodile-logo shirts, whose global success allowed Lacoste entrepreneurs Pierre and Denise Lévy to amass this outstanding collection. The highlights here are French paintings (including lots of fauvist works) created between 1850 and 1950, glass (especially the work of local glassmaker and painter Maurice Marinot) and ceramics. There's a remarkable portfolio of works by big-name artists including Degas, Rodin, Matisse, Modigliani, Picasso and Soutine.

Hôtel de Vauluisant MUSEUM

(4 rue de Vauluisant; adult/child €3/free; 10am-1pm & 2-6pm Wed-Sun Apr-Oct, to 5pm Nov-Mar) This haunted-looking, Renaissance-style mansion shelters a twinset of unique museums. The **Musée de l'Art Troyen** is a repository for the evocative paintings, stained glass and statuary (stone and wood) of the Troyes School, which flourished here during the economic prosperity and artistic ferment of the early 16th century. The **Musée de la Bonneterie** (Hosiery Museum) showcases the sock-strewn story of Troyes' 19th-century knitting industry, with exhibits from knitting machines and looms to bonnets and embroidered silk stockings. Plants used to make dyes and oil paints in the Middle Ages grow in the courtyard.

Église Ste-Madeleine CHURCH

(rue Général de Gaulle; 9.30am-12.30pm & 2-5pm Mon-Sat, 2-5pm Sun) Troyes' oldest and most interesting neighbourhood church has an early-Gothic nave and transept (early 13th century) and a Renaissance-style choir and tower. The highlights here are the splendid Flamboyant Gothic rood screen (early 1500s), dividing the transept from the choir, and the 16th-century stained glass in the presbytery portraying scenes from Genesis. In the nave, the statue of a deadly serious Ste-Marthe (St

Troyes

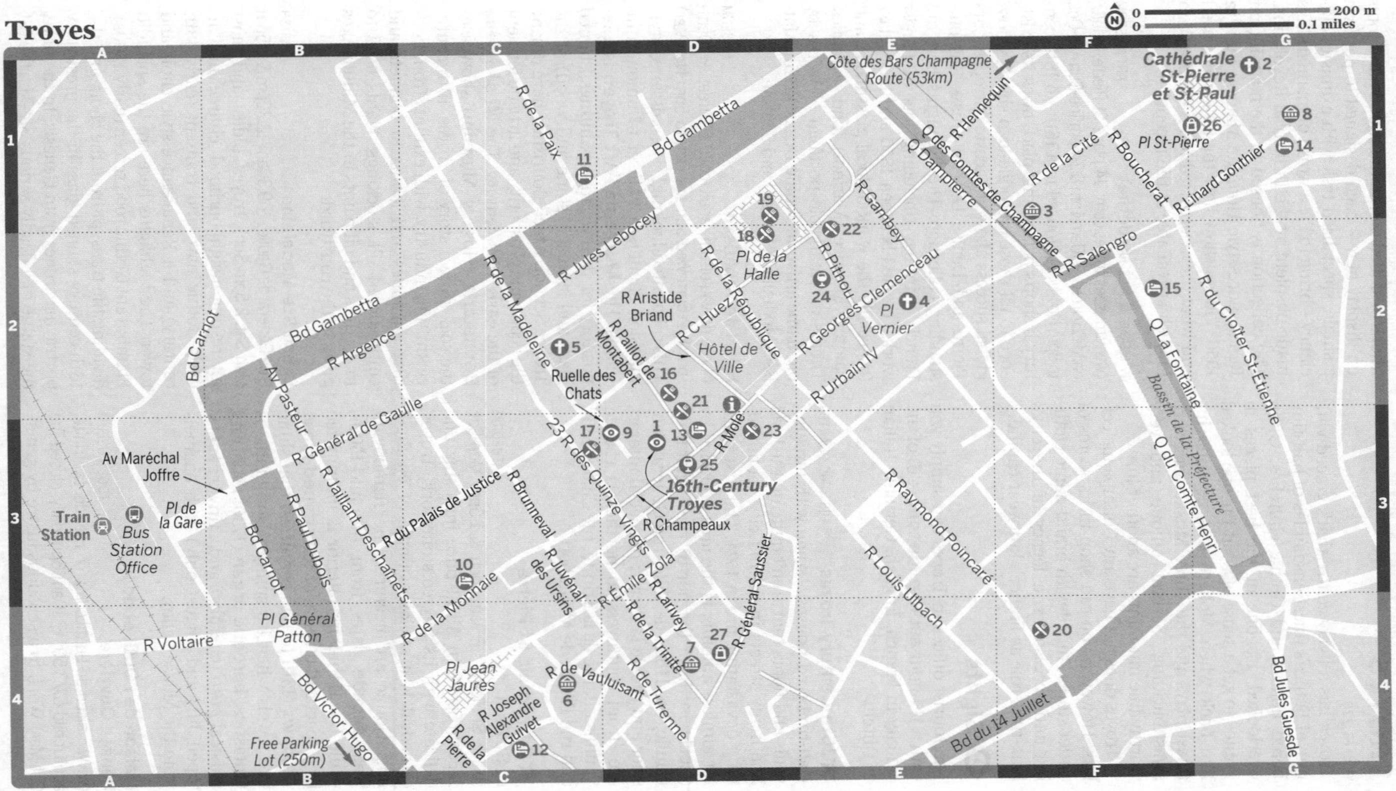
0 200 m
0 0.1 miles
Cathédrale St-Pierre et St-Paul
Côte des Bars Champagne Route (53km)
Pl St-Pierre
R de la Paix
Bd Gambetta
R Hennequin
Q des Comtes de Champagne
Q Dampierre
R de la Cité
R Boucherat
R Linard Gonthier
R Gambey
R R Salengro
R Jules Lebocey
R de la République
Pl de la Halle
R Pithou
R Georges Clemenceau
Pl Vernier
R du Cloîter St-Étienne
Q La Fontaine
Bassin de la Préfecture
Q du Comte Henri
R Aristide Briand
R C Huez
Hôtel de Ville
R de la Madeleine
R Argence
Bd Carnot
Av Pasteur
R Paillot de Montabert
Ruelle des Chats
R Urbain IV
R Général de Gaulle
R Mole
16th-Century Troyes
R Champeaux
23 R des Quinze Vingts
Av Maréchal Joffre
Train Station
Bus Station Office
Pl de la Gare
R Paul Dubois
R Jaillant Deschaînets
R du Palais de Justice
R Brunneval
R Juvénal des Ursins
R Émile Zola
R Larivey
R Général Saussier
R Raymond Poincaré
R Louis Ulbach
R de la Monnaie
R de la Trinité
R de Turenne
R de Vauluisant
Pl Général Patton
R Voltaire
Pl Jean Jaurès
R Joseph Alexandre Guivet
R de la Pierre
Bd Victor Hugo
Free Parking Lot (250m)
Bd du 14 Juillet
Bd Jules Guesde

Troyes

Top Sights
1 16th-Century Troyes D3
2 Cathédrale St-Pierre et St-Paul G1

Sights
3 Apothicairerie de l'Hôtel-Dieu-le-Comte F1
4 Basilique St-Urbain E2
5 Église Ste-Madeleine C2
6 Hôtel de Vauluisant C4
7 Maison de l'Outil et de la Pensée Ouvrière D4
8 Musée d'Art Moderne G1
9 Ruelle des Chats D3

Sleeping
10 Hôtel Les Comtes de Champagne C3
11 La Villa de la Paix C1
12 Le Clos Guivet C4
13 Le Relais St-Jean D3
14 Maison de Rhodes G1
15 Maison M F2

Eating
16 Au Jardin Gourmand D2
17 Aux Oiseaux de Passage C3
18 Claire et Hugo D2
19 Covered Market D1
20 Le Moine Gourmand F4
21 Le Valentino D2
22 Midi O Halles E2
23 Tout Simplement D3

Drinking & Nightlife
24 Dixi Café E2
25 Rouge et Noir D3

Shopping
26 Cellier St-Pierre G1
27 Sarah Dollé D4

Martha), around the pillar from the wooden pulpit, is considered a masterpiece of the 15th-century Troyes School.

Basilique St-Urbain CHURCH
(place Vernier; 9.30am-12.30pm & 2-6pm Mon-Sat, 2-6pm Sun, shorter hours Oct-Mar) Begun in 1262 by the Troyes-born Pope Urban IV, whose father's shoemaker shop once stood on this spot, this church is exuberantly Gothic both inside and out, and has some fine 13th-century stained glass. In the chapel off the south transept arm is **La Vierge au Raisin** (Virgin with Grapes), a graceful, early 15th-century stone statue of Mary and the Christ Child.

Ruelle des Chats HISTORIC STREET
Off rue Champeaux (between No 30 and 32), a stroll along tiny ruelle des Chats (Alley of the Cats), as dark and narrow as it was four centuries ago – the upper floors almost touch – is like stepping back into the Middle Ages. The stones along the base of the walls were designed to give pedestrians a place to stand when horses clattered by. See if you can spot the namesake cat in the stonework.

Apothicairerie de l'Hôtel-Dieu-le-Comte APOTHECARY MUSEUM
(www.musees-troyes.com; Quai des Comtes de Champagne; adult/child €3/free; 10am-1pm & 2-6pm Tue-Sun Apr-Oct, to 5pm Nov-Mar) If you come down with an old-fashioned malady – scurvy, perhaps, or unbalanced humours – the place to go is this fully outfitted, wood-panelled pharmacy from 1721. Rare majolica and earthenware pharmaceutical jars share shelf space with decorative pill boxes and bronze mortars.

Sleeping

Hôtel Les Comtes de Champagne HISTORIC HOTEL €
(03 25 73 11 70; www.comtesdechampagne.com; 56 rue de la Monnaie; r €69-105, apt €105-180;) The same massive wooden beams have kept this trio of pastel-hued half-timbered houses vertical since the 16th century. We love the bright courtyard lobby, the flower boxes and the 12th-century cellar. A huge and very romantic double goes for around €100. No lift.

★ **Le Relais St-Jean** HISTORIC HOTEL €€
(03 25 73 89 90; www.relais-st-jean.com; 51 rue Paillot de Montabert; d €98-157, ste €167-215; P) On a narrow medieval street in the heart of the old city, this hotel combines half-timbered charm with 24 contemporary rooms, a mini-tropical hothouse, a jacuzzi in the 16th-century cellar, a small fitness centre and facilities for the disabled. There's direct access from the underground car park (€10).

Le Clos Guivet B&B €€
(07 64 08 02 21; http://leclosguivet.fr; 7 rue Joseph Alexandre Guivet; s/d €100/115;) This beautifully restored house charms in its trio of large, individually designed rooms, stylishly decorated in muted colour schemes; all come with home comforts including Nespresso makers and bathrobes and slippers. Most romantic is La Driant up in the eaves. Breakfast is a terrific spread of local produce,

homemade preserves and fresh patisserie. Cots and high chairs are available on request.

Maison M B&B €€

(06 80 27 21 03, 03 25 46 30 97; http://maison-mtroyes.com; 3 quai de la Fontaine; d €100-130, q €150-180;) Michelle and Bruno are your kindly hosts at this boutique-flavoured guesthouse, which is a tasteful melange of 19th-century features and furnishings and eye-catching modern design. Most of the spacious, sunny, parquet-floored rooms face gardens and the canal, and breakfast is a small feast of local produce.

La Villa de la Paix BOUTIQUE HOTEL €€

(06 69 02 01 42; www.villapaix.com; 2 rue de la Paix; d €92-122, f €117-147;) This stout red-brick villa has a boutiquey flavour in its individually designed rooms, some with ornamental fireplaces and canopy beds. Family heirlooms, antiques and a flower-dotted garden given the place a delightfully homely feel, and breakfast comes with charcuterie, eggs, fruit, pastries – the works.

Maison de Rhodes HISTORIC HOTEL €€€

(03 25 43 11 11; www.maisonderhodes.com; 18 rue Linard Gonthier; d €199-265;) Once home to the Knights Templar, this half-timbered pile sits proudly on its 12th-century foundations. Creaking staircases lead to 11 spacious rooms, with beams and stone floors, which positively ooze medieval character; iPod docks and wi-fi suddenly wing you back into the 21st century. The gardens, courtyard and gourmet restaurant invite lingering. Breakfast will set you back an extra €20.

Eating

★ Claire et Hugo BURGERS €

(06 52 94 70 77; place de la Halle; mains €8-13; 12-2pm & 7-9pm Mon-Fri) Meet Claire and Hugo, the dynamic duo behind this double-decker-bus street food venture, which does the rounds in Troyes and its surrounds. Everything on the menu is homemade: from the burgers and *frites* to the bread, sauces, macarons and brownies. They pull up on place de la Halle on Mondays; see their Facebook page for other locations.

Midi O Halles DELI €

(11 place Saint Rémy; plat du jour €5.80, menus €8-10; 8am-7pm Tue-Sat) Whatever is fresh at the market that day lands on plates at this contemporary brick-walled bistro-cafe. Appetising no-nonsense *plats du jour* (€5.80) such as cheese-topped *tartiflette*, ratatouille and chicken curry are chalked up on the blackboard. They also do a fine line in coffee, teas, cakes and toasties, as well as wines in the adjacent bar.

Aux Oiseaux de Passage FRENCH €

(1 Cour du Mortier d'Or; menus €14-17.50; 11.30am-2.30pm Tue-Wed, 11.30am-2.30pm & 6.30-10pm Thu-Sat) Squirrelled away in an old-town backstreet, this artsy, family-friendly cafe brims with books, board games, quirky bird paintings and mismatched furniture. Come for the relaxed boho vibe, great coffee and homemade cake, tasty day specials (€12.50) prepared with market-fresh produce and chilled music. Look out for tapas nights and the odd gig at weekends.

Le Moine Gourmand FRENCH €

(03 25 73 77 23; 71 rue Raymond Poincaré; menus €13.50-27.50; noon-1.30pm & 7-9pm Mon, Tue & Thu-Sat, noon-1.30pm Wed;) It isn't in the prettiest part of town, but stick with this 'greedy monk' as he knows a thing or two about food. The vibe is welcoming in this modern-day bistro, which uses market-fresh veg, fish and meat in appetising dishes from classic *andouillette de Troyes* (coarse-grained tripe sausage) to duck breast in fig sauce.

★ Le Valentino MODERN FRENCH €€

(03 25 73 14 14; http://levalentino.com; 35 rue Paillot de Montabert; menus €28-58; noon-1.30pm & 7.30-9.30pm Tue-Sat) What could be more romantic than a *table à deux* in the cobbled courtyard of this rose-hued, 17th-century restaurant? The chef juggles flavours skilfully in market-driven specialities such as roasted monkfish with pak choi, ginger and pink pepper, and quail with red grape jelly and pear chutney.

Tout Simplement BISTRO €€

(03 25 40 83 72; www.resto-toutsimplement.fr; 29 place Alexandre Israël; mains €12-18; noon-2pm & 7-10pm Tue-Sat) Chipper staff keep the good vibes and food coming at this contemporary wine bar–bistro in the half-timbered heart of Troyes, which spills out onto a terrace in summer. Their famous *rillettes* (pâtés) – chicken, aubergine and grilled almonds, for instance – are a tasty prelude to mains such as creamy scallop risotto.

Au Jardin Gourmand FRENCH €€

(03 25 73 36 13; 31 rue Paillot de Montabert; mains €22-29; noon-1.30pm & 7.30-10pm Tue-Sat, 7.30-10pm Mon) Elegant without being overly formal, this intimate restaurant – with a summer terrace – uses only the fresh-

est ingredients for its classic French and *champenois* dishes; among the latter are no fewer than 11 varieties of *andouillette*. About 20 vintages from the estimable wine list are available by the glass.

Self-Catering

Covered Market FOOD MARKET €

(place de la Halle; 8am-12.45pm & 3.30-7pm Mon-Thu, 7am-7pm Fri & Sat, 9am-1pm Sun) Fruit, veggies, bread, charcuterie, fish and cheese glorious cheese.

Drinking & Nightlife

The hum of chatter fills the open-air bars and cafes around rue Champeaux and half-timbered place Alexandre-Israël on warm evenings.

Dixi Café BAR

(12 rue Pithou; 7pm-1.30am Mon, 5pm-1.30am Tue & Wed, 5pm-3am Thu-Sat) A convivial neighbourhood bar that draws an arty crowd, including students. The house speciality is *rhum arrangé* (fruit-infused rum). Has live music – rock, reggae, jazz, French *chansons* – at weekends from about 10pm.

Rouge et Noir WINE BAR

(13 rue Champeaux; 10.30am-2.30pm & 7-10pm Mon-Thu, 10.30am-2.30pm & 7-11pm Fri & Sat, 10.30am-3pm & 7-11pm Sun) Done out in red and grey hues as the name suggests, this smart stone-walled bar is an enticing pick for sampling local wines and Champagnes, perhaps accompanied by a tasting plate of regional specialities.

Shopping

In the city centre, handsome rue Émile Zola is lined with big-name high-street shops. Antique shops and galleries huddle along rue de la Cité.

Sarah Dollé FASHION & ACCESSORIES

(23 rue Larivey; 2-7pm Tue-Sat) Hidden down a narrow backstreet, this is where you will find Sarah's marvellous hat-making workshop. Squeeze into her tiny boutique, jam-packed with bonnets, woolly winter numbers, top hats and other fancy headwear, and slip back to a more glamorous age.

Cellier St-Pierre WINE

(www.celliersaintpierre.fr; 1 place St-Pierre; 10am-12.30pm & 2.30-7pm Tue-Fri, 10am-12.30pm & 2.30-7.30pm Sat) A fine place to purchase bubbly and Aube wines such as *rosé des Riceys*. The cellar has been used since 1840 to distil *Prunelle de Troyes*, a 40% liqueur made with sloe (blackthorn fruit) that's great on ice cream. The modest production facilities, which you can visit, are often fired up on Friday and Saturday mornings.

> **CITY PASS**
>
> **Le Pass' Troyes** (€12), sold at the tourist offices, gets you free entry to five of the big museums, a two-flute Champagne-tasting session, an old-city tour (with a guide or audioguide) and discounts at various factory outlet shops.

Information

Tourist Office (08 92 22 46 09; www.tourisme-troyes.com; 16 rue Aristide Briand; 9.30am-6.30pm Mon-Sat, 10am-1pm & 2-6pm Sun, shorter hours Oct-Mar) Sidling up to the town hall, this helpful bureau has stacks of info on Troyes, and free wi-fi.

Getting There & Around

BUS

The best way to get to Reims (€15, 2¼ hours, up to 13 daily) is by taking bus line 140 with **Courriers de l'Aube** (www.courriersdelaube.fr). Departures are from the very last bus berth to the right as you approach the train station; a schedule is posted. The **bus station office** (03 25 71 28 42; 8.30am-noon & 2-6.30pm Mon-Fri) is in the side of the train station.

TRAIN

Troyes is on the rather isolated train line that links Mulhouse (€47 to €110, four to six hours, 13 daily) in Alsace with Paris Gare de l'Est (€15 to €28, 1½ hours, 10 to 14 daily). To get to Dijon (€31 to €34, 2½ to 3½ hours), change in Culmont or Saint Florentin Vergigny.

CHAMPAGNE ROUTE OF THE CÔTE DES BAR

The 220km Côte des Bar Champagne Route does curlicues and loop-the-loops through austere fields, neat vineyards and forestland in an area 30km to 50km east and southeast of Troyes. Great for a deliciously leisurely drive, it passes through stone-built villages that are bedecked with flowers in the spring.

Although the Aube département is a major producer of Champagne, it gets a fraction of the recognition accorded to the Marne. Much of the acrimony dates back to 1909, when wine makers of the Aube were excluded from the growing area for

Champagne's AOC (Appellation d'Origine Contrôlée). Two years later, they were also forbidden to sell their grapes to producers up north, provoking a revolt by local *vignerons*, months of strikes and a situation so chaotic that the army was called in.

Today, Champagne production in the Aube is relatively modest in scale, though the reputation of the area's wines has been on an upward trajectory in recent years.

Colombey-les-Deux-Églises

POP 692

Charles de Gaulle lived in this village (www.colombey-les-deux-eglises.com) from 1934 – except, obviously, during WWII – until his death in 1970. It is named after two historic *églises* (churches), one a parish church, the other a Cluniac priory.

The hill just north of town (on D619) is crowned by a 43.5m-high Croix de Lorraine (Lorraine Cross), erected 1972, the symbol of France's WWII Resistance.

Sights

Mémorial Charles de Gaulle MEMORIAL

(http://memorial-charlesdegaulle.fr; adult/child €13.50/11; 9.30am-7pm daily May-Sep, 10am-5.30pm Wed-Mon Oct-Apr) The impressive Mémorial Charles de Gaulle presents graphic, easily digestible exhibits, rich in photos, which form an admiring biography of France's greatest modern statesman. Displays help visitors untangle such complicated mid-20th-century events as the Algerian war and the creation of the Fifth Republic, and consider the ways in which De Gaulle's years in power (1958–69) affected French culture, style and economic growth. Audioguides are available. The site affords breathtaking, sublime views of the Haute-Marne countryside.

DON'T MISS

PARTY TIME!

If you're in the Côte des Bar on the first weekend in August, you're in luck, as this is when the region hosts the Route du Champagne en Fête. A celebratory flute, costing €20 and sold at local tourist offices, is your ticket to free tastings at the *caves ouvertes* (open cellars) of more than 20 top Champagne houses. Exhibitions, live music, dinners and shows feature on the program.

La Boisserie MUSEUM

(www.charles-de-gaulle.org; adult/child €5.50/4; 10am-1pm & 2-6.30pm, shorter hours Oct-Mar) People flock by the coach-load to visit Charles de Gaulle's vine-swathed home, La Boisserie, its elegant antique furnishings unchanged since he was laid to rest in the village-centre *cimetière* (churchyard). Tours (English brochure available; price included in admission) begin at the ticket office, situated across D23 from the house, on the Colombey's southern edge.

Sleeping

Hostellerie La Montagne BOUTIQUE HOTEL €€

(03 25 01 51 69; www.hostellerielamontagne.com; 10 rue de Pisseloup; d €90-170) This boutique guesthouse exudes vintage-chic charm and offers quirky designer twists in its individually decorated rooms, some of which sport free-standing bath-tubs for a lingering soak. The big deal here, however, is its double act of excellent restaurants (*menus* €28 to €88), playing up winningly fresh seasonal produce – among them a Michelin-starred number with Jean-Baptiste Natali at the helm.

Information

The helpful **tourist information point** (03 25 03 12 42; http://colombey-les-deux-eglises.com; 10 place de l'Église; 9.30am-12.30pm & 2.30-6pm Thu-Mon) is located in the heart of town.

Bayel

POP 812

Crystal is the raison d'être of this dinky village, well off the tourist radar in the southeast of the Champagne-Ardenne region. Since the 17th century, Bayel has forged a reputation for producing some of France's finest glasswork.

Sights & Activities

Musée du Cristal GLASS MUSEUM

(www.bayel-cristal.com; 2 rue Belle Verrière; adult/child €5/3, with tour €7/4; 9am-12.30pm & 2-6pm Mon-Sat, closed Sat Oct-Mar) For insight into how crystal is made, visit the Musée du Cristal; a 15-minute film highlights the different stages involved in crystal production

Cristallerie Royale de Champagne Factory Tour GUIDED TOUR

(2 rue Belle Verrière; adult/child €5/3; 9.30am & 11am Mon-Fri) Thanks to the Cristallerie Royale de Champagne, established by a family of glass makers from Murano, Italy, the quiet village of Bayel has been a centre of crystal manufacture since 1678. To see

WORTH A TRIP

ABBAYE DE CLAIRVAUX

Bernard de Clairvaux (1090–1153), nemesis of Abelard and preacher of the Second Crusade, founded the hugely influential **Abbaye de Clairvaux Monastery** (www.abbayedeclairvaux.com; adult/child €7.50/free; ⏲tours 11am, 2.30pm & 4.30pm Mon & Tue, 10.30am, 11.45am, 1.30pm, 2.15pm, 3pm, 4.30pm & 5.15pm Wed-Sun late-Jun–early Sep, shorter hours rest of year) in 1115. Since Napoléon's time, the complex has served as one of France's highest-security prisons. Carlos the Jackal was among its past 'guests' and two prisoners who staged a revolt here in 1971 were guillotined. Several historic abbey buildings are open to the public. Tours take in 12th-century structures, built in the austere Cistercian tradition, but more interesting is the 18th-century Grand Cloître, where you can see collective 'chicken coop' cells (from the 1800s) and individual cells (used until 1971). For security reasons, visitors need to bring ID, mobile phones must be switched off, and photography is prohibited. The abbey is on D396, 8km south of Bayel and 6km north of A5 exit 23.

the production process, take a factory tour. The 1¼-hour tours are in French unless the group is predominantly English-speaking.

Information

Pick up info on Bayel and its surrounds at the **tourist information point** (☎03 25 92 42 68; www.tourisme.barsuraube.org; 2 rue de Belle Verrière; ⏲9.15am-1pm & 2.15-6pm Mon-Sat, 2.15-6pm Sun) in the Musée du Cristal.

Essoyes

POP 772

It's easy to see why Renoir loved Essoyes, so much that he spent his last 25 summers here: it's one of the area's comeliest villages, with neat stone houses, a riverfront that glows gold in the afternoon sun and landscapes of vineyards and flower-flecked meadows that unfold in a gentle, almost artistic way.

Sights & Activities

Espace des Renoir MUSEUM

(Renoir Centre; www.renoir-essoyes.fr; place de la Mairie; adult/child incl Atelier Renoir €8/4; ⏲10am-12.30pm & 2-6.30pm) The Renoir trail in Essoyes begins at the Espace des Renoir, which also houses the tourist office. Opened in 2011, the centre screens a 15-minute film about the artist and displays temporary exhibitions of mostly contemporary art.

Atelier Renoir HISTORIC BUILDING

(Renoir's Studio; www.renoir-essoyes.fr; 9 place de la Mairie; adult/child incl Espace des Renoir €8/4; ⏲10am-12.30pm & 2-6.30pm) The Atelier Renoir has displays zooming in on the hallmarks of Renoir's work (the female form, the vibrant use of colour and light), alongside original pieces such as his antiquated wheelchair and the box he used to carry his paintings to Paris. Perhaps loveliest of all is the studio garden, particularly in spring to early summer when it bursts forth with tulips, anemones and roses.

Circuit Découverte WALKING

You can slip into the shoes of great Impressionist Renoir on Essoyes' standout *circuit découverte*, a marked trail that loops around the village, taking in viewpoints that inspired the artist, the family home and the cemetery where he lies buried, his grave marked by a contemplative bronze bust. The trail begins at the Espace des Renoir.

Information

The **tourist office** (☎03 25 29 21 27; www.ot-essoyes.fr; place de la Mairie; ⏲9am-12.30pm & 1.30-5.30pm, closed Sat & Sun Oct-May) is housed in the Espace des Renoir.

Les Riceys

POP 1354

Running along both banks of the picturesque River Laigne, the commune of Les Riceys consists of three adjacent villages (Ricey-Bas, Ricey-Haute-Rive and Ricey-Haut). The commune is famous for its three churches, and for growing grapes belonging to three different AOC wines. Its best-known product is rosé des Riceys, an exclusive pinot noir rosé that can be made only in particularly sunny years and was a special favourite of Louis XIV. Annual production of this – when there is any – hovers around 65,000 bottles. Lots of Champagne wineries are nestled along and near D70.

Information

For details on walking circuits, contact the **tourist office** (☎03 25 29 15 38; www.les-riceys-champagne.com; 14 place des Héros de la Résistance, Ricey-Haut; ⏲9am-noon & 2-5pm).

Alsace & Lorraine

POP 4.2 MILLION

Includes ➡

Best Places to Eat

- ➡ 1741 (p326)
- ➡ Vince'Stub (p326)
- ➡ L'Imaginarium (p357)
- ➡ La Table du Brocanteur (p343)
- ➡ JY'S (p343)

Best Places to Sleep

- ➡ Villa Novarina (p324)
- ➡ Cour du Corbeau (p325)
- ➡ Villa Élyane (p342)
- ➡ Hôtel d'Haussonville (p351)
- ➡ Hôtel de la Cathédrale (p355)

Why Go?

Alsace is a cultural one-off. With its Germanic dialect and French sense of fashion, love of foie gras and *choucroute* (sauerkraut), fine wine *and* beer, this region often leaves you wondering quite where you are. Where are you? Why, in the land of living fairy tales, of course, where vineyards fade into watercolour distance, hilltop castles send spirits soaring higher than the region's emblematic storks and half-timbered villages garlanded with geraniums look fresh-minted for a Disney film set.

Lorraine has high culture and effortless grace thanks to its historic roll call of dukes and art-nouveau pioneers, who had an eye for grand designs and good living. The art and architecture in blessedly underrated cities like Nancy and Metz leave visitors spellbound, while the region's WWI battlefields render visitors speechless time and again with their painful beauty.

When to Go

Strasbourg

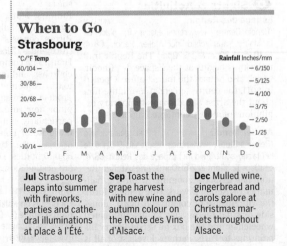

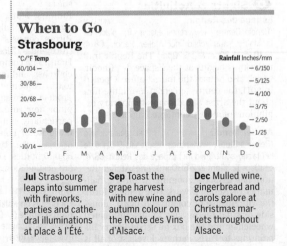

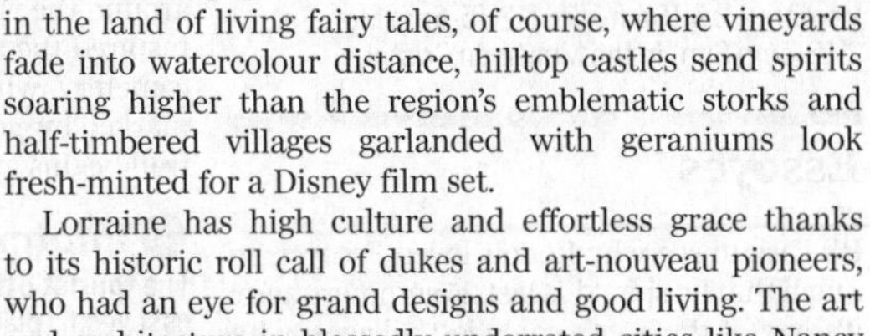

Jul Strasbourg leaps into summer with fireworks, parties and cathedral illuminations at place à l'Été.

Sep Toast the grape harvest with new wine and autumn colour on the Route des Vins d'Alsace.

Dec Mulled wine, gingerbread and carols galore at Christmas markets throughout Alsace.

ALSACE

Ask the French what they think of Alsace and watch them grow misty eyed with nostalgia and affection for this most idiosyncratic of regions, which borders Switzerland to the south and Germany to the east. So hard to nail in terms of its character, it proudly guards its own distinct identity, language, cuisine, history and architecture – part French, part German, 100% Alsatian. Here the candy-coloured towns and villages look as though they've popped up from a children's bedtime story, the gently rolling countryside, striped with vines, is nothing short of idyllic, and everywhere locals swear by centuries-old traditions.

> **FAST FACTS**
>
> **Area** 31,827 sq km
>
> **Local industry** Agriculture, tourism, industry
>
> **Signature drinks** Sylvaner white wine, Kronenbourg beer

History

Though settled since prehistoric times and cultivated by the Celts in 1500 BC, it wasn't until the Romans arrived in 58 BC that Alsace really made the history books. Alsace formed part of Germania Superior in the Roman Empire, and the Romans made their mark building forts and camps such as Argentoratum (modern-day Strasbourg).

As the influence of the Roman Empire waned, the Alemanni (Germanic tribes from the Upper Rhine) seized power, bringing with them the dialect that forms the basis of present-day Alsatian, but they were soon ousted by Frankish Merovingians in the 5th century.

Under Charlemagne (742–814), the church gained influence and Alsace flourished. Over the following eight centuries, Alsace prospered as part of the Holy Roman Empire. Thanks to the imperial clout of the Hohenstaufen emperors, the 12th and 13th centuries were a golden age, with the rise of guilds and a prosperous merchant class, the expansion of towns and cities, and the construction of Romanesque churches. Alsace became a cradle of intellectual and artistic activity in the 15th century. The final stone was laid on its Gothic crowning glory, Strasbourg's Cathédrale Notre-Dame, in 1439.

French influence in Alsace began during the Wars of Religion (1562–98) and increased during the Thirty Years War (1618–48). Most of the region was attached to France in 1648 under the Treaty of Westphalia.

By the time of the French Revolution, Alsatians felt more connected to France than to Germany, but time did little to dampen Germany's appetite for the region they called Elsass. When the Franco-Prussian War ended in 1871, an embittered France was forced to cede Alsace to the Kaiser. The region was returned to France following Germany's defeat in WWI, but it was re-annexed by Nazi Germany in 1940.

After WWII Alsace was once again returned to France. Intra-Alsatian tensions ran high, however, as 140,000 Alsatians – as annexed citizens of the Third Reich – had been conscripted into Hitler's armies. These conscripts were known as the 'Malgré-Nous' (literally 'despite ourselves') because the majority went to war against their will. To make Alsace a symbol of hope for future Franco-German (and pan-European) cooperation, Strasbourg was chosen as the seat of the Council of Europe (in 1949) and, later, of the European Parliament.

ℹ Getting There & Away

BICYCLE

Alsace is interwoven with 2500km of bike trails. Bicycles can be taken on virtually all regional TER trains (but not SNCF buses). A good resource for cyclists is **Alsace à velo** (www.alsaceavelo.fr), with maps, and itinerary and accommodation suggestions, plus practical info on where to rent and repair bikes.

CAR & MOTORCYCLE

From Strasbourg, the A4 heads northwest towards Metz and Paris, while from Mulhouse the A36 goes southwest towards the Jura and Dijon. The A31 connects Metz and Nancy with Luxembourg to the north and Dijon to the south. The Massif des Vosges gets snowy in winter, so winter tyres and/or chains may be required.

TRAIN

TER regional trains and TGV high-speed trains make up the region's fast and efficient rail network. Getting between major towns and cities is straightforward, but train services thin out in rural Alsace, where small towns and villages are connected by just a handful of buses, often making getting around by car a quicker, easier option.

Those aged 12 to 25 can get 50% off all regional rail travel with an annual Tonus Alsace pass (€19). The great-value Réflexe Alsace ticket, available for those aged 26 and over, costs €29 for a year and gets you a 30% discount on travel on weekdays and a huge 70% reduction at weekends.

Alsace & Lorraine Highlights

❶ **Petite Venise** (p339) Sauntering around this canal-laced area as Colmar starts to twinkle.

❷ **Cathédrale Notre-Dame** (p320) Getting a gargoyle's-eye view of Strasbourg from the platform of this Gothic cathedral.

❸ **Verdun Battlefields** (p360) Surveying the cross-studded lawn in the early-morning silence.

❹ **Musée de l'École de Nancy** (p348) Being amazed by art nouveau and rococo grace.

❺ **Château du Haut Kœnigsbourg** (p336) Gazing across the vines from giddy heights.

❻ **Hunawihr** (p336) Wishing for luck (or babies!) spotting storks.

❼ **Centre Pompidou-Metz** (p354) Contemplating modern art at this architecturally innovative gallery.

❽ **Massif des Vosges** (p344) Tiptoeing through the enchanting forests and mists.

❾ **Vallée de Munster** (p345) Going dairy-hopping in the verdant surrounds.

❿ **Riquewihr** (p337) Saving the storybook half-timbered lanes until dusk.

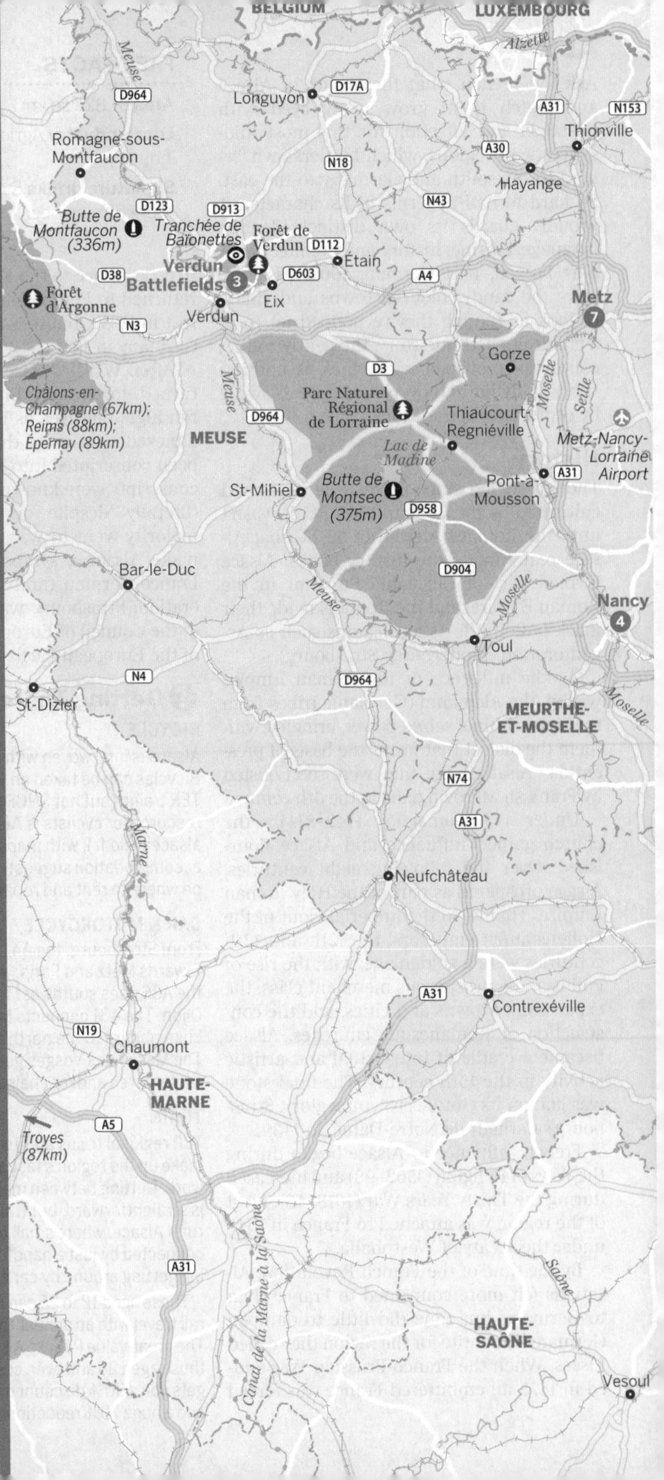

0 20 km
0 10 miles
Kaiserslautern
A6
GERMANY
Saar
Fort du Hackenberg
Veckring
D918
Saarbrücken
A4
St-Avold
MOSELLE
D910
Musée Lalique
D955
Château-Salins
Parc Naturel Régional de Lorraine
Bouxwiller
Haguenau
Rhine River
Karlsruhe/ Baden-Bade Airport
A4
BAS-RHIN
A35
A5
Marlenheim
Strasbourg
2
Lunéville
N4
Strasbourg Airport
Natzweiler-Struthof Concentration Camp
Mémorial de l'Alsace-Moselle
Meurthe
Obernai
Baccarat
Mont Ste-Odile
Mittelbergheim
Ill
N59
A35
Dambach-la-Ville
Lahr im Schwarzwald
Rambervillers
N57
St-Dié
N420
Kintzheim
Sélestat
Moselle
Haut Kœnigsbourg
5
Bergheim
Bruyères
Col du Bonhomme (949m)
Hunawihr
6
Ribeauvillé
Schnellenbuhl
Épinal
N415
Riegel
VOSGES
Kaysersberg
10
Riquewihr
Emmendingen
Lac Blanc
Katzenthal
Lac Noir
N57
Lac Vert
1
Colmar
Kaiserstuhl (560m)
Vallée de Munster
9
Rhine
Col de la Schucht (1139m)
GERMANY
Munster
Eguisheim
Neuf-Brisach
Parc Naturel Régional des Ballons des Vosges
D430
Petit Ballon (1267m)
Freiburg-im-Breisgau
A35
8
Route des Crêtes
Massif des Vosges
D431
N66
Grand Ballon (1424m)
Ungersheim
N66
N83
A5
St-Maurice
Luxeuil-les-Bains
D465
Ballon d'Alsace (1247m)
Willer-sur-Thur
Cernay
Thann
Mulhouse
A36
HAUT-RHIN
TERRITOIRE DE BELFORT
Lure
Basel-Mulhouse-Freiburg EuroAirport
Belfort
St-Louis
Doubs
7
Basel
DOUBS
SWITZERLAND

Strasbourg

POP 280,114

Strasbourg is the perfect overture to all that is idiosyncratic about Alsace – walking a fine tightrope between France and Germany and between a medieval past and a progressive future, it pulls off its act in inimitable Alsatian style.

Tear your gaze away from that mesmerising Gothic cathedral for just a minute and you'll be roaming the old town's twisting alleys lined with crooked half-timbered houses à la Grimm; feasting in the cosiest of *winstubs* (Alsatian taverns) by the canals in Petite France; and marvelling at how a city that does Christmas markets and gingerbread so well can also be home to the glittering EU Quarter and France's second-largest student population. But that's Strasbourg for you: all the sweeter for its contradictions and cross-cultural quirks.

Sights

★Cathédrale Notre-Dame CATHEDRAL

(www.cathedrale-strasbourg.fr; place de la Cathédrale; astronomical clock adult/child €2/1.50, platform adult/child €5/2.50; ⏲7-11.15am & 12.45-7pm, astronomical clock tickets sold 11.30am-12.25pm Mon-Sat, platform 9am-7.15pm; 🚊Grand'Rue) Nothing prepares you for your first glimpse of Strasbourg's Cathédrale Notre-Dame, completed in all its Gothic grandeur in 1439. The lace-fine façade lifts the gaze little by little to flying buttresses, leering gargoyles and a 142m spire. The interior is exquisitely lit by 12th- to 14th-century **stained-glass windows**, including the western portal's jewel-like rose window. The Gothic-meets-Renaissance **astronomical clock** strikes solar noon at 12.30pm with a parade of figures portraying the different stages of life and Jesus with his Apostles.

Victor Hugo declared it a 'gigantic and delicate marvel'; Goethe professed that its 'loftiness is linked to its beauty'; and, no matter the angle or time of day, you too will be captivated by this red-sandstone monolith that is at once immense and intricate.

A spiral staircase twists up to the 66m-high **viewing platform**, from which the tower and its Gothic openwork spire soar another 76m. As Hugo put it: 'From the belfry, the view is wonderful. Strasbourg lays at your feet, the old city of tiled triangular roof tops and gable windows, interrupted by towers and churches as picturesque as those of any city in Flanders'.

The **west façade**, most impressive if approached from rue Mercière, was completed in 1284, but the 142m spire – the tallest of its time – was not in place until 1439; its southern companion was never built.

To appreciate the cathedral in peace, visit in the early evening, when the crowds have thinned, and stay to see its façade glow gold at dusk.

★Grande Île HISTORIC SITE

(🚊Grand'Rue) History seeps through the twisting lanes and cafe-rimmed plazas of Grande Île, Strasbourg's Unesco World Heritage–listed island bordered by the River Ill. These streets – with their photogenic line-up of wonky, timber-framed houses in sherbet colours – are made for aimless ambling. They cower beneath the soaring magnificence of the cathedral and its sidekick, the gingerbready 15th-century Maison Kammerzell (p324), with its ornate carvings and leaded windows. The alleys are at their most atmospheric when lantern lit at night.

★Palais Rohan HISTORIC BUILDING

(2 place du Château; adult/child per museum €6.50/free, all 3 museums €12/free; ⏲10am-6pm Wed-Mon; 🚊Grand'Rue) Hailed a 'Versailles in miniature', this opulent 18th-century residence is replete with treasures. The basement **Musée Archéologique** takes you from the Palaeolithic period to AD 800. On the ground floor is the **Musée des Arts**

STRASBOURG SAVERS

The **Strasbourg Pass** (adult/child €18.90/9.45), a coupon book valid for three consecutive days, includes a visit to one museum, access to the cathedral platform and astronomical clock, half a day's bicycle rental and a boat tour, plus discounts on other tours and attractions.

The money-saving **Strasbourg Pass Musées** (day pass adult/child €12/6, 3-day pass €18/12; www.musees.strasbourg.eu) offers entry to all the Musées de la Ville de Strasbourg.

You can purchase both passes from the tourist office and the latter directly from the city's museums. Admission to all of Strasbourg's museums (www.musees-strasbourg.org) and the cathedral's platform is free on the first Sunday of the month.

Décoratifs, where rooms adorned with Hannong ceramics and gleaming silverware evoke the lavish lifestyle of the nobility in the 18th century. On the 1st floor, the **Musée des Beaux-Arts** collection of 14th- to 19th-century art includes El Greco, Botticelli and Flemish Primitive works.

Petite France AREA

(Grand'Rue) Criss-crossed by narrow lanes, canals and locks, Petite France is where artisans plied their trades in the Middle Ages. The half-timbered houses, sprouting veritable thickets of scarlet geraniums in summer, and the riverside parks attract the masses, but the area still manages to retain its Alsatian charm, especially in the early morning and late evening. Drink in views of the River Ill and the Barrage Vauban from the much-photographed **Ponts Couverts** (Covered Bridges; Musée d'Art Moderne) and their trio of 13th-century towers.

Musée d'Art Moderne et Contemporain ART MUSEUM

(MAMCS; www.musees.strasbourg.eu; 1 place Hans Jean Arp; adult/child €7/free; 10am-6pm Tue-Sun; Musée d'Art Moderne) This striking glass-and-steel cube showcases an outstanding fine-art, graphic-art and photography collection. Besides modern and contemporary works of the Kandinsky, Picasso, Magritte, Monet and Rodin ilk, you'll encounter pieces by Strasbourg-born artists, including the curvaceous creations of Hans Jean Arp and the evocative 19th-century works of Gustave Doré. The 1st-floor Art Café is graced by bold frescoes by Japanese artist Aki Kuroda and has a terrace overlooking the River Ill and Petite France.

Musée de l'Œuvre Notre-Dame ECCLESIASTICAL MUSEUM

(www.musees.strasbourg.eu; 3 place du Château; adult/child €6.50/free; 10am-6pm Tue-Sun; Grand'Rue) Occupying a cluster of sublime 14th- and 16th-century buildings, this museum harbours one of Europe's premier collections of Romanesque, Gothic and Renaissance sculpture (including many originals from the cathedral), plus 15th-century paintings and stained glass. *Christ de Wissembourg* (c 1060) is the oldest work of stained glass in France.

Barrage Vauban VIEWPOINT

(Vauban Dam; viewing terrace 7.15am-9pm, shorter hours winter; Faubourg National) FREE A triumph of 17th-century engineering, the Barrage Vauban bears the architectural imprint of the leading French military engineer of the age – Sébastien Le Prestre de Vauban. The dam was recently restored to its former glory and is now free to visit. Ascend to the terrace for a tremendously photogenic view that reaches across the canal-woven Petite France district to the Ponts Couverts and cathedral spire beyond.

THE LOCAL LINGO

The roots of Alsatian (Elsässisch) go back to the 4th century, when Germanic Alemanni tribes assimilated the local Celts (Gauls) and Romans. Similar to the dialects spoken in nearby Germany and Switzerland, it has no official written form (spelling is something of a free-for-all) and pronunciation varies considerably. Yet despite heavy-handed attempts by the French and Germans to impose their language on the region by restricting (or even banning) Alsatian, you'll still hear it used in everyday life by people of all ages, especially in rural areas.

Musée Historique HISTORY MUSEUM

(www.musees.strasbourg.eu; 2 rue du Vieux Marché aux Poissons; adult/child €6.50/free; 10am-6pm Tue-Sun; Grand'Rue) Trace Strasbourg's history from its beginnings as a Roman military camp called Argentoratum at this engaging museum, housed in a 16th-century slaughterhouse. Highlights include a painting of the first-ever performance of 'La Marseillaise', France's national anthem (which, despite its name, was written in Strasbourg in 1792); a 1:600-scale model, created in the 1720s to help Louis XV visualise the city's fortifications; and a Gutenberg Bible from 1485.

Musée Alsacien FOLK MUSEUM

(www.musees.strasbourg.eu; 23 quai St-Nicolas; adult/child €6.50/free; 10am-6pm Wed-Mon; Porte de l'Hôpital) Spread across three typical houses from the 1500s and 1600s, with creaky floors and beautifully restored wood-panelled interiors, this museum dips into rural Alsatian life over the centuries. Costumes, toys, ceramics, folk art, furniture and even a tiny 18th-century synagogue are on display in the museum's two dozen rooms.

Grande Mosquée de Strasbourg MOSQUE

(Strasbourg Grand Mosque; 6 rue Averroès; Laiterie) Designed by Italian architect Paolo

Strasbourg

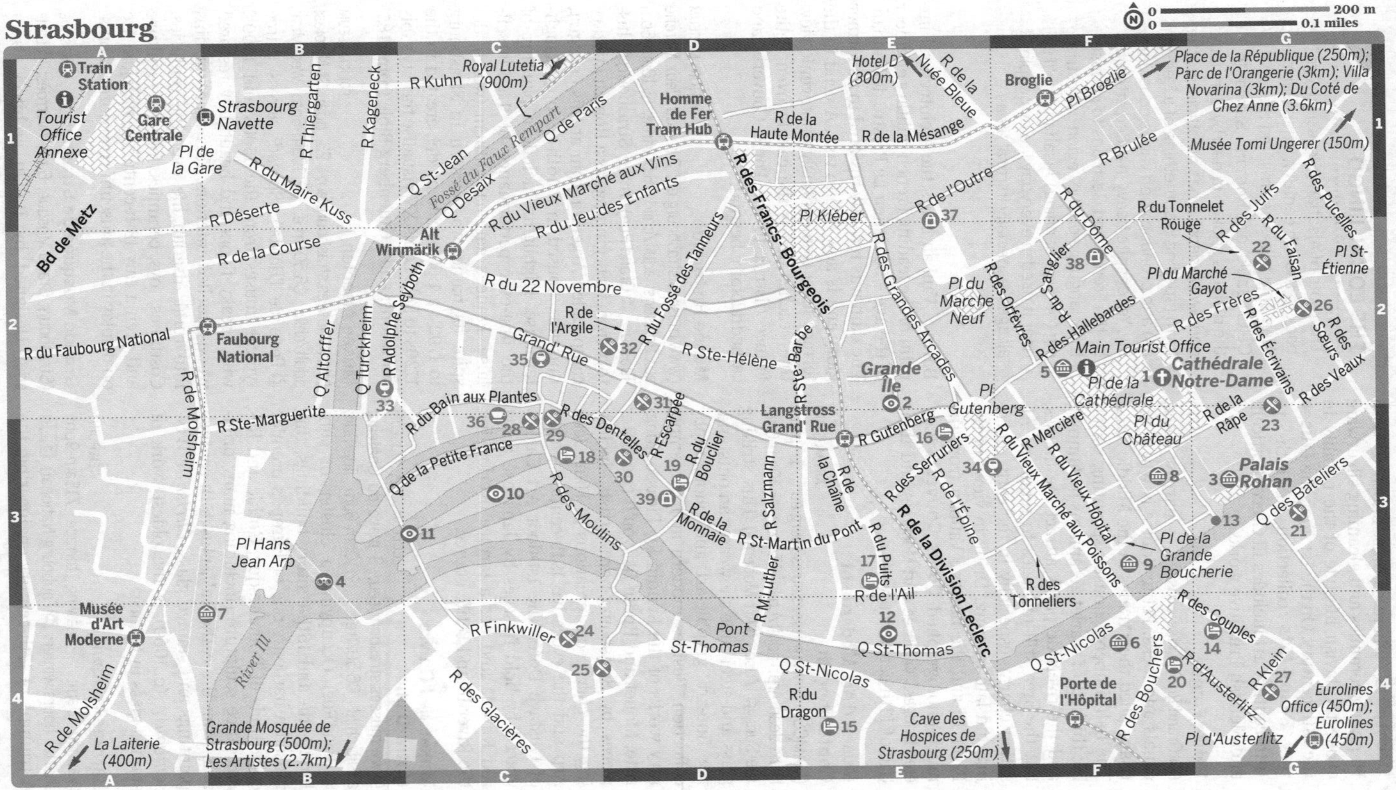
200 m
0.1 miles
A
B
C
D
E
F
G
1
2
3
4
Train Station
Tourist Office Annexe
Gare Centrale
Strasbourg Navette
Pl de la Gare
R Thiergarten
R Kageneck
R Kuhn
Royal Lutetia (900m)
Q St-Jean
Fossé du Faux Rempart
Q de Paris
Q Desaix
R du Maire Kuss
R Déserte
R de la Course
Bd de Metz
Alt Winmärik
R du Vieux Marché aux Vins
R du Jeu des Enfants
Homme de Fer Tram Hub
R de la Haute Montée
R de la Mésange
Hotel D (300m)
R de la Nuée Bleue
Broglie
Pl Broglie
Place de la République (250m); Parc de l'Orangerie (3km); Villa Novarina (3km); Du Coté de Chez Anne (3.6km)
Musée Tomi Ungerer (150m)
R Brulée
R de l'Outre
37
Pl Kléber
R des Francs- Bourgeois
R du Dôme
R du Tonnelet Rouge
R des Juifs
R du Faisan
R des Pucelles
Pl St-Étienne
22
Pl du Marché Gayot
R des Frères
26
R des Sœurs
R des Écrivains
R des Veaux
38
R du Sanglier
Pl du Marche Neuf
R des Orfèvres
R des Hallebardes
Main Tourist Office
5
Cathédrale Notre-Dame
1
Pl de la Cathédrale
R des Grandes Arcades
R du Faubourg National
Faubourg National
Q Altorffer
Q Turckheim
R Adolphe Seyboth
R du 22 Novembre
R de l'Argile
32
R du Fossé des Tanneurs
Grand' Rue
35
R Ste-Hélène
R Ste-Barbe
Grande Île
2
33
R de Molsheim
R Ste-Marguerite
R du Bain aux Plantes
36
28
29
R des Dentelles
31
R Escarpée
Langstross Grand' Rue
R Gutenberg
Pl Gutenberg
16
R Mercière
Pl du Château
R de la Râpe
23
Q de la Petite France
18
30
19
R du Boucier
39
10
R des Moulins
R de la Monnaie
R Salzmann
R de la Chaîne
R des Serruriers
R de l'Épine
34
R du Vieux Marché aux Poissons
R du Vieux Hôpital
8
Palais Rohan
3
13
Q des Bateliers
21
11
Pl Hans Jean Arp
4
R St-Martin du Pont
R M Luther
17
R du Puits
R de l'Ail
R de la Division Leclerc
R des Tonneliers
Pl de la Grande Boucherie
9
Musée d'Art Moderne
7
R Finkwiller
24
Pont St-Thomas
12
Q St-Thomas
Q St-Nicolas
6
R des Couples
14
River Ill
25
R des Glacières
R du Dragon
15
Cave des Hospices de Strasbourg (250m)
Porte de l'Hôpital
R des Bouchers
20
R d'Austerlitz
R Klein
27
Eurolines Office (450m); Eurolines (450m)
Pl d'Austerlitz
R de Molsheim
La Laiterie (400m)
Grande Mosquée de Strasbourg (500m); Les Artistes (2.7km)

Strasbourg

Portoghesi and opened in September 2012, France's biggest mosque (accommodating 1500 worshippers) sits on a bend in the River Ill and is topped by a copper dome and flanked by wings resembling a flower in bud. More than just another landmark, it took 20 years of political to-ing and fro-ing for this project to come to fruition and its completion is considered the beginning of a new era for Muslims and religious tolerance in France.

Musée Tomi Ungerer MUSEUM
(www.musees.strasbourg.eu; 2 av de la Marseillaise; adult/child €6.50/free; ⏱10am-6pm Wed-Mon; République) A tribute to one of Strasbourg's most famous sons – award-winning illustrator and cartoonist Tomi Ungerer – this museum, just northeast of Grande Île, is housed in the fetching Villa Greiner. The collection discloses the artist's love of dabbling in many genres, from children's-book illustrations to satirical drawings and erotica.

Parc de l'Orangerie PARK
(Droits de l'Homme) Across from the Council of Europe's Palais de l'Europe, 2km northeast of Grande Île, this flowery park, designed in the 17th century by Le Nôtre, of Versailles fame, is a family magnet with its playgrounds and swan-dotted lake. In summer you can rent **rowboats** on Lac de l'Orangerie. Kids can get up close to storks and goats at the park's mini **zoo** (free).

Le Vaisseau SCIENCE MUSEUM
(www.levaisseau.com; 1bis rue Philippe Dollinger; adult/child €8/7; ⏱10am-6pm Tue-Sun; Winston Churchill) Science is *never* boring at this interactive science and technology museum, 2.5km southeast of central Strasbourg. There are plenty of hands-on activities to amuse little minds, from crawling through an ant colony to creating cartoons and broadcasting the news. Take tram line B, C or F to the Winston Churchill stop.

Jardin des Deux Rives GARDENS
(Two-Shores Garden; ⏱9am-7pm; Aristide Briand) An expression of flourishing Franco-German friendship, Strasbourg and its German neighbour Kehl have turned former customs posts and military installations into this 60-hectare garden, whose play areas, promenades and parkland straddle both banks of the Rhine. The centrepiece is Marc Mimram's sleek (and hugely expensive) **suspension bridge**, which has proved a big hit with pedestrians and cyclists.

From the tram stop, walk east or take bus 21 for three stops. It is 3km southeast of central Strasbourg (Grande Île).

River Ill WATERFRONT

(Grand'Rue) The leafy paths that shadow the River Ill and its canalised branch, the Fossé du Faux Rempart, are great for an impromptu picnic or a romantic stroll.

Maison Kammerzell HISTORIC BUILDING

(rue des Hallebardes; Grand'Rue) The gingerbready 15th-century Maison Kammerzell has ornate carvings and leaded windows.

Tours

Take a DIY spin of Strasbourg's cathedral and the old city with one of the tourist office's 1½-hour **audioguides** (adult/child €5.50/2.75), available in five languages.

Batorama BOATING

(www.batorama.fr; rue de Rohan; adult/child €12.50/7.20; tours half-hourly 9.45am-9.15pm, shorter hours winter; Grand'Rue) This outfit runs scenic 70-minute boat trips, which glide along the storybook canals of Petite France, taking in the Barrage Vauban and the glinting EU institutions. Tours depart on rue de Rohan, the quay behind Palais Rohan.

Cave des Hospices de Strasbourg WINERY

(www.vins-des-hospices-de-strasbourg.fr; 1 place de l'Hôpital; 8.30am-noon & 1.30-5.30pm Mon-Fri, 9am-12.30pm Sat; Porte de l'Hôpital) FREE Founded in 1395, this brick-vaulted wine cellar nestles deep in the bowels of Strasbourg's hospital. A hospice back in the days when wine was considered a cure for all ills, today the cellar bottles first-rate Alsatian wines from rieslings to sweet muscats. One of its historic barrels is filled with a 1472 vintage. Take tram A or D to Porte de l'Hôpital. From here it is a three-minute walk south on rue d'Or.

LOCAL KNOWLEDGE

LADY LIBERTY

Prepare for *déjà vu* as you approach Colmar on the rte de Strasbourg (N83), 3km north of the old town, and spy the spitting image of the **Statue of Liberty**, albeit on a smaller scale. Bearing her torch aloft, this 12m-high, copper-green replica was erected to mark the centenary of the death of local lad Frédéric Auguste Bartholdi (1834–1904), creator of the NYC statue.

Festivals & Events

Place à l'Été CULTURAL

(www.ete.strasbourg.eu; late Jun-Aug) Strasbourg slides into summer with fireworks, fairs and striking cathedral illuminations at place à l'Été.

Marché de Noël CHRISTMAS

(Christmas Market; www.noel.strasbourg.eu; last Sat Nov-31 Dec) Mulled wine, spicy *bredele* (biscuits) and a Santa-loaded children's village are all part and parcel of Strasbourg's sparkly Marché de Noël.

Sleeping

It can be tricky to find last-minute accommodation from Monday to Thursday when the European Parliament is in plenary session (see www.europarl.europa.eu for dates). Book ahead for December, when beds are at a premium because of the Christmas market. The tourist office can advise about same-night room availability; if you drop by, staff are happy to help reserve a room.

Les Artistes GUESTHOUSE €

(03 88 77 15 53; http://chambre-hotes-les-artistes.fr; 22 rue Vermeer; d €60-80, tr €80-100; ; Elsau) Les Artistes offers clean, simple quarters and a good old-fashioned *bienvenue*. Rates include a fab breakfast, with fresh pastries and homemade jam. It's a homely pick, with a garden and barbecue area. Central Strasbourg, 3km away, can be reached on a cycle path or by tram (take B or C from rue du Faubourg National to the Elsau stop).

Hôtel Patricia HOTEL €

(03 88 32 14 60; www.hotelpatricia.fr; 1 rue du Puits; s €40, d €53-66, tr €60-74; ; Grand'Rue) The high-ceilinged, wood-floored rooms here are nothing fancy and the cheaper rooms have shared bathrooms, but you can't beat Hôtel Patricia for value. And given how central it is, this big, rambling townhouse bang in the heart of Grande Île is surprisingly quiet. Breakfast costs an extra €6.50.

★**Villa Novarina** DESIGN HOTEL €€

(03 90 41 18 28; www.villanovarina.com; 11 rue Westercamp; s €87-157, d €117-257, ste €237-537; P; Droits de l'Homme) New-wave design is pitched just right at this light-flooded 1950s villa near Parc de l'Orangerie. Slick without being soulless, rooms and suites are liberally sprinkled with art and overlook gardens. Breakfast places the accent on or-

DON'T MISS

BIENVENUE CHEZ LES EUROCRATS

Should the inner workings of the EU intrigue you, you can sit in on debates ranging from lively to yawn-a-minute at the **Parlement Européen** (European Parliament; www.europarl.europa.eu; rue Lucien Fèbvre; Parlement Européen); dates are available from the tourist office or on the website. For individuals it's first come, first served (bring ID).

A futuristic glass crescent, the Council of Europe's **Palais de l'Europe** (Palace of Europe; 03 88 41 20 29; www.coe.int; av de l'Europe; Droits de l'Homme) across the River Ill can be visited on free one-hour weekday tours; phone ahead for times and reservations.

It's just a hop across the Canal de la Marne to the swirly silver **Palais des Droits de l'Homme** (European Court of Human Rights; www.echr.coe.int; Allée des Droits de l'Homme; Droits de l'Homme), the most eye-catching of all the EU institutions.

The EU buildings sit 2km northeast of Grande Île (central Strasbourg), close to Parc de l'Orangerie. Take tram line E to the Droits de l'Homme stop.

ganic, regional produce. There's a heated pool, whirlpool and spa for quiet moments. It's a 10-minute walk south of Droits de l'Homme tram stop.

★Cour du Corbeau BOUTIQUE HOTEL €€
(03 90 00 26 26; www.cour-corbeau.com; 6-8 rue des Couples; r €145-175, ste €220-260; ; Porte de l'Hôpital) A 16th-century inn lovingly converted into a boutique hotel, Cour du Corbeau wins you over with its half-timbered charm and its location, just steps from the river. Gathered around a courtyard, rooms blend original touches such as oak parquet and Louis XV furnishings with mod cons including flat-screen TVs.

Hotel D BOUTIQUE HOTEL €€
(03 88 15 13 67; www.hoteld.fr; 15 rue du Fossé des Treize; d €129-189, ste €219-309; P; République) Splashes of bold colour and daring design have transformed this townhouse into a nouveau-chic boutique hotel. The slick, spacious rooms are dressed in soothing tones and no comfort stone has been left unturned – you'll find robes, Nespresso machines and iPod docks even in the standard ones. A fitness room and sauna invite relaxation.

Hôtel du Dragon HOTEL €€
(03 88 35 79 80; www.dragon.fr; 12 rue du Dragon; r €79-154; @; Porte de l'Hôpital) Step through a tree-shaded courtyard and into the, ahhh…blissful calm of this bijou hotel. The Dragon receives glowing reviews for its crisp interiors, attentive service and prime location near Petite France.

Romantik Hôtel Beaucour HISTORIC HOTEL €€
(03 88 76 72 00; www.hotel-beaucour.com; 5 rue des Bouchers; s €79-119, d €98-188, ste €149-256; @; Porte de l'Hôpital) With its antique flourishes and a cosy salon centred on a fireplace, this place positively oozes half-timbered romance. Rooms are stylishly decked out in warm colours and florals, and most feature (like it!) Jacuzzi bath-tubs.

Hôtel Gutenberg HISTORIC HOTEL €€
(03 88 32 17 15; www.hotel-gutenberg.com; 31 rue des Serruriers; r €109-221; @; Grand'Rue) Nestled in the flower-strewn heart of Petite France, this hotel is a harmonious blend of 250 years of history and contemporary design, combining clean lines, zesty colours and the occasional antique.

Le Bouclier d'Or BOUTIQUE HOTEL €€€
(03 88 13 73 55; www.lebouclierdor.com; 1 rue du Bouclier; d €198-234; ; Grand'Rue) This bijou family-run hotel nestles in a gorgeously restored 16th-century building in Petite France. It has been decorated with lots of loving care – whether you opt for an ever-so-snug 'Alsatian' room with beams and warm colours, or a grand, chandelier-lit 'bourgeoise' room furnished with antiques. After a day pounding the cobbles, your feet will be grateful for the spa.

Hôtel Régent Petite France DESIGN HOTEL €€€
(03 88 76 43 43; www.regent-hotels.com; 5 rue des Moulins; r €195-240; @; Alt Winmärik) Once an ice factory and now Strasbourg's hottest design hotel, this waterfront pile is quaint on the outside and uber-cool on the inside. The sleek rooms, dressed in muted colours and plush fabrics, sport shiny marble bathrooms. Work your relaxed look in the sauna, chic restaurant and Champagne bar with dreamy river views.

Eating

Crêperie Le Moulin du Diable CREPERIE €

(☎03 88 15 96 50; www.lemoulindudiable.com; 29 rue Finkwiller; crepes/galettes €3-10; ⏰11.30am-2pm & 6.30-11pm Tue-Fri, 6.30-11pm Sat & Sun; 🚋Faubourg National) *Ah oui*, there are crêpes and then there are proper Breton *crêpes* – and this nicely snug bolthole definitely falls into the second camp. Filled with a lifetime supply of nautical kitsch, it's a charming place to dig into a sweet *crêpe* or a cheese-filled buckwheat *galette* with a pitcher of cider. Service can be a tad slow.

Binchstub ALSATIAN €

(☎03 88 13 47 73; www.binchstub.fr; 6 rue du Tonnelet Rouge; tarte flambée €10-15; ⏰7pm-12.30am; 🚋Broglie) Cooked to thin, crisp perfection, the *Flammekueche (tarte flambée)* at Binchstub is in a league of its own. Locally sourced farm ingredients go into toppings such as goat's cheese, thyme and honey, and Bleu d'Auvergne cheese with pear and rocket.

Bistrot et Chocolat CAFE €

(☎03 88 36 39 60; www.bistrotetchocolat.net; 8 rue de la Râpe; snacks €7.50-11, brunch €18; ⏰11am-7pm Mon-Thu, 11am-9pm Fri, 10am-9pm Sat, 10am-7pm Sun; 🚋Grand'Rue) This chilled-out bistro is hailed for its solid and liquid organic chocolate (ginger is superb), day specials (€8.90) and weekend brunches.

★Vince'Stub FRENCH €€

(☎03 88 52 02 91; www.vincestub.com; 10 Petite rue des Dentelles; mains €14-17; ⏰11.30am-2pm & 7-10.30pm Tue-Sat; 🚋Grand'Rue) This sweet, petite bistro has a cosy beamed interior, a nicely down-to-earth vibe and a menu packed with Alsatian classics – see the blackboard for daily specials. It does a roaring trade in comfort food, from spot-on steak-*frites* to pork knuckles with Munster cheese.

Winstub S'Kaechele FRENCH €€

(☎03 88 22 62 36; www.skaechele.fr; 8 rue de l'Argile; mains €12-18.50; 🚋Grand'Rue) Traditional French and Alsatian grub doesn't come more authentic than at this snug, amiable *winstub* (wine tavern), run with love by couple Karine and Daniel. Cue wonderfully cosy evenings spent in stone-walled, lamp-lit, wood-beamed surrounds, huddled over dishes such as escargots oozing Roquefort, fat pork knuckles braised in pinot noir, and *choucroute garnie* (sauerkraut garnished with meats).

La Cuiller à Pot FRENCH €€

(☎03 88 35 56 30; www.lacuillerapot.com; 18b rue Finkwiller; mains €19.50-26.50; ⏰noon-2.30pm & 7-10.30pm Tue-Fri, 7-10.30pm Sat; 🚋Musée d'Art Moderne) Run by a talented husband-and-wife team, this little Alsatian dream of a restaurant rustles up fresh regional cuisine. Its well-edited menu goes with the seasons but might include such dishes as fillet of beef with wild mushrooms, and homemade gnocchi and escargots in parsley jus. Quality is second to none.

L'Oignon BISTRO €€

(☎03 88 16 59 81; www.restaurantloignon.fr; 4 rue des Moulins; mains €16.50-27.50; ⏰noon-2pm & 7-10pm; 🚋Grand'Rue) An enticing place to snuggle on chilly days, this beamed parlour is low-key rustic in look, with polished wood and banquette seating. It's an intimate spot for digging into spot-on bistro fare, along the lines of beef carpaccio with truffle oil, entrecôte and grilled scallops with Parmesan risotto – simply pair with Alsatian wines.

La Table Gayot FRENCH €€

(☎03 88 36 30 27; 8 place du Marché Gayot; mains €15-26; ⏰noon-2pm & 7-10pm Thu-Mon; 👪; 🚋Broglie) Sitting on one of Strasbourg's prettiest squares, surrounded by a veritable feast of half-timbered houses, this bistro is a fine pick for an alfresco lunch or a cosy dinner. On the meaty menu: nicely prepared dishes such as fillet of beef with pinot-noir sauce and lamb knuckles cooked with tarragon. There's a separate menu for *les petits*.

Maison des Tanneurs FRENCH €€

(☎03 88 32 79 70; 42 rue du Bain aux Plantes; mains €17-27; ⏰noon-1.45pm & 7.30-9.45pm Tue-Sat; 👪; 🚋Alt Winmärik) Even locals book ahead at this former tannery, bedecked with billowing geraniums and creaking under the weight of its 16th-century beams. *Choucroute* (sauerkraut) with fat pork knuckles and garlicky Alsatian-style escargot are matched with top-notch pinots and rieslings. Snag a window table for fine views of Petite France's canals.

★1741 GASTRONOMIC €€€

(☎03 88 35 50 50; www.1741.fr; 22 quai des Bateliers; lunch menu €38, 3-/5-course dinner menu €95-115; ⏰noon-2pm & 7-10pm Thu-Mon; 🚋Porte de l'Hôpital) Sparky young chef Guillaume Scheer runs the show at this Michelin-starred number facing the River Ill. Murals,

LOCAL KNOWLEDGE

PASS THE CHOCOLATE

Strasbourg is now sweeter than ever, as it's one of the main stops on **La Route du Chocolat et des Douceurs d'Alsace** (Alsace Chocolate and Sweets Road), stretching 80km north to Bad Bergzabern and 125km south to Heimsbrunn near Mulhouse. Pick up a map at the tourist office to pinpoint Alsace's finest patisseries, chocolateries, macaron shops and confectioners. The following are three sweet Strasbourg favourites to get you started.

Mireille Oster (www.mireille-oster.com; 14 rue des Dentelles; ⌚9am-7pm Tue-Sat; 🚊Grand'Rue) Cherubs adorn this heavenly shop where Strasbourg's *pain d'épices* (gingerbread) fairy Mireille Oster tempts with handmade varieties featuring figs, amaretto, cinnamon and chocolate. Have a nibble before you buy.

Christian (www.christian.fr; 12 rue de l'Outre; ⌚7am-6.30pm Mon-Sat; 🚊Broglie) Sumptuous truffles and pralines, weightless macarons and edible Strasbourg landmarks – renowned chocolatier Christian's creations are mini works of art.

Maison Alsacienne de Biscuiterie (www.maison-alsacienne-biscuiterie.com; 16 rue du Dôme; ⌚10am-6pm Mon-Thu & Sun, 9am-7pm Fri & Sat; 🚊Broglie) Bakes scrumptious Alsatian gingerbread, macarons, raisin-stuffed *kougelhopf* and *sablés* (butter cookies) flavoured with nuts and spices.

playful fabrics and splashes of colour add warmth to the dining room, where waiters bring well-executed, unfussy dishes, such as wild sea bass with Jerusalem artichoke and Alsatian venison with root vegetables, to the table. Service is excellent, as is the wine list.

Le Gavroche MEDITERRANEAN €€€

(☎03 88 36 82 89; www.restaurant-gavroche.com; 4 rue Klein; menus €37-90; ⌚noon-1.30pm & 7.30-9.30pm Mon-Fri; 👪; 🚊Porte de l'Hôpital) Nathalie and Benoît Fuchs give food a pinch of creativity and southern sunshine at intimate, softly lit Le Gavroche, awarded one Michelin star. Mains like veal in a mint crust with crispy polenta and coriander-infused artichoke tagine are followed by zingy desserts such as lime tart with lemon-thyme sorbet.

There's also a children's menu.

Umami FUSION €€€

(☎03 88 32 80 53; www.restaurant-umami.com; 8 rue des Dentelles; menus €50-70; ⌚7.30-9.30pm Mon, Tue & Fri, noon-1.15pm & 7.30-9.30pm Sat & Sun; 🚊Grand'Rue) Simplicity is the ethos at Michelin-starred Umami, loosely translated as 'savoury', the fifth taste in Japanese cuisine. A starkly minimalist, art-strewn bistro sets the scene for taste sensations like red-curry gambas ravioli, and fillet of wild cod with black rice sliding into an oyster and truffle sauce.

Drinking & Nightlife

Suspenders CAFE

(http://suspenders.fr; 36 rue du Bain aux Plantes; ⌚9am-7pm Tue-Sat; 🚊Alt Winmärik) The name is an attention-grabber, but you won't find sexy lingerie here, just Italian coffee worth raving about – served with an artistic flourish – chilled vibes and good music. The barista is a one-man band but knows his stuff when it comes to speciality coffees, which are best enjoyed with a slice of cake (around €3) or the homemade 'twix'.

La Popartiserie BAR

(www.lapopartiserie.com; 3 rue de l'Ail; ⌚2-10pm; 🚊Grand'Rue) Emerging urban artists from various countries showcase their edgy work at this gallery, wine bar and concert venue. There are regular free gigs, including pop and jazz Fridays and exhibitions, and the inner courtyard is a nicely chilled spot for drinks. Keep your eyes peeled for street art in this area, too.

L'Artichaut BAR

(www.lartichaut.fr; 56 Grand'Rue; ⌚11am-1am Tue-Sat, 1-8pm Sun; 📶; 🚊Grand'Rue) The 'artichoke' is the city's quirkiest arts and culture cafe, hosting free exhibitions, first-rate jazz concerts and jam sessions. The line-up is posted on the door and on the website.

Académie de la Bière PUB

(17 rue Adolphe-Seyboth; ⌚11am-4am; 📶; 🚊Alt Winmärik) Get the beers in at this chilled Petite France pub before a boogie in the

cellar disco. There are hundreds of brews on offer, from Kronenbourg to *krieks* (Belgian beers fermented with sour cherries).

Jeannette et les Cycleux BAR

(www.lenetdejeannette.com; 30 rue des Tonneliers; ⌚11.30am-1.30am Sun-Thu, to 3am Fri & Sat; 📶; 🚊Grand'Rue) Elvis lives on, baby, at this swinging 1950s-themed haunt, where classic motorbikes dangle from the chilli-red walls. We dig the good vibes, retro decor and music from rockabilly to Motown.

☆ Entertainment

Cultural event listings appear in the free monthly **Spectacles** (www.spectacles-publications.com, in French), available at the tourist office.

La Laiterie LIVE MUSIC

(www.artefact.org; 13 rue du Hohwald; 🚊Laiterie) Reggae, metal, punk, *chanson*, blues – Strasbourg's premier concert venue covers the entire musical spectrum and stages some 200 gigs a year. Tickets are available at the door and online. La Laiterie is just a five-minute walk (500m) south of Petite France along rue de Molsheim.

ℹ Information

The extremely helpful **main tourist office** (☎03 88 52 28 28; www.otstrasbourg.fr; 17 place de la Cathédrale; ⌚9am-7pm daily; 🚊Grand'Rue) should be your first port of call. A city-centre walking map with English text costs €1; bus/tram and cycling maps are free. You can pick up the money-saving Strasbourg Pass (p320) here.

There is also an **annexe** (⌚9am-7pm Mon-Sat, 9am-12.30pm & 1.45-7pm Sun; 🚊Gare Centrale) of the tourist office in the train station's south-ern wing.

WORTH A TRIP

MUSÉE LALIQUE

A stunning, romantic tribute to French art-nouveau designer René Lalique, the **Musée Lalique** (www.musee-lalique.com; rue du Hochberg, Wingen-sur-Moder; adult/child €6/3; ⌚10am-7pm daily, closed Mon Oct-Mar) harbours a collection assembling exquisite gem-encrusted and enamelled jewellery, perfume bottles, stoppers and sculpture. Complementing it are flower and wooded gardens, making the connection, as Lalique did, between art and the natural world. Located in the Northern Vosges, 60km north of Strasbourg, the museum can easily be visited on a half-day trip by taking the train to Wingen-sur-Moder (€10.60, 36 minutes). Alternatively, it's an hour's drive.

ℹ Getting There & Away

AIR

Strasbourg's international **airport** (www.strasbourg.aeroport.fr) is 17km southwest of the city centre (towards Molsheim), near the village of Entzheim. The airport is served by major carriers such as Air France, KLM, Iberia and budget airline Ryanair. Flights link Strasbourg to cities elsewhere in Europe, including London, Amsterdam, Madrid and Vienna, and domestic destinations including Paris, Nice, Lille and Lyon.

Ryanair links London Stansted with **Karlsruhe/Baden-Baden airport** (www.baden-airpark.de), across the Rhine in Germany, 58km northeast of Strasbourg.

BUS

The **Eurolines office** (☎08 92 89 90 91; www.eurolines.com; place de l'Étoile; ⌚9.30am-6.30pm Mon-Fri, to 4.30pm Sat; 🚊Étoile Bourse) is situated south of Grande Île on place de l'Étoile. Take tram line A or D to the Étoile Bourse stop. **Eurolines buses** (place de l'Étoile; 🚊Étoile Bourse) arrive and depart from the same square.

Strasbourg city bus 21 links the Jean Jaurès tram terminus with Kehl (€1.70, 13 minutes), the German town just across the Rhine.

TRAIN

Built in 1883, the Gare Centrale was given a 120m-long, 23m-high glass façade and underground galleries in order to welcome the new TGV Est Européen in grand style. On the Grande Île, tickets are available at the **SNCF Boutique** (www.voyages-sncf.com; 5 rue des Francs-Bourgeois; 🚊Grand'Rue).

Domestic

Destinations within France:

Lille €98 to €151, four hours, 17 daily
Lyon €38 to €182, 4½ hours, 14 daily
Marseille €88 to €199, 6¾ hours, 16 daily
Metz €27.10, 1½ hours, 16 daily
Nancy €26 to €31, 1½ hours, 12 daily
Paris €77 to €144, 2¼ hours, 19 daily

From Strasbourg, there are trains to Route des Vins destinations including the following:

Colmar €12.60, 32 to 41 minutes, 30 daily
Dambach-la-Ville €10.10, one hour, 12 daily
Obernai €6.40, 29 to 37 minutes, 20 daily
Sélestat €9, 20 minutes to one hour, 46 daily

International

If you take the Eurostar via Paris or Lille, London is just 5¼ hours away. Direct services include the following:

Basel SNCF €24.10 to €51.40, 1¼ hours, 25 daily

Brussels-Nord €80 to €181, 5¼ hours, three daily

Karlsruhe €25.40 to €29, 38 to 70 minutes, 16 daily

Stuttgart €42 to €83, 1¼ to two hours, four direct TGVs daily

Getting Around

TO/FROM THE AIRPORT

A speedy shuttle train links the airport to the train station (€4.30, nine minutes, four hourly); the ticket also covers your onward tram journey into the city centre.

Strasbourg Navette (www.strasbourg-navette.com) buses link place de la Gare in Strasbourg with Karlsruhe/Baden-Baden airport (€18 to €20, one hour), across the Rhine. Check timetables online.

BICYCLE

A world leader in bicycle-friendly planning, Strasbourg has an extensive and ever-expanding *réseau cyclable* (cycling network). The tourist office stocks free maps.

The city's 24-hour, self-rental **Vélhop** (www.velhop.strasbourg.eu; per hr/day €1/5) system can supply you with a bike. Pay by card and receive a code to unlock your bike. There's a refundable deposit of €150 per bike. Helmets are not available. There are 20 automatic rental points, plus outlets including the following:

City Centre (3 rue d'Or; 8am-7pm Mon-Fri, 9.30am-12.30pm & 2-5.30pm Sat; Porte de l'Hôpital)

Rotonde (rue de la Rotonde; Rotonde)

Train Station (8am-7pm Mon-Fri, 9.30am-12.30pm & 2-5.30pm Sat; Gare Centrale) Situated on Level -1. Adjacent is an 820-place bicycle parking lot (€1 for 24 hours).

PUBLIC TRANSPORT

Six super-efficient tram lines, A through F, form the backbone of Strasbourg's outstanding public-transport network, run by **CTS** (www.cts-strasbourg.fr). The main tram hub is Homme de Fer. Trams generally operate until 12.30am; buses – few of which pass through Grande Île – run until about 11pm. Night buses operate from 11.30pm to 5.30am on Friday and Saturday, stopping at nightlife hot spots.

Tickets, valid on both buses and trams, are sold by bus drivers and ticket machines at tram stops and cost €1.70 (€3.30 return). The 24h Individuel (for one person €4.30) and Trio (for two to three people €6.80) tickets, valid for 24 hours from the moment they are stamped, are sold at tourist offices and tram stops.

STORKS OF ALSACE

White storks *(cigognes)*, prominent in local folklore, are Alsace's most beloved symbols. Believed to bring luck (as well as babies), they winter in Africa and then spend summer in Europe.

In the mid-20th century, environmental changes reduced stork numbers catastrophically. By the early 1980s, only two pairs were left in the wild, so research and breeding centres were set up to establish a year-round Alsatian stork population. The program has been a huge success and today Alsace is home to more than 400 pairs – some of which you are bound to spot (or hear bill-clattering) on the Route des Vins d'Alsace.

Route des Vins d'Alsace

Green and soothingly beautiful, the Route des Vins d'Alsace (Alsace Wine Route, see p332) is one of France's most evocative drives. Vines march up the hillsides to castle-topped crags and the mist-enshrouded Vosges, and every mile or so there's a roadside *cave* (wine cellar) or half-timbered village inviting you to stop, raise a glass and enjoy. Corkscrewing through glorious countryside, the entire route stretches 170km from Marlenheim, 21km west of Strasbourg, southwards to Thann, 46km southwest of Colmar.

Local tourist offices can supply you with the excellent English-language map/brochure *The Alsace Wine Route*, and *Alsace Grand Cru Wines*, detailing Alsace's 50 most prestigious appellation d'origine contrôlée (AOC) winegrowing microregions.

Tours

For minibus tours of the Route des Vins try **Regioscope** (03 89 44 38 21, 06 88 21 27 15; www.regioscope.com; tours €105-115).

Getting There & Around

The Route des Vins comprises several minor, lightly trafficked roads (D422, D35, D18 and so on). It's signposted, but you might want to pick up a copy of Blay's colour-coded map *Alsace-Lorraine Touristique* (€5.95).

WORTH A TRIP

NATZWEILER-STRUTHOF

About 25km west of Obernai, off the D130, stands **Natzweiler-Struthof** (www.struthof.fr; Natzwiller; adult/child €6/3; ⏲9am-6.30pm, closed Christmas-Feb), the only Nazi concentration camp on French territory. Today the sombre remains of the camp are still surrounded by guard towers and concentric, once-electrified, barbed-wire fences. The four *crématoire* (crematorium ovens), the *salle d'autopsie* (autopsy room) and the *chambre à gaz* (gas chamber), 1.7km from the camp gate, bear grim witness to the atrocities committed here.

In all, some 22,000 of the prisoners (40% of the total) interned here and at nearby annexe camps died; many were shot or hanged. In early September 1944, as US Army forces approached, the 5517 surviving inmates were sent to Dachau.

The nearby **Centre Européen du Résistant Déporté** (⏲9am-6.30pm, closed Christmas-Feb) pays homage to Europe's Resistance fighters.

BICYCLE

Cyclists have a wide variety of on- and off-road options, which wend through some highly scenic countryside. Bike hire is available in all the major towns and cities. Expect to pay €10 per day.

CAR & MOTORCYCLE

Driving is undoubtedly the quickest and easiest way to reach villages and small towns on the Route des Vins, and the meandering country roads make for a memorable trip. Car hire is available at airports and in major cities. Parking can be a nightmare in the high season, especially in Ribeauvillé and Riquewihr; your best bet is to park a bit out of the town centre and walk for a few minutes.

TRAIN

It's entirely possible, if a bit cumbersome, to get around the Route des Vins by public transport, since almost all the main towns and villages are served by train from Strasbourg or by train and/or bus from Colmar. Bicycles can be taken on virtually all trains. A handy website for checking regional bus connections and timetables is www.vialsace.eu.

Obernai

POP 11,524

A vision of half-timbered, vine-draped, ring-walled loveliness, the wine-producing town of Obernai sits 31km south of Strasbourg. Give the summertime crowds the slip by ducking down cool, flower-bedecked alleyways, such as ruelle des Juifs, next to the tourist office.

Sights & Activities

A number of winegrowers have cellars a short walk from town (the tourist office has a map).

Place du Marché SQUARE

Life spirals around this market square, put to use each Thursday morning, where you'll find the 16th-century **hôtel de ville** (town-hall building) embellished with Baroque trompe l'œil; the Renaissance **Puits à Six Seaux** (Six Bucket Well), just across rue du Général Gouraud; and the bell-topped, 16th-century **Halle aux Blés** (Corn Exchange).

Ramparts HISTORIC SITE

Stretch your legs by strolling around Obernai's 13th-century ramparts, accessible from the square in front of twin-spired, neo-Gothic **Église St-Pierre et St-Paul.**

Sentier Viticole du Schenkenberg WALKING

This 1.5km wine route meanders through vineyards and begins at the hilltop cross north of town; to get there, follow the yellow signs from the cemetery behind Église St-Pierre et St-Paul.

Sleeping & Eating

Le Gouverneur HISTORIC HOTEL €

(☎03 88 95 63 72; www.hotellegouverneur.com; 13 rue de Sélestat; s €55-80, d €65-95, tr €75-120, q €85-130; P 📶) Overlooking a courtyard, this old-town hotel strikes perfect balance between half-timbered rusticity and contemporary comfort. Its petite rooms have a boutiquey feel, with bursts of vivid colour and art-slung walls. The family-friendly team can provide cots and high chairs free of charge.

La Villa du Coteau B&B €€

(☎06 32 58 00 61; www.villaducoteau.fr; 1 rue du Coteau; s €75-110, d €85-120; P 📶) This cute B&B sits a five-minute walk north of the centre. The spacious, wood-floored rooms are attractively beamed, and the pick of them have fine old-town views. Breakfast is great, with fresh pastries, fruit and juice. The kindly owners go out of their way to help and are happy to squeeze in a free cot if you need it.

Winstub La Dîme FRENCH €€
(☎03 88 95 54 02; 5 rue des Pélerins; menus €18-23; ⊙noon-2pm & 7-9pm Thu-Tue; 🚸) Precisely as an Alsatian *winstub* (wine tavern) should be: beamed and bustling with diners tucking into earthy dishes such as fat pork knuckles and *Zweibelkuchen* (onion tart). There's an €8 kids' menu.

La Fourchette des Ducs GASTRONOMIC €€€
(☎03 88 48 33 38; www.lafourchettedesducs.com; 6 rue de la Gare; menus €120-155; ⊙7-9.30pm Tue-Sat, noon-1.30pm Sun) A great believer in fastidious sourcing, chef Nicolas Stamm serves regional cuisine with gourmet panache and a signature use of herbs to a food-literate crowd at this two-Michelin-starred restaurant. The tasting *menus* go with the seasons, featuring specialities such as Alsatian pigeon with *baerewecke* (spiced fruit cake) and veal with truffles and Menton lemon jus – simple but sublime.

Information

The central **tourist office** (☎03 88 95 64 13; www.tourisme-obernai.fr; place du Beffroi; ⊙9am-noon & 2-5pm Mon-Fri) offers info on the town and its surrounds. You can also rent an electric bike here for €13/20 per half-/full day.

Getting There & Around

The train station is about 300m east of the old town. There are at least hourly TER train connections from Obernai to Colmar (€9.30 to €16.80, one hour to 70 minutes) and Strasbourg (€6.40, 29 to 37 minutes).

Mittelbergheim

POP 677

Serene, untouristy and set on a hillside, Mittelbergheim sits amid a sea of sylvaner grapevines and seasonal wild tulips, its tiny streets lined with sand-hued, red-roofed houses.

Activities

Sentier Viticole WALKING
From the car park on the D362 at the upper edge of the village next to the cemetery, a vineyard trail wriggles across the slopes towards the perky twin-towered **Château du Haut Andlau** and the lushly forested Vosges.

Domaine Gilg WINE
(www.domaine-gilg.com; 2 rue Rotland; ⊙8am-noon & 1.30-6pm Mon-Fri, to 5pm Sat, 9.30-11.30am Sun) Nip into this friendly, family-run winery to taste award-winning wines, including *grand cru* sylvaners, pinots and rieslings.

Sleeping

Private accommodation is good value and easy to come by – you'll see signs in windows all over town. For information, see www.pays-de-barr.com.

Hôtel Gilg HISTORIC HOTEL €
(☎03 88 08 91 37; www.hotel-gilg.com; 1 rte du Vin; r €68-98; 📶) For a dose of old-fashioned romance, check into this 17th-century half-timbered pile. A spiral staircase leads up to spacious, homey rooms in warm tones, some with wooden beams. The elegantly rustic restaurant (*menus* €35 to €56) serves classic French and Alsatian cuisine. Breakfast costs an extra €9.

Getting There & Away

The closest train station is in Barr, 1.5km north of town (approximately a 20-minute walk). From here, frequent trains run to Obernai (€2, 10 minutes), Sélestat (€4, 27 minutes) and Strasbourg (€7.50, 40 minutes).

Dambach-la-Ville

POP 2066

Ringed by vines and sturdy ramparts, this flowery village has some 60 *caves* but manages to avoid touristic overload. The renowned Frankstein *grand cru* vineyards cover the southern slopes of four granitic hills west and southwest of Dambach.

Sights & Activities

Some of the eye-catching half-timbered houses, painted in ice-cream colours like pistachio, caramel and raspberry, date from before 1500.

Ramparts HISTORIC SITE
A gentle stroll takes in the 14th-century, pink-granite ramparts, originally pierced by four gates, three still holding aloft watchtowers and bearing quintessentially Alsatian names: Ebersheim, Blienschwiller and Dieffenthal.

Sentier Viticole du Frankstein WALKING
It's a pleasant 1½-hour walk through the vineyards on this trail, which begins 70m up the hill from the tourist office on rue du Général de Gaulle. The path meanders among the hallowed vines, passing by hillside **Chapelle St-Sébastien** (⊙9am-7pm), known for its Romanesque tower and Gothic choir.

Place du Marché (p330), Obernai

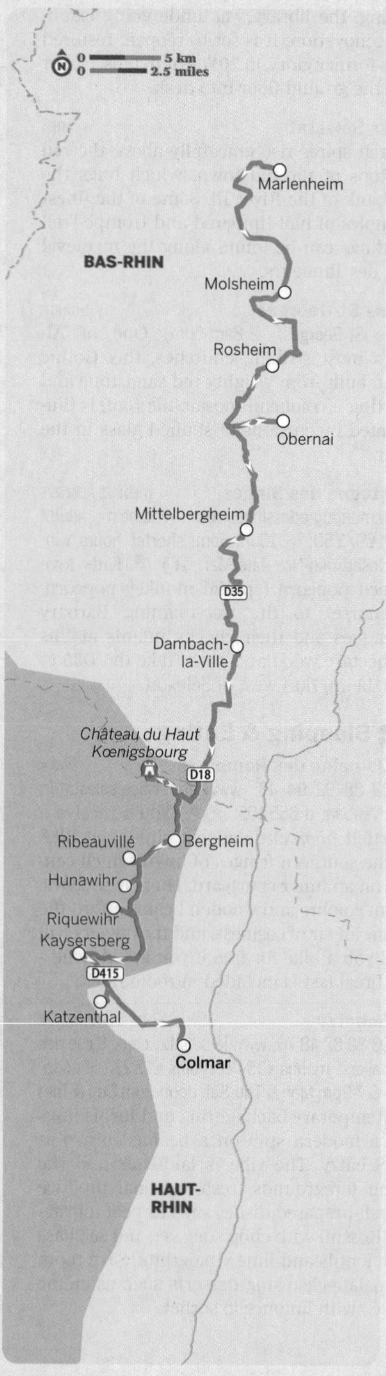

2 DAYS Route des Vins d'Alsace

Weaving through lyrical landscapes, this road trip takes in the best of the vine-strewn Route des Vins d'Alsace.

From the gateway town of **Marlenheim**, a well-marked lane leads through bucolic countryside to medieval **Molsheim**, centred on a square dominated by the step-gabled Renaissance *metzig* (butcher's shop). Continue south to **Rosheim**, where the striking Romanesque Église St-Pierre-St-Paul raises eyebrows with its, ahem, copulating gargoyles! Step inside for a moment of quiet contemplation before swinging south to pretty, half-timbered **Obernai** to explore the market square and château-topped vineyard trail. Views of the forest-cloaked Vosges unfold as you meander south to the sleepy hamlet of **Mittelbergheim**, pausing to taste the local *grand cru* wines at award-winning Domaine Gilg (p331). Even higher peaks slide into view as you cruise south to cellar-studded **Dambach-la-Ville**, embraced by 14th-century town walls, and catch your first tantalising glimpse of the turrets of 900-year-old Château du Haut Kœnigsbourg (p336). After detouring for astounding views from the castle ramparts – which reach to the Black Forest and Alps on cloudless days – rewind time roaming the cobbled streets in half-timbered **Bergheim**. Curving alleys hide cosy *winstubs* (wine taverns) in tower-speckled **Ribeauvillé** nearby. You'll definitely see storks in **Hunawihr** at the Centre de Réintroduction Cigognes & Loutres (p337); come in spring to coo over hatchlings. Allow time for serendipitous strolls in fairest-of-them-all **Riquewihr** – pure fairy-tale stuff with its procession of half-timbered houses painted pastel colours as bright as the macarons sold by its patisseries. Contemplate the Renaissance town hall and the house of Nobel Peace Prize–winner Albert Schweitzer (p338) in riverside **Kaysersberg**, then wend your way south to little-known **Katzenthal** for organic wine tasting and vineyard walks at family-run Vignoble Klur (p339). Wrap up your tour with culture and Michelin-starred dining in canal-woven **Colmar**, the enchanting Alsatian wine capital and birthplace of Statue of Liberty creator Frédéric Auguste Bartholdi (p340).

Sleeping & Eating

Le Vignoble HISTORIC HOTEL €

(☎03 88 92 43 75; www.hotel-vignoble-alsace.fr; 1 rue de l'Église; s/d €69/79;) Housed in a beautifully converted 18th-century barn, this hotel has comfortable wood-beamed rooms in fresh lemon and lime hues. It's well situated in the village centre. Breakfast will set you back an extra €9.

Le Pressoir de Bacchus REGIONAL CUISINE €€

(☎03 88 92 43 01; 50 rte des Vins, Blienschwiller; menus €15-48; noon-1.45pm Mon, 7-8.45pm Wed, noon-1.45pm & 7-8.45pm Thu-Sun) Good, honest Alsatian grub, cooked with passion and served with a smile, is the deal at this snug, wood-beamed bistro. Local wines marry well with classics like garlicky escargots and *choucroute garnie* (sauerkraut with smoked meats). It's 2.5km north of Dambach-la-Ville on the D35.

Information

Tourist Office (☎03 88 92 61 00; www.pays-de-barr.com; place du Marché; 9.30am-noon & 2-5.30pm Mon-Fri, 10am-noon Sat) In the Renaissance-style *hôtel de ville*. Hands out walking-tour maps and has details on cycling to nearby villages.

Getting There & Away

The train station is about 1km east of the old town. Dambach-la-Ville has hourly services to Sélestat (€2.20, 10 minutes), Colmar (€6.60, 40 minutes) and Strasbourg (€10.10, one hour).

Sélestat

POP 19,397

Wedged between Strasbourg, 50km to the north, and Colmar, 23km to the south, Sélestat is an enticing jumble of colourful half-timbered houses and church spires. The town's claim to cultural fame is its incomparable Bibliothèque Humaniste (Humanist Library).

Sights

Bibliothèque Humaniste LIBRARY

(Humanist Library; ☎03 88 58 07 20; 1 rue de la Bibliothèque; info desk 9am-noon & 2-5pm Mon-Fri) Founded in 1452, this library's stellar collection features a 7th-century book of Merovingian liturgy, a copy of *Cosmographiae Introductio* (printed in 1507), in which the New World is referred to as 'America' for the first time, and the first written mention of the Christmas tree (1521). At the time of writing, the library was undergoing extensive renovation; it is set to reopen, restored to its former glory, in 2017. For details, call or visit the ground-floor info desk.

Vieux Sélestat AREA

Church spires rise gracefully above the red rooftops of the old town, which hugs the left bank of the River Ill. Some of the finest examples of half-timbered and trompe-l'œil buildings can be found along the medieval quai des Tanneurs.

Église St-Georges CHURCH

(place St-Georges; 8am-6pm) One of Alsace's most striking churches, this Gothic giant, built from weighty red sandstone and sporting a colourful mosaic-tile roof, is illuminated by curtains of stained glass in the choir.

Montagne des Singes WILDLIFE RESERVE

(www.montagnedessinges.com; Kintzheim; adult/child €9/5.50; 10am-6pm, shorter hours winter, closed mid-Nov–late Mar;) Kids love to feed popcorn (special monkey popcorn, of course) to the free-roaming Barbary macaques and their cheeky infants at this 2.4-hectare woodland park. Take the D35 to Kintzheim, 7km west of Sélestat.

Sleeping & Eating

Le Domaine des Remparts B&B €

(☎03 88 92 94 43; www.gite-alsace-selestat.fr; 9 bd Vauban; d €55-105; P) You'll receive a heartfelt *bienvenue* at this pink-hued B&B on the southern fringes of town, which centres on an inner courtyard. Homely touches, warm colours and wooden beams afford the rooms an air of cosiness, and the owners will lend you a bike for free if you ask. A generous breakfast is included in room rates.

Le Schatzy INTERNATIONAL €€

(☎03 88 82 48 76; www.le-schatzy.com; 8 rue des Chevaliers; menus €15-45, mains €17-23; noon-2pm & 7-9pm Mon & Thu-Sat, noon-2pm Sun & Tue) Contemporary backlighting and furnishings put a modern spin on a beamed bistro at Le Schatzy. The vibe is laid-back and the menu foregrounds fresh seasonal produce in well-prepared dishes such as beef tournedos Rossini with chop suey veg and sea bass with lentils and lime vinaigrette. Save room for palate-cleansing desserts such as crème brûlée with limoncello sorbet.

Information

The **tourist office** (☎03 88 58 87 20; www.selestat-haut-koenigsbourg.com; 10 bd du Général Leclerc; ⏲9am-noon & 2-5.30pm Mon-Sat) is located on the edge of the town centre.

Getting There & Away

The train station is 1km west of the Bibliothèque Humaniste. Train is the fastest way to reach destinations including Strasbourg (€9, 20 minutes to one hour, twice hourly), Colmar (€5.10, 11 minutes, hourly) and Obernai (€5.30, 33 to 47 minutes, hourly).

Bergheim

POP 2038

Enclosed by a sturdy 14th-century ring wall, overflowing with geraniums and enlivened by half-timbered houses in vivid pastels, Bergheim is a joy to behold. But things have not always been so cheerful: overlords, stampeding invaders, women burnt at the stake for witchcraft – this tiny village has seen the lot.

Stroll the cobbled streets of the well-preserved medieval centre or follow the 2km path that circumnavigates the town's ramparts. Bergheim's *grand cru* wine labels are Kanzlerberg and Altenberg de Bergheim.

Sights

Medieval Centre AREA

A stroll through the cobbled streets of the well-preserved medieval centre takes in the early Gothic **church**; the wall-mounted **sundial** (44 Grand'Rue), dating from 1711; and the imposing, turreted **Porte Haute**, Bergheim's last remaining town gate.

Herrengarten Linden Tree LANDMARK

The gnarled Herrengarten linden tree was planted around 1300.

Sleeping & Eating

La Cour du Bailli HISTORIC HOTEL €€

(☎03 89 73 73 46; www.cour-bailli.com; 57 Grand'Rue; r €79-199; 🏊) Draped around a 16th-century courtyard, La Cour du Bailli has countrified studios and apartments, all of which have kitchenettes. Factor in downtime in the pool and stone-built spa, which pampers with luscious vinotherapy treatments. The atmospheric cellar restaurant (*menus* €30 to €50) serves wine-drenched specialities such as *coq au riesling*. There's no lift, so be prepared to lug your bags.

Wistub du Sommelier FRENCH €€

(☎03 89 73 69 99; www.wistub-du-sommelier.com; 51 Grand'Rue; menus €19-48; ⏲noon-2pm & 7-9.30pm Fri-Tue; 👪) Behind an ornate 18th-century façade lies this traditionally elegant bistro, where parquet floors, wooden beams and a *Kachelofen* (tiled oven) create a delightfully cosy ambience. The menu pairs fine regional wines with dishes from classic *choucroute garnie* (sauerkraut with smoked meats) to lighter flavours such as salmon with mussels in saffron sauce. The two-course €18 lunch including coffee is good value.

Information

Bergheim's little **tourist office** (☎03 89 73 31 98; 1 place du Dr Walter; ⏲9.30am-noon & 2-6pm Mon, 4-6pm Wed-Fri, 9am-noon & 2-7pm Sat, 10am-1pm & 5-7pm Sun, shorter hours low season) is situated right in the heart of town.

Getting There & Away

Bus 109 runs between Colmar's main train station and Bergheim (€4.05, 40 minutes) several times daily. Visit www.vialsace.eu for timetables and itineraries.

Ribeauvillé

POP 4957

Nestled snugly in a valley, presided over by a castle and with winding alleys brimming with half-timbered houses – medieval Ribeauvillé is a Route des Vins must. The local *grand cru* wines are Kirchberg de Ribeauvillé, Osterberg and Geisberg.

Sights & Activities

Vieille Ville AREA

Along the main street that threads through the old town, keep an eye out for the 17th-century **Pfifferhüs** (Fifers' House; 14 Grand'Rue), which once housed the town's fife-playing minstrels; the **hôtel de ville** and its Renaissance fountain; and the nearby, clock-equipped **Tour des Bouchers** (Butchers' Bell Tower).

★**Cave de Ribeauvillé** WINERY

(☎03 89 73 20 35; www.vins-ribeauville.com; 2 rte de Colmar; ⏲8am-noon & 2-6pm Mon-Fri, 10am-noon & 2-6pm Sat & Sun) FREE France's oldest winegrowers' cooperative, which brings together 40 vintners, was founded in 1895. The huge, contemporary building contains a viniculture museum, informative brochures and free tastings of its excellent wines, made with all seven of the grape varieties grown in

DON'T MISS

CHÂTEAU DU HAUT KŒNIGSBOURG

On its fairy-tale perch above vineyards and hills, the turreted red-sandstone **Château du Haut Kœnigsbourg** (www.haut-koenigsbourg.fr; Orschwiller; adult/child €9/5; ⌚9.15am-6pm, shorter hours winter) is worth a detour for the wraparound panorama from its ramparts, taking in the Vosges, the Black Forest and, on cloud-free days, the Alps. Audioguides delve into the turbulent 900-year history of the castle, which makes a very medieval impression despite having been reconstructed, with German imperial pomposity, by Kaiser Wilhelm II in 1908.

Alsace. You can also stock up on wine (from €6 per bottle) here. On weekends it's staffed by local winegrowers. It's just across two roundabouts north of the tourist office.

Castle Ruins WALKING
West and northwest of Ribeauvillé, the ruins of three 12th- and 13th-century hilltop castles – **St-Ulrich** (530m), **Giersberg** (530m) and **Haut Ribeaupierre** (642m) – can be reached on a hike (three hours return) beginning at place de la République (at the northern tip of Grand'Rue).

Sleeping

Camping Municipal Pierre de Coubertin CAMPGROUND €
(☎03 89 73 66 71; 23 rue Landau; 2 people, car & tent €14.50; 📶) This shady campground, with bike and canoe rental and a playground, is 500m east of the town centre.

Hôtel de la Tour HISTORIC HOTEL €€
(☎03 89 73 72 73; www.hotel-la-tour.com; 1 rue de la Mairie; s €79-104, d €85-112; 📶) Ensconced in a stylishly converted winery, this half-timbered hotel has quaint, comfy rooms, some with views of the Tour des Bouchers. Breakfast will set you back an extra €10.50.

Le Clos Saint Vincent BOUTIQUE HOTEL €€€
(☎03 89 73 67 65; www.leclossaintvincent.com; Osterbergweg; s €150-270, d €170-300, tr €280-320; P📶🏊) Gasp you might as you crest the hill and gaze out across the vines and the wooded peaks of the Vosges from this elegant guesthouse. The sound is silence and the smart, light-drenched rooms capitalise on those incredible views, as does the restaurant, serving French cuisine inspired by the seasons. An indoor pool and a little spa area invite relaxation.

Eating

Auberge du Parc Carola INTERNATIONAL €€
(☎03 89 86 05 75; www.auberge-parc-carola.com; 48 rte de Bergheim; menus €32-63, kids' menu €11.50; ⌚noon-1.30pm & 7-9.30pm Thu-Mon; 👪) Quaint on the outside, slick on the inside, this *auberge* (country inn) is all about surprises. Much-lauded chef Michaela Peters is behind the stove, and flavours ring clear and true in seasonal showstoppers such as hare fillet with chestnut-studded red cabbage and haddock with hazelnut risotto and pumpkin emulsion. Tables are set up under the trees in summer.

Wistub Zum Pfifferhüs FRENCH €€
(☎03 89 73 62 28; 14 Grand'Rue; menus €26-54; ⌚noon-1.30pm & 6.30-8.30pm Fri-Tue) If it's good old-fashioned Alsatian grub you're after, look no further than this snug wine tavern, which positively radiates rustic warmth with its beams, dark wood and checked tablecloths. Snag a table for copious dishes including *choucroute garnie* (sauerkraut with smoked meats), pork knuckles and *coq au riesling* (chicken braised in riesling and herbs).

Information

Tourist Office (☎03 89 73 23 23; www.ribeauville-riquewihr.com; 1 Grand'Rue; ⌚9.30am-noon & 2-6pm Mon-Sat, 9.30am-12.30pm Sun; 📶) At the southern end of one-way Grand'Rue. Free wi-fi.

Getting There & Away

A fairly frequent service runs from Ribeauvillé's central bus station to Route des Vins destinations including Colmar (€4.05, 25 minutes) and Riquewihr (€2.70, 13 minutes). Timetables are available online at www.vialsace.eu.

Hunawihr

POP 601

You're absolutely guaranteed to see storks in the quiet walled hamlet of Hunawihr, 1km south of Ribeauvillé. On a hillside just outside the centre, the 16th-century fortified church has been a simultaneum – serving both the Catholic and Protestant communities – since 1687.

Sights & Activities

Centre de Réintroduction Cigognes & Loutres WILDLIFE RESERVE
(Stork & Otter Reintroduction Centre; www.cigogne-loutre.com; rte des Vins; adult/child €9.50/8.50; 10am-6.30pm, closed Nov-Mar) About 500m east of Hunawihr, this delightful centre is home base for 200 free-flying storks; visit in spring to see hatchlings. Cormorants, penguins, otters and sea lions show off their fishing prowess several times each afternoon; see the website for times.

Jardins des Papillons GARDENS
(www.jardinsdespapillons.fr; adult/child €8/5.50; 10am-6pm, closed Nov-Easter) Stroll among exotic free-flying butterflies; the gardens are about 500m east of Hunawihr.

Sleeping & Eating

Chez Suzel APARTMENT €
(03 89 73 30 85; http://suzel-hunawihr.com; 2 rue de l'Église; apt €50; P) In the heart of town, this rustic *gîte* harbours sunny, wood-floored apartments with kitchenettes. The restaurant (*menus* €20 to €26) receives high praise for satisfying Alsatian grub along the lines of *Zwiebelkuchen* (dense onion tart) and wild boar cooked in pinot noir with *Spätzle* (egg noodles), washed down with local organic wines. Bag a spot on the terrace when the sun's out.

Getting There & Away

Bus 106 provides fairly frequent service between Hunawihr and Colmar (€4.05, 33 minutes).

Riquewihr

POP 1215

The competition is stiff, but Riquewihr is, just maybe, the most enchanting town on the Route des Vins. Medieval ramparts enclose its walkable centre, a photogenic maze of twisting lanes, hidden courtyards and half-timbered houses – each brighter and lovelier than the last. Of course, its chocolate-box looks also make it popular, so arrive in the early morning or the evening to appreciate the town at its peaceful best.

Sights & Activities

Dolder HISTORIC SITE
(www.musee-riquewihr.fr; €4, incl Tour des Voleurs €6; 2-6pm Sat & Sun Apr-Nov, daily Jul–mid-Aug) This late-13th-century stone and half-timbered gate, topped by a 25m bell tower, is worth a look for its panoramic views and small local-history museum.

Tour des Voleurs HISTORIC SITE
(Thieves' Tower; €4, incl Dolder €6; 10.30am-1pm & 2-6pm Easter-Oct) Rue des Juifs (site of the former Jewish quarter) leads down the hill to this medieval stone tower. Inside is a gruesome torture chamber with English commentary and an old-style winegrower's kitchen.

Sentier Viticole des Grands Crus WALKING
A yellow-marked 2km trail takes you out to acclaimed local vineyards Schœnenbourg (north of town) and Sporen (southeast of town), while a 15km trail with red markers takes you to five nearby villages. Both trails can be picked up next to Auberge du Schœnenbourg, 100m to the right of the *hôtel de ville*.

Sleeping & Eating

Sugary smells of traditional macarons and coconut macaroons – a tradition since coconuts were first brought here in the 1700s – waft through the centre, where you'll find confectioners, *winstubs* (wine taverns) and bakeries selling humongous pretzels.

Le Sarment d'Or HISTORIC HOTEL €€
(03 89 86 02 86; http://riquewihr-sarment-dor.fr; 4 rue du Cerf; d €73-88, tr €95) Yes, you'll have to schlep your bags up a spiral staircase, but frankly it's a small price to pay for staying at this 17th-century, rose-tinted abode. Rooms are simple with a dash of rusticity and the restaurant (mains €23 to €32) serves regional food cooked with precision and finesse.

Hôtel de la Couronne HISTORIC HOTEL €€
(03 89 49 03 03; www.hoteldelacouronne.com; 5 rue de la Couronne; s €57-71, d €65-135;) With its 16th-century tower and flowing wisteria, this central choice is big on old-world character. Rooms are country style with crisp floral fabrics, low oak beams and period furnishings; many have views over the rooftops to the hills beyond. There's no lift.

Au Trotthus MODERN FRENCH €€
(03 89 47 96 47; www.trotthus.com; 9 rue des Juifs; lunch menu €23, dinner menus €32-58; 7-10pm Mon, noon-2pm & 7-10pm Tue & Thu-Sat, noon-2pm Sun) Lodged in a 16th-century winemakers' house, this snug wood-beamed restaurant is overseen by a chef with exacting standards. The market-driven menu might include such delicacies as duck foie gras with spiced gingerbread and fig chutney,

and roast salmon with porcini mushrooms, chorizo chips and crustacean jus.

★ **Table du Gourmet** GASTRONOMIC €€€
(☎03 89 49 09 09; www.jlbrendel.com; 5 rue de la Première Armée; menus €38-115; ⏲noon-1.45pm & 7.15-9.15pm Fri-Mon, 7.15-9.15pm Wed & Thu) Jean-Luc Brendel is the culinary force behind this Michelin-starred venture. A 16th-century house given a slinky, scarlet-walled makeover is the backdrop for specialities made with herbs and little-heard-of vegetables from the restaurant's medieval garden. The menu swings with the seasons from asparagus to truffles, and dishes sing with intense, natural flavours – prepared with care, served creatively.

Information

Tourist Office (☎03 89 73 23 23; www.ribeauville-riquewihr.com; 2 rue de la Première Armée; ⏲9.30am-noon & 2-6pm Mon-Sat, 10.30am-1.30pm Sun, shorter hours winter; 📶) In the centre of the old town. Free wi-fi.

Getting There & Away

Bus 106 runs several times daily from Riquewihr to Ribeauvillé (€2.70, 18 minutes) and Colmar (€3.75, 25 minutes).

Kaysersberg

POP 2780

Kaysersberg, 10km northwest of Colmar, is an instant heart-stealer with its backdrop of gently sloping vines, hilltop castle and 16th-century fortified bridge spanning the gushing River Weiss.

Sights & Activities

Audioguides to the town (€5, 1½ to two hours) are available from the tourist office.

Vieille Ville AREA
An old-town saunter brings you to the ornate Renaissance **hôtel de ville** and the red-sandstone **Église Ste Croix** (⏲9am-4pm), whose altar has 18 painted haut-relief panels of the Passion and the Resurrection. Out front, a Renaissance **fountain** holds aloft a statue of Emperor Constantine.

Musée Albert Schweitzer MUSEUM
(126 rue du Général de Gaulle; adult/child €2/1; ⏲9am-noon & 2-6pm Easter-early Nov) The house where the musicologist, medical doctor and 1952 Nobel Peace Prize–winner Albert Schweitzer (1875–1965) was born is now a museum, with exhibits on the good doctor's life in Alsace and Gabon.

Sentiers Viticoles WALKING
Footpaths lead in all directions through glens and vineyards. A 10-minute walk above town, the remains of the massive, crenulated **Château de Kaysersberg** stand surrounded by vines; other destinations include Riquewihr and Ribeauvillé (four hours). These paths begin through the arch to the right as you face the entrance to the old town's *hôtel de ville*.

Sleeping & Eating

Hôtel Constantin HOTEL €
(☎03 89 47 19 90; www.hotel-constantin.com; 10 rue du Père Kohlmann; s €57, d €67-85, tr €98-110; P 📶) Originally a winegrower's house in the heart of the old town, this hotel has 20 clean and modern rooms with wood furnishings.

Le Chambard BOUTIQUE HOTEL €€€
(☎03 89 47 10 17; www.lechambard.fr; 9-13 rue du Général de Gaulle; d €174-299, ste €299-386; P ❄ 📶 🏊) A splash of minimalist cool in the heart of this little winegrowing village, Le Chambard offers contemporary digs with balcony or terrace, a spa and indoor pool for relaxing after exploring the Route des Vins, a cosy *winstub* (wine tavern) and gourmet restaurant, 64°.

64° GASTRONOMIC €€€
(☎03 89 47 10 17; www.lechambard.fr; 9-13 rue du Général de Gaulle; 5-course lunch menu €48, 5- to 7-course dinner menus €121-178; ⏲7-9pm Tue & Wed, noon-1.30pm & 7-9pm Thu-Sun) Chef Oliver Nasti helms this two-Michelin-starred restaurant at Le Chambard. Bronze-kissed chairs and lime drapes create a chic, contemporary backdrop for *menus* that spiral around what's in season – be it the signature egg cooked at 64° with chanterelles and cream of lemon and wood sorrel or Alsatian pigeon with roasted hazelnuts. The chef's precision, passion and eye for detail shine.

Information

Tourist Office (☎03 89 71 30 11; www.kaysersberg.com; 37 rue du Général de Gaulle; ⏲9am-12.30pm & 2-6pm Mon-Sat, 9am-12.30pm Sun; 📶) Inside the *hôtel de ville*; supplies walking-tour brochures as well as hiking and cycling maps, and makes bookings free of charge. Free internet access and wi-fi.

Getting There & Away

Bus 145 runs several times daily between Kaysersberg and Colmar (€3.75, 38 minutes).

Katzenthal

POP 551

Close-to-nature Katzenthal, 5km south of Kaysersberg, is great for tiptoeing off the tourist trail for a while. *Grand cru* vines ensnare the hillside, topped by the medieval ruins of Château du Wineck, where walks through forest and vineyard begin.

Sleeping & Eating

Vignoble Klur APARTMENT €

(☎03 89 80 94 29; www.klur.net; 105 rue des Trois Epis; 2-bed apt €82-96, 4-bed apt €105-120) Specialising in organic, biodynamic wines, family-run Vignoble Klur is a relaxed choice for tastings, Alsatian cookery classes and vineyard walks. The light-drenched, well-equipped apartments are great for back-to-nature holidays, and you can unwind in the organic sauna after a long day's walking and wine tasting. Le KatZ bistro pairs wines with dishes that make the most of local farm produce.

À l'Agneau FRENCH €€

(☎03 89 80 90 25; www.agneau-katzenthal.com; 16 Grand'Rue; menus €19-52, mains €16-28; ⏰noon-2pm & 7-10pm Fri-Tue, 7-10pm Thu; 👪) Market-driven *menus* and a cocoon-like setting of dark-wood panelling and lamp lighting draw locals to À l'Agneau. This friendly, family-run affair serves beautifully cooked food, whether you opt for Alsatian classics *such as* escargots and braised pork knuckles, or seasonal dishes such as pigeon cooked two ways with truffle jus or langoustines sliding into cream of asparagus. Wine pairing is reasonably priced.

Getting There & Away

Bus 145 operates several times a day between Colmar and Katzenthal. See www.vialsace.eu for timetables and itineraries. The village is 8km west of Colmar on the D415.

Colmar

POP 69,488

The capital of the Alsace wine region, Colmar looks for all the world as though it has been plucked from the pages of a medieval folk tale. At times the Route des Vins d'Alsace fools you into thinking it's 1454, and here, in the alley-woven heart of the old town, the illusion is complete. Half-timbered houses in chalk-box colours crowd dark cobblestone lanes and bridge-laced canals, which have most day-trippers wandering around in a daze of neck-craning, photo-snapping, gasp-eliciting wonder.

Quaintness aside, Colmar's illustrious past is clearly etched in its magnificent churches and museums, which celebrate local legends from Bartholdi (of Statue of Liberty fame) to the revered Issenheim Altarpiece.

Sights

Petite Venise AREA

(rowboats per 30min €6) If you see just one thing in Colmar, make it the Little Venice quarter. Canal connection aside, it doesn't resemble the Italian city in the slightest, but it's truly lovely in its own right, whether explored on foot or by rowboat (which depart next to Pont Rue de Turenne). The backstreets are punctuated by impeccably restored half-timbered houses in sugared-almond shades, many ablaze with geraniums in summer. Take a mosey around rue des Tanneurs, with its rooftop verandahs for drying hides, and quai de la Poissonnerie, the former fishers' quarter.

Pont Rue de Turenne BRIDGE

For photogenic views of Colmar's canal-woven Petite Venise district, head to this bridge at the top of rue de Turenne.

★ **Musée d'Unterlinden** ART MUSEUM

(www.musee-unterlinden.com; 1 rue d'Unterlinden; adult/child €13/8; ⏰10am-6pm Mon, Wed & Fri-Sun, to 8pm Thu) Gathered around a Gothic-style Dominican cloister, this recently revamped, expanded museum hides a prized medieval stone statue collection, late-15th-century prints by Martin Schongauer plus an ensemble of Upper Rhine Primitives. Its stellar modern-art collection contains works by Monet, Picasso and Renoir. The star attraction, however, is the late-Gothic Rétable d'Issenheim (Issenheim Altarpiece), by painter Mathias Grünewald and sculptor Nicolas of Haguenau. Hailed as one of the most profound works of faith ever created, the altarpiece realistically depicts New Testament scenes.

Église des Dominicains CHURCH

(place des Dominicains; adult/child €2/1; ⏰10am-1pm & 3-6pm Sun-Thu, 10am-6pm Fri & Sat

Colmar

0 200 m
0 0.1 miles

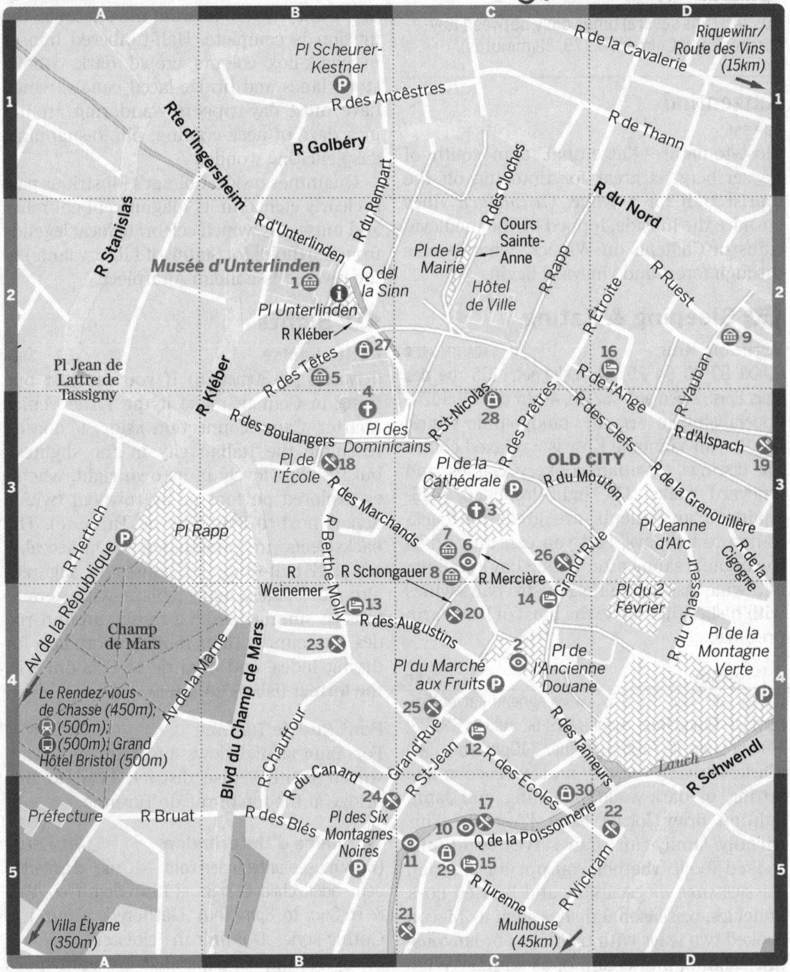

mid-Mar–Dec) Lit by late-medieval stained glass, this desanctified Gothic church shelters the celebrated triptych *La Vierge au Buisson de Roses* (The Virgin in the Rose Bush), painted by Martin Schongauer in 1473.

Musée Bartholdi MUSEUM

(www.musee-bartholdi.fr; 30 rue des Marchands; adult/child €5/free; ⏲10am-noon & 2-6pm Wed-Mon Mar-Dec) In the house where Frédéric Auguste Bartholdi was born in 1834, this museum pays homage to the sculptor who captured the spirit of a nation with his Statue of Liberty. Look out for the full-size plaster model of Lady Liberty's left ear (the lobe is watermelon-sized!) and the Bartholdi family's sparklingly bourgeois apartment. A ground-floor room shows 18th- and 19th-century Jewish ritual objects.

Maison des Têtes HISTORIC BUILDING

(House of the Heads; 19 rue des Têtes) True to its name, this step-gabled house, built in 1609 for a wealthy wine merchant, is festooned with 106 grimacing faces and heads of animals, devils and cherubs.

Colmar

Top Sights

1	Musée d'Unterlinden	B2

Sights

2	Ancienne Douane	C4
3	Collégiale St-Martin	C3
4	Église des Dominicains	B3
5	Maison des Têtes	B2
6	Maison Pfister	C3
7	Maison zum Kragen	C3
8	Musée Bartholdi	C3
9	Musée du Jouet	D2
10	Petite Venise	C5
11	Pont Rue de Turenne	C5

Sleeping

12	Gite L'Âme d'Antan	C4
	Hôtel les Têtes	(see 5)
13	Hotel Quatorze	B4
14	Hôtel St-Martin	C4
15	Le Colombier	C5
16	Maison Martin Jund	D2

Eating

17	JY'S	C5
18	La Cocotte de Grandmère	B3
19	La Table du Brocanteur	D3
	L'Arpège	(see 8)
20	L'Atelier du Peintre	C4
21	Le Caveau Saint Pierre	C5
22	L'Épicurien	D5
23	L'Un des Sens	B4
24	Palmyre	B5
25	Pâtisserie Gilg	C4
26	Sézanne	C3

Shopping

27	Choco en Têtes	B2
28	Fromagerie St-Nicolas	C3
29	Les Foie Gras de Liesel	C5
	Maison Martin Jund	(see 16)
30	Marché Couvert	C5

Ancienne Douane HISTORIC SITE
(place de l'Ancienne Douane) At the southern tip of rue des Marchands is this late-medieval customs house, with loggia and variegated tile roof, which now hosts temporary exhibitions and concerts.

Collégiale St-Martin CHURCH
(place de la Cathédrale; 8.30am-6.30pm) Delicate stonework guides the eye to the polychrome mosaic roof and Mongol-style copper spire of this Gothic church. Its jewel-like stained-glass windows cast kaleidoscopic patterns.

Musée du Jouet TOY MUSEUM
(www.museejouet.com; 40 rue Vauban; adult/child €5/3.90; 10am-5pm Wed-Mon) Kids of every age delight at the sight of toys from generations past – from demure 1950s Barbies to Gaultier-clad dolls and Hornby train sets – at this museum.

Maison Pfister HISTORIC SITE
(11 rue des Marchands) This Renaissance pile was built in 1537 for Ludwig Scherer, a wealthy hatter from Besançon. With its delicately painted panels, elaborate oriel window and carved wooden balcony, it is an immediate attention-grabber.

Maison zum Kragen HISTORIC BUILDING
(9 rue des Marchands) This 15th-century house is identifiable by its much-photographed sculpture of a *marchand* (merchant).

Festivals & Events

Festival International de Colmar CULTURAL
(www.festival-colmar.com; Jul) Orchestras strike up in historic venues across Colmar, including Musée d'Unterlinden, during the 10-day Festival International de Colmar.

Marché de Noël CHRISTMAS
(Christmas Market; www.noel-colmar.com) Colmar's snow globe of a Marché de Noël glitters from late November to 31 December. The entire city goes to town with festive sparkle, and five markets brim with gifts, hand-crafted decorations and gingerbread hearts. An open-air ice rink takes over place Rapp.

Sleeping

★ **Gite L'Âme d'Antan** APARTMENT €
(03 89 27 58 62; 1 rue des Écoles; apt €59-69, cleaning fee €45) Perched nest-like above the old-town bustle, this gorgeous attic apartment (sleeping three) is spacious, silent and equipped with dining area, kitchen and living room. The incredibly friendly owner, Annik, has furnished it with love, using family heirlooms and personal details – note the shutter headboard and her grandmother's hand-embroidered pillows. Towels and bed linen cost €20 extra per person.

Maison Martin Jund GUESTHOUSE €
(03 89 41 58 72; www.martinjund.com; 12 rue de l'Ange; r €39-55, apt €80-110;) Surrounding a courtyard in the backstreets of the old town,

this rosy half-timbered house shelters an organic winery and bright, well-kept studios, many with living rooms and kitchenettes. Breakfast is well worth the extra €7.50, with croissants, fresh-pressed juice, homemade jams and Vosges cheese.

★Villa Élyane B&B €€

(06 99 04 55 23; www.villa-elyane.com; 26a rue Camille Schlumberger; d €150-165, q €195-295; P) This graceful late-19th-century villa manages the careful balancing act of combining original art-nouveau features with modern comforts such as in-room iPod docks and espresso makers. Regional organic produce and fresh-squeezed juice make breakfast a delight. A garden, a sauna, a ping-pong table and bike rental boost the guesthouse's family appeal.

Le Colombier HISTORIC HOTEL €€

(03 89 23 96 00; www.hotel-le-colombier.fr; 7 rue Turenne; r €150-245, ste €295-318;) Behind the peach-hued, shuttered façade of a 16th-century townhouse in Petite Venise lies this truly welcoming hotel. The recently spruced-up rooms effortlessly bring together historic features such as exposed beams with contemporary design touches like backlighting. It works.

WORTH A TRIP

THE STAR OF CITADELS

Shaped like an eight-pointed star, the fortified town of Neuf-Brisach was commissioned by Louis XIV in 1697 to strengthen French defences and prevent the area from falling to the Habsburgs. It was conceived by Sébastien Le Prestre de Vauban (1633–1707).

A Unesco World Heritage Site since 2008, the citadel of Neuf-Brisach has remarkably well-preserved fortifications. The **Musée Vauban** (7 place de Belfort; adult/child €2.50/1.65; 10am-noon & 2-5pm Wed-Mon May-Oct), below the porte de Belfort gate, tells the history of the citadel through models, documents and building plans. Neuf-Brisach is just 4km from its German twin Breisach am Rhein on the banks of the Rhine.

To reach Neuf-Brisach, 16km southeast of Colmar, follow the signs on the D415. Buses 1076 and 301 also run between the town and Colmar's main station (€4.05, 40 minutes).

Hotel Quatorze DESIGN HOTEL €€

(03 89 20 45 20; www.hotelquatorze.com; 14 rue des Augustins; d €140-240, ste €260-360;) Bringing new-wave design to the heart of the old town, Hotel Quatorze occupies a lovingly transformed pharmacy dating from 1830. The 14 rooms and suites are streamlined and open plan, with wooden floors, and white walls enlivened by works by Spanish artist Alfonso Vallès. Details such as iPod docks, Aesop cosmetics and, in some suites, whirlpool tubs up the style ante.

Hôtel St-Martin HISTORIC HOTEL €€

(03 89 24 11 51; www.hotel-saint-martin.com; 38 Grand'Rue; d €75-140, f €120-160, ste €140-180;) What a location! Right on the place de l'Ancienne Douane, this 14th-century patrician house captures the elegance of yesteryear in rooms dressed with handcrafted furniture. Choose a top-floor room for rooftop views. Family rooms are available.

Hôtel les Têtes HISTORIC HOTEL €€

(03 89 24 43 43; www.maisondestetes.com; 19 rue des Têtes; r €160-305;) Luxurious but never precious, this hotel occupies the magnificent Maison des Têtes. Each of its 21 rooms has rich wooden panelling, an elegant sitting area, a marble bathroom and romantic views. The plushest rooms have their own Jacuzzis. With its wrought ironwork and stained glass, the restaurant provides a sumptuously historic backdrop for French-Alsatian specialities (*menus* €45 to €95).

Grand Hôtel Bristol HISTORIC HOTEL €€€

(03 89 23 59 59; www.grand-hotel-bristol.com; 7 place de la Gare; s €118-208, d €149-237, tr €160-304;) Historic meets contemporary at the century-old Bristol, which sits opposite the train station. A marble staircase sweeps up to modern rooms and a spa whose sundeck has fabulous city views. The big deal for gastronomes is the attached Michelin-starred **Le Rendez-vous de Chasse restaurant** (03 89 23 15 86; www.grand-hotel-bristol.com; 7 place de la Gare; menus €39-80; noon-2pm & 7-9.30pm Thu-Mon;).

Eating

The old town is liberally sprinkled with bistros and *winstubs*, especially place de l'Ancienne Douane, rue des Marchands and Petite Venise. And for a town of its moderate size, it packs a mighty gastronomic punch, with no fewer than three Michelin-starred restaurants.

Pâtisserie Gilg PATISSERIE €

(www.patisserie-gilg.com; 60 Grand'Rue; patisserie & desserts €3-5; ⌚9am-6.45pm Tue-Fri, to 6pm Sat, to 12.30pm Sun) Bitter-chocolate cake, desserts with fresh fruit, nuts or caramel, rainbow-hued macarons, magnificent millefeuilles – however will you choose? Gilg is Colmar's patisserie *par excellence*.

L'Un des Sens FRENCH €

(☎03 89 24 04 37; www.cave-lun-des-sens.fr; 18 rue Berthe Molly; light bites & mains €6.50-25; ⌚4-10pm Tue-Thu, 10am-10.30pm Fri & Sat) Lodged in a half-timbered house, this red-walled wine bar keeps the mood intimate and mellow. It speaks volumes that the owners know their suppliers by name, and regional charcuterie, cheese, pâté and tapas are expertly paired with wines (250 to choose from) that begin at a modest €3.50 per glass.

Sézanne BISTRO €

(www.sezanne.net; 30 Grand'Rue; light meals €10-15; ⌚10am-7pm Mon, 9am-7pm Tue-Sat) Buy local wine, pâté and charcuterie in the downstairs *épicerie* (specialist grocer) or dig into *tartines* (open-face sandwiches) and daily specials in the upstairs bistro.

La Cocotte de Grandmère FRENCH €

(☎03 89 23 32 49; www.lacocottedegrandmere.com; 14 place de l'École; lunch menus €13-15, mains 22-24; ⌚noon-2pm & 7-9pm Mon-Fri) Good, honest food and a warm ambience attract hungry locals to this sweet bistro. The three-course €15 *menu* hits the mark every time, with deeply satisfying home cooking from hearty casseroles to roast duck leg with creamy mash.

★**La Table du Brocanteur** FRENCH €€

(☎03 89 23 45 57; 23 rue d'Alspach; mains €20-23; ⌚noon-2pm & 7-9.30pm Tue-Sat, noon-2pm Sun) Tucked down a backstreet, this half-timbered house is decorated with milk pails, clogs and an attic's worth of other rustic knick-knacks. Bright flavours like scallop carpaccio and duck *magret* (breast of the foie-gras duck) with oranges and cumquats marry well with local wines. The €12 *menu du jour* is a bargain.

L'Arpège FRENCH €€

(☎03 89 24 29 64; www.larpegebio.com; 24 rue des Marchands; lunch menus €15-17, mains €16-24; ⌚noon-2pm Mon-Sat, plus 7-10pm Thu-Sat; 🖉) Discreetly tucked away at the back of a courtyard in a 15th-century house and with pretty garden seating when the weather is fine, L'Arpège places the accent on well-balanced, organic food. It's a convivial spot for dishes ranging from salads through to roast lamb with thyme jus and rabbit cooked in red wine. There's also a separate vegetarian menu.

Le Caveau Saint Pierre FRENCH €€

(☎03 89 41 99 33; http://lecaveausaintpierre-colmar.com; 24 rue de la Herse; menus €25-45; ⌚noon-2pm & 6.30-9.30pm Mon & Wed-Sat, noon-2pm Sun, 6.30-9.30pm Tue; 👪) Squirrelled away in the canal-laced heart of Petite Venise, this half-timbered restaurant is enticingly rustic, with low beams, stone walls and checked tablecloths. *Choucroutes* (such as with fresh fish or cider apples and blood sausage) and *tartes flambées* (thin Alsatian-style pizzas) are bang on the money, as are specialities such as pork cheeks in dark beer sauce. There's a €13 children's menu.

Palmyre MIDDLE EASTERN €€

(☎03 89 41 57 13; www.lepalmyre.com; 1 rue du Canard; menu €27.50, mains €13.50-17.50; ⌚11am-2pm & 5-10pm Mon-Sat; 👪) A sweet, simple choice, with stone walls and bistro tables, Palmyre does a roaring trade in Syrian and Lebanese cuisine. Take your pick from mezze, herby *tabouli* (bulgur-wheat salad) and slow-cooked, nicely spiced mechoui lamb.

L'Épicurien FRENCH €€

(☎03 89 41 14 50; www.epicurien-colmar.com; 11 rue Wickram; lunch menus €14.90-28, mains €23-28; ⌚noon-2pm & 7-9.30pm Tue-Sat; 👪) Hidden in a Petite Venise backstreet, this is a wine bar–bistro in the classic mould, with cheek-by-jowl tables and a good buzz. Whatever is fresh at the market goes into the pot, often with a generous pinch of spice – from filet of beef in red-wine sauce with *frites* to wild gambas poached in ginger and lemon with wok vegetables and fettuccine.

★**JY'S** GASTRONOMIC €€€

(☎03 89 21 53 60; www.jean-yves-schillinger.com; 17 quai de la Poissonerie; lunch menu €45, dinner menus €69-99; ⌚noon-2pm & 7-10pm) Jean-Yves Schillinger runs the stove at this Michelin-starred restaurant in Petite Venise. Behind a trompe-l'oeil façade lies an urban-cool, lounge-style restaurant, with flattering lighting and chesterfield sofas. Every flavour shines in seasonal dishes cooked with imagination and delivered with panache, be it trilogy of red tuna with tomato-olive tapenade or Alsatian pigeon breast with figs and foie gras.

L'Atelier du Peintre GASTRONOMIC €€€
(☎03 89 29 51 57; www.atelier-peintre.fr; 1 rue Schongauer; lunch menus €25-30, dinner menu €45; ⏱noon-1.30pm & 7-9.30pm Wed-Sat, 7-9.30pm Tue) With its art-slung walls and carefully composed cuisine, this Michelin-starred bistro lives up to its 'painter's studio' name. Seasonal masterpieces such as roast quail-breast fillets with hazelnut cream, fricassee of wild mushrooms and quince, salsify and oregano jus are cooked with verve and served with panache. The two-course lunch is a snip at €25.

ℹ Information

Tourist Office (☎03 89 20 68 92; www.tourisme-colmar.com; place Unterlinden; ⏱9am-6pm Mon-Sat, 10am-1pm Sun Apr-Oct, shorter hours rest of year; 📶) Can help find accommodation and supply information on hiking, cycling and bus travel (including schedules) along the Route des Vins and in the Massif des Vosges. Offers free wi-fi for 45 minutes.

ℹ Getting There & Away

AIR

Trinational **Basel-Mulhouse-Freiburg airport** (MLH or BSL; ☎+33 3 89 90 31 11; www.euroairport.com) is 60km south of Colmar.

BUS

Public buses are not the quickest way to explore Alsace's Route des Vins, but they *are* a viable option; destinations served include Riquewihr, Hunawihr, Ribeauvillé, Kaysersberg and Eguisheim.

The open-air bus terminal is to the right as you exit the train station. Timetables are posted and are also available at the tourist office or online (www.l-k.fr, in French).

Line 1076 goes to Neuf-Brisach (€3.75, 30 minutes), continuing on to the German city of Freiburg (€8.50, 1¼ hours, seven daily Monday to Friday, four daily weekends).

TRAIN

Colmar train connections:

Basel €14.10, 46 minutes, 25 daily
Mulhouse €8.70, 18 to 37 minutes, 38 daily
Paris Gare de l'Est; €86 to €102, three hours, 17 daily
Strasbourg €12.60, 32 to 41 minutes, 30 daily

Route des Vins destinations departing from Colmar include **Dambach-la-Ville** (€6.60, 27 to 40 minutes) and **Obernai** (€9.30, one hour), both of which require a change of trains at **Sélestat** (€5.10, 12 minutes, 30 daily).

About 20 daily TER trains (10 daily on weekends) link Colmar with the Vallée de Munster towns of **Munster** (€4.20, 19 to 33 minutes) and **Metzeral** (€5.30, 32 to 47 minutes).

CYCLING THE VINES

Colmar is a great base for slipping onto a bicycle saddle to pedal along the Route des Vins and the well-marked Franco-German trails of the nearby Rhine (www.2rives3ponts.eu, in French). Get your two-wheel adventure started by clicking onto www.haute-alsacetourisme.com and www.tourisme67.com, with detailed information on everything from bicycle hire to luggage-free cycling holidays, itinerary ideas and downloadable route maps.

If you'd rather join a group, **Bicyclette Go** (☎06 87 47 44 31; www.bicyclettego.com; 2 impasse du Tokay, Voegtlinshoffen), 12km south of Colmar, arranges all-inclusive half-day to two-week cycling tours in the region, many of which are customised. Half-day tours complete with wine tasting start at €40 per person.

ℹ Getting Around

TO/FROM THE AIRPORT

Frequent trains run between Colmar and St-Louis (€13.10, 37 minutes). An airport shuttle bus service operates between St-Louis and Basel-Mulhouse-Freiburg EuroAirport (€2.50, eight minutes, every 20 or 30 minutes).

BICYCLE

Colmarvélo (www.velodocteurs.com; 9 place de la Gare; city/mountain/e-bike per half-day €6/8/15, full day €8/12/20, deposit €150; ⏱8am-noon & 2-7pm Mon-Fri, 9am-7pm Sat & Sun) Municipal city bikes.

Massif des Vosges

The Vosges range is a little-known region of softly rounded, forest-cloaked heights and pastures interspersed with lakes and dairy farms. The secluded, 3000-sq-km **Parc Naturel Régional des Ballons des Vosges** (www.parc-ballons-vosges.fr) is surmounted by 1424m **Grand Ballon**, the highest peak in the range. Situated 20km southwest of Grand Ballon as the crow flies (by road, take the D465 from St-Maurice), the 1247m-high **Ballon d'Alsace** (www.ballondalsace.fr) marks the meeting point of the Alsace, Franche-Comté and Lorraine *régions*.

The **Vallée de Munster**, northeast of the park, is one of the region's loveliest valleys.

LOCAL KNOWLEDGE

THE EPICURE TOUR

Colmar is an exceptional city for all-out indulgence. So go, assemble your gourmet picnic:

Marché Couvert (rue des Écoles; ⏱8am-6pm Tue-Thu, to 7pm Fri, to 5pm Sat) Bag Munster cheese, pretzels, patisserie, wild-boar *saucisson* (dry-cured sausage or salami), foie gras and more at this 19th-century market hall.

Fromagerie St-Nicolas (www.fromagerie-st-nicolas.com; 18 rue St-Nicolas; ⏱2-7pm Mon, 10am-12.30pm & 2-7pm Tue-Fri, 9am-6.30pm Sat) Follow your nose to pungent Munster, Tomme and ripe Camembert. BYOB (bring your own baguette) and they'll make you a sandwich.

Les Foie Gras de Liesel (3 rue Turenne; ⏱9.30am-12.30pm & 2.30-6.30pm Tue-Sat) Marco and Marianne Willmann produce the silkiest, most subtly flavoured goose and duck foie gras in town.

Choco en Têtes (www.chocolat-en-tetes.com; 7 rue des Têtes; ⏱2-6.30pm Mon, 9.30am-12.45pm & 1.45-6.30pm Tue-Sat) Edible art describes this chocolatier's seasonally inspired truffles and pralines. Kids love the chocolate stork eggs.

Maison Martin Jund (www.martinjund.com; 12 rue de l'Ange; ⏱tastings 9am-noon & 2-6.30pm Mon-Sat) Need something to wash it all down? Head to this organic winery to taste home-grown pinots, rieslings and sylvaners.

Munster

POP 4828

Spread around gently rolling hills and famous for its notoriously smelly and eponymous cheese, streamside Munster, meaning 'monastery', is a relaxed base for exploring the valley (the long-distance hiking trail GR531 passes by here).

Sights & Activities

Enclos aux Cigognes WILDLIFE RESERVE

(Stork Enclosure; chemin du Dubach; ⏱24hr) FREE About 20 storks live year-round in the Enclos aux Cigognes, and more hang out on top of it. It's 250m behind the Renaissance *hôtel de ville;* on foot, cross the creek and turn left.

Cycle Hop Evasion CYCLING

(5 rue de la République; bike rental per day €14-18; ⏱9.30am-6.30pm Mon-Sat) Cycle Hop Evasion rents out mountain bikes, arranges guides and provides details on cycling routes.

Sleeping & Eating

Hôtel Deybach HOTEL €

(☎03 89 77 32 71; www.hotel-deybach.com; 4 chemin du Badischhof; s €52-66, d €60-80, tr €84-95; P ☎) You are made to feel instantly welcome at family-run Hôtel Deybach, which has fresh, simple rooms with town or country views and a flowery garden for relaxing moments. Breakfast costs an additional €10.

Salon de Thé Gilg CAFE €

(11 Grand'Rue; cakes & pastries €2-5; ⏱7.30am-6.30pm Tue-Fri, 7am-6pm Sat, 7.30am-12.30pm Sun) Skip dinner and go straight for dessert at this tearoom famous for its delectable *kougelhopf* (a ring-shaped marble cake), petits fours and pastries.

A l'Agneau d'Or REGIONAL CUISINE €€

(☎03 89 77 34 08; www.martinfache.com; 2 rue St-Grégoire; menus €37-48; ⏱noon-2pm & 7-9pm Wed-Sun) Brimming with bonhomie, A l'Agneau d'Or is a fine choice for robustly seasoned, attractively presented Alsatian dishes, such as *choucroute au gratin* with Munster cheese and pork cheeks slow braised in pinot noir.

Information

Maison du Parc Naturel Régional des Ballons des Vosges (☎03 89 77 90 34; www.parc-ballons-vosges.fr; 1 cour de l'Abbaye; ⏱10am-noon & 1.30-5.30pm Tue-Sun mid-Jun–mid-Sep, shorter hours rest of year) The regional park's visitors centre has ample information in English. To get there, walk through the arch from place du Marché.

Tourist Office (☎03 89 77 31 80; www.vallee-munster.eu; 1 rue du Couvent; ⏱9.30am-12.30pm & 2-6pm Mon-Fri, 10am-noon & 2-4pm Sat) Information on the Munster valley, including visits to cheesemakers. Sells hiking maps and topoguides in French. To get there, walk through the arch from place du Marché.

LOCAL KNOWLEDGE

HOLY CHEESE

Rich, white and creamy, with a pungent, earthy aroma when ripe and a mild flavour when fresh, Munster cheese has been made in this valley to the time-honoured methods of the Benedictine monks since the 7th century. Only the milk of the cows that lazily graze the Vosges' highest pastures is good enough for this semisoft cheese, delicious with cumin seeds, rye bread and a glass of spicy gewürztraminer. See www.vallee-munster.eu for details on dairy farms where you can taste and buy Munster and see it in the making.

Mulhouse

POP 112,523

The dynamic industrial city of Mulhouse (moo-looze), 57km south of Colmar, was allied with nearby Switzerland before voting to join Revolutionary France in 1798. Largely rebuilt after the ravages of WWII, it has little of the quaint Alsatian charm that you find further north, but the city's world-class industrial museums are well worth a stop.

Sights

Ecomusée d'Alsace MUSEUM

(www.ecomusee-alsace.fr; Ungersheim; adult/child €15/10; ⏲10am-6pm, closed Jan–mid-Mar) Ecomusée d'Alsace is a fascinating excursion into Alsatian country life and time-honoured crafts. Smiths, cartwrights, potters and coopers do their thing in and among 70 historic Alsatian farmhouses – a veritable village – brought here and painstakingly reconstructed for preservation (and so storks can build nests on them). Ungersheim is 17km northwest of Mulhouse. Take tram 1 to Rattachement, then bus 54 to the Ecomusée stop. The closest train station is in Bollwiller, 3km north.

Musée de l'Impression sur Étoffes TEXTILE MUSEUM

(Museum of Textile Printing; www.musee-impression.com; 14 rue Jean-Jacques Henner; adult/child €9/4.50; ⏲10am-noon & 2-6pm Tue-Sun) Once known as the 'French Manchester', Mulhouse is fittingly home to this peerless collection of six million textile samples – from brilliant cashmeres to intricate silk screens – which makes it a mecca for fabric designers. It's one long block northeast of the train station.

Musée du Papier Peint WALLPAPER MUSEUM

(www.museepapierpeint.org; 28 rue Zuber; adult/child €8/free; ⏲10am-noon & 2-6pm, closed Mon Nov-Apr) More stimulating than it sounds, this is a treasure trove of wallpaper (some of the scenic stuff is as detailed as an oil painting) and the machines used to produce it since the 18th century. To reach it, take bus 18 from the train station to Temple stop, or the Rixheim exit on the A36.

Cité de l'Automobile MUSEUM

(http://citedelautomobile.com; 192 av de Colmar; adult/child €12/9.50; ⏲10am-6pm) An ode to the automobile, this striking glass-and-steel museum showcases 400 rare and classic motors, from old-timers such as the Bugatti Royale to Formula 1 dream machines. There's a kids' corner for would-be mechanics. By car, hop off the A36 at the Mulhouse Centre exit. By public transport, take bus 10 or tram 1 from Mulhouse to the Musée de l'Automobile stop.

Cité du Train TRAIN MUSEUM

(www.citedutrain.com; 2 rue Alfred de Glehn; adult/child €12/9.50; ⏲10am-6pm) Trainspotters are in their element at Europe's largest railway museum, displaying SNCF's prized collection of locomotives and carriages. Take bus 20 from the train station or, if driving, the Mulhouse-Dornach exit on the A35.

Sleeping & Eating

Hotel du Musée Gare HOTEL €

(☎03 89 45 47 41; www.hotelmuseegare.com; 3 rue de l'Est; d €49-98, tr €105-198, q €115-218; P 📶) Sitting opposite the Musée de l'Impression sur Étoffes and very close to the station, this lovingly restored townhouse outclasses most of Mulhouse's hotels with its 19th-century flair, attentive service and spacious, high-ceilinged rooms. Free parking is a bonus. Buffet breakfast costs an extra €9.80.

Villa Eden VILLA €€€

(☎06 74 37 19 38, 03 89 44 50 72; www.villa-eden.fr; 99 av de la 1ère Division Blindée; s/d €170/195; P 📶 🏊) A far cry from the anonymity of many of Mulhouse's hotels, this shuttered villa sits above the city's zoo and botanical gardens. It's a secluded spot to escape the bustle of the centre, with gardens, an outdoor pool and individually designed rooms (from 'Zen' to 'sweet chocolate') with plenty of light, space and comfort.

Zum Sauwadala REGIONAL CUISINE €
(☎03 89 45 18 19; 13 rue Arsena; 2-course lunch €10, mains €12-21; ⌚noon-2pm & 7-11pm Tue-Sat) Two little pigs guide the way to this snug bistro – the very essence of Alsace quaintness with its dark timber, checked tablecloths and roll-me-out-the-door hearty grub. The menu is packed with classics – *Spätzle* (egg pasta), fat pork trotters and *choucroute* (garnished sauerkraut) – all of which marry nicely with a glass of the local pinot noir. The *plat du jour* goes for €8.50.

★**Chez Auguste** BISTRO €€
(☎03 89 46 62 71; www.chezauguste.com; 11 rue Poincaré; menus €20-25; ⌚noon-2pm & 7-10pm Tue-Sat) Overflowing with regulars, this casually sophisticated bistro always has a good buzz. The concise menu excels in classics including scallops with orange-infused carrot puree and pistachio, confit pork cheeks slow-cooked for six hours and chocolate fondant. Service is faultless.

Information

Mulhouse's helpful **tourist office** (☎03 89 35 48 48; www.tourism-mulhouse.com; 1 av Robert Schuman; ⌚10am-1pm & 2-6pm Mon-Sat, 10am-3pm Sun; 📶) is just north of the old town. Free wi-fi.

Getting There & Around

BICYCLE

Mulhouse has an automatic bike-rental system, **Velocité** (www.velocite.mulhouse.fr), with 40 stands across the city – the online map shows where. The first half-hour is free and it costs €1/3 per day/week thereafter (deposit €150).

TRAIN

France's second train line, linking Mulhouse with Thann, opened in 1839. The **train station** (10 av du Général Leclerc) is just south of the centre. Trains run at least hourly to Basel (€7.50, 23 to 31 minutes), Colmar (€8.70, 18 to 37 minutes), St-Louis (€5.50 to €6.10, 14 to 20 minutes) and Strasbourg (€18.70, 51 to 70 minutes).

LORRAINE

Lorraine, between the plains and vines of Champagne and the Massif des Vosges, is fed by the Meurthe, Moselle and Meuse Rivers – hence the names of three of its four *départements* (the fourth is Vosges).

Nancy

POP 106,342

Delightful Nancy has an air of refinement found nowhere else in Lorraine. With a resplendent central square, fine museums, formal gardens and shop windows sparkling with Daum and Baccarat crystal, the former capital of the dukes of Lorraine catapults you back to the riches of the 18th century, when much of the city centre was built.

Nancy has long thrived on a combination of innovation and sophistication. The art-nouveau movement flourished here (as the Nancy School) thanks to the rebellious spirit of local artists, who set out to prove that everyday objects could be drop-dead gorgeous.

OFF THE BEATEN TRACK

ROUTE DES CRÊTES

Partly built during WWI to supply French frontline troops, the **Route des Crêtes** (Route of the Crests) takes you to the Vosges' highest *ballons* (bald, rounded mountain peaks) and to several WWI sites. Mountaintop lookouts afford spectacular views of the Alsace plain, the Black Forest across the Rhine in Germany and – on clear days – the Alps and Mont Blanc.

From Col de la Schlucht, home to a small ski station, trails head off in various directions; walking north along the GR5 brings you to three pristine lakes: **Lac Vert**, **Lac Noir** and **Lac Blanc** (Green, Black and White Lakes).

At the dramatic, wind-buffeted summit of 1424m **Grand Ballon**, the highest point in the Vosges, a short trail takes you to an aircraft-radar ball and a weather station.

Roads swing up to several viewpoints, but for a truer sense of this mountainous, forest-cloaked corner of the Vosges, strike out on foot or with a mountain bike. Steep inclines and hairpin bends make the terrain challenging and exhilarating for cyclists.

For the lowdown on outdoor pursuits along the Route des Crêtes, visit www.parc-ballons-vosges.fr, www.tourismevosges.fr, and www.massif-des-vosges.com (in French).

Sights

The tourist office offers multilingual audioguide tours (€7.50) of the historic centre (two hours) and the art-nouveau quarters (up to three or four hours), or download a free MP3 tour online (www.nancy-tourisme.fr).

★Place Stanislas SQUARE

Nancy's crowning glory is this grand neoclassical square and Unesco World Heritage Site. Designed by Emmanuel Héré in the 1750s, it was named after the enlightened, Polish-born duke of Lorraine, whose statue stands in the middle. The square is home to an opulent ensemble of pale-stone buildings, including the **hôtel de ville** and the Opéra National de Lorraine (p352), as well as gilded wrought-iron gateways by Jean Lamour and rococo fountains by Guibal – look out for the one of a trident-bearing Neptune.

Place de la Carrière SQUARE

Adjoining place Stanislas – on the other side of Nancy's own **Arc de Triomphe**, built in the mid-1750s to honour Louis XV – is this quiet square. Once a riding and jousting arena, it is now graced by four rows of linden trees and stately rococo gates in gilded wrought iron.

★Musée des Beaux-Arts ART MUSEUM

(http://mban.nancy.fr; 3 place Stanislas; adult/child €6/4, audioguide €3; ⌚10am-6pm Wed-Mon) Lodged in a regal 18th-century edifice, Nancy's standout gallery occupies art lovers for hours. A wrought-iron staircase curls gracefully up to the 2nd floor, where a chronological spin begins with 14th- to 17th-century paintings by the likes of Perugino, Tintoretto and Jan van Hemessen. The 1st floor spotlights 17th- to 19th-century masterpieces of the Rubens, Monet, Picasso and Caravaggio ilk. A collection of Jean Prouvé furnishings, impressionist and modern art and a dazzling Daum crystal collection hide in the basement.

Highlights in the 1st- and 2nd-floor picture galleries include Mello da Gubbio's 14th-century altarpiece, Perugino's Renaissance *Madonna and Child with two Angels* (1505), Rubens' lucid, large-scale *Transfiguration* (1603), showing Jesus radiant on a mountain, and Caravaggio's dramatic chiaroscuro *Annunciation* (1607).

The basement **Jean Prouvé Collection** homes in on the pared-down aesthetic of Nancy-born architect and designer Jean Prouvé (1901–84), and displays a selection of Prouvé's furniture, architectural elements, ironwork and graphic works. Here you will also find the peerless **Daum Collection**, which is displayed in a dark, spotlit gallery that shows off the glassware to great effect and is cleverly set against the backdrop of Nancy's late-medieval city walls. Trace Daum through the ages – from the sinuous, naturalistic forms of art nouveau to the clean colours and restrained lines of contemporary crystal.

The downstairs picture gallery wings you into the 19th and 20th centuries with an excellent portfolio of works, among them Eugène Delacroix' *Battle of Nancy* (1831), Monet's dreamy *Étretat, Sunset* (1883) and Picasso's *Homme et femme* (1971), one of his final portraits.

Musée de l'École de Nancy MUSEUM

(School of Nancy Museum; www.ecole-de-nancy.com; 36-38 rue du Sergent Blandan; adult/child

ART-NOUVEAU TRAIL

In 1900, glassmaker and ceramist Émile Gallé founded the École de Nancy, one of France's leading art-nouveau movements, joining creative forces with masters of decorative arts and architecture such as Jacques Gruber, Louis Majorelle and the Daum brothers. Banks, villas, pharmacies, brasseries – wherever you wander in Nancy, you're bound to stumble across their handiwork, from sinuous grillwork to curvaceous stained-glass windows and doorways that are a profusion of naturalistic ornament.

Slip back to this genteel era by picking up the free *Art Nouveau Itineraries* brochure and map at the tourist office, covering four city strolls. Lucien Weissenburger's 1911 **Brasserie Excelsior** (p352) and the 1908 **Chambre de Commerce** with wrought iron by Louis Majorelle, both located on rue Henri Poincaré, are central standouts. Close to the Musée de l'École de Nancy lies the whimsical **Villa Majorelle** (p349), built by Henri Sauvage in 1901 and bearing the hallmarks of Majorelle (furniture) and Gruber (stained glass). The centrepiece is the Les Blés dining room with its vine-like stone fireplace. Advance telephone bookings are essential.

€6/4; ⏲10am-6pm Wed-Sun) A highlight of a visit to Nancy, the Musée de l'École de Nancy brings together an exquisite collection of art-nouveau interiors, curvaceous glass and landscaped gardens. It's housed in a 19th-century villa about 2km southwest of the centre; to get there take bus 6 (Painlevé stop) or bus 7 or 8 (Nancy Thermal stop).

Musée Lorrain MUSEUM
(www.musee-lorrain.nancy.fr; 64 & 66 Grande Rue; adult/child €6/4; ⏲10am-12.30pm & 2-6pm Tue-Sun) Once home to the dukes of Lorraine, the regal Renaissance Palais Ducal now shelters the Musée Lorrain. The rich fine arts and history collection spotlights medieval statuary, engravings and lustrous faience (glazed pottery). The regional art and folklore collection occupies a 15th-century former Franciscan monastery. Inside, the Gothic **Église des Cordeliers** and the 17th-century **Chapelle Ducale**, modelled on the Medici Chapel in Florence, served as the burial place of the dukes of Lorraine.

Villa Majorelle MUSEUM
(☎Mon-Fri 03 83 17 86 77, Sat & Sun 03 83 40 14 86; www.ecole-de-nancy.com; 1 rue Louis-Majorelle; adult/child €6/4; ⏲guided tours 2.30pm & 3.45pm Sat & Sun May-Oct) The whimsical Villa Majorelle, built by Henri Sauvage in 1901, bears the hallmarks of Majorelle (furniture) and Gruber (stained glass). The centrepiece is Les Blés dining room, with its vine-like stone fireplace. Advance telephone bookings are essential. At the time of writing, the façade was undergoing renovation.

Place de l'Alliance SQUARE
This lime tree–fringed square, World Heritage material, is graced by a **Baroque fountain** by Bruges-born Louis Cyfflé (1724–1806), inspired by Bernini's *Four Rivers* fountain in Rome's Piazza Navona.

Vieille Ville AREA
A saunter through the charming old town takes in the silver-turreted, 14th-century **Porte de la Craffe**, Nancy's oldest city gate, and **place St-Epvre**, dominated by ornate neo-Gothic **Basilique St-Epvre**.

Parc de la Pépinière PARK
(⏲6.30am-10.30pm, shorter hours winter) On a hot summer's day, escape the crowds in this formal garden, with ornamental fountains, a rose garden and a Rodin sculpture of Baroque landscape painter Claude Lorrain.

> **ℹ CITY PASS**
>
> The good-value **Nancy City Pass** (€12), valid for 10 days, gets you an audioguide tour of the city, a 24-hour transport ticket and a 50% discount on bike rental.

Cathédrale Notre-Dame-de-l'Annonciation CATHEDRAL
(place Monseigneur Ruch; ⏲8.45am-7pm Mon-Sat, 10.45am-8pm Sun) Crowned by a frescoed dome, Nancy's 18th-century cathedral is a sombre mixture of neoclassical and Baroque.

Festivals & Events

Jazz Pulsations MUSIC
(www.nancyjazzpulsations.com; ⏲Oct) Get your groove on to live jazz, blues and Latin at the 10-day Jazz Pulsations.

Marché de Nöel CHRISTMAS MARKET
The Christmas Market brings twinkle, carols and handicrafts to place André Maginot.

Sleeping

La Résidence HOTEL €
(☎03 83 40 33 56; www.hotel-laresidence-nancy.com; 30 bd Jean-Jaurès; d €73-84, q €115; P ☜) This convivial hotel is one of Nancy's best deals, with an inviting salon and a leafy courtyard for alfresco breakfasts. The snappy new rooms have ultramodern bathrooms and flat-screen TVs. The hotel is situated 1km south of the train station. Tram 1 stops at Mon Désert and Garenne, both a two-minute walk from the hotel.

Maison de Myon B&B €€
(☎03 83 46 56 56; www.maisondemyon.com; 7 rue Mably; s €115, d €135-140, apt €165-195; ☜) Slip behind the cathedral to reach this stately 17th-century house turned boutique B&B. A wrought-iron staircase leads to light-filled, wooden-floored rooms flaunting antique furnishings, one-of-a-kind art and ornamental fireplaces. Each room takes its name from its polished-concrete bathroom (sand, turquoise, mandarin and so on). The wisteria-draped courtyard is a calm breakfast spot.

La Villa 1901 B&B €€
(☎06 30 03 21 62; www.lavilla1901.fr; 63 av du Général Leclerc; s €145-165, d €165-185; ☜) Taking a leaf out of the chic interiors book, this B&B combines art nouveau with contemporary design flourishes and boho flair to

Nancy

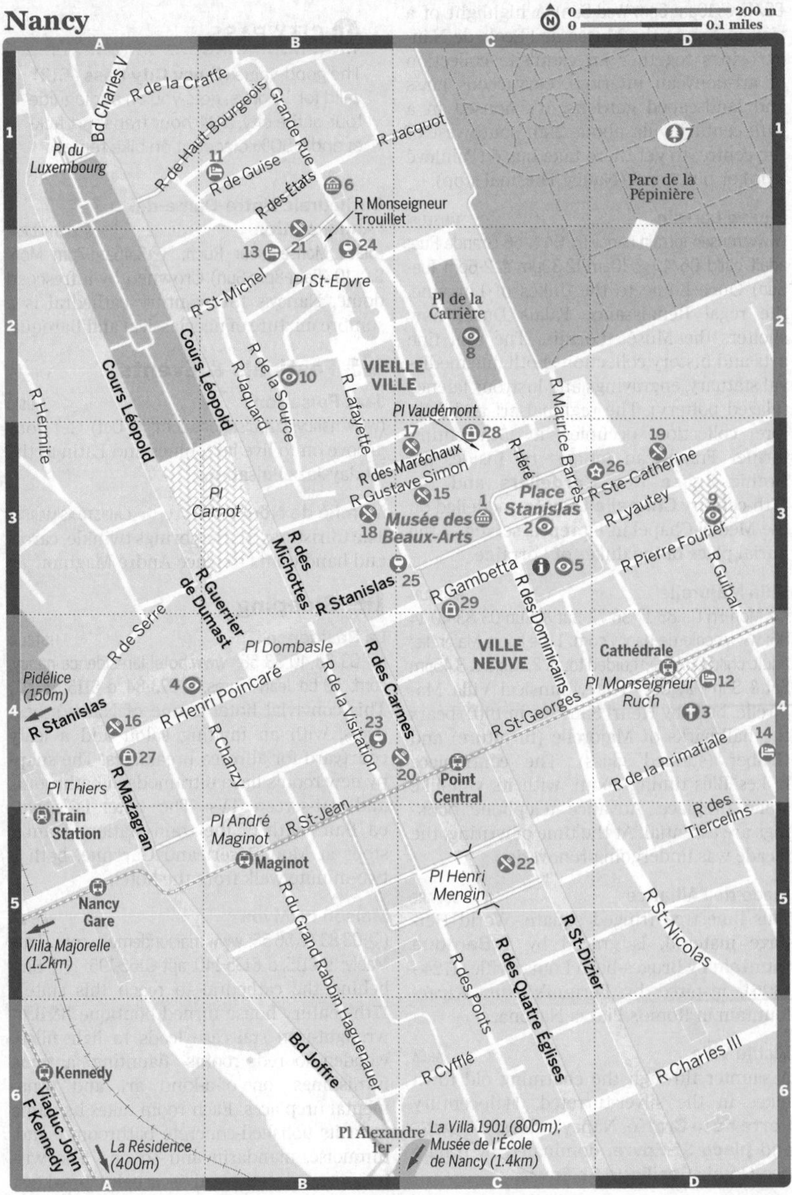

beautiful effect. The richly hued rooms and suites feature home-style touches like fireplaces and iPod docks, and there's a garden for quiet moments. Breakfast (included in the rate) is a treat, with fresh pastries, juice and preserves.

Hôtel des Prélats HISTORIC HOTEL **€€**
(☎03 83 30 20 20; www.hoteldesprelats.com; 56 place Monseigneur Ruch; s €79-125, d €119-145, ste €249; ❄📶) It's not every day you get to sleep in a 17th-century former bishop's palace right next to the cathedral. This elegant

Nancy

hotel plays up the romance in rooms with stained-glass windows, four-poster beds and shimmery drapes. Service is as polished as the surrounds.

Hôtel de Guise HISTORIC HOTEL €€
(☎03 83 32 24 68; www.hoteldeguise.com; 18 rue de Guise; s €69-95, d €77-129;) Boutique chic meets 17th-century elegance at this hotel, tucked down an old-town backstreet. A wrought-iron staircase sweeps up to old-fashioned rooms, with antique furnishings, inlaid parquet and heavy drapes. There's a walled garden for quiet moments.

★ **Hôtel d'Haussonville** HISTORIC HOTEL €€€
(☎03 83 35 85 84; www.hotel-haussonville.fr; 9 rue Monseigneur Trouillet; d €149-239;) Centred on an ornately carved courtyard, this sublime Renaissance mansion snuggles down a backstreet in the heart of Nancy's Vieille Ville. The seven individually designed rooms are decorated with impeccable taste, done out with parquet floors, elegant drapes and ornamental fireplaces. It's worth shelling out the extra €17 for breakfast.

Eating

Restaurant-speckled rue des Maréchaux dishes up everything from French to Italian, tapas, seafood, Indian and Japanese. Grande Rue is peppered with intimate bistros.

Le Bouche à Oreille BISTRO €
(☎03 83 35 17 17; http://restaurant-bouche-a-oreille.fr; 42 rue des Carmes; menus €11-24; 7-10pm Mon, noon-1.30pm & 7-10pm Tue-Thu, noon-1.30pm & 7-10.30pm Fri, 7-10.30pm Sat;) Resembling an overgrown doll's house, this knick-knack–filled bistro specialises in cheese-based dishes such as *raclette, tartiflette* (creamy, cheesy potato bake with onions and lardons) and fondue.

Pidélice SANDWICHES €
(25 rue Raymond-Poincaré; pidélices €6-8, menus €9.50-12; 11.30am-2.30pm & 6-10.30pm Mon-Fri, 6-10.30pm Sat & Sun) Is it a pizza? Is it a sandwich? Well, a *pidélice* is kind of both, served hot, crunchy and stuffed with gourmet fillings – from feta and olives to steak with melted cheese – prepared with organic ingredients. The walls are covered with quirky photos of moustaches; see if you can snap a better one.

Inévitable MODERN FRENCH €€
(☎03 83 36 36 36; www.bistorant-inevitable.fr; 17 rue Gustave Simon; menus €19-40; noon-2pm & 8-10pm Thu, Fri & Mon, 8-10pm Sat) You can expect a warm welcome at this slick, monochrome bistro, which keeps its menu seasonal, simple and regional, along the lines of market-fresh fish with braised fennel and bergamot confit.

À la Table du Bon Roi Stanislas FRENCH €€
(At the Table of Good King Stanislas; ☎03 83 35 36 52; http://tablestan.free.fr; 7 rue Gustave Simon; menus €19-43; ⏰7.15-9.30pm Mon & Wed, 12.15-1.30pm & 7.15-9.30pm Tue & Thu-Sat, 12.15-1.30pm Sun) À la Table du Bon Roi Stanislas dishes up good old-fashioned French food with lashings of bonhomie. Menu classics feature escargots with dill and duck cooked in red wine with fig confit. There's terrace seating in summer.

Le Gentilhommiere FRENCH €€
(☎03 83 32 26 44; www.lagentilhommierenancy.fr; 29 rue des Maréchaux; menus €25-40; ⏰noon-2pm & 7-10pm Mon-Fri, 7-10pm Sat) Warm-hued, subtly lit Le Gentilhommiere stands head and shoulders above most of the restaurants on rue des Maréchaux. Specialities like scallop tartlet with beetroot and liquorice vinaigrette and pike-perch fillets with Lorraine truffle risotto reveal true depth of flavour.

Le V-Four BISTRO €€
(☎03 83 32 49 48; www.levfour.fr; 10 rue St-Michel; menus €21-68; ⏰11.45am-1.30pm & 7.45-11.30pm Tue-Sat, 11.45am-1.30pm Sun) With just a handful of tables, this petite bistro is all about intimacy and understated sophistication. Mulberry chairs and crisp white tablecloths set the scene for original creations such as grilled scallops with Jerusalem artichoke and truffle. The three-course lunch is a steal at €21. Book ahead.

Brasserie Excelsior BRASSERIE €€
(☎03 83 35 24 57; www.brasserie-excelsior.com; 50 rue Henri Poincaré; menus €29-50; ⏰8am-12.30am Tue-Sat, to 11pm Sun & Mon) As opulent as a Fabergé egg with its stucco and stained glass, Excelsior whisks you back to the decadent era of art nouveau. Brusquely efficient waiters bring brasserie classics such as oysters (September through April), juicy steaks and banquet-like seafood platters to the table.

La Maison dans le Parc FRENCH €€€
(☎03 83 19 03 57; www.lamaisondansleparc.com; 3 rue Ste-Catherine; menus €69-98; ⏰noon-1.30pm & 7-9.30pm Wed-Sat, noon-1.30pm Sun) Shining with one Michelin star, this restaurant is Nancy's bastion of fine dining. Service is faultless and the ambience one of urban sophistication, with clean lines, monochrome hues and floor-to-ceiling windows. A smartly dressed crowd pours in for chef Françoise Mutel's artistically presented, intensely flavoured creations, simple as sea-bass tartare with oysters and caviar, and Iberian pork with sweet garlic.

Self-Catering

Marché Couvert FOOD MARKET €
(place Henri Mengin; ⏰7am-7pm Tue-Sat) A fresh-produce feast for the picnic basket, with several snack stands offering inexpensive lunches.

Drinking & Nightlife

Nancy's buoyant nightlife concentrates on bar-dotted Grande Rue; the spectacularly illuminated place Stanislas and laid-back place St-Epvre in the Vieille Ville are the best spots for sundowners.

Les Artistes BAR
(36 rue Stanislas; ⏰8am-2am Mon-Sat, 1pm-2am Sun) A young and lively crowd props up the bar and fills the pavement terrace at super-central Les Artistes. It's a chilled hangout for an afternoon coffee or something stronger as the night wears on.

Bab BAR
(29 rue de la Visitation; ⏰5pm-2am Tue-Sat) This fun-focused bar has a roster of events, from flamenco nights to gigs. The mojito list features its own creations laced with raspberry, melon and mint.

Le Ch'timi BAR
(17 place St-Epvre; ⏰9am-2am Mon-Sat, to 9pm Sun) On three brick-and-stone levels, Le Ch'timi is *the* place to go for beer. It's a beloved haunt of students, who come for the 150 brewskies, 16 of them on tap.

Entertainment

Details on cultural events appear in French in *Spectacles* (www.spectacles-publications.com).

Opéra National de Lorraine OPERA
(☎03 83 85 33 11; www.opera-national-lorraine.fr; 1 rue Ste-Catherine) A harmonious blend of neoclassical and art-nouveau styles, this is Nancy's lavish stage for opera and classical music. The resident orchestra performs at *concerts apéritifs* (€8), held roughly one Saturday a month.

Shopping

Nancy's grand thoroughfares are rue St-Dizier, rue St-Jean and rue St-Georges. Grande Rue is studded with idiosyncratic galleries and antique shops.

L'Épicerie du Goût FOOD & DRINKS
(www.epicerie-du-gout.fr; 4 place Vaudémont; ⏰10am-1pm & 3.30-8pm Mon-Fri, 10am-1pm &

2.30-8pm Sat) This family-run grocery store on the edge of the old town is crammed with Lorraine delicacies. Cheeses, smoked *saucisson*, macarons, *mirabelles* (plums) in every guise, beer, preserves – you'll find it all here.

Maison des Sœurs Macarons SWEETS
(www.macaron-de-nancy.com; 21 rue Gambetta; ⌚2-7pm Mon, 9.30am-12.30pm & 2-7pm Tue-Fri, 9am-7pm Sat) When Nancy's Benedictine nuns hit hard times during the French Revolution, they saw the light in heavenly macarons. They're still made to the original recipe (egg whites, sugar, Provençal almonds) at this old-world confectioner. A dozen box (€8) makes a great gift.

Lefèvre-Lemoine SWEETS
(47 rue Henri Poincaré; ⌚8.30am-7pm Mon-Sat, 9.30am-12.30pm Sun) They don't make sweet shops like this 1840s treasure any more, where a bird chirps a welcome as you enter. One of the old-fashioned sweet tins made a cameo appearance in the film *Amélie*. *Bergamotes de Nancy* (bergamot boiled sweets), caramels, nougat, gingerbread, glazed *mirabelles* (plums) – how ever will you choose?

Information

Tourist Office (☎03 83 35 22 41; www.nancy-tourisme.fr; place Stanislas; ⌚9am-7pm Mon-Sat, 10am-5pm Sun May-Sep, shorter hours rest of year; 📶) Inside the *hôtel de ville*. Has free brochures detailing walking tours of the city centre and art-nouveau architecture. Free wi-fi.

Getting There & Around

TRAIN

The **train station** (place Thiers) is on the line linking Paris with Strasbourg. Destinations:

Baccarat €11.40, 50 minutes, 15 daily
Metz €11.20, 38 to 53 minutes, 48 daily
Paris €62 to €88, 1½ hours, 13 daily
Strasbourg €26 to €31, 1½ hours, 12 daily

BICYCLE

Nancy is easy to navigate by bicycle. **Vélostan** (www.velostanlib.fr; per half-day/full day/week €2/3/8; ⌚24hr) has rental sites inside the train station and near the Musée de l'École de Nancy in Espace Thermal as well as 29 rental points where you can hire bikes 24/7. An €80 deposit is required.

Baccarat

POP 4668

The glitzy Baccarat *cristallerie* (crystal glassworks), founded in 1764, is 60km southeast of Nancy. Its famous crystal dazzles in the Musée Baccarat and Église St-Rémy.

Sights

Musée Baccarat CRYSTAL MUSEUM
(www.baccarat.fr; 2 rue des Cristalleries; adult/child €5/free; ⌚9am-noon & 2-6pm Tue-Sun) The Musée Baccarat displays 1100 exquisite pieces of handmade lead crystal. The boutique out front is almost as dazzling as the museum.

Église St-Rémy CHURCH
(1 av de Lachapelle; ⌚8am-5pm) On the bank of the park-lined River Meurthe, the dark concrete sanctuary of Église St-Rémy, built in the mid-1950s, is austere on the outside and kaleidoscopic on the inside – dramatically lit by 20,000 Baccarat crystal panels.

Information

The **tourist office** (☎03 83 75 13 37; www.ccvc54.fr; 13 rue du Port; ⌚9am-12.30pm & 1.30-6pm) has info on the surrounds and hiking maps.

Getting There & Away

Trains run from Baccarat to Nancy (€11.40, 48 minutes, 15 daily). By car, Baccarat makes an easy stop on the way from Nancy to Colmar via the Vosges' Col du Bonhomme.

Metz

POP 120,708

Sitting astride the confluence of the Moselle and Seille rivers, Lorraine's graceful capital, Metz, (pronounced 'mess') is ready to be feted. Though the city's Gothic marvel of a cathedral, superlative art collections and Michelin star–studded dining scene long managed to sidestep the world spotlight, all that changed with the show-stopping arrival of Centre Pompidou-Metz in 2010. Yet the Pompidou is but the prelude to Metz' other charms: buzzy pavement cafes and shady riverside parks, a beautiful old town built from golden Jeumont stone and a regal Quartier Impérial up for Unesco World Heritage status. Suddenly, everyone's talking about Metz, and rightly so.

Sights

★Centre Pompidou-Metz GALLERY

(www.centrepompidou-metz.fr; 1 parvis des Droits de l'Homme; adult/child €7/free; ⏲10am-6pm Mon & Wed-Thu, to 7pm Fri-Sun) Designed by Japanese architect Shigeru Ban, with a curved roof resembling a space-age Chinese hat, the architecturally innovative Centre Pompidou-Metz is the star of Metz' art scene. The satellite branch of Paris' Centre Pompidou draws on Europe's largest modern-art collection to stage ambitious temporary exhibitions, such as the deconstructive installations of Japanese artist and sculptor Tadashi Kawamata and the bold avant-garde works of German Bauhaus artist Oskar Schlemmer. The dynamic space also hosts cultural events, talks and youth projects.

★Cathédrale St-Étienne CATHEDRAL

(www.cathedrale-metz.fr; place St-Étienne; audioguide €7, combined ticket treasury & crypt adult/child €4/2; ⏲8am-6pm, treasury & crypt 9am-12.30pm & 1.30-6pm Mon-Sat, 1-6pm Sun) The lacy golden spires of this Gothic cathedral crown Metz' skyline. Exquisitely lit by kaleidoscopic curtains of 13th- to 20th-century stained glass, the cathedral is nicknamed 'God's lantern' and its sense of height is spiritually uplifting. Notice the flamboyant **Chagall windows** in startling jewel-coloured shades of ruby, gold, sapphire, topaz and amethyst in the ambulatory, which also harbours the **treasury**. A sculpture of the **Graoully** ('grau-lee'), a dragon said to have terrified pre-Christian Metz, lurks in the 15th-century **crypt**.

DON'T MISS

MARKET MAGNIFICENCE

If only every market were like Metz' grand **Marché Couvert** (Covered Market; place de la Cathédrale; ⏲7am-6.30pm Tue-Sat). Once a bishop's palace, now a temple to fresh local produce, this is the kind of place where you pop in for a baguette and struggle out an hour later with bags overflowing with charcuterie, ripe fruit, pastries and five different sorts of *fromage*.

Make a morning of it, stopping for an early, inexpensive lunch and a chat with the market's larger-than-life characters. **Chez Mauricette** (sandwiches €3-4.50, light meals €7-11) tempts with such Lorraine goodies as herby *saucisson*, local charcuterie and *mirabelle* (plum) pâté. Its neighbour, **Soupes á Soups** (soups €3-5), ladles out homemade soups, from mussel to creamy mushroom varieties.

Musée La Cour d'Or MUSEUM

(http://musee.metzmetropole.fr; 2 rue du Haut Poirier; adult/child €5/free; ⏲9am-12.30pm & 1.45-5pm) Delve into the past at this trove of Gallo-Roman antiquities, hiding remnants of the city's Roman baths and a statue of the Egyptian goddess Isis unearthed right here in Metz. Your visit continues with art from the Middle Ages, paintings from the 15th century onwards, and artefacts revealing the history of Metz' ancient Jewish community. A room-by-room brochure in English is available.

Quartier Impérial HISTORIC QUARTER

The stately boulevards and bourgeois villas of the German Imperial Quarter, including rue Gambetta and av Foch, are the brainchild of Kaiser Wilhelm II. Philippe Starck lamp posts juxtapose Teutonic sculptures, whose common theme is German imperial might, at the monumental Rhenish neo-Romanesque **train station**, completed in 1908. The massive main **post office**, built in 1911 of red Vosges sandstone, is as solid and heavy as the cathedral is light and lacy.

Built to trumpet the triumph of Metz' post-1871 status as part of the Second Reich, the architecture is a whimsical mix of art-deco, neo-Romanesque and neo-Renaissance influences. The area's unique ensemble of Wilhelmian architecture has made it a candidate for Unesco World Heritage status.

Place de la Comédie SQUARE

Bounded by one of the channels of the Moselle, this neoclassical square is home to the city's 18th-century **Théâtre**, France's oldest theatre still in use. During the Revolution, place de l'Égalité (as it was then known) was the site of a guillotine that lopped the heads off 63 'enemies of the people'. Only open during services, the neo-Romanesque **Temple Neuf** church was constructed under the Germans in 1904.

Église St-Pierre-aux-Nonains CHURCH

(Esplanade) Originally built around 380 as part of a Gallo-Roman spa complex, Église St-Pierre-aux-Nonains is a fine example of a pre-medieval basilica, tracing almost 2000 years of history. Now a cultural centre, it can only be admired from the exterior.

Place St-Louis SQUARE

On the eastern edge of the city centre, triangular place St-Louis is surrounded by medieval arcades and merchants' houses dating from the 14th to 16th centuries.

Riverside Park PARK

(quai des Régates) In summer, pedal boats and rowboats can be rented on quai des Régates. The promenade leads through a leafy riverside park, with statues, ponds, swans and a fountain. It's the ideal picnic spot.

Festivals & Events

Fête de la Mirabelle FOOD

(www.fetesdelamirabelle.fr; Aug) Sweet and juicy, the humble *mirabelle* (plum) has its day at the Fête de la Mirabelle.

Marché de Nöel CHRISTMAS

(www.noelmetz.com; Dec) Shop for stocking fillers at the illuminated Marché de Nöel (Christmas Market).

Sleeping

Les Chambres de l'Ile B&B €

(06 13 23 28 33; 15 rue de l'Horticulture, Longeville-lès-Metz; s/d/tr/q €70/80/100/120; P) You'll feel immediately *chez vous* (at home) at this sweet, friendly B&B on an island in the Moselle River. The parquet-floored, warm-coloured rooms overlook gardens, and homemade preserves, fresh-pressed juice and pastries feature at breakfast.

Péniche Alclair HOUSEBOAT €

(06 37 67 16 18; www.chambrespenichemetz.com; allée St-Symphorien; r incl breakfast €80;) What a clever idea: this old barge has been revamped into a stylish blue houseboat, with two cheerful wood-floored rooms and watery views. Breakfast is served in your room or on the sundeck. It's a 15-minute stroll south of the centre along the river.

Cécil Hôtel HOTEL €

(03 87 66 66 13; www.cecilhotel-metz.com; 14 rue Pasteur; s €62-75, d €72-90, tr €95-100; P) Built in 1920, this family-run hotel's smallish rooms are neat, petite and decorated in warm colours, though light sleepers should specify that they want a quiet room. Parking costs €10 per day.

★**Hôtel de la Cathédrale** HISTORIC HOTEL €€

(03 87 75 00 02; www.hotelcathedrale-metz.fr; 25 place de Chambre; d €75-120;) You can expect a friendly welcome at this classy little hotel, occupying a 17th-century townhouse in a prime spot right opposite the cathedral. Climb the wrought-iron staircase to your classically elegant room, with high ceilings, hardwood floors and antique trappings. Book well ahead for a cathedral view.

Hôtel L'Horizon HOTEL €€

(03 82 88 53 65; www.lhorizon.fr; 50 rte du Crève Coeur, Thionville; d €105-150; P) North of Metz, this romantic little hilltop hotel offers fine views across Thionville, a friendly welcome and homely, warm-hued rooms. There's also a restaurant, a sauna and a roof terrace. It's a good base for visiting nearby Fort du Hackenberg.

Eating

Metz has scores of appetising restaurants, many along and near the river. Place St-Jacques becomes one giant open-air cafe when the sun's out. Cobbled rue Taison and the arcades of place St-Louis shelter moderately priced bistros, pizzerias and cafes.

Pâtisserie Claude Bourguignon PATISSERIE €

(www.bourguignonmetz.fr; 31 rue de la Tête d'Or; snacks €3-8; 9.15am-7pm Tue-Sat, 9am-12.30pm Sun) Oh, the temptation! The window display says it all at this smart tearoom/chocolatier/patisserie, with an irresistible array of tarts (try *mirabelle* – plum), éclairs, quiches, ganaches and pralines.

Les Sans Culottes CRÊPERIE €

(03 72 13 55 72; http://lessansculottesmetz.wix.com; 31 place des Charrons; crêpes €3-7, galettes

WORTH A TRIP

FORT DU HACKENBERG

The largest single Maginot Line bastion in the Metz area was the 1000-man **Fort du Hackenberg** (www.maginot-hackenberg.com; adult/child €10/5; tours 2.30pm Mon-Fri, 2-3.30pm Sat & Sun late Mar–mid-Nov, shorter hours rest of year), whose 10km of galleries were designed to be self-sufficient for three months and, in battle, to fire 4 tonnes of shells a minute. An electric trolley takes visitors along 4km of tunnels – always at 12°C – past subterranean installations. Tours last two hours. The fort is around 35km northeast of Metz via the D2 or A35 and is probably best seen as a day trip from Metz – there's a smattering of places to eat in Thionville. Should you wish to stay the night, the Hôtel L'Horizon is nearby.

Metz

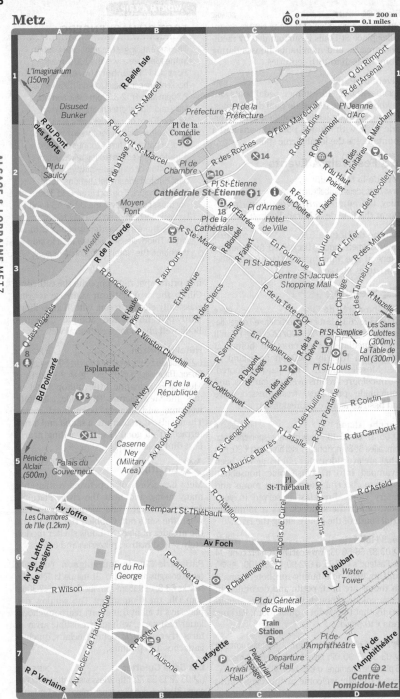

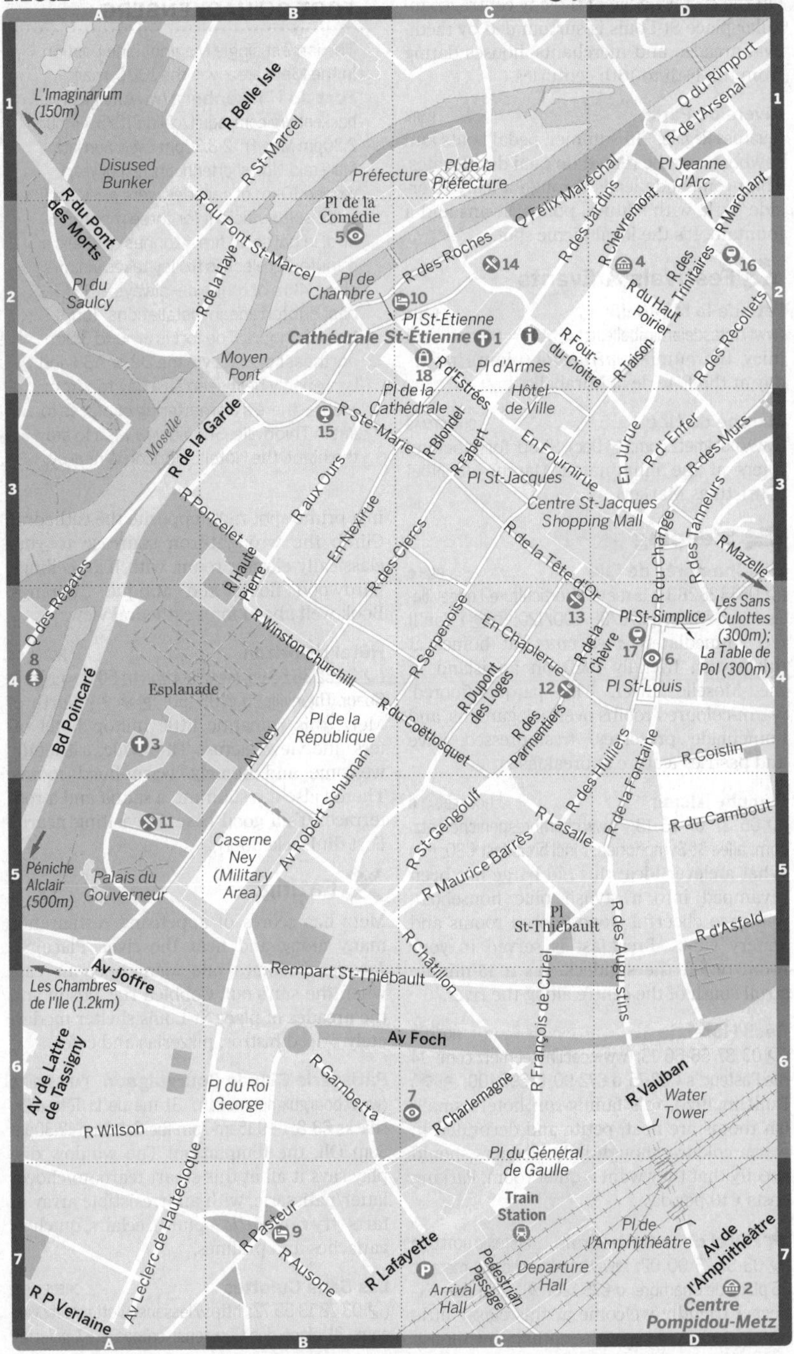

0 200 m
0 0.1 miles
L'Imaginarium (150m)
Disused Bunker
R Belle Isle
R St-Marcel
R du Pont des Morts
R du Pont St-Marcel
Préfecture
Pl de la Préfecture
Pl de la Comédie
5
Q Félix Maréchal
R des Jardins
R Chèvremont
Q du Rimport
R de l'Arsenal
Pl Jeanne d'Arc
R Marchant
R des Trinitaires
16
4
14
R des Roches
Pl de Chambre
10
Pl St-Étienne
Cathédrale St-Étienne
1
Pl du Saulcy
R de la Haye
Moyen Pont
18
R d'Estrées
Pl d'Armes
R Four-du-Cloitre
R Taison
R du Haut Poirier
R des Recollets
Hôtel de Ville
Pl de la Cathédrale
15
R Ste-Marie
R Blondel
R Fabert
En Fournirue
Pl St-Jacques
En Jurue
R d' Enfer
R des Murs
Moselle
R de la Garde
R Poncelet
R aux Ours
En Nexirue
R des Clercs
Centre St-Jacques Shopping Mall
R de la Tête d'Or
R du Change
R des Tanneurs
R Mazelle
Les Sans Culottes (300m); La Table de Pol (300m)
Q des Régates
R Haute Pierre
R Winston Churchill
R Serpenoise
En Chaplerue
13
Pl St-Simplice
17
6
R de la Chèvre
Pl St-Louis
8
Esplanade
12
R Dupont des Loges
Bd Poincaré
3
Av Ney
Pl de la République
R du Coëtlosquet
R des Parmentiers
R des Huilliers
R de la Fontaine
R Coislin
Av Robert Schuman
11
R St-Gengoulf
R Lasalle
R du Cambout
Caserne Ney (Military Area)
R Maurice Barrès
Péniche Alclair (500m)
Palais du Gouverneur
Pl St-Thiébault
R des Augustins
R d'Asfeld
R Châtillon
Av Joffre
Rempart St-Thiébault
Les Chambres de l'Ile (1.2km)
Av Foch
R François de Curel
Av de Lattre de Tassigny
R Gambetta
Pl du Roi George
7
R Charlemagne
R Vauban
Water Tower
R Wilson
Pl du Général de Gaulle
Av Leclerc de Hautecloque
Train Station
R Pasteur
9
Pl de l'Amphithéâtre
Av de l'Amphithéâtre
R Ausone
R Lafayette
Pedestrian Passage
Departure Hall
Arrival Hall
2
Centre Pompidou-Metz
R P Verlaine

Metz

Top Sights

Sights

Sleeping

Eating

Drinking & Nightlife

Shopping

€9-14.50; noon-2pm Mon, noon-2pm & 7-10pm Wed & Thu, noon-2pm & 7-10.30pm Fri & Sat;) Dishing up a nicely chilled vibe and just-right sweet and savoury crêpes, Les Sans Culottes is a great pit stop. Its *galettes* (buckwheat pancakes) are terrific, too, and come with toppings from *raclette* cheese to seafood and spinach. The *plat du jour* is good value at €9.50.

★ L'Imaginarium FRENCH €€

(03 87 30 14 40; http://imaginarium-restaurant.com; 2 rue de Paris; mains €20-23; noon-2pm & 7-10pm Wed-Sat, noon-2pm Sun & Tue) Decorated with one-of-a-kind artworks, this sleek, monochrome bistro by the river is one of Metz's top foodie addresses. The season-driven menu emphasises clean, bright flavours in dishes such as house-smoked salmon with beetroot-and-raspberry gazpacho, and duck breast in a peanut crust with artichoke.

Le Petit Frontalier FRENCH €€

(03 87 37 31 49; http://le-petit-frontalier.fr; 3 rue des Parmentiers; menus €33-46; noon-2pm & 7-10pm Wed-Sat, noon-2pm Sun) Huddled away in an old-town backstreet, this bright, modern bistro draws on the best of seasonal, regional produce. Dishes like hake fillet with sweet-potato millefeuille and lamb in a tangy Comté cheese crust are nicely cooked and presented. Save room for enticing desserts such as tarte tatin with *mirabelle* plums and almond cream.

La Table de Pol MODERN FRENCH €€

(03 87 62 13 72; www.latabledepol.fr; 1/3 rue du Grand Wad; menus €18-38.50, mains €19.50; noon-2pm & 7-9pm Tue-Sat) Intimate lighting and cheek-by-jowl tables keep the mood mellow in this friendly bistro, which serves winningly fresh dishes prepared with market produce, along the lines of lamb filet mignon in a herb crust and cod fillet with asparagus – all cooked to a T.

Restaurant Thierry INTERNATIONAL €€

(03 87 74 01 23; www.restaurant-thierry.fr; 5 rue des Piques; menus €23-40; noon-2.30pm & 7-10.30pm, closed Wed & Sun) Combining the historic backdrop of a 16th-century townhouse with the lighting, bohemian flair and subtly spiced cuisine of Morocco, this is one of Metz' most coveted tables. An aperitif in the candlelit salon works up an appetite for global flavours such as caramelised suckling-pig cheeks with basmati rice and cardamom, and tagine of lamb with olives and dried fruit.

Le Magasin aux Vivres GASTRONOMIC €€€

(03 87 17 17 17; 5 av Ney; menus €51-125; noon-2pm & 7.30-10pm Tue-Fri, 7.30-10pm Sat) Conjurer of textures and seasonal flavours chef Christophe Dufossé makes creative use of local produce at this sophisticated Michelin-starred restaurant. Moselle wines work well with specialities such as plump scallops with fresh truffle, Jerusalem artichoke millefeuille and roasted hazelnuts, and salt-crusted sea bass with seaweed and thyme and bay-leaf sauce.

Drinking & Nightlife

Some 22,000 resident students keep Metz' vibe young and upbeat after dark. For an alfresco sundowner or two, try the bars and open-air cafes lining place de Chambre and place St-Jacques.

Bazaar Sainte Marie BAR

(www.bsm-metz.com; 2bis rue Ste-Marie; 6pm-2am Mon-Sat) Retro-chic bar with red walls, vintage sofas, a relaxed vibe and old-school

music. Check the website for details of gigs, exhibitions and DJ nights.

Cafe Rubis BAR

(25 place St-Louis; ⌚8am-2am Mon-Sat) Cosy bar for a coffee or glass of wine, with a terrace under the arcades for summer drinks.

Café Jehanne d'Arc BAR

(place Jeanne d'Arc; ⌚11.30am-midnight Mon-Fri, 3pm-1am Sat) This 13th-century watering hole oozes history from every Gothic window, fresco and beam. The soundtrack skips from Gainsbourg to classical, and there's often free live jazz. The terrace is a chilled spot for summertime imbibing.

Information

Tourist Office (☎03 87 39 00 00; www.tourisme-metz.com; 2 place d'Armes; ⌚9am-7pm Mon-Sat, 10am-4pm Sun, shorter hours winter) In a one-time guardroom built in the mid-1700s. Free walking-tour and cycling maps, and free wi-fi. Can make room bookings for a €1.50 fee.

Getting There & Around

BICYCLE

Rent city and mountain bikes cheaply from non-profit **Mob d'Emploi** (www.mobemploi.com; 7 place du Général de Gaulle; per half-/full day/week €3/4/10, deposit per bike €250; ⌚8.30am-6.30pm Mon-Fri, 10am-6.30pm Sat, 2-8pm Sun). Helmets and locks are free; rental options include kids' bikes, electro bikes, child carriers and even a tandem.

TRAIN

Metz' ornate early-20th-century **train station** (place du Général de Gaulle) has a super-sleek TGV linking Paris with Luxembourg. Direct services:

Luxembourg €16.70, 55 minutes, 40 daily
Paris €33 to €81, 1½ hours, 15 daily
Nancy €11.20, 35 to 58 minutes, 48 daily
Strasbourg €27.10, 1½ hours, 16 daily
Verdun €15.40, 1½ hours, three direct daily

Verdun

POP 18,327

The unspeakable atrocities that took place in and around Verdun between 21 February and 18 December 1916, the longest battle of WWI, have turned the town's name into a byword for wartime slaughter and futile sacrifice.

Such a dark past means that Verdun always has an air of melancholy, even when the sun bounces brightly off the River Meuse and the town's shuttered houses. Go to the moonscape hills of the Verdun Battlefields, scarred with trenches and shells; walk through the stony silence of the cemeteries as the morning mist rises, and you will understand why. Time has healed and trees have grown, but the memory of *l'enfer de Verdun* (the hell of Verdun) has survived. And, some say, may it never be forgotten.

History

After the annexation of Lorraine's Moselle *département* and Alsace by Germany in 1871, Verdun became a front-line outpost. Over the next four decades it was turned into the most important and heavily fortified element in France's eastern defence line.

During WWI, Verdun itself was never taken by the Germans, but the evacuated town was almost totally destroyed by artillery bombardments. In the hills to the north and east of Verdun, the brutal combat – carried out with artillery, flame-throwers and poison gas – completely wiped out nine villages. During the last two years of WWI, more than 800,000 soldiers (some 400,000 French and almost as many Germans, along with thousands of the Americans who arrived in 1918) lost their lives in this area.

Sights

Citadelle Souterraine HISTORIC SITE

(☎03 29 84 84 42; www.citadelle-souterraine-verdun.fr; av du 5e RAP; adult/child €9/5; ⌚9am-6pm, closed Jan) Comprising 7km of underground galleries, this cavernous subterranean citadel was designed by military engineer Sébastien Le Prestre de Vauban in the 17th century and completed in 1838. In 1916 it was turned into an impregnable command centre in which 10,000 *poilus* (French WWI soldiers) lived, waiting to be dispatched to the front. About 10% of the galleries have been converted into an audiovisual re-enactment of Verdun's WWI history. Half-hour, battery-powered-car tours, available in six languages, should be booked ahead.

Centre Mondial de la Paix MUSEUM

(World Centre for Peace; www.cmpaix.eu; place Monseigneur Ginisty; adult/child €5.50/2.50; ⌚10am-12.30pm & 2-6pm) Set in Verdun's handsomely classical former bishop's palace, built in 1724, this museum's permanent exhibition touches upon wars, their causes and solutions; human rights; and the fragility of peace.

Cathédrale Notre Dame CATHEDRAL
(place Monseigneur Ginisty; ⌚9am-6pm) Perched on a hillside, this Romanesque-meets-Gothic cathedral shelters a gilded Baroque baldachin, restored after WWI damage. Much of the stained glass is from the inter-war period.

Monument à la Victoire MONUMENT
(Carrer de la Portella 5) Steep steps lead up to this austere 1920s monument commemorating war victims and survivors. The crypt hides a book listing the soldiers who fought in the Battle of Verdun.

Tours

The tourist office runs four one-hour tours of the **battlefields** (adult/child €10/7; hourly 2pm to 6pm early April to mid-November).

Braquier FOOD
(www.dragees-braquier.com; 50 rue du Fort de Vaux; ⌚9-11am & 2-6pm) FREE Braquier has been making Verdun's celebrated *dragées* (sugared almonds) since 1783 and offers free audioguide tours of its factory; see the website for further details.

Sleeping

Hôtel Montaulbain HOTEL €
(☎03 29 86 00 47; 4 rue de la Vieille Prison; d €85-96, f €140; 📶) It requires very little detective work to pin down this central hotel, which is run with charm and an eye for detail. Overlooking an inner courtyard, the 11 recently revamped rooms are compact, spotless and minimalist in look and feel.

Château des Monthairons HISTORIC HOTEL €€
(☎03 29 87 78 55; www.chateaudesmonthairons.fr; 26 rte de Verdun; d €110-250, apt €300-390; P📶) Reclining in its own beautifully tended grounds, this turreted vision of a 19th-century château has grand rooms dressed in flouncy florals and antique furnishings. Some have sweeping views of the Meuse Valley, others crank up the romance with four-poster beds. There's an excellent restaurant and spa on-site. It's a 15-minute drive south of Verdun via the D34.

Eating

Le Clapier BISTRO €
(☎03 29 86 20 14; 34 rue des Gros Degrés; menus €15-33; ⌚noon-2pm & 7-9pm Tue-Sat; 👪) The chef's penchant for Provence's balmy climes shines through on the menu at this cosy lime-walled bistro, whose name translates as 'the rabbit hutch'. Specialities like crumbly Brie tart and herb-infused leg of lamb are expertly paired with Meuse wines.

Chez Mamie FRENCH €€
(☎03 29 86 45 50; 52 av de la 42ème Division; menus €12-30; ⌚noon-2pm Mon, noon-2pm & 7-10pm Wed-Sun; 🌿👪) The clue's in the name: family-run Chez Mamie does indeed dish up the kind of wholesome, hearty grub your French gran might make. Pull up a chair at one of the checked-cloth tables for satisfying dishes such as scallops with bacon and fat, stubby pork trotters. Vegetarian and children's options are available.

Château des Monthairons FRENCH €€€
(☎03 29 87 78 55; www.chateaudesmonthairons.fr; 26 rte de Verdun; lunch menus €28-50, dinner menus €47-102; ⌚noon-2pm & 7-9pm Wed-Sun, 7-9pm Tue; 👪) It's not every day you get to dine at a bona-fide castle, so it's worth the 15-minute drive south of Verdun to this whimsically turreted château overlooking parkland. Chef Benoit Thouvenin puts his own creative spin on French cuisine in dishes such as confit pork cheeks with leeks and saffron-mustard sauce and iced parfait with Verdun *dragées* (sugared almonds).

Information

Tourist Office (☎03 29 86 14 18; www.tourisme-verdun.fr; place de la Nation; ⌚9am-12.30pm & 1.30-6pm Mon-Sat, 9am-1pm Sun, shorter hours winter; 📶) Friendly tourist office with guided tours, info on Verdun and the surrounding region, and free maps of the battlefields. Free wi-fi.

VERDUN CENT SAVER

Before heading to Verdun's sights and the Verdun Battlefields, visit the tourist office, where you can buy slightly discounted adult tickets for the Citadelle Souterraine (€7), Ossuaire de Douaumont audiovisual presentation (€4) and the Fort de Douaumont (€3).

Opposite the tourist office, the Maison du Tourisme sells the money-saving **Pass Musées Verdun 14/18** (adult/child €18/10), covering entry to the Ossuaire de Douaumont, Fort de Douaumont, Fort Vaux and the Citadelle Souterraine.

Getting There & Around

BICYCLE

Bikes are an excellent way to tour the Verdun battlefields. At the train station, **TiV' vélo** (www.bus-tiv.com; place Maurice Genevoix; half-day/day/week €1/2/5; ⏰9am-noon & 2-6pm Mon-Fri) rents out bicycles. You'll need to pay a €100 deposit.

CAR & MOTORCYCLE

You can park for free in the car parks south of the tourist office on av du 8 Mai 1945, rue des Tanneries and place de la Digne.

TRAIN

Verdun's poorly served train station, designed by Gustave Eiffel and built in 1868, has direct services to Metz (€15.40, 1½ hours, three direct daily). Five buses a day go to the Gare Meuse TGV station (€4.50, 30 minutes), from where direct TGVs whisk you to Paris' Gare de l'Est (€24 to €46, one hour).

Verdun Battlefields

Much of the Battle of Verdun was fought 5km to 8km (as the crow flies) northeast of Verdun. Today, the forested area – still a jumble of trenches and artillery craters – can be explored via signposted paths leading to dozens of minor remnants of the war. Site interiors are closed in January.

Sights

Mémorial de Verdun MEMORIAL
(www.memorial-de-verdun.fr; 1 av du Corps Européen, Fleury; adult/child €11/7; ⏰9.30am-7pm, shorter hours winter) The village of Fleury, wiped off the face of the Earth in the course of being captured and recaptured 16 times, is now the site of this memorial. It tells the story of '300 days, 300,000 dead, 400,000 wounded', with insightful displays of war artefacts and personal items. Downstairs you'll find a re-creation of the battlefield as it looked on the day the guns finally fell silent.

In the grassy crater-pocked centre of what was once Fleury, a few hundred metres down the road from the memorial, signs among the low ruins indicate the village's former layout.

Ossuaire de Douaumont MEMORIAL
(www.verdun-douaumont.com; ⏰9am-6pm Mon-Fri, 10am-6pm Sat & Sun, shorter hours winter) FREE Rising like a gigantic artillery shell above 15,000 crosses that bleed into the distance, this sombre, 137m-long ossuary, inaugurated in 1932, is one of France's most important WWI memorials. A ticket (adult/child €6/3) to the 20-minute **audiovisual presentation** on the battle also lets you climb the 46m-high **bell tower.** Out front, the French military **cemetery** is flanked by memorials to Muslim and Jewish soldiers (to the east and west, respectively) who died fighting for France in WWI.

The ossuary contains the bones of about 130,000 unidentified French and German soldiers collected from the Verdun battlefields and buried together in 52 mass graves according to where they fell. Each engraved stone denotes a missing soldier, while a touching display of photographs shows Verdun survivors – as they were in WWI and as they were later in life.

Fort de Douaumont FORT
(adult/child €4/2; ⏰10am-6.30pm, shorter hours winter) Sitting high on a hill, this is the strongest of the 38 fortresses and bastions built along a 45km front to protect Verdun. When the Battle of Verdun began, 400m-long Douaumont – whose 3km network of cold, dripping galleries was built between 1885 and 1913 – had only a skeleton crew. By the fourth day it had been captured easily, a serious blow to French morale; four months later, it was retaken by colonial troops from Morocco.

Charles de Gaulle, then a young captain, was wounded and taken prisoner near here in 1916. It's free to take in the sweeping country views from the fort's crater-pocked roof.

Fort Vaux FORT
(Vaux-devant-Damloup; adult/child €4/2; ⏰10am-6.30pm, shorter hours winter) Located in crater-scarred countryside 10km northeast of Verdun, this fort was constructed between

BATTLEFIELD OVERNIGHT

Housed in a bijou villa framed by gardens, **Villa Nantrise** (☎03 29 84 73 85; 46 rue de l'Argonne, Romagne-sous-Montfaucon; d €70; P 📶) is a B&B brilliantly placed for exploring the WWI American memorials around Romagne-sous-Montfaucon. Rooms are old-fashioned but spotlessly kept, and the welcome is heartfelt, with little touches including free bike rental and homemade jams at breakfast.

1881 and 1884. It was the second fort – Douaumont was the first – to fall in the Battle of Verdun, and became the site of the bloodiest battle for two months. Weak with thirst, Major Raynal and his troops surrendered to the enemy on 7 June 1916. You can gain an insight into past horrors by taking a tour of its dank interior and observation points.

Tranchée des Baïonnettes MEMORIAL

FREE On 12 June 1916, two companies of the 137th Infantry Regiment of the French army were sheltered in their *tranchées* (trenches), *baïonnettes* (bayonets) fixed, waiting for a ferocious artillery bombardment to end. It never did – the incoming shells covered their positions with mud and debris, burying them alive. They were found three years later, when someone spotted several hundred bayonet tips sticking out of the ground. Today the site is marked by a simple memorial that is always open. The tree-filled valley across the D913 is known as the **Ravin de la Mort** (Ravine of Death).

American Memorials

More than one million American troops participated in the Meuse-Argonne Offensive of late 1918, the last Western Front battle of WWI. The bloody fighting northwest of Verdun, in which more than 26,000 Americans died, convinced the Kaiser's government to cable US President Woodrow Wilson with a request for an armistice. The film *Sergeant York* (1941) is based on events that took place here. The website of the Meuse *département's* tourism board – www.tourisme-meuse.com – offers background on the region and its WWI sites.

Verdun also had considerable military presence from the end of WWII. This is commemorated at the Lorraine American Cemetery, Europe's biggest US WWII military cemetery.

Apart from Romagne '14-'18, all of the sites are managed by the **American Battle Monuments Commission** (www.abmc.gov) and are open from 9am to 5pm daily.

Sights

Meuse-Argonne American Cemetery CEMETERY

(Romagne-sous-Montfaucon) The largest US military cemetery in Europe is this WWI ground, where 14,246 soldiers lie buried – a sobering sea of white crosses reaching as far as the eye can see. The cemetery is located in Romagne-sous-Montfaucon, 41km northwest of Verdun along the D38 and D123.

Romagne '14-'18 WAR MUSEUM

(☎03 29 85 10 14; www.romagne14-18.com; 2 rue de l'Andon, Romagne-sous-Montfaucon; museum adult/child €5/free, guided walks €12.50; ⊙guided walks 9am-noon, museum noon-6pm Thu-Mon) The village of Romagne-sous-Montfaucon is home to this heart-rending museum, which, in the words of owner Jean-Paul de Vries, is all about 'life stories' and 'the human being behind the helmet'. Artefacts are shown in the state in which they were found – rust, dirt and all. Join Jean-Paul on one of his insightful morning walks of the battlefields – call ahead for an appointment. The museum is a 40-minute drive northwest of Verdun via the D964 and D123.

Lorraine American Cemetery CEMETERY

(St-Avold) Verdun had a significant military presence from the end of WWII until Charles de Gaulle pulled France out of NATO's integrated military command in 1966. Surrounded by woodland and set in landscaped grounds, this is the largest US WWII military cemetery in Europe. The cemetery is a 30-minute drive east of Metz via the A4 motorway.

St-Mihiel American Cemetery CEMETERY

(Thiaucourt-Regniéville) In this WWI cemetery, the graves of 4153 American soldiers who died in the 1918 Battle of St-Mihiel radiate towards a central sundial topped by a white American eagle. The cemetery is 40km southeast of Verdun on the outskirts of Thiaucourt-Regniéville.

Butte de Montsec MEMORIAL

(Montsec) This 375m-high mound, site of a US monument with a bronze relief map, is surrounded by a round neoclassical colonnade. The monument commemorates the achievements of the American soldiers who fought here in 1917 and 1918. It's a 50-minute drive south of Verdun via the D964.

Butte de Montfaucon MEMORIAL

(Montfaucon-en-Argonne) Commemorating the 1918 Meuse-Argonne Offensive, this 336m-high mound is topped by a 58m-high Doric column crowned by a statue symbolising liberty. Ascend 234 steps to reach the observation platform. The memorial is a 40-minute drive northwest of Verdun via the D38 and D19.

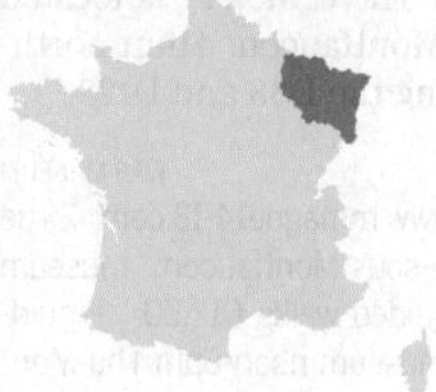

The Loire Valley

POP 2.6 MILLION

Includes ➡

Best Places to Eat

- ➡ Le Gambetta (p397)
- ➡ Les Années 30 (p393)
- ➡ Amboise Food Market (p384)
- ➡ Le Lièvre Gourmand (p369)
- ➡ Le Zinc (p380)

Best Places to Sleep

- ➡ Hôtel de l'Abeille (p368)
- ➡ Château de Beaulieu (p395)
- ➡ Demeure de la Vignole (p398)
- ➡ Château de Brissac (p403)
- ➡ Le Vieux Manoir (p384)

Why Go?

If it's French splendour, style and gastronomy you seek, the Loire Valley will exceed your expectations, no matter how great. Poised on the crucial frontier between northern and southern France, and just a short ride from Paris, the region was once of immense strategic importance. Kings, queens, dukes and nobles came here to establish feudal castles and, later on, sumptuous pleasure palaces – that's why this fertile river valley is sprinkled with hundreds of France's most extravagant fortresses. With crenellated towers, soaring cupolas and glittering banquet halls, the châteaux, and the villages and vineyards that surround them, attest to a thousand years of rich architectural, artistic and agrarian creativity. The Loire Valley – an enormous Unesco World Heritage Site – is also known for its outstanding wines and lively, sophisticated cities, including Orléans, Tours, Saumur and Angers.

When to Go

Tours

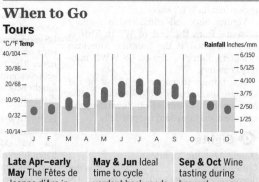

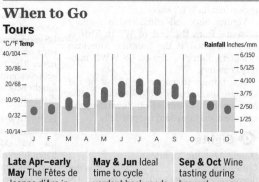

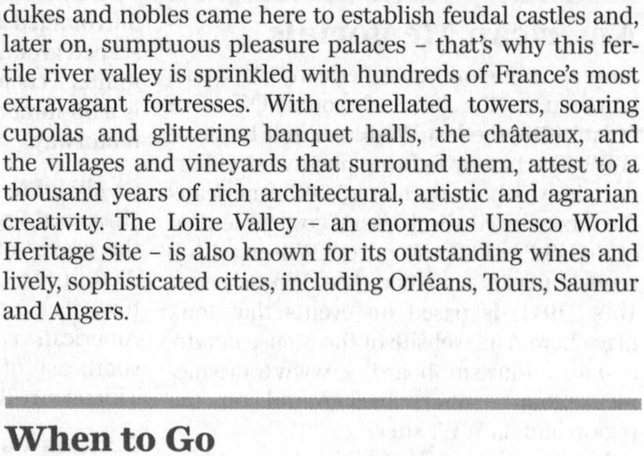

Late Apr–early May The Fêtes de Jeanne d'Arc in Orléans culminate with parades on 8 May.

May & Jun Ideal time to cycle verdant back roads and bike paths from château to château.

Sep & Oct Wine tasting during harvest season; the châteaux are less crowded.

History

The Loire Valley and its châteaux were the backdrop for some of the most dramatic events in French history. By Roman times the Loire was one of Gaul's most important transport arteries. The earliest châteaux were medieval fortresses established in the 9th century to fend off marauding Vikings. By the 11th century massive walls, fortified keeps and moats were must-haves for the region's potentates.

During the Hundred Years War (1337–1453), the Loire marked one of the boundaries between French and English forces and the area was ravaged by fierce fighting. After Charles VII regained his crown with the help of Joan of Arc, the Loire emerged as the centre of French court life. Charles took up residence in Loches with his mistress, Agnès Sorel, and the French nobility, and from then the aristocracy took to building extravagant châteaux as expressions of their wealth and influence.

François I (r 1515–47) made his mark by introducing ornate Renaissance palaces to the Loire. François' successor, Henri II (r 1547–59), his wife Catherine de Médicis and his mistress Diane de Poitiers fought their bitter personal rivalries from castle to castle, while Henri's son Henri III (r 1573–89) used Blois' castle to assassinate two of his greatest rivals before being assassinated himself eight months later.

Tours

Bus

If you don't have your own car, minibus tours are a good way to see the châteaux without being dependent on sometimes infrequent public transport. A variety of private companies offer well-organised itineraries, taking in various combinations of Azay-le-Rideau, Villandry, Cheverny, Chambord, Chenonceau and vineyards offering wine tasting. Many are also happy to create custom-designed tours. Half-day trips cost between €23 and €36 per person; full-day trips range from €50 to €54. These prices don't include admission to the châteaux, though you often get slightly discounted tickets. Reserve online or via the Tours (p381) or Amboise (p385) tourist offices, from where most tours depart.

Boat

The Loire offers few opportunities to get out on the water because its currents are often too unpredictable to navigate safely, but the river is not completely off limits. Check at tourist offices for boat excursions or kayak rentals; the Amboise and Saumur/Candes-St-Martin areas offer several options.

Specialised Tours

Tourist offices can supply details on **hot-air-balloon rides** (generally from April to October, weather permitting) run by a dozen companies, **helicopter rides** and specialised tours with themes such as cycling and wine tasting. Saumur is particularly rich in equestrian options.

Cheval et Châteaux HORSE RIDING
(www.cheval-et-chateaux.com; 4/7-day tours €1224/2448) Offers luxurious four- to seven-day horseback trips to some of the Loire's best-known châteaux, with overnights in castle-based B&Bs.

Art Montgolfières BALLOON TOUR
(☎02 54 32 08 11; www.art-montgolfieres.fr; per person from €159; ⏲Apr-Oct) Floating silently over fields, vineyards and châteaux in a hot-air balloon – what could be more romantic? Spend an hour aloft and then quaff a celebratory glass of bubbly (or two).

> **FAST FACTS**
>
> **Area** 40,440 sq km
>
> **Local industry** Viticulture
>
> **Signature drink** Cointreau, wine

Getting There & Away

AIR

Tours–Val de Loire Airport (www.tours.aeroport.fr) has Ryanair flights to London's Stansted airport and Dublin, while from **Angers Loire Airport** (www.angersloireaeroport.fr) British Airways goes to London-City Airport.

TRAIN

Tours is the Loire Valley's main rail hub. TGV trains connect St-Pierre-des-Corps (4km east of Tours) with Paris' Gare Montparnasse (one hour), Charles de Gaulle Airport (1¾ hours), Nantes (1½ hours) and Bordeaux (2¾ hours). Orléans, Blois, Amboise and other Loire towns also have fast rail links to Paris. TGVs from Angers to Paris' Gare Montparnasse (1¾ hours) go via Le Mans.

Getting Around

Most towns and a few châteaux are accessible by train and/or bus, but having your own wheels allows significantly more freedom.

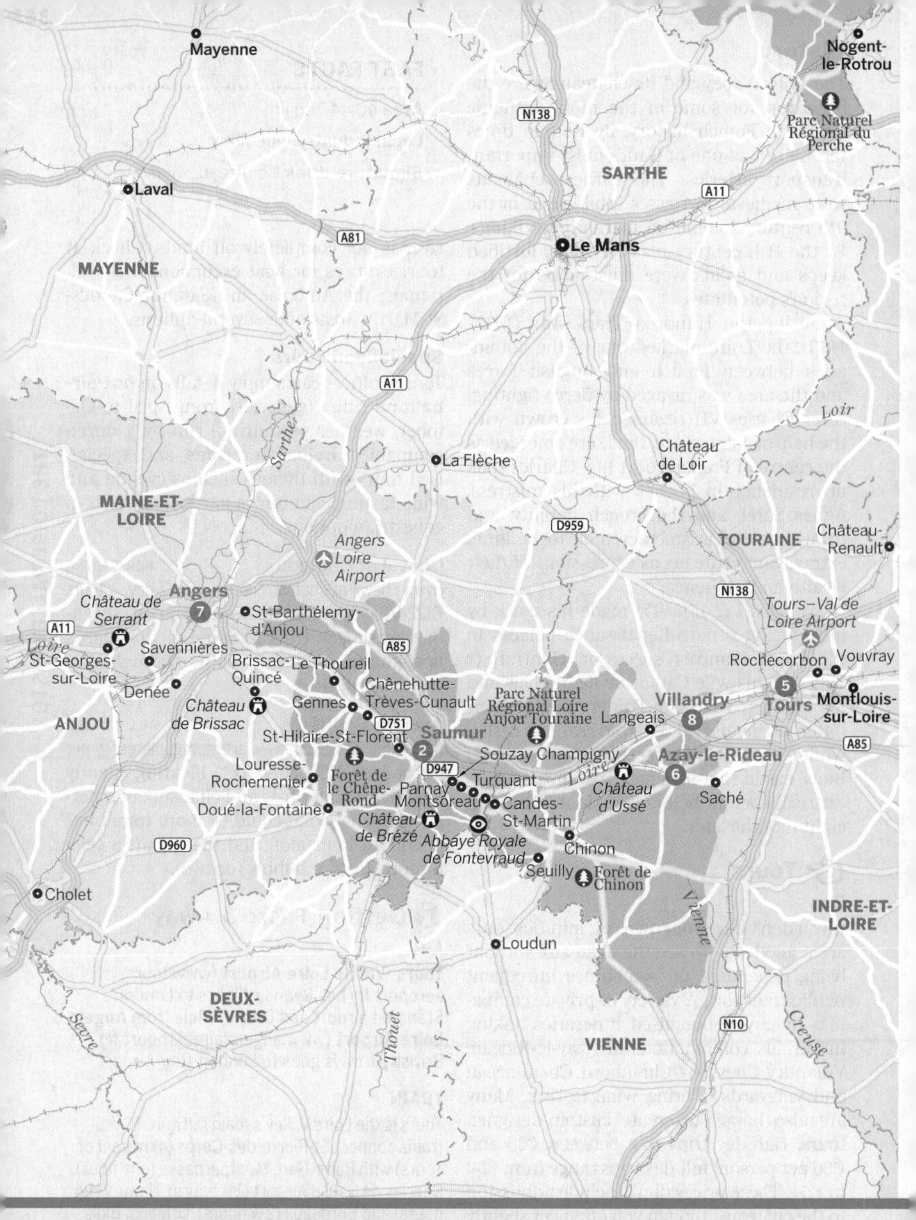

The Loire Valley Highlights

1. **Château de Chenonceau** (p382) Admiring elegant arches and fabulous art.
2. **Saumur** (p393) Enjoying fantastic food, great local wines and equestrian virtuosity.
3. **Le Clos Lucé** (p383) Exploring the final home of Leonardo da Vinci in Amboise.
4. **Château de Chambord** (p374) Climbing the double-helix stairway to the rooftop.
5. **Tours** (p376) Exploring super museums by day and partying by night.
6. **Azay-le-Rideau** (p389) Appreciating the furnishings of this serene island château.

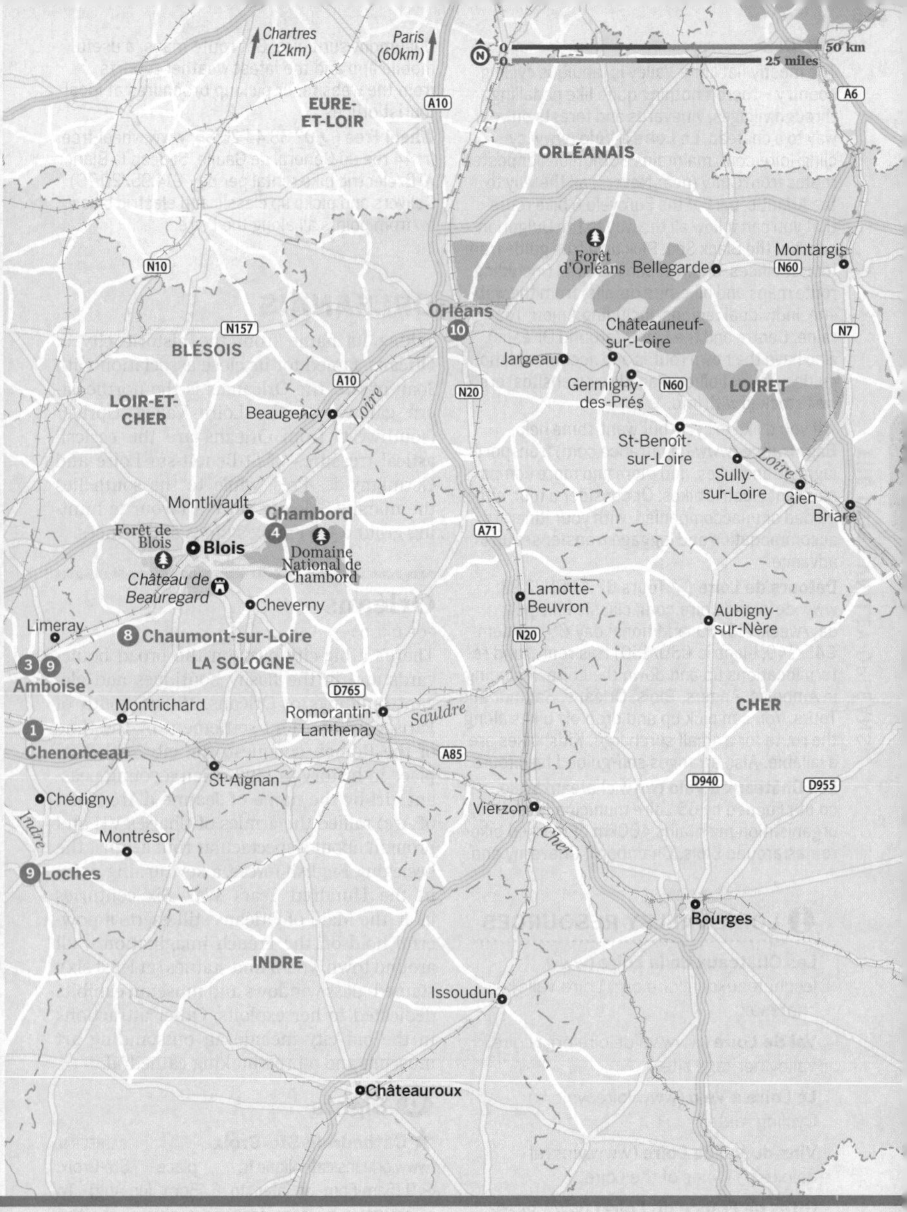

7 Château d'Angers (p400) Searching for dragons, angels and allegories in Angers' remarkable medieval Apocalypse tapestry.

8 Château de Villandry (p385) and **Château de Chaumont-sur-Loire** (p375) Wandering meticulously tended, flowery gardens.

9 Amboise's Sunday market (p384) Purchasing a picnic on the riverfront.

10 Orléans (p366) Taking in Joan of Arc lore and sampling top cuisine.

BICYCLE

The mostly flat Loire Valley is fabulous cycling country – there's nothing quite like pedalling through villages, vineyards and forests on your way to a château. **Le Loire à Vélo** (www.cycling-loire.com) maintains 800km of signposted routes from Cuffy (near Nevers) all the way to the Atlantic, part of the Eurovelo 6 bike route that you can follow all the way to the Bulgarian coast of the Black Sea. Pick up a free guide from tourist offices, or download material (including route maps and bike-hire details) from the website. Individual regions, including Anjou, Touraine, Centre and the Loiret (around Orléans), also have their own routes and accommodation guides. Tourist offices (and their websites) are well stocked with info.

If you'd like to cycle but want some help, **Bagafrance** (www.bagafrance.com) transports luggage and bikes, and more and more companies rent electric bikes. Or consider a tour, either guided or unaccompanied, with your itinerary, accommodation and luggage transfer set up in advance.

Détours de Loire (☎Tours 02 47 61 22 23; www.detoursdeloire.com; classic bike per day/week €15/60, additional day €5, tandem €45/140, electric €30/150) Has rental and return locations up and down the Loire, including in Amboise, Angers, Blois, Orléans, Saumur and Tours. You can pick up and drop off bikes along the route for a small surcharge. Kids' bikes are available. Also arranges self-guided bike tours.

Les Châteaux à Vélo (www.chateauxavelo.co.uk) Funded by 65 Loire municipalities, this organisation maintains 400km of marked bike routes around Blois, Chambord, Cheverny and Chaumont-sur-Loire. Get route maps, a useful mobile app and the latest weather reports from the website, or pick up brochures at local tourist offices.

Wheel Free (☎02 38 44 26 85; www.wheel-free.fr; 44 rue du Géneral de Gaulle, St-Jean le Blanc; ATB/electric bike rental per day €14.95/20.70) Delivers and picks up classic and electric bikes to/from points all along the Loire.

LOIRE VALLEY RESOURCES

Les Châteaux de la Loire (www.leschateauxdelaloire.org) Loire Valley châteaux.

Val de Loire (www.valdeloire.org) Loire Valley heritage site.

Le Loire à Vélo (www.loireavelo.fr) Cycling routes.

Vins du Val de Loire (www.vinsvaldeloire.fr) Wines of the Loire.

Gîtes de France du Loiret (www.gites-de-france-loiret.com) B&Bs, camping and vacation rentals.

Gîtes de France Loir et Cher (www.gites-de-france-blois.com) B&Bs, camping and vacation rentals.

destineo.fr (www.destineo.fr) Public-transport details.

ORLÉANAIS

Taking its name from the historic city of Orléans, famed for its close association with Joan of Arc, the Orléanais is the northeastern gateway to the Loire Valley. Upriver (southwest) from Orléans are the ecclesiastical treasures of St-Benoît-sur-Loire and Germigny-des-Prés, while to the south lies the marshy Sologne, once a favourite hunting ground for France's kings and princes.

Orléans

POP 114,300

There's a big-city buzz on the broad boulevards and in the flashy boutiques and elegant buildings of Orléans, 100km south of Paris. An important settlement by the time of the Roman conquest, the city sealed its place in history in 1429 when a young peasant girl by the name of Jeanne d'Arc (Joan of Arc) rallied the armies of Charles VII and brought about a spectacular rout against the besieging English forces, a key turning point in the Hundred Years War. Six centuries later, the Maid of Orléans still exerts a powerful hold on the French imagination – all around town, you'll find statues (at least six), stained-glass windows and museum exhibits dedicated to her exploits. Other attractions in the old city include an outstanding art museum and a breathtaking cathedral.

Sights

★**Cathédrale Ste-Croix** CATHEDRAL

(www.orleans.catholique.fr; place Ste-Croix; ⌚9.15am-5pm or later, to 6.45pm Jun-Aug) In a country of jaw-dropping churches, the Cathédrale Ste-Croix still raises a gasp. Towering above place Ste-Croix, Orléans' Flamboyant Gothic cathedral was originally built in the 13th century but later underwent tinkering by successive monarchs. Joan of Arc prayed here on 8 May 1429 and was greeted with a procession of thanks for saving the town.

★ Musée des Beaux-Arts ART MUSEUM
(02 38 79 21 55; www.orleans.fr; 1 rue Fernand Rabier; adult/child incl audioguide €4/free; 9.30am-6pm Tue-Sat, 2-6pm Sun) Orléans' five-storey fine-arts museum is a treat, with an excellent selection of Italian, Flemish and Dutch paintings (including works by Correggio, Velázquez and Bruegel) as well as a huge collection of work by French artists such as Léon Cogniet (1794–1880), Orléans-born Alexandre Antigna (1817–78), and Paul Gauguin (1848–1903), who spent some of his youth here. Other rare treasures include a set of 18th-century pastels by Maurice Quentin de la Tour and a self-portrait by Jean-Baptiste Chardin.

Hôtel Groslot HISTORIC BUILDING
(02 38 79 22 30; www.orleans.fr; place de l'Étape; 10am-noon & 2-6pm Oct-Jun, 7am-7pm Jul-Sep) FREE The Renaissance-style Hôtel Groslot was built between 1530 and 1550 as a private mansion for lawyer and bailiff Jacques Groslot. It became Orléans' town hall during the Revolution. The neo-Renaissance interior (1850s) is extravagant, especially the ornate bedroom – now used for wedding ceremonies – in which 17-year-old King François II died in 1560. The gardens behind the building are lovely.

Maison de Jeanne d'Arc MUSEUM
(02 38 68 32 63; www.jeannedarc.com.fr; 3 place du Général de Gaulle; adult/child €4/free; 10am-1pm & 2-6pm Tue-Sun Apr-Sep, afternoon only Oct-Mar) An excellent 15-minute movie (in French or English) tracing Joan of Arc's origins, accomplishments and historical impact is the main attraction at the Maison de Jeanne d'Arc, a reconstruction of the 15th-century house that hosted her between April and May 1429 (the original was destroyed by German bombing in 1940). Upstairs you can consult the archives of the world's largest Joan of Arc research centre.

Musée Historique et Archéologique MUSEUM
(02 38 79 25 60; www.orleans.fr; 21 rue Ste-Catherine; admission incl with Musée des Beaux-Arts ticket; 10am-1pm & 2-6pm Tue-Sun Apr-Sep, afternoon only Oct-Mar) The centrepiece of this museum, in the Renaissance-style Hôtel Cabu, is a collection of rare Celtic and Gallo-Roman bronzes recovered from the Loire's sandy bottom. The Salle Jeanne d'Arc displays artistic and popular representations of the Maid of Orléans, from a late 15th-century Swiss tapestry to 20th-century mustard jars.

Place du Martroi SQUARE
The focal point of central Orléans is place du Martroi, fed by rue Royale from the south and rue de la République from the north. In the centre is a bronze **statue** (1855) depicting St Joan atop a prancing steed. A food market sets up here on Friday evening from 5pm to 9.30pm.

CERCIL – Musée-Mémorial des Enfants du Vel d'Hiv MUSEUM
(02 38 42 03 91; www.cercil.fr; 45 rue du Bourdon-Blanc; adult/child €3/free; 2-8pm Tue, 2-6pm Wed-Fri & Sun) Between 1941 and 1943, more than 16,000 Jews were interned in two camps about 50km northeast of Orléans, Beaune-la-Rolande and Pithiviers. The adults were deported first, and only after authorisation had arrived from Berlin were 4400 parent-less, terrified children loaded on trains and sent to Auschwitz and Sobibor; only 26, all adolescents, survived. Exhibits (in French) document the deportation and serve as a moving memorial for the children. Exhibits include an original shack from Beaune-la-Rolande. A detailed guide booklet in English is available.

Festivals & Events

Fêtes de Jeanne d'Arc CULTURAL
(www.fetesjeannedarc.com; 29 Apr-10 May) The Orléanais have celebrated the liberation of their city by Joan of Arc since 1430. Festivities include a four-day medieval market, costume parades, concerts and, on 8 May (also a national holiday commemorating the surrender of Nazi Germany), a morning prayer service at the cathedral and a military parade (including tanks).

Sleeping

Les Trois Maillets B&B €
(06 28 43 29 14; www.troismailletsorleans.jimdo.com; 4 rue des Trois Maillets; d incl breakfast €85, additional person €17.50;) Charming rooms with space for up to four people, in a Renaissance-era building. Breakfasts are both delicious and copious.

Hôtel Archange BOUTIQUE HOTEL €
(02 38 54 42 42; www.hotelarchange.com; 1 bd de Verdun; d €55-90, 5-person ste €139;) Cherub murals and armchairs shaped like hands greet you at this exuberant hotel. Splashy colour schemes spice up the 22 themed rooms, whose wooden floors are kept clean by robots (yes, really). The double-thick windows are very effective against tram noise. Great value.

Orléans

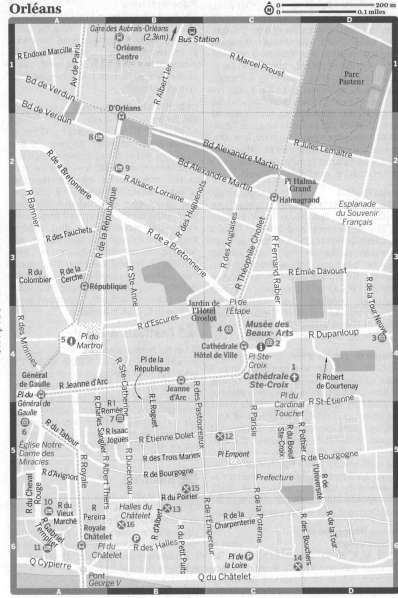

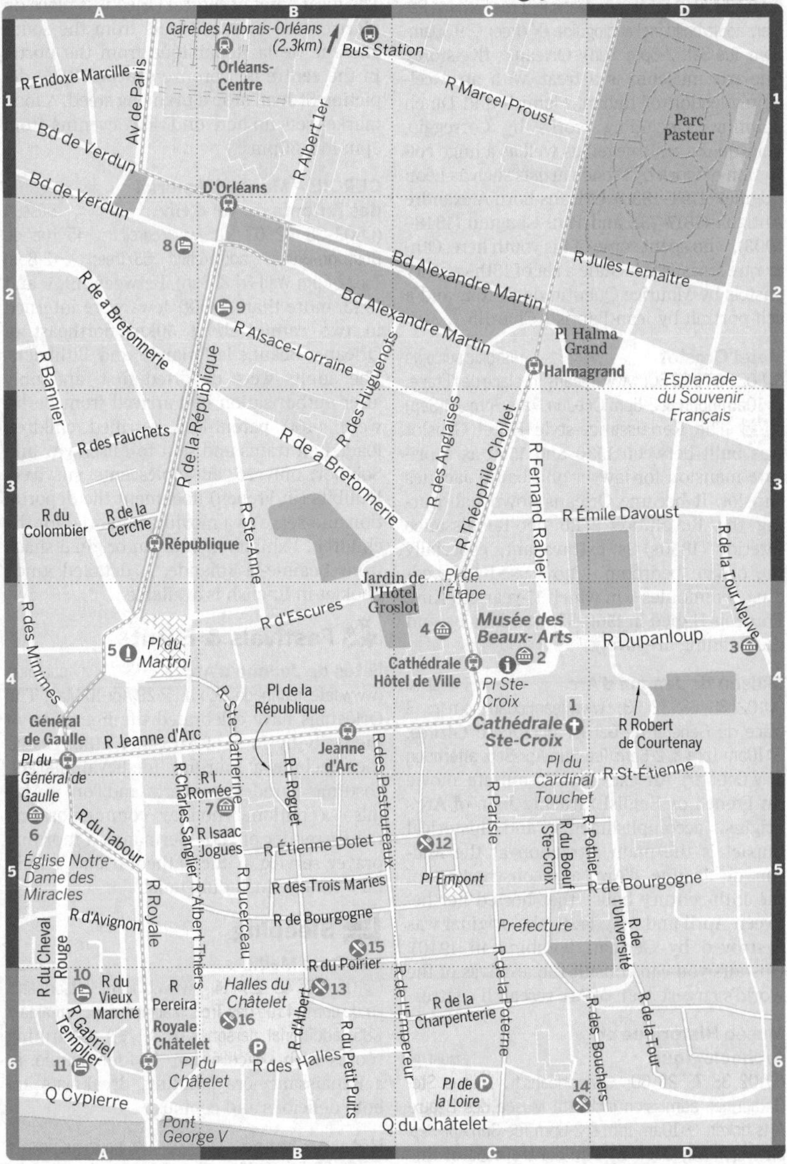

★**Hôtel de l'Abeille** HISTORIC HOTEL €€

(☎02 38 53 54 87; www.hoteldelabeille.com; 64 rue Alsace-Lorraine; d €98-135, q €180-210; @) Floorboards creak and vintage posters adorn the walls at this classic, 24-room hotel, built in 1903 and run by the same family since 1919 (that's four generations). The atmosphere is deliciously old-fashioned, from the real oak parquet and wildly ornate wallpapers to the hefty antique furniture. There's a beehive on the rooftop terrace. No lift.

Orléans

Top Sights
1 Cathédrale Ste-Croix C4
2 Musée des Beaux-Arts C4

Sights
3 CERCIL – Musée-Mémorial des Enfants du Vel d'Hiv D4
4 Hôtel Groslot C4
5 Joan of Arc Statue A4
6 Maison de Jeanne d'Arc A5
7 Musée Historique et Archéologique B5
Place du Martroi .... (see 5)

Sleeping
8 Hôtel Archange A2
9 Hôtel de l'Abeille B2
10 Hôtel Marguerite A6
11 Les Trois Maillets A6

Eating
12 La Dariole C5
13 La Parenthèse B6
14 Le Lièvre Gourmand C6
15 Les Fagots B5
16 Les Halles-Châtelet B6

Hôtel Marguerite HOTEL €€
(☎02 38 53 74 32; www.hotel-marguerite.fr; 14 place du Vieux Marché; d €70-105, q €125-145; @📶) This cheerful, 25-room establishment wins points for its friendly reception and central location. 'Superior' rooms are both more spacious and more modern. The bright breakfast room is presided over by a Sologne deer. Free locked bike parking.

Eating

Orléans has some great dining options. There's a cluster of midrange places at the northern end of rue Ste-Catherine.

Les Halles-Châtelet FOOD MARKET €
(place du Châtelet; ⌚7am or 8am-7.30pm Tue-Sat, 8am-1pm Sun) A covered food market with 35 stalls.

Les Fagots FRENCH €
(☎02 38 62 22 79; 32 rue du Poirier; menus €15-18; ⌚noon-2pm & 7.30-10pm Tue-Sat) Smokey barbecue smells welcome you to this unpretentious eatery, whose menu revolves around roasted meat and fish. The Breton chef cooks everything over an open fire, including baked potatoes slathered with crème fraiche and chives.

La Parenthèse MODERN FRENCH €€
(☎02 38 62 07 50; www.restaurant-la-parenthese.com; 26 place du Châtelet; lunch menus €18.50, dinner menus €26-30; ⌚noon-1.30pm & 7.30-9.30pm Tue-Sat) Youthful chef David Sterne turns fresh produce from nearby market stalls, including heritage vegetables, into old-fashioned, family-style French cuisine, creating a menu that changes continuously with the seasons. Choose from relaxed sidewalk seating or three more refined indoor dining rooms. Book well ahead.

La Dariole REGIONAL CUISINE €€
(☎02 38 77 26 67; 25 rue Étienne Dolet; menus €21-25.50; ⌚noon-1.30pm Mon-Fri, 7.30-10pm Tue & Fri) French cuisine made with fresh seasonal products: that's what so many locals come here for. Specialities include beef simmered in *sauce Bourguignonne* (Burgundy-style red-wine sauce) and desserts such as rum-flambéed-and-caramelised pineapple with vanilla butter and coconut ice cream.

★ **Le Lièvre Gourmand** GASTRONOMIC €€€
(☎02 38 53 66 14; www.lelievregourmand.com; 28 quai du Châtelet; menus €35-70; ⌚noon-12.45pm & 8-8.45pm Wed-Mon) You'll get a perfect amuse-bouche with your aperitif as you decide on a set of French, Asian and fusion courses, each a creative duo of hot and cold. Think delicate foams and infusions in unexpected combinations using seasonal ingredients, such as new asparagus in spring. It's a good idea to book ahead.

Information

Tourist Office (☎02 38 24 05 05; www.tourisme-orleans.com; 2 place de l'Étape; ⌚9.30am or 10am-1pm & 2-5pm or 6pm Mon-Sat, closed Mon morning Oct-Mar, open Sun Jul & Aug) Well stocked with English information, including cycling guides and a self-guided walking-tour brochure called *9 Walks Between the Sky & the Loire* (€0.50). Also has details on cultural events.

Getting There & Away

BUS

Ulys (☎08 00 00 45 00; www.ulys-loiret.com) links Orléans' **bus station** (2 rue Marcel Proust) with destinations in the Loiret *département*, including Châteauneuf-sur-Loire, Germigny-des-Prés, St-Benoît-sur-Loire and Sully-sur-Loire (all line 3); and Beaugency (line 9). Buy tickets (€2.40) on board.

OFF THE BEATEN TRACK

BEAUGENCY

Ready for a break from the château scene? Head over to wonderfully walkable Beaugency, a warren of medieval streets, towers, keeps and churches on the northern bank of the Loire. The **tourist office** (☎02 38 44 54 42; www.tourisme-beaugency.fr; 3 place du Dr Hyvernaud; ⏲9.30am or 10am-12.30pm & 2-5.30pm or 6.30pm Tue-Sat, plus Mon May–mid-Sep, plus 10am-1pm Sun early Jun–mid-Aug) has a walking-tour map and details on the two important 12th-century councils held here; the one in 1152 famously annulled the marriage of Louis VII and Eleanor of Aquitaine.

The town is 32km southwest of Orléans (towards Blois); it's served by train and Ulys (p369) bus 9.

TRAIN

The city's two stations, **Orléans-Centre** and **Gare des Aubrais-Orléans** (the latter is 2.5km to the north), are linked by tram and frequent shuttle trains; many trains stop at both.

Blois-Chambord €11.50, 40 minutes, 14 to 23 daily

Paris Gare d'Austerlitz €20.80, 65 minutes, hourly

Tours €20.70, 1½ hours, 13 to 17 daily

Getting Around

BICYCLE

Vélo+ (☎08 00 00 83 56; www.agglo-veloplus.fr; registration per 24hr €1, first 30min free, subsequent hours €1-2) On-street bike-hire system, with stations around town (eg at the train station and the cathedral). For rides out of town, try **Wheel Free** (p366), which rents, delivers and picks up classic and electric bikes.

BUS & TRAM

Trams – the two lines, A and B, intersect at place du Général de Gaulle – and buses are operated by **TAO** (☎08 00 01 20 00; www.reseau-tao.fr; 1/10 tickets €1.50/14, all-day ticket €3.90, weekend ticket €3.90). Information and tickets are available at tram-stop ticket machines, *tabacs* and TAO's **Agence Martroi** (rue de la Hallebarde; ⏲7.30am-7pm Mon-Fri, 8.30am-6pm Sat). Last-minute tickets (€1.60) are sold by bus drivers. Trams run until around 12.30am, buses till 9pm or a bit later.

East–west tram line B passes in front of the cathedral and tourist office. Navette O (€0.50), an electric shuttle, makes a circuit around the city centre four or five times an hour.

Orléans to Sully-sur-Loire

Upriver from Orléans a number of pretty towns – among them Châteauneuf-sur-Loire, Germigny-des-Prés, St-Benoît-sur-Loire and Sully-sur-Loire – make excellent day-trip destinations. North of Orléans lies the 350-sq-km **Forêt d'Orléans**, one of the few places in France where you can still spot wild ospreys.

Sights

Musée de la Marine de Loire MUSEUM

(☎02 38 46 84 46; www.chateauneuf-sur-loire.com; 1 place Aristide Briand, Châteauneuf-sur-Loire; adult/child €3.50/2; ⏲10am-6pm Wed-Mon Apr-Oct, 2-6pm Wed-Mon Nov-Mar) This well-presented museum tells the story of how a river that's basically non-navigable was used for commerce using ultra-shallow-draft (70cm) boats. Displays include a collection of model boats and riverine artefacts. An excellent English guide to the exhibits is available at the ticket counter. The museum occupies the former stables of the town's château (now the town hall).

★**Oratoire de Germigny-des-Prés** CHURCH

(☎tourist office 02 38 58 27 97; www.tourisme-loire-foret.com; Germigny-des-Prés; audioguide €3; ⏲9am-6.30pm Apr-Sep, 10am-5pm Oct-Mar) One of France's few Carolingian churches, this exceptional oratory, much of it rebuilt in the mid-1800s, is renowned for its unusual Maltese-cross layout and gilt-and-silver mosaic of the biblical Ark of the Covenant (806 AD; see Exodus 25:10-21). Audioguides are available across the square at the tourist office, or you can download the audio tour from its website.

Abbaye de Fleury MONASTERY

(☎02 38 35 72 43; www.abbaye-fleury.com; St-Benoît-sur-Loire; donation €4; ⏲6.30am-10pm year-round, guided visits 4pm Sat & 3.15pm Sun & holidays Mar-Oct) This Romanesque abbey, still home to 32 Benedictine brothers, is famous for its decorated portal and capitals and for the relics of St Benedict (480–547), brought from Montecassino, Italy, in 672. To get there, follow signs to the 'Basilique'.

Château de Sully-sur-Loire CHÂTEAU

(☎02 38 36 36 86; www.chateau-sully.com; Sully-sur-Loire; adult/child €7/3.50, with guided tour €8/4; ⏲10am-noon & 2-6pm Tue-Sun Feb-Dec, plus noon-2pm Apr-Sep, plus Mon Jul & Aug) With its machicolated ramparts, soaring round

turrets and steeply pitched roof, this is a grand example of a fairy-tale castle. Built from 1395, it was designed to defend one of the Loire's crucial crossings. The interior is richly furnished. One side of the glassy moat is lined by two-century-old bald cypresses, brought from the USA by General Lafayette, hero of the American Revolution, in the late 1700s.

Getting There & Away

Châteauneuf-sur-Loire, Germigny-des-Prés, St-Benoît-sur-Loire and Sully-sur-Loire are linked to Orléans by **Ulys** (p369) bus 3.

La Sologne

For centuries, the boggy wetland and murky woods of La Sologne have been one of France's great hunting grounds, with deer, boars, pheasants and stags roaming the woodland, and eels, carp and pike filling the deep ponds and rivers. François I established the region as a royal playground, but years of war and floods turned it into malaria-infested swamp; only in the mid-19th century, after it was drained under Napoléon III, did La Sologne regain its hunting prestige.

In winter La Sologne can be a desolate place, with drizzle and thick fog blanketing the landscape, but in summer it's a riot of wildflowers and makes for great country to explore on foot or horseback or by bike. Paths and trails, including the GR31 and the GR3C, criss-cross the area, but stick to the signposted routes during hunting season (late September to February) to avoid getting buckshot in your backside.

Sights

Maison des Étangs MUSEUM

(☎02 54 88 23 00; www.maison-des-etangs.fr; 2 rue de la Poste, St-Viâtre; adult/child €5/2.50; ⏲10am-noon & 2-6pm Apr-Oct, 2-6pm Wed, Sat & Sun Nov-Mar) Focuses on La Sologne's 3000 *étangs* (ponds).

Musée de Sologne MUSEUM

(☎02 54 95 33 66; www.museedesologne.com; Romorantin-Lanthenay; adult/child €6/4; ⏲10am-noon & 2-6pm Mon & Wed-Sat, 2-6pm Sun) Spotlights the history and ecology of La Sologne.

Information

Tourist Office (☎02 54 76 43 89; www.tourisme-romorantin.com; place de la Paix, Romorantin-Lanthenay; ⏲2-6pm or 6.30pm Mon, 9.30am-12.30pm & 2-6pm or 6.30pm Tue-Sat) Can supply you with info on hikes and walks in La Sologne.

Getting There & Away

Non-direct trains link Romorantin-Lanthenay with Tours (€16.50, 1½ hours, four to nine daily). **Route 41** (TLC; ☎02 54 58 55 44; www.route41.fr) bus 4 goes to Blois (€2, one hour, six daily Monday to Friday, two Saturday, one Sunday).

BLÉSOIS

The peaceful, verdant countryside around the former royal seat of Blois is home to some of France's finest châteaux, including graceful Cheverny, smaller Beauregard and the cupola-capped uber-château to top them all, Chambord.

Blois

POP 47,500

Towering above the northern bank of the Loire, Blois' royal château, one-time feudal seat of the powerful counts of Blois, offers a great introduction to some key periods in French history and architecture. The city makes an excellent base for visits to the châteaux, villages and towns of the central Loire Valley.

Sights

Blois' commercial centre – the partly pedestrianised area around rue Denis Papin – was heavily damaged by German bombs in 1940. From there, the château is 400m to the southwest and the old city is up the slope to the northwest. **Billets jumelés** (combo tickets; €11 to €16), sold at the château and Maison de la Magie, can save you some cash.

★**Château Royal de Blois** CHÂTEAU

(☎02 54 90 33 33; www.chateaudeblois.fr; place du Château; adult/child €10/5, audioguide €4/3; ⏲9am-6pm or 7pm Apr-Oct, 9am-noon & 1.30-5.30pm Nov-Mar) Seven French kings lived in Blois' royal château, whose four grand wings were built during four distinct periods in French architecture: Gothic (13th century), Flamboyant Gothic (1498–1501), early Renaissance (1515–20) and classical (1630s). You can easily spend a half-day immersing yourself in the château's dramatic and bloody history and its extraordinary architecture. In July and August there are free tours in English.

OFF THE BEATEN TRACK

BOURGES

Situated 110km southeast of Blois and Orléans, bustling Bourges has preserved its history well, with a maze of narrow, wonderful-to-explore medieval streets and the massively impressive **Cathédrale St-Étienne** (www.bourges-cathedrale.fr; church free, crypt & tower €7.50; ⌚8.30am-7.15pm Apr-Sep, 9am-5.45pm Oct-Mar). Bourges' **tourist office** (☎02 48 23 02 60; www.bourges-tourisme.com; 21 rue Victor Hugo; ⌚9am-6pm or 7pm Mon-Sat year-round, 10am-7pm Sun Apr-Sep, 2-5pm Sun Oct-Mar) has details on sights, activities and places to stay and eat. The historic centre is well signposted with French/English information placards.

The richly furnished complex's most famous Gothic feature is the richly painted **Hall of the States-General**, from the 13th century. In the **Renaissance wing**, the most extraordinary feature is the spiral **loggia staircase**, decorated with fierce salamanders and curly Fs, heraldic symbols of François I. Other château highlights include the **Queen's Chamber**, in which Catherine de Médicis (Henri II's machiavellian wife) died in 1589. According to Alexandre Dumas, the queen stashed her poisons in the adjacent **studiolo** in secret cupboards behind the elaborate wall panels (from the 1520s).

The 2nd-floor **King's Bedchamber** was the setting for one of the bloodiest episodes in the château's history. In 1588 Henri III had his arch-rival, Duke Henri I de Guise, murdered by royal bodyguards (the king is said to have hidden behind a tapestry while the dastardly deed was done). He had the duke's brother, the Cardinal de Guise, killed the next day. The bloodletting of the Wars of Religion continued when Henri III himself was murdered just eight months later by a vengeful monk. Dramatic and very graphic oil paintings illustrate these gruesome events next door in the **Council Room**.

The **Musée des Beaux-Arts** (Fine Arts Museum), in the Louis XII wing (look for his heraldic emblem, the porcupine), displays 300 16th- to 19th-century paintings, sculptures and tapestries.

In spring and summer, a **sound and light show** (☎02 54 90 33 33; adult/child €8.50/5; ⌚10pm late Mar-May & Sep, 10.30pm Jun-Aug) brings the château's history and architecture to life with dramatic lighting and narration. Tickets are sold at the château.

★**Maison de la Magie** MUSEUM
(☎02 54 90 33 33; www.maisondelamagie.fr; 1 place du Château; adult/child €9/5; ⌚10am-12.30pm & 2-6.30pm Apr-Aug & mid-Oct–2 Nov, 2-6.30pm 1st half Sep; 👪) Across the square from the château, this museum of magic occupies the one-time home of watchmaker, inventor and conjurer Jean Eugène Robert-Houdin (1805–71), after whom the American magician Harry Houdini named himself. Dragons emerge roaring from the windows every half-hour, while inside the museum has exhibits on Houdin and the history of magic, displays of optical trickery, and several daily magic shows.

Old City HISTORIC SITE
Blois' medieval and Renaissance old town is well worth a stroll, especially around 17th-century **Cathédrale St-Louis** (place St-Louis; ⌚9am or 10am-6pm or 7pm), whose lovely multistorey bell tower is dramatically floodlit after dark. Most of the stained glass inside was installed by Dutch artist Jan Dibberts in 2000. Across the square, the façade of **Maison des Acrobates** (3bis place St-Louis) – one of Blois' few surviving 15th-century houses – is decorated with wooden sculptures of figures from medieval farces. Another 15th-century townhouse, 50m from the cathedral's portal, is the **Hôtel de Villebrême** (13 rue Pierre de Blois).

Lovely panoramas unfold across town from the peaceful Jardins de l'Évêché (the gardens behind the cathedral) and from the top of the grand Escalier Dénis Papin staircase linking rue du Palais with rue Denis Papin.

Tours

The tourist office runs guided tours of Blois (in English on Friday in July and August) and sells walking-tour brochures (€2).

Carriage Rides CARRIAGE RIDE
(☎tourist office 02 54 90 41 42; www.attelagesdeblois.com; adult/child €7/4; ⌚2-6pm Apr-Jun & Sep, 11am-7pm Jul & Aug) Horse-drawn carriages clop around the town centre on a 25-minute circuit that begins in front of the château.

Boat Excursion BOAT TOUR
(☎02 54 56 09 24; www.observatoireloire.fr; Port de la Creusille, 5 quai Henri Chavigny; adult/child €9/7; ⌚departures 3pm & 4.15pm Tue-Sat May-

Sep, plus Sun Jul & Aug) Sail the Loire aboard a traditional *futreau* (flat-bottomed barge), run by a local NGO. Departures are right across the river from Blois' city centre.

Sleeping

Hôtel Anne de Bretagne HOTEL €
(☎02 54 78 05 38; www.hotelannedebretagne.com; 31 av du Dr Jean Laigret; s/d/q €60/69/95; P 📶) This ivy-covered hotel, in a great location midway between the train station and the château, has friendly staff, a cosy piano-equipped *salon* and 29 brightly coloured rooms with bold bedspreads. A packed three-course picnic lunch costs €11.50. It also rents out bicycles.

Côté Loire HOTEL €
(☎02 54 78 07 86; www.coteloire.com; 2 place de la Grève; r €59-97; @ 📶) This aptly named hotel, in a 15th- and 16th-century building facing the Loire, has eight spotless rooms decorated in subdued tones, some with 500-year-old beams and/or great Loire views. The restaurant (*menus* €21 to €31) serves French cuisine in a rustic dining room. No lift. Situated 400m due south of the château.

Les Salamandres B&B €
(☎02 54 20 69 55; www.salamandres.fr; 1 rue de St-Dyé, Montlivault; d incl breakfast €62-75) To get off the beaten path, head to this cheery, family-owned B&B, situated on an 18th-century wine estate 11km northeast of Blois and 7km northwest of Chambord. Martine and Jean-Claude offer simple, homey rooms and loads of regional knowledge.

★ **La Maison de Thomas** B&B €€
(☎09 81 84 44 59; www.lamaisondethomas.fr; 12 rue Beauvoir; s/d/tr incl breakfast €90/100/140; 📶) A friendly welcome and five spacious rooms with large windows, high ceilings and exposed beams await you at this beautiful B&B, on a pedestrianised street midway between the château and the cathedral. There's bike storage in the interior courtyard and a wine cellar where you can sample local vintages.

Eating

Food Market FOOD MARKET €
(place Louis XII; ⏲8am-1pm Sat) Blois' big weekly market is right below the château.

Les Planches ITALIAN €
(☎02 54 55 08 00; 5 rue Grenier à Sel; mains €10.50-15; ⏲noon-2pm & 7-10pm Mon-Sat; 🖉) Hidden away on a tiny square near lots of other dining options, Les Planches is a Blois favourite for its toasted bruschettas (open-faced Italian sandwiches) and meal-sized salads. Romantic, with a purple light on each table.

Les Banquettes Rouges MODERN FRENCH €€
(☎02 54 78 74 92; www.lesbanquettesrouges.com; 16 rue des Trois Marchands; lunch/dinner menus from €17.50/27.50; ⏲noon-1.30pm & 7-9.30pm Tue-Sat) In the St-Nicolas quarter below the château, this restaurant – easy to spot thanks to its bright-red façade – serves French *semi-gastronomique* cuisine. Favourites often available here include pan-fried veal liver with morello cherry and bitter-orange gravy, and *fondant au chocolat*.

L'Orangerie du Château GASTRONOMIC €€€
(☎02 54 78 05 36; www.orangerie-du-chateau.fr; 1 av Dr Jean Laigret; menus €38-84; ⏲noon-1.45pm & 7-9.15pm Tue-Sat; P) This Michelin-starred restaurant serves *cuisine gastronomique inventive* inspired by both French tradition and culinary ideas from faraway lands. The wine list comes on a tablet computer. For dessert try the speciality, soufflé.

Information

Tourist Office (☎02 54 90 41 41; www.bloischambord.co.uk; 23 place du Château; ⏲9am-7pm Easter-Sep, 10am-5pm Oct-Easter) Has town maps and sells châteaux combo and concert tickets. Download its smartphone app via the website. Situated across the square from the château.

Getting There & Around

BUS

The tourist office has a brochure detailing public-transport options to nearby châteaux.

CHÂTEAUX PASS

You can save money on visits to many Blésois châteaux – and avoid waiting in line – by buying a **Pass Châteaux** multi-site discount ticket. For information, contact the tourist offices in Blois and at Chambord, Chaumont and Cheverny. Popular combinations:

- Blois–Chambord–Cheverny €28.50
- Blois–Chenonceau–Chambord–Cheverny €40
- Blois–Chaumont–Chambord–Cheverny €38.50
- Blois–Chambord–Amboise–Clos Lucé €43

A *navette* (shuttle bus; €6) run by **Route 41** (p371) makes it possible to do a Blois-Chambord-Cheverny-Beauregard-Blois circuit on Wednesday, Saturday and Sunday from early April to 1 November; it also runs daily during school vacation periods and on holidays from early April to August.

A *navette* (one way/return €2.15/4.15) operated by **Azalys** (☎09 69 36 93 41; www.azalys-blois.fr) links Blois' train station and château with the Château de Chaumont twice a day on Saturday, Sunday and holidays from April to October (daily in July and August).

TRAIN

The **Blois-Chambord train station** (av Dr Jean Laigret) is 600m west (up the hill) from Blois' château.

Amboise €7.20, 15 minutes, 16 to 25 daily
Orléans €11.50, 33 to 43 minutes, 14 to 25 daily
Paris Gare d'Austerlitz €29.40, 1½ hours, five direct daily
Tours €11.20, 40 minutes, 14 to 22 daily

Chambord

One of the crowning achievements of French Renaissance architecture, the **Château de Chambord** (☎info 02 54 50 40 00, tour & show reservations 02 54 50 50 40; www.chambord.org; adult/child €11/9, parking near/distant €6/4; ⏲9am-5pm or 6pm; 👪) – with 440 rooms, 365 fireplaces and 84 staircases – is by far the largest, grandest and most visited château in the Loire Valley. Begun in 1519 by François I (r 1515–47) as a weekend hunting lodge, it quickly grew into one of the most ambitious – and expensive – architectural projects ever attempted by a French monarch.

Construction was repeatedly halted by financial problems, design setbacks and military commitments (not to mention the kidnapping of the king's two sons in Spain). Ironically, when Chambord was finally finished after 30-odd years of work, François found his elaborate palace too draughty, preferring instead the royal apartments in Amboise and Blois. In the end he stayed here for just 42 days during his entire reign!

Inside the château's main building, an interesting film (in five languages) relates the history of the castle's construction. The 1st floor is where you'll find the most interesting rooms, including the king's and queen's chambers, complete with interconnecting passages to enable late-night high jinks. Rising through the centre of the structure, the world-famous double-helix staircase – reputedly designed by the king's chum Leonardo da Vinci – ascends to the great lantern tower and the rooftop, where you can marvel at a veritable skyline of cupolas, domes, turrets, chimneys and lightning rods and gaze out across the vast grounds.

To get a sense of what you're looking at, it's well worth picking up an audioguide (1½ hours; €5) or a Histopad tablet computer (1½ hours; €8); the latter has a treasure hunt for kids, but the former has better information about the castle's history. In summer there may be hour-long guided tours (€5/3 per adult/child) in English – ask at the new Halle d'Acceuil (entrance pavilion). Outdoor spectacles held in the warm season include an **equestrian show** (☎02 54 50 40 00; www.chambord.org; adult/child €14.50/11; ⏲11.45am & 4pm Tue-Sun May-Sep, daily mid-Jul–early Sep).

From April to December there are several places to eat right around the château, including a cafe inside. In winter dress warmly – the castle is no easier to heat now than it was five centuries ago!

Chambord is 16km east of Blois, 45km southwest of Orléans and 18km northeast of Cheverny.

Domaine National de Chambord FOREST
(☎02 54 50 40 00; www.chambord.org) The 54-sq-km hunting reserve around the Château de Chambord – the largest walled park in Europe – is reserved for the exclusive use of very high-ranking French government officials (though it's difficult to imagine François Hollande astride a galloping stallion). About 10 sq km of the park, north and northwest of the château, is open to the public, with trails for walkers, cyclists and horse riders.

Hire bikes, pedal carts, electric golf carts, rowboats and electric boats at a **rental kiosk** (hire bicycle 1/4hr €6/15, rowboat 1hr €12, golf cart 45min €25; ⏲10am-7pm late Mar-early Nov), near the *embarcadère* (dock) midway between the château and its Halle d'Accueil.

The park is a great place for wildlife-spotting, especially during the deer mating season in September and October. Observation towers dot the perimeter of the park; set out at dawn or dusk to maximise your chances of spotting stags, boars and red deer. Or jump aboard a **Land Rover Safari tour** (adult/child €18/12; ⏲often 11am-5pm year-round) conducted by a French-speaking guide.

LUNCH BREAK

La Détente Gourmande (☎02 54 33 94 65; www.restaurant-chaumont-sur-loire.fr; 61 rue du Maréchal de Lattre de Tassigny, Chaumont-sur-Loire; mains €7-13; ⏰10.30am-approx 9pm Wed-Sun Mar–mid-Oct) For a light meal or a cup of tea or wine, drop by this quirky *salon de thé* (tearoom) and restaurant, on the D751 directly below the Château de Chaumont. Edibles include local charcuterie and cheeses and warm peach-and-pear pies.

La Madeleine de Proust (☎02 54 20 94 80; 33 rue du Maréchal Leclerc, Chaumont-sur-Loire; menus €21-28; ⏰noon-2pm & 7-9.30pm Wed-Sun) Excellent homemade French cuisine served impeccably and with a warm smile.

Max Vauché Chocolate Factory (☎02 54 46 07 96; www.maxvauche-chocolatier.com; 22 Les Jardins du Moulin, Bracieux; tour adult/child €4.50/3.60; ⏰10am-12.30pm & 2-7pm Tue-Sat, 3-6.30pm Sun Sep-Jun, plus Mon Jul & Aug) For scrumptious chocolate delicacies, head to sleepy Bracieux, 8km south of the Château de Chambord, where Max Vauché's chocolate factory has a shop and a *salon de chocolat* (chocolate cafe) and offers tours (in English at 11.30am and 2.30pm Monday to Saturday in July and August).

Cheverny

Perhaps the Loire's most elegantly proportioned château, **Château de Cheverny** (☎02 54 79 96 29; www.chateau-cheverny.fr; av du Château; château & gardens adult/child €10.50/7.50; ⏰9.15am-7pm Apr-Sep, 10am-5.30pm Oct-Mar) represents the zenith of French classical architecture: the perfect blend of symmetry, geometry and aesthetic order. Inside are some of the most sumptuous and elegantly furnished rooms anywhere in the Loire Valley, virtually unchanged for generations because the Hurault family has lived here, almost continuously, ever since the château's construction in the early 1600s by Jacques Hurault, an intendant to Louis XII.

Highlights include the formal dining room, with panels depicting the story of Don Quixote; the king's bedchamber, with ceiling murals and tapestries illustrating stories from Greek mythology; and a children's playroom complete with toys from the time of Napoléon III. The arms room is full of pikestaffs, claymores, crossbows and suits of armour – including a tiny gilded one made to measure for a four-year-old duke – and a magnificently preserved Gobelins tapestry (you can still see the reds).

The Huraults' fabulous art collection includes a portrait of Jeanne of Aragon by Raphael's studio, an 18th-century De la Tour pastel, and works by a who's who of court painters. Keep your eyes open for the certificate signed by US president George Washington.

Behind the main château, the 18th-century orangerie – where many priceless artworks, including (apparently) the *Mona Lisa,* were stashed during WWII – is now a tearoom (open April to November) with delicious hot chocolate.

In the gardens about 50m beyond the giant sequoia (planted around 1870), the kennels house around 100 hunting dogs, a cross between Poitevins and English foxhounds. Feeding time, known as the Soupe des Chiens, takes place at 11.30am daily from April to September and on Monday, Wednesday, Thursday and Friday (on other days the dogs are out hunting) from October to March.

Fans of Tintin might find the Château de Cheverny's façade oddly familiar: Hergé used it as a model (minus the two end towers) for Moulinsart (Marlinspike) Hall, the ancestral home of Tintin's irascible sidekick, Captain Haddock. Diehard devotees might enjoy **Les Secrets de Moulinsart** (combo ticket with château adult/child €15/11.40), which explores the world of Tintin with recreated scenes, thunder and other special effects.

Cheverny is 14km southeast of Blois and 18km southwest of Chambord.

Chaumont-sur-Loire

Set on a strategic bluff with sweeping views along the Loire, **Château de Chaumont-sur-Loire** (☎02 54 20 99 22; www.domaine-chaumont.fr; adult/child €12/7, during garden festival €18/11; ⏰10am-btwn 4.15pm & 6.30pm) combines a medieval defensive exterior, with cylindrical corner towers and a sturdy drawbridge, with an interior courtyard that is very much of the Renaissance. Most of the elegant furnishings inside date from the

19th century, a nice contrast with the exhibitions of striking contemporary art, which are as 21st century as can be. Chaumont's English-style gardens are at their finest during the annual **Festival International des Jardins** (adult/child €14/8.50; ⌚10am-7pm late Apr-Oct).

A defensive château was first built on this spot in the late 900s, but most of the present castle was constructed between 1468 and 1566. Following the death of Henri II in 1559, Catherine de Médicis (his widow) forced Diane de Poitiers (his mistress and her 2nd cousin) to accept Chaumont in exchange for the grander surroundings of Chenonceau. Savvy Diane earned considerable sums from Chaumont's vast landholdings but stayed here only occasionally.

In the second half of the 18th century, the château's owner, Jacques-Donatien Le Ray, a supporter of the American Revolution and an intimate of Benjamin Franklin, removed the decrepit north wing. In 1875 Princess de Broglie, heiress to the Say sugar fortune, bought the château and thoroughly renovated and furnished it.

The most impressive room is the Council Chamber, with its series of eight 16th-century tapestries (restored in 2015) and a 17th-century majolica-tiled floor from a palace in Palermo.

Don't miss the brick Écuries (stables), an outbuilding constructed in 1877 to house the Broglies' horses in equine luxury. A fine collection of 19th-century equestrian gear and horse-drawn carriages of surprisingly varied design is displayed inside.

It's a good idea to hire an informative audiovisual guide (a tablet computer; €4), available in a version for kids, or to download the app from iTunes (US$2.99) or Google Play (US$3.59).

The Château de Chaumont is 19km southwest of Blois. Trains link Onzain, a 2.5km walk across the Loire from the château, with Blois (€3.70, nine minutes, eight to 17 daily) and Tours (€8.80, 30 minutes, 10 to 17 daily).

TOURAINE

Often dubbed the 'Garden of France', the Touraine region is known for its rich food, tasty cheeses and famously pure French accent, as well as a first-rate line-up of glorious châteaux: some medieval (Langeais and Loches), others Renaissance (Azay-le-Rideau, Villandry and Chenonceau). The vibrant capital, Tours, offers plenty of château tours and public-transport options.

Tours

POP 135,000

Bustling Tours is a smart and vivacious city, with an impressive medieval quarter, fine museums, well-tended parks and a university of some 25,000 students. Combining the sophisticated style of Paris with the conservative sturdiness of central France, Tours makes an ideal staging post for exploring the castles of the Touraine.

Sights

Tours' focal point is grand, semicircular **place Jean Jaurès**, adorned with fountains, formal gardens and imposing public buildings (the town hall and the courthouse). **Vieux Tours** (the old city) occupies the narrow streets around place Plumereau (locally known as place Plum), about 400m west of boutique- and shop-lined **rue Nationale**.

★**Musée du Compagnonnage** MUSEUM

(☎02 47 21 62 20; www.museecompagnonnage.fr; 8 rue Nationale & 1 square Prosper Merimée; adult/child €5.50/3.80; ⌚9am-12.30pm & 2-6pm, closed Tue mid-Sep–mid-Jun) A highlight of a visit to Tours, this museum spotlights France's renowned *compagnonnages*, guild organisations of skilled craftspeople who have been responsible for everything from medieval cathedrals to the Statue of Liberty. Dozens of professions – from carpentry to saddle-making to locksmithery – are celebrated here with items handcrafted from wood, wrought iron, bronze, stone, brick, clay and leather; standouts include exquisite wooden architectural models. During nearby construction the entrance will be around the back, via the path opposite 23 rue Colbert.

★**Musée des Beaux-Arts** ART MUSEUM

(☎02 47 05 68 82; www.mba.tours.fr; 18 place François Sicard; adult/child €6/3; ⌚9am-12.45pm & 2-6pm Wed-Mon) This superb fine-arts museum, in a gorgeous 18th-century archbishop's palace, features paintings, sculpture, furniture and objets d'art from the 14th to 20th centuries. Highlights include paintings by Delacroix, Degas and Monet, a rare Rembrandt miniature and a Rubens *Madonna and Child*. Next to the flowery gardens is a massive ceder of Lebanon planted in 1804.

Cathédrale St-Gatien CHURCH
(place de la Cathédrale; ⌚9am-7pm) With its flying buttresses, gargoyles and twin Renaissance-style towers (70m) – and, inside, Gothic vaulting, dazzling stained glass and a huge Baroque organ – this cathedral cuts a striking figure. Near the entrance you can pick up an English brochure on its architecture and history; English signs in the choir explain the intricate stained glass. On the north side is **Cloître de la Psalette** (adult/child €3/free; ⌚9.30am-12.30pm & 2-5pm or 6pm, closed Sun morning, also closed Mon & Tue Sep-Mar), built from 1442 to 1524.

Basilique St-Martin CHURCH
(www.basiliquesaintmartin.fr; rue Descartes; ⌚7.30am-7pm, to 9pm Jul & Aug) In the Middle Ages, Tours was an important pilgrimage city thanks to the relics of soldier turned evangelist St Martin (c 317–97). In the 5th century a basilica was constructed above his tomb; in the 13th century it was replaced by an enormous Romanesque church, of which only the **Tour Charlemagne** and **Tour de l'Horloge** (Clock Tower) remain. Modern-day Basilique St-Martin, a domed, neo-Byzantine structure, was built from 1886 to 1925. The 1700th anniversary of St Martin's birth will be celebrated in 2017.

Down the block, the small **Musée St-Martin** (www.tours.fr; 3 rue Rapin; adult/child €2/1; ⌚10am-1pm & 2-5.30pm Wed-Sun mid-Mar–mid-Nov) displays artefacts relating to the lost churches and the life of the saint.

Jardin Botanique GARDENS
(www.tours.fr; 35 bd Tonnellé; ⌚7.45am-7.30pm Mar-Jun & Sep-Oct, to 9pm Jul & Aug, to 5.30pm Nov-Feb; 👪) Founded in 1843, Tours' lovely, 5-hectare botanical gardens have a tropical greenhouse, a medicinal herb garden, a petting zoo and children's playgrounds. Situated 2km west of place Jean Jaurès, the gardens are served by Fil Bleu bus 15 from place Jean Jaurès or bus 4 from the riverfront.

Tours

Lots of château tours begin in Tours – for details, contact the tourist office, which runs **guided city walks** (in French; adult/child €6/free, at night €9) and can supply you with a brochure for a self-guided walking tour.

La Calèche CARRIAGE RIDE
(☎02 47 66 70 70; www.filbleu.fr; €1.50; ⌚10am, 11am, 3pm, 4pm & 5pm Tue-Sat, 3pm, 4pm & 5pm Sun May-Sep) Run by the local public-transport company, La Calèche offers a 50-minute carriage ride for the price of a bus trip. Departures are from place François Sicard, near the cathedral. Drivers sell tickets.

> **OFF THE BEATEN TRACK**
>
> **BEAUREGARD**
>
> Smaller and less visited than the Blésois' more famous châteaux, peaceful **Château de Beauregard** (☎02 54 70 41 65; www.beauregard-loire.com; 12 chemin de la Fontaine, Cellettes; adult/child €12.50/5; ⌚10.30am-6.30pm or 7pm Apr-Sep, 1.30-5pm Mon-Fri & 10.30am-5pm Sat & Sun late Feb-Mar & Oct–mid-Nov) has charms all its own. Built as yet another hunting lodge by François I, the highlight is a portrait gallery depicting 327 notables of European royalty, clergy and intelligentsia who lived from 1328 to 1643. Famous faces to look for include Christopher Columbus, Sir Francis Drake, and Henry VIII of England and his doomed wife Anne Boleyn. English tours begin at noon from April to mid-November.
>
> The château's lovely 40-hectare park, well worth a stroll, encompasses various themed sections, including a rose garden. Beauregard is 8km southeast of Blois.

Sleeping

★**Hôtel l'Adresse** BOUTIQUE HOTEL €
(☎02 47 20 85 76; www.hotel-ladresse.com; 12 rue de la Rôtisserie; s from €55, d €78-105; ❄@📶) Looking for Parisian style in provincial Tours? L'Adresse is the address! On a pedestrianised street in the old quarter, this place has 17 rooms – finished in creams, tans and light browns – with designer sinks, sparkling bathrooms and, on the 3rd floor, 17th-century rafters.

★**Hôtel Ronsard** BOUTIQUE HOTEL €
(☎02 47 05 25 36; www.hotel-ronsard.com; 2 rue Pimbert; s €63-77, d €73-85; ❄@📶) A favourite of musicians and actors performing at the nearby Grand Théâtre, this quiet, 20-room hotel, built in 1920, offers easy comfort and good value. Staircases are lined with colourful photographs, while sleek rooms are decorated in muted tones of grey, brown and cream. No lift.

Hôtel des Arts HOTEL €
(☎02 47 05 05 00; www.hoteldesartstours.com; 40 rue de la Préfecture; s €35-51, d €50-56; 📶)

Tours

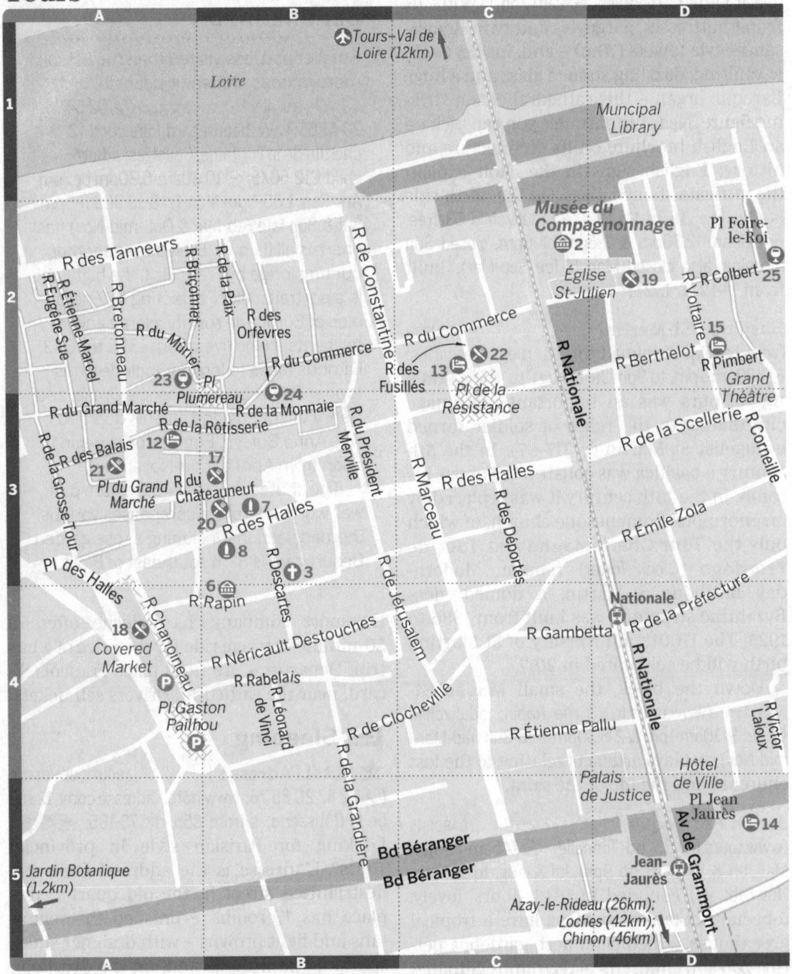

A delightful place with charming management, Hôtel des Arts has just 10 rooms, some of them pretty small, but all of them spotless, bright and cheery; oranges, yellows and greens predominate. Excellent value in a great location. No lift.

Hôtel Colbert HOTEL €

(☎02 47 66 61 56; www.tours-hotel-colbert.fr; 78 rue Colbert; s €47-64, d €53-76; 📶) In a great location near sights and restaurants, this family-run hotel offers a welcoming haven. The 15 rooms are smart, cheery and spacious. The quiet inner courtyard is a pleasant spot to relax or park bikes overnight. No lift.

Hôtel Val de Loire HOTEL €

(☎02 47 05 37 86; www.hotelvaldeloire.fr; 33 bd Heurteloup; d €52-82, q €98-108; 📶) Bright-red banisters, friendly management and cheery rooms welcome you to this very central hotel. The 14 well-kept rooms, four with (non-working) marble fireplaces, blend antique furnishings, modern touches and large, old-fashioned windows. No lift.

Hôtel Mondial HOTEL €

(☎02 47 05 62 68; www.hotelmondialtours.com; 3 place de la Résistance; d €64-105; 📶) In a fantastic city-centre location, this hotel has 20 rooms – six with balconies – decorated in

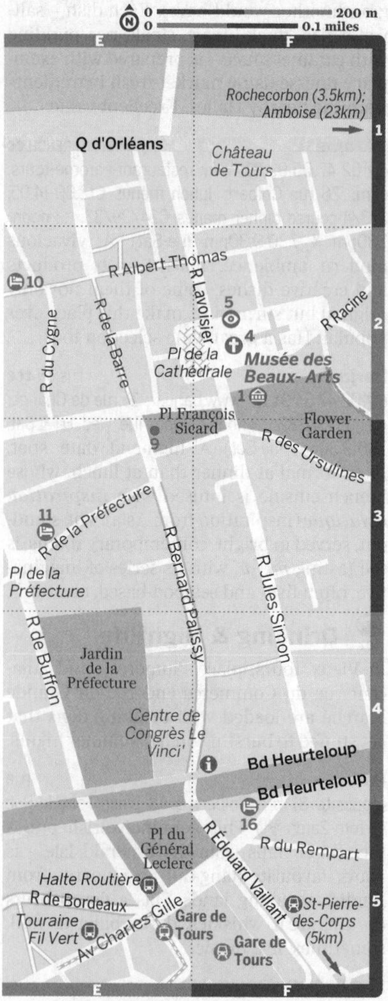

Tours

Top Sights
1 Musée des Beaux-Arts F2
2 Musée du Compagnonnage C2

Sights
3 Basilique St-Martin B3
4 Cathédrale St-Gatien F2
5 Cloître de la Psalette F2
6 Musée St-Martin B4
7 Tour Charlemagne B3
8 Tour de l'Horloge B3

Activities, Courses & Tours
9 La Calèche E3

Sleeping
10 Hôtel Colbert E2
11 Hôtel des Arts E3
12 Hôtel l'Adresse A3
13 Hôtel Mondial C2
14 Hôtel Oceania L'Univers D5
15 Hôtel Ronsard D2
16 Hôtel Val de Loire F5

Eating
17 Barju B3
18 Halles de Tours A4
19 L'Arôme D2
20 Le Timbre Poste B3
21 Le Zinc A3
22 Tartines & Co C2

Drinking & Nightlife
23 Excalibur A2
24 Les Trois Orfèvres B3
25 Pale D2

subdued greys, beiges and violets. Reception is on the 2nd floor; no lift.

Hôtel Oceania L'Univers HOTEL €€€
(02 47 05 37 12; www.oceaniahotels.com/hotel-lunivers-tours; 5 bd Heurteloup; d €200-245;) Everyone from Ernest Hemingway to Winston Churchill to Thomas Edison has bunked at L'Univers since it opened in 1846. Enjoy the lobby's frescoes and balconies before heading up to the 91 tasteful rooms, renovated in 2015. A pool and spa were added in 2016. Discounts available online.

Eating

Tours has two main dining zones: **Vieux Tours** and **rue Colbert**. Some of Tours' best restaurants are at **place du Grand Marché** (place du Monstre), but quality varies right around **place Plumereau** and adjacent, east–west-oriented rue du Grand Marché. About 1km east, rue Colbert has a selection of moderately priced restaurants serving international cuisines (eg Lebanese, Indian, Japanese).

Halles de Tours FOOD MARKET €
(www.halles-de-tours.com; place Gaston Pailhou; 7am-7.30pm Mon-Sat, 8am-1pm Sun;) Market stalls – 38 of them – sell everything you could want for a picnic, including cheese, wine and prepared dishes.

Le Timbre Poste CREPERIE €
(02 47 64 84 14; www.letimbreposte.fr; 10 rue du Châteauneuf; lunch menu €11.50, crêpes €3-11;

THE LOIRE VALLEY FOR CHILDREN

➡ Be razzle-dazzled by magic and illusions at Maison de la Magie (p372).

➡ Prowl through ancient cave dwellings at Rochemenier (p399) and Troglodytes et Sarcophages (p399).

➡ Celebrate comic-book character Tintin at the Château de Cheverny (p375).

➡ Visit the giant pandas at **ZooParc de Beauval** (☎02 54 75 50 00; www.zoobeauval.com; St-Aignan-sur-Cher; adult/child 3-10yr €29/23; ⊙9am-7pm or 8pm Mar-Oct, to 5.30pm Nov-Feb; 👪), one of Europe's most beautiful zoos.

➡ Book ahead for amazing horse acrobatics at Saumur's Cadre Noir public presentations (p394).

➡ Go on a tablet-computer treasure hunt at Château de Chambord (p374).

➡ Play games in the gardens of the Pagode de Chanteloup (p383).

⊙noon-2.30pm & 7-10pm Tue-Sat) Acclaimed by locals as one of Tours' best purveyors of savoury buckwheat galettes, sweet crêpes, apple *cidres* (€3.50/8 per glass/pitcher) from Normandy and Brittany, and creative salads, including one in which chèvre (goat's cheese) meets honey. The intimate dining room is decorated with old French postage stamps and postcards.

Tartines & Co SANDWICHES €
(☎02 47 20 50 60; 6 rue des Fusillés; sandwiches €7.90-14.40, lunch menus €10.50-15.50; ⊙noon-3.30pm & 7.15-10pm Mon-Sat; 🖉) This snazzy little cafe serves *tartines* (toasted or cold open-face sandwiches), made with scrumptious *pain Poilâne* (artisanal bread), amid jazz and friendly chatter. Toppings include smoked duck breast, tomato and red-pepper compote, beef carpaccio and foie gras with artichokes. Also has meal-size salads.

★**Le Zinc** FRENCH €€
(☎02 47 20 29 00; lezinc37@gmail.com; 27 place du Grand Marché; menus €20.90-25.90; ⊙noon-2pm Tue & Thu-Sat, 7.30-10pm Mon-Thu, to 11pm Fri & Sat; 📶🖉) This intimate restaurant, with just a dozen tables, garners rave reviews for its outstanding traditional French cuisine, prepared *à l'ancienne* (in the old style, like grandmother would have). Each dish – saltwater fish, duck breast, steak, rice pudding with caramel sauce – is prepared with exemplary finesse using market-fresh ingredients from the nearby Halles. Excellent value.

L'Arôme MODERN FRENCH €€
(☎02 47 05 99 81; www.restaurant-l-arome-tours.com; 26 rue Colbert; lunch menus €12.60-14.95, 2/3/4-course dinner menus €24/29/33; ⊙noon-1.30pm & 7.30-9.30pm Tue-Sat) A vivacious modern ambience, market-fresh products and creative dishes, some of them not only original but surprising, make this place ever popular. Has a great wine selection too.

Barju FUSION €€€
(☎02 47 64 91 12; www.barju.fr; 15 rue de Change; menus €42-82; ⊙noon-1.30pm Tue, Wed, Fri & Sat, 7.30-9.30pm Tue-Sat) A high-end date spot, more formal at dinner than at lunch, whose French cuisine is infused with *inspiration asiatique* (inspiration from Asia). The standout, served in bright, contemporary rooms, is the tasting *menu*, with its series of imaginative, often fish- and seafood-based, creations.

🍷 Drinking & Nightlife

In Vieux Tours, place Plumereau and adjacent rue du Commerce and rue du Grande Marché are loaded with drinking dens that get stuffed to bursting on hot summer nights.

Pale PUB
(opposite 81 rue Colbert & 18 place Foire-le-Roi; ⊙1pm-2am; 📶) This genuinely Irish pub – the owner hails from the Emerald Isle – is Tours' favourite hang-out for students from English-speaking lands. Has a dozen beers on tap, great whiskies, darts, billiards and, sometimes, live music.

Les Trois Orfèvres CLUB
(☎02 47 64 02 73; www.3orfevres.com; 6 rue des Orfèvres; Wed free, Thu-Sat €3; ⊙midnight-6am Wed-Sat) Underground (literally) nightspot where DJs (every night) and bands (one Friday a month from 7.30pm) lean towards pop and rock, and students hang out in force. Dress is very casual. Things really get going around 2am.

Excalibur CLUB
(☎02 47 64 76 78; www.facebook.com/excalibur.tours; 35 rue Briçonnet; Tue & Wed free, Thu & Fri €8, Sat €10; ⊙midnight-6am Tue-Sat) DJs spin the latest *musique commerciale* at this mainstream – if subterranean – disco, where student revellers hit the rhythmic groove

at about 1.30am or 2am. The dress code is casual.

Information

Tourist Office (☎02 47 70 37 37; www.tours-tourisme.fr; 78-82 rue Bernard Palissy; ⏱8.30am-7pm Mon-Sat, 10am-12.30pm & 2.30-5pm Sun Apr-Sep, 9am-12.30pm & 1.30-6pm Mon-Sat, 10am-1pm Sun Oct-Mar) Abundant info in English on cultural events and the Loire Valley; sells slightly reduced château tickets.

Getting There & Away

AIR

Tours–Val de Loire Airport (TUF; ☎02 47 49 37 00; www.tours.aeroport.fr), 6km northeast of the centre, is linked to London's Stansted and Dublin (Ireland) by Ryanair.

BUS

Touraine Fil Vert (☎02 47 31 14 00; www.tourainefilvert.com) operates buses to destinations around the Indre-et-Loire *département* from Tours' **Halte Routière** (place du Général Leclerc; ⏱office 7am-7pm Mon-Fri, to 6.30pm Sat). Destinations include Amboise (40 minutes, seven daily Monday to Saturday) and Chenonceau (1¼ hours, one or two daily Monday to Saturday), both served by line C. All fares are €2.40.

CAR & MOTORCYCLE

Tours' perplexing one-way streets make driving a headache. To park your car for more than two hours, use an underground garage; the one below the **Halles de Tours** (place Gaston Pailhou; per 1/24hr €1.80/12) also has some free spots at street level.

Avis (☎02 47 20 53 27; www.avis.com) and other rental companies have offices at Tours' train station, the St-Pierre-des-Corps TGV station and the airport (by reservation).

TRAIN

Tours is the Loire Valley's main rail hub. Regular trains and a few TGVs use the city-centre train station, **Tours-Centre** (place du Général Leclerc), while most TGV trains stop only at **St-Pierre-des-Corps**, 3km east and linked to Tours-Centre by frequent shuttle trains. Some destinations, including Paris, Angers and Orléans, are served by both stations.

Bicycles can be taken aboard almost all trains, so you can train it out and pedal back or vice versa.

Direct services from Tours-Centre include the following:

Amboise €5.70, 17 minutes, 13 to 23 daily

Angers €19, one hour, four to six daily

Azay-le-Rideau €5.90, 30/60 minutes by train/bus, five to 11 daily

Blois €11.20, 40 minutes, 12 to 23 daily

Chenonceaux €7, 25 minutes, nine to 12 daily

Chinon €9.90, 45 minutes by train, 1¼ hours by SNCF bus, five to 10 daily

Langeais €5.70, 17 minutes, six to 10 daily

Loches €9.60, one hour, one or two trains plus four to 15 SNCF buses daily

Orléans €20.70, 1½ hours, 13 to 17 daily

Paris Gare d'Austerlitz €36.20, 2¼ hours, four non-TGV daily

Paris Gare Montparnasse €53 to €69, 1¼ hours, six or seven TGVs daily

Saumur €12.30, 45 minutes, seven to 10 daily

Getting Around

BICYCLE

For bicycle hire, try **Détours de Loire** (p366).

BUS & TRAM

Local trams and buses are run by **Fil Bleu** (☎02 47 66 70 70; www.filbleu.fr; single/day ticket €1.50/3.90); many lines stop near the main hub, place Jean-Jaurès. Tickets are sold at tram stations, by bus drivers and at *tabacs*. The circular Citadine (C) line does a loop through the city centre, from the Grand Marché to the cathedral, four times an hour Monday to Saturday from 7.30am to 6.30pm.

Rochecorbon & Vouvray

Renowned chenin-blanc vineyards carpet the area around the small towns of Rochecorbon, Vouvray and Montlouis-sur-Loire, all about 10km east of Tours, and wine cellars sprinkle the region. Vouvray's tourist office (p382) has a list of cellars and details on walking trails through the vineyards.

Sights & Activities

Château de Moncontour WINERY

(☎02 47 52 60 77; www.moncontour.com; rue de Moncontour, Vouvray; ⏱9am-12.30pm & 1.30-6pm or 7pm daily Apr–mid-Sep, closed Sun mid-Sep–Mar, also closed Sat morning Jan-Mar) Has a small wine museum and also does tastings.

Cave de Vouvray WINE

(☎02 47 52 75 03; www.cavedevouvray.com; 38 rue de la Vallée Coquette, Vouvray; tours adult/child €2.60/1.50; ⏱9am or 10am-12.30pm & 2-6pm or 7pm daily year-round, no midday closure Jul & Aug) Created in 1953 by a group of Vouvray AOP *vignerons* (winemakers), this cooperative offers tastings and runs tours of its *caves* (cellars; in English at 11.30am and 4pm or 4.30pm from March to December, also at

2.30pm in July and August). Has a play area for kids.

NaviLoire BOAT TOUR
(☎02 47 52 68 88, 06 37 49 92 61; www.naviloire.com; 56 quai de la Loire, Rochecorbon; adult/child €10.50/7; ⊙Apr-Oct) Offers one of the few boat cruises (50 minutes) on the Loire proper, in a 66-seat vessel departing from Rochecorbon that sails past nature reserves and untamed islands. See the website for departure times.

Information

Vouvray Tourist Office (☎02 47 52 68 73; www.tourismevouvray-valdeloire.com; 12 rue Rabelais, Vouvray; ⊙9.30am-1pm & 2-5.30pm or 6.30pm Mon-Sat, 9.30am-12.30pm Sun mid-Apr–mid-Sep, Tue-Sat mid-Sep–mid-Apr) has a list of cellars and details on walking trails through the vineyards.

Getting There & Away

Fil Bleu (p381) bus 54 links Tours' riverside place Anatole France with Vouvray (€1.50, 25 minutes, hourly except Sunday morning).

Chenonceaux

Spanning the languid Cher River atop a supremely graceful arched bridge, **Château de Chenonceau** (☎02 47 23 90 07; www.chenonceau.com; adult/child €13/10, with audioguide €17.50/14; ⊙9am-7pm or later Apr-Sep, to 5pm or 6pm Oct-Mar) is one of France's most elegant châteaux. It's hard not to be moved and exhilarated by the glorious setting, the formal gardens, the magic of the architecture and the château's fascinating history, shaped by a series of powerful women. The interior is decorated with rare furnishings and a fabulous art collection that includes works by Tintoretto, Correggio, Rubens, Murillo, Van Dyck and Ribera (look for an extraordinary portrait of Louis XIV).

This spectacular complex is largely the work of several remarkable women (hence its nickname, Le Château des Dames). The initial phase of construction started in 1515 for Thomas Bohier, a court minister of King Charles VIII, although much of the work and design was actually overseen by his wife, Katherine Briçonnet.

The distinctive arches and the eastern formal garden were added by Diane de Poitiers, mistress of King Henri II. Following Henri's death Catherine de Médicis, the king's scheming widow, forced Diane (her 2nd cousin) to exchange Chenonceau for the rather less grand Château de Chaumont. Catherine completed the château's construction and added the yew-tree maze and the western rose garden. Louise of Lorraine's most singular contribution was her black-walled mourning room on the top floor, to which she retreated when her husband, Henri III, was assassinated in 1589.

Chenonceau had an 18th-century heyday under the aristocratic Madame Dupin, who made the château a centre of fashionable society; guests included Voltaire and Rousseau. During the Revolution, at the age of 83, she was able to save the château from destruction at the hands of angry mobs thanks to quick thinking and some strategic concessions.

The château's pièce de résistance is the 60m-long, chequerboard-floored Grande Gallerie over the Cher, scene of many an elegant party hosted by Catherine de Médicis and Madame Dupin. Used as a military hospital during WWI, from 1940 to 1942 it served as an escape route for *résistants*, Jews and other refugees fleeing from the German-occupied zone (north of the Cher) to the Vichy-controlled zone (south of the river). The upper level of the gallery, the Galerie Médicis, has a well-presented exhibition (in French and English) on the château's colourful history and the women who moulded it.

On summer nights the grounds are illuminated for the **Promenade Nocturne** (Night Walk; adult/child €6/free; ⊙9.30-11.30pm Jul & Aug).

The excellent audioguide, available in 11 languages, has a well-done version for kids aged seven to 12 (in French and English). There's a great deal to see, so plan on spending at least half a day here. From mid-March to mid-November, lunch choices include a gastronomic French restaurant called L'Orangerie (*menus* €31 to €40) and a cafeteria.

The château is 33km east of Tours, 13km southeast of Amboise and 40km southwest of Blois. From the town of Chenonceaux (spelt with an x), just outside the château grounds, trains go to Tours (€7, 25 minutes, nine to 12 daily).

Amboise

POP 13,200

Elegant Amboise, childhood home of Charles VIII and final resting place of the incompa-

rable Leonardo da Vinci, is gorgeously situated on the southern bank of the Loire, guarded by a towering château. With some seriously posh hotels, fine dining and one of France's most colourful weekly markets (on Sunday morning), Amboise is a convivial base for exploring the Loire countryside and nearby châteaux by car or bicycle.

Sights

As you walk up to Le Clos Lucé, keep an eye out for the **habitats troglodytiques** (cave houses) carved into the rock face overlooking rue Victor Hugo. Pedestrian-only **rue Nationale** is packed with attractive boutiques.

★Château Royal d'Amboise CHÂTEAU
(☎02 47 57 00 98; www.chateau-amboise.com; place Michel Debré; adult/child €11.20/7.50, incl audioguide €15.20/10.50; ⊙9am-6pm or 7.30pm Mar–mid-Nov, 9am-12.30pm & 2-5.15pm mid-Nov–Feb) Perched on a rocky escarpment above town, Amboise's castle was a favoured retreat for all of France's Valois and Bourbon kings. Only a few of the château's original structures survive, but you can still visit the furnished Logis (Lodge) – Gothic except for the top half of one wing, which is Renaissance – and the Flamboyant Gothic Chapelle St-Hubert (1493), where Leonardo da Vinci's presumed remains have been buried since 1863. The ramparts afford thrilling views of the town and river.

Charles VIII (r 1483–98), born and bred here, renovated parts in the radical new Renaissance style, imported from Italy. In 1560, an unsuccessful attempt by Huguenots to seize power from the ultra-Catholic Guise faction was brutally suppressed, with 1200 summary executions and rebel corpses hung on hooks from the château's façade. The defeated Algerian anti-colonial leader Abd el-Kader was imprisoned here with a large entourage from 1848 to 1852.

Brochures are available in 16 languages, audioguides in 12. An audioguide for children is available in English and French. Kids aged 10 to 15 may enjoy the interactive iPad circuit (in French with English subtitles; €5), set in the year 1518. Lots of cultural events are held here – you can download an extensive calendar from the website.

★Le Clos Lucé HISTORIC BUILDING
(☎02 47 57 00 73; www.vinci-closluce.com; 2 rue du Clos Lucé; adult/child €15/10.50; ⊙9am-7pm or 8pm Feb-Oct, 9am or 10am-5pm or 6pm Nov-Jan; 👪) It was on the invitation of François I that Leonardo da Vinci (1452–1519), aged 64, took up residence at this grand manor house (built 1471). An admirer of the Italian Renaissance, the French monarch named Da Vinci 'first painter, engineer and king's architect', and the Italian spent his time here sketching, tinkering and dreaming up ingenious contraptions. Fascinating models of his many inventions are on display inside the home and around its lovely 7-hectare gardens.

Visitors see rooms where Da Vinci worked and the bedroom where he drew his last breath on 2 May 1519. There is also a free iPhone/iPad app (see the website for links). From Monday to Friday in July and August, you can take an hour-long tour (€3.90) in English; call ☎02 47 57 55 78 for details. The 500th anniversary of Da Vinci's death will be commemorated in 2019.

Pagode de Chanteloup HISTORIC SITE
(www.pagode-chanteloup.com; adult/child €9.70/7.70; ⊙10am-6pm late Mar-Sep, 2-5pm Oct–mid-Nov; 👪) Three kilometres south of Amboise, this seven-storey, vaguely Asian 'pagoda' (44m) was built between 1775 and 1778, when blending classical French architecture and Chinese motifs was all the rage. Clamber to the top for glorious views. In summer, picnic hampers (adult/child €12.50/7) are available, and you can rent rowing boats (€5 per hour) and – great for kids – play free outdoor games.

TAKE A BREAK

Perched quietly beneath a dramatic 12th-century donjon (keep), the town of Montrichard, 9km east of Chenonceau, is a perfect spot for a fizzy break. Just outside town, Maison Monmousseau's extensive wine cellars, **Caves Monmousseau** (☎02 54 32 35 15; www.monmousseau.com; 71 route de Vierzon, Montrichard; ⊙10am-12.30pm & 1.30-6pm Apr-Oct, 10am-noon & 2-5pm Mon-Sat Nov-Mar), carved into the tufa stone, create the perfect 12°C environment for ageing *crémant* (sparkling wine). One-hour tours (adult/child €4/free), starting at 10am and 2pm, explain the *méthode traditionelle* (the traditional way to make bubbly) and end with a tasting.

LOCAL KNOWLEDGE

A COUNTRY LUNCH

Auberge de Launay (02 47 30 16 82; www.aubergedelaunay.com; 9 rue de la Rivière, Limeray; lunch/dinner menus €18.50/31; 12.15-1.30pm Sun-Fri, 7-9pm Mon-Sat, closed mid-Dec–mid-Jan;), a country inn 7.5km northeast of Amboise (just off the D952), is renowned for its traditional cuisine and cosy atmosphere. Herbs from the garden are used in classic French dishes, accompanied by libations from a superb wine list, local cheeses and scrumptious desserts. It also has 15 guestrooms (doubles €78 to €91) if you need to stay.

Sleeping

Camping Municipal de l'Île d'Or CAMPGROUND €
(02 47 57 23 37; www.camping-amboise.com; Île d'Or; sites per adult/child/tent €3.20/2.10/3.90; Apr-Sep;) Lovely 291-site campground on the Île d'Or, the island opposite the château. Facilities include pool, tennis courts, ping-pong and canoe hire.

Centre Charles Péguy-Auberge de Jeunesse HOSTEL €
(02 47 30 60 90; www.centrecharlespeguy.fr; Île d'Or; adult/child incl breakfast €22/13; reception 10am-noon & 2-8pm Mon-Fri;) An efficient if spartan 72-bed hostel at the downriver tip of the Île d'Or. Discounts for multi-night stays. Closed for repairs until at least mid-2017.

Hôtel Chaptal HOTEL €
(02 47 57 14 46; www.hotel-chaptal-amboise.fr; 11-13 rue Chaptal; s/d/q €54/67/91; reception 7.30am-9pm, closed Dec & Jan;) You don't have to have a big budget to enjoy the charms of Amboise. This friendly and very central hotel has 26 simple, clean rooms – great value! No lift.

Hôtel Le Blason HOTEL €
(02 47 23 22 41; www.leblason.fr; 11 place Richelieu; d €49-66, q €83-91, extra bed €10;) Quirky, creaky budget hotel on a quiet square with 27 higgledy-piggledy rooms wedged around corridors; most rooms are modern, smallish and timber beamed. Upstairs rooms under the eaves come with air-conditioning.

★**Le Vieux Manoir** B&B €€
(02 47 30 41 27; www.le-vieux-manoir.com; 13 rue Rabelais; d incl breakfast €150-220, f €330, cottages €260-310; late Mar-Oct;) Set in a lovely walled garden, this restored mansion has oodles of old-time charm. The six rooms and two cottages, decorated with antiques, get lots of natural light, and owners Gloria and Bob (expat Americans who once ran an award-winning Boston B&B) are generous with their knowledge of the area.

Le Clos d'Amboise HISTORIC HOTEL €€€
(02 47 30 10 20; www.leclosamboise.com; 27 rue Rabelais; r €189-239, 6-person ste €239-289;) Overlooking a lovely garden with 200-year-old fir trees and a heated pool, this posh pad – most of it built in the 17th century – offers country living in the heart of town. Stylish features abound, from luxurious fabrics to antique furnishings. Half of the 20 rooms still have their original, now non-functioning, fireplaces.

Le Manoir Les Minimes DESIGN HOTEL €€€
(02 47 30 40 40; www.manoirlesminimes.com; 34 quai Charles Guinot; d €97-235, ste €224-555;) This 15-room pamper palace will impress and delight even the most discerning of travellers. The best rooms in the stylish main building have tall windows opening onto Loire or château views (corner suite No 10 has both!).

Château de Pray HOTEL €€€
(02 47 57 23 67; www.chateaudepray.com; rue du Cèdre, Chargé; d €159-290, q €250-305; restaurant noon-1.30pm Thu-Sun & 7-9pm Wed-Sun, plus Tue evening Jun-Sep;) What better way to experience the Loire vibe than to stay in a 16th-century château? The 19 rooms here are full of old-fashioned charm and antique furnishings, and some have canopy beds. Has a Michelin-starred French *gastronomique* restaurant (four/five-course *menus* €58/71). Situated 3.5km northeast of Amboise's town centre, 300m off the D751.

Eating

In general, the restaurants around heavily touristed place Michel Debré, facing the château, are not Amboise's best.

★**Food Market** FOOD MARKET €
(quai du Général de Gaulle; 8am-1pm Sun) Voted France's *marché préféré* (favourite market) in 2015, this riverfront extravaganza, 400m southwest of the château, draws 200 to 300

stalls selling both edibles and durables. Worth timing your visit around.

Bigot PATISSERIE €
(☎02 47 57 04 46; www.maisonbigot-amboise.com; cnr rue Nationale & place du Château; breakfast €13, lunch menu €16; ⏰8.30am or 9am-7pm or 7.30pm Tue-Sun, to 8pm & open Mon Easter-Oct; 📶✎) Founded by Madame Bigot's grandfather in 1913, this *salon de thé*, *pâtisserie* and *chocolaterie* is known for its tarte tatin (€9), chocolates, homemade ice cream and light meals (omelettes, quiches, meal-size salads). Perfect for a sweet or savoury break.

Le Patio MODERN FRENCH €€
(☎02 47 79 00 00; www.facebook.com/lepatioamboise; 14 rue Nationale; lunch menus €19, dinner menus €30; ⏰noon-2pm & 7-9pm Thu-Mon, daily Jul & Aug; 📶) The friendly staff serves creative, beautifully presented French cuisine (eg slow-cooked shank of lamb) that garners rave reviews. Has a superb wine list.

La Fourchette FRENCH €€
(☎06 11 78 16 98; 9 rue Malebranche; lunch/dinner menus €17/30; ⏰noon-1.30pm Tue-Sat, 7-8.30pm Fri & Sat, plus Tue & Wed evenings summer) Hidden away in a back alley off rue Nationale, this is Amboise's favourite address for family-style French cooking – chef Christine will make you feel as though you've been invited to her house for lunch. The *menu* has just two entrées, two mains and two desserts. The restaurant is small, so reserve ahead.

L'Alliance MODERN FRENCH €€
(☎02 47 30 52 13; www.restaurant-amboise.com; 14 rue Joyeuse; lunch menus €18-21, dinner menus €31-48; ⏰noon-1.30pm Thu-Mon, 7-9.30pm Wed-Mon; 📶) Opened in 2015, this unpretentious restaurant has established a reputation for serving wonderfully fresh, traditional French *cuisine de saison* (cuisine based on the seasons). The *menu*, which changes four or five times a year, includes three fish options, three meat options and a great cheese plate (€12).

Drinking & Nightlife

Le Shaker BAR
(☎02 47 23 24 26; 3 quai François Tissard, Île d'Or; ⏰6pm-2am Sun, Tue, Wed & Thu, to 4am Fri & Sat) The big draw at this friendly bar on Amboise's mid-Loire island: supremely romantic views of the château. Serves beer (€3.50) and light meals, but the speciality is cocktails.

Information

Tourist Office (☎02 47 57 09 28; www.amboise-valdeloire.co.uk; cnr quai du Général de Gaulle & allée du Sergent Turpin; internet access per 30min €4; ⏰9am or 10am-6pm or 7pm Mon-Sat, 10am-12.30pm Sun Apr-Oct, 10am-12.30pm & 2-5pm Mon-Sat Nov-Mar; 📶) Has interesting walking-tour brochures and sells cycling maps and discount combo tickets for nine area châteaux. Its free app, called 'Val d'Amboise Tour', can be downloaded via the website. Situated across the street from the riverfront.

Getting There & Around

Amboise is 35km southwest of Blois and 24km east of Tours.

BICYCLE

Amboise is a great base for bike rides along the Loire. To rent a bike, try **Détours de Loire** (☎02 47 30 00 55; www.detoursdeloire.com; quai du Géneral de Gaulle; half-day/day/week €10/15/60; ⏰Jun-Sep), along the river, or **Cycles Richard** (☎02 47 57 01 79; 2 rue de Nazelles), directly across the river from the town centre.

BUS

Run by **Touraine Fil Vert** (p381), bus line C links Amboise's Théâtre with Tours' Halte Routière (bus station; €2.40, 50 minutes, eight daily Monday to Saturday) and Chenonceau (€2.40, 18 minutes, one or two daily Monday to Saturday).

CAR & MOTORCYCLE

There is free parking along quai du Général de Gaulle (along the river; parking is prohibited on Friday and Sunday mornings because of the market) and, a few blocks inland, at place Richelieu.

TRAIN

Amboise's **train station** (bd Gambetta) is 1.5km north of the château, on the opposite side of the Loire.

Blois €7.20, 15 minutes, 16 to 25 daily

Paris Gare d'Austerlitz €33.20, 1¾ hours, four direct daily

Tours €5.70, 17 minutes, 13 to 23 daily

Villandry

The six glorious landscaped gardens at **Château de Villandry** (☎02 47 50 02 09; www.chateauvillandry.com; 3 rue Principale; château & gardens adult/child €10.50/6.50, gardens only €6.50/4.50, audioguides €4; ⏰9am-btwn 5pm & 7pm year-round, château interior closed mid-Nov–mid-Dec & early Jan-early Feb) are some of the finest in France, with more than 6 hectares of cascading flowers, ornamental vines,

LEOKS / SHUTTERSTOCK ©

1. Formal gardens, Villandry (p385) 2. Moat-encircled Château de Sully-sur-Loire (p370) 3. Bedroom, Château de Chenonceau (p382) 4. Château d'Ussé (p389)

2

VIACHESLAV LOPATIN / SHUTTERSTOCK ©

4

Châteaux of the Loire Valley

The Loire Valley is the place to see castles, but with so many glorious options, what's the best way to spend your time?

For sheer architectural splendour, you can't top the big three: François I's country extravaganza Chambord (p374); Renaissance-era, river-spanning Chenonceau (p382); and the supremely graceful Cheverny (p375).

If you're looking for solitude, chances are that off-the-beaten-track châteaux, such as Brissac (p403), Brézé (p396) and Beauregard (p377), will be much quieter.

For historical significance, at the top of the list are the royal château of Blois (p371), spanning four distinct periods of French architecture; Amboise (p383), home to a succession of French monarchs; the Forteresse Royale de Chinon (p391), where Joan of Arc held her momentous first rendezvous with the future King Charles VII; the forbidding Château d'Angers (p400), with its fantastic tapestry of the Apocalypse; and pastoral Le Clos Lucé (p383), where Leonardo da Vinci spent his final years.

Looking for a picture-perfect setting? Our choices are the moat-ringed Château d'Azay-le-Rideau (p389) and the Château de Sully-sur-Loire (p370), and the stunning formal gardens at Villandry (p385) and Chaumont-sur-Loire (p375).

For literary connections, try Château d'Ussé (p389), the inspiration for Sleeping Beauty; or the Château de Montsoreau (p396), setting for a classic Alexandre Dumas novel.

TOP TIPS

➡ In the summer, go first thing or late in the day to avoid the coach-tour crowds.

➡ Buy multi-château combo tickets, or pre-purchase tickets at tourist offices, for slight savings and to avoid queues.

➡ Remember that château ticket offices close from 30 to 60 minutes before the châteaux themselves.

LOCAL KNOWLEDGE

TOP LOIRE VALLEY WINES

Ask a local chef, sommelier or oenophile about their favourite Loire Valley wines and you're likely to hear some astute recommendations. Ask two local wine experts the same question and you may spark a good-natured argument! If you prefer to get right down to tasting, you won't go wrong if you order wines by the following Loire Valley producers:

Château Pierre-Bise (02 41 78 31 44; www.chateaupierrebise.com; Beaulieu-sur-Layon) Claude Papin makes top Coteaux du Layon sweet whites, and Savenièrres and Anjou AOCs, at his family's winery south of Angers.

Domaine de Bablut (02 41 91 22 59; www.vignobles-daviau.fr; Brissac-Quincé) Christophe Daviau produces superb organic reds under the Anjou Villages Brissac AOC.

Domaine Cady (02 41 78 33 69; www.domainecady.fr; St-Aubin de Luigné) Alexandre Cady produces excellent Anjou AOC whites and sweet Coteaux du Layon AOC wines 28km southwest of Angers.

Domaine du Mortier (02 47 97 94 68; www.boisard-fils.com; St-Nicolas-de-Bourgueil) Cyril Boisard makes fine organic St-Nicolas-de-Bourgueil AOC and Bourgueil AOC reds 20km east of Saumur.

Domaine Wilfrid Rousse (02 47 58 84 02; http://chinonrousse.fr; Savigny-en-Véron) Wilfrid Rousse is known for his outstanding organic Chinon AOC reds and whites, grown 21km southeast of Saumur.

manicured lime trees, razor-sharp box hedges and tinkling fountains. Try to visit when the gardens are blooming, between April and October; midsummer is most spectacular.

The original gardens and château were built by Jean Le Breton, who served François I as finance minister and ambassador to Italy (and supervised the construction of Chambord). During his time as ambassador, Le Breton became enamoured with the art of Italian Renaissance gardening, later creating his own ornamental masterpiece at newly constructed Villandry. The current gardens were recreated starting in 1908.

Wandering the pebbled walkways, you'll see the classical Jardin d'Eau (Water Garden), the hornbeam Labyrinthe (Maze) and the Jardin d'Ornement (Ornamental Garden), which depicts various aspects of love (fickle, passionate, tender and tragic) using geometrically pruned hedges and coloured flowerbeds. The Jardin du Soleil (Sun Garden) is a looser array of gorgeous multicoloured and multiscented perennials. But the highlight is the 16th-century-style Jardin des Simples (Kitchen Garden), where cabbages, leeks and carrots are laid out to create nine geometrical, colour-coordinated squares.

After the gardens, the château (built 1530s) is a bit of a let-down. Nevertheless, highlights include the Oriental drawing room, with a gilded Moorish ceiling taken from a 15th-century palace in Toledo, and a gallery of Spanish and Flemish art. Best of all are the bird's-eye views across the gardens and the nearby Loire and Cher Rivers from the top of the donjon (the only remnant of the original medieval château) and the *belvédère* (panoramic viewpoint).

The château is 16km southwest of Tours and 11km northeast of Azay-le-Rideau. Fil Bleu (p381) bus 32 has a few runs a day to Tours (35 minutes). Trains link Savonnières, 4km northeast of Villandry, with Tours (€3.50, 13 minutes, two or three daily).

Langeais

POP 4300

No castle in the Loire is more authentically medieval in architecture and furnishings than the Château de Langeais, the focal point of a peaceful village with lovely walking streets and a bustling Sunday-morning market.

The most medieval of the Loire châteaux, **Château de Langeais** (02 47 96 72 60; www.chateau-de-langeais.com; adult/child €9/5; 9.30am-6.30pm Apr–mid-Nov, 10am-5pm mid-Nov–Mar) – built in the 1460s – is superbly preserved inside and out, looking much as it did at the tail end of the Middle Ages, with crenellated ramparts and massive towers dominating the surrounding village. Original 15th-century furniture fills its flagstoned chambers. In one room, a life-size wax-figure tableau portrays the marriage of Charles

VIII and Anne of Brittany, held here on 6 December 1491, which brought about the historic union of France and Brittany.

Langeais presents two faces to the world. From the town you see a fortified castle, nearly windowless, with machicolated walls rising forbiddingly from the drawbridge. But the sections facing the courtyard have large windows, ornate dormers and decorative stonework designed for more refined living.

Among the château's many fine, if faded, Flemish and Aubusson tapestries, look out for one from 1530 depicting astrological signs; three intricate panels with *mille-fleurs* ('thousand flowers') motifs; and the famous Les Neuf Preux series, whose nine 'worthy knights' represent the epitome of medieval courtly honour. In each room, plasticised sheets in eight languages provide information.

The Chemin de Ronde (Parapet Walk) gives you a knight's-eye view from the ramparts; gaps underfoot enabled boiling oil, rocks and ordure to be dumped on attackers. Across the château's courtyard, climb to the top of the ruined stone keep, constructed by great 10th-century builder Foulques Nerra (Fulk III), Count of Anjou.

Half a block from the entrance to the château, elegant **Au Coin des Halles** (☎02 47 96 37 25; www.aucoindeshalles.com; 9 rue Gambetta; lunch menus €16.50, dinner menus €26-55; ⏲12.15-2pm & 7.15-9pm Fri-Tue) is *mi-bistrot, mi-gastro* (half-bistro, half-gastronomic restaurant), serving delicious *cuisine du marché* (cuisine based on what's available fresh in the markets) grown and raised by local producers.

ℹ Getting There & Away

Langeais is 31km southwest of Tours and 10km west of Villandry. Its train station, 400m from the château, is on the line linking Tours (€5.70, 20 minutes, six or seven daily) with Saumur (€8.30, 25 minutes, six to 10 daily).

Azay-le-Rideau

Romantic, moat-ringed **Château d'Azay-le-Rideau** (☎02 47 45 42 04; www.azay-le-rideau.fr; adult/child €8.50/free, audioguide €4.50; ⏲9.30am-6pm Apr-Sep, to 7pm Jul & Aug, 10am-5.15pm Oct-Mar) is famed for its elegant turrets, perfectly proportioned windows, delicate stonework and steep slate roofs. Built in the early 1500s on a natural island in the middle of the Indre River, it is one of the Loire's loveliest castles: Honoré de Balzac called it a 'multifaceted diamond set in the River Indre'.

The château's most famous feature is the open, Italian-style loggia staircase overlooking the central courtyard, decorated with the salamanders and ermines of François I and Queen Claude.

The interior decor is mostly 19th century, created by the Marquis Charles de Biencourt (who bought the château after the Revolution) and his heirs. The Salon de Biencourt was given historically coherent furnishings – plucked from the extensive collection of the French government – and comprehensively restored to its 19th-century glory in 2016; other interiors will follow suit in 2017. The scaffolding should be off the exterior by the end of 2017, so the following July and August may see the return of the *son et lumière* (sound and light show; adult/child €11/3), one of the Loire's oldest and best, which is projected onto the castle wall. The lovely English-style gardens were restored and partly replanted in 2015.

SLEEPING BEAUTY

The creamy white towers and slate roofs of **Château d'Ussé** (☎02 47 95 54 05; www.chateaudusse.fr; Rigny-Ussé; adult/child €14/4; ⏲10am-6pm or 7pm, closed mid-Nov–Mar) jut out from the edge of the forest of Chinon, offering sweeping views across the flat Loire countryside, the flood-prone Indre River and the delightful formal gardens, designed by André Le Nôtre, landscape architect of Versailles. The château's main claim to literary fame is that it served as the inspiration for Charles Perrault's classic fairy tale, *La Belle au Bois Dormant*, known in English as *Sleeping Beauty*. Built on top of an 11th-century fortress, the modern-day château dates mainly from the 15th to 17th centuries. Some visitors come just for the gardens, in part because the furnished interior is not improved by a series of dodgy wax models recounting the tale of Sleeping Beauty. The château hosts annual exhibitions of clothing and fashion from centuries past.

The town of Rigny-Ussé is 12km northeast of Chinon.

Audioguides are available in five languages; one-hour guided tours in French are free. There's an **exposition** on the restoration of antique furnishings – the videos of experts at work are fascinating – in the outbuilding to the right as you exit the ticket-sales hall. A number of places to eat are located just a few hundred metres from the château.

Azay-le-Rideau is 26km southwest of Tours. The train station, 2.5km west of the château, is linked to Tours (€5.90, 30/60 minutes by train/bus, five to 11 daily) and Chinon (€5.30, 20 minutes, five to 11 daily). The D84 and D17, on either side of the Indre, are great for countryside cycling.

Loches

POP 7100

Loches, on the Indre River, spirals picturesquely up from the modern town – through ancient stone gates – to the citadel, a forbidding medieval stronghold established by Foulques Nerra in the 10th century and later updated by Charles VII. In 1429, Joan of Arc met with Charles VII here and persuaded him to march north to claim the French crown, but these days Loches is a sleepy place, great for a day of mellow exploration. The town is known for its bustling Wednesday- and Saturday-morning markets.

Sights

To reach Loches' fortress from the modern town centre, walk through **Porte Picois** and you'll be inside the **Ville-Basse** (lower city). Continue up rue du Château and through **Porte Royale** and you'll enter the Cité Royale (royal city), also known as the **Citadelle** (citadel) and the **Ville-Haute** (upper city).

Across the Indre River, **Beaulieu-lès-Loches** is home to the 11th-century abbey where citadel builder Foulques Nerra is buried. It can be reached on foot on a marked, 7.5km circuit (the tourist office has a map).

★Cité Royale de Loches — CITADEL

(☎02 47 59 01 32; www.chateau-loches.fr; 24hr) Loches' vast hilltop citadel is the size of a small town – a few lucky people even live here! Inside you can visit the Logis Royal and the Donjon – the same ticket is good for both – and a Romanesque church. The ensemble is great for kids who are into knights and castles.

➡ Donjon

(incl Logis Royal adult/child €8.50/6.50; 9am-7pm Apr-Sep, 9.30am-5pm Oct-Mar) The rectangular, 36m-high Tour Carrée (keep), at the southern end of the Cité Royale, was Loches' original medieval stronghold, built in the 10th century by Foulques Nerra. Though the interior floors have fallen away, you can still see various architectural details, including remnants of fireplaces and the original chapel. Climb dizzying catwalks for fantastic views.

Next door is the notorious Tour Louis XI, a tower built during the 15th century by Charles VII and Louis XI. In the basement, the circular Cachot (dungeon) is where the unfortunate Cardinal Balue was supposedly kept suspended from the ceiling in a wooden cage for betraying Louis XI. (In fact, this room was more likely a grain store, although you can see a replica of the cardinal's surprisingly spacious cage back in the entrance pavilion.) Other evidence of the darker aspects of the Donjon's past include the chilling Salle de Torture and traces of prisoners' graffiti etched into the walls. The rooftop terrace, once a platform for firing artillery, is now a fine viewpoint.

Reached from the courtyard, the 15th-century Martelet, 27m deep, houses additional dungeons and 11th-century tufa quarries.

➡ Logis Royal

(incl Donjon adult/child €8.50/6.50; 9am-7pm Apr-Sep, 9.30am-5pm Oct-Mar) At the northern end of the citadel stands the royal residence of Charles VII and his successors, originally built as a medieval fortress but later converted into a Renaissance-style hunting lodge. In May 1429, after her victory at Orléans, Joan of Arc famously met Charles VII here for the second time and nudged him towards coronation. Rooms are dedicated to some big personalities: Charles VII, Agnès Sorel, Anne of Brittany and Joan of Arc. English signs provide context.

➡ Collégiale St-Ours

(9am-7pm Apr-Sep, 9.30am-5pm Oct-Mar) This Romanesque church, in the citadel between the Logis Royal and the Donjon, contains the **tomb of Agnès Sorel**, Charles VII's mistress, who lived in the château during their long affair. For details in English on the richly coloured stained glass, pick up a plasticised sheet from a wall rack.

Fiercely intelligent and strikingly beautiful, Agnès earned many enemies at court because of her influence on the king. After bearing three daughters (among them an ancestor of former Spanish king Juan Carlos), she died in mysterious circumstances while pregnant with their fourth child. The official cause of

death was dysentery, but some scientists speculate that elevated levels of mercury in her body indicate she was poisoned.

➡ **Maison-Musée Lansyer**

(☎02 47 59 05 45; www.ville-loches.fr; 1 rue Lansyer; adult/child €2/free; ⏰10.30am-12.30pm & 2-6pm Wed-Mon Apr-Oct, plus Tue Jun-Aug) The family home of landscape painter Emmanuel Lansyer (1835–93) is now a museum displaying more than 100 of his paintings, his collection of Japanese art and works by Canaletto, Millet, Piranese, Manet and Corot. Situated in the citadel, left up the hill from the Porte Royale.

Sleeping & Eating

La Demeure Saint-Ours B&B €

(☎06 33 74 54 82; www.saintours.eu; 11 rue du Château; d incl breakfast €65-75; 📶) Ensconced in a 16th-century townhouse, this B&B has three attractive rooms with exposed wooden beams. The B&B is situated in the Ville-Basse midway between Porte Picois and Porte Royale; the entrance is at 18 rue des Fossés Saint-Ours.

La Gerbe d'Or MODERN FRENCH €

(☎02 47 91 67 63; www.restaurantlagerbedor.fr; 22 rue Balzac; lunch/dinner menus from €13.90/23.50; ⏰noon-2pm Tue-Sun, 7.30-9.30pm Wed-Sun; 🖉) Serves delicious dishes that bring together traditional French savoir faire, fresh local ingredients and flavours from Italy and East Asia. Lamb cutlets rubbed with fresh parsley and served with anise-flavoured oyster mushrooms and reduced juice of figs, anyone? For dessert, try dark-chocolate cake with ginger sorbet and orange jelly with pepper and turmeric.

Isabeau de Touraine CAFE €

(☎02 47 59 47 55; www.isabeaudetouraine.com; 33 Grand Rue; mains €4.50-13.90; ⏰9.30am-6pm, lunch noon-3pm Wed-Sun) Sandrine welcomes you to comfy plum-coloured couches or street-side tables, where she serves delicious home-baked cakes, quiches and meal-size salads.

Information

Tourist Office (☎02 47 91 82 82; www.loches-tourainecotesud.com; place de la Marne; ⏰9am or 10am-12.30pm & 2-5pm or 6pm Mon-Sat year-round, plus 10am-12.30pm & 2.30-5pm Sun Apr-Sep) Situated next to the river.

Getting There & Away

Loches is 68km southwest of Blois and 42km southeast of Tours. Trains and SNCF buses link the train station, across the Indre River from the tourist office, with Tours (€9.60, one hour, seven to 16 daily).

Chinon

POP 7900

Dominated by its towering medieval castle, the attractive town of Chinon is etched into France's collective memory both as the favourite fortress of Henry II (1133–89), King of England, and as the venue for Joan of Arc's first meeting with Charles VII in 1429. Below the château is an appealing medieval quarter, a warren of narrow lanes whose white tufa houses are topped with black slate roofs, giving the town its characteristic high-contrast aesthetic.

Surrounding the town is one of the Loire's main wine-producing areas, and Chinon AOC (www.chinon.com) cabernet-franc vineyards stretch along both banks of the Vienne River. Chinon makes a good base for wine-cellar visits.

Sights

★ **Forteresse Royale de Chinon** FORTRESS

(☎02 47 93 13 45; www.forteressechinon.fr; adult/child €8.50/6.50; ⏰9.30am-7pm May-Aug, to 5pm or 6pm Sep-Apr) Surrounded by massive walls, this hilltop castle – offering fabulous views across town, river and countryside – is split into three sections separated by dry moats. The ticket counter and shop are inside the 12th-century Fort St-Georges. Pass under the 14th-century Tour de l'Horloge (Clock Tower) and you come to the Château du Milieu (Middle Castle), vestige of a time when the Plantagenet court of Henry II and Eleanor of Aquitaine assembled here. Finally, Fort du Coudray sits on the tip of the promontory.

In the Château du Milieu, the restored south wing of the Logis Royaux (Royal Lodgings) has a multimedia exhibit, scale models of the castle, Joan of Arc memorabilia and archaeological finds. At the far end, the round, 13th-century Tour du Coudray was used to imprison Knights Templar in the early 1300s (find their graffiti inside) and hosted Joan of Arc in 1429.

The castle has neat booklets that activate audio and multimedia around the site, as well as iPad Mini audiovisual guides (€3; in French and English), with versions for adults and kids.

WORTH A TRIP

BALZAC IN SACHÉ

Meander down the Indre Valley along the tiny D84, passing mansions, villages and troglodyte caves, and 7km east of Azay-le-Rideau you come to sweet Saché. Once home to American sculptor Alexander Calder (one of his red-and-blue mobiles sits in the town square), it still celebrates the life of long-time resident Honoré de Balzac (1799–1850), author of *La Comédie Humaine*.

You don't have to be a French-literature major to enjoy the lovely **Musée Balzac** (☎02 47 26 86 50; www.musee-balzac.fr; adult/child €5.50/4.50; ⏲10am-6pm or 7pm daily Apr-Sep, 10am-12.30pm & 2-5pm Wed-Mon Oct-Mar), in the town's château, where Balzac was a frequent guest. On a quiet slope in the lush river valley, the museum has rooms furnished in the style of Balzac's time, manuscripts, letters, first editions and lithographs. You can easily imagine Balzac escaping his hectic Parisian life and reclining here in his cosy bed, a board on his knees, writing for 12 hours a day. An informative English brochure is available at the ticket desk.

Cité Médiévale HISTORIC SITE

(Medieval Town) François Rabelais (c 1494–1553), whose works include the Gargantua and Pantagruel series, grew up in Chinon; you'll see Rabelais-related names dotted all around the old town, whose narrow cobblestone streets and alleys present a fine cross-section of medieval architecture, best seen along rue Voltaire and its western continuation, rue Haute St-Maurice.

Structures to look out for include the 17th-century **Hôtel du Gouverneur** (48 rue Voltaire), an impressive townhouse whose double-flighted staircase is sheltered from the street by a carved gateway, and the Gothic **Palais du Bailliage** (73 rue Voltaire), the former residence of Chinon's bailiwick.

The tourist office has a free walking-tour leaflet and, from May to September, offers French-language tours (adult/child €4.70/2.50); some guides speak English – one is a New Yorker!

Activities

Loire Winery Tours WINE

(☎02 47 95 87 59; www.loirewinerytours.com; half-day tours per couple €85) Alain Caillemer, an excellent bilingual (French-English) guide, leads four- to five-hour customised wine tours near his native Chinon. Visit AOCs of your choice (Chinon, Cravant, Saumur, Champigny, St-Nicolas-de-Bourgueil or Touraine), stopping at his favourite vineyards, where you can meet producers, taste wine and make purchases.

Caves Paintes de Chinon WINE

(☎02 47 93 30 44; www.chinon.com; impasse des Caves Painctes; adult/child €3/free; ⏲tours 11am, 3pm, 4.30pm & 6pm Tue-Sun Jul & Aug) Hidden at the end of a cobbled alleyway off rue Voltaire, these former quarries were converted into wine cellars during the 15th century and written about by Rabelais. A *syndicat* (union) of local winegrowers runs tours and tastings in summertime.

Sleeping

Hôtel Le Plantagenêt HOTEL €

(☎02 47 93 36 92; www.hotel-plantagenet.com; 12 place Jeanne d'Arc; d €70-87, tr €97-105; P ❄ ᯤ) Halfway between the city centre and the train station, this hotel has 33 rooms, some with magnificent views of troglodyte dwellings, and a lovely garden. The original *maison bourgeoise* (mid-1800s) has more charm than the motel-style annexe out the back. Perks include (do-it-yourself) laundry (€10).

Hôtel Diderot HISTORIC HOTEL €

(☎02 47 93 18 87; www.hoteldiderot.com; 4 rue de Buffon; d €70-103, q €169; P ᯤ) This gorgeous townhouse is tucked amid luscious rose-filled gardens and crammed with polished antiques. The owners – Jean-Pierre, who's French, and Jamie, who hails from Florida – impart the sort of charm you'd expect for twice the price. The 26 cheerful rooms are all individually styled, some with flowery wallpaper. No lift. Situated 250m north of place Jeanne d'Arc.

Hôtel de France HOTEL €€

(☎02 47 93 33 91; www.bestwestern.fr/en/hotel-chinon,Best-Western-Hotel-De-France,93421; 47 place du Général de Gaulle, aka place de la Fontaine; d €99-139, apt €175; ❄ ᯤ) Run impeccably by the same couple since 1979, this Best Western–affiliated hotel, right in the centre of town, has 30 rooms arrayed around an

inner courtyard. Tastefully decorated in a contemporary style, many have views of the château – as does the magnificent, flowery terrace on the roof. Offers enclosed bicycle parking. No lift.

Eating

Food Market MARKET €

(place Jeanne d'Arc; ⏲7.45am-1.30pm Thu) Fruit, vegetables, cheeses and other picnic supplies.

★**Les Années 30** FRENCH €€

(☎02 47 93 37 18; www.lesannees30.com; 78 rue Haute St-Maurice; lunch/dinner menus from €18/27; ⏲12.15-1.45pm & 7.30-9.30pm Thu-Mon) Expect the kind of meal you came to France to eat, with exquisite attention to flavours and detail, served in relaxed intimacy. The *menu* ranges from traditional duck fillet to unusual choices such as pan-fried venison fillet with redcurrant sauce. The interior dining room is golden-lit downstairs and cool blue upstairs; in summer dine outside under the pergola.

La Part des Anges MODERN FRENCH €€

(☎02 47 93 99 93; www.lapartdesanges-chinon.com; 5 rue Rabelais; menus €18-29; ⏲noon-1.30pm & 7.30-8.15pm Wed-Sun) 'Between traditional and creative' – that's how Chef Virginie describes the delicious dishes she prepares using vegetables that are both local and organic. The wines are, too: almost all come from the Chinon AOC. Excellent value.

Au Chapeau Rouge GASTRONOMIC €€

(☎02 47 98 08 08; www.auchapeaurouge.fr; 49 place du Général de Gaulle, aka place de la Fontaine; lunch menus €22.50, dinner menus €29-58; ⏲noon-1pm Wed-Sun, 7.30-8.45pm Tue-Sat; 🛜) Secluded behind a red-and-gold awning, this sparkling and very elegant eatery makes top-quality French dishes using local products – look for Loire fish, lamb, asparagus and saffron, Touraine truffles, and Ste-Maure-de-Touraine, a delicious chèvre. In winter specialities include melt-in-your-mouth hare and foie-gras terrine. Has vegetarian options from June to August.

Information

Tourist Office (☎02 47 93 17 85; www.chinon-valdeloire.com; 1 rue Rabelais; ⏲10am-1.30pm & 2-7pm May-Sep, 10am-12.30pm & 2.30-6pm Mon-Sat Oct-Apr) Has a free walking-tour brochure and details on bike rental, kayaking, boat trips and hot-air balloons. Sells slightly reduced château tickets. Free smartphone app. Has a **summer kiosk** (⏲10am-1.30pm & 2.30-6pm mid-May–mid-Sep) up near the château.

Getting There & Away

The train station, 1km southeast of place du Général de Gaulle and the tourist office, is linked with Tours (€9.90, 45 minutes by train, 1¼ hours by SNCF bus, five to 10 daily) and Azay-le-Rideau (€5.30, 20 minutes, five to 11 daily). SNCF buses also stop in the centre of town.

ANJOU

As you float down the Loire and enter Anjou, fortified châteaux give way to chalky-white tufa cliffs concealing an astonishing subterranean world of wine cellars, mushroom farms and (literally) underground art. Up on the surface, black slate roofs pepper the vine-rich land, which grows some of the Loire's best wines.

Angers, the historic capital of Anjou, is famous for its powerful dukes, the fortified hilltop château they left behind, and the stunning medieval Apocalypse tapestry. Other architectural gems in Anjou include the medieval Abbaye Royale de Fontevraud, delightful riverside villages such as Candes-St-Martin, and some lovely châteaux. Europe's highest concentration of troglodyte dwellings dots the banks of the Loire around cosmopolitan Saumur.

To take in the Anjou wine country by car, head northwest from Saumur along route D751 towards Gennes, or southeast on route D947 through Souzay-Champigny and Parnay. From Angers cut southeast to Savennières.

Saumur

POP 27,500

There's an air of sparkly Parisian sophistication in Saumur but also a sense of laid-back contentment. The food is excellent, the local wine is even better, the spot is gorgeous – and the Saumurois know it. The town is renowned for the École Nationale d'Équitation, a national riding school that's home to the crack Cadre Noir equestrian corps. Soft white tufa cliffs stretch along the riverbanks east and west of town, pierced by *habitations troglodytes* (cave dwellings).

WORTH A TRIP

RABELAIS IN THE LOIRE

La Devinière, the prosperous farm where François Rabelais (c 1494–1553) – doctor, Franciscan friar, theoretician, author and all-around Renaissance man – grew up, inspired the settings for his five satirical, erudite Gargantua and Pantagruel novels. Surrounded by vineyards and open farmland, the farmstead contains **Musée Rabelais** (☎02 47 95 91 18; www.musee-rabelais.fr; 4 rue de la Devinière, Seuilly; adult/child €5.50/4.50; ⏲10am-7pm Jul & Aug, 10am-12.30pm & 2-6pm Apr-Sep, to 5pm Oct-Mar, closed Tue Oct-Mar), which has a few exhibits on Rabelais' life and genius, including early editions of his works and an original 1951 Matisse charcoal portrait (the other four portraits are facsimiles). Situated 8.5km southwest of Chinon and 1.4km northeast of the centre of Seuilly.

Sights & Activities

★École Nationale d'Équitation
RIDING SCHOOL

(☎02 41 53 50 60; www.cadrenoir.fr; av de l'École Nationale d'Équitation, St-Hilaire-St-Florent; tours adult/child €8/6; ⏲tours Mon-Sat early Feb-early Nov) One of the world's premier equestrian academies, the prestigious École Nationale d'Équitation is home to the Cadre Noir, an elite group of riding instructors that's also an equestrian display team. One-hour tours take you behind the scenes; kids will love to pat the horses in their spacious stalls – one stomps his feet insistently if passers-by don't caress him! Commentary is in French, but written information is available in five languages; call ahead for details on tours in English.

The riders and horses of the Cadre Noir, founded in 1825, are famous for their astonishing discipline and acrobatic prowess, all performed without stirrups. The school trains about 150 students – they're headed for careers as riding instructors – as well as their horses, 300 to 350 in number. Members of France's Olympic equestrian team also train at the spacious campus, built in 1980.

You can recognise members of the Cadre Noir by their distinctive black *(noir)* jackets and hats (*képis* for men, *bicornes* for women), gold spurs and the three golden wings on their whips. Look closely at their collar insignia: a grenade means they're members of the French military, a sun that they are civilians. Saumur has been an equestrian centre since 1593.

The school is 4.5km due west of Saumur, just outside sleepy St-Hilaire-St-Florent. There is no public transport.

Château de Saumur
CHÂTEAU

(☎02 41 40 24 40; www.chateau-saumur.com; adult/child €7/5; ⏲10am-1pm & 2-5.30pm Tue-Sun Apr-Oct, longer hours mid-Jun–mid-Sep, closed Nov-Mar) Soaring above the town's rooftops, Saumur's fairy-tale castle was largely built in the 13th century by Louis XI, and has served variously as a fortress for protection from the Normans, a Renaissance palace, a Protestant stronghold and an army barracks. An impressive collection of vintage equestrian gear is housed in the adjacent abbey church, and the museum also has a fine collection of faience (earthenware).

Musée des Blindés
MUSEUM

(☎02 41 83 69 95; www.museedesblindes.fr; 1043 rte de Fontevraud; adult/child €8/5; ⏲11am-5pm year-round) A century ago armoured vehicles replaced mounted cavalry on the field of battle, so it makes sense that Saumur should play host to more than 200 tanks and military vehicles – all in working order – from 17 countries. For fans of military history, this museum offers an exceptional opportunity to see tanks from all sides in WWI, WWII and the Cold War, including French models rarely seen overseas. Children can climb on some vehicles.

Musée de la Cavalerie
MUSEUM

(☎02 41 83 69 23; www.musee-cavalerie.fr; place Charles de Foucauld; adult/child €6/4; ⏲10am-noon & 2-6pm Mon, Wed, Thu & Fri, 2-6pm Sat & Sun late Mar-Jun & Sep–mid-Nov, 11am-6pm Jul & Aug) Housed in the Cadre Noir's one-time stables, this museum has exhibits on the history of the French cavalry from the 15th century to the age of tanks.

Langlois-Chateau
VINEYARD

(☎02 41 40 21 40; www.langlois-chateau.fr; 3 rue Léopold Palustre, St-Hilaire-St-Florent; tours adult/child €5/free; ⏲shop 10am-12.30pm & 2-6.30pm Apr–mid-Oct) Founded in 1885 and specialising in Crémant de Loire (sparkling wine) as well as still wines, this producer – one of six based in and around Saumur – is open for tours (reserve ahead), tastings and sales.

Distillerie Combier DISTILLERY
(☎02 41 40 23 02; www.combier.fr; 48 rue Beaurepaire; tours adult/child €4/free; ⊙tours 10.30am, 2.30pm & 4.30pm Tue-Sun Apr-Oct, plus Mon Jun-Sep, shop 10am-12.30pm & 2-6pm or 7pm Tue-Sat, plus Sun Apr-Oct & Dec, plus Mon Jun-Sep & Dec) In business since its invention of Triple Sec in 1834, this distillery has recently resurrected absinthe, the infamous firewater. Guided tours give you a behind-the-scenes look at the production facilities, with vintage architecture by Gustave Eiffel, gleaming century-old copper stills and fragrant vats full of Haitian bitter oranges. The shop offers free tastings.

Sleeping

Hôtel de Londres HOTEL €
(☎02 41 51 23 98; www.lelondres.com; 48 rue d'Orléans; d €74-114, q €125, apt €140; P❄@🛜) Built as an *hôtel de grand standing* (luxury hotel) and named in honour of the British capital in 1837, this family-run hotel – entirely renovated in 2016 – has 27 spacious rooms decorated in jolly colours and two family-friendly apartments, all with big windows and gleaming bathrooms. Lobby perks include afternoon tea (€2.50) and a well-stocked BD (comics) library. No lift (yet).

Camping l'Île d'Offard CAMPGROUND €
(☎02 41 40 30 00; www.saumur-camping.com; rue de Verden; 2-person sites €18-41, cabins without bathroom €45-50; ⊙mid-Mar–Oct; 🛜🏊) Well equipped and very pretty campground on an island opposite the château. Cyclists get discounts. Riverside and castle-view sites cost extra.

★**Château de Beaulieu** B&B €€
(☎02 41 50 83 52; www.chateaudebeaulieu.fr; 98 rte de Montsoreau; d incl breakfast €100-130, d/q €150/180; ⊙mid-Mar–mid-Nov; P🛜🏊) Irish expats Mary and Conor welcome you to their 1727 château with a glass of Crémant de Saumur (sparkling wine). Rooms are imaginatively and comfortably done up and the mood among gregarious guests is one of extended family. Sun yourself by the pool (next to the vineyard) or play billiards in the grand salon. Situated 2.5km southeast of Saumur.

Hôtel Saint-Pierre HISTORIC HOTEL €€
(☎02 41 50 33 00; www.saintpierresaumur.com; 8 rue Haute St-Pierre; r €110-190, ste €250; ❄🛜) A few steps from Église St-Pierre, this smart, 14-room hideaway mixes vintage style – pale stone walls, Persian rugs and antique furniture – with modern comforts. Black-and-white photos of the Cadre Noir adorn the delightfully colourful lobby, and there's a lovely glass-roofed breakfast room.

★**Château de Verrières** HERITAGE HOTEL €€€
(☎02 41 38 05 15; www.chateau-verrieres.com; 53 rue d'Alsace; r €180-240, ste €295-345; ⊙closed mid-Jan–mid-Feb; P@🛜🏊) This splendid 1890 château, surrounded by a 1.6-hectare English park, is sumptuous throughout, with wood-panelled salons, marble fireplac-

THE GREEN FAIRY: ABSINTHE

Some of France's most distinctive liqueurs are distilled in the Loire Valley, including the aniseedy (and allegedly hallucinogenic) brew known as absinthe. Distilled using a heady concoction of natural herbs, true absinthe includes three crucial components: green anise, fennel and the foliage of *Artemisia absinthium* (wormwood, used as a remedy since the time of the ancient Egyptians). Legend has it that modern-day absinthe was created by a French doctor (the wonderfully named Dr Pierre Ordinaire) in the late 1790s, and then the recipe was acquired by the father-and-son team who established the first major absinthe factory, Maison Pernod-Fils, in 1805.

The drink's popularity exploded in the 19th century, when it was discovered by bohemian poets and painters (as well as French troops, who were given it as an antimalarial drug). Seriously potent, absinthe's traditional green colour and supposedly psychoactive effects led to its popular nickname, 'the green fairy'; everyone from Rimbaud to Vincent van Gogh sang its praises. Ernest Hemingway invented his own absinthe cocktail, ominously dubbed 'Death in the Afternoon'.

But the drink's reputation was ultimately its downfall: fearing widespread psychic degeneration, governments around the globe banned it in the early 20th century (France in 1915). In the 1990s a group of dedicated absintheurs reverse-engineered the liqueur, chemically analysing century-old bottles that had escaped the ban. Absinthe was made legal once again in 2011; you can try it at **Distillerie Combier** in Saumur.

DON'T MISS

CHÂTEAUX TWINSET

Château de Montsoreau (☎02 41 67 12 60; www.chateau-montsoreau.com; passage du Marquis de Geoffre, Montsoreau; adult/child €9.20/5.50, adult incl Fontevraud €15; ⊙10am-7pm early Apr–mid-Nov, to 5pm mid-Dec–early Jan;) beautifully situated on the edge of the Loire, was built in 1455 by one of Charles VII's advisers and later became famous thanks to an Alexandre Dumas novel, *La Dame de Monsoreau*. Exhibits explore the castle's history, the novel and the river trade that once sustained the Loire Valley. There are spectacular river views from the rooftop.

Château de Brézé (☎02 41 51 60 15; www.chateaudebreze.com; 2 rue du Château, Brézé; adult/child €11.50/9.50, incl tour €14.50/12.50; ⊙10am-6pm or 7pm Feb-Dec) sits on top of a network of subterranean rooms and passages, 1.5km of which is open to the public, that include kitchens, wine cellars, defensive bastions and a troglodyte dwelling dating from at least the time of the Norman invasions in the 11th century. Above ground, much of the U-shaped château dates from the 19th century, as do the many intricately painted neo-Gothic and neo-Renaissance interiors. Brézé has been owned by the same family since 1682. Don't miss the top floor of the West Tower, used in the 1800s as quarters for lower-ranking servants. The only way to see four rooms in the Renaissance wing is to take a tour (at least four daily). The dry moat is the deepest (15m to 18m) in Europe that goes all the way around a castle. All signs are in English. Situated 12km south of Saumur.

es, original artwork, antique writing desks and cast-iron bath-tubs. Some of the 10 bedrooms, each different, offer views of the sun rising over Saumur's château.

Eating

Les Tontons BISTRO €

(☎02 41 59 59 40; www.bistrotlestontons.com; 1bis place St-Pierre; 2-/3-course lunch menus €14.80/18.80; ⊙noon-1.30pm & 7-9.30pm, closed Sun & Mon Nov-Mar;) There's a buzz about this tiny place, which serves excellent bistro fare (lamb shank, beef tartare) and 20 wines – most of them local – by the glass (€2.50 to €7.50). Run by Gérard, from an old Anjou winegrowing family, and Sarah-Jane, who hails from the Cotswolds (UK), it serves drinks and light meals throughout the afternoon from April to October.

Le 30 Février VEGETARIAN €

(☎02 41 51 12 45; 9 place de la République; mains €7.40-12.20; ⊙noon-2pm & 7-10.30pm Tue-Sat, plus Sun evening & Mon Jun-Sep;) A tiny, unpretentious place that serves up pizza, pasta and great-value vegetarian plates (€7.80) that consist of a cooked cereal (quinoa, rice or buckwheat) accompanied by raw veggies (eg carrots, cabbage and beets).

L'Escargot TRADITIONAL FRENCH €€

(☎02 41 51 20 88; 30 rue du Maréchal Leclerc; lunch/dinner menus from €20/30; ⊙noon-1.30pm Thu, Fri, Sun & Mon, 7.30-9.30pm Thu-Mon;) A Saumur fixture for more than half a century, this place is all about traditional recipes done really well, such as escargots with 'three butters' (flavoured with herbs, walnuts and Roquefort) or *carré d'agneau rôti à l'ail et au thym* (loin of lamb roasted with garlic and thyme).

Le Pot de Lapin MODERN FRENCH €€

(☎02 41 67 12 86; 35 rue Rabelais; mains €12-22; ⊙noon-2pm & 7-9.30pm Tue-Sat) Jazz wafts from the cheery dining room, decorated with tools of the winemaker's art, through the wine bar and onto the street-side terrace as Chef Olivier works the tables, proposing perfect wine pairings. Start with a local bubbly, then move on to foie gras with onion-and-fruit chutney or monkfish with cream. Situated 1km southeast along the river from the centre.

L'Aromate MODERN FRENCH €€

(☎02 41 51 31 45; www.laromate-restaurant.com; 42 rue du Maréchal Leclerc; lunch menus €16-20, 3-course dinner €22-36; ⊙noon-1.30pm & 7.30-9pm Tue-Sat;) L'Aromate is buzzy and bright, with changing *menus* – on chalkboards – that focus on traditional French cuisine but occasionally draw on Asian spices. Specialities include homemade foie gras accompanied by foie-gras ice cream made with vermouth and honey.

L'Amuse Bouche MODERN FRENCH €€

(☎02 41 67 79 63; www.lamusebouche.fr; 512 rte Montsoreau, Dampierre-sur-Loire; lunch/dinner menus €17.50/29.50; ⊙noon-1.30pm & 7.30-9.30pm Thu-Mon, plus Tue evening Jul & Aug) Tuck

into delicious, creative French meals, either under 18th-century beams in a stone-walled dining room or, in summer, on the terrace. Find it 4.5km southeast of Saumur on the D947.

★ **Le Gambetta** GASTRONOMIC €€€
(☎02 41 67 66 66; www.restaurantlegambetta.com; 12 rue Gambetta; lunch menus €28, dinner menus €35-109; ⌚noon-1.30pm Tue & Thu-Sun, 7.15-9pm Tue & Thu-Sat) This is one to write home about: a truly outstanding restaurant combining refined elegance and knock-your-socks-off creative French cuisine. Some *menus* include wine pairings perfectly chosen to complement the parade of gorgeously presented dishes, punctuated by surprise treats from the kitchen.

Entertainment

★ **Cadre Noir** EQUESTRIAN SHOW
(☎02 41 53 50 80; www.cadrenoir.fr; Présentation adult/child €19/13, Gala €30-65; ⌚specific dates Apr-Oct) The Cadre Noir equestrian display team puts on two types of astonishingly graceful show: Présentations Publiques, hour-long demonstrations with commentary, and – this is what it's most famous for – ballet-like Galas (in April, May, July, September and October) that showcase the extraordinary skills of the horses and riders. Reserve by phone or online.

Information

Tourist Office (☎02 41 40 20 60; www.saumur-tourisme.com; 8bis quai Carnot; ⌚9.15am-12.30pm & 2-6pm or 7pm Mon-Sat year-round, 10.30am-noon or 12.30pm Sun early Feb–mid-Nov, plus Sun afternoon May-late Sep;) Can supply you with a city map, details on bus transport, information on horse-riding options, a list of sites open in winter and slightly reduced-price châteaux tickets. Situated on the riverfront one block southwest of the bridge.

Maison des Vins (☎02 41 38 45 83; 7 quai Carnot; ⌚10am-1pm & 3-7pm Mon-Sat & 10am-1pm Sun Jun-Aug, 10am-12.30pm & 2.30-6pm Tue-Sat early Apr-May, Sep & Oct) This information centre for visiting Saumur-area vineyards is set to reopen under the auspices of a local winegrowers federation. Situated next to the tourist office.

Getting There & Around

BICYCLE

Détours de Loire (☎02 41 53 01 01; www.detoursdeloire.com; 10 rue de Rouen; half-day/day/week €10/15/60) Bike-rental outfit with locations all along the Loire.

BUS

Agglobus (☎02 41 51 11 87; www.agglobus.fr; single/day ticket €1.40/3.80) Saumur's local bus company (operating Monday to Saturday) runs *lignes estivales* (summer lines) linking the train station with Turquant and the Abbaye Royale de Fontevraud. The tourist office has details.

Anjou Bus (☎02 41 36 29 46; www.anjoubus.fr; tickets €1.90-5.90) Lines 4 and 17 serve Angers and intermediate points, including Chênehutte-Trèves-Cunault and Gennes. The tourist office has details.

TRAIN

Saumur's station is across the river from the town centre, 1.3km from the tourist office.

Angers €9.10, 21 to 32 minutes, eight to 20 daily

Paris Gare Montparnasse €62.50 to €84.30, two to three hours (requires one transfer)

Tours €12.30, 45 minutes, seven to 10 daily

East of Saumur

Some of the Loire's most exquisite scenery, including riverside tufa bluffs punctuated by cave houses, stretches along the D947 southeast of Saumur. Many of the renowned wine producers here, both small and large, offer free tastings at their cellars from spring to early autumn; see www.saumur-champigny.com (look for 'Annuaire des Vignerons') for details that include which growers speak English and whether you need to phone ahead. Note that winegrowers are especially busy during the *vendanges* (grape harvest) from mid-September to October.

Turquant

POP 600

Ten kilometres southeast of Saumur, the picturesque village of Turquant has one of the region's highest concentrations of troglodyte dwellings. Many have now been spruced up and converted into shops, galleries or restaurants.

Sights

Troglo des Pommes Tapées CAVE
(☎02 41 51 48 30; www.letroglodespommestapees.fr; 11 rue des Ducs d'Anjou; adult/child €6.50/4; ⌚10am-12.30pm & 2-6.30pm Apr-late Sep, 2-6pm Sat & Sun Oct–mid-Nov) One of the last places in France producing traditional dried apples known as *pommes tapées*. You can see dis-

plays on how it's done, sample the wares and buy some to take home.

Sleeping & Eating

★Demeure de la Vignole DESIGN HOTEL €€
(☎02 41 53 67 00; www.demeure-vignole.com; 3 impasse Marguerite d'Anjou; d €130-165, 4-person ste €270-290; ⊙closed mid-Nov–mid-Mar;) This swish hotel has 12 richly decorated rooms, five of them in caves. The 15m swimming pool is carved into the rock face, too. Very homey, and not just for hobbits. A wonderful change from the ordinary.

L'Hélianthe MODERN FRENCH €€
(☎02 44 10 12 39; www.restaurant-helianthe.fr; ruelle Antoine Cristal; mains €16; ⊙noon-2pm & 7-8.45pm Thu-Tue Apr–mid-Nov, Sat & Sun winter) Tucked into a cliff behind Turquant's *mairie* (town hall), this atmospheric restaurant has a hearty *menu* firmly based on local products and classic French flavours.

Bistroglo BISTRO €€
(☎02 41 40 22 36; www.bistroglo.com; Atelier 3, rue du Château Gaillard; mains €14-16.50; ⊙10.30am-9pm Tue-Sun Mar-Sep, Sat & lunch Sun Nov & Dec;) At this bistro-style restaurant, situated *en troglo* (in a cave) – thus the name – artisanal beers and local wines are an excellent prelude to traditional French cuisine, served with a smile.

Information

Parc Naturel Régional Loire-Anjou-Touraine Maison du Parc (☎02 41 38 38 88; www.parc-loire-anjou-touraine.fr; 15 av de la Loire, Montsoreau; ⊙9.30am-1pm & 2-6pm or 7pm daily Apr-Sep, Tue-Sun Oct, Sat & Sun Mar) The Maison du Parc provides maps and information on activities throughout the 2530-sq-km Parc Naturel Régional Loire-Anjou-Touraine, a regional park established to protect the landscape, extraordinary architectural patrimony and culture of this section of the Loire Valley.

Getting There & Away

Turquant is 10km southeast of Saumur along the riverfront D947.

Candes-St-Martin

POP 235

About 1.5km southeast of Montsoreau, the picturesque village of Candes-St-Martin occupies an idyllic spot at the confluence of the Vienne and Loire Rivers. St Martin died here in 397, turning little Candes into a major pilgrimage destination.

For great panoramas, climb the tiny streets above the church, past inhabited cave dwellings, or head down to the benches and path along the waterfront.

Collégiale St-Martin (place de l'Église; ⊙8.45am-5.30pm, to 6.45pm summer), the soaring village church built from 1175 to 1240, venerates the spot where St Martin died in 397 and was buried for a while (his body was later spirited off to Tours). Enter via the exceptional side porch.

Two traditional flat-bottomed boats known as *toues* depart from Candes-St-Martin and cruise the convergence of the

MUSHROOM MADNESS

Mushroom lovers – or those open to being seduced by the charms of *champignons* – can learn more, tour caves and taste samples in the Saumar area.

Musée du Champignon (☎02 41 50 31 55; www.musee-du-champignon.com; rte de Gennes, St-Hilaire-St-Florent; adult/child €8.40/6; ⊙10am-6pm early Feb–mid-Nov) Get acquainted with some fabulous fungi at this museum-producer, in a cave at the western edge of St-Hilaire-St-Florent, 4.5km northwest of Saumur. When you walk inside, try to resist declaring, 'there's a fungus among us!'

La Cave aux Moines (☎02 41 67 95 64; www.cave-aux-moines.com; Préban, Chênehutte-Trèves-Cunault; menus €20-24.90; ⊙lunch & dinner mid-Jun–mid-Sep, lunch Sat & Sun, dinner Fri-Sun rest of year;) Besides offering tours of the *champignonnière* (mushroom beds; adult/child €5.50/3), La Cave has a restaurant with all manner of 'shrooms, snails and *fouées*, the local fire-baked breads. Situated 10km northwest of Saumur.

Le Saut aux Loups (☎02 41 51 70 30; www.troglo-sautauxloups.com; av de la Loire, Montsoreau; menus €21-23; ⊙restaurant noon-3pm Mar–mid-Nov, dinner Jul & Aug;) Another great place to tour mushroom caves (adult/child €6.50/5; open 10am to 6pm March to mid-November) and tuck into *galipettes* (large stuffed mushrooms). Situated 11km southeast of Saumur.

DON'T MISS

TROGLODYTES: CAVE LIFE

For centuries the creamy-white tufa cliffs around Saumur have provided shelter and storage for local inhabitants, leading to the development of a unique *culture troglodyte* (cave-dwelling culture). The naturally cool caves were turned into houses *(habitations troglodytes)* and incorporated into castles (as at Brézé; p396) and are still very much used by vintners and mushroom farmers. Many of the Loire's grandest châteaux were built from white tufa, and the quarrying created caves.

Lots of caves can be found along the Loire east and west of Saumur, and around the village of Doué-la-Fontaine. Stop by the Saumur tourist office (p397) for a complete list. Bring something warm to wear as caves remain cool (13°C) year-round. The ones near Doué-la-Fontaine (a grim semi-industrial town) are best reached with your own wheels.

Rochemenier (☎02 41 59 18 15; www.troglodyte.fr; 14 rue du Musée, Louresse-Rochemenier; adult/child €6.10/3.70; ⏲9.30am-7pm Apr-Sep, 10am-6pm Tue-Sun Oct-Nov & Feb-Mar) Inhabited until the 1930s, this abandoned village, 6km north of Doué-la-Fontaine, is one of the best examples of troglodyte culture. Explore the remains of two farmsteads, complete with houses, stables and an underground chapel.

Troglodytes et Sarcophages (☎06 77 77 06 94; www.troglo-sarcophages.fr; 1 rue de la Croix Mordret, Doué-la-Fontaine; adult/child €4.90/3.30; ⏲2.30-7pm daily Jun-Aug, Sat & Sun May, tours 3pm daily Feb, Easter, All Saints Day & Christmas school holidays) A Merovingian mine where sarcophagi were produced from the 6th to the 9th centuries and exported via the Loire as far as England and Belgium. Reserve ahead for a 90-minute lantern-lit tour.

Les Perrières (☎02 41 59 71 29; www.les-perrieres.com; 545 rue des Perrières, Doué-la-Fontaine; adult/child €7/4.50; ⏲10am-12.30pm & 2-6pm Tue-Sun Mar-Oct) These one-time stone quarries are sometimes called 'cathedral caves' for their lofty, sloping walls, said to resemble Gothic arches.

Musée du Champignon Get acquainted with some fabulous fungus at this museum-producer, tucked into a cave at the western edge of St-Hilaire-St-Florent.

Loire and Vienne Rivers for 45 to 90 minutes. They're run by **CPIE Val de Loire** (☎02 47 95 93 15; www.cpie-val-de-loire.org; Candes-St-Martin; adult/child €11/7; ⏲3pm & 4.15pm Wed-Sun Jul & Aug), an NGO dedicated to sustainable development.

Getting There & Away

Candes-St-Martin is midway between Saumur and Chinon (about 14km from each) and about 2km southeast of Montsoreau. From Saumur take the scenic D947, from Chinon the D751.

Fontevraud-l'Abbaye

POP 1500

The quiet, stone-built town of Fontevraud-l'Abbaye, 15km southeast of Saumur, is famed for its medieval abbey.

Sights

★Abbaye Royale de Fontevraud HISTORIC SITE
(☎02 41 51 73 52; www.abbayedefontevraud.com; adult/child €11/7.50, audioguide €4.50; ⏲9.30am-6pm Apr-Oct, 10am-5pm Nov, Dec, Feb & Mar) The highlight of this 12th-century abbey complex is the huge but movingly simple church, notable for its soaring pillars, Romanesque domes and the polychrome stone tombs of four illustrious Plantagenets: Henry II, King of England (r 1154–89); his wife, Eleanor of Aquitaine (who retired to Fontevraud following Henry's death); their son Richard the Lionheart; and his brother King John's wife, Isabelle of Angoulème.

The cloister is surrounded by one-time dormitories, workrooms and prayer halls; the Salle Capitulaire (chapter room), with murals of the Passion of Christ by Thomas Pot; and a wonderful Gothic-vaulted refectory, where the nuns would eat in silence while being read the Scriptures. Both the nuns and the monks of Fontevraud were, exceptionally, governed by an abbess, generally a lady of noble birth who had retired from public life. Outside, there are medieval-style gardens and a multi-chimneyed, rocket-shaped kitchen, built entirely from stone to make it fireproof.

In 1804, by Napoleonic decree, Fontevraud was turned into a notoriously harsh prison, a role it played until 1963. Author

Jean Gênet was imprisoned for stealing (but not here) and, based on that experience, wrote *Miracle de la Rose* (1946), which is set at Fontevraud.

Sleeping & Eating

Fontevraud l'Hôtel DESIGN HOTEL €€

(☎02 46 46 10 10; www.hotel-fontevraud.com; d/q/ste Fri & Sat €155/175/199, Sun-Thu €139/155/170; ⊙restaurant 12.30-2pm Sun, 7.30-9.30pm Wed-Sat; @📶) Ultramodern meets medieval at this luxurious hotel, whose 34 sleek rooms are decorated in muted beiges and whites. It's a bit hard to find – occupying a one-time priory, it's around behind the main part of the abbey – but staff members are happy to help. Guests enjoy exclusive access to the abbey grounds at night.

The gastronomic restaurant (*menus* €55 to €95, with wine €83 to €135) serves seriously *haute* cuisine, conceived by award-winning chef Thibaut Ruggeri.

Chez Teresa CAFE €

(☎02 41 51 21 24; www.chezteresa.fr; 6 av Rochechouart; lunch menus €12.50; ⊙noon-8pm; 📶) English expats Teresa and Tony offer a welcome as cosy-warm as tea at this frilly little tearoom, stuffed with bric-a-brac from across the Channel. In the afternoon, pop by for a cuppa, little triangular sandwiches, scones with cream and jam, and cake (€9.80). The double room upstairs costs €65, breakfast included.

Getting There & Away

Fontevraud-l'Abbaye is 16km southwest of Saumur along the D947, whose most attractive section runs along the south bank of the Loire between Saumur and Montsoreau.

Angers

POP 149,000

An intellectual centre in the 1400s and a lively university city today, Angers – the historical seat of the Plantagenet dynasty and the dukes of Anjou – makes an engaging western gateway to the Loire Valley. The mostly pedestrianised old town supports a thriving cafe culture, thanks in part to the dynamic presence of 38,000 students, as well as some excellent places to eat. The city is famous for two sets of breathtaking tapestries: the 14th-century *Tenture de l'Apocalypse* in the city's medieval château, and the 20th-century *Chant du Monde* at the Jean Lurçat museum.

Sights

★Château d'Angers CHÂTEAU

(☎02 41 86 48 77; www.chateau-angers.fr; 2 promenade du Bout-du-Monde; adult/child €8.50/free, audioguide for 1/2 people €4.50/6; ⊙9.30am-6.30pm May-Aug, 10am-5.30pm Sep-Apr) Looming above the river, this forbidding medieval castle – seat of power of the once-mighty counts of Anjou – is ringed by moats, 2.5m-thick walls and 17 massive round towers. The centrepiece is the stunning **Tenture de l'Apocalypse** (Apocalypse tapestry), a 104m-long series of tapestries commissioned in 1375 to illustrate the story of the final battle between good and evil, as prophesied in the Bible's Book of Revelation.

The vivid scenes mix terror, pathos, extreme violence and humour, giving visitors an extraordinary peek into the medieval mind, its dreams and its deepest fears.

You can walk around the top of the castle's ramparts, which afford spectacular views, along the **Chemin de Rond** (Parapet Walk).

★Musée Jean Lurçat et de la Tapisserie Contemporaine MUSEUM

(☎02 41 24 18 45; www.musees.angers.fr; 4 bd Arago; adult/child €4/free; ⊙10am-6pm May–mid-Sep, 10am-noon & 2-6pm Tue-Sun mid-Sep–Apr) Inspired by *Tenture de l'Apocalypse* in the château, Jean Lurçat (1892–1966) began his epic tapestry masterpiece, *Chant du Monde* (Song of the World; 1957–61), 12 years after the end of WWII; scenes depict everything from the delights of Champagne to space exploration to nuclear holocaust. A quintessentially mid-20th-century meditation on the human condition, it is exuberant but contemplative, and only guardedly optimistic. The museum also exhibits other extraordinarily beautiful 20th-century and 21st-century tapestries. Situated 1.2km north of the château, on the opposite bank of the Maine.

Musée des Beaux-Arts ART MUSEUM

(☎02 41 05 38 00; www.musees.angers.fr; 14 rue du Musée; adult/child €4/free; ⊙10am-6pm daily May–mid-Sep, Tue-Sun mid-Sep–Apr) Has a section on the history of Angers and a superior 17th- to 20th-century collection (mainly paintings) that ranges from French masters Ingres, Fragonard and Watteau to the Florentine Lorenzo Lippi to Flemish and Dutch Golden Age painters such as Jacob Jordaens.

Angers

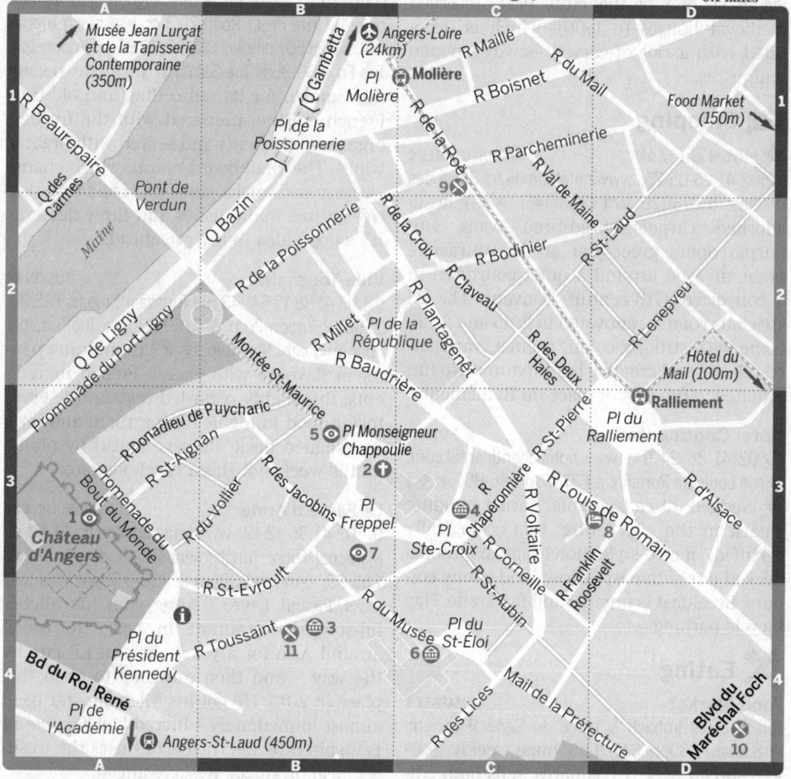

Angers

Top Sights

1 Château d'Angers A3

Sights

2 Cathédrale St-Maurice B3
3 Galerie David d'Angers B4
4 Maison d'Adam C3
5 Montée St-Maurice B3
6 Musée des Beaux-Arts C4
7 Quartier de la Cité B3

Sleeping

8 Hôtel Continental D3

Eating

9 Au Goût du Jour C1
10 Le Favre d'Anne D4
11 Villa Toussaint B4

Galerie David d'Angers MUSEUM

(☎02 41 05 38 90; www.musees.angers.fr; 33bis rue Toussaint; adult/child €4/free; ⏰10am-6pm daily May–mid-Sep, Tue-Sun mid-Sep–Apr) The Angers-born sculptor Pierre-Jean David (1788–1856), aka David d'Angers, is renowned for his lifelike sculptures, which adorn public monuments such as the Panthéon and can be seen in the Louvre and Paris' Père Lachaise cemetery. Here in the 12th-century Toussaint Abbey, flooded with light thanks to a striking glass-and-girder ceiling, you can admire models and moulds of most of his creations.

Quartier de la Cité HISTORIC SITE

One of the earliest examples of Angevin (Plantagenet) architecture in France, the Gothic **Cathédrale St-Maurice** (place Monseigneur Chappoulie; ⏰8am-7pm) is distinguished by its rounded ribbed vaulting, 15th-century stained glass and 12th-century portal depicting the Day of Judgement. From the square in front, a monumental staircase, **Montée St-Maurice**, leads down to a fountain and the river. Right behind the

cathedral stands the **Maison d'Adam** (place Ste-Croix), one of the city's best-preserved medieval houses (c 1500), which is decorated with a riot of carved, bawdy wooden sculptures.

Sleeping

★Hôtel du Mail HISTORIC HOTEL €
(☎02 41 25 05 25; www.hoteldumail.fr; 8 rue des Ursules; d €76-126, tr/q €136/146; P 📶) Rose-adorned carpets, bright-red walls and purple doors greet you at this attractive hotel, arrayed around a quiet courtyard in a converted 17th-century convent. The 25 spacious rooms, renovated in 2015 and 2016, come with striking colour themes, variegated pillows and creative light fixtures. No lift. Situated 250m east of place du Ralliement.

Hôtel Continental HOTEL €
(☎02 41 86 94 94; www.hotellecontinental.com; 14 rue Louis de Romain; s €77-87, d €86-90; ❄📶) Wedged into a triangular corner building smack in the city centre, this ecologically certified, metro-style hotel has 25 rooms decked out with cosy pillows and sunny colours. Breakfast is organic and fair trade. Has bicycle parking.

Eating

Food Market MARKET €
(place Louis Imbach & place du Général Leclerc; ⏲8.30am-1.30pm Sat) This huge weekly market, spread over two squares, sells both edibles and flea-market goods.

COINTREAU

Cointreau has its origins in the experiments of two brothers: sweet-maker Adolphe Cointreau, and Édouard-Jean Cointreau, who founded a **factory** (☎02 41 31 50 50; www.carre-cointreau.fr; 2 bd des Bretonnières, St-Barthélemy-d'Anjou; 2hr tours €10; ⏲boutique 11am-6pm Tue-Sat, tours by reservation) in Angers in 1849 to produce fruit-flavoured liqueurs. In 1875 Édouard-Jean's son (also called Édouard) hit upon a winning formula combining sweet and bitter oranges, flavoured with intensely orangey peel. Every one of the 15 million bottles produced annually is distilled according to the same top-secret recipe at this factory, 3km east of Angers' city centre (served by Irigo bus 6).

Au Goût du Jour MODERN FRENCH €
(☎02 41 23 73 19; restaurant.augoutdujour@gmail.com; 14 rue de la Roë; 2-/3-course lunch menus €14.50/16.50, dinner €18.90/21.90; ⏲noon-1pm Tue-Fri, 7.30-9pm Tue-Sat) An intimate restaurant known for its red ceiling and old-time French cuisine, prepared with the freshest organic ingredients and served with organic wines. The chalkboard *menu*, which changes every two weeks, consists of just three entrées, three main dishes and three desserts. It's a good idea to reserve ahead.

Villa Toussaint FUSION €€
(☎02 41 88 15 64; 43 rue Toussaint; mains €15.90-21.90; ⏲noon-2pm & 7.15-10.30pm Tue-Sat, bar noon-midnight May-Sep; 📶🖉) Combining pan-Asian flavours with classic French ingredients, this highly regarded restaurant serves fusion food in a chic dining room and on a tree-shaded deck. Reserve ahead by phone on the weekend. Has a Facebook page.

Le Favre d'Anne GASTRONOMIC €€€
(☎02 41 36 12 12; www.lefavredanne.fr; 21 bd du Maréchal Foch; lunch menus €49, dinner menus €65-95; ⏲noon-1.30pm & 7.30-9.30pm Wed-Sat) Chef Pascal Favre d'Anne shut his Michelin-starred restaurant in order to travel around Asia for a year – he's an LP fan, by the way – and then returned to open this place in 2015. He got his Michelin star back almost immediately – incredible! The *menu* is inspired by his travels but uses the freshest local products. Reserve ahead.

Information

Tourist Office (☎02 41 23 50 00; www.angersloiretourisme.com; 7 place du Président Kennedy; ⏲9am or 10am-5.30pm, 6pm or 7pm, closed Tue morning & Sun afternoon Oct-Apr) Very helpful, with luggage lockers big enough for backpacks, public toilets and loads of info on sights, activities (including cycling) and transport. Sells the **Angers City Pass** (€14/22/29 per 24/48/72 hours).

Getting There & Around

AIR

Angers Loire Airport (ANE; ☎02 41 36 29 46; www.angersloireaeroport.fr), 24km northeast of the city centre, has seasonal flights to London-City.

BICYCLE

The tourist office rents bikes (€15 per day) and has great cycling maps. The Cyclopédia smartphone app can be downloaded from www.anjou-cycling.co.uk.

BUS

Angers' **Gare Routière** (bus station) is next to the train station. **Anjou Bus** (p397) serves destinations within the Maine-et-Loire *département*, including Angers Loire Airport (bus 2), Saumur (lines 4 and 17), Brissac-Quincé (Château de Brissac; bus 5) and St-Georges-sur-Loire (Château de Serrant; bus 24). **Isilines** (www.isilines.fr) goes to Paris' Gallieni coach station (€12).

TRAIN

Angers-St-Laud Train Station is 600m south of the château and the tourist office.

Nantes €16 to €22, 40 minutes, at least 30 daily

Paris Gare Montparnasse €63 to €78, 1½ hours, hourly

Saumur €9.10, 21 to 32 minutes, eight to 20 daily

Tours €19, one hour, four to six daily

OFF THE BEATEN TRACK

A LUNCH TO REMEMBER

Pretty Le Thoureil is home to the excellent **La Route du Sel** (02 41 45 75 31; www.authoureil.fr; 55 quai des Mariniers; lunch/dinner menus from €17/32; noon-2.30pm & 7-9.30pm Wed-Sat, noon-2.30pm Sun;) which serves up French home cooking made with fresh Anjou products and accompanied by Saumur-brewed artisanal beer or wine from the family vineyards. Save room for the transcendent *gâteau de Marie*, a sesame-encrusted, gluten-free chocolate extravaganza.

Around Angers

South of Angers, the Maine joins the Loire for the final leg of its journey to the Atlantic. The river banks immediately west of this confluence remain the source of some of the valley's most notable wines, including Savennières (grown near a pretty village of the same name) and Coteaux du Layon. The area due south of Angers, between Gennes, Brissac-Quincé and Savennières, makes for great back-roads exploration.

Owned by the Brissac family since 1502 – 18 generations! – the seven-storey **Château de Brissac** (02 41 91 22 21; www.chateau-brissac.fr; Brissac-Quincé; adult/child incl tour €10/4.50, gardens only €5/free; tours 10am-noon & 2-5.30pm Wed-Mon Apr-Oct, 10am-5.30pm daily Jul & Aug, plus 2pm & 4pm Wed-Mon Feb & Christmas school holidays), the tallest in France, has 204 rooms, many of them sumptuously furnished with antique furniture, Flemish tapestries and twinkling chandeliers. The serene 70-hectare gardens have 19th-century stables, and vineyards boasting three AOC vintages. Guided tours are in French with an English reference text. From May to September, three of the château's bedrooms turn into an opulent **B&B** (€390 per room) – ideal for a honeymoon or a very special family vacation! Situated 21km southeast of Angers.

The elegant Renaissance-style **Château de Serrant** (02 41 39 13 01; www.chateau-serrant.net; St-Georges-sur-Loire; adult/child €10/6.50; tours hourly 9.30am-5.15pm daily Jul & Aug, shorter hours Wed-Sun early Feb-early Nov), owned and lived in by the same Irish family and its descendants since 1749, castle, built on medieval foundations, is notable for its 12,000-tome library, huge kitchens and the Chambre Empire, an extravagant domed bedroom designed for Napoléon (he stuck around for just two hours). Some areas can only be seen on a tour (in French with reference text in English), but you can visit the ground floor and the chapel on your own. Situated 20km southwest of Angers.

To experience rural France at its most pastoral, drop by **Auberge de Montrivet** (Ferme de Montrivet; 02 41 45 32 02; www.auberge-montrivet.fr; Montrivet, Denée; d/q €55/85; daily year-round) to sleep and/or dine – you're assured of a warm welcome at this working family farm. The four rooms are very simply furnished; the country-style French meals are made with duck, chicken and veggies grown right here. Phone or email a day ahead. Situated in the hamlet of Montrivet, 22km south of Angers and 5km southeast of the centre of Denée.

Getting There & Away

The towns and villages around Angers are served by **Anjou Bus** (p397). Services are limited, but it's often possible to get to Brissac-Quincé (Château de Brissac; bus 5) and St-Georges-sur-Loire (Château de Serrant; bus 24).

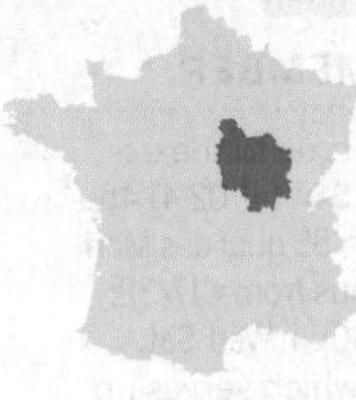

Burgundy

POP 1.64 MILLION

Best Places to Eat

- ➡ Au Fil du Zinc (p432)
- ➡ La Maison des Cariatides (p411)
- ➡ Le Millésime (p413)
- ➡ La Pause Gourmande (p429)

Best Places to Sleep

- ➡ Villa Louise Hôtel (p414)
- ➡ Côte Serein (p433)
- ➡ La Cimentelle (p435)
- ➡ Le Clos de l'Abbaye (p443)
- ➡ Moulin Renaudiots (p440)

Why Go?

Burgundy (Bourgogne in French) offers some of France's most gorgeous countryside: rolling green hills dotted with mustard fields and medieval villages. The region's towns and its dashingly handsome capital, Dijon, are heirs to a glorious architectural heritage that goes back to the Renaissance, the Middle Ages and into the mists of Gallo-Roman and Celtic antiquity. Two great French passions, wine and food, come together here in a particularly rich and enticing form. In 2015, Burgundy's vineyards were granted Unesco World Heritage status in recognition of the region's centuries-old history of viticulture, combined with the remarkable diversity of its winegrowing *terroir* (land).

Burgundy is also a paradise for lovers of the great outdoors. You can cycle through the Côte d'Or vineyards, hike the wild reaches of the Parc Naturel Régional du Morvan, glide along the Yonne's waterways in a canal boat, or float above it all in a hot-air balloon.

When to Go

Dijon

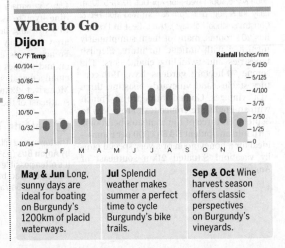

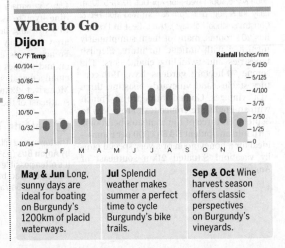

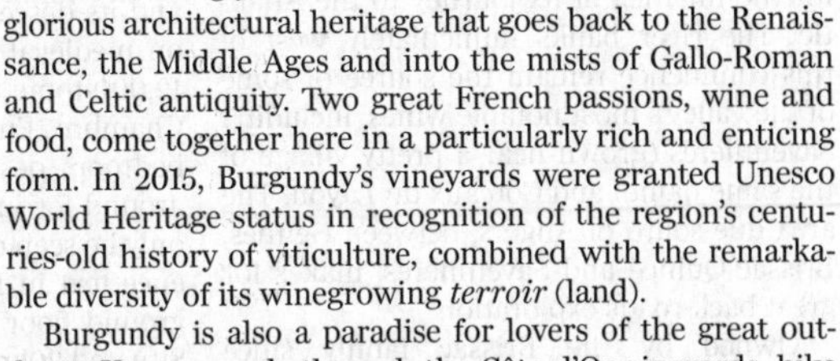

May & Jun Long, sunny days are ideal for boating on Burgundy's 1200km of placid waterways.

Jul Splendid weather makes summer a perfect time to cycle Burgundy's bike trails.

Sep & Oct Wine harvest season offers classic perspectives on Burgundy's vineyards.

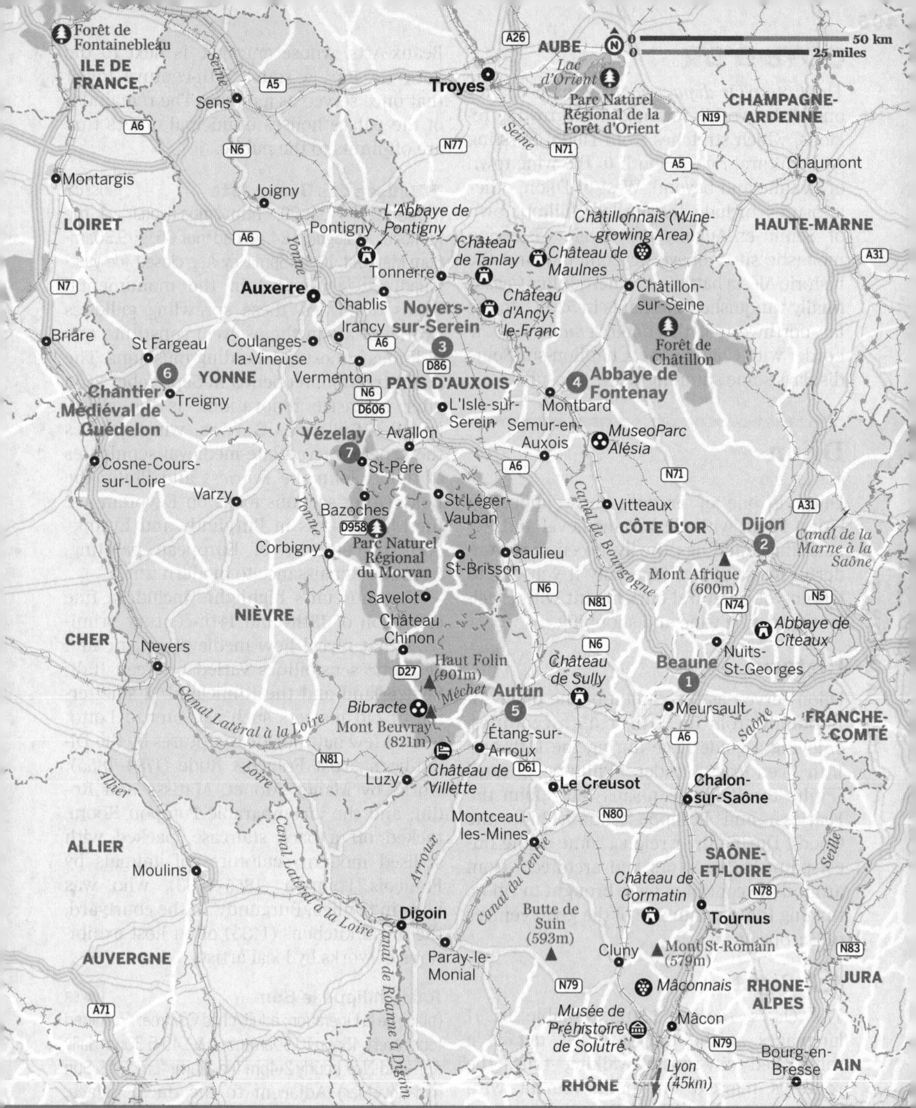

Burgundy Highlights

1. **Beaune** (p417) Sampling Burgundy's most renowned vintages in Beaune, heart of the Côte d'Or.
2. **Dijon** (p406) Basking in the reflected glory of the Burgundy dukes in this elegant historic city.
3. **Noyers-sur-Serein** (p433) Watching the mist rise off the river and the sun peek over the medieval battlements.
4. **Abbaye de Fontenay** (p425) Conjuring up monastic life at this Cistercian abbey.
5. **Musée Rolin** (p440) Gazing up at Gislebertus' *Last Judgment*, a masterpiece of 12th-century stone carving at this museum in Autun.
6. **Chantier Médiéval de Guédelon** (p430) Seeing a château being built with 13th-century technology at this medieval building site.
7. **Vézelay** (p436) Climbing through idyllic green countryside and cobblestoned lanes to reach the medieval basilica.

CÔTE D'OR

The Côte d'Or *département* is named after one of the world's foremost winegrowing regions, which stretches from Dijon, bursting with cultural riches, south to the wine town of Beaune and beyond. West of Dijon, other treasures include the walled, hilltop town of Semur-en-Auxois, the idyllic Cistercian monastic site Abbaye de Fontenay and the historic Alésia battlefield where Julius Caesar finally vanquished the Gauls in 52 BC. In the far northwest of the *département,* on the border with Champagne, Châtillon-sur-Seine displays some stunning Celtic treasures.

Dijon

POP 157,200

Dijon is one of France's most appealing cities. Filled with elegant medieval and Renaissance buildings, the lively centre is wonderful for strolling, especially if you like to leaven your cultural enrichment with excellent food, fine wine and shopping.

History

Dijon served as the capital of the duchy of Burgundy from the 11th to 15th centuries, enjoying a golden age during the 14th and 15th centuries under Philippe-le-Hardi (Philip the Bold), Jean-sans-Peur (John the Fearless) and Philippe-le-Bon (Philip the Good). During their reigns, some of the finest painters, sculptors and architects from around the continent were brought to Dijon, turning the city into one of the great centres of European art.

Sights

The Owl's Trail (€3.50), available in 11 languages at the tourist office, details a self-guided city-centre walking tour; the route is marked on the pavement with bronze triangles. All of Dijon's municipal museums are free except, occasionally, for special exhibitions. Major churches are open from 8am to 7pm.

Palais des Ducs et des États de Bourgogne PALACE
(Palace of the Dukes & States of Burgundy; place de la Libération) Once home to Burgundy's powerful dukes, this monumental palace with a neoclassical façade overlooks place de la Libération, Old Dijon's magnificent central square dating from 1686. The palace's eastern wing houses the outstanding Musée des Beaux-Arts, whose entrance is next to the **Tour de Bar**, a squat 14th-century tower that once served as a prison. The remainder of the palace houses municipal offices that are off-limits to the public.

★**Musée des Beaux-Arts** MUSEUM
(☎03 80 74 52 09; http://mba.dijon.fr; 1 rue Rameau; audioguide €4, guided tour €6; ⏱9.30am-6pm May-Oct, 10am-5pm Nov-Apr, closed Tue year-round) FREE Housed in the monumental Palais des Ducs, these sprawling galleries (works of art in themselves) constitute one of France's most outstanding museums. The star attraction, reopened in September 2013 after extensive renovations, is the wood-panelled **Salle des Gardes**, which houses the ornate, carved late-medieval sepulchres of dukes John the Fearless and Philip the Bold. Other sections focus on Egyptian art, the Middle Ages in Burgundy and Europe, and six centuries of European painting, from the Renaissance to modern times.

The museum's highlights include a fine collection of 13th- and 14th-century primitives that reveal how medieval artistic and aesthetic sensibilities varied between Italy, Switzerland and the Rhineland; a smattering of old masters such as Lorenzo Lotto; quite a few naturalistic sculptures by the Dijon-born artist François Rude (1784–1855); works by Manet, Monet, Matisse and Rodin; and the incomparable Pompon Room, tucked off a back staircase, packed with stylised modern sculptures of animals by François Pompon (1855–1933), who was born in Saulieu, Burgundy. In the courtyard, the ducal kitchens (1433) often host exhibitions of works by local artists.

Tour Philippe le Bon TOWER
(place de la Libération; adult/child €3/free; ⏱guided tours every 45min 10.30am-noon & 1.45-5.30pm daily Apr–mid-Nov, hourly 2-4pm Tue, 11am-4pm Sat & Sun mid-Nov–Mar) Adjacent to the ducal palace, this 46m-high, mid-15th-century tower affords fantastic views over the city. On a clear day you can see all the way to Mont Blanc. Dijon's tourist office handles reservations.

Église Notre Dame CHURCH
(place Notre-Dame; ⏱8am-7pm) A block north of the Palais des Ducs, this church was built between 1220 and 1240. Its extraordinary façade's three tiers are lined with leering gargoyles separated by two rows of pencil-thin columns. Atop the church, the 14th-century **Horloge à Jacquemart**, transported from

Flanders in 1383 by Philip the Bold who claimed it as a trophy of war, chimes every quarter-hour.

Rue de la Chouette STREET

Around the north side of Église Notre Dame, this street is named after the small stone *chouette* (owl) carved into the exterior corner of the chapel diagonally across from no. 24. Said to grant happiness and wisdom to those who stroke it, it has been worn smooth by generations of fortune-seekers.

Maison des Cariatides HISTORIC BUILDING

(28 rue Chaudronnerie) Maison des Cariatides, its façade a riot of stone caryatids, soldiers and vines, is one of Dijon's finest buildings.

Musée Archéologique MUSEUM

(03 80 48 83 70; www.dijon.fr; 5 rue Docteur Maret; 9.30am-12.30pm & 2-6pm Wed-Mon Apr-Oct, Wed, Sat & Sun Nov-Mar) FREE Truly surprising Celtic, Roman and Merovingian artefacts are displayed here, including a particularly fine 1st-century AD bronze of the Celtic goddess Sequana standing on a dual-prowed boat. Upstairs, the early-Gothic hall (12th and 13th centuries), with its ogival arches held aloft by two rows of columns, once served as the dormitory of a Benedictine abbey.

Musée de la Vie Bourguignonne MUSEUM

(03 80 48 80 90; www.dijon.fr; 17 rue Ste-Anne; 9.30am-12.30pm & 2-6pm Wed-Mon) FREE Housed in a 17th-century Cistercian convent, this museum explores village and town life in Burgundy in centuries past with evocative tableaux illustrating dress, customs and traditional crafts. On the 1st floor, a whole street has been re-created, complete with 19th-century pharmacy and numerous antique-filled shops (grocer, furrier, hat-maker, clock-maker, toy store and more).

Cathédrale St-Bénigne CHURCH

(place St-Philibert; 8am-7pm) Built over the tomb of St Benignus (believed to have brought Christianity to Burgundy in the 2nd century), Dijon's Burgundian Gothic-style cathedral was built around 1300 as an abbey church. Some of Burgundy's great figures are buried in its crypt.

Puits de Moïse SCULPTURE

(Well of Moses; Centre Hospitalier Spécialisé La Chartreuse, 1 bd Chanoine Kir; adult/child €3.50/free; 9.30am-12.30pm & 2-5.30pm Apr-Oct, to 5pm Nov-Mar) This famous grouping of six Old Testament figures, carved from 1395 to 1405 by court sculptor Claus Sluter and his nephew Claus de Werve, is on the grounds of a psychiatric hospital 1km west of the train station; by bus, take line 3 towards Fontaine d'Ouche.

FAST FACTS

Area 31,582 sq km

Local industry Viticulture

Signature drink White wine

Musée Magnin ART MUSEUM

(03 80 67 11 10; www.musee-magnin.fr; 4 rue des Bons-Enfants; adult/child incl audioguide €3.50/free; 10am-12.30pm & 1.30-6pm Tue-Sun) Jeanne and Maurice Magnin turned their historic townhouse over to the state to display their excellent art collection in perpetuity. Works include fine examples of the Italian Renaissance, and Flemish and medieval painting.

Jardin Darcy PARK

Dijon has plenty of green spaces that are perfect for picnics, including this inviting park between the train station and the historic centre.

Jardin de l'Arquebuse GARDENS

A delightful place for a Sunday stroll, this 5-hectare park south of the train station encompasses the colourful flower beds and rose trellises of Dijon's botanical gardens, along with an arboretum, a stream and pond.

Tours

The tourist office has scads of information on tours of the city and the nearby wine regions, and can make bookings.

Wine & Voyages WINE

(03 80 61 15 15; www.wineandvoyages.com; tours €58-114) Based in Nuits-St-Georges, this agency specialises in wine tours of the Côte de Nuits region.

Authentica Tours WINE

(06 87 01 43 78; www.authentica-tours.com; tours €65-130) Offers half- and full-day tours through the vineyards surrounding Dijon and Beaune.

Sleeping

Hôtel du Palais HOTEL €

(03 80 65 51 43; www.hoteldupalais-dijon.fr; 23 rue du Palais; s €59-79, d €65-95, q €109, breakfast €9.90;) Newly remodelled and

Dijon

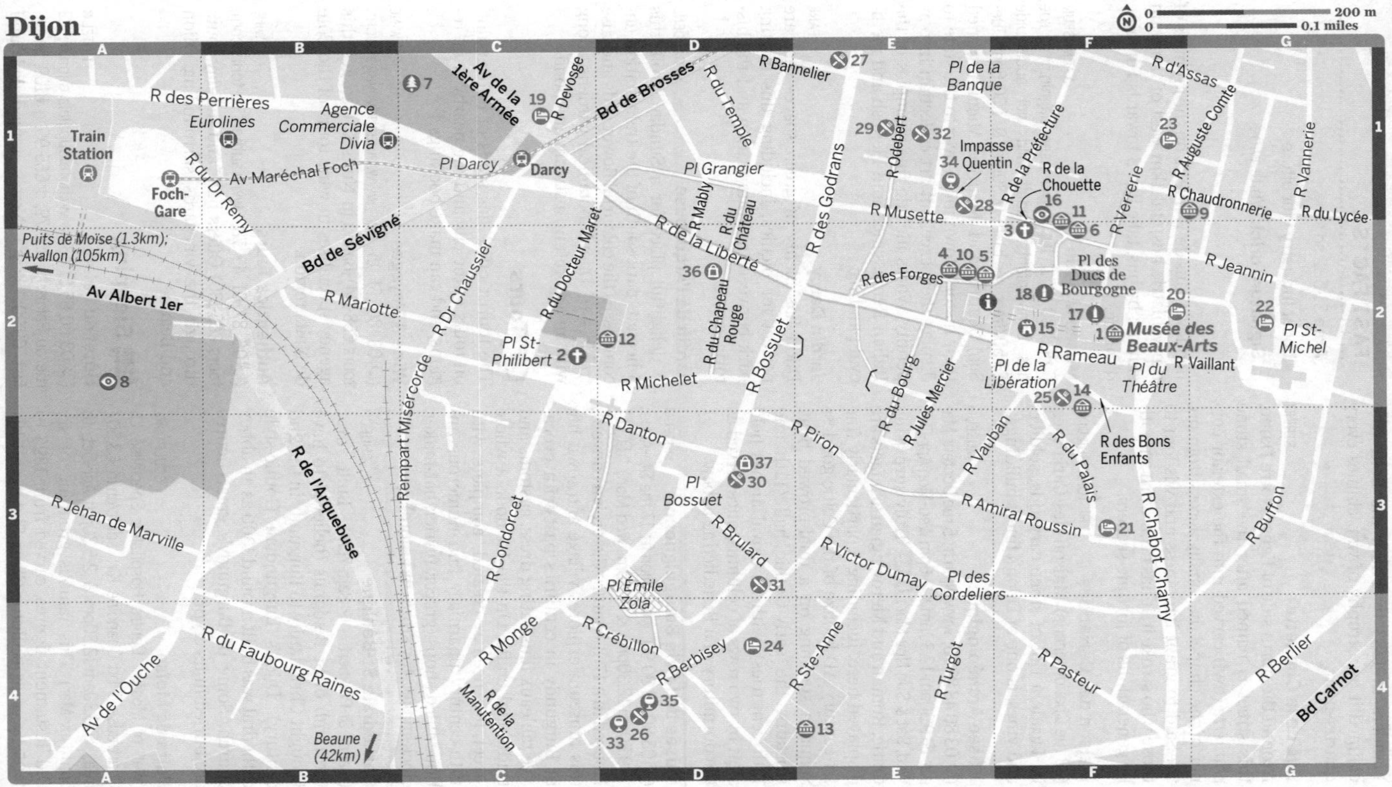
0 200 m
0 0.1 miles
Train Station
Foch-Gare
R des Perrières
Eurolines
Agence Commerciale Divia
R du Dr Remy
Av Maréchal Foch
Av de la 1ère Armée
7
19
R Devosge
Pl Darcy
Darcy
Bd de Brosses
R du Temple
R Bannelier
27
Pl de la Banque
R d'Assas
R Auguste Comte
23
R Vannerie
R du Lycée
R Chaudronnerie
9
R Verrerie
R de la Préfecture
R de la Chouette
16
11
6
3
Impasse Quentin
34
28
29
32
R Odebert
R Musette
R des Godrans
Pl Grangier
R Mably
R du Château
R de la Liberté
36
R du Chapeau Rouge
Puits de Moïse (1.3km); Avallon (105km)
Bd de Sévigné
Av Albert 1er
8
R Mariotte
R Dr Chaussier
R du Docteur Maret
12
Pl St-Philibert
2
R Michelet
R Bossuet
R des Forges
4
10
5
Pl des Ducs de Bourgogne
18
17
15
1
Musée des Beaux-Arts
R Jeannin
20
22
Pl St-Michel
R Rameau
R Vaillant
Pl du Théâtre
Pl de la Libération
25
14
R des Bons Enfants
R du Bourg
R Jules Mercier
R Piron
R Danton
37
30
Pl Bossuet
R Brulard
31
Rempart Miséricorde
R de l'Arquebuse
R Jehan de Marville
R Condorcet
R Victor Dumay
Pl des Cordeliers
R Amiral Roussin
R Vauban
R du Palais
21
R Chabot Chamy
R Buffon
Pl Émile Zola
R Monge
R Crébillon
R Berbisey
24
R Ste-Anne
13
R Turgot
R Pasteur
R Berlier
Bd Carnot
R du Faubourg Raines
Av de l'Ouche
R de la Manutention
35
26
33
Beaune (42km)

Dijon

upgraded to three-star status, this inviting hotel in a 17th-century *hôtel particulier* (private mansion) offers excellent value. The 13 rooms range from cosy, inexpensive 3rd-floor doubles tucked under the eaves to spacious, high-ceilinged family suites with abundant natural light. The location is unbeatable, on a quiet side street five minutes' walk from central place de la Libération.

Hôtel Le Chambellan HOTEL €
(03 80 67 12 67; www.hotel-chambellan.com; 92 rue Vannerie; s €50-55, d €55-60, s/d with shared bathroom €35/38;) For budget digs in the heart of medieval Dijon, it's hard to beat this small, unpretentious hotel in a building dating to 1730. Top-floor rooms under the rafters are a steal if you don't mind sharing a bath and climbing three flights of stairs.

Hôtel Le Jacquemart HOTEL €
(03 80 60 09 60; www.hotel-lejacquemart.fr; 32 rue Verrerie; s €56-69, d €65-79, s/d with shared bathroom €40/44;) In the heart of old Dijon, this two-star hotel has tidy, comfortable rooms and friendly staff. Rooms 5 and 6, in a 17th-century annexe just across the street, are larger and better equipped than those within the hotel's original core, and combine vintage touches (stone walls, beamed ceiling) with modern conveniences.

Hôtel des Ducs HOTEL €€
(03 80 67 31 31; www.hoteldesducs.com; 5 rue Lamonnoye; d €90-120, breakfast €11.50; P) A comfortable, convenient choice in the heart of medieval Dijon, this modern three-star hotel features fresh and airy rooms with a contemporary design scheme that's easy on the eye. Parking costs €12.50.

★ **La Cour Berbisey** B&B €€€
(03 45 83 12 38; www.lacourberbisey.fr; 31 rue Berbisey; r €129-159, junior ste €189-219, ste €249-279;) An arched red doorway in an ivy-draped wall leads to this luxurious B&B, easily Dijon's classiest midcity accommodation. Three enormous suites with parquet floors, beamed ceilings and tall French-shuttered windows are complemented by a lone junior suite and one smaller but equally comfortable double. Other upscale touches include an indoor swimming pool, sauna and antique-filled salon. Breakfast is included.

Grand Hôtel La Cloche HOTEL €€€
(03 80 30 12 32; www.hotel-lacloche.com; 14 place Darcy; s €165, d €195-379;) Well placed on a large park between the train station and Dijon's historic centre, this newly revamped historic five-star offers Dijon's most business-friendly accommodation. Sleek soundproofed rooms decorated with

DON'T MISS

ARCHITECTURAL GRAND DAMES: HÔTELS PARTICULIERS

Hôtel de Vogüé (8 rue de la Chouette) Behind Église Notre Dame, the 17th-century Hôtel de Vogüé is renowned for the ornate carvings around the arches of its exquisitely proportioned Renaissance courtyard. It's worth walking through the pink stone archway for a peek.

Hôtel Chambellan (34 rue des Forges) Go inside the splendid 17th-century Hôtel Chambellan, from whose courtyard a spiral stone staircase leads up to remarkable vaulting.

Hôtel Aubriot (40 rue des Forges) Originally built in the 13th-century, the Hôtel Aubriot's elegant façade owes some of its current splendour to restoration work completed in the early 1900s.

Maison Maillard (38 rue des Forges) This Renaissance-style gem sports a 16th-century façade richly ornamented with garlands, lions and other decorative motifs.

Maison Millière (10 rue de la Chouette) Figures of an owl and a cat perch high atop the roof of the 15th-century Maison Millière, which was a setting in the 1990 film *Cyrano de Bergerac* with Gérard Depardieu.

bold colour splashes offer every imaginable comfort, while the common spaces retain crystal chandeliers and other vintage touches. There's a brand-new restaurant, a spa, a pool and a garden out back.

Eating

Find loads of restaurants on buzzy rue Berbisey, around place Émile Zola, on rue Amiral Roussin and around the perimeter of the covered market. In warm months, outdoor cafes and brasseries (restaurants) fill place de la Libération.

Chez le Bougnat BURGUNDIAN €
(☎03 80 43 31 17; www.facebook.com/chezlebougnat; 53 rue Berbisey; menus €10.50-18; ⏰noon-2.30pm & 7pm-1am) Chef-owner (and former TV scriptwriter) Cyrille Doudies serves up copious plates of authentic Burgundian food at insanely low prices in this one-room eatery decorated with concert posters and old 45 RPM records. It's one of the few eateries in Dijon that opens dependably on Sundays.

Brasserie B9 BRASSERIE €
(☎03 80 38 32 02; www.brasserie-b9.com; 9 place de la Libération; mains €14-17; ⏰noon-2.30pm Tue-Sun, 6.30-9.45pm Tue-Sat) This brasserie on vast, sun-drenched place de la Libération serves up atmospheric views of the ducal palace and a €12 *plat du jour* (daily special).

Chez Nous BISTRO €
(impasse Quentin; plat du jour €10; ⏰5-10pm Mon, 11am-3pm & 6-10pm Tue-Thu, 10am-midnight Fri & Sat) This quintessentially French *bar du coin* (neighbourhood bar), often crowded, hides down an alleyway near the covered market. At lunchtime join the flock and go for the fabulous-value *plat du jour*. Wash it all down with glasses of local wine (€2).

Le Piano Qui Fume MODERN FRENCH €€
(☎09 70 35 84 63; www.lepianoquifume.com; 36 rue Berbisey; lunch menus €13-19.50, dinner menus €30-34; ⏰noon-1.45pm Mon, Tue & Thu-Sat, 7-9.45pm Thu-Sat) Market cuisine, carefully chosen ingredients, reasonably priced wines and a lovely contemporary dining room with traditional touches (exposed brick walls and beams) are the hallmarks of this popular hideaway. The lunchtime *plat du jour* is brilliant value at €9.90.

Chez Léon BURGUNDIAN €€
(☎03 80 50 01 07; www.restochezleon.fr; 20 rue des Godrans; mains €17-23, lunch menus €15-19, dinner menus €25-29; ⏰noon-2pm & 7-10.30pm Tue-Sat) From *bœuf bourguignon* (beef marinated in young red wine) to *andouillettes* (chitterling sausages), this family-run eatery offers the perfect primer course in hearty regional fare celebrated in a cosy and joyful atmosphere. There's outdoor seating in warmer months.

DZ'Envies MODERN BURGUNDIAN €€
(☎03 80 50 09 26; www.dzenvies.com; 12 rue Odebert; mains €16-22, lunch menus €13-20, dinner menus €29-36; ⏰noon-2pm & 7-10pm Mon-Sat) This zinging restaurant with cheery decorative touches is a good choice if you're tired of heavy Burgundian classics. The menu always involves seasonal, fresh ingredients, and dishes are imaginatively prepared and beautifully presented. At €18, the lunchtime 'I love Dijon' *menu* is a steal.

★ **La Maison des Cariatides** GASTRONOMIC €€€
(☎03 80 45 59 25; www.lamaisondescariatides.fr; 28 rue Chaudronnerie; lunch menus €21-27, dinner menu €58; ⏲noon-2pm & 7-10pm Tue-Sat; 📶) Basking in the glow of its newly acquired (2016) Michelin star, this renovated 17th-century mansion with exposed beams, stone walls and stellar period decor makes a delightful spot to savour top-of-the-line French and regional cuisine. There's also pleasant terrace seating out back. If you're on a budget, make a beeline for the lunch menu.

La Dame d'Aquitaine BURGUNDIAN €€€
(☎03 80 30 45 65; www.ladamedaquitaine.fr; 23 place Bossuet; menus from €37; ⏲noon-2pm Tue-Sat, 7-10pm Mon-Sat) Fine Dijonnais cuisine, accompanied by classical music and an extensive wine list, is served under the sumptuously lit bays of this 13th-century *cave* (wine cellar). The unconventional pricing concept involves paying a flat €29 fee, supplemented by small surcharges for each item ordered (€4 to €13 for appetisers, €5 to €12 for main courses and €4 to €5 for desserts).

Drinking & Nightlife

Lively bar-hopping neighbourhoods include rue Berbisey and the streets surrounding Les Halles.

L'Age de Raisin WINE BAR
(☎03 80 23 24 82; 67 rue Berbisey; ⏲6pm-2am Mon-Sat) With late hours and a welcoming ambience, this wine bar specialises in local vintages hand-selected by the knowledgeable and affable owners; it doubles as a bistro serving charcuterie and cheese platters alongside *plats du jour* built around locally sourced organic produce.

Le Quentin BAR
(☎03 80 30 15 05; www.facebook.com/bistrotquentin; 6 rue Quentin; ⏲4pm-1am Mon-Thu, 9am-2am Fri & Sat, 4-9pm Sun) This congenial drinking spot facing Les Halles overflows day and night with friendly regulars enjoying glasses of wine or fine aged rum from the wall-sized chalkboard menu. The streetside terrace allows for a dash of people-watching on market days.

L'Univers BAR
(☎03 80 30 98 29; 47 rue Berbisey; ⏲5pm-1am Mon-Sat) This energetic bar features extra-long happy hours (5pm to 10pm) and a cellar with live music on Friday and Saturday nights.

PICNIC PARADISE

Northwest of Palais des Ducs is Dijon's fabulous old covered market, **Les Halles** (rue Quentin; ⏲8am-1pm Tue & Thu-Sat). Abuzz with activity four mornings a week, it's the perfect place to stock up on fresh produce, cheeses and charcuterie for a picnic and to enjoy a spot of people-watching as you stroll among the dozens of stalls.

Shopping

The main shopping area is around rue de la Liberté and perpendicular rue du Bourg.

Mulot & Petitjean FOOD
(☎03 80 30 07 10; www.mulotpetitjean.fr; 13 place Bossuet; ⏲2-7pm Mon, 9am-noon & 2-7pm Tue-Sat) The sweet-toothed will lose all self-control at this Dijon institution dating to 1796. It's famous for its scrumptious *pain d'épices* (gingerbread made with honey and spices).

Moutarde Maille FOOD
(☎03 80 30 41 02; www.maille.com; 32 rue de la Liberté; ⏲10am-7pm Mon-Sat) When you enter the factory boutique of this mustard company, tangy odours assault your nostrils. Three-dozen varieties of mustard fill the shelves (cassis, truffle, celery etc), along with three rotating flavours on tap for you to sample.

Information

Tourist Office (☎08 92 70 05 58; www.visitdijon.com; 11 rue des Forges; ⏲9.30am-6.30pm Mon-Sat, 10am-6pm Sun Apr-Sep, 9.30am-1pm & 2-6pm Mon-Sat, 10am-4pm Sun Oct-Mar; 📶) Helpful office offering tours and maps. Also sells the €16 Dijon Côte de Nuits Pass, which offers free or reduced admission to Dijon city tours plus museums and attractions in the nearby Côte de Nuits vineyards.

Getting There & Away

BUS

Transco (☎03 80 11 29 29; www.cotedor.fr/cms/transco-horaires) Buses stop in front of the train station. Tickets are sold on-board (€1.50). Bus 44 goes to Nuits-St-Georges (45 minutes) and Beaune (1¼ hours).

Eurolines (☎08 92 89 90 91; www.eurolines.fr; 53 rue Guillaume Tell) International bus travel.

TRAIN

Connections from Dijon's train station include the following:

Lyon-Part Dieu Regional train/TGV from €32/39, two/1½ hours, 25 daily

Marseille TGV from €82, 3½ hours, six direct daily

Paris Gare de Lyon Regional train/TGV from €46/59, three/1½ hours, 25 daily

Getting Around

BICYCLE

Velodi (www.velodi.net; flat fee per week €1, rental per 30min €0.50-1), Dijon's version of Paris' Vélib' automatic rental system, has 400 city bikes at 40 sites around town.

BUS

Full details of Dijon's bus network, operated by Divia, are available online or at **Agence Commerciale Divia** (☎ 03 80 11 29 29; www.divia.fr; 16 place Darcy; ⏲ 9.30am-7pm Mon-Sat) near the train station.

CAR & MOTORCYCLE

All city-centre parking is metered. There's a free car park at place Suquet, just south of the police station.

TRAM

Divia's modern **tram system** (www.letram-dijon.fr; single ticket/day pass €1.20/3.60) has two lines, the T1 and T2. The four most helpful stops for travellers are served by both lines: Gare (train station), plus Darcy, Godrans and République stations along the northwestern edge of the Old Town.

Côte d'Or Vineyards

Burgundy's most renowned vintages come from the vine-covered Côte d'Or (literally Golden Hillside, but it is actually an abbreviation of Côte d'Orient or Eastern Hillside), the narrow, eastern slopes of a range of hills made of limestone, flint and clay that runs south from Dijon for about 60km. The exquisite terrain with its patchwork of immaculate hand-groomed vines is dotted with peaceful stone villages where every house seems to hold a vintner.

An oenophile's nirvana, the Côte d'Or vineyards are divided into two areas, Côte de Nuits to the north and Côte de Beaune to the south. The Côte de Nuits is noted for its powerful red wines, while the Côte de Beaune produces top-quality dry whites and delicate reds.

Côte de Nuits

The Côte de Nuits winegrowing area extends from Marsannay-la-Côte, just south of Dijon, to Corgoloin, a few kilometres north of Beaune. It includes the picturesque villages of Fixin, Gevrey-Chambertin, Morey-St-Denis, Chambolle-Musigny, Vougeot, Vosne-Romanée and Nuits-St-Georges.

Sights

Château du Clos de Vougeot MUSEUM, CASTLE
(☎ 03 80 62 86 09; www.closdevougeot.fr; Vougeot; adult/child €7.50/2.50; ⏲ 9am-6.30pm Sun-Fri & to 5pm Sat Apr-Oct, 10am-5pm Nov-Mar) A mandatory stop on your tour of Burgundy's vineyards, this magnificent wine-producing château (estate) provides a wonderful introduction to Burgundy's wine-making techniques. Originally the property of the Abbaye de Cîteaux, the 16th-century country castle served as a getaway for the abbots. Tours offer a chance to discover the workings of enormous ancient wine presses and casks.

Cassissium MUSEUM
(☎ 03 80 62 49 70; www.cassissium.fr; 8 passage Montgolfier, Nuits-St-Georges; adult/child €9/6.50; ⏲ 10am-1pm & 2-7pm Apr–mid-Nov, 10.30am-1pm & 2.30-5pm Tue-Sat mid-Nov–Mar) This museum and factory worships all things liqueur, with a particular focus on the blackcurrant, from which cassis is made. There's fun for the whole family: movies, displays, a 30-minute guided tour and a tasting with nonalcoholic fruit syrups for the kids. In the industrial area east of N74.

L'Imaginarium MUSEUM
(☎ 03 80 62 61 40; www.imaginarium-bourgogne.com; av du Jura, Nuits-St-Georges; adult incl basic/grand cru tasting €9/17, child €6; ⏲ 2-7pm Mon, 10am-7pm Tue-Sun) This gleaming modern museum is a good place to learn about Burgundy wines and wine-making techniques, with movies, exhibits and interactive displays, followed by a tasting.

Activities

Wine Tasting

The villages of the Côte de Nuits offer innumerable places to sample and purchase world-class wines (especially reds) a short walk from where they were made. Wine can be bought direct from the winegrowers, many of whom offer tasting, allowing you to sample two or three vintages, but at many places, especially the better-known ones, you have to make advance reservations. Lists of estates and *caves* open to the public are available from local tourist offices.

Walking

The GR7 and its variant, the GR76, run along the Côte d'Or from a bit west of Dijon to the hills west of Beaune, from where they continue southwards. The Beaune tourist office sells an excellent bilingual map, *Guide Rando Pédestre* (€3), which details 29 marked routes.

Sleeping

Maison des Abeilles B&B €

(☎03 80 62 95 42; www.chambres-beaune.fr; 4 rue Pernand, Magny-lès-Villers; d €68-78, q €113-128; 📶) New owner Céline maintains these six impeccably clean *chambres d'hôte* in Magny-lès-Villers, a small village off rte des Grands Crus, at the junction between Côte de Nuits, Haute Côte de Nuits and Côte de Beaune. Rooms have colourful linen, and breakfasts (included) are a feast of breads and homemade jams. The vast, flowery garden out back is another plus.

Hôtel de Vougeot HOTEL €€

(☎03 80 62 01 15; www.hotel-vougeot.com; 18 rue du Vieux Château, Vougeot; d €88-133; P📶) What's not to love in this gracious country manor? The 16 rooms are comfortable and impeccably maintained, many with rustically stylish features such as stone walls or exposed beams. Angle for one of the 10 rooms with a view of the Vougeot vineyards.

Les Deux Chèvres HOTEL €€€

(☎03 80 51 48 25; www.lesdeuxchevres.com; 23 rue de L'Eglise, Gevrey-Chambertin; r €175-275; 📶) Opened in 2013, this eight-room hotel occupies a renovated winery in the viticultural mecca of Gevrey-Chambertin. The varied room configurations include a lower-priced upstairs unit with vineyard views, a bright superior whose huge bathroom includes a claw-foot tub and modern shower, and a three-bedroom apartment. All guests share a fireplace room with massive stone walls and a spacious back patio.

Welsh-Polish owners Paul and Jolanta also offer weekly rentals and can organise tastings, talks on local wine history and tours of nearby vineyards.

Eating

★Le Millésime MODERN FRENCH €€

(☎03 80 62 80 37; www.restaurant-le-millesime.com; 1 rue Traversière, Chambolle-Musigny; lunch menu €20, dinner menus €32-50; ⏲noon-2pm & 7-9.30pm Tue-Sat) This renowned venture is located in an exquisitely renovated *maison de village*. The chef combines fresh local ingredients and exotic flavours in his excellent creations. Dark wood floors, well-spaced tables and a warm welcome create an easy air.

Le Chambolle BURGUNDIAN €€

(☎03 80 62 86 26; www.restaurant-lechambolle.com; 28 rue Caroline Aigle, Chambolle-Musigny; mains €17-20, menus €25-35; ⏲12.15-1.30pm & 7.15-8.30pm Thu-Tue) This unpretentious backroads gem creates traditional Burgundian cuisine with the freshest ingredients. On the D122, a bit west of Vougeot in gorgeous Chambolle-Musigny.

Chez Guy & Family MODERN FRENCH €€

(☎03 80 58 51 51; www.chez-guy.fr; 3 place de la Mairie, Gevrey-Chambertin; lunch menus €18-24, dinner menus €29-44; ⏲noon-2pm & 7-9.30pm) Its dining room is large and light, and there's a tempting choice of dishes on the fixed-price *menus*, complemented by one of the finest wine lists in the entire Côte de Nuits region. Signature seasonal specialities include tender duckling, rabbit leg and pollack.

La Cabotte MODERN FRENCH €€€

(☎03 80 61 20 77; www.restaurantlacabotte.fr; 24 Grande Rue, Nuits-St-Georges; lunch menu €19.50, dinner menus €30-57; ⏲12.15-1.30pm & 7.15-9pm Tue-Sat) This intimate restaurant serves up refined, inventive versions of French dishes. No artifice or posing here, just excellent, if sometimes surprising, food.

Shopping

Le Caveau des Musignys WINE

(☎03 80 62 84 01; 1 rue Traversière, Chambolle-Musigny; ⏲9.30am-6pm Wed-Sun, by appointment Mon & Tue) Directly below the fabulous Les Millésimes restaurant, this place represents more than 100 Côte de Nuits and Côte de Beaune winegrowers.

Getting There & Away

Transco (☎03 80 11 29 29; www.cotedor.fr/cms/transco-horaires) and **Transports Le Vingt** (☎03 80 11 29 29, 03 80 24 58 58; www.beaunecoteetsud.com/Guide-Horaires.html; tickets €1.50) offer bus services to several of the winegrowing villages.

Côte de Beaune

Welcome to one of the most prestigious winegrowing areas in the world. The Côte de Beaune area extends from Ladoix-Serrigny, just a few kilometres north of Beaune, to Santenay, about 18km south of Beaune. It

includes the delightful villages of Pernand-Vergelesses, Aloxe-Corton, Savigny-lès-Beaune, Chorey-lès-Beaune, Pommard, Volnay, Meursault, Puligny-Montrachet and Chassagne-Montrachet, which boast Burgundy's most fabled vineyards. If you're looking for an upscale wine château experience, you've come to the right place.

Sights

★Château de la Rochepot CASTLE

(☎03 80 20 04 00; www.larochepot.com; adult/child €8/6; ⏲10am-5.30pm Wed-Mon Easter-Nov) Conical towers and multicoloured tile roofs rise from thick woods above the ancient village of La Rochepot. This marvellous medieval fortress offers fab views of surrounding countryside and the interiors are a fascinating combination of the utilitarian (weapons) and the luxe (fine paintings).

Château de Meursault WINERY

(☎03 80 26 22 75; www.chateau-meursault.com; 5 rue du Moulin Foulot, Meursault; incl 7-wine tasting €21; ⏲10am-noon & 2-6pm Oct-Apr, 10am-6.30pm May-Sep) One of the prettiest of the Côte de Beaune châteaux, Château de Meursault has beautiful grounds and produces some of the most prestigious white wines in the world. Guided tours visit the estate's vast labyrinth of underground *caves*, the oldest dating to the 12th century; the 500-sq-metre 16th-century cellar is particularly impressive.

Château de Pommard WINERY

(☎03 80 22 12 59; www.chateaudepommard.com; 15 rue Marey Monge, Pommard; guided tour incl 4-wine tasting adult/child €25/free; ⏲9.30am-6.30pm Mar-Nov, to 5.30pm Dec-Feb) For many red-wine lovers, a visit to this superb château just 3km south of Beaune is the ultimate Burgundian pilgrimage. The impressive cellars contain many vintage bottles. If the tour has whetted your appetite, you can sample Burgundian specialities at the on-site restaurant.

Château Corton-André WINERY

(☎03 80 26 28 79; www.pierre-andre.com; rue Cortons, Aloxe-Corton; ⏲10am-1pm & 2.30-6pm) With its splendid cellars and colourful tiled roofs, this high-flying château is a wonderful place for a tasting session in atmospheric surrounds.

Activities

Cycling

The 20km **Voie des Vignes** (Vineyard Way), a bike route marked by rectangular green-on-white signs, goes from Beaune's Parc de la Bouzaize via Pommard, Volnay, Meursault, Puligny-Montrachet and Chassagne-Montrachet to Santenay, where you can pick up the Voie Verte (Green Way) to Cluny. Beaune's tourist office sells the detailed bilingual *Guide Rando Cyclo* map (€3).

Wine Tasting

You'll find plenty of wine-tasting opportunities in the wine-producing villages. You can stop at the famous wine châteaux or you may prefer to drop in at more laid-back wineries – look for signs.

Caveau de Puligny-Montrachet WINE

(☎03 80 21 96 78; www.caveau-puligny.com; 1 rue de Poiseul, Puligny-Montrachet; ⏲9.30am-7pm Easter-Oct, 10am-noon & 3-6pm Tue-Sun rest of year) Sample the town's namesake bijou appellation along with other fine local wines in this comfortable, relaxed wine bar and cellar in the lovely town of Puligny-Montrachet. Knowledgeable hosts Julien Wallerand and Emilien Masuyer provide excellent advice (in good English).

Sleeping

Côte de Beaune villages such as Meursault, Puligny-Montrachet, Aloxe-Corton and St-Romain offer charming accommodation in the heart of Burgundy's wine country.

★Villa Louise Hôtel HOTEL €€

(☎03 80 26 46 70; www.hotel-villa-louise.fr; 9 rue Franche, Aloxe-Corton; d €98-225; P@🛜🏊) In the pretty village of Aloxe-Corton, this tranquil mansion houses elegant, modern rooms, each of them dreamily different. The expansive garden stretches straight to the edge of the vineyard and a separate gazebo shelters the sauna and pool. Genteel Louise Perrin presides, and has a private *cave*, perfect for wine tastings. Breakfast costs €16.

Domaine Corgette RENTAL HOUSE €€

(☎03 80 21 68 08; www.domainecorgette.com; 14 rue de la Perrière, St-Romain; d or q €150; P🛜) Tucked in the centre of the quiet village of St-Romain, this renovated winery has five light and airy rooms with crisp linen and classic touches such as ornamental fireplaces and wood floors. Guests share access to a kitchen, a comfortable sitting area and a sun-drenched terrace. The rate is identical for two to four people, and there's a three-night minimum stay.

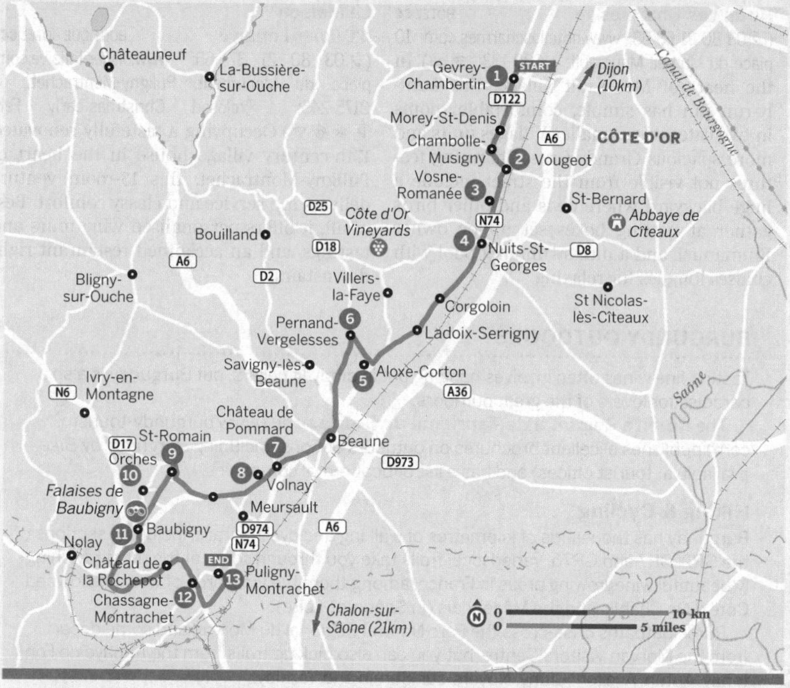

Driving Tour
Route des Grands Crus

START GEVREY-CHAMBERTIN
FINISH PULIGNY-MONTRACHET
LENGTH 55KM; ONE DAY

Burgundy's most famous wine route, the Route des Grands Crus (www.road-of-the-fine-burgundy-wines.com) follows the tertiary roads west of the N74, wending through seas of cascading vineyards dotted with stone-built villages, church steeples and château turrets. Signposted in brown, the route provides a grand tour of the world-renowned Côte de Nuits and Côte de Beaune.

Coming from Dijon, the Côte de Nuits begins in earnest just south of Marsannay-la-Côte. Most of the area's *grand cru* vineyards lie between 1 **Gevrey-Chambertin** and Vosne-Romanée. In 2 **Vougeot**, stop at the historic château. 3 **Vosne-Romanée** is famed for its Romanée Conti wines, among Burgundy's most prestigious and priciest. Continuing south, visit the Côte de Nuits' largest town, 4 **Nuits-St-Georges**, home to the Imaginarium wine museum.

On the Côte de Beaune, the impossibly steep coloured-tile roof of Château Corton-André in 5 **Aloxe-Corton** is easy to spot, just off the one-lane main street. 6 **Pernand-Vergelesses** is nestled in a little valley hidden from the N74.

South of Beaune, 7 **Château de Pommard**, surrounded by a stone wall, is on the D973 on the northeast edge of town. Wander quaint 8 **Volnay** to its hillside church. Off the main track, 9 **St-Romain** is a bucolic village situated right where vineyard meets pastureland, forests and cliffs. Hiking trails from here include the spectacular Sentier des Roches, a circuit that follows part of the GR7, and the D17I along the top of the Falaises de Baubigny (Baubigny cliffs), 300m above the Saône. Then, via the hillside hamlet of 10 **Orches**, which has breathtaking vineyard views, travel to the fantastic 15th-century 11 **Château de la Rochepot**. For a pretty finale to your journey, drive down to the villages of 12 **Chassagne-Montrachet** and 13 **Puligny-Montrachet**, where you'll have the chance to sample the world's most opulent whites.

Hotel Les Charmes HOTEL €€
(☎03 80 21 63 53; www.hotellescharmes.com; 10 place du Murger, Meursault; r €90-133;) In the heart of Meursault village, this family-run inn has simple, comfortable rooms in two categories: smaller Villages units and more spacious Grands Crus. Charming features not visible from the street include a huge backyard where owls and other birds gather at nesting boxes set up by owner Emmanuel, and a nice swimming pool with chaises longues for relaxing.

La Maison d'Olivier Leflaive BOUTIQUE HOTEL €€€
(☎03 80 21 37 65; www.olivier-leflaive.com; place du Monument, Puligny-Montrachet; d €175-245; closed Christmas-early Feb; P) Occupying a tastefully renovated 17th-century village house in the heart of Puligny-Montrachet, this 13-room venture delivers top service and classy comfort. Best of all, it offers personalised wine tours and tastings, and an acclaimed restaurant right downstairs.

BURGUNDY OUTDOORS

Tasting fine wines often involves hanging out in dimly lit cellars, but Burgundy is also a paradise for lovers of the great outdoors.

The **Comité Régional de Tourisme de Bourgogne** (www.burgundy-tourism.com) publishes excellent brochures on outdoors options (including *Burgundy by Bike*, available at tourist offices) and has a list of boat rental companies.

Hiking & Cycling

Burgundy has thousands of kilometres of walking and cycling trails, including sections of the GR2, GR7 and GR76. Varied local trails take you through some of the most ravishingly beautiful winegrowing areas in France, among them the vineyards of world-renowned Côte d'Or, Chablis and the Mâconnais (in Saône-et-Loire).

Rural footpaths criss-cross the Parc Naturel Régional du Morvan and some depart from the Morvan Visitors Centre, but you can also pick up trails from the Abbaye de Fontenay, Autun, Avallon, Cluny, Noyers-sur-Serein and Vézelay.

You can cycle on or very near the *chemin de halage* (towpath) of the Canal de Bourgogne all the way from Dijon to Migennes (225km). The section from Montbard to Tonnerre (65km) passes by Château d'Ancy-le-Franc; between Montbard and Pouilly-en-Auxois (58km), spurs go to the Abbaye de Fontenay and Semur-en-Auxois.

For details on Burgundy's planned 800km of *véloroutes* (bike paths) and *voies vertes* (green ways), including maps and guides, see www.burgundy-by-bike.com or stop at a tourist office.

Canal & River Boating

Few modes of transport are as relaxing as a houseboat on Burgundy's 1200km of placid waterways, which include the rivers Yonne, Saône and Seille and a network of canals, including the Canal de Bourgogne, the Canal du Centre, the Canal Latéral à la Loire and the Canal du Nivernais (www.canal-du-nivernais.com). Rental companies offer boats from late March to mid-November (canals close for repairs in winter).

France Afloat (Burgundy Cruisers; ☎03 86 81 54 55, in UK 08700 110 538; www.franceafloat.com; 1 quai du Port, Vermenton) Based in Vermenton (25km southeast of Auxerre), with a second base in Tonnerre.

Locaboat Holidays (☎03 86 91 72 72; www.locaboat.com; Port au Bois, Joigny) Based in Joigny (27km northwest of Auxerre), with additional bases in Montbard, Mâcon and St-Léger-sur-Dheune (27km southwest of Beaune).

Hot-Air Ballooning

From about April to October you can take a stunning *montgolfière* (hot-air balloon) ride over Burgundy. Book through the Beaune and Dijon tourist offices. Some veteran outfits:

Air Adventures (☎06 08 27 95 39; www.airadventures.fr; Pouilly-en-Auxois; Apr-Oct) Based just outside Pouilly-en-Auxois, 50km west of Dijon.

Air Escargot (☎03 85 87 12 30; www.air-escargot.com; Apr-Oct) In Remigny, 16km south of Beaune.

La Cueillette HERITAGE HOTEL €€€
(☎03 80 20 62 80; www.lacueillette.com; Château de Cîteaux, rue de Cîteaux, Meursault; r €150-360;) This grand old dame of a château, recently converted into a hotel and spa, provides luxurious digs on the edge of Meursault village. The best rooms have private terraces overlooking the vineyards, while even guests in simpler units have access to amenities including the swimming pool and the elegant downstairs bar-salon with plush leather couches and rich burgundy-tone walls.

Eating

Excellent restaurants are tucked away in the villages of the Côte de Beaune. Reserve ahead in high season.

Le Chevreuil – La Maison de la Mère Daugier MODERN FRENCH €€
(☎03 80 21 23 25; www.lechevreuil.fr; place de la République, Meursault; menus €24-60; ⏲noon-1.30pm & 7.15-9pm Mon, Tue & Thu-Sat) Chef Tiago is known for his creative take on regional staples. The dining room is country chic, and the menu takes the cream of traditional Burgundian and gives it a 21st-century spin. Try the *terrine chaude de la mère Daugier*, the house's signature offering (served here since 1870), and you'll see what we mean.

Le Cellier Volnaysien BURGUNDIAN €€
(☎03 80 21 61 04; www.le-cellier-volnaysien.com; place de l'Église, Volnay; menus €19.50-30.50; ⏲noon-1.30pm Thu-Tue, 7.30-9pm Sat) Solid Burgundian cooking in a cosy stone-walled, vaulted dining room in the heart of Volnay.

Les Roches BURGUNDIAN €€
(☎03 80 21 21 63; www.les-roches.fr; Bas Village, St-Romain; menus €29; ⏲noon-1.30pm & 7-8.30pm Thu-Mon) In the heart of the village, this sweet little spot with a pleasant outdoor setting serves farm-fresh fare and well-executed Burgundian specialities, including snails and *bœuf bourguignon*.

★ **Auprès du Clocher** GASTRONOMIC €€€
(☎03 80 22 21 79; www.aupresduclocher.com; 1 rue Nackenheim, Pommard; mains €24-37, lunch menu €26, dinner menus €32-72; ⏲noon-1.30pm & 7-9pm Thu-Mon) Celebrated chef Jean-Christophe Moutet rustles up unforgettable gastronomic delights at Auprès du Clocher, in the heart of Pommard. The ingredients are Burgundian, but imagination renders them into something new and elegant. The wine list is superb. The best tables enjoy direct views of the church bell tower for which the restaurant is named.

> **SHOPPING FOR WINE**
>
> **Domaines d'Aloxe-Corton** (☎03 80 26 49 85; place du Chapitre; ⏲10am-1pm & 3-7pm Thu-Mon Apr–mid-Nov), a polished wine shop in the charming village of Aloxe-Corton represents several makers of the excellent Aloxe-Corton appellation (terrific reds and whites).

La Table d'Olivier Leflaive BISTRO €€€
(☎03 80 21 37 65; www.olivier-leflaive.com; 10 place du Monument, Puligny-Montrachet; mains €24-26, dégustation menus €60-75; ⏲12.30-2pm & 7.30-9pm Mon-Sat early Feb–mid-Dec) This is *the* address in Puligny-Montrachet. The trademark four-course 'Repas Dégustation' (tasting menu) combines seasonal French classics with global flavours, and comes paired with six to nine wines served in 6cl glasses.

Le Charlemagne GASTRONOMIC €€€
(☎03 80 21 51 45; www.lecharlemagne.fr; 1 rte des Vergelesses, Pernand-Vergelesses; lunch menus Mon, Thu & Fri €32-39, dinner menus €63-105; ⏲noon-1.30pm & 7-9.30pm Thu-Mon) Vineyard views are perhaps even more mind-blowing than the imaginatively prepared dishes melding French cuisine with Asian techniques and ingredients. At the entrance of Pernand-Vergelesses.

Getting There & Away

Bus 20, operated by **Transports Le Vingt** (p413), runs between Beaune and several Côte d'Or wine villages, including Pommard, Meursault, St-Romain and La Rochepot.

Beaune

POP 22,540

Beaune (pronounced similarly to 'bone'), 44km south of Dijon, is the unofficial capital of the Côte d'Or. This thriving town's *raison d'être* and the source of its *joie de vivre* is wine: making it, tasting it, selling it, but most of all, drinking it. Consequently Beaune is one of the best places in all of France for wine tasting.

The jewel of Beaune's old city is the magnificent Hôtel-Dieu, France's most splendiferous medieval charity hospital.

Beaune

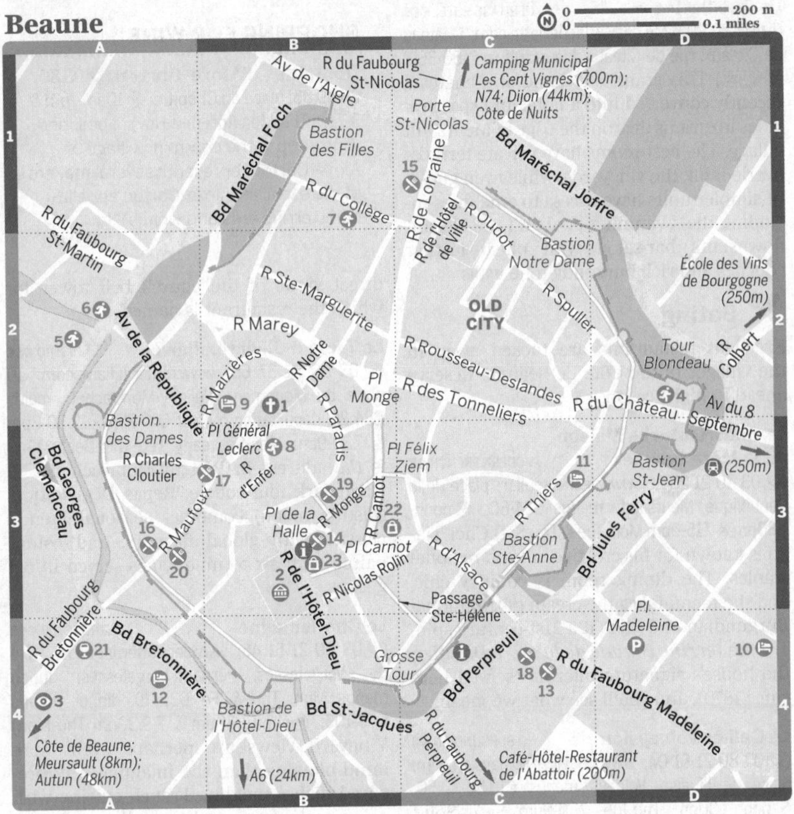

Beaune

Sights
1 Basilique Collégiale Notre Dame B2
2 Hôtel-Dieu des Hospices de Beaune B3
3 Moutarderie Fallot A4

Activities, Courses & Tours
4 Bouchard Père & Fils D2
5 Cellier de la Vieille Grange A2
6 La Cave de l'Ange Gardien A2
7 Patriarche Père et Fils B1
8 Sensation Vin B3

Sleeping
9 Abbaye de Maizières B2
10 Chez Marie D4
11 Hôtel des Remparts C3
12 Les Jardins de Loïs A4

Eating
13 Caves Madeleine C4
14 Food Market B3
15 La Ciboulette C1
16 La Lune A3
17 La Maison du Colombier B3
18 Le Bacchus C4
19 Le P'tit Paradis B3
20 Loiseau des Vignes A3

Drinking & Nightlife
21 La Dilettante A4

Shopping
22 Alain Hess Fromager B3
23 Athenaeum de la Vigne et du Vin B3

Sights

The amoeba-shaped old city is enclosed by thick stone ramparts and a stream, which is in turn encircled by a one-way boulevard with seven names. The ramparts, which shelter wine cellars, are lined with overgrown gardens and ringed by a pathway that makes for a lovely stroll.

Hôtel-Dieu des Hospices de Beaune HISTORIC BUILDING
(☎03 80 24 45 00; www.hospices-de-beaune.com; rue de l'Hôtel-Dieu; adult/child €7.50/3; ⏲9am-6.30pm mid-Mar–mid-Nov, 9-11.30am & 2-5.30pm mid-Nov–mid-Mar) Built in 1443, this magnificent Gothic hospital (until 1971) is famously topped by stunning turrets and pitched rooftops covered in multicoloured tiles. Interior highlights include the barrel-vaulted **Grande Salle** (look for the dragons and peasant heads up on the roof beams); the mural-covered **St-Hughes Room**; an 18th-century **pharmacy** lined with flasks once filled with elixirs and powders; and the multipanelled masterpiece **Polyptych of the Last Judgement** by 15th-century Flemish painter Rogier van der Weyden, depicting Judgment Day in glorious technicolour.

Moutarderie Fallot MUSTARD FACTORY
(Mustard Mill; ☎03 80 22 10 10; www.fallot.com; 31 rue du Faubourg Bretonnière; adult/child €10/8; ⏲tasting room 9.30am-6pm Mon-Sat, tours by arrangement) Burgundy's last family-run stone-ground-mustard company offers guided tours through its mustard museum, focusing on mustard's history, folklore and traditional production techniques, with kid-friendly opportunities for hand-milling mustard seeds. Another tour focuses on Fallot's modern mustard-production facility. Reserve tours ahead at Beaune's tourist office. Drop-ins can sample and purchase more than a dozen varieties in the *dégustation* room.

Basilique Collégiale Notre Dame CHURCH
(☎03 80 24 77 95; place Général Leclerc; ⏲9.30am-5.30pm) Built in Romanesque and Gothic styles from the 11th to 15th centuries, this church was once affiliated with the monastery of Cluny. It's notable for its extra-large porch and the 15th-century tapestries displayed inside, accessible by a €3 guided tour between April and December (schedules available at tourist office).

Activities

Underneath Beaune's buildings, streets and ramparts, millions of dusty bottles of wine are being aged to perfection in cool, dark cellars. Wine-tasting options abound.

La Cave de l'Ange Gardien WINE
(☎03 80 24 21 29; lacavedelangegardien@orange.fr; 38 bd Maréchal Foch) Beaune's most convivial wine-tasting experience is offered by the affable, bilingual Pierre and Nicole Jaboulet-Vercherre, whose family roots in the local winemaking business go back to 1834. Free tastings last two hours or longer, with plenty of good conversation thrown in as groups of a dozen people converge around round tables in the long cellar room.

Patriarche Père et Fils WINE
(☎03 80 24 53 01; www.patriarche.com; 7 rue du Collège; audioguide tour €17; ⏲9.30-11.30am & 2-5.30pm) Spanning 2 hectares and in business since 1780, Burgundy's largest cellars have 5km of corridors lined with about five million bottles of wine. (The oldest is a Beaune Villages AOC from 1904!) Visitors armed with multilingual audioguides can tour the premises in 60 to 90 minutes, tasting 13 wines along the way and taking the *tastevin* (tasting cup) home.

Bouchard Père & Fils WINE
(☎03 80 24 80 45; www.bouchard-pereetfils.com; 15 rue du Château; tours €25; ⏲10am-12.30pm & 2.30-6.30pm Tue-Sat year-round, plus 10am-12.30pm Sun Apr-Dec) These atmospheric cellars are housed in a former medieval fortress and feature plenty of prestigious *grands crus* from Côte de Nuits and Côte de Beaune. Visitors taste three reds and three whites on the one-hour tour (offered in French at 11am and English at 3pm).

Cellier de la Vieille Grange WINE
(☎03 80 22 40 06; www.bourgogne-cellier.com; 27 bd Georges Clemenceau; ⏲9am-noon & 2-6.30pm Mon-Sat, by appointment Sun) This no-frills wine shop is where locals come to buy Burgundy AOC wines for as little as €5.30 per litre. Tasting is free of charge.

Tours

The tourist office handles reservations for hot-air-balloon rides, and for vineyard tours run by the following companies: **Chemins de Bourgogne** (☎06 60 43 68 86; www.chemins-de-bourgogne.com), **Safari Tours** (☎03 80 24 79 12; www.burgundy-tourism-safaritours.com) and

> **DISCOUNT CARD**
>
> If you'll be taking in a lot of sights and activities, including wine tasting, in the Beaune area, consider picking up the **Pass Pays Beaunois** at the Beaune tourist offices. Ticket combos save 5% to 15% depending on the number of sights you plan to visit.

BUGUNDY WINE BASICS

Burgundy's epic vineyards extend approximately 258km from Chablis in the north to the Rhône's Beaujolais in the south and comprise 100 AOCs (Appellations d'Origine Contrôlée). Each region has its own appellations and traits, embodied by a concept called *terroir*, the earth imbuing its produce, such as grapes, with unique qualities. However, some appellations, such as Crémant de Bourgogne (a light, sparkling white or rosé) and Bourgogne Aligoté, are produced in several regions.

Wine Regions

Here's an ever-so-brief survey of some of Burgundy's major growing regions:

Côte d'Or vineyards The northern section, the Côte de Nuits, stretches from Marsannay-la-Côte south to Corgoloin and produces reds known for their robust, full-bodied character. The southern section, the Côte de Beaune, lies between Ladoix-Serrigny and Santenay and produces great reds and whites. Appellations from the area's hilltops are the Hautes-Côtes de Nuits and Hautes-Côtes de Beaune.

Chablis & Grand Auxerrois Four renowned chardonnay white wine appellations from 20 villages around Chablis. Part of the Auxerrois vineyards, Irancy produces excellent pinot noir reds. The Tonnerrois vineyards produce good, affordable reds, whites and rosés.

Châtillonnais Approximately 20 villages around Châtillon-sur-Seine producing red and white wines.

Côte Chalonnaise The southernmost continuation of the Côte de Beaune's slopes is noted for its excellent reds and whites.

Mâconnais Known for rich or fruity white wines, including the Pouilly-Fuissé chardonnay.

Want to Know More?

Tourist offices provide brochures including *The Burgundy Wine Road* and a useful map, *Roadmap to the Wines of Burgundy*. A handy website is www.bourgogne-wines.com. Lots of books are available at Beaune's Athenaeum de la Vigne et du Vin (p422).

Or take a class!

École des Vins de Bourgogne (☎03 80 26 35 10; www.ecoledesvins-bourgogne.com; 6 rue du 16e Chasseurs) Offers a variety of courses (from a three-hour, €75 fundamentals class to a three-day, €780 wine-taster's certificate program) to refine your viticultural vocabulary as well as your palate.

Sensation Vin (☎03 80 22 17 57; www.sensation-vin.com; 1 rue d'Enfer; ⌚10am-7pm) Offers a €35,1½-hour essentials class, half- and full-day tasting sessions and personalised wine-tasting circuits through the area's most famous vineyards.

Vinéatours (☎06 73 38 37 19; www.burgundy-wine-tour.com; 14 route de Monthélie, Meursault).

Bourgogne Evasion CYCLING
(☎06 64 68 83 57; www.bourgogne-evasion.fr) Offers half-day, full-day and multiday cycling tours through the vineyards, along with bike and trailer rentals. Tours meet at Beaune's tourist office on bd Perpreuil.

Festivals & Events

Festival International d'Opéra Baroque MUSIC
(www.festivalbeaune.com; ⌚Jul) Held over four weekends in July, this is one of the most prestigious baroque opera festivals in Europe. Performances (Friday to Sunday) are held at the Basilique Collégiale Notre Dame and the Hôtel-Dieu des Hospices de Beaune.

Vente aux Enchères des Vins des Hospices de Beaune WINE
(Hospices de Beaune Wine Auction; www.hospices-de-beaune.com; ⌚mid-Nov) On the third weekend in November, the Vente aux Enchères des Vins des Hospices de Beaune is the grandest of the Côte d'Or's many wine festivals. As part of this three-day extravaganza, the Hospices de Beaune holds a *vente aux enchères* (private auction) of wines from its endowment, 61 hectares of prime vineyards bequeathed by benefactors; proceeds go to medical facilities and research.

Sleeping

Camping Municipal Les Cent Vignes
CAMPGROUND €

(☎03 80 22 03 91; campinglescentvignes@mairie-beaune.fr; 10 rue Auguste Dubois; per adult/child/site €4.80/2.50/6.40; ⊙mid-Mar–Oct; 📶) A flowery, well-equipped campground 700m north of the centre.

Café-Hôtel-Restaurant de l'Abattoir
HOTEL €

(☎03 80 22 21 46; www.hotel-abattoir.fr; 19 rue du Faubourg Perpreuil; r €29, s/d incl half-board €48/78) If you don't need creature comforts and just want a central location at an unbeatable price, consider this unfussy hotel catering to local workers, with small, tidy rooms only a five-minute walk from the Hôtel-Dieu. Accommodation with half-board (breakfast and dinner) is also available. Note that reception is intermittently closed; call ahead.

★Les Jardins de Loïs
B&B €€

(☎03 80 22 41 97; www.jardinsdelois.com; 8 bd Bretonnière; r €160, ste €185-195, 2-/4-person apt €280/350; 📶) An unexpected oasis in the middle of the city, this luxurious B&B encompasses several ample rooms, including two suites and a 135-sq-metre top-floor apartment with drop-dead gorgeous views of Beaune's rooftops. The vast garden, complete with rose bushes and fruit trees, makes a dreamy place to sit and enjoy wine grown on the hotel's private domaine. Free parking.

Chez Marie
B&B €€

(☎06 64 63 48 20; www.chezmarieabeaune.com; 14 rue Poissonnerie; d €85-120, tr/q €145/170; 📶) At this peaceful haven on a residential street only a five-minute stroll from central Beaune, Marie and Yves make visitors feel right at home, sharing conversation and travel-planning advice (especially for cyclists) over breakfast in the sweet central garden. The four rooms, including two family-friendly apartments with kitchenettes, are impeccably simple and airy. Bikes (regular and electric) are available for rent.

Hôtel des Remparts
HISTORIC HOTEL €€

(☎03 80 24 94 94; www.hotel-remparts-beaune.com; 48 rue Thiers; d €97-129, ste €134-179; P❄📶) Set around two delightful courtyards, rooms in this 17th-century townhouse have red-tiled or parquet floors and simple antique furniture. Some rooms come with exposed beams and a fireplace while others have air-con. Most bathrooms have been renovated. Friendly staff can also hire out bikes. Parking costs €10.

Abbaye de Maizières
HISTORIC HOTEL €€€

(☎03 80 24 74 64; www.hotelabbayedemaizieres.com; 19 rue Maizières; d €180-245, ste €290-410; ❄@📶) This character-laden, four-star establishment inside a 12th-century abbey oozes history, yet all 12 rooms have been luxuriously modernised. Some rooms boast Cistercian stained-glass windows and exposed beams; those on the top floor offer views over Beaune's famed multicolour tile roofs. There's no lift, but the friendly staff will help haul your luggage upstairs.

Eating

Beaune harbours a host of excellent restaurants; you'll find many around place Carnot, place Félix Ziem and place Madeleine. Reserve ahead in high season.

La Maison du Colombier
TAPAS €

(☎03 80 26 16 26; www.maisonducolombier.com; 1 rue Charles Cloutier; tapas from €8) This supremely cosy 'gastro-bar' in candlelit 16th-century surrounds is the brainchild of Roland Chanliaud, former chef at the Michelin-starred Jardin des Remparts. Grab a seat beside the brick-walled open kitchen, on the sidewalk out front, or amid the labyrinth of stone-vaulted interior rooms to enjoy *tartines* (open-faced sandwiches), tapas-style cheese and charcuterie plates and an exceptional selection of Burgundian wines.

BRINGING IT ALL HOME

Dreaming of bringing a dozen or two bottles of Burgundian wine home with you, but running out of room in your suitcase? Help is at hand for overseas visitors who get a little carried away with their wine purchases. Companies such as **Côte d'Or Imports** (☎03 80 61 15 15; www.cotedorpdx.com) work with vineyards throughout Burgundy and can facilitate fully insured, door-to-door shipments to the United States or Canada for roughly €13 to €16 per bottle (depending on volume); shipments to Australia and New Zealand are also available for about €18 to €21 per bottle, plus duty – not a bad deal if you're buying the expensive stuff!

La Lune FUSION €

(☎03 80 20 77 42; la.lune.restaurant@gmail.com; 32 rue Maufoux; mains €10-22; ⏰6pm-1am Tue-Sat) Grab a counter seat and enjoy chef Seiichi Hirobe's one-man show as he prepares French-Japanese fusion treats such as tuna tartare with poached egg and lotus root, or grilled scallops with *umeboshi* (Japanese pickled plum) sauce. The abundance of fresh veggies offers a nice break from Beaune's normally richer cuisine, and long hours keep the place hopping well past midnight.

Le Bacchus MODERN BURGUNDIAN €€

(☎03 80 24 07 78; 6 rue du Faubourg Madeleine; lunch menus €14-16.50, dinner menus €29-31; ⏰noon-2pm & 7-10pm Tue-Sat) The welcome is warm and the food exceptional at this small restaurant just outside Beaune's centre. Multilingual co-owner Anna works the tables while her partner Olivier whips up market-fresh *menus* that blend classic flavours (steak with Fallot mustard) with tasty surprises (gazpacho with tomato-basil ice cream). Save room for desserts such as Bourbon vanilla crème brûlée, flambéed at your table.

La Ciboulette BURGUNDIAN €€

(☎03 80 24 70 72; 69 rue de Lorraine; menus €21-40; ⏰noon-1.30pm & 7.15-9.30pm Wed-Sun) Long popular with Beaune locals, but equally welcoming to tourists, this stone-walled, wood-beamed hideaway manages to feel both relaxed and refined, with smiling, efficient service and unpretentious but well-prepared dishes. Expect plenty of Burgundian classics, from pork cheeks in rich wine sauce to poached pears with cassis sorbet for dessert.

Caves Madeleine FRENCH €€

(☎03 80 22 93 30; 8 rue du Faubourg Madeleine; mains €19-27; ⏰noon-1.30pm & 7.15-9.45pm Mon, Tue & Thu-Sat) Focusing on fresh-from-the-farm meat and vegetables produced within a 100km radius of Beaune, this cosy little restaurant changes its menu daily. Reserve ahead for a private table, or enjoy a more convivial experience at the long shared table backed by well-stocked wine racks.

Le P'tit Paradis MODERN BURGUNDIAN €€

(☎03 80 24 91 00; www.restaurantleptitparadis.fr; 25 rue Paradis; menus €29-36; ⏰noon-1.30pm & 7.30-9.15pm Tue-Sat) This intimate restaurant on a narrow medieval street is known for *cuisine elaborée* (creatively transformed versions of traditional dishes) made with fresh local products. Summer terrace.

Loiseau des Vignes GASTRONOMIC €€€

(☎03 80 24 12 06; www.bernard-loiseau.com; 31 rue Maufoux; lunch menus €23-29, dinner menus €59-99; ⏰noon-2pm & 7-10pm Tue-Sat) For an upscale meal with your significant other, this Michelin-starred culinary shrine is the place to go. Expect exquisite concoctions ranging from caramelised pigeon to *quenelles de sandre* (pike-fish dumplings). At lunchtime even the most budget-conscious can indulge thanks to bargain-priced midday *menus*. In summer, the verdant garden is a plus.

Self-Catering

Food Market MARKET €

(place de la Halle; ⏰7am-1pm Wed & Sat) Beaune's Saturday food market is an elaborate affair, with vendors displaying their wares both indoors and on the cobblestones of Place de la Halle. There's a much smaller *marché gourmand* (gourmet market) on Wednesday morning.

Drinking & Nightlife

La Dilettante WINE BAR

(☎03 80 21 48 59; 11 rue du Faubourg Bretonnière; ⏰11am-midnight Mon, Tue & Thu-Sat) This relaxed wine bar serves a fabulous selection of wines along with soups, salads and Spanish-style tapas (small plates of cheese, Iberian ham and local charcuterie).

Shopping

Athenaeum de la Vigne et du Vin BOOKS

(☎03 80 25 08 30; www.athenaeumfr.com; 5 rue de l'Hôtel-Dieu; ⏰10am-7pm) This fabulous bookshop stocks thousands of titles, including many in English, covering everything from wine tasting to oenology (the art and science of winemaking) to gastronomy to wine literature and essays. There's also a nice selection of wine-related gifts.

Alain Hess Fromager FOOD

(☎03 80 24 73 51; www.fromageriehess.com; 7 place Carnot; ⏰9am-12.15pm & 2.30-7.15pm Mon-Sat year-round, 10am-1pm Sun Easter-Dec) This treasure trove of gourmet regional foodstuffs, including cheeses, mustards and wines will tempt the devil in you. Don't miss the Délice de Pommard, the house's signature cheese. Also look for Burgundy's famous Appellation d'Origine Protégée (AOP) cheeses: strong, creamy, orange-skinned Époisses, invented by 16th-century Cister-

cian monks; and elegant little wheels of soft white Chaource.

Information

Tourist Office (☎03 80 26 21 30; www.beaune-tourisme.fr; 6 bd Perpreuil; ⏲9am-6.30pm Mon-Sat, to 6pm Sun Apr-Oct, shorter hours Nov-Mar) Sells Pass Beaune and has lots of brochures about the town and nearby vineyards. An **annexe** (☎03 80 26 21 32; www.beaune-tourisme.fr; 1 rue de l'Hôtel-Dieu; ⏲10am-1pm & 2-6pm, closed Sun Nov-Mar) opposite the Hôtel-Dieu keeps shorter hours.

Getting There & Around

BICYCLE

Bourgogne Randonnées (☎03 80 22 06 03; www.bourgogne-randonnees.fr; 7 av du 8 Septembre; bikes per day/week €19/96; ⏲9am-noon & 1.30-6pm Mon-Sat, 10am-noon & 2-6pm Sun Mar-Oct) Rents everything you need to explore the area by bike (bikes, helmets, panniers, baby seats, tandems) and offers excellent advice on local cycling itineraries.

BUS

Bus 44, operated by Transco (www.cotedor.fr/cms/transco-horaires), links Beaune with Dijon (€1.50, 1¼ hours, two to seven daily), stopping at Côte d'Or villages such as Gevrey-Chambertin, Vougeot, Nuits-St-Georges and Aloxe-Corton. In Beaune, buses stop along the boulevards around the old city. Services are reduced in July and August. Get timetables online or at the tourist office.

TRAIN

Beaune's train station is located around 250m east of the old town along av du 8 Septembre. Trains connect the following places:

Dijon €8, 20 to 30 minutes, 40 daily
Lyon Part-Dieu from €27.20, 1¾ hours, 16 daily
Mâcon €16, 55 minutes, 19 daily
Nuits-St-Georges €3.70, 10 minutes, eight daily
Paris €50, 3½ hours, seven direct daily

Abbaye de Cîteaux

Set amid bucolic scenery between Dijon and Beaune, **Abbaye de Cîteaux** (☎03 80 61 32 58; www.citeaux-abbaye.com; D996, St-Nicolas-lès-Cîteaux; adult/child guided tour €7.50/5, video €3/1.50, tour & video €8.50/6; ⏲tours 10.30am-4.30pm Wed-Sat, 12.15-4.30pm Sun late Apr–early Oct) was founded in 1098 Cistercian monk. Nowadays you can visit the monastery on seasonal 1¼-hour guided tours in French, with printed English commentary. Tours depart hourly, and reservations are essential; phone or email ahead. There's also an audiovisual presentation available with or without the tour. The boutique sells edibles made at monasteries around France, including the abbey's own cheese.

In contrast to the showy Benedictines of Cluny, the medieval Cistercian order was known for its austerity, discipline and humility, and for the productive manual labour of its monks, one result of which was ground-breaking wine-producing techniques. The abbey enjoyed phenomenal growth in the 12th century under St Bernard (1090–1153), and some 600 Cistercian abbeys soon stretched from Scandinavia to the Near East. Cîteaux was virtually destroyed during the Revolution and the monks didn't return until 1898, but today it is home to about 35 monks. Visitors may attend daily prayers and Sunday Mass (10.30am) year-round.

DON'T MISS

KID-FRIENDLY BATTLE ZONE

Opened in 2012, the sensational **MuséoParc Alésia** (www.alesia.com; Alise-Ste-Reine; adult/child museum only €10/6, museum & Gallo-Roman site €12/7; ⏲10am-5pm mid-Feb–Mar & Nov, to 6pm Apr-Jun, Sep & Oct, to 7pm Jul & Aug) is well worth the drive from Dijon (67km) or Semur-en-Auxois (16km). This was the historic site of Alésia, the camp where Vercingétorix, the chief of the Gaulish coalitions, was defeated by Julius Caesar after a long siege. The defeat marked the end of the Gallic/Celtic heritage in France. You can visit the well-organised interpretative centre as well as the vestiges of the Gallo-Roman city that developed after the battle. It also offers entertaining programs and workshops for kids.

Pays d'Auxois

West of Dijon, along and around the Canal de Bourgogne, the Pays d'Auxois is verdant and rural. Broad mustard fields, wooded hills and escarpments are dotted with fortified hilltop towns, including Semur-en-Auxois. The excellent MuséoParc Alésia historical museum is another good reason to explore the area.

Semur-en-Auxois

POP 4510

Don't miss Semur-en-Auxois, an incredibly picturesque small fortress town. Perched on a granite spur and surrounded by a hairpin turn in the River Armançon, it is guarded by four massive pink-granite bastions, and the centre is laced with cobbled lanes flanked by attractive houses. At night the ramparts are illuminated, which adds to the appeal.

Sights

Most of the old city was built when Semur was an important religious centre boasting six monasteries. Just beyond the tourist office, pass through two concentric medieval gates, **Porte Sauvigne** (1417) and fortified **Porte Guillier** (14th century) to reach pedestrianised **rue Buffon**, lined with 17th-century houses. Further on, the **Promenade du Rempart** affords panoramic views from atop Semur's medieval battlements. Don't worry about the menacing cracks in the 44m-high **Tour de la Orle d'Or** – they've been there since 1589!

Collégiale Notre Dame CHURCH

(⏲9am-6.30pm Apr-Oct, to 5.45pm Nov-Mar) A stained-glass window (1927) and a plaque commemorating American soldiers who fell in France in WWI are inside this twin-towered, Gothic collegiate church.

> **CHEESE & WINE**
>
> What else would you pair with your glass of wine but one of Burgundy's Appellation d'Origine Protégé (AOP) cheeses?
>
> **Époisses** Invented in the 16th century by the monks at Abbaye de Cîteaux, Époisses is a soft, round, orange-skinned white cheese. It takes a month to make, using washes of salt water, rainwater and Marc de Bourgogne (local pomace brandy), resulting in a strong, creamy flavour.
>
> **Soumaintrain** Milder than Époisses, Soumaintrain has a spicy burst at the end of a tasting. Similar in appearance to Époisses.
>
> **Chaource** These elegant little wheels of soft white cheese can be quite fluid when young. A bit like Camembert, they are ideal with sparkling wines.

Sleeping

Hôtel des Cymaises HOTEL €

(☎03 80 97 21 44; www.hotelcymaises.com; 7 rue du Renaudot; s €67-73, d €73-77, tr/q €90/110; P 📶) In the heart of the old town, this grand 18th-century *maison bourgeoise* has comfortable, slightly worn rooms, some with exposed wooden beams, and a bright verandah for breakfast. There's free parking in the courtyard, and a relaxing garden out back.

★ **La Porte Guillier** B&B €€

(☎03 80 97 31 19; www.laporteguillier.com; 5bis rue de l'Ancienne Comédie; d €100-120; 📶) To really soak up the town's atmosphere, stay at this delightful B&B housed in a fortified stone gateway dating from the 14th century. Three generously sized rooms sport plenty of charming old furniture, and two enjoy stellar views of medieval Semur's main street. Nothing too standard, nothing too studied; a very personal home with good breakfasts brimming with organic specialities.

Eating

Pâtisserie Alexandre PATISSERIE €

(☎03 80 97 08 94; rue de la Liberté; ⏲7.30am-7pm Tue-Fri, 7am-1pm & 2-7pm Sat, to 1pm Sun) The speciality at this historic patisserie is *granit rose de l'auxois*, a pink confection laden with sugar, orange-infused chocolate, cherries, almonds and hazelnuts.

Le Saint-Vernier BURGUNDIAN €

(☎03 80 97 32 96; 13 rue Févret; mains €11-17, menus €16-30; ⏲noon-2pm & 7-10pm) This cosy bistro in the old town offers a variety of *menus* designed to satisfy your taste buds without spoiling your budget. Most specialities are made with locally sourced ingredients, such as Époisses cheese.

Information

The **tourist office** (☎03 80 97 05 96; www.tourisme-semur.fr/accueil-en; 2 place Gaveau; ⏲9.30am-12.15pm & 2-6pm Mon-Sat year-round, plus 10.30am-12.30pm & 2-6pm Sun Jun-Sep; 📶) has a free walking-tour brochure in English.

Getting There & Away

Transco (www.cotedor.fr/cms/transco-horaires) bus 49 (two to six daily) goes to Dijon (€1.50, 1½ hours) and Avallon (€1.50, 40 minutes). Bus 70 goes to Montbard (€1.50, 20 minutes, three to nine daily) on the Paris–Dijon rail line.

Abbaye de Fontenay

Idyllically set in a peaceful valley at road's end, **Abbaye de Fontenay** (Fontenay Abbey; ☎03 80 92 15 00; www.abbayedefontenay.com; adult/child self-guided tour €10/7, guided tour €12.50/7.90; ⏲10am-6pm Easter–mid-Nov, 10am-noon & 2-5pm mid-Nov–Easter) is a masterpiece of Cistercian monastic architecture that's well worth a short detour for anyone travelling north of Dijon.

Founded in 1118 and restored to its medieval glory a century ago, Fontenay Abbey offers a fascinating glimpse of the austere, serene surroundings in which Cistercian monks lived lives of contemplation and manual labour. Set in a bucolic wooded valley along a tranquil stream, the abbey, a Unesco World Heritage site, includes an unadorned Romanesque church, a barrel-vaulted monks' dormitory, landscaped gardens and Europe's earliest metallurgical forge, complete with a working reconstruction of the hydraulic hammer used by 13th-century monks.

A self-guided tour, with printed information in six languages, is available year-round; between Easter and mid-November, optional guided tours (in French with multilingual handout) are available every hour except 1pm.

From the parking lot, the GR213 trail forms part of two verdant walking circuits: one to Montbard (13km return), the other (11.5km) through Touillon and Le Petit Jailly. Maps and extensive guides to plant life are available in the abbey shop.

Getting There & Away

Fontenay is 25km north of Semur-en-Auxois. A taxi costs about €12 (30% more on Sunday and holidays) from the Montbard TGV station, where fast trains connect regularly with Dijon (€13.60, 35 minutes).

Châtillon-sur-Seine

POP 5940

On the northern outskirts of Burgundy, Châtillon-sur-Seine has a picturesque old quarter by the river, well-preserved buildings and a not-to-be-missed archaeology museum. It's also a good base if you want to explore the atmospheric Forêt de Châtillon and the Châtillonnais vineyards.

Sights

Musée du Pays Châtillonnais Trésor de Vix MUSEUM

(☎03 80 91 24 67; www.musee-vix.fr; 14 rue de la Libération; adult/child €7/3.50; ⏲10am-5.30pm daily Jul & Aug, closed Tue Sep-Jun) Châtillon's main claim to fame is the **Trésor de Vix** (Vix Treasure), a collection of Celtic, Etruscan and Greek objects from the 6th century BC on display at the Musée du Pays Châtillonnais. The outstanding collection includes an exquisitely ornamented, jaw-droppingly massive Greek krater; easily the largest known bronze vessel from the ancient world, it's 1.64m high, with a weight of 208.6kg and a capacity of 1100L!

The treasure was discovered in 1953 in the tomb of the Dame de Vix, a Celtic princess who controlled the trade in Cornish tin in the 6th century. Mined in Cornwall, the tin was brought by boat up the Seine as far as Vix and then carried overland to the Saône and the Rhône, whence river vessels conveyed it south to Marseille and its most eager consumers, the Greeks.

Activities

Wine Tasting

Among the wines produced in the Châtillonnais vineyards, north of town, is Burgundy's own bubbly, Crémant de Bourgogne (www.cremantdebourgogne.fr). Follow the 120km-long **Route du Crémant**, marked by white-on-brown signs to the vineyards, and allow plenty of time for a wine tasting. The tourist office can supply you with the useful map/brochure, *Route du Crémant* (free). The Champagne region's Côte des Bar vineyards are just a few kilometres further north.

Walking

The town's commercial centre, rebuilt after WWII, is bordered by two branches of the Seine, here hardly more than a stream. A short walk east, the idyllic **Source de la Douix** (dwee), a 600L-a-second artesian spring, flows from a 30m cliff. Perfect for a picnic, it is one of the oldest Celtic religious sites in Europe. Nearby, climb up to crenellated **Tour de Gissey** (c 1500s), for fine views.

The immense **Forêt de Châtillon** begins a few kilometres southeast of Châtillon. This peaceful haven is covered mainly by broadleaved trees, including beeches and hornbeams, and criss-crossed by walking trails.

Sleeping

Sylvia Hôtel HOTEL €
(☎03 80 91 02 44; www.sylvia-hotel.com; 9 av de la Gare; r €47-75; P @) At the western edge of town, this elegant mansion offers 16 simple yet welcoming rooms, a delightful garden and a bright upstairs sitting room with billiard table.

Hôtel de la Côte d'Or HOTEL €€
(☎03 80 91 13 29; www.hotel-delacotedor.fr; 2 rue Charles Ronot; d €70-110;) This atmospheric three-star in the city centre has rooms with antique furnishings, as well as a rustic restaurant (*menus* €22 to €45).

Information

Tourist Office (☎03 80 91 13 19; www.chatillonnais-tourisme.fr; 1 rue du Bourg; ⊙9am-noon & 2-6pm Mon-Sat, plus 10am-1pm Sun Jul & Aug)

Getting There & Away

Bus 50, operated by Transco (www.cotedor.fr/cms/transco-horaires), goes to Dijon (€1.50, 1¾ hours, two to four daily). SNCF buses go to the TGV train station in Montbard (€7.90, 40 minutes, three to five daily).

YONNE

The Yonne *département* (www.tourisme-yonne.com), roughly midway between Dijon and Paris, has long been Burgundy's northern gateway. The verdant countryside harbours the magical hilltop village of Vézelay, in the Parc Naturel Régional du Morvan, and the white-wine powerhouse, Chablis. Canal boats cruise from ancient river ports such as Auxerre.

Getting Around

Bus services in the Yonne are inexpensive (€2 per ride) but extremely limited. **TransYonne** (☎08 00 30 33 09; www.lyonne.com/Territoire-et-Economie/Transports-dans-l-Yonne) runs regularly scheduled buses no more than once or twice a day; additional services are available on demand, but you must reserve the day before, prior to 5pm, by internet or phone. Get timetables online or at local tourist offices.

Line 2 Links Auxerre with Pontigny.

Line 4 Links Auxerre with Chablis and Tonnerre.

Line 5 Links Avallon with Noyers-sur-Serein and Tonnerre.

Line 6 Links Auxerre with Avallon.

Auxerre

POP 36,860

The alluring riverside town of Auxerre (oh-sair) has been a port since Roman times. The old city clambers up the hillside on the west bank of the River Yonne. Wandering through the maze of its cobbled streets you come upon Roman remains, Gothic churches and timber-framed medieval houses. Views span a jumble of belfries, spires and steep tiled rooftops.

Auxerre makes a good base for exploring northern Burgundy, including Chablis, and is an excellent place to hire a canal boat.

Sights

Get wonderful city views from **Pont Paul Bert** (1857) and the arched footbridge opposite the main tourist office. For a self-guided architectural walking tour, pick up a copy of the *In the Steps of Cadet Roussel* brochure (€1.50) from the tourist office.

Abbaye St-Germain ABBEY
(☎03 86 18 02 98; www.auxerre.culture.gouv.fr; place St-Germain; abbey & museum free, crypt tours adult/child €6.90/free; ⊙10am-12.30pm & 1.45-6.30pm Apr-Sep, 10am-noon & 2-5pm Oct-Mar, closed Tue year-round) This ancient abbey with its dramatic flying buttresses began as a basilica above the tomb of St Germain, the 5th-century bishop who made Auxerre an important Christian centre. By medieval times it was attracting pilgrims from all over Europe. The **crypt**, accessible by tour (in French, with English handout), contains some of Europe's finest examples of Carolingian architecture. Supported by 1200-year-old oak beams, the walls and vaulted ceiling are decorated with 9th-century frescoes; the innermost sanctum houses St Germain's tomb.

Housed around the abbey's cloister, the **Musée d'Art et d'Histoire** displays rotating contemporary art exhibits, prehistoric artefacts and Gallo-Roman sculptures.

Cathédrale St-Étienne CATHEDRAL
(place St-Étienne; crypt adult/child €3/free, son et lumière show €5; ⊙cathedral 7.30am-6pm Mon-Fri, from 8.30am Sat & Sun, crypt 9am-1pm & 2-6pm Tue-Sat, 2-6pm Sun) This vast Gothic cathedral and its stately 68m-high bell tower dominate Auxerre's skyline. The choir, ambulatory and some of the vivid stained-glass windows date from the 1200s. The 11th-century Romanesque **crypt** is ornamented with remarkable frescoes, including a scene of

Auxerre

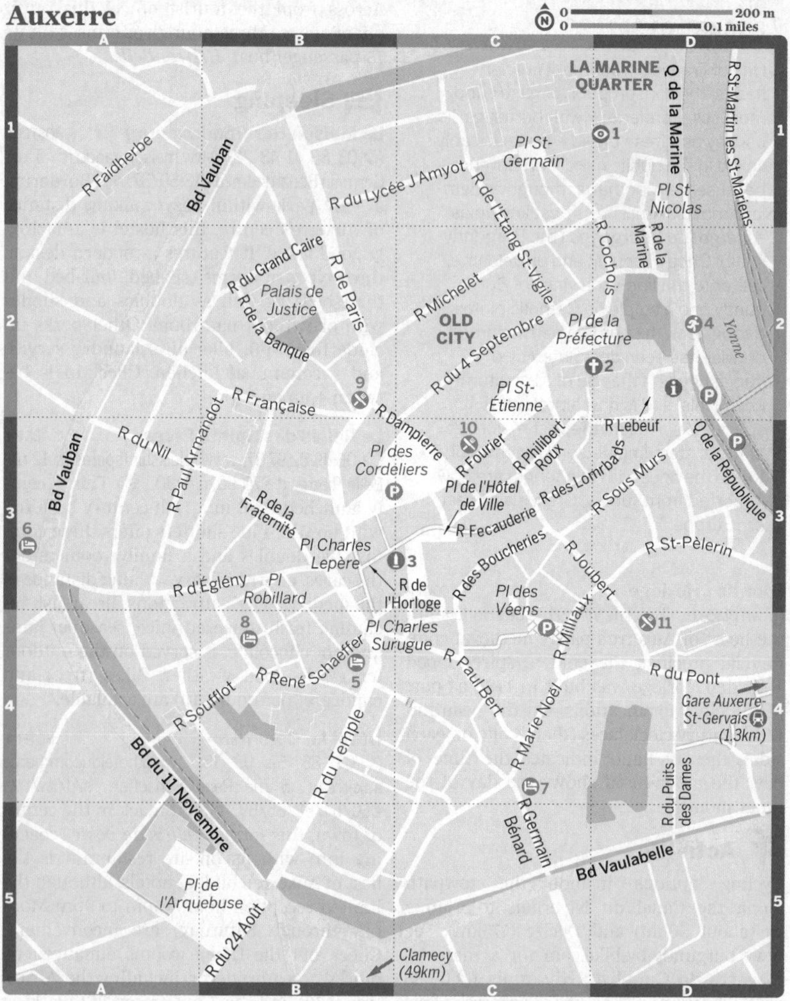

Auxerre

Sights

1 Abbaye St-Germain D1
2 Cathédrale St-Étienne D2
3 Tour de l'Horloge C3

Activities, Courses & Tours

Bateaux Touristiques de l'Auxerrois .... (see 4)
4 Boating D2

Sleeping

5 Hôtel Le Commerce B4
6 Hôtel Le Parc des Maréchaux A3
7 La Maison des Randonneurs C4
8 Le Relais des Saints Pères B4

Eating

9 L'1-Parfait B2
10 La Pause Gourmande C3
11 La P'tite Beursaude D4

Christ à Cheval (*Christ on Horseback*; late 11th century) unlike any other known in Western art. In July and August an hour-long **son et lumière** (sound-and-light) show is held Wednesday through Saturday at 10pm inside the cathedral.

ESCARGOTS

One of France's trademark culinary habits, the consumption of gastropod molluscs – preferably with butter, garlic, parsley and fresh bread – is inextricably linked in the public mind with Burgundy because *Helix pomatia*, though endemic in much of Europe, is best known as *escargot de Bourgogne* (the Burgundy snail). Once a regular, and unwelcome, visitor to the fine-wine vines of Burgundy and a staple on Catholic plates during Lent, the humble hermaphroditic crawler has been decimated by overharvesting and the use of agricultural chemicals, and is now a protected species. As a result, the vast majority of the critters impaled on French snail forks (the ones with two tongs) are now imported from Turkey, Greece and Eastern Europe.

Tour de l'Horloge TOWER
(btwn place de l'Hôtel de Ville & rue de l'Horloge) In the heart of Auxerre's partly medieval commercial precinct, the golden, spire-topped Tour de l'Horloge was built in 1483 as part of the city's fortifications. On the beautiful 17th-century clock faces (there's one on each side), the sun-hand indicates the time of day; the moon-hand shows the day of the lunar month.

Activities

Cycling options include the towpath along the Canal du Nivernais to Clamecy (about 60km) and Decize (175km); see www.burgundy-by-bike.com for a map. **La Navette du Canal du Nivernais** (☎03 86 46 24 99; www.navette-nivernais.fr; per cyclist from €45), a trailer-equipped minivan, is available to transport cyclists and their bikes back to their original starting point.

Boating BOATING
(☎03 86 52 06 19, 06 25 04 43 88; quai de la République; per 1hr/half-/full day €20/60/85; ⏲daily Easter–mid-Sep) The main tourist office rents electric boats. It takes at least 1½ hours to get to the locks on the Canal du Nivernais.

Bateaux Touristiques de l'Auxerrois BOATING
(☎09 75 23 27 89, 06 30 37 66 17; www.bateaux-auxerrois.com; 1 quai de la République; adult/child from €11/7; ⏲Tue-Sun mid-Apr–mid-Oct) Across from the tourist office, this outfit offers one- to three-hour river cruises on its 75-passenger boat, *L'Hirondelle*.

Sleeping

La Maison des Randonneurs HOSTEL €
(☎03 86 41 43 22; www.maison-rando.fr; 5 rue Germain Bénard; dm/d €18.50/37; wi-fi) Bordering a leafy park within easy walking distance of Auxerre's centre, this hostel is amazingly good value. It features a modern design, three types of dorms (six-bed, four-bed and three-bed) as well as doubles and singles with or without bathroom. Other perks include free wi-fi, bike hire, laundry service and a communal kitchen. Check-in is between 4pm and 7pm.

Le Relais des Saints Pères B&B €
(☎06 49 82 97 87; www.relaissaintsperes.fr; 12 rue Belle Pierre; d €70-90, q €130; wi-fi) This recently launched B&B in a 17th-century building with powder-blue shutters offers three comfortable doubles and a family room under the eaves, all within easy walking distance of the medieval city's attractions. Breakfast, including fresh-squeezed juice, seasonal jams and hot chocolate, is served on the outdoor terrace in good weather. Bikes (free) and childcare (per hour €10) are available.

Hôtel Le Commerce HOTEL €
(☎03 86 52 03 16; www.hotelducommerceauxerre.fr; 5 rue René Schaeffer; s/d/tw/tr/q €50/54/58/65/69; P wi-fi) Smack in the centre of town, this former *relais de poste* (coaching inn) with its on-site restaurant is the best of Auxerre's budget hotels, although the limited reception hours (5pm to 9pm Monday through Saturday) are inconvenient. Check out the theme rooms enhanced by quirkily creative decor, including the 'Africa' (room 12) and the 'Cow' (room 26). Parking costs €7.

Hôtel Le Parc des Maréchaux HISTORIC HOTEL €€
(☎03 86 51 43 77; www.hotel-parcmarechaux.com; 6 av Foch; s €91, d €121-156; P air-con wi-fi pool) Decorated in opulent 19th-century style and offering solid four-star amenities, this mansion of château-like proportions is a fine choice. The rooms, bar and common areas all brim with character. Opt for the quieter rooms that overlook the spacious private park out back. The pool is open from May to September.

Eating

★ La Pause Gourmande TEAROOM €€

(☎03 86 33 98 87; www.lapausegourmande-89.com; 1 rue Fourier; menu €25, incl 2 glasses of wine €32; ⏲9am-5.30pm Tue & Thu-Sat, to 2.30pm Wed) This sweet, unpretentious eatery near the cathedral features an ever-changing monthly menu built around fresh local produce and delectable desserts. Many of the gorgeously presented dishes come adorned with edible flowers from the greenhouse of friendly young owners David and Magali. Before noon and after 2.30pm, it doubles as a *salon de thé,* serving fine home-baked pastries.

La P'tite Beursaude BURGUNDIAN €€

(☎03 86 51 10 21; www.laptitebeursaude.fr; 55 rue Joubert; lunch menus €16-21, dinner menus €28-30; ⏲noon-2pm Fri-Mon, 7.15-9pm Wed-Mon) Waitresses wearing traditional Morvan dress serve excellent fish and meat dishes at this cosy eatery in the medieval centre. Ample dinner *menus* and bargain-priced lunches offer an introduction to Burgundian *cuisine du terroir* (traditional cuisine deeply connected to the land), which may include rib steak with Époisses cheese and *œufs en meurette* (poached eggs in red-wine sauce).

L'1-Parfait BISTRO €€

(☎03 86 40 35 03; www.1-parfait.fr; 65bis rue de Paris; lunch menu €16, dinner menus €18-31; ⏲noon-2pm & 7.30-9.30pm Tue-Sat) Popular with Auxerre's younger crowd and businesspeople in search of an affordable lunch, this trendy spot done up in red and black decor serves modern re-workings of traditional Burgundian classics: think snail tart with caramelised leeks and Chaource cheese or *poulet Gaston Gérard à la dijonnaise* (chicken stewed in a sauce of white wine, mustard and cream).

Information

Tourist Office (☎03 86 52 06 19; www.ot-auxerre.fr; 1-2 quai de la République; ⏲9.30am-12.30pm & 2-6pm Mon-Fri, to 6.30pm Sat, 10am-1pm Sun; 📶) The main branch of Auxerre's well-run tourist office is on the riverfront just below the cathedral. Offers bike and boat rentals and free wi-fi.

Getting There & Away

Trains run from **Gare Auxerre-St-Gervais** (rue Paul Doumer), 1km east of the centre:

Avallon €10.90, one hour, three daily

Dijon €29.40, two hours, 10 to 13 daily

Paris Gare de Bercy €29, 1¾ hours, 10 to 14 daily

Sermizelles-Vézelay €8.70, 40 minutes, three daily

Around Auxerre

Between the River Yonne and the Canal de Bourgogne lie the Auxerrois and the Tonnerrois, rural areas covered with forests, fields, pastures and vineyards. The quiet back roads and many of the walking trails make for excellent cycling. The standout attraction north of Auxerre is the serene 12th-century Cistercian abbey of Pontigny.

Founded in 1114, **Abbaye de Pontigny** (☎03 86 47 54 99; www.abbayedepontigny.com; Pontigny; guided tours €4.50; ⏲abbey 9am-7pm year-round, shop & grounds 10am-6pm Apr-Oct, 9.30am-4.30pm Nov-Mar) rises from the lush mustard fields 25km from Auxerre. The spectacular *abbatiale* (abbey church) is one of the last surviving examples of Cistercian architecture in Burgundy. The simplicity and purity of its white-stone construction reflect the austerity of the Cistercian order. On summer days sunshine filtering through the high windows creates an amazing sense of peace and tranquillity. *Discovering Pontigny* (€2.50), on sale in the gift shop, points out fascinating architectural details.

The Gothic sanctuary, 108m long and lined with 23 chapels, was built in the mid-12th century; the wooden choir screen, stalls and organ loft were added in the 17th and 18th centuries. Monks here were the first to perfect the production of Chablis wine.

The area south of Auxerre, anchored by the pretty town of Irancy, is known for its ruby red wines. Outlying villages have small restaurants where vineyard workers rub elbows with visitors in search of lesser-known local vintages.

In the heart of the winegrowing village of Coulanges-la-Vineuse, **Domaine Maltoff** (☎06 52 33 42 89; www.maltoff.com; 20 rue d'Aguesseau, Coulanges-la-Vineuse; r incl breakfast s €65-110; 📶) offers daily tastings along with accommodation. Rooms are simple but spacious and clean, with the nicest adjoining an upstairs terrace.

Domaine Dessus Bon Boire (☎03 86 53 89 99; www.dessusbonboire.com; 19 rue de Vallan, Vaux; s/d/tr/q incl breakfast €53/63/75/95; 📶) is a family-run B&B in sleepy riverside Vaux, 6km south of Auxerre. It offers impeccable

OFF THE BEATEN TRACK

WINE COUNTRY: IRANCY & COULANGES-LA-VINEUSE

Ask locals where they go to taste western Burgundy's wines and many say: **Irancy**. This relatively new AOC (Appellation d'Origine Contrôlée, as of 1999) predominantly uses a pinot noir grape, and the growing villages are extremely picturesque. Set in rolling hills and spring-blooming cherry orchards, Irancy and nearby **Coulanges-la-Vineuse**, which has its own appellation, lie 13km south of Auxerre. Explore and you'll find many domaines from which to sample. In Irancy you can visit organic producer **Thierry Richoux** (03 86 42 21 60; 73 rue Soufflot, Irancy; 9.30am-noon & 1.30-6pm). In Coulanges-la-Vineuse stop by **Clos du Roi** (03 86 42 25 72; www.closduroi.com; 17 rue André Vildieu, Coulanges-la-Vineuse; 8am-7pm Mon-Fri, 9am-7pm Sat, 10am-noon & 3-5pm Sun) or, in the heart of the village, Domaine Maltoff (p429), which is also a B&B. Just north of Irancy, another worthwhile stop is **Domaine Bersan** (03 86 53 33 73; www.bersan.fr; 20 rue du Docteur Tardieux, St-Bris-le-Vineux; 8.30am-noon & 1.30-6pm Mon-Sat, 10am-12.15pm Sun) in **St-Bris-le-Vineux**, a winery that's been in the same family for more than five centuries; ask to tour the medieval cellars below the tasting room.

rooms and plenty of peace and quiet. Friendly owners Catherine and André Donat, who have worked in organic viticulture since 2000, organise tours to local vineyards and share their extensive knowledge of the region's wines.

Getting There & Away

To properly explore the back roads of this area and soak up the rural beauty of the vineyards, you'll need your own set of wheels. Stray off main roads such as the D965 and onto narrower alternatives such as the D38 and D2 between Irancy and Chablis or the D124 northeast of Auxerre.

La Puisaye

The countryside west of Auxerre, known as La Puisaye, is a lightly populated landscape of woods, winding creeks and dark hills. The area is best known as the birthplace of Colette (1873–1954), author of *La Maison de Claudine* and *Gigi* (and 50 other novels) and is of particular interest because much of her work explores her rural Burgundian childhood.

Sights

Chantier Médiéval de Guédelon CASTLE

(03 86 45 66 66; www.guedelon.fr; D955, Treigny; adult/child €14/11; 10am-6pm Apr-Jun, to 7pm Jul & Aug, to 5.30pm Thu-Tue mid- to late-Mar, Sep & Oct) At this unique medieval building site, a team of skilled artisans, aided by archaeologists, has been diligently working since 1997 to build a fortified castle using only 13th-century techniques. No electricity or power tools here: stone is quarried on-site using iron hand tools forged by a team of blacksmiths, who also produce vital items such as door hinges. Clay for tiles is fired for three days using locally cut wood, and mortar is transported in freshly woven wicker baskets.

You can tour the site on your own or sign up for a guided visit (€3) in French or English. Wear closed shoes, as the site is often a sea of muck. Child-oriented activities include stone carving (using especially soft stone). Guédelon is 45km southwest of Auxerre and 7km southwest of St-Sauveur-en-Puisaye, with plenty of signposts to guide you as you draw near.

Château de Ratilly CASTLE

(03 86 74 79 54; www.chateauderatilly.fr; Treigny; adult/child €4/free; 10am-6pm late Jun–Sep, reduced hours rest of year) The elegant 13th-century Château de Ratilly sits in verdant countryside near Treigny. Interior rooms display a collection of pottery by the Pierlot family and host a changing series of excellent contemporary art exhibitions and concerts. Don't miss the magnificent 17th-century dovecote, with its original ladders and more than 1000 nesting holes for birds.

Musée Colette MUSEUM

(03 86 45 61 95; www.musee-colette.com; Château de St-Sauveur, St-Sauveur; adult/child €7/5; 10am-6pm Wed-Mon Apr-Oct) Colette, author of *La Maison de Claudine* and *Gigi*, lived till the age of 18 in the tiny town of St-Sauveur-en-Puisaye, 40km southwest of Auxerre. The Musée Colette, in the village château, displays letters, manuscripts, two furnished rooms from her apartment in Paris' Palais Royal and photos featuring her iconic hairdo.

Getting There & Away

To explore La Puisaye, you'll need your own vehicle. St-Sauveur is about 40km southwest of Auxerre via the D965 and D955. To reach Chantier Médiéval de Guédelon, continue 6km southwest of St-Sauveur on the D955; for Château de Ratilly, follow the series of signposted back roads 3.5km south from Guédelon.

Chablis

POP 2350

The well-to-do, picturesque town of Chablis, 20km east of Auxerre, has made its fortune growing, ageing and marketing the dry white wines that have carried its name to the four corners of the earth.

Chablis is made exclusively from chardonnay grapes and originated with the monks of Pontigny. Now it is divided into four AOCs: Petit Chablis, Chablis, Chablis Premier Cru and, most prestigious of all, Chablis Grand Cru. The seven *grands crus* are lovingly grown on just 1 sq km of land on the hillsides northeast of town.

Sights & Activities

Nearby villages worth exploring include Courgis, which offers great views; Chichée and Chemilly, both on the River Serein; and Chitry-le-Fort, famous for its fortified church. The gorgeous hillside village of Fleys has a number of wineries.

Southeast along rue Porte Noël are the twin bastions of Porte Noël (1778), formerly Chablis' southern town gate.

Wine Tasting

La Chablisienne WINE

(☎03 86 42 89 98; www.chablisienne.com; 8 bd Pasteur; ⏲9am-7pm Jul & Aug, 9am-12.30pm & 2-6pm Sep-Jun) To sample multiple vintages under one roof, try the cooperative cellar La Chablisienne, which carries six of Chablis' seven *grands crus*.

La Cave du Connaisseur WINE

(☎03 86 42 87 15; www.lacaveduconnaisseur.com; 6 rue des Moulins; ⏲10am-6pm, to 5pm mid-Nov–mid-Feb) In the heart of town, this place offers tastings of multiple local wines in atmospheric 13th-century cellars.

Defaix Winery WINE

(☎03 86 42 14 44; www.chablisdefaix.com; 14 rue Auxerroise; ⏲10am-2.30pm & 3.30-6pm Wed & Thu, to 9pm Fri & Sat, 10am-4pm Sun) One of Chablis' leading wineries, Defaix offers tastings and sales at its cellar wine bar in the heart of town.

Walking

An amble through Chablis' vineyard-cloaked hills is the perfect way to connect with the *terroir* before tippling. Vineyard walks from Chablis include the **Circuit des Grands Crus** (8km), the **Circuit des Clos** (13km to 24km, depending on your route) and the **Circuit du Moulin des Roches** (15.5km to 33km). The tourist office sells topoguides (€3.50) and IGN maps (€10.70).

Cycling

Cycling is a great way to tour the Chablis countryside. One flat, lush option is the 45km Chemin de Serein, which follows the old Tacot rail line southeast to Noyers-sur-Serein and L'Isle-sur-Serein. The tourist office hires **bikes** (per hour/half-day/full day €3/10/18) from May to September.

Tours

Au Coeur du Vin WINE

(☎03 86 18 96 35, 06 80 68 23 76; www.aucoeurduvin.com; tours €70-150) Tour the vineyards in a vintage Citroën 2CV.

Chablis Vititours WINE

(☎06 11 47 82 98; www.chablis-vititours.fr; tours €25-75) Tour the vineyards in an air-conditioned minibus.

Sleeping

La Menuiserie B&B €

(☎06 86 74 37 85, 03 86 18 86 20; http://lamenuiserie.pagesperso-orange.fr; 11 rue du Panonceau; s/d €75/85, q €125-145; P 📶) This is a peach of a B&B. Picture this: a former *menuiserie* (joiner's workshop) that has been renovated with a happy respect for the spirit of the place shelters one inviting room complete with exposed beams and stone walls. An upstairs mezzanine sleeps up to four additional people. Prices drop by 10% if you stay two nights or more.

Chambres d'Hôtes du Faubourg St-Pierre B&B €

(☎03 86 42 83 90; www.faubourg-saint-pierre.com; 17 rue Jules Rathier; d from €80; P 📶) Occupying a stately townhouse, this B&B is of a standard that puts many hotels to shame. The mansion's character has been lovingly preserved during refurbishment and the three rooms are large, bright and romantic.

Our choice is 'Pauline', with honey-coloured parquet flooring and a marble fireplace.

★**Maison du Moulin des Roches** B&B €€
(☎06 73 20 80 50; www.chablis-maisondumoulindesroches.fr; chemin du Moulin des Roches; d/q €125/195;) This lovingly renovated B&B, 1km outside Chablis beside an old mill on the Serein River, offers four spacious, elegantly appointed rooms. Downstairs, guests have access to a high-ceilinged fireplace room, a gym and (for a surcharge) a *hammam*. Owner Thierry, a dedicated marathon runner, prides himself on gourmet breakfasts featuring fresh-squeezed juice, local cheeses, home-grown fruit and more.

Hôtel du Vieux Moulin BOUTIQUE HOTEL €€
(☎03 86 42 47 30; www.larochehotel.fr; 18 rue des Moulins; d €120-190, ste €220-245; P) In a one-time mill smack in the centre of Chablis, the understated and very contemporary five rooms and two suites afford luscious views of a branch of the Serein. The breakfast room has *grand cru* views. Breakfast is €12.

Eating

Le Bistrot des Grands Crus BISTRO €
(☎03 86 42 19 41; www.bistrotdesgrandscrus.com; 10 rue Jules-Rathier; menus €11.50-22; noon-2pm & 7-9pm) A block southeast of Porte Noël, this hip place serves *cuisine du terroir* made with the freshest local ingredients. The €22 three-course *menu* changes three times weekly, while the €11.50 *formule* (main course plus glass of wine, available weekdays at lunch and dinner) is an excellent option for lighter eaters.

★**Au Fil du Zinc** MODERN FRENCH €€
(☎03 86 33 96 39; www.restaurant-chablis.fr; 18 rue des Moulins; menus €26-32; noon-1pm & 7.30-9pm Thu-Mon) At Chablis' newest culinary hot spot, exquisite *menus* with nods to Japanese cuisine are served in a long open dining area perched over the Serein River, and on the adjoining terrace in summer. A nine-page list of Chablis wines complements a menu that changes every 10 days, making abundant use of seasonal vegetables, local fish, meat and cheeses. Desserts are phenomenal.

Drinking & Nightlife

Wine bars and tasting rooms abound in the town centre.

S Chablis WINE BAR
(☎03 86 46 32 85; www.schablis.com; 8 rue Auxerroise; 10am-6pm Mon-Thu, to 7pm Fri & Sat, 9am-6pm Sun) English-speaking owners Arnaud and Guillaume run this combination wine shop, tasting room and self-proclaimed *oenobistro*, where you can enjoy 3cl sampler glasses (€1.25 to €4.75) or full 12cl glasses (€5 to €19) of Petit Chablis, Chablis, Premier Cru and Grand Cru wines accompanied by local cheeses, charcuterie, snails and other snacks (€5 to €15) .

Information

Tourist Office (☎03 86 42 80 80; www.chablis.net; 1 rue du Maréchal de Lattre de Tassigny; 10am-12.30pm & 1.30-6pm, closed Sun Nov-Easter) Has free maps of town and the surrounding vineyards.

Getting There & Away

Chablis is 20km (20 minutes) east of Auxerre via the D965. **TransYonne** (p426) offers very limited bus service between Auxerre and Chablis, but exploring the region is much more convenient with your own vehicle.

Tonnerre

POP 5180

The town of Tonnerre, on the Canal de Bourgogne, is best known for its Hôtel-Dieu. While the modern urban core is largely lacking in charm, the ancient Celtic spring at its heart is pure magic, making Tonnerre worth a brief visit for anyone passing near.

Sights

Fosse Dionne SPRING
(rue de la Fosse Dionne) Some 200L of water per second gushes from Fosse Dionne, a natural spring near the centre of Tonnerre that was sacred to the Celts and whose blue-green tint hints at its great depth. Legend has it that a serpent lurks at the bottom. The great circular pool is surrounded by a mid-18th-century washing house, a semi-circle of ancient houses and forested slopes.

Hôtel-Dieu HISTORIC BUILDING
(www.hoteldieudetonnerre.jimdo.com; rue de l'Hôpital; adult/child €5.50/free; 10am-noon & 2-6pm Apr–mid-Oct, 10am-noon & 2-5pm Tue & Thu-Sat rest of year) This charity hospital, founded in 1293 by Marguerite de Bourgogne (wife of Charles d'Anjou), is most famous for its vast, barrel-vaulted patients'

hall. Inside you'll find Marguerite's tomb, an unusual sculpture of the Virgin Mary with the Old Testament's Burning Bush, and an extraordinary 15th-century *Entombment of Christ*.

There's a small museum attached.

Information

The **tourist office** (03 86 55 14 48; www.tourisme-tonnerre.fr; place Marguerite de Bourgogne; 10am-noon & 2-6pm Apr–mid-Oct, 10am-noon & 2-5pm Tue & Thu-Sat rest of year), at the entrance to the Hôtel-Dieu, has maps of the Tonnerrois vineyards, walking tour info and bicycle rentals (per hour/day €3/18).

Getting There & Away

By rail, Tonnerre is linked to Dijon (€20.90, one hour, eight daily) and Auxerre (€11.70, one hour, two direct trains daily; otherwise transfer in Laroche-Migennes).

Noyers-sur-Serein

POP 670

A must-see on any Burgundy itinerary, the absolutely picturesque medieval village of Noyers (nwa-yair), 30km southeast of Auxerre, is surrounded by rolling pastureland, wooded hills and a sharp bend in the River Serein.

Stone ramparts and fortified battlements enclose much of the village and, between the two imposing **stone gateways**, cobbled streets lead past 15th- and 16th-century gabled houses, wood and stone archways and several art galleries.

Lines carved into the façade of the 18th-century **mairie** (town hall), next to the library, mark the level of historic floods.

Activities

Noyers is a superb base for walking. Just outside the clock-topped southern gate, **chemin des Fossés** leads northeastwards along the River Serein and the village's 13th-century fortifications; 19 of the original 23 towers are extant. A few hundred metres beyond the last tower, climb the marked trail to Noyers' utterly ruined hilltop château, then follow signs to the **Belvédère Sud** for spectacular perspectives on the town and the valley below.

There are also several longer hikes in the region; see the tourist office for details.

Festivals & Events

Rencontres Musicales de Noyers MUSIC
(03 86 75 98 16; www.musicalesdenoyers.com; Jul) For three weeks in July, Noyers' Église Notre-Dame hosts this series of classical concerts.

Sleeping

Le Tabellion B&B €
(06 86 08 39 92, 03 86 82 62 26; www.noyers-tabellion.fr; 5 rue du Jeu de Paume; d incl breakfast €92;) Friendly, knowledgeable and multilingual owner Rita Florin runs this attractive B&B in a former notary's office right next to the church. The three tastefully furnished and charmingly rustic rooms are rife with personality, and there's a delighful garden at the back.

La Vieille Tour B&B €
(03 86 82 87 69; place du Grenier à Sel; r incl breakfast €56-85; Apr-Sep;) In a rambling 17th-century house, this Dutch-run venture has several simply furnished *chambres d'hôte* of varying size and a cheerful garden. The best rooms, in a round medieval stone tower, have dreamy river views.

★ **Côté Serein** ACCOMMODATION SERVICES €€
(06 42 07 43 64; www.noyers-sur-serein.fr; 11 rue de Venoise; r €70-130;) Hosts Lionel and Marie-Noëlle rent out these 21 beautifully appointed rooms, suites and apartments in three historic Noyers buildings. Highlights include the Tour Madame, an atmospheric tower built into Noyers' medieval walls, complete with private panoramic terrace overlooking the Serein River, and the Loge, a two-level apartment in the town centre with its own full kitchen and plush living room.

Guests enjoy free use of rowboats and kayaks, and are welcomed (over a glass of Chablis) with oodles of tips for exploring the local area, including walking itineraries through the surrounding vineyards. Eleven of the rooms are housed within the charming Domaine de Venoise inside the old-town walls, while the Clos Malo, an additional ensemble of nine rooms outside the walls, comes with its own enclosed grassy courtyard and swimming pool.

Eating

Les Granges CAFE €
(03 86 55 45 91; www.lesgrangesnoyers.wix.com/les-granges; 7 promenade du Pré de l'Échelle; snacks from €5; 7-11pm Fri, noon-5pm Sat-Mon)

Harpist Haude Hodanger runs this inviting little tearoom between the river and the town's southern gate, serving sweet and savoury treats such as *boeuf bourguignon*, slow-roasted leg of lamb, trout with wild berries, zucchini tarts, fruit or chocolate charlottes and lemon pies, all accompanied by teas, coffees and local wines.

Restaurant La Vieille Tour MODERN FRENCH €€
(☎03 86 82 87 36; rue Porte Peinte; menus €18-25; ⊙noon-2pm Sat-Wed, 7.15-9pm daily Apr-Oct; ✎) Adjacent to the clock tower at the entrance to the historic centre, young chefs Laurens and Hélène serve a delicious, unpretentious and ever-changing menu featuring creative takes on Burgundian staples. Vegetarian options are also available.

Les Millésimes BURGUNDIAN €€
(☎03 86 82 82 16; www.maison-paillot.com; 14 place de l'Hôtel de Ville; menus €27-30; ⊙12.30-2.30pm Tue-Sun, 7-9.30pm Sat, closed Feb) This culinary haven in a meticulously restored medieval house complete with a large fireplace and sturdy wooden tables specialises in *terroir* creations ranging from *jambon au chablis* (ham flavoured with Chablis wine) to *tourte à l'Époisses* (pie with Époisses cheese). It's also renowned for its respectable wine list.

Shopping

Noyers has a sizeable population of local and expatriate artists.

DON'T MISS

GOURMET L'ISLE-SUR-SEREIN

You wouldn't necessarily expect to find a gastronomic gem in the modest village of L'Isle-sur-Serein, halfway between Avallon and Noyers-sur-Serein. But there's **Auberge du Pot d'Etain** (☎03 86 33 88 10; www.potdetain.com; rue Bouchardat, L'Isle-sur-Serein; menus €29-60; ⊙noon-1.30pm Wed-Sun, 7-8.30pm Tue-Sat, closed Feb & 2 weeks in Oct; ᯤ) , beating all the odds. The menu is classically Burgundian, built around fresh local meats, fish and vegetables, and the epic 60-page wine list has been recognised as one of France's top five. The *auberge* also shelters nine immaculate, comfy, country-style rooms (€65 to €98).

Illuminated Painting Studio ART
(Galerie Enluminures Medieval; ☎06 47 99 26 44, 06 76 31 64 26; www.diane-calvert.com; 47 place du Grenier à Sel; ⊙by appointment May-Sep) An interesting spot is Diane Calvert's illuminated painting studio where she grinds her own pigments from semi-precious stones and uses parchment and quill pens.

Création Maroquinerie LEATHER
(☎03 86 75 94 60; 24 place de l'Hôtel de Ville; ⊙10am-12.30pm & 2.30-6pm Wed-Sun) Among the town's quirky galleries is Création Maroquinerie, a fantastic leather shop full of chic belts and supple handbags. The proprietors, Yazmhil and Brice, do custom work and make everything on-site.

Information

Tourist Office (☎03 86 82 66 06; www.noyers-et-tourisme.com; place de l'Hôtel de Ville; ⊙10am-1pm & 2-5.30pm Mon-Sat year-round, plus 9.30am-1pm & 2-6pm Sun Jun-Sep)

Getting There & Away

The closest train stations are at Tonnerre (20 minutes by taxi) and Montbard (TGV station, 30 minutes by taxi).

TransYonne (p426) offers very limited bus links from Noyers to Avallon and Tonnere, but travel in the area is much more efficient with your own vehicle. Many of northern Burgundy's top attractions are within a 30- to 45-minute drive, including Auxerre, Vézelay, Abbaye de Fontenay and Semur-en-Auxois, making Noyers an excellent base for exploring the region by car.

Avallon

POP 7410

The once-strategic walled town of Avallon, on a picturesque hilltop overlooking the green terraced slopes of two River Cousin tributaries, was a stop on the coach road from Paris to Lyon in centuries past. At its most animated during the Saturday morning market, the city makes a good base for exploring Vézelay and the Parc Naturel Régional du Morvan.

Sights & Activities

A pathway descends from the ancient gateway **Petite Porte**, affording fine views over the Vallée du Cousin. You can walk around the walls, with their 15th- to 18th-century towers, ramparts and bastions. For a bucolic walk or bike ride in the **Vallée du Cousin**, take the shaded, one-lane D427, which fol-

DON'T MISS

TOP THREE: CHÂTEAU TRIPS

Château de Tanlay (☎03 86 75 70 61; www.chateaudetanlay.fr; Tanlay; adult/child €10/5; ⏲tours 10am, 11.30am, 2.15pm, 3.15pm, 4.15pm & 5.15pm Wed-Mon late-Mar–mid-Nov) The French Renaissance-style Château de Tanlay, an elegant product of the 17th century, is surrounded by a wide moat and elaborately carved outbuildings. Guided tours of the interior are offered in French and English; highlights include the **Grande Galerie**, whose walls and ceiling are completely covered with *trompe l'œil*. Find it 10km east of Tonnerre in the village of Tanlay.

Château d'Ancy-le-Franc (☎03 86 75 14 63; www.chateau-ancy.com; Ancy-le-Franc; adult/child €9/6, incl grounds $13/8, guided tour extra €1; ⏲10.30am-12.30pm & 2-5pm Tue-Sun late Mar–mid-Nov, to 6pm Apr-Sep, no midday closure Jul & Aug) The Italian Renaissance makes a cameo appearance at this imposing château, built in the 1540s by celebrated Italian architect Serlio. The richly painted interior, like the 32m-mural in the **Pharsale Gallery**, is mainly the work of Italian artists brought to Fontainebleau by François I. English-language handouts are available for self-guided tours. Don't miss Diane de Poitiers' private apartments on the ground floor, recently reopened after extensive restoration of their late-16th-century frescoes. The château is 19km southeast of Tonnerre.

Château de Maulnes (☎03 86 72 92 00; www.maulnes.fr; Cruzy-le-Châtel; adult/child €4/2; ⏲2.30-5.30pm Sat & Sun late Mar–Jun, Sep & Oct, daily Jul & Aug) The only château in France built on a pentagonal plan and buttressed by five towers, the Renaissance-era Château de Maulnes, 24km east of Tonnerre, is a fascinating sight, though fans of interior decoration may find it disappointing: the rooms are entirely bare, and parts of the structure are obscured by scaffolding due to ongoing restoration work.

lows the gentle rapids of the River Cousin through dense forests and lush meadows. The tourist office sells hiking maps and has information on Parc Naturel Régional du Morvan.

★Musée de l'Avallonnais MUSEUM
(☎03 86 34 03 19; museeavallonnais@ville-avallon.fr; 5 rue du Collège; adult/child €3/free, Wed free; ⏲2-6pm Wed-Mon Apr-Sep, Sat & Sun Oct, Feb & Mar, closed Nov-Jan) Founded in 1862, this wonderful small museum displays a series of expressionist watercolours by Georges Rouault (1871–1958) and an excellent art-deco silver collection by renowned designer and jeweller Jean Després (1889–1980). Upstairs, don't miss the permanent exhibition on the Yao people.

Collégiale St-Lazare CHURCH
(rue Bocquillot; ⏲9am-noon & 2-6pm) Eight centuries ago, masses of pilgrims flocked here thanks to a piece of the skull of St Lazarus, believed to provide protection from leprosy. The early-12th-century church once had three portals, but one was crushed when the northern belfry came a-tumblin' down in 1633; the two remaining portals are grandly decorated in Romanesque style, though much of the carving has been damaged.

Sleeping

Camping Municipal Sous Roche CAMPGROUND €
(☎03 86 34 10 39; www.campingsousroche.com; sites per adult/child/tent/car €3.70/2.10/2.90/2.90; ⏲Apr–mid-Oct; 📶) A verdant, well-maintained campground 2km southeast of the old city, just across the road from the Cousin River's forested banks. Has a play structure, RV hookups and wastewater disposal.

Hôtel Les Capucins HOTEL €
(☎03 86 34 06 52; www.avallonlescapucins.com; 6 av Président Doumer; d €54-68; ❄📶) On a quiet, plum-tree-lined side street near the train station, Avallon's best-value hotel has 25 spotless, well-appointed rooms. Cheapest are the recently updated 3rd-floor rooms under the eaves; most comfortable are the newer units out back. The attached **restaurant** (av Président Doumer; menus €18-39; ⏲noon-2pm & 7-9.30pm) serves up well-prepared Burgundian dishes. There's free parking adjacent to the small terrace and back garden. Breakfast costs €8.50.

★La Cimentelle B&B €€
(☎03 86 31 04 85; www.lacimentelle.com; 4 rue de la Cimentelle; s €80-110, d €95-125, q from €196, all

incl breakfast;) Situated on shady, extensive grounds 6km north of Avallon, this château houses two fantastic family apartments and three luxuriously appointed rooms, each one a bit different. One favourite, Hippolyte, has a free-standing claw-foot tub in front of a fireplace. Don't miss the spectacularly sited swimming pool and the sumptuous *tables d'hôte* (€46 including drinks). Nathalie, your amenable hostess, speaks English.

Le Moulin des Ruats HISTORIC HOTEL €€
(03 86 34 97 00; www.moulindesruats.com; D427; d €93-165; mid-Feb–mid-Nov;) This romantic former flour mill sits in a gorgeous wooded spot right on the River Cousin and has a ravishing waterside terrace. Cheaper rooms are a bit disappointing, but it's worth booking ahead for corner room 4, with its lovely mill and river views. Excellent Burgundian dishes are served at the peaceful riverside restaurant.

Eating

Le Vaudésir MODERN BURGUNDIAN €
(03 86 34 14 60; www.levaudesir.com; 84 rue de Lyon; mains €15-22, lunch menus €17-25; noon-2pm Tue-Sun, 7-9pm Tue & Thu-Sat) Freshness and value for money are the hallmarks of this sophisticated bistro, 800m from the centre on the road to Lyon. Quintessential dishes include *jambon à la chablisienne* (ham cooked in Chablis sauce) and *escargots en risotto*. There's outdoor seating in summer.

Dame Jeanne TEAHOUSE €
(03 86 34 58 71; www.damejeanne.fr; 59 Grande Rue Aristide Briand; snacks €7-13; 8am-7pm Fri-Wed Apr-Oct, closed Sun Nov-Mar;) Folks come from the countryside for delicious lunches or special pastry treats in the garden or 17th-century salon; it's just north of the tourist office.

Restaurant Le Moulin des Ruats BURGUNDIAN €€
(03 86 34 97 00; www.moulindesruats.com/fr/restaurant.html; D427; menus €27.50-35; noon-1.30pm Sun, 7.30-9pm Tue-Sun) This hotel restaurant is a real treat in warmer weather, when it serves its Burgundian specialities on an outdoor terrace beside the rushing Cousin River.

Information

Tourist Office (03 86 34 14 19; www.avallon-morvan.com; 6 rue Bocquillot; 9.30am-12.30pm & 2-6pm Mon-Sat Sep-Jun, 10am-6.30pm Mon-Sat, 10am-noon & 2-4pm Sun Jul & Aug;) Just south of the clock tower; has internet access.

Vézelay

POP 450

The tiny hilltop village of Vézelay – a Unesco World Heritage Site – is one of France's architectural gems. Perched on a rocky spur crowned by a medieval basilica and surrounded by a sublime patchwork of vineyards, sunflower fields and cows, Vézelay seems to have been lifted from another age.

One of the main pilgrimage routes to Santiago de Compostela in Spain starts here (see www.compostelle.asso.fr).

Sights & Activities

The **park** behind the Basilique Ste-Madeleine affords wonderful views of the Vallée de Cure and nearby villages. A dirt road leads north to the old and new **cemeteries**. **Promenade des Fossés** circumnavigates Vézelay's medieval ramparts. A footpath with fine views of the basilica links Porte Neuve, on the northern side of the ramparts, with the village of **Asquins** (ah-kah) and the River Cure. The GR13 trail passes by Vézelay.

★**Basilique Ste-Madeleine** CHURCH
(www.basiliquedevezelay.org; 7am-8pm) Founded in the AD 880s on a former Roman and Carolingian site, Vézelay's stunning hilltop basilica was rebuilt between the 11th and 13th centuries. On the famous 12th-century tympanum, visible from the narthex (enclosed porch), Romanesque carvings show an enthroned Jesus radiating his holy spirit to the Apostles. The nave has typically Romanesque round arches and detailed capitals, while the transept and choir (1185) have Gothic ogival arches. The mid-12th-century crypt houses a reliquary reputedly containing one of Mary Magdalene's bones.

The church has had a turbulent history. Damaged by the great fire of 1120, trashed by the Huguenots in 1569, desecrated during the Revolution and repeatedly struck by lightning, by the mid-1800s it was on the point of collapse. In 1840 the architect Viollet-le-Duc undertook the daunting task of rescuing the structure. His work, which included reconstructing the western façade and its doorways, helped Vézelay, previously a ghost town, spring back to life.

Visitors are welcome to observe prayers or Mass. Concerts of sacred music are held

in the nave from June to September; the tourist office and its website have details.

Musée Zervos ART MUSEUM
(☎03 86 32 39 26; www.musee-zervos.fr; 14 rue St-Étienne; adult/child €5/free; ⏰10am-6pm Wed-Mon mid-Mar–mid-Nov, daily Jul & Aug) This fantastic museum in the exquisite townhouse of Nobel Prize–winning pacifist writer Romain Rolland (1866–1944) holds the collection of Christian Zervos (1889–1970), an art critic, gallerist and friend of many modern art luminaries. He and his wife Yvonne collected paintings, sculptures and mobiles by Calder, Giacometti, Kandinsky, Léger, Mirò and Picasso (for whom he created a pivotal 22-volume catalogue).

Maison Jules Roy HISTORIC BUILDING
(☎03 86 33 35 01; rue des Écoles; ⏰2-6pm Wed-Sun, to 5pm Mon, closed mid-Nov–mid-Mar) FREE Up near the top of town, the former home of Algerian-born writer Jules Roy (1907–2000) is an enchanting spot with fine views of the basilica. Walk around the beautiful gardens and see the writer's study.

Festivals & Events

Rencontres Musicales de Vézelay MUSIC
(www.rencontresmusicalesdevezelay.com; ⏰Aug) This not-to-be-missed festival of classical music is held at various venues for four days in mid- to late August.

Sleeping

Centre Ste-Madeleine HOSTEL €
(☎03 86 33 22 14; accueil.fmj@vezelay.cef.fr; 26 rue St-Pierre; dm/s/d €18/24/42) First and foremost a pilgrims' hostel, this welcoming, well-run place reopened in 2013 after a major renovation. There are two large shared dorms, plus privates ranging from a four-bed family room to a cosy single-bed eyrie on the top floor. The location directly across from the basilica is unbeatable, and guests have access to a well-equipped shared kitchen.

Cabalus GUESTHOUSE €
(☎03 86 33 20 66; www.cabalus.com; rue St-Pierre; r €42-62) An atmospheric place to stay, Cabalus has four spacious rooms in a 12th-century building right next to the cathedral. They're sparsely decorated but come with sturdy beams, ancient tiles and stone walls. Note that the cheaper rooms have shared toilets. Organic breakfasts (€10) are served at the cafe downstairs.

WORTH A TRIP

VÉZELAY DAY TRIP

Le Château de Bazoches (☎03 86 22 10 22; www.chateau-bazoches.com; Bazoches; adult/child €9/4.50; ⏰2-6pm Feb & Mar, 9.30am-noon & 2.15-6pm Apr–mid-Nov, no midday closure Jul & Aug) sits magnificently on a hillside with views to Vézelay 12km to the north. Built in the 13th century and visited by royalty including Richard the Lionheart, it was acquired by field marshal and military strategist Marquis de Vauban in 1675. The château displays a decent collection of 17th- and 18th-century paintings and furniture.

The real appeal for French history buffs will be the chance to see the very room where Vauban, the most acclaimed military architect of his time, drafted plans for 300 fortified towns all over France. The château is still owned by his descendants.

Les Glycines BOUTIQUE HOTEL €€
(☎03 86 47 29 81; www.vezelay-laterrasse.com; rue St-Pierre; r €87-185; 📶) Named for the wisteria that cascades over the front terrace, this lovingly renovated 18th-century house near the hilltop, opened as a hotel in 2016, offers 13 rooms in various configurations. Most come with period features such as brick tile floors or exposed wood beams; some also have vintage mirrors, stone fireplaces, canopy beds or tapestries, and two boast basilica views.

The breakfast buffet features fresh-squeezed juice and treats from the Morvan park such as organic honey, preserves and *pain d'épices* (gingerbread made with honey and spices).

La Terrasse BOUTIQUE HOTEL €€
(☎03 86 33 25 50; www.vezelay-laterrasse.com; 2 place de la Basilique; r €104-143; 📶) Completely renovated in 2014, this six-room hotel enjoys a plum position opposite the basilica, complemented by numerous modern amenities: top-quality bedding, sparkling new bathroom fixtures and large flat-screen TVs. Unique touches include direct basilica views from the bath-tub in room 2 and a 12th-century stone window frame above the bed in room 4. The restaurant (p438) downstairs is among Vézelay's best.

BEYOND THE BASILICA: VÉZELAY'S HIDDEN CHAPEL

Vézelay's imposing hilltop basilica naturally commands the lion's share of tourists' attention, but a lesser-known treasure lies hidden just out back. Accessible by a lovely 15-minute stroll down a signposted trail behind the basilica, the Romanesque **Chapelle Ste-Croix** (affectionately nicknamed 'La Cordelle' after the rope belts of the Franciscan monks who adopted this spot in the 13th century) slumbers on an idyllic hillside, with espaliered grapevines climbing its stone façade. This beautiful, simple chapel was built to commemorate Bernard de Clairvaux' preaching of the Second Crusade on this very spot in 1146. Nowadays there's no sign of the throngs that filled the fields nearly nine centuries ago. Rather, the chapel has become an off-the-beaten-track refuge for pilgrims and others seeking a place for peaceful meditation in the heart of the Burgundian countryside.

Eating

À la Fortune du Pot BURGUNDIAN €
(☎03 86 33 32 56; www.fortunedupot.com; 6 place du Champ du Foire; menus €18.50-24; ⊙noon-2pm & 7-9pm) Well placed in the square at the foot of Vézelay's main street, this French-Colombian-run restaurant with English iPad *menus* is at its best in sunny weather, when tables spill out onto the terrace. Build your own two- to three-course menu featuring Burgundian classics such as escargots, *tarte à l'Époisses* (Époisses cheese tart) and bœuf bourguignon.

SY La Terrasse BISTRO €
(www.vezelay-laterrasse.com; place de la Basilique; mains €13-18, lunch menus €17-19.50; ⊙7-10pm Mon, noon-2pm & 7-10pm Tue-Sun) Stone walls, decorative tiled floors, smooth jazz and a roaring fire on chilly nights make this one of Vézelay's cosiest eateries. Menu options range from simple (the house special burger with pesto and parmesan) to fancier fare (wine-glazed scallops or rib steak with sautéed mushrooms). The bar, well-stocked with whiskeys, wines and rum, is a great spot for a nightcap.

Le Bougainville FRENCH €€
(☎03 86 33 27 57; 26 rue St-Etienne; menus €28-33.50; ⊙noon-2pm & 7-9pm Thu-Mon; ☑) The smiling owner serves rich French and Burgundian specialities such as Charolais beef and tripe sausages. If you're growing weary of heavy regional dishes, fear not – Le Bougainville is also noted for its *Menu du Jardinier* (€28), which features vegetarian options – a rarity in Burgundy!

Shopping

Vézelay has long attracted artists and writers. About half-a-dozen art galleries and several wine and crafts shops line rue St-Pierre and rue St-Étienne.

Domaine Maria Cuny (☎03 86 32 38 50; www.facebook.com/DomaineMariaCuny; 34 rue St-Étienne; ⊙by appointment), on Vézelay's main street, sells organic white wines from the tiny Bourgogne-Vézelay appellation. Owner Maria and her friendly daughter Julie can also organise vineyard tours in the region.

Information

Tourist Office (☎03 86 33 23 69; www.vezelaytourisme.com; 12 rue St-Étienne; ⊙10am-1pm & 2-6pm, closed Mon Oct-Apr & Sun mid-Nov–Easter; 📶) Sells hiking maps and offers free wi-fi.

Getting There & Away

CAR & MOTORCYCLE

Vézelay is 15km from Avallon (19km if you take the gorgeous D427 via Pontaubert). Car parks (€4 per day) are available at the base of town and behind the basilica.

TRAIN

Two daily SNCF buses link Vézelay with the nearby Sermizelles train station (€2.80, 15 minutes). From Sermizelles, trains run south to Avallon (€3.50, 10 minutes) or north to Auxerre (€8.70, 40 minutes) and Paris Gare de Bercy (€34, 2½ hours).

PARC NATUREL RÉGIONAL DU MORVAN

The 2990-sq-km Morvan Regional Park, bounded more or less by Vézelay, Avallon, Saulieu and Autun and straddling Burgundy's four *départements* (with the majority in the Nièvre), encompasses 700 sq km of dense woodland, 13 sq km of lakes, and vast expanses of rolling farmland broken by

hedgerows, stone walls and stands of beech, hornbeam and oak. The sharp-eyed can observe some of France's largest and most majestic birds of prey perched on trees as they scan for field rodents.

Sights

Several house museums and historic sites around the park, collectively known as the **Écomusée du Morvan**, explore traditional Morvan life and customs. The most important of these are located in the village of St-Brisson.

For spectacular panoramic views of the Morvan, climb to **Le Signal d'Uchon**, a 681m granite outcrop at the park's south-eastern corner, 22km south of Autun (a 30-minute drive).

Maison des Hommes et des Paysages MUSEUM
(☎03 86 78 79 10; www.parcdumorvan.org; St-Brisson; adult/child €3/2; ⏲10am-1pm & 2-6pm daily Jul & Aug, closed Sat morning & Tue mid-Apr–Jun & Sep–mid-Nov, closed mid-Nov–mid-Apr) With displays mainly in French, this thoughtfully organised museum invites visitors to contemplate the interplay between humans and the Morvan's landscapes over the centuries. Exhibits include a room-sized maquette of the park and the Salle des Panoramas, where touchscreens offer a chance to scan through photos of the region past and present.

Musée de la Résistance en Morvan MUSEUM
(☎03 86 78 72 99; www.museeresistancemorvan.fr; St-Brisson; adult/child €6.50/4; ⏲10am-1pm & 2-6pm daily Jul & Aug, closed Sat morning & Tue Apr-Jun & Sep-Nov, closed Dec-Mar) Commemorating the Morvan's role as a major stronghold for the Resistance during WWII, the Musée de la Résistance en Morvan chronicles key events and characters.

Maquis Bernard Résistance Cemetery CEMETERY
(www.ouroux-en-morvan.com/histoire/maquisfr.html) Seven RAF men (the crew of a bomber shot down near here in 1944) and 20 *résistants* are buried in the neatly tended Maquis Bernard Résistance Cemetery. It's surrounded by the dense forests in which British paratroops operated with Free French forces. The nearby drop zone is marked with signs. The cemetery is about 8km southwest of Montsauche-les-Settons (along the D977) and 5.6km east of Oroux-en-Morvan (along the D12), near the hamlet of Savelot.

Activities

The Morvan (a Celtic name meaning 'Black Mountain') offers an abundance of options to fans of outdoor activities. On dry land choose from **walking** (the park has more than 2500km of marked trails), **mountain biking**, **horse riding**, **rock climbing**, **orienteering** and **fishing.** On water, there's **rafting**, **canoeing** and **kayaking** on several lakes and the Chalaux, Cousin, Cure and Yonne rivers. Lac de Pannecière, Lac de St-Agnan and Lac des Settons have water-sports centres. Guided walks of the park, some at night (eg to observe owls), are available from April to October, and there are children's activities in July and August. **Boat tours** are available at Lac des Settons.

In the mood for **swimming**? Head for Lac des Settons or Lac de St-Agnan, which offer 'beaches' (a loose term by Morvan standards).

The **Morvan Visitors Centre** (☎03 86 78 79 57; http://tourisme.parcdumorvan.org; St-Brisson; ⏲10am-12.30pm & 2-5.30pm, closed Sat & Sun Nov-Easter) has a comprehensive list of outdoor operators.

Getting There & Away

Park headquarters in St-Brisson is 33km south of Avallon via the D10 and 45km north of Autun via the D980 and D20. The easiest way to reach the park is by private vehicle. Limited public transport from Autun to the park is sometimes available in July and August; see the Mobigo website (www.mobigo-bourgogne.com) for details.

SAÔNE-ET-LOIRE

In the southern Saône-et-Loire *département* (www.bourgogne-du-sud.com), midway between Dijon and Lyon, highlights include the Gallo-Roman ruins in Autun, Cluny's glorious Romanesque heritage and, around Mâcon, vineyards galore. Several rivers and the Canal du Centre meander among its forests and pastureland.

Autun

POP 15,210

Autun is a low-key town, but almost two millennia ago (when it was known as Augustodunum) it was one of the most important cities in Roman Gaul, boasting 6km of ramparts, four monumental gates, two theatres, an amphitheatre and a system of aqueducts. Beginning in AD 269, the city was repeatedly

DON'T MISS

CHÂTEAU SLEEP

Set in a 5-sq-km private estate 26km southwest of Autun, the delightful 16th- and 18th-century **Château de Villette** (03 86 30 09 13; www.chateaudevillette.eu; Poil; d/ste incl breakfast from €175/310, self-catering cottage €265;) offers a glimpse of the luxurious life of Burgundy's landed aristocracy. After waking up in a ravishingly furnished period room, suite or cottage, you can cycle or hunt escargots in the rolling countryside, play tennis or relax by the stress-melting pool. Reserve ahead. *Table d'hôte* dinners (€55; Wednesdays and Saturdays) receive warm praise.

sacked by barbarian tribes and its fortunes declined, but things improved considerably in the Middle Ages, making it possible to construct an impressive cathedral. The hilly area around Cathédrale St-Lazare, reached via narrow cobblestone streets, is known as the old city.

If you have a car, Autun is an excellent base for exploring the southern parts of the Parc Naturel Régional du Morvan.

Sights & Activities

For a stroll along the city walls (part-Roman but mostly medieval), walk from av du Morvan south to the 12th-century **Tour des Ursulines** and follow the walls to the north-east. The **chemin des Manies** leads out to the Pierre de Couhard, where you can pick up the **Circuit des Gorges**, three marked forest trails ranging from 4.7km to 11.5km (IGN map 2925 SB Autun – Le Creusot).

The **water-sports centre** based at Plan d'Eau du Vallon (an artificial lake east of the centre) rents kayaks, paddle boats and bikes.

★ **Cathédrale St-Lazare** CATHEDRAL

(place du Terreau; cathedral 8am-7pm Sep-Jun, plus 9-11pm Jul & Aug, chapter room summer only) Originally Romanesque, this cathedral was built in the 12th century to house the sacred relics of St Lazarus. Over the main doorway, the famous **Romanesque tympanum** shows the Last Judgment surrounded by zodiac signs, carved in the 1130s by Gislebertus, whose name is inscribed below Jesus' right foot. Ornamental capitals by Gislebertus and his school, described in a multilingual handout, adorn the columns of the nave; several especially exquisite capitals are displayed at eye level upstairs in the chapter room.

Musée Rolin MUSEUM

(03 85 52 09 76; 3 rue des Bancs; adult/child €6/free; 9.30am-noon & 1.30-6pm Wed-Mon Apr-Sep, shorter hours Mar, Oct & Nov, closed Dec-Feb) Don't miss this superb collection of Gallo-Roman artefacts, 12th-century Romanesque art, 15th-century paintings and modern art including work by Maurice Denis, Jean Dubuffet and Joan Mirò. The indisputable masterpiece here is the *Temptation of Eve*, an unusually sensual stone bas-relief by Gislebertus; sent to the Louvre for restoration in 2016, it's scheduled to return to Autun in 2017.

Théâtre Romain ARCHAEOLOGICAL SITE

(Roman Theatre; 24hr) FREE Let your imagination run wild at this ancient theatre, designed to hold 16,000 people; try picturing the place filled with cheering (or jeering), toga-clad spectators. From the top look south-west to see the **Pierre de Couhard** (Rock of Couhard), the 27m-high remains of a Gallo-Roman pyramid that was probably a tomb.

Temple de Janus ARCHAEOLOGICAL SITE

FREE Long associated (wrongly) with the Roman God Janus, this 24m-high temple in the middle of farmland 800m north of the train station is thought to have originally been a site for Celtic worship. It exudes an imposing, mysterious energy, despite the fact that only two of its massive walls still stand.

Sleeping

★ **Maison Sainte-Barbe** B&B €

(03 85 86 24 77; www.maisonsaintebarbe.com; 7 place Sainte-Barbe; s/d €80/85, ste €125-144;) Smack-dab in the old city in a 15th-century townhouse, this colourful, spotless B&B has five spacious, light-filled rooms, including one with fine views of the cathedral and a two-bedroom suite that's perfect for families. The icing on the cake? The friendly, knowledgeable owners prepare delicious breakfasts (included), and there's a verdant courtyard out back.

★ **Moulin Renaudiots** B&B €€

(03 85 86 97 10; www.moulinrenaudiots.com; chemin du Vieux Moulin; d incl breakfast €140-165; late Mar–mid-Nov;) The exterior of this old water mill is 17th-century stately; inside, it's a minimalist's dream, with vast bedrooms, tasteful colour schemes and luxurious linens. The large, gracious

garden comes complete with a swimming pool, perfect for an aperitif before enjoying a sumptuous *table d'hôte* meal (€52). The courteous hosts speak excellent English. About 3km from Autun off the road to Châlon-sur-Saône.

Eating

Le Petit Rolin CRÊPERIE, BURGUNDIAN €

(☎ 03 85 86 15 55; place St Louis; crêpes €5-11, menus €13-24; ⊙ noon-2pm & 7-9pm daily Apr-Sep, Tue-Sun Oct-Dec, closed Jan-Mar) At Le Petit Rolin, with its rustic interior dating back to the 15th century, the *bourguignonne galette* is filled with regional ingredients such as Époisses cheese and cured meat. Otherwise there are plenty of fish and meat dishes and salads to choose from. In summer, tables fill the square outside, opposite the cathedral's tympanum.

Le Monde de Don Cabillaud SEAFOOD €€

(☎ 07 60 94 21 10; 4 rue des Bancs; menus €28-33; ⊙ noon-1.30pm & 7-9pm Tue-Sat) This petite restaurant and oyster bar near Musée Rolin might not register high on the stylometer, but the convivial atmosphere makes up for it. The Breton owner serves a small but super-fresh selection of seafood dishes, prepared in a variety of styles and presented with a minimum of fuss.

Restaurant Le Chapitre MODERN FRENCH €€

(☎ 03 85 52 04 01; www.restaurantlechapitre.com; 13 place du Terreau; mains €15-25, lunch menus €15-20, dinner menus €31-40; ⊙ noon-1.30pm Wed-Sun, 7.30-9.30pm Tue-Sat) The intimate dining room in brushed-grey tones fills up with locals out for a quiet, elegant meal. Le Chapitre offers a creative French-inspired menu. Choose from the good selection of meat dishes such as Charolais beef and lamb shoulder confit, or opt for the *poisson du moment* (fish of the day). It's just behind the cathedral.

Information

Tourist Office (☎ 03 85 86 80 38; www.autun-tourisme.com; 13 rue Général Demetz; ⊙ 9.30am-12.30pm & 2-6pm Mon-Sat May, Jun & Sep, to 7pm Jul & Aug, 10am-12.30pm & 2-5.30pm Tue-Sat Oct-Apr) Sells a self-guided walking-tour brochure (€2) and hiking maps. Has information on the Parc Naturel Régional du Morvan. From June to September, it operates an annexe beside the cathedral.

Getting There & Away

For more convenient long-distance connections, **Buscéphale** (☎ 03 80 11 29 29; www.buscephale.fr) runs one to seven daily buses to the nearby Le Creusot TGV station (line 5; €1.50, 45 minutes), where TGVs depart regularly for Paris (from €66, 80 minutes) and Lyon (€36, 40 minutes).

Autun's downtown **train station** (av de la République) is on a slow tertiary line that requires a change of train to get almost anywhere. Destinations in Burgundy include Beaune (€16.20, 1¼ hours) and Dijon (€22.10, 1¾ hours).

Bibracte

For anyone who's ever read an Astérix comic book and wondered how France's Celtic people really lived, **Bibracte** (☎ 03 85 86 52 35; www.bibracte.fr; St-Léger-sous-Beuvray; ⊙ year-round) is a must-see. This hilltop stronghold of the ancient Gauls, together with the attached museum, offers a compelling portrayal of pre-Roman France.

The sprawling archaeological remains of Bibracte, capital of the Celtic Aedui people during the 1st and 2nd centuries BC, sit atop beautiful Mont Beuvray, 25km west of Autun. It was here, in 52 BC, that Vercingétorix was declared chief of the Gaulish coalition shortly before his defeat by Julius Caesar at Alésia. Caesar himself also resided here before the city decamped to Augustodunum (Autun). The site boasts expansive views, 1000 hectares of forest and numerous walking trails, including the GR13.

The excellent **Museum of Celtic Civilisation** (adult/child incl audioguide €7.50/5.50;

WORTH A TRIP

CHÂTEAU DE SULLY

This Renaissance-style **château** (☎ 03 85 82 09 86; www.chateaudesully.com; adult/child €8.80/5.60, gardens only €4.20/2; ⊙ 10am-5pm Apr-Oct, hourly guided tours in French 10.30am-4.30pm Sun Apr-Jun, Sep & Oct, daily Jul & Aug), on the outskirts of the village of Sully (15km northeast of Autun along the D973), has a beautifully furnished interior and a lovely English-style garden. It was the birthplace of Marshall MacMahon, Duke of Magenta and president of France from 1873 to 1879, whose ancestors fled Ireland several centuries ago and whose descendants still occupy the property. On Wednesday afternoons between June and September, guided visits in English can be arranged.

OFF THE BEATEN TRACK

CYCLING THE VOIE VERTE

An old railway line and parts of a former canal towpath have been turned into the **Voie Verte** (www.bourgogne-du-sud.com/index.php/la-voie-verte.html), a series of paved 'greenways' around the Saône-et-Loire *département* that have been designed for walking, cycling and in-line skating. From Cluny, the Voie Verte heads north, via vineyards and valleys, to Givry (42km) and Santenay.

10am-6pm mid-Mar–mid-Nov, to 7pm Jul & Aug) is housed in an impressive minimalist building designed by Pierre-Louis Faloci. Exhibits explain the technologies, such as a sophisticated system of ramparts, and culture of the Celtic Gauls throughout Europe and also display finds from the site. During the high season there are guided tours and lecture/workshop programs. A Zen-feeling cafe provides set meals and picnic baskets.

Walkers will also love Bibracte for its trails through high-altitude fields and forests.

Tournus

POP 6250

Tournus, on the Saône, is known for its 10th- to 12th-century Romanesque abbey church. The scenic roads that link Tournus with Cluny, including the D14, D15, D82 and D56, pass through lots of tiny villages, many with charming churches. The medieval hilltop village of **Brancion**, with its 12th-century church and **château** (03 85 32 19 70; www.chateau-de-brancion.fr; adult/child €6/3; 10am-12.30pm & 1-6.30pm Apr-Sep, to 5pm Oct–mid-Nov, closed mid-Nov–Mar), is a lovely place to wander, while **Chardonnay** is, as one would expect, surrounded by vineyards. There's a panoramic view from 579m **Mont St-Romain**.

A masterpiece of 10th- to 12th-century Romanesque architecture, **Abbatiale St-Philibert** (www.tournus.fr/le-site-abbatial-de-saint-philibert; 8am-6pm) has a beautiful 12th-century bell tower, along with some superb and extremely rare 12th-century mosaics of the calendar and the zodiac which were discovered by chance in 2002.

A few steps south of the abbey, **Le Bourgogne** (03 85 51 12 23; 37 rue du Dr Privey; menus €17-27; noon-2.30pm & 7-10pm Thu-Mon) serves delicious, authentic and well-priced *cuisine bourguignonne* (Burgundy cuisine), accompanied by an excellent selection of local wines.

Tournus' best bars are down by the Saône riverfront, along quai de Saône and quai du Midi.

Getting There & Away

The train station is just north and across the D906 from Tournus' abbey. Trains run north to Beaune (€10.90, 40 minutes) and Dijon (€16.60, one hour), and south to Mâcon (€7.40, 15 minutes) and Lyon (€18.60, 1¼ hours).

Cluny

POP 5090

The remains of Cluny's great abbey – Christendom's largest church until the construction of St Peter's Basilica in the Vatican – are fragmentary and scattered, barely discernible among the houses and green spaces of the modern-day town. But with a bit of imagination, it's possible to picture how things looked in the 12th century, when Cluny's Benedictine abbey, renowned for its wealth and power and answerable only to the pope, held sway over 1100 priories and monasteries stretching from Poland to Portugal.

Sights

★**Église Abbatiale** CHURCH

(03 85 59 15 93; www.cluny-abbaye.fr; place du 11 Août 1944; combined ticket with Musée d'Art et d'Archéologie adult/child €9.50/free; 9.30am-7pm Jul & Aug, to 6pm Apr-Jun & Sep, to 5pm Oct-Mar) Cluny's vast abbey church, built between 1088 and 1130, once extended all the way from the map table in front of the **Palais Jean de Bourbon** to the trees near the octagonal **Clocher de l'Eau Bénite** (Tower of the Holy Water) and the adjoining square **Tour de l'Horloge** (Clock Tower) – a staggering 187m! Virtual reality displays help modern-day visitors envision the grandeur of the medieval abbey while exploring its scant ruins. English-language audioguides and self-guided tour booklets are available.

Tour des Fromages TOWER

(rue Mercière; €2, combined ticket with Église Abbatiale & Musée d'Art et d'Archéologie adult/child €11/1; 9.30am-6.30pm May-Sep, shorter hours Oct-Apr) To better appreciate the abbey's vastness, climb the 120 steps to the top of this tower, once used to ripen cheeses. Access is through the tourist office.

Haras National FARM

(National Stud Farm; ☎03 85 59 85 19; www.ifce.fr/haras-nationaux/nos-sites/haras-national-de-cluny; 2 rue Porte des Prés; guided tour adult/child €6.50/free; ⏲Mar-Oct) Founded by Napoléon in 1806, the Haras National houses some of France's finest thoroughbreds, ponies and draught horses. A regular schedule of afternoon guided tours runs from March to October (see website for details). On Thursdays from mid-July through August, reserve ahead for the 'jeudis de Cluny' (adult/child €9/5), special weekly events that include music and expert riding demonstrations.

Musée d'Art et d'Archéologie MUSEUM

(rue de l'Abbatiale; combined ticket with Église Abbatiale adult/child €9.50/free; ⏲9.30am-7pm Jul & Aug, to 6pm Apr-Jun & Sep, to 5pm Oct-Mar) For an enlightening historical perspective on Cluny and its abbey, start your visit at this archaeological museum inside the Palais Jean de Bourbon. Displays include a model of the Cluny complex, a 10-minute computer-generated 3D 'virtual tour' of the abbey as it looked in the Middle Ages and some superb Romanesque carvings. A combined ticket covers the museum and abbey.

Sleeping

★Le Clos de l'Abbaye B&B €

(☎03 85 59 22 06; www.closdelabbaye.fr; 6 place du Marché; s/d €65/70, q €105-120; 📶) At this handsome old house directly adjoining the abbey, the three spacious, comfortable and stylishly decorated bedrooms and two family-friendly suites are flanked by a lovely garden with facilities for kids. Friendly, energetic owners Claire and Pascal are excellent tour advisers who direct guests to little-known treasures. There's a wonderful Saturday morning market just outside the front door.

Cluny Séjour HOSTEL €

(☎03 85 59 08 83; www.cluny-sejour.blogspot.com; 22 rue Porte de Paris; dm/s/d €20.50/22/41; ⏲mid-Jan–mid-Dec; P) Clean, bright two- to four-bed rooms, excellent showers and helpful staff make this simple, well-located hostel a real winner. Towels cost €2.70, and the optional breakfast costs €3.

La Pierre Folle B&B €

(☎03 85 59 20 14; www.lapierrefolle.com; D980; s/d/tr/q €70/80/100/120, ste s/d/tr/q €89/102/122/140; 📶) Surrounded by rolling fields just south of town, this immaculate B&B offers four spacious, comfortable rooms and one suite. Friendly owners Véronique and Luigi are generous with information about the local area, and serve delicious breakfasts (included) as well as Italian-influenced, four-course *table d'hôte* dinners (€28, book ahead).

Hôtel de Bourgogne HISTORIC HOTEL €€

(☎03 85 59 00 58; www.hotel-cluny.com; place de l'Abbaye; d €89-135, ste €159-165, 5-person apt €159-165; ⏲Feb-Nov; P📶) This family-run hotel sits right next to the remains of the abbey. Built in 1817, it has a casual lounge area, 13 antique-furnished rooms and three family-friendly apartments. Breakfast (€11) is served in an enchanting courtyard. Parking costs €10.

Eating

Le Pain sur la Table BAKERY €

(☎03 85 59 24 50; www.lepainsurlatable.fr; 1 Pont de l'Étang; daily specials €11, menus €15.50-23; ⏲bakery 8am-7pm Tue-Sat, lunch noon-2pm Tue-Sat; 🌿) A local favourite, this organic bakery near the bridge at Cluny's southern edge doubles as an informal restaurant serving healthy soups, sandwiches and other light meals. The daily-changing lunch menu always includes at least one vegetarian appetiser and main dish. Outside of the midday hours, it's a great spot for coffee and fresh-baked pastries.

Brasserie du Nord BRASSERIE €

(☎03 85 59 09 96; 1 place du Marché; mains €9.50-17.50; ⏲7am-11pm Mon-Sat, from 8am Sun) This brasserie boasts an expansive terrace in a top-notch location – just opposite the Église Abbatiale. The eclectic menu runs the

LOCAL KNOWLEDGE

ARTISAN BEER

Since 2012, **Brasserie de Vézelay** (☎03 86 34 98 38; www.brasseriedevezelay.com; rue du Gravier, St-Père-sous-Vézelay; ⏲11am-9pm daily May-Oct, 11am-5pm Mon-Fri, 2-6pm Sat Nov-Apr) near the Cure River has been brewing fine beers, all made according to Germany's strict purity law, using organic malt, hops, yeast and water from the adjoining Morvan park. Children can frolic on the big grassy lawn while their parents sample the award-winning stout, *hefeweizen* and *rauchbier*. There's live music on the outdoor terrace in summer.

gamut from salads and pasta to frogs' legs and meat dishes. Better still, it's well priced and stays open late (an exception in sedate Cluny).

Le Bistrot BISTRO €

(☎03 85 59 08 07; 14 place du Commerce; mains €10-19; ⊙8.30am-11pm Wed-Sun; 📶) This character-filled bistro whose walls are adorned with cool vintage posters and old clocks is a real charmer. The flavourful *ravioles* (ravioli with cheese filling) and frondy salads are the house specialities, but there are always imaginative daily specials scrawled on a chalkboard. It doubles as a bar (wine by the glass from €1.50).

★La Table d'Héloïse BURGUNDIAN €€

(☎03 85 59 05 65; www.hostelleriedheloise.com/restaurant-cluny; 7 rue de Mâcon; lunch menu €20, dinner menus €27-52; ⊙12.15-1.45pm Fri-Tue, 7.30pm-8.45pm Mon, Tue & Thu-Sat) South of town, this family-run restaurant with a charmingly cosy, newly remodelled interior is a terrific place to sample firmly traditional Burgundian specialities, from the dexterously prepared *fricassée d'escargots* (snail stew) to the tender Charolais rumpsteak to the ripe Époisses cheese and the devastatingly delicious homemade desserts. Book ahead for a table on the light-filled verandah overlooking the Grosne river.

La Halte de l'Abbaye BURGUNDIAN €€

(☎03 85 59 28 49; 3 rue Porte des Prés; daily specials €9.90, menus €16-30.50; ⊙8am-6pm Thu-Sun) Artisanal *andouillette* sausage, Charolais steak tartare and even *tête de veau* (calf's head) are among the classic Burgundian dishes on the menu at this family-run spot just outside the abbey gates. Hard-working owners Franck and Séverine offer nonstop service throughout the afternoon, making it a convenient break between sightseeing stints.

ℹ Information

Tourist Office (☎03 85 59 05 34; www.cluny-tourisme.com; 6 rue Mercière; ⊙9.30am-6.30pm May-Sep, shorter hours Oct-Apr; 📶) Has internet access.

ℹ Getting There & Around

BICYCLE

Ludisport (☎06 62 36 09 58, 07 83 91 62 59; www.ludisport.com; place des Martyrs de la Déportation; bike rental per day from €18; ⊙9am-noon & 2-5pm Jul & Aug, by arrangement rest of year) rents bicycles at the old train station, about 1km south of the centre.

BUS

The bus stop on rue Porte de Paris is served by **Buscéphale** (☎03 80 11 29 29; www.saoneetloire71.fr; tickets €1.50). Line 7 (€1.50, five to eight daily) goes to Mâcon (40 minutes), the Mâcon-Loché TGV station (25 minutes) and Cormatin (20 minutes). Line 9 also runs to Mâcon (€1.50, 30 minutes) once or twice daily. Schedules are posted at the bus stop and tourist office.

Mâcon & Around

POP 34,420

The town of Mâcon, 70km north of Lyon on the west bank of the Saône, is at the heart of the Mâconnais, Burgundy's southernmost winegrowing area, which produces mainly dry whites. The city has a pair of museums and a small but pleasant-enough historic centre consisting of a narrow strip of pedestrian-friendly streets near the riverfront. Beyond a meal at one of its fine restaurants, there's not much reason to linger.

⊙ Sights

Musée des Ursulines MUSEUM

(☎03 85 39 90 38; 5 rue des Ursulines; adult/child €2.50/free; ⊙10am-noon & 2-6pm Tue-Sat, 2-6pm Sun) Musée des Ursulines, housed in a 17th-century Ursuline convent, features Gallo-Roman archaeology, 16th- to 20th-century paintings, and displays about 19th-century Mâconnais life.

Musée Lamartine MUSEUM

(☎03 85 39 90 38; 41 rue Sigorgne; adult/child €2.50/free; ⊙10am-noon & 2-6pm Tue-Sat, 2-6pm Sun) Musée Lamartine explores the life and times of the Mâcon-born Romantic poet and left-wing politician Alphonse de Lamartine (1790–1869).

Maison de Bois HISTORIC BUILDING

(rue Dombey) The all-wood Maison de Bois, facing 95 rue Dombey and built around 1500, is decorated with carved wooden figures, some of them very cheeky indeed.

Musée Départemental de Préhistoire de Solutré MUSEUM

(☎03 85 35 85 24; www.musees-bourgogne.org; Solutré; adult/child €3.50/free; ⊙10am-6pm Apr-Sep, 10am-noon & 2-5pm Oct, Nov & Jan-Mar, closed Dec) The Musée de Préhistoire de Solutré displays finds from one of Europe's richest

prehistoric sites, occupied from 35,000 to 10,000 BC. A lovely 20-minute walk will get you to the top of the rocky outcrop known as the Roche de Solutré, from where Mont Blanc can sometimes be seen, especially at sunset. The museum is about 10km west of Mâcon.

Sleeping

There are a handful of B&Bs in Fuissé, Vinzelles and the other Mâconnais winegrowing towns. The tourist office in Mâcon can provide a list.

Hôtel du Nord HOTEL €

(03 85 38 08 68; www.hotel-dunord.com; 313 quai Jean-Jaurès; s/d/tw/q €78/87/90/155;) This solid, reasonably priced three-star hotel enjoys a prime location on Mâcon's riverfront.

Hôtel d'Europe et d'Angleterre HOTEL €€

(03 85 38 27 94; www.hotel-europeangleterre-macon.com; 92-109 quai Jean-Jaurès; r €78-145, ste €125-169; P) The inviting suites at this spiffy riverfront hotel overlook the Saône.

Eating

Mâcon boasts a bevy of excellent restaurants one block inland from the river, plus a lively Saturday-morning market.

If you're after top-quality Mâconnais wines, head to the nearby villages of **Fuissé**, **Vinzelles** and **Pouilly**, which produce the area's best whites.

Ma Table en Ville MODERN BURGUNDIAN €€

(03 85 30 99 91; www.matableenville.fr; 50 rue de Strasbourg; lunch menus €19-25, dinner menus €38-57; 12.15-1.30pm & 7.15-8.30pm Thu-Tue) Mâcon's up-and-coming favourite serves a weekly changing menu of market-fresh specials complemented by artisanal local wines in a bright dining room enlivened by colourful modern art.

L'Ethym' Sel BURGUNDIAN €€

(03 85 39 48 84; 10 rue Gambetta; menus €19-53; noon-1.45pm & 7-9.30pm Tue-Sat Jul & Aug, noon-1.45pm Thu-Tue, 7-9.30pm Mon & Thu-Sat Sep-Jun) Two blocks south of the tourist office, this modern bistro showcases French and Burgundian specialities including locally raised Charolais steak. The €19 three-course *menu*, available at both lunch and dinnertime on weekdays, offers spectacular value; local Mâcon wines are also attractively priced.

Restaurant Pierre GASTRONOMIC €€€

(03 85 38 14 23; www.restaurant-pierre.com; 7-9 rue Dufour; lunch menu €28, dinner menus €36-91; noon-1.30pm Wed-Sun, 7.30-9pm Tue-Sat) Mâcon's gastronomic sanctuary is Restaurant Pierre, where chef Christian Gaulin juggles creativity and tradition to conjure up sumptuous culinary surprises.

L'O des Vignes GASTRONOMIC €€€

(03 85 38 33 40; www.lodesvignes.fr; rue du Bourg, Fuissé; mains €30-35; noon-2pm & 7.30-10pm Thu-Mon) For a gastronomic experience among the Mâconnais vineyards, look no further than this gem of a restaurant, where Burgundy-born chef Sébastien Chambru builds his *menus* around seasonal produce, incorporates culinary influences from his wide-ranging international career, and complements it all with AOC white wines of the local Pouilly-Fuissé appellation.

Information

Across the street from the 18th-century town hall, the **tourist office** (03 85 21 07 07; www.macon-tourism.com; 1 place St-Pierre; 9.30am-12.30pm & 2-6pm daily Jun-Oct, Mon-Sat Apr & May, Tue-Sat Nov-Mar) has information on accommodation and visiting vineyards including the Route des Vins Mâconnais-Beaujolais.

Getting There & Away

BUS

Buscéphale (03 80 11 29 29; www.saoneet-loire71.fr; tickets €1.50) bus lines 7 and 9 (30 to 40 minutes, €1.50) serve Cluny six to 10 times daily.

TRAIN

The Mâcon-Ville train station is on the main line (18 daily) linking Dijon (€21.90, 1¼ hours), Beaune (€16, 55 minutes) and Lyon Part-Dieu (€13.60, 50 minutes). The fastest service to Paris (€70, 1¾ hours) is from Mâcon-Loché TGV station, 5km southwest of town.

1

Medieval Art & Architecture

Burgundy, once a powerful duchy and a major ecclesiastical centre, attracted the foremost European artists and builders of the Middle Ages. Now graced with a bounty of excellent museums and monumental architecture, Burgundy offers a trail of human accomplishment through its rolling emerald hills.

The Cistercians

Burgundy's clergy established a series of abbeys and churches that remain some of the world's best examples of Romanesque architecture. The austere Cistercian order was founded at the Abbaye de Cîteaux in 1098 by monks seeking to live St Benedict's teachings: *pax, ora et labora* (peace, pray and work). Their spectacular 1114 Abbaye de Pontigny (p429) is one of the finest surviving examples of Cistercian architecture in Burgundy – the purity of its white stone reflects the simplicity of the order.

The Benedictines

Cluny's 12th-century Benedictine abbey, now a sprawling ruin woven into the fabric of the town, once held sway over 1100 priories and monasteries stretching from Poland to Portugal. Aside from its imposing central towers, it's only a shell of its former self, but visitors can still conjure up its full original grandeur thanks to 3D virtual-reality screens sprinkled throughout the site. Further north, the much better preserved Abbaye de Fontenay (p425), founded in 1118, a Unesco World Heritage site, sits in a peaceful forested valley perfect for contemplation.

MICHAEL SHORT / GETTY IMAGES ©

SVETLANA BONDAREVA / SHUTTERSTOCK ©

RENAUD VISAGE / GETTY IMAGES ©

1. Abbaye de Pontigny (p429) **2.** Carved tympanum, Cathédrale St-Lazare (p440) **3.** Cloister, Abbaye de Fontenay (p425)

Autun & Vézelay

The 12th-century Cathédrale St-Lazare (p440) in Autun is world-renowned for its deceptively austere Gislebertus carvings: a fantastic tympanum of the Last Judgement and extraordinary capitals depicting Bible stories and Greek mythology. The adjacent Musée Rolin holds another Gislebertus masterpiece, *The Temptation of Eve*, whose sensitive (and sensual) portrayal of its female subject is nothing short of revolutionary for its time.

Vézelay's Basilique Ste-Madeleine (p436), another Unesco World Heritage Site, was founded in the 880s. A traditional starting point for the Chemin de St-Jacques trail to Santiago de Compostela, Spain, it is adorned with Romanesque carvings and attracts both religious and artistic pilgrims. Nearby, the medieval walls and turrets of Noyers-sur-Serein and Semur-en-Auxois are some of the finest remnants of Burgundy's more secular past.

The Dukes of Burgundy

Last but not least, let's not forget the royals. Dijon was home to the powerful Dukes of Burgundy (with fabulous names including John the Good, Philip the Bold and John the Fearless), and flourished into one of the art capitals of Europe. Explore the dukes' monumental palace (p406) in central Dijon, home to an excellent fine-arts museum. Or head south to Beaune, where Nicolas Rolin, chancellor to Philip the Good, established a hospital-cum-palace, Hôtel-Dieu des Hospices de Beaune (p419), that houses Rogier van der Weyden's fantastic (and fantastical) *Polyptych of the Last Judgement.*

Lyon & the Rhône Valley

POP 3.91 MILLION

Includes ➡

Best Places to Eat

- ➡ Au 14 Février (p468)
- ➡ Le Thou (p469)
- ➡ L'Ourson qui Boit (p461)
- ➡ Les Halles de Lyon Paul Bocuse (p460)
- ➡ Restaurant Pic (p472)
- ➡ L'Espace PH3 (p470)

Best Places to Sleep

- ➡ Auberge de Clochemerle (p468)
- ➡ Prehistoric Lodge (p473)
- ➡ Lyon Renaissance (p458)
- ➡ Cour des Loges (p458)
- ➡ La Maison de la Pra (p471)
- ➡ Hôtel de la Pyramide (p470)

Why Go?

At the crossroads of central Europe and the Atlantic, the Rhineland and the Mediterranean, grand old Lyon is France's third-largest metropolis and its gastronomic capital. Savouring timeless traditional dishes in checked-tableclothed *bouchons* (small bistros) creates unforgettable memories – as do the majestic Roman amphitheatres of Fourvière, the cobbled Unesco-listed streets of Vieux Lyon, and the audacious modern architecture of the new Confluence neighbourhood.

North of Lyon, Beaujolais produces illustrious wines, while the picturesque hilltop village of Pérouges is a perennial film location. Downstream, the Rhône forges past Vienne's Roman ruins and the centuries-old Côtes du Rhône vineyards, opening to sunny vistas of fruit orchards, lavender fields and the distant Alps as it continues south past Valence and Montélimar, eventually reaching the rugged Gorges de l'Ardèche, where the Ardèche River tumbles to the gates of Languedoc and Provence.

When to Go

Lyon

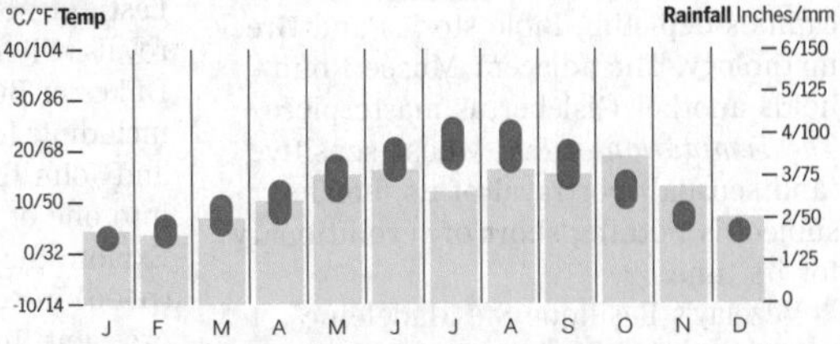

Jun & Jul Catch live performances in ancient Gallo-Roman theatres at Vienne's renowned jazz festival.

Nov Celebrate the tapping of the first bottles of Beaujolais Nouveau, the third Thursday in November.

Early Dec See Lyon spectacularly illuminated during the Fête des Lumières.

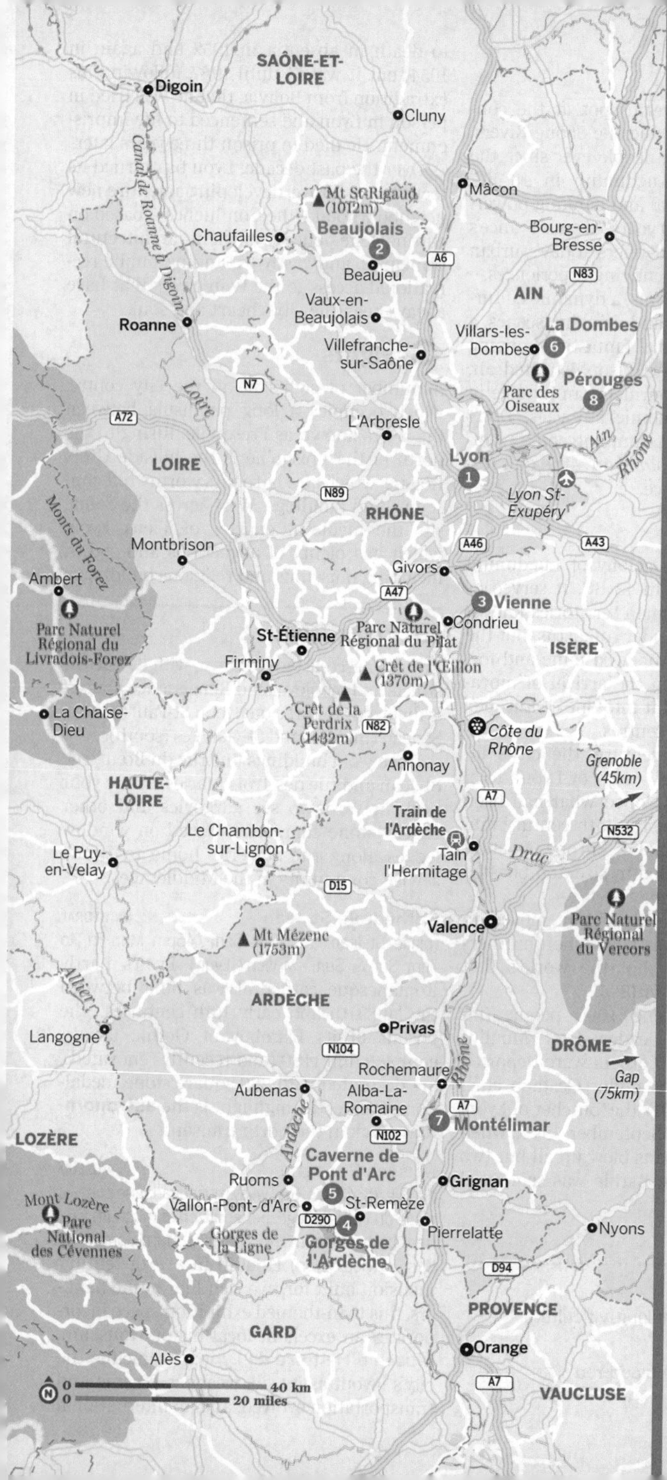

Lyon & the Rhône Valley Highlights

❶ **Lyon** (p450) Delving into Lyon's hidden labyrinth of *traboules* (secret passageways) and sampling Lyonnais specialities in a *bouchon*.

❷ **Beaujolais** (p466) Touring the vine-ribboned hills of this peaceful winegrowing region.

❸ **Vienne** (p470) Seeing dramatic Gallo-Roman ruins, including a perfectly preserved Corinthian-columned temple.

❹ **Gorges de l'Ardèche** (p473) Canoeing beneath the stunning natural stone bridge Pont d'Arc along these scenic gorges.

❺ **Caverne du Pont d'Arc** (p472) Being awed by this replica cave housing brilliantly reproduced prehistoric paintings.

❻ **La Dombes** (p469) Driving or biking around a lake-dotted region, famous for its great restaurants specialising in frogs' legs and carp.

❼ **Montélimar** (p470) Enjoying Provençale *joie de vivre* along tree-shaded avenues and sampling delectable nougat.

❽ **Pérouges** (p468) Strolling the cobbled alleyways of this achingly picturesque medieval village.

LYON

POP 509,000

Commanding a strategic spot at the confluence of the Rhône and the Saône Rivers, Lyon has been luring people ever since the Romans named it Lugdunum in 43 BC. Commercial, industrial and banking powerhouse for the past 500 years, Lyon is France's third largest city, and offers today's urban explorers a wealth of enticing experiences.

Outstanding museums, a dynamic cultural life, busy clubbing and drinking scenes, a thriving university and fantastic shopping lend the city a distinctly sophisticated air, while adventurous gourmets can indulge in their wildest gastronomic fantasies. Don't leave the city without sampling some Lyonnais specialities in a *bouchon* – the quintessential Lyon experience.

History

The Roman military colony of Lugdunum (Lyon) was founded in 43 BC. It served as the capital of the Roman territories known as the Three Gauls under Augustus, but the city had to wait for renewed fame and fortune until 1473, when the arrival of movable type transformed it into one of Europe's foremost publishing centres.

By the mid-18th century, the city's influential silk weavers – 40% of Lyon's total workforce – had developed what had been a textiles centre since the 15th century into the silk-weaving capital of Europe. A century on, Lyon had tripled in size and boasted 100,000 weaving looms.

In 1870, the Lumière family moved to Lyon, and cinema was born when brothers Louis and Auguste shot the world's first moving picture here in 1895.

During WWII some 4000 people (including Resistance leader Jean Moulin) were killed and 7500 others were deported to Nazi death camps under Gestapo chief Klaus Barbie (1913–91), the 'butcher of Lyon'. Nazi rule ended in September 1944, when the retreating Germans blew up all but two of Lyon's 28 bridges. Barbie was sentenced to death in absentia in 1952 and again in 1954, but it wasn't until 1987, following his extradition from Bolivia, that he was tried in person in Lyon and sentenced to life imprisonment. He died in prison three years later.

Over the past decade, Lyon has turned its focus to the future, developing an entire new neighbourhood – the Confluence – based on cutting-edge, energy-efficient architectural principles, and vastly expanding public recreational access to the twin rivers that have always been the city's heart and soul.

> **FAST FACTS**
>
> **Area** 25,851 sq km
>
> **Local industry** Banking, viticulture, fruit farming
>
> **Signature drink** A blood-red *Communard*

Sights

A number of sights lie in the city centre, which occupies a long peninsula between the rivers known as Presqu'île. Rising to the north of the Presqu'île is the hillside Croix Rousse, which also harbours worthwhile museums and buildings. West across the Saône sits the medieval quarter of Vieux Lyon, which has plenty of attractions and sights, including museums and religious buildings.

Vieux Lyon

Lyon's Unesco-listed old town, with its narrow streets and medieval and Renaissance houses, is divided into three quarters: St-Paul (north), St-Jean (middle) and St-Georges (south).

Lovely old buildings line rue du Bœuf, rue St-Jean and rue des Trois Maries. Crane your neck upwards to see gargoyles and other cheeky stone characters carved on window ledges along rue Juiverie, home to Lyon's Jewish community in the Middle Ages.

Cathédrale St-Jean CATHEDRAL
(place St-Jean, 5e; ⌚8.15am-7.45pm Mon-Fri, to 7pm Sat & Sun; Ⓜ Vieux Lyon) Lyon's partly Romanesque cathedral was built between the late 11th and early 16th centuries. The portals of its Flamboyant Gothic façade, completed in 1480 (and recently renovated), are decorated with 280 square stone medallions. Inside, the highlight is the **astronomical clock** in the north transept.

Musées Gadagne MUSEUM
(☎04 78 42 03 61; www.museegadagne.com; 1 place du Petit Collège, 5e; adult/child museum €6/free, both museums €9/free; ⌚11am-6pm Wed-Sun; Ⓜ Vieux Lyon) Housed in a 16th-century mansion built for two rich Florentine bankers, this twin-themed exhibition space incorporates an excellent local history museum, **Musée d'Histoire de Lyon**, chronicling the city's layout as its silk-weaving, cinema and transportation evolved, and an international

puppet museum, **Musée des Marionettes du Monde**, paying homage to Lyon's iconic puppet, Guignol. On the 4th floor, a cafe adjoins tranquil, terraced gardens, here since the 14th century.

Le Petit Musée Fantastique de Guignol MUSEUM
(☎04 78 28 62 04; www.le-petit-musee-fantastique-de-guignol.boutiquecardelli.fr; 6 rue St-Jean, 5e; adult/child €5/3; ⏲10.30am-1pm & 2-6.30pm Tue-Sun, 2-6pm Mon; Ⓜ Vieux Lyon) The star of this tiny, two-room museum is Guignol, the Lyonnais puppet famous for its slapstick antics and political commentary. Ask staff to set up the English soundtrack on the cute, sensor-activated exhibits.

Fourvière

More than two millennia ago, the Romans built the city of Lugdunum on the slopes of Fourvière. Today this prominent hill on the Saône's western bank is topped by a showy 19th-century basilica and the **Tour Métallique** (montée Nicolas de Lange; Minimes), an Eiffel Tower–like structure (minus its bottom two-thirds) built in 1893 and used as a TV transmitter.

Footpaths wind uphill to Fourvière from Vieux Lyon, but the funicular is the least taxing way up; catch it just up the escalators from the Vieux Lyon metro station.

Basilique Notre Dame de Fourvière CHURCH
(www.fourviere.org; place de Fourvière, 5e; rooftop tour adult/child €7/4; ⏲8am-6.45pm, guided tours Apr-Nov; Fourvière) Crowning the hill, with stunning city panoramas from its terrace, this superb example of late-19th-century French ecclesiastical architecture is lined with intricate mosaics. One-hour discovery visits take in the main features of the basilica and crypt; 75-minute rooftop tours ('Visite Insolite') climax on the stone-sculpted roof.

Musée Gallo-Romain de Fourvière ARCHAEOLOGICAL MUSEUM
(☎04 73 38 49 30; 17 rue Cléberg, 5e; adult/child €4/free, Thu free; ⏲10am-6pm Tue-Sun; Fourvière) For an enlightening historical perspective on the city's past, start your visit at this archaeological museum located on the hillside of Fourvière. It hosts a wide-ranging collection of ancient artefacts found in the Rhône Valley as well as superb mosaics.

Théâtre Romain ARCHAEOLOGICAL SITE
(rue Cléberg, 5e; Fourvière, Minimes) Lyon's Roman theatre, built around 15 BC and enlarged in AD 120, sat an audience of 10,000. Romans held poetry readings and musical recitals in the smaller, adjacent *odéon*.

LYON CITY CARD

The excellent-value **Lyon City Card** (www.en.lyon-france.com/Lyon-City-Card; 1/2/3 days adult €22/32/42, child €13.50/18.50/23.50) offers free admission to every Lyon museum, the roof of Basilique Notre Dame de Fourvière, guided city tours, Guignol puppet shows and river excursions (April to October), along with numerous other discounts. The card also includes unlimited city-wide transport on buses, trams, the funicular and metro. Full-price cards are available at the tourist office and some hotels, or save 10% by booking online and presenting your confirmation number at the tourist office.

Presqu'île

Lyon's city centre lies on this 500m- to 800m-wide peninsula bounded by the rivers Rhône and Saône.

Musée des Beaux-Arts MUSEUM
(☎04 72 10 17 40; www.mba-lyon.fr; 20 place des Terreaux, 1er; adult/child €8/free; ⏲10am-6pm Wed, Thu & Sat-Mon, 10.30am-6pm Fri; Ⓜ Hôtel de Ville) This stunning and eminently manageable museum showcases France's finest collection of sculptures and paintings outside of Paris from antiquity onwards. Highlights include works by Rodin, Rubens, Rembrandt, Monet, Matisse and Picasso. Pick up a free audioguide and be sure to stop for a drink or meal on the delightful stone terrace off its cafe-restaurant or take time out in its tranquil **cloister garden**.

Place des Terreaux SQUARE
(Ⓜ Hôtel de Ville) The centrepiece of the Presqu'île's beautiful central square is a 19th-century **fountain** made of 21 tonnes of lead and sculpted by Frédéric-Auguste Bartholdi (of Statue of Liberty fame). The four horses pulling the chariot symbolise rivers galloping seawards. The **Hôtel de Ville** fronting the square was built in 1655 but was given its present ornate façade in 1702. Daniel Buren's polka-dot 'forest' of 69 **granite fountains** are embedded in the ground across much of the square.

Lyon

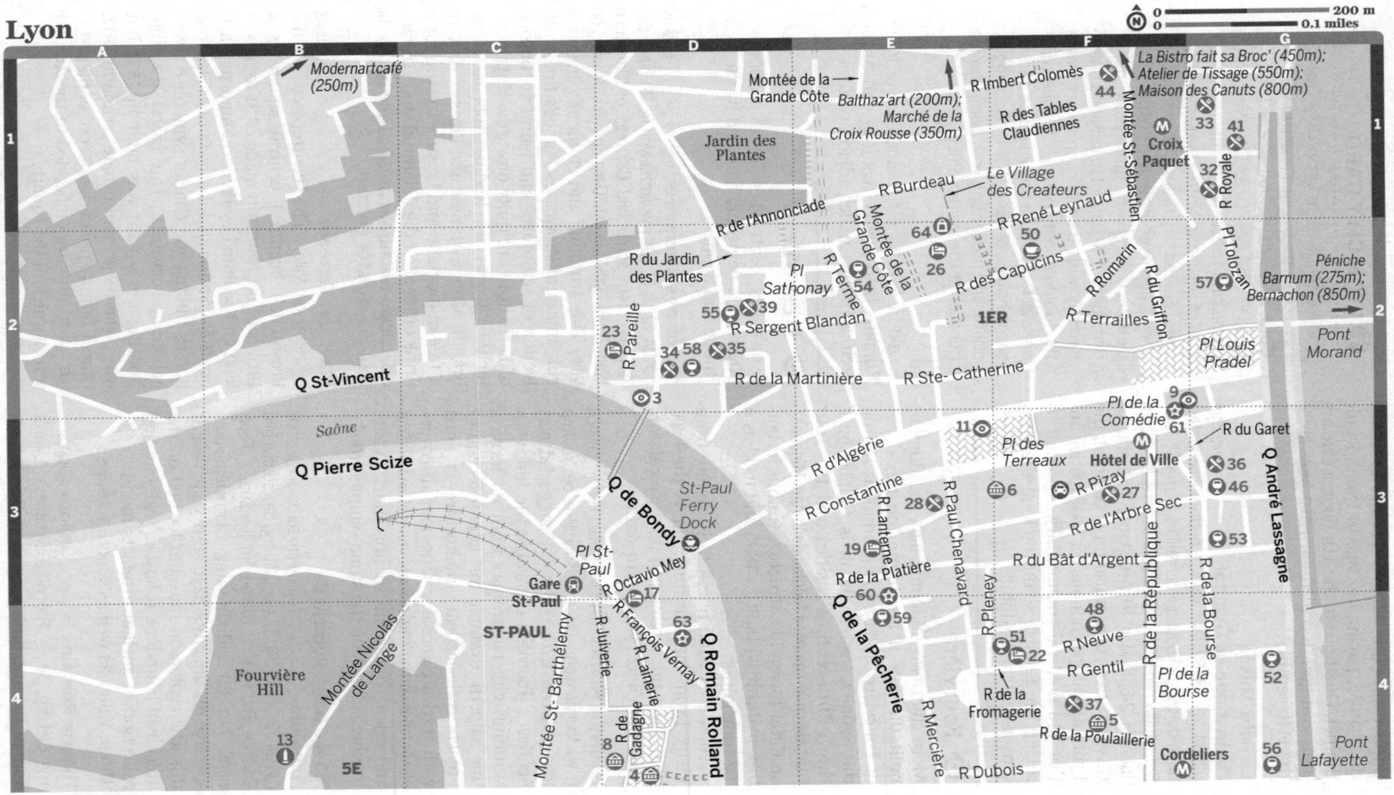
0 200 m
0 0.1 miles
Modernartcafé (250m)
Montée de la Grande Côte
Balthaz'art (200m); Marché de la Croix Rousse (350m)
R Imbert Colomès
La Bistro fait sa Broc' (450m); Atelier de Tissage (550m); Maison des Canuts (800m)
R des Tables Claudiennes
Montée St-Sébastien
Croix Paquet
R Royale
Jardin des Plantes
R Burdeau
Le Village des Createurs
R de l'Annonciade
Montée de la Grande Côte
R René Leynaud
Pl Tolozan
Péniche Barnum (275m); Bernachon (850m)
R du Jardin des Plantes
Pl Sathonay
R Terme
R des Capucins
R Romarin
R du Griffon
R Sergent Blandan
1ER
R Terrailles
Pont Morand
R Pareille
Pl Louis Pradel
Q St-Vincent
R de la Martinière
R Ste- Catherine
Pl de la Comédie
Saône
Pl des Terreaux
R du Garet
Hôtel de Ville
Q Pierre Scize
R d'Algérie
R Pizay
Q André Lassagne
St-Paul Ferry Dock
R Constantine
R Lanterne
R Paul Chenavard
R de l'Arbre Sec
Q de Bondy
R de la République
Pl St-Paul
R Octavio Mey
R du Bât d'Argent
R de la Platière
R de la Bourse
Gare St-Paul
Q de la Pêcherie
R Pleney
ST-PAUL
Montée St-Barthélemy
R Juiverie
R François Vernay
Q Romain Rolland
R Neuve
R Lainerie
R Gentil
Pl de la Bourse
Fourvière Hill
Montée Nicolas de Lange
R de la Fromagerie
R de Gadagne
R de la Poulaillerie
R Mercière
Cordeliers
Pont Lafayette
R Dubois
5E
A
B
C
D
E
F
G
1
2
3
4
3
4
5
6
8
9
11
13
17
19
22
23
26
27
28
32
33
34
35
36
37
39
41
44
46
48
50
51
52
53
54
55
56
57
58
59
60
61
63
64

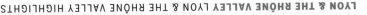

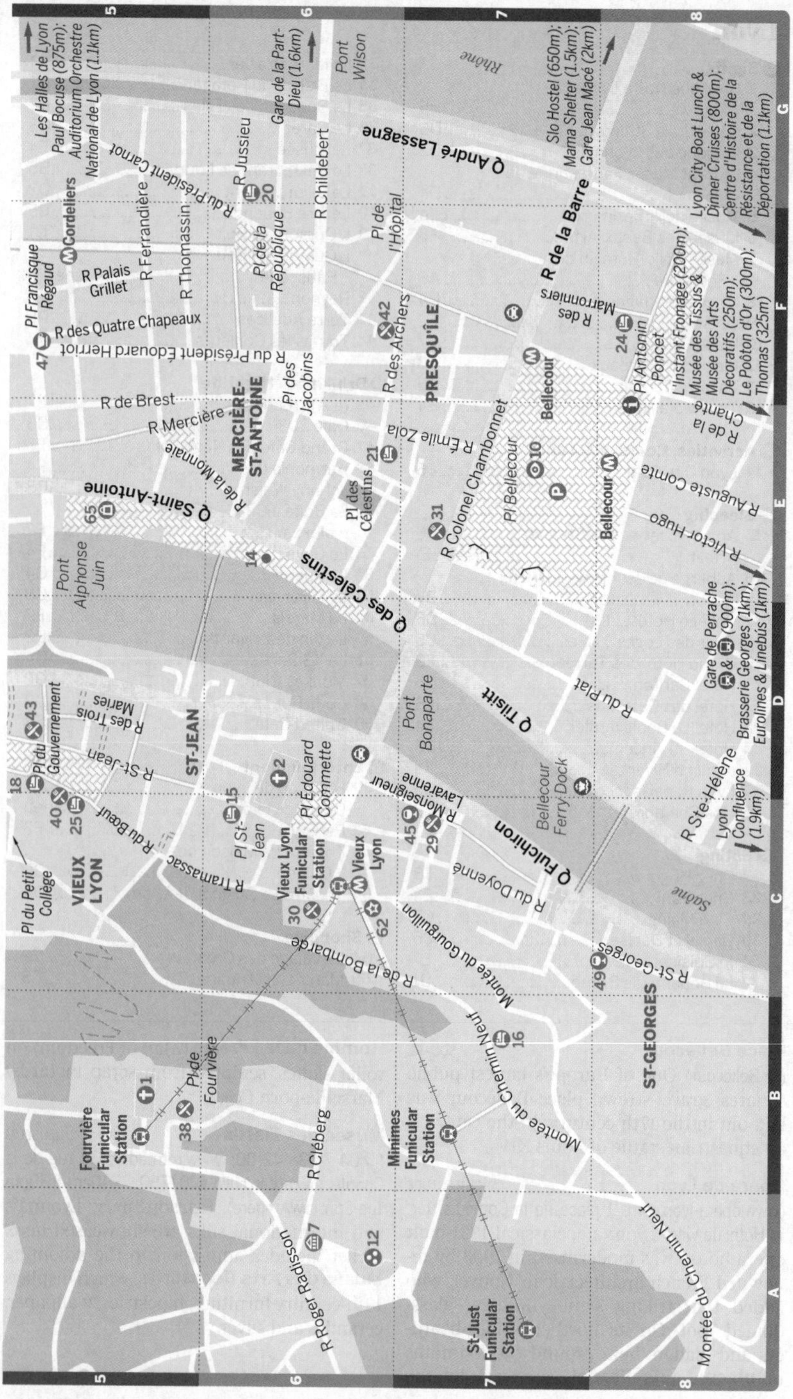

Les Halles de Lyon Paul Bocuse (875m); Auditorium Orchestre National de Lyon (1.1km)
Gare de la Part-Dieu (1.6km)
Slo Hostel (650m); Mama Shelter (1.5km); Gare Jean Macé (2km)
Lyon City Boat Lunch & Dinner Cruises (800m); Centre d'Histoire de la Résistance et de la Déportation (1.1km)
L'Instant Fromage (200m); Musée des Tissus & Musée des Arts Décoratifs (250m); Le Poêton d'Or (300m); Thomas (325m)
Gare de Perrache (900m); Brasserie Georges (1km); Eurolines & Linebús (1km)
Lyon Confluence (1.9km)
Rhône
Saône
Pont Wilson
Q André Lassagne
R du Président Carnot
Pl Francisque Régaud
Cordeliers
R Palais Grillet
R Ferrandière
R Thomassin
R Jussieu
R Childebert
Pl de la République
Pl de l'Hôpital
R de la Barre
R des Marronniers
R des Quatre Chapeaux
R du Président Édouard Herriot
R de Brest
R Mercière
MERCIÈRE-ST-ANTOINE
Pl des Jacobins
R des Archers
PRESQU'ÎLE
Bellecour
Pl Antonin Poncet
R de la Charité
R Émile Zola
R de la Monnaie
Q Saint-Antoine
Pl des Célestins
R Colonel Chambonnet
Pl Bellecour
R Auguste Comte
R Victor Hugo
Pont Alphonse Juin
Q des Célestins
Pont Bonaparte
Q Tilsitt
R du Plat
R Ste-Hélène
Bellecour Ferry Dock
Q Fulchiron
R du Doyenné
R Monseigneur Lavarenne
R St-Georges
ST-GEORGES
Montée du Gourguillon
Montée du Chemin Neuf
R des Trois Maries
Pl du Gouvernement
R St-Jean
ST-JEAN
Pl Édouard Commette
Pl St-Jean
R du Bœuf
R Tramassac
VIEUX LYON
Pl du Petit Collège
Vieux Lyon Funicular Station
Vieux Lyon
R de la Bombarde
Pl de Fourvière
Fourvière Funicular Station
R Cléberg
Minimes Funicular Station
R Roger Radisson
St-Just Funicular Station

Lyon

Sights
1 Basilique Notre Dame de Fourvière ... B5
2 Cathédrale St-Jean ... D6
3 Fresque des Lyonnais ... D2
4 Le Petit Musée Fantastique de Guignol ... D4
5 Musée de l'Imprimerie ... F4
6 Musée des Beaux-Arts ... F3
7 Musée Gallo-Romain de Fourvière ... A6
8 Musées Gadagne ... D4
9 Opéra de Lyon ... F2
10 Place Bellecour ... E7
11 Place des Terreaux ... E3
12 Théâtre Romain ... A6
13 Tour Métallique ... B4

Activities, Courses & Tours
14 Lyon City Boat ... E6

Sleeping
15 Apart'Observatoire St-Jean ... C6
Artelit ... (see 25)
16 Auberge de Jeunesse du Vieux Lyon ... B7
17 Collège Hotel ... D3
18 Cour des Loges ... D5
19 Grand Hôtel des Terreaux ... E3
20 Hotel Carlton ... G6
21 Hôtel des Célestins ... E6
22 Hôtel Le Boulevardier ... F4
23 Hôtel St-Vincent ... D2
24 Jardin d'Hiver ... F8
25 Lyon Renaissance ... C5
26 Nos Chambres en Ville ... E2

Eating
27 Chez Hugon ... F3
28 Chez Paul ... E3
29 Cinq Mains ... C7
30 Daniel et Denise ... C6
31 In Cuisine ... E7
32 La Bonâme de Bruno ... G1
33 La Mère Brazier ... G1
34 Le Bistrot du Potager ... D2
35 Le Bouchon des Filles ... D2
36 Le Garet ... G3
37 Le Musée ... F4
38 Le Restaurant de Fourvière ... B5
39 Le Saint Vincent ... D2
40 Le Tire Bouchon ... C5
41 L'Ourson qui Boit ... G1
L'Ourson qui Boit – Pâtisserie ... (see 41)
42 Reynon ... F6
43 Terre Adélices ... D5
44 Toutes les Couleurs ... F1

Drinking & Nightlife
45 (L'A)Kroche ... C7
46 Café 203 ... G3
47 Grand Café des Négociants ... F5
48 Harmonie des Vins ... F4
49 Johnny Walsh's ... C8
50 La Boite à Café – Café Mokxa ... F2
51 La Cave d'à Côté ... F4
52 La Ruche ... G4
53 Le L Bar ... G3
54 Le Marais ... E2
55 Le Vin des Vivants ... D2
56 Le XS Bar ... G4
57 Monkey Club ... G2
58 Soda Bar ... D2
59 United Café ... E4

Entertainment
60 Hot Club de Lyon ... E3
Opéra de Lyon ... (see 9)
61 Péristyle ... F3
62 Théâtre La Maison de Guignol ... C6
63 Théâtre Le Guignol de Lyon ... D4

Shopping
64 Le Village des Créateurs ... E2
65 Marché St-Antoine ... E5

Place Bellecour SQUARE
(Ⓜ Bellecour) One of Europe's largest public squares, gravel-strewn place Bellecour was laid out in the 17th century. In the centre is an equestrian statue of Louis XIV.

Opéra de Lyon ARCHITECTURE
(www.opera-lyon.com; 1 place de la Comédie, 1er; Ⓜ Hôtel de Ville) Lyon's neoclassical 1831-built opera house was modernised in 1993 by renowned French architect Jean Nouvel, who added the striking semi-cylindrical glass-domed roof. On its northern side, boarders and bladers buzz around the fountains of **place Louis Pradel**, surveyed by the **Homme de la Liberté** (Man of Freedom) on roller skates, sculpted from scrap metal by Marseille-born César.

Musée des Tissus MUSEUM
(☎04 78 38 42 00; www.mtmad.fr; 34 rue de la Charité, 2e; adult/child €10/7.50; ⏲10am-5.30pm Tue-Sun; Ⓜ Ampère) Extraordinary Lyonnais and international silks are showcased here. Ticket includes admission to the adjoining **Musée des Arts Décoratifs**, which displays 18th-century furniture, tapestries, wallpaper, ceramics and silver.

Musée de l'Imprimerie MUSEUM
(☎04 78 37 65 98; www.imprimerie.lyon.fr; 13 rue de la Poulaillerie, 2e; adult/child €5/free; ⏱10.30am-6pm Wed-Sun; Ⓜ Cordeliers) From early equipment through to computerised technology, this absorbing museum traces the history of the city's printing industry.

Croix Rousse

Independent until it became part of Lyon in 1852, and retaining its own distinct character with its bohemian inhabitants and lush outdoor food market, the hilltop quarter of Croix Rousse slinks north up the steep *pentes* (slopes) from place des Terreaux.

Following the introduction of the mechanical Jacquard loom in 1805, Lyonnais *canuts* (silk weavers) built tens of thousands of workshops in the area, with large windows to let in light and hefty wood-beamed ceilings more than 4m high to accommodate the huge new machines. Weavers spent 14 to 20 hours a day hunched over their looms breathing in silk dust. Two-thirds were illiterate and everyone was paid a pittance; strikes in 1830–31 and 1834 resulted in the deaths of several hundred weavers.

Hidden Croix Rousse gems include **place Bertone**, a leafy square that doubles as an open-air stage for ad-hoc summer entertainment; the **Jardin Rosa Mir** (http://rosa.mir.free.fr; enter via 87 Grande Rue de la Croix Rousse, 4e; ⏱3-6pm Sat Apr-Nov; Ⓜ Hénon), a walled garden decorated with thousands of seashells; and the panoramic **Parc de La Cerisaie** (rue Chazière, 4e; Ⓜ Croix Rousse).

Maison des Canuts SILK WORKSHOP
(☎04 78 28 62 04; www.maisondescanuts.com; 10-12 rue d'Ivry, 4e; adult/child €7/4; ⏱10am-6.30pm Mon-Sat, guided tours 11am & 3.30pm Mon-Sat; Ⓜ Croix Rousse) On a 50-minute guided tour, learn about weavers' labour-intensive life and the industry's evolution, see manual looms in use, and browse the silk boutique. Guided tours in English run at 11am on Monday and Saturday.

Atelier de Passementerie SILK WORKSHOP
(☎04 78 27 17 13; www.soierie-vivante.asso.fr; 21 rue Richan, 4e; guided tour adult/child €6/free, combined ticket with Atelier de Tissage €9/free; ⏱boutique 2-6.30pm Tue, 9am-noon & 2-6.30pm Wed-Sat, guided tours & demonstrations 2pm & 4pm Tue-Sat; Ⓜ Croix Rousse) Preserved for posterity by the Soierie Vivante association, this silk trimmings workshop functioned until 1979, weaving braids and intricate pictures. Browse fabrics in the attached boutique (admission free), or learn the history of the looms and see them at work on a 30-minute afternoon tour.

Atelier de Tissage SILK WORKSHOP
(☎04 78 27 17 13; www.soierie-vivante.asso.fr; 12bis rue Justin Godart, 4e; guided tour adult/child €6/free, combined ticket with Atelier de Passementerie €9/free; ⏱guided tours 3pm & 5pm Mon-Sat; Ⓜ Croix Rousse) Accessible strictly by guided tour, this wonderful old workshop houses looms that produce large fabrics. It's best visited in conjunction with the nearby Atelier de Passementerie.

La Confluence

Meet Lyon's newest neighbourhood: the Confluence (www.lyon-confluence.fr), where the Rhône and the Saône meet at Presqu'île's southern tip. This former industrial wasteland has recently been brought back to life by a multimillion-euro urban renewal project, recognised for its cutting-edge, environmentally sustainable design by the French government, the European Commission and the WWF.

During Phase One of the project, dozens of architecturally audacious, energy-efficient buildings sprang up, including the bizarre orange, Swiss-cheese-like office building **Le Cube Orange**, its sister **Le Cube Vert** and the **Pôle de Commerces et de Loisirs Confluence** (112 cours Charlemagne), an enormous shopping complex with an innovative, 2-hectare, transparent air-cushion roof. It has also seen the whimsical remodelling of existing buildings, including the **Pavillon des Douanes** (customs house), whose balconies are now surmounted by pairs of giant orange frogs, and **La Sucrerie**, a converted 1930s sugar warehouse that houses a nightclub on its top floor and hosts art exhibits during Lyon's **Biennale d'Art Contemporain** (www.labiennaledelyon.com).

Phase Two, which was initiated in 2015 by Swiss architects Herzog and de Meuron (of Tate Modern and Beijing Olympic Stadium fame), will make the neighbourhood more liveable, adding a residential and market district and linking the Confluence to the rest of Lyon with three new bridges, including a pedestrian-bike corridor, **La Transversale**, spanning both the Rhône and the Saône. The whole project should be completed by 2020.

DON'T MISS

LYON'S HIDDEN LABYRINTH

Deep within Vieux Lyon and Croix Rousse, dark, dingy *traboules* (secret passages) wind their way through apartment blocks, under streets and into courtyards. In all, 315 passages link 230 streets, with a combined length of 50km. A couple of Vieux Lyon's *traboules* date from Roman times, but most were constructed by *canuts* (silk weavers) in the 19th century to transport silk in inclement weather. Resistance fighters found them equally handy during WWII. Genuine *traboules* (derived from the Latin *trans ambulare,* meaning 'to pass through') cut from one street to another. Passages that fan out into a courtyard or cul-de-sac aren't *traboules* but *miraboules* (two of the finest examples are at 16 rue Bœuf and 8 rue Juiverie, both in Vieux Lyon).

Vieux Lyon's most celebrated *traboules* include those connecting 27 rue St-Jean with 6 rue des Trois Maries and 54 rue St-Jean with 27 rue du Bœuf (push the intercom button to buzz open the door). Step into Croix Rousse's underworld at 9 place Colbert, crossing cour des Voraces – renowned for its monumental seven-storey staircase – to 14bis montée St Sébastien, and eventually emerging at 29 rue Imbert Colomès. From here a series of other *traboules* zigzags down the slope most of the way to place des Terreaux.

For more detailed descriptions and maps of Lyon's *traboules,* visit www.lyontraboules.net or pick up a copy of the French-language guidebook *200 Cours et Traboules dans les Rues de Lyon* by Gérald Gambier (€9.95, available at Lyon's tourist office). The tourist office also includes *traboules* on many of its guided walking **tours** (☎04 72 77 69 69; www.lyon-france.com; tours adult/child €12/7; ⏲by reservation).

Musée des Confluences MUSEUM

(☎04 28 38 11 90; www.museedesconfluences.fr; 86 quai Perrache, 6e; adult/child €9/free; ⏲11am-6.15pm Tue, Wed & Fri, 11am-9.15pm Thu, 10am-6.15pm Sat & Sun; 🚊T1) Opened in late 2014, this building, designed by the Viennese firm Coop Himmelb(l)au, is the crowning glory of the Confluence. This ambitious science-and-humanities museum is housed in a futuristic steel-and-glass transparent crystal. Its distorted structure is one of the city's iconic landmarks.

Its permanent exhibitions are arranged thematically into four sections. The 'Origins' exhibition focuses on the origins of the Earth and the various theories of evolution; the 'Eternity' exhibition is devoted to death rites; the 'Societies' exhibition explores how human groups are organised and interact; and the 'Species' exhibition is devoted to natural history.

Aquarium du Grand Lyon AQUARIUM

(☎04 72 66 65 66; www.aquariumlyon.fr; 7 rue Stéphane Déchant, La Mulatière; adult/child €15/11; ⏲11am-6pm Wed-Sun Sep-Jun, daily Jul, Aug & school holidays; 🚌Maison du Confluent) Just west of the Confluence, Lyon's well-thought-out aquarium is home to some 280 marine species including more than 5000 fish. Bus 15 links it with place Bellecour. You get a 10% discount if you buy your ticket online.

Rive Gauche

The Rhône's Rive Gauche (Left Bank) harbours parks, museums and day-to-day Lyonnais amenities including the city's university and transport hubs.

Parc de la Tête d'Or PARK

(www.loisirs-parcdelatetedor.com; bd des Belges, 6e; ⏲6.30am-10.30pm mid-Apr–mid-Oct, to 8.30pm rest of year; 🚌C1, C5, Ⓜ Masséna) If you're museum-ed out, head to this lovely space north of the centre, which provides a green haven for nature lovers and families. Spanning 117 hectares, France's largest urban park was landscaped in the 1860s. It's graced by a lake (rent a row boat), botanic gardens with greenhouses, rose gardens, a zoo and a tourist train. Take bus C1 (from Part-Dieu train station) or bus C5 (from place Bellecour and Hôtel de Ville).

Musée d'Art Contemporain ART MUSEUM

(☎04 72 69 17 17; www.mac-lyon.com; 81 quai Charles de Gaulle, 6e; adult/child €9/free; ⏲11am-6pm Wed-Fri, 10am-7pm Sat & Sun; 🚌C1, C4, C5) Lyon's contemporary art museum mounts edgy temporary exhibitions and a rotating permanent collection of post-1960 art. It sometimes closes for several weeks between exhibitions, so check to make sure there's something on. Buses stop right out front.

Centre d'Histoire de la Résistance et de la Déportation MUSEUM
(☎04 78 72 23 11; www.chrd.lyon.fr; 14 av Berthelot, 7e; adult/child €4/free; ⏲10am-5.30pm Wed-Sun; Ⓜ Perrache, Jean Macé) The WWII headquarters of Gestapo commander Klaus Barbie evokes Lyon's role as the 'Capital of the Resistance' through moving multimedia exhibits. Extensively remodelled in 2012, the museum includes sound recordings of deportees and Resistance fighters, plus a varied collection of everyday objects associated with the Resistance (including the parachute Jean Moulin used to re-enter France in 1942).

Musée Lumière MUSEUM
(☎04 78 78 18 95; www.institut-lumiere.org; 25 rue du Premier Film, 8e; adult/child €6.50/5.50; ⏲10am-6.30pm Tue-Sun; Ⓜ Monplaisir-Lumière) Cinema's glorious beginnings are showcased at the art-nouveau home of Antoine Lumière, who moved to Lyon with sons Auguste and Louis in 1870. The brothers shot the first reels of the world's first motion picture, *La Sortie des Usines Lumières (Exit of the Lumières Factories)* here on 19 March 1895.

Tours

★ Walking Tours WALKING
(☎04 72 77 69 69; www.en.lyon-france.com/Guided-Tours-Excursions; adult/child €12/7; ⏲ by reservation) The tourist office organises a variety of excellent tours through Vieux Lyon and Croix Rousse with local English-speaking guides. Book in advance (online, by phone or in person at the tourist office).

Lyon City Tour BUS
(☎04 78 56 32 39; www.lyoncitytour.fr; adult 1-/2-day ticket €19/22, child 1 or 2 days €8; ⏲9.30am-6.30pm Apr-Oct, 9.45am-5.45pm Nov-Mar) Hop-on, hop-off double-decker bus tours. On Thursday and Sunday evenings from mid-June to mid-September, a Lyon by Night tour is also offered at 9.30pm.

Cyclopolitain CYCLING
(☎04 78 30 35 90; www.visite-insolite-cyclopolitain.com; tours 2 people €40-130; ⏲noon-7pm Tue-Fri, 10.30am-7pm Sat) Tiny and/or tired feet can rest aboard a cycle-taxi tour. Choose from nine different itineraries.

Lyon City Boat BOATING
(Navig'inter; ☎04 78 42 96 81; www.lyoncityboat.com; 2 quai des Célestins, 2e; river excursions adult/child €11.50/8; ⏲daily Apr-Oct; Ⓜ Bellecour, Vieux Lyon) From April to October, river excursions depart from Lyon City Boat's dock along the Saône. Advance bookings are essential for **lunch and dinner cruises** (3hr lunch cruise €50-59, 6hr lunch cruise €55-65, 3hr dinner cruise €59-69), which leave from a separate dock on the Rhône.

Festivals & Events

★ Fête des Lumières WINTER FESTIVAL
(Festival of Lights; www.fetedeslumieres.lyon.fr) Over four days around the Feast of the Immaculate Conception (8 December), magnificent sound-and-light shows are projected onto key buildings, while locals illuminate window sills with candles. This is Lyon's premier festival, and it's so colourful that it's worth timing your trip around it. Note that every hotel is fully booked.

Nuits de Fourvière PERFORMING ARTS
(Fourvière Nights; www.nuitsdefourviere.com) A diverse program of open-air theatre, music and dance concerts atmospherically set in Fourvière's Roman amphitheatre from early June to late July.

Sleeping

Lyon's tourist office runs a free **reservation service** (http://book.lyon-france.com/en/accommodation) and good-value package deals, including Les Weekends Fous de Lyon, a scheme that grants free breakfasts and 50% off the second night for guests booking a weekend hotel stay.

Chambres d'hôte (B&Bs) and rental apartments are also making headway; umbrella organisations include **Gîtes de France** (www.gites-bed-and-breakfast-rhone.com) and **Chambres Lyon** (www.chambreslyon.com). Other interesting websites include **Mon Hôtel Particulier Lyon** (www.mon-hotel-particulier-lyon.com) and **Loges Vieux Lyon** (www.loges-vieux-lyon.com).

Vieux Lyon

Auberge de Jeunesse du Vieux Lyon HOSTEL €
(☎04 78 15 05 50; www.hifrance.org; 41-45 montée du Chemin Neuf, 5e; dm incl breakfast €19.50-25.60; ⏲reception 7am-1pm, 2-8pm & 9pm-1am; @ 📶; Ⓜ Vieux Lyon, Minimes) Stunning city views unfold from the terrace of Lyon's HI-affiliated hostel, and from many of the (mostly four- and six-bed) dorms. Bike parking and kitchen facilities are available, and there's an on-site bar. Try for a dorm with city views. To avoid the tiring 10-minute climb from Vieux

Lyon metro station, take the funicular to Minimes station and walk downhill.

★Lyon Renaissance APARTMENT €€

(☎04 27 89 30 58; www.lyon-renaissance.com; 16 rue du Bœuf, 5e; apt €95-115; 📶; Ⓜ Vieux Lyon) Friendly owners Françoise and Patrick rent these two superbly situated Vieux Lyon apartments with beamed ceilings and kitchen facilities. The smaller 3rd-floor walk-up sleeps two, with windows overlooking a pretty tree-shaded square. A second unit, opposite Vieux Lyon's most famous medieval tower, has a spacious living room with ornamental fireplace and fold-out couch, plus a mezzanine with double bed.

Artelit APARTMENT €€

(☎04 78 42 84 83; www.dormiralyon.com; 16 rue du Bœuf, 5e; d €145-165, apt €150-250; 📶; Ⓜ Vieux Lyon) Run by Lyonnais photographer Frédéric Jean, the three spacious tower rooms and self-catering apartment of this delightful *chambre d'hôte* have centuries of history behind every nook and cranny. They're right in the heart of Vieux Lyon but still feel very quiet. If you fall in love with the artworks, you can buy them to take home. Good English is spoken.

Collège Hotel HOTEL €€

(☎04 72 10 05 05; www.college-hotel.com; 5 place St-Paul, 5e; d €130-165; P ❄ @ 📶; Ⓜ Vieux Lyon, Hôtel de Ville) With bright white, minimalist guestrooms and school-themed decor throughout, this four-star hotel is one of Vieux Lyon's unique lodging options. It shelters 40 luminous rooms, 10 of which come with balconies. Enjoy breakfast on the rooftop garden terrace, or in the *salle de classe petit dejeuner*, bedecked like a classroom of yesteryear. And yes, it has private parking (€16, 15 spaces).

Apart'Observatoire St-Jean APARTMENT €€

(☎06 30 95 59 30; www.gite-de-charme-lyon.com; 70 rue St-Jean, 5e; 2-person apt per night €105-145, per week €490-770; ❄📶; Ⓜ Vieux Lyon) It's worth braving the four-storey climb to these two historic, self-catering apartments, right in the heart of Vieux Lyon. The south-facing unit boasts full-on cathedral views, while the adjacent tower unit offers equally impressive perspectives towards Fourvière. Both have modern kitchen and laundry facilities, and Lyon's attractions are all accessible on foot or from the metro/funicular stop 200m south.

★Cour des Loges HOTEL €€€

(☎04 72 77 44 44; www.courdesloges.com; 2-8 rue du Bœuf, 5e; d €200-350, ste €250-600; ❄ @ 📶 ≋; Ⓜ Vieux Lyon) Four 14th- to 17th-century houses wrapped around a *traboule* (secret passage) with preserved features such as Italianate loggias make this an exquisite place to stay. Individually decorated rooms woo with designer bathroom fittings and bountiful antiques, while decadent facilities include a spa, a Michelin-starred restaurant (*menus* €95 to €115), a swish cafe and a cross-vaulted bar.

Presqu'île

Hôtel Le Boulevardier HOTEL €

(☎04 78 28 48 22; www.leboulevardier.fr; 5 rue de la Fromagerie, 1er; s €69-79, d €79; ❄📶; Ⓜ Hôtel de Ville, Cordeliers) Le Boulevardier is a bargain 14-room hotel with snug, spotless rooms, and sports quirky touches such as old skis and tennis racquets adorning the hallways. No two rooms are alike; some have exposed brick walls and wooden ceilings. It's up a steep spiral staircase above a cool little cafe, which doubles as reception.

Hôtel St-Vincent HOTEL €

(☎04 78 27 22 56; www.hotel-saintvincent.com; 9 rue Pareille, 1er; s/d €56/72; 📶; Ⓜ Hôtel de Ville) High-beamed ceilings, giant-sized windows, a couple of old stone walls and original wooden floors give this three-floor, 32-room hotel atmosphere to spare. The location halfway between Hôtel de Ville and Vieux Lyon is another big plus. There are plans to spruce up and modernise some rooms.

★Jardin d'Hiver B&B €€

(☎04 78 28 69 34; www.guesthouse-lyon.com; 10 rue des Marronniers, 2e; s/d incl breakfast €110/130, apt per week from €520; ❄📶; Ⓜ Bellecour) Chic and centrally located, this 3rd-floor B&B (no lift) has two spacious rooms replete with modern conveniences – one in understated purple and pistachio, the other in vivid purple and orange. Friendly owner Annick Bournonville serves 100% organic breakfasts in the foliage-filled breakfast room. In the same building, her son rents out apartments with kitchen and laundry facilities. English and Spanish are spoken. Prices drop by €10 if you stay three nights or more.

Hôtel des Célestins HOTEL €€

(☎04 72 56 08 98; www.hotelcelestins.com; 4 rue des Archers, 2e; d €91-199, ste €188-231; ❄📶; Ⓜ Bellecour) This cosy and classy hotel just

north of central place Bellecour is surrounded by designer boutiques. The priciest rooms have gorgeous (oblique) views of the theatre; the cheaper ones face a quiet courtyard. They all feature spotless albeit petite bathrooms that were modernised in 2015. The suites are particularly spacious and filled with character. Good English is spoken.

Grand Hôtel des Terreaux HOTEL €€
(☎04 78 27 04 10; www.hotel-lyon-grandhoteldesterreaux.fr; 16 rue Lanterne, 1er; s €98-114, d €114-135; ; Ⓜ Hôtel de Ville) This four-star venture ideally positioned southwest of place des Terreaux is a bargain, especially if you can score a promotional deal online. It offers neat, well-equipped rooms with a retro-chic decor. Its distinctive characteristic is the lovely indoor pool next to the breakfast room. No private parking.

Hotel Carlton HOTEL €€€
(☎04 78 42 56 51; www.sofitel.com; 4 rue Jussieu, 2e; r from €166; @; Ⓜ Cordeliers, Bellecour) After an extensive renovation in 2013, this vintage hotel tempts with soundproofed rooms done up in brilliant reds, lovingly restored with period furniture, mouldings and wallpaper. Options range from 15-sq-metre 'Cocoon' units to circular 40-sq-metre corner suites, many overlooking pedestrianised place de la République. A sauna, spa and sumptuous breakfast featuring traditional Lyonnais specialities add to the appeal.

Rive Gauche

Slo Hostel HOSTEL €
(☎04 78 59 06 90; www.slo-hostel.com; 5 rue Bonnefoi, 3e; dm €26.50-28.50, d with shared bathroom €65, d €77-87; ; Ⓜ Guillotière) Despite its slightly out-of-the-way location, Slo Hostel is a great port of call if you're counting the euros. It has a variety of rooms for every budget, including spacious, tidy four- to eight-bed dorms as well as modern doubles. There's a small communal kitchen, an inviting courtyard and bike rental. Breakfast is €5.

★**Mama Shelter** HOTEL €€
(☎04 78 02 58 00; www.mamashelter.com/en/lyon; 13 rue Domer, 7e; r €69-299; P@; Ⓜ Jean Macé) Lyon's branch of this trendy hotel chain has sleek decor, carpets splashed with calli-graffiti, firm beds, plush pillows, modernist lighting and big-screen Macs offering free in-room movies. A youthful crowd fills the long bar at the low-lit restaurant. The residential location 2km outside the centre may feel remote, but it's only three metro stops from Gare de la Part-Dieu and place Bellecour.

Péniche Barnum B&B €€
(☎09 51 44 90 18, 06 63 64 37 39; www.peniche-barnum.com; 3 quai du Général Sarrail, 6e; d €120-150; ; Ⓜ Foch) Moored on the Rhône between Pont Morand and the Passerelle du Collège footbridge, this unique B&B is a navy-and-timber barge with two smart en-suite guestrooms, a book-filled lounge, and a shaded deck terrace. Organic breakfasts cost €11.

Croix Rousse

Nos Chambres en Ville B&B €
(☎06 60 11 32 57, 04 78 27 22 30; www.chambres-a-lyon.com; 12 rue René Leynaud, 1er; s/d/tr incl breakfast €77/90/123; ⏱Sep-Jul; ; Ⓜ Croix Paquet, Hôtel de Ville) Graphic artist and jewellery designer Karine Sigiscar runs this three-room B&B in an 18th-century home midway between Croix Rousse and the Hôtel de Ville. It's on the ground floor. Rooms come with stone walls, exposed wood beams, low ceilings and parquet flooring. Common areas are limited, as half the building is the owner's personal living space.

Eating

A flurry of big-name chefs presides over a sparkling restaurant line-up that embraces all genres: French, fusion, fast and international, as well as traditional Lyonnais *bouchons* (small bistros).

Vieux Lyon

Vieux Lyon has a surfeit of restaurants, most aimed at tourists.

Terre Adélices ICE CREAM €
(☎04 78 03 51 84; www.terre-adelice.eu; 1 place de la Baleine, 5e; 1/2/3 scoops €2.60/4.70/6.50; ⏱10am-midnight Apr-Oct, noon-7pm Nov-Mar; Ⓜ Vieux Lyon) It's hard to resist the 150 flavours, both divine and daring, at this ice-cream shop on Vieux Lyon's main pedestrian thoroughfare. Play it safe with Valrhona dark chocolate, organic pistachio or vanilla from Madagascar, experiment gently with cardamom, Grand Marnier, or lavender, or take a walk on the wild side with a scoop of wasabi, yoghurt and pepper or tomato-basil.

★**Daniel et Denise** BOUCHON €€
(☎04 78 42 24 62; www.danieletdenise-stjean.fr; 36 rue Tramassac, 5e; mains €15-25, lunch menu

DON'T MISS

LYON FOOD MARKETS

Food shopping in Lyon is an unmissable part of the city's experience. And with so many urban spaces and parks, there are plenty of picnic spots too.

Lyon's famed indoor food market **Les Halles de Lyon Paul Bocuse** (04 78 62 39 33; www.hallespaulbocuse.lyon.fr; 102 cours Lafayette, 3e; 7am-10.30pm Tue-Sat, to 4.30pm Sun; M Part-Dieu) has more than 60 stalls selling their renowned wares. Pick up a round of impossibly runny St Marcellin from legendary cheesemonger Mère Richard, and a knobbly Jésus de Lyon from pork butcher Collette Sibilia. Or enjoy a sit-down lunch of local produce at the stalls, lip-smacking *coquillages* (shellfish) included.

Lyon has two main outdoor food markets: **Croix Rousse** (bd de la Croix Rousse, 1er; 6am-1pm Tue-Sun; M Croix Rousse) and **Presqu'île** (quai St-Antoine, 1er; 6am-1pm Tue-Sun; M Bellecour, Cordeliers). Each has more than 100 vendors.

€21, dinner menus €30-40; noon-2pm & 7.30-9.30pm Tue-Sat) One of Vieux Lyon's most dependable and traditional eateries, this classic spot is run by award-winning chef Joseph Viola, who was elected president of Lyon's *bouchon* association in 2014. Come here for elaborate variations on traditional Lyonnais themes.

★Cinq Mains BISTRO €€
(04 37 57 30 52; www.facebook.com/cinqmains; 12 rue Monseigneur Lavarenne, 5e; lunch menus €12-19, dinner menus €28-35; noon-2pm & 8-10pm daily) When young Lyonnais Grégory Cuilleron and his two friends opened this neobistro in early 2016, it was an instant hit. They're working wonders at this cool loft-like space with a mezzanine, serving up tantalising creations based on what they find at the market. A new generation of chefs and a new spin for Lyonnais cuisine.

Presqu'île

In the Presqu'Île, cobbled rue Mercière and rue des Marronniers – both in the 2e (metro Bellecour) – are chock-a-block with sidewalk terraces in summer. In the 1er, the tangle of streets south of the opera house, including rue du Garet, rue Neuve and rue Verdi, is equally jam-packed with eateries.

Reynon DELI €
(04 78 37 39 08; www.reynonlyon.com; 13 rue des Archers, 2e; 8.30am-1.30pm & 3-7.30pm Tue-Sat; M Bellecour) Since 1937, this *charcuterie-traiteur* has been one of Lyon's finest sources for sausages and prepared foods.

Le Bistrot du Potager NEOBISTRO, TAPAS €
(04 78 29 61 59; www.lebistrotdupotager.com; 3 rue de la Martinière, 1er; mains €12-17; noon-2pm & 7.30-9.30pm Tue-Sat; M Hôtel de Ville) An offshoot of the renowned Potager des Halles restaurant, this gourmet bistro and tapas bar is a dreamy spot for a tasty lunch or to while away an evening. Happy diners throng the high-ceilinged main dining room, cosy upstairs balcony and sidewalk tables opposite the Fresque des Lyonnais, lingering over wine and creative seasonal dishes.

In Cuisine CAFETERIA €
(www.incuisine.fr; 1 place Bellecour, 2e; mains €9, menus €14.90-16.20; 11am-noon & 2-6.30pm Mon, 10am-noon & 2-7pm Tue-Fri, 10am-7pm Sat; M Bellecour) This foodie haven has an astonishing selection of culinary, gastronomic and wine titles. It also offers demonstrations, tastings, cooking courses and lunch in its tearoom. The menu changes daily; it specialises in market-fresh cuisine with a twist.

L'Instant Fromage CHEESE €
(04 78 92 93 54; www.linstant-fromage.fr; 31 rue Ste-Hélène, 2e; lunch menu €11, mains €8-15; noon-2pm & 6-10pm Mon-Sat; ; M Ampère-Victor Hugo, Bellecour) This sweet hideaway with checked and polka-dotted tablecloths is a cheese-lover's dream. Sample individual portions of three-dozen French cheeses (cow, sheep and goat) from the chalkboard menu, or let them surprise you with an *ardoise découverte* (five cheeses for €13.50). There's also a nice selection of charcuterie, *tartines* (open-faced sandwiches) and salads.

★Le Musée BOUCHON €€
(04 78 37 71 54; 2 rue des Forces, 2e; lunch mains €14, lunch menus €19-26, dinner menus €23-32; noon-1.30pm & 7.30-9.30pm Tue-Sat; M Cordeliers) Housed in the stables of Lyon's former Hôtel de Ville, this delightful *bouchon* serves a splendid array of meat-heavy Lyonnais classics, including a divine *poulet au vinaigre* (chicken cooked in vinegar). The daily changing *menu* features 10 appetisers and 10 main dishes, plus five scrumptious desserts, all served on cute china plates at long family-style tables. After dinner, the gregarious owner offers history tours featuring the *traboule* out back.

★ Le Poêlon d'Or BOUCHON €€
(☎04 78 37 65 60; www.lepoelondor-restaurant.fr; 29 rue des Remparts d'Ainay, 2e; lunch menus €17-20, dinner menus €27-32; ⊙noon-2pm & 7.30-10pm Mon-Fri; Ⓜ Ampère-Victor Hugo) This upmarket *bouchon*, around the corner from the Musée des Tissus, is well known among local foodies who recommend its superb *andouillette* (chitterlings) and pike dumplings. Save room for the delicious chocolate mousse or the vanilla crème brûlée. Yummy. Well worth the detour.

Le Bouchon des Filles LYONNAIS €€
(☎04 78 30 40 44; 20 rue Sergent Blandan, 1er; menu €26; ⊙7-9.30pm Mon-Fri, noon-1.45pm & 7-9.30pm Sat & Sun; Ⓜ Hôtel de Ville) This contemporary ode to Lyon's legendary culinary *mères* (mothers) is run by an enterprising crew of young women with deep roots in the local *bouchon* scene and a flair for fine cooking. The light and fluffy quenelles are among the best you'll find in Lyon, and the rustic-chic decor, with wooden beams, is warm and welcoming.

Thomas MODERN FRENCH €€
(☎04 72 56 04 76; www.restaurant-thomas.com; 6 rue Laurencin, 2e; lunch menu €21, dinner menu €45; ⊙11am-2pm & 6-10pm Mon-Fri; Ⓜ Ampère) One of Lyon's savviest chefs, Thomas Ponson, infuses his cooking with a panoply of flavours. He gives taste buds the choice between formal dining at his eponymous restaurant; more casual fare in his Bouchon Thomas; and more casual still at his tapas-inspired Bistrot Thomas (both across the street).

Brasserie Georges BRASSERIE €€
(☎04 72 56 54 54; www.brasseriegeorges.com; 30 cours de Verdun, 2e; mains €17-24, menus €23-28; ⊙11.30am-11.15pm Sun-Thu, 11.30am-midnight Fri & Sat; Ⓜ Perrache) Opened as a brewery in 1836 (and still offering four homebrews on tap), Georges' enormous 1924 art-deco interior can feed 2000 a day! Famous customers include Rodin, Balzac, Hemingway, Zola, Verne and Piaf; food spans onion soup, sauerkraut, seafood, Lyonnais specialities as well as a smattering of vegetarian options.

Le Saint Vincent BOUCHON €€
(☎04 72 07 70 43; www.restaurant-saint-vincent.fr; 6 place Fernand Rey, 1er; lunch menu €17, dinner menu €25-30; ⊙noon-2pm & 8-10pm Mon-Sat; Ⓜ Hôtel de Ville) The ample three-course lunch *menu* of home-cooked soups and stews, fish and meat dishes and desserts is reason enough to visit this cosy neighbourhood eatery, but what really sets it apart is the outdoor seating at chartreuse chairs and tables on a pretty-as-a-picture, tree-shaded square – perfect on a sunny afternoon.

Croix Rousse

Croix Rousse is a great neighbourhood for foodies, with a range of affordable eateries with bags of character.

★ L'Ourson qui Boit FUSION €€
(☎04 78 27 23 37; 23 rue Royale, 1er; lunch/dinner menu €18/32; ⊙noon-1.30pm & 7.30-9.30pm Mon, Tue & Thu-Sat; Ⓜ Croix Paquet) On the fringes of Croix Rousse, Japanese chef Akira Nishigaki puts his own splendid spin on French cuisine, with plenty of locally sourced fresh vegetables and light, clean flavours. The ever-changing *menu* of two daily appetisers and two main dishes is complemented by good wines, attentive service and scrumptious desserts. Well worth reserving ahead.

In early 2016, Akira Nishigaki opened **L'Ourson qui Boit – Pâtisserie** (pastries €3.50) next door.

★ L'Instant CAFE €
(☎04 78 29 85 08; www.linstant-patisserie.fr; 3 place Marcel Bertone, 4e; breakfast €6.50, lunch mains €6.50-13, weekend brunch €20; ⊙8am-7pm Mon-Sat, to 1pm Sun; 📶; Ⓜ Croix Rousse) The best spot in Croix Rousse to start the day, this hybrid cafe–pastry shop overlooking lovely place Marcel Bertone packs a punch. The continental breakfast (and brunch on weekends) is the highlight, while the pastries and pies will leave your taste buds reeling. The wonderfully mellow setting and relaxed urban vibe add to the appeal. Ample outdoor seating on warm days.

Le Canut et Les Gones BISTRO €€
(☎04 78 29 17 23; www.lecanutetlesgones.com; 29 rue de Belfort, 4e; lunch mains €12-14, lunch menus €17-24, dinner menu €29; ⊙noon-1.30pm & 7.30-9pm Tue-Sat; Ⓜ Croix Rousse) With three cosy rooms and a funky retro decor featuring dozens of antique clocks, this laid-back neighbourhood eatery draws a savvy local crowd with creative cuisine built around produce from Croix Rousse's market.

Balthaz'art MODERN FRENCH €€
(☎04 72 07 08 88; www.restaurantbalthazart.fr; 7 rue des Pierres Plantées, 1er; lunch menus €17-20, dinner menus €29-34; ⊙noon-2pm Thu-Sat, 7.30-9.30pm Tue-Sat; Ⓜ Croix Rousse) A block south of Croix Rousse's central square, this cheerful

DON'T MISS

A BIRD'S-EYE VIEW

The views are so incredible that it'd be easy for **Le Restaurant de Fourvière** (☎04 78 25 21 15; www.restaurant-fourviere.fr; 9 place de Fourvière, 5e; mains €10-24, lunch menu €17, dinner menus €23-46; ⊙noon-2.30pm & 7-10.30pm) to be a tourist trap, so it's all the more impressive because it's not. Instead it concentrates on well-prepared French (and Lyonnais) specialities including sautéed scallops and pike perch cooked in red-wine sauce.

burgundy-red eatery draws animated crowds with its excellent-value lunches and sumptuous multicourse dinners. Inventive meat and fish dishes – including its signature *tartare de bœuf* with capers, olives, preserved lemon and coriander – come accompanied with plenty of seasonal vegetables.

Toutes les Couleurs VEGETARIAN €€
(☎04 72 00 03 95; www.touteslescouleurs.fr; 26 rue Imbert Colomès, 1er; mains €10-20, lunch menus €14-18, dinner menus €23-29; ⊙noon-2pm Tue-Sat, 7.30-10pm Fri & Sat; 🌶; Ⓜ Croix Paquet) Manna from heaven for Lyon's oft-neglected vegetarians, this place serves a fully meatless menu with abundant organic and gluten-free options.

La Bonâme de Bruno MODERN FRENCH €€
(☎04 78 30 83 93; www.restaurant-labonamedebruno.com; 5 Grande Rue des Feuillants; mains €13-18, lunch menus €15-18, dinner menus €28-36; ⊙noon-2pm Tue-Fri, 8-9.30pm Tue-Sat; Ⓜ Croix Paquet) Great food and atmosphere come together at this airy yet intimate eatery that's somewhere on the continuum between bistro and gastronomic. The high-ceilinged, parquet-floored dining room conjures the spirit of a 19th-century dance studio, while the *menus*, prepared with enthusiasm and creativity, change regularly based on Bruno's whims. Desserts are especially memorable.

La Mère Brazier GASTRONOMIC €€€
(☎04 78 23 17 20; www.lamerebrazier.fr; 12 rue Royale; lunch menus €57-70, dinner menus €100-155; ⊙noon-1.15pm & 7.45-9.15pm Mon-Fri Sep-Jul; Ⓜ Croix Paquet) Chef Mathieu Vianney has reinvented the mythical early-20th-century restaurant that earned Mère Eugénie Brazier Lyon's first trio of Michelin stars in 1933 (a copy of the original guidebook takes pride of place). Vianney is doing admirable justice to Brazier's legacy, claiming two Michelin stars himself for his assured cuisine accompanied by an impressive wine list.

Drinking & Nightlife

Lyon's beer-thirsty students keep the scene lively and the bars and clubs pumping at weekends. Vieux Lyon has an extraordinary concentration of British and Irish pubs. For off-beat bars, scout out alternative Croix Rousse. Many establishments start as a relaxed place for a drink, morphing into jam-packed bars and/or live-music and dancing venues as the night wears on.

Vieux Lyon

Johnny Walsh's PUB
(56 rue St-Georges, 5e; ⊙9pm-3am Tue-Sun; 📶; Ⓜ Vieux Lyon) Local connoisseurs claim this is the best pub in Lyon. It has live music four nights a week. At the south end of Vieux Lyon.

(L'A)Kroche BAR
(www.lakroche.wix.com/lakroche-bar; 8 rue Monseigneur Lavarenne, 5e; ⊙4pm-1am Tue-Sat, 4-9pm Sun & Mon; Ⓜ Vieux Lyon) Hip cafe-bar with six-dozen flavours of rum, daily happy hours and frequent live music with no cover charge.

Presqu'île

Harmonie des Vins WINE BAR
(www.harmoniedesvins.fr; 9 rue Neuve, 1er; ⊙10am-2.30pm & 6.30pm-1am Tue-Fri, 6.30pm-1am Sat; 📶; Ⓜ Hôtel de Ville, Cordeliers) Find out all about French wine at this charm-laden wine bar replete with old stone walls, contemporary furnishings and tasty food. A cheese or charcuterie platter will set you back €14.

Le Vin des Vivants WINE BAR
(www.levindesvivants.fr; 6 place Fernand Rey, 1er; ⊙6.30-9pm Tue & Wed, to 11.30pm Thu-Sat; Ⓜ Hôtel de Ville) This relaxed stone-walled corner bar on a pretty backstreet square specialises in organic wines.

Grand Café des Négociants CAFE
(www.lesnegociants.com; 1 place Francisque Régaud, 2e; ⊙7am-4am; Ⓜ Cordeliers) The tree-shaded terrace and Second Empire decor of chandeliers and mirror-lined walls are the big draws at this centrally located cafe-brasserie, a Lyonnais institution since 1864. Food is served from noon to midnight.

Soda Bar COCKTAIL BAR
(7 rue de la Martinière, 1er; ⊙6.30pm-1am Tue & Wed, to 3am Thu-Sat mid-Aug–mid-Jul; Ⓜ Hôtel de

LOCAL KNOWLEDGE

BOUCHONS FOR FOODIES

A *bouchon* might be a 'bottle stopper' or 'traffic jam' elsewhere in France, but in Lyon it's a small, friendly bistro that cooks up traditional cuisine using regional produce. *Bouchons* originated in the first half of the 20th century when many large bourgeois families had to let go of their in-house cooks, who then set up their own restaurant businesses. The first of these *mères* (mothers) was Mère Guy, followed by Mère Filloux, Mère Brazier (under whom Paul Bocuse trained) and others. Choose carefully – not all *bouchons* are as authentic as they first appear. Many of the best are certified by the organisation Les Authentiques Bouchons Lyonnais – look for the metal plate on their façades depicting traditional puppet Gnafron (Guignol's mate) with his glass of Beaujolais.

Kick-start a memorable gastronomic experience with a *communard*, a blood-red aperitif of Beaujolais wine mixed with *crème de cassis* (blackcurrant liqueur), named after the supporters of the Paris Commune killed in 1871. When ordering wine with your meal, ask for a *pot* – a classically Lyonnais 46cL glass bottle adorned with an elastic band to prevent wine drips – of local Brouilly, Beaujolais, Côtes du Rhône or Mâcon, costing around €9 to €12; a smaller, 25cL version called a *fillette* costs between €5 and €7.

Next comes the entrée, perhaps *tablier de sapeur* ('fireman's apron'; actually meaning breaded, fried tripe), *salade de cervelas* (salad of boiled pork sausage sometimes studded with pistachio nuts or black truffle specks), or *caviar de la Croix Rousse* (lentils in creamy sauce). Hearty main dishes include *boudin blanc* (veal sausage), *boudin noir aux pommes* (blood sausage with apples), quenelles (feather-light flour, egg and cream dumplings), *quenelles de brochet* (pike dumplings served in a creamy crayfish sauce), *andouillette* (sausage made from pigs' intestines), *gras double* (a type of tripe), *pieds de mouton/veau/couchon* (sheep/calf/pig trotters) and *poulet au vinaigre* (chicken cooked in vinegar).

For the cheese course, choose between a bowl of *fromage blanc* (a cross between cream cheese and natural yoghurt); *cervelle de canut* ('brains of the silk weaver'; *fromage blanc* mixed with chives and garlic), which originated in Croix Rousse and accompanied every meal for 19th-century weavers; or local St Marcellin ripened to gooey perfection.

Desserts are grandma-style: think *tarte aux pommes* (apple tart), or the Lyonnais classic *tarte aux pralines*, a brilliant rose-coloured confection made with crème fraiche and crushed sugar-coated almonds.

Little etiquette is required in *bouchons*. Seldom do you get clean cutlery for each course, and mopping your plate with a chunk of bread is fine. In the most popular and traditional spots, you'll often find yourself sitting elbow-to-elbow with your fellow diners at a long row of tightly wedged tables. Advance reservations are recommended.

Several classics worth seeking out:

Le Garet (☎04 78 28 16 94; 7 rue du Garet, 1er; lunch/dinner menus €20/26; ⊙noon-1.30pm & 7.30-9pm Mon-Fri; Ⓜ Hôtel de Ville)

Chez Hugon (☎04 78 28 10 94; www.bouchonlyonnais.fr; 12 rue Pizay, 1er; menu €27; ⊙noon-2pm & 7.30-9.30pm Mon-Fri; Ⓜ Hôtel de Ville)

Chez Paul (☎04 78 28 35 83; www.chezpaul.fr; 11 rue Major Martin, 1er; lunch menus €16-20, dinner menus €17-27; ⊙noon-2pm & 7.30-9.30pm Mon-Sat; Ⓜ Hôtel de Ville)

Le Tire Bouchon (☎09 83 22 88 47; www.facebook.com/restaurantletirebouchon; 16 rue du Bœuf, 5e; lunch menus €15-18, menus €21-32; ⊙noon-2pm Wed-Sun, 7-10pm Tue-Sat; Ⓜ Vieux Lyon)

Café des Federations (☎04 78 28 26 00; www.restaurant-cafedesfederations-lyon.com; 8-10 rue Major Martin, 1er; lunch/dinner menus €19.50/27; ⊙noon-1.30pm & 7.45-9pm Mon-Sat; Ⓜ Hôtel de Ville)

Ville) This hip bar is popular with a fashionable clientele. Choose from an inspired list of cocktails, or ask for the bar staff to surprise you with their own concoctions.

Monkey Club COCKTAIL BAR
(www.themonkeyclub.fr; 19 place Tolozan, 1er; ⊙6.30pm-1am Tue & Wed, to 3am Thu-Sat; Ⓜ Hôtel de Ville) This trendy, friendly cocktail bar with a retro feel is decked out with bright-

green walls, couches, and a youthful clientele. Good cocktails (from €10) as well as charcuterie and cheese platters (from €9).

Café 203 BAR
(9 rue du Garet, 1er; 7am-2am Mon-Sat, noon-1am Sun; ; Hôtel de Ville) This trendy corner resto-bar with sidewalk tables straddling both sides of a narrow backstreet buzzes day and night.

La Cave d'à Côté WINE BAR
(04 78 28 31 46; 7 rue Pleney, 1er; 11.30am-2pm & 6.30-11.30pm Mon-Sat; Cordeliers) Hidden in a tiny alleyway, this cultured bar and wine shop feels like a rustic English gentlemen's club with leather sofa seating and library.

Croix Rousse

Modernartcafé BAR
(http://modernartcafe.free.fr; 65 bd de la Croix Rousse, 4e; noon-2pm & 5pm-2am Sun-Fri, 5pm-2am Sat; ; Croix Rousse) Changing art on the walls, weekend brunch and various photography-, music- and video-driven events make this art bar a linchpin of Croix Rousse's creative community.

La Bistro fait sa Broc' BAR
(1-3 rue Dumenge, 4e; 5pm-1am Mon-Sat; Croix Rousse) A lime-green and candy-floss-pink façade greets you at this retro neighbourhood wine bar where no two chairs match. Occasional bands.

La Boite à Café – Café Mokxa CAFE
(www.cafemokxa.com; 3 rue Abbé Rozier, 1er; 8am-7pm Mon-Fri, 9am-7pm Sat, 11am-7pm Sun; ; Croix Paquet, Hôtel de Ville) A favourite haunt of Lyonnais caffeine fiends and students, this laid-back place on the Croix Rousse slopes roasts its own beans and serves Sunday brunch. In summer, tables spill onto charming, circular place du Forez. It also serves superb pastries.

WORTH A TRIP

GASTRONOMY KING

Some 7km up the Saône from central Lyon, triple-Michelin-starred **L'Auberge du Pont de Collonges** (04 72 42 90 90; www.bocuse.com; 40 quai de la Plage, Collonges au Mont d'Or; menus €165-260; noon-1.30pm & 8-9.30pm) is the flagship of the city's most decorated chef, Paul Bocuse. Classics include the likes of braised sweetbreads, thyme-roasted rack of lamb, Beaujolais winemaker's sherbet and Bocuse's signature *soupe VGE* (truffle soup created for French president Valéry Giscard d'Estaing in 1975).

Entertainment

★Le Sucre LIVE MUSIC
(www.le-sucre.eu; 50 quai Rambaud, 2e; 6pm-midnight Wed & Thu, 7pm-5am Fri & Sat) Down in the Confluence neighbourhood, Lyon's most innovative club hosts DJs, live shows and eclectic arts events on its super-cool roof terrace atop a 1930s sugar factory, La Sucrière.

Opéra de Lyon OPERA
(www.opera-lyon.com; place de la Comédie, 1er; Hôtel de Ville) Lyon's premier venue for opera, ballet and classical music.

Péristyle LIVE MUSIC
(Programme Jazz de l'Opéra de Lyon; www.opera-lyon.com; place de la Comédie, 1er; 7-10pm Mon-Sat mid-Jun–early Sep) Free summer concerts under the Opéra's arches, ranging from swing to blues and funk to jazz. Waiters circulate with drinks as the music plays. Hour-long sets start at 7pm, 8.15pm and 10pm; arrive early to snag a table.

Le Transbordeur LIVE MUSIC
(www.transbordeur.fr; 3 bd de Stalingrad, Villeurbanne; Wed-Sat; Cité Internationale/Transbordeur) In an old industrial building near the Parc de la Tête d'Or's northeastern corner, Lyon's prime concert venue draws international acts on the European concert-tour circuit.

Hot Club de Lyon LIVE MUSIC
(www.hotclubjazzlyon.com; 26 rue Lanterne, 1er; 8.30pm-1am Tue-Sat; Hôtel de Ville) Lyon's leading jazz club, around since 1948. Main acts take the stage at 9.30pm.

Hangar du Premier Film CINEMA
(www.institut-lumiere.org; 25 rue du Premier Film, 8e; Monplaisir-Lumière) This former factory and birthplace of cinema now screens films of all genres and eras in their original languages. From approximately June to September, the big screen moves outside.

Auditorium Orchestre National de Lyon CLASSICAL MUSIC
(04 78 95 95 95; www.auditorium-lyon.com; 149 rue Garibaldi, 3e; Sep-Jun; Part-Dieu, Part-Dieu-Servient, Part-Dieu-Villette) Built in

1975, this spaceship-like auditorium houses the National Orchestra of Lyon, along with workshops, jazz and world-music concerts.

Shopping

Vieux Lyon's narrow streets are dotted with galleries, and antiquarian and secondhand bookshops.

High-street chains line rue de la République and rue Victor Hugo, while upmarket boutiques and design houses stud rue du Président Édouard Herriot, rue de Brest and the streets between place des Jacobins and place Bellecour. More cluster between art galleries and antique shops around rue Auguste Comte, 2e.

Le Village des Créateurs FASHION & ACCESSORIES

(☎04 78 27 37 21; www.villagedescreateurs.com; Passage Thiaffait, 19 rue René Leynaud, 1er; ⊙workshop 2-7pm by reservation Wed-Sat, boutique 1-7pm Tue-Sat; Ⓜ Croix Paquet) Housed in an arcaded courtyard on the Croix Rousse *pentes*, this innovative cluster of workshop-boutiques showcases the artwork of a dozen up-and-coming local designers. The workshops can be visited with advanced reservation or you can pick up items from the adjacent shop, **VDC/B**, which serves as a sales outlet, specialising in clothing and accessories.

Les Puces du Canal MARKET

(www.pucesducanal.com; 3 rue Eugène Pottier, Villeurbanne; ⊙7am-noon Thu & Sat, to 3pm Sun; Le Roulet) With more than 400 exhibitors strung out along the canal banks in the northeastern suburb of Villeurbanne, France's second biggest flea market is a fun place to browse, especially for antiques and furniture. Sunday draws the biggest crowds.

DRINKS AFLOAT

Along quai Victor Augagneur on the Rhône's left bank, a string of *péniches* (barges with onboard bars) serve drinks from mid-afternoon onwards, many of them rocking until the wee hours with DJs and/or live bands. To study your options, stroll the quayside between Pont Lafayette and Pont de la Guillotière.

Information

Tourist Office (☎04 72 77 69 69; www.lyon-france.com; place Bellecour, 2e; ⊙9am-6pm; Ⓜ Bellecour) In the centre of Presqu'île, Lyon's exceptionally helpful, multilingual and well-staffed main tourist office offers a variety of city walking tours and sells the Lyon City Card. There's a smaller branch just outside the Vieux Lyon metro station.

Getting There & Away

AIR

Lyon-St-Exupéry Airport (www.lyonaeroports.com) Located 25km east of the city, with 40 airlines (including many budget carriers) serving more than 100 direct destinations across Europe and beyond.

BUS

International bus companies **Eurolines** (☎04 72 56 95 30, 08 92 89 90 91; www.eurolines.fr; Gare de Perrache, 2e; Ⓜ Perrache) and **Linebús** (☎04 72 41 72 27; www.linebus.com; Gare de Perrache) offer service to Spain, Portugal, Italy and Germany from the Centre d'Échange building at the north end of the Perrache train complex. Follow signs for 'Cars Grandes Lignes' and 'Galerie A: Gare Routière Internationale'.

LGBT LYON

Declared France's most gay-friendly city in 2014 by the magazine *Têtu*, Lyon has scads of venues. Guys' favourite places to party include **United Café** (www.united-cafe.com; impasse de la Pêcherie, 1er; ⊙midnight-5am; Ⓜ Hôtel de Ville), **Le XS Bar** (19 rue Claudia, 2e; ⊙5pm-3am; Ⓜ Cordeliers) and the city's oldest gay bar, **La Ruche** (22 rue Gentil, 2e; ⊙5pm-3am; Ⓜ Cordeliers). Lesbian venues include **Le L Bar** (19 rue du Garet, 1er; ⊙6pm-4am; Ⓜ Hôtel de Ville) and **Le Marais** (www.lemarais-lyon.fr; 3 rue Terme, 1er; ⊙9pm-3am Thu, 11pm-5am Fri & Sat; Ⓜ Hôtel de Ville, Croix Paquet).

For up-to-the-minute listings, visit Gay in Lyon (www.gayinlyon.com) and Hétéroclite (www.heteroclite.org), or check with the **Forum Gai et Lesbien de Lyon** (☎04 78 39 97 72; www.fgllyon.org; 17 rue Romarin, 1er; Ⓜ Croix Paquet), which organises social events. Lyon's **Lesbian & Gay Pride** (www.fierte.net) march and festivities hit the streets each year in June. In March, the city hosts a popular week-long LGBT film festival, **Écrans Mixtes** (www.festival-em.org).

TRAIN

Lyon has two main-line train stations: **Gare de la Part-Dieu** (place Charles Béraudier, 3e; Ⓜ Part-Dieu), 1.5km east of the Rhône, and **Gare de Perrache** (cours de Verdun Rambaud, 2e; Ⓜ Perrache). Some local trains stop at **Gare St-Paul** (www.ter.sncf.com/rhone-alpes; 11bis place St-Paul, 5e; Ⓜ Vieux Lyon) and **Gare Jean Macé** (www.ter.sncf.com/rhone-alpes; place Jean Macé, 7e; Ⓜ Jean Macé). There's also a TGV station at Lyon-St-Exupéry Airport. Buy tickets at the stations or at the **SNCF Boutique** (2 place Bellecour; ⏲10am-6.45pm Tue-Fri, to 5.45pm Sat; Ⓜ Bellecour) downtown.

Destinations by direct TGV include the following:

Dijon €37, 1½ hours, at least six daily
Lille-Europe €116, three hours, at least eight daily
Marseille €53, 1¾ hours, every 30 to 60 minutes
Paris Charles de Gaulle Airport €97, two hours, at least 11 daily
Paris Gare de Lyon €75, two hours, every 30 to 60 minutes

ℹ Getting Around

TO/FROM THE AIRPORT

The **Rhônexpress** (www.rhonexpress.fr; adult/youth/child €15.90/13.20/free) tramway links the airport with the Part-Dieu train station in under 30 minutes. It's a five- to 10-minute walk from the arrivals hall; follow the red signs with the Rhônexpress train logo. Trams depart every 15 minutes between 6am and 9pm, less frequently from 4.25am to 6am and 9pm to midnight. Online purchases and round-trip travel qualify for discounts.

By taxi, the 30- to 45-minute trip between the airport and the city centre costs around €50 during the day and €65 between 7pm and 7am.

BICYCLE

Pick up a red-and-silver bike at one of 200-odd bike stations throughout the city and drop it off at another with Lyon's **Vélo'v** (www.velov.grandlyon.com; 1st 30min free, next 30min €1, each subsequent 30min period €2) bike rental scheme. Start by paying a one-time flat fee for a *carte courte durée* (short-duration card, €1.50 for 24 hours, €5 for seven days). Once equipped with the card, you're entitled to unlimited rentals. Pay all fees with a chip-enabled credit card using machines installed at bike stations.

BOAT

Le Vaporetto (☎ 08 20 20 69 20; www.confluence.fr/W/do/centre/navette) operates *navettes* (passenger ferry boats) to Lyon's new Confluence neighbourhood. Boats (€2) depart hourly between 10am and 9pm from riverbank docks on the Saône near place St-Paul and place Bellecour, returning from the Confluence dock between 10.30am and 9.30pm. Travel time is 30 minutes from the **St-Paul dock** (quai de Bondy, 5e; Ⓜ Hôtel de Ville, Vieux Lyon) and 20 minutes from the **Bellecour dock** (quai Tilsitt, 2e; Ⓜ Bellecour, Vieux Lyon).

PUBLIC TRANSPORT

Buses, trams, a four-line metro and two funiculars linking Vieux Lyon to Fourvière and St-Just are operated by TCL (www.tcl.fr), which has information offices dispensing transport maps at major metro stations throughout Lyon. Public transport runs from around 5am to midnight.

Tickets valid for all forms of public transport cost €1.80 (€16.20 for a *carnet* of 10) and are available from bus and tram drivers as well as machines at metro entrances. Tickets allowing two consecutive hours of travel after 9am or unlimited travel after 7pm cost €3, and an all-day ticket costs €5.50. Bring coins, as machines don't accept notes (or some international credit cards). Time-stamp tickets on all forms of public transport or risk a fine.

Holders of the Lyon City Card (p451) receive free unlimited access to Lyon's transport network for the duration of the card's validity.

TAXI

Taxis hover in front of both train stations, on the place Bellecour end of **rue de la Barre (2e)**, at the northern end of rue du **Président Édouard Herriot (1er)** and along **quai Romain Rolland in Vieux Lyon (5e)**.

Allo Taxi (☎ 04 78 28 23 23; www.allotaxi.fr)
Taxis Lyonnais (☎ 04 78 26 81 81; www.taxilyonnais.com)

NORTH OF LYON

Lush green hills, lakes and vineyards unfold to the north of cosmopolitan Lyon.

Beaujolais

Ah, Beaujolais, where the unhurried life is complemented by rolling vineyards, beguiling villages, old churches, splendid estates and country roads that twist into the hills. This rural paradise is within easy reach of Lyon, which is a mere 50km to the southeast.

An oenophile's nirvana, the region is synonymous with its fruity red wines, especially its 10 premium *crus*, and the Beaujolais Nouveau, drunk at the tender age of just six weeks. Vineyards stretch south from Mâcon along the right bank of the Saône for some 50km. Renowned wine-producing villages include Brouilly, Villié-Morgon, Fleurie,

DON'T MISS

GUIGNOL: LYON'S HISTORIC PUPPET

The history of Lyon's famous puppet, Guignol, is intertwined with that of the city. In 1797, out-of-work silk-weaver Laurent Mourguet took up dentistry (ie pulling teeth). To attract patients, he set up a puppet show in front of his chair, initially featuring the Italian Polichinelle (who became Punch in England). Success saw Mourguet move into full-time puppetry, creating Guignol in about 1808 and devising shows revolving around working-class issues, the news of the day, social gossip and satire.

Today this little hand-operated glove puppet pops up all over his home town, including on the **Fresque des Lyonnais** (cnr rue de la Martinière & quai St-Vincent, 1er; M Hôtel de Ville) mural and at puppet museums.

Guignol's highly visual, slapstick-style antics appeal equally to children and adults (theatres also stage some adult-only evening performances). Shows are in French but also incorporate traditional Lyonnais dialect, such as the words *quinquets* (eyes), *picou* (nose), *bajafler* (talking nonstop) and *gones* (kids, and, by extension, all Lyonnais).

In addition to performances at **Parc de la Tête d'Or** (Le Véritable Guignol du Parc; ☎04 78 93 71 75; place de Guignol, 6e; adult/child €4/3; ⊙3pm, 4pm & 5pm Wed, Sat & Sun), Lyon has three dedicated Guignol theatres:

Théâtre La Maison de Guignol (☎04 72 40 26 61; www.lamaisondeguignol.fr; 2 montée du Gourguillon, 5e; tickets adult/child €11/9; ⊙Wed, Sat & Sun; M Vieux Lyon) Quaint St-Georges theatre.

Guignol, un Gone de Lyon (☎04 72 32 11 55; www.guignol-un-gone-de-lyon.com; 65 bd des Canuts, 4e; adult/child €9.50/7.50; ⊙performances 3.30pm Wed, Sat & Sun Oct-Jun; M Hénon) In Croix Rousse; puppeteers give audiences a behind-the-scenes peek at the props and puppets after certain performances.

Théâtre Le Guignol de Lyon (☎04 78 28 92 57; www.guignol-lyon.com; 2 rue Louis Carrand, 5e; adult/child €10/7.50; M Vieux Lyon) In Vieux Lyon.

Juliénas, Moulin-à-Vent and St-Amour Bellevue. Be sure to factor in plenty of time for wine tasting.

Sights

Salles-Arbuissonnas-en-Beaujolais Priory HISTORIC BUILDING
(☎04 74 07 31 94; rue du Chapitre, Salles-Arbuissonnas-en-Beaujolais; museum adult/child €4.50/free; ⊙museum 10am-12.30pm & 2-5pm Apr-Oct) For architecture buffs, this 10th-century priory founded by the monks of Cluny is a must. It's notable for its superb Roman cloister and elaborate porch. Adjacent to the building is a small museum that displays art exhibits and Gallo-Roman artefacts and also explores monastic life in past centuries in Salles-Arbuissonnas.

Activities

Château de Juliénas WINE
(☎04 74 04 49 98, 06 96 76 95 41; www.chateaudejulienas.com; Château de Juliénas, Juliénas; ⊙by reservation) A beauty of a castle, the 16th-century Château de Juliénas occupies a delightful estate; tours can be arranged by phoning ahead. No doubt you'll be struck by the cellars, the longest in the region. Tours can be followed by an *aperi'vin* (tasting and snacks; €10).

Château du Bourg WINE
(☎06 08 86 49 02, 04 74 69 81 15; www.chateau-du-bourg.com; Le Bourg, Fleurie; ⊙by reservation) A superb experience, Château du Bourg, run by the Matray brothers (ask for Denis, who speaks passable English), offers free tastings in a cool bistro-like setting and can arrange vineyard tours and cellar visits on request (€12). Tip: Grille-Midi, its signature vintage, is unforgettable.

Caveau de Morgon WINE
(☎04 74 04 20 99; www.morgon.fr; Château Fontcrenne, Rue du Château Fontcrenne, Villié-Morgon; ⊙10am-noon & 2-6pm Feb-Dec) Morgon wine, anybody? Expand your knowledge of the local appellation with a tasting session at this vaulted cellar, which occupies a grandiose 17th-century château in the heart of town – it can't get more atmospheric than that.

Domaine des Vignes du Paradis – Pascal Durand WINE
(☎03 85 36 52 97; www.saint-amour-en-paradis.com; En Paradis, St-Amour Bellevue; ⊙10am-6pm)

WORTH A TRIP

CELEBRITY PÉROUGES

French film buffs will recognise photogenic Pérouges. Situated on a hill 30km northeast of Lyon, this enchanting yellow-stone medieval village has long been used as a set for films such as *Les Trois Mousquetaires (The Three Musketeers)*. It's worth braving the summertime crowds to stroll its cobbled alleys, admire its half-timbered houses and liberty tree on place de la Halle (planted it 1792), and wolf down *galettes de Pérouges* (warm sugar-crusted tarts) with cider.

Not to be missed in St-Amour is this award-winning domaine run by the fifth generation of vintners. It welcomes visitors to its intimate cellars and sells St-Amour wines at unbeatable prices.

Caveau du Moulin à Vent WINE
(☎03 85 35 58 09; www.moulin-a-vent.net; 1673 rte du Moulin à Vent, Moulin à Vent, Romanèche Thorins; ⊙10am-12.30pm & 2.30-7pm daily Jul & Aug, 10am-12.30pm & 2.30-6pm Thu-Mon Sep–mid-Dec & Mar-Jun) Dubbed the 'King of Beaujolais', the Moulin à Vent ('windmill') *appellation* is a particularly charming wine to sample in situ: its Caveau du Moulin à Vent, across the road from the windmill, provides a prime wine-tasting opportunity.

Sleeping

★Les Buis du Chardonnet B&B €
(☎04 74 03 64 76; www.lesbuisduchardonnet.com; Chardonnet, 399 rte des Andrés, Cogny; s/d incl breakfast €75/88; P 📶) If you're after hush and seclusion, this B&B with a green ethos – it was built as a positive-energy home – is the answer. The trio of sunny rooms have great picture windows and command superlative views of the vineyards. Madame is a former English teacher and willingly shares her great knowledge of all things Beaujolais – in perfect English, of course. Bonus: there's a kitchen for guests' use.

Les Roulottes et les Folies de la Serve B&B €
(☎06 95 99 68 55; www.lesroulottes.com; La Serve, Ouroux; caravan/d incl breakfast €65/€95; ⊙Apr–mid-Nov; P 📶) Run by traditional caravan-maker Pascal and his wife Pascaline, this unique place has a trio of romantically furnished 1920s to 1950s gypsy caravans amid the B&B's fields (€3 to €5 extra per night for heating). Bathrooms are provided in the main farmhouse, which has two whimsical en-suite guestrooms. Reserve at least two days ahead for food baskets and picnic hampers (€15 per person). There's also a kitchen for guests' use.

★Le Trésor d'Alice B&B €€
(☎04 74 69 04 40; www.le-tresor-d-alice.com; Cherves, Quincié-en-Beaujolais; d incl breakfast €95-108; P 📶 🏊) Snug in a renovated farm nestled in a peaceful valley, this two-room B&B enchants. Rooms mix original features (including exposed stone walls) and period furniture with stylish contemporary fabrics and other decorative touches. Marie-Pascale, your gracious host, is very knowledgeable about Beaujolais wines and can arrange tasting sessions. Evening meals cost €22. The heated pool is another plus.

★Auberge de Clochemerle HOTEL €€
(☎04 74 03 20 16; www.aubergedeclochemerle.fr; 12 rue Gabriel Chevallier, Vaux-en-Beaujolais; d €60-185, q €200, restaurant menus €42-81; P 📶) A pleasant combination of modern and traditional, this atmospheric hotel smack dab in the centre of Vaux-en-Beaujolais has 12 stylishly refitted rooms, some with vineyard views. Dining at its Michelin-starred restaurant is a treat. Chef Romain creates elaborate Beaujolais meals using the best local ingredients, and his wife Delphine is a renowned sommelier – wine pairings are an adventure in themselves. Brilliant value.

Eating

La Terrasse du Beaujolais REGIONAL CUISINE €€
(☎09 70 35 32 27; www.la-terrasse-du-beaujolais.fr; La Terrasse, Chiroubles; mains €16-30, menus €26-58; ⊙noon-1.30pm & 7-8.30pm Mar-Aug, closed Mon & dinner Wed Sep-Nov, closed Mon-Thu Dec-Feb) That view! Perched high above Chiroubles at an altitude of 760m, this well-known venture offers a sensational panorama over the entire Beaujolais region, the Saône valley and the Alps. Food-wise, it's no less impressive, with hearty regional dishes, including *coq au beaujolais* (chicken cooked in Beaujolais wine) and *andouillette* (chitterlings). End on a sweet high with one of the excellent homemade desserts.

★Au 14 Février FUSION €€€
(☎03 85 37 11 45; www.sa-au14fevrier.com; Le Plâtre Durant, St-Amour Bellevue; menus €52-92; ⊙noon-2pm & 7.30-9pm Fri-Mon, 7.30-9pm Thu) For a gastronomic experience in the Beaujolais area, look no further than this gem of a

restaurant. A true alchemist, Japanese chef Masafumi Hamano has got the magic formula right, fusing French with Japanese to create stunning, colourful cuisine, perfectly matched with French wines. It's housed in a traditional *maison de village* that has been entirely refurbished and modernised.

Information

Tourist Office (☎04 74 69 22 88; www.beaujolaisvignoble.com; place de l'Hôtel de Ville, Beaujeu; ⊙9.30am-12.30pm & 2.30-6.30pm Mar-Nov) Beaujeu's tourist office provides information on wine cellars where you can taste and buy local wine. It can also help with accommodation.

Getting There & Away

To explore the delightful backroads and vineyards of Beaujolais, it's best to have your own set of wheels (and a non-drinking driver!).

For outdoorsy types, it's also possible to rent bikes at **La Maison du Terroir Beaujolais** (☎04 74 69 20 56; www.lamaisonduterroirbeaujolais.com; place de l'Hôtel de Ville, Beaujeu; ⊙10am-12.30pm & 2-6pm Wed-Mon Mar-Dec) in Beaujeu. It costs €12/17 for a half-/full day.

To get here by public transport, catch a train from Lyon to Belleville (€9.90, 35 minutes), where bus 235, operated by **Les Cars du Rhône** (☎0 800 10 40 36; www.carsdurhone.fr), connects hourly to Beaujeu (€2, 25 minutes).

La Dombes

La Dombes is a marshy area with hundreds of *étangs* (shallow lakes) that were created from malarial swamps over the past six centuries by farmers. They are used as fish ponds and then drained to grow crops on the fertile lake bed. While it's not big on sights, this rural territory has bags of bucolic panache. It's usually visited in conjunction with nearby Pérouges.

Sights

Parc des Oiseaux BIRD SANCTUARY

(☎04 74 98 05 54; www.parcdesoiseaux.com; RD 1083; adult/child €18/13; ⊙9.30am-6.30pm mid-Mar–mid-Nov) Observe local and exotic birds, including dozens of pairs of storks, at the Parc des Oiseaux, a landscaped bird park on the edge of Villars-les-Dombes.

Eating

La Dombes is heaven for foodies. People come from far and wide to sample frogs' legs, local chicken or carp at one of the area's many inns.

DON'T MISS

BEAUJOLAIS NOUVEAU

At the stroke of midnight on the third Thursday (ie Wednesday night) in November – as soon as French law permits – the *libération* (release) or *mise en perce* (tapping; opening) of the first bottles of cherry-bright Beaujolais Nouveau is celebrated around France and the world. In Beaujeu, 64km northwest of Lyon, there's free Beaujolais Nouveau for all as part of the **Sarmentelles de Beaujeu** (www.sarmentelles.com), a giant street party that kicks off the day before Beaujolais Nouveau for five days of wine tasting, live music and dancing.

L'Écu de France REGIONAL CUISINE €€

(☎04 74 98 01 79; www.lecudefrance.fr; 105 rue du Commerce; menus €26-38; ⊙noon-1.30pm Wed-Mon, 7-9pm Thu-Sun) Villars-les-Dombes' top table, L'Écu de France gets kudos for its refined, creative local cuisine made with fresh ingredients. When it comes to preparing savoury frogs' legs in butter sauce, chicken with morels or grilled pike perch, chef Pascal Gonin knows his stuff. Warm wood and stone walls make for a cosy dining room.

La Bicyclette Bleue REGIONAL CUISINE €€

(☎04 74 98 21 48; www.labicyclettebleue.fr; Le Pont, Joyeux; mains €17-26, lunch menu €12, dinner menus €22-46; ⊙noon-1.30pm & 7.30-9pm Thu-Mon, closed Dec-Feb) This laid-back family affair is 7.5km southeast of Villars-les-Dombes on the D61. It specialises in La Dombes staples, including frogs' legs and chicken. It also rents bicycles (per hour/day €4.50/16) to explore 12 mapped lakeland circuits, from 12km (one hour) to 59km (four hours).

★**Le Thou** REGIONAL CUISINE €€€

(☎04 74 98 15 25; www.lethou.com; Le Village, Bouligneux; mains €20-24, menus €29-62; ⊙noon-1.30pm & 7-8.30pm Wed-Sat, noon-1.30pm Sun) Occupying a lovingly restored inn, Le Thou is headed up by chef Stéphane Konig, who is known for his creative (and sometimes surprising) take on regional staples. Where else in the world could you sample a *tarte à la grenouille* (frog pie)? Well-spaced tables, colourful paintings adorning the walls and a warm welcome create an easy air.

Bonus: there's a garden terrace in the warm months. Find Le Thou about 4km northwest of Villars-les-Dombes.

Getting There & Away

Villars-les-Dombes' train station is linked to Lyon's Part-Dieu (€8, 40 minutes, at least hourly).

SOUTH OF LYON

South of Lyon, the Rhône flows past an incongruous mix of vineyards and nuclear power plants, but the landscapes grow more tantalising as you continue downriver towards Provence. Along the way there are several worthwhile stops for Lyon-based day-trippers.

Vienne

POP 30,100

France's Gallo-Roman heritage is alive and well in this laid-back riverfront city, whose compact old quarter hides a duo of spectacular Roman ruins, including a temple and a theatre. The theatre relives its glory days as a performance venue each summer during Vienne's two-week jazz festival.

Sights

Église & Cloître St-André Le Bas CHURCH
(Church & Cloister; 04 74 78 71 06; www.musees-vienne.fr; place du Jeu de Paume; adult/child €3/free; 9.30am-1pm & 2-6pm Tue-Sun) You can't miss this imposing church on the northern fringes of the old town. The back tower is decorated with tiny carved stone faces. In the cloister, which dates from the 12th century, look for the elaborate floral features and biblical scenes that adorn the columns.

Temple d'Auguste et de Livie HISTORIC SITE
(place Charles de Gaulle) FREE Best of all the Roman monuments in Vienne is this striking Roman temple right in the heart of the old town. Take a look at the superb Corinthian columns. It was built around 10 BC to honour Emperor Augustus and his wife, Livia.

Théâtre Romain THEATRE
(04 74 85 39 23; www.musees-vienne.fr; rue du Cirque; adult/child €3/free; 9.30am-1pm & 2-6pm Tue-Sun) This vast, well-preserved Roman amphitheatre was built around AD 40–50 at the base of Mt Pipet, on the eastern fringes of the old town. At that time, it was one of the largest theatres in the Roman empire – it was designed to seat 11,000 spectators.

Musée Gallo-Romain MUSEUM
(04 74 53 74 01; www.musees-gallo-romains.com; D502, St-Romain-en-Gal; adult/child €6/free; 10am-6pm Tue-Sun) Across the Rhône, the Musée Gallo-Romain highlights Vienne's historical importance, displaying several rooms full of dazzling mosaics and models of ancient Vienne, surrounded by the actual excavated remains of the Gallo-Roman city.

Festivals & Events

Jazz À Vienne MUSIC FESTIVAL
(www.jazzavienne.com) This two-week jazz festival held in late June/early July is said to be one of France's finest international jazz festivals, and it does attract some very big names, including Ibrahim Maalouf, Tonya Baker and Lisa Simone. Most concerts are held in the fabulous surrounds of the Roman theatre.

Sleeping & Eating

★**Hôtel de la Pyramide** HOTEL €€€
(04 74 53 01 96; www.lapyramide.com; 14 bd Fernand-Point; d €200-240, ste €350-420; P ❄ @ 🛜) Relax into the lap of luxury at this apricot-coloured villa overlooking La Pyramide (a 15.5m-tall obelisk dating from the Roman times). It shelters beautifully appointed rooms and a few top-notch suites. Foodies, rejoice: facilities include a gastronomic restaurant (*menus* €64 to €164). This tasteful haven is in a quiet neighbourhood on the southern outskirts of town.

★**L'Espace PH3** MODERN FRENCH €€
(04 74 53 01 96; www.lapyramide.com; 14 bd Fernand Point; mains €20-23, lunch menu €24; noon-1.30pm & 7.30-9.30pm) Overseen by two-Michelin-starred chef Patrick Henriroux, L'Espace PH3 offers an affordable gastronomic menu, serving a small selection of French classics with a creative twist. The lunch *menu* is an absolute steal. In summer, meals are served out on the superb garden terrace.

MONTÉLIMAR NOUGAT

In sunny Drôme Provençale, Montélimar, 46km south of Valence, is an appealing town, with an atmospheric old town and a tree-shaded, grassy promenade lined by cafe terraces carving a C-shape through its centre. An obligatory stop for sweet tooths, Montélimar is famous for its delectable nougat, which took off after WWII when motorists travelling to the French Riviera stopped here to buy the sweet treat to munch en route.

Information

Tourist Office (☎04 74 53 70 10; www.vienne-tourisme.com; 2 cours Brillier; ⊙9am-noon & 1.30-6pm Tue-Sat, 9am-noon & 2-6pm Sun, 10.30am-noon & 1.30-6pm Mon) Has details of museums and historical sites.

Getting There & Away

Trains link Vienne with Lyon's three main stations (€7.20, 20 to 30 minutes, at least hourly) as well as Valence Centre (€13.80, 50 minutes, at least hourly). All trains to Valence TGV station require changing at Valence Centre.

Valence

POP 65,000

Welcome to the Midi (as the French call the south)! With its warm weather, honey-coloured light, relaxed atmosphere and generous cuisine, it's easy to see why Valence advertises itself as the northern gateway to Provence. Its quaint old town is well endowed with eateries, convivial cafes and historic buildings, and the recently renovated Musée de Valence will appeal to culture aficionados.

Sights & Activities

Cathédrale St-Apollinaire CATHEDRAL

(place des Ormeaux; ⊙8am-6pm) A major landmark in the old town, this impressive cathedral dates from the late 11th century but was largely destroyed in the Wars of Religion and reconstructed in the 17th century. The square bell tower is a more recent addition – it was built in the 19th century.

Musée de Valence MUSEUM

(☎04 75 79 20 80; www.museedevalence.fr; 4 place des Ormeaux; adult/child €5/free; ⊙2-5.30pm Tue, 10am-5.30pm Wed-Sun) Renovated in 2014, this great museum adjoining the cathedral offers a comprehensive and well-organised collection of art and archaeology from the Rhône Valley. Of particular interest are the superb mosaics and artefacts dating from the Roman era, as well as the series of red chalk sketches and paintings of Hubert Robert (1733–1808). There is also a lovely vaulted gallery. For knockout views of the city and the Rhône Valley, head to the top floor, which has a *belvédère* (viewpoint).

L'École Scook COOKING

(☎04 75 44 14 14; www.anne-sophie-pic.com/scook; 243 av Victor Hugo; ⊙by reservation) Serious foodies will want to sign up at three-Michelin-star chef Anne-Sophie Pic's cutting-edge cooking school, Scook, with 1½-hour (€65) and half-day courses (€112), plus courses for kids from four years old upwards (€32 per 90 minutes). It also offers wine-tasting classes..

DON'T MISS

DEATH BY CHOCOLATE

Death by chocolate! On the main road in Tain l'Hermitage, **Cité du Chocolat Valrhona** (☎04 75 09 27 27; www.citeduchocolat.com; 12 av du Président Roosevelt; adult €7.80-9.20, child €6.60-7.20; ⊙9am-6pm Mon-Sat, 10am-5pm Sun) is a chocoholic's dream come true. This vast complex takes you through each stage of the production process thanks to interactive displays, workshops and hands-on exhibits. And yes, it includes tastings.

Sleeping & Eating

Valence is foodie heaven. Anne-Sophie Pic, France's only three-Michelin-star female chef, reigns over the city's gastronomy, as her father and grandfather did before her. There's a good range of eateries for every budget, including brasseries and snazzy neobistros. The city is also famed for its *suisse*, a crunchy, orange-rind-flavoured shortbread shaped like a Vatican Swiss guard to commemorate Pope Pius VI's imprisonment and death in Valence in 1799.

Les Négociants HOTEL €

(☎04 75 44 01 86; www.hotelvalence.com; 27 av Pierre Semard; d €45-69; P❄☜) This well-run venture with modernised rooms is definitely good value. The cheaper doubles have minuscule bathrooms and don't have air-con but are perfectly serviceable. It's just steps from the railway station and a five-minute stroll from the historic centre. There's private parking (€7) about 300m away. Another draw is the on-site restaurant.

★**La Maison de la Pra** B&B €€

(☎04 75 43 69 73; www.maisondelapra.com; 8 rue de l'Équerre; d €145-200, q €240; P❄☜) Such charm! If you've ever wanted to stay in a 16th-century *hôtel particulier* (master's house), this bijou B&B enticingly positioned in a quiet alley near the town hall is the real McCoy. It shelters five stadium-sized suites with beamed ceilings, period furniture and artworks. They're smack in the centre but still feel very quiet. Good English is spoken.

Maison Pic HOTEL €€€

(☎04 75 44 15 32; www.anne-sophie-pic.com; 285 av Victor Hugo; d €260-420, ste €390-600;

WORTH A TRIP

CONDRIEU & CÔTE RÔTIE

Wine buffs, take note: the Rhône Valley boasts two appellations that rank among the most prestigious in France: Condrieu and Côte Rôtie. While Condrieu is beloved of white-wine (viogner) aficionados, Côte Rôtie is a hallowed name among red-wine connoisseurs. Most of the Côte Rôtie vineyards, which extend over three villages, including Ampuis, are devoted to the syrah grape. Mixed with a bit of viognier, the Côte Rôtie produces rich reds, known for their robust, full-bodied character. A few kilometres further south, the Condrieu winegrowing area is a bit larger, and includes the small town of Condrieu. In all villages belonging to these appellations, you'll pass plenty of producers offering *dégustation* (tasting) en route. Both areas are within easy reach of Vienne.

Feb-Dec; P) The Pic family's truffle-coloured, 1889-established inn has ultrachic rooms mixing antique, contemporary and cutting-edge design. It is often fully booked with gastronomes, here for the three-Michelin-starred **Restaurant Pic** (lunch menu €110, menus €160-320) or the less formal bistro **André** (mains €24-54, menu €32). One downside: its location, on a busy road about 2km south of the old town, isn't exactly five-star.

Chez Grand Mère FRENCH €

(04 75 43 76 65; 5 place de la Pierre; mains €10-18, lunch menus €13-15, dinner menu €27; noon-2pm & 7.30-9.30pm) 'Grandma's place' stuns with its old-fashioned dining room decorated with a wide array of knick-knacks and retro junk. There's a heavy focus on regional cuisine; locals rave about the *ravioles fait maison* (homemade ravioli with cheese filling). The summer terrace on a delightful old-town *place* (square) is a winner.

Information

Tourist Office (04 75 44 90 40; www.valencetourisme.com; 11 bd Bancel; 9.30am-6.30pm Mon-Sat, 10am-3pm Sun;) Located two blocks north of the train station.

Getting There & Away

From Valence Centre station (also known as Valence-Ville), there are trains at least hourly to the following destinations; many also stop at Valence TGV Rhône-Alpes Sud station, 10km east:

Avignon Centre €21.90, about 1¼ hours
Grenoble €17.40, about 1¼ hours
Lyon (Gare Part-Dieu or Gare Jean-Macé) from €13.50, 35 minutes to 1¼ hours
Marseille from €37.50, one to 2½ hours
Montélimar €9.30, 30 minutes

Gorges de l'Ardèche

Be prepared to fall on your knees in awe: the steep and spectacular limestone Gorges de l'Ardèche cut a curvaceous swath through the high scrubland along the serpentine Ardèche River, a tributary of the Rhône. The main gorges begin near **Vallon-Pont-d'Arc** and empty into the Rhône Valley near **St-Martin-d'Ardèche**. En route, it passes beneath the Pont d'Arc, a sublimely beautiful stone arch created by the river's torrents.

From Vallon-Pont-d'Arc, the area's main hub, the scenic riverside D290 zigzags for 29km along the canyon's rim, with 29 *belvédères* revealing dazzling vistas of horseshoe bends, and kayakers in formation far below. However, it can turn into a chaotic traffic jam in midsummer. Vallon-Pont-d'Arc is also the main base for visiting the recent Caverne du Pont d'Arc, which houses replicas of amazing prehistoric paintings.

Sights

★Caverne du Pont d'Arc MUSEUM

(04 75 94 39 40; www.cavernedupontdarc.fr; Plateau du Razal; adult/child €13/6.50; 8.30am-8pm May-Sep, 9.30am-6.30pm Oct-Dec & Feb-Apr) Opened in 2015, this complex about 7km northeast of Vallon-Pont-d'Arc is an invitation to an incredible journey back in time. The biggest replica cave in the world, it was built a few kilometres north of the original Grotte Chauvet site and contains 1000 painstakingly reproduced paintings as well as around 450 bones and other debris. An hour-long tour (in various languages) takes visitors along a raised walkway, past panels displaying hundreds of breathtakingly sophisticated drawings of various animal species, including lions, panthers, rhinoceros and mammoths.

The original Grotte Chauvet, which was discovered in 1994 and is now a Unesco World Heritage Site, is not open to the public. It's the oldest known and the best preserved cave decorated by humans; the actual paintings date back 36,000 years. Specialists used 3D modelling techniques and a high-precision scanner to create a three-dimensional digital model of the original cave.

Due to visitor limits, it often sells out – buy your ticket online a few days in advance.

Grotte de la Madeleine CAVE
(☎04 75 04 22 20; www.grottemadeleine.com; D290, route touristique des Gorges; adult/child €9.50/5.50; ⏰10am-7pm Jul & Aug, to 6pm Mar-Jun & Sep, to 5pm Oct & Nov) The Ardèche plateau is riddled with caves. One of the most atmospheric ones in the area is Grotte de la Madeleine, which features impressive and colourful stalactite formations. A light and play show adds to the thrill. Near the ticket office you'll find one of the most spectacular *belvédères*, with awesome views of the gorges.

Activities

The best way to explore the gorges is on the water via kayak or canoe. It's also possible to walk into the gorges.

Base Nautique du Pont d'Arc WATER SPORTS
(☎04 75 37 17 79; www.canoe-ardeche.com; D290, rte touristique des Gorges, Vallon-Pont-d'Arc; per adult/child half-day €19/13, full day €29/19, 2-day €45/30; ⏰Apr-Nov) Hire canoes and kayaks through Base Nautique du Pont d'Arc. Options range from 8km half-day trips to 32km full-day or overnight camping trips. Minimum age is seven, and online discounts are available with advance booking.

Sleeping & Eating

★**Le Belvédère** HOTEL €
(☎04 75 88 00 02; www.hotel-ardeche-belvedere.com; D290, rte Touristique des Gorges; d €60-125; ⏰Apr-Oct; P❄📶🏊) Just 300m away from the Pont d'Arc, the aptly named Belvédère (Lookout) has 30 rooms that have been sleekly refitted. Half of the rooms have views of the Gorges, and some come with a balcony. Facilities include a swimming pool, a canoe/kayak rental outlet and a well-regarded on-site restaurant (*menus* from €23). Fancy a dip? There's direct access to the river just across the road.

★**Prehistoric Lodge** LODGE €€
(☎04 75 87 24 42; www.prehistoric-lodge.com; D290, rte touristique des Gorges; d €105-125, lodge d €115-165; ⏰Apr-Oct; P❄) By far the most unusual sleeping option in the Gorges de l'Ardèche, this good find offers eight luxury safari tents (called 'lodges') and four modern, snazzily decorated rooms with private terraces. Best of all, it's in a verdant property right on the river's edge, with direct access to a swimming area and superlative gorge views. Spacious and well designed, the tents are comfortable and appealing, although the open bathrooms might not be to everyone's taste. No wi-fi.

Hôtel Berneron HOTEL €€
(☎04 75 88 02 12; www.hotel-ardeche.com; 6 rue du Miarou, Vallon-Pont-d'Arc; d incl breakfast €99-150; P❄📶🏊) This renovated three-star venture not far from the town hall is now the nicest choice in Vallon-Pont-d'Arc, with 25 comfortable, light-filled and modern rooms. Those on the 3rd floor have great *colline* (hill) views. Precious perks include an atmospheric on-site restaurant, a heated pool and private parking.

★**Le Jardin d'Eden** MODERN FRENCH €€
(☎04 75 88 36 91; www.facebook.com/jardindedenrestaurant; 185 rue Henri Barbusse, Vallon-Pont-d'Arc; mains €16-21, menus €25-35; ⏰noon-2pm & 7-9pm Tue-Sun) Formerly a cinema, it's amazing what a renovation and an ownership change does for a place. The young team at the helm of this culinary outpost does a fine job at blending regional cuisine with contemporary style. Their risotto and tartares are especially good. Save a cranny for the splendid desserts – the *dôme royal* (a kind of chocolate cake) is amazing. Bonus: there's a lovely, plant-filled courtyard.

Information

Tourist Office (☎04 75 88 04 01; www.vallon-pont-darc.com; 1 place de l'Ancienne Gare; ⏰9am-12.30pm & 2-6pm Mon-Fri, to 5pm Sat, 9am-1pm Sun; 📶) Has some useful leaflets on walking itineraries and lists of canoeing and kayaking outlets. In the village centre.

Getting There & Away

Four daily SNCF buses link Vallon-Pont-d'Arc with Montélimar's train station (€12.20, 1½ hours) and Valence's TGV station (€20.90, 2½ hours).

ALL ABOARD

The scenic **Train de l'Ardèche** (☎04 75 06 07 00; www.trainardeche.fr; Gare de Tournon St-Jean, rte du Grand Pont, Tournon; adult €12-21, child €8-11; ⏰Apr-Oct) carves a sinuous route along the precipitous gorges of the Doux River. The train's three different itineraries – offering options to visit the cute mountain town of Colombier-le-Vieux or the market in Lamastre – all begin at the Tournon St-Jean station, just 5km off the A6.

French Alps & the Jura Mountains

POP 4.8 MILLION

Includes ➡

Best Places to Eat

- Yoann Conte (p499)
- Les Louvières (p530)
- Le Cap Horn (p484)
- Crèmerie du Glacier (p485)
- La Fruitière (p505)

Best Places to Sleep

- Petit Hôtel Confidentiel (p497)
- Hôtel de la Vallée Heureuse (p527)
- Hôtel Aiguille du Midi (p484)
- The Farmhouse (p489)

Why Go?

It took something as monumental as the collision of Africa and Europe to produce the Alps. Inconceivable forces buckled the land, driving it high into the sky, creating a place of enchantment and danger. And further north, where those forces finally reached their limit, the lower, lushly wooded ridges of the Jura mountains grew. What the geological millennia produced is a place where superlatives fail: colossal peaks thrusting upward into cobalt-blue skies, crevasse-fissured glaciers, tumbling crystal-clear rivers, sapphire lakes, and mountain passes blocked by snow for nine months a year.

In summer, all this can be explored on foot, or by bicycle, kayak or car. Then the return of the snow each year brings some of Europe's finest skiing: impossibly fast black runs and world-class off-piste routes, of course, but also plenty of fun for those just finding their feet. And, in the lush lowlands and stately medieval cities, you'll discover the rich culture, food and history of the folk who made these mountains home.

When to Go

Grenoble

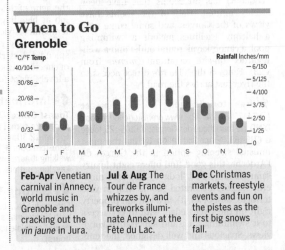

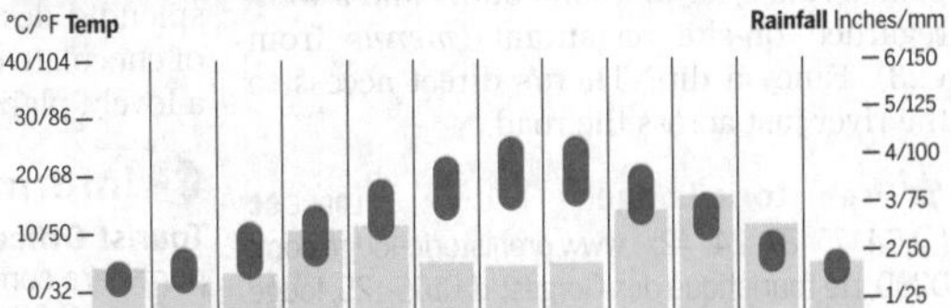

Feb-Apr Venetian carnival in Annecy, world music in Grenoble and cracking out the *vin jaune* in Jura.

Jul & Aug The Tour de France whizzes by, and fireworks illuminate Annecy at the Fête du Lac.

Dec Christmas markets, freestyle events and fun on the pistes as the first big snows fall.

Skiing & Snowboarding

The 200-plus resorts in the French Alps have earned a reputation for offering some of the best – perhaps *the* best – downhill skiing and snowboarding in Europe. In larger resorts, snowboarders are brilliantly catered for in snow parks kitted out with halfpipes, kickers and ramps.

At most stations, the ski season begins in early or mid-December and ends in mid- or late April, though the highest-altitude stations, such as Val Thorens (in Les Trois Vallées) and Val d'Isère (Espace Killy), open in mid- or late November and don't close until early or mid-May. Lots of people line up a chalet and go skiing for a week, staying from Saturday to Saturday.

Summer skiing on glaciers is possible from about 21 June to the end of August, and again for a week around 1 November, at two French ski stations: Les Deux Alpes and Val d'Isère/Tignes (Espace Killy).

The Jura is renowned for its selection of *ski de fond* (cross-country) trails, with Les Rousses at the centre. European downhill runs are colour-coded to indicate how kid-easy or killer-hard they are:

- **Green** Beginner
- **Blue** Intermediate
- **Red** Advanced
- **Black** Expert

AVALANCHES

Avalanches are a serious danger wherever deep snow meets steep slopes. You know the golden rule: never ski, hike or climb alone. Off-piste skiers should never head out without an avalanche pole, transceiver, shovel – and, most importantly, a professional guide. Ski resorts announce the daily risk level using signs and coloured flags: yellow (low risk), black and yellow (heightened risk) and black (severe risk). Henry's Avalanche Talk (www.henrysavalanchetalk.com) translates the daily avalanche forecast issued by Météo France into English during the ski season.

Ski Rental & Lessons

Skis (alpine, cross-country, telemark), snowboards, snowshoes, boots, poles and helmets can be hired at sport shops in every resort. All-inclusive rental costs around €35 per day for good-quality alpine equipment or snowboarding gear (about two-thirds of that for kids) and €18 for cross-country. Reserving ahead online can get you a 15% discount.

Every resort has a variety of ski schools with certified instructors; tourist offices have details. France's leading ski school, the **École du Ski Français** (www.esf.net) – its instructors distinctive in red jumpsuits – has a branch in every resort. Group lessons typically cost €60/200 for one/six half-days. Private instruction is also available (€182 per half-day). Kids can start learning from the age of four; from three years old they can play in the *jardin de neige* (snow garden).

Lift Passes

You will need a *forfait* (lift pass) to ride the various *remontées mécaniques* (lifts): *téléskis* (tow lines), *télésièges* (chairlifts), *télécabines* (gondolas), *téléphériques* (cable cars) and *funiculaires* (funicular railways). At the big resorts, passes cost €45 to €55 per day or €260 to €330 per week (reckoned as either six or seven days), about 40% less than at major US resorts. Everywhere in the Alps, lift tickets can be bought and recharged online.

At most stations, children aged three or four and under ski for free but still need a pass; bring along a passport as proof of age. Some places also offer free lift passes to skiers aged over 75. A few resorts (eg Val d'Isère and Les Deux Alpes) have several free lifts for beginners. Weeklong passes usually include limited access to a swimming pool, an ice-skating rink and indoor sports facilities.

You have to pay a *forfait* or *redevance* (fee), usually around €9 a day, to use *ski de fond* (cross-country) trails.

Insurance

Before you launch yourself like a rocket down that near-vertical black piste, make sure you're properly insured. Accidents happen, and expensive mountain-rescue costs (we're talking five figures here for a helicopter), medical treatment and repatriation add insult to injury.

Most ski packages include *assurance* (insurance), at least for evacuation and emergency first aid. If further treatment is required (eg you are evacuated to a hospital), your coverage may depend on your national or private health insurance. Note that some private insurance policies do not cover winter sports, especially off-piste, so check before you leave home.

French Alps & the Jura Mountains Highlights

1 **Portes du Soleil** (p488) Trying, just *trying*, to ski all the terrain at this vast, international ski area.

2 **Annecy** (p490) Exploring the stately city's medieval lanes, strongholds and crystal-clear waters.

3 **Lac Blanc** (p482) Hiking up to the turquoise lake for a breathtaking view of the Mont Blanc massif.

4 **Les Trois Vallées** (p503) Slaloming down legendary slopes, then partying away in après-ski bars.

5 **Parc Naturel Régional du Vercors** (p513) Communing with nature on a middle-of-nowhere farm.

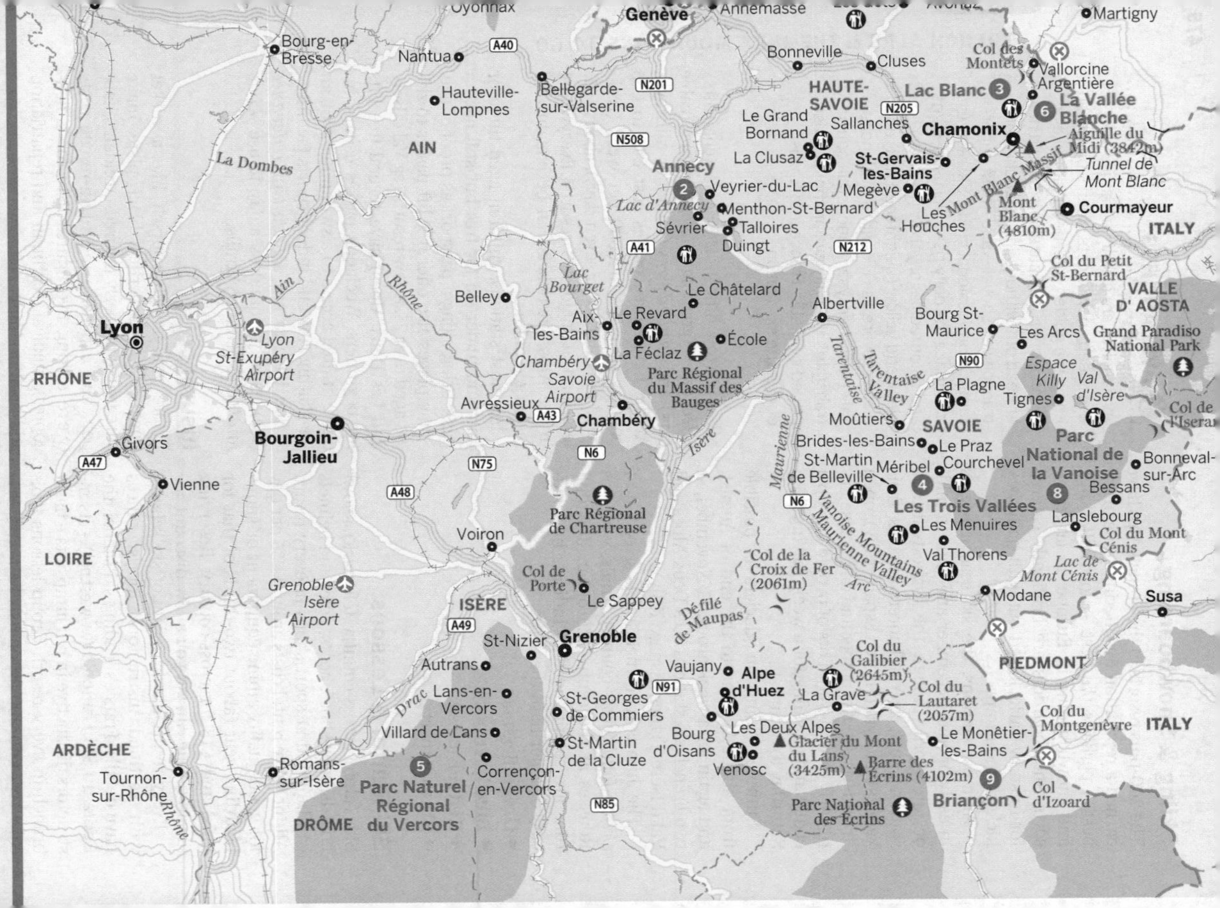

6 **La Vallée Blanche** (p482) Conquering the ultimate in Alpine off-piste skiing.

7 **Route des Vins du Jura** (p523) Sipping golden *vin jaune* amid bucolic vines.

8 **Parc National de la Vanoise** (p506) Hiking through glaciated grandeur.

9 **Parc National des Écrins** (p517) Getting buzzed on the dramatic winding drive to Briançon.

10 **Besançon** (p519) Walking the ramparts of the hilltop Vauban citadel.

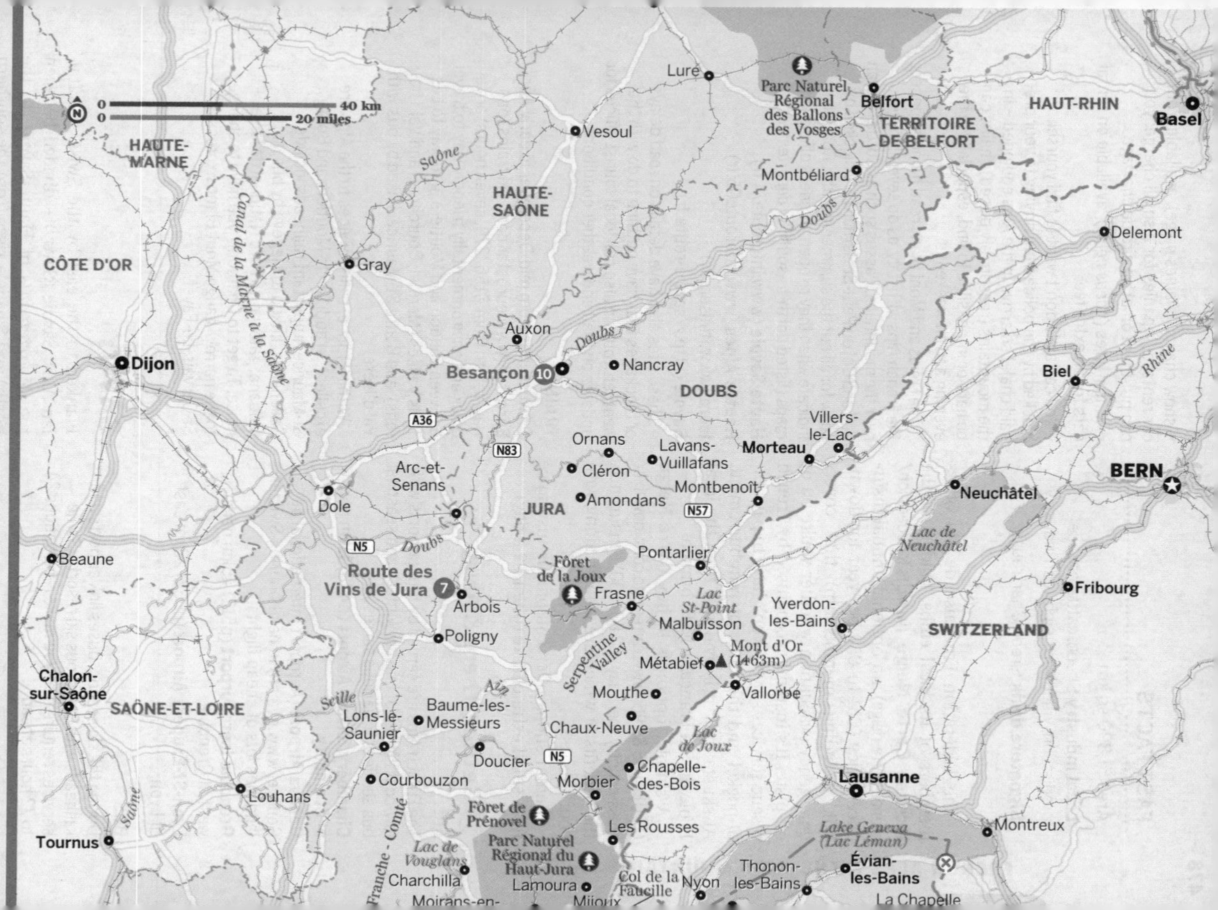

FAST FACTS

Area 51,890 sq km

Local industry Sheep, cattle, cheese production, viticulture, high-tech industry

Signature drink Green Chartreuse

The Fédération Française de Ski offers members of its local clubs, holders of the **License Carte Neige** (www.ffs.fr/federation/licence-carte-neige), an optional annual insurance policy (€31 to €50 per year for downhill, including membership) that covers emergency evacuation whether you're on or off-piste. It's instantly recognised by French rescue services so you won't have to pay out-of-pocket and then file for reimbursement. At ski stations, it is available from the local École du Ski Français (ESF) branch.

A simpler option is to buy **Carré Neige** (☎01 41 85 85 96; www.carreneige.com; downhill/cross-country per day €2.80/1.30) insurance, the benefits of which are similar, along with your lift pass.

Rental shops offer equipment insurance for a small extra charge (often €2 a day).

Getting There & Away

AIR

The French Alps are served by four airports with low-cost flights (at least in winter), and seasonal bus services to various ski resorts:

Chambéry Savoie Airport (p498) 11km north of Chambéry.

Geneva Airport (Aéroport International de Genève; www.gva.ch) In neighbouring Switzerland; has *lots* of cheap flights.

Grenoble Isère Airport (p512) 45km northwest of Grenoble.

Lyon-St-Exupéry Airport (p962) 28km east of Lyon.

BUS

During the ski season, buses link airports and railheads with numerous ski resorts. Some services require that you make reservations 24 to 72 hours ahead.

CAR & MOTORCYCLE

The roads up to many popular ski stations are narrow, steep and serpentine so in season (especially during French school holidays) traffic can be hellish, especially at weekends.

After a snowfall, local authorities may require that all cars have either:

- snow chains *(chaînes neige)*, available from car rental companies for a small charge; you can put them on at an *aire de chaînage*
- winter tyres *(pneus neige)*, available on rental cars for an extra fee.

You certainly don't want to find yourself blocked by the police from driving to your pre-paid chalet so arrive in the Alps equipped – in the mountains (reasonably priced) chains can be hard or impossible to find, especially in the evening and on weekends.

The Fréjus and Mont Blanc road tunnels connect the French Alps with Italy, as do several routes over the mountains. Passes such as Col de l'Iseran and and Col du Petit-St-Bernard are blocked by snow for all but the summer months. Road signs indicate when they're open, or check official online maps (listed north-to-south by *département*):

Haute Savoie (www.inforoute74.fr)

Hautes-Alpes (www.inforoute05.fr)

Isère (www.itinisere.fr)

Savoie (http://savoie-route.fr)

These sites also have details on road delays or blockages that have nothing to do with the weather. You can also call local tourist offices for updates on road and weather conditions.

TRAIN

On weekends from mid-December to early April, **Eurostar** (www.eurostar.com) ski trains (one way/return from €156/279, seven hours) are a quick and environmentally friendly way to travel between London and Moûtiers, gateway to Les Trois Vallées (Méribel, Courchevel and Val Thorens), and Bourg St-Maurice, linked by bus with Val d'Isère.

Within France, train services to the Alps are excellent. In addition to Moûtiers and Bourg St-Maurice, important railheads include Sallanches, linked to Megève by bus, and Modane, gateway to Parc National de la Vanoise. To get to Chamonix you have to change to the narrow-gauge Mont Blanc Express at St-Gervais-Le-Fayet.

SAVOY

Flanked to the east by the Swiss and Italian Alps, Savoie (Savoy) – divided between the *départements* of Haute-Savoie (to the north) and Savoie – rises from the southern shores of Lake Geneva, Europe's largest alpine lake, and culminates at the roof of Europe, mighty 4810m Mont Blanc. At higher elevations you'll find legendary ski resorts including Chamonix and Val d'Isère, with historical château towns such as Chambéry and lakeside Annecy to the west.

Rural life, unchanged for centuries, continues in the region's more remote corners, such as the Bauges massif and the wild Parc National de la Vanoise.

Chamonix

POP 9050 / ELEV 1037M

With the sheer white heights of the Mont Blanc massif as its sensational backdrop, the Chamonix Valley shows the Alps at their most dramatic. First 'discovered' as a tourist destination by Brits William Windham and Richard Pococke in 1741, it has become a wintertime playground of epic proportions, more than satisfying the most demanding skiers as well as the après-ski revellers who pack themselves into its boot-stompin' bars. In summer, lift-accessible highland trails offer thrilling panoramas to hikers, mountain bikers and other high-altitude thrill seekers.

Sights

★Aiguille du Midi VIEWPOINT

(information 04 50 53 22 75; www.compagniedumontblanc.co.uk) A great broken tooth of rock rearing among the Alpine fastness of the Mont Blanc massif, the Aiguille du Midi (3842m) is one of Chamonix' most distinctive geographical features. If you can handle the altitude, the 360-degree views of the French, Swiss and Italian Alps from the summit are (quite literally) breathtaking. Year-round, you can float in a cable car from Chamonix to the Aiguille du Midi on the vertiginous **Téléphérique de l'Aiguille du Midi** (place de l'Aiguille du Midi; adult/child return to Aiguille du Midi €58.50/49.70, to Plan de l'Aiguille summer €31/26.40, winter €17/14.50; 1st ascent btwn 7.10am & 8.30am, last btwn 3.30pm & 5pm).

Up top, you can take in the view in literally every direction, including straight down, thanks to the glass-floored **Step into the Void**. Halfway up, **Plan de l'Aiguille** (2317m) is a terrific place to start hikes or to paraglide.

Bring warm clothes, as even in summer the temperature at the top rarely rises above -10°C (in winter be prepared for -25°C).

From the Aiguille du Midi, between late May and September, you can continue for a further 50 minutes of mind-blowing scenery – think glaciers and spurs, seracs and shimmering ice fields – in the smaller bubbles of the **Télécabine Panoramique Mont Blanc** (adult/child return from Chamonix €80/68; last departure from Aiguille du Midi 2.30pm) to Pointe Helbronner (3466m) on the France–Italy border. A new **cable car** (www.montebianco.com; Pointe Helbronner; one way adult/child €36/25.20; 8.30am-4.30pm, earlier starts in summer) can then take you a further 4km to the Val d'Aosta ski resort of Courmayeur, on the Italian side of Monte Bianco.

Le Brévent VIEWPOINT

(information 04 50 53 22 75; www.compagniedumontblanc.co.uk) The highest peak on the western side of the Chamonix Valley, Le Brévent (2525m) has tremendous views of the Mont Blanc massif, myriad hiking trails through a nature reserve, ledges to para-

KIDDING AROUND CHAMONIX

There's plenty to amuse *les petits* (the little ones) around Chamonix. In the warm season, kids will love getting close to free-roaming chamois, ibex and whistling marmots at the **Parc de Merlet** (www.parcdemerlet.com; 2495 chemin de Merlet, Les Houches; adult/child €7/4; 10am-6pm Tue-Sun May, Jun & Sep, 9.30am-7.30pm Jul & Aug, by appointment 4 Jan–31 Mar), 13km by road (5km on foot) southwest of central Chamonix in Coupeau (across the River Arve from Les Houches). Or treat them to a fun-packed day on the trampolines and funfair rides at the **Parc de Loisirs de Chamonix** (04 50 53 08 97; www.chamonixparc.com; 351, chemin du Pied du Grépon; 1 day ski passes €21.90, 1/10 luge rides €5.50/45; 11.30am-6pm high season, reduced hours other times), near the chairlift in Les Planards, 500m east of Gare du Montenvers; the 1.3km luge winds through trees at mind-blowing speeds. **Cham' Aventure** (04 50 53 55 70; www.cham-aventure.com; 190 place de l'Église, Maison de la Montagne) has a wide variety of outdoor programs for children aged three to seven, eight to 12, and 13 to 17.

Back in Chamonix, the indoor **ice-skating rink** (04 50 53 12 36; 165 rte de la Patinoire; adult/child €6.20/4.60, skate hire €4.10) provides amusement when the weather packs up, as do sports activities at the adjacent **Centre Sportif Richard Bozon** (04 50 53 23 70; 214 av de la Plage; noon-7.30pm Mon-Fri, 2-7.30pm Sat & Sun), with indoor and (in summer) outdoor swimming pools.

Chamonix

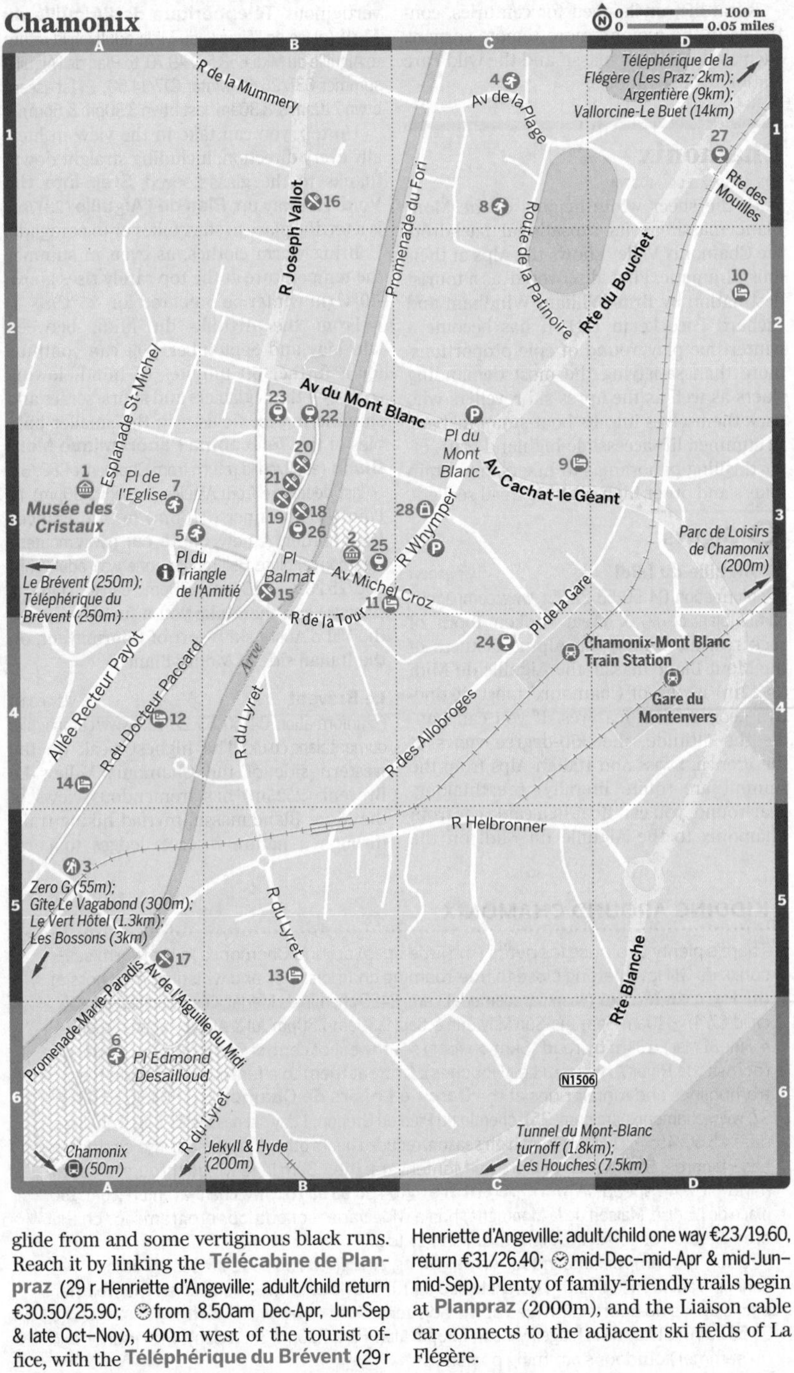

glide from and some vertiginous black runs. Reach it by linking the **Télécabine de Planpraz** (29 r Henriette d'Angeville; adult/child return €30.50/25.90; ⏲from 8.50am Dec-Apr, Jun-Sep & late Oct–Nov), 400m west of the tourist office, with the **Téléphérique du Brévent** (29 r Henriette d'Angeville; adult/child one way €23/19.60, return €31/26.40; ⏲mid-Dec–mid-Apr & mid-Jun–mid-Sep). Plenty of family-friendly trails begin at **Planpraz** (2000m), and the Liaison cable car connects to the adjacent ski fields of La Flégère.

Chamonix

Top Sights
1 Musée des Cristaux ... A3

Sights
2 Musée Alpin ... B3

Activities, Courses & Tours
3 Association Internationale des Guides du Mont Blanc ... A5
4 Centre Sportif Richard Bozon ... C1
5 Cham' Aventure ... A3
6 Chamonix Experience ... A6
7 Compagnie des Guides de Chamonix ... A3
École de Ski Français ... (see 5)
8 Ice-Skating Rink ... C1
Maison de la Montagne ... (see 7)
Office de Haute Montagne ... (see 5)

Sleeping
9 Auberge du Manoir ... C3
10 Chalet-Hôtel Hermitage ... D2
11 Club Alpin Français ... B3
12 Grand Hôtel des Alpes ... A4
13 Hotel L'Oustalet ... B5
14 Hôtel Richemond ... A4

Eating
15 Extreme Café ... B3
16 Hibou Deli ... B1
17 Le Bistrot ... A5
18 Le Cap Horn ... B3
19 Le Chaudron ... B3
20 Le GouThé ... B3
21 Munchie ... B3

Drinking & Nightlife
22 Bar'd Up ... B2
23 Bistrot des Sports ... B2
24 Chambre Neuf ... C4
25 Le Lapin Agile ... B3
26 Les Caves ... B3
27 MBC ... D1

Shopping
28 Cooperative Fruitière Val d'Arly ... C3

Mer de Glace VIEWPOINT
(information 04 50 53 22 75; www.compagniedumontblanc.fr) France's largest glacier, the 200m-deep 'Sea of Ice', flows 7km down the northern side of Mont Blanc, moving up to 1cm an hour (about 90m a year). The **Train du Montenvers** (35 place de la Mer de Glace; adult/child return €31/26.40; 10am-4.30pm), a picturesque, 5km-long cog railway opened in 1909, links Gare du Montenvers with Montenvers (1913m), from where a cable car takes you down to the glacier and the **Grotte de Glace** (closed last half of May & late Sep–mid-Oct). Your ticket also gets you into the Glaciorium, which looks at the birth, life and future of glaciers.

On foot, the Mer de Glace can be reached from **Plan de l'Aiguille** on the **Grand Balcon Nord trail**. The two-hour uphill trail from Chamonix starts near the summer luge track. Traversing the crevassed glacier requires proper equipment and an experienced guide.

★**Musée des Cristaux** MUSEUM
(04 50 55 53 93; www.mineralogie-chamonix.org; 615 allée Recteur Payot; adult/child €5.90/free; 2-6pm Sep-Jun, 10am-6pm Jul & Aug) Has a truly dazzling collection of crystals, rocks and minerals, many from around Mont Blanc. **L'Espace Alpinisme** focuses on the art and science of mountaineering with creative interactive displays and spectacular photos and videos of seemingly impossible ascents. Situated behind the church.

Musée Alpin MUSEUM
(04 50 53 25 93; 89 av Michel Croz; adult/child €5.90/free; 2-6pm Wed-Mon Sep-Jun, 10am-noon & 2-7pm Wed-Mon Jul & Aug) Perhaps better titled the Musée Chamonix-Mont Blanc, this engaging little collection richly illustrates the area's long history of Alpine adventure, including the cliff-hanging feats of crystal-hunter Jacques Balmat and the first ascent of Mont Blanc by a woman (Marie Paradis, a local maidservant, in 1808). Ask at the ticket counter for printed information in English.

Activities

Maison de la Montagne ADVENTURE SPORTS
(04 50 53 27 74; 190 place de l'Église; 8.30am-noon & 3-7pm) Get the Mont Blanc low-down here, opposite the tourist office. Inside is the highly regarded **Compagnie des Guides de Chamonix** (04 50 53 00 88; www.chamonix-guides.com; 8.30am-noon & 2.30-7.30pm, closed Sun & Mon late Apr–mid-Jun & mid-Sep–mid-Dec); the **École de Ski Français** (ESF; 04 50 53 22 57; www.esfchamonix.com; 8.15am-7pm ski season); and the **Office de Haute Montagne** (OHM; 04 50 53 22 08; www.ohm-chamonix.com; 9am-noon & 3-6pm), which has information on trails, hiking conditions, weather forecasts and *refuges* (mountain huts), and topoguides and maps that are free to consult.

Winter

Thrilling descents, glorious off-piste terrain and unbeatable Mont Blanc views – skiing in Chamonix is so darn fantastic that skiers don't even mind that accessing the slopes involves lots of land transport to and from the lifts. Of Chamonix' nine main areas, **Le Tour, Les Planards, Les Chosalets** and **La Vormaine** are best for beginners. For speed and challenge, it has to be **Brévent-Flégère**, above Chamonix, and **Les Grands Montets**, accessible from the attractive village of Argentière, 9km north of the town. Boarders seeking big air zip across to the kickers and rails at **Les Grands Montets snow park** and the natural halfpipe in **Le Tour.**

Chamonix' ski season runs from mid-December to mid-April.

La Vallée Blanche SKIING

(guided trips for 4 €310) This jaw-dropping 2800m descent is the off-piste ride of a lifetime. Beginning at the Aiguille du Midi, zipping over the crevasse-riddled Mer de Glace glacier and returning to Chamonix through the forest, it can only be tackled with a *guide de haute montagne* (specially trained mountain guide). Skiers should be red-piste level and in reasonable physical shape.

Huskydalen ADVENTURE SPORTS

(☎04 50 47 77 24; www.huskydalen.com; mushing per day adult/child €72/46; ⏲Nov-Apr) One of two Chamonix outfits offering introductory mushing (dog sledding) courses.

> **LIFT PASSES**
>
> Details of the following passes can be viewed and purchases made online at www.compagniedumontblanc.co.uk.
>
> **Chamonix Le Pass** (1/3/6 days €49/136/246) Gets you up to most Chamonix ski domains.
>
> **Mont Blanc Multipass** (1/3/6 days €61/86/124) In summer, this pass affords access to all operating lifts.
>
> **Mont Blanc Unlimited Pass** (1/3/6 days €60/176/293) A worthwhile investment for serious skiers, this pass grants access to 400km of runs, including all lifts in the Chamonix Valley, Courmayeur in Italy and Verbier in Switzerland, plus the Aiguille du Midi cable car and the Montenvers–Mer de Glace train.

Summer

When enough snow melts (usually sometime in June), hikers can take their pick of 350km of spectacular high-altitude trails, many easy to get to by cable car (running mid-June to September). In June and July there's enough light to walk until at least 9pm.

Balcon (literally 'balcony') trails, both *grand* and *petit,* run along both sides of the valley, the former up at around 2000m, the latter a bit above the valley's villages.

Lac Blanc Hike WALKING

(www.compagniedumontblanc.co.uk) Two gentle hours from **Télésiège de l'Index** (adult/child one way from Les Praz €23/19.60; ⏲Dec-Apr & Jun-Sep) leads along the western valley to stunning **Lac Blanc** (2352m). There's also the steeper trail from the **Téléphérique de la Flégère** (☎04 50 53 22 75; 35 rte des Tines; adult/child from Les Praz €13/11.70; ⏲8.45am-4pm Dec-Apr & Jun-Sep) or the even more challenging 1050 vertical-metre hike from Argentière (3½ hours one way). Reserve a place at the **Refuge du Lac Blanc** (☎04 50 53 49 14; refugedulacblanc@gmail.com; dm incl half-board €55; ⏲mid-Jun–Sep), a wooden chalet famed for its top-of-Europe Mont Blanc views.

Grand Balcon Sud Trail WALKING

This easygoing trail, linking **Col des Montets** (12km northeast of Chamonix) with **Les Houches** (8km southwest of Chamonix), skirts the western side of the valley at an altitude of around 2000m, commanding terrific views across the valley to Mont Blanc. To avoid hoofing it 900m up the slope, take the Téléphérique de la Flégère from Les Praz or the Télécabine de Planpraz (p480) from Chamonix; walking between the two takes about two hours. A variety of other great trails begins at the top of both these lifts.

Grand Balcon Nord Trail HIKING

Trails you can pick up at **Plan de l'Aiguille** – halfway up the Téléphérique de l'Aiguille du Midi (p479) – include the challenging Grand Balcon Nord, which takes you to the dazzling Mer de Glace, from where you can walk or take the Train du Montenvers (p481) down to Chamonix.

Cycling

Lower-altitude trails such as the Petit Balcon Sud from Argentière to Servoz are perfect for biking. Most outdoor-activity specialists arrange guided mountain-biking expeditions.

Zero G CYCLING
(☎04 50 53 01 01; www.zerogchamonix.com; 90 ave Ravanel-le-Rouge; ⏲9am-12.30pm & 3.30-7pm) Rents out good-quality mountain bikes, as well as snowboards and gear.

Paragliding

Come summer, the sky above Chamonix is speckled with colourful paragliders wheeling down from the heights. Tandem flights from Planpraz (2000m) cost €100 per person; from the Aiguille du Midi, count on paying €220.

Sleeping

You need to book ahead in winter and in July and August. Many places close for a while in the spring and autumn.

The prices quoted below are for the winter high season. Rates are significantly lower in July and August, and even lower in spring and autumn.

Club Alpin Français ACCOMMODATION SERVICES €
(☎04 50 53 16 03; www.clubalpin-chamonix.com; 136 av Michel Croz; ⏲4-6.45pm Tue-Sat) For details on staying in a *refuge* (mountain hut with bunk beds) high on the Mont Blanc massif, contact the Club Alpin Français. Expect to pay around €25 for a dorm bed and €40 to €50 for half-board. Meals are simple, hearty and prepared by the hut-keeper.

Gîte Le Vagabond HOSTEL €
(☎04 50 53 15 43; www.gitevagabond.com; 365 av Ravanel-le-Rouge; dm/sheets €21/5.50, d incl breakfast €101; ⏲reception 8-10am & 4.30-10.30pm; 📶) In the 150-year-old Le Brévent, once a stagecoach inn for travellers to Switzerland, Le Vagabond is Chamonix' hippest bunkhouse. It has rooms with four to six beds and a buzzing bar with a great log fire in winter. It's 850m southwest of the town centre.

★ **Hôtel Richemond** HOTEL €€
(☎04 50 53 08 85; www.richemond.fr; 228 rue du Docteur Paccard; s/d/tr €66.60/103.20/136.40; ⏲mid-Dec–mid-Apr & mid-Jun–mid-Sep; 📶) In a grand old building constructed in 1914 (and run by the same family ever since), this hotel – as friendly as it is central – has 52 spacious rooms with views of either Mont Blanc or Le Brévent; some are pleasantly old-fashioned (retaining original furniture and cast-iron bath-tubs), others are recently renovated in white, black and beige. Outstanding value.

> **ADVENTURE GUIDES**
>
> It takes three years of rigorous training to become an *accompagnateur en moyenne montagne* (mountain leader) and a full five years to be certified as a *guide de haute montagne* (high-mountain guide); only the latter are authorised to lead groups on to glaciers or on mountaineering climbs requiring specialised equipment. Recommended companies include the following:
>
> ➡ **Compagnie des Guides de Chamonix** (p481)
>
> ➡ **Association Internationale des Guides du Mont Blanc** (☎04 50 53 27 05; www.guides-du-montblanc.com; 9 passage de la Varlope)
>
> ➡ **Chamonix Experience** (☎09 77 48 58 69; www.chamex.com; 49 place Edmond Desailloud; ⏲8.30-11am & 3-7pm 1 Dec–5 May & 1 Jun–30 Sep)

Auberge du Manoir HOTEL €€
(☎04 50 53 10 77; www.aubergedumanoir.com; 8 rte du Bouchet; s/d/q €133/154/225; ⏲closed 2 weeks late Apr & 2 months autumn; 📶) This beautifully converted farmhouse, ablaze with geraniums in summer, offers 18 pine-panelled rooms that are quaint but never cloying, pristine mountain views, an outdoor hot tub, a sauna and a bar whose open fire keeps things cosy. It's family-owned, and prices fall during the week and in low season.

Le Vert Hôtel HOTEL €€
(☎04 50 53 13 58; www.verthotel.com; 964 rte des Gaillands; s/d/tr/q with breakfast €90/125/155/195; 📶) This lively, British-owned hotel has 21 compact rooms – all with new bathrooms, some with fantastic Aiguille du Midi views. There's also a more-than-decent restaurant (dinner *menu* €22.50), a bar that regularly hosts international acts (Gilles Peterson and Krafty Kutz, to name two) and in-house equipment rental. *Navettes* (shuttle buses) to central Chamonix, 2km to the northeast, stop right outside.

Grand Hôtel des Alpes HISTORIC HOTEL €€
(☎04 50 55 37 80; www.grandhoteldesalpes.com; 75 rue du Docteur Paccard; d/ste €171/350; ⏲closed mid-Apr–mid-Jun & late Sep–mid-Dec; @📶🏊) Established in 1840, this grand old dame and her 30 rooms exude timeless elegance. In winter a scrumptious and very

DON'T MISS

ROOM WITH A VIEW

Run by the same family since 1908, **Hôtel Aiguille du Midi** (☎04 50 53 00 65; www.hotel-aiguilledumidi.com; 479 chemin Napoléon, Les Bossons; d €77-158, q €198; ⏰mid-Dec–early Apr & mid-May–Sep; 📶🏊) has stunning views of the Aiguille du Midi and Mont Blanc. There are 39 cosy, pine-panelled rooms, an outdoor heated pool and a clay tennis court for summer fun, and a very good restaurant, accessible on half-board packages. Bus and train stops to Chamonix are right around the corner.

civilised teatime cake buffet (4pm to 6pm) greets skiers back from the slopes.

Hotel L'Oustalet HOTEL €€
(☎04 50 55 54 99; www.hotel-oustalet.com; 330 rue du Lyret; d/q €155/200; ⏰mid-Dec–mid-May & mid-Jun–mid-Oct; 📶🏊) A block from the Aiguille du Midi cable car, this lift-equipped hotel has 15 decent rooms, snugly built of thick pine, that open on to balconies with Mont Blanc views. To unwind, you can curl up by the fire with a *chocolat chaud* or loll about in the Jacuzzi, *hammam* or sauna – or, in summer, take a dip in the garden pool.

Chalet-Hôtel Hermitage HOTEL €€€
(☎04 50 53 13 87; www.hermitage-paccard.com; 63 chemin du Cé; d €216-275, ste €456; ⏰closed late Apr–mid-Jun & late Sep–mid-Dec; 📶) A family-run treasure, with an open fire crackling in the bar, a kids' playroom and flowery gardens. Decked out from tip to toe in larch wood, the 28 rooms blend traditional Alpine style with mod cons (eg two-person bathtubs) and afford mountain views. There's also a spa and bar to get you back into shape at the end of the day.

Eating

Hibou Deli DELI €
(☎04 50 96 65 13; www.hibou-chamonix.com; 416 rue Joseph Vallot; mains €8-10; ⏰11am-9pm mid-Dec–early May & mid-Jun–early Oct; 🌿) This tiny shopfront kitchen, owned by a British chef, pumps out fantastic Asian and North African-inflected dishes to takeaway. The lamb *mechoui* is rubbed with spices and cooked over 24 hours to an almost buttery consistency, the Bangkok chicken is fragrant with limes leaves and coconut, and there's always plenty of veggie options and an interesting *plat de jour*.

Le GouThé DELI €
(☎04 50 78 36 20; www.legouthe.weebly.com; 95 rue des Moulins; light mains €4-8; ⏰9am-7pm Jun-Apr; 🌿) This sweet tearoom serves tea, coffee and 15 kinds of hot chocolate as well salads, quiche, sweet and savoury crêpes, muffins and fruit tarts by the metre (apple and rhubarb, pear and cardamom and other combinations).

Extreme Café CAFE €
(☎04 50 21 99 45; 21 place Balmat; light meals €6-7; ⏰8am-7pm; 📶) If you're watching your pennies in Chamonix, this little snack bar is good for a cheap panino, glass of wine (from €2.90 a glass) or smoothie (€3.90). There's also free wi-fi and a terrace, heated in winter.

★ **Le Cap Horn** MODERN FRENCH €€
(☎04 50 21 80 80; www.caphorn-chamonix.com; 78 rue des Moulins; lunch menus €20, dinner menus €32-39; ⏰noon-3pm & 7-10.30pm) Housed in a gorgeous, two-storey chalet decorated with model sailing boats – joint homage to the Alps and Cape Horn – this highly praised restaurant, opened in 2012, serves French and Asian-inflected dishes such as pan-seared duck breast with honey and soy sauce, fisherman's stew and, for dessert, *souffle au Grand Marnier*. Reserve for dinner Friday and Saturday in winter and summer.

Le Chaudron FRENCH €€
(☎04 50 53 40 34; www.le-chaudron-chamonix.com; 79 rue des Moulins; menus €27-34; ⏰7-9.30pm or later mid-Dec–Apr & mid-Jun–Sep) Making stylish yet cosy use of a 100-year-old mule stable (the faux cowhide recalling its rustic origins) The Cauldron is guaranteed to give you a warm inner glow on a cold winter's day. Go-to dishes include terrine of Beaufort cheese and beef cheek, slow-cooked in red wine and served with creamy risotto.

Munchie FUSION €€
(☎04 50 53 45 41; www.munchie.eu; 87 rue des Moulins; mains €22-24; ⏰7pm-2am winter & summer) Franco-Asian-Scandinavian fusion may not be a tried-and-true recipe for success, but this casual, Swedish-skippered restaurant has been making diners happy since 1997. Dishes such as Sichuan-spiced lamb tataki, Japanese coconut rice with egg yolk confit and Thai 'pesto', and cod with ash and leek are so popular that reservations are recommended during the ski season.

Le Bistrot MODERN FRENCH €€€
(☎04 50 53 57 64; www.lebistrotchamonix.com; 151 av de l'Aiguille du Midi; lunch menus €20, dinner menus €55-85; ⊙noon-1.30pm & 7-9pm) Sleek and hushed, this is a real gastronome's paradise. Chef Daniele Raimondi, a protégé of Alain Ducasse, experiments with textures and seasonal flavours in creations such as duck breast with polenta, turnip and sour cherry sauce; pan-fried scallops with pumpkin, truffle and hazelnuts; and chocolate and coriander profiteroles with vanilla ice cream.

Drinking & Nightlife

Whether you're looking for a glammed-up cocktail bar, a spit-and-sawdust pub, or something in between, Chamonix nightlife rocks. For a bar crawl, head (along with the locals) to central rue des Moulins, where wall-to-wall watering holes keep buzzing until about 1am.

★**MBC** MICROBREWERY
(Micro Brasserie de Chamonix; ☎04 50 53 61 59; www.mbchx.com; 350 rte du Bouchet; ⊙4pm-2am winter & summer, to 1am spring & autumn) Run by the last man standing of four Canadian founders, this buzzing microbrewery is one of Chamonix' most unpretentious and gregarious watering holes. Be it with their phenomenal burgers (€10 to €15), chilli-licked wings (12 for €5.25 – half-price – on Monday), live music (from 9pm) or great craft beer, MBC delivers. Busiest from 5pm to 11pm.

Chambre Neuf BAR
(☎04 50 53 00 31; www.hotelgustavia.eu; 272 av Michel Croz; ⊙7am-1am;) Chamonix' most spirited après-ski party (4pm to 8pm), fuelled by a Swedish band and dancing on the tables, spills out the front door of Chambre Neuf. Wildly popular with seasonal workers, it opens its terrace in spring.

Bar'd Up BAR
(123 rue des Moulins; ⊙3pm-late) This 'Australian' dive bar is one of the friendliest, grungiest places in Cham. A pool table, scuffed arcade-game tables and low ceiling set the scene; the reasonable drinks, merry *seasonaires* and music (live and recorded) finish the job.

Les Caves BAR
(☎04 50 21 80 80; www.caphorn-chamonix.com; 80 rue des Moulins; ⊙6pm-2am mid-Dec–Oct) Spread over four levels, with cosy hidden corners and sheepskin seats, this futuristic/rustic disco chalet transforms itself from a quiet cocktail bar into a buzzing danceteria after 10.30pm. Hungry? Order food from adjacent Le Cap Horn.

Jekyll & Hyde PUB
(☎04 50 55 99 70; www.thejekyll.com; 71 rte des Pélerins, Chamonix Sud; ⊙4pm-2am Mon-Fri, opens earlier Sat & Sun;) This British-owned

LOCAL KNOWLEDGE

A TRADITIONAL FOREST LUNCH

A wooden forest chalet is the setting for Chef Claudy's world-famous *croûte aux fromages* (bread drenched in a secret white-wine sauce, topped with cheese and baked) at **Crèmerie du Glacier** (☎04 50 54 07 52; www.lacremerieduglacier.fr; 766 chemin de la Glacière; lunch menus €13, fondue €15-20; ⊙lunch & dinner mid-Dec–mid-May & late Jun–mid-Sep, closed Wed in winter). Other cheesy Savoyard delights here include nine kinds of fondue. Reserve by phone and follow the signpost from the roundabout near the bridge at the southern entrance to Argentière.

To get here, you have several options. In winter, ski down on Piste de la Pierre à Ric (red) or cross-country ski over on Piste de la Moraine. In summer, hike over from the Petit Balcon Nord trail, 15 minutes away. In winter or summer, walk or drive east for about 1km from the base of Téléphérique Lognan-Les Grands Montets; take one-lane chemin de la Glacière in summer and equally narrow chemin de la Rosière in winter.

Les Vieilles Luges (☎06 84 42 37 00; www.lesvieillesluges.com; Les Houches; menus €20-35; ⊙lunch daily winter, lunch & dinner by reservation summer, min 25 people) is an impossibly atmospheric 250-year-old farmhouse that can only be reached on skis or by a scenic 20-minute hike from the Maison Neuve chairlift. Hunker under low wood beams to savour dishes such as *grand-mère*'s bœuf bourguignon and creamy *farçon* (potato bake prepared with prunes, bacon and cream), washed down with *vin chaud* (mulled wine) warmed over a wood fire. Magic.

après-ski mainstay has a split personality: upstairs the 'Jekyll' has really good pub food (try the steak-and-Guinness pie), live music (Wednesday, Thursday and Sunday from 9.30pm) and DJs; downstairs, the 'Hyde' is cosier and more relaxed. Both have good Irish beer and a friendly vibe, and can be found 350m southwest of the Téléphérique de l'Aiguille du Midi.

Le Lapin Agile WINE BAR
(☎04 50 53 33 25; www.lelapinagile.fr; 11 rue Whymper; ⏰noon-3pm Wed-Sun, 7-10pm Tue-Sun early Dec–mid-May & late Jun–mid-Oct; 📶) This relaxed Italianate wine bar has an extensive choice of *vino* and a free *aperitivo* buffet from 6.30pm to 8pm daily. The Rabbit can also manage more substantial plates (mains €18 to €20), including plenty for vegetarians: perhaps a plate of charcuterie imported from Tuscany, or *fusilli* with mushrooms and Veronese radicchio.

Bistrot des Sports PUB
(☎04 50 53 00 46; 182 rue Joseph Vallot; ⏰8am-2am, when busy) Founded in 1878 to cater to muleteers, guides and other mountain folk, this classic pub-cum-bistro is where old-time climbing parties used to assemble before setting out to conquer Mont Blanc, and where many locals and seasonal workers still choose to unwind. The seating area was built for the 1924 Winter Olympics.

Cooperative Fruitière Val d'Arly FOOD
(☎04 50 93 15 89; www.coopflumet.com; 93 rue Whymper; ⏰9am-7.30pm) A shopfront for a venerable collective of more than 70 artisanal producers, this *fruitière* is the best place in Chamonix to stock up on Reblochon, *raclette*, Tomme de Savoie, Morteau sausage and all those other Savoyard delicacies.

ℹ Information

PGHM (☎04 50 53 16 89; www.pghm-chamonix.com; 69 rue de la Mollard) Mountain-rescue service for the Mont Blanc area.

Tourist Office (☎04 50 53 00 24; www.chamonix.com; 85 place du Triangle de l'Amitié; ⏰8.30am-7pm winter & summer, 9am-12.30pm & 2-6pm in low season; 📶) Information on accommodation, activities, the weather and cultural events.

ℹ Getting There & Away

BUS

Chamonix' **bus station** (☎04 50 53 01 15; 234 av Courmayeur, Chamonix Sud; ⏰8am-noon & 1.15-6.30pm in winter, shorter hours rest of year) has moved to av Courmayeur, Chamonix Sud.

Geneva, Switzerland (airport and bus station) One way/return €25/50, 1½ to two hours, eight daily in winter, six at other times. Operated by **Starshipper** (☎04 56 12 40 59; www.starshipper.com).

Courmayeur, Italy One way/return €15/21, 45 minutes, four daily. Run by **Savda** (☎+39 01 65 36 70 11; www.savda.it), with onward connections to Aosta and Milan.

See the websites or drop by the bus station for timetables and reservations (highly recommended).

CAR & MOTORCYCLE

Chamonix is linked to Courmayeur in Italy's Val d'Aosta by the 11.5km-long **Tunnel de Mont Blanc** (www.atmb.com; toll one way/return €43.40/54.30).

When the Col des Montets (between Argentière and Vallorcine) is closed by snow, signs will direct you to drive through the rail tunnel. Current conditions can be found at www.chamonix.com.

The valley's only car-hire company is **Europcar** (☎03 71 38 40 23 5; www.europcar.com; 36 place de la Gare; ⏰8.30am-noon & 2-6pm Mon-Sat).

TRAIN

The scenic, narrow-gauge **Mont Blanc Express** glides from St-Gervais-Le-Fayet to the Swiss town of Martigny, taking in Les Houches, Chamonix, Argentière and Vallorcine en route.

From St-Gervais-Le-Fayet, there are somewhat infrequent trains to cities around France, often with a change in Bellegarde or Annecy. Destinations include the following:

Annecy €15.70, 1½ hours, 12 daily

Lyon €36.60, 3½ to five hours, 10 daily

Paris €98.50 to €128, 4¾ to seven hours, 11 daily

ℹ Getting Around

BUS

Public buses run by **Chamonix Bus** (www.chamonix-bus.com) serve all the towns, villages, ski lifts and attractions in the Chamonix Valley, from Argentière (Col des Montets in summer) in the northeast, to Servoz and Les Houches in the southwest.

The buses all travel circuits that include the **bus station** in Chamonix Sud throughout the year, and have added destinations and are more frequent in winter (mid-December to mid-April) and summer (late June to early September).

All buses are free with a Carte d'Hôte (Guest Card), except the wintertime Chamo' Nuit night buses linking Chamonix with Argentière and Les Houches (last departures from Chamonix 11.30pm or midnight; €2).

Megève & St-Gervais

POP 8925

Megève, 20km due west of Mont Blanc, was developed in the 1920s for Baroness de Rothschild of the famous banking family, who found Switzerland's overcrowded St-Moritz frankly rather tiresome. Today this rustically charming ski village looks almost too perfect to be true: horse-drawn carriages and exquisitely arranged boutique windows spill into its cobbled, medieval-style streets lined with chalets. In winter, Megève attracts a well-off crowd (including lots of families), but the scene is more laid-back in summer.

Slightly lower down the valley, unpretentious St-Gervais-les-Bains is linked to Chamonix by the legendary Mont Blanc Express train. Most of the town is undistinguished 20th-century sprawl, but the lovely central square, with its baroque church, has a distinctly Alpine feel.

Activities

Megève's **Palais des Sports** (☎04 50 21 59 09; www.megeve.fr/index.php/sport; 247 rte du Palais des Sports, Megève; 1 session €11.50; ⌚9.30am-7pm Thu-Tue, to 8.30pm Wed) has plenty of active distractions, year-round, and the town is known for having lots of kid-friendly activities.

Bureau des Guides OUTDOORS
(☎04 50 21 55 11; www.guides-megeve.com; 76 rue Ambroise Martin, Maison de la Montagne, Megève; ⌚9.30am-12.30pm & 3-7pm, closed Sat & Sun low season) Open throughout the year, the Mountain Guides organise activities such as ice climbing, snowshoeing, rock climbing, canyoning and trail running.

Tramway du Mont Blanc CABLE CAR
(☎04 50 53 22 75; www.compagniedumontblanc.co.uk; rue de la Gare, St-Gervais; return to Bellevue/Nid d'Aigle €31/36; ⌚5 departures daily mid-Dec–early Apr, 8 daily early Jun-early Jul & late Aug–mid-Sep) Since 1907, France's highest rack-and-pinion railway has ascended from St-Gervais-Le-Fayet (590m) to Bellevue (1800m; one hour). In summer, when you can hike back down, it climbs all the way to Nid d'Aigle, on the cusp of the Bionnassay glacier (2482m; 80 minutes).

Winter

Having the Mont Blanc massif as a backdrop makes for fabulously scenic **skiing** in areas accessible both from Megève and, via the St-Gervais-Bettex cable car, from near the centre of St-Gervais (www.ski-saintgervais.com). Downhill runs are divided between three separate collections of slopes: **Mont d'Arbois-St-Gervais**, **Le Jaillet-Combloux-La Giettaz** and **Rochebrune-Cote 2000**. Skiing here is mostly for beginners and cruisy intermediates, though there are also some black runs – all told, the area has 445km of well-groomed pistes to play on. For a lift pass, go to www.ski-megeve.com.

> LOCAL KNOWLEDGE
>
> **THE POTTER BEHIND THE CHURCH**
>
> His name is Monsieur Baranger, but he prefers to be called 'the potter behind the church' – and that's precisely where you will find his rambling, poster-plastered **workshop and gallery** in the centre of St-Gervais. An eccentric and something of a local legend, M Baranger can often be seen at his wheel, where he throws pots, plates, ornaments and vases, which are then glazed in earthy shades of blue and cream. His workshop is open *quand vous voyez de la lumière* (when the lights are on).

Summer

In summer, both towns make superb bases for **hiking**, with trails for walkers and hikers of all levels, including young children. Panoramic trails abound, including many in the Bettex, Mont d'Arbois and Mont Joly (2525m) areas. Tourist offices sell IGN hiking maps (€6).

Some of the best **mountain-biking** terrain, with downhill runs accessible by lift, is between Val d'Arly, Mont Blanc and Beaufortain. Bikes can be rented in Megève.

Bungee Mont Blanc Elastique ADVENTURE SPORTS
(Viaduc de St-Gervais; 1/2 jumps €80/115; ⌚Sat & Sun Apr-Nov plus weekdays Jul & Aug) Plunge 65m from the new road bridge in St-Gervais, directly above a waterfall on the River Bonnant.

Information

Megève Tourist Office (☎04 50 21 27 28; www.megeve.com; 70 rue de Monseigneur Conseil; ⌚9am-7pm high season, 12.30pm & 2-6.30pm Mon-Sat other times; 📶) Can help with accommodation and reserve events tickets; it's situated in the pedestrian zone in the centre of town.

St-Gervais Tourist Office (☎04 50 47 76 08; www.saintgervais.com; 43 rue du Mont-Blanc; ⏰9am-12.30pm & 2-6pm or later Mon-Sat, also Sun high season; 📶) Can help find accommodation.

Getting There & Away

BUS

Geneva airport From late December to March, **Starshipper** (p486) links Megève with the airport (€25, 1½ hours, eight daily). Reserve at least 24 hours ahead.

Sallanches Bus 83 goes from Megève's bus station to this nearby railhead (€3.50, 25 minutes, six to nine daily Monday to Saturday, also Sunday in high season).

Les Portes du Soleil

Grandly dubbed 'the Gates of the Sun' (elevation 1000m to 2466m), this gargantuan ski area – the world's largest, if you accept their measurements – encompasses 12 villages on both sides of the unguarded France-Switzerland border. Access to Les Portes du Soleil is easy – by car, it's just 1¼ hours from Geneva airport.

The best known of the villages is **Morzine** (elevation 1000m), which retains some traditional Alpine charm, especially in summer, when visits to *fruitières* (cheese dairies) and traditional slate workshops are popular.

Small, trend-conscious **Avoriaz** (elevation 1800m), a purpose-built ski resort a few kilometres up the valley atop a rock, is completely free of cars. Horse-drawn sleighs (or snowcats) piled high with luggage romantically ferry new arrivals to and from the snowy village centre, enlivened by wacky 1960s architecture.

Arriving by road via Cluses, you hit the smaller ski station of **Les Gets** (elevation 1172m), a family favourite.

Activities

Bureau des Guides OUTDOORS

(☎04 50 75 96 65; www.guides-morzine.com/en; 23 Taille de Mas du Pleney, Morzine) The Bureau has all the information you need for guided off-piste skiing, and for warm-weather frolics such as hiking, biking, climbing, canyoning and paragliding, and **La Noire de Morzine**, Morzine's heart-stopping 3.2km, 500-vertical-metre bike descent from the top of the Pléney cable car. A high-mountain guide will set you back at least €360 per day.

Winter

Depending on how they're measured, between 450km and 650km of **downhill** slopes criss-cross Les Portes du Soleil, served by a whopping 199 lifts covered by a single transfrontier ski pass (per day/week €49.50/279; 30% off online passes for Tuesdays and Thursdays, January and late season). The area's most famous piste is **Le Pas de Chavanette**, better known as the Swiss Wall, which is so steep and moguled that on the European green-blue-red-black scale it's rated orange (double black).

Frequent powder, nursery slopes for little kids, toboggan runs, a new indoor swimming pool, children's clubs and snow play areas make Les Portes du Soleil a great choice for families. **Morzine** offers ideal beginner and intermediate terrain, with scenic runs through the trees for windy days. The snow-sure slopes of higher-elevation **Avoriaz** are great for intermediate skiers but can also challenge the more advanced. Plus, it's freestyle heaven for **snowboarders**, with five snow parks to play in and a fantastic superpipe near the top of the Prodains cable car.

Summer

In summer, the slopes attract **mountain bikers**, with invigorating routes such as the 90km circular Tour des Portes du Soleil,

TRAINS FROM MEGÈVE & ST-GERVAIS

The train station nearest Megève is 12km north in Sallanches; bus 83 connects the two towns. The St-Gervais-Le-Fayet train station is 2km northwest of the centre of St-Gervais. If you're heading to Chamonix, change here for the Mont Blanc Express. Destinations include the following:

TO	FARE (€)	TIME	FREQUENCY
Annecy	15.70	1½hr	4-7 daily
Chamonix	11.20	40min	almost hourly
Geneva (Cornavin)	23.50	2½hr	7-8 daily
Lyon	37	3½-4hr	14 daily
Paris Gare de Lyon	92-121	5-7hr	1-2 per hr

while **walkers** can pick and choose from 800km of marked trails. The extensive summer lift network (late June to early September, €24.50/110 per day/week) takes the slog out of reaching higher altitudes.

Plénéy Cable Car CABLE CAR
(summer day pass €24.50) Linking Morzine with Le Gets in the ski season, this gondola, opened in 2013, is also open to bikers and walkers from June to September.

Sleeping & Eating

Morzine, Avoriaz and Les Gets have the greatest range and extent of accommodation options. As always, book well ahead on weekends and during French school holidays.

Fleur des Neiges HOTEL €€
(04 50 79 01 23; www.hotel-fleur-des-neiges.fr; 227 Taille de Mas de Nant Crue, Morzine; per person per week incl breakfast/half-board €749/917; mid-Dec–mid-Apr & late Jun-early Sep;) A cheery welcome, 31 natural-timber rooms, a sauna, a pool and great food (cooked by long-term chef Patrick) await at this family-run chalet. Situated five long blocks northwest of the tourist office, it's within walking distance of the Super Morzine gondola. Prices drop by more than a third in low season.

★ **The Farmhouse** BOUTIQUE HOTEL €€€
(04 50 79 08 26; www.thefarmhouse.fr; Le Mas de la Coutettaz, Morzine; d incl half-board €224-478; mid-Dec–mid-Apr & Jun–mid-Sep;) This welcoming British-owned guesthouse has 11 rooms spread across a gorgeous pre-Revolutionary manor house and its delightful gardens. Dining is a lavish, candlelit affair around a banquet table; in summer it's a B&B, and in winter (when a one-week minimum applies) it offers half-board. Situated 600m southeast of Morzine's tourist office.

La Ferme de la Fruitière FRENCH €€
(04 50 79 77 70; www.alpage-morzine.com; 337 rte de la Plagne, Morzine; mains €18-22; 10am-2pm & 5pm-midnight) Attached to the Fruitière L'Alpage (a working dairy farm and cheese-maker) this top-notch Savoyard restaurant smells cheesy, in the best possible way. Either watch the golden wheels of Reblochon, Comté and Tomme ripening in the glass-walled downstairs dining room, or toast yourself by the upstairs fireplace as you tuck into the very best fondue, *crozets* and smoked Alpine sausage. Damaged by fire shortly after we visited, it was temporarily closed for repairs in 2016.

LES PORTES DU SOLEIL CENT SAVER

Les Portes du Soleil's hottest summer deal is the **Multipass**, which costs €2/8 per day/week if you're staying here and €8 for day-trippers. Available from early June to early September, the pass covers cable cars and chairlifts (some of which only run from late June) for hikers, as well as access to sporting facilities such as tennis courts, ice rinks and swimming pools.

Le Clin d'Oeil FRENCH €€
(04 50 79 03 10; www.restaurant-leclin.com; 63 rte du Plan, Morzine; menus €15-41; noon-2pm & 7-9.30pm Mon-Fri, 7-9.30pm Sat & Sun;) Brings the food of southwestern France to the Alps. The all-wood interior is inviting for rich, brothy *cassoulet* or duck leg with prunes and Armagnac in winter, while the flowery patio is ideal for lighter dishes such as risotto and seafood in summer. It's down the hill, near the church.

Information

Avoriaz Tourist Office (04 50 74 02 11; www.avoriaz.com; 44 promenade des Festivals, Avoriaz; 8.30am-12.30pm &1.30-7pm daily Dec-Mar, 9am-noon & 2-7pm daily Apr, 9am-12.30pm & 2-7pm daily Jul & Aug, 9am-midday & 2-5pm Mon-Fri May, Jun & Sep-Nov;) Can book self-catering chalets and studios.

Morzine Tourist Office (04 50 74 72 72; www.morzine-avoriaz.com; 26 place du Baraty, Morzine; 8.30am-7.30pm winter & summer, 8.30am-noon & 2-7.30pm Mon-Sat spring & autumn;) Has excellent brochures in English and can help find accommodation.

Getting There & Away

Les Portes du Soleil is easy to get to from Geneva airport, 83km to the west.

During the ski season **Altibus** (www.sat-leman.com) links the area's resorts with Geneva's airport and bus station (one way/return €30/55, two hours, three daily Friday to Monday, daily in school holidays) and the railheads of Thonon-les-Bains (one way/return €11/22, one hour, one to six daily) and Cluses (one way/return €11/22, one hour, four to 10 daily). To make reservations (required), call 08 20 32 03 68.

Within the Morzine area, free shuttle buses (seven lines in winter, one in summer) serve all the lifts.

Évian-les-Bains

POP 8527

The elegant belle-époque spa town of Évian, a favourite country retreat of the Dukes of Savoy, sits grandly on the southern shore of Lake Geneva. Its spas, flowery parks and stately buildings draw crowds mainly in summer.

Discovered in 1790 and bottled since 1826, the mineral water that has made the town famous takes at least 15 years to trickle down through the Chablais Mountains, gathering minerals en route, before emerging at 11.4°C.

Sights & Activities

Évian is compact and easily explored on foot. Facing the flowery **lakefront promenade** (along quai Baron de Blonay and quai Paul Léger) are a number of impressive Victorian and belle-époque buildings, including (from east to west): the **Palais Lumière** (☎04 50 83 15 90; www.ville-evian.fr/fr/culture/palais-lumiere; Quai Charles-Albert-Besson; ⏲Tue-Sun 10am-7pm, 2-7pm Mon); the **Villa Lumière** (☎04 50 83 10 00; www.ville-evian.fr; rue de la Source de Clermont; ⏲9-11am & 1.30-5pm Mon-Fri) FREE; the **Théâtre** (☎04 50 26 85 00; www.ville-evian.fr; quai Besson) and the **Casino** (☎04 50 26 87 87; www.casino-evian.com; quai Baron-de-Blonay; ⏲10am-2am Mon-Thu, to 3am Fri-Sun).

Source Cachat SPRING

(20 av des Sources; ⏲24hr) FREE Drink your fill of pure Évian at this outdoor tap, the original source of the world-famous water. In a little colonnaded pavilion painted pink and white, it's a block up the hill from 19 rue Nationale (Évian's pedestrianised main drag), to the right as you face the horseshoe-shaped staircase. The glass, wood and wrought-iron building across the street is the **Buvette Cachat**, an art-nouveau masterpiece from 1903.

Les Thermes Évian SPA

(☎04 50 75 02 30; www.lesthermesevian.com; place de la Libération; treatments from €35; ⏲9am-7.30pm Mon-Fri, to 6pm Sat) Ever dream of bathing in pure Évian mineral water? With medical spa treatments, fitness programs and a 'wellness centre' – all renovated in 2012 – these baths can make that luxurious dream come true. Reserve ahead, bring a swimsuit, bathing cap and flip-flops, and find the complex 700m east of the tourist office.

CGN Boats to Lausanne BOATING

(www.cgn.ch; return €33) Join local commuters for the scenic, 35-minute boat ride to the Swiss city of Lausanne. Boats depart from the Port de Commerce every hour or two.

Sleeping

Hôtel Continental HOTEL €

(☎04 50 75 37 54; www.hotel-continental-evian.com; 65 rue Nationale; s/d/tr €60/78/95; 📶) Owned by a Franco-American couple (Catherine is French, Mike is from North Carolina), this atmospheric hotel, built in 1868, has 32 rooms with belle-époque furnishings, chandeliers, high ceilings and a handsome central staircase connecting all four floors. It's very central (250m southeast of the tourist office) and excellent value.

Information

Tourist Office (☎04 50 75 04 26; www.evian-tourisme.com; place de la Port d'Allinges; ⏲9am-noon & 2-6pm Mon-Sat Sep-Apr, 9am-noon & 2-6pm daily May & Jun, 9am-6pm daily Jul & Aug; 📶) Has information on accommodation, activities, sights and historical walking tours, plus free wi-fi.

Annecy

POP 54,087 / ELEV 447M

Reclining gracefully by the shores of its mountain-fringed lake, cut by limpid canals, studded with geranium-bedecked houses, and dominated by its turreted château, Annecy is one of the ornaments of Savoie. Made great by the medieval Counts of Geneva, augmented by the Dukes of Savoy, it's kept much of its stunning *vieille ville* (old town), despite being capital of the modern *département* of Haute-Savoie.

The purity of the lake and the beauty of its setting compels Annéciens outdoors – in good weather it seems everyone is hanging out in pavement cafes, mountain-gazing along the lakefront, swimming in the lake, or just aimlessly cycling around it.

Sights

It's a pleasure simply to wander aimlessly around Annecy's medieval old town, a photogenic jumble of narrow pedestrians-only streets, crystal-clear canals – the reason Annecy is known as 'Venice of the Alps' – and colonnaded passageways. On the tree-fringed lakefront, the flowery Jardins de l'Europe are linked to the grassy Champ de

Annecy

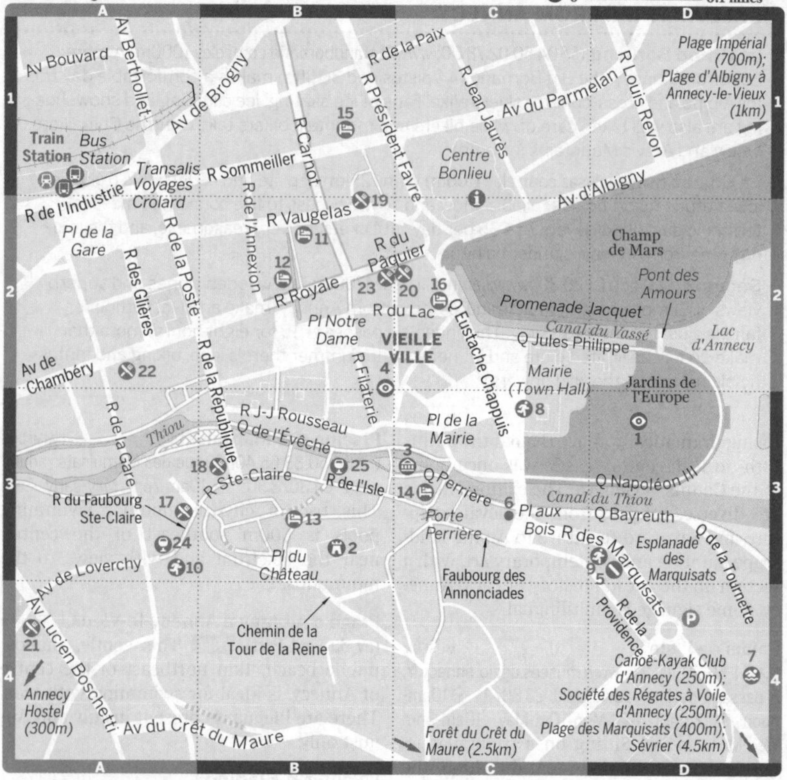

Annecy

Sights

1 Annecy Waterfront D3
2 Château d'Annecy B3
3 Palais de l'Isle C3
4 Vieille Ville B2

Activities, Courses & Tours

5 Annecy Plongée D3
6 Compagnie des Bateaux C3
7 Piscine des Marquisats D4
8 Roll'n Cy C3
9 Roul' ma Poule D3
10 Takamaka A3

Sleeping

11 Hôtel Alexandra B2
12 Hôtel Central B2
13 Hôtel du Château B3
14 Hôtel du Palais de l'Isle C3
15 Le Pré Carré B1
16 Splendid Hôtel C2

Eating

17 Creabistro A3
18 Food Market B3
19 La Ciboulette B2
20 La Cuisine des Amis C2
21 Le Denti A4
22 L'Esquisse A2
23 L'Étage B2

Drinking & Nightlife

24 Beer O'Clock A3
25 Captain Pub B3

Mars, a popular picnic spot, by the poetic iron arch of the Pont des Amours (Lovers' Bridge).

Château d'Annecy CASTLE
(www.musees.agglo-annecy.fr; rampe du Château; adult/child €5.20/2.60; ⏲10am-noon & 2-5pm Wed-Mon Oct-May, 10.30am-6pm daily Jun-Sep)

WORTH A TRIP

SKI DAY TRIPS FROM ANNECY

Le Grand Bornand (☎04 50 02 78 00; www.legrandbornand.com; elev 1000m) A mere hour from Annecy, the Big Bornand (44 pistes and 30 lifts) makes a comfortable day trip for Alpine and cross-country skiers alike. Fans of ice skating, ice climbing and snowshoeing are also well taken care of, while hikers and mountain bikers take over the Chinaillon Valley and Aravis Mountains in summer.

La Clusaz (www.laclusaz.com; elev 1100m) With 125km of piste and 49 lifts, this (relatively) low-altitude resort boasts reliable snow and – with access to five connected massifs – terrain to suit all skill levels. At €35 per day, lift tickets are very reasonable, and the journey time from Annecy is under an hour.

Semnoz (☎04 50 01 20 30; www.semnoz.fr; elev 1700m) The wooded slopes and superb views of Semnoz, less than 30 minutes' drive from Annecy, make an ideal setting for families just getting into skiing. The cheap ski passes (€15 for eight hours) more than make up for the limited piste and lift network. In summer there's luge, biking and fantastic hiking among the wild flowers.

Rising dramatically above the old town, this 13th- to 16th-century castle was once home to the Counts of Geneva. The exhibits inside are diverse, ranging from medieval sculpture and Savoyard furniture to Alpine landscape painting and contemporary art, with a section on the natural history of Lac d'Annecy. Some signage is multilingual.

Palais de l'Isle MUSEUM

(☎04 56 49 40 37; www.musees.agglo-annecy.fr; 3 passage de l'Île; adult/child €3.80/2; ⏱10am-noon & 2-5pm Wed-Mon Oct-May, 10am-5pm Wed-Mon Jun-Sep) Sitting on a triangular islet surrounded by the Canal du Thiou, the 12th-century Palais de l'Isle has been a lordly residence, a courthouse, a mint and a prison over the centuries. The central landmark of Annecy's gorgeous *vieille ville* (old town), it now houses permanent exhibits on local architecture and history, and temporary displays of art.

Activities

Sunbathing & Swimming

When the sun's out, the beaches fringing the lake beckon. Some are patrolled in summer, and can become very crowded.

Plage Impérial BEACH

(☎04 50 19 19 73; www.plage-imperial.com; 30 ave d'Albigny; per day €15; ⏱10am-7pm Sat & Sun May & Sep, daily Jun-Aug) This manicured private beach next to the elegant, pre-WWI Impérial Casino is part of the Plage de l'Impérial Complexe. Other family-friendly attractions include volleyball, badminton, *pétanque*, table tennis, minigolf and spaces for picnics and kids' swimming.

Piscine des Marquisats SWIMMING

(☎04 50 33 65 40; 29 rue des Marquisats; adult/child €4.30/3.30; ⏱10am-7pm May-early Sep) This trio of city-run outdoor swimming pools is 600m southeast of the centre, near the lakefront and with views to the mountains.

Plage d'Albigny à Annecy-le-Vieux BEACH

(av du Petit Port) FREE This gentle, shallow public beach, 1km northeast of the centre of Annecy, is ideal for swimming with kids. There are lifeguards present in July and August only.

Cycling & Blading

Biking and blading are big, with 46km of cycling track encircling the lake (there's a gap on the eastern shore between Menthon and Perroix), and another gentle path, once a railway grade, leading all the way to Albertville, 44km to the southeast. The tourist office (p495) has free maps.

Roll'n Cy SKATING

(☎06 28 34 66 34; www.roll-n-cy.org; ⏱8pm Fri) Strap on your skates for the weekly group rides organised by this local rollerblading club. The meeting point is in front of the *mairie* (town hall) at place de l'Hôtel de Ville. Call for updates from 7pm on Friday evening; rides may be cancelled due to rain.

Roul' ma Poule CYCLING

(☎04 76 39 77 20; www.roulemapoule.com; 4 rue des Marquisats; ⏱9.30am-7pm) This family bike shop rents rollerblades (€15/20 per half/full day), bicycles (€15/20), tandems (€34/44) and kids' trailers (€15/20), and is great source of day-trip recommendations.

Water Sports

The most relaxed way to see the lake is from the water. From sometime in March to October, pedal and motor boats can be hired for €15/50 per hour/day along the waterfront, at or near Jardins de l'Europe.

Canoë-Kayak Club d'Annecy KAYAKING
(☎04 50 45 03 98; www.kayak-annecy.com; 33 rue des Marquisats, Base Nautique; ⊙9am-noon Mon-Fri, 2-6pm Mon-Sat Apr-Jun & Sep-Nov, extended hours Jul & Aug) Offers kayaking courses.

Société des Régates à Voile d'Annecy BOATING
(☎04 50 45 48 39; www.srva.info; 31 rue des Marquisats, Base Nautique; ⊙10am-12.30pm & 1.30-7pm Mon-Sat, 10am-7pm Sun) Rents sailing boats starting at €44 for two hours on a single-person Laser dinghy; windsurfers are €28. Hours vary during school holidays.

Annecy Plongée DIVING
(☎04 50 45 40 97; www.annecyplongee.com; 6 rue des Marquisats; ⊙9am-noon & 2-7pm Mon-Fri, 9am-7pm Sat) Annecy Plongée can take you beneath the sparkling water of Lac d'Annecy. The highly experienced instructors have great enthusiasm for the lake and their sport.

Adventure Sports

Takamaka OUTDOORS
(☎40 50 45 60 61; www.takamaka.fr; 23 rue du Faubourg Ste-Claire; ⊙9am-noon & 2-6pm Mon-Fri, 10am-4pm Sat & Sun) Offers a wide range of outdoor adventures with licensed guides, including tandem paragliding (€95), rafting (€49), rock climbing (€49), mountain-bike free-riding (€59) and canyoning (€49 for a half-day).

Tours

Compagnie des Bateaux BOATING
(☎04 50 51 08 40; www.annecy-croisieres.com; 2 place aux Bois; 1hr lake cruises adult/child €14.2/9.60; ⊙late Mar–mid-Dec) The Boat Company runs lake cruises and, from mid-April to late September, trips to villages around the lake. For the romantically inclined there are also dinner cruises aboard the MS *Libellule* (€59 per person).

Festival & Events

Annecy celebrates the flamboyant **Venetian Carnival** in February (two weeks after its namesake in Venice, Italy); the **Fête du Lac**, with a spectacular 70 minutes of fireworks over the lake, on the first Saturday in August; and **Le Retour des Alpages**, when the cows come home from summer pasturage in the Alps, wreathed in flowers and bells, on the second Saturday in October. Street performers wow evening crowds at **Les Noctibules**, over four nights in July.

> **WORTH A TRIP**
>
> **YVOIRE**
>
> Officially one of 'The Most Beautiful Villages of France', sleepy, wisteria-wrapped Yvoire, 16km west of Thonon on the shores of Lake Geneva, makes for a great day trip. A former fishing village, fortified in the early 14th century, it's a riot of turrets, towers and old stone houses.
>
> Slumbering in the shadow of a 14th-century castle and enclosed by walls, the **Jardin des Cinq Sens** (Garden of Five Senses; ☎04 50 72 88 80; www.jardin5sens.net; rue du Lac; adult/child €12/7; ⊙10am-6.30pm early Apr–mid-Oct) is designed to be experienced through sight, touch, sound, scent and even (within reason!) taste. There's a maze, kids' activities, and more than 1300 plant species. It closes an hour early in the first and last two weeks of its opening period.

Sleeping

Annecy Hostel HOSTEL €
(☎09 53 12 02 90; www.annecyhostel.com; 32 av de Loverchy; dm from €22, d €56; @ 📶) Run by two well-travelled siblings, this friendly, 51-bed hostel has bright, funky dorm rooms with four to six beds, two shared kitchens, a TV lounge and bike rental (per day €12). The back garden – perfect for summer barbecues and meeting people – offers table tennis, a pool table, chickens and a bar with live music until 11pm.

★ **Hôtel Central** BOUTIQUE HOTEL €
(☎04 50 45 05 37; www.hotelcentralannecy.com; 6bis rue Royale; d/tr €70/80; P 📶) Forget the prosaic name – this splendid canalside hotel, occupying a late-17th-century building in the pedestrianised heart of the city, provides comfortably the most eccentric and visually entertaining digs in Annecy. Choose the Chambre Couture (complete with dressmaker's doll and antique sewing machine), the psychedelic Chambre Coco,

DON'T MISS

CHÂTEAU DE MENTHON-ST-BERNARD

The 1000-year-old **Château de Menthon-St-Bernard** (07 81 74 39 72; www.chateau-de-menthon.com; Menthon-St-Bernard; guided tours adult/child €8.50/4; 2-6pm Fri-Sun May, Jun & Sep, noon-6pm daily Jul & Aug) – one of the inspirations for Walt Disney's *Sleeping Beauty* castle (so they say) – was the birthplace of St Bernard in 1008. Tours of the medieval interior – courtesy of the 23rd generation of De Menthons to live here – take in tapestry-adorned *salons* and a magnificent library, stacked with more than 12,000 volumes dating to before the Revolution. But it's the sparkling Lac d'Annecy panorama that leaves many visitors speechless. Situated 8.5km southeast of Annecy.

the Chambre Orientale or any of the other 11 rooms: they're all delightful.

Hôtel du Château HOTEL €

(04 50 45 27 66; www.annecy-hotel.com; 16 rampe du Château; s/d/tr/q €59/85/95/110;) Just across the square from the château's imposing gatehouse, this family-run hotel has a sun-drenched, panoramic breakfast terrace and 16 neat, sweetly decorated rooms with rustic pine furniture and pastel walls. Four have lovely lake views.

Hôtel du Palais de l'Isle HISTORIC HOTEL €€

(04 50 45 86 87; www.palaisannecy.com; 13 rue Perrière; s/d €92/139;) In an 18th-century building right in the centre of the old town, this hotel has crisp contemporary decor and 34 minibar-equipped rooms with views of the *palais*, the château or the old town's rooftops. Breakfast – charcuterie, cheese and bread – is €12.

Splendid Hôtel BOUTIQUE HOTEL €€

(04 50 45 20 00; www.hotel-annecy-lac.fr; 4 quai Eustache Chappuis; s/d from €123/137;) This aptly named hotel, with green, breezy views of the adjacent Champ de Mars, has 47 classy, contemporary rooms with parquet floors. It's geared for families: whether you need an extra bed or a babysitter, the friendly staff will oblige.

Hôtel Alexandra HOTEL €€

(04 50 45 49 06; www.hotelannecy-alexandra.fr; 19 rue Vaugelas; s/d/ste €79/99/114;) The 25 smallish rooms, each unique, are sparely furnished, soundproof and spotless, and the welcome here is warm. Six rooms have balconies and a couple come with canal views.

Le Pré Carré BUSINESS HOTEL €€€

(04 50 52 14 14; www.hotel-annecy.net; 27 rue Sommeiller; s/d from €194/224;) This eight-storey hotel keeps things contemporary with 29 spacious, subdued, business-efficient rooms, almost all with a balcony or terrace. Amenities include a Jacuzzi, sauna and seminar room. Breakfast – a lavish affair starring regional and organic produce – can be taken at the buffet or in your room.

Eating

Food Market MARKET €

(cnr rues Ste-Claire & de la République; 7am-1am Sun, Tue & Fri) Growing organically through the picturesque arteries of the *vieille ville*, this sprawling market has all the Savoyard delicacies, fresh fruit and vegetables and cheap souvenirs you could possibly need.

Creabistro THAI €

(04 50 23 85 39; www.creabistro.com; 2 rue du Faubourg Ste-Claire; menus €9-18; noon-3pm & 6.30-10pm Thu-Tue) A fresh alternative to the weight of Savoyard cuisine, this build-your-own Thai noodle bar does a roaring trade from a small shopfront on the rue du Faubourg Ste-Claire. One bite of pad thai reveals the authenticity in the kitchen, and there are a few stools and a table or two for dining in.

La Cuisine des Amis FUSION €

(04 50 10 10 80; www.lacuisinedesamisannecy.fr; 9 rue du Pâquier; mains €17-20, lunch menus €14.80; noon-2pm & 7-10.30pm daily, closed dinner Sun & Mon Oct-May;) Welcoming clients like old *amis* (friends), this freshly remodelled bistro serves meat and fish with a creative, international twist. Alongside cheesy Savoyard specialities you'll find Moroccan classics such as couscous royale and *tajine* of lamb and figs.

Le Denti FRENCH €€

(04 50 64 21 17; 25bis av de Loverchy; lunch menus €22, dinner menus €32-42; noon-1.15pm Thu-Mon, 7.30-9.15pm Mon & Thu-Sat) A few blocks off the beaten track but worth seeking out, this unassuming restaurant serves traditional French cuisine – their speciality is fish – prepared so the taste of the super-fresh in-

gredients shines through. The menu changes twice a month according to the seasonal produce available in the markets.

L'Étage FRENCH €€

(☎04 50 51 03 28; www.letageannecy.com; 13 rue du Pâquier; lunch menus €13-16.50, other menus €19-36; ⊙noon-2.15pm & 7-10.30pm) Feast on local cheeses in the form of fondue or *raclette* (melted cheese, boiled potatoes, charcuterie and baby gherkins), or on French-style meat and fish dishes (eg steak with 'café de Paris' butter) in a building from the 1600s. Mellow music and the cheerful staff keep the ambience relaxed.

L'Esquisse GASTRONOMIC €€€

(☎04 50 44 80 59; www.esquisse-annecy.fr; 21 rue Royale; lunch menus €25, dinner menus €39-65; ⊙12.15-1.15pm & 7.30-9pm Mon, Tue & Thu-Sat) A talented husband-and-wife team runs the show at this intimate seven-table restaurant. Their passion shines through in the service, wine list and carefully composed *menus* dotted with delights such as pumpkin consommé with Beaufort cheese and roast scallops with brown butter. Reserve ahead.

La Ciboulette GASTRONOMIC €€€

(☎04 50 45 74 57; www.laciboulette-annecy.com; Cour du Pré Carré, 10 rue Vaugelas; menus €38-75; ⊙noon-1pm & 7.30-8.45pm Tue-Sat) Crisp white linen sets the scene at this elegant restaurant, where chef Georges Paccard prepares innovative delights such as veal sweetbreads with bitter gentian juice, and grilled turbot with pigs' trotter croquette and tarragon sauce.

Drinking & Nightlife

Captain Pub PUB

(☎04 50 45 79 80; www.captain-pub.fr; 11 rue du Pont Morens; ⊙11am-2.30am Wed-Mon; 📶) The Captain doesn't work too hard at being an 'Irish Pub', but does offer a warren of convivial nooks festooned with nauticalia, a plum riverside terrace, a great range of whiskys and draught beers, more-than-decent food and an atmosphere of genuine cheer.

Beer O'Clock BAR

(☎04 50 65 83 78; 18 rue du Faubourg Ste-Claire; 250mL beer €3-5.25; ⊙5pm-midnight Tue-Fri, to 1am Sat, to 11pm Sun; 📶) Opened in 2014, this laid-back, high-tech establishment serves beer like petrol stations sell gasoline: you only pay for what you pump. After buying credit on a computerised magnetic card, you can drink as much or as little of the 12 brews on offer as you like – a fantastic way to compare and savour lots of microbrews side-by-side.

Information

Tourist Office (☎04 50 45 00 33; www.lac-annecy.com; 1 rue Jean Jaurès, courtyard of Centre Bonlieu; ⊙9am-12.30pm & 1.45-6pm Mon-Sat year-round, plus 9am-12.30pm & 1.45-6pm Sun mid-May–mid-Sep, 9am-12.30pm Sun Apr–early Oct & Dec) Has free maps and brochures, and details on cultural activities all around the lake.

Getting There & Away

BUS

The ticket office for the **bus station** (Gare Routière; rue de l'Industrie) is inside the new train station.

Voyages Crolard (☎04 50 45 08 12; www.voyages-crolard.com) sends buses (every hour or two Monday to Saturday, fewer or none on Sunday) to villages around Lac d'Annecy, including Veyrier-du-Lac (€1.50, 15 minutes) and Talloires (€1.50, 30 minutes), as well as to the ski resorts of La Clusaz (€8, 45 minutes), Le Grand Bornand (€8, one hour) and Albertville (1½ hours). The company also has a service to Lyon's St-Exupéry airport (one way/return €36/54, 2¼ hours, four to six daily).

TRAINS FROM ANNECY

Direct services from Annecy's **train station** (place de la Gare), opened in 2012, include the following.

TO	FARE (€)	TIME	FREQUENCY
Aix-les-Bains	8.10	40min	hourly
Chambéry	10.30	50min	hourly
Lyon Part-Dieu	26-50	2hr	13 daily Mon-Fri, 8 daily Sat & Sun
Paris, Gare de Lyon	80-101	3¾hr	4-7 daily
St-Gervais-Le-Fayet (for Chamonix)	15.30	1½hr	5 daily Sun-Fri, 3 Sat

BEST FOOT FORWARD

Annecy is a real biped's town: you'll see large numbers of locals jogging serenely along their lakefront at all times of the year, and walking the *vieille ville* is a joy. From Jardins de l'Europe, you can amble along the lakefront northeast towards **Annecy-le-Vieux**, and southeast to **Esplanade des Marquisats** and beyond. Annecy's commercial centre is a few blocks north of the Canal du Thiou, around rue Royale.

Forêt du Crêt du Maure, about 3km due south of Annecy, has plenty of walking trails, as do the wildlife-rich wetlands of **Bout du Lac**, 20km from Annecy on the lake's southern tip, and the **Roc de Chère** nature reserve, 10km away on the eastern shore. The tourist office sells walking maps, including IGN's *Lac d'Annecy* (€12).

Transalis (✆ 04 50 51 08 51; www.transdevhautesavoie.com) handles services to Geneva's bus station (lines T72 and T73; €10.50, 1½ hours, 15 daily Monday to Friday, six to eight Saturday and Sunday), Thonon-les-Bains (€14, two hours, twice daily Monday to Friday) and Évian-les-Bains (€14, 2½ hours, twice daily Monday to Friday).

Getting Around

Bicycles can be hired from city-run **Vélonecy** (✆ 04 50 51 38 90; www.velonecy.com; place de la Gare; ⌚24hr), at the train station, for €20 per day (including a helmet); the deposit is €250. If you have a valid train ticket, the fee is only €6. In July and August reserve two or three days ahead. Staff can supply you with a bike-path map.

Chambéry

POP 56,500 / ELEV 270M

Located at the junction of two major Alpine valleys, the château town of Chambéry is an unjustly neglected gem. Twelve kilometres south of twinkling Lac du Bourget, it's within easy reach of two regional parks and preserves many signs of former glory (Chambéry was Savoy's capital from the 13th century until 1563, when the Dukes relocated to Turin). Its surprisingly few visitors are rewarded with crowd-free museums, lively cafes and serene strolls along arcaded streets.

Sights

★ Ville Ancienne HISTORIC SITE

Chambéry has one of the best-preserved medieval old towns this side of the Alps. Its hidden courtyards, cafe-rimmed squares and lanes flanked by 14th- to 18th-century *hôtels* are great for an aimless amble. Streets worth wandering include tiny **rue du Sénat de Savoie**, cobbled **rue Juiverie** and gallery-dotted **rue de la Métropole**. For a gorgeous perspective in every direction, stand at the intersection of arcaded **rue de Boigne** and long, handsome **place St-Léger**.

Once home to local aristocrats, **rue de la Croix d'Or** hides the Hôtel du Châteauneuf's rose-draped courtyard, with intricate wrought-iron grilles affording fine views of the castle. Winding to the base of the château's massive walls, 14th-century **rue Basse-du-Château** is most atmospheric when the afternoon sun warms its caramel-coloured façades.

Fontaine des Éléphants FOUNTAIN

(place des Éléphants) With its four intricately carved elephants, this fountain looks like the model for an old Indian postage stamp. It was sculpted in 1838 in honour of Général de Boigne (*bwan-y*; 1751–1830), who made his fortune in the East Indies. When he returned home he bestowed some of his wealth on the town and was honoured posthumously with this monument. The genteel arcaded street that leads from the fountain to Château des Ducs de Savoie, **rue de Boigne**, is one of his projects.

Château des Ducs de Savoie CASTLE

(✆ 04 79 70 15 94; place du Château; ⌚gardens 9am-6pm Mon-Fri mid-Feb–Jun & Sep-Dec, plus Sat & Sun Jul & Aug, exhibition 9am-noon & 1.30-6pm Tue-Fri, 10.30am-6pm Sat & Sun, closed Jan–mid-Feb) This forbidding medieval castle, once home to the counts and dukes of Savoy, now houses the Préfecture and Conseil Général of the Savoie *département*. The **gardens** and the **Cour d'Honneur** (courtyard) are open free-of-charge, but to see the 14th- and 15th-century **Tour Trésorerie** (Treasury Tower) and the stained glass inside the recently restored **Ste-Chapelle**, built in the 15th century to house the Shroud of Turin, you have to take a tour.

Guided tours (adult/child €6/4.50) depart at 2.30pm Tuesday to Sunday from May to September, and at 2.30pm Saturday and Sunday October to April. They begin at the château's Acceuil des Guides office in July

and August, and at the old town's **Hôtel de Condon** (71 rue St Réal), around the corner from the cathedral, the rest of the year.

In the small exhibition, scale models, engravings and paintings present the history and architecture of the château.

The chapel's 70-bell **Grand Carillon** (1993), one of the largest ensembles of bells in the world, peals in concert on the first and third Saturday of each month at 5.30pm (more frequently in summer).

Cathédrale St-François de Sales CATHEDRAL
(☎04 79 33 25 00; www.catholiques-chambery.paroisse.net; 6 rue Métropole; ⏲8.45am-noon & 3-5pm Mon-Sat, 9am-12.15pm & 3-8.15pm Sun except during Mass) Built as a Franciscan chapel in the 15th century, Chambéry's cathedral hides some surprises, including Europe's largest assemblage (occupying some 6000 sq metres) of *trompe l'œil* Gothic vaulting, painted by artists Sevesi and Vicario, and a 35m-long maze dating from the mid-19th century.

Musée Savoisien MUSEUM
(☎04 79 33 44 48; www.musee-savoisien.fr; sq de Lannoy de Bissy; ⏲10am-noon & 2-6pm Wed-Mon) Housed in a Franciscan monastery linked to the Cathédrale St-François de Sales by cloisters, this museum showcases the turbulent history, rich culture and diverse ethnography of Savoie. While the museum is closed for major renovations until 2017, the cloisters are accessible between 8.30am and noon then 2pm and 5pm Monday to Friday year-round, and between 10am and noon then 2pm and 5pm on weekends in December, January, July and August.

Musée des Beaux-Arts MUSEUM
(☎04 79 33 75 03; www.musees.chambery.fr; place du Palais de Justice; special exhibitions adult/child €3/1.50; ⏲10am-noon & 2-6pm Wed-Mon) FREE Occupying a former corn exchange, the light-flooded top-floor gallery showcases 14th- to 18th-century Italian works, with an emphasis on Florentine and Sienese paintings from the Renaissance, including pieces by Caravaggio, Titian and Ghirlandaio. Also worth a look are the many dramatic landscapes of Chambéry and the Alps painted between 1799 and 1975. Signs are in French.

Musée des Charmettes HISTORIC BUILDING
(☎04 79 33 39 44; www.chambery.fr/musees; 890 chemin des Charmettes; audioguides €3; ⏲10.30am-6pm Wed-Mon Apr-Nov, 10am-4.30pm Sat & Sun Dec-Mar) FREE Geneva-born philosopher, composer and writer Jean-Jacques Rousseau, a key figure of the Enlightenment and the French Revolution, lived with his lover, Baronne Louise Éléonore de Warens, at this charming, late-17th-century country house from 1736 to 1742. His passion for botany lives on in the peaceful garden, filled with medicinal herbs, aromatic flowers and heritage fruit trees and vines. Situated a steep 2km southeast of the centre, along rustic chemin des Charmettes.

Sleeping

Hôtel des Princes HOTEL €€
(☎04 79 33 45 36; www.hoteldesprinces.com; 4 rue de Boigne; s/d/tr/q from €88/98/123/143; 📶) The Shroud of Turin was once repaired in the late-15th-century convent that now houses this elegant family hotel in the old town. Renovated in 2015, the 45 medium-sized, modern rooms include chalet-style *chambres* on the top floor – room 11 (€193) is ideal for a family of five. There's also a spa and sauna, bookable for €16 per person per hour.

★ **Petit Hôtel Confidentiel** BOUTIQUE HOTEL €€€
(☎04 79 26 24 17; www.petithotelconfidentiel.com; 10 rue de la Trésorerie; ste €200-450; P❄📶) Starting from the ground-floor *épicerie* (grocery) where JJ Rousseau came a' courting in the 18th century, this elegant, family-run boutique hotel has steadily colonised an entire, 15th-century building in the lee of the château. Sophisticated and cosy, its 15 huge suites mostly come with two-person bath-tubs and ultramodern ethanol fireplaces, and all are individually decorated with panache. A five-star gem.

Eating

À l'Herboristerie VEGETARIAN €
(Café Botanique; ☎04 79 75 62 65; www.delabotanique.com; 193 rue Croix d'Or; mains €14; ⏲noon-2.30pm Tue-Sat; ✍) This gloriously old-fashioned herbalist's shop does a brisk

ℹ CHAMBÉRY CENT SAVER

Pick up the €2 **Chambéry Pass** at the tourist office from May to October for free entry to temporary exhibitions at the city's museums, substantial discounts on guided tours, 10% discounts at certain restaurants, and three hours of parking at the central Vinci Park garage.

trade in medicinal plants and herbal teas, many from the Alps, while the lunch-only restaurant next door serves up wholesome house-made salads, ravioli and quiches, some made with wild plants and mushrooms. The menu changes daily. The tearoom behind the shop is often open until 7pm.

La Fruitière d'Augustin CHEESE €
(☎04 79 33 77 17; 2 place de Genève; ⏲9am-12.30 & 3-7.15pm Tue-Fri, 7.30am-1pm & 2-7.15pm Sat) Specialising in the cheeses of Savoie, this outlet of the regional *fromagerie*, located just across the square from the **Marché des Halles** (Covered Market; place de Genève; ⏲7am-noon Tue, Wed, Fri & Sat), is the place for Reblochon, Tome des Bauges, Comté, Beaufort, Grand Colombier, bleu de Termignon and Persillé de Tignes.

★**Les Halles** FRENCH €€
(☎04 79 60 01 95; www.restaurant-les-halles-chambery.com; 15 rue Bonivard; lunch menus €15-18, dinner menus €26-36; ⏲noon-2pm & 7-10pm Tue-Sat; 👪) This ordinary-looking bistro, beloved by locals, combines gourmet panache with a warm welcome and faultless service. Try regional specialities including chicken stuffed with *diots* (Savoyard sausages) and creamy Beaufort polenta, or *tête de veau* (calf's head) with tangy/creamy *sauce gribiche.* But save room for *fondant au chocolat* with pecan ice cream!

L'Atelier FRENCH €€
(☎04 79 70 62 39; www.atelier-chambery.com; 59 rue de la République; lunch menus €21, dinner menus €32-40; ⏲noon-2.30pm & 7-10pm Tue-Sat) Chef Gilles Herard – who's worked in the kitchens of gastronomic princes such as Alain Ducasse and Paul Bocuse – works the stoves in this brick-vaulted wine bar-bistro. His daily menu shows some daring, and there are plenty of wines by the glass to match with unusual dishes such as lamb shank with pumpkin 'cappuccino' and *pain perdu*.

ℹ Information

Tourist Office (☎04 79 33 42 47; www.chambery-tourisme.com; 5bis place du Palais de Justice; ⏲9am-12.30pm & 2-6pm Mon-Sat, plus 10am-1pm Sun Jul & Aug) Can supply English brochures and details on Savoie's cheese and wine routes, and arranges guided old-town tours (in English in July and August), some at night. Staff are happy to help with room reservations (no charge). Situated just northwest of the old town, 300m south of the train station.

ℹ Getting There & Away

AIR

Chambéry Savoie Airport (☎04 79 54 49 54; www.chambery-airport.com; 73420 Viviers-du-Lac; 📶), 10km north of Chambéry at the southern tip of Lac du Bourget, has seasonal flights (mainly December to April) to various British regional airports.

BUS

While the train station was being renovated, the **bus station** (place Paul Vidal) was at place Paul Vidal, 300m southwest of the train station. It should have returned to place de la Gare in late 2016.

From late June to early September, the Ligne des Plages bus goes to Aix-les-Bains (50 minutes) via the beaches along Lac du Bourget.

TRAIN

Chambéry's **train station** (www.gares-sncf.com; place de la Gare) underwent a complete renovation through 2016. In the city centre, tickets are available at the **Boutique SNCF** (☎08 92 35 35 35; www.voyages-sncf.com; 21 place St-Léger; ⏲9am-noon & 2-5pm Mon-Fri, to 4pm Sat). Direct services include the following:

Annecy €10.20, 50 minutes, hourly

Geneva €17.70, 1¼ hours, four to six daily

Grenoble €11.90, one hour, at least hourly

Lyon (Part-Dieu) €18.40, 1½ hours, almost hourly

Paris Gare de Lyon €78 to €100, three hours, 10 daily Monday to Friday, seven Saturday, four Sunday

ℹ Getting Around

TO/FROM THE AIRPORT

Buses link the airport with various Alpine ski stations but not, unfortunately, with Chambéry's town centre. The 15-minute journey by taxi costs around €20 – call **Allo Taxi Chambéry** (☎04 79 69 11 12; www.taxi-chambery.com).

Lyon's St-Exupéry Airport Buses run by **Voyages Crolard** (☎04 50 51 08 51; www.voyages-crolard.com) link Chambéry with Lyon's airport (one way/return €24/36, one hour, four to six daily).

Geneva Airport Serviced by Aérocar (www.aerocar.fr) buses (one way/return €33.50/41.50, one hour, five daily).

BICYCLE

City-run **Vélostation** (☎04 79 96 34 13; www.velostation-chambery.fr; Parc du Verney; bike rental per hr/day €1.50/6; ⏲8am-noon & 2-7pm Mon-Fri, 1.30-7pm Sat Nov-Mar, plus 9am-7pm Sun & no midday closure Apr-Oct) rents out

WORTH A TRIP

LAKESIDE LEGENDS

Auberge du Père Bise (☎04 50 60 72 01; www.perebise.com; 303 rte du Port, Talloires; menus €85; ⊙12.30-2pm Wed-Mon & 7.30-9pm daily Jun-Sep, closed Wed late Sep–mid-Dec & mid-Feb–May) is never less than extraordinary. Chef Sophie Bise, a Lac d'Annecy local who comes from a long line of chefs, works wonders with top-notch local produce such as red-clawed crayfish, or lake fish, prepared *à la meunière*. Tea, coffee, pastries and sandwiches are served from 3pm to 6pm – no need to reserve. Situated in Talloires, 12km southeast of Annecy; follow the signs to 'Port-Plage'. Accommodation is available (doubles from €330).

Yoann Conte (☎04 50 09 97 49; www.yoann-conte.com; 13 Vieille rte des Pensières, Veyrier-du-Lac; lunch menus €85-126, dinner menus €189-220; ⊙noon-1.30pm & 7-8.30pm Wed-Sun, plus 7-8.30pm Tue in summer) is named afer the successor to French celebrity chef Marc Veyrat, who once ran the stoves in this delightful lakeside restaurant. Conte's regionalism shines through in dishes such as grilled sea bass in Savoyard Mondeuse wine, and *féra* (white fish from the adjacent lake) 'as Mr Sarvagnin liked it'. The baby-blue house on the lake also has eight wonderful rooms with magnificent views (doubles €235 to €435). To obtain a table, reserve a week ahead on holidays, for Saturday dinner and from June to early September. It's situated in Veyrier-du-Lac, a village across the lake from Annecy (6km by road). To get there by car from Annecy, follow the signs from the first roundabout you come to in Veyrier-du-Lac.

seven-speed city bikes. It was based next to the bus station (300m southwest of the train station) until late 2016, but should have returned to the train station. The greater Chambéry area has 80km of cycling lanes; staff can supply you with a cycling map.

Around Chambéry

Chambéry is wedged between two national parks, the Parc Naturel Régional du Massif des Bauges and the Parc Naturel Régional de Chartreuse. Both offer rich pickings for hikers, mountain bikers, snowshoers and cross-country skiers.

During the ski season, bus C8 runs from Chambéry's Bus Station to La Féclaz (€8, 50 minutes, two to four per day). Outside winter, you really need a car to explore the national parks around Chambéry properly.

Parc Naturel Régional de Chartreuse

The 690-sq-km **Chartreuse Regional Nature Park** encompasses the wild, forested slopes of the Chartreuse massif, dubbed the 'desert' by monks of the Carthusian Order who settled here in 1084. Today the **Grande Chartreuse monastery** is home to some 30 monks who have taken a vow of silence, and are known chiefly for distilling the famous Liqueurs Chartreuse. It is off-limits to visitors, but you can see it from above by hiking to the summit of 1867m **Charmant Som**; follow the signs for 'Col de Porte' on the D512. Or you can check out *Into Great Silence* (2007), an almost-silent film about the monastery. Underneath the park's limestone spine are some 280km of caves.

Sights

Musée de la Grande Chartreuse MUSEUM
(☎04 76 88 60 45; www.musee-grande-chartreuse.fr; La Correrie, St-Pierre-de-Chartreuse; adult/child €8.50/3.90; ⊙10am-6.30pm May-Sep, 1.30-6pm Mon-Fri, 10am-6pm Sat & Sun Apr & Oct) This intriguing museum explores the millennium-long history of the Grande Chartreuse monastery, some 2km away. Thirty-odd Carthusian monks reside there, withdrawn in silence from the world.

Information

Maison du Parc (Park Headquarters; ☎04 76 88 75 20; www.parc-chartreuse.net; place de la Mairie, Saint-Pierre-de-Chartreuse; ⊙9am-noon & 2-5pm Mon-Fri) Has information on the local environment, flora and fauna, and runs visits to the distillery where Chartreuse liqueur is produced. It closes for the Christmas/New Year's week, and two weeks in August. Located with the tourist office.

Parc Naturel Régional du Massif des Bauges

Hiking and biking enthusiasts can explore 900 sq km of pastures, plateaux and

wilderness in the little-known **Massif des Bauges Regional Nature Park**, northeast of Chambéry. Several marked trails set out from the **Maison Faune-Flore** (☎04 79 54 97 77; www.parcdesbauges.com; Chef Lieu, École; adult/child €2.50/1.50; ⏲10am-1pm & 2-6.30pm Wed-Mon Jul, Aug & daily in Christmas/New Year holidays, see website for other times) in École, where you can learn how to spot some of the many hundreds of chamois and mouflons inhabiting the park.

Chambéry's favourite weekend retreat for a little snow action is nearby **Savoie Grand Révard** (www.savoiegrandrevard.com; 1-day Nordic ski pass adult/child €8.20/4.80, 1-day Alpine ski pass €19/14.60).

Information

Le Châtelard Tourist Office (☎04 79 54 84 28; www.lesbauges.com; av Denis Therme, Le Châtelard; ⏲9am-noon & 2-6pm Mon-Sat May-Oct, to 5pm Mon-Wed & Fri Nov-Apr, see website for other times) The park's main tourist office, 36km northeast of Chambéry, has the low-down on all winter and summer activities.

La Féclaz Tourist Office (☎04 79 25 80 49; www.savoiegrandrevard.com; Station, La Féclaz; ⏲9am-noon & 3-7.30pm) The ski-station tourist office, 21km northeast of Chambéry, has information on accommodation and snow sports in the Bauges.

Aix-les-Bains

POP 28,700

With its leafy shores, grand casino and historic villas, Aix-les-Bains (*eks*-ley-bah), a small thermal spa 17km north of Chambéry, exudes an air of discreet gentility. Come to stroll, pedal, skate, sail, row or swim around France's largest natural lake, **Lac du Bourget**. The town centre is about 2.5km east of the lakefront.

Sights

Musée Faure MUSEUM
(☎04 79 61 06 57; www.aixlesbains.fr/culture/museefaure; 10 bd des Côtes; adult/child €5/free; ⏲10am-noon & 1.30-6pm Wed-Mon Apr-Oct, closed Mon & Tue Nov-Mar) This excellent little museum, housed in the former villa of collector Dr Jean Faure, is a must-see for fans of impressionism. And it's not all about Degas, Cézanne and Pissarro: the Faure's Rodin collection is perhaps only exceeded by the Rodin Museum in Paris.

Temple of Diana RUINS
(place Maurice Mollard, La Mairie) This 1st-century Roman temple – dedicated originally not to Diana, but probably a local Celtic god – is inside the town hall, a 16th-century château built over the ruin. To see it, and the accompanying archaeological collection, ask about guided tours at the tourist office.

LOCAL KNOWLEDGE

CHARTREUSE: THE MONASTIC LIQUEUR

Either acid green or radioactive yellow, Chartreuse may be the brightest, most shockingly hued herbal elixir of the cocktail and digestif world. Mixologists sing its praises and in ski resorts it adds a splash of Alpine fire to hot chocolate in Green Chaud. Its surge in global popularity over the past decade might have something to do with it being hailed as 'the only liqueur so good they named a colour after it' in Quentin Tarantino's 2007 thriller *Death Proof*. It certainly isn't because the Carthusian monks who make it have been brashly broadcasting its wonders, for this is a liqueur shrouded in secrecy and silence.

The production of Chartreuse began in 1737 and, at first, it was intended as a medicine. The green version, which celebrated its 250th birthday in 2014 (see www.chartreuse-verte250.com), is produced by macerating 130 hard-to-find mountain herbs, roots and plants in alcohol and leaving the mixture to age in oak casks.

Today, Chartreuse's exact ingredients remain a closely guarded secret, and word has it only two monks know the recipe. Perhaps closest to the original is the Elixir Végétal (69% alcohol), sold as a tonic, but potent, spicy, chlorophyll-rich Chartreuse Green (55% alcohol) and milder, sweeter Chartreuse Yellow (40% alcohol) are much better known. You can taste these otherworldly liqueurs, bone up on their history and tour barrel-lined cellars at the **Caves de la Chartreuse** (☎04 76 05 81 77; www.chartreuse.fr; 10 bd Edgar-Kofler, Voiron; ⏲9am-11.30am & 2-6pm daily Apr-Oct, Mon-Fri Nov-Mar) distillery, 45km southwest of Chambéry.

Information

Tourist Office (☎04 79 88 68 00; www.aixles-bains.com; place Maurice Mollard; ⏰9am-noon & 2-6pm Apr-Oct, 9am-12.30pm & 2-5.30pm Mon-Sat Nov-Mar) For details on what to see and do in the area, including lake cruises to the 12th-century Abbaye d'Hautecombe on the other side of the lake, contact the font of all things spa-, hike- and culture-related in Aix-le-Bains.

Getting There & Away

Aix-les-Bains is linked by train and SNCF bus (once or twice an hour) with Annecy (€8.10, 30 to 45 minutes) and Chambéry (€3.50, 11 to 23 minutes).

Les Trois Vallées

This is the big one you've heard all about: vast, fast and a contender for largest ski area in the world. It's impossible to tire of all this terrain: depending on how it's reckoned, there are more than 600km of pistes and 180 lifts linking eight resorts and three parallel valleys. Among these are **Val Thorens**, Europe's highest at a heady 2300m; wealthy and ever-so-British **Méribel** (elevation 1450m), founded by Scotsman Colonel Peter Lindsay in 1938; and playground of the super-rich **Courchevel**, which stretches over three purpose-built resorts at 1550m, 1650m and 1850m and is a fave of the Moët-at-five brigade and ultra-wealthy Russians. In between are a number of lesser-known Alpine villages – **Le Praz** (Courchevel-Le Praz; 1300m), **St-Martin de Belleville** (1450m) and *très anglais* **La Tania** (1400m); all are linked by speedy lifts to higher-elevation slopes.

Activities

Winter

Les Trois Vallées is blessed with some of the world's best skiable terrain – the pistes here are vast and varied enough to satisfy even the most demanding skiers. The season here is also among the longest in France, running from early December to late April (and even longer in Val Thorens). Save time queuing by buying your pass and lessons online at www.les3vallees.com.

Sunny, relaxed **Méribel** is intermediate heaven, with 150km of cruisy (mostly blue and red) runs, 46 ski lifts, two slalom stadiums, two (Albertville) Olympic runs, two **snow parks** with jumps, pipes and rails, and plenty of activities for kids. Packed with Brits and *seasonaires*, it's also famous for après-ski partying.

In glitzy **Courchevel** there's another 150km of well-groomed pistes, including some knee-trembling black *couloirs* (steep gullies), and excellent off-piste terrain. The 2.5km-long floodlit **toboggan run** through the forest, illuminated from 5pm to 7.30pm, is a fun après-ski alternative.

Watched over by glacier-licked peaks, **Val Thorens**, founded in 1972, enjoys a snow pack that's the envy of lower-altitude stations, superb **extreme skiing** and a **snow park**. Or bounce down the **toboggan run** (one run, with sledge and helmet, is €14.50 and takes 45 minutes), France's longest at 6km, with a drop of 700m.

Off-piste skiers seeking guidance should head for **La Croisette**, at the top of the Verdons ski lift: the **Maison de la Montagne** houses both the **ESF** (☎04 79 08 07 72; www.skischoolcourchevel.co.uk; rue du Forum, La Croisette; 2hr private lesson €135) and the **Bureau des Guides** (☎Courchevel 06 23 92 46 12, Méribel 04 79 00 30 38; www.guides-courchevel-meribel.com; Maison de la Montagne, La Croisette; ⏰9am-6pm).

La Tyrolienne ADVENTURE SPORTS

(www.la-tyrolienne.com; €50) Accessible only to skiers, this is the world's highest zip line. From the top of the Bouchet chair, those who dare fly 1300m in one minute and 45 seconds at speeds of up to 100km/h, dangling 200m from the ice below.

Summer

Summer in Les Trois Vallées – mid-June to mid-September – is a playground of stunning mountain scenery, hidden lakes and wild flower-strewn pastures. Diversions range from walking and hiking to rock climbing, paragliding and canyoning – tourist offices in the principal villages can help you find the right guides. Or you can clip on to two vertigo-inducing **via ferrata** fixed-cable routes: one at Levassaix (near Les Menuires), the other at Le Cochet (St-Martin de Belleville).

The resorts are criss-crossed by hundreds of kilometres of circuits and downhill runs for **mountain bikers**. IGN biking maps and details on bike rental outlets (there's at least one in each station) are available at tourist offices.

Sleeping & Eating

Tourist offices run accommodation services in **Courchevel** (☎04 79 08 00 29; www.courchevel.com; ⏰9am-noon & 2-6pm winter, 9am-noon & 2.30-6.30 Sat, Sun, Wed & Thu summer), **Méribel** (☎04 79 00 50 00; www.meribel.net; rte du Centre; ⏰9am-1pm & 2-7pm Mon-Fri, 9am-noon & 3-7pm Sat, 9am-noon Sun winter, reduced hours other seasons) and **Val Thorens** (☎04 79 00 01 06; www.valthorens.com; Grand Rue, Maison de Val Thorens; ⏰9am-8pm Mon-Fri, 10am-8pm Sat, to 7pm Sun winter & summer, 9am-noon & 2-6pm Mon-Fri spring & autumn).

Méribel

Le Roc HOTEL €€
(☎La Taverne 04 79 00 36 18; www.alpine-bars.com; rte du Centre, Méribel; d/tr €135/150; ⏰Dec-Apr, Jul & Aug) For some of the cheapest beds in central Méribel, this is the place to come. The smallish rooms have been recently refurbished but, situated directly over the late-opening and lively La Taverne bar, they're not recommended for families or light sleepers! Reception is in the bar.

La Fromagerie FRENCH €€
(☎04 79 08 55 48; Galerie des Cimes, Méribel; menus €19-28.50; ⏰fromagerie 9.30am-12.30pm & 3.30-7.30pm ski season, 7-10pm ski season, Jul & Aug) Only the tangiest, creamiest Alpine cheeses feature at this *fromagerie*-cum-restaurant, which serves Méribel's tastiest fondues and *raclette* in the rustic cellar. Book ahead for dinner, especially on Wednesday, Thursday and Friday. Situated 200m up the main drag from the tourist office.

Evolution INTERNATIONAL €€
(☎04 79 00 44 26; www.evolutionmeribel.com; rte de la Chaudanne, Méribel; menus €25-30; ⏰8.30am-1.30am; 📶✍) Brits, locals and seasonal workers flock to this charismatic cafe-brasserie for full English breakfasts, Sunday roasts and international fare such as curries, burgers and falafel. There's an eclectic live-music program (Tuesday, Saturday and Sunday from 10pm) and the whole outfit is only a 50m stumble from the Chaudanne ski lift.

Courchevel

Hôtel Tournier HOTEL €€
(☎04 79 04 16 35; www.hoteltournier.com; rue des Verdons, Courchevel 1850; d €139-179, extra bed €30; ⏰Dec–Apr; 📶) Decorated in kitschy 'chalet' accents (timber, taupe, and faux deer heads) the Tournier has 35 of the cheapest rooms in Courchevel 1850. It also has a lovely bar-bistro, L'Equipe, a bountiful breakfast buffet (7.30am to noon, €18 per person) and a central location, just a block from Parking La Croisette.

Le Chabichou HOTEL €€€
(☎04 79 08 00 55; www.chabichou-courchevel.com; rue des Chenus, Courchevel 1850; d incl breakfast 6 nights winter €640-900, 1 night summer €245; @📶) Washed as white as the goat's cheese for which it is named, this handsome, slopeside hotel and spa manages to quietly blend modern amenities with wood-panelled charm throughout its cosy public areas and 41 tasteful rooms. There's a six-night minimum stay during the ski season.

The hotel is open year-round, while the restaurants and spa close from late April to mid-June, and from early September to mid-December.

Val Thorens

Hotel des 3 Vallées HOTEL €€
(☎04 79 00 01 86; www.hotel3vallees.com; Grande Rue, Val Thorens; d incl half-board €120-308; ⏰late Nov–mid-May; 📶) The 28 rooms and four apartments here – half with balconies, almost all with great south-facing views – are wonderfully rustic, dressed with Christmassy bursts of red and green and wood reused from old barns. The traditional French cuisine is a treat (*menus* €23), as is the wellness area with Jacuzzi, sauna and *hammam*. Situated just 80m from the slopes.

Les Allues

La Croix Jean-Claude HOTEL €€
(☎04 79 08 61 05; www.croixjeanclaude.com; Les Allues; d/ste incl half-board €112/137; ⏰Jun-Apr; 📶) Far from the madding crowd, Les Allues' only hotel, built in 1848, combines the charm of a real Alpine village with quick access to Méribel's slopes via the Olympe bubble lift or a free shuttle. Florals lend a homey touch to the 15 cosy rooms, and market-fresh produce features on the menu.

La Tania

Le Farçon FRENCH €€€
(☎04 79 08 80 34; www.lefarcon.fr; Immeuble Le Kalinka, La Tania; lunch menus €38-68, dinner menus €62-110; ⏰noon-1.30pm & 7.30-9.30pm daily mid-Nov–Apr, Tue-Sun mid-Jun–mid-Sep) The

carefully crafted *menus* of Michelin-starred chef Julien Machet contain delights such as young leeks with *vin de Savoie* from Apremont, and free-range pork with sweet onions and Parmesan. All the produce is top-notch and local, and the walk-in wine cellar is a cave of delights. Reservations are a good idea, especially during school holidays.

Drinking & Nightlife

Hang out with the rich kids in Champagne-sipping Courchevel, slalom down to Méribel for the energetic après-ski scene or, until about 5pm, party it up high above Méribel and Val Thorens at the two incredibly popular piste-side branches of **La Folie Douce** (04 79 00 04 27; www.lafoliedouce.com; Piste Plein Sud, Val Thorens; 9am-5pm in high season;). Most places are open only during the ski season.

★ Le Rond Point BAR
(04 79 00 37 51; www.alpine-bars.com; near Meribel Rond Point; 9am-7.30pm ski season) This piste-side terrace café turns into a huge après-ski party at about 4pm. Shuffle in your ski boots and sing along to pumping live music (5pm to 7pm) between mouthfuls of chips and toffee vodka (the house speciality) at what *seasonaires* (seasonal workers) fondly call 'the Ronnie'.

La Taverne BAR
(04 79 00 30 94; www.alpine-bars.com; rte du Centre, Méribel; 8.30am-1.30am ski season, flexible hours rest of year;) Within a solid stone-and-timber building in the centre of Méribel sits this friendly, informal bar whose terrace, après-ski, is jam-packed with skiers and boarders talking epic descents. Has live music (in winter, Tuesday, Thursday, Friday and Sunday from 9.30pm), screens major sports events and serves pub food from 6.30pm to 10pm.

Information

Courchevel 1850 Tourist Office (04 79 08 00 29; www.courchevel.com; 9am-noon & 2-6pm winter, 9am-noon & 2.30-6.30 Sat, Sun, Wed & Thu summer;) Has other offices at Courchevel 1650m, 1550m and 1300m.

Méribel Tourist Office (04 79 08 60 01; www.meribel.net; rte du Centre; 9am-7pm in winter, closed midday in summer & weekends in spring & autumn) Has the low-down on winter and summer activities.

Val Thorens Tourist Office (04 79 00 08 08; www.valthorens.com; Grand Rue, Maison de Val Thorens; 8.30am-7pm winter & summer, closed midday & weekends spring & autumn) Has plenty of information in English.

Getting There & Away

TO/FROM THE AIRPORT

For all airport buses, reserve 48 hours ahead.

In winter, **Altibus** (Chambéry office 08 20 32 03 68; www.altibus.com; call centre 8am-6pm Mon-Sat, midday closure Apr-Nov) links all three Les Trois Vallées resorts with the following airports:

Chambéry one way/return €37/61, 2½ to four hours

Geneva one way/return €85/144, 3½ hours, three daily Sunday to Friday, six Saturday

Lyon St-Exupéry one way/return €73/115, 3¼ to four hours

The nearest railway station is in Moûtiers. From there, during the ski season, **Belle Savoie** (Altibus in Chambéry 08 20 32 03 68, Méribel 04 79 08 54 90; www.altibus.com) runs buses to Val Thorens, Méribel and Courchevel (lines T3, T4 and T5, respectively, one way/return €12.30/21).

TAXI

Taxis wait at Moûtiers' train station for the trip up to Méribel (€60), Courchevel (€70 to €80) and Val Thorens (€110).

TRAIN

Moûtiers (Moûtiers-Salins-Brides-les-Bains) is the nearest railhead, with services to/from:

Chambéry €14.50, 1½ hours, hourly Monday to Friday, 13 per day Saturday and Sunday

Paris Gare de Lyon €90 to €124, 4½ to six hours, hourly Monday to Friday, four Saturday and Sunday

On weekends from mid-December to early April, **Eurostar** (www.eurostar.com) operates direct overnight and day trains from London to Moûtiers (one way/return from €165/290, seven hours).

Val d'Isère

POP 1637 / ELEV 1850M

Accessible only by a sinuous access road clinging to the heights of the upper Tarentaise Valley, Val d'Isere is enchanting and challenging in equal measure. Drawn by the abundance of skiing and boarding terrain, including plenty of off-piste action, devotees also rave about the culture – either slopeside partying, or the quieter charms of a real Alpine village, huddled around the 16th-century Église St-Roch.

The mighty dam walls of the Lac du Chevril loom large on the approach to Val d'Isère, 32km southeast of Bourg St-Maurice. **Tignes** (elevation 2100m), a purpose-built lakeside village, and nearby Val d'Isère form the gargantuan **Espace Killy** skiing area, named after Jean-Claude Killy, who grew up in Val d'Isère and won three slalom and downhill golds at the 1968 Winter Olympics in Grenoble. The area is especially popular with Brits, Danes and Swedes.

Activities

Centre Aquasportif SPA

(☎04 79 04 26 01; www.centre-aquasportif.com; rte de la Balme; 1 entry, multiple facilities €18.40; ⏱10am-9pm) Situated next to the Téléphérique Olympique, this glass-and-stone complex is great for a postslope unwind. Besides pools with jets and bubble beds, it offers first-class sports facilities, a climbing wall, and a spa area with saunas, steam rooms and whirlpools.

Espace Killy SKIING

(www.espacekilly.com) Killy's ski season runs from very late November until very early May, offering a great mix of beginner, intermediate and advanced skiing on 300km of pistes between 1550m and 3456m – and miles of glorious off-piste. Its height makes summer skiing possible, on the Grande Motte and Pissaillas glaciers.

Bureau des Guides OUTDOORS

(☎03 77 08 09 76; www.guides-montagne-valdisere.com) Be it for canyoning, mountaineering or off-piste winter adventures, this office can arrange experienced local guides. Ask at the Mountain Proshop, Galerie des Cimes, av Olympique.

Top Ski SKIING

(☎07 82 85 88 89; www.topski.fr; av Olympique, Immeuble Les Andes) This highly regarded independent ski school arranges one-to-one and group tuition in on- and off-piste skiing, boarding, ski touring, heliskiing and snowshoeing with expert guides. They're the ideal companions with which to explore Espace Killy.

ESF SKIING

(☎04 79 06 02 34; www.esfvaldisere.com; place des Dolomites, Val Village; ⏱9.30am-12.30pm & 2.30-5pm in high season) Based in Val Village, the ESF can help skiers and boarders of all levels progress, from €45 for two hours.

Village des Enfants OUTDOORS

(☎04 79 40 09 81; www.valdisere-levillagedesenfants.com; Rond Point des Pistes; child 3-13yr half/full day with lunch €46.50/66.50; ⏱9am-5.30pm Sun-Fri) Nursery and activities for children aged 6 months to 13 years. Booking at least a month in advance is advisable.

Winter

Ski touring in the area is fabulous, especially in Parc National de la Vanoise. The many ski schools include well-regarded Top Ski and the ESF.

At 2300m, the **snow park** is on the back of Bellevarde mountain. Graded from green (easy) to black (experts only), it has rails, jumps, hips, quarters and a boardercross – everything an aficionado of freestyle (skiing or snowboarding) could ask for. Other winter options range from ice climbing to mushing, and ice skating to winter paragliding – or you can head to the Centre Aquasportif for swimming pools (great for kids), sports facilities and a spa. For more children's activities, head to the Village des Enfants.

You can buy lift passes online or in person from **STVI** (☎04 79 06 32 32; www.valdiserepass.com; Gare Centrale; adult/reduced per day €54/43.50, 6 days €270/216; ⏱8.30am-5pm in high season). Five free lifts on the lower slopes let novices find their feet without having to purchase a lift ticket.

Summer

Espace Killy is one of only two places in France (the other is Les Deux Alpes) that still has **summer skiing**: here it's on the Grande Motte and Pissaillas glaciers, which are near Tignes and Val d'Isère, respectively.

The valleys and trails that wend their way from Val d'Isère into the nearby Parc National de la Vanoise are a hiker's dream. If you fancy more of a challenge, you can play (safely) among the cliffs at La Daille's two via-ferrata fixed-cable routes. For canyoning, mountaineering or rock climbing with a guide, contact the Bureau des Guides.

Mountain biking (Vélo Tout Terrain, or VTT) is big in Val (but forbidden within the national park), with an assortment of downhill (green, blue, red and black), endurance and cross-country circuits. Bikes can be rented at local sport shops. Five lifts are open for no charge to downhill cyclists as well as hikers.

The summer season runs from late June to the first weekend in September. Stop by

the tourist office for details on family-friendly activities, including pony rides.

Sleeping

To rent an apartment or a chalet, contact tourist-office-run **Val Location** (04 79 06 74 32; www.valdisere-reservation.com). To buy a four-bedroom apartment in the centre of town, bring at least €2 million.

Hôtel L'Avancher HOTEL €€
(04 79 06 02 00; www.hotel-lavancher.com; rte du Prariond; d €144-183, tr/q €231/280;) The welcome is always warm and attentive at this hotel, one of the oldest in the valley. Its 17 snug rooms are sweetly decorated, chalet style (hearts jigsawed into wood panels, faux-fur bedspreads), plus there's a small lounge with board games and a piano, and a ski/mountain bike workshop.

★**Les Cinq Frères** BOUTIQUE HOTEL €€€
(04 79 06 00 03; www.les5freres.com; rue Nicolas Bazile; d incl breakfast €240-355, q incl breakfast €495; ski season & mid-Jun–Aug;) Situated 150m up the main street from the tourist office, this family hotel has been going strong since 1936. Named for the five sons of its founder, it offers rustic-chic luxury with a lovely lounge area, a playroom for kids and 17 tasteful yet character-filled rooms, some with giant old-style bath-tubs.

Eating

Le Salon des Fous CAFE €
(04 79 00 17 92; www.lesalondesfous.com; 10 av Olympique, Centre Village; light mains €7-10; 8am-10.30pm mid-Nov–Apr & mid-Jun–late Sep) With regular live acts and understated style, the 'Fool's Salon' is one of Val d'Isere's most relaxing boltholes. Light meals served throughout the day – salads, quiches, cheesecake crêpes and the like (€3.50 to €13) – pair nicely with teas such as the 'Secret Tibétain' (jasmine, lavender, ginger, ginseng and vanilla).

★**La Fruitière** MODERN FRENCH €€
(04 79 06 07 17; www.lafoliedouce.com; mains €18-29; noon-3pm Dec-May) At the top of the La Daille gondola (and next to La Folie Douce, the famous piste-side bar), this *restaurant d'altitude* is legendary for its fine dining and breathtaking mountain views. The creative cuisine is prepared with farm-fresh produce and paired with top wines. Save room for the Savoyard cheese plate.

DON'T MISS

ALPINE CHEESE

Part of Val d'Isère's charm is that it's a real village with year-round residents. Claudine is one of them and she runs **La Fermette de Claudine** (04 79 06 13 89; www.lafermettedeclaudine.com; Val Village, Val d'Isère; 7am-8pm Dec-May, Jul & Aug). Walk in the door of this *fromagerie*-cum-delicatessen and you'll be enveloped by the heady odours of Alpine cheeses and artisanal sausages.

Claudine's family dairy farm, **La Ferme de l'Adroit** (04 79 06 13 02; www.lafermedeladroit.com; Val d'Isère; fromagerie 9am-noon & 3-7pm Mon-Sat year-round), is also open to the public. All that dairy goodness is served up at the adjacent **L'Étable d'Alain** (04 79 06 13 02; www.lafermedeladroit.fr; Val d'Isère; menus €40-45; noon-2pm Tue-Sun, 7-10pm daily;).

L'Edelweiss MODERN FRENCH €€
(06 10 28 70 64; www.restaurant-edelweiss-valdisere.com; Piste Mangard, Le Fornet; 2-/3-course menus €24/28.50; 9.30am-4pm Dec-Apr) Perched halfway up Le Fornet's Mangard blue run, this wood-and-stone chalet has wondrous views around the valley. And the food matches the prospect: duck breast with honey and Sichuan pepper, veal with morels and spot-on tarte Tatin. It's good value, and reservations are recommended.

★**L'Atelier d'Edmond** MODERN FRENCH €€€
(04 79 00 00 82; www.atelier-edmond.com; rue du Fornet, Le Fornet; menus €95-155; lunch Wed-Sun, dinner Tue-Sun Dec-early May) Candlelight bathes stone walls, low beams and family heirlooms in this gorgeous double-Michelin-starred restaurant, where locally sourced ingredients are imaginatively transformed into dishes such as smoked pigeon with cocoa beans and pumpkin. Call ahead to secure one of the Atelier's limited seats, and find it 2km east of Val Village, across from the Téléphérique du Fornet ski lift.

Drinking & Nightlife

The après-ski scene in Val d'Isère is way up there with the craziest in the French Alps.

★**La Folie Douce** BAR
(www.lafoliedouce.com; La Daille; 9am-5pm Dec-Apr) Why wait until you're back down in the

village to party? From 2.30pm every day, DJs, singers, choreographed dancers and live bands fuel a riotous après-ski bash on this outdoor terrace at the top of the La Daille cable car. Ibiza in the snow!

La Cave...sur le Comptoir WINE BAR
(☎04 79 22 27 81; www.cuisinaval.com; av Olympique; ⊙7pm-1am) One of the most relaxed spots to raise a glass in the valley, this convivial bar offers not only 30 wines by the glass (€5 to €8; *grand cru* wines €9 to €12) but also delightful ballast in the form of *fromage* and charcuterie. Situated 100m down the hill from the bus station.

Moris Pub PUB
(☎06 19 20 16 80; av du Prariond, Centre Village; ⊙4pm-1.30am Mon-Fri, 1pm-1.30am weekends Dec-Apr) A scuffed timber interior and tattooed staff belie the warm welcome at this buzzy British pub. There are also big-screen sports, gourmet burger deals, regular live music (5pm to 7pm and 11pm to 1.30am) and the occasional fancy-dress theme party. Go easy on the toffee vodka.

Dick's Tea Bar CLUB
(☎06 51 39 99 81; www.dicksteabar.com; rue du Parc des Sports; after 1am €10; ⊙11pm-5am) Val d'Isère's party HQ and the fabled home of *vodka pomme* (vodka with apple juice), Dick's has been catering to the valley's night owls since 1979. Live music (sax with percussion) from 11pm gives way to resident and international DJs in the small hours. Dress is 'smart casual'.

Le Petit Danois BAR
(☎04 79 06 27 97; www.lepetitdanois.com; rue du Coin, Centre Village; ⊙9.30am-1.30am Dec-Apr) Live music and free shots between 5pm and 7pm, €7.50 cocktails, unlimited popcorn and revved-up partygoers dancing on the tables – lucky this Danish-owned party bar serves a full English breakfast the next morning to mop up the mess (€13). Situated 100m behind the bus station.

ℹ Information

Tourist Office (☎04 79 06 06 60; www.valdisere.com; place Jacques Mouflier, Centre Village; ⊙8.30am-7.30pm daily Dec-Apr & Jun-Aug, 9am-noon & 2-6pm Mon-Fri low season; 📶) Can supply you with lots of excellent brochures on winter and summer activities, including several for families with kids, and *ValScope*, a weekly schedule of cultural events that comes out each Friday. Internet computers and wi-fi cost €5 per hour.

ℹ Getting There & Away

TO/FROM THE AIRPORT

Chambéry airport Direct buses during the ski season (one way/return €32/51, two hours, six daily Thursday, Saturday and Sunday).

Geneva airport Aérobus (www.altibus.com; www.alpski-bus.com) has direct services (one way/return €68/115, four hours, at least three daily from early December to mid-April). A cheaper ski season option (one way/return €44/75, Saturday and Sunday morning) is run by Ben's Bus (www.bensbus.co.uk), which also serves Grenoble airport.

Lyon St-Exupéry airport Seasonal services run by **Altibus** (☎08 20 32 03 68; www.altibus.fr) (one way/return €73/115, 3½ hours, three or four daily Friday, Saturday and Sunday). Another option is to take the train to Bourg St-Maurice (4½ hours) and then bus T14.

Advance reservations are essential during school holiday periods and can be made online or by phone. Tickets are slightly cheaper if bought online.

BUS

From December to May, **Belle Savoie Express** (☎08 20 20 53 30; www.mobisavoie.fr) links the railhead of Bourg St-Maurice, 32km northwest of Val d'Isére, with Val d'Isère and Tignes.

CAR & MOTORCYCLE

The roads up to Val d'Isère, outfitted with lots of *paravalanche* (avalanche protection) shelters, are narrow, winding and can get traffic-clogged. **Col de l'Iseran** (2764m), on the D902 southeast to Bonneval-sur-Arc, and **Col du Petit-St-Bernard** (2188m), which leads from Bourg St-Maurice northeast to the Aosta valley in Italy, are blocked by snow for all but the summer months.

TRAIN

Bourg St-Maurice, the nearest railhead, has train connections to destinations all over France (eg Chambéry and Lyon-Part Dieu) and seasonal bus links to Val d'Isère.

From mid-December to early April on weekends, **Eurostar** (www.eurostar.com) operates direct daytime and overnight services between Bourg St-Maurice and London (one way/return from €156/279, 7½ to nine hours).

Parc National de la Vanoise

Rugged snowcapped peaks, mirrorlike lakes and an incredible 53 sq km of glaciers are just a few of the sublime natural attractions in the 529-sq-km Parc National de la Vanoise, neatly sandwiched between the

Tarentaise and Maurienne Valleys. This incredible swathe of wilderness was designated France's first national park in 1963. Five nature reserves and 28 villages border the highly protected core of the park, where marmots, chamois and France's largest colony of *bouquetins* (Alpine ibexes) – around 1600 of them – graze freely and undisturbed beneath the larch trees. Overhead, 20 pairs of golden eagles and the odd bearded vulture fly in solitary wonder.

You can base yourself in **Lanslebourg-Mont-Cénis** or **Bonneval-sur-Arc**, two pretty villages along the southern edge of the park (note that the road north to Val d'Isère is open only in summer).

Activities

The park is hiker's heaven, although heavy snow can make walking trails inaccessible for all but a fraction of the year – June to late September, usually. The **Grand Tour de Haute Maurienne** (www.hautemaurienne.com), a hike of seven days or more around the upper reaches of the valley, takes in national-park highlights. The GR5 and GR55 cross it, and other trails snake south to the Park National des Écrins and east into Italy's Grand Paradiso National Park.

Information

The tourist offices in **Lanslebourg** (04 79 05 23 66; www.haute-maurienne-vanoise.com; 89 rue du Mont-Cenis, Lanslebourg; 9am-noon & 2-6.30pm mid-Dec–mid-Apr & mid-Jun–Aug, to 5pm Tue, Thu, Fri & Sat May–mid-Jun) and **Bonneval-sur-Arc** (04 79 05 95 95; www.bonneval-sur-arc.com; Bonneval-sur-Arc; 9am-noon & 2-6pm late Dec–mid-Apr) stock practical information on walking, limited skiing (cross-country and downhill) and other activities in and around the park. **Termignon-la-Vanoise**, 6km southwest of Lanslebourg, houses the national park's small information centre, the **Maison de la Vanoise** (04 79 20 51 67; www.parcnational-vanoise.fr; place de la Vanoise, Termignon; 9am-noon & 2-6pm late Jun-early Sep, to 5pm Mon-Fri low season, Tue-Sat shoulder season).

Getting There & Away

Trains serving the Arc River valley leave from Chambéry and run as far as Modane, 23km southwest of Lanslebourg, from where **Transdev Savoie** (Altibus 08 20 32 03 68; www.altibus.com) runs three to four daily buses (one or none in the low season) to/from Termignon (€7.40, 35 minutes), Val Cénis-Lanslebourg (€12.30, 45 minutes) and Bonneval-sur-Arc (€12.30, 1¼ hours).

DAUPHINÉ

Named for the dolphin *(dauphin)* that leapt joyously across the coat of arms of its prior rulers, the historic region of Dauphiné encompasses the territories south and southwest of Savoy, stretching from the River Rhône in the west to the Italian border in the east. It roughly corresponds to the *départements* of Isère, Drôme and – in the *région* of Provence-Alpes-Côte d'Azur, which stretches south to the Mediterranean – Hautes-Alpes. It includes the city of Grenoble (the former capital) and, southeast of there, the mountainous Parc National des Écrins. The relatively gentler terrain of western Dauphiné is typified by the Parc Naturel Régional du Vercors, much loved by cross-country skiers. In the southeast, the bastion town of Briançon stands sentinel near the Italian frontier.

Grenoble

POP 160,215 / ELEV 215M

Known as the 'Capital of the Alps', Grenoble boasts great museums, excellent dining, effervescent nightlife, outstanding quality of life and a superb public transport system. Home to a slew of high-tech industries, the 1968 Winter Olympic City is the focal point for a wider metropolitan area of more than 650,000 Grenobloises and Grenoblois, nearly 10% of them students.

The city is dramatically sited among the looming massifs of the Parc Naturel Régional de Chartreuse and Parc Naturel Régional du Vercors, with clear sight lines to Mont Blanc itself. Cut by the swift-flowing River Isère, Grenoble delivers mostly mild weather thanks to its low elevation.

Sights

The pedestrian-friendly city centre is on the left (south) bank of the River Isère, between the Musée de Grenoble (to the east) and Pont de la Porte de France (a bridge). To the north, Fort de la Bastille, a vast hilltop fortress, towers over the area from across the river. The train and bus stations are 500m southwest of Pont de la Porte de France.

★ **Musée de Grenoble** MUSEUM

(04 76 63 44 44; www.museedegrenoble.fr; 5 place de Lavalette; adult/child €8/free; 10am-6.30pm Wed-Mon) It's worth a trip to Grenoble just to experience this grand tour of Western art from the 13th century, which includes 20th-century luminaries such as Bonnard,

Grenoble

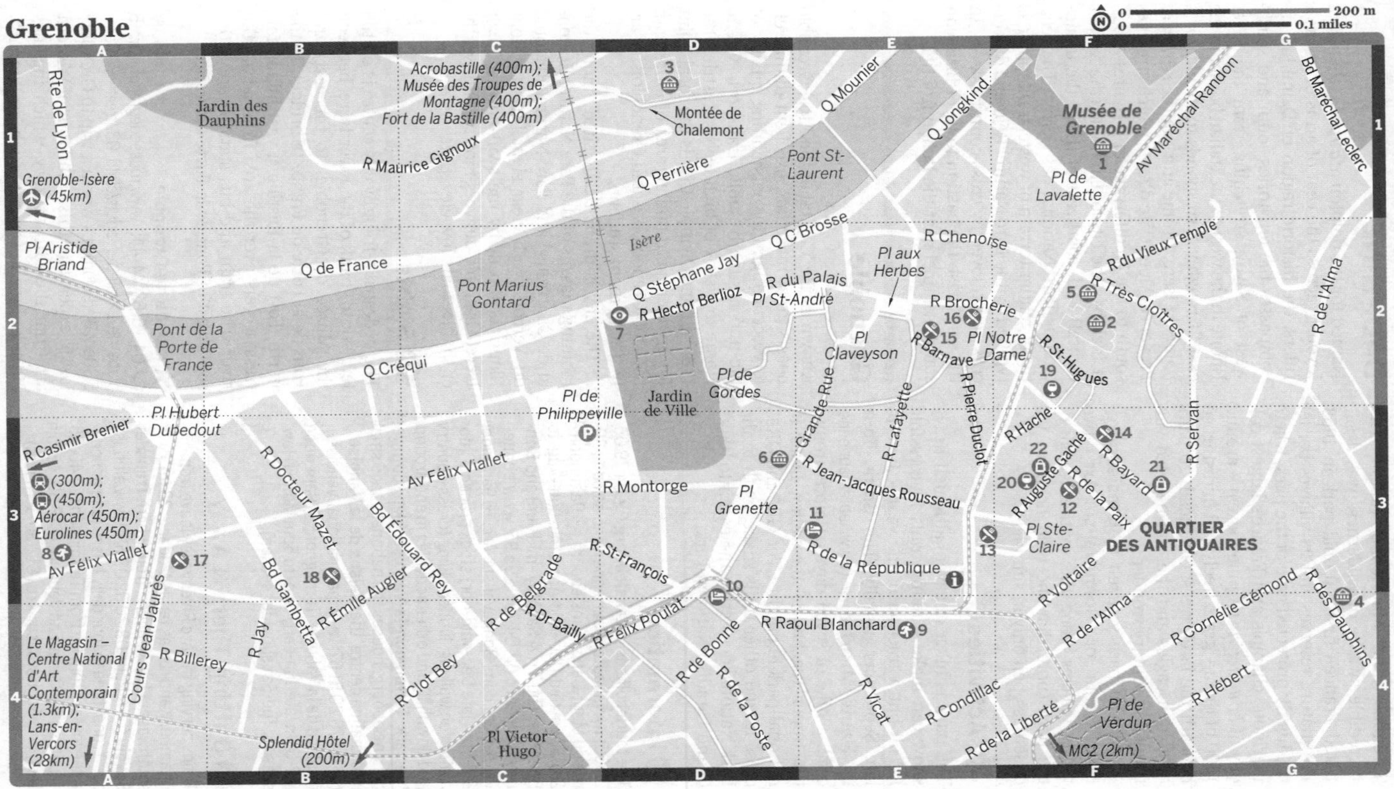
0 200 m
0 0.1 miles
Jardin des Dauphins
Rte de Lyon
Grenoble-Isère (45km)
Acrobastille (400m); Musée des Troupes de Montagne (400m); Fort de la Bastille (400m)
R Maurice Gignoux
Montée de Chalemont
Q Perrière
Q Mounier
Q Jongkind
Pont St-Laurent
Musée de Grenoble
Av Maréchal Randon
Bd Maréchal Leclerc
Pl de Lavalette
Isère
Pl Aristide Briand
Q de France
Pont Marius Gontard
Q C Brosse
Q Stéphane Jay
R Hector Berlioz
R du Palais
Pl St-André
Pl aux Herbes
R Chenoise
R du Vieux Temple
R Très Cloîtres
R de l'Alma
R Brocherie
Pl Notre Dame
R Barnave
R St-Hugues
Pont de la Porte de France
Q Créqui
Pl Claveyson
Pl de Gordes
Jardin de Ville
Pl de Philippeville
Grande Rue
R Lafayette
R Pierre Duclot
R Servan
R Hache
R Bayard
Pl Hubert Dubedout
R Casimir Brenier
(300m); (450m); Aérocar (450m); Eurolines (450m)
Av Félix Viallet
R Docteur Mazet
Bd Édouard Rey
R Montorge
Pl Grenette
R Jean-Jacques Rousseau
R Auguste Gaché
R de la Paix
Pl Ste-Claire
QUARTIER DES ANTIQUAIRES
R de la République
R St-François
R de Belgrade
R Dr Bailly
R Émile Augier
Bd Gambetta
R Jay
Cours Jean Jaurès
R Billerey
R Félix Poulat
R Raoul Blanchard
R Voltaire
R de l'Alma
R Cornélie Gémond
R des Dauphins
R Hébert
R de Bonne
R de la Poste
R Vicat
R Condillac
R de la Liberté
Pl de Verdun
MC2 (2km)
R Clot Bey
Pl Victor Hugo
Le Magasin – Centre National d'Art Contemporain (1.3km); Lans-en-Vercors (28km)
Splendid Hôtel (200m)

Grenoble

Calder, Giacometti, Léger, Magritte, Miró, Modigliani, Picabia, Soutine, de Staël and Van Dongen. Among the other highlights: superb 19th-century landscapes of the Dauphiné region; four absolutely huge canvases by the 17th-century Spaniard Zurbarán; and the gorgeous, light-filled building itself, opened in 1994. Audioguides (€2) are available in French, English and Italian.

Fort de la Bastille FORTRESS
(www.bastille-grenoble.com) Built to defend France against the Duchy of Savoy, its great Alpine rival of the early 1800s, this massive fortress sprawls 300m atop the limestone outcrop dominating Grenoble, incorporating earlier defences. From February to December the **Téléphérique Grenoble-Bastille** (quai Stéphane Jay; adult/child one way €5.50/3.35, return €8/4.70; 11am-6.30pm Tue-Sun Feb-Apr & Oct-Dec, 9.30am or 11am-7.30pm daily May-Sep, closed Jan) leads directly from the south bank of the Isère to the fortress; alternatively, there are paths for the steep hour-long hike. At the top, a number of walking trails, including the GR9, start or pass by.

From the top, the views are spectacular: on clear days you can see not only the peaks of the Vercors but also the snowy hump of Mont Blanc. On the viewing platform known as the **Belvédère Vauban**, panels (in French and English) indicate what you're looking at. The fort complex has five places to eat, a **tourist office** (04 76 89 46 45; 1.30-6.30pm Wed, Sat & Sun May-Sep, to 5.30pm Oct-Apr, daily in school holidays), and the absorbing **Musée des Troupes de Montagne** (French Alpine Troops Museum; 04 76 44 33 65; www.bastille-grenoble.fr; adult/child €3/free; 11am-6pm Tue-Sun Oct-Dec & Feb-Apr, 9am-6pm daily May-Sep).

Le Magasin – Centre National d'Art Contemporain MUSEUM
(04 76 21 95 84; www.magasin-cnac.org; 155 cours Berriat; adult/child €4/2.50; 2-7pm Wed-Sun) A cavernous glass-and-steel warehouse built by Gustave Eiffel has been turned into one of France's leading centres of contemporary art. Many of the cutting-edge temporary exhibitions were designed specifically for this space. It's situated about 2km west of the centre; to get there, take tram A to the Berriat–Le Magasin stop.

Musée Dauphinois MUSEUM
(04 57 58 89 01; www.musee-dauphinois.fr; 30 rue Maurice Gignoux; 10am-6pm Wed-Mon Sep-May, to 7pm Jun-Aug) FREE Occupying a 17th-century convent, this *département*-run museum has examined the people, cultures, crafts and traditions of the Dauphiné highlands since 1906. Permanent exhibitions in French and English – tracing subjects such as the history of skiing (from the Stone Age to the snowboard age) – are complemented by well-curated temporary displays. It's situated on the hillside below Fort de la Bastille, 300m up the hill from Pont St-Laurent over the River Isère.

GRENOBLE CENT SAVER

The pick-and-mix **Grenoble Pass** (2/3 attractions €12.50/16.50), sold at the tourist office, can save you money if you'll be visiting the Grenoble or Stendhal museums, travelling by cable car up to Fort de la Bastille, or taking a guided or audioguide tour of the city.

Musée de l'Ancien Évêché MUSEUM
(04 76 03 15 25; www.ancien-eveche-isere.fr; 2 rue Très Cloîtres; 9am-6pm Mon, Tue, Thu & Fri, 1-6pm Wed, 11am-6pm Sat & Sun) The 13th-century Bishops' Palace now houses a rich collection tracing the area's development from prehistory, through Gallo-Roman and medieval times to the early 20th century. Underneath place Notre Dame you can see part of Roman Grenoble's 3rd-century defensive walls and a 4th-century baptistery, discovered in the late 1980s during tram-line construction. Tours are free, and some signage is in English.

Musée de la Résistance et de la Déportation de l'Isère MUSEUM
(04 76 42 38 53; www.resistance-en-isere.fr; 14 rue Hébert; 9am-6pm Mon & Wed-Fri, 1.30-6pm Tue, 10am-6pm Sat & Sun) FREE This emotive, finely curated museum presents the history of Grenoble's famously vigorous resistance to Italian and then German forces during WWII, and of the deportation of a thousand local Jews – including 80 children – to Nazi camps. There are temporary exhibitions and signs in French, English and German.

Musée Stendhal MUSEUM
(04 76 86 52 08; www.bm-grenoble.fr/1083-musee-stendhal.htm; 20 Grande Rue; admission with audioguide/videoguide €3/5; 10am-noon & 2-6pm Sat, 2-6pm 1st Sun of month) This modest museum, housed in the restored apartment of his maternal grandfather, Docteur Gagnon, celebrates the milieu and work of the author of *The Red and the Black*. Correspondence, lithographs, statuary and other mementos of his life are on display. Contact the museum in advance for guided tours during the week (available from 10am to noon and 2pm to 6pm Tuesday to Friday).

Activities

Grenoble is well set up for exploring on two wheels: bikes can easily be hired from 32 Métrovélo (p513) stations across the city.

★Acrobastille ADVENTURE SPORTS
(04 76 59 30 75; www.acrobastille.fr; Fort de la Bastille; adult/child €27/19; Mar-Nov) Adrenaline junkies should head up to the Bastille (p509) and hop on one of Acrobastille's two 300m-long zip lines, plunge into the Spéléobox (caving simulator) or try out the new Mission Bastille (a labyrinth worthy of Indiana Jones). Check the website for reservations and opening hours (subject to change due to weather conditions). Admission includes all a trip up and back in the cable car.

Maison de la Montagne OUTDOORS
(04 76 44 67 03; www.grenoble-montagne.com; 3 rue Raoul Blanchard; 9.30am-12.30pm & 1-6pm Mon-Fri, 10am-1pm & 2-5pm Sat) This city-run centre provides advice on the perennial action of the Dauphiné Alps – including ski touring, ice climbing (on frozen waterfalls), hiking, rock climbing, biking, canyoning, paragliding and caving – plus weather and avalanche bulletins, and help planning overnight stays in the mountains. It also has all the maps you'll need, including the free METROPOLE guide to nature walks around Grenoble.

Bureau des Guides et Accompagnateurs de Grenoble OUTDOORS
(04 38 37 01 71; www.guide-grenoble.com; 3 rue Raoul Blanchard, Maison de la Montagne; 9.30am-12.30pm & 1-6pm Mon-Fri, 10am-1pm & 2-5pm Sat) The dedicated guides from this bureau can help climbers, hikers, rafters and high-altitude thrill seekers of all levels explore Les Alpes.

Club Alpin Français OUTDOORS
(04 76 87 03 73; www.cafgrenoble.com; 32 av Félix Viallet; 3-5pm Tue & Fri, 5-7pm Wed & Thu, reduced days in Jul & Aug) The French Alpine Club runs outings and mountain day trips: details are posted in its front window and on its website, and casual purchasers of a €6 'Discovery Card' can join in. This branch runs most of the *refuges* (overnight mountain stays) in the Isère *département*.

Festivals & Events

Les Détours de Babel WORLD MUSIC
(04 76 89 07 16; www.detoursdebabel.fr; late Mar–mid-Apr) A three-week festival of jazz and world music with some innovative ticketing ideas: it's possible to buy a 'solidarity ticket' for someone who can't afford to attend, or to pay what you feel selected events are worth (to you).

Vues d'en Face FILM
(www.vuesdenface.com; ⏲early Apr) The rainbow flag flies high for this 10-day gay and lesbian film fest.

Cabaret Frappé MUSIC
(www.cabaret-frappe.com; 3 nights €39; ⏲late Jul) This much-loved festival, free in 2016, brings a week of fresh-air concerts to the Jardin la Ville.

Sleeping

Many of Grenoble's hotels cater to the business trade, meaning prices are initially reasonable, then drop considerably on the weekend (Friday, Saturday and Sunday nights) and in August. A number of inexpensive hotels can be found right around the train station.

Hôtel de l'Europe HISTORIC HOTEL €
(☎04 76 46 16 94; www.hoteleurope.fr; 22 place Grenette; s/d/tr/q from €82/87/94/104;) On the city centre's liveliest square, this hotel occupies two historic buildings – one from 1820, the other from 1905. All but a few of the 39 immaculately kept rooms have wrought-iron balconies (ask for a mountain view) and a family of parakeets lives on the *entresol* floor. Breakfast is €9.50 and off-site parking is available at a 50% discount. Rates drop on weekends.

Hostel Grenoble HOSTEL €
(☎04 76 09 33 52; www.hihostels.com; 10 av du Grésivaudan, Échirolles; dm incl breakfast €20; ⏲reception 24hr; @) Grenoble's ultramodern, ecoconscious hostel, with 126 beds, is set in parkland in the suburb of Échirolles, 5km southwest of the centre. The top-notch facilities include a bar, kitchen, games room, sun deck and laundry.

Served by bus 1; get off at 'La Quinzaine' stop. Non-HI-members must buy a full membership to stay.

Splendid Hôtel HOTEL €€
(☎04 76 46 33 12; www.splendid-hotel.com; 22 rue Thiers; d €99-149, f €149; @) Its lobby and 45 rooms jazzed up with funky and disparate designs, this charismatic place is a welcome break from Grenoble's workaday hotel scene. Some of the cosy rooms have hydromassage showers, and studio apartments can also be had for a week or more. Enclosed parking costs €5.90, or take trams A, B or E.

Le Grand Hôtel HOTEL €€
(☎04 76 51 22 59; www.grand-hotel-grenoble.fr; 5 rue de la République; s/d from €99/118; @) This family-run affair, the only four-star hotel in central Grenoble, makes great use of a stately, late-19th-century building. Beyond the sleek, colourful reception and 'Stendahl' bar are well-appointed, monochromatic rooms with spacious bathrooms, triple-pane soundproof windows and video-on-demand. From the upper floors, balconies look out across the city to the Alps beyond.

Eating

As the one-time capital of Dauphiné, Grenoble is the place to sample *gratin dauphinois* (finely sliced potatoes oven-baked in cream with a pinch of nutmeg).

Halles Ste-Claire MARKET €
(place Ste-Claire; ⏲7am-1pm Tue-Sun, 3-7pm Fri & Sat) Pick up picnic fixin's or fresh meat, vegetables and pasta at this covered food market, built in 1874.

La Ferme à Dédé FRENCH €
(☎04 76 54 00 33; www.restaurantlafermeadede.com; 24 rue Barnave; mains €18; ⏲noon-2.30pm & 7-11.30pm) One of three 'farms' Dédé keeps in Grenoble and nearby Sassenage, this is a good place to get up to speed on what eating in the Dauphiné is all about. Grilled hanger steak with morel mushrooms and *gratin dauphinois* is a good place to start.

La Petite Idée FRENCH €
(☎04 76 47 52 95; www.la-petite-idee.fr; 7 cours Jean Jaurès; lunch menus €14-18, dinner menus €18-30; ⏲noon-2pm & 7-10pm Tue-Sun;) At this convivial restaurant, the traditional French *menu* changes two or three times a year but always features market-fresh, seasonal dishes such as rosemary-rubbed lamb with creamy *gratin dauphinois*. The €10 lunchtime *plat du jour* is great value.

Le Petit Bouche BISTRO €€
(☎04 76 43 10 39; 16 rue Docteur Mazet; lunch plats du jour €8.50, menus €27-32; ⏲noon-2pm & 7-9pm Mon-Fri) Festooned with vintage bric-a-brac, with time-scuffed floors and a narrow open bar-kitchen, Le Petit Bouche enjoys a loyal following. Its classic bistro fare, such as *boudin noir* with apple, is great value.

Ciao a Te ITALIAN €€
(☎04 76 42 54 41; 2 rue de la Paix; lunch menus €16 & €22, mains €12-29; ⏲noon-2pm & 7.30-10pm Tue-Sat Sep-Jul) Emilian and Pugliese

dishes jostle with the food of Naples and Sicily in this perennially popular trattoria. Enter through the kitchen and loosen your belt for freshly made pasta, crispy *panzerotti* (deep-fried calzone), or veal stuffed with mozzarella and napped with tomato sauce. Dinner bookings are advisable.

La Cuisine des Tontons FRENCH €€
(☎04 76 25 25 00; www.lacuisinedestontons.fr; 9 rue Bayard; menus €19.90-29.90; ⊙noon-2pm & 7.30-10pm Tue-Sat) One for those with a 'meat tooth', this whimsically decorated bistro – decked out in homage to the 1963 French caper flick *Les Tontons Flingeurs* – does no fewer than eight different versions of *tartare*: alongside the classic, others involve Roquefort, nuts and other innovations.

La Fondue FRENCH €€
(☎04 76 15 20 72; www.lafonduegrenoble.fr; 5 rue Brocherie; mains €16-22; ⊙noon-1.30pm & 7pm-1am Mon-Sat) Faced with slightly kitsch wood panelling and serving 17 kinds of cheese and meat fondue, this is a great place to warm your insides on a cold Grenoble evening. *Raclette* and *tartiflette* round out the Savoyard offerings, and, for dessert, there's chocolate fondues laced with Génépi or Chartreuse.

Drinking & Nightlife

There's a cluster of cafes and pubs a couple of blocks south of the river, on and around place aux Herbes, adjacent place Claveyson and nearby place St-André. When it's warm enough, place Grenette, three blocks further southwest, fills with cafe tables.

Le Tord Boyaux WINE BAR
(☎04 76 44 18 90; www.tord-boyaux.fr; 4 rue Auguste Gaché; ⊙6pm-1am Tue & Wed, to 2am Thu-Sat) This unique establishment, popular with students, features 40+ *vins aromatisés* (flavoured wines; €2.50) that, believe it or not, you drink on the rocks. Some of them are quite extravagant: *chataigne* (chestnut), *Génépi-fraise* (Génépi-strawberry), *mangue pimentée* (spicy mango) and the mysterious *p'tite pillule bleu* (little blue pill). Come during *les heures joyeuses* (6pm to 9pm) and put your taste buds through their paces.

Le 365 WINE BAR
(☎04 76 51 73 18; 3 rue Bayard; ⊙6pm-1am or 2am Tue-Sat) A clutter of oversized glass bottles, oil paintings and candles create a relaxed setting for sipping wine – about 30 are available by the glass (€2.50 to €6). You can snack on cheese, sausages and terrines, wig out to live bands (two Wednesdays per month) or get into the spirit of monthly themed parties.

Shopping

Épicerie Fine J.P. Bresson FOOD & DRINKS
(☎04 76 44 42 08; 2 rue Auguste Gâche; ⊙8.30am-12.30pm & 2.30-7pm Tue-Sat) An irresistible trove of comestibles, this handsome wooden-shuttered *épicerie* (grocer's) is stuffed rigid with wines, confectionery, *confits des fleurs* (preserves made from violet, rose, jasmine and other petals) and Grenobloise specialities such as hazelnut oil.

Cave de la Laiterie Bayard FOOD & DRINKS
(☎09 60 40 27 13; 17 rue Bayard; ⊙7am-12.30pm & 3-7pm Mon-Sat) Established in 1931, this richly lactic-smelling dairy shop does a roaring trade in Alpine cheeses, fresh milk, yoghurt, butter, wine and spirits. The milk-bottle door handles and Alpine scenes on the walls ensure there's no confusion as to their line of business.

Information

Tourist Office (☎04 76 42 41 41; www.grenoble-tourisme.com; 14 rue de la République; ⊙1-6pm Mon, 9am-6pm Tue-Sat, 9am-noon Sun Oct-Apr, to 7pm Mon-Sat May-Sep; 🛜) Has very useful free maps and guides in English.

Getting There & Away

AIR

During the ski season, a clutch of budget airlines, including easyJet, Ryanair and Jet2.com, link **Grenoble Isère Airport** (☎04 76 65 48 48; www.grenoble-airport.com), 45km northwest of Grenoble, with major British airports.

BUS

Eurolines (www.eurolines.com; 11 place de la Gare; ⊙6am-8pm Mon-Sat, 7am-8pm Sun), which connects with most European countries, has a desk at Grenoble bus station

Transaltitude (☎08 20 08 38 38; www.transaltitude.fr) has frequent buses to various ski stations during the ski season, including Alpe d'Huez and Les Deux Alpes (€18, 95 minutes, three to nine per day) and Chamrousse (€14, 75 minutes, one to six per day).

Transisère (www.transisere.fr) can get you to Bourg d'Oisans (bus 3000; €6.50, 1¾ hours, at least five daily).

VFD (www.vfd.fr; www.bus-et-clic.com) goes – faster than the train – to Briançon (€30.50, 2½ hours, one to three daily).

TRAIN

Train station (1 place de la Gare) About 1km west of the centre; linked to the centre by tram lines A and B.

SNCF boutique (www.sncf.com/fr; 15 rue de la République; ⌚10am-6pm Mon-Sat) Sells train tickets in the city centre, right across the street from the tourist office.

Getting Around

TO/FROM THE AIRPORT

The intercity train and **bus stations** (11 place de la Gare; ⌚6am-8pm Mon-Sat, 7am-8pm Sun) are adjacent to one another, 1km northwest of the town centre. Take trams A or B, or walk 15 minutes, to the city centre.

Grenoble Isère Airport is 45km north of the city, accessible by **shuttle bus** (☎04 76 06 48 66; www.actibus.com/aeroport) or taxi. Shuttles also run to and from Lyon St-Exupéry and Geneva airports, run by **Faure Vercors** (☎08 25 82 55 36; www.faurevercors.fr) and **Aérocar** (☎09 74 50 07 50; www.aerocar.fr), respectively.

For details on seasonal buses from Grenoble Isère Airport to various ski stations, see www.actibus.com/aeroport, www.bensbus.co.uk and www.mobsavoie.fr.

BICYCLE

Compact, and with extensive cycle infrastructure, Grenoble is great for two-wheeled exploration. Pick up *Les Itinéraires Cyclables*, a free map of Grenoble-area cycling routes, from **Métrovélo** (☎08 20 22 38 38; www.metrovelo.fr; place de la Gare) or the **tourist office**.

Around Grenoble

Grenoble is within striking distance of two gorgeous, mountainous national parks: Parc Naturel Régional du Vercors and Parc National des Écrins. Both are wonderful for cross-country skiing, walking, caving, wildlife and just generally immersing yourself in the unhurried culture of the region.

Parc Naturel Régional du Vercors

The gently rolling pastures, highland plateaux, chiselled limestone peaks and pastoral hamlets of this 2062-sq-km nature park, southwest of Grenoble, are quieter and cheaper than the Alps' high-profile resorts. The wildlife-rich park draws families seeking fresh air and low-key activities such as cross-country skiing, snowshoeing, hiking (on a whopping 3000km of trails), mountain biking and caving. Topping it all is the Réserve Naturelle des Hauts-Plateaux, at 170 sq km, France's largest terrestrial nature reserve.

Sights & Activities

Grotte de la Luire CAVE
(www.grottedelaluire.com; Le passage, 26420 Saint Agnan en Vercors; adult/child €8.50/6; ⌚Dec 17–Nov 13) Filled with karst springs and enormous, spectacularly lit chambers, the Grotte de la Luire was used as an emergency hospital during WWII. Up to five tours depart daily, but days of operation vary greatly throughout the year: check the website to be certain.

Les Accompagnateurs Nature et Patrimoine WALKING
(☎04 76 95 08 38; www.accompagnateur-vercors.com; ⌚year-round) Leaving from the tourist offices of Villard de Lans (p514) or Lans-en-Vercors, Les Accompagnateurs walks in the Vercors park are conducted by knowledgeable guides. In spring, summer and autumn they offer half-day (adult/child €17/11) and day walks (adult/child €27/20) among Alpine wild flowers and wildlife, while half-day snowshoeing tours (adult/child €20/15) are offered in winter.

Gorges du Furon CANYON
Canyoning, abseiling and walking are all popular in the spectacular Gorges du Furon, carved through the Vercors limestone by the rushing River Furon. You'll see the gorges (in fact, pass through them) just before you reach Lans-en-Vercors, on the D531 from Grenoble.

Sleeping & Eating

À la Crécia B&B €
(☎04 76 95 46 98; www.gite-en-vercors.com; 436 chemin des Cléments, Les Clements, Lans-en-Vercors; s/d/tr/q incl breakfast €58/63/78/93) Renovated by Véronique and Pascal, this ecoconscious 16th-century farm, home to goats, pigs and poultry, has five large guest rooms panelled in spruce and pine. Dinner is a feast of farm-fresh produce, with wine included (*menus* €19). You'll find it 1.8km south of Lans-en-Vercors' church, on the far outskirts of the village.

Au Gai Soleil de Mont-Aiguille HOTEL €
(☎04 76 34 41 71; www.hotelgaisoleil.com; Chichilianne; d/superior €48/73;) At the foot of striking Mont Aiguille, this simple inn has fabulous views, superb access to local hiking routes, a rustic country restaurant, a spa and

two massage rooms for treating weary muscles at trail's end.

Gîte d'Alpage de la Molière FRENCH €
(☎06 09 38 42 42; http://gitedelamoliere.aufilduvercors.org; 41 impasse des Frênes, Les Eperouses, Autrans; menus €15-28; ⊙lunch daily Jun-Sep) High above Lans-en-Vercors, this welcoming trail-side *refuge* with incomparable views serves simple mountain fare (savoury vegetable tarts, salad with smoked trout, and raspberry, blueberry and walnut pies) on umbrella-shaded picnic tables astride an Alpine meadow. The picnic hampers, only €12 per adult, are a great option for ramblers.

Information

Tourist Office (Villard de Lans) (☎04 76 95 10 38; www.villarddelans.com; 101 place Mure-Ravaud, Villard de Lans; ⊙9am-noon & 2.30-6.30pm daily Jul & Aug, other times hours vary; 📶) Villard de Lans' tourist office has an online service for booking hotels and *chambres d'hôte*, and should be your first port of call for information on outdoor activities and local guides. Its opening hours follow a complicated seasonal pattern, so check online before visiting!

Getting There & Away

Buses 5100 and 5110, run by **Transisère,** (☎08 20 08 38 38; www.transisere.fr) link Grenoble with Lans-en-Vercors (€5.90, 45 minutes, seven to 10 daily) and Villard de Lans (€5.90, one hour, four to seven daily). The trip, which passes through the looming **Gorges du Furon** (p513), is quite beautiful.

Les Deux Alpes

POP 2200 / ELEV 1600M

Les Deux Alpes were once a brace of quiet mountain hamlets. Today, with glorious powder for off-piste fans, summer skiing on a glacier, thrilling mountain-bike descents and a party to rival anywhere in the French Alps, this buzzing resort brings as much attitude as altitude.

Sights & Activities

Contact the Bureau des Guides for ice climbing, snowshoeing and off-piste skiing in winter, and rock climbing, canyoning and biking expeditions in summer.

Grotte de Glace CAVE
(Ice Cave; adult/child €5/4; ⊙10am-3.30pm winter & summer) Ice statues representing creatures from prehistory glisten in this ice cave, carved 30m deep into the Glacier des Deux Alpes. To get there, take the Jandri Express lift to 3200m.

Winter

Les Deux Alpes' winter season runs from December to April. The main **skiing** domain lies below (ie west of) the summit of **La Meije** (3983m), one of the highest peaks in the Parc National des Écrins. Lots of lifts (per day/week €47.50/268.10 for an adult, €38.10/214.50 for a child) come right into the village, making ski-in ski-out a cinch; five beginners' lifts – great for kids – are free. The higher you go, the easier the pistes are.

Free-riders come from far and wide to tackle the breathtaking, near-vertical **Vallons de la Meije** descent in La Grave, 24km (by road) east of Les Deux Alpes on the other side of the mountain. The stuff of myth, the off-piste run plummets from 3800m to 1400m – that's 2400 vertical metres! – and is strictly for the crème de la crème of off-piste riders.

Other winter options include ice skating, careening around on an ice bumper car (for kids) and going on a *motoneige* (snowmobile) expedition; the tourist office has details.

La Grave SKIING
(☎04 76 79 91 09; www.la-grave.com) One gondola from the charming stone village of La Grave (€47.50 for a day pass, 30 minutes) drops the adventurous off at 3200m, from where they find their way down unmarked and unpatrolled slopes. It's possible to link by foot with Les Deux Alpes, at 3500m; a guide is strongly recommended.

Summer

Thanks to the **Glacier des Deux-Alpes** (2900m to 3600m), Les Deux Alpes is one of only two places in France where you can **ski** (or learn to ski) on a glacier in summer (the other is Espace Killy, above Val d'Isère and Tignes). When it's clear, the 360-degree panorama takes in much of southeastern France, including Mont Blanc, the Massif Central and Mont Ventoux. The season runs from about 21 June to August and reopens for a week in late October/early November; a day pass, valid for skiing and the **snow park** from 7.15am to 12.30pm (and for other activities in the afternoon), costs €38.50/31 for an adult/child.

You can combine morning skiing with **mountain biking** on scores of nail-biting

descents (in winter they're ski pistes) and cross-country trails. A pass to seven bike-accessible lifts costs €20/24.50 for a half-/full day. Les Deux Alpes also offers numerous **hiking trails** and plenty of opportunities for **paragliding** as well as ice skating, swimming, summer luge, tennis etc.

Many ski shops rent out Alp-ready mountain bikes in the summer.

Sleeping & Eating

Hotel Serre-Palas HOTEL €

(☎04 76 80 56 33; www.hotelserre-palas.fr; 13 place de Venosc; d incl breakfast €55-143) With 24 bright, quiet rooms, a snug bar for après-ski and marvellous views of the Écrins national park, this spick-and-span chalet is excellent value. Lionel, your affable host, is a ski instructor and can give you plenty of insider tips. It's situated at the southern edge of town, near the gondola to Venosc.

★**Hotel Côte Brune** HOTEL €€€

(☎04 76 80 54 89; www.hotel-cotebrune.fr; 6 rue Côte Brune; d incl half-board €170-260;) You can ski in and out of this hotel, with its swanky new spa and sprawling slopeside terrace bar. The 18 wood-panelled rooms radiate Alpine charm, the south-facing ones have balconies, and some are geared for families.

Le Raisin d'Ours FRENCH €€

(☎04 76 79 29 56; www.leraisindours.fr; 98 av de la Muzelle; menus €26-40; noon-2pm & 7-10pm) This stylishly rustic restaurant serves French Alpine cuisine – *diots* (Savoyard sausages), ravioli in cream, and similarly sustaining fare – accompanied by wines from every region of France (the owner, Aurélie, is a sommelier). The mood is relaxed, the service attentive.

Drinking & Nightlife

Smithy's Tavern BAR

(☎04 76 11 36 79; www.smithystavern.com; 7 rue du Cairou;) Doing its best to live up to the clunky motto 'The Avoidance of Sameness', this rocking, English-owned pub is one of the premier party spots in the Deux Alpes. The low, timbered ceiling and long, battle-scarred bar downstairs oversee regular gigs, DJ nights and head-spinning parties, while the upstairs grill pumps out fajitas, burgers and steaks.

Smokey Joe's BAR

(place des Deux Alpes; 9am or 10am-midnight late Nov–late Apr & mid-Jun–Aug;) A daily happy hour (4pm to 7pm), spicy Tex-Mex food, pizzas and dice shots are bound to get you grooving in your snow boots at this British-owned hang-out very near the base of the Jandri lift. There's also foosball, pool, and a staff of native English speakers.

Information

Maison des Deux Alpes (4 place des Deux Alpes; 8am-7pm in high season) is home to the **Tourist Office** (☎04 76 79 22 00; www.les2alpes.com; 4 place des Deux Alpes; 8am-7pm late Nov–late Apr & mid-Jun–Aug, 9am-noon & 2-6pm Mon-Fri in low season;), **ESF** (☎04 76 79 21 21; www.esf2alpes.com; Maison des Deux Alpes; 8.30am-6.30pm in high season) and **Bureau des Guides** (☎04 76 11 36 29; www.guides2alpes.com; 4 place des Deux Alpes; 3.30-6.30pm).

Getting There & Away

Les Deux Alpes is 67km southeast of Grenoble and 19km southeast of Bourg d'Oisans. Airport transfers are available from Grenoble and Lyon airports, and **Transaltitude** (☎08 20 08 38 38; www.transaltitude.fr) buses connect to Grenoble, in high season.

Book online or at **Agence Transisère VFD** (☎04 76 80 51 22; 112 av de la Muzelle).

Alpe d'Huez

POP 1700 / ELEV 1860M

The Alpe d'Huez Grand Domaine Ski Area combines the resorts of Alpe d'Huez, Auris-en-Oisans, Huez-en-Oisans, Oz-en-Oisans, Vaujany and Villard Reculas. Ranging from 1250m to 3330m, it boasts 250km of well-groomed pistes that range from dead easy to death-defying. The ski season lasts from early December to late April, when the sun on its south-facing slopes can become a problem.

Summer (July and August) brings a mix of hikers and mountain bikers – and, often, the Tour de France.

Activities

For adventure activities such as ice climbing, mountain climbing, via ferrata and glacier hiking, contact the Bureau des Guides.

Bureau des Guides OUTDOORS

(☎04 76 80 42 55; www.guidesalpedhuez.com; Rond-Point des Pistes, Chalet ESF; 9.30am-12.30pm & 2.30-5.30pm) This should be your first port of call for off-piste, back-country and guided skiing, and for mountaineering

and climbing in the warmer months. A half-day's guided skiing costs €250.

ESF SKIING
(☎04 76 80 31 69; www.esf-alpedhuez.com; place Paganon, La Maison de l'Alpe; ⏰9am-7pm ski season, 9am-noon & 1.30-5.30pm rest of year) Housed in the same building as the principal tourist office in Alpe d'Huez, the French Ski School has lessons for skiers and boarders of all levels. A one-hour lesson for one or two people costs €48.

Skiing

The **Pic Blanc** (3330m), Alpe d'Huez' highest point, commands magical panoramas that reach across one-fifth of France. Accessible winter and summer via the Tronçon and Pic Blanc cable cars, it's possible to ski over two vertical kilometres from this awesome eyrie. Then there's Europe's longest black run, the breathtakingly sheer, 16km, **La Sarenne** (also accessed from the Pic Blanc car).

Hiking & Biking

In summer, marked **hiking trails** lead up and across the slopes to jewel-like lakes such as the **Lac Blanc**, **Lac de la Fare** and **Lac du Milieu**.

For **mountain-biking** enthusiasts, the area is downhill heaven, with more than 260km of trails to rattle and roll down, and four bike parks. A one-day summertime lift pass costs €16 for both pedestrians and cyclists.

Alpe d'Huez is (in)famous for its incredibly steep, 14km access road, whose 21 hairpin curves are a regular highlight of the Tour de France.

Sleeping & Eating

Few places to stay are ski-in ski-out, but the free Télécentre lift connects the village with Rond-Point des Pistes at the village's upper edge, departure point for lots more lifts. Stay in central Alpe d'Huez to be close to the action, or consider a quieter billet in one of the outlying villages.

Le Tremplin FRENCH €
(☎04 76 80 33 99; Centre de Jour, Bergers; mains €10-22; ⏰8am-10pm in high season) Dominating the northern side of the Commercial Centre in the Quartier des Bergers is this briskly efficient, all-purpose brasserie, ideal for post-piste pizzas, *galettes* every-which-way, traditional Alpine dishes, or a warming après-ski *vin chaud* on the decking.

Le Passe-Montagne FRENCH €€
(☎04 76 11 31 53; www.lepasse-montagne.com; 122 rte de la Poste; menus lunch/dinner €19.50/32.50; ⏰11.45am-1.30pm & 6.30-9.30pm; 👪) An open fire burns in the beamed dining room of this stylish wooden chalet, a fine place for a tête-á-tête over *ravioles du royans* (Comte-stuffed pasta squares, perhaps with cream and snails) or a steak, hot-stone grilled at your table.

Information

Information hub **Maison de l'Alpe** (place Paganon; ⏰8.45am-7pm Dec-Apr, 9am-noon & 2-5pm Mon-Fri Sep-Nov; 📶) sells ski passes and houses the helpful **tourist office** (☎04 76 11 44 44; www.alpedhuez.com; place Paganon; ⏰8.45am-7pm Dec-Apr, 9am-noon & 2-5pm Mon-Fri Sep-Nov; 📶), **accommodation reservation centre** (☎04 76 11 59 90; www.reservation.alpedhuez.com; place Paganon, La Maison de l'Alpe) and ESF.

Getting There & Away

Alpe d'Huez is 64km southeast of Grenoble. From late December to March, **Transaltitude** (☎08 20 08 38 38; www.transaltitude.fr) buses link Alpe d'Huez with Grenoble's train and bus stations (€6.50, two hours, at least three daily) via Bourg d'Oisans.

Bourg d'Oisans

POP 3228 / ELEV 720M

A gateway to several world-famous resorts, the valley village of Bourg d'Oisans – starting point for the serpentine, 23km road to Alpe d'Huez – makes an excellent base for hiking, mountain biking and snow sports.

Sights & Activities

For information on the area, check out http://oisans.com and www.bikes-oisans.com, which have details on trails, maps and bike hire. For details on activities such as kayaking on the Drac's turquoise waters, rock climbing, via-ferrata routes and paragliding, contact the tourist office.

Musée des Minéraux et de la Faune des Alpes MUSEUM
(☎04 76 80 27 54; www.musee-bourgdoisans.fr; place de l'Église; adult/child €5.15/2.30; ⏰2-6pm Sat & Sun mid-Dec–mid-Nov, 2-6pm Wed-Mon Apr-Jul & school holidays) Bone up on the national park's fascinating geology, flora and fauna, including ibex and chamois, at this nature-savvy museum.

Cycles et Sports CYCLING
(☎04 76 79 16 79; www.cyclesetsports.com; place du Docteur Faure; ⊙9am-noon & 2-6pm Mon-Sat Oct-Apr, 8.30am-7pm daily May-Sep) For those mad enough to tackle the remorseless climb up Alpe d'Huez (21 bends, an ascent of nearly 1220m, and an average gradient of 7.9%) this boutique operation hires out high-end road bikes for between €42 and €90 per day.

Sleeping & Eating

Aside from brasseries and restaurants serving robust Alpine fare, pizza is the most widely available food in Le Bourg. Establishments fan out from the junction of av de la République and rue du Général de Gaulle, and there's an outdoor **food market** in the village centre on Saturday, from 7am to 1pm, plus Wednesdays in July and August.

Ferme Noémie B&B €
(☎04 76 11 06 14; www.fermenoemie.com; chemin Pierre Polycarpe, Les Sables; apt per week €375-1500, luxury tents per day/week €65/450, camp sites €10.50-25; ⊙campground Apr-Oct) Run by a British couple, Melanie and Jeremy Smith, Ferme Noémie has barn-conversion apartments with four to six beds, four-bed luxury tents and old-fashioned camp sites. Prices depend on seasonal demand. To get there from the D1091, follow the signs for about 500m.

Information

The **Maison du Parc** (☎04 76 80 00 51; www.ecrins-parcnational.fr; 120 rue Gambetta; ⊙1.30-5pm Mon-Thu Sep-Jun, 10am-noon & 3-6.30pm daily Jul & Aug) is great for information on the Parc National des Écrins, while the **Tourist Office** (☎04 76 80 03 25; www.bourgdoisans.com; quai Girard; ⊙9am-noon & 2-6pm Mon-Sat Sep-Jun, 9am-6pm Jul & Aug; ☎) is good for everything else.

Getting There & Away

During the ski season, **Transaltitude** (☎08 20 08 38 38; www.transaltitude.fr) runs buses from Grenoble's bus station, through Bourg d'Oisans, to Alpe d'Huez and Les Deux Alpes (€18, 95 minutes, three to nine per day). During the same period, **LER** (☎08 21 20 22 03; www.info-ler.fr) operates buses to/from Bourg, on the way between Grenoble and Briançon (€20, three hours, four daily).

Briançon

POP 11,570 / ELEV 1320M

Briançon's Cité Vauban (walled old town), perched high on a hill, is straight out of a fairy tale, with sweeping views of nearby Vauban fortifications and the snowcapped Écrins peaks. The Italian vibe is no coincidence – Italy is just (a dizzying) 20km away. Briançon is proud of its 300 sunny days a year.

No matter whether you come by bus or car, it feels like a long, long way to Briançon – but it's worth every horn-tooting, head-spinning, glacier-gawping minute. The road from Grenoble is pure drama, and not just because of the scenery. The locals adopt a nonchalant attitude to driving, the general consensus being: overtaking on hairpin bends, *pas de problème*! But brave it behind the wheel and you'll be richly rewarded with views of thundering falls, sheer cliffs and jagged peaks razoring above thick larch forests as you drive from Isère into the sunny and distinctly southern Hautes-Alpes *département*.

Sights

Cité Vauban HISTORIC SITE
(Vieille Ville) Surrounded by mighty starburst-shaped ramparts, Briançon's hilltop old town looks much as it did centuries ago, its winding cobbled lanes lined with Italianate, pastel-painted townhouses. The steep main street, the **Grande Rue** – also known as the Grande Gargouille (Great Gargoyle) because of its gushing rivulet – was laid out in 1345. You can walk all the way around the interior of Vauban's upper ramparts, enjoying spectacular views, by following the streets marked as the **chemin de Ronde**.

Vauban Fortifications HISTORIC SITE
Three centuries ago, Briançon – situated at the confluence of five river valleys – was highly vulnerable to attack by France's Alpine arch-rival of the era, the Duchy of Savoy. Under Louis XIV and his successors, vast effort was expended on constructing hilltop fortresses to defend the remote town, marvels of military engineering that, along with a dozen other Vauban sites in France, were given Unesco World Heritage status in 2008.

Perched atop a rocky crag high above the Cité Vauban, the **Fort du Château** (1326m) can be visited on foot from late April to November. Across the 55m-high **Pont d'Asfeld** (erected 1720), a graceful stone bridge over the River Durance, **Fort des Trois Têtes**

(1435m) can be seen on a walking tour in the warm season and on snowshoes in winter (€25; most Thursdays at 1.50pm). Also accessible on foot and by snowshoes is **Fort des Salettes** (1400m).

For details on tours, contact the **Service du Patrimoine** (☎04 92 20 29 49; www.ville-briancon.fr; Porte de Pignerol, Cité Vauban; tours adult/child €6.20/4.60; ⊙10am-noon & 2-5.30pm Tue-Fri & Sun Sep-Jun, Mon-Sat Jul & Aug), inside the Cité Vauban's main gate.

Activities

For information on hiking in the **Parc National des Écrins**, ie in the mountains west of town, stop by the **Maison du Park** (☎04 92 21 42 15; www.ecrins-parcnational.fr; place du Médecin Général Blanchard; ⊙10.30am-6.30pm Jul & Aug, 2-6pm Mon-Fri Sep-Jun), a three-storey visitor centre situated at the bottom of the Cité Vauban's Grande Rue.

Serre Chevalier SKIING

(www.serre-chevalier.com; ⊙Dec-Apr) The Serre Chevalier ski area, properly called Le Grand Serre Chevalier, links 13 villages and 250km of pistes along the Serre Chevalier Valley between Briançon and Le Monêtier-les-Bains, 15km northwest. To get to the slopes (and warm-season trails) directly from Briançon, take the **Télécabine du Prorel** lift, located 1.8km across the valley – on the western edge of Ste-Catherine – from the Cité Vauban.

Bureau des Guides et Accompagnateurs de Briançon OUTDOORS

(☎04 92 20 15 73; www.guides-briancon.fr; 24 rue Centrale; ⊙10am-noon & 3-7pm Mon-Fri, 3-7pm Sat, 10am-1pm Sun in summer, 4-7pm rest of year) Organises off-piste outings, snowshoeing and ice climbing in winter; and trekking, mountain climbing, mountaineering, via-ferrata climbs, glacier traverses, mountain biking and canyoning in summer.

Sleeping & Eating

Hôtel de la Chaussée HISTORIC HOTEL €

(☎04 92 21 10 37; www.hotel-de-la-chaussee.com; cnr av de la République & rue Centrale, Ste-Catherine; s/d/tr €80/88/135; 📶) The Bonnaffoux family has run this place with charm and efficiency for five generations – since 1892, in fact. The 16 rooms fulfil every Alpine chalet fantasy: wood panelled, beautifully furnished and oh so cosy.

Au Plaisir Ambré MODERN FRENCH €€

(☎04 92 52 63 46; www.auplaisirambre.com; 26 Grande Rue; menus €23-32; ⊙noon-1.15pm by reservation & 7-9.15pm Fri-Tue year-round, plus Wed Jul & Aug) At this Alpine-chic bistro, French dishes with Italian and Asian touches are perfectly matched with wines and followed by indulgent desserts such as *soufflé glacé à la Chartreuse.*

Information

The **tourist office** (☎04 92 21 08 50; www.ot-briancon.fr; Maison des Templiers, 1 place du Temple, Cité Vauban; ⊙9am-noon & 2-6pm Mon-Sat, 10am-noon & 2-5pm Sun; 📶) can help with last-minute accommodation. Room availability information is posted on the door.

Getting There & Away

BUS

The bus station is next to the train station. **LER** (☎08 21 20 22 03; www.info-ler.fr) bus 35, run by the Provence-Alpes-Côte d'Azur *région,* links Briançon with Grenoble (€30.50, 2½ hours, one to three daily) via Bourg d'Oisans. LER bus 29 goes to Gap (€13.90, two hours, six daily Monday to Saturday), Aix-en-Provence (€37.80, five hours, two daily Monday to Saturday) and Marseille (€42, 5½ hours, two daily Monday to Saturday).

CAR & MOTORCYCLE

The **Col de Montgenèvr**e (1850m), linking Briançon with neighbouring Italy, is kept open year-round, as is the **Col du Lautaret** (2058m) between Briançon and Grenoble. Both, though, occasionally get snow-bogged.

TRAIN

The **train station** (av du Général de Gaulle), terminus of a rail spur that heads northwestward from Gap, is 1.8km southwest the Cité Vauban and 1km south of Ste-Catherine (the city centre). It is linked to the rest of town by local TUB buses 1 and 3. To Grenoble, the bus is much faster than the train.

To get to Paris (€95 to €116, seven to nine hours), you can either take an overnight train to Gare d'Austerlitz, or a day train to Gare de Lyon; the latter requires changing in Grenoble, Valence TVG and/or Gap. But the fastest way to get to Paris is to take a bus to the Italian town of Oulx (€10, one hour, six daily from December to mid-April) – reserve 36 hours ahead on ☎04 92 50 25 05 or via www.05voyageurs.com – and then a TGV to Paris' Gare de Lyon (€113, 4½ hours).

Other destinations:

Grenoble €33.40, 4½ hours, five daily

Gap €14.80, 1¼ hours, at least nine daily

Marseille €45, 4½ hours, five daily

TOUR DE FRANCE

No event gets the wheels of the cycle-racing world spinning quite as fast as the Tour de France, or 'Le Tour' as it is popularly known in France. This is the big one: one prologue, 21 stages, some 3500km clocked in three weeks by about 180 riders, an entire country – and, often, bits of its neighbours – criss-crossed by bicycle. Broadcast around the world every July, it is a spectacle of epic determination and endurance, of mountain passes steep enough to turn thighs to rubber, of hell-for-leather sprints, of tears and triumph.

The brainchild of journalist Géo Lefèvre, the race was first held in 1903 to boost sales of *L'Auto* newspaper, with 60 trailblazers pedalling through the night to complete the 2500km route in 19 days. Since then, the Tour has become *the* cycling event. And despite headlines about skulduggery, doping and scandal, the riders' sheer guts and hard-won triumphs never fail to inspire.

THE JURA MOUNTAINS

The dark wooded hills, limestone plateaux, rolling dairy country and vine-wreathed villages of the Jura Mountains stretch for about 250km from Lake Geneva northeast to Belfort, along both sides of the Franco-Swiss border. Rural, deeply traditional and *un petit peu* eccentric, the Jura – from a Gaulish word meaning 'forest' – is ideal if you're seeking serenity, authentic farmstays and the simple pleasures of mountain life. Wayside farms invite you to stop, relax and sample the tangy delights of Comté cheese and *vin jaune* (yellow wine) – a sure way to experience those 'ahhh, *c'est la vie...*' moments.

The Jura – after which the Jurassic period in geology is named – is France's premier cross-country skiing area. The region is dotted with small ski stations, and every year it hosts the **Transjurassienne** (www.transjurassienne.com; ⏲ Feb), one of the world's toughest cross-country skiing events.

Besançon

POP 116,353 / ELEV 262M

Hugging a *bouclé* (hairpin curve) of the River Doubs, the cultured and very attractive capital of Franche-Comté remains refreshingly modest and untouristy, despite charms such as a monumental Vauban citadel, a graceful 18th-century old town and France's first public museum.

In Gallo-Roman times, Vesontio (over the centuries, the name evolved to become Besançon) was an important stop on the trade routes linking Italy, the Alps and the Rhine, and some striking remains of this period survive.

Sights

For a lovely stroll, you can walk paths along either bank of the River Doubs, where it encircles the old city.

★Citadelle de Besançon CITADEL
(www.citadelle.com; 99 rue des Fusillés de la Résistance; adult/child €10.60/8.50; ⏲10am-5pm Jan-Mar & Oct-Dec, 9am-6pm Apr-Jun & Sep, 9am-7pm Jul & Aug, closed early Jan) Dominating the city from Mt St Etienne, 120 vertical metres above the old town, the 17th-century Citadelle de Besançon – designed by Vauban for Louis XIV – commands sweeping views of the city and the serpentine River Doubs. Along with 11 other Vauban works, it was recognised as a Unesco World Heritage site in 2008.

The entry fee includes two audioguides, available in French, English and German. Two cafes serves edibles.

For an introduction to the citadel's architecture, head to **Espace Vauban**, where exhibits include a fascinating 3D film (14 minutes). Booklets in English and German are available at the entrance. The **chemin de Rond** lets you walk along two sections of the citadel's outer ramparts.

The **Musée de la Résistance et de la Déportation** is one of France's most in-depth and comprehensive WWII museums. Each room is supposed to have an information sheet in English (look for a wall-mounted holder) but the 20 rooms of evocative photos, documents and artefacts are best visited with a free audioguide. Some of the photographs are unsuitable for young children. During WWII, the Germans imprisoned British civilians in the citadel, and German firing squads executed about 100 resistance fighters here. Nearby, the **Musée Comtois** presents local life in centuries past.

Kids are sure to be fascinated by the **Insectarium**, with creepy-crawlies such as tarantulas, scorpions and stick insects; the small **Aquarium**, where you can pet the koi; the ho-hum **Noctarium**, where a few of the Jura's nocturnal rodents snuffle around; and, at the southeast end, the **zoo**, home base for the free-range peacocks that strut their stuff around the fort.

If you don't fancy the uphill trudge, take Ginkobus' bus 17 (€1.30) from the city centre or Parking Rodia, which runs one to five times an hour from April to mid-October.

★Musée des Beaux-Arts et d'Archéologie MUSEUM

(☎03 81 87 80 67; www.mbaa.besancon.fr; 1 place de la Révolution; adult/child €5/free; ⏰9.30am-noon & 2-6pm Mon & Wed-Fri, 9.30am-6pm Sat & Sun) France's oldest public museum, founded in 1694, is famous for its stellar collection of local Gallo-Roman archaeology; its Cabinet des Dessins, with some 6000 drawings from the 15th to 20th centuries, including masterpieces by Dürer, Delacroix and Rodin; and its 14th- to 20th-century paintings, with standouts by Titian, Rubens, Goya and Matisse. The museum will be closed for renovations until mid-2018.

FRAC Franche-Comté MUSEUM

(☎03 81 87 87 40; www.frac-franche-comte.fr; 2 passage des Arts, Cité des Arts; adult/child €4/2; ⏰2-6pm Wed-Fri, to 7pm Sat & Sun) Bringing contemporary art to the Franche-Comté region is the *raison d'être* of this museum, which opened in 2013. The riverside building, with its distinctive chequerboard timber façade, was designed by the Japanese architect Kengo Kuma.

Horloge Astronomique MONUMENT

(☎03 81 81 12 76; http://horloge-besancon.monuments-nationaux.fr; rue du Chapitre; adult/child €3/free; ⏰guided tours hourly 9.50-11.50am & 2.50-5.50pm Wed-Mon Apr-Sep, Thu-Mon Oct-Mar) The base of 18th-century **Cathédrale St-Jean's** (☎03 81 83 34 62; www.cathedrale-besancon.fr; 10ter rue de la Convention; ⏰9am-7pm, to 6.15pm winter) bell tower houses an incredible astronomical clock, powered by 11 weights, that has run the church's bells since its installation in 1860. The ornate gadget has 30,000 moving parts and 57 clock faces and, among other things, tells the time in 16 places around the world and indicates the tides in eight different French ports.

Porte Noire HISTORIC SITE

(Black Gate; square Castan) Erected in AD 175 in honour of Marcus Aurelius, this Roman triumphal arch stands very near where the columns of a Roman theatre and the vestiges of an aqueduct (all still visible) were discovered in 1870. The site, which attests to the importance of Besançon as a site of Gallo-Roman civilisation, was restored as an 'English-style architectural garden' in 2006.

Musée du Temps MUSEUM

(☎03 81 87 81 50; www.mdt.besancon.fr; 96 Grande Rue; adult/child €5/free; ⏰9.15am-noon & 2-6pm Tue-Sat, 10am-6pm Sun) Housed in the grand 16th-century Palais Granvelle, this museum testifies to the proud history of *horologie* (watchmaking) in Besançon. Astrological clocks, watches, cabinet clocks, watchmaking tools: the beauty and precision of the artefacts on display is arresting.

Maison Natale de Victor Hugo MUSEUM

(☎03 81 41 53 65; 140 Grande Rue; adult/child €2.50/1.50; ⏰10.30am-5.30pm Wed-Mon Nov-Mar, to 6pm Apr-Oct) Victor Hugo, famous for masterpieces such as *Les Misérables* and *Notre-Dame de Paris* (The Hunchback of Notre Dame), was born here in 1802. Exhibits focus on the great man's public life and political activism.

Parc Micaud PARK

(av Édouard Droz) For that must-have snapshot of the hilltop citadel with the swiftly flowing Doubs in the foreground, take a stroll along this leafy riverside promenade, a great spot for a picnic with a view. A carousel, a playground and donkey rides keep kids entertained.

Tours

Vedettes de Besançon BOATING

(☎06 64 48 66 80; www.vedettesdebesancon.com; Pont de la République; adult/child €12/9; ⏰2-3 launches daily Apr-Jun, Sep & Oct, 5 daily Jul & Aug; 👪) This 1¼-hour river cruise is a relaxed way to see Besançon from the Doubs' hairpin curve and the 375m-long boat tunnel that goes underneath the citadel. *Menus* (€16 to €50) are served on some launches and only bespoke bookings are taken between November and March.

Sleeping

Most hotels lower their rates on Friday, Saturday and Sunday nights, when business demand dwindles. There are a number of reasonably priced hotels facing the train station.

★Residence Charles Quint APARTMENT €
(☎03 81 82 00 21; www.residence-charlesquint.com; 3 rue du Chapitre; d/apt €80/110;) Slumbering behind the cathedral, in the shade of the citadel, this discreetly grand 18th-century townhouse is now a sublime 'residence' featuring period furniture, sumptuous fabrics, a peaceful private garden and a wood-panelled dining room.

Parking (€5 per night) is available and a buffet breakfast (€13.50) can be taken at the nearby Hotel Sauvage. Minimum three-night stay.

★Hôtel de Paris DESIGN HOTEL €€
(☎03 81 81 36 56; www.besanconhoteldeparis.com; 33 rue des Granges; s/d €71/90;) Housed in an 18th-century coaching inn that has hosted luminaries such as the novelist Colette and the historian Jules Michelet (coiner of the word 'Renaissance'), this stylishly refurbished establishment is ideally placed in the heart of the old city. Of the 50 spacious rooms, a few open, motel-style, on to the enclosed parking lot (€8 per night) and three are wheelchair-accessible.

Eating

There are a number of small restaurants in the northwest corner of the old town, along rue Claude Pouillet. Across the river, cheap ethnic eats can be found on and near rue Battant.

Marché Beaux-Arts MARKET €
(☎03 81 87 81 86; place de la Révolution; ⊙7am-7pm Tue-Sat, 8am-1pm Sun) This covered food market has a lively outdoor extension on Wednesday morning, Friday morning and Saturday. Grab half a dozen super-fresh oysters (€8.25) at the tiny central 'restaurant' while shopping for charcuterie, fresh produce and cheese.

Le Mascareigna MADAGASCAN €
(☎03 81 50 53 89; 21 rue du Lycée; menus €15; ⊙noon-3pm & 6.30-10pm Tue-Sun) If you've ever wanted to try *cuisine réunionnaise* (the food of the Francophone tropical island of Réunion), this pleasant little neighbourhood restaurant, decked out like an island hut, is a great place to start. Samosas, curries, pickles and delicious rum-based ti' punch await.

La Petite Adresse BISTRO €
(☎03 81 82 35 09; 28 rue Claude Pouillet; lunch/dinner menus €11/18; ⊙noon-2pm & 7-10.30pm Mon-Sat;) A little address that's big on cheese dishes such as *boîte chaude* (hot box; two-person minimum), made with seasonal Vacherin Mont d'Or, and another Jura speciality, *saucisse de Morteau* (Morteau sausage).

Le Poker d'As FRENCH €€
(☎03 81 81 42 49; www.restaurant-lepokerdas.fr; 14 square St-Amour; menus €23.50-55; ⊙noon-1.30pm & 7.30-9.30pm Tue-Sat) With its thoughtful blend of traditional and creative French fare – trout tartare with top-grade olive oil and fine herbs; chicken with morels and *vin jaune*; cod with puy lentils and black radish cream – the 'Poker Ace' usually wins.

Brasserie 1802 BRASSERIE €€
(☎03 81 82 21 97; www.restaurant-1802.fr; place Granvelle; 3-course menus €29; ⊙noon-2pm & 7-10pm;) With a terrace spilling out on to tree-shaded place Granvelle, this glass-fronted brasserie serves up French classics such as Charolais rib steak, plus such Franc-Comtois specialities as trout with savagnin *(vin jaune) beurre blanc*.

Hambourgeois BURGERS €€
(☎03 81 57 59 49; 2 rue Jean Petit; menus €22; ⊙11am-2pm & 6-11pm Mon-Sat) Trying to up the ubiquitous burger a notch, Hambourgeois uses good-quality ingredients in its five different offerings, with unusual inclusions such as *cabécou*, a soft goat's cheese. The *menu* includes a burger, salad, fries, wine and dessert.

★Le Saint-Pierre MODERN FRENCH €€€
(☎03 81 81 20 99; www.restaurant-saintpierre.com; 104 rue Battant; menus €40-75; ⊙noon-1.30pm Mon-Fri, 7.30-9pm Mon-Sat) Crisp white tablecloths, exposed stone and subtle lighting are the backdrop for intense flavours, such as lobster lasagne with spinach and lobster bouillon, which are expertly paired with regional wines. At €40 the three-course *menu du marché*, which includes wine and coffee, is excellent value.

Drinking & Nightlife

Students spice up the nightlife in Besançon. Pubs can be found around the northern end of the Grande Rue (eg along tiny rue Claude Pouillet) and, across the river, in the more diverse and gritty Battant quarter.

Green Man BAR
(☎03 81 50 99 59; 21 rue Pasteur; ⊙7am-midnight Mon-Fri, 10am-midnight Sat) Technically an Irish bar (some effort has been made to invoke the Emerald Isle through decor, although the instruments hanging on the walls could be from many European countries) this convivial little bar really marches to a Gallic

Besançon

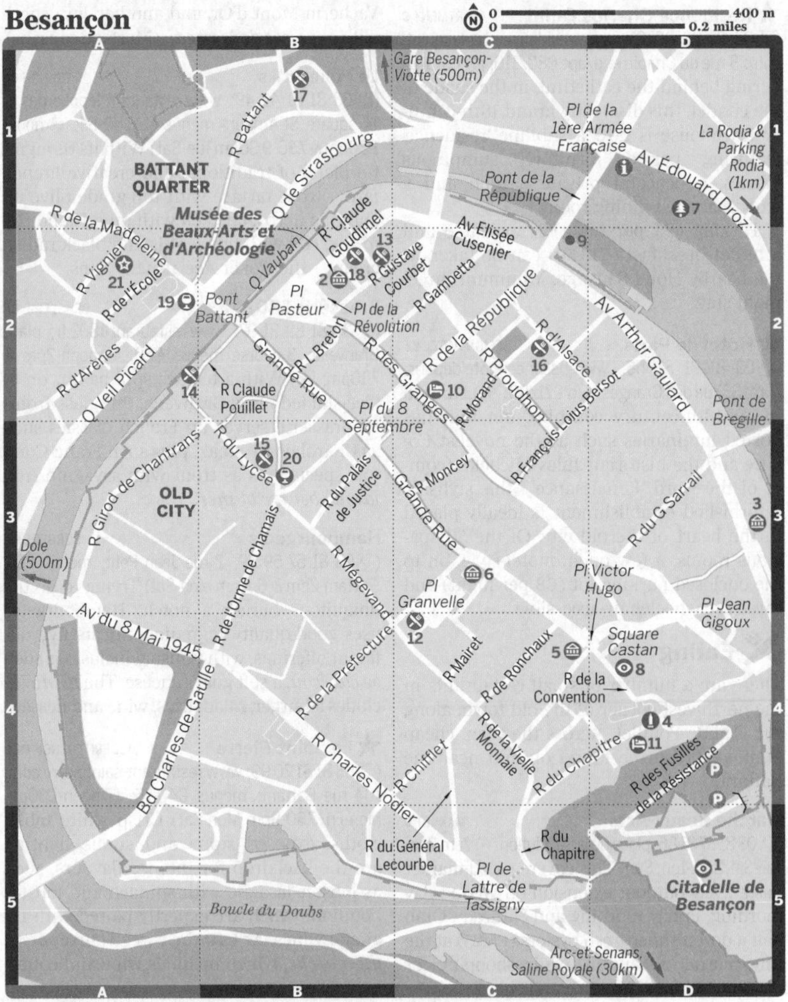

beat: coffee and food during the day, and aperitifs and conversation later on.

Brass'éliande PUB

(☎03 81 81 15 25; www.brasseliandecafe.fr; 1 place Jouffroy d'Abbans; ⏰11am-1am) Beer is the first order of business at this quayside pub with a handsome stone exterior and woodsy interior, complete with faux foliage. *Tartines* (open sandwiches) with *fromage blanc*, ham and other toppings (€4 to €6) provide the ballast for a broad range of draught and bottled beers, while pints are half price between 7pm and 9pm every day but Saturday.

☆ Entertainment

Les Passagers du Zinc LIVE MUSIC

(☎03 81 81 54 70; www.lespassagersduzinc.com; 5 rue Vignier; €5; ⏰4pm-1am Tue & Wed, to 2am Thu-Sat) You'd never guess that behind an anonymous, black-shuttered shopfront lies one of Besançon's best venues for live music. Opening only when a gig's on (usually between 9pm and midnight on Thursday, Friday or Saturday – it could be rock, hardcore, synth-pop or electro), it has battered leather sofas and a suitably grungy vibe.

Besançon

Top Sights
1 Citadelle de Besançon D5
2 Musée des Beaux-Arts et d'Archéologie B2

Sights
Cathédrale St-Jean .... (see 4)
3 FRAC Franche-Comté D3
4 Horloge Astronomique D4
5 Maison Natale de Victor Hugo C4
6 Musée du Temps C3
7 Parc Micaud D1
8 Porte Noire D4

Activities, Courses & Tours
9 Vedettes de Besançon C2

Sleeping
10 Hôtel de Paris C2
11 Residence Charles Quint D4

Eating
12 Brasserie 1802 .... C4
13 Hambourgeois B2
14 La Petite Adresse A2
15 Le Mascareigna B3
16 Le Poker d'As C2
17 Le Saint-Pierre B1
18 Marché Beaux-Arts B2

Drinking & Nightlife
19 Brass'éliande A2
20 Green Man B3

Entertainment
21 Les Passagers du Zinc A2

Information

Following a suspected arson attack on the Hôtel de Ville, the **tourist office** (☎ 03 81 80 92 55; www.besancon-tourisme.com; 2 place de la 1ère Armée Française, Parc Micaud; ⏲10am-12.30pm & 1.30-6pm Mon-Sat, 10am-1pm Sun Sep-Jun, 10am-6pm daily Jul & Aug; 📶) is now located at the northwestern end of the Parc Micaud.

Getting There & Around

BICYCLE

VéloCité (www.velocite.besancon.fr; per hr/day €1/4) Besançon's credit-card-operated automatic bike-rental system has 30 pick-up and drop-off sites across the city.

TRAIN

The train station, **Gare Besançon-Viotte** (Besançon Train Station; 2 av de la Paix; ⏲4.30am-12.15am), refurbished in 2014, is 800m north (up the hill) from northern edge of the city centre. Services include the following:

Arc-et-Senans €7.50, 25 minutes, 18 daily

Arbois €9.90, 40 minutes, 13 daily

Belfort €14.70 to €25.50, one hour, one or two per hour

Dijon €16.50 to €22, one hour, two or three per hour

Paris-Gare de Lyon €66 to €90, 2½ to 3¼ hours, 14 daily, including three direct

Connections to major cities are often cheaper and/or quicker from Gare TGV Besançon Franche-Comté, on the TGV line linking Dijon with Mulhouse. Situated 10km northwest of the centre, it's a 15-minute hop by hourly shuttle train from Gare Besançon-Viotte.

Buy tickets at the **Boutique SNCF** (2 ave de la Paix; ⏲7am-7.30pm Mon-Fri, to 7pm Sat, 10am-7pm Sun).

Southwest of Besançon

Southwest of Besançon is wine and cheese country, home of the Route des Vins du Jura, the golden elixir *vin jaune*, and sweet, nutty Comté cheese. It's also strongly identified with the scientific pioneer Louis Pasteur, who was born in Dole, raised in Arbois, and who taught in Besançon itself. It's a peaceful region of vineyards, rolling dairy farms, and old stone villages.

Arbois

The Route des Vins du Jura (Jura Wine Trail) is a delightful 80km of chardonnay, savagnin and pinot poir vineyards, time-worn stone villages and darkly wooded slopes. It begins in Arbois, a beautiful Jurassien, wine-producing village.

Sights & Activities

The 2.5km-long **Chemin des Vignes** walking trail and the 8km-long **Circuit des Vignes** mountain-bike route meander through the vines. Both trails (marked with orange signs) begin at the top of the steps next to Arbois' Château Pécauld; a booklet with details is available at the tourist office.

High above Arbois is tiny **Pupillin**, a cute yellow-brick village famous for its wine production. Some 10 different *caves* (wine cellars) are open to visitors.

MAREMAGNUM / GETTY IMAGES ©

1. Château de Menthon-St-Bernard (p496) 2. Hiking in Parc National des Écrins (p518) 3. Skiing, La Vallée Blanche (p484) 4. Paragliding over Lake Annecy (p492)

GUIZIOU FRANCK / HEMIS.FR / GETTY IMAGES ©

Mountain Highs

You're tearing down the Alps on your mountain bike, a deep blue sky overhead; you're hiking through flowery pastures tinkling with cowbells; you're slaloming on a glacier while it slowly slithers down the flanks of Mont Blanc – everywhere the scenery makes you feel glad to be alive!

Downhill Skiing

Glide to off-piste heaven on the legendary Vallée Blanche (p482), zigzag like an Olympic pro down black pistes in Val d'Isère (p503), or take your pick of Les Portes du Soleil's (p488) 650km of runs.

Magical Views

Take in breathtaking panoramas of shimmering Mont Blanc from the Aiguille du Midi (p479) or contemplate the ethereal loveliness of the Grand Balcon Sud trail (p482). Lake Annecy spreads out like a mirror before the fairest castle of them all: Château de Menthon-St-Bernard (p494).

Sky High

The sky is blue, the mountain air brisk and pure – just the day to go paragliding or hang-gliding above glistening Lake Annecy (p493).

Alpine Hiking

There's nothing quite like donning a backpack and hitting the trails in the Alps' national parks. The rugged wilderness of Parc National des Écrins (p518) and the snowcapped majesty of Parc National de la Vanoise (p506) will leave you awestruck.

On the Edge

For an adrenaline buzz, few adventures beat racing down Morzine's heart-pumping mountain-bike route, La Noire de Morzine (p488). Not enough of a challenge? Head to Chamonix (p479) to summit one of the area's spectacular 'four-thousanders'.

WORTH A TRIP

ROYAL SALTWORKS

Envisaged by its designer, Claude-Nicolas Ledoux, as the 'ideal city', the 18th-century **Saline Royale** (Royal Saltworks; ☎03 81 54 45 45; www.salineroyale.com; Grande Rue; adult/child €8.80/4.50; ⏰10am-noon & 2-5pm Nov-Mar, 9am-noon & 2-6pm Apr, May & Oct, 9am-6pm Jun & Sep, to 7pm Jul & Aug) is a showpiece of early Industrial Age town planning. Although his urban dream was never fully realised, Ledoux's beautifully symmetrical creation has been a Unesco World Heritage Site since 1982. Arc-et-Senans is 35km southwest of Besançon, on route D17. Three-star accommodation is available here (single €84, double €113).

Musée de la Vigne et du Vin du Jura MUSEUM
(☎03 84 66 40 45; www.arbois.fr; adult/child €3.50/free; ⏰10am-noon & 2-6pm Wed-Mon Mar-Oct, 2-6pm Wed-Mon Nov-Feb) The history of the precious yellow wine is told in this understated museum, housed in the turreted Château Pécauld. A short video, in French, includes footage of the tasting of *vin jaune* laid down before the Revolution.

Festivals & Events

La Percée du Vin Jaune WINE
(www.percee-du-vin-jaune.com; entry & 14 tasting tickets €14; ⏰Feb) The festival of the 'Opening of the Yellow Wine' brings a little sunshine to the Jura wine region in early February, when the vintage produced six years and three months earlier is cracked out. Villages take turns holding the two-day celebration, during which the new vintage is blessed and rated and *vin jaune* aficionados enjoy street tastings, cooking competitions, cellar visits and auctions.

Sleeping & Eating

Sampling the local wines, both in the glass and on the plate, is made easy by the region's abundance of excellent restaurants and brasseries. *Coq au vin jaune* with morel mushrooms is a local classic that goes spectacularly with a glass of Arbois Savagnin.

★Closerie les Capucines B&B €€
(☎03 84 66 17 38; www.closerielescapucines.com; 7 rue de Bourgogne, Arbois; d/q incl breakfast from €125/250; ⏰Feb-Dec; @ 📶 🏊) A 17th-century stone convent has been lovingly transformed into this boutique B&B, with five rooms remarkable for their pared-down elegance, a tree-shaded garden by the river and a plunge pool.

★Bistrot des Claquets FRENCH €
(☎03 84 66 04 19; www.bistrot-des-claquets.com; 33 rue de Faramand; 2-/3-course menus €13/16; ⏰7.30am-9pm Tue-Sat; 👪) Loved by *vignerons* (winegrowers) and other locals, this unpretentious, convivial little *bistrot* serves fantastic French country fare, but only at lunchtime! If you miss the *petit salé* (lentils with salt pork), *blanquettes de veau* (poached veal in white sauce) or whatever else is cooking that day, it's still worth popping in to sample the *vin jaune* and happy chatter.

La Balance Mets et Vins FRENCH €€
(☎03 84 37 45 00; www.labalance.fr; 47 rue de Courcelles, Arbois; weekday lunch menus €16.30-19.80, other menus €24-67; ⏰noon-2pm & 7-9pm Tue-Sat Feb-Jun & Sep–mid-Dec, Tue-Sun Jul & Aug; 🌿 👪) La Balance uses local, organic produce to produce signature dishes such as *coq au vin jaune* with morel mushrooms and crème brûlée with *vin jaune*. Accompanying wines can be had for €24 (*vin du Jura*) or €29 (*vin jaune*) and youngsters and teetotallers can enjoy three organic grape juices for €9. Reserve ahead on Saturday and holidays, especially from May to August.

Information

Arbois' **tourist office** (☎03 84 66 55 50; www.arbois.com; 17 rue de l'Hôtel de Ville, Arbois; ⏰10am-12.30 & 2-5.30pm Mon-Sat year-round, 10am-noon Sun May–late Jun, 10am-noon & 3-5.30pm Sun late Jun–mid-Sep) is located on the southern side of the main bridge over La Cuisance, in the centre of town.

Getting There & Away

Car This is excellent driving country, and having your own transport brings more villages and wineries into play.

Trains Run between Arbois and Besançon (€9.90, 40 minutes, one per hour between 6am and 8pm).

Poligny

POP 4158

The small town of Poligny, 60km southwest of Besançon, is the centre of the Jura's hugely important Comté cheese industry. Dozens of *fruitières* (cheese cooperatives) are open to the public.

Activities

Maison du Comté FOOD
(☎03 84 37 78 40; www.maison-du-comte.com; av de la Résistance; adult/child €5/3; ⏲2-5pm Tue-Sun Apr-Jun, Sep & Oct, 10am-noon & 2-5.30pm Jul & Aug) Learn how 450L of milk is transformed into a 40kg wheel of tangy Comté cheese and have a nibble at the Maison du Comté. Between two and nine guided tours leave per day, depending on the season, while tours for 10 or more can be arranged at any time of the year. Check the website for 'exceptional' opening times.

Sleeping & Eating

You can't leave the area without sampling the AOC-protected Comté. Made exclusively from the milk of Montbeliarde and Simmental cows in the Franche-Comté region, the real thing is aged for four, 18 or 24 months, in which time its sweet, nutty flavour intensifies remarkably. Luckily, there's an abundance of *fruitières* and factory shops in Poligny, eager for you to try their wares.

Hôtel de la Vallée Heureuse HOTEL €€
(☎03 84 37 12 13; www.hotelvalleeheureuse.com; rte de Genève; s/d/q €99/133/185;) In a beautifully converted 18th-century mill by a rushing stream, this serene country retreat has 11 large, tastefully decorated rooms and a restaurant (lunch menus €29, dinner menus €42 to €70) specialising in traditional French cuisine. Run by the welcoming Isabelle and Patrice, it's on the road from the centre of town towards Champagnole and Geneva (N5), 400m past the sign indicating that you're leaving Poligny.

Shopping

Caveau des Jacobins WINE
(☎03 84 37 14 58; 1 rue Hyacinthe Friant; ⏲10am-noon & 2.30-6.30pm Mon-Sat) This 13th-century Gothic church, abandoned by the Jacobins (Dominicans) after the Revolution and nabbed by the vignerons of Poligny in 1907, makes for an unforgettably atmospheric place to sample the wines of Jura. Gone is the religious statuary, and in its place are not only colossal barrels of savagnin, chardonnay and *vin jaune*, but also expositions of local art.

Information

Tourist Office (☎03 84 37 24 21; www.poligny-tourisme.com; 20 place des Déportés; ⏲10am-12.30pm & 1.30-5.30pm Mon-Fri, 10am-12.30pm & 2-5pm Sat) Has details on cheesemakers and wineries in the region, plus accommodation, *restauration*, and cultural events.

Getting There & Away

Poligny's train station is about 15 minutes' walk northwest of the centre. There are regular trains to Besançon (€11.90, 45 minutes, 13 per day) and Lons-le-Saunier (€6.40, 20 minutes, 16 per day).

Baume-les-Messieurs

POP 182

Nestled at the foot of towering, lushly wooded limestone cliffs and wedged between three glacial valleys, Baume-les-Messieurs is a picturesque village of honey-coloured

LIQUID GOLD

Château-Chalon, a quiet medieval village of yellow stone atop a rocky prominence in a sea of vineyards, is reputed to produce the best *vin jaune*.

Legend has it that *vin jaune* (yellow wine) was invented when a winemaker came across a forgotten barrel, six years and three months after he'd filled it, and discovered that its contents had been miraculously transformed into gold-coloured wine.

A long, undisrupted fermentation process gives Jura's signature wine its unique characteristics. Savagnin grapes are harvested late and their sugar-saturated juice left to ferment for a minimum of six years and three months in oak barrels. A thin layer of yeast forms over the wine, preventing oxidisation; there are no top-ups to compensate for wine that evaporates (known as *la part des anges*, 'the angels' share'). In the end, 100L of grape juice ferments down to just 62L of *vin jaune* (lucky angels!) which is then bottled in a special 0.62L bottle called a *clavelin*.

Vin jaune is renowned for ageing extremely well, with prime vintages easily keeping for more than a century. A 1774 vintage was a cool 220 years old when sipped by an awestruck committee of experts in 1994.

Visit www.jura-tourism.com to plan your sojourn in the land of *vin jaune*.

ROUTE PASTEUR

The Route Pasteur tracks significant landmarks in the life of pioneering biochemist Louis Pasteur (1822-95), who developed the first rabies vaccine and, of course, pasteurisation, meandering through very pleasant wine and dairy country as it does so. It begins in the handsome medieval city of **Dole**, his birthplace and former capital of Franche-Comté, 20km west of Arc-et-Senans along the D472. A scenic stroll along the **Canal des Tanneurs** brings you to his childhood home, which now houses the **Musée Pasteur** (La Maison de Natale Pasteur; ☎03 84 72 20 61; www.musee-pasteur.com; 43 rue Pasteur, Dole; adult/child €5/free; ⏲2-6pm Feb-Apr, Oct & Nov, 9.30am-12.30pm & 2-6pm May-Sep), an atmospheric museum whose exhibits include his cot, first drawings and university cap and gown.

From here, the route wends 47km southeast through Franche-Comté, taking in smaller sites such as Salins-les-Bains and the village of Aiglepierre, and ending, happily, in the major wine-producing town of Arbois, 35km southeast of Dole, where Louis Pasteur's family settled in 1827. His laboratory and workshops here can be seen at the **Maison de Louis Pasteur** (☎03 84 66 11 72; www.terredelouispasteur.fr; 83 rue de Courcelles, Arbois; adult/child €6.50/4; ⏲2-6pm Feb-Apr, Oct & Nov, 9.30am-12.30pm & 2-6pm May-Sep), still decorated with original 19th-century fixtures and fittings.

stone houses and red-tiled rooftops. It's located 20km south of Poligny.

Sights

Grottes de Baume CAVE

(Baume Caves; ☎03 84 48 23 02; www.baumelesmessieurs.fr; adult/child €8/4; ⏲guided tours 10.30am-12.30pm & 1.30-5pm, 6pm or 7pm Apr-Sep, no midday closure Jul & Aug) About 2km south of Baume-les-Messieurs, the 30-million-year-old Grottes de Baume feature some impressive stalagmites and stalactites, arrayed in more than a kilometre of accessible galleries. If you plan on visiting the Abbaye Impériale too, a combined ticket costs €10/5 per adult/child.

Abbaye Impériale MONASTERY

(Imperial Abbey; www.baumelesmessieurs.fr; adult/child €6/4; ⏲guided tours Mar-Sep) Baume-les-Messieurs' abandoned Benedictine Abbaye Impériale has an exquisite polychrome Flemish altarpiece dating from the 16th century (the time when the abbey, which grew from a simple 7th-century monastic cell, was at its apogee). Combined tickets to the Grottes de Baume and the abbey cost €10/5 per adult/child.

Sleeping & Eating

Le Grand Jardin B&B €

(☎03 84 44 68 37; www.legrandjardin.fr; 6 place Guillaume de Poupet; d incl breakfast €68-99; ⏲closed Tue & Wed Sep-Jun) This delightful, family-run *chambre d'hôte,* opposite the abbey, has three sunny, wood-floored rooms in a 16th-century house backed by carefully tended gardens. French and Franc-Comtoise dishes such as slow-cooked pork fillet with Comtoise polenta feature on the restaurant menu (*menus* €25 to €45).

Getting There & Away

Baume-les-Messieurs isn't on the train line from Besançon to Lons-le-Saunier, but there are occasional buses from Voiteur, which is on it (see www.jurago.fr).

Belfort

POP 50,196

Once part of Alsace's Haut-Rhin *département,* Belfort put up 229 days of tenacious resistance to the Prussian siege of 1870–71, thanks to which it managed to remain French after the rest of Alsace was annexed to Germany. Today, the city is neither Alsatian nor Jurassien but rather its own *territoire* (territory), known for its Vauban-built **Citadelle** and its role in producing super-speedy TGV trains.

Belfort makes a convenient stopover on the way from Alsace to Paris, Burgundy or the Alps.

Sights

Musée de l'Aventure Peugeot MUSEUM

(☎03 81 99 42 03; www.museepeugeot.com; Carrefour de l'Europe, Sochaux; adult/child €8.50/4.50; ⏲10am-6pm) Gleaming old-timers, concept cars and thumb-size miniatures – it's Peugeots *à gogo* at this automobile museum, 18km south of Belfort (towards Besançon) in So-

chaux. Reserve ahead for a weekday tour of the ultramodern Peugeot factory, one of Europe's largest car plants (adult/child €18/12, no children younger than 12).

Festivals & Events

★ Les Eurockéennes MUSIC
(www.eurockeennes.fr; Jul) A huge, three-day open-air alternative rock festival held on the first weekend in July. Three nights of thoughtfully curated music, plus camping, will set you back only €115.

Sleeping & Eating

Don't leave Belfort without biting into a *Belflore,* a scrumptious almond-flavoured pastry filled with raspberries and topped with hazelnuts.

Hôtel Vauban HOTEL €
(03 84 21 59 37; www.hotel-vauban.com; 4 rue du Magasin; s/d/tr €70/75/88, breakfast €8.50;) This friendly, great-value hotel, built as a house in 1902, has 14 midsized en-suite rooms decorated in crisp, sometimes whimsical modern styles. There are also colourful oil paintings (by the owner's husband, Guy) to admire, and a lovely back garden, complete with koi pond.

Situated one long block northeast, along the river, from the tourist office.

Grand Hôtel du Tonneau d'Or HISTORIC HOTEL €€
(03 84 58 57 56; www.tonneaudor.fr; 1 rue du Général Reiset; d/tr €105/133;) A grand belle époque hotel right in the city centre, the 'Golden Barrel' combines its original Corinthian columns, coffered ceilings and a sweeping central staircase with 52 large, modern rooms. Rates drop 25% from Friday to Sunday.

Information

Tourist Office (03 84 55 90 90; www.belfort-tourisme.com; 2bis rue Clémenceau; 9am-12.30pm & 2-6pm Mon-Sat year-round, plus 10am-1pm Sun Jul & Aug) Has city, cycling and hiking maps, plus details on cultural activities and local producers.

Getting There & Away

Belfort's train station (6 av Wilson) has direct links to Besançon (€17.40, 1¼ hours, up to three per hour), and direct and indirect TGVs and TERs to Paris-Gare de Lyon (from €79, 2½ to four hours, one or two every hour).

Belfort-Montbéliard TGV station, 12km southeast of the city centre, is a stop on the LGV Rhin-Rhône service linking Marseille with Strasbourg and Frankfurt.

Parc Naturel Régional du Haut-Jura

To experience the Jura in all of its upland beauty, head to the Haut-Jura Regional Park, whose 1780 sq km – in the *départements* of Ain, Doubs and Jura – stretch from Chapelle-des-Bois southward almost to the western tip of Lake Geneva. The park's prime sports hub, in both winter (skiing) and summer, is **Les Rousses**.

Col de la Faucille (1323m; open year-round), a serpentine 13km east of Lajoux and 29km north of Geneva Airport, has incredible views across Lake Geneva to the snowy Alps beyond.

Sights & Activities

Maison du Parc du Haut-Jura MUSEUM
(03 84 34 12 30; www.parc-haut-jura.fr; 29 Qua le Village, Lajoux; adult/child €5/3; 9am-12.30pm & 1.30-6pm Tue-Sun Jun & school holidays, Tue-Fri other times) The park's visitor centre has interactive, tactile exhibits on the Jura's flora and fauna that kids will love, as well as temporary displays, literature and regional products. It's in Lajoux, 19km east of the park's largest town, St-Claude.

Sleeping

There are seven or eight hotels in Les Rousses, mainly two- and three-star. Mijoux and

DON'T MISS

RONCHAMP

Le Corbusier designed the surreal modernist **Chapelle de Notre-Dame du Haut** (03 84 20 65 13; www.colline-notredameduhaut.com; rue de la Chapelle; adult/child €8/4; 9am-7pm Apr-Oct, 10am-5pm Nov-Mar) on this age-old site of Marian pilgrimage, 22km northwest of Belfort. With a sweeping concrete roof, dazzling stained-glass windows and plastic features, it's considered a masterpiece of mid-20th-century architecture. There's also a convent and a visitor centre (La Porterie) set into the hillside, both designed by Renzo Piano.

St-Claude are two other centres with multiple options, including *chambres d'hôte.*

Le Clos d'Estelle B&B €
(☎03 84 42 01 29; www.leclosdestelle.com; 1 La Marcantine, Charchilla; d/q incl breakfast €85/140; @) Surrounded by fields and sheep, Christine and Jean-Pierre warmly welcome guests to four very spacious, wood-built *chambres d'hôte* (B&B) in their mid-19th-century farmhouse. Situated in Charchilla (shar-*shiy*-a), 200m down the hill behind the church.

La Mainaz CHALET €€
(☎04 50 41 31 10; www.la-mainaz.com; Col de la Faucille; d/q from €150/285;) This charming high-end chalet, run by the same family since 1945, has spectacular panoramas of Lake Geneva and Mont Blanc, 21 rooms and excellent French and regional cuisine (*menus* €20 to €50). Situated 800m towards Geneva from Col de la Faucille.

Eating

Soufflé au Comté, Potée Franc-Comtoise (salt pork and Morteau sausage simmered with vegetables) and other highlights of Jurassien cuisine will never taste as good as they do at a restaurant in the High Jura, after a stiff walk in the woods.

Les Louvières INTERNATIONAL €€
(☎03 84 42 09 24; www.leslouvieres.fr; Pratz; 2/3-course menus €40/48; ⊙noon-2pm Wed-Sun, 7.30-9pm Wed-Sat) The 'wolf's lair' is both elegant and creatively modern, with gorgeous Jura views and delicious, *gastronomique* cuisine. Chef Philippe Vaufrey is fond of adding coriander, ginger, lychees and other Asian touches to distinguish his use of prime local ingredients.

Reserve ahead and find the lair between Pratz (pronounced 'prah') and Moirans, 1.8km along a one-lane road from the D470 (follow the signs).

Information

Tourist Office (Station des Rousses; ☎03 84 60 02 55; www.lesrousses.com; 495 rue Pasteur, Les Rousses; ⊙hours vary, see website for details) The go-to source for information on culture, activities and accommodation in the park.

Getting There & Away

Public transport is scant in the High Jura. The local bus network, **Jurago** (www.jurago.fr), connects Lons-le-Saunier with St-Claude, then with smaller destinations within the park. It's a flat €2 per journey.

Métabief & Around

POP 1089 / ELEV 1000M

Métabief vies with Les Rousses for the honour of Jura's leading cross-country ski resort. Winter and summer lifts take you almost to the top of Mont d'Or (1463m), the area's highest peak, where a fantastic 180-degree panorama stretches over the foggy Swiss plain to Lake Geneva (Lac Léman) and all the way from the Matterhorn to Mont Blanc.

Sights & Activities

Château de Joux CASTLE
(☎03 81 69 47 95; www.chateaudejoux.com; La Cluse-et-Mijoux; adult/child €7.50/4.20; ⊙10am-noon & 2-4.30pm Apr-Jun & Sep-Nov, 10am-5.30pm Jul & Aug) Clinging to a picturesque limestone

DON'T MISS

HOT BOX & JÉSUS

It's hot, it's soft and it's packed in a box. Vacherin Mont d'Or is the only French cheese to be eaten with a spoon – hot. Made between 15 August and 15 March with *lait cru* (unpasteurised milk), it derives its unique nutty taste from the spruce bark in which it's wrapped. Connoisseurs top the soft-crusted cheese with chopped onions, garlic and white wine, wrap it in aluminium foil and bake it for 45 minutes to create a *boîte chaude* (hot box). Only 11 factories in the Jura are licensed to produce Vacherin Mont d'Or.

Mouthe, 15km south of Métabief Mont d'Or, is the mother of *liqueur de sapin* (fir-tree liqueur). *Glace de sapin* (fir-tree ice cream) also comes from Mont d'Or, known as the North Pole of France due to its seasonal subzero temperatures (record low: -38°C). Sampling either is rather like ingesting a Christmas tree. Then there's *Jésus* – a small, fat version of *saucisse de Morteau* (Morteau sausage), easily identified by the wooden peg on its end, attached after the sausage is smoked with pinewood sawdust in a traditional *tuyé* (mountain hut).

outcrop, Château de Joux, 10km north of Métabief, used to guard the route between Switzerland and France. Today it houses France's most impressive arms museum and a 147m-deep well. Guided tours are gripping, full of anecdotes and stories, and available in English (ring ahead). In summer, torch-lit night-time tours are organised for extra spookiness.

Parc Polaire WILDLIFE RESERVE

(☎03 81 69 20 20; www.parcpolaire.com; Cernois Veuillet et les Fo, Chaux-Neuve; adult/child €9/7.50; ⏲10am-5.30pm late Dec-Oct, to 6.30pm in summer holidays) The closest you'll get to the North Pole in these parts is the Christmassy Parc Polaire in Chaux-Neuve, where the friendly team will introduce you to huskies, reindeer and some mighty hairy yak, on a 1½-hour guided tour.

Sleeping

Hôtel Étoile des Neiges HOTEL €€

(☎03 81 49 11 21; www.hoteletoiledesneiges.fr; 4 rue du Village; d/f €60/108;) Family-run Hôtel Étoile des Neiges has bright, well-kept rooms, including great mezzanine family rooms. There's an indoor pool, a sauna, a tiny fitness centre and a canteen-style restaurant.

Getting There & Away

Métabief is 58km east of Arbois and 75km south-east of Besançon, on the main road to Lausanne (Switzerland). There is no train station, but SNCF runs an *autocar* (bus) service to Frasne, which is on the TGV line from Lausanne to Paris.

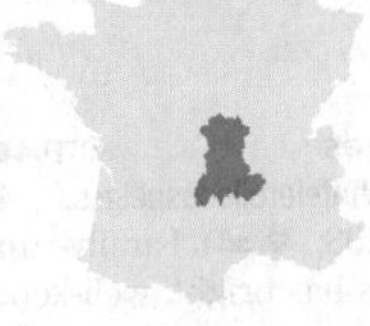

Auvergne

Includes ➡

Best Places to Eat

- ➡ L'Air 2 Rien (p543)
- ➡ Auberge de la Forge (p550)
- ➡ Le Flamboyant (p538)
- ➡ Le Chaudron (p550)
- ➡ La Golmotte (p547)
- ➡ Le Sisisi (p536)

Best Places to Sleep

- ➡ Le Diapason (p542)
- ➡ Alta Terra (p548)
- ➡ Hôtel Notre Dame (p545)
- ➡ Auberge de la Petite Ferme (p548)
- ➡ L'Epicurium (p554)

Why Go?

The land-locked Auvergne is a mosaic of volcanic cones, hilltop villages and bucolic farmland, at the centre of France's Massif Central mountain range. Two great green lungs of protected land extend across this sparsely populated region: to the west, the Parc Naturel Régional des Volcans d'Auvergne is puckered with slumbering volcanoes and winter sports hubs; to the east lies the wilder, wooded Parc Naturel Régional Livradois-Forez. Tumbling between the two is the Allier River, which bisects the colourful Pays d'Issoire and carves out rafting country in the Gorges de l'Allier. East of here, petrified lava plumes tower over pilgrimage town Le Puy-en-Velay.

Cultural splendours range from Romanesque churches to treasured regional cuisine, including five Appellation d'Origine Protégée (AOP) cheeses, world-famous Le Puy lentils, and Salers beef. Mirroring the region's rough charisma, meals are hearty, simple and utterly free of pretension – you won't be able to resist digging in.

When to Go

Clermont-Ferrand

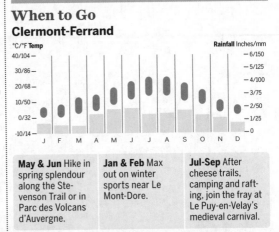

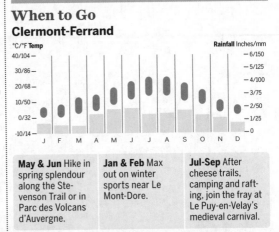

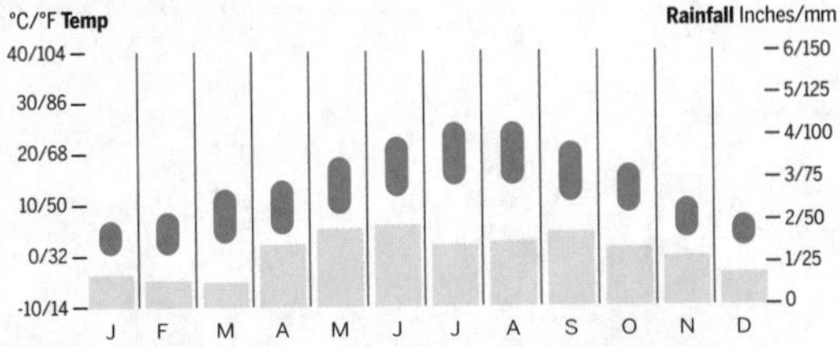

May & Jun Hike in spring splendour along the Stevenson Trail or in Parc des Volcans d'Auvergne.

Jan & Feb Max out on winter sports near Le Mont-Dore.

Jul-Sep After cheese trails, camping and rafting, join the fray at Le Puy-en-Velay's medieval carnival.

Auvergne Highlights

1 **Panoramique des Dômes** (p544) Trundling up to volcanic views on a cog railway

2 **Clermont-Ferrand** (p537) Admiring fountains, black stone architecture and cosmopolitan nightlife

3 **Chapelle St-Michel d'Aiguilhe** (p551) Panting up to remarkable views at this cave chapel near Le Puy-en-Velay

4 **Vichy** (p538) Sliding into thermal waters after a day belle-époque buildings

5 **Pays d'Issoire** (p542) Overloading your senses with churches and gastronomy

6 **Cheese Trail** (p547) Driving between dairy farms to buy cheese right at the source

7 **Le Mont-Dore** (p546) Pounding pistes or hiking hills around this grand spa town

8 **Musée de la Coutellerie** (p550) Watching artisans at work in this knife-making capital

9 **Gorges de l'Allier** (p556) Rafting between jewel-like villages

10 **Riom** (p537) Exploring the historic nucleus of a former regional capital

CLERMONT-FERRAND

POP 141,500

Surrounded by snoozing ancient volcanoes, the skyline of Clermont-Ferrand bears a strong imprint of geological drama. Its twin-turreted cathedral, dozens of fountains and treasury of 18th-century mansions are primarily constructed from black volcanic stone, giving a smouldering air to the old town.

Beyond its cobblestoned centre, the Auvergne's capital is an industrial powerhouse, home to the Michelin empire. Nonetheless, its blend of Gothic buildings and vibrant bars, plus the growing band of restaurants serving modernised Auvergnat cuisine, make Clermont-Ferrand an utterly refreshing city break and a great base for day trips into the wilds of the Parc Naturel Régional des Volcans d'Auvergne.

Sights

Visitors ambling through Clermont-Ferrand's shaded laneways won't fail to notice the city's more than 40 fountains, with cherubs and animals sculpted in lava stone. For a self-guided watery walking tour, you can download a free app (iOS/Android); search for 'Clermont Fontaines' (French) or 'Clermont Fountains' (English).

Clermont-Ferrand

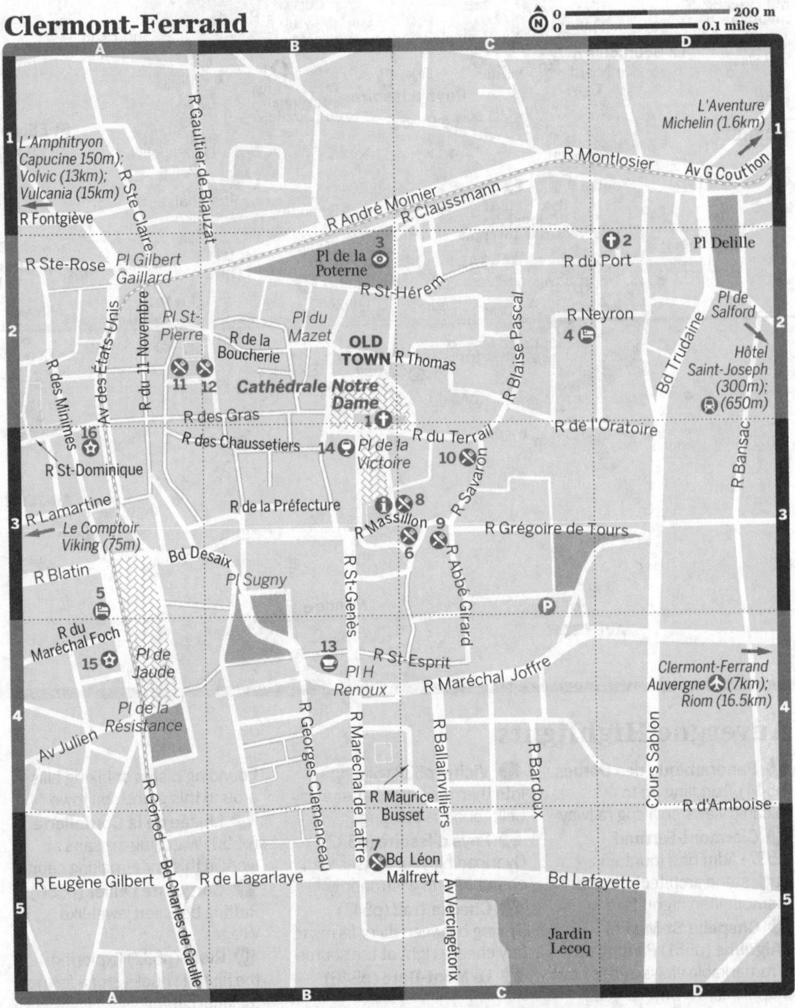

★ Cathédrale Notre Dame CATHEDRAL
(place de la Victoire; tower €2; ⏲7.30am-noon & 2-6pm Mon-Sat, 9.30am-noon & 3-7.30pm Sun) Clermont-Ferrand's skyline broods with dark volcanic stone, but most impressive is Cathédrale Notre-Dame, whose 108m spires pierce the sky like blackened spears. Its façade, with snarling gargoyles and Gothic tracery, was constructed between the 13th and 19th centuries. Within, sunlight glancing through the 20th-century stained-glass windows dapples its bare stone walls with colour. For fantastic views east to Thiers and west to Puy de Dôme, climb up **Tour de la Bayette** (summer only).

Fontaine d'Amboise FOUNTAIN
(place de la Poterne) Two blocks north of the cathedral, this early-16th-century fountain is the focal point of a pretty park with views towards Puy de Dôme.

Basilique Notre Dame du Port CHURCH
(rue du Port; ⏲8am-noon & 2-6pm Mon-Sat, 9am-noon & 3-8pm Sun) This architectural gem has all the key elements of a Romanesque church: semi-circular arches, bulky silhouette and a broad headpiece. But its distinctive decorations set it apart, and strengthened the case for granting it Unesco World Heritage status back in 1998. Floral and geometric patterns of black volcanic stone are smoothly set in the church's peachy sandstone. Its exterior playfully combines neoclassical columns, terracotta tiles and medieval reliefs. The church's exterior is best admired from the *belvédère* (follow signs across the street).

L'Aventure Michelin MUSEUM
(www.laventuremichelin.com; 32 rue du Clos Four; adult/child €9.50/5.50, audioguide €2; ⏲10am-6pm Tue-Sun Sep-Dec & Feb-Jun, 10am-7pm daily Jul & Aug; 👪) Next door to Clermont's mammoth Michelin factory lies an engaging museum dedicated to this locally grown rubber empire, including its impact on the region and contribution to aviation, rail, maps, restaurant guides and GPS technology. Entertaining for both adults and kids, it's got some great hands-on interactive exhibits and advertising retrospectives. Allow at least a couple of hours; last entry is 90 minutes before closing. Take Tram A to Stade Marcel Michelin.

Clermont-Ferrand

Top Sights
1 Cathédrale Notre Dame B2

Sights
2 Basilique Notre Dame du Port D2
3 Fontaine d'Amboise B2

Sleeping
4 5 Chambres en Ville C2
5 Hôtel Le Lion A3

Eating
6 Avenue C3
7 Bougnat Burger B5
8 La Table au Plafond C3
9 Le Sisisi C3
10 Les Arcandiers C3
11 Marché St-Pierre A2
12 Myrtille B2

Drinking & Nightlife
13 Australian Coffee House B4
14 Café Pascal B3

Entertainment
15 Ciné Capitole A4
16 Cinéma Les Ambiances A3

Sleeping

Hôtel Saint-Joseph HOTEL €
(☎04 73 92 69 71; www.hotelsaintjoseph.fr; 10 rue de Maringues; s/d/tr/f €41/53/77/79; @📶) The double-glazed rooms at this small hotel near the Friday morning St-Joseph market offer the best budget value in Clermont.

★ 5 Chambres en Ville B&B €€
(☎07 81 16 60 95; www.5-chambresenville.com; 8 rue Neyron; r incl breakfast €90-130; P❄📶) This classy B&B offers pristine, design-conscious rooms in a convenient central location. All five units come with ample beds, quality linens, dependable wi-fi and plenty of natural light; the more expensive pair on the top floor offer romantic features, especially the 'zen' room with its recessed, candlelit, slate-walled bath-tub. Parking costs €9.

Hôtel Le Lion HOTEL €€
(☎04 73 17 60 80; www.hotel-le-lion-clermont.fr; 16 place de Jaude; s/d/f from €91/101/141; ❄📶) Rooms with fresh, monochrome decor, coffee makers and comfy beds fill this design-conscious three-star on Clermont-Ferrand's grandest square. Downstairs, the brasserie spilling onto the square is good for a drink. Ask about discounted parking near the hotel (€9.50 per night).

Eating

Place de Jaude and the area north around rue St-Dominique are filled with inexpensive eateries. Cafe terraces ring place de la Victoire just south of the cathedral; Clermont's

covered market (www.marche-saint-pierre.com; place St-Pierre; ⏲7am-7.30pm Mon-Sat) is a few blocks northwest.

Le Sisisi BISTRO €

(☎04 73 14 04 28; www.lesisisi.com; 14 rue Massillon; mains €17-19, lunch menu €14.80; ⏲noon-1.30pm Tue-Fri, 8-10pm Tue-Sat) Looking for gastronomic excellence without white tablecloths and sniffy waiters? Inventive dishes are served in a well-worn bistro backdrop at this restaurant just off Clermont's cathedral square. Tuck into mains such as roast chicken and tagliatelle strewn with mushrooms, honey-roasted pork with truffled potatoes, or delectable deserts including *mille-feuille* of salted caramel and cocoa nibs.

Bougnat Burger BURGERS €

(☎07 60 12 00 63; www.bougnatburger.fr; 10 bd Léon Malfreyt; mains €11; ⏲noon-2pm & 7-10pm Mon-Sat) Plump organic burgers are served with occasional Auvergnat flourishes, such as Bleu d'Auvergne cheese dipping sauce, at this deservedly busy diner. Wash it down with local microbrews including Le Plan B.

Myrtille CAFE €

(☎04 73 39 09 97; www.cafemyrtille.com; 4 petite rue Saint Pierre; menus €15; ⏲9am-6pm Tue-Sat; 🌱) This minimalist cafe facing Clermont-Ferrand's covered market specialises in all things organic, whipping up seasonal soups, roasted veggie dishes and a pleasing array of cakes (some vegan or gluten-free). Whether you're nibbling their fresh apple fondant over a green tea or staying for lunch, it's a calming space to escape the market bustle.

Les Arcandiers BISTRO €

(☎04 73 92 21 50; 10 place du Terrail; mains €11; ⏲noon-2pm & 6.30-10pm Wed-Sat) Illuminated globes and model planes hang from vaulted ceilings, and jazz album covers plaster the walls at this nostalgically decorated bistro. Les Arcandiers doubles as a relaxing lunch spot and an alluring evening hangout for glass after glass of local wine.

La Table au Plafond AUVERGNAT, TAPAS €€

(☎09 83 01 57 15; http://latableauplafond.wix.com; 7 place de la Victoire; menus from €21; ⏲noon-2pm & 7-10pm Tue-Sat) Stop for a lunch special or evening tapas-style nibbles at this innovative spot and you'll be rewarded with fish seared to perfection, thoughtfully curated platters of Auvergnat cheeses and dessert plates speckled with lemon curd, meringues and nuggets of chocolate. And yes – look up and you'll see the table on the ceiling after which this free-spirited little restaurant is named.

Avenue MODERN FRENCH €€

(☎04 73 90 44 64; www.restaurant-avenue.fr; 10 rue Massillon; lunch menu €15, mains €18-22; ⏲noon-2pm & 7.30-9.30pm Tue-Sat) The ever-changing menu at this chic restaurant is a roll-call of inventive ensembles like goat's-cheese crème brûlée, marmalade-roasted veal, and pineapple with rum and hazelnut. There's always a *plat du jour* (€9.50) at lunchtime.

L'Amphitryon Capucine GASTRONOMIC €€€

(☎04 73 31 38 39; www.amphitryoncapucine.com; 50 rue Fontgiève; lunch menus €21, dinner menus €31-85; ⏲noon-1.30pm & 7.30-9.30pm Tue-Sat) Wear your spiffiest suit for this sophisticated restaurant, 800m northwest of the cathedral. Its multicourse *menus* overflow with seasonal dishes such as bream fragranced with yuzu. The three-course lunch menu is the best bargain, but foodies might want to plump for the decadent evening *menu gourmand*.

AUVERGNE MOVIE MAGIC

With its youthful population and open-minded spirit, it's no surprise that Clermont-Ferrand is a city of film fanatics. One of the world's most respected short film festivals, the **Festival International du Court Métrage** (www.clermont-filmfest.com; ⏲Feb), unfolds here each year, with competitions for international and domestic shorts. Check schedules on the festival website or enquire at the tourist office, just make sure you book accommodation well in advance.

Outside film-festival season, join Clermont-Ferrand's lovers of the silver screen at **Ciné Capitole** (www.cine-capitole.fr; 32 place de Jaude) or **Cinéma Les Ambiances.** (www.cinema-les-ambiances.fr; 7 rue St-Dominique)

Drinking & Nightlife

Australian Coffee House COFFEE

(☎04 63 22 63 49; 35 rue Saint-Esprit; ⏲8am-7pm Tue-Sat) We know, you're travelling *à la française*, but this Aussie-inspired coffee place pours the best brews in Clermont-Ferrand (from €3). The interior is bare with schoolroom seating, so let the flat whites do the talking. Homemade cakes, including the moist banana cake with toffee frosting, are served in generous wedges.

Le Comptoir Viking BAR
(www.lecomptoirviking.fr/clermont.html; 38 rue Lamartine; 5pm-1am Tue-Sat) While there are no longboats or horned helmets, this wood-walled rock bar is one of the friendliest bars in town, with an energising heavy-metal soundtrack. Check ahead on their Facebook page for themed nights and sports screenings, or just wriggle into your most skull-adorned T-shirt and join in.

Café Pascal BAR
(http://cafepascal.com; 4 place de la Victoire; 8.30am-1.30am) This late-opening sport and beer bar is the liveliest haunt on cathedral square, attracting a raucous crowd of locals to its mixed soundtrack of rock 'n' roll and Irish folk. Chug a beer or better yet, a beer cocktail; or toast Clermont-Ferrand's most famous polymath with a 'Sexy Pascal' cocktail (€7.50) of peach and passionfruit.

Information

Tourist Office (04 73 98 65 00; www.clermont-fd.com; place de la Victoire; 9am-7pm daily Jul & Aug, 9am-6pm Mon-Fri, 10am-1pm & 2-6pm Sat & Sun rest of year) Opposite the cathedral, chock full of city maps and free literature.

Getting There & Away

AIR

Clermont-Ferrand Auvergne airport (www.clermont-aeroport.com), 6km east of the city centre, is an Air France hub. Domestic destinations include Paris, Nice and Ajaccio; international flights go to Porto and Amsterdam.

TRAIN

Clermont is the region's main rail and long-distance bus hub. You can buy tickets at the **boutique SNCF** (premium rate 08 92 35 35 35; 43 rue du 11 Novembre; 9am-6pm Mon-Fri, 10am-1pm & 2-5.50pm Sat) in the city centre. Long-haul destinations:

Le Mont-Dore €14.50, 1¾ hours, two direct SNCF buses daily

Le Puy-en-Velay €27.20, 2¼ hours, three or four daily (direct or via St-Étienne)

Lyon €35.50, 2½ hours, more than eight daily

Nîmes €45, 4½-5 hours, three direct trains daily (more via Lyon)

Paris €61, 3½ hours, six to 10 daily to Bercy (direct) and Gare de Lyon (via Lyon)

Frequent, direct short-hauls also run to the following:

Riom €3.50, 10 minutes

Thiers €9.50, 45 minutes

Vichy €10.90, 30 minutes

Volvic €4.80, 25 minutes

> **CENT SAVERS**
>
> Planning to visit L'Aventure Michelin, take a ride on the Panoramique des Dômes, and check out one of Clermont-Ferrand's city art or science museums? Save money by grabbing the 72-hour **Clermont Pass** (€18), available at the tourist office, which grants access to all three, and throws in a guided city tour and public transport. If you prefer to gallery-hop, there's a **museum pass** (€9) giving entry to Clermont-Ferrand's three major museums over the space of a month.

Getting Around

TO/FROM THE AIRPORT

Bus 20 travels to/from the airport several times daily Monday to Saturday (€1.50); a **taxi** (04 73 19 53 53; www.allotaxiradio-clermontferrand.fr) costs between €20 and €30.

BICYCLE

C.vélo (04 73 92 65 08; www.c-velo.fr; per day €5) hires bikes at more than 20 self-service stations around town, including the train station and place de Jaude.

BUS & TRAM

Clermont's public-transport system is handled by **T2C** (www.t2c.fr; single ticket/24hr pass/carnet of 10 €1.50/4.60/12.60). Buses link the city and station, while tram A connects place de Jaude with Montferrand (every eight minutes between 9am and 6pm).

AROUND CLERMONT-FERRAND

Riom

POP 18,675

Zooming along the A89 road between Clermont-Ferrand and Vichy, you risk missing out on an elegant former capital of the Auvergne, the historic town of Riom. A pilgrimage stop during the Middle Ages thanks to relics of Riom-born St Amable, the town grew into an administrative capital and steadily acquired *hôtels particuliers* during the Renaissance and into the 18th century.

The fortifications enclosing Riom were demolished in the 18th century to allow

FAST FACTS

Area 26,013 sq km

Local industry Dairy farming, cutlery

Signature drink Verveine

expansion. Still, the town centre retains a wistful air: 17th-century fountains carved from dark volcanic stone still trickle, statues of saints gaze beatifically down from eaves, and the skyline is a pleasing assortment of pointed church roofs and Riom's unmistakeable belltower.

Sights

★Musée Mandet ART MUSEUM
(14 rue de l'Hôtel de Ville; adult/child €3/free, Wed free; ⏲10am-noon & 2-5.30pm Tue-Sun, to 6pm Jul & Aug) Since 1866, this fabulous museum has been showcasing art from medieval European statues to cutting-edge modern graphics. Room 4 is a highlight for its sculptures from Renaissance to present day, while room 9's recreations of 18th-century salons create a wonderfully immersive experience.

Tour de l'Horloge CLOCK TOWER
(rue de l'Horloge; adult/child €1/free, Wed free; ⏲10am-noon & 2-5pm Tue-Sun, to 6pm daily Jul & Aug) This Renaissance belfry hosts a few simple displays on the town's history and development, but the real pleasure is climbing its 128 stairs to panoramic views of Riom's dark volcanic-stone houses and rippling hills.

Église Notre Dame du Marthuret CHURCH
(rue du Commerce; ⏲9am-6pm) Peer into this shadowy late-14th-century church to see Riom's most prized relics. The *Vierge Noire* (Black Madonna) dates to the 13th or 14th century, while the Vierge à l'Oiseau statue, depicting the Virgin and Child accompanied by a fluttering bird, is a copy of the 14th-century original (which is kept under lock and key). The latter icon was inspired by legends that young Jesus modelled birds in clay and brought them to life.

Musée Régional d'Auvergne MUSEUM
(☎0473381731; www.ville-riom.fr/Musee-regional-d-Auvergne; 10bis rue Delille; adult/child €3/free; ⏲guided tours 2.30pm & 4pm Tue-Sun, closed mid-Nov–mid-May) Customs and traditions of life in the Auvergne are explored at this excellent museum (visitable by guided tour only).

Sleeping & Eating

Hotel Pacifique HOTEL €
(☎04 73 38 15 65; www.hotel-lepacifique-riom.com; 52 av de Paris; s/d/tr/q €59/67/85/98; P ᯤ) This welcoming three-star has bold, colourful rooms and cosy common areas decorated with velvet armchairs and chintzy relics of Auvergne's past. With Riom's historic centre packed with paid parking, Hotel Pacifique's out-of-town location, a 15-minute walk north, is a boon if you're driving.

L'Antre 2 AUVERGNAT €
(☎04 73 63 11 06; www.lantre2.fr; 15 rue du Marthuret; mains 15; ⏲noon-2pm & 7-10pm Tue-Sun) This historic grocer's shop has been transformed into an understated eatery where you can happily binge on Auvergnat belly-busters like fondue of St-Nectaire cheese, steaks with beer and honey sauce, or lighter choices such as char with toasted almonds.

★Le Flamboyant MODERN FRENCH €€
(☎04 73 63 07 97; www.restaurant-le-flamboyant.com; 21bis rue de l'Horloge; mains €30; ⏲noon-2pm & 7-10pm Tue-Sat, noon-2pm Sun) Experience a smorgasbord of local flavours at this gem of a restaurant near the clock tower. Set *menus* offer superb value for their range; try the 'Sens et saveurs' *menu* for Moroccan-style chicken *pastilla* (light flaky pie), roasted lamb with orange and carrot jus, and a spread of cheeses. Better yet, be guided by the seasonal dishes, built around whatever is freshest.

Information

The cheerfully staffed **tourist office** (☎04 73 38 59 45; www.tourisme-riomlimagne.fr; 27 place de la Fédération; ⏲9.30am-12.30pm & 2-5.30 Mon-Sat, to 6.30pm Jul & Aug, 10am-12.30pm Sun, shorter hours Nov-Mar) is close to the Église St-Amable.

Getting There & Away

Riom is 14km north of Clermont-Ferrand, served by frequent trains (€3.50, 10 minutes). The station, Riom-Châtel-Guyon, is 1km southeast of the tourist office.

Vichy

POP 25,325

Cradled in a bend in the Allier River, Vichy has plenty of belle-époque sparkle. During the heyday of this Auvergne spa town, visitors flocked to sip its reputedly healing waters and plunge into thermal springs. Vichy has

Vichy

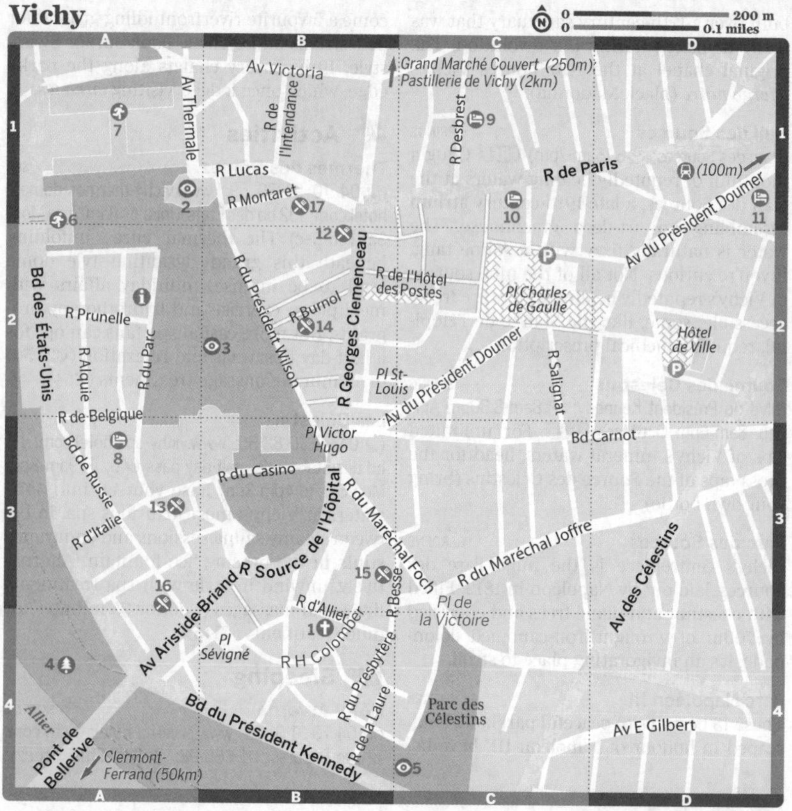

kept its reputation as a health retreat, helped along by the reputation of the cosmetic brand named for the town, which prides itself on using local mineral water in products.

Tree-lined boulevards laid out in the 19th century, and art-deco buildings such as the Opéra de Vichy, add to the town's nostalgic feel. Among Vichy's mansions and riverside parks, there's a rich seam of confectionery shops. As a result, there are plenty of opportunities to be marvellously unhealthy right in the midst of this whimsical wellness capital.

Sights

Église St-Blaise CHURCH

(rue d'Allier) From the outside, grey concrete and brutalist angles make this 1931 church resemble something of a Soviet space rocket. Nonetheless, its interior is aglow with 20th-century stained glass and bronzed mosaics, as well as frescoes of some of France's famous churches. Église St-Blaise (the church's patron is the saint of healing) was

Vichy

Sights

1 Église St-Blaise ... B4
2 Hall des Sources ... A1
3 Parc des Sources ... B2
4 Parc Napoléon III ... A4
5 Source des Célestins ... C4

Activities, Courses & Tours

6 Les Célestins ... A1
7 Thermes des Dômes ... A1

Sleeping

8 Aletti Palace Hôtel ... A3
9 Hôtel Arverna ... C1
10 Hôtel de Naples ... C1
11 La Demeure d'Hortense ... D1

Eating

12 Aux Marocains ... B2
13 Brasserie du Casino ... A3
14 La Table d'Antoine ... B2
15 Les Caudalies ... B3
16 L'Hippocampe ... A3
17 Vichy-Prunelle ... B1

built over a 17th-century sanctuary that was badly damaged during the revolution. The original chapel at the rear houses Vichy's *Vierge noire* (black Madonna).

Hall des Sources SPRINGS

(Parc des Sources; ⏲6.15am-7pm) FREE Chug a mouthful of reputedly healing waters at the Hall des Sources, a late-19th-century atrium resembling an art-deco greenhouse. The water is naturally fizzy with a saline tang, if you're curious. Not all of the nine sources of Vichy's reputedly healing waters are freely accessible: some, like the Source de l'Hôpital, require a medical prescription.

Source des Célestins SPRING

(blvd du Président Kennedy; ⏲8am-8.30pm Apr-Sep, 8am-6pm Oct-Mar) FREE For unlimited sips of Vichy's mineral waters, head for the brass taps of the Source des Célestins (bring your own bottle).

Parc des Sources GARDENS

Vichy's centrepiece is the huge Parc des Sources, laid out by Napoléon in 1812. Filled with chestnut and plane trees and encircled by 700m of wrought-iron-canopied colonnade, it's an invigorating place to stroll.

Parc Napoléon III PARK

These 13 hectares of peaceful parkland, landscaped in honour of Napoléon III, have become a favourite riverfront idling ground for pedestrians and cyclists. Look out for Swiss-style, 19th-century chalets along the park's edge, which once lodged visiting *curistes*.

Activities

Thermes des Dômes SPA

(☎04 70 97 39 59; www.vichy-thermes-domes-hotel.com; 132 bd des États-Unis; ⏲8am-7pm Mon-Sat Feb-Dec) The thermal 'cures' unfolding beneath this grand Byzantine-style dome tend to be intense, multiday affairs with meal plans, exercise and hydrotherapy programs. But more casual spa fans can opt for a half-day of saunas and relaxation (€21.50) or 15-minute massage treatments (€54).

Les Célestins SPA

(☎04 70 30 82 35; www.vichy-spa-hotel.com; 111 bd des États-Unis; half-day pass €40; ⏲9am-8pm Mon-Sat, to 4pm Sun) Ease yourself into 34°C waters at Vichy's most luxurious spa, in between steamy sauna sessions and endurance stints in the bracing 'ice fountain'. Alternatively, unwind in style with spa treatments like facial massages (€66 for 25 minutes) or mud treatments (€145).

Sleeping

Hôtel Arverna HOTEL €

(☎04 70 31 31 19; www.arverna-hotels-vichy.com; 12 rue Desbrest; d €66-98; ❄📶) This breezy,

SWEET VICHY

If sugary treats make you weak at the knees, you may have found your dream destination in Vichy. What began with *pastilles de Vichy*, grew into a confectionery trade that has allowed *chocolateries*, patisseries and sweet boutiques to bloom across Vichy.

The town's signature sweeties, *pastilles de Vichy*, are octogonal pastilles dating to 1825. They were originally made with bicarbonate of soda to soothe digestive troubles. Hype grew when Eugénie, wife of Napoléon III, developed a passion for these moreish sweets. Salts extracted from local mineral water were soon included in the recipe, mixed with sugar and flavoured with mint, lemon or aniseed, and *pastilles* remain firmly established as an after-dinner refresher across the Auvergne.

In their traditional blue-checked tins, *pastilles* are a favourite gift or souvenir. Numerous confectioners around Vichy sell them, but dedicated sugar-fiends can take a pilgrimage to their birthplace, the **Pastillerie de Vichy** (☎04 70 30 94 70; www.pastille-vichy.fr; 94 Allée des Ailes; ⏲9am-noon & 1.30-3pm Mon-Fri Apr–mid-Nov), a sweet factory 2.5km north of town.

But don't limit yourself to *pastilles*. Other regional delights include *carreaux de Vichy*, layers of almond paste and fruit jelly pressed into colourful cubes, as well as homemade *guimauves* (marshmallows) in flavours from blackcurrant to vanilla; head to **Vichy-Prunelle** (☎04 70 98 20 02; www.vichy-prunelle.com; 36 rue Montaret; ⏲9am-noon & 2-7pm Mon-Sat, from 10am Sun) for a mouth-watering assortment. Another sugary trove is **Aux Marocains** (☎04 70 98 30 33; www.auxmarocains.com; 33 rue Georges Clemenceau; ⏲9.45am-12.15pm & 2.30-7pm Tue-Sat, 10.30am-12.15pm & 3-7pm Sun, 3-7pm Mon), with its dilemma-inducing range of artisan chocolates, liqueur-soaked cherries and *pâte de fruits* (sugared jellies made from real fruit).

central hotel has enjoyed a makeover and now boasts a charming lounge room and mini-library to relax in, when you aren't snoozing in one of its 23 well-furnished rooms. The larger rooms have sofas that fold out into an extra bed. Breakfast (€9) is a well-chosen buffet of bouncy fresh breads, jams and freshly squeezed orange juice.

Hôtel de Naples HOTEL €

(☎04 70 97 91 33; www.hoteldenaples.fr; 22 rue de Paris; d €47, tr €57/68; P 📶) Perfectly located between the train station and the Parc des Sources, this family-run hotel has 28 simple rooms, each decorated individually, from rock 'n' roll vinyl themes to pretty floral touches. The tucked-away car park costs an extra €6 per day. In summer, breakfast (€8) is served on the grassy back terrace.

La Demeure d'Hortense B&B €€

(☎04 70 96 73 66; www.demeure-hortense.fr; 62 ave du Président Doumer; s €105, d €115-130, ste €145; ❄📶) This stately 19th-century mansion with parquet floors, marble staircases and vintage stained glass has been lovingly refurbished with modern comforts. Three rooms and two luxurious suites come with ultracomfy beds, classy antique and designer furniture and spacious bathrooms. Common areas include an elegant salon and a relaxing back patio. Breakfast is included.

★**Aletti Palace Hôtel** HOTEL €€€

(☎04 70 30 20 20; www.hotel-aletti.fr; 3 place Joseph Aletti; d €160-195, ste €250; ❄📶🏊) Time travel to more glamorous era at this luxurious hotel overlooking the Parc des Sources. Cosy up in the downstairs bar, where stained-glass windows cast a soft light over sleek leather sofas, or plunge into the heated outdoor pool (summer only). Either way, you'll retreat to romantic lodgings with marbled bathrooms, warm maroon decor, and plenty of space. The downstairs Véranda Restaurant serves fine Auvergnat cuisine with set *menus* from €17 to €24. Breakfast is an additional €14.

Eating

For inexpensive sidewalk dining, check out the cluster of brasseries at the intersection of rue de Paris and rue Georges Clemenceau. Vichy's **covered market** (☎04 70 30 55 75; www.legrandmarchecouvert-vichy.fr; place PV Léger; ⏰7am-1pm Tue-Sun, plus 4-7pm Fri & Sat) is 500m northwest of the train station.

★**La Table d'Antoine** GASTRONOMIC €€

(☎04 70 98 99 71; www.latabledantoine.com; 8 rue Burnol; mains €30, lunch menus €23, dinner menus €31-69; ⏰12.15-2pm & 7.30-9pm Tue-Sat, 12.15-2pm Sun) Abstract portraits and high-backed chairs create a boutique feel at this high-class temple to French fine dining. Choose from flavour pairings like fillet of brill with pink grapefruit butter, or beef stewed in local Saint-Pourçain wine. Tasting *menus* cost up to €69 and are worth every cent. Reserve well ahead.

L'Hippocampe SEAFOOD €€

(☎04 70 97 68 37; www.restaurant-poisson-hippocampe-vichy.fr; 3 bd de Russie; mains €25, menus €22-45; ⏰noon-2pm & 7.30-10.30pm Wed-Sat) This award-winning restaurant wows diners with its succulent seafood, thoughtfully paired with sauces and terrines fit for Neptune's table; try the seared scallops with beetroot confit. The weekday lunch *menu* is good value at €22, though you won't regret spending a little more on the summertime lobster *menu* (€45). Desserts such as Grand Marnier soufflé and a reimagined lemon meringue pie make a lip-smacking finish.

Brasserie du Casino BRASSERIE €€

(☎04 70 98 23 06; www.brasserie-du-casino.fr; 4 rue du Casino; lunch/dinner menus €21/32; ⏰noon-1.30pm & 7.30-9.30pm Thu-Mon) All shiny brass, faded wood and squeaky leather, this timeless haunt and local favourite has a wall of photos

BLACK MADONNAS OF THE AUVERGNE

There are hundreds of 'black Madonna' icons across Europe, and these medieval depictions of the Virgin Mary – usually painted wooden statues less than 1m in height – are numerous in the Auvergne. Their colour has a variety of explanations, from depictions of Middle Eastern skin tones to gradual darkening over centuries due to incense smoke or the oxidising of lead-based paints. While some have suggested that they are linked to older traditions involving the Egyptian goddess Isis or a pagan Mother Goddess, most historians have discounted these theories. The Auvergne's *Vierges noires* (black Madonnas) attract pilgrims from across Europe to sights including Le Puy-en-Velay's **Cathédrale Notre Dame** (p552), Vichy's **Église St-Blaise** (p539), and Besse-et-Saint-Anastasie, whose black Madonna is processed to neighbouring village Vassivière each year for the feast known as the **Transhumance de la Vierge Noire** (⏰Jul-Sep).

featuring the actors and *chanteurs* who've stopped by from the opera house. The food is substantial (duck confit, beef tartare) and the feel unmistakably French.

Les Caudalies GASTRONOMIC €€€
(☎04 30 22 03 40; www.les-caudalies-vichy.fr; 9 rue Besse; lunch menus €23-27, dinner menus €33.50-90; ⊙noon-2pm Tue-Sun, 7-9.30pm Tue-Sat) Chef Emmanuel Bosset creates masterfully inventive twists on traditional French cuisine, from starters such as escargots (snails) in hazelnut and anise liqueur-scented butter to Champagne sorbet with raspberries for dessert. The weekday lunchtime *jéroboam menu*, including three courses and a glass of wine, is good value at €26.50.

Information

Pick up a map of historic buildings at the **tourist office** (☎04 70 98 71 94; www.vichy-tourisme.com; 19 rue du Parc; ⊙9.30am-noon & 1.30-6pm Mon-Sat year-round, plus 3-6pm Sun Apr-Sep) next to the Parc des Sources for a self-guided tour of Vichy's belle-époque architecture.

Getting There & Around

Near the station, **Établissement Gaillardin** (☎04 70 31 52 86; www.scooters-gaillardin-vichy.fr; 48 bd Gambetta; bike rental half-day/day/week €25/8/5; ⊙8.45am-noon & 2-7pm Tue-Sat, 2-7pm Mon) rents bikes.

Train destinations include the following:

Clermont-Ferrand €10.90, 35 minutes, half-hourly

Lyon €28.90, two hours, five to eight daily

Paris Gare de Bercy €54, three hours, six to eight daily

Riom €8.70, 25 minutes, half-hourly

Pays d'Issoire

The sun-drenched Pays d'Issoire is the most colourful strip of the Auvergne, nestled between the green expanses of the two regional natural parks. In the middle of a tapestry of meadows with iron-tinged soil is main town Issoire, home to the Auvergne's most fabulously decorated Romanesque church. Equally as dazzling is the Vallée des Saints, a geological marvel of ochre and red fairy chimneys. Fortified village Montpeyroux and tiny Le Broc each have remarkable views over pastures and rolling hills. Meanwhile the cuisine is easily as colourful as its surroundings, with hubs of experimental gastronomy popping up in even the most bucolic spots.

Sights & Activities

Abbatiale Saint-Austremoine CHURCH
(place Saint-Paul, Issoire; ⊙8am-7pm) Issoire is the proud home to the Auvergne's most richly decorated Romanesque church. The exterior of this 12th-century edifice is festooned with geometric decorations in white and black lava stone, dappled across its ornamental arches. Twelve signs of the zodiac in stone relief have been beautifully restored. Inside, blood-red columns are crowned with depictions from Christ's life, from the Last Supper to the Resurrection, all painted in vivid colour.

Donjon de Montpeyroux HISTORIC BUILDING
(rue de la Grande Charreyre, Montpeyroux; adult/child €2.50/free; ⊙10am-1pm & 2-6pm Apr-Jun & Sep, to 7pm Jul & Aug, 2-6pm Oct) This castle keep is the stocky centrepiece of the medieval walled town of Montpeyroux, built as a safe haven from fires and attacks. From the top of its 33m-high tower, built in the 12th century, feast your eyes on panoramic views over the Chaines des Puys and Monts du Cantal. It's also a fine vantage point over the labyrinth of blonde sandstone lanes in the village below.

Vallée des Saints Circuit WALKING
Rock formations rise like flames along this 6km walking circuit from the village of Boudes. The palette of sunset orange and sienna, with stony chimneys towering up to 30m high, conjures a US national park, and thatches of forest are a-flutter with birds. Boudes is a 17km drive southwest of Issoire. Park in the lot next to the tourist information point, off the D48 as you enter the village, where you'll find trail maps. Only set out in good weather and well before sundown.

Sleeping & Eating

Travelling gastronomes, you're in the right place. Issoire is spangled with independent restaurants that specialise in reinvented Auvergnat flavours, with excellent choices in tiny Montpeyroux and Le Broc too.

Le Diapason BOUTIQUE HOTEL €€
(☎04 73 71 71 71; www.lediapason.fr; rue du plateau de la Chaux, Le Broc; s/d €115/130; P ❄ 📶) Five kilometres south of Issoire, this luxurious retreat creates a curious silhouette: the ultramodern building with an industrial iron exterior towers above the coral rooftops of Le Broc village. Its six light-filled rooms are decked out with wood panels, sleek white furnishings and marbled bathrooms. Its

attached restaurant (lunch/dinner *menus* €25/31) is a regional standout.

L'Air 2 Rien AUVERGNAT €€

(☎04 73 71 16 21; 3 rue Notre Dame du Ponteil, Issoire; mains €16-20; ⊙noon-2pm Tue-Sat, 8-10pm Thu-Sat) This special spot is warm and welcoming in ambience, but acidly modern in style. The restaurant's ancient interior has been whitewashed and decked out with red picture frames and mirrors, while a hip alt-rock soundtrack ensures you tap your toes between sips of Sancerre. House specials, including lightly sautéed scallops in lemongrass vinaigrette and entrecôte (recommended rare), are whipped up by a lone chef before your eyes.

Le Bistrot Zen AUVERGNAT €€

(☎04 73 96 95 36; http://lebistrotzen.com; rue de la Grande Charreyre, Montpeyroux; lunch/dinner menus €21/30; ⊙Wed-Mon noon-2pm & 7-9pm Jul & Aug, closed Mon & Tue Apr-Jun, Sep & Oct, shorter hours rest of year, closed Jan) This bistro in the romantic walled town of Montpeyroux is a culinary breath of fresh air. Regional flavours like bleu d'Auvergne cheese find expression in homemade savoury tarts, while entrées such as salmon tartare with apple and citrus cleanse the palate before the house take on English fish and chips.

ℹ Information

The helpful **tourist office** (☎04 73 89 15 90; www.issoire-tourisme.com; 9 place Saint-Paul; ⊙9am-12.30pm & 2-6pm, longer hours in Jul & Aug) is full of suggestions on where to eat and sleep. Ask about summer guided tours of the Abbatiale Saint-Austremoine.

ℹ Getting There & Away

Regular direct trains serve Issoire from Clermont-Ferrand (€7.90, 40 minutes) and there are some direct train links from Le Puy-en-Velay (€19.90, 1¾ hours, three daily). To explore beyond Issoire, you're best off with your own wheels; the D909 is the main artery through Montpeyroux in the northern Pays d'Issoire, running through Issoire town towards Le Broc.

PARC NATUREL RÉGIONAL DES VOLCANS D'AUVERGNE

The Auvergne's most exhilarating views are to be found among the volcanic cones, snow-lashed peaks and crater lakes of its Parc Naturel Régional des Volcans. One of France's largest regional natural parks at 3897 sq km, this photogenic swathe of the Massif Central mountains has countless places to hike, bike and (erratic snowfall permitting) ski, particularly around the Massif du Sancy. Toasty thermal waters fuel numerous spas, some of them dating back to Roman times, ensuring that muscles stiffened by long hikes are quickly soothed.

Though outdoor activity is the primary touristic drive here, there is also a scattering of noteworthy architecture, particularly in Besse-et-Saint-Anastaise and Orcival.

> **LOCAL KNOWLEDGE**
>
> **WILD ART IN THE SANCY**
>
> Each summer, imagination-firing creations by local and international artists are carefully installed at different locations in the Sancy wilds, as part of the **Horizons Sancy project** (www.horizons-sancy.com). Displays and locations change annually, so check the website or at local tourist offices to seek out these edifying sights.

Volvic

POP 4425

Volvic is caught between its world-famous mineral water brand and an old-timey town centre, packed with regal grey buildings and fountains of volcanic stone. A number of excellent walks spider out from this peaceable town, which is tucked inside the Parc Naturel Régional des Volcans d'Auvergne's northeastern boundary. It's a refreshing stop but there's little to detain you beyond a day.

Beyond the water-bottling plant, Volvic is overlooked by a medieval fortress, **Château de Tournoël** (☎04 73 33 53 06; www.tournoel.com; adult/child €8/3; ⊙10.30am-12.30pm & 2-6pm Jul & Aug), which is a stopping point along the scenic GR441 walking trail. Parts of the crumbling château date as far back as the 9th century. During high summer you can visit the kitchens, kitchen gardens and the 14th-century defensive round tower, but it's an impressive photo-op from the outside too.

At the glossy visitors centre, **Espace d'Information** (☎04 73 64 51 24; www.espaceinfo.volvic.fr; rue des Sources; ⊙10am-12.15pm & 2-6pm Mon-Fri, 2.30-6pm Sat & Sun Apr-Sep, shorter hours Oct, closed Nov-Mar), you can learn about Volvic's world-famous mineral water, a 10-minute walk west of Volvic's tourist office. Outside, walking trails (from 45 minutes to

FIERY FURNACES

Gazing at the *parc naturel*'s still lakes and wildflower meadows, it's hard to imagine that this pastoral part of the Auvergne was forged by volcanic activity. The 80-odd cones of the **Chaîne des Puys**, in the northernmost part of the region, were created by volcanic blasts nearly 10,000 years ago. But the Chaîne des Puys' volcanic hills are young whippersnappers compared to the craggy **Massif du Sancy**, formed nearly five million years ago, and the **Monts du Cantal** further south, formed by a nine-million-year-old volcano that collapsed inwards.

There hasn't been a rumble in seven millennia, but traces of the region's explosive beginnings are everywhere, from the geothermal springs that bubble into the spas of La Bourboule and Le Mont-Dore, to the black stone that gives a distinctively Auvergnat air to nearby Clermont-Ferrand's most celebrated buildings.

two hours) fan into the lush surrounds, linking with the GR441. Free hour-long factory tours of its nearby bottling facility are available between mid-April and early September.

The **tourist office** (☎04 73 33 58 73; www.volvic-tourisme.com; place de l'Église; ⊙9am-noon & 1.30-5pm Tue-Sat) is on the village's central square; find info on accommodation and walking trails within.

Trains connect **Volvic station** (3km west of the centre) with Clermont-Ferrand (€4.80, 30 minutes, six daily). If you're driving, pick up a blue parking disc from a *tabac* (€2.50) to allow you to leave your car in the blue spaces in central Volvic.

Puy de Dôme & Around

Puy de Dôme (1465m) is the best-known of the Auvergne's slumbering Chaîne des Puys, a 40km chain of cones and craters in the Massif Central mountain range. The Chaîne des Puys' distinctive silhouettes make it easy to imagine the geological drama that forged them. But these days, cauldrons of rock are carpeted in green, while maars – valleys carved out by explosions – gleam as crater lakes.

A relative youngster (in geological terms, at least) at 10,000 years old, Puy de Dôme has long acted as a spiritual lightning rod. The remains of a Gallo-Roman temple stand on the summit, though its glinting TV antennae are more noticeable from afar. The summit can be reached on foot or by cog railway, and it's a favourite spot for paragliders. Whether you visit during a summer sunset or in midwinter, when the hills are kissed by snow, you are guaranteed one of France's prettiest panoramas.

Sights

Temple de Mercure RUIN, MUSEUM

(☎04 73 62 21 46; ⊙mid-Mar–Dec) FREE An enigmatic imprint of the distant past stands atop the summit of Puy de Dôme: a 1st-century Gallo-Roman temple undergoing gradual restoration. The ruins, discovered in the 19th century, are an intriguing photo-op, plus there's a visitors centre that explains the region's Roman history.

Vulcania AMUSEMENT PARK

(☎04 73 19 70 00; www.vulcania.com; rte de Mazayes, Saint-Ours-les Roches; adult/child €28/19.50; ⊙10am-6pm mid-Mar–mid-Nov, closed Mon & Tue Mar & Sep-Nov; 👪) The Auvergne's long-extinct volcanoes are brought back to life in spectacular style at Vulcania volcanic theme park, 15km west of Clermont on the D941. Combining educational museum with thrills and spills, highlights include the 'dynamic 3D' film *Awakening of the Auvergne Giants*, depicting volcanic eruptions complete with air blasts and water spray, a Dragon Ride – not very scientific, but good fun all the same – and the Cité des Enfants (Kids' City), with activities specially geared for three- to seven-year-olds.

Vulcania was dreamt up by French geologists Katia and Maurice Krafft, who were tragically killed in a volcanic eruption on Mt Unzen in Japan a year before its 1992 opening.

Volcan de Lemptégy AMUSEMENT PARK

(☎04 73 62 23 25; www.auvergne-volcan.com; adult/child €10.50/8.50, by train €14.50/11.50; ⊙10am-6pm mid-Apr–Sep, longer hours Jul & Aug, shorter hours Mar–mid-Apr & Oct) At Volcan de Lemptégy, just across the D941B from Vulcania amusement park, you can set off on foot or aboard a little motorised 'train' to discover volcanic landscapes (chimneys, lava flows and more). The intense 'dynamic 3D' exploding mine film makes a fitting finale, though it's not suitable for littlies. Last entry is 2½ hours before closing.

Activities

Be uplifted by views of volcanic cones and meadows on **Panoramique des Dômes**

(www.panoramiquedesdomes.fr; adult/child one way €9.80/4.90, return €12.30/6.20; ⏲10am-7pm Apr-Jun & Sep, 9am-9pm Jul & Aug, 10am-5pm Wed-Sun Oct-Mar), a rattling cog railway ride to the top of Puy de Dôme, a 15-minute journey from a station at the base of the mountain. Departures are three times per hour (or every 40 minutes in winter).

Some walkers skip the cog railway and hike to the top of Puy de Dôme along the Chemin des Muletiers. It's a steep climb (400m elevation gain over 1.8km) but the recent addition of wooden stairs has made it easier on the hiking boots. Much less strenuous are the walking paths that spiral around the summit. For bird's-eye views, consider booking a hang-gliding adventure with **Aero Parapente** (☎06 61 24 11 45; www.aeroparapente.fr; adult €150; ⏲Feb-Oct).

Getting There & Away

It's a 13km drive west from Clermont-Ferrand to the Puy de Dôme (follow signs for Orcines, then Panoramique des Dômes). Between mid-April and late September, you can take the **shuttle bus** (☎04 73 44 68 68; www.smtc-clermont-agglo.fr; €1.50) that runs from platform 1 at Clermont-Ferrand's SNCF station or place de Jaude to the foot of the Panoramique train (€1.50, 20 minutes, six daily).

Orcival

POP 233 / ELEV 870M

Since the 6th century, pilgrims have flooded into tiny Orcival, halfway between Puy de Dôme and Le Mont-Dore. Within the magnificent stone basilica that towers over the village lies a 12th-century icon, the Virgin of Orcival, the focal point of veneration each Ascension Day.

Hikers also find their way to this romantic village of stone houses that hug the rushing River Sioulet. Beyond the basilica and a huddle of welcoming restaurants, Orcival opens out to verdant (and often precipitous) hiking terrain. It may only justify an overnight stop, but waystations are rarely as scenic as this.

Its stately 12th-century Romanesque **Basilique Notre-Dame** (⏲8.30am-6pm Oct-Mar, to 7.30pm Apr-Sep) is one of the most graceful churches in all of the Auvergne. The church you see today was built over holy tombs laid waste by Norman invaders. The highlight is the Virgin of Orcival icon, displayed in the choir and the focus of Ascension Day pilgrimages since the 6th century. Inside, take time to admire the carved capitals on top of graceful stone pillars, and a shadowy crypt below.

Just north of town off the D27 is the 15th-century **Château de Cordès** (☎04 73 21 15 89; www.chateau-cordes-orcival.com; garden & chateau/garden only €8/4, child free; ⏲10am-noon & 2-6pm daily Jul & Aug, & 2-6pm Sun in Jun), not to be missed by Fans of French gardens. Visitors can tour the magnificent formal grounds laid out by Versailles' garden designer Le Nôtre in 1695, as well as peep inside the château's fairy-tale towers on guided tours.

Right in front of Orcival's mighty basilica, delightful family-run **Hôtel Notre Dame** (☎04 73 65 82 02; www.hotelnotredame-orcival.com; s/d/f €48/59/63; ⏲Feb-Dec; wi-fi) offers an effusive welcome. Five of its seven clean, comfortable rooms have glorious views over the basilica. Family rooms are vast, and each has a kettle, TV and wi-fi. Generous breakfasts (€9.50) consist of local cheeses, homemade jams, plus fresh bread and cakes. The attached restaurant cheerfully serves up filling mountain cuisine.

The tiny **tourist office** (☎04 73 65 89 77; www.terresdomes-sancy.com; ⏲10am-noon & 2-5pm Tue-Sat May-Sep; shorter hours winter; wi-fi), opposite the basilica, can suggest hiking routes in the surrounding wilds.

Orcival is not served by public transport so you'll need your own wheels. If it's crowded in the tiny town centre, there is a well-signposted overflow car park just off the D27 as you drive into town.

DON'T MISS

WALK ON THE WILD SIDE

Experience the Auvergne's wild side with outdoor experts Christophe and Isabelle from **Aluna Voyages** (☎06 78 40 36 79; www.aluna-voyages.com), who lead superb excursions from Nordic walking (June to September) to multiday donkey treks and winter snowshoe adventures. The wild plant tours (three days from €360, May to September) are an eye-opener: groups explore the meadows around Orcival, hunting for berries, mushrooms and more. They can also arrange self-guided trips in the region. Book in advance.

Col de Guéry

Towering above spa-and-ski havens Le Mont-Dore and La Bourboule is the Col de Guéry. Wild hiking and snowshoeing territory

extends from this mountain pass, punctuated by rocky crags including the formidable **Roche Tuillière** (1288m) and **Roche Sanadoire** (1286m), dormant volcanoes eroded by the movement of ancient glaciers.

Above the pass gleams the **Lac de Guéry**, the highest lake in the Auvergne at 1268m, filled with trout and perch. This is the only lake in France that allows *pêche blanche* (ice-fishing).

Le Mont-Dore

POP 1347 / ELEV 1050M

Le Mont-Dore is the Auvergne's prime winter sports base. Nestled in a narrow valley 44km southwest of Clermont-Ferrand, and 4km north of Puy de Sancy (1886m), the town is quieter than the Alps' adrenaline-pumped resorts (and not as snow-sure). Nonetheless, its charisma amply outweighs identikit Alpine ski villages: the historic bathhouse and grand 19th-century mansions add a glint of belle-époque glamour among its fondue restaurants and gear-hire shops. After sundown, the focus is local gastronomy rather than unbridled après-ski, so the town draws a loyal following of hikers and snow-sports fans seeking lower-key mountain thrills.

Sights & Activities

Thermes du Mont-Dore SPA

(04 73 65 05 10; 1 place du Panthéon; 6.30am-12.30pm & 2-5.30pm Mon-Fri, 6.30am-12.30pm Sat mid-Apr–early Nov) Le Mont-Dore's graceful 19th-century buildings grew from its centuries-old spa heritage, which long predates the town's reputation as a ski hub. See the source of its famous hot springs on a 45-minute guided tour of the grand bathhouses (French only; adult/child €3.50/2.50; 2pm, 3pm and 4pm Monday to Friday). You'll admire neo-Byzantine architecture, including tilework dappled with gold leaf, be shown 'treatment rooms' (the vapours are thought to cure respiratory ailments), and take a sip of the water – brace yourself for a warmish, metallic-flavoured mouthful.

Station du Mont-Dore SKIING

(www.sancy.com/commune/mont-dore; day pass adult/child €31/21.70; 9am-5pm mid-Dec–mid-Apr) Four kilometres from Le Mont-Dore extend the winter sports fields of Station du Mont-Dore (and connected to it, Super-Besse), 84km of downhill runs for beginners through to intermediate skiers (hardened snow-heads venture off-piste). Rise early if you're skiing during local school holidays: lift queues can be enormous. Parking places close to the lifts fill quickly; consider the free shuttle bus from Le Mont-Dore instead.

Espace Nordique Sancy SKIING

(Dec-Apr) Glide along 250km of cross-country ski trails at this Nordic-skiing space north of Super-Besse. Prices depend on which of the nine sectors of trails you want to tackle (from adult/child €7.70/3.50); find maps on www.sancy.com. Ask about snow conditions locally (or check the '*bulletin de neige*' on www.sancy.com) before you set your heart on schussing among frost-rimmed forests.

Funiculaire du Capucin FUNICULAR

(rue René Cassin; one way/return adult €4.50/5.90, child €3.70/4.50; 10am-12.10pm & 2-5.40pm Wed-Sun May-early Oct, to 6.40pm daily Jul & Aug) Built in 1898, France's oldest funicular railway (and listed historic monument) sets off every 20 minutes, crawling at 1m per second up to the plateau of Les Capucins, 1245m above town. Various trails lead off the plateau, including the 2km trail to Pic du Capucin (1319m), the GR30, which wends southward towards the Puy de Sancy, and the steep 1km downhill back to town.

Téléphérique du Sancy CABLE CAR

(one way/return adult €7.30/9.70, child €5.50/7.30; 9am-12.10pm & 1.30-5pm mid-Nov–Jun & Sep, 9am-6pm Jul & Aug) From this cable car's upper station, it's a short climb along a maintained trail and staircase to Puy de Sancy's snowcapped summit, where fabulous views unfold over the northern *puys* and the Monts du Cantal.

Sleeping & Eating

★**Grand Hôtel** HOTEL €

(04 73 65 02 64; www.hotel-mont-dore.com; 2 rue Meynadier; s €53-63, d €63-73, q €93-103; mid-Dec–mid-Nov; P) The romantic ambience of this turreted 1850 hotel is amply delivered within its rooms, which have a sharp modern design and comfortable wrought-iron beds. The best have balconies looking towards the mountains. Meanwhile, time spent in the spa (€5) is the perfect balm for calf muscles that sting from exertion up in the mountains.

Les Mancelles HOTEL €

(04 73 65 03 66; www.auberge-sancy.fr; rte du Sancy; d/tr €40/50, with shared bathroom €30/40; P) Flanked by cow-filled pastures up near Le Mont-Dore's ski lifts, this old-school,

family-run hotel offers low-priced rooms upstairs (the cheapest with shared bathroom), and a convivial restaurant downstairs with checked tablecloths, beamed ceilings and hearty Auvergnat *menus*. There are reasonable guest rates for breakfast (€6), half-board (€22.50) or full board (€34).

Auberge de Jeunesse Le Grand Volcan HOSTEL €
(☎04 73 65 03 53; www.auberge-mont-dore.com; rte du Sancy; per person incl breakfast/half-board/full board €20.20/32.80/45.40; ⊗mid-Dec–mid-Nov; 📶) Usually jammed with skiers and hikers, this excellent hostel is right below the Puy de Sancy cable car, 3.5km south of town. Facilities include squeaky-clean two- to six-bed dorms with en-suite bathrooms, a guest kitchen and laundry, ski and snowshoe rentals, and an in-house bar. Book way ahead in winter, especially for one of the seven double rooms.

Camping Domaine de la Grande Cascade CAMPGROUND €
(☎04 73 65 06 23; www.camping-grandecascade.com; rte de Besse; 2-person site €13.20; ⊗late May-late Sep; 📶) At 1250m elevation, this campground is on the chilly side, but it's a stupendous spot to pitch a tent, just 15 minutes' walk from a 30m waterfall, with marvellous views of the surrounding mountains. Head 3km south of town on the D36.

Café de Paris BISTRO €
(Chez Mimi; ☎04 73 65 01 77; rue Jean-Moulin; mains €10-16; ⊗10am-8pm Fri-Wed) Channeling a merrily retro vibe with its peeling paintwork, flower boxes, glass chandeliers and Jazz photographs, this Parisian-style bistro gets busy with locals clamouring for the enormous salads, omelettes and fondues.

Twenty One Café CREPERIE €
(☎04 73 65 99 94; 21-23 rue Jean Moulin; mains €10; ⊗noon-2.30pm Tue-Sun, 7-9pm Tue-Sat, closed Nov–mid-Dec) Gobble *galettes* (savoury buckwheat pancakes) in the glimmer of fairylights at this cosy crêperie in central Le Mont-Dore. Roast salmon and Cantal cheese are among the waist-thickening *galette* fillings, or you can opt for a hefty 'St Nectairade', gratinated potatoes drowned in local cheese. Lunch *menus* (€12.50) give you the best of both worlds with one savoury *galette* plus a sweet wheat crêpe.

★La Golmotte AUVERGNAT €€
(☎04 73 65 05 77; www.aubergelagolmotte.com; rte D996; menus €18-39; ⊗noon-2pm Wed-Sun, 7-9pm Wed-Sat) The excellent regional cuisine at this mountainside inn is worth the 3km trek up the main road towards Orcival and Murol. Tuck into mouth-watering country pâté sweetened with onion relish, bream lavished in tarragon butter, and Auvergnat classics *such as truffade* and *pounti* (a prune-studded savoury cake). La Golmotte has four simple but snug *chambres d'hôte* (doubles from €58).

LOCAL KNOWLEDGE

AUVERGNE'S CHEESE TRAIL

Among countless dairy delights produced in the Auvergne's fragrant pastures are five Appellation d'Origine Protégée (AOP) cheeses. In order of increasing intensity, these are semihard, cheddar-like Cantal and nutty Salers; St-Nectaire, rich, flat and semisoft; Fourme d'Ambert, a mild, smooth blue cheese; and Bleu d'Auvergne, a powerful blue cheese. A road trip along part of the Routes des Fromages is an excellent way to tour regional cheese producers: you can tramp merrily across fields to buy hunks of cheese right at the source, witness early-morning milkings, or indulge in tasting tours. The Auvergne's cheese trail is best explored during the summer, when many local producers open their doors to tourists; find maps on www.fromages-aop-auvergne.com.

ℹ Information

Tourist Office (☎04 73 65 20 21; www.sancy.com; av de la Libération; ⊗9am-12.30pm & 2-6pm; 📶) Free wi-fi and tons of local info, including hiking maps and guides. Continuous opening hours during school holidays.

ℹ Getting There & Away

SNCF buses connect Le Mont-Dore with Clermont-Ferrand (€14.50, 1½ hours, two to five daily).

Around Le Mont-Dore

Le Mont-Dore is the Auvergne's focal point for winter sports and spa breaks. But the villages in its surrounds also demand attention for their historic charms, gastronomy and fresh-air pursuits.

La Bourboule, 7km west of Le Mont-Dore, is the most glamorous base, with thermal waters and belle-époque buildings to inspire nostalgic daydreams. Little

WORTH A TRIP

BESSE-ET-SAINT-ANASTAISE

Life in Besse-et-Saint-Anastaise may dawdle at a small-town pace, but this mountain village accesses some of the most pulse-quickening territory in the Auvergne. A crater lake, Lac Pavin, shimmers 6km west of Besse; 1km beyond here, winter brings skiers and snowboarders flocking to the slopes of Super-Besse.

The village of Besse is a dream of pebbled lanes and basalt-brick cottages. Once enclosed by 6m-high walls, only one monumental gateway remains today, crowned by an octagonal 16th-century tower. Lift your gaze to the top and you'll see an old wolf's-head weathervane still trembling in the wind.

A handful of quaint hotels huddle in the centre of Besse, but winter-sports fans tend to opt for lodgings around Lac des Hermines, right by the Super-Besse ski lifts (7km west of town). Or you can fling open your window shutters to views of rolling pastures from one of 32 snug rooms at **Auberge de la Petite Ferme** (☎04 73 79 51 39; www.auberge-petite-ferme.com; Le Faux; s/d/ste from €58/65/120; P ☎), a converted farmhouse, 800m from Besse's historic centre. You can almost taste fresh air in the breakfast buffet (€11.50) of cheeses, yoghurts and local honey.

Besse-et-Saint-Anastaise is also a good spot for admirers of architecture, though most visit in winter for the ski station Super-Besse.

Pristine lakes offer a serene contrast to thundering down snowy pistes; head north from Le Mont-Dore to **Lac du Guéry** for fishing, or east to **Lac Pavin** and **Lac Chambon** for walking or sunbathing. Continuing east, rural **St-Nectaire** is most famous for its cheese, though its caves and stunning Romanesque church shouldn't be missed.

Murat & the Monts du Cantal

The Monts du Cantal, at the southern end of Parc Naturel Régional des Volcans d'Auvergne, constitute one of the most wild and beautiful landscapes in the Auvergne. Most dramatic are the peaks of **Puy Mary** (1787m), **Plomb du Cantal** (1858m) and **Puy de Peyre Arse** (1806m), last vestiges of an exploded supervolcano that was once the largest in all of Europe.

At the Cantal massif's eastern edge, tumbling down a steep basalt crag topped by a statue of the Virgin Mary, Murat (930m) makes an excellent base for exploring the area. Its cluster of dark stone houses huddled beneath the Rocher Bonnevie make it one of the southern Auvergne's prettiest towns and a popular hiking and skiing hub.

The twisting streets and stone cottages of Murat's old town make an enjoyable afternoon stroll, but most people are here for gorge walks and snowy thrills on the pistes of **Le Lioran** (www.lelioran.com; day pass adult/child €30.20/20.70; ⏲mid-Dec–early Apr). This 150-hectare ski station, 12km west of Murat, is geared towards middle-of-the-road skiers, with just over half of its 44 pistes rated as blue (intermediate) or red (advanced). Ask locally about snow conditions before you head out.

Sleeping

★ Alta Terra B&B €
(☎04 71 20 83 03; www.altaterra-cantal.com; Pradel, Lavigerie; s/d/tr/q €65/70/90/110; P ☎) Antique skis and creaking wooden eaves give a charming chalet feel to this friendly, family-run B&B in Lavigerie, a 16km drive northwest of Murat. Slide into the outdoor Nordic hot tub (especially satisfying with snow outside), or soothe your muscles in the *hammam* and sauna (no extra charge).

Auberge d'Aijean INN €
(☎04 71 20 83 43; www.auberge-puy-mary.com; La Gandilhon, Lavigerie; d €65-70, 4-person ste €100-125; P ☎) Sublime Monts du Cantal views and cosy, well-outfitted rooms are reason enough to stay at this welcoming mountain inn 15km west of Murat on the road to Puy Mary. The four-course dinners (€23), served in front of a blazing fire in the huge stone fireplace and featuring local specialties like lentil soup, Salers beef, and Auvergnat cheeses, are icing on the cake.

Instants d'Absolu Ecolodge & Spa BOUTIQUE HOTEL €€
(☎04 71 20 83 09; www.ecolodge-france.com; Lac du Pêcher, Chavagnac; d/ste €125/154; ⏲mid-Apr–mid-Nov & mid-Dec–mid-Mar; P ❄ ☎) This 300-year-old lakeside farm, in the peaceful wilds 16km north of Murat, was remodelled with sustainability in mind – carpets from

recycled fibres, ecologically sound paintwork, and meticulous recycling. So with a clear conscience, slide into an outdoor hot tub, stretch out in the sauna, or flop onto a bed in one of 12 individually designed rooms (deliberately TV-free).

Information

Get walking maps, volcanic history and access to the **Mémorial des Déportés de Murat** (Memorial to Murat's Deported People) at the **tourist office** (Maison du Tourisme et du Parc des Volcans d'Auvergne; ☎04 71 20 09 47; www.officedetourismepaysdemurat.com; 1 place de l'Hôtel de Ville; ⏲9.30am-12.30pm & 2-6pm Mon-Sat Sep-Jun, daily Jul & Aug) in the heart of Murat.

Getting There & Away

Regional trains connect Murat with Clermont-Ferrand (€21.20, 1¾ hours, four to six daily).

Salers

POP 350 / ELEV 830M

One of the Auvergne's most attractive towns, Salers sits at the western edge of the Monts du Cantal, looking up towards the Puy Violent (1592m) and Puy Mary (1787m), making it the perfect base for exploring the mountains' western slopes. Spreading out from its compact core of 16th-century stone buildings are rolling meadows filled with horned brown cows that create its eponymous Salers Appellation d'Origine Protégée (AOP) cheese.

Sights

Salers' picturesque central square, place Tyssandier d'Escous, is named for the 19th-century agronomist who developed the Salers breed of cattle. Surrounding his statue is a harmonious collection of turreted lava-rock buildings that date from Salers' 16th-century heyday as a regional administrative centre. From here you can walk up to the leafy **Esplanade de Barrouze belvédère** (panoramic viewpoint), or descend into the town's tangle of cobbled streets filled with shops selling cheese, knives and Auvergnat knick-knacks.

Musée de Salers — MUSEUM

(☎04 71 40 75 97; rue des Templiers; adult/child €5/free; ⏲10am-12.30 & 2-5.30pm Mon-Thu & Sun, 2-5.30pm Sat mid-Apr–mid-Oct) Uncover Salers' history in one of the most charming buildings in town. This former Knights Templar house exposes local history and traditions among its Gothic vaults and echoing stone walls.

Sleeping & Eating

Hôtel Saluces — HOTEL €€

(☎04 71 40 70 82; www.hotel-salers.fr; rue de la Martille; d €78-95, tr/q from €125/150; ⏲mid-Dec–mid-Nov; @📶) Half a block below the square, the delightful Hôtel Saluces offers nine spacious and individually decorated rooms with modern amenities, in an ancient stone building with a sunny interior courtyard. There's an adjoining crêperie and *salon de thé* to unwind in.

La Diligence — AUVERGNAT €

(☎04 71 40 75 39; www.ladiligence-salers.com; rue de Beffroi; mains €15; ⏲noon-3.30pm & 7-10.30pm Tue-Sat late-Mar–Oct) Wear your loose pants for filling regional cuisine such as *boudin noir* (blood sausage), *pounti* (a prune-studded savoury cake) and expertly cooked omelettes at this welcoming restaurant in the centre of Salers.

Le Drac — CREPERIE €

(☎04 71 40 72 12; www.ledrac.supersite.fr; place Tyssandier d'Escous; mains €10; ⏲noon-2pm & 7-9pm) Neatly folded *galettes* (buckwheat flour pancakes) bulge with St-Nectaire cheese, garlic, and a host of local hams and veggies at this main-square restaurant named after a gnome.

Information

The **tourist office** (☎04 71 40 58 08; www.salers-tourisme.fr; place Tyssandier d'Escous; ⏲9.30am-noon & 2-5.30pm), on the main square, offers information, maps and books about local hikes.

Getting There & Away

Salers is on the D680, 43km west of Murat and 21km west of the Pas de Peyrol at the foot of Puy Mary. You'll need your own vehicle to get here.

PARC NATUREL RÉGIONAL LIVRADOIS-FOREZ

The Parc Naturel Régional Livradois-Forez is the more easterly of the Auvergne's two expanses of protected land. Though it doesn't have the striking geology of the western Auvergne, its pine-forested swathes of raw nature, stretching from the plains of Limagne in the west to the Monts du Forez in the east, are rousing hiking terrain. Woodlands are cut through with babbling streams. The occasional Romanesque church or elegantly

ramshackle village interrupts miles of solitary roads that curl among the hills. Formerly a centre for logging and agriculture, it's now a haven for nature lovers and weekend walkers.

Information

The **Maison du Parc** (Park Information Office; 04 73 95 57 57; www.parc-livradois-forez.org; Le Bourg; 9am-12.30pm & 1.30-5.30pm Mon-Thu, to 4.30pm Fri) is off the D906 in St-Gervais-sous-Meymont, halfway between Thiers and Ambert. It's stocked with leaflets detailing local honey shops, lace-makers and perfumers, walking trails and mountain-bike routes.

Thiers

POP 11,308 / ELEV 340M

Six centuries of cutlery production may not seem the most enticing legacy. But Thiers' living industrial heritage makes this riverside town a superb day trip. Thanks to power from the gushing River Durolle, medieval Thiers became a knife-making powerhouse. The town still produces around 70% of France's knives, which remain famous across the country and popular gifts among Auvergnat locals. Weathered stone houses and swinging knife signs make Thiers' centre a charming area to explore, though beyond this tangle of historic streets, the town is sprawling and industrial.

Split over two buildings along rue de la Coutellerie, the **Musée de la Coutellerie** (Cutlery Museum; www.musee-coutellerie-thiers.com; 23 & 58 rue de la Coutellerie; adult/child €5.70/2.80, combined ticket with Vallée des Rouets €6.90/3; 10am-noon & 2-6pm, closed Mon Oct-May) explores the history of cutlery-making and showcases knives past and present. The crowning moment is seeing sparks fly during a knife-making demonstration on centuries-old equipment (French only; written information in other languages on request). In summer, you can pair a visit to the museum with the open-air Vallée des Rouets, 4km northeast of Thiers. A free shuttle-bus operates between the two museums.

The **Vallée des Rouets** (Valley of the Waterwheels; adult/child €4.10/1.85; noon-2pm & 2-6pm Jun & Sep, to 7pm Jul & Aug) is an open-air museum dedicated to the knife-makers who once toiled here in front of water-driven grindstones.

You can even fashion your very own knife in Thiers under the tutelage of master cutlery-maker **Robert David Coutellerie** (04 73 80 07 77; www.robert-david.com; 94 ave des États Unis; adult/child €30/15; 10am, 2pm & 4pm Mon-Sat by reservation).

Twenty kilometres southwest of town, rich Auvergnat flavours find lighter expression at superb restaurant **Auberge de la Forge** (04 73 73 41 80; www.aubergedelaforgeglainemontaigut.com; Le Bourg, Glaine-Montaigut; mains €20; noon-1.30pm & 7-8.30pm Mon, Tue, Thu-Sat, noon-1.30pm Sun Apr-Oct, noon-1.30pm Mon, Tue, Thu-Sun, 7-8.30pm Fri & Sat Nov-Mar). Sea bream with star anise and snail linguini accompany baskets of local cheese, served by attentive staff in a dining area flooded with natural light.

Alternatively, test the limits of your cheese threshold at friendly **Le Chaudron** (04 73 80 09 67; 10 rue Denis Papin; mains €12; noon-2pm & 7-9pm Tue-Sat, noon-2pm Sun) in the thick of historic Thiers. The *fondant St-Nectaire* is an entire baked cheese, served with morsels of potato, salad and cured meat, while the *truffade* (cheese and potato bake) is marvellously garlicky. There's an open terrace in summer, but the stone-walled interior is just as atmospheric.

Learn where to shop for knives, and get the latest hotel and restaurant info, from the **tourist office** (04 73 80 65 65; www.thiers-tourisme.fr; 1 place du Pirou; 10am-noon & 2-5pm Mon-Sat Oct-Apr, longer hours May-Sep;).

Thiers is easily reached by direct trains from Clermont-Ferrand (€9.50, 45 minutes, up to 13 daily) and Vichy (€8.80, 45 minutes, six daily). Thiers' **train station** is a 1km walk north of the tourist office.

DON'T MISS

TIP-TOP EAT-SLEEP

Bed down in one of the well-kept rooms at **Auberge du Ripailleur** (04 73 72 83 20; www.auberge duripailleur.com; Le Bourg, Dore-l'Église; s/d/tr €55/65/85;), a cheerful inn within the enchanting hamlet of Dore-l'Église, 8km north of La Chaise-Dieu. Cosy, wooden-floored rooms roost above an excellent restaurant that prides itself on Auvergnat nosh such as confit duck and an enticing crème brûlée flavoured with verveine.

La Chaise-Dieu

POP 800 / ELEV 1082M

The centrepiece of historic La Chaise-Dieu, 40km north of Le Puy-en-Velay, is its monumental **Église Abbatiale de St-Robert**

OFF THE BEATEN TRACK

LA MONTAGNE PROTESTANTE

Driving east from Le Puy-en-Velay, roads begin to meander among thick expanses of evergreen forest. These windblown highlands, nicknamed 'La Montagne Protestante' on account of their historic Protestant majority, have as their most distinctive landmarks the peaks of **Le Testavoyre** (1436m) and **Mont Mézenc** (1753m), whose summit is accessible via the GR73 and GR7 hiking trails.

The region around **Le-Chambon-sur-Lignon**, 45km east of Le Puy-en-Velay, is renowned for its residents' courageous (and often ingenious) resistance during World War II. Residents succeeded in saving more than 3000 refugees from deportation by the Nazis, and their feats of bravery are honoured at a museum-memorial.

A 20km drive northeast of here lies **Saint-Bonnet-le-Froid**. This village may seem far-flung, but it's marked firmly on the maps of French foodies, thanks to Michelin-starred celebrity chef Régis Marcon setting up restaurants and lodgings here.

La Coulemelle (04 71 65 63 62; www.regismarcon.fr; place de l'Église, Saint-Bonnet-le-Froid; mains €25; noon-2pm & 7.30-10pm Wed-Mon, mid-Feb–Dec) Renowned French chef Régis Marcon has a glittering trio of Michelin stars and operates a clutch of eateries in Saint-Bonnet-le-Froid. At this bistro, earthy flavours come to the fore in dishes such as duck with bilberries. With the restaurant's name (a mushroom) and the Maison du Champignon (Mushroom House) next door, it's no surprise which ingredient features most prominently on the menu.

(www.abbaye-chaise-dieu.com; 9.30am-noon & 2-5.30pm). This mighty 14th-century church makes the small town a worthy stop before you venture out to explore the verdant walking trails of the Parc Naturel Régional Livradois-Forez. Built atop an earlier abbey chapel by Pope Clement VI, who served here as a novice monk, the gorgeous Gothic church dominates La Chaise-Dieu.

Highlights include the massive 17th-century organ (a focal point of the town's Sacred Music Festival), Clement VI's marble tomb and the celebrated *Danse Macabre* fresco, in which Death dances a mocking jig around members of 14th-century society. During our visit, the church and its surrounds were undergoing significant renovation, due to be unveiled in 2017.

Behind the church is the **Salle de l'Echo** – an architectural oddity that allows people on opposite sides of the chamber to hear each other talking, without being overheard by those in between. It's thought to have been built to enable monks to hear lepers' confessions without contracting the dreaded disease.

The **tourist office** (04 71 00 01 16; www.la-chaise-dieu.info; rue St-Esprit; 10am-noon & 2-5pm Tue-Sat;) has a free English-language leaflet outlining a walking tour of the village.

SNCF buses run once or twice each weekday between La Chaise-Dieu and Le Puy-en-Velay (€9.60, one hour).

LE PUY-EN-VELAY

POP 18,619 / ELEV 630M

It's hard to top the drama of Le Puy-en-Velay's skyline. Volcanic stone pillars thrust skywards, crowned by a trio of sacred monuments: a vermillion statue of the Virgin Mary, an imposing cathedral, and a 10th-century church. Le Puy is the starting point of the Via Podiensis, the oldest French route on the Way of St James' pilgrimage.

For pilgrims passing through, the town is a pleasant surprise. Le Puy has a fine slew of restaurants dotted around the cobbled lanes of its old town. It's the proud home of two of the Auvergne's major gastronomic boasts: lentils grown in the region's rich volcanic soil – gilded with Appellation d'Origine Protégée designation – and verveine du Velay, an aromatic green liqueur. Le Puy was also a historic centre for lace-making; this local craft remains greatly admired and fuels a modest souvenir trade.

Sights

Between April and mid-November, three of Le Puy's major sights (Chapelle St-Michel d'Aiguilhe, the Rocher Corneille and the Forteresse de Polignac) can be visited on the joint **Pass'Espace museum pass** (adult/child €9.50/5.50). Buy it at any of the sights or from the tourist office.

★**Chapelle St-Michel d'Aiguilhe** CHURCH
(www.rochersaintmichel.fr; adult/child €3.50/2; 9am-6.30pm May-Sep, shorter hours rest of year,

Le Puy-en-Velay

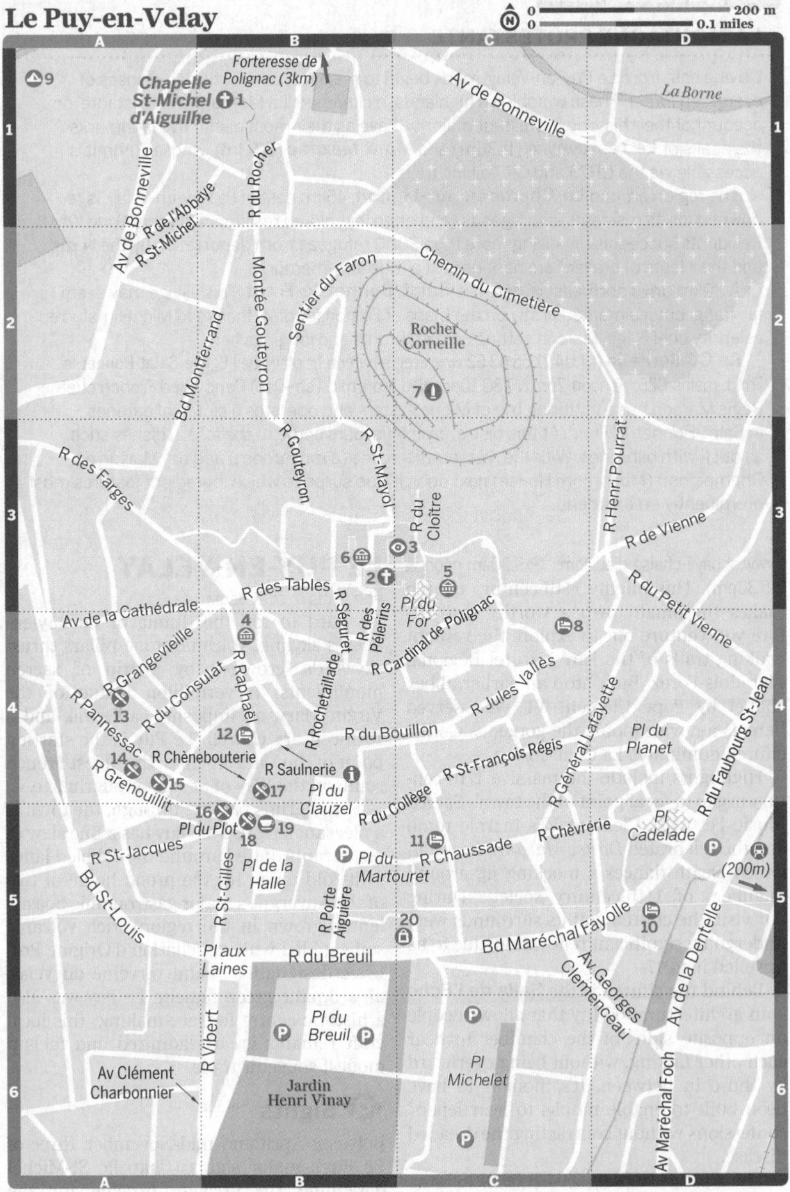

closed mid-Nov–Jan) Le Puy's oldest chapel (first established in the 10th century, and rebuilt several times since) teeters atop an 85m-high volcanic plug, reached by climbing 268 craggy stairs. Stepping through its exquisite polychrome doorway into the cavelike interior is a near-mystical experience – the chapel follows the natural contours of the rock, and the unusual carvings and 12th-century frescos create an otherworldly atmosphere.

Cathédrale Notre Dame CATHEDRAL
(www.cathedraledupuy.org; rue de la Manécanterie; ⏲6.30am-7pm) Le Puy's Unesco-listed cathe-

Le Puy-en-Velay

Top Sights

1 Chapelle St-Michel d'Aiguilhe ... B1

Sights

2 Cathédrale Notre Dame ... B3
3 Cathédrale Notre Dame Cloister ... C3
4 Centre d'Enseignement de la Dentelle au Fuseau ... B4
5 Le Camino ... C3
6 Musée Interactif Hôtel-Dieu ... B3
7 Rocher Corneille & Notre Dame de France ... C2

Sleeping

8 Auberge de Jeunesse ... C4
9 Camping Bouthezard ... A1
10 Hôtel Le Régina ... D5
11 L'Epicurium ... C5
12 Une Coquille Sous l'Oreiller ... B4

Eating

13 Bambou et Basilic ... A4
14 Entrez les Artistes ... A4
15 Fromagerie Coulaud ... A4
16 La Table du Plot ... B5
17 Restaurant Tournayre ... B4
18 Saturday Market ... B5

Drinking & Nightlife

19 Café Alami ... B5

Shopping

20 Espace Pagès Maison Verveine du Velay ... C5

dral is an exquisite checkerboard of grey and white stone, inspiring immediate awe in visitors who climb the stairs to reach it. Symmetry radiates from its Romanesque arches, while the interior is awash in neck-craning Roman-era frescoes, some 5.5m high. The cathedral houses one of the Auvergne's most famous *Vierges noires* (black Madonnas). This 11th-century icon was replaced with a 17th-century statue after the original was burned by revolutionaries, but the new model inspires much the same devotion among pilgrims. The cathedral opens an hour later outside high season.

Cathédrale Notre Dame Cloister CLOISTER
(http://cathedrale-puy-en-velay.monuments-nationaux.fr; rue du Cloître; adult/child €5.50/free; ⏲9am-noon & 2-6.30pm mid-May–mid-Sep, to 5pm rest of year) A peaceful 12th-century cloister adjoins Le Puy's cathedral, its multicoloured bricks and columns alluding to strong Moorish influences. Upstairs is a fine collection of embroidered religious artwork and vestments, accompanied by absorbing audiovisual displays about their origins.

Rocher Corneille & Notre Dame de France MONUMENT
(adult/child €4/2; ⏲9am-7pm May-Sep, 10am-5pm Feb-Apr & Oct–mid-Nov) At 16m tall and weighing a svelte 110 tonnes, this crimson Notre Dame de France (Virgin Mary) statue makes an imposing guardian over Le Puy. Since 1860, she has been watching over the city from the Rocher Corneille, a 757m-high volcanic pillar, and you can share her lofty view by climbing up to her haloed head. The statue was fashioned from 213 cannons captured during the Crimean War.

Le Camino MUSEUM
(Musée de St-Jacques de Compostelle; www.lecamino.org; 2 rue de la Manécanterie; adult/child €3/1.50; ⏲2-6pm Apr-Jun & Sep–mid-Oct, 12.30-8pm Jul & Aug) Interesting for armchair travellers, as well as committed walkers about to undertake the multiweek journey to Santiago de Compostela, this museum in the restored 16th-century Hôtel St-Vidal traces every stage of the 1700km Chemin de St-Jacques (Way of Saint James) pilgrimage route, in exhibits spread out over a dozen rooms on four floors.

Centre d'Enseignement de la Dentelle au Fuseau MUSEUM
(☎04 71 02 01 68; www.ladentelledupuy.com; 38-40 rue Raphaël; adult/child €4.50/free; ⏲8am-noon & 1.30-6pm Mon-Fri year-round, plus 9.30am-4.30pm Sat Apr-Oct) Le Puy is famed for the intricacy and beauty of its lace, and this workshop-museum – led by formidable lace expert Mick Fouriscot – showcases remarkable examples of the delicate craft, plus old photographs of the region's lace-makers across centuries. Nimble-fingered travellers can sign up for lace-making classes (book well in advance), which you can continue at home via the centre's correspondence courses. There's an adjoining shop filled with pretty souvenirs and books.

Musée Interactif Hôtel-Dieu MUSEUM
(www.hoteldieu.info; 2 rue Becdelièvre; adult/child €6/4; ⏲10am-12.30pm & 1.30-6.30pm Jul & Aug, 10am-noon & 2-6pm Tue-Sat Mar-Jun &

Sep–mid-Nov) The highlight of this museum inside Le Puy's historic hospital is the 19th-century pharmacy, elegantly panelled in walnut and wild cherry wood. Upstairs, French-language interactive exhibits focus on the architecture, history and natural history of the Haute-Loire region.

Forteresse de Polignac CASTLE
(www.forteressedepolignac.fr; adult/child €5/3.50; ⏲10am-7pm Jul & Aug, 10am-noon & 1.30-6pm Apr-Jun, Sep & Oct, 1.30-5.30pm Feb, Mar & early Nov) Dramatically perched atop a volcanic dome just 5km northwest of Le Puy, this 11th-century castle was built by the powerful Polignac family, who once controlled access to the city from the north. It's ringed by a practically continuous wall dotted with lookout towers and a 32m-high rectangular keep.

Festivals & Events

Fête du Roi de l'Oiseau STREET CARNIVAL
(www.roideloiseau.com; ⏲mid-Sep) This week-long street party harks back to a 16th-century competition in which Le Puy's most skilled archer, the first to shoot a straw bird from a high tower, would be rewarded with year-long tax exemption, dining with the nobles, and the title of '*roi de l'oiseau*' (bird king). The festival was resurrected in modern times with less emphasis on archery and more on outlandish costumes and street parties. Book accommodation well ahead, don a wimple or wig, and hurl yourself into the fray.

DON'T MISS

VERVEINE DU VELAY

Sip free samples of Le Puy's famous green liqueur and buy a bottle of your preferred drop at **Espace Pagès Maison Verveine du Velay** (☎04 71 02 46 80; www.verveine.com; 29 place du Breuil; ⏲10am-12.30pm & 2.30-7pm Tue-Sat, to 6pm Oct-Mar, plus Mon in Jul & Aug) First concocted in 1859 as a digestive tonic, the liqueur is a top-secret mix of 32 plants and herbs. These days verveine is glugged across the world as an aperitif or stirred into cocktails. Let your taste buds decide between the 55%-proof original, honeyed yellow verveine, a cognac-strengthened 'Extra' variety, or refreshing citrus-scented 'Petite Verte'.

In summer, take a 45-minute guided tour of the **distillery** (☎04 71 03 04 11; St-Germain Laprade; tours adult/child €6.20/2.50; ⏲10.30am, 2.30pm, 3.30pm & 4.30pm Mon-Sat), 7km east along the N88 in St-Germain Laprade.

Sleeping

★ **L'Epicurium** GUESTHOUSE €
(☎06 24 41 56 10; 5 rue du Bessat; s/d/tr incl breakfast from €58/64/99; 📶) This gastronomy-obsessed guesthouse in the city's historic centre is Le Puy-en-Velay's trendiest address. Its five spacious rooms have been freshly renovated in minimalist chic: ceilings are high, bathrooms are vast, breakfast involves a toothsome range of fancy jams, and you can add a three-course meal of local specialities to your stay (€18). Wooden floors are rather creaky, but background din is part of L'Epicurium's old-world charm.

Une Coquille Sous l'Oreiller B&B €
(☎06 95 43 97 03; www.unecoquillesousloreiller.com; 15 rue Raphaël; d/ste €59-65/75; 📶) The name of this guesthouse, 'a shell under your pillow', is a nod to myth that pilgrims sleeping rough along the Way of St James would protect their ears with a scallop shell. These *chambres d'hôte* are a good deal comfier, with simple individually decorated rooms, some with fine views of the historic town centre, accessed via a creaking, 300-year-old staircase.

Auberge de Jeunesse HOSTEL €
(☎04 71 05 52 40; www.hifrance.org/auberge-de-jeunesse/le-puy-en-velay.html; 9 rue Jules Vallès; dm €15; P📶) Austere but clean, this hostel offers great value for its prime position just below the cathedral. Dorms sleep three to nine people, there are facilities for disabled travellers, plus there are washing machines to blitz the trail dust from your clothes. Simple breakfasts of cereals, bread and orange juice cost €4.50 per head, and there's free on-site parking. Note that reception is closed at lunch and dinnertime; gates close at 11.30pm.

Camping Bouthezard CAMPGROUND €
(☎04 71 09 55 09; www.aquadis-loisirs.com/camping-de-bouthezard; chemin de Bouthezard; pitch/adult/child from €16.90/3.50/1.60; ⏲late Mar–mid-Oct; P📶) Le Puy's campground enjoys an attractive berth beside the River Borne, overlooked by the towering Chapelle St-Michel d'Aiguilhe across the road. Facilities include washing machines, kids club (July and August), and wi-fi in the reception area. Take bus 5 to the Parc Quincieu stop.

Hôtel Le Régina HOTEL €€

(☎04 71 09 14 71; www.hotelrestregina.com; 34 bd Maréchal Fayolle; s €67-74, d €83-104, ste €119; P ❄ ☎) Pop-art themes enliven the rooms of this well-run hotel, a five-minute walk from Le Puy's train station. Individually decorated bedrooms feature Coke bottles, New York City's Chrysler building, and murals of Marilyn Monroe in a saccharin-decorated suite complete with violet sinks and Jacuzzi. Private garage parking is an extra €7.50 per night.

Eating

Dubbed 'vegetarian caviar' by locals, the local *lentille verte du Puy* (green Puy lentil; www.lalentillevertedupuy.com) is something of a superfood. Granted Appellation d'Origine Protégée (AOP) classification, this versatile pulse pops up most frequently as a well-seasoned side dish, but you'll also find chefs baking *sablés* (shortbread biscuits) and macarons from lentil flour. Rich in protein, vitamin B and iron, Le Puy's lentils are adored by chefs because they're comparatively less starchy than other lentils and cook quickly.

La Table du Plot AUVERGNAT €

(☎04 71 57 05 28; 6 place du Plot; mains €16; ⊙noon-2pm Thu-Tue, 7-10pm Mon & Thu-Sat; 🖉) This reliable spot on the market square whips up filling regional dishes, like steak with nostril-singeing Bleu d'Auvergne cheese (€19.50), and there's usually one meat-free option, like their pleasing vegetable *mille-feuille* with parmesan (€13.50).

Entrez les Artistes AUVERGNAT €

(☎04 71 09 71 78; 29 rue Pannessac; mains €16; ⊙noon-2pm Tue-Sat, 7-9pm Tue-Fri) Chef Pascale Suc pours heart, soul and lovingly selected local ingredients into the meals at this amiable restaurant. The atmosphere is jolly and inviting, Le Puy lentils are served seasoned to perfection, portions are ample from steaks to homemade *mousse au chocolat*, and there's a healthy wine cellar awash with fine French drops.

★ **Restaurant Tournayre** AUVERGNAT €€

(☎04 71 09 58 94; www.restaurant-tournayre.com; 12 rue Chênebouterie; mains €25; ⊙noon-1.30pm & 7.30-9.30pm Wed-Sat, noon-1.30pm Sun) This is one of the best addresses in Le Puy for food and form. Its atmospheric setting, within a 12th- to 16th-century *hôtel particulier* (historic town house), sets the tone. But the four-course *menus* will dominate conversation. Savour seared cod or succulent lamb on the great-value lunchtime *menu du marché* (€29) or try the 'Compostelle *menu*', featuring scallops and zander with gnocchi (€42).

AMBERT: A CHEESY MUST

Creamy blue Fourme d'Ambert cheese stands regally in dairy counters across the Auvergne, noticeable for its tall, cylindrical shape. There is no better spot to pay homage to this *fromage*, one of the Auvergne's five Appellation d'Origine Protégée (AOP) cheeses, than its home town of Ambert. The **Maison de la Fourme d'Ambert** (www.maison-fourme-ambert.fr; 29 rue des Chazeaux; adult/child €6/4.50; ⊙10am-noon & 2-6pm Tue-Sat) has displays on the history and manufacture of this unctuous blue. Three-cheese tastings (including a glass of wine or apple juice) cost an additional €3. This emporium of cheese history is a 50km drive south of Thiers, 60km east of Issoire or 30km north of La Chaise-Dieu.

Bambou et Basilic MODERN FRENCH €€

(☎04 71 09 25 59; www.bambou-basilic.com; 18 rue Grangevieille; mains €20; ⊙noon-1.30pm & 7.15-9pm Wed-Sun Mar-Nov, noon-1.30pm & 7.15-9pm Wed-Sat, noon-1.30pm Sun Dec-Feb) Creative dishes and elegant service have brought local gourmands flocking since Bambou et Basilic opened its doors in 2011. From herb-crusted pork to roasted zander on artichoke purée, dishes are cooked with finesse and sculpted prettily on plates. Desserts such as Bourbon-cream *mille-feuille* (pastry) are worth saving room for, plus there's a good wine selection.

Self-Catering

Fromagerie Coulaud CHEESE €

(24 rue Grenouillit; ⊙8.30am-12.30pm & 2-7pm Tue-Sat) Floral milk jugs and farming tools bedeck the interior of this periwinkle-blue cheese shop. It's been running since 1925 and the produce is mercifully unchanged since then. Choose from goat and sheep's cheeses, homemade jams and local honeys.

Saturday Market MARKET €

(place du Plot; ⊙8am-1pm Sat) Shop for fresh produce at Le Puy's excellent Saturday market. Some of the local cheeses aren't sold anywhere else.

THE VIA PODIENSIS PILGRIMAGE ROUTE

Ever since the 9th century, when a hermit named Pelayo stumbled across the tomb of the Apostle James (brother of John the Evangelist), the Spanish town of Santiago de Compostela has been one of Christendom's holiest sites. The pilgrimage to Santiago de Compostela is traditionally known as the Camino de Santiago (Way of St James). There are many different routes from London, Germany and Italy; of the French routes, the oldest (and most frequented) is the 736km Via Podiensis from Le Puy-en-Velay to St-Jean-Pied-de-Port via Figeac, Cahors and Moissac, established in AD 950–951 by Le Puy's first bishop. Early pilgrims were inspired to undertake the arduous journey in exchange for fewer years in purgatory. Today the reward is more tangible: walkers or horse riders who complete the final 100km to Santiago (cyclists the final 200km) qualify for a Compostela Certificate, issued on arrival at the cathedral.

The modern-day GR65 roughly follows the Via Podiensis route. Plenty of organisations can help you plan your adventure: contact Le Puy's tourist office, or, in Toulouse, the **Association de Coopération Interrégionale: Les Chemins de Saint-Jacques de Compostelle** (05 62 27 00 05; www.chemins-compostelle.com). For a useful English-language website, see www.csj.org.uk.

Drinking & Nightlife

Le Puy does post-dinner *digestifs* better than raucous nightclubs. Find bars along rue Saint-Pierre and off the main D88 road opposite the train station. For coffee, **Café Alami** (place du Plot; 8am-12pm & 2-5.30pm) is an Aladdin's cave for coffee fans. Beans originating from Ethiopia, the Caribbean and beyond are displayed on its packed shelves and lovingly ground on-site by the gregarious owner (cups from €2.50).

Information

Tourist Office (04 71 09 38 41; www.ot-lepuy envelay.fr; 2 place du Clauzel; 8.30am-7pm daily Jul & Aug, 8.30am-noon & 1.30-6.15pm daily Apr-Jun & Sep, 8.30am-noon & 1.30-6.30 Mon-Sat Oct-Mar;) Stop by for free wi-fi and local information.

Getting There & Away

SNCF operates direct trains from Le Puy to Clermont-Ferrand (€24.80, 2¼ hours, four to six daily). There are direct trains to Lyon as well as services via St Étienne (€24.70, two to 3½ hours, five to 10 daily). Connections to Paris transit via Lyon or St Étienne.

GORGES DE L'ALLIER

One of the prettiest stretches of the Allier River, which gushes through central France for 410km, is south of Clermont-Ferrand. Here the water teems with salmon and tumbles prettily between sharp cliffs and wild tangles of scrub, drawing white-water enthusiasts and walkers to the languid villages on its banks. With campgrounds and activities galore, the Gorges de l'Allier makes a refreshing region to explore *en famille*.

Brioude, 50km northwest of Le Puy-en-Velay, is a fine place to start a Gorges de l'Allier odyssey. This town of 7000 has a riveting array of architectural styles, from candy-coloured walls and stone turrets to its famous basilica. Discover more cultural treasures in **Lavaudieu**, home to a Benedictine abbey. Twenty kilometres further south, seize some oars in **Langeac**, an excellent base for white-water rafting and canyoning.

To admire the valley at a gentler pace, take a ride on the **Train des Gorges de l'Allier** (04 71 77 70 17; www.train-gorges-allier.com; adult €18-24, child €12-14; May-Sep) scenic rail. The longest route, from Langeac to Langogne, allows you to whistle along the entire length of the gorge. Days and itineraries vary, so plan ahead. Tickets are available from Langeac's **tourist office** (04 71 77 05 41; www.haut-allier.com; place Aristide Briand, Langeac; 9am-12.30pm & 1.30-6pm Tue-Sat;).

Campgrounds and simple B&Bs, especially in Langeac and Saugues, cater to an outdoorsy crowd of rafters and hikers who venture to the Allier River from April to October. Outside this season, many accommodation options hibernate. **Le Moulin Ferme-Auberge** (04 71 74 03 09; www.gite-aubergedumoulin.com; St-Arcons-d'Allier; dm/d/tr/q incl breakfast €25/60/95/105; P), 6km south of Langeac, offers charmingly renovated stone and wood cottages on a verdant farmstead.

Trains reach Brioude from Le Puy-en-Velay (€14.20, one hour, four daily). From there, you can catch a train to Langeac (€7.20, 30 minutes, three daily). It's easier by car, a 40km drive from Le Puy-en-Velay along the N102.

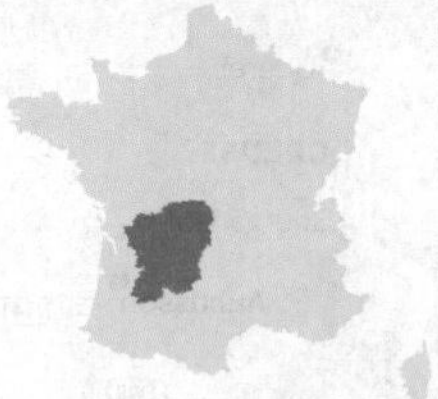

Dordogne, Limousin & the Lot

POP 1.33 MILLION

Includes ➡

Best Places to Eat

- ➡ Le Vieux Logis (p568)
- ➡ Les Truffieres (p568)
- ➡ Le Petit Paris (p571)
- ➡ La Tour des Vents (p565)

Best Places to Sleep

- ➡ Hôtel La Grézalide (p601)
- ➡ Manoir de Malagorse (p599)
- ➡ Château de Maraval (p571)
- ➡ Château les Merles (p564)

Why Go?

Dordogne, Limousin and the Lot are the heart and soul of *la belle France,* a land of dense oak forests, winding rivers, emerald-green fields and famously rich country cooking. It's the stuff of which French dreams are made: turreted châteaux and medieval villages line the riverbanks, wooden-hulled *gabarres* (traditional flat-bottomed, wooden boats) ply the waterways, and market stalls overflow with pâté, truffles, walnuts, cheeses and fine wines.

The Dordogne *département* has a bevy of *bastides* (fortified towns) and fantastic medieval castles, as well as Europe's most spectacular cave paintings, and probably the best cuisine. To the northeast, the Limousin *région* – encompassing the Haute-Vienne, Creuse and Corrèze *départements* – is the most rural, strewn with farms and hamlets, as well as the porcelain centre, Limoges. To the south, the Lot *département* is ribboned with rivers to cruise and caverns to explore, plus dramatic hilltop villages, and medieval settlements.

When to Go

Limoges

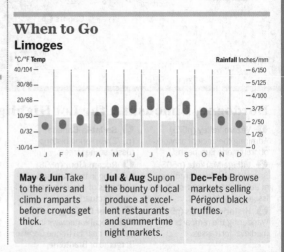

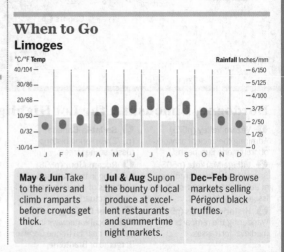

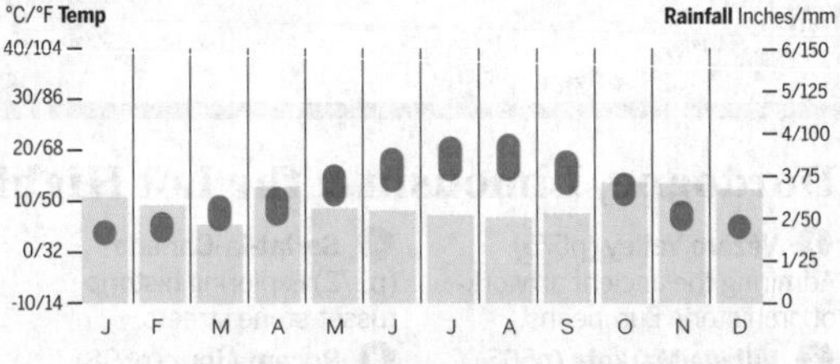

May & Jun Take to the rivers and climb ramparts before crowds get thick.

Jul & Aug Sup on the bounty of local produce at excellent restaurants and summertime night markets.

Dec–Feb Browse markets selling Périgord black truffles.

Dordogne, Limousin & the Lot Highlights

1. **Vézère Valley** (p575) Admiring the ancient artwork of prehistoric Europeans.
2. **Village Markets** (p566) Sampling rich local produce at abundant markets, such as Issigeac's or Martel's.
3. **Historic Castles** (p569) Wandering the ramparts of medieval fortresses.
4. **Sarlat-la-Canéda** (p572) Exploring historic russet-stone streets.
5. **Rocamadour** (p598) Following in the footsteps of centuries of pilgrims at the cliff-face sanctuaries.
6. **River Cruising** (p573) Plying local waterways in a *gabarre* near La Roque Gageac, Bergerac or Brantôme.
7. **Musée Gallo-Romain Vesunna** (p561) Strolling a 1st-century Roman villa.
8. **Limoges** (p588) Shopping for French porcelain at renowned china factories.
9. **Medieval Cities** (p601) Traipsing through still-vibrant towns from the Middle Ages, including Figeac and Cahors.

THE DORDOGNE

Few regions sum up the attractions of France better than the Dordogne. With its rich food, heady history, château-studded countryside and picturesque villages, the Dordogne has long been a favourite getaway for French families on *les grandes vacances*. It's also famous for having some of France's finest prehistoric cave art, which fill the caverns and rock shelters of the Vézère Valley.

Part of the historic area that was called Aquitaine, its strategic importance through the ages is illustrated by the many *bastides* (fortified towns) and fortresses throughout. Today it's known to the French as the Périgord, and is divided into four colour-coded areas: Périgord Pourpre (purple) for the wine-growing regions around Bergerac; Périgord Noir (black) for the dark oak forests around the Vézère Valley and Sarlat-la-Canéda; Périgord Blanc (white) after the limestone hills around the capital, Périgueux; and Périgord Vert (green) for the forested regions of the north.

Périgueux

POP 31,531

Founded by Gallic tribes, and later developed by the Romans into the important city of Vesunna, Périgueux remains the Dordogne's biggest (and busiest) town, with a lively cafe and restaurant scene, and plenty of shopping. Get past its suburban sprawl to its centre, and you discover a thoroughly charming old town dotted with medieval buildings and Renaissance mansions, radiating out from the Gothic Cathédrale St-Front.

Reminders of the city's Roman past fill the Cité quarter – the original 'old town'. You can visit a ruined garden-filled amphitheatre and triumphal tower, as well as a grand villa at the city's excellent Gallo-Roman museum.

Sights

The tourist office has a great walking tour map (€0.50) and offers guided tours (adult/child €6/3).

Puy St-Front

The area around the cathedral, known as Puy St-Front, encompasses most of the city's most impressive medieval streets and buildings.

★Cathédrale St-Front CATHEDRAL
(place de la Clautre; ⌚8.30am-7pm) Périgueux' most distinctive landmark is most notable for its five creamy Byzantine tower-topped domes (inspired by either St Mark's Basilica in Venice or the church of the Holy Apostles of Constantinople, depending on whom you ask). Built in the 12th century on the site of two earlier basilicas, it was sacked in the Wars of Religion, and redesigned and rebuilt by Abadie (the architect of Paris' Sacré Cœur) in the late 19th century.

A striking bell tower remains from the 12th-century church, and informed the design of Abadie's domes. The interior is laid out in a Greek cross, and the cloisters date from the 12th to 16th centuries.

The best views of the cathedral are from **Pont des Barris** just to the east.

★St-Front Quarter HISTORIC QUARTER
North of the cathedral, Périgueux' broad boulevards give way to a tangle of cobblestone streets lined with medieval houses. The best examples are along rue du Plantier, rue de la Sagesse, rue de la Miséricorde and rue Aubergerie, and many are marked with French/English placards.

Rue Limogeanne, a super shopping street, has graceful Renaissance buildings at nos 3, 5 and 12. Around the corner, the 15th-century **Maison du Pâtissier** (17 rue Éguillerie) is elaborately carved. Nearby **Galerie Daumesnil** is a series of linked courtyards within 15th- to 17th-century townhouses.

Puy St-Front used to be surrounded by medieval fortifications. Now, only the 15th-century Tour Mataguerre remains.

★Musée d'Art et d'Archéologie du Périgord MUSEUM
(www.perigueux-maap.fr; 22 cours Tourny; adult/child €5.50/free; ⌚10.30am-5.30pm Mon & Wed-Fri, 1-6pm Sat & Sun) The city's museum displays fine Roman mosaics, prehistoric scrimshaw, medieval stonework from the Cathédrale St-Front, and interesting art (mainly from the 19th and 20th centuries).

★Tour de Vésone ROMAN SITES
(⌚park 7.30am-9pm Apr-Sep, to 6.30pm Oct-Mar) FREE This 24.5m-high *cella* (shrine) is the

FAST FACTS

Area 31,219 sq km

Local industry Goose and duck husbandry

Signature drink *Eaux de noix* (walnut liqueur)

Périgueux

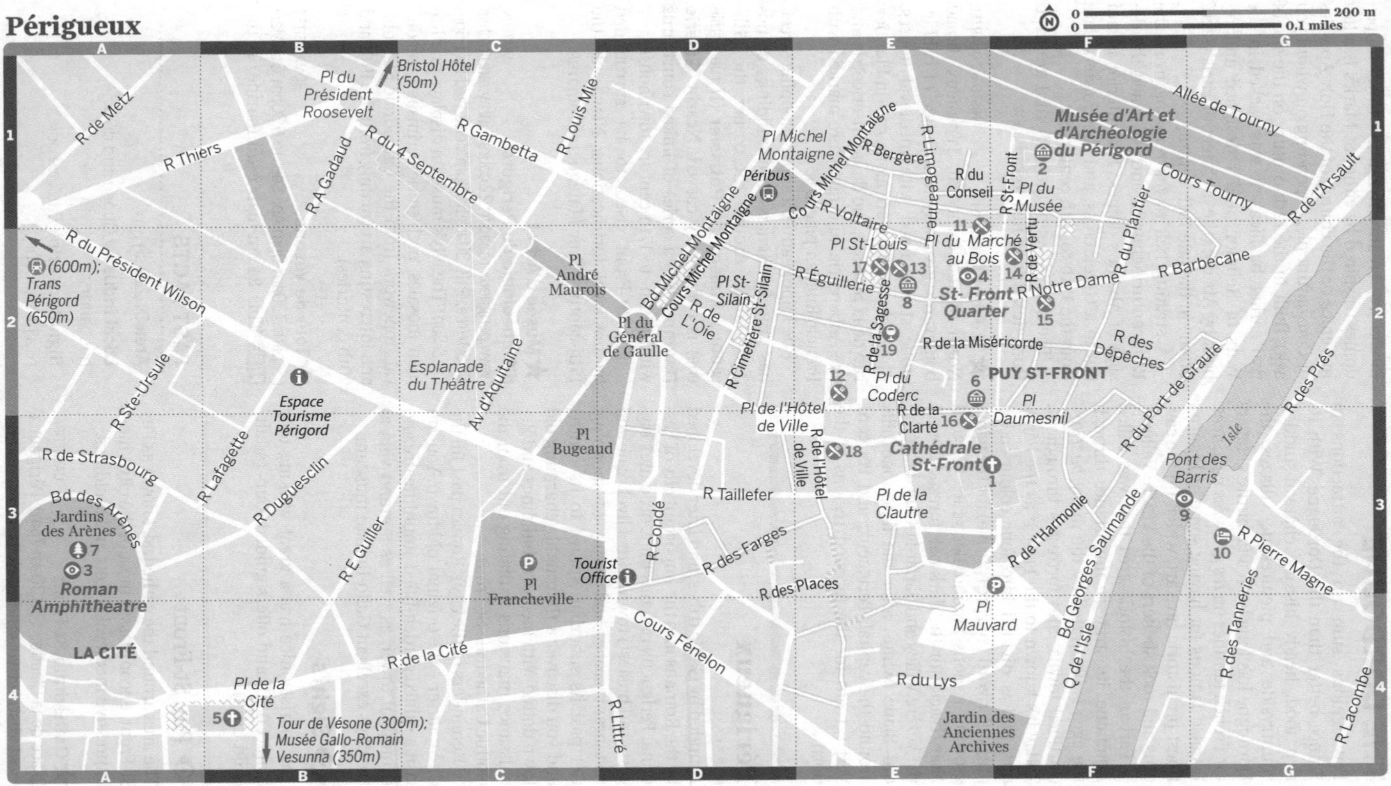
200 m
0.1 miles
Bristol Hôtel (50m)
Pl du Président Roosevelt
R de Metz
R Thiers
R A Gadaud
R du 4 Septembre
R Gambetta
R Louis Mie
Pl Michel Montaigne
Péribus
Cours Michel Montaigne
R Bergère
R Limogeanne
R du Conseil
R St-Front
Pl du Musée
Musée d'Art et d'Archéologie du Périgord
2
Allée de Tourny
Cours Tourny
R de l'Arsault
R du Président Wilson
(600m); Trans Périgord (650m)
Pl André Maurois
Bd Michel Montaigne
R Voltaire
Pl St-Louis
17
13
11
Pl du Marché au Bois
4
14
R de Vertu
R du Plantier
R Barbecane
R Éguillerie
8
St- Front Quarter
R Notre Dame
15
Pl St-Silain
R de L'Oie
R Cimetière St-Silain
R de la Sagesse
19
R de la Miséricorde
R des Dépêches
Pl du Général de Gaulle
Esplanade du Théâtre
Av d'Aquitaine
Espace Tourisme Périgord
12
Pl du Coderc
PUY ST-FRONT
6
R de la Clarté
16
Pl Daumesnil
R du Port de Graule
R des Prés
Isle
R Ste-Ursule
Pl de l'Hôtel de Ville
R de l'Hôtel de Ville
18
Cathédrale St-Front
1
Pont des Barris
9
Pl Bugeaud
R de Strasbourg
R Lafagette
R Duguesclin
R Taillefer
Pl de la Claustre
Bd des Arènes
Jardins des Arènes
7
3
Roman Amphitheatre
R E Guiller
Pl Francheville
Tourist Office
R Condé
R des Farges
R des Places
R de l'Harmonie
Bd Georges Saumande
10
R Pierre Magne
Pl Mauvard
LA CITÉ
R de la Cité
Cours Fénelon
R du Lys
Q de l'Isle
R des Tanneries
Pl de la Cité
5
Tour de Vésone (300m); Musée Gallo-Romain Vesunna (350m)
R Littré
Jardin des Anciennes Archives
R Lacombe

Périgueux

Top Sights
1 Cathédrale St-Front F3
2 Musée d'Art et d'Archéologie du Périgord F1
3 Roman Amphitheatre A3
4 St-Front Quarter E2

Sights
5 Église St-Étienne de la Cité B4
6 Galerie Daumesnil E2
7 Jardin des Arènes A3
8 Maison du Pâtissier E2
9 Pont des Barris F3

Sleeping
10 Hôtel des Barris G3

Eating
11 Café de la Place E2
12 Covered Market E2
13 La Ferme St-Louis E2
14 Le Clos St-Front F2
15 Le Troquet F2
16 L'Essentiel E3
17 Marchés au Gras E2
18 Pierrot Gourmet E3

Drinking & Nightlife
19 Le Chai Bordin E2

last remaining section of a massive 2nd-century Gallo-Roman temple dedicated to Roman goddess Vesunna.

La Cité

The La Cité neighbourhood, west of the modern-day city centre, is the site of ancient Vesunna, among the most important cities in Roman Gaul.

★ Musée Gallo-Romain Vesunna — ROMAN SITES

(05 53 53 00 92; www.perigueux-vesunna.fr; 20 rue du 26e Régiment d'Infanterie, Parc de Vésone; adult/child €6/4, audioguide €1; 9.30am-5.30pm Tue-Fri, 9.30am-12.30pm & 2.30-6pm Sat & Sun Apr-Jun & Sep, 10am-7pm daily Jul & Aug, shorter hours rest of year) Part of the park that contains the Tour de Vésone, this sleek museum designed by French architect Jean Nouvel encompasses a 1st-century Roman villa uncovered in 1959. Light floods in through the glass-and-steel structure, and walkways circumnavigate the excavated villa; it's still possible to make out the central fountain, supporting pillars and the underfloor hypocaust system, as well as original mosaic murals, jewellery, pottery and even a water pump.

A joint ticket with the Musée d'Art et d'Archéologie du Périgord costs €9/6 per adult/child.

★ Roman Amphitheatre — ROMAN SITES

FREE The ruins of the city's amphitheatre, designed to hold more than 20,000 baying spectators, was one of the largest such structures in Gaul. Today the tops of the arches have been revealed and embrace a peaceful park and fountain, the **Jardin des Arènes** (7.30am-9pm Apr-Sep, to 6.30pm Oct-Mar), popular with local families.

Église St-Étienne de la Cité — CHURCH

(place de la Cité; 8am-6pm) The Église St-Étienne de la Cité was built in the 11th century on the site of the Roman temple to Mars. Périgueux' cathedral until 1669, it only has two of its original four powerfully built domed bays (each different from the others).

Sleeping

The choice of hotels in Périgueux leaves a lot to be desired, with chain hotels often being the best bet – you might find it better to visit on a day trip. The tourist office has lists of B&Bs and campgrounds.

Hôtel des Barris — HOTEL €

(05 53 53 04 05; www.hoteldesbarris.com; 2 rue Pierre Magne; s €49, d €55, f €62-82;) Beside the broad River Isle with a cute waterside terrace, this Logis hotel is the best value in Périgueux, as long as you can get a river-view room (the ones by the main road can be noisy). Higher-end rooms have air-conditioning, but only two have cathedral views. Reception closes in the middle of the day.

Bristol Hôtel — HOTEL €

(05 53 08 75 90; www.bristolfrance.com; 37-39 rue Antoine Gadaud; d €62-96, f €80-100;) The Bristol's boxy façade has little appeal, but look beyond the exterior and you'll find serviceable, spacious rooms with all the mod cons, super-friendly staff, and a central location. Find it half a block north of rue Gambetta, on the western edge of the Puy St-Front quarter. There's free parking.

Eating

★ Café de la Place — BRASSERIE, CAFE €

(05 53 08 21 11; http://www.cafedelaplace24.com; 7 place du Marché au Bois; menus €15-28; restaurant noon-2.30pm & 7-10.30pm, bar 8am-2am) You simply couldn't hope to find a more lively Gallic spot. Cutlery clatters

DON'T MISS

MARKETS IN PÉRIGUEUX

Folks come from far and wide for Périgueux' bustling markets, and the winter Marchés au Gras is tops for truffles.

Wednesday & Saturday Market (8am-1pm) Périgueux' wonderful street markets explode into action twice a week, taking over place du Coderc, place de la Clautre and place de l'Hôtel de Ville.

Marchés au Gras (p565) Browse local winter delicacies, such as truffles (December to February), wild mushrooms and foie gras.

Covered Market (place du Coderc; 8am-1pm) The covered market is a year-round staple.

beneath classic brasserie trappings – spinning fans, shiny brass fittings, burnished wooden bar – and there's nowhere better in town for people-watching over a *petit café* or perfectly decadent *steak-frites*.

Pierrot Gourmet DELI €
(05 53 53 35 32; www.pierrotgourmet.com; 6 rue de l'Hôtel de Ville; mains €9.50, menus €14.50; noon-5pm Tue-Sat) This lovely deli serves regional dishes canteen-style in the buzzy dining room, or boxed up to go for the perfect gourmet picnic. Specialities include cep (mushroom) flans, duck parmentier, Périgueux pâté, and sinful gingerbread tiramisu.

La Ferme St-Louis REGIONAL CUISINE €€
(05 53 53 82 77; 2 place St-Louis; lunch/dinner menus €16/30; noon-2pm & 7-9.30pm daily Apr-Sep, closed Sun, Mon & Wed Oct-Mar) Specialising in local products such as duck foie gras. Dine in the intimate stone room with the tinkle of glasses, or under plane trees on the square.

Le Troquet BISTRO €€
(05 53 35 81 41; www.letroquet-perigueux.fr; 4 rue Notre Dame; mains €15-16; noon-2pm Tue-Fri, 7.30-10pm Tue-Thu, to 11pm Fri & Sat) Locals in the know reserve ahead at this shoebox-small alleyway bistro great for authentic market cuisine.

★L'Essentiel GASTRONOMIC €€€
(05 53 35 15 15; www.restaurant-perigueux.com; 8 rue de la Clarté; lunch menus €29-47, dinner menus €43-78; noon-1.30pm & 7.30-9.30pm Tue-Sat) At Michelin-starred L'Essentiel, it feels like you're dining inside an aristocratic friend's living room, with floral wallpaper and orange velour chairs providing a suitably posh setting for Périgueux' top gourmet cuisine. Chef Eric Vidal, a Tulle native, prepares meals steeped in local flavours: Quercy lamb, cockerel and local rare-breed pigs regularly feature on the *menu*, often with a truffly, nutty touch.

Le Clos St-Front GASTRONOMIC €€€
(05 53 46 78 58; www.leclossaintfront.com; 12 rue St-Front; lunch menus €33, dinner menus €44-68; noon-1.30pm Tue-Sun, 7.30-9.30pm Tue-Sat) Inside a 16th-century *hôtel particulier*, Patrick Feuga applies a creative approach to traditional Périgordine ingredients, with a seasonal *menu* that changes every month and a half. The tree-shaded garden is a dreamy, much sought-after place to eat in summer; book ahead.

Drinking & Nightlife

Le Chai Bordin WINE BAR
(09 81 89 40 65; www.lechaibordin.com; 8 rue de la Sagesse; 10am-12.30pm & 3-8pm Tue-Thu, to 10pm Fri & Sat) Convivial hole in the wall crammed with wines.

Information

Espace Tourisme Périgord (05 53 35 50 24; www.dordogne-perigord-tourisme.fr; 25 rue du Président Wilson; 9am-noon & 2-5pm Mon-Fri) Dordogne *département* information.

Tourist Office (05 53 53 10 63; www.tourisme-perigueux.fr; 26 place Francheville; 9am-7pm Mon-Sat, 10am-6pm Sun Jul & Aug, shorter hours rest of year;) Helpful, with loads of info and a smartphone app.

Getting There & Away

BUS

Péribus (05 53 53 30 37; www.peribus.fr; 22 cours Montaigne; tickets €1.25) operates local buses, including a shuttle that runs from place Faidherbe to St-Front on Wednesday and Saturday market days.

Further afield, **Trans Périgord** (05 53 08 43 13; www.transperigord.fr; 19 rue Denis Papin; 1/10 tickets €2/14) runs school buses to destinations including Sarlat (line 7; 1½ hours, four daily Monday to Friday), Montignac (line 7 and 8A; 1¾ hours, four daily Monday to Friday), Bergerac (line 3; 1¼ hours, four daily Monday to Friday), and Brantôme centre (line 1; 50 minutes, two daily Monday to Friday)

TRAIN

The **train station** (rue Denis Papin), 1km northwest of the old town, is served by Péribus lines

GBE, 4 and 5. Getting to Bergerac (€25.70, 12 daily) requires a change in Libourne, and Sarlat-la-Canéda (€16.30, five daily) requires a change in Le Buisson.

Bordeaux €22, 1½ hours, 10 to 12 daily

Brive-la-Gaillarde €14, one hour, seven daily

Les-Eyzies-de-Tayac-Sireuil €8.50, 35 minutes, six daily

Limoges €18, one hour, nine daily

Brantôme

POP 2181

Beautiful Brantôme sits on a small island in a bend in the River Dronne, with five medieval bridges and romantic riverfront architecture, thus earning its tagline 'Venice of the Périgord'. Its impressive abbey is built into a mainland cliff face, and it's surrounded by parks and willow-filled woodland, making Brantôme an enchanting spot to while away an afternoon or embark on a boat ride.

Sights

Abbaye de Brantôme ABBEY

(☎05 47 45 30 12; bd Charlemagne; church & cloister adult/child €7/5; ⏲10am-noon & 2-5pm Oct-May, to 6pm or 7pm Jun-Sep) Brantôme's most illustrious landmark is the former Benedictine Abbey, built and rebuilt from the 11th to 18th centuries and now occupied by the town hall and an **art museum**. Look out for the abbey's spectacular detached 11th-century Romanesque bell tower, built into the rock, and the oldest in the Limousin style. Next door is the Gothic **abbey church**.

A joint ticket with the Grottes de l'Abbaye costs €8.50/5 per adult/child.

Grottes de l'Abbaye CAVE

(☎05 47 45 30 12; bd Charlemagne; adult/child €5/2; ⏲10am-noon & 2-5pm Oct-May, to 6pm or 7pm Jun-Sep) Behind the modern-day abbey lie moody caves, originally a place of pagan worship and then part of Brantôme's first 8th-century abbey. Its most famous feature is a 15th-century rock frieze thought to depict the Last Judgment.

Activities

Plenty of outfitters hire out one-person kayaks and multi-person canoes for a trip down the Dronne. They also offer half-day trips from Fontaine (4km upriver), Verneuil (8km upriver) and Bourdeilles (12km downriver), as well as a full-day trip from Verneuil to Bourdeilles (20km).

> WORTH A TRIP
>
> **EAT-SLEEP AU CHÂTEAU**
>
> **Bistro La Verrière** (☎05 53 03 53 59; www.chateau-hotel-perigord.com; 15 ave des Reynats, Chancelade; lunch menus €19, dinner menus €26-44; ⏲noon-2pm & 7-9.30pm; P 📶), a glass-encased bistro attached to the grand **Château des Reynats**, 8km northeast of Perigueux, creates refined seasonal cuisine in a relaxed atmosphere surrounded by verdant gardens. A high-end gastronomic restaurant, **L'Oison** (menus €77 to €99) opens at the château for dinner, and you can stay in unique castle rooms (doubles from €130). Rooms in the detached *orangerie* run to the bland (doubles €81).

Brantôme Croisières BOATING

(☎05 53 04 74 71; www.brantomecroisieres.com; rue Pierre de Bourdeille; adult/child €7.50/5.50; ⏲Apr-Oct) Pleasure boats depart from the banks of the river in front of the abbey at Pont Coudé, and cruise Brantôme's waterways. Cruises last about 50 minutes, with up to five trips per day.

Sleeping & Eating

Hostellerie du Périgord Vert HOTEL €

(☎05 53 05 70 58; www.hotel-hpv.fr; 7 av André Maurois; d €66-87, f €120; P 📶) The ivy-covered façade promises period charm, but inside the rooms are rather modern and bland. Still, bathrooms are sleek, rates are reasonable, and the restaurant (*menus* €19 to €39) serves reliable local cuisine.

★**Hostellerie Les Griffons** HOTEL €€

(☎05 53 45 45 35; www.griffons.fr; Bourdeilles; d from €95; 📶) In the riverside town of Bourdeilles, 9km southwest of Brantôme along the D78, this charming converted mill perched over the river drips character. Medieval fireplaces, solid beams and higgledy-piggledy layouts characterise the rooms. Its riverside **restaurant** (3-course menus €32-45) opens onto a lovely waterfront terrace, and is renowned throughout the region. It's walking distance to Bourdeilles' château.

Moulin de l'Abbaye GASTRONOMIC €€€

(☎05 53 05 80 22; www.moulinabbaye.com; 1 rte de Bourdeilles; lunch/3-course/5-course menus €29/38/65; ⏲noon-1.40pm Thu-Sun, 7.30-9.30pm Wed-Mon Feb-Oct) At this carefully converted water mill at the foot of the abbey, choose between its extravagant gastronomic restaurant

OFF THE BEATEN TRACK

REGIONAL NATURE PARKS

This corner of France is renowned for its unspoilt natural beauty, with huge swathes protected in three *parcs naturels régionaux:* **Périgord-Limousin** (www.pnr-perigord-limousin.fr) in the northwest, **Millevaches en Limousin** (www.pnr-millevaches.fr) in the east and **Causses de Quercy** (www.parc-causses-du-quercy.org) in the south. All three offer a wealth of outdoor activities. Tourist offices stock walking leaflets, mountain-bike guides, and horseback-riding information.

and its two sister bistros: **Au Fil de l'Eau** (quai Bertin 21; menus €26), specialising in fish, and **Au Fil du Temps** (1 chemin du Vert Galant; menus €24) with traditional Périgordian roasted meats. At the main restaurant, terraces overlook the river, and 19 equally luxe rooms are on offer upstairs (rooms €170 to €260).

Information

Tourist Office (05 53 05 80 63; www.perigord-dronne-belle.fr; 10am-6pm Apr-Sep, shorter hours rest of year) Large office across the bridge from the abbey in Église Notre-Dame.

Getting There & Away

Brantôme is 27km north of Périgueux along the D939. From Monday to Friday, two **Trans Périgord** (www.transperigord.fr) buses per day run from the police station in Brantôme centre to Périgueux (€2, 50 minutes).

Bergerac

POP 29,058

Rich vineyards and rolling fields surround pretty cream-stone Bergerac, a good gateway to the Dordogne and one of the most prestigious winegrowing areas of the Aquitaine. The sweet town's main claim to fame is dramatist and satirist Savinien Cyrano de Bergerac (1619–55), whose romantic exploits – and oversized nose – have inspired everyone from Molière to Steve Martin. Despite the legend (largely invented by 19th-century playwright Edmond Rostand), Cyrano's connection with the town is tenuous – he's thought to have stayed here only a few nights, if at all. Bergerac's riverfront old town and lively cafe scene make it fun to explore.

Sights & Activities

The prettiest parts of Bergerac's fine old town are place de la Mirpe, with its tree-shaded square and timber houses, and place Pelissière, where a jaunty **statue of Cyrano de Bergerac** gazes up at the nearby **Église St-Jacques**, a former pilgrimage point. The **ancien port** wraps beautifully along the river. Rue St-Clar arcs inland and is lined with half-timbered houses. The tourist office has a good free walking-tour map.

Musée du Vin et de la Batellerie MUSEUM
(05 53 57 80 92; 5 rue des Conférences; adult/child €3/2; 10am-noon & 1-6pm Jun-Sep, shorter hours rest of year) Wonderfully musty displays of vintage winemaking equipment and scale models of local river boats.

Gabarres de Bergerac BOATING
(05 53 24 58 80; www.gabarres.fr; quai Salvette; adult/child €9/6; Easter-Oct) Atmospheric 50-minute cruises from the Ancien Port.

Sleeping

Le Colombier de Cyrano et Roxane B&B €
(05 53 57 96 70; www.lecolombierdecyrano.fr; place de la Mirpe; d €77-87;) One of several sweet *chambres d'hôte* in Bergerac's old town, this 16th-century blue-shuttered stone building has three colourful rooms and a flower-filled terrace where you can doze in the hammock.

★ **Château Les Farcies du Pech'** B&B €€
(05 53 74 16 11, 06 75 28 01 90; www.farciesdupech.com; Farcies Nord, Pécharmant; d incl breakfast €100; mid-Mar–mid-Nov) Part of a group of four renowned wineries (www.vignobles-dubard.com), this beautiful château-vineyard 2km north of Bergerac is definitely the choice for oenophiles. All five rooms scream rustic chic, with original stonework and vintage character. The proprietor Marie serves a lovely home-cooked French brekkie in the dining room and can arrange tours of the vineyards.

★ **Château les Merles** BOUTIQUE HOTEL €€€
(05 53 63 13 42; www.lesmerles.com; Tuilières, Mouleydier; d €190-210, ste €250, apt €350; @) Behind its 19th-century neoclassical façade, this château 15km east of Bergerac is a study in modish minimalism. Monochrome colour schemes including black-and-white sofas and artfully chosen antiques run throughout the rooms, most of which would look more at home in Paris than deep in the Dordogne. From the nine-hole golf course to

the ravishing fusion restaurant (lunch/dinner *menus* from €20/30), it's a royal retreat.

Eating

Bergerac and the surrounding wine country are loaded with great eateries to fit any budget. Market days are Wednesday and Saturday, and they are abundant. The central **covered market** (place Louis de la Bardonnie; ⌚7am-1pm) operates daily, and is surrounded by bistros.

La Désirade ICE CREAM €

(☎05 53 58 27 50; place Pélissière; per scoop €2.50; ⌚10am-11pm May-Sep) Lick a scoop of homemade ice cream on one of the benches on the square.

★ Villa Laetitia REGIONAL CUISINE €€

(☎05 53 61 00 12; laetitiajustino@hotmail.com; 21 rue de l'Ancien Port; lunch menus €17-22, dinner menus €25-38; ⌚noon-2pm Tue-Sun, 7-9pm Tue-Sat) Book ahead for a seat with in-the-know locals in the soft, cream-stone dining room where charming waitstaff serve delicious local cuisine, made in the open kitchen at the rear. Expect farm-fresh ingredients and delicious Périgord classics exquisitely presented.

L'Imparfait REGIONAL CUISINE €€

(☎05 53 57 47 92; www.imparfait.com; 8-10 rue des Fontaines; lunch menus €29, 6-course dinner menus €49; ⌚noon-2pm & 7-10pm) Chef Hervé Battiston has made this sweet little restaurant a favourite, thanks to artful French food served up in a pretty 12th-century cloister. Reserve ahead.

La Ferme de Biorne REGIONAL CUISINE €€

(☎05 53 57 67 26; www.biorne.com; Lunas; menus €19-24; ⌚Tue-Sun Apr-Oct by reservation; 👪) 🌿 This rural *ferme auberge* (farm restaurant), 12km northwest of Bergerac, raises its own birds for the restaurant table, including goose, quail and duck for its foie gras. Cosy *gîtes* (€980 for four people per week in summer) are also available.

La Tour des Vents GASTRONOMIC €€€

(☎05 53 58 30 10; www.tourdesvents.com; Le Moulin de Malfourat, Monbazillac; lunch menus €29, dinner menus €44-77; ⌚noon-1.15pm Wed-Sun, 7.30-9.15pm Tue-Sat; 🖉) Chef Marie Rougier Salvat

BLACK PEARLS OF PÉRIGORD

While the Dordogne is famed for all of its gourmet goodies, for some culinary connoisseurs there's only one that matters: the black Périgord truffle (*Tuber melanosporum*), often dubbed *le diamant noir* (black diamond) or, hereabouts, *la perle noire du Périgord*.

A subterranean fungus that grows naturally in chalky soils (in the Dordogne around the roots of oak or hazelnut trees), it is notoriously capricious: a good truffle spot one year can be inexplicably bare the next, which makes large-scale farming practically impossible. The art of truffle hunting is a matter of luck, judgment and hard-earned experience, with specially trained dogs (and sometimes pigs) helping in the search.

The height of truffle season is between December and March, when you'll find them on local menus and when special **truffle markets** are held around the Dordogne, such as Périgueux' **Marchés au Gras** (place St-Louis; ⌚8am-1pm Wed & Sat mid-Nov–early-Mar) 🌿, **Brantôme** (⌚6am-noon Fri Dec-Feb) and **Sarlat** (p572). Leading local chefs head 35km south of Périgueux to St-Alvère's **marché aux truffes** (⌚from 10am Mon Dec-Feb) where top harvests fetch as much as €1000 a kilogram, a bargain by retail standards. Truffles are classified by quality and size, with the *brumale* species of truffles garnering lower prices.

Alternatively, book with local truffle expert Edouard Aynaud at **Truffière de Péchalifour** (☎05 53 29 20 44; www.truffe-perigord.com; tours adult €8-10, child free-€5; ⌚tours 10.45am Wed-Sat Jul & Aug, by reservation rest of year) for a truffle-hunting tour, meal or stay at his *truffière* (truffle-growing area), just north of St-Cyprien.

Sorges, 23km northeast of Périgueux, has an **Écomusée de la Truffe** (☎05 53 05 90 11; www.sorges-perigord.com; Le Bourg, Sorges; adult/child €5/2.50; ⌚9.30am-6.30pm Mon-Fri, 9.30am-12.30pm & 2.30-6.30pm Sat & Sun mid-Jun–Sep, shorter hours rest of year) and a 3km trail through the local *truffières*, while **La Truffe Noire de Sorges** (☎06 08 45 09 48; www.truffe-sorges.com; Domaine de Saleix, Sorges; tours €10-25; ⌚by reservation Dec-Feb & Jun-Sep) runs truffle-themed tours followed by a tasting (tour in English on request). Sample the local speciality, or stay over, at **Auberge de la Truffe** (☎05 53 05 02 05; www.auberge-de-la-truffe.com; 21 rue Nationale, Sorges; lunch/dinner menus from €19.50/26.50; ⌚noon-2pm Wed-Sun, 7.30-9.30pm daily Easter-Oct; 📶).

OFF THE BEATEN TRACK

AROUND BERGERAC: WINE COUNTRY

The broad, flat area south of Bergerac is covered in vineyards. Seven Appellation d'Origine Contrôlées (AOCs) hale from this region, which abuts Bordeaux wine country to the west, and represent some of the Dordogne's best wines. Pick up the *Wines of Bergerac* guide-map from local tourist offices or the **Maison des Vins** (☎05 53 63 57 55; www.vins-bergerac.fr; Cloître des Récollets; ⏰10am-12.30pm & 2-7pm Tue-Sat Feb-Jun & Sep-Dec, daily Jul & Aug, closed Jan) in Bergerac, and hit the wine-tasting trail.

Château Montdoyen (☎05 53 58 85 85; www.chateau-montdoyen.com; Le Puch, Monbazillac; ⏰9.30am-1pm & 2-7pm) This fun family-run winery makes a full range of excellent wines, from Bergerac AOC reds, to whites with intriguing names such as Divine Miséricorde (sauvignon blanc and sauvignon gris), to a delicious rosé and outstanding Monbazillac sweet white. Find it 10km south of Bergerac, off the D933.

Château d'Elle (☎05 53 61 66 62; www.chateaudelle.com; 323 chemin de la Briasse, Bergerac; ⏰10am-8pm) Jocelyne Pécou, one of the few Bergerac female vintners (hinted at in the winery's name), produces robust red Pécharmant AOC, 5km east of Bergerac centre.

Château de la Jaubertie (☎05 53 58 32 11; www.chateau-jaubertie.com; Colombier; ⏰10am-5pm Mon-Sat May–mid-Sep) This historic monument and former royal hunting lodge in pretty fields off the N21 south of Monbazillac produces a range of organic AOC Bergerac wines.

Château de Monbazillac (☎05 53 63 65 00; www.chateau-monbazillac.com; Monbazillac; château adult/child €7.50/3.75; ⏰10am-noon & 2-5pm Jun-Sep, shorter hours rest of year, closed Dec & Jan) Often crowded because of its grand 16th-century château (best seen from outside), this vineyard specialises in sweet white Monbazillac AOC.

creates eleborate *périgourdine* meals using the freshest seasonal ingredients, and friendly staff serves them to the dining room or terrace with panoramic views of Bergerac wine country. Dishes include foie gras with local strawberries, port gelée and balsamic vinegar.

Information

Tourist Office (☎05 53 57 03 11; www.bergerac-tourisme.com; 97 rue Neuve d'Argenson; ⏰9.30am-1pm & 2-6.30pm Mon-Sat Sep-Jun, plus Sun Jul & Aug; 📶)

Getting There & Around

AIR

Bergerac's **airport** (EGC; www.bergerac.aeroport.fr), 4km southeast of town, is served by Air France and budget carriers including Ryanair. Destinations include Paris Orly, Bristol, Brussels Charleroi, Edinburgh, London Stansted, London Gatwick, East Midlands, Liverpool, Birmingham, Exeter, Leeds Bradford, Southampton and Rotterdam.

Taxis (☎05 53 23 32 32), which cost about €15, and rental cars are the only option for getting into town.

BUS

Trans Périgord (www.transperigord.fr) line 3 connects Bergerac with Périgueux (€2, 1¼ hours, four to five Monday to Friday).

TRAIN

Bergerac is on the regional line between Bordeaux (€17.70, 1½ hours, 11 daily) and Sarlat (€13.20, 1½ hours, five daily). For other destinations, change at Le Buisson or Libourne.

Issigeac

POP 728

Bastides (fortified towns) abound in the area southeast of Bergerac, and one of the best is wonderful Issigeac. Its high stone walls encircle a medieval village that is a joy to explore, especially at its magnificent Sunday morning market. An agricultural area as well, it produces everything from foie gras to three AOC strawberry varieties. Look out for the delicious walnut-rind cheese, called *echourgnac*, made by nuns at Abbaye d'Echourgnac.

Issigeac's predominantly 13th- to 18th-century historic buildings were constructed on top of a former 4th-century Roman villa, later a 7th-century Benedictine abbey. The tourist office has a free walking-tour leaflet. There's also an antique fair in August.

Another top *bastide* to explore nearby is **Beaumont-du-Périgord** with its large central square, fortified church, and Monday night market. One of its *bastide* gates leads

straight into the countryside, and the tourist office has lists of walks and maps.

Sleeping & Eating

Passé et Présent B&B €
(☎05 53 63 35 31; www.passe-et-present.com; 14 Grand Rue, Issegiac; d incl breakfast €48-55; ❄) Impeccably done antique-filled rooms fill a pretty ancient townhouse in Issegiac's centre. Take your tea in a rose-filled courtyard.

★ **Shabby Chic Corner** CAFE €
(☎05 53 57 88 20; www.boheme-est-la-marquise.com; 3 rue Ernest Esclangon; ⏲9.30am-6pm Sun) Wonderful Nathalie has a lovely sewing atelier and shop around the corner, and a quaint, country-French-style *salon de thé* (tearoom) here. She bakes everything from scratch, and the place is open (and packed) for Sunday market days.

El Borini GASTRONOMIC €€
(Restaurant Chez Alain; ☎05 53 58 06 03; http://elborini.com; Tour de Ville; lunch menus €18, dinner menus €28-40; ⏲noon-2pm daily, 7-10pm Mon-Sat; 👪) Choose between the garden terrace surrounding a fountain on the edge of the medieval fortifications or the elegant white-linen dining room, and then tuck into chef Christian Borini's recipes designed to highlight the market-fresh ingredients from the region.

Information

Tourist Office (☎05 53 58 79 62; www.pays-des-bastides.com; place du Château; ⏲10am-noon & 2-5pm Tue-Sat, 10am-12.30pm Sun; 📶) Loads of info on *bastide* country.

Getting There & Away

Issigeac is located 18km south of Bergerac on the D14, and is best reached with your own wheels.

Monpazier

POP 506

One of the Dordogne's best-preserved *bastides* is beautiful Monpazier. Founded in 1284 by a representative of Edward I (King of England and Duke of Aquitaine), it had a turbulent time during the Wars of Religion and the Peasant Revolts of the 16th century, but despite numerous assaults and campaigns, the town has survived wonderfully intact, with original walls, gates and a church.

Other top villages nearby are **Belvès** (16km northeast), with its yellow-gold houses strung across a gorgeous hilltop, and **Villefranche-du-Périgord** (20km southeast), another *bastide* with an enormous covered market in the central square. Teeny **Prats-du-Périgord** is for Romanesque architecture lovers, with its moody, fortified Église St-Maurice.

Sights

★ **Place des Cornières** SQUARE
From the town's three gateways, Monpazier's flat, grid-straight streets lead to the arcaded market square (also known as place Centrale), surrounded by an ochre-hued collection of stone houses that reflect centuries of building and rebuilding. In one corner is an old *lavoir* once used for washing clothes. Thursday is market day, as it has been since the Middle Ages.

Château de Biron CHÂTEAU
(☎05 53 63 13 39; www.semitour.com; D53; adult/child €8.20/5.30, joint ticket with Cadouin €11.90/7; ⏲10am-7pm daily Jul & Aug, 10am-1pm & 2-6pm Apr-Jun, Sep & Oct, Tue-Sun Nov-May, closed Jan) Eight kilometres south of Monpazier, this much-filmed château is a glorious mishmash of styles, having been fiddled with by eight centuries of successive heirs. The castle was finally sold in the early 1900s to pay for the extravagant lifestyle of a particularly irresponsible son. It's notable for its slate turrets and double loggia staircase, supposedly modelled on one at Versailles.

Sleeping & Eating

Chez Edèll B&B €
(☎05 53 63 26 71; www.chezedell.com; 2 rue Notre Dame; d incl breakfast €63, cottage €70; 📶) Cozy up in this diminutive but welcoming guesthouse in the middle of Monpazier. Rooms have balconies with sweeping country views, and a refrigerator – perfect for stocking up at the weekly market. A self-catering cottage is a superb deal.

Hôtel Edward 1er HOTEL €€
(☎05 53 22 44 00; www.hoteledward1er.com; 5 rue St-Pierre; d €108-140, ste €150-170; ⏲7.30-9pm Thu-Tue Sep-Jun, daily Jul & Aug; 📶🏊) Rooms in this tower-topped mansion get more luxurious the more you pay: top-of-the-line suites have a choice of Jacuzzi or Turkish bath, and views of surrounding hills. It feels slightly dated considering the price, but the owners are fun, and there's an excellent restaurant (*menus* €30 to €50), for which you should book ahead.

Bistrot 2 BISTRO €€
(☎05 53 22 60 64; www.bistrot2.fr; Foirail Nord; lunch/dinner menus from €16/22; ⏰9am-10pm Sat-Thu) Modern dining in an old-town setting with a wisteria-covered terrace right opposite a medieval gateway. Food is French with an adventurous slant.

Information

The **tourist office** (☎05 53 22 68 59; www.pays-des-bastides.com; place des Cornières; ⏰10am-12.30pm & 2-6pm Jun-Sep, reduced hours rest of year) is in the southeastern corner of the square.

Getting There & Away

Monpazier is 50km southwest of Sarlat and 50km southeast of Bergerac. There is no public transport.

The Dordogne Valley

Lush meadows and green woods roll out along the meandering banks of the Dordogne, one of France's most iconic and idyllic rivers. In centuries gone by, the valley marked an important frontier during the Hundred Years War, and the hilltops are studded with defensive châteaux, as well as heavily fortified towns. These days it's a picture of French tranquillity, perfect country to explore by bike or, better still, by paddle.

Trémolat & Around

Little Trémolat sits in a dramatic bend of the River Dordogne. Besides the beautiful, forested landscape, the area is home to several top restaurants and wine experiences, and there are a handful of interesting sights nearby.

Sights

Cloître de Cadouin CLOISTER
(☎05 53 63 36 28; www.semitour.com; Cadouin; adult/child €6.80/4, joint ticket with Château de Biron €11.90/7; ⏰10am-7pm Tue-Sun Jul & Aug, 10am-1pm & 2-6pm Tue-Sun Apr-Jun, Sep & Oct, shorter hours rest of year) This Unesco-listed 12th-century Cistercian abbey and its Gothic cloister hide in the forest just south of the Dordogne, along the River Bélingou.

Château de Lanquais CHÂTEAU
(☎06 10 79 12 69; http://chateaudelanquais.fr; Lanquais; adult/child €8/6; ⏰10am-7pm Jul & Aug, 2.30-6.30pm Wed-Mon Apr-Jun & Sep) This château, with portions dating from as early as the 12th century, though much of it is in the later Italian Renaissance style, is notable for being fully kitted out with period furnishings.

Eating

Chai Monique WINE BAR €
(☎05 53 07 29 84; 3 rue de Paris, Le Bugue; dishes €9-10; ⏰11am-8pm Tue, Fri & Sat, 11am-6pm Wed & Thu) An easy, light-hearted spot to grab a bite of local charcuterie, cheese and a glass of wine, all day long, in Le Bugue, 13km northwest of Trémolat.

★**Au Fil de l'Eau** REGIONAL CUISINE €€
(☎05 53 61 79 76; www.au-fil-de-leau.net; 32 av de Cahors, Couze St-Front; lunch menus €15, dinner menus €24-45; ⏰noon-2pm Wed-Fri & Sun, 7.30-9pm Wed-Sat) It's well worth stopping in the nondescript village of Couze St-Front for the warm welcome and riverside dining at Au Fil de l'Eau. Jazzy tunes tinkle as a parade of fresh, seasonal dishes is served; super-popular with locals. Reserve ahead to get a seat at the giant windows overlooking the river.

★**Les Truffieres** REGIONAL CUISINE €€
(☎05 53 27 30 44; www.auberge-les-truffieres.fr; Bosredon, Trémolat; lunch/dinner menus from €22/31; ⏰noon-1.30pm Tue-Sun, 7.30-9.30pm Tue-Sat May–mid-Sep, dinner only mid-Sep–Apr) Reserve ahead for fantastic local cuisine prepared by lively Yanick and his son Aurélian on a farm in the hills above Trémolat. The dining room feels like the country home it is, and the dishes are tops: from classic garlic soup to homemade foie gras.

★**Le Vieux Logis** GASTRONOMIC €€€
(☎05 53 22 80 06; www.vieux-logis.com; Trémolat; lunch menus €49, 4-course menus from €70; ⏰noon-1.30pm & 7.30-9pm, closed Wed & Thu mid-Oct–mid-Apr) Folks come from far and wide for chef Vincent Arnould's refined, beautifully presented creative cuisine of the Périgord. The ceiling soars over the elegant dining room, or dine alfresco under a canopy of sculpted trees. Every dish is a surprising treat, and the wine list matches. There's also excellent **Bistrot de la Place** (*menus* lunch/dinner from €17/23).

The Logis offers beautiful rooms (€210 to €385), creating the perfect peaceful retreat.

Shopping

Julien de Savignac WINE
(☎05 53 07 10 31; www.julien-de-savignac.com; av de la Libération, D51, Le Bugue; ⏰9am-7pm Tue-Sat, to noon Sun) One of Dordogne's best wine shops – spoiled for choice in Le Bugue, just

south of the town centre. Check the website for other branches.

Getting There & Away

Trémolat is 35km east of Bergerac and 44km west of Sarlat, and best reached with your own wheels.

Beynac-et-Cazenac & Around

Beynac, as it is known by locals, and its environs make up one of the Dordogne's most dramatic landscapes, with the two opposing fortresses of Beynac and Castelnaud, facing off across the gloriously broad river, plied by pleasure craft in summer.

Scenes from the Lasse Hallström-directed movie *Chocolat* (2000), starring Johnny Depp and Juliette Binoche, were filmed along rue de l'Ancienne Poste in Beynac, and part of Luc Besson's *The Messenger: The Story of Joan of Arc* (1999) was filmed in the fortress.

Sights

★Château de Castelnaud CASTLE

(www.castelnaud.com/uk; Castelnaud-la-Chapelle; adult/child €9.60/4.80; ⏲9am-8pm Jul & Aug, 10am-5pm Feb-Jun & Sep–mid-Nov, 2-5pm mid-Nov–Jan) The massive ramparts and metre-thick crenellated walls of this quintessential medieval fortress (occupied by the English during the Hundred Years War) contain an elaborate **museum of medieval warfare** with displays of daggers, spiked halberds, archaic cannons and enormous crossbows. Climb the dark 16th-century **artillery tower** stairs to see the exhibits and reach the rugged 13th-century donjon (keep). From the upper terrace a fantastic view encompasses the Dordogne Valley all the way to Castelnaud's arch-rival, the Château de Beynac, 4km to the north.

Daily demonstrations of giant trebuchets and a forge bring the fortress to life, and events including one-hour guided evening tours by costumed actors or mock battles are staged mid-July to August (check the website).

★Château de Beynac CHÂTEAU

(☎05 53 29 50 40; www.beynac-en-perigord.com; Beynac-et-Cazenac; adult/child €8/3.50; ⏲10am-6.30pm May-Aug, to 5pm Jan-Apr, Sep & Oct, closed Nov & Dec) Towering gloriously atop a limestone bluff, this 12th-century fortress' panoramic position above the Dordogne made it a key defensive position during the Hundred Years War. Apart from a brief interlude under Richard the Lionheart, Beynac remained fiercely loyal to the French monarchy, often placing it at odds with the English-controlled stronghold of nearby Castelnaud. Protected by 200m cliffs, a double wall and double moat, it presented a formidable challenge for would-be attackers, though it saw little direct action.

Highlights include the château's Romanesque **keep**, a grand **Salle des États** (State Room) and frescoed 15th-century **chapel**, and the 16th- and 17th-century **apartments** built to lodge castle barons. From the battlements, there's a fantastic view along the Dordogne.

The impressive fortress is rather bare-bones inside; buy the information booklet to add context. Parking slips (€2) are also good for town parking below.

Château des Milandes MUSEUM

(☎05 53 59 31 21; www.milandes.com; Castelnaud-la-Chapelle; adult/child €10/6.50; ⏲9.30am-7.30pm Jul & Aug, 10am-6.30pm Apr-Jun & Sep–mid-Nov) This 15th-century château, 3km southwest of Beynac, is famous for its fabulous former owner: glamorous dancer, singer and music-hall star Josephine Baker (1906–75), who took Paris by storm in the 1920s with her risque performances. Baker purchased the castle in 1936 and lived here

TOP MARKETS

Throughout the region local markets fill medieval cobbled streets and overflow with winter-time black truffles, walnuts, chestnuts, cheese, honey and seasonal produce. Baskets and clothing also feature at some. Summertime night markets are fantastic: bring your own plates and cutlery and dine at tables under the stars.

Monday St-Alvère, Beaumont-du-Périgord (night), Montignac (night)

Tuesday Beaumont-du-Périgord, Brive-la-Gaillarde, Le Bugue

Wednesday Périgueux, Sarlat-la-Canéda, Bergerac, Martel, Cahors, Cadouin

Thursday Monpazier, Issigeac (night)

Friday Brantôme, St-Pompon

Saturday Périgueux, Sarlat-la-Canéda, Brive-la-Gaillarde, Bergerac, Beaumont-du-Périgord, Villefranche-du-Périgord, Martel, Cahors, Figeac, St-Pompon (night)

Sunday Issigeac, St-Cyprien, Daglan

until 1958. It houses a super museum documenting her life with original photos and memorabilia including a fantastic costume collection, and her songs play throughout.

Baker was awarded the Croix de Guerre and the Legion of Honour for her work with the French Resistance during WWII, and was later active in the US civil-rights movement. She is also remembered for her 'Rainbow Tribe' – 12 children from around the world adopted as 'an experiment in brotherhood'.

From April to October free 30-minute daily **birds of prey displays** feature the château's owls, falcons and eagle.

Activities

Montgolfière Châteaux BALLOONING

(☎06 71 14 34 96; www.montgolfiere-chateaux.com; 1hr aloft adult/child from €180/120) Lovely Monsieur Lionel Druet takes you soaring over Dordogne châteaux in hot-air balloons.

Gabarres de Beynac BOATING

(☎05 53 28 51 15; www.gabarre-beynac.com; Beynac-et-Cazenac; adult/child €8/4.50; ⌚every 30min 10am-6pm May-Sep) Gabarres de Beynac does flat-bottomed boat trips departing from Beynac-et-Cazenac; kids cruise for free in the mornings.

Information

Tourist Office (☎05 53 29 43 08; www.sarlat-tourisme.com; Beynac; ⌚10am-1pm & 2-6pm Jul & Aug, shorter hours rest of year)

Getting There & Away

Beynac is 12km southwest of Sarlat, and there is no public transport.

La Roque Gageac & Around

La Roque Gageac's row of amber buildings and flourishing gardens built into the cliff face along the River Dordogne live up to all the adjectives: stunning, breathtaking! And it's an idyllic launch pad for a cruise or canoe trip.

Sights

★ **Jardins de Marqueyssac** GARDENS

(☎05 53 31 36 36; www.marqueyssac.com; Vézac; adult/child €8.80/4.40; ⌚9am-8pm Jul & Aug, 10am-7pm Apr-Jun & Sep, 10am-6pm Feb, Mar & Oct–mid-Nov) Garden fans won't want to miss these famous manicured gardens, stretching along a rocky bluff overlooking the Dordogne Valley. Signposted paths lead through painstakingly clipped box hedges and decorative topiary to the gardens' breathtaking *belvédère* (viewpoint), with sightlines to area castles, the Dordogne and La Roque Gageac. Thursday nights in July and August, the entire place is alight with candles (adult/child €13/6.50). Find the entrance 3km west of La Roque Gageac.

Fort Troglodyte FORT

(La Roque Gageac; adult/child €5/2; ⌚10am-6pm) A warren of meandering lanes leads up to La Roque's dramatic fort, where a series of defensive positions constructed by medieval engineers have been carved out of overhanging cliffs.

Activities

Paddling along the river, especially along this particular stretch, offers a changing panorama of soaring cliffs, castles and picturesque villages. Several canoe operators are based near La Roque Gageac and Cenac, including **Canoë Vacances** (☎05 53 28 17 07; www.canoevacances.com; Lespinasse, La Roque Gageac; self-guided canoeing per person €14-22), **Canoë Loisirs** (☎05 53 28 23 43; www.canoes-loisirs.com; Pont de Vitrac, Vitrac; self-guided canoe & kayak trips €8-25) and **Canoë Dordogne** (☎05 53 29 58 50; www.canoesdordogne.fr; La Roque Gageac; canoeing per person €7-24), which offer self-guided trips of between one and five hours from various points upriver.

La Roque Gageac's quay is also a launch point for short river cruises (p573) aboard a traditional *gabarre*.

Sleeping & Eating

La Belle Étoile HOTEL €

(☎05 53 29 51 44; www.belleetoile.fr; La Roque Gageac; d €80, ste €150; ⌚Apr-Oct; 📶) This riverside hotel has a prime position in La Roque, in an amber stone building with views across the water from higher-priced rooms (others overlook the village). Expect traditional wooden furniture and understated fabrics. The **restaurant** (menus from €32; ⌚noon-1.30pm Tue & Thu-Sun, 7.30-9.30pm Tue-Sun) is renowned for its sophisticated French food, and opens onto a vine-shaded terrace with a fabulous view.

Hôtel La Treille REGIONAL CUISINE €€

(☎05 53 28 33 19; www.latreille-perigord.com; Vitrac; menus €31-62; ⌚12.30-2pm Wed-Sun & 7.30-9pm daily Apr–mid-Nov; 📶) One of the few local restaurants open on Sunday and Monday nights, gourmet food is dished up river-

side at this sweet, small hotel (double/triple rooms from €54/73), in Vitrac, 6.5km east of La Roque Gageac.

Getting There & Away

La Roque Gageac is 15km south of Sarlat, via the D46 and D703. There's no public transport.

Domme & Around

Commanding an unparalleled view across the surrounding countryside from a dizzying outcrop above the Dordogne, Domme was a perfect defensive stronghold – a fact not lost on Philippe III of France, who founded the town in 1281 as a bastion against the English. Still one of the area's best preserved *bastides,* Domme retains most of its 13th-century ramparts and three original gateways. The imposing cliff-top position is best appreciated from esplanade du Belvédère and the adjacent promenade de la Barre, which offer panoramic views across the valley.

Domme can be overrun in high season, so plan to see the town and view and get out quick. Twelve kilometres south, beautifully preserved **Daglan** (population 550) and other villages hide some of the area's top restaurants.

Sights & Activities

Grottes Naturelles CAVE
(www.perigordnoir-valleedordogne.com; adult/child incl museum €8.50/6; ⌚4-20 tours daily Feb-Oct) Honeycombing the stone underneath the village is a series of large caves decorated with ornate stalactites and stalagmites. Get tickets, which include admission to the small **Musée d'Arts et Traditions Populaires** (⌚10.30am-12.30pm & 2.30-6pm Apr-Sep), a folk museum, at the tourist office opposite the entrance to the caves.

Prison des Templiers TOWER
(adult/child €7/5; ⌚Apr-Sep) Many Knights Templar were imprisoned in Domme in 1307 while they awaited trial. Loads of Templar graffiti in their code system still marks their prison. Ask at the tourist office for information.

★**Fabrice le Chef** COOKING
(☎06 83 22 61 92; www.fabricelechef.fr; Daglan; 2-3hr class per person €50) Learn how to cook delicious Périgord cuisine from Fabrice, or have him come cook for you! He also has a great restaurant (lunch/dinner *menus* from €15/25) in Daglan, serving seasonal, creative cuisine.

Sleeping

The Dordogne in general and the area around Domme in particular is loaded with vacation rentals, easy to find on sites such as http://vrbo.com: from simple cottages to 13th-century dream hilltop Château Peyruzel. B&Bs in this area are generally of a high quality.

La Tour de Cause B&B €€
(☎05 53 30 30 51; www.latourdecause.com; Pont de Cause, Castelnaud-la-Chapelle; d/studio incl breakfast €100/110; P ⊗ 📶 ≋) Nico and Igor have painstakingly renovated an historic manor house and barn into a comfortable B&B with modern bathrooms and luxe linens. Find it 6km east of Domme on the D50, or 2.5km south of Castelnaud on the D57.

La Guérinière B&B €€
(☎05 53 29 91 97; www.la-gueriniere-dordogne.com; Cénac et St-Julien; d incl breakfast €105, q €175; 📶 ≋) 🍃 Surrounded by 6 hectares of grounds in the valley 5km south of Domme along the D46, this family-friendly B&B's rooms are all named after flowers: our faves are Mimosa, with its sloping roof and chinoiserie wardrobe, and the supersized Bleuet room. Book ahead for *tables d'hôte* (set *menus;* €28 including wine) that use mostly organic produce.

★**Château de Maraval** DESIGN HOTEL €€€
(☎06 06 94 37 61; www.chateaudemaraval.fr; Cénac-et-Saint-Julien; d €195; ⌚Feb-Dec; P ❄ 📶 ≋) Here's your chance to combine historic elegance (a grand château in lush grounds) with contemporary luxury (mod rooms kitted out with design tapestries, sleek furnishings and high-concept bathrooms). This friendly escape just south of Domme in Cénac pampers with high-threadcount linens, spa facilities and an idyllic pool.

Eating

★**Le Petit Paris** REGIONAL CUISINE €€
(☎05 53 28 41 10; www.le-petit-paris.fr; Daglan; menus €29-39; ⌚noon-1.30pm Tue-Sun, 7-8.45pm Tue-Sat late-Feb–mid-Nov) Friendly staff serve you on little Daglan's central square, promoting an elegant 'there's all the time in the world' feel, while wowing with impeccable seasonal local cuisine. Spring brings lovely asparagus, the rest of the year find tender Limousin beef,

falling off the bone, or foie gras that melts in your mouth. It's 11km south of Domme.

L'Envie des Mets MODERN FRENCH €€
(☎05 53 31 94 01; www.lenvie-des-mets-resto.com; St-Pompon; menus €32; ⊙noon-3pm Tue-Sat, 7.30-10.30pm Thu-Sat) Reserve ahead for the popular restaurant where a young chef whips up cutting-edge seasonal *périgourdine* cuisine in St-Pompon, 16km southwest of Domme. Naturally, the *menu* changes weekly.

★**Le Saint Martial** GASTRONOMIC €€€
(☎05 53 29 18 34; www.lesaintmartial.com; St-Martial-de-Nabirat; menus €36-75; ⊙noon-1.30pm & 7.30-9pm Wed-Sun; ❄ 👪) Details, details, details. Valérie and Jean-Marc Réal get them all right at this small restaurant in low-key St-Martial-de-Nabirat, 8km south of Domme. The church bells chime lightly and the terrace stretches out in the sun as you enjoy a steady procession of beautifully presented local dishes. Book well ahead.

Information

Tourist Office (☎05 53 31 71 00; www.tourisme-domme.com; place de la Halle; ⊙9.30am-6.30pm May-Sep, 10-12.30pm & 1.30-5pm Mar-Apr & Oct)

Getting There & Away

Domme is 18km south of Sarlat along the D46. There are no public transport options. In high season, park at the edge of the village and walk in, or take the **mini-train** (www.domme-perigord.com; adult/child €5/2) from the Porte des Tours parking lot.

Sarlat-la-Canéda

POP 9414

A picturesque tangle of honey-coloured buildings, alleyways and secret squares make up the beautiful town of Sarlat-la-Canéda. Boasting some of the region's best-preserved medieval architecture, it's a popular base for exploring the Vézère Valley, and a favourite location for film directors. It's also firmly on the tourist radar, and you might find it difficult to appreciate the town's charms among the summer throngs, especially on market days.

Well-known markets sell a smorgasbord of goose-based products, and Sarlat hosts an annual goose festival, the Fest'Oie (late February/early March), when live birds and market stalls fill the streets, and Sarlat's top chefs prepare an outdoor banquet.

Sights

★**Weekly Markets** MARKET
(place de la Liberté & rue de la République; ⊙8.30am-1pm Wed, 8.30am-6pm Sat) For an introductory French market experience, visit Sarlat's heavily touristed Saturday market, which takes over the streets around Cathédrale St-Sacerdos. Depending on the season, delicacies include local mushrooms and duck- and goose-based products such as foie gras. The Wednesday version is a smaller affair. An atmospheric largely organic **night market** (⊙6-10pm) operates on Thursdays.

Marché aux Truffes TRUFFLE MARKET
(⊙from 9am Sat Dec-Feb) Get *truffe noir* (black truffle) at the winter morning Marché aux Truffes.

★**Place du Marché aux Oies** SQUARE
(Goose Market Sq) A life-size statue of three bronze geese stands in the centre of beautiful place du Marché aux Oies, where live geese are still sold during the Fest'Oie.The square's architecture is exceptional.

★**Église Ste-Marie** CHURCH, MARKET
(place de la Liberté) Église Ste-Marie was ingeniously converted by acclaimed architect Jean Nouvel, whose parents still live in Sarlat, into the town's touristy **Marché Couvert** (Covered Market; ⊙8.30am-2pm daily mid-Apr–mid-Nov, closed Mon, Thu & Sun rest of year). Its panoramic lift offers 360-degree views across Sarlat's countryside.

★**Cathédrale St-Sacerdos** CATHEDRAL
(place du Peyrou) Once part of Sarlat's Cluniac abbey, the original abbey church was built in the 1100s, redeveloped in the early 1500s, and remodelled again in the 1700s, so it's a real mix of styles. The belfry and western façade are the oldest parts of the building, while the nave, organ and interior chapels are later additions.

Jardin des Enfeus PARK
Behind the cathedral, the Jardin des Enfeus was Sarlat's first cemetery. The rocket-shaped **Lanterne des Morts** (Lantern of the Dead) may have been built to honour a visit by St Bernard in 1147, one of the founders of the Cistercian order.

Manoir de Gisson HISTORIC BUILDING
(☎05 53 28 70 55; www.manoirdegisson.com; place des Oies; adult/child €6/3.50; ⊙10am-6.30pm Apr-Sep, reduced hours rest of year) Tour this mansion, dating from the 13th century,

in the heart of Sarlat to get a taste of how the bourgeoisie lived. There's a cabinet of curiosities in the basement to entertain the kids.

Out of Town

Château de Puymartin CHÂTEAU
(05 53 59 29 97; www.chateau-de-puymartin.com; adult/child €8/4; 10am-6.30pm Jul & Aug, 10am-11.30am & 2-6pm Apr-Jun & Sep, 2-5.30pm Oct–mid-Nov) This impressive turreted château, 8km northwest of Sarlat, was first built in 1270, destroyed in 1358 during the Hundred Years War, and rebuilt around 1450. The ornate interior is furnished lavishly with mostly 19th-century decor.

Moulin de la Tour FARM
(05 53 59 22 08; www.moulindelatour.com; Ste-Nathalene; 9.30am-noon & 2-6.30pm Mon, Wed & Fri, 2-6.30pm Sat Apr-Sep, Wed & Fri only rest of year) One of the Dordogne's most distinctive flavours is the humble *noix* (walnut). It's been a prized product of the Dordogne for centuries, and is still used in many local recipes – cakes, puddings, pancakes and breads, as well as liqueurs and *huile de noix* (walnut oil). At the Moulin de la Tour, the region's last working watermill, you can watch walnut oil being made and stock up with nutty souvenirs. Don't miss the *cerneaux de noix au chocolat* (chocolate-covered walnuts) and *gâteau de noix* (walnut cake).

L'Elevage du Bouyssou FARM
(05 53 31 12 31; www.elevagedubouyssou.com; Le Bouyssou, Carsac-Aillac; shop 8am-6pm, tours 6.30pm daily Jul & Aug, Mon-Sat rest of year) The Dordogne is famous for its foie gras (fattened goose liver). You'll see duck and goose farms dotted throughout the countryside, many of which offer guided tours and *dégustation* (tasting). L'Elevage du Bouyssou is a family-run farm to the north of Carsac-Aillac. Owners Denis and Nathalie Mazet run tours and demonstrate *la gavage* – the controversial force-feeding process (p926) that helps fatten up the goose livers. You can also buy homemade foie gras in the shop.

Festivals & Events

Fest'Oie FOOD
(late Feb or early Mar) Sarlat hosts an annual goose festival, the Fest'Oie, when live birds and market stalls fill the streets, and Sarlat's top chefs prepare an outdoor banquet.

DON'T MISS

GABARRE CRUISES

One of the best ways to explore the gorgeous scenery of the Dordogne River is aboard a *gabarre*, a flat-bottomed, wooden boat used to transport freight up and down the rivers of the Périgord and Lot Valley. *Gabarres* were a common sight in this part of France until the early 20th century, when they were eclipsed by the rise of the railway and the automobile.

From April to October, traditional *gabarres* cruise from several points along the river, including Bergerac, Brantôme, Beaulieu-sur-Dordogne and the quay at La Roque Gageac.

La Roque Gageac's operators include **Gabarres Caminade** (05 53 29 40 95; http://gabarrecaminade.fr) and **Gabarres Norbert** (05 53 29 40 44; www.gabarres.com). Standard trips last about an hour and cost around €9/7 per adult/child; advance reservations are recommended. Gabarres de Beynac (p570) does slightly shorter, cheaper trips departing from Beynac-et-Cazenac, and kids cruise free in the mornings.

Sleeping

Hôtel Les Remparts HOTEL €
(05 53 59 40 00; www.hotel-lesremparts-sarlat.com; 48 av Gambetta; d €71-78, tr/q €88/110;) Just outside the old town centre on a busyish one-way street, this simple stone hotel has to be one of the best deals in Sarlat. Rooms lack sparkle; simple furniture and the odd reclaimed roof beam are all you should expect.

Hôtel La Couleuvrine HOTEL €
(05 53 59 27 80; www.la-couleuvrine.com; 1 place de la Bouquerie; d €80-100;) Originally part of Sarlat's city wall, this rambling hotel with a sunny terrace has rooms jammed along creaky corridors. Superior and family rooms are more spacious.

Hôtel Le Mas de Castel HOTEL €
(05 53 59 02 59; www.hotel-lemasdecastel.com; rte du Sudalissant; d €80-95, f €110-125;) This former farmhouse 3km south of town makes a delightful escape from the hectic hum of central Sarlat. Some of its 14 sunny rooms open to the flower-filled courtyard and pool; one has self-catering facilities.

Sarlat-la-Canéda

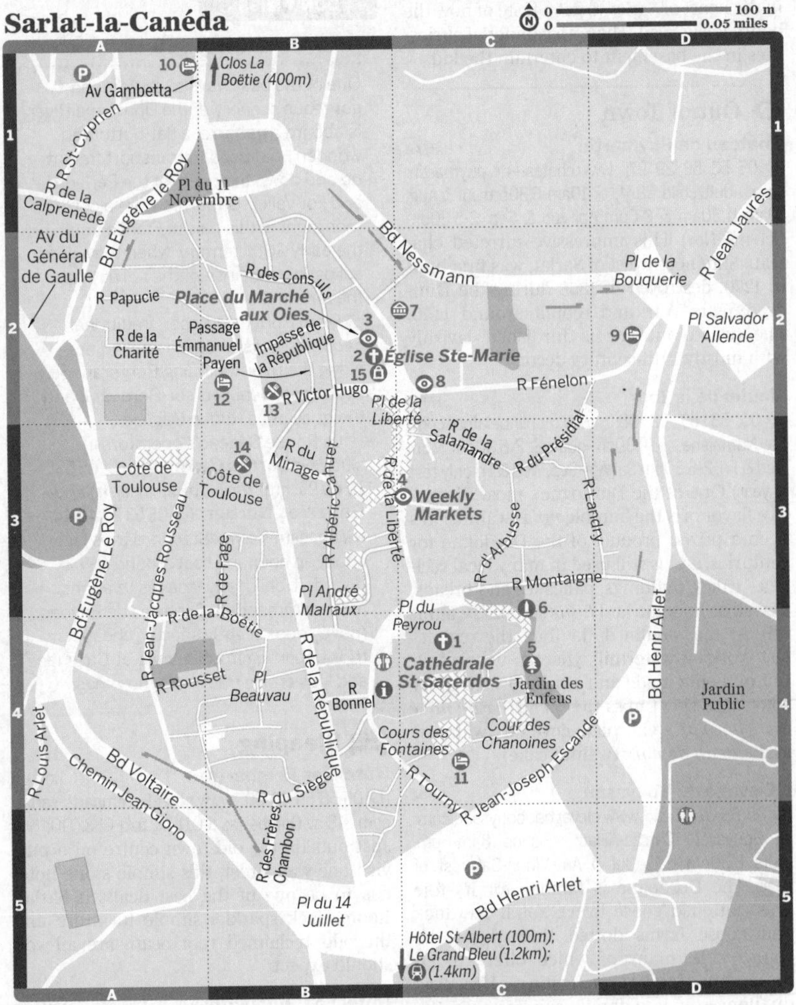

★ Villa des Consuls B&B €€

(☎ 05 53 31 90 05; www.villaconsuls.fr; 3 rue Jean-Jacques Rousseau; d €95-110, apt €150-190; @ 📶) Despite its Renaissance exterior, the enormous rooms here are modern through and through, with shiny wood floors and sleek furnishings. Several delightful self-contained apartments dot the town, all offering the same mix of period plushness – some also have terraces overlooking the town's rooftops.

★ La Maison des Peyrat HOTEL €€

(☎ 05 53 59 00 32; www.maisondespeyrat.com; Le Lac de la Plane; r €70-112) This beautifully renovated 17th-century house, formerly a nuns' hospital and later an aristocratic hunting lodge, is set on a hill about 1.5km from Sarlat centre. Eleven generously sized rooms are decorated in modern farmhouse style; the best have views over gardens and the countryside beyond. Good restaurant, too.

Le Porche de Sarlat APARTMENT €€

(☎ 06 80 15 27 21; www.appart-hotel-sarlat.fr; 6 cour des Fontaines; apt €125-175; ❄ 📶) Superb modern apartments fill this townhouse as central as could be in medieval Sarlat. Some have views of the cathedral or the cours des Fontaines, and small private gardens or ter-

Sarlat-la-Canéda

Top Sights
1 Cathédrale St-Sacerdos C4
2 Église Ste-Marie B2
3 Place du Marché aux Oies B2
4 Weekly Markets C3

Sights
5 Jardin des Enfeus C4
6 Lanterne des Morts C3
7 Manoir de Gisson C2
8 Marché aux Truffes C2

Sleeping
9 Hôtel La Couleuvrine D2
10 Hôtel Les Remparts A1
11 Le Porche de Sarlat C4
12 Villa des Consuls B2

Eating
13 Le Petit Manoir B2
14 Le Quatre Saisons B3

Shopping
15 Marché Couvert B2

races. All have full kitchens and high-quality fittings. There is a €50 cleaning charge.

Clos La Boëtie BOUTIQUE HOTEL €€€
(☎05 53 29 44 18; www.closlaboetie-sarlat.com; 95-97 av de la Selves; d €250-310; ❄@📶🏊) Supremely luxurious rooms in a 19th-century mansion, with a price tag to match. It's 400m north of the centre.

Eating

Le Petit Manoir REGIONAL CUISINE €€
(☎05 53 29 82 14; 13 rue de la République; mains €20; ⏰12.40-2pm & 7-9pm Tue-Sun; 📶🖋) Book ahead for a seat in the ornate 15th-century mansion where the cuisine combines creative Dordogne specialities with a touch of Asian fusion. The Vietnamese chef creates a *menu* that changes with the seasons, and there are always vegetarian options (*menu* €27).

Le Quatre Saisons REGIONAL CUISINE €€
(☎05 53 29 48 59; 2 côte de Toulouse; menus from €26; ⏰12.30-2pm & 7.30-9.30pm Thu-Mon; 🖋👪) A reliable local favourite, hidden in a beautiful stone house on a narrow alley leading uphill from rue de la République. The food is honest and unfussy, taking its cue from market ingredients and regional flavours. The most romantic tables have cross-town views.

★**Le Grand Bleu** GASTRONOMIC €€€
(☎05 53 31 08 48; www.legrandbleu.eu; 43 av de la Gare; lunch menus €36, dinner menus €54-125; ⏰12.30-2pm Thu-Sun, 7.30-9.30pm Tue-Sat) This eminent Michelin-starred restaurant run by chef Maxime Lebrun is renowned for its creative cuisine with elaborate *menus* making maximum use of luxury produce: truffles, lobster, turbot and scallops, with a wine list to match. Cooking courses (€40) are also available. Located 1.5km south of the centre.

Information

Tourist Office (☎05 53 31 45 45; www.sarlat-tourisme.com; 3 rue Tourny; ⏰9am-7pm Mon-Sat, 10am-1pm & 2-6pm Sun May-Sep, shorter hours Oct-Apr; 📶) Sarlat's tourist office is packed with info, but often gets overwhelmed by visitors; the website has it all.

Getting There & Around

BICYCLE

Hire bikes for around €17 for half a day from **Liberty Cycle** (☎07 81 24 78 79; www.liberty-cycle.com; D704; half-day bicycle/electric-cycle €17/30; ⏰10am-6pm Apr-Oct).

CAR

Cars are banned in the medieval centre from June to September, and rue de la République, the main street that bisects the centre, is pedestrianised in July and August. Find two large, free car parks on av Général de Gaulle, northwest of the old town. Europcar is near the train station.

TRAIN

The **train station** (av de la Gare) is 1.3km south of the old city. Many destinations require a change at Le Buisson or Libourne.

Bergerac €13.20, 1½ hours, five daily
Bordeaux €27.70, 2¾ hours, six daily
Les Eyzies €10.10, 1½ to two hours depending on connections, four daily
Périgueux €16.30, 1½ to 2½ hours depending on connections, five daily

The Vézère Valley

North of the Dordogne, the placid River Vézère winds through lush green meadows and softly blowing willow trees, creating a gorgeous tiny valley flanked by limestone cliffs that conceal dozens of subterranean caverns and indented *abris* (shelters). This tiny Vézère Valley is world famous for its wonderfully preserved prehistoric sites, and especially for its incredible collection of cave paintings – the highest concentration of

Stone Age art found in Europe. The paintings and etchings were mostly created by Cro-Magnon people between around 15,000 BC and 10,000 BC, and range in style and artistry from simple scratched lines to complex multicoloured frescos.

Most of the key sites are around the towns of Les Eyzies-de-Tayac-Sireuil and Montignac, though Montignac is by far the more charming. Neither has particularly good restaurants. Visits can also be done as day trips from elsewhere in the Dordogne.

Les Eyzies-de-Tayac-Sireuil & Around

At the heart of the Vézère Valley, Les Eyzies (as it's known locally) makes an uninspiring introduction to the wonders of the Vézère, with postcard sellers and souvenir shops lining the small main street. Still, the town has an excellent museum, and many major sites are within a short drive.

Sights

LES EYZIES TOWN

★Musée National de Préhistoire MUSEUM

(☎05 53 06 45 65; www.musee-prehistoire-eyzies.fr; 1 rue du Musée; adult/child €6/4.50, 1st Sun of month free; ⏲9.30am-6.30pm daily Jul & Aug, 9.30am-6pm Wed-Mon Jun & Sep, 9.30am-12.30pm & 2-5.30pm Wed-Mon Oct-May) Inside a marvellous modern building alongside the cliffs, this museum provides a fine prehistory primer (providing your French is good) with the most comprehensive collection of prehistoric finds in France. Highlights include a huge gallery of Stone Age tools, weapons and jewellery, and skeletons of some of the animals that once roamed the Vézère (including bison, woolly rhinoceros, giant deer and cave bears). A collection of carved reliefs on the 1st floor includes a famous frieze of horses and a bison licking its flank.

Abri Pataud HISTORIC SITE

(☎05 53 06 92 46; www.mnhn.fr; 20 rue du Moyen Âge; adult/child €5/free; ⏲10am-noon & 2-6pm Sun-Thu May & Jun, daily Jul & Aug, Mon-Fri Apr & early-Oct, closed mid-Oct–Mar) About 250m north of the Musée National de Préhistoire, this Cro-Magnon *abri* (shelter) was inhabited over a period of 15,000 years starting some 37,000 years ago and now displays bones and other excavated artefacts. The ibex carved into the ceiling dates from about 19,000 BC. Admission includes a one-hour guided tour (some in English).

EAST OF LES EYZIES

★Grotte de Font de Gaume HISTORIC SITE

(☎05 53 06 86 00; www.eyzies.monuments-nationaux.fr; 4 av des Grottes; adult/child €7.50/free; ⏲guided tours 9.30am-5.30pm Sun-Fri mid-May–mid-Sep, 9.30am-12.30pm & 2-5.30pm Sun-Fri mid-Sep–mid-May) This extraordinary cave contains the only original polychrome (as opposed to single colour) paintings still open to the public. About 14,000 years ago, prehistoric artists created the gallery of more than 230 figures, including bison, reindeer, horses, mammoths, bears and wolves, although only about 25 are included in the fantastically atmospheric tour. Look out for the famous **Chapelle des Bisons**, a scene of courting reindeer and stunningly realised horses, several caught in mid-movement. Try to reserve ahead by phone as far in advance as you can.

Font de Gaume is such a rare and valuable site that there is always talk of the cave being closed for its own protection. Visitor numbers are currently limited to 78 per day, and after the few tickets available for advance reservation are gone, you must line up very, very early on the day to get one. The small 45-minute guided tours are occasionally in English. Find the ticket office and cave 1km northeast of Les Eyzies on the D4.

★Grotte des Combarelles HISTORIC SITE

(☎05 53 06 86 00; www.eyzies.monuments-nationaux.fr; adult/child €7.50/free; ⏲guided tours 9.30am-5.30pm Sun-Fri mid-May–mid-Sep, 9.30am-12.30pm & 2-5.30pm Sun-Fri mid-Sep–mid-May) This narrow, very long cave 1.5km east of Font de Gaume was the first rediscovered in the valley, in 1901, and is renowned for its animal engravings, many of which cleverly use the natural contours of the rock to sculpt the animals' forms. Look out for mammoths, horses and reindeer, and human figures, as well as a fantastic mountain lion that seems to leap from the rock face. Reserve ahead or go early on the day to buy tickets at the Font de Gaume ticket office for 45-minute, seven-person tours.

★Abri de Cap Blanc HISTORIC SITE

(☎05 53 06 86 00; www.eyzies.monuments-nationaux.fr; adult/child €7.50/free; ⏲guided tours 10am-6pm Sun-Fri mid-May–mid-Sep, 10am-12.30pm & 2-5.30pm Sun-Fri mid-Sep–mid-May) While most of the Vézère's caves contain engravings and paintings, unusually, this rock shelter contains only evocatively carved sculptures, shaped using simple flint tools some 14,000

Vézère & Dordogne Valleys

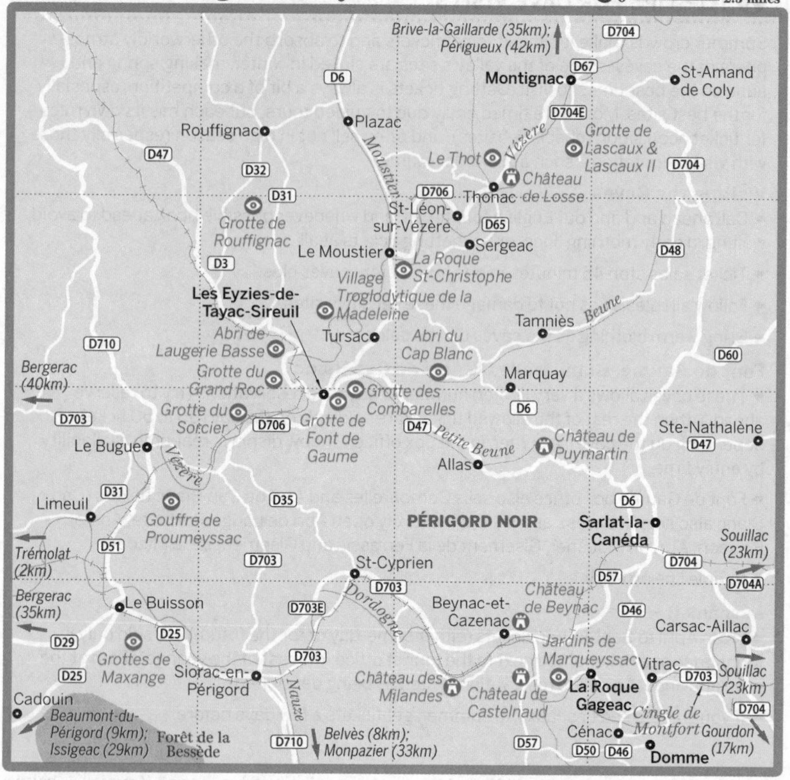

years ago. The 40m frieze of horses and bison is impressive, especially when the guide plays the flashlight over its contours. It's 7km east of Les Eyzies. Tickets available on-site or at Font de Gaume ticket office.

NORTHWEST & WEST OF LES EYZIES

★Grotte de Rouffignac HISTORIC SITE

(☎05 53 05 41 71; www.grottederouffignac.fr; Rouffignac-St-Cernin-de-Reilhac; adult/child €7.50/4.80; ⏲9-11.30am & 2-6pm Jul & Aug, 10-11.30am & 2-5pm Apr-Jun, Sep & Oct, closed Nov-Mar) Hidden in pretty woodland 15km north of Les Eyzies, this enormous tri-level cave is one of the most complex and rewarding to see in the Dordogne. Board an electric train to explore a 1km maze of tunnels in the massive cavern plunging 8km into the earth.

Highlights include the frieze of 10 mammoths in procession, one of the largest cave paintings ever discovered, and the awe-inspiring Great Ceiling, with more than 65 figures from ibex to aurochs. You'll also see nests of long-extinct cave bears, and 17th-century graffiti.

Tickets are sold at the cave but can't be reserved and do sell out, so arrive by 9am in July and August to get tickets for any time that day. March to June and September to October, afternoon tickets are only available after 2pm.

Grotte du Grand Roc CAVE

(☎05 53 06 92 70; www.semitour.com; adult/child €7.50/5; ⏲10am-7pm Jul & Aug, 10am-1pm & 2-6pm Apr-Jun, Sep & Oct, shorter hours rest of year) Around 3km northwest of Les Eyzies along the D47, this cave contains an array of glittering stalactites and stalagmites. A joint ticket (adult/child €9.50/6) includes adjacent **Abri de Laugerie Basse**, a rock shelter originally occupied by Cro-Magnon people and still used until recent times.

Grotte du Sorcier HISTORIC SITE

(☎05 53 07 14 37; www.grottedusorcier.com; St-Cirq; adult/child €7/3.50; ⏲10am-7.30pm Jul &

TOP TIPS FOR CAVE VISITS

Summer crowds make it difficult to get tickets and to absorb the otherworldly atmosphere of the caves; some of the valley's sites are closed in winter, making spring and autumn the best times to visit. Getting tickets is always a bit of a competition, especially for the best sites. Most have timed entry due to guided tours, but each has its own rules for ticket acquisition (check websites), and often sell out in high season (especially those with visitor limitations, such as Font de Gaume).

Visiting the Caves

- Call ahead and find out English tour times, and whenever possible book ahead to avoid waiting in early morning lines, or not getting tickets at all.
- Ticket sales stop 45 minutes to one hour before caves close.
- Follow all rules so as not to damage these sensitive sites.
- Bring warm clothing as the caves can be cold.

Font de Gaume, Combarelles & Abri de Cap Blanc

- These caves allows a very limited number of advance reservations (try to reserve ahead!), then the rest of the allowed tickets are *sold only on the day* (35 to 50 tickets, depending on the cave). A screen in the box office window displays real-time availability by entry time.
- Font de Gaume box office also sells Combarelles and Abri de Cap Blanc tickets (Cap Blanc also sold at caves), as a well as the rarely open Abri de Laugerie-Haute, Abri du Poisson, Abri du Moustier, Gisement de la Ferrassie and Gisement de la Micoque.
- People line up *early*.

Lascaux II

- From April to September, tickets (either same-day or for the future) are sold only in Montignac at a ticket office next to the tourist office; the rest of the year get them at the cave entrance. An online reservation system is being developed.
- If you want to see Lascaux II in summer, get tickets a few days before.

Aug, 10am-6pm Apr-Jun & Sep–mid-Nov) About 8km west of Les Eyzies, near the hamlet of St-Cirq, this privately owned cave features several animal engravings dating from around 15,000 BC to 17,000 BC, but it's best known for a male human figure known as the *Sorcier* (Sorceror), who's endowed with a phallus of truly enormous proportions, possibly indicating his shamanic status...

Activities & Tours

Prehistoric Art & Cave Tour CAVE TOUR
(☎05 53 07 26 04; www.caveconnection.fr; per day for 1 person €270, per additional person €20, maximum €370) Expert prehistoric anthropologist Christine Desdemaines-Hugon tailors cave tours for everyone from the Smithsonian to private individuals. She writes about Dordogne cave art in *Stepping-Stones: A Journey through the Ice Age Caves of the Dordogne*. Cave tickets not included, but she helps to acquire the often-hard-to-get tickets.

Animation Vézère Canoë Kayak BOATING
(☎05 53 06 92 92; www.vezere-canoe.com; Les Eyzies; adult/child from €9/4.50; ⏰Apr-Oct) Canoe and kayak rentals with minibus transport, at Les Eyzies bridge.

Canoës Vallée Vézère BOATING
(☎05 53 05 10 11; www.canoesvalleevezere.com; 1-3 promenade de la Vézère, Les Eyzies; self-guided trips €16-24; ⏰Apr-Sep) Organises 10km to 26km self-guided canoe and kayak trips including minibus transport. Multiday trips stop at campgrounds or hotels.

Sleeping & Eating

Camping La Rivière CAMPGROUND €
(☎05 53 06 97 14; www.lariviereleseyzies.com; campsites per adult/child €7.20/5.56; ⏰Apr–mid-Oct; P@🛜🏊) The nearest campground to Les Eyzies, just west of town beside the river. Facilities include a restaurant, bar, laundry and grocery. There's also a small hotel (doubles/quads €55/72).

Hôtel Le Cro-Magnon HOTEL €
(☎05 53 06 97 06; www.hostellerie-cro-magnon.com; 54 av de la Préhistoire; d €85-100; ⊙Mar-Nov;) This pretty wisteria-clad hotel has been around since the 1850s and was often used as a base by pioneering prehistorians. Flowery rooms are a touch bland, but corridors built straight into the rock face add quirky appeal. Dining is good value in the lovely beam-ceilinged restaurant.

Hôtel des Glycines HOTEL €€
(☎05 53 06 97 07; www.les-glycines-dordogne.com; 4 av de Laugerie; d €144-199, ste €270-345; ⊙Jan–mid-Nov;) Les-Eyzies' top posh pad: plush rooms range from cream-and-check 'classics' to full-blown suites with terraces and garden views. Beware 'courtyard rooms', which overlook the main road. The hotel's gastronomic restaurant (lunch *menus* €19, dinner *menus* €62 to €110) is a pampering affair.

Moulin de la Beaune REGIONAL CUISINE €€
(Au Vieux Moulin; ☎05 53 06 94 33; www.moulindelabeune.com; menus €21-58; ⊙mid-Apr–Oct) Reserve ahead for a spot at one of the riverfront terrace tables at this renovated water mill converted into a lovely restaurant and hotel (doubles €70 to €80). The most charming family-run establishment in Les-Eyzies, it's also the most beautifully situated, and serves up authentic, seasonal local fare.

Information

Tourist Office (☎05 53 06 97 05; www.lascaux-dordogne.com; 19 av de la Préhistoire, Les Eyzies; ⊙9am-6.30pm Jul & Aug, shorter hours rest of year) Small office with maps and local walk information.

Getting There & Away

Les Eyzies is 21km west of Sarlat, on the D47. The train station is 700m north of town, with connections to Sarlat (change at Le Buisson or Libourne; €10.10, 1½ to two hours depending on connections, four daily), and direct trains to Périgueux (€8.50, 35 minutes, six daily).

Les Eyzies to Montignac

The majority of sights are along the main road (D706) linking Les Eyzies with Montignac.

Sights

Le Thot MUSEUM
(☎05 53 50 70 44; www.semitour.com; Thonac; adult/child €9/5.90, joint ticket with Lascaux II €14.50/9.80; ⊙10am-7pm Jul & Aug, to 6pm Apr-Jun, Sep & Oct, shorter hours rest of year) In an effort to bring the prehistoric age to life, Le Thot, 8km southwest of Montignac, places reproduced Lascaux cave scenes alongside displays about Cro-Magnon life and art, as well as real-life descendants of the animals the art depicts (reindeer, stags, ibex and European bison), which roam the grounds.

Le Village Troglodytique de la Madeleine HISTORIC SITE
(☎05 53 46 36 88; www.la-madeleine-perigord.com; adult/child €6/3.50; ⊙9.30am-8pm Jul & Aug, 10am-7pm May, Jun & Sep, 10am-6pm Apr & Oct, Sat & Sun only Nov-Mar) Many of the Vézère's caves were used for storage, defence or protection as recently as the Middle Ages. This cave village 8km northeast of Les Eyzies was carved from the cliff face above the Vézère River, and its lower level was occupied by prehistoric people 10,000 to 14,000 years ago, but its upper level was used as a fortified village by medieval settlers.

La Roque St-Christophe HISTORIC SITE
(☎05 53 50 70 45; www.roque-st-christophe.com; Peyzac-le-Moustier; adult/child €8/4.50; ⊙10am-8pm Jul & Aug, to 6.30pm Apr-Jun & Sep, reduced hours rest of year) On a sheer cliff face 80m above the Vézère, this 900m-long series of terraces and caves has been a practically unassailable natural fortress for almost 50 millennia – initially used by Mousterian (Neanderthal) people 50,000 years ago, followed by successive generations until the 16th century. Sweeping views are stunning, though the caverns themselves are largely empty and some of the plastic reconstructions are decidedly lame. Located 10km northeast of Les Eyzies.

Montignac

POP 2917

The charming auburn-stone riverside town of Montignac has become famous for the nearby Grottes de Lascaux, hidden in wooded hills just outside town. Montignac itself, with its crumbling medieval fortress and arching bridges, drapes beautifully along both banks of the Vézère, and is a more peaceful base than Les Eyzies for exploring the valley.

The tiny lanes of the old city sit on the river's west bank; many hotels are on the east bank, near the Lascaux ticket office and place Tourny.

Vézère Valley Cave Art

Deep in the Vézère Valley, prehistoric Cro-Magnon artists worked by the light of primitive oil torches, creating some of Europe's first art. Today in the Vézère caves you can see what they created: from simple scratched lines and hand-tracings to complex multicoloured frescos of leaping horses, mammoths, ibex, aurochs, reindeer and bulls.

Who were the artists?

Most of the Vézère Valley's cave paintings date from the end of the last ice age, between 20,000 BC and 10,000 BC, and were painted by Cro-Magnon people. Until around 20,000 BC much of northern Europe was still covered by vast glaciers and ice sheets, so people lived a hunter-gatherer lifestyle, using the mouths of the natural caves as temporary shelters while they followed the migration routes of prey.

The paintings seem to have come to an abrupt halt around 10,000 BC, around the same time the last ice sheets disappeared and humans hereabouts established a more fixed agricultural lifestyle.

What did they create?

Using flint tools for engraving, natural fibre brushes, pads or sponges for painting, and pigments derived from minerals including magnesium and charcoal (black), ochre (red/yellow) and iron (red), Cro-Magnon artists usually depicted animals, though there are occasional mysterious geometric shapes and symbols.

The earliest known cave art in the area is from the Gravettian period, from before 22,000 BC, consisting of abstract engravings, paintings of female genitalia, or 'Venus' figures. It then developed into complex animal figures and friezes such as those at Lascaux, Rouffignac and Font de Gaume, which date from around 17,000 BC to 10,000 BC. These early artists also created jewellery from shells, bones, antlers and scrimshaw, decorated with animal scenes and geometric patterns.

Theories abound as to why Cro-Magnons made this often elaborate art, but in reality, no one knows.

1

1. Viewing cave art in the Great Hall of the Bulls, Lascaux II (p582)
2. Hunting scene, Grotte de Lascaux (p582)
3. Cave art detail, Lascaux II (p582)

3

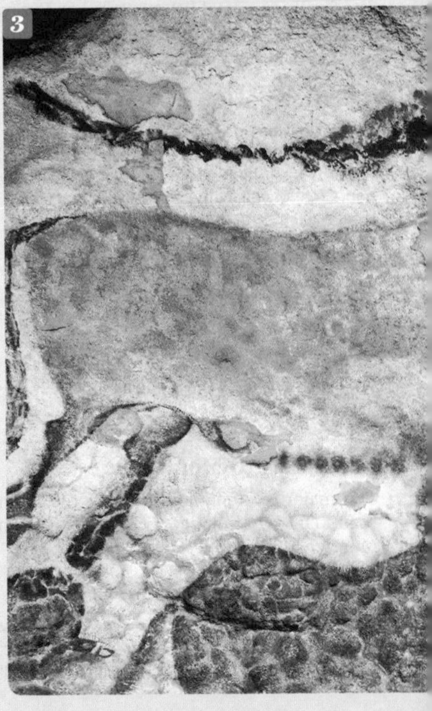

2

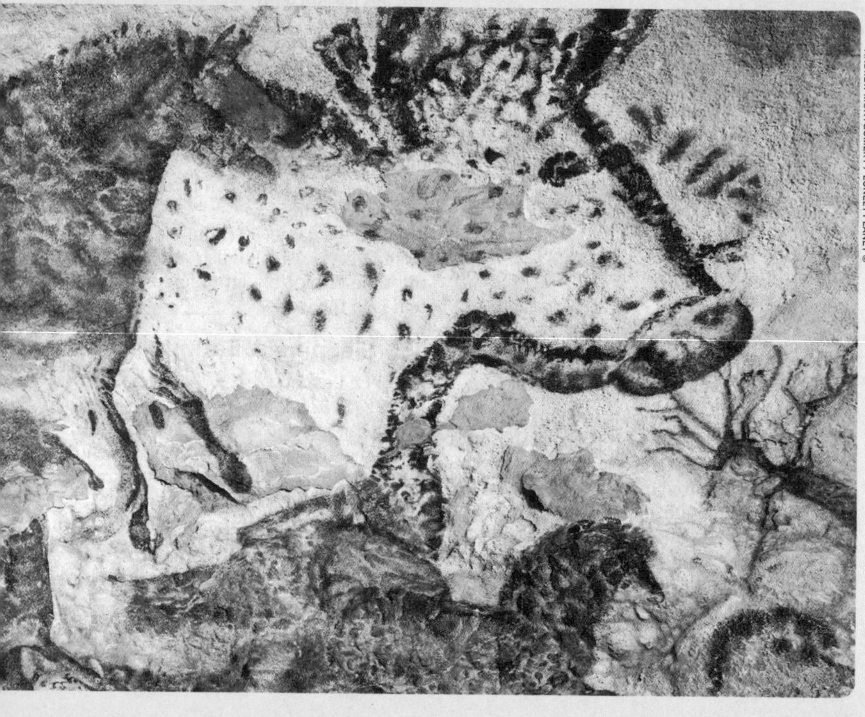

DON'T MISS

A NEW, SMARTER LASCAUX

Lascaux IV (☎05 53 50 15 63, reservations 05 53 05 65 60; www.lascaux.fr; adult/child €16/10.40; ⏲9am-10pm Jul & Aug, 9.30am-8pm Apr-Jun & Sep,10am-5pm rest of the year) will open its digitally smart doors in Montignac on 15 December 2016. Slated as France's biggest cultural opening of the year, the site will exhibit – for the first time ever – the complete collection of prehistoric paintings uncovered in the original Grotte de Lascaux. The latest in laser technology has been used to recreate the rock paintings in what feels like a real cave – muffled sounds, semi-darkness, damp smells, prehistoric fauna etc. The cave lies hidden in a strikingly contemporary building, partly submerged in the hillside where the original Lascaux lies. Six interactive zones treat visitors to hands-on Paleolithic-art workshops, an immersive theatre, art galleries, 3D cinema, 3D real-time cave trips and video games – all geared to exploring the incredible history, culture, environmental fragility and artistic significance of Lascaux's world-class, prehistoric-art collection. Find Lascaux IV, also known as the Centre International de l'Art Pariétal Montignac-Lascaux, at the foot of the hill leading up to Lascaux II (which is expected to remain open only for small-group, bespoke tours). For ticketing and tour information, see the website. The temperature inside the cave is a chilly 13°C – dress warmly.

Sights

★Grotte de Lascaux & Lascaux II HISTORIC SITE

(☎05 53 51 95 03; www.semitour.com; Montignac; adult/child €9.90/6.40, combined ticket with Le Thot €13.50/9.40; ⏲guided tours 9am-7pm Jul & Aug, 9.30am-6pm Apr-Jun, Sep & Oct, 10am-12.30pm & 2-5pm Nov, Dec & Mar, closed Jan) France's most famous prehistoric cave paintings are at Grotte de Lascaux, 2km southeast of Montignac. Completely sealed and protected for ages, it was discovered in 1940 by four teenage boys searching for their lost dog. It contains a vast network of chambers adorned with the most complex prehistoric paintings ever found.

From April to September, tickets (either same-day or for the future) are sold *only* in Montignac at a ticket office next to the tourist office; the rest of the year, get them at the cave.

The original cave was opened to visitors in 1948, but within a few years it became apparent that human breath, temperature changes and introduced elements were causing irreparable damage, and the cave was closed in 1963. A replica of the most famous sections of the original cave was created a few hundred metres away – a massive undertaking requiring the skills of some 20 artists over 11 years.

Lascaux has often been referred to as the prehistoric equivalent of the Sistine Chapel, and it's a fitting comparison. Renowned for their artistry, the 600-strong menagerie of animal figures are depicted in technicolor shades of red, black, yellow and brown, ranging from reindeer, aurochs, mammoths and horses to a monumental 5.5m-long bull, the largest single cave drawing ever found. After a visit in 1940, Picasso allegedly muttered, 'We have invented nothing'.

Carbon dating has shown that the paintings are between 15,000 and 17,000 years old, but it's still a mystery why the prehistoric painters devoted so much time and effort to their creation, and why this particular site seems to have been so important.

Although the idea may sound contrived, the reproductions are beautifully done using the original techniques, and they are certainly better than nothing. But, inevitably, they can't quite match the thrill of seeing original paintings.

Frequent, large 50-minute guided tours include several in English and Spanish. At the time of writing, an online booking system is in the works.

Sleeping & Eating

Hotel Le Lascaux HOTEL €

(☎05 53 51 82 81; http://hotel-lascaux.jimdo.com; 109 av Jean-Jaurès; d €73-95; ⏲Apr-Sep; 📶) Despite the old-timey candy-stripe awnings, rooms at this family-owned hotel are bang up to date, with cool colour schemes, distressed wood furniture and sparkling bathrooms. Superior rooms have more space, and some overlook the shady back garden.

Hostellerie La Roseraie HOTEL €€

(☎05 53 50 53 92; www.laroseraie-hotel.com; 11 place des Armes; d €80-164, ste/q from €200/220;

Apr-Oct;) This mansion in Montignac boasts its own gorgeous rose garden, set around a palm-fringed pool. Rococo rooms are lovely if you like rosy pinks, floral patterns and garden views. Truffles, chestnuts, pork and guinea fowl find their way onto the seasonal *menu* in the restaurant, and on warm summer nights the terrace is a delight.

La Chaumière REGIONAL CUISINE €
(05 53 50 14 24; 53 rue du 4 Septembre; menu €18.90; noon-2pm Sun-Tue, Thu & Fri, 7.30-9.30pm Wed-Mon) A simple *menu* of charcuterie, cut by the friendly proprietor at the back of the small dining room, or large portions of duck confit, *cassoulet* and duck-fat roasted potatoes are the order of the day.

Information

Tourist Office (05 53 51 82 60; www.lascaux-dordogne.com; place Bertran de Born; 9am-6.30pm Jul & Aug, 9.30am-12.30pm & 2-6pm Mon-Sat, 9.30am-12.30pm Sun May, Jun & Sep, shorter hours rest of year;) Around 200m west of place Tourny, next to 14th-century Église St-Georges le Prieuré.

Getting There & Away

Montignac is 25km northeast of Les Eyzies on the D706. Buses are inconveniently geared around school times, so you'll need your own car.

LIMOUSIN

With its rolling pastures and little-visited villages, Limousin might be the most overlooked area of southwestern France. It's not nearly as exciting as the Dordogne to the south or the Loire to the north, but it does offer a chance to get off the beaten path, and aficionados will like Limoges for its porcelain and Aubusson for its tapestries.

Technically the Limousin *région* is made up of three *départements:* Haute-Vienne, in the west, the capital of which is lively Limoges; the rural Creuse, in the northeast; and, in the southeast, perhaps the most interesting area, the Corrèze, home to Brive-la-Gaillarde and the region's most beautiful villages.

Limoges

POP 140,100

Porcelain connoisseurs will already be familiar with the legendary name of Limoges. For more than 200 years, the city has thrived as the top producer of excellent hard-paste porcelain (china) in France. Several factories continue to make 'limoges' and stunning examples fill city museums and galleries.

Limoges is on the site of the 10 BC Roman city Augustoritum, which took advantage of this strategic position on the River Vienne. The modern-day centre is compact and easy to explore: historic buildings and museums cluster in the medieval Cité quarter, alongside the river, and the partly pedestrianised Château quarter, just to the west.

If you come by train you'll be arriving in style at the city's grand art-deco Gare des Bénédictins.

> LOCAL KNOWLEDGE
>
> **WHAT A BOAR!**
>
> See wild boars being raised in semi-freedom on **Les Sangliers de Mortemart** (05 53 03 21 30; www.elevage-sangliers-mortemart.com; St-Felix-de-Reilhac; adult/child €3/1.50; 10am-7pm Jul & Aug, 1-5pm Sep-Jun), a farm just outside Mortemart. These porky cousins of the modern pig were once common across France, but their numbers have been reduced by habitat restriction and hunting. The boars are fed a rich diet of *châtaignes* (chestnuts), which gives the meat a distinctive nutty flavour. It's a key ingredient in the hearty stew *civet de sanglier*, as well as pâtés and country terrines. There's a farm shop where you can buy boar-themed goodies.

Sights

Château Quarter

This bustling corner of Limoges is the heart of the old city, and is the modern-day shopping centre. It gets its name from the fortified walls that once enclosed the ducal castle and medieval St-Martial abbey, both long gone.

★ **Rue de la Boucherie** HISTORIC SITE
Pedestrianised rue de la Boucherie was named for the butchers' shops that lined the street in the Middle Ages. Today it has many attractive medieval half-timbered houses, and the **Maison de la Boucherie** (36 rue de la Boucherie; 10am-1pm & 2-7pm Jul-Sep) FREE operates a small history museum. Tiny 1475 **Chapelle St-Aurélien** (place St-Aurélien; 7am-7pm), dedicated to the patron saint of butchers, is maintained by the butchers' guild.

Limoges

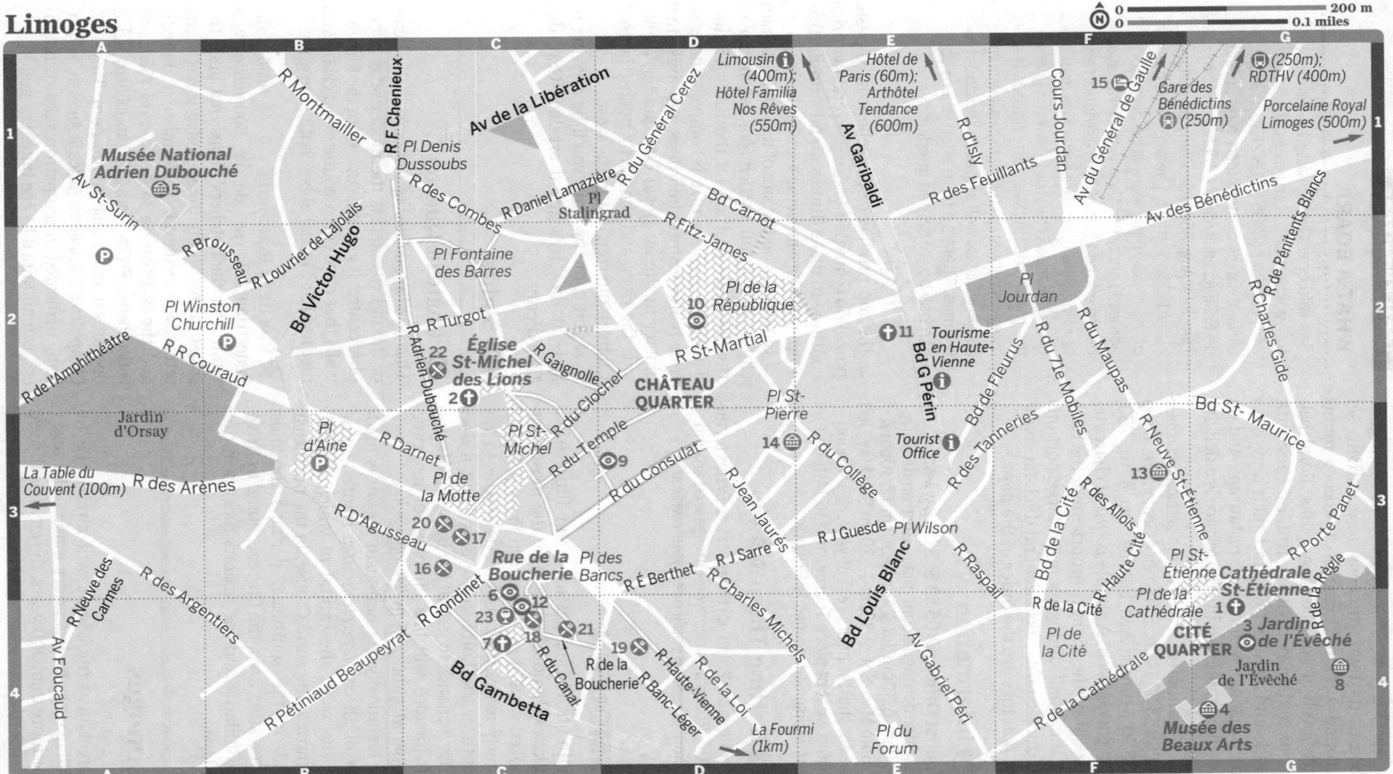
0 200 m
0 0.1 miles
N
A
B
C
D
E
F
G
1
2
3
4
Musée National Adrien Dubouché
5
Av St-Surin
R Montmailler
R F Chenieux
Pl Denis Dussoubs
Av de la Libération
R des Combes
R Daniel Lamazière
Pl Stalingrad
R du Général Cerez
Limousin (400m); Hôtel Familia Nos Rêves (550m)
Hôtel de Paris (60m); Arthôtel Tendance (600m)
Av Garibaldi
R d'Isly
Cours Jourdan
15
Av du Général de Gaulle
Gare des Bénédictins (250m)
(250m); RDTHV (400m)
Porcelaine Royal Limoges (500m)
R des Feuillants
Av des Bénédictins
R de Pénitents Blancs
Bd Carnot
R Fitz-James
R Brousseau
R Louvier de Lajolais
Bd Victor Hugo
Pl Fontaine des Barres
Pl de la République
10
Pl Jourdan
R Charles Gide
Pl Winston Churchill
R Turgot
Église St-Michel des Lions
22
2
R Gaignolle
R St-Martial
11
Tourisme en Haute-Vienne
Bd G Périn
R du 71e Mobiles
R du Maupas
R de l'Amphithéâtre
R R Couraud
R Adrien Dubouché
R du Clocher
CHÂTEAU QUARTER
Pl St-Pierre
Bd de Fleurus
Bd St-Maurice
Jardin d'Orsay
Pl d'Aine
R Darnet
Pl St-Michel
R du Temple
9
14
R du Collège
Tourist Office
R des Tanneries
R Neuve St-Étienne
La Table du Couvent (100m)
R des Arènes
Pl de la Motte
R du Consulat
R Jean Jaurès
13
R des Allois
R Porte Panet
R D'Agusseau
20
17
16
Rue de la Boucherie
Pl des Bancs
R É Berthet
R J Sarre
R J Guesde
Pl Wilson
R Raspail
Bd de la Cité
R Haute Cité
Pl St-Étienne
Cathédrale St-Étienne
R de la Règle
R Neuve des Carmes
R des Argentiers
R Gondinet
6
12
23
18
21
R Charles Michels
Bd Louis Blanc
R de la Cité
Pl de la Cathédrale
1
Av Foucaud
7
19
R du Canal
R de la Boucherie
R Haute-Vienne
R de la Loi
Av Gabriel Péri
Pl de la Cité
CITÉ QUARTER
3
Jardin de l'Évêché
Jardin de l'Évêché
8
R Pétiniaud Beaupeyrat
Bd Gambetta
R Banc-Léger
La Fourmi (1km)
Pl du Forum
R de la Cathédrale
4
Musée des Beaux Arts

Limoges

Top Sights

1	Cathédrale St-Étienne	G4
2	Église St-Michel des Lions	C2
3	Jardin de l'Évêché	G4
4	Musée des Beaux Arts	G4
5	Musée National Adrien Dubouché	A1
6	Rue de la Boucherie	C3

Sights

7	Chapelle St-Aurélien	C4
8	Cité des Métiers et des Arts	G4
9	Cour du Temple	D3
10	Crypt of St Martial	D2
11	Église St-Pierre du Queyroix	E2
12	Maison de la Boucherie	C4
13	Musée de la Résistance	F3
14	Pavillon du Verdurier	D3

Sleeping

15	Villa 13	F1

Eating

16	Chez Alphonse	C3
17	Halles Centrales	C3
18	L'Amphitryon	C4
19	Le 27	D4
20	Le Bistrot d'Olivier	C3
21	Les Petits Ventres	C4
22	Philippe Redon	C2

Drinking & Nightlife

23	Le Duc Étienne	C4

★Église St-Michel des Lions CHURCH
(rue Adrien Dubouché; 9am-6pm) Named for the two granite lions flanking its door, Église St-Michel des Lions was built between the 14th and 16th centuries. It contains the relics (including his skull) of St Martial, Limoges' first bishop, who converted the city to Christianity. Look for the huge copper ball perched atop its 65m-high spire.

Cour du Temple SQUARE
Tucked away between rue du Temple and rue du Consulat, this tiny enclosed courtyard is surrounded by 16th-century *hôtels particuliers* (private mansions). Look out for coats of arms and the 16th-century stone staircase around the edge of the courtyard.

Église St-Pierre du Queyroix CHURCH
(place St-Pierre; 9am-6pm) The moody Église St-Pierre du Queyroix is notable for its characteristic Limousin belfry and stained glass.

Crypt of St Martial TOMB
All that remains of the once-great pilgrimage point St-Martial abbey, founded in AD 848, is a faint outline on place de la République, and an underground tomb dedicated to the city's patron saint. Entry is by tourist office tours in July and August.

West of Château Quarter

★Musée National Adrien Dubouché MUSEUM
(05 55 33 08 50; www.musee-adriendubouche.fr; 8bis place Winston Churchill; adult/child €6/free; 10am-12.30pm & 2-5.45pm Wed-Mon) This museum, founded in 1845, has one of France's two outstanding ceramics collections (the other is in Sèvres, southwest of Paris), so it's a must for ceramics lovers. Displays illustrate the evolution from earthenware to Limoges hard-paste porcelain, and include 12,000 pieces from Limoges makers as well as Meissen, Royal Doulton, Royal Worcester and others.

Cité Quarter

★Musée des Beaux Arts ART MUSEUM
(05 55 45 98 10; www.museebal.fr; 1 place de l'Evêché; adult/child €5/free; 10am-6pm Wed-Mon Apr-Sep, to noon Mon & Wed-Sat, 2-5pm Wed-Mon Oct-Mar) The city's wonderful art museum is inside the beautifully restored 18th-century bishops' palace. Come either to explore the exquisite building or the excellent collections of Limoges porcelain and enamel, fine paintings from 14th-century Italian masterpieces to Renoir, and displays on the city's history.

★Cathédrale St-Étienne CHURCH
(place St-Étienne; 9am-6pm Mon-Sat, 2-6pm Sun Apr-Oct, to 5pm Nov-Mar) Built between 1273 and 1888, Limoges' Gothic cathedral is worth a visit for the Flamboyant-style Portail St-Jean, as well as a glorious rose window, a Renaissance choir screen (beneath the organ loft), and three ornate tombs in the chancel. The bell tower's lower three stories are part of the few remaining Romanesque portions of the cathedral; its top four storeys are Gothic.

★Jardin de l'Évêché GARDENS
FREE Alongside Cathédrale St-Étienne, Limoges' beautiful botanical garden terraces down to the river, with super views. Medicinal and toxic herbs have been grown here since medieval times.

LIMOUSIN RESOURCES

Region-wide tourism sites offer loads of accommodation, map, transport and activities information.

Corrèze Tourist Board (www.vacances-en-correze.net; smartphone site www.tourismecorreze.mobi).

Creuse Tourism (www.tourisme-creuse.com)

Limousin Tourism Board (www.tourismelimousin.com)

Tourisme en Haute-Vienne (www.tourisme-hautevienne.com)

Musée de la Résistance MUSEUM
(☎05 55 45 84 44; http://resistance-massif-central.fr; 7 rue Neuve-Ste-Étienne; adult/child €4/free; ⊙10am-6pm Wed-Mon mid-Jun–mid-Sep, 9.30am-5pm Wed-Mon mid-Sep–mid-Jun) The Limousin was a stronghold of the Resistance during WWII, and this museum explores the story of their struggle against German occupation through archive film, photography and wartime memorabilia, including photos, letters, diaries and military hardware.

Cité des Métiers et des Arts MUSEUM
(☎05 55 32 57 84; www.cma-limoges.com; 5 rue de la Règle; adult/child €4.50/2.50; ⊙2.30-7pm daily mid-Jun–mid-Sep, shorter hours rest of year) Showcases work by top members of France's craft guilds.

Sleeping

Hôtel de Paris HOTEL €
(☎05 55 77 56 96; www.hoteldeparis-limoges.com; 5 cours Vergniaud; d €60-75; 📶) Basic but good-value rooms spread out over several floors of a tall townhouse. Floors are squeaky, doors are creaky and the spiral staircase will give you a good workout, but it's equally handy for town and station.

Hôtel Familia Nos Rêves HOTEL €
(☎05 55 77 41 43; www.hotelfamilia.fr; 16 rue du Général du Bessol; s €55, d €69, q €99; 📶) This small family-run hotel is the pick of the budget places near the station. Forget frills – easy-clean fabrics and pastel colours are the order of the day – but it's good value, especially if you get a room over the back garden. Parking costs €5.

Villa 13 APARTMENT €€
(☎06 77 56 32 55; www.villa13.fr; 13 av du Général de Gaulle; apt €120-150; 📶) Swanky contemporary apartments fill this townhouse near the train station. Bathrooms are spacious, linens of high quality, and kitchenettes well furnished.

Eating

Halles Centrales FOOD MARKET €
(place de la Motte; ⊙6am-1pm Mon-Thu & Sat, 6am-6pm Fri, 8am-1pm Sun) Limoges' central market runs the gourmet gamut from local cheese to Limousin beef.

Chez Alphonse REGIONAL CUISINE €
(☎05 55 34 34 14; www.chezalphonse.fr; 5 place de la Motte; menus €13-20; ⊙noon-2pm & 7.30-10.30pm Mon-Sat) Checked tablecloths, laughing locals and blackboards stuffed with regional dishes: what more could you want from a Limoges bistro?

Le Bistrot d'Olivier REGIONAL CUISINE €
(☎05 55 33 73 85; Halles Centrales; menus €12-16; ⊙7am-2pm Mon-Sat) For an authentic lunch, you can't do much better than this chaotic little place inside the market, where folks sit at communal wooden tables and share hearty, no-fuss portions of French food chosen straight from the blackboard.

★**Philippe Redon** MODERN FRENCH €€
(☎05 55 79 37 50; www.philippe-redon.com; 14 rue Adrien Dubouché; lunch/dinner menus from €13/48; ⊙noon-2pm & 8-10pm) Book ahead for a spot at this romantic modern restaurant that serves some of the best food in the region. Dishes incorporate fresh seasonal produce from truffles to Limousin beef, and service is snappy and welcoming. Leave room for decadent desserts.

★**La Table du Couvent** FRENCH €€
(☎05 55 32 30 66; www.latableducouvent.com; 15 rue Neuve des Carmes; mains €10-20, lunch/dinner menus from €17/25; ⊙noon-2pm Wed-Sun, 7-10pm Tue-Sat) This modish restaurant in a former Carmelite convent is one of the city's most popular eateries, with tables set among rough brick walls. Sit at the open kitchen counter to watch meals being prepared, including locally sourced steaks cooked over an open hearth. Cooking courses (€60) are available.

L'Amphitryon TRADITIONAL FRENCH €€
(☎05 55 33 36 39; www.amphitryon-limoges.fr; 26 rue de la Boucherie; lunch menus €23, dinner menus €28-65; ⊙noon-1.15pm & 7.45-9.15pm Tue-Sat) One of Limoges' top tables for years, it's in a delightful medieval timbered building and serves classically rich French cuisine, creat-

ed by renowned head chef Richard Lequet. The dining room is suitably smart too.

Le 27 MODERN FRENCH €€
(☎05 55 32 27 27; www.le27.com; 27 rue Haute-Vienne; lunch/dinner menu €17/27; ⊙noon-2pm & 7.45-10.30pm Mon-Sat) A contemporary bistro with quirky decor to match the inventive cuisine. Teardrop lanterns cast moody lighting, and one wall is taken up by wine. Dishes are French classics with a contemporary spin.

Les Petits Ventres REGIONAL CUISINE €€
(☎05 55 34 22 90; www.les-petits-ventres.com; 20 rue de la Boucherie; lunch menus €18, dinner menus €20-33; ⊙noon-2pm & 7.30-9.30pm Tue-Sat;) At this cosy, family-friendly eatery, tuck into Limousin's famous carnivorous cuts such as the eponymous beef or *andouillettes* (sausages). Other bits are grand as well, such as the generous, excellent cheese platter.

Drinking & Nightlife

The large student crowd keeps Limoges' nightspots ticking; you'll find most action around rues Haute-Vienne and Charles Michels.

Le Duc Étienne BAR
(place St-Aurélien; ⊙11am-2am Mon-Sat, 6pm-2am Sun) Hip little bar supplying beers and late-night coffee to a pre-club crowd. In summer, things spill onto the terrace in front of Église St-Aurélien.

Entertainment

La Fourmi LIVE MUSIC
(www.lafourmi87.net; 3 rue de la Font Pinot) The best place for live music, with breaking acts, alternative bands and theatrical spectacles in a twin-floored warehouse-style space. One kilometre south of the cathedral.

Information

Tourist Office (☎05 55 34 46 87; www.limoges-tourisme.com; 12 bd de Fleurus; ⊙10am-6pm Mon-Sat, plus 10am-1pm Sun May-Sep;) Loads of info on what's on, transport and maps.

Getting There & Away

AIR

Just off the A20, 10km west of the city, **Limoges Airport** (LIG; ☎05 55 43 30 30; www.aeroportlimoges.com) is a major UK gateway, served by budget carriers including Ryanair and Flybe, as well as Air France. Domestic destinations include Paris Orly, Lyon, Nice and Ajaccio (Corsica).

Taxis (☎05 55 38 38 38; www.taxis87.com) from the airport charge a flat-rate fare of €24 during the day, and €34 after 7pm and on Sundays.

BUS

Limoges' bus station is across the tracks from the train station. **RDTHV** (Régie Départementale des Transports de la Haute-Vienne; ☎05 55 10 31 00; www.rdthv.com; place des Charentes; ticket €2) buses are geared towards school timetables, so there's only one or two per day during the week. Information and timetables are also available from the tourist office or **Haute-Vienne en Car** (http://hautevienneencar.cg87.fr). SNCF runs additional buses; a map is available at www.regionlimousin.fr.

TRAIN

Limoges' beautiful Gare des Bénédictins is on the Paris–Toulouse and Bordeaux–Clermont Ferrand lines.

Bordeaux €35.40, three hours, four direct daily

Paris' Gare d'Austerlitz €35 to €63, three hours, nine daily

Périgueux €17.70, one hour, eleven daily

Toulouse €25 to €51, 3½ hours, five daily

Aubusson

POP 3898

Quaint riverside Aubusson has become synonymous with fine tapestries. It was the clacking centre of French production during the 19th century (rivalled only by the Gobelins factories in Paris), producing elegant tapestries renowned for vivid colours, fine detail and exquisite craftsmanship. An exploration of Aubusson's beautiful terraced streets rising above the River Creuse, and its modern-day tapestry museums and studios, is a must for any lover of the art.

Sights

★Cité Internationale de la Tapisserie MUSEUM
(Musée de la Tapisserie; ☎05 55 83 08 30; www.cite-tapisserie.fr; rue des Arts; adult/child €7/free; ⊙9.30am-noon & 2-6pm Wed-Mon Feb-Jun & Sep-Dec, 10am-6pm Jul & Aug, closed Jan) In 2016, the excellent Musée de la Tapisserie moved to grand new space at the colourfully striped former National School of Decorative Arts. The building has been completely redesigned to explore tapestry worldwide, Aubusson's particular history and contribution, as well as contemporary tapestry, including

artists in residence. It is the premier place to get both an historical overview as well as see intricate examples of both antique and modern tapestries produced in Aubusson.

Maison du Tapissier MUSEUM

(05 55 66 32 12; 63 rue Vieille; adult/child €5/4; 10am-noon & 2-5pm Mon-Sat) Next to the tourist office, this 16th-century building holds a recreation of a 17th-century weaver's workshop, with tools, original furniture and vintage tapestries.

Exposition-Collection Fougerol MUSEUM

(34 rue Jules Sandeau; adult/child €3/free; 10am-1pm & 2-6pm Mon-Sat, 10am-noon & 2.30-5.30pm Sun Jun-Sep) About 135 tapestries from the 16th to 19th centuries from Aubusson and Flanders.

Sleeping & Eating

Daytime eateries gear towards the tour-bus crowd, but there are several *boulangeries* and the hotel restaurants are good value.

Hôtel La Beauze BOUTIQUE HOTEL €

(05 55 66 46 00; www.hotellabeauze.fr; 14 av de la République; d €70-90; P) This renovated 19th-century townhouse on the edge of the old town is one of Aubusson's comfiest places to stay. Stylishly furnished rooms have peaceful views across a grassy garden.

L'Hôtel de France HOTEL €€

(05 55 66 10 22; www.aubussonlefrance.com; 6 rue des Déportés; d €78-106;) This upmarket Logis hotel has 21 plush rooms: some modern, some old fashioned and frilly, some tucked into the attic with sloping ceilings. Its restaurant (three-course *menus* €22 to €39) is the best in town, with Limousin dishes served to the tunes of a tinkling piano.

Information

Tourist Office (05 55 66 32 12; www.tourisme-aubusson.com; 63 rue Vieille; 10am-noon & 2-6pm;) Tapestry, transport and lodging info.

LIMOGES CHINA

For more than 300 years, the name of Limoges has been synonymous with *les arts du feu* (literally 'the fire arts'), especially the production of *émail* (enamel) and *porcelaine* (porcelain).

Limoges had been producing enamel since at least the 12th century, but its fortunes were transformed by the discovery of an extremely pure form of kaolin near St-Yrieix-La-Perche in 1768. This fine white clay, a vital ingredient in porcelain manufacture (along with quartz and feldspar), had previously been imported at huge expense from Asia (the recipe was originally from China, hence porcelain's alternate name). Its discovery on home soil, plus the ease of getting wood on barges on the Vienne to fire kilns, led to an explosion of porcelain production in Limoges in the late 18th and 19th centuries. Three factors distinguish porcelain from other clay-baked ceramics: it's white, extremely hard and translucent. Buildings around Limoges are often decorated with porcelain and enamel tiles. Check out the **Halles Centrales** (p586) and the **Pavillon du Verdurier** (place St-Pierre), a beautiful octagonal building dating from 1900 that now hosts art exhibitions.

Many of the city's porcelain makers have factory shops, and outstanding city museums focus on the industry. The tourist office has complete lists.

Porcelaine Royal Limoges (05 55 33 28 74; www.royal-limoges.fr; 28 rue Donzelot; guided tour €7; tours 10am-5pm, shop 10am-6pm Mon-Sat) One of the oldest factories, dating from 1797, offers guided tours by reservation, and has the 19.5m-high **Four des Casseaux** (www.museedescasseaux.com; adult/child €4.50/2.50; 10am-5.30pm Mon-Sat), the only surviving 18th-century brick kiln. It's 500m southeast of the train station.

Bernardaud (05 55 10 55 91; www.bernardaud.fr; 27 av Albert Thomas; tours adult/child €4.50/free; 9.45am-11.15am & 1.30-4.30pm Mon-Sat Jun-Sep) Offers guided tours of porcelain production, from raw material to finished pieces. The factory is 1km northwest of Limoges' centre.

Haviland (05 55 30 21 86; www.haviland.fr; 3 av du Président Kennedy; 10.30am-1pm & 2-6.30pm Mon-Sat) FREE Screens a short film and has a small museum; 3km southeast of Limoges' centre.

Getting There & Away

Aubusson is 88km east of Limoges. Trains (and SNCF buses) link Aubusson with Limoges (€20.90, 1¾ hours, two to five direct daily Monday to Saturday, one on Sunday). The station is about 400m from town. **Trans Creuse** (☎05 44 30 27 23; www.creuse.fr) buses serve the area around Aubusson.

Rochechouart

POP 3946

Meteorites and modern art might be an unlikely combination but they're the twin draws of the pretty walled town of Rochechouart, 45km west of Limoges. It's a fun stop for a quick walk with its beautiful château and church with a special spiralling spire.

Housed in the town's striking château, which overlooks the confluence of two small rivers, the **Musée Départemental d'Art Contemporain** (☎05 55 03 77 77; www.musee-rochechouart.com; place du Château; adult/child €4.60/3, 1st Sun of month free; ⏲10am-12.30pm & 1.30-6pm Wed-Mon, closed mid-Dec–Feb) includes a collection of works by acclaimed Dadaist Raoul Haussman and a room decorated by 16th-century frescos.

Two hundred million years ago, a 1.5km-radius intergalactic rock slammed into Earth 4km west of Rochechouart at 72,000km/h with the force of 14 million Hiroshima bombs, creating a crater 20km wide and 6km deep. A small geological museum, **Éspace Météorite Paul Pellas** (☎05 55 03 02 70; www.espacemeteorite.com; 16 rue Jean-Parvy; adult/child €4/2; ⏲10am-12.30pm & 1.30-6pm Mon-Fri, 2-6pm Sat & Sun mid-Jul–mid-Aug, shorter hours rest of year), explores it through minerals, models and videos.

Limoges RDTHV (www.rdthv.com) bus 21 (80 minutes, two daily Monday to Friday, one on Saturday) serves Rochechouart.

Solignac

POP 1543

In the thickly wooded Briance Valley, 10km south of Limoges, the tiny medieval village of Solignac was a major stop on the pilgrimage route to Santiago de Compostela. Its sweet village is made of golden-coloured granite typical of the Limousin and the 11th-century church, **L'Abbaye St-Pierre de Solignac** (⏲9am-6pm), is a Romanesque wonder.

Still operational, the church is renowned for its 14m-wide domed roof. The stalls in the nave are decorated with carved wooden sculptures of human heads, fantastical animals and a monk mooning the world, while the columns depict human figures being devoured by dragons.

Five kilometres southeast of Solignac are the moody ruins of the **Château de Chalucet**, a 12th-century keep occupied by the English during the Hundred Years War. The spot, along a pretty little brook with forested hills and tweeting birds, makes a fine picnic stop, with valley views from the tumble-down keep.

Hôtel Le St-Eloi (☎05 55 00 44 52; www.lesainteloi.fr; 66 av St-Eloi, Solignac; d €93-104) has 15 sunny rooms inside a quaint shuttered building opposite the church. The ones with Jacuzzis and terraces are good value, and half board is available at the restaurant (*menus* €19 to €39).

The Solignac–Le Vigen **train station** is on the Limoges (€3.20, 10 minutes) to Brive-la-Gaillarde (€15.90, 1¼ hour) line with five trains daily.

Uzerche

POP 3013

Breathtakingly situated on a spur above the glistening River Vézère, the walled town of Uzerche is one of the Limousin's prettiest hilltop hamlets. Spiky turrets top the walls of 15th- and 16th-century **maisons à tourelles** (turret houses) like witches' hats, and the **Porte Bécharie**, one of the nine original 14th-century gates, remains remarkably intact.

Uzerche's single street leads uphill past vibrant cafes to the **Église St-Pierre**, a fortified church with an 11th-century crypt – one of the oldest in the Limousin. From the front, there are fabulous panoramas of the river valley from **place de la Lunade** (which takes its name from a pagan summer solstice festival now rejigged as a Christian procession). Nearby, the **tourist office** (☎05 55 73 15 71; www.pays-uzerche.fr; 10 place de la Libération; ⏲10am-noon & 2-5.30pm Mon-Sat; 📶) sells local art, chutneys and honeys.

Sleeping & Eating

Hôtel Ambroise HOTEL €
(☎05 55 73 28 60; www.hotel-ambroise.com; 34 av Charles de Gaulle; d €50-60, tr/q €65/75; ⏲closed mid-Oct–mid-Apr; 📶) Hôtel Ambroise is nicer inside than outside: snug, simple rooms

WORTH A TRIP

ORADOUR-SUR-GLANE

On the afternoon of 10 June 1944, the little town of Oradour-sur-Glane, 21km northwest of Limoges, witnessed one of the worst Nazi war crimes committed on French soil. German lorries belonging to the SS 'Das Reich' Division surrounded the town and ordered the population onto the market square. The men were divided into groups and forced into barns, where they were machine-gunned before the structures were set alight. Several hundred women and children were herded into the church, which was set on fire, along with the rest of the town. Only one woman and five men who were in the town that day survived the massacre; 642 people, including 193 children, were killed. The same SS Division committed a similarly brutal act in Tulle two days earlier, in which 99 Resistance sympathisers were strung up from the town's balconies as a warning to others.

Since these events, the entire village has been left untouched, complete with prewar tram tracks and electricity lines, the blackened shells of buildings and the rusting hulks of 1930s automobiles – an evocative memorial to a village caught up in the brutal tide of war. At the centre of the village is an **underground memorial** inscribed with the victims' names and displaying their recovered belongings, including watches, wallets, hymnals from the burnt church and children's bikes. Victims were buried in the nearby **cemetery**.

Entry is via the modern **Centre de la Mémoire** (☎05 55 43 04 30; www.oradour.org; Oradour-sur-Glane; adult/child €7.80/5.20; ⏱9am-7pm May–mid-Sep, to 5pm or 6pm rest of year, closed mid-Dec–Jan), which does an excellent job contextualising the massacre using historical exhibitions, videos and survivors' testimonies. Various theories have been put forward to try to explain the event – perhaps a reaction to the Allied landings four days earlier, or reprisal for sabotage raids committed by the Resistance, or the Resistance's hostage-taking of an SS officer. Those who were ultimately accused of the crime were tried at a 1953 military tribunal in Bordeaux, with outcomes ranging from a death sentence to amnesty (much to the chagrin of Oradour survivors and relatives).

After the war, a new Oradour was rebuilt a few hundred metres west of the ruins. **RDTHV** (www.rdthv.com) bus 12 serves the Limoges bus station (45 minutes, three daily Monday to Saturday).

(some with river views) and a restaurant (*menus* €14 to €27). Parking costs €8.

Hôtel Joyet de Maubec BOUTIQUE HOTEL €€
(☎05 55 97 20 60; www.hotel-joyet-maubec.com; place des Vignerons; d/ste from €138/250) Sleek, contemporary design meets French country living at this fine hotel in Uzerche, set above the River Vézère. The elegant restaurant (*menus* €27 to €36) serves elaborate local cuisine, and also has a pastoral terrace.

Le Table de M REGIONAL CUISINE €€
(☎05 55 98 17 80; place Alexis Boyer; lunch menus €14, dinner menus €25-39; ⏱noon-1.30pm & 7.30-9.30pm) Sup on dishes created from locally sourced ingredients, such as Limousin beef, served by friendly staff on a lively terrace, or in a contemporary dining room dressed in slate grey and rose.

Getting There & Away

Uzerche's train station, 2km north of the old city along the N20, is on the Limoges (€11-16, 40 minutes, nine daily) to Brive-la-Gaillarde (€9–13, 30 minutes, nine daily) line.

Brive-la-Gaillarde

POP 48,110

Busy Brive-la-Gaillarde is the main commercial and administrative centre for the agricultural Corrèze *département*. Get through its busy outskirts and a ring of boulevards encloses the golden sandstone central village, an interesting maze of walking streets and cafe life. The bustling weekly markets draw folk from all around.

Sights

Collégiale St-Martin CHURCH
(place Charles de Gaulle) In the heart of town, the Romanesque Collégiale St-Martin dates from the 11th century. Original parts include the transept and a few decorated columns depicting fabulous beasties and biblical scenes.

Maison Denoix DISTILLERY
(☎05 55 74 34 27; www.denoix.com; 9 bd du Maréchal Lyautey; ⏱9am-noon & 2.30-7pm Tue-Sat) FREE Since 1839, this traditional distillery has produced the favourite Corrèze

firewater, *l'eau de noix* (walnut liqueur), alongside concoctions such as chocolate and quince liqueurs. See the copper stills and sample the wares, including grape mustard, or take a summer-only guided tour.

Musée Labenche MUSEUM
(http://museelabenche.brive.fr; 26bis bd Jules-Ferry; adult/child €5/2.70; ⌚10am-12.30pm & 1.30-6pm Wed-Mon) The town's main museum is in the beautiful Renaissance Hôtel de Labenche. Exhibits explore local history and archaeology, and there's a collection of accordions and unique 17th-century English tapestries.

Sleeping

Brive has a good collection of hotels of all types. It makes a useful, if busy, base for exploring the region, especially if you need to use trains to get around, since it is well connected.

Auberge de Jeunesse HOSTEL €
(☎05 55 24 34 00; www.fuaj.org; 56 av Maréchal Bugeaud; dm €15.60; ⌚reception 8am-noon & 4-8pm Feb-Nov; 📶) Brive's hostel makes a striking first impression, with reception inside a former mansion, however, most dorm rooms are actually in a modern annexe. It's 1.5km from the station.

Hôtel Le Coq d'Or HOTEL €
(☎05 55 17 12 92; www.hotel-coqdor.fr; 16 bd Jules Ferry; s/d/tr from €60/65/88; 📶) This stone townhouse sits on the ring boulevard around the centre, with a sunny terrace and quaint old-fashioned rooms.

Hôtel le Collonges HOTEL €€
(☎05 55 74 09 58; www.hotel-collonges.com; 3-5 place Winston Churchill; d €69-79, tr €89; ❄📶) Modern rooms are in tip-top condition at this smart hotel in the centre of Brive. Rooms upstairs under the eaves can sleep three, and the breakfast buffet (€9) is grand.

Château de Castel-Novel HOTEL €€€
(☎05 55 85 09 03; www.castelnovel.com; Varetz; d €170-360, ste €590; ❄📶🏊) About 10km northwest of Brive-la-Gaillarde, this grand château was immortalised by Colette who wrote *Le Blé en Herbe* and *Chéri* here. Topped by turrets and gables, it's filled with idiosyncratic rooms with patterned wallpapers (including Colette's Louis XVI apartment) and surrounded by sweeping grounds. Equally inspired is the château's gastronomic restaurant (*menus* lunch €49, dinner €63 to €98).

Eating

Food Market MARKET €
(place du 14 Juillet; ⌚Tue & Sat) Bustling Tuesday and Saturday morning market on the main square, with a smaller market on Thursday morning. Stock up on Limousin goodies: goose products, plum brandy and *galette corrézienne* (walnut and chestnut cake).

En Cuisine BISTRO €€
(☎05 55 74 97 53; www.encuisine.net; 39 av Edmond-Herriot; lunch/dinner menus from €24/31; ⌚noon-2pm & 7.30-9.30pm Tue-Sat) A young chef creates hearty, beautifully presented dishes based on the produce of the season. Warm wood and stone walls make for a cosy dining room. Find it near the train station.

★ **La Table d'Olivier** GASTRONOMIC €€€
(☎05 55 18 95 95; 3 rue St-Ambroise; lunch/dinner menus from €26/41; ⌚noon-1.30pm Thu-Sun, 7.30-9.30pm Wed-Sun) Reserve ahead for a seat at Brive's top table, where refined, creative local cuisine is served with charm. Dishes arrive looking like small works of art. Save room for delicate desserts.

Information

The **tourist office** (☎05 55 24 08 80; www.brive-tourisme.com; place du 14 Juillet; ⌚9am-12.30pm & 1.30-6.30pm Mon-Sat) is housed in a former water tower, locally known as the *phare* (lighthouse), overlooking the market square.

Getting There & Around

AIR

Brive-Vallée de la Dordogne Airport (BVE; ☎05 55 22 40 00; www.aeroport-brive-vallee-dordogne.com), about 10km south of town, has budget flights to Paris-Orly and London City Airport. The only airport transport is taxi or rental car.

WORTH A TRIP

ALL ABOARD!

Clamber aboard carriages pulled by a 1932 steam engine on the **Chemin de Fer Touristique Limousin–Périgord** (www.trainvapeur.com) to watch the Limousin's fields and forests roll by. The trains run certain days and routes from Limoges and Eymoutiers, late May to August. Reservations are essential; make them online or at the tourist office in Limoges, Eymoutiers, Guéret, Pompadour or St-Yrieix.

BUS

The **bus station** (place du 14 Juillet) is next to the tourist office. **Trans Périgord** (www.trans-perigord.fr) connects Brive with Montignac (€2, 1¼ hours, one daily Monday to Friday).

CFTA (www.cftaco.fr) Regional buses, including a service to Tulle (€2, 45 minutes, six daily Monday to Friday, one Saturday).

Libéo (☎05 55 74 20 13; www.libeo-brive.fr; ticket €1) Local buses around town; lines 3, N and D serve the train station.

TRAIN

The **train station** (av Jean Jaurès) is located at a major confluence of rail lines 900m southwest of Brive centre. There are lines north to Limoges and Paris, south to Toulouse, west to Périgueux, east to Clermont-Ferrand, and southeast to Figeac.

Cahors €13 to €23, 1¼ hours, seven daily

Limoges €15 to €23, one hour, 19 daily

Paris' Austerlitz €36 to €73, 4¼ hours, eight daily

Périgueux €14, one hour, seven daily

South of Brive

Rolling countryside unfolds south of Brive to the banks of the Dordogne and the border of the northern Lot. Some of the Limousin's most picturesque villages dot the region.

WORTH A TRIP

TULLE ACCORDIONS

The industrial town of Tulle, 28km north-east of Brive, is renowned as the world's accordion capital. A single accordion consists of between 3500 and 6800 parts and making one requires up to 200 hours' labour. The very best instruments fetch upwards of a staggering €9000.

One of the last remaining traditional accordion makers, **Maugein** (☎05 55 20 08 89; www.accordeons-maugein.com; D1089, Zone Industrielle Mulatet; adult/child €5/free; ⊙tours by reservation 2.30pm Tue-Thu), runs guided factory tours, where you can see the craftspeople at work and browse the accordion museum.

Accordions take centre stage during mid-September's four-day street music festival Nuits de Nacre; Tulle's **tourist office** (☎05 55 26 59 61; www.tulle-en-correze.com) has details. Regular trains run to Tulle from Brive (€5.90, 30 minutes).

Turenne

POP 810

Rising up from a solitary spur of rock, the hilltop village of Turenne is an arresting sight: honey-coloured stone cottages and slanted houses are stacked up like dominoes beneath the towering château from which viscounts ruled a huge portion of the Limousin, Périgord and Quercy for almost 1000 years.

The **tourist office** (☎05 55 24 12 95; www.turenne.fr; guided visits adult/child €4/free; ⊙10am-12.30pm & 3-6pm Tue-Sun Easter-Sep) at the base of the village runs guided visits and costumed night-time promenades in summer.

The **Château de Turenne**, (☎05 55 85 90 66; www.chateau-turenne.com; adult/child €5/free; ⊙10am-noon & 2-6pm Apr-Oct, 2-5pm Sun Nov-Mar) built to protect the feudal seat of the powerful viscounts of Turenne, has beautiful views of the surrounding countryside from the 12th-century **Tour de César**, the arrow-straight tower. Apart from a few ramparts and a 14th-century guard room, the rest of the lordly lodgings have crumbled away, and are now occupied by an ornamental garden.

Behind the 16th-century Flamboyant Gothic façade of Turenne's only hotel, **La Maison des Chanoines** (☎05 55 85 93 43; www.maison-des-chanoines.com; rue Joseph Rouveyrol; d €90-105; ⊙mid-Apr–mid-Oct; 📶), you'll find sparingly decorated countrified rooms and a good restaurant (dinner *menus* €38 to €54).

Turenne is 15km south of Brive. Public transport is limited: there are **CFTA** (www.cftaco.fr) buses from Brive (€2, 30 minutes, three daily Monday to Friday) and trains (€3.70, 15 minutes, four daily) that stop 3km southeast of the village.

Collonges-la-Rouge

POP 502

Collonges centres on its church and covered market. Rue Noire is the oldest part of town, loaded with turrets and towers. The 1583 fortified Castel de Vassinhac is one of the grandest manor houses. Shops fill the entire area, offering everything from silk and leather products to local mustards. The **tourist office** (☎05 55 25 32 25; www.ot-collonges.fr; ⊙9.30am-7pm) can arrange guided tours (adult/child €4/free) of the village.

The fortified **St-Pierre church**, constructed from the 11th to the 15th centuries on the site of an 8th-century Benedictine

WORTH A TRIP

CHÂTEAU DE POMPADOUR

Equine aficionados won't want to miss the **Château de Pompadour** (☎05 55 98 55 47; www.pompadour-tourisme.fr; adult/child €9.50/7; ⊙10am-6.30pm Jul–mid-Sep, reduced hours rest of year), home to one of France's foremost national *haras* (stud farms). Established in the 18th century by the mistress of Louis XV, Madame de Pompadour (born Jeanne-Antoinette Poisson), it's particularly known for its Anglo-Arab pedigrees. Admission to the château includes a stable visit; an additional charge applies for high-season equine spectacles (also available as separate admission adult/child €5/4). Check the website for schedules.

You can grab a bite to eat on the terrace at **Auberge du Château** (☎05 55 73 33 74; www.auberge-du-chateau.net; 5 av du Limousin; lunch/dinner menus from €13.50/24; ⊙noon-2pm & 7.30-9.30pm), which serves classic French cuisine.

In the château's right tower, the **tourist office** (☎05 55 98 55 47; www.pompadour.net; Château de Pompadour; ⊙10am-6pm Jul–mid-Sep, reduced hours rest of year) details forthcoming equestrian demonstrations and races, as well as local horse-riding options.

Arnac-Pompadour is on the train line, 60km south of Limoges (€12.80, 1¼ hours, three daily).

priory, is an important stop on the pilgrimage to Santiago de Compostela. In an unusual show of unity during the late 16th century, local Protestants held prayers in the southern nave and their Catholic neighbours prayed in the northern nave. The 12th-century **tympanum** is made from white Turenne limestone, and the bell tower is in the Limousin style.

The basic rooms at **Relais St-Jacques** (☎05 55 25 41 02; www.hotel-stjacques.com; d €73-98; ⊙Mar-Nov) are nothing to write home about, but this hotel is in the centre of Collonges and its **restaurant** (*menus* €26 to €38) is one of the town's best.

Collonges' top table for locally sourced ingredients, creativity and a relaxed ambience is **Auberge de Benges** (☎05 55 85 76 68; www.aubergedebenges.com; menus €28-35; ⊙noon-2pm Fri-Wed & 7-9pm Wed-Sat Mar-Dec). Step through the wisteria-clad entry to a terrace with sweeping views from the foot of the village.

Collonges is linked by **CFTA** (www.cftaco.fr) bus 4 with Brive (€2, 30 minutes, four to six daily Monday to Friday, one on Saturday), 18km to the northwest along the D38.

Beaulieu-sur-Dordogne

POP 1220

On a tranquil bend of the Dordogne surrounded by agricultural fields, Beaulieu was once an important stop for Compostela pilgrims. Its beautifully preserved medieval quarter is one of the region's finest: a network of curving lanes lined with timber-framed houses and smart mansions, many dating from the 14th and 15th centuries. Its church is tops.

Sights

★Abbatiale St-Pierre CHURCH

(⊙9am-7pm) Beaulieu's most celebrated feature is this 12th-century Romanesque abbey church, with a wonderful tympanum (c 1130) depicting incredible scenes from the Last Judgment, including dancing apostles and resurrected sinners. Also look for its small treasury case filled with 10th- to 13th-century masterworks.

Chapelle des Pénitents CHURCH

(⊙mid-Jun–mid-Sep) The pretty riverside Chapelle des Pénitents was built to accommodate pious parishioners – access to the abbey church was strictly reserved for monks and paying pilgrims. Now it hosts temporary exhibitions.

Château de Castelnau-Bretenoux FORTRESS

(☎05 65 10 98 00; www.castelnau-bretenoux.fr; Prudhomat; adult/child €7.50/free, parking €2; ⊙10am-7pm daily Jul & Aug, 10am-12.30pm & 2-5.30pm Sep-Apr, to 6.30pm May & Jun, closed Tue Oct-Mar) Not to be confused with the Château de Castelnaud, Castelnau-Bretenoux was constructed in the 12th century and saw heavy action during the Hundred Years War, before being redeveloped in the Middle Ages for newer forms of artillery. It is beautifully (and strategically) set on a promontory above the broad valley. Much of the fortress is in ruins, but you can climb the 15th-century **artillery tower**, which has

RICHARD THE LIONHEART

The swashbuckling spectre of Richard Cœur de Lion (Richard the Lionheart) looms over the Haute-Vienne *département*. The crusading king waged several bloody campaigns here in the 12th century before meeting his end at the now-ruined keep of **Château de Chalûs-Chabrol**, 40km west of Limoges, where he was mortally wounded by a crossbowman in 1199.

Many other sites share a Lionheart connection: they're signposted along the **Route de Richard Cœur de Lion** (www.routerichardcoeurdelion.com). Pick up the English-language map from tourist offices.

great views, and visit 17th- and 18th-century residential rooms (by guided tour).

Castelnau-Bretenoux fell into disrepair in the 19th century and was refurbished around the turn of the 20th century by Parisian opera singer Jean Mouliérat.

It's about 11km south of Beaulieu-sur-Dordogne off the D940.

Sleeping & Eating

Beaulieu's **market** is on Wednesday and Saturday mornings. On the second Sunday in May the **Fête de la Fraise** (Strawberry Festival) is held.

Camping des Îles CAMPGROUND €
(05 55 91 02 65; www.campingdesiles.com; bd de Turenne; sites for 2 adults, tent & car €26-32; May-Sep;) Well-equipped riverside campground on an island between two branches of the Dordogne.

La Ferme du Masvidal CAMPGROUND, B&B €
(05 55 91 53 14; www.lafermedumasvidal.fr; bd de Turenne, Bilhac; sites for 2 adults, tent & car €14, d incl breakfast €70; Apr-Sep;) This lovely working farm, about 10km southwest of Beaulieu in Bilhac, offers shady camping, B&B rooms and home-cooked meals (per adult/child from €23/10) made with their own produce.

Auberge de Jeunesse HOSTEL €
(05 55 91 13 82; www.hifrance.org; place du Monturuc; dm €15.75; Apr-Oct;) Parts of this quirky 28-bed hostel date from the 15th century: latticed windows and a miniature turret. Inside find a cosy lounge, well-stocked kitchen and dinky four-bed rooms, all with private bathrooms.

Le Beaulieu HOTEL €€
(05 55 91 01 34; www.hotelbeaulieudordogne.com; 4 place du Champ-de-Mars; r €90-105, ste €130;) Half old-fashioned *auberge*, half smart hotel, rooms mix the best of old and new: wood floors, glass sinks and flat-screen TVs meet solid furniture, velvet armchairs, and the odd vintage piece. Plus a courtyard restaurant (*menus* €19 to €44).

Information

Beaulieu-sur-Dordogne Tourist Office (05 55 91 09 94; www.beaulieu-tourisme.com; place Marbot; 9.30am-12.30pm & 2.30-5pm Mon-Sat Sep-Jun, also 9.30am-12.30pm Sun Jul & Aug) is on the main square with local and regional maps.

Getting There & Away

CFTA (www.cftaco.fr) bus 9 links Beaulieu with Brive (€2, one hour, one to three daily) from Monday to Saturday.

THE LOT

Stretching from the River Dordogne in the north to the serpentine River Lot near busy Cahors (and its renowned vineyards) and beyond, the Lot *département* (www.tourisme-lot.com) offers an arresting landscape of limestone cliffs and canyons, hilltop towns and undulating hills carpeted in forests, fields or vines. Formerly the northern section of the old province of Quercy, the modern Lot is part of the Midi-Pyrénées *region* (www.tourisme-midi-pyrenees.com), and makes for great exploring, especially if you have your own wheels.

Cahors

POP 20,764

In a U-shaped curve in the River Lot, Cahors combines the feel of the sunbaked Mediterranean with an alluring old town. Pastel-coloured buildings line the shady squares of the ancient medieval quarter, criss-crossed by a labyrinth of alleyways and cul-de-sacs, and bordered by scenic quays.

Slicing through the centre of Cahors, bd Léon Gambetta – named after the French statesman who was born in Cahors in 1838 – neatly divides Vieux Cahors (old Cahors) to the east and the new city to the west.

Cahors

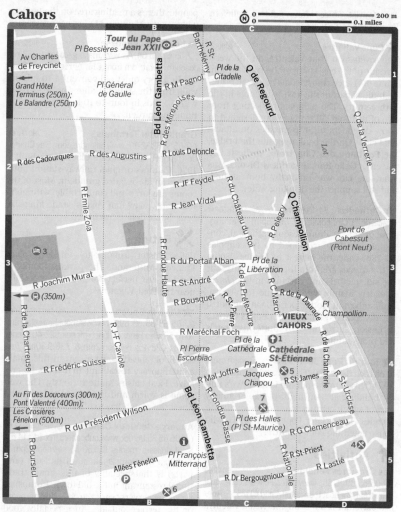

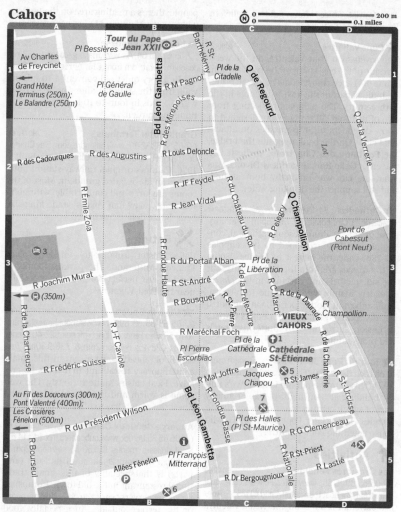

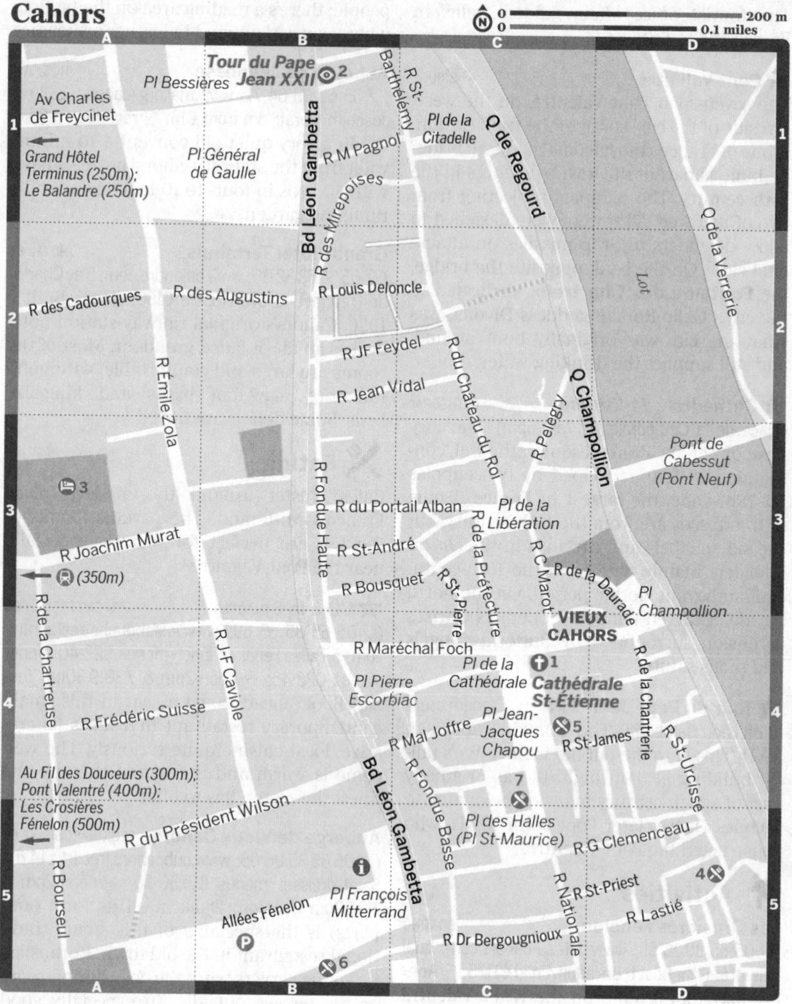

Sights

In the Middle Ages, Cahors was a prosperous commercial centre, and the old city is densely packed with timber-fronted houses and galleried mansions built by the city's medieval merchants. Wandering the old town is a real highlight, with fascinating ancient details around every corner. Don't-miss streets include Dr Bergougnioux, Lastié, St-Priest and St-Urcisse.

Get a copy of *Gardens of Cahors*, a superb free booklet that highlights a walking tour of the town, including many secret gardens.

Cahors

Top Sights

1 Cathédrale St-Étienne C4
2 Tour du Pape Jean XXII B1

Sleeping

3 Auberge de Jeunesse A3
Hôtel Jean XXII .... (see 2)

Eating

4 Auberge de Vieux Cahors D5
5 Le Marché C4
6 L'Ô à la Bouche B5
7 Marché Couvert C4

The tourist office offers guided walks in French (€5 to €6).

★**Pont Valentré** BRIDGE

The seven-span Pont Valentré, on the western side of the city, south of the train station, is one of France's most iconic medieval bridges, built as part of the town's defences in the 14th century. The parapets projecting from two of its three tall towers were designed to allow defenders to drop missiles on attackers below. On the bank opposite the bridge, the **Fontaine des Chartreux**, dedicated to the city's Gallo-Roman goddess Divona, was what the city was originally built around, and still supplies the drinking water.

★**Cathédrale St-Étienne** CATHEDRAL

(place de la Cathédrale; 7am-6pm) The airy nave of Cahors' Romanesque cathedral, consecrated in 1119, is topped by two cupolas (at 18m wide, the largest in France). Some of the frescos are from the 14th century, but the side chapels and carvings in the *cloître* (cloister) mainly date from the 16th-century Flamboyant Gothic period. On the north façade, a carved tympanum depicts Christ's ascension surrounded by fluttering angels and pious saints.

★**Tour du Pape Jean XXII** ARCHITECTURE

(3 bd Léon Gambetta) The Tour du Pape Jean XXII (closed to the public) is the town's tallest building at 34m high. It was originally part of a 14th-century mansion belonging to Jacques Duèse (later Pope John XXII), who constructed the Pont Valentré.

Activities

Les Crosières Fénelon BOATING

(05 65 30 16 55; www.bateau-cahors.com; quai Valentré; 1¾hr boat tours adult/child €11/5; Apr–mid-Oct) Tool around on the River Valentré by boat, some going as far as St-Cirq Lapopie (adult/child €62/37) or the vineyards to the west of Cahors (adult/child €59/35), or catch the tourist train around Cahors (€7.50/4).

Sleeping

★**Hôtel Jean XXII** HOTEL €

(05 65 35 07 66; www.hotel-jeanxxii.com; 2 rue Edmond-Albé; s €57, d €68-77, q €89; reception closes 10.30am-4.30pm;) Next to the Tour du Pape Jean XXII, this excellent nine-room hotel mixes original stone, greenery and well-worn wood with a dash of metropolitan minimalism. Rooms sleep one to four people; there's a reading area on the 1st floor where you can unwind in leather armchairs.

Auberge de Jeunesse HOSTEL €

(05 65 35 64 71; www.fuaj.org/cahors; 222 rue Joachim Murat; dm from €16; reception 5-9pm;) In a very quiet old convent a 10-minute walk from the station, Cahors' hostel is basic with 50 beds in four- to 10-bed dorms and a rambling garden.

Grand Hôtel Terminus HOTEL €€

(05 65 53 32 00; www.balandre.com; 5 av Charles de Freycinet; d €75-115, ste €150;) Built c 1920, Cahors's original railway-station hotel evokes an air of faded grandeur. Most of the rooms are large and comfortable, with hefty radiators, claw-foot baths and king-size beds. Some details are frayed.

Eating

Cafes cluster around the modern place François Mitterand. The parklike banks of the Lot are perfect for picnics, especially near the Pont Valentré.

★**L'Ô à la Bouche** MODERN FRENCH €€

(05 65 35 65 69; www.loalabouche-restaurant.com; 56 allée Fénelon; lunch menus €22-40, dinner menus €28-45; noon-2pm & 7.30-9.30pm Tue-Sat) Book ahead to get a seat in this small, contemporary restaurant that takes its creative, local cuisine quite seriously. The welcome is warm and the ingredients are the finest the region has to offer.

Auberge de Vieux Cahors REGIONAL CUISINE €€

(05 65 35 06 05; www.aubcahors.free.fr; 144 rue Saint-Urcisse; menus €19.50-36; noon-2pm & 7-9.30pm Thu-Mon) Duck in all its form (and parts) is the speciality of this small, traditional restaurant in the old town. Enthusiastic young servers work the cosy dining room or the terrace outside. An especially good choice on Sunday night when other local options are few.

Au Fil des Douceurs REGIONAL CUISINE €€

(05 65 22 13 04; 32 av André Breton; lunch menu from €15, dinner menus €25-70; noon-2pm & 7-9.30pm Tue-Sat) From top locally sourced foods to a superb regional wine list, this elegant but fun restaurant serves excellent – and ever-changing – *menus*. Dine inside the modern two-level restaurant or outside on the terrace, with a fabulous view of Pont Valentré.

Le Marché REGIONAL CUISINE €€

(05 65 35 27 27; www.restaurantlemarche.com; 27 place Jean-Jacques Chapou; lunch menu from

€20, dinner menus €27-42; ⏲noon-2pm & 7.30-9pm Tue-Sat) Food sourced from the region stars at this urbane bistro. Puce-and-cream armchairs set the designer tone; the short *menu* changes with the seasons.

Le Balandre GASTRONOMIC **€€€**
(☎05 65 53 32 00; www.balandre.com; 5 av Charles de Freycinet; lunch menus €23-47, dinner menus €47-62; ⏲noon-1.30pm & 7.30-9.15pm Tue-Sat) With chandeliers and stained glass, the deeply traditional family-run restaurant at Grand Hotel Terminus commands a devoted following, especially for its foie gras and *confit de canard*. Also offers monthly cooking courses (€50 to €100) with chef Alexandre Marre.

Self-Catering

The city's main **covered market** (place des Halles; ⏲7.30am-12.30pm & 3-7pm Tue-Sat, 9am-noon Sun) is often simply called Les Halles. There's a not-to-be-missed **open-air market** on Wednesday and Saturday mornings around the covered market and on place Jean-Jacques Chapou. Excellent food shops cluster around the market and along rue Nationale.

ℹ Information

Tourist Office (☎05 65 53 20 65; www.tourisme-cahors.com; place François Mitterrand; ⏲9am-7pm daily Jun-Aug, 9.30am-12.30pm & 2-6pm Mon-Sat Sep-May; 📶)

ℹ Getting There & Away

Cahors is on the main line between Paris' Gare d'Austerlitz (€35 to €127, 5½ hours, four to six daily), Limoges (€22 to €37, 2¼ hours, four daily) and Toulouse (€16.50 to €24, 1½ hours, eight to 10 daily).

North of Cahors

Some of the Lot's most striking sights lie north of Cahors near Limousin and the Dordogne, including the celebrated pilgrimage site of Rocamadour. Public transport is virtually nonexistent: you'll need your own wheels to get around.

Rocamadour

POP 666

There are certain places in the world you just may remember for your whole life, and Rocamadour is one of them. From the dramatic silhouette of Rocamadour's steeples and pale stone chapels clamped to 150m of vertical cliffside beneath the ramparts of a 14th-century château, to the magically evocative feeling as you explore this ancient pilgrimage site, this spot makes an impression.

A hugely venerated pilgrimage place through the ages, on holy days as many as 30,000 people would stream into the valley to seek favours from the miraculous statue of the Virgin housed within. Henry Plantagenet (1133–89), King of England and Count of Anjou, was miraculously cured here. Always an important financial and symbolic spot, Rocamadour suffered during the Wars of Religion, when everything was razed. Miraculously the icon and one bell survived, and they remain today in the rebuilt sanctuaries, which are still an active pilgrimage point.

Pedestrianised Rocamadour climbs the face of a cliff above the River Alzou, ascending from the Cité (old city) to the Sanctuaires (sanctuaries) to the château on top. You can approach from below or above; each area has car parks, and it's all connected by elevators.

The château on top is connected to the sanctuaries by the switchbacked but pretty, tree- and cave-lined **Chemin de Croix pathway** (Stations of the Cross) or by **ascenseur incliné** (cable car; ☎05 65 33 67 79; www.ascenseurincline-rocamadour.com; one way/return €2.60/4.20; ⏲9am-8pm Jul & Aug, to 6pm or 7pm Apr-Jun, Sep & Oct, reduced hours rest of year). The sanctuaries and the Cité below are connected by **Escalier des Pelerins** (223 stairs that the pious once traversed on their knees) or another **ascenseur** (one way/return €2.10/3.10; ⏲9am-6.50pm May-Sep, to 4.50pm Feb-Apr & Oct, closed Nov-Jan). A small **tourist train** (www.lepetittrainderocamadour.com; adult/child from €3.50/2; ⏲10.30am-7.30pm Apr-Sep) goes from the lower parking lot about 150m to the Cité.

On the top side of Rocamadour, 1.5km across a spur of the hill, sits the modern conglomeration of shops, hotels and restaurants at touristy hamlet **L'Hospitalet**.

◉ Sights

You can reserve ahead with the *ascenseur incliné* staff for a one-hour French-only **guided tour** (€8.80) of the site.

In the pedestrianised Cité below the Sanctuaires, the commercial thoroughfare **Grande Rue** is crammed (just as in the pilgrims' heyday) with souvenir shops and touristy restaurants. **Porte du Figuier**, one of the city's original medieval gateways, still exists at the street's far end.

In L'Hospitalet, a cliffside **park** with perfect picnic benches enjoys excellent views

to Rocamadour. Nearby the evocative **ruins of an ancient chapel** recall how this was pilgrims' first stop, where they healed and prepared themselves before going to Rocamadour's sanctuary.

★Sanctuaires RELIGIOUS SITE
(⏲9am-6.30pm) FREE The Sanctuaires are seven beautiful 12th- to 14th-century chapels built into the rockface and surrounding a central courtyard. You can see worn stones where pilgrims cycled between the churches. **Chapelle Notre Dame** is the highlight, containing the magical **Vierge Noire** (Black Madonna). Carved from walnut in the 12th century, she drew worshippers from across Europe in the Middle Ages. Overhead, the 9th-century iron bell is said to have rung on its own when somewhere in the world the Virgin performed a miracle.

Outside the chapel are the sites where it is said that the original hermit, St Amadour, was buried, and where **Durandal**, Roland's famous sword, was embedded in the wall. Rocamadour is still an active site; dress appropriately.

Château FORTRESS
(€2; ⏲8am-8pm) Perched atop Rocamadour, the château is a series of 14th-century protective ramparts with excellent views of the valley. Exact change is required for the machine operating the entrance.

Grotte des Merveilles CAVE
(☎05 65 33 67 92; www.grotte-des-merveilles.com; adult/child €7/4.50; ⏲hourly guided visits Apr-mid-Oct) Natural cave with stalactites and 20,000-year-old cave art; in L'Hospitalet.

Sleeping

★Moulin de Latreille B&B €
(☎05 65 41 91 83; www.moulindelatreille.com; Calès; d incl breakfast €90; ⏲mid-Mar–Oct; 📶) British expats Giles and Fi Stonor have painstakingly restored this 12th-century water mill on the banks of the River Ouysse, using the mill to power the whole tastefully done property. Situated 2km down a dirt road from the hilltop village of Calès (17km west of Rocamadour on the D673).

Hôtel Le Troubadour HOTEL €€
(☎05 65 33 70 27; www.hotel-troubadour.com; Belveyre; d €120-145; ⏲mid-Feb–mid-Nov; P📶🏊) Rooms in the renovated stone house at this 17th-century farmstead are comfortably kitted out with unique furnishings and modern bathrooms. Grounds are extensive, with a big pool, and half-board (€72) is available. Find it 2km northeast of Rocamadour, off the D673.

Information

Cité Tourist Office (Grand Rue, Rocamadour; ⏲9.30am-1pm & 2-6.30pm; 📶) Small branch in the old city.

Main Tourist Office (☎05 65 33 22 00; www.vallee-dordogne.com; L'Hospitalet; ⏲9.30am-1pm & 2-6.30pm Mon-Sat, 10am-1pm Sun; 📶) In L'Hospitalet. Has smartphone app.

Getting There & Around

Rocamadour is 59km north of Cahors and 51km east of Sarlat. There is no public transport.

Carennac

POP 421

Tiny Carennac is a sweet cluster of amber houses secluded on the left bank of the emerald Dordogne. Above the square is the Tour de Télémaque, named after the hero of Fénelon's *Les Aventures de Télémaque*, written here in 1699.

Just inside the castle gateway sit the priory and the Romanesque **Église St-Pierre** (⏲10am-7pm) with a remarkable Romanesque **tympanum** of Christ in Majesty. Off the *cloître* (cloister), still beautiful despite being heavily damaged in the Revolution, is a dramatic late-15th-century **Mise au Tombeau** (Statue of the Entombment).

The town's main landmark is the 16th-century Château du Doyen, which houses a heritage centre and a free museum, **L'Espace Patrimoine** (www.pays-vallee-dordogne.com; ⏲10am-noon & 2-6pm Mon-Fri, 2-6pm Sat & Sun Jul-Sep, Tue-Fri Easter-Jun & Oct), showcasing the art and history of the region.

Information

Tourist Office (☎05 65 33 22 00; www.vallee-dordogne.com; ⏲9.30am-1pm & 2-6.30pm Mon-Sat) Next to the church.

Getting There & Away

Carennac is 58km east of Sarlat-la-Canéda and 38km southeast of Brive-la-Gaillarde. Visit by car.

Martel

POP 1690

Marvellous Martel is known as *la ville aux sept tours* (the town of seven towers) for its turret-topped skyline. This vibrant pale-stone village was the ancient capital of the Vicomtes

de Turenne, and a prosperous judicial centre, and it retains its medieval architecture and charm in its pedestrianised centre.

Sights & Activities

Place des Consuls SQUARE

Martel's central square, place des Consuls, is home to the former fortress of the viscounts, **Hôtel de la Raymondie**, and is filled by a great **market** on Wednesday and Saturday. Truffle markets feature in December and January.

Chemin de Fer Touristique du Haut-Quercy RAIL

(☎05 65 37 35 81; www.trainduhautquercy.info; adult/child diesel train €8/5, steam train €10.50/6.50; ⏰Apr-Sep) Runs one-hour trips from Martel east along the precipitous cliff face to St-Denis. It used to transport truffles.

Sleeping & Eating

Château de Termes HOTEL €

(☎05 65 32 42 03; www.chateau-de-termes.com; St-Denis-lès-Martel; r from €74, cabin €90-130; ⏰mid-Mar–Nov;) This family-friendly cottage complex is set around a manor that originally belonged to winemakers and truffle growers. It has something for everyone: lovely, spacious rooms, two- to six-person cabins, badminton and a heated pool, and the owners organise canoe hire and horse riding. It's 5.3km northwest of Martel.

★**Manoir de Malagorse** B&B €€

(☎05 65 27 14 83; www.manoir-de-malagorse.fr; Cuzance; d incl breakfast €160-200, ste €290-320; ⏰mid-Mar–mid-Dec;) In quiet Cuzance, 8km northwest of Martel, this beauty of a B&B offers luxury normally reserved for top-end hotels. Owners Anna and Abel's period house is a chic combo of sleek lines, soothing colours and fluffy fabrics. It's surrounded by 4 private hectares, and the four-course home-cooked dinner (€42) is superb. Winter truffle weekends.

Relais Sainte-Anne HOTEL €€

(☎05 65 37 40 56; www.relais-sainte-anne.com; rue du Pourtanel; d €139-185, ste €230-280; ⏰Apr–mid-Nov;) The pick of places to stay in Martel village, on a quiet lane with 16 individually decorated rooms that blend country comforts with contemporary flair. Its excellent **restaurant** (menus from €30; ⏰noon-1.30pm Sun Nov-Mar, 7.30-9.30pm daily Apr-Oct) uses produce directly from Martel's markets.

DON'T MISS

GOUFFRE DE PADIRAC

Discovered in 1889, the spectacular **Gouffre de Padirac** (☎05 65 33 64 56; www.gouffre-de-padirac.com; adult/child €12/8.50; ⏰hours vary, approximately 9.30am-7pm Apr–mid-Nov) features some of France's spangliest underground caverns. The cave's navigable river, 103m below ground level, is reached through a 75m-deep, 33m-wide chasm. Boat pilots ferry visitors along 1km of subterranean waterways, visiting a series of glorious floodlit caverns, including the soaring **Salle de Grand Dôme** and the **Lac des Grands Gours**, a 27m-wide subterranean lake. You can book online; except for same-day tickets, which must be purchased at the cave. From Rocamadour, the caverns are 15km northeast.

★**Au Hasard Balthazar** REGIONAL CUISINE €€

(☎05 65 37 42 01; www.auhasardbalthazar.fr; rue Tournemire; lunch/dinner menus from €19/28; ⏰noon-1.30pm Tue-Sun, 7.30-9.30pm Tue-Sat May-Aug, shorter hours Apr & Sep) Local farm Les Bouriettes operates this wonderful shop and restaurant filled with their super products. Friendly proprietors serve regional specialities in the courtyard below the Tour Tournemire, or in the intimate stone dining room. Imagine ingredients such as walnut oil, pigeon confit, foie gras and wine mustard.

Information

Buried deep within the pedestrianised centre, the **tourist office** (☎05 65 37 43 44; www.martel.fr; place des Consuls; ⏰9.30am-1pm & 2-6.30pm Mon-Sat;) has a booklet (€.50) and maps of architectural and historical highlights.

Getting There & Away

Martel is 43km east of Sarlat-la-Canéda and 36km south of Brive-la-Gaillarde. Regional buses (www.lot.fr) are geared towards schoolkids. It's best to have your own wheels.

East of Cahors

Some of the Lot's best scenery, with limestone cliffs along the river valley and undulating fields on its hilltops, is criss-crossed by narrow roads east of Cahors. For example, the D662 tracks the banks of the River Lot east from Cahors towards Figeac. This wonderfully scenic region calls for

WORTH A TRIP

GROTTE DU PECH MERLE

Discovered in 1922, the 1200m-long **Grotte du Pech Merle** (☎05 65 31 27 05; www.pechmerle.com; adult/child €11/7; ⌚9.30-noon & 1.30-5pm Apr-Oct, greatly reduced hours rest of year) is one of the few decorated caves found around the Lot Valley. It has several wonderful galleries of mammoths, bison and dappled horses, as well as unique hand tracings, fingerprints and human figures. Look out for the beautifully preserved adolescent footprint, clearly imprinted in the clay floor.

Entry is by guided tour (reserve ahead for English) and includes a museum and 20-minute film (French and English). Reserve ahead by phone or online in peak season; visitors are limited to 700 per day. Find it perched high on the hills above the riverside town of Les Cabrerets, 30km northeast of Cahors.

digressions on peaceful back roads as you travel remarkable, wonderful villages including St-Cirq-Lapopie, Figeac and Najac.

St-Cirq-Lapopie

POP 221

Teetering at the crest of a sheer cliff high above the River Lot, minuscule St-Cirq-Lapopie's terracotta-roofed houses and vertiginous streets tumble down the steep hillside, affording incredible valley views. It's one of the most magical settings in the Lot, but in high summer it's packed, and in winter it's mostly closed.

Sights & Activities

St-Cirq has one long main street leading up to its highlights: the early 16th-century **Gothic church** and a ruined **château**, where you'll be rewarded with a jaw-dropping panorama across the Lot Valley. Many of the village's houses are now artists' shops producing pottery, leatherwork and jewellery.

Musée Rignault ART MUSEUM
(☎05 65 31 23 22; http://musees.lot.fr; adult/child €2/free; ⌚10am-12.30pm & 2.30-6pm Wed-Mon Mar-Oct) Eclectic collection of French furniture, African and Chinese art, and rotating exhibitions. Delightful garden.

Les Croisères de St-Cirq-Lapopie BOATING
(☎05 65 31 72 25; www.croisieres-saint-cirq-lapopie.com; Bouziès; 1hr tour adult/child €11/8) Runs regular river cruises on its small fleet of boats, including aboard an open-topped *gabarre*, a flat-bottomed barge that was once the traditional mode of river transport in this region of France.

Kalapca OUTDOORS
(☎05 65 24 21 01; www.kalapca.com/uk; Bouziès; half-/full day €30/45; ⌚Apr-Sep) Hires out kayaks and canoes, perfect for experiencing the gorgeous river scenery at your own pace. Trip lengths range from 4km to 22km; rates include minibus transport to your chosen starting point. Also caving, canyoning, climbing and other outdoor activities.

Sleeping & Eating

Auberge de Sombral HOTEL €
(☎05 65 31 26 08; www.lesombral.com; r €60-80;) This central, pretty sienna-stone townhouse has seven cosy doubles and a titchy attic room with modern decor. The **restaurant** (*menus* €16 to €30; noon-2pm Fri-Wed, 7.30-9.30pm Fri & Sat) offers Quercy cuisine, including lamb and trout. Best of all, you'll have the village practically to yourself after dark.

La Plage CAMPGROUND €
(☎05 65 30 29 51; www.campingplage.com; sites for tent & 1 person €17; ⌚mid-Apr–mid-Oct;) Riverside campground on the southern bank of the Lot near a small swimming beach, with a slew of amenities including canoe and kayak rental. Also tents and cabanas (€53 to €71).

★**Hôtel Le Saint Cirq** HOTEL €€
(☎05 65 30 30 30; www.hotel-lesaintcirq.com; Tour de Faure; s €88-128, d €108-148, f/ste from €158/218;) This luxurious hotel in the valley below St-Cirq boasts one of the best views of its hilltop profile. Lovely, traditional rooms have terracotta-tiled floors and French windows onto the garden. 'Seigneurale' rooms boast sunken baths, slate bathrooms and the like.

Le Gourmet Quercynois REGIONAL CUISINE €€
(☎05 65 31 21 20; www.restaurant-legourmet-quercynois.com; rue de la Peyrolerie; menus €21-38; ⌚noon-2pm & 7.30-9.30pm mid-Feb–Dec) St-Cirq's top table offers an enormous *menu*, ranging from *nougat de porc* (pork medallions) to country *cassoulet* (stew). Escape to the little patio to catch evening rays setting over town.

Information

The **tourist office** (☎05 65 31 31 31; www.saint-cirqlapopie.com; place du Sombral; ⊙10am-1pm & 2-6pm; 📶) is in the village hall.

Getting There & Away

St-Cirq is 25km east of Cahors and 44km southwest of Figeac.

BUS

SNCF buses between Cahors (€6.60, 45 minutes) and Figeac (€9.10, one hour, four to five daily) stop at Tour-de-Faure; from there it's 3km uphill to St-Cirq.

Figeac

POP 10,580

The buoyant riverside town of Figeac, 70km northeast of Cahors on the River Célé, has a vibrant charm steeped in history. Traffic zips along river boulevards and the fantastic medieval old town has an appealingly lived-in feel. Winding streets are lined with medieval and ornate Renaissance houses, many with open-air galleries on the top floor (once used for drying goods). Founded by Benedictine monks, the town was later an important medieval trading post and pilgrims' stopover.

Sights

The tourist office offers a changing schedule of **tours** (adult/child €6/free; Apr-Oct) of the old town and nearby countryside.

★Medieval Figeac HISTORIC SITE

Enter the historic centre of Figeac at place Vival, where the tourist office and a history **museum** occupy the **Hôtel de la Monnaie**, an arcaded 13th-century building where money was exchanged. Purchase the excellent leaflet *Les Clefs de la Ville* (€0.30) for a guide to Figeac's medieval and Renaissance architecture.

Rue de Balène and rue Caviale have the best examples of 14th- and 15th-century houses, many with wooden galleries, timber frames and original stone carvings, while rue de Colomb has fine Renaissance *hôtels particulier*.

Place Champollion is in the heart of the quarter, and behind Musée Champollion, **place des Écritures** is surrounded by medieval buildings and features a modern art replica of the Rosetta Stone by Joseph Kosuth.

★Musée Champollion MUSEUM

(☎05 65 50 31 08; www.musee-champollion.fr; place Champollion; adult/child €5/2.50; ⊙10.30am-6.30pm daily Jul & Aug, shorter hours rest of year) This museum is named after Figeac-born Egyptologist and linguist Jean-François Champollion (1790–1832), whose efforts in deciphering the Rosetta Stone provided the key for cracking Egyptian hieroglyphics. The lavishly restored mansion where he was born is now devoted to the history of writing, with exhibits ranging from illustrated medieval manuscripts to Chinese writing tools.

★Église St-Sauveur CHURCH

(place de la Raison; ⊙9am-6pm) This soaring spot on the Compostela pilgrims' trail, the 11th-century former Benedictine Abbey church, features the exquisite **Notre-Dame-de-Pieté chapel**, a 17th-century wood-working masterpiece.

Sleeping & Eating

Figeac's lively **Saturday morning market** takes place under the 19th-century cast-iron arcade on place Carnot, with stalls also filling place Champollion and place Vival.

Hôtel des Bains HOTEL €

(☎05 65 34 10 89; www.hoteldesbains.fr; 1 rue Griffoul; d €54-83, f €75-115; ❄📶) Basic riverfront hotel with 19 rooms; the best have balconies overlooking the river.

★Hôtel La Grézalide HOTEL €€

(☎05 65 11 20 40; www.grezalide.com; Grèzes; d €105-188, tr/f €145/185; P📶🏊🐾) You'll need a car to reach this beautiful country estate, 21km west of Figeac in the quaint village of Grèzes, but it's worth the drive. Rooms in the 17th-century manor make maximum use of its architecture, with solid stone and original floorboards. Public rooms display art collections, and the courtyard garden, pool, and fantastic regional restaurant (*menus* €26 to €45) round it all out.

Hôtel Le Quatorze HOTEL €€

(☎05 65 14 08 92; www.le-quatorze.fr; 14 place de l'Estang; d €90-100; ⊙closed Sat & Sun Nov-Jan; 📶) This welcoming hotel is run by friendly proprietors who run a tight ship: super-tidy rooms are warmly and cleanly decorated. The more spacious rooms have long desks, since the hotel stays open year-round, focusing on business travellers.

LOCAL KNOWLEDGE

WEST OF CAHORS: WINE COUNTRY

Downstream from Cahors, the lower River Lot twists its way through the rich vineyards of the Cahors Appellation d'Origine Contrôlée (AOC) region (www.vindecahors.fr). Pick up the super, free *Vignobles de Cahors et du Lot* map for a comprehensive list of wineries, or visit www.vignobles.tourisme-lot.com and download the map. Malbecs predominate, with some merlot and tannat here and there, and you'll find they're best aged. Local whites don't carry the Cahors AOC.

Snake along the river's northern bank on the D9 for superb views of the vines and the river's many twists and turns. As you go west of Cahors, you'll pass **Luzech**, the medieval section of which sits at the base of a donjon, and **Castelfranc**, with a dramatic suspension bridge. Many wineries cluster around **Puy l'Évêque**.

Château de Cèdre (☎05 65 36 53 87; www.chateauducedre.com; Vire-sur-Lot; ⏰9am-noon & 2-6pm Mon-Sat) Casual, organic vineyard in the countryside, 5.5km west of Puy l'Évêque, with award-winning AOC Cahors malbecs.

Château Chambert (☎05 65 31 95 75; www.chambert.com; Floressas; ⏰10am-12.30pm & 2-5.30pm Mon-Fri, plus Sat Jun-Sep) Absolutely iconic château rising above organic vines, 8.5km south of Puy l'Évêque.

Clos Triguedina (☎05 65 21 30 81; www.jlbaldes.com; Vire-Sur-Lot; ⏰9am-noon & 2-6pm Mon-Sat) In the Baldès family since 1830, this place 5.5km west of Puy l'Évêque produces everything from straight-up malbecs to rosé and a new 'black' vintage.

Take a Break

Domaine Le Peyrou (☎05 65 30 51 98; www.lepeyrou.com; Luzech; d incl breakfast €68-78, studio/house per week from €395/525; P 📶 🏊) This former vineyard turned B&B is popular for its relaxed country setting in the heart of the Cahors wine country. There are also studios and houses for rent.

Le Dodus en Ville (☎05 65 22 91 82; http://auxdodus.free.fr; rue Ernest-Marcouly, Puy l'Évêque; menus from €14; ⏰noon-2.30pm Tue-Fri, 7-9pm Tue-Sat) Choose from bright chairs out on the main street of Puy l'Évêque or inside the glass-fronted, jaunty dining room and tuck into locally sourced, seasonal dishes created by friendly Mimie de Lestrade. Save room for her homemade ice cream.

Le Sarrasin CREPERIE €
(☎05 65 34 76 44; 6 rue Balène; mains €9-16; ⏰noon-2pm & 7.30-9.30pm Tue-Sat) This favourite among locals specialises in all sorts of crêpes: savoury to sweet. Book ahead to get a spot, and dig in.

★**La Dinée du Viguier** GASTRONOMIC €€
(☎05 65 50 05 05; www.chateau-viguier-figeac.fr; 4 rue Boutaric; lunch menus €23, dinner menus €32-80; ⏰noon-2pm & 7.45-9pm) Figeac's top table is a must for foodies into creative cuisine incorporating fresh, regional ingredients. Choose between beautifully prepared dishes including lobster, oysters and locally reared duck.

ℹ Information

Tourist Office (☎05 65 34 06 25; www.tourisme-figeac.com; place Vival; ⏰9am-7pm Jul & Aug, 9am-12.30pm & 2-6pm Mon-Sat Sep-Jun; 📶) Helpful. Has smartphone app, walking tours, transport and activities info.

ℹ Getting There & Away

BUS

SNCF buses run west to Cahors (€13.80, 1¾ hours, five daily) via Tour-de-Faure.

TRAIN

Figeac's train station, on the south side of the river and served by local bus 7, is at a junction. One key line runs north to Brive-la-Gaillarde (€16, 1¼ hours, six daily) and south to Najac (€10.40, 50 minutes, six daily) and Toulouse (€27.10, 2¼ hours, six daily).

Najac

POP 740

Magical Najac unfurls like a slender ribbon of stone along a rocky saddle high above a bend in the River Aveyron. Its soaring, tur-

reted fortress is a must: an evocative journey into the past, with superb views from the central keep.

Sights

The top of the village revolves around central **place du Faubourg**, a beguiling broad square surrounded by timber-framed houses, some from the 13th century. A pedestrianised lane leads 1.2km down the saddle of the hill to the **Porte de la Pique**, near the fortress. Drivable av de la Gare skirts the edge of town to Église St-Jean and the valley and train station below.

★Forteresse Royale de Najac FORTRESS
(☎05 65 29 71 65; adult/child €5.50/4; ⊙10.30am-7pm Jul & Aug, 10.30am-1pm & 3-5.30pm Mar-Jun, Sep & Oct) High on a hilltop 150m above a hairpin bend in the River Aveyron, Najac's fortress looks as if it's fallen from the pages of a fairy tale: slender towers and fluttering flags rise from crenellated ramparts, surrounded on every side by dizzying *falaises* (cliffs) dropping to the valley floor below. Its crumbling architecture is somehow beautifully preserved, and the view from the central keep is unsurprisingly superb.

Look for the **secret passage** leading out of **St Julian's Chapel**, the **dungeon**, which imprisoned Knights Templar, and **symbols** carved in walls by stone masons.

A masterpiece of medieval military planning (check out the **extended loopholes** that allowed two archers to fire at once), and practically unassailable thanks to its position, Najac was a key stronghold during the Middle Ages, and was hotly contested by everyone from English warlords to the powerful counts of Toulouse. Richard the Lionheart signed a treaty here in 1185.

Reach the fortress via a steep path from the bottom of town.

Église St-Jean CHURCH
(rue de l'Église; ⊙10am-noon & 2-6pm daily May-Sep, Sat & Sun only Apr & Oct) Two hundred metres below the Forteresse Royale de Najac is the austere 13th-century Église St-Jean, constructed and financed by local villagers on the orders of the Inquisition as punishment for their heretical tendencies.

Sleeping & Eating

★Oustal del Barry HOTEL €
(☎05 65 29 74 32; www.oustaldelbarry.com; place du Faubourg; s €54, d €65-70; ❄📶) The best hotel in town is this wonderfully worn and rustic *auberge,* with haphazard rooms filled with trinkets and solid furniture to match its venerable timber-framed façade. Try for a room with a balcony. Visit its renowned country restaurant (*menus* €22 to €56) for traditional southwest cuisine.

La Salamandre REGIONAL CUISINE €
(☎05 65 29 74 09; rue du Barriou; lunch/dinner menus from €12.50/19; ⊙10.30am-2.30pm Fri-Wed, 6.30-9.30pm Tue, Wed, Fri & Sat) Simple but charming, this little restaurant is best not for its basic local cuisine, but for its wonderful panoramic terrace overlooking the fortress.

Information

Najac's tiny **tourist office** (☎05 65 29 72 05; www.tourisme-villefranche-najac.com; 25 place du Faubourg; ⊙9.30am-noon & 2-6pm Mon-Fri, 9.30am-noon Sat & Sun, closed Jan, Sun & Mon Oct-Apr) is on the southern side of the main square. It offers occasional French-language **tours** (adult/child €3/free).

Getting There & Away

The train station, served by an automatic machine, is in the valley 1.2km below Najac. Trains go to Figeac (€10.40, 50 minutes, six daily) and Toulouse (€21.80, 1¾ hours, six daily)

Atlantic Coast

POP 6,128,712

Includes ➡

Why Go?

With quiet country roads winding through vine-striped hills and wild stretches of coastal sand interspersed with misty islands, the Atlantic coast is where France gets back to nature. Much more laid-back than the Med (but with almost as much sunshine), this is the place to slow the pace right down.

But the Atlantic coast can do cities and culture as well. There's bourgeois Bordeaux with its wonderful old centre, extraordinary wine culture and dynamic dining scene; studenty Nantes with its wealth of fascinating museums; and seafaring La Rochelle with its breathtaking aquarium, beautiful old port and bucolic offshore islands.

A love of the finer things in life unites people in this region, a part of France where *art de vivre* means appreciating exceptional wine, famous worldwide, and feasting on an ocean of oysters and other fresh, salt-of-the-earth seafood.

Best Places to Eat

- ➡ Magasin Général (p628)
- ➡ Pickles (p609)
- ➡ Potato Head (p629)
- ➡ La Co(o)rniche (p637)
- ➡ Café Lavinal (p633)

Best Places to Sleep

- ➡ Château Cordeillan-Bages (p633)
- ➡ Hôtel Le Sénéchal (p618)
- ➡ L'Hôtel Particulier (p625)
- ➡ Le B d'Arcachon (p636)
- ➡ Quai des Pontis (p620)

When to Go

Bordeaux

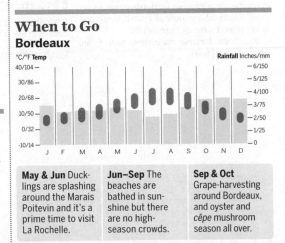

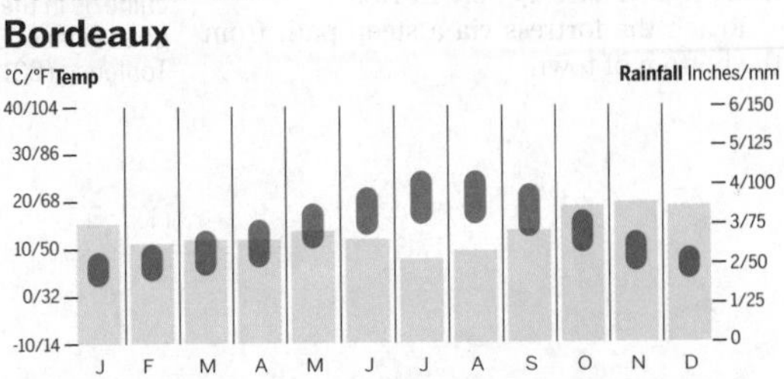

May & Jun Ducklings are splashing around the Marais Poitevin and it's a prime time to visit La Rochelle.

Jun–Sep The beaches are bathed in sunshine but there are no high-season crowds.

Sep & Oct Grape-harvesting around Bordeaux, and oyster and *cêpe* mushroom season all over.

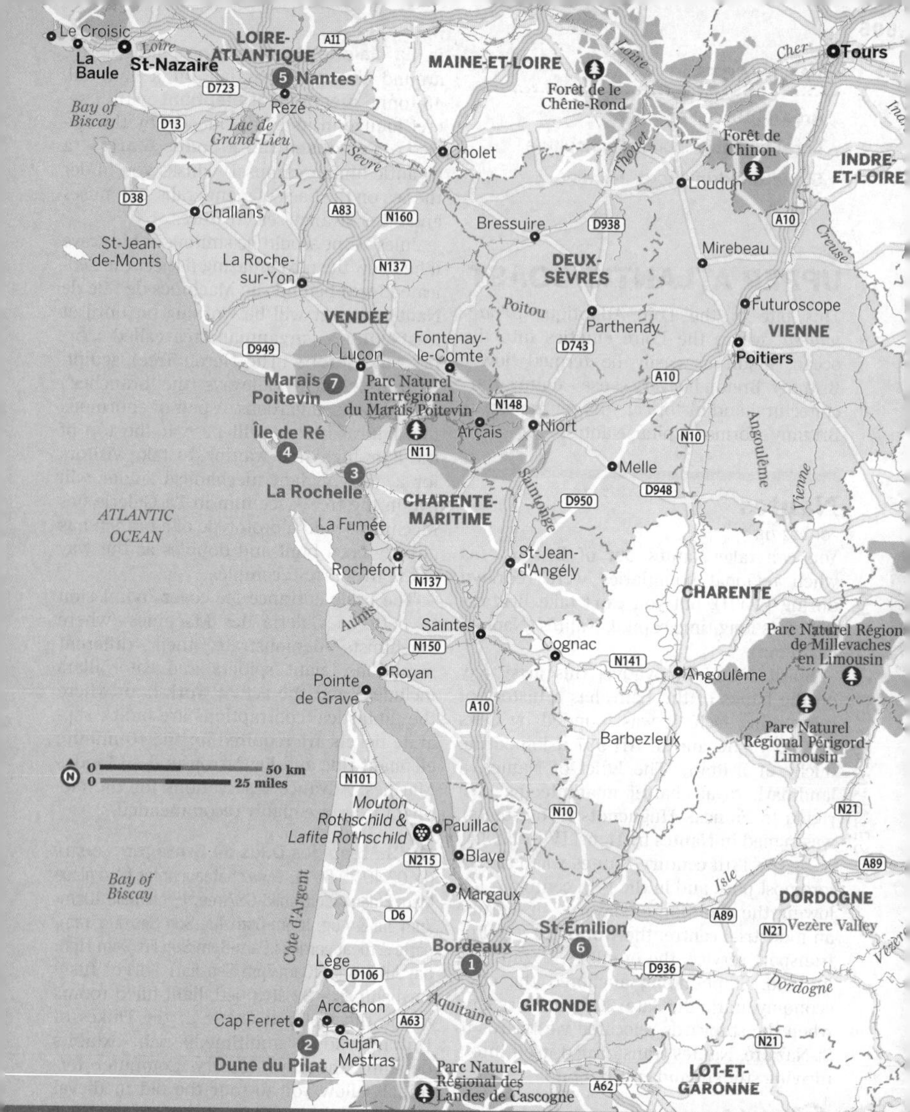

Atlantic Coast Highlights

1 Bordeaux (p622) Gorging on exceedingly fine architecture, art, food and wine in the Unesco-listed city that can do no wrong.

2 Dune du Pilat (p637) Romping atop Europe's highest sand dune, followed by lunch with sensational sea-and-sand view at La Co(o)rniche.

3 La Rochelle (p613) Scaling ancient defensive towers, sailing to Fort Boyard and encountering sharks in this port city's incredible aquarium.

4 Île de Ré (p617) Cycling smooth bike paths past oyster farms and ancient salt pans.

5 Nantes (p606) Riding on the back of a giant heron in flight or a lumbering 60-tonne mechanical elephant.

6 St-Émilion (p633) Learning about and tasting some of the world's most famous wines.

7 Marais Poitevin (p613) Gliding through the emerald-green waterways of western France's 'Green Venice'.

FAST FACTS

Area 44,113 sq km

Local industry Tourism, agriculture

Signature drink Bordeaux wine, cognac

UPPER ATLANTIC COAST

This bite of the Loire-Atlantique *département,* where the Loire empties into the ocean, might as easily be termed 'lower Brittany'. Breton in every sense – cultural, architectural and historical – its centrepiece is Brittany's former capital, Nantes.

Nantes

POP 292,718

You can take Nantes out of Brittany (as when regional boundaries were redrawn during WWII), but you can't take Brittany out of its long-time capital, Nantes (Naoned in Breton).

Spirited and innovative, this artsy city on the banks of the Loire has a history of reinventing tself. It was founded by Celts around 70 BC and in AD 937 it joined the duchy of Brittany. The Edict of Nantes, a landmark royal charter guaranteeing civil rights to France's Huguenots (Protestants), was signed in Nantes by Henri IV in 1598.

By the 18th century Nantes was France's foremost port, and in the 19th century – following the abolition of slavery – it became an industrial centre; the world's first public transport service, the omnibus, began here in 1826. Shipbuilding anchored the city's economy until the late 20th century and when the shipyards relocated westwards to St-Nazaire, Nantes transformed itself into a thriving student and cultural hub.

Sights

★Les Machines de l'Île de Nantes AMUSEMENT PARK

(☎02 51 17 49 89, 08 10 12 12 25; www.lesmachines-nantes.fr; blvd Léon Bureau, Parc des Chantiers; adult/child €8.50/6.90, elephant ride €8.50/6.90, carousel €6.40/4; ⊙10am-7pm Jul & Aug, 10am-6pm Apr-Jun, Sep & Oct, 2-5pm or 6pm Nov, Dec, Feb & Mar) Nantes' quirkiest sight is this fantasy world – a serious and seriously wacky workshop with mechanical contraptions galore displayed in plant-filled hothouses – where you can fly giant herons in **La Galerie des Machines** and prance around like a maharajah on a 12m-tall, 48-tonne **mechanical elephant** with a secret lounge in its belly. Outside, by the river, **Le Carrousel des Mondes Marins** (a gigantic funfair carousel) whisks you under the sea on the back of giant crabs, octopuses and other strange sea creatures.

Jules Verne would be smiling in his grave if he knew the next amazing project the dedicated team behind the Machines de l'Île de Nantes project will be working on until at least 2018: a gargantuan tree called **L'Arbre aux Hérons** (The Heron Tree), sculpted from 22 steel walkways (the 'branches') and suspended gardens. A pair of enormous mechanical herons will nest at the top of the 36m-high tree waiting to take visitors for a ride. A giant mechanical spider will live in the tree – see him in La Galerie des Machines – and a prototype of a branch has already been built and doubles as the way out of the current complex.

The basic entrance fee covers admission to both La Galerie des Machines (where machinists demonstrate their different inventions, giant spiders and caterpillars included) and the actual workshop (where the fantastical contraptions are built); separate tickets are required for the 40-minute elephant ride and Le Carrousel des Mondes Marines. Advance reservations for the elephant rides are highly recommended.

★Château des Ducs de Bretagne CASTLE

(☎02 40 20 60 11; www.chateaunantes.fr; 4 place Marc Elder; adult/child €8/free; ⊙château 10am-7pm Jul & Aug, 10am-6pm Tue-Sun Sep-Jun, ramparts & moat gardens 9am-8pm Sun-Fri, 9am-11pm Sat Jul & Aug, 10am-7pm Sep-Jun) Forget fusty furnishings – 32 stripped, light-filled rooms inside the restored Castle of the Dukes of Brittany house multimedia-rich exhibits detailing the city's history. Computer terminals allow you to tour the old medieval city, juxtaposed with images of today. Other exhibits to look out for include sobering documentation of the slave trade, and vintage scale models of Nantes' evolving cityscape. Admission includes temporary exhibitions too; audioguides cost €2. The grassy moat gardens and rampart walk are free to meander and picnic in at leisure.

Musée Jules Verne MUSEUM

(☎02 40 69 72 52; www.julesverne.nantes.fr; 3 rue de l'Hermitage; adult/child €6/2.50; ⊙10am-7pm Jul & Aug, 10am-noon & 2-6pm Wed-Sat, 10am-noon Sun Sep-Jun) Overlooking the river, this is a

magical museum with 1st-edition books, hand-edited manuscripts and cardboard theatre cut-outs. Child-friendly interactive displays introduce or reintroduce you to the work of Jules Verne, who was born in Nantes in 1828. Signs are in French but Verne's books, such as *Around the World in 80 Days,* are so well known that it's worthwhile visiting regardless. The museum is a 2km walk down river from the town centre.

Cathédrale St-Pierre et St-Paul CATHEDRAL
(place St-Pierre; ⏲9am-7pm Apr-Sep, to 6pm Oct-Mar, garden 8.45am-8pm) Inside Nantes' Flamboyant Gothic cathedral, the tomb of François II (r 1458–88), Duke of Brittany, and of his second wife, Marguerite de Foix, is a masterpiece of Renaissance art. Enjoy a moment of peace afterwards in **Jardin de la Psallette**, the secret cathedral garden out back.

Jardin des Plantes PARK
(bd Stalingrad; ⏲8.30am-8pm Mar-Oct, shorter hours rest of year) Opened in 1860, this exquisitely landscaped city park is one of France's most interesting botanical gardens. Century-old magnolia and mulberry trees, Japanese maples, tulip trees, redwoods (sequoias) and magnificent cedars tower above beautiful flower beds, duck ponds, fountains and the enchanting **Serre de l'Île de Palmiers**, a glass 19th-century hothouse filled with palm trees and decked out out with tables and chairs for lounging on. There is a **children's playground** and goats to pet at the park's northern end, near the train station.

Sleeping

Hôtel du Château HOTEL €
(☎02 40 74 17 16; 5 place de la Duchesse Anne; s/d from €46/53; ⏲reception 7.30am-1.30pm & 5.30-10pm Mon-Fri, from 9am Sat & Sun; ᯤ) This cosy two-star address, tucked down an alley opposite the château, actually thinks it is a castle. Short histories of various kings and queens grace the doors to the rooms, and the bedrooms themselves have an equally royal flavour with elegant bedspreads and old-fashioned bedside tables. Some rooms have views of the château. Breakfast costs €6.90.

Hôtel Pommeraye BOUTIQUE HOTEL €€
(☎02 40 48 78 79; www.hotel-pommeraye.com; 2 rue Boileau; s/d €94/99; ❄ᯤ) Young and chic, the Pommeraye is more art gallery than hotel. Each year a Nantais artist takes up residence here – think retro art-house cinema, architect musings, hedgehog-like lamps and pop-art faces – and once a month, room 108 becomes a radio recording studio. Evolving eye-catching art aside, expect friendly service and comfortable rooms in shades of grey, gold, chocolate and violet. Breakfast costs €10.75.

Hôtel La Pérouse DESIGN HOTEL €€
(☎02 40 89 75 00; www.hotel-laperouse.fr; 3 allée Duquesne; d €99-179, tr €109-189; ❄@ᯤ) Built in 1994 by French architects Barto & Barto, this four-star design hotel is a historical monument. Its distinctive slit windows evoke the city's shipbuilding heritage and a 2016 makeover has injected a zesty dose of contemporary chic into the striking vintage ensemble. Minimalist rooms are cream with dark wood floors, glass cupboards and zig-zag chairs. Breakfast – wholly organic – costs €14.

The ground-floor lobby – with designer furniture, honesty bar, free tea and coffee, iMac, and artwork for sale – is a stylish place to lounge.

LOCAL KNOWLEDGE

A UNIQUE TREASURE

Within the one-time LU biscuit factory (crowned by an iconic angel-sculpted, domed tower, which you can ascend for €2), industrial-chic **Le Lieu Unique** (The Unique Place; ☎02 40 12 14 34; www.lelieuunique.com; quai Ferdinand Favre; ⏲bar 11am-8pm Mon, 11am-1am Tue & Wed, 11am-2am Thu, 11am-3am Fri & Sat, 3-8pm Sun, hammam 11am-9pm) is a cutting-edge venue for dance and theatre, eclectic and electronic music, philosophical sessions and art exhibitions. It's also a buzzing cafe-bar and restaurant (mains €8 to €12). Deckchairs lounge by the water in summer.

A decadent *hammam* (Turkish bath) complex in the basement tops off the edgy ensemble. From the quayside, walk around the building onto rue de la Biscuiterie to admire **Le Grenier du Siècle**, a treasure trove of tin boxes built into the wall. The tins, sealed on 31 December 1999, contain 12,000 different objects contributed by the city's inhabitants in a nod to local history. They will only be opened on 1 January 2100.

Nantes

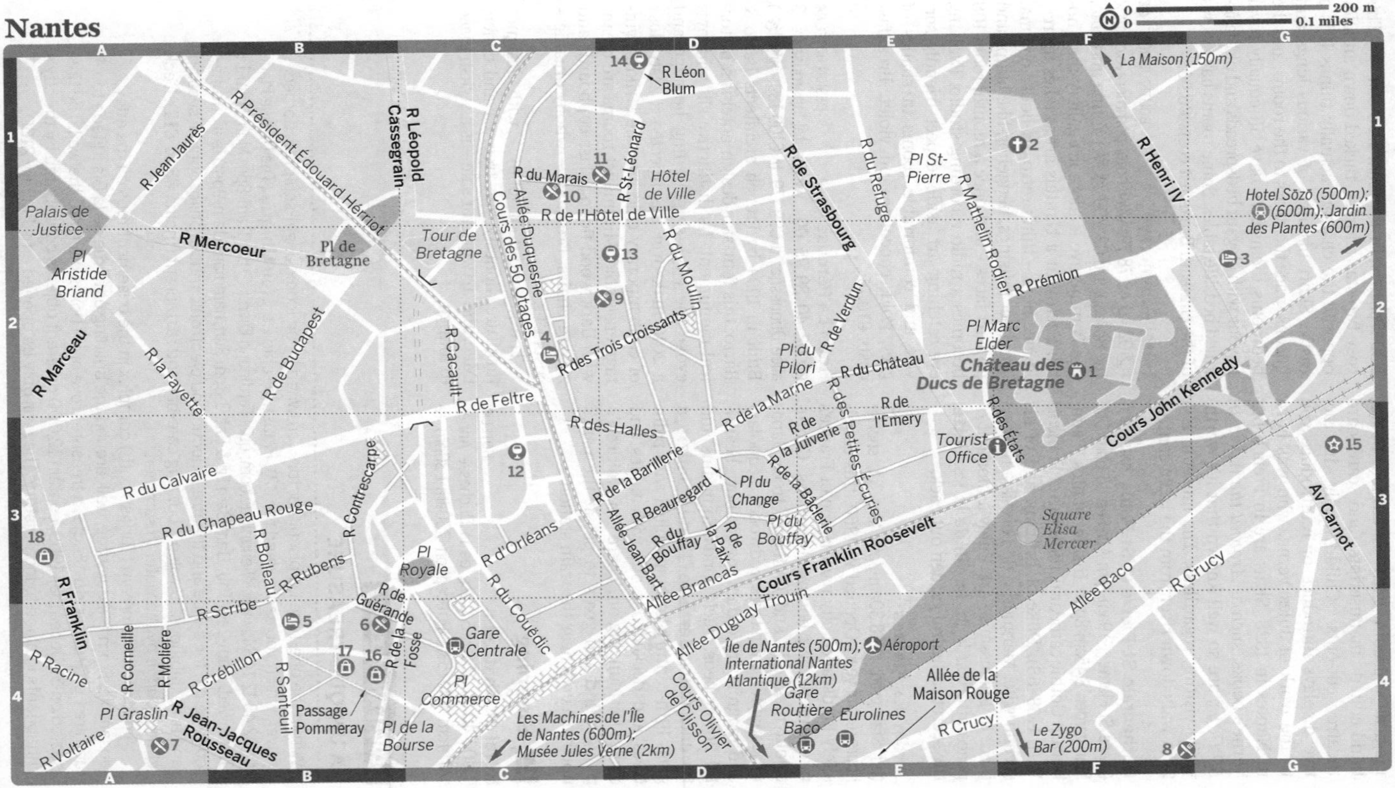
0 200 m
0 0.1 miles
La Maison (150m)
R Léon Blum
R Président Édouard Herriot
R Léopold Cassegrain
R Jean Jaurès
R du Marais
R St-Léonard
Hôtel de Ville
R de l'Hôtel de Ville
R de Strasbourg
R du Refuge
Pl St-Pierre
R Mathelin Rodier
R Henri IV
Hotel Sōzō (500m); (600m); Jardin des Plantes (600m)
Palais de Justice
Pl Aristide Briand
R Mercoeur
Pl de Bretagne
Tour de Bretagne
Cours des 50 Otages
Allée Duquesne
R du Moulin
R Prémion
R de Verdun
Pl Marc Elder
R des Trois Croissants
Pl du Pilori
R du Château
Château des Ducs de Bretagne
Cours John Kennedy
R Marceau
R la Fayette
R de Budapest
R Cacault
R de Feltre
R des Halles
R de la Marne
R de la Juiverie
R des Petites Écuries
R de l'Emery
Tourist Office
R des États
R de la Barillerie
Pl du Change
R de la Bâclerie
R du Calvaire
R Contrescarpe
R Beauregard
R du Bouffay
R de la Paix
Pl du Bouffay
Square Elisa Mercœr
Av Carnot
R du Chapeau Rouge
R Boileau
R Rubens
Pl Royale
R d'Orléans
Allée Jean Bart
Cours Franklin Roosevelt
Allée Brancas
Allée Baco
R Crucy
R Franklin
R Scribe
R de Guérande
R du Couëdic
Allée Duguay Trouin
Gare Centrale
R de la Fosse
R Racine
R Corneille
R Molière
R Crébillon
R Santeuil
Pl Commerce
Cours Olivier de Clisson
Île de Nantes (500m); Aéroport International Nantes Atlantique (12km)
Allée de la Maison Rouge
Gare Routière Baco
Eurolines
Pl Graslin
R Jean-Jacques Rousseau
Passage Pommeray
Pl de la Bourse
Les Machines de l'Île de Nantes (600m); Musée Jules Verne (2km)
Le Zygo Bar (200m)
R Voltaire

Nantes

Top Sights

Sights

Sleeping

Eating

Drinking & Nightlife

Entertainment

Shopping

Hotel Sōzō DESIGN HOTEL €€€
(☎02 51 82 40 00; www.sozohotel.fr; 16 rue Frédéric Cailliand; d €127-347; ❄@📶) The architects who designed this place must have been in seventh heaven when asked to transform a graceful old chapel into a luxury boutique hotel. The main features of the chapel have been retained, including the stained-glass windows, but sitting happily alongside are dozens of virgin-white angel wings, garish cartoon art and purple and red lights.

Eating

★**Crêperie de Brucéliande** CREPERIE €
(☎02 40 89 04 03; 3 rue de Guerande; crêpes €3-13; ⊙noon-2.30pm & 7-10.30pm Tue-Sat) There is no denying the city's Breton roots with crêpes and *galettes de blé noir* (savoury buckwheat crêpes) like this. Both come generously brushed in Breton butter – unsalted for sweet, salted for savoury. The Fondante – a *galette* filled with *andouille* (tripe sausage), melted curé Nantais cheese and creamed leeks – is the local tip-off, washed down of course with a bowl or bottle of artisanal cider or apple juice.

★**Pickles** MODERN FRENCH €€
(www.pickles-restaurant.com; 2 ru du Marais; 2-/3-course lunch menu €15.50/19.50, dinner menu €32; ⊙noon-2pm Tue, noon-2pm & 7-10pm Wed-Fri, 7-10pm Sat) This buzzing neobistro would be right at home in Paris. Market-sourced, modern and wholly creative cuisine by English chef Dominic Quirke (a Newcastle lad wed to a French lass) is sensational – and extraordinarily good value to boot. Dining is around tightly packed bistro tables or at a *table d'hôte*–style bar, and don't be surprised if Dom comes to chat with you. Advance reservations are absolutely essential.

★**LuluRouget** MODERN FRENCH €€
(☎02 40 47 47 98; 1 rue du Cheval Blanc; 2-/3-course lunch menu €19/23, dinner menus €49 & €59; ⊙noon-2.30pm & 7.45-9.45pm Tue-Sat) Local foodies pile into this contemporary bistro with steel grey façade and designer interior to gorge on some of the most creative and gastronomic, homemade cuisine in the city. Young chef Ludovic Pouzelgues cooks up some fabulous combinations, best experienced with one of his *'yeux fermés'* fixed *menus* – a succession of four or five surprise tasting courses.

Les Chants d'Avril BISTRO €€
(☎02 40 89 34 76; www.leschantsdavril.fr; 2 rue Laennec; 2-/3-course lunch menu €19/22.50, dinner menu €26.50; ⊙noon-2pm Mon-Wed, noon-2pm & 7.30-10.30pm Thu & Fri) Follow locals to the iconic bistro of *'chef magicien'* Christopher François, who runs this hugely successful 'locavore' address with wife Véronique. Everything bar the bread is *fait maison* (homemade) and there is an exceptional list of natural wines (by the glass €4.50 to €6.50, bottles from €25) to accompany the hearty, five-star fare.

Mademoiselle B FRENCH €€
(☎02 40 41 17 21; 13 rue Armand Brossard; 2-/3-course menu €14.50/18.50; ⊙8-11pm Tue, noon-2.30pm & 8-11pm Wed-Sat) This backstreet favourite, with potted plants on its window sills and the day's *menu* chalked on a blackboard outside, enchants. Pick from two different entrées and main courses – salmon with vegetable risotto and lime dressing or curried pork with sesame-peppered noodles, perhaps – and save space for dessert. Mademoiselle B's homemade *riz au lait* (rice pudding) with salted butter caramel is a local legend.

NANTES CITY PASS

The **Pass Nantes** (24/48/72 hours €25/35/45), available from the tourist office, includes unlimited bus and tram transport as well as entry to museums and monuments, and extras such as a free guided tour and shopping discounts.

★**La Cigale** BRASSERIE €€€
(☎02 51 84 94 94; www.lacigale.com; 4 place Graslin; lunch menus €15 & €25.60, mains €15.50-27; ⌚7.30am-12.30am, kitchen from 11.45am) No visit to Nantes is complete without breakfast, brunch, lunch or afternoon tea at the city's legendary brasserie, a dazzling riot of gilded tile work and frescoed ceilings in a series of historic salons dating to 1895. Fresh seafood (platters from €39) and French classics such as snails, pan-fried calf kidneys and steak in pepper sauce are served nonstop from 11.30am, making it a great place to hit between official mealtimes.

Drinking & Nightlife

Nantes has no shortage of lively spots for a drink. Prime areas are the medieval Bouffay quarter; rue Olivettes heading towards the river; and the rejuvenated industrial riverbanks of Île de Nantes. The latter buzzes with atmosphere after dark when the 18 metal rings of **Anneaux de Buren** – a contemporary art installation by French artist Daniel Buren – plot out the water's edge in a rainbow of dazzling colour.

★**Le Jéroboam** WINE BAR
(☎02 72 02 30 47; 21 rue Léon Blum; ⌚6pm-2am Tue-Sat) This enchanting *bar à vin* with vintage green wood façade is the best spot in town to taste regional wines and feast on well-thought-out *tartines* (toasts), served on slate platters and featuring some wonderful combos: think curried fish with raisins and a citrus onion chutney, grilled *boudin* (black blood sausage) with caramelised shallots, and so on. Arrive early to snag a seat.

La Verre Bouteille WINE BAR
(☎02 40 20 10 96; 23 rue St-Léonard; ⌚6pm-midnight Tue-Sat) Contribute to the mountain of corks stashed high in the window at the Glass Bottle, a popular wine bar with more than 350 wine references to choose from. A tasty choice of cheese, charcuterie, foie gras, homemade *rillettes de poisson* (fish paste) and so on make for the perfect marriage.

Hangar à Bananes BAR, CLUB
(www.hangarabananes.com; 21 quai des Antilles; ⌚daily till late) This former banana-ripening warehouse on Île de Nantes is home today to a line-up of trendy restaurants, bars and clubs, each hipper than the next. Pavement terraces lounge by the water's edge and are particularly atmospheric after dark when Daniel Buren's riverside rings glow a rainbow of bright colours.

Le Zygo Bar BAR
(☎02 51 83 51 34; www.facebook.com/zygo.bar; 35 rue des Olivettes; ⌚5pm-2am Wed-Sun) This funky music bar, a student favourite, is one of a handful of buzzing after-dark drinking addresses away from the centre on rue Olivettes. Folk, rock, afro, reggae and blues are the among the eclectic mix of live sounds that blast out here. Sessions start most evenings at 9pm. Check its Facebook page for events.

Fées Maison BAR
(☎02 40 48 44 42; 3 rue du Pré Nian; ⌚6pm-2am Wed-Sat) Follow a hip local crowd to this *café curiosités,* a characterful and eclectic bar packed with vintage and often kitsch curiosities – think garden gnomes, flowery teapots, potted roses, anything goes. Seating is a retro mix of baggy sofas draped in crocheted rugs and low faux-fur armchairs.

Shopping

Pedestal statues symbolise traditional Nantais industries inside the ornate three-tiered shopping arcade **Passage Pommeray** (www.passagepommeraye.fr; off rue de la Fosse; ⌚variable), built in 1843.

★**Vincent Guerlais** CHOCOLATE
(☎02 40 08 08 79; www.vincentguerlais.com; 11 rue Franklin; ⌚10am-7.30pm Tue-Fri, 9.30am-7.30pm Sat) Nantes' self-proclaimed *'agitateur de papilles'* (taste-bud agitator) lures locals into his flamboyant violet-coloured boutique with silky-smooth chocolate squares, pralines, exquisite cakes too beautiful to eat and – drum roll – shimmering gold, chocolate versions of Nantes' signature Petit Beurre biscuits that every French person knows. His 1m-long box of shaped chocolates is the perfect souvenir.

★**Gautier-Debotté** CHOCOLATE
(☎02 40 48 23 19; www.patisserie-debotte.com; 9 rue de la Fosse; ⌚9am-7.15pm Tue-Sat, 2-7pm Mon) A young Jules Verne was awed by this beautiful chocolate shop's chandeliers, marble floors and circular velvet banquette

where Nantais have lingered amid the sweet aroma of chocolate since 1823. Handmade specialities include *Le Mascaron Nantais* (a crunchy hazelnut praline in a dark-chocolate shell; €8.30 per 100g) and a rainbow of *berlingots* (fruit-flavoured hard-boiled sweets; €1.80 per 100g).

Information

Tourist Office (02 72 64 04 79; www.nantes-tourisme.com; 9 rue des États; 9am-7pm Jul & Aug, 10am-6pm Mon-Sat, 10am-5pm Sun Sep-Jun) Gen up at the helpful tourist office on **Le Voyage de Nantes** (www.levoyageanantes.fr), an annual summer project that brings a bounty of contemporary art and installations to the city's streets and squares, linked by a 12km-long walking trail marked in green; the tourist office has free maps. Book excellent themed guided walking tours (€7 or €9 per person) in advance online or by telephone.

Getting There & Away

AIR

Aéroport International Nantes-Atlantique (www.nantes.aeroport.fr) The airport is 12km southeast of town.

BUS

Lila (http://lila.loire-atlantique.fr) buses cover the surrounding Loire-Atlantique *département*. Tickets cost €2 per ride.

Eurolines (08 92 89 90 91; www.eurolines.com; allée de la Maison Rouge) has an office in town, with buses arriving/departing from the **Gare Routière Baco** (Bus Station; allée de la Maison Rouge) near the train station.

TRAIN

The **train station** (27 bd de Stalingrad), with two entrances (north and south) in the city centre, is well connected to most of the country. Destinations include the following:

Bordeaux (€52.20, 4¼ hours, three or four daily)

La Rochelle (€29.60, 2¼ hours, three or four daily)

Paris Gare Montparnasse (€85, 2¼ hours, 15 to 20 daily)

Tickets and information are also available at the **SNCF ticket office** (12 place de la Bourse; 10am-6.30pm Mon-Fri, to 6pm Sat) in the city centre.

Getting Around

TO/FROM THE AIRPORT

A *navette* (shuttle bus) links the airport with the train station's southern entrance (€8, 20 minutes) and place du Commerce every 20 minutes from about 5.30am until 11pm. Buy tickets in advance online at www.tan.fr, from the machine by the bus stop or direct from the driver.

BUS & TRAM

The **TAN network** (www.tan.fr) includes three tram lines that intersect at the **Gare Centrale** (place du Commerce) on place du Commerce, the main bus/tram transfer point. Buses run from 6.45am to 10pm. Night services continue until 12.30am.

Bus/tram tickets (€1.60 or €14.50 for a *carnet* of 10) can be individually purchased online, by smartphone, or from bus (but not tram) drivers and at tram-stop ticket machines. They're valid for one hour after being time-stamped. A *ticket journalier*, good for 24 hours, costs €5 or €8 for a ticket valid for four people travelling together; time-stamp it only the first time you use it.

CENTRAL ATLANTIC COAST

The Poitou-Charentes region, midway along the Atlantic Coast, scoops up a pot-pourri of attractions – from the history-rich capital, Poitiers, to the portside panache of La Rochelle, the languid beaches of Île de Ré, and the eponymous home of Cognac.

Poitiers

POP 87,427

Inland from the coast, history-steeped Poitiers was founded by the Pictones, a Gaulish tribe. The city rose to prominence as the former capital of Poitou, the region governed by the Counts of Poitiers in the Middle Ages. A pivotal turning point came in AD 732, when somewhere near Poitiers (the exact site is not known) the cavalry of Charles Martel defeated the Muslim forces of Abd ar-Rahman, governor of Córdoba, thus ending Muslim attempts to conquer France. Until the Revolution, this sublimely beautiful city was known as the 'town of 100 bell towers'; the remarkable Romanesque churches that remain today are in part a legacy of Eleanor of Aquitaine's financial support.

Poitiers has one of the oldest universities in the country, established in 1432 and today a linchpin of this lively city: students make up 25% of the population.

Sights

Église St-Hilaire le Grand CHURCH
(rue St-Hilaire; 9am-6.30pm) Consecrated in 1049, used as a warehouse during the Revolution and partly rebuilt in the 19th century,

WORTH A TRIP

TIME TRAVEL

Futuristic theme park **Futuroscope** (☎05 49 49 11 12; www.futuroscope.com; av René Monory, Chasseneuil-du-Poitou; adult/child €43/35; ⊙10am-11.15pm Jul, 9am-11.15pm Aug, shorter hours rest of year, closed Jan–mid-Feb) takes you whizzing through space, diving into the deep-blue ocean depths, and racing around city streets and on a close encounter with creatures of the future, among many other space-age cinematic experiences. To keep things cutting edge, one-third of the attractions change annually. Many are motion-seat set-ups requiring a minimum height of 120cm, but there's a play area for younger children with miniature cars and so on.

Allow at least five hours to see the major attractions; two days to see everything. Futuroscope's numerous hotels are bookable through the website, or directly at the lodging desk. Futuroscope is 10km north of Poitiers in Jaunay-Clan (take exit 28 off the A10). TGV trains link the park's TGV station with cities including Paris and Bordeaux; times and prices are similar to those to/from Poitiers. Local Vitalis buses 1 and E link Futuroscope (Parc de Loisirs stop) with Poitiers' train station (€1.50, 30 minutes, twice hourly).

this grandiose Romanesque church appears on Unesco's list of World Heritage sites as a treasured stop on the Chemin de St-Jacques de Compostelle. The remains of 11th-century decorative paintings – in rich ochre, ginger and gold tones – in its ornate sculpted interior are justifiably striking.

Église Notre Dame la Grande CHURCH
(place Charles de Gaulle; ⊙9am-7pm, light show 10.30pm 21 Jun-Aug, 9.30pm until 3rd weekend in Sep) FREE The celebrated west façade of this Romanesque church was exquisitely sculpted in soft gold stone between 1115 and 1130. Spot the temptation of Adam and Eve, the Nativity, the 12 Apostles and many other biblical scenes – at their most spectacular in summer when a colourful 15-minute light show, evoking the medieval tradition of painting churches, is projected onto the façade. The painted columns inside the church today date to 1851.

Palais de Justice HISTORIC BUILDING
(Palais des Comtes de Poitou; ☎05 49 50 22 00; place Alphonse Lepetit; ⊙8.30am-noon & 1.30-5.30pm Mon-Fri) FREE Today it houses the law courts, but nearly a thousand years ago this stunning building was the seat of the Counts of Poitou and Dukes of Aquitaine. Its most impressive feature is the dining hall constructed in the late 12th century by that local lass with big dreams, Eleanor of Aquitaine.

Cathédrale St-Pierre CATHEDRAL
(place de la Cathédrale et du Cardinal Pré; ⊙9am-7pm summer, to 5pm winter) FREE The town's grand Gothic cathedral safeguards beautiful 13th-century oak-carved choir stalls, an 18th-century organ with more than 3000 pipes and exceptional stained glass: the 12th-century window (1160–70) illustrating the Crucifixion and the Ascension at the far end of the choir is one of the oldest in France. It was given to the cathedral by Eleanor of Aquitaine and Henry II Plantagenet, King of England, who wed here in 1152.

Musée Ste-Croix MUSEUM
(☎05 49 41 07 53; www.musees-poitiers.org; 3bis rue Jean Jaurès; adult/child Mon-Sat €4.50/free, Sun €2; ⊙10am-noon & 1.15-8pm Tue, to 6pm Wed-Fri, 10am-noon & 2-6pm Sat & Sun Jun-Sep, shorter hours rest of year) The 1970s Brutalist architecture of this art museum, built from reinforced concrete, comes as a shock after the elegance of its ancient episcopal neighbours. Inside, prehistoric, Roman and medieval artefacts mingle with art from the 14th to 20th centuries. Jean-Baptiste Pierre's magnificent *Aurore et Tithon* (1747) and several signed statues by sculptor Camille Claudel (1864–1943), artist model and companion to Renoir, are highlights. Occasional temporary exhibitions too.

Sleeping & Eating

Hôtel de l'Europe HOTEL €
(☎05 49 88 12 00; www.hotel-europe-poitiers.com; 39 rue Sadi Carnot; d/tr from €60/115; @ 🛜) Be sure to ask for a room in the original main building of this period, two-star hotel with a history harking back to 1710. Refined communal areas, including stylish lounge with fireplace and sweeping staircase, compensate for the simplicity of the rooms. Those in the modern annexe just don't have the same appeal. Breakfast costs €9.50.

Jasmine Citronelle FRENCH €
(☎05 49 41 37 26; 32 rue Gambetta; mains €9.50-11.50; ⊙noon-6.30pm Tue-Fri, noon-7pm Sat) Parisian Mariage Frère teas served in bone china teapots, old-fashioned hot chocolate and flavoured milks are perfect companions to the delicious English-styled cakes, crumbles and gourmandises served at this utterly charming tearoom. Find it secreted away in a tiny flowery courtyard with easily the best summer terrace in town. Lunch here is equally idyllic; reservations essential.

La Serrurerie FRENCH €
(☎05 49 41 05 14; www.laserrurerie.com; 28 rue des Grandes Écoles; menu €13, mains €10-17.50; ⊙7.30am-2am) Lap up local life at this fabulous industrial-styled lounge restaurant with zinc bar, scrubbed ginger-brick walls and a vintage curiosities collection that would put your grandmother's to shame. Service is swift, and the kitchen caters to most tastes and ages: interesting meal-sized salads, gorgonzola burgers, Brighton-style fish and chips (yes, battered, in paper) and French classics such as *magret de canard* (duck), steaks and pan-fried liver.

Information

Tourist office (☎05 49 41 21 24; www.ot-poitiers.fr; 45 place Charles de Gaulle; ⊙10am-7pm Mon-Sat, to 6pm Sun mid-Jun–mid-Sep, 9.30am-6pm Mon-Sat rest of year) Opposite the sculpted west façade of Église Notre Dame la Grande.

Getting There & Away

The **train station** (☎36 35; bd du Grand Cerf) has direct links to Bordeaux (€42, 1¾ hours), La Rochelle (€25.10, 1½ hours) and many other cities including Paris' Gare Montparnasse (€58, 1¾ hours, 12 daily).

Marais Poitevin

From Poitiers town, an hour's drive southwest along the A10 to Niort and beyond plunges you into the heart of the Marais Poitevin. This *marais* (marshland) – an enchanting web of pea-green waterways overlooked by quaint villages – is a protected nature park. For those seeking somewhere to melt into rural life, there is no finer spot.

Parc Naturel Interrégional du Marais Poitevin (www.parc-marais-poitevin.fr) is a tranquil bird-filled wetland dubbed the Venise Verte (Green Venice) due to the duckweed that turns its maze of waterways emerald green each spring and summer. Covering some 800 sq km of wet and drained marsh, the marshlands are interspersed with villages and woods threaded by canals and bike paths. There are two main bases from which to punt out across the waterways: the small honey-coloured town of **Coulon** and the romantic village of **Arçais**.

Boating and cycling are the only way to satisfactorily explore the area and there is no shortage of operators hiring out bikes and flat-bottomed boats or kayaks for watery tours. Rental outlets in both towns offer identical services for the same price: single kayak per hour/half-day from €12/35, three-place canoe from €15/40, six-person wooden boat €10/45. Guided tours are also possible. Bikes can be hired from several operators in both towns for €5/12/18 per hour/half-day/day.

Getting to either Coulon or Arçais is difficult in anything other than your own car.

La Rochelle

POP 77,294

Known as La Ville Blanche (the White City), La Rochelle's luminous limestone façades glow in the bright coastal sunlight. One of France's foremost seaports from the 14th to 17th centuries, the city has arcaded walkways, half-timbered houses (protected from the salt air by slate tiles), ghoulish gargoyles and a fabulous collection of lighthouses – all rich reminders of its magnificent seafaring heritage. The early French settlers of Canada, including the founders of Montreal, set sail from here in the 17th century.

This 'white city' is also commendably green, with innovative public transport, open spaces and plenty of activities and attractions for families visiting with children.

La Rochelle's late-20th-century district of Les Minimes was built on reclaimed land, and now has one of the largest marinas in the country. Unlike the Med with its motor cruisers, the 3500 moorings here are mostly used by yachts, which fill the harbour with billowing spinnakers.

Sights

★**Aquarium La Rochelle** AQUARIUM
(www.aquarium-larochelle.com; quai Louis Prunier; adult/child €16/12; ⊙9am-11pm Jul & Aug, 9am-8pm Apr-Jun & Sep, 10am-8pm Oct-Mar) La Rochelle's state-of-the-art, family-friendly aquarium is home to 12,000 marine animals and 600 different species. Visits begin by descending in a clunky old 'submarine' to the

La Rochelle

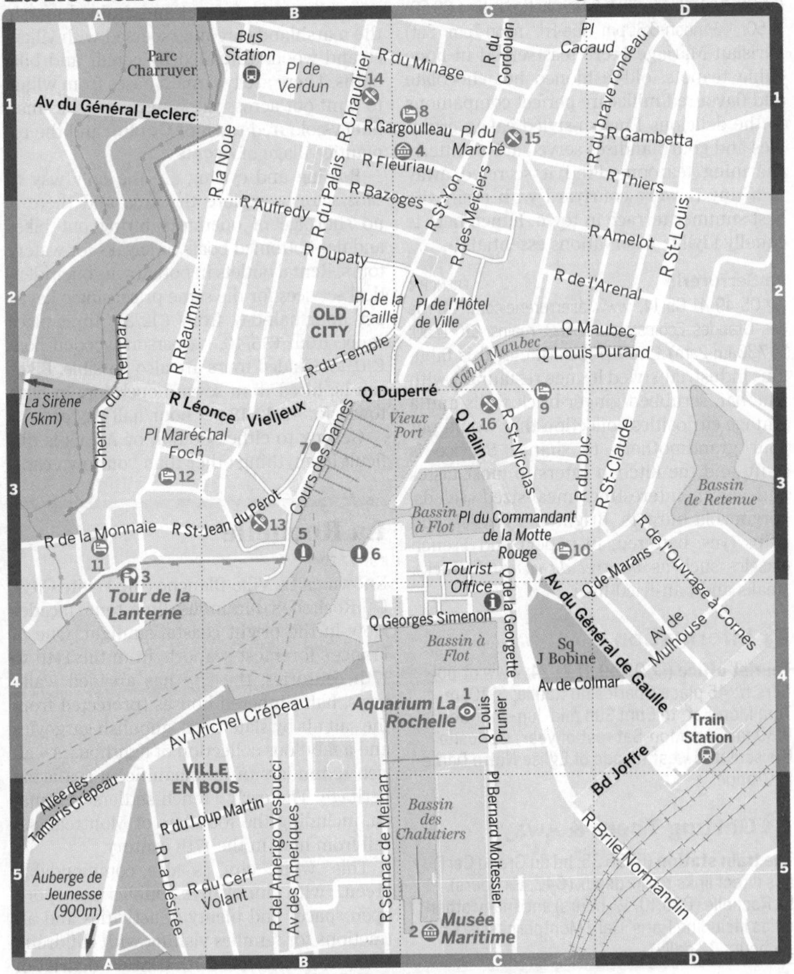

ocean floor, where, serenaded by the sound of crashing waves and classical music, you're greeted by the pouting fish of the North Atlantic. After this you swim through the oceans and seas of the world learning about all its diverse lifeforms. One floor up, the Galerie des Lumières (Gallery of Lights) is particularly magical.

★Musée Maritime MUSEUM

(Maritime Museum; ☎05 46 28 03 00; www.museemaritimelarochelle.fr; place Bernard Moitessier; adult/child €8/5; ⏲10am-7pm Jul & Aug, to 6.30pm Apr-Jun & Sep, shorter hours rest of year) In a series of canopied hangars at the Bassin à Flot, the Maritime Museum evokes the history of La Rochelle port, from the days when Parisians would arrive by train in La Rochelle to then set sail on a steamer to South America and Africa, to the present day.

There are plenty of model ships and short films to entertain younger minds, but the real highlight is the trio of retired boats moored here: meteorological research ship *France 1*, in service from 1958 until 1985, a *chalutier* (fishing boat) and a tug.

La Rochelle

Musée du Nouveau Monde MUSEUM
(New World Museum; 10 rue Fleuriau; adult/child €5/free; ⏲10am-12.30pm & 1.45-6pm Mon & Wed-Sat, 2-6pm Sun) La Rochelle's role as a departure point for North America is interpreted at this museum, housed in an 18th-century mansion.

Activities

Several islands are scattered around La Rochelle, including nearby **Île de Ré** and a trio further south. Accessible only by boat, tiny crescent-shaped **Île d'Aix** (eel dex), 16km due south of La Rochelle, has some blissful beaches and lovely windswept walking. Neighbouring **Île d'Oléron** is larger and is linked to the mainland by a free bridge.

From La Rochelle Vieux Port, it is an invigorating 3km-long bike ride or walk along the coast to sandy **Plage des Minimes**; by the beach pick up the path to **Cap Horn** to admire the enchanting **Phare du Bout du Monde**, a replica of the 16-sided wooden lighthouse that glowed with the light of seven oil lamps from 1894 until 1902.

Croisières Inter-Îles BOATING
(☎08 25 13 55 00; www.inter-iles.com; cours des Dames) Inter-Îles has sailings from Easter to early November to Fort Boyard (adult/child €20/12.50), Île d'Aix (€29.90/18.50) and Île d'Oléron (€25.50/17.50), plus sailings to Île de Ré (€22/14.50) in July and August. A couple of other companies with kiosks on the same quayside offer identical boat trips.

Sleeping

Hôtel de la Paix HOTEL €
(☎05 46 41 33 44; www.hotelalarochelle.com; 14 rue Gargoulleau; d/tr from €74/105; 📶) In a lovely 18th-century building, a sweeping staircase of polished wood leads to 19 good-value rooms, some of which have open stone walls and all of which have plenty of splashes of colour and character. There are also rooms that sleep five (from €129), which are good for families.

Un Hôtel en Ville BOUTIQUE HOTEL €
(☎05 46 41 15 75; www.unhotelenville.fr; 20 place du Maréchal Foch; s/d €79/89; P❄📶) Everything about this smart, 11-room boutique hotel at the Vieux Port screams quality. Moderately sized rooms are painted in a startling white, with white bed linens, dark stone furnishings and decorative chocolate, beige and zinc cushion fabrics. Count an extra €10 per person for *le petit dej* or €12 should you fancy breakfasting on your own private terrace.

Auberge de Jeunesse HOSTEL €
(☎05 46 44 43 11; www.aj-larochelle.fr/hostel; av des Minimes; dm €16.30-22, tw €65-74; ⏲reception 8am-noon, 2-7pm & 9-10pm) This popular HI hostel is 2km southwest of the train station in the seaside suburb of Les Minimes. Dorms sport four to six places in bunk beds – or bunk up in a twin. Rates include breakfast, and dinner is available for an additional fee.

★**Hôtel St-Nicolas** BOUTIQUE HOTEL €€
(☎05 46 41 71 55; www.hotel-saint-nicolas.com; 13 rue Sardinerie et place de la Solette; d/tr €125/145; P❄📶) This stylish hotel, tucked in a peaceful courtyard with delightful summer terrace, has smart comfortable rooms with ultramodern bathrooms – think giant rain showers, heated towel rails and sweet-smelling welcome products. A handful of rooms are across the courtyard in an equally inviting annexe, and breakfast (€12) is served in an indoor tropical garden. Check its website for excellent-value deals.

La Monnaie DESIGN HOTEL €€
(☎05 46 50 65 65; www.hotelmonnaie.com; 3 rue de la Monnaie; d/tr from €144/234; P❄📶) This fabulous boutique hotel, tucked in a 17th-century manor house, markets itself as

'art hotel and spa' – for good reason. Its interior is a virtual art gallery of contemporary artworks, sculptures and subtle lighting. Rooms are four-star comfortable, with cutting-edge bathrooms. If you need pampering there's a gym, a spa and an uber-cool bar open to nonguests too.

Ibis La Rochelle Vieux Port HOTEL €€
(☎05 46 41 60 22; place du Commandant de la Motte Rouge; d €68-135, tr €78-145; P ❄ @ ☜) Unusually, the 79 bright modern rooms of this chain hotel hide behind the extraordinary façade of an elegant 17th-century chapel, built in a Jesuit style in 1628. The church was deconsecrated in 1887 and later became a warehouse then hotel. The lobby lounge is red, steel grey and black, and the sofa-strewn patio in an alfresco interior courtyard is an utter delight. The excellent buffet breakfast costs €9.90.

Eating

★**À la Gerbe de Blé** SEAFOOD €
(☎05 46 41 05 94; rue Thiers; sandwiches €5.50, mains €10.50-17.50; ⊙10am-1pm) Lunch local. Buy a dozen oysters from the oyster stand in front of the **Marché Central** (rue Thiers, place du Marché; ⊙7am-1.30pm), ask to have them shucked, then head around the corner to Chez Geff and Christine, a buzzing cafe-bar built into the red-brick market wall. Tables on the pavement terrace enjoy the morning sun, and a simple *menu* of steak and fries, omelettes and sandwiches complement the bring-your-own seafood.

Prao MODERN FRENCH €€
(☎05 46 37 85 46; http://prao.biz/; 10 rue St-Nicolas; 2-/3-course lunch €22/27, mains €16; ⊙noon-2pm & 7.30-10.30pm Mon-Sat, 11am-2.30pm Sun; ☜) Named after the multi-hull proa (*prao* in French) sailboat typical to the Pacific and Indian Oceans, this funky bistro takes great pride in the products it cooks with, all sourced locally from small, often artisan, producers. The result is a light, healthy cuisine packed with lots of vegetables, herbs, seeds and pulses to accompany the daily *effet mer* (fish dish) and *effet terre* (meat dish). Sunday brunch (€12 to €22) is particularly popular.

La Fleur de Sel BISTRO €€
(☎05 46 41 17 06; 5 rue St-Jean du Pérot; 2-/3-course lunch menu €16/19.80, dinner menu €28, mains €16.50-27; ⊙noon-2pm & 7-10pm) A favourite Sunday-lunch address with discerning locals, Delphine and Bruno's whitewashed bistro on two floors has a signature mini wooden trough of rock salt on each table. Cuisine is modern French with dishes such as fish crumble, and pan-fried squid with chorizo risotto on the interesting *menu*. The lunchtime *menu* is unbeatable value.

Café de la Paix BRASSERIE €€
(☎05 46 41 39 79; 54 rue Chaudrier; mains €13.50-15.50; ⊙7am-10pm Mon-Sat) Meal-sized salads, hand-cut tartares, steaks, foie gras, duck and other classic French brasserie fare is the order of the day at this historic belle-époque cafe, an address that is more about oggling at soaring frescoed ceilings and splendid gold-edged arched mirrors than fine food. Tourists love it.

★**André** SEAFOOD €€€
(☎05 46 41 28 24; www.barandre.com; 5 rue St-Jean du Pérot, place de la Chaîne; menus €22 & €36.90, mains €13-90; ⊙noon-4pm & 7pm-midnight) Opened in the 1950s as a waterfront seafood cafe, André grew so popular it began buying adjacent shops. It is now an eye-catching maze of eight different interconnecting rooms, each with its own individual ambience (dinner in a port-holed cabin, anyone?) but all serving the same succulent seafood caught the night before.

Expect luxuriant seafood platters (€19.70 to €59), local sole and moules simmered in sweet Pineau des Charentes. Service is equally exceptional.

Information

Tourist Office (☎05 46 41 14 68; www.larochelle-tourisme.com; 2 quai Georges Simenon; ⊙9am-7pm Jul & Aug, 9am-5pm Apr-Jun & Sep, shorter hours rest of year) Sells the Pass' Rochelais, offering various discounts for public transport, sights and activities.

Getting There & Away

AIR

La Rochelle Airport (www.larochelle.aeroport.fr), north of the city centre off the N237, has a variety of flights to Lyon, Ajaccio and Brussels, and several British and Irish airports.

BUS

From the **bus station** (Gare Routière; place de Verdun), **Les Mouettes** (☎08 11 36 17 17; www.lesmouettes-transports.com) runs services to regional destinations. Year-round buses to/from Île de Ré depart from in front of the train station, stopping at place de Verdun en route.

DEFENSIVE TOWERS

La Rochelle's waterfront is dominated by four gigantic defensive towers that once helped to protect the town. Enchanting **Rue sur les Murs** was built along the ramparts between 1352 and 1387 to link two of the towers. Buy individual tickets or visit all of them on a single joint ticket.

Tour de la Lanterne (rue sur les Murs; adult/child €6/free, 3 towers €8.50/free; ⏲10am-1pm & 2.15-6.30pm Apr-Sep, to 5.30pm Oct-Mar) Easily mistaken as an ornate church spire, the conical 15th-century Tour de la Lanterne is La Rochelle's beauty queen. It was so named because of its role as the harbour's lighthouse (lit by an enormous candle) and is one of the oldest of its kind in the world. It is sometimes referred to as Tour des Quatre Sergents in memory of four local sergeants, two of whom were held here for plotting to overthrow the newly reinstated monarchy before their execution in Paris in 1822.

Tour de la Chaîne (cours des Dames; adult/child €6/free, 3 towers €8.50/free; ⏲10am-1pm & 2.15-6.30pm Apr-Sep, to 5.30pm Oct-Mar) To protect the harbour at night in times of war, an enormous chain was raised between the two 14th-century stone towers at the harbour entrance to La Rochelle, giving rise to the name Tour de la Chaîne (Chain Tower). There are superb views from the top and an insightful exhibition on French migration to the New World, hence Quebec, in the 17th and 18th centuries.

Tour St-Nicolas (rue de l'Armide; adult/child €6/free, 3 towers €8.50/free; ⏲10am-6.30pm Apr-Sep, 10am-1pm & 2.15-5.30pm Oct-Mar) The only tower to be decked out like a house, this 37m-high pentagonal stone tower has leaned slightly to one side ever since building was complete in 1376. It was originally used for both defensive purposes and as a royal residence, and the different rooms can still be visited. City views from the rooftop terrace are predictably fine – count 120 odd steps in total to the top.

TRAIN

The **train station** (place Pierre Semard) is linked by TGV to Paris' Gare Montparnasse (from €70, 3¼ hours). Other destinations served by regular direct trains include Nantes (€29, 1¾ hours), Poitiers (from €28, 1½ hours) and Bordeaux (from €31, 2¼ hours).

Getting Around

TO/FROM THE AIRPORT

Yélo Bus 7 links the airport with place de Verdun in the town centre every 30 minutes; journey time is 15 minutes and a ticket costs €1.30. In summer there are direct **Les Mouettes** buses from the airport to/from Île de Ré.

BICYCLE

Pick up a set of wheels from **Greenbike** (☎05 46 29 31 03; www.location-greenbike.com; 41 quai du Gabut; 4/24hr from €11/18; ⏲9am-1pm & 2-7pm Jul & Aug, 10am-noon & 2-6.30pm Sep-Nov & Apr-Jun) near Tour St-Nicolas or from the seasonal **Point Vélo Jaune** (place de la Motte Rouge; per hour €1.30; ⏲9am-8pm Jul & Aug, 9am-12.30 & 1.30-8pm Apr & Sep, weekends only May & Jun) opposite the tourist office. To rent a canary-yellow bike from this unbeatable-value, city-run outlet – the tourist service of the city's Yélo bike-sharing scheme – you'll need to leave your passport and a €250 credit-card deposit (no negotiation). Rental costs €1.30 per hour.

Île de Ré

POP 17,723

Bathed in the southern sun, drenched in a languid atmosphere and scattered with villages of green-shuttered, whitewashed buildings with terracotta roof tiles, Île de Ré is one of the most delightful places on France's west coast. The island spans 30km from its most easterly and westerly points, and just 5km at its widest section. In July and August it is almost impossible to move around and even harder to find a place to stay.

On the northern coast, about 12km from the toll bridge that links the island to La Rochelle, is main town **St-Martin-de-Ré** (population 2600), a quaint fishing port. Surrounded by 17th-century star-shaped fortifications and a citadel (today a prison) built by Vauban, the port town is a mesh of streets filled with Paris-chic fashion boutiques, art galleries and salty sea views. St-Martin's tourist office (p619) has information for the entire island.

Sights & Activities

St-Martin de Ré tourist office has plenty of information on water sports, including windsurfing, kite-surfing, paddle-boarding, sailing and canoeing.

★Phare des Baleines LIGHTHOUSE
(www.lepharedesbaleines.fr; adult/child €3.20/1.70, lighthouse & museum €4.50/2.20; 9.30am-9pm Jun–mid-Sep, shorter hours rest of year) For an overview of the island, follow the crowds to Phare des Baleines, the island's scarlet-tipped, 59m-tall lighthouse on its northwestern tip. Scale the dizzying, 257-step spiral staircase inside the 19th-century lighthouse (1854) for a sweeping coastal panorama and learn its history in the neighbouring **Musée de la Mer**, snug against a second older lighthouse (1682), now defunct and hence called the **Vieille Tour** (old tower). The latter is only open to visitors in July and August.

Clocher Observatoire TOWER
(05 16 19 81 96; 1 rue du Palais; adult/child €1.85/free; 10am-11pm Jul & Aug, to 7pm Sep–mid-Nov & Feb-Jun) A hike up the 117 steps inside the bell stone of fortified Église St-Martin rewards with a mighty fine panorama of St-Martin de Ré and the coast. The well-used wooden staircase twists up past the bell tower's trio of bells, the largest of which dates to 1890 and weighs a mighty 1140kg. Be warned: the bells ring for a few minutes every half-hour, in addition to a deafening 10 minutes at 7am, noon and 7pm each day to announce the traditional call to prayer.

Maison du Fier BIRDWATCHING
(05 46 29 50 74; lilleau.niges@espace-naturels.fr; Les Portes-en-Ré; museum adult/child €5/4; 10am-1pm & 2.30-7pm Sun-Fri, 2.20-7pm Sat Jul & Aug, shorter hours rest of year, closed Dec–mid-Mar) A short bike ride from the village of Les Portes en Ré brings you to this wooden building, surrounded by marshes and ancient salt pans in the **Reserve Naturelle Lilleau des Niges**. Some 300 different bird species frequent this soggy, sun-flooded nature reserve and sightings of kestrels, red shanks, blue throats et al are common. Bring binoculars or rent some for €5/3 per day/half-day. The Maison du Fier runs a small nature museum and organises excellent guided nature walks and activities for both adults and children.

LOCAL KNOWLEDGE

AN OYSTER FARMER'S LUNCH

For an authentic taste of island life, spurn St-Martin's portside restaurants and pick up the cycling path to Ars-en-Ré – either on foot or by bike. Within seconds of hitting the coast, the path brushes past a twinset of oyster farmer *cabanes* (huts), whose doors are open to the culinary curious. Grab a straw hat to keep off the sun, snag a table overlooking oyster beds and tuck into freshly shucked oysters courtesy of **Auberge de la Mer** (06 83 08 20 38; chemin de la Galère, St-Martin-de-Ré; oysters per dozen €12-19). Or kick back next door on a brightly coloured bar stool facing the sea at **Ré Ostréa** (06 63 91 80 19; www.degustationhuitres-iledere.fr; chemin de la Galère, St-Martin-de-Ré; oysters per dozen €12-19; 10am-8pm Apr-Sep), a super-friendly oyster bar with fresh prawns, whelks, clams and dozens of island oysters (€12 to €19 per dozen) to tempt.

Sleeping

★Hôtel Le Sénéchal BOUTIQUE HOTEL €€
(05 46 29 40 42; www.hotel-le-senechal.com; 6 rue Gambetta, Ars en Ré; d €79-349;) The stunning creation of a Parisian architect, this 22-room boutique hotel on the church square in Ars-en-Ré languishes luxuriantly in several traditional old-stone *maisons de village* and exudes panache and good taste. Scrubbed wooden floorboards, exposed stone walls, designer bathrooms and beautiful fabrics dress each room. Breakfast is served in a flowery courtyard and there's a pocket-sized heated pool.

Hotel La Jetée HOTEL €€
(05 46 09 36 36; www.hotel-lajetee.com; 23 quai Clémenceau, St-Martin-de-Ré; d €99-195;) In the heart of pretty St-Martin-de-Ré, this smart and comfortable portside hotel offers good value for Île de Ré. Stylish rooms enjoy a nautical, beach-chic decor with vintage 'gone fishing' signs and seafaring lamps; some peep out over St-Martin's picture-postcard Vieux Port.

Eating

Waterfront quays in every village are laden with cafes, bistros and restaurants cooking up a mix of local fish and seafood dishes and classic French fare. Dining is pricier than elsewhere in western France – count around €30 for an unstartling three-course *menu*.

PEDALLING AROUND

Criss-crossed by an extensive network of smooth, well-signposted and scenic *pistes cyclables* (bicycle paths) well away from motorised traffic, pancake-flat Île de Ré is a cycling paradise. In **St-Martin de Ré** pick up a free cycling map (marked with trails, distances and times, online at www.cdciledere.fr) at the tourist office and a pair of chic polka-dotted wheels across the road at **Yoo Too** (05 46 68 08 09; www.cycles-yootoo.com; 9 av Victor Bouthillier, St-Martin de Ré; per half-day/24hr from €7.50/10; 9am-8pm Jul & Aug, to 7pm Apr-Jun & Sep, shorter hours rest of year), open year-round; advance reservations are essential for July and August.

In summer, practically every village has somewhere to hire bikes, including trailers and seats for young children. From early July until the end of August, shuttle buses transport cyclists and their bikes between four cycling information points on the island.

From St-Martin, a fabulous 14km (one hour) trail follows the coast west past working oyster beds, before crossing the island past ancient salt pans to the pretty village of **Ars-en-Ré** where you can buy local rock salt and *fleur de sel* from the island's salt-producers cooperative. From here, it's another 7km to **Phare des Baleines**, the island's 59m-tall lighthouse on its northwestern tip.

From the lighthouse, a shady 5.5km trail ducks through the protected forest of the **Foret Dominiale du Lizay** to the north-coast village of **Les Portes en Ré**. Birdwatching enthusiasts (bring binoculars) should not miss the trail from here, via the **Maison du Fier**, into the marshes and salt pans of the **Reserve Naturelle Lilleau des Niges** and beyond to Ars-en-Ré. Time the ride with a memorable guided nature walk or activity (for adults and children) organised by the Maison du Fier.

When thirst strikes on a hot day, consider a chilled bottle of *biére de Ré* (www.bieres-dere.fr), artisan beer brewed on the island in St-Martin de Ré.

★ **La Martinière** ICE CREAM €

(05 46 09 20 99; www.la-martiniere.fr; 17 quai de la Poithevinière, St-Martin-de-Ré; 1-/2-/3-/4-scoop cones €3/3.70/4.20/4.70; 10.30am-11pm Jul & Aug, to 9.30pm Sep-Jun) No trip to St-Martin de Ré is complete without an ice-cream cone from this *glacier* extraordinaire. There are between 250 and 300 incredible flavours to choose from, including madras, caviar and oyster, salted caramel, potato and caramel or rice pudding alongside strawberry, mango, passion fruit, peach and lavender, and other more traditional fruit flavours. Each season a new ice cream is launched (a creamy kulfi flavour perfumed with cardamon, pistachio and praliné in 2016).

Information

St-Martin's **tourist office** (05 46 09 20 06; www.iledere.com; 2 av Victor Bouthillier, St-Martin de Ré; 9.30am-1pm & 2-6.30pm Mon-Sat, 9.30am-1.30pm Sun Jul & Aug, shorter hours rest of year), next to the bus stop at the entrance to the Vieux Port, has information on the entire island.

Getting There & Away

A return ticket to drive across the Pont de Île de Ré (www.pont-ile-de-re.com), the bridge connecting the mainland and island, costs €8 (mid-June to mid-September €16); pay on your way to the island from La Rochelle.

Year-round **Les Mouettes** (p616) buses link La Rochelle train station and place de Verdun with all the major towns on the island; a single fare to St-Martin (one hour) or a *forfait journée* covering unlimited travel all day (including the return trip) costs €5.

Cognac

POP 18,626

On the banks of the River Charente amid vine-covered countryside, Cognac is known worldwide for the double-distilled spirit that bears its name, and on which the local economy thrives. Most visitors head here to visit the famous cognac houses; however, it's a picturesque stop even if you don't happen to be a huge fan of the local firewater.

Cognac centres on a cafe-ringed central roundabout, place François Ier. From here, the old town and most of the Cognac distilleries are downhill towards and along the river.

Sights & Activities

Musée des Arts du Cognac MUSEUM

(MACO; 05 45 36 21 10; www.musees-cognac.fr; place de la Salle Verte; adult/child €4/1; 10am-noon & 2-6pm Jul & Aug, 2-6pm Tue-Sun Jun-Sep) This museum, inside a contemporary building set into the ramparts alongside 19th-century Hôtel Perrin de Boussac, explains the production of Cognac from vine to bottle. In the adjoining **Espace Decouverte** (admission free) is a model of Château de Cognac, the castle where François I was born in 1494. Just a fraction of the original riverside edifice remains, today home to the Otard Cognac house.

Musée d'Art et d'Histoire de Cognac MUSEUM

(MAH; 05 45 32 07 25; www.musees-cognac.fr; 48 bd Denfert-Rochereau; adult/child €4/1; 10am-noon & 2-6pm Jul & Aug, 2-6pm Wed-Mon Jun-Sep) In the southern corner of the grotto- and pond-clad **Jardin Public**, Cognac's Art and History Museum showcases the town's history. Its interior – magnificent 19th-century Hôtel Dupuy d'Angec (1837) – is as interesting as the painting, sculptures and decorative arts on display.

La Dame Jeanne BOATING

(05 45 82 10 71; quai des Flamands; adult/child €8.25/5.25; May-Sep;) Float with the sticklebacks down the River Charente on *La Dame Jeanne*, a re-creation of one of the flat-bottomed cargo boats known as *gabarres* that were once the lifeblood of trade along the river. The trip lasts 90 minutes; reserve through the tourist office.

Sleeping

★**Quai des Pontis** HOTEL €

(05 45 32 47 40; www.quaidespontis.com; 16 rue des Pontis; d/tr from €75/80) At home in a former wood factory, this riverside estate is a leafy delight. Pick from one of seven design rooms in the attractive hotel building, an enchanting wooden cabin on stilts right by the water's edge or a romantic *roulotte* (caravan) for two. *Roulottes* and cabins have modern bathrooms, kitchenettes and a serenely peaceful outlook over the River Charente. Breakfast costs €9.50.

DON'T MISS

THE HOME OF COGNAC

According to local lore, divine intervention plays a role in the production of Cognac. Made of grape *eaux-de-vie* (brandies) of various vintages, Cognac is aged in oak barrels and blended by an experienced *maître de chai* (cellar master). Each year some 2% of the casks' volume – *la part des anges* (the angels' share) – evaporates through the pores in the wood, nourishing the tiny black mushrooms that thrive on the walls of Cognac warehouses. That 2% might not sound like much, but it amounts to around 20 million bottles a year.

The best-known Cognac houses are open to the public, running tours of their cellars and production facilities, and ending with a tasting session. Opening times vary annually; it's a good idea to reserve in advance.

Camus (05 45 32 72 96; www.camus.fr; 29 rue Marguerite de Navarre; adult/child from €8.50/free; 2-6pm Mon, 10.30am-12.30pm & 2-6pm Tue-Sat May-Sep) Located 250m northeast of the Jardin Public.

Hennessy (05 45 35 72 68; www.lesvisites.hennessy.com; 8 rue Richonne; adult/child €16/8; 10am-5pm Apr-Oct) Situated 100m uphill from quai des Flamands; tours include a film (shown in English) and a boat trip across the Charente to visit the cellars.

Martell (05 45 36 33 33; www.martell.com; place Édouard Martell; 10am-6pm Mar-Oct) Found 250m northwest of the tourist office.

Otard (05 45 36 88 86; www.otard.com; 127 bd Denfert-Rochereau; adult/child €10/4.50; 10am-noon & 1.30-6pm Jul & Aug, shorter hours rest of year) Housed in the 1494 birthplace of King François I, the Château de Cognac, 650m north of place François 1er.

Rémy Martin (05 45 35 76 66; www.visitesremymartin.com) Two locations: the estate, 4km southwest of town towards Pons; and, in town, the house, for intimate tastings in groups of up to eight.

The tourist office has a list of smaller Cognac houses near town; most close between October and mid-March.

FORT BOYARD

The stuff of cinema, Fort Boyard is a 20m-high iceberg of a fortress island lording over the ocean midway between Île d'Aix and Île d'Oléron. It was dreamt up in the 1700s to defend the Bay of Rochefort against the English, but construction of the extraordinary 'stone ship' only began a century later – and even then it took 19th-century builders 62 years to complete. The first building materials were hauled out to sea in 1802 and the fort was finally completed under Napoléon III (1851–70). At the end of the Second Empire it became a prison for Prussian soldiers, and was subsequently abandoned. Since 1990 the dramatic construction has been the TV studio and film location of the French TV game show *Fort Boyard*. Closed to visitors today, the unique fort is best admired on a boat trip or, in summer, close-up aboard a sea kayak with **Antioche Kayak** (☎06 63 20 51 44; www.antioche.kayak.com; Port Sud, Fouras), kayak and stand-up paddle guides based 30km south of La Rochelle in Fouras.

Hôtel Le Cheval Blanc HOTEL €
(☎05 45 82 09 55; www.hotel-chevalblanc.fr; 6 place Bayard; d/tr €71/79; ⏲reception 7am-9.30pm Mon-Fri, 8am-12.30pm & 3-9.30pm Sat, 8am-12.30pm & 5-9.30pm Sun; P❄📶) A flowery courtyard out back and stylish family rooms are highlights of this unpretentious 27-room hotel, run with passion by Parisian couple Mylène and Frédéric Personyre, who clearly delight in Cognac's small-town *art de vivre* after fast-paced life in the capital. Rooms are immaculate, with white linens and bright colours; nine open onto the table-bedecked patio garden. Breakfast costs €8.80.

Hôtel Spa François Premier HISTORIC HOTEL €€
(☎05 45 80 80 80; www.hotelfrancoispremier.fr; 3 place François 1er; d from €165; ❄📶) This grand four-star hotel lords over Cognac's main cafe-clad square. Twenty-six comfortable, carpeted rooms are dressed in regal shades of bordeaux, violet or blue. The courtesy tray with kettle is a welcome touch and facilities – the hotel spa, patio garden and bar with tempting choice of Cognac-based cocktails – are excellent. Breakfast costs €18.

Eating

★**L'Arty Show** INTERNATIONAL €
(☎06 80 43 78 53; www.facebook.com/lartyshowcognac; 23 rue du Pont Faumet; 2-/3-course menu €16/18; ⏲noon-2pm Mon-Thu, noon-2pm & 7.30pm-midnight Fri) Cognac invariably stars in the inventive, veg- and pulse-packed dishes of chefs Nathalie and Delphine at L'Arty Show, an edgy bistro with vintage flea-market furnishings and a name that sounds like *artichaut* ('artichoke' in French). The duo work with local, seasonal and often organic market products and there is no menu: be prepared for a delicious surprise.

In summer, dining is outside around a linden tree, beside Cognac's covered market on place d'Armes. Reserve in advance or arrive on the dot of noon to snag a spot.

Poulpette NEOBISTRO €€
(☎05 45 82 22 08; www.facebook.com/poulpette.cognac; 46 av du Maréchal de Lattre-de-Tassigny; menu €26; ⏲noon-2pm Mon & Tue, noon-2pm & 7.30-11pm Wed-Fri) Well away from the tourist crowd, across the river, Poulpette is a deliciously urban neobistro with a minimalist, faintly industrial interior and an outstanding no-choice *menu* that changes daily. Cuisine is young and inventive, with an abundance of fresh herbs and unexpected combos. The day's *menu* reads like a shopping list of seasonal products.

Drinking

Tasting Cognac in the town's famous Cognac houses is the main drinking that goes on in small provincial Cognac. Cafe terraces abound on main square place François 1er and the length of rue Grande.

★**La Gabare** BAR
(39 rue de Bellefonds; ⏲10am-12.30pm & 3-8pm Tue & Wed, 3-8pm Thu, 10am-12.30pm & 3-11pm Fri & Sat) Follow knowing locals away from the old town to this superb *cave à bières*, a contemporary beer bar with spartan interior dedicated to the serious business of *dégustation* (tasting). It stocks some 300 different world beers, including several brewed in southwest France: try non-filtered Aliénor beers made in St-Caprais de Bordeaux or beers from the La Debauche brewery in Angoulême.

Information

Tourist Office (☎05 45 82 10 71; www.tourism-cognac.com; 16 rue du 14 Juillet;

⌚9am-7pm Mon-Sat, 10am-5pm Sun Jul & Aug, shorter hours rest of year) Pick up a map and the excellent *Promenades Cognac* brochure outlining signposted walks in Cognac at the super-friendly tourist office. It also has information on canoeing on the river.

Getting There & Away

Cognac's **train station** (av du Maréchal Leclerc), 1km south of the town centre, has regular trains to/from Bordeaux (€25.40, 2¼ hours) and La Rochelle (€17.70, 1¼ hours).

LOWER ATLANTIC COAST

At the lower edge of the Atlantic coast, the expansive Aquitaine region extends to the Dordogne in the east and the Basque Country in the south. The gateway to the region's wealth of attractions, set amid glorious vine-ribboned countryside, is its capital, Bordeaux.

Bordeaux

POP 242,945

The city of Bordeaux is among France's most exciting, vibrant and dynamic cities. In the last decade and a half, it's shed its languid, *Belle au Bois Dormant* (Sleeping Beauty) image thanks to the vision of city mayor Alain Juppé who has pedestrianised boulevards, restored neoclassical architecture, created a high-tech public transport system and reclaimed Bordeaux's former industrial wet docks at Bassin à Flots. Half the city (18 sq km) is Unesco-listed, making it the largest urban World Heritage site; while world-class architects have designed a bevy of striking new buildings – the Herzog & de Meuron stadium (2015), decanter-shaped La Cité du Vin (2016) and Jean-Jacques Bosc bridge (2018) across the Garonne River included.

Bolstered by its high-spirited university-student population and 5½ million visitors annually, La Belle Bordeaux scarcely sleeps: think barista-run coffee shops, super-food food trucks, an exceptional dining scene and more fine wine than you could ever possibly drink. *Santé!*

Sights

★La Cité du Vin MUSEUM

(☎05 56 81 38 47; www.laciteduvin.com; 1 Esplanade de Pontac; adult/child €20/free; ⌚9.30am-7.30pm daily Apr-Oct, 9.30am-7.30pm Tue-Sun Nov-Mar) The complex world of wine is explored in depth at ground-breaking La Cité du Vin, a stunning piece of contemporary architecture resembling a wine decanter on the banks of the River Garonne. The curvaceous gold building glitters in the sun and its 3000 sq metres of exhibits are equally sensory and sensational. Digital guides lead visitors around 20 different themed sections covering everything from vine cultivation, grape varieties and wine production to ancient wine trade, 21st-century wine trends and celebrated personalities.

Tours end with a glass of wine – or grape juice for the kids – in the panoramic Belvedere, with monumental 30m-long bar and chandelier made out of recycled wine bottles, on the 8th floor. Watch too for temporary art exhibitions, cultural events and brilliant, themed 1½-hour tasting workshops – for adults and children. To get here, take tram B (direction Bassins à Flots) from Esplanade des Quinconnes or walk 2.5km north along the river.

★Miroir d'Eau FOUNTAIN

(Water Mirror; place de la Bourse; ⌚10am-10pm summer) FREE A fountain of sorts, the Miroir d'Eau is the world's largest reflecting pool. Covering an area of 3450 sq metres of black granite on the quayside opposite the imposing Palais de la Bourse, the 'water mirror' provides hours of entertainment on warm sunny days when the reflections in its thin slick of water – drained and refilled every half-hour -- are stunning. Every 23 minutes a dense fog-like vapor is ejected for three minutes to add to the fun (and photo opportunities).

Musée du Vin et du Négoce MUSEUM

(☎05 56 90 19 13; www.museeduvinbordeaux.com; 41 rue Borie; adult/child incl tasting €10/free; ⌚10am-6pm) This small Wine and Trade Museum, hidden in one of the city's oldest buildings – an Irish merchant's house dating to 1720 in the ancient trading district of Chartrons – offers a fascinating insight into the historic origins of Bordeaux's wine trade and the importance of the *négociant* (merchant trader) in the 19th century. The vaulted cellars, 33m long, display dozens of artefacts, including hand-crafted stave oak barrels and every size of wine bottle from an Avion to a Melchior.

Visits end with tasting of wine by small, lesser-known producers. To find the museum, walk north along rue Notre Dame then turn left onto rue Borie.

Cathédrale St-André CATHEDRAL
(www.cathedrale-bordeaux.fr; place Jean Moulin; ⌚2-6pm Mon, 10am-noon & 2-6pm Tue-Sun) Lording over the city, and a Unesco World Heritage site prior to the city's classification, the cathedral's oldest section dates from 1096; most of what you see today was built in the 13th and 14th centuries. Enjoy exceptional masonry carvings in the north portal.

Even more imposing than the cathedral itself is the gargoyled, 50m-high Gothic belfry, **Tour Pey-Berland** (place Jean Moulin; adult/child €5.50/free; ⌚10am-1.15pm & 2-6pm Jun-Sep, 10am-12.30pm & 2-5.30pm Oct-May), erected between 1440 and 1466.

Musée d'Aquitaine MUSEUM
(☎05 56 01 51 00; www.musee-aquitaine-bordeaux.fr; 20 cours Pasteur; adult/child €4/2; ⌚11am-6pm Tue-Sun) Gallo-Roman statues and relics dating back 25,000 years are among the highlights at this bright and spacious, well-curated history and art museum. Grab a bilingual floor plan at the entrance and borrow an English-language catalogue to better appreciate the exhibits that span prehistory through to 18th-century Atlantic trade and slavery, world cultures and the emergence of Bordeaux as a world port in the 19th century.

Musée d'Art Contemporain ART MUSEUM
(CAPC; ☎05 56 00 81 50; www.capc-bordeaux.fr; 7 rue Ferrère; adult/child €4/2; ⌚11am-6pm Tue & Thu-Sun, to 8pm Wed) Built in 1824 as a warehouse for French colonial produce such as coffee, cocoa, peanuts and vanilla, the cavernous Entrepôts Lainé creates a dramatic backdrop for cutting-edge modern art at Bordeaux's Museum of Contemporary Art. Highlights include works by Keith Haring and photographs of the derelict warehouse interior in the 1980s by Parisian photographer Georges Rousse. Temporary exhibitions command a higher admission fee (adult/child €6.50/3.50).

Musée des Beaux-Arts ART MUSEUM
(☎05 56 96 51 60; www.musba-bordeaux.fr; 20 cours d'Albret; adult/child €4/2; ⌚11am-6pm mid-Jul–mid-Aug, closed Tue rest of year) The evolution of Occidental art from the Renaissance to the mid-20th century is on view at Bordeaux's Museum of Fine Arts, which occupies two wings of the 1770s-built Hôtel de Ville, either side of elegant city park Jardin de la Mairie. The museum was established in 1801; highlights include 17th-century Flemish, Dutch and Italian paintings. Temporary exhibitions are regularly hosted at its nearby annexe, **Galerie des Beaux-Arts** (place du Colonel Raynal; adult/child €6.50/3.50).

> **BORDEAUX CITY PASS**
>
> Consider investing in a **Bordeaux City Pass** (www.bordeauxcitypass.com). A one-/two-/three-day card costs €26/33/40 and covers admission to many museums and monuments, unlimited public transport and various other discounts. The tourist office sells it.

Jardin Public GARDENS
(cours de Verdun) Landscaping is artistic as well as informative at the Jardin Public. Established in 1755 and laid out in the English style a century later, the grounds incorporate duck ponds, the meticulously catalogued **Jardin Botanique** dating from 1629, and the city's **Musée d'Histoire Naturelle** (5 place Bardineau) (Natural History Museum). It is closed for renovation work and slated to open again in late 2017.

Tours

The tourist office (p631) runs a packed program of city tours in English, including **gourmet** and **wine tours**, **river cruises** in the warmer months, and **child-friendly tours**. All tours take a limited number of participants; reserve ahead on the tourist office website or in situ.

Sleeping

Hôtel Notre Dame HOTEL €
(☎05 56 52 88 24; 36-38 rue Notre Dame; s/d €54/63; 📶) Location is the key selling point of this good-value hotel. It's within an easy stroll of the town centre, just back from the river and in the middle of a trendy village-like neighbourhood of antique shops, fashion boutiques, cafes and restaurants. It also has a wheelchair-accessible room. Breakfast costs €8.

Auberge de Jeunesse HOSTEL €
(☎05 56 33 00 70; www.auberge-jeunesse-bordeaux.com; 22 cours Barbey; dm incl sheets & breakfast €24; 📶) Bordeaux's only hostel is housed in an ultramodern building with a self-catering kitchen, good wheelchair access and table football to boot. From the train station, follow cours de la Marne northwest for 300m and turn left opposite the park; the hostel is about 250m ahead on your left.

Bordeaux

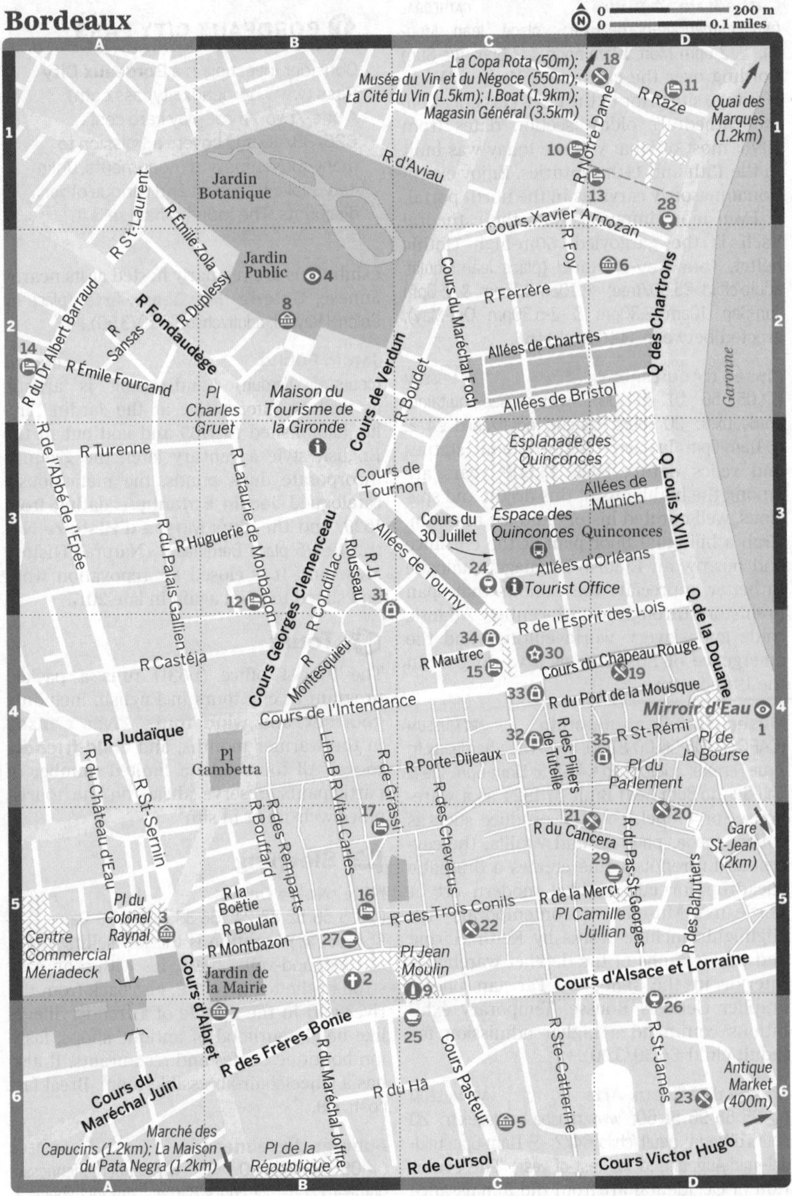

Hôtel La Cour Carrée BOUTIQUE HOTEL €€
(☎ 05 57 35 00 00; www.lacourcarree.com; 5 rue de Lurbe; d €125-300; ❄@📶) Bright white, contemporary rooms ensure the day starts well at La Cour Carrée, a stylish design-driven hotel that takes its name from the delightful interior *cour* (courtyard) the soft stone, vintage building squirrels away. In warm weather, wooden decking, tables and chairs transform the space into a much-appreciated outdoor lounge. Breakfast costs €10.

Bordeaux

Mama Shelter DESIGN HOTEL €€
(☎05 57 30 45 45; www.mamashelter.com/en/bordeaux; 19 rue Poquelin Molière; d/tr from €79/129) With personalised iMacs, video booths and free movies in every room, Mama Shelter leads the way in cutting-edge sleep. Crisp white rooms come in small, medium or large, with family-friendly XL doubles touting a sofa bed. The ground-floor restaurant (mains €13 to €29) sports the same signature rubber rings strung above the bar as other Philippe Starck–designed hotels, and weekends usher concerts, gigs and other cultural happenings onto the small stage.

Chez Dupont B&B €€
(☎05 56 81 49 59; www.chez-dupont.com; 45 rue Notre Dame; s/d from €85/100) Five impeccably decorated rooms, peppered with a wonderful collection of vintage curiosities, inspires love at first sight at this thoroughly contemporary, design-driven B&B in the trendy former wine-merchant quarter of Chartrons. Across the road from, and run by, the bistro of the same name, Chez Dupont is one of the best deals in town.

Ecolodge des Chartrons B&B €€
(☎05 56 81 49 13; www.ecolodgedeschartrons.com; 23 rue Raze; s €100-125, d €106-145; 📶) Veronique and Yann have stripped back and lime-washed the stone walls of an old house, scrubbed the wide floorboards and brought in recycled antique furniture to create a highly memorable place to stay in the atmospheric wine-merchant district of Chartrons. Ecofriendly initiatives include a solar-powered hot-water system, energy-efficient gas heating and hemp-based soundproofing. Rates include breakfast.

★ **L'Hôtel Particulier** BOUTIQUE HOTEL €€€
(☎05 57 88 28 80; www.lhotel-particulier.com; 44 rue Vital-Carles; d €189-299; 📶) Step into this fabulous boutique hotel and be wowed by period furnishings mixed with contemporary design, extravagant decorative touches and an atmospheric courtyard garden. Its five individually designed hotel rooms (breakfast €12) match up to expectations with vintage fireplaces, carved ceilings and bath-tubs with legs. Exceptional value are the suite of equally well-furnished self-catering apartments, sleeping one (€89), two (€109) or four people (€179).

La Maison Bord'eaux BOUTIQUE HOTEL €€€
(☎05 56 44 00 45; www.lamaisonbord-eaux.com; 111-113 rue du Dr Albert Barraud; d from €180; ⌚reception 8am-9pm Mon-Sat, 8.30am-8pm Sun; P❄📶) You'd expect to find a sumptuous 18th-century château with a conifer-flanked courtyard and stable house in the countryside, but this stunning *maison d'hôte*

1

2

JUSTIN FOULKES / LONELY PLANET ©

1. Vineyard near St-Émilion (p633) **2.** Châteaux and vineyard in the Médoc region (p632) **3.** Boxed Bordeaux wines

Wine, Glorious Wine

The countryside around the Bordeaux region is full of renowned vineyards and legendary châteaux, many of which can be visited. Venture a little further north and the Cognac region offers a totally different sort of tipple.

Cognac

Bordeaux isn't the only wine party in town. Cognac produces a drink so heavenly that even the angels are said to partake. Learn all about it during a visit to the Musee des Arts du Cognac (p620).

St-Émilion

The quintessential French wine town and the oldest French wine region, St-Émilion (p633) has robust and generous wines that tickle the taste buds and any number of wine-related tours (available through the tourist office) to get the most from it.

Bordeaux

No wine-tasting tour is complete without an exploration at the groundbreaking La Cité du Vin (p622) and a tasting workshop at the École du Vin de Bordeaux (p628). Built on the wealth of the grape, Bordeaux lives up to its bourgeois reputation, but today an army of students gives the city a lighter edge.

The Médoc

The Médoc region (p632) encompasses some of the finest wine territory in France, with such grand names as Mouton Rothschild, Latour and Lafite Rothschild hailing from this area. Numerous wine-themed tours are available.

Oysters & Wine

One of the most pleasurable ways of enjoying the region's wines is at Bordeaux's Marché des Capucins (p631), with a glass of chilled white wine in one hand and a fresh, raw oyster in the other.

hidden behind a high stone wall is right in the middle of the city. It is part of the prestigious Châteaux & Hotels Collection, with sumptuous rooms to match. Public areas include a lovely library. Breakfast costs €16 (€14 November to April).

Eating

Bordeaux cooks up excellent dining. Iconic addresses mingle with new openings in the tasty tangle of pedestrian streets around place du Parlement; place St-Pierre is perfect for cheaper eats alfresco.

North along the river, quai des Chartons is laced with waterfront restaurants and bars – enchanting at sunset. Wine aficionados adore panoramic restaurant **Le 7** inside La Cité du Vin (p622).

★ Magasin Général INTERNATIONAL **€**
(☎05 56 77 88 35; www.magasingeneral.camp/; 87 quai des Queyries; 2-/3-course menu €14/18, mains €9-19; ⏲8.30am-6pm Wed-Fri, 8.30am-midnight Sat, 10am-midnight Sun, kitchen noon-2.15pm & 7-10pm; 📶) Follow the hip crowd across the river to this huge industrial hangar on the right bank, France's biggest and best organic restaurant with gargantuan terrace complete with vintage sofa seating, ping-pong table and table football. Everything here, from the vegan burgers and super-food salads to smoothies, pizzas, wine and French bistro fare, is *bio* (organic) and sourced locally. Sunday brunch (€24) is a bottomless feast.

★ Seasons INTERNATIONAL **€**
(www.seasonsfoodtruck.fr; mains €5-6, menus €8-10) This retro food truck – a French-manufactured Citroën HY no less – is worth tracking down; the week's planning is on its website. Sydney chef Tristan and savvy sous-chef Margot cook up a homemade health-busting cuisine using local seasonal produce: think homemade wraps, muffins with creative toppings (the coriander- and date-laced marinated pork is outstanding), vitamin-packed soups and salads.

La Copa Rota MEXICAN **€**
(☎06 37 77 04 58; www.facebook.com/lacoparot; 87 rue Notre Dame; tacos & quesadillas €2-6, plat du jour €10; ⏲noon-3pm & 7-10pm Tue-Sat, 7-10pm Sun) This tiny but colourful *taquería* on trendy rue Notre Dame in the Chartrons district heaves with students feasting on its excellent-value, seriously authentic tacos, quesadillas and other Mexican dishes – washed down, of course, with margeritas and other boozy tequila-based cocktails. Reservations recommended.

ON THE WINE TRAIL

Thirsty? The 1000-sq-km winegrowing area around the city of Bordeaux is, along with Burgundy, France's most important producer of top-quality wines.

The Bordeaux region is divided into 57 appellations (production areas whose soil and microclimate impart distinctive characteristics to the wine produced there) that are grouped into seven *familles* (families), and then subdivided into a hierarchy of designations (eg *premier grand cru classé,* the most prestigious) that often vary from appellation to appellation. The majority of the Bordeaux region's reds, rosés, sweet and dry whites and sparkling wines have earned the right to include the abbreviation AOC (Appellation d'Origine Contrôlée) on their labels, indicating that the contents have been grown, fermented and aged according to strict regulations that govern such viticultural matters as the number of vines permitted per hectare and acceptable pruning methods.

Bordeaux has more than 5000 châteaux (also known as *domaines* or *clos*), referring not to palatial residences but rather to the properties where grapes are raised, picked, fermented and then matured as wine. Smaller châteaux sometimes accept walk-in visitors, but at many places, especially the better-known ones, you have to make advance reservations. Many close during the *vendange* (grape harvest) in October.

Whet your palate with the tourist office's city tour, a two-hour session (€14) starting at 10am daily, which includes wine tasting. Or go for the Urban Wine Tour (€49), which introduces wine lovers to châteaux and *bars à vin* (wine bars) in the city, or a 1½-hour river cruise with oysters and wine tasting (€15).

Serious students of the grape can enrol at highly regarded wine school **École du Vin de Bordeaux** (Bordeaux Wine School; ☎05 56 00 22 85; www.bordeaux.com; 3 cours du 30 juillet), inside the Maison du Vin de Bordeaux (Bordeaux House of Wine).

Plume FRENCH €

(☎09 81 18 69 55; www.plume.coffee; 32 rue Cheverus; salads €7-13.50, sandwiches €5.90; ⏲10am-7pm Tue-Sat, to 3pm Sun) For super-food salads bursting with veggies, homemade soups, creative sandwiches (hot or cold) and completely irresistible cakes, look no further than this hip coffee shop and bistro. Eating is pretty much all day, the ginger iced tea and cakes are superb, and weekend brunch (€20) is among the best in town. Summer sees the eating and drinking action spill onto the pavement terrace outside.

★**Le Petit Commerce** SEAFOOD €€

(05 56 79 76 58; 22 rue Parlement St-Pierre; 2-course lunch menu €14, mains €15-25; ⏲noon-midnight) This iconic bistro, with dining rooms both sides of a narrow pedestrian street and former Michelin-starred chef Stéphane Carrade in the kitchen, is the star turn of the trendy St-Pierre quarter. It's best known for its excellent seafood *menu* that embraces everything from Arcachon sole and oysters to eels, lobsters and *chipirons* (baby squid) fresh from St-Jean de Luz.

End your meal, as locals do, with a bowl of *riz au lait à l'orange* (orange-perfumed rice pudding).

★**Potato Head** MODERN FRENCH €€

(http://potatoheadbordeaux.com/; 27 rue Buhan; mains lunch €13, dinner €18-25, 5-course tasting menu €41; ⏲11am-3pm Sun) With its eclectic mix of seating (bar stool, bistro and armchair), moss-clad vegetal wall and industrial-style lighting, this trendy bistro is a fabulous space to dine in. Throw in a creative kitchen known for surprise combos (foie gras, beetroot, ginger and chocolate, anyone?) and the finest summer garden in the city and, well, you need to reserve well in advance. Sunday brunch (€24) in the garden is a languid and sensational affair.

Miles MODERN FRENCH €€

(☎05 56 81 18 24; http://restaurantmiles.com/; 33 rue du Cancera; 3-/4-course lunch menu €24/29, 5-course dinner menu €43; ⏲12.15-2pm & 7.30-10pm Tue-Fri, 7.30-10pm Sat) This contemporary oyster-grey space is the creation of four young chefs from France and Vietnam, Israel, Japan and New Caledonia, whose innovative, creative and wholly seasonal kitchen reflects their mixed roots. There's no menu – rather a series of tasting courses. Think monkfish with beetroot, *nori* (seaweed) and citrus fruits perhaps, or pork, leek, lemon and smoked dates.

WORTH A TRIP

COOKING WITH SAINT JAMES

Memorable cooking courses are organised at **Côté Cours**, the prestigious but highly accessible cooking school of chic lifestyle hotel **Le Saint James** (☎05 57 97 06 00; www.saintjames-bouliac.com; 3 place Camille Hostein), a stunning piece of architecture by Jean Nouvel, between vines in the village of Bouliac, 10km southeast of Bordeaux. Themed classes last three to 3½ hours and cost €75 to €155 per person. Afterwards indulge in a drink at **Café de l'Esperance**, Bouliac's uber-cool village cafe also run by Le Saint James.

Bocca a bocca ITALIAN €€

(☎05 57 83 69 66; 75 rue Notre Dame; mains €12-15, salads €8.50-12; ⏲noon-2.30pm & 7.15-10.15pm Tue-Sat) Locals can't get enough of this candlelit trattoria with summer terrace on Chartron's trendiest foodie street. Meal-sized salads bursting with grilled aubergines, creamy mozzarella, San Daniele cured meat and other typical Italian products vie for attention with cold-meat platters and tempting *primi* such as gorgonzola-laced polenta with pancetta and baby spinach leaves.

If the queue's too long, try to snag a seat at La Bocca's equally mouth-watering *épicerie* (gourmet grocery) opposite.

La Boîte à Huîtres OYSTERS €€

(☎05 56 81 64 97; 36 cours du Chapeau Rouge; 12 oysters €14-36; ⏲noon-2pm & 7-11pm) The Oyster Box is the best place in Bordeaux to munch on fresh Arcachon oysters. Traditionally they're served with sausage but you can have them in a number of different forms, including with that other southwest delicacy, foie gras. They'll also pack them up so you can take them away for a riverfront picnic.

★**La Tupina** REGIONAL CUISINE €€€

(☎05 56 91 56 37; www.latupina.com; 6 rue Porte de la Monnaie; lunch menu €18, dinner menus €39 & €74; ⏲noon-2pm & 7-11pm Tue-Sun) Filled with the aroma of soup simmering inside a *tupina* ('kettle' in Basque) over an open fire, this iconic bistro is feted for its seasonal southwestern French fare: think foie gras and egg *cassoullette* (mini casserole), milk-fed lamb, tripe and goose wings. Hopefully nothing will change following the retirement of the

gregarious Jean-Pierre Xiradakis, life and soul of La Tupina since 1968.

Drinking & Nightlife

Bordeaux places great importance on drinking – be it tasting extraordinary vintages in a *bar à vin*, guzzling *cacolac* (chocolate milk made in Bordeaux since 1954) in a cafe or glugging local Darwin beer in an industrial hangar. Find picture-postcard cafe terraces on place Pey Berland, place St-Pierre and place Fernand-Lafargue. Student pubs, coffee shops and wine bars pepper rue St-James.

★Symbiose COCKTAIL BAR

(Old-fashioned Stories; ☎05 56 23 67 15; www.facebook.com/symbiosebordeaux/; 4 quai des Chartrons; ⏰noon-2.30pm Mon, noon-2.30pm & 6.30pm-2am Tue-Fri, 6.30pm-2am Sat) There is something eminently inviting about this clandestine address with soft green façade across from the river on the fringe of the Chartrons district. This is the secret speakeasy that introduced good cocktails with gastronomic food pairings to Bordeaux. The chef uses locally sourced, artisan products, and cocktails rekindle old-fashioned recipes packed with homemade syrups and 'forgotten', exotic or unusual ingredients.

★Black List COFFEE

(☎06 89 91 82 65; www.facebook.com/blacklist-cafe; 27 place Pey Berland; ⏰8am-6pm Mon-Fri, 9.30am-6pm Sat) For serious coffee lovers, nothing beats the beans that arrive at this coffee shop freshly roasted from Paris' Belleville Brûlerie. In a tiny but stylishly retro, ceramic-tiled interior, barista Laurent Pierre serves espresso and filtered *grand cru* coffee to a discerning Bordelais crowd. Granola breakfasts, veggie-packed salads and creative sandwiches (lunch *menus* €8.50 to €11.50), and fresh organic juices complement the fantastic coffee.

Once a month Black List teams up with the Seasons (p628) food truck to serve a super-food brunch (€21).

★Bar à Vin WINE BAR

(☎05 56 00 43 47; http://baravin.bordeaux.com; 3 cours du 30 Juillet; ⏰11am-10pm Mon-Sat) This ultrastylish but very accessible wine bar, inside the hallowed halls of the Maison du Vin de Bordeaux, is the designer hot spot to tipple with Bordelais who really know their wine. Lounge between walls of stacked bottles, on armchairs or at the bar, and allow gracious sommeliers guide you through the choice of 30-odd different Bordeaux wines by the glass (€3 to €8).

There is also sparkling grape juice, local *bien sûr*, and a select choice of cheese, charcuterie and chocolate platters (€6 to €8).

★Utopia CAFE, BAR

(www.cinemas-utopia.org; 3 place Camille Jullian; ⏰10am-1am summer, to 10.30pm winter) At home in an old church, this much-venerated art address is a local institution. Art-house cinema, mellow cafe, hot lunch spot and bar rolled into one, it is one of the top addresses in the city to mingle over a drink, *tartine* (open sandwich, €7) or good-value meal (mains €13 to €15) with local Bordelais at any time of day. Its atmospheric pavement terrace on a car-free square catches the morning sun.

L'Apollo BAR

(www.apollobar.fr; 19 place Fernand Lafargue; ⏰11.30am-1.30am Mon-Sat; 📶) No place buzzes with a local Bordelais crowd quite like the Apollo, a fabulous neighbourhood bar with burnt-orange, paint-peeling façade and busy pavement terrace. In the best of pub fashion, it has a pool table and a fantastic line-up of DJ sets, music parties and '*apéro* mix' soirées belting out funk, soul and reggae.

Les Mots Bleues CAFE

(☎05 56 90 01 93; 40 rue Poquelin Molière; ⏰10am-7pm Tue-Sun) When respite from the urban crowds beckons, duck into this peaceful coffee shop and *salon de thé* near the cathedral. Books to tempt and be browsed casually sit on shelves in the contemporary blue-and-white interior, filled each morning with the comforting aroma of baking from the tiny kitchen. The homemade cakes, cookies, crumbles and other sweet treats are among the best in town.

★I.Boat CLUB

(☎05 56 10 48 35; www.iboat.eu; quai Armand Lalande, Bassins à Flot 1; ⏰7pm-6am) Hip hop, rock, indie pop, psyche blues rock, punk and hardcore are among the varied sounds that blast out of this fun nightclub and concert venue, afloat a decommissioned ferry moored in the increasingly trendy, industrial Bassins à Flot district in the north of the city. Live music starts at 7pm, with DJ sets kicking in on the club dance floor from 11.30pm.

Entertainment

Gen up on the month's cutural events, concerts and happenings with *Sortir* (www.

bordeaux.sortir.eu) and *Clubs & Concerts* (www.clubsetconcerts.com), two freebie listings mags available at the tourist office. For non-dubbed art-house films, follow the hip brigade to the cinema inside Utopia.

Rock School Barbey LIVE MUSIC
(☎05 56 33 66 00; www.rockschool-barbey.com; 18 cours Barbey; admission €10-25; ⏰variable) Catch live bands at Rock School Barbey, funky host to a stream of up-and-coming French and international indie bands. Admission prices vary depending on the gig. And yes, this happening space really is a rock school too.

Grand Théâtre THEATRE, OPERA
(☎05 56 00 85 95; www.opera-bordeaux.com; place de la Comédie) Designed by Victor Louis (of Chartres Cathedral fame), this grand 18th-century theatre stages operas, ballets and concerts of orchestral and chamber music.

Shopping

Europe's longest pedestrian shopping street, rue Ste-Catherine, stretches north from place de la Victoire to place de la Comédie, with 19th-century shopping arcade **Galerie Bordelaise** (rue de la Porte Dijeaux & rue Ste-Catherine) nearby. Luxury fashion boutiques lace *le triangle* formed by cours Georges Clemenceau, cours de l'Intendance and allées de Tourny.

Trendy independent boutiques and design shops are concentrated on hip rue St-James in the St-Pierre quarter and rue Notre-Dame in Chartrons.

★**Le Comptoir Bordelaise** FOOD & DRINKS
(www.lecomptoirbordelais.com; 1 rue Piliers de Tutelle; ⏰9am-7.30pm) Rev up your taste buds in this gourmet boutique selling local and regional food and drink specialities. Be tempted by local cheese, *canalés* (sandcastle-shaped cakes from Bordeaux), *bouchons de Bordeaux* (cork-shaped pastries filled with almonds), *raisins au Sauternes* (chocolate-enrobed raisins soaked in Sauternes wine), salted caramels, chocolate sardines, olive oils, sauces and condiments, artisan beers, the list is endless. Then, of course, there is wine...

★**w.a.n.** HOMEWARES
(☎05 56 48 15 41; www.wanweb.fr; 1 rue des Lauriers; ⏰10am-7pm Mon-Sat) 'Slow design' is the driver behind this Pandora's Box of a boutique, packed to the rafters with innovative design objects, homewares, clothing, knick-knacks and trinkets – all made in France or, as the shop motto explains, 'Made in *pas trop loin*' (not too far away). It's a lovely space to browse for gifts.

★**Beillevaire** FOOD
(☎09 54 86 80 03; www.fromagerie-beillevaire.com; 8 rue Michel Montaigne; ⏰8.30am-7.30pm Tue-Sat) This artisan *fromager* and *crémier* is a sheer delight for local foodies who shop here for boutique cheeses and creamy yellow butter hand-moulded in fat curvaceous patties near Nantes. Don't miss the *demi-sel croquant* butter, studded with crunchy crystals of rock salt. If you want to take some cheese home with you, ask for it to be vacuum-packed.

Marché des Capucins MARKET
(http://marchedescapucins.com; place des Capucins; ⏰6am-1pm Tue-Sun) A classic Bordeaux experience is a Saturday morning spent slurping oysters and white wine from a seafood stand in the city's legendary covered food market. Stalls overflowing with fruit, veg, cheese, meats, fish and all sorts fill the space to bursting. Walk south down cours Pasteur to place de la Victoire, then turn left onto rue Élie Gintrec.

L'Intendant WINE
(www.intendant.com; 2 allées de Tourny; ⏰10am-7.30pm Mon-Sat) A central spiral staircase climbing four floors is surrounded by cylindrical shelves holding 15,000 bottles of regional wine at this highly respected *caviste* (wine cellar). Watch for tastings most Saturdays.

Quai des Marques MALL
(www.quaidesmarques.com/bordeaux; quai des Chartrons; ⏰10am-7pm Tue-Sun) Walk 2km north along the river to find this shopping mall, inside a series of hangars on the waterfront. Some 30 different outlet stores are here, including many big-name brands such as Hugo Boss, Reebok and Swiss chocolate-maker Lindt.

Information

Tourist Office (☎05 56 00 66 00; www.bordeaux-tourisme.com; 12 cours du 30 Juillet; ⏰9am-7.30pm Mon-Sat, 9.30am-6.30pm Sun Jul & Aug, shorter hours Sep-Jun) Runs an excellent range of city and regional tours; reserve in advance online or in situ. It also rents pocket modems to hook you up with wi-fi. There's a small but helpful **branch** (☎05 56 91 64 70; rue Charles Domercq, Parvis Louis Armand;

LOCAL KNOWLEDGE

A DRINK WITH A VIEW

No public work of art turns heads quite like **Sanna** (2013), a striking modern sculpture on place de la Comédie in Bordeaux by Spanish artist Jaume Plensa. Grab a seat on a cafe pavement terrace on the square to admire the 7m-high cast-iron woman's head. Or head up to the stunning rooftop terrace of the luxurious 18th-century **Le Grand Hôtel** (☎05 57 30 44 44; www.ghbordeaux.com; 2-5 place de la Comédie; d from €350), on the same square, for a cocktail with bird's-eye view of *Sanna* and her beautiful adopted city. Should you fancy dining in serious style post drink, reserve a table in advance at Gordon Ramsay's Michelin-starred **Le Pressoir d'Argent** restaurant – named after the silver lobster press, one of five in the world, it proudly owns – inside the landmark hotel. Fishy gastronomic *menus* start at €90.

⏲9am-noon & 1-6pm Mon-Sat, 10am-noon & 1-3pm Sun Jul & Aug, shorter hours rest of year) at the train station.

Maison du Tourisme de la Gironde (☎05 56 52 61 40; www.tourisme-gironde.fr; 9 rue Fondaudège; ⏲9am-6pm Mon-Fri, 10am-1pm & 2-6.30pm Sat) Information on the surrounding Gironde *département*.

Getting There & Away

AIR

Aéroport de Bordeaux (www.bordeaux.aeroport.fr) is in Mérignac, 10km southwest of the city centre, with domestic and increasing numbers of international flights to many western European and North African destinations.

TRAIN

Bordeaux is one of France's major rail-transit points. The station, **Gare St-Jean** (cours de la Marne), is about 3km from the city centre at the southern terminus of cours de la Marne.

Bayonne (€31.90, 1¾ hours, at least 10 daily)

La Rochelle (€31.50, 2¼ hours, six daily)

Nantes (€52.40, five hours, three daily)

Paris Gare Montparnasse (€79, 3¼ hours, at least 16 daily)

Poitiers (€42, 1¾ hours, at least hourly)

Toulouse (€40 to €50, 2¼ hours, hourly)

Getting Around

TO/FROM THE AIRPORT

The train station, place Gambetta and urban transport hub Esplanade des Quinconces are connected to the airport by an hourly shuttle bus (www.navetteaeroport-bordeaux.com; €7.20, 30 minutes). Alternatively, hop aboard urban bus line 1 that runs every 10 minutes or so from the airport to the train station; journey time is 40 minutes (longer at rush hour) and a ticket costs €1.50. Both services operate from 6am to 11pm. A taxi between the city centre and airport costs around €50.

BICYCLE

Public bike-sharing scheme VCub (www.vcub.fr) has 1700 bicycles available for use at 166 stations all over the city. Pay €1.50 to access a bike for 24 hours, plus €2 per hour after the first 30 minutes (free) is up; you'll need to initially register online or with your credit card at a VCub station.

BOAT

Batcub boats (www.batcub.fr) shuttle between quai des Maréchal Lyautey (by Palais de la Bourse), quai de Bacalan (by Quai des Marques shopping mall and La Cité du Vin) and quay des Queyries on the right bank (near Magasin Général). Tickets cost €1.50.

BUS & TRAM

Urban buses and trams are run by **TBC** (www.infotbc.com). Get timetable information and tickets from its **Espace des Quinconces** (☎05 57 57 88 88; www.infotbc.com; Esplanade des Quinconces; ⏲7am-7.30pm Mon-Fri, 9am-6pm Sat) information office on Esplanade des Quinconces, the main bus and tram hub. Tram line C links the latter with the train station via the riverside; tram B cruises north along the river to Bassins à Flot and La Cité du Vin.

Single tickets (€1.50) are sold onboard buses, and from machines at tram stops (stamp your ticket onboard); tickets are valid for one hour, but not for transfers. You can also buy a *carnet* of 10 tickets (€12.40) or a one-day ticket covering unlimited travel (€4.60).

TAXI

To order a taxi call ☎05 56 29 10 25.

The Médoc

Northwest of Bordeaux, along the western shore of the Gironde Estuary – formed by the confluence of the Garonne and Dordogne Rivers – lie some of Bordeaux's most celebrated vineyards. To their west, fine-sand beaches, bordered by dunes and lagoons, stretch from Pointe de Grave south along

the Côte d'Argent (Silver Coast) to the Bassin d'Arcachon and beyond, with great surf.

On the banks of the muddy Gironde, the port town of Pauillac (population 1300) is at the heart of the wine country, surrounded by the distinguished Haut-Médoc, Margaux and St-Julien appellations. Extraordinary châteaux pepper these parts, from the world-famous Château Ducru-Braucaillou on its southeast fringe to Château Margaux, with striking cellars designed by Lord Norman Foster in 2015. The Pauillac wine appellation encompasses 18 *crus classés*, including the world-renowned Mouton Rothschild, Latour and Lafite Rothschild. Pauillac tourist office houses the **Maison du Tourisme et du Vin** (☎05 56 59 03 08; www.pauillac-medoc.com; La Verrerie, Pauillac; ⊙9.30am-7pm Mon-Sat, 10am-1pm & 2-6pm Sun), with information on visiting châteaux.

Sights & Activities

★Château Lynch-Bages WINERY

(☎05 56 73 19 31; www.jmcazes.com/en/chateau-lynch-bages; Craste des Jardins, Pauillac; 1hr visit with tasting €9, 2½hr bespoke tastings €75; ⊙9.30am-1pm & 2.30-6pm) Château Lynch-Bages, gracefully set in the wealthy hamlet of Bages, 2km southwest of Pauillac, is one of the best-known Médoc wineries – due in no small part to the extraordinary energy, passion and charisma of the Cazes family who have owned the estate since 1939. It is one of the region's oldest, its wine being among the 18 prestigious *Cinquièmes Crus* classified for the first time in 1855. Each year a contemporary artist is invited to the château to create a work of art for it.

Admission to the seasonal art exhibition (May to October) is free. Guided tours, which must be booked in advance, take in the 19th-century vat house where winemakers once crushed grapes by foot, the cellars and tastings of two wines. Wine enthusiasts can also reserve bespoke tastings. There is no lovelier end to a château visit than a meal or drink at neighbouring **Café Lavinal** (www.jmcazes.com/en/cafe-lavinal; Passage du Desquet, Bages; menus €28 & €38, mains €12-25; ⊙8am-2pm & 7.30-9pm; ❄📶), Bages' chic village bistro run by the same family and named after Jean-Michel Cazes' grandmother.

★La Winery WINE

(☎05 56 39 04 90; www.winery.fr; rte du Verdon, Rond-point des Vendangeurs, Arsac-en-Médoc; ⊙10.30am-7.30pm Tue-Sun, boutique 10am-8pm Jun-Sep, to 7.30pm Oct-May) Don't miss Philippe Raoux's vast glass-and-steel wine centre, which mounts concerts and contemporary-art exhibits alongside various fee-based tastings, including innovative tastings that determine your *signe œnologique* (wine sign), costing from €25 (booking required). Its boutique stocks more than 1000 different wines.

Sleeping

Le Pavillon de Margaux HOTEL €€

(☎05 57 88 77 54; www.le-pavillon-de-margaux.fr; 3 rue Georges Mandel, Margaux; d €99-129; 📶) This welcoming, family-run address has 14 country-chic rooms styled according to famous local châteaux; several have their own little *salon* (sitting-room area) and they all come with a much-appreciated courtesy tray with kettle, tea and coffee. Breakfast (€12) with vineyard view and taste local wine over dinner in the hotel restaurant (*menus* €35 and €50).

★Château Cordeillan-Bages DESIGN HOTEL €€€

(☎05 56 59 24 24; www.cordeillanbages.com; rte des Châteaux, Bages; d from €259; ⊙Mar-Nov; ❄@📶🏊) 'A delight for hedonists' is how this luxurious 19th-century mansion describes itself – understandably so. Plump in the heart of Médoc wine country, this Relais & Châteaux hotel-restaurant is the ultimate splurge in viticulture and gastronomic luxury. Twenty-eight modern rooms with designer furniture gaze brazenly at vines, wine tasting is an essential part of every stay, and chef Jean-Luc Rocha has two Michelin stars.

Getting There & Away

The lack of public transport to most of the châteaux means this area is best explored by car.

St-Émilion

POP 1930

The medieval village of St-Émilion perches above vineyards renowned for producing full-bodied, deeply coloured red wines and is easily the most alluring of all the region's wine towns. Named after Émilion, a miracle-working Benedictine monk who lived in a cave here between AD 750 and 767, it soon became a stop on pilgrimage routes, and the village and its vineyards are now Unesco-listed. Today, despite masses of tourists descending onto the town, it's well worth venturing 40km east from Bordeaux to experience St-Émilion's magic, particularly

when the sun sets over the valley and the limestone buildings glow with halo-like golden hues.

Sights

Clocher de l'Église Monolithe TOWER
(Bell Tower; place des Créneaux.; adult/family €1.50/5) For captivating views of the hilltop hamlet, borrow one of three keys from the tourist office to scale the 196 steps of this bell tower, built to crown subterranean rock church Église Monolithe (only open to guided tours) during the 12th to 15th centuries.

Tour du Roy CASTLE
(rue du Couvent; adult/family €1.50/5; 2-5.30pm Mon-Fri, 11am-12.15pm & 2-5.30pm Sat & Sun Jul & Aug, shorter hours rest of year, closed Jan) Climb 118 steps inside this sturdy square tower – what's left of a 13th-century donjon – for a 360-degree panorama of the town, Dordogne River and its bucolic valley.

Activities

A variety of **hiking and cycling circuits** loop through the greater World Heritage jurisdiction; the tourist office has maps. The tourist office also rents bicycles (€15 to €18); in high season reserve your wheels in advance online.

★ **Maison du Vin de St-Émilion** WINE
(05 57 55 50 55; www.maisonduvinsaintemilion.com; place Pierre Meyrat; 9.30am-12.30pm & 2-6.30pm) As much information centre and wine school as shop, this excellent wine cellar is owned by the 250 winegrowers whose wines it sells at cellar-door prices. Begin with the small exhibition on the different St-Émilion appellations and test your tasting skills by guessing 12 different aromas: roast coffee, smoked or toasted? Rose, lilac or violet? Advance reservations are essential for its highly recommended introductory wine-tasting courses (in French and English), held weekends year-round and daily in summer (€25 per person, 1½ hours).

It also hosts themed six-wine discovery (€50, 1½ hours) and blending tastings (€45, two hours).

Festivals & Events

St-Émilion Jazz Festival MUSIC
(www.saint-emilion-jazz-festival.com; tickets €25-75) In July the soothing tones of jazz take over the town during this fabulous three-day jazz fest; find ticketing information online.

Grandes Heures de St-Émilion MUSIC
(www.grandesheuresdesaintemilion.fr; tickets €37) Classical concerts are held at various châteaux between March and December and naturally include wine tasting. Tickets must be booked in advance; the program and ticketing information is online.

Sleeping & Eating

The village and its vineyard-stitched surrounds have some charming, if expensive, hotels and luxury *chambres d'hôtes*. If you're on a budget and don't want to camp, consider a day trip from Bordeaux.

Yelloh! Villlage Saint Émilion CAMPGROUND €
(05 57 24 75 80; www.camping-saint-emilion.com; rte de Montagne; campsite €20-40; late Apr–late-Sep;) This family-friendly campground is about 2km north of St-Émilion on the D122. It has three different pools, a water slide, mini golf and bags of other outdoor fun for kids. Pitch up beneath trees or rent a wooden cabin sleeping two to six people. For a tad more solitude, reserve the floating wood cabin moored on the campsite's small lake.

Palais Cardinal HISTORIC HOTEL €€
(05 57 24 72 39; www.palais-cardinal.com; place du 11 Novembre 1918; s/d from €75/94;) Run by the same family for five generations, this historic hotel from 1878 puts a little more thought into its dress sense than the other 'budget' hotels in St-Émilion. The heated pool is set in flower-filled gardens and framed by sections of the original medieval town-wall fortifications, dating from the 13th century. Its 24 rooms are comfortable and quietly elegant. Breakfast costs €14.

Grand Barrail CHÂTEAU €€€
(05 57 55 37 00; www.grand-barrail.com; rte de Libourne; d €320;) Grand doesn't even begin to describe this immense château, built in 1850, with its 46 antique-dressed rooms, spa, stone-flagged heated swimming pool, vast park and helipad on the front lawn. Undoubtedly the best seat in its gastronomic restaurant (*menus* €55 and €65) is the corner table framed by exquisite 19th-century stained glass. Find the castle 3km from St-Émilion village, signposted off the D243. Breakfast costs €24.

★ **L'Envers du Decors** FRENCH €€
(06 57 74 48 31; www.envers-dudecor.com; 11 rue du Clocher; mains €17.50-35; noon-2.30pm & 7-10.30pm) A few doors down from the tourist office, this wine bar is one of the best places

DON'T MISS

LUNCH BY DESIGN

Knowing foodies adore **La Terrasse Rouge** (☎05 57 24 47 05; www.laterrasserouge.com; lunch menu €28; ⊙noon-2.30pm & 7-11pm Jun-Sep, noon-2.30pm & 7-11pm Fri & Sat, noon-2.30pm Sun-Thu Oct-May), a spectacular vineyard restaurant borne out of Jean Nouvel's designer revamp of Château La Dominique's wine cellars. Chefs work exclusively with small local producers to source the seasonal veg, fruit and so on used in their creative cuisine. Oysters are fresh from Cap Ferret, delicious French caviar comes from Neuvic in the Dordogne and the iPad mini wine list is naturally extraordinary.

Dining on the uber-chic terrace overlooking a field of dark-red glass pebbles – one of several contemporary art installations on the wine-producing estate – and a sea of vine beyond is nothing short of sublime. Watch for the monthly cooking classes held here, built around lunch and *dégustation* (tasting) of two St-Émilion wines. Advance reservations essential.

to eat – and inevitably drink – in this tasteful wine town. The kitchen cooks up fabulous local classics including *lamproie à la Bordelaise* (a local eel-like fish simmered in red wine), duck liver pan-fried in Sauternes and oysters by the dozen. Summer-time dining spills into a beautiful cobbled courtyard and garden hidden out back.

Information

Tourist office (☎05 57 55 28 28; www.saint-emilion-tourisme.com; place des Créneaux; ⊙9.30am-7.30pm Jul & Aug, shorter hours rest of year) Upon arriving in town, make this your first port of call – to reserve a spot on one of the tourist office's excellent, themed *visites guidées* (guided tours). Staff are super-friendly and have plenty of maps and brochures on where to wine-taste in both the village and surrounding vineyards.

Getting There & Away

From Bordeaux, a handful of direct trains run daily to/from St-Émilion (€9.50, 35 minutes). St-Émilion train station is a scenic 1.7km walk from town.

Arcachon

POP 10,830

A long-time oyster-harvesting area on the south side of the tranquil, triangular Bassin d'Arcachon (Arcachon Bay), this seaside town lured bourgeois Bordelaise at the end of the 19th century. Its four little quarters are romantically named for each of the seasons, with villas that evoke the town's golden past amid a scattering of 1950s architecture.

Arcachon's generous swathe of golden-sand beach seethes with sun-seekers in summer, but there are plenty of equally sandy but less-crowded beaches, including the lovely Plage des Arbousiers, just a short bike ride away.

Sights & Activities

Beautiful cycling paths wind along the waterfront and through scented pine forests to link Arcachon with the Dune du Pilat (8km), Biscarosse (30km south) and east to La Teste de Buch (4.5km), Gujan Mestras (15km) and Le Teich (20km). In Arcachon get a free *carte des pistes cyclables* from the tourist office showing all the trails around the Bassin d'Arcachon and rent wheels at **Locabeach** (☎05 56 83 79 11; www.locabeach.com; 34 av du Général de Gaulle; 4hr/1 day €10/13; ⊙10am-6pm) near the train station or **Dingo Vélos** (☎05 56 83 44 09; www.dingo-velo.com; 1 rue Grenier; 4hr/1 day €10/13) by the beachfront.

Plage d'Arcachon BEACH

In the delightful **Ville d'Été** (Summer Quarter), Arcachon's deep sandy beach, Plage d'Arcachon, is flanked by two piers. Lively **Jetée Thiers** is at the western end, from where boats yo-yo across the water to Cap Ferret. The eastern pier, **Jetée d'Eyrac**, is lauded over by an old-fashioned carousel, a vintage Big Wheel and the town's turreted casino. The sheltered basin in which Arcachon sits means the water is always absolutely flat calm and ideal for families – a far cry from most Atlantic beaches.

Ville d'Hiver AREA

On the tree-covered hillside south of the Ville d'Été, the century-old Ville d'Hiver (Winter Quarter) has more than 300 villas, many decorated with delicate wood tracery, ranging in style from neo-Gothic through to colonial. It's an easy stroll or a short ride up the (free) art-deco public lift in Parc Mauresque.

Les Bateliers Arcachonnais BOATING
(☎08 25 27 00 27; www.bateliers-arcachon.com; 75 bd de la Plage; 👪) Year-round boats sail around **Île aux Oiseaux**, the uninhabited 'bird island' in the middle of the bay. It's a haven for tern, curlew and redshank, so bring your binoculars; tours last 1¾ hours and cost €16/11 for adults/children. In July and August there are all-day excursions (11am to 5.30pm; adult/child €26/17.50) to the **Banc d'Arguin**, the sand bank off the Dune du Pilat, and some fabulous themed trips afloat – sunset sailing, gastronomic catamaran cruises, oyster brunches and so forth. Buy tickets at the Les Bateliers Arcachonnais wooden huts, next to the jetty from where boats set sail.

Sleeping

Hôtel le Dauphin HISTORIC HOTEL €
(☎05 56 83 02 89; www.dauphin-arcachon.com; 7 av Gounod; s/d €95/105; ❄📶🅿) This late-19th-century gingerbread house with patterned red-and-cream brickwork is very twee, but it's a badge it wears with pride. An icon of its era, it's graced by twin semicircular staircases, magnolias and palms. Plain but spacious rooms are well set up for families. Parking is free. The beach is five minutes' walk away.

★**Le B d'Arcachon** DESIGN HOTEL €€
(☎05 56 83 99 91; www.hotel-b-arcachon.com; 4 rue du Professeur Jolvet; r €80-225; ❄@📶) A skip from the waterfront, overlooking Arcachon's vintage Big Wheel, Le B can do no wrong. Its 56 spacious rooms feel more like five- than three-star, with a beautiful colour palette, quality fabrics and big walk-in showers. Superior rooms have a balcony with sea views. Late check-out (noon), excellent service and a delicious breakfast buffet (€15) earn it yet more brownie points.

Families note: incredibly, children aged up to 16 stay in well-sized triple and quadruple rooms for free; the third and/or fourth adult pays €27 per person on top of the room rate.

★**Hôtel Villa d'Hiver** BOUTIQUE HOTEL €€
(☎05 56 66 10 36; www.hotelvilledhiver.com; 20 av Victor Hugo; d from €165; ⏰reception 8am-10pm; ❄@📶🅿) In the heart of Arcachon's stylish 1860s Ville d'Hiver district, this 12-room boutique hotel seduces with a trio of garden-clad houses a 10-minute walk from the train station. Pricier, balcony-clad rooms on the 1st floor can glimpse the sea, and the hotel's pop-up Club Plage Pereire is one of the hottest addresses in town.

Eating

★**Club Plage Pereire** SEAFOOD €€
(☎05 57 16 59 13; www.clubplagepereire.com; 12 bd de la Mer; mains €20; ⏰10am-midnight Apr-Oct) Each year this pop-up beach hut on sandy Plage Pereire is built afresh, much to the joy of local foodies and bons vivants who flock here for tasty seafood cuisine, the buzzing beach vibe, impossible romantic drinks on the sand and stunning sunset views. To get here from Jetée Thiers, follow the coast west along bd de la Plage and bd de l'Océan for 2km. Reservations essential.

★**Chez Pierre** SEAFOOD €€
(☎05 56 22 52 94; www.cafe-plage-restaurant-pierre.fr; 1 bd Veyrier Montagnères; 2-/3-course menu €27/32, mains €25-30; ⏰noon-3pm & 7-10.30pm) Stunning shellfish and seafood to suit most budgets, gracious service and an elegant terrace on the seafront with white tablecloths makes this contemporary address the top dining choice in Arcachon. Its fixed *menus* are excellent value and sunset views – over a dozen deftly shucked oysters from the bay (from €24) or a shellfish platter (€30 to €62) fit for a king and queen – are impossibly romantic.

★**Le Bikini** SEAFOOD €€
(☎05 56 83 91 36; 18 allée des Arbousiers, Plage des Arbousiers; mains €22-27; ⏰12.15-2.30pm & 8pm-midnight, cafe-bar from 9am) With comfy, candy-striped cushioned seating overlooking kitesurfers on sandy Plage des Arbousiers and an atmospheric bar wrapped around a tree, the Bikini buzzes year-round with energy, fun and locals. Its kitchen cooks up first-class shellfish and seafood, fresh from the ocean – the *barbu* (brill) *à la plancha* is superb. Between meals (reservations essential), it morphs into a hip cafe-bar and waterfront hangout.

To get here, follow the cycling path from Arcachon along the coast towards Dune du Pilat for 4km.

Information

Tourist office (☎05 57 52 97 97; www.arcachon.com; Esplanade Georges Pompidou; ⏰9am-7pm Jul & Aug, shorter hours rest of year) A five-minute walk back from the beach, near the train station.

Getting There & Away

There are frequent trains between Bordeaux and Arcachon (€11.50, one hour) **train station** (bd du Général Leclerc), a five-minute walk from the seafront along av de la Gaulle. To continue to the Dune du Pilat, take local bus line 1 from in front of Arcachon train station (€1).

Shuttle boats run by **Les Bateliers Arcachonnais** sail daily across the water to/from Cap Ferret (adult/child €7.50/5, 30 minutes, at least hourly).

Around Arcachon

When the weather allows, Arcachon's watery surrounds are an absolute delight to explore by bicycle. Cycling paths are abundant and cruise along the coast or through scented pine forest: remember water, sun hat and map (free from the tourist office).

Dune du Pilat

This colossal sand dune (sometimes referred to as the Dune de Pyla because of its location 4km from the small seaside resort town of Pyla-sur-Mer), 8km south of Arcachon, stretches from the mouth of the Bassin d'Arcachon southwards for 2.7km. Already Europe's largest, the dune is growing eastwards 1.5m a year – it has swallowed trees, a road junction and even a hotel, so local lore claims.

The view from the top – approximately 115m above sea level – is magnificent. To the west you see the sandy shoals at the mouth of the Bassin d'Arcachon, including Cap Ferret and the **Banc d'Arguin** bird reserve where up to 6000 couples of Sandwich terns nest each spring. Dense dark-green forests of maritime pines, oaks, ferns and strawberry trees (whose wood is traditionally used to build oyster-farmer shacks) stretch from the base of the dune eastwards almost as far as the eye can see.

Cycling is the most invigorating way to get to/from the dune, although there is one hill on the final approach; a beautiful bike path cruises along the waterfront and through scented pine forests to link Arcachon with the Dune du Pilat (8km). Alternatively, local bus line 1 links Arcachon train station with the Dune du Pilat (€1).

Cap Ferret

POP 8100

Hidden within a canopy of pine trees at the tip of the Cap Ferret peninsula, the tiny and deliciously oyster-rich village of Cap Ferret spans a mere 2km between the tranquil bay and the crashing Atlantic waves. The easiest and most invigorating way to get around its seafaring quarters is by bicycle; **Locabeach** (☎05 56 60 49 46; www.locabeach.com; 4hr/1 day €10/13; ⏲9.30am-7pm Apr–mid-Nov), by the Bélisaire boat jetty, rents wheels.

Sights & Activities

Phare du Cap Ferret LIGHTHOUSE

(☎05 57 70 33 30; adult/child €6/4; ⏲10am-7.30pm Jul & Aug, 10am-12.30pm & 2-6.30pm Apr-Jun & Sep, 2-5pm Wed-Sun Oct-Mar) Scale 258 steps inside the cape's 53m-tall, red-and-white lighthouse for a stunning view of Cap Ferret, the Bassin d'Arcachon and the stunning Dune du Pilat. Interactive exhibits inside the lighthouse complement the climb. In the surrounding park, a small exhibition inside the **Blockhaus du Parc du Phare** – a concrete bunker with 2m-thick walls built by occupying Germans in 1940 – explains how the original lighthouse was destroyed by dynamite in 1944. The current lighthouse was built in 1947.

DON'T MISS

LUNCH WITH A VIEW

There's no more glamorous address on the Atlantic coast than **La Co(o)rniche** (☎05 56 22 72 11; www.lacoorniche-pyla.com; 46 av Louis Gaume, Pyla-sur-Mer; 2-/3-course lunch menu €53/58, seafood platters €40-85). This 1930s hunting lodge, reinvented by French designer Philippe Starck is perfectly placed for a meal or tapas-fuelled drink after a sandy walk on Dune du Pilat and the sensational seaside address is beach chic at its best. Feasting here on incredible views of the dune and the chef's modern French cuisine is unforgettable. Snag a table by the infinity pool or, should you prefer a cheaper or lighter dine (€12 to €20), flop with a cocktail and seafood tapas in a cushioned canapé in the bar. Should you fall madly in love with the place and find yourself unable to leave, doubles in the designer five-star hotel start at €255.

LOCAL KNOWLEDGE

LOCAL LIFE

As seafront cafes go, you can't do better than stylish **Café de la Plage** (☎05 56 22 52 94; www.cafedelaplage.com; 1 bd Veyrier Montagnères, Arcachon; ⏲8am-2am). From sunrise to sunset and beyond, this gourmet cafe and bar by the vintage Big Wheel on the seafront buzzes with local life – in the company of exceptionally charming and super-efficient waiting staff. The all-day *menu* includes fresh sushi, seafood platters and oysters, salads, crêpes and ice-cream sundaes.

L'École Surf Center SURFING
(☎05 56 60 61 05; www.surf-center.fr; 22 allées des Goëlands; lessons from €25; ⏲Easter-Sep) This surfing school rents out surfboards and runs surfing and bodyboarding lessons on Plage de l'Horizon, a sandy beach on the cape's western coast, near La Pointe du Cap Ferret (the southernost tip of the cape).

Eating

Restaurants line the waterfront and main village streets. But for a more authentic, memorable experience, rent a bicycle and pedal south along bd de la Plage and rue de la Conche to the oyster-fishing hamlet of **L'Escourre du Jonc**. Equally magnificent are the wooden *cabane* (fishermen's huts) restaurants lacing the seashore in a string of remote *villages ostréicole* (oyster fishing villages) north of Cap Ferret.

★ **La Canfouine** SEAFOOD €
(☎06 64 33 23 85; 75 rue Sainte-Catherine, Le Canon; dozen oysters €12-14; ⏲noon-3pm & 6-9pm Apr-Sep, Sat & Sun Oct-Dec & Mar) Expect local products the whole way at La Canfouine ('hut' in local dialect), an upmarket 'hut' on the seashore in the fishing village of Le Canon, about 7km north of Cap Ferret along cycling trails. Order oysters, whelks and nail-sized prawns with a Bordeaux rosé or Graves white, and kick back on black sofa seating with world-class views of oyster beds and the Dune du Pilat beyond. Heaven.

Information

The **tourist office** (☎04 93 76 08 90; www.saintjeancapferrat.fr; 5 av Denis Séméria; ⏲9am-5pm Mon-Fri, 10am-5pm Sat) organises a variety of guided tours in English and French, including a themed one exploring the cape during the belle époque. Watch for a new tourist office to open at no. 59 on the same street.

Getting There & Away

Cap Ferret is a scenic drive around Bassin d'Arcachon. Alternatively, drive here directly from Bordeaux (72km) along the D106.

Boats run by **Les Bateliers Arcachonnais** (www.bateliers-arcachon.com) sail to Cap Ferret's Jetée Bélisaire year-round from Arcachon (adult/child €7.50/5, 30 minutes, at least hourly). In summer, seasonal boats link Cap Ferret with the Dune du Pilat (adult return €26, 45 minutes, three daily).

Gujan Mestras

POP 20,136

Picturesque oyster ports are dotted around the town of Gujan Mestras, which sprawls along 9km of coastline.

The small but fascinating **Maison de l'Huître** (House of the Oyster; ☎05 56 66 23 71; www.maison-huitre.fr; rue du Port de Larros; adult/child €5.80/3.80; ⏲10am-12.45pm & 2.15-6.30pm Jul & Aug, 10am-12.30pm & 2.30-6pm Mon-Sat Sep-Jun) at Port de Larros explains how oysters are farmed in the Bassin d'Arcachon – from the baby beginnings when oyster larvae stick themselves to terracotta half-pipes laid out in rows by *ostréiculteurs* (oyster farmers) in shallow waters near the seashore, to their removal a year later to oyster banks in deeper waters where they mature and acquire their distinctive taste over a two- or three-year period.

A series of scenic and peaceful walking trails – 6km in all – wind through and around the swamps, lakes and woodlands of the idyllic **Réserve Ornithologique du Teich** (Bird Reserve; ☎05 56 22 80 93; www.reserve-ornithologique-du-teich.com; adult/child €8.90/6.70; ⏲10am-8pm Jul & Aug, to 7pm mid-Apr–Jun & 1-15 Sep, to 6pm mid-Sep–mid-Apr; 👪) in Le Teich, 5km east of Gujan Mestras. There are plenty of hides to watch birds up close: some 260 species of migratory and nonmigratory birds call the reserve home. Bring binoculars, water and a camera, and time your visit for high tide *(marée haute)*, when birds are most abundant.

Gujan Mestras' train station is on the line linking Bordeaux with Arcachon; count 45 minutes to/from Bordeaux (€10.10) and 11 minutes to/from Arcachon (€2.60).

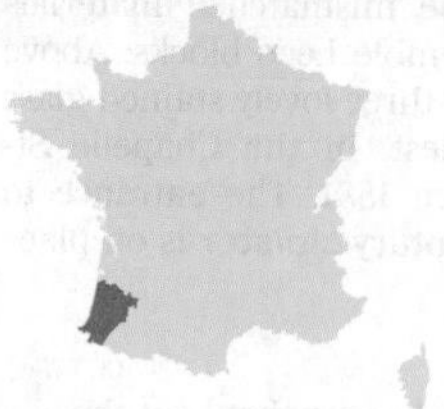

French Basque Country

POP 272,100

Includes ➡

Best Places to Eat

- ➡ Table de Pottoka (p642)
- ➡ Restaurant Le Pim'pi (p650)
- ➡ L'Etable (p650)
- ➡ Ithurria (p661)
- ➡ Le Kaiku (p659)

Best Places to Sleep

- ➡ Hôtel de Silhouette (p649)
- ➡ Hôtel Villa Koegui (p649)
- ➡ La Devinière (p658)
- ➡ Hôtel Balea (p655)
- ➡ Hôtel Restaurant Euzkadi (p661)

Why Go?

Jammed between the brilliant blue Bay of Biscay and the craggy foothills of the Pyrenees, the Pays Basque (Basque Country) feels one step removed from the rest of France – hardly surprising, since it's been an independent nation for much of its history and has more in common with the nearby Basque regions of Spain. Proud, independent and fiery, the people of the Basque Country are fiercely protective of their history and culture, whether it's their passion for *pelota* or their fondness for their spicy chilli pepper, *le piment d'Espelette*. It's a fascinating place.

The region's biggest town is the glitzy beach resort of Biarritz, famous for its sweeping beaches and thriving surf scene. Nearby Bayonne is considered the true capital of the Basque Country, and hosts a major Basque festival every July. Along the coast you'll find surf towns and fishing ports, while lots of sleepy hilltop villages nestle among the hills towards the Spanish border.

When to Go

Bayonne

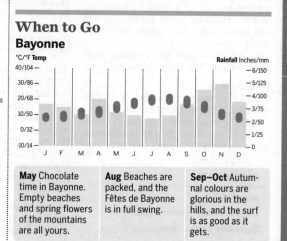

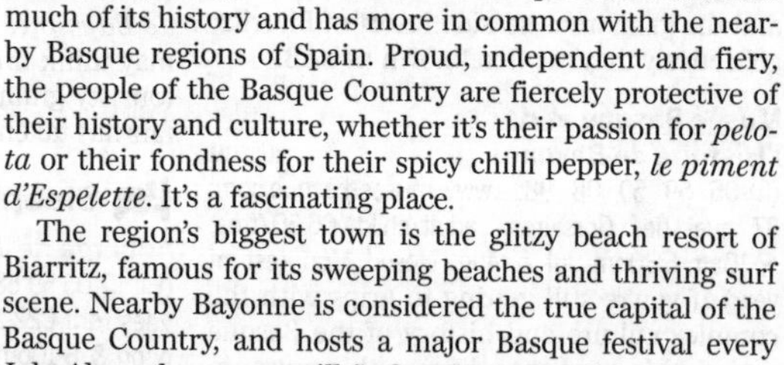

May Chocolate time in Bayonne. Empty beaches and spring flowers of the mountains are all yours.

Aug Beaches are packed, and the Fêtes de Bayonne is in full swing.

Sep–Oct Autumnal colours are glorious in the hills, and the surf is as good as it gets.

Bayonne

POP 46,200

Stretching along the banks of the Rivers Adour and Nive, the waterside city of Bayonne is one of the prettiest in southwest France, and the capital of the French Basque Country. It's been a strategic stronghold since medieval times, and the old ramparts are still visible around the outskirts of the old town, but it's Bayonne's pretty half-timbered buildings, riverside restaurants and shady cobbled streets that make it worthy of exploration.

Sights

The Rivers Adour and Nive split central Bayonne into three: St-Esprit, the area north of the Adour; Grand Bayonne, the oldest and most attractive part of the city, on the western bank of the Nive; and the rather grungy but very Basque quarter of Petit Bayonne to the east. To the west, Bayonne meets the suburban sprawl of Anglet (famed for its beaches) and the glamorous seaside resort of Biarritz; collectively they're often known as BAB.

Musée Basque et de l'Histoire de Bayonne MUSEUM

(☎05 59 59 08 98; www.musee-basque.com; 37 quai des Corsaires; adult/child €6.50/free; ⏰10am-6.30pm Jul & Aug, closed Mon rest of year) If you're still getting to grips with the complex culture and history of the Basque region, this excellent ethnographic museum makes a great place to start. It's crammed with artefacts, from traditional costumes, artwork and archaeological ephemera to a reconstruction of a typical Basque *etxe* (home). Labelling is in French, Spanish and Basque only – but English information sheets are available.

In July and August free 'nocturnal' visits are possible on Thursday evenings at 8.30pm.

Cathédrale Ste-Marie CATHEDRAL

(place Louis Pasteur; ⏰10-11.45am & 3-6.15pm Mon-Sat, 3.30-6.15pm Sun, cloister 9am-12.30pm & 2-6pm) The twin towers of Bayonne's Gothic cathedral soar above the city. Construction began in the 13th century, and was completed in 1451; the mismatched materials in some ways resemble Lego blocks. Above the north aisle are three lovely stained-glass windows; the oldest, in the Chapelle St-Jérôme, dates from 1531. The entrance to the stately 13th-century **cloister** is on place Louis Pasteur.

Ramparts CITY WALL

Once the defensive barrier that kept the city safe from attack, Bayonne's 17th-century fortifications are now covered in grass and enveloped in pretty parks. You can walk the stretches of the ramparts that rise above bd Rempart Lachepaillet and rue Tour de Sault.

> **FAST FACTS**
>
> **Area** 3039 sq km
>
> **Local industry** Tourism, agriculture
>
> **Signature drinks** Cider, Izarra

Festivals & Events

Fêtes de Bayonne CULTURAL

(www.fetes.bayonne.fr; ⏰early Aug) A five-day extravaganza of food, drink, dance and fireworks. See p644 for more information.

Foire au Jambon FOOD

(Ham Fair; ⏰Mar/Apr) During Easter week, the town hosts a Ham Fair, honouring *jambon de Bayonne*, the acclaimed local ham. You may think this is just a recently thought up touristy gimmick to sell ham, but no – this fair has taken place annually since 1462!

Sleeping

Auberge de Jeunesse HOSTEL €

(HI; ☎05 59 58 70 00; www.fuaj.org; 19 rte des Vignes; dm €22-26; ⏰mid-Apr–Sep, reception 9am-noon & 6-10pm; @📶) The nearest hostel is actually in Anglet, but it's not for wallflowers – with droves of surfers and backpackers passing through, it's a real party place, complete with its own Scottish pub and surf-film screenings. Rooms are mostly seven-bed dorms, and in summer it doesn't accept families. Catch bus 4 from outside Bayonne's town hall, then walk the last 500m.

Hôtel des Arceaux BOUTIQUE HOTEL €

(☎05 59 59 15 53; www.hotel-arceaux.com; 26 rue Port Neuf; d €69-89; 📶) On the pretty street of Port-Neuf, this simple hotel offers colourful, no-frills rooms, some of which share a bathroom, some of which are suited to families; they're all different, so ask to see a few. It's a jumble of old furniture, faded prints and chaise longues; there's even a vintage rocking horse in the lounge. Head to the 1st floor for reception.

Péniche Djébelle HOUSEBOAT €€

(☎05 59 25 77 18; www.djebelle.com; face au 17 Quai de Lesseps; d incl breakfast €150; ⏰closed

Oct-Apr; 📶) For something completely different, a stay on this *péniche* (houseboat) definitely fits the bill. There are just two rooms, each with roughly half the boat: one has a Moroccan theme and the other, which has the boat's steering wheel built into the bathroom, is themed after tropical islands. A lavish breakfast is included.

Hôtel Côte Basque HOTEL €€
(☎05 59 55 10 21; www.hotel-cotebasque.fr; 2 rue Maubec; d €63-119, tr & f €75-155; ❄📶) A real Bayonne bargain – an old hotel just steps from the station, set around an enclosed courtyard that would once have divided the nearby houses. There's a clanky old lift that rattles up between the floors, leading to simple but comfy rooms, most of which have a view towards the River Nive and the cathedral's spires.

Le Grand Hôtel HISTORIC HOTEL €€
(☎05 59 59 62 00; www.legrandhotelbayonne.com; 21 rue Thiers; d €89-169, tr & f €120-189; P❄📶) This old building was once a convent, but when they ran out of nuns someone turned it into a hotel – the poshest in town. It's a Best Western, so the decor tends towards the generic and modern, but the lobby and public areas have a dash of minimalist glamour. Parking is €15.

Eating

Bayonne has some superb places to eat, and costs are generally much lower than in nearby Biarritz. The **covered market** (quai Commandant Roquebert; ⏰7am-1.30pm Mon-Fri, 6am-1.30pm Sat, 8am-1.30pm Sun) sits on the riverfront. There are a number of tempting food shops and delicatessens along rue Port Neuf and rue d'Espagne.

Xurasko TAPAS €
(☎05 59 59 21 77; 16 rue Poissonnerie; tapas from €2.50; ⏰noon-11pm) Rough and ready, and all the better for it, this atmospheric corner bar near the market is guaranteed to be packed with a mix of after-dinner drinkers, market-workers and tourists. Pull up a stool by the zinc bar or grab a table on the street and tuck into tapas plates accompanied by a glass of bubbly Txakoli wine or a Bob's beer.

Ibaia TAPAS €
(45 quai Amiral Jauréguiberry; mains from €8; ⏰noon-2pm & 7-10pm Tue-Sat) This is the place to come to join the Bayonnais for some authentic tapas – there's a huge selection, from chorizo sausage to spicy prawns, and loads of

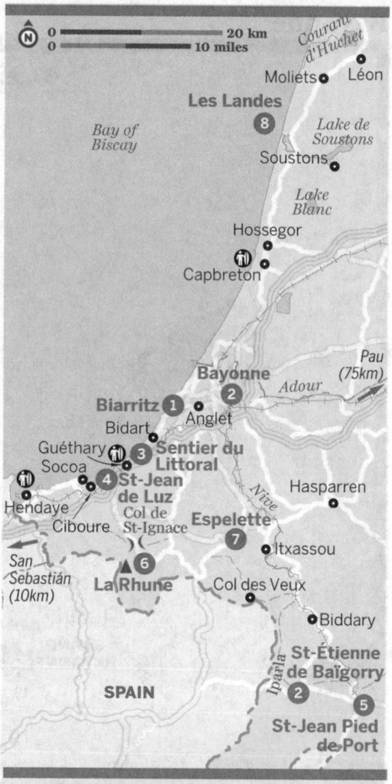

French Basque Country Highlights

1 **Biarritz** (p645) Joining the hordes of surfers and sunbathers on the seafront.

2 **Bayonne** (p645) Sampling at one of Bayonne's celebrated chocolate shops.

3 **Sentier du Littoral** (p659) Hiking along the wild coast path between Bidart and Hendaye.

4 **St-Jean de Luz** (p655) Seeking out some shade along the backstreets of this seaside town.

5 **St-Jean Pied de Port** (p662) Heading for the hills around this old pilgrimage town.

6 **La Rhune** (p660) Catching an antique train to the summit of La Rhune.

7 **Espelette** (p661) Picking up some of the Basque Country's famous powdered pimento pepper.

8 **Les Landes** (p648) Seeking out remote beaches along the coastline of Les Landes.

Bayonne

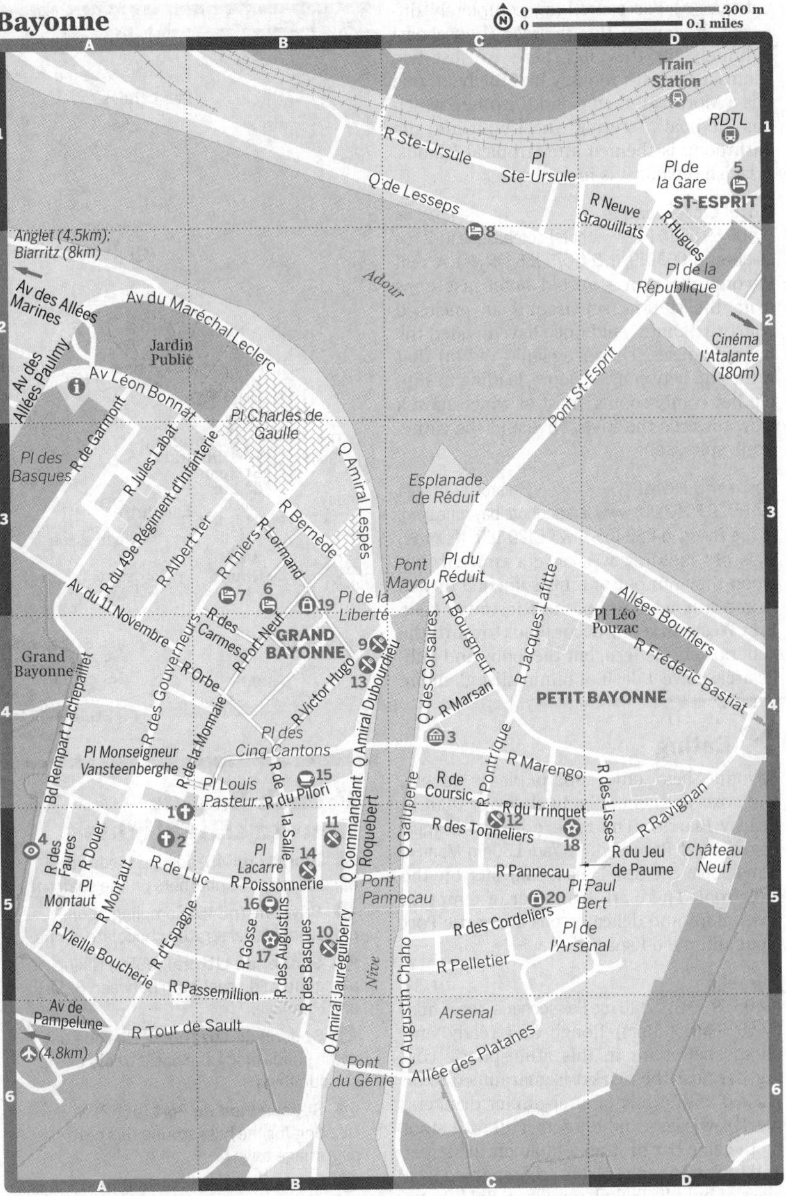

local wines by the glass. The riverfront patio is a super spot to linger on hot summer days.

★ **Table de Pottoka** GASTRONOMIC €€
(☎ 05 59 46 14 94; www.pottoka.fr; 21 quai Amiral Dubourdieu; menu lunch/dinner €15/35, à la carte mains €20; ⊙ noon-2pm & 7-10pm Mon-Tue & Thu-Sat) Run by renowned chef Sebastien Gravé (who also runs a place in Paris), this is Bayonne's hottest new table. It's committed to big Basque flavours, but explores them in all kinds of innovative ways. Inside things are sleek and minimal, with plain wooden

Bayonne

Sights
1 Cathédrale Ste-Marie A5
2 Cloister A5
3 Musée Basque et de l'Histoire de Bayonne C4
4 Ramparts A5

Sleeping
5 Hôtel Côte Basque D1
6 Hôtel des Arceaux B3
7 Le Grand Hôtel B3
8 Péniche Djébelle C2

Eating
9 À Table! B4
10 Ibaia B5
11 Les Halles B5
12 Restaurant Bakera C5
13 Table de Pottoka B4
14 Xurasko B5

Drinking & Nightlife
15 Bar François B4
16 Chai Ramina B5

Entertainment
17 La Luna Negra Music B5
18 Trinquet St-André C5

Shopping
19 Cazenave B3
Daranatz .... (see 19)
20 Pierre Ibaïalde C5

tables and pop-art prints on the walls, and there are dreamy river views through the plate-glass windows.

Restaurant Bakera BASQUE €€
(☎05 59 25 51 68; 15 rue des Tonneliers; mains €15-18; ⊙noon-2pm & 7-10pm Tue-Sat) It might not look like much from the outside, but this is a great place to try classic bistro dishes shot through with some southwest flavours. It's in a slightly grubby area of town, so it's probably not the place for alfresco dining, but the food is big, bold and very Basque.

À Table! MODERN FRENCH €€
(☎05 59 56 79 22; 27 quai Amiral Dubourdieu; mains €12-16; ⊙noon-2pm & 7-10pm Tue-Sat) Watch your elbows! There's barely enough room to avoid knocking over your neighbour's *pichet* of wine at this quayside restaurant, but that doesn't seem to deter the diners. It's ever-popular for bistro staples, especially at lunchtime, and the cheery decor (all stripes and primary colours) makes it a fun place to dine.

Drinking & Nightlife

Petit Bayonne is awash with pubs and bars (all generally open from noon to 2am Monday to Saturday), especially along rue Pannecau, rue des Cordeliers and quai Galuperie.

Bar François CAFE
(☎05 59 59 10 38; 14 rue Guilhamin; ⊙7am-11pm) As French as a string of onions, this is the classic pavement cafe: tables strewn out over the cobbles, waiters rushed off their feet, and more wines by the glass than you could drink in a week's worth of trying. Next to the covered market, this is *the* place to just watch town life roll by.

Chai Ramina BAR
(☎05 59 59 33 01; 11 rue Poissonnerie; ⊙10am-11pm) When there's a big rugby match on (the local club is one of the biggest in France) and the weather is fine, rue Poissonnerie is completely blocked by the huge crowds spilling out of Chai Ramina.

Entertainment

Upcoming cultural events are listed in *À l'Affiche* and the trimestrial *Les Saisons de la Culture,* both available free at the tourist office. At 9.30pm every Thursday in July and August, there's free traditional **Basque music** in place Charles de Gaulle.

Trinquet St-André SPECTATOR SPORT
(☎05 59 59 18 69; rue des Tonneliers; adult/child €10/2; ⊙matches 4pm Thu Oct-Jun) Hidden down a backstreet, this atmospheric *trinquet* (indoor court) stages *main nue pelota* (bare hand *pelota*) matches under an impressive timber-framed roof. There's also a lively bistro and bar for post-match discussion.

La Luna Negra Music LIVE MUSIC
(www.lunanegra.fr; rue des Augustins; ⊙7pm-2am Wed-Sat) Down an alley in the old town, this venerable late-night cabaret venue serves up a mixed program of comedy, world music, salsa and live jazz.

Shopping

Bayonne is famous for two premium products – handmade chocolates, which have been made here for centuries, and the cured ham known as *jambon de Bayonne.* One

other local souvenir that you probably won't be able to get through customs is a *baïonnette* (bayonet), developed here in 1640 on rue des Faures (Blacksmiths St).

Pierre Ibaïalde DELI

(☎05 59 25 61 54; www.pierre-ibaialde.com; 41 rue des Cordeliers) This is the address to buy Bayonne's celebrated *jambon* – traditionally served wafer thin, and claimed by locals to be every bit as good as *pata negra* or prosciutto. There are afternoon tours of the shop and drying room in summer (in French) if you really want to understand what makes the ham special.

Information

Tourist Office (☎08 20 42 64 64; www.bayonne-tourisme.com; place des Basques; ⏲9am-7pm Mon-Sat, 10am-1pm Sun Jul & Aug, 9am-6.30pm Mon-Fri, 10am-1pm & 2-6pm Sat Mar-Jun, Sep & Oct, shorter hours rest of year) Efficient office providing stacks of informative brochures and bike rental, plus guided city tours.

Getting There & Away

AIR

Biarritz-Anglet-Bayonne airport (☎05 59 43 83 83; www.biarritz.aeroport.fr) is 5km southwest of central Bayonne and 3km southeast of the centre of Biarritz. It's served by low-cost carriers including EasyJet, Flybe and Ryanair, as well as Air France, British Airways, SAS, Voltea and others, with daily domestic flights and flights to the UK and most other areas of Europe.

BUS

Chronoplus (☎05 59 52 59 52; www.chronoplus.eu) buses link Bayonne, Biarritz and Anglet. Services run several times an hour; a single ticket costs €1, while a 24-hour pass is €2. Bus A2 runs between Bayonne and Biarritz, stopping at the Hôtels de Ville and train stations in both towns.

For longer journeys, **ATCRB** (☎09 70 80 90 74; www.transports-atcrb.com) buses leave from place des Basques to the Spanish border. The 816 travels to St-Jean de Luz (€2, 40 minutes, at least hourly Monday to Saturday, every two hours on Sunday) and Hendaye (€2, one hour). Summer beach traffic can double journey times.

Transportes Pesa (www.pesa.net) buses leave place des Basques twice a day Monday to Saturday for Bilbao (€20.50) in Spain, calling at Biarritz, St-Jean de Luz, Irún and San Sebastián (€8.05).

Starshipper (www.starshipper.com) also runs long-distance buses between Bordeaux and San Sebastian, stopping at Bayonne, Biarritz and St-Jean de Luz en route. There are four daily Monday to Saturday and two on Sunday. The one-way fare from Bayonne is €7.

RDTL (www.rdtl.fr) runs services northwards into Les Landes, including Capbreton/Hossegor (€2, 40 minutes, six daily Monday to Saturday, four on Sunday).

FÊTES DE BAYONNE

Beginning on either the first Wednesday in August or occasionally the last in July, the Fêtes de Bayonne attracts thousands of people from across France and Spain for a five-day orgy of drinking, dancing, processions, fireworks and bulls. In many ways it's like a less commercialised version of the famous San Fermín festival in Pamplona (Spain) and, just like in Pamplona, Bayonne also holds bull running. However, here the bulls are actually cows – though they still have horns and they still hurt when they mow you down – and they don't run down the streets, but are instead released on the crowd in front of the Château Neuf. During the *fête*, real bullfights also take place.

One of the biggest highlights of the *fête* is the **opening ceremony**, when huge crowds gather in front of the town hall at 10pm on the Wednesday night for an impressively noisy firework display and the arrival of a 'lion' (the town's mascot).

While the nocturnal activities might be a bit much for children, the daytime processions, marching bands, organised children's picnics and even a children's 'bull' run are tailor-made for the delight of little ones. Thursday daytime has the most child-friendly activities.

If you're planning on attending the *fête*, you'll need to book at least six to eight months in advance for hotel accommodation anywhere in the vicinity of Bayonne. A number of temporary campgrounds (€60 for six days) are erected in and around Bayonne to ease the pressure; otherwise you can just do what most people do and sleep in the back of a car (camping outside one of the campgrounds is forbidden).

Finally, unless you want to stand out like a sore thumb, don't forget to dress all in white with a red sash and neck-scarf. For dates and other *fête* information, see www.fetes.bayonne.fr.

DON'T MISS

BAYONNE CHOCOLATE

Bayonne's long association with chocolate stems from a rather unlikely source – the Spanish Inquisition. Fleeing persecution, Jewish chocolate-makers fled their Spanish homeland in Bayonne's St-Esprit neighbourhood, establishing the town's reputation for producing some of the finest chocolate anywhere in France. By 1870, Bayonne boasted 130 chocolatiers, more than in all of Switzerland – although now only around a dozen remain.

The town's premium makers are **Daranatz** (☎05 59 59 03 05; www.chocolat-bayonne-daranatz.fr; 15 rue Port Neuf; ⊙9am-noon & 2-7pm Tue-Sat) and **Cazenave** (☎05 59 59 03 16; www.chocolats-bayonne-cazenave.fr; 19 rue Port Neuf; ⊙9.15am-noon & 2-7pm Tue-Sat), who are based next door to each other on rue Port Neuf, but there are plenty more to try. You can see chocolate being made during a tour at **L'Atelier du Chocolat** (☎05 59 55 00 15; www.atelierduchocolat.fr; 1 allée de Gibéléou; adult/child €6/3; ⊙9.30am-6.30pm Mon-Sat), which includes a historical overview of chocolate in Bayonne and, of course, the chance to taste the goods. Bayonne also hosts its own chocolate-themed weekend in May, **Les Journées du Chocolat**.

TRAIN

TGVs run between Bayonne and Paris Gare Montparnasse (€69 to €109, five to six hours, eight daily). Other destinations include Bordeaux and Toulouse.

For travel to Biarritz, you're better off catching a bus, as Biarritz' TGV station at La Négresse is way out of town. For destinations further south, trains run at least hourly including services to St-Jean de Luz (€4.50, 20 minutes) and Hendaye (€6, 28 minutes), and twice daily to Irún (€6.50, 43 minutes).

There are also four trains daily to St-Jean Pied de Port (€8, 1¼ hours).

Getting Around

TO/FROM THE AIRPORT

Chronoplus bus 14 links Bayonne with the airport (€1, buses depart roughly hourly). A taxi from the town centre costs around €20.

BICYCLE

Bayonne's tourist office lends out bikes for free (not overnight); you simply need to leave some ID as a deposit.

BUS

A free *navette* (shuttle bus) loops around the heart of town.

Biarritz

POP 26,000

Half ritzy coastal resort, half summer surfer's hang-out, the seaside resort of Biarritz has been a favourite seaside getaway ever since Napoléon III and his Spanish-born wife Eugénie arrived during the mid-19th century. It's been a glamorous spot ever since, lined with elegant villas and heritage-listed residences that glitter with belle époque and art deco details. Unfortunately the 20th century wasn't quite so kind, and the seafront is blessed with its fair share of concrete carbuncles that have done little to enhance its aesthetic appeal. Nevertheless, Biarritz remains one of the southwest's seaside gems – so long as you can cope with the summer crowds and seasonal prices, that is.

Sights & Activities

From art deco mansions to Russian Orthodox churches and 1970s tower-block disasters, Biarritz has a fantastic mish-mash of architectural styles.

Musée de la Mer MUSEUM

(☎05 59 22 75 40; www.museedelamer.com; esplanade du Rocher de la Vierge; adult/child/family €14.50/9.80/50, joint ticket with Cité de l'Océan €18.50/13/63; ⊙9.30am-midnight Jul & Aug, 9.30am-8pm Apr, Jun, Sep & Oct, shorter hours rest of year) Housed in a wonderful art deco building near the old port, Musée de la Mer is seething with underwater life from the Bay of Biscay and beyond, including huge aquariums of sharks, playful grey seals and tropical reef fish, as well as exhibits exploring Biarritz' whaling past. In high season it's possible to have the place almost to yourself by visiting late at night.

Cité de l'Océan MUSEUM

(☎05 59 22 75 40; www.citedelocean.com; 1 av de la Plage; adult/child/family €11.50/7.50/39, joint ticket with Musée de la Mer €18.50/13/63; ⊙10am-10pm Jul & Aug, 10am-7pm Easter, Apr-Jun, Sep & Oct, shorter hours rest of year) Biarritz' newest sea-themed attraction is part museum, part theme park, part educational centre. It takes

Biarritz

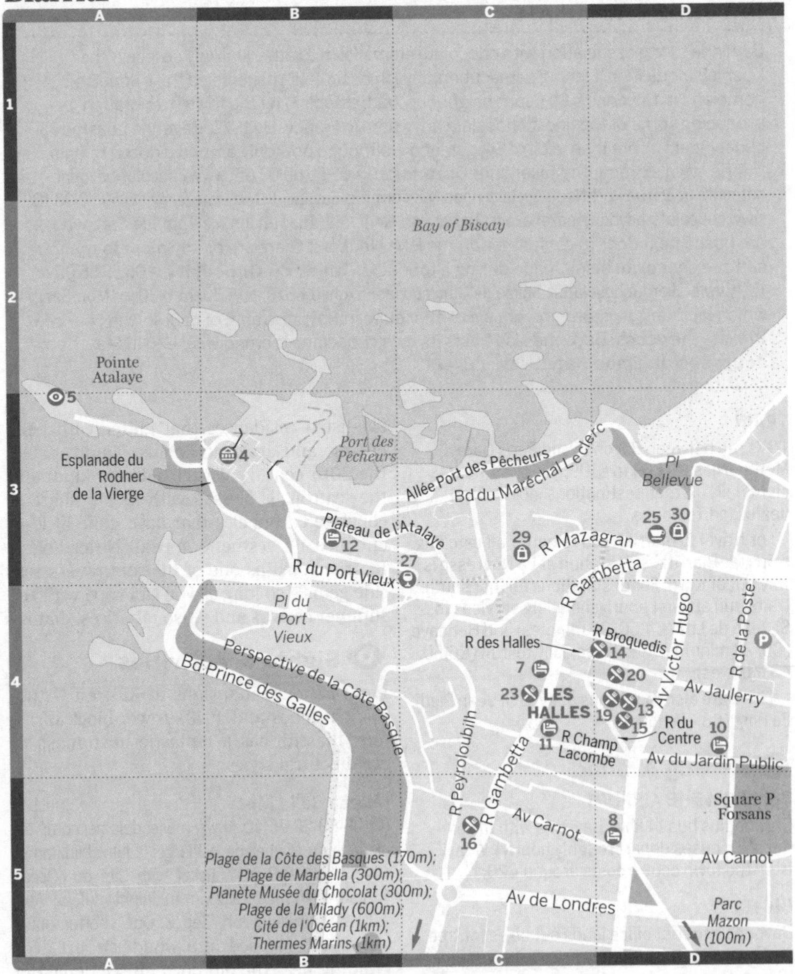

a fun approach to learning about the sea in all its forms – attractions range from a chance to explore a marine lab to a simulated dive into the depths in an underwater bathysphere. It's good fun, but probably more of interest to older kids.

In July and August a free *navette* (shuttle bus) runs between Musée de la Mer and the Cité de l'Océan. Tickets can be booked online in advance.

Chapelle Impériale CHURCH

(☎05 59 22 37 10; 15 rue des 100 Gardes; €3; ⏰2.30-6pm) Built in 1864 on the instructions of Empress Eugénie, this glitzy church mixes Byzantine and Moorish styles, and the plaza in front has a great view of the Grande Plage. You can buy tickets online at the tourist office to avoid queues.

Rocher de la Vierge VIEWPOINT

(Rock of the Virgin) If the swell's big, you might get a drenching as you cross the twee, toy-town-like footbridge at the end of Pointe Atalaye to Rocher de la Vierge, named after its white statue of the Virgin and child. Views from this impressive outcrop extend to the mountains of the Spanish Basque Country.

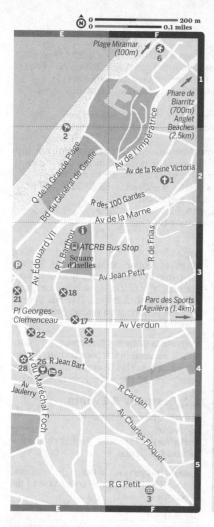

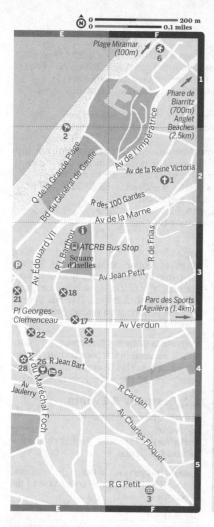

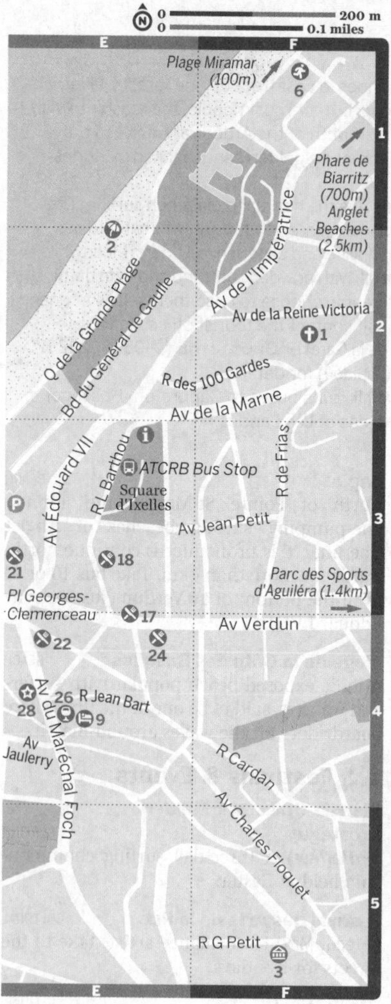

Biarritz

Sights
1 Chapelle Impériale.......F2
2 Grande Plage.......E2
3 Musée d'Art Oriental Asiatica.......F5
4 Musée de la Mer.......B3
5 Rocher de la Vierge.......A3

Activities, Courses & Tours
6 Thalassa Biarritz.......F1

Sleeping
7 Hôtel de Silhouette.......C4
8 Hôtel Edouard VII.......D5
9 Hôtel Villa Koegui.......E4
10 Maison du Lierre.......D4
11 Maison Garnier.......C4
12 Villa Le Goëland.......B3

Eating
13 Bar du Marché.......D4
14 Bar Jean.......D4
15 Bistrot des Halles.......D4
16 CAB (Comptoir à Burger).......C5
17 Fumoir au Marin.......E4
18 Le Clos Basque.......E3
19 Le Comptoir du Foie Gras/Maison Pujol.......D4
20 Les Halles.......D4
21 L'Etable.......E3
22 Milwaukee Café.......E4
23 Puig & Daro.......C4
24 Restaurant le Pim'pi.......E4

Drinking & Nightlife
25 Miremont.......D3
26 Red Café.......E4
27 Ventilo Caffé.......C3

Entertainment
28 Cinéma Le Royal.......E4

Shopping
29 Les Sandales d'Eugénie.......C3
30 Robert Pariès.......D3

Phare de Biarritz LIGHTHOUSE
(adult/child €2.50/2; ⏲9am-6pm) Climbing the 258 twisting steps inside the 73m-high Phare de Biarritz, the town's 1834 lighthouse, rewards you with sweeping views of the Basque coast.

Musée d'Art Oriental Asiatica MUSEUM
(☎05 59 22 78 79; www.museeasiatica.com; 1 rue Guy Petit; adult/child €10/2; ⏲10.30am-6.30pm Mon-Fri, 2-7pm Sat & Sun Jul, Aug & during French school holidays, shorter hours rest of year) Out on the edge of town is this unexpected treasure trove of ancient Indian, Chinese and Tibetan statues, monuments and temple artwork. The layout is a bit haphazard, but the information cards (in several languages) clearly explain the significance of the objects. It's generally considered the finest collection of its type outside Paris.

Planète Musée du Chocolat MUSEUM
(☎05 59 23 27 72; www.planetemuseeduchocolat.com; 14 av Beau Rivage; adult/child €6.50/5; ⏲10am-7pm Jul & Aug, shorter hours rest of year) It's certainly not planet-sized, but this small museum still makes an intriguing detour for chocophiles, exploring the Basque Country's long association with the cacao bean. Attractions include vintage chocolate-making

WORTH A TRIP

LES LANDES

North of Bayonne is the *département* of Les Landes, a vast tract of pine forests, lakes and seaside towns. It's great for hiking and biking, but for most people, the reason to visit is its seemingly never-ending beaches. From the mouth of the Ardour at Anglet to the mouth of the Gironde stretches a ribbon of shimmering golden sand, backed by dunes and basking under a deep blue sky.

The combination of sand and waves has made this the heartland of French surfing. The action centres on the small beach towns of **Capbreton** and **Hossegor**, where there are numerous surf schools offering lessons for both novice and experienced riders. Meanwhile the tiny village of **Moliets** has the best beach of all, with powder-soft sand and safe bathing.

Local hotels tend to be overpriced, so most people choose to base themselves at one of the area's many campgrounds or 'surf-camps'; contact the tourist offices in **Hossegor** (☎05 58 41 79 00; www.hossegor.fr; 166 ave de la Gare) or **Capbreton** (☎05 58 72 12 11; www.capbreton-tourisme.com; ave du Président Pompidou) for details.

From Bayonne's train station, **RDTL** (www.rdtl.fr) runs buses to Capbreton/Hossegor (€2, 40 minutes, six or seven daily) and other areas of Les Landes.

equipment, vintage posters and various other bits of ephemera – but it's the handmade chocs and frothy hot-chocolate conclusion that always bring the biggest grins. Bus 9 runs past the front gate.

Beaches

Once the almost exclusive haunt of the rich and pampered, Biarritz is now known more as the capital of European **surfing** (although in truth, the real centre of European surfing is the small town of Hossegor around 25km to the north). The city's main beach, **Grande Plage**, is good from mid-low tide on a moderate swell, but the 4km-long stretch of beaches that make up **Anglet** to the south are usually more consistent.

There are plenty of surf schools around town that offer lessons from around €35 per hour; the tourist office keeps a list. Make sure your school is registered with the **Féderation Française de Surf** (FFS; www.surfingfrance.com) to make sure you get the best standard of training.

Grande Plage BEACH

Grand by name, grand by nature, Biarritz' vast main beach has been the place to be seen in since the days of Napoléon II and Eugénie. It's wall-to-wall with bodies on summer days, and eerily deserted in winter. Stripy 1920s-style beach tents can be hired for €9.50 per day.

Plage Miramar BEACH

A little way north of the Grande Plage, on the way to the lighthouse, plage Miramar is packed on summer days.

Anglet BEACH

North of Pointe St-Martin, the adrenaline-pumping surfing beaches of Anglet (the final 't' is pronounced) continue northwards for more than 4km. Take bus 10 or 13 from the bottom of av Verdun (just near av Édouard VII).

Plage de la Côte des Basques BEACH

A long, exposed beach popular with surfers and walkers, said to be one of the first where boardriders hit the waves around Biarritz.

Festivals & Events

Biarritz Quiksilver Maider Arosteguy SURFING

(⌚Mar/Apr) A three-day surfing championship held at Easter.

Festival des Arts de la Rue CULTURAL

(⌚early May) Performance artists take to the streets for five days.

Big Festival MUSIC

(www.bigfest.fr; ⌚mid-Jul) As its name implies, this is Biarritz' largest music festival, attracting big mainstream acts.

Roxy Jam SURFING

(⌚mid-Jul) A major female surfing championship.

Le Temps d'Aimer DANCE

(www.letempsdaimer.com; ⌚mid-Sep) A two-week celebration of dance in all its forms.

Festival de Biarritz Amérique Latine FILM

(www.festivaldebiarritz.com; ⌚late Sep-early Oct) This film and culture festival brings some Latin spice to Biarritz.

Sleeping

Auberge de Jeunesse de Biarritz HOSTEL €
(☎05 59 41 76 00; www.hihostels.com; 8 rue Chiquito de Cambo; dm incl sheets & breakfast €26.40; ⊙reception 9am-noon & 6-10pm, closed mid-Dec–early Jan; @) This popular, well-run place has a lot going for it: clean dorms, a lively cafe-bar and a sunny terrace for summer barbecues, but it's a bit pricey as HI hostels go. From the train station, follow the railway line westwards for 800m.

Maison du Lierre HERITAGE HOTEL €€
(☎05 59 24 06 00; www.hotel-maisondulierre-biarritz.com; 3 av du Jardin Public; d €129-169;) What a beauty this mansion is, impressively detached, with a balcony and park view from nearly every room (apart from the very cheapest, which overlook a neighbouring building). It's elegantly simple – wooden floors, cool furnishings, rooms named after flowers – and the central staircase is a listed monument. It's not even expensive for Biarritz. Recommended.

Hôtel Mirano BOUTIQUE HOTEL €€
(☎05 59 23 11 63; www.hotelmirano.fr; 11 av Pasteur; d €79-139; P) Wow, it's like stepping into a frame from *Boogie Nights* at this '70s retro palace, where everything looks like it's been picked up from the glory days of disco – from the orange perspex light fittings to the leather lounge chairs and squiggly wallpaper (oh, and there's a Betty Boop in the bar). Camp, fun and decently priced too.

To get here take the D910 southeast out of town, turn left onto av de Grammont and then right onto av Pasteur. It's a good 10-minute walk from the centre.

Hôtel Edouard VII HISTORIC HOTEL €€
(☎05 59 22 39 80; www.hotel-edouardvii.com; 21 av Carnot; d €140-190;) In a cream-coloured 19th-century mansion that once belonged to one of Biarritz' mayors, this heritage hotel has a touch of old-fashioned grandeur about it – from the tick-tocking clocks in the lobby to its antique furniture and floral rugs. There are four room categories – 'Confort' offers the best space–price ratio.

Maison Garnier BOUTIQUE HOTEL €€
(☎05 59 01 60 70; www.hotel-biarritz.com; 29 rue Gambetta; d from €79-139;) This corner townhouse has a super location: walk out the door and you'll be right in the thick of the tapas bars around the covered market. It feels soothingly old-world inside, even a touch austere, and still has lots of original features like fireplaces, cornicing and carvings. Reception isn't always staffed, so it's worth ringing ahead.

★**Hôtel de Silhouette** BOUTIQUE HOTEL €€€
(☎05 59 24 93 82; www.hotel-silhouette-biarritz.com; 30 rue Gambetta; d from €200;) The address if you want to splash out in Biarritz, just steps from the covered market, but surprisingly secluded thanks to its set-back-from-the-street setting. It's full of fun, from the weird faces on the wallpaper to the odd sculptures of bears and sheep dotted round, and there's a gorgeous garden. The building dates from 1610, but it's metropolitan modern in style.

★**Villa Le Goëland** B&B €€€
(☎05 59 24 25 76; www.villagoeland-biarritz.com; 12 plateau de l'Atalaye; r €160-250; P) With its château-like spires, this stunning mansion perched high on a plateau above Pointe Atalaye is one of the most notable buildings in town. It's now a swish B&B – all four rooms, tastefully furnished with antiques, family photos and mementos, have panoramic views. The pick of the bunch is 'chambre Goëland' with its huge private terrace.

Hôtel Villa Koegui BOUTIQUE HOTEL €€€
(☎05 59 50 07 77; www.hotel-villakoegui-biarritz.fr; 7 rue de Gascogne; r from €200;) Big-city style in Biarritz, with cool and minimal rooms spread out over a modern building brimming with quirky furnishings and decor (look out for the pair of fibreglass flamingos in the window). The central courtyard garden is a big plus, but the backstreet location makes parking a pain.

SEA HEALING

Thalassotherapy ('sea healing'), using the restorative properties of seawater (along with seaweed and mud), has been popular in Biarritz since the late 18th century and continues to serve as an antidote to 21st-century ailments such as stress and insomnia.

In Biarritz, put thalassotherapy's curative powers to the test – or simply bliss out – at the following:

Thalassa Biarritz (☎05 59 41 30 00; www.accorthalassa.com; 11 rue Louison-Bobet)

Thermes Marins (☎08 25 12 64 64; www.biarritz-thalasso.com; 80 rue de Madrid)

Eating

Biarritz has a great range of restaurants, from fine-dining to beachfront cafes, as well as a cracking tapas culture – check out the area around Les Halles.

Les Halles MARKET €
(www.halles-biarritz.fr; rue des Halles; 7am-1.30pm) Biarritz' lovely covered market is the place to come for picnic ingredients.

★ **Restaurant Le Pim'pi** FRENCH €€
(05 59 24 12 62; 14 av Verdun; menus €14-28, mains €15-18; noon-2pm Tue, noon-2pm & 7-9.30pm Wed-Sat) A small and resolutely old-fashioned place unfazed by all the razzamatazz around it. The daily specials are chalked up on a blackboard – most are of the classic French bistro style but are produced with such unusual skill and passion that many consider this one of the town's better places to eat.

Fumoir au Marin SEAFOOD €€
(05 59 22 09 26; 13 ave de Verdun; lunch menu €15, dinner mains €16-20; noon-2pm & 7-10.30pm) There's a theme to everything that's on the table at this bistro – nearly everything's been smoked in some way, with fish and seafood taking top billing. But this is no rustic smokehouse – it's stylish and smart, with blonde-wood tables and a great wine choice. The smoked scallops and the tuna with pink peppercorns are highlights, if they're on offer.

L'Etable BASQUE €€
(05 59 22 10 11; 6 rue Lavernis; mains €16-24; 7pm-midnight Wed-Mon) This is one of those places, hidden down an alley and in a cave-like building, that's so discreet that only a local could have pointed it out to you. Despite the less-than-obvious look to the place, it has a stellar reputation for assured, traditional local dishes, featuring lots of duck, chilli and seafood.

Le Clos Basque BASQUE €€
(05 59 24 24 96; 12 rue Louis Barthou; menus €26, mains €14.50; noon-1.30pm & 7.45-9.30pm Tue-Sat, noon-1.30pm Sun) One of Biarritz' more traditional tables, with a sweet front patio sheltered by climbing plants and an awning. The menu is proudly Basque, so expect classic dishes such as *axoa* (mashed veal, onions and tomatoes spiced with red Espelette chilli). It gets very busy, so service can be slow.

Milwaukee Café CAFE €€
(05 59 54 17 04; 2 rue du Helder; lunch mains €8-12; 9am-6.30pm) A little dose of Americana cafe culture is on offer here – burgers, salads, smoothies and health shakes, followed up by delicious cupcakes and proper barista-made coffees. It's light, fresh and bright inside, and popular with local office workers and ladies-who-lunch. The name is a reference to the owner's family – she's a Milwaukee native but grew up in Biarritz.

Bistrot des Halles BASQUE €€
(05 59 24 21 22; 1 rue du Centre; mains €17-19; noon-2pm & 7.30-10.30pm Tue-Sat) One of a cluster of restaurants along rue du Centre that get their produce directly from the nearby covered market, this bustling place stands out from the pack for serving excellent fish and other market fare from a blackboard menu. The interior is adorned with old metallic advertising posters. Open daily during Easter and the summer holidays.

THE BASQUE LANGUAGE

According to linguists, Euskara, the Basque language, is unrelated to any other tongue on Earth, and is the only tongue in southwestern Europe to have withstood the onslaught of Latin and its derivatives.

Basque is spoken by about a million people in Spain and France, nearly all of whom are bilingual. In the French Basque Country, the language is widely spoken in Bayonne and the hilly hinterland. However, while it is an official language in Spain, it isn't recognised as such in France (although some younger children are educated in Basque at primary-school level). The language also has a higher survival rate on the Spanish side.

But you'll still encounter the language in France on Basque-language TV stations, and see the occasional sign reading *'Hemen Euskara emaiten dugu'* (Basque spoken here) on shop doors. You'll also see the Basque flag (similar to the UK's but with a red field, a white vertical cross and a green diagonal one) flying throughout the region, as well as another common Basque symbol, the *lauburu* (like a curly four-leaf clover), signifying prosperity, or life and death.

DON'T MISS

TAPAS IN BIARRITZ

Like Bayonne, tapas (or *pintxos* as it's known in the Basque Country) is an ever-popular way to eat in Biarritz. Whether it's a quick snack over drinks or a slap-up feast, there are plenty of places to indulge, especially around the covered market.

La Cave à Manger des Contrabandiers (☎05 59 24 02 27; 20 ave Victor Hugo; tapas €6-11; ⊙noon-2pm & 7-10pm Tue-Fri, noon-3pm & 7-11pm Sat & Sun) Attached to a wine shop, this trendy spot is great for an imaginative spin on tapas traditionals – try the Txirula sausage and the *jambon/lomo/*chorizo platter.

Le Comptoir du Foie Gras/Maison Pujol (☎05 59 22 57 42; www.comptoir-foie-gras-biarritz.com; 1 rue du Centre; tapas from €1; ⊙8am-2pm & 5-11pm) Foie-gras specialist by day, tapas hang-out by night, on a corner next to the covered market. The tapas tends to be heavy on foie gras, but there are other options too.

Bar du Marché (☎05 59 23 48 96; 8 rue des Halles; tapas €1-3.50; ⊙8am-3pm & 6pm-2am) Established in 1938, this sunny yellow bar is as good for sit-down meals as for its late-night tapas selection.

Puig & Daro (☎05 59 23 30 45; rue Gambetta; mains €8-13; ⊙10am-11pm) Take a seat on the wooden pavement patio and dine on a comprehensive tapas selection, from local cheeses to Cantabrian anchovies and sardines in olive oil.

Bar Jean (☎05 59 24 80 38; www.barjean-biarritz.fr; 5 rue des Halles; tapas €2-6; ⊙noon-3.30pm & 6.30pm-midnight) One of the oldest tapas venues in town, traditional and full of atmosphere – from the flamenco soundtrack to the Andalucian tiles. Try the calamari rings wrapped around a stack of lardons and drizzled in olive oil.

CAB (Comptoir à Burger) BURGERS €
(☎05 59 51 07 10; 62 rue Gambetta; burgers €8-12; ⊙noon-2pm & 7-10pm) Burgers are big in Biarritz these days, just like everywhere, and this place is the locals' tip for the best in town. Options range from a classic burger with Emmental cheese to a chicken burger spiced with Espelette pepper – or you could just trust the grillsters and go for whatever the 'Burger au Moment' happens to be that week.

Drinking & Nightlife

The area around rue du Port Vieux and the covered market tend to be the hot spots for Biarritz' nightlife. Most places will stay open till around 2am, unless otherwise indicated.

Miremont CAFE
(☎05 59 24 01 38; www.miremont-biarritz.com; 1bis place Georges-Clemenceau; hot chocolate from €5; ⊙9am-8pm) Operating since 1880, this *grande dame* harks back to the time when belle époque Biarritz was the beach resort of choice for the rich and glamorous. Today it still attracts perfectly coiffed hairdos (and that's just on the poodles) but it's the fine tea and cakes that draw in the well-heeled punters – none of whom seem to mind the sky-high prices.

Red Café BAR
(☎05 59 24 21 02; 9 av du Maréchal Foch; ⊙Tue-Sun) Rugby is a religion in Biarritz, and this place is themed around the colours of Biarritz Olympique (red and white). It gets lively on match days, but it's a chilled hang-out when the boys aren't playing.

Ventilo Caffé BAR
(rue du Port Vieux; ⊙closed Tue Oct-Easter) One of several options along the street leading up from the old port, this is a good place for wine by the glass and plates of tapas. It gets packed in summer, when the sliding doors are opened up and the action spills out onto the street.

Entertainment

Free classical-music concerts take place in high summer at various outdoor venues around town; the tourist office has the program. There are a couple of cheesy nightclubs and lounge bars just behind Grande Plage.

Cinéma Le Royal CINEMA
(www.royal-biarritz.com; 8 av du Maréchal Foch) Screens a good selection of nondubbed films.

Parc des Sports d'Aguiléra SPECTATOR SPORT
(av Henri Haget) Regular professional *pelota* matches (admission €10 to €20) are held

Basque Culture

Call a Basque French or Spanish and it's almost certain you'll receive a glare and a stern 'I'm Basque!' in return. It's no surprise, as the Basques *are* different, with their own unique culture and history, and a language – Euskara – unrelated to any other European language. Basque people are genetically different, too: many share the same blood group which can be traced back to Europe's earliest settlers.

Pelote Basque

Pelote Basque (pelota) is the catch-all name for around 16 traditional Basque ball games. The most well-known has players using a scoop-like basket called a *chistera,* while *main nue* is played with an open hand; *jaï alaï* is the most high-octane variant, and has a professional league with games screened on local TV. Every village has its own *pelota* court, called a *fronton.*

Festivals

Basque festivals are the best place to see traditional dress: even if you're not in costume, wearing red and white is mandatory. The big seasonal celebration is the Fêtes de Bayonne, held in July, but there are many smaller celebrations too.

Lauburu

The most visible symbol of Basque culture is the *lauburu,* also known as the Basque cross. Regarded as a symbol of prosperity, it's also used to signify life and death.

Basque Eats

The Basque version of tapas is called *pintxos;* two or three dishes per person is usually enough. Look out for local specialities:

Le Piment d'Espelette This little chilli pepper is an essential spice in cooking.

Fromage des Pyrénées Local cheeses are best bought straight from the farm: look out for varieties such as Ossau-Iraty.

Jambon de Bayonne The Basque version of *pata negra,* sliced wafer-thin.

Axoa Mashed veal with tomato, onions and *le piment d'Espelette.*

Izarra A fiery herb-flavoured liqueur that comes in green and yellow versions.

1. Drying chillies **2.** Traditional *pelota* game (p643)
3. Crowds celebrating the Fêtes de Bayonne (p644)

2

DELPIXEL / SHUTTERSTOCK ©

at 9pm at this sports complex, 2km east of central Biarritz, between mid-June and mid-September.

Shopping

Robert Pariès CHOCOLATE
(☎05 59 22 07 52; 1 place Bellevue; ⌚9am-7.30pm) Scrumptious chocolates and Basque sweets, including *canougas* (chocolate-covered caramels) and *gateaux basques* (cream-filled cake, often flavoured with cherries).

Les Sandales d'Eugénie SHOES
(18 rue Mazagran; ⌚10am-1pm & 3-6.30pm) Vincent Corbun continues his grandfather's business, established in 1935, making and selling espadrilles in a rainbow of colours and styles (customised with ribbons and laces while you wait).

Information

Tourist Office (☎05 59 22 37 10; http://tourisme.biarritz.fr; square d'Ixelles; ⌚9am-7pm Jul & Aug, shorter hours rest of year) In July and August there are tourist-office annexes at the airport and train station, and at the roundabout just off the Biarritz *sortie* (exit) 4 from the A63.

Getting There & Away

AIR

To reach BAB (Biarritz-Anglet-Bayonne) airport by bus, **Chronoplus** (☎05 59 52 59 52; www.chronoplus.eu) has a couple of possible options: Line C is the most useful, as it runs from the train station in Biarritz, while Line 14 leaves from a stop near the Biarritz tourist office. Both run every half-hour or so, with a journey time of about 10 minutes. A single fare costs €1.

BUS

Buses run frequently between Bayonne and Biarritz; they work out much cheaper than taking the train as you'll pay the same to get from Biarritz' train station to its town centre as you will to get from Bayonne to Biarritz directly on the bus.

ATCRB (☎09 70 80 90 74; www.transports-atcrb.com) line 816 buses travel down the coast to St-Jean de Luz, Urrugne and Hendaye; there's also an express service that runs three times daily. The fare is a flat-rate €2, and buses leave from the stop just near the tourist office beside square d'Ixelles.

Buses to Spain, including San Sebastián and Bilbao, also depart from the same stop.

TRAIN

All trains to Biarritz now only stop at La Négresse train station, about 3km south of the town centre (the old Gare du Midi station was closed some years ago, and is now a cultural centre). Chronoplus bus A1 runs regularly into the city centre.

Times, fares and destinations are much the same as for Bayonne, a nine-minute train journey away. There is an **SNCF boutique** (13 av du Maréchal Foch; ⌚9am-12.30pm & 1.30-6pm Mon-Sat) in downtown Biarritz.

Getting Around

There is a free Chronoplus shuttle bus that trundles around central Biarritz. There are two lines, one which travels around the town centre, the other which runs north–south along the coast between Plage Miramar, Grande Plage and Plage de la Milady. It runs roughly every 20 minutes Monday to Saturday.

LOCAL KNOWLEDGE

TOP SURF SPOTS – BASQUE & ATLANTIC COASTS

France's Basque and Atlantic coasts have some of Europe's best surf. Autumn is prime time, with warm(ish) water temperatures, consistently good conditions and few(er) crowds. The big-name spots are **Biarritz** and **Hossegor**, where you can watch pro surfers battling it out for world-title points during September/October's World Surf League (www.worldsurfleague.com) event. In fact, decent surf can usually be found almost anywhere between St-Jean de Luz in the south and Soulac-sur-Mer in the north.

The reef breaks around **Guéthary**, just to the south of Biarritz, are also popular, or you could join Bordeaux' surfers on the beaches around **Lacanau**.

Lesser-frequented spots can be found around the pine-forested **Cap Ferret** peninsula, along with various other remote areas along the coastline of Les Landes.

For beginners, the mellow waves at **Hendaye**, just to the south of St-Jean de Luz, are tailor-made for learners. There are plenty of surf schools; lessons start at around €35. Contact local tourist offices for details.

OFF THE BEATEN TRACK

ESCAPE INTO THE HILLS

There's no doubting the Basque Country's beauty, but unfortunately its good looks mean it's far from a well-kept secret. The coast can be horrendously crowded in summer, but with your own wheels it's possible to escape into the hills to find some of the area's less-frequented corners.

Itxassou This hilltop village is famous for its cherries, and its scenic surrounds.

La Bastide-Clairence With whitewashed houses brushed in lipstick red, this is arguably the most beautiful of all Basque mountain villages.

Bidarray A pretty riverside village famed for its white-water-rafting opportunities.

Forêt d'Iraty A vast beech forest that turns the high mountain slopes fire-orange in autumn. A web of walking trails allows for easy exploration.

Larrau This quaint village surrounded by monster hills is another hiker's favourite, with gorges and a monstrous cavern nearby.

Guéthary

POP 1365

Halfway between Biarritz and St-Jean de Luz and handy for both is the little seaside village of Guéthary, once a whaling station, but now a swish getaway for the Basque Coast's jet set. Set out along a steep hillside that leads down to the attractive harbour and seafront – it's a pretty spot for an afternoon stroll, with a couple of small sandy beaches tucked in under the breakwater and some grand art deco architecture set out along its winding walkways.

Sights

Musée d'Art Moderne et Contemporain MUSEUM
(☎05 59 54 86 37; www.musee-de-guethary.fr; 117 Ave du Général de Gaulle; €2; ⌚10.30am-12.30pm & 2.30-6.30pm Mon & Wed-Sat Jul & Aug, 2.30-6.30pm Mon & Wed-Sat May, Jun, Sep & Oct) Housed inside the magisterial Villa Saraleguinea, this intriguing little art museum is based around the collection of local poet Paul-Jean Toulet, who lived in Guéthary during the last years of his life, and the sculptor Georges Clément de Swiecinski. It's an eclectic mix that takes in everything from Roman ephemera to abstract sculptures, as well as changing exhibitions of contemporary art, photography and ceramics – but it's the house and grounds that really steal the show.

Sleeping

★Hôtel Balea BOUTIQUE HOTEL €€
(☎05 59 26 08 39; www.hotel-balea-guethary.com; 106 Rue Adrien Lahourcade; d €89-159; P❄📶) Pay attention, class – this cracking hotel receives top marks. It's housed in Guéthary's former public schoolhouse, and the decor echoes its educational heritage in entertaining ways – from an original playground mural and arithmetical room numbers to the vintage maps and pots of pens adorning the breakfast room. It's cool, fun and reasonably priced, even in season. A+.

Information

Guéthary Tourist Office (☎05 59 26 56 60; www.guethary-tourisme.com; 74 rue du Comte de Swiecinski; ⌚9am-12.30pm & 2-6.30pm Jun-Sep, closed Sun Oct-May) Located right beside the tiny train station.

Getting There & Away

BUS

Chronoplus buses travelling between Biarritz and St-Jean de Luz stop off on the main road in Guéthary; the fare is a flat-rate €2 for anywhere along the coast.

TRAIN

There are several trains an hour from Guéthary's tiny station south to St-Jean de Luz (€2, seven minutes) and north to Bayonne (€3.50, 15 minutes). It's easier to take a bus to Biarritz as the SNCF station is way out of town.

St-Jean de Luz & Ciboure

POP 14,200

If you're searching for the quintessential Basque seaside town – complete with atmospheric narrow streets, a lively harbour and a sparkling sandy beach, you've found it.

The attractive town of St-Jean de Luz, 24km southwest of Bayonne, grew up

St-Jean de Luz

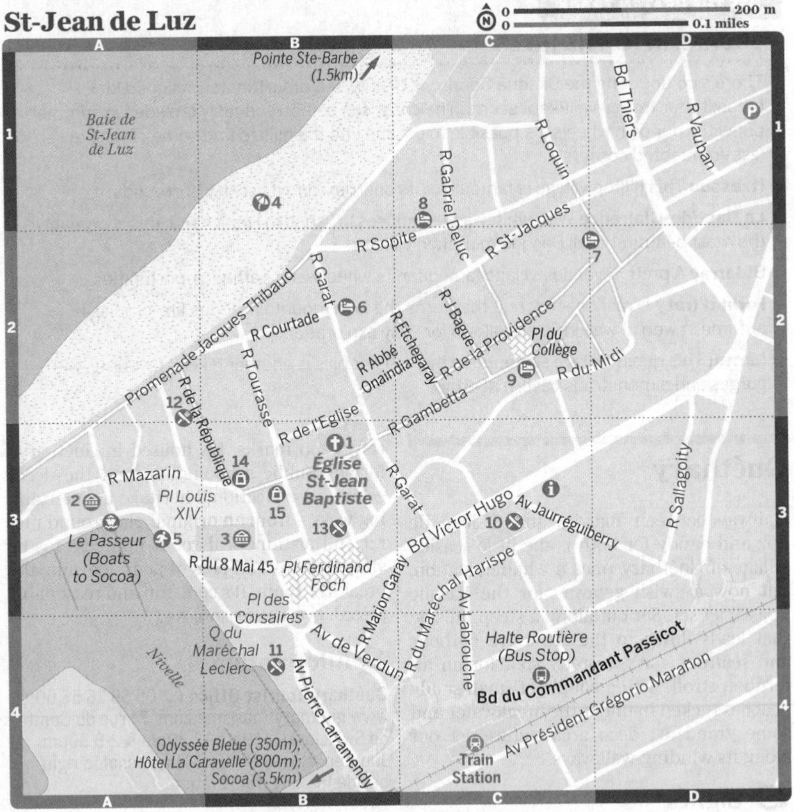

around the mouth of the River Nivelle as a fishing port, pulling in large catches of sardines, anchovies and, rather less salubriously, whales in bygone days. Later, like the rest of the Basque coastline, it became a fashionable resort for well-to-do French, English and Spanish tourists in the late 19th century, but the town still maintains a sizable fishing fleet.

St-Jean and its sleepy sister town of Ciboure are linked by busy Pont Charles de Gaulle, which overlooks the fishing port. In summer, the best way to cross the river mouth is to catch one of the regular ferries that chug between the two.

Sights

St-Jean's shady backstreets are great for a wander, especially along the main shopping thoroughfare, rue Gambetta. The grandest buildings are around place Louis XIV.

★Église St-Jean Baptiste CHURCH
(rue Gambetta, St-Jean de Luz; ⏲8.30am-noon & 2-7pm) The plain façade of France's largest and finest Basque church conceals a splendid interior with a magnificent baroque altarpiece. It was in front of this very altarpiece that Louis XIV and María Teresa, daughter of King Philip IV of Spain, were married in 1660. After exchanging rings, the couple walked down the aisle and out of the south door, which was then sealed to commemorate peace between the two nations after 24 years of hostilities.

Maison Louis XIV HISTORIC BUILDING
(☎05 59 26 27 58; www.maison-louis-xiv.fr; 6 place Louis XIV, St-Jean de Luz; adult/child €6/4; ⏲10.30am-noon & 2.30-6.30pm Wed-Mon Jul & Aug, 11am-3pm & 4-5pm Wed-Mon Easter, Jun & Sep–mid-Oct) The grandest house in town was built in 1643 by a wealthy shipowner, but its main claim to fame is as the house where Louis XIV lived out his last days of

St-Jean de Luz

bachelorhood before marrying María Teresa. It's awash with period detail and antiques. Half-hour guided tours (with English text) depart several times daily in July and August. Alongside is St-Jean de Luz' Hôtel de Ville, built in 1657.

Maison de l'Infante HISTORIC BUILDING
(☎05 59 26 36 82; quai de l'Infante, St-Jean de Luz; adult/child €2.50/free; ⏱11am-12.30pm & 2.30-6.30pm Tue-Sat, closed mid-Nov–May) In the days before her marriage to Louis XIV, María Teresa stayed in this brick-and-stone mansion (like the temporary home of her husband-to-be, it was owned by a shipowner) with fine architectural detail, just off place Louis XIV.

Socoa OLD TOWN
The heart of Socoa is about 2.5km west of Ciboure along the continuation of quai Maurice Ravel (named for the *Boléro* composer, who was born in Ciboure in 1875). Its prominent **fort** was built in 1627 and later improved by Vauban. You can walk out to the Digue de Socoa breakwater or climb to the **lighthouse** via rue du Phare, then out along rue du Sémaphore for fabulous coastal views.

L'Écomusée Basque Jean Vier MUSEUM
(☎05 59 51 33 23; www.ecomusee-basque.com; adult/child €7.50/3.20; ⏱10am-6.30pm Jul & Aug, 10-11.15am & 2.30-5.30pm Mon-Sat Apr-Jun, Sep & Oct, closed Nov-Apr) Basque traditions are brought to life at this illuminating multimedia museum, which explores everything from *pelota* and Basque architecture to the art of making Izarra (Basque for 'star'), a liqueur made from 20 different local plants. It's around 2km north of St-Jean de Luz beside the N10.

Château d'Urtubie CASTLE
(☎05 59 54 31 15; www.chateaudurtubie.net; rue Bernard de Coral; adult/child €6.50/3.50; ⏱10.30am-6.30pm mid-Jul–Aug, 10.30am-12.30pm & 2-6.30pm Apr-Jun, Sep & Oct) This small château was constructed in the 13th century and has been in the hands of the same family ever since. Rooms are decorated in period style and are stuffed full of antiques and other treasures. You can even stay overnight (rooms €85 to €175). To get there follow the D704 and D810 about 3km southwest of St-Jean de Luz, in the direction of Spain, and you'll find it sitting pretty just off the D810 road.

St-Jean Plage BEACH
St-Jean de Luz' beautiful banana-shaped beach sprouts stripy bathing tents from June to September. It's protected from the wrath of the Atlantic by breakwaters and jetties, and is one of the more child-friendly beaches in the Basque Country.

Plage de Socoa BEACH
Ciboure has its own modest beach, Plage de Socoa, 2km west of Socoa on the corniche (the D912); it's served by ATCRB buses en route to Hendaye and, in high season, by boats.

Activities

Odyssée Bleue DIVING
(☎06 63 54 13 63; www.odyssee-bleue.com; chemin des Blocs, hangar 4, Ciboure) The Basque coast is a great place to learn to dive, and this school comes highly recommended. A 20-minute 'baptism' dive costs €55, with longer courses starting from €180. It also offers snorkelling expeditions in summer for €25.

Nivelle V CRUISE
(☎06 09 73 61 81; www.croisiere-saintjeandeluz.com; quai de l'Infante, St-Jean de Luz; adult/child €17/13; ⏱Apr–mid-Oct) Between April and October, the *Nivelle V* runs out along the surrounding coastline all the way towards Spain at 2pm daily, with extra cruises at 10.30am on Tuesdays, Wednesdays and Thursdays from mid-July to mid-September. Shorter cruises on the *Nivelle IV* (adult/child €10/7) depart at 4pm daily, with an extra tour at

5pm daily and at 11am on Sundays in July and August. Also offers sea-fishing trips.

Festivals & Events

Fêtes de la St-Jean CULTURAL

(Jun) Bonfires, music and dancing take place on the weekend nearest 24 June.

Danses des Sept Provinces Basques DANCE

Folk dancers from across the Spanish and French Basque Country meet in early summer.

Régates de Traînières SPORTS

(Jul) A weekend of boat races on the first weekend in July.

La Nuit de la Sardine CULTURAL

(Jul & Aug) The Night of the Sardine – a night of music, folklore and dancing – is held twice each summer, on a Saturday in early July and the Saturday nearest 15 August.

La Fête du Thon FOOD

(Jul) The Tuna Festival, on a weekend in July, fills the streets with brass bands, Basque music and dancing, while stalls sell sizzling tuna steaks.

Sleeping

July to mid-September are packed and advance reservations are essential; low-season prices can drop significantly. There are a couple of cheap and cheerful places opposite the train station.

Between St-Jean de Luz and Guéthary, 7km northeast up the coast, are no fewer than 16 camping grounds. ATCRB's Biarritz and Bayonne buses stop within 1km of them all.

★ **Les Almadiès** HOTEL €€

(05 59 85 34 48; www.hotel-les-almadies.com; 58 rue Gambetta, St-Jean de Luz; d €100-135;) Summer bargains are hard to come by in St-Jean de Luz, but this pretty little streetside hotel definitely ranks as one. It's in a great location on the lively thoroughfare of rue Gambetta, overlooking a little square, and though the rooms are a bit generic – beige carpets, white bathrooms, identikit furniture – there's no doubting the deal here.

La Devinière BOUTIQUE HOTEL €€

(05 59 26 05 51; www.hotel-la-deviniere.com; 5 rue Loquin, St-Jean de Luz; d €120-180;) You have to love a place that forsakes TVs for antiquarian books (room 11 even has its own mini-library). Beyond the living room, with its piano and comfy armchairs, there's a delightful small patio equipped with lounges and the rooms are stuffed full of antique and replica antique furnishings. The garden rooms are worth the extra.

Hôtel La Caravelle BOUTIQUE HOTEL €€

(05 59 47 18 05; www.hotellacaravelle.com; bd Pierre Benoît, Ciboure; d with sea view €75-145, d without sea view €45-90, f €80-165;) Stylish and shipshape, this elegant hotel is one step removed from the summertime buzz in St-Jean de Luz, overlooking the water on the opposite side of the port in Ciboure. Originally two fishermen's cottages, it's been spruced up with cream-and-blue colour

CROSS-BORDER ENCOUNTERS: A DAY IN SAN SEBASTIÁN

Just 33km southwest of St-Jean de Luz, the elegant, sexy and seriously Spanish city of San Sebastián makes a perfect day trip from the French Basque Country. With its twin beaches, lively nightlife and lovely old town, San Sebastian is worth a day of anyone's time, but it's the sensational food that really makes the trip worthwhile. The town has some of the best tapas (or *pintxos*, as it's known here) bars anywhere in Spain, not to mention more Michelin-starred restaurants per capita than anywhere else in the world – including thrice-starred **Arzak**, the flagship establishment of acclaimed chef Juan Mari Arzak, who frequently features in lists of the world's best chefs.

From St-Jean de Luz, it's just a short 20-minute jump down the A64 (and its many toll-booths); the N10 is toll-free but turns into one long traffic jam in summer. In high season, it's better to catch a bus or train; trains run from St-Jean de Luz to Hendaye (and occasionally onto Irun) roughly hourly (€3.50, 12 minutes), from where you can board one of the frequent Eusko Trens for the ride into San Sebastián (€1.80, 30 minutes). Otherwise, Transportes Pesa (p644) and Starshipper (p644) buses run regularly to San Sebastián.

For further information, head to www.lonelyplanet.com to purchase a PDF of the Bilbao, Basque Country & La Rioja chapter from Lonely Planet's *Spain* guide.

LOCAL KNOWLEDGE

SENTIER DU LITTORAL

Running for 25 breezy kilometres between Bidart and Hendaye is one of the Basque Country's best-kept secrets – the **Sentier du Littoral**, a coastal hiking trail that passes through some of the region's most beautiful seaside scenery. Though much of the coastline between Biarritz and the Spanish border has been heavily built up over the last century, a few wild stretches still remain, carpeted with fragrant maquis and pockmarked by rocky coves, all backed by the shimmering blue line of the Atlantic horizon. Walking through the stunning coastal scenery, it's possible to get a glimpse of the natural splendour that first attracted tourists here in the late 19th century.

There are access points at various places along the route, including at Bidart, Guéthary, St-Jean de Luz, Socoa and Hendaye; interpretative panels are positioned along the trail, and a downloadable route map is available from the Guéthary tourist office website (www.guethary-tourisme.com/discover-guethary/path-of-the-coast.php).

It's perfectly feasible to just do a couple of sections and then catch a bus or train back to Biarritz or St-Jean de Luz. Bring plenty of water and sunscreen, and aim to do your walking early morning or late afternoon, as the summer sun can be relentless.

schemes and nautical knick-knacks. Needless to say, a sea view is a must here. There's free street parking outside.

La Marisa Hôtel HOTEL €€
(☎05 59 26 95 46; www.hotel-lamarisa.com; 16 rue Sopite, St-Jean de Luz; r €128-178;) With its scarlet timbers and shutters, this tall townhouse is typical of the architecture in St-Jean de Luz. The rooms are split into three categories: Classic, Comfort and Extra Comfort, all tinted in the same sunny shades, decorated in the same genteel fashion, and with a choice of bath or shower – so essentially you're paying extra solely for the space. Elsewhere around the hotel there's lots of books, antiques and wood-panelling, plus a pleasant courtyard garden.

Hôtel Ohartzia HOTEL €€
(☎05 59 26 00 06; www.hotel-ohartzia.com; 28 rue Garat, St-Jean de Luz; d €85-95, f €120;) If you really want to be in the heart of town (and steps from the beach), this cute little hotel is a good bet. Outside, it's covered with balconies and flowers; inside, smart rooms of varying sizes, and a secret shady garden where breakfast is served in summer.

Eating

★Buvette des Halles SEAFOOD €
(☎05 59 26 73 59; bd Victor Hugo, St-Jean de Luz; dishes €7-14; ⊙6am-2pm & dinner, closed Tue Sep-Jun) For the full-blown French market experience, this tiny corner restaurant hidden away in Les Halles is a must. Pull up a stool at the counter under its collection of vintage teapots, and tuck into plates of Bayonne ham, grilled sardines, mussels, fish soup and local cheeses. In summer there are tables outside.

Grillerie du Port SEAFOOD €
(☎05 59 51 18 29; quai du Maréchal Leclerc, St-Jean de Luz; mains €7.50-9.50; ⊙noon-2.30pm & 7-10.30pm daily Jun-Sep) It won't take long to peruse the menu at this old port-side classic. It's essentially a choice of grilled sardines or grilled tuna – all freshly caught that morning and utterly delicious.

Xaya FRENCH €€
(☎05 59 47 75 48; www.restaurant-saint-jean-de-luz.com; 5 rue St-Jean, St-Jean de Luz; 2-course lunch menu €14, mains €13.50-20; ⊙noon-2pm & 7.30-9.45pm Tue-Sun) Duck down a little alley into this stone-vaulted restaurant for French food with a Basque twist. There are two options: order grilled fish or steaks à la carte, or just delve into tapas for the whole table to share. Inside it feels bright and modern, with mirrors, upcycled barrels and blonde wood, and a photo mural of fishing scenes.

★Le Kaiku GOURMET €€€
(☎05 59 26 13 20; www.kaiku.fr; 17 rue de la République, St-Jean de Luz; menu lunch/dinner €32/64, mains €26-38; ⊙12.30-2pm & 7.30-10pm Thu-Mon) For a spoil, Nicholas Borombo's stellar address is the place to dine in St-Jean. Known for his modern interpretation of Basque classics, his dishes are full of unusual ingredients, from Asian spices to edible flowers. The setting is lovely too, in an old-town location on a cobbled street near the beach. Non-French speakers might struggle with the complicated menu. Reservations and smart attire essential.

Entertainment

Jaï Alaï Compos Berri SPECTATOR SPORT
(rte de Bayonne, N10, St-Jean de Luz) In summer, frequent *pelota* matches take place at Jaï Alaï Compos Berri, 1km northeast of the train station. The tourist office can supply times and prices.

Shopping

Maison Adam FOOD
(05 59 26 03 54; 6 rue de la République, St-Jean de Luz; 8am-12.30pm & 2-7.30pm) This renowned shop, selling delicious macarons (melt-in-the-mouth biscuit-like delicacies), hams and other regional foods, has been trading since 1666 – longer than many a nation has been in existence!

Sandales Concha SHOES
(05 59 51 07 56; 2 rue Gambetta, St-Jean de Luz; 9am-noon & 2-7pm Tue-Sat) The traditional shoe of the Basque Country is the espadrille and here you can choose from a huge range of handmade shoes starting from €10.

Information

Tourist Office (05 59 26 03 16; www.saint-jean-de-luz.com; 20 bd Victor Hugo, St-Jean de Luz; 9am-12.30pm & 2-7pm Mon-Sat, 10am-1pm Sun) Runs an extensive program of French-language tours around the town and across the Spanish border; ask about English-language tours in summer.

DON'T MISS

GROTTES DE SARE

Who knows what the first inhabitants of the **Grottes de Sare** (www.grottes-desare.fr; adult/child €8.50/4.50; 10am-7pm Aug, 10am-6pm Apr-Jul & Sep, closed Jan–mid-Feb), some 20,000 years ago, would make of today's whiz-bang technology that now lights up the stygian gloom at these stunning subterranean caves? Multilingual 45-minute tours take you through a gaping entrance via narrow passages to a huge central cavern, where impressive shows of holograms and laser lights are staged.

Follow the D306, 6km south of the village of Sare. Le Basque Bondissant (www.basquebondissant.com) runs buses from St-Jean de Luz to the caves (€2; bus 868) a couple of times a day in summer.

Getting There & Away

BUS

ATCRB (p644) buses stop near the train station on their way northeast to Biarritz (30 minutes, hourly) and Bayonne (40 minutes). Southwest, there are around 10 services daily to Hendaye (35 minutes). All journeys cost a flat-rate €2.

Transportes Pesa (p644) and **Starshipper** (p644) buses stop in St-Jean de Luz en route to San Sebastián and Bilbao.

TRAIN

There are frequent trains to Bayonne (€4.50, 20 to 35 minutes) via Biarritz (€3, 10 to 20 minutes) and to Hendaye (€3.50, 20 to 40 minutes), with onward connections to Spain.

Getting Around

BOAT

The good ship **Le Passeur** plies between the jetty on the northern edge of St-Jean's beach, quai de l'Infante and Socoa (adult/child one way €2.50/2) hourly between April and September.

TAXI

Call 05 59 47 38 38.

La Rhune

Traditionally considered the first mountain of the Pyrenees, the 905m-high, antenna-topped and border-straddling La Rhune ('Larrun' in Basque), 10km south of St-Jean de Luz, has always been considered sacred by Basques, though today people come for the spectacular views rather than religious or cultural reasons.

The mountain is best approached from **Col de St-Ignace**, 3km northwest of Sare on the D4 (the St-Jean de Luz road). From here, you can take a fairly strenuous five-hour (return; about 11km) hike, or have all the hikers curse you by hopping on **Le Petit Train de la Rhune** (www.rhune.com; single/return adult €15/18, child €8/11; mid-Feb–mid-Nov). This charming little wooden train takes 35 minutes to haul itself up the 4km to the summit. In July and August departures are every 35 minutes, the rest of the time they are limited to two to four times a day (see website for exact times). Outside high season, prices are a few euros cheaper. Be prepared for a wait of up to an hour in high summer.

A free *navette* (shuttle bus) runs from St-Jean de Luz several times daily in summer, and leaves from outside the train station.

Ainhoa

POP 686

'Un des plus jolis villages de la France', says the sign as you enter this, indeed, very pretty village.

Ainhoa's elongated main street is flanked by imposing 17th-century houses, half-timbered and brightly painted. Look for the rectangular stones set above many of the doors, engraved with the date of construction and the name of the family to whom the house belonged. The fortified church has the Basque trademarks of an internal gallery and an embellished altarpiece.

For a memorable Basque meal, stop at the Michelin-starred **Ithurria** (☎05 59 29 92 11; www.ithurria.com; place du Fronton; menus €42-88, mains €19-35; ⏱restaurant noon-2pm Fri-Tue, 7.30-9pm Thu-Tue; P ❄ 📶), established by the Isabal family in an old pilgrims' hostel and now run by Maurice Isabal's two sons (one the sommelier, the other the chef). To make a night of it, Ithurria's rainbow-hued rooms (doubles from €140) and dreamy swimming pool complement the food perfectly.

If the restaurant is too extravagant for you there's a bistro where you can get a sense of what you're missing (mains €11 to €17; open for lunch Monday to Saturday in high season).

Espelette

POP 2000

The whitewashed Basque town of Espelette is famous for its dark-red chillies, an integral ingredient in traditional Basque cuisine. So prized is *le piment d'Espelette* that it's been accorded Appellation d'Origine Contrôlée (AOC) status, like fine wine. In autumn you can scarcely see the walls of the houses under rows of chillies drying in the sun. The last weekend in October marks Espelette's **Fête du Piment**, with processions, a formal blessing of the chilli peppers and the ennoblement of a *chevalier du piment* (a knight of the pimento).

Sleeping & Eating

Maison d'hôte Irazabala B&B €

(☎06 07 14 93 61; www.irazabala.com; 155 Mendiko Bidea; d incl breakfast €77-87; P 📶) This beautiful Basque farmhouse is situated in the middle of wild flower meadows. With views over green mountains, it is a bucolic place to rest up. The four rooms are easily the equal of the setting and you'll struggle to tear yourself away from the garden. There are no TVs in the rooms, but when the setting is as lovely as this, who cares?

It's a couple of kilometres out of town (follow signs for the campsite and it's signed just on from there).

★**Hôtel Restaurant Euzkadi** RESTAURANT €

(☎05 59 93 91 88; www.hotel-restaurant-euzkadi.com; 285 Karrika Nagusia; menus €20-36, mains €12-18; ⏱12.30-2pm & 7.30-9.30pm; 📶) This red-and-white half-timbered hotel is characteristic of the architecture of the Basque Country, and its food is equally classic – *piment d'Espelette* figures heavily in many dishes, and you can try local specialities like *axoa* (tender minced veal simmered with onions and fresh chillies).

Rooms are surprisingly modern too (three comfort categories to choose from; double €79 to €92, triple €100 to €115 and quad €130 to €150), and there's a lovely pool.

Shopping

L'Atelier du Piment FOOD

(☎05 59 93 90 21; www.atelierdupiment.com; ⏱9am-8pm Apr-Oct, 9am-6pm Nov-Mar) FREE

LOCAL KNOWLEDGE

LARRESSORE

At the **L'Atelier Anciart Bergara** (☎05 59 93 03 05; www.makhila.com; Larressore; ⏱8am-noon & 2-6pm Mon-Fri, to 5pm Sat) workshop in the little village of Larressore, around 6km north of Espelette, craftsmen make the traditional wooden walking sticks known as *makhila*, which have been carried by shepherds, farmers and hillspeople in the Basque Country for as long as anyone cares to remember. Customarily made from medlar wood and topped by a decorative leather pommel capped with steel, bone, horn or bronze, each one is made to order to suit its owner and can take several weeks of work to complete.

Most *makhilas* also have a hidden secret – the hand-grip can be slipped off to reveal a sharp spike, effectively turning a walking stick into a deadly weapon. The workshop offers three core models costing from €280 to €650, or you can order your own custom version for considerably more. Either way, it's a fascinating art that's well worth watching.

This shop on the edge of the village sells a huge variety of chilli-pepper products, from jams to chocolate.

Information

Tourist Office (05 59 93 95 02; www.espelette.fr; 9am-12.30pm & 2-6.30pm Mon-Fri, 9.30am-12.30pm & 2-6pm Sat Jul & Aug, shorter hours rest of year) Helpful office situated within a small stone château.

Getting There & Away

Le Basque Bondissant (www.basquebondissant.com) runs buses between St-Jean de Luz and Espelette a couple of times a day in summer and less frequently in winter.

St-Jean Pied de Port

POP 1700

At the foot of the Pyrenees, the town of St-Jean Pied de Port (St-Jean at the Foot of the Pass), 53km southeast of Bayonne, was for centuries the last stop in France for pilgrims heading south over the Spanish border, a mere 8km away, and on to Santiago de Compostela in western Spain. Today it remains a popular waypoint for hikers attempting the pilgrim trail – you're bound to see a few of them wandering along the main cobbled street of rue de la Citadelle.

The walled town itself is beautifully preserved, ringed by ramparts and topped off by a sturdy citadel. It's an ideal day trip from Bayonne, particularly on Monday when the market is in full swing.

Sights

Walled Town HISTORIC QUARTER

Though modern St-Jean has expanded considerably, during medieval times, the entire town was enclosed by defensive ramparts, guarding France's southwestern corner against incursions from across the Spanish border. The town's four original *portes* (gates) are still in situ, including one at either end of the cobbled rue de la Citadelle.

The traditional entry point for pilgrims is via the **Porte St-Jacques**, at the top end of the street, while at the other, the **Porte Notre-Dame** stands next to the town's most famous landmark – the **Pont Romain**, a photogenic arched bridge spanning the River Nive. Despite the name, it's not actually Roman – it was built sometime around 1720.

As you walk along rue de la Citadelle, look out for the dates of construction carved into the lintels above the doorways (the oldest we found was 1510). Also keep your eyes peeled for the motif of the scallop shell – the traditional symbol of the Santiago de Compostela, as pilgrims who completed the route would take a souvenir shell home from the Spanish coast.

La Citadelle FORTRESS

From the top of rue de la Citadelle, a rough cobblestone path ascends to the massive citadel itself, from where there's a spectacular panorama of the town and the surrounding hills. Constructed in 1628, the fort was rebuilt around 1680 by military engineers of the Vauban school. Nowadays it serves as a secondary school and is closed to the public.

If you've got a head for heights, descend by the steps signed *'escalier poterne'* (rear stairway). Steep and slippery after rain, they plunge beside the moss-covered ramparts to **Porte de l'Échauguette** (Watchtower Gate).

Prison des Évêques MONUMENT

(Bishops' Prison; 41 rue de la Citadelle; adult/under 15yr €3/free; 10.30am-7pm mid-Jul–Aug, 11am-12.30pm & 2.30-6.30pm Wed-Mon Apr–mid-Jul, Sep & Oct) Dating back to the 14th century, this vaulted cellar served as the town jail from 1795, as a military lock-up in the 19th century, then as a place of internment during WWII for those caught trying to flee to nominally neutral Spain. The lower section dates from the 13th century, when St-Jean Pied de Port was a bishopric of the Avignon papacy; the building above it dates from the 16th century. Inside can be found seasonal exhibitions.

Activities

St-Jean makes a great base for hiking, even if you're not up for trudging the whole Santiago de Compostela route. Two GRs (*grandes randonnées;* long-distance hiking trails) pass through town: the **GR10** (the trans-Pyrenean long-distance trail running from the Atlantic to the Mediterranean over the course of 45 days) and the **GR65** (the Chemin de St-Jacques pilgrim route).

Shorter sections of each route make for a great day-hike from St-Jean; ask at the tourist office for route maps.

Sleeping & Eating

Much of the accommodation is geared towards pilgrims on the long hike to Santiago de Compostela in Galicia, Spain. This means it's always very basic; normally it consists of just dorm beds, but it's cheap (€10 to €15 per person). At many places non-pilgrims will

be turned away. Note that if you're staying inside the old town, you'll have to lug your luggage on foot from wherever you park.

Itzalpea B&B €

(☎05 59 37 03 66; www.hotel-itzalpea.com; 5 place du Trinquet; incl breakfast s €49-55, d €66-69, tr €89; ❄📶) Outside the walled town, above a popular tearoom, this simple hotel makes a good base, with seven rooms eclectically decorated with puffy bedspreads, vintage furniture and splashes of modern art. It's basic but good for those on a budget. Not all rooms have air-con, and front-facing ones suffer from a bit of road noise.

Hôtel Ramuntcho HOTEL €€

(☎05 59 37 03 91; www.hotel-ramuntcho.com; 1 rue de France; r €70-106; 📶) In the same hands for generations – and with a suitably old-fashioned feel – this is the only hotel proper inside the walled town. It's in a typical Béarn half-timbered house, with plain, peach-coloured rooms, some of which look over the street, others which have views over the Pyrenean foothills. There's also a restaurant on the ground floor. It's part of the Logis de France chain.

Maison E Bernat B&B €€

(☎05 59 37 23 10; www.ebernat.com; 20 rue de la Citadelle; d €85-95; 📶) On the main street through the old town, this old pilgrim's hostel makes a pleasant overnight stay. There are four rooms squeezed between stone walls and rafters, each with a double and a single bed, although unsurprisingly they're on the small side. The owners run a little on-site restaurant in season (*menus* from €20).

Chez Arrambide GASTRONOMIC €€€

(☎05 59 37 01 01; www.hotel-les-pyrenees.com; 19 place Charles de Gaulle; menus €42-110, mains €34-52; ⊙12.15-1.45pm & 7.45-9pm Jul & Aug, Wed-Mon Sep-Jun) This two-Michelin-starred restaurant at the Hôtel des Pyrénées is renowned for miles around, and is where chef Firmin Arrambide works wonders with market produce. It's a high-class treat, where dishes are as arty as they are edible. Pricey rooms (€105 to €225) are available upstairs.

☆ Entertainment

Year-round, variants of *pelota* (admission €7 to €10), including a bare-handed *pelota* tournament, are played at the *trinquet, fronton* municipal and *jaï alaï* courts. In summer, these tend to take place at 5pm on a Friday.

In high summer, traditional Basque music and dancing takes place in the *jaï alaï* court or the church. Confirm schedules with the tourist office.

ℹ Information

Tourist Office (☎05 59 37 03 57; www.saint-jeanpieddeport-paysbasque-tourisme.com; place Charles de Gaulle; ⊙9am-7pm Mon-Sat, 10am-1pm & 2-7pm Sun Jul & Aug, 9am-noon & 2-6pm Mon-Sat Sep-Jun)

ℹ Getting There & Away

Train is the only option to travel to or from Bayonne (€8, 1¼ hours, four daily).

St-Étienne de Baïgorry

The village of St-Étienne de Baïgorry and its outlying hamlets straddle the Vallée de Baïgorry. Tranquillity itself after busy St-Jean Pied de Port, the pretty village is stretched thinly along a branch of the River Nive. Like so many Basque settlements, the village has two focal points: the church and the *fronton* (*pelota* court). It makes a good base for hikers, as a couple of spectacular walks start close by (although you'll still need a car to reach many of the trailheads). Tourist offices in St-Étienne de Baïgorry or St-Jean Pied de Port should be able to supply route suggestions. Even if you're not a hiker, you can't fail to be impressed by the area's beauty, so an overnight stay is recommended.

A couple of kilometres north of St-Étienne de Baïgorry in the hamlet of Urdos, rural **Hôtel-Restaurant Manechenea** (☎05 59 37 41 68; www.hotel-saint-etienne-de-baigorry.com; s €55-65, d €60-80) has butter-yellow rooms that overlook green fields and a bubbling mountain-fed brook. You can eat some of the denizens of said brook, such as delicious trout, for lunch at the in-house restaurant (two-/three-course *menu* €20/28).

Impressive **Hôtel-Restaurant Arcé** (☎05 59 37 40 14; www.hotel-arce.com; d €140-180, ste €170-290; ⊙closed Nov-mid-Apr; 📶🏊) has a stunning riverside location and spacious rooms with old-style furnishings. To reach the pool, you must stroll past the orange trees and cross the river via a little humpback bridge. The in-house restaurant (menus from €32; open for lunch Tuesday and Friday to Sunday, dinner daily) is highly regarded by locals, and the half-board deals offer good value (per person double €130, suite €150 to €190).

The Pyrenees

POP 480,000

Includes ➡

Best Places to Eat

- Le Viscos (p673)
- L'Héptaméron des Gourmets (p683)
- Le Poulet à Trois Pattes (p668)
- Les Papilles Insolites (p668)

Best Places to Sleep

- Le Castel de la Pique (p682)
- Hôtel des Rochers (p673)
- Auberge les Myrtilles (p685)
- L'Abbaye de Camon (p686)
- Le Balcon de l'Ossau (p679)

Why Go?

Spiking the skyline for 430km along the Franco-Spanish border, the snow-dusted Pyrenees offer a glimpse of France's wilder side. This serrated chain of peaks contains some of the country's most pristine landscapes and rarest wildlife, including endangered species such as the griffon vulture, izard (a type of mountain goat) and brown bear. Since 1967, 457 sq km has been protected as the Parc National des Pyrénées, ensuring its valleys, tarns and mountain pastures are preserved for future generations.

Rural and deeply traditional, the Pyrenees' wild landscapes now provide a paradise for skiers, climbers, hikers and bikers. But there's more to the mountains than just outdoor thrills: there are mountain villages to wander, hilltop castles to admire and ancient caves to investigate. They might not be on quite the same scale as the Alps, but the Pyrenees are every bit as stunning. Strap on your boots – it's time to explore.

When to Go

Pau

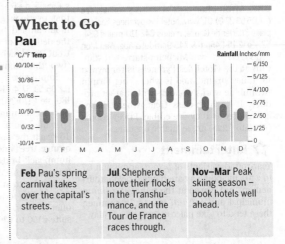

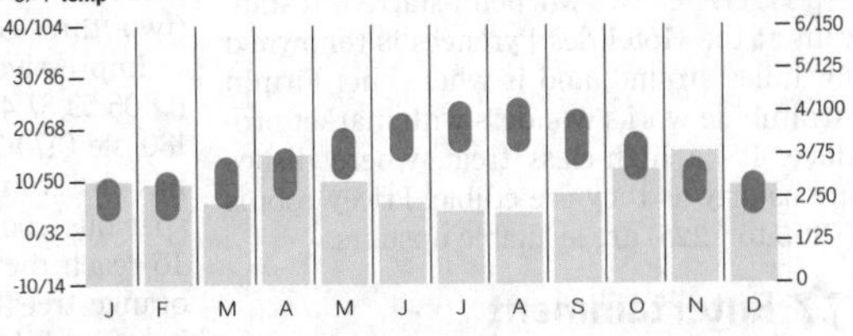

Feb Pau's spring carnival takes over the capital's streets.

Jul Shepherds move their flocks in the Transhumance, and the Tour de France races through.

Nov–Mar Peak skiing season – book hotels well ahead.

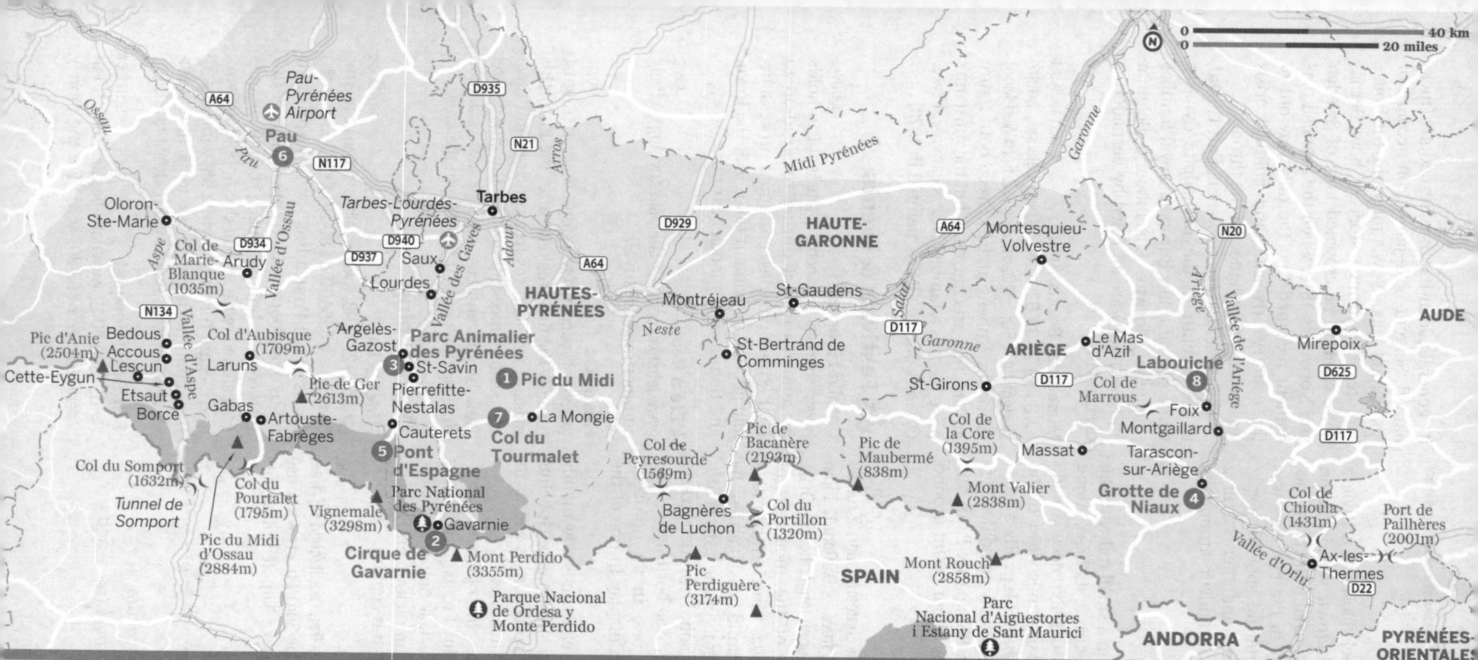

The Pyrenees Highlights

1 **Pic du Midi** (p681) Admiring the views from the sky-top observatory.

2 **Cirque de Gavarnie** (p676) Trekking to the mountain amphitheatre.

3 **Parc Animalier des Pyrénées** (p674) Seeing endangered Pyrenean wildlife.

4 **Grotte de Niaux** (p685) Marvelling at the prehistoric cave-paintings.

5 **Pont d'Espagne** (p679) Tackling the trails around Cauterets.

6 **Pau's old town** (p666) Exploring winding lanes and chocolate shops.

7 **Col du Tourmalet** (p681) Driving over the Pyrenees' highest road pass.

8 **Labouiche** (p684) Floating through the underworld on a subterranean river.

Pau

POP 78,000

In many ways, Pau feels closer to a Riviera resort than a mountain town, with its grand villas, public parks and palm-lined promenades. The largest city in the Pyrenees was once a favourite wintering spot for expat British and Americans, and there's still a touch of fin-de-siècle grandeur around its well-kept streets.

Sights

The town centre sits on a small hill with the Gave de Pau (River Pau) at its base. Along its crest stretches bd des Pyrénées, a wide promenade offering panoramic views of the mountains. A creaky **funicular railway** dating from 1908 clanks down from bd des Pyrénées to av Napoléon Bonaparte. Pau's tiny old centre extends for about 500m around the château.

Château de Pau CHÂTEAU

(05 59 82 38 00; www.chateau-pau.fr; 2 rue du Château; adult/child €7/free; 9.30am-12.15pm & 1.30-5.45pm, gardens open longer hours) Originally the residence of the monarchs of Navarre, Pau's castle was transformed into a Renaissance château amid lavish gardens by Marguerite d'Angoulême in the 16th century. Marguerite's grandson, Henri de Navarre (the future Henri IV), was born here – cradled, so the story goes, in an upturned tortoise shell (still on display in one of the museum's rooms).

Much restored, the château is now mainly worth visiting for its collections of Gobelins tapestries and Sèvres porcelain, as well as its fine Renaissance architecture.

Admission includes an obligatory one-hour guided tour in French (departing every 15 minutes; the last one commences at 5.45pm), but you can pick up an English-language guide sheet at reception.

Musée Bernadotte MUSEUM

(05 59 27 48 42; 8 rue Tran; adult/child €3/free; 10am-noon & 2-6pm Tue-Sun) This townhouse is the birthplace of one of Napoléon's favourite generals, Jean-Baptiste Bernadotte (nicknamed 'Sergent belle-jambe', on account of his shapely legs). Now a museum, the house explores the strange story of how Bernadotte came to be crowned king of Sweden and Norway in 1810, when the Swedish parliament reckoned that the only way out of the country's dynastic and political crisis was to stick a foreigner on the throne.

The present king of Sweden, Carl Gustaf, is the seventh in the Bernadotte dynasty, while several other European royal families (including Norway, Luxembourg, Belgium and Denmark) are all ruled by Bernadotte's descendants.

Musée des Beaux-Arts ART MUSEUM

(05 59 27 33 02; rue Mathieu Lalanne; adult/student €4/1.50; 10am-noon & 2-6pm Wed-Mon) Works by Rubens and El Greco both figure at Pau's fine-arts museum, but the museum's prize piece is a famous Degas canvas, *A New Orleans Cotton Office,* painted in 1873.

Festivals & Events

Carnival Biarnés CARNIVAL

(www.carnavalbiarnes.com; late Feb) Pau holds its annual carnival during the lead-up to Lent. Street parades, costumed processions and general merriment takes over the town, and there's even a mock bear hunt.

L'Été à Pau MUSIC

(www.leteapau.com; late Jul-early Aug) Lively summer music festival.

Hestiv'Òc MUSIC

(www.hestivoc.com) Over four days in August (usually the first weekend after the 15th), this massive fest features free concerts and theatre performances all around the city centre. Pau's biggest and best event is always a good time, so don't miss it if you're in the area.

Sleeping

Hôtel Bristol HOTEL €€

(05 59 27 72 98; www.hotelbristol-pau.com; 3 rue Gambetta; s €55-100, d €80-110, f €120-130; P) A classic old French hotel with surprisingly up-to-date rooms, all wrapped up in a fine 19th-century building. Each room is uniquely designed, with stylish decor, bold artwork and elegant furniture, while big windows fill the rooms with light. Ask for a mountain-view room with balcony. Breakfast is €12.

Brit Hôtel Bosquet HOTEL €€

(05 59 11 50 11; www.hotel-bosquet.com; 11 Rue Valéry Meunier; r €63-80;) For the money,

FAST FACTS

Area 9942 sq km

Local industry Agriculture

Signature dish *Garbure* (meat and vegetable hotpot)

Pau

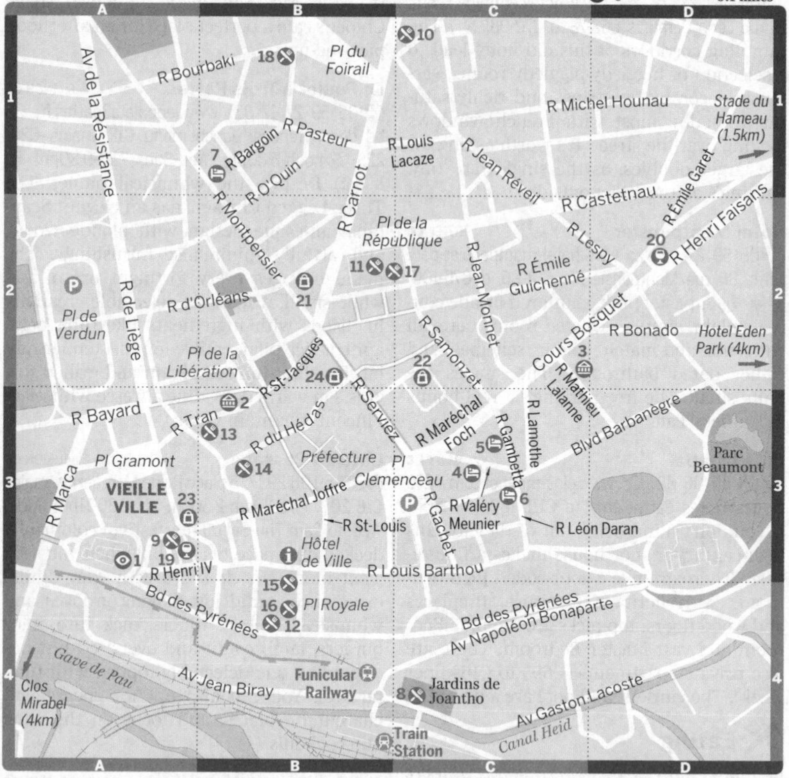

Pau

Sights

1 Château de Pau A3
2 Musée Bernadotte B3
3 Musée des Beaux-Arts C2

Sleeping

4 Brit Hôtel Bosquet C3
5 Hôtel Bristol C3
6 Hôtel Central C3
7 Hôtel Montpensier B1

Eating

8 Au Fin Gourmet C4
9 Café du Passage A3
10 Chez Chloée C1
11 Halles de Pau B2
12 La Brasserie Royale B4
13 La Fiancée du Desert B3
14 Le Lavoir B3
15 Le Majestic B4
16 Le Poulet à Trois Pattes B4
17 L'Emporte Pièce B2
18 Les Amants du Marché B1
Les Papilles Insolites .... (see 22)

Drinking & Nightlife

19 Au Grain de Raisin A3
20 Le Garage D2

Shopping

21 Au Parapluie des Pyrénées B2
22 BricOTruc C2
23 Francis Miot A3
24 Josuat B2

this is one of the best-value lodging options in the historic centre. Rooms are a mix of cheery yellow sponge-painting and exposed stone walls, along with oversized mirrors, touches of artwork and bright bathrooms (with blue and yellow ceramic tiles), though some rooms could use more natural light. Service is friendly.

Hôtel Central HOTEL €€
(☎05 59 27 72 75; www.hotelcentralpau.com; 15 rue Léon Daran; s €62-78, d €72-98;) The rambling corridors of this old hotel lead to a selection of higgledy-piggledy rooms, variously decorated in stripes and richly saturated shades, most with French windows looking over the street. It's worth asking for the larger doubles, as the singles are tiny. Parking's on the street outside.

Hôtel Montpensier HOTEL €€
(☎05 59 27 42 72; www.hotel-montpensier-pau.com; 36 rue Montpensier; s €61-85, d €75-100;) A pastel pink, shuttered façade conceals plain, simple carpeted rooms here, all with mix-and-match colour schemes and rather dated bathrooms. The singles are quite small. The free parking's a real bonus in trafficky Pau.

Clos Mirabel B&B €€€
(☎05 59 06 32 83; www.clos-mirabel.com; 276 av des Frères Barthélémy; d €110-160;) If you don't mind being out of the city, this 18th-century manor house makes a fine retreat. There are five colour-coded B&B bedrooms with heritage furniture, fireplaces and wood floors: top picks are the Blue Bedroom and vast Master Bedroom. There are also private apartments (€695 to €1695 per week). The gardens and pool are a bonus.

Eating

La Fiancée du Desert MIDDLE EASTERN €
(☎05 59 27 27 58; www.la-fiancee-du-desert.com; 21 rue Tran; mains around €9, menus €13-19; ⊙noon-2pm & 7-9.30pm Tue-Sat) Colourful tapestries, fairy lights and Moroccan lamps set the scene at this rustically chic spot that seems to be everyone's favourite eatery *du jour*. The small plates are best – order a platter with tabouli, hummus, babaganoush, felafel and many other Lebanese delicacies and taste everything. End with mint tea and heavenly baklava.

Halles de Pau MARKET €
(Covered Market; place de la République; ⊙6am-1pm Mon-Sat) The brutalist concrete-loving building is an eyesore, but culinary goodness lies within. Pau's main market is great for picnic supplies. You can also dine at good-value spots like **L'Emporte Pièce** (mains €9-12; ⊙6am-2pm).

Chez Chloée CAFE €
(☎05 59 27 71 83; 60 rue Carnot; cakes €3-6; ⊙9am-1pm & 3-7pm Tue-Sat, 8am-1pm Sun) Fine teas, gourmet coffees and deliciously naughty patisseries (all made in-house) make Chloée's cafe a perfect place for an afternoon pick-me-up.

Le Poulet à Trois Pattes FRENCH €€
(☎05 59 27 17 33; www.lepouleta3pattes.fr; 26 bd des Pyrénées; lunch menu €18, mains €20-22; ⊙noon-6.30pm Wed-Sun, 7.30-9.30pm Fri & Sat) Despite the whimsical name, 'The Three-Legged Chicken' has an elegant Scandinavian-esque design with blonde woods and artfully minimalist furnishings. The menu changes every fortnight or so, and while small, it features delectable creativity in dishes with ingredients like tuna belly, apricot rice pilaf, endive fondue, tender rabbit, hazelnut-infused cream and grilled foie gras. On warm days, dine alfresco with magnificent mountain views.

Café du Passage FUSION €€
(☎05 59 06 29 17; 5 place Reine Marguerite; mains €16-20; ⊙9.30am-2.30pm & 6.30-11pm Mon-Wed, to 2am Thu-Sat) This festive, colourfully decked-out space fits the bill when you seek a bit more *joie de vivre* with your dining experience. Amid low-playing grooves and whimsical murals, diners tuck into juicy burgers, lamb confit and oversized tartines (including one delectably topped with tuna tartare). You can also opt for cheese and charcuterie plates, and focus on the wine and cocktails.

Les Amants du Marché VEGETARIAN €€
(☎05 59 02 75 51; www.lesamantsdumarche.fr; 1 rue Bourbaki; menu €15-26, mains around €13; ⊙noon-2pm & 7.30-10pm Tue-Sat) Vegetarians have much to celebrate at this delightful little eatery across from the organic market. The chalkboard menu changes regularly and showcases ingredients often overlooked in traditional French cooking. You'll find deliciously creative dishes along the lines of broccoli and split-pea terrine; bok choy with chickpeas, cumin and peanut sauce; and arancini with squash, feta, sun-dried tomatoes and fennel.

Les Papilles Insolites BISTRO €€
(☎05 59 71 43 79; www.lespapillesinsolites.blogspot.co.uk; 5 rue Alexander Taylor; lunch/dinner menu €22/45, mains around €23; ⊙12.15-2pm & 8-9.30pm Wed-Sat) Run by a former Parisian sommelier, this cosy bar-bistro pitches itself between a bistro and a wine shop. It serves beautifully prepared, ingredient-rich dishes like Galician-style octopus with potatoes, fennel and olive tapenade, or beef with

leeks, tempura and lemongrass-raspberry reduction. Complete the experience with the owner's choice of one of the 350-odd wines stacked around the shop. Gorgeously Gallic.

Le Lavoir BRASSERIE €€
(☎05 59 83 32 62; 3 rue du Hédas; mains €16-17; ⏲7-10.30pm Mon-Sat) Lost among the alleys of the old town, this small brasserie run by chef Brice Gabenisch is known for its simple, classically presented French cuisine. The stone-walled dining room is intimate, with blackboards and old wooden tables, and Brice often pops his head out of the kitchen to check his clients are happy.

La Brasserie Royale BRASSERIE €€
(☎05 59 27 72 12; www.brasserie-royale.com; 5 place Royale; menus €24-29, mains €17-21; ⏲noon-2pm daily & 7.30-10pm Mon-Sat) This busy brasserie on place Royale is ideal for an early-evening beer and a quick *steak-frites* (steak and chips), *magret de canard* (duck breast) or the hearty Pyrenean soup of *garbure*.

Le Majestic TRADITIONAL FRENCH €€€
(☎05 59 27 56 83; 9 place Royale; menus lunch €16-25, dinner €27-42; ⏲noon-1.30pm & 7.30-9pm Tue-Sat, noon-1.30pm Sun) This smart restaurant serves top-notch French cuisine. It's formal inside – ice-white tablecloths, razor-sharp napkins, twisted willow – but it suits the sophisticated food, heavy on premium ingredients such as turbot, sea bass, Bigorre pork and Pyrenean lamb. If the sun's out, sit at a table beneath the trees on leafy place Royale.

Au Fin Gourmet GASTRONOMIC €€€
(☎05 59 27 47 71; www.restaurant-aufingourmet.com; 24 av Gaston Lacoste; standard menus €28-39, tasting menus €62-76; ⏲noon-1.30pm Wed-Sun, 7.30-9.30pm Tue-Sat) For old-school fine French dining, this *restaurant gastronomique* is Pau's premier address. It's run by the Ithurriague brothers, Patrick and Laurent, known for their Michelin-style food and fondness for sauces, creams, foams and garnishes. It's in the Jardins de Joantho, near the funicular.

Drinking & Nightlife

Pau's bars generally open from 10am to 2am. 'Le Triangle', bounded by rue Henri Faisans, rue Émile Garet and rue Castetnau, is the centre of student nightlife, and a string of bars extends along bd des Pyrénées.

Le Garage BAR
(www.le-garage-bar.fr; 49 rue Émile Garet; ⏲noon-2am Mon-Fri, from 3pm Sat & Sun) Le Garage plays heavily on the filling-station theme, with road signs, rockabilly tunes and dangling motorbikes overhead (choose your table carefully). It draws a young and lively crowd, and there's often live music on weekends – and sports shown on multiple screens at other times.

Au Grain de Raisin WINE BAR
(11 rue Sully; ⏲5pm-1am Wed-Sun) A welcoming wine bar near the château, which serves a good selection of continental beers and local wines by the glass, accompanied by plates of tapas.

Shopping

Pau is famous for its *chocolatiers* (chocolate shops): the top names are **Josuat** (23 rue Serviez; ⏲9.30am-12.15pm & 2.30-7.15pm Mon-Sat) and **Francis Miot** (48 rue Maréchal Joffre; ⏲10am-7pm Mon-Sat).

BricOTruc VINTAGE
(5 rue Taylor) After browsing the boutiques of nearby rue Serviez, stop by BricOTruc, which has a delightful assortment of recycled jewellery, picture frames, toys, artwork, vases and other assorted bric-a-brac, all handsomely displayed.

Au Parapluie des Pyrénées FASHION & ACCESSORIES
(12 rue Montpensier; ⏲8am-noon & 2-7pm Tue-Sat) This lovely old shop makes beech-handled, rattan-ribbed umbrellas traditionally used by Pyrenean shepherds. Also specialises in the anachronistic art of umbrella repair.

Information

Tourist Office (☎05 59 27 27 08; www.pau-pyrenees.com; place Royale; ⏲9am-6pm Mon-Sat, 9.30am-1pm Sun) Stocked with useful information on local transport and the Pyrenees generally.

Getting There & Away

AIR

Aéroport Pau-Pyrénées (☎05 59 33 33 00; www.pau.aeroport.fr) The airport is 7km northwest of town. There are currently six daily flights to Paris Orly, three daily to Paris Charles de Gaulle and Lyon, and nine per week to Marseille.

BUS

Bus services are very limited, although there are at least a couple of daily services to Agen and Mont de Marsan. Contact **Cars Région Aquitaine** (☎0 800 64 40 47; www.car.aquitaine.fr) for timetables.

TRAIN

Trains are the quickest way to get to Pau. There are currently four TGVs daily from Paris; note that travel times will shorten (to 4½ hours) by late 2017. In summer, SNCF buses run from Oloron-Ste-Marie into the Vallée d'Aspe.

Bayonne €19 to €24, 1½ hours

Oloron-Ste-Marie €8, 40 minutes

Paris Montparnasse €80 to €110, 5½ hours via direct TGV

Toulouse €35, two to 2½ hours

Getting Around

TO/FROM THE AIRPORT

Idelis (05 59 14 15 16; www.reseau-idelis.com) runs a shuttle to Pau's train station and town centre. From the airport, buses run roughly hourly from 7.40am to 7.40pm; from the train station, buses run from 6.30am to 7.50pm. Tickets cost €1, and the journey time is half an hour. Note that buses don't run on Sunday, so you'll need to reserve a taxi at the airport **information desk** (05 59 33 33 00); expect to pay between €32 and €38.

CAR & MOTORCYCLE

Most streets in central Pau are *payant* (metered), but there's free parking on place de Verdun and the street leading west of there (av du 18 Régiment d'Infanterie). Major car-rental firms have kiosks at the airport.

PUBLIC TRANSPORT

Public transport in Pau is handled by Idelis. Single/day tickets cost €1/2.80. Pau's bike-sharing network, **IDEcycle** (www.idecycle.com; per day/week €1/5) is handy for zipping around town.

Lourdes

POP 15,800 / ELEV 400M

The sprawling town of Lourdes, 43km southeast of Pau, has been one of the world's most important pilgrimage sites since 1858, when 14-year-old Bernadette Soubirous (1844–79) is believed to have been visited 18 times in a rocky grotto by the Virgin Mary. The visions were subsequently acknowledged by the Vatican, and Bernadette was beatified in 1933.

Now known as the Sanctuaires Notre Dame de Lourdes, the grotto is considered one of the holiest sites in Christendom. Over six million people arrive in Lourdes every year hoping to be healed by the holy waters, but the modern town of Lourdes itself can feel rather dispiriting, with a tatty tangle of neon-signed hotels and souvenir shops selling everything from plastic crucifixes to Madonna-shaped bottles.

Outside the theme-park-like atmosphere of the town, you'll find some intriguing sites, including a hilltop castle and various humble abodes where Soubirous resided – which more than anything illustrate the many hardships the lower classes endured in the late 19th century.

Sights & Activities

★Sanctuaires Notre Dame de Lourdes CAVE

(www.fr.lourdes-france.org; Porte St-Michel & Porte St-Joseph 5am-midnight, grotte 24hr, baths 8.30am-12.30pm & 1.30-6pm Mon-Sat, 10am-noon & 2-4pm Sun, shorter hours Nov-Mar) The spiritual centre of Lourdes is the subterranean grotto where Bernadette Soubirous experienced her visions in 1858. From the **Porte St-Michel**, a broad boulevard sweeps towards the gilded spires of the **Basilique du Rosaire** and the **Basilique Supérieure** (Upper Basilica). Underneath is the fabled **Grotte de Massabielle**, where people queue for hours to enter and take a blessed dip in the cave's icy-cold baths, while other pilgrims content themselves by lighting candles of remembrance outside.

From Palm Sunday to mid-October, nightly torchlight processions start from the Massabielle Grotto at 9pm, while at 5pm there's the Procession Eucharistique (Blessed Sacrament Procession) along the Esplanade des Processions.

Château Fort MUSEUM

(www.chateaufort-lourdes.fr; adult/child €7/3.50; 10am-7pm mid-Apr–mid-Oct, to 6pm mid-Oct–mid-Apr) Lourdes' imposing castle stands on a sheer hill just behind the town. There's been a stronghold here since Roman times, but the present building combines a medieval keep with fortifications added during the 17th and 18th centuries. Since the 1920s, the castle has housed the **Musée Pyrénéen**, which displays local artefacts and folk art.

A free **lift** (Rue Baron Duprat) takes you up to the castle.

Pic du Jer VIEWPOINT

(05 62 94 00 41; www.picdujer.fr; bd d'Espagne; funicular return adult/child €11/9; 9.30am-6pm late Mar–mid-Nov, to 7pm Jul & Aug) Panoramic views of Lourdes and the central Pyrenees are on offer from this rocky outcrop just outside town. There are two routes to the top: a punishing three-hour hike (ideal for

penitents) or a speedy six-minute ride on the funicular (ideal for everyone else).

There's a choice of routes back down: a black-run mountain-bike trail, or a more family-friendly option along the **Voie Verte des Gaves**, a decommissioned railway that finishes up at the lower funicular station.

To get to the lower funicular, take bus 2 from place Monseigneur Laurence.

Musée de Lourdes MUSEUM
(05 62 94 28 00; www.musee-lourdes.fr; 11 rue de l'Égalité; adult/child €6.50/3.50; 10am-noon & 2-6pm Mar-Oct;) The kitsch factor is high at this whimsical museum near the cemetery. On a 40-minute self-guided audio tour (during which you'll receive a small portable boombox rather than headphones), you'll get an overview of Lourdes' life c 1858, with life-size mannequins and their recreated work and living environments telling about the toil of the baker, the blacksmith, the miller, and so on. Kids will undoubtedly get a kick out of it.

Moulin de Boly MUSEUM
(Boly Mill; 12 rue Bernadette Soubirous; 9am-noon & 2-6.30pm late Mar-Oct, 3-5pm Nov-late Mar) FREE Bernadette was born in this millhouse on 7 January 1844, one year after the marriage of her parents Louise Castérot and François Soubirous. She lived here for the first 10 years of her life; it's still possible to see her childhood bedroom, along with the house's mill machinery.

Le Cachot HISTORIC SITE
(15 rue des Petits Fossés; 9am-noon & 2-6.30pm Apr-Oct, shorter hours rest of year) FREE In 1857 Bernadette Soubirous' family fell on hard times and were forced to move to this dingy prison, where they lived communally in a room measuring just 16 sq metres. It was while living here that Bernadette stumbled across the Grotte de Massabielle, having been sent out to collect firewood.

Grottes de Bétharram CAVE
(05 62 41 80 04; www.betharram.com; Chemin Léon Ross, St-Pé-de-Bigorre; adult/child €14/9; 9am-noon & 1.30-5.30pm late Mar-Oct) Along the D937, 14km west of Lourdes, a network of subterranean caverns have been carved out from the limestone, glittering with impressive formations of stalactites and stalagmites. Visits to the cave aboard a combination of minitrain and barge last around 1½ hours, but be warned: the site gets extremely busy in high summer.

Chemin de Croix WALKING
(Way of the Cross; 6am-10pm) The Chemin de Croix (sometimes known as the Chemin du Calvaire) leads for 1.5km up the hillside from the Basilique Supérieure past 14 life-size bronze-painted figures representing Stations of the Cross. Seriously devout pilgrims climb to the first station on their knees.

Festivals & Events

Festival International de Musique Sacrée MUSIC
(www.festivaldelourdes.fr) Lourdes' renowned week of sacred music is held around Easter.

Sleeping

Lourdes has an enormous number of hotels (second only to Paris in terms of bed space, believe it or not), but most of them are chronically overpriced and generally of a disappointing standard. You'll be better off basing yourself outside town.

Lourdes

Hôtel Saint-Avit HOTEL €
(05 62 94 06 35; hotel-saint-avit.com; 32 rue de l'Egalité; r €35-55;) In a peaceful part of town (overlooking a cemetery), this good-value, family-run guesthouse has bright, simply furnished rooms, the best of which have views over the rolling hills beyond town. There's also a restaurant with a pleasant terrace.

Hôtel Majestic HOTEL €€
(05 62 94 27 23; www.hotel-lourdes-majestic.com; 9 ave Maransin; d/tr/q from €50/60/70) Although it's on a busy avenue, the friendly Hôtel Majestic is worth considering for its bright, attractive rooms, with polished wood floors and big windows that let in ample light (but little street noise). It's also quite central, and an easy 300m (downhill) walk from the train station.

Around Lourdes

Eth Béryè Petit B&B €€
(05 62 97 90 02; www.beryepetit.com; 15 rte de Vielle; s/d from €70/75; P) Twelve kilometres south of Lourdes, off the N21 near Beaucens, this 17th-century farmhouse offers country charm and knockout mountain views. There are three rooms: the most spacious is Era Galeria, which has French windows onto a private balcony, while Poeyaspé and Bédoret are tucked into the beamed attic. Rates are cheaper for subsequent nights. Cash only.

Lourdes

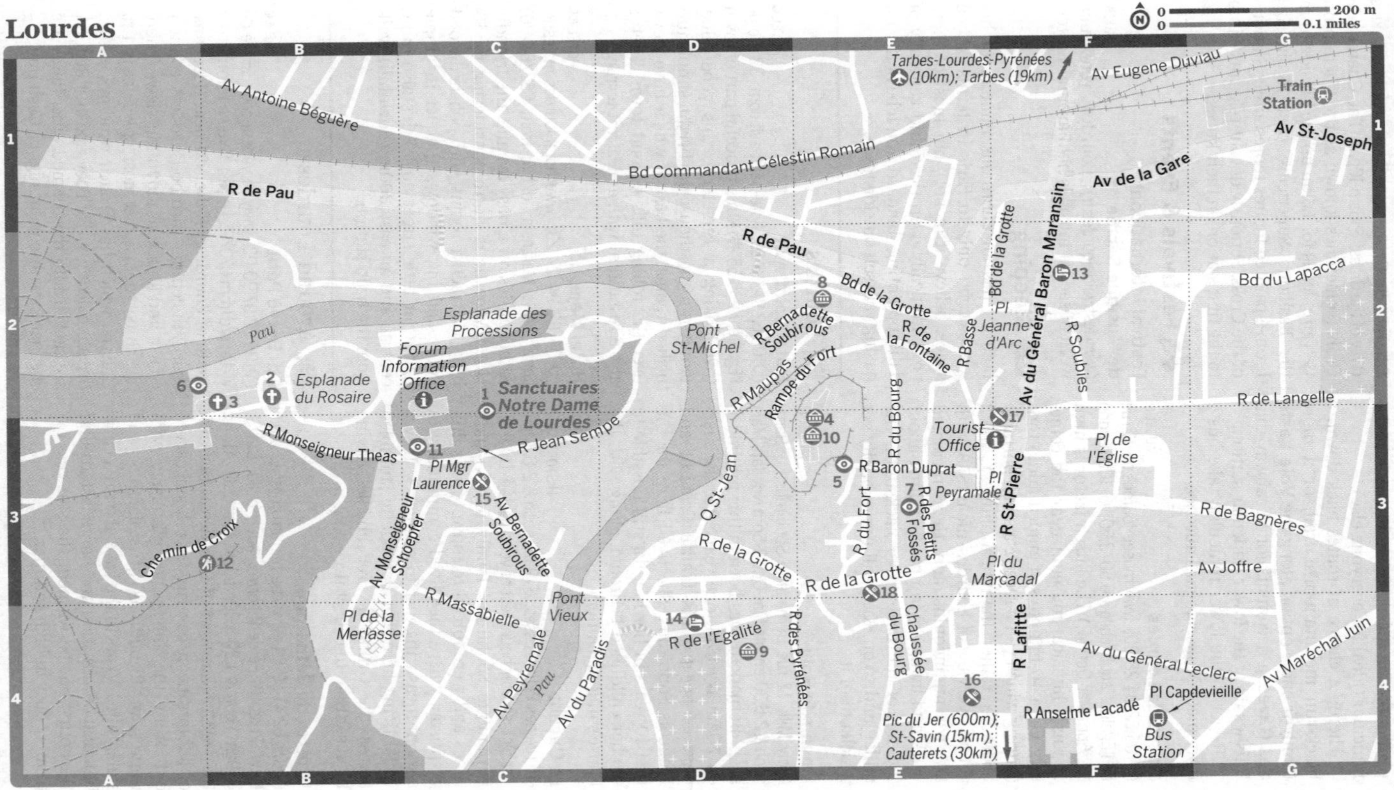
0 200 m
0 0.1 miles
A
B
C
D
E
F
G
1
2
3
4
Tarbes-Lourdes-Pyrénées (10km); Tarbes (19km)
Av Eugene Duviau
Train Station
Av St-Joseph
Av Antoine Béguère
Bd Commandant Célestin Romain
R de Pau
Av de la Gare
R de Pau
Bd de la Grotte
Av du Général Baron Maransin
13
Bd du Lapacca
8
Bd de la Grotte
Pl Jeanne d'Arc
R Basse
R Soubies
R de la Fontaine
Esplanade des Processions
Pau
Pont St-Michel
R Bernadette Soubirous
Forum
Information Office
Rampe du Fort
R Maupas
6
2
3
Esplanade du Rosaire
1
Sanctuaires Notre Dame de Lourdes
4
10
R du Bourg
17
R de Langelle
Tourist Office
R Monseigneur Theas
11
R Jean Sempe
Pl Mgr Laurence
15
R Baron Duprat
5
Pl de l'Église
7
Pl Peyramale
R des Petits Fossés
R St-Pierre
Q St-Jean
R du Fort
R de Bagnères
Av Bernadette Soubirous
Av Monseigneur Schoepfer
Chemin de Croix
12
R de la Grotte
R de la Grotte
Pl du Marcadal
Av Joffre
R Massabielle
Pont Vieux
18
14
R de l'Egalité
R des Pyrénées
Chaussée du Bourg
R Lafitte
Pl de la Merlasse
9
Av du Général Leclerc
Av Maréchal Juin
Av Peyremale
Pau
Av du Paradis
16
Pl Capdevieille
R Anselme Lacadé
Pic du Jer (600m); St-Savin (15km); Cauterets (30km)
Bus Station

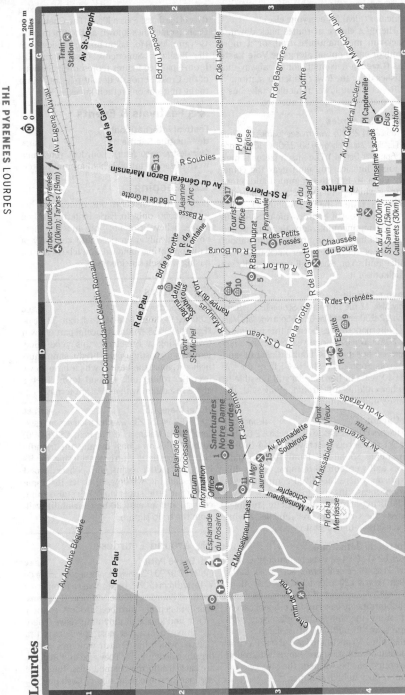

Lourdes

Top Sights

1 Sanctuaires Notre Dame de Lourdes ... C2

Sights

2 Basilique du Rosaire ... B2
3 Basilique Supérieure ... B2
4 Château Fort ... E3
5 Château Fort Elevator ... E3
6 Grotte de Massabielle ... A2
7 Le Cachot ... E3
8 Moulin de Boly ... E2
9 Musée de Lourdes ... D4
10 Musée Pyrénéen ... E3
11 Porte St-Michel ... C3

Activities, Courses & Tours

12 Chemin de Croix ... B3

Sleeping

13 Hôtel Majestic ... F2
14 Hôtel Saint-Avit ... D4

Eating

15 Le Majorelle ... C3
16 Les Halles de Lourdes ... E4
17 Lung Ta ... F3
18 O Piment Rouge ... E3

Hôtel des Rochers HOTEL €€
(05 62 97 09 52; www.lesrochershotel.com; 1 place du Castillou; d €60-68, tr €95-100; P) In the idyllic village of St-Savin, 16km south of Lourdes, this handsomely landscaped hotel makes a perfect mountain retreat. It's run by an expat English couple, John and Jane, who have renovated the rooms in clean, contemporary fashion – insist on one with a mountain view. Half-board is available.

Relais de Saux B&B €€
(05 62 94 29 61; www.lourdes-relais.com; d €80-96; P) Ruched curtains, antique wardrobes and canopy beds abound at this ivy-covered mansion, about a mile north of Lourdes. The period house is beautiful, but it's the surroundings that sell the place: grassy lawns and tree-filled gardens set against snowy Pyrenean peaks.

Eating

Les Halles de Lourdes MARKET €
(place du Champ Commun; 6.30am-1pm daily in summer, closed Sun in winter) Lourdes' covered market occupies most of the square.

Lung Ta TIBETAN €
(05 62 92 80 45; www.restaurantlungta.fr; 8 rue des Quatre Frères Soulas; mains €7-10; noon-2.30pm & 7-9pm Wed-Mon;) This cosy and warmly lit Tibetan eatery is a surprising find in Lourdes. Amid rice-paper lamps, Tibetan prayer flags and a small Buddha shrine, diners tuck into the fragrant dishes from the mountain kingdom. Rich soups like Tsel Thuk (with vegetables and housemade noodles) are quite good. Good vegetarian choices.

O Piment Rouge BASQUE €€
(05 62 41 47 87; 37 rue de la Grotte; mains €16-21; noon-2pm Thu-Tue, 7-10pm Thu-Mon) Dining out can be decidedly hit-and-miss in Lourdes, which makes this delightful eatery a doubly good find. It serves up delicacies from the Basque Country, including squid cooked in ink, tender stewed lamb and a decadent custard sponge cake.

★ **Le Viscos** GASTRONOMIC €€€
(05 62 97 02 28; www.hotel-leviscos.com; 1 rue Lamarque, St-Savin; menus €49-75; 12.30-2.30pm Tue-Sun, 7.30-9.30pm daily; P) Ex-TV chef Jean-Pierre St-Martin has established his own gastronomic hideaway in St-Savin, 16km south of Lourdes. Known for blending Basque, Breton and Pyrenean cuisine, as well as his unshakable passion for foie gras, he's now assisted by his son Alexis. Expect very rich, very traditional fine-dining food. If you over-indulge, there are country-styled rooms upstairs (€99 to €123, with full board €67 extra per person).

Le Majorelle FRENCH €€€
(05 62 94 12 32; www.grandhotelmoderne.com; 21 av Bernadette Soubirous; menus €24-60; noon-2pm & 7.30-9.30pm) The restaurant at the Grand-Moderne hotel makes quite a first impression, with its art nouveau architecture, wood-panelled walls and sparkling chandeliers. It's a sight straight out of a Fitzgerald novel, and the food is fittingly classic, focusing on rich French and Italian cuisine. Dress smartly and enjoy a bit of luxury *a l'ancienne*.

Information

Forum Information Office (05 62 42 20 08; www.lourdes-france.com; Esplanade des Processions; 9am-noon & 1.30-5.30pm) For information on the Sanctuaires Notre Dame de Lourdes.

Tourist Office (05 62 42 77 40; www.lourdes-infotourisme.com; place Peyramale; 9am-6.30pm) Lourdes' main tourist office has general information on the Pyrenees and advice on accommodation, transport and activities.

WORTH A TRIP

NATURE WATCH

Thirteen kilometres south of Lourdes, off the D821 near Argelès-Gazost, fantastic animal park **Parc Animalier des Pyrénées** (☎05 62 97 91 07; www.parc-animalier-pyrenees.com; adult/child €18/13; ⏲9.30am-6pm or 7pm Apr-Oct) is home to many species which were once commonly sighted across the Pyrenees. The animals live on special 'islands' designed to mirror their natural habitat: marmots, chamoix and ibex inhabit rocky hills; beavers and giant otters dart along wooded waterways; and brown bears lord it over their own boulder-strewn mountain kingdom.

There are also flying displays by birds of prey and the park's resident vultures. You can even spend the night in a trapper's cabin (double €300), with windows looking into the wolves' enclosure or sleep in Le Refuge, a dome-shaped cabin with a floor-to-ceiling window overlooking the bears' habitat (double €350).

The park is doubly important given that many of the species here have either disappeared in the wild or are teetering on the brink of extinction – most notably the brown bear (known in the US as the grizzly), which has all but vanished in the Pyrenees as a result of hunting and habitat loss. Despite fierce opposition from local farmers, a reintroduction program using wild bears from Slovenia has attempted to re-establish a breeding population, and it's thought that there are now around 30 bears roaming wild across the mountains – including a 26-year-old alpha male called Pyros.

Getting There & Away

AIR

Tarbes-Lourdes-Pyrénées Airport (www.tlp.aeroport.fr) is 10km north of Lourdes on the N21. There are three daily flights to Paris Orly (Air France), plus three weekly flights to London Stansted and two to Milan (both Ryanair), and several a week to Brussels (Brussels Airlines and Jetairfly), Rome and Milan (AlbaStar).

BUS

The small **bus station** (place Capdevieille) has services northwards to Pau (though trains are much faster and the recommended way to go). Buses running between Tarbes and Argelès-Gazost (at least eight daily), the gateway to the Pyrenean communities of Cauterets, Luz-St-Sauveur and Gavarnie, also stop here.

SNCF buses to Cauterets (€8.20, 55 minutes, at least five daily) leave from the train station.

CAR & MOTORCYCLE

Lourdes has a befuddling one-way system, so leave your car on the outskirts; there's free parking near the train and bus stations.

TRAIN

Lourdes has regular train connections, including direct TGVs to Pau and Paris Montparnasse. Trains to Toulouse often connect through Tarbes.

Bayonne €25 to €35, two hours via Pau

Paris Montparnasse €80 to €133, four hours via TGV

Pau €8.30, 25 minutes

Toulouse €30, 2¼ hours

Parc National des Pyrénées

Sprawling for 100km across the Franco-Spanish border, the Parc National des Pyrénées conceals some of the last pockets of true wilderness left in France. In partnership with the 156-sq-km Parque Nacional de Ordesa y Monte Perdido, on the Spanish side of the border, this mountain landscape is a haven for rare flora and fauna, and remains fiercely proud of its culture and heritage: traditional hill-farming and shepherding are still practised here in much the same way as they were a century ago.

Within the park's boundaries are the highest peaks in southwest France, including the loftiest of all, Vignemale (3298m).

Activities

Walking

Three hundred and fifty kilometres of waymarked trails (including the Mediterranean-to-Atlantic GR10) criss-cross the park. Within the park are about 20 *refuges* (mountain huts), primarily run by the Club Alpin Français (CAF). Most are staffed only from July to September but maintain a small crew year-round.

Each of the six park valleys (Vallée d'Aure, Vallée de Luz, Vallée de Cauterets, Val d'Azun, Vallée d'Ossau and Vallée d'Aspe) has a national park folder or booklet in French, *Randonnées dans le Parc National des Pyrénées,* describing 10 to 15 walks.

White-Water Sports

The Gave d'Aspe, Gave d'Oloron and Gave d'Ossau offer excellent white-water rafting. There are several companies based around Oloron-Ste-Marie, including Gaïa Aventure (p677) and **Centre Nautique de Soeix** (05 59 39 61 00; http://soeix.free.fr; quartier Soeix), which both offer canoeing, kayaking and rafting trips. Prices start at between €25 and €35 for a two-hour session.

Mountain Biking

Once the last snows melt around mid-April to May, many of the Pyrenean ski stations open up their trails to VTTs (*vélos tout-terrains;* mountain bikes).

Val d'Azun, Bagnères du Bigorre, Barrousse, Barèges, Ax and several other places all have extensive areas of *sentiers balisés* (marked trails). **Pyrénées Passion** (www.pyrenees-passion.info/VTT.php) lists the main VTT areas on its website.

There's also a large mountain-bike park near Aude, offering over 900km of trails. Visit **Espace VTT-FFC Aude en Pyrénées** (www.vtt-pyrenees.com/espace-vtt) for directions, trail maps and other details.

Bikes are widely available, and specialist companies such as **La Rébenne** (05 61 65 20 93; www.larebenne.com; chemin de Malet, Foix) offer guided mountain-biking expeditions.

Skiing

While the Pyrenees' best skiing is across the border at the Spanish resorts (around Baqueira-Beret and Andorra), the French-side resorts still offer good skiing, snowboarding, *ski nordique* (cross-country skiing) and *raquette à neige* (snowshoeing).

Cauterets SKIING
(www.cauterets.com) The best known of the French resorts, with well-groomed runs and a slightly longer snow season than other areas. It's also renowned for its summer hiking.

Val d'Azun SKIING
(www.valdazun.com) The best cross-country skiing in the Pyrenees, 30km southwest of Lourdes.

Barèges La Mongie SKIING
(www.n-py.com) Grand Tourmalet Barèges La Mongie is the largest resort in the Pyrenees, with runs tracing their way around Col du Tourmalet and the Pic du Midi.

Ax Trois Domaines SKIING
(www.ax-ski.com) Above Ax-les-Thermes, gentle runs snake through pine forest and, higher up, the open spaces of Campels. In summer its trails offer excellent hiking and cycling.

Information

For general information, the **PNR Pyrenees** (www.parc-pyrenees.com) website, the park's official tourist site, is the place to start. It has comprehensive information on activities, accommodation and sights.

There are also small park visitor centres in Etsaut, Laruns, Arrens-Marsous, Cauterets, Luz-St-Sauveur, Gavarnie and St-Lary-Soulan.

Vallée d'Aspe

The westernmost of the main Pyrenean valleys, the Vallée d'Aspe has been an important thoroughfare since Julius Caesar's Roman legionnaires marched this way. Later, during medieval times, the valley became one of the main routes for pilgrims on the Chemin de St-Jacques, seeking a way across the mountains en route to Santiago de Compostela.

Fewer than 3000 people now live in the valley's 13 villages, and its upper reaches are still among the most remote corners of the French Pyrenees. But for many the valley's seclusion is a thing of the past thanks to the controversial Tunnel de Somport, an 8km-long road tunnel across the Spanish border, which opened in 2003.

The small town of Oloron-Ste-Marie stands at the valley's northern end. From here, the N193 runs south, roughly following the course of the River Aspe for about 50km to the border, passing through the villages of Sarrance, Bedous, Accous, Cette-Eygun and Etsaut en route.

Sights

Écomusée de la Vallée d'Aspe MUSEUM
(http://ecomusee.vallee-aspe.com) FREE Four sites around the valley, collectively known as the Écomusée de la Vallée d'Aspe, explore the area's heritage and agricultural traditions. Opening hours vary by the season. See the website for details. There are small folk museums in the villages of Sarrance, Lourdios-Ichère and Borcé, but the most interesting site is Les Fermiers Basco-Béarnais.

Les Fermiers Basco-Béarnais FARM SHOP
(05 59 34 76 06; rue Gambetta, Accous; 9am-noon Mon, 9am-1pm & 3-7pm Tue-Fri, 10am-12.45pm & 3-7pm Sat) At this farmers' co-op and *fromagerie* (cheese shop), you can sample cheese made from the milk of local ewes, goats and cows.

WORTH A TRIP

CIRQUE DE GAVARNIE

Fifty-two kilometres south of Lourdes on the D921 you'll find three of the most breathtaking vistas in the Pyrenees: a trio of natural mountain amphitheatres, carved out by ancient glaciers and framed by sawtoothed, snow-dusted peaks – many of which top out at over 3000m.

The easiest of the three amphitheatres to reach – and consequently the most popular – is the **Cirque de Gavarnie**, with a panorama of spiky mountains that provides one of the Pyrenees' most famous vistas. It's especially dramatic after heavy rain, when waterfalls cascade down the mountainsides. The Cirque is about 1½ hours' walk from Gavarnie village; wear proper shoes, as the trail can be slippery and rocky. Between Easter and October you can clip-clop along on a horse or donkey (around €25 for a round-trip).

A second spectacular amphitheatre, the **Cirque de Troumouse**, can be reached via the minor D922 and a hair-raising 8km toll road near Gèdre, 6.5km northeast of Gavarnie. The toll-road itself is steep and quite exposed, with hairpin turns and no barriers, so take it slow. Snows permitting, it's usually open between April and October; the toll is €4 per vehicle.

Hidden among the mountains between Troumouse and Gavarnie is the third amphitheatre, **Cirque d'Estaubé**. It's much wilder and more remote, and only accessible on foot. The trail starts from the turn-off to the barrage des Gloriettes, which you pass on the D922 en route to Troumouse. It's about a 3½-hour return walk; pack proper boots, water and snacks.

Activities

Hiking

For most people, the main reason to visit the Vallée d'Aspe is the chance to tramp the trails. Route suggestions and planning tools are available from the useful **Caminaspe** (www.caminaspe.com) website.

The GR10 long-distance trail (part of the iconic Chemin St-Jacques) winds through the valley via the high-altitude village of Lescun, 5.5km from Bedous, which offers westerly views of the stunning **Cirque de Lescun** and the 2504m **Pic d'Anie**. Another popular route follows the GR10 south from Borce or Etsaut to **Fort du Portalet**, a 19th-century fortress used as a WWII prison.

The Bedous tourist office sells maps and the locally produced guidebook, *Le Topo des 45 Randonnées en Vallée d'Aspe*.

Mountain Biking

Rando Bike MOUNTAIN BIKING
(☎05 59 34 79 11; www.rando-bike.fr; adult/child half-day €23/18, full day €30/23) On Bedous' main street, this experienced firm rents out bikes and also runs its own half- and full-day *randonées VTT* (mountain-bike trips). If you're here in winter, they'll also teach you how to snowshoe.

Horse Riding & Donkey Trekking

In the days before road and rail, the only way to transport goods over the mountains was using mule-power, and donkey trekking is still a great way to experience the mountains.

Randonnés à Cheval
Auberge Cavalière HORSE RIDING
(☎05 59 34 72 30; www.auberge-cavaliere.com; Accous; 4-/7-day trip €690/1150) The main centre for horse trips in the valley, run by experienced horse-wranglers Eric and Michel Bonnemazou from their family farm near Accous. It offers five or six guided expeditions throughout the summer, including a four- or seven-day tour of the national park, and a seven-day tour of Languedoc's Cathar castles. There's a special expedition during the spring and autumn transhumance.

Le Parc Aux Ânes DONKEY TREKKING
(☎05 59 34 88 98; www.garbure.net/ane_rando.htm; 4-day trip incl meals adult/child €245/175, plus €131 per donkey) Run by the owners of La Garbure *gîte*, this donkey-trekking outfit offers a range of guided trips, staying at remote mountain *gîtes* (self-catering cottages) – or, if you wish, wild camping. It's a fabulous experience, far removed from the modern world of wi-fi and mobile phones – and best of all, thanks to your new donkey pal, you don't even have to carry your baggage.

Paragliding

There are several paragliding schools in Accous, which offer tandem *baptême* (introductory) rides with an instructor from €70.

White-Water Sports

Gaïa Aventure WATER SPORTS

(☎06 18 58 08 69; www.gaiaaventure.com; Oloron-Ste-Marie) This outfit leads white-water rafting trips on the rivers around Oloron-Ste-Marie. Prices start at between €25 and €35 for a two-hour session.

Festivals & Events

The valley holds three annual markets in celebration of its local produce: an Easter market in Bedous, a summer market in Aydius on the first Sunday of August, and an autumn food fair in Sarrance.

Other events to look out for are **Le Transhumance de Lourdios** in early June, and the **Fête du Fromage d'Etsaut**, a cheese fair on the last Sunday in July.

Sleeping

Accommodation is mainly geared towards walkers, with several seasonal campgrounds and *gîtes d'étapes* (walkers' lodges) operating on a *demi-pension* (half-board) basis.

Camping Le Gave d'Aspe CAMPGROUND €

(☎05 59 34 88 26; www.campingaspe.com; Urdos; per adult/child/tent €4.95/2.50/4.95; ⊙May-Sep) Beautifully situated alongside the clattering River Aspe, in a forested site near the mountain village of Urdos, this is a superb family-friendly campground. There's a choice of timber bungalows or canvas-roofed chalets, or you can pitch your own tent.

Camping du Lauzart CAMPGROUND €

(☎05 59 34 51 77; www.camping-lescun.com; per adult/tent/child/car €3.50/4.50/2.50/1.50) Twenty-seven spacious sites pitched under the trees with full-blown mountain views, in a secluded spot just outside Lescun. There's an on-site cafe and fresh bread is delivered daily.

La Garbure GÎTE €

(☎05 59 34 88 98; www.garbure.net; per adult €19, half-board €32) Rustic *gîte* accommodation in a stone farmhouse in Etsaut.

Maison de la Montagne GÎTE €

(☎05 59 34 79 14; http://gite-lescun.perso.sfr.fr; per person €19, half-board €38) A sweet *gîte* in a converted Lescun barn, set in its own delightful flower-filled garden. The owner runs guided walks.

La Toison d'Or B&B €€

(☎06 08 70 75 18; www.aubergetoisondor.com; place de l'Église de Cette, Cette-Eygun; r €76-87; P 📶) You'll keep expecting members of Monty Python to pop their heads round the corner at this bizarrely brilliant medieval-era *auberge* (country inn), where the rooms hunker behind arches, block-stones and carved wooden doors. It's been gradually renovated by owner Julie; the breakfast room is the highlight, with its vaulted ceiling and monumental mountain view. It's a 2km drive from Cette-Eygun.

Auberge Cavalière B&B €€

(☎05 59 34 72 30; www.auberge-cavaliere.com; Accous; d/tr/f incl breakfast €72/105/135; P 📶) You'll really feel part of valley life at this rambling old horse farm 3km south of Accous, which offers five floral rooms and a cosy family *gîte*. The stone house is a picture of rustic character. Dinner and picnic baskets can also be arranged.

Les Estives B&B €€

(☎05 59 34 77 60; www.estives-lescun.com; Lescun; s/d/tr/f €46/55/72/88) A former barn renovated in 2006 with ecofriendly materials and timber cladding. The four rooms are cute and feminine: some have spotty wallpaper, others shades of peach or duck-egg blue. There's a kitchen for guests' use, or you can dine *chez maison*. It's 300m from Lescun.

Information

Tourist Office (☎05 59 34 57 57; www.tourisme-aspe.com; place Sarraillé, Bedous; ⊙9am-12.30pm & 2-5.30pm Mon-Sat) The valley's main tourist office.

Maison du Parc National des Pyrénées (☎05 59 34 88 30; Etsaut; ⊙10.30am-12.30pm & 2-6.30pm May-Oct) Housed in Etsaut's disused train station.

Getting There & Away

SNCF buses and trains connect Pau and Oloron-Ste-Marie up to 10 times daily.

Citram Pyrenees (☎05 59 27 22 22; www.citrampyrenees.fr) runs a regular bus (three to five daily Monday to Saturday, two daily at weekends) from Oloron into the valley, stopping at all the main villages en route to Somport.

Vallée d'Ossau

Running parallel to the Vallée d'Aspe, about 10km further east, the Vallée d'Ossau tracks its namesake river from its confluence with the Aspe at Oloron-Ste-Marie all the way to the watershed at Col du Pourtalet (1794m), some 60km to the south. The entrance to the valley as far as Laruns is green and pastoral,

carpeted with lush fields and farms. Further south, the mountains stack up as the valley draws ever closer to the Spanish border.

There are 18 tiny villages dotted along the valley. The main focus is Laruns, 37km from Pau, a sturdy hamlet which has an excellent tourist office and national park centre, both stocked with information on hiking, mountain biking, rafting and other outdoor pursuits. Ossau is known for its tangy cheese, *fromage d'Ossau*, made from ewe's milk. It's sold all over the place in summer, and the valley holds an annual **Foire au Fromage** (cheese fair) in October.

Sights & Activities

Falaise aux Vautours WILDLIFE RESERVE

(Cliff of the Vultures; ☎05 59 82 65 49; www.falaise-aux-vautours.com; adult/child €6/4; ⏲10.30am-12.30pm & 2-6.30pm Jul & Aug, 2-5.30pm Apr-Jun & Sep) The griffon vulture *(Gyps fulvus)* was once a familiar sight over the Pyrenees, but habitat loss and hunting have taken their toll on these strange, majestic birds. Now legally protected, over 100 nesting pairs roost around the limestone cliffs of this 82-hectare reserve. It's a thrill watching them swoop and wheel from their nests above the valley, and strategically placed CCTV cameras allow you to see inside their nests from the visitor centre. Keep an eye out for the other species, the Egyptian vulture now confined to just a few small areas of the Alps.

Bielle VILLAGE

The former 'capital' of the valley, Bielle is a beautiful village with many fine 15th- and 16th-century houses, linked together via a guided walk.

Rébénacq VILLAGE

Rébénacq is one of the few *bastides* (fortified towns) of the Pyrenees, built in 1347 by a lieutenant of Gaston Fébus, the 11th Count of Foix. Like all *bastides*, it's set around a central square, the place de la Bielle, whose buildings and dimensions have barely changed in seven centuries.

Castet VILLAGE

Perched precariously on a glacial outcrop, this hilltop village boasts a 12th-century keep and a truly magnificent valley view. From the *belvédère* (panoramic viewpoint) known as Port de Castet (868m), hiking and biking trails wind along the hillside, and you can hire donkeys in the village.

Eaux-Bonnes HOT SPRINGS

During the 19th century, the village of Eaux-Bonnes (literally, Good Waters) flourished as a spa resort thanks to its geothermal hot springs, which fed public baths frequented by many illustrious figures including the Empress Eugénie. If you're aching after too much hiking, you can enjoy a spa treatment and a soak at the **Thermes des Eaux Bonnes** (☎05 59 05 34 02; eauxbonnes@valvital.fr; spa pass adult child €15/7).

★**Le Petit Train d'Artouste** TOURIST TRAIN

(☎05 59 05 36 99; www.altiservice.com/excursion/train-artouste; adult/child €25/21; ⏲Jun–mid-Sep) Six kilometres east of Gabas, near the ski resort of Artouste-Fabrèges (1250m), a cable car cranks up the Pic de la Sagette (2032m) to reach the start of one of France's most scenic train journeys. The toy-sized Train d'Artouste (affectionately known as Le Petit Train) was built for dam workers in the 1920s, but now trundles its way for 10km to Lac d'Artouste, offering heart-stopping views over the valley and the spiky Pic du Midi d'Ossau.

The train gets very busy in summer, carrying over 100,000 passengers in the three-and-a-half months it's open – try to visit at

THE TRANSHUMANCE

If you're travelling through the Pyrenees between late May and early June and you happen to find yourself stuck behind an enormous cattle-shaped traffic jam, there's a good chance you may have just got caught up in the age-old tradition of the Transhumance, in which shepherds move their flocks from their winter pastures up to the high grass-rich meadows of the mountain uplands.

This ancient custom has been a fixture on the Pyrenean calendar for hundreds of years, and is still regarded as one of the most important events of the year in the Pyrenees. The Transhumance is carried on in the time-honoured way – usually on foot, assisted by the occasional sheepdog or quad-bike – and several of the valleys host lively festivals to mark the occasion. The whole show is repeated in October, when the flocks are brought back down to the valleys before the snows of winter descend in earnest.

the start and end of the season, when it's usually quieter. Tickets can be bought in advance online and by phone. Trains run half-hourly in July and August, hourly at other times. The round-trip lasts about four hours. You can also buy a Billet Randonneur (Walkers' Ticket), which allows you to get off the train and hike the trails, then get a train back.

Sleeping

Aux Pieds des Pics B&B €
(☎05 59 05 22 68; Bescat; s/d from €55/62, f €85-107; P 📶) With its blue shutters, cute rooms and mountain-view balcony, this village B&B in Bescat is a beauty. Stripy bedspreads and pale-wood floors define the simply furnished rooms, and owners Delphine and Benoît are full of knowledge on the area. For breakfast, you might even get eggs from their own hens.

Casa Paulou GUESTHOUSE €
(☎05 59 05 35 98; 6 rue Bourgneuf Claa, Laruns; s/d from €45/60; P 📶) In the town of Laruns, the friendly Casa Paulou makes a great base for outdoor adventures in the surrounding countryside. Its five comfy rooms are quite large and painted in cheerful colours; some have magnificent views of the mountains. It's within walking distance of the restaurants of Laruns.

Le Balcon de l'Ossau GUESTHOUSE €
(☎05 59 21 05 46; www.chambres-hotes-ossau.fr; 17 rue du Bourg, Bescat; s/d/tr €60/64/80; 📶) In Bescat, the owners Kathrin and Michel roll out the welcome mat, with three handsomely set rooms and a peaceful garden where you can take in the views. Outdoor lovers can get loads of tips on hikes and other activities in the area.

Hotel de France HOTEL €€
(☎05 59 05 60 16; www.hotel-arudy-pyrenees.fr; 1 place de l'Hôtel de Ville, Arudy; s/d/tr/f €58/67/83/90; 📶) In Arudy, this hotel looks like it's appeared from a vintage postcard. It's on a quiet street leading to the church; outside there are pale green shutters and a pebbledash-and-wood frontage, while inside are pleasant, no-frills rooms and a good country bistro serving regional dishes such as *garbure béarnaise*.

Information

La Maison de la Vallée d'Ossau Office de Tourisme (☎05 59 05 31 41; www.valleedossau-tourisme.com; Laruns; ⏲9am-noon & 2-6pm) Located on the square.

National Park Visitor Centre (☎05 59 05 41 59; www.parc-pyrenees.com; Laruns; ⏲9am-noon & 2-5.30pm) Beside the tourist office.

Cauterets

POP 1300 / ELEV 930M

It might not have the altitude of its sister ski stations in the Alps, but in many respects Cauterets is a more pleasant place to hit the slopes. While many of the Alpine resorts have been ruthlessly modernised and are crammed to capacity during the winter and summer seasons, Cauterets has clung on to much of its fin-de-siècle character, with a stately spa and grand 19th-century residences dotted round town.

Snow usually lingers here until early May, returning in late October or early November. In summer the landscape around Cauterets transforms into a hikers' paradise, with trails winding their way into the Parc National des Pyrénées.

Sights & Activities

Cauterets' two ski areas are the Pont d'Espagne and Cirque du Lys, both great for hiking once the snows melt. Local guides offer outdoor activities including paragliding, rock-climbing, fishing and via ferrata. Ask at the Cauterets tourist office, or consult the Cauterets website (www.cauterets.com).

Pavillon des Abeilles BEEHIVES
(www.pavillondesabeilles.com; 23bis av du Mamelon Vert; ⏲10.30am-12.30pm & 2.30-7pm Wed-Sat, open Mon-Sat during school holidays, plus Sun in summer) FREE This educational attraction explores the wonderful world of the bee, with a glass-sided hive, video and honey of every possible flavour.

Pont d'Espagne HIKING
(cable cars adult/child €13/10.50) The most popular hike in Cauterets leads to the sparkling **Lac de Gaube**, a brilliantly blue mountain lake cradled by serrated peaks, while another trail winds up the **Vallée de Marcadau** to the high-altitude Refuge Wallon-Marcadau (1866m). From the giant car park at Pont d'Espagne, four miles above Cauterets, a combination *télécabine* (cable car) and *télésiege* (chairlift) provides easy access to the trailheads. Shuttle buses (adult/child return €7.50/4.50) run between Cauterets and the Pont d'Espagne car park every couple of hours in July and August. The car park costs €5.50 for up to 12 hours, or €8 for longer stays.

Cirque du Lys OUTDOORS
(cable car adult/child €12/10; 9am-noon & 1.45-5.15pm Jul & Aug) Cauterets' second most popular hiking area is this mountain amphitheatre, 1850m above sea-level. The best route is to catch the cable car and chairlift from Cambasque up to **Crêtes du Lys**, and walk back down the mountain for 1½ hours via the **Lac d'Ilhéou**, where there's a handy lakeside refuge for lunch. From there it's another 1½ hours back to Cambasque.

A joint cable-car ticket is available with the Pont d'Espagne if you want to do both hiking routes, costing adult/child €22/20.

The valley is also home to Cauterets' **mountain-bike park** (one-day pass adult/child €17.50/14.50; Jul & Aug), with three routes and a drop of 1500m to test your skills.

Bains du Rocher SPA
(05 62 92 14 20; www.bains-rocher.fr; ave du Docteur Domer; 2-hour pass adult/child €18/9; 10am-9pm daily May-Sep, 2-7.15pm Mon-Fri, 10am-12.45pm & 2-7.45pm Sat & Sun Oct & Dec-Apr, closed Nov) It wasn't snow which attracted the first tourists to Cauterets – it was the area's hot springs, which bubble up at temperatures between 36°C and 53°C. The waters are rumoured to have numerous healing properties. At this bath complex, you can treat yourself to a sauna, *hammam* (Turkish steambath) or Jacuzzi, and enjoy the lovely view of the mountains while basking in the pool. There's also an outdoor swimming pool open in the summer.

Sleeping

Camping GR10 CAMPGROUND €
(06 20 30 25 85; www.gr10camping.com; rte de Pierrefitte Quartier Concé; site for 2 adults €19; May-Sep;) Two-and-a-half kilometres north of town on the D920, this is the pick of Cauterets' campgrounds. It's tucked in a flat, grassy site cradled by mountains and forest, and has 69 spacious sites plus great facilities (hook-ups, *pétanque*, tennis courts and heated bathrooms). It even has its own adventure park with a via ferrata.

★**Hôtel du Lion d'Or** HOTEL €€
(05 62 92 52 87; www.liondor.eu; 12 rue Richelieu; s €76-86, d €80-162, s/d with half-board from €119/144;) This Heidi-esque hotel oozes mountain character from every nook and cranny. In business since 1913, it is deliciously eccentric, with charming old rooms in polkadot pinks, sunny yellows and duck-egg blues, and mountain-themed knick-knacks dotted throughout, from antique sleds to snowshoes. Breakfast includes homemade honey and jams, and the restaurant serves hearty Pyrenean cuisine.

Hôtel Le Bois-Joli HOTEL €€
(05 62 92 53 85; www.hotel-leboisjoli.com; 1 place du Maréchal-Foch; d €90-130, f €115-170;) Above a popular cafe right in the middle of Cauterets, this attractive hotel makes a good central base, with rooms in rich hues of blue, red or green, and mountain views from the upper floors. Breakfast is available in the wood-filled cafe downstairs, but it's a bit steep at €11.

Hôtel-Restaurant Astérides-Sacca HOTEL €€
(05 62 92 50 02; www.asterides-sacca.com; 11 bd Latapie-Flurin; r €72-120) Three adjoining buildings, each with an elegant balcony-clad façade, set the stage for a comfy overnight at this centrally located option. Rooms are a mishmash of styles; the best are wood-panelled chambers, which lend an Alpine feel. Others are a touch on the business bland side. There's a sauna and a decent restaurant (mains €12 to €18).

Eating

Les Halles de Cauterets MARKET €
(3 av Leclerc; 8am-noon & 2-6pm Mon-Sat) Cauterets' covered market is a turn-of-the-century beauty, and a great place to assemble a picnic.

La Fruitière TRADITIONAL FRENCH €€
(05 62 42 13 53; menus lunch €12, dinner from €20; noon-3pm & 7-9pm mid-Apr–Oct) For dining with a view, nowhere beats the Fruitery. It sits at the head of the Lutour Valley, and has a mountain-view terrace that'll blow your thermal socks off. The food is traditional and delicious: tuck into baked trout or grilled duck with a cream of foie gras, and follow with blueberry tart. It's 7km south from town along the D920.

Lau Tant'hic BISTRO €€
(05 62 92 02 14; Galerie Aladin, rue de Belfort; mains €15-20, menus €21-27; noon-2.30pm & 7-10pm) Owner Gérant adds his own twist to mountain dishes at his little restaurant, but still favours local ingredients, especially lamb, duck, cured sausages and cheeses. His presentation shows a bit of big-city flair, too, and the wine list is great. This is a fine place to try the Pyrenean dish of *garbure*.

MOUNTAIN PASSES

High road passes link the Vallée d'Ossau, the Vallée d'Aspe and the Vallée de Gaves (all of which have regularly featured as punishing mountain stages during the Tour de France). The altitude means that they're often blocked by snow well into summer; signs indicate whether they're *ouvert* (open) or *fermé* (closed).

Col d'Aubisque (1709m; open May to October) The D918 links Laruns in the Vallée d'Ossau with Argèles-Gazost in the Vallée de Gaves. An alternative that's open year-round is the D35 between Louvie-Juzon and Nay.

Col de Marie-Blanque (1035m; open most of year) The shortest link between the Aspe and Ossau valleys is the D294, which corkscrews for 21km between Escot and Bielle.

Col du Pourtalet (1795m; open most of year) The main crossing into Spain generally stays open year-round except during exceptional snowfall.

Col du Tourmalet (2115m; open June to October) Between Barèges and La Mongie, this is the highest road pass in the Pyrenees. If you're travelling east to the Pic du Midi (for example from Cauterets), the only alternative is a long detour north via Lourdes and Bagnères-de-Bigorre.

La Grande Fache TRADITIONAL FRENCH €€
(☎06 08 93 76 30; 5 rue Richelieu; fondue per person €18-23; ⊙noon-2.30pm & 7-10pm) You're in the mountains, so really you should be eating artery-clogging, cheese-heavy dishes such as *tartiflette* (potatoes, cheese and bacon baked in a casserole), *raclette* and fondue. This family-run restaurant will oblige, served in a dining-room crammed with mountain memorabilia.

La Reine Hortense FRENCH €€
(☎06 75 67 01 50; Chemin Rural de la Reine Hortense; mains €12-20; ⊙10am-7pm Mar-Oct) Although you can drive here, the best way to arrive at this rustic mountaintop eatery is on foot. Take the marked walking path just behind the Thermes de César; it's about 2½ hours return. Once there, you can dine on grilled meats and crêpes while enjoying spectacular views from the outdoor tables.

Information

Cauterets Tourist Office (☎05 62 92 50 50; www.cauterets.com; place Maréchal Foch; ⊙9am-12.30pm & 2-7pm) A helpful office on the main square.

Maison du Parc National des Pyrénées (☎05 62 92 52 56; place de la Gare; ⊙9.30am-noon & 3-7pm) Sells walking maps and guidebooks, and organises guided walks in summer.

Office de la Montagne (☎05 62 91 02 83; place Maréchal Foch; ⊙8.30am-12.30pm & 5-7.30pm daily Jun-Sep, 4-6.30pm Fri, 9am-12.30pm & 4-6.30pm Sat & Sun Oct-May) On the main square, this handy office is the best place to pick up trail maps and get tips on scenic walks in the area.

Getting There & Away

Sadly the last train steamed out of Cauterets' magnificent station in 1947. It now serves as the **bus station** (☎05 62 92 53 70; place de la Gare), with SNCF buses running between Cauterets and Lourdes train station (€8.20, one hour, four to six daily).

Vallée des Gaves & Around

Gentle and pastoral, the Vallée des Gaves (Valley of the Mountain Streams) extends south from Lourdes to Pierrefitte-Nestalas. Here the valley forks: the narrow, rugged eastern tongue twists via Gavarnie while the western tongue corkscrews up to Cauterets.

Sights

★**Pic du Midi** VIEWPOINT
(www.picdumidi.com; adult/child €36/23; ⊙9am-7pm Jun-Sep, 10am-5.30pm Oct-Apr, closed Nov & May) If the Pyrenees has a mustn't-miss view, it's the one from the Pic du Midi de Bigorre (2877m). Once accessible only to mountaineers, since 1878 the Pic du Midi has been home to an important observatory, and on a clear day the sky-top mountain views are out of this world. A cable car climbs to the summit from the nearby ski resort of La Mongie (1800m). Early morning and late evenings generally get the clearest skies and fewest crowds. At the top, there are several viewing terraces, all offering a different perspective on the serrated mountain landscape. There's also a sandwich shop and restaurant (*menus* €18 to €30).

Check the website for closures due to bad weather or periodic closures. If you're travelling from the western valleys via the Col du Tourmalet, double-check the road is open before you set out.

Le Donjon des Aigles BIRD PARK

(☎05 62 97 19 59; www.donjon-des-aigles.com; adult/child €14/8.50; ⊙10am-noon & 2.30-6.30pm Apr-Sep) Some 15km south of Lourdes, in the spectacular surroundings of the 11th-century Château de Beaucens, you can see one of the world's largest collections of birds of prey. Among the taloned residents are bald eagles, fish eagles, horned owls, vultures and a collection of parrots: flying displays are held at 3.30pm and 5pm (3pm, 4.30pm and 6pm in August).

Vallée de Garonne

Located in a central swath of the Pyrenees, this picturesque region is home to a few old-fashioned villages. You'll also find one of the most popular ski resorts in the Pyrenees, which doubles as a gateway to fantastic trekking in the summer.

Bagnères de Luchon

POP 3100 / ELEV 630M

Bagnères de Luchon (or simply Luchon) is a trim little town of gracious 19th-century buildings, expanded to accommodate the *curistes* who came to take the waters at its splendid spa. It's now one of the Pyrenees' most popular ski areas, with the challenging runs of Superbagnères right on its doorstep.

> **OFF THE BEATEN TRACK**
>
> **ST-BERTRAND DE COMMINGES**
>
> On an isolated hillock, St-Bertrand and its **Cathédrale Ste-Marie** (www.cathedrale-saint-bertrand.org; adult/child incl audioguide €5/1.50; ⊙9am-6pm Mon-Sat, 2-6pm Sun May-Sep, 10am-noon & 2-5pm Oct-Apr) loom over the Garonne Valley and the much-pillaged remains of the Gallo-Roman town of **Lugdunum Convenarum**. The cathedral has been an important pilgrimage site since medieval times, and you'll still see their modern-day descendants wandering round – although these days they'll be equipped with hiking gear and walking poles.

Activities

★**Le Vaporarium** BATHHOUSE

(☎05 61 94 52 52; www.luchon-bien-etre.fr; parc des Quinconces; from €15; ⊙3-7.30pm Mon-Sat, 10am-5pm Sun, longer hours during winter school holidays) You can't leave Luchon without visiting its *vaporarium*, said to be the only natural *hammam* in Europe. The experience takes place amid 160m of underground rock-walled corridors where you can sit on (admittedly uncomfortable) benches and breathe in the scented, steamy air. Afterwards, dunk yourself in the warm-water pool, naturally heated to 34°C, then repeat. It's located in a modern-looking building at the southern end of allée d'Étigny.

Inside the *vaporarium*, Luchon's thermal waters filter through the rocks creating a temperature between 38°C and 42°C. There are lots of spa packages available, but the basic €15 fee gives you unlimited access for each visit.

Superbagnères SKIING, CYCLING

(www.uk.luchon-superbagneres.com; adult/child one-way €7.90/5.90, all day access €9.50/7.50; ⊙ski-lifts 9am-12.30pm & 2-6pm Jul & Aug, 1.30-6pm weekends May-Jun & Sep, 8.45am-6pm or 7pm in winter) Luchon's *télécabine* (ski lift) whisks you up to the mountain plateau known as Superbagnères (1860m), the starting point for the area's winter ski-runs and summer walking trails. The tourist office has lots of information on possible routes, and sells maps and guides.

Sleeping

★**Le Castel de la Pique** HOTEL €€

(☎05 61 88 43 66; www.castel-pique.fr; 31 cours des Quinconces; r €75-98; P ≋) There's a bit of storybook charm to this hotel, with its château corner-turrets and 19th-century façade. Once inside, the lovely rooms don't disappoint, with wood floors, mantelpieces and French windows opening onto decorative balconies: mountain views are practically universal. Owner Alain is a character, and a mine of local knowledge. All in all, it's a bargain – especially with breakfast at €7.50.

Hospice de France GUESTHOUSE €€

(☎06 88 32 40 64; www.hospicedefrance.com; dm/s/d from €19/50/50, incl half-board from €44/78/106; ⊙mid-Apr–early Nov) Set high in the mountains some 11km southeast of Bagnères de Luchon, the Hospice de France has been welcoming travellers since the 17th century. Today, its comfortable but simply

designed rooms make a great base for spectacular hikes and mountain-bike adventures in the region. The on-site restaurant serves traditional Pyrenean cuisine, while access to trails lies right outside the door.

Alti Hôtel HOTEL €€
(☎05 61 79 56 97; www.actaluchon.com; 19 allée d'Étigny; s €78-88, d €93-109, tr €113-136; P 📶) This brilliantly central, balcony-clad hotel straddles the corner of two pretty streets and a lively cafe in the old town. Despite its vintage exterior, it's resolutely modern inside: expect glossy wood floors and generic modern furniture.

Eating

This mountain town is a fine spot to try Pyrenean dishes like *garbure* as well as classic French bistro fare. The best place to browse for a meal is along restaurant-lined allée d'Etigny.

Covered Market MARKET €
(rue Docteur Germès; ⏲daily Apr-Oct, Wed & Sat Nov-Mar) Luchon's covered market was established in 1897 and is still going strong.

Le Baluchon BISTRO €€
(☎05 61 88 91 28; 12 av du Maréchal Foch; menus lunch €16, dinner €27-33; ⏲12.30-2pm & 7.30-10pm) In contrast to the traditional fare on many Luchon menus, this bistro takes its cue from a more contemporary cookbook. It's run by husband and wife team Laura and Thomas, who favour seasonal ingredients and stripped-back presentation: expect local meats and river trout partnered by a swirl of sauce or a delicate vegetable mousseline.

L'Arbesquens REGIONAL CUISINE €€
(☎05 61 79 33 69; 47 allée d'Étigny; fondue per person €19-25; ⏲noon-2pm Thu-Tue, 7-10pm Mon-Sat) Cheesy *raclettes* and fondues are the mainstay at this zero-fuss brasserie – there are more than 15 on offer, all served to share, and you can add meats for a full-meal experience.

L'Héptaméron des Gourmets GASTRONOMIC €€€
(☎05 61 79 78 55; www.heptamerondesgourmets.com; 2 bd Charles de Gaulle; menu €60, with wines €90; ⏲7-10.30pm Tue-Sat) This swish restaurant is the address for traditional French fine dining. Start with an aperitif in the salon, with its book-lined shelves and leather armchairs, then graduate to the kitschy conservatory for rich cuisine drowned in creamy sauces and truffle butters. Chef Jean-Luc Danjou can also accommodate vegetarian and vegan diners with advance notice. Reserve ahead.

> OFF THE BEATEN TRACK
>
> **EUROPE'S LARGEST CAVE SYSTEM**
>
> Twenty-two kilometres north of Ax-les-Thermes on the N20 near Ussat-les-Bains, **Lombrives** (☎06 70 74 32 80; www.grotte-lombrives.fr; standard tour adult/child €8/5; ⏲9am-7pm Jul & Aug, 10am-5pm Jun & Sep, 2-5pm May & Oct) burrows its way through the soft limestone rock beneath the Pyrenees' peaks. Guided tours take in more than 200 stalactite-lined tunnels, grottoes and galleries, including a sandy expanse known as the Sahara Desert, and limestone columns variously resembling a mammoth, a wizard and the Virgin Mary. Standard tours last an hour, but multi-hour expeditions are available for the adventurous (and non-claustrophobic).

Information

Tourist Office (☎05 61 79 21 21; www.luchon.com; 18 allée d'Étigny; ⏲9am-7pm Jul & Aug, shorter hours rest of year) Helpful office with loads of info on activities in the surrounding area. On Luchon's main restaurant- and shop-lined strip.

Getting There & Away

SNCF trains and coaches run between Luchon and Montréjeau (€8, 50 minutes, six daily), which has frequent connections to Toulouse (€18.50) and Pau (€21).

Vallée de l'Ariège

On the eastern side of the French Pyrenees, the sleepy Vallée de l'Ariège is awash with prehistoric interest: it's home to some of Europe's most impressive underground rivers and subterranean caverns, many of which are daubed with cave paintings left behind by prehistoric people.

The most useful bases are **Foix**, former seat of the Comtes de Toulouse, and **Mirepoix**, a well-preserved *bastide*.

Sights

Information on the main sights in the Ariège Valley is available from the Sites Touristiques Ariège (www.sites-touristiques-ariege.fr).

If you're visiting several sights, it's worth picking up the free **Pass Multi-Sites** at the first place you visit, which gives discounts at all the subsequent places you go to.

Château de Foix CHÂTEAU
(☎05 61 05 10 10; adult/child €5.60/3.80; ⏰9am-6pm in summer, shorter hours rest of year) The Ariège's most unmistakeable landmark is Foix' triple-towered castle, the stronghold of the powerful Comtes de Foix. Built in the 10th century, it survived as their seat of power throughout the medieval era, and served as a prison from the 16th century onwards.The castle is approached via a cobbled causeway from the old town. The interior is rather bare, but the view from the battlements is wonderful. In July and August there is at least one guided tour in English offered daily (at 1pm).

Parc de la Préhistoire MUSEUM
(☎05 61 05 10 10; Tarascon-sur-Ariège; adult/child €11/8.30; ⏰10am-7pm Jul & Aug, to 6pm or 7pm rest of year, closed Nov-Mar) Eighteen kilometres south of Foix, near Tarascon-sur-Ariège, this excellent museum-park provides a useful primer on the area's prehistoric past. The centrepiece is the **Grand Atelier**, which uses film, projections and an audio-visual commentary to explain the story of human settlement. There are also many animal skeletons, including a cave bear and a mammoth, as well as a full-scale reproduction of the Salon Noir in the Grotte de Niaux (see box, right).

DON'T MISS

TO ST-GIRONS MARKET

One of the biggest and best markets outside of Paris happens in the village of St-Girons along a picturesque stretch of the river Le Salat. At this **market** (rue du Champ de Mars, St-Girons; ⏰8am-1pm Sat), you'll find beautiful fruits and vegetables, bakery items, cheeses, smoked meats, freshly baked tarts, craft beers and more – nearly all of which are produced in the surrounding region. Among the food stalls you'll find vendors whipping up delicious galettes, meaty sandwiches, crêpes and Asian-style dumplings. Edibles aside, this Saturday extravaganza also has antiques, crafts, clothes, sheepskins, natural beauty products, baskets, books, records and plenty of other finds.

Outside you can follow a trail around the park's grounds, explore a selection of prehistoric tents and learn how to use an ancient spear-thrower.

Grotte du Mas d'Azil CAVE, MUSEUM
(☎05 61 05 10 10; www.sites-touristiques-ariege.fr; adult/child €9/5.50; ⏰caves 10am-12.30pm & 1.30-6pm, museum 2-6pm, 9.30am-8pm Jul & Aug) Twenty-five kilometres northwest of Foix, near Le Mas d'Azil, this rock shelter is famous for its rich finds of prehistoric tools, as well as its cave art. Two galleries are open to the public: in the Galerie Breuil you can see engravings of bison, horses, fish, deer and what appears to be a cat, while in the Oven Room, there's a rare – and haunting – depiction of a human face. The ticket also includes entry to the site's museum.

Les Forges de Pyrène MUSEUM
(☎05 34 09 30 60; adult/child €9/6; ⏰10am-noon & 1-6.30pm, 10am-7pm Jul & Aug, closed Nov-Mar) In Montgaillard, 4.5km south of Foix, this 'living museum' explores Ariège folk traditions, with live displays of ancient trades such as blacksmithing, shoe-making, bread baking, tanning and thatching.

Rivière Souterraine de Labouiche UNDERGROUND RIVER
(☎05 61 65 04 11; www.labouiche.com; adult/child €10.80/8.80; ⏰10-11am & 2-4.30pm Apr-Jun & Sep-mid-Nov, 9.30am-5pm Jul & Aug, closed mid-Nov–Mar & Mon Oct–mid-Nov) Deep beneath the village of Labouiche, 6km northwest of Foix, flows Europe's longest navigable underground river. Discovered in 1908 by a local doctor, it's been open to the public since 1938. Barge trips run for about 1.5km along its underground course, with guides pulling the boats along by ropes attached to the ceiling, and walkways entering more caverns and eerie chambers.

The highlight of the visit is saved for the end: a clattering waterfall known as the **Cascade Salette** which tumbles into a sparkling turquoise pool. Depending on rainfall, the waterfall's speed can vary anywhere from 100 to 1500 litres per second. It's all quite touristy, but the kids are bound to love it. Best of all on a blazing summer's day, the caves hover at a cool constant temperature of 13°C.

Château de Montségur CHÂTEAU
(www.montsegur.fr; adult/child Jul & Aug €6.50/3.50, other times €5.50/3; ⏰9am-7pm Jul & Aug, 10am-6pm Apr-Jun & Sep, 10am-5pm Mar

DON'T MISS

PREHISTORIC PAINTERS OF THE PYRENEES

Most people know about the prehistoric artworks of the Dordogne, but far fewer realise that ancient painters left their mark in caves all across the Pyrenees. Halfway up a mountainside about 12km south of Foix, the **Grotte de Niaux** (05 61 05 50 40; www.sites-touristiques-ariege.fr; adult/child €12/8; tours hourly 10.15am-4.15pm, extra tours in summer) is the most impressive, with a fabulous gallery of bison, horses and ibex adorning a vast subterranean chamber called the **Salon Noir**. There's also one tiny depiction of a weasel – the only cave painting of the animal yet found.

The Salon Noir is reached via an 800m underground trek through pitch darkness. To preserve the paintings, there's no lighting inside the cave, so you'll be given a torch as you enter. On the way, look out for graffiti left by previous visitors, some of which dates back to the 17th century.

The cave can only be visited with a guide. From April to June and in September and October there's usually one English-language tour a day at 1.30pm. In July and August, English-language tours happen at 9.45am and 12.15pm. Visitor numbers are limited, so call or go online to reserve a place.

& Oct, 11am-4pm Nov-Feb) For the full Monty Python medieval vibe, tackle the steep 1207m climb to the ruins of this hilltop fortress, 32km east of Foix (and don't forget to bring your own water). It's the westernmost of the string of Cathar castles stretching across into Languedoc; the original castle was razed to rubble after the siege, and the present-day ruins largely date from the 17th century.

It was here, in 1242, that the Cathars suffered their heaviest defeat; the castle fell after a gruelling nine-month siege, and 220 of the defenders were burnt alive when they refused to renounce their faith. A local legend claims that the Holy Grail was smuggled out of the castle in the days before the final battle.

Sleeping

Florivalier GUESTHOUSE €
(05 61 04 86 75; www.florivalier.fr; Route de Sentaraille, Lorp-Sentaraille; d/tr incl breakfast €60/80; P 🛜) This delightful four-room guesthouse has comfortably furnished rooms and a pretty garden strung with hammocks, from where you can admire the jagged mountain peaks in the distance. It's run by a friendly Dutch couple, who have a wealth of tips on exploring the area. Good home-cooked meals can also be arranged here. You'll need a car to get here and around.

Les Minotiers HOTEL €
(05 61 69 37 36; www.hotelmirepoix.com; Mirepoix; r €51-66; P ❄ 🛜) This affordable hotel in Mirepoix has clean and simple rooms with big windows, located just a short stroll to the village centre. Though the design is fairly uninspiring, it's hard to beat the prices. The on-site restaurant (mains €15 to €22) earns high marks for its Pyrenees-inspired fare (try the pastry-covered lamb with morels).

★ **Auberge les Myrtilles** B&B €€
(05 61 65 16 46; www.auberge-les-myrtilles.com; Salau; d €67-105; P 🛜) You'll feel rather like you're staying in the Canadian wilderness here, with its timber-framed chalet cabins and forested hillside setting. It's a wonderful place to settle yourself: despite the rustic style, there are lots of luxury spoils, including a covered swimming pool with a knockout view, a Swedish-style sauna and, of course, mountain panoramas on every side. It's about 20km west of Foix on the D17.

The restaurant (*menu* €26) is great for local cuisine – don't miss the Azinat (a duck, sausage and vegetable hotpot).

Hôtel Eychenne HOTEL €€
(05 61 65 00 04; www.hotel-eychenne.com; 11 rue Peyrevidal, Foix; s/d €50/60; 🛜) In a good location in the centre of Foix, Hôtel Eychenne has simple, carpeted rooms with wooden shutters and bathrooms of a vaguely futuristic (c 1960s) design, with capsule-like showers. There's an easygoing bar downstairs.

Hôtel Restaurant Lons HOTEL €€
(05 34 09 28 00; www.hotel-lons-foix.com; 6 place Dutilh, Foix; r €79-103) One of the better hotels in Foix, this is an old-fashioned affair with rambling corridors and functional but comfy rooms, some of which look onto the river, while the others face Foix' shady streets. The riverside restaurant offers good-value half-board (*menus* €18 to €36).

Maison des Consuls HOTEL €€
(☎05 61 68 81 81; www.maisondesconsuls.com; 6 place du Maréchal Leclerc, Mirepoix; d €95-135; P 📶) This offbeat hotel has themed all its rooms after notable figures from Mirepoix' past. The best ones are the Louis XV–style Monseigneur room, with windows overlooking the main square, and the Dame-Louise room, decorated in Louis XIII–style, with a four-poster bed and a superb view over the cathedral. There's also a room with its own small balcony (but twin beds).

Hôtel les Remparts HOTEL €€
(☎05 61 68 12 15; www.hotelremparts.com; 6 cours Louis Pons Tarde, Mirepoix; s €68-78, d €82-98; 📶) Built into the *bastide* architecture of Mirepoix, this is a smart option, with a mixed-bag of nine rooms that combine modern design with the building's centuries-old heritage – a patch of exposed stone here, a wonky wooden doorway there. The excellent restaurant is one of Mirepoix' best, serving fine French cuisine (*menus* €26 to €37) under stone arches and great oak beams.

Château de Beauregard HOTEL €€
(☎05 61 66 66 64; www.chateaubeauregard.net; av de la Résistance, St-Girons; r €100-220, d incl half-board €180-300; P 📶 🏊) In St-Girons, halfway between St-Gaudens and Foix along the D117, this grand château is ideal for playing lord of the manor: the house is topped by turrets and surrounded by 2.5 hectares of gardens, with grand rooms named after writers (some have their bathrooms hidden in the castle's corner towers). There's also a pool, spa and a great Gascon restaurant.

★**L'Abbaye de Camon** B&B €€€
(☎05 61 60 31 23; www.chateaudecamon.com; 3 place Philippe de Lévis, Camon; d €135-200; ⏲Apr-Oct; P 📶 🏊) Wow – what a spot. Founded as a Benedictine abbey in the 12th century, this is now possibly the poshest B&B anywhere in the Pyrenees. The building's decor puts most châteaux to shame, with vaulted archways, winding staircases, a Renaissance-style drawing room, ravishing gardens and a lovely pool – plus five regal rooms oozing antique grandeur. It's 13km southeast of Mirepoix.

ℹ Information

Tourist Office (☎05 61 65 12 12; www.tourisme-foix-varilhes.fr; 29 rue Delcassé, Foix; ⏲9am-noon & 2-6pm Mon-Sat year-round, plus 10am-12.30pm & 2-6pm Sun mid-Jun–Aug) A good place to get info on walks and other activities in the area.

ℹ Getting There & Away

Regular trains connect Toulouse and Foix (€15.30, 1¼ hours).

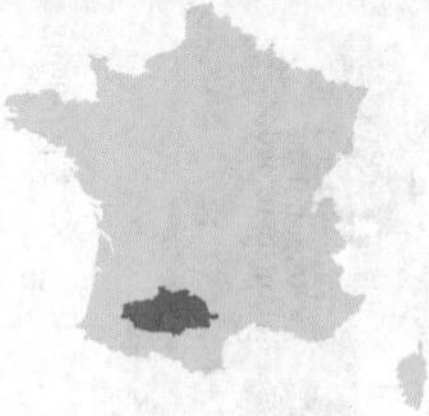

Toulouse Area

Includes ➡

Best Places to Eat

➡ Les Halles Victor Hugo (p694)

➡ Le Genty-Magre (p696)

➡ L'Epicurien (p700)

➡ La Table des Cordeliers (p705)

➡ La Table d'Oste (p704)

Best Places to Sleep

➡ Les Bruhasses (p706)

➡ La Maison (p699)

➡ Lacassagne (p706)

➡ Hôtel Albert 1er (p694)

➡ Au Château (p702)

Why Go?

Gastronomy and good living are the passions underpinning this sun-kissed corner of southwestern France. At the heart of the region's farms and flower-sprinkled meadows is Toulouse, a city of pink stone invigorated by bustling *salons de thé* (tearooms), galleries and nightlife aplenty. Beyond here, stocky *bastides* (fortified towns), like hilltop Cordes-sur-Ciel and pint-sized Fourcès, snooze between vineyards and rolling pastures. Slicing through is the formidable Canal du Midi, a 17th-century feat of engineering now plied by idling houseboaters. Meanwhile tables groan under hefty dishes like *cassoulet* and confit duck, with splashes of complex Gaillac wine.

Once you've enjoyed your fill of Toulouse's festivals, music and cutting-edge art, it's time to slow down. Meander under monastery arches in Valence-sur-Baïse or La Romieu, sip fiery mouthfuls in Armagnac distilleries and bunk down in creaky converted farmhouses. If at all possible, lose track of time: this delightful region is best experienced at a dawdle.

When to Go

Toulouse

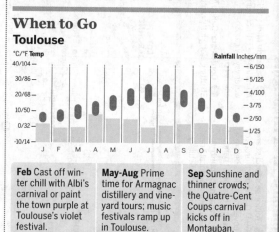

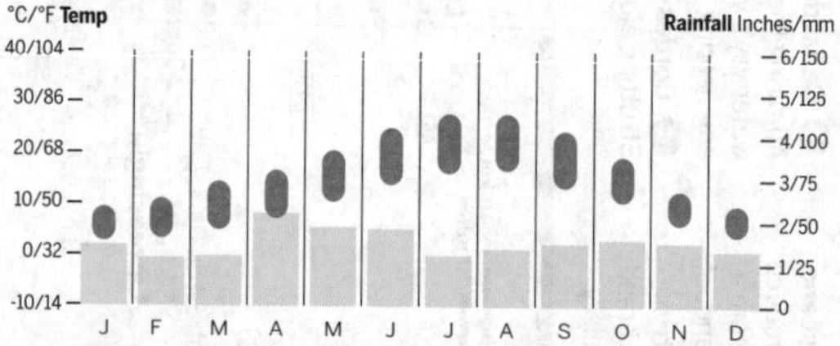

Feb Cast off winter chill with Albi's carnival or paint the town purple at Toulouse's violet festival.

May-Aug Prime time for Armagnac distillery and vineyard tours; music festivals ramp up in Toulouse.

Sep Sunshine and thinner crowds; the Quatre-Cent Coups carnival kicks off in Montauban.

Toulouse Area Highlights

1. **Toulouse's food scene** (p694) Ogling fresh produce in covered markets before a duck and *cassoulet* banquet.
2. **Armagnac country** (p706) Swigging local brandy in a centuries-old distillery.
3. **Canal du Midi** (p695) Admiring the 17th-century waterway's virtuoso engineering.
4. **Cordes-sur-Ciel** (p700) Strutting along lofty ramparts.
5. **Abbaye St-Pierre** (p701) Wandering rose-tinted cloisters in Moissac's 12th-century abbey.
6. **Gers' romantic B&Bs** (p706) Bedding down in historic farmhouses.
7. **Larressingle's medieval warfare** (p705) Standing back as trebuchets are armed for battle in this Lilliputian village.
8. **Vieil Albi** (p698) Weaving through medieval laneways to Albi's gargantuan cathedral.
9. **Beaumont-de-Lomagne's maths hero** (p702) Furrowing your brow at geometry puzzles in the hometown of Fermat.
10. **Escalier Monumental** (p703) Gazing at expansive views in Auch.

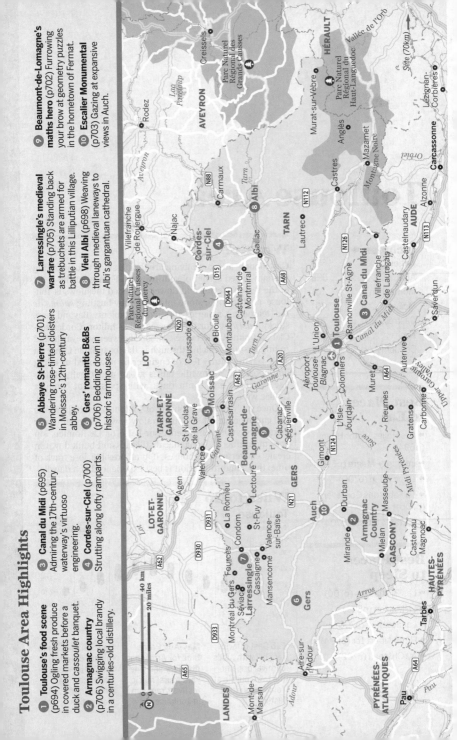

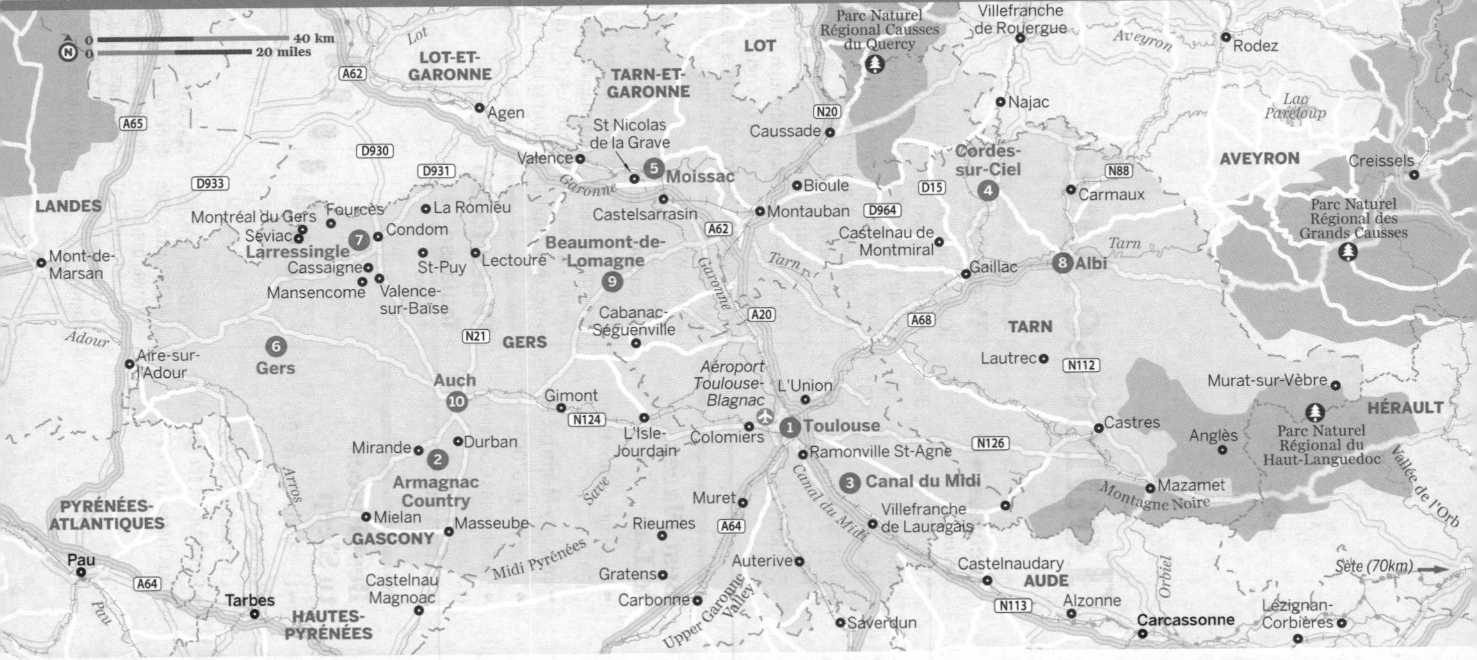

Toulouse

POP 458,298

Ochre rooftops and blushing brick churches earned Toulouse the nickname 'La Ville Rose' (the pink city). Its enchanting Vieux Quartier (Old Quarter) is a dreamy jumble of coral-coloured shopfronts and churches. Beyond the old town, Toulouse sprawls into France's fourth-largest metropolis. It's an animated, hectic place, but Toulouse – nestled between a bend in the Garonne River and the mighty Canal du Midi – is invigorated by its waterways.

Toulouse has one of the largest universities outside Paris: at its core this southwestern French city is home to students and scientists. French aeronautical history continues to be innovated in the Airbus factory outside town. But Toulouse knows how to have a good time, whether in teeming food markets, *salons de thé* or the thick of its smouldering jazz, techno and rock scenes. From the tips of dusky pink spires to its loudest bars, time spent in Toulouse truly has a rose-tinted sheen.

FAST FACTS

Area 18,324 sq km

Local industry Manufacturing, wine-making

Signature drink Armagnac

Sights

Lavish place du Capitole is the classic starting point to explore, before wandering south into the pedestrianised Vieux Quartier (Old Quarter). Most major galleries, museums and religious architecture are easily accessed from metro stops Esquirol, Jean Jaurès and Jeanne d'Arc, all on the red A line.

Place du Capitole SQUARE

Toulouse's magnificent main square is the city's literal and metaphorical heart, where Toulousiens turn out en masse on sunny evenings to sip a coffee or an early aperitif at a pavement cafe. On the eastern side is the 128m-long façade of the **Capitole** (9am-7pm), the city hall, built in the 1750s. Inside is the **Théâtre du Capitole**, one of France's most prestigious opera venues, and the over-the-top, late 19th-century **Salle des Illustres** (Hall of the Illustrious). To the south of the square is the city's **Vieux Quartier** (Old Quarter), a tangle of lanes and leafy squares brimming with cafes, shops and eateries.

Basilique St-Sernin CHURCH

(place St-Sernin; ambulatory €2.50; 8.30am-6pm Mon-Sat, to 7.30pm Sun) This well-preserved Romanesque edifice is built from golden and rose-hued stonework up to the tip of the octogonal bell tower. Entry is free, but it's worth the additional charge to explore the **ambulatory**, where marble statues stare out from alcoves in the pink brick walls. The tomb of the basilica's namesake St Sernin (also known as St Saturnin) has pride of place: he was Toulouse's first bishop and met a gruesome end when pagan priests tied him to a bull. Down in the **crypt** (accessed from the ambulatory), you can tiptoe among the shadowy rib vaults to view reliquaries containing venerable bones from the likes of St Papoul, another southern French martyr. Entry to the ambulatory and crypt has shorter hours from October to May (10am to noon and 2pm to 5.30pm).

★**Couvent des Jacobins** CHURCH, MONASTERY

(www.jacobins.mairie-toulouse.fr; rue Lakanal; cloister adult/child €4/2; 9am-6pm Tue-Sun) Fresh from celebrating its eighth centenary, this elegant ecclesiastical structure is the mother church of the Dominican order, founded in 1215. First admire the **Église des Jacobins**' ornate stained-glass windows before wandering through the **Cloitre des Jacobins**, in which graceful russet-brick columns surround a green courtyard. Pause in chapels and side rooms along the way, like the echoing **Salle Capitulaire**, a 14th-century hall ornamented with a haloed lamb. Don't miss **Chapelle St-Antonin**, with its 14th-century ceiling frescoes showing apocalyptic scenes.

Musée des Augustins ART MUSEUM

(www.augustins.org; 21 rue de Metz; adult/child €5/free; 10am-6pm Thu-Mon, to 9pm Wed) Located within a former Augustinian monastery, this fine-arts museum spans the Roman era through to the early 20th century. Echoing stairwells and high-vaulted chambers are part of the fun, but artistic highlights include the French rooms – with works by Delacroix, Ingres and Courbet – and works by Toulouse-Lautrec and Monet, among the standouts from the 20th-century collection. Don't skip the 14th-century **cloister gardens**, with gurning gargoyle statues that seem to pose around the courtyard. Temporary exhibitions are €4 extra.

Toulouse

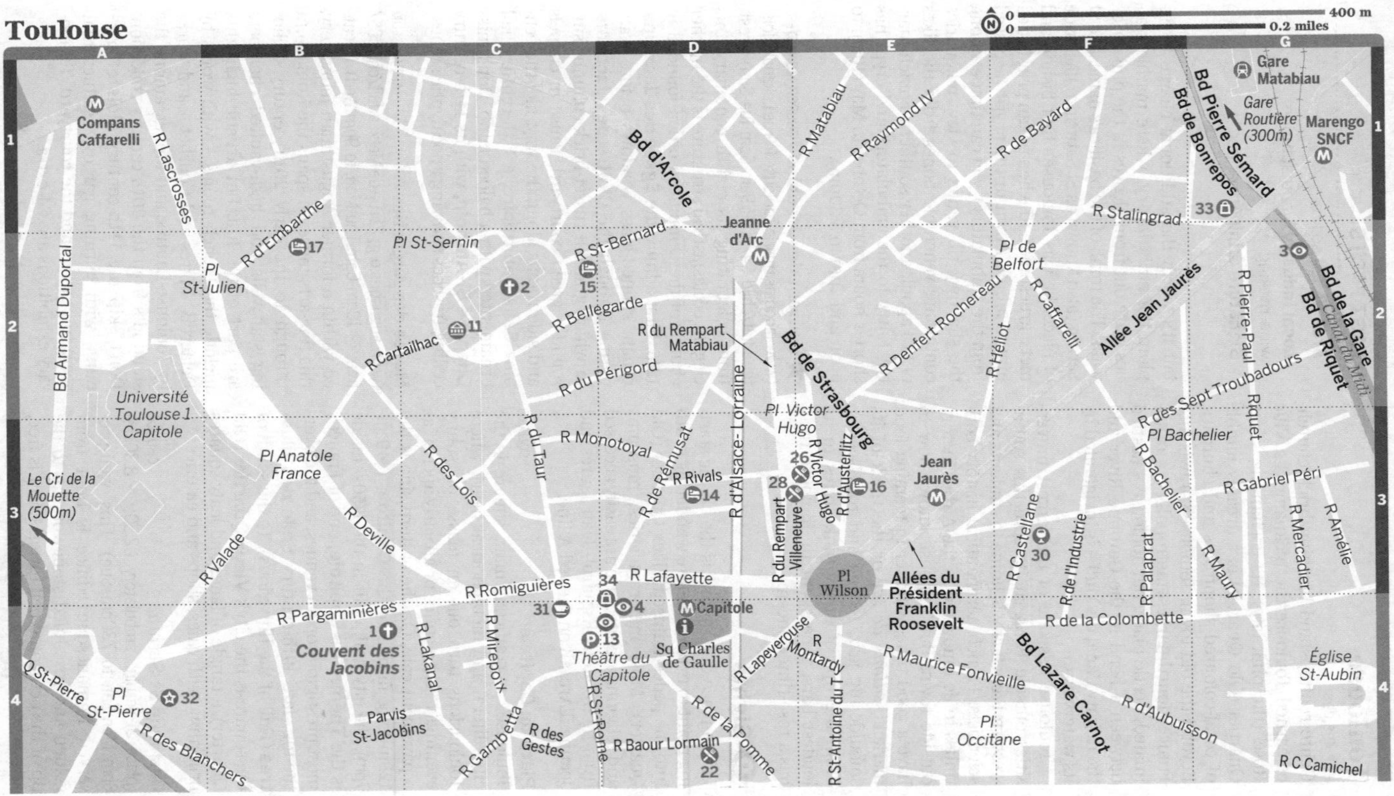
0 400 m
0 0.2 miles
N
A
B
C
D
E
F
G
1
2
3
4
Gare Matabiau
Gare Routière (300m)
Marengo SNCF
Compans Caffarelli
Bd Pierre Sémard
Bd de Bonrepos
33
R Lascrosses
Bd d'Arcole
R Matabiau
R Raymond IV
R de Bayard
R Stalingrad
Jeanne d'Arc
R d'Embarthe
17
Pl St-Sernin
R St-Bernard
15
Pl St-Julien
2
11
R Bellegarde
R Cartailhac
Bd Armand Duportal
R du Rempart Matabiau
Bd de Strasbourg
R du Périgord
R Denfert Rochereau
Pl de Belfort
R Caffarelli
R Héliot
Allée Jean Jaurès
3
Bd de la Gare
Bd de Riquet
Canal du Midi
R Pierre-Paul Riquet
R des Sept Troubadours
Pl Bachelier
Université Toulouse 1 Capitole
Pl Anatole France
R des Lois
R du Taur
R Monotoyal
R de Rémusat
R Rivals
14
R d'Alsace-Lorraine
Pl Victor Hugo
26
R Victor Hugo
28
R d'Austerlitz
16
Jean Jaurès
R Bachelier
R Gabriel Péri
Le Cri de la Mouette (500m)
R Deville
R Valade
R du Rempart Villeneuve
Pl Wilson
Allées du Président Franklin Roosevelt
R Castellane
30
R de l'Industrie
R Palaprat
R Maury
R Mercadier
R Amélie
R Romiguières
34
R Lafayette
31
4
Capitole
R Pargaminières
1
Couvent des Jacobins
R Lakanal
R Mirepoix
13
Théâtre du Capitole
Sq Charles de Gaulle
R Lapeyrouse
R Montardy
R Maurice Fonvieille
R de la Colombette
Bd Lazare Carnot
Église St-Aubin
Q St-Pierre
Pl St-Pierre
32
R des Blanchers
Parvis St-Jacobins
R Gambetta
R des Gestes
R St-Rome
R Baour Lormain
22
R de la Pomme
R St-Antoine du T
Pl Occitane
R d'Aubuisson
R C Camichel

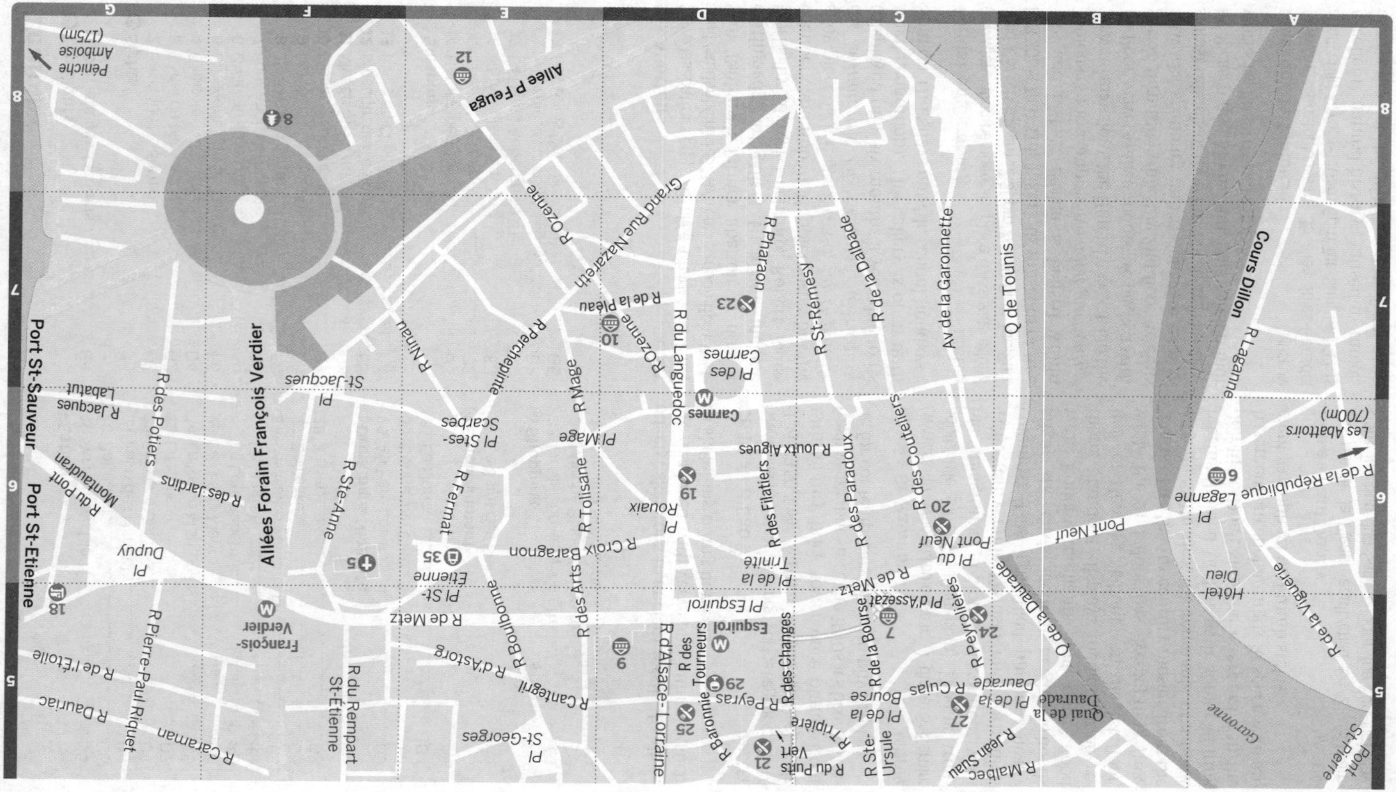
Port St-Sauveur
Port St-Étienne
Allées Forain François Verdier
Allée P Feuga
Péniche Amboise (175m)
Les Abattoirs (700m)
R Jacques Labatut
R des Potiers
R des Jardins
R du Pont Montaudran
Pl Dupuy
R Pierre-Paul Riquet
R de l'Étoile
R Dauriac
R Caraman
François-Verdier
R du Rempart St-Étienne
Pl St-Georges
R Cantegril
R d'Astorg
R Boulbonne
R de Metz
Pl St-Étienne
R Ste-Anne
Pl St-Jacques
R Fermat
Pl Stes-Scarbes
R Ninau
R Perchepinte
R des Arts
R Tolisane
R Mage
Pl Mage
R Croix Baragnon
Pl Rouaix
R d'Alsace-Lorraine
R du Languedoc
Carmes
Pl des Carmes
R de la Pleau
R Ozenne
R Ozenne
Grand Rue Nazareth
R Pharaon
R St-Rémesy
R de la Dalbade
Av de la Garonnette
Q de Tounis
Cours Dillon
R Laganne
R de la République
Pl Laganne
Pont Neuf
Pl du Pont Neuf
R des Couteliers
R des Paradoux
R Joutx Aigues
R des Filatiers
Pl de la Trinité
Pl Esquirol
Esquirol
R des Tourneurs
R Baronnie
R Peyras
R des Changes
R Tripière
R du Puits Vert
R Ste-Ursule
Pl de la Bourse
R de la Bourse
Pl d'Assezat
R de Metz
R Cujas
Pl de la Daurade
R Peyrolières
Q de la Daurade
Quai de la Daurade
R Jean Suau
R Malbec
Garonne
Hôtel-Dieu
R de la Viguerie
Pont St-Pierre
1
5
6
7
8
9
10
12
18
19
20
21
23
24
25
27
29
35
A
B
C
D
E
F
G

Toulouse

Top Sights
1 Couvent des Jacobins B4

Sights
2 Basilique St-Sernin C2
3 Canal du Midi G2
4 Capitole D4
5 Cathédrale de St-Étienne F6
6 Château d'Eau A6
7 Fondation Bemberg C5
8 Jardin des Plantes F8
9 Musée des Augustins D5
10 Musée Paul Dupuy D7
11 Musée St-Raymond C2
12 Muséum de Toulouse E8
13 Place du Capitole D4

Sleeping
14 Hôtel Albert 1er D3
15 Hôtel St-Sernin C2
16 Hôtel Wilson Square E3
17 La Petite Auberge de St-Sernin B2
18 Les Bains Douches G5

Eating
19 Au Poussin Bleu D6
20 Balthazar C6
21 Faim des Haricots D5
22 Flower's Café D4
23 La Braisière D7
24 La Reine Margot C5
25 Le Genty Magre D5
Le Louchebem ..... (see 26)
Le Magret ..... (see 26)
26 Les Halles Victor Hugo E3
27 Solilesse C5
28 Xavier D3

Drinking & Nightlife
29 Au Père Louis D5
30 Connexion Café F3
31 Le Florida C4

Entertainment
32 Le Saint des Seins A4

Shopping
33 La Maison de la Violette G1
34 Marché Place du Capitole D3
35 Marche St-Étienne E6

Les Abattoirs GALLERY
(www.lesabattoirs.org; 76 allée Charles de Fitte; adult/student/child €7/4/free; noon-6pm Wed-Sun) Toulouse's former abattoir is now a cutting-edge art gallery. Highlights include works by Marcel Duchamp, Robert Rauschenberg and Robert Mapplethorpe, but the showpiece is a huge Picasso, *La Dépouille du Minotaure en Costume d'Arlequin* (displayed only six months a year due to its fragile condition). The gallery is open until 8pm on Thursdays outside school holidays.

Fondation Bemberg MUSEUM
(www.fondation-bemberg.fr; place d'Assézat; adult/child €8/5; 10am-12.30pm & 1.30-6pm Tue-Sun, to 8.30pm Thu) This luxurious museum of fine arts and historic design is housed within Toulouse's most impressive *hôtel particulier* (private mansion), the Hôtel d'Assézat. On the 1st floor, velvet-walled rooms are packed with period furniture, while the 2nd floor exhibits artworks spanning impressionist to expressionist schools of thought. There are sketches by Picasso and Modigliani, plus some minor works by Pissarro and Egon Schiele.

Muséum de Toulouse MUSEUM
(www.museum.toulouse.fr; 35 allée Jules-Guesde; adult/child €7/5; 10am-6pm Tue-Sun) This excellent natural-history museum ranges across the epochs, with exhibits from pterodactyl skeletons to ancient fossils. Exhibits are displayed with verve and humour (such as skeletons riding horses).

Château d'Eau GALLERY
(www.galeriechateaudeau.org; 1 place Laganne; adult/child €3.50/free; 1-7pm Tue-Sun Feb-Dec) This 19th-century brick tower once pumped out fresh water, but since the 1970s it's been a venue for contemporary photography displays.

Musée St-Raymond MUSEUM
(www.saintraymond.toulouse.fr; 1 place St-Sernin; adult/child €4/2; 10am-6pm) Having trouble imagining Toulouse decorated with 4th-century nude Venuses and Corinthian columns? This light-filled museum neatly aligns the city's modern neighbourhoods with Roman remnants that once stood there. Standout displays include stone reliefs of Hercules' labours on the 1st floor, while the 2nd floor has eye-popping fragments of a 4th–5th-century mosaic from the villa de St-Rustice, the remnants of a huge, marine-themed design with somersaulting dolphins. Don't skip the **necropolis** in the basement, an enchantingly lit space with ancient sarcophagi and tomb steles.

Musée Paul Dupuy MUSEUM
(13 rue de la Pléau; adult/child €4/2; 10am-6pm Tue-Sun Jun-Sep, to 5pm Tue-Sun Oct-May)

Browse a treasure trove of religious art and pharmaceutical items, lovingly assembled by local collector Paul Dupuy and housed within a 17th-century mansion. Ceramic medicine jars and medical tools will make you grimly ponder the prospect of being lanced or sliced open before modern medicine. Highlights are a wooden bench (circa 1500) ornamented with scenes from the life of St Étienne, and a 1320 tapestry illustrating stories from Christ's life in silken thread.

Cathédrale de St-Étienne CATHEDRAL
(place St-Étienne; ⌚8am-7pm Mon-Sat, from 9am Sun) The city cathedral dates mainly from the 12th and 13th centuries, and has a gorgeous rose window. It's also the burial place of Pierre-Paul Riquet, the master architect behind the Canal du Midi.

Aeroscopia MUSEUM
(www.musee-aeroscopia.fr; allée André Turcat; adult/child under under 6yrs €11.50/free; ⌚9.30am-6pm, closed early Jan; Beauzelle) This aviation museum was built on the very spot the A380 Airbus was first completed. Here you can admire commercial and military aircraft and learn behind-the-scenes knowledge about the industry, as well as clamber inside certain vessels.

Jardin des Plantes PARK
(allée Frédéric Mistral; ⌚7.45am-9pm summer, to 6pm winter) These 200-year-old sculpted gardens are a refreshing place to take a breather from hectic central Toulouse. Find the entrance to this 7-hectare park a 500m-walk south from place St-Jacques.

Tours

Airbus Factory Tours TOURS
(05 34 39 42 00; www.manatour.fr; allée André Turcat, Blagnac; tours adult/child €15.50/13; ⌚Mon-Fri) Hardcore plane-spotters can arrange a guided tour of Toulouse's massive JL Lagardère Airbus factory, near the airport in Blagnac, 10km northwest of the city centre. The main factory tour includes a visit to the A380 production line; there's also a longer 'Panoramic Tour', which takes in other sections of the 700-hectare site via bus. All tours must be booked in advance, and non-EU visitors must book at least two days ahead. Bring a passport or photo ID. For security reasons, cameras aren't allowed, and you'll have to leave bulky bags behind.

Festivals & Events

Festival de la Violette CULTURAL
(⌚early Feb) Since the 19th century, this street parade and its accompanying revelry have been painting the town purple in a celebration of Toulouse's favourite flower. Everything from sweet and savoury food to liqueurs and wines will have the unmistakable scent of violet. Dress accordingly.

Sleeping

Hôtel Wilson Square HOTEL €
(05 61 21 67 57; www.hotel-wilson.com; 12 rue d'Austerlitz; r €69-98;) It won't win interior design awards, but this friendly two-star hotel is perched right by the edge of the action – five minutes' walk to Capitole and the Vieux Quartier, with Jean Jaurès metro just steps away. Staff are off-the-charts helpful, while rooms are neat and comfy.

La Petite Auberge de St-Sernin HOSTEL €
(09 81 26 63 00; www.lapetiteaubergedesaint-sernin.com; 17 rue d'Embarthe; dm €22, r €45-55;) No-frills but friendly, this backpacker-filled hostel offers boxy dorm rooms of four, six and eight beds, plus a few doubles (winter only). The decor's plain – tiled floors,

DON'T MISS

SPACE TRIP

The fantastic space museum, **Cité de l'Espace** (www.cite-espace.com/en; av Jean Gonord; adult €21-25.50, child €15.50-19; ⌚10am-7pm daily Jul & Aug, to 5pm or 6pm Sep-Dec & Feb-Jun, closed Mon in Feb, Mar & Sep-Dec, closed Jan;), on the city's eastern outskirts brings Toulouse's aeronautical history to life through hands-on exhibits, including a moon-running simulator, a rotating pod to test your tolerance for space travel, a planetarium and an observatory, plus a vast cinema to immerse you in a space mission. The showpieces are the full-scale replicas of iconic spacecraft, including the Mars Rover and a 52m-high Ariane 5 space rocket. Since WWII, Toulouse has been the centre of France's aerospace industry, developing many important aircraft as well as components for international space programs. To reach the museum, catch bus 15 from allée Jean Jaurès to the last stop, from where it's a 500m walk. To avoid queuing, buy your tickets in advance online or at the tourist office.

bare walls – but there's a garden for barbecues, and you're only a minute's walk from the Basilique St-Sernin. Some rooms have air-conditioning; ask when you book.

Auberge de Jeunesse HOSTEL €
(Habitat Jeunes O Toulouse; 05 34 30 42 80; www.otoulouse.org; 2 ave Yves Brunaud; dm from €19; reception 2-11pm; @) It won't win any beauty contests, but Toulouse's main hostel is functional, friendly and great value. Dorms are simple and clean, there's a cafe for casual dining, and you can connect to free wi-fi on the ground floor. The hostel is about 1km northeast of Gare Matabiau along av Georges Pompidou – but take care around the station after dark.

★**Hôtel Albert 1er** HOTEL €€
(05 61 21 47 49; www.hotel-albert1.com; 8 rue Rivals; d €65-145;) The Albert's central location and eager-to-please staff are a winning combination. A palette of maroon and cream, with marble flourishes here and there, bestows a regal feel on comfortable rooms. Bathrooms are lavished with ecofriendly products. The breakfast buffet is largely organic. Some rooms have mod cons such as USB ports and coffee makers.

LOCAL KNOWLEDGE

LUNCH AT THE MARKET

A morning spent admiring fresh cheeses, fruits and jars of homemade *cassoulet* at **Les Halles Victor Hugo** (www.marchevictorhugo.fr; place Victor Hugo; 7am-1.30pm Tue-Sun) certainly fires the appetite. Fortunately the upper floor of this covered market houses a handful of lunch places that source their ingredients directly from the produce below. Expect simple, hearty Toulouse fare, served up in a hectic setting where you brush elbows with other diners.

Le Louchebem (menus €18-26; noon-2pm Tue-Sun) is the top choice for local favourites like *cassoulet*, while **Le Magret** (www.restaurant-lemagret.com; menus €14-27; 11.45am-2pm Tue-Fri, to 3pm Sat & Sun) is known for its expertly seared fish and great-value *menus*. Arrive a few minutes before noon if you want to snag a table, as hungry Toulousiens descend en masse by 1pm.

Péniche Amboise B&B €€
(06 50 77 64 58; www.peniche-amboise.com; 17 bd Griffoul Dorval; s €75, d €89-105, tr €115;) Love life on the river? Then how about staying aboard a genuine *péniche* (barge) moored on the banks of the Canal du Midi? There are four cosy, colour-coded rooms, all with private bathrooms and porthole windows. The best is 'Amboise', with cool cabin-beds and wood floors. Huge fun.

Hôtel St-Sernin BOUTIQUE HOTEL €€
(05 61 21 73 08; www.hotelstsernin.com; 2 rue St-Bernard; d €79-119; P) Red-velvet furnishings and white walls give a classic feel to this hotel's small-but-sleek rooms. The best rooms have floor-to-ceiling windows overlooking the Basilique St-Sernin. Ask in advance about parking; there's limited spaces.

Les Bains Douches HOTEL €€€
(05 62 72 52 52; www.hotel-bainsdouches.com; 4 & 4bis rue du Pont Guilhemery; d €140-210, ste €280-330; P) If it's style you want, let the colourful modernist murals on this former bathhouse draw you, moth-like, into Toulouse's flashiest address. Depending on your tastes, you'll either adore the shimmering chrome and subdued lighting in the rooms, or you'll dream of more homely comforts. Parking is an additional €12.

Eating

Unmissable regional dishes include curly *saucisse de Toulouse* (Toulouse sausage); *cassoulet* (bean stew), preferably with confit duck; and a dessert of *galette des rois* (frangipane tart). For atmospheric dining, head to half-timbered rue Perchepinte for a clutch of classy restaurants. Boulevard de Strasbourg, place Wilson and the western side of place du Capitole are one long cafe-terrace line-up (though quality varies). Hit rue Pargaminières for kebabs, burgers and other late-night student grub.

Balthazar BISTRO €
(05 62 72 29 54; 50 rue des Couteliers; mains €12-15; noon-2pm & 8-9.30pm Wed-Fri, 8-9.30pm Sat) Ask around about where's best for lunch and someone will point you in the direction of Balthazar. It's a modern take on an old-style bistro, with classic Gascon cuisine crafted only from seasonal, market-fresh and organic ingredients. Wooden furniture matches the honest food, and the wine list is great.

DON'T MISS

CANAL DU MIDI

Stretching for 241km between Toulouse and the southern port of Sète, the **Canal du Midi** (www.canaldumidi.com) is the queen of French canals. A waterway connecting the Atlantic and Mediterranean seas had been dreamed of since Roman times, and was finally realised in the 17th century under engineering mastermind Pierre-Paul Riquet. It was constructed as the first stretch of the mighty 'Canal des Deux Mers' (Canal of the Two Seas).

With an eye on invigorating the Languedoc wine and wheat trades – and dodging the pirate-ridden transport routes around Spain – Louis XIV commissioned the canal in 1666. Riquet, a Languedoc tax farmer and mathematical genius, painstakingly devised a system of dams, bridges, aqueducts, tunnels and locks to overcome the region's difficult terrain. After years of toil by a workforce of 12,000 women and men, spiralling debts and a loss of faith among Riquet's sponsors, the canal opened in 1681. Riquet died a few months before the official opening of his life's work. Between Toulouse and Castres, in Revel, the **Musée et Jardin Canal du Midi** (www.museecanaldumidi.fr; blvd Pierre-Paul Riquet, Revel; adult/child €5/free; ⏲10.30am-12.30pm & 2-6pm daily late-Feb–Oct, 2-5pm Sat & Sun Nov & Dec) explores the waterway's remarkable construction and Riquet's life.

Though its commercial importance was eclipsed by the railway in the 19th century, these days the canal, a Unesco World Heritage site since 1996, is enormously popular with pleasure-boaters. It takes several weeks to sail the whole length, but it's possible to do shorter sections, with especially scenic stretches near Agde, Béziers and Narbonne. Alternatively, hire a bike and appreciate the canal's tranquil, tree-lined scenery from its towpaths.

Locaboat (☎03 86 91 72 72; www.locaboat.com) and **Caminav** (☎03 85 53 76 74; www.caminav.com; Carnon; weekend/five-day rental from €660/1101; ⏲Mar-Oct) loan small motorboats, while **Minervois Cruisers** (☎UK +44 19 26 81 18 42; www.minervoiscruisers.com; ⏲Mar-Oct) offers narrowboats. Prices vary depending on season and boat size, but expect to pay between €900 and €1400 a week for a standard four-berth. *Péniches* (motorised, live-aboard barges) are more expensive – around €360 per day.

Flower's Café CAFE €

(☎05 34 44 93 66; www.theflowerscafe.com; 6 pl Roger Salengro; cakes €4; ⏲10am-8pm Mon-Sat, 2-8pm Sun) Beside a tinkling fountain, this busy cafe is a cake lover's dream – though deciding between glistening raspberry tarts, pavlova or New York–style cheesecake is an exquisite nightmare. Arrive mid-morning for the best chance of grabbing a table. Lunch service is between noon and 3pm from Monday to Saturday only.

La Reine Margot CAFE €

(☎09 86 20 55 69; 13 rue Peyrolières; mains €8.50, menus €12.50; ⏲10am-7pm Mon-Sat; 🌿) This welcoming *salon de thé* specialises in fresh, healthy set lunches – like goat's-cheese tarts and coconut-carrot soups – within a simple but cosy brick-walled space. The homemade cakes are a delight, and there are ample choices for vegetarians and gluten-free diners.

Faim des Haricots VEGETARIAN €

(☎05 61 22 49 25; www.lafaimdesharicots.fr; 3 rue du Puits Vert; menus €12-14; ⏲noon-3pm & 6-10pm; 🌿) With confit duck and pâté featuring prominently on restaurant menus across Toulouse, this budget vegetarian canteen provides a much-needed palate cleanser. Faim des Haricots serves everything *à volonté* (all you can eat); simply choose whether you'd prefer to tuck into salads, quiches or the dish of the day.

Solilesse BISTRO €€

(☎09 83 34 03 50; www.solilesse.com; 40 rue Peyrolières; 3-course menu lunch/dinner €17.50/29; ⏲noon-2.30pm Tue-Fri, 7.30-10.30pm Mon-Fri) Punky chef Yohann Travostino has turned his bistro into one of the city's hottest dining addresses. He previously worked in Mexico and California, so his food blends French style with zingy West Coast flavours. Staff radiating enthusiasm hustle modern French dishes to tables, with surprise ingredients like popcorn or candied citrus guest-starring alongside pan-fried salmon and duck.

La Braisière BISTRO €€

(☎05 61 52 37 13; www.labraisiere.fr; 42 rue Pharaon; mains €14-22; ⏲noon-2.30pm & 6.30-10pm Mon-Sat, 6.30-11pm Sun) This carnivorous bistro flame-grills beef to perfection, lavishing fine cuts of meat with sauces from green pepper to pungent Roquefort. Right in the middle of one of Toulouse's most historic streets, its interior decorated with watercol-

DISCOUNT CARDS

The **Pass Tourisme Toulouse** (www.toulouse-visit.com/all-events/pass-tourisme; 24/48/72hr €15/22/29) entitles you to free public transport and entry to various sights, including the Musée des Augustins, the Muséum de Toulouse, Les Abattoirs and Fondation Bemberg. Pass-holders can also enjoy discounts on Cité de l'Espace and Aeroscopia, and in several shops. There's also a **premium pass** (24/48/72hr €20/27/35), which includes a river cruise and ride on the tourist train. Buy it at the tourist office or Tisséo agencies at the airport and train station.

ours of Toulouse's past, La Braisière exudes comfort and nostalgia. Come hungry.

★ **Le Genty Magre** FRENCH €€€
(☎05 61 21 38 60; www.legentymagre.com; 3 rue Genty Magre; mains €18-30, menu €38; ⊙12.30-2.30pm & 8-10pm Tue-Sat) Classic French cuisine is the order of the day here, but lauded chef Romain Brard has plenty of modern tricks up his sleeve, too. The dining room feels inviting, with brick walls, burnished wood and sultry lighting. It's arguably the best place in the city to try rich, traditional dishes such as *confit de canard* (duck confit) or *cassoulet*.

Self-Catering

Xavier CHEESE €
(☎05 34 45 59 45; www.xavier.fr; place Victor Hugo; cheese from €5; ⊙9.30am-1.15pm & 3.30-7.15pm Tue-Sat, afternoon only Mon) Follow the tangy scent of ripe Brie into this exceptional cheese shop. Browse for good-value selections of *raclette* (from €5.50), designed for melting onto potatoes. Die-hard *fromage* fans will be all too happy to stump up for rich, truffled Brie (from €18).

Au Poussin Bleu BOULANGERIE €
(☎05 61 52 01 70; 45 rue du Languedoc; sweets from €1.80; ⊙8am-7.15pm Mon-Sat, 8am-12.45pm Sun) Succumb to sweet temptation at this cake and chocolate specialist, well-known for the quality of their buttery frangipane tarts, preservative-free chocolates made on-site, and melt-in-your-mouth macarons. Pillowy sugar buns start at €1.80; a whole *galette des rois,* Toulouse's favourite tart, is €17 – and worth every cent.

Drinking & Nightlife

Almost every square in the Vieux Quartier has at least one cafe, busy day and night. Other areas lively after dark include rue Castellane, rue Gabriel Péri and near the river around place St-Pierre.

Le Florida CAFE
(☎05 61 23 94 61; www.leflorida-capitole.fr; 12 place du Capitole; ⊙7am-1am) Perfectly positioned for people-watching on Toulouse's grandest square, this busy cafe gleams with belle-époque trimmings that hark back to its 19th-century beginnings. There's a pleasing range of teas, wines by the glass (from €4), and cocktails (€10). Check its Facebook page for details on swanky soirées in **Le Roof**, the jazz lounge above the cafe.

Connexion Café BAR
(www.connexion-cafe.com; 8 rue Gabriel Péri; ⊙5.30pm-late Mon-Sat) A mash-up of cocktail bar, nightclub and tapas bar in a converted industrial space, this popular spot also hosts live gigs straddling genres from hip-hop to jazz to metal. When the weather's warm, the action spills onto the outdoor terrace.

Au Père Louis WINE BAR
(www.au-pere-louis.fr; 45 rue des Tourneurs; ⊙9am-2.30pm & 6-11.30pm Mon-Sat) This unashamedly retro bar/brasserie in maroon and gold trim has been here since 1889. The left-hand entrance panel reads *'vin blanc'*; the right, *'vin rouge'*. But you needn't pick a side with such a large wine list to choose from. Sip the house speciality, *quinquina,* a powerful fortified wine flavoured with cinchona bark (the source of quinine, the antimalarial treatment).

Entertainment

Toulouse has a cracking live-music and clubbing scene. Check www.toulouse.sortir.eu for the latest events.

Le Saint des Seins LIVE MUSIC
(www.lesaintdesseins.com; 5 place St-Pierre; ⊙6pm-2am Mon-Fri, noon-3am Sat) Grungy posters, pop art and tongue-in-cheek etiquette tips promise an edgier nightspot than average. Follow the thud of rock and indie inside this live-music haunt for an eye-opening night, whether the theme is beer pong or burlesque.

Le Bikini LIVE MUSIC
(☎05 62 24 09 50; www.lebikini.com; rue Théodore Monod, Ramonville-St-Agne; ⊙from 8pm) This

concert hall has been vibrating with the sounds of rock, pop, world music and DJ sets for more than 30 years. It's at the southern end of metro line B (Ramonville stop).

Le Cri de la Mouette LIVE MUSIC
(www.lecridelamouette.com; 78 allée de Barcelone; ⌚10pm-late Thu-Sat) Party hard on a converted canal boat, with regular electro, disco and rock nights. Check its website for events (timings vary depending on the gig).

Shopping

In addition to the fantastic covered markets, Toulouse's outdoor shopping opportunities include a midweek **market** (place du Capitole; ⌚7am-7pm Wed) packed with jewellery, clothing and vintage memorabilia, an antiquarian **book market** (place St-Étienne; ⌚9.30am-6pm Sat), and a **flea market** (⌚7am-1.30pm Sat & Sun) by place St-Sernin.

La Maison de la Violette GIFTS, SOUVENIRS
(☎05 61 99 01 30; www.lamaisondelaviolette.com; riverbank, opposite allée Jean Jaurès; ⌚10am-12.30pm & 2-7pm Tue-Sat) This button-cute *péniche* (river barge) sells everything from herbal tea to bath soaps scented with Toulouse's trademark flower, the violet. It's moored opposite the corner of bd Bonrepos and allée Jean Jaurès

Information

Tourist Office (☎€0.45/min 08 92 18 01 80; www.toulouse-tourisme.com; square Charles de Gaulle; ⌚9am-7pm Mon-Sat, 10.30am-5.15pm Sun Jun-Sep, 9am-6pm Mon-Fri, 9am-12.30pm & 2-6pm Sat, 10am-12.30pm & 2-5pm Sun Oct-Mar) The modern, multilingual tourist office is housed within a spiky 16th-century belfry.

Getting There & Away

AIR

Eight kilometres northwest of the centre, **Toulouse-Blagnac Airport** (TLS; www.toulouse.aeroport.fr/en) has frequent flights to Paris and other large French cities, as well as major hub cities in the UK, Italy and Germany.

BUS

Long-distance bus services are provided by several private operators; destinations include Bordeaux and Paris (overnight coach). Find routes on **Eurolines** (www.eurolines.fr). All services run to/from Toulouse's **Gare Routière** (Bus Station; bd Pierre Sémard).

TRAIN

Toulouse is served by frequent fast TGVs, which run west to Montauban, Agen and Bordeaux (which has connections to Bayonne and the southwest, plus Paris), and east to Carcassonne, Narbonne, Montpellier and beyond.

Buy tickets at the **SNCF boutique** (9.30am-6.30pm Mon-Sat) within Jean Jaurès metro station in town or at Toulouse's main train station, **Gare Matabiau** (bd Pierre Sémard), 1km northeast of the centre.

Albi €14.10, one hour, 11 to 16 daily
Auch €16, 1½ hours (direct or with bus), 10 daily
Bordeaux €26 to €44 via TGV, two hours, 15 daily
Carcassonne €16.50 to €22, 45 minutes to 1 hour, 12 to 20 daily
Castres €15.70, 1¾ hours, 10 to 18 daily
Montauban €10.30 to €14.90, 30 minutes, 20 daily
Pau €34.20, 2¼ to 3 hours, 10 daily

Getting Around

TO/FROM THE AIRPORT

Toulouse airport is linked to the city's metro network (single ticket €1.60); change at Arènes station for the red A line to central Toulouse (Capitole) or Matabiau (the main train station).

Alternatively, the **Navette Aéroport Flybus** (Airport Shuttle; www.tisseo.fr; single/return €8/15) links the airport with central Toulouse. The service runs every 20 minutes from 5am to 9.20pm from town, and from 5.30am to 12.15am from the airport. From the airport, shuttle buses depart next to the metro stop. From town, catch the bus in front of the bus station, outside the Jean Jaurès metro station or at place Jeanne d'Arc. The trip takes between 20 and 40 minutes, depending on traffic.

Taxis (☎05 61 30 02 54) to/from town cost from €25 to €30.

BICYCLE

The city's bike-hire scheme **Vélô Toulouse** (www.velo.toulouse.fr) has pick-up/drop-off stations dotted every 300m or so round the city. Tickets cost €1.20 a day or €5 a week, plus a €150 credit-card deposit. For one- to seven-day bike hire, you'll just need a chip-and-pin card. (Longer subscriptions can be bought online, but you'll still need a chip-and-pin card to work the automated machines.)

BUS & METRO

Local buses and the two-line metro are run by **Tisséo** (www.tisseo.fr). There are ticket kiosks at the airport, place Jeanne d'Arc and metro stops. A single ticket costs €1.60, a 10-ticket *carnet* (book of tickets) is €13.40 and a one-/two-day pass is €5.50/8.50. Most bus lines run daily until at least 8pm. Night bus lines run from 10pm to midnight.

Albi

POP 49,342

The bustling provincial town of Albi has two main claims to fame: a truly mighty cathedral and a truly marvellous painter. Looming up from the centre of the old town, the Cathédrale Ste-Cécile is one of France's most monumental Gothic structures. Next door is the fantastic Musée Toulouse-Lautrec, dedicated to the groundbreaking artist Henri de Toulouse-Lautrec, who was born here in 1864 and went on to depict the bars and brothels of turn-of-the-century Paris in his own inimitable style. Albi's old town is also well worth a wander, although it's surprisingly small given the town's sprawling suburbs.

Sights & Activities

The **Albi City Pass** (€12), sold at the tourist office, gives free admission to the Musée Toulouse-Lautrec and Cathédrale Ste-Cécile's *grand chœur,* and offers discounts at local shops and restaurants.

★ Cathédrale Ste-Cécile CHURCH

(place Ste-Cécile; adult/child €2/free; ⏲9.30am-6pm Mon-Sat, 9.30-10.15am & 2-5.15pm Sun) Resembling a castle more than a cathedral, this grand edifice in orange brick rises above Vieil Albi like an apparition. Its defensive walls hark back to the many religious wars that scarred medieval Albi. Begun in 1282, the cathedral took well over a century to complete; eight centuries later, it's still one of the world's largest brick buildings, and has been on Unesco's World Heritage list since 2010.

★ Musée Toulouse-Lautrec ART MUSEUM

(www.museetoulouselautrec.net; place Ste-Cécile; adult/student €8/free; ⏲9am-6pm Jun-Sep, closed noon-2pm rest of year & all day Tue Oct-Mar) Lodged inside the Palais de la Berbie (built in the early Middle Ages for the town's archbishop), this wonderful museum offers an overview of Albi's most celebrated son. The museum owns more than 1000 original works by Toulouse-Lautrec – the largest collection in France outside the Musée d'Orsay – spanning the artist's development, from his early neo-impressionist paintings to his famous Parisian brothel scenes and poster art.

Of particular interest are the early portraits of some of Toulouse-Lautrec's friends and family – including his mother, the Comtesse Adèle de Toulouse-Lautrec, his cousin Gabriel Tapié de Celeyran, and his close friend, Maurice Joyant. They clearly demonstrate the artist's wry eye and playful sense of humour. There are also some delicate animal studies (especially of horses).

Inevitably, however, it's the later works that draw the eye. Toulouse-Lautrec's lifelong fascination with the Parisian underworld, particularly the lives of dancers and prostitutes, is brilliantly represented. Look out for key works including *L'Anglaise du Star au Havre* (Englishwoman of the Star Harbour) and *Les Deux Amies* (The Two Friends), which depicts two prostitutes embracing while they wait for their clients. Pride of place goes to two versions of one of his most famous canvases, *Au Salon de la rue des Moulins,* hung side-by-side to illustrate changes in the artist's technique.

Toulouse-Lautrec's skills as a cartoonist and caricaturist also made him a pioneer of poster art, and the museum has a fantastic collection of his most famous designs in its permanent collection. On the top floor is a small collection of works by some of his contemporaries, including Pierre Bonnard, Maurice de Vlaminck and Henri Matisse.

Maison du Vieil Alby MUSEUM

(1 rue de la Croix Blanche; adult/child €2/free; ⏲10.30am-12.30pm & 2.30pm-6.30pm Mon-Sat Jun-Aug, 2-5pm Mon-Sat Sep-Apr) This museum houses a small exhibition on the city's history and its connections with Toulouse-Lautrec.

Musée de Lapérouse MUSEUM

(www.laperouse-france.fr; 41 rue Porta; adult/child €3.50/free; ⏲9am-noon & 2-6pm Tue-Sun, to 7pm Jul & Aug, reduced hours Nov-Feb) This intriguing museum explores the adventures of Albi-born explorer Jean-François de Galaup (aka the Comte de Lapérouse), who made several pioneering naval expeditions around the Pacific between 1785 and 1788. Mysteriously, his ships disappeared without a trace towards the end of their voyage; subsequent expeditions suggested they may have been wrecked on reefs near the island of Vanikoro, halfway between the Solomon Islands and Vanuatu.

Albi Croisières BOATING

(☎05 63 43 59 63; www.albi-croisieres.com; ⏲May-Oct) Glide down the Tarn River aboard a traditional *gabarre* (flat-bottomed barge). There are regular 30-minute cruises (adult/child €7.50/5) between 11am and 6pm, a 1½-hour lunchtime cruise (€12/8) leaving at 12.30pm, and full-day return trips (€24/15) to the village of Aiguelèze, near Gaillac.

Albi

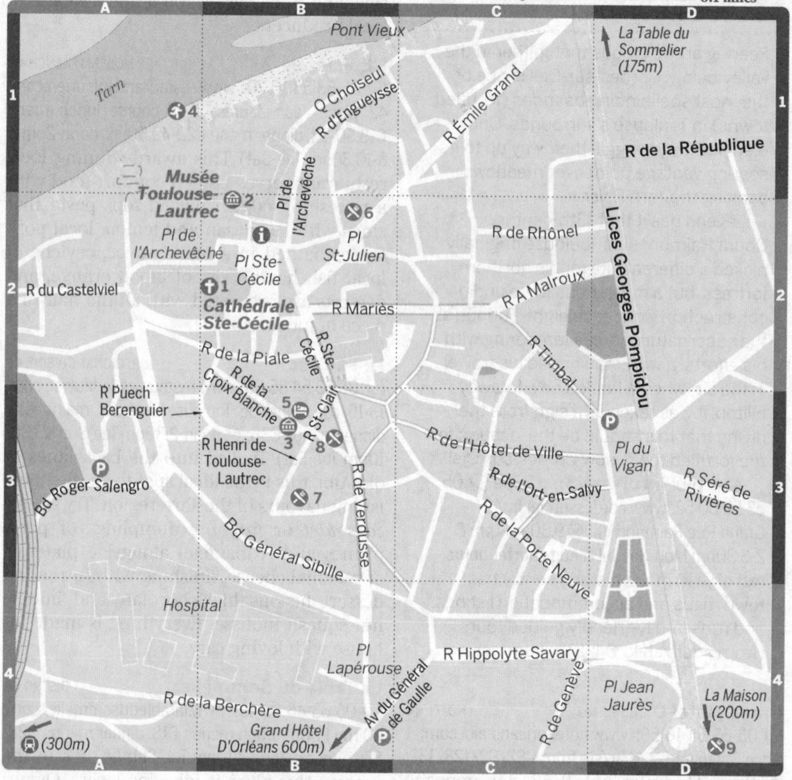

Albi

Top Sights
1 Cathédrale Ste-Cécile ... B2
2 Musée Toulouse-Lautrec ... B2

Sights
3 Maison du Vieil Alby ... B3

Activities, Courses & Tours
4 Albi Croisières ... A1

Sleeping
5 Hôtel St-Clair ... B3

Eating
6 Covered Market ... B2
7 Le Lautrec ... B3
8 Le Papillon ... B3
9 L'Epicurien ... D4

Sleeping

Hôtel St-Clair HOTEL €

(05 63 54 25 66; www.hotel-albi-saintclair.com; 8 rue St-Clair; s €40-65, d €48-75, f €90; P) A real rabbit's warren of a hotel – thrillingly creaky rooms with brassy-bordered mirrors fill an old house slap-bang in the middle of old Albi. The carpark has three spaces (€8 per night); if they're full you'll have to park on the edge of the old city and walk.

La Maison B&B €€

(05 63 38 17 35; www.chambre-hote-albi.com; 40 bd Andrieu; s €85-95, d €100-110 incl breakfast; P) In contrast to Albi's 'olde worlde' feel, this B&B is a model of modernity. The Velours and Métal rooms glimmer with glossy wood floors and designer furniture, while Ficelle feels more classic, with neutral colours, oil paintings and distressed furniture. It's a 700m walk south from the old city, but you get a garden and parking.

WORTH A TRIP

CORDES-SUR-CIEL

Peering above clouds that gather in the valley below, Cordes-sur-Ciel is one of the most spellbinding *bastides* (fortified towns) in Toulouse's surrounds. Cobbled pathways wiggle their way up to its soaring vantage point over meadows banking the Tarn River.

Legend has it that 13th-century Count Raimon VII of Toulouse originally picked a different site for his northern fortress, but a mysterious force undid construction work each night. Furious at the supernatural forces tampering with his efforts, a workman hurled his trowel in the air; when it landed on a faraway hilltop, it was taken as a sign from the divine that this should be the location for the fortified town, now Cordes-sur-Ciel.

A helpful **information office** (☎05 63 56 00 52; www.cordessurciel.fr; 42 Grand Rue Raimond VII; ⊙9.30am-1pm & 2-6.30pm Mon-Sat Jul & Aug shorter hours rest of year) in the historic centre has town maps and accommodation listings, and runs family-friendly guided tours (from adult/child €4/3) in summer.

Grand Hôtel D'Orléans HOTEL €€
(☎05 63 54 16 56; www.hotel-orleans-albi.com; 1 place Stalingrad; s/d/tr/ste from €82/92/128/132; P ❄ 📶) This pleasant three-star opposite Albi's train station, less than 1km south of the old town, has trim, tidy rooms and friendly service. There's covered parking (€10 per night) but there's usually space to leave your car at the train station.

Eating

Le Papillon REGIONAL CUISINE €
(☎05 63 43 10 77; 1bis rue Henri de Toulouse Lautrec; mains €16; ⊙noon-2pm & 7.30-9.30pm Fri-Wed) Duck three ways and (of course) foie gras dominate a fowl-heavy and good-value menu, alongside regional favourite *cassoulet* and salads strewn with farmhouse cheese. There's usually at least one veggie option. Check ahead for the timing of its regular blues and jazz nights.

Covered Market SELF-CATERING €
(place St-Julien; ⊙8am-2pm Tue-Sun) Albi's triangular turn-of-the-century covered market is a delight, built by the celebrated architect Thierry Bourdois and engineer André Michelin between 1901 and 1905. Behind its steel-and-brick façade you'll find a wealth of local producers.

L'Epicurien MODERN FRENCH €€
(☎05 63 53 10 70; www.restaurantlepicurien.com; 42 place Jean Jaurès; 2-/3-course lunch menu €18.50/21, dinner menu €29-49.50; ⊙noon-2pm & 8-10.30pm Tue-Sat) This award-winning local restaurant serves French comfort food with a refreshing edge. Chicken tops pasta that zings with Parmesan and lemon, local pork comes bathed in a morel sauce, ceviche of local fish has a twist of blood orange, and desserts are presented with all the flair of a piece of modern art.

Le Lautrec REGIONAL CUISINE €€
(☎05 63 54 86 55; www.restaurant-le-lautrec.com; 13-15 rue Henri de Toulouse-Lautrec; mains €18, dinner menus €36; ⊙noon-2.30pm Tue-Sun & 7.30-10pm Tue-Sat) Tucked into the back lanes of old Albi, this is the ideal spot to guzzle nourishing flavours of the Tarn region. Try smoky *cassoulet* or *farçous* (dumplings of pork, prunes and Armagnac) alongside platefuls of regional cheese, finishing with intriguing dessert fusions like chocolate and butternut squash mousse. Everything is made in-house with loving care.

La Table du Sommelier BISTRO €€
(☎05 63 46 20 10; www.latabledusommelier.com; 20 rue Porta; lunch menus €18, dinner menus €28-55; ⊙noon-2pm, 7-10pm Tue-Sat; 🖉) It's in the name – this place is for wine lovers. Owner Daniel Pestre is an experienced sommelier, with an infectious passion for his local vintages: dinner *menus* are themed around wines. The outdoor patio shaded by huge umbrellas is a great spot when the sun shines. It's on the northern bank of the Tarn, 10 minutes' walk from the tourist office.

Information

Tourist Office (☎05 63 36 36 00; www.albi-tourisme.fr; place Ste-Cécile; ⊙9am-12.30pm & 1.30-6pm Mon-Sat, 10am-6pm Sun Oct–mid-Jun, 9am-6pm Mon-Sat, 10am-6pm Sun mid-Jun–Sep) Next door to the Toulouse-Lautrec Museum. Ask for one of the themed walking leaflets around Old Albi.

Getting There & Away

BUS

TarnBus (☎08 11 99 00 81; http://tarnbus.tarn.fr) lines include the 703 to Castres (€3, 50 minutes, at least hourly Monday to Saturday) and the 707 to Cordes-sur-Ciel (€2, 35 minutes,

four to six Monday to Saturday, three on Sunday). Most leave from place Jean Jaurès.

TRAIN

Destinations include Gaillac (€4.80, 20 minutes, frequent service), Rodez (€15.30, 1½ hours, seven to 10 daily) and Toulouse (€14.10, one hour, 11 to 15 daily). For trains to Castres, change at St-Sulpice Tarn station.

Montauban

POP 56,271

Bastides litter the landscape of southwest France. Montauban, nestled on the banks of the Tarn River, is a fine example: founded in 1144, it is southern France's second-oldest *bastide* (the oldest is Mont-de-Marsan).

In the historic upper town, all roads lead to **place Nationale**, hemmed in on every side by arcaded walkways and tall pink buildings. The town was battered during both the Hundred Years' War and the Wars of Religion, and famously withstood an 86-day siege imposed by Louis XIII in 1621, during which the defenders resorted to eating horses, rats and dogs to survive. Encircling Montauban's distinguished centre are busy main roads and less-than-inspiring urban sprawl.

The main focus of Montauban is this fine-arts museum, **Musée Ingres** (☎05 63 22 12 91; www.museeingres.montauban.com; 19 rue de l'Hôtel de Ville; adult/child €7/3.50; ⊙10am-6pm daily Jul & Aug, 10am-noon & 2-6pm Tue-Sun Sep-Jun), which centres on the work of the neoclassical painter (and accomplished violinist) Jean-Auguste-Dominique Ingres, who was born in Montauban in 1780. Inspired by Poussin and David, Ingres became one of the most celebrated portrait painters of his day, and the museum houses many of his key works alongside old masters such as Tintoretto, Van Dyck and Gustave Courbet.

Another Ingres masterpiece, *Le Vœu de Louis XIII*, depicting the king pledging France to the Virgin, hangs in the 18th-century **Cathédrale Notre Dame de l'Assomption** (place Franklin Roosevelt; ⊙8.30am-noon & 2-7pm Mon-Fri, 3-7pm Sat, 8.30am-noon Sun).

Wine lovers will adore **Mas des Anges** (☎05 63 24 27 05; www.lemasdesanges.com; route de Verlhac Tescou; s/d incl breakfast €75/80; 📶🏊), a 4.5-hectare vineyard 8km south of Montauban. It's run by Sophie and Juan Kervyn, a friendly couple who've made wine-making into a lifelong passion. The three ground-floor rooms each have a slightly different theme (African, Latin, Marine). Tree-filled grounds, a fine pool and guest barbecues are the icing on the cake.

Book accommodation and grab some local maps at the **tourist office** (☎05 63 63 60 60; www.montauban-tourisme.com; 4 rue du Collège; ⊙9.30am-6.30pm Mon-Sat, 10am-12.30pm Sun Jul-Aug, 9.30am-noon & 2-6.30pm Mon-Sat Sep-Jun) in Montauban's old town.

From the Montauban Ville Bourbon **train station** (av Mayenne), about 1km from place Nationale across the Tarn River, direct services reach Toulouse (€10.30, 40 minutes, half-hourly) and Moissac (€6.40, 20 minutes, six daily).

> **WORTH A TRIP**
>
> **COUNTRY DINING ALFRESCO**
>
> By far the best place to eat around Montauban is **Les Boissières** (☎05 63 24 50 02; www.lesboissieres.com; 708 route de Caussade, Bioule; 2-/3-course lunch menu €20/23, dinner menus €32-60; ⊙noon-2pm & 8-9.30pm Tue-Fri, 8-9.30pm Sat, noon-2pm Sun), where chef Cyril Rosenberg blends regional cuisine with contemporary style. Savour duck sautéed in garlic and Chardonnay or lamb saddle with chestnut purée in the stone-walled dining room. On warm afternoons, the garden terrace is the place to be. It's 22km northeast of Montauban, in Bioule.

Moissac

POP 12,470

Riverside Moissac has been an important stop-off on the Santiago de Compostela trail since the 12th century, thanks to the glorious Abbaye St-Pierre. This standout religious complex is resplendent with some of France's finest Romanesque architecture, especially the apocalyptic scene on its tympanum.

Beyond the abbey, Moissac is a quiet spot best known for *chasselas de Moissac* grapes. First cultivated by medieval monks, these succulent globes find their way into everything from baked goods to detox remedies.

Rosy brick characteristic of the Toulouse area heightens the majesty of **Abbaye St-Pierre** (place Durand de Bredon; adult/child €6.50/4; ⊙9am-7pm Jul & Aug, 9am-noon & 2-7pm Sep-Jun) and its Romanesque cloister. Awarded Unesco World Heritage status in part for its significance along the Way of St

James pilgrimage route, the abbey contains some compelling religious art, in particular a frieze of St John's vision of the apocalypse above the south portal. The **cloister** was completed in 1100, followed a few years later by the **Tour-Porche bell tower** (mind your step on the way up).

The cloister is worth scrutinising on account of the carved capitals topping its slender stone columns: many of them depict biblical scenes in tender detail, such as Samuel pouring holy oil over a kneeling David. Some sculptures were smashed during the Revolution and are yet to be identified, like the delicate *'petite tête'* (little head). Inside the bell tower, keep your eyes peeled for faint initials carved into the stone – graffiti by the original stone masons.

Entry to the abbey is via the **tourist office** (☎05 63 04 01 85; http://tourisme.moissac.fr; 6 place Durand de Bredon; 9am-7pm Jul & Aug, shorter hours rest of year).

Sleeping & Eating

Le Moulin de Moissac HOTEL €€
(☎05 63 32 88 88; www.lemoulindemoissac.com; 1 promenade Sancert; d €105-179, ste from €164; P ❄ 📶) Housed in a 15th-century grain mill overlooking the Tarn, this hotel is a riverside treat. Rooms with distressed wallpaper, lovingly painted furniture and tall French windows open onto river-view balconies. The restaurant (lunch/dinner *menu* €25.50/43) dishes up duck tartare and beef in miso soup, among other French-Asian fusions. There's a smart sauna-spa and a romantic Jacuzzi, too.

Au Château B&B €€
(☎05 63 95 96 82; www.au-chateau-stn.com; 1 bd des Fossés de Raoul, St Nicolas de la Grave; d €70-90, f €85-130; P ❄ 📶 🏊) This B&B 10km south of Moissac offers five enormous rooms blending modern touches such as flat-screen TVs with the house's 18th-century château shell, while retaining original features like marble fireplaces and a regal hallway. There's a heated pool (open April to October), grounds shaded by olive trees, and a sand pit, play area and enclosed garden for kids.

Le Table de Nos Fils FRENCH €€
(www.le-pont-napoleon.com; 2 allée Montebello; menus €29-45; ⏰noon-1.30pm & 7.30-10.30pm; 🖉) The restaurant attached to hotel **Le Pont Napoléon** (☎05 63 04 01 55; r/ste €62/75; P 📶) is one of the best addresses in town to dig into beautifully presented Tarn produce, such as duck nestled in a bed of artichokes or scallops surfing an asparagus risotto. Talented chef Patrick Delaroux runs occasional Saturday **cooking courses** (€55), from Lebanese food to the art of macaron-making; enquire in advance via the website.

ℹ Getting There & Away

There are regular direct trains from Moissac to Toulouse (€14.70, one hour, up to seven daily) and Montauban (€6.40, 20 minutes, frequent service).

WORTH A TRIP

BEAUMONT-DE-LOMAGNE

In a region of identically pretty towns, whose timbered houses doze under the afternoon sun, Beaumont-de-Lomagne's mathematical heritage offers something a little different. Yes, this town between Toulouse and Condom is blessed with creaky *hôtels particuliers* (private mansions), russet church towers and a garlic festival in late July – **La Fête de l'Ail Blanc de Lomagne** (www.club.quomodo.com/fetedel-ail) – but Beaumont is most famous as the birthplace of 17th-century maths genius and polymath Pierre de Fermat. In honour of Fermat's colossal contribution to world thought – including laying the groundwork for analytic geometry and pioneering probability theory with his contemporary, Blaise Pascal – visitors to his hometown will find maths and puzzle trails galore.

The works of Fermat spring to life at **Maison Natale de Pierre Fermat** (Association Fermat-Science; www.fermat-science.com; 3 rue Pierre de Fermat; ⏰9am-noon & 2-5pm Mon-Fri, 9am-noon Sat Jun-Sep, to 6pm Mon-Fri, 2-5pm Sat Jul & Aug, 2-5pm Mon-Fri Oct-May; 👪), a small museum within his birth house. His breakthroughs in geometry and collaborations with contemporaries like Descartes and Pascal are explained with hands-on displays. Try the countless maths games or take the spiral staircase up the 15th-century tower for sublime views over Beaumont's tiled roofs. Only 60km northwest of Toulouse, Beaumont makes for an agreeable and family-friendly detour.

Castres

POP 41,600

Local descriptions of Castres, 70km east of Toulouse, as a 'little Venice' do slightly oversell its charms. But not only does the town have political pedigree as the birthplace of French Socialism's founding father Jean Jaurès, it also has a superb museum of Spanish art and a landscaped park laid out by the designer of Versailles' gardens. With former tanneries casting fetching reflections in the Agout River flowing through town, Castres is a scenic spot to take a breather from Toulouse.

Settled since the Iron Age, Castres rose to prominence with the construction of a Benedictine abbey in the 9th century. Much of its architectural finery dates to the 17th century, and several *hôtels particuliers* (private mansions) from this era remain.

Sights

Admire the best views in town from **quai des Jacobins**, which overlooks bridges and historic houses clustered at the river's edge, and the **Jardin de l'Évêché**, laid out by Le Nôtre, architect of Versailles' park.

If you're planning to visit both the Musée Goya and Centre Jean Jaurès, it's cheaper with Castres' museum pass (€6.50), available at the tourist office.

Centre Jean Jaurès MUSEUM
(2 place Pélisson; adult/child €3/1.50; ⌚10am-noon & 2-6pm Tue-Sat Sep-Jun, 10am-noon & 2-6pm Mon-Sat Jul-Aug) If you're wondering why almost every French town seems to have a 'rue Jean Jaurès', this museum has everything you need to know about the father of French Socialism. Castres-born Jean Jaurès lifted the movement for the emancipation of working people into the mainstream. The museum pays tribute to his life and works (most information is in French), while contextualising principles that remain cherished in modern France: press freedom, the right to strike, and the importance of leisure for working people.

Musée Goya ART MUSEUM
(goya@ville-castres.fr; rue de l'Hôtel de Ville; adult/child €5/free; ⌚10am-6pm Jul & Aug, 10am-noon & 2-5pm Tue-Sun Sep-Jun) This excellent gallery on the 1st floor of Castres' Hôtel de Ville has a collection of mostly Spanish art, including work by Picasso, Rusiñol, Velázquez and, of course, several works by Goya (including the vast *La Junte des Philippines*). The museum's arms room has interesting collections of old weapons, helmets and fragments of WWII resistance history.

Information

Tourist Office (☎05 63 62 63 62; www.tourisme-castres.fr; 2 place de la République; ⌚9.30am-6.30pm Mon-Sat, 10.30am-noon & 2.30-4.30pm Sun Jul & Aug, 9.30am-12.30pm & 2-6pm Mon-Sat, 2.30-4.30pm Sun Sep-Jun) Get your hands on hotel and transport information, plus a money-saving museum pass, at this tourist office overlooking the sculpted Jardin de l'Évêché.

Getting There & Away

Direct trains and SNCF buses reach Castres from Toulouse (€15.70, one to 1½ hours, 10 to 14 daily).

Auch

POP 22,000

Quaint Auch (rhymes with 'gauche') is a tangle of narrow lanes and half-timbered houses, with architectural treasures that hint at its former glory. Capital of the Gers *département,* named for the river sloshing through the Hautes Pyrénées, Auch was formerly a seat of power for Armagnac's counts.

One monument to Auch's stately past and strategic importance is the 40m **Tour d'Armagnac**, a 14th-century tower and former prison. Auch's snug historic centre, dotted with Gascon restaurants and easy-going bars, is an agreeable day trip and an ideal way station between Toulouse and the west coast of France.

The 374 stone steps of **Escalier Monumental** flow luxuriantly from place Salinis, behind Auch's cathedral, to bd Sadi Carnot by the Gers River, over a drop of 35m. Scenic lookouts from this 1863 staircase overlook Auch's lower town and the surrounding hills. Halfway up there's a chest-puffing statue of Gers-born d'Artagnan, the 17th-century king's guard immortalised in Alexandre Dumas' *The Three Musketeers,* and a modern installation by Catalan artist Jaume Plensa, with metallic lettering that tells the Biblical story of the flood.

Even travellers weary of traipsing around yet another French church will be delighted by Auch's Unesco World Heritage–listed **Cathédrale Ste-Marie** (rue Arnaud de Moles; ⌚9.30am-7pm Jul & Aug, 9.30am-noon & 2-5.50pm Sep-Jun), a flamboyant late-Gothic to

DON'T MISS

A GASCON FEAST

Duck features heavily on the menu at cosy **La Table d'Oste** (☎05 62 05 55 62; www.latabledoste.com; 7 rue Lamartine; menus lunch €18, dinner €25-43; ⏲noon-2pm & 7-9pm Tue-Fri, noon-2pm Sat, 7-9pm Mon) – you could eat several courses dedicated to Gascony's favourite bird, roasted to succulence and lavished with local red wine or Gascon mustard. In the *hamburger Gascon*, different preparations of duck replace both bun and burger. Refresh yourself after the meat feast with prune-and-Armagnac ice cream.

Renaissance building with limestone towers rising imperiously from Auch's main square. Don't miss the **choir** (€2), where intricate wood carvings depict apostles, saints, Greek sages and pagan prophetesses. Look for Judith nonchalantly decapitating Holopherne, and St Martha with a tamed *tarasque* (dragon) by her feet. Eighteen impressive stained-glass windows, dating to 1513, beam from above.

The **tourist office** (☎05 62 05 22 89; www.auch-tourisme.com; 1 rue Dessoles; ⏲9.30am-6.30pm Mon-Sat, 10am-12.30pm & 3-5.30pm Sun Jul & Aug, 10am-12.15pm & 2-6pm Mon-Fri, to 5pm Sat Sep-Jun) is opposite the cathedral in a 15th-century half-timbered building. Pick up a trail map for a self-guided walking tour around Auch's historic buildings; if the office is closed, you can scan QR codes on display with your smartphone to access info and trails.

Direct trains or SNCF buses link Auch with Toulouse (€16, 1½ to two hours, six daily). Local buses serve Condom (€7, one hour, two to three daily). The train and bus stations are 1km east of the town centre.

Condom

POP 7000

Somewhere between pacing medieval streets and standing beneath a superb Gothic cathedral, amusement over Condom's unfortunate town name quickly turns to awe. It actually derives from the Gallo-Roman word 'Condatomagus', meaning a market town at a river confluence (Condom is situated where the Baïse and Gèle Rivers meet). Locals are well aware of the name's contraceptive meaning, which elicits sniggers among English-speakers; town signs are firmly nailed down, to avoid falling prey to souvenir-hunters.

While the historic centre needs only a day to explore, Condom is in the midst of Armagnac country, where a potent local brandy has been produced for centuries. This mellow town is a superb base from which to visit distilleries, abbeys and historic ramparts.

Sights & Activities

Cathédrale St-Pierre CHURCH

(place St-Pierre; ⏲8am-6pm daily) The foundations of this formidable cathedral date back to 1011, when the site hosted a Benedictine abbey. The cathedral was rebuilt in Flamboyant Gothic style with a lofty nave and elaborate chancel. The 16th-century **cloister**, accessed from rue de l'Evêché, was designed to offer wet-weather protection for Compostela pilgrims; note the weathered scallop shell, emblem of St James, in stone relief on the wall.

Musée de l'Armagnac MUSEUM

(2 rue Jules Ferry; adult/child €2.20/1.10; ⏲10am-noon & 3-6pm Wed-Mon Apr-Oct, 2-5pm Wed-Sat Nov & Dec, Feb & Mar, closed Jan) Located in a turn-of-the-century cellar, this museum is dedicated to the fine art of Armagnac production; it houses a modest collection of vintage bottles, agricultural tools and an 18-tonne press dating from the 19th century.

Gascogne Navigation BOATING

(☎05 62 28 46 46; www.gascogne-navigation.com; 3 av d'Aquitaine) From April to October, Gascogne Navigation runs one-hour river cruises (adult/child €8/6) and 2½-hour lunch cruises (€39/26) along the Baïse River, departing from quai Bouquerie. It also rents small motorboats (€35/82/120 per hour/half-day/full day).

Sleeping & Eating

Hôtel Continental HOTEL €

(☎05 62 68 37 00; www.lecontinental.net; 20 rue Maréchal Foch; r €65-98, ste €148; P Wi-Fi) This lemon-yellow heritage hotel set along the riverfront has small but immaculately clean rooms, all decorated in a palette of cream with occasional vintage flourishes. The quietest rooms overlook the garden. Hotel parking, just across the road, is €5 per night; otherwise leave your car a little further away along av Général de Gaulle.

The restaurant (mains €16) stands out as one of the best in town, serving regional flavours like bean-and-sausage stew alongside nicely cooked Charolais beef and coconut-mango *clafoutis* (flan).

Les Trois Lys HOTEL €€
(☎05 62 28 33 33; www.lestroislys.com; 38 rue Gambetta; d €80-180; P ❄ 📶 🏊) This 18th-century mansion has been transformed into an aristocratic hotel. Rooms range in style and size, but most have antique furniture and vintage rugs; some have shuttered windows overlooking the pool. The restaurant serves suitably upmarket French cuisine.

★ **La Table des Cordeliers** GASTRONOMIC €€€
(☎05 62 68 43 82; www.latabledescordeliers.com; 1 rue des Cordeliers; menus €23-75; ⏲noon-2pm & 7-9pm Tue-Sat) Condom's premier restaurant is run by Michelin-starred Eric Sampietro, a culinary magician known for seasonal ingredients assembled in surprising combinations. Tasting *menus* come at a price, but the adjoining bistro offers a three-course *menu* for just €23, with beguiling dishes such as ricotta-and-lobster ravioli. The setting is gorgeous: it's inside a 13th-century chapel, complete with cloister garden.

Information

Tourist Office (☎05 62 28 00 80; www.tourisme-condom.com; 5 place Saint-Pierre; ⏲9am-noon & 2-6.30pm Mon-Sat) Opposite the cathedral. Ask about guided cathedral tours and seasonal opening times for Armagnac distilleries.

Getting There & Around

Condom's bus links are limited but local services run to Auch (€1.50, one hour, two daily Monday to Friday), while local and SNCF buses reach Agen (€3.50 to €8.70, 50 minutes, one to three daily Monday to Saturday), from where you can catch trains to Toulouse.

To park on the street, you'll need a blue timed disc, available from the tourist office, but there are free car parks near the cathedral and off rue Jean Jaurès.

Around Condom

A carpet of meadows and vineyards unfurls beyond the town of Condom. This northern expanse of the Gers *département* is renowned for its centuries-old Armagnac distilleries. The terrain is ideal for unchallenging road trips: long boulevards lined with birch trees connect regal châteaus with villages of ancient stone.

During the Hundred Years' War, the area was pinched between strongholds of the French and English armies, based in Toulouse and Bordeaux, respectively. This past tumult has bequeathed it a number of *bastides*, created by wealthier villages as protection against attack.

May to September is prime visitor season; at either end of that period you'll enjoy fewer crowds.

Sights

Ensemble Collégiale St-Pierre CHURCH, MONASTERY
(www.la-romieu.com; La Romieu; adult/child €5.10/free; ⏲9.30am-7pm Mon-Sat, 2-7pm Sun May-Sep, 10am-12.30pm & 1.30-6pm Mon-Sat, 2-6pm Sun Oct-Apr) A twin-towered medieval church and cloisters are the focal point of tiny La Romieu, 12km northeast of Condom. This lonely village outpost first sprang up as a priory, founded in 1062 by two Benedictine monks returning from a pilgrimage to Rome via Toulouse (the name comes from *roumieu*, meaning 'Roman pilgrim'). The church interior is lavished with colourful decorations dating to the 19th century; ascend one of the towers (watch your step) for panoramic views of the Gers countryside.

Cité des Machines du Moyen Age OPEN-AIR MUSEUM
(http://larressingle.free.fr; Larressingle; adult/child €8.20/5.20; ⏲10am-7pm Jul & Aug, 2-6pm Mar-Jun, Sep & Oct, closed Nov-Feb; 👪) Would you have withstood the hardships of medieval

OFF THE BEATEN TRACK

ABBAYE DE FLARAN

Serene Cistercian abbey **Abbaye de Flaran** (☎05 62 28 50 19; www.fources.fr/abbayeflaran.html; Valence-sur-Baïse; adult/child €5/2; ⏲9.30am-7pm Jul-Aug, 9.30am-12.30pm & 2-6pm Sep-Jun) is one of the loveliest in the Gers *département*. Founded in 1151 and guarded by a 14th-century fortress door, it was abandoned after the Revolution but the building is remarkably well preserved. Among the rooms on show are the monks' cloister, refectory and sleeping cells, and there's a herb garden out back. It's near Valence-sur-Baïse, 10km south of Condom. Last entry is 30 minutes before closing time.

DON'T MISS

ARMAGNAC COUNTRY

Armagnac is best understood as Cognac's sophisticated older sister. While Cognac is world-renowned, Armagnac brandy is produced in smaller quantities for a rapt audience of European *digestif* connoisseurs. Distilled from white grapes in oaken barrels, Armagnac has the longest history of any French brandy – references to its medicinal qualities date back to the 14th century. There are several atmospheric locations within easy reach of Condom where you can sniff, sample and buy Armagnac. If you're sipping for the first time, keep breathing through your nose to allow its aromas to flood your senses.

Armagnac Ryst-Dupeyron (☎05 62 28 08 08; 36 rue Jean Jaurès; ⊙10am-noon & 2-5pm Mon-Fri) A turn-of-the-century cellar in Condom offering 45-minute tours and tasting sessions, with commentary in French, English, Spanish or Dutch; you can also buy bottles on-site. Arrive an hour before closing time (better yet, call ahead).

Château de Cassaigne (☎05 62 28 04 02; www.chateaudecassaigne.com; tours adult/child €2.50/free; ⊙9am-noon & 2-7pm Jul & Aug, 9am-noon & 2-6pm Tue-Sat Sep-Jun) Fine Armagnac and other regional drops are produced within this beautiful 13th-century château, 6.5km southwest of Condom (off the D931 to Éauze). It's particularly known for its Floc de Gascogne, an aperitif fortified with Armagnac.

Château du Busca Maniban (☎05 62 28 40 38; www.buscamaniban.com; Mansencôme; ⊙9am-noon & 2-6pm Mon-Thu, 9am-noon Fri) This magnificent château, 10km south of Condom on the D229, has been distilling Armagnac since the mid-17th century. It's not the place for a distillery tour, but you can sample and buy fantastic Armagnac in its shop.

warfare, and looked dapper in a chainmail tunic? Find out in Larressingle, the smallest fortified town in France, where replica war machines from the 13th and 14th centuries, including trebuchets and *bombardelle* cannons, are set up around the ramparts and shown off with flash-bang demonstrations.

Sleeping & Eating

Outstanding *chambres d'hôte* with warm-hearted hospitality can be found in historic buildings around the region, especially near Larressingle.

La Lumiane B&B €

(☎05 62 28 95 95; www.lalumiane.com; St Puy; s €66-76, d €69-79; ⊙Mar-Dec; 📶🏊) Bubbly host Mireille (and her canine sidekick Admiral Nelson) aim to please at this cheery B&B between Condom and Auch. Housed in a 17th-century cottage, the interior has been redecorated in bold shades from chocolate to violet, adding a dash of modern flair among the creaking wooden beams and stone walls. There are shady gardens to relax in, plus a small pool with views of the village church. There's wi-fi in common areas. Reserve a few days ahead for an evening meal of rustic Gers cuisine (three courses €30).

★**Les Bruhasses** B&B €€

(☎05 62 68 38 35; www.lesbruhasses.fr; off D931, Condom; d €85, ste €95-150 incl breakfast; ⊙mid-Jan–mid-Dec; 🅿📶) This turreted 1750 building 5km south of Condom once hosted an Armagnac producer, and has since been converted into a comfortable family-run guesthouse with plenty of period detail. Local gastronomy is a passion for the owners, who prepare meals on-site and source wines from barely 20 minutes down the road (three courses with aperitif, wine and coffee costs €32).

Lacassagne B&B €€

(☎05 62 28 26 89; www.lacassagnechambresd-hotes.fr; Laressingle; d incl breakfast €65-105; 🅿📶) Set in oak-filled countryside just outside Laressingle, this delightful, one-storey hilltop house has shuttered French doors looking out onto the garden, four simple rooms with romantic trimmings, and lounge with fireplace. Owner Maïder Papelorey is a fantastic cook; enquire about her €28 *menus*, featuring locally sourced produce. House dogs Bobby and Jacky guarantee a loud welcome.

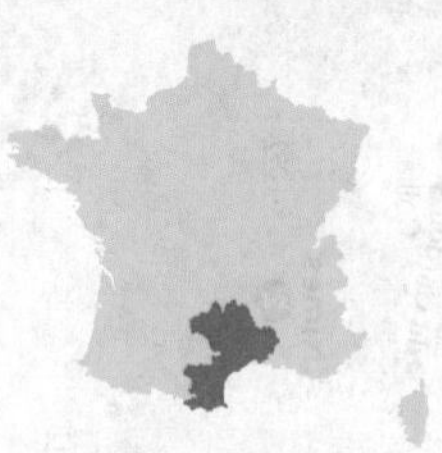

Languedoc-Roussillon

POP 2.7 MILLION

Includes ➡

Best Places to Eat

- ➡ L'Esprit des Mets (p716)
- ➡ La Mangeoire (p742)
- ➡ La Barbacane (p733)
- ➡ Le Marin (p727)

Best Places to Sleep

- ➡ Hôtel de la Cité (p731)
- ➡ Château de Creissels (p741)
- ➡ Rivages (p725)
- ➡ La Sousta (p714)

Why Go?

Stretching from Provence to the Pyrenees, this sultry, sun-baked region feels like a country in its own right. It's been a strategic border since Roman times and is awash with historical reminders, from Roman aqueducts to hilltop Cathar castles. These days it's best known for its vineyards, which produce a third of France's wines, and the busy beaches sprawling along its Mediterranean shore.

Each of Languedoc-Roussillon's three main areas has its own distinct landscape and character. Coastal Bas-Languedoc is home to the biggest beaches and the captivating cities of Montpellier and Nîmes. Inland lies the high, wild country of the Haut-Languedoc, home to the Parc National des Cévennes' hills, caves, gorges and forests. To the southwest is Roussillon, which shares close ties with Catalonia just across the Spanish border, including traditional *sardanes* folk dances and a passion for rugby, bullfights and vibrant summer *férias*.

When to Go

Montpellier

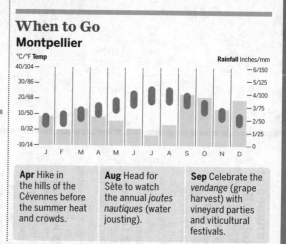

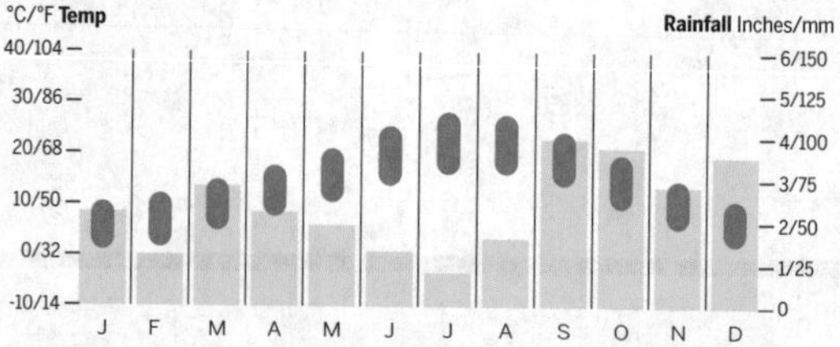

Apr Hike in the hills of the Cévennes before the summer heat and crowds.

Aug Head for Sète to watch the annual *joutes nautiques* (water jousting).

Sep Celebrate the *vendange* (grape harvest) with vineyard parties and viticultural festivals.

Languedoc-Roussillon Highlights

1 Musée Fabre (p717) Contemplating one of France's richest collections of European art in the exquisite city of Montpellier.

2 Les Arènes (p710) Visiting Nîmes' monumental twin-tiered amphitheatre dating from c 100 BC.

3 Pont du Gard (p714) Marvelling at the Romans' architectural ambition at this towering aqueduct.

4 Parc National des Cévennes (p733) Trekking in Robert Louis Stevenson's footsteps with a donkey through wild, rugged countryside.

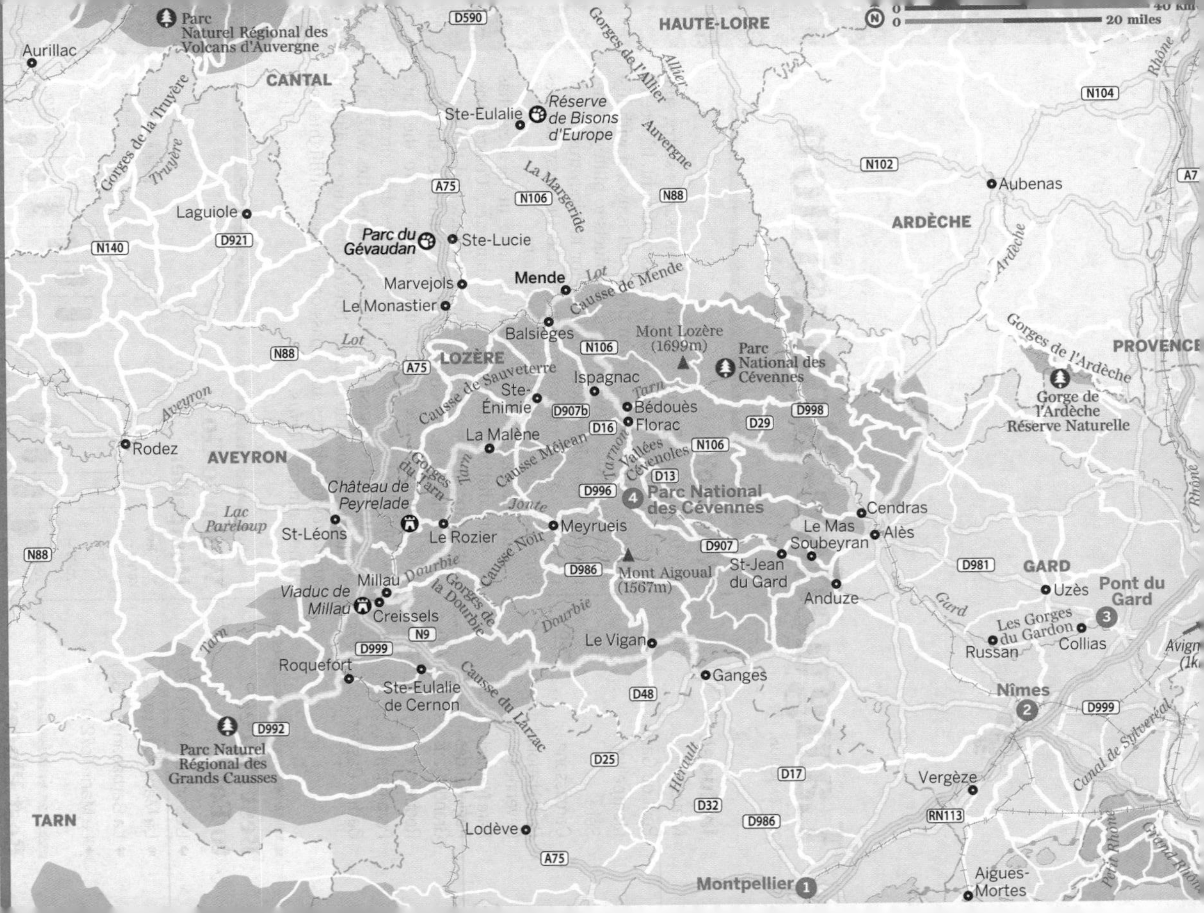

5 Bouzigues (p726) Viewing shellfish beds aboard a cruise before tasting the town's famous oysters and mussels.

6 Cathar castles (p749) Time-travelling back to the Middle Ages among the crumbling Cathar fortresses.

7 La Cité (p729) Strolling through Carcassonne's fairy-tale fortress, ringed by battlements and towers topped by witch's-hat turrets.

8 Parc des Dinosaures (p726) Being dwarfed by life-size dinosaur models at the site where Europe's biggest cache of dinosaur eggs was discovered.

FAST FACTS

Area 27,376 sq km

Local industry Winemaking, agriculture, tourism

Signature drink Red wine

BAS-LANGUEDOC

The broad, flat plains of Bas-Languedoc take in all of the Languedoc's main towns, as well as its best beaches and richest Roman remains, along with outstanding wines and gourmet produce.

During the Middle Ages, Bas-Languedoc was largely the property of the counts of Toulouse, but it now forms the modern-day *départements* of Gard and Hérault.

Nîmes

POP 154,000

Nîmes is a lively commercial centre these days, but two millennia ago it was one of the most important cities of Roman Gaul, as evidenced by its incredible collection of Roman buildings, including a magnificent amphitheatre and a 2000-year-old temple.

There are plenty of museums and markets to explore in Nîmes' palm-tree-lined streets, as well as a host of high-profile festivals throughout the year. The city is famed for the hard-wearing twill fabric known as *serge de Nîmes,* traditionally worn by agricultural labourers and now universally known as denim.

Sights

Save money by purchasing a **Pass Nîmes Romaine** (Roman Nîmes Pass; adult/child €12/10), which covers admission to Les Arènes, Maison Carrée and Tour Magne, and remains valid for three days.

★Les Arènes ROMAN SITE

(www.arenes-nimes.com; place des Arènes; adult/child incl audioguide €10/8; 9am-8pm Jul & Aug, shorter hours Sep-Jun) Nîmes' twin-tiered amphitheatre is the best preserved in France. Built around 100 BC, the arena once seated 24,000 spectators and staged gladiatorial contests and public executions, and it's still an impressive venue hosting gigs, events and summer bullfights (during which it's closed for visits). An audioguide provides context as you explore the arena, seating areas, stairwells and corridors (known to Romans as *vomitories*), and afterwards you can view replicas of gladiatorial armour and original bullfighters' costumes in the museum.

At 133m long, 101m wide and 21m high, with an oval arena encircled by two tiers of arches and columns, the amphitheatre is a testament to the skill and ingenuity of Roman architects. Despite being adapted, plundered for stone and generally abused over many centuries, the structure of the amphitheatre is still largely intact, and it's not hard to imagine what the atmosphere must have been like when it was filled to capacity.

The seating is divided into four tiers and 34 rows; the posher you were, the closer you sat to the centre. The amphitheatre's oval design meant everyone had an unrestricted view. A system of trapdoors and hoist-lifts beneath the arena enabled animals and combatants to be put into position during the show. Originally, the amphitheatre would have had a canopy that protected spectators from the weather.

Maison Carrée ROMAN SITE

(place de la Maison Carrée; adult/child €6/5; 9.30am-8pm Jul & Aug, shorter hours Sep-Jun) Constructed in gleaming limestone around AD 5, this temple was built to honour Emperor Augustus' two adopted sons. Despite the name, the Maison Carrée (Square House) is actually rectangular – to the Romans, 'square' simply meant a building with right angles. The building is beautifully preserved, complete with stately columns and triumphal steps. There's no need to go inside unless you're interested in the relatively cheesy 22-minute 3D film.

Jardins de la Fontaine ROMAN SITES

(quai de la Fontaine; garden free, Tour Magne adult/child €3.50/3; 9am-8pm Jul & Aug, shorter hours Sep-Jun) Roman remains in these elegant gardens include the 30m-high **Tour Magne**, raised around 15 BC – the largest of a chain of towers conveying imperial power that once punctuated the city's 7km-long Roman ramparts. At the top of its 140 steps, an orientation table interprets the panoramic views over Nîmes. The gardens also shelter the **Source de la Fontaine** – once the site of a spring, temple and baths – and the crumbling **Temple de Diane**, located in the northwest corner.

Carré d'Art ART MUSEUM

(www.carreartmusee.com; 16 place de la Maison Carrée; permanent collection free, exhibitions

adult/child €5/3.70; ⏲10am-6pm Tue-Sun) The striking, glass-and-steel Carré d'Art was designed by British architect Sir Norman Foster. Inside is the **municipal library** and the **Musée d'Art Contemporain**, with permanent and temporary exhibitions covering art from the 1960s onwards. The rooftop restaurant makes a lovely spot for a drink.

Musée du Vieux Nîmes MUSEUM
(www.carreartmusee.com; place aux Herbes; ⏲10am-6pm Tue-Sun) FREE Inside Nîmes' 17th-century episcopal palace, the town museum delves into the history of Nîmes from Roman times through to the modern era, with lots of period costumes and a display of denim-wearing celebrities including Elvis and Marilyn Monroe.

Nîmes

0 — 200 m
0 — 0.1 miles

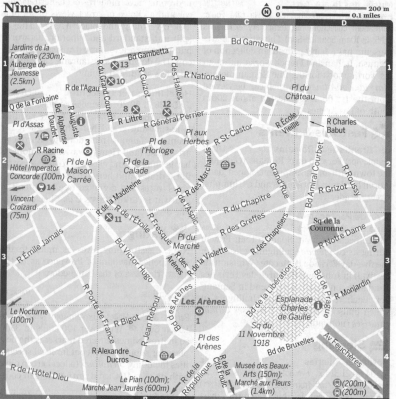

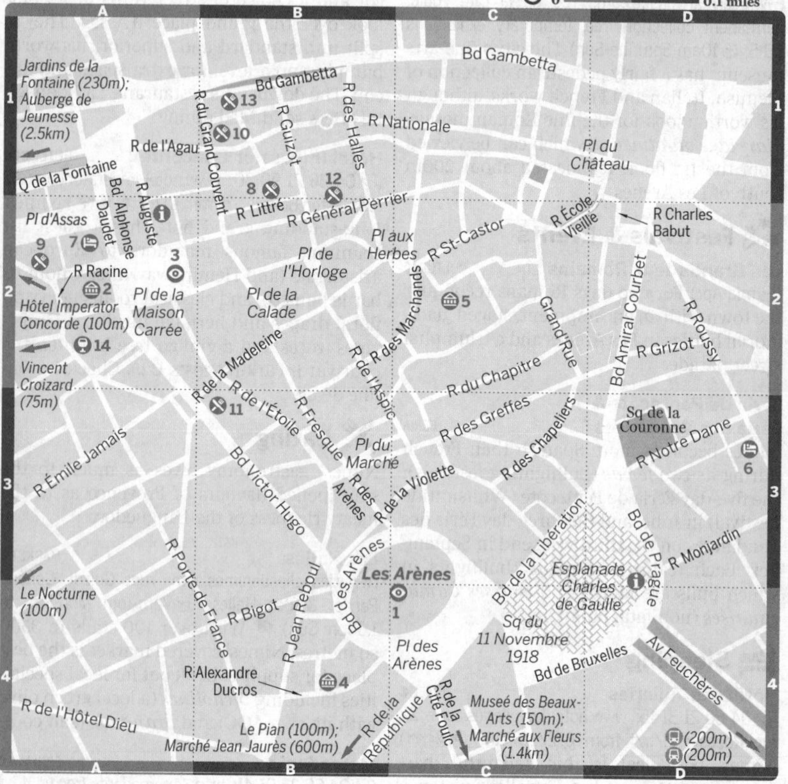

Nîmes

Top Sights
1 Les Arènes C4

Sights
2 Carré d'Art A2
3 Maison Carrée A2
4 Musée des Cultures Taurines B4
5 Musée du Vieux Nîmes C2

Sleeping
6 Hôtel des Tuileries D3
7 Royal Hôtel A2

Eating
8 Aux Plaisirs des Halles B1
9 Carré d'Art A2
10 La Petite Fadette B1
11 Le Cerf à Moustache B3
12 Les Halles B1
13 Mercadante B1

Drinking & Nightlife
14 L'Instant T A2

Musée des Cultures Taurines MUSEUM
(☎04 30 06 77 07; www.ot-nimes.fr; 6 rue Alexandre Ducros; permanent collection free, temporary exhibitions adult/child €5/3.70; ⊙10am-6pm Tue-Sun May-Oct) Learn about the origins of bullfighting at Nîmes' bullfighting museum, footsteps from Les Arènes. Over 8000 pieces make up the collection, including costumes, fans, photos, figurines and trophy (ie bull) heads.

Musée des Beaux-Arts ART MUSEUM
(www.carreartmusee.com; rue de la Cité Foulc; permanent collection free, temporary exhibitions €3-5; ⊙10am-6pm Tue-Sun) The city's fine-arts museum has a fairly pedestrian collection of Flemish, Italian and French works, although it's worth a look for the fine Roman mosaic, *Marriage of Admetus,* which can be viewed from the 1st floor. It's located about 200m south of Les Arènes.

Festivals & Events

Les Grands Jeux Romains CULTURAL
(⊙mid-Apr) For two days Romans reconquer the town with an encampment, staged gladiatorial battles in Les Arènes and a triumphal street parade.

Féria de Pentecôte & Féria des Vendanges FERIA
Nîmes becomes more Spanish than French during its two *férias* (bullfighting festivals): the five-day Féria de Pentecôte (Whitsuntide Festival) in June, and the three-day Féria des Vendanges on the third weekend in September. Each features *corridas* (bullfights in which bulls are killed) and *courses Camarguaises* (non-fatal bullfights).

Sleeping

Hôtel des Tuileries HOTEL €
(☎04 66 21 31 15; www.hoteldestuileries.com; 22 rue Roussy; d/tr/f from €72/90/115; P❄📶) Nîmes' best deal is this delightful, bargain-priced 11-room hotel strolling distance from Les Arènes. Individually decorated rooms are spacious and spotless, and some have covered balconies. Breakfast costs €8. Its private parking garage (€10) is located just down the street, but there are only five car spaces, so reserve ahead.

Auberge de Jeunesse HOSTEL €
(☎04 66 68 03 20; www.hifrance.org; 257 chemin de l'Auberge de Jeunesse, La Cigale; dm/d/f from €16.90/39/75; ⊙reception 7.30am-1am, hostel closed Nov & Dec; P📶) It's out in the sticks, 4km northwest of the bus and train stations, but this hostel has lots in its favour: spacious dorms, family rooms, a large garden with room to kick a football around and a self-catering kitchen and cafe. Take bus I, direction Alès or Villeverte, and get off at the Stade stop.

Royal Hôtel HOTEL €€
(☎04 66 58 28 27; www.royalhotel-nimes.com; 3 bd Alphonse Daudet; d €85-105, f €190; ❄📶) This upmarket hotel offers grace and style. Bedrooms have modern-meets-heritage decor and a choice of street views or an outlook over the grand place d'Assas. They're split into standard and superior; it's worth bumping up a level for extra space and air-con. The downstairs restaurant, La Boduegita, offers solid Med dining.

Hôtel Imperator Concorde HOTEL €€€
(☎04 66 21 90 30; www.hotel-imperator.com; 15 rue Gaston Boissier; d from €170; P❄📶) Nîmes' long-standing grand hotel has a guest list spanning famous matadors to European aristocrats (and Hemingway, after whom its bar is named), and classical rooms heavy on floral drapes and heritage furniture. Grapevines, roses and a ginkgo tree brighten the courtyard. Parking costs €25. Check for online deals.

Eating

Nîmes' gastronomy owes as much to the sun-ripened flavours of Provence as to the meaty richness of the Languedoc.

Les Halles MARKET €
(www.leshallesdenimes.com; rues Guizot, Général Perrier & des Halles; ⊙7am-1pm Mon-Sat, to 1.30pm Sun) 🌿 With over 100 stalls in 3500 sq metres, Nîmes' covered market is the best place for supplies. Look out for local specialities including *picholines* (a local green olive with its own AOC) and *brandade* (salt cod).

Mercadante SICILIAN €
(☎04 66 23 01 41; http://mercadante.free.fr; 4 bd Gambetta; 2-/3-course menus €14.50/19.50, mains €12-15; ⊙11.45am-2pm & 6-10pm Tue-Sat) Sicilian brothers Fabio and Salvo Mercadante serve the classic flavours of their homeland at their little gem of a restaurant: aubergine filled with pine nuts and raisins, lemon-stuffed sardines with olive oil, skewers of veal, cured ham and cheese, squid-ink spaghetti with fresh tomatoes and tuna, and swordfish in basil-laced tomato stew.

La Petite Fadette CAFE €
(☎04 66 67 53 05; 34 rue du Grand Couvent; menus €10-14.50, tapas €3.30-7.50; ⊙11am-2.30pm

Mon-Wed, 11am-2.30pm & 6-10.30pm Thu-Sat) *Tartines* (open-face toasted sandwiches) such as smoked salmon or cured ham and goat's cheese, as well as huge salads, are specialities of this cosy cafe, which has a cute rococo interior lined with vintage photos, and outside tables on a small courtyard. Contemporary tapas takes over the menu of an evening: crispy duck hearts, mini burgers, courgette *frites* (fries)...

★ Le Cerf à Moustache BISTRO €€
(☎09 81 83 44 33; www.lecerfamoustache.com; 38 bd Victor Hugo; 2-/3-course menus lunch €15.80/19.90, dinner €25.90/30.90; ⊙11.45am-2pm & 7.45-10pm Mon-Sat) The Deer with the Moustache has established itself as one of Nîmes' best bistros, with quirky decor (including reclaimed furniture and a wall of sketch-covered old books), matched by chef Julien Salem's creative take on the classics (Aveyronnais steak with St-Marcellin cream, rabbit ballotine with crushed potatoes and garlic, white-chocolate mousse with mandarin meringue) and 60 wines by the glass.

Carré d'Art GASTRONOMIC €€
(☎04 66 67 52 40; www.restaurant-lecarredart.com; 2 rue Gaston Boissier; lunch/dinner menu €19.50/26, mains €22-26; ⊙noon-3pm & 7.30-10pm Tue-Sat) Open since 1989, this heavy hitter is still one of Nîmes' top fine-dining addresses. The setting is elegant, in an abstract-art-adorned 19th-century town house with a gorgeous shaded courtyard, and the seasonal dishes give traditional French cuisine a modern spin: sole *meunière* with candied ginger, duck fillet with spiced honey *jus*, chocolate profiteroles with tonka-bean sauce, and chestnut tiramisu.

Le Nocturne BISTRO €€
(☎04 66 67 20 28; www.restaurant-le-nocturne.com; 29bis rue Benoit Malon; mains €30-40; ⊙8pm-1am Wed-Sun) Late-opening Le Nocturne is a fine place to dine on rich southwest flavours. Duck dominates the menu, whether duck breast with a choice of four sauces (raspberry, apple, cep or morel), classic *confit de canard* (duck cooked in its own fat) or *au tartare* (served raw), but there are also fish options. There are just 26 seats, so book ahead.

Aux Plaisirs des Halles TRADITIONAL FRENCH €€
(☎04 66 36 01 02; www.auxplaisirsdeshalles.com; 4 rue Littré; 2-course lunch menu €23, 2-/3-/4-course dinner menus €25/30/48; ⊙noon-2pm Tue & Sun, noon-2pm & 7.30-10pm Wed-Sat; 👪) Market-fresh dining is the order of the day here (red-mullet salad, beef with Jerusalem artichoke purée and grapefruit and red-pepper *jus*), served with an excellent choice of Languedoc wines. The mains are quite expensive, so consider swinging by for the good-value lunch *menu* or tapas.

Vincent Croizard GASTRONOMIC €€€
(☎04 66 67 04 99; www.restaurantcroizard.com; 17 rue des Chassaintes; lunch menus €23-28, dinner menus €48-70, mains €28; ⊙7.45-9.30pm Tue, noon-1.45pm & 7.45-9.30pm Wed-Sat, noon-1.45pm Sun) From its discreet facade on a quiet side street you'd never guess that this restaurant is home to an impossibly romantic lamplit courtyard garden and some of Nîmes' most inventive and artistic high-end cooking. Dishes use premium produce (black truffles, Aveyron suckling lamb, milk-fed veal and Bouzigues oysters); rare vintages and limited releases from small-scale producers make up the wine list.

Drinking & Nightlife

Place aux Herbes, place de l'Horloge and place du Marché are packed with busy cafes. Late-night bars and clubs congregate on rue Jean Reboul.

★ Le Pian WINE BAR
(www.bistrot-le-pian.jimdo.com; 20bis rue Bourdaloue; ⊙6.30pm-midnight Wed-Sat) Le Pian's vaulted cellar-like surrounds are an atmospheric setting for sampling some of its 500-plus wines and 80 whiskies, accompanied by cheese and charcuterie platters. It's set back from the street behind a rustic courtyard with bucolic murals and hefty timber beams that hosts jazz, blues, folk and world music. Glass doors lead to its state-of-the-art **wine shop** (⊙9.30am-7pm Tue, to 10pm Wed-Sat).

L'Instant T BAR
(www.linstantt-nimes.com; 2 rue Racine; ⊙11.30pm-1am Mon-Fri, 3.30pm-1am Sat, 5pm-midnight Sun) There's something happening most nights at this lively bar, from concerts (rock, folk, blues and traditional French *chansons*) to DJs, debates, cocktail events and beer and wine tastings. Over 90 beers are on the drinks menu, along with local wines.

Information

Tourist Office (☎04 66 58 38 00; www.ot-nimes.fr; 6 rue Auguste; ⊙9am-7.30pm Mon-Fri, 9am-7pm Sat, 10am-6pm Sun Jul & Aug, shorter hours rest of year; 📶) Also has a seasonal **annexe** (esplanade Charles de Gaulle;

⌚10am-5pm Jul & Aug) on esplanade Charles de Gaulle.

Getting There & Around

AIR

Aéroport de Nîmes Alès Camargue Cévennes (FNI; ☎04 66 70 49 49; www.aeroport-nimes.fr) Nîmes' airport, 10km southeast of the city on the A54, is served only by Ryanair, which flies to/from London Luton, Liverpool, Brussels and Fez.

An airport bus (€6.50, 30 minutes) to/from the train station connects with all flights.

BUS

The **bus station** (rue Ste-Félicité) is next to the train station. A bus journey anywhere within the Gard département costs a flat-rate €1.50. Local buses are run by Edgard (www.edgard-transport.fr).

Alès Line A10, €1.50, 1¼ hours, two to four Monday to Saturday

Pont du Gard Line B21, €1.50, 40 minutes, hourly Monday to Saturday, two on Sunday

Uzès Line E52, €1.50, 45 minutes, eight to 10 daily Monday to Friday, three or four at weekends

TRAIN

TGVs run hourly to/from Paris' Gare de Lyon (€77, three hours) from the **train station** (bd Sergent Triaire). Local destinations, with at least hourly departures, include the following:

Alès €9.90, 35 minutes

Arles €8.80, 35 minutes

Avignon €10.60, one hour

Montpellier €9.90, 30 minutes

Sète €13.10, 45 minutes

WORTH A TRIP

THE TRACTOR

A converted warehouse in Argilliers, 8km southeast of Uzès via the D981, is the setting for an offbeat and brilliant, dining destination – **Le Tracteur** (☎04 66 62 17 33; www.lucietestud.com/letracteur; Argilliers; 3-course menus lunch/dinner €25/29.50; ⌚kitchen noon-2pm Mon-Thu, noon-2pm & 7-10pm Fri, 7-10pm Sat). It's part wine shop, part art gallery, part deli, part bistro, and has a tree-shaded courtyard. Filled with battered furniture and abstract art, it's a fantastic space for dining on inspired Mediterranean creations. Look out for the namesake tractor outside.

Pont du Gard

Southern France has some fine Roman sites, but nothing can top the Unesco World Heritage-listed Pont du Gard.

Sights

★Pont du Gard ROMAN SITE

(☎04 66 37 50 99; www.pontdugard.fr; car & up to 5 passengers €18, after 8pm €10, by bicycle or on foot €7, after 8pm €3.50; ⌚site 24hr year-round, visitor centre & museum 9am-8pm Jul & Aug, shorter hours Sep–mid-Jan & mid-Feb–Jun) The extraordinary three-tiered Pont du Gard, 21km northeast of Nîmes, was once part of a 50km-long system of channels built around 19 BC to transport water from Uzès to Nîmes. The scale is huge: the bridge is 48.8m high, 275m long and graced with 52 precision-built arches. It was sturdy enough to carry up to 20,000 cu metres of water per day.

Each block was carved by hand and transported from nearby quarries – no mean feat, considering the largest blocks weighed over 5 tonnes. The height of the bridge descends by 2.5cm across its length, providing just enough gradient to keep the water flowing – an amazing demonstration of the precision of Roman engineering. The **Musée de la Romanité** provides background on the bridge's construction, and the **Ludo play area** helps kids to learn in a fun, hands-on way; both are closed from mid-January to mid-February.

You can walk across the tiers for panoramic views over the Gard River, but the best perspective on the bridge is from downstream, along the 1.4km **Mémoires de Garrigue walking trail**. Early evening is a good time to visit, as admission is cheaper and the bridge is stunningly illuminated after dark.

Sleeping & Eating

Pont du Gard has an on-site restaurant and cafe on opposite sides of the river operating seasonal hours, but they're often busy and not great value. Your best bet is to bring a picnic; alternatively, there are dining options in the nearby towns of Collias, Remoulins and Vers-Pont-du-Gard, and there's an outstanding restaurant, Le Tracteur, in Argilliers.

★La Sousta CAMPGROUND €

(☎04 66 37 12 80; www.lasousta.com; 28 av du Pont du Gard, Remoulins; camping per 2 people & tent €30, car €8, cabins per week from €825;

WORTH A TRIP

CANOEING ON THE GARD RIVER

For a unique perspective on the Pont du Gard, see it from the water. The Gard River flows from the Cévennes mountains all the way to the aqueduct, passing through the dramatic Gorges du Gardon en route. The best time to do it is early spring between April and June, as winter floods and summer droughts can sometimes make the river impassable.

Most of the local hire companies are based in Collias, 8km from the bridge, a journey of about two hours by kayak. Depending on the season and the height of the river, you can make a longer journey by being dropped upstream at Pont St-Nicholas (19km, four to five hours) or Russan (32km, six to seven hours); the latter option also includes a memorable trip through the Gorges du Gardon. There's a minimum age of six. Life jackets are always provided, but you must be a competent swimmer.

In addition to canoe rental, **Canoë Le Tourbillon** (04 66 22 85 54; www.canoeletourbillon.com; 3 chemin du Gardon, Collias; adult/child from Collias €23/17, from Russan €36/24; 9am-7pm Apr-Sep) also offers transport and equipment for via ferrata climbs on the nearby Gardon massif (€15 for two hours). Picnic lunches are available on request.

Kayak Vert (04 66 22 80 76; www.kayakvert.com; 8 chemin de St-Vincent, Collias; adult/child from Collias €23/19, from Russan €41/37; 9am-6pm mid-May–Oct) has one- to four-person boats.

Mar-Oct; P) As close to the Pont du Gard as it's possible to stay, only 100m from the car park, La Sousta has shady, well-spaced sites and good facilities including a laundry, barbecues, tennis courts, ping-pong tables and its own private beach on the river, with patrolled swimming areas during summer. Wi-fi's available at the kitchen block, pool and grocery shop.

Getting There & Away

There are large car parks on both banks of the river that are a 400m level walk from the Pont du Gard.

Several buses stop nearby, including Edgard bus B21 (€1.50, hourly Monday to Saturday, two or three on Sunday) between Nîmes and Alès.

Uzès

POP 8573

Storybook-pretty Uzès is renowned for its Renaissance architecture, a reminder of the days when it was an important trading centre – especially for silk, linen and liquorice. But it also has strong Roman links: water was delivered here via the Pont du Gard aqueduct en route to Nîmes, 25km to the southwest.

Highlights here include the ducal palace, the cathedral and the arcaded central square, place aux Herbes, which hosts a lively farmers market every Wednesday and Saturday. For foodies, Uzès' biggest appeal is its cache of sublime places to dine.

Sights

★Cathédrale St-Théodont CATHEDRAL

(www.nimes.catholique.fr; place de l'Évêché; 9am-6pm May-Sep, to 5pm Oct-Apr) Built in 1090 on the site of a Roman temple, Uzès' cathedral was partially destroyed in both the 13th and 16th centuries and stripped during the French Revolution. All that remains of the 11th-century church is its 42m-high tower, Tour Fenestrelle, the only round bell tower in France, which resembles an upright Leaning Tower of Pisa. The neo-Romanesque façade was built in the 19th century and was listed as a national monument in 1862.

The church's Baroque 17th-century organ, built in 1670, is the only one in the country to retain its original grey-painted, gilded shutters. Concerts take place in summer – check with the tourist office for dates and tickets.

★Duché CHÂTEAU

(www.duche-uzes.fr; place du Duché; €13, incl tour €18; 10am-12.30pm & 2-6.30pm Jul & Aug, 10am-noon & 2-6pm Sep-Jun) This fortified château belonged to the House of Cressol, who were the dukes of Uzès for over 1000 years until the French Revolution. The building is a Renaissance wonder, with a majestic 16th-century façade showing the three orders of classical architecture (Ionic, Doric and Corinthian). Inside, guided tours (in French) take in the lavish ducal apartments and 800-year-old cellars; you can climb the 135-step Bermonde tower for wraparound town views. On Sunday, tour prices drop to €10.

WORTH A TRIP

LUNCH IN ALÈS

Industrial Alès – and especially its business park 3km south of the centre across the river – is the last place you'd expect to find a fine-dining diamond, but foodies flock to **L'Esprit des Mets** (☎04 66 52 21 80; 148 av d'Anduze; 2-course lunch menu €16, 2-/3-course dinner menus €24/29, mains €18-25; ⊙noon-2pm & 7.30-9.30pm Tue-Sat;), so book ahead. In his open kitchen, chef Christian Achour creates masterpieces including his signature *tournedos rossini* (filet mignon and pan-fried foie gras) with black-truffle *jus*. All wines are local.

Jardin Médiéval GARDENS
(Medieval Garden; http://jardinmedievaluzes.com; rue Port Royal; adult/child garden & Tour du Roi €6/3.50, garden only €4.50/2; ⊙10.30am-12.30pm & 2-6pm Jul & Aug, shorter hours Apr-Jun, Sep & Oct, closed Nov-Mar) This delightful garden contains a wealth of plants and flowers that served a variety of purposes for their medieval planters: medicinal, nutritional and symbolic. Climbing 100 steps inside the Tour du Roi (King's Tower) rewards with panoramic views over Uzès' rooftops.

Musée du Bonbon Haribo MUSEUM
(Sweets Museum; www.museeharibo.fr; Pont des Charrettes; adult/child €7/5; ⊙9.30am-7pm Jul & Aug, 10am-1pm & 2-6pm Tue-Sun Sep-Jun) Uzès' history as a centre for confectionery continues at this Wonka-esque museum, which explores the sweet-making process from the early 20th century through to the present day. There's a collection of antique advertising posters and vintage confectionery machinery, but inevitably it's the rainbow-coloured sweet shop that takes centre stage. It's 4km southeast of town.

Festivals & Events

Foire Aux Truffes FOOD
(⊙late Jan) A full-blown truffle fair, held on the third Sunday in January.

Foire à l'Ail FOOD
(⊙24 Jun) Heady scents fill Uzès during its garlic fair.

Nuits Musicales d'Uzès MUSIC
(www.nuitsmusicalesuzes.org; ⊙Jul) This international festival of baroque music and jazz takes place during the second half of July.

Sleeping

La Maison Rouge B&B €€
(☎09 50 25 91 06; www.maison-rouge-uzes.com; 6 rue de la Perrine; d €135-160;) The Red House was built from scarlet brick in 1830 for a gentleman-about-town on the edge of old Uzès. Despite its vintage trappings (balconies, stone staircase), the house has been beautifully modernised, with wooden floors, walk-in showers and swish furniture. Shutters open out to the back-garden pool; on a clear day you can see Mont Ventoux.

Hostellerie Provençale HOTEL €€
(☎04 66 22 11 06; www.hostellerieprovencale.com; 1-3 rue de la Grande Bourgade; d €130-155, tr €175;) This old-style hotel is a trip back in time: the nine rooms of varying size are a mix of wonky floors, sloping ceilings, antique dressers and exposed stone, giving the place a bygone-era vibe. The downstairs restaurant, La Parenthèse, serves good regional cuisine (*menus* €22 to €46). Parking costs €15; breakfast is €14.

★**La Maison d'Uzès** BOUTIQUE HOTEL €€€
(☎04 66 20 07 00; www.lamaisonduzes.fr; 18 rue du Dr Blanchard; d €270-310;) Occupying a 17th-century *hôtel particulier* (historic mansion) in Uzès' historic centre, this jewel has beautiful rooms filled with light-toned vintage and contemporary furnishings, and a Michelin-starred restaurant, La Table d'Uzès, opening to a gorgeous linden-tree-shaded courtyard with a fountain at its centre. The pièce de résistance is the in-house spa with swimming pool set in an old Roman cellar.

Eating

La Fabrique Givrée ICE CREAM €
(www.lafabriquegivree.com; 27 place aux Herbes; 1/2/3/4 scoops €2.50/4.50/6/7; ⊙10am-1am Jun-Sep, 11am-10pm Oct-May) Exquisite seasonal flavours at this late-opening artisanal *glacier* (ice-cream maker) range from chestnut, salted caramel, and white peach to exotic Iranian pistachio, Indian sesame, Ethiopian coffee, Libyan tangerine, basil and Lebanon orange flower, and Italian lemon and mint.

La Nougatine BOULANGERIE, TEAROOM €
(25 bd Gambetta; dishes €1.80-6; ⊙6am-7.30pm Tue-Sun) Uzès' best *boulangerie*-patisserie makes the town speciality *croquignole:* shortbread made from sugar syrup, icing sugar and flour, with an almond or hazelnut at its centre, and coated in an orange glaze after baking. It also makes mouth-watering pastries as well as savoury quiches, gourmet

sandwiches and crunchy breads, and serves hot chocolate in winter. There's an elegant on-site tearoom.

La Table d'Uzès GASTRONOMIC €€
(☎04 66 20 07 00; www.lamaisonduzes.fr; 18 rue du Dr Blanchard; lunch/dinner menus from €29/59; ⌚12.15-1.45pm & 7.30-8.45pm Wed-Sun) Chef Christophe Ducros works his magic with seasonal sun-ripened local produce such as peaches, apricots, courgettes, aubergines, tomatoes, green beans, line-caught Mediterranean fish, truffles, Lozère lamb, wild trout, pigeon and mushrooms foraged from the Parc National des Cévennes at his Michelin-starred restaurant inside La Maison d'Uzès. Book ahead and be sure to request a courtyard seat in fine weather.

MilléZime MODERN FRENCH €€
(☎04 66 22 27 82; http://restaurant-millezime.fr; 6 bd Gambetta; 2-/3-course menus lunch €16/19, dinner €20/25; ⌚noon-3pm & 7-10pm Jul & Aug, noon-2pm & 7-9pm Tue-Sun Sep-Jun) MilléZime's barrel-vaulted dining room is a romantic setting for enjoying local specialities such as snail *cassoulet,* sea bream with truffled crushed potatoes, filet mignon with roast mushrooms and red-wine *jus,* and pigeon with artichokes. Order the signature Grand Marnier soufflé at the start of your meal so it's ready by the end. In winter, the four-course truffle menu (€48) is fantastic value.

ℹ Information

Tourist Office (☎04 66 22 68 88; www.uzes-tourisme.com; place Albert 1er; ⌚10am-6pm Mon-Fri, 10am-1pm & 2-5pm Sat & Sun Jun-Sep, shorter hours Oct-May) Just outside the old quarter.

ℹ Getting There & Away

Local buses are run by **Edgard** (www.edgard-transport.fr).

Alès Line A15, €1.50, one hour, five daily Monday to Friday, three on weekends

Avignon Line A15, €1.50, one hour, five daily Monday to Friday, three on weekends

Nîmes Line E52, €1.50, one hour, eight to 10 daily Monday to Friday, three or four on weekends

Montpellier

POP 272,000

Graceful and easy-going, Montpellier is a stylish metropolis with elegant buildings, grand *hôtels particuliers* (private mansions), stately boulevards and shady backstreets, and gorgeous white-sand beaches on its doorstep.

Unlike many southern towns, Montpellier has no Roman heritage. Instead it was founded in the 10th century by the counts of Toulouse and later became a prosperous trading port as well as a scholarly centre – Europe's first medical school was established here in the 12th century.

The population swelled in the 1960s when many French settlers left independent Algeria and relocated here, and it's now France's fastest-growing city and one of its most multicultural. Students make up over a third of the population, giving it a spirited vibe.

Sights

Montpellier's beating heart is the huge open square of place de la Comédie. The city's finest period architecture and *hôtels particuliers* are around the old quarter, which lies to the northeast, bordered by the main roads of bd Henri IV, rue Foch and bd Louis Pasteur.

City Centre

★**Musée Fabre** GALLERY
(www.museefabre.fr; 39 bd de Bonne Nouvelle; adult/child €6/4, with Département des Arts Décoratifs €7/5, 1st Sun of month free; ⌚10am-6pm Tue-Sun) Founded in 1825 by painter François-Xavier Fabre, this exceptional museum houses one of France's richest collections of European art. The galleries are split into three main sections: Old Masters, Modern Movements and Decorative Arts, collectively representing the last 600 years of artistic activity in Europe. Most of the big names are represented, and the renovation has transformed the museum into a light, airy and engaging space.

Highlights of the Old Masters include three paintings by Rubens, a dreamy Venus and Adonis by Nicholas Poussin, and a

> **ℹ CENT SAVER**
>
> The **Montpellier City Card** (1/2/3 days €13.50/19.80/25.20, children half-price) allows unlimited travel on trams and buses, discounts at shops, a guided walking tour and free admission to several museums – with the notable exception of the Musée Fabre. It must be pre-booked on the tourist-office website and collected in person.

Montpellier

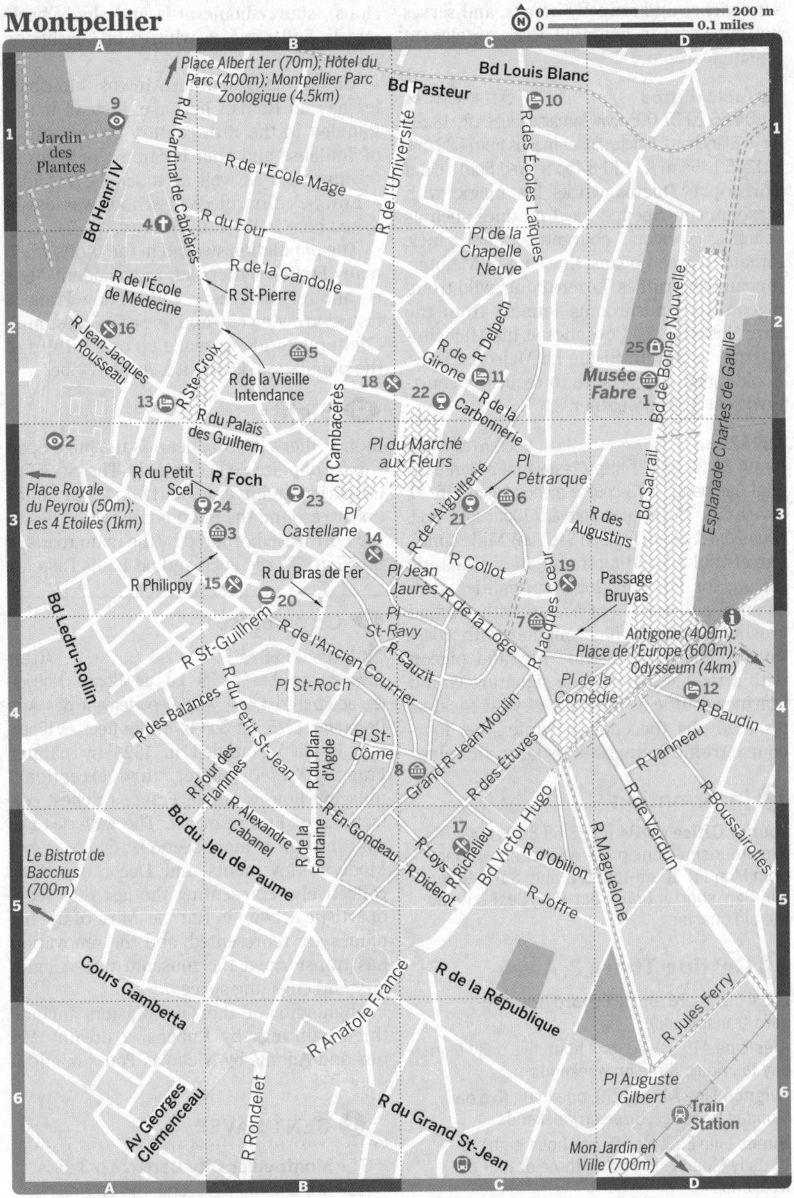

collection of works by Jacques-Louis David. The Romantic section is strong on French artists – particularly Delacroix, Géricault and Courbet – while Manet, Degas and Delaunay are among the standouts of the modern section.

Of particular local interest are the works of Marseille-born artist Fréderic Bazille (1841–70), a close contemporary of Monet, Sisley and Manet. The artist has a whole room devoted to him: look out for his portrait of Renoir, seated on a chair with

Montpellier

Top Sights

1 Musée Fabre D2

Sights

2 Arc de Triomphe A3
3 Carré Sainte-Anne B3
4 Cathédrale St-Pierre A1
5 Hôtel de la Vieille Intendance B2
6 Hôtel de Varennes C3
7 Hôtel des Trésoriers de France C4
8 Hôtel St-Côme C4
9 Jardin des Plantes A1
L'Hôtel de Cabrières-Sabatier d'Espeyran .... (see 1)

Sleeping

10 Auberge de Jeunesse C1
11 Baudon de Mauny C2
12 Hôtel de la Comédie D4
13 Hôtel du Palais A2

Eating

14 Halles Castellane B3
15 La Fine Mouche B3
16 Le Petit Jardin A2
17 Les Bains de Montpellier C5
18 Les Vignes B2
L'Heure Bleue .... (see 11)
19 Tripti Kulai C3

Drinking & Nightlife

20 Café Solo B3
21 Chez Boris C3
22 Le Café de la Mer C2
23 Le Rebuffy B3
24 Papa Doble B3

Shopping

25 Le Boutik R D2

legs tucked up beneath him, and a moody portrait of the artist himself by a very young Monet. Tragically, Bazille's potential was never fulfilled: he died aged just 28 in a battle during the Franco-Prussian War.

Attached to the museum is **L'Hôtel de Cabrières-Sabatier d'Espeyran** (2-5pm Tue-Sun late-Jun–mid-Sep, 2-5pm Tue, Sat & Sun mid-Sep–late-Jun), a lavish Montpellier mansion that belonged to local notable Madame Frédéric Sabatier d'Espeyran. The interior of the house is filled with incredible ceramics, furniture and objets d'art – an evocative reminder of the fabulous wealth enjoyed by Montpellier's elite during the late 19th century.

Carré Sainte-Anne GALLERY
(04 67 60 82 11; www.montpellier.fr; 2 rue Philippy; 11am-1pm & 2-7pm Apr-Sep, 10am-1pm & 2-6pm Tue-Sun Oct-Mar) FREE This landmark neogothic St Anne's church, with dazzling stained-glass windows, was deconsecrated in the 1980s and is now a spectacular setting for contemporary-art exhibitions and site-specific installations. High-profile artists to have featured here include Marc Desgrandchamps, Véronique Pagès, Hervé Di Rosa, Manuel Ocampo, Robert Combas and Gérard Garouste. Hours can vary depending on the program.

Cathédrale St-Pierre CATHEDRAL
(www.cathedrale-montpellier.fr; 1 rue St-Pierre; 9.30am-6pm) Montpellier's monumental Cathédrale St-Pierre began life as a church attached to the 14th-century monastery of St-Benoît; it was raised to cathedral status in 1536. Heavily rebuilt after the Wars of Religion, it's now the seat of the city's archbishops.

Place Royale du Peyrou GARDENS
(place Royale du Peyrou; 7am-midnight Jun-Aug, to 9.30pm Mar-May, Sep & Oct, to 8pm Nov-Feb) At the eastern end of this wide, tree-lined esplanade is the 1692 **Arc de Triomphe** (rue Foch; tours adult/child €6.50/5.50; tours in English 10am Tue Jul & Aug). From the **Château d'Eau**, an elaborate hexagonal water tower at its western limit, stretches the **Aqueduc de St-Clément**, spectacularly illuminated at night.

Jardin des Plantes GARDENS
(bd Henri IV; noon-8pm Tue-Sun Jun-Sep, to 6pm Tue-Sun Oct-May) North of place Royale du Peyrou is one of Montpellier's hidden gems, the Jardins des Plantes – the oldest botanical garden in France. Established in 1593, it was used as a model for the much better-known Jardin des Plantes in Paris, laid out nearly 30 years later. Along its shady paths you'll find more than 2500 species, including nine varieties of palm, 250 medicinal plants and an arboretum of rare trees, as well as a glorious greenhouse dating from 1860.

Outskirts

Montpellier Parc Zoologique ZOO
(www.zoo.montpellier.fr; 50 av Agropolis; zoo free, Serre Amazonienne adult/child €6.50/3; 9.30am-6.30pm Tue-Sun Easter-Sep, 10am-6pm Tue-Sun Feb, Mar & Oct, 10am-5pm Tue-Sun

OFF THE BEATEN TRACK

STEAM TRAIN THROUGH THE CÉVENNES

Chugging along a 13km stretch of track between St-Jean du Gard and Anduze (40 minutes one way), **Train à Vapeur des Cévennes** (☎04 66 60 59 00; www.trainavapeur.com; adult/child/bike return €15.50/10.50/3; ⏱Apr-Oct) follows an old line through the Gardon Valley that was in operation between 1909 and 1971. Restored by enthusiasts, the train is a marvellous way to see the scenery, traversing several arched viaducts and subterranean tunnels, including the 833m-long Tunnel d'Anduze.

Nov-Jan) FREE Four kilometres north of the city centre, this excellent zoo – France's second-largest, covering 60 hectares – has an enormous population of wild residents that spans the world's continents, including a rare white rhinoceros, three leopard brothers (called Tao, Tango and Twist) and a family of Atlas lions. It's laid out like a safari park, with most of the animals roaming free in open enclosures – so be prepared for walking. Take tram 1 to the St-Eloi stop, from where you can either walk to the zoo or catch the free Line 13 shuttle bus (labelled 'La Navette').

Aquarium Mare Nostrum AQUARIUM
(www.aquariummarenostrum.fr; Odysseum; adult/child €15.50/10.50; ⏱10am-8pm Jul & Aug, to 7pm Sep-Jun) Part of the Odysseum shopping centre, this aquarium recreates 15 aquatic environments, from polar waters to tropical forests. Imaginative tanks include an Ocean Balcony, where you stare down over submarine cliffs patrolled by sharks and rays, and a huge Amphitheatre, the largest covered tank in France, with 1.8 million litres of seawater. Kids will also love the interactive displays, such as a simulated cargo ship battling through stormy seas. Take tram 1 to the Odysseum station Place de France.

Sleeping

Hôtel de la Comédie HOTEL €
(☎04 67 58 43 64; www.hotel-montpellier-comedie.com; 1bis rue Baudin; s/d €52/75; ❄📶) What you lose in luxury here you more than make up for in location: the lively and central place de la Comédie is mere seconds away. Rooms are basic but comfy, with crimson bedspreads and double glazing keeping out street noise, and breakfast (€8) is served in a smart salon next to reception. There's a lift (elevator) but no car access.

Auberge de Jeunesse HOSTEL €
(☎04 67 60 32 22; www.fuaj.org; 2 impasse de la Petite Corraterie; dm incl breakfast €22.50; 📶) Montpellier's HI-affiliated hostel feels very institutional, with spartan dorms and bare decor, but there's a lounge downstairs with table football and pool, and a small garden. Take the tram to the Louis Blanc stop.

★**Hôtel du Palais** HOTEL €€
(☎04 67 60 47 38; www.hoteldupalais-montpellier.fr; 3 rue du Palais des Guilhem; s €75, d €85-100, tr €130; 📶) Superbly located near the Arc de Triomphe, this charming hotel has small but beautifully furnished rooms (some with wrought-iron balconies and window boxes), local art on the walls, and a resident cat. The setting on a quiet square is delightful; try to get a front-facing room if you can. The nearest car park is on rue Foch. Breakfast costs €10.

Les 4 Étoiles B&B €€
(☎04 67 02 47 69; www.les4etoiles.com; 3 rue Delmas; s €98-105, d €125-135; P📶) A great city base, this 1930s family house has been converted into a contemporary B&B, with four rooms named after constellations individually styled by a local interior designer. They share the same clean-lined character: sharp furniture, flat-screen TVs, retro design pieces and gorgeous tiled floors. It's 1km east from bd Henri IV. On-site parking costs €10, but spaces are limited.

Hôtel du Parc HOTEL €€
(☎04 67 41 16 49; www.hotelduparc-montpellier.com; 8 rue Achille-Bégé; s €79-92, d €89-112, tr €129; P❄📶) It's a 500m walk from the old quarter, but this charming 18th-century *hôtel particulier* (private mansion) offers peace and tranquillity. Set around its own garden, it has 19 regal rooms, accessed via plush carpeted corridors and a sweeping central staircase. There's plenty of free parking inside the house's gates. Head north from place Albert 1er along av Faubourg Boutonnet.

Baudon de Mauny B&B €€€
(☎04 67 02 21 77; www.baudondemauny.com; 1 rue de la Carbonnerie; d €170-335; ⏱reception 4-10pm; 📶) A cross between a palatial B&B and a boutique hotel, with eight rooms, this 18th-century house has been given the full

designer overhaul: original fireplaces, oak doors and sash windows sit alongside modern furniture, anglepoise lamps and butterfly wallpaper. The most convenient parking is at Parking du Corum, 500m northeast.

Eating

Halles Castellane MARKET €

(rue de la Loge; 7am-8pm Mon-Sat, to 1.30pm Sun) The city's main covered market is stocked to the rafters with local goodies. There are lots of Languedoc wines on offer, as well as copious fish and shellfish from the ports at Sète and Agde.

★ **La Fine Mouche** CHEESE €

(12 rue Ste-Anne; lunch menus €9-17, mains €6-19, platters per person €12.50; 11am-3pm & 6-11pm Wed-Sat, 6-11pm Sun) Heavenly French cheeses star at this *bar à fromage* (cheese bar), whether in pungent Roquefort or runny St-Marcellin tartines (toasted open-faced sandwiches), rich dishes such as Camembert baked with Champagne, or assorted cheese platters served on wooden planks. Its outdoor terrace sits opposite the shopfront under the eaves of church-turned-gallery Carré Sainte-Anne. You can also stock up at its deli.

L'Heure Bleue CAFE €

(1 rue de la Carbonnerie; dishes €3-5; 9am-5pm Tue-Sat) Scrumptious pastries and fine teas served in china teapots are on offer at this cute cafe.

Les Vignes MODERN FRENCH €€

(04 67 60 48 42; www.lesvignesrestaurant.com; 2 rue Bonnier d'Alco; menus lunch €15-23, dinner €29-49; noon-1.30pm & 7.45-9.30pm Mon & Wed-Sat) Thierry Germain is passionate about local produce and Provençal cooking, which come to the fore at his smart restaurant. Cévennes lamb, Mediterranean seafood and bull meat from the Camargue are among the ingredients you might find on the menu. The interior is suitably chic – white tablecloths, table lamps, Provençal colours – but the little terrace is the place in warm weather.

Le Bistrot de Bacchus BISTRO €€

(09 50 08 00 54; www.bistrot-bacchus.com; 8 rue Marioge; mains €16-22; noon-2.30pm & 7-10.30pm Mon & Thu-Sat) There's no menu at this little neobistro in the Arceaux district – just a blackboard chalked up with the day's dishes, which incorporate what's available at the markets. The open kitchen smokes its own salmon and turns out hearty country cooking, such as *poule au pot* (pot-boiled chicken) and beefsteak with thick-cut chips. Worth the walk.

Les Bains de Montpellier SEAFOOD €€

(04 67 60 70 87; www.les-bains-de-montpellier.com; 6 rue Richelieu; mains €18-31.50; noon-2pm & 8-11pm Mon-Sat;) A former public bathhouse is now a hip restaurant that's especially strong on seafood and Italian-influenced dishes. Tables are set around the old perimeter bathrooms, with plush purple chairs and overhead chandeliers, but the best are in the interior courtyard, surrounded by ponds and palms.

Le Petit Jardin MODERN FRENCH €€

(04 67 60 78 78; www.petit-jardin.com; 20 rue Jean-Jacques Rousseau; 2-/3-course lunch menus

LOCAL KNOWLEDGE

MONTPELLIER'S BEACHES

Strolling around the winding lanes of the old quarter, it's easy to forget that Montpellier is actually a coastal city. Most beaches can be reached in about half an hour by bus or car via the D21, or via the new purpose-built cycling track. The sands run for around 10km between the concrete-heavy (and pretty ghastly) beach resorts of **Palavas-les-Flots** and **La Grande-Motte**, and are generally packed in summer.

For a real local's tip (not to mention much quieter shores), head a few kilometres southeast of La Grande-Motte to **Plage de l'Espiguette**, by far Montpellier's best beach. On the western side of an isolated headland, the beach is a designated nature reserve, with dune systems providing a habitat for endangered birds and insects (as well as naturists). It's often windy, which makes it popular with kitesurfers and kite-buggiers, but it's usually much, much emptier than the fleshpot beaches to the west.

Another tip for wildlife spotters is to explore the area of wetlands and coastal lagoons around the small town of **Villeneuve-lès-Maguelone**, on the coastal road to Sète. This is often a good area for **flamingo spotting**; the birds regularly stop off here en route from the Camargue, some 30km to the east.

€21/28, 3-course dinner menu €37, mains €23-49; noon-1.30pm & 7.30-9pm Tue-Sun;) Without doubt, the 'Little Garden' has one of the city's most romantic dining settings – a charmingly green, glass-enclosed secret garden, hidden away behind the amber façade of a typical town house in the old quarter. It also has a more relaxed, cheaper bistro (mains €15 to €19); either way, the food is fresh, seasonal and very French.

Tripti Kulai VEGETARIAN €€

(04 67 66 30 51; www.triptikulai.com; 20 rue Jacques Cœur; 2-/3-course menus lunch €13/17.50, dinner €18/23, mains €9.50-18; noon-3pm & 6-10pm Mon-Sat;) Ideal for lunch, this all-organic cafe has vegetarian, vegan and gluten-free dishes, from pastries, quiches and salads to gratinées, savoury polenta cakes, soups and stews, along with desserts such as fruit crumble or tiramisu. The fresh fruit juices are great, but – this being France – it also serves wine (and beer).

Drinking & Nightlife

You'll find plenty of bars around rue En-Gondeau, off Grand Rue Jean Moulin, around place Jean Jaurès, and around the intersection of rue de l'Université and rue de la Candolle.

For nightlife listings, check *Sortir à Montpellier* (www.sortiramontpellier.fr) in print or online. The big clubs are around Espace Latipolia, 10km out of town on rte de Palavas, served by night buses.

Le Rebuffy PUB

(Pink Elephant; 2 rue Rebuffy; 10am-1am Mon & Thu, 11am-1am Tue, Wed, Fri & Sat, 3pm-1am Sun) One of Montpellier's most atmospheric terraces, shaded by plane trees strung with fairy lights, and some of the cheapest drinks in town make this vibrant pub locally known as the Pink Elephant a virtual extension of the university campus. 'Extracurricular activities' here include live gigs (mainly folk, blues and rock) and timeless board games. It's tucked down a cobbled laneway.

Papa Doble COCKTAIL BAR

(www.papadoble.fr; 6 rue du Petit Scel; 6pm-1am Mon-Sat) The menu at this Hemingway-themed underground bar is printed to form the outline of the legendary writer's face, and cocktails created in his honour include the Hemingway Daiquiri (Havana Club rum, maraschino liqueur, grapefruit and fresh lime juice), Papa's Summer Cup (gin, Pimms, curaçao and ginger beer; traditionally consumed during Wimbledon) and the Last Word (gin, lime and green chartreuse).

Café Solo CAFE

(www.cafesolomontpellier.fr; 30 rue St-Guilhem; 9am-7pm Mon-Sat) Perfect for a caffeine hit, Café Solo roasts its own beans and serves its brews, along with teas, hot chocolate and freshly squeezed juices, in its split-level interior with mezzanine seating or out on its street terrace with mismatched furniture and warm blankets to wrap up in when it's chilly.

Chez Boris WINE BAR

(04 67 02 13 22; www.chezboris.com; 20 rue de l'Aiguillerie; noon-2.30pm & 7.30-10.30pm;) Boris Leclercq's wine bar proved so popular he also opened a restaurant at 17 bd Sarrail and another in Paris' ritzy 8e. It's relaxed and friendly, with wines served by the glass, accompanied by plates of Iberico ham and Aubrac beef if you're peckish. Check out previous guests' comments on the ceiling.

Le Café de la Mer BAR, GAY

(5 place du Marché aux Fleurs; 8am-1am Mon-Sat, 3pm-1am Sun) One of the city's oldest gay bars now has a mixed clientele along with Montpellier's best, sunniest terrace. Ask at the bar for info about where else is hot (or not).

DON'T MISS

GOURMET SHOPPING

Stock up on delicious regional products at **Le Boutik R** (www.leboutikr.fr; 41 bd Bonne Nouvelle; 10am-7pm Tue-Sat): Cévennes chestnut, lavender and garrigue honey, nougat, olives, truffles, olive oils, vinegars, Camargue salt, *Grisettes de Montpellier* (local-speciality sweets incorporating liquorice powder, honey and sugar), wines and liqueurs.

Information

Tourist Office (04 67 60 60 60; www.montpellier-tourisme.fr; 30 allée Jean de Lattré de Tasigny; 9.30am-6pm Mon-Sat, 10am-5pm Sun) Sells the Montpellier City Card (p717) and runs guided tours.

Getting There & Away

AIR

Montpellier Airport (MPL; 04 67 20 85 00; www.montpellier.aeroport.fr) Mont-

DON'T MISS

HÔTELS PARTICULIERS IN MONTPELLIER

During the 17th and 18th centuries, Montpellier's rich merchants built themselves grand *hôtels particuliers* (private mansions) to show off their power and prodigious wealth. The most important houses are marked by a descriptive plaque in French; you can pick up a map in the tourist office. Many of the houses have fabulous inner courtyards (mostly, alas, closed to the public).

Among the most notable are the **Hôtel de Varennes** (2 place Pétrarque), just off place Pétrarque, a mix of medieval and Renaissance architecture, which now contains the Musée du Vieux Montpellier.

A short walk south on rue Jacques Coeur is the 17th-century **Hôtel des Trésoriers de France** (7 rue Jacques Cœur). Just west is the **Hôtel St-Côme** (Grand Rue Jean Moulin), a suitably grand building for the city's Chamber of Commerce.

Further west near the Cathédrale St-Pierre is the early-17th-century **Hôtel de la Vieille Intendance** (rue de la Vieille Intendance), built during the reign of Louis XIII for the queen mother and his niece Marie Louise d'Orléans (coloquially known as 'La Grande Mademoiselle'). The house was later occupied by the city's *intendant* (governor), by philosopher Auguste Comte and by Sète-born poet Paul Valéry.

pellier's airport, 8km southeast of town, has regular connections to most French and many European cities.

BUS

The **bus station** (☎ 04 67 92 01 43; rue du Grand St-Jean) is an easy walk from the train station. Most regional services provided by **Hérault Transport** (☎ 04 34 88 89 99; www.herault-transport.fr) cost a flat-rate €1.60. Destinations include the following:

La Grande-Motte (20 minutes, half-hourly Monday to Saturday, every 15 minutes on weekends) Catch bus 106 from place de France, in the Antigone quarter. Several buses a day continue to Aigues-Mortes.

Palavas-les-Flots (10 to 20 minutes, at least hourly) Catch the tram to Station Étang l'Or – the last stop before the coastline, just south of the airport, 11km southeast of the city centre – then take bus 131.

Sète (55 minutes, hourly Monday to Saturday, three on Sunday) Take bus 102 from Sabines tram station, 4km southwest of the city centre.

TRAIN

Trains run from Montpellier to Barcelona on to Madrid up to four times daily.

Work started on the city's stunning new pleated-concrete and glass TGV station, designed by French architect Marc Mimram, in 2015. It's due to open in late 2017 in the Odysseum quarter, some 4km east of the city centre towards the coast, cutting travel time to Paris to three hours and eventually offering a high-speed link to Madrid.

Meanwhile, there's at least one hourly connection from the current **station** (place Auguste Gibert) to the following cities:

Carcassonne €26, 1½ hours

Narbonne €15, one hour

Nîmes €9.90, 30 minutes

Paris Gare de Lyon €77, 3½ hours by TGV

Perpignan €21.80, 1¾ hours

Getting Around

The city's public transport system is run by **TaM** (☎ 04 67 22 87 87; www.tam-voyages.com). There's a flat rate of €1.50 per journey.

TO/FROM THE AIRPORT

Navette Aéroport (Airport Shuttle; one way €1.60) The airport bus (line 120) runs hourly between the airport and the place de l'Europe tram stop. Buses from the city to the airport run from 5.15am to 8.30pm, and from 9am to 11pm from the airport to the city.

The standard bus fare to place de l'Europe is €1.60, or you can buy an onward tram/bus pass for €2.60.

BICYCLE

Montpellier is hugely bicycle-friendly.

VéloMagg (per hour €0.50) The city's automated bike-hire system has 51 stations across town; you'll need a credit or bank card to hire, or you can buy an access card for €5 from the tourist office.

TRAM & BUS

Christian Lacroix contributed designs for Montpellier's funky, four-line tram system. Single tickets (valid on trams and buses) cost €1.50; a one-day pass costs €4. There are ticket machines at most tram stops, or you can buy them at the tourist office or newsagents.

Sète

POP 45,200

Set alongside the saltwater lagoon of Étang du Thau, Sète is a gritty and not-always-pretty port, somewhat oversold by its local moniker of the 'Little Venice of Languedoc' – a reference to the many canals that run through town, including the Canal du Midi, which terminates its 240km journey here from Toulouse, and the Canal du Rhône, whose 98km journey from Beaucaire also ends here. But its honest, workaday atmosphere makes a refreshing change from the built-up tourist towns of the rest of the Languedoc coast – and if you like seafood, this is the place to indulge: Sète has the largest working fishing fleet anywhere on France's Mediterranean coast. Sète's beaches begin 3km southwest of the town centre.

Sète is also France's gateway to Africa by sea, with ferries to Tangier and Nador in Morocco docking here.

Sights

Musée Paul Valéry MUSEUM
(www.museepaulvalery-sete.fr; 148 rue François Desnoyer; adult/child €5.50/3, incl temporary exhibitions €8/4; ⌚9.30am-7pm Apr-Oct, 10am-6pm Tue-Sun Nov-Mar) Sète was the birthplace of symbolist poet Paul Valéry (1871–1945), and the town's main museum houses a huge collection of his works, along with over 700 paintings and 1000 drawings and diverse temporary exhibitions. Sète's local area features heavily – especially the sea, Valéry's main poetic inspiration. He is buried in the Cimitière Marin across the street.

Espace Georges Brassens MUSEUM
(www.espace-brassens.fr; 67 bd Camille Blanc; adult/child €5.50/2; ⌚10am-6pm Jun-Sep, 10am-noon & 2-6pm Tue-Sun Oct-May) Sète was the childhood home of singer and poet Georges Brassens (1921–81), whose mellow voice still speaks at this multimedia space.

Musée International des Arts Modestes ART MUSEUM
(MIAM; www.miam.org; 23 quai Maréchal de Lattre de Tassigny; adult/child €5.50/2.50; ⌚9.30am-7pm Apr-Sep, 10am-noon & 2-6pm Tue-Sun Oct-Mar) This offbeat gallery is refreshingly free of big names – here the emphasis is on the art of everyday objects, curated by local artists Hervé di Rosa and Bernard Belluc. From religious icons to kitsch china and travel souvenirs, it's like wandering round a jumble sale curated by an art critic.

Activities

Between April and October, boats run by **Sète Croisières** (☎04 67 46 00 46; www.sete-croisieres.com; quai Général Durand; port & coast tour adult/child €10/8.50, Étang du Thau tour €12/9.50, town tour €9/7.50) cruise around the town, port and coast, and the Étang du Thau and the local mussel and oyster farms, which you can peer at through the boat's glass-bottomed hulls. All trips leave from quai Général Durand.

Rent kayaks and SUPs (stand-up paddleboards) or take a guided tour of Sète's wa-

OCCITAN

The Languedoc's distinctive language of Occitan is an ancient tongue that is closely related to Catalan. The *langue d'oc* was once widely spoken across most of southern France, while the *langue d'oïl* was the predominant language spoken in the north (the words *oc* and *oïl* meant 'yes' in their respective languages).

Occitan reached its zenith during the 12th century, but it was dealt a blow when Languedoc was annexed by the French kingdom. *Langue d'oïl* became the realm's official language, effectively relegating Occitan to the status of a language spoken only by the poor and uneducated. Despite the best efforts of the ruling elite to wipe it out, Occitan survived as a distinct language, largely thanks to rural communities keen to hold on to their own regional identity. It enjoyed a literary revival in the 19th century, spearheaded by the poet Frédéric Mistral, who wrote in Occitan's Provençal dialect.

Today Occitan is still widely spoken across southern France, with an estimated 610,000 native speakers and around a million others who have a basic working knowledge. There are six officially recognised dialects: Languedocien *(lengadocian)*, Limousin *(lemosin)*, Auvergnat *(auvernhat)*, Provençal *(provençau)*, Vivaro-Alpine *(vivaroaupenc)* and Gascon *(gascon)*; the latter includes the Aranese sub-dialect spoken in parts of Spanish Catalonia.

terways with local outfit **Kayak Med** (☎06 95 63 12 75; www.kayakmed.com; Le Môle St-Louis; kayak/SUP rental per 3hr €25/30, kayak & SUP tours per 2½ hrs from €35; ⏲8am-6pm Apr-Sep). Life jackets and waterproof containers are provided. Cash only.

For a spin around the port and coastline, **Bike Med** (☎06 69 32 74 13; www.bikemed.fr; 19 quai de la Consigne; bike rental per 4hr/day €8/12, electric-bike rental €18/30; ⏲10am-1pm & 2-6pm Apr-Sep) offers bicycle and electric-bike rental. Child seats are available for €4 per rental; helmets for adults and children are included. You'll need to leave a €200 deposit.

Festivals & Events

Joutes Nautiques SPORTS
(⏲mid-Jun–Aug) The *joutes nautiques,* when boat crews joust with long poles in an attempt to knock each other into the harbour, run from mid-June, culminating in late August, when the centrepiece La Saint Louis event takes place on quai du Canal Royal.

Sleeping

Auberge de Jeunesse Sète HOSTEL €
(☎04 67 53 46 68; www.hifrance.org; 7 rue Général Revest; dm incl breakfast from €23.40; ⏲Apr-Oct; 📶) An elegant 19th-century building with harbour views houses two small dorms, sleeping four people each, and a self-catering kitchen. It's 500m west of town and 3km east of the Sète beaches.

★**Rivages** B&B €€
(☎07 61 46 65 68; www.rivages-sete.com; 22 chemin des Ivrognes; d €95-133; P ❄ 📶 🏊) With its hilltop setting, secluded garden and timber-decked swimming pool lined by sunloungers, this B&B is the kind of place you won't want to leave. The three rooms all have a keynote colour – rich gold, cool blue or papal purple – with a panoramic lounge offering distant harbour views through floor-to-ceiling glass. Breakfast is served on the shady terrace.

Grand Hôtel HOTEL €€
(☎04 67 74 71 77; www.legrandhotelsete.com; 17 quai Maréchal de Lattre de Tassigny; d/f/ste from €106/131/206; P ❄ 📶) As its name suggests, this 19th-century harbourfront hotel is grand, from the gleaming marble lobby, filled with palms and modern art, all the way through to the stylish rooms, arranged around a palm-filled, glass-roofed interior courtyard. Family rooms sleep up to four. The best rooms overlook the harbour.

DON'T MISS

A FISHY AFFAIR

To really see what makes Sète tick, head for **La Criée** (Fish Auction; www.sete.port.fr; quai Maximin Licciardi; tours adult/child €7/3.60; ⏲tours 4pm Mon-Fri Feb-Oct), when fishers sell off their day's catch to the highest bidder. This is no free-for-all; it's a highly organised process that takes place in its own miniature theatre, with buyers placing bids on crates of fish via handheld electronic devices. It's normally off limits to visitors, but one-hour guided tours (in French) depart from Sète's tourist office; confirm ahead that the trawlers are in the day you visit.

Eating

Fish restaurants line quai Durand and quai Maximin Licciardi, but the quality can be variable, so choose carefully.

Look out for local specialities such as *rouille sétoise* (a rich tomato sauce made with cuttlefish) and *la tielle* (tomato-and-octopus pie), as well as oysters.

La Méditerranéenne SEAFOOD €€
(☎04 67 74 38 37; www.la-mediterraneenne-sete.com; 3 quai Maximin Licciardi; mains €14-20, platters €35-78; ⏲noon-2.30pm & 7-11pm) Sète is awash with seafood restaurants, but this quayside bistro by local chef Fouzia Sakrani scores highly on friendliness and freshness. Simple but delicious food spans sea bream, red mullet, sardines and swordfish, as well as vast shellfish platters – all served with copious amounts of crusty bread to soak up the rich fish juices.

La Péniche SEAFOOD €€
(☎04 67 48 64 13; www.restaurant-peniche-sete.fr; 1 quai des Moulins; 2-/3-course menus €26/32, mains €22; ⏲11am-3pm & 7-10pm Mon-Sat, 11am-3pm Sun; 👪) Dine on classic Sètoise seafood on this converted barge, which looks more like a big-city bistro inside, with its sharp tables and shiny wooden floor. The Languedoc's Spanish influence is clear – lots of dishes are cooked *à la plancha* (grilled on a hot plate). Fish fingers are a favourite on the children's menu.

★**La Coquerie** SEAFOOD, GASTRONOMIC €€€
(☎06 47 06 71 38; www.annemajourel.fr; 1 chemin du Cimetière; 6-course menu €65, mains €18-26; ⏲noon-1.15pm & 8-9.30pm Mon-Sat Jun-Sep, noon-1.15pm & 8-9.30pm Thu-Sat, noon-1.15pm

Sun Oct-May) Michelin-starred chef Anne Majourel shuns *menus* in favour of what's fresh from the fish auction. Dishes might include smoked bonito with pistachio oil; sea bream, gurnard, monkfish and mussel bouillabaisse; squid stuffed with red pepper; and cod served with turnip mousse. The best views over the harbour aren't from the terrace but inside the dining room opposite the open kitchen.

Information

Tourist office (04 99 04 71 71; www.tourisme-sete.com; 60 Grand Rue Mario Roustan; 9.30am-7pm Jul & Aug, 9.30am-6pm Mon-Sat, 10am-5pm Sun Apr-Jun & Sep, 9.30am-5.30pm Mon-Sat, 10am-1pm Sun Oct-Mar) Just back from the waterfront.

Getting There & Away

The regular 102 bus (€1.60, hourly Monday to Saturday, three on Sunday) runs between Sète and Montpellier in just under an hour via Montpellier's beaches, or you can catch a train (€6.10, 25 minutes, hourly).

Italian ferry company **Grandi Navi Veloci** (GNV; Italy contact centre +39 010 2094591; www.gnv.it; rte de Pont Martin; seat/cabin/car Sète-Tangier from €64/77/200, Sète-Nador from €69/87/200) operates ferries between Sète and the Moroccan ports of Tangier (32 hours) and Nador (29 hours). There are two sailings per week, usually on Monday, Tuesday or Wednesday, from Sète.

Bouzigues

POP 1398

Oyster and mussel beds occupy the waters of the shimmering Étang de Thau lagoon, which surrounds this little village 15km northwest of Sète, while vineyards criss-cross the hillsides above town. Although wine has been produced here since the 6th century, shellfish farming only started in 1925, but it now anchors Bouzigues' economy.

Sights & Activities

★ Parc des Dinosaures — MUSEUM

(www.dinosaure.eu; Mèze; Musée des Dinosaures or Musée de l'Évolution adult/child €9.80/8.50, both museums €16.50/14; 10am-7pm Jul & Aug, 2-6pm Feb-Jun, Sep & Oct, 2-5pm Jan, Nov & Dec, closed Jan) Signs warning of dinosaurs line the drive up, but this dinosaur park is no gimmick – the biggest cache of dinosaur eggs ever discovered in Europe was found here in 1996 and ongoing archaeological digs are unearthing more fossils and footprints. Life-size dinosaur models stand in the parkland surrounding the two museums; a complete original brachiosaurus skeleton resides in the standout Musée des Dinosaures, where bilingual signs bring exhibits to life. The park's 11km west of Bouzigues via the D613.

Musée de Site Gallo-Romain Villa Loupian — ROMAN SITE

(04 67 18 68 18; www.loupian.fr; Loupian; adult/child €5/3.50; 11am-7pm Jul & Aug, 1.30-6pm Wed-Mon Sep-Dec & Feb-Jun, closed Jan) Dating from the 1st century AD, this extraordinary Roman villa was built on the Via Domitia road linking Italy and Spain, and it was occupied for 600 years. Highlights include its dazzling preserved mosaics, with Syrian and Aquitaine influences, covering 13 ground-floor rooms, and its wine cellar, which could store 150,000L. Audioguides are included with admission; free tours take place at 11am Thursday in French, with translation sheets available. The site is 4.5km southwest of Bouzigues off the D613.

Musée de l'Étang de Thau — MUSEUM

(www.bouzigues.fr/musee; quai du Port; adult/child €5/3.50; 10am-12.30pm & 2-7.30pm Jul & Aug, shorter hours Sep-Jun) The Musée de l'Étang de Thau has aquarium tanks, sepia photos, vintage fishing equipment and models of the lagoon.

★ Bateau Promenade — BOATING

(06 03 31 44 90; www.promenade-bouzigues.fr; quai du Port; adult/child €12/8; tours 11am, 2.30pm & 5.30pm Jul & Aug, 11am & 2.30pm May, Jun & Sep, 3pm Apr & Oct) Bateau Promenade takes you out on the water aboard the semi-covered *Bleu Marin* on one-hour cruises to view the shellfish beds; cruises pass the Roquérols lighthouse.

Sleeping & Eating

Lou Labech — CAMPGROUND €

(04 67 78 30 38; www.lou-labech.fr; chemin du Stade; tent, 2 people & car €16.50-30, chalets, cabins & safari tents from €123; Apr-Oct; P) It's worth paying more for a waterfront pitch at this well-spaced beachside campground, which also has chalets and cabins sleeping up to five people and safari tents sleeping up to four (minimum rental of three nights). There's an on-site shop and bar serving *moules-frites* (mussels and fries) of an evening. Wi-fi's available in the bar and self-catering kitchen area only.

À La Voile Blanche HOTEL €€
(☎04 67 78 35 77; www.alavoileblanche.fr; 1 av Louis Tudesq; d €85-110, ste €190; ❄📶) Higher-priced rooms at this family-run waterfront hotel have balconies and panoramic views across the lagoon, marina and oyster beds to Mont St-Clair rising above Sète. All rooms are spacious, with streamlined, contemporary styling and comfortable beds. Its seafood restaurant downstairs is excellent.

★**Le Marin** SEAFOOD €€
(☎04 67 18 10 39; www.lemarin34.com; 8 place de la Golette; 3-course lunch menu €16.50, dinner menus €18-41, mains €15-25, oysters per half-dozen from €8; ⊙noon-9.30pm Jul & Aug, noon-2.30pm & 7-9.30pm Sat & Sun Sep-Jun) *Producteur d'huîtres* (oyster producer) Le Marin has its own shellfish beds right out front, and its delicacies – oyster gratin, stuffed mussels, bouillabaisse, grilled cuttlefish, monkfish and rosemary skewers – are served in its cosy dining room and out on its wonderful lagoon-facing terrace, which adjoins a small waterside park.

Getting There & Away

Buses are operated by Hérault Transport (www.herault-transport.fr). Buses 104 and 103 link Bouzigues with Montpellier (€1.60, 40 minutes, at least three daily). Bus 320 links Bouzigues with Sète (€1.60, 10 minutes, at least three daily).

Agde

POP 24,500

There are really three Agdes: Vieux Agde, the original settlement beside the Hérault River; the fishing port of Grau d'Agde; and Cap d'Agde, a built-up summer playground.

For most people, the only real reason to stop in Agde is for some swimming and sunbathing, but **Vieux Agde** is worth a wander, with some imposing *hôtels particuliers* (private mansions) and a pretty riverside setting; half-day cruises along the waterways are run by **Bateaux du Soleil** (☎04 67 94 08 79; www.bateaux-du-soleil.com; 8 rue André Chassefières; half-day cruises adult/child €20/10; ⊙Apr-Sep).

If you're here to sunbathe, **Cap d'Agde** is the place. Beaches sprawl around the headland; the nicest areas are on the far west (especially around La Tamarissière and St-Vincent) and the far east, home to France's (and the world's) largest nudist colony.

Situated 8km northeast of Agde in the fishing port of Marseillan is the **Noilly-Prat Factory** (☎04 67 77 20 15; www.noillyprat.com; 1 rue Noilly; ⊙10am-noon & 2.30-7pm May-Sep, shorter hours Oct, Nov, Mar & Apr, closed Dec-Feb) FREE, which has been making its famous dry vermouth to the same secret recipe since 1813.

At Cap d'Agde, the **tourist office** (☎04 67 62 91 99; www.capdagde.com; Rond-Point du Bon Accueil; ⊙9am-8pm Jul & Aug, shorter hours Sep-Jun) has information on activities and water sports.

The Cap d'Agde coast is best accessed with your own wheels. Agde's **train station** (rue de la Digue) is on the northern side of the Hérault River, 300m northwest of Vieux Agde. Hourly-or-better services include Montpellier (€10.10, 30 minutes), Perpignan (€19.80, 1¼ hours) and Sète (€5.30, 10 minutes).

Narbonne

POP 51,306

The picturesque Canal de la Robine runs right through the centre of elegant Narbonne and connects the Étang de Bages-Sigean with the Canal du Midi. These days it's a charming midsize Languedoc market town, but wind the clock back two millennia and you'd be in a major Roman city: the capital of the province of Gallia Narbonensis. Exceptional sights include its cathedral and former archbishops' palace, and the town is now a popular stop-off for boaters.

Sights

Palais des Archevêques PALACE
(Archbishops' Palace; place de l'Hôtel de Ville; all museums €9, single museum €4; ⊙10am-6pm Jun-Sep, 10am-noon & 2-5pm Wed-Mon Oct-May) The former archbishops' palace houses several archaeological museums. Roman mosaics and stucco paintings are on display at the **Musée d'Art et d'Histoire** and **Musée Archéologique**, along with an underground gallery of Gallo-Roman shops in the **Horreum**, and a collection of impressive Roman masonry in the **Musée Lapidaire**.

Cathédrale St-Just CATHEDRAL
(entry on rue Armand Gauthier; ⊙9am-noon & 2-6pm) Narbonne's most distinctive landmark is actually only half-finished: construction was halted in the 14th century, and only the towers and choir reached final completion. Its treasury has a beautiful Flemish tapestry of the Creation, while grotesque gargoyles leer down upon the 16th-century cloister.

Activities

In the heart of Narbonne, **Les Petits Bateaux du Canal** (☎06 15 65 12 51; 32 cours de la République; 5-/7-seater boat rental per hour €29/33, each additional hour €20/25; ⊙10am-7pm late Mar–mid-Oct) rents electric boats to explore the waterways under your own steam. No boat licence is required; life jackets are provided.

For a spin along the towpaths, **Mellow Vélos** (☎04 68 43 38 21; www.mellowvelos.com; rte Neuve, Paraza; adult/child per day from €20/10, per week €86/43; ⊙8am-7pm Fri-Wed) rents bikes. It's located in Paraza, 20km northwest of Narbonne, off the D124, and will deliver bikes to your door (free within a 10km radius, or anywhere in Bas-Languedoc for a small charge). Electric bikes are also available. Cash only.

Sleeping & Eating

Will's Hotel HOTEL €
(☎04 68 90 44 50; www.willshotel-narbonne.com; 23 av Pierre Semard; s/d/q €61/69/99; ❄📶) Once a merchant's house dating from 1860, this basic corner hotel just 150m from the train station is a decent base for overnighting in Narbonne. Some of the rooms are shoebox-sized, however, so insist on a 'Double Confort' room. There's a bike garage; parking is available at a nearby municipal car park.

Demeure de Roquelongue B&B €€
(☎04 68 45 63 57; www.demeure-de-roquelongue.com; 53 av de Narbonne, St-André-de-Roquelongue; d €110-135, f €200; P📶🏊) In the village of St-André-de-Roquelongue, 19km southwest of Narbonne, this *maison vigneronne* (winemakers' house) dating from 1870 makes a beautiful base, with five royally decorated rooms. Cers has its original fireplace and garden view, Espan a vintage bathtub screened by curtains, and family-friendly Eole has two connecting bedrooms sleeping up to five, and its own lounge area and patio.

Les Halles MARKET €
(www.narbonne.halles.fr; 1 cours Mirabeau; ⊙7am-1pm) Narbonne's covered market is one of the most beautiful in France. Built at the turn of the 20th century, it's a masterpiece of art-nouveau style, with panels of frosted glass, decorative stonework and a wonderful cast-iron roof. Inside, over 70 stalls sell cheese, charcuterie, poultry, meat and fish as well as fruit, flowers and wine.

★**À La Table du Marché** MODERN FRENCH €€
(☎04 68 43 19 27; 8 rue Émile Zola; 2-/3-course menus €24/29, mains €18-26; ⊙noon-2pm & 7.30-10pm Wed-Sun) Inspired flavour combinations on the daily-changing menu, sourced from Les Halles directly opposite, might include duck with truffled polenta, merlot-braised beef cheeks with lentils and heirloom carrots, and lemon sole with asparagus and saffron risotto, but the showstoppers are desserts like dark-chocolate ganache with raspberry sauce and hazelnut meringue or bourbon-vanilla-marinated pineapple crumble with chestnut ice cream.

WORTH A TRIP

NARBONNE DAY TRIPPER

Abbaye de Fontfroide (☎04 68 45 11 08; www.fontfroide.com; chemin de Fontfroide; adult/child abbey, garden & museum €19/15, abbey & gardens only €11/7, cash only; ⊙9.30am-7pm Jul & Aug, 11am-6pm Apr-Jun, Sep & Oct, 10am-12.30pm & 1.30-5pm Nov-Mar) is 15km southwest of Narbonne via the D613. Founded by Cistercian monks in 1093, it became one of southern France's most powerful ecclesiastical centres during the Middle Ages. Highlights include the tranquil chapter hall, refectory and monks' dormitory, as well as a rose garden added during the 18th century. Fontfroide also produces its own renowned wine, which you can sample in the on-site wine shop or in the vaulted **restaurant** (☎04 68 41 02 26; 2-/3-course lunch menus €21/25, 3-/4-course dinner menus €35/39).

The **Réserve Africaine de Sigean** (www.reserveafricainesigean.fr; 19 chemin Hameau du Lac; adult/child €32/23; ⊙9am-6.30pm Easter-early Sep, shorter hours rest of year) is 17km south of Narbonne, off the A9. Opened in 1974, this excellent 300-hectare wildlife reserve aims to recreate the atmosphere of the African savannah – a climate not all that different from the Languedoc's dry and dusty plains. Lions, white rhinos, warthogs, giraffes and zebras are just a few of the 160 species on show, with some 3800 animals here in all. Some areas are drive-through, while others you explore on foot.

Information

Tourist Office (☎04 68 65 15 60; www.narbonne-tourisme.com; 31 rue Jean Jaurès; ⏰9am-7pm Apr–mid-Sep, 10am-12.30pm & 1.30-6pm Mon-Sat, 9am-1pm Sun mid-Sep–Mar) Can advise on canal cruises and water sports on the nearby Étang de Bages-Sigean lagoon.

Getting There & Away

Frequent trains serve Narbonne en route from Béziers (€6.10, 15 minutes), Montpellier (€15, one hour) and Perpignan (€15.50, one hour).

Carcassonne

POP 49,400

Perched on a rocky hilltop and bristling with zigzag battlements, stout walls and spiky turrets, the fortified city of Carcassonne looks like something out of a children's storybook when it's seen from afar. A Unesco World Heritage Site since 1997, it's most people's idea of the perfect medieval castle.

La Cité, as the old walled town is now known, attracts over four million visitors every year, peaking in high summer. Time your visit for late in the day (or better still for spring and autumn) to truly appreciate the old town's medieval charm.

Sights

Beneath Carcassonne's fortified castle La Cité, on the left bank of the Aude River, is the city's second half, **Ville Basse**. It's a mostly modern town that conceals a medieval heart: the Bastide St-Louis, which was built during the 13th century using the characteristic grid of streets set around a central square, place Carnot.

The lower town was later redeveloped during the 18th and 19th centuries, and is home to several impressive *hôtels particuliers* (private mansions) and religious buildings, as well as Carcassonne's marvellous covered market, dating from 1768.

★La Cité WALLED CITY

(Map p730; enter via Porte Narbonnaise or Porte d'Aude; ⏰24hr) Built on a steep spur of rock, Carcassonne's rampart-ringed fortress dates back over two millennia. The fortified town is encircled by two sets of battlements and 52 stone towers, topped by distinctive 'witch's hat' roofs (added by architect Viollet-le-Duc during 19th-century restorations). A drawbridge can still be seen in the main gate of **Porte Narbonnaise** (Map p730), which leads into the citadel's interior, a maze of cobbled lanes and courtyards, now mostly lined by shops and restaurants.

The hill on which La Cité stands has been fortified many times across the centuries – by Gauls, Romans, Visigoths, Moors, Franks and Cathars, to name a few. Following the annexation of Roussillon by France in 1659, the castle's usefulness as a frontier fortress declined and it slowly crumbled into disrepair, but it was saved from destruction by Viollet-le-Duc, who left his mark on many of France's medieval landmarks, including Notre Dame in Paris and Vézelay in Burgundy.

The castle is laid out in a concentric pattern, with the double wall and defensive towers designed to resist attack from siege engines. The castle's second gate, **Porte d'Aude** (Map p730), was partly destroyed in 1816 and no longer has its drawbridge.

In between the walls, an interior space known as **Les Lices** runs for just over 1km around the castle. Though designed as a defensive space to delay would-be attackers, during the medieval era the city's poorest residents would have built a shanty-town of houses and workshops here, which were cleared out during Viollet-le-Duc's restorations. It's now the best place to escape the crowds and properly appreciate the castle's martial architecture.

To actually walk on the ramparts, you have to pay to enter the **Château Comtal** (Map p730; place du Château; adult/child €8.50/free; ⏰10am-6.30pm Apr-Sep, 9.30am-5pm Oct-Mar), a keep built for the viscounts of Carcassonne during the 12th century. Admission includes access to the keep's rooms and a section of the battlements, with fabulous views over the surrounding countryside and the distant Pyrenees. Guided tours in several languages are available in summer; check with the tourist office for schedules. It's free on the 1st Sunday of the month from November to March.

Before you leave, visit the lovely **Basilique St-Nazaire** (Map p730; place St-Nazaire; ⏰9am-7pm Jul & Aug, to 6pm Sep-Jun) next to place du Château, notable for its Gothic transept and vivid rose windows. Often, traditional plain chant can be heard inside.

Pont-Vieux BRIDGE

(Map p732) Though it's only one of several bridges spanning the Aude River, the Pont-Vieux is by far the oldest and prettiest. It was built during the 14th century to provide a quick link between Carcassonne's lower and upper towns, and rebuilt in the 19th

Carcassonne (La Cité)

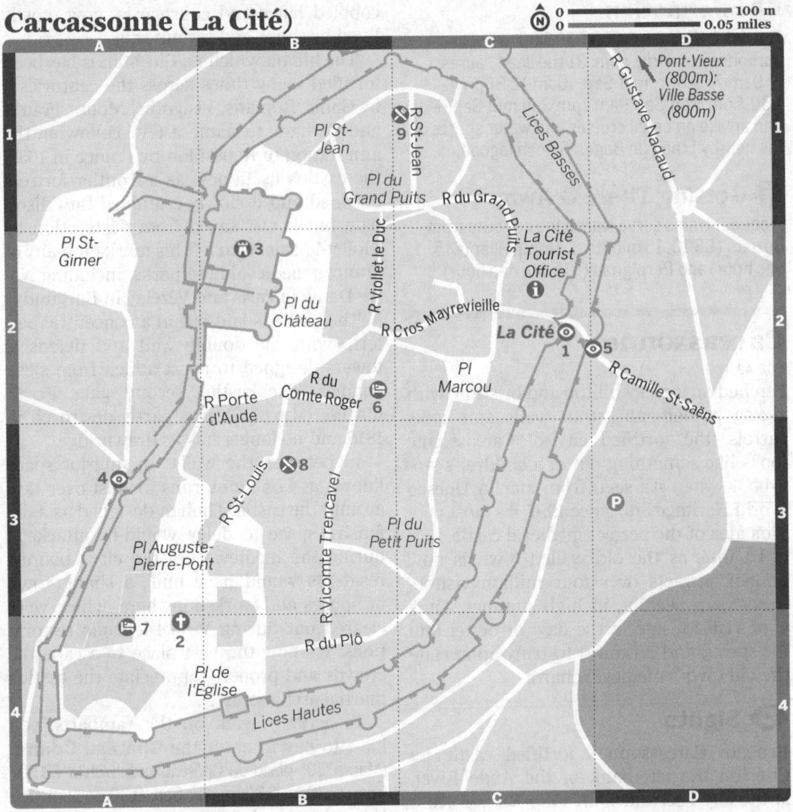

Carcassonne (La Cité)

century. It's one of the few surviving medieval bridges in France, prized for its graceful arches and compact dimensions, and is only open to pedestrians.

Activities

When you've had your fill of architecture, take a canal cruise, go cycling or sample the local wines.

Boat Tours

Several companies offer cruises along the Canal du Midi, also a Unesco-listed wonder, providing a beautiful way to appreciate Carcassonne's architecture from afar surrounded by gorgeous countryside.

The main operators are **Carcassonne Croisières** (Map p732; ☎06 80 47 54 33; www.carcassonne-navigationcroisieres.com; Port de Plaisance; 1¼-hr cruise adult/child €8.50/6.50; ⊙10.30am & 2pm Jul & Aug, 10.30am & 2.30pm Apr-Jun, Sep & Oct) and **Le Cocagne** (Map p732; ☎06 50 40 78 50; www.bateau-cocagne-canal-carcassonne.fr; Port de Plaisance; 1¼-hr cruise adult/child €8/6; ⊙2pm & 6pm daily Jul & Aug, 2pm & 6pm Wed-Mon Apr-Jun, Sep & Oct). Standard cruises last around 1¼ hours, but there are

longer trips available. All trips leave from the Port de Plaisance in the Ville Basse.

Wine Tasting

Experienced English-speaking company **Vin en Vacances** (Map p732; ☎06 42 33 34 09; www.vinenvacances.com; 10 rue du Pont Vieux; day tours €125-145) runs scheduled minibus tours of local vineyards from Carcassonne.

In town, most of the wines at cellar/wine-tasting establishment **Vins & Vinos** (Map p732; ☎04 68 10 97 04; www.vinsvinos.com; 38 rue Barbès; tastings from €15; ⊙10am-6pm Tue-Fri, 9.30am-5pm Sat) come from the south of France but especially the Languedoc-Roussillon and Toulouse areas. Learn more about the *terroirs* and meet the winemakers during tastings and other events; check the program online.

Sleeping

Sleeping inside the old city may seem romantic, but you might think twice once you've lugged your bags through the alleyways. As vehicles are banned, if you're driving you'll have to leave your car outside the city walls overnight. Staying outside the walled city is more practical (and invariably cheaper).

Auberge de Jeunesse HOSTEL €
(Map p730; ☎04 68 25 23 16; www.hifrance.org; rue du Vicomte Trencavel, La Cité; dm incl breakfast €25; ⊙closed mid-Dec–Jan & weekends Feb; @ 📶) This HI hostel is smack bang in the centre of La Cité – great for atmosphere, not great if you're arriving at the train station 4km downhill to the northwest. Facilities include four- to six-bed dorms, a spacious kitchen, an outside terrace and bike rental. It's very popular, so book well ahead.

Hôtel Astoria HOTEL €
(Map p732; ☎04 68 25 31 38; www.astoriacarcassonne.com; 18 rue Tourtel; d €39-77, tr €65-89, q €81-99, 5-person r €91-115; P ❄ 📶) It's not going to win any style awards, but this 22-room budget hotel is great value for Carcassonne. Rooms are small and bathrooms are basic, but it's just 500m east of the train station, and the private parking (€5 outside, €8 under cover) is a bonus. Bike rental is available for €10 per day.

La Maison Vieille B&B €€
(☎06 23 40 65 34; www.la-maison-vieille.com; 8 rue Trivalle; d €90-95, f €105-125; 📶) As charming a B&B as you'll find in Carcassonne, this old mansion's beautiful rooms include Barbacane in blues, Cité with exposed brick, Prince Noir with an in-room bath, and vintage-furnished Dame Carcas. Filled with fig trees, olive trees and lavender, its walled courtyard is idyllic for breakfast. It's handy for the walled city and Ville Basse; families are warmly welcomed.

★**Hôtel de la Cité** HISTORIC HOTEL €€€
(Map p730; ☎04 68 71 98 71; www.hoteldelacite.fr; place Auguste-Pierre-Pont, La Cité; s/d/f from €230/270/350; ❄ 📶 🏊) Built in the 19th century in the Gothic Revival style, this is Carcassonne's most magnificent place to stay. Palatial rooms are individually appointed, many with wood panelling and/or timber beams, and some have panoramic private terraces. Floor-to-ceiling bookshelves line the private library, which has its own bar, and there's a topiary-flanked swimming pool. Its Michelin-starred restaurant, La Barbacane (p733), is sublime.

Eating

Restaurants in La Cité tend to be touristy; you'll find more authentic fare at better value in the Ville Basse.

On menus you'll often see *cassoulet* – a stew of vegetables, white beans and meat that is said to have been invented in the nearby village of Castelnaudry. Quality varies, so be choosy about where you try it.

Markets take place in Ville Basse on place Carnot on Tuesday, Thursday and Saturday mornings.

Les Halles FOOD MARKET €
(Map p732; place Eggenfelden; ⊙7.30am-1.30pm Tue-Sat) Carcassonne's beautiful stone-columned covered market, dating from 1768, sells local wines, cheeses, shellfish and produce.

L'Artichaut BISTRO €
(Map p732; ☎09 52 15 65 14; 14 place Carnot; mains €12-22; ⊙noon-2pm Mon-Wed, noon-2pm & 7-9.30pm Thu-Sat; 👪) This lively local hangout is full of office workers at lunchtime, so you know you're in good hands. It's great for no-fuss bistro standards, such as roast Camembert, classic *steak-frites* and tapas platters, and the location on place Carnot is a winner. The children's menu offers petite versions of main dishes.

La Marquière BISTRO €€
(Map p730; ☎04 68 71 52 00; www.lamarquiere.com; 13 rue St-Jean, La Cité; 2-/3-course menus €32/44; ⊙noon-2.30pm & 7-10.30pm Fri-Tue)

Carcassonne (Ville Basse)

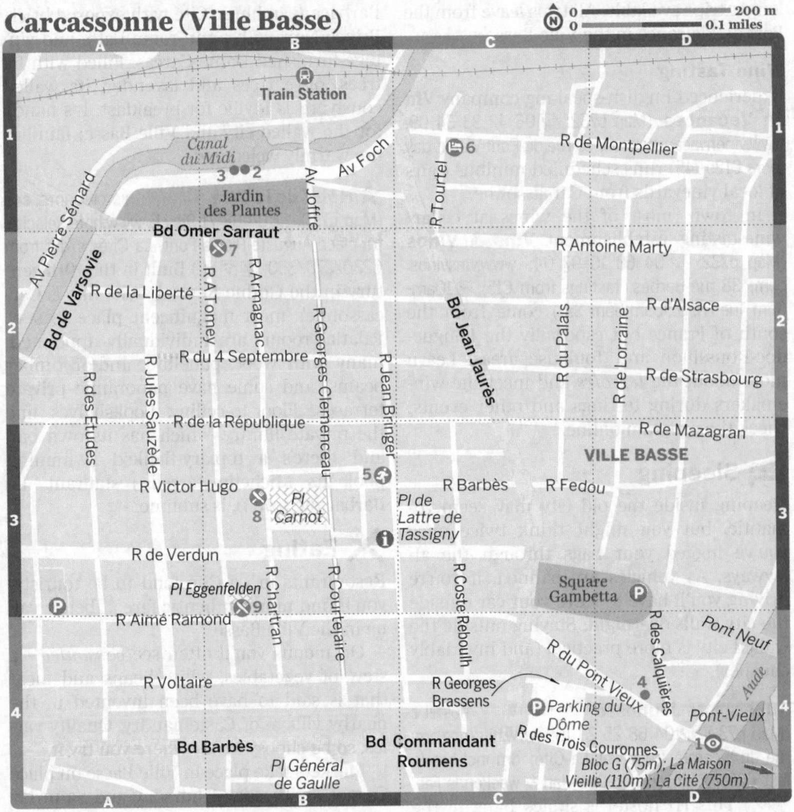

Carcassonne (Ville Basse)

Sights

Activities, Courses & Tours

Sleeping

Eating

In an old shuttered *auberge* (country inn), complete with beams and original hearth, this family-run bistro serves meaty *cassoulet*, along with Mediterranean-influenced dishes such as lamb with parsnip gnocchi, foie gras ravioli, aubergine and spinach cannelloni, and sea bass with squid-ink spaghetti. Ask for a table in the courtyard if it's sunny.

Au Comte Roger MODERN FRENCH €€

(Map p730; ☎04 68 11 93 40; www.comteroger.com; 14 rue St-Louis, La Cité; 2-/3-course lunch menus €24/30, 3-course dinner menu €41, mains €20-32; ⊙noon-1.30pm & 7-9.30pm Tue-Sat) The citadel location bumps up the prices considerably, but this is one of the better establishments for traditional *cassoulet*. The restaurant's smart dining room has cream-coloured chairs and tables and polished wooden floors, but the best seats are in the vine-draped courtyard beside an old well.

Bloc G BISTRO €€

(☎04 68 47 58 20; www.bloc-g.com; 112 rue Barbacane; 3-course lunch menu €15, dinner mains €15-25; ⊙noon-2.30pm Tue, noon-2.30pm & 7-10.30pm Wed-Sat) A modern dining space of

white walls, white chairs and white tables is reflected in the short lunch menu of salads and *tartes salées* (savoury tarts), and creative versions of southwestern French classics such as *l'ouillade* (hearty soup made from pig's trotters, cabbage and turnips) of an evening, along with great local wines by the glass. Also has guest rooms (doubles €10).

Chez Fred BISTRO €€
(Map p732; ☎04 68 72 02 23; www.chez-fred.fr; 31 bd Omer Sarraut; 2-/3-course menus lunch €15/22, dinner €22/28, mains €16-22; ⏰noon-1.45pm & 7-9.45pm Tue-Fri, 7-9.45pm Sat-Mon Jul & Aug, closed Sun & Mon Sep-Jun; 👪) Accessed via antique gates, Fred's Place is a relaxed bistro set around a courtyard. Tuck into sensational *cassoulet* or adventurous dishes such as plum-marinated pork, pumpkin risotto or roast chicken with olive tapenade. Kids get a pared-down version of adults' cuisine on the children's menu.

★**La Barbacane** GASTRONOMIC €€€
(Map p730; ☎04 68 71 98 71; www.hoteldelacite.fr; place Auguste-Pierre-Pont, La Cité; 3-course lunch menu €38, 6-course dinner menu €85, mains €40-60; ⏰12.30-2pm & 7.30-9.30pm) Carcassonne's finest dining is inside the Hôtel de la Cité (p731) at chef Jérôme Ryon's Michelin-starred premises. Opulent carved woodwork and stained glass set the stage for unforgettable dishes utilising some of France's finest produce: poached Bouzigues oysters with preserved lemon; Charolais beef with potato churros and Perigord sauce; and Languedoc-grown saffron, white asparagus and black-garlic risotto with Cévennes goat's cheese.

ℹ Information

La Cité Tourist Office (Map p730; ☎04 68 10 24 30; www.tourisme-carcassonne.fr; Porte Narbonnaise, La Cité; ⏰9.30-7.30pm Jul & Aug, 9.30am-6.30pm Apr-Jun, Sep & Oct, 9.30am-1pm & 1.30-5.30pm Tue-Sun Nov-Mar)

Ville Basse Tourist Office (Map p732; ☎04 68 10 24 30; www.tourisme-carcassonne.fr; 28 rue de Verdun; ⏰9.30am-7.30pm Jul & Aug, 9.30am-6.30pm Mon-Sat, 10am-1pm Sun Apr-Jun, Sep & Oct, 9.30am-5.30pm Mon-Sat Nov-Mar)

ℹ Getting There & Away

AIR

Carcassonne Airport (CCF; ☎04 68 71 96 46; www.aeroport-carcassonne.com) Carcassonne's airport, 5.5km west of town, is used by a handful of carriers, currently Ryanair, Iberia and Atlas Atlantic. It serves several UK cities, including London Stansted, plus Cork, Dublin, Brussels and Porto.

TRAIN

Carcassonne is on the main line from Toulouse. Buses are geared to school timetables, so it's much easier and quicker to catch a train.

Montpellier €26, 1½ hours, up to three hourly

Narbonne €11.50, 30 minutes, up to three hourly

Perpignan €21.20, two hours; change in Narbonne, up to three hourly

Toulouse €16, 50 minutes, up to three hourly

ℹ Getting There & Away

TO/FROM THE AIRPORT

The Navette Aéroport runs to and from the airport (€5, 25 minutes), leaving the train station hourly April to October; from November to March it only serves arriving and departing flights.

BUS

In July and August there's a little tourist-train shuttle (on wheels) between the Ville Basse and the old city every 10 minutes; a one-way ticket is €2, while a day-return ticket is €3.

At other times of year, Agglo (www.carcassonne-agglo.fr) bus 4 runs every 30 minutes Monday to Saturday, hourly on Sunday, from the train station to La Cité's main entrance at Porte Narbonnaise. Journey time is 10 minutes. A single ticket costs €1; a day ticket is €2.60.

HAUT-LANGUEDOC

Haut-Languedoc is a world away from the towns, vineyards and beaches of the coastal plain. It's sparsely populated, and much of the area is now taken up by the Parc National des Cévennes, a land of craggy gorges, windswept plateaux and dense forest, ideal for getting out in the open air.

Parc National des Cévennes

Dotted with hamlets and cut through by rivers and ravines, this expanse of protected landscape was created in 1970 in an attempt to bring ecological stability to an area that had been heavily exploited for agriculture, logging, cattle farming and mining.

The park has subsequently been expanded, and the Cévennes has become a figurehead for French conservation: it's famous for its biodiversity, with 2300 plant species and

1

2

COLIN MCKIE / GETTY IMAGES ©

1. Château Royal (p751), Collioure 2. Palais des Rois de Majorque (p744), Perpignan 3. La Cité (p729), Carcassonne

Languedoc-Roussillon Architecture

The Languedoc landscape is strewn with spectacular structures that provide a fascinating insight into the region's past.

During the 2nd century AD, the Languedoc was part of the province of Gallia Narbonensis, a strategically important region of Roman Gaul. As its name suggests, the province's capital was Narbonne, but the most impressive Roman ruins are in Nîmes, including a wonderfully preserved **Roman temple** and a 20,000-seat amphitheatre now known as **Les Arènes** (p710). Just outside the city, the three-tiered Pont du Gard (p714) aqueduct was built to transport water between Uzès and Nîmes, and ranks as one of the great achievements of Roman engineering.

Long after the Romans, the Languedoc remained a strategically important frontier. The legacy of this can be seen in the region's numerous castles and fortified towns – most notably the fortress of **Carcassonne** (p729), with its distinctive 'witch's hat' turrets, and the lonely hilltop castles left behind by the Cathars, an ultra-devout Christian sect persecuted by Rome during the 13th-century Albigensian Crusade.

For much of the medieval era, the neighbouring province of Roussillon was Catalonian rather than French. In 1231, Perpignan became capital of the Kingdom of Mallorca, and it still has a mighty Spanish-style castle, the **Palais des Rois de Majorque** (p744), where the kings and their families lived. A smaller fortress, the **Château Royal** (p751), can be seen in nearby Collioure. Even today, Roussillon still shares strong ties with Catalonia, with bullfights and *férias* an important part of the festive calendar.

2410 animal species so far recorded. Many animals that were previously extinct – including vultures, beavers, otters, roe deer and golden eagles – have been reintroduced, either by conservationists or by natural migration. Now spanning 937 sq km at its core, the Cévennes is the only national park in France that's largely covered by forest, mostly beech, oak and sweet chestnut. In recognition of its precious natural assets, it's been a Unesco Biosphere Reserve since 1985, and a World Heritage Site since 2011.

Sights & Activities

The park provides a wealth of opportunity for outdoor activities. In winter there's cross-country skiing on Mont Aigoual and Mont Lozère, while donkey treks are popular in the park in warmer months. The rest of the park is criss-crossed by over 600km of trails, including 200km of mountain-biking trails and a dozen GR (Grandes Randonnées; hiking) footpaths – most notably, the GR70, aka the Chemin de Stevenson.

Mont Aigoual Observatory OBSERVATORY, VIEWPOINT
(☎04 67 42 59 83; www.aigoual.fr; ⏰10am-7pm Jul & Aug, 10am-1pm & 2-6pm May-Jun & Sep, by reservation Oct-Apr) FREE Looming 37km south of Florac off the D18 is the prominent peak of Mont Aigoual (1567m). Its lofty 1894-opened observatory is the last remaining mountain-based meteorological station in France. Inside, you can learn the science behind weather forecasting and cloud formation and take in the wraparound views of the central Cévennes.

★**Les Ânes de Vieljouvès** DONKEY TREKKING
(☎04 66 94 04 12; www.vieljouves-gite-cevennes.fr; St-André-de-Lancize; donkey trekking per day €50; ⏰Apr-Sep) Organic picnics incorporating local specialities (per person €8.50) are the perfect accompaniment to the donkey treks offered by Les Ânes de Vieljouvès. It also has guest rooms (per person €33, half-board €51.50) featuring organic meals too. It's located 28km east of Florac off the N106.

Le 107 ADVENTURE SPORTS
(☎06 87 17 12 12; www.le107.com; Le Cirque des Baumes, La Malène; bungee jump €90; ⏰by reservation Thu-Sun Jul & Aug, Sun Apr-Jun, Sep & Oct) It's a 20-minute uphill walk to the 107m-high teetering metal platform from which you hurtle yourself off, attached to a bungee cord. The majestic scenery here makes it a spectacular place to take the plunge. Look for Le 107's car park signposted 20km southwest of Ste-Énimie.

Cavalcatore HORSE RIDING
(☎04 66 44 22 21; 37 rte de Salenson, Ispagnac; 2/3hr ride €27/37, full day €75; ⏰Apr-Sep) Located between Mont Lozère and the northern edges of the Parc National des Cévennes, 9.5km northwest of Florac, Cavalcatore organises treks for beginners through to experienced riders.

WORTH A TRIP

CHEMIN DE STEVENSON (GR70)

Famously, the writer Robert Louis Stevenson trekked across the Cévennes in 1878 with his donkey Modestine, a journey recounted in his classic travelogue, *Travels with a Donkey in the Cévennes*. His route now provides the backbone of the GR70 long-distance trail, which runs for 252km from Le Puy-en-Velay to Alès (slightly longer than Stevenson's original route). It's the Cévennes' most famous walk, and one of the best long-distance routes in France, travelling from the forests of the Cévennes across the Mont Lozère massif into the farmland and valleys of Gévaudan and Velay.

The useful Chemin Stevenson (www.chemin-stevenson.org) and GR70 Stevenson (www.gr70-stevenson.com) websites provide planning information. Free pamphlets and trail maps are widely available once you arrive, or you can rely on the excellent *The Robert Louis Stevenson Trail* guidebook, written by Alan Castle and published by Cicerone.

You don't even need a donkey to carry your baggage these days, as several local companies provide luggage-transfer services:

La Malle Postale (☎04 71 04 21 79, 06 67 79 38 16; www.lamallepostale.com)

Stevenson Bagages (Taxi Genestier; ☎06 07 29 01 23, 04 66 47 04 66; www.stevenson-bagages.com)

Sleeping

★ La Ferme des Cévennes FARMSTAY €

(☎04 66 45 10 90; www.lafermedescevennes.com; La Borie; s/d €39/51, f €61-83; ⏱Apr-Oct; P) Organic farmer Jean-Christophe Barthes cooks up meals using home-grown produce (breakfast €7, packed lunch €8, dinner €20; cheaper rates apply for kids according to their ages). Depending on the season, you can help make traditional cheese, jams, sausages and pâté, join the chestnut and apple harvests and milk goats. It's 5km southeast of Florac just off the N106.

Camping Chantemerle CAMPGROUND €

(☎04 66 45 19 66; www.camping-chantemerle.com; Lieu dit la Pontèze, Bédouès; sites for 2 people €18; ⏱Apr-Oct; P 📶) Riverside pitches, a private sandy beach and an on-site grocery store, restaurant and bar are highlights of this secluded campground 4.5km northeast of Florac in the village of Bédouès on the banks of the Tarn River. Canoeing, kayak rental, horse riding, donkey trekking and hiking trips can be organised through reception.

La Ferme de Vimbouches FARMSTAY €

(☎04 66 31 56 55; www.causses-cevennes.com/ferme-vimbouches; St-Frézal de Ventalon; d €60; ⏱Apr-Oct; P) Immerse yourself in everyday Cévennes life at this rural property with four rustic, cosy farmhouse rooms. You can borrow a donkey for a day's trekking, visit the pig pen and chicken run, or help out with resident horses, rabbits and goats. Children's beds are available; half-/full board costs €50/60 (€30/40 for kids). It's 38km east of Florac off the D29.

Information

Maison du Parc National des Cévennes

(☎04 66 49 53 00; www.cevennes-parcnational.fr; 6bis place du Palais; ⏱9am-noon & 2-6pm Mon-Fri, 10am-1pm & 3-6pm Sat & Sun Apr-Sep, shorter hours Oct-Mar) This Florac-based information centre should be your first port of call for general information on things to see and do inside the park. Its office and website provide comprehensive information on accommodation, activities, nature and much more.

Getting There & Around

Public transport is very limited in the Cévennes: about the only options are the daily bus that shuttles between Alès and Ispagnac, stopping at Florac en route; and the daily service linking Florac with Mende. From Mende you can connect to Ste-Énimie.

By car, the most spectacular route from the east is the Corniche des Cévennes, a ridge road that winds along the mountain crests of the Cévennes for 56km from St-Jean du Gard to Florac.

If you're approaching Florac from Mende and the north, leave the N106 at Balsièges and drive the much quieter, even prettier D31. This crosses the wild, upland Causse de Sauveterre, then descends to Ispagnac, where you turn left to rejoin the main N106.

Note that petrol stations are few and far between – there are service stations in Florac and Ste-Énimie, but prices here inevitably tend to be high – so it's a good idea to fuel up before you enter the park.

Florac

POP 2014

In a forested valley 79km northwest of Alès and 38km southeast of Mende, the pretty, peaceful rural village of Florac sits at the confluence of three rivers, the Tarnon, Mimente and Tarn. It's the most useful base for exploring the Parc National des Cévennes and the upper reaches of the Gorges du Tarn.

Activities

Florac marks the start of numerous walks. The national park has published 20 'topoguides' covering around 275 *petites randonnées* (PR) trails, most ranging from just a few kilometres up to full-day hikes. Five Grandes Randonnées (GR) trails also cross the park, including GR4, 6, 7, 70 and 700. The IGN Top25 map series covers most of the national-park area.

One of the most popular options from Florac is the **Sentier de Gralhon** (6km, two hours), an easy walk that climbs up to the old Gralhon manor and Monteil village before looping back to Florac, but the visitor centre in Florac has lots more ideas.

Longer routes take in the nearby peaks, including **Mont Lozère** (1699m), 14km to the northeast of Florac, the highest peak in the Cévennes.

Tourisme-Actif OUTDOORS

(☎06 83 41 73 08; www.sport-nature-lozere.com; 11 place de l'Esplanade; caving €35-75, canyoning €50-70, via ferrata €35-49; ⏱10am-6pm Apr-Sep) All equipment is provided on half- and full-day trips organised by Florac-based adventure company Tourisme-Actif, which can

WORTH A TRIP

MICHELIN-STAR SUPPERS

If you're looking for a once-in-a-lifetime meal, two chefs tucked away in the countryside have won the hallowed three Michelin stars. Both also have accommodation.

Bras (05 65 51 18 20; www.bras.fr; Laguiole; menus €140-220, mains €45-90; 7-9.30pm Tue & Wed, 11.30am-1.30pm & 7-9.30pm Thu-Sun early Apr-Nov, closed Dec-early Apr;) Michel Bras has been based at the eponymous Bras in the village of Laguiole since 1999. His food is steeped in the rustic, country flavours of his youth, reinvented in all kinds of outlandish ways. It's worth a trip for the restaurant alone: a modernist, plate-glass marvel, with views over Aubrac's green hills. Double rooms start at €310. Unusually for a superstar chef, Michel Bras is self-made: he's never strayed from his home on the Aubrac plateau, between the Massif Central and the Cévennes, and he learned many of his skills from his mother. He's now handed over the reins to his son, Sébastien, but still makes regular appearances.

Auberge du Vieux Puits (04 68 44 07 37; www.aubergeduvieuxpuits.fr; Fontjoncouse; menus €110-190; noon-1.30pm & 8-9.30pm Wed-Sat, noon-1.30pm Sun Mar-Dec, closed Jan & Feb;) Gilles Goujon's wonderfully relaxed Auberge du Vieux Puits is tucked away in the hilltop village of Fontjoncouse, between Narbonne and Perpignan. Goujon's known for his fondness for humble ingredients such as Bigorre pork, woodcock, hare, boar and pigeon. The menus stretch between four and seven courses and include a 'chariot of cheese' that defies belief. Double rooms start at €165.

take you on caving, canyoning and via ferrata expeditions of varying levels of difficulty.

Cévennes Évasion HIKING
(04 66 45 18 31; www.cevennes-evasion.com; 6 place Boyer; 3-night hiking or mountain-biking trips from €230; Apr-Sep) Based in the centre of Florac, Cévennes Évasion runs multiday guided hiking and mountain-biking trips.

Sleeping & Eating

Rue du Pêcher and av Jean Monestier have the greatest concentration of restaurants and cafes.

Camping Le Pont du Tarn CAMPGROUND €
(04 66 45 18 26; www.camping-florac.com; rte du Pont de Montvert; sites for 2 people €12.50-22; Apr-Oct;) Here you can swim in either the heated pool or the Tarn River, which runs right by this shady 5-hectare campsite 2km north of Florac beside the D998. Stylish canvas bungalows sleeping two to four (per week from €246), and simpler cabins with private terraces sleeping two to eight (per week from €196), can be rented on a weekly basis.

La Carline HOSTEL €
(04 66 45 24 54; www.gite-florac.fr; 18 rue du Pêcher; dm €18, incl breakfast €24; Apr–mid-Sep) In an 18th-century house in the centre of Florac, this cute little travellers' *gîte* is run by welcoming hosts Monette and Alain Lagrave. Rooms are very simple and share bathrooms, but there are lots of maps and guidebooks to browse, and Alain makes his own jams for the breakfast table.

Au Pêcher Mignon CRÊPERIE €
(04 66 45 14 28; 13ter place Louis Dides; crêpes & galettes €2-7.50; noon-10.30pm mid-Jun–Aug, noon-2pm Tue-Thu, noon-2pm & 6-9pm Fri & Sat May–mid-Jun & Sep, noon-2pm Tue-Sat Apr, closed Oct-Mar) Savoury *galettes* made from buckwheat flour include fillings such as locally smoked trout and chive cream, walnut and Roquefort, and local ham and Cévennes goat's cheese, while sweet crêpe options span salted-butter caramel to apple and raisin, and local blueberry or chestnut jam with Chantilly cream at this lime-green-hued crêperie. Tables on the awning-shaded terrace overlook a splashing fountain.

Le Camisard TRADITIONAL FRENCH €
(04 30 43 42 13; 12 rue du Pêcher; 3-course lunch menu €14, mains €7.50-12; noon-2pm Mon, Tue & Thu, noon-2pm & 7-9pm Wed & Fri, 6-9pm Sat) The apricot-shaded exterior might be plain and the white-tiled interior even plainer, but Le Camisard is a locals' favourite for hearty Cévennes fare – veal bourguignon, line-caught trout tournedos, red-wine-braised beef with locally farmed potatoes, and courgette, leek and goat's cheese quiche – that offers the best value for money in town.

★ **Les Tables de la Fontaine** TRADITIONAL FRENCH €€
(☎04 66 65 21 73; www.tables-de-la-fontaine.com; 31 rue du Therond; 2-/3-course menus €21/24; ⏲noon-2pm & 7-9.30pm Mon-Sat, noon-2pm Sun Apr-Sep; 👪) Red-umbrella-shaded tables are scattered around a natural spring in the courtyard adjoining this ivy-clad restaurant. River trout with preserved lemon, Lozère lamb with potato gratin, vegetable tart with Cévennes goat's cheese, and red-wine-marinated pears are among the daily-changing dishes incorporating locally sourced produce. Wines are also local and beers are artisanal. Live music often plays of an evening.

Upstairs are four simple but comfortable guest rooms (doubles including breakfast €65 to €85; half-board available).

Information

Tourist Office (☎04 66 45 01 14; www.vacances-cevennes.com; 33 av Jean Monestier; ⏲9am-12.30 & 2-6.30pm Mon-Sat, 10am-1pm Sun Jul & Aug, shorter hours Sep-Jun) Beside the Tarnon River.

Getting There & Away

Voyages Boulet (☎04 66 65 19 88; www.voyages-boulet.com) runs one daily bus from Alès to Florac (€15.50, 65 minutes) Monday to Saturday from mid-April to September.

Local bus line 8 links Florac with Mende (€2, 50 minutes) three times daily Monday to Friday and once Saturday mid-April to October, once daily Monday to Saturday November to mid-April.

Gorges du Tarn

Slicing down the flanks of Mont Lozère, the plunging canyons of the Gorges du Tarn wind for some 50km through the Parc National des Cévennes southwest from Florac, marking the boundary between the Causse Méjean to its south and the Causse de Sauveterre to the north.

Steep cliffs carve through sparkling blue-green waters and limestone escarpments. As the narrow, twisting riverside road is notorious for summer traffic jams, the best way to explore is on the water in a kayak or canoe.

Ste-Énimie

POP 563

Clinging to the cliffside, teeny Ste-Énimie is a charming village with a cobbled quarter full of restored timber houses and stone cottages, along with the 12th-century **Église de Ste-Énimie** and the old Halle aux Blés (Flour Market).

Situated 27km west of Florac and 56km northeast of Millau, it's the most central base for exploring the Gorges du Tarn, within the Parc National des Cévennes. Bear in mind that most activities, accommodation and dining options are only open between April and October.

Sleeping & Eating

Camping Couderc CAMPGROUND €
(☎04 66 48 50 53; www.campingcouderc.fr; rte des Gorges du Tarn; sites for 2 people €14-25, yurts €35-45, cabins €45-55; ⏲Apr-Sep; 🅿🏊) Although they're packed in pretty tightly, the 130 pitches at this riverside campground 2.5km southwest of Ste-Énimie are mostly beneath trees, so they stay shady and cool. Canvas-sided yurts and cabins (minimum two-night stay) sleep up to four people. Fantastic facilities include restaurant, bar and heated swimming pool, as well as on-site kayak hire (per day €22).

Yelloh Village Camping Nature et Rivière CAMPGROUND €
(☎04 66 48 57 36; www.camping-nature-riviere.com; St-Chély du Tarn; sites for 2 people €15-39, 4-/6-person chalets €111/137; ⏲late Apr-early Sep; 🅿@📶) It's worth paying extra for a riverside site at this small forest campground 3km southwest of Ste-Énimie. Its 57 pitches spread out below beech trees with plenty of space set aside for each site; families also have the option of timber chalets, high chairs and cots. There's a bar and grocery store, and a multimedia area; fridge hire is available.

Maison de Marius B&B €€
(☎04 66 44 25 05; www.maisondemarius.fr; 8 rue Pontet, Quézac; d €70-95, tr €120, f €165; 🅿) In Quézac, 17km east of Ste-Énimie, this cosy place is a proper home from home. Owner Dany has individually decorated the countrified bedrooms with floral fabrics, watercolours, old luggage and roll-top baths – the Pompeii Suite even has its own Jacuzzi, complete with Roman murals. A garden chalet is available for weekly stays (from €600 per week).

★ **Château de la Caze** HOTEL €€€
(☎04 66 48 51 01; www.chateaudelacaze.com; rte des Gorges du Tarn, La Malène; castle d €134-200, house ste €256-266, house apt €294-320; ⏲early Apr-early Nov; 🅿❄📶🏊) Rising unexpectedly in the middle of the gorge, this château

DON'T MISS

CANOEING IN THE GORGES DU TARN

Riding the Tarn is best in high summer, when the river is usually low and the descent a lazy trip over mostly calm water. You can canoe as far as the impassable Pas de Soucy, a barrier of boulders about 9km downriver from La Malène. You'll have to arrange for your canoe to be transported beyond the barrier if you want to carry on further.

Tariffs and trip durations depend on how far you want to travel. From Ste-Énimie, destinations include La Malène (€21, 12km, four hours) and Les Baumes Basses (€26, 22km, six hours). If you want a longer trip, buses can transport you upriver to start in Prades, Montbrun or Ispagnac. Return transport is included in rental prices.

Dozens of companies in Ste-Énimie and La Malène provide canoe and kayak rental from around mid-April to September, including **Canoë 2000** (04 66 48 57 71; www.canoe2000.fr; La Malène; single kayak/2-person canoe rental from €17/32), **Locanoë** (04 66 48 55 57; www.gorges-du-tarn.fr; Castelbouc; canoe & kayak rental per person from €15), **Méjean Canoë** (04 66 48 58 70; www.canoe-mejean.com; Ste-Énimie; canoe & kayak rental from €13; 9am-6.30pm May-Sep) and **Le Canophile** (04 66 48 57 60; www.canoe-tarn.com; Ste-Énimie; canoe & kayak rental per person from €10; daily Jul & Aug, Sat & Sun May, Jun & Sep). It's worth asking about seasonal offers and package prices.

If you'd rather someone else did the hard work, **Les Bateliers de la Malène** (04 66 48 51 10; www.gorgesdutarn.com; La Malène; per 4 people €88; 9am-noon & 1.30-5pm Apr-early Oct) will punt you down an 8km stretch of the gorge from La Malène in a traditional barge, then drive you back.

comes complete with fortified towers, landscaped gardens, flagstone halls and even the odd suit of armour. Rooms are split between the main castle (some with bathrooms inside the turrets) and the Maison de la Martine, a smaller house positioned across the gardens with luxurious suites and four-person apartments.

The château has its own private beach, spa, gym, heated swimming pool and helipad. Breakfast costs €16; half-board at its restaurant costs €60 per person in addition to the room rate.

Restaurant du Nord TRADITIONAL FRENCH €
(04 66 48 53 46; rue Principale; menus €11-25; noon-9pm Jul & Aug, noon-2pm & 7-9pm Mar-Jun & Sep-Nov;) A canopied 20-seater terrace overlooks a stone bridge spanning the Tarn River outside this traditional restaurant, which serves classics including *cassoulet* (rich meat and white-bean stew), onion soup, grilled mushrooms stuffed with Pélardon goat's cheese and meal-sized salads. A pared-down kids' menu is available for €8.

Information

Tourist office (04 66 48 53 44; www.gorgesdutarn.net; rte de Mende; 9.15am-12.15pm & 2-6pm Mon-Sat, 9am-1pm Sun Jul & Aug, shorter hours Apr-Jun & Sep, closed Oct-Mar) Has info on the Gorges du Tarn and the entire Parc National des Cévennes.

Parc Naturel Régional des Grands Causses

The Grands Causses are part of the same geological formation as the Massif Central to the north. Scorched in summer and windswept in winter, these harsh plateaux hold little moisture, as water filters through the limestone to form an underground world, ideal for cavers.

The rivers Tarn, Jonte and Dourbie have sliced deep gorges through the 5000-sq-km plateau, creating four *causses* ('plateaux' in the local lingo): Sauveterre, Méjean, Noir and Larzac, each slightly different in its geological make-up. All are eerily empty, save for the occasional shepherd and flock – making them perfect for hikers and bikers who like nothing better than to go hours without seeing another soul on the trail.

The Gorges de la Jonte, where birds of prey wheel and swoop, skim the park's eastern boundary.

Sights

Causse de Sauveterre PLATEAU
The northernmost of the *causses* is a gentle, hilly plateau dotted with a few isolated farms and traversed by hiking trails. Every possible patch of fertile earth is cultivated, creating irregular, intricately patterned wheat fields.

Causse Méjean PLATEAU

Causse Méjean, the highest of the *causses*, is also the most barren and isolated. Defined to the north by the Gorges du Tarn and to the south by the Gorges de la Jonte, it looms over Florac, on its eastern flank. It's a land of poor pasture enriched by fertile depressions, where streams gurgle down into the limestone through sinkholes, funnels and fissures.

This combination of water and limestone has created some spectacular underground scenery. Within the cavern of **Aven Armand** (www.aven-armand.com; Hures-la-Parade; adult/child €11.50/8.60, combination ticket with Chaos de Montpellier-le-Vieux €15.80/11.50; ⏲9.30am-6pm Jul & Aug, 10am-noon & 1.30-5pm late Mar-Jun & Sep-early Nov) is the world's greatest concentration of stalagmites, including a gallery of stone columns known as the Forêt Vierge (Virgin Forest). The cave is accessed via a funicular that drops 75m into the gloom. Guided visits last about 45 minutes. Combination tickets with the Chaos de Montpellier-le-Vieux canyons are available.

Causse Noir PLATEAU

Rising immediately east of Millau, the Black Causse is best known for the **Chaos de Montpellier-le-Vieux** (www.montpellierlevieux.com; Montpellier-le-Vieux; adult/child €6.80/5.40, combination ticket with Aven Armand €15.80/11.50; ⏲9am-7pm Jul & Aug, 9.30am-5.30pm late Mar-Jun & Sep-early Nov), 18km northeast of Millau, overlooking the Gorges de la Dourbie. Water erosion has created more than 120 hectares of tortured limestone formations with fanciful names such as the Sphinx and the Elephant. Three trails, lasting one to three hours, cover the site – or you can take a trip aboard the **tourist train** (adult/child €4.40/3.60; ⏲9am-7pm Jul & Aug, 9.30am-5.30pm late Mar-Jun & Sep-early Nov).

Causse du Larzac PLATEAU

The Causse du Larzac is the largest of the four *causses*. An endless sweep of distant horizons and rocky steppes broken by medieval villages, it's known as the 'French Desert'. You'll stumble across venerable fortified villages such as **Ste-Eulalie de Cernon**, long the capital of the Larzac region, and **La Cavalerie**, both built by the Knights Templar, a religious military order that distinguished itself during the Crusades.

Causse de la Jointe PLATEAU

The 15km-long Gorges de la Jonte cleave east–west from Meyrueis to Le Rozier, dividing Causse Noir from Causse Méjean.

Just south of the Gorges de la Jonte, **Grotte de Dargilan** (www.grotte-dargilan.com; Dargilan; adult/child €9.50/6.10; ⏲10.15am-6pm Jul & Aug, 10.30am-5pm Apr-Jun & Sep, 2-4pm Oct) is known as La Grotte Rose (Pink Cave) for its rosy colouring. The most memorable moment of the one-hour, 1km tour through this vast chasm is a sudden, dazzling exit onto a ledge, with a dizzying view of the gorge way below.

Birdwatchers won't want to miss the **Belvédère des Vautours** (Vulture Viewing Point; ☎05 65 62 69 69; www.vautours-lozere.com; Le Truel; adult/child €6.70/3; ⏲9.30am-7pm Jul & Aug, 9.30am-7pm Tue-Sun May, Jun & Sep, 10am-6pm Tue-Sun Apr & Oct), just west of Le Truel on the D996, where a population of more than 200 reintroduced vultures now thrives on the sheer limestone cliffs. You can watch the birds gliding through the *causse* from the viewing point, which also has a live video feed from the nesting sites.

Activities

Activities abound in the Parc Naturel Régional des Grands Causses, with hang-gliding, paragliding, rock climbing, walking and cycling opportunities all accessible from Millau.

Information

Parc Naturel Régional des Grands Causses Office (☎05 65 61 35 50; www.parc-grands-causses.fr; 71 bd de l'Ayrolle, Millau; ⏲9am-noon & 2-5pm Mon-Fri) Provides maps and information on hiking, cycling and adventure activities in the park.

Millau

POP 22,000

Famous within France for glove-making, Millau (pronounced mee-yo) squeezes between the Parc Naturel Régional des Grands Causses' Causse Noir and Causse du Larzac at the confluence of the Tarn and Dourbie Rivers. The town is an ideal jumping-off point for hiking and adventure sport – particularly hang-gliding and paragliding, exploiting the uplifting thermals.

Sleeping & Eating

★**Château de Creissels** HOTEL €€

(☎05 65 60 16 59; www.chateau-de-creissels.com; place du Prieur, Creissels; d €86-120, ste €132; ⏲early Mar-late Dec; P❄📶🏊) In Creissels, 2km southwest of Millau on the D992, this castle's rooms are split between the 12th-century tower (parquet floors, fireplaces, oil

DON'T MISS

VIADUC DE MILLAU

The gravity-defying toll bridge **Viaduc de Millau** (www.leviaducdemillau.com; A75, Millau; toll Jul & Aug €9.80, Sep-Jun €7.80; 24hr) hovers 343m above the Tarn valley, making it one of the world's highest road bridges. Designed by British architect Sir Norman Foster and opened in 2004, it's a work of imagination as much as engineering: seven slender pylons support 2.5km of the A75 motorway, and despite its heavyweight construction (127,000 cu metres of concrete, 19,000 tonnes of steel, 5000 tonnes of cable), the bridge looks as delicate as a gossamer thread.

At ground level beneath the viaduct on the D992, the **Viaduc Espace** (05 65 61 61 54; D992; guided tours adult/child €6/3.50; 10am-7pm Apr-Oct, to 5pm Nov-Mar) explores the story of the bridge's construction and offers 45-minute guided visits around its exhibition garden under the bridge.

To truly appreciate the bridge's astonishing dimensions, take a 1½-hour boat trip with **Bateliers du Viaduc** (05 65 59 12 41; www.bateliersduviaduc.com; adult/child €24/16.50; every 45min 9am-5.30pm Apr-Oct) along the Tarn from the nearby village of Creissels.

paintings) and modern wings (sleek showers, stripped-wood floors, designer lamps; some have balconies overlooking the large garden). Excellent regional cuisine is served in the restaurant's brick-vaulted cellar and panoramic terrace. Breakfast costs €11.50; half-board is €74 per person.

★ La Mangeoire REGIONAL CUISINE €€
(05 65 60 13 16; www.restaurantmillau.com; 10 bd de la Capelle; 2-/3-course lunch menus €16/23, 3-/4-/5-course dinner menus €24/33/49.50, mains €17-26; noon-2pm & 7-10pm Tue-Sun) Fronted by a shady pavement terrace strung with fairy lights and opening to a romantic vaulted-stone dining room, Millau's best restaurant refines the rich flavours of the region: wood-fire-grilled Trénels sheep-stomach sausage with *aligot* (mashed potato and melted sheep's cheese); Aubrac beef ribs with Roquefort sauce; spicy spit-roasted local hare; lamb sweetbreads in parsley-butter sauce; and chestnut sorbet in Armagnac.

Getting There & Away

Public transport to and from Millau is severely limited; your own wheels are a much better bet.

Mende

POP 12,300

On the northern edge of the Parc National des Cévennes, Mende is the capital of Lozère, France's least populous *département*. It's a peaceful, rural town with a lovely medieval quarter that would once have been surrounded by defensive walls.

A few half-hidden towers are all that remain of the ramparts, but some interesting medieval buildings still exist. A busy farmers market takes over place Urbain V in front of the cathedral on Saturday morning.

During WWII, Mende (like much of Lozère) was a hotbed of the French Resistance, and local Resistance fighters scored several important victories against the Vichy regime – mainly blowing up railways and disrupting transport links during the run-up to D-Day. Panels around town commemorate several key fighters, including former Mende mayor Henri Bourrillon, the chief of the Lozère Resistance, who was captured in 1944 and died in a Nazi concentration camp.

Sleeping & Eating

★ La Grange d'Emilie B&B €€
(04 66 47 30 82; www.chambrehote-emilie.com; Fontans; s €95-115, d €105-125; May-Oct; P) An old Lozèrois farm 30km north of Mende is now a seriously luxurious retreat, with five stunning rooms that still retain rustic character. Old meets new with wood, stone and beams offset by rendered surfaces, reclaimed furniture and freestanding baths (including one made from a cow's watering trough). *Table d'hôte* dinners cost €35 per person.

Hôtel de France HOTEL €€
(04 66 65 00 04; www.hoteldefrance-mende.com; 9 bd Lucien Arnault; d €98-105; P) Clad in shutters and slate, this renovated coaching inn is the best place to stay in Mende, with 31 rooms, all huge and some with sweeping views over the garden and valley (two have their own roof terrace). It's modern, despite the heritage exterior, and the restaurant (*menus* €31 to €56) is a

fine-dining treat. Covered/uncovered parking costs €7/5.

La Cantine BISTRO €€

(☎04 66 32 86 12; 8 rue St-Privat; 2-/3-course menus lunch €17/19, dinner €20/22; ⏰noon-1.30pm & 7.30-9.30pm Tue-Sun, noon-1.30pm Mon; 🌿👶) A daily market-sourced menu incorporating local organic ingredients is served on antique crockery at this locals' favourite down a cobbled laneway. Depending on the season, dishes might include parsnip and pumpkin gratin with veal steak, roast beetroot stuffed with Roquefort and almonds, courgette and chicken pie or pigeon with carrot crumble, accompanied by natural wines and *bio* beer. Book ahead.

ℹ Information

Tourist Office (☎04 66 94 00 23; www.ot-mende.fr; place du Foirail; ⏰9am-7pm Mon-Sat, 10am-5pm Sun Jul & Aug, 9am-noon & 2-6pm Mon-Fri, 9am-noon Sat May, 9am-noon & 2-6pm Mon-Sat Jun & Sep, closed Oct-Apr; 📶) Has free audioguides for city sightseeing walks.

ℹ Getting There & Away

BUS

Buses leave from the train station. Most pass by place du Foirail, beside the tourist office. Timetables change during school holidays.

Florac Line 8, €2, 50 minutes, two daily Monday to Saturday mid-April to September, one daily Monday to Friday October to mid-April

Le Puy-en-Velay Line 3, €2, two hours, one bus on weekdays

Ste-Enimie Line 11, €2, 45 minutes, one bus on Friday

TRAIN

The train station is 1km north of town across the Lot River.

Alès €20.20, 2½ hours, four daily

Le Puy-en-Velay €30.20, 1¾ hours, one daily

Roquefort

POP 685

Twenty-five kilometres southwest of Millau, the village of Roquefort (full name Roquefort-sur-Soulzon) is synonymous with its famous blue cheese, produced from ewe's milk in nearby caves.

There are seven AOC-approved producers in Roquefort, two of which (Gabriel Coulet and La Société) offer cellar visits. The cellars of five other producers (Roquefort Carles, Le Vieux Berger, Vernières Frères, Le Papillon and Les Fromageries Occitanes) aren't open to the public, but they all have shops where you can sample and buy cheeses.

Activities

Gabriel Coulet CHEESE TASTING

(☎05 65 59 24 27; www.gabriel-coulet.fr; 3 av de Lauras; ⏰9am-7pm Jul & Aug, 9.30am-6pm Apr-Jun & Sep, 9.30am-noon & 1.30-5pm Oct-Mar) FREE This is the more intimate of Roquefort's two cellars open for visits (the other, La Société, is the world's largest producer of the cheese). You're free to explore the penicillin-streaked caves below the shop, then head upstairs for a tasting.

La Société CHEESE TASTING

(☎05 65 58 54 38; www.roquefort-societe.com; 2 av François Galtier; adult/child €5/3; ⏰10am-noon & 1.30-5pm Apr-Oct, 10am-noon & 1.30-4.30pm Nov-Mar) Established in 1842, this is the largest, flashiest producer of Roquefort, churning out 60% of the world's supply. One-hour tours of the caves (where the temperature is a nippy 10°C; bring warm clothes) include sampling the company's three main varieties. Its on-site restaurant overlooks the valley.

THE KING OF CHEESES: ROQUEFORT

Marbled with blue-green veins caused by microscopic fungi known as *Penicillium roqueforti* (which are initially grown on leavened bread), pungent Roquefort is one of the region's oldest cheeses. In 1407 Charles VI granted exclusive Roquefort cheesemaking rights to the villagers, and in the 17th century the Sovereign Court of the Parliament of Toulouse imposed severe penalties on cheesemakers fraudulently trading under the Roquefort name. Roquefort was the first cheese in France to be granted its own Appellation d'Origine Contrôlée (AOC) – in 1925. Legend claims the cheese was discovered by accident, when a local lad became distracted by a beautiful girl and left a wheel of cheese behind in one of the village caves. When he returned, it was covered in mould that turned out to be surprisingly tasty. It's now France's second-most-popular cheese after Comté, with an annual production of around 18,000 tonnes.

WORTH A TRIP

MICROPOLIS

Creepy-crawly-loving kids can indulge their insectivorous interests at the excellent 'Insect City' **Micropolis** (La Cité des Insectes; ☎05 65 58 50 50; www.micropolis-aveyron.com; Le Bourg, St-Léons; adult/child €13.80/9.50; ⊙10am-7pm Jul & Aug, to 6pm Apr-Jun, to 5pm Wed-Sun mid-Feb–Mar, Sep & Oct), 19km northwest of Millau. This high-tech centre brings the world of insects impressively to life: you can peer inside ant colonies, see the inner workings of beehives and explore the wonderful butterfly pavilion. Audioguides are included in admission. Afterwards kids can burn off steam at the insect-themed adventure playground while adults unwind in the cafe.

Information

Tourist office (☎05 65 58 56 00; www.ot-du-saintaffricain.com; av de Lauras; ⊙9.30am-6.30pm Mon-Sat, 11am-6pm Sun Jul & Aug, shorter hours Sep-Jun) Has free cheese tastings and information on the town's cellars.

Getting There & Away

There is no direct transport to Roquefort. Trains from Millau (€5.70, 25 minutes, three daily) or Béziers (€16.80, 1½ hours, three daily) stop 3km east at Tournemire. From here, a **taxi** (☎05 65 46 27 39) costs €6.

ROUSSILLON

Dusty scrubland, crimson towns and scorching summer temperatures give Roussillon a distinctly Spanish flavour. Also known as French Catalonia, it incorporates busy beach towns and coastal villages along the Mediterranean as well as the abandoned abbeys and crumbling Cathar strongholds inland among the fragrant maquis.

Howling down from the Pyrenees, the violent Tramontane wind cuts to the bone in winter and in summer is strong enough to overturn a caravan.

Roussillon's only city is Perpignan, capital of the Pyrénées-Orientales *département* and a useful base for exploring the region.

History

Roussillon's history is inextricably linked with Spain's. After flourishing as the capital of the kingdom of Mallorca, it fell under Aragonese rule for much of the late Middle Ages.

In 1640 the Catalans on both sides of the Pyrenees revolted against the rule of distant Madrid. Peace came in 1659 with the Treaty of the Pyrenees, defining the border between Spain and France once and for all and ceding Roussillon (until then the northern section of Catalonia) to the French, much to the indignation of the locals.

Although it's no longer officially part of Catalonia, Roussillon retains much of its Catalan identity. The *sardane* folk dance is still performed, and the Catalan language, closely related to Provençal, is still commonly spoken.

Perpignan

POP 123,000

Framed by the peaks of the Pyrenees 13km west of the Mediterranean coastline and just 38km north of the Spanish border, Perpignan radiates out from the tight knot of the old town's warren of alleys, palm-shaded squares and shabby tenements painted in shades of lemon, peach and tangerine.

Historically, Perpignan (Perpinyà in Catalan) was capital of the kingdom of Mallorca, a Mediterranean power that stretched northwards as far as Montpellier and included all the Balearic Islands; the Mallorcan kings' palace still stands guard at the southern end of the old town.

Its proximity to Spain means the town is strong on fiestas.

Sights

Perpignan's old town is roughly contained within the main ring roads of bd des Pyrénées in the west, bd Thomas Wilson in the north, bd Anatole France in the east, and bd Henri Poincaré in the south. Its shallow canal skirts its western edge. Cars are banned in the centre, so if you're driving you'll have to park in one of the large municipal car parks on the edges of the old town.

★**Palais des Rois de Majorque** PALACE
(☎04 68 34 96 26; www.ledepartment66.fr; 4 rue des Archers; adult/child €4/2; ⊙10am-6pm Jun-Sep, 9am-5pm Oct-May) Perpignan's most dominant monument, the Palace of the Kings of Mallorca sprawls over a huge area to the south of the old town. Built in 1276, the castle was later refortified with massive red-brick walls by Louis XIV's military engineer, Vauban. These days the star-shaped

citadel is sparsely furnished, but its great battlements and strategic defences still give a sense of the Mallorcan kings' might. Views from the ramparts stretch over Perpignan's terracotta rooftops to the coast.

Le Castillet & Casa Païral GATE, MUSEUM
(place de Verdun; adult/child €2/free; ⏲10am-6.30pm Tue-Sun) Like many medieval towns, Perpignan was once encircled by defensive walls. Today all that remains is the red-brick town gate of **Le Castillet**, at the northern end of the old town. Inside the gateway is the **Casa Païral museum**, displaying Catalan ephemera from traditional bonnets and lace mantillas to an entire 17th-century kitchen.

Cathédrale St-Jean CATHEDRAL
(place Gambetta; ⏲8am-7pm Mon-Fri, 10.30am-6.30pm Sat & Sun Jun-Sep, 8am-6pm Mon-Fri, 11am-5.30pm Sat & Sun Oct-May) Perpignan's old town has several intriguing churches, but the most impressive is the Cathédrale St-Jean, begun in 1324 and not completed until 1509. Topped by a Provençal wrought-iron bell cage, the cathedral has a flat façade of red brick and smooth, zigzagging river stones.

Inside, the fine carving and ornate altarpiece are characteristically Catalan, and the simple statue of the Virgin and child in the north aisle is a venerated relic.

Festivals & Events

Fête de la Sant Joan CULTURAL
(⏲mid-Jun) A sacred flame that's maintained all year at the town gate of Le Castillet is taken to the top of Mont Canigou for a Midsummer bonfire. Afterwards, the flame is brought back to Le Castillet, where fireworks are set off and children light lanterns.

Nuit et Fête du Vin Primeur WINE
(⏲Oct) On the third Thursday in October, a barrel of the year's new wine production is ceremonially paraded through the streets to Cathédrale St-Jean to be blessed. Wine tasting (accompanied by local charcuterie) later takes place all over the city, along with samba, jazz and blues performances.

Sleeping

Hôtel de la Loge HOTEL €
(☎04 68 34 41 02; www.hoteldelaloge.com; 1 rue des Fabriques Nabot; s/d from €63/78; ❄📶) The best option inside the old town is this 22-room former merchant's house footsteps from the Castillet tower. It now feels like an upmarket antique shop: its staircase and hallways are filled with Catalan furniture and quirky objets d'art and rooms are furnished in old-fashioned style. Rooms 106 and 206 overlook place de la Loge.

Auberge de Jeunesse HOSTEL €
(☎04 68 34 63 32; www.hifrance.org; 3 allée Marc Pierre; dm/tw/q incl breakfast €19.30/42.60/77.20; ⏲reception 8-11am & 5-9pm mid-Apr–mid-Oct, hostel closed mid-Oct–mid-Apr; ❄📶) Built in hacienda style, with a central courtyard that's ideal for summer-night barbecues, and interior and exterior arches, Perpignan's modern, well-run HI-affiliated hostel has a handy location just north of Parc de la Pépinière 300m west of the bus station. Single-sex dorms are spartan but well kept; private rooms have showers (but not toilets) and there's a self-catering kitchen.

★**Nyx** BOUTIQUE HOTEL €€
(☎04 68 34 87 48; www.nyxhotel.fr; 62bis av Général de Gaulle; s/d/f from €89/106/135; ❄📶)

WORTH A TRIP

MENDE DAY TRIPPER

Réserve de Bisons d'Europe (☎04 66 31 40 40; www.bisoneurope.com; Ste-Eulalie; adult/child horse-drawn carriage €13.50/7, sleigh €16/8.50, walking path €6/4; ⏲10am-6pm Jul & Aug, to 5pm May, Jun & Sep, to 5pm Tue & Thu Jan-Apr & Oct-early Nov, closed early Nov-Dec) is a vast 200-hectare nature reserve near the small village of Ste-Eulalie, 45km north of Mende, which contains over 80 free-roaming bison. Visits to are by horse-drawn carriage or, in winter, by sleigh. From mid-June to September, you can follow a self-guided 1km walking path around the periphery.

Wolves once prowled freely through the Lozère forests, but today you'll see them only in **Les Loups du Gévaudan** (www.loupsdugevaudan.com; Ste-Lucie; guided tours adult/child €8/5; ⏲10am-11.30pm mid-Jul–mid-Aug, shorter hours mid-Aug–Dec & Feb–mid-Jul, closed Jan), a sanctuary in Ste-Lucie, 7km north of Marvejols and 36km northeast of Mende off the D809. This 25-hectare park sustains around 100 Mongolian, Canadian, Siberian and Polish wolves living in semi-freedom. The only way to visit is on a guided tour during the day or on special nocturnal visits in high summer. Feedings take place at 4pm.

Brilliantly located 500m east of the train station, a 10-minute stroll to the historic centre, Perpignan's standout hotel is this 17-room boutique gem with small but supremely comfortable rooms featuring iridescent fabrics, and themed around the sun, moon, day and night. Two have huge 20-sq-metre terraces, one includes an in-room Jacuzzi. Breakfast (€9.50) includes bacon and eggs and homemade jam.

Eating

Perpignan's dining scene is a melange of French and Spanish cuisines, along with

Perpignan

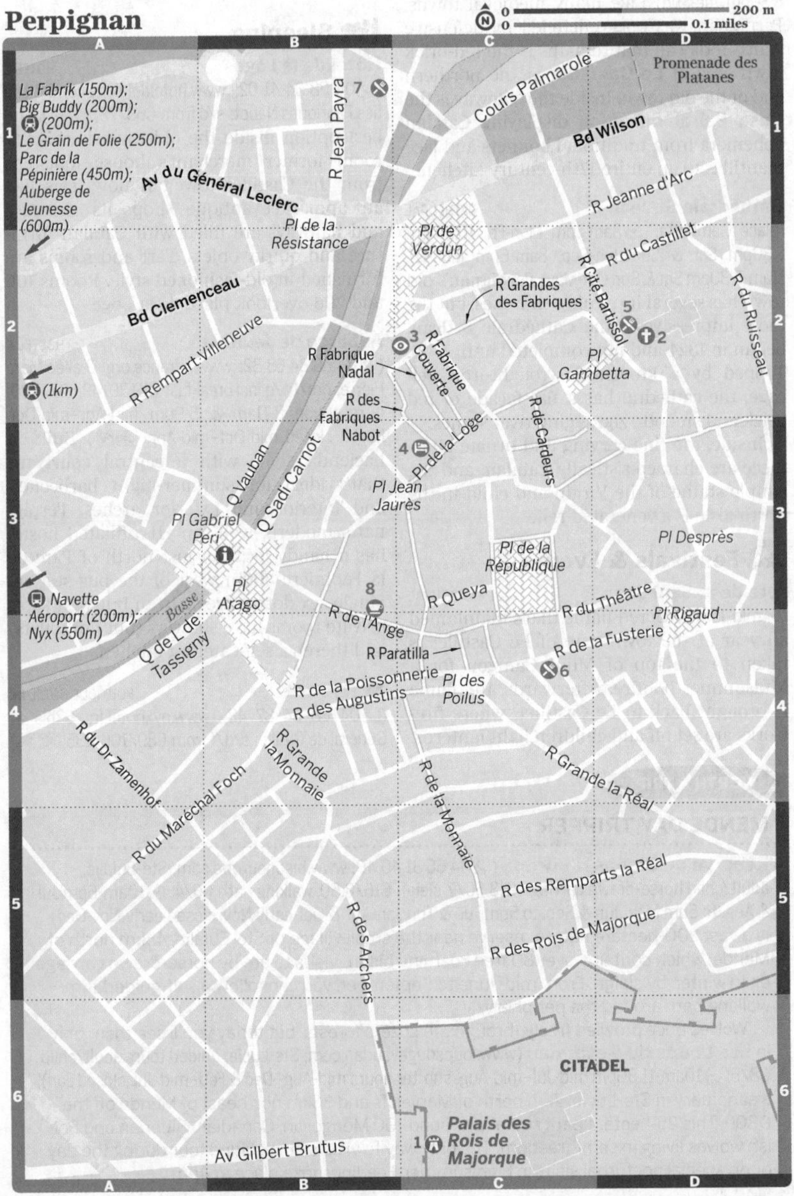

wider Mediterranean influences. Rue Paratilla, known to locals as rue des Épices (Spice St), has an aromatic concentration of foodie shops (delis, greengrocers, charcuteries, fishmongers and, yes, spice shops).

Spaghetteri Aldo ITALIAN €
(☎04 68 61 11 47; www.spaghetteri-aldo-perpignan.fr; 1 rue des Variétés; pasta €9.50-13.50, mains €17.50-19.50; ⊙noon-2pm & 7-11.30pm Tue-Sat) International rugby stars fuel up on the ultrafresh homemade pasta dishes (incorporating 15 pasta styles) at this authentic wood-beamed Italian restaurant. Favourites include langoustine ravioli, gnocchi Gorgonzola, salmon lasagne, and olive, basil and bresaola (aged, air-dried salted beef) pappardelle. Mains span anchovy-stuffed veal to juicy, grilled, sliced beef tagliata, but don't expect pizza, which it resolutely doesn't serve.

Big Buddy BURGERS €
(☎04 68 73 96 83; 63 av du Général Leclerc; burgers €12-16; ⊙noon-2pm Mon & Tue, noon-2pm & 8-10pm Wed-Sat) Reservations are essential at this burger bar, which is the hottest ticket in town. Burgers such as Mont d'Or (beef and bacon with mushroom sauce), Triple Cheese (cheddar, Mimosette and Tomme de Brebis, with Jack Daniels BBQ sauce) and Chabry (grilled aubergine and courgette, goat's cheese, sundried tomato and honey) come with fries (twice-cooked in beef dripping) and salads.

★**Le St-Jean** MODERN FRENCH €€
(☎04 68 51 22 25; www.lesaint-jean.com; 1 rue Cité Bartissol; tapas €7-14, 2-/3-course lunch menus €15/19, 3-course dinner menu €32, mains €21-32; ⊙noon-2pm & 7-10.30pm Mon-Sat mid-Jun–mid-Sep, noon-2pm Mon-Wed, noon-2pm & 7-10.30pm Thu-Sat mid-Sep–mid-Jun) Atmospherically set in the shadow of its namesake cathedral, opening to a charming magnolia-shaded cobbled courtyard, Le St-Jean is Perpignan's top address for inventive French fare: red mullet with fennel cream; rabbit pâté and orange salad; walnut-crusted scallops with parsnip purée and leek pesto sauce; veal steak stuffed with sage and apple; and a meringue-encased raspberry dome with blackberry coulis.

Le Grain de Folie BISTRO €€
(☎04 68 51 00 50; 71 av du Général Leclerc; 2-/3-course menus lunch €16.50/20, dinner €30/40; ⊙noon-2pm & 7.30-9.30pm Mon-Sat, noon-2pm Sun;) On up-and-coming av du Général Leclerc, this is one of Perpignan's best-value bistros, run with care by a husband-and-wife team. It's classic in style and strong on southern French flavours: tuck into rib-eye fillet with girolle mushrooms or sea bass with roasted artichoke. The kids' menu includes local sausages and battered fish.

Les Frères Mossés TRADITIONAL FRENCH €€
(☎04 68 80 63 31; 14 rue de la Fusterie; 2-/3-course lunch menu €17/19, mains €16-25; ⊙noon-2pm & 8-10.30pm Tue-Sat) Warm colours, tinkling jazz and walls covered in vintage signs give this cosy place the air of an old-time Parisian bistro. It's a great bet for French favourites *(confit de canard; steak-frites)* and you can watch the chef at work in the semi-open kitchen.

Drinking & Nightlife

Cafes and bars cluster on and around place de la République and on both banks of the canal. Av du Général Leclerc has an emerging drinking and nightlife scene.

La Cafetière COFFEE
(www.lacafetiere66.com; 17 rue de l'Ange; ⊙1.30-7pm Mon, 8am-7pm Tue-Sat) Freshly-ground-coffee aromas waft from this wonderful roastery, which sells beans to take away and brews fantastic espressos to drink at its counter or on the trio of cherry-red pavement tables. Loose-leaf teas are also a speciality, along with gourmet chocolates.

La Fabrik BAR
(53 av du Général Leclerc; ⊙11.30am-2am Mon-Fri, 5pm-2am Sat) Local Roussillon wines, French and Spanish beers, rum cocktails and classic

Perpignan

Top Sights
1 Palais des Rois de Majorque C6

Sights
2 Cathédrale St-Jean D2
3 Le Castillet & Casa Païral C2

Sleeping
4 Hôtel de la Loge C3

Eating
5 Le St-Jean D2
6 Les Frères Mossés C4
7 Spaghetteri Aldo B1

Drinking & Nightlife
8 La Cafetière B3

Spanish tapas are served inside this cavernous bar with gorgeous tiled floors and on its glass-screened, umbrella-shaded pavement terrace, which overflows with revellers on warm evenings.

Information

Tourist office (☎04 68 66 30 30; www.perpignantourisme.com; place François Arago; ⌚9am-7pm Mon-Sat, 10am-5pm Sun Jun-Sep, 9am-6pm Mon-Sat, 10am-1pm Sun Oct-May) Just west of the historic centre atop a covered section of the canal.

Getting There & Around

AIR

Perpignan's **airport** (PGF; ☎04 68 52 60 70; www.aeroport-perpignan.com; av Maurice Bellonte) is 5km northwest of the town centre. Destinations include London Stansted, Birmingham, Brussels (Ryanair); Southampton (Flybe); Dublin (Aer Lingus); Paris and Lille (Air France).

The **Navette Aéroport bus 7** (Airport Shuttle; one way €1) links the airport with place de Catalogne on the northwestern edge of the old town (25 minutes, every 30 minutes Monday to Saturday, two services Sunday).

BUS

Buses anywhere in the Pyrénées-Orientales *département* cost a flat-rate €1 (see www.cg66.fr/252-les-bus-departementaux.htm). Perpignan's **bus station** is on av du Général Leclerc.

Côte Vermeille (hourly Monday to Saturday, one on Sunday) Bus 400/404 trundles to Collioure (50 minutes), Port-Vendres (65 minutes) and Banyuls-sur-Mer (80 minutes).

Tech Valley (hourly Monday to Saturday, four on Sunday) Buses 300/341/342 run regularly to Céret (50 minutes).

Têt Valley (every two hours Monday to Saturday, two on Sunday) Regular buses to Prades (one hour) and Vernet-les-Bains (1½ hours); buses are numbered 200/210/220/260 depending on the route.

TRAIN

Frequent direct trains serve destinations in France and across the border in Spain.

Banyuls-sur-Mer €7.70, 30 minutes
Barcelona €37.10, 1½ hours
Carcassonne €21.20, two hours
Collioure €6.10, 20 minutes
Montpellier €21.80, 1¾ hours
Narbonne €15.50, one hour
Paris Gare de Lyon €105, 5½ hours

Céret

POP 7885

Tucked in the Pyrenean foothills just off the Tech Valley, the little town of Céret conceals an unexpected surprise – one of southern France's best modern-art museums, with a collection of stellar canvases donated by some of the 20th century's foremost names from cubism to neorealism. Lively festivals also take place in spring and summer.

Sights & Activities

★**Musée d'Art Moderne** ART MUSEUM
(www.musee-ceret.com; 8 bd Maréchal Joffre; adult/child €5.50/3.50, incl temporary exhibitions €8/6; ⌚10am-7pm Jul-Sep, to 5.30pm Tue-Sun Oct-Jun) Roussillon had its artistic heyday around the turn of the 20th century, when Fauvist and cubist artists flocked here, attracted by the searing colours and sun-drenched landscapes. This wonderful museum was created in 1950 by Pierre Brune and Frank Burty Haviland, who convinced friends including Picasso, Matisse, Chaïm Soutine and Georges Braque to donate works. The result is one of the finest collections of modern art outside Paris. Take your time – this place is a real treat.

Céret's artistic connections stretch back to 1910, when Catalan sculptor Manolo Hugué, painter Frank Burty Haviland and composer Déodat de Séverac settled here. They were followed in 1911 by Pablo Picasso and Georges Braque, along with other significant figures from the cubist and Fauvist movements, mostly escaping the spiralling rents and stifling atmosphere of the Montmartre art scene.

All the big names passed through Céret, sometimes staying for a short while, sometimes for extended periods. Reading like a who's who of modern art, the list includes André Masson, Max Jacob, Juan Gris, Raoul Dufy, Jean Cocteau, Chaïm Soutine, Amedeo Modigliani, Marc Chagall, Salvador Dalí and Joan Miró among them.

After the museum's formation in 1950, many of these artists (or their estates) chose to donate their works for free in recognition of Céret's importance to their artistic development (Picasso alone donated 57 pieces, although only one painting, a still life of a dead crane and a jug).

Standout works include a moving *Crucifixion* (1925) by Marc Chagall, *Woman, Bird, Stars* by Joan Miró, and a famous cub-

ist view of Céret by Chaïm Soutine, painted in 1919 – but there are many more to discover.

Aquacanyon ADVENTURE SPORTS
(☎07 62 92 34 99; www.aquacanyon.fr; 21 rue Aristide Maillol; canyoning/via ferrata/rafting/rock climbing from €35/47/30/45; ⏲9am-10pm) Canyoning and via ferrata trips in the Pyrenees are organised year-round by Aquacanyon; in summer it also offers white-water rafting, while in the cooler winter months you can go rock climbing.

Sleeping & Eating

There are several places to sleep in and around the town, but Céret's proximity to Perpignan, 30km to the northeast, means it's easy to visit as a day trip.

★**Le Relais des Chartreuses** B&B €€
(☎04 68 83 15 88; www.relais-des-chartreuses.fr; 106 av d'en Carbonner, Le Boulou; s €70-80, d €80-187, ste €210-273; P ❄ 📶 ≋) A glorious getaway 12.5km east of Céret via the D618, Le Relais des Chartreuses has 15 glossy rooms inside a Catalan-style house dating from the 17th century. Clutter has been stripped out in favour of a few key antiques, and there's a designer pool and a *table d'hôte* restaurant. Half-board costs €45 per person; breakfast is €15.

Al Catalā CATALAN €€
(☎04 68 87 07 91; www.restaurantalcatalaceret66.com; 15 av Georges Clemenceau; menus €15-36, mains €14-21; ⏲noon-2pm & 7.30-9.30pm Tue-Sat, noon-2pm Sun) Classic Catalan dishes – monkfish with chorizo, duck stew, Pyrenees veal steak with courgette and fiery peppers – are artistically presented and served in a colourful red and hot-pink dining room, but they're best enjoyed in the bamboo-screened, umbrella-shaded courtyard garden.

Information

Tourist office (☎04 68 87 00 53; www.ot-ceret.fr; 1 av Georges Clemenceau; ⏲9am-12.30pm & 2-5pm Mon-Sat) Can suggest hiking itineraries in the region.

Getting There & Away

Buses 340, 341 and 342 run to/from Perpignan (€1, 35 minutes, up to 12 daily Monday to Saturday, up to three Sunday).

There's a large car park next to the Musée d'Art Moderne.

Cathar Castles

Dotted across the parched plains of Roussillon and Languedoc are many castles left behind by the Cathars, an ultra-devout Christian sect who were persecuted during the 12th century, and eventually crushed by the forces of Pope Innocent III during the Albigensian Crusade.

Perched on rocky outcrops surrounded by orange scrubland, the castles are hugely atmospheric, but many are fast crumbling into dust. They can be explored in a long day's drive from Perpignan – but pack plenty of water and a hat, as temperatures soar out here in summer. If you're crossing into the Pyrenees, it's also worth making the trip to the Château de Montségur (p684), another classic (and important) Cathar stronghold.

Perched 728m up on a rocky hill, **Château de Quéribus** (☎04 68 45 03 69; www.cucugnan.fr; Cucugnan; adult/child €6.50/3.50; ⏲9am-8pm Jul & Aug, shorter hours rest of year) was the site of the Cathars' last stand in 1255. Its structure is well preserved: the *salle du pilier* inside the central keep still features Gothic pillars, vaulting and archways. Mind-blowing views stretch to the Mediterranean and Pyrenees from the top. In the theatre, a short film documents the castle's history, seen through the eyes of one of its curates. An audioguide costs €4. It's 42km northwest of Perpignan via the D117.

Château de Peyrepertuse (☎04 82 53 24 07; www.chateau-peyrepertuse.com; Duilhac-sous-Peyrepertuse; adult/child Jul & Aug €9/3.50, rest of year €6.50/3.50; ⏲9am-8pm Jul & Aug, shorter hours rest of year) is the largest of the Cathar castles, teetering on a sheer spur of rock with a drop of 800m on either side. Several of the original towers and many sections of ramparts are still standing. It's well worth renting an audioguide (€4) for an insight into its history. In mid-August, the castle holds falconry displays and a two-day medieval festival, complete with knights in armour. It's 51km northwest of Perpignan via the D117.

In a lofty location 63km northwest of Perpignan via the D117, turreted **Château de Puilaurens** (☎04 68 20 65 26; www.pays-axat.org; Lapradelle; adult/child €5/3; ⏲9am-8pm Jul & Aug, shorter hours Sep–mid-Nov & Feb-Jun) Puilaurens is perhaps the most dramatic of the Cathar fortresses. It has the full range of medieval defences: double walls, four corner towers and crenellated battlements. The views from the castle are particularly grand,

stretching across sun-baked plains and pine woodland. It's also said to be haunted by the White Lady, a niece of Philippe le Bel.

Built during the late 12th century on a 605m-high promontory 58km southwest of Carcassonne via the D118 and D620, **Château de Puivert** (☎04 68 20 81 52; www.chateau-de-puivert.com; Puivert; adult/child €5/3; ⏰9am-7pm Easter–mid-Nov, 10am-5pm Sun-Fri mid-Dec–Easter) Puivert belonged to the aristocratic Congost family, who were high-profile members of the Cathar movement. It was besieged in 1210 by Thomas Pons de Bruyères-le-Chatel, who took control of the castle and oversaw its redevelopment. Today it retains much of its medieval footprint.

Têt Valley

Fruit orchards carpet the lower reaches of the Têt Valley. Beyond the strategic fortress town of Villefranche-de-Conflent, the scenery becomes wilder, more open and undulating as the valley climbs towards Spanish Catalonia and Andorra.

Villefranche-de-Conflent

POP 223

The Unesco-listed town of Villefranche-de-Conflent sits in a breathtaking spot, hemmed in by tall cliffs, at the strategic confluence of the valleys of the Têt and Cady Rivers.

It's still possible to walk along much of Villefranche's **ramparts** (adult/child €4.50/free; ⏰10am-8pm Jun-Aug, shorter hours rest of year). Built in stages between the 11th and 19th centuries, they have survived remarkably intact.

Villefranche's mighty **Château-Fort Liberia** (www.fort-liberia.com; adult/child €7/3.80; ⏰9am-8pm Jul & Aug, 10am-7pm Jun & Sep, 10am-6pm Apr & May, 10am-5pm Oct-Mar) dominates the skyline above town. Built by Vauban in 1681, it was heavily refortified by Napoléon III between 1850 and 1856. You can wander around its corner turrets and battlements, as well as the defensive keep and a former prison. A shuttle bus from town (adult/child return €10/5.10) saves you a climb up 734 steps.

The bright-yellow mountain railway **Le Train Jaune** (☎04 68 96 63 62; www.tersncf.com; adult/child one way €10/5) trundles from Villefranche-de-Conflent (427m) through spectacular Pyrenean scenery to Latour de Carol (1231m). One of France's most famous train trips, it doesn't take bookings, so arrive a good hour before departure. It makes scheduled stops at eight of its 22 stations; you can alight at the others on request. At Latour de Carol you can return to Villefranche or change for Toulouse or Barcelona.

Bus 240 links Villefranche-de-Conflent with Perpignan (€1, 1¼ hours, five daily Monday to Saturday, no services Sunday). Buses 240 and 241 serve Vernet-les-Bains (€1, 15 minutes, seven daily Monday to Saturday, no services Sunday).

Vernet-les-Bains

POP 1430

Busy in summer and a ghost town for the rest of the year, the little spa town of Vernet-les-Bains was frequented by the British aristocracy in the late 19th century. Vernet has the status of 'village arboretum' in recognition of the more than 300 varieties of tree that flourish on its slopes, many brought here as seeds by overseas visitors.

Vernet is a great base for mountain biking and hiking, particularly for tackling Mont Canigou (2784m). You can get a head start by catching a 4WD up the mountain as far as Les Cortalets (2175m), from where the summit is a three-hour return hike. The **tourist office** (☎04 68 05 55 35; www.vernet-les-bains.fr; 2 rue de la Chapelle; ⏰9am-noon & 2-5pm Mon-Fri) can provide plenty of advice.

Local 4WD operators include **Garage Villacèque** (☎04 68 05 51 14; louis.villaceque@orange.fr; rue du Conflent; one way per person €30; ⏰Jun-Sep) and **Jeeps du Canigou** (☎04 68 05 99 89; jpbtransports@bbox.fr; 17 bd des Pyrénées; one way per person €29; ⏰Jun-Sep).

Bus 240 links Vernet-les-Bains with Perpignan (€1, 1½ hours, four daily Monday to Saturday, no services Sunday). Buses 240 and 241 serve Villefranche-de-Conflent (€1, 15 minutes, seven daily Monday to Saturday, no services Sunday).

Côte Vermeille

Named for its red rock, the Côte Vermeille (Vermilion Coast) runs south from Collioure to Cerbère on the Spanish border, where the Pyrenees foothills dip to the sea. Against a backdrop of vineyards and pinched between the Mediterranean and the mountains, it's riddled with small, rocky bays and little ports.

The main town here is Collioure. Three kilometres to its south, Port-Vendres, Roussillon's only natural harbour and

deep-water port, has been exploited ever since Greek mariners roamed the rocky coastline. Until the independence of France's North African territories in the 1960s, it was an important port linking them with the mainland. It's still a significant cargo and fishing harbour, however, with everything from small coastal chuggers to giant deep-sea vessels bristling with radar. There's also a large leisure marina, and lots of pleasant walks around the coastline nearby.

Getting There & Away

Buses and trains run regularly along the coast from Perpignan. If you're driving, you can follow the lovely coastal roads all the way to Banyuls-sur-Mer.

Collioure

POP 3096

Colliourе, where boats bob against a backdrop of houses washed in soft pastel colours, is the smallest and most picturesque of the Côte Vermeille resorts. Once Perpignan's port, it found fame in the early 20th century when it inspired the Fauvist artists Henri Matisse and André Derain and later both Picasso and Braque.

Today the town has more than 30 galleries and workshops, including many on rue de la Fraternité. Collioure is also famed for its wine and its prized Collioure anchovies. Like most beaches along the Côte Vermeille, Collioure's main town beach is shingly, but pleasant enough for a paddle.

Sights

Château Royal CHÂTEAU

(☎04 68 82 06 43; www.cg66.fr; Port Plaisance; adult/child €4/2; ⏲10am-7pm Jul & Aug, 9am-5pm Sep-Jun) Collioure's seaside castle was mostly built between 1276 and 1344 by the counts of Roussillon and the kings of Aragon, and was later occupied by the Mallorcan court, although the outer wall was the work of Vauban in the 17th century. Interior furnishings are minimal, but the hybrid Spanish-French architectural styles are striking and the coastal views lovely. Markets, concerts and theatre performances take place in the grounds throughout the year.

Musée d'Art Moderne ART MUSEUM

(4 rte de Port-Vendres; adult/child €3/free; ⏲10am-noon & 2-6pm Jun-Sep, 10am-noon & 2-6pm Wed-Mon Oct-May) Boat sketches by Matisse and Edouard Pignon along with coastal canvases by Henri Martin and Henri Marre are among the highlights of this small but worthwhile museum. It has a good collection of mainly 20th-century canvases and holds regular exhibitions by local artists.

Moulin de la Cortina LANDMARK

(Parc Pams) The most scenic way to reach this 14th-century windmill is a 950m walk through olive and almond groves from Fort St-Elme along the Cami del Port de Sant Telm (about 20 minutes). Alternatively, it's a steep 150m walk from the Musée d'Art Moderne. Mediterranean views of boats, rocky coast and brilliant blue sea extend from the mill's raised base.

Fort St-Elme FORTRESS

(www.fortsaintelme.fr; rte Stratégique; adult/child €6/free; ⏲10.30am-7pm Apr-Sep, to 5pm mid-Feb–Mar & Oct-early Nov) Built in 1552 by Spanish king Charles V between Collioure and Port-Vendre, this hilltop fort was designed as a key piece of the coastal defence system. It's now mainly used as an exhibition centre.

Activities

Le Chemin de Fauvisme WALKING

During the early 20th century, Collioure's vibrant coastal hues and piercing light attracted a group of artists known as the Fauves (the Wild Animals), whose focus was pure colour. The tourist office has a free map

---

WORTH A TRIP

PREHISTORIC DAY OUT

The cave-riddled cliffs above Tautavel, 34km northwest of Perpignan along the D117, have yielded a host of prehistoric finds, most notably a human skull unearthed in the Arago Cave that's estimated to be 450,000 years old (one of Europe's oldest such discoveries). The fascinating **Musée de Préhistoire de Tautavel** (Tautavel Prehistory Museum; ☎04 68 29 07 76; www.450000ans.com; av Jean Jaurès, Tautavel; adult/child incl audioguide €8/4; ⏲10am-7pm Jul & Aug, 10am-12.30pm & 2-6pm Sep-Jun) here delves into the area's prehistoric past, with a full-size cave reproduction, displays of fossilised bones and tools, and multimedia exhibits. Admission includes a secondary exhibition at Musée des Premiers Habitants d'Europe, 500m southeast.

There's no public transport, so you'll need your own wheels.

of the Chemin de Fauvisme, a walking trail taking in 19 locations that featured in works by Henri Matisse and his younger colleague André Derain.

Cellier des Dominicains WINE TASTING
(☎04 68 82 05 63; www.cellierdominicain.com; place Orphila; cellar tours €2; ⏰9am-noon & 2-6pm Mon-Sat Apr-Sep) This former monk's cellar now showcases vintages from more than 150 local *vignerons* (winegrowers). Cellar tours lasting 40 minutes, followed by a tasting, take place at 4pm Thursday June to September in French and English.

Sleeping

Hôtel Princes des Catalognes HOTEL €
(☎04 68 98 30 00; www.hotel-princescatalogne.com; rue des Palmiers; d €83-93, f €165-185;) While it doesn't have much of a sea view, this modern hotel makes up for it by offering some of the most reasonable rates in Collioure, even in high summer. The decor is clean and fresh, if a touch bland, but with only 15 rooms it doesn't feel crowded even when full. Family rooms sleep up to four people.

Villa Miranda B&B €€
(☎04 68 98 03 79; www.villamiranda.fr; 15 rte du place de les Forques; d €105-115; P) Simple but sweet, this B&B has five rooms decked out in cheery stripes, with blonde-wood floors and bright bathrooms; Xalac, Marinade and Migjorn have their own private sea-view patios, and there's a shared panoramic terrace on the 1st floor.

Casa Pairal HOTEL €€
(☎04 68 82 05 81; www.hotel-casa-pairal.com; rue des Palmiers; d €127-207, ste €307; P@) Set around a secluded jasmine- and rose-perfumed garden sheltering a heated swimming pool and a fountain, this 18th-century house has 27 heritage-style rooms. Moving up the price scale buys extra space and balconies overlooking the garden, vineyards and mountains beyond. Breakfast is served beneath a century-old magnolia tree. It's conveniently situated in the town centre, a 250m stroll from the beach.

Eating

Casa Leon BISTRO €€
(☎04 68 82 10 74; 2 rue Rière; menus €28-36, mains €16.50-25; ⏰noon-2pm & 7-10.30pm) Lost in the tangled old quarter, this simple Catalan bistro relies on the quality of its ingredients: grilled half-lobster and langoustines, cod with mussels and oysters, or king scallops in creamy sauces, along with Collioure's celebrated anchovies.

La 5ème Péché FUSION €€
(☎04 68 98 09 76; www.le-cinquieme-peche.com; 16 rue Fraternité; 2-/3-course lunch menus €19/25, 3-course/tasting dinner menus €39/62; ⏰12.15-1.45pm & 7.30-9pm Wed-Sat, 12.15-1.45pm Sun, 7.30-9pm Mon & Tue) Japan meets France at this creative fusion restaurant. Chef Masashi Iijima utilises locally caught seafood in artistic dishes such as scallop sashimi with seaweed, langoustines in mussel broth, and swordfish with bamboo-shoot mousse. The dining room is small and very popular with locals and visitors alike – book ahead.

Le Neptune GASTRONOMIC €€€
(☎04 68 82 02 27; www.leneptune-collioure.com; 9 rte de Port-Vendres; 3-course lunch menu €29, 3-/4-/5-course dinner menus €39/59/79; ⏰noon-2pm & 7-10pm Jul-Sep, noon-2pm & 7-10pm Tue-Sun Apr-Jun & Oct, noon-2pm & 7-9.30pm Thu-Sun Nov-Mar;) It's a toss-up whether the setting or the food steals the show here. Overlooking Collioure's brilliant blue bay and red rooftops, the panoramic seaside terrace (covered and heated in winter) is an absolute stunner, while local ingredients span just-landed turbot to just-cooked lobster. The style is formal, so you'll need to dress up. A four-course vegetarian menu is available for €39.

Information

Tourist office (☎04 68 82 15 47; www.collioure.com; place du 18 juin; ⏰9.15am-6.45pm Jul-Sep, 9.15am-6.45pm Mon-Sat, 10am-5.30pm Sun Apr-Jun & Oct) On the northern side of town next to quai de l'Amirauté.

Banyuls-sur-Mer

POP 4749

Just 14km north of the Spanish border, Banyuls is a small coastal town that began life as a fishing port but is now best known for its wines (Banyuls, Banyuls Grand Cru and Collioure). Grapes grow on the slopes around town on steep, rocky terraces divided by drystone walls, which help retain water and prevent soil erosion.

It's a lovely spot, with three shingly but superb beaches (Centrale, Les Elmes and Centre Hélio Marin) with translucent turquoise waters, and an important marine reserve, the **Réserve Naturelle Cerbère-Banyuls**, 6km southeast of town, where you can snorkel and scuba dive. Banyuls is also a

convenient stop-off if you're heading over the border into Spain.

At the southern end of Banyuls' seafront promenade is France's oldest aquarium, the **Biodiversarium** (☎04 68 88 73 39; www.biodiversarium.fr; av du Fontaulé; adult/child aquarium €5/2.50, joint ticket with Jardin Méditerranéen €7.50/4; ⊙10am-12.30pm & 2-6pm). Built in 1885 as the oceanographic research station of Paris' Université Pierre et Marie Curie, the Laboratoire Arago houses an intriguing collection of Mediterranean marine life, from seahorses to sea anemones. Combination tickets are available with the **Jardin Méditerranéen du Mas de la Serre** (☎04 68 88 73 39; www.biodiversarium.fr; rte des Crêtes; adult/child garden only €5/2.50; ⊙10am-12.30pm & 2-6pm Jul & Aug, 2-6pm Wed-Sun Apr-Jun & Sep).

Paulilles Director's House (www.ledepartement66.fr; D914; ⊙9am-noon & 2-5pm Apr-Oct, 9am-noon & 2-5pm Wed-Mon Nov-Mar), 3.2km north of Banyuls-sur-Mer, is part industrial relic, part nature walk. This 35-hectare coastal site is remote, as you'd expect of a one-time dynamite factory. It was set up by Nobel Prize founder Alfred Nobel in 1870 and subsequently abandoned in 1984. Haunting photos inside the former director's house depict the hard lives and close community of Catalan workers, whose explosives helped to blast the Panama Canal, Trans-Siberian Railway and Mont Blanc Tunnel.

The Réserve Naturelle Cerbère-Banyuls is a favourite with underwater photographers for its crabs, lobsters, starfish, groupers, anemones, ballan wrasse, damselfish, octopuses, sea bream, wolf fish, eels, orange gorgonians and jellyfish. Immerse yourself in its crystalline waters with **Aquableu Plongée** (☎04 68 88 17 35; www.aquableu-plongee.com; 5 quai Georges Petit; diving from €26, gear rental per dive from €5, snorkelling trips from €20; ⊙Apr-early Nov), which offers diving and snorkelling as well as multiday live-aboard trips and PADI courses for beginners through to experienced divers.

The best place to try Banyuls wines is **Cellier des Templiers** (☎04 68 98 36 92; www.terresdestempliers.fr; rte du Mas Reig; ⊙10am-7.30pm late Mar-early Nov), 1.5km west of the seafront via the D86. Free 30-minute guided tours take in the vineyards and the century-old oak vats. Tours in English depart at 2.30pm, 4pm and 5.30pm.

Banyuls' **tourist office** (☎04 68 88 31 58; wwwbanyuls-sur-mer.com; 4 av de la République; ⊙9am-7pm Jul & Aug, 9am-noon & 2-6pm Mon-Sat Sep-Jun) is midway along the beachfront.

DON'T MISS

LUNCH WITH SEA VIEW

Bang on the beach, with a sun-drenched glass-enclosed terrace, **La Littorine** (☎04 68 88 03 12; www.restaurant-la-littorine.fr; Plage des Elmes; 2-/3-course lunch menus €24/32, mains €28-60; ⊙noon-1.45pm & 7-8.45pm) is the pick of Banyuls' restaurants. It stocks over 400 Languedoc-Roussillon wines to complement flavour-packed Mediterranean dishes: Collioure anchovies marinated in olive oil, scallops with beetroot carpaccio and walnut vinaigrette, octopus with Espelette peppers, tuna with foie-gras sauce and heirloom vegetables, and Roussillon apricot tart with mascarpone sorbet.

Provence

POP 2.67 MILLION

Includes ➡

Best Places to Eat

- ➡ L'Atelier Jean-Luc Rabanel (p784)
- ➡ Le Mazet du Vaccarès (p787)
- ➡ La Table de Ventabren (p782)

Best Places to Sleep

- ➡ Mama Shelter (p764)
- ➡ Le Cloître (p783)
- ➡ Hôtel Edmond Rostand (p764)
- ➡ Sous les Figuiers (p790)

Why Go?

Provence evokes picture-postcard images of lavender fields, medieval hilltop villages, bustling markets and superb food and wine. Less expected is Provence's incredible diversity. The Vaucluse and Luberon epitomise the Provençal cliché. But near the mouth of the Rhône in the Camargue, craggy limestone yields to bleached salt marshes specked pink with flamingos, and the light, which so captivated Van Gogh and Cézanne, begins to change. Then there's the serpentine Gorges du Verdon, its pea-green water lorded over by half-mile-high limestone walls and craggy mountain peaks beyond. The region's other belle surprises are its cities: sultry Marseille and Roman Arles.

Constant across the region is the food – clean, bright flavours, as simple as sweet tomatoes drizzled with olive oil and sprinkled with *fleur de sel* (sea salt) from the Camargue.

When to Go

Marseille

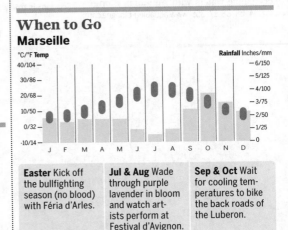

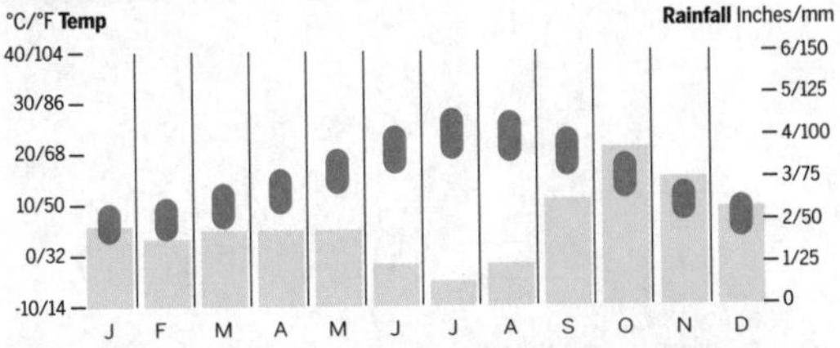

Easter Kick off the bullfighting season (no blood) with Féria d'Arles.

Jul & Aug Wade through purple lavender in bloom and watch artists perform at Festival d'Avignon.

Sep & Oct Wait for cooling temperatures to bike the back roads of the Luberon.

MARSEILLE

POP 858,902

For many years, the busy port city of Marseille has suffered from a serious image problem. Dismissed for its down-at-heel reputation, urban decay and often alarming crime statistics, it's long been the black sheep of the Provençal coastline. But while it's gritty, and not always pretty – Cannes or St-Tropez, it's not – Marseille is a dynamic, edgy, bustling city that's rich with more than 1500 years of history. And since its stint as the European Capital of Culture in 2013 and the addition of a brace of swanky new museums, the city has sparkled with a new sense of optimism and self-belief. At long last, everyone seems to be waking up to the fact that France's second-biggest city might have been unfairly maligned all along.

The heart of the city is the vibrant Vieux Port (old port), mast-to-mast with yachts and pleasure boats. Just uphill is the ancient Le Panier neighbourhood, the oldest section of the city. Also worth an explore is the République quarter, with its stylish boutiques and Haussmannian buildings, and the Joliette area, centred onMarseille's famous striped Cathédrale de la Major.

History

Around 600 BC, Greek mariners founded Massilia, a trading post, at what is now Marseille's Vieux Port. In the 1st century BC, the city lost out by backing Pompey the Great rather than Julius Caesar: Caesar's forces captured Massilia in 49 BC and directed Roman trade elsewhere.

Marseille became part of France in the 1480s, but its citizens embraced the Revolution, sending 500 volunteers to defend Paris in 1792. Heading north, they sang a rousing march, ever after dubbed 'La Marseillaise' – now the national anthem. Trade with North Africa escalated after France occupied Algeria in 1830 and the Suez Canal opened in 1869. After the World Wars, a steady flow of migration from North Africa began and with it the rapid expansion of Marseille's periphery.

Sights

Greater Marseille is divided into 16 *arrondissements* (districts), which are indicated in addresses (eg 1er for the first *arrondissement* and so on). The city's main thoroughfare, La Canebière (from the Provençal word *canebe,* meaning 'hemp', after the city's traditional rope industry), in the 1st *arrondissement,* stretches eastwards from the Vieux Port towards the train station, a 10-minute walk or two metro stops from the water. North is Le Panier, Marseille's oldest quarter; south is the bohemian concourse of cours Julien; and southwest is the start of the coastal road.

The **Marseille City Pass** (www.resamarseille.com; 24/48/72hr €24/31/39) covers admission to city museums, public transport, a guided city tour, a Château d'If boat trip and more, plus other discounts. It's not necessary for children under 12, as many attractions are greatly reduced or free. Buy it online or at the tourist office.

Central Marseille

★Vieux Port HISTORIC SITE

(Map p766; Ⓜ Vieux Port) Ships have docked for more than 26 centuries at the city's birthplace, the colourful old port. The main commercial docks were transferred to the Joliette area north of here in the 1840s, but the old port remains a thriving harbour for fishing boats, pleasure yachts and tourists. Guarding either side of the harbour are **Fort St-Nicolas** (Map p766; ⏲8am-7.45pm May-Aug, shorter hours rest of year) and **Fort St-Jean** (Map p766; Ⓜ Vieux Port), founded in the 13th century by the Knights Hospitaller of St John of Jerusalem (and now home to the city's flagship MuCEM museum).

The port's southern quay is dotted with bars, brasseries and cafes, and there are more to be found around place Thiars and cours Honoré d'Estienne d'Orves, where the action continues until late. For supremely lazy sightseers, there's also a **cross-port ferry** (Map p766; ⏲10am-1.15pm & 2-7pm).

Perched at the edge of the peninsula, the **Jardin du Pharo** (Map p762) is a perfect picnic and sunset spot.

★Le Panier HISTORIC SITE

(Map p766; Ⓜ Vieux Port) From the Vieux Port, hike north up to this fantastic history-woven quarter, which is fabulous for a wander with its artsy ambience, cool hidden squares and

> **FAST FACTS**
>
> **Area** 15,579 sq km
>
> **Local Industry** Fruit farming, fishing, viticulture, tourism
>
> **Signature drink** Pastis (aniseed liqueur)

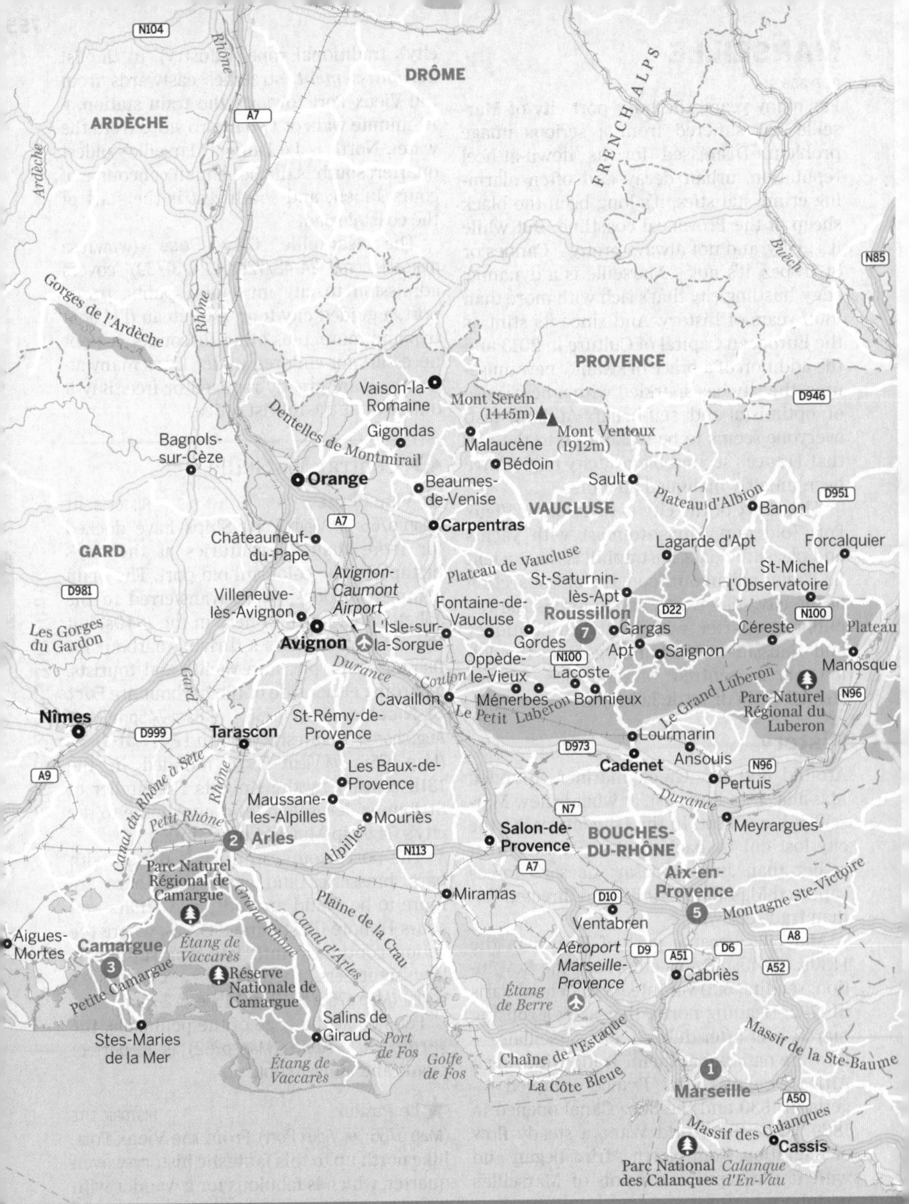

Provence Highlights

1 Marseille (p755) Soaking up this seething, heady city with ancient port, stunning contemporary architecture and bags of character.

2 Arles (p778) Trailing Van Gogh around town, from the state-of-the-art Fondation Vincent Van Gogh to spots where he painted some of his best-known canvases.

3 Camargue (p785) Spotting pink flamingos and riding white horses.

4 Gorges du Verdon (p816) Experiencing white-water thrills in vertigo-inducing gorges.

5 Aix-en-Provence (p773)
Shopping at the market, boutique browsing and strutting fountain-peppered streets in the south's most elegant city.

6 The Luberon (p813)
Pedalling around hilltop villages, cherry orchards and vineyards in picture-postcard Provence.

7 Roussillon (p811)
Learning about ochre and hiking between fantastical fiery-red rock formations.

Vieux Port

AN ITINERARY

Start with an early morning coffee on the balcony at La Caravelle, with views of the boats bobbing in the harbor and Basilique Notre Dame de la Garde across the way.

Mosey down the quay to the sparkling **MuCEM** ❶ and its cantilevered neighbour **Villa Méditerranée** ❷ for a morning of art and culture. You'll enter through Fort St-Jean, and wind through roof-top gardens to reach the state-of-the-art museums.

Alternatively, take in green-and-white striped **Cathédrale de la Major** ❸ then explore the apricot-coloured alleys of **Le Panier** ❹, browsing the exhibits at the **Centre de la Vieille Charité** ❺, and shopping in the neighbourhood's tiny boutiques.

In the afternoon, hop on the free cross-port ferry to the harbour's south side and take a **boat trip** ❻ to Château d'If, made famous by the Dumas novel *The Count of Monte Cristo*.

Or stroll under Norman Foster's mirrored pavilion, then wander into the **Abbaye St-Victor** ❼, to see the bones of martyrs enshrined in gold.

As evening nears, you can catch the sunset from the stone benches in the **Jardin du Pharo** ❽. Then as the warm southern night sets in, join the throngs on cours Honoré d'Estienne d'Orves, where you can drink pastis and people-watch beneath a giant statue of a lion devouring a man – the **Milo de Croton** ❾.

Cathédrale de la Major
The striped facade of Marseille's cathedral is made from local Cassis stone and green Florentine marble. Its grand north staircase leads from Le Panier to La Joliette quarter

Musée des Civilisations de l'Europe et de la Méditerranée (MuCEM)
Explore the icon of modern Marseille, this stunning museum designed by Rudy Ricciotti and linked by vertigo-inducing footbridge to 13th-century Fort St-Jean. You'll get stupendous views of the Vieux Port and the Mediterranean.

Centre de la Vieille Charité

Before the 18th century, beggar hunters rounded up the poor for imprisonment. The Vieille Charité almshouse, which opened in 1749, improved their lot by acting as a workhouse. It's now an exhibition space and only the barred windows recall its original use.

Le Panier

The site of the Greek town of Massilia, Le Panier woos walkers with its sloping streets. Grand Rue follows the ancient road and opens out into place de Lenche, the location of the Greek market. It is still the place to shop for artisanal products.

GARDEL BERTRAND/GETTY IMAGES ©

Frioul If Express

Catch the Frioul If Express to Château d'If, France's equivalent to Alcatraz. Prisoners were housed according to class: the poorest at the bottom in windowless dungeons, the wealthiest in paid-for private cells, with windows and a fireplace.

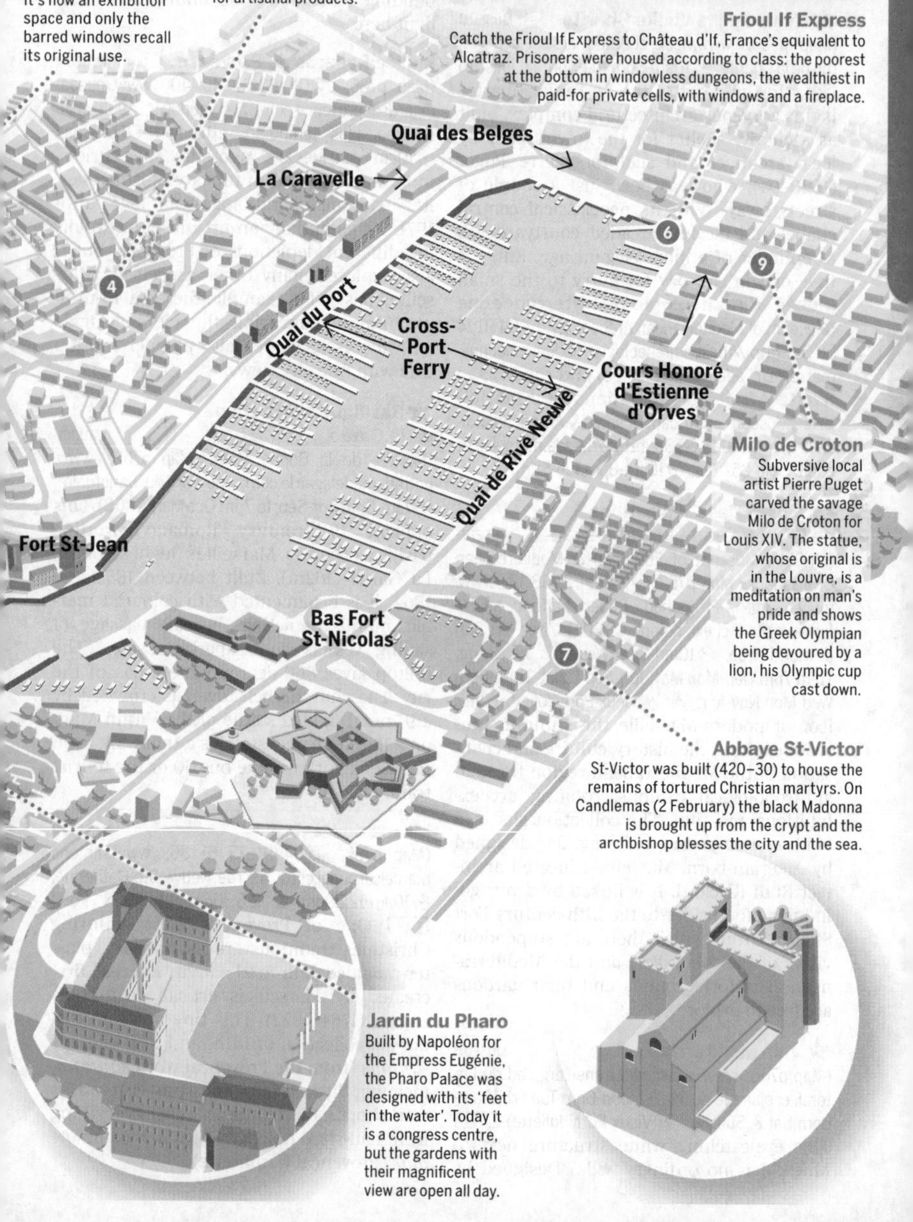

Milo de Croton

Subversive local artist Pierre Puget carved the savage Milo de Croton for Louis XIV. The statue, whose original is in the Louvre, is a meditation on man's pride and shows the Greek Olympian being devoured by a lion, his Olympic cup cast down.

Abbaye St-Victor

St-Victor was built (420–30) to house the remains of tortured Christian martyrs. On Candlemas (2 February) the black Madonna is brought up from the crypt and the archbishop blesses the city and the sea.

Jardin du Pharo

Built by Napoléon for the Empress Eugénie, the Pharo Palace was designed with its 'feet in the water'. Today it is a congress centre, but the gardens with their magnificent view are open all day.

sun-baked cafes. In Greek Massilia it was the site of the *agora* (marketplace), hence its name, which means 'the basket'. During WWII the quarter was dynamited and afterwards rebuilt. Today it's a mishmash of lanes hiding artisan shops, *ateliers* (workshops) and terraced houses strung with drying washing.

★Centre de la Vieille Charité MUSEUM
(Map p766; www.vieille-charite-marseille.com; 2 rue de la Charité; ⏲10am-6pm Tue-Sun; Ⓜ Joliette) **FREE** In the heart of the Le Panier quarter is this gorgeous architectural complex, built as a charity shelter for the town's poor by local architect and sculptor Pierre Puget (1620–94), who was born just a couple of streets away. With its neoclassical central chapel and elegant arcaded courtyard, it's a reminder of a more elegant age. Entry is free, or you can pay for entry to the small **Musée d'Archéologie Méditerranéenne** (Museum of Mediterranean Archeology; ☎04 91 14 58 59; http://musee-archeologie-mediterraneenne.marseille.fr; adult/child €5/free) and the **Musée d'Arts Africains, Océaniens et Amérindiens** (Museum of African, Oceanic & American Indian Art; ☎04 91 14 58 38; http://maaoa.marseille.fr; adult/child €5/free; ⏲10am-6pm Tue-Sun).

★Musée des Civilisations de l'Europe et de la Méditerranée MUSEUM
(MuCEM, Museum of European & Mediterranean Civilisations; Map p762; ☎04 84 35 13 13; www.mucem.org; 7 Promenade Robert Laffont; adult/family/child incl exhibitions €9.50/14/free, 1st Sun of month free; ⏲10am-8pm Wed-Mon Jul & Aug, 11am-7pm Wed-Mon May, Jun, Sep & Oct, 11am-6pm Wed-Mon Nov-Apr; 👪; Ⓜ Vieux Port, Joliette) The icon of modern Marseille, this stunning museum explores the history, culture and civilisation of the Mediterranean region through anthropological exhibits, rotating art exhibitions and film. The collection sits in a bold, contemporary building, J4, designed by Algerian-born, Marseille-educated architect Rudi Ricciotti. It is linked by a vertigo-inducing footbridge to the 13th-century Fort St-Jean, from which there are stupendous views of the Vieux Port and the Mediterranean. The fort grounds and their gardens are free to explore.

★Villa Méditerranée MUSEUM
(Map p766; www.villa-mediterranee.org; bd du Littoral, esplanade du J4; ⏲noon-6pm Tue-Fri, 10am-6pm Sat & Sun; 👪; Ⓜ Vieux Port, Joliette) **FREE** This eye-catching white structure next to MuCEM is no ordinary 'villa'. Designed by architect Stefano Boeri in 2013, the sleek white edifice sports a spectacular cantilever overhanging an ornamental pool. Inside, a viewing gallery with glass-panelled floor (look down if you dare!), and two or three temporary multimedia exhibitions evoke aspects of the Mediterranean, be they sea life, history or environmental. But it's the building itself that's the undisputed highlight here.

Musée Regards de Provence MUSEUM
(Map p766; ☎04 96 17 40 40; www.museeregardsdeprovence.com; ave Vaudoyer; adult/child €4/free, plus temporary exhibition €8.50/free; ⏲10am-6pm Tue-Sun; Ⓜ Joliette) This curious museum is housed in the city's former sanitary station, operational from 1948 until 1971. It's essentially an art museum exploring different depictions of Provence, but it also explores many other aspects of Marseille's past – for example, there's a 45-minute film documenting the city's struggle with diseases! There's also a super rooftop cafe with fine city views.

★Basilique Notre Dame de la Garde CHURCH
(Montée de la Bonne Mère; Map p762; www.notredamedelagarde.com; rue Fort du Sanctuaire; ⏲7am-8pm Apr-Sep, to 7pm Oct-Mar; 🚌60) This opulent 19th-century Romano-Byzantine basilica occupies Marseille's highest point, La Garde (162m). Built between 1853 and 1864, it is ornamented with coloured marble, murals depicting the safe passage of sailing vessels and superb mosaics. The hilltop gives 360-degree panoramas of the city. The church's bell tower is crowned by a 9.7m-tall gilded statue of the Virgin Mary on a 12m-high pedestal. It's a 1km walk from the Vieux Port, or take bus 60 or the tourist train.

Musée du Santon MUSEUM
(Map p766; ☎04 91 13 61 36; www.santonsmarcelcarbonel.com; 49 rue Neuve Ste-Catherine; ⏲10am-12.30pm & 2-6.30pm; Ⓜ Vieux Port) **FREE** One of Provence's most enduring Christmas traditions are its *santons* (plaster-moulded, kiln-fired nativity figures), first created by Marseillais artisan Jean-Louis Lagnel (1764–1822). This tiny museum displays a collection of 18th- and 19th-century *santons* (from the Provençal word *santoun*, meaning 'little saint'), and runs visits to its workshops. Its boutique sells everything from nail-sized dogs and pigs to a complete *mas* (Provençal farmhouse).

Musée d'Histoire de Marseille MUSEUM

(Map p766; ☎04 91 55 36 00; http://musee-histoire.marseille.fr; 2 rue Henri-Barbusse; adult/child €5/free; ⏰10am-6pm Tue-Sun; Ⓜ Vieux Port) In a completely renovated, 15,000-sq-metre modern space within the Centre Bourse shopping centre, this museum offers fascinating insight into Marseille's long history. Highlights include the remains of a 3rd-century AD merchant vessel, discovered in the Vieux Port in 1974. To preserve the soaked and decaying wood, it was freeze-dried where it now sits behind glass.

Musée des Beaux Arts MUSEUM, PALACE

(☎04 91 14 59 30; http://musee-des-beaux-arts.marseille.fr; 7 rue Édouard Stephan; adult/child €5/free; ⏰10am-6pm Tue-Sun; 👪; Ⓜ Cinq Avenues-Longchamp, 🚋 Longchamp) Spectacularly set in the colonnaded Palais de Longchamp, Marseille's oldest museum is a treasure trove of Italian and Provençal painting and sculpture from the 17th to 21st centuries. The palace's shaded park is one of the centre's few green spaces, and is popular with local families. The spectacular fountains were constructed in the 1860s, in part to disguise a water tower at the terminus of an aqueduct from the River Durance.

La Cité Radieuse ARCHITECTURE

(The Radiant City; L'Unité d'Habitation; ☎04 91 16 78 00; www.marseille-citeradieuse.org; 280 bd Michelet; ⏰9am-6pm; 🚌83 or 21, stop Le Corbusier) FREE Visionary international-style architect Le Corbusier redefined urban living in 1952 with the completion of his vertical 337-apartment 'garden city', popularly known as La Cité Radieuse. Today it is mostly private apartments, plus a hotel, Hôtel Le Corbusier, the high-end restaurant Le Ventre de l'Architecte and a rooftop terrace. Architecture buffs can book guided tours (adult/child €10/5) that include a model apartment; contact the tourist office. It's about 5km south of the centre along av du Prado.

Along the Coast

Mesmerising views of another Marseille unfold along **corniche Président John F Kennedy**, the coastal road that cruises south to small, beach-volleyball-busy **Plage des Catalans** (Map p762; 3 rue des Catalans; ⏰8.30am-6.30pm; 🚌83) and fishing cove **Vallon des Auffes** (Map p762; 🚌83), crammed with boats.

Further south, the vast **Prado beaches** are marked by Jules Cantini's 1903 marble replica of Michelangelo's *David*. The beaches, all gold sand, were created from backfill from the excavations for Marseille's metro. They have a world-renowned **skate park**. Nearby lies expansive Parc Borély.

Promenade Georges Pompidou continues south to **Cap Croisette**, from where the beautiful Calanques (p772) can be reached on foot.

To head down the coast, take bus 83 from the Vieux Port. At av du Prado switch to bus 19 to continue further. La Navette Maritime (p772) runs boats between the Vieux Port and La Pointe-Rouge, just to the south of the Prado beaches; the City Pass does not cover the ticket.

Château d'If ISLAND, CASTLE

(www.if.monuments-nationaux.fr; adult/child €5.50/free; ⏰10am-6pm Apr-Oct, to 5pm rest of year) Located 3.5km west of the Vieux Port, this island fortress-prison was immortalised in Alexandre Dumas' classic 1844 novel *The Count of Monte Cristo*. Many political prisoners were incarcerated here including the Revolutionary hero Mirabeau and the Communards of 1871. Other than the island itself there's not a great deal to see, but it's worth the trip just for the views of the Vieux Port. **Frioul If Express** (Map p766; www.frioul-if-express.com; 1 quai des Belges) runs boats (€10.50 return, 20 minutes, around nine daily) from the quay.

Îles du Frioul ISLAND

A few hundred metres west of Île d'If are the Îles du Frioul, the barren, dyke-linked, white-limestone islands of Ratonneau and Pomègues. Sea birds and rare plants thrive on these tiny islands, which are each about 2.5km long, totalling 200 hectares. Ratonneau has three beaches. Frioul If Express boats to Château d'If also serve the Îles du Frioul (one/two islands €10.50/15.60 return, 35 minutes, around 20 daily).

Festivals & Events

Fiesta des Suds MUSIC

(www.dock-des-suds.org; ⏰Mar) World music at Dock des Suds (p770), with performances from across the globe – from Malian musicians to reggae, bangra and more.

Carnaval de Marseille CARNIVAL

(⏰Mar or Apr) Marseille's version of Carnival, with mad costumes and decorated floats.

Lesbian & Gay Parade LGBT

(www.pride-marseille.com; ⏰Jul) Marseille's annual pride festival.

Marseille

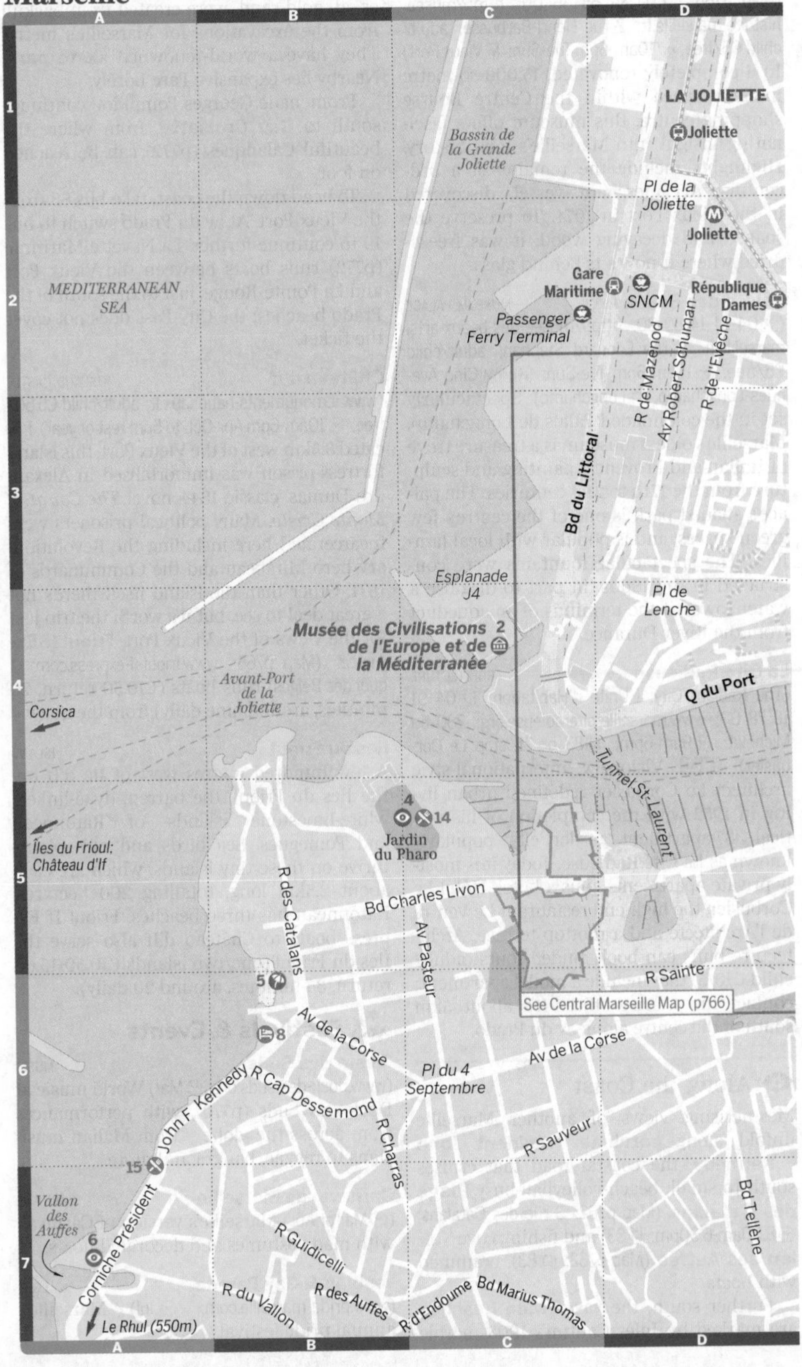

LA JOLIETTE
Joliette
Bassin de la Grande Joliette
Pl de la Joliette
Joliette
Gare Maritime
SNCM
République Dames
MEDITERRANEAN SEA
Passenger Ferry Terminal
R de Mazenod
Av Robert Schuman
R de l'Evêche
Bd du Littoral
Esplanade J4
Pl de Lenche
Musée des Civilisations de l'Europe et de la Méditerranée
2
Avant-Port de la Joliette
Q du Port
Corsica
Tunnel St-Laurent
4
14
Jardin du Pharo
Îles du Frioul; Château d'If
R des Catalans
Bd Charles Livon
Av Pasteur
5
R Sainte
See Central Marseille Map (p766)
Av de la Corse
8
Pl du 4 Septembre
Av de la Corse
R Cap Dessemond
John F Kennedy
R Charras
R Sauveur
15
Vallon des Auffes
6
Corniche Président
R Guidicelli
Bd Tellène
R du Vallon
R des Auffes
R d'Endoume
Bd Marius Thomas
Le Rhul (550m)

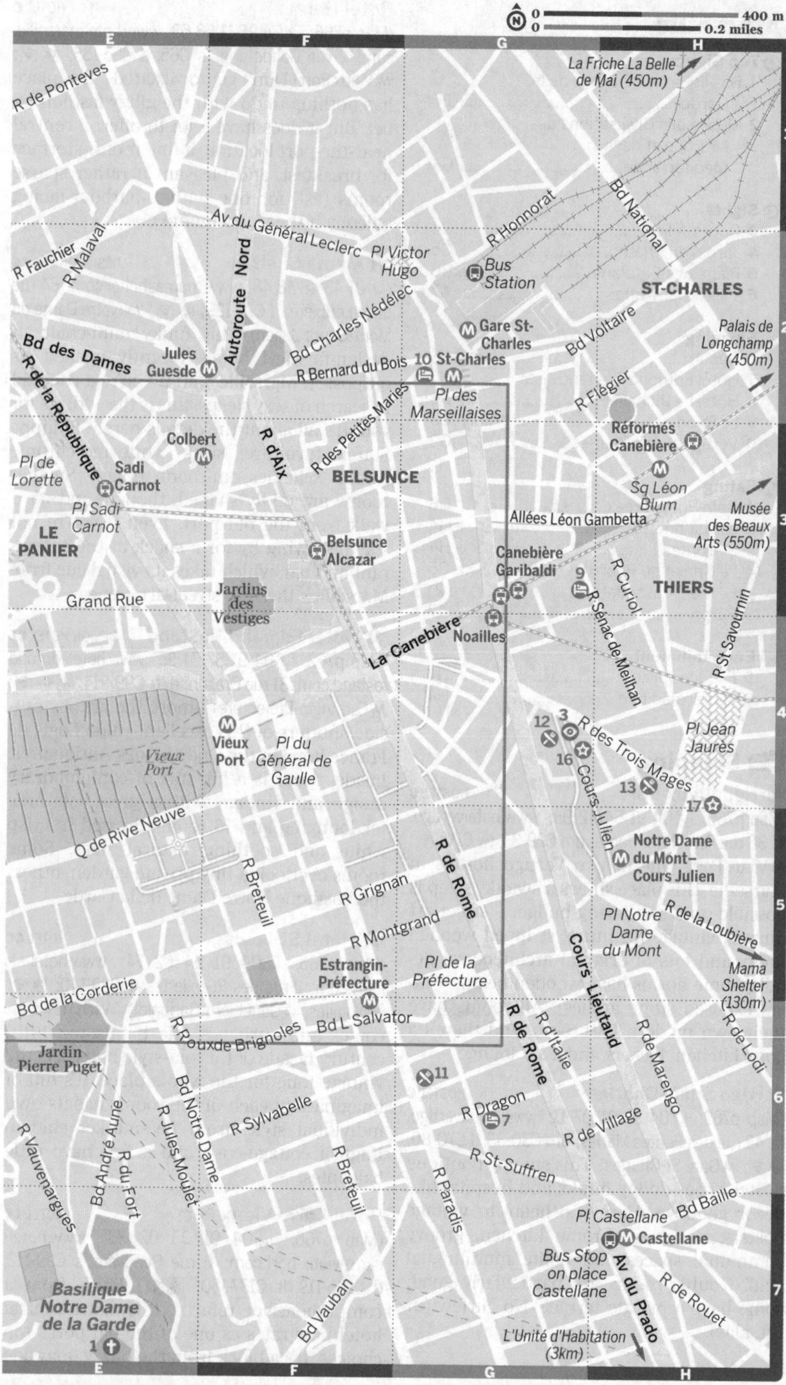

0 400 m
0 0.2 miles
E
F
G
H
1
2
3
4
5
6
7
La Friche La Belle de Mai (450m)
R de Ponteves
Bd National
R Honnorat
Av du Général Leclerc
Pl Victor Hugo
Bus Station
ST-CHARLES
R Fauchier
R Malaval
Autoroute Nord
Bd Charles Nédélec
Gare St-Charles
Bd Voltaire
Palais de Longchamp (450m)
Bd des Dames
Jules Guesde
R Bernard du Bois
10
St-Charles
Pl des Marseillaises
R Flégier
R de la République
Colbert
R d'Aix
R des Petites Maries
Réformés Canebière
Pl de Lorette
Sadi Carnot
BELSUNCE
Sq Léon Blum
Musée des Beaux Arts (550m)
Pl Sadi Carnot
Allées Léon Gambetta
LE PANIER
Belsunce Alcazar
Canebière Garibaldi
R Curiol
9
THIERS
Jardins des Vestiges
Grand Rue
R Sénac de Meilhan
R St Savournin
La Canebière
Noailles
12
3
R des Trois Mages
Vieux Port
Vieux Port
Pl du Général de Gaulle
16
Cours Julien
Pl Jean Jaurès
13
17
Q de Rive Neuve
R Breteuil
R de Rome
Notre Dame du Mont–Cours Julien
R Grignan
Pl Notre Dame du Mont
R de la Loubière
R Montgrand
Cours Lieutaud
Mama Shelter (130m)
Estrangin-Préfecture
Pl de la Préfecture
Bd de la Corderie
Bd L Salvator
R de Rome
R d'Italie
R de Marengo
R de Lodi
R Rouxde Brignoles
Jardin Pierre Puget
11
Bd Notre Dame
R Sylvabelle
R Dragon
7
R de Village
R Jules Moulet
R Vauvenargues
Bd André Aune
R du Fort
R Breteuil
R Paradis
R St-Suffren
Pl Castellane
Bd Baille
Castellane
Bus Stop on place Castellane
Av du Prado
R de Rouet
Basilique Notre Dame de la Garde
1
Bd Vauban
L'Unité d'Habitation (3km)

Marseille

Top Sights

Sights

Sleeping

Eating

Entertainment

Sleeping

Vertigo Vieux-Port HOSTEL €

(Map p766; ☎04 91 54 42 95; www.hotelvertigo.fr; 38 rue Fort Notre Dame; dm €29-33, tw €70; ; M Vieux Port) One of two Vertigo hostels in Marseille, this place shows a swanky sleep is possible on a shoestring budget – street-art murals, vintage furniture, stripped wooden floors and lots of original architectural details (some dorms have wooden beams, others exposed stone arches). All rooms have their own modern bathroom, and there's a good kitchen, lockers and a TV lounge.

Vertigo Saint-Charles HOSTEL €

(Map p762; ☎04 91 91 07 11; www.hotelvertigo.fr; 42 rue des Petites Maries; dm €30-33, d €70-80; @; M Gare St-Charles) This snappy boutique hostel kisses dodgy bunks and hospital-like decor goodbye. Here it's 'hello' to vintage posters, designer chrome kitchen, groovy communal spaces and polite multilingual staff. Double rooms are particularly good; some have a private terrace. No curfew (or lift, alas).

Hôtel Hermès HOTEL €

(Map p766; ☎04 96 11 63 63; www.hotelmarseille.com; 2 rue Bonneterie; s €65, d €85-135; ; M Vieux Port) Don't get too excited – this place has nothing to do with the glitzy fashion label. But it does have a lot to offer: a central near-the-port location, a fine rooftop terrace for breakfast, and pleasant if rather sparse rooms (ask for one with a harbour-facing balcony if the views matter).

★ **Mama Shelter** DESIGN HOTEL €€

(☎01 43 48 48 48; www.mamashelter.com; 64 rue de la Loubière; d €79-129; ; M Notre Dame du Mont-Cours Julien) This funky mini-chain of design-forward hotels recently opened its outpost in Marseille, and if you're a cool kid in search of sexy sleeps, this is the address for you. It's all about the details here – Philippe Starck furniture, sleek white-and-chrome colour schemes, in-room iMacs. Smaller rooms are oddly shaped, though, and it's a walk from the old port. Even if you're not staying, swing by for a snack at the restaurant and bar, which takes its visual cue from Marseille's thriving street-art scene.

★ **Hôtel Edmond Rostand** DESIGN HOTEL €€

(Map p762; ☎04 91 37 74 95; www.hoteledmondrostand.com; 31 rue Dragon; d/tr €99/114; @; M Estrangin-Préfecture) Ignore the grubby outside shutters of this excellent-value Logis de France hotel in the Quartier des Antiquaires. Inside, decor is a hip mix of contemporary design and vintage, with a great sofa area for lounging and 16 rooms dressed in crisp white and soothing natural hues. Some rooms overlook a tiny private garden, others the Basilique Notre Dame de la Garde.

★ **Hôtel St-Louis** HOTEL €€

(Map p766; ☎04 91 54 02 74; www.hotel-st-louis.com; 2 rue des Récollettes; r €89-140; ; M Noailles, Canebière Garibaldi) With its balconies and curlicues, the handsome 19th-century façade of this old-style hotel sets the vintage tone for the whole place. It's full of imagination: each of the rooms has its own individual style, from flea-market chic to English cottage-cosy, and a few have little balconies.

Hotel Carré Vieux Port HOTEL €€

(Map p766; ☎04 91 33 02 33; www.hotel-carre-vieux-port.com; 6 rue Beauvau; s €99-112, d €106-119, tr €137-150;) Fresh from a comprehensive refurb, this ultra-central hotel now rates as one of the old port's top choices. It's a block from the buzzy quayside

of the Vieux Port, and its rooms are bright, spacious and comfortable, with nice touches like frying-pan-sized shower heads, cube-shaped bath goodies, kettles in every room, and – er – a fibreglass bull in reception.

Decoh APARTMENT €€
(Map p762; 04 91 37 74 95; www.decoh.fr; 31-33 rue Dragon; apt & studios per night €125-180; ; M Estrangin-Préfecture) The creative, vintage-loving team at the Edmond Rostand hotel are behind this appealing, hotel-serviced self-catering accommodation on rue Paradis, rue Dragon and rue Albert. Studios sleep two people and apartments four; the super-stylish antique furniture recalls eras from the 1950s to '70s. Stay a night, week or month. Cook for yourself, or breakfast at the Hôtel Edmond Rostand.

Hôtel La Résidence du Vieux Port DESIGN HOTEL €€
(Map p766; 04 91 91 91 22; www.hotel-residence-marseille.com; 18 quai du Port; d €185-205; ; M Vieux Port) The building is about as attractive as a municipal car park, but this portside hotel scores big on design and views. Its rooms are self-consciously retro – bold primary colours, '60s-style furniture, anglepoise lamps – and most come with a port-view balcony. The ultimate is the 8th-floor Suite Ciel (Sky Suite).

Hôtel Le Richelieu HOTEL €€
(Map p762; 04 91 31 01 92; www.lerichelieu-marseille.com; 52 corniche Président John F Kennedy; d €89-142; ; 83) A long walk out of town beside the plage des Catalans, this old beachside hotel has a lot going for it – super sea views, a prow-like breakfast patio and very friendly owners – but the odd-shaped rooms, erratic bathrooms and occasionally shabby decor won't be to everyone's liking. It spans several floors and there's no lift.

Le Ryad BOUTIQUE HOTEL €€
(Map p762; 04 91 47 74 54; www.hoteldemarseille.fr; 16 rue Sénac de Meilhan; s €55-121, d €65-134, ste €120-190; ; M Noailles, Canebière Garibaldi) Morocco comes to Marseille at this stylish hotel, which (as its name suggests) takes its decorative inspiration from the riads of North Africa, all woven cushions, patterned rugs and colourful throws. There's a lovely garden, and the top-floor room has its own mini-roof terrace. Unfortunately the neighbourhood remains sketchy, and there was building work nearby when we visited.

★ **Casa Honoré** B&B €€€
(Map p766; 04 96 11 01 62; www.casahonore.com; 123 rue Sainte; d €150-200; ; M Vieux Port) Los Angeles meets Marseille at this four-room *maison d'hôte,* built around a central courtyard with a lap pool shaded by banana trees. The fashion-forward style reflects the owner's love for contemporary interior design, using disparate elements like black wicker and the occasional cow skull, which come together in one sexy package.

Eating

The Vieux Port and surrounding pedestrian streets teem with cafe terraces, but choose carefully. For world cuisine, try cours Julien and nearby rue des Trois Mages. For pizza, roast chickens, and Middle Eastern food under €10, nose around the streets surrounding **Marché des Capucins** (Map p766; place des Capucins; 8am-7pm Mon-Sat; M Noailles, Canebière Garibaldi).

★ **Les Buffets du Vieux Port** FRENCH €
(Map p766; 04 13 20 11 32; www.clubhouse-vieuxport.com; 158 quai du Port; adult/child menu €23/13; noon-2.30pm & 7.30-10.30pm; ; M Vieux Port) What a great idea – a high-class, on-trend self-service canteen, with a vast array of starters, mains, salads and desserts laid out like a banquet for diners to help themselves to. Premium cold cuts, fresh seafood, bouillabaisse, mussels, fish soup – it's all here and more. Portside tables go fast, but there's plenty of room inside.

BOUILLABAISSE

Originally cooked by fishermen from the scraps of their catch, bouillabaisse is Marseille's signature dish. True bouillabaisse includes at least four kinds of fish, and sometimes shellfish. Don't trust tourist traps that promise cheap bouillabaisse; the real deal costs at least €50 per person. It's served in two parts: the *soupe de poisson* (broth), rich with tomato, saffron and fennel; and the cooked fish, de-boned tableside and presented on a platter. On the side are croutons, *rouille* (a bread-thickened garlic-chilli mayonnaise) and grated cheese, usually Gruyère. Spread *rouille* on the crouton, top with cheese, and float it in the soup. Be prepared for a huge meal and tons of garlic.

Central Marseille

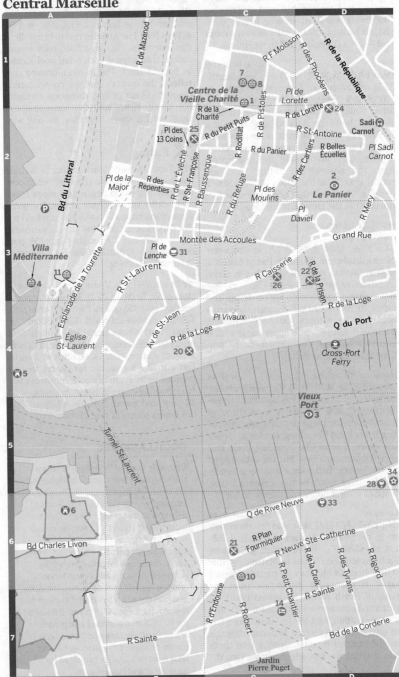

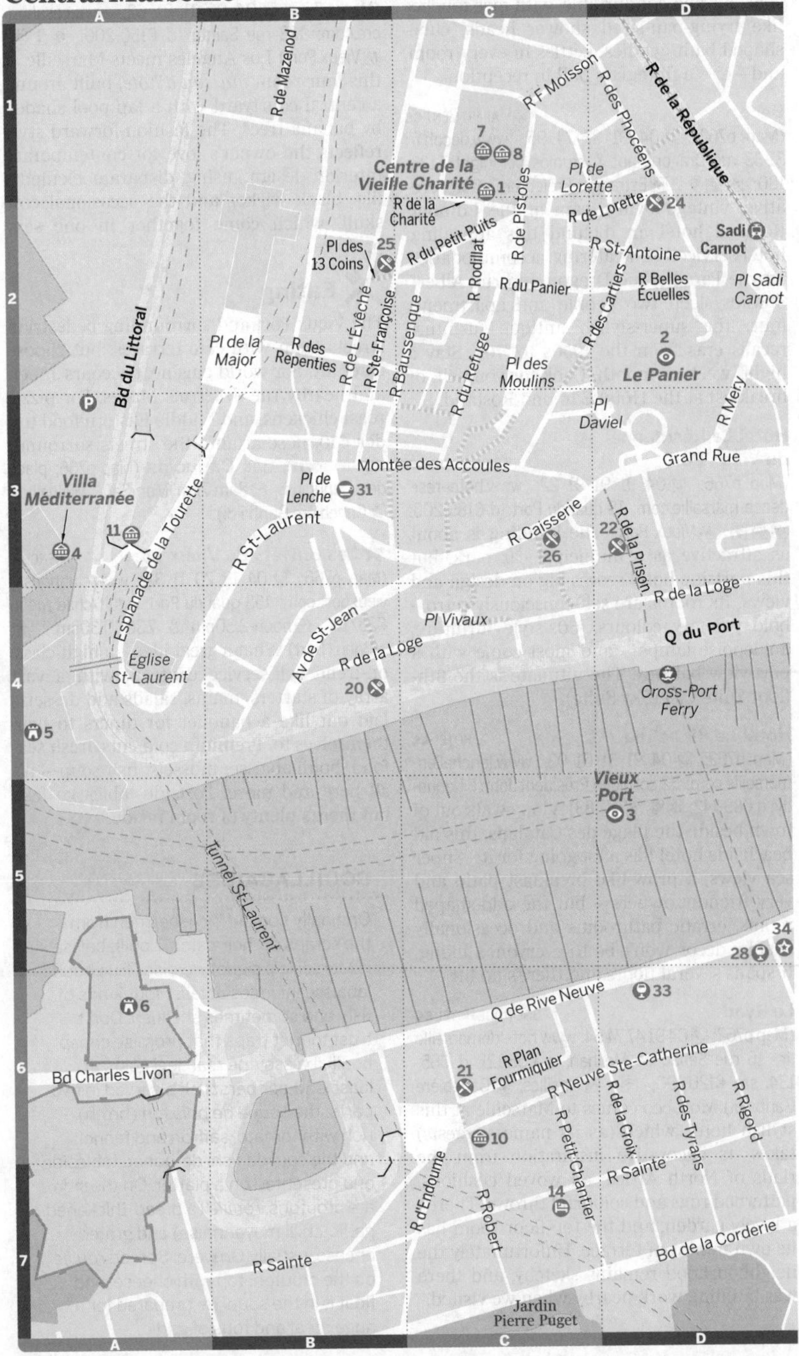
A
B
C
D
1
2
3
4
5
6
7
R de Mazenod
R F Moisson
R des Phocéens
R de la République
Centre de la Vieille Charité
7
8
1
R de la Charité
Pl de Lorette
R de Pistoles
R de Lorette
24
Sadi Carnot
Pl des 13 Coins
25
R du Petit Puits
R Rodillat
R St-Antoine
R du Panier
R Belles Écuelles
Pl Sadi Carnot
R des Cartiers
2
Le Panier
Bd du Littoral
Pl de la Major
R des Repenties
R de L'Évêché
R Ste-Françoise
R Baussenque
R du Refuge
Pl des Moulins
Pl Daviel
R Mery
Montée des Accoules
Grand Rue
Villa Méditerranée
Pl de Lenche
31
R St-Laurent
Esplanade de la Tourette
11
4
R Caisserie
22
26
R de la Prison
R de la Loge
Av de St-Jean
Pl Vivaux
Q du Port
Église St-Laurent
R de la Loge
20
Cross-Port Ferry
5
Vieux Port
3
Tunnel St-Laurent
34
28
33
6
Q de Rive Neuve
Bd Charles Livon
21
R Plan Fourmiquier
R Neuve Ste-Catherine
R de la Croix
R des Tyrans
R Rigord
10
R d'Endoume
R Robert
R Petit Chantier
R Sainte
14
R Sainte
Bd de la Corderie
Jardin Pierre Puget

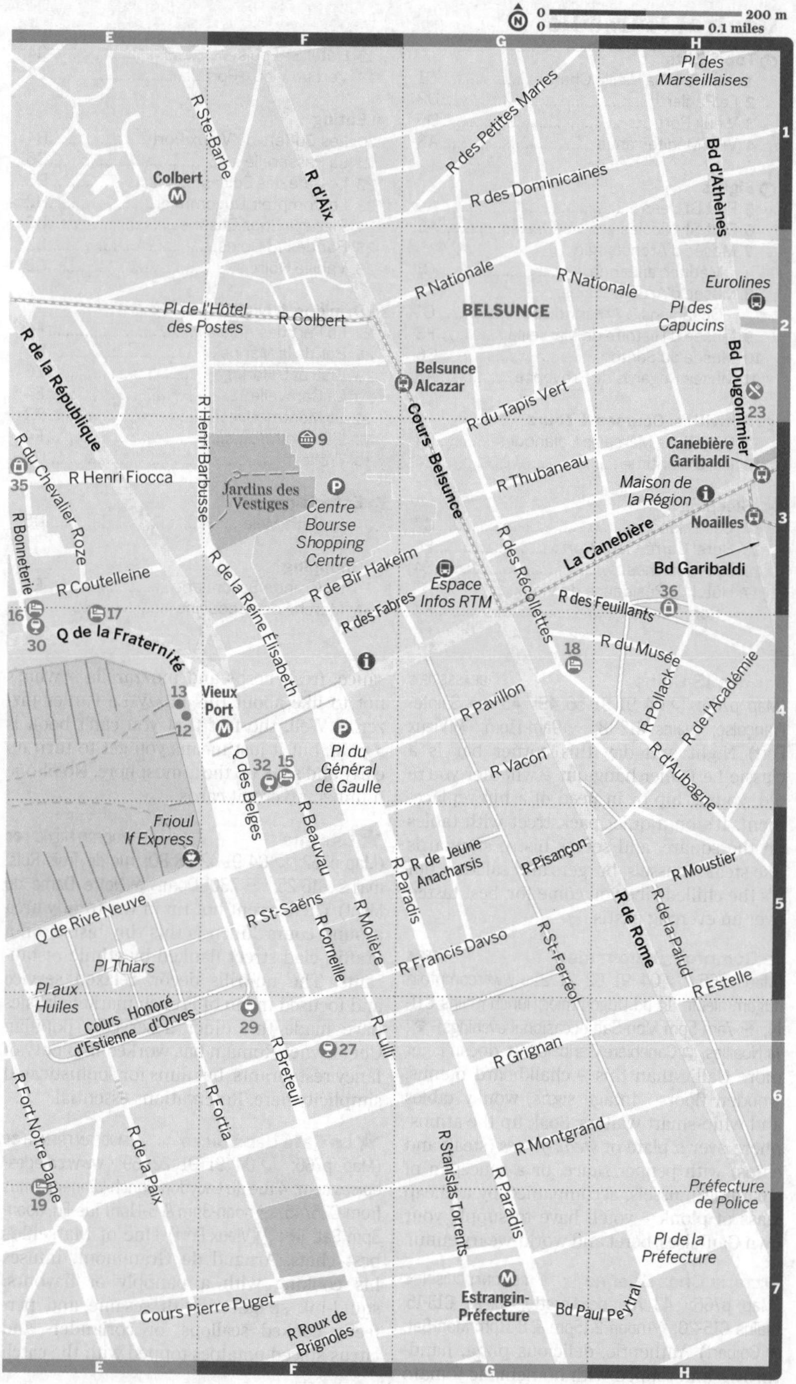
0
200 m
0
0.1 miles
E
F
G
H
1
2
3
4
5
6
7
Pl des Marseillaises
R Ste-Barbe
R des Petites Maries
Bd d'Athènes
Colbert
R d'Aix
R des Dominicaines
R Nationale
R Nationale
Eurolines
BELSUNCE
Pl des Capucins
Pl de l'Hôtel des Postes
R Colbert
R de la République
Bd Dugommier
Belsunce Alcazar
R Henri Barbusse
R du Tapis Vert
23
Cours Belsunce
9
Canebière Garibaldi
R du Chevalier Roze
R Thubaneau
35
R Henri Fiocca
Jardins des Vestiges
Maison de la Région
Centre Bourse Shopping Centre
Noailles
R Bonneterie
La Canebière
R de la Reine Elisabeth
R des Récollettes
R de Bir Hakeim
Bd Garibaldi
R Coutelleine
Espace Infos RTM
36
16
17
R des Fabres
R des Feuillants
30
Q de la Fraternité
R du Musée
18
13
Vieux Port
R Pavillon
R Pollack
R de l'Académie
12
32
15
Pl du Général de Gaulle
R Vacon
R d'Aubagne
Q des Belges
R Beauvau
Frioul If Express
R de Jeune Anacharsis
R Pisançon
R Moustier
R Paradis
Q de Rive Neuve
R St-Saëns
R Molière
R Corneille
R de Rome
R de la Palud
R St-Ferréol
R Francis Davso
Pl Thiars
R Estelle
Pl aux Huiles
Cours Honoré d'Estienne d'Orves
29
R Lulli
27
R Grignan
R Breteuil
R Fort Notre Dame
R Fortia
R de la Paix
R Montgrand
R Stanislas Torrents
R Paradis
Préfecture de Police
19
Pl de la Préfecture
Estrangin-Préfecture
Bd Paul Peytral
Cours Pierre Puget
R Roux de Brignoles

Central Marseille

Bar des 13 Coins BRASSERIE €
(Map p766; ☎04 91 91 56 49; 45 rue Sainte-Françoise; mains €12-18; ⌚9am-11pm; Ⓜ Vieux Port) Night and day this corner bar is a classic Le Panier hang-out – whether you're old, young, hip or in need of a hip replacement. It's on a quiet backstreet with tables on the square, and serves bistro standards like steak, mussels, burgers and salads – but it's the chilled vibe you come for, best tasted over an evening pastis.

Le Comptoir Dugommier CAFE €
(Map p766; ☎04 91 62 21 21; www.comptoir-dugommier.fr; 14 bd Dugommier; lunch mains €11-14; ⌚7am-5pm Mon-Sat, occasional evenings; 📶; Ⓜ Noailles, 🚊 Canebière Garibaldi) It doesn't get more Gallic than this – chalkboard menus, wooden floors, vintage signs, wonky tables and whip-smart waiters. Soak up the atmosphere over a plate of *steak-frites* (steak and chips) with pepper sauce, or a saucepan of steaming mussels, accompanied by a cheap glass of plonk – you'll have to supply your own Gauloises, beret and world-weary ennui.

Pizzaria Chez Étienne REGIONAL CUISINE €
(Map p766; 43 rue de Lorette; pizza €13-15, mains €15-20; ⌚noon-2.15pm & 8-11pm Mon-Sat; Ⓜ Colbert) Authentic, delicious pizza, hand-thrown and topped with homemade tomato sauce, fresh herbs and mozzarella – what's not to like about this buzzy Le Panier pizzeria? Well, the fact that you can't book is a pain, but it just means you get to turn up early and soak up the atmosphere. No phone number, no credit cards.

★ **L'Arome** MODERN FRENCH €€
(Map p762; ☎04 91 42 88 80; rue de Trois Rois; mains €16-25; ⌚7.30-10pm; Ⓜ Notre Dame du Mont) The current hot tip in the trendy area around cours Julien is this tiny bistro, on a graffiti-clad street flanked by ethnic restaurants. The no-frills decor, relaxed service and focused menu of French market classics have made this diner deservedly popular. Chef-owner Romain has worked in plenty of fancy restaurants, but aims for sophisticated simplicity here. Reservations essential.

★ **Le Café des Épices** MODERN FRENCH €€
(Map p766; ☎04 91 91 22 69; www.cafedes-epices.com; 4 rue du Lacydon; lunch/dinner menus from €25/45; ⌚noon-3pm & 6-11pm Tue-Fri, noon-3pm Sat; 👪; Ⓜ Vieux Port) One of Marseille's best chefs, Arnaud de Grammont, infuses his cooking with a panoply of flavours: squid-ink spaghetti with sesame and perfectly cooked scallops, or coriander- and citrus-spiced potatoes topped with the catch

of the day. Presentation is impeccable, the decor playful, and the colourful outdoor terrace between giant potted olive trees nothing short of superb.

★**Café Populaire** BISTRO €€
(Map p762; ☎04 91 02 53 96; www.cafe-populaire.com; 110 rue Paradis; tapas €6-16, mains €17-22; ⏰noon-2.30pm & 8-11pm Tue-Sat; Ⓜ Estrangin-Préfecture) Vintage furniture, old books on the shelves and a fine collection of glass soda bottles lend a retro air to this trendy, 1950s-styled *jazz comptoir* (counter) – a restaurant despite its name. The crowd is chic and smiling chefs in the open kitchen mesmerise with daily specials like king prawns *à la plancha* (grilled) or beetroot and coriander salad.

La Cantinetta ITALIAN €€
(Map p762; ☎04 91 48 10 48; 24 cours Julien; mains €12-19; ⏰noon-2pm & 7.30-10.30pm Mon-Sat; Ⓜ Notre Dame du Mont-Cours Julien) Top-class Italian trattoria on the buzzy setting of cours Julien. All the pasta here is homemade, and ingredients are sourced from top Italian suppliers. Ask for a table on the lovely little garden, paved with terracotta tiles and shaded by palms. The *bresaola* (air-dried beef) and parma ham platter are superb.

Le Chalet du Pharo MEDITERRANEAN €€
(Map p762; ☎04 91 52 80 11; www.le-chalet-du-pharo.com; Jardin du Pharo, 58 bd Charles Livon; mains €18-30; ⏰noon-3pm daily, 7.30-9.30pm Mon-Sat; Ⓜ Vieux Port) Only Marseillais and those in the know are privy to this little chalet with a very big view, secreted in the Jardin du Pharo. Its hillside terrace, shaded by pines and parasols, stares across the water at Fort St-Jean, MuCEM and the Villa Méditerranée beyond. Grilled fish and meat dominate the menu. Online reservations are essential. No credit cards.

La Passarelle PROVENCAL €€
(Map p766; ☎04 91 33 03 27; www.restaurantlapassarelle.fr; 52 rue Plan Fourmiguier; mains €16-22; ⏰noon-2.30pm & 8-10.30pm May-Oct, shorter hours rest of year; Ⓜ Vieux Port) This admirably unpretentious bistro grows most of its organic veggies in its own *potager* (kitchen garden), from tomatoes to courgettes, salad leaves and aubergines. It's a cosy, friendly place for sampling delicious Mediterranean flavours, with mix-and-match tables and chairs arranged on a decked terrace beneath a spreading sail. Charming and simple.

DON'T MISS

BLACK ICE

There are plenty of ice-cream shops around Marseille, but there's only one that sells black ice cream: **Vanille Noire** (Map p766; ☎07 77 33 68 19; 13 rue Caisserie; ice cream €2; ⏰12.30-6.45pm; Ⓜ Vieux Port). The colour comes from vanilla pods, which also give it a unique bittersweet, custardy flavour. Plenty of other flavours on offer here too, all made on-site with organic ingredients.

Le Môlé Passédat MODERN FRENCH €€€
(Map p762; www.passedat.fr; 1 esplanade du J4, MuCEM; La Table lunch/dinner menus from €52/73, La Cuisine 2-/3-course menus €22/35; ⏰12.15-2.30pm & 7.30-10.30pm Mon & Wed-Sat, lunch only Sun; Ⓜ Vieux Port, Joliette) Few kitchens are so stunningly located as this one. On the top floor of Marseille's flagship museum, MuCEM, Michelin-starred chef Gérald Passédat cooks up exquisite French fare alongside big blue views of the Mediterranean and Marseillais coastline. **La Table** is the gastronomic restaurant; **La Cuisine** (open noon to 4pm), with self-service dining around shared tables (no sea view), is the cheaper choice. Reserve both online.

Péron SEAFOOD €€€
(Map p762; ☎04 91 52 15 22; www.restaurant-peron.com; 56 corniche Président John F Kennedy; menus from €69; ⏰noon-2pm & 8-10.15pm; 🚌83) Another premium address for seafood, with the advantage of sea views to boot. Vast seafood platters, proper bouillabaisse (€57) and various fish dishes, served in a slightly starchy and old-school setting.

Le Rhul SEAFOOD €€€
(☎04 91 52 01 77; www.hotel-restaurant-le-rhul.com/le-restaurant; 269 corniche Président John F Kennedy; bouillabaisse €53; ⏰noon-2pm & 5-9pm; 🚌83) This long-standing classic has atmosphere (however kitschy): it's a 1940s seaside hotel with Mediterranean views. Although this is one of the most reliably consistent spots for authentic bouillabaisse, go the classic one better and get the *bourride* (minimum two people), a hard-to-find variation brimming with garlic in white sauce.

🍷 Drinking & Nightlife

In the best tradition of Mediterranean cities, Marseille embraces the cafe-lounger lifestyle. Near the Vieux Port, head to place

SHOPPING FOR SOAP

Soapmaking has been a Marseille tradition since the 18th century, but much of the stuff for sale at the city's markets is made elsewhere (sometimes not even in Provence). That's not the case at **La Grande Savonnerie** (Map p766; ☎09 50 63 80 35; www.lagrandesavonnerie.com; 36 Grande Rue; soaps from €2.50; ⏲10am-7pm Mon-Sat; Ⓜ Vieux Port) – all of its products are produced in a mini-factory just outside town. It specialises in the genuine Marseillais article, made with olive oil and no added perfume, and shaped into cubes.

Thiars and cours Honoré d'Estienne d'Orves for cafes that bask in the sun by day and buzz into the night. Cours Julien is a fine place on a sunny day to watch people come and go at the many characterful shops, cafes and restaurants in one of Marseille's most interesting neighbourhoods. Up in Le Panier, place de Lenche and rue des Pistoles are ideal places to while away an afternoon while soaking up the area's boho charms.

La Part des Anges WINE BAR
(Map p766; ☎04 91 33 55 70; www.lapartdesanges.com; 33 rue Sainte; ⏲9am-2am Mon-Sat, 9am-1pm & 6pm-2am Sun; Ⓜ Vieux Port) No address buzzes with Marseille's hip, buoyant crowd more than this fabulous all-rounder wine bar, named after the alcohol that evaporates through a barrel during wine or whisky fermentation: the angels' share. Take your pick of dozens of wines by the glass.

La Caravelle BAR
(Map p766; www.lacaravelle-marseille.com; 34 quai du Port; ⏲7am-2am; Ⓜ Vieux Port) Look up or miss this standout upstairs hideaway, styled with rich wood and leather, a zinc bar and yellowing murals. If it's sunny, snag a coveted spot on the portside terrace. On Friday there's live jazz from 9pm.

Bar de la Marine BAR
(Map p766; ☎04 91 54 95 42; 15 quai de Rive Neuve; ⏲7am-1am; Ⓜ Vieux Port) Though it is often erroneously thought that Marcel Pagnol filmed the card-party scenes in *Marius* at this Marseille institution, it did figure in the film *Love, Actually*. Come for a drink, not the food, and a lounge on this simple bar's waterside pavement along the Vieux Port. Don't leave without peeking at the original vintage interior.

Bistrot L'Horloge BAR
(Map p766; ☎09 50 41 39 66; 11 cours Honoré d'Estienne d'Orves; ⏲9am-1pm Mon-Sat; Ⓜ Vieux Port) A local favourite with parasol-shaded table and chairs at the lion-statue end of cours Honoré d'Estienne d'Orves, this *bistrot*-bar rocks. In summer live music entertains in the early evening while punters chat over mint and ice-jammed mojitos, pots of black olive tapenade and charcuterie platters. And yes, it does have an *horloge* (clock) above its wine-barrel-ramed entrance.

Le Montmartre CAFE
(Map p766; ☎04 91 56 03 24; 4 place de Lenche; mains from €6; ⏲9am-11pm; Ⓜ Vieux Port, Joliette) Place de Lenche is a lovely, small square in Le Panier with glimpses of the Vieux Port. Among several cafes here, this one captures the neighbourhood vibe and is a fine place to hang out with a drink on a lazy afternoon.

L'Endroit GAY BAR
(Map p766; ☎04 91 33 97 25; www.lendroitrestoclub.fr; 8 rue Bailli de Suffren; ⏲7pm-6am Tue-Sat; Ⓜ Vieux Port) Dive through the tiny door to the Vieux Port's only gay bar. Theme nights include karaoke.

Trolleybus CLUB
(Map p766; ☎04 91 54 30 45; www.letrolley.com; 24 quai de Rive Neuve; ⏲midnight-6am Thu-Sat; Ⓜ Vieux Port) Shake it to techno, funk and indie in between games of *pétanque* at this mythical Marseillais club with four *salles* (rooms) beneath 17th-century stone vaults at the Vieux Port.

☆ Entertainment

La Friche La Belle de Mai CULTURAL CENTRE
(☎04 95 04 95 04; www.lafriche.org; 41 rue Jobin; ⏲information & ticket kiosk 11am-6pm Mon, to 7pm Tue-Sun; 🚌49, stop Jobin) This former sugar-refining plant and subsequent tobacco factory is now a vibrant arts centre with a theatre, artists' workshops, cinema, multimedia displays, skateboard ramps, electro and world-music parties et al. Check its program online. The quickest way by public transport is to catch the metro to Gare St-Charles and walk along rue Guibal, or take line M2 to Cinq Avenues Longchamp, cross Parc Longchamp and then take Rue Bénédit.

Dock des Suds LIVE MUSIC
(☎04 91 99 00 00; www.dock-des-suds.org; 12 rue Urbain V; ⏲closed Aug; Ⓜ National, 🚌 Arenc le Silo)

Eclectic live music in a large venue in the Joliette neighbourhood north of the Vieux Port.

L'Intermédiaire LIVE MUSIC
(Map p762; ☎06 87 87 88 21; 63 place Jean Jaurès; ⏲9pm-2am Wed-Sun; Ⓜ Notre Dame du Mont-Cours Julien) This grungy venue with graffitied walls is one of the best for DJs and live bands (usually techno or alternative).

Espace Julien LIVE MUSIC
(Map p762; ☎04 91 24 34 10; www.espace-julien.com; 39 cours Julien; Ⓜ Notre Dame du Mont-Cours Julien) Rock, *opérock,* alternative theatre, reggae, hip-hop, Afro groove and other cutting-edge entertainment all appear on the bill. The website lists gigs.

Le Pelle Mêle JAZZ
(Map p766; ☎04 91 54 85 26; 8 place aux Huiles; ⏲5.30pm-2am Tue-Sat; Ⓜ Vieux Port) Jive to jazz or fill the busy pavement terrace. Live bands every evening at 7.30pm (except Tuesday), but drinks are pricey.

Information

Tourist Office (Map p766; ☎04 91 13 89 00; www.marseille-tourisme.com; 11 La Canebière; ⏲9am-7pm Mon-Sat, 10am-5pm Sun; Ⓜ Vieux Port) Marseille's useful tourist office has plenty of information on everything, including guided city tours on foot or by bus, electric tourist train or boat, as well as to the Calanques. Has free wi-fi too.

Maison de la Région (Map p766; www.regionpaca.fr; 61 La Canebière; ⏲11am-6pm Mon-Sat; Ⓜ Noailles) Info on Provence and the Côte d'Azur.

Marseille Expos (www.marseilleexpos.com) The outstanding arts organisation Marseille Expos distributes an excellent map of hot galleries and sponsors the festival Printemps de l'Art Contemporain each May. Its website lists what's on.

Getting There & Away

AIR

Aéroport Marseille-Provence (Aéroport Marseille-Marignane; MRS; ☎04 42 14 14 14; www.marseille.aeroport.fr) is located 25km northwest of Marseille in Marignane. There are regular year-round flights to nearly all major French cities, plus major conurbations in the UK, Germany, Belgium, Italy and Spain.

BOAT

The **passenger Ferry terminal** (Map p762; www.marseille-port.fr; Ⓜ Joliette) is located 250m south of place de la Joliette.

SNCM (Map p762; ☎08 91 70 18 01; www.sncm.fr; 61 bd des Dames; Ⓜ Joliette) has regular ferries from Nice and Marseille to Corsica and Sardinia, plus long-distance routes to Algeria and Tunisia.

BUS

The **bus station** (Map p762; www.lepilote.com; 3 rue Honnorat; Ⓜ Gare St-Charles) is located on the northern side of the train station. Buy tickets here or from the driver. Services to some destinations, including Cassis, use the **stop on place Castellane** (Map p762; Ⓜ Castellane), south of the centre.

For most destinations along the Côte d'Azur, it's faster and easier to catch the train, but for some smaller towns and villages (especially inland) buses are an alternative. There are several different companies, but you can find comprehensive timetable information on Le Pilote (www.lepilote.com). Sample destinations:

Aix-en-Provence (€6, Cartreize Line 50, 40 minutes, every 10 minutes Monday to Saturday, less frequent Sunday) Express bus leaves from Marseille St-Charles. Line 51 also runs frequently to Aix-en-Provence.

Barcelonette (€33.50, LER Line 28, two daily)

Cassis (€2, La Marcouline Line M06, 45 minutes, hourly Monday to Saturday)

Forcalquier (€16.40, LER Line 50, 30 minutes, six daily Monday to Saturday, three Sunday)

Eurolines (Map p766; www.eurolines.com; 3 allées Léon Gambetta; Ⓜ Noailles) also has international services.

TRAIN

Eurostar (www.eurostar.com) has services one to five times weekly between Marseille and London (from €99, 6½ hours) via Avignon and Lyon. As always, the earlier you book, the cheaper the potential fare.

Regular and TGV trains serve **Gare St-Charles** (⏲ticket office 5.15am-10pm; Ⓜ Gare St-Charles SNCF), which is a junction for both metro lines. The **left-luggage office** (⏲8.15am-9pm) is next to platform A. Sample fares:

Avignon €17 to €20.50, 35 minutes

Nice €28, 2½ hours

Paris Gare de Lyon from €75, three hours on TGV

Getting Around

TO/FROM THE AIRPORT

Navette Marseille (www.navettemarseilleaeroport.com; ⏲4.30am-11.30pm) buses link the airport and Gare St-Charles (adult/child €8.20/4.10) every 15 to 20 minutes.

The airport's train station has direct services to several cities including Arles and Avignon; a free shuttle bus runs to/from the airport terminal.

WORTH A TRIP

LES CALANQUES

Marseille abuts the wild and spectacular **Parc National des Calanques** (www.calanques-parcnational.fr), a 20km stretch of high, rocky promontories, rising from brilliant-turquoise Mediterranean waters. The sheer cliffs are occasionally interrupted by small idyllic beaches, some impossible to reach without a kayak. The Marseillais cherish the Calanques, and come here to soak up the sun or take a long hike. The promontories have been protected since 1975 and shelter an extraordinary wealth of flora and fauna: 900 plant species, Bonelli's eagle, and Europe's largest lizard (the 60cm eyed lizard) and longest snake (the 2m Montpellier snake).

From October to June the best way to see the Calanques (including the 500 sq km of the rugged inland Massif des Calanques) is to hike the many maquis-lined trails. Marseille's **tourist office** (p771) leads guided walks (no kids under eight) and has information about trail and road closures. It also has an excellent hiking map of the various *calanques*, as does Cassis' **tourist office** (☎08 92 39 01 03; www.ot-cassis.com; quai des Moulins; ⏲9am-7pm Mon-Sat, 9.30am-12.30pm & 3-6pm Sun Jul & Aug, shorter hours rest of year; 📶), and their websites.

Of the many *calanques* along the coastline, the most easily accessible are **Calanque de Sormiou** and **Calanque de Morgiou**, while remote inlets such **Calanque d'En Vau** and **Calanque de Port-Miou** take dedication and time to reach – either on foot or by kayak.

In July and August trails close due to fire danger: the only option then is to take a boat tour with **Croisières Marseille Calanques** (Map p766; ☎04 91 33 36 79; www.croisieres-marseille-calanques.com; Vieux Port; Ⓜ Vieux Port) from Marseille or Cassis. Check in advance if you're hoping to be able to stop for a swim, as only a few tours allow this, such as the one offered by **Icard Maritime** (Map p766; ☎04 91 333 679; www.visite-des-calanques.com; quai des Belges; Ⓜ Vieux Port).

Otherwise, you'll have to drive, cycle or take public transport, though roads are rough, parking scarce and the going slow. The roads into each *calanque* are often closed to drivers, unless they have a reservation at one of the *calanque* restaurants. You must instead park at a public lot, then walk the rest of the way in.

The best way to reach the *calanques* is by sea – either by boat, or by hiring a kayak from Marseille or Cassis. Operators such as **Destination Calanques Kayak** (☎06 07 15 63 86; www.destination-calanques.fr; half-/full day €35/55; ⏲Apr-Oct) and **Raskas Kayak** (☎04 91 73 27 16; www.raskas-kayak.com; half-/full day €35/65) organise sea-kayaking tours; local tourist offices have details of lots of other hire companies. **Calanc'O** (☎06 25 78 85 93; www.calanco-kayak-paddle.com; half-/full day €35/55) also offers paddle boarding.

For access to the *calanques* closest to Marseille, drive or take bus 19 down the coast to its terminus at **La Madrague**, then switch to bus 20 to **Callelongue**, a small *calanque* with restaurants (note that the road to Callelongue is open to cars weekdays only mid-April to May and closed entirely June to September). From there you can walk to **Calanque de la Mounine** and **Calanque de Marseilleveyre** along spectacular trails over the clifftops. **Calanque de Sugiton** is also easy to access without a car. Take bus 21 from av du Prado, at Castellane, towards Luminy and get off at the last stop. From there follow the path (about a 45-minute walk).

BICYCLE

With the **Le Vélo** (www.levelo-mpm.fr) bike-share scheme, you can pick up/ and drop off bikes from 100-plus stations across the city and along the coastal road to the beaches. Users must subscribe online first (€1/5 a week/year), after which the first 30 minutes is free, then €1 per hour. Stations only take credit cards with chips.

BOAT

Boats run from the old port to the Îles du Frioul, as well as to the Parc National des Calanques.

PUBLIC TRANSPORT

Marseille has two metro lines (Métro 1 and Métro 2), two tram lines (yellow and green) and an extensive bus network. Bus, metro or tram tickets (per hour/day €1.60/5.20) are available from machines in the metro, at tram stops and on buses. Most buses start in front of the **Espace Infos RTM** (6 rue des Fabres; Ⓜ Vieux Port), where you can obtain information and tickets.

The metro runs from 5am to 10.30pm Monday to Thursday, and until 12.30am Friday to Sunday. Trams run 5am to 1am daily.

AIX-EN-PROVENCE

POP 145,300

A pocket of left-bank Parisian chic deep in Provence, Aix (pronounced like the letter X) is all class: its leafy boulevards and public squares are lined with 17th- and 18th-century mansions, punctuated by gurgling moss-covered fountains. Haughty stone lions guard its grandest avenue, cafe-laced cours Mirabeau, where fashionable Aixois pose on polished pavement terraces sipping espresso. While Aix is a student hub, its upscale appeal makes it pricier than other Provençal towns.

The part pedestrianised centre of Aix' old town is ringed by busy boulevards, with several large car parks dotted on the edge of town. Whatever you do, don't try and drive into the centre.

Sights

The **Aix City Pass** (http://booking.aixenprovencetourism.com; 24/48/72hr €25/34/43) covers entry to all the major museums and Cézanne sights, plus public transport and a guided walking tour.

Cours Mirabeau HISTORIC SITE

No avenue better epitomises Provence's most graceful city than this fountain-studded street, sprinkled with Renaissance *hôtels particuliers* (private mansions) and crowned with a summertime roof of leafy plane trees. Named after the revolutionary hero Comte de Mirabeau, it was laid out in the 1640s. Cézanne and Zola hung out at Les Deux Garçons (p776), one of a clutch of busy pavement cafes.

★Musée Granet MUSEUM

(04 42 52 88 32; www.museegranet-aixenprovence.fr; place St-Jean de Malte; adult/child €5/free; 11am-7pm Tue-Sun) This fabulous art museum sits right near the top of France's artistic must-sees, housing works by some of the most iconic artists associated with Provence, including Picasso, Léger, Matisse, Monet, Klee, Van Gogh and, perhaps most importantly of all in Aix, nine works by local boy Cézanne. The collection is named after the Provençal painter François Marius Granet (1775–1849), who donated a large number of works, and housed inside a dramatic 17th-century priory.

Vieil Aix HISTORIC SITE

The centre of Aix's old town is a wonderful place for a stroll. The heart of town is the graceful public square of cours Mirabeau. South of cours Mirabeau, **Quartier Mazarin** was laid out in the 17th century, and is home to some of Aix' finest buildings. **Place des Quatre Dauphins** is particularly enchanting and has a fountain (1667) with water-spouting dolphins.

★Caumont Centre d'Art HISTORIC BUILDING

(04 42 20 70 01; www.caumont-centredart.com; 3 rue Joseph Cabassol; temporary exhibitions €8.50-11; 10am-7pm May-Sep, to 6pm Oct-Apr) Aix' newest pride and joy is also one of its oldest: a stellar art space housed inside the Mazarin quarter's grandest 17th-century *hôtel particulier*. There are three exhibitions every year exploring the region's rich artistic and cultural heritage, but it's the building itself that's the star of the show. Built from honey-coloured stone, its palatial rooms are stuffed with antiques and objets d'art that illustrate the aristocratic lifestyle of the house's most celebrated owner, the Marquise de Caumont.

Festivals & Events

★Festival d'Aix-en-Provence PERFORMING ARTS

(04 34 08 02 17; www.festival-aix.com; Jul) World-renowned month-long festival of classical music, opera, ballet and buskers.

Sleeping

Aix has a good choice of hotels, but they are on the expensive side, and most are booked up solid during the summer. Very few have their own car parks, so if you're driving you'll have to park in one of the car parks around the ring road and walk into town.

Hôtel Paul HOTEL €

(04 42 23 23 89; www.aix-en-provence.com/hotelpaul; 10 av Pasteur; s/d/tr from €55/65/77; P) On the edge of Vieil Aix, this faded hotel is hardly luxurious, but it's a bit of a bargain as long as you can put up with the no-frills decor. There's a pleasant garden and breakfast is a very reasonable €5. It doesn't take credit cards.

Hôtel Cardinal HOTEL €

(04 42 38 32 30; www.hotel-cardinal-aix.com; 24 rue Cardinale; s €69, d €79-119;) Pleasantly removed from the hustle and bustle of central Aix, this quaint Mazarin Quarter hotel is surprisingly elegant considering the price, with heritage rooms featuring original fireplaces, antiques and a surfeit of swag curtains.

Aix-en-Provence

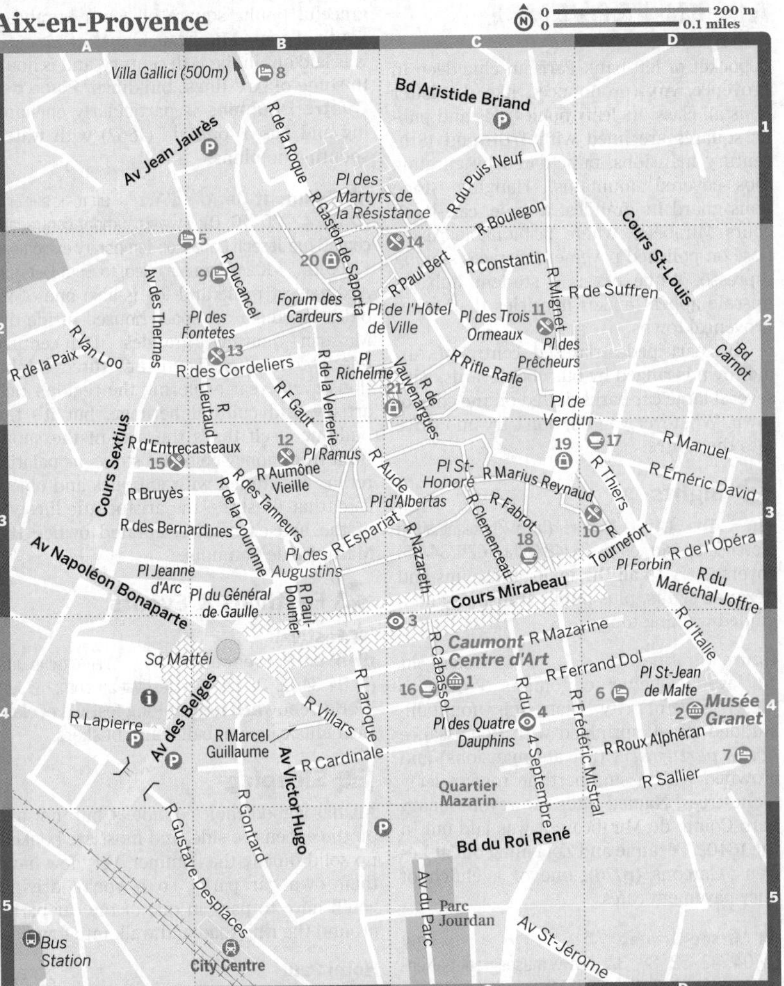

There are also six large suites in the annexe up the street, each with a kitchenette and dining room – ideal for longer stays.

★**L'Épicerie** B&B €€

(☎06 08 85 38 68; www.unechambreenville.eu; 12 rue du Cancel; d €100-140; 📶) This intimate B&B on a backstreet in Vieil Aix is the creation of born-and-bred Aixois lad Luc. His breakfast room re-creates a 1950s grocery store, and the flowery garden out the back is perfect for excellent evening dining and weekend brunch (book ahead for both). Breakfast is a veritable feast. Two rooms accommodate families of four.

Hôtel La Caravelle HOTEL €€

(☎04 42 21 53 05; www.lacaravelle-hotel.com; 29 bd du Roi René; s €69, d €79-99, f €109-119; ❄📶) On the southern side of the Mazarin Quarter, this solid, friendly family-run hotel represents super value in Aix – the rates hardly vary across the seasons, making it a real bargain in summer. The decor's nothing to get excited about – white walls, grey bedspreads, functional bathrooms – but rooms are quite comfortable.

Ask for one on the garden side if you're a light sleeper.

Aix-en-Provence

Top Sights
1 Caumont Centre d'Art C4
2 Musée Granet D4

Sights
3 Cours Mirabeau C4
4 Place des Quatre Dauphins C4

Sleeping
5 Hôtel Aquabella B2
6 Hôtel Cardinal D4
7 Hôtel La Caravelle D4
8 Hôtel Paul B1
9 L'Épicerie B2

Eating
10 Bistrot Petit Pierre D3
11 Farinoman Fou C2
12 Jacquou Le Croquant B3
13 La Bidule B2
14 Le Bistrot C2
15 Le Petit Verdot A3

Drinking & Nightlife
16 Book in Bar C4
17 La Mado D3
18 Les Deux Garçons C3

Shopping
19 Flea Market C3
20 La Maison du Roy René B2
21 Morning Market C2

Hôtel Aquabella HOTEL €€
(☎04 42 99 15 00; www.aquabella.fr; 3 rue des Étuves; d from €130) Attached to Aix' thermal spa, this four-star hotel pulls out all the stops to pamper you during your stay: rates include access to the Sensory spa, which includes a Finnish sauna and two *hammams* (Turkish steam). The modern building itself hasn't much charm, but the rooms are contemporary and comfortable.

★ **Villa Gallici** HISTORIC HOTEL €€€
(☎04 42 23 29 23; www.villagallici.com; 18 av de la Violette; r from €350; P ❄ 📶 ≋) Baroque and beautiful, this fabulous villa was built as a private residence in the 18th century, and it still feels marvellously opulent. Rooms are more like museum pieces, stuffed with gilded mirrors, toile de Jouy wallpaper and filigreed furniture. There's a lovely lavender-filled garden to breakfast in, plus a super pool for lazy evening swims. It even has its own wine cellar.

Eating

Aix excels at Provençal cuisine, and restaurant terraces spill out across dozens of charm-heavy old-town squares, many pierced by an ancient stone fountain: place des Trois Ormeaux, place des Augustins, place Ramus and vast Forum des Cardeurs are particular favourites.

★ **Farinoman Fou** BOULANGERIE €
(www.farinomanfou.fr; 3 rue Mignet; breads €1-3; ⊙7am-7pm Tue-Sat) Tucked just off place des Prêcheurs is this truly phenomenal bakery, with a constant queue outside its door. The different crunchy breads baked by artisanal *boulanger* Benoît Fradette are reason enough to sell up and move to Aix. The bakery has no shop as such; customers jostle for space with bread ovens and dough-mixing tubs.

Le Bistrot BISTRO €
(☎04 42 23 34 61; 5 Rue Campra; plat du jour €9.90, 2-course lunch menu €15.90, mains €13-17; ⊙noon-2.30pm & 7.30-10pm Tue-Sat) Locals pack into the minuscule dining room of this ultra-traditional diner for the superb-value lunch menus. All the bistro boxes are ticked: red-and-white tablecloths, friendly old-school service, a chuffing coffee machine and a menu of classics like *daube provencal* (meat stew), chicken hotpot and grilled entrecôte. Extra points for the witty names: the chocolate mousse is called 'Look out, moustache-wearers.'

DON'T MISS

SWEET TREATS

Aix' sweetest treat since King René's wedding banquet in 1473 is the marzipan-like local speciality, *calisson d'Aix*, a small, diamond-shaped, chewy delicacy made on a wafer base with ground almonds and fruit syrup, and glazed with icing sugar. Traditional *calissonniers* still make them, including **La Maison du Roy René** (www.calisson.com; 13 rue Gaston de Saporta; ⊙9.30am-1pm & 2-6.30pm Mon-Sat, 9am-4pm Sun), which has a tiny museum, and whose factory on the edge of town is open for tours (€5).

La Bidule BISTRO €

(☎04 42 26 87 75; www.brasserielebidule.fr; 8 rue Lieutaud; 2-course lunch menu €13, mains €12.50-15; ⏲9am-11.30pm) The long square of Forum des Cardeurs has plenty of places to choose from, but 'The Thingy' is an old favourite: cheap and cheerful, with flowery PVC tablecloths, a vast blackboard menu and a fairy-lit terrace. Expect filling pastas, copious salads, big burgers and a classic *plat du jour* (dish of the day). Bargain lunch *menus* include a glass of wine or coffee.

Jacquou Le Croquant PROVENCAL €

(☎04 42 27 37 19; www.jacquoulecroquant.com; 2 rue de l'Aumône Vielle; plat du jour €11, 2-/3-course menu €20/25; ⏲noon-3pm & 7-11pm) Smack bang in the centre of old Aix, this jolly little restaurant specialises in southwestern cuisine, which means copious amounts of duck, rabbit and foie gras on the menu. There's a pleasing patio for sunny days.

★Bistrot Petit Pierre BISTRO €€

(Petit II R; ☎04 82 75 72 81; www.bistrotpetitpierre.com; 11 Petite Rue St-Jean; 2-course menus €19-34, 3-course menus €27-39; ⏲noon-2.30pm & 7.30-10.30pm Tue-Sat) Now that his flagship address has a new château location outside town, Pierre Reboul's Vieil Aix bistro is a must-visit for his innovative interpretations of French cuisine. The decor is playful (think acid-bright fabrics and lampshades made from pencils), and the menu ranges from 'southwest' burgers to shell-on scallops with asparagus risotto and saffron butter.

AIX-ELLENT MARKETS

At the daily **food market** (place Richelme; ⏲7am-noon), trestle tables groan under the weight of marinated olives, goat's cheese, garlic, lavender, honey, peaches, melons, cherries and a bounty of other sun-kissed seasonal food. Plane trees provide ample shade on the T-shaped square, endowed with a couple of corner cafes where Aixois catch up on the gossip over *un café* once their shopping is done.

Flower markets fill place des Prêcheurs (Sunday morning) and place de l'Hôtel de Ville (Tuesday, Thursday and Saturday mornings).

The **flea market** (place de Verdun; ⏲Tue, Thu & Sat mornings) has quirky vintage items three mornings a week.

★Le Petit Verdot FRENCH €€

(☎04 42 27 30 12; www.lepetitverdot.fr; 7 rue d'Entrecasteaux; mains €19-25; ⏲7pm-midnight Mon-Sat) Great Provençal food and great Provençal wines – really, what more do you want from a meal in this part of France? It's all about hearty, honest dining here, with table tops made out of old wine crates, and a lively chef-patron who runs the place with huge enthusiasm. Expect slow-braised meats, seasonal veg, sinful desserts and some super wines to go with.

Restaurant Pierre Reboul GASTRONOMIC €€€

(☎04 82 75 72 60; www.restaurant-pierre-reboul.com; 11 Petite Rue St-Jean; lunch menu €44, dinner menus €59-139; ⏲noon-2pm & 7-10pm) Pierre Reboul's renowned restaurant has moved out to a new location at the Château de la Pioline, a suitably smart location for his high-class cuisine. His rich, indulgent French fare meets flavours and ingredients cherry-picked from across the globe (like orange and pepper-infused lamb with a soy-ginger dressing). Rooms are sumptuous too. It's 8km southwest of town on the D65 towards the TGV station.

Drinking & Nightlife

The scene is fun but fickle. For nightlife, hit the student-friendly drinking dens on rue de la Verrerie and place Richelme. Open-air cafes crowd the city's squares, especially Forum des Cardeurs, place de Verdun and place de l'Hôtel de Ville (our favourite, for its more intimate scale and shady trees).

★Book in Bar CAFE

(☎04 42 26 54 41; www.bookinbar.com; 4 rue Joseph Cabassol; ⏲9am-7pm Mon-Sat) Bibliophiles rejoice: this brilliant Anglophile bookshop has a huge selection of English-language books for sale and a thoroughly pleasant tearoom. Look out for occasional book readings, jazz evenings etc.

La Mado CAFE

(Chez Madeleine; ☎04 42 38 28 02; 4 place des Prêcheurs; ⏲7am-2am) This smart cafe, with steel-grey parasols and box-hedged terrace on a busy square, is unbeatable for coffee and fashionable-people watching. Its food (lunch/dinner *menus* €18/32) is equally excellent.

Les Deux Garçons CAFE

(☎04 42 26 00 51; http://lesdeuxgarcons.fr; 53 cours Mirabeau; ⏲7am-2am) Cézanne and Zola once lingered in this classic brasserie-cafe, complete with snooty waiters in waistcoats

DON'T MISS

CÉZANNE SIGHTS

Circuit de Cézanne (Cézanne Trail) The life of local lad Paul Cézanne (1839–1906) is treasured in Aix. To see where he ate, drank, studied and painted, follow the Circuit de Cézanne, marked by bronze plaques embedded in the footpath. The essential English-language guide to the plaques and other artist-related sites, *In the Steps of Cézanne*, is free at the **tourist office** (p777).

Atelier Cézanne (☎04 42 21 06 53; www.atelier-cezanne.com; 9 av Paul Cézanne; adult/child €6/free; ⏰10am-6pm Jul & Aug, shorter hours Sep-Jun) Cézanne's last studio, 1.5km north of the tourist office on a hilltop, was painstakingly preserved (and re-created: not all the tools and still-life models strewn around the room were his) as it was at the time of this death. Though the studio is inspiring, none of his works hang there. Take bus 1 or 20 to the Atelier Cézanne stop or walk from town.

Terrain des Peintres A wonderful terraced garden perfect for a picnic, from where Cézanne, among others, painted the Montagne Ste-Victoire. The view of the jagged mountain is inspirational. The gardens are opposite 62 av Paul Cézanne. You'll find it a 10-minute walk uphill from the Atelier Cézanne stop (bus 1 or 20).

Carrières de Bibemus (Bibémus Quarries; ☎04 42 16 11 61; 3090 chemin de Bibémus; adult/child €6/free; ⏰tours from 9.45am daily Jun-Sep, from 10.30am Mon, Wed, Fri & Sun Apr-May & Oct, from 3pm Wed & Sat Nov-Mar) In 1895, Cézanne rented a *cabanon* (cabin) at the Carrières de Bibemus, on the edge of town, where he painted prolifically. Atmospheric one-hour tours of the ochre quarry take visitors on foot through the dramatic burnt-orange rocks that Cézanne captured so vividly on canvas. Book tours in advance at the tourist office, wear sturdy shoes and avoid wearing white. English-language tours usually run at 10.30am.

Bastide du Jas de Bouffan (☎04 42 16 11 61; adult/child €6/free; ⏰guided tours from 10.30am daily Jun-Sep, Tue, Thu & Sat May & Oct, Wed & Sat Nov-Mar) In 1859, Cézanne's father bought Le Jas de Bouffan, a country manor 4.5km west of Aix where Cézanne painted furiously, producing 36 oils and 17 watercolours in the decades that followed, depicting the house, farm, chestnut alley, green park and so forth. Visits are by guided tour only and should be reserved in advance at the tourist office. From April to October, there's an English-language tour at 2pm (or noon at other times of year). Take bus 6 from La Rotonde (av Victor Hugo) to the Corsy stop or walk the 20 minutes from town.

Montagne Ste-Victoire East of Aix towers Cézanne's favourite haunt, the magnificent silvery ridge of Montagne Ste-Victoire, its dry slopes carpeted in *garrigue* (scented scrub), lush pine forests, burnt-orange soil and Coteaux d'Aix-en-Provence vineyards. Many hike the mountain's north side, but the south side, though steeper, is quite beautiful. The mountain is closed July and August due to the threat of forest fire (though roads remain open). Driving the loop around Ste-Victoire is gorgeous, or catch bus 110 (www.lepilote.com) from La Rotonde in Aix to Payloubier/St-Antonin-sur-Bayon.

and a huge, chronically overpriced menu of bistro standards. Ignore the slow service and just enjoy sipping a *petit café* or, better still, a pastis sundowner.

ℹ Information

Tourist Office (☎04 42 16 11 61; www.aixenprovencetourism.com; 300 av Giuseppe Verdi; ⏰8.30am-7pm Mon-Sat, 10am-1pm & 2-6pm Sun, to 8pm Mon-Sat Jun-Sep; 📶) Touch screens add a high-tech air to the usual collection of brochures. Sells tickets for guided tours and cultural events, and has a shop selling regional souvenirs.

ℹ Getting There & Around

Consult www.lepilote.com for timetables, fares and itineraries for public transport journeys to/from Aix and www.navetteaixmarseille.com for shuttle buses to/from Marseille.

TO/FROM THE AIRPORT

Bus 40 runs from Aix to Aéroport Marseille Provence (€8.20, 40 minutes, every 30 minutes).

BICYCLE

Opposite the train station, **Electric Cycles** (☎04 42 39 90 37; www.aixenvelo.com; 12 rue Gustave Desplaces; per half-/full day €23/35; ⏰8.30am-5pm Mon-Sat) rents bikes with electrical motors and has mapped several itineraries around town.

BUS

Aix' **bus station** (☎04 42 91 26 80, 08 91 02 40 25; place Marius Bastard) is a 10-minute walk southwest from La Rotonde. Sunday service is limited. Most of the following services are run by LER (www.info-ler.fr):

Avignon (Line 23, €17.40, 1¼ hours, six daily)

Marseille (Line 20, €5.60, 25 minutes, every 10 minutes, five daily, three on Sunday)

Nice (Line 20, €29.40, 3¼ hours, five daily, three on Sunday)

Toulon (Line 19, €13.90, one hour, seven daily)

TRAIN

The **city centre train station**, at the southern end of av Victor Hugo, serves Marseille (€6.50, 45 minutes).

Aix' **TGV station**, 15km from the centre, is a stop on the high-speed Paris–Marseille line. Bus 40 runs from the TGV station to Aix' bus station (€4.10, 15 minutes, every 15 minutes).

Note that the direct Eurostar that connects London, Lyon, Avignon and Marseille does not stop at Aix' TGV station; to get to Aix, you have to change onto a connecting TGV at Lille or Paris.

ARLES & THE CAMARGUE

Forget all about time in this hauntingly beautiful part of Provence roamed by black bulls, white horses and pink flamingos. This is slow-go Provence, a timeless wetland chequered with silver salt pans, waterlogged rice paddies and movie-style cowboys. Birds provide the most action on this 780-sq-km delta wedged between the Petit Rhône and Grand Rhône. Grab your binoculars, squat in a shack between bulrushes and know, as another flamingo flits across the setting sun, that these magnificent waters, steeped in legend and lore, have a soul of their own.

The main town of the region, diminutive Arles, is a show-stopper. Wander the narrow golden-hued streets that inspired Van Gogh to find the town's lovely restored Roman amphitheatre, top-notch art and history museums, and world-class restaurants. It'll be hard to tear yourself away.

Arles

POP 53,600

Roman treasures, shady squares and plenty of Camarguais culture make Arles a seductive stepping stone into the Camargue. And if its colourful sun-baked houses evoke a sense of déjà vu, it's because you've seen them already on a Van Gogh canvas – the artist painted 200-odd works around town, but sadly his famous little 'yellow house' on place Lamartine, which he painted in 1888, was destroyed during WWII. Happily, the Fondation Vincent van Gogh brings in at least one work each season for its annual exhibition. Arles' Saturday market is also a must-see – it's one of Provence's best.

Sights

★Les Arènes ROMAN SITE

(Amphithéâtre; ☎08 91 70 03 70; www.arenes-arles.com; Rond-Point des Arènes; adult/child €6/free, incl Théâtre Antique €9/free; ⏲9am-8pm Jul & Aug, to 7pm May, Jun & Sep, shorter hours Oct-Apr) During the heyday of Roman Gaul, every important town had an amphitheatre, where gladiators fought to the death and wild animals met their (usually grisly) end. Few have survived, but Arles (like nearby Nîmes) has preserved its colosseum largely intact. At 136m long, 107m wide and 21m tall, built around AD 90, the oval-shaped amphitheatre would have held 21,000 baying spectators, and though the structure has suffered down the centuries, it's still evocative of the might and ambition of the Roman Empire.

★Fondation Vincent Van Gogh ART MUSEUM

(☎04 90 49 94 04; www.fondation-vincentvangogh-arles.org; 35ter rue du Docteur Fanton; adult/child €9/4; ⏲11am-7pm Tue-Sun Apr–mid-Sep, to 6pm mid-Sep–Mar) This Van Gogh–themed gallery is a must-see, as much for its contemporary architecture and design, as for the art it showcases. It has no permanent collection; rather, it hosts one or two excellent exhibitions a year, always with a Van Gogh theme and always including at least one Van Gogh masterpiece. Architectural highlights include the rooftop terrace and the coloured-glass bookshop ceiling. A joint ticket with the Musée Réattu is available for €12.

★Musée Réattu ART MUSEUM

(☎04 90 49 37 58; www.museereattu.arles.fr; 10 rue du Grand Prieuré; adult/child €8/free; ⏲10am-6pm Tue-Sun, to 5pm Dec-Feb) This splendid modern-art museum is housed in the exquisitely renovated 15th-century Grand Priory of the Knights of Malta. Among its collections are works by 18th- and 19th-century Provençal artists and two paintings and 57 sketches by Picasso. It hosts wonderfully curated cutting-edge exhibitions. A joint

Arles

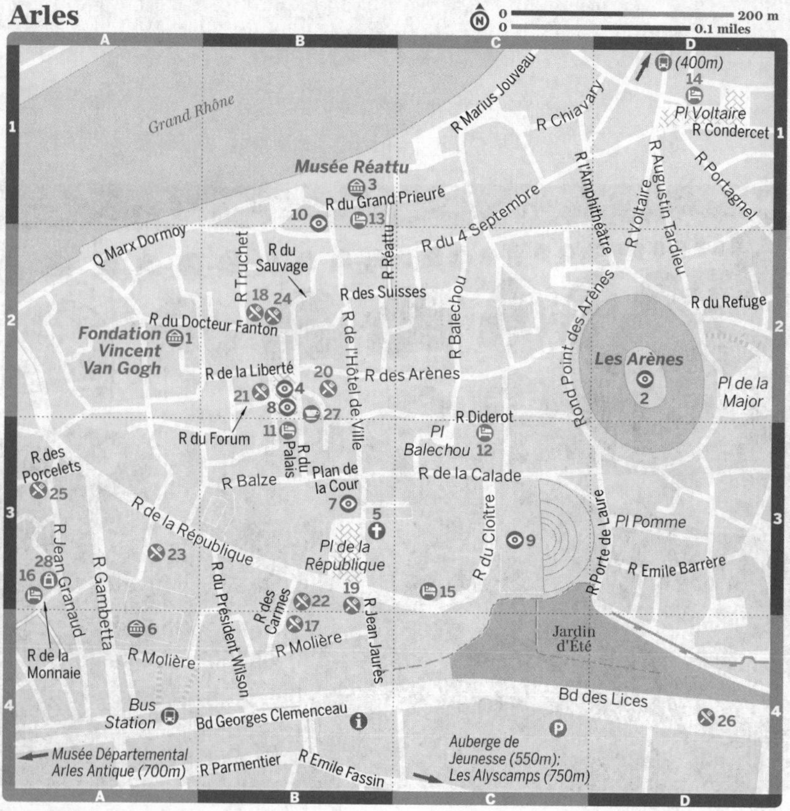

Arles

Top Sights
1 Fondation Vincent Van Gogh............... A2
2 Les Arènes D2
3 Musée Réattu...................................... B1

Sights
4 Cryptoportiques B2
5 Église St-Trophime............................ B3
6 Espace Van Gogh A4
7 Hôtel de Ville B3
8 Place du Forum................................... B2
9 Théâtre Antique.................................. C3
10 Thermes de Constantin B1

Sleeping
11 Grand Hôtel Nord Pinus..................... B3
12 Hôtel de l'Amphithéâtre..................... C3
13 Hôtel du Musée.................................. B1
14 Le Belvédère Hôtel D1
15 Le Cloître C3
16 L'Hôtel Particulier A3

Eating
17 À Côté.. B4
18 Au Brin de Thym................................. B2
19 Comptoir du Sud B3
20 Fad'Ola B2
21 Glacier Arlelatis B2
22 L'Atelier Jean-Luc Rabanel................ B3
23 L'Autruche A3
24 Le Galoubet B2
25 Le Gibolin A3
L'Ouvre Boîte...................................(see 15)
26 Marché d'Arles D4

Drinking & Nightlife
27 Café Van Gogh..................................... B2

Shopping
28 La Botte Camarguaise......................... A3

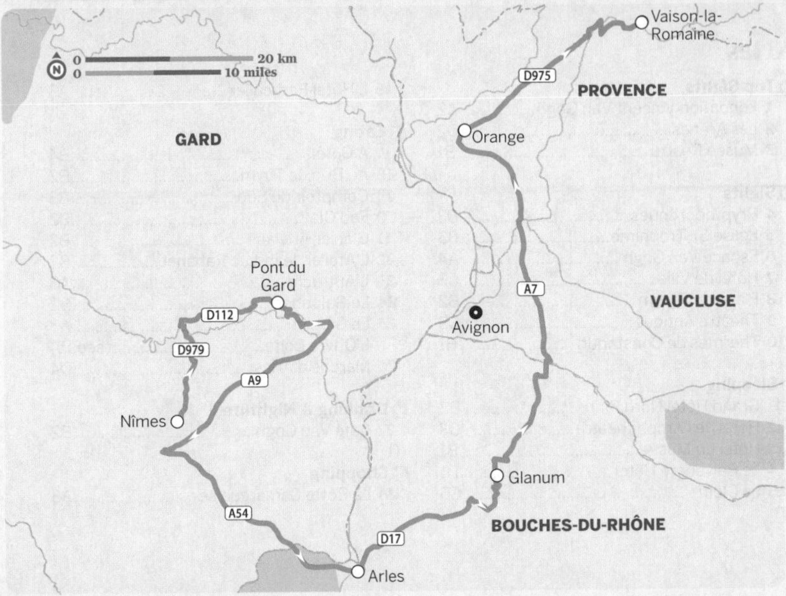
0 — 20 km
0 — 10 miles
Vaison-la-Romaine
D975
PROVENCE
Orange
GARD
A7
VAUCLUSE
Pont du Gard
D112
Avignon
D979
A9
Nîmes
Glanum
A54
BOUCHES-DU-RHÔNE
D17
Arles

PICAVET / GETTY IMAGES ©

PHILIP LANGE / SHUTTERSTOCK ©

Top: Pont du Gard (p714) Bottom: Roman obelisk in Place de la Republique, Arles (p778)

3 DAYS Roman Provence

Rome really flexed its imperial muscles in Southern France. Roman roads duck and dive across Roman bridges to theatres and arenas where you can grab a seat in the bleachers and watch the curtain rise. Let the show begin!

Though not technically in Provence, **Nîmes'** incredible Roman monuments are essential viewing (p710). The town's coat of arms – a crocodile chained to a palm tree – recalls the region's first sun-worshipping retirees: Julius Caesar's loyal legionnaires were granted land here to settle after hard years on the Nile campaigns. Two millennia later, Nîmes' intact 1st-century-AD amphitheatre and temple blend seamlessly with the modern town.

The Romans didn't do anything on a small scale and Unesco-listed **Pont du Gard** (p714), 21km northeast along the D9086, is no exception. At 50m this is the world's highest Roman monument. Traverse its awe-inspiring arches, and swim upstream for unencumbered views, or downstream to shaded wooden platforms made for flopping between dips.

Overnight in Uzès, returning south next morning along the D979 to Nîmes and A54 to **Arles** (p778) – count on an hour. Part of the Roman Empire from the 2nd century BC, Roman Arelate has a splendid amphitheatre, theatre and baths. Grab a coffee or ice on place du Forum, the hub of Roman social, political and religious life.

From Arles follow the D17, D78F and D5 north to **Glanum** (p789). Park by the roadside triumphal arch and spend the afternoon exploring the Roman archaeological site. Overnight 2km north in St-Rémy de Provence.

Day three, motor 50km along the A7 to **Orange** (p800). Roman monuments here are stunning and unusually old – from Augustus Caesar's rule (27 BC–AD 14). The stage wall of the Théâtre Antique dominates.

Push on along the D975 to **Vaison-la-Romaine** (p802) for a late lunch. Park on the river banks next to the Roman bridge (Pont Romain). Explore the ruins of the city that flourished here between the 6th and 2nd centuries BC and end with the archaeological museum which revives Vaison's Roman past with incredible swag.

WORTH A TRIP

A HILLTOP LUNCH

Reason enough to visit medieval Ventabren, a hilltop village 16km west of Aix-en-Provence, is Michelin-starred **La Table de Ventabren** (☎04 42 28 79 33; www.latabledeventabren.com; 1 rue Cézanne; lunch menu Wed-Sat €39, multi-course menus €65-92; ⏰noon-1.15pm Wed-Sun, 7.45-9.15pm Tue-Sun May-Sep, shorter hours rest of year), with its canvas-canopied terrace, magical on summer evenings. Inside find exposed stone and design-led details. Chef Dan Bessoudo creates inventive French dishes and out-of-this-world desserts. Afterwards, hike to the ruined Château de la Reine Jeanne for panoramic views.

ticket with the Fondation Vincent Van Gogh is available for €12.

Musée Départemental Arles Antique MUSEUM
(☎04 13 31 51 03; www.arles-antique.cg13.fr; av de la Première Division Française Libre; adult/child €8/5; ⏰10am-6pm Wed-Mon) This striking, state-of-the-art cobalt-blue museum perches on the edge of what used to be the Roman chariot-racing track (circus), 1.5km southwest of the tourist office. The rich collection of pagan and Christian art includes stunning mosaics and an entire wing dedicated to archaeological treasures highlighting Arles' commercial and maritime past.

Théâtre Antique ROMAN SITE
(☎04 90 96 93 30; bd des Lices; adult/child €6/free, joint ticket with Les Arènes €9/free; ⏰9am-7pm May-Sep, shorter hours rest of year) Still used for summertime concerts and plays, this outdoor theatre dates to the end of the 1st century BC. For hundreds of years it was a source of construction materials, with workers chipping away at the 102m-diameter structure (the column on the right-hand side near the entrance indicates the height of the original arcade). Enter on rue de la Calade.

Église St-Trophime CHURCH
(place de la République; church free, cloister adult/child €5.50/free; ⏰9am-7pm May-Sep, shorter hours rest of year) Arles was an archbishopric from the 4th century until 1790, and this Romanesque-style church was once a cathedral. Built in the late 11th and 12th centuries, it's named after St Trophime, an Arles bishop from the 2nd or 3rd century AD. On the western portal, the intricately **sculpted tympanum** depicts St Trophime holding a spiral staff. Inside, the **treasury** contains bone fragments of Arles' bishops. Occasional exhibitions are hosted in neighbouring cloister, **Cloître St-Trophime**.

Les Alyscamps CEMETERY
(av des Alyscamps; adult/child €4/free; ⏰9am-7pm May-Sep, shorter hours rest of year) Van Gogh and Gauguin both painted this necropolis, founded by the Romans 1km southwest of the city centre.

Thermes de Constantin ROMAN SITE
(rue du Grand Prieuré; adult/child €4/free; ⏰9am-7pm Jul & Aug, shorter hours rest of year) Partly preserved Roman baths that were built for Emperor Constantin's private use in the 4th century.

Place du Forum ROMAN SITE
Just as social, political and religious life revolved around the forum in Roman Arles so this busy plane-tree-shaded square buzzes with cafe life today. Underneath it lies the underground galleries of **Cryptoportiques** (adult/child €4.50/free; ⏰9am-noon & 2-7pm) – the forum's subterranean foundations and buried arcades (89m long and 59m wide). These were carved out – the plaza was lower in Roman times – in the 1st century BC.

Access is from the **Hôtel de Ville** (Town Hall; place de la République).

Espace Van Gogh GALLERY
(☎04 90 49 39 39; place Félix Rey) The former hospital where Van Gogh had his ear stitched and was later locked up – not to be confused with the asylum Monastère St-Paul de Mausole (p790) – hosts the occasional exhibition. Other times, its small courtyard garden is worth a peek.

Festivals & Events

Féria d'Arles BULLFIGHTING
(Féria de Pâques; www.feriaarles.com; ⏰Easter) Festival heralding the start of bullfighting season, with bullfighting in Les Arènes most Sundays in May and June.

Fête des Gardians CULTURAL
(⏰1 May) Mounted Camargue cowboys parade and hold games during this festival. It's an old and renowned event, and a fascinating insight into the tradition of the Camargue.

Fêtes d'Arles PERFORMING ARTS
(www.festivarles.com; ⊙ late Jun-early Jul) Dance, theatre, music and poetry over two weeks starting around late June.

L'Abrivado des Bernacles BULL PARADE
(www.feriaarles.com; ⊙ 1st Mon in Jul) Camargue *gardians* shepherd bulls for 15km from paddock to Les Arènes for the season's most prestigious *course Camarguaise* (p788), the **Cocarde d'Or**. Hundreds of aficionados on bike, scooter, foot and horseback follow the *gardians*.

Sleeping

Le Belvédère Hôtel BOUTIQUE HOTEL €
(04 90 91 45 94; www.hotellebelvedere-arles.com; 5 place Voltaire; s €50, d €57-95;) Prim, plain and proper, this straightforward hotel has some of the most reasonable rates in town. Downstairs, a striking scarlet-and-black lobby and breakfast room, lit by sculptural chandeliers; upstairs, smallish rooms in red, chocolate brown and grey, with arty photographic flower prints.

Hôtel du Musée BOUTIQUE HOTEL €
(04 90 93 88 88; www.hoteldumusee.com; 11 rue du Grand Prieuré; s/d/q from €65/75/120; ⊙ mid-Mar–Oct;) In a fine 17th- to 18th-century building, this impeccable hotel has comfortable rooms, a checkerboard-tiled breakfast room (breakfast €9.50) and a sweet patio garden brimming with pretty blossoms. Parking €12.

Auberge de Jeunesse HOSTEL €
(04 90 96 18 25; www.fuaj.org; 20 av Maréchal Foch; dm incl breakfast & sheets €20.10; ⊙ mid-Feb–mid-Dec, reception closed 10am-5pm) Modern, sheeny and spic-and-span, this efficient if rather characterless hostel is 10 minutes' walk from the city centre. The usual Fédération Unie des Auberges de Jeunesse (FUAJ) facilities are on offer – kitchen, lounge, cafe and dorms of varying sizes, plus a bar. Doors are locked at 11pm.

★ **Le Cloître** DESIGN HOTEL €€
(04 88 09 10 00; www.hotel-cloitre.com; 18 rue du Cloître; s €105, d €130-185;) Proving you don't need to spend a fortune for originality and imagination, the 19 rooms at this zingy hotel next to the Cloître Ste-Trophime combine history and modern design to winning effect: bold colours, funky patterns and retro furniture abound, and the rooftop terrace is a stunning sundowner spot. The lavish breakfast spread is (unusually) worth the €14 price tag. No elevator. Free bikes.

★ **Hôtel de l'Amphithéâtre** HISTORIC HOTEL €€
(04 90 96 10 30; www.hotelamphitheatre.fr; 5-7 rue Diderot; s €65, d €85-119, tr/ste €139/159;) This elegant address is quite a bargain: the standard of design here far outreaches the reasonable price tag. Antiques, rugs, fireplaces and staircases speak of the building's history, while minimal rooms nod to modern trends, and several have super views over Arles' rooftops (although you'll pay for the privilege).

★ **Grand Hôtel Nord Pinus** HERITAGE HOTEL €€€
(04 90 93 44 44; www.nord-pinus.com; place du Forum; r €170-420) An Arlésian landmark, this classy hotel has been frequented by everyone from famous bullfighters to artists and writers like Picasso, Hemingway, Jean Cocteau and Fritz Lang. It's chock-full of heritage: wrought-iron beds, art deco sinks, 20th-century furniture and vintage *féria* posters, as well as black-and-white photographs by Peter Beard downstairs. Room 10 is the grandest, and the bullfighters' favourite.

L'Hôtel Particulier BOUTIQUE HOTEL €€€
(04 90 52 51 40; www.hotel-particulier.com; 4 rue de la Monnaie; d/ste from €315/455; ⊙ Easter-Oct) This former private mansion has an air of aristocratic exclusivity around it, from the luminous all-white rooms to the rococo detailing, original fireplaces, elegant staircase and gorgeous *hammam* (Turkish steambath). The restaurant is top-class, too.

Eating

★ **Marché d'Arles** FOOD MARKET €
(bd des Lices; ⊙ 7am-1pm Sat) At Arles' enormous Saturday-morning market, Camargue salt, goats' milk cheese and *saucisson d'Arles* (bull-meat sausage) scent the air. The scene shifts to bd Émile Combes on Wednesday morning.

Fad'Ola SANDWICHES €
(04 90 49 70 73; 40 rue des Arènes; sandwiches €3.80-6.50, salads €4.50-15; ⊙ 11.30am-3pm & 7-10pm, shorter hours low season) Well-stuffed sandwiches – made to order, *frotté à l'ail* (rubbed with garlic) and dripping with silken AOC Vallée des Baux olive oil – lure the crowds to this tiny sandwich shop with a hole-in-the-wall takeaway counter. It also sells olive oil by the litre (€12 to €25). Find it footsteps from central 'cafe' square, place du Forum.

ROMAN COMBO PASS

Buy a pass for multiple sights at the Arles tourist office or any Roman site: **Passeport Avantage** (€16) covers the museums, both theatres, the baths, crypt, Les Alyscamps and the Cloître St-Trophime; the **Passeport Liberté** (€12) gives you the choice of a total of six sights, including two museums.

Glacier Arlelatis ICE CREAM €
(8 place du Forum; 1/2 scoops €2/4; ⏲12.30-11pm) Creamy, artisanal ice cream is the mainstay of this *glacier* on busy place du Forum. Buy a cone to take away or treat yourself to a magnificent whipped-cream-topped sundae sitting down. Flavours change but there's always a few distinctly Provençal ones: lavender honey, chestnut and so forth.

Comptoir du Sud CAFE €
(☎04 90 96 22 17; 2 rue Jean Jaurès; sandwiches €4.50-6; ⏲9am-5pm Tue-Fri) A great lunch option, with a counter brimming with picnicky treats – homemade pâtés, chutneys and cheeses, top-class charcuterie and bite-sized salads. There are a few bar stools to perch on, but most people order to go.

★Le Gibolin BISTRO €€
(☎04 88 65 43 14; 13 rue des Porcelets; lunch menu €16, dinner menus €27-34; ⏲12.15-2pm & 8-10.30pm Tue-Sat) After spending three decades plying Paris with their passion for organic wines, owners Brigitte and Luc decided to head south and open a new bistro and wine bar in Arles. Unsurprisingly, it's become a much-loved local fixture, known for its hearty home cooking and peerless wine list (mostly available by the glass).

À Côté BISTRO €€
(☎04 90 47 61 13; www.bistro-acote.com; 21 rue des Carmes; menus €32; ⏲noon-1.30pm & 7.30-9pm) A meal at Rabanel's high-flying *haute cuisine* restaurant may be a little rich for some budgets, but the grand chef knows how to do solid, no-fuss bistro dining too. It's reassuringly casual here, with wooden chairs and terrace-style tables, and the blackboard menu is solid bistro through and through – go for something like roast chicken or *brandade de morue* (salted cod, olive oil and garlic).

L'Ouvre Boîte TAPAS €€
(☎04 88 09 10 10; 22 rue du Cloître; dishes €6-12; ⏲7.30-9.30pm Thu-Sat) Alexandre's little joint (the 'Open Box') may only be open a few nights a week, but that hasn't prevented it from becoming a locals' favourite for chilled evening eats. He specialises in tapas-like 'little plates' – oysters, octopus in herby tomato sauce, pork in Asian broth – ordered to share. Arrive early for a prime table on the tiny, tree-shaded square.

Au Brin de Thym BISTRO €€
(☎04 90 97 85 18; brindethym@gmail.com; 22 rue du Docteur Fanton; menus from €25; ⏲noon-2pm & 7-9pm daily Apr-Sep, Thu-Mon Oct-Mar) A favourite recommendation for bistro dining, chilled in vibe and creative in execution. The menu is dictated by seasons and the best produce on offer from the market, so the choice can be limited, but everything's guaranteed fresh. Bull steak, grilled fish, lamb cutlets and sardine tart were the specials on the day we visited.

Le Galoubet BISTRO €€
(☎04 90 93 18 11; 18 rue du Docteur Fanton; menus €26-31; ⏲noon-2.30pm Mon-Sat, 7-9pm Tue-Sat) Stone walls, wooden bar, fireplace, friendly staff and dishes with a Provençal-Asian twist – what's not to like about this romantic, reliable bistro? Céline works the magic in the kitchen, while owner Franck runs the show. It's busy and buzzy, and usually full.

L'Autruche MODERN FRENCH €€
(☎04 90 49 73 63; 5 rue Dulau; lunch menus €18, mains €29; ⏲lunch & dinner Tue-Sat) This modern, inviting restaurant run by husband-and-wife team Fabien and Ouria assembles market-fresh dishes to perfection. For example, the Michelin-experienced chef layers thin strips of Granny Smith apple chutney with a superbly prepared foie gras. Extravagant desserts are a treat.

★L'Atelier Jean-Luc Rabanel GASTRONOMIC €€€
(☎04 90 91 07 69; www.rabanel.com; 7 rue des Carmes; menus €85-145; ⏲sittings begin noon-1pm & 8-9pm Wed-Sun) Offering as much an artistic experience as a meal (and graced with double Michelin stars), this is the gastronomic home of charismatic chef Jean-Luc Rabanel. Many products are sourced from the chef's veggie patch and wine pairings are an adventure in themselves. Half-day cooking classes are also available, with/without

lunch €200/145. Next door, Rabanel's À Côté offers bistro fare.

Drinking & Nightlife

Café Van Gogh CAFE

(11 place du Forum) The Roman place du Forum, shaded by outstretched plane trees, turns into a giant dining table at lunch and dinner during summer. It's also where you'll find Café la Nuit, thought to be the subject of Van Gogh's *Café Terrace at Night* (1888), painted bright yellow to re-create Vincent's depiction of night-time lights.

Shopping

La Botte Camarguaise SHOES

(☎06 16 04 08 14; 22 rue Jean Granaud; ⏰9am-12.30pm & 2-6.30pm Mon-Fri, 7am-noon Sat) Buy a pair of handmade Camargue-style cowboy boots.

Information

Tourist Office (☎04 90 18 41 20; www.arlestourisme.com; esplanade Charles de Gaulle, Blvd des Lices; ⏰9am-6.45pm Apr-Sep, 9am-4.45pm or 5.45pm Mon-Fri, 10am-1pm Sun Oct-Mar; 📶) Sells Arles' two sightseeing passes, and also has some useful leaflets on cycling and walking itineraries.

Getting There & Around

BICYCLE

Europbike (☎06 38 14 49 50; www.europbike-provence.net; per day adult €10-18, child €8, electric e-bike €35; ⏰8am-6pm) Rents bikes and runs tours.

BUS

Most buses leave from the central **bus station** (☎08 10 00 08 16; www.lepilote.com; 24 bd Georges Clemenceau): there are three different companies, so for up-to-date timetables, consult www.lepilote.com, www.edgard-transport.fr or www.envia.fr. Destinations include the following:

Aix-en-Provence (€11, AllôCartreize Line 18, 1¼ hours, two hourly Monday to Friday, four daily on weekends)

Nîmes (€1.50, Edgard Line C30, one hour, hourly Monday to Saturday, two on Sunday)

Stes Marie-de-la-Mer (€2.50, Envia Line 20, one hour, six daily Monday to Saturday)

TRAIN

The **train station** (av Paulin Talabot) has services to Nîmes (from €7.50, 30 to 60 minutes), Marseille (€13, one hour) and Avignon (€6, 20 minutes). The closest TGV stations are in Avignon and Nîmes.

Camargue Countryside

Just south of Arles, Provence's rolling landscapes yield to the flat, marshy wilds of the Camargue, famous for teeming birdlife – roughly 500 species, from grey herons and little egrets to avocets and oystercatchers, as well as the candy-pink flamingo, which enjoys the mild winters of these expansive wetlands. Equally famous are the Camargue's small white horses, watched over by local cowboys known as *gardians*.

It's a great area for wildlife-watching and birdspotting, particularly within the boundaries of the 850-sq-km **Parc Naturel Régional de Camargue** (www.parc-camargue.fr) and the 600-sq-km lagoon Étang de Vaccarès. Bring binoculars and plenty of mosquito repellent – the still marshes might be beautiful, but they're a perfect breeding ground for the biting blighters.

The Camargue's two largest towns are the seaside pilgrim's outpost Stes-Maries-de-la-Mer and, to the northwest, the walled town of Aigues-Mortes.

Sights & Activities

The Camargue is a traditional region, and that's reflected in its food: it's hearty and bold in flavours, with some unusual ingredients on the menu, such as *taureau* (bull) and locally farmed salt. Seafood is a highlight, particularly on the coast.

★Parc Ornithologique du Pont de Gau PARK

(☎04 90 97 82 62; www.parcornithologique.com; D570, Pont du Gau; adult/child €7.50/5; ⏰9am-sunset Apr-Sep, from 10am Oct-Mar) For that pink flamingo photo op, this wetland is the place. It's home to all the Camargue's big-ticket birds, including herons, storks, egrets, teals and grebes, as well as those fabulous flamingos. The reserve has 7km of trails, although what you see depends on the time of year and your own bird-spotting skills. Flamingo breeding season is between April and June, but with luck, you should spot them until September. The reserve is on the D570 4km north of Stes-Maries-de-la-Mer.

★Domaine de la Palissade PARK

(☎04 42 86 81 28; www.palissade.fr; rte de la Mer; adult/child €3/free; ⏰9am-6pm mid-Jun–mid-Sep, to 5pm Mar–mid-Jun & mid-Sep–Oct, 9am-5pm Wed-Sun Feb & Nov, closed Dec-Jan) This remote nature centre, 12km south of Salin de Giraud, organises fantastic forays through

marshland, scrubby glasswort, flowering sea lavender (August) and lagoons, on foot and horseback; call ahead to book horse treks (€18 per hour). Before hitting the scrub, rent binoculars (€2) and grab a free map of the estate's three marked walking trails (1km to 8km) from the office.

Musée de la Camargue MUSEUM
(Musée Camarguais; ☎04 90 97 10 82; www.parc-camargue.fr; D570, Mas du Pont de Rousty; adult/child €5/free, free 1st Sun of month; ⏲9am-12.30pm & 1-6pm Wed-Mon Apr-Oct, 10am-12.30pm & 1-5pm Nov-Mar) Inside a 19th-century sheep shed 10km southwest of Arles, this museum evokes traditional life in the Camargue, with exhibitions covering history, ecosystems, farming techniques, flora and fauna. *L'Oeuvre Horizons* by Japanese artist Tadashi Kawamata – aka a wooden observatory shaped like a boat – provides a bird's-eye view of the agricultural estate, crossed by a 3.5km walking trail. The headquarters of the Parc Naturel Régional de Camargue are also based here.

La Capelière PARK
(☎04 90 97 00 97; www.reserve-camargue.org; La Capelière; permits adult/child €3/1.50; ⏲9am-1pm & 2-6pm daily Apr-Sep, 9am-1pm & 2-5pm Wed-Mon Oct-Mar;) This information centre for the **Réserve Nationale de Camargue** (www.reserve-camargue.org) sells permits for the observatories and 4.5km of nature trails at the wild **Salin de Badon**, former royal salt pans 7km south. True birders must not miss a night in its **gîte** (dm €12), a cottage with 20 beds over seven rooms, kitchen, toilet and solar electricity. BYO food, drinking water, bedding and mosquito spray. At La Capelière's 1.5km-long **Sentier des Rainettes** (Tree-Frog Trail) discover flora and fauna native to freshwater marshes.

Manade des Baumelles BULL FARM
(☎04 90 97 84 14; www.manadedesbaumelles.com; D38; bull-farm tour with/without lunch €45/25) The *manade* (bull farm) provides an authentic opportunity to spend a morning with Camargue 'cowboys', learn about farm life and bull breeding, and watch cowboys at work in the field from the safety of a tractor-pulled truck. Tours end with an optional farm lunch. Find the *manade* a few kilometres north of Stes-Maries-de-la-Mer, at the end of a gravel track off the D38 towards Aigues-Mortes.

Cabanes de Cacharel HORSE RIDING
(☎04 90 97 84 10, 06 11 57 74 75; www.cabanes-decacharel.com; rte de Cacharel, D85A; 1/2/3hr horse trek €20/30/40) Farms along rte d'Arles (D570) offer *promenades à cheval* (horseback riding) astride white Camargue horses, but a more authentic experience can be had at these stables, just north of Stes-Maries-de-la-Mer along the parallel rte de Cacharel (D85A). It also offers one-hour horse-and-carriage rides (€15) and can arrange tours where you get to experience the life of a traditional *gardian* (Camargue cowboy).

Kayak Vert Camargue CANOEING
(☎04 66 73 57 17; www.kayakvert-camargue.fr; Mas de Sylvéréal; kayak 1hr/day €10/32; ⏲7am-7pm Mar-Oct) For canoeing and kayaking on the Petit Rhône, contact Kayak Vert Camargue, 14km north of Stes-Maries-de-la-Mer off the D38.

Sleeping

★**Cacharel Hotel** HOTEL €€
(☎04 90 97 95 44; www.hotel-cacharel.com; rte de Cacharel, D85A; s/d/tr/q €132/144/156/178, horse riding per hour €32; ⏲year-round;) This isolated farmstead, 400m down an unpaved track off the D85A just north of Stes-Maries-de-la-Mer, perfectly balances modern-day comforts with rural authenticity. Photographic portraits of the bull herder who created the hotel in 1947 (son Florian runs the three-star hotel with much love today) give the vintage dining room soul. Rooms sit snug in whitewashed cottages, some overlooking the water.

Swings in the paddock, horse riding with a *gardian* (cowboy), boules to play *pétanque* and bags of open space make it a perfect family choice.

★**Mas de Calabrun** HOTEL €€
(☎04 90 97 82 21; www.mas-de-calabrun.fr; rte de Cacherel, D85A; d €129-169, wagons from €139; ⏲mid-Feb–mid-Nov;) From the striking equestrian sculpture in its front courtyard to the swish pool, stylish restaurant terrace and fabulous views of open Camargue countryside, this hotel thoroughly deserves its three stars. The icing on the cake, however, is its trio of *roulottes* (old-fashioned 'gypsy' wagons), which promise the perfect romantic getaway. Breakfast buffet €15.

★**Le Mas de Peint** BOUTIQUE HOTEL €€€
(☎04 90 97 20 62; www.masdepeint.com; Le Sambuc; d from €245; ⏲mid-Mar–mid-Nov;) This genteel farmhouse-hotel is very upmar-

ket, but has retained design elements that nod to its rural roots: solid beams, wooden furniture, saddles on the walls, a bull's head in the lobby. But it's the rustic **restaurant** (lunch/dinner menus from €41/59, mains €17-35; ⌚lunch Sat & Sun, dinner Fri-Wed) most people come for – you can watch chefs work from the dining room, or eat on the lovely poolside terrace.

The hotel also has horses to ride, and offers flamenco, bull-herding and birdwatching weekends.

Eating

★Le Mazet du Vaccarès CAMARGUAIS €€

(Chez Hélène et Néné; ☎04 90 97 10 79; www.mazet-du-vaccares.fr; south of Méjanes; 3-course menu €35; ⌚10am-11pm Fri-Sun, closed mid-Aug–mid-Sep & mid-Dec–mid-Jan) Gorging on fish in this legendary lakeside cabin is a feast for the eyes and belly. Memorabilia from Hélène and Néné's days as lighthouse keepers in Beauduc fill the restaurant with soul. The jovial couple cook up one fixed *menu* built from the catch of local fishers. From Domaine Paul Ricard, it is a signposted 2.5km drive south along potholed gravel.

★La Telline CAMARGUAIS €€

(☎04 90 97 01 75; www.restaurantlatelline.fr; rte de Gageron, Villeneuve; mains €24-35; ⌚noon-1.15pm & 7.30-9pm Fri-Mon) A true local favourite, this isolated cottage restaurant with sage-green wooden shutters could not be simpler or more authentic. Summer dining is in a small and peaceful flower-filled garden, and the no-frills menu cooks up a straightforward choice of *tellines* (edible molluscs), salad or terrine as starter followed by grilled fish or meat, or a beef or bull steak. No credit cards.

Chez Bob CAMARGUAIS €€

(☎04 90 97 00 29; www.restaurantbob.fr; Mas Petite Antonelle, rte du Sambuc, Villeneuve; menu €45; ⌚noon-2pm & 7.30-9pm Wed-Sun) This house restaurant is an iconic address adored by Arlésians. Feast on grilled bull chops, duck breasts and lamb beneath trees or inside between walls plastered in photos, posters and other memorabilia collected over the years by Jean-Guy alias 'Bob'. Find his pad 20km south of Arles in Villeneuve, 800m after the crossroads on the D37 towards Salin. Reserve online.

★La Chassagnette GASTRONOMIC €€€

(☎04 90 97 26 96; www.chassagnette.fr; rte du Sambuc; 7-course menu €95, 5-course menu with wine €125, mains €36-42; ⌚noon-1.30pm & 7-9.30pm Thu-Mon Mar-Jun, Sep & Oct, daily Jul & Aug, reduced hours Nov-Mar) Surrounded by a vast *potager* (kitchen garden), which supplies practically all the restaurant's produce, this renowned gourmet table is run by Armand Amal, a former pupil of Alain Ducasse. The multi-course *menus* are full of surprises, and the bucolic setting is among the loveliest anywhere in the Camargue. It's 12km southeast of Arles on the D36.

Getting There & Around

Touring the tiny roads criss-crossing this flat, wild region is best done by car or bicycle. For the Marseille-bound, the Bac de Barcarin provides a car ferry (€5) across the Grand Rhône from Salin de Giraud.

Stes-Maries-de-la-Mer

POP 2400

This remote seaside outpost has a rough-and-tumble holidaymaker feel, with white-washed buildings crowding dusty streets. During its Roma pilgrimages, street-cooked pans of paella fuel chaotic crowds of carnivalesque guitarists, dancers and mounted cowboys. Tickets for bullfights and *courses Camarguaises* are sold at the seafront village arena.

Sights & Activities

Stes-Maries-de-la-Mer is fringed by 30km of fine-sand beaches, easily reached by bicycle. Nudist beaches surround the Gacholle lighthouse off the Digue à la Mer.

Église des Stes-Maries CHURCH

(www.sanctuaire-des-saintesmaries.fr; place Jean XXIII; rooftop €2.50; ⌚rooftop 10am-noon & 2-5pm Mon-Sat, 2-5pm Sun) This 12th- to 15th-century church, with its dark, hushed, candle-wax-scented atmosphere, draws legions of pilgrim Roma to venerate the statue of Sara, their revered patron saint, during the Pèlerinage des Gitans. The relics of Sara and those of Marie-Salomé and Marie-Jacobé, all found in the crypt by King René in 1448, are enshrined in a wooden chest, stashed in the stone wall above the choir. Don't miss the panorama from the rooftop terrace.

Digue à la Mer DIKE

FREE This 2.5m-high dike was built in the 19th century to cut the delta off from the sea. A 20km-long walking and cycling track runs along its length linking Stes-Maries with the solar-powered **Phare de la Gacholle** (1882),

a lighthouse automated in the 1960s. Footpaths cut down to lovely sandy beaches and views of pink flamingos strutting across the marshy planes are second to none. Walking on the fragile sand dunes is forbidden.

Le Vélo Saintois CYCLING
(☎04 90 97 74 56; www.levelosaintois.camargue.fr; 19 rue de la République; per day adult/child €15/13.50, tandem €30; ⏰9am-7pm Mar-Nov) This bike-rental outlet has bikes of all sizes, including tandems and kids' wheels. Helmets cost an extra €1 per day and a free brochure details four circular cycling itineraries (26km to 44km, four hours to eight hours) starting in Stes-Maries-de-la-Mer. Free hotel delivery.

Le Vélociste CYCLING
(☎04 90 97 83 26; www.levelociste.fr; place Mireille; per day adult/child €15/13.50; ⏰9am-7pm Mar-Nov) This bike-rental shop rents wheels, advises on cycling itineraries (24km to 70km, four hours to nine hours) and organises fun one-day combined cycling and horse-riding (€30/40 with one-/two-hour horse ride) or cycling and canoeing packages (€30). Free hotel delivery.

Les Quatre Maries BOATING
(☎04 90 97 70 10; www.bateaux-4maries.camargue.fr; 36 av Théodore Aubanel; adult/child per 90min €12/6; ⏰mid-Mar–Oct) Power-boat company offering trips through the marshy Camargue.

Sleeping

Most places operate April to October.

Hôtel Méditerranée HOTEL €
(☎04 90 97 82 09; www.hotel-mediterranee.camargue.fr; 4 av Frédéric Mistral; d/tr/q from €48/75/85; ⏰mid-Mar–mid-Nov; ❄) This whitewashed cottage hotel, festooned with an abundance of flower pots steps from the sea, is truly a steal. Its 14 rooms – three with their own little terrace garden – are spotlessly clean, and breakfast (€7) is served in summer on a pretty vine-covered patio garden – equally festooned with strawberry plants, geraniums and other potted flowers. Bike rental costs €15 per day.

Camping Le Clos du Rhône CAMPGROUND €
(☎04 90 97 85 99; www.camping-leclos.fr; rte d'Aigues Mortes; tent, car & 2 adults €26.50; ⏰Apr-Oct; @📶🏊) Right by the beach, this large and well-equipped camping ground sports the whole range of accommodation options: tent pitches, wooden chalets, self-catering cottages. The pool with two-lane water slide and a beachside spa with Jacuzzi and *hammam* make it a real family favourite.

★**Lodge Sainte Hélène** BOUTIQUE HOTEL €€€
(☎04 90 97 83 29; www.lodge-saintehelene.com; chemin Bas des Launes; d €150-190; ❄@📶🏊) These designer-chic, pearly white terraced cottages strung along a lake edge are prime real estate for birdwatchers and romance seekers. The mood is exclusive, remote and so quiet you can practically hear flamingo wings flapping overhead. Each room comes with a birdwatchers' guide and binoculars, and dynamic owner Benoît Noel is a font of local knowledge. Breakfast €15.

CAMARGUE CULTURE

The *course Camarguaise* is a local Camargue variation of the bull fight, but one in which the bulls aren't harmed. It sees amateur *razeteurs* (from the word 'shave') wearing skin-tight white shirts and trousers, get as close as they dare to the *taureau* (bull) to try to snatch rosettes and ribbons tied to the bull's horns, using a *crochet* (a razor-sharp comb) held between their fingers. Their leaps over the arena's barrier as the bull charges make spectators' hearts lurch.

Bulls are bred on a *manade* (bull farm) by *manadiers*, who are helped in their daily chores by *gardians* (Camargue cattle-herding cowboys). These mounted herdsmen parade through Arles during the **Fête des Gardians** (p782) in May.

Many *manades* also breed the creamy white *cheval de Camargue* (Camargue horse) and some welcome visitors; ask at tourist offices in Arles and Stes-Maries-de-la-Mer.

A calendar of *courses Camarguaises* is online at the **Fédération Française de la Course Camarguaise** (French Federation of Camargue Bullfights; ☎04 66 26 05 35; www.ffcc.info), with many occurring at the arena in Stes-Maries-de-la-Mer. *Recortadores* (a type of bull-baiting with lots of bull-jumping) also happens during the bullfighting season (Easter to September).

Eating

★Ô Pica Pica SEAFOOD €€

(☎06 10 30 33 49; www.degustationcoquillages-lessaintesmariesdelamer.com; 16 av Van Gogh; mains €17-25; ⊙noon-3pm & 7-11pm Mar-Nov) Fish and shellfish do not come fresher than this. Watch them get gutted, filleted and grilled in the 'open' glass-walled kitchen, then devour your meal on the sea-facing pavement terrace or out the back in the typically Mediterranean white-walled garden. Simplicity is king here: plastic glasses, fish cooked *à la plancha* and shellfish platters. No coffee and no credit cards.

★La Cabane aux Coquillages SEAFOOD €

(☎06 10 30 33 49; www.degustationcoquillages-lessaintesmariesdelamer.com; 16 av Van Gogh; shellfish €8.50-12.50; ⊙noon-3pm & 5-11pm Apr-Nov) Seafood is the only thing worth its salt in Stes-Maries. Part of the excellent Ô Pica Pica restaurant, this attractive little shack specialises in *coquillages* (shellfish), including oysters, *palourdes* (clams), *coques* (cockles), *tellines* (a type of local shellfish known elsewhere in France as *pignons*) and *fritures* (deep-fried and battered baby prawns, baby squid or anchovies).

Information

Tourist Office (☎04 90 97 82 55; www.saintesmaries.com; 5 av Van Gogh; ⊙9am-7pm) Guided walking tours (€7) depart 2pm Tuesday and Friday.

Getting There & Away

Buses to/from Arles (Line L20; www.lepilote.com; €2.90, one hour, four to eight daily depending on school term times) use the bus shelter at the northern entrance to town on av d'Arles (the continuation of rte d'Arles and the D570).

LES ALPILLES

This silvery chain of low, jagged mountains strung between the Rivers Durance and Rhône delineates a *très* chic side of Provence, notably around upmarket St-Rémy-de-Provence, known for fine restaurants and summertime celebrity-spotting. The entire region is full of gastronomic delights – AOC olive oil, vineyards and Michelin-starred restaurants. History comes to life at magnificent ruined castles and at one of Provence's best Roman sites, the ancient city of Glanum.

WORTH A TRIP

AIGUES-MORTES

The picturesque town of Aigues-Mortes sits 28km northwest of Stes-Maries-de-la-Mer at the western extremity of the Camargue. Set in flat marshland and encircled by high stone walls, the town was established in the mid-13th century by Louis IX to give the French crown a Mediterranean port under its direct control. Scaling the ramparts rewards you with sweeping views, and cobbled streets inside the walls are lined with restaurants, cafes and bars, giving it a festive atmosphere and making it a charming spot from which to explore the Camargue.

The **tourist office** (☎04 66 53 73 00; www.ot-aiguesmortes.fr; place St-Louis; ⊙9am-6pm) is inside the walled city.

St-Rémy-de-Provence

POP 10,826

See-and-be-seen St-Rémy has an unfair share of gourmet shops and restaurants – in the spirit of the town's most famous son, prophecy-maker Nostradamus, we predict you'll need to let your belt out a notch. Come summer, the jet set wanders the peripheral boulevard and congregates at place de la République, leaving the quaint historic centre strangely deserted. The low season is quiet.

Sights

Pick up the free **Carte St-Rémy** at the first sight you visit, get it stamped, then benefit from reduced admission at St-Rémy's other sights.

★Site Archéologique de Glanum ROMAN SITES

(☎04 90 92 23 79; www.site-glanum.fr; rte des Baux-de-Provence; adult/child €7.50/free, parking €2.70; ⊙9.30am-6.30pm Apr-Sep, 10am-5pm Oct-Mar, closed Mon Sep-Mar) Though Provence's other Roman sites often take precedence, you'll get a better sense of the reality of everyday life in Gaul by wandering around the ruined Gallo-Roman city of Glanum. Established around a sacred spring in the 3rd century, the remains of this once-thriving town are still clear to see – complete with baths, forum, columns, marketplace, temples and houses. A triumphal arch (AD 20)

and mausoleum (30 to 20 BC) mark the entrance, 2km south of St-Rémy.

★Monastère St-Paul de Mausole HISTORIC SITE
(☎04 90 92 77 00; www.saintpauldemausole.fr; adult/child €5/free; ⏲9.30am-6.30pm Apr-Sep, 10.15am-4.30pm Oct-Mar, closed Jan–mid-Feb) This monastery turned asylum is famous for one of its former residents – the ever-volatile Vincent van Gogh, who admitted himself in 1889. Safe within the monastery's cloistered walls, Vincent enjoyed his most productive period, completing 150-plus drawings and around 150 paintings, including his famous *Irises*. A reconstruction of his room is open to visitors, as are a Romanesque **cloister** and **gardens** growing flowers that feature in his work.

From the monastery entrance, a **walking trail** is marked by colour panels, showing where the artist set up his easel.

St-Paul remains a psychiatric institution: an exhibition room sells artwork created by patients.

Festivals & Events

Fête de la Transhumance EVENT
(⏲May/Jun) On Pentacost Monday thousands of sheep pack the streets before departing to the mountains for summer.

Sleeping

Le Sommeil des Fées HOTEL €
(☎04 90 92 17 66; www.angesetfees-stremy.com; 4 rue du 8 Mai 1945; r incl breakfast €65-85) Upstairs from La Cuisine des Anges, this cosy B&B has five rooms all named after characters from Arthurian legend, blending Provençal and Andalucian decorative details.

Hôtel Canto Cigalo HOTEL €
(☎04 90 92 14 28; www.cantocigalo.com; 8 chemin Canto Cigalo; d €75-98; ❄@📶🏊) Staying in St-Rémy is pricey, which makes this cute little apricot-coloured hotel a bit of a bargain. It's frill and feminine in style, with rooms decorated in dusty rose, with wicker and white-wood furniture, and sky-blue shutters. The pool is lovely too. Breakfast is €9.50; there's a gluten/lactose-free option for €11.

★Sous les Figuiers BOUTIQUE HOTEL €€
(☎04 32 60 15 40; www.hotelsouslesfiguiers.com; 3 av Gabriel St-René Taillandier; d €99-121, tr €189; P❄@📶) A five-minute walk from town, this country-chic house hotel has 14 art-filled rooms facing a leafy garden – lovely for unwinding after a day's explorations. The owner is a painter (who runs half-day classes costing €85 per person) and has exquisite taste, marrying design details like velvet and distressed wood, Moroccan textiles and rich colour palettes. Breakfast €13.50.

Eating

St-Rémy has some superb cafes and bakeries, but restaurant prices tend to be on the high side. Market day is on Wednesday and is a magnet for sightseers and locals alike.

Maison Cambillau BOULANGERIE €
(1 rue Carnot; fougasses & sandwiches €2.60-3; ⏲7.30am-1.30pm & 3-7.30pm Fri-Wed) Well-stuffed *fougasse* (Provençal flatbread) and baguettes with a variety of tasty fillings make this well-established *boulangerie* (bakery) the perfect spot to stock up on a picnic. Complete the takeaway feast with a feisty meringue, bag of nougat, nutty florentine or almond- and pistachio-studded *crousadou*.

Les Filles du Pâtissier CAFE €
(☎06 50 61 07 17; 3 place Favier; mains €15-20; ⏲10am-10pm, closed Wed Apr-Oct) Particularly perfect on sultry summer nights, this upbeat, colourful cafe has vintage tables filling one corner of a delightful car-free square in the old town. Its daily-changing menu features market-driven salads and tarts, and come dusk it morphs into a wine bar with charcuterie plates and occasional live music. Don't miss the homemade *citronnade* (lemonade) and melon-fizz soda.

La Cuisine des Anges BISTRO €€
(☎04 90 92 17 66; www.angesetfees-stremy.com; 4 rue du 8 Mai 1945; 2-course menu €25-27, 3-course menu €29; ⏲noon-2.30pm & 7.30-11pm

WORTH A TRIP

THE ALCHEMIST'S GARDEN

Eleven kilometres east of St-Rémy, the fascinating **Jardin de l'Alchimiste** (☎04 90 90 67 67; www.jardin-alchimiste.com; Mas de la Brune, Eygalières; adult/child €8/3; ⏲10am-6pm daily May, 10am-6pm Sat & Sun Jun-Sep), inspired by the nearby 16th-century house of an alchemist, is planted in arcane medieval patterns and filled with blossoming trees and herbs reputed to hold mystical properties. It's a magical destination for a Sunday-afternoon drive.

LOCAL KNOWLEDGE

SUPER-STYLISH BOUTIQUE SHOPPING

Joël Durand (☎04 90 92 38 25; www.joeldurand-chocalatier.fr; 3 bd Victor Hugo; ⏲9.30am-12.30pm & 2.30-7.30pm) Among France's top chocolatiers, using Provençal herbs and plants – lavender, rosemary, violet and thyme – with unexpected flavours such as Earl Grey.

Espace Anikado (☎04 90 94 53 22; www.anikado.canalblog.com; 1 bd Marceau; ⏲10.30am-6.30pm) There is no finer shop for vibrant local art, craft and design than Espace Anikado. The hybrid boutique-gallery showcases fashion, jewellery, shoes, furniture and more by local designers. It also hosts Provençal art exhibits.

Moulin à Huile du Calanquet (☎04 32 60 09 50; www.moulinducalanquet.fr; Vieux Chemin d'Arles; ⏲9am-noon & 2-6.30pm Mon-Sat, plus Sun Apr-Oct) Brother-and-sister-run olive-oil mill located 4.5km southwest of St-Rémy, with tastings and homemade tapenade, fruit juice and jam.

Mon, Wed, Sat & Sun, 7.30-11pm Thu & Fri; ❄📶) Packed with locals and tourists, this casual *maison d'hôte* (B&B) has been around for an age and just doesn't lose its edge. Light Provençal dishes are derived from organic local ingredients and served in the interior patio or wooden-floored dining room with textured paintings and zinc-topped tables. Upstairs is a cute B&B, Le Sommeil des Fées.

★**Maison Drouot** MODERN FRENCH €€€
(☎04 90 15 47 42; www.maisondrouot.blogspot.fr; 150 rte de Maillane/D5; menus lunch €23-49, dinner €45-65; ⏲12.30-2.30pm & 7.30-11pm Wed-Sun) Stuck on where to head for lunch? Stop fretting and head five minutes out of town to this 19th-century oil mill, now a charming country bistro where nearly every dish is based on ingredients sourced from local suppliers. The interior is contemporary, the architecture is classic and the terrace, shaded by a vine-covered pergola, is irresistibly seductive. Look out for the turning opposite supermarket Intermarché on the D5 towards Maillane.

ℹ Information

Tourist Office (☎04 90 92 05 22; www.saintremy-de-provence.com; place Jean Jaurès; ⏲9.15am-12.30pm & 2-6.30pm Mon-Sat, 10am-12.30pm Sun mid-Apr–mid-Oct, shorter hours rest of year) Helpful, with transport schedules, walking maps of town and Van Gogh sites, and summertime guided tours (book ahead).

ℹ Getting There & Around

BICYCLE

Rentals and free delivery within a 20km radius of St-Rémy from **Telecycles** (☎04 90 92 83 15; www.telecycles-location.fr; per day €20) and **Vélo-Passion** (☎04 90 92 49 43; www.velopassion.fr; per day €15-20). Or add a zip to your pedal power with a battery-assisted electric bike from **Sun e-Bike** (☎04 32 62 08 39; www.location-velo-provence.com; 16 bd Marceau; per day €36; ⏲9am-6.30pm Apr-Sep, shorter hours rest of year).

BUS

Allô Cartreize (☎08 10 00 13 26; www.lepilote.com) buses depart from place de la République. Line 54 stops in St-Rémy on its way from Cavaillon (€1.80, 30 minutes, three daily Monday to Saturday) to Arles (€2.50, 50 minutes). Line 57 runs to Avignon (€3.60, one hour, at least one every two hours including on Sunday).

Les Baux-de-Provence

POP 450

Clinging precariously to an ancient limestone *baou* (Provençal for 'rocky spur'), this fortified hilltop village is one of the most visited in France (best seen as a day trip, and avoid the summer crowds if you can). It's easy to understand its popularity: narrow cobbled streets wend car-free past ancient houses, up to a splendid ruined castle.

👁 Sights

Château des Baux CASTLE, RUIN
(☎04 90 54 55 56; www.chateau-baux-provence.com; adult/child Apr-Sep €10/8, Oct-Mar €8/6; ⏲9am-8pm Jul & Aug, to 7pm Apr-Jun & Sep, reduced hours Oct-Mar) Crowning the village of Les Baux, these dramatic maze-like ruins date to the 10th century. The clifftop castle was largely destroyed in 1633, during the reign of Louis XIII, and is a thrilling place to explore – particularly for rambunctious kids. Climb crumbling towers for incredible views, descend into disused dungeons, and

flex your knightly prowess with giant medieval weapons dotting the open-air site. Medieval-themed entertainment and hands-on action – shows, duels, catapult demonstrations and so on – abound in summer.

Carrières de Lumières LIGHT SHOW
(☎04 90 54 55 56; www.carrieres-lumieres.com; rte de Maillane; adult/child €12/10; ⊙9.30am-7.30pm Apr-Sep, 10am-6pm Oct-Dec & Mar) Inside the chilly galleries of a former limestone quarry, this peculiar but intriguing attraction is like an underground audiovisual art gallery, with giant projections illuminating the walls, floor and ceiling, accompanied by oration and swelling music. Programs change annually and there are joint tickets with the Château des Baux. Dress warmly.

Eating

★L'Oustau de Baumanière GASTRONOMIC€€€
(☎04 90 54 33 07; www.oustaudebaumaniere.com; lunch/dinner menus from €90/160, mains €65-100; ❄📶) Twice Michelin-starred and luxurious with a capital L, this legendary hotel-restaurant is the most exclusive – and expensive – place to dine in this corner of Provence. Head chef Jean-André Charial revels in the rich flavours of classical French cooking, and at one of the *table d'hôte* sessions (€150) you can watch the chef work and share lunch with him.

The restaurant also hosts weekend cooking classes (€170 including lunch) and wine discovery courses (€190 with lunch). Upstairs there are luxurious hotel rooms (doubles from €203).

Information

Tourist Office (☎04 90 54 34 39; www.lesbauxdeprovence.com; Maison du Roy; ⊙9.30am-5pm Mon-Fri, 10am-5.30pm Sat & Sun)

Getting There & Around

BUS

Allô Cartreize (☎08 10 00 13 26; www.lepilote.com, www.cartreize.com) has services to St-Rémy-de-Provence (€2.40, 15 minutes) and Arles (€2.40, 30 minutes) on weekends from May to September and daily in July and August.

CAR

Driving is easiest, but parking is hellish. Find metered spaces (€5 per day) far down the hill at the village's edge; there's free parking outside Carrières de Lumières. Good luck.

THE VAUCLUSE

The Vaucluse is like every Provençal cliché rolled into one: lavender fields, scenic hills, rows upon rows of vineyards, enchanting villages, picturesque markets, traditional stone houses, beating summer sun and howling winter mistral. At the heart of Vaucluse, which means 'closed valley', is the exquisite town of Avignon.

A car is the ideal way to cover the Vaucluse, but it's possible (if not expedient) to get around by bus.

Avignon

POP 91,250

Attention, quiz fans: name the city where the pope lived during the early 14th century. Answered Rome? Bzzz: sorry, wrong answer. For 70-odd years of the early 1300s, the Provençal town of Avignon served as the centre of the Roman Catholic world, and though its stint as the seat of papal power only lasted a few decades, it's been left with an impressive legacy of ecclesiastical architecture, most notably the soaring, World Heritage–listed fortress-cum-palace known as the Palais des Papes.

Avignon is now best known for its annual arts festival, the largest in France, which draws thousands of visitors for several weeks in July. The rest of the year, it's a lovely city to explore, with boutique-lined streets, leafy squares and some excellent restaurants – as well as an impressive medieval wall that entirely encircles the old city.

History

Avignon first gained its ramparts – and reputation for arts and culture – during the 14th century, when Pope Clement V fled political turmoil in Rome. From 1309 to 1377, seven French-born popes invested huge sums in the papal palace and offered asylum to Jews and political dissidents. Pope Gregory XI left Avignon in 1376, but his death two years later led to the Great Schism (1378–1417), during which rival popes (up to three at one time) resided at Rome and Avignon, denouncing and excommunicating one another. Even after the matter was settled and an impartial pope, Martin V, established himself in Rome, Avignon remained under papal rule. Avignon and Comtat Venaissin (now the Vaucluse *département*) were ruled by papal legates until 1791.

Sights

★Palais des Papes PALACE
(Papal Palace; www.palais-des-papes.com; place du Palais; adult/child €11/9, with Pont St-Bénezet €13.50/10.50; ⏲9am-8pm Jul, to 8.30pm Aug, shorter hours Sep-Jun) The largest Gothic palace ever built, the Palais des Papes was erected by Pope Clement V, who abandoned Rome in 1309 as a result of violent disorder following his election. It served as the seat of papal power for seven decades, and its immense scale provides ample testament to the medieval might of the Roman Catholic church. Ringed by 3m-thick walls, its cavernous halls, chapels and antechambers are largely bare today, but an audioguide (€2) provides a useful backstory.

Place du Palais SQUARE
This impressive vast square surrounding Palais des Papes provides knockout photo ops. On top of the Romanesque 17th-century **cathedral** stands a golden statue of the Virgin Mary (weighing 4.5 tonnes), while next to the cathedral, the hilltop **Rocher des Doms** gardens provide great views of the Rhône, Mont Ventoux and Les Alpilles. Opposite the palace is the 17th-century **Hôtel des Monnaies**, once the papal mint, and festooned with elaborate carvings and heraldic beasts.

★Pont St-Bénezet BRIDGE
(bd du Rhône; adult/child 24hr ticket €5/4, with Palais des Papes €13.50/10.50; ⏲9am-8pm Jul, to 8.30pm Aug, shorter hours Sep-Jun) Legend says Pastor Bénezet had three saintly visions urging him to build a bridge across the Rhône. Completed in 1185, the 900m-long bridge with 20 arches linked Avignon with Villeneuve-lès-Avignon. It was rebuilt several times before all but four of its spans were washed away in the 1600s.

If you don't want to pay to visit the bridge, admire it for free from Rocher des Doms park or Pont Édouard Daladier or on Île de la Barthelasse's chemin des Berges.

Don't be surprised if you spot someone dancing: in France, the bridge is known as Pont d'Avignon after the nursery rhyme: 'Sur le pont d'Avignon/L'on y danse, l'on y danse...' (On Avignon Bridge, all are dancing...).

Musée Calvet ART MUSEUM
(☎04 90 86 33 84; www.musee-calvet.org; 65 rue Joseph Vernet; adult/child €6/3, joint ticket with Musée Lapidaire €7/3.50; ⏲10am-1pm & 2-6pm Wed-Mon) The elegant Hôtel de Villeneuve-Martignan (built 1741–54) provides a fitting backdrop for Avignon's fine-arts museum, with 16th- to 20th-century oil paintings, compelling prehistoric pieces, 15th-century wrought iron, and the elongated landscapes of Avignonnais artist Joseph Vernet.

★Musée du Petit Palais MUSEUM
(☎04 90 86 44 58; www.petit-palais.org; place du Palais; adult/child €6/free; ⏲10am-1pm & 2-6pm Wed-Mon) The archbishops' palace during the 14th and 15th centuries now houses outstanding collections of primitive, pre-Rennaissance, 13th- to 16th-century Italian religious paintings by artists including Botticelli, Carpaccio and Giovanni di Paolo – the most famous is Botticelli's *La Vierge et l'Enfant* (1470).

Musée Angladon ART MUSEUM
(☎04 90 82 29 03; www.angladon.com; 5 rue Laboureur; adult/child €8/6.50; ⏲1-6pm Tue-Sun Apr-Sep, 1-6pm Tue-Sat Oct-Mar) Tiny Musée Angladon harbours an impressive collection of impressionist treasures, including works by Cézanne, Sisley, Manet and Degas – but the star piece is Van Gogh's *Railway Wagons*, the only painting by the artist on display in Provence. Impress your friends by pointing out that the 'earth' isn't actually paint, but bare canvas.

Collection Lambert ART MUSEUM
(☎04 90 16 56 20; www.collectionlambert.com; 5 rue Violette; adult/child €10/8; ⏲11am-6pm Tue-Sun Sep-Jun, to 7pm daily Jul & Aug) Reopened in summer 2015 after significant renovation and expansion, Avignon's contemporary-arts museum focuses on works from the 1960s to the present. Work spans from minimalist and conceptual to video and photography – in stark contrast to the classic 18th-century mansion housing it.

Musée Lapidaire MUSEUM
(☎04 90 85 75 38; www.musee-lapidaire.org; 27 rue de la République; adult/child €2/1, joint ticket with Musée Calvet €7/3.50; ⏲10am-1pm & 2-6pm Tue-Sun) Housed inside the town's striking Jesuit Chapel is the archaeological collection of the Musée Calvet, newly displayed since 2015. There's a good display of Greek, Etruscan and Roman artefacts, but it's the Gaulish pieces that really draw the eye – including some grotesque masks and deeply strange figurines.

Avignon

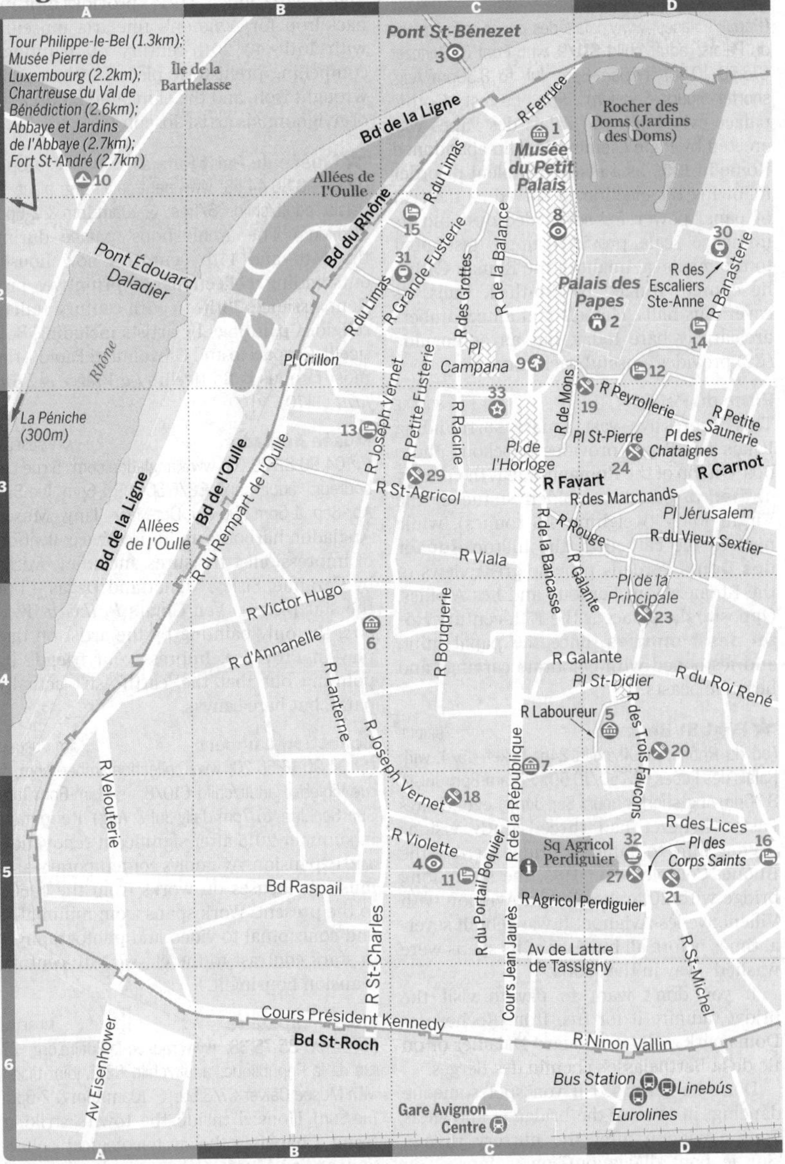

Activities

Le Carré du Palais WINE TASTING

(04 90 27 24 00; www.carredupalaisavignon.com; 1 place du Palais) The historic Hôtel Calvet de la Palun building in central Avignon has been renovated into a wine centre promoting and serving Côtes du Rhône and Vallée du Rhône appellations. Stop in to get a taste of the local vintages.

Avignon Wine Tour TOURS

(06 28 05 33 84; www.avignon-wine-tour.com; per person €80-100) Visit the region's vine-

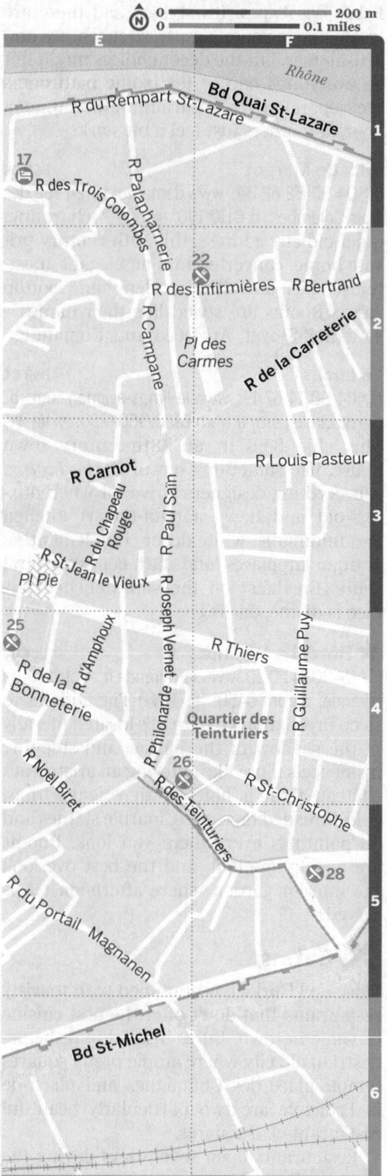

Avignon

Top Sights
1 Musée du Petit Palais ... C1
2 Palais des Papes ... D2
3 Pont St-Bénezet ... C1

Sights
4 Collection Lambert ... C5
5 Musée Angladon ... D4
6 Musée Calvet ... B4
7 Musée Lapidaire ... C4
8 Place du Palais ... C2

Activities, Courses & Tours
9 Le Carré du Palais ... C2

Sleeping
10 Camping & Auberge Bagatelle ... A1
11 Hôtel Boquier ... C5
12 Hôtel La Mirande ... D2
13 Hôtel Mignon ... B3
14 La Banasterie ... D2
15 Le Limas ... C2
16 Les Jardins de Baracane ... D5
17 Villa de Margot ... E1

Eating
18 83.Vernet ... C5
19 Christian Etienne ... D3
20 Fou de Fafa ... D4
21 Ginette et Marcel ... D5
22 Le Barrio ... F2
23 Le Potard ... D4
24 L'Épicerie ... D3
25 Les Halles ... E4
26 L'Ubu ... E4
27 Maison Violette ... D5
28 Numéro 75 ... F5
29 Restaurant L'Essentiel ... C3

Drinking & Nightlife
30 La Manutention ... D2
31 L'Esclave ... C2
32 Milk Shop ... D5

Entertainment
Cinéma Utopia ... (see 30)
33 Opéra Théâtre d'Avignon ... C3

yards with a knowledgeable guide, leaving you free to enjoy the wine.

Festivals & Events

★ **Festival d'Avignon** PERFORMING ARTS
(www.festival-avignon.com; Jul) The three-week annual Festival d'Avignon is one of the world's great performing-arts festivals. Over 40 international works of dance and drama play to 100,000-plus spectators at venues around town. Tickets don't go on sale until springtime, but hotels sell out by February.

Festival Off PERFORMING ARTS
(www.avignonleoff.com; Jul) The Festival d'Avignon is paralleled by a simultaneous fringe event, Festival Off, with eclectic experimental programming.

Sleeping

Hôtel Mignon HOTEL €
(☎04 90 82 17 30; www.hotel-mignon.com; 12 rue Joseph Vernet; s €40-60, d €65-77, tr €80-99, q €105;) Cute by name and nature, this little hotel is a sweet place to stay. Its slightly faded rooms are good value and the location on Avignon's smartest shopping street is great, but bathrooms are tiny, stairs are steep and sound-proofing leaves something to be desired. Breakfast €7.

Hôtel Boquier HOTEL €
(☎04 90 82 34 43; www.hotel-boquier.com; 6 rue du Portail Boquier; s €55-77, d €55-80, tr €73-86, q €80-99;) It sits on a rather shabby side street, but the owners' infectious enthusiasm and the colourful rooms at this small hotel compensate; try for themed rooms Morocco or Lavender. Breakfast €9.

La Péniche HOUSEBOAT €
(☎06 62 37 25 17, 04 90 25 40 61; www.chambre-peniche.fr; chemin île Piot, Île de la Barthelasse; houseboats €80-95;) Rock to sleep aboard Avignon's most unique *chambre d'hôte*. Moored across the river, a 10-minute walk on Île de la Barthelasse, this four-room barge-houseboat gleams and has a small self-catering kitchen. Extras include a wading pool and free bikes.

Camping & Auberge Bagatelle CAMPGROUND €
(☎04 90 86 30 39; www.campingbagatelle.com; Île de la Barthelasse; sites for tent, car & 2 people €24.47, dm incl breakfast from €21.21; ⌚reception 8am-9pm;) Shaded and just 20 minutes' walk from the city centre on an adjacent small island in the Rhône. It also has basic two- to eight-bed dorms.

Les Jardins de Baracane B&B €€
(☎06 11 14 88 54; www.lesjardinsdebaracane.fr; 12 rue Baracane; r €125-205;) This 18th-century house near place des Corps-Saints is owned by an architect, so it's been sensitively and tastefully renovated. Wood beams, stone walls and period detailing feature in all rooms, but the best are the two suites, which are posh enough for a pope. There's a great pool, and breakfast is served in the garden under a huge wisteria tree.

La Banasterie B&B €€
(☎06 87 72 96 36; www.labanasterie.com; 11 rue de la Banasterie; r €125-180;) Heritage meets contemporary at this B&B, offering five spacious rooms in a building behind the Palais des Papes. It's stylish, and there are treats like in-room Nespresso machines and artisan teas, but the decor choices might not be everyone's cup of tea: some bathrooms are separated by a curtain rather than a door, and others just feel a bit stark.

Villa de Margot B&B €€
(☎04 90 82 62 34; www.demargot.fr; 24 rue des Trois Colombes; d €110-190;) A charming, quiet old-city address, this 19th-century private home, converted into an elegant guesthouse, has a walled garden and rooftop views. Rooms are styled like their names – 'Oriental', 'Royal', 'Art Deco' and 'Romantic'.

Le Limas B&B €€
(☎04 90 14 67 19; www.le-limas-avignon.com; 51 rue du Limas; s/d/tr from €130/150/250;) This chic B&B in an 18th-century town house, like something out of *Vogue Living*, is everything designers strive for when mixing old and new: state-of-the-art kitchen and minimalist white decor complementing antique fireplaces and 18th-century spiral stairs. Breakfast on the sun-drenched terrace is divine, darling.

★Hôtel La Mirande HOTEL €€€
(☎04 90 14 20 20; www.la-mirande.fr; 4 place de la Mirande; d from €450;) The address to sleep in Avignon *en luxe*. It's located literally in the shadow of the palace, and stepping inside feels more like entering an aristocrat's château than a hotel, with oriental rugs, gold-threaded tapestries, marble statues and oil paintings everywhere you look. Rooms are equally opulent, and the best overlook the interior garden where afternoon tea is served.

Eating

Place de l'Horloge is crammed with touristy restaurants that don't offer the best cuisine or value in town. Delve instead into the pedestrian old city where ample pretty squares tempt: place des Châtaignes and place de la Principle are two particularly beautiful restaurant-clad squares.

Restaurants open seven days during the summer festival season, when reservations become essential.

Les Halles MARKET €
(www.avignon-leshalles.com; place Pie; ⌚6am-1.30pm Tue-Fri, to 2pm Sat & Sun) Over 40 food stalls showcase seasonal Provençal ingredients. Cooking demonstrations are held at

11am Saturday. Outside on place Pie, admire Patrick Blanc's marvellous vegetal wall.

Maison Violette BOULANGERIE €

(☎ 06 59 44 62 94; place des Corps Saints; ⏰ 7am-7.30pm Mon-Sat) We simply defy you not to walk into this bakery and not instantly be tempted by the stacks of baguettes, *ficelles* and *pains de campagnes* loaded up on the counter, not to mention the orderly ranks of eclairs, *millefeuilles*, fruit tarts and cookies lined up irresistibly behind the glass. Go on, a little bit of what you fancy does you good, *non*?

Le Barrio BISTRO €

(☎ 04 90 27 00 45; 13 rue des Infirmières; 2-course lunch €14, mains €10-19; ⏰ 11am-2pm & 7-10pm Tue-Sat) In the town's studenty quarter near elegant place des Carmes, this no-fuss hangout is ideal for solid, unpretentious grub like stir-fries, crusted cod, burgers and hotpots. It attracts a young crowd – note the vintage vinyl hanging on the walls and shabby-chic tables – and there's a choice of inside or outside dining. Head here for a laid-back lunch.

Le Potard BURGERS €

(☎ 04 90 82 34 19; www.lepotard.com; 19-21 place de la Principale; burgers €14-18; ⏰ noon-2.30pm Tue-Sat, 6.30-10pm Wed-Sat) Gourmet brioche-based burgers in a multitude of guises, loaded with tempting goodies from smoked bacon and St-Nectaire cheese to caramelised onions, crunchy rocket and sundried tomato caviar. There's also a range of salad plates served with mini-burgers. In case you're wondering, the name refers to the dial on a guitar (sometimes called a 'pot' in English).

Ginette et Marcel CAFE €

(☎ 04 90 85 58 70; 27 place des Corps Saints; tartines €4.30-6.90; ⏰ 11am-11pm Wed-Mon; 👪) Set on one of Avignon's most happening plane-tree-shaded squares, this vintage cafe styled like a 1950s grocery is a charming spot to hang out and people-watch over a *tartine* (open-face sandwich), tart, salad or other light dish – equally tasty for lunch or an early-evening *apéro*. Kids adore Ginette's cherry- and violet-flavoured cordials and Marcel's glass jars of old-fashioned sweets.

★ Restaurant L'Essentiel FRENCH €€

(☎ 04 90 85 87 12; www.restaurantlessentiel.com; 2 rue Petite Fusterie; menus €32-46; ⏰ noon-2pm & 7-9.45pm Tue-Sat) Snug in an elegant, caramel-stone *hôtel particulier*, the Essential is one of the finest places to eat in town – inside or in the wonderful courtyard garden.

LOCAL KNOWLEDGE

DYERS' STREET

Canal-side **rue des Teinturiers** (literally 'street of dyers') is a picturesque pedestrian street known for its alternative vibe in Avignon's old dyers' district. A hive of industrial activity until the 19th century, the street today is renowned for its bohemian bistros, cafes and gallery-workshops. Stone 'benches' in the shade of ancient plane trees make the perfect perch to ponder the irresistible trickle of the River Sorgue, safeguarded since the 16th century by Chapelle des Pénitents Gris. Those in the know dine at **L'Ubu**, with a tiny, daily-changing menu chalked on the blackboard.

Begin with courgette flowers poached in a crayfish and truffle sauce, then continue with rabbit stuffed with candied aubergine, perhaps.

L'Ubu BISTRO €€

(☎ 04 90 80 01 01; 13 rue des Teinturiers; starters/mains €7.50/16.50; ⏰ noon-2.30pm & 7-10.30pm) This hipster place is a little tricky to find, hidden away on the cobbled street of rue des Teinturiers. Wholefood and organic features strongly on the tiny menu, and there's a choice of sleek interior or tables overlooking the water. It's a bistro, but with a trendy twist.

L'Épicerie BISTRO €€

(☎ 04 90 82 74 22; www.restaurantlepicerie.fr; 10 place St-Pierre; lunch/dinner menus from €16/23; ⏰ noon-2.30pm & 8-10pm) Traditional and unashamedly so, this cosy bistro is a fine spot for hearty French dishes, from homemade foie gras to a mixed platter of Provençal produce (€19). All the bistro boxes receive a big tick: checked tablecloths, vintage signs, friendly waiters, great local wines by the glass.

83.Vernet MODERN FRENCH €€

(☎ 04 90 85 99 04; www.83vernet.com; 83 rue Joseph Vernet; 2-course lunch menu €17, 2-/3-course dinner menu €24/30; ⏰ noon-3pm & 7pm-1am Mon-Sat) Forget flowery French descriptions. The menu is straightforward and to the point at this bistro-bar, where the stark white furniture and studiously minimal decor counterpoints the heritage architecture of a medieval college. Expect pan-seared

OFF THE BEATEN TRACK

OLIVE-OIL MILLS

The Alpilles' southern edge contains some of Provence's best-known *moulins d'huile* (oil mills), where four types of olive, freshly harvested from November to January, are pummelled and pressed into silken AOC Vallée des Baux-de-Provence oil.

In Maussane-les-Alpilles, the cooperative **Moulin Jean-Marie Cornille** (☎04 90 54 32 37; www.moulin-cornille.com; rue Charloun Rieu, Maussane-les-Alpilles; ⏰9.30am-6.30pm Mon-Sat, 11am-6pm Sun) sells direct to the public, though its 200,000L sell out by mid-August. You can tour the mill at 11am on Tuesday and Thursday June to September.

At Mouriès, 6km southeast of Maussane, pop in for tastes of exceptional oils milled at **Moulin Coopératif de Mouriès** (☎04 90 47 53 86; www.moulincoop.com; Quartier du Mas Neuf, Mouriès; ⏰9am-noon & 2-6pm Mon-Sat). The village celebrates a **Fête des Olives Vertes** (Green Olive Festival) in mid-September, and the arrival of the year's new oil with the **Fête des Huiles Nouvelles** in early December.

scallops, squid *à la plancha* and beef steak in pepper sauce on the menu, and hipster cocktails served till late.

Fou de Fafa BISTRO €€
(☎04 32 76 35 13; 17 rue des Trois Faucons; 2-/3-course menu €25/31; ⏰6.30-11pm Wed-Sun; 👪) A typical French bistro, Fou de Fafa's strength lies in simplicity – fresh ingredients, bright flavours, convivial surroundings (and a notably early opening time handy for families with young children). Dining is between soft golden-stone walls and the chef gives a fresh spin to classics. *Magret de canard* (duck breast) in a strawberry and balsamic reduction, anyone?

Numéro 75 MODERN FRENCH €€
(☎04 90 27 16 00; www.numero75.com; 75 rue Guillaume Puy; 2-/3-course menus from €30/37; ⏰noon-2pm & 7.30-9.35pm Mon-Sat) The chic dining room, in the former mansion of absinthe inventor Jules Pernod, is a fitting backdrop to the stylised Mediterranean cooking. *Menus* change nightly and include just a handful of mains, but brevity guarantees freshness. Starter/main-course-sized *salades goumandes* (€9/18), served only at lunchtime, are good value. On balmy nights, reserve a table in the elegant courtyard garden.

★**Christian Etienne** PROVENÇAL €€€
(☎04 90 86 16 50; www.christian-etienne.fr; 10 rue de Mons; lunch/dinner menus from €35/75; ⏰noon-2pm & 7.30-10pm Tue-Sat) One of Avignon's top tables, this much-vaunted restaurant occupies a 12th-century palace with a leafy outdoor terrace, adjacent to Palais des Papes. Interiors feel slightly dated, but the refined Provençal cuisine remains exceptional, and the restaurant has earned a Michelin star.

Drinking & Nightlife

Chic yet laid-back Avignon is awash with gorgeous, tree-shaded pedestrian squares buzzing with cafe life. Favourite options, loaded with pavement terraces and drinking opportunities, include place Crillon, place Pie, place de l'Horloge and place des Corps Saints. Students tend to favour the many bars dotted along the aptly named rue de la Verrerie (Glassware St).

La Manutention BAR
(4 rue des Escaliers Ste-Anne; ⏰noon-midnight) No address better reflects Avignon's artsy soul than this bistro-bar at cultural centre La Manutention. Its leafy terrace basks in the shade of Palais des Papes' stone walls and, inside, giant conservatory-style windows open onto the funky decor of pocket-size bar Utopia. There's a cinema too.

Milk Shop CAFE
(☎09 82 54 16 82; www.milkshop.fr; 26 place des Corps Saints; ⏰7.45am-7pm Mon-Fri, 9.30am-7pm Sat; 📶) Keen to mingle with Avignon students? Make a beeline for this *salon au lait* ('milk bar') where super-thick ice-cream shakes (€4.50) are slurped through extra-wide straws. Bagels (€5 to €7), cupcakes and other American snacks create a deliberate US vibe, while comfy armchairs and wi-fi encourage hanging out.

L'Esclave GAY
(☎04 90 85 14 91; 12 rue du Limas; ⏰11.30pm-7am Tue-Sun) Avignon's inner-city gay bar rocks well into the wee hours, pulling a clientele that is not always that quiet, based on dozens of neighbour-considerate 'be quiet' signs plastered outside.

☆ Entertainment

Avignon is one of the premier cities for theatre in France; tickets for concerts and events are sold at the tourist office *billetterie* (box office).

Cinéma Utopia CINEMA
(☎04 90 82 65 36; www.cinemas-utopia.org; La Manutention, 4 rue des Escaliers Ste-Anne) Four-screen art-house cinema at cultural centre La Manutention; shows films in their original language.

Opéra Théâtre d'Avignon PERFORMING ARTS
(☎04 90 82 81 40; www.operagrandavignon.fr; place de l'Horloge; ⌚box office 11am-6pm Tue-Sat) Built in 1847, Avignon's main classical venue presents operas, plays, chamber music and ballet from October to June.

Information

Tourist Office (☎04 32 74 32 74; www.avignon-tourisme.com; 41 cours Jean Jaurès; ⌚9am-6pm Mon-Sat, 10am-5pm Sun Apr-Oct, shorter hours Nov-Mar) Offers guided walking tours and information on other tours and activities, including boat trips on the River Rhône and wine-tasting trips to nearby vineyards. Smartphone apps too.

Tourist Office Annexe (Gare Avignon TGV; ⌚Jun-Aug) During summer, Avignon has an information booth at the TGV station.

Getting There & Away

The TGV has pretty much eliminated the need to fly to Avignon from anywhere in mainland France; it's nearly always easier, cheaper (and in many cases faster) to take the train than fly.

AIR

Aéroport Avignon-Provence (AVN; ☎04 90 81 51 51; www.avignon.aeroport.fr) In Caumont, 8km southeast of Avignon. Direct flights to London, Birmingham and Southampton in the UK.

BUS

The **bus station** (bd St-Roch; ⌚information window 8am-7pm Mon-Fri, to 1pm Sat) is next to the central train station. Tickets are sold on board. For schedules, see www.lepilote.com, www.info-ler.fr and www.vaucluse.fr. Long-haul companies **Linebus** (☎04 90 85 30 48; www.linebus.com) and **Eurolines** (☎04 90 85 27 60; www.eurolines.com) have offices at the far end of bus platforms and serve places like Barcelona.

Aix-en-Provence (€17.40, LER Line 23, 1¼ hours, six daily Monday to Saturday, two on Sunday)

Arles (€7.10, LER Line 18, 50 minutes, at least seven daily)

Carpentras (€2, TransVaucluse Line 5.1, 45 minutes, two or three hourly Monday to Saturday, every two hours Sunday)

Orange (€2, TransVaucluse Line 2.1, one hour, hourly Monday to Saturday, five on Sunday)

TRAIN

Avignon has two train stations: **Gare Avignon Centre** (42 bd St-Roch), on the southern edge of the walled town, and **Gare Avignon TGV**, 4km southwest in Courtine. Local shuttle trains link the two every 20 minutes (€1.60, five minutes, 6am to 11pm). Note that there is no luggage storage at the train station.

Destinations served by TGV include Paris Gare du Lyon (€35 to €80, 3½ hours), Marseille (€17.50, 35 minutes) and Nice (€31 to €40, 3¼ hours). **Eurostar** (www.eurostar.com) services operate one to five times weekly between Avignon TGV and London (from €59.50, 5¾ hours) en route to/from Marseille.

Arles €6.50, 20 minutes

Marseille €17.50, 1¼ to two hours

Marseille airport (Vitrolles station) €14.50, one to 1½ hours

Nîmes €8, 30 minutes

Orange €5.50, 22 minutes

Getting Around

TO/FROM THE AIRPORT

From the airport, TCRA bus 30 (www.tcra.fr; €1.30, 25 minutes, Monday to Saturday) goes to the post office and LER bus 22 (www.info-ler.fr; €1.50) goes to the Avignon bus station and TGV station.

BICYCLE

Vélopop (☎08 10 45 64 56; www.velopop.fr) Shared-bicycle service, with 17 stations around town. The first half-hour is free; each additional half-hour is €1. Membership per day/week is €1/5.

Provence Bike (☎04 90 27 92 61; www.provence-bike.com; 7 av St-Ruf; bicycles per

AVIGNON PASS

An excellent-value discount card, **Avignon Passion** yields cheaper admission to big-hitter museums and monuments in Avignon and Villeneuve-lès-Avignon. The first site visited is full price, but each subsequent site is discounted. The pass is free, is valid 15 days, covers a couple of tours too, and is available at the tourist office and at museums.

day/week from €12/65, scooters €25/150; ⏲9am-6.30pm Mon-Sat, plus 10am-1pm Sun Jul) Rents city bikes, mountain bikes, scooters and motorcycles.

BUS

TCRA (Transports en Commun de la Région d'Avignon; ☎04 32 74 18 32; www.tcra.fr) Tickets (€1.30) are sold on board. Buses run from 7am till about 8pm. The main transfer points are Poste (main post office) and place Pie. For Villeneuve-lès-Avignon, take bus 5.

Villeneuve-lès-Avignon

POP 12,872

Across the Rhône from Avignon, compact Villeneuve-lès-Avignon has monuments to rival Avignon's but none of the crowds. Meander the cloisters of a medieval monastery, take in hilltop views from Fort St-André and lose yourself in spectacular gardens at Abbaye St-André – reason enough to visit.

Sights

The Avignon Passion discount pass is valid here.

★Abbaye et Jardins de l'Abbaye MONASTERY, GARDENS
(☎04 90 25 55 95; www.abbayesaintandre.fr; Fort St-André, rue Montée du Fort; adult/child abbey €13/free, garden €6/free; ⏲10am-6pm Tue-Sun May-Sep, 10am-1pm & 2-5pm Tue-Sun Mar & Oct, to 6pm Apr) The resplendent vaulted halls of this 10th-century abbey, within Fort St-André, can only be visited by guided tour. The stunning terrace gardens, however – built atop the abbey vaults and classed among France's top 100 gardens – can be freely roamed. Pathways meander among fragrant roses, iris-studded olive groves, wisteria-covered pergolas and the ruins of three ancient churches. The views of Avignon and the Rhône are spectacular.

Fort St-André FORT
(☎04 90 25 45 35; rue Montée du Fort St-André; adult/child €5.50/free; ⏲10am-6pm Jun-Sep, 10am-1pm & 2-5pm Oct-May) King Philip the Fair (aka Philippe le Bel) wasn't messing around when he built defensive 14th-century Fort St-André on the then border between France and the Holy Roman Empire: the walls are 2m thick! Today you can walk a small section of the ramparts and admire 360-degree views from the **Tour des Masques** (Wizards' Tower) and **Tours Jumelles** (Twin Towers).

Chartreuse du Val de Bénédiction MONASTERY
(☎04 90 15 24 24; www.chartreuse.org; 58 rue de la République; adult/child €8/free; ⏲9.30am-6.30pm May-Sep, to 5pm Oct-Mar) Shaded from the summer's heat, the three cloisters, 24 cells, church, chapels and nook-and-cranny gardens of the Chartreuse du Val de Bénédiction make up France's biggest Carthusian monastery, founded in 1352 by Pope Innocent VI, who was buried here 10 years later in an elaborate mausoleum.

Tour Philippe-le-Bel LANDMARK
(☎04 32 70 08 57; Montée de la Tour; adult/child €2.60/free; ⏲10am-12.30pm & 2-6pm Tue-Sun May-Oct, 2-5pm Feb-Apr) King Philip commissioned the Tour Philippe-le-Bel, 500m outside Villeneuve, to control traffic over Pont St-Bénézet to and from Avignon. The steep steps spiralling to the top reward climbers with stunning river views.

Musée Pierre de Luxembourg MUSEUM
(☎04 90 27 49 66; 3 rue de la République; adult/child €3.60/free; ⏲10am-12.30pm & 2-6pm Tue-Sun May-Oct, 2-5pm Nov-Apr) Inside a 17th-century mansion, this museum's masterwork is Enguerrand Quarton's *The Crowning of the Virgin* (1453), in which angels wrest souls from purgatory. Rounding out the collection are 16th- to 18th-century paintings.

Getting There & Away

TCRA bus 5 links Villeneuve-lès-Avignon with Avignon (it's only 2km, but dull walking).

Orange

POP 29,645

Considering the exceptional beauty of its Roman theatre and monumental archway – both Unesco World Heritage sites – Orange is surprisingly untouristy, and eerily quiet in winter. Accommodation is good value for the region, but it's nearly impossible to find dinner Sunday or Monday nights.

Sights

★Théâtre Antique ROMAN SITES
(Ancient Roman Theatre; ☎04 90 51 17 60; www.theatre-antique.com; rue Madeleine Roch; adult/child €9.50/7.50; ⏲9am-7pm Jun-Aug, to 6pm Apr, May & Sep, 9.30am-5.30pm Mar & Oct, 9.30am-4.30pm Nov-Feb) Orange's monumental Roman theatre is unquestionably one of France's most impressive Roman sights. It's one of only three intact Roman theatres

left in the world (the others are in Syria and Turkey), and its sheer size is awe-inspiring: designed to seat 10,000 spectators, its stage wall towers 37m high, 103m wide and 1.8m thick. Little wonder that Louis XIV called it 'the finest wall in my kingdom'.

Admission includes an audioguide and entry to the Musée d'Art et d'Histoire.

★Colline St-Eutrope GARDENS

For bird's-eye views of the theatre – and phenomenal vistas of Mont Ventoux and the Dentelles de Montmirail – follow montée Philbert de Chalons or montée Lambert up Colline St-Eutrope (St Eutrope Hill; elevation 97m), once the Romans' lookout point. En route, pass ruins of a 12th-century **château**, once the residence of the princes of Orange.

Musée d'Art et d'Histoire MUSEUM

(www.theatre-antique.com; rue Madeleine Roch; entry included with admission to Théatre Antique; 9.15am-7pm Jun-Aug, to 6pm Apr, May & Sep, shorter hours Oct-Mar) This small museum contains various finds relating to the theatre's history, including plaques and friezes that once formed part of the scenery, a range of amphora, busts, columns and vases, and a room displaying three rare engraved *cadastres* (official surveys) dating from 77 BC.

Arc de Triomphe ROMAN SITES

Orange's 1st-century-AD monumental arch, the Arc de Triomphe – 19m high and wide, and 8m thick – stands on the Via Agrippa. Restored in 2009, its brilliant reliefs commemorate 49 BC Roman victories with carvings of chained, naked Gauls.

Festivals & Events

Les Chorégies d'Orange PERFORMING ARTS

(www.choregies.asso.fr; Jul & Aug) The Théatre Antique comes alive with all-night concerts, weekend operas and choral performances. Reserve tickets months ahead, and rooms the year before.

Sleeping & Eating

It's worth wandering away from the line-up of cafe terraces opposite the Théatre Antique on place des Frères Mounet to delve into the pedestrian squares of Orange's softly hued old town. Market stalls spill across streets in the town centre every Thursday.

Hôtel Saint Jean HOTEL €

(04 90 51 15 16; www.hotelsaint-jean.com; 1 cours Pourtoules; s/d/tr/q €75/85/105/125; P ❄) A cosy, rather old-timey hotel on the side of the Colline St-Eutrope, dead handy for the theatre. Rooms are small and decorated in warm Provençal colours, and a few feature exposed rock walls from the attached hill. The terrace is a lovely spot for breakfast (€9). Parking €7.

Camping Manon CAMPGROUND €

(04 32 81 94 96; www.camping-manon.com; 1321 rue Alexis Carrel, Quartier Le Jonquier; sites for 2 people €14-27; Apr-Sep; @) This good camping ground has been recently overhauled and has pool, hot tub, tennis, laundry and a minimart. Camping sites are available both with and without electricity.

Les Saveurs du Marché FRENCH €

(06 14 44 26 63; 24 place Sylvain; 2-/3-/4-course lunch menu €12.50/15.50/23, dinner menu €29; noon-2pm Tue-Sun, 7-9pm Tue-Sat) The clue's in the name: market flavours underpin the menu here, from delicious homemade tapenades made with locally grown olives, to pan-seared red mullet drizzled with olive oil and fragrant pesto. The menu changes regularly – the four-course lunch is a steal – but quality can suffer a bit when it gets overbusy, so it's usually best to arrive early.

La Grotte d'Auguste TRADITIONAL FRENCH €€

(04 90 60 22 54; www.restaurant-orange.fr; Théatre Antique, rue Madeleine Roch; lunch/dinner menu from €16/21; noon-2pm & 7-10pm Tue-Sat) Locations don't come much more perfect in Orange than at Auguste's Grotto, hidden away beneath the Roman theatre (although for sunny-day dining, there's also an outside space overlooking a ruined temple). The food's rich, filling and unabashedly meaty.

Information

Tourist Office (04 90 34 70 88; www.otorange.fr; place des Frères Mounet; 9am-6.30pm Mon-Sat, 9am-1pm & 2-6.30pm Sun, closed Sun Oct-Mar) Has lots of brochures and handles hotel bookings, and also sells the Roman Pass (see box).

ROMAN PASS

The **Roman Pass** is a joint ticket that allows access to Orange's Roman theatre and museum, plus Les Arènes, the Maison Carrée and Tour Magne in Nîmes. It's valid for seven days, and you can buy it at any of the venues.

Getting There & Around

BICYCLE

Sport Aventure (☎04 90 34 75 08; 1 place de la République; half-day/day/week €12/18/69) Central bike shop; delivers within 20km radius.

BUS

Useful lines operated by **TransVaucluse** (www.vaucluse.fr) serve Avignon (€2, Line 2.1, 45 minutes, two hourly Monday to Saturday, five or six on Sunday) and Vaison-la-Romaine (€2, Line 4, 45 minutes, every two hours Monday to Friday, two or three daily on weekends).

Most buses depart from Orange's **bus station** (☎04 90 34 15 59; 201 cours Pourtoules).

TRAIN

Orange's **train station** (av Frédéric Mistral) is 1.5km east of the town centre.

Arles €9, 40 minutes
Avignon €5.50, 22 minutes
Marseille €15.50 to €28, 1¾ hours
Marseille airport (Vitrolles station) €18, 1¼ hours

Vaison-la-Romaine

POP 6275

Tucked between seven hills, Vaison-la-Romaine has long been a traditional exchange centre, and it still has a thriving Tuesday market. The village's rich Roman legacy is obvious – 20th-century buildings rise alongside France's largest archaeological site. A Roman bridge crosses the River Ouvèze, dividing the contemporary town's pedestrianised centre and the spectacular walled, cobbled-street hilltop Cité Médiévale – one of Provence's most magical ancient villages – where the counts of Toulouse built their 12th-century castle. Vaison is a good base for jaunts into the Dentelles de Montmirail or Mont Ventoux, but tourists throng here in summer: reserve ahead.

Sights

★Gallo-Roman Ruins ROMAN SITES

(☎04 90 36 50 48; www.provenceromaine.com; adult/child incl all ancient sites, museum & cathedral €8/4; ⏲9.30am-6.30pm Jun-Sep, 9.30am-6pm Apr & May, 10am-noon & 2-5.30pm Oct-Mar) The ruined remains of Vasio Vocontiorum, the Roman city that flourished here between the 6th and 2nd centuries BC, fill two central Vaison sites. Two neighbourhoods of this once opulent city, Puymin and La Villasse, lie on either side of the tourist office and av du Général de Gaulle. Admission includes entry to the 12th-century Romanesque cloister at **Cathédrale Notre-Dame de Nazareth** (cloister only €1.50; ⏲10am-12.30pm & 2-6pm Mar-Dec), a five-minute walk west of La Villasse and a soothing refuge from the summer heat.

In **Puymin**, see houses of the nobility, mosaics, workers' quarters, a temple, and the still-functioning, 6000-seat **Théâtre Antique** (c AD 20). To make sense of the remains (and collect your audioguide; €3), head for the **Musée Archéologique Gallo-Roman**, which revives Vaison's Roman past with incredible swag – superb mosaics, carved masks and statues that include a 3rd-century silver bust and marble renderings of Hadrian and wife Sabina.

The Romans shopped at the colonnaded boutiques and bathed at **La Villasse**, where you'll find **Maison au Dauphin**, which has splendid marble-lined fish ponds.

★Cité Médiévale HISTORIC SITE

Wandering around Vaison-la-Romaine's wonderful medieval quarter, you could be forgiven for thinking you've stepped into a forgetten set from *Monty Python and the Holy Grail*. Ringed by ramparts and accessed via the pretty Pont Romain (Roman bridge), it's a fascinating place to explore, criss-crossed by cobbled alleyways. Look out for the elaborate carvings around many of the doorways as you climb up towards the 12th-century **château** and its wraparound vistas.

Festivals & Events

Festival des Chœurs Lauréats MUSIC

(www.festivaldeschoeurslaureats.com; ⏲late Jul) The best choirs in Europe.

Festival de Vaison-la-Romaine DANCE

(www.vaison-danses.com; ⏲Jul) Three-week-long festival held at the Roman Théâtre Antique. Book by April.

Sleeping

★Hôtel Burrhus HOTEL €

(☎04 90 36 00 11; www.burrhus.com; 1 place de Montfort; d €65-98, apt €140; P ❄ ☜) As much art gallery as hotel, this imaginative and exciting place zings with modern artwork, sculptures, funky furniture and fun decorative details, like the terracotta pot suspended above the interior patio. Rooms are divided into three size categories, all brimming with interest. Breakfast is copious, and good value at €9.

For three days every December during the Supervues art festival (www.supervues.com), the hotel's rooms are occupied by artists who create work during their stay.

L'École Buissonière B&B €
(☎04 90 28 95 19; www.buissonniere-provence.com; D75, Buisson; s/d/tr/q incl breakfast from €53/65/82/100;) Five minutes north of Vaison, in the countryside between Buisson and Villedieu, hosts Monique and John have transformed their stone farmhouse into a tastefully decorated three-bedroom B&B, big on comfort. Breakfast features homemade jam, and there's an outdoor summer kitchen.

Camping du Théâtre Romain CAMPGROUND €
(☎04 90 28 78 66; www.camping-theatre.com; chemin de Brusquet; sites per 2 people with tent & car €25.90; mid-Mar–mid-Nov;) Opposite the Théâtre Antique. Very sunny, and there's a pool.

L'Évêché B&B €€
(☎04 90 36 13 46; http://eveche.free.fr; rue de l'Évêché; r €87-145) There's atmosphere galore in this rambling, regal B&B in the old medieval city, once the bishop's residence. Rooms are huge and packed with period detail, from wonky beams to nooks and crannies. Owners Jean-Loup and Aude know practically everyone in town, and will happily lend you bikes for exploring.

Eating

Maison Lesage BOULANGERIE €
(2 rue de la République; sandwiches €4-6; 7am-1pm & 3-5pm Mon, Tue & Thu-Sat, 7am-1pm Sun) For picnics by the river, this excellent bakery has no shortage of foodie fare: big baguettes, homemade pastries and nougat, and the house speciality, bun-sized meringues in a rainbow of flavours.

★**Bistro du'O** BISTRO €€
(☎04 90 41 72 90; www.bistroduo.fr; rue du Château; lunch/dinner menus from €19/32; noon-2pm & 7.30-10pm Tue-Sat) Gosh, this place knows how to impress. First the setting: a vaulted cellar in the medieval city (once the château stables). Then the food: local and seasonal, rooted in the classics but contemporary in style, and dictated by what talented young chef Philippe Zemour has found in the market. The menu's short, but full of surprises: we loved it.

La Lyriste PROVENÇAL €€
(☎04 90 36 04 67; 45 cours Taulignan; menus €14.50-28; noon-2.30pm & 7-9.30pm Tue & Thu-Sun;) Nothing world-changing here, but tasty regional food from *bourride* (fish stew) to *brandade de cabillaud* (cod kebabs), laced with lashings of olive oil, tomatoes and Provençal herbs. Unusually, there's generally a good choice of veggie options on offer. The plane-tree-shaded terrace tables are the ones to ask for.

Information

Tourist Office (☎04 90 36 02 11; www.vaison-ventoux-tourisme.com; place du Chanoine Sautel; 9.30am-noon & 2-5.45pm Mon-Sat year-round, plus 9.30am-noon Sun mid-Mar–mid-Oct) Helps book rooms, organise activities, and sells concert and event tickets.

Getting There & Away

Bus timetables are available at **TransVaucluse** (www.vaucluse.fr). The bus stop is on av des Choralies, 400m east of the tourist office.

Carpentras (€2, Line 11, 45 minutes, four or five daily)

Orange (€2, Line 4, 45 minutes, every two hours Monday to Friday, two or three daily on weekends)

Mont Ventoux

Visible for miles around, Mont Ventoux (1912m) stands like a sentinel over northern Provence. From its summit, accessible by road between May and October, vistas extend to the Alps and, on a clear day, the Camargue.

Because of the mountain's dimensions, every European climate type is represented here, from Mediterranean on its lower southern reaches to Arctic on its exposed northern ridge. As you climb, temperatures can plummet by 20°C, and the fierce mistral wind blows 130 days a year, sometimes at speeds of 250km/h. Bring warm clothes and rain gear, even in summer. You can ascend by road year-round, but you cannot traverse the summit from 15 November to 15 April.

The mountain's diverse fauna and flora have earned the mountain Unesco Biosphere Reserve status. Some species live nowhere else, including the rare snake eagle.

Three gateways – Bédoin, Malaucène and Sault – provide services in summer, but they're far apart.

WORTH A TRIP

CHÂTEAUNEUF-DU-PAPE WINES

Carpets of vineyards unfurl around tiny, medieval Châteauneuf-du-Pape, epicentre of one of the world's great wine-growing regions. Only a small ruin remains of the château, once the summer residence of Avignon's popes, dismantled for stone after the Revolution, and ultimately bombed by Germany in WWII. Now it belongs to picnickers and day hikers, who ascend the hill for 360-degree panoramas of the Rhône Valley. It's an ideal half-day trip for wine tasting and lunch before continuing to Orange.

Thank geology for these luscious wines: when glaciers receded, they left a thick layer of *galets* scattered atop the red-clay soil; these large pebbles trap the Provençal sun, releasing heat after sunset, helping grapes ripen with steady warmth.

The Romans first planted vines here 2000 years ago, but wine-growing took off after Pope John XXII built a castle in 1317, planting vineyards to provide the court with wine. From this papally endorsed beginning, wine production flourished.

Most Châteauneuf-du-Pape is red; only 6% is white (rosé is forbidden). Strict regulations – which formed the basis for the *appellation d'origine contrôlée* (AOC) system – govern production. Reds come from 13 grape varieties – grenache is the biggie – and should age five years minimum. The full-bodied whites drink well young (except for all-roussanne varieties) and make an excellent, mineral-y aperitif that's hard to find elsewhere (but taste before buying; some may lack acidity).

The **Tourist Office** (☎04 90 83 71 08; www.ot-chateauneuf-du-pape.mobi; place du Portail; ⏲9.30am-6pm Mon-Sat, closed lunch & Wed Oct-May) has loads of advice on wine tasting and visiting local vineyards, including ones that offer English-language tours. It can also make appointments for you.

Hiking

The GR4 crosses the Dentelles de Montmirail before scaling Mont Ventoux' northern face, where it meets the GR9. Both traverse the ridge. The GR4 branches eastwards to Gorges du Verdon; the GR9 crosses the Vaucluse Mountains to the Luberon. The essential map for the area is *3140ET Mont Ventoux*, by IGN (www.ign.fr). Bédoin's tourist office stocks maps and brochures detailing walks for all levels.

In July and August tourist offices in Bédoin and Malaucène facilitate night-time expeditions up the mountain to see sunrise (participants must be over 15 years old).

Les Ânes des Abeilles TOURS
(☎04 90 64 01 52; http://abeilles.ane-et-rando.com; rte de la Gabelle, Col des Abeilles; day/weekend from €50/95) A novel means of exploring the Gorges de la Nesque, a spectacular limestone canyon, or nearby Mont Ventoux, is alongside a donkey from Les Ânes des Abeilles. Beasts carry up to 40kg (ie small children or bags).

Cycling

Tourist offices distribute *Les Itinéraires Ventoux*, a free map detailing 11 itineraries – graded easy to difficult – and highlighting artisanal farms en route. For more cycling trails, see www.lemontventoux.net. Most cycle-hire outfits also offer electric bikes.

Station Ventoux Sud Bike Park CYCLING
(☎04 90 61 84 55; www.facebook.com/VentouxBikePark; Chalet Reynard; half-/full day €10/14; ⏲10am-5pm Sat & Sun, weekday hours variable) Near the Mont Ventoux summit, at Chalet Reynard, mountain bikers ascend via rope tow (minimum age 10 years), then descend ramps and jumps down three trails (5km in total). In winter it's possible to mountain bike on snow. Bring bike, helmet and gloves or rent all gear at Chalet Reynard. Call to check opening times, which are highly weather dependent.

ℹ Information

Sault Tourist Office (☎04 90 64 01 21; www.saultenprovence.com; av de la Promenade; ⏲9.30am-12.30pm & 1.30-6.30pm Mon-Fri, 10am-12.30pm & 2-6.30pm Sat & Sun Jun-Aug, 9am-12.30pm & 2.30-5pm or 6pm Mon-Sat Sep-Mar) Good resource for Mont Ventoux information.

Malaucène Tourist Office (☎04 90 65 22 59; http://villagemalaucene.free.fr; place de la Mairie; ⏲9.15am-12.15pm & 2.30-5.30pm Mon-Fri, 9am-noon Sat) Small village office with info on Mont Ventoux, but otherwise rather limited on other areas.

Bédoin Tourist Office (☎04 90 65 63 95; www.bedoin.org; Espace Marie-Louis Gravier, 1 rte de Malaucène; ⏲9.30am-12.30pm & 2-6pm Mon-Sat, 9.30am-12.30pm Sun mid-Jun–Aug, reduced hours rest of year) Excellent source of information on all regional activities; also helps with lodging.

Getting There & Away

Getting up the mountain by public transport isn't feasible – you'll need a car or if you're feeling fit, a bike.

Carpentras

POP 29,600

Try to visit Carpentras on a Friday morning, when the streets spill over with more than 350 stalls laden with bread, honey, cheese, olives, fruit and a rainbow of *berlingots*, Carpentras' striped, pillow-shaped hard-boiled sweets. During winter the pungent **truffle market** murmurs with hushed-tone transactions. The truffle season is kicked off by Carpentras' biggest fair, held during the **Fête de St-Siffrein** on 27 November, when more than 1000 stalls spread across town.

Markets aside, this slightly rundown agricultural town has but a handful of historic sights. A Greek trading centre and later a Gallo-Roman city, it became papal territory in 1229, and was also shaped by a strong Jewish presence, as Jews who had been expelled from French crown territory took refuge here.

Sights

★Synagogue de Carpentras SYNAGOGUE
(☎04 90 63 39 97; place Juiverie; ⏲10am-noon & 3-4.30pm Mon-Thu, 10-11.30am & 3-3.30pm Fri) Carpentras' remarkable synagogue dates to 1367 and is the oldest still in use in France. Although Jews were initially welcomed into papal territory, by the 17th century they had to live in ghettos in Avignon, Carpentras, Cavaillon and L'Isle-sur-la-Sorgue: the synagogue is deliberately inconspicuous. The wood-panelled prayer hall was rebuilt in 18th-century baroque style; downstairs are bread-baking ovens, used until 1904. For access, ring the doorbell on the half-hour.

Alternatively, join the excellent 1½-hour **guided tour** (adult/child €5/3.50) organised by the tourist office every Tuesday at 10.30am from April to September.

★Arc Romain ROMAN SITES
Hidden behind Cathédrale St-Siffrein, the Arc Romain was built under Augustus in the 1st century AD and is decorated with worn carvings of enslaved Gauls.

Cathédrale St-Siffrein CATHEDRAL
(place St-Siffrein; ⏲8am-noon & 2-6pm Mon-Sat) Carpentras' cathedral was built between 1405 and 1519 in meridional Gothic style but is crowned by a distinctive contemporary bell tower. Its **Trésor d'Art Sacré** (Treasury of Religious Art) holds precious 14th- to 19th-century religious relics that you can only see during the Fête de St-Siffrein (27 November) and on guided walks with the tourist office.

Sleeping

Le Malaga HOTEL €
(☎06 16 59 85 59, 04 90 60 57 96; www.hotel-malaga-carpentras.fr; 37 place Maurice-Charretier; s/d/q €42/48/72; 📶) Plus points for this no-frills hotel: it's cheap as chips and dead central. Minus points: rooms are basic bordering on spartan, and can be prone to noise from the brasserie bar downstairs.

Hôtel du Fiacre HOTEL €€
(☎04 90 63 03 15; www.hotel-du-fiacre.com; 153 rue Vigne; d €70-150; P📶) Frills, swags and canopies abound at this grand old dame of a hotel, where the old-style decor takes its cue from the 18th-century architecture. Contemporary it ain't, but charming it most surely is. The marble staircase is a thing of beauty, too.

★Methamis B&B €€€
(☎04 90 34 46 84; www.metafort-provence.com; 31 Montée du Vieil Hôpital, Méthamis; d €165-215; ❄📶🏊) Wow. This palatial pad pulls out all the stops in terms of architecture, design and out-and-out luxury. It's in a 17th-century village house in Methamis, 17km southeast of Carpentras, but the design is unabashedly 21st-century: strikingly minimal rooms, modern art, Scandi-style furniture and an eye-popping rooftop pool overlooking the rocky, maquis-covered hills of the Nesque Valley. Stunning is an understatement.

Eating

★La Maison Jouvaud PATISSERIE €
(40 rue de l'Évêché; boxes of sweets from €10; ⏲10am-7pm Mon, 8am-7pm Tue-Fri, 9am-7pm Sat & Sun) From mountains of meringues to divine cakes, sweets, chocolates and candied fruits, this vintage cake shop and tearoom is the place to indulge your sweet tooth. Try

the house speciality *chocolat à l'ancienne* (old-fashioned hot chocolate).

Chez Serge PROVENÇAL €€
(☎04 90 63 21 24; www.chez-serge.com; 90 rue Cottier; lunch/dinner menus from €17/27; ⊙noon-2pm & 7.30-10pm Jun-Sep, noon-1.30pm & 7.30-9.30pm Oct-May;) You're in rural Provence, yes, but at Serge's place, it feels almost like you're in a fashionable brasserie in downtown Paris. It's effortlessly elegant – distressed wood, designer lights, exposed stone, an elephant mural – and the menu blends modern flavours with a passion for Provençal flavours (especially truffles).

La Galusha PROVENÇAL €€
(☎06 62 79 25 42, 04 90 60 75 00; www.galusha.fr; 30 place de l'Horloge; lunch/dinner menus from €14.50/24; ⊙noon-1.30pm & 7.30-9.30pm Tue-Sun) Venetian lamps and whimsical Arcimboldo paintings fill the romantic interior of this village town house, but it's the gorgeous flower-filled patio out the back where you'll find the best tables. For lunch there are 'gargantuan salads' (€14.50), while for dinner you'll tuck into hearty dishes like duck breast, scallops and veal à la provençale.

Drinking & Nightlife

En Face WINE BAR
(☎06 37 34 32 58; 54 rue Raspail; ⊙6pm-1am Mon, 8am-2.30pm & 6pm-1am Tue-Sat) En Face (literally 'Opposite') is a no-frills wine bar and *bistrot* with well-worn wooden floor, vintage posters on the walls and an appealing choice of tapas-style dishes (tapas €1.50 to €6, platters €6 to €10) chalked on the blackboard out the front.

Angel'Art Galerie COCKTAIL BAR
(☎06 10 13 41 94; www.facebook.com/AngelArtGalerie; 59 rue Raspail; ⊙6pm-1am Mon, 9am-1am Tue-Sat) This hybrid art gallery–cocktail lounge is one of the hippest spaces in town – alongside its equally trendy neighbours, with whom it shares brightly coloured sunshade sails, strung from one side of the tiny pedestrian street to the other.

Shopping

Friday Market MARKET
If you do nothing else in Carpentras, make sure you find time to visit the fabulous Friday market, when several hundred stalls fill Rue d'Inguimbert, ave Jean Jaurès and many side streets. It's an institution, and as Provençal as they get – not to be missed.

Information

Tourist Office (☎04 90 63 00 78; www.carpentras-ventoux.com; 97 place du 25 Août 1944; ⊙9.30am-12.30pm & 2-7pm Mon-Sat, plus 3-7pm Tue) Excellent website, guided tours in English (adult/child €5/3.50), helpful staff and an adjoining boutique of local culinary products.

Getting There & Away

BUS

The **bus station** (place Terradou) is 150m southwest of the tourist office, which has schedules, as does TransVaucluse (www.vaucluse.fr).

Nearly all local destinations cost a flat-rate €2.

Avignon (Line 5.1, 45 minutes, two or three per hour Monday to Saturday, six on Sunday)

Cavaillon (Line 12.1, one hour, every two hours Monday to Saturday)

Orange (Line 10, 55 minutes, every two hours Monday to Saturday)

Vaison-la-Romaine (Line 11, 45 minutes, four or five daily)

TRAIN

Local trains connect Carpentras' **train station** (av de la Gare) to Avignon Centre station (€5, 30 minutes, hourly) and Avignon TGV station (38 minutes).

Fontaine-de-Vaucluse

POP 661

France's most powerful spring surges from beneath the pretty village of Fontaine-de-Vaucluse, at the end of a U-shaped valley beneath limestone cliffs. The rain that falls within 1200 sq km gushes out here as the River Sorgue. The miraculous appearance of this crystal-clear flood draws 1.5 million tourists each year – aim to arrive early in the morning before the trickle of visitors becomes a deluge; avoid it Sundays in summer.

Stroll beyond the village's tourist distractions and you quickly sense the peace and beauty that inspired Italian poet Petrarch (1304–74), who wrote his most famous works here – sonnets to his unrequited love, Laura.

Sights & Activities

★**La Fontaine** SPRING
At the foot of craggy cliffs, an easy 1km walk from the village, the River Sorgue surges from the earth's depths. The spring is most dazzling after heavy rain, when water glows azure blue, welling up at an incredible 90 cu metres per second. Jacques Cousteau was among those who attempted to plumb the

spring's depths, before an unmanned submarine touched base (315m down) in 1985.

Musée d'Histoire Jean Garcin: 1939–1945 MUSEUM
(04 90 20 24 00; chemin de la Fontaine; adult/child €3.50/free; 10am-6pm Wed-Mon Apr-Oct & Jan-Feb, Sat & Sun Mar, Nov & Dec) A small museum exploring the harsh realities of life in occupied France during WWII.

Maison de la Rose PERFUMERY
(06 87 65 25 47; www.lesartsdelarose.com; 2-4pm) The façade of this eye-catching *hôtel particulier* dating from 1900 is pure romance. Sitting pretty in pink on the left as you walk from the car park to village centre, the mansion's sculpted floral façade shields an elegant interior dressed with original furnishings. Its boutique sells rose-scented cosmetics and other skin products crafted in the perfumery's laboratory, alongside edible rose products, rose plants and so on.

Canoe to L'Isle-sur-la-Sorgue CANOEING
There is no more enchanting means of meandering from Fontaine-de-Vaucluse 8km downstream to neighbouring L'Isle-sur-la-Sorgue (or it can be done in reverse) than in a canoe or kayak. Take guided or self-guided two-hour trips (adult/child €17/11) from late April to October with **Canoë Évasion** (04 90 38 26 22; www.canoe-evasion.net; rte de Fontaine-de-Vaucluse/D24) or **Kayak Vert** (04 90 20 35 44; www.canoe-france.com; Quartier la Baume). Life jackets are provided, but children must be able to swim 25m. Afterwards you're returned by minibus to your car.

Sleeping

Hôtel du Poète HISTORIC HOTEL €€
(04 90 20 34 05; www.hoteldupoete.com; d €98-325; Mar–Nov;) Drift to sleep to the sound of rushing water at this elegant small hotel, inside a restored mill on the river's banks. By day, lie poolside in the sun-dappled shade among the parklike grounds. Breakfast €17.

Information

Tourist Office (04 90 20 32 22; www.oti-delasorgue.fr; Résidence Jean Garcin; 9am-1pm & 2.30-6pm Mon-Sat, 9.30am-1pm Sun) By the bridge, mid-village.

Getting There & Away

Voyages Raoux (www.voyages-raoux.fr) buses serve Avignon (€2, one hour) and L'Île-sur-la-Sorgue (€1.50, 15 minutes).

WORTH A TRIP

GIGONDAS

Wine cellars and cafes surround the sun-dappled central square of Gigondas, famous for prestigious red wine. Wine tasting here provides an excellent counterpoint to Châteauneuf-du-Pape: both use the same grapes, but the soil is different. In town, **Caveau de Gigondas** (04 90 65 82 29; www.caveau-dugigondas.com; place Gabrielle Andéol; 10am-noon & 2-6.30pm) represents 100 small producers and offers free tastings – most bottles cost just €12 to €17. The **tourist office** (04 90 65 85 46; www.gigondas-dm.fr; rue du Portail; 9am-12.30pm & 2.30-6.30pm Mon-Sat, 10am-1pm Sun Jul & Aug, shorter hours rest of year) has a complete list of wineries.

Above the central square, along the Cheminement de Sculptures, enigmatic outdoor sculptures line narrow pathways, leading ever upward to castle ruins, campanile, church and cemetery with stunning vistas.

A tourist-office brochure details three easy back-roads cycling routes. Bike shops in L'Isle-sur-la-Sorgue deliver to Fontaine.

THE LUBERON

Named after the mountain range running east–west between Cavaillon and Manosque, the Luberon is a Provençal patchwork of hilltop villages, vineyards, ancient abbeys and mile after mile of fragrant lavender fields. It's a rural, traditional region that still makes time for the good things in life – particularly fine food and even finer wine. Nearly every village hosts its own weekly market, packed with stalls selling local specialities, especially olive oil, honey and lavender.

Covering some 600 sq km, the Luberon massif itself is divided into three areas: the craggy Petit Luberon in the west, the higher Grand Luberon mountains, and the smaller hills of the Luberon Oriental in the east. They're all worth exploring, but whatever you do, don't rush – part of the fun of exploring here is getting lost on the back lanes, stopping for lunch at a quiet village cafe, and taking as much time as you possibly can to soak up the scenery.

Apt

POP 11,500

The Luberon's principal town, Apt is edged on three sides by sharply rising plateaux surrounding a river that runs through town – the gateway to Haute-Provence. Its Saturday-morning market is full of local colour (and produce), but otherwise Apt is mainly a place you pass through to get somewhere else. Nonetheless, it makes a decent base, if only for a night or two.

Apt is known throughout France for its *fruits confits* (candied fruits, sometimes also known as glacé or crystallised fruit). Strictly speaking, they're not sweets: they're actually made with real fruit, in which the water is removed and replaced with a sugar syrup to preserve them. As a result, they still look (and more importantly taste) like pieces of the original fruit. There are several makers around town where you can try and buy straight from the source.

It's also a hub for the 1650-sq-km **Parc Naturel Régional du Luberon** (www.parcduluberon.fr), a regional nature park and an official Unesco Biosphere Reserve, criss-crossed by hiking trails.

Sights & Activities

Musée de l'Aventure Industrielle du Pays d'Apt MUSEUM

(Industrial History Museum; ☎04 90 74 95 30; 14 place du Postel; adult/child €4/free; ⏲10am-noon & 2-6.30pm Mon-Sat Jun-Sep, to 5.30pm Tue-Sat Oct-May) Gain an appreciation for Apt's artisanal and agricultural roots at this converted *fruits confits* (candied fruits) factory. The well-curated museum interprets the fruit and candying trade, as well as ochre mining and earthenware production from the 18th century.

Confiserie Kerry Aptunion TOURS

(☎04 90 76 31 43; www.lesfleurons-apt.com; D900, Quartier Salignan; ⏲shop 9am-12.15pm & 1.30-6pm Mon-Sat, no lunch break Jul & Aug) Allegedly the largest *fruits confits* maker in the world, this factory 2.5km outside of Apt produces sweets under the prestigious Les Fleurons d'Apt brand. Free tastings are offered in the shop, and you can watch the process in action on guided factory tours; they run at 2.30pm Monday to Friday in July and August, with an extra tour at 10.30am in August. The rest of the year there's just one weekly tour, usually on Wednesday at 2.30pm; confirm ahead.

Sleeping

Hôtel le Palais HOTEL €

(☎04 90 04 89 32; www.hotel-restaurant-apt.fr; 24bis place Gabriel-Péri; s/d/tr/q €55/67/75/90; 📶) Young, friendly owners lend a real air of dynamism to this veteran cheap-as-chips hotel, right in the heart of town. Rooms are on the poky side, but breakfast is a bargain at €5.

★**Le Couvent** B&B €€

(☎04 90 04 55 36; www.loucouvent.com; 36 rue Louis Rousset; d €98-130; @📶🏊) Hidden behind a wall in the old town, this enormous five-room *maison d'hôte* occupies a 17th-century former convent. Staying here is as much architectural experience as accommodation: soaring ceilings, stonework, grand staircase, plus five palatial rooms (one has a sink made from a baptismal font). There's a sweet garden, and breakfast is served in the old convent refectory. It's tricky to find, so phone ahead for directions.

Hôtel Sainte-Anne HOTEL €€

(☎04 90 74 18 04; www.apt-hotel.fr; 62 place Faubourg-du-Ballet; d €119-139; ❄@📶) This lovely seven-room hotel in a 19th-century dwelling has been completely renovated. Spotless, crisp-at-the-edges rooms mix modern and traditional furnishings, with exceptional beds and big bathtubs (though small toilets). Little extras include homemade jams and breads, made by the charming owner, served as part of the copious breakfast (€10).

Eating

Grand Marché MARKET €

Apt's huge Saturday-morning market attracts hordes of locals and tourists alike. If you really want to see what a *marché* Provençal is all about, then make it a date in your diary.

L'Auberge Espagnole TAPAS €

(www.laubergeespagnole-apt.com; 1 rue de la Juiverie; tapas €4.50-8, lunch menu €13.50) Dominated by an ancient plane tree, the old-town square onto which this colourful tapas bar spills could not be more enchanting – or typically Provençal. Take your pick from the Spanish-inspired tapas chalked on the board, and soak up the atmosphere on the square.

Thym, Te Voilà BISTRO €€

(☎04 90 74 28 25; www.thymtevoila.com; 59 place St-Martin; menus lunch €17.50-22, dinner €22-26; ⏲noon-2pm & 7.30-10pm Tue-Sat; 🖉) *Cuisine du monde* is what's on offer at this charming little bistro – in other words, a little bit of

everything, from a splash of Asian spice to a traditional Hungarian goulash. It's on a lovely square in the old town, with outside tables next to the tinkling fountain in summer.

Information

Tourist Office (04 90 74 03 18; www.luberon-apt.fr; 20 av Philippe de Girard; 9.30am-1pm & 2.30-7pm Mon-Sat, 9.30am-12.30pm Sun Jul & Aug, 9.30am-12.30pm & 2-6pm Mon-Sat Sep-Jun) Excellent source of information for activities, excursions, bike rides and walks.

Maison du Parc du Luberon (04 90 04 42 00; www.parcduluberon.fr; 60 place Jean Jaurès; 8.30am-noon & 1.30-6pm Mon-Fri, 9am-noon Sat Apr-Sep, shorter hours rest of year) A central information source for the Parc Naturel Régional du Luberon, with maps, walking guides and general info. There's also a small fossil museum.

Getting There & Around

BICYCLE

Bike hire and general cycling supplies and services are available from **Luberon Cycles** (04 86 69 19 00; 86 quai Général-Leclerc; per half-day/day from €12/16; 9am-noon & 2-6pm Mon-Sat).

BUS

The **bus station** (250 av de la Libération) is just a few blocks east of the city centre. Trans-Vaucluse (www.vaucluse.fr) buses leave from here to the following towns, and charge a flat-rate €2 to most destinations:

Aix-en-Provence (Line 9.1, two hours, two or three daily, one on Sunday) Via Bonnieux, Lourmarin and Lauris.

Avignon (Line 15.1, 1½ hours, every two hours Monday to Saturday, two on Sunday) Travels via the Pont Julien near Bonnieux, Cavaillon and Avignon's TGV station.

Banon (Line 16.2, 1¾ hours, two daily Monday to Saturday) Via Caseneuve and Simiane-la-Rotonde; an extra bus runs on Wednesday and Sunday.

Cavaillon (Line 15.2, 45 minutes, one to three daily depending on school term times) Via Bonnieux, Ménerbes and Oppède; extra buses run during school terms.

North of Apt

Some of Provence's quintessential sights – impossibly pretty villages, beehive-shaped *bories* (primitive dry-limestone dwellings), lavender fields and a stunning Cistercian abbey – lie just a few kilometres apart on the rugged northern side of the Luberon.

Make reservations as far ahead as possible for lunch and dinner, lest you go hungry. Every table fills in high season.

Gordes & Around

Like a giant wedding cake rising over the Rivers Sorgue and Calavon, the tiered village of Gordes juts spectacularly out of the white-rock face of the Vaucluse plateau. Gordes is high on many tourists' must-see lists (notably celebrity Parisians): summer brings a cavalcade of buses, and car parks are choked. Arrive early or late, or expect to be crammed onto narrow footpaths, dodging tourists and buses. Come sunset, the village glows gold – an eye-popping sight.

Sights

★ Abbaye Notre-Dame de Sénanque CHURCH

(04 90 72 05 72; www.abbayedesenanque.com; adult/child €7.50/3.50; 9.45-11am Mon-Sat, tours by reservation) Situated 4km northwest of Gordes off the D177, this supremely peaceful spot provides one of the classic postcard images of this part of Provence: a graceful Cistercian abbey surrounded by swathes of purple lavender. The best displays are usually in July and August. You can wander around the grounds on your own from 9.45am to 11am, but at other times (and to visit the abbey's cloistered interior) you must join a guided tour.

Musée de la Lavande MUSEUM

(04 90 76 91 23; www.museedelalavande.com; D2, Coustellet; adult/child €6.80/free; 9am-7pm May-Sep, 9am-noon & 2-6pm Oct-Apr) To get to grips with Provence's most prestigious crop, this excellent eco-museum makes an ideal first stop. An audioguide and video (in English) explain the lavender harvest, and giant copper stills reveal extraction methods. Afterwards you can take a guided tour of the fields (1pm and 5pm daily May to September). The on-site boutique is an excellent (if pricey) one-stop shop for top-quality lavender products. There's also a picnic area in the lavender-festooned garden. It's located about 7.5km southwest of Gordes on the D2, in the direction of Coustellet.

Moulin des Bouillons DISTILLERY

(04 90 72 22 11; www.moulindesbouillons.com; rte de St-Pantaléon; adult/child €5/3.50; 10am-noon & 2-6pm Wed-Mon Apr-Oct) Heading 3.5km south from Gordes along rte de St-Pantaléon (D148), you hit this marvellous rural

museum: an olive-oil mill with a 10m-long Gallo-Roman press weighing 7 tonnes – reputedly the world's oldest. The adjoining stained-glass museum showcases beautiful translucent mosaics; a joint ticket costs adult/child €7.50/5.50.

Village des Bories ARCHITECTURE
(04 90 72 03 48; adult/child €6/4; 9am-8pm, shorter hours winter) Beehive-shaped *bories* (stone huts) bespeckle Provence and at the Village des Bories, 4km southwest of Gordes, an entire village of them can be explored. Constructed of slivered limestone, *bories* were built during the Bronze Age, inhabited by shepherds until 1839, then abandoned until their restoration in the 1970s. Visit early in the morning or just before sunset for the best light. Note that the lower car park is for buses; continue to the hilltop car park to avoid hiking uphill in the blazing heat.

Sleeping

★**Les Balcons du Luberon** B&B €€
(06 38 20 42 13; www.lesbalconsduluberon.fr; rte de Murs; d €110-170;) Uphill from Gordes' centre on the D15, this ravishing five-room B&B makes a wonderful bolthole. It's in an 18th-century stone farmhouse, but the decor is totally 21st century – all designer furniture, funky lights and minimal clutter. There's a gorgeous pool, and owner Étienne Marty (a trained chef) offers a lavish dinner by reservation (€35).

Mas de la Régalade B&B €€
(04 90 76 90 79; www.masregalade-luberon.com; D2, Quartier de la Sénancole; d €130-160; mid-Apr–mid-Nov;) A stone farmhouse on a grassy plain surrounded by oak woodlands, 3.5km south of Gordes, Mas de la Régalade's four rooms artfully blend mod cons with playful antiques. In the garden, a vintage blue Citroën peeks between scented hedgerows of lavender and rosemary, beyond the big pool. Discounts for longer stays.

★**Auberge de Carcarille** HOTEL €€
(04 90 72 02 63; www.auberge-carcarille.com; rte d'Apt; d from €81-130;) Old outside, new inside: this country hotel marries the atmosphere of a traditional *bastide familiale* (family house) with spotless, modern rooms. There's a delightful garden to wander, and the restaurant serves superior Provençal food (lunch/dinner *menu* €25/40); half-board deals are great value. It's 3km from Gordes, at the bottom of the valley.

Le Mas de la Beaume B&B €€
(04 90 72 02 96; www.labeaume.com; rte de Cavaillon, Gordes; d €160-230;) In a visually stunning hilltop locale at the edge of the village, this impeccable five-room *maison d'hôte* is like a Provençal postcard come to life, with yellow-washed stone-wall rooms decorated with bunches of lavender hanging from wood-beamed ceilings. Beds are dressed in high-thread-count linens, and breakfast is delivered to your room.

Eating

Le Gordes-Manger CAFE €
(04 90 72 08 01; rue André Lhote; mains €8-14; noon-3pm & 7-9pm) For a no-fuss, good-value lunch, make a beeline for this fine little hole-in-the-wall cafe run by a husband-and-wife team. Nothing fancy here, just solid, delicious Provençal market-driven food: a rich octopus stew, perhaps, or a fresh tomato, burrata and aubergine salad drizzled with lashings of local olive oil. Tables are limited (a few inside, a few more outside under umbrellas), so arrive early.

★**Le Mas Tourteron** GASTRONOMIC €€€
(04 90 72 00 16; www.mastourteron.com; chemin de St-Blaise les Imberts; menu lunch/dinner €48/57; 7.30-9.30pm Wed-Sat, 12.30-2pm Sun Apr-Oct) A longstanding gourmet table, where chef Elisabeth Bourgeois-Baique showcases her passion for traditional Provençal dishes like roast guinea-fowl and herb-crusted lamb, spiced with occasionally exotic ingredients (her assistant chef is Japanese). It's in an attractive country house,

WORTH A TRIP

L'ISLE-SUR-LA-SORGUE

A moat of flowing water encircles the ancient and prosperous town of L'Isle-sur-la-Sorgue, 7km west of Fontaine-de-Vaucluse. This 'Venice of Provence' is home to several antiques villages, housing 300 dealers between them. Sunday is the big market day, with antique vendors participating as well, while Thursday offers a smaller market through the village streets.

L'Isle dates to the 12th century, when fishermen built huts on stilts above what was then a marsh. By the 18th century, canals lined with 70 giant wheels powered silk factories and paper mills.

DON'T MISS

PROVENCE'S COLORADO

Reds and oranges, scarlets and yellows, purples and crimsons – the fiery colours burned into the earth between Roussillon and Rustrel are astonishing. They're the result of the area's rich mineral deposits, especially hydrated iron oxide, otherwise known as **ochre**, which has been mined in this part of the Luberon since Roman times. Traditionally used to colour earthenware and paint buildings, around the late 18th century, the extraction process was industrialised, and large mines and quarries sprang up. In 1929, at the peak of the ochre industry, some 40,000 tonnes of ochre was mined around Apt.

There are several ochre-themed sites to visit around Roussillon, but for the full technicolour experience, head for the **Colorado Provençal** (04 32 52 09 75; www.colorado-provencal.com; 9am-dusk), a quarry site where ochre was mined from the 1880s until 1956. With its weird rock formations and rainbow colours, it's like a little piece of the Southwest USA plonked down amongst the hills of Provence.

Colour-coded trails lead from the car park, signposted south of Rustrel village, off the D22 to Banon. Parking costs €4 (free November to March), or you can walk down from the village. The site gets blazingly hot in summer: start early, carry water and wear hiking boots and a hat – and don't be surprised if you take some ochre home with you on your clothes (the best idea is to wait till it dries and brush it off).

For extra thrills, try the treetop assault courses on offer at nearby **Colorado Aventures** (06 78 26 68 91; www.colorado-adventures.fr; adult/child €19/14; 9.30am-7.30pm Jul & Aug, 10am-7pm Mar-Jun, Sep & Nov).

3.5km south of Gordes off the D2: aim for one of the lovely garden tables if you can.

Information

Tourist Office (04 90 72 02 75; www.gordes-village.com; place du Château; 9am-noon & 2-6pm Mon-Sat, 10am-noon Sun) Located inside Gordes' medieval château, which was enlarged and given its defensive Renaissance towers in 1525.

Roussillon

POP 1353

Red by name, red by nature, that's Roussillon – once the centre of local ochre mining, and still unmistakably marked by its crimson colour (villagers are required to paint their houses according to a prescribed palette of some 40 tints). Today it's home to artists' and ceramicists' workshops, and its charms are no secret: arrive early or late.

During WWII the village was the hideout for playwright Samuel Beckett, who helped the local Resistance by hiding explosives at his house and occasionally going on recce missions. Parking (€3 March to November) is 300m outside the village.

Sights & Activities

Conservatoire des Ocres et de la Couleur ARTS CENTRE
(L'Usine d'Ocre Mathieu; 04 90 05 66 69; www.okhra.com; rte d'Apt; guided tours adult/student €6.50/5; 10am-7pm Jul & Aug, to 6pm Sep-Jun, closed Mon & Tue Jan & Feb;) This art centre is a great place to see ochre in action. Occupying a disused ochre factory on the D104 east of Roussillon, it explores the mineral's properties through hands-on workshops and guided tours of the factory. The shop upstairs stocks paint pigments and other artists' supplies. The centre also rents bikes (adult/child €28/22).

Mines de Bruoux HISTORIC SITE
(04 90 06 22 59; www.minesdebruoux.fr; rte de Croagnes; adult/child €8.10/6.50; 10am-7pm Jul & Aug, to 6pm Apr-Jun, Sep & Oct) In Gargas, 7km east of Roussillon, this former mine has more than 40km of underground galleries where ochre was once extracted. Around 650m are open to the public, some of which is as much as 15m high. Visits are only by guided tour; reserve ahead as English-language tours are at set times.

The caverns sometimes provide a stunning setting for concerts; check the website for schedules.

★**Sentier des Ocres** HIKING
(Ochre Trail; adult/child €2.50/free; 9.30am-5.30pm;) In Roussillon village, groves of chestnut and pine surround sunset-coloured ochre formations, rising on a clifftop. Two circular trails, taking 30 or 50 minutes to complete, twist through mini-desert landscapes – it's like stepping into a Georgia

LOCAL KNOWLEDGE

PICNIC PERFECT

Those short of time or money in Gordes should follow the locals downhill along rue Baptistin Picca to **La Boulangerie de Mamie Jane** (☎04 90 72 09 34; rue Baptistin Picca; lunch menus from €6.50; ⏲6.30am-1pm & 2-6pm Thu-Tue), which has been in the same family for three generations. Mamie Jane cooks up outstanding bread, pastries, cakes and biscuits, including lavender-perfumed *navettes* and delicious peanut-and-almond brittle known as *écureuil* (from the French for squirrel).

O'Keeffe painting. Information panels highlight 26 types of flora to spot, the history of local ochre production, and so on. Wear walking shoes and avoid white!

Information

Tourist Office (☎04 90 05 60 25; www.roussillon-provence.com; place de la Poste; ⏲9am-noon & 1.30-5.30pm Mon-Sat) General information on the village's history and suggestions for walking routes through the surrounding area.

St-Saturnin-lès-Apt & Around

POP 2479

About 9km north of Apt and 10km northeast of Roussillon, St-Saturnin-lès-Apt is refreshingly ungentrified and just beyond the tourist radar. Shops (not boutiques), cafes and bakeries line its cobbled streets. It has marvellous views of the surrounding Vaucluse plateau – climb to the ruins atop the village for knockout views. Or find the photogenic 17th-century windmill, Le Château les Moulins, 1km north, off the D943 towards Sault.

Sleeping & Eating

Le Saint Hubert HOTEL €

(☎04 90 75 42 02; www.hotel-saint-hubert-luberon.com; d €57-63, tr €73) Charm personified, this quintessential village *auberge* (country inn) has welcomed travellers since the 18th century and is a gorgeous spot to stay. Rooms are simple but elegant, and the sweeping view of the southern Luberon from valley-facing rooms is breathtaking – especially considering the bargain-basement rates.

The restaurant (two-/three-course lunch menu €16.50/20.50, dinner menu €30) is also well worth a visit, with a truly glorious panoramic terrace. If you're staying, ask about half-board.

Le Mas Perréal B&B €€

(☎04 90 75 46 31; www.masperreal.com; Quartier la Fortune; d €130-140, self-catering studio €100-150;) Surrounded by vineyards, lavender fields and cherry orchards, on a vast 7-hectare property outside St-Saturnin-lès-Apt, this farmhouse B&B offers a choice of cosy rooms or self-catering studios, both filled with country antiques and Provençal fabrics. There's a heavenly pool and big garden with mountain views. Elisabeth, a long-time French teacher, offers cooking and French lessons. It's 2km southwest of town along the D2.

Au Point de Lumière B&B €€

(☎04 90 04 83 14; www.aupointdelumiere.com; 771 chemin de Perréal; d €120-135;) What a find this stylish B&B is. The three rooms all have their own theme – choose from soothing Alizarine, cool Zen or exotic Sienne – and all come with luxurious spoils like Italian showers and private terraces overlooking the garden. There's a lovely pool shaded by trees, and owner Jean-Claude gets breakfast goodies straight from the market every day.

★**La Coquillade** FRENCH €€€

(☎04 90 74 71 71; www.coquillade.fr; Le Perrotet, Gargas; menus lunch €39, dinner €72-90; ⏲12.30-1.30pm & 7.30-9.30pm mid-Apr–mid-Oct) Overnighting at this luxurious hilltop estate won't suit everyone's budget, but everyone should try to fork out for the great-value Bistrot lunch menu. Michelin-starred and run by renowned chef Christophe Renaud, it'll be one of the most memorable meals you'll have in the Luberon. It's a 13km drive west from St-Saturnin, near the village of Lioux; there are plenty of signs, but phone ahead to confirm directions.

The hotel itself is a stunner, with luxurious rooms (doubles €325 to €390) overlooking a sea of vines.

Le Petit Luberon

The westernmost extent of the Luberon massif, the Petit Luberon's craggy hills are interspersed with wooded valleys, vineyards and rural farms. It's separated from the Grand Luberon by the slash of the Combe de Lourmarin, which cuts north–south through the mountains and is tracked by the D943 between Bonnieux and Lourmarin.

Bonnieux

Settled during the Roman era, Bonnieux is another bewitching hilltop town that still preserves its medieval character. It's intertwined with alleys, cul-de-sacs and hidden staircases: from place de la Liberté, 86 steps lead to 12th-century Église Vieille du Haut. Look out for the alarming crack in one of the walls, caused by an earthquake.

The pleasure here is just to wander – especially if you time your visit for the lively Friday market, which takes over most of the old town's streets.

In the scrubby hills about 6km south of Bonnieux, a twisty back road slopes up to the wonderful **Fôret des Cèdres** (Cedar Forest; ⌚dawn-dusk), whose spreading boughs provide welcome relief from Provence's punishing summer heat. Various paths wind through the woods, including a new nature trail that's accessible for wheelchairs. The trip up to the forest is worth the drive by itself: the wraparound views of the Luberon valley and its *villages perchés* (hilltop towns) are out of this world. Take the D36 towards Buoux and look out for the signs.

Sleeping & Eating

La Couleur des Vignes B&B €€
(☎06 77 85 97 92; www.lacouleurdesvignes.com; r €120-140; P 📶 🏊) On the edge of the village, this is the kind of place that inspires serious life envy. It feels wonderfully secluded, with fragrant lavender-filled gardens overlooking the Luberon hills, and five rooms named after local villages and stuffed with rustic-chic (thick walls, beams, tiles, fireplaces). But it's the eye-popping 20m infinity pool that has the real wow factor.

★ **Maison Valvert** B&B €€€
(☎06 72 22 37 89; www.maisonvalvert.com; rte de Marseille; d €200-225, tree house €290; 📶 🏊) Wow – for our money, this could well be the most stylish B&B in the Luberon. On an 18th-century *mas* (farm) and lovingly renovated by Belgian owner Cathy, it's straight out of a designer magazine: neutral-toned rooms, natural fabrics, solar-heated pool and fabulous buffet breakfast. For maximum spoils, go for the ultra-romantic tree house.

Market MARKET
Bonnieux' huge Friday-morning market is (along with Apt's) one of the biggest and best in the Luberon. It sprawls over several streets in the village centre, with local farmers and producers selling everything from local cheeses, hams and charcuterie to the reddest, ripest tomatoes you could ever hope to see.

Lacoste

Situated 6.5km west of Bonnieux, Lacoste has nothing to do with the designer brand – although it does have couturier connections. In 2001 designer Pierre Cardin purchased the 9th-century **Château de Lacoste** (☎04 90 75 93 12; www.chateau-la-coste.com), and much of the village, where the Marquis de Sade (1740–1814) retreated in 1771, when his writings became too scandalous for Paris. The château was looted by revolutionaries in 1789, and the 45-room palace remained an eerie ruin until Cardin arrived. He created a 1000-seat theatre and opera stage adjacent, only open during the month-long **Festival de Lacoste** (www.festivaldelacoste.com; ⌚Jul). Daytime visits are possible only by reservation.

PEDAL POWER

Don't be put off by the hills – the Luberon is a fantastic destination for cyclists. Several bike routes criss-cross the countryside, including **Les Ocres à Vélo**, a 51km route that takes in the ochre villages of Apt, Gargas, Rustrel, Roussillon and Villars, and the **Véloroute du Calavon**, a purpose-built bike path that follows the route of a disused railway line for 28km between Beaumettes in the west (near Coustellet), via Apt, to La Paraire in the west (near St-Martin-de-Castillon). Plans are underway to extend the trail all the way from Cavaillon to the foothills of the Alps, but it'll be a while before it's completed.

For longer trips, **Le Luberon à Vélo** (☎04 90 76 48 05; www.leluberonavelo.com; 203 rue Oscar Roulet, Robion) has mapped a 236km itinerary that takes in pretty much the whole Luberon. Tourist offices stock detailed route leaflets and can provide information on bike rental, luggage transport, accommodation and so on.

Several companies offer e-bikes, which have an electric motor. They're not scooters – you still have to pedal – but the motor helps on the ascents.

Ménerbes

Hilltop Ménerbes is another wonder for wandering, with a maze of cobbled alleyways that afford sudden glimpses over the surrounding valleys. It became famous as the home of ex-pat British author Peter Mayles, whose books *A Year in Provence* and *Toujours Provence* recount his tales of renovating a farmhouse just outside the village in the the late 1980s. Monsieur Mayle now lives in Lourmarin.

A shrine to corkscrews, quirky **Musée du Tire-Bouchon** (☎04 90 72 41 58; www.domaine-citadelle.com; adult/child €5/free; ⏲9am-noon & 2-7pm Apr-Oct, 10am-noon & 2-5pm Mon-Sat Nov-Mar) displays over 1000 of them at Domaine de la Citadelle, a winery on the D3 toward Cavaillon, where you can sample Côtes du Luberon.

Opposite the town's 12th-century church, **Maison de la Truffe et du Vin** (☎04 90 72 38 37; www.vin-truffe-luberon.com; place de l'Horloge; ⏲10am-noon & 2.30-6pm daily Apr-Oct, Thu-Sat Nov-Mar) is home to the Brotherhood of Truffles and Wine of the Luberon, and represents 60 local *domaines*. From April to October, there are free wine-tasting sessions daily, and afterwards you can buy the goods at bargain-basement prices. Winter brings truffle workshops.

Oppède-le-Vieux

Jutting from a craggy hilltop 3km from the modern town of Oppède, Oppède-le-Vieux was abandoned in 1910, when villagers moved down the hill to the valley to cultivate the plains.

From the car parks (€3), a wooded path leads up to the village's snaking, atmospheric alleyways. At the very top of town, the village's ruined castle provides a formidable vantage point over the surrounding valley – although the ruins themselves are off limits while the village raises funds for the castle's restoration.

Several artists and ceramicists have set up their studios here, and sell their wares during the summer. Signs from the car parks also direct you to the **Sentier Vigneron**, a 1½-hour viticulture trail through olive groves, cherry orchards and vineyards.

For lunch, **Le Petit Café** (☎04 90 76 74 01; www.lepetitcafe.fr; place de la Croix; menus €18-25; ⏲8.30am-11.30pm) serves inventive Provençal dishes on the village square.

Le Grand Luberon

Divided from the hills of the Petit Luberon to the west by a deep river canyon, the Combe de Lourmarin, the scenic hills of the Grand Luberon are made for exploring. The main villages of note are Buoux, known for its small medieval fort, and Saignon, a sleepy place with impressive views. Take your time along the winding back roads: the scenery deserves to be savoured.

Buoux

Dominated by the hilltop ruins of Fort de Buoux, the tiny village of Buoux (the 'x' is pronounced) sits across the divide from Bonnieux, 8km south of Apt. The village itself is little more than a collection of a few tumbledown houses, but the **fort** is worth walking up to for the views – be careful, as the path is badly worn and crumbling in places. Signs show you the way, but ask anywhere in the village for directions.

You won't get a more honest Provençal lunch than at Maurice Leporati's roadside inn, **Auberge de la Loube** (☎04 90 74 19 58; lunch/dinner menu from €25/33; ⏲by reservation noon-3pm & 7.30-9pm), where the feast always starts with wicker trays filled with hors d'oeuvres such as tapenade and *anchöiade* (olive and anchovy dips), quail's eggs, braised artichokes, aïoli and hummus. The showpiece Sunday lunch is legendary.

Saignon

Even in a land of heart-stoppingly pretty villages, little Saignon still manages to raise an admiring eyebrow. Perched high on a rocky flank, surrounded by lavender fields and overlooked by the crumbling remains of a medieval castle, its cobbled streets and central square (complete with cascading fountain) are the stuff of which Provençal dreams are made.

A short trail leads up to the castle ruins and the aptly titled **Rocher de Bellevue**, a fabulous viewpoint overlooking the entire Luberon range, stretching north to Mont Ventoux on a clear day.

Above the village, the D113 climbs to the **Distillerie Les Agnels** (☎04 90 74 34 60; www.lesagnels.com; rte de Buoux, btwn Buoux & Apt; adult/child €6/free; ⏲10am-7pm Apr-Sep, to 5.30pm Oct-Mar), which uses locally grown lavender, cypress and rosemary in its fragrant products. It also rents three gorgeous

self-contained cottages (€1300 to €2000 per week) that share a glorious heated pool covered by a greenhouse roof.

There's one reason to make a detour to hilltop Caseneuve, 10km east of Saignon, and that's to eat at **Le Sanglier Paresseux** (04 90 75 17 70; www.sanglierparesseux.com; Caseneuve; menus lunch €25, dinner €35-49; noon-2pm Tue-Sun, 7-9pm Tue-Sat). Run by Brazilian chef Fabricio Delgaudio, it's one of the Luberon's most talked about tables. Cuisine is inventive, unfussy, seasonal and the perfect showcase for regional ingredients – and the view from the vine-shaded terrace is unforgettable. Reservations essential.

NORTHEASTERN PROVENCE & THE SOUTHERN ALPS

Haute-Provence's heady mountain ranges arc across the top of the Côte d'Azur to the Italian border, creating a far-flung crown of snowy peaks and precipitous valleys. To the west, a string of sweet, untouristy hilltop villages and lavender fields drape the Vallée de la Durance. Magical Moustiers Ste-Marie is a gateway to the plunging white waters of Europe's largest canyon, the Gorges du Verdon. In the east, the Vallée des Merveilles wows with 36,000 Bronze Age rock carvings. In the far north are the winter ski slopes and summer mountain retreats of the Ubaye and Blanche Valleys. Outside of ski areas, many establishments close in winter.

Pays de Forcalquier

Beyond the radar of most tourists, the area around Forcalquier is great for leisurely exploring: wildflower-tinged countryside, isolated villages, lavender farms and the spectre of the mountains never too far away. You'll pass through as you travel east from the Luberon towards the Alps.

Sights

★Prieuré de Salagon MONASTERY, GARDENS
(04 92 75 70 50; www.musee-de-salagon.com; adult/child/family €8/6/22; 10am-8pm Jun-Aug, to 7pm May & Sep, to 6pm Oct–mid-Dec & Feb-Apr;) Situated 4km south of Forcalquier near Mane, this peaceful priory dates from the 13th century. It's worth a visit to wander around its medieval herb gardens, fragrant with native lavender, mint and mugwort, and a show garden of world plants. There are also regular workshops on topics ranging from foraging to paper-making.

Old Town AREA
To reach the citadel and its little octagonal chapel, it's a 20-minute walk uphill via shady backstreets and winding steps. At the top there's a viewing platform offering panoramic views. On the way back down, keep an eye out for some of the town's impressive wooden doorways, dating from the days when Forcalquier was the pre-Revolutionary seat of power for the Comtes de Provence.

Ecomusée l'Olivier MUSEUM
(04 92 72 66 91; www.ecomusee-olivier.com; adult/child €4/free; 10am-6pm Mon-Fri, 1.30-6pm Sat) If all the olive groves around Forcalquier have inspired your curiosity, head 15km southeast to Volx, where this intriguing eco-museum explains the extraction process and the olive tree's importance to Mediterranean culture. There's also a posh shop where you can pick up souvenirs, and taste various olive-oil varieties, as well as an excellent Provençal restaurant, **Les Petites Tables** (04 86 68 53 14; lespetitestables@gmail.com; lunch mains €10-16; noon-3pm Tue-Sat), that's perfect for lunch.

Sleeping & Eating

★Relais d'Elle B&B €
(04 92 75 06 87, 06 75 42 33 72; http://relais-delle.com; rte de la Brillane, Niozelles; s/d/tr/q from €60/75/90/115;) What a stunner of a B&B this is, 8km from Forcalquier in a delightful ivy-covered farmhouse dating from 1802, surrounded by tended gardens, bucolic countryside and a grand pool. The sweet, feminine rooms all have views – we liked Collines for its cosiness and Pierres for its atmosphere. The owners are passionate about horses. They also offer a delicious dinner by reservation.

Couvent des Minimes HOTEL €€€
(04 92 74 77 77; www.couventdesminimes-hotelspa.com; chemin des Jeux de Maï, Mane; r from €275;) A real budget-buster, but boutique in every sense of the word. Housed in a converted convent, it pulls out all the luxury stops: beautiful rooms, an indulgent spa and a superb restaurant, all wrapped up in wonderful medieval architecture. Low-season and last-minute deals often bring prices down a notch. It's in the village of Mane on the D4100.

Café de Niozelles PROVENCAL, ITALIAN €€
(☎04 92 73 10 17; http://bistrot.niozelles.net; place du Village, Niozelles; set menu €26; ⏰12.30-2.30pm & 7-9pm Fri-Wed; ❄) For just-like-mama-made-it French cuisine, it's worth the 5km drive to this unashamedly old-fashioned bistro in Niozelles. You'll need an appetite, and a taste for all the traditional trimmings, like offal, tripe and sheep trotters, but you won't find a more authentic French meal in the Pays de Forcalquier.

Information

Tourist Office (☎04 92 75 10 02; www.forcalquier.com; 13 place du Bourguet; ⏰9am-noon & 2-6pm Mon-Sat) Information on walks, cycling routes, hot-air ballooning and other activities in the Forcalquier area. Useful iPhone app: 'visit 04.'

Getting There & Around

Various bus routes stop in Forcalquier on the way to the Alps.

Bachelas Cycles (☎04 92 75 12 47; www.bachelas-cycles.com; 5 bd de la République; per day/week from €19/81; ⏰9am-12.30pm & 2-7pm Mon-Wed, Fri & Sat) Bike hire (standard and e-bike) in Forcalquier. Also has a branch in Manosque (☎04 92 72 15 84; 24 bd de la Plaine; per day/week from €19/81; ⏰8.30am-12.30pm & 2-8pm Mon-Sat).

Vallée de la Durance

Halfway between the Luberon and the high Alps lies the broad, flat floodplain of the River Durance. Centuries ago, this natural pass was crossed by the Via Domitia – the main road that enabled Roman legionnaries and traders to travel through the south of Gaul. It's now crossed by a more modern equivalent: the A8 motorway.

The area is also famous for its lavender fields, especially around Manosque and the nearby Plateau de Valensole. Many growers offer guided visits and sell products direct: ask in any local tourist office for one of the free *Routes de la Lavande* leaflets. There's also a new lavender museum in Digne-les-Bains.

Travelling north from Forcalquier towards Sisteron, you can't miss the mysterious **Rochers des Mées**: rows and rows of rocky pinnacles, some as high as 100m. Legend claims they were once monks, turned to stone for lusting after Saracen women. A loop trail travels through the formations, taking around 3½ hours from end to end.

Ganagobie's otherworldly **Monastère Notre Dame de Ganagobie** (☎04 92 68 00 04; www.ndganagobie.com; Ganagobie; ⏰3-5pm Tue-Sun, shop 10.30am-noon & 2.30-6pm Tue-Sun) is another essential stop. Founded in the 10th century, it's still home to a working Benedictine community, who produce products including soaps, honey, jam and beer, all for sale in the monastery shop. The chapel (worth a visit for its fabulous 12th-century floor mosaics) is the only area open to the public, but you're free to wander around most of the grounds.

It's located at the end of a winding 4km lane; look out for signs on the D4096 as you travel between Forcalquier and Sisteron. Note that the monastery is closed during times of monastic retreat.

To get around town, **Bachelas Cycles** rents mountain, road, tandem and electric bicycles, and **LER Buses** (Lignes Express Régionales; ☎08 21 20 22 03; www.info-ler.fr) connect Forcalquier, Mane and St-Michel l'Observatoire with Apt, Avignon, Digne-les-Bains, Sisteron, Manosque, Aix-en-Provence and Marseille. The Forcalquier tourist office has complete info.

Gorges du Verdon

For sheer, jaw-dropping drama, few sights in France can match the epic Gorges du Verdon. The 'Grand Canyon of Europe' slices a 25km swath through Haute-Provence's limestone plateau all the way to the foothills of the Alps. Etched out over millions of years by the Verdon River, the gorges have formed the centrepiece of the Parc Naturel Régional du Verdon since 1997. With their sheer, plunging cliffs – in some places 700m high, twice the height of the Eiffel Tower – the gorges are a haven for birds, including a colony of reintroduced *vautours fauves* (griffon vultures).

From the top of the cliffs, the Verdon River itself seems little more than a silver trickle, but down at gorge level it takes on a different character: it's one of France's best spots for white-water rafting. The canyon floors are only accessible by foot or raft, and it's worth experiencing the gorges from both bottom and top to get a proper sense of their brain-boggling size.

The main gorge begins at Rougon, near the confluence of the Verdon and Jabron Rivers. The most useful jumping-off points are Moustiers Ste-Marie, in the west, and Castellane, in the east.

Activities

Cycling & Driving

A complete circuit of the Gorges du Verdon from Moustiers Ste-Marie involves 140km of driving, not to mention a relentless series of hairpin turns. There's a cliffside road on either side of the gorges, but passing spots are rare, roads are narrow and rockfalls are possible – so take it slow and enjoy the scenery.

Spring and autumn are ideal times to visit: the roads can be traffic-clogged in summer and icy in winter. The Route des Crêtes is snowbound from mid-November to mid-March.

The only village en route is La Palud-sur-Verdon (930m), so make sure you've got a full tank of gas before setting out.

Route des Crêtes DRIVING TOUR
(D952 & D23; closed mid-Nov–mid-Mar) A 23km-long loop with 14 lookouts along the northern rim with drop-dead vistas of the plunging Gorges du Verdon. En route the most thrilling view is from **Belvédère de l'Escalès** – one of the best places to spot vultures overhead.

Outdoor Sports

Castellane is the main water-sports base (April to September); its tourist office has lists of local operators. Most charge similar rates for rafting, canyoning, kayaking and hydrospeed expeditions: around €35 for two hours, €55 for a half-day and €75 for a full day. Safety kit is provided, but you'll get (very) wet, so dress appropriately. Reservations are required.

Lac de Castillon's beaches are popular for swimming and paddle boating, while St-André-les-Alpes, on the lakeshore, is France's leading paragliding centre.

Latitude Challenge ADVENTURE SPORTS
(04 91 09 04 10; www.latitude-challenge.fr; bungee jumps €115) Bungee jumps from Europe's highest bungee site, the 182m Pont de l'Artuby (Artuby Bridge). Also offers skydiving.

Aqua Viva Est WATER SPORTS
(04 92 83 75 74, 06 82 06 92 92; www.aquavivaest.com; 12 bd de la République, Castellane; 10.30am-1.30pm & 4-6.30pm Mon-Sat) With an office handily placed across from the main square in Castellane, Aqua Viva Est organises rafting, canyoning, hydrospeed and kayaking expeditions.

Aérogliss PARAGLIDING
(04 92 89 11 30; www.aerogliss.com; chemin des Iscles, St-André-les-Alpes; intro flights from €75) Offers 'baptism' flights for novice paragliders, as well as catering to more experienced fliers.

Via Ferrata du Rocher de Neuf Heures CLIMBING
(www.ot-dignelesbains.fr; 6am-8pm high season, 8am-5pm low season) Inspired by the system of fixed ladders and cables that Italian troops used to travel through the Dolomites in WWII, Digne's via ferrata course allows you all the thrill of rock climbing without the need for experience. If you've done it before, you can rent the necessary kit at the tourist office – or arrange a guide if it's your first time.

Walking

Dozens of blazed trails traverse the wild countryside around Castellane and Moustiers. Tourist offices carry the excellent, English-language *Canyon du Verdon* (€4.70), detailing 28 walks, as well as maps of five principal walks (€2.40).

Note that wild camping anywhere in the gorges is illegal. Don't cross the river, except at bridges, and always stay on marked trails, lest you get trapped when the upstream dam opens, which happens twice weekly. Check water levels and the weather forecast with local tourist offices before embarking.

Sortie de Découverte des Vautours du Verdon WILDLIFE WATCHING
(04 92 83 61 14; adult/child €10/6; 9.30am & 6pm Tue, Wed & Fri mid-Jun–mid-Sep) Guided tours to watch vultures in the Gorges du Verdon. Book through Castellane's tourist office.

Sleeping & Eating

Mas du Verdon B&B €
(04 92 83 73 20; www.masduverdon.com; Quartier d'Angles; r €59-67, apt €84; Apr-Oct;) A peaceful farmhouse retreat, hidden away 1km south of town on the Verdon's banks. It's lodged inside an attractive 18th-century farmhouse, and offers four rooms named after herbs and flowers, as well as a self-catering apartment. *Table d'hôte* dinners (€24 per person, or €30 with wine) are available by reservation from May to September.

Gîte de Chasteuil B&B €
(04 92 83 72 45; www.gitedechasteuil.com; Hameau de Chasteuil; incl breakfast d €73-89, tr €103-117; Mar-Nov) Around 12km west of Castellane, this excellent-value *chambre d'hôte* run by Nancy and Pascal resides in a former schoolhouse with gorgeous mountain views. It is an ideal stop for hikers along

the GR4. Excellent *table d'hôte* (€20/24 on Tuesday/Friday) are available by reservation.

Auberge du Teillon PROVENÇAL, GASTRONOMIC €€ (☎04 92 83 60 88; www.auberge-teillon.com; D4805/rte Napoléon, La Garde; d €65-80, menus €29-59) Located 5km east of Castellane on the road to Grasse, this much-loved roadside hotel has a handful of simple rooms up top, but it's the restaurant that's the main draw. Cuisine is 'Provençal classic' and the atmosphere is formal: the Sunday lunch is a feast to be remembered.

Information

Castellane Tourist Office (☎04 92 83 61 14; www.castellane-verdontourisme.com; rue Nationale; 9am-7.30pm daily Jul & Aug, 9am-noon & 2-6pm Mon-Sat & 10am-1pm Sun May-Jun & Sep, closed Sun rest of year) The best source for info on river trips and the eastern side of the Gorges du Verdon.

Moustiers Ste-Marie Tourist Office (☎04 92 74 67 84; www.moustiers.eu; 9.30am-7pm Mon-Fri, 9.30am-12.30pm & 2-7pm Sat & Sun Jul & Aug, 10am-noon & 2-6pm Apr-Jun & Sep, closes around 5pm rest of year;) Excellent service, general info on the Gorges du Verdon and free wi-fi.

Getting There & Away

Public transport in the gorges is limited, but the useful **Navette Gorges du Verdon** (☎04 92 34 22 90; autocars.delaye@orange.fr) shuttle bus links Castellane with Point Sublime, La Palud and La Maline (but not Moustiers). Services run twice-daily in July and August and weekends April to June and in September. The fare costs between €2 and €6.

There's also a daily LER Bus from Marseille to Riez (€16.90), Moustiers (€18.30) and Castellane (€25.80). The single fare from Moustiers to Castellane is €7.10.

Moustiers Ste-Marie & Around

POP 710 / ELEV 634M

Dubbed 'Étoile de Provence' (Star of Provence), jewel-box Moustiers Ste-Marie crowns towering limestone cliffs, which mark the beginning of the Alps and the end of Haute-Provence's rolling prairies. A 227m-long chain, bearing a shining gold star, is stretched high above the village – a tradition, legend has it, begun by the Knight of Blacas, who was grateful to have returned safely from the Crusades. Twice a century, the weathered chain snaps, and the star gets replaced, as happened in 1996. In summer, it's clear that Moustiers' charms are no secret.

Sights & Activities

Chapelle Notre Dame de Beauvoir CHURCH (guided tours adult/child €3/free) Lording over the village, beneath Moustiers' star, this 14th-century church clings to a cliff ledge like an eagle's nest. A steep trail climbs beside a waterfall to the chapel, passing 14 stations of the cross en route. On 8 September, Mass at 5am celebrates the nativity of the

OFF THE BEATEN TRACK

PARC NATIONAL DU MERCANTOUR

Created in 1979, this vast national park covers seven separate alpine valleys and a total area of 685 sq km. Pocked by deep valleys and spiked with jagged peaks, and dominated by the Cime du Gélas (3143m), the third-highest mountain in the Alps-Maritimes, it's a haven for outdoor activities: skiing and snowboarding in winter, hiking and biking in summer, and pretty much everything else besides.

It's also celebrated for its flora and fauna, including rare species such as the ibex, the mouflon, the golden eagle and even a few wild grey wolves, which you can see roaming semi-wild at the excellent **Alpha wolf park** (☎04 93 02 33 69; www.alpha-loup.com; Le Boréon; adult/child €12/10; 10am-5pm or 6pm Apr-Oct;) near the mountain village of St-Martin-Vésubie. Nearby, the remote **Vallée des Merveilles** has many Bronze Age rock carvings, and can only be visited on foot during the summer months.

The area's deep, high-sided gorges also make for spectacular driving, especially along plunging canyons such as the **Gorges de Daluis**, where the rock glows red from mineral deposits. Note that several of the high mountain passes between the valleys are closed by seasonal snows from October to May.

Les Guides RandOxygène (www.randoxygene.org) has indispensable activity guides.

Virgin Mary, followed by flutes, drums and breakfast on the square.

Musée de la Faïence MUSEUM

(☎04 92 74 61 64; rue Seigneur de la Clue; adult/student/under 16yr €3/2/free; ⊙10am-12.30pm Jul & Aug, to 5pm or 6pm rest of year, closed Tue year-round) Moustiers' decorative *faïence* (glazed earthenware) once graced the dining tables of Europe's most aristocratic houses. Today each of Moustiers' 15 ateliers has its own style, from representational to abstract. Antique masterpieces are housed in this little museum, adjacent to the town hall.

Des Guides pour l'Aventure OUTDOORS

(☎06 85 94 46 61; www.guidesaventure.com) Offers activities including canyoning (from €45 per half-day), rock climbing (€40 for three hours), rafting (€45 for 2½ hours) and 'floating' (€50 for three hours) – which is like rafting, except you have a buoyancy aid instead of a boat.

Sleeping

★ **Ferme du Petit Ségriès** FARMSTAY €

(☎04 92 74 68 83; www.chambre-hote-verdon.com; d incl breakfast €74-84;) Friendly hosts Sylvie and Noël offer five colourful, airy rooms in their rambling farmhouse, 5km west of Moustiers on the D952 to Riez. Family-style *tables d'hôte* (€30 with wine, served daily except on Wednesday and Sunday) are served at a massive chestnut table, or outside beneath a foliage-covered pergola in summer. Bikes are available for hire (from €15 per day). Noël is a mountain-bike guide and runs excellent tours (from €78).

Clos des Iris HOTEL €

(☎04 92 74 63 46; www.closdesiris.fr; chemin de Quinson; d €75-89, f €110-160; ⊙Jan-Sep; P) A sweet, simple family hotel, shaded by shutters and pergolas, and surrounded by lovely leafy gardens. There are nine bedrooms, and the owners also run a self-catering cottage down the road.

La Ferme Rose HOTEL €€

(☎04 92 75 75 75; www.lafermerose.com; chemin de Quinson; d €85-159;) This Italianate terracotta-coloured farmhouse, signposted off the D952 to Ste-Croix de Verdon, is as eclectic and charming as it gets in Provence.

SHOPPING FOR LAVENDER

When shopping for lavender, it's worth knowing that the most sought-after product is fine lavender (in French, *lavande fine;* in Latin, *Lavandula angustifolia, L vera, L officinalis*), not spike lavender (*L latifolia*) or the hybrid lavandin (*L hybrida*). The latter are high in camphor and are used in detergents and paint solvents, not perfume.

Its interior is crammed with quirky collectibles – including a Wurlitzer jukebox, a display case of coffee grinders, and vintage steam irons on the turquoise-tiled staircase. Colourful, airy rooms look out onto unending flowery gardens. Breakfast €12.

Eating

★ **La Grignotière** PROVENCAL €

(☎04 92 74 69 12; rte de Ste-Anne; mains €6-15; ⊙11.30am-10pm May-Sep, to 6pm Feb–mid-May) Hidden behind the soft pink facade of Moustiers' Musée de la Faïence is this utterly gorgeous, blissfully peaceful garden restaurant. Tables sit between olive trees and the colourful, eye-catching decor – including the handmade glassware – is the handiwork of talented, dynamic owner Sandrine. Cuisine is 'picnic chic', meaning lots of creative salads, tapenades, quiches and so on.

La Treille Muscate PROVENCAL €€

(☎04 92 74 64 31; www.restaurant-latreillemuscate.fr; place de l'Église; lunch/dinner menus from €24/32; ⊙noon-2pm Fri-Wed, 7.30-10.30pm Fri-Tue) The top place to eat in the village proper: classic Provençal cooking served with panache, either in the stone-walled dining room or on the terrace with valley views. Expect tasty dishes like oven-roasted lamb served with seasonal veg and rainbow trout with *sauce vierge.* Reservations recommended.

Getting There & Away

A car makes exploring the gorges much more fun, though if you're very fit, cycling is an option too. Bus services run to Castellane and Moustiers, but there's scant transport inside the gorges.

The French Riviera & Monaco

POP 2.90 MILLION

Includes ➡

Best Places to Eat

- ➡ Café de la Fontaine (p862)
- ➡ Le Mirazur (p870)
- ➡ Le Bistrot d'Antoine (p830)
- ➡ Bobo Bistro (p837)
- ➡ Philcat (p837)

Best Places to Sleep

- ➡ Nice Excelsior (p829)
- ➡ Les Rosées (p844)
- ➡ Les Cabanes d'Orion (p848)
- ➡ Hôtel Le Canberra (p837)
- ➡ La Maison du Frêne (p847)

Why Go?

With its glistening seas, idyllic beaches and fabulous weather, the Riviera (known as Côte d'Azur to the French) encapsulates many people's idea of the good life. The beauty is that there is so much more to do than just going to the beach – although the Riviera does take beach-going very seriously: from nudist beach to secluded cove or exclusive club, there is something for everyone.

Culture vultures will revel in the region's thriving art scene: the Riviera has some fine museums, including world-class modern art, and a rich history to explore in Roman ruins, WWII memorials and excellent museums.

Foodies for their part will rejoice at the prospect of lingering in fruit and veg markets, touring vineyards and feasting on some of France's best cuisines, while outdoor enthusiasts will be spoilt for choice with coastal paths to explore, and snorkelling and swimming galore.

When to Go

Monaco

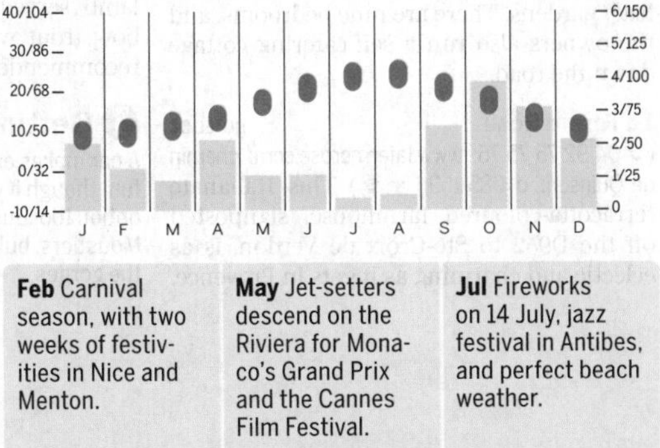

Feb Carnival season, with two weeks of festivities in Nice and Menton.

May Jet-setters descend on the Riviera for Monaco's Grand Prix and the Cannes Film Festival.

Jul Fireworks on 14 July, jazz festival in Antibes, and perfect beach weather.

Nice

POP 343,000

With its mix of real-city grit, old-world opulence, year-round sunshine and stunning seaside location, Nice is the unofficial capital of the Côte d'Azur, and a must-see for every visitor. A magnet for sunseekers and high-rollers since the 19th century, this bewitching coastal city has so much going for it, it's almost embarrassing – fabulous markets, an enticing old town, glorious architecture and a wealth of super restaurants. It's far from perfect – it's scruffy in spots, the traffic's horrendous and the beach is made entirely of pebbles – but if you really want to soak up the Riviera vibe, there's really no better place to do it.

Orientation

Av Jean Médecin runs south from near the main train station to place Masséna, close to the beach and old town. The bus station is two blocks east of place Masséna.

From the airport, 6km west, promenade des Anglais runs along the curving beachfront (Baie des Anges), becoming quai des États-Unis near the old town. Vieux Nice (Old Nice) is crunched into a 500-sq-metre area enclosed by bd Jean Jaurès, quai des États-Unis and the hill known as Colline du Château. The increasingly trendy Port Lympia area lies to the east of Colline du Château. The wealthy residential neighbourhood of Cimiez, home to some outstanding museums and belle-époque architecture, is north of the centre.

Sights

All museums in the city are free, with the exception of Musée Chagall.

★Vieux Nice — HISTORIC SITE

Getting lost among the dark, narrow, winding alleyways of Nice's old town is a highlight. The layout has barely changed since the 1700s, and it's now packed with delis, restaurants, boutiques and bars, but the centrepiece remains **cours Saleya**: a massive market square that's permanently thronging in summer. The **food market** (cours Saleya; 6am-1.30pm Tue-Sun) is perfect for fresh produce and foodie souvenirs, while the flower market is worth visiting just for the colours and fragrances. A **flea market** (cours Saleya; 8am-5pm Mon) is held on Monday.

Baroque aficionados will adore architectural gems **Cathédrale Ste-Réparate** (place Rossetti), honouring the city's patron saint; exuberant 16th-century **Chapelle de la Miséricorde** (cours Saleya); and 17th-century **Palais Lascaris** (04 93 62 72 40; 15 rue Droite; guided visit €6; 10am-6pm Wed-Mon) FREE, a frescoed riot of Flemish tapestries, faience (tin-glazed earthenware), gloomy religious paintings and 18th-century pharmacy.

There's also a lively – and very smelly – fish market (p832) on place St-François.

★Parc du Château — GARDENS

(8.30am-8pm Apr-Sep, to 6pm Oct-Mar) FREE For the best views over Nice's red-tiled rooftops, climb the winding staircases up to this wooded outcrop on the eastern edge of the old town. It's been occupied since ancient times; archaeological digs have revealed Celtic and Roman remains, and the site was later occupied by a medieval castle that was razed by Louis XIV in 1706 (only the 16th-century Tour Bellanda remains). There are various entrances, including one beside the tower, or you can cheat and ride the free **lift** (Ascenseur du Château; rue des Ponchettes; 9am-8pm Jun-Aug, 9am-7pm Apr, May & Sep, 10am-6pm Oct-Mar).

★Promenade des Anglais — ARCHITECTURE

The most famous stretch of seafront in Nice – if not France – is this vast paved promenade, which gets its name from the English expat patrons who paid for it in 1822. It runs for the whole 4km sweep of the Baie des Anges with a dedicated lane for cyclists and skaters; if you fancy joining them, you can rent skates, scooters and bikes from Roller Station (p825).

★Musée Masséna — MUSEUM

(04 93 91 19 10; 65 rue de France; adult/child €6/free; 10am-6pm Wed-Mon) Originally built as a holiday home for Prince Victor d'Essling (the grandson of one of Napoleon's favourite generals, Maréchal Massena), this lavish belle-époque building is another of the city's iconic architectural landmarks. Built between 1898 and 1901 in grand neoclassical style with an Italianate twist, it's now a

> **FAST FACTS**
>
> **Area** 10,272 sq km
>
> **Local industry** Services, technology, tourism
>
> **Signature drink** Rosé

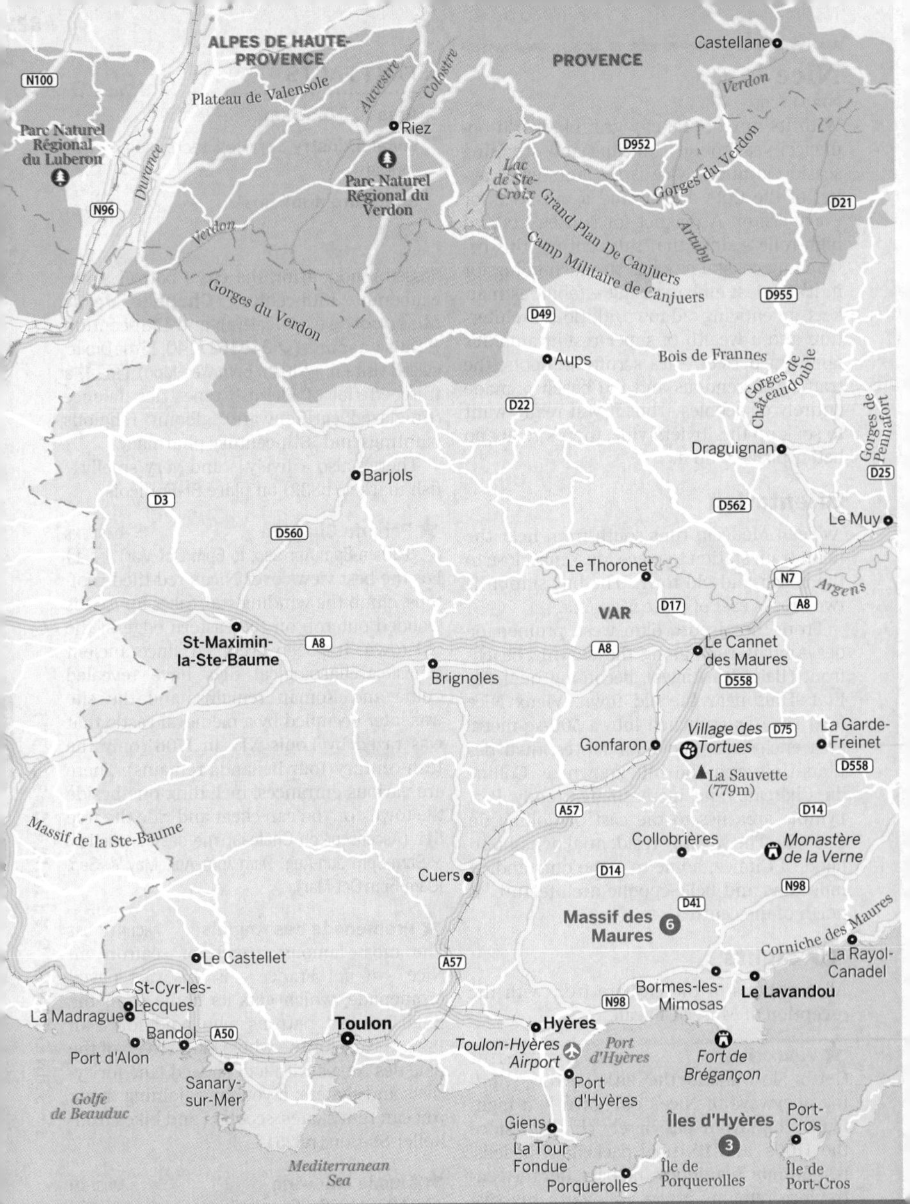

French Riviera & Monaco Highlights

❶ **Grande Corniche** (p862) Taking a scenic drive for jaw-dropping views of the Med.

❷ **Vieux Nice** (p821) Losing yourself in labyrinthine Vieux Nice and enjoying a picnic on Parc du Château.

❸ **Îles d'Hyères** (p858) Sailing a ferry through pristine Mediterranean seascapes to these beautiful islands.

❹ **St-Tropez** (p851) Hobnobbing with hipsters in the Riviera's chic port town.

❺ **St-Paul de Vence** (p848) Admiring seminal 20th-century art at Fondation Maeght.

❻ **Massif des Maures** (p854) Hiking through thick forests and scented chestnut

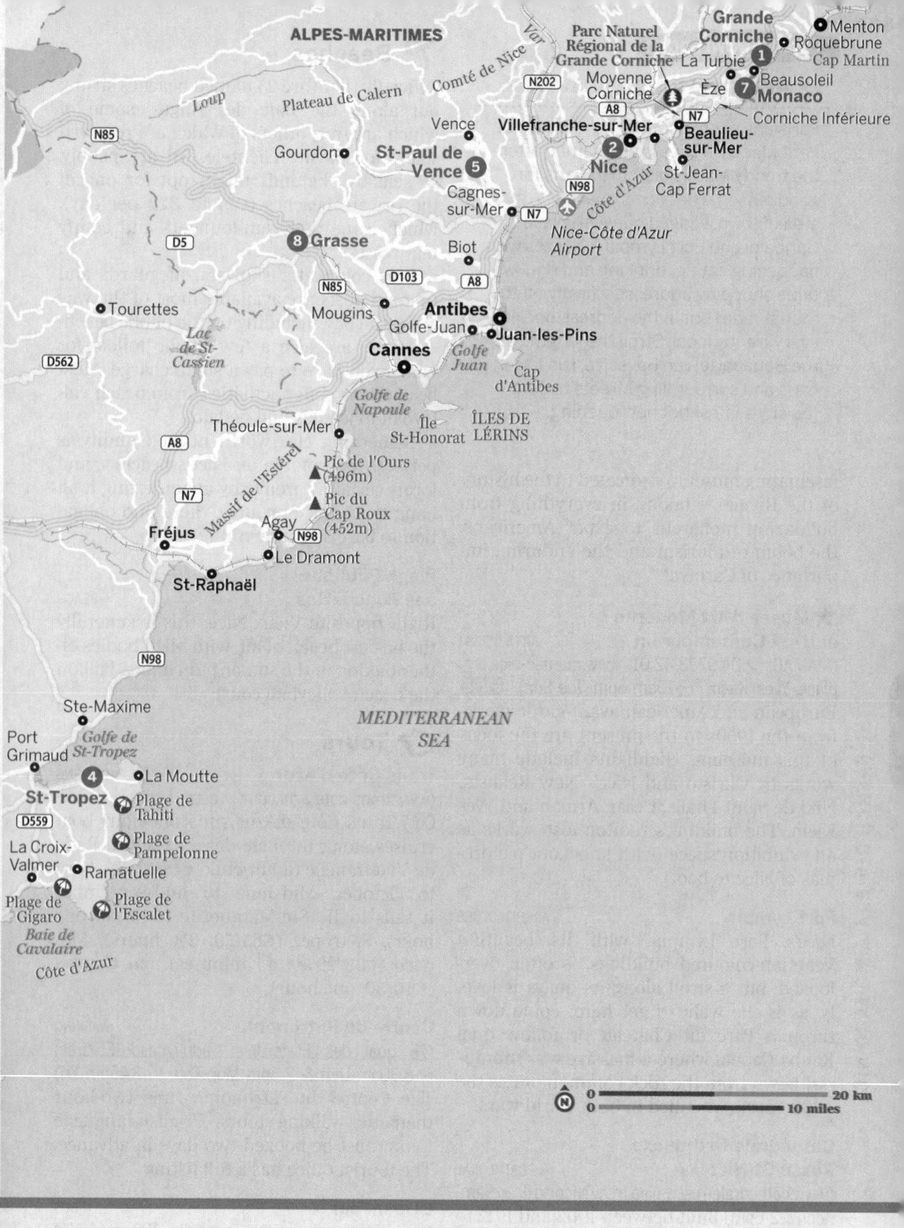

groves *sans crowds* in this wild part of southern France.

7 Monaco (p862) Trying your luck at Monte Carlo's opulent casino

8 Grasse (p845) Discovering the world of perfumery and even crafting your own scent in this celebrated perfurme-making town.

LOCAL KNOWLEDGE

LE PETIT MARAIS

Parisians might scoff at the idea, but Le Petit Marais in Nice is nicknamed after the trendy Marais district in Paris for good reason. The Niçois *quartier* – the area of town wedged between place Garibaldi and Port Lympia – buzzes with happening eating, drinking and boutique shopping addresses, firmly off the tourist radar but in the address book of every trendy local. Stroll the lengths of rue Bonaparte, rue Bavestro, rue Lascaris and surrounding streets to catch the city's latest hot new opening.

fascinating museum dedicated to the history of the Riviera – taking in everything from holidaying monarchs to expat Americans, the boom of tourism and the enduring importance of Carnival.

★Musée d'Art Moderne et d'Art Contemporain ART MUSEUM

(MAMAC; 04 97 13 42 01; www.mamac-nice.org; place Yves Klein; 10am-6pm Tue-Sun) FREE European and American avant-garde works from the 1950s to the present are the focus of this museum. Highlights include many works by Christo and Nice's New Realists: Niki de Saint Phalle, César, Arman and Yves Klein. The building's rooftop also works as an exhibition space (with knockout panoramas of Nice to boot).

Port Lympia ARCHITECTURE

Nice's Port Lympia, with its beautiful Venetian-coloured buildings, is often overlooked, but a stroll along its quays is lovely, as is the walk to get here: come down through Parc du Château or follow quai Rauba Capeu, where a massive **war memorial** hewn from the rock commemorates the 4000 Niçois who died in both world wars.

Cathédrale Orthodoxe Russe St-Nicolas CATHEDRAL

(www.cathedrale-russe-nice.fr; av Nicolas II; 9am-noon & 2-6pm) Built between 1902 and 1912 to provide a big enough church for the growing Russian community, this cathedral, with its colourful onion domes and rich, ornate interior, is the biggest Russian Orthodox church outside Russia. The cathedral boasts dozens of intricate icons – unfortunately, there is very little in the way of explanation for visitors.

Beaches

Officially there are 25 named beaches strung out along the Baie des Anges, some of which are free, others of which are reserved solely for paying clientele. All are pebbly, so sensitive behinds might opt for one of the private beaches (€15 to €22 per day), which come with sun-loungers and comfy mattresses.

Free cold-water showers, lifeguards and first-aid posts are available most of the way along the bay, including on the public beaches; there are also a few public toilets for which you have to pay a small charge. Most beaches also offer activities, from beach volleyball to jet-skis and pedalos.

Something else worth noting: nudity is perfectly acceptable on Nice's beaches, and locals certainly aren't shy about letting it all hang out – but of course, there's no obligation to bare all (or anything).

Plage Publique des Ponchettes BEACH

Right opposite Vieux Nice, this is generally the busiest beach of all, with oiled bodies either baking in the sun or punching a ball on the beach-volleyball court.

Tours

Trans Côte d'Azur BOATING

(www.trans-cote-azur.com; quai Lunel; Apr-Oct) Trans Côte d'Azur runs one-hour boat cruises along the Baie des Anges and Rade de Villefranche (adult/child €18/12.50) April to October. Mid-June to mid-September it sails to Île Ste-Marguerite (€40/30, one hour), St-Tropez (€65/50, 2½ hours), Monaco (€38/29.50, 45 minutes) and Cannes (€40/30, one hour).

Centre du Patrimoine WALKING

(75 quai des Etats-Unis; adult/child €5/free; 8.30am-1pm & 2-5pm Mon-Thu, to 3.45pm Fri) The Centre du Patrimoine runs two-hour thematic walking tours. English-language tours must be booked two days in advance. The tourist office has a full listing.

L'OpenTour BUS

(www.nice.opentour.com; opposite 109 quai des États-Unis; 1-/2-day pass adult €22/25, child €8) With headphone commentary in several languages, the open-topped bus tours (1½ hours) give you a good overview of Nice. Hop on or off at any one of 14 stops.

Activities

Roller Station SKATING
(☎04 93 62 99 05; www.roller-station.fr; 49 quai des États-Unis; skates, boards & scooters per hr/day €5/10, bicycles €5/15; ⏰9am-8pm Jul & Aug, 10am-7pm Sep-Jun) For a fantastic family outing, rent inline skates, skateboards, scooters and bicycles at this rental outlet to whizz along Nice's silky smooth Promenade des Anglais. You'll need some ID as a deposit. Count an extra €1/2 per hour/day for protective gear (helmet and pads).

Mobilboard Nice SEGWAY
(☎04 93 80 21 27; www.mobilboard.com/nice-promenade; 2 rue Halévy; 30min initiation €17, 1/2hr tour €30/50) For an effortless cruise along Promenade des Anglais, hop aboard an electric Segway. Rental includes a 15-minute lesson on how to ride the two-wheeled, battery-powered 'vehicle,' protective helmet and audioguide.

Festivals & Events

Carnaval de Nice CARNIVAL
(www.nicecarnaval.com; ⏰Feb) Held around Mardi Gras (Shrove Tuesday) since 1294. Highlights include the *batailles de fleurs* (battles of flowers), and the ceremonial burning of the carnival king on Promenade des Anglais, followed by a fireworks display.

Nice Jazz Festival MUSIC
(www.nicejazzfestival.fr; ⏰Jul) France's original jazz festival has taken on a life of its own, with fringe concerts popping up all around the venue, from Vieux Nice to Massena and the shopping streets around rue de France.

Sleeping

Accommodation is excellent and caters to all budgets, unlike many cities on the Côte d'Azur. Hotels charge substantially more during the Monaco Grand Prix. Book well in advance in summer.

Hôtel Solara HOTEL €
(☎04 93 88 09 96; www.hotelsolara.com; 7 rue de France; s €60-80, d €60-110, f €150; ⏰reception 8am-9pm; ❄📶) Were it not for its fantastic location on pedestrian rue de France and the sensational terraces that half the rooms boast, we'd say the Solara was an honest-to-goodness steal. But with those perks (and did we mention the small fridges in each room for that evening rosé?), it is budget gold. Rooms are small, but you're right in the heart of the action here.

Villa Saint-Exupéry Beach Hostel HOSTEL €
(☎04 93 16 13 45; www.villahostels.com; 6 rue Sacha Guitry; dm €40-50, d/tr €120/150; ❄@📶) It's actually a few blocks from the beach, but this longstanding city hostel has plenty of other pluses: bar, kitchen, free wi-fi, gym, games room etc, plus friendly multilingual staff and a great location. The downside? High prices (at least for a hostel) and occasionally drab decor. All dorms have a private en-suite bathroom, and sleep from three to 14.

★**Nice Pebbles** SELF-CONTAINED €€
(☎04 97 20 27 30; www.nicepebbles.com; 1-/2-/3-bedroom apt from €110/130/200; ❄📶) Nice Pebbles offers nearly a hundred apartments and villas to choose from, from one to five bedrooms: all chosen for quirkiness

DON'T MISS

MODERN ART IN CIMIEZ

Musée Matisse (☎04 93 81 08 08; www.musee-matisse-nice.org; 164 av des Arènes de Cimiez; ⏰10am-6pm Wed-Mon), 2km north in the leafy Cimiez quarter, houses a fascinating assortment of works by Matisse, including oil paintings, drawings, sculptures, tapestries and Matisse's famous paper cut-outs. The permanent collection is displayed in a red-ochre 17th-century Genoese villa in an olive grove. Temporary exhibitions are in the futuristic basement building. Matisse is buried in the **Monastère Notre Dame de Cimiez** (place du Monastère; ⏰8.30am-12.30pm & 2.30-6.30pm) cemetery, across the park from the museum.

The strange, dreamlike and often unsettling work of the Belarusian painter Marc Chagall (1887–1985) is displayed at the small **Musée National Marc Chagall** (☎04 93 53 87 20; www.musee-chagall.fr; 4 av Dr Ménard; adult/child €9/7; ⏰10am-6pm Wed-Mon May-Oct, to 5pm Nov-Apr) , which owns the largest public collection of the painter's work. The main hall displays 12 huge interpretations (1954–67) of stories from Genesis and Exodus. From the city centre, allow about 20 minutes to walk to the museum (signposted from av de l'Olivetto).

Nice

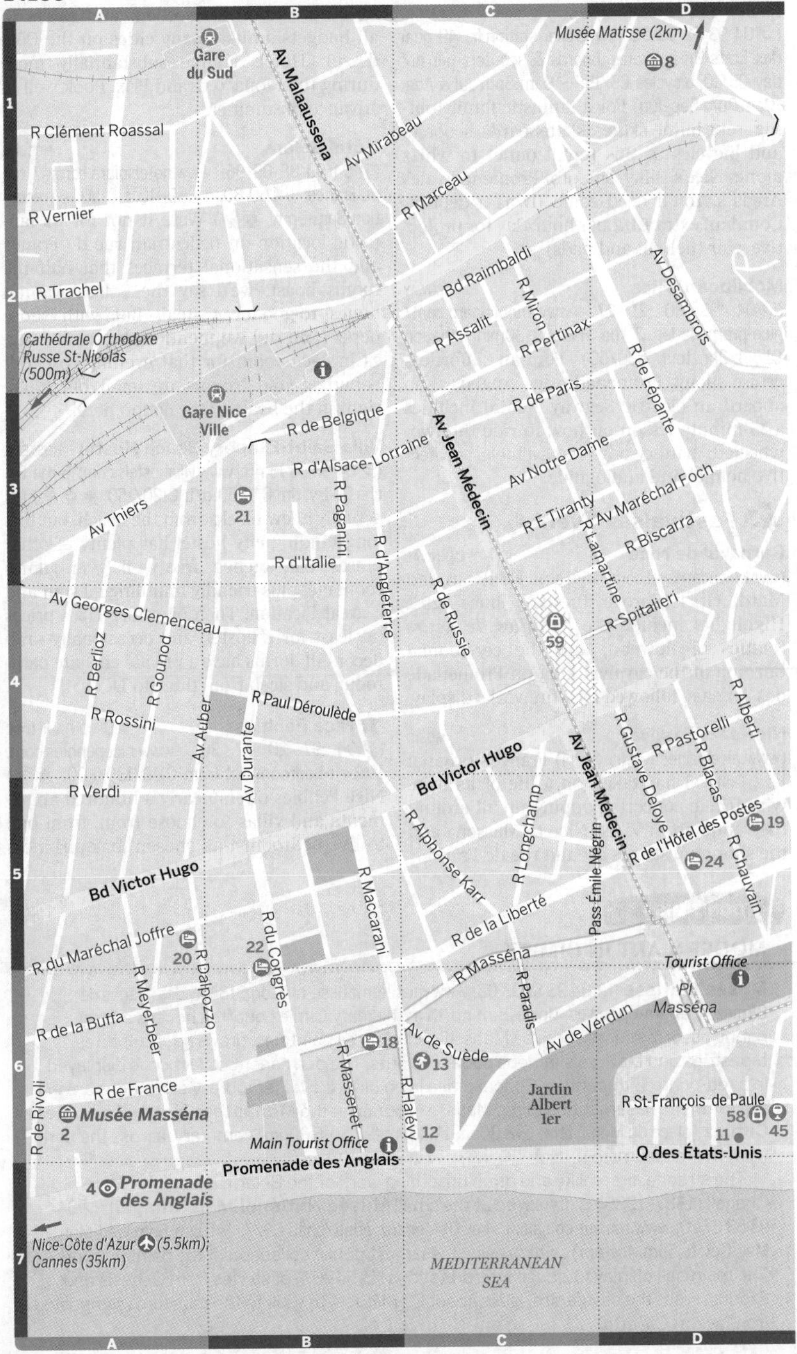

Musée Matisse (2km)
8
Gare du Sud
Av Malaaussena
Av Mirabeau
R Clément Roassal
R Marceau
R Vernier
Bd Raimbaldi
R Miron
Av Desambrois
R Trachel
R Assalit
R Pertinax
Cathédrale Orthodoxe Russe St-Nicolas (500m)
R de Lépante
R de Paris
Gare Nice Ville
R de Belgique
Av Jean Médecin
R d'Alsace-Lorraine
Av Notre Dame
Av Maréchal Foch
R Paganini
R E Tiranty
21
Av Thiers
R Biscarra
R Lamartine
R d'Italie
R d'Angleterre
R de Russie
Av Georges Clemenceau
R Spitalieri
59
R Berlioz
R Gounod
R Paul Déroulède
R Rossini
Av Auber
Av Durante
R Gustave Deloye
R Alberti
R Pastorelli
Bd Victor Hugo
R Blacas
R Verdi
R Alphonse Karr
R Longchamp
Pass Émile Négrin
R de l'Hôtel des Postes
19
R Chauvain
24
R Maccarani
R de la Liberté
R du Maréchal Joffre
20
22
R du Congrès
R Dalpozzo
R Meyerbeer
R Masséna
R Paradis
Tourist Office
Pl Masséna
R de la Buffa
Av de Verdun
18
Av de Suède
13
R Massenet
R Halévy
R de France
Jardin Albert 1er
R St-François de Paule
R de Rivoli
Musée Masséna
2
12
58
45
11
Main Tourist Office
Q des États-Unis
Promenade des Anglais
4
Nice-Côte d'Azur (5.5km); Cannes (35km)
MEDITERRANEAN SEA
A
B
C
D
1
2
3
4
5
6
7

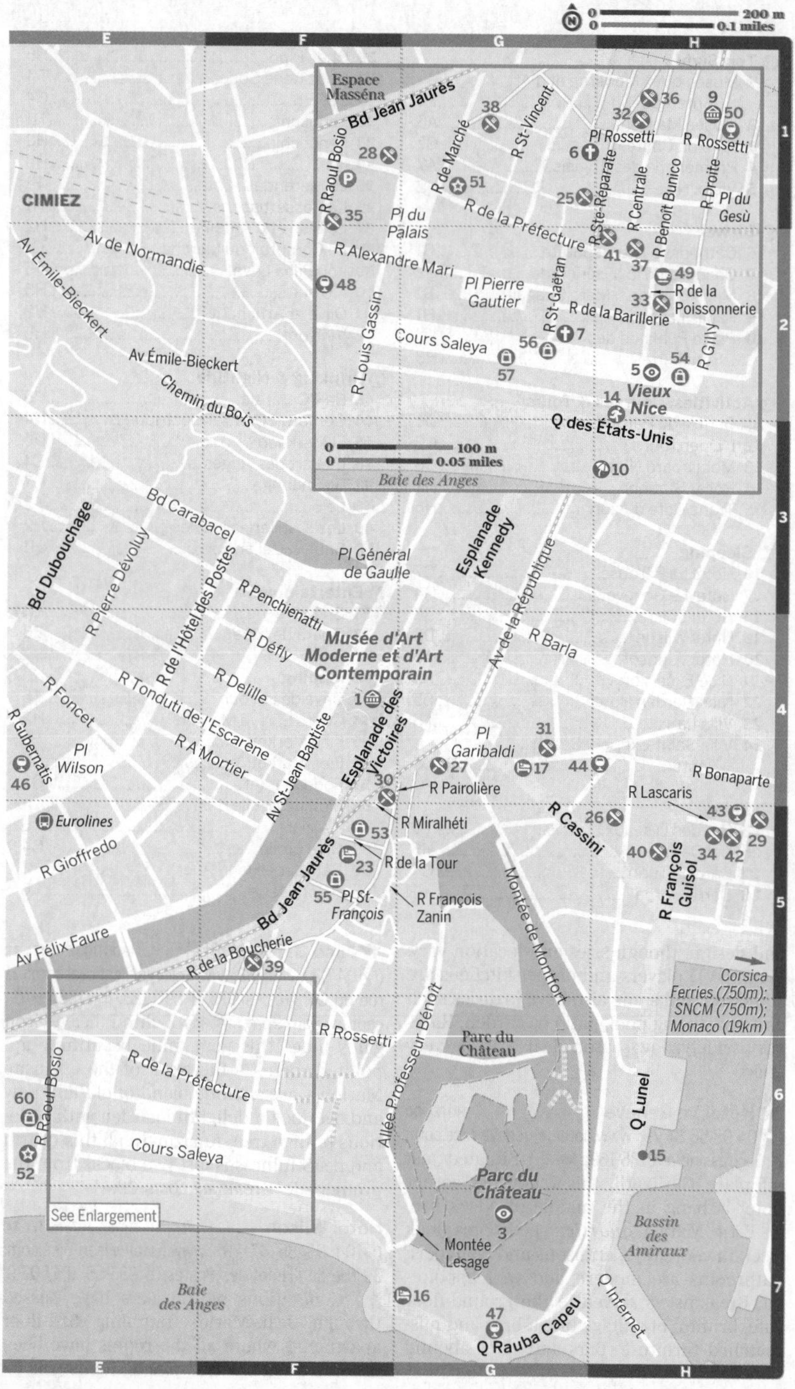

Espace Masséna
Bd Jean Jaurès
CIMIEZ
Av de Normandie
Av Émile-Bieckert
Chemin du Bois
Bd Carabacel
Bd Dubouchage
R Pierre Dévoluy
R de l'Hôtel des Postes
R Penchienatti
R Défly
R Delille
R Tonduti de l'Escarène
R A Mortier
R Foncet
R Gubernatis
Pl Wilson
Eurolines
R Gioffredo
Av Félix Faure
Av St-Jean Baptiste
Pl Général de Gaulle
Esplanade Kennedy
Musée d'Art Moderne et d'Art Contemporain
Esplanade des Victoires
Av de la République
R Barla
Pl Garibaldi
R Pairolière
R Miralhéti
R de la Tour
R François Zanin
Pl St-François
R de la Boucherie
R Rossetti
R de la Préfecture
Cours Saleya
R Raoul Bosio
See Enlargement
Allée Professeur Bénoît
Montée de Montfort
Parc du Château
Montée Lesage
Baie des Anges
Q Rauba Capeu
Q Infernet
Bassin des Amiraux
Q Lunel
R Cassini
R François Guisol
R Lascaris
R Bonaparte
Corsica Ferries (750m); SNCM (750m); Monaco (19km)
R de Marché
R St-Vincent
Pl Rossetti
R Rossetti
R Ste-Réparate
R Centrale
R Benoît Bunico
R Droite
Pl du Gesù
Pl du Palais
R Alexandre Mari
Pl Pierre Gautier
R St-Gaëtan
R de la Barillerie
R de la Poissonnerie
R Louis Gassin
R Gilly
Vieux Nice
Q des États-Unis
Baie des Anges
0 200 m
0 0.1 miles
0 100 m
0 0.05 miles

Nice

Top Sights
1 Musée d'Art Moderne et d'Art Contemporain ... F4
2 Musée Masséna ... A6
3 Parc du Château ... G7
4 Promenade des Anglais ... A7
5 Vieux Nice ... H2

Sights
6 Cathédrale Ste-Réparate ... G1
7 Chapelle de la Miséricorde ... G2
8 Musée National Marc Chagall ... D1
9 Palais Lascaris ... H1
10 Plage Publique des Ponchettes ... H3

Activities, Courses & Tours
11 Centre du Patrimoine ... D6
12 L'OpenTour ... C6
13 Mobilboard Nice ... C6
14 Roller Station ... H2
15 Trans Côte d'Azur ... H6

Sleeping
16 Hôtel La Pérouse ... G7
17 Hôtel Le Genève ... G4
18 Hôtel Solara ... B6
19 Hôtel Wilson ... D5
20 Hôtel Windsor ... A5
21 Nice Excelsior ... B3
22 Nice Garden Hôtel ... B5
23 Villa La Tour ... F5
24 Villa Saint-Exupéry Beach Hostel ... D5

Eating
25 Bar des Oiseaux ... G1
26 Bel Oeil ... H5
27 Café de Turin ... G4
28 Carré Llorca ... F1
29 Chez Pipo ... H5
30 Chez René Socca ... F4
31 Déli Bo ... G4
32 Fenocchio ... H1
33 Fenocchio ... H2
34 Jan ... H5
35 La Merenda ... F1
36 La Rossettisserie ... H1
37 Le Bistrot d'Antoine ... H2
38 Le Comptoir du Marché ... G1
39 Lou Pilha Leva ... F5
40 L'Uzine ... H5
41 Olive et Artichaut ... H2
42 Vinivore ... H5

Drinking & Nightlife
43 BaR'Oc ... H5
44 Comptoir Central Électrique ... H4
45 El Merkado ... D6
46 La Part des Anges ... E4
47 La Shounga ... G7
48 Le 6 ... F2
49 Les Distilleries Idéales ... H2
50 Snug & Cellar ... H1

Entertainment
51 Chez Wayne's ... G1
52 Opéra de Nice ... E6

Shopping
53 Cave de la Tour ... F5
54 Cours Saleya Markets ... H2
55 Fish Market ... F5
56 Flea Market ... G2
57 Food Market ... G2
58 Moulin à Huile d'Olive Alziari ... D6
59 Nice Étoile ... C4
60 Pâtisserie Henri Auer Confiserie ... E6

and design, though sizes and location vary. Wi-fi, DVD players and proper kitchens are standard, and some also have luxuries such as a swimming pool, patio or garden. Rates vary widely; low-season deals can be very good.

★Hôtel Le Genève HOTEL €€
(☎04 93 56 84 79; www.hotel-le-geneve-nice.com; 1 rue Cassini; r €135-169; ❄📶) Situated just off place Garibaldi, this renovated corner hotel is bang in the middle of Nice's lively Petit Marais *quartier*. Bedrooms look sleek in cool greys, crimsons and charcoals; bathrooms are modern and well appointed. Breakfast is served in the ground-floor cafe, brimful of vintage bric-a-brac and mismatched furniture. Bars and cafes abound here.

★Nice Garden Hôtel BOUTIQUE HOTEL €€
(☎04 93 87 35 62; www.nicegardenhotel.com; 11 rue du Congrès; s €75, d €90-123, tr €138; ⏲reception 8am-9pm; ❄📶) Behind heavy iron gates hides this gem: nine beautifully appointed rooms – the work of the exquisite Marion – are a subtle blend of old and new and overlook a delightful garden with a glorious orange tree. Amazingly, all this charm and peacefulness is just two blocks from the promenade. Breakfast costs €9.

Hôtel Wilson HOTEL €€
(☎04 93 85 47 79; www.hotel-wilson-nice.com; 39 rue de l'Hôtel des Postes; s €35-55, d €50-79; 📶) Generations of travellers have passed through Jean-Marie's rambling 3rd-floor apartment, where all the rooms have been decorated with potted plants, items collect-

ed on his travels and a faintly bohemian, hippie-hangover style (one room's styled after Frida Kahlo, another stuffed with '70s kitsch, while others have African and Asian flavours). It's a bit faded in spots, and cheaper rooms share bathrooms.

Villa La Tour BOUTIQUE HOTEL €€
(☎04 93 80 08 15; www.villa-la-tour.com; 4 rue de la Tour; d €82-350; ❄📶) This old-town favourite has 17 lovely rooms, each individually decorated to evoke a different artist – Niki de Saint Phalle, Vaco, Klein and so forth. Riviera history buffs will appreciate the Queen Victoria room. A diminutive flower-decked roof terrace is complemented by a street terrace, ideal for watching Vieux Nice go by. Breakfast costs €12.50.

Hôtel Windsor BOUTIQUE HOTEL €€
(☎04 93 88 59 35; www.hotelwindsornice.com; 11 rue Dalpozzo; d €89-290; ❄@📶🏊) Don't be fooled by the staid stone exterior: inside, many of the rooms are all surprising, with several treated as experimental painterly palettes by well-known artists. Some are frescoed, others are festooned with experimental chandeliers or photographic murals. The little garden and pool are delightful. Breakfast is overpriced at €14.

★**Nice Excelsior** DESIGN HOTEL €€€
(☎04 93 88 18 05; www.excelsiornice.com; 19 av Durante; d €169-229; ❄📶) This 1892 building is a belle-époque beauty. Inside, the hotel has been entirely refurbished, with the designers finding inspiration in Nice as a popular travel destination: the furniture has been custom-made based on old travel trunks, but with a modern, colourful twist, and rooms are decorated with postcard-like sketches of the city.

Hôtel La Pérouse BOUTIQUE HOTEL €€€
(☎04 93 62 34 63; www.hotel-la-perouse.com; 11 quai Rauba Capeu; d from €333; ❄@📶🏊) Built into the rock cliff next to Tour Bellanda, La Pérouse evokes the spirit of a genteel villa. Lower-floor rooms face a lemon-tree-shaded courtyard and pool; upper-floor rooms have magnificent sea vistas. Smart accent colours add flair to the traditional decor. Online bookings include breakfast.

Eating

Booking is advisable at most restaurants, particularly during the busy summer season. To lunch with locals, grab a pew in the midday sun on one of the many place Garibaldi cafe terraces. There are lots of restaurants on cours Saleya, but quality can be variable, so choose carefully.

★**La Rossettisserie** FRENCH €
(☎04 93 76 18 80; www.larossettisserie.com; 8 rue Mascoïnat; mains €13.50-14.50; ⊙noon-2pm & 7.30-10pm Mon-Sat) Roast meat is the order of the day here: make your choice from beef, chicken, veal or lamb, and pair it with a choice of mashed or sautéed potatoes and ratatouille or salad. Simple and sumptuous, and the vaulted cellar is a delight.

Chez Pipo NIÇOIS €
(☎04 93 55 88 82; 13 rue Bavastro; socca €2.70; ⊙11.30am-2.30pm & 5.30-11pm Tue-Sun) Everyone says the best *socca* (chickpea-flour pancakes) can be found in the old town, but don't believe them – this place near Port Lympia has been in the biz since 1923 and, for our money, knocks *socca*-shaped spots off anywhere else in Nice.

Déli Bo CAFE, BISTRO €
(☎04 93 56 33 04; 5 rue Bonaparte; mains €12-20; ⊙7am-8pm) This hybrid coffee shop–bistro is the current hang-out for discerning Niçois hipsters. It's good for lunchtime salads and other light bites, but it's the sumptuous cakes and superb coffee that ensures it's always packed. It does a great Sunday brunch too.

La Merenda NIÇOIS €
(www.lamerenda.net; 4 rue Raoul Bosio; mains €14-16; ⊙noon-2pm & 7-10pm Mon-Fri) Simple, solid Niçois cuisine – stockfish, calf tripe à la Niçoise with *panisse* (chunky, pan-fried sticks of chickpea-flour batter) and the like – by former Michelin-starred chef Dominique Le Stanc draws the crowds to this pocket-sized bistro where diners rub shoulders, literally. The tiny open kitchen stands proud at the back of the room, and the equally small menu is chalked on the board. No phone, no credit cards.

★**Olive et Artichaut** PROVENCAL €€
(☎04 89 14 97 51; www.oliveartichaut.com; 6 rue Ste-Réparate; 3-course menu €32, mains €16-22; ⊙noon-2pm & 7.30-10pm Wed-Sun) There's barely enough room to swing a pan in this tiny street bistro, especially when it's full of diners (as it often is), but it doesn't seem to faze young Niçois chef Thomas Hubert and his friendly team. He sources as much produce as possible from close-to-home suppliers (Sisteron lamb, Niçois olives, locally caught fish) and likes to give the old classics his own individual spin. Wise diners reserve.

NIÇOIS SPECIALITIES

Niçois specialities include *socca* (a savoury, griddle-fried pancake made from chickpea flour and olive oil, sprinkled with a liberal dose of black pepper), *petits farcis* (stuffed vegetables), *pissaladière* (onion tart topped with black olives and anchovies) and the many vegetable *beignets* (fritters). Try them at **Chez René Socca** (04 93 92 05 73; 2 rue Miralhéti; small plates €3-6; 9am-9pm Tue-Sun, to 10.30pm Jul & Aug, closed Nov;) or **Lou Pilha Leva** (04 93 13 99 08; 10 rue du Collet; small plates €3-5; 9am-midnight;).

★Le Bistrot d'Antoine MODERN FRENCH €€
(04 93 85 29 57; 27 rue de la Préfecture; menus €25-43, mains €15-25; noon-2pm & 7-10pm Tue-Sat) A quintessential French bistro, right down to the checked tablecloths, streetside tables and impeccable service – not to mention the handwritten blackboard, loaded with classic dishes such as rabbit pâté, pot-cooked pork, blood sausage and duck breast. If you've never eaten classic French food, this is definitely the place to start; and if you have, you're in for a treat.

Bel Oeil BISTRO €€
(09 80 33 08 38; 12 rue Emmanuel Philibert; mains €16-35; 7-11.30pm Tue-Sat, noon-2pm Sun) Light, bright and very contemporary, the Handsome Eye is a hot new local's tip in the Port Lympia area. Run by Jeanne and Christophe, it's a modern bistro with a taste for fresh and floral flavours, such as beetroot risotto with aniseed cream, or lemon-scented cod kebabs. It draws a lively after-work crowd, and the Sunday brunch is deservedly popular with Niçois in the know.

Bar des Oiseaux FRENCH €€
(04 93 80 27 33; 5 rue Saint-Vincent; mains €16-25; noon-1.45pm & 7.15-9.45pm Tue-Sat) An old town classic, in business since 1961 on a corner of a shady backstreet (expect to get lost en route). It's been various things down the years, including a bar and nightclub, and still has a few of its original saucy murals left in situ. But today it's a lively bistro serving trad French cuisine spiced up with a modern twist or two. Bookings recommended.

It's owned by local entrepreneur Armand Crespo, who also runs Le Bistrot d'Antoine.

L'Uzine MEDITERRANEAN €€
(04 93 56 42 39; 18 rue François Guisol; mains €14-20; 11am-11pm Tue-Sat) The pop art prints and artfully distressed decor set the tone at this hip little Port Lympia place (the name means 'The Factory'), which is equally popular for weekend drinks as for its bistro food. There are bands at the weekend and a predictably trendy clientele.

Vinivore BISTRO €€
(04 93 14 68 09; www.vinivore.fr; 10 rue Lascaris; dinner menu €32-25, mains €18-25; noon-2pm & 7.30-10.30pm Tue-Fri, 7.30-10.30pm Sat) The name gives it away: this place is for carnivores with a penchant for fine *vin*. There's a choice of more than 200 wines, many of which are organic and small-scale, plus a daily changing menu of four starters, four mains and three desserts. It's particularly good value at lunchtime.

Café de Turin SEAFOOD €€
(04 93 62 29 52; www.cafedeturin.fr; 5 place Garibaldi; seafood platters from €24.90; 8am-10pm) For a lavish seafood platter loaded with oysters, lobster, crab, cockles and more, this is the place to come. You can also buy individual oysters from the takeaway counter. It's also a good place to try local specialities such as *aïoli* (cod with vegetables and garlic mayonnaise) and bouillabaisse (seafood stew).

Carré Llorca BISTRO €€
(04 93 92 95 86; www.carrellorca.com; 3 rue de la Préfecture; mains €16-28; noon-10.30pm Mon-Sat) The menu at this contemporary urban bistro is signed off by Michelin-starred chef Jean-Michel Llorca. Neutral hues add an understated elegance to the clean-cut space, and the cuisine is Mediterranean with a generous dash of Niçois – lots of cooking *à la plancha* (grilling). The *pulpe* (octopus) served with new potatoes and Niçois sauces is delicious.

Jan MODERN FRENCH €€€
(04 97 19 32 23; www.restaurantjan.com; 12 rue Lascaris; 2-/3-course lunch menu €30/35, dinner menu €75; 6.30-10pm Tue-Sat, noon-2pm Fri & Sat) For the full-blown fine-dining experience, Jan Hendrik's restaurant is the top table in town. Born in South Africa, Jan's dishes are laced with Antipodean and New World flavours and crackle with artistic and culinary flair. There's nothing à la carte – Jan decides his *menus* on the day. It's high-end (dress smart) and sought after; reservations essential.

Drinking & Nightlife

La Part des Anges WINE BAR

(☎04 93 62 69 80; www.la-part-des-anges-nice.fr; 17 rue Gubernatis; ⏲10am-8.30pm Mon-Sat) The focus at this classy wine shop–bar is organic wines – a few are sold by the glass, but the best selection is available by the bottle, served with homemade tapenades and charcuterie platters. The name means the 'Angel's Share,' referring to the alcohol that evaporates as wines age.

There are only a few tables, so arrive early or reserve ahead.

Les Distilleries Idéales CAFE

(☎04 93 62 10 66; www.lesdistilleriesideales.fr; 24 rue de la Préfecture; ⏲9am-12.30am) The most atmospheric spot for a tipple in the old town, whether you're after one of the many beers on tap or a local wine by the glass. Brick-lined and set out over two floors (with a little balcony that's great for people-watching), it's packed until late.

Happy hour is from 6pm to 8pm.

El Merkado BAR

(www.el-merkado.com; 12 rue St-François de Paule; ⏲11am-1.30am) Footsteps from cours Saleya, this hip tapas bar (strapline: 'In Sangria We Trust') struts its vintage stuff on the ground floor of a quintessential Niçois townhouse. Lounging on its pavement terrace or a sofa with an after-beach cocktail is the thing to do here.

Snug & Cellar PUB

(☎04 93 80 43 22; www.snugandcellar.com; 22 rue Droite; ⏲noon-12.30am) A more chilled retreat than many of the pubs in the old town, especially if you can bag one of the prime tables in the cosy cellar. Quizzes, bands and one-off events keep the interest going.

Happy hour is from 8pm to 10pm.

Comptoir Central Électrique BAR

(☎04 93 14 09 62; www.comptoircentralelectrique.fr; 10 rue Bonaparte; ⏲8.30am-12.30am Mon-Sat) Once a lighting factory (check out the lighbulb collection inside), now a hip-and-happening Port Lympia bar with slouchy sofas, industrial-chic decor and loads of beers and wines by the glass. There's a blackboard menu of snacks to share too.

BaR'Oc WINE BAR

(☎06 43 64 68 05; 10 rue Bavastro; ⏲7pm-12.30am) Fine wine and even finer tapas – from parma ham to oven-baked *figatelli* (a type of salami from Corsica) – plus tasting platters of cheese and cold cuts.

DON'T MISS

THE BEST ICE IN TOWN

There's no shortage of ice-cream sellers in the old town, but **Fenocchio** (www.fenocchio.fr; 2 place Rossetti; 1/2 scoops €2.50/4; ⏲9am-midnight Feb-Oct) has been king of the scoops since 1966. The array of flavours is mind-boggling – olive, tomato, fig, beer, lavender and violet are just a few to try. Dither too long over the 70-plus flavours and you'll never make it to the front of the queue. For a Niçois twist, ask for *tourte de blette* (a sweet chard tart with raisins, pine kernels and parmesan). The queues are long on hot summer days, but they're generally shorter at the **second branch** (6 rue de la Poissonerie; ⏲9am-midnight Wed-Mon) around the corner.

La Shounga COCKTAIL BAR

(☎04 92 27 75 93; http://shounga.bar; 12 place Guynemer; ⏲8.30am-12.30am; 📶) Decadent, all-day desserts, ice-cream sundaes and cocktails (€8.50) are the reason to hit the sea-facing terrace of this vibrant mojito bar.

Le 6 GAY BAR

(☎0 493 626 664; www.le6.fr; 6 rue Raoul Bosio; ⏲10pm-5am Tue-Sat) Primped and pretty A-gays crowd shoulder to shoulder at Nice's compact, perennially popular gay bar. Le 6 keeps a busy event and party schedule: guest DJs, karaoke and shower shows.

Entertainment

Nice has a strong live-music tradition, from pop rock to jazz and cabaret; many bars regularly host bands.

Opéra de Nice OPERA

(www.opera-nice.org; 4-6 rue St-François de Paule) The vintage 1885 grande dame hosts operas, ballets and orchestral concerts.

Chez Wayne's LIVE MUSIC

(www.waynes.fr; 15 rue de la Préfecture; ⏲10am-2am) One of a strip of raucous drinking holes on the edge of the old town, Wayne's Place is a proper pub, through and through: plenty of beers on tap, a nightly roster of bands and big-screen sports action. Scruffy as it

DON'T MISS

THE PINE CONE TRAIN

Chugging between the mountains and the sea, the **Train des Pignes** (Pine Cone Train; www.trainprovence.com; one way/return fare Nice to Digne €23.30/46.60) is one of Provence's most picturesque train rides. The 151km track between Nice and Digne-les-Bains rises to 1000m for breathtaking views as it passes through Haute-Provence's scarcely populated backcountry.

The service runs four times a day and is ideal for a day trip inland. The beautiful medieval village of Entrevaux is just 1½ hours from Nice (return €23.60), perfect for a picnic and a wander through its historic centre and citadel.

comes, but great fun if that's what you're in the mood for.

Shopping

Shops abound in Nice, ranging from the touristy boutiques of Vieux Nice to the designer temples to fashion around rue de France and the enormous **Nice Étoile** (www.nicetoile.com; av Jean Médecin) shopping mall. For vintage (fashion and objects) and contemporary art, meander the hip Petit Marais north of Port Lympia. For gourmet gifts to take home, head for the market, where you'll find olive oil, wine, biscuits, candied fruits and much more.

Cours Saleya Markets MARKET
(cours Saleya; ⌚6am-5.30pm Tue-Sat, to 1.30pm Sun) Split between its beautiful flower market and rightly famous food market. On Mondays from 6am to 6pm, flowers and food make way for an antiques market.

Fish Market MARKET
(place St-François; ⌚6am-1pm Tue-Sun) Pick up freshly caught fish from Nice's fish market.

Cave de la Tour WINE
(☎04 93 80 03 31; www.cavedelatour.com; 3 rue de la Tour; ⌚7am-8pm Tue-Sat, 7am-12.30pm Sun) Since 1947, locals have been trusting this atmospheric *cave* (wine seller) to find the best wines from across the Alpes Maritimes and Var. It's a ramshackle kind of place, with upturned wine barrels and blackboard signs, and a loyal clientele, including market traders and fishmongers getting their early-morning wine fix. Lots of wines are available by the glass.

Moulin à Huile d'Olive Alziari FOOD
(☎04 93 62 94 03; www.alziari.com.fr; 14 rue St-François de Paule; ⌚8.30am-12.30pm & 2.15-7pm Mon-Sat) Superb (but very expensive) hand-pressed olive oil, fresh from the mill on the outskirts of Nice. It comes in several flavours of differing fruitiness. The shop also sells delicious tapenades, jams, honeys and other goodies. From Monday to Friday, you can visit the mill to see the process in action: catch bus no 3 to the Terminus stop.

Pâtisserie Henri Auer Confiserie FOOD
(☎04 93 85 77 98; www.maison-auer.com; 7 rue St-François de Paule; ⌚9am-6pm Tue-Sat) With its gilded counters and mirrors, this looks more like a 19th-century boutique than a sweet shop, but this is where discerning Niçois have been buying their *fruits confits* (crystallised fruit) since 1820.

Information

Tourist Office (Promenade des Anglais; ☎08 92 70 74 07; www.nicetourisme.com) Nice's main tourist office was closed for renovations at the time of research, but should have re-opened by now. There are two smaller alternative branches on **Promenade du Paillon** (☎08 92 707 407; Promenade du Paillon; ⌚9am-6pm Mon-Sat) and outside the **train station** (Gare de Nice; ☎08 92 70 74 07; av Thiers; ⌚9am-7pm daily Jun-Sep, 9am-6pm Mon-Sat & 10-5pm Oct-May).

Nice Tourisme (http://en.nicetourisme.com) Informative city website with info on accommodation and attractions.

Getting There & Away

AIR

Nice-Côte d'Azur Airport (☎08 20 42 33 33; www.nice.aeroport.fr; 📶) is France's second-largest airport and has international flights to Europe, North Africa and the US, with regular and low-cost airlines. The airport has two terminals, linked by a free shuttle bus.

BOAT

Nice is the main port for ferries to Corsica. **SNCM** (www.sncm.fr; quai du Commerce) and **Corsica Ferries** (www.corsicaferries.com; quai du Commerce) are the two main companies.

BUS

There is an excellent intercity bus service from Nice; tickets cost just €1.50.

Bus 100 To Menton (1½ hours) via the Corniche Inférieure and Monaco (40 minutes).

Bus 200 To Cannes (1½ hours).

Bus 400 To Vence (1¼ hours) via St-Paul de Vence (one hour).

Bus 500 To Grasse (1½ hours).

Eurolines (www.eurolines.com; 27 rue de l'Hôtel des Postes) serves long-haul European destinations.

Getting Around

TO/FROM THE AIRPORT

Nice is relatively spread out, but since the weather is often good and the city beautiful and pedestrian-friendly, walking is the best way to get around.

BICYCLE

Vélo Bleu (☎04 93 72 06 06; www.velobleu.org) is Nice's shared-bicycle service. It's great value and very convenient for getting round town, with 100-plus stations around the city – pick up your bike at one, return it at another.

One-day/week subscriptions costs €1/5, plus usage: free for the first 30 minutes, €1 the next 30, then €2 per hour thereafter. Some stations are equipped with terminals to register directly with a credit card; otherwise you'll need a mobile phone (beware of roaming charges).

The handy Vélo Bleu app allows you to find your nearest station, gives real-time information about the number of bikes available at each and calculates itineraries.

BUS & TRAM

Buses and trams in Nice are run by **Lignes d'Azur** (www.lignesdazur.com). Tickets cost just €1.50 (or €10 for a 10-journey pass) and include one connection, including intercity buses within the Alpes-Maritimes *département*.

Buses are particularly handy to get to Cimiez and the port. Night buses run from around 9pm until 2am.

CAR & MOTORCYCLE

Traffic, a confusing one-way system, and pricey parking mean driving in Nice is a bad idea – it's better to explore the city first, then head back out to the airport and rent your car there instead.

Holiday Bikes (☎04 93 160 162; http://loca-bike.fr; 23 rue de Belgique; ⏲9.30am-12.30pm & 2.30-6.30pm Mon-Sat, 10am-noon & 5-6.30pm Sun) rents 50cc scooters/125cc motorcycles for €30/55.

Cannes

POP 74,626

There are few places in the world where you can go from showbiz glitz and opulent luxury to remote rural life within 45 minutes. This is one of them. Glamorous Cannes sets camera flashes popping at its film festival in May, when stars pose in tuxes and full-length gowns on the red carpet of La Croisette – you could fine dine alongside the famous and drink until dawn in the seaside town's designer bars. A 'take two' scenario could find you fleeing the congested city to walk along peaceful trails and wander farmers' flower-filled fields by day and dine decadently by night.

Equally compelling is the region's art heritage: Matisse, Picasso and Renoir all stopped here for inspiration, and the works they left behind are superb. Then there's the Massif de l'Estérel, with its rugged, flaming, red-rock beauty and top-rated walks.

As you walk among the couture shops and palaces of La Croisette, the wealth and glamour of it all cannot fail to impress: admiring Ferraris and Porsches cruising by and celebrity spotting on the glitzy sunlounger-striped beaches and liner-sized

TRAINS FROM NICE

Nice has excellent train connections to pretty much everywhere on the coast, and many towns further afield too.

DESTINATION	FARE (€)	DURATION	FREQUENCY
Cannes	5.90	40min	hourly
Grasse	9.30	1¼hr	hourly
Marseille	35-38	2½hr	hourly
Menton	4.60	35min	half-hourly
Monaco	3.30	25min	half-hourly
Paris	66-140	5¾hr	hourly
St-Raphaël	11.50	1¼hr	hourly

Cannes

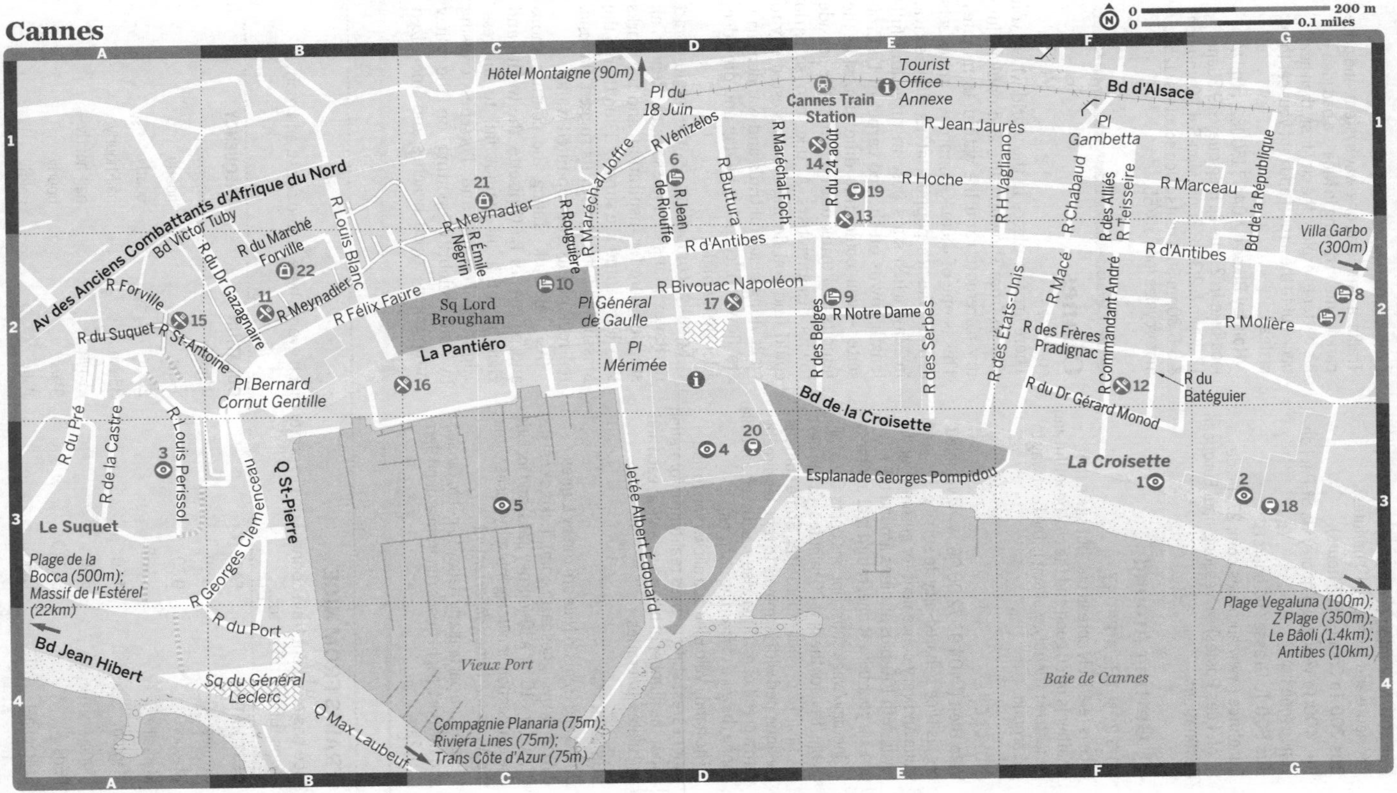
0 200 m
0 0.1 miles
Hôtel Montaigne (90m)
Pl du 18 Juin
Cannes Train Station
Tourist Office Annexe
Bd d'Alsace
R Jean Jaurès
Pl Gambetta
R Vénizélos
R Maréchal Joffre
R Jean de Riouffe
R Buttura
R Maréchal Foch
R du 24 août
R Hoche
R H Vagliano
R Chabaud
R des Alliés
R Teisseire
R Marceau
Bd de la République
Villa Garbo (300m)
R d'Antibes
R Molière
Av des Anciens Combattants d'Afrique du Nord
Bd Victor Tuby
R du Marché Forville
R du Dr Gazagnaire
R Louis Blanc
R Meynadier
R Émile Négrin
R Rouguière
R Forville
R du Suquet
R St-Antoine
R Félix Faure
Sq Lord Brougham
La Pantiéro
Pl Général de Gaulle
R Bivouac Napoléon
R des Belges
R Notre Dame
R des Serbes
R des États-Unis
R Macé
R Commandant André
R des Frères Pradignac
R du Batéguier
R du Dr Gérard Monod
Pl Mérimée
Pl Bernard Cornut Gentille
Bd de la Croisette
Esplanade Georges Pompidou
La Croisette
R du Pré
R de la Castre
R Louis Perissol
Q St-Pierre
R Georges Clemenceau
Le Suquet
Jetée Albert Édouard
Plage de la Bocca (500m); Massif de l'Estérel (22km)
R du Port
Bd Jean Hibert
Sq du Général Leclerc
Vieux Port
Q Max Laubeuf
Compagnie Planaria (75m); Riviera Lines (75m); Trans Côte d'Azur (75m)
Baie de Cannes
Plage Vegaluna (100m); Z Plage (350m); Le Bâoli (1.4km); Antibes (10km)

Cannes

yachts moored at the port are hot Cannes pastimes.

Whether Cannes' soul has managed to survive its celebrity-playground status is another question, but, there's still enough natural beauty to make a trip worthwhile: the harbour, the bay, the clutch of islands off the coast and the old quarter, Le Suquet, all spring into life on a sunny day.

Sights

★La Croisette — ARCHITECTURE

The multi-starred hotels and couture shops lining the iconic bd de la Croisette (aka La Croisette) may be the preserve of the rich and famous, but anyone can enjoy strolling the palm-shaded promenade – a favourite pastime among Cannois at night, when it twinkles with bright lights. Views of the Baie de Cannes and nearby Estérel mountains are beautiful, and seafront hotel palaces dazzle in all their stunning art-deco glory.

Palais des Festivals et des Congrès — LANDMARK

(Festival & Congress Palace; 1 bd de la Croisette; guided tour adult/child €4/free) Posing for a selfie on the 22 steps leading up to the main entrance to this concrete bunker – unlikely host to the world's most glamorous film festival – at the western end of La Croisette is a Cannes essential. Afterwards, wander along the **Allée des Étoiles du Cinéma**, a footpath of 46 celebrity hand imprints in the pavement – pick up the start of it with the hands of Meryl Streep in front of the tourist office.

The only way to enter the festival building and walk into the auditorium, tread the stage and learn about cinema's most glamorous event is with a Palais des Festivals guided tour organised by the Cannes tourist office (p841). Tours can only be booked in person at the tourist office; check dates on its website.

La Malmaison — NOTABLE BUILDING

(☎04 97 06 44 90; 47 bd de la Croisette) Walk a few blocks along La Croisette to La Malmaison, a seaside pavilion in the former games and tea room of Cannes' grandest hotel of the 1860s, the Grand Hôtel (opened in 1864, shut in 1950, demolished and rebuilt in the 1960s). Modern art exhibitions fill part of La Malmaison today.

Vieux Port — PORT

(Old Port) The celebrity yachts that line the port are here to remind you of Cannes' celebrity status, lest you forget it.

Le Suquet — HISTORIC SITE

Follow rue St-Antoine and snake your way up Le Suquet, Cannes' oldest district, for great views of the bay.

Beaches

Z Plage — SWIMMING

(☎04 93 90 12 34; La Croisette; ⏲9.30am-6pm May-Sep) Expect to pay €36/32/42 for the blue sunloungers on the front row/other rows/pier of the super-stylish Z Plage, the beach of Hôtel Martinez. Booking ahead is advised.

Plage Vegaluna — SWIMMING

(☎04 93 43 67 05; www.vegaluna.com; La Croisette; sunloungers €15-25; ⏲9.30am-7pm; 👪) Family-friendly private beach.

DON'T MISS

ÎLES DE LÉRINS

Although just 20 minutes away by boat, these tranquil islands feel far from the madding crowd. **Île Ste-Marguerite**, where the mysterious Man in the Iron Mask was incarcerated during the late 17th century, is known for its bone-white beaches, eucalyptus groves and small marine museum. Tiny **Île St-Honorat** has been a monastery since the 5th century: you can visit the church and small chapels and stroll through the monks' vineyards. Boats leave Cannes from quai des Îles on the western side of the harbour. **Riviera Lines** (04 92 98 71 31; www.riviera-lines.com; quai Max Laubeuf) runs ferries to Île Ste-Marguerite and **Compagnie Planaria** (www.cannes-ilesdelerins.com; quai Max Laubeuf) covers Île St-Honorat.

Tours

Trans Côte d'Azur BOATING

(04 92 98 71 30; www.trans-cote-azur.com; quai Max Laubeuf) June to September, this boat company sails to St-Tropez (adult/child return €49/39), Monaco (€53/39) and the Île Ste-Marguerite (€40/30). Shorter, two-hour cruises (€27/18) take in the dramatic contrasts of the Estérel's red cliffs, green forests and intense azure waters.

Festivals & Events

Cannes lives for music in the summer, so come prepared to party hard.

Festival de Cannes FILM

(www.festival-cannes.com; May) Cannes' world-famous celebration of cinema. You won't get in to any of the premiers, but it's fun because you see all the celebs walking around.

Festival d'Art Pyrotechnique FIREWORKS

(www.festival-pyrotechnique-cannes.com) Around 200,000 people cram onto La Croisette every summer to admire the outstanding fireworks display over the Baie de Cannes. Magical. Held on six nights from July to August.

Les Plages Électroniques MUSIC

(www.plages-electroniques.com; 1-day pass €16.10, 2-/3-day pass €31.10/51.28) DJs spin on the sand at the Plage du Palais des Festivals during this relaxed festival. Held July to August, once a week for five or six weeks.

Festival Pantiero MUSIC

(www.festivalpantiero.com; tickets €25-30; early Aug) Electronic-music and indie-rock festival on the terrace of the Palais des Festivals; very cool.

Sleeping

During festival season you won't be able to find a bed for love nor money, and many hotels are booked up in summer too. You can always stay in nearby Nice and catch the train to Cannes.

Hôtel Alnea HOTEL €

(04 93 68 77 77; www.hotel-alnea.com; 20 rue Jean de Riouffe; s €61-75, d €70-99;) At this breath of fresh air in a town of stars, Noémi and Cédric have put their heart and soul into this hotel, offering bright, colourful two-star rooms, original paintings and numerous little details, such as the afternoon coffee break, the honesty bar, and the bike or boules (to play *pétanque*) loans. Breakfast costs €8.50.

Hôtel de Provence HOTEL €€

(04 93 38 44 35; www.hotel-de-provence.com; 9 rue Molière; s €126-147, d €169-317;) This traditional Provençal townhouse with buttermilk walls and lavender-blue shutters disguises a minimalist-chic interior. Almost every room sports a balcony, climaxing with a 7th-floor suite with stunning rooftop terrace. The Provence also has self-catering studios in the neighbourhood for three to six people. Breakfast costs €9.80.

Hôtel Splendid HOTEL €€

(04 97 06 22 22; www.splendid-hotel-cannes.com; 4-6 rue Félix Faure; d from €162;) A proper old-fashioned hotel, and an architectural landmark, this gleaming white supertanker of a hotel was built in 1871, and it's still an address of note. As you'd expect, the styling is traditional (some might say dated) – tasteful tones of cream, yellow and peach, wooden furniture, monogrammed bath towels. Sea-facing rooms (preferably with balcony) are essential here.

Hôtel Montaigne BOUTIQUE HOTEL €€

(04 97 06 03 40; www.hotel-montaigne.eu; 4 rue Montaigne; d from €119-179, f €208-238;) An address for the aesthetes, prime for pampering. It's loaded with luxuries: *hammam*, spa, heated pool and plenty of wellbeing packages – and the styling throughout is clean and minimal, with a faint art-deco touch. There are wheelchair-accessible rooms, plus family suites

with interconnecting rooms and kitchenettes. Lovely garden too – and not overpriced for the facilities.

Hôtel Le Mistral BOUTIQUE HOTEL €€

(☎04 93 39 91 46; www.mistral-hotel.com; 13 rue des Belges; s €89-109, d €99-129; ❄📶) For super-pricey Cannes, this little 10-roomer is quite amazing value. Rooms are small but decked out in flattering red and plum tones – Privilege rooms have quite a bit more space, plus a fold-out sofa bed. There are sea views from the top floor, and the hotel is just 50m from La Croisette. There's no lift, though.

Villa Garbo BOUTIQUE HOTEL €€€

(☎04 93 46 66 00; www.villagarbo-cannes.com; 62 bd d'Alsace; d from €230; ❄@📶) For a taste of Cannes' celeb lifestyle, this indulgent stunner is hard to beat. Rooms are more like apartments, offering copious space, plus kitchenettes, king-size beds, sofas and more. The style is designer chic – acid tones of puce, orange and lime contrasted with blacks and greys, supplemented by quirky sculptures and objets d'art. Unusually, rates include breakfast. You also get free sunloungers on a private beach.

Hôtel Le Canberra BOUTIQUE HOTEL €€€

(☎04 97 06 95 00; www.hotel-cannes-canberra.com; 120 rue d'Antibes; d from €221; ❄@📶🏊) This boutique stunner, just a couple of blocks back from La Croisette, is the epitome of Cannes glamour: designer grey rooms with splashes of candy pink, sexy black-marble bathrooms with coloured lighting, heated pool (April to October) in a bamboo-filled garden, intimate atmosphere (there are just 35 rooms) and impeccable service. Rooms overlooking rue d'Antibes are cheapest.

Eating

Most private beaches have restaurants, particularly delightful on warm sunny days, although you pay for the privilege of eating *les pieds dans l'eau* (by the sea). Expect to pay around €25 to €30 for a main of grilled fish or meat, or a gourmet salad.

Cheaper eats can be found in and around the atmospheric Marché Forville (p840).

★PhilCat SANDWICHES €

(Promenade de la Pantiéro; sandwiches & salads €3.50-6; ⊙7am-7pm Mar-Oct; 🥄) Phillipe and Catherine's prefab cabin on the waterfront is a perfect lunch spot. This is fast-food, Cannes-style – giant salads, toasted panini and the best *pan bagna* (€5; a gargantuan bun filled with tuna, onion, red pepper, lettuce and tomato, and dripping in olive oil) on the Riviera. The 'super' version (€5.30) throws anchovies into the mix.

★La Boulangerie par Jean-Luc Pelé BOULANGERIE €

(☎04 93 38 06 10; www.jeanlucpele.com; 3 rue du 24 août; lunch menus €6-9.50; ⊙7.30am-7.30pm Mon-Sat) This swanky bakery by Cannois *chocolatier* and *pâtissier* Jean-Luc Pelé casts a whole new spin on eating cheap in Cannes. Creative salads, sandwiches, wraps and bagels – to eat in or out – burst with local flavours and provide the perfect prelude to the utterly sensational cakes and desserts Pelé is best known for. Gourmets note: macarons, unusually, come in sweet and savoury flavours. Foie gras and fig, anyone?

★Bobo Bistro MEDITERRANEAN €

(☎04 93 99 97 33; 21 rue du Commandant André; pizza €12-16, mains €15-20; ⊙noon-3pm & 7-11pm Mon-Sat, 7-11pm Sun) Predictably, it's a 'bobo' (bourgeois bohemian) crowd that gathers at this achingly cool bistro in Cannes' fashionable Carré d'Or (Golden Sq). Decor is stylishly retro, with attention-grabbing objets d'art including a tableau of dozens of spindles of coloured yarn. Cuisine is local, seasonal and invariably organic: artichoke salad, tuna carpaccio with passion fruit, roasted cod with mash *fait masion* (homemade).

La Meissounière FRENCH €€

(☎04 93 38 37 76; www.lameissouniere.com; 15 rue du 24 Août; 1-/2-course lunch menu €16/22, mains €15-22; ⊙noon-2pm Tue-Sat, 7-10pm Thu-Sat; 🥄) This honest, no-fuss little diner seems

FRENCH RIVIERA PASS

Although most museums in Nice are free, there are still plenty of attractions that you have to pay for in Nice and along the Riviera. The **French Riviera Pass** (www.frenchrivierapass.com; 1-/2-/3-day pass €26/38/56) includes access to a number of these sights. It is available online or at the Nice tourist office.

Included in the price of the pass are: in Nice, the Musée National Marc Chagall, Nice Le Grand Tour bus and guided walking tours; along the coast, the Musée Renoir in Cagnes, the Musée National Fernand Léger in Biot, the Jardin Exotique d'Èze, and the Jardin Exotique and Musée Océanographique in Monaco.

1

2

MAREMAGNUM / GETTY IMAGES ©

3

BRIAN LAWRENCE / GETTY IMAGES ©

1. La Promenade des Anglais (p821), Nice
Pictured with a dusting of winter snow, this promenade is one of the most famous seafronts in France.

2. Cathédrale Ste-Réparate (p821), Vieux Nice
A Baroque gem that honours the city's patron saint.

3. Cap d'Antibes (p841), Cote d'Azur
An exclusive promontory with several kilometres of walking trails.

4. Antibes (p841)
This quintessential Mediterranean town has captivated artists and writers for the past century.

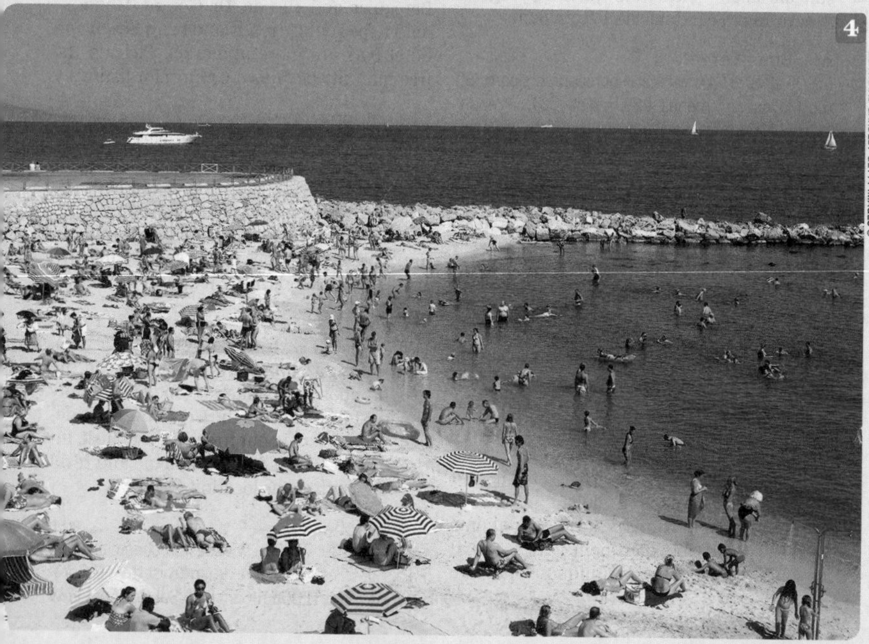

4

BERTRAND GARDEL / GETTY IMAGES ©

DON'T MISS

CHEESE, GLORIOUS CHEESE

With cowbells strung from the wooden ceiling, and a stunning array of cheeses, **Fromagerie Ceneri** (☎04 93 39 63 68; www.fromagerie-ceneri.com; 22 rue Meynadier; ⏰10am-6pm Mon, 8am-7.30pm Tue-Sat, 8.30am-12.30pm Sun) is the only place to shop for dairy products in Cannes. A master *fromager-affineur* (cheesemonger and ripener) in business since 1968, Ceneri is a rare and precious breed on the Riviera. Its selection of *chèvre* (goat's cheese) from Provence is second to none.

somewhat out of place among the glitz and glam of Cannes. It's perfect for French classics, such as steak, duck breast, calf's liver and salmon tartare, and there's always a pan-fried fish of the day. Lunch gets busy, so arrive early.

Petit Paris BRASSERIE €€
(☎04 93 38 88 60; www.le-petitparis.fr; 13 rue des Belges; mains €18-29; ⏰8am-midnight; 📝) Little Paris smacks of the French capital city with its quintessential Parisian brasserie decor. Like any brasserie worth its French fries, it serves food all day as well as sterling breakfasts to suit all suits – pick from Parisian, English, American or Scandinavian – from 8am.

Aux Bons Enfants FRENCH €€
(☎06 18 81 37 47; www.aux-bons-enfants.com; 80 rue Meynadier; menus €29, mains €16; ⏰noon-2pm & 7-10pm Tue-Sat) A people's-choice place since 1935, this informal restaurant cooks up regional dishes, such as *aïoli garni* (garlic and saffron mayonnaise served with fish and vegetables), *daube* (a Provençal beef stew) and *rascasse meunière* (pan-fried rockfish), all in a convivial atmosphere. No credit cards or reservations.

★**Mantel** MODERN EUROPEAN €€€
(☎04 93 39 13 10; www.restaurantmantel.com; 22 rue St-Antoine; menus €35-80, mains €34-45; ⏰noon-2pm Fri-Mon, 7.30-10pm Thu-Tue) Discover why Noël Mantel is the hotshot of the Cannois gastronomic scene at his refined old-town restaurant. Service is stellar and the seasonally inspired cuisine divine – Mantel's food maximises local ingredients but isn't afraid to experiment with unusual flavours and cooking techniques. Spot the classic film stars on the walls, from Cary Grant to Alfred Hitchcock.

Sea Sens FUSION €€€
(☎04 63 36 05 06; www.five-hotel-cannes.com; 1 rue Notre Dame; lunch menus €29 & €39, dinner menus €65-115; ⏰7.30-11pm Tue-Sat; 📶) Perched on the 5th floor of the Five Seas Hotel, this single-Michelin-starred restaurant blends French gastronomy and Asian elegance with panoramic views of Le Suquet and Cannes' rooftops. Pastry chef Jerôme De Oliveira's champion desserts are the sweet highlight. Lunch is excellent value.

Shopping

Marché Forville MARKET
(rue du Marché Forville; ⏰7am-1pm Tue-Sun) For local folklore, head to Cannes' busy food market, a couple of blocks back from the port. In the biz since 1934, it is one of the most important markets in the region and the supplier of choice for restaurants – and for your beach picnic! On Monday the food stalls are replaced by an all-day *brocante* (flea market).

Drinking & Nightlife

Going out in Cannes is taken seriously: dress to impress. Bars around the Carré d'Or (Golden Sq) – bordered by rue Commandant André, rue des Frères Pradignac, rue du Batéguier and rue du Dr Gérard Monod – tend to be young, trendy and busy. Beach and hotel bars are more upmarket. Pick up the free monthly *Le Mois à Cannes* for listings.

L'Epicurieux WINE BAR
(☎06 64 50 11 82; 6 rue des Frères Casanova; ⏰10am-11pm) A cosy little spot for a glass or two of a local vintage – the wine list here is great, with hand-picked choices from local domains including Côtes de Provence and Côtes du Rhône. Bistro snacks and live bands at weekends make it doubly attractive.

JW Grill LOUNGE
(☎04 92 99 70 92; 50 bd de la Croisette; ⏰11am-11pm) This dazzling white lounge bar on the ground floor of the Marriott hotel is possibly the most beautiful on the Croisette, with designer sofas facing out to sea. Come dusk, indulge in a €16 glass of Champagne and revel in the chic five-star location.

Les Marches CLUB
(☎04 93 39 77 21; www.lesmarches-club.com; Palais des Festivals, 1 bd de la Croisette; ⏰8pm-6am May-Sep, 11.30pm-6am Fri & Sat Oct-Apr) Few

hobnobbing spots in Cannes are as sweet as the rooftop terrace of this chic club in Palais des Festivals.

Gotha Club CLUB
(☎04 93 45 11 11; place Franklin Roosvelt, Casino Palm Beach; cover €25-50; ⏰midnight-dawn May, Jul & Aug) Only open in May during the film festival and again in July and August, this club is a hot ticket in DJ land. Bringing together some of the most happening names in music with a spectacular setting at the seafaring end of La Croisette, Gotha is a glitzy VIP favourite. Door policy is tight: no guys without girls and only fabulous-looking people.

Le Bâoli CLUB
(☎04 93 43 03 43; www.lebaoli.com; Port Pierre Canto, bd de la Croisette; ⏰8pm-6am Thu-Sat) This is Cannes' coolest, trendiest and most selective nightspot – so selective, in fact, that your entire posse might not get in unless you're dressed to the nines. It's part club, part restaurant, so one way to ensure you'll get in is to book a table and make a night of it. Located at the eastern end of La Croisette.

Information

Tourist Office (☎04 92 99 84 22; www.cannes-destination.fr; 1 bd de la Croisette; ⏰9am-8pm Jun-Aug, 9am or 10am-7pm Sep-May; 📶)

Tourist Office Annexe (☎04 93 99 19 77; rue Jean Jaurès; ⏰9am-1pm & 2-6pm Mon-Sat)

Getting There & Around

BICYCLE

Mistral Location (☎04 93 39 33 60; www.mistral-location.com; 4 rue Georges Clémenceau) rents out bicycles/scooters for €16/35 per day.

BUS

Transport Alpes-Maritimes (TAM) runs express services to Nice (bus 200; €1, 1½ hours, every 15 minutes), Nice-Côte d'Azur airport (bus 210; one way/return €22/33, 50 minutes, half-hourly), Mougins (bus 600; €1, 20 minutes, every 20 minutes) and Grasse (bus 600; €1, 45 minutes). The electric Elo Bus (€1) follows a loop that takes in the bus station, the Croisette, rue d'Antibes and the train station. It has no set stops, just flag it down as it passes.

TRAIN

Cannes' gleaming white train station is well connected with other towns along the coast.

Antibes (€2.50, 12 minutes, at least twice hourly)

Marseille (€25, two hours, half-hourly)

Monaco (€8, one hour, at least twice hourly)

Nice (€6, 40 minutes, every 15 minutes)

St-Raphaël (€6, 30 minutes, every 20 minutes)

Antibes & Juan-les-Pins

With its boat-bedecked port, 16th-century ramparts and narrow cobblestone streets festooned with flowers, it's little wonder that lovely Antibes has stolen the hearts of so many artists and writers: including Graham Greene, Max Ernst and Picasso, who featured the town in many paintings and now has a museum dedicated to him.

Nearby **Cap d'Antibes**, a wooded cape studded with seaside mansions and the 2km beach resort of **Juan-les-Pins**, was famously the home of F Scott Fitzgerald, who lived here with his wife Zelda and daughter Scottie until 1927 (their house is now a posh hotel).

Only Antibes' attractive old town would be recognisable to any of its famous former residents. The modern town, like many along the Riviera, has sprawled rather unbecomingly along the coast and inland, so the best vantage point is from the sea – ideally in one of the many posh yachts that pull into port throughout summer.

Sights & Activities

Vieil Antibes HISTORIC SITE
Ringed by sturdy medieval walls and criss-crossed with lanes and shady squares, old Antibes is a delightful place for a wander. The wonderful Marché Provençal (p843) is old Antibes' beating heart, sheltered by a 19th-century cast-iron roof and packed with stalls selling olives, cheese, vegetables, tapenades and other Provençal goodies until around 1pm every day.

Along the edge of the old town, views from the sea walls stretch all the way to Nice (spot the runway) and inland to the snowy Alps. There's one section of the ramparts overlooking place du Verdun where you can walk along and imagine yourself operaing a medieval cannon.

Musée Picasso MUSEUM
(☎04 92 90 54 20; www.antibes-juanlespins.com/culture/musee-picasso; Château Grimaldi, 4 rue des Cordiers; adult/concession €6/3; ⏰10am-6pm Tue-Sun mid-Jun–mid-Sep, 10am-noon & 2-6pm Tue-Sun mid-Sep–mid-Jun) Picasso himself said, 'If you want to see the Picassos from Antibes, you have to see them in Antibes'. The 14th-century Château Grimaldi was

Picasso's studio from July to December 1946 and now houses an excellent collection of his works and fascinating photos of him. The sheer variety – lithographs, paintings, drawings and ceramics – shows how versatile and curious an artist Picasso was. The museum also has a room dedicated to Nicolas de Staël, another painter who adopted Antibes as home.

Fort Carré MONUMENT

(rte du Bord de Mer; guided tour adult/child €3/free; ⏲10am-6pm Tue-Sun Jul & Aug, to 4.30pm Tue-Sun Sep-Jun) The impregnable 16th-century Fort Carré, enlarged by Vauban in the 17th century, dominates the approach to Antibes from Nice. It served as a border defence post until 1860, when Nice, until then in Italian hands, became French. Tours depart half-hourly; some guides speak English.

Bastion St-Jaume MONUMENT

(quai Henri Rambaud; ⏲10am-11pm Jun-Aug, to 6pm Sep-May) FREE Stroll along the rampart walkway, **Promenade des Arts**, to the harbour, where luxury yachts jostle for the limelight with *Nomade* (2010), an 8m-tall sculpture of a man looking out to sea. The work of Catalan artist Jaume Plensa, the mirage-like piece is built from thousands of white letters and is lit at night – a magnificent sight. It squats on the terrace of the Bastion St-Jaume, the site of a Roman temple, a 17th-century fortified tower and, until 1985, a shipyard.

Jardin Botanique de la Villa Thuret GARDENS

(☎04 97 21 25 00; www6.sophia.inra.fr/jardin_thuret/infos-pratiques; 90 chemin Raymond; ⏲8am-6pm Mon-Fri Jun-Sep, 8.30am-5.30pm Mon-Fri Oct-May) FREE In the centre of Cap d'Antibes, this serene, 3.5-hectare botanical garden was created in 1856 and showcases 2500 species – the perfect opportunity to study the sun-rich cape's lush and invariably exotic flora up close.

Villa Eilenroc HISTORIC BUILDING

(☎04 93 67 74 33; av Mrs Beaumont, Cap d'Antibes; adult/child €2/free; ⏲2-5.30pm Wed, plus 1st & 3rd Sat of month) This beautiful Cap d'Antibes villa, designed in 1867 for a Dutchman who scrambled the name of his wife, Cornélie, to come up with the villa's name, has seen better days – its scantily furnished interior lacks glamour. But a stroll around its 11-hectare park with rosary, olive grove and aromatic garden is evocative of its belle-époque heyday. Down by the water below the villa, **Plage de Galets** is a bijou pebble cove well worth a dip and/or sun-kissed siesta.

Cap d'Antibes WALKING

Cap d'Antibes' 4.8km of wooded shores are the perfect setting for a walk-swim-walk-swim afternoon. Paths are well marked. The tourist office maps show itineraries.

Beaches

Plage de la Garoupe SWIMMING

This stretch of Cap d'Antibes was first raked clear of seaweed in 1922 by Cole Porter and American artist Gerald Murphy to create a sandy beach. Its golden sand is shared today by a small public beach overlooked by the excellent-value terrace of Le Rocher and the private **Plage Keller** (with white-tablecloth dining, and sun loungers on a jetty).

Plage de la Gravette SWIMMING

(quai Henri Rambaud) Right in the centre of Antibes, you'll find Plage de la Gravette, a small patch of sand by the *remparts* (ramparts).

Festivals & Events

Jazz à Juan MUSIC

(www.jazzajuan.com; ⏲mid-Jul) This major festival, celebrated in Juan-les-Pins, has been running for more than 50 years. Every jazz great has performed here, and the festival continues to attract big music names.

Sleeping

Relais International de la Jeunesse HOSTEL €

(☎04 93 61 34 40; www.clajsud.fr; 272 bd de la Garoupe; dm €20; ⏲Apr-Oct; 📶) With sea views the envy of neighbouring millionaires, this basic-but-friendly hostel is particularly popular with 'yachties' looking for their next job in Antibes' port. Rates include sheets and breakfast. Daily lockout 11am to 5pm.

Hôtel La Place HOTEL €€

(☎04 97 21 03 11; www.la-place-hotel.com; 1 av du 24 août; d €99-180; ❄@📶) It's rare to find contemporary chic next to a city bus station, but The Place does it awfully well. Its 14 rooms are spacious, stylish and dressed in soothing taupe and aubergine or aniseed green. Three have bijou balconies, and breakfast (€13) is served in the airy lounge. It's squeezed into a tall, narrow building, but unfortunately there's no lift.

Le Relais du Postillon HOTEL €€
(☎04 93 34 20 77; www.relaisdupostillon.com; 8 rue Championnet; d €83-149; ⊙reception 7.30am-11pm; ❄📶) This former coaching hotel is a bit of a steal, all things considered; it's got a great location on the edge of the old town, it overlooks a pretty square and park, and the rooms are rather charming, especially if you bag one at the front, which have their own dinky balconies overlooking the square. The ground-floor cafe is a lovely spot for breakfast, too.

Hôtel La Jabotte B&B €€
(☎04 93 61 45 89; www.jabotte.com; 13 av Max Maurey; d from €120; ❄@📶) A couple of kilometres south of the old town on the coastal bd James Wyllie towards Cap d'Antibes, this pretty little hideaway makes a cosy base. Hot pinks, sunny yellows and soothing mauves dominate the homey, feminine decor, and there's a sweet patio where breakfast is served on sunny days. There's a minimum stay of three nights in summer.

Eating

By the water on quai des Pêcheurs, fishers sell their morning's catch from 9am to 12.30pm. For picnic goodies, hit Antibes' **Fromagerie l'Etable** (1 rue Sade; ⊙8am-1pm & 4-7pm Tue-Sat, 8am-1pm Sun) for cheese and deli products, and dazzling morning market **Marché Provençal** (cours Masséna; ⊙7am-1pm Tue-Sun Sep-Jun, daily Jul & Aug) for everything else.

★**L'Atelier Jean-Luc Pelé** SANDWICHES €
(☎04 92 95 78 21; 27 rue de la République; sandwiches from €5; ⊙9am-7.30pm Mon-Sat, to 7pm Sun) This branch of Jean-Luc Pelé's stellar Cannes bakery is a welcome addition to Antibes' lunch counter. Gourmet bagels and wraps (from €5) come in all kinds of creative combos, and for €9.50 you can add a drink and a sinful cake from the patisserie counter. Divine.

La Badiane FUSION €
(☎04 93 34 45 41; 3 traverse du 24 Août; lunch menus €17-18.50, mains €13-15; ⊙lunch Mon-Fri) This little side street behind Antibes' bus station has a clutch of great lunchtime restaurants, including this exotic Moroccan-tinged diner, which serves up yummy treats such as chicken tagine, crispy *pastillas* (filled pastries) and spicy quiches. Shame it's only open for lunch on weekdays.

WORTH A TRIP

MUSÉE RENOIR

Le Domaine des Collettes (as the property was known in the artist's time) was home and studio to an arthritis-crippled Renoir (1841–1919) from 1907 until his death. He lived there with his wife and three children, and the house is wonderfully evocative, despite being sparsely furnished. Newly reopened in 2013, **Musée Renoir** (☎04 93 20 61 07; www.cagnes-tourisme.com; chemin des Colettes, Cagnes-sur-Mer; adult/child €6/free; ⊙10am-1pm & 2-6pm Jun-Sep, 10am-noon & 2-5pm Oct-Mar, to 6pm Apr & May) contains a handful of original paintings, including a version of *Les Grandes Baigneuses* (The Women Bathers; 1892), as well as a number of sculptures, letters, photos and documents. The villa's gardens are delightful too, awash with colourful flowers and olive and citrus groves. Many visitors set up their own easel to paint.

Le Rocher BEACH RESTAURANT €
(☎04 93 67 51 36; 925 chemin de la Garoupe, Plage de la Garoupe; mains €17-22) At weekends and in high season, reservations are essential at this good-value beach restaurant with waterside terrace overlooking Cap d'Antibes' legendary Plage de la Garoupe. Giant salads and gargantuan *galettes* (savoury buckwheat pancakes) filled with ham and cheese provide beachside sustenance alongside fishier *plats du jour* (dishes of the day).

★**Nacionale** INTERNATIONAL €€
(☎04 93 61 77 30; www.restaurant-nacional-antibes.com; 61 place Nationale; plat du jour & glass of wine €17, tapas €9-21, mains €19-45; ⊙noon-2pm & 7-10pm Tue-Sat, noon-2pm Sun) 'Beef & Wine' is the strapline of this contemporary wine bar–styled space, so that should give you some idea of the focus here. It's popular for its burgers, steaks in pepper or port sauce, and other grilled meats. The in-crowd adores it for aperitifs and tapas, best sampled on the walled patio garden hidden away at the back.

Big Moustache BURGERS €
(☎04 93 34 31 20; 30 rue Fourmillière; burgers €15; ⊙8.30am-5pm Tue-Sat) Artisanal bread, homemade sauces, veg 'fresh from the earth' and the pick of epicurean cheeses go into the gourmet burgers at Big Moustache. There

are generally four or five meaty choices and two veggie burgers chalked on the *ardoise* (blackboard) each day, always with plenty of rocket, spinach leaves and other freshly picked seasonal goodies. Kids *menu* €6.

Information

Accueil Touristique du Vieil Antibes (04 93 34 65 65; 32 bd d'Aguillon; 10am-noon & 1-6pm Mon-Sat Jul & Aug, to 5pm Tue-Sat Sep-Jun) Old-town info point, steps from the water.

Tourist Office (04 22 10 60 10; www.antibesjuanlespins.com; 42 av Robert Soleau; 9am-7pm daily Jul & Aug, 9am-12.30pm & 1.30-6pm Mon-Fri, 9am-noon & 2-6pm Sat, 9am-1pm Sun Sep-May) By Antibes train station; excellent source of tourist information and guided walking tours of Old Antibes and 'Painters on the French Riviera' (adult/child €7/3.50).

Getting There & Away

BUS

The Nice–Cannes service (www.envibus.fr; bus 200, €1.50) stops by the tourist office. Local bus services (€1) for Opio, Vence and St-Paul de Vence leave from the **bus station** (04 89 87 72 01; place Guynemer; ticket office 9am-12.30pm & 2-5pm Mon-Sat).

TRAIN

Antibes' train station is on the main line between Nice (€3, 30 minutes, five hourly) and Cannes (€2.50, 10 minutes, five hourly).

Mougins & Mouans-Sartoux

Pinprick Vieux Mougins looks almost too perfect to be real. Picasso discovered the medieval village in 1935 with lover Dora Marr and lived here with his final love, Jacqueline Roque, from 1961 until his death. Mougins has since become something of an elite location, with prestigious hotel-restaurants, the country's most sought-after international school and Sophia Antipolis (France's Silicon Valley) nearby.

Nearby Mouans-Sartoux also has a clutch of excellent museums to explore.

Sights

Musée d'Art Classique de Mougins ART MUSEUM
(04 93 75 18 65; www.mouginsmusee.com; 32 rue Commandeur; adult/child €12/5; 10am-6pm) The brainchild of compulsive art collector and British entrepreneur Christian Levett, this outstanding museum contains 600 works spanning 5000 years. The collection aims to show how ancient civilisations inspired neoclassical, modern and contemporary art, thus the collection is organised by civilisations – Rome, Greece and Egypt – with antiquities juxtaposed with seminal modern works. The top floor is dedicated to armoury, with excellent interactive displays bringing to life the helmets, spears and shields. There's also a fascinating Roman and Greek coin collection.

Espace de l'Art Concret ART MUSEUM
(www.espacedelartconcret.fr; place Suzanne de Villeneuve; adult/child €7/free; 11am-7pm Jul & Aug, 1-6pm Wed-Sun Sep-Jun) Modern-art and architecture lovers shouldn't miss Mouans-Sartoux' contemporary-art centre, housed in the 16th-century Château de Mouans and the purpose-built Donation Albers-Honegger extension, a brilliant and brilliantly controversial lime-green concrete block ferociously clashing with its historic surroundings. All the old familiars (Eduardo Chillida, Yves Klein, Andy Warhol, César, Philippe Starck) are here, along with lesser-known practitioners and temporary exhibitions.

Musée de la Photographie André Villers PHOTOGRAPHY MUSEUM
(Porte Sarrazine, rue de L'Église, Mougins; 10am-noon & 2-6pm Tue-Fri, 11am-7pm Sat & Sun) FREE The small but perfectly formed Musée de la Photographie has some fascinating B&W photos of Picasso, snapped by celebrated photographers such as André Villers and Jacques Henri Lartigue. It also hosts regular exhibitions on anything from fashion to war photography.

Sleeping & Eating

★**Les Rosées** B&B €€€
(04 92 92 29 64; www.lesrosees.com; 238 chemin de Font Neuve, Mougins; d €220-302; P ❄ ☜ ≋) You know that dreamy Provençal getaway you've been looking for? The one in the little village, set among gardens filled with lavender and honeysuckle, and peaceful wood-beamed rooms looking out over Provençal hills? Well, this place is it. Throw in luxuries including Bose sound systems, designer bathrooms, home-cooked food and a gorgeous pool, and you really won't ever want to leave.

★**Le Sot l'y Laisse** PROVENCAL €€
(04 93 75 54 50; place Suzanne de Villeneuve; lunch menu €15, dinner menu €29, mains €14-23;

noon-2pm & 8-10pm Wed-Sun) On the shady town square of Mouans-Sartoux, you won't find a more authentic Provençal restaurant than this place. The signature dish, a hearty chicken stew, gives the place its name (it means 'the fool leaves it there,' referring to the juicy oyster of meat most people miss in poultry).

Information

Tourist Office (04 92 92 14 00; www.mougins-tourisme.com; 39 place des Patriotes, Mougins; 9.30am-6pm or 7pm Mon-Sat, 10am-2pm Sun Jul & Aug, shorter hours rest of year) Located at the entrance of the old village. Pick up the free map to the town's historic centre.

Getting There & Away

Bus 600 (€1.50, every 20 minutes) runs between Cannes (20 minutes) and Grasse (35 minutes) stopping in Mougins and Mouans-Sartoux.

Grasse

POP 52,212

Up in the hills to the north of Nice, the town of Grasse has been synonymous with perfumery since the 16th century, and the town is still home to around 30 makers – a few of which offer guided tours of their factories, and the chance to hone your olfactory skills. The perfumes of Provence are something that lingers long after you leave for home – especially if you happen to have bought a few soaps, body sprays and eaux de toilettes to take home with you.

Sights

Attractions in Grasse focus on its celebrated perfume industry, a refreshing change from traditional sights and activities.

If you're planning to visit both the Musée International de la Parfumerie and the Jardins du MIP in Mougins, you can buy a combined ticket for €5, which includes a bus ticket between Grasse and the gardens (bus 20 or 21).

★Musée International de la Parfumerie MUSEUM

(MIP; 04 97 05 58 11; www.museesdegrasse.com; 2 bd du Jeu de Ballon; adult/child €4/free; 10am-7pm May-Sep, 10.30am-5.30pm Oct-Apr;) This whiz-bang museum is a work of art: housed in an 18th-century mansion, daringly enlarged with a modern glass structure, it retraces three millennia of perfume history through beautifully presented artefacts, bottles, videos, vintage posters, olfactive stations and explanatory panels. The museum offers interesting insights into how the industry developed in Grasse. Kids are well catered for with dedicated multimedia stations, a fragrant garden, a film testing sense of smell and the reproduction of a 19th-century perfume shop.

★Les Jardins du MIP GARDENS

(04 92 98 62 69; www.museesdegrasse.com; 979 chemin des Gourettes, Mouans-Sartoux; adult/child €4/free; 10am-7pm May-Aug, 10am-5.30pm mid-Mar–Apr & Sep–mid-Nov, closed mid-Nov–mid-Mar) These gorgeous gardens belonging to the Musée International de la Parfumerie showcase plants used in scent-making. Half the garden is displayed as fields to show how roses, jasmine and lavender are grown; the other half is organised by olfactory families (woody, floral, amber etc), which you can rub and smell on your way around. The gardens are 10km southwest of town on the edge of the village of Mouans-Sartoux. It's half-price if you show your ticket for the perfume museum. Take bus 20 or 21 from Grasse bus station.

Villa Musée Jean-Honoré Fragonard ART MUSEUM

(04 93 36 52 98; www.fragonard.com; 14 rue Jean Ossola; adult/child €2/free; 1-7pm Jul-Sep) On Grasse's main pedestrian street, this small museum explores the work of

WORTH A TRIP

FLOWER FARM

For a different spin on Grasse's perfume production, a trip to **Domaine de Manon** (06 12 18 02 69; www.le-domaine-de-manon.com; 36 chemin du Servan, Plascassier; adult/child €6/free) is a great option. Centifolia rose and jasmine have been cultivated here for three generations, and the farm now supplies Dior exclusively. Tours only take place during flowering, on Tuesday at 9am from early May to early June for roses, and on Tuesday at 9am from August to mid-October for jasmine; ring ahead to double-check, since exact times vary from year to year. The farm is 7km southeast of the centre of Grasse. Head in the direction of Valbonne along the D4 as you leave Grasse, and then follow signs for 'Vieux Village' when you get to Plascassier. The *domaine* will be on your left.

Grassois painter Jean-Honoré Fragonard (1732–1806), whose risqué paintings of love scenes shocked and titillated 18th-century France with their licentious love scenes. This elegant 18th-century villa was Fragonard's home for a year in 1790, and contains several of his major paintings, as well as a stunning *trompe l'œil* fresco in the stairwell by his equally gifted son. Admission also includes entry to the **Musée d'Art et d'Histoire de Provence** (☎04 93 36 80 20; 2 rue Mirabeau; adult/child €2/free; ⏲10am-7pm May-Sep, to 5.30pm Oct-Apr).

Fragonard's Usine Historique & Musée du Parfum MUSEUM
(☎04 93 36 44 65; www.fragonard.com; 20 bd Fragonard; ⏲9am-7pm Jul & Aug, 9am-12.30pm & 2-6pm Sep-Jun) FREE At the entrance to the old town, next to the Jardin des Plantes, this ochre-coloured mansion is where the Fragonard perfumery began in 1926 – though perfumers were at work here as early as 1782. Visits take in the original equipment used for extraction and distilling, include a small **Musée du Parfum** (Perfume Museum) on the 1st floor, and end at the shop where you can buy Fragonard scents. Perfume-making workshops are available; book ahead.

Tours

Several well-known perfumeries run free tours of their modern, out-of-town facilities. Tours take visitors through every stage of production, from extraction and distillation to the work of the 'nose.' Tours leave every 15 to 30 minutes and are available in a number of languages. Visits end in the factory shops, where you can buy fragrances (much cheaper than couture perfumes, where some 60% of what you pay is packaging).

Fragonard TOUR, WORKSHOP
(La Fabrique des Fleurs; ☎04 93 77 94 30; www.fragonard.com; Les 4 Chemins, rte de Cannes; ⏲9am-6pm Feb-Oct, 9am-12.30pm & 2-6pm Nov-Jan) Grasse's most famous perfumery runs free guided tours of its modern, out-of-town *usine* (factory), covering extraction, distillation, the science of scent creation and, of course, the chance to buy some perfume. Perfume-making workshops are run at its older factory in town (20 bd Fragonard).

Sleeping & Eating

Le Mas du Naoc B&B €€
(☎04 93 60 63 13; www.lemasdunaoc.com; 580 chemin du Migranié, Cabris; d/tr €160/230;) This vine-covered, 18th-century *chambre d'hôte,* 4km southwest of Grasse, slumbers in the shade of century-old olive, jasmine, fig and orange trees. Soft natural hues dress Sandra and Jérôme Maingret's four lovely rooms, and the coastal panorama from the pool is inspirational. Find the *mas* signposted off the D4 to Cabris. No children under seven; minimum two-night stay April to October.

Café des Musées MODERN FRENCH €
(1 rue Jean Ossola; lunch menus €12-16, mains €10-23; ⏲9am-6pm) This stylish cafe is the perfect stop for lunch (creative salads, carefully crafted daily specials, soup or pasta of the day) or a gourmet coffee break (pastry with coffee or tea €7.50), ice cream or crêpes between sights.

MAKE YOUR OWN PERFUME

It can take months for a *nez* (nose or perfumer who, after 10 years' training, can identify up to 3000 smells) to create a perfume. And you'll understand why the instant you plant yourself in front of a nose's organ – a line-up of miniature ginger-glass bottles containing 127 'notes' ranging from green amber, sandalwood, vanilla, hyacinth, lily of the valley and civet (nose shock or what) to hare, rose petals and sandalwood. The fact that many bottles contain not one but several essences pre-mixed only adds to the olfactory bewilderment. The number of combinations is dizzying.

Perfume workshops won't turn you into a perfumer overnight, but the olfactory education they offer is fascinating – and great fun for adults and kids alike. **Molinard** (☎04 93 36 01 62; www.molinard.com; 60 bd Victor Hugo; 30min/1hr workshops €30/69; ⏲9.30am-6.30pm) runs several different workshops, ranging in length from 30-minute sessions to two-hour epics, during which you get to create your own custom perfume from the essences on offer; you get to take it home with you at the end. **Galimard** (☎04 93 09 20 00; www.galimard.com; 73 rte de Cannes; workshops from €49; ⏲9am-12.30pm & 2-6pm) and **Fragonard** offer similar workshops.

Information

Tourist Office (☎04 93 36 66 66; www.grasse.fr; place de la Buanderie; ⏰9am-1pm & 2-5pm Mon-Fri, 10am-1pm & 2-5pm Sat; 📶) Takes reservations for guided tours and workshops of the perfume factories, and provides maps and information on the town. Located at the Grasse bus station.

Getting There & Away

BUS

Bus 600 goes to Cannes (50 minutes, every 20 minutes) via Mouans-Sartoux (25 minutes) and Mougins (30 minutes). Bus 500 goes to Nice (1½ hours, hourly). All buses leave from the **bus station** (place de la Buanderie); fares are a flat-rate €1.50.

TRAIN

The station is a short distance downhill from the centre; shuttle buses (€1.50) to 'Centre Ville' depart from in front of the train station. There are regular rail services to Nice (€8, 1¼ hours, hourly) via Cannes (€3.50, 30 minutes).

Vence

POP 19,180

Despite its well-preserved medieval centre, visitors often skip Vieux Vence altogether to head straight to Matisse's otherworldly Chapelle du Rosaire. Yet Vence deserves more than a flying visit, to appreciate its comparatively quiet medieval streets and enjoy some of its gastronomic talent. A fruit-and-veg market fills place du Jardin several mornings a week, with antiques on Wednesday.

Sights

★Chapelle du Rosaire ARCHITECTURE
(Rosary Chapel; ☎04 93 58 03 26; 466 av Henri Matisse; adult/child €6/3; ⏰2-5.30pm Mon, Wed & Sat, 10-11.30am & 2-5.30pm Tue & Thu, closed mid-Nov–early Dec) An ailing Henri Matisse moved to Vence in 1943 to be cared for by his former nurse and model, Monique Bourgeois, who'd since become a Dominican nun. She persuaded him to design this extraordinary chapel for her community. The artist designed everything from the decor to the altar and the priest vestments. From the road, you can see the blue-and-white ceramic roof tiles, wrought-iron cross and bell tower. Inside, light floods through the glorious blue, green and yellow stained-glass windows.

Vieux Vence HISTORIC SITE
Much of the historical centre dates back to the 13th century. The **Romanesque cathedral** on the eastern side of the square was built in the 11th century on the site of an old Roman temple. It contains Chagall's mosaic of Moses (1979), appropriately watching over the baptismal font.

Apart from the town itself, there are plenty of galleries to explore, plus an interesting art museum, the **Fondation Émile Hugues** (☎04 93 24 24 23; www.museedevence.com; 2 place du Frêne; adult/child €8/free; ⏰11am-6pm Tue-Sun). Housed inside a former château, it focuses on 20th century art.

Sleeping & Eating

Le 2 B&B €€
(☎04 93 24 42 58; www.le2avence.fr; 2 rue des Portiques; d incl breakfast €105-125; ❄📶) This 'bed and bistro,' as it's tagged itself, is a welcome addition to staid Vence. Nicolas and his family have turned this medieval townhouse into a hip new establishment offering four very modern rooms and a pocket-sized cellar featuring local musicians one night a week. Value and atmosphere guaranteed.

★La Maison du Frêne B&B €€€
(☎04 93 24 37 83; www.lamaisondufrene.com; 1 place du Frêne; d €165-185; ⏰Feb-Dec; ❄📶) This arty guesthouse is quite astonishing. Yes, that Niki de Saint Phalle is an original. And yes, the César too. It's an essential sleepover for true art-lovers, if only to enjoy the superb rooms with their classic or contemporary looks and original works. Owners and avid art collectors Thierry and Guy are a mine of information on the local art scene.

Le Michel Ange MEDITERRANEAN €
(☎04 93 58 32 56; 1 place Godeau; 2-/3-course menu €17/22, mains €14-18; ⏰noon-2.30pm & 6.30-9.30pm Tue-Sat, noon-2.30pm Sun) With tables beneath a leafy tree on a fountain-clad square behind the cathedral, this casual eatery gets top billing among locals. Families with kids swarm here at weekends for its car-free outdoor space and easy, excellent-value cuisine that embraces everything from pizza to stockfish. Reservations recommended. Check its Facebook page for weekly *menus*.

Information

Tourist Office (☎04 93 58 06 38; www.vence-tourisme.fr; 8 place du Grand Jardin;

9am-5pm Mon-Sat) Has several good leaflets on self-guided tours in and around Vence.

Getting There & Away

Lignes d'Azur (www.lignesdazur.com) bus 400 to/from Nice (€1.50, 1¼ hours, at least hourly) stops on place du Grand Jardin. Medieval Vence is pedestrian; park on place du Grand Jardin or in the streets leading to the historical centre.

St-Paul de Vence

POP 3600

Once upon a time, St-Paul de Vence was a small medieval village atop a hill looking out to sea. Then came the likes of Chagall and Picasso in the postwar years, followed by showbiz stars such as Yves Montand and Roger Moore, and St-Paul shot to fame. The village is now home to dozens of art galleries as well as the exceptional Fondation Maeght.

The village's tiny cobbled lanes get overwhelmingly crowded in high season – come early or late to beat the rush.

Sights

Strolling the narrow streets is how most visitors pass time in St-Paul. The village has been beautifully preserved and the panoramas from the ramparts are stunning. The main artery, rue Grande, is lined with art galleries. The highest point in the village is occupied by the Église Collégiale; the adjoining Chapelle des Pénitents Blancs was redecorated by Belgian artist Folon.

Many more artists lived in or passed through St-Paul de Vence, among them Soutine, Léger, Cocteau, Matisse and Chagall. The latter is buried with his wife, Vava, in the cemetery at the village's southern end (immediately to the right as you enter). The tourist office runs a **guided tours** (adult/child €5/free; 1½hr).

★Fondation Maeght MUSEUM
(04 93 32 81 63; www.fondation-maeght.com; 623 chemin des Gardettes; adult/child €15/10; 10am-7pm Jul-Sep, to 6pm Oct-Jun) For an overview of some of the key 20th-century artists – including many who found inspiration along the Côte d'Azur – this fabulous museum is absolutely unmissable. From pieces by Georges Braque, Vassily Kandinsky and Marc Chagall to spooky sculptures by Giacometti and glassworks by Miró, it is a treasure trove. The innovative building designed by Josep Lluís Sert is fittingly experimental, and the gardens are a delight. The museum is a 500m walk downhill from the village.

Sleeping & Eating

Hostellerie Les Remparts HOTEL €€
(04 93 24 10 47; www.hostellerielesremparts.com; 72 Grande Rue; d €65-120;) Right in the heart of the *vieux* (old) village, in an old medieval building, this family-run hotel is a charming address. The rooms are spacious and furnished in traditional French style (solid wood furniture and flowery spreads) and those overlooking the valley have fantastic views. The bathrooms are dated but functional.

★Les Cabanes d'Orion B&B €€€
(06 75 45 18 64; www.orionbb.com; Impasse des Peupliers, 2436 chemin du Malvan; d from €260;) Dragonflies flit above water lilies in the natural swimming pool, while guests slumber amid a chorus of frogs and cicadas in luxurious cedar-wood tree houses perched in the trees at this enchanting, ecofriendly B&B. Children are well catered for with mini-*cabanes* in two of the tree houses. There's a minimum three-night stay from April to October.

★Le Tilleul MODERN FRENCH €€
(04 93 32 80 36; www.restaurant-letilleul.com; place du Tilleul; lunch menus €25-29, mains €14-25; 8.30am-10.30pm;) Considering its location on the *remparts,* this place could have easily plumbed the depths of a typical tourist trap. But it hasn't. Instead, divine and beautifully presented dishes grace your table at Le Tilleul and the all-French wine list includes a generous selection of options by the glass. Sit under the shade of a big lime-blossom tree. Open for breakfast and afternoon tea too.

Information

Tourist Office (04 93 32 86 95; www.saint-pauldevence.com; 2 rue Grande; 10am-7pm Jun-Sep, to 6pm Oct-May, closed 1-2pm weekends) Runs a series of informative, themed guided tours that delve into the village's illustrious past. Some tours are also available in English. Book ahead. Also organises *pétanque* lessons (€5 per person, plus €2 ball rental; reserve in advance).

Getting There & Away

St-Paul is served by bus 400 (www.lignesdazur.com) running between Nice (€1.50, one hour, at least hourly) and Vence (€1.50, 15 minutes, hourly). The town is closed to traffic, but there

WORTH A TRIP

BIOT

This 15th-century hilltop village was once an important pottery-manufacturing centre specialising in earthenware oil and wine containers. Metal containers brought an end to this, but Biot is still active in handicraft production, especially glass making.

You can see the blowers in action and pick up some premium glassware at the renowned **Verrerie de Biot** (☎04 93 65 03 00; www.verreriebiot.com; chemin des Combes; museum adult/child €3/1.50; ⏲9.30am-7.30pm Mon-Sat, 10.30am-1pm & 2.30-7.30pm Sun Apr-Sep, to 6pm Oct-Mar), at the foot of the village. One and a half kilometres south of town, there's also a **museum** (☎04 92 91 50 30; www.musee-fernandleger.fr; chemin du Val de Pome; adult/child €5.50/free; ⏲10am-6pm Tue-Sun May-Oct, to 5pm Nov-Apr) devoted to the experimental artist Fernand Léger, a major inspiration for pop art.

Biot's dynamic **tourist office** (☎04 93 65 78 00; www.biot.fr; 46 rue St-Sébastien; ⏲9am-noon & 2-6pm Mon-Fri, 2-6pm Sat & Sun) has plenty of information on the town; ask about its various art-heritage discovery itineraries (downloadable as the *Visit Biot* app).

are several car parks (€2.70 per hour) surrounding the village.

Corniche de l'Estérel

A walk or drive along the winding Corniche de l'Estérel (also called the Corniche d'Or, 'Golden Coast'; the N98), opened by the Touring Club de France in 1903, is an attraction in its own right. Views are spectacular and small summer resorts and dreamy inlets (perfect for swimming), all accessible by bus or train, dot its 30km length. The most dramatic stretch is between Anthéor and Théoule-sur-Mer, where the tortuous, narrow N98 skirts through sparsely built areas.

Activities

With its lush green Mediterranean forests, intensely red peaks and sterling sea views, the Estérel is a walker's paradise. Local tourist offices have leaflets detailing the most popular walks, including Pic de l'Ours (496m) and Pic du Cap Roux (452m). Buy IGN's Carte de Randonnée (1:25,000) No 3544ET *Fréjus, Saint-Raphaël & Corniche de l'Estérel* for more serious walks.

Those preferring a more informed hike can sign up for a three-hour guided walk with a forest ranger from the Office National des Forêts (National Forestry Office) or nature guide at **St-Raphaël tourist office** (☎04 94 19 52 52; www.saint-raphael.com; 99 quai Albert 1er; ⏲9am-7pm Jul & Aug, 9am-12.30pm & 2-6.30pm Mon-Sat Sep-Jun). Access to the range is prohibited on windy or particularly hot days because of fire risks; check with the tourist office before setting off.

With its 36km of coastline, the corniche has more than 30 beaches running the gamut of possibilities: sandy, pebbly, nudist, cove-like, you name it. But wherever you go, the sea remains that crystal-clear turquoise and deep blue, an irresistible invitation to swim.

The Estérel is also a leading dive centre, with numerous WWII shipwrecks and pristine waters. Much of the coast is protected, meaning its fauna and flora are among the best around.

Sentier du Littoral HIKING

Running 11km between Port Santa Lucia (the track starts behind the naval works) and Agay, this coastal path (yellow markers) takes in some of the area's most scenic spots. It takes roughly 4½ hours to complete, but from May to October you could make a day of it by stopping at some of the idyllic beaches scattered along the way.

You can choose to walk smaller sections; the most scenic is around **Cap du Dramont**, crowned by a signal station, which you can do as a loop from **Plage du Débarquement**. This long, sandy beach is where the US 36th Infantry Division landed on 15 August 1944 as part of Operation Dragoon (Provence landing). The large memorial park has a car park easily accessible from the N98.

Fréjus

POP 53,298

Once an important province of Roman Gaul (when it was known as Forum Julii), the little town of Fréjus is a quiet spot that has some surprisingly big attractions – including some Roman ruins, a chapel decorated by the filmmaker-artist Jean Cocteau (of *Les Enfants du Paradis* fame), and an impressive Gothic cathedral with some of the most

outlandish medieval frescos you could ever hope to see. It's particularly worth a visit on Wednesday and Saturday morning, when the old-town market is in full swing.

Sights

★Cloître de la Cathédrale de Fréjus CATHEDRAL
(04 94 52 14 01; www.cloitre-frejus.fr; 58 rue de Fleury; adult/child €5.50/free; 10am-12.30pm & 1.45-6.30pm Jun-Sep, 10am-1pm & 2-5pm Tue-Sat Oct-May) Fréjus' star sight is its 11th- and 12th-century cathedral, one of the region's first Gothic buildings. Its **cloister** features rare 14th- and 15th-century painted wooden ceiling panels depicting angels, devils, hunters, acrobats and monsters in vivid comic-book fashion. The meaning and origin of these are unknown. Only 500 of the original 1200 frames survive. Afterwards, peek at the octagonal 5th-century **baptistery**, which incorporates eight Roman columns; it's one of the oldest Christian buildings in France and is exceptionally well preserved.

Musée Archéologique MUSEUM
(place Calvini; adult/child €2/free; 9.30am-12.30pm & 2-6pm Tue-Sun Apr-Sep, 9.30am-noon & 2-4.30pm Tue & Thu-Sat Oct-Mar) Fréjus' Roman remains have seen better days, so the town's archaeological museum makes a useful accompaniment. There are some fascinating treasures on display dating all the way back to the town's Grecian and Roman beginnings, from everyday objects to rare finds, such as a double-faced marble statue of Hermes, a head of Jupiter and a stunning 3rd-century mosaic depicting a leopard.

Sleeping

Domaine du Colombier CAMPGROUND €
(04 94 51 56 01; www.domaine-du-colombier.com; 1052 rue des Combattants en Afrique du Nord; tent sites €22-64, cottages €64-416;) This is camping the way French families like to do it: in fully equipped self-catering cottages, surrounded by restaurants, sportsgrounds, play areas and a landscaped lagoon complete with waterslides. Lowly tent-pitchers will find just a couple of dozen spaces, hardly surprising given the sky-high prices.

Auberge de Jeunesse Fréjus-St-Raphaël HOSTEL €
(04 94 53 18 75; www.fuaj.org; chemin du Counillier; dm €19; Mar-Oct;) A rambling, pretty basic HI-affiliated hostel set in 10 hectares of pine trees, where you can also pitch your tent. Take bus 7 from St-Raphaël or Fréjus train stations to stop Les Chênes, then cross the roundabout and take chemin du Counillier on your left (600m). Daily lockout between noon and 5.30pm; rates include breakfast and sheets.

Hôtel L'Aréna HOTEL €€
(04 94 17 09 40; www.hotel-frejus-arena.com; 145 rue du Général de Gaulle; d €63-201, tr €97-253, f €104-298;) One of Fréjus' fanciest options, a traditional family hotel bedecked in Provençal decor complete with garden, pool and upmarket restaurant. The duplexes are ideal for families (with two single beds on a mezzanine). Breakfast is a juicy €17.

Eating

★Mon Fromager DELI €
(04 94 40 67 99; www.mon-fromager.fr; 38 rue Sieyès; plat du jour €13.90, 5-cheese platter €10.90; shop 9am-7pm Tue-Sat, lunch noon-2pm Tue-Sat;) Enterprising cheesemonger Philippe Daujam not only sells cheese – he also cooks it into tasty lunches in his deli-style restaurant arranged in front of the cheese counter and on the street outside. Locals flock for the excellent-value *plat du jour* and can't-go-wrong cheese platters with salad. The faux cow-skin table mats are a fun touch, and Philippe is a font of *fromage* knowledge.

Maison de la Tarte BOULANGERIE €
(04 94 51 17 34; 33 rue Jean Jaurès; tart slices €2.80; 7am-7pm Mon-Sat Aug-Jun;) If you're planning a picnic, stop at this mouth-watering bakery. Tarts of every kind (lemon meringue, pear and chocolate, raspberry and almond etc), sold by the slice, fill the front window and back shelves. Sandwiches and quiches are equally good.

Information

Tourist Office (04 94 51 83 83; www.frejus.fr; 249 rue Jean Jaurès; 9.30am-7pm Jul & Aug, 9.30am-12.30pm & 2.30-6.30pm Mon-Sat Jun & Sep, 9am-noon & 2-6pm Mon-Sat Oct-May)

Getting There & Away

BUS

Bus 4 links Fréjus' little **bus station** (rue Gustave Bret) with St-Raphaël (€1.10).

TRAIN

From Fréjus' small train station, in summer there are hourly services to/from Cannes (€7.90, 40 minutes), St-Raphaël (€1.40, three minutes) and Nice (€12, 70 minutes).

St-Tropez

POP 4903

Pouting sexpot Brigitte Bardot came to St-Tropez in the '50s to star in *Et Dieu Créa la Femme* (*And God Created Woman*; 1956) and overnight transformed the peaceful fishing village into a sizzling jet-set favourite. Tropeziens have thrived on their sexy image ever since: at the Vieux Port, yachts like spaceships jostle for millionaire moorings, and infinitely more tourists jostle to admire them.

Yet there is a serene side to this village trampled by 60,000 summertime inhabitants and visitors on any given day. In the low season, the St-Tropez of mesmerising quaint beauty and 'sardine scales glistening like pearls on the cobblestones' that charmed Guy de Maupassant (1850–93) comes to life. Meander cobbled lanes in the old fishing quarter of La Ponche, sip pastis at a place des Lices cafe, watch old men play *pétanque* beneath plane trees, or walk in solitary splendour from beach to beach along the coastal path.

Sights

Vieux Port PORT

Yachts line the harbour and visitors stroll the quays at the picturesque old port. In front of the sable-coloured townhouses, the **Bailli de Suffren statue** (quai Suffren), cast from a 19th-century cannon, peers out to sea. The bailiff (1729–88) was a sailor who fought with a Tropezien crew against Britain and Prussia during the Seven Years' War.

★Musée de l'Annonciade ART MUSEUM

(place Grammont; adult/child €6/free; ⏲10am-1pm & 2-6pm Wed-Mon) In a gracefully converted 16th-century chapel, this small but famous museum showcases an impressive collection of modern art infused with that legendary Côte d'Azur light. Pointillist Paul Signac bought a house in St-Tropez in 1892 and introduced other artists to the area. The museum's collection includes his *St-Tropez, Le Quai* (1899) and *St-Tropez, Coucher de Soleil au Bois de Pins* (1896).

★La Ponche HISTORIC SITE

Shrug off the hustle of the port in St-Tropez's historic fishing quarter, La Ponche, northeast of the Vieux Port. From the southern end of quai Frédéric Mistral, place Garrezio sprawls east from 10th-century **Tour Suffren** to place de l'Hôtel de Ville. From here, rue Guichard leads southeast to sweet-chiming **Église de St-Tropez** (place de l'Ormeau), a St-Trop landmark built in 1785 in Italian baroque style. Inside is a bust of St Torpes, honoured during Les Bravades in May.

Place des Lices SQUARE

St-Tropez' legendary and very charming central square is studded with plane trees, cafes and *pétanque* players. Simply sitting on a cafe terrace watching the world go by or jostling with the crowds at its extravaganza of a twice-weekly market (p854), jam-packed with everything from fruit and veg to antique mirrors and sandals, is an integral part of the St-Tropez experience.

Artists and intellectuals have met for decades in St-Tropez's famous Café des Arts, now simply called Le Café (p853) – and not to be confused with the newer, green-canopied Café des Arts on the corner of the square. Aspiring *pétanque* players can borrow a set of boules from the bar.

★Citadelle de St-Tropez MUSEUM

(✆04 94 54 84 14; admission €3; ⏲10am-6.30pm Apr-Sep, to 5.30pm Oct-Mar) Built in 1602 to defend the coast against Spain, the citadel dominates the hillside overlooking St-Tropez to the east. The views are fantastic. Its dungeons are home to the excellent **Musée de l'Histoire Maritime**, an all-interactive museum inaugurated in July 2013 retracing the history of humans at sea, from fishing, trading, exploration, travel and the navy.

Beaches

★Plage de Pampelonne BEACH

The 5km-long, celebrity-studded Plage de Pampelonne sports a line-up of exclusive beach restaurants and clubs in summer. Find public access (and parking for €5.50) near Moorea Plage; otherwise, join the crowds at one of the beach clubs. The northern edge of the beach begins 4km southeast of St-Tropez with **Plage de Tahiti**.

Plage des Salins BEACH

(rte des Salins) Just east of St-Tropez, Plage des Salins is a long, wide sandy beach at the southern foot of Cap des Salins. At the northern end of the beach, on a rock jutting out to sea, is the tomb of Émile Olivier (1825–1913), who served as first minister to Napoleon III until his exile in 1870. It looks out towards **La Tête de Chien** (Dog's Head), named after the legendary dog who declined to eat St Torpes' remains.

DON'T MISS

LUNCH BREAK

The tastiest dine on the Estérel coast road is **Villa Matuzia** (☎04 94 82 79 95; www.matuzia.com; 15 bd Ste Guitte, Agay; mains €20, menus €27-47; ⊙lunch & dinner Wed-Sun, closed Sun evening Oct-May; ❄📶), 200m from the sea. It serves elaborate Mediterranean cuisine (fabulous catch of the day) and the setting is charming: a cosy dining room in winter and a lush summer terrace. Its two bedrooms (doubles including breakfast €75) each have a little patio.

Activities

Sentier du Littoral WALKING

A spectacular coastal path wends past rocky outcrops and hidden bays 35km south from St-Tropez, around the peninsula to the beach at Cavalaire-sur-Mer. In St-Tropez the yellow-flagged path starts at **La Ponche**, immediately east of Tour du Portalet, and curves around Port des Pêcheurs, past St-Tropez' citadel. It then leads past the walled **Cimitière Marin** (Marine Cemetery), **Plage des Graniers** and beyond.

The tourist office has maps with distances and walking times (eg to Plage des Salins: 8.5km, 2½ hours).

Les Bateaux Verts BOATING

(☎04 94 49 29 39; www.bateauxverts.com; quai Jean Jaurès) Les Bateaux Verts offers trips around Baie des Cannebiers (dubbed 'Bay of Stars' after the celebrity villas dotting its coast) April to September (adult/child €11/6), as well as seasonal boats to Cannes (€38.50/24.80) and Porquerolles (€43/28.20), and regular shuttle boats to Marines de Cogolin, Port Grimaud, Ste-Maxime and Les Issambres.

Sleeping

St-Tropez is home to celebrity-studded hangs, with prices to match – this is no shoestring destination, though campgrounds do sit southeast along Plage de Pampelonne. Most hotels close occasionally in winter; the tourist office lists what's open and also has a list of B&Bs. If you're driving, double-check the parking arrangements.

Hôtel Lou Cagnard HOTEL €€

(☎04 94 97 04 24; www.hotel-lou-cagnard.com; 18 av Paul Roussel; d €83-176; ⊙Mar-Oct; ❄📶) This old-school hotel stands out in stark contrast against most of the swanky hotels around St-Tropez. Located in an old house shaded by lemon and fig trees, its rooms are unashamedly frilly and floral, but some have garden patios, and the lovely jasmine-scented garden and welcoming family feel make it a home away from home. The cheapest rooms share toilets.

Hôtel Le Colombier HOTEL €€

(☎04 94 97 05 31; http://lecolombierhotel.free.fr; impasse des Conquettes; d €105-185, tr €235-285; ⊙mid-Apr–mid-Nov; ❄📶) An immaculately clean converted house, a five-minute walk from place des Lices, the Colombier's fresh, summery decor is feminine and uncluttered. Rooms are in shades of white and furnished with vintage furniture.

Hôtel Les Palmiers HOTEL €€

(☎04 94 97 01 61; www.hotel-les-palmiers.com; 26 bd Vasserot; d €146-285; ❄📶) What a great spot this simple hotel has, in an old villa on the edge of place des Lices. Rooms are plain and bright, the best of which overlook the hotel's gated courtyard. Choose one in the main building rather than the annexe.

Pastis DESIGN HOTEL €€€

(☎04 98 12 56 50; www.pastis-st-tropez.com; 61 av du Général Leclerc; d from €325; ❄📶🏊) This stunning townhouse turned hotel is the brainchild of an English couple besotted with Provence and passionate about modern art. You'll die for the pop art–inspired interior, and long for a swim in the emerald-green pool. Every room is beautiful, although those overlooking av du Général Leclerc are noisy. It's very expensive in high season, but in low season there are often deals.

Hôtel Ermitage BOUTIQUE HOTEL €€€

(☎04 94 81 08 10; www.ermitagehotel.fr; av Paul Signac; r €160-850; ❄📶) Well, if you really want to hang with the jet set, the hip hermitage is your kind of place. Self-consciously retro, the decor draws inspiration from St-Tropez's midcentury heyday: bold primary colours, vintage design pieces and big prints of '60s icons on the walls. The bar's as cool as they come, with sweeping views over St-Trop.

Hôtel Byblos HOTEL €€€

(☎04 94 56 68 00; www.byblos.com; av Paul Signac; r/ste from €340/875; ⊙mid-Apr–Sep; P@📶🏊) Hôtel Byblos remains a perennial favourite among Hollywood A-listers, who come for the exclusive atmosphere, smack

in the centre of St-Tropez. Renowned Alain Ducasse restaurant Rivea and Byblos' **Les Caves du Roy** (www.lescavesduroy.com; ⌚7pm-5am Fri & Sat Apr-Oct, nightly Jul & Aug) club scene round out the fun.

Eating

Prices are high: the glamour dust sprinkled on fish and chips doesn't come cheap! Quai Jean Jaurès is lined with mediocre restaurants with great portside views. Cheaper eats cluster near quai de l'Épi and the new port. Many restaurants close in winter. Reservations are essential in high season.

Don't leave town without sampling *tarte Tropézienne,* an orange blossom–flavoured double sponge cake filled with thick cream, created by Polish baker A Mickla in 1955.

★La Tarte Tropézienne CAFE €
(☎04 94 97 04 69; www.latartetropezienne.fr; place des Lices; mains €13-15, cakes €3-5; ⌚6.30am-7.30pm & noon-3pm) This newly renovated cafe-bakery is the creator of the eponymous sugar-crusted, orange-perfumed cake. There are smaller branches at **36 rue Clémenceau** (☎04 94 97 71 42; ⌚7am-7pm) and near the **new port** (☎04 94 97 19 77; 9 bd Louis Blanc; ⌚6.30am-7.30pm).

La Pesquière SEAFOOD €
(☎04 94 97 05 92; 1 rue des Remparts; menu €29, mains €14-20; ⌚9am-midnight daily mid-Mar–Nov) This is the kind of place you wouldn't think could still exist in swanky St-Tropez – a down-to-earth, honest-as-they-come seafood restaurant, which has been been serving up bowls of mussels, stuffed sardines and Provençal vegetables for going on five decades. It's near the old fishing quays of La Ponche, so the fish is guaranteed fresh – but don't expect any frills.

La Ramade BISTRO €
(☎04 94 81 58 67; 3 rue du Temple; menus €16; ⌚noon-2pm & 7-10.30pm Feb–mid-Nov) Just what you might not expect to dig up in St-Tropez – an honest, down-to-earth, unpretentious bistro, pleasantly removed from busy place des Lices. Tuck into rabbit, duck, grilled fish and steaks on the peaceful terrace, washed down with a crisp glass of a local white, and you could almost believe you were in rural Provence.

Bistro Canaille FUSION €€
(☎04 94 97 75 85; 28 rue des Remparts; plates €8-24; ⌚7-11pm Fri & Sat Mar-May & Oct-Dec, 7-11pm Tue-Sun Jun-Sep) Probably the pick of the places to eat in town – creative, cosy and great value while still hitting the gourmet heights. It's got the soul of a bistro, but specialises in fusion-style tapas dishes inspired by the owners' travels. More filling mains are chalked on the board. It's on the street leading up to the château.

Le Café CAFE €€
(☎04 94 97 44 69; www.lecafe.fr; place des Lices; lunch/dinner menus €18/32; ⌚8am-11pm) Whetting whistles since 1789, this historic cafe is where artists and painters preferred to hang out back in the days when St-Trop was still a sleepy port. Happily, it's clung on to its no-nonsense roots – you'll find solid dishes such as pot-roasted chicken, mussels and grilled fish on the menu, as well as a lovely interior bar with globe lights and wooden fixtures that still give it a cosy *fin-de-siècle* vibe. They'll lend you a set of boules if you want to take on some *pétanque* players on the square.

Le Sporting BRASSERIE €€
(place des Lices; lunch menu €13, mains €16-30; ⌚8am-1am) The locals' hang-out of choice at any time of day: a knockabout bistro-bar where everyone know everyone and the patio overlooking place des Lices is packed with evening pastis-drinkers. Expect simple brasserie grub – entrecôte, hamburgers, salads.

La Table du Marché BISTRO €€
(☎04 94 97 01 25; www.christophe-leroy.com; 11 rue des Commerçants; lunch/dinner menu €19.50/29, mains €15.50-29; ⌚noon-2pm & 7-10pm Apr-Oct; ☞) Local chef Christophe Leroy has a good thing going with his 'Market Table' bistros, which now exist in various Moroccan towns as well as the original one here. The concept combines a bistro with a patisserie, *salon de thé* and posh grocery shop in an elegant village house. Dishes are fairly straightforward but efficiently done, and the setting is full of charm.

★La Vague d'Or GASTRONOMIC €€€
(☎04 94 55 91 00; www.residencepinede.com; Résidence de la Pinède, Plage de la Bouillabaisse; menus from €205; ⌚7.30-10pm mid-Apr–mid-Oct) Wonder-chef Arnaud Donckele has established a gastronomic temple with three Michelin stars at the Résidence de la Pinède: expect Mediterranean ingredients and flavours, with a one-of-a-kind twist.

Shopping

St-Tropez is loaded with couture boutiques, gourmet food shops and art galleries.

Market MARKET

(place des Lices; ⏱8am-1pm Tue & Sat) Forget the fancy side of St-Tropez for a while, and re-enter a more traditional Provence at this twice-weekly market, offering everything from cheese trucks and veg stalls to bric-a-brac sellers, sandal-makers and vintage clothes.

K Jacques SHOES

(16 rue Seillon; ⏱10am-1pm & 3-7pm Mon-Sat, 10.30am-1pm & 3.30-7pm Sun) Outlet for St-Tropez hand-crafted sandals (€145 to €220). K Jacques has been around since 1933, serving such clients as Picasso and Brigitte Bardot.

Atelier Rondini SHOES

(☎04 94 97 19 55; www.rondini.fr; 16 rue Georges Clémenceau; ⏱9.30am-6.30pm Tue-Sat, 10.30am-1.30pm & 3.30-6.30pm Sun) Colette brought a pair of sandals from Greece to Atelier Rondini (open since 1927) to be replicated. It's still making the iconic sandals for about €135.

Information

Tourist Office (☎08 92 68 48 28; www.sainttropeztourisme.com; quai Jean Jaurès; ⏱9.30am-1.30pm & 3-7.30pm Jul & Aug, 9.30am-12.30pm & 2-7pm Apr-Jun, Sep & Oct, to 6pm Mon-Sat Nov-Mar) Runs occasional walking tours April to October, and also has a kiosk in Parking du Port in July and August. Rather stingily, you have to pay for a town map (€2).

Getting There & Away

BICYCLE

Rolling Bikes (☎04 94 97 09 39; www.rolling-bikes.com; 14 av du Général Leclerc; per day bikes/scooters/motorcycles from €17/46/120, plus deposit; ⏱10am-6pm Mon-Sat, to 5pm Sun) Do as the locals do and opt for two wheels.

BOAT

Services are reduced or cut in winter.

Les Bateaux Verts (p852) Runs shuttle boats connecting St-Tropez with Ste-Maxime (one way/return €7.50/13.50, 15 minutes), Les Issambres (€8.50/15, 25 minutes), Marines de Cogolin (€7/12.30, 15 minutes) and Port Grimaud (€7/12.30, 20 minutes).

Les Bateaux de St-Raphaël (☎04 94 95 17 46; www.bateauxsaintraphael.com) Connects St-Tropez (Nouveau Port) and St-Raphaël (adult/child €15/10, one hour) mid-April to October. The train station in St-Raphaël is 200m from the dock.

Sea taxi (☎06 12 40 28 05; www.taxi-boat-saint-tropez.com) Boat taxis can be booked for anywhere around St-Tropez.

BUS

VarLib (☎04 94 24 60 00; www.varlib.fr) tickets cost €3 from the **bus station** (☎04 94 56 25 74; av du Général de Gaulle) for anywhere within the Var département (except Toulon-Hyères airport), including Ramatuelle (35 minutes), St-Raphaël (1¼ hours to three hours, depending on traffic) via Grimaud and Port Grimaud, and Fréjus. Buses to Toulon (two hours, seven daily, less in summer) stop at Le Lavandou (one hour) and Hyères (1½ hours).

Buses serve Toulon-Hyères airport (€15, 1½ hours), but some require a transfer.

TRAIN

By train, the most convenient station is in St-Raphäel, which is served by **Les Bateaux de St-Raphaël** boats in high season, or a slower **VarLib** bus. There is no luggage storage at the train station (or any public place in the Var).

Massif des Maures

A wild range of wooded hills rumpling the landscape inland between Hyères and Fréjus, the Massif des Maures is a pocket of surprising wilderness just a few miles from the summer hustle of the Côte d'Azur. Shrouded by pine, chestnut and cork oak trees, its near-black vegetation gives rise to its name, derived from the Provençal word *mauro* (dark pine wood).

Traditional industries (chestnut harvests, cork, pipe-making) are still practised here, and the area is criss-crossed by hiking trails that offer spectacular views of the surrounding coastline.

Local tourist offices can supply trail guides and route suggestions, but note that from June to September, access to many areas is limited due to the risk of forest fire. Depending on the risk, trails are graded yellow, orange, red and black, with yellow meaning some minor restrictions at certain times of day, and black meaning total closure. It's worth asking at a local tourist office before you set out.

Sights

Hidden in the forest, the leafy village of Collobrières is *the* place to taste chestnuts. Across the 11th-century bridge, the tourist office can help you participate in the Octo-

ber chestnut harvest, celebrated with the Fête de la Châtaigne, or join a guided forest walk.

★ **Monastère de la Verne** MONASTERY
(☎ 04 94 43 45 51; http://la.verne.free.fr; off D14; adult/child €6/3; ⏲ 11am-6pm Wed-Mon Jun-Aug, to 5pm Wed-Mon Feb-May & Sep-Dec) The majestic 12th- to 13th-century Monastère de la Verne perches unbelievably on the hip of a mountain deep in the forest, but with a view to the sea. The Carthusian monastery was founded in 1170, possibly on the site of a temple to the goddess Laverna, protector of the bandits who hid in the Maures. The Huguenots destroyed most of the original charterhouse in 1577. Since 1982 the solitary complex has been home to 24 nuns of the Sisters of Bethlehem.

The monastery's restoration has been a labour of love. A 20-minute video details the work. Highlights include the austere Romanesque church, the prior's cell, complete with a small formal garden and workshop, the bakery and the olive mill. The shop (closed Sunday) is full of excellent artisanal food, soaps, art and crafts made by the nuns. Walking trails lead from the monastery into its forested surroundings.

From Collobrières, follow rte de Grimaud (D14) east for 6km, then turn right (south) on to the D214 and drive another 6km to the monastery; park at the lot and walk the final section, which is unpaved.

Village des Tortues WILDLIFE RESERVE
(☎ 04 94 78 26 41; www.villagetortues.com; Gonfaron; adult/child €12/8; ⏲ 9am-7pm Mar-Nov, to 6pm Dec-Feb) About 20km north of Collobrières, this sanctuary protects one of France's most endangered species, the Hermann tortoise (*Testudo hermanni*). Once common along the Mediterranean coast, it is today found only in the Massif des Maures and on Corsica. In summer the best time to see the tortoises is in the morning and late afternoon. Watch them hatch from mid-May to the end of June; they hibernate from November through early March. A great palaeontology trail has vicious-looking models of the tortoise's ancestors lurking among the bushes.

Fôret des Maures HIKING
The Collobrières tourist office gives hiking directions to the **Châtaignier de Madame**, the biggest chestnut tree in Provence, with a mighty 10.4m circumference; and the two biggest menhirs (each over 3m) in the Var region, now Heritage-listed monuments, which were raised between 3000 BC and 2000 BC. Three shorter walking trails are mapped on the noticeboard outside the office.

Eating

Traditional country cuisine dominates local menus. In season, you might have the chance to sample some wild boar.

Auberge de la Môle REGIONAL CUISINE €€€
(☎ 04 94 49 57 01; place de l'Église, La Môle; lunch/dinner menus €23/55; ⏲ noon-2pm & 7-9pm Tue-Sat, noon-2pm Sun) Tradition rules fierce and strong at this no-frills village inn, which doubles as the local *bar-tabac* (cafe-tobacconist). For locals, Auberge de la Môle is *the* place to appease hearty appetites with legendary terrines, pâtés and feisty jars of pickles. Find the inn next to the church in the hamlet of La Môle.

★ **La Petite Fontaine** TRADITIONAL FRENCH €€
(☎ 04 94 48 00 12; place de la République, Collobrières; 3-/5-course menu €27/33; ⏲ noon-2.30pm Tue-Sun, 7-10pm Tue-Sat Apr-Sep, noon-2.30pm Tue-Sun, 7-10pm Fri & Sat Oct-Mar) Locals throng from miles around to sit at a tree-shaded table and feast on seasonal forest mushrooms and chestnuts at one of southern France's most charming, relaxed village inns. The walls inside are exposed stone, and the fruit tarts for dessert are…out of this world. Reservations essential. No credit cards.

Information

Tourist Office (☎ 04 94 48 08 00; www.collobrieres-tourisme.com; bd Charles Caminat; ⏲ 9am-12.30pm & 2-5.30pm Tue-Sun, closed Sun & Mon Sep-Jun) Has maps for local walks, and lists *gîtes* and B&Bs in the area online.

Corniche des Maures

The Corniche des Maures (D559) unwinds beautifully southwest from La Croix-Valmer to Le Lavandou along a shoreline trimmed with sandy beaches ideal for swimming, sunbathing and windsurfing.

Tiny **Plage du Rayol** and **Plage de l'Escale** are particularly enchanting beaches: they're backed by pine trees and have a restaurant on the sand. As the D559 hugs the coast going west, you'll reach **Plage du Layet**, the beautiful beach at **Cavalière** (not to be confused with Cavalaire-sur-Mer).

Once a fishing village, **Le Lavandou** is now an overbuilt family-oriented beach

resort with a small but intact old town and 12km of golden sand.

Sights & Activities

★Domaine du Rayol GARDENS

(☎04 98 04 44 00; www.domainedurayol.org; av des Belges, Rayol-Canadel-sur-Mer; adult/child €10.50/7.50; ⊙9.30am-7.30pm Jul & Aug, to 6.30pm Apr-Jun, Sep & Oct, to 5.30pm Nov-Mar) This stunning, lush garden, with plants from all Mediterranean climates the world round, is wonderful for a stroll or a themed nature walk. The dense flora cascades down the hillside from a villa to the sea, and while the flowers are at their best in April and May, it's always worth a visit. In summer, at the estate's gem of a beach, you can snorkel around underwater flora and fauna with an experienced guide; bookings are essential.

Fort de Brégançon FORT

(www.bormeslesmimosas.com; Hameau de Cabasson, Bormes-les-Mimosas; adult/child €10/free; ⊙9am-7pm Jul-Sep, shorter hours rest of year) A private state residence for the president of the republic since 1968, the Fort de Brégançon opened to the public for the first time in July 2014. Located on a scenic peninsula in Bormes-les-Mimosas, the imposing fort dates back to the 11th century and has featured in numerous conflicts since, from the tensions between Provence and France to the French Revolution and WWI. Tickets must be booked in advance at the Bormes tourist office, either in person or online.

Sleeping & Eating

There are a few hotels dotted along the coastal road, but the hillside village of Bormes-les-Mimosas makes a more pleasant base.

DON'T MISS

LUNCH IN BORMES-LES-MIMOSAS

Jérôme Masson rules over the kitchen, and his wife, Patricia, over the dining room at **La Rastègue** (☎04 94 15 19 41; www.larastegue.com; 48 bd du Levant; menus €35-49; ⊙7-9pm Tue-Sat, noon-1.45pm Sun Apr-Nov), where they sure do excel. They have earned a Michelin star with their ever-changing menu of superb Provençal fare, inviting dining room and sea-view terrace. The open kitchen allows you to see the chef at work.

★Hôtel Bellevue HOTEL €

(☎04 94 71 15 15; www.bellevuebormes.com; place Gambetta, Bormes-les-Mimosas; r €72-112; ⊙Jan-Sep; ❄📶) As its name suggests, this charming salmon-pink village hotel boasts sensational views, stretching over the village's jumbled rooftops all the way to the glittering blue. There are a couple of cheap not-yet-renovated rooms, plus a couple more that are wheelchair accessible. There's also a pleasant restaurant (lunch *menu* €16.80): arrive early for a prime valley-view table.

Le Relais des Maures INN €€

(☎04 94 05 61 27; www.lerelaisdesmaures.fr; av Charles Koeklin, Rayol-Canadel-sur-Mer; r €105) This inn, tucked just off the southern side of the D559, has homey guest rooms, some with sea views. The excellent restaurant (*menus* from €32) here is worth a stop in its own right for its seasonally changing *menus* of locally sourced produce.

Chez Jo SEAFOOD €€

(☎04 94 05 85 06; Plage du Layet, Cavalière; mains €20-30; ⊙noon-2pm May-Sep) Buzzing with barefoot, overly bronzed, sarong-clad beach-lovers with unexpected piercings and a fondness for nude bathing, this beach restaurant grills everything straight from the sea. It's bare bones and without a sign in sight to tell you it's here; dining is around a few tables on the sand or on a wooden deck above the water. No credit cards.

Information

Tourist Office (☎04 94 01 38 38; www.bormeslesmimosas.com; 1 place Gambetta, Bormes-les-Mimosas; ⊙9am-12.30pm & 2.30-7pm Jul & Aug, shorter hours rest of year; 📶) Organises local walks.

Le Lavandou Tourist Office (☎04 94 00 40 50; www.ot-lelavandou.fr; quai Gabriel Péri; ⊙9am-noon & 2.30-6pm Mon-Sat) The tourist office is the faux castle on the seafront. Boats sail to the Îles des Hyères from the ferry dock opposite.

Hyères

POP 56,600

Driving down the busy streets of Hyères, lined by stately palm trees and a big casino, you could be forgiven for completely missing the medieval old town on which the modern conurbation is founded. Its shady lanes are worth a wander, but the main reason for stopping actually lies to the south – a

WORTH A TRIP

ROUTE DES CRÊTES

For breathtaking views of the islands, follow rte des Crêtes as it winds its way through maquis-covered hills some 400m above the sea. From Bormes-les-Mimosas, follow the D41 uphill (direction Collobrières) past the Chapelle St-François and, 1.5km north of the village centre, turn immediately right after the sign for Col de Caguo-Ven (237m).

Relais du Vieux Sauvaire (☎04 94 05 84 22; rte des Crêtes; mains €17-32; ⏲noon-2.30pm & 7-9.30pm Jun-Sep) is the hidden gem of these hills. With 180-degree views you could only dream of, this restaurant and pool (most people come for lunch and then stay all afternoon) is one of a kind. The food is as sunny as the views: pizzas, melon and Parma ham, or whole sea bass in salt crust.

Past the restaurant, rte des Crêtes joins the final leg of the panoramic Col du Canadel road. On the *col* (mountain pass), turn left to plunge into the heart of the forested Massif des Maures or right to the sea and the coastal Corniche des Maures (D559).

T-shaped peninsula known as the Presqu'île de Giens (Giens Peninsula), which is fantastic for water sports and birdwatching, not to mention trips to the lovely Îles d'Hyères.

Hyères' attractive **Vieille Ville** (old town) begins on the western side of place Georges Clemenceau at the 13th-century **Porte Massillon** (look for the clock). West along cobbled rue Massillon is rue des Porches, with its polished flagstones and shady arcades. The rambling hillside grove of **Parc St-Bernard** abuts the striking Villa Noailles. Back downhill, **Parc Castel Ste-Claire**, a 17th-century convent converted into a private residence, was home to American writer Edith Wharton from 1927.

If you don't have time to visit the Camargue, **Presqu'île de Giens** might well be your next-best bet for flamingo-spotting. Several large lagoons lie at the centre, visited by many seasonal species including herons, egrets, teals, cormorants and Provence's famous flamingos. A **Sentier du Littoral** (Coastal Path) loops the peninsula; bring binoculars. The peninsula is well signposted from the old town. It's about 9km drive to the end of the point along the D197.

Several pleasant beaches are scattered around the edge of the peninsula, and the little port is the launch pad for day trips to the Îles d'Hyères.

Pink flamingos also add a splash of colour to the otherwise barren landscape of **La Capte**, two narrow sand bars supporting the Salins des Presquiers salt pans and a lake 4km south of Hyères' centre. A 1½-hour cycling itinerary (12.5km) loops the salt pans, and the Hyères tourist office runs guided bird-discovery **nature walks** (adult/child €5/free).

The western sand-bar road dubbed the rte du Sel (Salt Rd) is particularly spectacular. It's accessible only in summer.

The **tourist office** (☎04 94 01 84 50; www.hyeres-tourisme.com; Rotonde du Park Hôtel, av de Belgique; ⏲9am-6pm Mon-Fri, to 4pm Sat, plus Sun Jul & Aug) offers guided birdwatching walks to Hyères' lagoons.

From the **Hyères train station** (place de l'Europe), destinations include Toulon (€4.60, 23 minutes) and Marseille Blancarde (€15.30, 1¼ hours). Most trains also stop in Cassis, La Ciotat, Bandol and Ollioules-Sanary.

Toulon

POP 167,200

Rough-round-the-edges Toulon just doesn't fit in with the glittering Côte d'Azur. Built around a *rade* (a sheltered bay lined with quays), France's second-largest naval port has a certain rough charm, and isn't quite as terrible as it once was, though most visitors wisely just pass through.

North of the city, **Mont Faron** (584m) towers over Toulon, and the views are, as you would expect, epic. Near the summit, **Mémorial du Débarquement de Provence** (☎04 94 88 08 09; adult/child €4/free; ⏲10am-noon & 2-4.30pm Tue-Sun) commemorates the Allied landings of Operation Dragoon, which took place along the coast here in August 1944. There are pleasant walks in the surrounding forest. To get here, catch a ride on the **Téléphérique du Mont Faron** (☎04 94 92 68 25; www.telepherique-faron.com; return adult/child €7.50/5.50; ⏲10am-6pm) cable car. The one-day Toulon Pass (p859) includes a trip on the Mont Faron cable car.

From the port you can take a guided boat tour around **Les Bateliers de la Rade** (☎04

DON'T MISS

ÎLES D'HYÈRES

Shimmering temptingly on the horizon as you drive the coast road from Toulon to Hyères, the Îles d'Hyères are often known locally as the Îles d'Or (Islands of Gold) – a reference not just to their mica-rich rock, but also the golden beaches that fringe their rocky shorelines. In July and August, they're overrun, but for much of the rest of the year you might well find you have them largely to yourself.

Île de Porquerolles, at 7km long and 3km wide, is the largest; Île de Port-Cros, in the middle, is a national park with fantastic submarine snorkelling; and its eastern sister, Île du Levant, is both an army camp and a nudist colony. Wild camping and cars are forbidden throughout the archipelago.

Bendor and Embiez lie to the west, and are jointly known as the Îles Paul Ricard – a reference to the famous pastis maker, who purchased the islands in the 1950s. Both have been heavily developed, so you're better off keeping your island exploring to the Îles d'Hyères.

The main ports for travelling to the islands are La Tour Fondue, Port d'Hyères and Le Lavandou, but from June to September, seasonal ferries also run from other locations including Toulon and St-Tropez.

Transport Littoral Varois (✆ 04 94 58 21 81; www.tlv-tvm.com) Runs year-round ferries to the Île de Porquerolles (return €19.50, 20 minutes), Île de Port-Cros (return €28.10, one hour) and Île du Levant (return €28.10, 1½ hours). Boats run from the jetties at Port d'Hyères and Tour Fondue. There's also a two-island day trip (return €31.50) to Port-Cros and Le Levant; it runs only from the Port d'Hyères.

Vedettes Îles d'Or et Le Corsaire (✆ 04 94 71 01 02; www.vedettesilesdor.fr; 15 quai Gabriel Péri) Runs boats to the Îles d'Hyères from its bases at Le Lavandou, Cavalaire and La Croix Valmier. From Le Lavandou, boats go to Île du Levant (return €28, 35 to 55 minutes), Île de Port-Cros (€28, 35 to 55 minutes) and Île de Porquerolles (€30, 50 minutes); trips from Cavalaire and La Croix Valmier cost about €5 extra.

There are also multi-island cruises (€48) on high-speed La Croisière Bleue vessels, which stop at both Porquerolles and Port-Cros. You can catch these from any of the three mainland ports.

94 46 24 65; www.lesbateliersdelarade.com; quai de la Sinse; adult/child €10/6; ⊙ May-Sep), with a commentary on the local events of WWII (the commentary is in French, but there are leaflets in English).

Sleeping & Eating

Hôtel Little Palace HOTEL €

(✆ 04 94 92 26 62; www.hotel-littlepalace.com; 6-8 rue Berthelot; s €50, d €55-90, tr €75-80; ❄ @ 📶) The over-the-top, Italian-inspired decor lacks authenticity and the lighting could be nicer, but Little Palace is well run and friendly. No lift.

Les P'tits Pins FRENCH €€

(✆ 04 94 41 00 00; www.lesptitspins.com; 237 place de la Liberté; 2-/3-course menu €19/27; ⊙ 11.30am-2pm Mon-Sat, 7.30-10pm Fri & Sat; ✎) This is the restaurant that shows that Toulon is a town that, slowly but surely, is shaking off its down-at-heel image. With its crisp white tablecloths, sparkling glasses and banquette seats, it's an elegant setting for elegant food: steamed skate, Charolais beef, white onion soup and the like.

L'Aromate Provençale PROVENCAL €€

(✆ 04 94 29 73 87; 32 rue Gimelli; lunch €17, dinner menu €27; ⊙ noon-2pm & 7-10pm Tue-Sat) Traditional Provençal flavours get a modern twist at this little side-of-the-street brasserie, run by enterprising young entrepreneurs Pierre Andreini and Martial Merlino. The space is small, but the flavours are big: zingy tomato sauces, citrus and herbal overtones, lashings of olive oil. The location is great too, near the opera house.

Information

Tourist Office (✆ 04 94 18 53 00; www.toulontourisme.com; 12 place Louis Blanc; ⊙ 9am-6pm Mon-Sat, 9.30am-12.30pm Sun Apr-Oct, shorter hours rest of year) Has maps and walking-tour brochures, and sells tickets for sights including the Mont Faron cable car.

Getting There & Around

AIR

Toulon-Hyères Airport (TLN; ☎08 25 01 83 87; www.toulon-hyeres.aeroport.fr; 📶), 25km east of Toulon, currently offers flights (some seasonal) to Brussels, Rotterdam, London, Southampton, as well as French cities including Paris Orly, Brest, Lyon, Bordeaux and Corsica.

Reseau Mistral bus 102 runs at least five times daily to Toulon's train and bus stations (30 minutes) via Hyères' port and bus stations (10 minutes); the fare costs flat-rate €1.40. **VarLib** (www.varlib.fr) runs a shuttle bus to St-Tropez (€3, 1½ hours).

BOAT

Corsica Ferries (www.corsica-ferries.fr; Port de Commerce, 2 av de l'Infanterie-de-Marine) has services to both Corsica and Sardinia, and **SNCM** (www.sncm.fr; Port de Commerce, 2 av de l'Infanterie-de-Marine) to Corsica.

In summer, **Bateliers de la Côte d'Azur** (☎04 94 05 21 14; www.bateliersdelacotedazur.com; quai Cronstadt) goes to the Îles d'Hyères, including Porquerolles (adult/child €28/18), Port-Cros (€29.50/20) or a combined two-island cruise (€36/19). Ferry services also run to St-Tropez in season, and there are cruises around the bay too.

BUS

VarLib (www.varlib.fr) buses (€3) operate from the **bus station** (☎04 94 24 60 00; bd de Tessé), next to the train station. Buses to St-Tropez (six daily) go via Hyères (35 minutes) and Le Lavandou (one hour).

The tourist office sells a one-day **Toulon Pass** (www.reseaumistral.com; per person €6) that includes unlimited travel on local **Le Réseau Mistral** (☎04 94 03 87 00; www.reseaumistral.com) buses and commuter boats, and a return ticket for the Mont Faron Téléphérique.

TRAIN

Toulon has frequent connections to Marseille (€10, 50 minutes), St-Raphaël (€12, 50 minutes), Cannes (€14.50, 1¼ hours) and Nice (€17, one hour 50 minutes). Fastest trips are by TGV.

Bandol & Around

Bandol's old fishing-port charm has long since been swallowed up by its high-rise seaside apartment blocks, but the plentiful restaurants, cheap-and-cheerful shops and copious beach facilities make it a favourite for holidaymakers from nearby Toulon and Marseille. For everyone else, it's probably best for a quick lunch stop or a spot of wine tasting rather than an overnight stay.

Activities

Bandol's 49 vineyards carefully manage their prized production of red, rosé and white. The Bandol appellation comprises eight neighbouring communities, including Le Castellet, Ollioules, Évenos and Sanary-sur-Mer. Most vineyards require an appointment.

Maison des Vins WINE

(Oenothèque des Vins du Bandol; ☎04 94 29 45 03; www.maisondesvins-bandol.com; place Lucien Artaud, Bandol; ⏰10am-1pm & 3-6.30pm Mon-Sat, 10am-1pm Sun) Pascal Perier, the manager at the Maison des Vins, is a living Bandol encyclopaedia. He provides tastings, keeps a well-supplied shop and can direct you to surrounding vineyards.

Sentier du Littoral WALKING

This yellow-marked coastal trail runs 12km (allow 3½ to four hours) from Bandol's port to La Madrague in St-Cyr-les-Lecques, with the beautiful Calanque de Port d'Alon roughly halfway.

Sleeping

Golf Hôtel HOTEL €€

(☎04 94 29 45 83; www.golfhotel.fr; 10 promenade de la Corniche; d/q from €80/120; ⏰Jan-Nov; ❄📶) A prime address for beachside sleeping; some of the rooms have terraces facing the sea.

Key Largo HOTEL €€

(☎04 94 29 46 93; www.hotel-key-largo.com; 19 corniche Bonaparte; d €90-125; ❄📶) Bandol's hotels are short on charm, but this small place on the point between the port and Renécros beach is one of the better options. Rooms are decorated in mauves, greys and sea blues, and the out-of-town setting ensures a peaceful vibe.

Eating

L'Espérance BISTRO €€

(☎04 94 05 85 29; 21 rue du Dr Marçon; lunch menu €25, dinner menus €29-58; ⏰noon-1.30pm Wed-Thu, Sat & Sun, 7-9pm Tue-Sun) Reserve ahead to get a spot in this tiny Provençal restaurant run ably by a husband-and-wife team.

L'Ardoise MEDITERRANEAN, BISTRO €€

(☎04 94 32 28 58; 25 rue du Dr Marçon; lunch menu €16, dinner menus €27-41; ⏰noon-2pm & 7.30-10.30pm Wed-Sun) Set back from the port's hustle, this stylish place is good for gourmet Mediterranean cuisine. The best tables are on the streetside terrace, or there's a cosy dining room for chilly nights.

Information

Tourist Office (☎04 94 29 41 35; www.bandol.fr; allées Vivien; ⏰9am-noon & 2-6pm Mon-Sat) Offers the usual information on hotels, restaurants and activities, plus a town guide in English.

Getting There & Away

Bandol has direct rail links from Marseille to all stations along the coast as far as Ventimiglia.

The Three Corniches

This trio of *corniches* (coastal roads) hugs the cliffs between Nice and Monaco, each higher than the last, with dazzling views of the Med. For the grandest views, it's the Grande Corniche you want, but the Moyenne Corniche runs a close scenic second. The lowest of all, the Corniche Inférieure, allows access to a string of snazzy coastal resorts.

Corniche Inférieure

Skimming the villa-lined waterfront between Nice and Monaco, the Corniche Inférieure, built in the 1860s, passes through the towns of Villefranche-sur-Mer, St-Jean-Cap Ferrat, Beaulieu-sur-Mer, Èze-sur-Mer and Cap d'Ail.

Walk down from the hilltop village of Èze to its coastal counterpart, Èze-sur-Mer, via the steep chemin de Nietzsche, a 45-minute footpath named after the German philosopher Nietzsche, who started writing *Thus Spake Zarathustra* while staying in Èze (and enjoying this path).

Getting There & Around

Bus 100 (€1.50, every 15 minutes from 6am to 8pm) runs the length of the Corniche Inférieure between Nice and Menton, stopping at all the villages along the way, including Villefranche-sur-Mer (15 minutes), Beaulieu-sur-Mer (20 minutes) and Cap d'Ail (35 minutes). Bus 81 serves Villefranche (20 minutes) and St-Jean-Cap Ferrat (30 minutes).

From Nice, trains to Ventimiglia in Italy (half-hourly 5am to 11pm) stop at Villefranche-sur-Mer (€1.20, seven minutes), Beaulieu-sur-Mer (€1.60, 10 minutes) and Cap d'Ail (€2.80, 18 minutes).

VILLEFRANCHE-SUR-MER

POP 5400

Heaped above a idyllic harbour, this picturesque village with imposing citadel overlooks the Cap Ferrat peninsula and, thanks to its deep harbour, is a prime port of call for cruise ships. The 14th-century old town, with its tiny, evocatively named streets broken by twisting staircases and glimpses of the sea, is a delight to amble (preferably broken with a long lazy lunch on the water's edge or a bijou old-town square).

BEAULIEU-SUR-MER & ST-JEAN-CAP FERRAT

The seaside holiday town of Beaulieu-sur-Mer is well known for its well-preserved belle-époque architecture. It sits at the beginning of Cap Ferrat, a wooded peninsula laden with millionaires' villas and home to the small village of St-Jean-Cap Ferrat.

Sights & Activities

Villa Ephrussi de Rothschild HISTORIC BUILDING

(☎04 93 01 33 09; www.villa-ephrussi.com/en; St-Jean-Cap Ferrat; adult/child €13/10; ⏰10am-7pm Jul & Aug, 10am-6pm Feb, Mar, Sep & Oct, 2-6pm Mon-Fri, 10am-6pm Sat & Sun Nov-Jan) An over-the-top, belle-époque confection, this villa was commissioned by Baroness Béatrice Ephrussi de Rothschild in 1912. She was an avid art collector and the villa is filled with Fragonard paintings, Louis XVI furniture and Sèvres porcelain. From its balcony, nine exquisite themed gardens appear like a ship's deck. Stunning in spring, the Spanish, Japanese, Florentine, stone, cactus, rose and French gardens are delightful to stroll through – sea views are supreme and fountains 'dance' to classical music every 20 minutes. An audioguide helps make sense of the show

Bus 81, which links Nice and St-Jean-Cap Ferrat, stops at the foot of the driveway leading to the villa; the stop is called 'Passable.'

★Cap Ferrat WALKING

This dreamy peninsula is laced with 14km of eucalyptus-scented walking paths, all with magnificent views and wonderful coastline all the way. There are various itineraries, all easygoing; tourist offices have maps.

Information

Tourist Office (☎04 93 01 01 21; www.otbeaulieusurmer.com; place Georges Clémenceau, Beaulieu-sur-Mer; ⏰9am-6.30pm Mon-Sat, 9am-12.30pm Sun Jul & Aug, shorter hours rest of year) Beaulieu's tourist office is town-focused, but keeps current lists of events, accommodation and bars.

Tourist Office (☎04 93 76 08 90; www.saintjeancapferrat-tourisme.fr; 5 & 59 av

WORTH A TRIP

ROQUEBRUNE-CAP MARTIN

Beautiful Cap Martin nestles its languid shores into the sea of crystalline water between Monaco and Menton. The village of Roquebrune-Cap-Martin is actually centred on the medieval village of Roquebrune, which towers over the cape (the village and cape are linked by innumerable *very* steep steps). The amazing thing about this place is that, despite Monaco's proximity, it feels a world away from the urban glitz of the principality: the coastline around Cap Martin remains relatively unspoiled and it's as if Roquebrune had left its clock on medieval time.

Roquebrune The medieval chunk of Roquebrune-Cap-Martin, Roquebrune sits 300m high on a pudding-shaped lump crowned by 10th-century **Château de Roquebrune** (☎04 93 35 07 22; www.roquebrune-cap-martin.com; place William Ingram, Roquebrune; adult/child €5/3; ⊙10am-1pm & 2.30-7pm Jun-Sep, shorter hours rest year) – an atmospheric place with simple but evocative props of life in medieval times. Of all the steep and tortuous streets leading up to the château, rue Moncollet, with its arcaded passages and rock-carved stairways, is the most impressive. Architect Le Corbusier is buried in the village cemetery (section J; he designed his own tombstone). Sensational sea views unfold from place des Deux Frères.

Cabanon Le Corbusier (☎06 48 72 90 53; www.capmoderne.com; Promenade Le Corbusier; guided tours adult/child €15/10; ⊙guided tours only 10am & 3pm Tue-Sun Jul & Aug, 10am & 2pm Tue-Sun May, Jun & Sep–mid-Oct) The only building French architect Le Corbusier (1887–1965) ever built for himself is this rather simple – but very clever – beach hut on Cap Martin. The *cabanon* (small beach hut), which he completed in 1952, became his main holiday home until his death. The hut can be visited on excellent 2½-hour guided tours run by the Association Cap Moderne; tours depart on foot from Roquebrune-Cap-Martin train station and must be reserved in advance by phone or email.

Sentier du Littoral With the exception of in Monaco, you can walk the 13km between Cap d'Ail and Menton without passing a car. The Sentier du Littoral follows the rugged coastline from the hedonistic **Plage Mala** (a tiny gravel cove where a couple of restaurants double as private beach and cocktail bars) in Cap d'Ail to **Plage Marquet** in the Fontvieille neighbourhood of Monaco. The path then picks up at the other end of Monaco, in **Larvotto**, from where you can walk to Menton along the beaches and wooded shores of Cap Martin, including the beautiful **Plage Buse**.

The walk is easy going, but visitors should note that the stretch of coast between Monaco and Cap d'Ail is inaccessible in bad weather. The path is well signposted and you can easily walk small sections or make a day trip out of it, including beach stops and lunch in Monaco. If you don't fancy walking through Monaco, you can catch bus 6 from Larvotto to Fontvieille.

Denis Séméria, St-Jean-Cap Ferrat; ⊙9.30am-6.30pm Mon-Sat, 10am-5pm Sun Jul & Aug, shorter hours rest of year) Efficient tourist office with well-informed staff, with lots of information on walks, activities and water sports.

Moyenne Corniche

Cut through rock in the 1920s, the Moyenne Corniche takes drivers from Nice past the Col de Villefranche (149m), Èze and Beausoleil (the French town bordering Monaco's Monte Carlo).

Bus 82 serves the Moyenne Corniche from Nice all the way to Èze (20 minutes); bus 112 carries on to Beausoleil (40 minutes, Monday to Saturday).

ÈZE

POP 2600

This rocky little village perched on an impossible peak is the jewel in the Riviera crown. The main attraction is the medieval village itself, with small higgledy-piggledy stone houses and winding lanes (and plenty of galleries and shops), and the mesmerising views of the coast.

You'll get the best panorama from **Jardin Exotique d'Èze** (☎04 93 41 10 30; adult/child €6/2.50; ⊙9am-7.30pm Jul-Sep, to 6.30pm Apr-May & Jun, to 5.30pm rest of year), a cactus garden at the top of the village where you'll also find the old castle ruins. Take time to sit there or in the garden's Zen area to contem-

DON'T MISS

GOURMET ICE

When you start to feel the heat, follow locals away from the tourist crowd to the kitchen boutique of **Pierre Geronoli** (☎97 98 69 11; 36 bd d'Italie, Monaco; 1/2/3 scoops €3.8/7/10.10). This Corsican master ice-cream maker, the darling of every gastronomic chef around, crafts extraordinary flavours: beetroot and raspberry, pistachio and almond, chestnut cream and honey, tomato and basil, and champagne. Buy his creations straight in a cone or tub, or as a gourmet cocktail in a super-stylish *verrine* (glass jar).

plate the stunning view: few places on earth offer such a wild panorama.

The village gets very crowded during the day; for a quieter wander, come early in the morning or late afternoon. Or even better, stay overnight. Five-star boutique **Château Eza** (☎04 93 41 12 24; www.chateaueza.com; rue de la Pise; d from €360; ❄📶) has 12 sumptuous rooms and a Michelin-starred gastronomic **restaurant** (☎04 93 41 12 24; www.chateaueza.com; rue de la Pise; mains €45-67), with a dreamy panoramic bar for an unforgettable aperitif.

Bus line 82 travels between Nice and Èze (hourly Monday to Saturday, every two hours Sunday) via Villefranche-sur-Mer. The fare is a flat-rate €2.

Grande Corniche

Views from the spectacular cliff-hanging Grande Corniche are mesmerising, and if you're driving, you'll probably want to stop at every bend to admire the unfolding vistas. Hitchcock was sufficiently impressed by Napoléon's Grande Corniche to use it as a backdrop for his film *To Catch a Thief* (1956), starring Cary Grant and Grace Kelly. Ironically, Kelly died in 1982 after crashing her car on this very same road.

There are no villages of note along the Grande Corniche until you reach hilltop La Turbie, best known for its monumental Roman triumphal monument.

Those not in the know wouldn't give inconspicuous **Café de la Fontaine** (☎04 93 28 52 79; 4 av Général de Gaulle, La Turbie; mains €18-25; ⏰noon-2.30pm & 7-11pm) a second glance. What they don't know is that it is Michelin-starred chef Bruno Cirino's baby – somewhere for him to go back to his culinary roots with simple yet delicious dishes reflecting *le terroir* (land) and season. Blackboard *plats* (dishes) are a perfect reflection of what's at the market.

Monaco

POP 37,800 / ☎377

Squeezed into just 200 hectares, this principality might be the world's second-smallest country (the Vatican is smaller), but what it lacks in size it makes up for in attitude. A magnet for high-rollers and hedonists since the early 20th century, it's also one of the world's most notorious tax havens (residents pay no income tax). It's also famous for its annual Formula 1 Grand Prix, held every year in May since 1929.

Despite its prodigious wealth, Monaco itself is a long way from the prettiest town on the French Riviera: it's basically an ode to concrete and glass, dominated by high-rise hotels and apartment blocks that rise into the hills like ranks of dominos, not to mention an utterly bewildering street layout that seems solely designed to confound lowly pedestrians.

It's a rather different story on the rocky outcrop known as Le Rocher, which juts out on the south side of the port and is home to the royal palace, as well as a rather charming little old town which feels a world away from Monte Carlo's skyscrapers and super yachts.

History

Since the 13th century, Monaco's history has been that of the Grimaldi family, whose rule began in 1297. Charles VIII, king of France, recognised Monégasque independence in 1489. But during the French Revolution, France snatched Monaco back and imprisoned its royal family. Upon release, they had to sell the few possessions they still owned and the palace became a warehouse.

The Grimaldis were restored to the throne under the 1814 Treaty of Paris. But in 1848 they lost Menton and Roquebrune to France, and Monaco swiftly became Europe's poorest country. In 1860, Monégasque independence was recognised for a second time by France and a monetary agreement in 1865 sealed the deal on future cooperation between the two countries.

Rainier III (r 1949–2005), nicknamed *le prince bâtisseur* (the builder prince), ex-

panded the size of his principality by 20% in the late 1960s by reclaiming land from the sea to create the industrial quarter of Fontvieille. In 2004 he doubled the size of the harbour with a giant floating dyke, placing Port de Monaco (Port Hercules) among the world's leading cruise-ship harbours. Upon Rainier's death, son Albert II became monarch.

Sights & Activities

A major construction project is underway on the the north side of the port, where the foundations for Monaco's brand new Museum of the Automobile and a large car park are currently being laid; the work is expected to continue until at least 2019.

Save a few cents by buying a combined ticket (adult/child €19/9) covering same-day admission to both the Palais Princier de Monaco and the Musée Océanographique de Monaco; both sights sell it.

★Musée Océanographique de Monaco — AQUARIUM

(☎93 15 36 00; www.oceano.mc; av St-Martin; adult €11-16, child €7-12; ⏲9.30am-8pm Jul & Aug, 10am-7pm Apr-Jun & Sep, to 6pm Oct-Mar) Stuck dramatically to the edge of a cliff since 1910, the world-renowned Musée Océanographique de Monaco, founded by Prince Albert I (1848–1922), is a stunner. Its centrepiece is its **aquarium** with a 6m-deep lagoon where sharks and marine predators are separated from colourful tropical fishes by a coral reef. Upstairs, two huge colonnaded rooms retrace the history of oceanography and marine biology (and Prince Albert's contribution to the field) through photographs, old equipment, numerous specimens and interactive displays.

★Le Rocher — HISTORIC SITE

Monaco Ville, also called Le Rocher, is the only part of Monaco to have retained its original old town, complete with small, windy medieval lanes. The old town thrusts skywards on a pistol-shaped rock, its strategic location overlooking the sea that became the stronghold of the Grimaldi dynasty. There are various staircases up to Le Rocher; the best route up is via Rampe Major, which starts from place aux Armes near the port. On your way up, look out for the statue of the late Prince Rainier looking down on his beloved Monaco, created by Dutch artist Kees Verkade.

★Casino de Monte Carlo — CASINO

(☎98 06 21 21; www.montecarlocasinos.com; place du Casino; 9am-noon €10, from 2pm Salons Ordinaires/Salons Privées €10/20; ⏲visits 9am-noon, gaming 2pm-2am or 4am or when last game ends) Peeping inside Monte Carlo's legendary marble-and-gold casino is a Monaco essential. The building, open to visitors every morning, is Europe's most lavish example of belle-epoque architecture. Prince Charles III came up with the idea of the casino and in 1866, three years after its inauguration, the name 'Monte Carlo' – Ligurian for 'Mount Charles' in honour of the prince – was coined. To gamble or watch the poker-faced play, visit after 2pm (when a strict over-18s-only admission rule kicks in).

Jardin Exotique — GARDENS

(☎93 15 29 80; www.jardin-exotique.mc; 62 bd du Jardin Exotique; adult/child €7.20/3.80; ⏲9am-7pm May-Sep, to 6pm Feb-Apr & Oct, to 5pm Nov-Jan) Home to the world's largest succulent and cactus collection, from small echinocereus to 10m-tall African candelabras, the gardens tumble down the slopes of Moneghetti through a maze of paths, stairs and bridges. Views of the principality are spectacular. Admission includes the **Musée d'Anthropologie**, which displays prehistoric remains unearthed in Monaco, and a 35-minute guided tour of the **Grotte de**

LOCAL KNOWLEDGE

SECRET BEACH

A peaceful, panoramic alternative to the sweaty busy hike with the crowds up Rampe Majeur to Le Rocher is via the **Digue de Monaco** (Monaco Dyke) – the world's largest flloating dyke, 28m wide and 352m long. Scale the steps at the end of quai Antoine 1er and detour left along the dyke's smooth concrete walkway to the viewpoint next to the cruise-ship terminal. The Monte Carlo panorama from here is the best there is. Backtrack to **Esplanade Stefano Casiraghi** and recharge batteries on the vast, designer sundeck here – ladders allow you to dip into the water. Then weave your way along the coastal path and up through the shady **Jardins St-Martin** to Le Rocher. En route, watch for old stone steps careering steeply down to the water and a secret shingle beach only locals know about.

Monaco

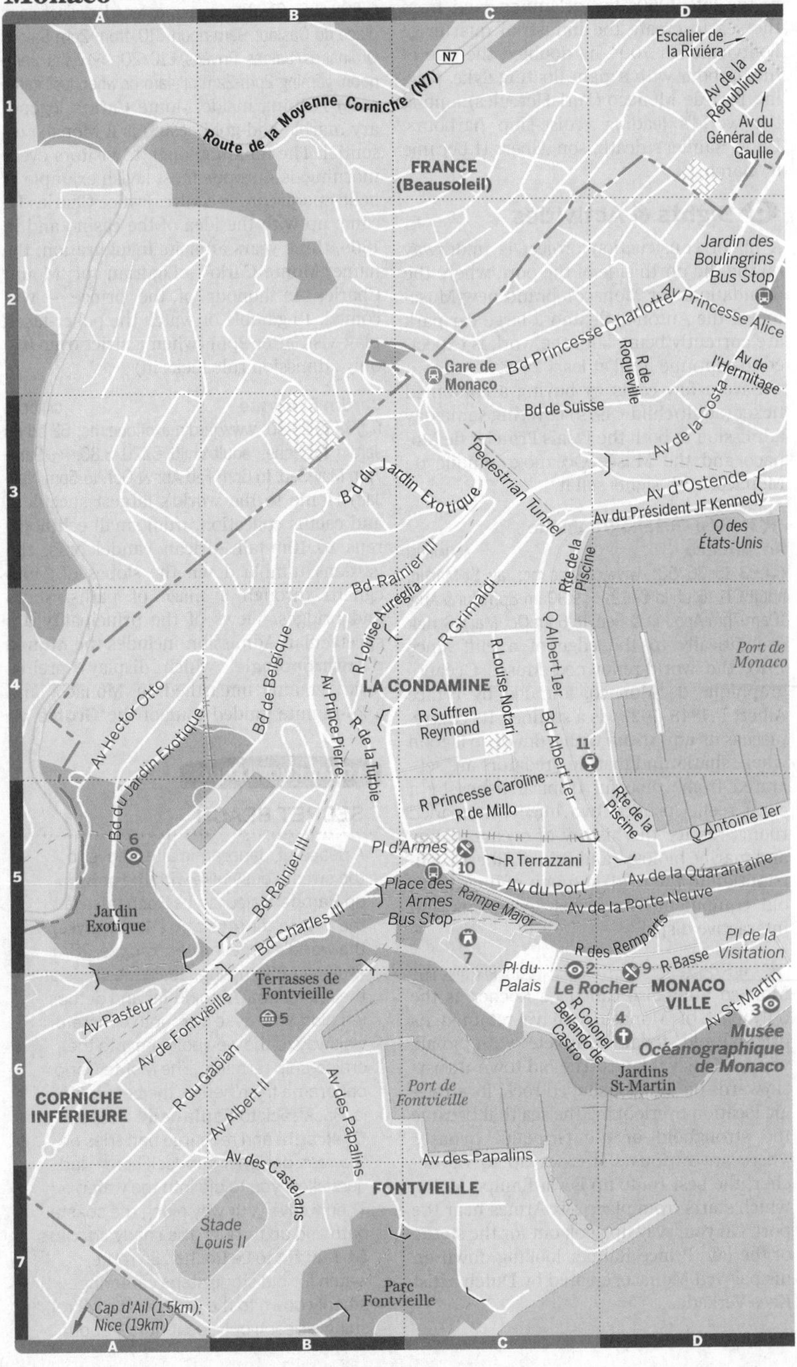

A
B
C
D
1
2
3
4
5
6
7
N7
Route de la Moyenne Corniche (N7)
FRANCE (Beausoleil)
Escalier de la Riviéra
Av de la République
Av du Général de Gaulle
Jardin des Boulingrins Bus Stop
Bd Princesse Charlotte
Av Princesse Alice
Av de l'Hermitage
R de Roqueville
Gare de Monaco
Bd de Suisse
Av de la Costa
Pedestrian Tunnel
Bd du Jardin Exotique
Av d'Ostende
Av du Président JF Kennedy
Q des États-Unis
Rte de la Piscine
Bd Rainier III
R Louise Auréglia
R Grimaldi
R Louise Notari
Q Albert 1er
Port de Monaco
Bd de Belgique
Av Prince Pierre
LA CONDAMINE
Av Hector Otto
Bd du Jardin Exotique
R de la Turbie
R Suffren Reymond
Bd Albert 1er
11
R Princesse Caroline
R de Millo
Rte de la Piscine
Q Antoine 1er
6
Pl d'Armes
10
R Terrazzani
Bd Rainier III
Av de la Quarantaine
Place des Armes Bus Stop
Av du Port
Rampe Major
Av de la Porte Neuve
Jardin Exotique
Bd Charles III
7
R des Remparts
Pl de la Visitation
Pl du Palais
2
9
R Basse
Terrasses de Fontvieille
Le Rocher
MONACO VILLE
Av St-Martin
3
Av Pasteur
Av de Fontvieille
5
R Colonel Bellando de Castro
4
Musée Océanographique de Monaco
R du Gabian
Jardins St-Martin
Av des Papalins
Port de Fontvieille
CORNICHE INFÉRIEURE
Av Albert II
Av des Castelans
Av des Papalins
FONTVIEILLE
Stade Louis II
Parc Fontvieille
Cap d'Ail (1.5km); Nice (19km)

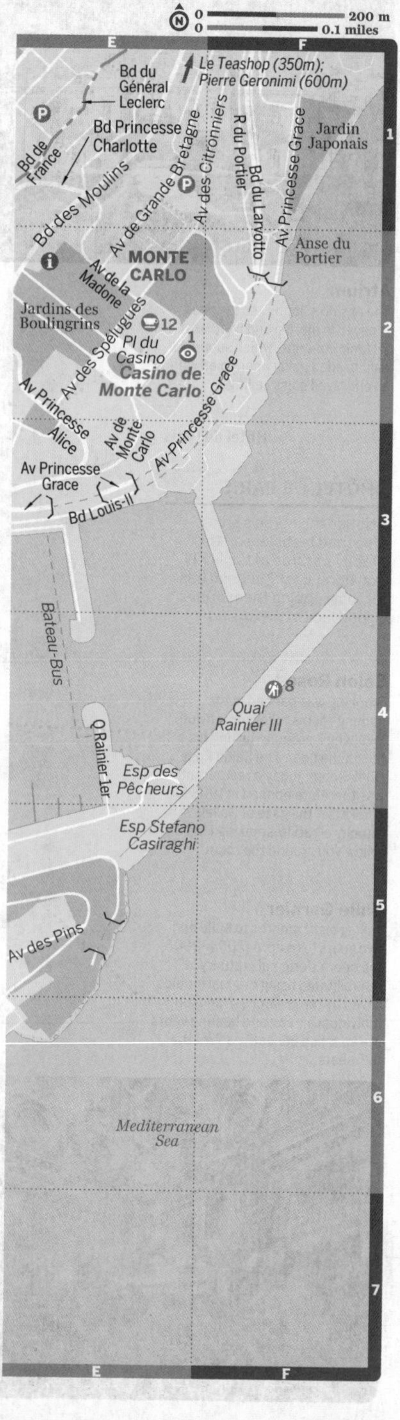

Monaco

Top Sights

1 Casino de Monte Carlo.......................E2
2 Le Rocher..C6
3 Musée Océanographique de Monaco...D6

Sights

4 Cathédrale de Monaco.......................D6
5 Collection de Voitures Anciennes.......................................B6
6 Jardin Exotique...................................A5
7 Palais Princier de Monaco C5

Activities, Courses & Tours

8 Digue de Monaco..................................F4

Eating

9 La Montgolfière...................................D6
10 Marché de la Condamine..................C5

Drinking & Nightlife

11 Brasserie de Monaco C4
12 Café de Paris.......................................E2

l'Observatoire. The prehistoric, stalactite- and stalagmite-laced cave is bizarre: it's the only cave in Europe where the temperature rises as you descend. Bus 2 links Jardin Exotique with the town centre.

Palais Princier de Monaco PALACE

(☎93 25 18 31; www.palais.mc; place du Palais; adult/child €8/4, incl Car Museum €11.50/5; ⏰10am-6pm Apr-Jun, Sep & Oct, to 7pm Jul & Aug) Built as a fortress atop Le Rocher in the 13th century, this palace is the private residence of the Grimaldi Family. It is protected by the blue-helmeted, white-socked Carabiniers du Prince; **changing of the guard** takes place daily at 11.55am, when crowds gather outside the gates to watch.

Most of the palace is off limits, but you can get a glimpse of royal life on a tour of the glittering **state apartments**, where you can see some of the lavish furniture and priceless artworks collected by the family over the centuries. It's a good idea to buy tickets online in advance to avoid queuing.

There's also a joint ticket available that buys entry to see the Prince's **classic car collection** (☎92 05 28 56; mtcc@mtcc.mc; Terrasses de Fontvieille; ⏰10am-6pm).

Cathédrale de Monaco CATHEDRAL

(4 rue Colonel Bellando de Castro; ⏰8.30am-6.45pm, closed 1st Thu of month Sep-May) FREE An adoring crowd continually shuffles past Prince Rainier's and Princess Grace's

Monte Carlo Casino

TIMELINE

1863 Charles III inaugurates the first Casino on Plateau des Spélugues. The **atrium** ❶ is a small room with a wooden podium from which an orchestra entertains while punters purchase entrance tickets.

1864 Hôtel de Paris opens and the area becomes known as the 'Golden Square'.

1865 Construction of **Salle Europe** ❷. Cathedral-like, it is lined with onyx columns and lit by eight Bohemian crystal chandeliers weighing 150kg each.

1868 The steam train arrives in Monaco and **Café de Paris** ❸ is completed.

1878–79 Gambling moves to Hôtel de Paris while Charles Garnier is charged with building a new casino with a miniature replica of the Paris Opera House, **Salle Garnier** ❹.

1890 The advent of electricity casts a glow on architect Jules Touzet's newly added **gaming rooms** ❺ for high rollers.

1903 Inspired by female gamblers, Henri Schmit decorates **Salle Blanche** ❻ with caryatids and the painting *Les Grâces Florentines*.

1904 Smoking is banned in the gaming rooms and **Salon Rose** ❼, a new smoking room, is added.

1910 **Salle Médecin** ❽, immense and grand, hosts the high-spending Private Circle.

1966 Celebrations mark 100 years of uninterrupted gambling despite two world wars.

TOP TIPS

➡ After 2pm when gaming begins, admission is strictly for 18 years and over. Photo ID is obligatory.

➡ Don't wear trainers. A jacket for men is not obligatory (but is recommended) in the gaming rooms.

➡ In the main room, the minimum bet is €5/25 for roulette/blackjack.

➡ In the Salons Privés, the minimum bet is €15, with no maximum.

SLOW IMAGES/GETTY IMAGES ©

Atrium
The casino's 'lobby', so to speak, is paved in marble and lined with 28 Ionic columns, which support a balustraded gallery canopied with an engraved glass ceiling.

HÔTEL DE PARIS

Notice the horse's shiny leg (and testicles) on the lobby's statue of Louis XIV on horseback? Legend has it that rubbing them brings good luck in the casino.

Salon Rose
Smoking was banned in the gaming rooms following a fraud involving a croupier letting his ash fall on the floor. The Salon Rose (Pink Room; today a restaurant) was therefore opened in 1903 for smokers – the gaze of Gallelli's famous cigarillo-smoking ladies follow you around the room.

Salle Garnier
Taking eight months to build and two years to restore (2004–2006), the opera's original statuary is rehabilitated using original moulds saved by the creator's grandson. Individual air-con and heating vents are installed beneath each of the 525 seats.

DEA/G. DAGLI ORTI/GETTY IMAGES ©

Salle Europe

The oldest part of the casino, where they continue to play *trente-et-quarante* and European roulette, which have been played here since 1865. Tip: the bull's-eye windows around the room originally served as security observation points.

Café de Paris

With the arrival of Diaghilev as director of the Monte Carlo Opera in 1911, Café de Paris becomes the go-to address for artists and gamblers. It retains the same high-glamour ambience today. Tip: snag a seat on the terrace and people-watch.

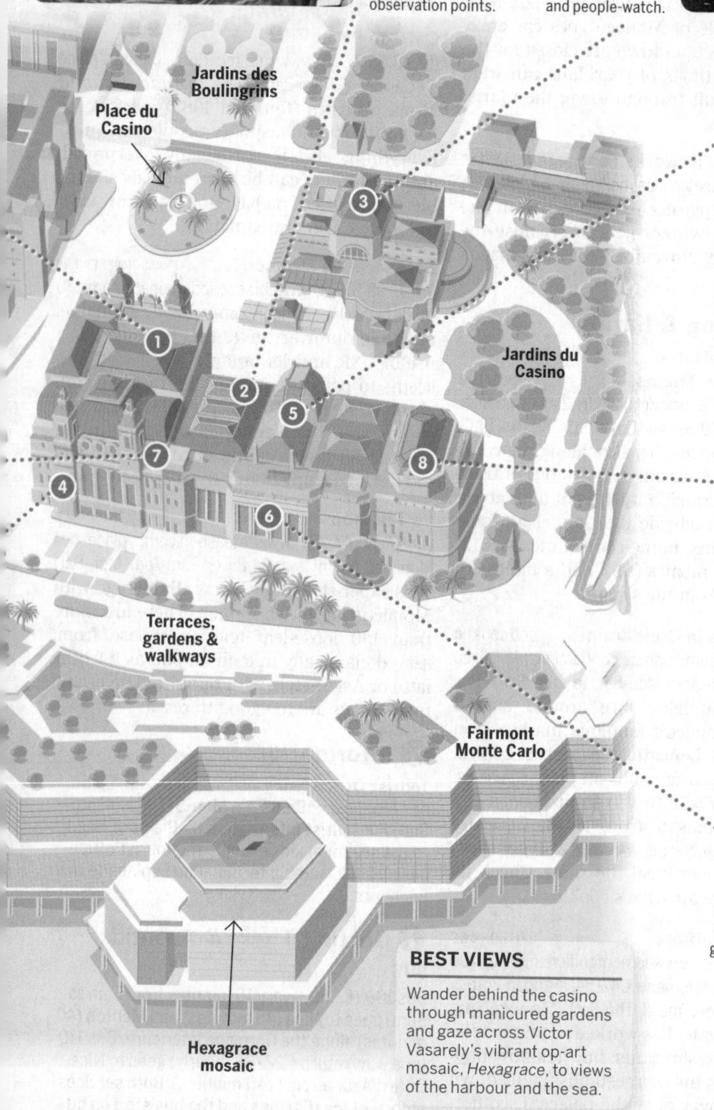

Salles Touzet

This vast partitioned hall, 21m by 24m, is decorated in the most lavish style: oak, Tonkin mahogany and oriental jasper panelling are offset by vast canvases, Marseille bronzes, Italian mosaics, sculptural reliefs and stained-glass windows.

Salle Médecin

Also known as Salle Empire because of its extravagant Empire-style decor, Monégasque architect François Médecin's gaming room was originally intended for the casino's biggest gamblers. Part of it still remains hidden from prying eyes as a Super Privé room.

Salle Blanche

Today a superb bar-lounge, the Salle Blanche (White Room) opens onto an outdoor gaming terrace, a must on balmy evenings. The caryatids on the ceiling were modelled on fashionable courtesans such as La Belle Otéro, who placed her first bet here aged 18.

BEST VIEWS

Wander behind the casino through manicured gardens and gaze across Victor Vasarely's vibrant op-art mosaic, *Hexagrace*, to views of the harbour and the sea.

flower-adorned graves, located inside the cathedral choir of Monaco's 1875 Romanesque-Byzantine cathedral. The Monaco boys' choir, **Les Petits Chanteurs de Monaco**, sings Sunday Mass at 10.30am between September and June.

Festivals & Events

Formula One Grand Prix SPORTS
(www.formula1monaco.com; late May) Formula One's most iconic race kicks off in late May, when the whole of Monaco goes car crazy and all the streets in town are closed for the race. At other times of year, fans can walk the 3.2km circuit through town; the tourist office has maps.

International Fireworks Festival EVENT
(www.monaco-feuxdartifice.mc/en; Jul & Aug) A showdown of pyrotechnic expertise in the port area. The winner gets to organise the fireworks on 18 November, eve of Monaco's national holiday.

Sleeping & Eating

Relais International de la Jeunesse Thalassa HOSTEL €
(04 93 78 18 58; www.clajsud.fr; 2 av Gramaglia, Cap d'Ail; dm €20; Apr-Oct) This hostel isn't actually in Monaco, it's 2km along the coast at Cap d'Ail, but it's only a quick bus or train ride into the principality. It's got a lot going for it: a fab beachside location, clean four- to 10-bed dorms, home-cooked meals (€12) and takeaway picnics (€9), and a handy location 300m from the station.

★ **Marché de la Condamine** FOOD COURT €
(www.facebook.com/marche.condamine; 15 place d'Armes; 7am-3pm Mon-Sat, to 2pm Sun) For tasty, excellent-value fare around shared tables, hit Monaco's fabulous market food court, tucked beneath the arches behind the open-air market stalls on place d'Armes. Fresh pasta (€5.50 to €9) from Maison des Pâtes, truffle cuisine from Truffle Gourmet and traditional Niçois *socca* (€2.80 per slice) from Chez Roger steal the show. Check its Facebook page for what's cooking.

★ **La Montgolfière** FUSION €€€
(97 98 61 59; www.lamontgolfiere.mc; 16 rue Basse; 3-/4-course menu €47/54; noon-2pm & 7.30-9.30pm Mon, Tue & Thu-Sat) Monegasque chef Henri Geraci has worked in some of the Riviera's top restaurants, but he's now happily settled at his own establishment down a shady alleyway near the palace. Escoffier-trained, he's faithful to the French classics, but his travels have given him a taste for Asian flavours too, so expect some exotic twists. The restaurant's small and sought after, so reserve ahead.

Drinking & Nightlife

Much of Monaco's superchic drinking goes on in its designer restaurants and the bars of luxury hotels, but you'll find a bunch of less sophisticated bars located behind the port.

Café de Paris CAFE
(98 06 77 77; www.montecarloresort.com; place du Casino; 7am-2am) The *grande dame* of Monaco's cafes (founded 1882), perfect for *un petit café* and a spot of people-watching. Everything else is chronically overpriced, and the waiters can be horrendously snooty, but it's the price you pay for a front-row view of Monte Carlo's razzamatazz.

Brasserie de Monaco MICROBREWERY
(97 98 51 20; www.brasseriedemonaco.com; 36 rte de la Piscine; noon-2pm) Having Monaco's only microbrewery gives this portside bar a useful USP, and its organic lagers and ales seems to pack the punters in. Inside it's all chrome, steel and big-screen TVs, and live sports and DJs keep the weekends extra busy. Head for the patio out front if it gets too hectic. Happy hour's from 6pm to 8pm.

Le Teashop TEAROOM €
(97 77 47 47; www.leteashop.com; place des Moulins; pot of tea €4-8; 9am-7pm Mon-Sat) This super-stylish tea bar is all the rage with Monaco's ladies who lunch. There are more than 130 loose-leaf teas to choose from, served classically in a china pot, as a frothy latte or Asian-style with bubbles. The home-made cakes are too good to resist.

Information

Tourist Office (www.visitmonaco.com; 2a bd des Moulins; 9am-7pm Mon-Sat, 11am-1pm Sun) For tourist information by the port, head to the seasonal kiosk run by the tourist office near the cruise-ship terminal on Esplanade des Pêcheurs.

Getting There & Around

BUS

Bus 100 (€1.50, every 15 minutes from 6am to 9pm) goes to Nice (45 minutes) and Menton (40 minutes) along the Corniche Inférieure. Bus 110 (one way/return €22/33, hourly) goes to Nice-Côte d'Azur airport (40 minutes). Both services stop at **place d'Armes** and the **bus stop** on bd

des Moulins opposite Jardins des Boulingrins. Night services run Thursday to Saturday.

TRAIN

Services run about every 20 minutes east to Menton (€2, 15 minutes) and west to Nice (€3, 25 minutes). Access to the station is through pedestrian tunnels and escalators from 6 av Prince Pierre de Monaco, pont Ste-Dévote, place Ste-Dévote and bd de la Belgique. The last trains leave around 11pm.

Menton

POP 29,670

Last stop on the Côte d'Azur before Italy, the seaside town of Menton offers a glimpse of what the high life on the Riviera must have been like before the developers moved in. With its sunny climate, shady streets and pastel mansions – not to mention a lovely old port – it's one of the most attractive towns on the entire coast. Menton's old town is a cascade of pastel-coloured buildings. Add a fantastic museum dedicated to the great artist and film director Jean Cocteau, as well as several excellent restaurants, and Menton really is a must.

To French people, the town is also known for its lemons, which are renowned for their flavour and celebrated every February with a big lemon-themed party.

DON'T MISS

LEMON FEST

Menton's quirky two-week **Fête du Citron** (Lemon Festival; www.feteducitron.com; Feb) sees sculptures and decorative floats made from tonnes of lemons weave along the seafront. Afterwards, the monumental lemon creations are dismantled and the fruit sold off at bargain prices in front of Palais de l'Europe. Each year the festival follows a different theme.

Sights & Activities

The town's epicentre is the bustling, pedestrianised rue St-Michel and its ice-cream parlours and souvenir shops.

★Musée Jean Cocteau Collection Séverin Wunderman GALLERY
(04 89 81 52 50; www.museecocteaumenton.fr; 2 quai de Monléon; adult/child €8/free; 10am-6pm Wed-Mon) Art collector Séverin Wunderman donated some 1500 Cocteau works to Menton in 2005 on the condition that the town build a dedicated Cocteau museum. And what a museum Menton built: this futuristic, low-rise building is a wonderful space to make sense of Cocteau's eclectic work. Its collection includes drawings, ceramics, paintings and cinematographic work. Admission includes the Cocteau-designed Musée du Bastion.

Musée du Bastion ART MUSEUM
(quai Napoléon III; adult/child €8/free; 10am-6pm Wed-Mon) Cocteau loved Menton. It was following a stroll along the seaside that he got the idea of turning a disused 17th-century bastion (1636) on the seafront into a monument to his work. He restored the building himself, decorating the alcoves, outer walls, reception hall and floors with pebble mosaics. The works on display change regularly. Admission includes entry to the Musée Jean Cocteau.

Jardin de la Serre de la Madone GARDENS
(04 93 57 73 90; www.serredelamadone.com; 74 rte de Gorbio; adult/child €8/4; 10am-6pm Tue-Sun Apr-Oct, to 5pm Jan-Mar, closed Nov & Dec) Beautiful if slightly unkempt, this garden was designed by American botanist Lawrence Johnston. He planted dozens of rare plants picked up from his travels around the world. Abandoned for decades, it has been mostly restored to its former glory. Guided tours (1½ hours) take place daily at 3pm. Take bus 7 to the Serre de la Madone stop.

Sleeping

Hôtel Lemon HOTEL €
(04 93 28 63 63; www.hotel-lemon.com; 10 rue Albert 1er; s/d/tr/q €65/76/91/125;) Hôtel Lemon sits in an attractive 19th-century villa with pretty garden, opposite a school. Its spacious minimalist rooms are decked out in shades of white with bright red or lemon-yellow bathrooms. Breakfast costs €6.50.

★Hôtel Napoléon BOUTIQUE HOTEL €€
(04 93 35 89 50; www.napoleon-menton.com; 29 porte de France; d €95-330;) Standing tall on the seafront, the Napoléon is Menton's most stylish sleeping option. Everything from the pool, the restaurant-bar and the back garden (a heaven of freshness in summer) has been beautifully designed. Rooms are decked out in white and blue, with Cocteau drawings on headboards. Sea-facing rooms have balconies but are a little noisier because of the traffic.

Eating

★ Au Baiser du Mitron BOULANGERIE
(☎04 93 57 67 82; www.aubaiserdumitron.com; 8 rue Piéta; cakes €2-5; ⏲8am-7pm Tue-Sat) A Kiss from the Baker is no ordinary *boulangerie*. It showcases breads from the Côte d'Azur, inland Provence and places elsewhere in the world that innovative baker Kevin Le Meur has travelled to. Everything is baked in a traditional *four à bois* (wood bread oven) from 1906, using 100% natural ingredients and no preservatives. The *tarte au citron de Menton* (Menton lemon tart) is the best there is.

Eric Kayser BOULANGERIE, CAFE €
(☎04 93 28 25 81; www.maison-kayser.com; 1 rue Partouneaux; sandwiches €4-6; ⏲7am-7pm) Fortunately for the rest of France, this Parisian baker has spread his wings to the Mediterranean, where deeply satisfying breads and pastries titillate local taste buds. Half-baguettes filled with different sandwich fillings, generously topped focaccia slices and *pain citron* (lemon bread) ensure the perfect picnic. Eat in or takeaway. Find a smaller branch in Menton's indoor **Halles Municipales** (quai de Monléon; ⏲7.15am-1pm), a food market by the seafront.

Le Cirke SEAFOOD €€
(☎04 89 74 20 54; www.restaurantlecirke.com; 1 square Victoria; menus lunch €26 & €29, dinner €30 & €45, mains €18-35; ⏲noon-1.30pm & 7.15-9.30pm Wed-Mon) From paella to bouillabaisse, grilled fish to fried calamari, this smart Italian-run restaurant is the place to turn to for delicious seafood. The wine list is a mix of Italian and French wines, and the service is as sunny as Menton itself.

★ Le Mirazur GASTRONOMIC €€€
(☎04 92 41 86 86; www.mirazur.fr; 30 av Aristide Briand; lunch menu €47, dinner menus €85-140; ⏲12.15-2pm & 7.30-10pm Wed-Sun Mar-Dec) Design, cuisine and sea view (the full sweep of the Med above Menton town below) are all spectacular at this 1930s villa with a twinset of Michelin stars. This is the culinary kingdom of daring Argentinian chef Mauro Colagreco, who flavours dishes not with heavy sauces, but with herbs and flowers from Le Mirazur's dazzling herb and flower garden, citrus orchard and vegetable patch.

Find it 3km northeast of Menton off the coastal D6007 to Italy. Cooking classes too.

Information

Tourist Office (☎04 92 41 76 76; www.tourisme-menton.fr; 8 av Boyer; ⏲9am-12.30pm & 2-6pm Mon-Sat)

Getting There & Away

Bus 100 (€1.50, every 15 minutes) goes to Nice (1½ hours) via Monaco (40 minutes) and the Corniche Inférieure. Bus 110 links Menton with Nice-Côte d'Azur airport (one way/return €22/33, one hour, hourly).

There are regular train services (half-hourly) to Ventimiglia in Italy (€2.50, nine minutes), Monaco (€2, 11 minutes) and Nice (€4, 35 minutes).

Corsica

POP 316,257

Includes ➡

Best Places to Eat

- La Sassa (p879)
- Le Matahari (p875)
- A Pignata (p898)
- U Casanu (p883)
- Pasquale Paoli (p881)

Best Places to Sleep

- Hôtel Demeure Les Mouettes (p887)
- Au Vieux Moulin (p878)
- Domaine de Croccano (p890)
- Auberge U n'Antru Versu (p898)
- Les Roches Rouges (p882)

Why Go?

Jutting out of the Med like an impregnable fortress, Corsica resembles a miniature continent, with astounding geographical diversity. Within half an hour, the landscape morphs from glittering bays, glitzy coastal cities and fabulous beaches to sawtooth peaks, breathtaking valleys, dense forests and enigmatic hilltop villages. Holidays in Corsica will therefore be incredibly varied: from hiking and canyoning to working your tan, enjoying a leisurely cruise, delving into the island's rich history and sampling local specialities.

Though Corsica has officially been part of France for more than 200 years, it feels different from the mainland in everything from customs and cuisine to language and character, and that's part of its appeal. Locals love talking about their Corsican identity so plenty of engaging evenings await, especially if the holy trilogy of food, wine and melodious Corsican music are involved.

When to Go

Ajaccio

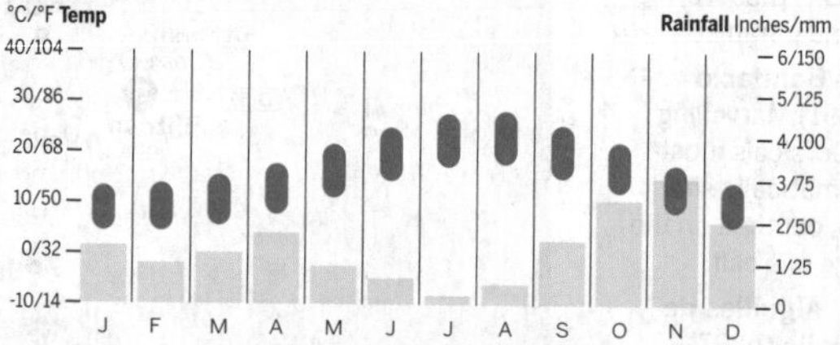

Easter Marked by solemn processions and colourful passion plays.

May & Jun The maquis is in blossom and it's warm enough to swim but not too hot to hike.

Jul–Sep Enjoy the summer party vibe at beach restaurants and nightclubs.

Corsica Highlights

1. **Réserve Naturelle de Scandola** (p885) Cruising the sapphire waters off Corsica's western coast.
2. **Cap Corse** (p874) Exploring this wild and remote area by way of winding coastal roads.
3. **Les Calanques de Piana** (p882) Seeing red, blazing red, between fantastic rock formations.
4. **Vallée du Tavignano** (p900) Hiking through this gorgeous, traffic-free valley near Corte.
5. **Plage de Palombaggia** (p895) Slipping into serene turquoise waters at Corsica's prettiest beach.
6. **Filitosa** (p891) Admiring the work of prehistoric people – see where they lived and what they built.
7. **Ajaccio** (p886) Boning up on Bonaparte around Napoléon's home town.
8. **Îles Lavezzi** (p894) Discovering island paradise.
9. **Bonifacio** (p891) Marvelling at Corsica's most dramatically sited city, perched on the edge of a cliff.
10. **Aiguilles de Bavella** (p897) Walking and canyoning among the rocky spires of this breathtaking massif.

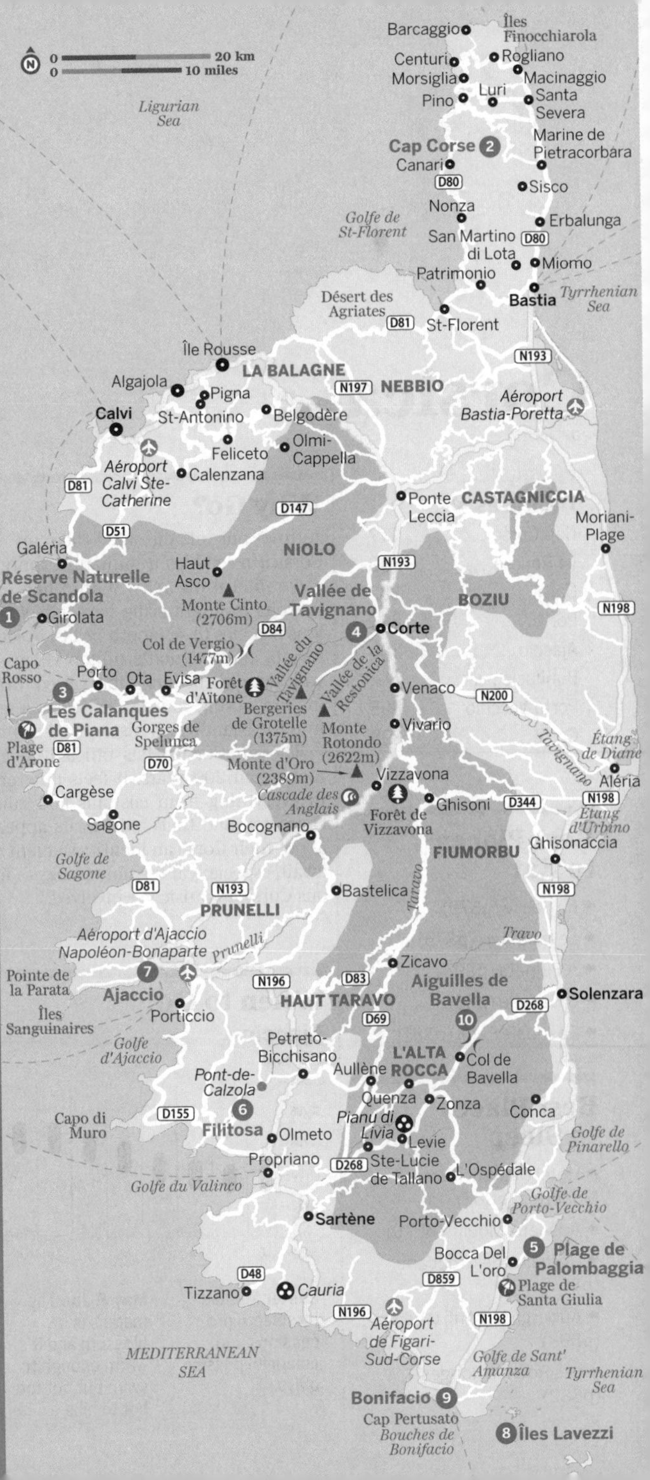

History

From the 11th to 13th centuries, Corsica was ruled by the city-state of Pisa, superseded in 1284 by its arch-rival, Genoa. To prevent seaborne raids, a massive system of coastal citadels and watchtowers was constructed, many of which still ring the coastline.

In 1755, after 25 years of sporadic warfare against the Genoese, Corsicans declared their independence, led by Pascal Paoli (1725–1807). Under Paoli's rule they established the National Assembly and founded the most democratic constitution in Europe.

Corsicans made the inland town of Corte their capital, but the island's independence was short-lived. In 1768, the Genoese ceded Corsica to Louis XV, whose troops crushed Paoli's army in 1769. The island has since been part of France, except for 1794–96, when it was briefly under English domination.

A movement for Corsican autonomy was formed in the 1960s to combat what some perceived as France's 'colonialist' policy towards the island. In 1976, the Front de Libération Nationale de la Corse (FLNC) was created, and talk of autonomy increasingly turned to claims for full independence.

By the 1990s, the FLNC had broken into multiple splinter groups, most armed and violent. Meanwhile, there remained many Corsicans who did not support the separatist movements. In 2003 a long-awaited referendum, which would have granted the island greater autonomy, was rejected despite a nail-biting electoral race.

Nevertheless, the nationalist issue remains a burning topic: in April 2014, the Corsican assembly adopted the *Statut de Résident,* a law requiring at least five years of residency on the island to be able to buy a property; and in December 2015, Corsican nationalists – led by Gilles Simeoni, mayor of Bastia – shocked the nation by winning 24 of 51 seats in departmental elections, establishing Simeoni as president of Corsica's executive council for the next two years.

Getting There & Away

AIR

Corsica has four airports: Ajaccio, Bastia, Calvi and Figari (north of Bonifacio), served by regular flights year-round from many French mainland airports. From May to September there are also frequent flights to Europe and elsewhere with low-cost airlines; you'll likely need to fly via mainland France if you're heading internationally at other times of the year.

> **SEASONAL WARNING**
>
> Corsica's tourism is heavily seasonal with most hotels, restaurants and sights opening only from Easter to October. Winter visitors will need patience, a good book and an enjoyment of walking...

BOAT

To/from Mainland France

Corsica's six ferry ports (Ajaccio, Bastia, Calvi, Île Rousse, Porto-Vecchio and Propriano) can be reached from Nice, Marseille and Toulon. Journeys last between 5½ and 13½ hours, depending on the route and the size of the vessel.

There are numerous crossings in summer, but far fewer in winter. Whatever the time of year, however, book ahead. The fare structure varies dramatically – anything from €30 to €100 for a foot passenger – depending on route, crossing time, class of comfort and size of vehicle (if any). In July and August expect to pay around €500 return for a car and two passengers from Nice to Ajaccio.

Ferry companies include **Corsica Ferries** (☎ 08 25 09 50 95; www.corsica-ferries.fr), **La Méridionale** (☎ 08 10 20 13 20, 04 91 99 45 09; www.lameridionale.fr) and **Corsica Linea** (☎ 08 25 88 80 88; www.corsicalinea.com).

To/from Italy

Ferries operated by **Corsica Ferries**, **La Méridionale** and **Moby** (☎ 04 95 34 84 94; www.mobycorse.com) link Corsica with the Italian ports of Genoa, Livorno and Savona on the mainland and Porto Torres in Sardinia year-round. Moby and **Blu Navy** (☎ 04 95 73 00 96; www.blunavy-traghetti.com) also run seasonal routes between Bonifacio and Santa Teresa di Gallura in Sardinia from April to October.

Getting Around

By far the best way to get around Corsica is by car, but car hire and fuel can quickly add up over a holiday. A detailed road map is an indispensable companion, such as Michelin's yellow-jacketed *Corse-du-Sud, Haute-Corse* (map 345), covering the entire island in a scale of 1:150,000.

Getting around by public transport (bus or train) is only possible between large towns and cities. Local exploration will then have to be done on foot or by bike or scooter (which are readily available for hire). The **train** (www.train-corse.com) is an attractive, if limited option, running through stunning countryside between Bastia and Ajaccio, with a branch route to Calvi and Île Rousse. The bus network is more comprehensive but there is often just one bus a day, and generally none on Sunday.

Corsica Bus & Train (www.corsicabus.org) is a tip-top one-stop website for viewing current bus and train timetables island-wide.

BASTIA & CAP CORSE

Seen on the map, Bastia and Cap Corse may look like an insignificant fraction of the island, yet Corsica's second city and the enchanting peninsula next door pack in an amazing variety of attractions. You could easily spend a week here, hiking Cap Corse's trails, gawking at the spectacular coastal scenery, exploring small towns such as Nonza, Centuri and Erbalunga, and rubbing elbows with locals in the markets and narrow lanes of Bastia's Terra Vecchia neigbourhood.

Bastia

POP 42,948

Filled with heart, soul and character, the bustling old port of Bastia is a good surprise. Sure, it might not measure up to the sexy style of Ajaccio or the architectural appeal of Bonifacio, but it has an irresistible magnetism. Bastia is an authentic snapshot of modern-day Corsica, a lived-in city that's resisted the urge to polish up its image just to please the tourists. The historical neighbourhoods of Terra Vecchia and Terra Nova are especially vibrant – allow yourself a day to take in the sights and mosey around atmospheric streets and boutiques.

Sights

★Terra Vecchia HISTORIC SITE

A spiderweb of narrow lanes, Terra Vecchia is Bastia's heart and soul. Shady **place de l'Hôtel de Ville** hosts a lively morning market on Saturday and Sunday. One block west, baroque **Chapelle de l'Immaculée Conception** (rue des Terrasses), with its elaborately painted barrel-vaulted ceiling, briefly served as the seat of the short-lived Anglo-Corsican parliament in 1795. Further north is **Chapelle St-Roch** (rue Napoléon), with an 18th-century organ and *trompe l'œil* roof.

★Vieux Port HARBOUR

Bastia's Vieux Port is ringed by pastel-coloured tenements and buzzy brasseries, as well as the twin-towered **Église St-Jean Baptiste** (4 rue du Cardinal Viale Préla). The best views of the harbour are from the Citadelle or from the hillside park of **Jardin Romieu**, reached via a gorgeous old stately staircase that twists uphill from the waterfront.

★Terra Nova HISTORIC SITE

Above Jardin Romieu looms Bastia's amber-hued citadel, built from the 15th to 17th centuries as a stronghold for the city's Genoese masters. Inside, the Palais des Gouverneurs houses the **Musée de Bastia** (☎04 95 31 09 12; www.musee-bastia.com; place du Donjon; adult/child €5/2.50, Oct-Apr free; ⊙10am-6.30pm Tue-Sun May-Sep, daily Jul & Aug, shorter hours rest of year), which retraces the city's history. A few streets south, don't miss the majestic **Cathédrale Ste-Marie** (rue de l'Évêché) and nearby **Église Ste-Croix** (rue de l'Évêché), featuring gilded ceilings and a mysterious black-oak crucifix found in the sea in 1428.

Place St-Nicolas SQUARE

Bastia's buzzing focal point is 19th-century place St-Nicolas, a gigantic asphalt-covered square that sprawls along the seafront between the ferry port and the harbour. Named after the patron saint of sailors – a nod to Corsica's seagoing heritage – the square is lined with plane trees and a string of attractive terrace cafes along its western edge, as well as a **statue of Napoléon Bonaparte**.

Sleeping

Staying near central place Nicolas puts you within walking distance of Bastia's restaurants, nightlife and other attractions. For rural souls who prefer 'in the sticks' to 'urban', several lovely addresses accessed via the coastal road that snakes north towards Cap Corse offer an agreeable alternative.

Hôtel Central HOTEL €€

(☎04 95 31 71 12; www.centralhotel.fr; 3 rue Miot; s €80-90, d €90-110, apt €130;) From the vintage, black-and-white tiled floor in the entrance to the sweeping staircase and eclectic jumble of plant pots in the minuscule interior courtyard, this family-run address oozes 1940s grace. The hotel's pedigree dates to 1941 and the vintage furnishings inside the 19th-century building don't disappoint. The three apartments, with fully equipped kitchen, are great for longer stays.

Hôtel Les Voyageurs HOTEL €€

(☎04 95 34 90 80; www.hotel-lesvoyageurs.com; 9 av Maréchal Sébastiani; s €65-134, d €75-134, ste €117-159; P@) This modern three-star hotel has been entirely refurbished with travel as the main theme. Each room represents a different destination and there is a very cosy lounge on the ground floor reminiscent of an explorer's library. The hotel has a private car park, unusual for city-centre hotels.

Hôtel L'Alivi HOTEL €€€

(☎04 95 55 00 00; www.hotel-alivi.com; rte du Cap; d €160-220, tr €190-250, ste €270-400;

mid-Mar–Oct;) The building does need to be dragged kicking and screaming into the 21st century but the location, right on the beach and off the northbound coastal road from Bastia to Cap Corse, is unrivalled, as is the sensational pool and terrace. All rooms have sea views and balconies.

Eating

★Raugi ICE CREAM €
(04 95 31 22 31; www.raugi.com; 2 rue du Chanoine Colombani; ice cream from €2; 9.30am-midnight Tue-Sat, 9.30am-noon Sun Oct-May, 9.30am-12.30pm & 4.30pm-1am Tue-Sun Jun-Sep) Going strong since 1937, Raugi is a Bastia institution. Flavours range from bog-standard raspberry, lemon and so on to Corsican chestnut, mandarin, fig, aromatic *senteur de maquis* (scent of Corsican herbal scrubland) and sweet *myrte* (myrtle). The *verrines glacées* (ice-cream desserts, €5) are fantastic.

Chez Vincent PIZZA, FRENCH €
(04 95 31 62 50; www.facebook.com/chez.vincent.1; 12 rue St-Michel; pizzas €10-12, mains €17-26; noon-2pm Mon-Fri, 6.30-11pm Mon-Sat;) Chez Vincent's unique selling point is its location: on the edge of the citadel with glorious views of the port. The wide-ranging menu includes a solid selection of well-executed French fare – mussels, steaks etc – and excellent pizzas.

Col Tempo SEAFOOD €€
(04 95 58 14 22; www.facebook.com/coltempobastia; 4 rue St-Jean, Vieux Port; mains €20-28; noon-2pm Tue-Sun, 7-10pm Tue-Sat) This relative newcomer overlooking Bastia's Vieux Port earns kudos from locals for its scrumptious market-fresh cuisine. Gaze at the boats bobbing in the harbour as you tuck into specialities such as *rillettes de crabe au citron vert* (lime-marinated crabmeat pâté), *risotto 'retour de la pêche'* (risotto studded with fresh-caught seafood) or codfish fillet with truffled polenta and asparagus-leek fondue.

Chez Huguette SEAFOOD €€
(04 95 31 37 60; www.chezhuguette.fr; rue de la Marine; mains €20-37; noon-2.30pm & 7.30-10.30pm Mon-Sat, 7.30-10pm Sun) If fresh seafood is your muse, bag a table by the water at Chez Huguette. It's set a little apart from the line-up of restaurants at the Vieux Port and rightly so: posher than the rest, this is white-tablecloth dining enjoyed by Bastians since 1969. For a real treat, go for the locally caught *langouste* (spiny lobster; €20 per 100g).

DON'T MISS

PLAGE DE L'ARINELLA

If there is one crescent of sand in Corsica you must not miss, it's Plage de l'Arinella, a serene, rock-clad cove with dramatic views of the citadel of Calvi and one of the finest beach-dining experiences on Corsica.

Wooden tables, strung along the sand and topped with straw parasols, immediately evoke a tropical paradise at **Le Matahari** (04 95 60 78 47; www.lematahari.com; Plage de l'Arinella; mains €25-35; noon-3pm mid-Apr–Sep, 7-10.30pm Tue-Sun late May–mid-Sep). From the stylish, shabby-chic interior to the waiters dressed in white and boaters, this is one special hideaway. Cuisine is Mediterranean fusion: *penne à la langouste*, tuna steak in sesame coating, fish teriyaki. Opening hours are weather-dependent and reservations are essential.

A Scudella CORSICAN
(04 95 46 25 31, 09 51 70 79 46; 10 rue Pino; menu €25; 7pm-2am Tue-Sat) Tucked down a back alley between place de l'Hôtel de Ville and the Vieux Port, this is a superb spot to sample traditional mountain fare, from appetisers of fine Corsican charcuterie and *beignets de brocciu* (fritters filled with *fromage frais*) to *veau aux olives* (stewed veal with olives) to *flan à la châtaigne* (chestnut flan).

Shopping

★LN Mattei FOOD & DRINKS
(15 bd Général de Gaulle; 9.30am-12.30pm & 2-7pm Mon-Sat) This iconic boutique for visiting gourmets has the look and feel of a 1900 grocer. Choose from locally milled chestnut flour, *sel à la figue* (fig-scented salt), Corsican *marrons* (chestnuts) preserved in *eau-de-vie* (brandy) or a bottle of Mattei's signature aperitif, Cap Corse.

Santa Catalina FOOD
(04 95 32 30 69; 8 rue des Terrasses; 9am-12.45pm & 3-7.45pm Mon-Sat) In season, fresh Brocciu cheese is among the many delicious local delicacies stocked at this packed, pocket-size culinary boutique.

Information

Tourist Office (04 95 54 20 40; www.bastia-tourisme.com; place St-Nicolas; 8am-

Bastia

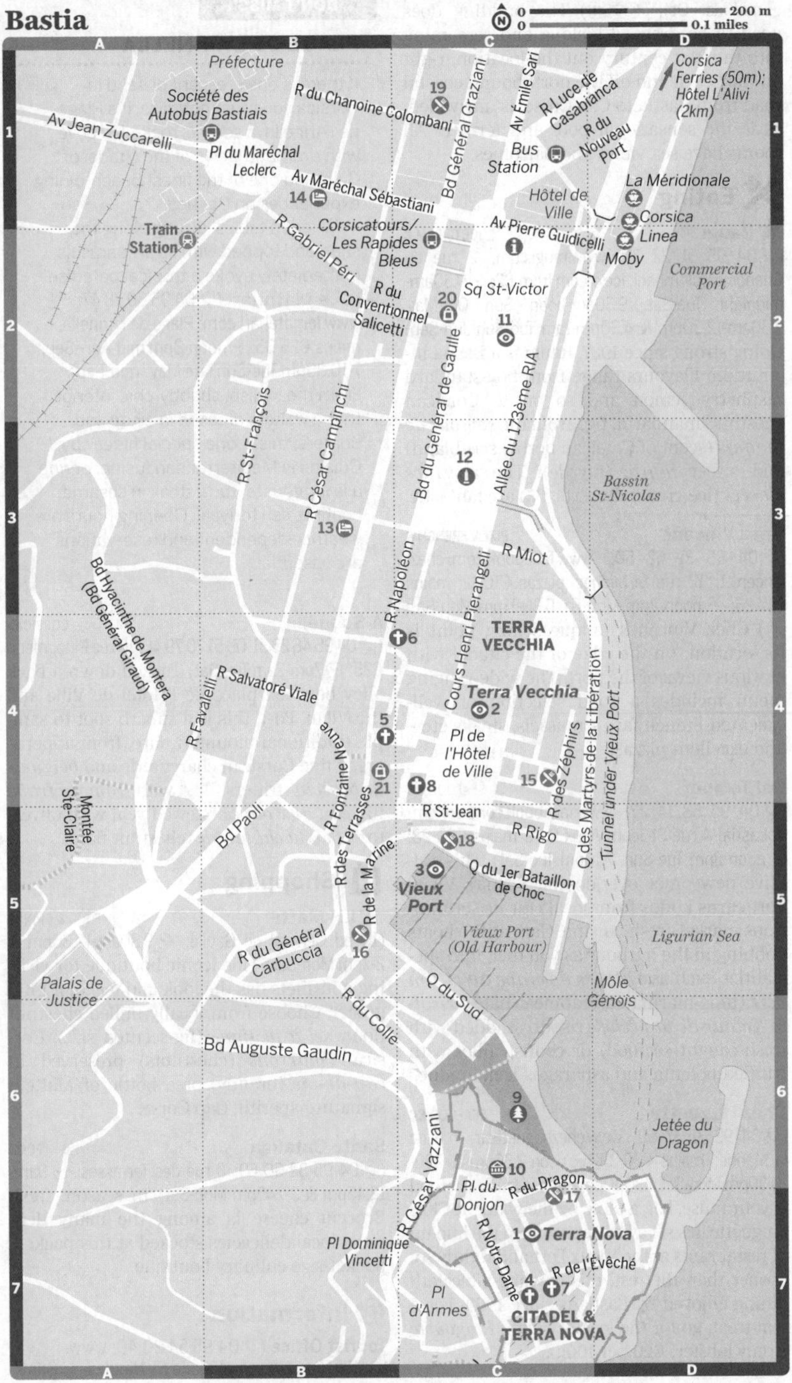
0 200 m
0 0.1 miles
A
B
C
D
1
2
3
4
5
6
7
Préfecture
Société des Autobus Bastiais
Av Jean Zuccarelli
Pl du Maréchal Leclerc
R du Chanoine Colombani
19
Bd Général Graziani
Av Émile Sari
R Luce de Casabianca
R du Nouveau Port
Corsica Ferries (50m); Hôtel L'Alivi (2km)
Bus Station
Av Maréchal Sébastiani
14
Hôtel de Ville
La Méridionale
Corsica
Linea
Moby
Train Station
R Gabriel Péri
Corsicatours/ Les Rapides Bleus
Av Pierre Guidicelli
Commercial Port
R du Conventionnel Salicetti
20
Sq St-Victor
11
R St-François
R César Campinchi
Bd du Général de Gaulle
Allée du 173ème RIA
12
Bassin St-Nicolas
13
R Miot
R Napoléon
Cours Henri Pierangeli
Bd Hyacinthe de Montera (Bd Général Giraud)
6
TERRA VECCHIA
R Salvatoré Viale
Terra Vecchia
2
R Favalelli
Q des Martyrs de la Libération
Tunnel under Vieux Port
R Fontaine Neuve
5
Pl de l'Hôtel de Ville
21
8
15
R des Zéphirs
Montée Ste-Claire
Bd Paoli
R des Terrasses
R St-Jean
R Rigo
18
R de la Marine
3
Vieux Port
Q du 1er Bataillon de Choc
Vieux Port (Old Harbour)
Ligurian Sea
16
R du Général Carbuccia
Palais de Justice
R du Collé
Q du Sud
Môle Génois
Bd Auguste Gaudin
9
Jetée du Dragon
R César Vazzani
10
Pl du Donjon
R du Dragon
17
R Notre Dame
1
Terra Nova
Pl Dominique Vincetti
R de l'Évêché
4
7
Pl d'Armes
CITADEL & TERRA NOVA

Bastia

Top Sights
1 Terra Nova C7
2 Terra Vecchia C4
3 Vieux Port C5

Sights
4 Cathédrale Ste-Marie C7
5 Chapelle de l'Immaculée Conception B4
6 Chapelle St-Roch C4
7 Église Ste-Croix C7
8 Église St-Jean Baptiste C4
9 Jardin Romieu C6
10 Musée de Bastia C6
11 Place St-Nicolas C2
12 Statue of Napoléon Bonaparte C3

Sleeping
13 Hôtel Central B3
14 Hôtel Les Voyageurs B1

Eating
15 A Scudella C4
16 Chez Huguette B5
17 Chez Vincent C7
18 Col Tempo C5
19 Raugi C1

Shopping
20 LN Mattei C2
21 Santa Catalina B4

6pm Mon-Sat, to noon Sun;) Organises guided tours of the city and has plenty of information about Cap Corse.

Getting There & Around

GETTING TO/FROM THE AIRPORT

Aéroport Bastia-Poretta (www.bastia.aeroport.fr) is 24km south of the city. **Société des Autobus Bastiais** (04 95 31 06 65; bastiabus.com) operates shuttles (€9, 35 minutes) every hour or two between the airport and Bastia's downtown Préfecture building. **Taxi Aéroport Poretta** (04 95 36 04 65; www.corsica-taxis.com) charges €48/66 by day/night.

BOAT

Ferry companies including **Corsica Ferries** (p873), **Corsica Linea** (08 25 88 80 88; www.corsicalinea.com), **La Méridionale** (08 10 20 13 20, 04 91 99 45 09; www.lameridionale.fr) and **Moby** (p873) have information offices at **Bastia Port** (www.bastia.port.fr); they are usually open for same-day ticket sales a couple of hours before sailings. Ferries sail to/from Marseille, Toulon and Nice (mainland France), and Livorno, Savona and Genoa (Italy).

TRAIN

From the **train station** (av Maréchal Sébastiani), there are daily services to Ajaccio (€21.60, 3¾ hours, four daily) via Corte (€10.10, 1¾ hours), and Calvi (€16.40, 3¼ hours, two daily) via Île Rousse (€13.50, 2¾ hours).

BUS

The **bus station** (1 rue du Nouveau Port) is north of place St-Nicolas, behind the Hôtel de Ville (town hall). Additional bus stops are scattered around town. There are buses to the airport, and to **Calvi** (€16, 2¼ hours, one to two daily Monday to Friday from the train station), **Macinaggio – Cap Corse** (€7, one hour, one daily Monday to Friday from the bus station), **Porto-Vecchio** (€25, three hours, two daily Monday to Saturday from place St-Nicolas) and **Île Rousse** (€14, 1¾ hours, one to two daily Monday to Friday from the train station), among other destinations.

Buses to Porto-Vecchio are run by **Corsicatours/Les Rapides Bleus** (04 95 31 03 79; www.rapides-bleus.com). Note that there are no intercity buses on Sunday.

Cap Corse

This spiny northeastern peninsula stands out from the rest of Corsica. About 40km long and 10km wide, Cap Corse resembles a giant geographical finger poked towards Italy. The west coast is famed for its dramatic, rugged beauty with rocky cliffs, perched villages and strong winds, whereas the east coast has a more languorous feel with rolling green hills, beautiful beaches and pretty seaside villages.

Be prepared for some adventurous driving: although the peninsula is only 40km long, the narrow road that rounds its coast (the D80) crams in 120km of switchback curves and breathtaking drops into the sea.

Erbalunga

From Bastia, the coast unfurls through seaside resorts and tiny beaches towards this quaint harbour village, 9km to the north. Wander down to Erbalunga's cute village square and quayside, casually strewn with well-used fishing boats and tempting restaurant terraces. Narrow alleys lead through shady courtyards to a romantic, 16th-century **Genoese tower** by the water.

WORTH A TRIP

AROUND BASTIA: SAN MARTINO DI LOTA

Perched high in the hilltop village of San Martino di Lota, **Hôtel-Restaurant La Corniche** (☎04 95 31 40 98; www.hotel-lacorniche.com; San Martino di Lota; d €78-106; ⊙mid-Feb–Dec; ❄📶🏊) is a brilliant halfway house between city convenience (it's 8km from Bastia) and Cap Corse wilderness: the sea views will leave you smitten. A family-run hotel since 1934, it woos travellers with its fabulous location and gourmet food.

Summertime ushers in dreamy lounging in the back garden, by the pool or on the front porch terrace that stares out to sea. Perfect the experience with dinner in the much-lauded restaurant (mains €18 to €29, *menus* €24.50 to €31.50), where produce is locally sourced. Advance reservations recommended.

Sleeping & Eating

★Hôtel Demeure Castel Brando BOUTIQUE HOTEL €€
(☎04 95 30 10 30; www.en.castelbrando.com; rte Principale, Erbalunga; d €160-220; ⊙late Mar-Oct; ❄📶🏊) Overlooking the main road through the village, the Castel Brando is a dreamy, creamy, mid-19th-century mansion, with sage-green shutters and lush palm-shaded gardens wrapped around a heated pool and Jacuzzi. The atmosphere is rustic chic meets cool and fashionable.

A Piazzetta BISTRO €€
(☎04 95 33 28 69; place d'Erbalunga; mains €13-23; ⊙noon-2pm & 7-10pm daily Jul & Aug, Wed-Mon Mar-Jun, Sep & Oct, Thu-Sun Nov & Dec, closed Jan & Feb) With its cosy stone-walled interior and a summertime terrace beneath an ancient plane tree on the plaza, A Piazzetta is a good-value choice with a quintessential, traditional village-square vibe. It serves Corsican bistro fare: stuffed mussels, steaks, pizzas, pasta and salads.

Le Pirate MODERN CORSICAN €€€
(☎04 95 33 24 20; www.restaurantlepirate.com; Erbalunga; lunch menu €42, dinner menus €75-90; ⊙noon-2pm & 7.30-10pm Jun-Sep, closed Mon & Tue Apr, May & Oct) For a meal to remember, dine at this award-winning, Michelin-starred restaurant, with a terrace overlooking the harbour – magic on starry summer evenings.

Centuri

Lobster, anyone? The tiny, boat-crammed harbour of Centuri is home to one of Europe's most important *langouste* (European spiny lobster or rock lobster) fleets: eight boats worked by three rival lobster-fishing families. Among the cluster of seafood eateries on the waterfront, you'll find a couple of addresses stand out for their legendary *pâtes à la langouste* (pasta with lobster), a local dish in season early April to early October.

Sleeping & Eating

Hôtel du Pêcheur HOTEL €
(☎04 95 35 60 14; Port de Centuri; d €65-85; ⊙May-Oct) Right by the water at the Vieux Port, Hôtel du Pêcheur sits snug in an old building with Bordeaux shutters, vintage in age and oozing retro charm. Rooms are without pretension (no TV, air-con or wi-fi, and old-fashioned bathrooms) but they are cheap as chips for this pricey neck of the woods.

Au Vieux Moulin HOTEL €€
(☎04 95 35 60 15; www.le-vieux-moulin.net; Port de Centuri; d €130-225) Hobnob with a chichi set at this upmarket hotel-restaurant just above the harbour. The two lovely rooms upstairs in the old mansion are especially classy; those in the annexe are less original but sport fabulous balconies with views of the water.

The hotel's **terrace restaurant** (mains €28-42; ⊙noon-2.30pm & 7.30-10pm Apr-Oct; ❄📶) also overlooks the port, making it a delightful dining spot in warm weather. The signature *pâtes à la langouste* follows the owner's grandmother's recipe, which has remained unchanged for more than 50 years.

La Bella Vista SEAFOOD €€
(☎04 95 35 62 60; Port de Centuri; menus €21-40; ⊙noon-2pm & 7-10pm Apr–mid-Nov) Run by one of Centuri's fishing families and sporting a sweet sunny terrace directly above the boats in the harbour, this is a great spot for fresh seafood. Specialities include bouillabaisse and the Misto Bella Vista, a smorgasbord of squid, scallops, shrimp, grilled fish and – of course – locally caught lobster.

Nonza

Clinging to the flanks of a rocky pinnacle crowned with a Genoese watchtower, Nonza is easily the most attractive village on the cape's western coast. With its jumble of schist-roofed stone houses looking ready

to tumble down the steep hillside onto the black-pebble beach far below, it fits the picture-postcard ideal. Scramble down the rocky path, past walled lemon groves, to the black beach, a legacy of the asbestos mine that operated on the coast here between 1941 and 1965. The beach's polluted past does little to inspire confidence, but locals certainly do not seem worried about it given the summertime crowds that pack out its pebbly shoreline.

Nonza's picture-postcard church, **Église Ste-Julie**, is impossible to miss on the tiny village square. It's well worth a peek for its polychrome marble altar created in Florence in 1693. From here, weave your way up between rocks and sun-warmed cacti to the **Tour de Nonza**. The old Genoese watchtower, one of Corsica's best-kept, boasts staggering coastal views (and a ticky-tacky souvenir shop inside its thick stone walls).

Sleeping & Eating

Casa Lisa B&B €
(06 11 70 45 73, 04 95 37 83 52; www.casalisa.fr; Nonza; r €55-75;) Park in Nonza's town square and walk three minutes downhill via a series of signposted staircases to this simple, immaculate B&B. Delightful views down to the shoreline unfold from the garden patio and several of the five rooms. Breakfast costs €7 extra.

Le Relais du Cap B&B €
(04 95 37 86 52; www.relaisducap.com; Marine de Negru; s €55-70, d €60-75, all with shared bathroom; Apr-Oct;) For the ultimate rustic seaside escape, this is hard to beat. Tucked improbably between a towering cliff and a pocket-size pebble beach, this pert little B&B features four unpretentious yet neat doubles (with shared bathroom), all with staggering sunset-facing sea views. No air-con here, but who needs it with the sea breezes puffing in? It's 4km south of Nonza.

Casa Maria B&B €€
(04 95 37 80 95; www.casamaria-corse.com; chemin de la Tour; d/q €95/165; Apr-Oct;) A bewitching little hideaway in the heart of the village, this five-room *chambre d'hôte* sits snug in a coolly refurbished 18th-century mansion. Four of its five rooms revel in sea views, and three – including a great one for families – sit harmoniously beneath the sloping roof. In summer, enjoy breakfast beneath a vine-wrapped pergola in the bijou back garden.

★ **La Sassa** GRILL €€
(04 95 38 55 26; www.lasassa.com; Tour de Nonza; mains €17-30; noon-3pm & 7.30-midnight Apr-Sep) Few addresses are as inspirational. Built atop cliffs in the shade of Nonza's Genoese watchtower, this strictly alfresco diner – it has no interior – cooks up succulent meat on an open Argentinian-style grill. The site is beautifully illuminated at night with coloured spotlights, and there's frequent live music, with an emphasis on jazz. The sea views and sunsets are unforgettable.

Boccafine FUSION €€
(06 80 95 85 07; www.boccafine.fr; mains €28-32; noon-2pm & 7.30-9.30pm Wed-Sun Apr-Oct) For a fine-dining experience in Nonza, make a beeline for the vine-shaded terrace at Boccafine, where up-and-coming, internationally trained chef Clement Collet creates a monthly changing menu of three starters, three mains and three desserts, all built around locally sourced seasonal produce. Asian and Mediterranean influences intermingle with classic Corsican ingredients to sublime effect.

L'Auberge du Chat Qui Pêche CORSICAN €€
(04 95 37 81 52; www.aubergeduchatquipeche.com; Abro, Canari; mains €17-25) Local seafood and Corsican charcuterie take centre stage at this roadside eatery perched on steep

DON'T MISS

VILLAGE LIFE

For dreamy views and an authentic taste of rural life, check out the two *chambres d'hôte* (B&B rooms) hidden inside this beautiful old, golden-stone **Maison Battisti** (04 95 35 10 40; www.maisonbattisti.com; Conchiglio, Barrettali; r incl breakfast €85) in the hamlet of Conchiglio. Furnishings in the house, and an old *miellerie* (honey-maker's workshop), win vintage lovers over with historical romance. The two adjacent *gîtes* (self-catering cottages), available by the week, are equally enchanting.

A 1.5km trail leads directly from the B&B down to the beach below. The Battisti family also runs the gorgeous adjacent shop that sells local products and photo books about Corsica. Conchiglio is located on the wiggly and alarmingly narrow D133, signposted off the coastal D80 between Nonza and Centuri.

slopes 8km north of Nonza. The stone-and-brick interior dining room makes a pleasant place to indulge in *gambas à la paysanne* (prawns sautéed with parsley, garlic, olive oil and pancetta), but the real show-stopper here is the outdoor terrace, with jaw-dropping sea and mountain views.

LA BALAGNE

This striking region blends history, culture and beach, with a dash of Mediterranean glam sealing the deal. Refine your art of sampling *la dolce vita* in Calvi and Île Rousse before venturing inland in search of that picture-postcard-perfect village.

Île Rousse

POP 3609

Sun-worshippers, celebrities and holidaying yachties create a buzz in the busy beach town of Île Rousse, straddling a long, sandy curve of land backed by maquis-cloaked mountains. Founded by Pascal Paoli in 1758 as a rival port to pro-Genoese Calvi, the town was later renamed after the offshore russet-coloured rock of Île de la Pietra (now home to the town's ferry port and lighthouse).

Sights & Activities

Old Town HISTORIC SITE

Île Rousse's old town is a delight. The covered food market abuts **place Paoli**, Île Rousse's central tree-shaded square.

DON'T MISS

THE TREMBLER

You may well tremble as the *trinighellu* (trembler) – as the train service between Île Rousse and Calvi is affectionately called – trundles close to the shore along sand-covered tracks. The dinky little **train** (☎04 95 32 80 57; www.cf-corse.fr; one way €6) is the easiest way to access the numerous hidden coves and beaches sprinkled along the coast: no traffic jams and a low-key, scenic journey. The train runs six to seven times daily, calling at 15 stations en route, all by request only. Hop off at an intermediate rocky cove or, for fine golden sand, leave the train at Algajola or Plage de Bodri, the last stop before Île Rousse.

Promenade a Marinella BEACH

Starting in the heart of town, this coastal promenade follows Île Rousse's sandy beaches east along the seafront. Less-crowded beaches around Île Rousse include **Plage de Bodri**, immediately southwest of town; **Algajola**, 7km southwest; or the magnificent **Plage de Lozari**, 6km east.

Île de la Pietra ISLAND

For an easy stroll, head over the short umbilical causeway that links rocky Île de la Pietra to the mainland, past a **Genoese watchtower** and up to the **lighthouse**.

Parc de Saleccia GARDENS

(☎04 95 36 88 83; www.parc-saleccia.fr; rte de Bastia, N197; adult/child €9/7; ⏲9.30am-7pm Jul & Aug, 10am-7pm Tue-Sun, 2-7pm Mon Apr-Jun & Sep, closed Mon & Sat Oct) Wander the 7 hectares of these landscaped gardens to explore the flora of Corsica – the tough plants of the maquis, pines, myrtles, fig trees and more than 100 varieties of olive trees. The gardens are 4.5km from town on the road to Bastia.

Club Nautique d'Île Rousse WATER SPORTS

(☎04 95 60 22 55; www.cnir.org; rte du Port; ⏲9am-6pm Jul & Aug, by arrangement Sep-Jun) Club Nautique d'Île Rousse rents out water-sports equipment (kayaks, sailboards, stand-up paddleboards, catamarans) and organises two-hour sea-kayak trips (€35) around the promontory and its islets.

Sleeping

Hôtel Le Splendid HOTEL €

(☎04 95 60 00 24; www.le-splendid-hotel.com; av Comte Valéry; s/d €73/89; ⏲Apr–mid-Nov; ❄@🛜🏊) You'll be hard-pushed in Corsica to find better value: Le Splendid is splendid in value, in attitude (all smiles and helpfulness) and in proximity to the beach (footsteps away). Rooms are clean, and vary in size and outlook, and those that sleep four – perfect for families – are unusually spacious. The generous breakfast buffet is the icing on the cake.

L'Escale Côté Sud HOTEL €€

(☎04 95 63 01 70; www.hotel-ilerousse.com/escale-cote-sud; 22 rue Notre-Dame; r €95-195) Open year-round, this centrally located, recently remodelled three-star with attached restaurant is an excellent midrange option, especially if you can snag one of the four sea-facing rooms with dreamy views of limpid turquoise waters lapping the beach across the street.

WORTH A TRIP

LA BALAGNE INTERIOR

Hidden among the countless valleys and spurs of La Balagne's spectacular interior you'll find cute-as-can-be hilltop villages, Romanesque chapels, olive groves and lush vineyards. The Balagne hinterland is also a source of inspiration for many artisans. A signposted route, the **Strada di l'Artigiani** (www.routedesartisans.fr), links the region's most attractive villages and details local workshops; pick up a route map from the Calvi or Île Rousse tourist offices.

Particularly charming is **Pigna**, a mirage of burnt-orange rooftops and blue-shuttered houses 8km south of Île Rousse via the D151. The village has become something of a music destination for Corsican music thanks to its high-profile auditorium, **Centre Culturel Voce** (☎04 95 61 73 13; www.ccvoce.org; Pigna; tickets €10-15). Artisan workshops are scattered among the sweet cobbled streets both here and in the cute hamlet of **Sant'-Antonino**, precariously perched on a rocky outcrop that commands incredible views.

Hôtel Perla Rossa BOUTIQUE HOTEL €€€
(☎04 95 48 45 30; www.hotelperlarossa.com; 30 rue Notre-Dame; d €190-350, ste €370-490; ⏲late Apr-Oct; ❄📶) With its enchanting soft-apricot façade and oyster-grey shutters, this cocoon adds a real touch of glam to the hotel scene. Its refined interior would be right at home in the latest edition of *Elle,* and its 10 rooms – all suites – completely spoil guests. The best have balconies with swoon-inducing sea views.

Eating

★**A Casa Corsa** CORSICAN €
(☎04 95 60 23 63; 6 place Paoli; sandwiches & salads €5-10; ⏲8am-11pm Tue-Sun mid-Mar–Oct; 🍷) With a prime location on the gorgeous place Paoli, this wine bar makes a brisk trade in salads, cheese and charcuterie platters and other stalwart Corsican fare. As expected, the wine selection, including by the glass, and advice are excellent and all Corsican.

Food Market MARKET €
(place Paoli; ⏲8am-1pm mid-Apr–Sep, shorter hours rest of year) With its 21 classical columns, Île Rousse's covered food market resembles a Greek temple. Outside the summer months, it's busiest on Fridays.

★**Pasquale Paoli** GASTRONOMIC €€
(☎04 95 47 67 70; www.pasquale-paoli.fr; 2 place Paoli; 3-course lunch/dinner menu €26/55; ⏲noon-2pm & 8-10pm daily Jun-Sep, Tue-Sat Apr, May & Oct-Dec) The town's most gastronomic restaurant, Michelin star and all, cooks up a sophisticated dining experience inside a whitewashed, vaulted dining room. Or dine alfresco on the wood-decked terrace on place Paoli. Each main is expertly introduced by the maître d' (including the origin of the main ingredients). Considering the quality, prices are extremely reasonable.

L'Osteria MODERN CORSICAN €€
(☎04 95 31 90 90; place Santelli; mains €17-32, menus from €22; ⏲noon-2pm & 7-10pm daily Jun-Sep, closed Wed & lunch Thu Oct-May) With its young and funky vibe, and excellent €22 three-course *menu,* L'Osteria has become popular among locals. Visitors should follow suit. The cuisine features local products (seafood, veal etc) in modern renditions of Corsican classics, along with dishes inspired by the wider Mediterranean culinary repertoire.

Drinking & Nightlife

Café des Platanes CAFE
(place Paoli; ⏲6am-2am Jun-Sep, 7am-8.30pm Oct-May) Watch nightly boules contests courtesy of the local gents while you sip an aperitif on the terrace of venerable Café des Platanes – it can't get more Île Rousse than that.

Information

Tourist Office (☎04 95 60 04 35; www.ilerousse-tourisme.com; av Calizi; ⏲9am-7pm Mon-Sat, 10am-1pm & 3-6pm Sun mid-Jun–mid-Sep, 9am-noon & 2-6pm Mon-Fri rest of year) Has information on the wider Balagne area.

Getting There & Away

BOAT

Corsica Linea (☎08 25 88 80 88; www.corsicalinea.com) and **Corsica Ferries** (☎04 95 60 44 11; www.corsica-ferries.fr) offer ferry service from Île Rousse to the mainland French ports of Marseille, Nice and Toulon.

BUS

There are one or two buses a day to Calvi (€4, 30 minutes) and Bastia (€14, 1¾ hours).

TRAIN

Twice-daily trains to Bastia (€13.50, 3½ hours) and Ajaccio (€22.20, 4½ hours) require a change of train in Ponte Leccia. There are four or five services a day to Calvi (€6, 40 minutes).

Algajola

POP 308

Just 7km from Île Rousse and 16km from Calvi, Algajola is a lovely alternative to its larger neighbours with its 16th-century historic centre and long, golden sandy beach.

Sleeping & Eating

L'Escale BUNGALOW €

(04 95 60 60 80; www.hotel-corse-lescale.com; Plage d'Aregno; d €59-89, 4-person bungalow per week €490-791; late Apr-Oct) Beach bums, rejoice! This cluster of 20 self-catering apartments and 50 spick-and-span rooms – with bathroom, comfy bed, terrace and five-star sea views – sits inside low-lying beige bungalows plump on the sand, at the northern end of Algajola on Alegno Beach.

★U Castellu B&B €€

(04 95 36 26 13; www.ucastelluchambresdhotes.com; 8 place du Château; d €90-166; Apr-Oct;) U Castellu will win you over with its location on the village's square in the shade of the ancient castle. Set in an old village home, the five rooms are a wonderful blend of old and new. Maud's welcome is another drawcard, as is the panoramic rooftop terrace where the copious buffet breakfast is served.

The adjoining **restaurant** (04 95 60 78 75; mains €12-20, menus €20-25; noon-2.30pm & 7-10.30pm Apr-Sep) comes equally recommended for its sunny, reliable Mediterranean cuisine.

Le Padula SEAFOOD, PIZZA €€

(04 95 60 75 22; Plage d'Aregno; pizza from €10, mains €15-24; 8am-11pm Easter-Oct) Spectacular views and tasty, unpretentious food are the twin drawcards at this informal beach terrace restaurant on Plage d'Aregno, just east of Algajola. The menu ranges from pizza (served day and night) to the daily *plat du jour* (€14.90) to classic seafood snacks such as *moules marinière* (mussels cooked with garlic, shallots and white wine) and *friture de calamars* (fried squid).

Calvi

POP 5503

Basking between the fiery orange bastions of its 15th-century citadel and the glittering waters of a moon-shaped bay, Calvi feels clos-

DON'T MISS

LES CALANQUES DE PIANA

No amount of hyperbole can capture the astonishing beauty of Les Calanques de Piana (E Calanche in Corsican), sculpted cliffs above the Golfe de Porto that rear up from the sea in staggering scarlet pillars, teetering columns, towers and irregularly shaped boulders of pink, ochre and ginger. Flaming red in the sunlight, this natural ensemble is one of Corsica's most awe-inspiring sights. And as you sway around switchback after switchback along the rock-riddled 10km stretch of the D81 between Porto and the village of Piana, one mesmerising vista piggybacks on another.

There are two ways to discover the Calanques: by boat or on foot. Numerous companies offer boat trips from Porto; allow €25 for the 1½-hour excursion. For a different perspective, don your walking boots. Several trails wind their way around these dramatic rock formations. Many start near Stade Municipal (stadium) about 3km north of Piana on the D81 (signposted). The **tourist office** (09 66 92 84 42; www.otpiana.com; place de la Mairie; 9am-5pm Mon-Fri, 9am-1pm Sat & Sun Jul & Aug, shorter hours rest of year;) in Piana stocks the leaflet *Piana: Sentiers de Randonnée* (€1), detailing six walks.

Afterwards, flop on the sand on the idyllic beaches of **Ficajola** or **Arone**, 5km and 11km southwest respectively. The **Camping de la Plage d'Arone** (04 95 20 64 54; Plage d'Arone, Piana; 2 people with tent & car €26-29; mid-May–Sep) is one of the most tranquil campgrounds you'll find in Corsica. Or splurge on lunch (mains €35, lunch *menu* €25) or sundowners with epic views at Corsica's original luxury hotel, **Les Roches Rouges** (04 95 27 81 81; www.lesrochesrouges.com; D81; s €130, d €125-145; Apr-Oct;). Built in 1912, it remains one of the island's quirkiest vintage addresses.

A couple of daily buses link Piana with Ajaccio and Porto.

er to the chichi sophistication of a French Riviera resort than a historic Corsican port. Palatial yachts and private cruisers jostle for space along its harbourside, lined with upmarket brasseries and cafes, while high above the quay the watchtowers and battlements of the town's Genoese stronghold stand guard, proffering sweeping views inland to Monte Cinto (2706m). Unsurprisingly, Calvi is one of Corsica's most popular tourist spots and in summer it's crammed to bursting.

Sights & Activities

★Citadel HISTORIC SITE

Crowning a lofty promontory, Calvi's massive fortified citadel offers superb wraparound views from its five bastions. Built by the town's Genoese governors, it has fended off everyone from Franco-Turkish raiders to Anglo-Corsican armies. Inside the battlements, don't miss the well-proportioned **Caserne Sampiero**, a military barracks that once served as the Genoese administration's seat of power, and the 13th-century **Cathédrale St-Jean Baptiste**, whose most celebrated relic is the ebony *Christ des Miracles,* credited with saving Calvi from Saracen invasion in 1553.

Plage de Calvi BEACH

Calvi's stellar 4km-long sandy beach has some of the best views of Calvi's citadel. It begins at the marina and runs east around the Golfe de Calvi. Rent kayaks and windsurfing sailboards on the sand, and hook up with local diving schools by the tourist office at the marina.

Colombo Line BOATING

(04 95 65 32 10; www.colombo-line.com; quai Landry, Port de Plaisance; Apr-Sep) At the marina, Colombo Line runs a bevy of seasonal boat trips along the coast – a fine way to beat the summer traffic. Highlights include day trips to the Réserve Naturelle de Scandola with a beach stopover at Girolata (adult/child €64/32) or Ajaccio (€90/45).

Festivals & Events

Rencontres Polyphoniques MUSIC

(www.facebook.com/rencontrespolyphoniquescalvi) Catch traditional Corsican chants at this five-day music festival in September.

Sleeping

Camping La Pinède CAMPGROUND €

(04 95 65 17 80; www.camping-calvi.com; rte de la Pinède; tent, car & 2 adults €29.50-44; Apr-Oct;) Handy for town and beach, with good facilities including a shop, a laundry, a pool and play areas; mobile homes and chalets too.

Hôtel Le Magnolia HOTEL €€

(04 95 65 19 16; www.hotel-le-magnolia.com; rue Alsace Lorraine; d €110-155; Apr-Oct;) An oasis from the harbourside fizz, this attractive mansion sits behind a beautiful high-walled courtyard garden pierced by a handsome magnolia tree. Pretty much every room has a lovely outlook – Calvi rooftops, garden or sea – and connecting doubles make it an instant hit with families.

Hôtel La Villa LUXURY HOTEL €€€

(04 95 65 10 10; www.hotel-lavilla.com; chemin Notre-Dame de la Serra; d from €360, ste from €760; late Apr-early Oct; @) If you want to do Calvi in style, head straight for this lavish hilltop hideaway, brimming with boutique trappings. Clean lines, cappuccino-and-chocolate colour schemes, designer fabrics and minimalist motifs distinguish the rooms, while the exterior facilities include a pool, a spa, tennis courts and a Michelin-starred restaurant with the most fabulous views of Calvi.

Eating

Mar A Beach MEDITERRANEAN €

(06 33 62 17 64; Plage de l'Alga; mains €12-25; restaurant noon-4pm May-Oct, bar noon-7pm May-Oct) Tucked into a pretty cove 3km west of Calvi, this Robinson Crusoe–style beach hut in a turquoise-water creek makes a dreamy spot for lunch. It's a 20-minute walk downhill from the turn-off for Pointe de la Ravelleta. Book ahead.

Annie Traiteur DELI €

(04 95 65 49 67; www.annietraiteur.com; 5 rue Clémenceau; snacks from €3; 8.30am-7pm Sep-Jun, 6am-midnight Jul & Aug) This beautifully stocked deli is the perfect place to get provisioned for a picnic lunch by the pier. The dazzling range of Corsican charcuterie, cheeses, prepared deli foods, jams, wines, liqueurs, olive oils and chestnut flour cakes will keep even the most die-hard foodie happy.

★U Casanu CORSICAN €€

(04 95 65 00 10; 18 bd Wilson; mains €15-22; noon-1.30pm & 8-10pm Mon-Sat Jan-Oct) For an unforgettable lunch, grab a booth at this cosy hole-in-the-wall, decorated in cheery yellow and green, and hung with watercol-

ours painted by septuagenarian artist-owner Monique Luciani. Tuck into home-cooked fish couscous, roast lamb, codfish aioli or octopus salad, and don't miss the exquisite *fiadone*, a classic Corsican cheesecake made with lemon-scented *brocciu* cheese soaked in *eau de vie* (brandy).

A Candella CORSICAN €€

(☎04 95 65 42 13; 9 rue St-Antoine; mains €16-25; ⌚noon-2pm & 7-10pm mid-May–Sep) One of a handful of addresses at which to eat within the citadel, A Candella stands out for its romantic, golden-hued terrace of stone strung with pretty flowers in pots and olive trees. The food is Corsican hearty, and the sea view is the most marvellous you could hope for.

Drinking & Nightlife

There are plenty of places around town at which to wet your whistle. The best after-dark buzz is quayside.

★Chez Tao BAR

(www.cheztao.com; rue St-Antoine; ⌚6pm-5am Jun-Sep) You won't find cooler than this (or more amazing sea views with cocktail in hand). Up high within the citadel, this super-smooth piano bar is an institution. Find it in a lavishly decorated vaulted room, founded in 1935 by White Russian émigré Tao Kanbey de Kerekoff. Eight decades on, hedonistic hipsters continue to flock here.

Information

Tourist Office (☎04 95 65 16 67; www.balagne-corsica.com; Port de Plaisance; ⌚9am-6.30pm Mon-Sat, 9am-1pm Sun mid-Jun–mid-Sep, shorter hours rest of year; 📶) Very dynamic, with excellent resources on La Balagne, including detailed walk itineraries complete with maps (€2 for one itinerary, €6 for four).

Getting There & Away

AIR

Calvi's **Aéroport Calvi Ste-Catherine** (www.calvi.aeroport.fr), 7km southeast of the city centre, has flights to mainland France, Switzerland, Belgium and Germany. Count on paying €25 for a taxi in to town.

BOAT

Corsica Ferries (☎04 95 65 43 21; www.corsica-ferries.fr) sails to Nice (5¾ hours) between May and September from Calvi's **ferry terminal** (quai Landry).

BUS

There is a solitary weekday bus (two daily in summer) to Bastia (€16, 2½ hours) via Île Rousse (€4, 30 minutes). From May to mid-October there's also a bus to Porto (€16, 2½ hours, one daily July and August, Monday through Saturday rest of year).

TRAIN

From Calvi train station, south of the harbour, there are at least two departures daily to Bastia (€16.40, 3¼ hours) and Ajaccio (€25.10, 4¾ hours) via Ponte Leccia, and four or five services to Île Rousse (€6, 40 minutes).

PORTO TO AJACCIO

The drive from Porto to Ajaccio is a majestic one that is blessed with bags of beaches, wild rock formations aka the iconic Calanques de Piana, and, last but not least, the irresistible boutique and restaurant of Corsica's most famous *maître glacier* (master ice-cream chef), **Glaces Geronimi** (☎04 95 28 04 13; rte de Cargèse, Sagone; ⌚9am-11pm Jul & Aug, shorter hours rest of year), in the small town of Sagone. Violet tutti-frutti, Camembert or artichoke ice cream (yes, really), anyone?

Porto

POP 605

The setting couldn't be more grandiose. The crowning glory of the west coast, the seaside town of Porto sprawls at the base of a thickly forested valley trammelled on either side by crimson peaks. Buzzing in season and practically deserted in winter, it's a fantastic spot for exploring the shimmering seas around the Unesco-protected marine reservation of the Réserve Naturelle de Scandola, the astonishing Calanques de Piana and the rugged interior.

The village is split by a promontory, topped by a restored Genoese square tower, erected in the 16th century to protect the gulf from Barbary incursions.

Sights & Activities

Waterfront PORT

Porto's main sights are at the harbour. Once you've climbed the russet-coloured rocks up to the **Genoese tower** (€2.50; ⌚9am-6pm mid-Apr–mid-Oct), you can stroll round to the bustling marina, from where an arched footbridge crosses the estuary to an impressive eucalyptus grove and Porto's pebbly beach.

Réserve Naturelle de Scandola NATURE RESERVE

There's no vehicle access or footpath into the magnificent, protected Réserve Naturelle de Scandola – the only way to get here is by sea. As a result, Scandola, a Unesco World Heritage Site, is blessed with exceptional wilderness both above and below the waterline: the gulf boasts fantastic marine biodiversity, with a jaw-dropping topography – just as on land. Various operators, including **Via Mare** (☎06 09 51 15 25, 06 07 28 72 72; www.viamare-promenades.com), **L'Eivissa** (☎07 85 97 26 50, 06 75 30 96 27; www.portoeivissa.com), and **Corse Émotion** (☎06 68 58 94 94; www.corse-emotion.com), offer boat trips into the reserve, charging €38 to €45 for a three-hour excursion.

★ **Gorges de la Spelunca** HIKING

One of Corsica's deepest natural canyons, the Gorges de Spelunca offer splendid hiking opportunities and freshwater swimming on hot summer days. The signposted 45-minute trail through the heart of the gorge (marked with orange blazes) starts at the road bridge over the Porto River, 2km east of Ota on the D124, and continues east to the Pont de Zaglia, an 18th-century Genoan stone bridge; alternatively, hike the longer section connecting the towns of Ota and Evisa (2½ hours each way).

Sleeping

Camping Les Oliviers CAMPGROUND €

(☎04 95 26 14 49; www.camping-oliviers-porto.com; Pont de Porto; per adult/child/tent or car €10.80/5.50/4; ⏲late Mar-early Nov; @🛜🏊) Idyllically set among overhanging olive trees, this steeply terraced site climaxes with a swimming pool surrounded by rocks. You can also swim in the river. There are wooden chalets and *roulottes* (caravans) to rent by the week.

Le Bon Accueil HOTEL €

(☎04 95 26 19 50; www.bonaccueilporto.com; rte de la Marine; s €50-60, d €55-65; ❄🛜) With Brutus the miniature dog running the reception desk, and owners Didier and Claire warmly welcoming visitors, this family hotel upstairs from a *tabac* (tobacco shop) on the road to the port offers simple, well-priced rooms, a guest fridge and a sweet upstairs terrace ideal for picnics and alfresco drinks.

Hôtel-Restaurant Le Belvédère HOTEL €€

(☎04 95 26 12 01; www.hotelrestaurant-lebelvedere-porto.com; Porto Marine; r €65-135, q €116-146; 🛜) Brilliantly located down by Porto's harbour, near the steps to the Genoese watchtower, this small hotel has many rooms with direct sea views, including some with private terraces. Family rooms sleep up to five, with a double bed, two bunks and a trundle bed.

Eating

Le Moulin CORSICAN €

(☎04 95 26 12 09; D84; mains €14-20, menus €17.50; ⏲noon-9.30pm Apr-Oct) Pleasantly situated above a rushing river, south of the bridge on the D84 towards Evisa, 'The Mill' serves solid Corsican fare in an unpretentious, family-friendly setting. Specialities include zucchini *beignets*, Corsican bean and vegetable soup, polenta, local cheese and charcuterie, cannelloni and grilled meats.

Le Maquis CORSICAN €€

(☎04 95 26 12 19; cnr D124 & D81; mains €19-24, menus €23-25; ⏲noon-2pm & 7-10pm, closed Dec) This character-filled eatery in a granite house high above the harbour is much loved by locals and tourists alike. The food's a delight, with a tempting menu based on traditional Corsican cooking. Sit in the cosy wood-beamed interior or reserve a table on the balcony for brilliant views.

OFF THE BEATEN TRACK

OTA & EVISA

The picturesque villages of Ota and Evisa, high up in the hills above Porto, make for a fabulous day trip. Ota is in fact part of the same municipality as Porto but has a completely different feel: quiet, mountainous and unperturbed by the ebb and flow of seasonal visitors. There are spectacular views of the village from across the valley, on the D84.

Further up the mountain on the D84, Evisa is something of a trekking hot spot. The village features on several long-distance trails and it gets a regular flow of hikers from April to October. It's also well known for its chestnuts, which are turned into flour, jam and candied sweets.

The scenic and informative **Sentier des Châtaigniers** crosses some of the village's chestnut groves – find the start opposite local restaurant **A Tràmula** (☎04 95 26 24 39; D84, Evisa; mains €14, menu €18; ⏲noon-3pm & 7-10pm).

Information

Tourist Office (☎04 95 26 10 55; www.porto-tourisme.com; place de la Marine; ⏰9am-6pm Mon-Sat, to 1pm Sun May-Sep, 9am-5pm Mon-Fri Oct-Apr)

Getting There & Away

Face it: there is no fast or easy way to reach Porto. Whether you're driving from Calvi (75km to the north) or Ajaccio (80km to the south), expect two hours of switchbacks and jaw-dropping vistas as you navigate the coastal D81.

Bus services:

Ajaccio €12, two hours, two daily

Calvi €16, 2½ hours, one daily

Piana €3, 20 minutes, two daily

Ajaccio

POP 68,265

Ajaccio is all class and seduction. Commanding a lovely sweep of bay, the city breathes confidence and has more than a whiff of the Côte d'Azur. Everyone from solo travellers to romance-seeking couples and families will love moseying around the centre, replete with mellow-toned buildings and buzzing cafes – not to mention its large marina and the trendy rte des Sanguinaires area, a few kilometres to the west.

The spectre of Corsica's general looms over Ajaccio. Napoléon Bonaparte was born here in 1769, and the city is dotted with sites relating to the diminutive dictator, from his childhood home to seafront statues, museums and street names.

Sights

Palais Fesch – Musée des Beaux-Arts ART MUSEUM

(☎04 95 26 26 26; www.musee-fesch.com; 50-52 rue du Cardinal Fesch; adult/child €8/5; ⏰10.30am-6pm Mon, Wed & Sat, noon-6pm Thu, Fri & Sun May-Sep, to 5pm Oct-Apr) One of the island's must-sees, this superb museum established by Napoléon's uncle has France's largest collection of Italian paintings outside the Louvre. Mostly the works of minor or anonymous 14th- to 19th-century artists, there are also canvases by Titian, Fra Bartolomeo, Veronese, Botticelli and Bellini. Look out for *La Vierge à l'Enfant Soutenu par un Ange* (Mother and Child Supported by an Angel), one of Botticelli's masterpieces. The museum also houses temporary exhibitions.

Chapelle Impériale CHAPEL

(Imperial Chapel; admission €3; ⏰by arrangement) Several members of the imperial family lie entombed in the crypt of this chapel, just across the courtyard from the Palais Fesch. Constructed in 1860, it recently reopened after extensive renovations. Visitors can see the tombs of Napoléon's parents and other relatives, but don't expect to find the man himself – he's buried in Les Invalides in Paris. Pay admission at the Musée des Beaux-Arts; chapel visits are available upon request whenever the museum is open.

Maison Bonaparte MUSEUM

(☎04 95 21 43 89; www.musees-nationaux-napoleoniens.org; rue St-Charles; adult/child €7/free; ⏰10.30am-12.30pm & 1.15-6pm Tue-Sun Apr-Sep, to 4.30pm Oct-Mar) Napoléon spent his first nine years in this house. Ransacked by Corsican nationalists in 1793, requisitioned by English troops from 1794 to 1796, and eventually rebuilt by Napoléon's mother, the house became a place of pilgrimage for French revolutionaries. It hosts memorabilia of the emperor and his siblings, including a glass medallion containing a lock of his hair. A comprehensive audioguide (included in admission price for adults, €2 for children) is available in several languages.

Salon Napoléonien MUSEUM

(☎04 95 51 52 62; www.musee-fesch.com; Hôtel de Ville, av Antoine Sérafini; adult/child €2.50/free; ⏰9-11.45am & 2-5.45pm Mon-Fri mid-Jun–mid-Sep, to 4.45pm rest of year) Fans of Napoléon will make a beeline for this tiny museum on the 1st floor of the Hôtel de Ville. It exhibits Napoléonic medals, busts and portraits, Napoléon's death mask and a fabulously frescoed ceiling of the general and his entourage.

Cathédrale Ste-Marie CATHEDRAL

(rue Forcioli Conti; ⏰8-11.30am & 2.30-5.45pm Mon-Sat) The 16th-century cathedral contains Napoléon's baptismal font and the *Vierge au Sacré-Cœur* (Virgin of the Sacred Heart) by Eugène Delacroix (1798–1863).

Plage de Porticcio BEACH

Beach bums will prefer the sands of Porticcio to the busier city beaches. It's 17km across the bay from Ajaccio and accessible four to nine times daily by a 20-minute **ferry** (Navette Maritime; ☎04 95 52 95 00, 04 95 52 53 37; www.promenades-en-mer.org/Navettes-maritimes_a1.html; tickets €5).

Activities

Kiosks on the quayside opposite place du Maréchal Foch sell tickets for seasonal **boat trips** around the Golfe d'Ajaccio and Îles Sanguinaires (adult/child €25/15), and excursions to the Réserve Naturelle de Scandola (adult/child €55/35).

Pointe de la Parata WALKING

This cape, about 12km west of Ajaccio, is a magnet for walkers. A much-trodden walking trail leads around the promontory, which rewards with great sea views and tantalising close-ups of the four islets of the **Îles Sanguinaires** (Bloody Islands), so named because of their crimson-coloured rock. Bus 5 (€1, 30 minutes) runs between town and the trailhead.

LSP 2 Roues CYCLING

(☎06 07 28 84 81; www.lsp2roues.com; 13 bd Sampiero; bike/electric bike/scooter per day €20/30/54; ⏰9am-noon & 3-7pm Mon-Fri, by arrangement Sat & Sun) To pedal to the Pointe de la Parata from downtown Ajaccio, pick up two wheels from LSP 2 Roues.

Festivals & Events

St Érasme RELIGIOUS

Street and boat procession on 2 June in honour of St Érasme, patron saint of *pêcheurs* (fishermen).

Ajaccio Fête le Printemps CULTURAL

(www.ajaccio-tourisme.com) For two weeks in late April, Ajaccio and the surrounding areas host a raft of events – concerts, workshops, outdoor activities, guided tours – to celebrate the start of the *beaux jours* (long sunny days).

Fêtes Napoléoniennes STREET CARNIVAL

Ajaccio's biggest bash celebrates Napoléon's birthday on 15 August (which coincides with the Assumption of Mary, a national bank holiday) with military-themed parades, street spectacles and a huge fireworks display.

Sleeping

Hôtel Marengo HOTEL €

(☎04 95 21 43 66; www.hotel-marengo.com; 2 rue Marengo; d €78-98; ⏰Apr-Oct; ❄📶) For something near to the sand, try this charmingly eccentric small hotel. Rooms have a balcony, there's a quiet flower-filled courtyard and reception is an agreeable clutter of tasteful prints and personal objects. Find it down a cul-de-sac off bd Madame Mère.

Hôtel Napoléon HOTEL €€

(☎04 95 51 54 00; www.hotel-napoleon-ajaccio.fr; 4 rue Lorenzo Vero; d €118-139; ❄📶) The warmth of a family-run hotel, coupled with prime location on a side street in the heart of town, make the Napoléon an excellent mid-range choice. Rooms are clean, bright and comfortable, despite the rather uninspiring decor; some of the nicest are on the 7th floor, with high ceilings and tall shuttered windows looking out on a leafy backyard.

Hôtel San Carlu Citadelle HOTEL €€

(☎04 95 21 13 84; www.hotel-sancarlu.com; 8 bd Danièle Casanova; d €85-157, f €158-248; ❄📶) Located smack opposite the citadel, this cream-coloured townhouse with oyster-grey shutters is a solid bet. Rooms are clean and modern and views get better with every floor. Traffic noise could be an issue for light sleepers. The family room sleeps up to five comfortably.

★Hôtel Demeure Les Mouettes BOUTIQUE HOTEL €€€

(☎04 95 50 40 40; www.hotellesmouettes.fr; 9 cours Lucien Bonaparte; d €170-520; ⏰Apr-Oct; ❄📶🏊) This peach-coloured 19th-century colonnaded mansion right on the water's edge is a dream. Views of the bay of Ajaccio from the (heated) pool and terrace are exquisite: dolphins can often be spotted very early in the morning or in the evenings. Inside, the decor is one of understated elegance and service is four stars.

Eating

★L'Altru Versu BISTRO €€

(☎04 95 50 05 22; rte des Sanguinaires; mains €20-29; ⏰12.30-2pm Thu-Mon, 7.30-10.30pm daily mid-Jun–mid-Oct, 12.30-2pm Thu-Tue, 7.30-10.30pm Mon, Tue & Thu-Sat rest of year) A phoenix rising from the ashes, this perennial favourite reopened in 2015 on Ajaccio's western waterfront after suffering two devastating winter storms and a fire. Magnificent sea views complement the exquisite gastronomic creations of the Mezzacqui brothers (Jean-Pierre front of house, David powering the kitchen), from crispy minted prawns with pistachio cream to pork with honey and clementine zest.

The Mezzacqui brothers are also noteworthy for their musical talents – after serving customers at L'Altru Versu each Friday, they hop on their motorscooters, hitch on their guitars and join their father in serenading

Ajaccio

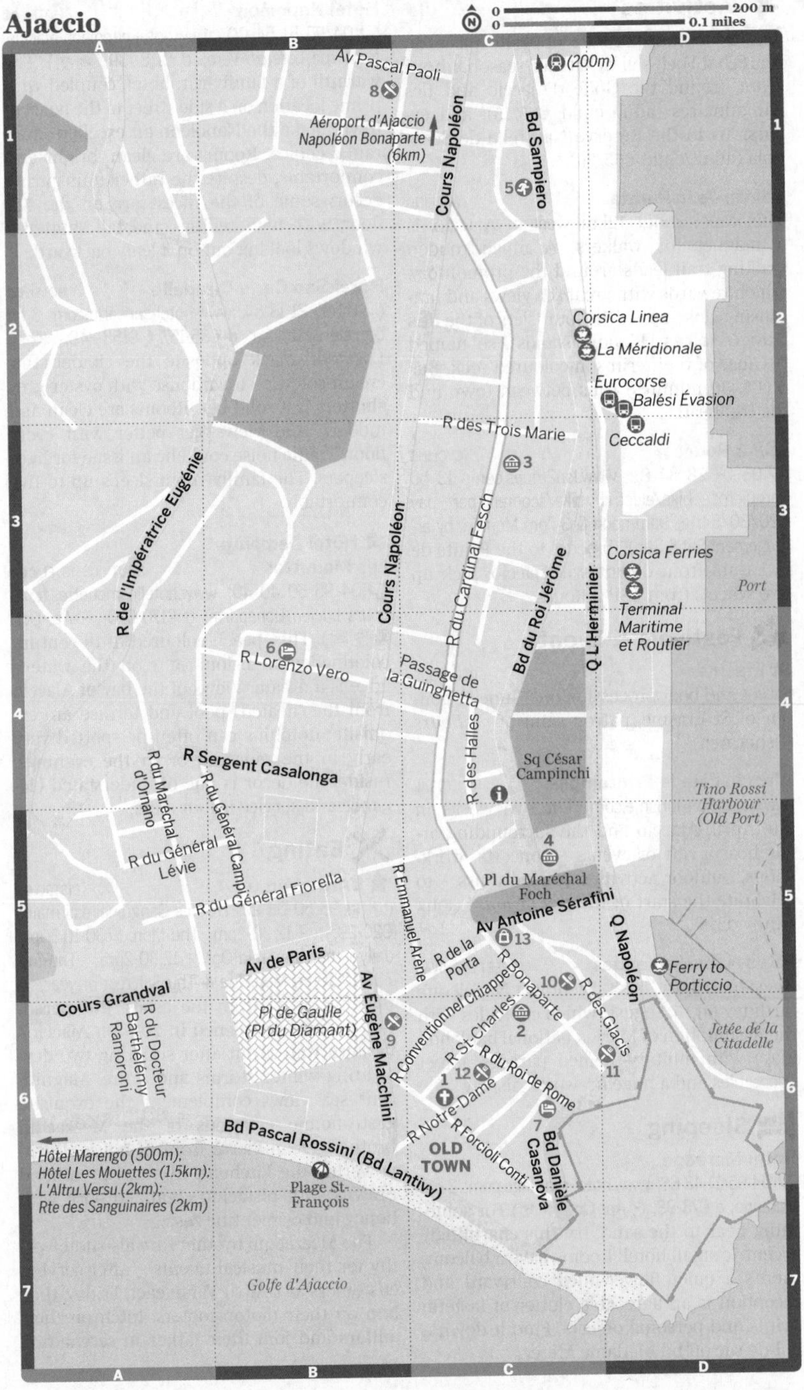
0 200 m
0 0.1 miles
A
B
C
D
1
2
3
4
5
6
7
Av Pascal Paoli
8
Aéroport d'Ajaccio Napoléon Bonaparte (6km)
(200m)
Cours Napoléon
Bd Sampiero
5
Corsica Linea
La Méridionale
Eurocorse
Balési Évasion
Ceccaldi
R des Trois Marie
3
R de l'Impératrice Eugénie
Cours Napoléon
R du Cardinal Fesch
Bd du Roi Jérôme
Q L'Herminier
Corsica Ferries
Terminal Maritime et Routier
Port
6
R Lorenzo Vero
Passage de la Guinghetta
R des Halles
R Sergent Casalonga
R du Maréchal d'Ornano
R du Général Campi
Sq César Campinchi
Tino Rossi Harbour (Old Port)
R du Général Lévie
R du Général Fiorella
R Emmanuel Arène
4
Pl du Maréchal Foch
Av Antoine Sérafini
13
Q Napoléon
Ferry to Porticcio
Av de Paris
R de la Porta
R Bonaparte
10
R des Glacis
Cours Grandval
R du Docteur Barthélémy Ramoroni
Pl de Gaulle (Pl du Diamant)
Av Eugène Macchini
9
R Conventionnel Chiappe
R St-Charles
2
11
Jetée de la Citadelle
12
1
R du Roi de Rome
R Notre-Dame
7
R Forcioli Conti
Bd Danièle Casanova
OLD TOWN
Bd Pascal Rossini (Bd Lantivy)
Hôtel Marengo (500m); Hôtel Les Mouettes (1.5km); L'Altru Versu (2km); Rte des Sanguinaires (2km)
Plage St-François
Golfe d'Ajaccio

Ajaccio

Sights

1 Cathédrale Ste-Marie C6
Chapelle Impériale .... (see 3)
2 Maison Bonaparte C6
3 Palais Fesch – Musée des Beaux-Arts C3
4 Salon Napoléonien C5

Activities, Courses & Tours

5 LSP 2 Roues C1

Sleeping

6 Hôtel Napoléon B4
7 Hôtel San Carlu Citadelle C6

Eating

8 A Nepita B1
9 Le 20123 .... B6
10 Le Bilboq – Chez Jean Jean C5
11 Le Cabanon D6
12 Le Roi de Rome C6

Shopping

13 U Stazzu C5

guests at their other restaurant across town, the Bistrotello.

Le 20123 TRADITIONAL CORSICAN €€
(☎04 95 21 50 05; www.20123.fr; 2 rue du Roi de Rome; menu €35; ⏰7-11pm Tue-Sun) This fabulous, one-of-a-kind eatery started life in the village of Pila Canale (postcode 20123, get it?), and when the owner upped sticks to Ajaccio, he decided to take the old village with him – water pump, washing line, life-sized dolls in traditional dress, central square and all. It may sound tacky, but you won't find many more character-filled places in Corsica.

Everyone feasts on the same four-course *menu*, built solely from local produce and traditional recipes, and, amazingly, unchanged for 25 years.

Le Roi de Rome CORSICAN €€
(☎04 95 21 32 88; 14 rue du Roi de Rome; lunch menu €18, mains €14-32; ⏰noon-3pm Mon-Sat, 7-11pm daily) This buzzy venue on a back street near the Citadel is half wine bar, half convivial neighbourhood eatery. Stop in for an early evening aperitif, choosing from a vast array of Corsican wines by the glass, and linger for dinner. Meats are the house speciality, from Charolais beef carpaccio to Corsican veal with olives to lamb shank or pork tenderloin.

A Nepita BISTRO €€
(☎04 95 26 75 68; 4 rue San Lazaro; 2-/3-course menus lunch €24/29, dinner €35/40; ⏰noon-1.30pm Mon-Fri, 8-9.30pm Thu-Sat) Ajaccio's rising culinary star keeps winning plaudits and loyal followers for its modern French cuisine and elegant setting. It's a nice change from hearty traditional Corsican fare, although the island isn't forgotten. The straightforward menu of two appetisers, two mains and two desserts changes daily and uses only the freshest local products, including seasonal seafood and vegetables.

Le Cabanon FRENCH €€
(☎04 95 22 55 90; 4 bd Danièle Casanova; mains €18-28; ⏰noon-2pm & 7.30-10pm Tue-Sat) Loïc fishes, Nadine cooks – a winning combination if there ever was one. Nestled in the old town near the citadel, Le Cabanon (The Shed) offers a sunny cuisine inspired by Loïc's catch of the day in a charming bistro-like dining room. On summer evenings, the most prized seats are those on the sidewalk terrace facing the citadel.

Le Bilboq – Chez Jean Jean SEAFOOD €€€
(☎04 95 51 35 40; 1 rue des Glacis; mains €60; ⏰8-11pm daily Jun-Sep, closed Mon Oct-May) This decades-old Ajaccio icon is famous for two things: grilled lobster flambéed in cognac, and *spaghettis à la langouste* (spaghetti with lobster), savoured alfresco in a cobblestoned square or in two cosy upstairs rooms spread with colourful carpets and hung with vintage photos of Ajaccio celebrities. Don't miss peeking into the kitchen, housed in a 17th-century brick-vaulted former Genoese stable.

Shopping

U Stazzu FOOD & DRINKS
(www.ustazzu.com; 1 rue Bonaparte; ⏰9am-7pm Mon-Sat Jun-Sep, 9am-noon & 2.30-6.30pm Mon-Sat Oct-May) For Corsican goodies, there's only one address that matters: U Stazzu, famous for its handmade charcuterie and Corsican delicacies (olive oil, jams, liqueurs, honey) crafted by small producers. Owner Paul Marcaggi has been honored multiple times as the best charcutier in Corsica, and once as best charcutier in France. In summer, people line up just to get in the door.

Information

Tourist Office (☎04 95 51 53 03; www.ajaccio-tourisme.com; 3 bd du Roi Jérôme; ⏰8am-7pm Mon-Sat, 9am-1pm Sun Apr-Oct, shorter hours Nov-Mar; 📶)

Getting There & Away

AIR

Aéroport d'Ajaccio Napoléon Bonaparte (☎04 95 23 56 56; www.2a.cci.fr/Aeroport-Napoleon-Bonaparte-Ajaccio.html), 7km east of town, is linked by bus 8 (€4.50, 15 minutes) with Ajaccio's train station (bus stop marked Marconajo). Count on around €25 for a taxi into town.

BOAT

Corsica Linea (☎08 25 88 80 88, 04 95 29 66 65; www.corsicalinea.com), **Corsica Ferries** (☎04 95 50 78 82; www.corsica-ferries.fr) and **La Méridionale** (p873) offer ferry services to the French mainland ports of Toulon, Nice and Marseille from Ajaccio's **Terminal Maritime et Routier** (☎04 95 51 55 45; quai L'Herminier). Buy tickets before sailings inside the combined bus and ferry terminal.

BUS

Local bus companies, including **Ceccaldi** (☎04 95 21 01 24; www.autocars-ceccaldi.com), **Eurocorse** (☎04 95 21 06 30; www.eurocorse.com) and **Balési Évasion** (☎04 95 70 15 55; www.balesievasion.com), have ticket kiosks inside the terminal building, which is the arrival/departure point for buses. As always in Corsica, expect reduced services on Sunday and during the winter months. Destinations include the following:

Bonifacio €20, 3 hours, two daily Monday to Saturday

Porto €12, 2 hours, two daily Monday to Saturday

Porto-Vecchio €20, 3¼ hours, two daily Monday to Saturday

Zonza €12, 2 hour, two daily Monday to Saturday

TRAIN

From the **train station** (place de la Gare), 500m north of town, services include the following:

Bastia €21.60, 3¾ hours, five daily

Calvi €25.10, 4¾ hours, two daily (change at Ponte Leccia)

Corte €11.50, two hours, five daily

THE SOUTH

A microcosm of Corsica itself, the South boasts the island's most beautiful beach (Palombaggia), its most remarkable archaeological site (Filitosa), some of its most breathtaking mountains (Aiguilles de Bavella) and two of its most alluring urban centers: the cliff-hugging citadel of Bonifacio and the refined coastal resort of Porto-Vecchio.

Sartène

POP 3534

With its grey granite houses, secretive dead-end alleys and sombre, introspective air, Sartène has long been said to encapsulate Corsica's rugged spirit (French novelist Prosper Mérimée dubbed it the 'most Corsican of Corsican towns'). There's no doubt that Sartène feels a long way from the glitter of the Corsican coast; the hillside houses are endearingly ramshackle, the streets are shady and scruffy, and life still crawls along at a traditional tilt. It offers a much more convincing glimpse of how life was once lived in rural Corsica than any of the island's more well-heeled towns.

Notorious for its banditry and bloody vendettas in the 19th century, Sartène has more recently found fame thanks to the annual **Procession du Catenacciu**, a re-enactment of the Passion that has taken place here every Good Friday since the Middle Ages. Barefoot, wearing red robes and cowled (to preserve his anonymity), the Catenacciu (literally 'chained one'; penitent) – chosen by the parish priest to atone for a grave sin – lugs a massive 35kg wooden cross through town in a re-enactment of Christ's journey to Calvary.

View the cross and 17kg chain the penitent wears inside Sartène's granite **Église Ste-Marie** (place Porta).

For those seeking end-of-the-road tranquillity **Domaine de Croccano** (☎04 95 77 11 37; www.corsenature.com; rte de Granace/D148, km 3; d €92-120, q €142-180; ⊙Jan-Nov; ❄📶) makes a blissful getaway. Set in a charming stone farmhouse among 10 hectares of rolling maquis, its rooms are very old-fashioned but the welcome couldn't be warmer and the pastoral views are stunning. The Domaine also offers picnic facilities and horse-riding excursions for guests. From Sartène's town square, follow the green signs 3.5km towards Granace.

At cheerful **Le Jardin de l'Echauguette** (☎04 95 77 12 86; place de la Vardiola; menu €22; ⊙noon-2pm & 7-10pm mid-Apr–Sep), just down the stairs from Sartène's main square, Corsican specialities such as *beignets de courgette* (zucchini fritters), *cannelloni au brucciu* (pasta tubes stuffed with sheep's-milk cheese) or *daube de veau* (veal stew) are served on a dreamy walled garden terrace overhung by trees.

WORTH A TRIP

PREHISTORIC CORSICA: FILITOSA & CAURIA

Southern Corsica boasts the island's most astonishing prehistoric sites, which are must-sees for anyone who has an interest in Corsica's ancient civilisations (and even those who don't – the surrounding landscapes are stunning).

Some time around 4000 BC to 3000 BC, Corsica developed its own megalithic faith (possibly imported by seafaring settlers from mainland Europe); most of the island's standing stones and menhirs date from this period. The most important and impressive site is **Filitosa** (☎ 04 95 74 00 91; www.filitosa.fr; D57; €7; ⏲ 9am-sunset Apr-Oct), northwest of Propriano, where a collection of extraordinary carved menhirs was discovered in 1946. The Filitosa menhirs are highly unusual: several have detailed faces, anatomical features (such as ribcages) and even swords and armour, suggesting that they may commemorate specific warriors or chieftains.

About 10km south of Sartène, the desolate and beautiful **Cauria** plateau is home to three megalithic curiosities: the *alignements* (lines) of **Stantari** and **Renaju**, several of which show similar anatomical details and weaponry to those of Filitosa; and the **Fontanaccia dolmen**, one of Corsica's few burial chambers, with its supporting pillars and capstones. The sites are signposted as *sites préhistoriques* about 2km south of Sartène off the N196. What did these strange sites signify for their megalithic architects? Were they ritual temples? Sacred graveyards? Mythical armies? Or even celestial timepieces? Despite countless theories, no one has the foggiest idea.

Both sites can easily be visited from Sartène; alternatively, **U Mulinu di Calzola** (☎ 04 95 24 32 14, 06 84 79 21 86; www.umulinu.net; Pont de Calzola, Casalabriva; d €82-99, tr €92-108; ⏲ May–Oct) is a gorgeous inn located right on the banks of the Taravo river, less than 10 minutes' drive from Filitosa. Dinner on the shaded terrace is certain to win you over after a day sightseeing.

Information

Tourist Office (☎ 04 95 77 15 40; www.lacorsedesorigines.com; cours Sœur Amélie; ⏲ 9am-6pm Mon-Fri, 10am-5pm Sat Jun-Sep, 10am-5pm Mon-Fri Oct-May)

Getting There & Away

By car, Sartène is 80km (1½ hours) south of Ajaccio and 50km (one hour) north of Bonifacio. Twice-daily (except Sunday) Eurocorse buses head for Ajaccio, Bonifacio and Porto-Vecchio.

Bonifacio

POP 3016

With its glittering harbour, dramatic perch atop creamy white cliffs, and stout citadel above the cornflower-blue waters of the Bouches de Bonifacio, this dazzling port is an essential stop. Just a short hop from Sardinia, Bonifacio has a distinctly Italianate feel: sun-bleached town houses, dangling washing lines and murky chapels cram the web of alleyways of the old citadel; down below on the harbourside, brasseries and boat kiosks tout their wares to the droves of day trippers. Bonifacio's also perfectly positioned for exploring the island's southerly beaches and the Îles Lavezzi.

Sights

★ Citadel HISTORIC SITE

(Haute Ville) Much of Bonifacio's charm comes from strolling the citadel's shady streets, several spanned by arched aqueducts designed to collect rainwater to fill the communal cistern opposite **Église Ste-Marie Majeure**. From the marina, the paved steps of **montée du Rastello** and **montée St-Roch** bring you up to the citadel's old gateway, **Porte de Gênes**, complete with an original 16th-century drawbridge.

Inside the gateway is the 13th-century **Bastion de l'Étendard** (adult/child €2.50/free, incl Escalier du Roi d'Aragon €3.50/free; ⏲ 9am-8pm mid-Apr–Sep, 10am-5pm rest of year), home to a small history museum exploring Bonifacio's past. Stroll the ramparts to **place du Marché** and **place de la Manichella** for jaw-dropping views over the Bouches de Bonifacio.

On the other side of the citadel, the **Escalier du Roi d'Aragon** (adult/child €2.50/free, incl Bastion de l'Étendard €3.50/free; ⏲ 9am-sunset Apr-Oct) cuts down the southern cliff-face.

West along the limestone headland is the **Église Ste-Dominique**, one of Corsica's few Gothic churches and, a little further, Bonifacio's eerily quiet but beautiful **marine cemetery**. At the western tip of the penin-

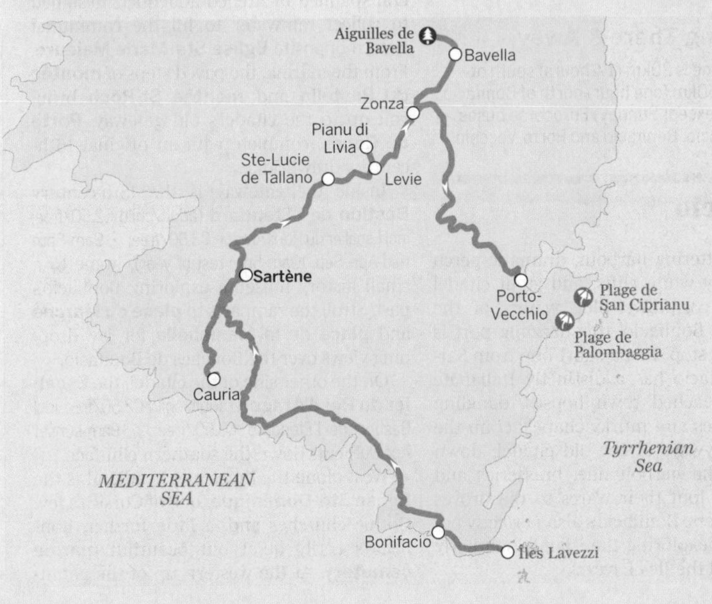
Aiguilles de
Bavella
Bavella
Zonza
Pianu di
Livia
Levie
Ste-Lucie
de Tallano
Sartène
Porto-
Vecchio
Plage de
San Ciprianu
Plage de
Palombaggia
Cauria
Tyrrhenian
Sea
MEDITERRANEAN
SEA
Bonifacio
Îles Lavezzi

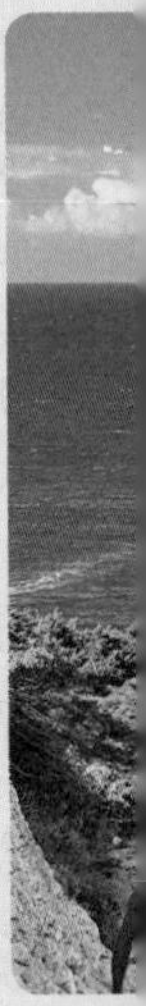

Top: Canyoning near Bavella (p897)
Bottom: Limestone cliffs, Bonifacio (p891)

1 WEEK Exploring Southern Corsica

Southern Corsica is a concentrate of the very best the island has to offer: mountains and beaches, culture, history and plenty of fabulous addresses for epicurean travellers.

Start off your trip in **Bonifacio** (p891): perched dramatically on chalky cliffs that plunge into the sea, it is undoubtedly Corsica's most spectacular city. Allow a day to mosey about the streets of the citadel, descend (and then ascend!) the spectacular Escalier du Roi d'Aragon and walk to the Phare de Pertusato for breathtaking views of the city.

The next day, pack a picnic and your snorkelling gear and join a boat trip to **Îles Lavezzi** (p894), an idyllic archipelago southeast of Bonifacio, where you can walk the island paths and swim among schools of fish in dazzling turquoise waters.

On the third day, head north from Bonifacio towards **Sartène** (p890) – taking a small detour to the beautiful prehistoric sites of **Cauria** (p891) on your way to a late lunch on the panoramic terrace at Le Jardin de l'Echauguette. Continue to **Levie** (p898), up in the mountainous region of Alta Rocca. Your final destination that day is the exquisite boutique inn A Pignata (p898).

The next morning, visit the prehistoric sites of **Pianu di Livia** (p898), just five minutes' drive from the hotel. The rest of the day can be spent exploring the picturesque villages of Levie and **Ste-Lucie de Tallano** or simply enjoying the creature comforts and views of A Pignata.

On day five: action! Go canyoning, hiking or mountain biking in the **Aiguilles de Bavella** (p897), a stunning mountain range characterised by steep, serrated peaks, forested slopes and deep canyons. Spend the night in **Zonza** (p897) to recover, before driving down to **Porto-Vecchio** (p895) the next day and flopping on one its paradisiacal beaches: Plage de Palombaggia or Plage de San Ciprianu get our vote.

For your last day, enjoy a spot of shopping in Porto-Vecchio's pretty boutiques, feast on fresh pasta or a *tartare* (a dish of seasoned raw meat or fish) at the harbourside U Molu and check out the beaches you missed out on the day before.

sula, an underground passage dug by hand during WWII leads to the **Gouvernail de la Corse**, a rudder-shaped rock about 12m from the shore.

Îles Lavezzi ISLAND

Paradise! This protected clutch of uninhabited islets were made for those who love nothing better than splashing in tranquil lapis-lazuli waters. The 65-hectare Île Lavezzi, which gives its name to the whole archipelago, is the most accessible of the islands.

In summer, various companies organise **boat trips** here; buy tickets at the booths located on Bonifacio's marina and bring your own picnic lunch. Boats also sail to the island from Porto-Vecchio.

Activities

Bonifacio's town beaches are a little underwhelming. **Plage de Sotta Rocca** is a small pebbly cove below the citadel, reached by steps from av Charles de Gaulle. For something nicer, explore **Plage Fazzio** and the other sandy inlets on the northern side of Bouches de Bonifacio, accessed via a 3km footpath marked 'Sentier des Plages'; look for the trailhead along av Sylvère Bohn, just north of the Esso petrol station at the harbour's eastern edge. The finest stretches of sand are 8km east of Bonifacio in **Sperone**.

SPMB BOATING

(Société des Promenades en Mer de Bonifacio; ☎04 95 10 97 50; www.spmbonifacio.com; Port de Bonifacio) Don't leave Bonifacio without taking a boat trip around its extraordinary coastline, where you'll get the best perspective of the town's precarious position atop the magnificent chalky cliffs. The basic one-hour itinerary (adult/child €17.50/9) includes several *calanques* (deep rocky inlets), views of the Escalier du Roi d'Aragon and the **Grotte du Sdragonato** (Little Dragon Cave), a vast watery cave with a natural rooftop skylight. A slightly more leisurely, 1¼-hour circuit explores the same attractions in a glass-bottomed boat (adult/child €22.50/13).

Phare de Pertusato WALKING

If you're after that perfect picture, don't miss the easy walk along the cliffs to the Pertusato Lighthouse, from where you'll enjoy spectacular, seamless views of the cliffs, Îles Lavezzi, Bonifacio and Sardinia. Pick up the trail just to the left of the sharp bend on the hill up to Bonifacio's citadel. Count on 2½ hours for the 5.6km round trip.

Bonif' Kayak KAYAKING

(☎06 27 11 30 73; www.bonifacio-kayak.com; Plage de Piantarella; kayak rental per hr from €8, excursions per person from €35) Rents kayaks and stand-up paddleboards and organises guided sea-kayaking excursions.

Sleeping

Hôtel Le Colomba HOTEL €€

(☎04 95 73 73 44; www.hotel-bonifacio-corse.fr; 4-6 rue Simon Varsi; d €112-167; ❄📶) Occupying a tastefully renovated 14th-century building, this hotel enjoys a prime location on a picturesque (steep) street, bang in the heart of the old town. Rooms are simple and smallish, but fresh and individually decorated with amenities including wrought-iron bedsteads, country fabrics, carved bedheads and/or checkerboard tiles. Other pluses include friendly staff and breakfast served in a medieval vaulted cellar.

Hôtel Genovese HOTEL €€€

(☎04 95 73 12 34; www.hotel-genovese.com; place de l'Europe, Haute-Ville; d €210-310, ste €255-420; ❄📶🏊) Chic and stylish, this ultra-cool hotel built on Bonifacio's northern ramparts is hard to resist. Its rooftop swimming pool and bijou garden are stunning and the interior is bright and fresh. Standard rooms are comfortable if a bit underwhelming, while the poolside terrace and some of the better rooms and suites offer spectacular views over town and the harbour below.

Eating

★**Kissing Pigs** CORSICAN €

(☎04 95 73 56 09; 15 quai Banda del Ferro; mains €11-23, menus €20-22; ⏰noon-2.30pm & 7-10.30pm Tue-Sun) Soothingly positioned by the harbour, this widely acclaimed restaurant and wine bar serves savoury fare in a seductively cosy interior, complete with wooden fixtures and swinging sausages. It's famed for its cheese and charcuterie platters; for the indecisive, the combination *moitié-moitié* (half-half) is perfect. The Corsican wine list is another hit.

La Bodega CORSICAN €

(☎06 73 75 94 70; www.facebook.com/LaBodegaBonifacio; place Bonaparte; mains €13.50-19; ⏰noon-10pm Mon-Sat Mar-Oct) At this cute wood-beamed hole-in-the-wall near the tourist office, gregarious owner Jean-Marie whips up no-nonsense Corsican classics, from veal with olives to *civet de sanglier* (wild boar stew). Don't miss his *aubergine à la boni-*

facienne (eggplant roasted and stuffed with garlic, breadcrumbs, egg, and two kinds of cheese) or sample a bit of everything with an *assiette dégustation* (€19).

Sorba BOULANGERIE €
(☎06 22 51 70 12; 3 rue St-Erasme; ⏰8am-12.30pm & 3-6pm Tue-Sun Apr-Oct) Before setting off on a boat trip, visit this artisan patisserie-gelateria down by the water, run by the same family since 1921. Splash out on a bag of sweet lemon- or aniseed-flavoured *canistrelli* (Corsican biscuits), a loaf of *pain des morts* (literally 'death bread' but actually sweet nut-and-raisin bread) or some giant-sized chestnut and orange *fugazzi* (cookies) to nibble aboard.

Cantina Doria CORSICAN €
(☎04 95 73 50 49; 27 rue Doria; mains €10-16, menu €16-21; ⏰noon-2.30pm & 7-11pm Apr–mid-Oct) A Bonifacio institution, this cavernous joint has a tantalising menu showcasing the great classics of Corsican cuisine in a rustic setting.

L'An Faim CORSICAN €€
(☎04 95 73 09 10; 7 montée Rastello; lunch menus €15-20, dinner mains €28-34; ⏰noon-3pm & 7.30-11.30pm Thu-Tue) Straddling the steps that climb from Bonifacio's port to the citadel, this relative newcomer has been wowing visitors since 2015 with its exquisite market-sourced cuisine. Seasonally changing specials run the gamut from bouillabaisse to Corsican veal chops (from the striped *vache tigre* cow) to appetisers of purple artichokes, slow-roasted peppers and artisanal sausages.

ℹ Information

Tourist Office (☎04 95 73 11 88; www.bonifacio.fr; 2 rue Fred Scamaroni; ⏰9am-8pm Jul & Aug, shorter hours rest of year; 📶)

ℹ Getting There & Away

AIR

A taxi into town from **Aéroport de Figari-Sud-Corse** (☎04 95 71 10 10; www.2a.cci.fr/Aeroport-Figari-Sud-Corse.html), 20km northwest of town, costs about €45. Seasonal shuttle-bus service from the airport had been indefinitely discontinued at the time of research.

BOAT

Italian ferry operators **Moby** (☎04 95 73 00 29; www.mobycorse.com) and **Blu Navy** (p873) run seasonal boats between Bonifacio and Santa Teresa Gallura (Sardinia); sailing time is 50 minutes.

BUS

Eurocorse Voyages (☎04 95 21 06 30; www.eurocorse.com) runs daily services to Porto-Vecchio (€8, 30 minutes) and Ajaccio (€20, 3¼ hours).

Porto-Vecchio & Around

POP 11,574

Shamelessly seductive and fashionable, Porto-Vecchio is dubbed the Corsican St-Tropez, and it's no wonder. Sitting in a marvellous bay, it's the kind of place that lures French A-listers and wealthy tourists. Its picturesque backstreets, lined with restaurant terraces and designer shops, have charm in spades, and are presided over with grace by the photogenic ruins of an old Genoese citadel. Although there is no beach in the town proper, some of the island's best, and most famous, beaches are close by.

Lapped by turquoise waters, fringed with pine trees and graced with gorgeous views of the Îles Cerbicale, the long sandy crescent of **Plage de Palombaggia** is considered by many to be Corsica's most beautiful beach.

South of Plage de Palombaggia, **Plage de la Folacca** (also known as Plage de Tamariciu) is no less impressive. Continue a few kilometres further south over a pass called Bocca di L'Oru and you'll come across another gem of a beach, the gently curving **Plage de Santa Giulia**. From Porto-Vecchio, follow the N198 to the south and turn left onto rte de Palombaggia (it's signposted), which winds around the coast.

To the north, the coast is also sprinkled with scenic expanses of sand. The gorgeous, translucent depths of the beaches at **Cala Rossa** and **Baie de San Ciprianu** are sure to set your heart aflutter. Further to the north is the stunning **Golfe de Pinarello**, with its Genoese tower and yet more beautiful expanses of sand lapped by shallow waters.

In town at the marina, various operators offer boat excursions to the Îles Lavezzi and Bonifacio.

🛏 Sleeping

A Littariccia B&B €€
(☎04 95 70 41 33; www.littariccia.com; rte de Palombaggia; d €100-215; ❄📶🏊) This B&B's trump card is its *fabulous* location, in the hills overlooking Plage de Palombaggia, with a dreamy pool. The rooms are pretty but simple and not all come with a sea view – or wi-fi.

Le Belvédère HOTEL €€€

(☎04 95 70 54 13; www.hbcorsica.com; rte de Palombaggia; d €250-300, ste €380-510; ⏱May-Nov; ❄📶🏊) Built out of an old family estate tucked between eucalyptus, palm and pine on the seashore, this 15-room hotel is quite divine, darling. Decor is modern and exotic: a gregarious mix of traditional stone, wood, marble and wrought iron. Public areas lounge between natural rock and sand, and as for the sea-facing pool, you'll be hard-pushed to move.

Eating

A Cantina di l'Orriu CORSICAN €

(☎04 95 25 95 89; www.orriu.com; 5 cours Napoléon; mains €15-29; ⏱noon-2pm Wed-Sun, 7-10pm Tue-Sun mid-Mar–Oct) Gourmets will be in heaven at this wonderful *bar à vin*, its atmospheric old-stone interior packed to the rafters with sausages and cold meats hung up to dry, cheeses, jars of jam and honey, and other tasty Corsican produce. Lunch platters range from light to feisty – raviolis are one of the house specialities – and desserts are sumptuous.

La Table de Nathalie BISTRO €€

(☎04 95 71 65 25; www.facebook.com/restaurant-latabledenahalie; 4 rue Jean Jaures; mains €21-29; ⏱noon-2pm & 7-11pm Tue-Sat Mar-Nov, plus 7-11pm Sun & Mon Jul & Aug) Locals and tourists alike pile onto the front terrace of this chic little bistro just south of Porto-Vecchio's tourist office. The menu abounds in seasonally inspired, locally sourced treats such as slow-cooked fish of the day in citrus-herb crust, terrine of rabbit with Cervione hazelnuts or homemade foie gras with muscat from Cap Corse.

Tamaricciu MEDITERRANEAN €€

(☎04 95 70 49 89; www.tamaricciu.com; Plage de Palombaggia; mains €16-32; ⏱12.30-6pm May-mid-Jun & Sep–mid-Oct, to 10.30pm mid-Jun–Aug) Among the various beach restaurants scattered along the Palombaggia sands south of Porto-Vecchio, Tamaricciu has that hip St-Tropez-chic touch. With its wooden decking terrace and first-class views of the turquoise surf, dining really does not get better than this. Cuisine is Mediterranean, with lots of grilled fish and meat and pasta, all beautifully presented.

Drinking & Nightlife

Le Glacier de la Place BAR

(place de la République; ⏱8am-11pm Jun-Aug, shorter hours rest of year) It may be called 'ice-cream parlour' but this place on Porto-Vecchio's main square is more famous for its staggering selection of beers from all over the world (130 in total), as well as its numerous rums and whiskies.

Via Notte CLUB

(☎04 95 72 02 12; www.vianotte.com; rte de Porra; ⏱8pm-5am daily Jun-Sep) On the southern outskirts of Porto-Vecchio, Via Notte is Corsica's hottest club, Europe's largest open-air disco and one of the most famous nightspots in the Med. With up to 5000 revellers and superstar DJs most nights in summer, it has to be seen to be believed.

Information

Tourist Office (☎04 95 70 09 58; www.ot-portovecchio.com; rue Général Leclerc; ⏱9am-11pm Jul & Aug, to 8pm Jun & Sep, shorter hours rest of year; 📶)

Getting There & Away

AIR

From **Aéroport de Figari-Sud-Corse** (p895), about 25km from Porto-Vecchio, the cheapest way into town is the shuttle bus (€4, 30 minutes, two to four daily) operated by **Transports Rossi** (☎04 95 71 00 11), which drops you at Porto-Vecchio's bus station. A taxi will cost around €50.

BOAT

Corsica Linea (p873) and **Corsica Ferries** (www.corsica-ferries.fr) operate seasonal ferries to Porto-Vecchio from the mainland French ports of Marseille, Nice and Toulon.

BUS

All buses leave from the bus station, Gare Routière, at the northern end of the harbour.

Balési Évasion (☎04 95 70 15 55; www.balesievasion.com; rte de Bastia) Buses to Ajaccio (€20, three hours) via Zonza (€8, one hour).

Eurocorse (☎04 95 71 24 64; www.eurocorse.com) Operates twice-daily services to Bonifacio (€8, 30 minutes) and to Ajaccio (€20, 3½ hours) via Sartène. Also runs summer-only shuttles to Plage de Palombaggia (€9 return).

Corsicatours/Les Rapides Bleus (☎04 95 70 96 50; www.rapides-bleus.com) Operates two daily services to Bastia (€25, three hours) and summer-only shuttles to Plage de Santa Giulia (€9 return).

L'Alta Rocca

If you've had a temporary surfeit of superb seascapes, take a couple of days to explore L'Alta Rocca, north of Porto-Vecchio. Here

you can really feel a sense of wilderness, a world away from the bling-bling and bustle of the coast. At the south of the long spine that traverses the island, it's a beguiling combination of dense, mixed evergreen-deciduous forests and granite villages strung over rocky ledges.

The Col de Bavella (Bavella Pass; 1218m) is overlooked by the imposing silhouette of one of southern Corsica's most striking and beautiful landscape features: the sharp points of the **Aiguilles de Bavella** (Bavella Needles). If you're lucky you may spot a few of the *mouflons* (wild mountain sheep) that sashay around the area.

The peaks, which rise to a height of more than 1600m and which are also known as the Cornes d'Asinao (Asinao Horns), are jagged points whose colour ranges from grey to ochre to golden depending on the position of the sun in the sky. Behind these stone 'needles' looms the profile of Monte Incudine (2134m), which the GR20 links to the Col de Bavella. From the pass you can see the statue of **Notre Dame des Neiges** (Our Lady of the Snows). The Bavella massif is a wonderful place for climbing, canyoning and walking. There is a high-mountain spur of the GR20 that splits off north beyond Notre Dame des Neiges and allows you to approach the peaks. Alternatively, follow the red-marked trail one hour south to the **Trou de la Bombe**, a giant hole in the rock accessed mostly by a wide dirt road, with a last-minute scramble up the rocks.

Bavella is one of the best spots to do canyoning in Corsica; for an exhilarating day out walking, jumping and sliding through mountain gorges, contact local agencies such as **Corsica Canyon** (☎06 22 91 61 44; www.canyoncorse.com; Bavella, D268) and **Bavella Canyon** (☎06 20 27 49 41; www.bavellacanyon.com).

Outdoor action done, feast on roasted baby goat, wild boar stew and other hearty Corsican fare at **Auberge du Col de Bavella** (☎04 95 72 09 87; www.auberge-bavella.com; Col de Bavella, D268; mains €11-23, menu €24; ⊙noon-3pm & 7-9.30pm Apr-Oct), a rustic roadside inn near the summit. The central fireplace is particularly welcome on cooler spring and autumn days. Should you want to stay overnight, it has impeccable four- to eight-bed dorms with en-suite facilities (per person €20, with breakfast/half-board/full board €26/40/49).

Zonza & Around

The village of Zonza (pronounced 'tzonz') is the perfect base for exploring L'Alta Rocca, with a good range of restaurants and accommodation options. Another little charmer is the nearby village of **Quenza**, cradled by thickly wooded mountains and the Aiguilles de Bavella looming on the horizon.

Sleeping

Hameau de Cavanello B&B €
(☎04 95 78 66 82; www.locationzonza.com; Hameau de Cavanello, Zonza; s €72-87, d €79-94; ⊙May-mid-Oct; ❄📶🏊) For a rural setting, Hameau de Cavanello, 2km towards the Col de Bavella, has a handful of cosy rooms (equipped with fridges and TVs) and a pool nesting in hectares of green meadows and forests with magical views of the Aiguilles de Bavella.

Le Pré aux Biches CAMPGROUND €
(☎06 27 52 48 03; Zonza; d/tr/q yurt €50/60/80; ⊙May-Sep) Plump for a stylish Mongolian yurt between trees on an organic farm at Le Pré aux Biches. Each yurt has its own toilet and shower cubicle in the bathroom block; evening meals (€18) with products from the farm are available.

Chez Pierrot B&B €€
(☎04 95 78 63 21; www.gitechezpierrot.free.fr; Plateau de Ghjallicu, Quenza; dm/d incl half-board €45/120) If you're after a typically Corsican atmosphere and the most tranquil location imaginable, at an altitude of about 1200m, bookmark Chez Pierrot, southern Corsica's most idiosyncratic venture. This multifaceted place – *gîte*, B&B, restaurant and equestrian centre – is run by charismatic Pierrot, a local character who's been living here since his early childhood. It's on Plateau de Ghjallicu, about 5km uphill from Quenza.

Eating

A Stadda PIZZA, CORSICAN €
(☎04 95 25 45 33, 06 11 03 99 28; D268; pizzas €8.50-13, mains €17-20; ⊙noon-2pm & 7-10pm Apr-Oct) With its pair of oak-fired ovens always blazing, this roadside joint near Zonza's southern entrance specialises in pizzas, grilled meat and Corsican classics such as white-bean stew, lasagne with fresh ricotta-like *brocciu* cheese, or stuffed vegetables cooked *au feu de bois* (over the wood fire). In good weather, sit on the outdoor patio overlooking the fields of the attached farm.

Eternisula CAFE €
(☎04 95 27 44 71; www.facebook.com/leternisula; rte de Quenza, Zonza; sandwiches, soups & snacks €6-18.50; ⏰11am-10pm Tue-Sat, to 5pm Sun late Apr-Oct) For sustenance, drop by Eternisula, a gorgeous cafe-cum-gourmet shop. The brainchild of an Anglo-Corsican couple, it offers charcuterie and cheese platters, sandwiches, soups and a suggestion of the day, served in the pretty dining room or on the terrace.

Levie & Around

For culture vultures, Levie makes a great stop for its museum and the nearby archaeological sites.

About 7km north of Levie, **Pianu di Livia** (Site Archaéologique Cucuruzzu Capula; ☎04 95 78 48 21; adult/child €4/free; ⏰9.30am-7pm Jun-Sep, to 6pm Apr, May & Oct), comprises two archaeological sites, the *castelli* (fortified places made up of menhirs and boulders) of **Cucuruzzu** and **Capula**. Archaeologists believe they were erected during the Bronze Age, around 1200 BC. The *castelli* are located in a beautiful forest, with an easy 2.5km loop trail connecting the sites and information centre.

Multilingual interpretive booklets are available along with audioguides (€3) in English, German or Italian. The site is signposted off the D269 between Levie and Ste-Lucie de Tallano.

The well-organised **Musée de l'Alta Rocca** (☎04 85 78 00 78; www.cg-corsedusud.fr/patrimoine-et-culture/musee-de-levie; av Lieutenant de Peretti; adult/child €4/free; ⏰10am-5pm Tue-Sat Oct-May, to 6pm daily Jun-Sep) does a good job of elucidating Corsican geology, climate, flora and fauna. It also features ethnology and archaeology sections.

Sleeping

★**Auberge U n'Antru Versu** B&B €€
(☎04 95 78 31 47; www.aubergeunantruversu.com; San Gavinu di Carbrini; d €75-115, q €135-155, all incl breakfast; ⏰Mar-Dec; ❄📶) This unexpected family-run boutique B&B hides in a pretty village house in the hamlet of San Gavinu di Carbrini, between Levie and Zonza. The decor is absolutely exquisite, blending modern fittings, antique furniture and plenty of colourful soft furnishings. The downstairs restaurant (mains €15 to €20) serves French cuisine and delicious pizzas.

★**A Pignata** BOUTIQUE HOTEL €€€
(☎04 95 78 41 90; www.apignata.com; rte du Pianu; d €200-360, ste €280-400, all incl half-board; ⏰late Mar-Dec; ❄📶🏊) A family affair fronted by brothers Antoine and Jean-Baptiste, this boutique farmhouse with vegetable garden and herd of pigs (that end up as the most divine charcuterie) is pure class. Despite its rural setting, its 16 rooms and two family-friendly treehouse cabins perched on stilts are thoroughly contemporary, while its rustic restaurant (*menu* €48) is among Corsica's finest.

Shopping

Atelier du Lotus ARTS & CRAFTS
(☎04 95 74 05 13; www.u-lotus.com; ⏰9am-6pm daily Apr–mid-Nov, closed Sun mid-Nov–Mar) This workshop-cum-shop in the village, sells hand-forged traditional knives (from €100).

CORTE

POP 7500

Secretive. Inward looking. Staunchly Corsican. In many ways, the mountain town of Corte feels different from other Corsican cities. This is the heart and soul of Corsica. It has been at the centre of the island's fortunes since Pascal Paoli made it the capital of his short-lived Corsican republic in 1755, and it remains a nationalist stronghold. It is also Corsica's only university town, with a youthful energy that sets it apart. In summer it's a popular base for those eager to canyon, hike, rock climb and mountain bike in the nearby **Restonica** and **Tavignano** valleys.

Sights & Activities

Citadel HISTORIC SITE
(adult/child incl Museu di a Corsica €5.30/1.50; ⏰10am-5pm Tue-Sun Apr-Jun & Oct, to 7pm daily late Jun-late Sep, shorter hours in winter) Jutting out above the Tavignano and Restonica Rivers, and the cobbled alleyways of the **Haute Ville**, the citadel's oldest part is the **château** – known as the Nid d'Aigle, meaning 'Eagle's Nest' – built in 1419. The 19th-century barracks now houses the tourist office and the **Museu di a Corsica** (☎04 95 45 25 45; www.musee-corse.com; ⏰10am-6pm Tue-Sun Apr-Oct, to 8pm daily late Jun-late Sep, shorter hours in winter), a must-see for Corsica culture buffs.

Belvédère VIEWPOINT
FREE For stunning views of the city, the citadel and surrounding valleys without paying the citadel/museum admission charge, head to the *belvédère* (viewing platform) south of the citadel, reached via a signposted staircase just outside the ramparts.

Place Gaffory SQUARE

From the citadel, meander downhill to place Gaffory, a lively square lined with restaurants and cafes and dominated by the 15th-century **Église de l'Annonciation**. The walls of nearby houses are pock-marked with bullet holes, reputedly from Corsica's war of independence.

Cours Paoli STREET

A gentle wander along the main strip makes a pleasant prelude to an aperitif or a fine meal at one of the town's good restaurants. Start from place Paoli, Corte's focal point, which is dominated by a **statue of Pascal Paoli**, and stroll down the *cours*.

Sleeping & Eating

L'Albadu B&B €

(☎04 95 46 24 55; www.hebergement-albadu.fr; ancienne rte d'Ajaccio; d incl half-board per person €60, camping adult/tent/car €6/3/3) On the outskirts of Corte, the friendly owners of this horse farm offer a variety of accommodations – camping, dorms and double rooms – at bargain prices. Abundant *table d'hôte* dinners (included with half-board, €25 otherwise) come with appetiser, main course, cheese, dessert, aperitif, wine and coffee. Horseback excursions into the surrounding countryside are icing on the cake.

★**Osteria di l'Orta** B&B €€

(☎04 95 61 06 41; www.osteria-di-l-orta.com; av du Pont de l'Orta; d €100, ste €130-180; ❄@🛜🏊) Inside a powder-blue town house on the edge of town, this peach of a B&B is run by a charming couple, Marina and Antoine. The three rooms and two suites (named after local notables) are lovely, with polished wood floors, gleaming walls and great showers. The guest kitchen, dining room and DVD lounge are a real bonus.

The Guelfucci family also farm the surrounding land, and Marina is a mean cook, so make sure you treat yourself to a delicious (and copious) dinner (€25 to €35) of Corsican specialities with products from the farm. The family started making their own aperitifs and wine in 2015, and is expanding their agricultural endeavours again in 2017 with a brand new roof garden.

Hôtel Duc de Padoue HOTEL €€

(☎04 95 46 01 37; www.ducdepadoue.com; 2 place Padoue; s €92-102, d €92-123, tr €125-135, q €140-150; ❄🛜) The Duc de Padoue may lack soul, but compensates with a central location, charming staff and rooms that are comfortable, clean and well equipped.

La Rivière des Vins BISTRO €

(☎04 95 46 37 04; 5 rampe Ste-Croix; mains €10-19, menus €12-19; ⏲noon-2pm & 7-10.30pm Mon-Fri, 7-10.30pm Sat; 🖉) Diners flock to this fab bistro on a side terrace off Corte's main street for the relaxed atmosphere, unbeatable value and tasty food – the *patatines* (roasted potatoes) are to die for, as are the *brochettes* (skewered meat) cooked in the fireplace. The copious salads and omelettes will have vegetarians crying for joy. Excellent selection of wines (including by the glass/jug).

Le 24 TAPAS €

(☎04 95 46 02 90; 24 cours Paoli; tapas €10-17; ⏲noon-2.30pm & 7-11pm Mon-Sat) Rustic stone walls and contemporary decor come together at this ever-popular, newly remodeled wine bar on the main drag. There's an innovative menu of tapas made with top-quality, seasonally changing ingredients, and an excellent selection of Corsican wines.

Café Le Bip's CORSICAN €€

(☎04 95 46 06 26; 14 cours Paoli; mains €12-28) Want to know where students from Corsica's only university go when they fancy going out for dinner? To this old stone candlelit cellar, famed across town for its gargantuan portions of traditional Corsican fare. Find it on the vast square behind cours Paoli. In winter, by the fireplace is the place to be.

Drinking & Nightlife

Thanks to Corte's student population, there's a lively bar scene along cours Paoli.

La Vieille Cave WINE BAR

(☎04 95 46 33 79; 2 ruelle de la Fontaine; ⏲11am-7pm, later if it's busy) Sit round a barrel on a low stool in this jewel of a wine cellar and let the formidable Emmanuel Simonini guide you through the innumerable vintages on offer – to sip right there and then with a charcuterie platter or take home as a souvenir.

Le Cyrnéa BAR

(www.facebook.com/ACyrnea; rue Prof Santiaggi; ⏲11am-1am) This archetypal village bar is where students and oldies alike gather over pastis (aniseed-flavoured aperitif), myrtle liqueur, and cheap wine and beer. No points for decor (neon lighting and formica tables) but plenty for atmosphere and the spacious patio out back.

LOCAL KNOWLEDGE

LONG-DISTANCE TRAIL TASTER

Corsica's long-distance trails, especially the north–south, two-week GR20, are legendary. But fitting two weeks of walking into a holiday may not be possible (or desirable!) for everyone. Spending a night in a *refuge* (mountain hut) is a great experience, however, and **Refuge A Sega** (☎09 88 99 35 57, 06 10 71 77 26; www.parc-corse.org; dm €14; ⊙Jun-Sep) is a great option to get a taste of the hiker's life and to combine two of central Corsica's most scenic valleys in one easy, two-day itinerary.

Day one is a five-hour walk from Corte up the stunning Vallée du Tavignano, following the orange waymarks for Corsica's famous cross-island Mare a Mare itinerary. You can break for a picnic at the Passerelle de Rossolino. Upon arriving at the *refuge* (spaces must be booked in advance online), take a dip in the natural pools nearby before enjoying a three-course home-cooked Corsican dinner.

After breakfast on day two, head east to the Bergeries d'Alzu (sheepfold, two hours), before heading down to the Vallée de la Restonica (one hour) and then back to Corte along the scenic D623 (two hours).

Café du Cours CAFE
(22 cours Paoli; ⊙7am-10pm) This unfussy cafe is a great place to watch the world go by.

Information

Tourist Office (☎04 95 46 26 70; www.centru-corsica.com; Citadel; ⊙9am-6pm daily Jul–mid-Sep, shorter hours rest of year)

Getting There & Away

Five daily trains (three on Sunday) serve Bastia (€10.10, 1¾ hours) and Ajaccio (€11.50, two hours).

AROUND CORTE

The spectacular mountains and valleys surrounding Corte are a paradise for outdoors enthusiasts. Prime destinations include the Tavignano and Restonica river valleys and the mountain town of Vizzavona, all easily accessible as day trips from Corte.

Vallée de la Restonica

Just south of Corte's city limits, the Vallée de la Restonica is one of the prettiest spots in all of Corsica. The river, rising in the grey-green mountains, has scoured little basins in the rock, offering sheltered pinewood settings for bathing and sunbathing. From Corte, the D623 winds its way through the valley for 15km to the Bergeries de Grotelle (1375m), where a car park (€5) and a huddle of shepherds' huts (three of which offer drinks, local cheeses and snacks) marks the end of the road. From them, a path leads to a pair of picture-pretty glacial lakes, Lac de Melu (1711m), reached after about one hour, and Lac de Capitellu (1930m), 45 minutes' walk further on. Depending on snowfall, the first lake can usually be reached from April to October, the second from May onwards. Always check the weather with the tourist office before setting off.

Vallée du Tavignano

If you have a day to spare, don't miss the opportunity to hike into this deliciously peaceful, car-free wonderland. Corsica's deepest gorge is only accessible on foot and remains well off the beaten track, despite being on Corte's doorstep. From Corte, the signposted track leads to the Passerelle de Rossolino footbridge, reached after about 2½ hours. It's an idyllic spot for a picnic, and there are plenty of transparent green natural pools in which you can dunk yourself. The valley can also be explored on horseback with the outdoorsy folks behind the lovely B&B and camping *à la ferme*, L'Albadu (p899).

Vizzavona

South of Corte, the N193 climbs steeply in the shadow of Monte d'Oro (2389m) before arriving at the cool mountain hamlet of Vizzavona. A mere cluster of houses around a train station, Vizzavona is an ideal base from which to explore the Forêt de Vizzavona, where the 1633 hectares are covered mainly by beech and laricio pines. A magnet for walkers, it features lots of excellent hikes. Look for the signpost indicating a short, gentle path that meanders down through a superb forest to **Cascades des Anglais**, a sequence of gleaming waterfalls.

Understand France

France Today

France has not escaped economic crisis, terrorism and the unexpected rise of the far right in Europe. But this ancient country of Gallic pride and tradition has weathered greater storms and it's far from sunk. Wine tourism is on the up, politicians have redrawn the local-government map and across the board, French people are turning to grass-roots culture and gastronomy for strength and inspiration.

Best on Film

La Môme (La Vie en Rose; 2007) Story of singer Edith Piaf starring French actress Marion Cotillard.

Coco Avant Chanel (Coco Before Chanel; 2009) Compelling life story of orphan turned fashion designer Coco Chanel, with Audrey Tautou.

Hugo (2011) Martin Scorsese's Oscar-winning children's film pays tribute to Parisian film pioneer Georges Méliès through the adventure of an orphan boy in the 1930s who tends clocks at a Paris train station.

Marseille (2016) Comedy about just that, starring French-Algerian actor and film-maker Kad Merad.

Best in Print

Paris (Edward Rutherford; 2013) Eight centuries of Parisian history.

A Moveable Feast (Ernest Hemingway; 1964) Beautiful evocation of 1920s Paris.

The Hundred Foot Journey (Richard C Morais; 2010) Culinary warfare between two restaurant owners: a boy from Mumbai and a famous chef!

The Fruits of the Land

French wine growers are riding high. In 2015 fabled vineyards in the ancient wine-growing regions of Champagne and Burgundy were inscribed on the Unesco World Heritage list as extraordinary world treasures – think exceptional scenery, unique know-how shared between generations and a remarkable cultural heritage. And with the French more passionate than ever about their *terroir* (land) and the fruits it bears, it is with a celebratory pop of corks that *viticulteurs* (wine growers) in Champagne prepare to plant new vines in 40 new Champagne-producing villages in 2017: such is the growing global demand for the prestigious bubbly that Champagne has been given the official go-ahead to expand its production area for the first time since 1927.

Developments in the urban wine world are equally exciting – and a gentle reminder of just how intrinsic wine culture is to contemporary life in France. In the city of Bordeaux in southwest France, the fabulously flamboyant and sassy, €81 million La Cité du Vin opened to much fanfare in 2016, its mission: to explore the global world of wine, its history, geography, culture, myths, rites, artistic expression and technical nous included. Avignon's new Le Carré du Palais does the same for Provence's fabled Côtes du Rhône and Vallée du Rhône appellations, albeit not on quite the same ambitious scale. In the vine-laced countryside around Bordeaux meanwhile, world-class architects are designing state-of-the-art wine cellars, cooking schools and urban-chic dining spaces for ancient châteaux whose daily existence has, for centuries, been charted by the seasons and languid rhythm of nature. Wine tourism in France is the new gold.

A Shift to the Right

As the country gears up for presidential elections in May 2017, all eyes are on the increasingly powerful Front National (FN; National Front), known for its fervent

anti-immigrant stance. In 2014 municipal elections, the far-right party led by Marine Le Pen won 7% of votes, trumping the ruling left-centre Socialists in several towns. In European elections a month later the FN won a quarter of votes, ahead of the main opposition party UMP (21%) and governing left-wing Socialists (14%). Prime Minister Manuel Valls was reported in the press as describing the victory as a political 'earthquake'. The ultimate humiliation came during parliamentary elections a few months later: the FN won its first ever two seats in the French Senate and the Socialists lost majority control of the Upper Chamber.

French president François Hollande's popularity hovers at a record all-time low. The Socialists and its allies managed to keep the FN at bay in 2015 regional elections, but it's clear that Marine Le Pen and the FN has one goal in mind: the Élysée Palace.

Terrible Times

On 7 January 2015, the Paris offices of newspaper *Charlie Hebdo* were attacked in response to satirical images it had published of the prophet Muhammad. Eleven staff and one police officer were killed and a further 22 people injured. #JeSuisCharlie ('I am Charlie') became a worldwide slogan of support. Worse followed. On 13 November 2015 terrorist attacks occurred in Paris and St-Denis. During a football match watched by 80,000 spectators, three explosions were heard outside the stadium. Soon after, gunmen fired on customers drinking on pavement terraces outside several cafes and restaurants in Paris' 10e and 11e *arrondissements*. At 9.40pm three gunmen stormed concert hall Le Bataclan and fired into the audience. In all that evening 130 people lost their lives and 368 were injured. Months later, during festive Bastille Day celebrations in Nice on 14 July 2016, a lorry ploughed at high speed through crowds watching fireworks on Promenade des Anglais. The driver subsequently got out and started shooting into the crowd before being shot himself by police. Death toll: +80.

Tossed But Not Sunk

Fluctuat nec mergitur (tossed but not sunk) has been the motto of the French capital since 1853 when Baron Haussmann etched it for eternity onto the city coat of arms. And since the fatal terrorist attacks on Paris in November 2015, it has become the rallying cry of French people countrywide who stand in complete solidarity with Parisians; who tenaciously cling more than ever to their grass-roots culture that sees the French shop for food at the weekly market and chit-chat in all weathers over coffee or an *apéro* on cafe pavement terraces. Little wonder that a love for local, seasonal and organic – *'locavore'* is the new buzz word in French foodie circles – is taking off at such a terrific pace.

POPULATION: **64.4 MILLION**

AREA: **551,000 SQ KM**

GDP: **€2183 BILLION**

INFLATION: **0.9%**

UNEMPLOYMENT: **10.4%**

if France were 100 people

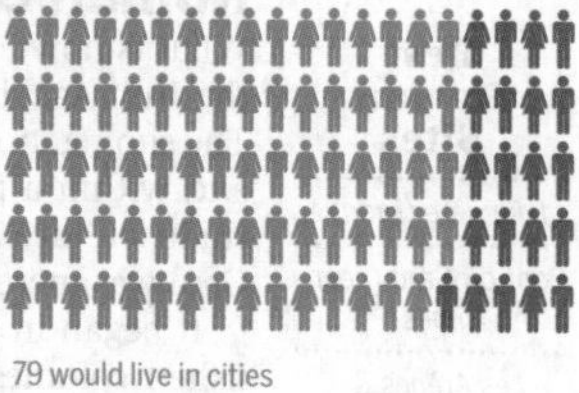

79 would live in cities
21 would live in rural areas

belief systems

(% of population)

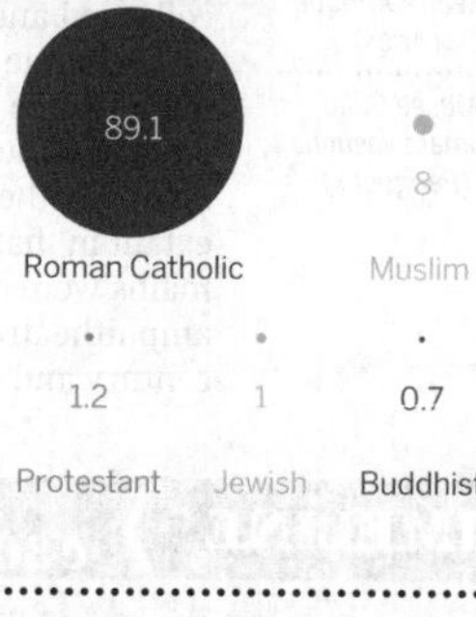

population per sq km

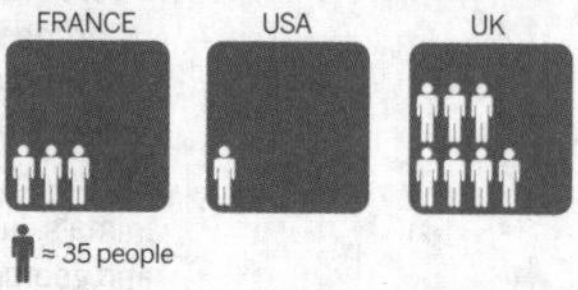

History

The history of France mirrors that of much of Europe. Its beginnings saw the mass migration of the nomadic Celts, the subjugation by the Romans, and their civilising influence, and the rise of a local nobility. Christianity brought a degree of unity, but nowhere else would such a strongly independent church continue to coexist under a powerful central authority (think Charles 'The Hammer' Martel or Louis XIV's claim to be the state itself). This is the essence of France's story.

Roman Gaul

Best Roman Sites

- *Fourvière (Lyon)*
- *Pont du Gard (near Nîmes)*
- *Les Arènes & Maison Carrée (Nîmes)*
- *Musée Gallo-Romain & Théâtre Romain (Vienne)*
- *Théâtre Antique (Orange)*
- *Théâtre Antique (Arles)*
- *Musée Gallo-Romain Vesunna (Périgueux)*

What is now France was settled by several different groups of people in the Iron Age, but the largest and most organised were the Celtic Gauls. The subjugation of these people and their territory by Rome was gradual, and within a few centuries Rome had imposed its government, roads, trade, culture and even language. A Gallo-Roman culture emerged and Gaul was increasingly integrated into the Roman Empire.

It began in the 1st millennium BC as the Greeks and Romans established colonies on the Mediterranean coast, including Massilia (Marseille). Centuries of conflict between the Gauls and the Romans ended in 52 BC when Julius Caesar's legions crushed a revolt by many Gallic tribes led by Celtic Arverni tribe chief Vercingétorix at Gergovia, near present-day Clermont-Ferrand – no site better evokes the drama and bloodshed of this momentous point in history than the MuséoParc Alésia in Burgundy. For the next couple of years, during the Gallic Wars, the Gauls hounded the Romans with guerrilla warfare and fought them in several match-drawn pitched battles. But gradually Gallic resistance collapsed and the Romans reigned supreme.

The stone architecture left by the occupiers was impressive and Roman France is magnificent, climaxing with the mighty Pont du Gard aqueduct, built to bring water to the city of Nîmes in southern France. Splendid theatres and amphitheatres dating from this period are still extant in that city as well as at Autun, Arles and Orange. Some Roman remains were reused: in an early form of recycling, the 1st-century Roman amphitheatre at Périgueux in the Dordogne was dismantled in the 3rd century and its stones used to build the city walls.

TIMELINE

c 30,000 BC

During the middle Palaeolithic period, Cro-Magnon people start decorating their homes in the Vézère Valley of the Dordogne with colourful scenes of animals, human figures and geometric shapes.

c 7000 BC

Neolithic people turn their hands to monumental menhirs and dolmen during the New Stone Age, creating a fine collection in Brittany that continues to baffle historians.

1500–500 BC

Celtic Gauls move into the region and establish trading links with the Greeks, whose colonies included Massilia (Marseille) on the Mediterranean coast; the latter bring grapes and olives.

PRIMITIVE ART

The Cro-Magnons, a *Homo sapiens* variety who arrived in what is now France about 35,000 years ago, had larger brains than their ancestors, the Neanderthals, long and narrow skulls, and short, wide faces. Their hands were nimble, and with the aid of improved tools they hunted reindeer, bison, horses and mammoths to eat. They played music, danced and had fairly complex social patterns.

Those agile hands were not just used to make tools and hunt; Cro-Magnons were also artists. A tour of Grotte de Lascaux – a replica of the real Lascaux cave in which one of the world's best examples of Cro-Magnon drawings was found in 1940 – demonstrates how initial simplistic drawings and engravings of animals gradually became more detailed and realistic. Dubbed 'Périgord's Sistine Chapel', the Lascaux cave contains some 2000 paintings of human figures and abstract signs, as well as animals, and is one of 25 known decorated caves in Dordogne's Vézère Valley.

The Neolithic period produced France's incredible collection of menhirs and dolmens: Brittany's Morbihan Coast is awash in megalithic monuments.

Sophisticated urban centres with markets and baths of hot and cold running water began to emerge. The Romans planted vineyards, notably in Burgundy and Bordeaux; introduced techniques to process wine; and introduced the newfangled faith of Christianity.

Later the Franks would adopt these important elements of Gallo-Roman civilisation (including Christianity), and their eventual assimilation resulted in a fusion of Germanic culture with that of the Celts and the Romans.

Medieval Agony & Ecstasy

When the Roman Empire collapsed, the gates to a wave of Franks and other Germanic tribes under Merovius opened to the north and northeast. Merovius' grandson, Clovis I, converted to Christianity, giving him greater legitimacy and power over his Christian subjects, and made Paris his seat; his successors founded the abbey of St-Germain des Prés in Paris and later the one at St-Denis to the north, which would become the richest, most important monastery in France and the final resting place of its kings.

No single museum evokes medieval France more beautifully than Paris' Musée National du Moyen Age, aptly located in the capital's finest civil medieval building, the 15th-century Hôtel Cluny.

The Frankish tradition, by which the king was succeeded by all of his sons, led to power struggles and the eventual disintegration of the kingdom into a collection of small feudal states. The dominant house to emerge was that of the Carolingians.

Carolingian power reached apogee under Charlemagne, who extended the boundaries of the kingdom and was crowned Holy Roman Emperor (Emperor of the West) in AD 800. But during the 9th century Scandinavian Vikings (also called Norsemen, thus Normans) raided France's west-

3rd century BC
The Celtic Parisii tribe builds a handful of wattle-and-daub huts on what is now the Île de la Cité in Paris; the capital city is christened Lutetia by the Romans.

121 BC
The Romans begin taking Gallic territory, annexing southern Gaul as the province of Gallia Narbonensis, with its capital at the present-day town of Narbonne.

55–52 BC
Julius Caesar launches his invasion of Britain from the Côte d'Opale in far northern France; the Gauls defeat the Romans at Gergovia near present-day Clermont-Ferrand.

AD 100–300
The Romans go on a building spree throughout France, erecting magnificent baths, temples and aqueducts of almighty proportions such as the Pont du Gard near Nîmes in southern France.

ern coast, settling in the lower Seine Valley and later forming the duchy of Normandy. This would be a century of disunity in France, marked politically by the rise of Norman power and religiously by the foundation of influential abbeys such as the Benedictine one at Cluny. By the time Hugh Capet ascended the throne in 987, the king's domain was a humble parcel of land around Paris and Orléans.

The tale of how William the Conqueror and his forces mounted a successful invasion of England from their base in Normandy in 1066 is told on the Bayeux Tapestry, showcased inside Bayeux' Musée de la Tapisserie de Bayeux. In 1152 Eleanor of Aquitaine wed Henry of Anjou, bringing a further third of France under the control of the English crown. The subsequent rivalry between France and England for control of Aquitaine and the vast English territories in France lasted three centuries.

Best Walled Towns

- *Carcassonne*
- *Avignon*
- *St-Malo*
- *Domme (Dordogne)*
- *Uzerche (Limousin)*

Hundred Years War

In 1337 hostility between Capetians and Anglo-Normans degenerated into the Hundred Years War, fought on and off until the middle of the 15th century. The Black Death, which broke out a decade after the hostilities began and lasted more than two years, killed more than a third (an estimated 80,000 souls) of Paris' population alone.

The French suffered particularly nasty defeats at Crécy and Agincourt. Abbey-studded Mont St-Michel in present-day Normandy was the only place in northern and western France not to fall into English hands. The dukes of Burgundy (allied with the English) occupied Paris and in 1422 John Plantagenet, duke of Bedford, was made regent of France for England's King Henry VI, then an infant. Less than a decade later Henry was crowned king of France.

Luckily for the French, 17-year-old Jeanne d'Arc (Joan of Arc) came along with the outlandish tale that she had a divine mission from God to expel the English from France and bring about the coronation of French Charles VII in Reims.

The Rise of the French Court

With the arrival of Italian Renaissance culture during the reign of François I (r 1515–47), the focus of French attention became the Loire Valley. Italian artists decorated royal castles at Amboise, Azay-le-Rideau, Blois, Chambord and Chaumont.

Renaissance ideas of scientific and geographic scholarship and discovery assumed a new importance, as did the value of secular matters over religious life. Writers such as Rabelais, Marot and Ronsard of La Pléiade were influential, as were artist and architect disciples of Michelangelo and Raphael. Evidence of this architectural influence can be seen in François I's château at Fontainebleau – where superb artisans, many

c 455–70

France remains under Roman rule until the 5th century, when the Franks (hence the name 'France') and the Alemanii invade and overrun the country from the east.

732

Somewhere near Poitiers, Charles Martel and his cavalry repel the Muslim Moors. His grandson, Charlemagne, extends the boundaries of the kingdom and is crowned Holy Roman Emperor.

800–900

Scandinavian Vikings (also called Norsemen, thus Normans) raid France's western coast and settle in the lower Seine Valley where they later form the Duchy of Normandy.

987

Five centuries of Merovingian and Carolingian rule ends with the crowning of Hugh Capet; a dynasty that will rule one of Europe's most powerful countries for the next eight centuries is born.

of them brought over from Italy, blended Italian and French styles to create the First School of Fontainebleau – and the Petit Château at Chantilly, both near Paris. This new architecture reflected the splendour of the monarchy, which was fast moving towards absolutism. But all this grandeur and show of strength was not enough to stem the tide of Protestantism that was flowing into France.

The Reformation swept through Europe in the 1530s, spearheaded by the ideas of Jean (John) Calvin, a Frenchman born in Picardy but exiled to Geneva. Following the Edict of January 1562, which afforded the Protestants certain rights, the Wars of Religion broke out between the Huguenots (French Protestants who received help from the English), the Catholic League (led by the House of Guise) and the Catholic monarchy, and lasted three dozen years.

Henri IV, founder of the Bourbon dynasty, issued the controversial Edict of Nantes in 1598, guaranteeing the Huguenots civil and political

THE VIRGIN WARRIOR

Many stories surround the origins of Jeanne d'Arc (Joan of Arc), the virgin warrior burned at the stake by the English, and France's patron saint. Some say she was the bastard child of Louis d'Orléans, King Charles VI's brother. The more accurate account pinpoints Domrémy in northeastern France (Domrémy-la-Pucelle today) as the place where she was born to a peasant family in 1412.

Revelations delivered by the Archangel Michael prompted Jeanne d'Arc to flee the fold in 1428. Her mission: to raise a siege against the city of Orléans and see the future Charles VII crowned king of France. An enquiry conducted by clergy and university clerks in Poitiers tried to establish if Jeanne d'Arc was a fraud or a gift, as she claimed, from the king of Heaven to the king of France. Her virginity was likewise certified. Following the six-week interrogation Jeanne was sent by Charles VII to Tours, where she was equipped with intendants, a horse, a sword and her own standard featuring God sitting in judgement on a cloud. In Blois the divine warrior collected her army, drummed up by Charles VII from his Royal Army Headquarters there. In April 1429, Jeanne d'Arc started her attack on Orléans, besieged by the English from October of the previous year. On 5 and 6 May the French gained control of Bastille St-Loup and Bastille des Augustins, followed the next day by Fort des Tourelles – a fort guarding the only access to the city from the left bank. This last shattering defeat prompted the English to lay down the siege on 8 May and was a decisive turning point in the Hundred Years War.

From Orléans Jeanne d'Arc went on to defeat the English at Jargeau, Beaugency and Patay. Despite Charles' promised coronation in July 1429, battles between the English and the French waged until 1453, by which time the virginal warrior responsible for turning the war around was dead: Jeanne d'Arc was captured by the Burgundians, sold to the English, convicted of witchcraft and heresy in Rouen in 1431 and burned at the stake. She was canonised in 1920.

1066

Duke of Normandy William the Conqueror and his Norman forces occupy England, making Normandy and, later, Plantagenet-ruled England formidable rivals of the kingdom of France.

1095

Pope Urban II preaches the First Crusade in Clermont-Ferrand, prompting France to take a leading role and giving rise to some splendid cathedrals, including those at Reims, Strasbourg and Metz.

1152

Eleanor of Aquitaine weds Henry of Anjou, bringing a further third of France under the control of the English crown and sparking a French–English rivalry that will last three centuries.

1163

Two centuries of nonstop building in the capital reaches its zenith with the start of Notre Dame Cathedral under Maurice de Sully, the bishop of Paris; construction continues for 150-odd years.

rights, notably freedom of conscience. Ultra-Catholic Paris refused to allow the new Protestant king to enter the city, and a siege of the capital continued for almost five years. Only when Henri IV embraced Catholicism at the cathedral in St-Denis did the capital submit to him.

France's most famous king of this or any other century, Louis XIV (r 1643–1715), called Le Roi Soleil (the Sun King), ascended the throne at the tender age of five. Bolstered by claims of divine right, he involved the kingdom in a series of costly wars with Holland, Austria and England, which gained France territory but nearly bankrupted the treasury. State taxation to refill the coffers caused widespread poverty and vagrancy. In Versailles, Louis XIV built an extravagant palace and made his courtiers compete with each other for royal favour, thereby quashing the ambitious, feuding aristocracy and creating the first centralised French state. In 1685 he revoked the Edict of Nantes.

The Seven Years War (1756–63) was one of a series of ruinous military engagements pursued by Louis XV, the Sun King's grandson. It led to the loss of France's flourishing colonies in Canada, the West Indies and India. It was in part to avenge these losses that his successor Louis XVI sided with the colonists in the American War of Independence a dozen years later. But the Seven Years War cost France a fortune and, more disastrously for the monarchy, it helped to disseminate at home the radical democratic ideas that were thrust upon the world stage by the American Revolution.

Revolution to Republic

Paris Revolution Encounters

- *Jeu de Paume*
- *Place de Bastille*
- *Hôtel des Invalides*
- *Place de la Concorde*
- *Conciergerie*

At the beginning of the 18th century, new economic and social circumstances began to render the *ancien régime* (old order) dangerously out of step with the needs of the country. The regime was further weakened by the anti-establishment and anticlerical ideas of the Enlightenment, whose leading lights included Voltaire, Rousseau and Diderot. But entrenched vested interests, a cumbersome power structure and royal lassitude prevented change from starting until the 1770s, by which time the monarchy's moment had passed.

By the late 1780s, the indecisive Louis XVI and his dominating consort, Marie Antoinette, had managed to alienate virtually every segment of society, and the king became increasingly isolated as unrest and dissatisfaction reached boiling point. When he tried to neutralise the power of the more reform-minded delegates at a meeting of the États-Généraux (States-General) in Versailles in May and June 1789, the masses took to the streets of Paris. On 14 July, a mob raided the armoury at the Hôtel des Invalides for rifles, seizing 32,000 muskets, then stormed the prison at Bastille – the ultimate symbol of the despotic *ancien régime*. The French Revolution had begun.

1309

French-born pope Clément V moves papal headquarters from Rome to Avignon, where the Holy Seat remains until 1377; 'home' is the resplendent Palais des Papes built under Benoît XII.

1337

Incessant struggles between the Capetians and England's King Edward III, a Plantagenet, over the powerful French throne degenerate into the Hundred Years War, which will last until 1453.

1358

The war between France and England and the devastation and poverty caused by the plague lead to the ill-fated peasants' revolt led by Étienne Marcel.

1422

John Plantagenet, duke of Bedford, is made regent of France for England's King Henry VI, then an infant; in less than a decade Henry is crowned king of France at Paris' Notre Dame.

A DATE WITH THE REVOLUTION

Along with standardising France's system of weights and measures with the now almost universal metric system, the revolutionary government adopted a new, 'more rational' calendar from which all 'superstitious' associations (ie saints' days and mythology) were removed. Year 1 began on 22 September 1792, the day the First Republic was proclaimed.

The names of the 12 months – Vendémaire, Brumaire, Frimaire, Nivôse, Pluviôse, Ventôse, Germinal, Floréal, Prairial, Messidor, Thermidor and Fructidor – were chosen according to the seasons. The autumn months, for instance, were Vendémaire (derived from *vendange*, grape harvest), Brumaire (from *brume*, mist or fog) and Frimaire (from *frimas*, wintry weather). In turn, each month was divided into three 10-day 'weeks' called *décades*, the last day of which was a rest day. The five remaining days of the year were used to celebrate Virtue, Genius, Labour, Opinion and Rewards. These festivals were initially called *sans-culottides* in honour of the *sans-culottes*, the extreme revolutionaries who wore pantaloons rather than the short breeches favoured by the upper classes.

While the republican calendar worked well in theory, it caused no end of confusion for France in its communications and trade abroad because the months and days kept changing in relation to those of the Gregorian calendar. The revolutionary calendar was abandoned and the old system restored in 1806 by Napoléon Bonaparte.

At first, the Revolution was in the hands of moderate republicans called the Girondins. France was declared a constitutional monarchy and various reforms were introduced, including the adoption of the Déclaration des Droits de l'Homme et du Citoyen (Declaration of the Rights of Man and of the Citizen) modelled on the American Declaration of Independence. But as the masses armed themselves against the external threat to the new government – posed by Austria, Prussia and the exiled French nobles – patriotism and nationalism mixed with extreme fervour, popularising and radicalising the Revolution. It was not long before the Girondins lost out to the extremist Jacobins, who abolished the monarchy and declared the First Republic after Louis XVI proved unreliable as a constitutional monarch. The Assemblée Nationale (National Assembly) was replaced by an elected Revolutionary Convention.

In January 1793, Louis XVI was convicted of 'conspiring against the liberty of the nation' and guillotined on place de la Révolution, today's place de la Concorde, in Paris. Two months later the Jacobins set up the Committee of Public Safety to deal with national defence and to apprehend and try 'traitors'. This body had dictatorial control over the country during the so-called Reign of Terror (September 1793 to July 1794), which saw religious freedoms revoked and churches desecrated, cathedrals

1431

Jeanne d'Arc (Joan of Arc) is burned at the stake in Rouen for heresy; the English are not driven out of France until 1453.

1515

With the reign of François I the royal court moves to the Loire Valley, where a rash of stunning Renaissance châteaux and hunting lodges is built.

1530s

The Reformation, spurred by the writings of French Jean (John) Calvin, sweeps through France, pitting Catholics against Protestants and eventually leading to the Wars of Religion (1562–98).

1572

Some 3000 Huguenots visiting Paris to celebrate the wedding of the Protestant Henri of Navarre (the future Henri IV) are slaughtered on 23–24 August, in the so-called St Bartholomew's Day Massacre.

turned into 'Temples of Reason', and thousands incarcerated in dungeons in Paris' Conciergerie on Île de la Cité before being beheaded.

After the Reign of Terror faded, a five-man delegation of moderate republicans set itself up to rule the republic as the Directoire (Directory).

Napoléon & Empire

Under Napoléon, France enjoyed significant economic growth. Paris was transformed under urban planner Baron Haussmann (1809–91), who created the 12 huge boulevards radiating from the Arc de Triomphe. Napoléon III threw glittering parties at the royal palace in Compiègne, and breathed in fashionable sea air at Biarritz and Deauville.

It was true happenstance that brought dashing young Corsican general Napoléon Bonaparte to the attention of France. In October 1795 a group of royalist youths bent on overthrowing the Directoire were intercepted on rue St-Honoré in Paris by forces under Bonaparte, who fired into the crowd. For this 'whiff of grapeshot' he was put in command of the French forces in Italy, where he was particularly successful in the campaign against Austria.

In 1799 Napoléon overthrew the Directoire and assumed power as First Consul, chosen by popular vote. A referendum three years later declared him 'Consul for Life' and his birthday became a national holiday. In 1804, when he crowned himself 'Emperor of the French' in the presence of Pope Pius VII at Notre Dame in Paris, the scope of Napoléon's ambitions were obvious to all.

To legitimise his authority, Napoléon needed more battlefield victories. So began a series of wars and victories by which France would come to control most of Europe. In 1812 his troops captured Moscow, only to be killed off by the Russian winter. Two years later Allied armies entered Paris, exiled Napoléon to Elba in the Mediterranean and restored the House of Bourbon to the French throne at the Congress of Vienna.

In early 1815 Napoléon escaped Elba, landed in southern France and gathered a large army as he marched towards Paris. On 1 June he reclaimed the throne. But his reign ended just three weeks later when his forces were defeated at Waterloo in Belgium. Napoléon was exiled again, this time to St Helena in the South Atlantic, where he died in 1821. In 1840 his remains were moved to the Hôtel des Invalides in Paris.

Although reactionary in some ways – he re-established slavery in France's colonies in 1802, for example – Napoléon instituted a number of important reforms, including a reorganisation of the judicial system; the promulgation of a new legal code, the Code Napoléon (or civil code), which forms the basis of the French legal system to this day; and the establishment of a new education system. More importantly, he preserved the essence of the changes brought about by the Revolution.

A struggle between extreme monarchists seeking a return to the *ancien régime,* people who saw the changes wrought by the Revolution as irreversible, and the radicals of the poor working-class neighbourhoods of Paris dominated the reign of Louis XVIII (r 1815–24). His successor Charles X responded to the conflict with ineptitude and was overthrown

1588

The Catholic League forces Henri III (r 1574–89), the last of the Valois kings, to flee the royal court at the Louvre; the next year he is assassinated by a fanatical Dominican friar.

1589

Henri IV, the first Bourbon king, ascends the throne after renouncing Protestantism; *'Paris vaut bien une messe'* (Paris is well worth a Mass), he is reputed to have said upon taking communion.

1598

Henri IV gives French Protestants freedom of conscience with the Edict of Nantes – much to the horror of staunchly Catholic Paris, where many refuse to acknowledge the forward-thinking document.

1635

Cardinal Richelieu, de-facto ruler during the reign of Henri IV's son, Louis XIII, founds the Académie Française, the first and best known of France's five institutes of arts and sciences.

THE KINDEST CUT

Hanging, then drawing and quartering – roping the victim's limbs to four oxen, which then ran in four different directions – was once the favoured method of publicly executing commoners. In a bid to make public executions more humane, French physician Joseph Ignace Guillotin (1738–1814) came up with the guillotine.

Several tests on dead bodies down the line, highwayman Nicolas Jacques Pelletie was the first in France to have his head sliced off by the 2m-odd falling blade on 25 April 1792 on place de Grève (today's place de l'Hôtel de Ville) in Paris. During the Reign of Terror, at least 17,000 met their death by guillotine.

By the time the last person in France to be guillotined (murderer Hamida Djandoubi in Marseille) was given the chop in 1977 (behind closed doors – the last public execution was in 1939), the lethal contraption had been sufficiently refined to slice off a head in 2/100 of a second. A real McCoy guillotine is displayed in the Galerie de la Méditerraneé of Marseille's MuCEM.

France abolished capital punishment in 1981.

in the so-called July Revolution of 1830. Those who were killed in the accompanying Paris street battles are buried in vaults under the Colonne de Juillet in the centre of place de la Bastille. Louis-Philippe, a constitutional monarch of bourgeois sympathies who followed him, was subsequently chosen as ruler by parliament, only to be ousted by the 1848 Revolution.

The Second Republic was established and elections brought in Napoléon's inept nephew, the German-reared (and accented) Louis Napoléon Bonaparte, as president. In 1851 he staged a coup d'état and proclaimed himself Emperor Napoléon III of the Second Empire, which lasted until 1870.

Like his uncle before him, Napoléon III embroiled France in a number of costly conflicts, including the disastrous Crimean War (1854–56). In 1870, Otto von Bismarck goaded Napoléon III into declaring war on Prussia. Within months the thoroughly unprepared French army was defeated and the emperor had been taken prisoner.

The Belle Époque

Though it ushered in the glittering belle époque (beautiful age), there was little else attractive about the start of the Third Republic. Born as a provisional government of national defence in September 1870, it was quickly besieged by the Prussians, who laid siege to Paris and demanded National Assembly elections be held. The first move made by the resultant monarchist-controlled assembly was to ratify the Treaty of Frankfurt. The terms of the treaty – a huge war indemnity and surrender of the

1643

The Roi Soleil (Sun King), Louis XIV, all of five years old, assumes the French throne. In 1682 he moves his court – lock, stock and satin slipper – from Paris' Palais des Tuileries to Versailles.

1756–63

The Seven Years War against Britain and Prussia sees Louis XV engage in several ruinous wars resulting in the loss of France's colonies in Canada, the West Indies and India.

1789

The French Revolution begins when a mob arms itself with weapons taken from the Hôtel des Invalides and storms the prison at Bastille, freeing a total of just seven prisoners.

1793

Louis XVI is tried and convicted as citizen 'Louis Capet' (as all kings since Hugh Capet were declared to have ruled illegally) and executed; Marie Antoinette's turn comes nine months later.

Paris in the 1920s and '30s was a centre of the avant-garde, with painters pushing into new fields of art such as cubism and surrealism, Le Corbusier rewriting the architecture textbook, foreign writers such as Ernest Hemingway drawn by the city's liberal atmosphere (and cheap booze), and nightlife establishing a cutting-edge reputation.

provinces of Alsace and Lorraine – prompted immediate revolt (known as the Paris Commune), during which several thousand Communards were killed and another 20,000 executed.

The belle époque launched art-nouveau architecture, a whole field of artistic 'isms' from impressionism onwards, and advances in science and engineering, including the construction of the first metro line in Paris. World Exhibitions were held in the capital in 1889 (showcased by the Eiffel Tower) and again in 1901 in the purpose-built Petit Palais.

But all was not well in the republic. France was consumed with a desire for revenge after its defeat by Germany, and looking for scapegoats. The so-called Dreyfus Affair began in 1894 when Jewish army captain Alfred Dreyfus was accused of betraying military secrets to Germany; he was then court-martialled and sentenced to life imprisonment on Devil's Island in French Guiana. Liberal politicians succeeded in having the case reopened despite opposition from the army command, right-wing politicians and many Catholic groups, and Dreyfus was vindicated in 1900. This resulted in more rigorous civilian control of the military and, in 1905, the legal separation of church and state.

The Two World Wars

Central to France's entry into war against Austria-Hungary and Germany had been its desire to regain Alsace and Lorraine, lost to Germany in the Franco-Prussian War – but it would prove to be a costly piece of real estate in terms of human life. By the time the armistice was signed in November 1918, some 1.3 million French soldiers had been killed and almost one million crippled. At the Battle of Verdun alone, the French (under the command of General Philippe Pétain) and the Germans each lost about 400,000 men.

The naming of Adolf Hitler as Germany's chancellor in 1933 signalled the end of a decade of compromise between France and Germany over border guarantees. Initially the French tried to appease Hitler, but two days after Germany invaded Poland in 1939 France joined Britain in declaring war on Germany. By June 1940 France had capitulated. The Maginot Line had proved useless, with German armoured divisions outflanking it by going through Belgium.

The Germans divided France into a zone under direct German rule (along the western coast and the north, including Paris), and a puppet-state based in the spa town of Vichy and led by General Pétain, the ageing WWI hero of the Battle of Verdun. The Vichy regime was viciously anti-Semitic, and local police helped the Nazis in rounding up French Jews and others for deportation to Auschwitz and other death camps. While many people either collaborated with the Germans or passively waited out the occupation, the underground movement known as the

1795

A five-man delegation of moderate republicans led by Paul Barras sets itself up as the Directoire (Directory) and rules the First Republic for five years.

1799

Napoléon Bonaparte dismisses the Directoire and seizes control of the government in a coup d'état, opening the doors to 16 years of despotic rule, victory and then defeat on the battlefield.

1815

British and Prussian forces under the Duke of Wellington defeat Napoléon at Waterloo; he is exiled to a remote island in the South Atlantic where he dies six years later.

1851

Louis Napoléon leads a coup d'état and proclaims himself Emperor Napoléon III of the Second Empire (1852–70), a period of significant economic growth and building under Baron Haussmann.

THE MAGINOT LINE

The Ligne Maginot, named after France's minister of war from 1929 to 1932, was one of the most spectacular blunders of WWII. This elaborate, mostly subterranean defence network, built between 1930 and 1940 (and, in the history of military architecture, second only to the Great Wall of China in sheer size), was the pride of prewar France. It included everything France's finest military architects thought would be needed to defend the nation in a 'modern war' of poison gas, tanks and aeroplanes: reinforced concrete bunkers, subterranean lines of supply and communication, minefields, antitank canals, floodable basins and even artillery emplacements that popped out of the ground to fire and then disappeared. The only things visible above ground were firing posts and lookout towers. The line stretched along the Franco-German frontier from the Swiss border all the way to Belgium where, for political and budgetary reasons, it stopped. The Maginot Line even had a slogan: *Ils ne passeront pas* (They won't get through).

'They' – the Germans – never did. Rather than attack the Maginot Line straight on, Hitler's armoured divisions simply circled around through Belgium and invaded France across its unprotected northern frontier. They then attacked the Maginot Line from the rear.

Résistance, or Maquis, whose active members never amounted to more than about 5% of the French population, engaged in such activities as sabotaging railways, collecting intelligence for the Allies, helping Allied airmen who had been shot down, and publishing anti-German leaflets.

An 80km-long stretch of beach was the site of the D-Day landings on 6 June 1944, when more than 100,000 Allied troops stormed the coastline to liberate most of Normandy and Brittany. Paris was liberated on 25 August by a force spearheaded by Free French units, sent in ahead of the Americans so the French would have the honour of liberating their own capital.

The war ruined France. More than one-third of industrial production fed the German war machine during WWII, the occupiers requisitioning practically everything that wasn't (and was) nailed down: ferrous and nonferrous metals, statues, iron grills, zinc bar tops, coal, leather, textiles and chemicals. Agriculture, strangled by the lack of raw materials, fell by 25%.

In their retreat, the Germans burned bridges (2600 destroyed) and the Allied bombardments tore up railroad tracks (40,000km). The roadways had not been maintained since 1939, ports were damaged, and nearly half a million buildings and 60,000 factories were destroyed. The French had to pay for the needs of the occupying soldiers to the tune of 400 million francs a day, prompting an inflation rip tide.

Published posthumously, the award-winning *Suite Française* (2004) by Ukrainian-born author Irène Némirovsky, who was murdered at Auschwitz in 1942, evokes the horror of Nazi-occupied Paris from June 1940 until July 1941.

1871

The Treaty of Frankfurt is signed, the harsh terms of which (a 5-billion-franc war indemnity, surrender of the provinces of Alsace and Lorraine) prompt immediate revolt.

1903

The world's biggest sporting event after the Olympics and the World Cup sprints around France for the first time; Tour de France riders pedal throughout the night to cover 2500km in 19 days.

1904

Colonial rivalry between France and Britain in Africa ends with the Entente Cordiale (Cordial Understanding), marking the start of a cooperation that continues, more or less, to this day.

1905

The emotions aroused by the Dreyfus Affair and the interference of the Catholic Church lead to the promulgation of *lăcité* (secularism), the legal separation of church and state.

Rebuilding & the Loss of the Colonies

The magnitude of France's postwar economic devastation required a strong central government with broad powers to rebuild the country's industrial and commercial base. Soon after liberation most banks, insurance companies, car manufacturers and energy-producing companies fell under government control. Other businesses remained in private hands, the objective being to combine the efficiency of state planning with the dynamism of private initiative. But progress was slow. By 1947 rationing remained in effect and France had to turn to the USA for loans as part of the Marshall Plan to rebuild Europe.

One aim of the plan was to stabilise postwar Europe financially and politically, thus thwarting the expansion of Soviet power. As the Iron Curtain fell over Eastern Europe, the pro-Stalinist bent of France's Communist Party put it in a politically untenable position. Seeking at once to exercise power within the government and at the same time oppose its measures as insufficiently Marxist, the communists found themselves on the losing end of disputes involving the colonies, workers' demands and American aid. In 1947 they were booted out of government.

The economy gathered steam in the 1950s. The French government invested in hydroelectric and nuclear-power plants, oil and gas exploration, petrochemical refineries, naval construction, auto factories and building construction to accommodate a boom in babies and consumer goods. The future at home was looking brighter; the situation of *la France d'outre-mer* (overseas France) was another story altogether.

France's humiliation at the hands of the Germans had not been lost on its restive colonies. As the war economy tightened its grip, native-born people, poorer to begin with, noticed that they were bearing the brunt of the pain. In North Africa the Algerians coalesced around a movement for greater autonomy, which blossomed into a full-scale independence movement by the end of the war. The Japanese moved into strategically important Indochina in 1940. The Vietnamese resistance movement that developed quickly took on an anti-French, nationalistic tone, setting the stage for Vietnam's eventual independence.

The 1950s spelled the end of French colonialism. When Japan surrendered to the Allies in 1945, nationalist Ho Chi Minh launched a push for an autonomous Vietnam that became a drive for independence. Under the brilliant General Giap, the Vietnamese perfected a form of guerrilla warfare that proved highly effective against the French army. After their defeat at Dien Bien Phu in 1954, the French withdrew from Indochina.

The struggle for Algerian independence was nastier. Technically a French *département*, Algeria was in effect ruled by a million or so French settlers who wished at all costs to protect their privileges. Heads stuck firmly in the Saharan sands, the colonial community and its supporters

Key War Museums

Mémorial de la Shoah (Paris)

Centre d'Histoire de la Résistance et de la Déportation (Lyon)

Mémorial – Un Musée pour la Paix (Caen)

Musée Mémorial de la Bataille de Normandie (Bayeux)

1918

The armistice ending WWI signed at Fôret de Compiègne near Paris sees the return of lost territories (Alsace and Lorraine), but the war brings about the loss of more than a million French soldiers.

1920s

Paris sparkles as the centre of the avant-garde. The luxurious Train Bleu (Blue Train) makes its first run, and Sylvia Beach of the Shakespeare & Company bookshop publishes James Joyce's *Ulysses*.

1939

Nazi Germany occupies France and divides it into a zone under direct German occupation (along the north and western coasts), and a puppet state led by General Pétain, based in the spa town of Vichy.

1944

Normandy and Brittany are the first to be liberated by Allied troops following the D-Day landings in June, followed by Paris on 25 August by a force spearheaded by Free French units.

THE BIRTH OF THE BIKINI

Almost called *atome* (atom) rather than bikini, after its pinprick size, the scanty little two-piece bathing suit was the 1946 creation of Cannes fashion designer Jacques Heim and automotive engineer Louis Réard. It made its first appearance poolside in Paris at the Piscine Molitor, an art deco pool complex that reopened in 2014 – with original pool – as the stunning Hôtel Molitor.

Top-and-bottom swimsuits had existed for centuries, but it was the French duo who made them briefer than brief and plumped for the name 'bikini' – after Bikini, an atoll in the Marshall Islands chosen by the USA in the same year as the testing ground for atomic bombs.

Once wrapped top and bottom around the curvaceous 1950s sex-bomb Brigitte Bardot on St-Tropez' Plage de Pampelonne, there was no looking back. The bikini was here to stay.

in the army and the right wing refused all Algerian demands for political and economic equality.

The Algerian War of Independence (1954–62) was brutal. Nationalist rebel attacks were met with summary executions, inquisitions, torture and massacres, which made Algerians more determined to gain their independence. The government responded with half-hearted reform. International pressure on France to pull out of Algeria came from the UN, the USSR and the USA, while *pieds noirs* (literally 'black feet', as Algerian-born French people are known in France), elements of the military and extreme right-wingers became increasingly enraged at what they saw as defeatism in dealing with the problem. A plot to overthrow the French government and replace it with a military-style regime was narrowly avoided when General Charles de Gaulle, France's undersecretary of war who had fled Paris for London in 1940 after France capitulated and had spent more than a dozen years in opposition to the postwar Fourth Republic, agreed to assume the presidency in 1958.

The French invented the first digital calculator, the hot-air balloon, Braille and margarine, not to mention Grand Prix racing and the first public interactive computer network.

De Gaulle's initial attempts at reform – according the Algerians political equality and recognising their right in principle to self-determination – infuriated right-wingers without quenching the Algerian thirst for independence. Following a failed coup attempt by military officers in 1961, the Organisation de l'Armée Secrète (OAS; a group of French settlers and sympathisers opposed to Algerian independence) resorted to terrorism. It tried to assassinate de Gaulle several times and in 1961 violence broke out on the streets of Paris. Police attacked Algerian demonstrators, killing more than 100 people. Algeria was granted independence the following year.

1949

France signs the Atlantic Pact uniting North America and Western Europe in a mutual defence alliance (NATO); the Council of Europe, of which France is part, is born.

1951

Fear of communism and a resurgent Germany prompts the first steps towards European integration with the European Coal and Steel Community and military accords three years later.

1946–62

French colonialism ends with war in Indochina (1946–54) followed by the Algerian War of Independence (1954–62), brought to a close with the signing of the Accord d'Évian (Evian Accord) in Évian-les-Bains.

1966

France withdraws from NATO's joint military command in 1966; it has maintained an independent arsenal of nuclear weapons since 1960. A year later NATO moves out of its headquarters near Paris.

The Road to Prosperity & Europe

The turbulent mood and politics of Paris from 1968 until the mid-1970s is poignantly portrayed in Olivier Assayas' film, *Après Mai* (*Something in the Air*, 2012), a semi-autobiographical tale of a young man's artistic awakening in the face of revolution.

In the late 1960s Charles de Gaulle was appearing more and more like yesterday's man. Loss of the colonies, a surge in immigration and rise in unemployment had weakened his government. De Gaulle's government by decree was starting to gall the anti-authoritarian baby-boomer generation, now at university and agitating for change. Students reading Herbert Marcuse and Wilhelm Reich found much to admire in Fidel Castro, Che Guevara and the black struggle for civil rights in America, and vociferously denounced the war in Vietnam.

Student protests of 1968 climaxed with a brutal overreaction by police to a protest meeting at the Sorbonne, Paris' most renowned university. Overnight, public opinion turned in favour of the students, while the students themselves occupied the Sorbonne and erected barricades in the Latin Quarter. Within days a general strike by 10 million workers countrywide paralysed France.

But such comradeship between workers and students did not last long. While the former wanted a greater share of the consumer market, the latter wanted to destroy it. After much hesitancy de Gaulle took advantage of this division by appealing to people's fear of anarchy. Just as the country seemed on the brink of revolution and an overthrow of the Fifth Republic, stability returned. The government decentralised the higher-education system and followed through in the 1970s with a wave of other reforms (lowering the voting age to 18, instituting legalised abortion and so on). De Gaulle meanwhile resigned from office in 1969 and suffered a fatal heart attack the following year.

Georges Pompidou stepped onto the presidential podium in 1969. Despite embarking on an ambitious modernisation program, investing in aerospace, telecommunications and nuclear power, he failed to stave off inflation and social unrest following the global oil crisis of 1973. He died the following year.

France today maintains a rigid distinction between church and state. The country is a secular republic, meaning there can be no mention of religion on national school syllabuses.

In 1974 Valéry Giscard d'Estaing inherited a deteriorating economic climate and sharp divisions between the left and the right. His friendship with emperor and alleged cannibal Jean-Bédel Bokassa of the Central African Republic did little to win him friends, and in 1981 he was ousted by long-time head of the Parti Socialiste (PS; Socialist Party), François Mitterrand.

Despite France's first socialist president instantly alienating the business community by setting out to nationalise several privately owned banks, industrial groups and other parts of the economy, Mitterrand gave France a sparkle. Potent symbols of France's advanced technological savvy – the Minitel, a proto-personal computer in everyone's home, and high-speed TGV train service between Paris and Lyon – were launched in 1980 and 1981 respectively; a clutch of *grands projets* were embarked

1968

Large-scale anti-authoritarian student protests (known as 'May 1968'), aimed at Charles de Gaulle's style of government by decree, escalate into a countrywide protest that eventually brings down the president.

1994

The 50km-long Channel Tunnel linking France with Britain opens after seven years of hard graft by 10,000 workers.

1995

After twice serving as prime minister, Jacques Chirac becomes president of France, winning popular acclaim for his direct words and actions in matters relating to the EU and the war in Bosnia.

1998

After resuming nuclear testing in the South Pacific in the early 1990s, France signs the worldwide test-ban treaty, bringing an end to French nuclear testing once and for all.

upon in the French capital. The death penalty was abolished, homosexuality was legalised, a 39-hour work week was instituted, annual holiday time was upped from four to five weeks and the right to retire at 60 was guaranteed.

But by 1986 the economy was weakening and in parliamentary elections that year the right-wing opposition, led by Jacques Chirac (mayor of Paris since 1977), won a majority in the National Assembly. For the next two years Mitterrand worked with a prime minister and cabinet from the opposition, an unprecedented arrangement known as *cohabitation*. The extreme-right Front National (FN; National Front) meanwhile quietly gained ground by loudly blaming France's economic woes on immigration.

Presidential elections in 1995 ushered Chirac (an ailing Mitterrand did not run and died the following year) into the Élysée Palace. However, Chirac's attempts to reform France's colossal public sector in order to meet the criteria of the European Monetary Union (EMU) were met with the largest protests since 1968, and his decision to resume nuclear testing on the Polynesian island of Mururoa and a nearby atoll was the focus of worldwide outrage. Always the maverick, Chirac called early parliamentary elections in 1997 – only for his party, the Rassemblement pour la République (RPR; Rally for the Republic), to lose out to a coalition of socialists, communists and greens. Another period of *cohabitation* ensued.

The 2002 presidential elections surprised everybody. The first round of voting saw left-wing PS leader Lionel Jospin eliminated and the FN's Jean-Marie Le Pen win 17% of the national vote. But in the subsequent run-off ballot, Chirac enjoyed a landslide victory, echoed in parliamentary elections a month later when the president-backed coalition UMP (Union pour un Mouvement Populaire) won a healthy majority, leaving Le Pen's FN without a seat in parliament and ending years of *cohabitation*.

France has always drawn immigrants: 4.3 million from Europe between 1850 and WWI, and another three million between the world wars. Post-WWII, several million unskilled workers followed from North Africa and French-speaking sub-Saharan Africa.

Sarkozy's France

Presidential elections in 2007 ushered out old-school Jacques Chirac (in his 70s with two terms under his belt) and brought in Nicolas Sarkozy. Dynamic, ambitious and media savvy, the former interior minister and chairman of centre-right party UMP wooed voters with policies about job creation, lower taxes, crime crackdown and help for France's substantial immigrant population – issues that had particular pulling power coming from the son of a Hungarian immigrant father and Greek Jewish–French mother. However, his first few months in office were dominated by personal affairs as he divorced his wife Cecilia and wed Italian multimillionaire singer Carla Bruni a few months later.

The 2008 global banking crisis saw the government inject €10.5 billion into France's six major banks. Unemployment hit the 10% mark in

Best History Museums

- *MuCEM (Marseille)*
- *Musée Carnavalet (Paris)*
- *Musée d'Art et d'Histoire (Bayeux)*
- *Mémorial – Un Musée pour la Paix (Caen)*
- *Centre d'Histoire de la Résistance et de la Déportation (Lyon)*

2001
Socialist Bertrand Delanoë becomes the first openly gay mayor of Paris (and any European capital); he is wounded in a knife attack by a homophobic assailant the following year.

2002
The French franc, first minted in 1360, is thrown onto the scrap heap of history as the country adopts the euro as its official currency along with 14 other EU member-states.

2005
The French electorate overwhelmingly rejects the EU Constitution. Parisian suburbs are wracked by rioting Arab and African youths.

2011
French parliament bans burkas in public. Muslim women publicly wearing the face-covering veil can be fined and required to attend 'citizenship classes'.

2010 and in regional elections the same year, Sarkozy's party lost badly. The left won 54% of votes and control of 21 out of 22 regions on mainland France and Corsica. Government popularity hit an all-time low.

The President of the Republic has a website (www.elysee.fr), posts regularly on his Facebook page and is active on Twitter @elysee.

Riots ripped through the Alpine town of Grenoble in 2010 after a 27-year-old man was shot dead by police while allegedly trying to rob a casino. The incident echoed bloodshed five years earlier in a Parisian suburb following the death of two teenage boys of North African origin, electrocuted after hiding in an electrical substation while on the run from the police. In Grenoble the burning cars and street clashes with riot police were seen as a measurement of just how volatile France had become.

Hollande's France

Presidential elections in 2012 ushered in France's first socialist president since François Mitterand left office in 1995. Nicolas Sarkozy ran for a second term in office, but lost against left-wing candidate François Hollande (b 1954) of the Socialist party whose ambitious talk of reducing unemployment, clearing the country's debts, upping tax on corporations and salaries over €1 million per annum and increasing the minimum salary clearly won over the electorate. Parliamentary elections a month later sealed Hollande's grip on power: the Socialists won a comfortable majority in France's 577-seat National Assembly, paving the way for Hollande to govern France during Europe's biggest economic crisis in decades.

His term got off to a rocky start. Scandal broke in 2013 after finance minister Jerome Cahuzac admitted to having a safe-haven bank account in Switzerland and was forced to resign. Two months later France officially entered recession again. France's AA+ credit rating was downgraded still further to AA and unemployment dipped to 11.1% – the highest in 15 years. Rising anger at Hollande's failure to get the country's economy back on track saw his popularity plunge fast and furiously, and his Socialist party was practically wiped out in the 2014 municipal elections as the vast majority of the country swung decisively to the right. Paris, with the election of Spanish-born socialist Anne Hidalgo as Paris' first female mayor, was one of the few cities to remain on the political left.

Hollande's handling of his personal affairs proved equally inelegant. The same year French tabloid magazine *Closer* published photographs of the French president arriving at the Paris apartment of his alleged mistress, actress Julie Gayet, on a scooter – prompting public concern about both presidential security (or rather, lack of) and the well-being of the president's relationship with long-term partner and official First Lady, journalist Valérie Trierweiler. The presidential couple soon after announced the end of their relationship. Hollande's popularity plummeted to a new rock-bottom.

Keep tabs on the moves and motions of France's National Assembly at www.assemblee-nat.fr.

2012

France loses its top AAA credit rating. Economic policy is the big issue in presidential elections which usher in François Hollande, France's first Socialist president in 17 years.

2013

Same-sex marriage is legalised in France. By the end of the year, 7000 gay couples have tied the knot.

2015

Deadly terrorist attacks in Paris: on staff at satirical newspaper *Charlie Hebdo* on 7 January and on civilians at multiple locations including mythical Parisian concert hall Le Bataclan on 13 November.

2016

As of 1 January, France's 22 administrative *régions* are reduced to 13 in a bid to reduce the reams of bureaucracy, paperwork and admin France is famous for. On the ground, French people are less impressed.

The French

Stylish, sexy, chic, charming, arrogant, rude, bureaucratic, chauvinistic... France is a country whose people attract more stubborn myths and stereotypes than any other. Over the centuries dozens of tags, true or otherwise, have been pinned on the garlic-eating, beret-wearing, *sacrebleu*-swearing French. (The French, by the way, don't wear berets or use old chestnuts like *sacrebleu* anymore.) So what precisely does it mean to be French?

Superiority Complex

Most French people are proud to be French and are staunchly nationalistic a result of the country's republican stance that places nationality – rather than religion, for example – atop the self-identity list. This has created an overwhelmingly self-confident nation, culturally and intellectually, that can appear as a French superiority complex.

Such natural confidence is the backbone to being French. Never was this demonstrated more passionately or fervently than during the terrorist attacks that rocked the French capital in November 2015. Far from cowering in a corner, the shock attacks – repeated in Brussels, Belgium, just a few months later – prompted the French to get out there and defiantly brandish their culture and national pride as their greatest weapon against terrorism: while the hashtag slogan #JeSuisEnTerrasse spread like wildfire on the internet, Parisians took to cafe pavement terraces and public spaces in typical quiet and elegant defiance.

Sixty Million Frenchmen Can't Be Wrong: What Makes the French so French ask Jean-Benoît Nadeau and Julie Barlow in their witty, well-written and at times downright comical musings on the French.

Many French speak a foreign language fairly well, travel, and are happy to use their language skills should the need arise. Of course, if monolingual English-speakers don't try to speak French, there is no way proud French linguists will reveal they speak English! Many French men, incidentally, deem an English-speaking gal's heavily accented French as irresistibly sexy as many people deem a Frenchman speaking English.

Tradition vs Innovation

Suckers for tradition, the French are slow to embrace new ideas and technologies: it took the country an age to embrace the internet, clinging on to its own at-the-time-advanced Minitel system. Yet the French innovate. They came up with microchipped credit cards long before anyone else. The lead pencil, refrigerator, tinned foods, calculator, spirit level and little black dress *(merci,* Chanel) are all French inventions.

FRENCH MANNERS

- Splitting the bill is deemed the height of unsophistication. The person who invites pays, although close friends often go Dutch.
- Fondle fruit, veg, flowers or clothing in shops and you'll be greeted with a killer glare from the shop assistant.
- Take flowers (not chrysanthemums, which are only for cemeteries) or Champagne when invited to someone's home.
- Never, ever, discuss money over dinner.

FRENCH KISSING

Kissing French-style is not straightforward, 'how many' and 'which side first' being potentially problematic. In Paris it is two: unless parties are related, *very* close friends or haven't seen each other in an age, anything more is deemed affected. That said, in hipster 20-something circles, friends swap three or four cheek-skimming kisses.

Travel south and *les bises* (kisses), or *les bisous* as the French colloquially say, multiply; three or four is the norm in Provence. The bits of France neighbouring Switzerland around Lake Geneva tend to be three-kiss country (in keeping with Swiss habits); and in the Loire Valley it is four. Corsicans, bizarrely, stick to two but kiss left cheek first – which can lead to locked lips given that everyone else in France starts with the right cheek.

Naturally Sexy

When it comes to sex, not all French men ooze romance or light Gitane cigarettes all day. Nor are they as civilised about adultery as French cinema would have you believe. Adultery, illegal in France until 1975, was actually grounds for automatic divorce until as late as 2004. Today, 55% of marriages in France end in divorce – with women being the ones to file for divorce in three out of four cases. As with elsewhere in Europe, couples are marrying later – at the average age of 32 and 30 for men and women respectively, compared to 30 and 28 a decade ago. Fifty-seven percent of babies in France are born out of wedlock, and one-fifth are raised by a single parent.

Kissing is an integral part of French life. (The expression 'French kissing' doesn't exist in French, incidentally.) Countrywide, people who know each other reasonably well, really well, a tad or barely at all greet each other with a glancing peck on each cheek. Southern France aside (where everyone kisses everyone), two men rarely kiss (unless they are related or artists) but always shake hands.

Gay & Married

The French capital has long been known as 'gay Paree', with an openly proud gay mayor for 13 years (until 2014) and a gay and lesbian scene so open that there is far less of a defined 'scene' than in many other European cities where gay and lesbian life remains somewhat underground. Yet despite all this, reactions to the legalisation of same-sex marriage in France in 2013 were mixed and at times extreme, exposing a deeply conservative streak in some French people that few expected or anticipated.

After gay marriage was legalised, 7000 couples – 3% of all marriages in France – wed in 2013 and another 10,000 in 2014.

Lifestyle

Be a fly on the wall in the 5th-floor bourgeois apartment of Monsieur et Madame Tout le Monde and you'll see them dunking croissants in bowls of *café au lait* for breakfast, buying a baguette every day from the boulangerie and recycling nothing bar a few glass bottles and the odd cardboard box. They go to the movies once a month, work 35 hours a week (many French still toil 39 hours or more a week – employers can enforce a 39-hour work week for a negotiable extra cost), and enjoy five weeks' holiday and almost a dozen public holidays a year.

The couple view the web-radio production company their 24-year-old son set up and heads in Paris with a mix of pride, amusement and scepticism. Their 20-year-old daughter is a student: France's crowded state-run universities are free and open to anyone who passes the baccalaureate. Then there's their youngest, aged 10 and one of France's many children who have Wednesday afternoons off school – the four-and-a-half day week is a ball for kids, but not so easy for working parents who have to sort out childcare for that half-day each week.

Madame buys hot-gossip weekly magazines, Monsieur meets his mates to play boules, and the first two weeks of August is the *only* time to go on a summer holiday. Dodging dog poo on pavements is a sport and everything goes on the *carte bleue* (credit or debit card) when shopping. The couple have a landlord: with a tradition of renting rather than buying, home ownership is low (63% of households own their own home; the rest rent).

One of the bestsellers addressing French culture in recent years is Pamela Druckerman's *French Children Don't Throw Food* (2012), a witty and entertaining look at how French parents in Paris raise their kids, written by an American living in the city.

Les Femmes

Women were granted suffrage in 1945, but until 1964 a woman needed her husband's permission to open a bank account or get a passport. Younger French women in particular are quite emancipated. But this self-confidence has yet to translate into equality in the workplace, where women hold few senior positions. Sexual harassment is addressed with a law imposing financial penalties on the offender. A great achievement in the last decade has been *Parité,* the law requiring political parties to fill 50% of their slates in all elections with female candidates.

Abortion is legal during the first 12 weeks of pregnancy, and girls under 16 do not need parental consent provided they are accompanied by an adult: 30 abortions take place in France for every 100 live births.

Above all else French women are known for their natural chic, style and class. And there's no doubt that contemporary French women are sassier than ever. Take the Rykiel women: in the 1970s, legendary Parisian knitwear designer Sonia Rykiel designed the skin-tight, boob-hugging sweater worn with no bra beneath. In the new millennium, daughter Nathalie created Rykiel Woman, a sensual label embracing everything from lingerie to sex toys and aimed squarely at women who know what they want.

Then, of course, there is Spanish-born Anne Hidalgo, Paris' first ever female mayor, elected in 2014. *Allez les femmes!*

Linguistic Patriotism

Speaking a language other than their own is an emotional affair for the French, memorably illustrated a few years back when the then French president Jacques Chirac walked out of an EU summit session after a fellow countryman had the audacity to address the meeting in English. French newspapers and the French blogosphere seethed with debate on linguistic patriotism the following day, French bloggers – many of whom write in English – rightly pointing out that French has not been the primary international language for a long, long time.

Former president Nicolas Sarkozy fared marginally better than his monolingual predecessor. Yet Sarkozy also stuck to what he knew best in public, so much so that the couple of lines he did utter in English were instantly plastered over the internet as a video link and swiftly went viral. Then there was the famous letter from President François Hollande to US president Barack Obama which ended 'Friendly, François

FROGS VS ROSBIFS

In the finest of traditions, tales of the rivalry between *rosbifs* (the English) and frogs (the French) sell like hotcakes. Our favourites:

- *1000 Years of Annoying the French* (Stephen Clarke, 2011) A comic look at French-Anglo history by the man who launched his career with *A Year in the Merde* (A Year in the Shit).
- *Cross Channel* (Julian Barnes, 1996) Classic short stories set either side of the Channel.
- *More France Please! We're British!* (Helen Frith-Powell, 2004) France from the perspective of Brits who choose to live there permanently.
- *Dirty Bertie: An English King in France* (Stephen Clarke, 2014) Apparently, fervent Francophile Edward VII learnt everything there is to know about life from the French...

Hollande' – a plain embarrassing mistranslation of *amicalement* used to sign off letters in French.

This said, in 2015, France's École Nationale d'Adminstration (National School of Administration) in Strasbourg – the elite university attended by Jacques Chirac, François Hollande et al – did finally make English an admission requirement for students aspiring to study at the school, the unspoken entry point for the French civil service and government.

With English words like 'weekend', 'jogging', 'stop' and 'OK' firmly entrenched in daily French usage, language purists might just have lost the battle. One look at the many Anglo-American shop and restaurant signs featured in the online Musée des Horreurs (Museum of Horrors) on the website of the Paris-based Défense de la Langue Française (DLF; Defence of the French Language; www.langue-francaise.org) says it all.

French was the main language of the EU until 1995 when Sweden and Finland came into the EU fold. French broadcasting laws restrict the amount of airtime radio and TV stations can devote to non-French music, but nothing can be done to restrict who airs what on the internet.

France maintains a rigid distinction between church and state. The country is a secular republic, meaning there can be no mention of religion on national school syllabuses.

Multiculturalism

France is multicultural (immigrants make up around 9% of the population), yet its republican code, while inclusive and nondiscriminatory, has been criticised for doing little to accommodate a multicultural society (and, interestingly, none of the members of France's National Assembly represents the immigrant population, first or second generation). Nothing reflects this dichotomy better than the law, in place since 2004, banning the Islamic headscarf, Jewish skullcap, crucifix and other religious symbols in French schools.

Some 90% of the French Muslim community – Europe's largest – are noncitizens. Most are illegal immigrants living in poverty-stricken *bidonvilles* (shanty towns) around Paris, Lyon, Marseille and other

FRANCE'S NORTH–SOUTH DIVIDE

No film better illustrates what southerners think of those from 'the sticks' in the far north than Dany Boon's *Bienvenue chez les Ch'tis* (Welcome to the Sticks; 2008), a classic commentary on France's north–south divide.

For starters, the weather in the cold rainy north is revolting. So no surprise that post-office chief Philippe, upon setting off north from his native Salon-de-Provence on the sun-drenched Côte d'Azur, dons a puffer jacket and scarf as he bids farewell to bronzed wife Julie. The weather changes when he passes the 'Nord-Pas de Calais' sign – at which point it doesn't just rain but slashes down beyond windscreen-wiper control. Even the gendarme on the autoroute, upon stopping him for driving too slowly, lets him off with a sympathetic smile and his deepest condolences when he hears where he's heading: Bergues, an ex-mining town of 4300 inhabitants, 9km from Dunkirk.

Bienvenue chez les Ch'tis is a kaleidoscope of comic scenes that slowly chip away at the deeply entrenched prejudices surrounding this northern land of redundant coal mines and its unemployed, impoverished, pale, unhealthy and 'uncultured' inhabitants who drink too much beer and speak like this – *'Ej t'ermerci inne banes'* (that means *Merci beaucoup*).

Yes, their thick Ch'timi dialect (old Picard peppered with Flemish) is incomprehensible to outsiders. Yes, they dunk stinky Maroilles cheese and bread in *chicorée café* (chicory-flavoured instant coffee) for breakfast. Yes, they skip the traditional French three-course lunch for an alfresco round of *frites fricadelle, sauce picadilly* (chips 'n' meatballs) – eaten with their fingers. And yes, their very nickname (les Ch'tis) was borne out of prejudice during WWI when French soldiers mocked the thickly accented way their northern comrades spoke – *'ch'est ti, ch'est mi'* (*c'est toi, c'est moi* – it's you, it's me), hence 'Ch'ti'.

The north and its regional characteristics are no mystery to director Boon, a born-and-bred northerner who grew up in Armentières, near Lille.

A NEW MAP OF FRANCE

On 1 January 2016 a new map of France was unveiled on which the country's traditional 22 administrative *régions* were reduced to 13. The new regions have until July 2016 to come up with their new names, currently a simple, if wordy, amalgamation of the original region names – in strict alphabetical order to avoid appearing to favour one historic region over another.

Naturally, such a *redécoupage territorial* sparked off a flurry of regional sentiment and emotion among the French, notably in northeastern France where Germanic Alsace is suddenly wed to dramatically different Lorraine and Champagne; and in Languedoc-Roussillon which is now joined at the hip with the Midi-Pyrénées, despite the natural inclination of main town Nîmes and surrounds to be in completely the opposite direction, towards Provence.

Yet for tourists in France, not an awful lot changes. Tourist boards for each historical region remain firmly independent, with each French region continuing to enjoy and promote its unique identity, culture and gastronomy.

metropolitan centres. Many are unemployed (youth unemployment in many suburbs is as high as 40%) and face little prospect of getting a job.

Good Sports

Most French wouldn't be seen dead walking down the street in trainers and tracksuits. But contrary to appearances, they love sport. Shaved-leg cyclists toil up Mont Ventoux, football fans fill stadiums and anyone who can flits off for the weekend to ski or snowboard.

France's traditional ball games include *pétanque* and the more formal boules, which has a 70-page rule book. Both are played by men on a gravel pitch.

Les 24 Heures du Mans and the F1 Grand Prix in Monaco are the world's raciest dates in motor sports; the French Open, aka Roland Garros, in Paris in late May to early June is the second of the year's four grand-slam tennis tournaments; and the Tour de France is – indisputably – the world's most prestigious bicycle race. Bringing together 189 of the world's top male cyclists (21 teams of nine) and 15 million spectators in July each year for a spectacular 3000-plus-kilometre cycle around the country, the three-week race always labours through the Alps and Pyrenees and finishes on Paris' Champs-Élysées. The route in between changes each year but wherever it goes, the French systematically turn out in droves – armed with tables, chairs and picnic hampers – to make a day of it. The serpentine publicity caravan preceding the cyclists showers roadside spectators with coffee samples, logo-emblazoned balloons, pens and other free junk-advertising gifts and is easily as much fun as watching the cyclists themselves speed through – in 10 seconds flat.

France's greatest moment in soccer history came at the 1998 World Cup, which the country hosted and won. But the game has produced no stars since, losing to Italy in the final of the 2006 World Cup and and only making it as far as the quarter-finals in the 2014 World Cup in Brazil. Indeed, football fans look back with fondness at the days of France's golden boy of football, now retired, Marseille-born midfielder Zinedine Zidane (b 1972). The son of Algerian immigrants, Zidane wooed the nation with a sparkling career of goal-scoring headers and extraordinary footwork that unfortunately ended with him head-butting an Italian player during the 2006 World Cup final. But such was the power of his humble Marseillais grin (since used to advertise Adidas sports gear, Volvic mineral water and Christian Dior fashion) that the French nation instantly forgave him.

France was not only the host country to the UEFA Euro 2016. With Real Madrid centre-back Raphaël Varane (b 1993) – a French lad from Lille – firmly at the heart of France's defence, *Les bleues* went into the tournament as the hot favourite to win the international championship. The team went the whole way through the final, only to lose 1-0 to Portugal.

The French Table

Few Western cuisines are so envied, aspired to or seminal. The freshness of ingredients, natural flavours, regional variety and range of cooking methods is phenomenal. The very word 'cuisine' was borrowed from the French – no other language could handle all the nuances. The French table waltzes taste buds through a dizzying array of dishes sourced from aromatic street markets, seaside oyster farms, sun-baked olive groves and ancient vineyards mirroring the beauty of each season. Discovering these varied regional cuisines is an enriching, essential experience.

Foodie Towns

- *Le Puy-en-Velay (lentils)*
- *Dijon (mustard)*
- *Privas (chestnuts)*
- *Cancale (oysters)*
- *Espelette (red chillies)*
- *Colmar (chocolate stork eggs)*
- *Lyon (piggy-part cuisine)*

Terroir

No country so blatantly bundles up cuisine with its *terroir* (land). *'Le jardin de France'* (the garden of France), a poetic phrase coined by the French writer Rabelais in the 16th century to describe his native Touraine in the Loire Valley, has been exploited ever since. Yet it is the serene valley tracing the course of the River Loire west of the French capital, which remains most true to the Rabelais image of a green and succulent landscape laden with lush fruits, flowers, nuts and vegetables.

It was in the Renaissance kitchens of the Loire's celebrated châteaux that French cooking was refined: *coq au vin* (chicken in wine) and *cuisses de grenouilles* (frogs' legs) were common dishes, and poultry and game dishes were the pride and joy. Once or twice a year a fattened pig was slaughtered and prepared dozens of different ways – roasts, sausages, *boudin noir* (black pudding), charcuterie (cold meats), pâtés and so on. No single part, offal et al, was wasted.

Sauces

With plenty of game and poultry going into châteaux kitchens, it was natural that medieval cooks should whip up a sauce to go with it. In the 14th to 16th centuries, *sauce verte* (green sauce) – a rather crude, heavily spiced mix of vinegar and green grape juice – accompanied meat dishes. In 1652 François-Pierre de la Varenne published his cook book *Le Cuisinier François* in which he dismissed bread and breadcrumbs as thickening agents in favour of *roux* (a more versatile mixture of flour and fat). This paved the way for the creation, a century later, of classic French sauces such as béchamel (a milk-based sauce thickened with *roux*) and *velouté* (a velvety mix of chicken or other stock and melted butter, seasoned and thickened with *roux*) a century later. *Velouté* is the base for dozens of other sauces made to accompany meat, fish and game dishes today.

A CAKE FOR KINGS

On Jour des Rois (Day of the Kings; 6 January), or Epiphany, when the Three Wise Men paid homage to the infant Jesus, a *galette des rois* (literally 'kings' cake'; a puff-pastry tart with frangipane cream) is placed in the centre of the table and sliced while the youngest person ducks under the table, calling out who gets each slice. The excitement lies in who gets *la fève* (literally 'bean', which translates these days as a miniature porcelain figurine) hidden inside the tart; whoever does is crowned king with a gold paper crown that's sold with the *galette*.

Bread

In northern France wheat fields shade vast swathes of agricultural land a gorgeous golden copper, and nothing is more French than *pain* (bread). Starved peasants demanded bread on the eve of the French Revolution when the ill-fated Queen Marie Antoinette is purported to have said 'let them eat cake'. And bread today – no longer a matter of life or death but a cultural icon – accompanies every meal. It's rarely served with butter, but when it is, the butter is always *doux* (unsalted).

Every town and almost every village has its own *boulangerie* (bakery) which sells bread in all manner of shapes, sizes and variety. Artisan *boulangeries* bake their bread in a wood-fired, brick bread oven pioneered by Loire Valley châteaux in the 16th century.

Plain old *pain* is a 400g, traditional-shaped loaf, soft inside and crusty out. The iconic classic is *une baguette,* a long thin crusty loaf weighing 250g. Anything fatter and it becomes *une flûte,* thinner *une ficelle.* While French baguettes are impossibly good, they systematically turn unpleasantly dry within four hours, unbelievably rock-hard within 12.

Charcuterie & Foie Gras

Charcuterie, the backbone of every French picnic and a bistro standard, is traditionally made from pork, though other meats are used in making *saucisse* (small fresh sausage, boiled or grilled before eating), *saucisson* (salami), *saucisson sec* (air-dried salami), *boudin noir* (blood sausage or pudding made with pig's blood, onions and spices) and other cured and salted meats. Pâtés, terrines and rillettes are also considered charcuterie. The difference between a pâté and a terrine is academic: a pâté is removed from its container and sliced before it is served, while a terrine is sliced from the container itself. Rillettes, spread cold over bread or toast, is potted meat or even fish that has been shredded with two forks, seasoned and mixed with fat.

The key component of *pâté de foie gras* is foie gras which is the liver of fattened ducks and geese. It was first prepared *en croûte* (in a pastry crust) around 1780 by one Jean-Pierre Clause, chef to the military governor of Alsace, who was impressed enough to send a batch to the king of Versailles. Today, it is a traditional component of celebratory or festive meals – particularly Christmas and New Year's Eve – in family homes countrywide, and is consumed with relish year-round in regions in southwest France where it is primarily made, namely Aquitaine (the Dordogne), Limousin, Auvergne and the Midi-Pyrénées.

Cooking Classes

La Terrasse Rouge (St-Émilion)

Le St-James (near Bordeaux)

Le Mirazur (Menton)

Le Grand Bleu (Sarlat-la-Canéda)

La Table du Couvent (Limoges)

Patisserie

Patisserie is a general French term for pastries and includes *tartes* (tarts), *flans* (custard pies), *gâteaux* (cakes) and *biscuits* (cookies) as well as traditional croissants, *pains au chocolats* and other typical pastries. *Sablés* are shortbread biscuits, *tuiles* are delicate wing-like almond cookies, madeleines are small scallop-shaped cakes often flavoured with a hint of vanilla or lemon, and *tarte tatin* is an upside-down caramelised apple pie that's been around since the late 19th century. Louis XIV (1643–1715), known for his sweet tooth, is credited with introducing the custom of eating dessert – once reserved for feast days and other celebrations – at the end of a meal.

No sweet treat evokes the essence of French patisserie quite like the elegant, sophisticated and zany macaron, a legacy of Catherine de Médicis who came to France in 1533 with an entourage of Florentine chefs and pastry cooks adept in the subtleties of Italian Renaissance cooking and armed with delicacies such as aspic, truffles, quenelles (dumplings), artichokes – and macarons. Round and polished smooth like a giant

Smartie, the macaron (nothing to do with coconut) is a pair of crisp-shelled, chewy-inside discs – egg whites whisked stiff with sugar and ground almonds – sandwiched together with a smooth filling. Belying their egg-shell fragility, macarons are created in a rainbow of lurid colours and flavours, wild and inexhaustible: rose petal, cherry blossom, caramel with coconut and mango, mandarin orange and olive oil…

Cheese

No French food product is a purer reflection of *terroir* than cheese, an iconic staple that – with the exception of most coastal areas – is made all over the country, tiny villages laying claim to ancient variations made just the way *grand-père* (grandfather) did it. France boasts more than 500 varieties, made with *lait cru* (raw milk), pasteurised milk or *petit-lait* ('little-milk', the whey left over after the fats and solids have been curdled with rennet).

Classic cheese and wine pairings: Alsatian gewürztraminer and Munster; Côtes du Rhone and Roquefort; Côte d'Or (Burgundy) and Brie or Camembert; Bordeaux and emmental or Cantal; and Champagne and Chaource.

Chèvre, made from goat's milk, is creamy, sweet and faintly salty when fresh, but hardens and gets saltier as it matures. Among the best is Ste-Maure de Touraine, a mild creamy cheese from the Loire Valley; Cabécou de Rocamadour from Midi-Pyrénées, often served warm with salad or marinated in oil and rosemary; and Lyon's St-Marcellin, a soft white cheese that should be served impossibly runny.

Roquefort, a ewe's-milk veined cheese from Languedoc, is the king of blue cheeses and vies with Burgundy's pongy Époisses for the strongest taste award. Soft, white, orange-skinned Époisses, created in the 16th century by monks at Abbaye de Cîteaux, takes a month to make, using washes of saltwater, rainwater and Marc de Bourgogne – a local pomace brandy and the source of the cheese's final fierce bite.

Equal parts of Comté, Beaufort and Gruyère – a trio of hard fruity, cow's milk cheeses from the French Alps – are grated and melted in a garlic-smeared pot with a dash of nutmeg, white wine and *kiersch* (cherry liqueur) to create fondue Savoyarde. Hearty and filling, this pot of melting glory originated from the simple peasant need of using up cheese scraps. It is now the chic dish to eat on the ski slopes.

Wine

Viticulture in France is an ancient art and tradition that bears its own unique trademark. The French thirst for wine goes back to Roman times when techniques to grow grapes and craft wine were introduced, and *dégustation* (tasting) has been an essential part of French wine culture ever since.

LE GAVAGE

Fattened duck and goose liver have been enjoyed since time immemorial, but it wasn't until the 18th century that it was introduced on a large scale. France today produces 20,000 tonnes of foie gras – 80% of world production – a year, fattening the livers of 37 million ducks and 700,000 geese on farms, primarily in southwest France, to do so.

Traditionally, back in the 11th century, local farmers in the Dordogne would slaughter the farm goose then pluck out its liver and soak it in warm milk to ensure a succulent swollen liver, ripe for feasting on with a chilled glass of sweet Monbazillac white. Today, in order to fatten the livers, ducks and geese are controversially force-fed twice a day for two or three weeks with unnatural amounts of boiled corn. During *le gavage* (force-feeding), a tube is threaded down the throat into the bird's stomach, enabling 450g or so of boiled corn to be pneumatically pumped into the bird in just a few seconds. Fattened livers are up to 10 times larger than their natural size. A fattened duck is slaughtered at three weeks, a goose at four.

Force-feeding is illegal in 12 countries in the EU, Norway, Switzerland, Israel and the USA; and foie gras imports are forbidden in many countries. Within France itself, there is a growing movement to end *le gavage*.

THE PERFECT CHEESEBOARD

Treat your taste buds to the perfect balance of cheese by taking at least one of each type from the cheeseboard:

Goat's cheese *(fromage de chèvre)* Made from goat's milk.

Blue cheese *(fromage à pâté persillée)* 'Marbled' or with veins resembling *persil* (parsley).

Soft cheese *(fromage à pâté molle)* Moulded or rind-washed, the classic soft cheese that everyone knows is Camembert from Normandy made from unpasteurised cow's milk. Munster from Alsace is a fine-textured, rind-washed cheese.

Semihard cheese *(fromage à pâté demi-dure)* Among the finest uncooked, pressed cheese is Tomme de Savoie, made from pasteurised or unpasteurised cow's milk near the Alps; and St-Nectaire, a strong-smelling pressed cheese with a complex taste.

Hard cheese *(fromage à pâté dure)* Must-taste cooked and pressed cheeses are Beaufort, a fruity cow's-milk cheese from Rhône-Alpes; Comté, made with raw cow's milk in Franche-Comté; emmental, a cow's-milk cheese made all over France; and Mimolette, an Edam-like bright-orange cheese from Lille aged for as long as 36 months.

Quality wines in France are designated as Appellation d'Origine Contrôlée (AOC; literally, 'label of inspected origin'), equivalent since 2012 to the European-wide Appellation d'Origine Protégée (AOP). Both labels mean the same: that the wine has met stringent regulations governing where, how and under what conditions it was grown and bottled. French AOC can cover a wide region (such as Bordeaux), a sub-region (such as Haut-Médoc), or a commune or village (such as Pomerol). Some regions only have a single AOC (such as Alsace), while Burgundy has dozens.

Some viticulturists have honed their skills and techniques to such a degree that their wine is known as a *grand cru* (literally 'great growth'). If this wine has been produced in a year of optimum climatic conditions, it becomes a *millésime* (vintage) wine. *Grands crus* are aged in small oak barrels then bottles, sometimes for 20 years or more, to create those memorable bottles (with price tags to match) that wine experts enthuse about with such passion.

There are dozens of wine-producing regions throughout France, but the principal ones are Burgundy, Bordeaux, the Rhône and Loire Valleys, Champagne, Languedoc, Provence and Alsace. Wines are generally named after the location of the vineyard rather than the grape varietal. Organic and biodynamic wines are increasingly popular.

The Food of France by Waverley Root, first published in 1958, remains the seminal work in English on *la cuisine française*, with a focus on historical development, by a long-time Paris-based American foreign correspondent.

Red

France's most respected reds are from Burgundy (Bourgogne in French), Bordeaux and the Rhône Valley.

Monks in Burgundy began making wine in the 8th century during the reign of Charlemagne. Today vineyards remain small, rarely more than 10 hectares, with vignerons (winegrowers) in Côte d'Or, Chablis, Châtillon and Mâcon producing small quantities of excellent reds from pinot noir grapes. The best Bourgogne vintages demand 10 to 20 years to age.

In the sun-blessed south, Bordeaux has the perfect climate for producing wine: its 1100 sq km of vineyards produce more fine wine than any other region in the world. Well-balanced Bordeaux reds blend several grape varieties, predominantly merlot, cabernet sauvignon and cabernet franc. The Médoc, Pomerol, St-Émilion and Graves are key winegrowing areas.

The most renowned red in the Côtes du Rhône appellation from the Rhône Valley – a vast 771-sq-km winegrowing area with dramatically different soils, climates, topography and grapes – is Châteauneuf du Pape,

APERITIFS & DIGESTIFS

Meals in France are preceded by an aperitif such as a *kir* (white wine sweetened with a sweet fruit syrup like blackcurrant or chestnut), *kir royale* (Champagne with blackcurrant syrup), *pineau* (cognac and grape juice) or a glass of sweet white Coteaux du Layon from the Loire Valley. In southern France aniseed-flavoured pastis (clear in the bottle, cloudy when mixed with water) is the aperitif to drink alfresco; in the southwest, go local with a Floc de Gascogne, a liqueur wine made from Armagnac and red or white grape juice. In Corsica, Cap Corse Mattei – a fortified wine whose recipe has stood the test of time (nearly 150 years!) – is the choice *apéro*.

After-dinner drinks accompany coffee. France's most famous brandies are Cognac and Armagnac, both made from grapes in the regions of those names. *Eaux de vie* (literally 'waters of life') can be made with grape skins and the pulp left over after being pressed for wine (Marc de Champagne, Marc de Bourgogne), apples (Calvados) and pears (Poire William), as well as such fruits as plums *(eau de vie de prune)* and even raspberries *(eau de vie de framboise)*. In the Loire Valley a shot of orange (aka a glass of local Cointreau liqueur) ends the meal.

When in Normandy, do as the festive Normans do: refresh the palate between courses with a *trou normand* (literally 'Norman hole') – traditionally a shot of *calva* (Calvados) or a contemporary scoop of apple sorbet doused in the local apple brandy.

a strong full-bodied wine bequeathed by the Avignon popes who planted the distinctive stone-covered vineyards.

Further south on the coast near Toulon, deep-flavoured Bandol reds have been produced from dark-berried mourvèdre grapes since Roman times. These wines were famous across Gaul, their ability to mature at sea ensuring they travelled far beyond French shores in the 16th and 17th centuries.

Britons have had a taste for Bordeaux' full-bodied wines, known as clarets in the UK, since the 12th century when King Henry II, who controlled the region through marriage, gained the favour of locals by granting them tax-free trade status with England.

White

Some of France's finest whites come from the Loire Valley. This large winegrowing region produces the country's greatest variety of wines, and light delicate whites from Pouilly-Fumé, Vouvray, Sancerre, Bourgueil and Chinon are excellent. Muscadet, cabernet franc and chenin blanc are key grape varieties, contrasting with the chardonnay grapes that go into some great Burgundy whites.

Vines were planted by the Greeks in Massilia (Marseille) around 600 BC and crisp Cassis whites remain the perfect companion to the coast's bounty of shellfish and seafood.

Alsace produces almost exclusively white wines – mostly varieties produced nowhere else in France – that are known for their clean, fresh taste. Unusually, some of the fruity Alsatian whites also go well with red meat. Alsace's four most important varietal wines are riesling (known for its subtlety), gewürztraminer (pungent and highly regarded), pinot gris (robust and high in alcohol) and muscat d'Alsace (less sweet than muscats from southern France).

Rosé

Chilled, fresh pink rosé wines – best drunk alfresco beneath a vine-laced pergola – are synonymous with the hot south. Côtes de Provence, with 20 hectares of vineyards between Nice and Aix-en-Provence, is the key appellation (and France's sixth-largest).

Other enticing rosé labels include Coteaux d'Aix-en-Provence, Palette and Coteaux Varois of Angelina Jolie and Brad Pitt fame – the former celebrity pair owned Château de Miraval, an organic wine-producing estate in Correns where Pink Floyd recorded part of *The Wall* in 1979.

Champagne

Champagne has been produced northeast of Paris since the 17th century when innovative monk Dom Pierre Pérignon perfected a technique for making sparkling wine. It's made from the white chardonnay, red pinot noir or black pinot meunier grape. Each vine is vigorously pruned and trained to produce a small quantity of high-quality grapes.

If the final product is labelled *brut*, it is extra dry, with only 1.5% sugar content. *Extra-sec* means very dry (but not as dry as *brut*), *sec* is dry and *demi-sec* slightly sweet. The sweetest Champagne is labelled *doux*. Whatever the label, it is sacrilege to drink it out of anything other than a traditional Champagne flute, narrow at the bottom to help the bubbles develop, wider in the middle to promote the diffusion of aromas, and narrower at the top again to concentrate those precious aromas.

For excellent, practical guides – full of background information, tasting notes and eating/sleeping/drinking recommendations – to France's wine regions, peruse the Wine Travel Guides (www.winetravelguides.com) website.

Beer & Cider

Alsace, with its close ties to Germany, produces some excellent local beers such as Bière de Scharrach, Schutz Jubilator and Fischer. The north, close to Belgium and the Netherlands, has equally tasty beers, including Saint Sylvestre Trois Ponts, Colvert and Terken Brune. Brewers around the city of Lille produce *bières de garde* (literally 'keeping beers'), strong and fruity in taste. They are bottled in what look like Champagne bottles, corked and wired. Popular among young Bretons is a crop of beers made by boutique breweries, including Lancelot barley beer and Telenn Du buckwheat beer. Corsica has its own unique brews, including the light herby lager, Colomba, and La Pietra, a full-bodied beer made from the island's abundance of chestnuts.

Cidre (apple cider) is made in many areas, including Savoy, Picardy and the Basque Country where it is called *sagarnoa*. But cider's real home is Normandy and Brittany where it is traditionally served in tea cups – with crêpes. Top ciders include Cornouaille (AOC) and those produced in the towns of Morlaix, Hennebont and the Val de Rance.

The Arts

France's vast artistic heritage is the essence of French *art de vivre*. Contemporary French writers might struggle to be published abroad, but Voltaire, Victor Hugo, Marcel Proust and Simone de Beauvoir walk the hall of fame. Music is embedded in the French soul, with world-class rap, dance and electronica coming out of Paris. French painting, with its roots in prehistoric cave art, continues to break new ground with provocative street art, while French film is enjoying a marvellous renaissance.

Literature

Modern Literature

The world's longest novel – a seven-volume 9,609,000-character giant by Marcel Proust (1871–1922) – dominated the early 20th century. *À la Recherche du Temps Perdu* (Remembrance of Things Past) explores in evocative detail the true meaning of past experience recovered from the unconscious by involuntary memory.

Surrealism proved a vital force until WWII. André Breton (1896–1966) captured the spirit of surrealism – a fascination with dreams, divination and all manifestations of the imaginary – in his autobiographical narratives. In Paris the bohemian Colette (1873–1954) captivated and shocked with her titillating novels detailing the amorous exploits of heroines such as schoolgirl Claudine. In New York meanwhile, what would become one of the bestselling French works of all time was published in 1943: *Le Petit Prince* (The Little Prince), by Lyon-born writer and pilot, Antoine de Saint-Exupéry (1900–44). He captured the hearts of millions with his magical yet philosophical tale for children about an aviator's adventures with a little blonde-haired Prince from Asteroid B-612.

When Besancon-born Victor Hugo (1802–85) died, his coffin was laid beneath Paris' Arc de Triomphe for an all-night vigil. His work remains a hot topic in French schools – to the horror of some students whose abusive tweets after sitting the 2014 baccalaureate exam went so far as saying the writer would be a dead man if crossed in the street by one of them.

After WWII, existentialism developed around the lively debates of Jean-Paul Sartre (1905–80), Simone de Beauvoir (1908–86) and Albert Camus (1913–60) in Paris' Left Bank cafes.

The *nouveau roman* of the 1950s saw experimental young writers seek new ways of organising narratives, with Nathalie Sarraute slashing identifiable characters and plot in *Les Fruits d'Or* (The Golden Fruits). *Histoire d'O* (Story of O), an erotic sadomasochistic novel written by Dominique Aury under a pseudonym in 1954, sold more copies outside France than any other contemporary French novel.

Another writer to turn heads was radical young writer Françoise Sagan (1935–2004) who shot to fame at the age of 18 with her first novel, *Bonjour Tristesse* (Hello Sadness; 1954). The hedonistic lifestyle pursued by the bourgeois-born writer kept her in the spotlight until her death in 2004.

Courtly Love to Symbolism

Troubadours' lyric poems of courtly love dominated medieval French literature, while the *roman* (literally 'romance', now meaning 'novel') drew on old Celtic tales. With the *Roman de la Rose,* a 22,000-line poem by Guillaume de Lorris and Jean de Meung, allegorical figures like Pleasure, Shame and Fear appeared.

French Renaissance literature was extensive and varied. La Pléiade was a group of lyrical poets active in the 1550s and 1560s. The exuber-

ant narrative of Loire Valley–born François Rabelais (1494–1553) blends coarse humour with encyclopedic erudition in a vast panorama of every kind of person, occupation and jargon in 16th-century France. Michel de Montaigne (1533–92) covered cannibals, war horses, drunkenness and the resemblance of children to their fathers and other themes.

The *grand siècle* (golden age) ushered in classical lofty odes to tragedy. François de Malherbe (1555–1628) brought a new rigour to rhythm in poetry, and Marie de La Fayette (1634–93) penned the first French novel, *La Princesse de Clèves* (1678).

The philosophical Voltaire (1694–1778) dominated the 18th century. A century on, Besançon gave birth to French Romantic Victor Hugo (1802–85). The breadth of interest and technical innovations exhibited in his poems and novels – *Les Misérables* and *The Hunchback of Notre Dame* among them – was phenomenal.

In 1857 literary landmarks *Madame Bovary* by Gustave Flaubert (1821–80), and Charles Baudelaire's (1821–67) poems *Les Fleurs du Mal* (The Flowers of Evil), were published. Émile Zola (1840–1902) saw novel-writing as a science in his powerful series, *Les Rougon-Macquart*.

Contemporary Literature

Marc Levy is France's bestselling writer. The film rights of his first novel were snapped up for the Stephen Spielberg box-office hit, *Just Like Heaven* (2005), and his novels have been translated into 42 languages. *Une Autre Idée de Bonheur* (Another Idea of Happiness; 2013), was published a year later in English, as will his latest – *L'Horizon à l'Envers* (2016) – in due course no doubt.

No French writer better delves into the mind, mood and politics of France's notable ethnic population than Faïza Guène (b 1985), who writes in a notable 'urban slang' style. Born and bred on a ghetto housing estate outside Paris, she stunned critics with her debut novel, *Kiffe Kiffe Demain* (2004), sold in 27 countries and published in English as *Just Like Tomorrow* (2006). Faïza Guène's father moved from a village in western Algeria to northern France in 1952, aged 17, to work in the mines. Only in the 1980s could he return to Algeria. There he met his wife, whom he brought back to France, to Les Courtillières housing estate in Seine-St-Denis, where 6000-odd immigrants live in five-storey, high-rise blocks stretching for 1.5km. Such is the setting for Guène's first book and her second semi-autobiographical novel, *Du Rêve pour les Oeufs* (2006), published in English as *Dreams from the Endz* (2008). Her third novel, *Les Gens du Balto* (2008), published in English as *Bar Balto* (2011), is a series of colloquial, first-person monologues by various characters who live on a street in a Parisian suburb. Her more recent work, *Un Homme ça ne Pleure Pas* (Real Men Don't Cry, 2014), shifts to Nice in southern France.

Another French writer to address ethnic issues engagingly is Jean-Marie Gustave Le Clézio, born during WWII in Nice to a Niçois mother and Mauritian father. The bulk of his childhood was spent in Nigeria and he

FRENCH CINEMA

1920s

French film flourishes. Sound ushers in René Clair's (1898–1981) world of fantasy and satirical surrealism. **Watch** Abel Gance's antiwar blockbuster *J'Accuse!* (I Accuse!; 1919), filmed on WWI battlefields.

1930s

WWI inspires a new realism: portraits of ordinary lives dominate film. **Watch** *La Grande Illusion* (The Great Illusion; 1937), a devastating evocation of war's folly based on the trench warfare experience of director Jean Renoir.

1940s

Surrealists eschew realism. **Watch** Jean Cocteau's *La Belle et la Bête* (Beauty and the Beast; 1945) and *Orphée* (Orpheus; 1950). WWII saps the industry of talent and money.

1950s

Nouvelle Vague (New Wave) sees small budgets, no stars and real-life subject matter. **Watch** A petty young criminal on the run in Jean-Luc Godard's *À Bout de Souffle* (Breathless; 1958) and adolescent rebellion in François Truffaut's *Les Quatre Cents Coups* (The 400 Blows; 1959).

1960s

France as the land of romance. **Watch** Claude Lelouch's *Un Homme et une Femme* (A Man and a Woman; 1966) and Jacques Demy's bittersweet *Les Parapluies de Cherbourg* (The Umbrellas of Cherbourg; 1964).

READING LIST

One way of ensuring your beach reading is right up to the minute is to plump for the latest winner of the Prix Goncourt, France's most prestigious literary prize awarded annually since 1903 and reflective, in recent years, of the occupation in contemporary French literature with issues of race, multiculturalism and immigration.

Winners include Marcel Proust in 1919 for *À l'Ombre des Jeunes Filles en Fleurs* (Within a Budding Grove, 1924); Simone de Beauvoir in 1954 for *Les Mandarins* (The Mandarins, 1957); and, more recently, French-Senegalese novelist-playwright Marie NDiaye with *Trois Femmes Puissantes* (Three Strong Women, 2009). The first black woman to win the award, NDiaye stunned the literary world at the age of 21 with *Comédie Classique* (1988), a 200-page novel comprising one single sentence. In 2015 the prize went to Mathias Énard, a Persian and Arabic scholar from southwest France whose winning novel *Boussole* addresses relations between Europe and the Middle East.

Add to your reading list the laureate of France's other big literary award, the Grand Prix du Roman de l'Académie Française, around since 1918. The 2009 Grand Prix winner, *Les Onze,* by French novelist Pierre Michon (b 1945), published in English as *The Eleven* (2013), portrays a humble Parisian painter who decorates the homes of Louis XIV's mistresses and goes on to create a *Mona Lisa*–type masterpiece. Michon's earlier novels, *Small Lives* (2008) and *Master and Servants* (1997), come equally recommended. It has been known for the jury to be split, as was the case in 2015 when two winners were announced: French writer Hédi Kaddour with *Les Prépondérants* and Algerian writer Boualem Sansal with his Orwellian and apocalyptic *2084: la Fin du Monde* (2084: The End of the World).

studied in Bristol, England, and Aix-en-Provence. In 2008 he won the Nobel Prize in Literature,

Music

Classical

French Baroque music heavily influenced European musical output in the 17th and 18th centuries. French musical luminaries – Charles Gounod (1818–93), César Franck (1822–90) and *Carmen* creator Georges Bizet (1838–75) among them – were a dime a dozen in the 19th century. Modern orchestration was founded by French Romantic Hector Berlioz (1803–69). He demanded gargantuan forces: his ideal orchestra included 240 stringed instruments, 30 grand pianos and 30 harps.

Claude Debussy (1862–1918) revolutionised classical music with *Prélude à l'Après-Midi d'un Faune* (Prelude to the Afternoon of a Fawn), creating a light, almost Asian musical impressionism. Impressionist comrade Maurice Ravel (1875–1937) peppered his work, including *Boléro*, with sensuousness and tonal colour. Contemporary composer Olivier Messiaen (1908–92) combined modern, almost mystical music with natural sounds such as birdsong. His student Pierre Boulez (b 1925) works with computer-generated sound.

Best Literary Sights

- *Maison de Victor Hugo (Paris)*
- *Sartre and de Beauvoir's graves, Cimetière du Montparnasse (Paris)*
- *Oscar Wilde's grave, Cimetière du Père Lachaise (Paris)*
- *Musée Colette (Burgundy)*
- *Château d'If (Marseille)*
- *Musée Jules Verne (Nantes & Amiens)*

Jazz & French Chansons

Jazz hit 1920s Paris in the banana-clad form of Josephine Baker, an African American cabaret dancer. Post-WWII ushered in a much-appreciated bunch of musicians, mostly black Americans who opted to remain in Paris' bohemian Montmartre rather than return to the brutal racism and segregation of the US: Sidney Bechet called Paris home from 1949, jazz drummer Kenny 'Klook' Clarke followed in 1956, pianist Bud Powell in 1959, and saxophonist Dexter Gordon in the early 1960s.

In 1934 a chance meeting between Parisian jazz guitarist Stéphane Grappelli and three-fingered Roma guitarist Django Reinhardt in a Montparnasse nightclub led to the formation of the Hot Club of France quintet. Claude Luter and his Dixieland band were hot in the 1950s.

The *chanson française,* a French folk-song tradition dating from the troubadours of the Middle Ages, was eclipsed by the music halls and burlesque of the early 20th century, but was revived in the 1930s by Édith Piaf and Charles Trenet. In the 1950s, Paris' Left Bank cabarets nurtured *chansonniers* (cabaret singers) such as Léo Ferré, Georges Brassens, Claude Nougaro, Jacques Brel and the very charming, very sexy, very French Serge Gainsbourg. A biopic celebrating his life, *Serge Gainsbourg: Une Vie Héroïque* (Serge Gainsbourg: A Heroic Life), was released in 2009 to wide acclaim.

Jazz fans will adore the gypsy jazz style of young French pop singer Zaz – an experimental voice from Tours in the Loire Valley, often compared to Edith Piaf – who stormed to the top of the charts with her debut album *Zaz* (2010). Her subsequent third album, *Paris* (2014) is a musical ode to the French capital with 13 songs evoking Paris' irresistible charm and romance. Her first live album, *Sur la Route* (2015) only confirms that Zaz is one of France's hottest contemporary female voices.

Rap

France is known for its rap, an original 1990s sound spearheaded by Senegal-born, Paris-reared rapper MC Solaar and Suprême NTM (NTM being an acronym for a French expression far too offensive to print). Most big-name rappers are French twenty-somethings of Arabic or African origin whose prime preoccupations are the frustrations and fury of fed-up immigrants in the French *banlieues* (suburbs).

Disiz La Peste, born in Amiens to a Senegalese father and French mother, portrayed precisely this in his third album, aptly entitled *Histoires Extra-Ordinaires d'un Jeune de Banlieue* (The Extraordinary Stories of a Youth in the Suburbs; 2005), as did his 'last' album *Disiz the End* (2009), after which he morphed into Peter Punk (www.disizpeterpunk.com) and created a very different rock-punk-electro sound. In 2011 he returned as rap artist Disiz La Peste, releasing a rash of albums culminating in 2015 with *Rap Machine,* his 10th album.

France's other big rap band is Marseille's homegrown IAM (www.iam.tm.fr), around since 1989 and enjoying a comeback since their release of two albums in the space of one year: despite rumours that *Arts Martiens* (2013) would be their last album, music label Def Jam subsequently announced it had signed up the Marseillais band to record two further albums, the first of which is slated for 2017.

Rock & Pop

One could be forgiven for thinking that French pop is becoming dynastic. The distinctive M (for Mathieu) is the son of singer Louis Chédid; Arthur H is the progeny of pop-rock musician Jacques Higelin; and Thomas Dutronc is the offspring of 1960s idols Jacques and Françoise Hardy. Serge Gainsbourg's daughter with Jane Birkin, Charlotte Gainsbourg (b 1971) made her musical debut in 1984 with the single *Lemon Incest*

1970s

The limelight baton goes to lesser-known directors like Éric Rohmer (b 1920), who make beautiful but uneventful films in which the characters endlessly analyse their feelings.

1980s

Big-name stars, slick production values and nostalgia: generous state subsidies see film-makers switch to costume dramas and comedies in the face of growing competition from the USA. **Watch** Luc Besson strikes box-office gold with *Subway* (1985) and *Le Grand Bleu* (The Big Blue; 1988).

1990s

French actor Gérard Depardieu wins huge audiences in France and abroad. **Watch** *Cyrano de Bergerac* (1990) and *Astérix et Obélix: Mission Cléopâtre* (2002). Besson continues to stun with *Nikita* (1990) and *Jeanne d'Arc* (Joan of Arc; 1999).

New Millennium

'New French Extremity' is the tag given to the socially conscious, transgressive films of Paris-born, Africa-raised film-maker Claire Denis. **Watch** *Chocolat* (1988) and *Matériel Blanc* (White Material; 2009), scripted by Parisian novelist Marie NDiaye, to explore the legacy of French colonialism.

2011

Renaissance of French film. **Watch** *The Artist* (2011), a silent B&W, French-made romantic comedy set in 1920s Hollywood that scooped five Oscars and seven BAFTAs to become the most awarded film in French film history.

2014

Female film-maker Pascale Ferrari (b 1960) makes her mark with *Bird People* (2014), set in and around a hotel at Paris' Charles de Gaulle airport.

and – several albums later – released a cover version of the song *Hey Joe* as soundtrack to the film *Nymphomaniac* (2013) in which she also starred as the leading lady. For her latest album, to be released in 2016, she collaborated with Guy Man from Daft Punk and French electronic music producer SebastiAn.

Noir Désir was the sound of French rock until its lead vocalist, Bertrand Cantat (b 1964), was imprisoned in 2003 for murdering his girlfriend. Following his release from prison, Noir Désir limped along until 2010. The controversial singer, who's been called France's Jim Morrison, later formed the band Détroit with instrumentalist Pascal Humbert. Cantat's powerfully husky voice instantly won fans over: Détroit's only album to date, *Horizons* (2013), sold 160,000 copies in just six months.

Always worth a listen is Louise Attaque (http://louiseattaque.com) who, after a 10-year break, released its new album, *L'Anomalie,* with huge success in early 2016. Nosfell (www.nosfell.com), one of France's most creative and intense musicians, sings in his own invented language called *le klokobetz*. His third album, *Armour Massif* (2014), opens and closes in *le klokobetz* but otherwise woos listeners with powerful French love lyrics. In 2015 Nosfell wrote the music for *Contact,* a musical comedy by French dancer and choreographer Philippe Decouflé.

Best Musical Sights

- *Serge Gainsbourg's grave, Cimetière du Montparnasse (Paris)*
- *Jim Morrison's grave, Cimetière du Père Lachaise (Paris)*
- *Château des Milandes (Dordogne)*
- *Espace Georges Brassens (Sète)*
- *Juan-les-Pins (French Riviera)*

Christophe Maé mixes acoustic pop with soul, with stunning success. His jazzy third album, *Je Veux du Bonheur* (2013), was heavily influenced by the time the Provence-born singer spent travelling in New Orleans. Travels abroad likewise provide the inspiration for the 2016 album *Palermo Hollywood*, by talented singer-songwriter Benjamin Biolay (b 1973).

Marseille-born Marina Kaye (b 1998) won *France's Got Talent* TV show at the age of 13, as well as huge acclaim with her debut single 'Homeless', and released her first album *Fearless* in 2015. Celebrity singer Nolwenn Leroy (b 1982) performs in Breton, English and Irish as well as French, while Paris' very own Indila (b 1984) woos France with her edgy pop and *rai* (a style derived from Algerian folk music).

Dance & Electronica

France does dance music well: computer-enhanced Chicago blues and Detroit techno are often mixed with 1960s lounge music and vintage tracks from the likes of Gainsbourg and Brassens to create a distinctly urban, highly portable sound.

Internationally successful bands like Daft Punk and Justice head the scene. Daft Punk (www.daftalive.com), originally from Versailles, adapts first-wave acid house and techno to its younger roots in pop and indie rock. Its debut album *Homework* (1997) fused disco, house funk and techno, while *Random Access Memories* (2013) boldly ditched computer-generated sound for a strong disco beat played by session musicians. The album's lead single, 'Get Lucky', featuring US singer-songwriter Pharrell Williams, sold more than 9.3 million copies and made it in into the Top 10 in over 30 countries.

Electronica band Justice, aka talented duo Gaspard Michel Andre Augé and Xavier de Rosnay, burst onto the dance scene in 2007 with a debut album that used the band's signature crucifix as its title. Raved about for its rock and indie influences, Justice has released several albums since, most recently *D.Y.S, Jsc* (Do You Some Justice; 2015). Electronica duo AIR (an acronym for 'Amour, Imagination, Rêve' meaning 'Love, Imagination, Dream') and M83 (named after the Messer 83 galaxy) from Antibes are two other electronica bands to listen out for.

David Guetta, Laurent Garnier, Martin Solveig and Bon Sinclair – originally nicknamed 'Chris the French Kiss' – are top Parisian electronica music producers and DJs who travel the international circuit. In the late 1990s David Guetta, with his wife Cathy, directed Paris' mythical nightclub Les Bains Douches, today a trendy club-hotel in Le Marais.

World

With styles from Algerian *rai* to other North African music (artists include Cheb Khaled, Natacha Atlas, Jamel, Cheb Mami) and Senegalese *mbalax* (Youssou N'Dour), West Indian zouk (Kassav', Zouk Machine) and Cuban salsa, France's world beat is strong. Manu Chao (www.manuchao.net), the Paris-born son of Spanish parents, uses world elements to stunning effect.

Magic System from Côte d'Ivoire popularised *zouglou* (a kind of West African rap and dance music) with its album *Premier Gaou*, and Congolese Koffi Olomide still packs the halls. Also try to catch blind singing couple, Amadou and Mariam; Rokia Traoré from Mali; and Franco-Algerian DJ turned singer Rachid Taha (www.rachidtaha.fr) whose music mixes Arab and Western musical styles with lyrics in English, Berber and French.

No artist has sealed France's reputation in world music more than Paris-born, Franco-Congolese rapper, slam poet and three-time Victoire de la Musique–award winner, Abd al Malik (www.abdalmalik.fr). His albums *Gibraltar* (2006), *Dante* (2008) and *Château Rouge* (2010) are classics, as will his latest effort, *Scarifications* (2015), no doubt be.

Painting

Prehistoric to Landscape

France's oldest known prehistoric cave paintings (created 31,000 years ago) adorn the Grotte Chauvet-Pont-d'Arc in the Rhône Valley and the underwater Grotte Cosquer near Marseille; neither can be visited. In the Dordogne, it is the prehistoric art in caves at Lascaux that stuns.

According to Voltaire, French painting proper began with Baroque painter Nicolas Poussin (1594–1665), known for his classical mythological and biblical scenes bathed in golden light. Wind forward a couple of centuries and modern still life popped up with Jean-Baptiste Chardin (1699–1779). A century later, neoclassical artist Jacques Louis David (1748–1825) wooed the public with vast history paintings.

While Romantics like Eugène Delacroix (1798–1863; buried in Paris' Cimetière du Père Lachaise) revamped the subject picture, the Barbizon School effected a parallel transformation of landscape painting. Jean-François Millet (1814–75), the son of a peasant farmer from Normandy, took many of his subjects from peasant life, and reproductions of his *L'Angélus* (The Angelus; 1857) – the best-known painting in France after the *Mona Lisa* – are strung above mantelpieces all over rural France. The original hangs in Paris' Musée d'Orsay.

Realism & Impressionism

The Realists were all about social comment: Édouard Manet (1832–83) evoked Parisian middle-class life and Gustave Courbet (1819–77) depicted working-class drudgery.

It was in a flower-filled garden in a Normandy village that Claude Monet (1840–1926) expounded Impressionism, a term of derision taken from the title of his experimental painting *Impression: Soleil Levant* (Impression: Sunrise; 1874). A trip to the Musée d'Orsay unveils a rash of other members of the school – Boudin, Sisley, Pissarro, Renoir, Degas and more.

An arthritis-crippled Renoir painted out his last impressionist days in a villa on the French Riviera, a part of France that inspired dozens of artists: Paul Cézanne (1839–1906) is particularly celebrated for his post-impressionist still lifes and landscapes done in Aix-en-Provence, where he was born and worked; Paul Gauguin (1848–1903) worked in Arles; while Dutch artist Vincent van Gogh (1853–90) painted Arles and St-Rémy de Provence. In St-Tropez pointillism took off: Georges Seurat (1859–91) was

Setting the Trends

- *Palais de Tokyo (Paris)*
- *Centre Pompidou (Paris)*
- *Fondation Louis Vuitton (Paris)*
- *Fondation Maeght (St-Paul de Vence)*
- *Centre Pompidou-Metz (Metz)*
- *Musée d'Art Moderne et d'Art Contemporain (Nice)*

Modern Art Hubs

- *Monet's garden (Giverny)*
- *Musée Renoir (Cagnes-sur-Mer)*
- *Musée Picasso (Paris & Antibes)*
- *Musée Matisse & Musée Chagall (Nice)*
- *Musée Jean Cocteau Collection Séverin Wunderman (Menton)*
- *Atélier Cézanne (Aix-en-Provence)*
- *Chemin de Fauvisme (Collioure)*

the first to apply paint in small dots or uniform brush strokes of unmixed colour, but it was his pupil Paul Signac (1863–1935) who is best known for pointillist works.

20th Century to Present

Twentieth-century French painting is characterised by a bewildering diversity of styles, including cubism, and Fauvism, named after the slur of a critic who compared the exhibitors at the 1906 autumn Salon in Paris with *fauves* (wild animals) because of their radical use of intensely bright colours. Spanish cubist Pablo Picasso (1881–1973) and fauvist Henri Matisse (1869–1954) both chose southern France to set up studio, Matisse living in Nice and Picasso in Antibes.

No literary genre has a bigger cult following in France than *bandes dessinées* (comic strips) – Paris even has a museum, Art Ludique-Le Musée, dedicated to the art. Originally written for children, comic strips for adults burst onto the scene in 1959 with René Goscinny and Albert Uderzo's now-iconic *Astérix* series.

The early 20th century also saw the rise of the Dada movement, and no piece of French art better captures its rebellious spirit than Marcel Duchamp's *Mona Lisa,* complete with moustache and goatee. In 1922 German Dadaist Max Ernst moved to Paris and worked on surrealism, a Dada offshoot that drew on the theories of Freud to reunite the conscious and unconscious realms and permeate daily life with fantasies and dreams.

With the close of WWII, Paris' role as artistic world capital ended. The focus shifted back to southern France in the 1960s with new realists such as Arman (1928–2005) and Yves Klein (1928–62), both from Nice. In 1960 Klein famously produced *Anthropométrie de l'Époque Bleue,* a series of imprints made by naked women (covered from head to toe in blue paint) rolling around on a white canvas, in front of an orchestra of violins and an audience in evening dress.

Artists in the 1990s turned to the minutiae of everyday urban life to express social and political angst. Conceptual artist Daniel Buren (b 1938) reduced his painting to a signature series of vertical 8.7cm-wide stripes that is applied to any surface imaginable – white marble columns in the courtyard of Paris' Palais Royal included. The painter (who in 1967, as part of the radical *groupe BMPT,* signed a manifesto declaring he was not a painter) was the *enfant terrible* of French art in the 1980s. Partner-in-crime Michel Parmentier (1938–2000) insisted on monochrome painting – blue in 1966, grey in 1967 and red in 1968.

Paris-born conceptual artist Sophie Calle (b 1953) brazenly exposes her private life in public with eye-catching installations such as *Prenez Soin de Vous* (Take Care of Yourself; 2007), a compelling and addictive work of art in book form exposing the reactions of 107 women to an email Calle received from her French lover, dumping her. Her *Rachel, Monique* (2010) evoked the death and lingering memory of her mother in the form of a photographic exhibition first shown at Paris' Palais de Tokyo, later as a live reading performance at the Festival d'Avignon, and most recently in a chapel in New York. In 2015 *Suite Vénitienne* was published, a beautiful hard-back rendition, on gilt-edged Japanese paper, of her first art book in 1988 in which she followed Henri B around Venice for two weeks, anonymously photographing the enigmatic stranger.

Street art is big, thanks in part to the pioneering work of Blek Le Rat (http://bleklerat.free.fr) in the 1980s. The Parisian artist, born as Xavier Prou, began by spraying tiny rats in hidden corners of the streets of Paris, went on to develop stencil graffiti as a recognised form, and notably inspired British street artist Banksy.

Then there is digital art. In 2013 the world's largest collective street-art exhibition, La Tour Paris 13 (www.tourparis13.fr), opened in a derelict apartment block in Paris' 13e *arrondissement.* Its 36 apartments on 13 floors showcased works by 100 international artists. The blockbuster exhibition ran for one month, after which the tower was shut and demolished. Itself an art work, the three-day demolition was filmed and streamed live on the internet – where the street artworks remain.

Architecture

From prehistoric megaliths around Carnac in Brittany to Vauban's 33 star-shaped citadels dotted around France to defend its 17th-century frontiers, French architecture has always been of *grand-projet* proportions. In the capital, the skyline shimmers with Roman arenas, Gothic cathedrals, postmodernist cubes and futuristic skyscrapers, while provincial France cooks up the whole gamut of mainstream architectural styles along with regional idiosyncrasies.

Prehistoric to Roman

No part of France better demonstrates the work of the country's earliest architects than Brittany, which has more megalithic menhirs (monumental upright stones), tombs, cairns and burial chambers than anywhere else on earth. Many date from around 3500 BC and the most frequent structure is the dolmen, a covered burial chamber consisting of vertical menhirs topped by a flat capstone. Bizarrely, Brittany's ancient architects had different architectural tastes from their European neighbours – rather than the cromlechs (stone circles) commonly found in Britain, Ireland, Germany and Spain, they were much keener on building arrow-straight rows of menhirs known as *alignements*. And, indeed, Carnac's monumental Alignements de Carnac is the world's largest known prehistoric structure.

Catch up with southern France's prehistoric architects at Marseille's Centre de la Vieille Charité, Quinson's Musée de Préhistoire des Gorges du Verdon, and the beehive-shaped huts called *bories* at the Village des Bories near Gordes in the Luberon.

The Romans left behind a colossal architectural legacy in Provence and the French Riviera. Thousands of men took three to five years to haul the 21,000 cu metres of local stone needed to build the Pont du Gard near Nîmes. Other fine pieces of Roman architecture, still operational, include amphitheatres in Nîmes and Arles, open-air theatres in Orange and Fréjus, and Nîmes' Maison Carrée.

Romanesque

A religious revival in the 11th century led to the construction of Romanesque churches, so-called because their architects adopted many architectural elements (eg vaulting) from Gallo-Roman buildings still standing at the time. Romanesque buildings typically have round arches, heavy walls, few windows and a lack of ornamentation that borders on the austere.

Romanesque masterpieces include Toulouse's Basilique St-Sernin, Poitiers' Église Notre Dame la Grande, the exquisitely haunting Basilique St-Rémi in Reims, Caen's twinset of famous Romanesque abbeys, and Provence's trio in the Luberon (Sénanque, Le Thoronet and Silvacane). In Normandy the nave and south transept of the abbey-church on Mont St-Michel are beautiful examples of Norman Romanesque.

Then there is Burgundy's astonishing portfolio of Romanesque abbeys, among the world's finest: Abbaye de Pontigny, Abbaye de Cîteaux and Vézelay's Basilique Ste-Madeleine are highlights.

Gothic

Avignon's pontifical palace is Gothic architecture on a gargantuan scale. The Gothic style originated in the mid-12th century in northern France,

FRANCE'S MOST BEAUTIFUL VILLAGES

One of French architecture's signature structures popped up in rural France from the 13th century, 'up' being the operative word for these *bastides* or *villages perchés* (fortified hilltop villages), built high on a hill to afford maximum protection for previously scattered populations. Provence and the Dordogne are key regions to hike up, down and around one medieval hilltop village after another, but you can find them in almost every French region. Many of the most dramatic and stunning are among Les Plus Beaux Villages de France (The Most Beautiful Villages in France; www.les-plus-beaux-villages-de-france.org).

where the region's great wealth attracted the finest architects, engineers and artisans. Gothic structures are characterised by ribbed vaults carved with great precision, pointed arches, slender verticals, chapels (often built or endowed by the wealthy or by guilds), galleries and arcades along the nave and chancel, refined decoration and large stained-glass windows. If you look closely at certain Gothic buildings, however, you'll notice minor asymmetrical elements introduced to avoid monotony.

The world's first Gothic building was the Basilique de St-Denis near Paris, which combined various late-Romanesque elements to create a new kind of structural support in which each arch counteracted and complemented the next. The basilica served as a model for many other 12th-century French cathedrals, including Notre Dame de Paris and Chartres' cathedral – both known for their soaring flying buttresses. No Gothic belfry is finer to scale than that of Bordeaux' Cathédrale St-André.

In the 14th century, the Radiant Gothic style developed, named after the radiating tracery of the rose windows, with interiors becoming even lighter thanks to broader windows and more translucent stained glass. One of the most influential Rayonnant buildings was Paris' Ste-Chapelle, whose stained glass forms a curtain of glazing on the 1st floor.

Renaissance

Renaissance architecture stamped châteaux with a new artistic form: the monumental staircase. The most famous of these splendid ceremonial (and highly functional) creations are at Azay-le-Rideau, Blois, and Chambord in the Loire Valley.

The Renaissance, which began in Italy in the early 15th century, set out to realise a 'rebirth' of classical Greek and Roman culture. It had its first impact on France at the end of that century, when Charles VIII began a series of invasions of Italy, returning with some new ideas.

To trace the shift from late Gothic to Renaissance, travel along the Loire Valley. During the very early Renaissance period, châteaux were used for the first time as pleasure palaces rather than defensive fortresses. Many edifices built during the 15th century to early 16th century in the Loire Valley – including Château d'Azay-le-Rideau and Château de Villandry – were built as summer or hunting residences for royal financiers, chamberlains and courtiers. Red-patterned brickwork – such as that on the Louis XII wing of Château Royal de Blois – adorned the façade of most châteaux dating from Louis XII's reign (1498–1515).

The quintessential French Renaissance château is a mix of classical components and decorative motifs (columns, tunnel vaults, round arches, domes etc) with the rich decoration of Flamboyant Gothic. It ultimately showcased wealth, ancestry and refinement. Defensive towers (a historical seigniorial symbol) were incorporated into a new decorative architecture, typified by its three-dimensional use of pilasters and arcaded loggias, terraces, balconies, exterior staircases, turrets and gabled chimneys. Heraldic symbols were sculpted on soft stone façades, above doorways and fireplaces, and across coffered ceilings. Symmetrical floor plans broke new ground and heralded a different style of living: Château de Chambord contained 40 self-contained apartments, arranged on five

floors around a central axis. This ensured easy circulation in a vast edifice that many rank as the first modern building in France.

Mannerism

Mannerism, which followed the Renaissance, was introduced by Italian architects and artists brought to France around 1530 by François I, whose royal château at Fontainebleau was designed by Italian architects. Over the following decades, French architects who had studied in Italy took over from their Italian colleagues.

The Mannerist style lasted until the early 17th century, when it was subsumed by the Baroque style.

Hotels for Architecture Buffs

Les Bains & Hôtel Molitor (Paris)

Hôtel Le Corbusier (Marseille)

Hôtel Oscar (Le Havre)

Hotel Sōzō (Nantes)

La Co(o)rniche (Pyla-sur-Mer)

Baroque

During the Baroque period (the tail end of the 16th to late 18th centuries), painting, sculpture and classical architecture were integrated to create structures and interiors of great subtlety, refinement and elegance. Architecture became more pictorial, with the painted ceilings in churches illustrating the Passion of Christ to the faithful, and palaces invoking the power and order of the state.

Salomon de Brosse, who designed Paris' Palais du Luxembourg in 1615, set the stage for two of France's most prominent early-Baroque architects: François Mansart (1598–1666), who designed the classical wing of Château Royal de Blois, and his younger rival Louis Le Vau (1612–70), who worked on France's grandest palace at Versailles.

Neoclassicism

Nancy's place Stanislas in northern France is the country's loveliest neoclassical square. Neoclassical architecture, which emerged in about 1740 and remained popular until well into the 19th century, had its roots in the renewed interest in the classical forms and conventions of Greco-Roman antiquity: columns, simple geometric forms and traditional ornamentation.

Among the earliest examples of this style is the Italianate façade of Paris' Église St-Sulpice, designed in 1733 by Giovanni Servandoni, which took inspiration from Christopher Wren's St Paul's Cathedral in London; and the Petit Trianon at Versailles, designed by Jacques-Ange Gabriel for Louis XV in 1761. France's greatest neoclassical architect of the 18th century was Jacques-Germain Soufflot, the man behind the Panthéon in Left Bank Paris.

Neoclassicism peaked under Napoléon III, who used it extensively for monumental architecture intended to embody the grandeur of imperial

VAUBAN'S CITADELS

From the mid-17th century to the mid-19th century, the design of defensive fortifications around the world was dominated by the work of one man: Sébastien Le Prestre de Vauban (1633–1707).

Born to a relatively poor family of the petty nobility, Vauban worked as a military engineer during almost the entire reign of Louis XIV, revolutionising both the design of fortresses and siege techniques. To defend France's frontiers, he built 33 immense citadels, many of them shaped like stars and surrounded by moats, and he rebuilt or refined more than 100.

Vauban's most famous citadel is situated at Lille, but his work can also be seen at Antibes, Belfort, Belle Île, Besançon, Concarneau, Neuf-Brisach (Alsace), Perpignan, St-Jean Pied de Port and St-Malo. The Vauban citadel in Verdun comprises 7km of underground galleries. A dozen sites (www.sites-vauban.org) star on Unesco's World Heritage Site list under a 'Vauban Fortifications' banner.

France and its capital: the Arc de Triomphe, La Madeleine, the Arc du Carrousel at the Louvre, the Assemblée Nationale building and the Palais Garnier. It was during this period moreover that urban planner Baron Haussmann, between 1850 and 1870 as Prefect of the Seine, completely redrew Paris' street plan, radically demolishing the city's maze of narrow, cramped medieval streets and replacing it with wide boulevards, sweeping parks and attractive *passages couverts* (covered passages).

The true showcase of this era though is Casino de Monte Carlo in Monaco, created by French architect Charles Garnier (1825–98) in 1878.

Art Nouveau

Art nouveau (1850–1910) combined iron, brick, glass and ceramics in ways never before seen. The style emerged in Europe and the US under various names (Jugendstil, Sezessionstil, Stile Liberty) and caught on quickly in Paris. The style was characterised by sinuous curves and flowing asymmetrical forms reminiscent of creeping vines, water lilies, the patterns on insect wings and the flowering boughs of trees. Influenced by the arrival of exotic objets d'art from Japan, its French name came from a Paris gallery that featured works in the 'new art' style. True buffs should make a beeline for the art nouveau tourist trail in Nancy.

Belle Époque

The glittering belle époque, hot on the heels of art nouveau, heralded an eclecticism of decorative stucco friezes, *trompe l'œil* paintings, glittering wall mosaics, brightly coloured Moorish minarets and Turkish towers. Immerse yourself in its fabulous and whimsical designs with a stroll along promenade des Anglais in Nice, where the pink-domed Hôtel Negresco (1912) is the icing on the cake, or, up north, around the colourful Imperial Quarter of Metz. Or flop in a beautiful belle époque spa like Vichy.

Architecture et Musique (www.architecmusique.com) is a fine concept: enjoy a classical-music concert amid an architectural masterpiece; the annual program is online.

Modern

The Fondation Victor Vasarely, by the father of op art Victor Vasarely (1908–97), was an architectural coup when unveiled in Aix-en-Provence in 1976. Its 14 giant monumental hexagons reflected what Vasarely had already achieved in art: the creation of optical illusion and changing perspective through the juxtaposition of geometrical shapes and colours.

France's best-known 20th-century architect, Charles-Édouard Jeanneret (better known as Le Corbusier; 1887–1965), was born in Switzerland but settled in Paris in 1917 at the age of 30. A radical modernist, he tried to adapt buildings to their functions in industrialised society without ignoring the human element, thus rewriting the architectural style book with his sweeping lines and functionalised forms adapted to fit the human form. No single building has redefined urban living more than Le Corbusier's vertical 337-apartment 'garden city' known as La Cité Radieuse (the Radiant City) – today Hôtel Le Corbusier – that he designed on the coast in Marseille in 1952.

Most of Le Corbusier's work was done outside Paris, though he did design several private residences and the Pavillon Suisse, a dormitory for Swiss students at the Cité Internationale Universitaire in the 14e *arrondissement* of the capital. Elsewhere, Chapelle de Notre-Dame du Haut in the Jura and Couvent Ste-Marie de la Tourette near Lyon are 20th-century architectural icons.

Until 1968, French architects were still being trained almost exclusively at the conformist École des Beaux-Arts, reflected in most of the acutely unimaginative and impersonal 'lipstick tube' structures erected in the Parisian skyscraper district of La Défense, the Unesco building (1958) in the 7e, and Montparnasse's ungainly 210m-tall Tour Montparnasse (1973).

BIG-NAME BUILDINGS

Frank Gehry La Cinémathèque Française (Paris), Cité de la Vigne (Gruissan), Fondation Louis Vuitton (Paris), Luma Fondation (Arles)

Jean Nouvel Institut du Monde Arabe and Fondation d'Art pour l'Art Contemporain (Paris), Les Docks Vauban (Le Havre), Église Ste-Marie (Salat-la-Canéda), Musée Gallo-Romain (Périgueux), Château La Dominique (St-Émilion)

Lord Norman Foster Carrée d'Art (Nîmes), Viaduc de Millau (Languedoc), Musée de la Préhistoire des Gorges du Verdon (Quinson), Château Margaux (The Médoc)

Contemporary

For centuries French political leaders sought to immortalise themselves through the erection of huge public edifices (aka *grands projets*) in Paris. Georges Pompidou commissioned the once reviled, now much-loved Centre Pompidou (1977) in which the architects – in order to keep the exhibition halls as uncluttered as possible – put the building's insides out. His successor, Valéry Giscard d'Estaing, was instrumental in transforming the derelict Gare d'Orsay train station into the glorious Musée d'Orsay (1986). And François Mitterrand commissioned the capital's best-known contemporary architectural landmarks (taxpayers' bill: a whopping €4.6 billion), including the Opéra Bastille, the Grande Arche in La Défense, the four glass towers of the national library, and IM Pei's glass pyramid at the hitherto sacrosanct and untouchable Louvre (an architectural cause célèbre that paved the way, incidentally, for Mario Bellini and Rudy Ricciotti's magnificent flying carpet roof atop the Louvre's Cour Visconti in 2012).

No single museum presents a finer overview of French architecture than Paris' Cité de l'Architecture et du Patrimoine inside the 1937-built Palais de Chaillot.

Jacques Chirac's only *grand projet* was the riverside Musée du Quai Branly, an iconic glass, wood-and-sod structure with a 3-hectare experimental garden designed by Jean Nouvel (b 1945). France's leading and arguably most talented architect, Jean Nouvel was also the creative talent behind the Institut du Monde Arabe (1987), a highly praised structure in Paris that successfully mixes modern and traditional Arab and Western elements, and is considered one of the most beautiful and successful of France's contemporary buildings.

Nouvel also designed the Philharmonie de Paris, an experimental concert hall for the city's symphonic orchestra in Parc de la Villette. Birds flutter across its glittering metallic façade and a unique auditorium of 2400 terrace seats ensnare the orchestra pit inside the curvaceous, dramatically contemporary building. Initially approved as a €200 million project, the controversial concert hall ended up costing €387 million. To add insult to injury, Jean Nouvel personally boycotted its official opening in 2015 after submitting a court order (which he subsequently lost) asking for his name to be removed from the building which, the architect said, did not comply with his original design.

Drawing on the city's longstanding tradition of glass in its architecture, Canadian architect Frank Gehry used 12 enormous glass sails to design the extraordinary Fondation Louis Vuitton pour la Création in the Bois de Bologne in 2014. Glass likewise dominates the Forum des Halles in the 1er, a 1970s-eyesore shopping centre transformed in 2016 by architects Patrick Berger and Jacques Anziutti. The new radically curvaceous, curvilinear Les Halles is topped by a vast gold-coloured canopy made of 18,000 glass shingles weighing 7000 tonnes.

In the 15e, a shimmering slug of a contemporary building courtesy of Italian architect Renzo Piano breathtakingly emerges between two his-

toric buildings (with façades sculpted by Auguste Rodin no less) at the stunning Fondation Jérôme Seydoux-Pathé (2014).

Notable pieces of architecture in the provinces include Lyon's sparkling glass-and-steel cloud on the confluence of the Rhône and Saône Rivers, aka the cutting-edge Musée des Confluences (2014); Strasbourg's European Parliament; Jean Nouvel's glass-and-steel Musée Gallo-Romain Vesunna in Périgueux, Dutch architect Rem Koolhaas' Euralille and a 1920s art-deco swimming pool turned art museum in Lille; and the fantastic Louvre II in Lens, 37km south of Lille. Also noteworthy are an 11th-century abbey turned monumental sculpture gallery in Angers and Le Havre's rejuvenated 19th-century docks.

Then, of course, there's one of the world's tallest bridges, the stunning Viaduc de Millau in Languedoc, designed by Sir Norman Foster. Other bridges worth noting for their architectural ingenuity are Normandy's Pont de Normandie (1995) near Le Havre and Paris' striking Passerelle Simone de Beauvoir (2006). Both cross the Seine.

In Strasbourg, Italian architect Paolo Portoghesi designed France's biggest mosque, large enough to seat 1500 worshippers. Topped by a copper dome and flanked by wings resembling a flower in bud, the riverside building took 20 years of political to-ing and fro-ing for the groundbreaking project – a landmark for Muslims in France – to come to fruition.

The daring duo Shigeru Ban (Tokyo) and Jean de Gastines (Paris) is the tour de force behind the very white, bright Centre Pompidou-Metz (2010). Looking south, Frank Gehry is the big-name architect behind Arles' innovative new cultural centre: all ashimmer in the bright southern sun, rocklike Luma Fondation will evoke the nearby Alpilles mountain range with its two linked towers topped with aluminium when it opens in 2018.

Other striking works of contemporary architecture to grace future France include a futuristic concert and exhibition hall by Bernard Tschumi Architects in Rouen; and a new building for Monaco's car museum. In Paris Jean Nouvel will head a €600 million renovation of Gare d'Austerlitz (with one-third of the budget going on restoring the amazing glass roof); and Amanda Levete's London-based architectural studio, AL_A, will redesign Paris' famous Galeries Lafayette department store in 2017. In Lyon meanwhile, Swiss architects Herzog and de Meuron (of Tate Modern and Beijing National Stadium fame) are hard at work on phase two of the exciting Confluence project, begun in 2016, which will add a notable residential district, market and new bridges to the former wasteland.

Landscapes & Wildlife

France is a land of art. Fantastic portraits adorn the walls of galleries, villages resemble oil paintings plucked from a bygone rural age, and the people are naturally stylish. But as gorgeous as the art of France is, it fades when compared to the sheer beauty of the countryside itself.

The Land

Hexagon-shaped France, Europe's third-largest country, is fringed by water or mountains along every side except in the northeast. The country's 3200km-long coastline is incredibly diverse, ranging from white-chalk cliffs (Normandy) and treacherous promontories (Brittany) to broad expanses of fine sand (Atlantic coast) and pebbly beaches (the Mediterranean coast). Western Europe's highest peak, Mont Blanc (4810m), spectacularly crowns the French Alps, which stagger along France's eastern border. North of Lake Geneva, the gentle limestone Jura Mountains run along the Swiss frontier to reach heights of around 1700m, while the rugged Pyrenees guard France's 450km-long border with Spain and Andorra, peaking at 3404m.

Follow the progress of France's precious wolf, bear and lynx populations with Ferus (www.ferus.org), France's conservation group for these protected predators.

Five major river systems crisscross the country: the Garonne (which includes the Tarn, the Lot and the Dordogne) empties into the Atlantic; the Rhône links Lake Geneva and the Alps with the Mediterranean; Paris is licked in poetic verse by the Seine, which slithers through the city en route from Burgundy to the English Channel; and tributaries of the North Sea–bound Rhine drain much of the area north and east of the capital. Then there's France's longest river, the château-studded Loire, which meanders through history from the Massif Central to the Atlantic.

Wildlife

France is blessed with a rich variety of flora and fauna, although few habitats have escaped human impacts: intensive agriculture, wetland draining, urbanisation, hunting and the encroachment of industry and tourism infrastructure menace dozens of species.

WILDLIFE WATCH

The national parks and their regional siblings are great for observing animals in their natural habitat. The following are also worth a gander:

Flamingos The Camargue, France's best-known wetland site, attracts 10,000 pink flamingos and over 400 other bird species including rollers and glossy ibises.

Vultures Found in the Pyrenees at Falaise aux Vautours, the Vallée d'Ossau and in Languedoc at the Belvédère des Vautours in the Parc Naturel Régional des Grands Causses.

Storks In Alsace at the Centre de Réintroduction Cigognes & Loutres, in Hunawihr, and the Enclos aux Cigognes in Munster; on the Atlantic coast at Réserve Ornithologique du Teich, near Arcachon; and at the Parc des Oiseaux outside Villars-les-Dombes near Lyon.

Dolphins and whales Playful bottlenose dolphins splash around in the Mediterranean, and whales are sometimes sighted, too. Prime viewing from boat trips on the French Riviera and Corsica.

Animals

France has more mammal species (around 135) than any other European country. Couple this with around 500 bird species (depending on which rare migrants are included), 40 types of amphibian, 36 varieties of reptile and 72 kinds of fish, and wildlife-watchers are in seventh heaven. Of France's 40,000 identified insects, 10,000 creep and crawl in the Parc National du Mercantour in the southern Alps.

High-altitude plains in the Alps and the Pyrenees shelter the marmot, which hibernates from October to April and has a shrill and distinctive whistle; the nimble chamois (mountain antelope), with its dark-striped head; and the *bouquetin* (Alpine ibex), seen in large numbers in the Parc National de la Vanoise. Mouflons (wild mountain sheep), introduced in the 1950s, clamber over stony sunlit scree slopes in the mountains, while red and roe deer and wild boar are common in lower-altitude forested areas. The Alpine hare welcomes winter with its white coat, while 19 of Europe's 29 bat species hang out in the dark in the Alpine national parks.

The *loup* (wolf), which disappeared from France in the 1930s, returned to the Parc National du Mercantour in 1992 – much to the horror of the mouflon (on which it preys) and local sheep farmers. Dogs, corrals and sound machines have been used as an effective, nonlethal way of keeping the growing free-roaming wolf population of the Mercantour and other Alpine areas from feasting on domesticated sheep herds. Nonetheless, in late 2014 desperate farmers descended on the capital's Eiffel Tower with a flock of 250 sheep which they herded around the Champs de Mars to draw attention to their plight: the wolf is a government-protected species, hence farmers are powerless to shoot an attacking wolf.

A rare but wonderful treat is the sighting of an *aigle royal* (golden eagle): 40 pairs nest in the Mercantour, 20 pairs nest in the Vanoise, 30-odd in the Écrins and some 50 in the Pyrenees. Other birds of prey include the peregrine falcon, the kestrel, the buzzard and the bearded vulture – Europe's largest bird of prey, with an awe-inspiring wingspan of 2.8m. More recently, the small, pale-coloured Egyptian vulture has been spreading throughout the Alps and Pyrenees.

Even the eagle-eyed will have difficulty spotting the ptarmigan, a chickenlike species that moults three times a year to ensure a foolproof seasonal camouflage (brown in summer, white in winter). It lives on rocky slopes and in Alpine meadows above 2000m. The nutcracker, with its loud, buoyant singsong and larch-forest habitat, the black grouse, rock partridge, the very rare eagle owl and the three-toed woodpecker are among the other 120-odd species keeping birdwatchers glued to the skies in highland realms.

Elsewhere, there are now 12,000 pairs of white storks; 10% of the world's flamingo population hangs out in the Camargue; giant black cormorants – some with a wingspan of 1.7m – reside on an island off Pointe du Grouin on the north coast of Brittany; and there are unique seagull and fishing-eagle populations in the Réserve Naturelle de Scandola on Corsica. The *balbuzard pêcheur* (osprey), a migratory hunter that flocks to France in February or March, today only inhabits two regions of France: Corsica and the Loire Valley.

BROWN BEARS

The brown bear disappeared from the Alps in the mid-1930s. The 150-odd native bears living in the Pyrenees a century ago had dwindled to one orphaned cub following the controversial shooting of its mother – the last female bear of Pyrenean stock – by a hunter in 2004. However, between 18 and 22 bears of Slovenian origin also call the French and Spanish Pyrenees home, though the most famous, Balou, was found dead in 2014. The reintroduction program has faced fierce opposition from sheep herders.

LIFE & DEATH OF THE IBEX

Often spotted hanging out on sickeningly high crags and ledges, the nippy *bouquetin des Alpes* (Alpine ibex), with its imposingly large, curly-wurly horns, is the animal most synonymous with the French Alps. Higher altitudes were loaded with the handsome beast in the 16th century but, three centuries on, its extravagant horns had become a must-have item in any gentleman's trophy cabinet, and within a few years it had been hunted to the brink of extinction.

In 1963 the Parc National de la Vanoise was created in the Alps to stop hunters in the massif from shooting the few Alpine ibex that remained. The creation of similar nature reserves and rigorous conservation campaigns have seen populations surely and steadily recover – to the point where today the Alpine ibex is thriving. Not that you're likely to encounter one: the canny old ibex has realised that some mammals are best avoided.

Plants

About 140,000 sq km of forest – beech, oak and pine in the main – covers 20% of France, and there are 4900 different species of native flowering plants countrywide (2250 alone grow in the Parc National des Cévennes).

The Alpine and Pyrenean regions nurture fir, spruce and beech forests on north-facing slopes between 800m and 1500m. Larch trees, mountain and arolla pines, rhododendrons and junipers stud shrubby subalpine zones between 1500m and 2000m; and a brilliant riot of spring and summertime wildflowers carpets grassy meadows above the treeline in the alpine zone (up to 3000m).

Of France's 150 orchids, the black vanilla orchid is one to look out for – its small red-brown flowers exude a sweet vanilla fragrance.

Alpine blooms include the single golden-yellow flower of the arnica, long used in herbal and homeopathic bruise-relieving remedies; the flame-coloured fire lily; and the hardy Alpine columbine, with its delicate blue petals. The protected 'queen of the Alps' (aka the Alpine eryngo) bears an uncanny resemblance to a purple thistle but is, in fact, a member of the parsley family (to which the carrot also belongs).

Corsica and the Massif des Maures, west of St-Tropez on the Côte d'Azur, are closely related botanically: both have chestnut and cork-oak trees and are thickly carpeted with garrigues and maquis – heavily scented scrubland, where dozens of fragrant shrubs and herbs find shelter.

National Parks

The proportion of protected land in France is surprisingly low: seven *parcs nationaux* (www.parcsnationaux.fr) fully protect just 0.8% of the country. Another 13% (70,000 sq km) in metropolitan France and its overseas territories is protected to a substantially lesser degree by 48 *parcs naturels régionaux* (www.parcs-naturels-regionaux.tm.fr), and a further few per cent by 320 smaller *réserves naturelles* (www.reserves-naturelles.org), some of them under the eagle eye of the Conservatoire du Littoral.

While the central zones of national parks are uninhabited and fully protected by legislation (dogs, vehicles and hunting are banned and camping is restricted), their delicate ecosystems spill over into populated peripheral zones in which economic activities, some of them environmentally unfriendly, are permitted and even encouraged.

Most regional nature parks and reserves were established not only to maintain or improve local ecosystems, but also to encourage economic development and tourism in areas suffering from hardship and diminishing populations (such as the Massif Central and Corsica).

Select pockets of nature – the Pyrenees, Mont St-Michel and its bay, part of the Loire Valley, the astonishingly biodiverse Cévennes, a clutch of capes on Corsica and vineyards in Burgundy and Champagne – have been declared Unesco World Heritage Sites.

HIGH-FACTOR PROTECTION BY THE SEA

Over 10% of the coastline of mainland France and Corsica is managed by the Conservatoire du Littoral (www.conservatoire-du-littoral.fr), a public coastal-protection body. Among the *conservatoire's* rich pageant of *espaces naturels protégés* (protected natural areas) are the rare-orchid-dotted sand dunes east of Dunkirk, the Baie de Somme with its ornithological park, several wet and watery pockets of the horse-studded Camargue, and a Corsican desert. France also sports 43 Ramsar Convention wetland sites (www.ramsar.org).

Environmental Issues

Wetlands in France – incredibly productive ecosystems essential for the survival of birds, reptiles, fish and amphibians – are shrinking. More than 20,000 sq km (3% of French territory) are considered important wetlands but only 4% of this land is protected.

Great tracts of forest burn each summer, often because of careless day trippers but occasionally, as is sometimes reported on the Côte d'Azur, because they're intentionally torched by people hoping to get licences to build on the damaged lands. Since the mid-1970s, between 31 sq km and 615 sq km of land has been reduced to black stubble each year by an average of 540 fires. However, as prevention and fire-fighting improve, the number of fires is falling, according to the Office National des Forêts (www.onf.fr), the national forestry commission.

Dogs and guns also pose a threat to French animal life, brown bears included. While the number of hunters has fallen by more than 20% in the last decade, there are still more hunters in France (1.3 million) than in any other Western European country. Despite the 1979 Brussels Directive for the protection of wild birds, their eggs, nests and habitats in the EU, the French government has been very slow to make its provisions part of French law, meaning birds that can fly safely over other countries can still be hunted as they cross France.

Green initiatives in Paris include the creation of 100 hectares of green roofs, façades and vertical walls in the capital city, a third of which will be devoted to urban agriculture.

The state-owned electricity company, Electricité de France, has an enviable record on minimising greenhouse-gas emissions – fossil-fuel-fired power plants account for just 4.6% of its production. Clean, renewable hydropower, generated by 220 dams, comprises 8.8% of the company's generating capacity but this does affect animal habitats. And no less than 75% (the highest in the world) of France's electricity comes from another controversial carbon-zero source: nuclear power, generated by 59 nuclear reactors at 20 sites. When François Hollande came to power in 2012, he pledged to reduce France's reliance on nuclear energy to 50% by 2025. Meanwhile the world's most ambitious nuclear-power program continues to grow. Costing an extraordinary €10.5 billion, the country's most recent nuclear reactor, Flamanville 3 on Normandy's west coast near Cherbourg, is due for completion in 2018 – seven years later than planned.

Europe's largest solar-powered electricity-generating farm sits 1000m-high on a south-facing slope near the village of Curbans in Provence. The 150-hectare array of photovoltaic cells – 145,000 panels – removes 120,000 metric tonnes of carbon dioxide from the French annual energy bill. Global warming might translate as a shorter and riskier season for skiers in the Alps as snowfall becomes erratic and avalanches occur more often. But for Alpine flora and fauna, it is even more serious. Alpine plants are fleeing up the warming mountainsides at between 0.5m and 4m per decade, reports the WWF, making way for invasive species and the pathogens and animals that come with them. France's largest glacier, the Mer de Glace near Chamonix, is retreating by 4m to 5m per year. No wonder, therefore, that at the United Nations Climate Change Conference (COP21), held in Paris in 2015, world leaders reached an agreement to limit global warming to less than 2°C by the end of the century.

Survival Guide

Directory A–Z

Accommodation

As a rule of thumb, budget covers everything from basic hostels to small family-run places; midrange means a few extra creature comforts such as an elevator; while top-end places stretch from luxury five-star palaces with air-conditioning, swimming pools and restaurants to boutique-chic Alpine chalets.

Costs

Accommodation costs vary wildly between seasons and regions: what will buy you a night in a romantic *chambre d'hôte* (B&B) in the country-side may get a dorm bed in a major city or high-profile ski resort.

Reservations

Midrange, top-end and many budget hotels require a credit card number to secure an advance reservation made by phone; some hostels do not take bookings. Many tourist offices can advise on availability and reserve for you, often for a fee of €5 and usually only if you stop by in person. In the Alps, ski-resort tourist offices run a central reservation service for booking accommodation.

Seasons

➡ In ski resorts, high season is Christmas, New Year and the February–March school holidays.

➡ On the coast, high season is summer, particularly August.

➡ Hotels in inland cities often charge low-season rates in summer.

➡ Rates often drop outside the high season – in some cases by as much as 50%.

➡ In business-oriented hotels in cities, rooms are most expensive from Monday to Thursday and cheaper over the weekend.

➡ In the Alps, hotels usually close between seasons, from around May to mid-June and from mid-September to early December; many addresses in Corsica only open Easter to October.

B&Bs

For charm, a heartfelt *bienvenue* (welcome) and solid home cooking, it's hard to beat France's privately run *chambres d'hôte* (B&Bs) – urban rarities but as common as muck in rural areas. By law a *chambre d'hôte* must have no more than five rooms and breakfast must be included in the price; some hosts prepare a meal *(table d'hôte)* for an extra charge of around €30 including wine. Pick up lists of *chambres d'hôte* at tourist offices, or find one to suit online.

Bienvenue à la Ferme (www.bienvenue-a-la-ferme.com)

Chambres d'Hôtes France (www.chambresdhotesfrance.com)

Fleurs de Soleil (www.fleursdesoleil.fr) Selective collection of 550 stylish *maisons d'hôte*, mainly in rural France

Gîtes de France (www.gites-de-france.com) France's primary umbrella organisation for B&Bs and self-catering properties *(gîtes);* search by region, theme (charm, with kids, by the sea, gourmet, great garden etc.), activity (fishing, wine tasting etc.) or facilities (pool, dishwasher, fireplace, baby equipment etc.)

SLEEPING PRICE RANGES

The following price ranges refer to a double room in high season, with private bathroom (any combination of toilet, bath-tub, shower and washbasin), excluding breakfast unless otherwise noted. Breakfast is assumed to be included at a B&B. Where half-board (breakfast and dinner) and full board (breakfast, lunch and dinner) is included, this is mentioned with the price.

€ less than €90 (less than €130 in Paris)

€€ €90–190 (€130–250 in Paris)

€€€ more than €190 (more than €250 in Paris)

THE FINE ART OF SLEEPING

A château, a country manor, Parisian opulence in the shade of the Eiffel Tower – whether you want to live like a lord, sleep like a log or blow the budget, there's a room with your name on it.

Alistair Sawday's (www.sawdays.co.uk) Boutique retreats and *chambres d'hôte*, placing the accent on originality and authentic hospitality.

Châteaux & Hôtels Collection (www.chateauxhotels.com) Châteaux and other historic properties, now boutique hotels, with a thousand tales to tell.

Grandes Étapes Françaises (www.grandesetapes.fr) Beautiful châteaux-hotels and multistar residences.

iGuide (www.iguide-hotels.com) Abbeys, manors, châteaux – a real mixed bag of charming hotels.

Logis de France (www.logis-de-france.fr) Small, often family-run hotels with charm and a warm welcome.

Relais & Châteaux (www.relaischateaux.com) Seductive selection of top-end villas, châteaux and historic hotels.

Relais du Silence (www.relaisdusilence.com) Fall asleep to complete silence in a gorgeous château, spa-clad *auberge* (country inn), or vineyard hotel.

Small Luxury Hotels of the World (www.slh.com) Super-luxurious boutique hotels, chalets and resorts.

iGuide (www.iguide-hotels.com) Gorgeous presentation of France's most charming and often-times most upmarket B&Bs, organised by region and/or theme (romantic, gastronomic, green, oenological and so forth)

Samedi Midi Éditions (www.samedimidi.com) Country, mountain, seaside...choose your *chambre d'hôte* by location or theme (romance, golf, design, cooking courses)

Camping

Be it a Mongolian yurt, boutique treehouse or simple canvas beneath stars, camping in France is in vogue. Thousands of well-equipped campgrounds dot the country, many considerately placed by rivers, lakes and the sea.

➡ Most campgrounds open March or April to late September or October; popular spots fill up fast in summer so it is wise to call ahead.

➡ 'Sites' refer to fixed-price deals for two people including a tent and a car. Otherwise the price is broken down per adult/tent/car. Factor in a few extra euro per night for *taxe de séjour* (holiday tax) and electricity.

➡ Euro-economisers should look out for local, good-value but no-frills *campings municipaux* (municipal campgrounds).

➡ Many campgrounds rent mobile homes with mod cons such as heating, fitted kitchen and TV.

➡ Pitching up 'wild' in nondesignated spots *(camping sauvage)* is illegal in France.

➡ Campground offices often close during the day.

➡ Accessing many campgrounds without your own transport can be slow and costly, or simply impossible.

Websites with campsite listings searchable by location, theme and facilities:

Bienvenue à la Ferme (www.bienvenue-a-la-ferme.com)

Camping en France (www.camping.fr)

Camping France (www.campingfrance.com)

HPA Guide (http://camping.hpaguide.com)

Gîtes de France (www.gites-de-france.com)

Homestays

One of the best way to brush up your *français* and immerse yourself in local life is by staying with a French family under an arrangement known as *hôtes payants* or *hébergement chez l'habitant*. Popular among students and young people, this set-up means you rent a room and usually have access (sometimes limited) to the bathroom and the kitchen; meals may also be available.

If you are sensitive to smoke or pets, make sure you mention this.

France Lodge Locations (☎01 56 35 85 80; www.apartments-in-paris.com) Accommodation in private Parisian homes; €36 to €78 a night for a single, €56 to €95 for two or three people.

Gîtes de France (www.gites-de-france.com) Handles some of the most charming *gîtes ruraux* (self-contained holiday cottages) in rural areas.

Homestay.com (www.homestay.com) Homestays in major cities.

WHICH FLOOR?

In France, 'ground floor' refers to the floor at street level; the 1st floor – what would be called the 2nd floor in the US – is the floor above that.

Hostels

Hostels in France range from funky to threadbare, although with a wave of design-driven, up-to-the-minute hostels opening in Paris, Marseille and other big cities, hip hang-outs with perks aplenty seem to easily outweigh the threadbare these days.

➡ In university towns, *foyers d'étudiant* (student dormitories) are sometimes converted for use by travellers during summer.

➡ A dorm bed in an *auberge de jeunesse* (youth hostel) costs €20 to €50 in Paris, and anything from €15 to €40 in the provinces, depending on location, amenities and facilities; sheets are always included, breakfast more often than not.

➡ To prevent outbreaks of bed bugs, sleeping bags are not permitted.

➡ Hostels by the sea or in the mountains sometimes offer seasonal outdoor activities.

➡ French hostels are 100% nonsmoking.

HOSTELLING CARD

Official *auberges de jeunesse* affiliated to the Fédération Unie des Auberges de Jeunesse (www.fuaj.org) or Ligue Française pour les Auberges de la Jeunesse (www.auberges-de-jeunesse.com) require guests to have an annual Hostelling International (HI) card (€7/11 for under/over 26s) or a nightly Welcome Stamp (up to €3, maximum of six per year).

Hotels

Hotels in France are rated with one to five stars, although the ratings are based on highly objective criteria (eg the size of the entry hall), not the quality of the service, the decor or cleanliness.

➡ French hotels almost never include breakfast in their rates. Unless specified, prices quoted don't include breakfast, which costs around €8/12/25 in a budget/midrange/top-end hotel.

➡ When you book, hotels usually ask for a credit card number; some require a deposit.

➡ A double room generally has one double bed (sometimes two singles pushed together!); a room with twin beds *(deux lits)* is usually more expensive, as is a room with a bath-tub instead of a shower.

➡ Feather pillows are practically nonexistent, even in top-end hotels.

➡ All hotel restaurant terraces allow smoking; if you are sensitive to smoke, you may need to sit inside.

Refuges & Gîtes d'Étape

➡ *Refuges* (mountain huts or shelters) are bog-basic cabins established along walking trails in uninhabited mountainous areas and operated by national-park authorities, the **Club Alpin Français** (www.ffcam.fr) or other private organisations.

➡ *Refuges* are marked on hiking and climbing maps.

➡ A bunk in a dorm generally costs €10 to €25. Hot meals are sometimes available and, in a few cases, mandatory, pushing the price up to €30 or beyond.

➡ Advance reservations and a weather check are essential before setting out.

➡ *Gîtes d'étape*, better equipped and more comfortable than *refuges* (some even have showers), are situated along walking trails in less remote areas, often in villages.

➡ Drop by **Gîtes d'Étape et Refuges** (www.gites-refuges.com), an online listing of 4000 *gîtes d'étape* and *refuges* in France.

Rental Accommodation

If you are planning on staying put for more than a few days or are travelling in a group, then renting a furnished studio, apartment or villa can be an economical alternative. You will have the chance to live like a local, with trips to the farmers market and the *boulangerie* (bakery).

Finding an apartment for long-term rental can be gruelling. Landlords, many of whom prefer locals to foreigners, usually require substantial proof of financial responsibility and sufficient funds in France; many ask for a *caution* (guarantee) and a hefty deposit.

➡ Cleaning, linen rental and electricity fees usually cost extra.

➡ Classified ads appear in *De Particulier à Particulier* (www.

GLAMPING

Farewell clammy canvas, adieu inflatable mattress... Glamping in France is cool and creative, with *écolo chic* (ecochic) and adventurous alternatives springing up all the time. If you fancy doing a Robinson Crusoe by staying in a treehouse with an incredible view over the treetops, visit Cabanes de France (www.cabanes-de-france.com), which covers leafy options between branches all over France. Prefer to keep your feet firmly on the ground? Keep an eye out for ecoconscious campsites where you can snooze in a *tipi* (tepee) or in a giant hammock.

pap.fr, in French), published on Thursday and sold at newsstands.

- For apartments outside Paris it's best to search at your destination.
- Check places like bars and *tabacs* (tobacconists) for free local newspapers (often named after the number of the *département*) with classifieds listings.

Customs Regulations

Goods brought in and out of countries within the EU incur no additional taxes provided duty has been paid somewhere within the EU and the goods are for personal consumption. Duty-free shopping is available only if you are leaving the EU.

Duty-free allowances (for adults) coming from non-EU countries (including the Channel Islands):

- 200 cigarettes or 50 cigars or 250g tobacco
- 1L spirits or 2L of sparkling wine/other alcoholic drinks less than 22% alcohol
- 4L still wine
- 16L beer
- other goods up to the value of €300/430 (€150 for under 15 year olds)

Higher limits apply if you are coming from Andorra; anything over these limits must be declared. For further details, see www.douane.gouv.fr.

Discount Cards

Discount cards yield fantastic benefits and easily pay for themselves. As well as the card fee, you'll often need a passport-sized photo and ID with proof of age (eg passport or birth certificate).

People over 60 or 65 are entitled to discounts on things like public transport, museum admissions and theatres.

Discount card options:

- **Camping Card International** (www.campingcardinternational.com; €10) Used as ID for checking into campsites; the annual card includes third-party liability insurance and covers up to 11 people in a party; it usually yields up to 20% discount. Available at automobile associations, camping federations and campgrounds.
- **European Youth Card** (www.euro26.org, http://kiosk.eyca.org; €14) Wide range of discounts for under-26-year-olds. Available online.
- **International Student Identity Card** (www.isic.org; €15) Discounts on travel, shopping, attractions and entertainment for full-time students. Available at ISIC points listed online.
- **International Teacher Identity Card** (www.isic.org; €18) Travel, shopping, entertainment and sightseeing discounts for full-time teachers.
- **International Youth Travel Card** (www.isic.org; €13) Discounts on travel, tickets and so forth for under 26 year olds.

Electricity

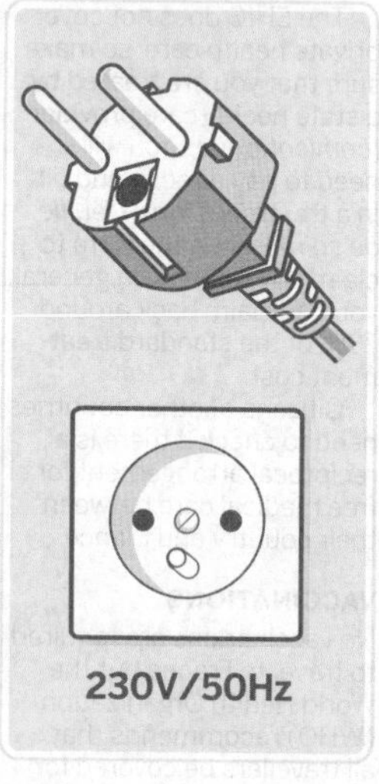

Embassies & Consulates

All foreign embassies are in Paris.

- Many countries – including Canada, Japan, the UK, USA and most European countries – also have consulates in other major cities such as Bordeaux, Lyon, Nice, Marseille and Strasbourg.
- To find a consulate or an embassy, visit www.embassiesabroad.com or look up '*ambassade*' in the super user-friendly Pages Jaunes (www.pagesjaunes.fr).

Gay & Lesbian Travellers

The rainbow flag flies high in France, a country that left its closet long before many of its European neighbours. *Laissez-faire* perfectly sums up France's liberal attitude towards homosexuality and people's private lives in general; in part because of a long tradition of public tolerance towards unconventional lifestyles.

- Paris has been a thriving gay and lesbian centre since the late 1970s, and most major organisations are based there today.
- Bordeaux, Lille, Lyon, Montpellier, Toulouse and many other towns also have an active queer scene.
- Attitudes towards homosexuality tend to be more conservative in the countryside and villages.
- France's lesbian scene is less public than its gay male counterpart and is centred mainly on women's cafes and bars.
- Same-sex marriage has been legal in France since May 2013.
- Gay Pride marches are held in major French cities mid-May to early July.

EATING PRICE RANGES

Price indicators refer to the average cost of a two-course meal, be it an *entrée* (starter) and *plat* (main course) or main and dessert, or a two- or three-course *menu* (set meal at a fixed price).

€ less than €20

€€ €20–40

€€€ more than €40

Publications

- **Damron** (www.damron.com) Has published English-language travel guides since the 1960s, including *Damron Women's Traveller* for lesbians and *Damron Men's Travel Guide* for gays.
- **Spartacus International Gay Guide** (www.spartacus-world.com) A male-only guide to just about every country in the world, with more than 70 pages devoted to France, almost half of which cover Paris. There's a smartphone app too.

Websites

- **Gaipied** (www.gayvox.com/guide3) Online travel guide to France, with listings by region, by Gayvox.
- **Gay Travel & Life in France** (www.gay-france.net) Insider tips on gay life in France.
- **Tasse de Thé** (www.tassedethe.com) A *webzine lesbien* with lots of useful links.

Health

France is a healthy place, so your main risks are likely to be sunburn, foot blisters, insect bites and mild stomach problems from eating and drinking with too much gusto.

Before You Go

- Bring your medications in their original, clearly labelled, containers.
- A signed and dated letter from your physician describing your medical conditions and medications, including generic names (French medicine names are often completely different from those in other countries), is also a good idea.
- Dental care in France is usually good; however, it is sensible to have a dental check-up before a long trip.

HEALTH INSURANCE

Citizens of the EU, Switzerland, Iceland, Norway or Liechtenstein receive free or reduced-cost, state-provided health care cover with the European Health Insurance Card (EHIC) for medical treatment that becomes necessary while in France. Each family member will need a separate card. UK residents can get application forms from post offices, or download them from the Department of Health website (www.dh.gov.uk), which has comprehensive information about the card's coverage.

The EHIC does not cover private health care, so make sure that you are treated by a state health-care provider (*conventionné*). You will need to pay directly and fill in a treatment form (*feuille de soins*); keep the form to claim any refunds. In general, you can claim back around 70% of the standard treatment cost.

Citizens of other countries need to check if there is a reciprocal arrangement for free medical care between their country and France.

VACCINATIONS

No vaccinations are required to travel to France but the World Health Organization (WHO) recommends that all travellers be covered for diphtheria, tetanus, measles, mumps, rubella and polio, regardless of their destination.

In France

AVAILABILITY & COST OF HEALTH CARE

Visitors to France can get excellent health care from hospital *(hôpital)* emergency rooms/casualty wards *(salles des urgences)* and at a doctors' office *(cabinet médical)*.

- For minor illnesses, trained staff in pharmacies – in every village and town with a green-cross sign outside that flashes when open – give valuable advice, sell medications, can tell you when more specialised help is needed and will point you in the right direction.
- You will need to pay upfront for any health care you receive, be it at a doctor's surgery, pharmacy or hospital, unless your insurance plan makes payments directly to providers.
- The standard rate for a consultation with a GP/specialist is €30 to €50.
- Emergency contraception is available with a doctor's prescription. Condoms *(les préservatifs)* are readily available.

Insurance

- Comprehensive travel insurance to cover theft, loss and medical problems is highly recommended.
- Some policies specifically exclude dangerous activities such as scuba diving, motorcycling, skiing and even trekking: read the fine print.
- Check that the policy covers ambulances or an emergency flight home.
- Find out in advance if your insurance plan will make payments directly to providers or reimburse you later for overseas health expenditures.

➡ If you have to claim later, make sure you keep all documentation.

➡ Paying for your airline ticket with a credit card often provides limited travel accident insurance – ask your credit card company what it is prepared to cover.

➡ Worldwide travel insurance is available at www.lonelyplanet.com/travel-insurance. You can buy, extend and claim online anytime – even if you're already on the road.

Internet Access

➡ Wi-fi (pronounced 'wee-fee' in French) is available at major airports, in most hotels, and at many cafes, restaurants, museums and tourist offices.

➡ Free public wi-fi hot spots are available in cities and many towns: Paris alone has 400 public hot spots in 26 different locations citywide (www.paris.fr/wifi), including parks, libraries and municipal buildings. In parks look for a purple 'Zone Wi-Fi' sign near the entrance and select the 'PARIS_WI-FI_' network to connect.

➡ To search for free wi-fi hot spots in France, visit www.hotspot-locations.com.

➡ Tourist offices is some larger cities, including Lyon and Bordeaux, rent out pocket-sized mobile wi-fi devices that you carry around with you, ensuring a fast wi-fi connection while roaming the city.

➡ Alternatively, rent a mobile wi-fi device online before leaving home and arrange for it to be delivered by post to your hotel in France through HipPocketWifi (http://hippocketwifi.com), Travel WiFi (http://travel-wifi.com) or My Webspot (http://my-webspot.com).

➡ Internet cafes are increasingly rife; at least one can usually be tracked down in cities. Prices range from €2 to €6 per hour.

Legal Matters

Police

➡ French police have wide powers of search and seizure and can ask you to prove your identity at any time – whether or not there is 'probable cause'.

➡ Foreigners must be able to prove their legal status in France (eg with a passport, visa or residency permit) without delay.

➡ If the police stop you for any reason, be polite and remain calm. Verbally (and of course physically) abusing a police officer can lead to a hefty fine, and even imprisonment.

➡ You may refuse to sign a police statement, and have the right to ask for a copy.

➡ People who are arrested are considered innocent until proven guilty, but can be held in custody until trial.

Drugs & Alcohol

➡ French law does not distinguish between 'hard' and 'soft' drugs.

➡ The penalty for any personal use of *stupéfiants* (including cannabis, amphetamines, ecstasy and heroin) can be a one-year jail sentence and a €3750 fine but, depending on the circumstances, it might be anything from a stern word to a compulsory rehab program.

➡ Importing, possessing, selling or buying drugs can get you up to 10 years in prison and a fine of up to €500,000.

➡ Police have been known to search chartered coaches, cars and train passengers for drugs just because they're coming from Amsterdam.

➡ *Ivresse* (drunkenness) in public is punishable by a fine.

WHAT THE [wi-fi icon] ICON MEANS

Only accommodation providers that have an actual computer that guests can use to access the internet are flagged with an internet icon, @.

The wi-fi icon, [wi-fi icon], indicates anywhere with wi-fi access. Where this icon appears, assume the wi-fi is free unless otherwise specified.

Money

ATMs

Automated Teller Machines (ATMs) – known as *distributeurs automatiques de billets* (DAB) or *points d'argent* in French – are the cheapest and most convenient way to get money. ATMs connected to international networks are situated in all cities and towns and usually offer an excellent exchange rate.

AMERICANS, TAKE NOTE

Travellers with credit cards issued in the US, be aware that you might well find yourself occasionally stuck when it comes to paying with your card: certain places in France – notably, Vélib in Paris and bike-share schemes in other cities, self-service toll booths on the autoroute (highway), and garages with self-service petrol (gas) pumps – only accept credit cards with chips and PINs. There is no solution to this bar ensuring you always have an emergency stash of cash on you.

Credit & Debit Cards

➡ Credit and debit cards, accepted almost everywhere in France, are convenient, relatively secure and usually offer a better exchange rate than travellers cheques or cash exchanges.

➡ Credit cards issued in France have embedded chips – you have to type in a PIN to make a purchase.

➡ Visa, MasterCard and Amex can be used in shops and supermarkets and for train travel, car hire and motorway tolls.

➡ Don't assume that you can pay for a meal or a budget hotel with a credit card – enquire first.

➡ Cash advances are a supremely convenient way to stay stocked up with euros, but getting cash with a credit card involves both fees (sometimes US$10 or more) and interest – ask your credit-card issuer for details. Debit-card fees are usually much less.

LOST CARDS

For lost cards, these numbers operate 24 hours:

Amex (☎01 47 77 72 00)

MasterCard (☎08 00 90 13 87)

Visa (Carte Bleue; ☎08 00 90 11 79)

Currency

You always get a better exchange rate in-country but it is a good idea to arrive in France with enough euros to take a taxi to a hotel if you have to.

Money Changers

➡ Commercial banks charge up to €5 per foreign-currency transaction – if they even bother to offer exchange services any more.

➡ In Paris and major cities, *bureaux de change* (exchange bureaus) are faster and easier, open longer hours and often give better rates than banks.

➡ Some post-office branches exchange travellers cheques and banknotes in a variety of currencies but charge a commission for cash; most won't take US$100 bills.

Taxes & Refunds

The standard value-added tax (VAT) rate of 20% is levied on most goods and services in France. Restaurants and hotels must always include 10% VAT in their prices.

Non-EU residents can claim a VAT refund on same-day purchases over €175, providing the goods are for personal consumption and are being personally transported home; retailers have details.

Tipping

By law, restaurant and bar prices are *service compris* (ie they include a 15% service charge), so there is no need to leave a *pourboire* (tip). If you were extremely satisfied with the service, however, you can – as many locals do – show your appreciation by leaving a small 'extra' tip for your waiter or waitress.

WHERE/WHO	CUSTOMARY TIP
bar	None at the bar; round to nearest euro for table service
cafe	5-10%
hotel porter	€1-2 per bag
restaurant	10%
taxi	10-15%
toilet attendant	€0.50
tour guide	€1-2 per person

Travellers Cheques

Travellers cheques, a 20th-century relic, cannot be used to pay French merchants directly – change them into euro banknotes at banks, exchange bureaux or post offices.

Opening Hours

French business hours are regulated by a maze of government regulations, including the 35-hour working week.

➡ The midday break is uncommon in Paris but common elsewhere; in general, the break gets longer the further south you go.

➡ French law requires that most businesses close on Sunday; exceptions include grocery stores, *boulangeries* (bakeries), florists and businesses catering to the tourist trade.

STANDARD HOURS

BUSINESS	OPENING HOURS
Banks	9am–noon and 2pm–5pm Monday to Friday or Tuesday to Saturday
Restaurants	Noon–2.30pm and 7pm–11pm six days a week
Cafes	7am–11pm
Bars	7pm–1am
Clubs	10pm–3am, 4am or 5am Thursday to Saturday
Shops	10am–noon and 2pm–7pm Monday to Saturday

- In many towns and villages, shops close on Monday.
- Many service stations open 24 hours a day and stock basic groceries.
- Restaurants generally close one or two days of the week, chosen according to the owner's whim. Opening days/hours are only specified if the restaurant isn't open for both lunch and dinner daily.
- Most (but not all) national museums are closed on Tuesday; most local museums are closed on Monday, though in summer some open daily. Many museums close at lunchtime.

Post

French post offices are flagged with a yellow or brown sign reading 'La Poste'. Since La Poste (www.laposte.fr) also has banking, finance and bill-paying functions, queues can be long but automatic machines dispense postage stamps.

Public Holidays

The following *jours fériés* (public holidays) are observed in France:

New Year's Day (Jour de l'An) 1 January

Easter Sunday & Monday (Pâques & Lundi de Pâques) Late March/April

May Day (Fête du Travail) 1 May

Victoire 1945 8 May

Ascension Thursday (Ascension) May; on the 40th day after Easter

Pentecost/Whit Sunday & Whit Monday (Pentecôte & Lundi de Pentecôte) Mid-May to mid-June; on the seventh Sunday after Easter

Bastille Day/National Day (Fête Nationale) 14 July

Assumption Day (Assomption) 15 August

All Saints' Day (Toussaint) 1 November

Remembrance Day (L'onze Novembre) 11 November

Christmas (Noël) 25 December

The following are *not* public holidays in France: Shrove Tuesday (Mardi Gras; the first day of Lent); Maundy (or Holy) Thursday and Good Friday, just before Easter; and Boxing Day (26 December).

Note: Good Friday and Boxing Day *are* public holidays in Alsace.

Safe Travel

France is generally a safe place in which to live and travel despite crime and terrorism rising dramatically in the last few years. Although property crime is a problem, it is extremely unlikely that you will be physically assaulted while walking down the street. Always check your government's travel advisory warnings.

Because of the threat of terrorism, French police are very strict about security. Do not leave baggage unattended, especially at airports or train stations: suspicious objects may be summarily blown up. In large museums and monuments, it is fairly routine for bags to be checked upon entering.

The France hunting season runs from September to February. If you see signs reading *'chasseurs'* or *'chasse gardée'* strung up or tacked to trees, think twice about wandering into the area. As well as millions of wild animals, some 25 French hunters die each year after being shot by other hunters. Hunting is traditional and commonplace in all rural areas in France, especially the Vosges, the Sologne, the southwest and the Baie de Somme.

STATE OF EMERGENCY

Following the fatal terrorist attacks on the capital in November 2015, France declared a state of emergency. An attack on Bastille Day in Nice the following year prompted the French president to extend the state of emergency for a further three months. At the time of writing, France remained in an official 'state of emergency', meaning authorities are able to carry out police raids and place suspects under house arrest without prior court authorisation.

Natural Dangers

- There are powerful tides and strong undertows at many places along the Atlantic coast, from the Spanish border north to Brittany and Normandy.
- Only swim in *zones de baignade surveillée* (beaches monitored by life guards).
- Be aware of tide times and the high-tide mark if walking or sleeping on a beach.
- Thunderstorms in the mountains and the hot southern plains can be extremely sudden and violent.
- Check the weather report before setting out on a long walk and be prepared for sudden storms and temperature drops if you are heading into the high country of the Alps or Pyrenees.
- Avalanches pose a significant danger in the French Alps.

Theft

Pickpocketing and bag/phone snatching (for example, in dense crowds and public places) are as prevalent in big French cities – Paris, Marseille and Nice in particular – as in other cities in Europe. There's no need whatsoever to travel in fear. A few simple precautions will minimise your chances of being ripped off.

- On trains, avoid leaving smartphones and tablets lying casually on the table in front of you and keep bags as close to you as possible: luggage racks at the ends of carriages are easy prey for thieves; in sleeping compartments, lock the door carefully at night.
- Be especially vigilant for bag/phone snatchers at train stations, airports, fast-food outlets, outdoor cafes, beaches and on public transport.
- Break-ins to parked cars are a widespread problem. Never, ever leave anything valuable – or not valuable – inside your car, even in the boot (trunk).
- Aggressive theft from cars stopped at red lights is occasionally a problem, especially in Marseille and Nice. As a precaution, lock your car doors and roll up the windows.

Strikes

France is the only European country in which public workers enjoy an unlimited right to strike. Aggrieved truck drivers block motorways from time to time, and farmers agitating for more government support have been known to dump tonnes of produce on major arteries. Sporadic train strikes and striking taxi drivers can sometimes disrupt travel.

Getting caught in one of the 'social dialogues' that characterise labour relations in France can put a serious crimp in your travel plans. It is best to leave some wriggle room in your schedule, particularly around departure times.

Telephone

Mobile Phones

- French mobile phone numbers begin with 06 or 07.
- France uses GSM 900/1800, which is compatible with the rest of Europe and Australia but not with the North American GSM 1900 or the totally different system in Japan (though some North Americans have tri-band phones that work here).
- Check with your service provider about roaming charges – dialling a mobile phone from a fixed-line phone or another mobile can be incredibly expensive.
- It is usually cheaper to buy a local SIM card from a French provider such as Orange, SFR, Bouygues or Free Mobile, which gives you a local phone number. To do this, ensure your phone is unlocked.
- If you already have a compatible phone, you can slip in a SIM card (from €3.90) and rev it up with prepaid credit, though this is likely to run out fast as domestic prepaid calls cost about €0.50 per minute.
- Recharge cards are sold at most *tabacs* (tobacconist-newsagents), supermarkets and online through websites such as Topengo (www.topengo.fr) or Sim-OK (https://recharge.sim-ok.com).

Phone Codes

Calling France from abroad Dial your country's international access code, then 33 (France's country code), then the 10-digit number *without* the initial zero.

Calling internationally from France Dial 00 (the international access code), the *indicatif* (country code), the area code (without the initial zero if there is one) and the local number. Some country codes are posted in public telephones.

Directory inquiries For national *service des renseignements* (directory inquiries) dial 11 87 12 or use the service for free online at www.118712.fr.

International directory inquiries For numbers outside France, dial 11 87 00.

Phonecards

- Public phones still exist, although they are increasingly hard to find when you need one. In France they are all phonecard-operated, but in an emergency you can use your credit card to call.
- Emergency numbers (p19) can be dialled from public phones without a phonecard.
- Public phones can receive both domestic and

CHARGING DEVICES

Carrying your own charger and cable is the only sure way of ensuring you don't run out of juice. Don't be shy to ask in cafes and restaurants if you can plug in and charge – if you ask nicely, most will oblige. In Paris the odd cafe lends cables to customers, savvy taxi drivers stock a selection of smartphone-compatible cables and chargers for passengers to use, and new RATP bus stops are equipped with USB ports (bring your own cable).

On TGV trains, all 1st-class carriages (and occasionally 2nd-class depending on how new the train is) have plugs. On every TGV irrespective of age, there is at least one 'office' space between carriages with mini-desk and double plug. Otherwise, upon arrival, an increasing number of SNCF train stations have charging stations: in Paris, Gare de Nord, Gare de Montparnasse and Gare de St-Lazare all have pedal-powered charging stations operated by Belgium-based We-Bike, as do several other stations countrywide including Lille, Lyon, Strasbourg and Avignon TGV.

PRACTICALITIES

Classifieds Surf FUSAC (www.fusac.fr) for classified ads about housing, babysitting, jobs and language exchanges in and around Paris.

Laundry Virtually all French cities and towns have at least one *laverie libre-service* (self-service laundrette). Machines run on coins.

Newspapers and magazines Locals read their news in centre-left *Le Monde* (www.lemonde.fr), right-leaning *Le Figaro* (www.lefigaro.fr) or left-leaning *Libération* (www.liberation.fr).

Radio For news, tune in to the French-language France Info (105.5MHz; www.franceinfo.fr), multilanguage RFI (738kHz or 89MHz in Paris; www.rfi.fr) or, in northern France, the BBC World Service (648kHz) and BBC Radio 4 (198kHz). Popular national FM music stations include NRJ (www.nrj.fr), Virgin (www.virginradio.fr), La Radio Plus (www.laradioplus.com) and Nostalgie (www.nostalgie.fr).

TV and DVD TV is Secam; videos work on the PAL system.

Smoking Illegal in all indoor public spaces, including restaurants and pubs (though, of course, smokers still light up on the terraces outside).

Weights and measures France uses the metric system.

international calls. If you want someone to call you back, just give them France's country code (☎33) and the 10-digit number, usually written after the words 'Ici le...' or 'No d'appel' on the tariff sheet or on a little sign inside the phone box. Remind them to drop the initial '0' of the number. When there's an incoming call, the words *décrochez – appel arrive* (pick up receiver – incoming call) will appear in the LCD window.

➡ Public phones require a credit card or *télécarte* (phonecard; €7.50/15 for 50/120 calling units), sold at post offices, *tabacs*, supermarkets, SNCF ticket windows, Paris metro stations and anywhere you see a blue sticker reading '*télécarte en vente ici*' (phonecard for sale here).

➡ Prepaid phonecards with codes *(tickets téléphones)* can be up to 60% cheaper for calling abroad than a standard *télécarte*. When purchasing, *tabacs* can tell you which type is best for the country you want to call. Or simply buy online at www.topengo.fr (click on *cartes appels internationaux* and select the *ticket téléphone* for the geographic zone you'll call).

Using phonecards from a home phone is much cheaper than using them from public phones or mobile phones.

➡ Hotels, *gîtes*, hostels and *chambres d'hôte* are free to meter their calls as they like. The surcharge is usually around €0.30 per minute but can be higher.

Time

France uses the 24-hour clock and is on Central European Time, which is one hour ahead of GMT/UTC. During daylight-saving time, which runs from the last Sunday in March to the last Sunday in October, France is two hours ahead of GMT/UTC.

The following times do not take daylight saving into account:

PARIS	NOON
Auckland	11pm
Berlin	noon
Cape Town	noon
London	11am
New York	6am
San Francisco	3am
Sydney	9pm
Tokyo	8pm

Toilets

Public toilets, signposted WC or *toilettes*, are not always plentiful in France, especially outside the big cities.

Love them (as a sci-fi geek) or loathe them (as a claustrophobe), France's 24-hour self-cleaning toilets are here to stay. Outside Paris these mechanical WCs are free, but in Paris they cost around €0.50 a go. Don't even think about nipping in after someone else to avoid paying unless you fancy a *douche* (shower) with disinfectant. There is no time for dawdling either: you have precisely 15 minutes before being (ooh-la-la!) exposed to passers-by. Green means *libre* (vacant) and red means *occupé* (occupied).

Some older establishments and motorway stops still have the hole-in-the-floor *toilettes à la turque* (squat toilets). Provided you hover, these are actually very hygienic, but take care not to get soaked by the flush.

Keep some loose change handy for tipping toilet attendants, who keep a hawk-like eye on many of France's public toilets.

The French are completely blasé about unisex toilets,

so save your blushes when tiptoeing past the urinals to reach the ladies' loo.

Tourist Information

Almost every city, town and village has an *office de tourisme* (a tourist office run by some unit of local government) or *syndicat d'initiative* (a tourist office run by an organisation of local merchants). Both are excellent resources and can supply you with local maps as well as details on accommodation, restaurants and activities. If you have a special interest such as walking, cycling, architecture or wine sampling, ask about it.

➡ Many tourist offices make local hotel and B&B reservations, sometimes for a nominal fee.

➡ *Comités régionaux de tourisme* (CRTs; regional tourist boards), their *départemental* analogues (CDTs) and their websites are a superb source of information and hyperlinks.

➡ French government tourist offices (usually called Maisons de la France) provide every imaginable sort of tourist information on France.

Useful websites include:

French Government Tourist Office (www.france.fr) The low-down on sights, activities, transport and special-interest holidays in all of France's regions. Brochures can be downloaded online.

French Tourist Offices (www.tourisme.fr) Website of tourist offices in France, with mountains of inspirational information organised by theme and region.

Travellers with Disabilities

While France presents evident challenges for *visiteurs handicapés* (disabled visitors) – cobblestones, cafe-lined streets that are a nightmare to navigate in a wheelchair *(fauteuil roulant)*, a lack of kerb ramps, older public facilities and many budget hotels without lifts – don't let that stop you from visiting. Efforts are being made to improve the situation and with a little careful planning, a hassle-free accessible stay is possible. Download Lonely Planet's free Accessible Travel guide from http://lptravel.to/AccessibleTravel.

➡ Paris tourist office runs the excellent 'Tourisme & Handicap' initiative whereby museums, cultural attractions, hotels and restaurants that provide access or special assistance or facilities for those with physical, mental, visual and/or hearing disabilities display a special logo at their entrances. For a list of qualifying places, go to www.parisinfo.com and click on 'Practical Paris'.

➡ Paris metro, most of it built decades ago, is hopeless. Line 14 of the metro was built to be wheelchair-accessible, although in reality it remains extremely challenging to navigate in a wheelchair – unlike Paris buses which are 100% accessible.

➡ Parisian taxi company Horizon, part of Taxis G7 (www.taxisg7.fr), has cars especially adapted to carry wheelchairs and drivers trained in helping passengers with disabilities.

➡ Countrywide, many SNCF train carriages are accessible to people with disabilities. A traveller in a wheelchair can travel in both the TGV and in the 1st-class carriage with a 2nd-class ticket on mainline trains provided they make a reservation by phone or at a train station at least a few hours before departure. Details are available in the SNCF booklet *Le Mémento du Voyageur Handicapé (Handicapped Traveller Summary)* available at all train stations.

Accès Plus (☎09 69 32 26 26, 08 90 64 06 50; www.accessibilite.sncf.com) The SNCF assistance service for rail travellers with disabilities. Can advise on station accessibility and arrange a *fauteuil roulant* or help getting on or off a train.

Access Travel (☎in UK 01942-888 844; www.access-travel.co.uk) Specialised UK-based agency for accessible travel.

Infomobi.com (☎09 70 81 83 85; www.infomobi.com) Has comprehensive information on accessible travel in Paris and the surrounding Île de France area.

Mobile en Ville (☎09 52 29 60 51; www.mobile-en-ville.asso.fr; 8 rue des Mariniers, 14e) Association that works hard to make independent travel within Paris easier for people in wheelchairs. Among other things it organises some great family *randonnées* (walks) in and around Paris.

Tourisme et Handicaps (☎01 44 11 10 41; www.tourisme-handicaps.org; 43 rue Marx Dormoy, 18e, Paris) Issues the 'Tourisme et Handicap' label to tourist sites, restaurants and hotels that comply with strict accessibility and usability standards. Different symbols indicate the sort of access afforded to people with physical, mental, hearing and/or visual disabilities.

Resources

➡ SNCF's French-language booklet *Guide des Voyageurs Handicapés et à Mobilité Réduite*, available at train stations, gives details of rail access for people with disabilities.

➡ Michelin's *Guide Rouge* uses icons to indicate hotels with lifts (elevators) and facilities that make them at least partly accessible to people with disabilities.

➡ *Handitourisme* (€16), a national guide in French, is published by Petit Futé (www.petitfute.fr).

➡ Jaccede.com (www.jaccede.com) is an excellent interactive accessibility

Régions & Départements

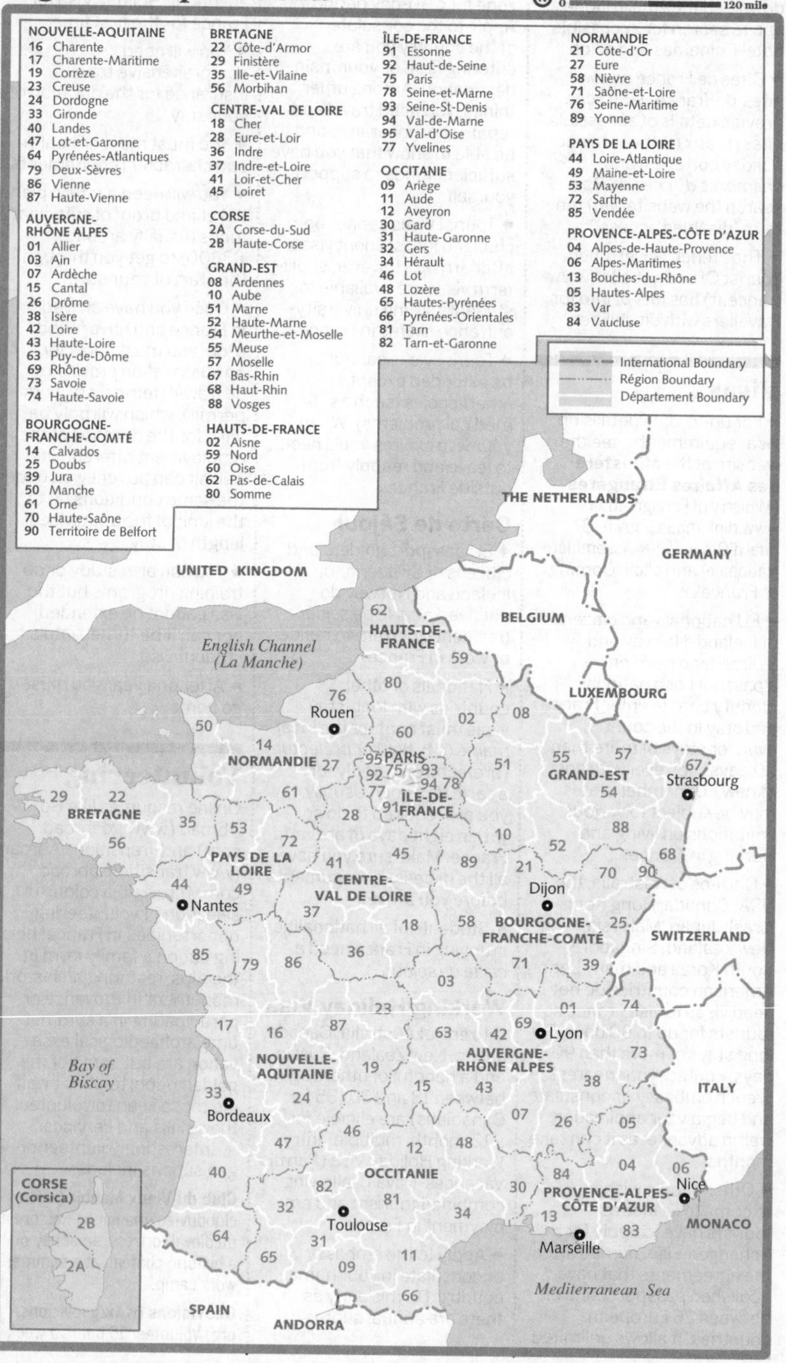
0 200 km
0 120 miles
NOUVELLE-AQUITAINE
16 Charente
17 Charente-Maritime
19 Corrèze
23 Creuse
24 Dordogne
33 Gironde
40 Landes
47 Lot-et-Garonne
64 Pyrénées-Atlantiques
79 Deux-Sèvres
86 Vienne
87 Haute-Vienne
AUVERGNE-RHÔNE ALPES
01 Allier
03 Ain
07 Ardèche
15 Cantal
26 Drôme
38 Isère
42 Loire
43 Haute-Loire
63 Puy-de-Dôme
69 Rhône
73 Savoie
74 Haute-Savoie
BOURGOGNE-FRANCHE-COMTÉ
14 Calvados
25 Doubs
39 Jura
50 Manche
61 Orne
70 Haute-Saône
90 Territoire de Belfort
BRETAGNE
22 Côte-d'Armor
29 Finistère
35 Ille-et-Vilaine
56 Morbihan
CENTRE-VAL DE LOIRE
18 Cher
28 Eure-et-Loir
36 Indre
37 Indre-et-Loire
41 Loir-et-Cher
45 Loiret
CORSE
2A Corse-du-Sud
2B Haute-Corse
GRAND-EST
08 Ardennes
10 Aube
51 Marne
52 Haute-Marne
54 Meurthe-et-Moselle
55 Meuse
57 Moselle
67 Bas-Rhin
68 Haut-Rhin
88 Vosges
HAUTS-DE-FRANCE
02 Aisne
59 Nord
60 Oise
62 Pas-de-Calais
80 Somme
ÎLE-DE-FRANCE
91 Essonne
92 Haut-de-Seine
75 Paris
78 Seine-et-Marne
93 Seine-St-Denis
94 Val-de-Marne
95 Val-d'Oise
77 Yvelines
OCCITANIE
09 Ariège
11 Aude
12 Aveyron
30 Gard
31 Haute-Garonne
32 Gers
34 Hérault
46 Lot
48 Lozère
65 Hautes-Pyrénées
66 Pyrénées-Orientales
81 Tarn
82 Tarn-et-Garonne
NORMANDIE
21 Côte-d'Or
27 Eure
58 Nièvre
71 Saône-et-Loire
76 Seine-Maritime
89 Yonne
PAYS DE LA LOIRE
44 Loire-Atlantique
49 Maine-et-Loire
53 Mayenne
72 Sarthe
85 Vendée
PROVENCE-ALPES-CÔTE D'AZUR
04 Alpes-de-Haute-Provence
06 Alpes-Maritimes
13 Bouches-du-Rhône
05 Hautes-Alpes
83 Var
84 Vaucluse
International Boundary
Région Boundary
Département Boundary
THE NETHERLANDS
GERMANY
UNITED KINGDOM
BELGIUM
LUXEMBOURG
English Channel
(La Manche)
HAUTS-DE-FRANCE
NORMANDIE
PARIS
ÎLE-DE-FRANCE
GRAND-EST
Rouen
Strasbourg
BRETAGNE
PAYS DE LA LOIRE
CENTRE-VAL DE LOIRE
Nantes
Dijon
BOURGOGNE-FRANCHE-COMTÉ
SWITZERLAND
Bay of Biscay
NOUVELLE-AQUITAINE
AUVERGNE-RHÔNE ALPES
Lyon
ITALY
Bordeaux
OCCITANIE
Toulouse
PROVENCE-ALPES-CÔTE D'AZUR
Marseille
Nice
MONACO
CORSE
(Corsica)
2B
2A
Mediterranean Sea
SPAIN
ANDORRA

guide; before arrival download the smartphone app to search for accessible hotels, cinemas and so on.

➡ Gîtes de France (www.gites-de-france-var.fr) can provide details of accessible *gîtes ruraux* (self-contained holiday cottages) and *chambres d'hôte* (B&Bs); search the website with the term 'disabled access'.

➡ The French Government Tourist Office website (www.france.fr) has lots of info for travellers with disabilities.

Visas

➡ For up-to-date details on visa requirements, see the website of the **Ministère des Affaires Étrangères** (Ministry of Foreign Affairs; www.diplomatie.gouv.fr; 37 quai d'Orsay, 7e; Ⓜ Assemblée Nationale) and click 'Coming to France'.

➡ EU nationals and citizens of Iceland, Norway and Switzerland need only a passport or a national identity card to enter France and stay in the country, even for stays of more than 90 days. However, citizens of new EU member states may be subject to various limitations on living and working in France.

➡ Citizens of Australia, the USA, Canada, Hong Kong, Israel, Japan, Malaysia, New Zealand, Singapore, South Korea and many Latin American countries do not need visas to visit France as tourists for up to 90 days. For long stays of more than 90 days, contact your nearest French embassy or consulate and begin your application well in advance, as it can take months.

➡ Other people wishing to come to France as tourists have to apply for a Schengen Visa, named after the agreements that have abolished passport controls between 26 European countries. It allows unlimited travel throughout the entire zone for a 90-day period. Apply to the consulate of the country you are entering first, or your main destination. Among other things, you need travel and repatriation insurance and to be able to show that you have sufficient funds to support yourself.

➡ Tourist visas cannot be changed into student visas after arrival. However, short-term visas are available for students sitting university-entrance exams in France.

➡ Tourist visas cannot be extended except in emergencies (such as medical problems). When your visa expires you'll need to leave and reapply from outside France.

Carte de Séjour

➡ EU passport holders and citizens of Switzerland, Iceland and Norway do not need a *carte de séjour* (residence permit) to reside or work in France.

➡ Nationals of other countries with long-stay visas must contact the local *mairie* (city hall) or *préfecture* (prefecture) to apply for a *carte de séjour*. Usually, you are required to do so within eight days of arrival in France. Make sure you have all the necessary documents before you arrive.

➡ Students of all nationalities studying in France need a *carte de séjour*.

Working Holiday Visa

Citizens of Australia, Canada, Japan, New Zealand, Russia and a handful of others aged between 18 and 30 (35 for Canadians) are eligible for a 12-month, multiple-entry Working Holiday Visa (Permis Vacances-Travail), allowing combined tourism and employment in France.

➡ Apply to the embassy or consulate in your home country. Do this early as there are annual quotas.

➡ You must be applying for a Working Holiday Visa for France for the first time.

➡ You will need comprehensive travel insurance for the duration of your stay.

➡ You must meet all health and character requirements.

➡ You will need a return plane ticket and proof of sufficient funds (usually around €3800) to get you through the start of your stay.

➡ Once you have arrived in France and have found a job, you must apply for an *autorisation provisoire de travail* (temporary work permit), which will only be valid for the duration of the employment offered. The permit can be renewed under the same conditions up to the limit of the authorised length of stay.

➡ You can also study or do training programs but the visa cannot be extended, nor can it be turned into a student visa.

➡ After one year you *must* go home.

Volunteering

Online resources like Go Abroad (www.goabroad.com) and Transitions Abroad (www.transitionsabroad.com) throw up a colourful selection of volunteering opportunities in France: helping out on a family farm in the Alps, restoring an historic monument in Provence or participating in a summertime archaeological excavation are but some of the golden opportunities awaiting those keen to volunteer their skills and services.

Interesting volunteer organisations include:

Club du Vieux Manoir (www.clubduvieuxmanoir.fr) Restore a medieval fortress, an abbey or a historic château at a summer work camp.

GeoVisions (www.geovisions.org) Volunteer 15 hours a week

to teach a French family English in exchange for room and board.

Rempart (www.rempart.com) Brings together 170 organisations countrywide committed to preserving France's religious, military, civil, industrial and natural heritage.

Volunteers For Peace (www.vfp.org) US-based nonprofit organisation. Can link you up with a voluntary service project dealing with social work, the environment, education or the arts.

World Wide Opportunities on Organic Farms (WWOOF; www.wwoof.org) Work on a small farm or other organic venture (harvesting chestnuts, renovating an abandoned olive farm near Nice etc).

Work

- EU nationals have an automatic right to work in France.
- Most others will need a hard-to-get work permit, issued at the request of your employer, who will have to show that no one in France – or the entire European Economic Area – can do your job.
- Exceptions may be made for artists, computer engineers and translation specialists.
- Working 'in the black' (that is, without documents) is difficult and risky for non-EU nationals.
- The only instance in which the government might turn a blind eye to workers without documents is during fruit harvests (mid-May to November) and the *vendange* (grape harvest; mid-September to mid- or late October). Though, of course, undocumented workers harvest at their own risk.
- Au pair work is also very popular and can be done legally even by non-EU citizens. To apply, contact a placement agency at least three months in advance.

Transport

GETTING THERE & AWAY

Flights, cars and tours can be booked online at www.lonelyplanet.com/bookings.

Entering the Country

Entering France from other parts of the EU is usually a breeze – no border checkpoints and no customs – thanks to the Schengen Agreement, signed by all of France's neighbours except the UK, the Channel Islands and Andorra. For these three entities, old-fashioned document and customs checks are still the norm when exiting France (when entering France from Andorra).

Air

Airports & Airlines

Air France (www.airfrance.com) is the national carrier, with plenty of both domestic and international flights in and out of major French airports.

Smaller provincial airports with international flights, mainly to/from the UK, continental Europe and North Africa, include Paris-Beauvais, Bergerac, Biarritz, Brest, Brive-la-Gaillarde (Vallée de la Dordogne), Caen, Carcassonne, Clermont-Ferrand, Deauville, Dinard, Grenoble, La Rochelle, Le Touquet (Côte d'Opale), Limoges, Montpellier, Nîmes, Pau, Perpignan, Poitiers, Rennes, Rodez, St-Étienne, Toulon and Tours.

Aéroport de Charles de Gaulle, Paris (CDG; ☎01 70 36 39 50; www.aeroportsdeparis.fr)

Aéroport d'Orly, Paris (ORY; ☎01 70 36 39 50; www.aeroportsdeparis.fr)

Aéroport de Bordeaux (www.bordeaux.aeroport.fr)

Aéroport de Lille (www.lille.aeroport.fr)

Aéroport International Strasbourg (www.strasbourg.aeroport.fr)

Aéroport Lyon-St Exupéry (www.lyonaeroports.com)

Aéroport Marseille-Provence (Aéroport Marseille-Marignane; MRS; ☎04 42 14 14 14; www.marseille.aeroport.fr)

Aéroport Nantes Atlantique (www.nantes.aeroport.fr)

Aéroport Nice Côte d'Azur (☎08 20 42 33 33; www.nice.aeroport.fr; 📶)

Aéroport Toulouse-Blagnac (TLS; www.toulouse.aeroport.fr/en)

EuroAirport, Basel (MLH or BSL; ☎+33 3 89 90 31 11; www.euroairport.com)

Land

Bicycle

Transporting a bicycle to France is a breeze.

On **Eurotunnel Le Shuttle** (☎in France 08 10 63 03 04, in UK 08443 35 35 35; www.eurotunnel.com) trains through the Channel Tunnel,

CLIMATE CHANGE & TRAVEL

Every form of transport that relies on carbon-based fuel generates CO_2, the main cause of human-induced climate change. Modern travel is dependent on aeroplanes, which might use less fuel per kilometre per person than most cars but travel much greater distances. The altitude at which aircraft emit gases (including CO_2) and particles also contributes to their climate change impact. Many websites offer 'carbon calculators' that allow people to estimate the carbon emissions generated by their journey and, for those who wish to do so, to offset the impact of the greenhouse gases emitted with contributions to portfolios of climate-friendly initiatives throughout the world. Lonely Planet offsets the carbon footprint of all staff and author travel.

the fee for a bicycle, including its rider, is from £20 one way.

A bike that's been dismantled to the size of a suitcase can be carried on-board a **Eurostar** (☎in France 08 92 35 35 39, in UK 08432 186 186; www.eurostar.com) train from London or Brussels just like any other luggage. Otherwise, there's a £30 charge and you'll need advance reservations. For links relevant to taking your bike on other international trains to France, see **RailPassenger Info** (www.railpassenger.info).

On ferries, foot passengers – where allowed – can usually (but not always) bring along a bicycle for no charge.

European Bike Express (☎in UK 01430 422 111; www.bike-express.co.uk) transports cyclists and their bikes from the UK to places around France.

Bus

Eurolines (☎08 92 89 90 91; www.eurolines.eu), a grouping of 32 long-haul coach operators (including the UK's National Express), links France with cities all across Europe, Morocco and Russia. Discounts are available to people under 26 and over 60. Make advance reservations, especially in July and August.

A single Paris–London fare is between €18 and €40, including a Channel crossing by ferry or the Channel Tunnel. Book as far ahead as possible to bag the cheapest ticket.

Car & Motorcycle

A right-hand-drive vehicle brought to France from the UK or Ireland must have deflectors affixed to the headlights to avoid dazzling oncoming traffic. In the UK, information on driving in France is available from the **RAC** (www.rac.co.uk/driving-abroad/france) and the **AA** (www.theaa.com).

A foreign motor vehicle entering France must display a sticker or licence plate identifying its country of registration.

EUROTUNNEL

The Channel Tunnel (Chunnel), inaugurated in 1994, is the first dry-land link between England and France since the last ice age.

High-speed **Eurotunnel Le Shuttle** (☎in France 08 10 63 03 04, in UK 08443 35 35 35; www.eurotunnel.com) trains whisk bicycles, motorcycles, cars and coaches in 35 minutes from Folkestone through the Channel Tunnel to Coquelles, 5km southwest of Calais. Shuttles run 24 hours a day, with up to three departures an hour during peak periods. LPG and CNG tanks are not permitted, meaning gas-powered cars and many campers and caravans have to travel by ferry.

Eurotunnel sets its fares the way budget airlines do: the further in advance you book and the lower the demand for a particular crossing, the less you pay; same-day fares can cost a small fortune. Fares for a car, including up to nine passengers, start at £23/€32.

Train

Rail services link France with virtually every country in Europe.

➡ Book tickets and get train information from **Rail Europe** (www.raileurope.com). In the UK contact **Railteam** (www.railteam.co.uk).

➡ A very useful train-travel resource is the information-packed website **The Man in Seat 61** (www.seat61.com).

Certain rail services between France and its continental neighbours are marketed under a number of unique brand names:

Elipsos Luxurious, overnight 'train-hotel' from Paris to Madrid and Barcelona in Spain; book through France's **SNCF** (Société Nationale des Chemins de fer Français, French National Railway Company; ☎from abroad +33 8 92 35 35 35, in France 36 35; http://en.voyages-sncf.com).

TGV Lyria (high-speed train; www.tgv-lyria.fr) To Switzerland.

Thalys (www.thalys.com) Thalys trains pull into Paris' Gare du Nord from Brussels, Amsterdam and Cologne.

Thello (www.thello.com) Overnight train service from Paris to Milan, Brescia, Verona and Venice in Italy.

SAMPLE TRAIN FARES

ROUTE	FULL FARE (€)	DURATION (HR)
Amsterdam-Paris	95	3¼
Berlin-Paris	189	8
Blois-London	90	5½
Brussels-Paris	60	1½
Dijon-Milan	108	7
Marseille-Barcelona	70	4½
Paris-Venice	121	11¾
Vienna-Strasbourg	182	9¾

EURAIL PASS

Rail passes are worthwhile if you plan to clock up the kilometres.

Available only to people who don't live in Europe, the **Eurail Pass** (www.eurail.com) is valid in up to 21 countries, including France. People 25 and under get the best deals. Passes must be validated at a train-station ticket window before you begin your first journey.

EUROSTAR

The **Eurostar** (☎in France 08 92 35 35 39, in UK 08432 186 186; www.eurostar.com) whisks you from London to Paris in 2¼ hours.

Except late at night, trains link London (St Pancras International) with Paris (Gare du Nord; hourly), Calais (Calais-Fréthun; one hour, three daily), Lille (Gare Lille-Europe; 1½ hours, eight daily), Disneyland Resort Paris (2½ hours, one direct daily), Lyon (4¾ hours, one to five per week), Avignon (5¾ hours, one to five per week) and Marseille (6½ hours, one to five per week), with less frequent services departing from Ebbsfleet and Ashford in Kent. Weekend ski trains connect England with the French Alps late-December to mid-April. Potential future routes include a direct London–Bordeaux service.

Eurostar offers a bewildering array of fares. A semi-flexible 2nd-class one-way ticket from Paris to London costs €66.50; super-discount fares start at €39.

For the best deals, buy a return ticket, stay over a Saturday night, book up to 120 days in advance and don't mind non-exchangeability and non-refundability. Discount fares are available for under 26s or over 60s.

Sea

Some ferry companies have started setting fares the way budget airlines do: the longer in advance you book and the lower the demand for a particular sailing, the less you pay. Seasonal demand is a crucial factor (Christmas, Easter, UK and French school holidays, July and August are especially busy), as is the time of day (an early-evening ferry can cost much more than one at 4am). People under 25 and over 60 may qualify for discounts.

To get the best fares, check **Ferry Savers** (☎in UK 0844 371 8021; www.ferrysavers.com).

Foot passengers are not allowed on Dover–Boulogne, Dover–Dunkirk or Dover–Calais car ferries except for daytime (and, from Calais to Dover, evening) crossings run by P&O Ferries. On ferries that do allow foot passengers, taking a bicycle is usually free.

Several ferry companies ply the waters between Corsica and Italy.

GETTING AROUND

Driving is the simplest way to get around France but a car is a liability in traffic-plagued, parking-starved city centres, and petrol bills and *autoroute* (dual carriageway/divided highway) tolls add up.

France is famous for its excellent public-transport network, which serves everywhere bar some very rural areas. The state-owned Société Nationale des Chemins de Fer Français (SNCF) takes

INTERNATIONAL FERRY COMPANIES

COMPANY	CONNECTION	WEBSITE
Brittany Ferries	England-Normandy, England-Brittany, Ireland-Brittany	www.brittany-ferries.co.uk; www.brittanyferries.ie
Condor Ferries	England-Normandy, England-Brittany, Channel Islands-Brittany	www.condorferries.co.uk
CTN	Tunisia-France	www.ctn.com.tn
DFDS Seaways	England-Normandy	www.dfdsseaways.co.uk
Grandi Navi Veloci (GNV)	Morocco-Sète (Languedoc-Roussillon)	www.gnv.it
Irish Ferries	Ireland-Normandy, Ireland-Brittany	www.irishferries.com
Manche Îles Express	Channel Islands-Normandy	www.manche-iles-express.com
My Ferry Link	Dover-Calais	www.myferrylink.fr
Norfolk Line (DFDS Seaways)	England-Channel Ports	www.norfolkline.com
P&O Ferries	England-Channel Ports	www.poferries.com
SNCM	Algeria-France, Sardinia-France, Tunisia-France	www.sncm.fr
Stena Line Ferries	Ireland-Normandy	www.stenaline.ie

care of almost all land transport between *départements* (counties). Transport within *départements* is handled by a combination of short-haul trains, SNCF buses and local bus companies.

Air

France's high-speed train network renders rail travel between some cities (eg from Paris to Lyon and Marseille) faster and easier than flying.

Airlines in France

Air France (www.airfrance.com) and its subsidiaries **Hop!** (www.hop.com) and **Transavia** (www.transavia.com) control the lion's share of France's domestic airline industry.

Budget carriers offering flights within France include **EasyJet** (www.easyjet.com), **Twin Jet** (www.twinjet.net) and **Air Corsica** (www.aircorsica.com).

Bicycle

France is great for cycling. Much of the countryside is drop-dead gorgeous and the country has a growing number of urban and rural *pistes cyclables* (bike paths and lanes; see **Voies Vertes**, www.voievertes.com) and an extensive network of secondary and tertiary roads with relatively light traffic.

French law requires that bicycles must have two functioning brakes, a bell, a red reflector on the back and yellow reflectors on the pedals. After sunset and when visibility is poor, cyclists must turn on a white headlamp and a red tail lamp. When being overtaken by a vehicle, cyclists must ride in single file. Towing children in a bike trailer is permitted.

Never leave your bicycle locked up outside overnight if you want to see it – or at least most of its parts – again. Some hotels offer enclosed bicycle parking.

Transportation

The SNCF does its best to make travelling with a bicycle easy; see www.velo.sncf.com for full details.

Bicycles (not disassembled) can be taken along on virtually all intraregional TER trains and most long-distance intercity trains, subject to space availability. The charge for TER and Corail Intercité trains is either free, €5 or €10 depending on the route; TGV, Téoz and Lunéa trains require a €10 reservation fee that must be made when you purchase your passenger ticket. Bike reservations can be made by phone (☎36 35) or at an SNCF ticket office but not via the internet.

Bicycles that have been partly disassembled and put in a box *(housse)*, with maximum dimensions of 120cm by 90cm, can be taken along for no charge in the baggage compartments of TGV, Téoz, Lunéa and Corail Intercité trains.

In the Paris area, bicycles are allowed aboard Transilien and RER trains except Monday to Friday during the following times:

➡ 6.30am to 9am for trains heading into Paris

➡ 4.30pm to 7pm for trains travelling out of Paris

➡ 6am to 9am and 4.30pm to 7pm on RER lines A and B

With precious few exceptions, bicycles are not allowed on metros, trams and local, intra-*département* and SNCF buses (the latter replace trains on some runs).

Bike Rental

Most French cities and towns have at least one bike shop that rents out *vélos tout terrains* (mountain bikes; around €15 a day), known as VTTs, as well as more road-oriented *vélos tout chemin* (VTCs), or cheaper city bikes. You usually have to leave ID and/or a deposit (often a credit-card slip of €250) that you forfeit if the bike is damaged or stolen.

A growing number of cities – including Paris, Lyon, Aix-en-Provence, Amiens, Besançon, Bayonne, Bordeaux, Caen, Clermont-Ferrand, Dijon, La Rochelle, Lille, Marseille, Montpellier, Mulhouse, Nancy, Nantes, Nice, Orléans, Rennes, Rouen, Toulouse, Strasbourg and Vannes – have automatic bike-rental systems, intended to encourage cycling as a form of urban transport, with computerised pick-up and drop-off sites all over town. In general, you have to sign up either short term or long term, providing credit-card details, and can then use the bikes for no charge for the first half-hour; after that, hourly charges rise quickly.

Boat

There are boat services along France's coasts and to its offshore islands, and ferries aplenty to/from Corsica.

Canal Boating

Transportation and tranquillity are usually mutually exclusive – but not if you rent a houseboat and cruise along France's canals and navigable rivers, stopping at whim to pick up supplies, dine at a village restaurant or check out a local château by bicycle. Changes in altitude are taken care of by a system of *écluses* (locks).

Boats generally accommodate from two to 12 passengers and are fully outfitted with bedding and cooking facilities. Anyone over 18 can pilot a riverboat, but first-time skippers are given a short instruction session so they qualify for a *carte de plaisance* (a temporary cruising permit). The speed limit is 6km/h on canals and 8km/h on rivers.

Prices start at around €650 a week for a small boat and easily top €3000 a week for a large, luxurious craft. Except in July and August, you can often rent over a weekend.

Advance reservations are essential for holiday periods, over long weekends and in July and August, especially for larger boats.

Rental agencies:

Canal Boat Holidays (www.canalboatholidays.com) Australia-based, European canal-boating specialist.

France Afloat (www.franceafloat.com) Anglophone, canal-boat specialist in France.

Free Wheel Afloat (www.freewheelafloat.com) UK-based, self-drive barge specialist.

H2olidays (www.barginginfrance.com) Hotel barges, river cruises and self-drive barges.

Worldwide River Cruise (www.worldwide-river-cruise.com) River-cruiser rental, price-comparison website.

Bus

Buses are widely used for short-distance travel within *départements*, especially in rural areas with relatively few train lines (eg Brittany and Normandy). Unfortunately, services in some regions are infrequent and slow, in part because they were designed to get children to their schools in the towns rather than transport visitors around the countryside.

Over the years, certain uneconomical train lines have been replaced by SNCF buses, which, unlike regional buses, are free if you've got a rail pass.

Car & Motorcycle

Having your own wheels gives you exceptional freedom and makes it easy to visit more remote parts of France. Depending on the number of passengers, it can also work out cheaper than the train. For example, by *autoroute*, the 930km drive from Paris to Nice (9½ hours of driving) in a small car costs about €75 for petrol and another €75 in tolls – by comparison, a one-way, 2nd-class TGV ticket for the 5½-hour Paris to Nice run costs anything from €45 to €140 per person.

In the cities, traffic and finding a place to park can be a major headache. During holiday periods and bank-holiday weekends, roads throughout France also get backed up with traffic jams *(bouchons)*.

Motorcyclists will find France great for touring, with winding roads of good quality and lots of stunning scenery. Just make sure your wet-weather gear is up to scratch.

France (along with Belgium) has the densest highway network in Europe. There are four types of intercity roads:

Autoroutes (highway names beginning with A) Multilane divided highways, usually (except near Calais and Lille) with tolls *(péages)*. Generously outfitted with rest stops.

Routes Nationales (N, RN) National highways. Some sections have divider strips.

Routes Départementales (D) Local highways and roads.

Routes Communales (C, V) Minor rural roads.

For information on *autoroute* tolls, rest areas, traffic and weather, go to the **Sociétés d'Autoroutes** (www.autoroutes.fr) website.

Bison Futé (www.bison-fute.gouv.fr) is also a good source of information about traffic conditions. Plot itineraries between your departure and arrival points, and calculate toll costs with an online mapper such as **Via Michelin** (www.viamichelin.com) or **Mappy** (www.mappy.fr).

Theft from cars is a major problem in France, especially in the south.

Hire

To hire a car in France, you'll generally need to be over 21 years old, have had a driving licence for at least a year, and have an international credit card. Drivers under 25 usually have to pay a surcharge *(frais jeune conducteur)* of €25 to €35 per day.

Car-hire companies provide mandatory third-party liability insurance but things such as collision-damage waivers (CDW, or *assurance tous risques*) vary greatly from company to company. When comparing rates and conditions (ie the fine print), the most important thing to check is the *franchise* (deductible/excess), which for a small car is usually around €600 for damage and €800 for theft. With many companies, you can reduce the excess by half, and perhaps to zero, by paying a daily insurance supplement of up to €20. Your credit card may cover CDW if you use it to pay for the rental but the car-hire company won't know anything about this – verify conditions and details with your credit-card issuer to be sure.

Arranging your car hire or fly/drive package before you leave home is usually considerably cheaper than a walk-in rental, but beware of website offers that don't include a CDW or you may be liable for up to 100% of the car's value.

International car-hire companies:

Avis (☎08 21 23 07 60, from abroad 01 70 99 47 35; www.avis.com)

Budget (☎08 25 00 35 64; www.budget.fr)

EasyCar (☎in France 08 26 10 73 23, in the UK 0800 640 7000; www.easycar.com)

Europcar (☎08 25 35 83 58; www.europcar.com)

Hertz (☎01 41 91 95 25, 08 25 86 18 61; www.hertz.com)

Sixt (☎08 20 00 74 98; www.sixt.fr)

French car-hire companies:

ADA (☎08 99 46 46 36; www.ada.fr)

DLM (www.dlm.fr)

France Cars (www.francecars.fr)

Locauto (☎04 93 07 72 62; www.locauto.fr)

Renault Rent (☎08 25 10 11 12; www.renault-rent.com)

Rent a Car (☎08 91 700 200; www.rentacar.fr)

Deals can be found on the internet and through companies such as the following:

Auto Europe (☎in USA 888-223-5555; www.autoeurope.com)

DriveAway Holidays (☎in Australia 1300 363 500; www.driveaway.com.au)

Holiday Autos (☎in UK 020 3740 9859; www.holidayautos.co.uk)

Rental cars with automatic transmission are very much the exception in France; they usually need to be ordered well in advance and are more expensive than manual cars.

For insurance reasons, it is usually forbidden to take rental cars on ferries, eg to Corsica.

All rental cars registered in France have a distinctive number on the licence plate, making them easily identifiable – including to thieves. *Never* leave anything of value in a parked car, even in the boot (trunk).

Purchase-Repurchase Plans

If you don't live in the EU and will need a car in France (or Europe) for 17 days to six months (up to one year if you'll be studying), by far the cheapest option is to 'purchase' a new one and then 'sell' it back at the end of your trip. In reality, you pay only for the number of days you have the vehicle but the 'temporary transit' (TT) paperwork means that the car is registered under your name – and that the whole deal is exempt from all sorts of taxes.

Companies offering purchase-repurchase *(achat-rachat)* plans:

Eurocar TT (www.eurocartt.com)

Peugeot OpenEurope (www.peugeot-openeurope.com)

Renault Eurodrive (www.eurodrive.renault.com)

Eligibility is restricted to people who are not residents of the EU (citizens of EU countries are eligible if they live outside the EU); the minimum age is 18 (in some cases 21). Pricing and special offers depend on your home country. All the plans include unlimited kilometres, 24-hour towing and breakdown service, and comprehensive insurance with absolutely

ROAD DISTANCES (KM)

	Bayonne	Bordeaux	Brest	Caen	Cahors	Calais	Chambéry	Cherbourg	Clermont-Ferrand	Dijon	Grenoble	Lille	Lyon	Marseille	Nantes	Nice	Paris	Perpignan	Strasbourg	Toulouse
Bordeaux	184																			
Brest	811	623																		
Caen	764	568	376																	
Cahors	307	218	788	661																
Calais	164	876	710	339	875															
Chambéry	860	651	120	800	523	834														
Cherbourg	835	647	399	124	743	461	923													
Clermont-Ferrand	564	358	805	566	269	717	295	689												
Dijon	807	619	867	548	378	572	273	671	279											
Grenoble	827	657	1126	806	501	863	56	929	300	302										
Lille	997	809	725	353	808	112	767	476	650	505	798									
Lyon	831	528	1018	698	439	755	103	820	171	194	110	687								
Marseille	700	651	1271	1010	521	1067	344	1132	477	506	273	999	314							
Nantes	513	326	298	292	491	593	780	317	462	656	787	609	618	975						
Nice	858	810	1429	1168	679	1225	410	1291	636	664	337	1157	473	190	1131					
Paris	771	583	596	232	582	289	565	355	424	313	571	222	462	775	384	932				
Perpignan	499	451	1070	998	320	1149	478	1094	441	640	445	1081	448	319	773	476	857			
Strasbourg	1254	1066	1079	730	847	621	496	853	584	335	551	522	488	803	867	804	490	935		
Toulouse	300	247	866	865	116	991	565	890	890	727	533	923	536	407	568	564	699	205	1022	
Tours	536	348	490	246	413	531	611	369	369	418	618	463	449	795	197	952	238	795	721	593

no deductible/excess, so returning the car is hassle-free, even if it's damaged.

Extending your contract (up to a maximum of 165 days) after you start using the car is possible, but you'll end up paying about double the prepaid per-day rate.

Purchase-repurchase cars, which have special red licence plates, can be picked up at about three-dozen cities and airports all over France and dropped off at the agency of your choosing. For a fee, you can also pick up or return your car in certain cities outside France.

Driving Licence & Documents

An International Driving Permit (IDP), valid only if accompanied by your original licence, is good for a year and can be issued by your local automobile association before you leave home.

Drivers must carry the following at all times:

- passport or an EU national ID card
- valid driving licence (*permis de conduire;* most foreign licences can be used in France for up to a year)
- car-ownership papers, known as a *carte grise* (grey card)
- proof of third-party liability *assurance* (insurance)

Fuel

Essence (petrol), also known as *carburant* (fuel), costs around €1.28 per litre for 95 unleaded (Sans Plomb 95 or SP95, usually available from a green pump) and €1 to €1.30 for diesel (*diesel, gazole* or *gasoil,* usually available from a yellow pump). Check and compare current prices countrywide at www.prix-carburants.gouv.fr.

Filling up *(faire le plein)* is most expensive at *autoroute* rest stops, and usually cheapest at hypermarkets.

Many small petrol stations close on Sunday afternoons and, even in cities, it can be hard to find a staffed station open late at night. In general, after-hours purchases (eg at hypermarkets' fully automatic, 24-hour stations) can only be made with a credit card that has an embedded PIN chip, so if all you've got is cash or a magnetic-strip credit card, you could be stuck.

Insurance

Third-party liability insurance *(assurance au tiers)* is compulsory for all vehicles in France, including cars brought in from abroad. Normally, cars registered and insured in other European countries can circulate freely in France, but it's a good idea to contact your insurance company before you leave home to make sure you have coverage – and to check whom to contact in case of a breakdown or accident.

If you get into a minor accident with no injuries, the easiest way for drivers to sort things out with their insurance companies is to fill out a Constat Aimable d'Accident Automobile (European Accident Statement), a standardised way of recording important details about what happened. In rental cars it's usually in the packet of documents in the glove compartment. Make sure the report includes any information that will help you prove that the accident was not your fault. Remember, if it *was* your fault you may be liable for a hefty insurance deductible/excess. Don't sign anything you don't fully understand. If problems crop up, call the police (☎17).

French-registered cars have details of their insurance company printed on a little green square affixed to the windscreen.

Parking

In city centres, most on-street parking places are *payant* (metered) from about 9am to 7pm (sometimes with a break from noon to 2pm) Monday to Saturday, except bank holidays.

Road Rules

Enforcement of French traffic laws (see www.securiteroutiere.gouv.fr) has been stepped up considerably in recent years. Speed cameras are common, as are radar traps and unmarked police vehicles. Fines for many infractions are given on the

PRIORITY TO THE RIGHT

Under the *priorité à droite* (priority to the right) rule, any car entering an intersection (including a T-junction) from a road (including a tiny village backstreet) on your right has the right of way. Locals assume every driver knows this, so don't be surprised if they courteously cede the right of way when you're about to turn from an alley onto a highway – and boldly assert their rights when you're the one zipping down a main road.

Priorité à droite is suspended (eg on arterial roads) when you pass a sign showing an upended yellow square with a black square in the middle. The same sign with a horizontal bar through the square lozenge reinstates the *priorité à droite* rule.

When you arrive at a roundabout at which you do not have the right of way (ie the cars already in the roundabout do), you'll often see signs reading *vous n'avez pas la priorité* (you do not have right of way) or *cédez le passage* (give way).

SPEED FIENDS: TAKE NOTE

When it comes to catching and punishing speed fiends, France has upped its act in recent years. Automatic speed cameras, not necessarily visible, are widespread and the chances are you'll get 'flashed' at least once during your trip. Should this occur, a letter from the French government (stamped 'Liberté, Egalité, Fraternité – Liberty, Equality, Fraternity') will land on your door mat informing you of your *amende* (fine) and, should you hold a French licence, how many points you have lost. Motorists driving up to 20km/h over the limit in a 50km/h zone are fined €68 and one point; driving up to 20km/h over the limit in a zone with a speed limit of more than 50km/h costs €135 and one point.

There is no room for complacency. Moreover, should you be driving a rental car, the rental company will charge you an additional fee for the time they spent sharing your contact details with the French government.

spot, and serious violations can lead to the confiscation of your driving licence and car.

Speed limits outside built-up areas (except where signposted otherwise):

Undivided N and D highways 90km/h (80km/h when raining)

Non-autoroute divided highways 110km/h (100km/h when raining)

Autoroutes 130km/h (110km/h when raining, 60km/h in icy conditions)

To reduce carbon emissions, *autoroute* speed limits have recently been reduced to 110km/h in some areas.

Unless otherwise signposted, a limit of 50km/h applies in *all* areas designated as built up, no matter how rural they may appear. You must slow to 50km/h the moment you come to a white sign with a red border and a place name written on it; the speed limit applies until you pass an identical sign with a horizontal bar through it.

Other important driving rules:

➡ Blood-alcohol limit is 0.05% (0.5g per litre of blood) – the equivalent of two glasses of wine for a 75kg adult. Police often conduct random breathalyser tests and penalties can be severe, including imprisonment.

➡ All passengers, including those in the back seat, must wear seat belts.

➡ Mobile phones may be used only if they are equipped with a hands-free kit or speakerphone.

➡ Turning right on a red light is illegal.

➡ Cars from the UK and Ireland must have deflectors affixed to their headlights to avoid dazzling oncoming motorists.

➡ Radar detectors, even if they're switched off, are illegal; fines are hefty.

➡ Children under 10 are not permitted to ride in the front seat (unless the back is already occupied by other children under 10).

➡ A child under 13kg must travel in a backward-facing child seat (permitted in the front seat only for babies under 9kg and if the airbag is deactivated).

➡ Up to age 10 and/or a minimum height of 140cm, children must use a size-appropriate type of front-facing child seat or booster.

➡ All vehicles driven in France must carry a high-visibility reflective safety vest (stored inside the vehicle, not in the trunk/boot), a reflective triangle, and a portable, single-use breathalyser kit.

➡ If you'll be driving on snowy roads, make sure you have snow chains (*chaînes neige*), required by law whenever and wherever the police post signs.

➡ Riders of any type of two-wheeled vehicle with a motor (except motor-assisted bicycles) must wear a helmet. No special licence is required to ride a motorbike whose engine is smaller than 50cc, which is why rental scooters are often rated at 49.9cc.

Hitching

Hitching is never entirely safe in any country in the world, and we don't recommend it. Travellers who decide to hitch should understand that they are taking a small but potentially serious risk. Remember that it's safer to travel in pairs and be sure to inform someone of your intended destination. Hitching is not really part of French culture.

Hitching from city centres is pretty much hopeless, so your best bet is to take public transport to the outskirts. It is illegal to hitch on *autoroutes*, but you can stand near an entrance ramp as long as you don't block traffic. Hitching in remote rural areas is better, but once you get off the *routes nationales*, traffic can be light and local. If your itinerary includes a ferry crossing, it's worth trying to score a ride before the ferry since vehicle tickets usually include a number of passengers free of charge. At dusk, give up and think about finding somewhere to stay.

LEFT-LUGGAGE FACILITIES

Because of security concerns, few French train stations have *consignes automatiques* (left-luggage lockers). In larger stations you can leave your bags in a *consigne manuelle* (staffed left-luggage facility) where items are handed over in person and X-rayed before being stowed. Charges are around €5 for up to 10 hours and €8 for 24 hours; payment must be made in cash.

Ride Share

A number of organisations around France arrange *covoiturage* (car sharing), that is, putting people looking for rides in touch with drivers going to the same destination. The best known is **Allo Stop** (www.allostop.net) where you pay €3/5/8/10 for a single journey up to 50/100/150/200km. You might also try **Covoiturage** (www.covoiturage.fr), **Bla Bla Car** (www.blablacar.fr) or, for international journeys, **Karzoo** (www.karzoo.eu).

Local Transport

France's cities and larger towns have world-class public-transport systems. There are *métros* (underground subway systems) in Paris, Lyon, Marseille, Lille and Toulouse and ultramodern light-rail lines *(tramways)* in cities such as Bordeaux, Grenoble, Lille, Lyon, Nancy, Nantes, Nice, Reims, Rouen and Strasbourg, as well as parts of greater Paris.

In addition to a *billet à l'unité* (single ticket), you can purchase a *carnet* (booklet or bunch) of 10 tickets or a *pass journée* (all-day pass).

Taxi

All medium and large train stations – and many small ones – have a taxi stand out front. In small cities and towns, where taxi drivers are unlikely to find another fare anywhere near where they let you off, one-way and return trips often cost the same. Tariffs are about 30% higher at night and on Sundays and holidays. A surcharge is usually charged to get picked up at a train station or airport, and there's a small additional fee for a fourth passenger and/or for suitcases.

Train

Travelling by train in France is a comfortable and environmentally sustainable way to see the country. Since many train stations have car-hire agencies, it's easy to combine rail travel with rural exploration by car.

The jewel in the crown of France's public-transport system – alongside the Paris *métro* – is its extensive rail network, almost all of it run by **SNCF** (Société Nationale des Chemins de fer Français, French National Railway Company; ☎from abroad +33 8 92 35 35 35, in France 36 35; http://en.voyages-sncf.com). Although it employs the most advanced rail technology, the network's layout reflects the country's centuries-old Paris-centric nature: most of the principal rail lines radiate out from Paris like the spokes of a wheel, the result being that services between provincial towns situated on different spokes can be infrequent and slow.

Up-to-the-minute information on *perturbations* (service disruptions), for example because of strikes, can be found on www.infolignes.com.

Since its inauguration in the 1980s, the pride and joy of SNCF is the **TGV** (Train à Grande Vitesse; www.tgv.com), pronounced 'teh zheh veh', which zips passengers along at speeds of up to 320km/h.

The main TGV lines (or LGVs, short for *lignes à grande vitesse*, ie high-speed rail lines) head north, east, southeast and southwest from Paris (trains use slower local tracks to get to destinations off the main line):

➡ **TGV Nord, Thalys and Eurostar** Link Paris Gare du Nord with Arras, Lille, Calais, Brussels (Bruxelles-Midi), Amsterdam, Cologne and, via the Channel Tunnel, Ashford, Ebbsfleet and London St Pancras.

➡ **LGV Est Européene** (www.lgv-est.com) Connects Paris Gare de l'Est with Reims, Nancy, Metz, Strasbourg, Zurich and Germany, including Frankfurt and Stuttgart. The super-high-speed track stretches as far east as Strasbourg.

➡ **TGV Sud-Est and TGV Midi-Méditerranée** Link Paris Gare de Lyon with the southeast, including Dijon, Lyon, Geneva, the Alps, Avignon, Marseille, Nice and Montpellier.

➡ **TGV Atlantique Sud-Ouest and TGV Atlantique Ouest** Link Paris Gare Montparnasse with western and southwestern France, including Brittany (Rennes, Brest, Quimper), Tours, Nantes, Poitiers, La Rochelle, Bordeaux, Biarritz and Toulouse.

➡ **LGV Rhin-Rhône** High-speed rail route bypasses Paris altogether in its bid to better link the provinces. Six services a day speed between Strasbourg and Lyon, with most continuing south to Marseille or Montpellier on the Mediterranean.

TGV tracks are interconnected, making it possible to go directly from, for example, Lyon to Nantes or Bordeaux to Lille without having to switch trains in Paris or

Trains & Ferries

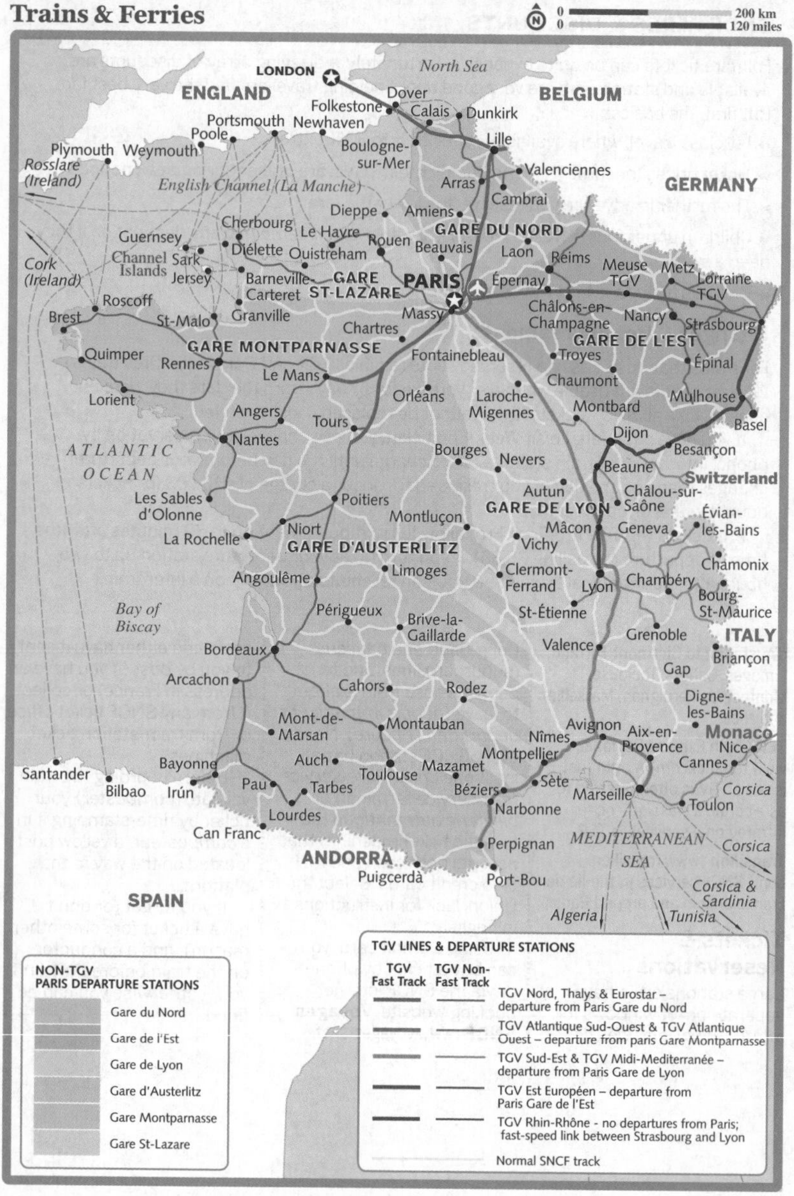

transfer from one of Paris' six main train stations to another. Stops on the link-up, which runs east and south of Paris, include Charles de Gaulle airport and Disneyland Resort Paris.

Long-distance trains sometimes split at a station – that is, each half of the train heads off for a different destination. Check the destination panel on your car as you board or you could wind up very far from where you intended to go.

Other types of train:

Téoz (www.corailteoz.com) Especially comfortable trains that run southward from Paris Gare

SNCF FARES & DISCOUNTS

Full-fare tickets can be quite expensive. Fortunately, a dizzying array of discounts are available and station staff are very good about helping travellers find the very best fare. But first, the basics:

- 1st-class travel, where available, costs 20% to 30% extra.
- Ticket prices for some trains, including most TGVs, are pricier during peak periods.
- The further in advance you reserve, the lower the fares.
- Children under four travel for free, or €9 with a *forfait bambin* to any destination if they need a seat.
- Children aged four to 11 travel for half-price.

Changes & Reimbursements

For trains that do not assign reserved seats (such as TER and Corail Intercités trains), full-fare tickets are usable whenever you like for 61 days from the date they were purchased. Like all SNCF tickets, they cannot be replaced if lost or stolen.

If you have a full-fare Loisir Week-End ticket, you can change your reservation by phone, internet or at train stations for no charge until the day before your departure; changes made on the day of your reserved trip incur a charge of €10 (€3 for tickets bought with a discount card).

Pro tickets (eg TGV Pro, Téoz Pro) allow full reimbursement up to 30 minutes *after* the time of departure (by calling 36 35). If you turn up at your departure station up to two hours after your original travel time, you can reschedule your trip on a later train.

d'Austerlitz to Clermont-Ferrand, Limoges, Cahors, Toulouse, Montpellier, Perpignan, Marseille and Nice.

TER (Train Express Régional; www.ter-sncf.com) A train that is not a TGV is often referred to as a *corail*, a *classique* or, for intraregional services, a TER.

Transilien (www.transilien.com) SNCF services in the Île de France area in and around Paris.

Tickets & Reservations

Large stations often have separate ticket windows for *international, grandes lignes* (long-haul) and *banlieue* (suburban) lines, and for people whose train is about to leave (*départ immédiat* or *départ dans l'heure*). Nearly every SNCF station has at least one *borne libre-service* (self-service terminal) or *billeterie automatique* (automatic ticket machine) that accepts both cash and PIN-chip credit cards. Select the Union Jack for instructions in English.

Using a credit card, you can buy a ticket by phone or via the SNCF internet booking website, **Voyages SNCF** (www.voyages-sncf.com), and either have it sent to you by post (if you have an address in France) or collect it from any SNCF ticket office or from train-station ticket machines.

Before boarding the train, validate *(composter)* your ticket by time-stamping it in a *composteur,* a yellow post located on the way to the platform.

If you forget (or don't have a ticket for some other reason), find a conductor on the train before they find you – otherwise you can be fined.

Language

Standard French is taught and spoken throughout France. This said, regional accents and dialects are an important part of identity in certain regions, but you'll have no trouble being understood anywhere if you stick to standard French, which we've also used in this chapter.

The sounds used in spoken French can almost all be found in English. There are a couple of exceptions: nasal vowels (represented in our pronunciation guides by o or u followed by an almost inaudible nasal consonant sound m, n or ng), the 'funny' *u* (ew in our guides) and the deep-in-the-throat *r*. Bearing these few points in mind and reading our pronunciation guides below as if they were English, you'll be understood just fine.

BASICS

French has two words for 'you' – use the polite form *vous* unless you're talking to close friends, children or animals in which case you'd use the informal *tu*. You can also use *tu* when a person invites you to use *tu*.

All nouns in French are either masculine or feminine, and so are the adjectives, articles *le/la* (the) and *un/une* (a), and possessives *mon/ma* (my), *ton/ta* (your) *and son/sa* (his, her) that go with the nouns. In this chapter we have included masculine and femine forms where necessary, separated by a slash and indicated with 'm/f'.

WANT MORE?

For in-depth language information and handy phrases, check out Lonely Planet's *French Phrasebook*. You'll find it at **shop.lonelyplanet.com**, or you can buy Lonely Planet's iPhone phrasebooks at the Apple App Store.

Hello.	*Bonjour.*	bon·zhoor
Goodbye.	*Au revoir.*	o·rer·vwa
Excuse me.	*Excusez-moi.*	ek·skew·zay·mwa
Sorry.	*Pardon.*	par·don
Yes.	*Oui.*	wee
No.	*Non.*	non
Please.	*S'il vous plaît.*	seel voo play
Thank you.	*Merci.*	mair·see
You're welcome.	*De rien.*	der ree·en

How are you?
Comment allez-vous? ko·mon ta·lay·voo

Fine, and you?
Bien, merci. Et vous? byun mair·see ay voo

You're welcome.
De rien. der ree·en

My name is ...
Je m'appelle ... zher ma·pel ...

What's your name?
Comment vous appelez-vous? ko·mon voo·za·play voo

Do you speak English?
Parlez-vous anglais? par·lay·voo ong·glay

I don't understand.
Je ne comprends pas. zher ner kom·pron pa

ACCOMMODATION

Do you have any rooms available?
Est-ce que vous avez des chambres libres? es·ker voo za·vay day shom·brer lee·brer

How much is it per night/person?
Quel est le prix par nuit/personne? kel ay ler pree par nwee/per·son

Is breakfast included?
Est-ce que le petit déjeuner est inclus? es·ker ler per·tee day·zher·nay ayt en·klew

KEY PATTERNS

To get by in France, mix and match these simple patterns with words of your choice:

Where's (the entry)?
Où est (l'entrée)? — oo ay (lon·tray)

Where can I (buy a ticket)?
Où est-ce que je peux (acheter un billet)? — oo es·ker zher per (ash·tay un bee·yay)

When's (the next train)?
Quand est (le prochain train)? — kon ay (ler pro·shun trun)

How much is (a room)?
C'est combien pour (une chambre)? — say kom·buyn poor (ewn shom·brer)

Do you have (a map)?
Avez-vous (une carte)? — a·vay voo (ewn kart)

Is there (a toilet)?
Y a-t-il (des toilettes)? — ee a teel (day twa·let)

I'd like (to book a room).
Je voudrais (réserver une chambre). — zher voo·dray (ray·ser·vay ewn shom·brer)

Can I (enter)?
Puis-je (entrer)? — pweezh (on·tray)

Could you please (help)?
Pouvez-vous (m'aider), s'il vous plaît? — poo·vay voo (may·day) seel voo play

Do I have to (book a seat)?
Faut-il (réserver une place)? — fo·teel (ray·ser·vay ewn plas)

campsite	*camping*	kom·peeng
dorm	*dortoir*	dor·twar
guest house	*pension*	pon·syon
hotel	*hôtel*	o·tel
youth hostel	*auberge de jeunesse*	o·berzh der zher·nes
a ... room	*une chambre ...*	ewn shom·brer ...
single	*à un lit*	a un lee
double	*avec un grand lit*	a·vek un gron lee
twin	*avec des lits jumeaux*	a·vek day lee zhew·mo
with (a)...	*avec ...*	a·vek ...
air-con	*climatiseur*	klee·ma·tee·zer
bathroom	*une salle de bains*	ewn sal der bun
window	*fenêtre*	fer·nay·trer

DIRECTIONS

Where's ...?
Où est ...? — oo ay ...

What's the address?
Quelle est l'adresse? — kel ay la·dres

Could you write the address, please?
Est-ce que vous pourriez écrire l'adresse, s'il vous plaît? — es·ker voo poo·ryay ay·kreer la·dres seel voo play

Can you show me (on the map)?
Pouvez-vous m'indiquer (sur la carte)? — poo·vay·voo mun·dee·kay (sewr la kart)

at the corner	*au coin*	o kwun
at the traffic lights	*aux feux*	o fer
behind	*derrière*	dair·ryair
in front of	*devant*	der·von
far (from)	*loin (de)*	lwun (der)
left	*gauche*	gosh
near (to)	*près (de)*	pray (der)
next to ...	*à côté de ...*	a ko·tay der...
opposite ...	*en face de ...*	on fas der ...
right	*droite*	drwat
straight ahead	*tout droit*	too drwa

EATING & DRINKING

What would you recommend?
Qu'est-ce que vous conseillez? — kes·ker voo kon·say·yay

What's in that dish?
Quels sont les ingrédients? — kel son lay zun·gray·dyon

I'm a vegetarian.
Je suis végétarien/végétarienne. — zher swee vay·zhay·ta·ryun/vay·zhay·ta·ryen (m/f)

I don't eat ...
Je ne mange pas ... — zher ner monzh pa ...

Cheers!
Santé! — son·tay

That was delicious.
C'était délicieux! — say·tay day·lee·syer

Please bring the bill.
Apportez-moi l'addition, s'il vous plaît. — a·por·tay·mwa la·dee·syon seel voo play

I'd like to reserve a table for ...	*Je voudrais réserver une table pour ...*	zher voo·dray ray·zair·vay ewn ta·bler poor ...
(eight) o'clock	*(vingt) heures*	(vungt) er
(two) people	*(deux) personnes*	(der) pair·son

Key Words

appetiser	*entrée*	on·tray
bottle	*bouteille*	boo·tay
breakfast	*petit déjeuner*	per·tee day·zher·nay
children's menu	*menu pour enfants*	mer·new poor on·fon
cold	*froid*	frwa
delicatessen	*traiteur*	tray·ter
dinner	*dîner*	dee·nay
dish	*plat*	pla
food	*nourriture*	noo·ree·tewr
fork	*fourchette*	foor·shet
glass	*verre*	vair
grocery store	*épicerie*	ay·pees·ree
highchair	*chaise haute*	shay zot
hot	*chaud*	sho
knife	*couteau*	koo·to
local speciality	*spécialité locale*	spay·sya·lee·tay lo·kal
lunch	*déjeuner*	day·zher·nay
main course	*plat principal*	pla prun·see·pal
market	*marché*	mar·shay
menu (in English)	*carte (en anglais)*	kart (on ong·glay)
plate	*assiette*	a·syet
spoon	*cuillère*	kwee·yair
wine list	*carte des vins*	kart day vun
with/without	*avec/sans*	a·vek/son

Meat & Fish

beef	*bœuf*	berf
chicken	*poulet*	poo·lay
crab	*crabe*	krab
lamb	*agneau*	a·nyo
oyster	*huître*	wee·trer
pork	*porc*	por
snail	*escargot*	es·kar·go
squid	*calmar*	kal·mar
turkey	*dinde*	dund
veal	*veau*	vo

Fruit & Vegetables

apple	*pomme*	pom
apricot	*abricot*	ab·ree·ko
asparagus	*asperge*	a·spairzh
beans	*haricots*	a·ree·ko
beetroot	*betterave*	be·trav
cabbage	*chou*	shoo
cherry	*cerise*	ser·reez
corn	*maïs*	ma·ees
cucumber	*concombre*	kong·kom·brer
grape	*raisin*	ray·zun
lemon	*citron*	see·tron
lettuce	*laitue*	lay·tew
mushroom	*champignon*	shom·pee·nyon
peach	*pêche*	pesh
peas	*petit pois*	per·tee pwa
(red/green) pepper	*poivron (rouge/vert)*	pwa·vron (roozh/vair)
pineapple	*ananas*	a·na·nas
plum	*prune*	prewn
potato	*pomme de terre*	pom der tair
prune	*pruneau*	prew·no
pumpkin	*citrouille*	see·troo·yer
shallot	*échalote*	eh·sha·lot
spinach	*épinards*	eh·pee·nar
strawberry	*fraise*	frez
tomato	*tomate*	to·mat
vegetable	*légume*	lay·gewm

Other

bread	*pain*	pun
butter	*beurre*	ber
cheese	*fromage*	fro·mazh
egg	*œuf*	erf
honey	*miel*	myel
jam	*confiture*	kon·fee·tewr
lentils	*lentilles*	lon·tee·yer
pasta/noodles	*pâtes*	pat
pepper	*poivre*	pwa·vrer
rice	*riz*	ree
salt	*sel*	sel
sugar	*sucre*	sew·krer
vinegar	*vinaigre*	vee·nay·grer

SIGNS

Entrée	Entrance
Femmes	Women
Fermé	Closed
Hommes	Men
Interdit	Prohibited
Ouvert	Open
Renseignements	Information
Sortie	Exit
Toilettes/WC	Toilets

Drinks

beer	*bière*	bee·yair
coffee	*café*	ka·fay
(orange) juice	*jus (d'orange)*	zhew (do·ronzh)
milk	*lait*	lay
tea	*thé*	tay
(mineral) water	*eau (minérale)*	o (mee·nay·ral)
(red) wine	*vin (rouge)*	vun (roozh)
(white) wine	*vin (blanc)*	vun (blong)

EMERGENCIES

Help!
Au secours! — o skoor

I'm lost.
Je suis perdu/perdue. — zhe swee·pair·dew (m/f)

Leave me alone!
Fichez-moi la paix! — fee·shay·mwa la pay

There's been an accident.
Il y a eu un accident. — eel ya ew un ak·see·don

Call a doctor.
Appelez un médecin. — a·play un mayd·sun

Call the police.
Appelez la police. — a·play la po·lees

I'm ill.
Je suis malade. — zher swee ma·lad

It hurts here.
J'ai une douleur ici. — zhay ewn doo·ler ee·see

I'm allergic to ...
Je suis allergique ... — zher swee za·lair·zheek ...

SHOPPING & SERVICES

I'd like to buy ...
Je voudrais acheter ... — zher voo·dray ash·tay ...

May I look at it?
Est-ce que je peux le voir? — es·ker zher per ler vwar

I'm just looking.
Je regarde. — zher rer·gard

I don't like it.
Cela ne me plaît pas. — ser·la ner mer play pa

How much is it?
C'est combien? — say kom·byun

It's too expensive.
C'est trop cher. — say tro shair

Can you lower the price?
Vous pouvez baisser le prix? — voo poo·vay bay·say ler pree

There's a mistake in the bill.
Il y a une erreur dans la note. — eel ya ewn ay·rer don la not

ATM	*guichet automatique de banque*	gee·shay o·to·ma·teek der bonk
credit card	*carte de crédit*	kart der kray·dee
internet cafe	*cybercafé*	see·bair·ka·fay
post office	*bureau de poste*	bew·ro der post
tourist office	*office de tourisme*	o·fees der too·rees·mer

QUESTION WORDS

How?	*Comment?*	ko·mon
What?	*Quoi?*	kwa
When?	*Quand?*	kon
Where?	*Où?*	oo
Who?	*Qui?*	kee
Why?	*Pourquoi?*	poor·kwa

TIME & DATES

What time is it?
Quelle heure est-il? — kel er ay til

It's (eight) o'clock.
Il est (huit) heures. — il ay (weet) er

It's half past (10).
Il est (dix) heures et demie. — il ay (deez) er ay day·mee

morning	*matin*	ma·tun
afternoon	*après-midi*	a·pray·mee·dee
evening	*soir*	swar
yesterday	*hier*	yair
today	*aujourd'hui*	o·zhoor·dwee
tomorrow	*demain*	der·mun

Monday	*lundi*	lun·dee
Tuesday	*mardi*	mar·dee
Wednesday	*mercredi*	mair·krer·dee
Thursday	*jeudi*	zher·dee
Friday	*vendredi*	von·drer·dee
Saturday	*samedi*	sam·dee
Sunday	*dimanche*	dee·monsh

January	*janvier*	zhon·vyay
February	*février*	fayv·ryay
March	*mars*	mars
April	*avril*	a·vreel
May	*mai*	may
June	*juin*	zhwun
July	*juillet*	zhwee·yay
August	*août*	oot
September	*septembre*	sep·tom·brer
October	*octobre*	ok·to·brer
November	*novembre*	no·vom·brer
December	*décembre*	day·som·brer

TRANSPORT

Public Transport

boat	*bateau*	ba·to
bus	*bus*	bews
plane	*avion*	a·vyon
train	*train*	trun

I want to go to ...
Je voudrais aller à ... zher voo·dray a·lay a ...

Does it stop at (Amboise)?
Est-ce qu'il s'arrête à (Amboise)? es·kil sa·ret a (om·bwaz)

At what time does it leave/arrive?
À quelle heure est-ce qu'il part/arrive? a kel er es kil par/a·reev

Can you tell me when we get to ...?
Pouvez-vous me dire quand nous arrivons à ...? poo·vay·voo mer deer kon noo za·ree·von a ...

I want to get off here.
Je veux descendre ici. zher ver day·son·drer ee·see

first	*premier*	prer·myay
last	*dernier*	dair·nyay
next	*prochain*	pro·shun
a ... ticket	*un billet ...*	un bee·yay ...
1st-class	*de première classe*	der prem·yair klas
2nd-class	*de deuxième classe*	der der·zyem las
one-way	*simple*	sum·pler
return	*aller et retour*	a·lay ay rer·toor

aisle seat	*côté couloir*	ko·tay kool·war
delayed	*en retard*	on rer·tar
cancelled	*annulé*	a·new·lay
platform	*quai*	kay
ticket office	*guichet*	gee·shay
timetable	*horaire*	o·rair
train station	*gare*	gar
window seat	*côté fenêtre*	ko·tay fe·ne·trer

Driving & Cycling

I'd like to hire a ...	*Je voudrais louer ...*	zher voo·dray loo·way ...
4WD	*un quatre-quatre*	un kat·kat
car	*une voiture*	ewn vwa·tewr
bicycle	*un vélo*	un vay·lo
motorcycle	*une moto*	ewn mo·to
child seat	*siège-enfant*	syezh·on·fon
diesel	*diesel*	dyay·zel
helmet	*casque*	kask
mechanic	*mécanicien*	may·ka·nee·syun
petrol/gas	*essence*	ay·sons
service station	*station-service*	sta·syon·ser·vees

Is this the road to ...?
C'est la route pour ...? say la root poor ...

(How long) Can I park here?
(Combien de temps) Est-ce que je peux stationner ici? (kom·byun der tom) es·ker zher per sta·syo·nay ee·see

The car/motorbike has broken down (at ...).
La voiture/moto est tombée en panne (à ...). la vwa·tewr/mo·to ay tom·bay on pan (a ...)

I have a flat tyre.
Mon pneu est à plat. mom pner ay ta pla

I've run out of petrol.
Je suis en panne d'essence. zher swee zon pan day·sons

I've lost my car keys.
J'ai perdu les clés de ma voiture. zhay per·dew lay klay der ma vwa·tewr

NUMBERS

1	*un*	un
2	*deux*	der
3	*trois*	trwa
4	*quatre*	ka·trer
5	*cinq*	sungk
6	*six*	sees
7	*sept*	set
8	*huit*	weet
9	*neuf*	nerf
10	*dix*	dees
20	*vingt*	vung
30	*trente*	tront
40	*quarante*	ka·ront
50	*cinquante*	sung·kont
60	*soixante*	swa·sont
70	*soixante-dix*	swa·son·dees
80	*quatre-vingts*	ka·trer·vung
90	*quatre-vingt-dix*	ka·trer·vung·dees
100	*cent*	son
1000	*mille*	meel

GLOSSARY

(m) indicates masculine gender, (f) feminine gender and (pl) plural

accueil (m) – reception
alignements (m pl) – a series of standing stones, or menhirs, in straight lines
AOC – Appellation d'Origine Contrôlée; system of French wine and olive oil classification showing that items have met government regulations as to where and how they are produced
AOP – Appellation d'Origine Protégée; Europe-wide equivalent to *AOC*
arrondissement (m) – administrative division of large city; abbreviated on signs as 1er (1st arrondissement), 2e (2nd) etc
atelier (m) – workshop or studio
auberge – inn
auberge de jeunesse (f) – youth hostel

baie (f) – bay
bassin (m) – bay or basin
bastide (f) – medieval settlement in southwestern France, usually built on a grid plan and surrounding an arcaded square; fortified town; also a country house in Provence
belle époque (f) – literally 'beautiful age'; era of elegance and gaiety characterising fashionable Parisian life in the period preceding WWI
billet (m) – ticket
billetterie (f) – ticket office or counter
bouchon – Lyonnais bistro
boulangerie (f) – bakery or bread shop
boules (f pl) – a game similar to lawn bowls played with heavy metal balls on a sandy pitch; also called *pétanque*
brasserie (f) – restaurant similar to a *café* but usually serving full meals all day (original meaning: brewery)
bureau de change (m) – exchange bureau
bureau de poste (m) – post office
carnet (m) – a book of five or 10 bus, tram or metro tickets sold at a reduced rate
carrefour (m) – crossroad
carte (f) – card; menu; map
cave (f) – wine cellar
chambre (f) – room
chambre d'hôte (f) – B&B
charcuterie (f) – butcher's shop and delicatessen; the prepared meats it sells
cimetière (m) – cemetery
col (m) – mountain pass
consigne or **consigne manuelle** (f) – left-luggage office
consigne automatique (f) – left-luggage locker
correspondance (f) – linking tunnel or walkway, eg in the metro; rail or bus connection
cour (f) – courtyard
crémerie (f) – dairy or cheese shop

dégustation (f) – tasting
demi (m) – 330mL glass of beer
demi-pension (f) – half board (B&B with either lunch or dinner)
département (m) – administrative division of France
donjon (m) – castle keep

église (f) – church
épicerie (f) – small grocery store
ESF – École de Ski Français; France's leading ski school

fest-noz or **festoù-noz** (pl) – night festival
fête (f) – festival
Fnac – retail chain selling entertainment goods, electronics and tickets
forêt (f) – forest
formule or **formule rapide** (f) – lunchtime set similar to a *menu* but with two of three courses on offer (eg starter and main or main and dessert)
fromagerie (f) – cheese shop
FUAJ – Fédération Unie des Auberges de Jeunesse; France's major hostel association
funiculaire (m) – funicular railway
galerie (f) – covered shopping centre or arcade
gare or **gare SNCF** (f) – railway station
gare maritime (f) – ferry terminal
gare routière (f) – bus station
gendarmerie (f) – police station; police force
gîte d'étape (m) – hikers accommodation, usually in a village
golfe (m) – gulf
GR – *grande randonnée;* long-distance hiking trail
grand cru (m) – wine of exceptional quality

halles (f pl) – covered market; central food market
halte routière (f) – bus stop
horaire (m) – timetable or schedule
hostellerie – hostelry
hôtel de ville (m) – city or town hall
hôtel particulier (m) – private mansion

intra-muros – old city (literally 'within the walls')

jardin (m) – garden
jardin botanique (m) – botanic garden

laverie (f) or **lavomatique** (m) – laundrette
libre – vacant, available

mairie (f) – city or town hall
maison du parc (f) – a national park's headquarters and/or visitors centre
marché (m) – market
marché aux puces (m) – flea market
marché couvert (m) – covered market
mas (m) – farmhouse in southern France
menu (m) – fixed-price meal with two or more courses
mistral (m) – strong north or northwest wind in southern France
musée (m) – museum

navette (f) – shuttle bus, train or boat

occupé – occupied

palais de justice (m) – law courts

parapente – paragliding

parlement (m) – parliament

parvis (m) – square

patisserie (f) – cake and pastry shop

pétanque (f) – a game similar to lawn bowls played with heavy metal balls on a sandy pitch; also called *boules*

petit déjeuner – breakfast

place (f) – square or plaza

plage (f) – beach

plan (m) – city map

plan du quartier (m) – map of nearby streets (hung on the wall near metro exits)

plat du jour (m) – daily special in a restaurant

pont (m) – bridge

porte (f) – gate in a city wall

poste (f) – post office

préfecture (f) – prefecture (capital of a *département*)

presqu'île (f) – peninsula

puy (m) – volcanic cone or peak

quai (m) – quay or railway platform

quartier (m) – quarter or district

refuge (m) – mountain hut, basic shelter for hikers

région (f) – administrative division of France

rond point (m) – roundabout

salon de thé – tearoom

sentier (m) – trail

service des urgences (f) – casualty ward

ski de fond – cross-country skiing

SNCF – Société Nationale des Chemins de Fer; state-owned railway company

SNCM – Société Nationale Maritime Corse-Méditerranée; state-owned ferry company linking Corsica and mainland France

sortie (f) – exit

square (m) – public garden

tabac (m) – tobacconist (also selling bus tickets, phonecards etc)

table d'hôte – set menu at a fixed price

taxe de séjour (f) – municipal tourist tax

télécarte (f) – phonecard

télécabine – gondola

téléphérique (m) – cableway or cable car

téléski (m) – chairlift

téléski (m) – ski lift or tow

terroir – land

TGV – *Train à Grande Vitesse;* high-speed train or bullet train

tour (f) – tower

vallée (f) – valley

VF (f) – *version française*; a film dubbed in French

vieille ville (f) – old town or old city

ville neuve (f) – new town or new city

VO (f) – *version originale*; a nondubbed film with French subtitles

VTT – *vélo tout terrain;* mountain bike

winstub – traditional Alsatian eatery

Behind the Scenes

SEND US YOUR FEEDBACK

We love to hear from travellers – your comments keep us on our toes and help make our books better. Our well-travelled team reads every word on what you loved or loathed about this book. Although we cannot reply individually to your submissions, we always guarantee that your feedback goes straight to the appropriate authors, in time for the next edition. Each person who sends us information is thanked in the next edition – the most useful submissions are rewarded with a selection of digital PDF chapters.

Visit **lonelyplanet.com/contact** to submit your updates and suggestions or to ask for help. Our award-winning website also features inspirational travel stories, news and discussions.

Note: We may edit, reproduce and incorporate your comments in Lonely Planet products such as guidebooks, websites and digital products, so let us know if you don't want your comments reproduced or your name acknowledged. For a copy of our privacy policy visit lonelyplanet.com/privacy.

OUR READERS

Many thanks to the travellers who used the last edition and wrote to us with helpful hints, useful advice and interesting anecdotes:

James Ritchie, John Reilly, Linda DesBarres, Lucy & Stuart Stirland, Peter Woods, Remi Favier, Robert van Barlingen, Robyn Stokes, Ted Bailey, Terri Christensen, Vanessa Vizi, Yong-cheol Lee

WRITER THANKS

Nicola Williams

Un grand merci to the many who aided and abetted in tracking down the very best, including in Nantes, Katia Forte, @Rachelwill and rapidly rising chef Dominic Quirke at neobistro Pickles; Pascale Chaillot in Cognac; and in Bordeaux, wine expert Jane Anson, Kirsty Curtis (Musée du Vin et du Négoce) and Sophie Gaillard (Bordeaux Tourisme). At home, sweet thanks to *belle-mère* Christa Luefkens and my highly experienced trilingual 'family travel' research team, Niko, Mischa and Kaya.

Alexis Averbuck

Once again my journey through the Dordogne was made magnificent by the generosity of the gorgeous Janice Bowen. She shared her home, her fantastic knowledge of the region, and her enthusiastic heart. A million thanks to wonderful Alexandra Miliotis for her top tips on travelling the back roads of Brittany. The pink granite coast, walled city of St-Malo and the sumptuous seafood of Brittany wouldn't have been nearly as delicious without my darling Ryan Ver Berkmoes: husband, friend, travel genie and joy.

Oliver Berry

For this edition I would like to thank Didier Lafarge, Jean Dubarry, Eloise Guilmard and Agnes Tilleul for help during research and write-up. I would also like to send special thanks to Susie and Gracie Berry for receiving all the postcards, and to Rosie Hillier for love, late-night correspondence, and making the road a lot less lonely.

Jean-Bernard Carillet

Big thanks to Christine for joining me for a few days in Beaujolais, and to all the people I met while on the road for their tips and recommendations. Last but not least, a *gros bisou* to my half-Parisian, half-Lorraine daughter Eva.

Kerry Christiani

I'd like to say a big *merci* to all the wonderful locals I met on my travels, as well as to the tourist boards who made the road to research silky smooth. A special thank you goes to Jeal-Paul de Vries at Romagne '14-'18 for the behind-the-scenes battlefields tour.

Gregor Clark

Un grand merci to the countless locals who shared their knowledge of Burgundy and Corsica with me. Special thanks to Claire Beuvrot in Cluny for the cloves that cured my toothache. And big hugs to Gaen, Meigan and Chloe, who always make coming home the best part of the trip.

Anita Isalska

Enormous thanks to the friends and colleagues who shared insider insights, tips and support for this project. Special thank yous go to Thomas Ducloutrier, Bill Lehane, Vanessa Michy, Pascale Suc, Jean-Paul Grimaud, Kate Morgan, Melissa Buttelli, and friendly tourist offices along the Tarn. And to Normal Matt, who drove from London to Vichy in a beat-up Toyota just to cheer me on.

Catherine Le Nevez

Un grand merci to my Paris co-writers Chris and Nicola. *Merci mille fois* to Julian, and everyone in and around Paris and in Languedoc-Roussillon who offered insights and inspiration. In particular, *merci beaucoup* to Laurent for going above and beyond, and to Laurence for the same. Huge thanks also to Helen Elfer, Kate Morgan and everyone at LP. A heartfelt *merci encore* to my parents, brother, *belle-sœur* and *neveu* for sustaining my lifelong love of Paris and France.

Hugh McNaughtan

Thanks to Helen Elfer and to my ever-understanding family.

Christopher Pitts

Special thanks to my two great co-authors for their advice and input and to all the crew at LP who have put much hard work into making this book what it is. *Bises* as well to the Pavillards and my dearest partners in crime: Perrine, Elliot and Celeste.

Daniel Robinson

Special thanks to (from north to south): Anny Monet (Lille), Virginie Debret (Lens' 14-18 museum), Rodney and Philippe (Arras), Carole Lefebvre and Corinne Vasseur (Parc du Marquenterre Bird Sanctuary), Thapedi Masanabo (South African National Memorial), Lauren Tookey (Amiens and UK) and Madame Thion (Cercil, Orléans). This project would not have been possible without the support, enthusiasm and forbearance of my wife Rachel and our sons Yair and Sasson (Orléans, Tours and New London, Connecticut).

Regis St Louis

I'm particularly grateful to the tourism officials, innkeepers, booksellers, baristas, priests, hitch-hikers and assorted other locals who shared tips and advice along the way. Special thanks to Penny, Thierry and Olivier in Honfleur; Marion and Hans at Florivalier, and the mysterious but kind-hearted vegan galette maker in Foix. Lastly, *gros bisous* to my partner in crime, Cassandra, and daughters Magdalena and Genevieve.

ACKNOWLEDGEMENTS

Climate map data adapted from Peel MC, Finlayson BL & McMahon TA (2007) 'Updated World Map of the Köppen-Geiger Climate Classification', Hydrology and Earth System Sciences, 11, 163344.

Paris metro system map © RATP – CML Agence Cartographique.

Illustrations pp70-1, pp84-5, pp88-9, pp164-5, pp246-7, pp758-9 and pp866-7 by Javier Zarracina.

Cover photograph: Ville-Dommange and vineyards, Champagne-Ardenne, Matteo Colombo/AWL ©.

THIS BOOK

This 12th edition of Lonely Planet's *France* guidebook was researched and written by Nicola Williams, Alexis Averbuck, Oliver Berry, Jean-Bernard Carillet, Kerry Christiani, Gregor Clark, Anita Isalska, Catherine Le Nevez, Hugh McNaughtan, Christopher Pitts, Daniel Robinson and Regis St Louis. The previous edition was written by Nicola Williams, Alexis Averbuck, Oliver Berry, Stuart Butler, Jean-Bernard Carillet, Kerry Christiani, Gregor Clark, Emilie Filou, Catherine Le Nevez and Daniel Robinson. This guidebook was produced by the following:

Destination Editors Helen Elfer, Daniel Fahey

Product Editor Catherine Naghten

Senior Cartographers Mark Griffiths, Valentina Kremenchutskaya

Book Designer Wibowo Rusli

Assisting Editors Sarah Bailey, Imogen Bannister, Bridget Blair, Andrea Dobbin, Samantha Forge, Carly Hall, Gabrielle Innes, Helen Koehne, Ali Lemer, Rosie Nicholson, Kristin Odijk, Monique Perrin, Gabrielle Stefanos, Fionnuala Twomey

Cover Researcher Naomi Parker

Thanks to Carolyn Boicos, Rosie Draffin, Liz Heynes, Lauren Keith, Kate James, Andi Jones, Kate Kiely, Kate Morgan, Claire Naylor, Karyn Noble, Kirsten Rawlings, Kathryn Rowan, Tony Wheeler

Index

B

Map Pages **000**
Photo Pages **000**

Map Pages **000**
Photo Pages **000**

M

Map Pages **000**
Photo Pages **000**

N

Map Pages **000**
Photo Pages **000**

Y

Z

Map Legend

Sights
- Beach
- Bird Sanctuary
- Buddhist
- Castle/Palace
- Christian
- Confucian
- Hindu
- Islamic
- Jain
- Jewish
- Monument
- Museum/Gallery/Historic Building
- Ruin
- Shinto
- Sikh
- Taoist
- Winery/Vineyard
- Zoo/Wildlife Sanctuary
- Other Sight

Activities, Courses & Tours
- Bodysurfing
- Diving
- Canoeing/Kayaking
- Course/Tour
- Sento Hot Baths/Onsen
- Skiing
- Snorkelling
- Surfing
- Swimming/Pool
- Walking
- Windsurfing
- Other Activity

Sleeping
- Sleeping
- Camping

Eating
- Eating

Drinking & Nightlife
- Drinking & Nightlife
- Cafe

Entertainment
- Entertainment

Shopping
- Shopping

Information
- Bank
- Embassy/Consulate
- Hospital/Medical
- Internet
- Police
- Post Office
- Telephone
- Toilet
- Tourist Information
- Other Information

Geographic
- Beach
- Gate
- Hut/Shelter
- Lighthouse
- Lookout
- Mountain/Volcano
- Oasis
- Park
- Pass
- Picnic Area
- Waterfall

Population
- Capital (National)
- Capital (State/Province)
- City/Large Town
- Town/Village

Transport
- Airport
- Border crossing
- Bus
- Cable car/Funicular
- Cycling
- Ferry
- Metro station
- Monorail
- Parking
- Petrol station
- S-Bahn/Subway station
- Taxi
- T-bane/Tunnelbana station
- Train station/Railway
- Tram
- Tube station
- U-Bahn/Underground station
- Other Transport

Note: Not all symbols displayed above appear on the maps in this book

Routes
- Tollway
- Freeway
- Primary
- Secondary
- Tertiary
- Lane
- Unsealed road
- Road under construction
- Plaza/Mall
- Steps
- Tunnel
- Pedestrian overpass
- Walking Tour
- Walking Tour detour
- Path/Walking Trail

Boundaries
- International
- State/Province
- Disputed
- Regional/Suburb
- Marine Park
- Cliff
- Wall

Hydrography
- River, Creek
- Intermittent River
- Canal
- Water
- Dry/Salt/Intermittent Lake
- Reef

Areas
- Airport/Runway
- Beach/Desert
- Cemetery (Christian)
- Cemetery (Other)
- Glacier
- Mudflat
- Park/Forest
- Sight (Building)
- Sportsground
- Swamp/Mangrove

Daniel Robinson

Lille, Flanders & the Somme, Loire Valley Co-author (with Tony Wheeler) of Lonely Planet's first *Paris* guide, Daniel has been writing about France for over 25 years. Passionate about history, he is always moved by the grand châteaux of the Loire, the sombre cemeteries of the Somme, and the dramatic and tragic events that both embody. Daniel's travel writing has appeared in the *New York Times*, *National Geographic Traveler* and many other publications, and has been translated into 10 languages. He holds degrees in history from Princeton and Tel Aviv University.

Regis St Louis

Pyrenees, Normandy Regis' French ancestry fuelled an early interest in all things francophone, which led to Serge Gainsbourg records, François Truffaut films and extensive travels around France. For his latest journey, Regis walked the drizzly beaches of Normandy, explored Joan of Arc lore in Rouen and idled behind sheep-powered roadblocks in the Pyrenees. A full-time travel writer since 2003, Regis has covered numerous destinations for Lonely Planet, including Montreal, Senegal and New York City. Follow his latest posts on Twitter @regisstlouis.

PLAN YOUR TRIP

VINEYARD, ST-ÉMILION P633

JUSTIN FOULKES / LONELY PLANET ©

ROUSSILLON P744

LOTTIE DAVIES / LONELY PLANET ©

ON THE ROAD

lonely planet

France

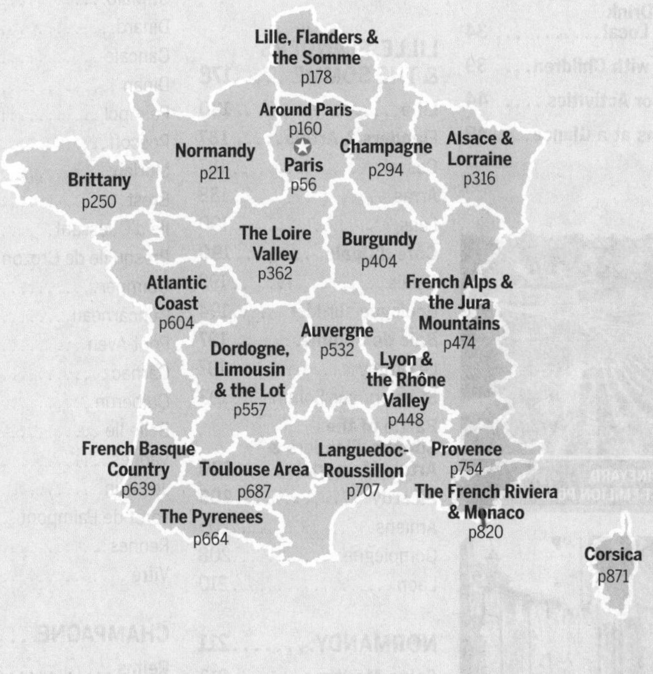

THIS EDITION WRITTEN AND RESEARCHED BY

Nicola Williams,

Alexis Averbuck, Oliver Berry, Jean-Bernard Carillet,

Kerry Christiani, Gregor Clark, Anita Isalska, Catherine Le Nevez,

Hugh McNaughtan, Christopher Pitts, Daniel Robinson and Regis St Louis